NIC 2004-05   October 2004

Tracking the Dragon

National Intelligence Estimates on China During the Era of Mao, 1948-1976

This paper was prepared under the auspices of
Ambassador Robert L. Hutchings, Chairman,
National Intelligence Council. Inquiries may be directed
to the Chairman on (703) 482-6724.

Preface

The National Intelligence Council is pleased to issue this collection of over seventy National Intelligence Estimates on China—the largest such release ever made at one time. These formerly classified documents represent the most authoritative assessments of the United States Government and so constitute a unique historical record of a momentous era in China's modern history.

The collection spans the pivotal period from the final stages of the Chinese civil war and the consolidation of the Communist regime through the upheavals of the Great Leap Forward and Cultural Revolution. It chronicles the struggles within the top leadership, the buildup of the Chinese military, and the evolution of the Sino-Soviet split. With the benefit of hindsight, we can now study the assessments of these developments with a degree of historical perspective, while still feeling the excitement of reading "history as it happens."

The collection was truly a collaborative undertaking. The editors of this volume—John K. Allen, John Carver, and Tom Elmore—did a masterful job of selecting and editing the documents to be included. Robert Suettinger drew on his experience in the intelligence, policy, and scholarly worlds to write a superb introduction. Within the National Intelligence Council, Mathew Burrows and his analytic and production staff expertly turned the raw documents into a finished book, which we unveiled at a major international conference held in partnership with the Woodrow Wilson International Center for Scholars and its Cold War International History Project. Finally and most importantly, the volume was made possible by the contributions of a whole generation of analysts and senior officers from the many agencies of the United States Intelligence Community.

Ambassador Robert L. Hutchings

Chairman, National Intelligence Council

序言

国家情报委员会很高兴发行共收录七十余份有关中国的国家情报评估文件的汇编,这是有史以来一次发行规模最大的汇编集.这些曾经列为机密的文件代表美国政府最具有权威性的评估,是有关中国近代史上一个重要时代的绝无仅有的历史记录.

本汇编涵盖了包括中国国内战争,共产政权的巩固,以及大跃进和文化革命时期的动乱的关键时期,它记录最高领导层的斗争,中国的军队建设,和中苏决裂的演变.我们事后可以用一定程度的历史眼光研究这些事态的发展,同时还感觉到阅读"历史正在发生"的那种兴奋.

本汇编是真正通过同心协力而完成的.编纂本汇编的编辑人员约翰.K.艾伦,约翰.卡弗,汤姆,尔摩出色地完成了选录和编辑所要收录的文件.苏葆立利用其在情报界,决策界,和学术界的经验写出极佳的绪论.在国家情报委员会里,马修.伯罗斯和他的情报分析与生产人员精巧地将原始文件编制成一本书,我们将这本书在和伍德罗.威尔逊国际学者中心与其冷战国际历史项目共同举办的一次重大国际会议上公诸于众,最后和最重要的一点,本汇编是因为来自美国情报界的整整一代的分析家和高级官员所做出的贡献才编写成的.

罗伯特.哈钦斯大使

国家情报委员会主席

Contents

Note: Sections are complete unless otherwise noted.

This publication is also available on the NIC Public Web site at: www.cia.gov/nic under Declassified NIC Publications.

Forward

This collection of declassified intelligence Estimates on China is the first such release by the CIA of analytic products exclusively on China. The inspiration for this undertaking came from National Intelligence Council (NIC) Chairman Robert Hutchings and Herb Briick of CIA's Information Management Services (IMS). Upon reviewing outstanding requests for NIC documents received though Freedom of Information and Executive Order channels, both noted a critical mass of requests on China. The 71 documents in the collection—37 of which are printed in whole or part in this volume and all 71 of which are on the accompanying CD in their entirety—also include some Estimates which have been previously declassified and released either to individual requesters or as part of periodic voluntary releases undertaken by CIA's Historical Review Group.

The production of the collection was a joint effort by the NIC and IMS. Beginning in early 2004, a small team under a project manager was formed on the staff of the DCI's Information Review Office. The team included three editors, all with analytic experience on China (see biographic sketches below), who reviewed, selected and declassified the documents, assisted on a part time basis by two experts on the declassification process and a specialist on electronic management of documents.

During the period 1948-1976, some 240 Estimates dealing in some degree or another with China were produced. Owing to time and space constraints, the editors made a representative selection from this total. The editors' aim was to include Estimates that tracked the general trends of China's internal politics, foreign relations, national economy, and the growth of its military establishment. Redundant Estimates and those that dealt with topics peripheral to China were omitted. The largest category not chosen was Estimates on the Communist Bloc as a whole. Most of these Estimates were devoted primarily to the Soviet Union, and many of these had already been released.

John K. Allen, Jr.

Mr. Allen is a 30-year veteran of CIA, having served in operations, analysis, and the management of analysis. As an analyst, he followed China during the 1970s, focusing on China's foreign policy. He served on the NIC as National Intelligence Officer in 1994 and 1995. He studied Chinese affairs at Harvard University (MPA, 1977).

John Carver

Mr. Carver is a 40-year CIA veteran with an additional 10 years on contract. His work on China began in 1954 and has included translation of Chinese documents and analysis of China's internal politics and leaders, economy, and science and technology. He lectured on China at the CIA in the 1970s. He graduated from the University of Pennsylvania with a BA in International Relations.

Tom Elmore

Mr. Elmore also is a 40-year veteran of the CIA, having served primarily in analysis and the management of analysis. As an analyst, he followed China during 1968-1975 and again in 1982-1993, focusing on both China's domestic and foreign policy. He also taught Chinese foreign policy at The George Washington University while serving as Intelligence Officer in Residence. He studied Chinese affairs at Harvard University (1967-1968).

Introduction

By Robert L. Suettinger

A 24-year career intelligence analyst, Robert L. Suettinger served as Deputy National Intelligence Officer for East Asia on the National Intelligence Council from 1989 to 1994 and as National Intelligence Officer for East Asia from 1997 to 1998. He also was Director of Asian Affairs on the National Security Council from 1994 to 1997. His book on U.S.-China relations, *Beyond Tiananmen: The Politics of U.S.-China Relations, 1989-2000*, was published by The Brookings Institution in 2003.

This volume, consisting of 37 declassified National Intelligence Estimates (NIEs) and Special National Intelligence Estimates (SNIEs) on China, along with the CD-ROM containing these and 34 other such documents, is a welcome addition to the study of intelligence and policy in the United States Government. It joins several other noteworthy collections by CIA's Center for the Study of Intelligence, including *Watching the Bear: Essays on CIA's Analysis of the Soviet Union* (2003), *CIA's Analysis of the Soviet Union, 1947-1991* (2001), *At Cold War's End: U.S. Intelligence on the Soviet Union and Eastern Europe, 1989-91* (1999), and *CIA Assessments of the Soviet Union: The Record Versus the Charges* (1996)[1] as rich sources of information for historians and political scientists interested in how the intelligence process works, how well it performs its tasks, and what impact it has on policy. The documents in this volume played an essential role in helping U.S. Government leaders and officials formulate policy toward the Communist Party of China during the Chinese civil war and the government of the People's Republic of China (PRC) after its founding in 1949 and during Mao Tse-tung's (Mao Zedong's)[2] leadership.

Equally important, in my view, is the significance of these papers as source documents in our ongoing efforts to understand the PRC, its politics, economics, and foreign policy. Unlike the collections on the Soviet Union, which are retrospectives on a failed Soviet Union and a Cold War now over, these papers contain formative thinking on an existing state, an ongoing challenge to American interests and security. They are, in a sense, some of the foundation stones for a work that is still in progress. Papers on Communist Party leadership issues of 50 years ago remain pertinent to an understanding of how leadership succession and transition issues are carried out in contemporary Beijing. The studies of the Taiwan Strait crises of the 1950s are relevant to the cross-Strait tensions of today, which still see the United States in the middle of the remnants of China's civil war. Echoes of China's involvement in the Korean War can be heard in the Six-Party Talks currently under way to resolve tensions between the United States and North Korea over its nuclear program. And China's economy—now one of the world's largest—is clearly a product of its struggles with industrialization and agricultural modernization, tracked in the Estimates published in this volume.

---

[1] These and other documents are most easily accessed through the CSI Web site at http://www.cia.gov/csi/index.html.

[2] During this period, the US government used the Wade-Giles Romanization system for Chinese names. Later, it adopted the *pinyin* system used in China. In referring to individual Chinese leaders, I will use the Wade-Giles system first, followed by the current spelling in *pinyin*.

On the Subject of Estimates

Before going into details about the papers and their significance, however, it is important to note that all but a few of the papers in this collection were published originally in the form of National Intelligence Estimates or Special National Intelligence Estimates. Unlike other intelligence reports, which focus on current intelligence, Estimates are forward-looking assessments. Such Estimates, from the earliest days of the modern U.S. intelligence system—the product of the National Security Act of 1947—have been considered to be the best analysis of specific issues of national importance or of national crisis situations that could be brought to bear by the Director of Central Intelligence (DCI), with the concurrence of the other intelligence organizations of the United States Government. As DCI Walter Bedell Smith put it in a 1950 meeting of the Intelligence Advisory Council,

> A national intelligence estimate . . . should be compiled and assembled centrally by an agency whose objectivity and disinterestedness are not open to question. . . Its ultimate approval should rest upon the collective judgment of the highest officials in the various intelligence agencies. . . [I]t should command recognition and respect throughout the Government as the best available and presumably the most authoritative estimate. …It is … the clear duty and responsibility of the Central Intelligence Agency under the statute to assemble and produce such coordinated and authoritative Estimates.[3]

Accordingly, the responsibility for drafting Estimates, after briefly being assigned to CIA's Office of Research and Estimates (ORE), was located in CIA's Office of National Estimates (ONE) as of November 1950. ONE performed its estimative task fully, preparing more than 1,500 of them until the office was disestablished in November 1973.[4] ONE was a small organization, consisting of a Board of National Estimates of between five and twelve senior experts, a professional staff of 25-30 regional and functional specialists, and a support staff.[5]

Estimates could be requested (tasked) by the President, members of the National Security Council, any member of the United States Intelligence Board (USIB—predecessor of the National Foreign Intelligence Board, discussed below), or by the leadership of ONE itself. Upon completion by ONE—a process that averaged about 6-8 weeks, Estimates were forwarded to the DCI, who presented them to a USIB meeting for final concurrence. At this point, if individual bureaucracies had specific objections to judgments made in the Estimate, they would be discussed, registered, and entered into the final draft. Final copies of Estimates were disseminated by ONE to 100-300 individuals or offices within the U.S. Government, depending upon classification levels, subject and relevance. After publication, many Estimates also were subjected to a formal review of "intelligence gaps" or shortfalls of information it was hoped could be addressed by intelligence collectors.[6]

---

[3] Quotations from Sherman Kent, *The Law and Custom of the National Intelligence Estimate*, available at http://www.cia.gov/csi/books/shermankent/5law.html.

[4] *Ibid.* The numbering system for Estimates in this collection reflects this organizational history. Estimates produced by ORE bear the office's abbreviated designator. National Intelligence Estimates (NIEs) and Special National Intelligence Estimates (SNIEs) were produced by ONE or the NIO system.

[5] *Ibid.* See also Sherman Kent, *The Making of an NIE*, which is available at http://www.cia.gov/csi/books/shermankent/making.html. This is a particularly valuable essay by the individual who was head of ONE from 1952 to 1967. It discusses in detail the ONE process of preparing an Estimate from beginning to end.

[6] *Ibid.*

To improve responsiveness to intelligence needs and to better engage the Intelligence Community members[7] in the drafting of estimative intelligence, the ONE was succeeded in 1973 by National Intelligence Officers. This group of substantive experts became the National Intelligence Council in 1979.[8] Only two of the papers in this volume and three in the entire collection were produced under the auspices of the NIO system. The final approval for NIEs currently is the responsibility of the National Foreign Intelligence Board, which is chaired by the DCI or Deputy DCI, and consists of the heads of the principal intelligence collection and analytic services in the US Government.[9]

To this day, Estimates remain controversial. Yet for all their controversy they are not always the most critical components of the foreign policy making process. Again, to paraphrase Sherman Kent, estimating is what you do when you do not know something with exactitude or confidence. In discussing large or complex topics, formal intelligence Estimates necessarily have to delve into a realm of speculation, a dense process of trying to separate out the probable from the possible from the impossible, and of providing answers to difficult but important questions with an appropriate degree of uncertainty about incomplete information.

In the course of a 24-year career in the U.S. Government, I have been both a producer and a consumer of intelligence Estimates,[10] and can attest to the variegated role they play in the policy making process. If they are written at the specific request of a policy principal, or focused on an ongoing crisis, Estimates are likely to be read avidly and be an important factor in crisis management and decisionmaking. If they are highly technical and involve weapons of mass destruction, they will be read carefully and be factored into long-range planning processes, particularly by military consumers. If they are more general overviews of internal politics, economic development, or even foreign policy, they are less likely to be read by key policymakers, but they may be highly useful in educating middle-level officials and other members of the Intelligence Community on general policy issues and potential problems just over the (invariably short) horizon of the policy players.

In any case, Kent's advice to those charged with preparing Estimates remains sound. An Estimate,

> …should be relevant within the area of our competence, and above all it should … be credible. Let things be such that if our policymaking master is to disregard our knowledge and wisdom, he will never do so because our work was inaccurate, incomplete, or patently biased. Let him disregard us only when he must pay greater heed to someone else. And let him be uncomfortable—thoroughly uncomfortable— about his decision to heed this other.[11]

Equally important, in my view, NIEs are documents of record, contributions to institutional, and perhaps national, history. Current intelligence analysis disappears quickly and even more thoroughly than yesterday's newspaper. Mid-range analysis is usually remembered only if it's

---

[7] As currently constituted, the Intelligence Community consists of the Central Intelligence Agency; Defense Intelligence Agency, National Security Agency, National Geospatial-Intelligence Agency; National Reconnaissance Office; the State Department's Bureau of Intelligence and Research; Air Force, Army, Coast Guard, Marine Corps and Navy Intelligence; the Federal Bureau of Investigation; Department of Homeland Security; Department of Energy, and the Treasury Department.

[8] For a full description of the NIC, its organization, history, mandate and a selection of its products, go to http://www.cia.gov/nic/NIC_home.html.

[9] This structure was authorized under Director of Central Intelligence Directive 3/1, of January 14, 1997, which can be found at http://www.fas.org/irp/offdocs/dcid3-1.html.

[10] See biographic note at the beginning of this essay.

[11] "Estimates and Influence," Sherman Kent, available at http://www.cia.gov/csi/books/shermankent/4estimates.html

wrong. But Estimates put the big judgments on the record, they represent the collective knowledge of hundreds of intelligence analysts, and they are intended to stand a test of time—in most cases, two to five years. So in a sense, they are written for historians as well as policymakers.

Domestic Politics—The Mao Years

In considering how to divide up and comment on the rather large and unwieldy body of analytical literature provided in this collection, I thought it might be useful to adopt the overall structure of some of the Estimates themselves, particularly the generic overview Estimates, such as NIE 13-58 and NIE 13-60, both entitled *Communist China*. Their usual analytical line of march was to comment on the leadership situation within the party, then move on to economic matters, including sources of public discontent, military capabilities, then foreign policy, finishing with an outlook. I will follow that pattern, looking at what intelligence estimators had to say about China's domestic political environment, economic developments, military capabilities, and finally foreign affairs, specifically Sino-Soviet relations and the Taiwan issue.

People outside the intelligence business often assume that intelligence analysts have unique sources of information—classified data and secret reports—and that therefore their assessments should be more insightful, accurate and predictive; in other words, truer. The documentation provided in this volume leaves little doubt that, at least in the early years of the PRC, intelligence analysts enjoyed few advantages over their academic and journalistic counterparts on the question of the inner workings of the Chinese Communist Party. Beginning with the first post-1949 Estimate on Communist China in 1951, NIE 10, *Communist China*, the estimators came up with a firm judgment about the leadership that scarcely wavered for a decade:

> For the foreseeable future, the Chinese Communist regime will probably retain exclusive governmental control of Mainland China. Although there is undoubtedly much dissatisfaction with the Communist regime in China, it does enjoy a measure of support or acquiescence and is developing strong police controls. No serious split in the Communist regime itself is now indicated.[12]

Three years later, in the more comprehensive NIE 13-54, *Communist China's Power Potential Through 1957*, published in June 1954, it was noted that while a February central committee plenary meeting suggested that "differences and rivalries" appeared to exist within the leadership group led by Mao Tse-tung (Mao Zedong), no "clearly established factions" existed, and the leadership was characterized by "cohesion and stability." The plenum had, in fact, overseen the first major party purge, that of Politburo member Kao Kang (Gao Gang) and Organization Department director Jao Shu-shih (Rao Shushi), but the information would not become public knowledge for another year.

It should come as no surprise that hard information sources during this early period would be sparse. The United States and China did not have formal diplomatic relations, a trade embargo kept commercial contacts to a bare minimum, and a state of extreme ideological hostility permeated the relationship in the wake of the Korean War. Information from Taiwan was not always considered accurate or reliable. Moreover, the PRC itself had put together an extremely effective propaganda and information control operation that kept stories of its internal politics and policy deliberations strictly confidential. Even in 1979, after extensive investigation of party documents and other

---

[12] NIE 10, *Communist China*, January 17, 1951, page 1. All pages cited in NIEs and SNIEs refer to the page numbers of the original documents.

materials released during the Cultural Revolution, Frederick Teiwes would note that the causes and outcomes of the Kao Kang purge remained obscure.[13]

By 1960, evidence of discontent within the upper ranks of the party had grown, and NIE 13-60 noted that the purge of Defense Minister P'eng Te-huai (Peng Dehuai) and several others in 1959 was "probably the result of their questioning of party policies."[14] But the overall judgment of the Estimate was that Mao's authority and support base were such that his views would prevail in party councils, and "factionalism will not be a serious issue while he lives."[15] Three years later, NIE 13-63, *Problems and Prospects in Communist China,* would note that, while the regime's economic policies and the cutoff of Soviet assistance had done "grievous" damage to the Chinese economy and further reduced popular support, Mao retained "ultimate power," along with the core of individuals who had led the party since the 1930s. While the estimators doubted that factionalism would become a problem, the NIE raised "actuarial" concerns about Mao and his colleagues, most of whom were in their late 60s or older.[16]

NIE 13-7-65, *Political Problems and Prospects in Communist China,* represents something of a watershed and is one of the most remarkable documents in the collection. Relentlessly pessimistic, the paper focuses on evidence of ineffective political and economic policies, reduced morale among lower-level party members, increased tensions and attacks on intellectuals in the "socialist education campaign," and a top-level leadership that is "increasingly inflexible and dogmatic." Mao is described as "fearful and suspicious," sensitive to criticism, and increasingly focused on personal loyalty above all else. He "shows a tendency to look back upon his years as a guerrilla leader for methods of coping with modern-day problems" which the writers believe will bring more unworkable policies. Yet the Estimate notes—again accurately—that factionalism, while possible, has not yet become serious enough to "crack the discipline under which the leaders have so long operated."[17]

Nine months later, the "Great Proletarian Cultural Revolution" was in full swing, instigated by Mao against his designated successor Liu Shao-ch'i (Liu Shaoqi) and his cohorts, who were now accused, *inter alia,* of disloyalty, trying to restore capitalism, and practicing factionalism. What ensued was a confusing and chaotic decade-long political struggle that did enormous damage to China's social stability, political system, economy, and foreign policy. In its initial phases, students and analysts of China were often at odds over what appeared to be remarkably self-destructive policies and actions. Two senior CIA analysts wrote articles in *The China Quarterly* during 1967-68, presenting contrasting perspectives on what the raucous and increasingly violent internal political struggle was all about.[18]

One of the unintended consequences of the Cultural Revolution was an explosion of previously unknown documentary material being published in various Chinese newspapers and journals. As members of the Red Guard and Cultural Revolution Group radicals denounced and sought to justify the purges of veteran Party leaders, they published speeches, exposés, articles and other materials that shed considerable light on earlier periods of the party's history. The Foreign Broadcast

---

[13] Frederick C. Teiwes, *Politics & Purges in China: Rectification And The Decline Of Party Norms, 1950-1965,* (New York: M.E. Sharpe, Inc., 1979), pages 166 ff.

[14] NIE 13-60, *Communist China,* December 6, 1960, page 9.

[15] *Ibid.*

[16] NIE 13-63, *Problems and Prospects in Communist China,* May 1, 1963, page 4.

[17] NIE 13-7-65, *Political Problems and Prospects in Communist China,* August 5, 1965, pages 3, 9.

[18] See Philip Bridgham, *Origin and Development [of the Great Proletarian Cultural Revolution]* in *The China Quarterly* No. 29 (January-March 1967), pages 1-35; Philip Bridgham, *Mao's Cultural Revolution in 1967: The Struggle to Seize Power* in *The China Quarterly* No. 34 (April-June 1968), pages 6-37; and Charles Neuhauser, *The Chinese Communist Party in the 1960s: Prelude to the Cultural Revolution* in *The China Quarterly* No 32 (October-December 1967), pages 3-36.

Information Service, Joint Publications Research Service, and the Hong Kong consulate's Survey of Chinese Mainland Publications translated and published extra editions to try to keep up, providing a treasure trove for intelligence analysts and academic specialists alike.[19] In some ways, experts had a glut of information.

But that didn't necessarily make the job of estimating any easier. NIE 13-7-67, *The Chinese Cultural Revolution*, is a carefully balanced effort to try to make some sense of the conflicting information. It is blunt in its evaluation of the unknowns and risks inherent in predicting outcomes. It states, "The political crisis in China continues. No end is in sight. Among the several possible outcomes, no one is distinctly more likely than others."[20] The paper is prophetic in noting that civil war or fragmentation along regional lines was unlikely and in assessing the probability that a cautious group within the military would be inclined to find common ground with moderate political leaders in the post-Mao era. And it reaches careful, but appropriate conclusions about where the movement would go.

> There will probably continue to be fluctuations between more radical initiatives and periods of consolidation or retreat. We cannot predict precise tactics or individual victims at the top. But we can be fairly confident that as long as Mao is capable of political command, China's situation will probably be tense and inherently unstable.[21]

After Mao, the estimators expected a "disorderly and contentious" succession struggle, followed by the gradual abandonment of his "discredited" political and economic policies, with military and civilian leaders attempting to find common ground and restore policies that might "secure modest economic growth."[22] What the Estimate drafters could not know, of course, is that Mao would live for another nine years.

Unfortunately, the collection provides only a few examples of this kind of cogent analysis on China's leadership situation. In NIE 13-9-68, which weighed the impact of the Cultural Revolution on Mao and his adherents, the opposition to Mao and the instruments of power in China were again examined. Also in NIE 13-3-72, *China's Military Policy and General Purpose Forces*, there is considerable discussion of the political turmoil within the military following the purge of Defense Minister Lin Piao (Lin Biao), who was later accused of trying to engineer a coup against Mao.[23] But that carefully constructed tale—still something of a mystery—was not completed at the time of the Estimate, which in any case was devoted to a more thorough discussion of PLA strengths and capabilities. Thus, a discussion of the late phases of the Cultural Revolution is not available among these papers. Part of the reason may lie in the fact that the newly organized National Intelligence Officer system (instituted in 1973) had not put together a research or analytical program on China's internal political situation that was comparable to that of ONE. And perhaps during that period of nascent U.S.-China friendship and relationship-building, there was less call for gloomy assessments of China's muddled political situation. But the tale of the Mao years seems strangely unfinished.

---

[19] Roderick MacFarquhar, in his monumental three-volume study, *The Origins of the Cultural Revolution*, published by Columbia University, makes extensive use of the documentary material released during this period to put together a detailed history of leadership interactions during the 1950s and early 1960s. Although evaluation of the origins of the Cultural Revolution and its political goals remains controversial, NIE 13-7-67 holds up very well both as an accurate accounting of a tumultuous period, and in comparison with some press and academic analysis done during the time.

[20] NIE 13-7-67, *The Chinese Cultural Revolution*, May 25, 1967, page 1.

[21] *Ibid.*, pages 10-11.

[22] *Ibid.*, page 12.

[23] According to later accounts, Lin was killed on September 12, 1971, while trying to flee to the Soviet Union in a commandeered military airliner. Lin's principal lieutenants—who dominated the 9th Central Committee Politburo elected in 1969—and many other military officers were arrested and removed from power in a massive purge of the People's Liberation Army.

The record is nonetheless an impressive one. Of course, it is easy to find mistakes and missed calls, as in any retrospective on estimative material. But the fundamentals are consistently right. The drafters of NIEs during this period had an understanding of Chinese history, a good grasp of the dynamics of a Soviet-style politburo system, and a growing base of information about the personalities and policies of the Beijing government. Their judgments were very general, focused on the threats presented by "Communist China"[24] to U.S. interests, especially in Asia. But they were objective, non-ideological, and balanced, at least in my view. The more important judgment that the Estimates consistently got right was that the Communist Party was never challenged—from 1948 onward—in its predominance of power on the Chinese Mainland, and that Mao was never effectively challenged from within the party. Even when his unrealistic economic policies brought on the disaster of the Great Leap Forward—which the ONE analysts initially underestimated, both in terms of its economic and social impact—or when his ideologically ambitious programs and propaganda led to a split with the Soviet Union, even when his jealous paranoia nearly destroyed the Communist Party during the Cultural Revolution, Mao's leadership was never really in doubt. And even today, Mao's reputation is not open to question within the Communist Party.

Measuring China's Economy

From the period following the Korean War armistice, when "Communist China's" survival as a state seemed assured, the papers provided in this collection make clear that evaluating China's economic policies and performance was an important part of the task of estimating China's performance and prospects. Earlier Estimates, such as the strongly ideological and apparently inaccurate ORE 89-49, *The Food Outlook for Communist China,* and NIE 10, *Communist China*, only looked at economic issues insofar as they might be liabilities to regime survival—and even then warned against trying to use them to undermine the new Communist government. Beginning with NIE 13-54, *Communist China's Power Potential Through 1957*, estimators tried to evaluate and measure China's economic performance and to develop understandable statistical standards. This effort was hampered by the slow development of an economic statistical system in China. The targets of the first five-year plan (1952-57), for example, were not announced until 1955 and were revised almost continuously after that.

The estimators took stock of what was known of China's preliminary economic plan, clearly saw that it was modeled on Soviet lines, and drew their conclusions accordingly.

> Emphasis is placed upon increasing the output of the industrial sector, particularly heavy industry and transport. Fulfillment of the regime's plan depends upon increasing agricultural output while rigorously restricting consumption so as to provide the resources needed to support the industrial investment and military programs. A large part of the capital goods needed to fulfill the program will have to be obtained from the rest of the Soviet bloc in return for Chinese exports.

The Estimate drafters fully recognized the enormity of the tasks facing China and credited the regime with making significant progress in reconstituting an economy shattered by civil war, social turmoil, and decades of mismanagement. They added that China also was faced with serious

---

[24] The use of ideologically-backed terms like "Communist China," rather than "China" or "PRC," or until the 1960s, "Peiping" (Beiping)—the Nationalist Chinese term—rather than Peking (Beijing) does not imply an ideologically biased perspective in these papers. With a few exceptions, they are carefully neutral and non-ideological in their judgments of Chinese actions and accomplishments. They do not shrink from the view that, as part of the international Communist movement, China's goals and practices were intrinsically hostile to the United States. But they do not reflect some of the more extreme perspectives (or terminology) used elsewhere in the public domain— e.g. "Red China," "Chicoms," etc.—during this period.

shortages of technically skilled economic managers and administrators, a costly over-concentration on military production, and a rapidly growing population, all of which would limit growth. Nonetheless, the Estimate concluded that China was likely to achieve a 20-25 percent growth in total output over the course of the first five-year plan. [25]

The next major look at China's economic performance came in NIE 13-58, *Communist China*, which included a five-page annex on the first five-year plan, detailed analysis of central budgetary expenditures, and an assessment of key economic sectoral growth rates. Again, the overall Estimate was upbeat, a carefully nuanced evaluation that concluded China's ambitious goals for its second five-year plan were within reach, if difficult, and dependent upon a number of non-economic variables. One of the most important of these was the very narrow margin of difference between the overall rate of population growth and the growth of agricultural production. In a cautionary footnote, the Estimate added,

> Chinese Communist statistics on which the data and analyses throughout this Estimate are based are subject to the same reservations as those of other Bloc countries, but to a somewhat greater extent, in view of the inexperience on the part of the newly established Chinese Communist statistical collection system. . . . Chinese Communist statistics are the basis for the regime's planning and we believe are not, in general, misrepresented. [26]

In retrospect, the Estimate's economic projections proved to be substantially wrong, and China's economy suffered catastrophic setbacks in the following two years. While the Estimate's analysis represented good-faith and methodologically sound attempts to draw on existing quantitative data for estimates of future performance, the drafters underestimated the degree of political interference that Mao would introduce into the economic planning and production system. And although they tried to factor in statistical inaccuracies, they could not have predicted the massive and deliberate misrepresentation of production data that characterized the "Great Leap Forward" from its inception. They were not alone in that error; not only other Western academic experts, but the entire Chinese economic planning system seemed disoriented and unable to comprehend the scale of China's economic problems during those years.

By 1963, the regime's economic travails were better understood, even if the political struggles that lay behind them remained opaque. NIE 13-63, *Problems and Prospects in Communist China*, presented a harsh assessment of the Great Leap and its aftermath: "During the past five years, . . . Communist China's economy has been grievously mismanaged. The leadership has been handicapped by inadequate economic training and experience, limited by a narrow doctrine, and misled by fanaticism."[27] It attributed a considerable degree of the damage to China's economy to the withdrawal of Soviet aid and expertise that accompanied the Sino-Soviet split. (See section that follows on Sino-Soviet Relations.) The paper also included a lengthy annex analyzing China's economic performance in 1962—a very general, sectoral evaluation based on non-Chinese statistics or internal CIA estimates. It held out the possibility of a continuing recovery—perhaps to the general level of productivity achieved in 1957—if the regime focused its attention on improving agricultural production and continued "to pursue relatively moderate and reasonable policies and if it has reasonable luck with the weather." It warned, however, that the margin between success and failure remained so slim as to render any estimate of China's economic future "general and tentative."[28]

China's economic problems remained the focus of Estimates in the following three years, and ONE analysts saw their worst-case scenarios coming true. NIE 13-5-67, *Economic Outlook for*

---

[25] NIE 13-54, *Communist China's Power Potential Through 1957*, June 3, 1954, page 1.
[26] NIE 13-58, *Communist China*, May 23, 1958, page 22 footnote 1.
[27] NIE 13-63 *Problems and Prospects in Communist China*, May 1, 1963, page 5.
[28] *Ibid.*, page 6.

Communist China, reflects an implicit sense of frustration at the continuing failure of the economy to fulfill its potential. It states,

> There seems little doubt that economic performance has declined this year, but it is impossible to quantify the decline. . . Peking has published little useful data since 1960. With economic planning in a state of suspended animation, it seems likely that major economic initiatives will be postponed until some resolution of the political struggle is achieved.

Nonetheless, the Estimate judged that efforts were being made to insulate basic economic production from the worst excesses of the Cultural Revolution, and an economic crisis did not appear to be imminent.[29]

The NIE collection does not provide any further examples of focused economic analysis. Part of the reason is perhaps organizational—CIA's Directorate of Intelligence formed an Office of Economic Research in 1966, and it assumed the task of providing detailed and statistical analysis of China's economy, developing sophisticated techniques and models to compensate for the paucity of official economic statistics but for the most part reporting its findings through channels other than ONE. Another reason is that China's economy continued to stumble along for the next ten years, and the policy community's interests shifted to more urgent issues involving China's strategic weapons programs and its foreign policies toward the Soviet Union and the United States.

In looking at the extraordinary "takeoff" of the Chinese economy of the last 20 years, its rapid achievement of global significance and the changes it has brought to ordinary Chinese, it is difficult to see how it might have emerged from the economic shambles described in these Estimates. It is worth noting, however, that for a significant percentage of China's population—those dwelling in the rural areas away from the coast—real economic conditions may not have changed so radically from what is depicted in these Estimates. Agricultural production still lags urban industrial development, excess farm population remains a serious drag on the economy, and rural discontent continues to challenge the political leadership, echoing developments described in these Estimates. China may be under new economic management, but some of the old problems linger.

The Military Challenge and China's Strategic Weapons Programs

Very few of the Estimates in this collection failed to take account of, and several focused exclusively on, the development of the People's Liberation Army (PLA), in earlier years referred to as the "Chinese Communist army," into an effective fighting force and a threat to the security interests of the United States. Irrespective of the variations of ideological concern evident in these papers—and it varied in interesting ways—the notion that Chinese military capabilities merited respect and concern is evident throughout.

- In describing the shocking collapse of the Nationalist Chinese in the civil war, ORE 77-48 observed in 1948: "The strength and tactical success of the Chinese Communist [Armed] Forces have been the chief instruments in the ascent of the Communist Party, and will continue to be so . . ."[30]

- On the eve of China's entry into the Korean War in 1950, another NIE stated: "The Chinese Communist Forces are . . . believed capable either of: a) halting further UN advance northward

---

[29] NIE 13-5-67, *Economic Outlook for Communist China*, June 29, 1967, page 4.
[30] ORE 77-48, *Communist Capabilities for Control of All China*, December 10, 1948, page 1.

by matching any foreseeable UN buildup with piecemeal commitment of forces . . . ; or b) forcing UN withdrawal further south through a powerful assault."[31]

- NIE 13-54 considered In 1954: "The internal control and international power position enjoyed by the Communist regime rest largely upon the power potential of China's military establishment, at present the largest of any Asian nation."[32]

- In the 1958 Quemoy-Matsu crisis, SNIE 100-9-58 warned: "If opposed only by Chinese Nationalist forces, the Chinese Communists have the capability to deny the Taiwan Strait to the Chinese Nationalist air force, interdict supply of the offshore islands, or seize these islands."[33]

- Assessing China's strategic aspirations after it tested both fission and fusion weapons in the mid-1960s, NIE 13-8-67 observed: "The present leaders probably believe that the successful development of strategic weapons would greatly enhance their prestige and strengthen their claims to leadership in Asia and their status as a great power . . . the Chinese may believe the ability to strike the U.S. and targets in Asia with nuclear weapons would serve to limit U.S. military operations in Asia and to keep any confrontation at the level of conventional arms where the Chinese would expect to enjoy many advantages."[34]

A corollary to the assessment that the Beijing regime was reliant on its military forces and had invested significant economic resources into their development was the observation in several of the papers in this collection that Beijing's leaders were chary of risking a direct military confrontation with the United States, either strategic or conventional. This was probably partly the result of the Korean War, when Mao did throw enormous numbers of troops into a conventional war against American troops and suffered heavy casualties only to bring about an indeterminate result—the tense armistice that continues today. That reluctance may also have been a result of the 1954-55 Quemoy-Matsu crisis when U.S. President Dwight Eisenhower threatened the use of tactical nuclear weapons against Mainland targets if the PRC attacked the Nationalist-controlled offshore islands of Quemoy (Chin-men or Jinmen) or Matsu (Mazu).[35] Most importantly, however, Beijing's caution was part of Mao's own military doctrine, which stressed defense of Chinese territorial integrity and sovereignty, "People's War," and a prudent approach to a militarily superior American foe. NIE 13-3-67 put this succinctly:

> Although the threat of force and its actual use beyond China's borders are significant elements in Peking's outlook, Chinese military strategy places primary emphasis on defense. With the possible exception of their nuclear/missile activities, we do not see in train the general programs, the development or deployment of forces, or the doctrinal discussions which would suggest a more forward strategy. At least for the short term, the high-priority nuclear program is probably viewed by the Chinese as primarily for deterrence . . .[36]

---

[31] NIE 2, *Chinese Communist Intervention in Korea*, November 6, 1950 (two weeks before the "Chinese People's Volunteers" entered the war in force), page 3.

[32] NIE 13-54, *op.cit.*, page 2.

[33] SNIE 100-9-58, *Probable Developments in the Taiwan Strait Area*, August 26, 1958, page 2.

[34] NIE 13-8-67, *Communist China's Strategic Weapons Program*, August 3, 1967, page 3.

[35] See Robert Accinelli, *Crisis And Commitment: United States Policy toward Taiwan, 1950-1955*, (Chapel Hill, NC: University of North Carolina Press, 1996) and Thomas E. Stolper, *China, Taiwan, and the Offshore Islands: Together with an Implication for Outer Mongolia and Sino-Soviet Relations*, (Armonk, NY: M. E. Sharpe, Inc., 1985).

[36] NIE 13-3-67, *Communist China's Military Policy and Its General Purpose and Air Defense Forces*, April 6, 1967, page 1.

Two SNIEs on China's response and involvement in the Vietnam War and three on the Taiwan Strait Crisis of 1958 make clear the different estimators were certain of their analysis that China would not risk an open confrontation with the United States. In 1966, for example, after the United States Air Force had expanded and intensified its bombing of North Vietnamese targets near Hanoi and Haiphong, ONE was asked to evaluate the prospects for China becoming more actively involved in combat operations. SNIE 13-66 declared: "At present levels of U.S. action against [North Vietnam], we continue to believe that China will not commit its ground or air forces to sustained combat against the U.S. In our view, neither the Chinese nor the North Vietnamese regard the present situation as critical enough to justify outside intervention with its attendant risks of a much wider war, ultimately including the threat of nuclear war . . . ."[37] They believed China would continue to be involved in helping North Vietnam resist American military pressure—including the deployment of some support troops—but would not engage as they had done in Korea.

Likewise in the Taiwan Strait situation, the baseline estimate in May 1958 had been that China would "not resort to military action to seize Taiwan, so long as this would involve risk of war with the U.S."[38] It did hold out the possibility that China would take a "more aggressive" approach to the offshore islands. When the PLA artillery units across from Chin-men began shelling the island heavily in late August 1959, the National Security Council requested an Estimate on Chinese Communist intentions. SNIE 100-9-58 reiterated that the actions were intended to test U.S. and "Republic of China" government intentions, but that China's armed forces, while they had the capability to attack the offshore islands, were "probably deterred because of their fear of U.S. intervention."[39]

When the PRC upped the ante by declaring it would interdict Nationalist resupply of the Chin-men garrison and would fire on any ships in its territorial waters, another Estimate was prepared. This one, SNIE 100-11-58, hedged a bit, saying the PRC seemed to be displaying a greater willingness to risk war with the United States. It predicted that, should Washington choose to use the U.S. Navy to resupply the island or escort Nationalist shipping into PRC territorial waters, China "would probably attack the U.S. force." However, the estimators reiterated that it still did not appear as though either China or the Soviet Union were preparing for a large-scale conflict.[40] President Dwight Eisenhower chose to have the U.S. Navy escort Nationalist resupply ships up to the three-mile limit of PRC territorial waters, while at the same time again threatening nuclear attacks against PRC forces should the war widen, and reopening diplomatic talks with China in Warsaw. In early October, Chinese artillery barrages were lifted for a week to allow resupply without interference, and the crisis gradually wound down. Follow-up SNIEs in late October 1958 and in February 1959 reiterated the point that the Chinese backed down in the face of U.S. resolve to defend the offshore islands.

In retrospect, China's inability to counter either U.S. conventional or nuclear capabilities in the Taiwan Strait, and the clearly limited Soviet willingness to back up its Chinese ally during the crisis (a point also noted in the Estimates) no doubt contributed both to the increase in Sino-Soviet tensions and to China's decision to accelerate its own program to develop strategic weapons. After 1960, that program became the focus of increasing attention for estimators, who produced thirteen Estimates on the subject between 1962 and 1974. Knowledge of the Chinese program was driven largely by increasingly sophisticated intelligence collection programs, particularly satellite imagery, which began to be available in the early 1960s. The nature of those programs—and their continuing relevance to collection and analysis of intelligence today—accounts for the heavy redaction to be found in most of the papers dealing with China's efforts to develop its nuclear program.

---

[37] SNIE 13-66, *Current Chinese Communist Intentions in the Vietnam Situation*, August 4, 1966, page 5.
[38] NIE 13-58, *op.cit.*, page 19.
[39] SNIE 100-9-58, *op.cit.*, page 5.
[40] SNIE 100-11-58, September 16, 1958, pages 1-2.

Viewing heavily redacted documents can be a frustrating process and will not yield many unique insights into the nature of either China's nuclear weapons or strategic missile programs. The redacted documents do demonstrate the intense interest and concern that the programs generated in both the United States and the Soviet Union. They also reveal that estimating a country's nuclear capabilities—much less intentions—on the basis of a few photographs and other scarce clues has been an imprecise science from the start. In the first major Estimate on China's strategic weapons program, NIE 13-2-60[41], ONE estimators judged that the first nuclear detonation would most probably occur in 1963, though possibly in 1964 or 1962 depending on the degree of Soviet assistance. On the other hand, SNIE 13-4-64, *The Chances of an Imminent Chinese Communist Nuclear Explosion*, for example, published in late August 1964, noted the apparent readiness of the test site at Lop Nor (now Lop Nur), but saw few indications that a sufficient amount of fissionable material was available for a bomb, and concluded a test was unlikely before the end of the year. The test took place on October 16, 1964.

The speed with which the Chinese nuclear program developed remains a matter of surprise. Two years after its first atmospheric test, China announced it had tested a nuclear weapon aboard a guided missile, and in June 1967, it conducted its first test of a thermonuclear weapon. This impressive progress took place despite significant weakness in the Chinese economy and amid growing chaos in the political system caused by the Cultural Revolution. The apparent insulation of China's strategic weapons programs from the turmoil of the larger society impressed the drafters of NIE 13-8-67, *Communist China's Strategic Weapons Program*, with the sense of determination that lay behind the program. But the speed of its development had left the estimators with "little evidence on Chinese thinking with respect to the role of nuclear weapons in [China's] overall strategy."[42] They did not appear to believe China was going to attempt to match U.S. or Soviet strategic programs in scale or lethality, and pointed out that substantial technical and logistical problems remained to be resolved. They concluded that the Chinese program "will be limited in scope, and in qualitative and quantitative achievements over the next decade, by the industrial, technological and skilled manpower weaknesses of China."[43]

Nonetheless, the program was alarming, particularly to the USSR, during a period when Chinese foreign as well as domestic policy was in an extraordinarily radical phase. The Sino-Soviet dispute deteriorated into open hostility and hatred during the mid-1960s, and finally into armed conflict in 1969, when Chinese and Soviet troops fought pitched battles at several places along their border. NIE 11/13-69, *The USSR and China*, speculated that the Soviet leadership showed signs of thinking about and preparing for a military showdown with China, one goal of which might be "using their air superiority to knock out Chinese nuclear and missile installations, while blocking Chinese retaliatory attacks on the ground with their own theater forces."[44] The estimators viewed that as being unlikely to achieve Moscow's goals, and as having extremely grave consequences, but could not rule out the possibility. In the end, cooler heads prevailed and the dispute eased somewhat, but the importance of China's strategic weapons—and also their vulnerability—was a key factor in U.S. strategic assessments of China that followed.

By 1974, the new NIO system had produced an Estimate that had somewhat firmer judgments about both the intentions and the scope of China's strategic programs. The program was judged to have slowed—owing to political, economic and technical constraints—and was aimed at developing a "token nuclear capability to strike the USSR west of the Urals and the continental U.S."[45] Rather than being a headlong rush to develop strategic weapons at all costs, the programs were now

---

[41] NIE 13-2-60, *The Chinese Communist Atomic Energy Program*, 13 December 1969, page 3.
[42] NIE 13-8-67, *op.cit.*, page 3.
[43] *Ibid.*, page 13.
[44] NIE 11/13-69, *The USSR and China*, August 12, 1969, page 7.
[45] NIE 13-8-74, *China's Strategic Attack Programs*, page 3.

considered to reflect both the domestic political realities of a chastened military (in the wake of the Lin Biao purges), and a less alarmed perception of their international situation, both in terms of a reduced threat from the USSR as well as improved ties to the United States. China was judged to have about 130 missiles and bombers capable of carrying nuclear weapons, and was expected to have as many as six intercontinental ballistic missiles capable of targeting the United States by the end of the decade, along with some submarine-launched missiles.[46]

China's military capabilities, including its strategic weapons programs, remain a topic of intense interest to U.S. Government policymakers. In some ways, little in the strategic relationship between China and the United States has changed in the nearly 30 years since the last Estimate in this collection was written. China maintains a small but credible nuclear force invulnerable to a first strike, has a full array of missiles capable of hitting U.S. bases or allies in East Asia, and a few weapons with sufficient range to strike the continental United States. The nature of the U.S.-China relationship has undergone fundamental changes for the better, largely because of the changes tracked through these Estimates in China's foreign policy. Few would argue, however, that it would make sense to ease or discontinue efforts to understand the People's Liberation Army and its conventional and strategic capabilities.

Sino-Soviet Relations in American Eyes

From the earliest papers in this collection, the close affiliation between the Communist Party of China and the party-government of the Soviet Union was taken for granted, and was deemed to be inimical to American interests. ORE 45-48, looking at the perilous position of the Nationalist Government of Chiang Kai-shek in July 1948, judged that a Nationalist collapse and replacement by a Chinese Communist Party "under Soviet influence if not under Soviet control," was the "worst prospect," but one increasingly likely.[47] Six months later, after Communist armies had defeated the Nationalists in Jinan, Jinzhou, Shenyang and other key cities, the estimators knew the outcome was no longer in doubt: "There are no effective Nationalist forces" capable of sustained resistance, they judged. As for the Communist Party of China,

> It shares with the USSR a common ideology, a common political organization, common strategies and techniques, and at present, a common goal. The Chinese Communist Party has never publicly deviated from the Soviet Party line, has never publicly criticized any Soviet action or representative, and has never publicly given any indication whatsoever that it could be oriented away from the USSR and toward the United States. It is certain that the Chinese Communist Party *has been and is an instrument of Soviet policy.*

There was "no chance of a split," at least for the present.[48]

The equation of Chinese and Soviet systems, policies and interests was fully justified in the wake of the establishment of the People's Republic in 1949. Beijing made its allegiance to Moscow perfectly clear in its political structure and practices, as well as its policies. The Treaty of Friendship, Alliance and Mutual Assistance signed in February 1950 linked the two countries in what looked to be a strong defense pact. China's intervention in the Korean War in 1950 was assumed to be an example of doing Moscow's bidding.

---

[46] *Ibid.*, There was some dispute within the intelligence community on the numbers, with both the Navy and Air Force taking footnotes to the quantitative estimate of China's future weapons development.

[47] ORE 45-48, *The Current Situation in China*, July 22, 1948, page 2.

[48] ORE 77-48, *Chinese Communist Capabilities for Control of All China*, December 12, 1948, pages 3, 8, emphasis added.

Nonetheless, watching for a split or strain in what was perceived to be a critical relationship became a consistent theme of estimators looking at both the PRC and the Soviet Bloc as a whole. They shared this interest with academic observers as well. With the benefit of hindsight, it is tempting to compare them, to see who, if anyone, "got it right" first. That is not a particularly fruitful exercise. As early as 1952, the drafters of NIE 58, *Relations Between the Chinese Communist Regime and the USSR*, identified areas to watch for possible strain in relations, including efforts by the USSR to intensify its control over China, military and economic assistance, border demarcation issues, relations with other Communist movements in Asia, and Mao's ideological role in the overall Communist movement. They concluded, however, that the mutual interests of the two countries and parties—and particularly the shared goal of eliminating American influence in Asia—would outweigh factors that might drive them apart.[49] Academic experts, writing slightly later, drew similar conclusions.[50]

The strains began in 1956, with Nikita Khrushchev's denunciation of Stalin at the 20th Congress of the Communist Party of the Soviet Union in February (which the Chinese resented), grew with Soviet contempt for Mao's decision to form "communes" during the Great Leap Forward in 1958, and reached a serious stage with Moscow's reluctance to back China during the 1958 Quemoy-Matsu crisis, and with Khrushchev's efforts to develop a closer relationship with Washington. But the strains remained hidden beneath a continuing patina of socialist solidarity for more than a year, only breaking into open polemics in April 1960.[51] In August, NIE 100-3-60, *Sino-Soviet Relations*, noted a "sharp increase in discord," between the "two voices of authority" within the Communist movement. The paper thoroughly examined all aspects of the increasingly complex Sino-Soviet relationship, and concluded: "We believe the cohesive forces in the Sino-Soviet relationship are stronger than the divisive forces and are likely to remain so throughout the [five-year] period of this estimate, at least." Nonetheless, while an open break was unlikely, so was a fundamental reconciliation of their increasingly divergent views.[52]

In November 1960, Moscow convened a major international conference of communist parties, in hopes of restoring a semblance of discipline within the movement. But the long and contentious meeting, which ended up merely exacerbating the split between the Chinese and Soviet parties, did not result in an open break. An Estimate done the following year, NIE 10-61, *Authority and Control in the Communist Movement*, summed up the increasingly tattered state of the movement, but did not alter the judgment of the previous year that the Sino-Soviet dispute would persist but would not necessarily worsen. And indeed, after the removal of Khrushchev in 1964, Soviet leaders did appear to be trying to patch up the relationship with China. But everyone misjudged Mao and his ability to impose his views on Chinese policy, including its foreign policy. In his increasingly sharp disputes with his domestic adversaries, Mao used accusations of support for Soviet "revisionism" to

---

[49] See NIE 58, *Relations Between the Chinese Communist Regime and the USSR: Their Present Character and Probable Future Course*, September 10, 1952, pages 2-5.

[50] See, for example, Howard L. Boorman, Alexander Eckstein, Philip E. Mosely, and Benjamin Schwartz, *Moscow-Peking Axis: Strengths and Strains*, (New York: Harper & Brothers Publishers, 1957); W. W. Rostow, *The Prospects for Communist China*, (Cambridge, MA: Technology Press of the Massachusetts Institute of Technology, 1954), particularly chapter 4.

[51] For an excellent summary of the entire range of CIA analysis of the Sino-Soviet split, including some of the estimates included in this collection, see Harold P. Ford, "Calling the Sino-Soviet Split," in *Studies in Intelligence*, Winter 1998-1999, available at http://www.cia.gov/csi/studies/winter98_99/art05.html.

[52] NIE 100-3-60, *Sino-Soviet Relations*, August 9, 1960, page 14. Some academic studies during the period did see a more direct tie between domestic politics and the Sino-Soviet rift. See, for example, Donald S. Zagoria, *The Sino-Soviet Conflict: 1956-1961* (Princeton: Princeton University Press, 1962), William E. Griffith, *The Sino-Soviet Rift* (Cambridge, MA: The MIT Press, 1964), and David Floyd, *Mao Against Khrushchev: A Short History of the Sino-Soviet Conflict* (New York: Praeger, 1964).

undermine Liu Shaoqi, Deng Xiaoping and others, and attacks on the Soviet Union became even more venomous.

By 1966, ONE was ahead of the curve in understanding the fact that the volatility of China's domestic politics would also affect its foreign policy. "Sino-Soviet relations will continue to deteriorate so long as the Mao Tse-tung – Lin Piao leadership group retains authority," the estimators concluded in an overview of the bilateral relationship that year. While the estimators still thought an open break in state relations was unlikely, they stated

> ...we cannot completely exclude a sudden explosion of the dispute into a new and more virulent form. . . . If China's power began to give punch to its national assertiveness, serious trouble could develop, particularly over the frontiers.[53]

Three years later, clashes along the Sino-Soviet border in Heilongjiang and Xinjiang took the relationship to its lowest state, and estimators observed that it was "reasonable to ask whether a major Sino-Soviet war could break out in the near future." Again, with a balanced perspective on the interests of both sides and the seriously damaging repercussions of a deepening of the conflict, they concluded that a war would not be initiated by China, and that the Soviet Union might consider a preemptive strike against China's strategic weapons facilities but probably would decide against it.[54] As to whether the antagonistic state of relations between the USSR and China might induce either to alter policies toward Washington, the Estimate was downbeat. Moscow might be "accommodating on minor issues . . . We are not suggesting that the Soviets presently contemplate any sacrifice of essential positions—e.g. the division of Germany and the legitimacy of a Soviet sphere in Eastern Europe. Even less likely is a major revision of China's anti-U.S. stance."[55] On September 11, 1969, Soviet Premier Alexei Kosygin stopped off in Beijing on his way back from Ho Chi Minh's funeral in Hanoi and conferred with Premier Zhou Enlai at the airport about the prospect of re-opening negotiations to resolve the border dispute. Zhou was non-committal, and reportedly warned Kosygin against a Soviet strike against Chinese nuclear bases. In late September, China exploded two thermonuclear devices at Lop Nur, one of them estimated to be more than three megatons. On October 7, China agreed to resume border negotiations, thereby easing the crisis considerably.[56]

The final Sino-Soviet Estimate in this collection was done in 1973 and concluded that

> The Sino-Soviet relationship, while it will continue to move through varying degrees of tension, is more likely to move toward lessened tension than toward war.

The paper looked at the prospects for and implications of both possibilities, and noted that a continuation of the troubled peace, with neither war nor reconciliation, seemed the most likely prospect. It again cautioned against any expectation that the West might be able to benefit from either an improvement or deterioration of the Sino-Soviet relationship.[57]

---

[53] NIE 11/12-66, *The Outlook for Sino-Soviet Relations,* December 1, 1966, pages 1-2.

[54] NIE 11/13-69, *op. cit.*, pages 1, 8.

[55] *Ibid.,* page 10. See Patrick E. Tyler, *A Great Wall: Six Presidents and China—An Investigative History,* (New York: Public Affairs Press, 1999), pages 61-69 for an interesting, if speculative account of how the Sino-Soviet border clashes affected the Nixon Administration's strategic thinking with respect to China, the USSR, and North Vietnam.

[56] China's Foreign Ministry account of the Zhou-Kosygin meeting can be found at http://www.fmprc.gov.cn/eng/ziliao/3602/3604/t18005.htm; Chinese nuclear test information is available at http://fas.org/nuke/guide/china/nuke/tests.htm.

[57] NIE 11/13/6-73, *Possible Changes in the Sino-Soviet Relationship*, October 25, 1973.

Overall, the papers on Sino-Soviet relations represent sound, cautious examination of complex issues, characteristic of inter-bureaucratic analysis in their nuanced evaluations of scenarios and possibilities, and their propensity to predict a continuation of the status quo. In many cases, that approach correctly predicted the outcome. In all cases, the Estimates presented the available evidence in useful summaries that enabled policy-level readers to understand the background of the evolving relationship. They fell short, in my view, in three areas: 1) over-estimating the importance of ideological solidarity and other centripetal forces within the Communist Bloc—at least in the 1950s; 2) having insufficient evidence of the impact of domestic politics on foreign policy in China; and 3) not being able (authorized) to evaluate fully the impact of U.S. policy choices on the foreign affairs decisions of the People's Republic of China or the Soviet Union. The last consideration is no fault of the estimators but was and still is a function of the need to maintain strict boundaries between intelligence analysis and policymaking.

The PRC-ROC-US Triangle

For the last of the three reasons cited above, the papers on the complex relationship among the United States, the People's Republic of China, and the Republic of China (ROC) are the least illuminating of the collection. For 25 of the 28 years covered by these Estimates, the United States and China were locked in an implacably hostile relationship, in which no change was sought or expected. "The Chinese Communists are following a course of action designed to destroy U.S. strategic interests in the Far East and to reduce the worldwide power position of the U.S. and its allies," asserted NIE 10 in 1951,[58] and that judgment remained remarkably consistent for the ensuing two decades. Whether focused on Southeast Asia, Korea/Japan, or the Taiwan issue, Communist China's hostility to the United States, its interests and allies was taken for granted by ONE estimators. It was also axiomatic that China's strategic goal was to become the most powerful force in Asia. According to NIE 13-60: "A basic tenet of Communist China's foreign policy—to establish Chinese hegemony in the Far East—almost certainly will not change appreciably [for the next five years]."[59] NIE 13-9-65 took the case even further:

> For both ideological and nationalistic reasons, China regards the U.S. as its primary enemy. Peiping's immediate security interests and the short reach of its military power lead it to concentrate its main foreign policy efforts on undermining the US position in the Far East.[60]

Even in the wake of the obvious failures of China's foreign policy during the Cultural Revolution, NIE 13-69 (an excellent summary of 20 years of Chinese foreign policy) would insist, "Almost all Chinese—whether in Peking or on Taiwan—would agree that China's rightful position is one of political dominance on the Asian mainland, and ultimately throughout East and Southeast Asia."[61]

One could find fault with this kind of approach, on the grounds that it appears somewhat ideological—Cold War-like—and is seldom backed up with substantiating quotes from Chinese leaders about their own strategic goals. But the available facts suggest that the Estimates were well-grounded in reality. It may seem like a distant and strange memory today, but the Cold War was real in the 1950s and 1960s. Chinese official statements and rhetoric about the United States during that period are remarkably negative, shrill, and hostile. Nothing in them could be seen as accommodating or even vaguely desirous of improving bilateral relations. Estimative analysis of China's foreign policy aspirations, in fact, seems generally understated, or at least low-key. And the

---

[58] NIE 10, *op.cit.*, page 2.
[59] NIE 13-60, op.cit., page 2.
[60] NIE 13-9-65, *Communist China's Foreign Policy*, May 5, 1965, page 1.
[61] NIE 13-69, *Communist China and Asia*, March 6, 1969, pages 6-7.

standards of objectivity, even on subjects relevant to American interest, were quite high in the papers in this collection.

That is particularly true with regard to the Taiwan issue. Even though the subject was not often raised, the papers in this collection are crisp and objective, and were not without controversy when they were written. The early ORE papers are particularly intriguing, especially when read in the context of the times—when China's civil war and American involvement in it were coming to an unhappy end, when controversy over China policy was swirling between the Departments of Defense and State, and between the executive and legislative branches, when anti-Communism was rising to a fever pitch in the United States. In July 1948, just after Congress had passed the China Aid Act, appropriating an additional $125 million for Chiang Kai-shek's government to use to procure additional military equipment, ORE 45-48, *The Current Situation in China*, delivered bleak news:

> The position of the current Nationalist Government is so precarious that its fall may occur at any time … Even with the current US aid program, the present Nationalist Government has little prospect of reversing or even checking these trends of disintegration. The power and prestige of Chiang Kai-shek is steadily weakening because of the unsuccessful prosecution of the war and his apparent unwillingness and inability to accomplish positive reforms.[62]

The paper probably played a role in buttressing those in the State Department, including Secretary George Marshall and head of Policy Planning George Kennan, who were arguing for limiting the U.S. commitment of more aid to Chiang Kai-shek.[63] It certainly was not in agreement with U.S. military estimates that more effective supply of American arms would enable the Nationalists to hold out.

In early December 1948, on the eve of a visit to the United States by Madame Chiang Kai-shek to plead for more military and economic aid, ORE 77-48 *Chinese Communist Capabilities*, predicted that Nationalist resistance would collapse within a matter of months. Once the collapse had been completed, Communist forces would mop up all further local resistance "at leisure" and proceed to establish a nominal coalition government, dominated entirely by the Communist Party. The paper credited the Communist Party with effective military and logistical work, noted that it was pursuing "moderate" land reform policies in areas it already controlled, and faulted the Nationalist Government for its inability to undertake any meaningful economic or political reform.[64] Comparable objectivity on the part of State Department desk officers would draw accusations from some members of Congress that they were a "Red cell" of Communist sympathizers within the Far Eastern Bureau. The controversy eventually cost several China experts within the State Department their jobs and reputations.[65]

In selecting the Estimates for this collection, the editors chose not to include those that dealt with the government of the Republic of China (GRC) after Chiang Kai-shek set it up on Taiwan in 1949. The Estimates on the Taiwan Strait crises of the 1950s were included because of their attention to Peiping's role. Hopefully, those Estimates dealing with the Nationalists post-1949 will be included in later collections. In the Estimates on the Strait crises we have here, ONE analysts maintained a scrupulously objective approach to the issues at hand. NIE 100-9-58, *Probable Developments in the Taiwan Strait Area*—disseminated during the high point of the crisis in August 1958—speculated that the renewed attacks on the offshore islands were in part motivated by frustration on the part of

---

[62] ORE 45-48 *The Current Situation in China*, published July 22, 1948.
[63] See *Foreign Relations of the United States, 1948, Vol. VII, The Far East: China*, pages 118-154.
[64] ORE 77-48, *Chinese Communist Capabilities for Control of All China*, December 10, 1948.
[65] Tang Tsou, *America's Failure in China, 1941-50* (Chicago: University of Chicago Press, 1963), page 466.

"Chinese Communist" leaders that their efforts have "failed to visibly advance them toward their goal of ending the existence of the GRC [Government of the Republic of China]," nor have they prevented "wider international acceptance of a *de facto* 'two China' situation," or displaced the GRC at the United Nations. Nationalist objectives were equally frankly described as maintaining GRC prestige, keeping alive hope of returning to the Mainland, sustaining public morale, gaining more U.S. aid and a firmer commitment to Taiwan's defense and—for some unnamed officials—embroiling the United States in a war with Communist China.[66] The Estimate concluded with what came very close to being policy recommendations, judging that "lesser measures" by the United States, such as deploying more ships, providing Taiwan with more weapons, or issuing "warnings in general terms" would not deter the Chinese from their pressure campaign against the offshore islands.

In the end, the U.S. commitment to Taiwan was demonstrated conclusively to both Taiwan and the mainland, despite the Eisenhower Administration's obvious reluctance to be drawn into a costly war over indefensible and strategically valueless offshore islands. And despite the fact that Moscow made explicit threats to Washington to retaliate with nuclear weapons should the United States use them against China—Khrushchev's letter of September 19—its willingness to come to Beijing's aid was perceived to be hollow and conditional both by the United States and by China.

Although the subject of Taiwan in the relationship between the PRC and the United States would become a central issue in the negotiations that attended the visit of President Richard Nixon to China in 1972 (and remains the most sensitive issue in bilateral relations to this day), the topic never gets more than a passing notice in other Estimates in this collection. This is in some ways a result of the enhanced capabilities of policymakers, who no longer felt obligated to buttress their own appraisals of China's policies toward the United States with intelligence community papers. And it is in some ways a reflection of the growth in overall U.S.-China relations. No longer distant, dimly-perceived antagonists, Chinese leaders, in the mid-1970s, became frequent interlocutors of American presidents, national security advisers and secretaries of state, who began to understand their opinions, goals and intentions—so they believed—better than a committee made up of cautious generalists in the CIA headquarters.

Nevertheless, this collection reminds us once again of the value of Estimates for a long-range understanding of China and its policies. Combining historical appraisals and summaries with current events and a willingness to speculate about future contingencies, Estimates at their best were critical roadmaps for important issues confronting policymakers. They provided context, background, trends, predictions, and the observations and judgments of seasoned experts on the vital issues of the day. They offered important opportunities for members of the IC to focus their attention and pool their wisdom on issues of policy significance. And in retrospect, they make for fascinating reading for those who want to know more about intelligence analysis, the U.S. policy process, the People's Republic of China, and the early years of the U.S.-China relationship. I commend and thank the National Intelligence Council and the editors and declassification experts of CIA's Information Management Services for making this unique collection of papers available to the general public.

---

[66] SNIE 100-9-58, *op.cit.*, pages 5-6.

苏葆立

作者为职业情报分析家,从事情报分析工作长达二十四年,1989年至1994年,在国家情报委员会担任主管东亚事务的副国家情报官,1997年至1998年,担任主管东亚事务的国家情报官,1994年至1997年,在国家安全委员会担任亚洲事务部主任. 曾著有*天安门事件之后:有关美中关系的政治, 1989-2000*, 由布鲁金斯学会2003年出版.

本汇编收录了有关中国的销密国家情报评估与特别国家情报评估共三十七份,包括存有七十一份相关文件的只读光盘一张. 为研究美国政府情报工作与政策提供了一份备受欢迎的补充资料. 中央情报局的情报研究中心所编纂的其他优秀汇编, 如*观熊:中央情报局对苏联的分析文章(2003), 中央情报局对苏联的分析, 1947-1991 (2001), 冷战结束之际: 美国有关苏联与东欧的情报, 1989-91 (1999)*, 和*中央情报局对苏联的评估: 成绩相对于指责(1996)*(注1), 与本集一道将为对情报作业程序, 任务执行情况, 与其对政策所产生的影响感兴趣的历史学家和政治学家提供丰富的原始资料. 这些文件在美国政府领导人与官员制定有关中国国内战争时期的中国共产党以及 1949 年后成立的和在毛泽东(注2)领导下的中华人民共和国政府的政策过程中起到了至关重要的作用.

本人认为, 同样重要的是, 这些文件作为原始资料对于我们目前了解中华人民共和国, 包括其政治, 经济, 和外交政策, 所进行的努力具有重要意义. 有关苏联的汇编是对垮掉了的苏联和已结束的冷战进行回顾, 而这些文件却体现了对一个现实存在的国家正在成形的思维, 这个国家正在对美国的利益和安全构成挑战. 在某种意义上, 这些文件构成一件在制品的部分基石, 有关五十年前共产党领导层问题的文件仍然有助于了解当今北京领导层更替与权力交接问题. 有关五十年代台湾海峡危机的研究在当今紧张的海峡两岸关系中有其针对性, 而美国则被卷入中国内战余留下来的问题之中. 中国卷入朝鲜战争的回声在目前所进行的旨在解决美国与北韩因后者的核计划而产生紧张关系的六方会谈可以听得到. 中国的经济目前是世界上最强大的经济之一, 它很明显是经过艰苦的工业化和农业现代化后而产生的, 本汇编将对其进行探讨.

有关评估的问题

在对这些文件与其重要意义作详细的阐述之前,必须指出,除了一小部分的文件外,所有其他被收录到本汇编的文件当初是以国家情报评估或特别国家情报评估的形式印行的.评估不同于其他情报报告,这些报告注重现况情报,而评估则着眼于未来,美国现代情报系统是1947通过的国家安全法的产物,而情报评估在美国现代情报系统建立的最初时期就被认为是中央情报主任,经过美国政府其他情报机构的同意,所运用的对国家有重要影响的具体问题与国家危机情况之最佳分析,正如中央情报主任沃尔特贝德儿史密斯在1950年举行的情报咨询委员会的一次会议上所说,

> 一份国家情报评估应该由一个机构统一汇集和编制,而这个机构的客观性和无偏见性应该是毋庸置疑的,这份评估最终由各情报机构最高领导官员作出集体论断后通过...它应该在所有政府部门作为可以获得的最佳评估,而且可能是最有权威性的评估而受到承认与尊敬.在该条法律下,中央情报局有明确的责任和义务汇集和制作协调一致和具有权威性的评估(注3).

因此,起草评估的责任短暂地交给中央情报局的研究与评估办公室后,于1950年十一月,转交给中央情报局的国家评估办公室,该办公室充分履行其评估任务,准备了一千五百余份情报评估,直到它在1973年十一月解散为止(注4).该办公室是一个小规模的机构,设有由五到十二名高级专家组成的国家评估委员会,并雇用二十五到三十名具有地区与职务专长的专业人员以及后勤职工(注5).

总统,国家安全委员会成员,美国情报部(下面所讨论的国家对外情报部的前身)任何成员,或国家评估办公室领导本身可以要求(下达任务)进行评估.评估过程平均为六到八周,国家评估办公室完成评估后,由中央情报主任提交美国情报部每周一次的会议取得最后同意.届时,如个别部门对评估里的论断提出具体异议,将对其进行讨论,并记录和记载于最后的草稿中.评估的最后稿件由国家评估办公室,根据机密级别,评估议题,以及针对性传送到美国政府内的一百至三百个人员或办公室.许多评估经过发表后,还接受正式的复核以便情报搜集人员对"情报缺欠"或信息不足加以纠正(注6).

为了更好地满足对情报的需求和更好地使情报界人员(注7)参加起草评估性的情报,国家评估办公室于1973年由国家情报官接替.1979年成立的国家情报委员会(注8)由这批具有实质性知识的专家组成.本集汇编中由国家情报官系统主持下编制的只有两份文件,而全部汇编中只有三份文件是由国家情报官系统主持下编制的,国家对外情报部目前负有对国家情报评估予以最后批准的责任,该部由中央情报主任或副主任主持,并由美国政府主要情报搜集与分析部门的领导人组成(注9).

情报评估至今仍引起争论.这些评估虽然有其争议性,但它们未必是外交决策过程中的最关键性的组成部分,再者,正如薛曼肯特说,当你对谋事情没有准确的了解或没有把握时,你会对它进行评估.在讨论重大或复杂的议题时,正式的情报评估有必要在臆测的范畴内进行钻研,这是一个繁密的过程,在这过程中,从不可能的事情中筛选出可能的事情,再从可能的事

情中筛选出很可能的事情, 以及对重要难题提供答案, 而这答案是由于缺乏完整的信息而有一定程度的不确定性.

本人任职于美国政府长达二十四年, 既是情报评估的生产者, 又是情报评估的消费者(注10). 本人可以证实这些评估在决策过程中发挥多方面的作用. 若评估是因为主要决策者具体要求或针对正在发生的危机而编写的, 则它们很可能被兴致勃勃地阅读, 而且成为危机处理与决策过程中的重要因素. 若评估非常专业化和涉及大规模杀伤性武器, 则将被仔细阅读, 而且将被纳入长期规划过程中, 这对军事情报消费者而言, 更是如此. 若评估是对国内政治, 经济发展, 甚至外交政策的综述, 则它们不太可能被主要决策者阅读, 而是非常有助于对中级官员和情报界其他人员就一般政策问题和决策制定者面临的(始终是逼近的)潜在问题进行教育.

总之, 肯特给为评估作准备的人员的忠告仍然是正确的. 他说, 一份评估

> ...应该在我们评估权限内有其针对性, 尤其应该具有可靠性. 如果我们作决策的主人, 无视我们的知识与智慧, 他如此做并不是因为我们的工作不准确, 不完整, 或者有明显的偏见, 而是因为他需要更注意别人的话. 要让他因为决定听从别人的话而感到不安, 而且是十足的不安(注11).

本人认为, 同样重要的是, 国家情报评估是记录文件, 为建制史, 也许亦为国家历史, 作出贡献. 现况情报分析很快就消失, 而且比昨天的报纸消失的更彻底. 中程分析往往是因为错误才被记住. 但是评估记载着重要论断, 代表着数百名情报分析家的集体学识, 而且准备经受时间的考验, 在大多数的情况下, 经得住两年到五年的时间考验. 在某种意义上, 它们是为历史学家与决策者编写的.

国内政治--毛年代

在考虑如何将本汇编所收录的大量的分析文献进行划分和予以评论, 本人认为应该采取某些评估本身的总体结构, 尤其是综述性的评估, 如编号为 NIE13-58 和 NIE13-60, 标题均为*中共* 的评估. 这样做会很有助益. 这些评估通常所采用的分析方式是先评论党内领导状况, 进而评论经济事务, 包括造成群众不满的根源, 军事力量, 外交政策, 最后以对未来展望作结论. 本人将按照这个模式, 将情报评估员对中国国内政治环境, 经济发展, 军事力量, 以及最后对其外交事务, 尤其是中苏关系和台湾问题, 所作的评估加以讨论.

非从事情报事业的人员经常认为情报分析家有独特的信息来源, 如机密资料, 秘密报告等. 因此认为他们的评估应该是更有见解的, 准确的, 和有预测性的. 换言之, 应该是更为确实的. 从本汇编所收录的文件看, 几乎可以肯定, 相对于学者和记者, 情报分析家对中国共产党的内部运作进行了解时所占的优势并不多, 至少在中华人民共和国建立之初是如此. 从 1951年编制的首篇有关 1949 年后的中共之评估, 即编号为 NIE10, 题为*中共的评估*

开始,评估员就斩钉截铁地作出有关领导层的论断,而这论断在以后十年内没有动摇,论断称:

> 在可见的未来,中共政权很有可能对中国大陆维持绝对的控制权.虽然在中国对共产政权的确存在许多不满的情绪,但这政权享有一定程度的支持或默认,而且正在采取强硬的治安管理措施.目前没有迹象显示该共产政权内有严重的分裂(注12).

三年以后,一份于1954年六月发行,编号为 NIE13-54,题为*中共到1957年的潜在权力*的更为全面之评估称,虽然在二月举行的一次中央委员会全体会议上有迹象显示毛泽东领导的领导班子里存在"分歧与对抗",但没有"明确建立起来的派系,"而领导层被描述为"具有凝聚力和稳定性."事实上,该全会主导了党的第一次重大清算,清算的对象是政治局委员高岗和组织部长饶漱石,然而有关消息一年以后才为外人所知.

早期缺乏铁一般消息来源并不稀奇.美国与中国当时没有正式的外交关系,商业制裁将商业来往减少到最低限度,朝鲜战争以后极端的敌视意识形态贯穿着双边关系,台湾方面的信息不被认为准确或可靠,而且中华人民共和国本身组织了非常有效的宣传与新闻管制作业以便严守有关内部政治和政策讨论的机密.泰伟斯在1979年对文化革命期间公布的党的文献与其他资料进行广泛研究后,对有关高岗的清算的原因和结果仍表示费解(注13).

到了1960年,有更多证据表明对党的高层存在不满的情绪,编号为 NIE13-60 的评估认为在1959年对国防部长彭德怀和其他人员展开的清算"很有可能是因为他们置疑党的政策(注14)."但评估的总体论断是,由于毛拥有权力和支持根基,他的意见在党委会占优势,"在他有生之年党派主义不会成为严重的问题(注15)."三年以后,另一份编号为 NIE13-63,题为*中共的问题与前景*的评估称,虽然该政权的经济政策和苏联停止援助造成"严重"的损害和进一步削弱群众对它的支持,毛和从三十年代开始一直领导党的核心分子一道仍保持"最终权力."虽然评估员对派别主义会成为问题保持怀疑的态度,但评估对毛与他的同僚表示基于"寿命估算"的关注,因为他们大部分已经六十多岁,有的年龄更大(注16).

题为*中共的政治问题与前景*,编号为 NIE13-7-65 的评估代表某种程度的转折点,它是本汇编中最令人注目的文件.该文件发表极为悲观的看法,重点讨论了有关政治与经济失策的证据,低层党员士气低落,在"社会主义教育运动"中与知识分子的紧张关系加剧和对知识分子加大攻击,以及"日益僵化和独断的"最高领导层.毛被描述为"不安和多疑,"对批评敏感,和越来越把个人忠诚置于一切之上.他"倾向于回想当年担游击队队长的日子,以便寻求解决当今问题的办法."评估的作者相信这种作法会产生更不切实际的政策.然而,这份评估又一次准确地表示,派别主义虽然可能存在,但还没有严重到"打破领导人长期运作的纪律(注17)."

九个月以后,"文化大革命"如火如荼地展开,这场由毛煽动发起的运动是针对他的指定接班人刘少奇和他的同夥而展开的,他们被指控不忠,试图恢复资本主义,和实行党派主义.继而发生的是长达十年的混乱和动乱,这场政治斗争给中国社会稳定,政治制度,经济,和外交造成巨大的损害.起初研究中国的学生与分析家对这些明显的自我毁灭性的政策和行动发生意见不和. 两名中央情报局的高级分析家于1967-68年在*中国季刊* 发表文章, 对这场闹哄哄而日益激烈的国内政治斗争发表截然不同的意见(注18).

文化革命造成的一个意外的结果是, 许多鲜为人知的文献资料被刊登在中国各报刊. 为了谴责和清算党的元老提供依据, 红卫兵与文革小组的激进分子发表言论, 攻讦性报道, 文章, 和其他相当程度上阐明党史早期的资料. 为了跟上事态的发展, 国外广播资讯服务处, 联合刊物研究服务处, 和香港领事馆的中国大陆报刊查阅处翻译和发行特辑, 这些特辑成为情报分析家与学术界专家的宝库(注19). 在某些方面, 专家们所掌握的信息是绰绰有余的.

不过评估工作并不因此变得更加容易. 题为*中国文化革命*, 编号为 NIE13-7-67 的评估采取仔细和平衡的态度对互相矛盾的信息进行了解. 它对预测结果进程中固有的未知因素与风险直言不讳地说:"中国的政治危机继续进展, 它不会即将结束, 在它可能产生的几种结果中, 没有一个结果比其他的结果有更明显的可能性. (注20)." 该文件作出有预言性的评估, 表示国内战争发生或国家分裂成不同地区的可能性不大, 认为军中的一个小心谨慎的集团会倾向于和后毛时代的温和派政治领导人寻找共同点. 并对运动的方向作出慎重而适当的结论.

> 局势很可能在更偏激的措施和巩固或撤退的时段间摇摆不定. 我们不能准确地预测所要采取的策略或在最高层的受害者. 但我们有相当的把握认为只要毛能够掌握政治指挥权, 中国的局势很可能会紧张和基本上不稳定(注21).

评估员预料毛以后, 会有"混乱和有争议的"为接替权力而展开的斗争. 然后毛的"失去信用"的政治与经济政策会逐渐被放弃. 军方和文人领导将试图寻找共同点和恢复可能有助于"取得适度经济增长"的政策(注22). 评估起草者并不知道毛会再活九年.

不幸的是, 本汇编只提供若干对中国领导层情况进行有说服力分析的例子. 编号为 NIE13-9-68 的评估在衡量文化革命对毛和他的追随者所造成的影响时, 再次研究毛所遭到的反对以及在中国的权力工具. 题为*中国军事政策与多功能部队*, 编号为 NIE13-3-72 的评估相当详尽地讨论了国防部长林彪被清算后军队内部的政治动乱. 林彪是后来被控企图向毛策划政变(注23). 但那精心编造的故事至今仍然是个谜. 在进行评估时故事还没有编造完毕. 评估是对人民解放军的军事力量与能力进行更深入的讨论. 因此这些文件对文化革命后期没有进行讨论. 而造成这种情况的部分原因可能是刚成立的国家情报员系统(于1973年成立)还没有制定和国家情报办公室可以相提并论的研究或分析中国国内政治局势的计划. 也许在美中友谊与关系正在发展的时期, 没有必要对中国混乱的政治局势作出悲观的评估. 可是说也奇怪, 毛时代的故事似乎还没有结束.

然而所取得的成绩却给人深刻的印象. 当然事后总是从评估性的资料中找到错误和失误. 但评估的基本论点始终是正确的. 在那段时期, 国家情报评估的起草者了解中国历史, 对苏联式的政治局体制有深刻的了解, 并且掌握日益增加的有关北京政府人士与政策的信息. 他们的论断是非常笼统, 主要讨论"中共"(注24)对美国的利益所造成的威胁, 尤其在亚洲. 但是论断是客观的, 没有受到意识形态的影响, 是平衡的, 至少本人是如此认为. 评估作出的一条更重要的, 始终准确的论断是, 共产党在中国大陆所掌握的权力自1948年以来始终没有受到挑战, 毛也从来没有在党内受到真正的挑战. 他不切实际的经济政策造成大跃进的灾害, 但国家评估办公室的分析家当初低估了大跃进对经济和社会所造成的影响, 毛在意识形态领域中雄心勃勃的计划和宣传导致与苏联分裂, 而他猜疑和多疑的性格在文化革命中几乎毁灭了共产党, 但他的领导地位从来没有受到怀疑. 即使今天, 毛的声望在共产党内是不容置疑的.

衡量中国的经济

朝鲜战争停战后, 当"中共"作为一个国家存续的可能性被确定时, 这集汇编中的文件明确表示要对中国的经济政策与效益进行评估, 作为对中国的整体运作与前景进行评估的重要组成部分. 早期的评估, 如编号为 ORE89-49, 题为*关于中共的粮食展望* 和编号为 NIE10, 题为*中共* 的评估, 意识色彩浓厚而且显然不准确. 这些评估只研究经济问题对政权存续造成的妨碍, 甚至警告不要企图利用这些问题暗中破坏新的共产政府. 编号为 NIE13-54, 题为*中共到1957年的潜在权力* 的评估制定人员试图评估和衡量中国的经济效益, 并尝试制定让人能够了解的统计标准. 但这方面的努力由于中国的经济统计制度发展滞后而受到阻碍. 例如, 第一个五年计划(1952-57)的对象到1955年才宣布, 而且之后还不断地修改.

评估员对当时他们对中国的初步经济计划所能了解的情况进行估计. 发现该计划仿效苏联模式, 从而作出相应的结论.

> 对增加工业产量重视, 尤其是重工业与交通业, 该政权的计划之实现有赖于增加农业产量, 同时严格抑制消费, 为支持对工业的投入和进行军事项目提供必要的资源. 大部分为实现计划所需要的生产资料是从苏联集团的其他国家获得的, 以中国向那些国家出口为交换.

评估的起草者充分认识到中国所面临的艰巨任务, 认为该政权在重建被国内战争, 社会动乱, 和数十年管理不善破坏了的经济方面取得重大进展. 他们还说, 中国严重缺乏经济经营与管理方面的专业人才, 过渡集中精力于开销庞大的军工生产, 而且人口快速增长, 这些将限制中国的增长. 然而评估还是作出结论认为在第一个五年计划期间, 中国的总产量很可能增加百分之二十到二十五(注25).

下一篇有关中国经济效益的分析文件刊登在编号为NIE13-58, 题为*中共* 的评估. 这份文件附有长达五页的有关第一个五年计划的附件, 对中央预算支出进行详细的分析, 对主要经济部门的增长率进行评估. 评估总体上是乐观的, 它谨慎而精细地认定中国有能力实现第二个五年计划所确定的宏伟目标, 虽然实现这些目标很困难而且有赖于若干非经济变数. 其中最重要的是人口总体增长率与农业生产增长之间的极小的差距. 评估在脚注中加以警告说:

这份评估里的数据与分析是基于中共方面的统计, 评估对这些统计数据持保留态度. 正如对其他集团国家一样, 而且是更有所保留, 这是由于刚成立的对中共进行搜集统计数据的系统缺乏经验... 中共的统计数据是该政权制定计划的基础, 我们相信一般而言是不会被歪曲的(注26).

现在看来, 当时评估所作的经济预测是有实质性的错误. 中国的经济在以后的两年受到灾难性的挫折, 虽然评估里的分析是运用健全的方法和利用现有的数据诚心诚意地对未来效益进行估计, 但评估起草者低估了毛对经济计划和生产体系的政治干预. 虽然他们把统计误差加以考虑, 但他们不可能料想到"大跃进"刚开始生产数据就被大规模和故意地扭曲. 这方面的失误不仅限于他们, 不但西方学术界的专家, 而且整个中国经济计划体系显得迷惑和不了解当时中国面临的巨大经济问题.

到1963年, 外界加深了对该政权经济痛楚的了解, 即使对其背后的政治斗争不清楚. 编号为NIE13-63, 题为 *中共的问题与前景* 的评估对大跃进和其所造成的后果进行严厉的评析指出: "过去五年, 中共的经济管理严重失当, 领导层缺乏经济方面的训练和经验, 受狭隘的教条局限, 被狂热主义引入歧途(注27)." 评估认为中国经济遭受重大损害是因为苏联和中国决裂以后停止向中国提供援助和专业指导(参阅以下讨论). 该文件还附有长篇附件对中国在1962年的经济效益进行分析. 该分析基于非从中国获得的统计数据和中央情报局的内部估算进行非常笼统的产业评估. 它不排除经济继续复苏的可能性, 认为该政权如果把注意力集中到改善农业生产和继续"执行比较温和与合理的政策, 如果在天气方面有适当的运气, " 则可能恢复1957年所取得的总体生产力水平. 不过评估也警告说, 由于成功和失败之间, 犹如薄纸一隔, 有关中国经济前景的估计只能是"笼统而暂时性的(注28)."

中国经济问题仍然是以后三年评估的重点. 国家评估办公室的分析家发现他们对最坏情况的假设正成为事实. 编号为 NIE13-5-67, 题为 *中共的经济展望* 暗示对中国继续不能发挥其经济潜力的失望. 该评估表示:

今年的经济效益似乎毫无疑问有所下降, 不过对下降的幅度不可能进行量化... 自从1960年, 北京很少公布有助益的数据. 在经济计划暂时被搁置的情况下, 重大经济措施很可能推迟到对政治斗争取得某种程度的解决后才出台.

尽管如此, 评估研判中国正在努力使基本经济生产免遭文化革命最严重的破坏. 经济危机似乎不会即将发生(注29).

国家情报分析汇编没有列举重点经济分析的例子. 其中部分原因可能是组织性的, 中央情报局情报处于1966年设立经济研究办公室, 承担对中国经济进行详细的统计分析, 发展先进技术与模式来弥补官方经济统计数据的不足. 以及主要通过国家评估办公室以外的其他管道报告其研究结果的任务. 另外一个原因是以后十年中国经济情况继续摇晃不定, 决策圈的兴趣转移到更迫切的问题, 这些问题牵涉到中国的战略性武器计划以及它对苏联与美国的外交政策.

过去二十年,中国取得了惊人的经济"起飞"和重要的国际地位,这些给中国的老百姓带来变化,难以想象当时中国是如何从这些评估所描写的疮痍满目的经济废墟中崛起.值得注意的是中国大部分的人口仍然居住在远离海岸的农村,他们的经济情况可能与这些评估所描绘的状况没有根本的不同.农业生产仍滞后于工业发展,农业富余人口严重阻碍经济发展,农村群众的不满继续对政治领导层构成挑战.这些是评估所描写的事态的重演.虽然中国出现了新的经济管理人员,但一些旧问题仍然存在.

军事挑战与中国战略性武器计划

本汇编所收录的评估中很少没有考虑到人民解放军发展成为一支有效的战斗部队,对美国的利益构成威胁,一些评估甚至进行这方面的专门讨论,人民解放军早期被称为"中国共军."尽管这些文件表示不同的意识形态领域的关注,,认为中国的武力值得重视与关注的观念在全集中是显而易见的.这些关注以有趣的方式呈现变化.

- 编号为 ORE77-48 的评估在1948年叙述国民党在国内战争遭受令人震惊的战败时,评述道:"中国共军的力量与战术方面的成功是共产党崛起的主要工具,这种情况将继续下去...(注30)"

- 另外一份评估在中国于1950年加入朝鲜战争前夕写道:"我们相信中国共军能够停止联合国部队往北的推进,他们根据可预见的联合国部队的集结,零星地投入部队,他们也能够猛烈攻击迫使联合国部队进一步往南撤退(注31)."

- 编号为 NIE13-54 的评估在1954年写道:"共产政权所享有的内部控制与国际上的权力地位很大程度上有赖于中国军队的潜在权力,而这支军队目前是亚洲国家中最大的部队(注32)."

- 编号为 SNIE100-9-58 评估在1958年的金门和马祖危机期间警告说:"如果只遭到国民党部队的反击,中国共产党人有能力将台湾海峡不让给国民党空军,堵截向外岛的补给,或者攻占这些外岛(注33)."

- 在评析中国在六十年代试验裂变和聚变武器后的战略野心,编号为 NIE13-8-67 的评估写道:"当前的领导人可能相信,如果成功地发展战略性武器,他们的声望就会大大提高,他们在亚洲的领导权与大国地位将增强...中国可能相信能够以核武器攻击美国与其在亚洲的目标可以限制美国在亚洲的军事行动,可以将对抗维持在常规武器层面上,因为中国在这方面享有许多优势(注34)."

本汇编里的几篇文件所发表的意见是有关北京政权依赖和投入大量经济资源发展其军队的评估的引申,这些意见认为北京领导人谨防冒险与美国发生直接军事对抗,无论是战略性或常规性对抗,这可能一部分是朝鲜战争的结果,在朝鲜战争中,毛投入大量部队与美国部队进行常规战争, 但仍然遭受惨重的伤亡,而且因此产生的结果是不确定的,即延续至今的充满紧张的停战.这方面的不愿意也可能是因为1954年和1955年发生的金门和马祖危机,危机期间,美国总统艾森豪威胁道,如果中华人民共和国攻击国民党控制的金门或马祖外岛,美国将对大陆目标使用战术性核武器(注35).最重要的是,北京方面的谨慎源于毛自己的军事学说,该学说强调"人民战争"以保卫中国的领土完整与主权,以及对占军事优势的美国敌军采取慎重的态度.编号为NIE13-3-67的评估扼要地指出:

> 虽然在中国境外威胁使用和实际使用武力构成北京的观点之组成部分,但中国军事策略的主要重点是防卫.可能除了涉及核武器或导弹的活动外,我们没有看见意味着更有前瞻性的策略的综合计划,兵力发展或部署,或学说方面的讨论.至少在短期内,中国可能视优先发展核计划主要为达成其威慑目的而进行...(注36).

两份有关中国对越南战争的反应和卷入越战的特别国家情报评估与三份有关 1958 年的台湾海峡危机的特别国家情报评估明确地表示评估员确信他们有关中国不会冒险与美国公开对抗的分析是准确的.比如,在1966年,美国空军扩编和加大对在河内与海防附近的北越目标进行轰炸后,国家评估办公室被要求对中国更积极卷入军事行动的可能性进行评估.编号为 SNIE13-66 的评估称:"就目前美国对北越的军事行动的层次看,我们继续相信中国不会投入其陆军或空军部队与美国持续作战.我们认为,无论是中国或北越都不认为目前局势已到需要外部介入的危急地步,外部介入会带来扩大战争的危险,最终带来核战争的威胁...(注37)."他们相信中国会继续帮助北越抵抗美国的军事压力,包括部署部分支援部队,但不会像在朝鲜那样,参与战争.

同样在台湾海峡,1958年五月的基线推断认为只要有与美国发生战争的危险,中国"不会使用军事行动攻占台湾(注38)."不过推断没有排除中国可能对外岛采取"更有侵略性"的态度.当人民解放军在金门对岸的炮兵部队在 1959 年八月下旬开始猛烈炮击该岛时,国家安全委员会要求对中共的意图进行评估.编号为 SNIE100-9-58 的评估重申炮击行动的目的是要试探美国与"中华民国"政府的意图.虽然中国的武装力量有能力攻击外岛,但"很可能因为怕美国干预而不敢冒动(注39)."

当中华人民共和国提高赌注宣称会堵截国民党对金门卫戍部队进行补给和向在其领海的船舰开火时,我方准备了另一份评估.这份编号为 SNIE100-11-58 的评估留有余地地表示中华人民共和国似乎越来越愿意冒险与美国进行战争.评估预测,如华府选择使用美国海军向该外岛进行补给或护卫国民党船舰进入中华人民共和国领海.中国"可能袭击美国部队."然而评估员重申中国或苏联似乎没有正在为大规模的冲突进行准备(注40).总统艾森豪选择使用美国海军护卫国民党补给舰到距离中华人民共和国领海三英里以外之处.同时再威胁如果战争扩大,将向中华人民共和国部队进行核攻击.在华沙重开与中国的外交谈判.十月初,中国停止炮击一个星期,让补给不受干扰地进行,危机因此逐渐缓和.于1958年十月下旬和1959年二月发表的后续特别国家情报评估重申有关中国在美国决心保卫外岛面前退让的论点.

回顾过去,中国在台湾海峡不能反击美国常规或核能力,而且苏联在危机期间很明显不愿意支持它的中国盟友(评估指出这一点),这无疑导致中苏的紧张关系,使中国决定加快发展其战略性武器计划.该计划1960年后成为评估员日益关注的重点问题,1962年到1974年间,他们编写十三份有关这问题的评估.日益先进的情报搜集计划,尤其在六十年代开始可供使用的卫星图像技术,有助于从事有关中国计划的人员获得更多对中国的知识.由于这些计划的性质和它们与当今情报的搜集和分析继续有关系,大部分有关中国发展核计划的文件都被大量修改.

阅读被大量修改过的文件是令人有挫折感的过程,不会让人对中国的核武器或战略导弹计划的性质产生许多独特的见解.不过被修改过的文件表明这些计划在美国与苏联产生极大的兴趣和关注,也表明基于一些照片和其他不足够的线索对一个国家的核能力进行评估从一开始就不是一门精确的科学,更何况对它的核意向进行评估.国家评估办公室的评估员在编号为 NIE13-2-60 (注41)的首份有关中国战略性武器计划的重大评估中,研判第一个核爆炸很可能在1963年进行,也可能在1964年或1962年进行,这有赖于苏联的援助.另一方面,于1964年八月下旬发布的,编号为SNIE13-4-64,题为*中共即将进行核爆炸的可能性*的评估指出在罗布泊的试验场明显地已经准备就绪,同时指出很少迹象显示有足够的可裂变物质可供制造炸弹,在年底之前不可能完成试验.然而试验在1964年十月十六日进行.

中国核计划的发展速度始终是一件出乎意料的事情.在进行首次大气层中的试验两年后,中国宣布进行导弹核武器试验,而且于1967年六月,首次进行热核武器试验.这些惊人的进展是在中国经济相当疲弱和政治制度因文化革命日趋混乱的背景下取得的. 整个社会的动乱似乎未殃及中国的战略性武器计划,这给编写编号为 NIE13-8-67, 题为*中共的战略性武器计划* 的评估的起草者深深地感觉到计划背后的决心.但是发展速度给评估员留下"极少有关中国对核武器在整体战略中地位的思维方面的证据(注42)."他们似乎不相信中国将试图在战略计划的规模或毁灭性方面争取与美国或苏联势均力敌,并指出在技术和保障方面持续存在的问题有待解决.他们作出结论说,中国的计划"在未来十年内,将由于中国在工业,技术,与人才方面的薄弱,受到有关范围,质量,和数量方面的限制(注43)."

然而该计划却令人担忧,尤其对苏联而言,当时中国的外交和国内政策处于非常激进的阶段.在六十年代,中苏争端演变成公开的敌视和仇恨,于1969年,终于演变成武装冲突.在该场冲突中,中国与苏联的部队在其边界多处进行激战.编号为 NIE11/13-69, 题为*苏维埃社会主义共和国联盟与中国* 的评估揣测说,有迹象显示苏联领导层正在考虑和准备与中国进行一场军事决战.这样做的其中一个目的是"利用其空中优势破坏中国的核设施与导弹设施,同时阻止中国使用其战区部队展开地面上的报复性攻击(注44)."评估员认为莫斯科不太可能实现它的目标,而且认为这样做会产生非常严重的后果,不过他们不排除这个可能性.最后由于比较冷静的头脑占了上风,争端有所缓和,但是中国的战略性武器的重要性和弱点成为随后美国对中国进行战略评估的主要因素.

到 1974 年,新成立的国家情报官系统编写一篇评估对中国战略计划的意向和范围作出稍微更坚定的论断.由于政治,经济,和技术方面的约束,计划被认为已经减速,而转为旨在发展"对乌拉尔山脉以西的苏维埃社会主义共和国联盟以及美国大陆进行袭击的象征性核能力(注45)."计划被认为不是不惜任何代价,仓促和轻率地发展战略性武器,而是体现(在林彪被清算后)军队被制服了的国内政治现实,以及对国际局势不认为那么令人不安的看法,这种看法是来自苏维埃社会主义共和国联盟的威胁减轻和与美国的关系改善的结果.中国被认为拥有130枚导弹和可以携带核武器的轰炸机,而且被预料在十年内会拥有六枚能够瞄准美国的洲际弹道导弹,以及一些潜艇发射的导弹(注46).

中国的军事能力,包括其战略性武器计划,仍然是美国政府决策者极为关注的议题.在某些方面,这汇编所收录的最后一份评估编写将近三十年以来,中美战略关系没有发生多大的变化.中国维持可靠的小规模核部队,这支部队经得住第一袭击,配备着一整套的能够击中美国在亚洲的基地或盟国的导弹,以及少数有足够射程袭击美国大陆的武器.美中关系的性质向好的方向发生根本性变化,主要是因为这些评估所探讨的中国外交政策上的变化.不过很少人会认为有理由放松或停止对人民解放军和它的常规和战略能力进行了解的努力.

在美国眼里的中苏关系

本汇编所收录的最早的文件理所当然地认为中国共产党与苏联的政党和政府之间存在着密切的关系.这种关系被认为对美国的利益有害.编号为 ORE45-48 的评估考虑到 1948 年七月蒋介石的国民党政府地位岌岌可危,便推断国民党会垮台和被"即使不受控于苏联也将受苏联影响"的中国共产党取代.评估认为这将是越来越可能发生的"最坏的事情(注47)."六个月以后,共军在济南,锦州,沈阳,与其他重要城市击败国民党部队,评估员对事态的后果再也不怀疑了.他们推断"没有具有实际战斗力的国民党部队"可以持续抵抗.至于中国共产党,他们写道:

> 它与苏维埃社会主义共和国联盟有共同的意识形态,共同的政治组织,以及共同的战略与策略,就目前而言,它们还有共同的目标.中国共产党从来没有公开偏离苏联党的路线,从来没有公开批评苏联的任何行动或代表,从来没有表示可能将其导向从苏维埃社会主义共和国联盟转向美国.可以肯定中国共产党*曾经和仍然是苏联政策的工具*.

没有"分裂的可能性,"至少就目前而言(注48).

在人民共和国1949年成立以后,将中国与苏联的制度,政策,和利益等同起来是完全有道理的.北京在其政治结构,作法,与政策上非常明确地表示它对莫斯科的忠诚.于1950年二月签署的友谊,同盟,互助条约将两国联系在看似强大的国防协定之下.中国在1950年加入朝鲜战争被认为是苏联授意的.

然而注意被认为是非常重要的关系中是否出现分裂或紧张的迹象始终成为对中华人民共和国与整个苏联集团进行评估的人员的工作主题,他们与学术界的观察家在这方面有共同的兴趣.事后回顾当时的情况,让人很想对他们作个比较,看他们之间谁首先对事情"弄对."这是效果不特别大的作法.早在1952年,起草编号为 NIE58, 题为*中共政权与苏维埃社会主义共和国联盟的关系* 的评估人员就确定对中苏关系中可能出现的紧张迹象应该注意的事项,包括苏维埃社会主义共和国联盟对中国加强控制所进行的努力,它对中国提供的军事和经济援助,有关划分边界的问题,与在亚洲的其他共产主义运动的关系,以及毛在整个共产主义运动中所扮演的意识形态领域的角色.但他们作出结论说,两国与两党的共同利益,尤其是它们消除美国在亚洲的影响力的共同目标,超过可能使它们疏远的因素(注49).学术界的专家稍后撰文作出类似的结论(注50).

1956 年双边关系开始紧张,赫鲁晓夫在二月举行的苏共第二十次党代表大会上谴责斯大林
(中方对此表示不满),紧张的关系随着苏联对毛在1958年的大跃进中设立"公社"的决定表
示轻蔑而升级,紧张的关系由于莫斯科在 1958 年金门和马祖危机爆发时不愿意支持
中国和赫鲁晓夫试图与华府建立更密切的关系而达到严重的地步.但是紧张的关系被仍然
光泽鲜明的社会主义团结的外表隐藏了一年,到 1960 年四月才爆发成为公开的争辩
(注51).八月份,编号为 NIE100-3-60, 题为*中苏关系* 的评估指出共产主义运动中的"
两个权力声音"之间"纷争急剧上升." 该文件对中苏日益复杂的关系的各方面进行详尽
的研究,并作出结论说:"我们相信中苏关系里的凝聚力比分化力强大,这种情况至少在这份
评估所涵盖的五年内很可能继续存在."然而即使公开的决裂不可能发生,双方之间越来越
大的分歧亦不可能调和(注52).

1960 年十一月,莫斯科举办一场重大的共产党国际会议,希望借此使该运动恢复表面的
纪律.该会议会期长,且争论不休,最后加剧了中国与苏联政党之间的分裂,但没有导致公开
的决裂.次年编写的编号为 NIE10-61, 题为*共产主义运动中的权力与控制*
的评估对越来越支离破碎的运动作了总结,评估没有改变一年前所作的论断,这论断认为中
苏争端会持续下去,但不一定会恶化.在赫鲁晓夫于1964年被撤职后,苏联领导人的确似乎
试图与中国言归于好.不过大家误判了毛和他将他的意见强加于中国政策的能力,这些政
策包括外交政策,毛在他和他国内的敌人间越来越激烈的争论中,用支持苏联"修正主义"的
指控来伤害刘少奇,邓小平,和其他人.并对苏联进行更加恶毒的攻击.

到1966年,国家评估办公室超前地了解到中国动荡不安的国内政治局势会影响它的外交政
策.评估员总结当年的双边关系时作出结论说:"只要毛泽东和林彪领导班子保持权力,中苏
关系将继续恶化."虽然评估员认为不可能发生公开的决裂,他们还是写道:

> ...我们不能完全排除争端突然爆发,而以新的,更恶毒的形式体现...如果中国的权力
> 加强其民族专断性,严重的麻烦可能出现,尤其在边境地区(注53).

三年后,在黑龙江与新疆的中苏边境发生冲突,使双边关系达到最低点.评估员评述说"提出
重大的中苏战争会否在短期内爆发的问题是合理的." 评估员们再次对双方的利益和冲突
深化所带来的严重损害性的后果采取平衡的看法,作出结论说中国不会发动战争,苏联可能
会考虑先发制人攻击中国的战略性武器设施,但很可能决定不这样做(注54).至于苏维埃社
会主义共和国联盟和中国之间的敌对关系会否促使其中一方调整对华府的政策,评估员对
此并不乐观.莫斯科可能"在小问题上作一些让步...但我们不认为苏联目前正在考虑牺牲
它至关重要的立场..例如,德国的分割和在东欧的苏联圈子的合法性.更不可能的是中国反
美立场的重大改变(注55)." 1969 年九月十一日,苏联总理科锡金在河内出席胡志明
的葬礼后返回途中停留北京,与周恩来总理在机场商谈重启谈判解决边界问题.周的态度不
明确,据说他向科锡金提出警告说苏联不要攻击中国的核基地.九月下旬,中国在罗布泊引
爆两个热核爆炸装置,其中一个装置的威力在三百万吨级当量.十月七日,中国同意恢复边
界谈判.从而大大地缓和危机(注56).

本汇编有关中苏的最后评估在1973年编写,评估作出结论说:

虽然中苏关系将继续呈现不同程度的紧张,但可能会往紧张缓和的方向发展,而不是往战争方向发展.

该文件讨论这两个可能性的展望与含义,指出最大的可能性是不安的和平将延续,战争不会爆发,但也不会有和解.评估再警告西方国家不要期望因中苏关系改善或恶化而受益(注57).

有关中苏关系的文件总体上对复杂的问题进行合理,谨慎的分析,这是跨部门分析的特点,这种分析对可能发生的局面与事情作精细的评估,倾向于预测现状将延续.在很多情况下,这种作法对后果作出正确的预测.在所有的情况下,评估在其有助益的摘要中提出证据使决策层的读者了解正在演变中的关系之背景.本人认为这些评估有以下三方面的不足之处:1)高估了至少在五十年代中意识形态的团结以及共产集团内其他向心力的重要性;2)没有足够有关国内政治对中国外交政策造成影响的证据;3)不能(没有被允许)对美国的政策选择对中华人民共和国或苏联的外交决定所造成的影响进行充分的评估.最后的因素不是评估员的过错,是被需要保持情报分析与决策之间严格的界线所决定的.

中华人民共和国,中华民国,美国的三角关系

由于上面所列举的三个原因中最后一个原因,这些文件,与本集汇编其他方面比较,最不能阐明美国,中华人民共和国,和中华民国之间的复杂关系.这些评估所涉及的时间长达二十八年,其中美国和中国处于不能消解的敌视关系长达二十五年,双方没有寻求或期望改变这种状况.编号为NIE10的评估在1951年宣称,"中共所采取的行动是为了破坏美国在远东的战略利益以及削弱美国与其盟国在世界范围内的权力地位(注58)."该论断在以后二十年保持显著的连贯性.不管他们研究的重点是东南亚,朝鲜,日本,或台湾问题,国家评估办公室的评估员都理所当然地认为中共对美国与其利益和盟国采取敌视的态度.而且认为中国想成为亚洲最强大的力量之战略目标是不言而喻的.编号为 NIE13-60 的评估称,"中共外交政策的一个基本原则是中国在远东称霸.这个原则几乎不会(在未来五年)发生明显的改变(注59)."编号为 NIE13-9-65 的评估进一步说:

> 由于意识形态和民族主义原因,中国把美国视为它的头号敌人.北平当前的安全利益和其有限的军事力量范围导致它在外交上集中主要精力破坏美国在远东的地位(注60).

即使在文化革命期间中国在外交政策上遭到明显的失败后,编号为NIE13-69的评估(这是一分极佳的对中国外交政策二十年的总结)仍坚称:"几乎所有的中国人,无论是在北京或台湾,都一致认为中国的正当地位应该通过在亚洲大陆,最终在整个东亚和东南亚,取得政治主宰权来建立(注61)."

这种看法可能被认为有缺点,因为它显得受意识形态的,冷战式的影响,而且中国领导人关于他们战略目标的谈话很少被引用来作根据.不过现有事实表明这些评估在现实中是有充分根据的.冷战现在回忆起来似乎是遥远和不可思议的事,但是在五十年代和六十年代它

是真实的事情. 中国在那个时期有关美国的官方谈话与言论很明显是有反抗性的, 尖锐的, 和富有敌意的, 没有妥协的迹象或隐隐约约显示出改善双边关系的意愿. 事实上, 有关中国外交政策意愿的评估性分析文章一般都是轻描淡写或至少是低调处理. 本汇编所收录的文件有比较高的客观性, 即使在讨论涉及美国利益的问题时亦如此.

尤其在台湾问题上更是如此. 虽然这问题没有经常被提到, 本汇编所收录的文件表现出干净利落和客观的一面. 这些文件编写的时候并不是无争议的. 研究与评估办公室早期的文件尤其在其时代背景下阅读时显得颇有兴味, 当时中国国内战争和美国对此的卷入正在以不幸的结局收场. 国防部与国务院之间以及行政部门与立法部门之间爆发有关中国政策的争论, 反共情绪在美国达到狂热的地步. 1948年七月, 国会通过援助中国法案, 该法案追加拨款1.25亿美元让蒋介石政府购买额外武器装备, 在国会刚通过该法案后, 编号为 ORE45-48, 题为 *中国目前的局势* 的评估就发表一则令人丧气的消息说:

> 当前国民党政府的地位岌岌可危, 它可能随时会垮台... 即使在美国目前的援助计划下, 现在的国民党政府似乎没有希望扭转或停止走向解体的趋势. 由于战争失败和他显然不愿意和不能完成有建设性的改革, 蒋介石的权力与声望不断地在下降(注62).

该文件可能为国务院的论点提供了依据, 当时国务卿乔治. 马歇尔与政策计划主任乔治. 凯南赞成限制美国向蒋介石提供更多的援助(注63). 这无疑与美国军事评估的论点有出入, 这些评估认为更有效地提供美国武器会让国民党支撑下去.

蒋介石夫人于1948年十二月初访问美国请求更多的军事与经济援助. 在她访问前夕, 编号为 ORE77-48, 题为 *中共的能力* 的评估预言国民党的抵抗将在数月内被粉碎. 一旦完成粉碎行动, 共军会"从容不迫"地进一步肃清所有地方反抗力量, 进而建立完全由共产党主导的名义上的联合政府. 该文件认为共产党展开有效的军事和后勤工作, 指出它在其控制的地区推行"适度"的土地改革政策, 责备国民党政府不能进行有意义的经济和政治改革(注64). 当国务院的司务官表现出类似的客观性时, 被一些国会议员指责为远东局内同情共产党人的"红色小组." 这方面的争议最后使国务院的几位中国专家失去工作和声望(注65).

在为本汇编选录评估文件时, 编辑人员决定不收录有关蒋介石在1949年于台湾建立的中华民国政府的讨论. 关于五十年代台湾海峡危机的评估被收录是因为它们与北平所扮演的角色有关. 希望以后的汇编会收录与1949年后的国民党有关的评估文件. 就我们现有的关于海峡危机的评估而言, 国家评估办公室的分析家对所评估的问题保持严谨客观的态度. 编号为 NIE100-9-58, 题为 *台湾海峡地区可能的事态发展* 的评估揣测说, 对外岛恢复进攻部分原因是"中共"领导人对于他们"未能为实现结束中华民国政府存在的目标而取得明显的进长," 未能防止"国际上更广泛地接受实际上存在' 两个中国'的状况," 以及未能在联合国取代中华民国政府而感到不满, 该评估于1958年八月危机高峰时期发布. 评估对国民党的目的进行同样坦率的分析, 认为它设法保持中华民国政府的威信, 使返回大陆的希望之火不熄灭, 维持民众的士气, 以及从美国获得更多的援助和保卫台湾的更坚定的承诺, 一些未指名的官员还认为它设法将美国卷入与中共的战争(注66). 该评估提出近乎政策建议的结论说, 美国如果采取"次要的措施," 如部署更多的船舰, 向台湾提供更多的武器, 或提出"一般的警告," 这不会阻止中国对外岛施加压力.

虽然艾森豪政府明显地不愿意卷入一场为保卫难以防守和无战略价值的外岛进行代价高的战争,虽然莫斯科通过赫鲁晓夫九月十九日的一封信明确地威胁华府说,如果美国向中国使用核武器, 莫斯科将进行核报复,但最后美国还是向台湾和大陆明确地表示其对台湾的承诺.美国和中国都认为莫斯科表示愿意帮助北京的言论是空洞和有条件的.

虽然在中华人民共和国与美国的关系中的台湾问题日后成为尼克松在1972年访华时谈判的中心问题(而且至今仍然是双边关系中最敏感的问题),但本汇编所收录的评估只是顺便提到这议题.在某些方面,这是因为决策者加强自身的能力,不再认为必须用情报界的文件为自己对中国有关美国的政策的评估提供依据.在某些方面,这反映了整个美中关系的发展.在七十年代中,中国领导人已经不是遥远和模糊不清记忆中的对手,而是美国总统,国家安全顾问, 和国务卿的对话者,他们相信他们开始了解中国领导人的主张,目的,和意图,甚至比由中央情报局总部的小心翼翼的通才组成的委员会了解更深.

尽管如此,本汇编再度提醒我们评估文件对中国与其政策的长远了解具有价值.评估文件将历史评析和总结与时事结合,愿意揣测未来可能发生的事情,在最佳状态下的评估文件为决策者面临的重要问题提供至关重要的路线图.它们阐明当今极其重要的问题的环境,背景,和趋势,对这些问题进行预测, 以及提供富有经验的专家的观点和论断.它们为情报界人员在具有重大政策意义的问题上集中注意力和集思广益提供重要机会.纵观过去,它们为希望多了解情报分析, 希望多了解美国的决策过程,中华人民共和国,以及早期的美中关系的人士提供极为有趣的读物.本人赞扬和感谢国家情报委员会以及中央情报局信息管理人员中的编辑人员和销密专家将这独特的文件汇编提供给广大群众.

注释

注1: 这些和其他文件很容易在情报研究中心的网站http://www.cia.gov/csi/index.html取阅.
注2: 当时美国政府使用威妥玛拼音法翻译中文名字,后来改用中国使用的拼音法.在提及中国领导人时,本人将先使用威妥玛法,然后再使用目前的拼音法.
注3: 引自薛曼肯特的*有关国家情报分析的法律与惯例*. 该著作可在http://www.cia.gov/csi/books/shermankent/5law.html查阅.
注4: 同上.本汇编所收录的评估使用的编号体现了这组织历史.研究与分析办公室所编写的评估编有该办公室的名称缩写.编号为 NIE和 SNIE的评估则由国家评估办公室编制.
注5: 同上.参阅薛曼肯特的*一份国家情报评估的制作过程*. 该著作可在http://www.cia.gov/csi/books/shermankent/making.html查阅.这是一篇特别有价值的文章.作者从1952至1967年主管国家评估办公室.该文章详细讨论了国家评估办公室准备评估的全部过程.
注6: 同上.
注7: 情报界目前由中央情报局,国防情报局,国家安全局,国家地理空间情报局,国家侦察办公室,国务院情报与研究局,空军,陆军,海岸防卫队,海军陆战队情报处,联邦

调查局，本土安全部，能源部，和财政部组成.

注8：欲获得有关国家情报委员会的详细叙述以及了解其组织结构，历史，授权任务，和其制作的一部分作品，可到http://www.cia.gov/nic/NIC_home.html.查阅.

注9：该结构是中央情报主任根据1997年一月十四日的3/1命令授权建立的.有关信息可在http://www.fas.org/irp/offdocs/dcid3-1.html查阅.

注10：参阅刊载于本文开端的简历.

注11：参阅薛曼肯特的*评估与影响*.该著作可在 http://www.cia.gov/csi/books/shermankent/4estimates.html查阅.

注12：NIE10，*中共*，第一页，1951年一月十七日.所有被引述的国家情报评估与特别国家情报评估的页码均为原文的页码.

注13：泰伟斯，*中国的政治与清算：整改与党的准则的衰退, 1950-1965*，第166页，（纽约：M.E.夏普出版社1979年出版）.

注14：NIE13-60，*中共*，第九页，1960年十二月六日.

注15：同上.

注16：NIE13-63，*中共的问题与前景*，第四页，1963年五月一日.

注17：NIE13-7-65，*中共的政治问题与前景*，第三页和第九页，1965年八月五日.

注18：参阅刊载于*中国季刊* 第二十九期（1967年一月至三月）第一页到第三十五页，菲利普.布里奇哈姆著作的*(文化大革命的)起源与发展*;刊载于*中国季刊* 第三十四期（1968年四月至六月）第六页到第三十七页，菲利普.布里奇哈姆著作的*1967年毛的文化革命：为夺取权力而展开的斗争*;以及刊载于*中国季刊* 第三十二期（1967年十月至十二月）第三页到第三十六页，查儿斯.纽豪萨儿著作的*六十年代的中国共产党：文化革命的序曲*.

注19：由哥伦比亚大学出版，罗德里克·麦克法夸尔(马若德)著作的三卷本巨著*文化大革命的起源* 利用该时期公布的大量文献资料编写一部五十年代和六十年代初领导层互动的详细历史.虽然有关文化革命的起源和政治目标的评估仍有争议，编号为 NIE13-7-67 的评估所提出的论据无论作为该动乱时期的准确叙述或与当时的报刊和学术界分析文章相比都是非常站得住脚的.

注20：NIE13-7-67，*中国文化革命*，第一页，1967年五月二十五日.

注21：同上，第十页和十一页.

注22：同上，第十二页.

注23：据后来的报道说，林是于1971年九月十二日乘坐军用飞机逃往苏联时被杀害.林的主要助手主导1969年选出的第九届中央委员会政治局，他们和很多其他军官在一次对人民解放军的大规模清算中被逮捕和撤职.

注24：这些文件使用意识形态领域的用语，如"中共"而非"中国"或"中华人民共和国，"以及到六十年代使用国民党所用的"北平，"这并不意味这些文件有意识形态的偏见.除了个别例子外，这些文件对中国的行动和成就作论断时采取谨慎中立和非意识形态的态度.它们毫不讳言地指出中国作为国际共产主义运动的一部分，其目的和做法本质上对美国具

有敌意的，但它们没有体现当时公共范畴里所见到的其他更为极端的看法(用语)，如"红色中国"或"赤共."

注25：NIE13-54, *中共到1957年的潜在权力*, 第一页，1954年六月三日.

注26：NIE13-58, *中共*, 第二十二页，注1，1958年五月二十三日.

注27：NIE13-63, *中共的问题与前景*, 第五页，1963年五月一日.

注28：同上，第六页.

注29：NIE13-5-67, *中共的经济展望*, 第四页，1967年六月二十九日.

注30：ORE77-48, *共产党控制全中国的能力*, 第一页，1948年十二月十日.

注31：NIE2, *中共对朝鲜的干涉*,
第三页，1950年十一月六日("中国人民志愿军"全面加入战争两周前).

注32：NIE13-54,前引书，第二页.

注33：SNIE100-9-58, *台湾海峡地区可能的事态发展*, 第二页，1958年八月二十六日.

注34：NIE13-8-67, *中共的战略性武器计划*, 第三页，1967年八月三日.

注35：参阅罗伯特.艾辛奈里的 *危机与承诺：美国对台政策, 1950-1955*,
(北卡罗来纳，查普希尔：北卡大学出版社1996年出版)，和托马斯.施托尔珀的
中国，台湾，与外岛：一起对外蒙和中苏关系的影响
(纽约，阿蒙克：M.E.夏普出版社1985年出版).

注36：NIE13-3-67, *中共的军事政策，总目标，与防空部队*, 第一页，1967年四月六日.

注37：SNIE13-66, *中共目前对越南局势的意图*, 第五页，1966年八月四日.

注38：NIE13-58,前引书，第十九页.

注39：SNIE100-9-58,前引书，第五页.

注40：SNIE100-11-58,第一页和第二页，1958年九月十六日.

注41：NIE13-2-60, *中共的原子能计划*, 第三页，1969 年十二月十三日.

注42：NIE13-8-67,前引书，第三页.

注43：同上，第十三页.

注44：NIE11/13-69, *苏维埃社会主义共和国联盟与中国*, 第七页，1969 年八月十二日.

注45：NIE13-8-74, *中国的战略攻击计划*, 第三页.

注46：同上，这些数量在情报界引起争论，海军和空军对中国未来武器发展方面的数量估计提出脚注.

注47：ORE45-48, *中国目前的局势*, 第二页，1948年六月二十二日.

注48：ORE77-48, *中共控制全中国的能力*, 第三页和第八页，1948年十二月十二日,着重部分由作者标明.

注49：参阅NIE58, *中共政权与苏维埃社会主义共和国联盟的关系：目前的性质与未来的可能方向*, 第二页到第五页，1952年九月十日.

注50：参阅，如包华德，亚利山大·艾克斯坦，菲利普.莫斯利，本杰明·史华兹的 *莫斯科与北京的轴线：强大和紧张之处*, (纽约，哈伯特兄弟出版社 1957 年出版)，以及W.W.罗斯托的 *中共的前景* (麻省，剑桥：麻省理工学院理工出版社1954年出版)，尤其参阅第四章.

注51：如欲阅读有关中央情报局对中苏决裂的全部分析文章之极佳的概述，包括本汇编所收录的评估文件，参阅刊载于1998年至1999年冬天的 *情报研究*, 哈罗德.福特的 *识别中苏决裂*, 该文可在
http://www.cia.gov/csi/studies/winter98_99/art05.html查阅.

注52：NIE100-3-60, *中苏关系*, 第十四页, 1960 年八月九日. 当时有些学术界的研究认为国内政治与中苏决裂有更直接的关系. 参阅, 如唐纳德.柴哥利亚的 *中苏冲突：1956-1961年*（普林斯顿：普林斯顿大学出版社 1962 年出版），威廉.格里菲思的 *中苏决裂*（麻省，剑桥：麻省理工学院出版社 1964 年出版），以及戴维.弗洛伊德的 *毛对赫鲁晓夫：中苏冲突的简史*(纽约：普瑞爵 1964 年出版)

注53：NIE11/12-66, *中苏关系的展望*, 第一页和第二页, 1966年十二月一日.

注54：NIE11/13-69, 前引书, 第一页和第八页.

注55：同上, 第十页. 如欲阅读有关中苏边界冲突对尼克松政府关于中国, 苏维埃社会主义共和国联盟, 和北越之战略思维所造成的影响的揣测性的, 有趣的报道, 参阅郜培德的 *一道长城：六位总统与中国--调查性历史*(纽约：公共事务出版社1999年出版), 第六十一页到六十九页.

注56：中国外交部有关周与科锡金的会晤的报道可在http://www.fmprc.gov.cn/eng/ziliao/3602/3604/t18005.htm查阅;有关中国试验的信息可从http://fas.org/nuke/guide/china/nuke/tests.htm取阅.

注57：NIE11/13/6-73, *中苏关系中可能发生的变化*, 1973 年十月二十五日.

注58：NIE10, 前引书, 第二页.

注59：NIE13-60, 前引书, 第二页.

注60：NIE13-9-65, *中共的外交政策*, 第一页, 1965 年五月五日.

注61：NIE13-69, *中共与亚洲*, 第六页和第七页, 1969 年三月六日.

注62：ORE45-48, *中国目前的局势*, 于1948 年六月二十二日出版.

注63：参阅 *美国的对外关系, 1948年*, 第七卷, 远东：中国, 第118 页到第154 页.

注64：ORE77-48, *中共控制全中国的能力*, 1948 年十二月十日.

注65：邹谠 *美国在中国的失败, 1941-50*（芝加哥：芝加哥大学出版社1963年出版），第466页.

注63：SNIE100-9-58, 前引书, 第五页和第六页.

SECTION 1

ORE 45-48

The Current Situation in China

22 July 1948

CONFIDENTIAL

COPY NC. 82
FOR THE ASSISTANT DIRECTOR
FOR REPORTS AND ESTIMATES

40443

THE CURRENT SITUATION
IN CHINA

CIA HISTORICAL REVIEW PROGRAM
RELEASE IN FULL

ORE 45-48

Published 22 July 1948

Document No. 051
NO CHANGE in Class. ☐
DECLASSIFIED
Class. CHANGED TO: TS S C
DDA Memo, 4 Apr 77
Auth: DDA REG. 77/1763
Date: By:

CENTRAL INTELLIGENCE AGENCY

320064

ORE 45-48   SECRET

THE CURRENT SITUATION IN CHINA

SUMMARY

The position of the present National Government is so precarious that its fall may occur at any time. It is quite likely, however, that it may survive with diminishing power for some time, but soon become only one of several regimes exercising governmental powers independently in Nationalist China. Even with the current US aid program, the present National Government has little prospect of reversing or even checking these trends of disintegration. The increasing instability in Nationalist China will facilitate the extension of Chinese Communist military and political influence.

Within Nationalist China the power and prestige of Chiang Kai-shek is steadily weakening because of the unsuccessful prosecution of the war under his leadership and his apparent unwillingness and inability to accomplish positive reforms. Opposition, both within the Kuomintang and among dissident elements, centered chiefly in Hong Kong, is gathering strength. In addition, deteriorating economic conditions are exerting a cumulative impact on the political structure of the National Government. Furthermore, the military forces of the Chinese Communists have been able to seize the tactical initiative on an increasingly large scale. Even with current US assistance, it is improbable that the Nationalist Army can successfully defend all of its present territories.

In foreign relations, questions concerning the neighboring states of Japan and the USSR are of paramount interest to China for reasons of security. Chinese opinion favors a "hard" peace settlement with Japan so as to prevent the resurgence of that country as a Great Power. It is equally important for China to maintain correct and if possible friendly relations with the USSR, for China unaided cannot match Soviet power. Implementation of US aid to China is complicated by the question of the extent of US controls and supervision, and US insistence upon accompanying economic, political, and military reforms. The USSR thus far has refrained from overt material assistance to the Chinese Communists and continues to recognize the National Government, but it is apparent, nevertheless, that Soviet sympathies lie with the Chinese Communists. Even if US aid should prove effective, this might prove to be only a temporary advantage for the National Government, since it might be offset by Soviet counter-aid to the Chinese Communists.

The prospect for the foreseeable future in China is at best an indefinite and inconclusive prolongation of the civil war, with the authority of the National Government limited to a dwindling area in Central and South China and isolated major cities in north and northeast China, and with political and economic disorder spreading throughout the country except possibly in Communist-held areas. The worst prospect is complete collapse of the National Government, and its replacement by a Chinese

Note: The information in this report is as of 11 June 1948.
The intelligence organizations of the Departments of State, Army, Navy, and the Air Force have concurred in this report.

1   SECRET

SECRET

Communist-controlled regime, under Soviet influence if not under Soviet control, and uncooperative toward the US if not openly hostile. The latter development would result in an extensive loss of US prestige and increased Communist influence throughout the Far East, as well as an intensification of threat to US interests in the Western Pacific area.

SECRET   2

SECTION 2

ORE 12-48

Prospects for a Negotiated
Peace in China

3 August 1948

APPROVED FOR RELEASE
DATE: MAY 2004

SE~~CRET~~

PROSPECTS FOR A NEGOTIATED PEACE IN CHINA

ORE 12-48
Published August 3, 1948

CENTRAL INTELLIGENCE AGENCY

SE~~CRET~~

ORE 12-48   SECRET

PROSPECTS FOR A NEGOTIATED PEACE IN CHINA

SUMMARY

The prospects for a negotiated peace in the near future between the Chinese National Government under its present leadership and the Chinese Communists appear remote. This does not preclude, however, an early cessation of hostilities in some of the presently active military theaters as a result of regional arrangements between opposing commanders.

War-weariness and defeatism are widespread throughout Nationalist China, and although these sentiments have not yet been crystallized into a strong political force, no Nationalist leader can afford to ignore them. So long as Chiang Kai-shek remains in office, however, compromise between the National Government and the Communists appears virtually impossible, Chiang being opposed to negotiations with the Communists and they with him.

Chiang's position is steadily deteriorating, and his Government is in such a precarious situation that its collapse or overthrow could occur at any time. His ultimate fall is apparently inevitable, but the prospects of any single leader succeeding to a position with power comparable to that which Chiang now holds are remote. Any successor to Chiang, in order to secure peace, would have to be willing to negotiate on the terms the Communists would demand, and would have to possess the leadership and military support to hold the central government together while promoting such a policy. At the present time, although Li Chi-shen has been attempting to ride into power on the strength of a professed determination to seek an accommodation with the Communists, no such leader has appeared. Assuming that Chiang will not be replaced by any effective successor, and assuming further deterioration of the National Government's position, the probability is that before any peace negotiations can be undertaken, the Government will split into regional factions which will be forced to capitulate separately to the Communists.

While the bulk of the people in Nationalist China feel that continued resistance against the Communists is hopeless and therefore pointless, to Chiang and his immediate followers, the fortunes of the Government may appear in a different light. It may be a matter of years before the Communists can achieve total military victory, and before that time comes, Chiang probably feels that he can count on the incentive of presently guaranteed US aid, possible increased aid that might come from a new US administration, and an "inevitable" US-Soviet war in which the US would become his active ally.

The Soviet Ambassador has already made some overtures concerning a peace settlement to certain National Government officials. Given an opportune moment, the USSR would undoubtedly extend its good offices and attempt to exploit the dual

---

Note: The information in this report is as of 12 July 1948.

The intelligence organizations of the Departments of State, Army, Navy, and the Air Force have concurred in this report.

SECRET

SECRET

advantages of a peacefully communized China, and the propaganda value accruing from apparent advocacy of world peace.

A negotiated peace would have real advantages for the Communists, but since they hold the military initiative and feel sure of final victory, they would probably insist on terms that woud ensure their ultimate control of China.

2

SECRET

SECRET

PROSPECTS FOR A NEGOTIATED PEACE IN CHINA

1. **WAR-WEARINESS IN NATIONALIST CHINA.**

    Large numbers of people throughout Nationalist China blame the civil conflict for their present misfortunes. The internal struggle has already dashed the hope of peace and stability which the end of the war with Japan held out. The apparent hopelessness of ultimate victory for the Nationalists contributes heavily to the low morale of the common soldier, the civil servant, and the peasantry; and makes continued military operations against the Communists seem pointless. (See ORE 45-48.)

    The bulk of the common people in Nationalist areas have become apathetic; their aspirations and hopes for a brighter future under either a Nationalist or Communist regime have been dissipated. The peasants are told that the Government is in favor of agrarian reform, but except in certain Communist areas little substantial reform has been carried out. The students and intellectual groups have been pauperized by the inflation, and this has intensified their bitterness, frustration, and despair. Some students, in the face of severe and arbitrary police measures, are championing the Communist cause in Nationalist universities. Even many businessmen of Nationalist China are resigned to the prospects of living under Communist domination if that is prerequisite to the restoration of peace. Inflation, the complex and discriminatory Government controls, and the feeling of uncertainty have brought much of China's private enterprise to a standstill. It is significant to note that many foreign businessmen, including Americans, are reported to favor peace now under the Chinese Communists rather than continued and inconclusive fighting. These groups would probably support any program holding out hope for their continued existence and economic betterment, and they would be indifferent as to whether such a program would be to the advantage of the National Government as a political entity.

    This widespread feeling of war-weariness has also penetrated the ranks of Government civil and military officials, a number of whom are believed to favor an immediate settlement with the Communists. This desire, however, is and will continue to be largely ineffectual until it finds expression through a strong political organization with effective military support.

2. **NATIONAL GOVERNMENT ATTITUDE TOWARD PEACE.**

    a. *Chiang Kai-shek's Opposition to Negotiations.*

    Chiang Kai-shek and his closest personal adherents in the inner circle of powerful military and political figures are the key to the Nationalist position, and they remain adamant in their opposition to a compromise peace. The conservative CC Clique and the Whampoa Military Clique, in particular, so long as they see any hope in the continuation of the military struggle, will give the Generalissimo staunch support in his refusal to consider a political accommodation with the Communists.

    The National Government under Chiang has reasons for holding out as long as possible. The US aid program alone is a strong inducement and there is further hope that a new administration may increase the program. Since it may well be years before the Communists can achieve total military victory, the National Government may be able to maintain itself as a significant political entity longer by continu-

3

SECRET

SECRET

ing its present course than by engaging in peace negotiations with them. The long-range hopes of many Nationalist officials, furthermore, hinge upon their expectation of an inevitable war between the US and the USSR, in which the US would be an active war ally of the National Government in a struggle against international Communism.

In order that the National Government may continue to exist as now constituted it might withdraw to South China where its prospects for continued resistance, however, are not bright (see ORE 30-48).

b. *Forces Working for Chiang's Removal.*

Defeatism has to some extent penetrated those groups close to the Generalissimo, and, while this may not result in peace overtures to the Communists, it may provide tacit approval, in high circles, of such a move. Even certain high military figures feel that the Nationalist military position is almost hopeless.

There has not yet emerged any leader capable of directly challenging Chiang as head of the state but there are some who are working for his removal. Li Tsung-jen, the new Vice-President, is a potential threat to Chiang and reportedly hopes to induce him to accept a far-reaching reform program, failing which Li might try to force Chiang into the background and assume the presidential powers. Since his election in April, however, Li has had little opportunity to influence the political scene. In assessing the elements relating to Li which will influence the prospects for peace, it is important to note that he may be as unacceptable to the Communists as Chiang, inasmuch as their propaganda has recently classed him with the Generalissimo as an enemy of the Chinese people and a tool of US imperialism. In addition Li has publicly professed his opposition to peace talks with the Communists.

Li Chi-shen and his Kuomintang Revolutionary Committee in Hong Kong are openly attempting to displace Chiang, and plan to establish soon a new "provisional government", probably somewhere in Southwest China. In addition to the fact that he believes peace is necessary to a stable National Government, Li Chi-shen feels that the faction which brings peace to China will gain immense popular support. He has been cooperating with Communists in Hong Kong with the hope that such cooperation will place him in a key position for any future peace negotiations and the establishment of a coalition government. At the same time, however, he maintains that he is anti-Communist and that he intends to retain the upper hand over the Communists in such a government. Li Chi-shen is essentially an opportunist and will probably accept any offer from any source that would assist him in attaining a position of power. While Li may have considerable popular support, the extent of his organized political and military backing is probably small.

3. CHINESE COMMUNIST POSITION.

The Communists, since the collapse of negotiations in early 1947, have reiterated their refusal to deal with the Generalissimo and his followers. Any discussion of peace on the part of the Communists, therefore, presupposes the removal of Chiang. They continue to stress in their propaganda that they favor the establishment of a coalition government of all democratic elements, under firm Communist leadership.

4

SECRET

SECRET

· Despite their favorable military position, the object of the Chinese Communists, which is the control of all China, could probably be achieved sooner and more easily through peaceful channels than by continuance of the war. The Communists could demand that they be given legal status in the government of China, and such status would probably facilitate the extension of their control over all China. By taking over the remainder of the country before it is further disorganized or damaged by fighting, they would have fewer problems in creating a stable China.

4. SOVIET POSITION IN PEACE OVERTURES.

The USSR is the most likely external medium through which the two sides can be brought together because it is in the unique position of maintaining treaty relationships with the National Government while giving ideological, if not material support to the Chinese Communists.

Roshchin, Soviet Military Attache, gave added impetus to the movement toward a compromise peace by his unofficial overture to certain National Government officials several months ago. He was subsequently recalled to Moscow (in January 1948) and was appointed in late February 1948 as Soviet Ambassador to China. In mid-July Roshchin reopened the discussion when he approached another Nationalist official. This has added strength to the opinion that the USSR may offer a specific mediation proposal at a time judged propitious by Moscow.

A peace settlement mediated by the Soviets would be advantageous to them since it would present an opportunity to counteract US influence in Nationalist China. In addition, by shifting the Communist revolt from a military to a political sphere, the USSR could vitiate the influence of the present Chinese Communist leadership which the USSR may distrust. A Communist China would be an immense advantage to the USSR and would be important in spreading Soviet influence over the entire Far East. Even if Soviet efforts to bring about an end to the war were unsuccessful, the USSR would gain prestige, and the propaganda value of having attempted to bring peace to China. The USSR has already exploited and aggravated the current disunity in the National Government by bringing up the question of mediation.

5. NEGOTIATIONS FOR PEACE.

The 1945-46 peace negotiations between the Kuomintang and the Chinese Communist Party were broken off because of failure to reach agreement on (1) the reorganization and disposition of the armed forces, (2) local government and territorial control, (3) representation in a coalition government, and (4) problems relating to the calling of a National Assembly for the adoption of a Constitution. These questions would necessarily constitute the basis for any future negotiations.

Because the Communists are now in a position to resume the military offensive at any time, they can insist on much more extreme terms. These demands, which would undoubtedly include the removal of Chiang, would be in excess of the maximum concessions that the Nationalists would be prepared to make at this time.

In the event of Chiang's fall, there may be no single leader in Nationalist China, with the possible exception of Li Tsung-jen, with sufficient support to form an effective successor Government. If no qualified successor to Chiang should emerge, several

5

SECRET

SECRET

more or less independent regional regimes would come into existence. The Communists could enter into separate negotiations with the leaders of these local regimes who would be forced to deal with them in order to preserve, if only temporarily, some vestige of their personal power.

If, upon the removal of Chiang, a leader or group should emerge with sufficient political and military backing to unite the diverse elements of the Kuomintang into an effective successor Government, negotiations for peace might follow. Such negotiations would be colored by the fact that the new National Government would probably be in an even weaker bargaining position than the present Government under Chiang. In the negotiations, the Communists might satisfy themselves initially with either a territorial settlement or a controlling position in a "coaliton" government. Although the former type of settlement would afford the Communists legal recognition of the areas they now occupy and permit them to consolidate their administration and reconstruct these areas, it would by no means satisfy the ultimate aspirations of the Chinese Communist Party. A territorial settlement would, therefore, be honored by the Communists only so long as it was to their advantage.

The ultimate goal of the Communists would be better served through the inclusion of that Party within a "liberal front" coalition government. In such a government the Communists would obviously have a powerful, if not a dominating, voice. They could force through a new National Assembly a new or revised Constitution and a new election, all of which would aid them in seizing virtual control of China.

SECRET

SECTION 3

ORE 77-48

Chinese Communist Capabilities for
Control of All China

10 December 1948

APPROVED FOR RELEASE
DATE: MAY 2004

 SECRET

CHINESE COMMUNIST CAPABILITIES FOR CONTROL OF ALL CHINA

ORE 77-48

Published 10 December 1948

CENTRAL INTELLIGENCE AGENCY

 SECRET

ORE 77-48   SECRET

CHINESE COMMUNIST CAPABILITIES FOR CONTROL OF ALL CHINA

SUMMARY

The rapid disintegration of the Nationalist Army indicates that organized resistance to the military forces of the Chinese Communist Party will probably cease within a few months. When there is no further Nationalist resistance directed from a central headquarters, Communist forces will proceed at leisure to the reduction of anti-Communist forces in Inner Mongolia and South and western China.

The Communists are not, as yet, officially advancing a program of radical reform. Their measures in newly acquired territory have been moderate and conciliatory, gaining them increased popular support. The Communists have exploited the hopeless economic situation in North and Central China to the point where any Communist program appears more desirable to the people than a Nationalist survival.

A Communist-dominated government will probably come to power as a result of what is in effect the surrender of the National Government. This government will probably be proclaimed as a "coalition," and it will include many non-Communists, among them members of the present National Government. As a "coalition" it will have the advantage of not necessarily forfeiting international recognition. It is almost certain, however, that Communist officials will dictate the policies of such a government.

There is no doubt that the Chinese Communist Party has been and is an instrument of Soviet policy. While there is no guarantee that the USSR will always find the Chinese Communists dependable, there appears to be no chance of a split within the Party or between the Party and the USSR until the time of Communist domination of China.

Note: The information in this report is as of 1 December 1948.
    The intelligence organizations of the Departments of State, Army, Navy, and the Air Force
    have concurred in this report.

SECRET

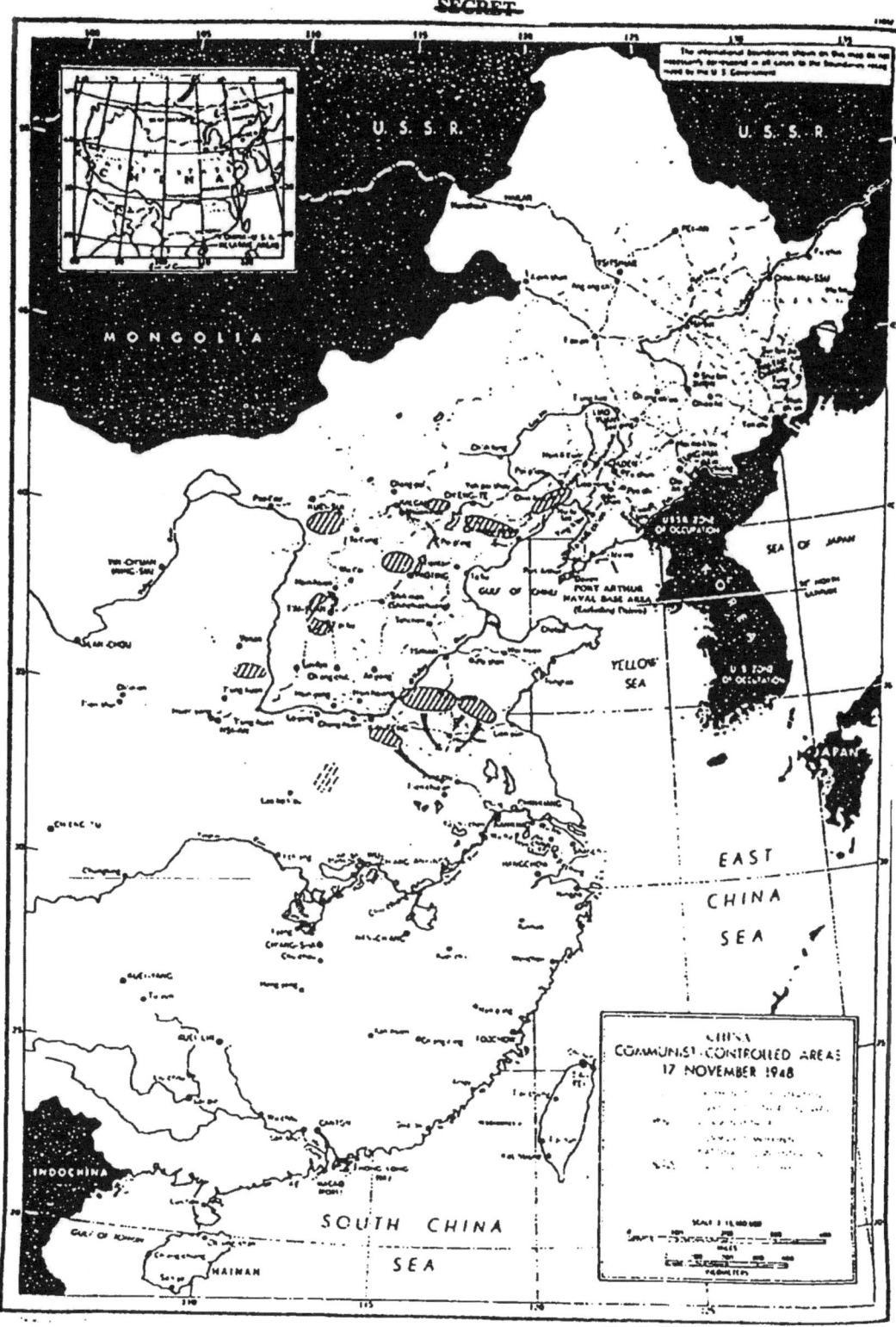

CHINESE COMMUNIST CAPABILITIES FOR CONTROL OF ALL CHINA

This paper assumes that the intention of the Chinese Communist Party is to gain absolute control of all China. It is the purpose of this paper to determine whether the Chinese Communists are capable of so doing.

The Military Phase

The strength and the tactical success of the Chinese Communist Forces have been the chief instruments in the ascent of the Communist Party, and will continue to be so until all organized resistance by the Nationalist Army has been overcome. As the Nationalist Army is the major obstacle to that ascent, the mission of the Communist Forces will be to proceed with the annihilation of the Nationalists' vital strength. The Communist Forces, through extremely able use of available human resources, through support (derived or extracted) from the populace in Communist-held areas, and through a clever use of propaganda, have overcome initial limitations in the materials of war and have reached or exceeded parity with the Nationalists in numbers, weapons, and equipment. The Communists' greatest advantage over their opponent is found in this expert exploitation of human resources, and their prospect of eventual victory rests upon that ability.

    a.   *The Human Factor.*

High morale and excellent leadership, repetitive and finally credible propaganda themes, plus a well-developed sense of purpose, have elevated the once materially weak Communist Forces to their present position of superiority in the civil conflict. The morale of the opposing Nationalists is excessively low, and is reflected not only in a marked preference for passive tactics but often in a wholesale refusal to fight. Entire armies surrender *en masse*, and even those units which choose to fight often find that the defections of neighboring units have rendered their position tactically untenable. As continued resistance appears pointless, and as Communist propaganda emphasizes this, the defenses soon collapse. Further, the loss of such defense centers as Chin-hsien, Mukden, or Tsinan, has the same effect in an over-all strategic sense as do local defections in a tactical sense.

Communist propaganda is aimed both at strengthening internal Communist morale and at weakening the morale of National Government supporters. A simple theme, constantly repeated—things are better under the Communists—creates in time, and under the proper circumstances, a conviction in the minds of the Nationalist officers and men that this is true. The Communists have offered equivalent grades to those who "come over"; they offer food as a lure; they reiterate the essential brotherhood of all Chinese and the futility of internecine warfare (especially the futility of continued resistance to the Communist tide); they point out corruption and discrimination within the Nationalist Forces; in fact there is, in Communist propaganda, something for everybody. It is effective, for the will of the Nationalists to resist has been

1

SECRET

SECRET

so weakened as to make highly improbable any continued effective resistance over a significant period of time. The insidious effects of the Communist Fifth Column and the obvious superiority of Communist intelligence, contribute heavily both to the Communists' military and political successes. Nationalist counter-efforts in each of these fields have been puerile failures.

b. *The Material Factor.*

It is estimated that the strength of the Communist Forces is about 1,500,000, the great majority being combat effectives. In addition, they possess a strategic reserve. They are opposed by slightly over a million Nationalists, the great majority of whom will offer only token resistance before defecting to the Communists. It is unnecessary for the Communists to integrate the growing number of Nationalist renegades into their army inasmuch as present Communist combat forces are sufficiently large to fulfill their mission; if they were to absorb large numbers of defected Nationalist Forces, they would probably dilute their real strength. In addition to their first-line troops, the Communists can, when necessary, call upon the combat services of some 2,000,000 irregulars, whose indoctrination, from the Communist viewpoint, is superior to that of disaffected Nationalists.

The Communists' logistic position is such that they now have a marked advantage over the Nationalist Army. The former, with Japanese, Chinese, and US arms garnered from a variety of sources, can now outgun the latter at almost any point. As neither combatant can supply itself from current arsenal production, each must remain dependent upon outside supply. The US has supplied, and again is supplying, arms and ammunition to the National Government, while the chief source of supply for the Communist Forces remains the capture of matériel from the Nationalists. The USSR allowed the Communists to take over the large stocks of the Japanese Kwantung Army in Manchuria (which matériel is probably only now running out), and even now may be extending them technical advice, but no concrete evidence exists to support the contention that the USSR is currently supplying Japanese or Soviet matériel to the Chinese Communists.

The Communists control the great majority of the rural, food-producing areas of North and Northeast China, and are thereby enabled to employ food as a weapon in the civil contest. Shortages of food, later starvation, in Nationalist-held cities, surrounded and cut off from the normal sources of food, play an important role in their eventual capitulation. By making effective use of all means of transport available to them, and by conditioning tactics to their limitations in this regard, the Communists have enjoyed a relative advantage in combat supply. More recently the railways of Manchuria have lent the Communists a new and apparently devastating mobility and striking power. Nationalist transport has, on the contrary, gone from bad to worse, and is now reduced to short stretches of highway and railway within or leading into the combat areas. These truncated channels are supplemented by waterborne and aerial transportation, which are, though inadequate, the most important available to the Nationalists.

SECRET

2

SECRET

The Nationalists possess the only extant navy and air force, and thus enjoy certain limited tactical advantages. The Nationalist Air Force, however, has shown itself to be an ineffective organization in the fields of bombing and fighter support. In addition, shortages of almost all materials required to operate an air force have reduced the Nationalist Air Force to a primary function of transport.

c. *Strategy and Probable Future Trends.*

A shift in the Communist tactical emphasis has paralleled the growth of its army. At first tentatively, but lately with assurance, the Communists have assaulted large, comparatively well-defended cities. Although this has produced a portion of the Communist Army, which, departing from the traditional Communist concept of guerrilla warfare, is probably capable of taking any Nationalist-held city, there remains a considerable section of Communist units still operating primarily along guerrilla lines. The latter groups will be principally employed in the initial phases of any new operations. The assault troops will undertake to reduce Nationalist-held pockets which have been encircled and are about to fall. Communist strategy will continue to invite Nationalist defections and will probably be highly successful.

At present the principal areas of Nationalist resistance are in the Tientsin-Kalgan area of North China, and the Central China area around Hsuchou. Greatly superior Communist forces are moving into position to attack the former region, while a strong Communist drive in the Hsuchou area is well under way. This drive, which threatens to engulf all Nationalist units in the area and open a clear pathway to lightly defended Nanking, might well prove the *coup de grace* to organized resistance by the Nationalist Army. Other areas of Nationalist resistance, at Sian, Kueisui, Taiyuan, and Hankow, are now being reduced or can be reduced later without much difficulty by the Communists. There are no effective Nationalist forces, nor are there any local troops that could successfully resist the Communists, in South, Southwest, or West China, and it can be assumed that the extension of Communist authority into these areas will inevitably follow the termination of organized military operations by the Nationalist Army.

The Economic Phase.

The Chinese Communist Party will not be faced with any economic problems which in scope or kind will prevent it from attaining its immediate military and political goals. As the military program of the Communist Army nears completion, and the islands of Nationalist resistance are reduced, the pattern of the Communist economy will gradually develop from a loose federation of relatively self-sufficient and economically independent regions into a structure with increased integration and interdependence.

a. *Agricultural Factor.*

The food situation, in areas occupied by the Communists, will not be serious. Although agricultural prospects are not favorable, the food situation in Communist areas should not be worse than it has been under the Nationalists. Insect plagues in

3

SECRET

SECRET

southern Manchuria have reduced the normally large grain surplus from Manchuria, but the outlook for North China is good, and production should be close to that of prewar. In North China there will be, as always, a few famine areas, notably in parts of Shansi and the flooded areas of the Huai River and the Hungtze and Weishan Lakes, but this may be partly overcome by moving food from areas of more adequate production. The unification of the economic regions of North China may have an immediate salutary effect on the distribution system which formerly linked the farmers and the numerous small towns dotting the North China plains. The problem of feeding the large cities which have come under Communist control, or which will fall to the Communists in the near future, will be offset by possession of through rail connections which will permit transportation of food from surplus areas. While the obligation of feeding these additional cities will strain the Communists' food resources, the standard of living in the cities will probably not be reduced under Communist rule.

b. *The Industrial Factor*.

The Chinese Communists have thus far exploited the resources and industry of Manchuria only to a limited extent, and further rehabilitation of transportation, mining, and industry in Communist areas will probably prove difficult. There has been no large-scale resumption of the heavy iron and steel industry once built up in this region. With the exception of a few consumer items, such as textiles, the present limited production of small-scale home industries, augmented by the smuggling of goods from Nationalist areas, apparently meets the immediate needs of the Communists' economy.

North China would have a possible excess of industrial capacity over the Chinese Communists' immediate requirements if the Communists acquire control of the large textile and other industrial installations in North China cities; textile shortages in Manchuria could thus be eased.

By capturing Tsinan and Mukden intact, the Communists have gained possession of large industrial installations and stocks of raw materials and finished goods. This may establish a precedent, and, if Tientsin or other large cities fall to the Communists, the industrial installations, power plants, and railway networks may be taken over by them in a comparatively undamaged state. In attempting to rehabilitate the industry of newly won areas, the Communists will necessarily be faced with the problem of replacing worn-out machinery and equipment, but in the immediate future, all of the Communists' industrial needs can be met even with the plants in their present under-maintained and obsolete condition. The Communists will not be faced with any large-scale shortages of skilled personnel, for most of the technicians operating Nationalist factories probably can be induced to stay on the job under a Communist regime.

The large arsenal at Mukden has fallen to the Communist Forces and will add to the Communist military potential. Furthermore, the Communists have acquired such a vast stock of weapons and equipment in their capture of Nationalist military units that, even without the arsenal, the Communist Forces would have an adequate supply of munitions.

SECRET

4

SECRET

There is no shortage of coal in Manchuria, mining capacity being well in excess of requirements for power plants, railroads, and fuel. When the Kailan mines (north of Tientsin) fall into Communist hands, there will be a surplus of coal over and above Communist domestic requirements in North China.

The transportation system in North China and Manchuria, although under-maintained and in most cases seriously deteriorated, will be of great benefit to the Communists in their consolidation of the areas of North and Northeast China. Through rail routes are already in operation, and several more seem about to be. In addition, the capture of the North China ports might give the Communists a number of small vessels, totaling perhaps 100,000 tons, which would provide adequate shipping for coastal requirements.

    c. *Possible Future Trends.*

A basic advantage which the Communists possess derives from the fact that the economic situation under the Nationalists in North and Central China has so com-pletely deteriorated that any change for the better, no matter how slight, will afford the Communists great psychological benefits. By re-establishing normal relationships between the major cities of North China and Manchuria and their surrounding coun-tryside, the wartime barriers to trade and communication will be eliminated, and the Communists' opportunity for consolidating their gains in this part of China will be immeasurably advanced.

The Political Phase.

In the period during which the Communist political effort will be parallel to, and dependent upon, the military effort, the Chinese Communist Party will simultaneously: (a) consolidate its control over areas which it already occupies, (b) prepare to admin-ister areas which will presently be under its control, and (c) continue to erect a frame-work for a Communist-dominated government for all of China.

    a. *Consolidation of Control.*

Within China, the Communist Party has derived its principal popular sup-port from the peasant masses, and to a lesser extent from industrial workers and urban intelligentsia. The Communist Party has skillfully exploited three major and genuine grievances: peasant misery, affronts to national sovereignty, and the corruption and ineptitude of the National Government. By carrying out, on a larger scale than has the National Government, such basic agrarian reforms as redistribution of land and reduction of rent and taxes, the Communist Party apparently has demonstrated, to the majority of the populace in Communist-controlled areas, its practical superiority to the National Government. The promise of the CCP to defend China against foreign aggression has in some quarters been received with favor, despite the Chinese Communists' affinity with the USSR. The character of the National Government, a government which not only has not solved but has refused even to attack the basic economic and political problems of China, has of course been a major asset to the Communists. The peasant masses have never supported the National Government

5

SECRET

26

SECRET

and do not now resist the advances of the Communists. The latter are, furthermore, attracting increasingly large numbers of urban workingmen, businessmen, intellectuals, and officials.

The various areas of China occupied by the Communists have in the past been administered through the Central Executive Committee of the Chinese Communist Party; this body does not, however, fully perform the functions of a central government, and unconsolidated areas are apparently permitted to exercise some degree of administrative autonomy. About three months ago the Communist Party proclaimed a "North China People's Government," formalizing the previous unification of two northern border region governments. This North China government may be the prototype for a number of other "People's Governments," to be formally established elsewhere in China as rapidly as the Communist Party consolidates its control. It is further possible that these various regional governments will be administered by a central government, but public proclamation of such a government would not be necessary to the Communist plan for effecting a "coalition" with other dissident groups and various elements of the present National Government. In the meantime, it is probable that the various regional governments will be permitted to pursue policies best adapted to the particular area.

b. *Preparations for Control.*

At present the Communists are pursuing a policy of moderation both in the areas which they control and toward the areas which they are preparing to control. Before Communist Forces enter a besieged city, the Communist Party promises to cooperate with businessmen, landlords, and Nationalist troops, and appeals to the people of the city to maintain order, preserve the governmental apparatus, and remain on the job; the Communist Party promises that it will be lenient with all elements which "cooperate" with it. These tactics appear to indicate that the Communists, because they lack trained personnel, must rely in part upon Nationalist urban administrations, but in any case this practice enables the Communists to control any given city rapidly and to administer it efficiently. Political officers accompany Communist troops into the city; the military administration is replaced by a civil body as soon as practicable. The maintenance of order and the restoration of the municipal government and economy, can be presented by the Communists as a favorable contrast to the disorder and confusion which preceded its entry and which exist in many Nationalist-occupied cities not yet threatened by the Communists. The Communists even claim that they will protect the interests of private industry so long as such industries "cooperate." The Communists lack experience and personnel for the operation of large industries, and they are apparently willing, temporarily, to accept assistance from any quarter. Thus the above claim certainly encourages propertied elements in their hope of survival in health under a Communist government. It is highly probable, however, that the Communist will assume complete control of all enterprises when they are prepared to do so.

The Communist Party also is following a moderate policy toward rural areas. The practice of outright expropriation of land, liquidation of landlords, and terroriza-

6

SECRET

tion of the populace as a whole, has been officially condemned by the Communist Party as "extremist." Agrarian reform, especially in areas occupied by the Communists in the past several months, has apparently become cautious and gradual. The program of rapid agrarian reform in Central China has been postponed indefinitely; at present, only the reduction of rent and interest rates is being effected. The Communists claim that the peasant masses are not yet "ideologically prepared" for a swift and complete reformation. This is apparently an admission that the Communist Party faces real problems in consolidating its control, but it also means that, by pursuing a moderate policy, the Communists will considerably broaden their support in rural areas.

c. *Government for All China.*

In planning for a government for all of China, the Communist Party must choose one of the following alternatives: (a) to establish a "coalition" government in the area which it already controls, this government to include the various Communist regional governments, with the anti-Nationalist Kuomintang Revolutionary Committee (KMTRC), the Democratic League, and other dissident groups; or (b) to continue to plan, together with the above groups, a government which will proceed toward control of all of China, and which will probably be proclaimed as a "coalition," to include elements of the National Government. (It is not necessary that the Communists proclaim a "coalition"; but it would probably appear to them desirable.)

It does not seem likely that the Communists will choose the first course cited above. A premature "coalition" government, merely with the KMTRC and Democratic League, and merely in areas already held by the Communists, would have few positive advantages, and the great disadvantage of necessarily forfeiting international recognition. In addition, it is probable that the Nationalists will soon have no alternative to that of attempting to negotiate with the Communists, perhaps through the good offices of the USSR, for a "coalition" government for all of China, such "coalition" to be dominated by the Communists.

It is probable that a Communist-dominated government will come to power as a result of, perhaps at the time of, what is in effect the surrender of the National Government, but that the new government will be proclaimed as a "coalition," which would *not* necessarily forfeit international recognition. This government will include representatives of the KMTRC, the Democratic League, and elements of the present National Government. It is quite possible that the Communists will prefer to have a non-Communist as titular head of the government, and to have non-Communists as titular heads of a number of departments of government; but it is almost certain that genuine authority, at every level of the government, will in time be exercised by the Communist Party alone.

The subsequent relations of the Communist-dominated "coalition" government with the USSR and the US will be a matter of considerable complexity. In accordance with the present strategy of the Soviet-directed international Communist movement, the Chinese Communist Party presents itself to Chinese primarily in terms of national interest, rather than in its role in the international Communist movement. The pol-

7

SECRET

SECRET

icy of both the Chinese Communists and the USSR, moreover, in emphasizing the former's positive achievements in China, has been extremely effective, in that only a small proportion of Chinese realize fully the implications of a Soviet-oriented Communist government. The Communist Party shares with the USSR a common ideology, a common political organization, common strategies and techniques, and, at present, a common goal. The Chinese Communist Party has never publicly deviated from the Soviet Party line, has never publicly criticized any Soviet action or representative, and has never publicly given any indication whatsoever that it could be oriented away from the USSR and toward the United States. It is certain that the Chinese Communist Party has been and is an instrument of Soviet policy. While it is not certain that the Communist Party is or will be an absolutely reliable instrument, there appears to be no chance of a split within the Chinese Communist Party or between the USSR and the Chinese Communists, until at least such time as a Communist-dominated government of China comes to power.

SECRET   8

SECTION 4

ORE 29-49

Prospects for Soviet Control
of a Communist China

15 April 1949

APPROVED FOR RELEASE
DATE: MAY 2004

SE~~CRET~~

PROSPECTS FOR SOVIET CONTROL OF A COMMUNIST CHINA

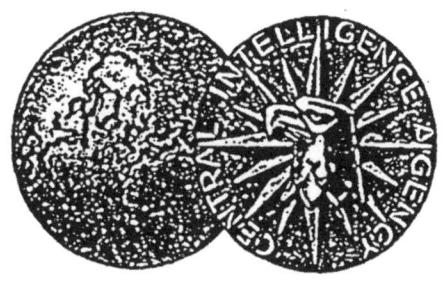

ORE 29-49

Published 15 April 1949

CENTRAL INTELLIGENCE AGENCY

SE~~CRET~~

ORE 29-49

SECRET

PROSPECTS FOR SOVIET CONTROL OF A COMMUNIST CHINA *

SUMMARY

It is the intention of the Soviet Union to advance toward its goal of eventual world domination by adding to the Soviet orbit the enormous territory and population of China, and by employing China to facilitate Soviet expansion into other Far Eastern areas.

A coalition government formed by the Chinese Communists, while representing a temporary tactical maneuver, will contain no elements capable of offering real opposition to the Communists.

A moderate Chinese Communist policy toward small business proprietors, landowners, and peasants will help to gain popular support, at least until the government feels strong enough to launch into the more vigorous phases of communization.

The Communist timetable in China will be flexible and will be influenced by internal conditions in China generally, as well as by the international situation. The complexities of ruling a country like China will, undoubtedly, retard the consolidation of Communist control, but these complexities in themselves probably cannot, in the long run, prevent it.

The Chinese Communists will support Soviet foreign policy by diplomatic moves calculated to embarrass the Western Powers, by blatant anti-Western propaganda, and by assistance to the Communist parties and nationalist movements of Asia.

Foreign loans which involve no political commitments will be negotiated by the Chinese Communists wherever possible, and foreign trade (under state supervision) will undoubtedly be continued with non-Communist countries. This policy does not imply permanent benevolence toward foreign business interests in China.

The Soviet Union will attempt to use the CCP as its chief instrument to consolidate control over China as it has successfully used the various national Communist parties of Eastern Europe. The strong influence exerted by the Soviet Union over the Chinese Party has been variously revealed and provides ample indication that the present leadership of the Chinese Communists identifies itself solidly with international Communism as promulgated by Moscow. The Kremlin will endeavor to prevent possible cleavages in the Party leadership from jeopardizing eventual Soviet control over China.

The present Sino-Soviet Treaty can be directed at the US and its allies, and other agreements may provide for a high degree of economic and military integration between the USSR and China. At the same time, in accordance with its strategy of creating on its borders easily dominated political entities, the Soviet Government will probably press for political autonomy in all present Chinese border areas adjacent to the USSR.

Note: The intelligence organizations of the Departments of State, Army, Navy, and the Air Force have concurred in this report. The information herein is as of 12 April 1949.

* This paper discusses a pattern of developments which should become apparent prior to 1951.

1

SECRET

SECRET

It must be emphasized that the process of consolidation of Soviet control over China will unquestionably encounter considerable difficulty, in view of the many potential points of conflict between the USSR and the Chinese Communists, e.g., the issues of US aid, control of peripheral areas, control of assistance to Communist movements in other Far Eastern areas, and the subservience which Moscow will undoubtedly demand of the CCP. While some opposition to Moscow control probably exists in the CCP, for such opposition to be effective the dissident groups must wrest the control apparatus from the pro-Moscow leadership, or that leadership itself must change its policy toward Moscow. Until evidence is available that an effective opposition is developing, it is concluded that the CCP will remain loyal to Moscow.

SECRET

2

SECTION 5

ORE 45-49

Probable Developments in China

16 June 1949

APPROVED FOR RELEASE
DATE: MAY 2004

 SECRET

PROBABLE DEVELOPMENTS
IN CHINA

ORE 45-49

Published 16 June 1949

CENTRAL INTELLIGENCE AGENCY

 SECRET

S~~E~~C~~R~~ET

PROBABLE DEVELOPMENTS IN CHINA

SUMMARY

Introductory Note: The purpose of the following discussion is to present probable developments in China which will affect US interests during the next six to twelve months.

1. Communist military forces are capable during the summer months of 1949 of destroying all semblance of unity in the National Government of China; and before the year is out, the Communists will have formed a central government which will seek international recognition.

2. The US cannot reverse or significantly check this course of events, nor is there any prospect that the Soviet orientation of the Chinese Communists can be altered in the immediate future. However, during the coming months, developments in China will raise a number of problems on which the US may either take action advancing, or avoid action compromising, its interests in China and elsewhere. Chief among these are the formation of a Communist central government claiming international recognition, Communist aims regarding Taiwan and Hong Kong, the Communist need for foreign trade, and US aid to anti-Communist groups in China. In addition, US interests probably will be affected adversely by the expansion of Communist influence throughout the Far East, particularly if a Chinese Communist regime gains seats on the Far Eastern Commission and the Allied Council for Japan, and acquires China's claims regarding a future Japanese peace treaty.

3. The government to be organized by the Chinese Communists will be proclaimed as a "coalition," but actually will be a Communist dictatorship. In foreign affairs the Communists during the coming months will continue to be solidly aligned with the USSR. The new regime will honor the Sino-Soviet Treaty of 1945 and its attitude in international relations will be governed by the Moscow line. It will probably maintain an unfriendly attitude toward the US in particular and all other governments that impede the world Communist movement, as well as denounce China's existing international agreements with those governments.

4. Communist armed forces, now decisively superior to the Nationalists, will continue their program of area-by-area acquisition. They are capable of eliminating all effective military resistance in the south, southwest, and northwest by the end of 1950.

5. The Chinese Communists will probably not be faced with serious food shortages during the next year. Some progress will be made in reviving transportation and industry, and the Communists will have a relatively stable currency. The Communists' principal economic problem in the coming months will be that of acquiring petroleum, machinery, and perhaps cotton. There is little prospect of substantial Soviet aid, and domestic resources must be supplemented by these essential imports. Therefore, China's economic recovery during the next year will probably depend on active Western trade and close ties with occupied Japan.

Note: The intelligence organizations of the Departments of Army, Navy, and the Air Force have concurred in this report; for a dissent of the Intelligence Organization of the Department of State, see Enclosure A, p. 21. This report contains information available to CIA as of 2 June 1949.

S E C~~R~~E T

1

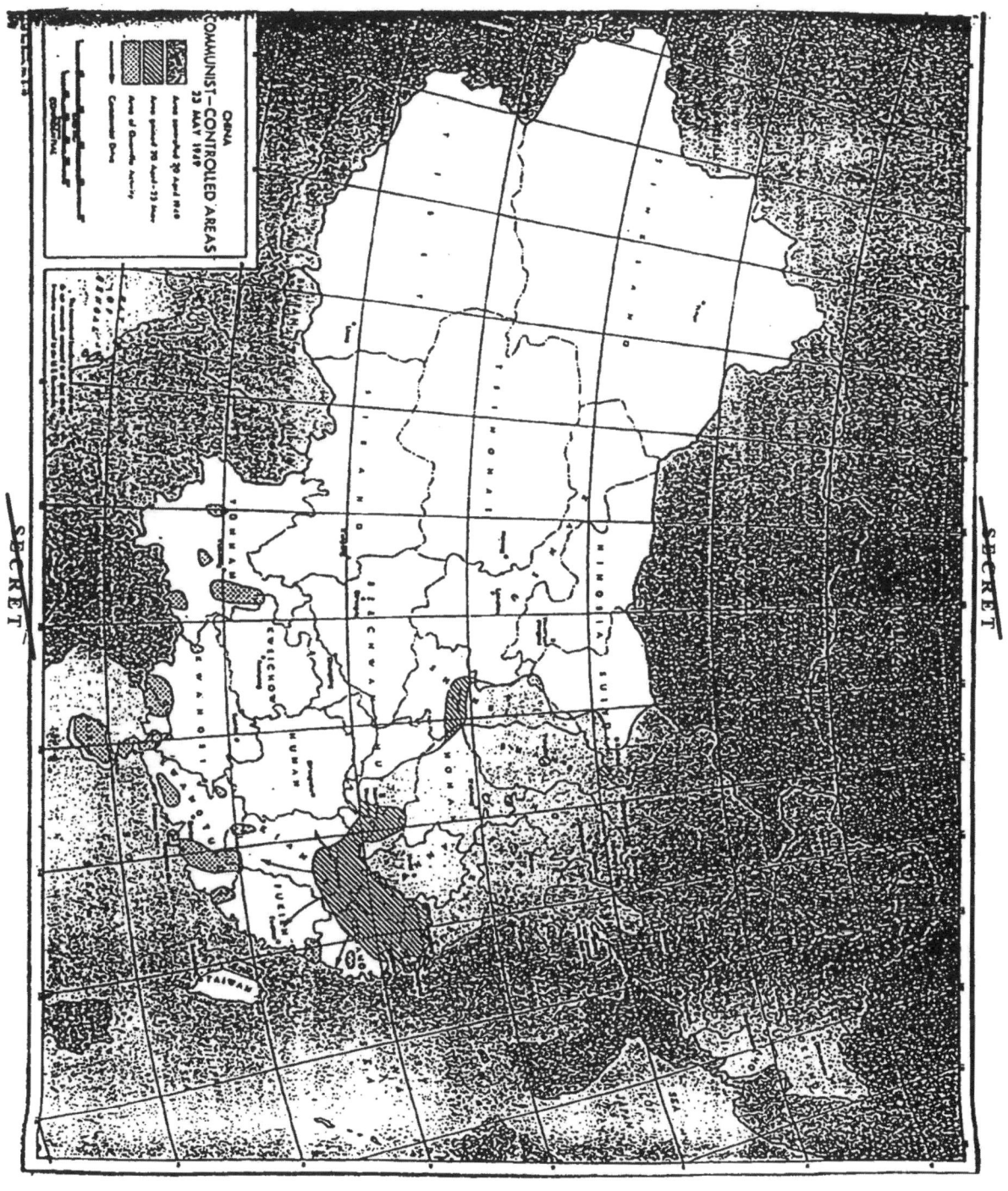

SECRET

PROBABLE DEVELOPMENTS IN CHINA

Introductory Note: The purpose of the following discussion is to present probable developments in China which will affect US interests during the next six to twelve months.

1. Imminent Problems for the US Arising out of Developments in China.

The Chinese Communist armies have the capability, during the summer months of 1949, of completing their campaign in the Yangtze Valley, from the eastern border of Szechwan to the sea, and of dislodging the Nationalists from Canton and other ports on the southeast coast during this same period. Their military operations in this period will destroy all semblance of unity in the present National Government, the remnants of which will seek refuge in Taiwan, southwest and northwest China, or in flight abroad. In late summer or early autumn, the Chinese Communist Party will convoke a Political Consultative Conference to form and proclaim a Communist-controlled government for all China before the end of 1949. At that time, Communist China will contain more than half of China's people, and, if not more than half of China's territory, at least the larger part of its most productive areas. The Communist Government then will seek recognition as the national government of China.

The US cannot reverse the course of the Chinese civil conflict nor induce the Chinese Communists to modify their intention to establish a Communist dictatorship over China. Also, there is no prospect that the US can alter the Soviet orientation of the Chinese Communists in the immediate future. During the next few months, however, there will be a number of developments in China affecting US interests such as: (1) possible incidents involving US armed forces, officials, and nationals; (2) sharpening of the Communist-Nationalist struggle for Taiwan, where US strategic interests are involved; (3) Chinese Communist designs on Hong Kong and Macao; (4) US aid to anti-Communist groups in China; (5) the Communist need for foreign trade; (6) the establishment of a Communist central regime seeking international recognition, and; (7) the expansion of Chinese Communist influence throughout the Far East.

It is known that the leaders of the Chinese Communists desire international recognition for their regime, and that they also desire commercial relations with the West and with Japan. These facts may permit the US, in the course of the next several months, either to take action advancing or to avoid action compromising certain of its interests in China and elsewhere in the Far East.

a. Possible Incidents.

In firing upon British warships in the Yangtze, the Communists demonstrated that they are prepared to risk reprisals in order to substantiate their promise to protect China from "imperialist aggression." The Chinese Communist Party (CCP) undoubtedly gained face within China and elsewhere in Asia by this action, and it is possible that the Communists will again take advantage of any opportunities which arise for military action against foreign armed forces. The opportunities for local incidents involving foreign officials and nationals have become much more numerous with the CCP occupation of major cities—as suggested by the forced entry of the US Ambassador's residence by Communist soldiers during their occupation of Nanking. Incidents involving the mistreatment of foreign nationals and the destruction or seizure of foreign property are likely. If the Communist regime should request, and be refused recognition, it is highly probable that such incidents will multiply, with CCP connivance. If the US should extend further support to the Nationalists, such incidents can reach serious proportions.

b. Taiwan.

There is no doubt that the CCP desires to extend its control over the island of Taiwan.

SECRET

3

4

SECRET

where Chiang Kai-shek is preparing for a last stand, hoping to survive until reinforced by the US at the outbreak of a world conflict which he believes inevitable. The Communist-Nationalist contest for control of the island will become more sharply drawn in the near future, when Chiang Kai-shek and his Nationalist followers will be forced to establish headquarters there.

The CCP is not capable, at the present time, of successfully undertaking an amphibious operation against Taiwan. In the next few months, however, the CCP will not only acquire the mainland coastal ports and shipping to make such an operation possible but also will be able to infiltrate the island, attempt to subvert Nationalist officials there, and exploit the widespread native resentment of Nationalist rule. These developments will improve CCP chances of taking control of Taiwan. The Communist-controlled regime certainly will assert sovereignty over Taiwan, and the leaders of Taiwanese native groups in time may support them in that claim. While civil disorders on Taiwan will probably not be sufficiently serious to wrest the island from Nationalist control, any insurrection which develops on Taiwan is likely to further the purposes of the CCP. There is a prospect of lengthy propaganda warfare, with increasingly successful subversion of Nationalist officials and armed forces, and increasingly damaging civil disorders, which may set the stage for Communist military occupation.

US economic and military aid, short of armed intervention, would probably not significantly assist the Nationalists in holding Taiwan, any more than such aid has helped the Nationalist cause on the mainland of China. Taiwan's economic problem is principally that of Nationalist inefficiency in management, not deficiency in resources; and extensive stocks of military equipment are already stored on the island. Furthermore, such an aid program would make it difficult, if not impossible, to establish normal diplomatic and consular relationships with the Communists, in the event that the US should decide on a policy of recognition of a central government established by the Communists on the mainland.

c. *Western Possessions of Hong Kong and Macao.*

Although Hong Kong, under British control, offers Communist China certain advantages in foreign trade, nationalistic sentiment will almost certainly impel the CCP to press for the return of this colony, as well as Portuguese Macao. The British Government, determined to defend Hong Kong against a possible Communist military assault, is dispatching considerable reinforcements to the colony, thus reducing its capability to meet military commitments in Europe and elsewhere and to maintain a strategic reserve in Great Britain. In addition, the UK is seeking at least moral support from the US for its Hong Kong defense plans. However, Communist military action against Hong Kong and Macao, while possible, is not likely. It is more probable that one of the early acts of the Communist regime will be that of initiating discussions with the British and Portuguese governments in regard to the transfer of authority in Hong Kong and Macao. If the UK and Portugal should withhold *de facto* recognition from the Communist Government, or in some other manner refuse to enter into such negotiations, the CCP will retaliate. The CCP, which presumably does not fear Portugal, may choose to exert military pressure on Macao, as well as to work through the Communist underground. In Hong Kong, rather than taking military action, the CCP will propably choose to operate through the strong Communist underground, which already constitutes a serious threat to the colony and which will become increasingly active. The Communists could cripple Hong Kong by fomenting strikes in transportation and communication facilities, could restrict or cut off food supplies from the Chinese mainland, could sabotage water supplies, could resort to unrestricted piracy against shipping, and could create an exchange rate between the currencies of Hong Kong and Communist China to weaken the economy of Hong Kong. The eventual return of Hong Kong to China, thereby depriving the UK (and indirectly the US) of a valuable but vulnerable Far Eastern naval base, appears probable, but not within the calendar year of 1949.

SECRET

5

d. US Aid to Anti-Communist Groups.

The US is the best available source for the small arms, artillery and ammunition desired by the remaining anti-Communist forces, and it may be anticipated that such forces, individually or in the name of the National Government, will appeal to the US to supply such materiel. However, major anti-Communist forces controlled by Chiang Kai-shek, Chang Chun, and the Moslem leaders of the northwest, Ma Pu-fang and Ma Hung-kuei, even now are located either off the mainland or in the peripheral areas of China. In addition, there is some doubt as to whether any of those forces, except those of the two Mas, could usefully employ further US aid. Chiang's forces on Taiwan already have extensive military and economic resources. Chang Chun's forces in Szechwan do not need economic aid. Moreover, it is improbable that military aid to these forces can prevent the Communists from extending their control over Szechwan at any time they choose to do so.

The Mas of the Northwest (the provinces of Ningsia, Kansu, and Tsinghai) with the advantages of forbidding terrain, excellent organization, and hardy troops, are in the strongest defensive position of any of the remaining anti-Communist forces in China. Moreover, on the basis of past performance, the Mas, as compared with other anti-Communist groups, would make the most effective use of any aid which they might be given. However, their bases in the provinces of Tsinghai and Ninghsia are the most difficult to reach with US aid, which probably would have to be transported by air. The Northwest area is self-sufficient in food, and may hold out for several years even without US aid, either because the Communists will be reluctant to attack or will favor its development as a buffer against the expansion of the USSR into China through Sinkiang.

Overt US aid to anti-Communist forces in China would compromise the maintenance of normal diplomatic and commercial relations with the Communist-controlled regime, in the event that the US should choose to follow a policy of recognizing such a regime. Furthermore, US military aid to any anti-Communist forces other than the Mas, might well go the way of the bulk of US aid supplied to the Nationalists in the past—to the Communists. Aid of the type and proportions extended hitherto to the National Government, at best, could delay but will fail to prevent the extension of Communist rule through all China.

A further consideration is the continuation of US aid to Nationalist China, as provided for in the China Aid Program. With Nationalist-held areas soon to be limited to Taiwan and the western provinces of China, it will be difficult to justify the US program on humanitarian grounds as aid to the Chinese people as a whole. Thus the US would become increasingly vulnerable to Communist propaganda, attacking the US aid program as designed solely to bolster and prolong resistance on the part of anti-Communist remnants.

e. Communist Need for Foreign Trade.

Communist import requirements provide the US with a possible weapon against Communist China. Depriving the Communists of essential imports would retard the rehabilitation of China and increase the economic difficulties that will confront the CCP. Some essential imports, chiefly petroleum products and items of capital equipment, can be obtained in quantity only from the US or UK. The USSR, without some sacrifices in its domestic economy, will be unable to supply many kinds of equipment, will provide inferior goods in other cases, and will probably make heavy demands on China in exchange for its assistance.

The controls to be used would probably not be effective if they were so severe as to be in fact an embargo. It is doubtful if the US could arrange for concerted support for an embargo among the Western Powers, and the Communists would gain sympathy and support within China by representing an embargo as "imperialist" persecution. Limited export controls on selected commodities such as petroleum and capital goods probably would be acceptable to the UK, which has the largest economic interests of any Western Power in China, and would probably serve US purposes just as well as a complete embargo.

SECRET

6

SECRET

On the other hand, there are advantages the US may gain from free trade with Communist China. *Quid pro quo* concessions, such as regularization of the position of US consulates in Communist-held areas of China, might be obtained. The promotion of commerce between Communist China and Japan, furthermore, in addition to being valuable to China, would significantly assist Japan economically and thereby reduce the drain of US support of the Japanese economy.

f. The Communist Desire for International Recognition.

The Communist-controlled regime will seek international recognition as the National Government of China as soon as it is formed and proclaimed—an event which will probably occur near the end of 1949. The attitude of this regime toward the US will be unfriendly, if not frankly and actively hostile. For the purposes of this discussion, it is assumed that the US, when confronted with the Communist regime's request for recognition, will pursue one of three courses: (1) non-recognition, i.e., neither *de facto* nor *de jure* recognition for an indefinite period; or (2) immediate *de jure* recognition, which the Communists presumably desire; or (3) delayed *de jure* recognition, e.g., early *de facto* recognition, but a delay of several months to a year or more in according *de jure* recognition. The consequences of each of these three courses of action are estimated briefly below.

Obviously, the international act of granting or withholding recognition would not effect any genuine change in the ideological hostility of the CCP toward the non-Communist world. So long as the Chinese Communists regard the USSR as the leader of world Communism, and the USSR regards the US as its principal enemy, the conduct of the CCP toward the US will continue to be governed by the international Communist line, as promulgated by the USSR.

(1) *Non-Recognition.*

For the US to refuse recognition to a Communist China would entail a number of unfavorable consequences. There is no prospect that the Nationalists can be restored to authority over any large part of China; the Na-tionalist leaders, their authority progressively restricted to their place of refuge, are doomed to exile or extinction. In addition, it is improbable that many foreign governments will withhold for a prolonged period recognition of the Communist regime in China; thus, the official representatives and private citizens of governments withholding recognition would find themselves at a disadvantage as compared with the nationals of governments extending recognition. Moreover, the Communist regime, strengthened by recognition by one or more major powers, would claim seats in the UN, other international organizations, and on the Far Eastern Council, and would be supported in its claim by members of such bodies. It is further probable that the Communist regime, if the US were to withhold recognition, would in turn refuse to regularize the position of US consulates in China, and would even force them out of China.

(2) *Immediate De Jure Recognition.*

Immediate *de jure* recognition of the Communist regime, which almost certainly is the CCP's objective, would avoid certain of the adverse consequences of non-recognition. The CCP presumably would be opposed to any international relations short of full *de jure* recognition, because mere *de facto* recognition would permit the Western Powers openly to support anti-Communist elements in China, and because *de facto* recognition has been associated in Chinese eyes with the 1911-27 period of warlordism. Immediate recognition, however, would not alter the basic hostility of the CCP toward the US, and might even encourage the Chinese Communists in their arrogant and intransigent attitude toward the US and toward other powers which followed the US lead, perhaps to the extent that they would follow the Soviet lead in restricting the number and location of US consular offices, particularly in Manchuria. In addition, immediate recognition would probably not cause the Communists to withdraw their threat to repudiate existing Sino-US treaties, or to refrain from obstructing US policies on international issues such as the Japanese peace settlement.

SECRET

45

SECRET

(3) Delayed Recognition.

Should the US delay, for a period of several months to a year or more, in according de jure recognition to the Communist regime in China, some of the disadvantages of both non-recognition and immediate recognition might be obviated. Since the Communists are interested in obtaining de jure recognition as soon as possible, they might be inclined to discuss, and to reach some prior understanding with the US regarding present and future treaties and the number and location of US consular offices in China. This period would also afford other Western governments an opportunity to bring political and economic pressure on the Communist regime. Concerted action by Atlantic Pact powers, which have indicated a desire to maintain a common front, can be anticipated if the delay in according de jure recognition is not prolonged to the point where it would become inimicable to their interests. Through the period of a common front, however, there would always be the risk that other governments, seeking special advantage by early action, would proceed unilaterally to extend de jure recognition. The Communists can be expected to follow, and probably to improve upon, the traditional Chinese diplomatic practice of playing one power against another.

g. Chinese Communist Influence throughout the Far East.

The CCP has indicated its interest in uniting one billion Orientals in a Communist Asia. To this end, the CCP industriously propagates the view that Communism is inevitable in Asia, and that only the Communists are the champions of Asian "independence." The prestige of Communism will increase enormously as the CCP extends its control over all of China.

(1) Japan and Korea.

The CCP has stated that China and Japan "can and should establish close friendship" and has warned that Japan must conclude a peace treaty with a Communist-controlled government of China. The CCP is attempting to open trade with Japan, and the Japanese Communist Party echoes the CCP line that only "democratic" forces can successfully conduct commercial and political relations with China. In Korea, the CCP's successes have contributed greatly to the confidence of the North Korean regime and to the feeling of defeatism in the Republic of Korea. Through its relationship with North Korean leaders, the CCP is capable of providing significant military and economic aid to North Korea. The opportunity of South Korean leaders to offset the development of such an adverse trend has largely passed and it now appears that South Korea can do little to forestall such a development. Recognition by the Western Powers of the CCP's regime would be to the advantage of Communist China both politically and economically, insofar as it permitted trade between China and Japan. De jure recognition would give the Chinese Communists further opportunity to claim seats on the Far Eastern Commission and on the Allied Council for Japan, as well as weaken further the position of the Korean Republic's government.

(2) Southeast Asia.

The CCP is extending its influence throughout Southeast Asia by identifying itself with native independence movements, by denouncing "reactionary" colonial governments, by threatening "fascist" non-colonial governments, and by promising protection to overseas Chinese communities. De facto recognition of the Communist regime by the Western Powers would tend to increase the political and economic influence of the CCP in Southeast Asia. To withhold de jure recognition would make the CCP's work in Southeast Asia somewhat more difficult, but the governments and the Chinese overseas communities in that area would pay little heed to such a legalism. The Chinese communities will tend to orient themselves toward the CCP as it acquires control of China although there may be significant resistance elements among the overseas Chinese. Likewise the governments in Southeast Asia will adjust themselves to these new circumstances, whether for accommodation or resistance. The CCP will probably not employ military force to gain its objectives in Southeast Asia and it has no significant economic resources with which to maneuver. Its success in China, however, will

SECRET

6   SECRET

permit strong and unremitting political pressure on Southeast Asia.

2. Political Situation.

a. Communist China.

(1) Extension of Control.

(a) Present Extent of Communist China. Communist China now is divided into six administrative areas: (1) Northeast China, having an Administrative Council but as yet no "People's Government"; (2) Inner Mongolia with an Inner Mongolian Autonomous Government; (3) North China (Hopeh, southeast corner of Chahar, eastern Shansi, western Shantung) having a North China People's Government; (4) Central Plains (Honan, most of Anhuei, northeast corner of Hupeh) with a Central Plains People's Government; (5) East China (Kiangsu and eastern Shantung) with as yet no People's Government; (6) Northwest China (western Shansi, eastern Shensi, eastern Suiyuan, eastern tips of Kansu and Ningsia) with as yet no People's Government. The Communists do not yet have a central government, so that whatever centralized control there is, is exercised by the Central Committee of the Chinese Communist Party, at present located in Peiping.

(b) Intended Extent of Communist China. In its New Year's Message for 1949, the CCP stated that its armies would cross the Yangtze in 1949 and that the Party would convoke a Political Consultative Conference to form and proclaim a Communist-controlled government. Without pretending that this government would actually control all China by the end of 1949, the CCP statement strongly implied that the new regime would nonetheless seek recognition as the national government. Subsequent statements have reiterated that it is the CCP's firm intention to extend its control over all China and to destroy all significant political and military opposition. The CCP has announced that, in the interest of preserving the manpower and material resources of the nation, it prefers to negotiate a peaceful transfer of military and political power wherever possible; but that the Communist armies are prepared to effect such transfer of power by military force where Na-

tionalist leaders and forces refuse to cooperate in a peaceful transfer of power.

(c) Lack of Popular Resistance. The resumption of the military offensive by the Communist armies has forced the CCP to offer the war-weary people of China some justification for this action. Before and during the April peace negotiations in Peiping, the CCP repeatedly accused the Nationalists of insincerity, at the same time claiming that the people of China did not desire an uneasy truce with the Yangtze as a boundary-line. In their order to continue the drive into South China, Chairman Mao Tse-tung and Commander Chu Teh again accused the Nationalists of negotiating only to gain time for a comeback designed "to destroy the revolution." Although no amount of propaganda can persuade the people of China that the Communists are everything they pretend to be, the bulk of the people in Nationalist China are probably not dismayed by the prospect of a change of government, and may even welcome the prospect of Communist rule, believing that it will bring a greater degree of security and a lesser degree of exploitation.

(2) Transfer of Political Authority.

(a) A New Central Government. Because the CCP has not formed or proclaimed a central government asserting authority over all of China, decisions on the question of international recognition of such a government thus far have been postponed. Diplomatic officials in Nanking and consular officials elsewhere in Communist China are regarded by the local Communist authorities as private citizens rather than as the representatives of their governments. This situation is likely to continue until the proclamation of a Communist-controlled government, at which time the question of de facto recognition will arise. For the next few months, the CCP will be absorbing large numbers of lower and middle echelon National Government personnel—by far the greater part of these officials stay on the job—thus avoiding a complete break in continuity with the old order. The CCP probably will take the stand that, if foreign powers wish to continue operations in China, either through official representatives or as private

SECRET

47

SECRET   9

citizens, they must give at least *de facto* recognition to the regime.

(b) *The "Coalition" Pattern.* The CCP has promised to convoke a Political Consultative Conference in 1949 to form and proclaim a "coalition" government. The Kuomintang as a Party will be excluded from this new "coalition." The CCP has frankly stated that the intended "coalition" government will be "under the firm leadership of the CCP." The concept of "coalition" derives from the larger concept of Chairman Mao's "new democracy," the name given to the transitional stage from today's "capitalist" society to the later "socialist" society. In structure, the "coalition" will include three major blocs: (1) the CCP; (2) non-Communist "democratic parties" which follow the CCP line, such as the Democratic League and the Kuomintang Revolutionary Committee and; (3) "democratic elements," occupational and functional groups which invariably support the CCP's position. While this government will permit some degree of popular participation in the election of representative bodies, all real power will be concentrated in the CCP, whose function it is to "guide" the backward masses.

(c) *Political Consultative Conference.* The Political Consultative Conference will be the medium for creating a new constitutional system and for obtaining some degree of domestic sanction for the new regime, just as the Political Consultative Conference held in 1946 was a symbol of potential National unity. The Chinese Communist Party will convoke this Conference in its own name and in the name of minority parties and functional groups which follow the Communist line, probably in the late summer or early autumn of 1949, after they have consolidated their control of the Yangtze valley. It is not known whether the Conference will consist of a few dozen or several hundred persons; in either case, the Communists will control it firmly. The Conference will either draft and ratify a constitution, or, possibly working through a committee established for that purpose, draft a constitution and set a date for elections to a "constitutional convention." In the latter event, promulgation of the constitution and formal establishment of a constitutional gov-

ernment would be delayed until 1950. In any case, the Conference will simply be a rubber-stamp congress summoned to approve in the name of "the people" policies predetermined by the Communists while its constitution, formally providing for various rights, will, in fact, bestow no rights which the Communists cannot take away.

(d) *Domestic Sanction for the New Order.* In order to gain domestic sanction for the Communist-controlled regime, the CCP, in conjunction with the Political Consultative Conference, will probably exploit the alleged affinities of Communist doctrine and practice with the theories of Sun Yat-sen, generally regarded within China as the "father" of the Republic. The CCP claims that Sun's famous Three People's Principles—"nationalism, democracy, livelihood"—have been more closely followed by the Communists than by the Kuomintang. It points to Sun's advocacy, in the 1920's, of "alliance with the Soviet Union, alliance with the Communists, alliance with the workers and peasants." The CCP may also cite the 1924-27 period, when the Communists were admitted to the Kuomintang by Sun himself, and insist that only the CCP has truly carried out the terms of Sun's will by ushering in the constitutional stage of government which he demanded. The CCP will by no means deify Sun Yat-sen, but his tradition can be very useful in smoothing the Party's path.

(3) *Foreign Relations.*

(a) *Sino-Asian.*

(i) *Japan and Korea.* The CCP, in a broadcast attempting to influence the Japanese elections of January 1949, stated that China and Japan "can and should establish close friendship," and pointed out that Japan must conclude a peace treaty with a Communist-controlled government of China and establish economic and political relations with it. More recently, the CCP has been attempting to open trade with Japan. There is little doubt that China will exert economic pressure and political influence on both Japan and Korea, possibly with a view to subordinating those countries to itself in a Communist Asia. The CCP maintains close relations with Com-

SECRET

10

SECRET

munist leaders in Japan and Korea, and there is reason to believe that at least some of those leaders are oriented as much toward Communist China as toward the USSR.

(ii) *Southeast Asia.* In recent months, the CCP: (1) has told the Indonesian Republican leaders that they cannot succeed without Communist leadership; (2) has denounced the British and French governments for their activities in China, Malaya, and Indochina; and (3) has threatened retaliation against the "fascist" governments of the Philippines and Siam for "persecuting" overseas Chinese. Assistance to revolutionary movements throughout Southeast Asia, pressure upon the colonial governments concerned, and influence within overseas Chinese communities will certainly increase as the CCP extends its control throughout China and obtains international recognition of its "coalition" government. However, the extension of CCP influence in southeast Asia will not be unopposed, because of the deep-seated fear of "Chinese imperialism" in these countries.

(b) *Sino-Soviet.* Chinese Communist relations with the USSR should continue to be extremely cordial. In major policy statements of the past year, the CCP has endorsed the Cominform's denunciation of Tito, called upon "revolutionary forces" throughout the world to unite under Soviet leadership against "American imperialism" and promised that China will be the ally of the USSR in any West-provoked war. The CCP's tactical procedures have found orthodox justification in Lenin's and Stalin's expositions of the principles governing "colonial" revolutions, and the CCP is now bringing its policies more nearly into accord with those of more "advanced" revolutions. There are points of potential conflict between the USSR and the CCP—such as possible Soviet inability to assist in China's industrialization, Soviet designs in China's border regions, the CCP's intentions toward Communist movements in Asia, and the general issue of subservience to Moscow—but none of these issues seems likely to cause serious friction in the near future. The "coalition" government will certainly give the USSR preferential status in China, perhaps by expanding the Sino-Soviet Treaty of

1945—which the CCP has repeatedly endorsed—to provide for a high degree of military and economic integration between the USSR and China's border regions. For the present, CCP leadership appears genuinely to feel that China's best interests will be served by close Sino-Soviet cooperation.

(c) *Sino-US.*

(i) *"Traitorous" Treaties.* The CCP position, in regard to treaties concluded by the National Government since early 1946, has been that such treaties were concluded without the knowledge and consent of the parties—among them the CCP—participating in the Political Consultative Conference of 1946, and that the CCP therefore does not recognize their validity and "absolutely will not bear any obligation" for them. The CCP has stated that "all those (treaties and agreements) detrimental to the Chinese people and nation, especially those which sell out national rights, should be abrogated, revised or reconcluded, according to the circumstances." The Sino-Soviet Treaty of 1945 has been specifically excluded by the CCP from those treaties which "sell out national rights." The Sino-US treaties which the CCP regards as "traitorous" are those which provide for economic and military aid to the National Government and the stationing of US armed forces in China. The CCP view appears to be that, first, the post-1946 Sino-American treaties are "traitorous" simply because they were concluded with the US, the principal enemy of world Communism, and, second, that US economic and military aid to the National Government was employed principally in the struggle against the Communists. In addition, the CCP has indicated its intention of repudiating the existing Sino-US "Treaty of Friendship, Commerce and Navigation" (1948), on the grounds that this agreement is an instrument of US "imperialism" in China. In order to develop trade with the US, however, the CCP may come to see the desirability of negotiating a new agreement of this nature.

(ii) *The US as an Enemy.* As the CCP has proclaimed the USSR as China's principal friend, the US has been portrayed with equal

SECRET

SECRET

11

fervor as China's outstanding enemy. The CCP has represented the US as the leader and supporter of all "imperialist" and "reactionary" forces in the world, as forcing "traitorous" treaties upon China in exchange for financing the Nationalists in the civil conflict, as directing the military operations of the Nationalists and encouraging them to reject the Communist-dictated "peace agreement," and as plotting with forces inside and outside China to destroy the CCP and keep the Orient in permanent slavery.

While the CCP has understandable grounds for resenting the US contribution to the Nationalists' military operations, the CCP's present anti-Americanism is primarily dictated by the opposite CCP and US positions regarding the USSR and world Communism. US official representatives and private citizens in Communist China, although not subjected to physical violence, have been restricted in their movements and in the discharge of their consular, commercial, or educational functions, while the CCP is exploiting the US loss of prestige in China and enhancing its own prestige by an intransigent attitude toward the Western Powers. The "coalition" government will presumably invite US recognition and attempt to conclude commercial treaties with the US but the CCP can be expected to give aggressive support to Soviet and satellite diplomacy, to continue its vigorous and irresponsible anti-American propaganda, to bring pressure upon the US to withdraw its assistance to Nationalist remnants on Taiwan and to make the work of US diplomatic missions difficult. At present, there is little chance of orienting the CCP away from the USSR.

(d) *Other Foreign Relations.* The CCP has adopted an attitude toward foreign governments hostile in proportion to the degree that those governments are impeding the world Communist movement, regardless of whether such governments have or have not supported the Nationalists in the Chinese civil conflict. The fact that the UK has been of service to the CCP, in affording sanctuary and an operating base to CCP leaders in Hong Kong, did not restrain Communist forces from firing upon British warships in the Yangtze. Neither will it prevent the CCP from demanding the return of Hong Kong to China nor will it obviate the possibility of giving support to terrorist bands operating against the British in Malaya.

The CCP undoubtedly intends to deprive Portugal of the colony of Macao, by negotiations, if possible, but by military action if necessary. The French Government has been denounced by the CCP for encouraging US "imperialism" in China and for its actions in Indochina. The Netherlands Government has been similarly castigated by the CCP in regard to Indonesia. All other Atlantic Pact states have been the targets of CCP propaganda abuse, both for joining the Pact and for other "reactionary" activities. India, which is probably recognized by the CCP as its principal rival for leadership in Asia, is characterized as remaining under the influence of British "imperialism."

Representatives of the Commonwealth countries and of a number of European governments in China have expressed a desire to become accredited to the Communist regime soon after it is proclaimed. These representatives would like to regularize their status by early recognition of the Communists in order to protect and perhaps expand their present interests in China. They have not regarded the prospect of applying economic sanctions to China with favor and they apparently anticipate profitable commercial relations with the new regime in varying degrees. At the same time, the governments of most Commonwealth and Atlantic Pact nations have admitted the desirability of maintaining a united front on the question of recognition.

b. *Nationalist China.*

Nationalist China is virtually bankrupt and the National Government is in its death-throes. The process of disintegration and fragmentation is so far advanced as to render almost impossible the establishment of a functioning government or even a loosely organized coalition capable of offering resistance to the Communists.

The National Government no longer functions as an organized administration even on

SECRET

12

SECRET

a regional basis. Since Chiang Kai-shek's retirement from the presidency in January, there has been little evidence of leadership or central direction of the Government. (Acting President Li Tsung-jen has little power and his effectiveness has been little greater than that of a well-meaning warlord.) The Executive Yuan has accomplished little for months; even the basic ministries are limping along ineffectually. The Legislative, Control and Judicial Yuan in Canton are rump organs with slight influence. Political power is largely in the hands of provincial or regional bodies. Taxation and other basic governmental functions are localized.

The Nationalist split into factions headed by Chiang and Li has hastened the process of disintegration and fragmentation. Although Chiang retired as President without resigning, he has continued to control armies, military and financial resources, the secret police, the party agencies, and many leading officials. Acting President Li nominally heads the Government, but, in his weakness and frustration, has done little else than conduct the abortive peace negotiations which ended on 20 April. The struggle between Li and Chiang is so intense that any significant rapprochement or compromise appears improbable. Li controls Kwangsi and has the support of Pai Chung-hsi, various southern warlords, and many peace-seeking officials. He will probably continue his nominal leadership of the Canton Government until Communist military pressure compels Nationalist leaders to seek refuge elsewhere, at which time Li will probably try to maintain a government in Southwest China.

Chiang Kai-shek controls Taiwan and adjacent areas on the southeast coast, and has a diminishing influence in the southwestern provinces. Chiang has been transferring Nationalist resources systematically to Taiwan, which is being prepared as the final refuge to which many Nationalist officials in Canton will flee when the city is threatened by the Communists. Large numbers of refugees from mainland China are already in Taiwan and the provincial administration is headed by Chiang's appointee, General Chen Cheng. Although Nationalist rule is increasingly unpopular with the oppressed, unorganized native population, the Nationalists probably will be able to maintain a regional regime in Taiwan for at least the remainder of the year 1949. The major threat to their position will come from mainland Communist forces rather than from the local people.

As in the recent past, the National Government's foreign relations during coming months will be dominated by issues concerning the US and the USSR. Nationalist China has depended greatly on US economic and military aid, which still continues in diminishing quantities, although no future US military commitments are in prospect. Despite repeated failures to obtain additional aid, the National Government and Nationalist regional regime will continue their appeals to the US and claim that such aid will be used to resist the Communists.

In Taiwan, the Nationalists have an important bargaining point. Aware of US interest in that island, they will present themselves as a means and perhaps the sole means of preventing its communization, and will offer various inducements and assurances in return for US aid and US moral support for a regional Chinese regime. They will also argue the legality of such a Chinese administration despite the fact that Taiwan's status has not been formalized by conclusion of a peace treaty with Japan.

The National Government will strive to keep its international status despite its growing weakness. Depending chiefly on what future Communist policies may be, that status might not be seriously challenged for several months and foreign recognition of the National Government will probably continue so long as it stays in Canton.

Chiang Kai-shek and other Nationalist leaders are embittered toward the USSR, which they feel is at least partly responsible for their misfortunes. The idea of appealing to the UN has been seriously considered in Nationalist circles and the matter may be brought up again before the Nationalists lose their international status. If made, this maneuver would be accompanied by denunciation of the Sino-Soviet Treaty of 1945, governing the status of Manchuria and Outer Mongolia.

SECRET

SECRET

13

While such antagonistic measures might be directed against the USSR on the one hand, the National Government might at the same time effect an apparent rapprochement with the Soviet Union and conclude agreements involving further concessions, particularly in Sinkiang and the Northwest provinces.

In its last stages of existence, Nationalist China may turn its wrath against the US. In Nationalist thinking, the US is largely responsible for the Yalta agreement, and the US postwar policy of mediation in the civil war and intermittent limited assistance have facilitated the Communist triumph. Such feelings will be intensified if the US rejects further appeals for aid and evidences interest in recognizing a future Communist-dominated Chinese Government.

3. Military Situation.

a. General Strategy.

The objective of the Chinese Communist forces is the elimination of all anti-Communist armed resistance in China. To attain this objective the Chinese Communist Party has employed the strategy of using military force as a medium of realizing their political objectives. Communist control over the remainder of China will be accomplished by means of an area-by-area program of military acquisition, dictated to a large degree by the state of their political preparedness for administering these areas.

The remaining Nationalist or anti-Communist forces have now adopted the strategy of avoiding decisive military action, while at the same time attempting to deny territory to the Chinese Communists as long as possible.

b. Communist Armed Forces.

The Chinese Communist Forces possess sufficient wealth in material and manpower to overcome all anti-Communist remnants in China. Having already eliminated the majority of the best Nationalist armies, the CCP is now in the process of consolidating its recent virtually unopposed military conquest of the Yangtze valley. In consequence, Communist armies, free to accelerate their movements to the south and the west, appear to be headed toward Kwangtung. As elsewhere, however, the speed and magnitude of this operation

probably will be limited in some degree by the abilities of the CCP political organization to assume the additional administrative responsibilities.

Recent CCF victories have brought with them the new responsibility of protecting communications, urban life, and industry. Consequently a considerable portion of CCF must be utilized to garrison "liberated" areas and maintain lines of communication.

(1) Strength and Disposition of Communist Ground Forces.

The Communist regular forces comprised of the field forces and Military District troops now total approximately 2,017,000 (see Table, p. 14), thus giving the CCF a decisive numerical superiority over the Nationalists in combat strength. These regular forces, particularly the field forces, are characterized by good leadership, good equipment, high morale and discipline, as well as excellence in intelligence and the employment of propaganda. In addition to the regulars, there are irregular forces, known as the People's Militia, generally local in character and function, totalling perhaps 2,000,000. Such forces, on occasion in the past, have supplemented the regulars during a campaign. In the future, they will probably be occupied largely with the task of policing CCP areas. A third potential source of manpower comes from Nationalist troops which have fallen into Communist hands. Of these, approximately 90,000 have been integrated into the CCF. Communist regulars will also be greatly assisted in their drive south by dissidents, bandits, and irregular Communist bands, already in control of wide rural stretches in the southern provinces.

(2) Air Force.

The Chinese Communist Air Force made its first public appearance during 1949 May Day celebrations in the Mukden area. Both B-25 and F-51 type aircraft participated in the air parade. The Communists are known to have obtained by defection or capture at least 38 operational aircraft including bombers, fighters, transports, and trainers. The actual number of pilot defections is believed to be substantially greater than the 20 known cases although the Communist claim of 2,000 is con-

SECRET

14

SECRET

ORGANIZATION OF CHINESE COMMUNIST FORCES, 25 MAY 1949

REGULAR FORCES

New Unit Designation	Old Unit Designation	Commander	Strength	Areas
1st Field Army	Northwest People's Liberation Army	Peng Teh-huai	158,000	Shensi-Shansi
2nd Field Army	Central Plains People's Liberation Army	Liu Po-cheng	321,000	Yangtze and South China
3rd Field Army	East China People's Liberation Army	Chen Yi	400,000	Yangtze
4th Field Army	Northeast People's Liberation Army	Lin Piao	720,000	Yangtze and North China
5th Field Army	North China People's Liberation Army	Nieh Jung-chen	383,000	North China
Undesignated Regulars in South China			35,000	South China
Regular Forces Total			2,017,000	
IRREGULAR FORCES: The People's Militia			2,000,000	

CAPTURED NATIONALIST TROOPS: Only the approximately 90,000 troops in the units enumerated above have been included in CCF strength. Remainder are not yet believed to have been integrated into the CCF order of battle.

Note: The total regulars includes an estimated 636,600 Military District Troops and former Nationalist troops of the ex-Nationalist 38th, 59th, 60th and 77th Armies, and 84th and 110th Divisions with an aggregate total of approximately 90,000 troops.

sidered to be greatly exaggerated. There is no evidence that Soviet aircraft observed in CCP areas of Manchuria have been there in any but a transient capacity. No Communist aircraft have been used in the combat areas and lack of aviation fuel will drastically limit the CCP capability for air operations.

(3) Navy.

The CCP has acquired by defection and capture upwards of 63 Nationalist naval vessels. The following is a breakdown, as to types, that may be operational in Communist hands as of 31 May 1949:

- 3 Destroyer escorts (DE)
- 1 Mine-sweeper (AM)
- 7 Gunboats (PG)
- 1 Repair Ship, light (ARL)
- 1 Icebreaker (AGB)
- 1 Landing Ship, medium (LSM)
- 1 Landing Craft, Infantry (LCI)
- 17 Landing barges
- 17 Armed motorboats
- 14 Small patrol boats

For the most part, crews of the foregoing craft and those of other naval craft which have been disabled or destroyed are available to the Communists. These craft, plus merchant shipping which may be captured or otherwise acquired, will provide the Communists with a growing capability for short over-water operations.

(4) Logistics.

The CCF, hitherto almost solely dependent on animal transport, makeshift machine-shop arsenals, and captured Nationalist stores for logistic support, has now overcome this earlier handicap. In addition to substantial Japanese stockpiles turned over to them in Manchuria during 1945-46, the CCF, having captured tremendous Nationalist stocks which were largely US-supplied—now enjoys superiority in materiel over the Nationalists. In addition, the CCF has acquired most of the industrial centers of North and Central China—including the Mukden arsenal, which alone produced some 60-70 percent of the total Nationalist ordnance output. This and other installations taken over by the CCF can supply all the materiel needed for future mainland operations. In place of horse-cart methods of supply, the Communists now control and are rapidly rehabilitating most of China's rail and

SECRET

SECRET

water transport net. A north-south rail line from Manchuria to the Yangtze has already been opened.

c. Anti-Communist Armed Forces.

The Chinese Nationalist armed forces, although defeated by the Communists and lacking cohesive command structure at present, were not beaten by the sheer force of arms. Very few major battles, such as those witnessed in World War II, were fought. From the resumption of Nationalist-Communist hostilities in May 1946 until September 1948, the Chinese Communists employed guerrilla tactics of hit, ruin and run, with resultant minor but effective actions. In September 1948, the Chinese Communists stormed Nationalist Tsinan, where, much to the Communists' surprise, key Nationalist defections brought about by the disintegration of local troop morale led to the collapse of government resistance. The debacle at Tsinan established the pattern for subsequent defections; from September 1948 to May 1949, a rising wave of mass defections, sell-outs, and general unwillingness to fight swept through the Nationalist armed forces. The defeat of the Chinese Nationalist Army, therefore, can be attributed basically to internal decay. Although the strategic error of over-extension of forces contributed in part, the basic reasons for Nationalist defeat were, and continue to be: (1) army politics, which kept militarily incompetent officers in positions of high command; (2) the personal command of all combat areas exercised by Chiang Kai-shek, which prevented independent tactical action by field commanders; (3) accelerating economic decay, which resulted in inadequate pay, food, clothing, and equipment for the troops; and (4) graft and corruption, practiced by senior officers at the expense of their troops.

In consequence of these conditions, Nationalist morale disintegrated from top to bottom and Nationalist forces lost the all-important "will to fight." Nationalist armed forces, today, have ceased to be an organized, cohesive and centrally directed military machine. They now exist as a group of widely scattered, disorganized, and uncoordinated regional anti-Communist "warlord" forces.

(1) Strength and Disposition of Nationalist Ground Forces.

The strength of the remaining anti-Communist armies in China totals approximately 720,000 regular combat troops. In addition, there are some 500,000 service troops dispersed throughout the remaining areas of Nationalist operation (see Table, p. 16).

The "combat" forces listed in the accompanying table include a high percentage of poorly trained and ill-equipped provincial levies. Not included are an undetermined number of local (Peace Preservation Corps) troops.

At present, there are basically four separate centers of potential anti-Communist resistance in China. These are: (1) the southeast (including Taiwan) directly under Chiang Kai-shek—approximate strength, 300,000; (2) the southern provinces of Kwangtung and Kwangsi, under Li Tsung-jen and Pai Chung-hsi—approximate strength, 200,000 plus; (3) the southwest, under Chang Chun (possibly including the troops of Hu Tsung-nan)—approximate strength 225,000; and (4) the northwest, under Ma Pu-fang and Ma Hung-kwei—approximate strength, 100,000.

(2) Air Force.

The Nationalist Air Force has from 85,000–100,000 men and approximately 1000 aircraft, of which 600 are reportedly operational. The potential of the CAF has also been reduced by losses through defection and capture. Five-sixths of the CAF's total of 1,000 aircraft have been transferred to Taiwan. Because of maintenance difficulties and operational accidents only 35 percent of the operational aircraft are effective. The morale of the air forces, although somewhat higher than the ground forces due to differences in pay scales, is still very low. Consequently, CCP propaganda has found and continues to find a receptive audience in the ranks of the air force.

(3) Navy.

The Nationalist Navy, lately weakened by the loss of upwards of 63 craft (of which at least a light cruiser, destroyer escort, and a gunboat have been destroyed or disabled) has approximately 150 ships, not including harbor craft, and about 30,000 men. Navy morale, as

SECRET

15

SECRET

ORGANIZATION OF ANTI-COMMUNIST FORCES, 15 MAY 1949

Commander	Strength	Loyalty	Present Area	Future (?)
Tang En-po	250,000 *	Chiang Kai-shek	Unknown *	Fukien, Taiwan
Pai Chung-hsi	150,000	Li Tsung-jen	Hunan, Kwangsi	Kwangsi
Hu Tsung-nan	175,000	Chiang Kai-shek	South Shensi	Szechwan
Ma Pu-fang Ma Hung-Kwei	120,000	Self	Northwest	Northwest
Chang Chun	40,000	Chiang Kai-shek	Taiwan	Taiwan
Hsueh Yueh	50,000	Undetermined	Kwantung	Kwantung
Chen Cheng	30,000 **	Chiang Kai-shek	Taiwan	Taiwan
Liu An-chi	30,000	Chiang Kai-shek	Tsingtao	Taiwan (?)
Total Combat Forces	845,000			
Service and Miscellaneous Troops	500,000			
Total	1,345,000			

Note: * Subject to revision when Nationalist withdrawal from Shanghai is clarified—last estimate of strength in Shanghai was 100,000. The other troops under Tang (150,000) are withdrawing southward from Nanking-Shanghai area.

** Number could be augmented by Nationalist withdrawals from the mainland.

in the other services, is extremely low and Communist infiltration of the navy continues.

(4) Logistics.

The Nationalist field forces have been depleted in numbers and deprived of the larger part of their weapons, transportation, and equipment. Their central supply organization is now defunct and, more important, their central supply base, from which unit materiel replacements had previously been obtained, is now non-existent. The Nationalist field commanders find themselves facing logistics similar to those encountered by Communist field commanders a year ago. The Nationalists must now depend largely upon their own private resources and ingenuity for logistic support. The anti-Communist forces, largely confined to marginal regions, will hold only two areas which can presently contribute substantial logistic support. These are Szechwan, with some 13 major arsenals as well as rich agricultural resources, and Taiwan. Taiwan, which produces an agricultural surplus, has lately received US military aid shipments as well as arsenal installations transferred from the lower Yangtze Valley.

The northwest, in contrast, requires air supply, and the entire sweep of southern China is incapable of supporting large armies and broad-scale military operations over an extended period. Long-term resistance in these areas, therefore, would require a steady flow of supplies, both military and economic, from outside China. Communication in the south and southwest can be kept open only so long as the loyalty of the people in those areas is retained.

d. Present and Future Operations.

The objective of the latest Chinese Communist offensive, begun on 20 April, is to secure the lower Yangtze Valley from Szechwan to the sea and at the same time drive a wedge deep into south China in order to separate the forces of Pai Chung-hsi and Li Tsung-jen in Kwangsi from those of Chiang Kai-shek in the southeast. The southern drive on Canton and Foochow, additionally, will accelerate fragmentation of the Nationalist Government by forcing further flight to Taiwan or Chungking or possibly to both.

The primary Communist objective probably will be realized by the end of August. At no time from now on can the Nationalists be expected to put up more than token resistance, since their first concern will be withdrawal of their remaining troops intact to Taiwan and the more remote areas of the southwest. By the end of 1949, in consequence, the Chinese Communists probably will exercise military control over all of mainland China from Man-

SECRET

SECRET

17

churia south to Kwangtung and from the eastern border of Szechwan to the sea.

(1) *Communist Military Problems.*

Although the Communist forces have all the advantages at present, when they move to eliminate the last areas of resistance they will face certain entirely new problems. The Communist armies will be moving into extremely rough mountainous terrain in their drive to the southwest and the northwest. In order to support their occupation armies adequately, they must of necessity greatly extend their lines of supply and communication into these food-deficit areas. Although Communist forces will be greatly assisted by dissidents, bandits, and irregular CCP bands in the south and southwest provinces, they will, particularly in the northwest, be moving into a great expanse of territory where the local populace is either actively or potentially hostile. The expanding Communist armies will also face the problem of how to feed, clothe, indoctrinate, and otherwise dispose of captured or defected anti-Communist forces.

The acquisition of Taiwan is another problem for the CCP: The Communist armies have no amphibious experience or training. At present, they lack the requisite shipping to undertake an assault on Taiwan. The lack of amphibious experience, moreover, may force the CCP to be satisfied with the much slower political methods of underground action to accomplish their conquest of the island.

Perhaps the largest problem facing the CCP lies in preventing the military machine from outrunning their abilities for political consolidation. To halt their victorious armies would not only belie CCP propaganda but would probably shake troop morale from top to bottom. Over-all success, therefore, depends upon the maintenance of a very delicate balance between CCP military acquisitions and political preparedness.

(2) *Nationalist Problems.*

Problems currently facing the remaining Nationalist Armed Forces appear to be insurmountable. The present centrifugal tendency in Nationalist China is a recreation of conditions once almost nation-wide, which the surviving warlords understand well, but which

makes central planning and control virtually impossible. The remaining Nationalist troops are desperately in need of re-equipping, re-training, re-vitalizing, and re-organizing under a competent and effective central command. It appears unlikely that these basic Nationalist needs will be fulfilled. Consequently, anti-Communist forces in China when threatened by the Communist armies, must further withdraw, capitulate, or be annihilated.

(3) *Estimate of Capabilities.*

(a) *Nationalist.* Remaining Nationalists or anti-Communist forces cannot, in the foreseeable future, effectively resist the Communist military machine. Even if it were possible to cure existing military ills by means of outside assistance, superficial reforms would be ineffectual unless the ailment is also treated—the troops must be re-instilled with the will to fight. This can only be accomplished by paying the troops in accordance with the cost of living, by feeding and clothing them properly and, above all, by giving them something to fight for. This obviously is impossible under present conditions. The CCP, therefore, can and probably will eradicate any and all regional anti-Communist armed resistance whenever it chooses to do so.

(b) *Communist.* The CCP is currently capable of launching simultaneous operations to the south, southwest, and northwest and eliminating all effective military resistance by the end of 1950. However, in view of Communist logistic and morale problems which undoubtedly would result from too fast a take-over, the CCP will probably continue its methodical area-by-area conquest and it may be 2 to 3 years before the final liquidation of all anti-Communist resistance in China. The south and southwest will probably be the first two entries on the CCP military time-table and the *coup de grace* reserved for the Mas in the Northwest.

4. Economic Situation.

a. *Nationalist China.*

The economic activities of the National Government in Canton and of each provincial government (except Taiwan and Szechwan) are largely confined to the search for sufficient

SECRET

18   SECRET

revenue to maintain their military and political power. Economic and commercial paralysis throughout most of non-Communist China has pauperized both the National and most provincial governments.

The financial position of the National Government at Canton is desperate. It has suffered from a serious decrease in revenue because of its inability to collect taxes, the widespread repudiation of the national currency, and the virtual elimination of customs duties. In addition, State-owned industries and enterprises have largely ceased to operate and the profits of many remaining plants are no longer available to any but local political administrations. Reserves of gold and silver still under Canton's control are very limited and most provincial governments are reported to be in a similarly serious fiscal situation.

While most of non-Communist China is impoverished, Szechwan and Taiwan are exceptions. Both areas possess a relatively sound economy. Other important Nationalist assets are a considerable amount of coastal and ocean shipping and the gold bullion in Taiwan.

b. Communist China.

(1) Internal Problems.

(a) *Economic Objectives.* The first economic objectives of the Communists will be: (1) the acquisition of all assets owned by the National Government and "bureaucratic capitalists"; (2) the preservation of governmental financial and commercial institutions; and (3) obtaining the support of productive elements of society. The Nationalist assets least accessible to the Communists are the three million-odd ounces of gold controlled by Chiang Kai-shek, the overseas assets and holdings of the Government and its "war criminal" officials, private holdings and the million tons of shipping now in Nationalist hands. It is unlikely that an appreciable amount of industrial plant will be removed to Nationalist areas, and the Communists should inherit Nationalist industries largely intact.

(b) *Food Problems.* While the possibility exists that the Communists may not be able to overcome the war's disruption of marketing facilities in a short time and that Manchurian surpluses may be pre-empted by the USSR,

no starvation is expected in Communist areas before the June harvests, except in some flooded or war-desolated localities.

Although the coastal cities long have imported rice, grains and vegetable oils, because of the high costs of transport from inland areas of production to coastal consumption centers, there is probably enough food in the Yangtze Valley to supply these cities, if the CCP can solve the problems of collection and distribution.

(c) *Development of Transportation and Industry.* That some progress in industrial reconstruction has begun is indicated by reports from Manchuria, Tsinan, Peiping, Tientsin, and many towns in North China which show that the reopening of industries and railroad reconstruction in liberated towns is a high-priority task. Shortages of raw material, power, and skilled labor will continue to limit Communist development of industry after control over Central China is consolidated but, with the exception of petroleum and possibly cotton which must be imported, there will be sufficient resources to run most existing industry at a high level of capacity.

The need for petroleum in Central China will decrease as coal becomes available in larger quantities and as such large oil consumers as power companies are reconverted to coal. Domestic collection of cotton for textiles, China's chief industry, will be large and, together with present stocks in Shanghai, should be nearly adequate for this year's needs. Rehabilitated railroads, together with captured junks and barges on the Yangtze River and its tributaries, should provide adequate internal transportation for essential marketing purposes.

(d) *Gaining Support of Productive Elements.* The CCP will try to gain the active support of productive elements in the middle classes who may not yet be entirely convinced of the bountiful life which is promised under the Communist order. The Communists have declared that taxes must not be confiscatory, that governmental enterprises harmful to private enterprises shall not be permitted, that workers must not demand excessively high wages, and generally that all means will be utilized to encourage private industrial pro-

SECRET

57

SECRET

19

duction. While these promises have largely remained unfulfilled, they have gained wide support for the CCP among Shanghai and Nanking businessmen. Among the middle classes, those most actively wooed by the Communists are the technicians. They are offered high pay (in Mukden reportedly twice that of government officials) and the chance to be leaders in China's reconstruction. The CCP has apparently gained the support of responsible technical and managerial groups in other Communist areas in China and may do so in Central China as well.

Urban workers and the farmers may not be as strenuously recruited, both because their support is already assumed and because increased rewards to the middle classes must frequently be made at the expense of the lower income groups. While continued lip service will be paid to better living standards, workers will be told that, as the "leading" political group, they must carry the burden of economic reconstruction and development. Similarly, few promises, other than reduced rents and interest rates, may be made to the tenant farmers, since landlords have already been promised that the country is too "backward economically" for immediate drastic land redistribution.

(e) *Financial and Commercial Problems.* The CCP has shown considerable concern over the establishment of internal financial stability and the resumption of domestic commerce. The lack of financial experts will seriously hinder the Communists in the establishment of a stable and flexible currency which will be adequate for the commercial and industrial needs of North and Central China. Conditioned by the recent Nationalist experience with paper currency, the Communists in the immediate present may continue to rely on a less flexible exchange system based on barter and tax payments in grain and other commodities. To date, the Communists have been sufficiently successful in collecting agricultural output, which has provided them with a substantial source of revenue.

Although transportation and marketing difficulties will hinder domestic trade, both state and, to a lesser degree, private commerce

has been encouraged by the CCP's commercial policy and probably will continue to be. "Liberation" of the Yangtze Valley will probably yield to the Communists the huge collection-and-sale apparatus of the Central Trust and other National Government agencies, thus reenforcing and firmly establishing the Communist state trading base.

Further, CCP acquisition of the Yangtze region will be an important factor in curing the present paralysis of internal commerce by restoring the normal integration of the Central and North China economies.

(2) *External Problems.*

(a) *Requirements in Foreign Trade.* Petroleum, cotton, and the railroad, factory, and power equipment needed for reconstruction are the principal imports that the Communists will require during the next year. Inadequate amounts of any of these items will seriously hamper economic recovery. Fuel-oil requirements can be met in part by the substitution of coal, which should be available in quantity to the Communists. But kerosene, gasoline, lubricants and other petroleum products which have no substitutes must be imported. Current Chinese consumption, including aviation gasoline, is 15-20 million barrels annually and 10-12 million barrels would probably be a minimum continuing annual requirement, with full utilization of coal and with no increase in the level of economic activity.

Reconstruction requirements for China are enormous. A minimum reconstruction program, calling for rebuilding China's prewar industry and railroads and perhaps one-half of Manchuria's peak industrial capacity, would require imports of US $300-$500 million in China and a similar amount in Manchuria. The bulk of the expense would be for railroad equipment; the remainder would largely be textile, mining, and power machinery and equipment. Reconstruction offers special difficulties to the Communists since substantial credits or investments from the USSR are unlikely and there are severe political obstacles in the way of Western investments. In the next few years, the Chinese Communists will be confronted with the problem of paying for

SECRET

SECRET

20

their rehabilitation through their own efforts.

(b) *Trade with the USSR.* Soviet domination of Manchuria will be a major factor in directing the course of China's foreign trade in the next year. The Soviet Union will continue to take most of Manchuria's grain and soybean crops to meet the deficits of edible oils throughout the USSR and of food in the Soviet Far East. The total value of these imports from Manchuria may well be in excess of US $100 million annually, at world market prices. In China Proper, the USSR does not have the same dominant position with respect to foreign trade that it enjoys in Manchuria. The foreign trade of China Proper is more likely to be directed to the non-Soviet countries because of the limited market in the USSR for such important Chinese exports as bristles, processed eggs, handicrafts, and coal.

The disadvantages to China of the Manchurian trade with the USSR derive largely from the cheap monopoly price that the Soviets have been able to obtain on soybeans, the chief Manchurian export. Through its control of the Manchurian railroads and the port of Dairen, the USSR has been able to prevent the export of Manchurian products to world markets. Necessarily, trade with the Soviet Union on such unfavorable terms tends to impair China's ability to finance her essential import requirements. In China Proper, the Communists will be freer to maximize their return by directing their exports to whatever country offers the highest prices. Exports to non-Soviet countries will provide the Chinese directly with the means needed to obtain essential imports, such as petroleum, railroad equipment, electrical and other industrial machinery, and chemicals—products which can be obtained from these countries more readily than from the USSR.

(c) *Trade with the US.* The advantage of CCP trade with the West and with Japan lies in the character of China's import requirements and her export markets. These advantages particularly apply to US trade, which, in the postwar period, has been the largest of any country's with China.

The US would be a major source for petroleum, certain types of capital equipment, and vehicles. If the US alone were excluded from trade, Japan, the UK, and other Western countries might fill a portion of China's reconstruction needs but it is unlikely that these countries can make sufficient capital goods exports in the next year to satisfy all of China's requirements.

Not only will China probably be forced to depend on the US for essential imports, but the market for many Chinese commodities, such as handicrafts, tung oil, and animal products is determined by US demand. Were the US market eliminated, China's exports would be reduced substantially, her export industries depressed, and her ability to pay for needed imports greatly restricted. China's chances for economic recovery in such circumstances would be small.

(d) *Trade with Japan.* Smaller transportation costs would permit Japan to outbid the world market for many of China's exports. In the case of China's export of such bulk commodities as coal, iron ore, and salt, Japan would be the only commercially important feasible market. In return, Japan could sell to China machinery and railroad equipment which significantly would aid the CCP rehabilitation program. Trade, profitable to both countries, could in a few years total US $3-400,000,000 annually, an amount which would be a substantial portion of China's total foreign trade.

Although Chinese antipathy toward the industrial revival of Japan is a political factor militating against such large-scale trade, it is very likely that the urgent economic considerations of recovery will override such an objection. Indeed, the CCP's Ministry of Industry and Commerce in Tientsin suggested resumption of Japan trade in April and Premier Yoshida has repeatedly declared that Japan "will and must" trade with China. Japan's market, as well as that of the US, is very important in the long run for the achievement of Chinese economic independence and recovery.

SECRET

SECRET

ENCLOSURE A

DISSENT OF THE INTELLIGENCE ORGANIZATION, DEPARTMENT OF STATE

The Intelligence organization of the Department of State dissents from the subject report on the grounds that it does not give adequate treatment to the implications of the anticipated desire of a Communist China for international recognition. The treatment herein accorded this highly complex and technical subject makes for an over-simplification which is considered unsatisfactory in view of the important policy decisions inevitably involved in the present Chinese situation.

SECTION 6

ORE 89-49

The Food Outlook for Communist China

3 February 1950

APPROVED FOR RELEASE
DATE: MAY 2004

SECRET

THE FOOD OUTLOOK FOR COMMUNIST CHINA

ORE 89-49

Published 3 February 1950

CENTRAL INTELLIGENCE AGENCY

SECRET

SECRET

THE FOOD OUTLOOK FOR COMMUNIST CHINA

SUMMARY

Widespread droughts and floods during 1949 will cause severe famine in China in 1950. Serious food shortages in the rural areas of poor harvests are a foregone conclusion. Although famine is a common historical experience in China, the new Communist regime will be put in a disadvantageous light by any comparison of 1949 harvests with the more favorable harvests of recent years under the Nationalists. Food shortages furthermore will delay the fulfillment of Communist promises to the rural population. Peasant rebellions, although not well organized and not ideologically inspired, already have been reported in several areas. Such uprisings may be further encouraged by the famine. Rural unrest may impede the establishment of political and economic stability in China, but it cannot be considered a serious threat to the power of the Communist regime. Continued peasant rebellion, however, may force the Communists to maintain larger armed forces than they had anticipated.

Despite Communist efforts to assure adequate food supply to key urban areas, the problem of shortages has tended to defeat Communist attempts at urban price control. Because wage payments are geared to food prices, the famine will result in increased prices of manufactured goods.

The Communists will not wish to utilize their meager foreign exchange resources for the purchase of food from the west. It is also unlikely that the Communists will seriously approach the US or other non-Communist countries for aid in meeting their current food deficits.

The Soviet-Manchurian trade pact concluded in July 1949 requires the export of Manchurian foodstuffs to the USSR. In an effort to counter unfavorable Chinese reaction, however, the USSR might relax these requirements for food exports or, more likely, might make highly publicized token relief shipments to China.

Note: The intelligence organizations of the Departments of State, Army, Navy and the Air Force have concurred in this report. It contains information available to CIA as of 23 January 1950.

SECRET

1

SECRET

THE FOOD OUTLOOK FOR COMMUNIST CHINA

As a result of widespread droughts and floods during 1949, the year 1950 should bring an exceptionally severe famine to China. While some areas have enjoyed a good harvest, others will suffer from serious food shortages, and many will face famine conditions.*

North China suffered a particularly poor crop year in 1949, but droughts and floods also cut into harvests in many areas of Manchuria, Central China, and South China and drove millions of families from their homes. North China's production of food crops in 1949 was about 20 percent below the level of the previous year, with the lower Yellow River valley and eastern Hopei hard hit by drought in early summer and floods later in the year. Other areas in China which suffered poor harvests include the lake areas of the Central Yangtze Valley, northern Kiangsu, northern Anhwei, parts of Honan, Shansi, and Chahar, northern Manchuria and the lower Liao River valley of Manchuria. Because of their comparative isolation and insufficient modern transport facilities, many distressed localities will be unable to count on a sufficient quantity of commercial or relief shipments from food surplus areas. (For a more detailed discussion of the areas affected, see Appendix.)

The Chinese Communists are thus likely to be faced with peasant unrest in 1950. Peasant rebellions, although not well organized and not ideologically inspired, have already been reported in several areas and may be encour-

aged further by the disappointments and pressure on living standards resulting from poor harvests. In some areas, peasant hostility will take the form of passive resistance and non-cooperation. In a few localities resistance to increased tax burdens may take such overt forms as the murder of tax collectors and open insurrection. The Communists will have to postpone complete pacification in traditionally bandit-ridden areas because of the high cost of policing them.

Despite such patterns of unrest it is not likely that Chinese Communist political control will be seriously threatened. Famine is a common occurrence in China, and consequent disorders are traditionally localized in character. The Communists must necessarily suffer, however, from any comparison of current harvests with those in recent years under the Nationalists; and Chinese peasants, prone to regard omens and auguries seriously, will inevitably make the comparison. Food shortages will delay both the fulfillment of Communist promises to the peasantry and the agricultural programs. In order to cope with peasant unrest in and out of the bandit areas, the Communist government must keep, at some cost, a large armed force in being which it will employ against any resistance that may develop. In their concern about feeding the urban populations, as well as their increased military forces, the Communists may be forced to make increased levies on the peasantry.

In 1948 the difficulties besetting the Nationalists in bringing food to the cities were alleviated by CRM and ECA which supplied nearly three-fourths of China's rice and the bulk of its wheat flour imports. With this assistance now cut off, the Communists must mobilize and transport supplies from the countryside—a task, however, that they are performing with more efficiency than did the Nationalists. It is probable that the most serious food shortages in 1950 will occur, not in the cities, but

---

* Some light is thrown on the extent and seriousness of the famine threat by recent broadcasts over the Communist radio. According to a Peiping report in October, about 10 million peasants in North China alone had been affected by drought, storms, floods, and insect pests. Calamities in Manchuria and in several areas of Central China are affecting many millions more. To meet the famine threat, the Communists are reportedly mobilizing women and children for the collection of grass under the stimulus of such slogans as, "Mix bran and grass to tide over the famine," and "Eat leaves and grass this year, then grain may be eaten next year."

SECRET

in those rural areas which suffered poor harvests and are relatively isolated by the lack of modern transport facilities.

Some of the hardships arising from the food shortages could be alleviated through commercial food imports. Because of their meager resources in foreign exchange, however, and their determination to use this foreign exchange as far as possible to import industrial goods, the Communists will keep food imports to a minimum. The Nationalist blockade, if it continues with moderate effectiveness in 1950, will also constitute a deterrent to food imports. It is highly improbable that the Communists will make a serious approach to the US or other non-Communist countries for aid in meeting their current food deficits.

Probably the most serious problems for the Communists in the cities will be those involving price control. Food shortage in China has tended to defeat all Communist measures to control prices. Upward pressure in the early fall of 1949 was disguised in part by the fact that crops currently being harvested were moving into the cities, in part by Communist skill in collecting supplies and dumping them on the market whenever prices threatened to rise rapidly. With supplies becoming scarcer, however, dumping has already become ineffectual as a means of controlling speculation. A rise in food prices is especially significant in China because wage payments are linked closely to the price of food; poor harvests will

thus tend to increase the costs of manufacture and undermine the competitive position of such Chinese exports as textiles.

Poor harvests, furthermore, will impede initiation of Communist plans for industrialization. With agricultural exports necessarily reduced, Chinese ability to earn foreign exchange will be impaired, and foreign purchases will have to be deferred. If the reduced exports are directed in substantial part to the USSR at terms less favorable than offered on world markets, China's exchange earnings will be even further reduced.

The famine during 1950 may have some effect on Chinese relations with the USSR. Under the terms of the Soviet-Manchurian trade pact concluded in July 1949, Manchuria is required to ship food to the Soviet Union. Although this treaty has been publicized in the Chinese press as an example of mutually beneficial Chinese-Soviet trade, there is evidence of suspicion among many Chinese that the treaty actually favors the USSR at the expense of China. Should the USSR insist on continuation of food shipments from Manchuria, such suspicions would grow, and the whole Soviet policy toward China would become suspect among more and more Chinese. In an effort to counter unfavorable Chinese reaction, however, the USSR might relax these requirements for food exports, or, more likely, might make highly publicized token relief shipments to China.

SECRET

SECTION 7

NIE-2

Chinese Communist
Intervention in Korea

6 November 1950

APPROVED FOR RELEASE
DATE: MAY 2004

(b)(1)
(b)(3)

NATIONAL INTELLIGENCE ESTIMATE

Number 2

8 NOV 1950

COPY NO. 51
FOR CENTRAL RECORDS, CIA FOR FILE

CENTRAL INTELLIGENCE AGENCY

SECRET

NATIONAL INTELLIGENCE ESTIMATE

CHINESE COMMUNIST INTERVENTION IN KOREA

NIE-2

6 November 1950

Advance Copy

In order to expedite delivery, this estimate is
being given a special preliminary distribution.
The final printed copy will be disseminated as
soon as available.

The intelligence organizations of the Departments of State,
the Army, the Navy, and the Air Force participated in the
preparation of this estimate and concur in it. This paper
is based on information available on 6 November 1950.

SECRET

SECRET

CHINESE COMMUNIST INTERVENTION IN KOREA

THE PROBLEM

1. To estimate the scale and purpose of Chinese Communist intervention in North Korea and Chinese Communist capabilities and intentions.

SUMMARY and CONCLUSIONS

2. Present Chinese Communist troop strength in North Korea is estimated at 30,000 to 40,000. Chinese Communist ground units are engaging UN forces at various points ranging from 30 to 100 miles south of the Korean-Manchurian border. Recent action has been marked also by the appearance of Soviet-type jet fighters in combat with US aircraft over Korea.

3. Present Chinese Communist troop strength in Manchuria is estimated at 700,000. Of this number, there are at least 200,000 regular field forces. These troop strengths, added to the forces already in Korea, are believed to make the Chinese Communists capable of: (a) halting further UN advance northward, through piecemeal commitment of troops; or (b) forcing UN withdrawal to defensive positions farther south by a powerful assault.

4. The objective of the Chinese Communist intervention appears to be to halt the advance of UN forces in Korea and to keep a Communist regime in being on Korean soil. In accomplishing this purpose, the Chinese Communists would: (a) avert the psychological and political consequences of a disastrous outcome of the Korean venture; (b) keep UN forces away from the actual frontiers of China and the USSR; (c) retain an area in Korea as

- i -

SECRET

SECRET

a base of Communist military and guerrilla operations;
(d) prolong indefinitely the containment of UN, especially
US, forces in Korea; (e) control the distribution of hydroelectric power generated in North Korea and retain other
economic benefits; and (f) create the possibility of a favorable political solution in Korea, despite the military defeat
of the North Koreans.

5. The Chinese Communists thus far retain full freedom of
action with respect to Korea. They are free to adjust their
action in accordance with the development of the situation.
If the Chinese Communists were to succeed in destroying
the effective strength of UN forces in northern Korea, they
would pursue their advantage as far as possible. If the military situation is stabilized, they may well consider that, with
advantageous terrain and the onset of winter, their forces now
in Korea are sufficient to accomplish their immediate purposes.

6. A likely and logical development of the present situation
is that the opposing sides will build up their combat power
in successive increments to checkmate the other until forces
of major magnitude are involved. At any point in this development, the danger is present that the situation may get out of
control and lead to a general war.

7. The Chinese Communists, in intervening in Korea, have
accepted a grave risk of retaliation and general war. They
would probably ignore an ultimatum requiring their withdrawal.
If Chinese territory were to be attacked, they would probably
enter Korea in full force.

8. The fact that both the Chinese Communists and the USSR
have accepted an increased risk of a general war indicates
either that the Kremlin is ready to face a showdown with the
West at an early date or that circumstances have forced them
to accept that risk.

- ii -

SECRET

SECRET

DISCUSSION

9. Actual Development of Intervention to Date.

Prior to mid-October, Chinese Communist support of the
North Koreans consisted solely of logistical aid and moral support. Since that time, however, the Chinese Communists have
been committing troops in increasing number so that at present
UN forces are being engaged by Chinese Communist ground units
in varying penetrations, ranging from 30 to 100 miles south of
the Manchurian-Korean border.

To date, elements taken from the Chinese Communist 38th,
39th, 40th, and 42nd armies of the Fourth Field Army have been
identified in the combat zone of Korea. Units of approximately
battalion size from each division of three or more of the Chinese
Communist armies along the Korean border in Manchuria have
been combined to form units of approximately division size. One
regular Chinese Communist division has been tentatively identified. Present Chinese Communist troop strength in North Korea
is estimated to number from 30,000 to 40,000. This number, combined with an estimated 45,000 North Korean troops, constitutes
an over-all enemy strength of 75,000 to 85,000. Of this total, an
estimated 52,000 are in contact with UN forces.

The arrival of Chinese Communist ground units in the Korean
fighting has been accompanied by a marked stiffening of North
Korean resistance. The previously confused and disorganized
North Korean units now appear to be in process of recommitment
as reorganized and re-equipped combat units. There are indications that Chinese Communist forces in Korea are being reinforced.

Although the nationality of the hostile aircraft involved in
recent incidents over the Korean-Manchurian border has not been
definitely established, the fact that Soviet-type jet aircraft were

- 1 -

SECRET

SECRET

involved indicates that the North Koreans are receiving air assistance from Manchuria in addition to direct ground force support from the Chinese Communists.

10. Chinese Communist Capabilities for Armed Intervention.

The over-all strength of the Chinese Communist ground forces is estimated at 2,800,000. Of this number, 1,770,000 are well-trained and well-equipped regular field forces, and the remainder are fairly well-trained and well-equipped military district troops. In addition, there are approximately 2,000,000 poorly-trained and poorly-equipped provincial troops.

Since Spring 1950, there has been a general build-up of Chinese Communist tactical troop strength in Manchuria to a point which exceeds normal security needs. The movement of numerous major units from south and central China is estimated to have brought current Chinese Communist strength in Manchuria to approximately 700,000. Of this number, there are at least 200,000 regular field forces, comprising possibly eight to ten armies, plus elements of at least four other armies.

The Chinese Communist Air Force, not tested in combat to date, is believed to consist of 200 combat aircraft in tactical units. Of this 200, 40 are TU-2 light bombers, 40 are IL-10 ground attack, and 120 are LA-9 fighters. It is possible that the CCAF may include 30-40 Soviet-type swept-wing jet fighters formerly stationed in the vicinity of Shanghai, some of which are believed to have been the jet aircraft which have appeared in recent operations in North Korea.

With these ground forces and this air strength, the Chinese Communists could probably make available as many as 350,000 troops within 30 to 60 days for sustained ground operations in

- 2 -

SECRET

SECRET

Korea and could provide limited air support and some armor.
This could be done without jeopardizing their internal control
in Manchuria or China proper. The Chinese Communist Forces
are therefore believed capable either of: (a) halting further UN
advance northward by matching any foreseeable UN build-up
with piecemeal commitment of forces presently along the Yalu
River; or (b) forcing UN withdrawal to defensive positions further
south through a powerful assault.

11. Chinese Communist Motives for Intervention.

The Chinese Communist decision to commit troops in North
Korea, entailing as it does the serious risk of widening the Korean
conflict, would not have been taken by Communist China without
Soviet sanction or possibly direction. It must therefore be assumed that both parties consider the anticipated benefits to justify
the acceptance of the calculated risk of precipitating a general war
in China which could eventually involve the Soviet Union. This
calculated risk includes the possibility of a reaction on the part
of the US directly to meet the broader issue with the USSR rather
than to allow itself to become involved in an expensive and indecisive war with Communist China.

The immediate occasion for Communist Chinese armed assistance appears to have been the crossing of the 38th Parallel
by US forces and the consequent swift collapse of North Korean
resistance. Unless the Chinese had intervened, UN forces would
soon have reached and secured the Yalu River line. The Korean
People's Republic would have ceased to exist except as a govern-
ment-in-exile and as a guerrilla movement. Confronted with this
possibility, the Chinese Communists have apparently determined
to prevent an early UN military victory in Korea and to keep a
Communist regime in being on Korean soil.

- 3 -

SECRET

SECRET

It is significant that the Chinese Communists refrained from committing troops at two earlier critical phases of the Korean war, namely when the UN held no more than a precarious toehold in the Pusan perimeter and later when the UN landings were made at Inchon. The failure to act on those occasions appears to indicate that Peiping was unwilling to accept a serious risk of war, prior to the US crossing of the 38th Parallel. Since the crossing of the Parallel, Chinese Communist propaganda has increasingly identified the Peiping cause with the cause of the North Koreans.

The immediate objective of the Chinese Communist intervention in Korea appears to have been to halt the advance of UN forces. Chinese Communist military operations to date, including the nature of the forces employed, suggest an interim military operation with limited objectives. This view is strengthened by consideration of the limitations imposed on military operations by winter weather in this mountainous area.

In assisting the North Koreans, the Chinese Communists can derive several advantages for themselves, the Soviet Union, and world Communism. They are:

a.. <u>To avert the psychological and political consequences of a disastrous outcome of the Korean venture.</u>

The prestige of the world Communist movement and, more particularly, the domestic and international political position of the Chinese Communist regime, are linked with the fate of the North Korean satellite. A complete UN victory in Korea would adversely affect the power of international Communism to attract and hold adherents. For the Chinese regime itself, the total elimination of a satellite state in Korea

- 4 -

SECRET

SECRET

would mean a serious loss of political face in China and in
the world at large, most notably in the Asiatic areas that
have probably been selected by the Chinese Communists as
their primary sphere of influence.

b. **To keep UN forces away from the actual frontiers
of China and the USSR.**

The establishment of a Western-oriented and US-
supported regime on the south bank of the Yalu River is
probably viewed by Peiping as a threat to the security of the
Communist regime in China. The USSR would likewise be
sensitive to the advance of UN forces to the northeastern tip
of Korea. The Chinese Communists apparently regard the
US as a hostile power, determined to bring about their eventual
overthrow.

c. **To retain an area in Korea as a base of Communist
military and guerrilla operations.**

The terrain of North Korea adjacent to the Manchurian
border is especially suitable for such a base.

d. **To prolong indefinitely the containment of UN, especially
US, forces in Korea.**

Prolonged involvement of UN and US forces in Korea
is favorable for Communist global strategy. The containment
of these forces in Korea prevents their redeployment to Germany, or to other areas where they might be required to oppose
Communist aggression.

- 5 -

SECRET

SECRET

e. **To control the distribution of hydroelectric power generated in North Korea and retain other economic benefits.**

Peiping has an immediate economic stake in the preservation of a friendly state south of the Yalu. The hydroelectric installations in North Korea, particularly the Suiho plant, are important sources of power for South Manchuria. The port of Antung in Manchuria is part of an economic entity that embraces the Korean city of Sinuiju across the river; trade in the area would be hampered severely if no arrangements existed for the operation of the Antung-Sinuiju port as a single unit. River traffic on the Yalu and the Tumen Rivers is dependent upon workable agreements between political authorities in Manchuria and Korea.

f. **To create the possibility of a favorable political solution in Korea, despite the military defeat of the North Koreans.**

It is possible that the Chinese Communists and the USSR hope to establish a military situation that will make the UN willing to negotiate a settlement of the Korean conflict in preference to a long drawn-out and expensive campaign.

12. **Possible Developments.**

The Chinese Communists thus far retain full freedom of action with respect to Korea. They are free to adjust their actions in accordance with the development of the situation. Their current violent propaganda--centering as it has on (a) the "will of the Chinese people" (rather than the government) to supply "people's volunteers" to aid the North Koreans and "defend China"; and (b) America's "use of Japanese" and

- 6 -

SECRET

SECRET

"aping of Japan" in its "aggression against China"--is
excellently adapted for preserving maneuverability. It
could mean equally: whipping up of public opinion that
seems chilly toward any Korean venture; a part of a general war of nerves; a real intention to organize an anti-UN
military campaign on a "people's volunteer" basis; or a
psychological preparation of the Chinese people for hostilities with the US, if not a world war.

If the Chinese Communists were to succeed in destroying the effective strength of UN forces in northern Korea,
the Chinese Communists would probably pursue that advantage as far as possible, bringing in reinforcements from
Manchuria to exploit the opportunity.

If the military situation is stabilized, the Chinese Communists might well consider that, with advantageous terrain
and the onset of winter, their forces now in Korea are
adequate to prevent a military decision favorable to the UN,
at least until spring. Such a military deadlock would contain
UN forces in Korea and expose them to attrition. It would
also permit the reconstitution of North Korean forces and
facilitate the development of guerrilla operations behind the
UN lines. In these circumstances, the possibility of a political solution as the most convenient means of bringing the
situation in Korea to a conclusion would be increased.

A likely and logical development of the present situation
is that the opposing sides will build up their combat power
in successive increments to checkmate the other until forces
of major magnitude are involved. At any point in this development the danger is present that the situation may get out of
control and lead to a general war.

- 7 -

SECRET

SECRET

The Chinese Communists appreciate that in intervening in Korea they have incurred grave risks of retaliation and general war, but have accepted the risk. They would probably ignore a UN ultimatum requiring their withdrawal. If Chinese territory were to be attacked, they could and probably would enter Korea in full force, with the purpose of expelling UN forces altogether.

The fact that both the Chinese Communists and the USSR have accepted an increased risk of a general war indicates either that the Kremlin is ready to face a showdown with the West at an early date or that circumstances have forced them to accept that risk.

- 8 -

SECRET

SECTION 8

NIE-10

Communist China

17 January 1951

APPROVED FOR RELEASE
DATE: MAY 2004

(b)(3)

COPY NO. 234

~~SECRET~~

NATIONAL INTELLIGENCE ESTIMATE

COMMUNIST CHINA

NIE-10

Published 17 January 1951

CENTRAL INTELLIGENCE AGENCY

~~SECRET~~

SECRET

COMMUNIST CHINA

THE PROBLEM

To estimate the stability of the Chinese Communist regime, its relations with the USSR, and its probable courses of action toward the non-Communist world.

DISCUSSION

Stability of the Chinese Communist Regime.

1. For the foreseeable future the Chinese Communist regime will probably retain exclusive governmental control of mainland China. Although there is undoubtedly much dissatisfaction with the Communist regime in China, it does enjoy a measure of support or acquiescence and is developing strong police controls. No serious split in the Communist regime itself is now indicated. In particular, the regime has effective control of the Chinese Communist army. There are no indications that current anti-Communist efforts can achieve a successful counter-revolution. On the basis of the slight evidence available, it is estimated that about 700,000 men may be engaged in active resistance operations, ranging from local banditry to organized guerrilla warfare. There is insufficient evidence either to substantiate or deny Nationalist claims that a considerable number of these are associated with the Nationalist regime on Taiwan. These forces are creating widespread disorders and are handicapping the Chinese Communist program despite the fact that they are uncoordinated, lack effective top-level leadership, and so far have developed no constructive political program. By themselves and under present conditions these resistance forces do not constitute a major threat to the Chinese Communist regime.

General Objectives of Communist China.

2. The main objectives of the Chinese Communist regime are to establish and perpetuate its own control over all Chinese territory and to construct in China a Communist economic and social order. The Chinese Communists aim at eliminating Nationalist Chinese and Western power from China and contiguous territories as rapidly as possible. With support of the USSR, they aim further at the final victory of world communism and at Chinese leadership of a Communist Far East.

Sino-Soviet Relations.

3. The Chinese Communists are clearly coordinating policy and acting in close cooperation with the USSR. There is between Peiping and Moscow a defense treaty. There is also at the present time a strong bond of mutual interest in jointly protecting the security of the two regimes, in eliminating Western influence from Asia, and in furthering the success of international communism.

4. The current Soviet program of economic and military assistance is contributing to Communist China's ability to progress toward its military objectives. Western countermeasures against Chinese Communist advances would render Communist China more dependent on the USSR for such further economic and military support as the USSR might be able or willing to provide. It is possible that such measures would result in Communist China becoming an economic liability to the USSR.

5. Latent possibilities of conflict between Peiping and Moscow exist in such questions as: (a) control of Chinese border territories like Sinkiang and Manchuria; (b) ultimate control over Korea; (c) Soviet efforts to infiltrate and control the Chinese Communist government; and (d) failure of the USSR to meet the economic and military requirements

SECRET

1

SECRET

2

of Communist China. But these elements of potential conflict between Chinese national interests and Soviet imperialistic policy and tactics are unlikely to develop at least so long as Communist military operations against the "common enemy" continue to be successful.

6. If Soviet strength should decline sharply in relation to that of the US and its allies, and if, at the same time, the Chinese Communist regime became convinced that it could remain in power through an accommodation with the US and its allies, the Chinese Communist regime might conceivably attempt to break its association with the USSR. This situation is unlikely to develop in the foreseeable future.

Immediate Chinese Communist Threats To US Security Interests.

7. The Chinese Communists are following a course of action designed to destroy US strategic interests in the Far East and to reduce the worldwide power position of the US and its allies in relation to the joint power position of the USSR and China.

8. The scale of the Chinese Communist operations in Korea and the unwillingness of the Chinese Communists to discuss a diplomatic settlement except on their own terms indicate that they intend to drive UN forces out of Korea; they have already committed a large proportion of their best troops for this purpose, and are prepared to commit additional forces.

9. The Chinese Communists have indicated their firm intention of capturing Taiwan in order to complete the conquest of Chinese territory and eliminate the last stronghold of the Nationalist regime. The Chinese Communists have the capability for mounting an amphibious attack on Taiwan. So long as the US Seventh Fleet is available to protect the island, however, it is unlikely that the Chinese Communists would undertake such an operation.

10. The Chinese Communists at present also have the capability of intervening effectively in Indochina. They have been supporting the Viet Minh for some time. Direct intervention in strength is almost certain to occur

whenever there is danger either that the Viet Minh will fail to attain its military objective of driving the French out of Indochina, or that the Bao Dai government is succeeding in undermining the support of the Viet Minh. Even if they do not openly intervene in Indochina, they can and probably will increase military assistance to the Viet Minh in an effort to make the French position untenable.

11. The Chinese Communists are also capable of securing Honk Kong at any time, and they are likely to do so whenever they have convinced themselves that there is no longer any advantage in leaving Hong Kong in British hands and whenever they are willing to accept the consequences of hostile action against British territory. Similar considerations apply to Macao. In the case of Hong Kong, they might stay their hand so as to utilize the Hong Kong problem as a continuing wedge between the US and UK or to preserve the flow of trade through Hong Kong.

12. The Chinese Communists have further capabilities of attacking Burma and of carrying on subversive activities in other countries of Southeast Asia. It is estimated that at present they do not have the capabilities for military attack upon Japan.

13. Under present circumstances, the Chinese Communists probably have the military capability of concurrently carrying on their operations in Korea, intervening effectively in Indochina and Tibet, attacking Burma, and capturing Hong Kong, while continuing to contain opposition groups within China.

Vulnerabilities of Communist China.

14. Because of Communist China's well recognized enormous numbers of ground forces, the great extent of its territory, and the inadequacy of its communication routes for large-scale Western-type military ground operations, the counter-measures to which Communist China is most vulnerable are the following:

(a) Support of Resistance Forces.

By supplying the active anti-Communist forces already present in mainland China with effective communications, military equipment, and logistical support, Communist mili-

SECRET

SECRET

3

tary strength could be sapped, and their capabilities for operations elsewhere could be reduced. Even under these circumstances, these opposition groups would be unlikely to overthrow the Chinese Communist regime in the absence of an effective counter-revolutionary movement, a political program, a clearcut organization, competent leadership and a plan for action.

(b) Use of Nationalist Forces.

The Nationalist Chinese Government on Taiwan has an army in being of approximately 428,000 troops. There is considerable doubt, however, as to the reliability and effectiveness of the Nationalist forces under present Nationalist leadership. The morale and combat efficiency of these forces could doubtless be substantially improved under US training and supervision. Given adequate logistic support, a large portion of these forces could be landed on the mainland. There is considerable question as to whether the Nationalists could mobilize popular support on the mainland or command the effective cooperation of present guerrilla forces. They might, however, be able to capitalize on existing discontent with the Communist regime. Such an operation would for a time occupy considerable Communist military strength.

(c) Economic Warfare and Limited Military Action.

Although the economy of China is mainly rural and operates at the subsistence level, the urban segment of the economy is largely dependent on overseas and coastal trade, and by reason of its concentration in a few localities, is particularly vulnerable to bombardment and blockade. Curtailment of foreign trade by Western economic controls, embargos, or by naval blockade, would create urban unemployment and unrest, hinder industrial production and development, and create serious financial difficulties. A campaign of aerial and naval bombardment against selected ports, rail systems, industrial capacity and storage bases, in addition to economic warfare measures, would seriously reduce the military capabilities of Communist China for sustained operations, would impair the ability of the regime to maintain internal controls and conceivably might imperil the stability of the regime itself.

(d) Continuation of UN Operations in Korea.

The continued maintenance of UN military operations in Korea would result in a significant drain on the Chinese Communists, would pin down a large portion of their crack troops and reduce their war-making capabilities elsewhere. It could have other far-reaching effects, such as weakening the present feeling of invincibility, reducing the prestige the regime is gaining from current successes, encouraging internal opposition and straining relations with the Kremlin.

(e) Effect of Counter-Measures.

The measures outlined in (a), (b), (c) and (d) above, if applied in combination, would imperil the Chinese Communist regime. These actions would, however, create a grave danger of Soviet counteraction and would increase the danger of a global war.

SECTION 9

NIE-58

Relations Between the Chinese
Communist Regime and the USSR:
Their Present Character and
Probable Future Courses

10 September 1952

APPROVED FOR RELEASE
DATE: MAY 2004

~~SECRET~~
~~SECURITY INFORMATION~~

(b)(3)

COPY NO. 53

~~RECORD COPY~~

NATIONAL INTELLIGENCE ESTIMATE

RELATIONS BETWEEN THE CHINESE COMMUNIST REGIME AND THE USSR: THEIR PRESENT CHARACTER AND PROBABLE FUTURE COURSES

Superseded by 13-56

NIE - 58

Published 10 September 1952

The following member organizations of the Intelligence Advisory Committee participated with the Central Intelligence Agency in the preparation of this estimate: The intelligence organizations of the Departments of State, the Army, the Navy, the Air Force, and the Joint Staff.

All members of the Intelligence Advisory Committee concurred in this estimate on 4 September 1952. See, however, the reservation of the Special Assistant, Intelligence, Department of State, to paragraphs 5 and 26.

CENTRAL INTELLIGENCE AGENCY

~~SECRET~~

APPROVED FOR RELEASE
DATE: MAY 2004

SECRET

RELATIONS BETWEEN THE CHINESE COMMUNIST REGIME AND THE USSR: THEIR PRESENT CHARACTER AND PROBABLE FUTURE COURSES

THE PROBLEM

To estimate the present nature and state of relations between Communist China and the USSR and to estimate the probable courses of these relations over the next two years.

CONCLUSIONS

1. The Peiping regime accepts Moscow leadership in the world Communist movement, and is becoming increasingly dependent on the USSR economically and militarily. However, we believe that the Peiping regime retains some capability for independent action, and is in a position to influence the formulation of Communist policy in the Far East.

2. We believe that Moscow will try to extend and intensify its control over Communist China. However, we believe it unlikely that, at least during the period of this estimate, the Kremlin will be able by nonmilitary means to achieve a degree of control over Communist China comparable to that which it exercises over the European Satellites. We believe it is almost certain that the Kremlin will not attempt to achieve such control by military force.

3. Over the long run, Sino-Soviet solidarity might be weakened as a result of efforts by the USSR to intensify and extend its control over Communist China,

disputes over Soviet economic and military assistance to Communist China, divergent views concerning the border areas, Communist Chinese efforts to control and direct Far Eastern "liberation movements," or divergent views over the priority of Far Eastern Communist objectives in relation to other world Communist objectives.

4. We believe that during the period of this estimate these factors will be far outweighed by close ideological ties and continuing mutual involvement in the pursuit of common objectives, particularly the elimination of Western influence from the Far East.

5. Although the Peiping regime will undoubtedly continue to attempt to gain legal recognition internationally, to secure Formosa, and to resume trade and commerce with the West, we do not believe that the existing Sino-Soviet solidarity can be weakened by non-Communist concessions to Communist China.

SECRET

1

SECRET   2

Moreover, as we have previously estimated, we believe that Western pressures against Communist China, while weakening her, would not disrupt Sino-Soviet solidarity during the period of this estimate.[1]

DISCUSSION

Introduction

6. Communist China and the USSR present a united front to the world. Since the establishment of the Chinese Communist regime in 1949 there has been no reliable indication that either country has adopted any important course of action of joint concern without the consent of the other. In February 1950, the Chinese Communists and the USSR signed a 30-year treaty of friendship, alliance, and mutual assistance, and this treaty provides the formal basis for current relations between the two states. [2]

CURRENT STATUS OF SINO-SOVIET RELATIONSHIP

Soviet Communism and the Chinese Communist Party

7. The Chinese Communist Party (CCP), unlike the Communist parties of the European Satellites, gained power with little assistance from the Soviet Army. The Chinese Communist claims of independent achievement which allow the USSR credit only for ideological and moral support until the formation of the Peiping regime in October 1949, have some basis in fact although they underestimate the assistance given by the USSR during the period from 1945 to 1949.

8. The high command of most Communist parties in the world has undergone frequent and violent changes, which are believed to have been dictated from Moscow. In contrast, the CCP has exhibited unique stability and continuity in its leadership. This leadership undoubtedly takes pride in its independent rise to power and recognizes that it possesses a capacity for independent action.

9. The Chinese Communists claim for Mao Tse-tung authority in his own right as a Communist theoretician. This claim has been accepted in part by Moscow, and the prestige accorded Mao in this respect goes far beyond that accorded any other contemporary non-Soviet Communist. However, even those Chinese who would place Mao near Stalin in authority profess allegiance to the Marxist-Leninist-Stalinist doctrine held by the rulers in Moscow. The CCP leaders have repeatedly and emphatically proclaimed their adherence to Stalinism, their rejection of the "national selfishness" of Titoism, and their debt to the inspiration and example of the Russian leaders and the October Revolution. Common ideology is thus a strong force binding together the Chinese and Soviet regimes. Peiping and Moscow both aim at expelling all Western influence from Asia and at extending Communist control over the entire area. Both desire to spread the Communist world revolution.

---

[1] The Special Assistant, Intelligence, Department of State, believes that the difficult and complex problem of the possible effect of Western actions on Sino-Soviet solidarity requires more thorough study than has been possible in the course of preparing this or earlier national intelligence estimates. He therefore reserves judgment on the validity of paragraph five, preferring to state simply that a significant weakening of Sino-Soviet solidarity is unlikely during the period of this estimate.

[2] The published text of the treaty is appended as Annex "A." The more important clauses of this brief and general treaty provide that: (a) in the event one party is attacked by Japan or any state allied with it and thus is involved in a state of war, the other will immediately render military and other assistance by all means at its disposal; (b) the two parties will consult with each other in regard to all important international problems affecting their common interests; and (c) each party undertakes, in conformity with the principles of equality, mutual benefit, and mutual respect for the national sovereignty and territorial integrity and noninterference in the internal affairs of the other, to develop and consolidate economic and cultural ties.

SECRET

SECRET   3

Other Soviet Influences in Communist China

10. Soviet political and economic "advisors" are stationed in China at various governmental and party levels. We do not believe that these advisors issue direct orders, but the Chinese have been receptive to their advice, which seems to be given through Chinese intermediaries. Soviet advisors are not only attached to the government and the party and to certain economic and security organs, but are also assigned to specific engineering, industrial, and cultural projects. Neither these advisors nor the Kremlin has criticized, at least publicly, the internal policies of Communist China or the implementation of these policies.

11. The Korean war greatly increased Communist China's economic dependence on the USSR. The adoption of more severe Western trade controls in July 1951 has accelerated the orientation of Communist China's trade to the Soviet Bloc. Although Communist Chinese economic dependence on the Bloc increases Soviet influence in Communist China, the USSR does not directly control the Chinese economy or operate any of the industry of mainland China (outside of Manchuria and Sinkiang).

12. The Korean war appears to be directed from joint Sino-Soviet military headquarters. The Chinese Communists are undoubtedly strongly influenced by Soviet military advisors, and it is probable that no major decisions are made in the Korean war without Soviet approval.

13. Except for captured equipment, the Chinese Communist forces are wholly dependent on the USSR for heavy items of military equipment, and the large scale of Soviet logistic support has presumably further increased Moscow's influence with the Chinese military. The Chinese Communist Air Force is largely a Soviet creation and is wholly dependent upon the USSR for equipment and supply.

Situation in the Border Areas

14. In Manchuria, the influence of Chinese Communist political and military leaders appears to outweigh that of the Soviet personnel in the area. Economic policies also reflect the central planning and directives of Peiping. Nevertheless, the USSR exerts great influence over economic and strategic developments in the area through its military and economic advisors, its intelligence activities, its supervision of rail lines, and its control of the Port Arthur naval base area. According to the Sino-Soviet agreements,[3] Soviet control over Port Arthur and participation in the administration of Manchurian rail lines is scheduled to be terminated in 1952; however, it is probable that such termination would not greatly lessen Soviet influence in Manchuria.

15. Soviet advisors and commercial enterprises in Inner Mongolia have economic and political influence, particularly in Eastern Inner Mongolia which borders on the USSR. However, Peiping has at least administrative control, and the strength of Chinese influence appears to be growing.

16. In Sinkiang, Peiping has stationed 70,000 troops and appears to exercise effective administrative control. For geographic reasons, however, Sinkiang's trade is chiefly with the USSR, and the Chinese need Soviet assistance to develop the resources of the area. The USSR exerts great influence through three Sino-Soviet companies and through Soviet citizens in the service of the provincial government.

17. Soviet influence in the border areas, political as well as economic, is extensive. At the same time, Chinese Communist political and territorial interests have apparently not been sacrificed in the interest of Soviet expansion. The trend since 1950 appears to be towards an increase in Chinese Communist administrative control.

The Character of Current Sino-Soviet Relations

18. From a consideration of the available evidence, we conclude that the Peiping regime — unlike the European Satellites — is not directly and completely controlled by the Kremlin. Sino-Soviet cooperation is based upon Chinese Communist acceptance of Moscow leadership

---

[3] See Annex "B" for the published text of the agreement between Communist China and the USSR on the Chinese-Changchun Railway, Port Arthur, and Dairen.

SECRET

SECRET

4

in the world Communist movement, a common ideology, and the common objective of eliminating Western influence from the Far East. This relationship is further solidified by common hostility to a resurgent and non-Communist Japan and to US power in the western Pacific. It is greatly reinforced by the Kremlin's need for an ally in the Far East, and by Communist China's need for Soviet assistance in training and equipping its armed forces and in developing its economy.

19. We believe also that the size and potential of China, the strength and cohesion of the Chinese Communist Party, the traditional Chinese xenophobia, and the inherent difficulties encountered by foreigners in exercising control in China, have permitted the Chinese Communists to retain some capability for independent action and a capability to exert an influence upon the shaping of Communist policy in the Far East.

20. The Chinese Communist regime appears willing to subordinate, at least temporarily, those Chinese national interests which are incompatible with the interests of the USSR, to submerge any fears it may have of Soviet expansion at China's expense, and to substitute for China's traditional unilateral policy of playing foreign powers against one another, a joint Sino-Soviet policy of endeavoring to eliminate Western influence from Asia. Chinese Communist leaders probably estimate that close Sino-Soviet collaboration will ensure Chinese security from Western counteraction, and ensure Soviet economic and military aid without ending China's independence.

21. The Kremlin appears to recognize that Communist China now possesses the determination and some capacity to pursue its own interests. Moreover, the Kremlin almost certainly sees in the present relationship the opportunity to use Communist China to weaken the Western position in Asia. On the other hand, the Kremlin probably views the relationship also as an opportunity to extend Soviet domination over Communist China by subversion, by making Communist China economically and militarily dependent upon the USSR, and by Soviet pressure upon the

borderlands. Furthermore, a friendly Communist China provides the USSR with a defense in depth, constitutes a valuable potential source of manpower and other resources, and is an important political and psychological asset.

Future Course of Sino-Soviet Relations

22. We believe that the following factors will tend to ensure the continuation of Sino-Soviet solidarity during the period of this estimate:

a. The cohesive force of common ideology will probably continue to bind the two regimes together.

b. The military and economic dependence of Communist China upon the USSR will increase, at least for as long as the Korean war continues without settlement.

c. Continued US assistance to the Nationalist Government on Taiwan, the US-Japan Security Pact, and the ever-present apprehension of US action against Communist China itself will tend to draw Communist China and the USSR together.

d. Neither the USSR nor Communist China now appears capable of altering the current relationship to its advantage without jeopardizing the attainment of its own objectives. A Chinese Communist effort unilaterally to revise the relationship or to leave the Bloc would result in the cessation of Soviet economic and military aid and support and in serious dissension within the Chinese Communist Party and the armed forces. It might lead to armed conflict with the USSR. Similarly, a Kremlin effort to reduce Communist China to the status of the European Satellites might lead to armed conflict with Communist China and would divide and confuse the international Communist movement.

23. On the other hand, the following factors may, sooner or later, weaken Sino-Soviet solidarity:

a. The history of Sino-Russian relations is full of conflicts over Sinkiang, Mongolia, and Manchuria. During the last century there has been almost continuous Russian encroachment on Chinese interests in those areas. The Sino-Soviet Treaty of 1950 temporarily

SECRET

93

SECRET   5

ended such border disputes. It is difficult to believe, however, that such longstanding disputes have been permanently settled. We think that they are likely to recur, in one form or another, and that they must be considered in assessing the probable course of Sino-Soviet relations in the future.

b. Having provided assistance and advice to the "liberation" movements of other countries in the Far East, Peiping may attempt to extend its own sphere of influence. China has traditional aspirations to primacy in the Far East, and there is evidence that the Chinese Communist role in other Far Eastern "liberation" movements has been increasing but has not been permanently defined.

c. At present, the interests of China are for the most part confined to the Far East; those of the Kremlin are world-wide. Hence, the Chinese Communists may view the accomplishment of Far Eastern objectives with more urgency and impatience than do the Soviets, who might postpone action in the Far East because of situations elsewhere in the world. The Chinese Communists might make demands upon the USSR, or even take action, incompatible with long-range Soviet global interests. This is applicable to the Korean conflict which is a potential source of friction to the two regimes.

d. The Chinese Communist program of industrialization and military modernization increasingly depends on Soviet material and technical assistance. Frictions might arise because of Soviet inability or disinclination to supply capital equipment. Soviet conditions for such supply might be offensive to Chinese national pride.

e. We have estimated that the ultimate objective of the Kremlin is the establishment of a Communist world dominated from Moscow. We do not believe, however, that the leaders of Communist China would accept complete Soviet domination of China.

Whether future leaders of China will do so is a question; if they do not, a serious clash of interests is certain.

24. We believe that Moscow will try to extend and intensify its control over Communist China. However, we believe it unlikely that, at least during the period of this estimate, the Kremlin will be able by nonmilitary means to achieve a degree of control over Communist China comparable to that which it exercises over the European Satellites. We believe it is almost certain that the Kremlin will not attempt to achieve such control by military force. The military conquest of China would be a long, difficult, and expensive process.

25. We believe that for the period of this estimate the factors tending to divide the USSR and Communist China will be far outweighed by close ideological ties and continuing mutual involvement in the pursuit of common objectives, particularly the elimination of Western influence from the Far East.

26. Although the Peiping regime will undoubtedly continue to attempt to gain legal recognition internationally, to secure Formosa, and to resume trade and commerce with the West, we do not believe that the existing Sino-Soviet solidarity can be weakened by non-Communist concessions to Communist China. Moreover, as we have previously estimated, we believe that Western pressures against Communist China, while weakening her, would not disrupt Sino-Soviet solidarity during the period of this estimate. [4]

---

[4] The Special Assistant, Intelligence, Department of State, believes that the difficult and complex problem of the possible effect of Western actions on Sino-Soviet solidarity requires more thorough study than has been possible in the course of preparing this or earlier national intelligence estimates. He therefore reserves judgment on the validity of paragraph twenty-six, preferring to state simply that a significant weakening of Sino-Soviet solidarity is unlikely during the period of this estimate.

SECRET

SECRET

6

ANNEX "A"

THE TREATY OF FRIENDSHIP, ALLIANCE, AND MUTUAL ASSISTANCE BETWEEN THE PEOPLE'S REPUBLIC OF CHINA AND THE SOVIET UNION

The Central People's Government of the People's Republic of China and the Presidium of the Supreme Soviet of the Union of Soviet Socialist Republics, fully determined to prevent jointly, by strengthening friendship and cooperation between the People's Republic of China and the Union of Soviet Socialist Republics, the rebirth of Japanese imperialism and the resumption of aggression on the part of Japan or any other state that may collaborate in any way with Japan in acts of aggression; imbued with the desire to consolidate lasting peace and universal security in the Far East and throughout the world in conformity with the aims and principles of the United Nations; profoundly convinced that the consolidation of good neighbourly relations and friendship between the People's Republic of China and the Union of Soviet Socialist Republics meets the vital interests of the peoples of China and the Soviet Union, have towards this end decided to conclude the present treaty and have appointed as their plenipotentiary representatives: Chou En-lai, Premier of the Government Administration Council and Minister of Foreign Affairs, acting for the Central People's Government of the People's Republic of China; and Andrei Yanuarjevich Vyshinsky, Minister of Foreign Affairs, acting for the Presidium of the Supreme Soviet of the Union of Soviet Socialist Republics. Both plenipotentiary representatives upon exchanging their credentials, found to be in good and due form, have agreed upon the following:

Article 1

Both contracting parties undertake jointly to adopt all necessary measures at their disposal for the purpose of preventing the resumption of aggression and violation of peace on the part of Japan or any other state that may collaborate with Japan directly or indirectly in acts of aggression. In the event of one of the contracting parties being attacked by Japan or any state allied with it and thus being involved in a state of war, the other contracting party shall immediately render military and other assistance by all means at its disposal.

The contracting parties also declare their readiness to participate in a spirit of sincere cooperation in all international actions aimed at ensuring peace and security throughout the world and to contribute their full share to the earliest implementation of these tasks.

Article 2

Both contracting parties undertake in the spirit of mutual agreement to bring about the earliest conclusion of the peace treaty with Japan jointly with other powers which were Allies during the Second World War.

Article 3

Each contracting party undertakes not to conclude any alliance directed against the other contracting party and not to take part in any coalition or in any actions or measures directed against the other contracting party.

Article 4

Both contracting parties, in the interests of consolidating peace and universal security, will consult with each other in regard to all important international problems affecting the common interests of China and the Soviet Union.

Article 5

Each contracting party undertakes, in the spirit of friendship and cooperation and in conformity with the principles of equality, mutual benefit and mutual respect for the national sovereignty and territorial integrity and non-interference in the internal affairs of the other contracting party, to develop and

SECRET

SECRET

7

consolidate economic and cultural ties between China and the Soviet Union, to render the other all possible economic assistance and to carry out necessary economic cooperation.

Article 6

The present treaty comes into force immediately upon its ratification; the exchange of instruments of ratification will take place in Peking.

The present treaty will be valid for thirty years. If neither of the contracting parties gives notice one year before the expiration of this term of its intention to renounce the treaty, it shall remain in force for another five years and will be further extended in compliance with this rule.

Done in Moscow on February 14, 1950, in two copies, each in the Chinese and Russian languages, both texts being equally valid.

On the authorization of the Central People's Government of the People's Republic of China

CHOU EN-LAI

On the authorization of the Presidium of the Supreme Soviet of the Union of Soviet Socialist Republics

A. Y. VYSHINSKY

SECRET

SECRET

8

ANNEX "B"

THE AGREEMENT ON CHINESE CHANGCHUN RAILWAY, PORT ARTHUR, AND DAIREN BETWEEN THE PEOPLE'S REPUBLIC OF CHINA AND THE UNION OF SOVIET SOCIALIST REPUBLIC

The Central People's Government of the People's Republic of China and the Presidium of the Supreme Soviet of the Union of Soviet Socialist Republics declare that since 1945, fundamental changes have occurred in the situation in the Far East, namely: imperialist Japan has suffered defeat; the reactionary Kuomintang Government has been overthrown; China became a People's Democratic Republic; a new people's government has been formed in China which has united the whole of China and has carried out a policy of friendship and cooperation with the Soviet Union and has proved its ability to defend the national independence and territorial integrity of China and the national honour and dignity of the Chinese people.

The Central People's Government of the People's Republic of China and the Presidium of the Supreme Soviet of the Union of Soviet Socialist Republics declare that this new situation permits a new approach to the question of the Chinese Changchun Railway, Port Arthur, and Dairen.

In conformity with these new circumstances the Central People's Government of the People's Republic of China and the Presidium of the Supreme Soviet of the Union of Soviet Socialist Republics have decided to conclude the present agreement on the Chinese Changchun Railway, Port Arthur, and Dairen:

Article 1

Both contracting parties agree that the Soviet Government transfer without compensation to the Government of the People's Republic of China all its rights in the joint administration of the Chinese Changchun Railway with all the property belonging to the Railway. The transfer will be effected immediately on the conclusion of the peace treaty with Japan, but not later than the end of 1952.

Pending the transfer, the existing Sino-Soviet joint administration of the Chinese Changchun Railway shall remain unchanged. After this engagement becomes effective, posts (such as manager of the Railway, chairman of the Central Board, etc.) will be periodically alternated between representatives of China and the U.S.S.R.

As regards concrete methods of effecting the transfer, these will be agreed upon and determined by the Governments of both contracting parties.

Article 2

Both contracting parties agree that Soviet troops be withdrawn from the jointly-utilized naval base Port Arthur, and that the installations in this area be handed over to the Government of the People's Republic of China immediately on the conclusion of the peace treaty with Japan, but not later than the end of 1952. The Government of the People's Republic of China will compensate the Soviet Union for expenses which it has incurred in restoring and constructing installations since 1945.

For the period pending the withdrawal of Soviet troops and the transfer of the above-mentioned installations, the Governments of China and the Soviet Union will each appoint an equal number of military representatives to form a joint Chinese-Soviet military commission which will be alternately presided over by each side and which will be in charge of military affairs in the area of Port Arthur; concrete measures in this sphere will be drawn up by the joint Chinese-Soviet military commission within three months after the present agreement becomes effective and shall be put into force upon approval of these measures by the Governments of both countries.

SECRET

SECRET   9

The civil administration in the aforementioned area shall be under the direct authority of the Government of the People's Republic of China. Pending the withdrawal of Soviet troops, the zone for billetting Soviet troops in the area of Port Arthur will remain unaltered in conformity with existing frontiers.

In the event of either of the contracting parties becoming the object of aggression on the part of Japan or any state that may collaborate with Japan, and as a result thereof becoming involved in hostilities, China and the Soviet Union may, on the proposal of the Government of the People's Republic of China and with the agreement of the Government of the U.S.S.R., jointly use the naval base Port Arthur for the purpose of conducting joint military operations against the aggressor.

Article 3

Both contracting parties agree that the question of Dairen harbour be further considered on the conclusion of the peace treaty with Japan. As regards the administration of Dairen, it fully belongs to the Government of the People's Republic of China. All the property in Dairen now provisionally administered by or leased to the Soviet Union, shall be taken over by the Government of the People's Republic of China. To carry out the transfer of the aforementioned property, the Governments of China and the Soviet Union will appoint three representatives each to form a joint commission which, within three months after the present agreement comes into effect, shall draw up concrete measures for the transfer of the property; and these measures shall be fully carried out in the course of 1950 after their approval by the Governments of both countries upon the proposal of the joint commission.

Article 4

The present agreement comes into force on the day of its ratification. The exchange of instruments of ratification will take place in Peking.

Done in Moscow on February 14, 1950, in two copies, each in the Chinese and Russian languages, both texts being equally valid.

On the authorization of the Central People's Government of the People's Republic of China

CHOU EN-LAI

On the authorization of the Presidium of the Supreme Soviet of the Union of Soviet Socialist Republics

A. Y. VYSHINSKY

SECRET

SECTION 10

NIE 13-54

Communist China's Power
Potential Through 1957

3 June 1954

APPROVED FOR RELEASE
DATE: MAY 2004

COPY NO. 1

(b) (3)

~~SECRET~~

NATIONAL INTELLIGENCE ESTIMATE

COMMUNIST CHINA'S POWER POTENTIAL THROUGH 1957

NIE 13–54

Approved 25 May 1954

Published 3 June 1954

The Intelligence Advisory Committee concurred in this estimate on 25 May 1954. The AEC and FBI abstained, the subject being outside of their jurisdiction.

The following member organizations of the Intelligence Advisory Committee participated with the Central Intelligence Agency in the preparation of this estimate: The intelligence organizations of the Departments of State, the Army, the Navy, the Air Force, and The Joint Staff.

CENTRAL INTELLIGENCE AGENCY

~~SECRET~~

SECRET

COMMUNIST CHINA'S POWER POTENTIAL THROUGH 1957

THE PROBLEM

To estimate the political, economic, and military development of Communist China through 1957.

CONCLUSIONS

1. The Chinese Communists[1] have as their long-range goal the development of a Soviet-style state in China, with its own bases of economic and military strength, and dominant in eastern and southern Asia. To this end they will proceed, as rapidly as possible, through the forced and ruthless measures characteristic of Communist regimes, to reorganize the social structure along Communist lines, improve the effectiveness of the administrative system, and develop the economy to the extent feasible. The regime will devote substantial resources to modernizing and strengthening its armed forces as a power base for its foreign policy.

2. Although the Chinese plans for economic development are not known in detail, it appears that these plans comtemplate an increase in total output in 1957 to 20–25 percent above the 1952 level. Emphasis is placed upon increasing the output of the modern industrial sector, particularly heavy industry and transport. Fulfillment of the regime's economic plans depends upon increasing agricultural output while rigorously restricting consumption so as to provide the resources needed to support the industrial investment and military programs. A large part of the capital goods needed to fulfill the program will have to be obtained from the rest of the Soviet Bloc in return for Chinese exports. Available resources will have to be efficiently allocated to ensure that crucial sectors of the economy, such as transport, meet the demands generated by increasing production.

3. Barring a major crisis or other unpredictable event, we estimate that China will have attained by 1957 a gross national product of roughly US $32 billion, an increase of 20–25 percent over the 1952 figure. We estimate that agricultural output will be about 10 percent higher than in 1952, and the output of the modern industrial sector of the economy 70–100 percent higher. The increases in individual industries (including transportation) will of course vary widely from this over-all rate of increase. Even by 1957, however, the Communists will only have begun the modernization of China's economy. The country will as a whole remain agrarian and underdeveloped.

[1] Except where otherwise indicated explicitly or by context, "China" and "Chinese," as used hereafter, refer to Communist China and the Chinese Communists.

SECRET

1

SECRET

2

4. We believe that by 1957 the Chinese regime will have increased its administrative efficiency and have further tightened its control over its people and resources, but the regime will not have been able substantially to alter traditional social patterns or to obtain more than passive acceptance from the bulk of the population. However, we believe that the regime's ability to direct and control China will not be significantly impaired. Furthermore, we believe that the regime will be able to master leadership problems that are likely to arise, even in the event of the death or retirement of Mao Tse-tung.

5. The internal control and the international power position enjoyed by the Communist regime rest largely upon the power potential of China's military establishment, at present the largest of any Asian nation. We believe that the military establishment will gain in strength and effectiveness during the period of this estimate through the regime's program of modernization and training. Soviet assistance will continue to be essential to the fulfillment of this program.

6. We believe China's dependence on the USSR will not be significantly lessened during the period of this estimate, and that maintenance of the alliance with the USSR will continue to be a dominant aspect of China's foreign policy. The Communist Chinese regime will continue to consolidate its political position, to gain in economic and military strength, and by 1957 will be a more powerful force in world affairs than at present. Certain aspects of China's development will be used to support claims that time is on the Communist side in Asia. China's increased power and prestige will present a challenge to the influence of the Western nations in Asia, and to the Asian leadership aspirations of India and Japan.

DISCUSSION

I. INTRODUCTION

7. Since their assumption of power in 1949, the Chinese Communists have, with Soviet assistance, built up a powerful military establishment. The Communists have undertaken a political and social revolution of vast proportions, and they have virtually eliminated effective opposition. They have largely rehabilitated and established control over the country's economy.

8. The Communist regime has accomplished the foregoing in the face of serious obstacles and at great economic and human cost. In 1949 the regime was confronted by widespread economic disruption, and general weariness resulting from 12 years of virtually continuous war. The regime has had to impose its will on 500,000,000 Chinese people and over an area approximately as large as the US, Mexico, and Alaska combined. The bulk of the people are illiterate; communication and transportation facilities are rudimentary or inadequate in many areas. Formidable problems must still be overcome before the Chinese reach the ambitious goals set by the regime.

II. PRESENT SITUATION IN CHINA

9. The Chinese Communist regime has undertaken to create an industrialized and militarily powerful state. At present, the energies of the regime appear to be devoted to the consolidation and expansion of China's economic strength, modernization of military forces, and the transformation of China's political and social structure. To these ends, the regime is creating a more effective administration of government, intensifying its con-

SECRET

103

SECRET

3

trols, and undertaking to eliminate or neutralize institutions or individuals which stand in the way of its goals.

Political Development

10. *Administration and leadership.* The Chinese Communists have adapted Soviet administrative and political institutions and techniques to Chinese conditions. The highly centralized and dictatorial government has instituted effective measures to suppress traditional regional, clan, and ethnic loyalties, and has imposed a unitary state structure with direct lines of command down to the village level.

11. Ultimate power in China resides in the Communist party and is vested in the Political Bureau (Politburo) of the Party's Central Committee. Under Mao Tse-tung's leadership each of the five principal members of the Politburo appears to have certain general areas of responsibility, in addition to collective responsibility in the Politburo: Liu Shao-ch'i, party affairs; Chou En-lai, operation of the government; Chu Teh, military; and Ch'en Yun and Kao Kang, economic affairs.

12. The decisions of the Politburo are transmitted through a governmental structure patterned on that of the USSR. (See Chart I.) The highest place in the governmental structure is reserved for the All China People's Congress, a body to be chosen by national elections now promised for 1954. Until this event takes place the top governmental body is the Central People's Government Council, headed by the Chairman (Mao Tse-tung) and six vice-chairmen. To bolster the fiction that the government is a coalition, three of the six vice-chairmen are "democratic personages" representing other political groups such as the Chinese Democratic League and the Kuomintang Revolutionary Committee. The principal administrative bodies — the Government Administration Council and the People's Revolutionary Military Council — are nominally responsible to the Central People's Government Council. However, since the principal members of the Politburo are also members of these administrative bodies, the authority of the Communist party is brought to bear

directly upon the administration of the state. Decisions made by the national authority are implemented in each of the administrative regions of China by a regional organization composed of party, government, and military organs. A similar pattern of integrations of party and government is repeated down to local government level.

13. Chinese leadership is marked by the cohesion and stability of the party elite. The Communist leaders have been closely knit by their common experience in revolution and war since the party's founding in 1921. As in any group, however, there have been rivalries for power in the past and some almost certainly exist at present. Party pronouncements such as the February 1954 warning by the Central Committee on existing dangers to party unity suggest the existence of differences and rivalries, and there are hints of the existence of ill-defined groupings about Liu Shao-ch'i and Chou En-lai. There is no firm evidence, however, of clearly established factions among the upper echelons. There have been no major purges in the past 16 years.

14. The precise manner in which Soviet influence or control finds its way into Chinese policies is not known. The USSR apparently treats its Chinese ally with deference. Soviet advisers almost certainly are in contact with the highest level of Chinese party and government leadership, but we do not believe that these Soviet officials issue direct orders. We believe the USSR is able to exert influence over Chinese policies primarily by virtue of their common ideology and China's economic and military dependence on the USSR.

15. *Political Controls.* The Communist regime has vigorously and ruthlessly set about establishing political control over the Chinese people. To do this, it has employed a wide array of programs, ranging from inducements and patriotic appeals to coercion and terror.

16. The Chinese Communists have developed an elaborate system of persuasion, involving social, economic, legal, and psychological pressures, and the operations of an extensive and highly coordinated propaganda apparatus. The Communists have sought to instill in the people a sense of participation in

SECRET

104

Chart 1

COMMUNIST CHINA
PARTY AND GOVERNMENT ORGANIZATION

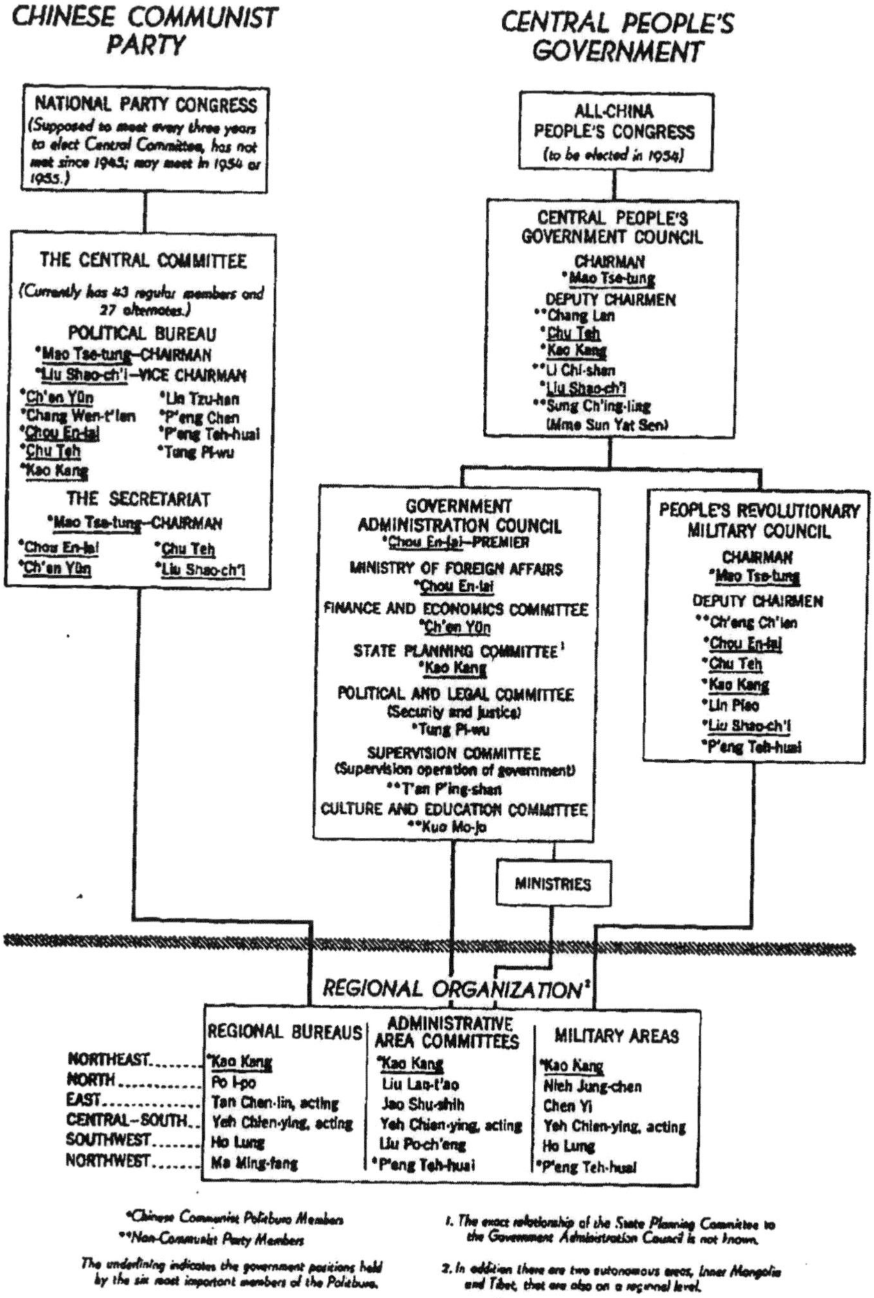

CHINESE COMMUNIST PARTY

CENTRAL PEOPLE'S GOVERNMENT

NATIONAL PARTY CONGRESS
(Supposed to meet every three years to elect Central Committee, has not met since 1945; may meet in 1954 or 1955.)

ALL-CHINA PEOPLE'S CONGRESS
(to be elected in 1954)

THE CENTRAL COMMITTEE
(Currently has 43 regular members and 27 alternates.)
POLITICAL BUREAU
*Mao Tse-tung—CHAIRMAN
*Liu Shao-ch'i—VICE CHAIRMAN

*Ch'en Yün	*Lin Tzu-han
*Chang Wen-t'ien	*P'eng Chen
*Chou En-lai	*P'eng Teh-huai
*Chu Teh	*Tung Pi-wu
*Kao Kang	

THE SECRETARIAT
*Mao Tse-tung—CHAIRMAN

*Chou En-lai	*Chu Teh
*Ch'en Yün	*Liu Shao-ch'i

CENTRAL PEOPLE'S GOVERNMENT COUNCIL
CHAIRMAN
*Mao Tse-tung
DEPUTY CHAIRMEN
**Chang Lan
*Chu Teh
*Kao Kang
**Li Chi-shen
*Liu Shao-ch'i
**Sung Ch'ing-ling
(Mme Sun Yat Sen)

GOVERNMENT ADMINISTRATION COUNCIL
*Chou En-lai—PREMIER

MINISTRY OF FOREIGN AFFAIRS
*Chou En-lai

FINANCE AND ECONOMICS COMMITTEE
*Ch'en Yün

STATE PLANNING COMMITTEE[1]
*Kao Kang

POLITICAL AND LEGAL COMMITTEE
(Security and Justice)
*Tung Pi-wu

SUPERVISION COMMITTEE
(Supervision operation of government)
**T'an P'ing-shan

CULTURE AND EDUCATION COMMITTEE
**Kuo Mo-jo

PEOPLE'S REVOLUTIONARY MILITARY COUNCIL
CHAIRMAN
*Mao Tse-tung
DEPUTY CHAIRMEN
**Ch'eng Ch'ien
*Chou En-lai
*Chu Teh
*Kao Kang
*Lin Piao
*Liu Shao-ch'i
*P'eng Teh-huai

MINISTRIES

REGIONAL ORGANIZATION[2]

	REGIONAL BUREAUS	ADMINISTRATIVE AREA COMMITTEES	MILITARY AREAS
NORTHEAST	*Kao Kang	*Kao Kang	*Kao Kang
NORTH	Po I-po	Liu Lan-t'ao	Nieh Jung-chen
EAST	Tan Chen-lin, acting	Jao Shu-shih	Chen Yi
CENTRAL—SOUTH	Yeh Chien-ying, acting	Yeh Chien-ying, acting	Yeh Chien-ying, acting
SOUTHWEST	Ho Lung	Liu Po-ch'eng	Ho Lung
NORTHWEST	Ma Ming-fang	*P'eng Teh-huai	*P'eng Teh-huai

*Chinese Communist Politburo Members
**Non-Communist Party Members

The underlining indicates the government positions held by the six most important members of the Politburo.

1. The exact relationship of the State Planning Committee to the Government Administration Council is not known.

2. In addition there are two autonomous areas, Inner Mongolia and Tibet, that are also on a regional level.

13123 CIA. 5-54

SECRET   4

the "new China" and, through exaggerated claims of China's military and diplomatic accomplishments, to stimulate Chinese national pride. The regime has attempted to win public support by extensive campaigns against corruption and nepotism and by promising increased opportunity to the peasantry and urban proletariat. The regime has tried in particular to win the loyalties of youth.

17. The Communists have had considerable success in winning support from certain segments of the population. Some of the initial revolutionary zeal remains. In particular, a large portion of China's youth is impressed by the regime's achievements. Other important and energetic elements of support are found among members of the armed forces, government workers, skilled industrial workers, and a considerable proportion of the women.

18. Through terror and force, the Communists have eliminated the landlord class and thousands of businessmen, professionals, and former government officials. There is no evidence of significant organized resistance to the regime. To insure its control, the regime has established extensive security and police forces in addition to the army. In addition to these organized forces, the regime's ability to ferret out dissenters has been augmented by a pervasive system of vigilance committees and volunteer informers.

19. However, much of the voluntary support the regime received in 1949 has been dissipated. The regime's coercive measures have created an atmosphere of fear among many segments of the population. Many Chinese have probably become increasingly suspicious that the USSR is encroaching upon China's sovereignty. In some instances, strong adverse reactions have resulted from attacks on religious and traditional institutions. Increased taxation and regimentation have caused an adverse reaction among the farmers. Dissatisfaction has arisen among workers as a result of the failure of real income to rise. Merchants and petty shopkeepers are resentful of heavy taxes and government competition. Dissatisfaction has grown among intellectual and professional groups as

a result of the drop in their living standards and of the regime's unrelenting pressure toward literal conformity.

20. However, such dissatisfaction as now exists in China has neither the universality, the intensity, nor the physical means by which to transform itself into effective resistance.

Economic Situation

21. China is an underdeveloped agricultural country with a population of 500 million. China's estimated gross national product of approximately US $27 billion [*] is less than one-third of Soviet and about one-fourteenth of US GNP. China's per capita gross national product of roughly US $54 is about equal to that of India but only about one-quarter that of Japan. While there are the beginnings for a modern industrial development the present contribution of the industrial sector to total output is small. The regime faces a formidable task in achieving its long-term goal of a modern industrialized economy. To accomplish this, the Communists are developing their organization for planning and for controlling the economy.

22. As in any planned economy, the national budget is the major instrument for channeling resources to implement the regime's programs. By 1952, the Chinese national budget had risen to about a third of the gross national product, a substantially lower proportion than in the case of the USSR. The two most important categories of budget expenditures during this period have been military outlay and capital investment. (See Chart II for breakdown of the budget.)

23. In 1949, when the Communists undertook the task of rehabilitating and expanding the Chinese economy after 12 years of wartime disruption, production was extremely low. At that time, the production of electric power was only about two-third's of the peak production under the Japanese, coal roughly two-

---

[*] Estimates based on 1952 data are used generally throughout. Changes since 1952 are believed not to have altered the general order of magnitudes or the relationships.

SECRET

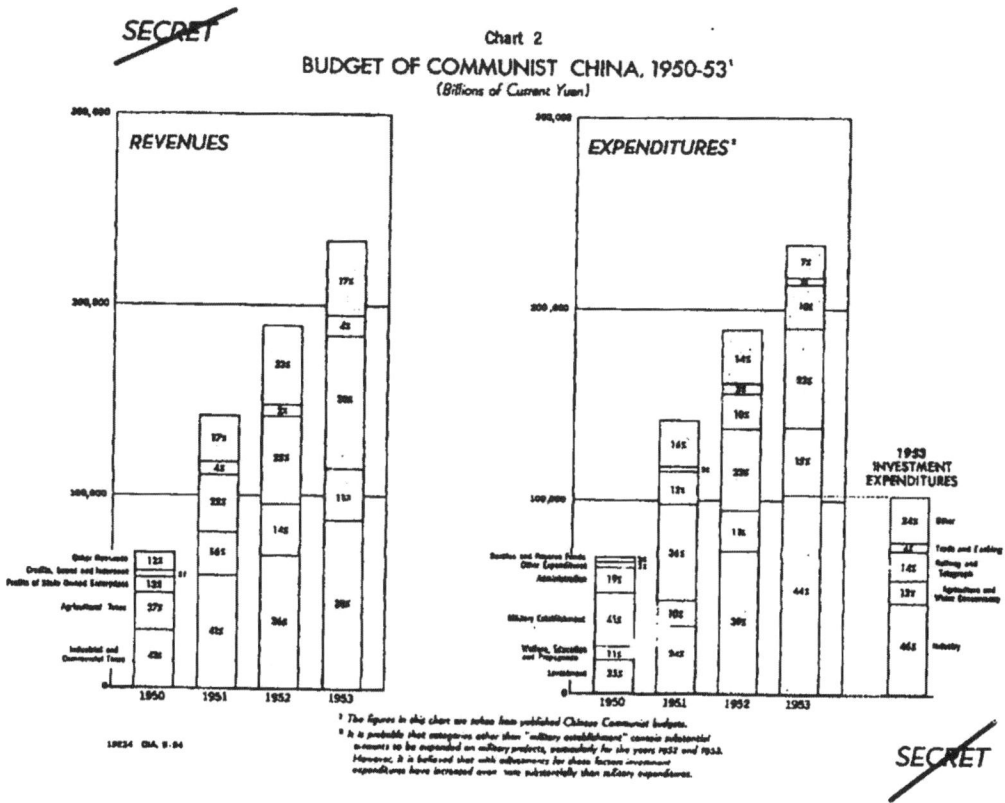

Chart 2
BUDGET OF COMMUNIST CHINA, 1950-53'
(Billions of Current Yuan)

SECRET

5

fifth's, and finished steel about one-sixth. (See Table I.) By the end of 1952, the Chinese had succeeded in general in rehabilitating the economy. Steel production exceeded by roughly one-quarter the highest levels reached between the years 1937 and 1945; grain and power production were slightly above this level; and coal output was about three-quarters of this level. (See Chart III for comparison of Chinese production in 1952 with highest 1937–1945 levels and with production in US and USSR.)

TABLE I

ESTIMATED PRODUCTION OF SELECTED KEY COMMODITIES IN CHINA, 1952

Commodity	Units	1937–1945 Peaks		1952
		Year	Quantity	
Food Grains	million metric tons	1939	106	112
Electric Power	billion KWH	1944	7	8
Crude Steel	million metric tons	1943	0.9	1.1
Crude Oil	thousand metric tons	1943	260	315
Coal	million metric tons	1942	65	50

24. The general rise in domestic production and trade, the great expansion of overland trade between the Soviet Bloc and China, and the movement of military supplies to Korea have increased demands on Chinese transport capacity. The regime has almost restored the rail net developed by the Chinese Nationalists and the Japanese in their respective zones prior to 1945. The Communists have also brought to completion about 800 miles of new lines. (For major transport lines see Map 1 at end of estimate.) However, the rail net is still inadequate in many areas. Lack of rail transportation has greatly hampered the exploitation of strategic minerals in western China, including such key projects as the development of the Yumen oil fields. Moreover, the Chinese have not yet restored the prewar supply of freight cars and loco-

motives. Largely because of the increased transport demand and shortages of rolling stock, the rail system is currently operating under considerable strain. Drastic measures are being employed to stretch present capacity by intensifying the utilization of equipment.

25. Other forms of transport have played a smaller part in the regime's program. There is still relatively little motor transport. Long distance motor transport has not been feasible in most areas because of poor roads and shortages of fuel. Transport via inland waterways is not utilizing the full capacity of available shipping, apparently in part because of the significant change in the pattern of trade. Cargo junks make up the bulk of China's inland and coastal water transport capacity, though the Chinese ocean-going merchant fleet of 101 small slow ships plays an important part in coastal trade from Shanghai northward. China is dependent on non-Chinese shipping for almost all of her seaborne foreign trade. Civil aviation is little developed and has been used primarily as an adjunct of military air transport, especially during the Korean War.

26. Although the Communists have made considerable progress in rehabilitating the Chinese economy, the basic pattern remains unchanged. Agriculture is still the primary activity and per capita production is still low. The major sector contributions to gross national product are shown in Chart IV. Moreover, the geographic concentrations of economic activity within China remain substantially unchanged. (See Map 1 at end of text.)

27. On the other hand, the Communists have made a major change in the direction and composition of China's foreign trade. In 1938 practically all of this trade was with countries not now in the Soviet Bloc, while in 1952 the Soviet Bloc accounted for about 70 percent of China's foreign trade. In terms of constant dollars, China's total foreign trade in 1952 was roughly the same as in 1938. However, imports in constant dollars were considerably less in 1952 than in 1938 when a large import surplus was financed by Japa-

SECRET

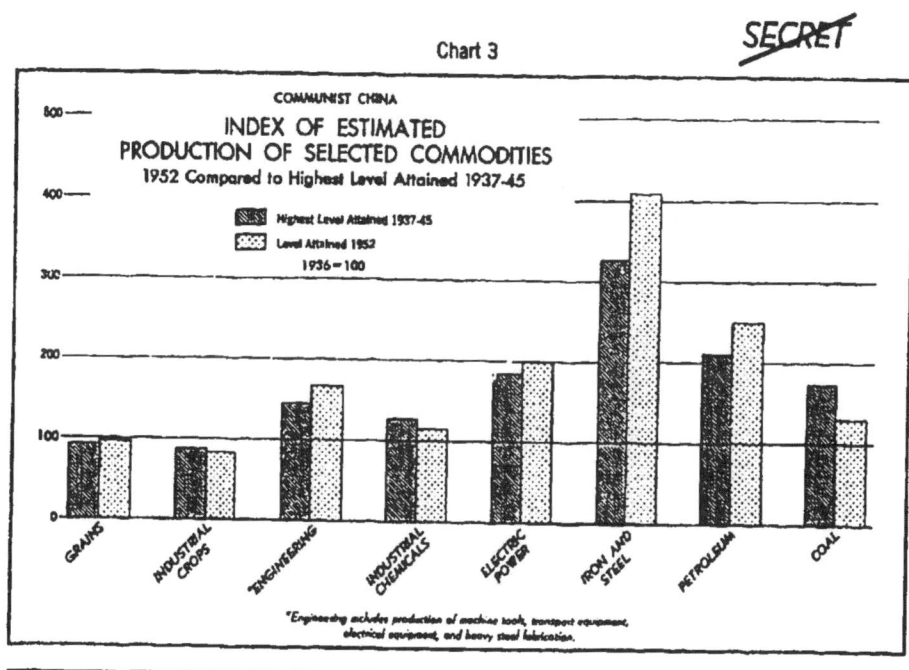

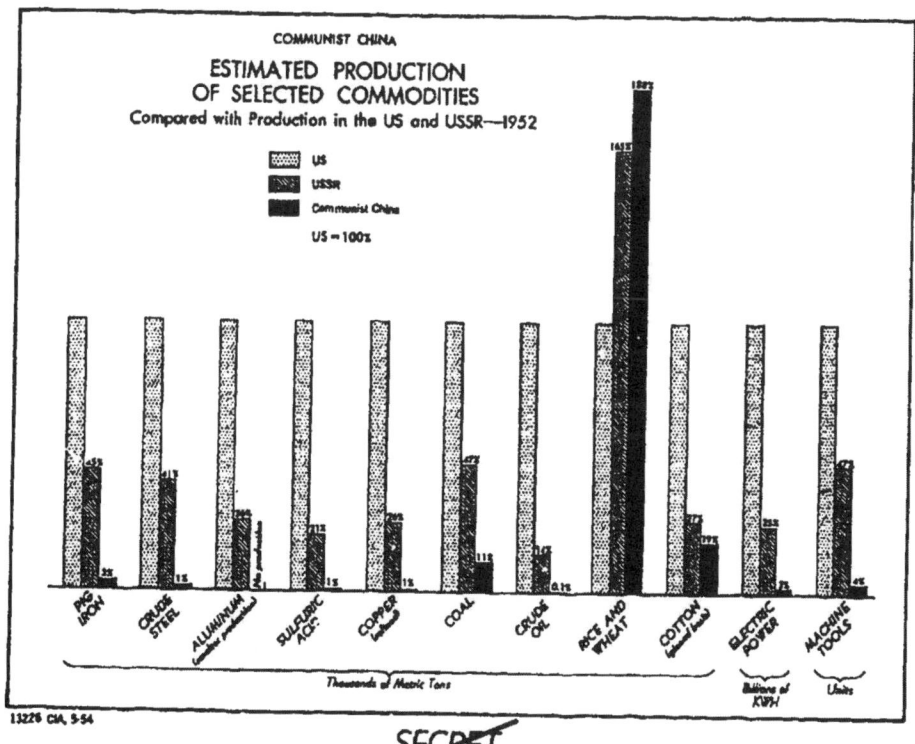

SECRET

Chart 4

COMMUNIST CHINA

GROSS NATIONAL PRODUCT
ESTIMATED PERCENTAGE CONTRIBUTION OF SECTORS
1952

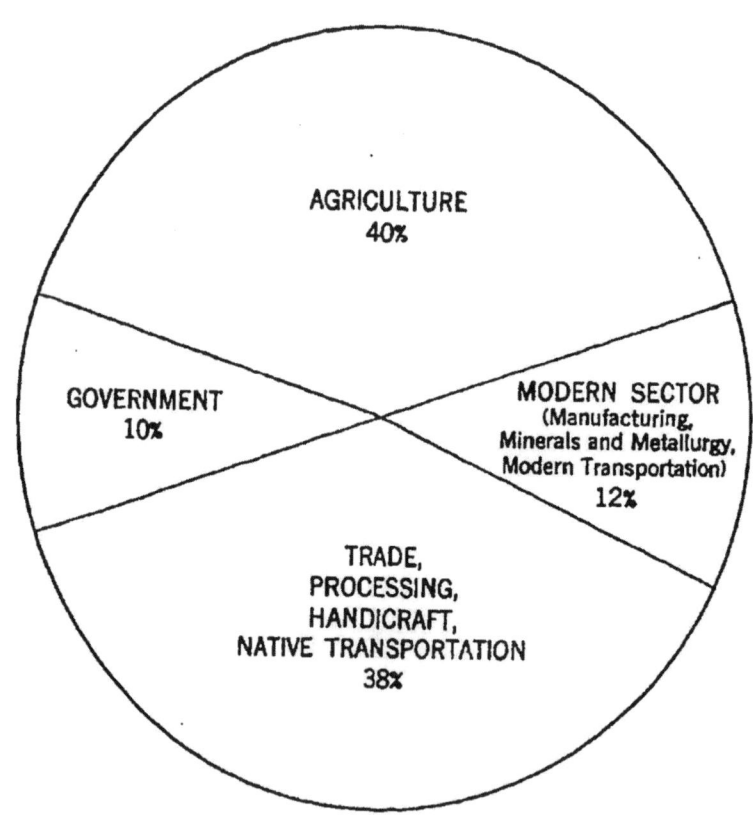

Total GNP—$27 billion
Per capita—$54

13227 CIA, 5-54

SECRET

SECRET   6

nese investment in Manchuria. Imports of consumer goods in 1952 constituted a smaller proportion of the total than in 1938. Imports of military supplies in 1952 constituted a much greater proportion of the total than in 1938. Imports of capital goods and industrial raw materials constituted about the same proportion in 1952 as in 1938. These changes in direction and composition have come about in part because of China's new political relationship with the Soviet Bloc, in part because of Western trade restrictions, and in part because of the requirements of China's programs of economic and military development.

Chinese Communist Armed Forces

28. The internal control and the international power position enjoyed by the Communist regime rest largely upon the power potential of China's military establishment. Within China, the armed forces have held a position of unique privilege and power in the state hierarchy since Mao Tse-tung assumed leadership of the party. The loyalty of the military forces adds greatly to the regime's power to coerce the people. The Chinese military establishment is at present the largest of any Asian nation, with over 2¼ million men in the field forces and an actual aircraft strength of more than 1,500. (See Table II.) These forces, supported by the USSR and greatly improved by the Korean War, have given the Communists an overwhelming military advantage over the countries of non-Communist Asia and have profoundly affected the over-all balance of power in Asia.

TABLE II

CHINESE COMMUNIST MILITARY STRENGTH

Army		Air Force		Naval Air		Navy	
Total Strength	3,300,000	Total Strength	64,000	Total Strength	1,200	Total Strength	60,000
Field Force	2,300,000	Total Aircraft Strength		Total Plane Strength		Naval Vessels¹	
		TO & E	Actual	TO & E	Actual		
160 Infantry Div.		1,980 — 1,500		160 — 80		1 Light Cruiser	
5 Armored Div.		930 —	720 Jet Fgts.	80 — 40 Piston Fgt.		17 Frigate/Gunboats	
3 Parachute Div.		280 —	170 Piston Fgts.	40 — 10 Jet Lgt. Bmb.		3 Old Gunboats	
6 Cavalry Div.		200 —	150 Ground Att.	40 — 30 Piston Lgt. Bmb.		4 Motor Gunboats	
19 Artillery Div.		200 —	120 Jet Lgt. Bmb.			40–50 Motor Torpedo Boats	
40 Independent Reg.		240 —	220 Piston Lgt. Bmb.			16 River Gunboats	
35 Independent Bn.						45 (or more) Amphibious	
		10 —	10 Piston Med. Bmb.			vessels of all kinds	
		120 —	110 Transports			11 (or more) Auxiliaries	

Public Security Forces 1,000,000²

18 Security Div.
16 Independent Security Reg.

¹ The light cruiser is believed to be nonoperational. In addition to the vessels listed the CCN has from 250 to 300 armed motor junks and district patrol craft. It is known that some Chinese personnel have undergone submarine training and one ex-Soviet submarine, possibly of the "medium-range" type, is in Chinese hands at Tsingtao. This submarine is believed to be in a "training status" and is not operational.
² Identified units constitutes only a small portion of total estimated strength. In addition to others as yet unidentified divisions and regiments, there are an unknown number of small local units of varying size scattered throughout China.

SECRET

111

SECRET

7

29. The Chinese Army, with its heavy emphasis on the foot soldier and human or animal transport, would be less deterred by formidable terrain and extremes of weather than would a mechanized army. On the other hand, deficiencies in logistics, communications, heavy equipment, and combined arms technique would put the Chinese Army in a disadvantageous position in dealing with a modern Western army under conditions where heavy equipment and modern techniques could be used.

30. The Chinese air capability was not fully tested in Korea. Combat activity was limited almost entirely to an air defense role, and the air force operated as one component of the Communist Air Force, which also included Soviet and Korean units. The Chinese have a fair capability in air defense under good visibility conditions, but they have little capability at present for combat operations at night or in marginal weather. Although tactical support operations were not undertaken in Korea, the Chinese Air Force has some capability for such operations. Likewise, although the Chinese bombing capability was not tested in Korea, they have a sizable force of light bombers, both jet and piston, and a few medium bombers.

31. The Chinese Navy has a low over-all operational effectiveness by US standards. Not only is its equipment scanty but its mission and interests are subordinated to those of the army and the air forces. However, the Chinese Navy has the capability for carrying out limited surface combat operations in the coastal waters off the China mainland. These could include raids, coastal security patrols and escort operations, mine laying and mine sweeping, and amphibious assault over a short distance. While the naval air force is still in its formative phase, it has a limited capability of supporting surface combat operations by mine laying and by low altitude attacks against surface elements.

32. The major weakness of the Chinese armed forces is their lack of domestic supply facilities and their concomitant dependence upon the Soviet Union for such items as tanks, aircraft, military transport, naval vessels, POL, electronic equipment, and spare parts. At the present time this weakness would become critical in the event of a general war in the Far East which involved both the Soviet Union and China. In such a circumstance, the ability of the Soviet Union to supply China with military goods would be limited by the capacity of the Trans-Siberian railway, in view of the demand on this capacity entailed in supplying Soviet forces in the Far East. Chinese arsenals at the present time are capable of producing small arms, light and heavy machine guns, mortars, light artillery, and ammunition for these weapons, but not in sufficient quantities to supply the present needs of the modernization program.

Chinese Communist Foreign Policy

33. The task of carrying out a political, social, and economic revolution within China along Communist lines is complicated by China's international relationships. China's alliance with, and dependence on the USSR as well as their common ideology have led China to subordinate some of its interests to broader Bloc interests. Mainly as a result of China's aggressive posture and actions toward non-Communist states, China has largely been cut off from non-Communist economic relations and diplomatic support.

34. The Peiping regime has embarked upon a program to make China the dominant power in a Communist Asia. An intrinsic part of this program is a strengthening of China's military establishment. Partly in pursuit of its long-range objective and partly in response to Soviet policy, Peiping has assumed a leading role in furthering international Communist policy in Asia.

35. China's domestic interest, international relationships, and long-term aspirations have resulted in a foreign policy along these broad lines: (a) maintenance of the alliance with the USSR; (b) aid to indigenous Communist parties and groups in non-Communist Asian countries; (c) continued application of political warfare pressure against non-Communist Asia; and (d) diplomatic and propaganda

SECRET

SECRET   8

efforts designed to enhance China's prestige and world status. Such a policy appears to be designed to further China's domestic and international objectives without provoking open conflict with the West. It also appears to be based on the belief that time will work to the Communist advantage in achieving China's international aspirations.

III. PROBABLE TRENDS IN CHINA THROUGH 1957

Long-Range Objectives and Plans

36. The Chinese Communists have as their long-range goal the development of a Soviet-style state in China with its own bases of economic and military strength, and dominant in eastern and southern Asia. To this end they will continue to reorganize the social structure, improve the administrative system, and modernize the economy as rapidly as possible. They will continue gradually to enlarge the state sector of the economy, curtailing and subjugating private enterprise, and establishing large cooperative and collective farms. They will continue to give first priority to basic industrial and transport development. The regime will also devote substantial resources to modernizing and strengthening its armed forces as a power base for its foreign policy.

Problems of Leadership and Control

37. Within recent months, there have been increasing indications that the party leadership is dissatisfied with the performance of various high officials. The current emphasis on the need for party unity and collective leadership, while directed immediately at individual dissidents, appear ultimately directed to improvement of collective planning and management. It also seeks to minimize personal differences among party leaders in the event of Mao's death. Disagreement over Soviet aid and the pace of socialization may constitute an obstacle to the success of the economic program.

38. It is possible that China will be faced with a "succession" problem between now and 1957. Mao, now 60 years old, is reported to be in poor health. If he were to retire or die during this period, a collegial succession, at least initially, would be more probable. If a single leader were chosen either Liu Shaoch'i or Chou En-lai would appear to be the most likely successor. In any event, Mao's disappearance from the scene would probably have an adverse effect upon China's ruling group, and would almost certainly have an adverse effect upon China's relative prestige within the Sino-Soviet partnership. We believe, however, that the problems arising out of possible need to choose a successor to Mao will not seriously impair the dictatorship or the regime's ability to direct and control China.

39. The regime must also overcome its acute shortages of qualified technical, managerial, and administrative personnel. Such shortages affect all sectors of the regime's efforts to administer, control, and develop China. The capacity of Chinese middle schools and institutions of higher education will be adequate to graduate only a fraction of the approximately 600,000 technicians, teachers, medical personnel, and trained workers in government and commerce which the regime has announced it will require by 1957 to carry out its national economic programs. The effects of this shortage in trained personnel will be aggravated by widespread Chinese technical inexperience and by the high degree of illiteracy (80 percent). China will therefore probably attempt during the period of this estimate to deal with shortages of trained personnel by lowering educational standards, by sending greater numbers of Chinese students to the USSR for training, and by utilizing Soviet advisers and technicians. By such measures, China will probably be able to avoid any serious breakdown of its political and economic programs. Nevertheless, the shortage of trained personnel will continue to be an important retarding factor in the regime's over-all progress.

40. The regime will continue to have difficulty in maintaining its present degree of support while pushing forward with its programs. Political and economic pressures will tend to

SECRET

SECRET

9

antagonize the peasantry and certain other groups, and all classes will increasingly resent the use of force. Government appeals to nationalism as well as efforts to persuade the people of the necessity for Soviet advice and guidance may backfire by fostering resentment of Soviet influence in China, and thereby increase dissatisfaction with the regime. The regime's attacks on traditional Chinese values will continue to encounter increased resistance, particularly in rural areas. In any case, the regime will be unable to offer significant incentives to mitigate these adverse reactions because of the pressure on available resources entailed in fulfillment of its military and investment programs.

41. However, in some segments of the population certain other factors will be working in the regime's favor. By 1957, a substantial portion of China's population will have matured under Communist indoctrination. National pride may be stimulated by propaganda extolling real and imaginary achievements of a "new China." A sense of participation in China's national life will be increased by the activities of elective local, regional, and national bodies, even though these bodies will in fact have no real authority.

42. In sum, we believe that during the period of this estimate the regime will not have greatly changed the prevailing social customs and practices, nor will it have gone far in reducing illiteracy. We believe that while the regime will continue to receive the support of some and face the hostility of other portions of the population, the bulk of the people will continue to accept Communist leadership passively. In any event, because the efficiency of governmental control apparatus will probably improve, the degree of control exercised by the regime over the people will probably increase. Finally, we believe that the leadership will continue to resolve any personal differences which might significantly impair its ability to direct and control China.

Economic Problems and Programs

43. Although the Chinese plans for economic development are not known in detail, the regime in May 1953 announced a substantial

reduction of its goals in the first year of the five-year program. The program now appears to be to increase the gross national product in 1957 to 20–25 percent above the 1952 level. Emphasis is placed upon increasing the output of the modern industrial sector, particularly heavy industry and transport. Plans for industrial development appear to be directed in particular toward continued rehabilitation and expansion of the Manchurian plant, with some expansion of industry in the rest of China.

44. The central economic problem confronting the regime in carrying out its plans is to accumulate capital resources and to allocate such resources in a way most conducive to a rapid and efficient implementation of its programs. The major domestic determinant in the success of the programs will be the extent to which the regime is able to increase agricultural output to feed the growing population, to provide raw materials for industry, and to provide exports to pay for essential capital goods imports. At the same time, in restricting consumption the regime must avoid destroying production incentives. The regime must also avoid disrupting production by pressing too aggressively with its political, social, and economic reforms. The task of allocation will require the development of an effective administrative apparatus, despite the obstacles faced in the lack of trained personnel, poor communications, the low level of literacy, and the awkwardness of the written language. Allocation decisions must be made between the competing claims on the resources and energies of the regime for the economic, military, political, and social programs.

45. Aside from domestic considerations, the most important factor determining the rate of industrial development in China will be the volume of goods and services made available to China by the USSR. While China's ability to export commodities in demand by the Soviet Union and the European Satellites is an essential element, of equal significance is the availability in the Bloc of desired goods and services and the policy of the USSR with respect to building a strong China.

SECRET

SECRET   10

46. China's agricultural system, involving about three-quarters of the total population, has basic weaknesses. There is a low ratio of cultivated land to the population. The farmers lack knowledge of new techniques; they lack capital with which to purchase fertilizers, insecticides, and equipment; individual holdings are generally too small to permit the introduction of mechanization even if capital were available. These factors result in inefficient use of manpower and low output per man.

47. Taking into account the many problems involved, we believe agricultural production will have increased by about 10 percent between 1952 and 1957. These gains in output are expected to result from expansions of acreage under cultivation, extension and repair of irrigation facilities, increased use of chemical fertilizers, and the additional incentive to intensive and diversified production induced by the expansion of urban and export markets. However, weather and other unpredictable factors may prevent the Communists from achieving such an increase. The regime may also encounter difficulties in its efforts to reorganize agricultural production and to enforce crop collection. The emphasis will be placed on cooperative action rather than on the formation of state farms. However, implementation of the regime's plan to organize some 20 percent of the farmers into producers' cooperatives by 1957, may have disruptive effects on agricultural production.

48. In order to provide capital from increased production to support industrial expansion and increased imports of capital goods, the Communists must maintain control over the rate of consumption. Pressures for increased consumption will come from the farmers, increased numbers of industrial workers, and the over-all rise in total population. The population increase, in part a result of improved public health measures and in part a result of more stable conditions, will tend to be concentrated, by migration, in the large urban areas where per capita consumption is about twice that of the rural areas. Because of this, a population growth projected at less than one percent per year, would increase total consumption by five to eight percent between 1952 and 1957 even in the absence of any change in urban and rural living standards. Although the regime will be faced with many difficulties in restricting consumption, particularly in rural areas, we believe that its control mechanism is adequate to restrict consumption to roughly half of the expected 20-25 percent increase in total output by 1957 The remaining proportion could provide sufficient investment resources to permit achievement of the regime's estimated industrial and military programs.

49. Another crucial problem in fulfilling the industrial program will be the supply of capital goods. Domestic capital goods output is small, of poor quality, and of limited variety, and the Chinese Communists must depend on foreign trade — particularly with the Soviet Bloc — for the bulk of their supply of capital goods. Although the USSR provided US $300 million in credits to China in the 1950–1954 aid agreement, the Soviet Union probably will not grant substantial further credits to China for capital goods and therefore we believe that China's imports with the possible exception of some military items are likely to be approximately limited to the amount which can be financed through exports. Moreover, since import programs from Bloc countries are determined in annual barter contracts and since transport between China and these countries is difficult, deliveries of capital goods are likely to be uncertain, with resulting adverse effects on the development program.

50. In view of the current deficiencies in rail transport and the large prospective increase in traffic requirements, the Communists will have to make strenuous efforts to insure that the rate of increase in transport capacity, particularly railroads, keeps abreast of the demands generated by the increase in production. The most urgent need will continue to be rolling stock. Locomotive and freight cars cannot be produced domestically in adequate quantities and therefore will have to be imported. Thus a crucial area of investment required for the fulfillment of the Chinese economic program will be the expansion of railroad capacity. The regime has recognized

SECRET

SECRET

11

the importance of this problem and we believe that it will continue to give it high priority.

51. The Chinese will divert substantial resources to building up a modern military force. Over and above the funds allocated in announced national budgets for military expenditures (see Chart II), substantial funds for military purposes, such as arsenal construction, are concealed in other categories of the budget. We believe that at present something over US $3 billion, about one-third of the national budget, is being expended on military items and that this level will not change substantially during the period of this estimate. Moreover, since China's armaments industry does not produce heavy equipment such as tanks and artillery or aircraft, a major share of foreign exchange earnings must be used for military end-items as well as equipment for expanding China's armament production. We believe the Chinese will utilize roughly one-third of total export earnings for the import of military end-items and POL during the period of this estimate. This does not include possible imports of military supplies given to China by the USSR on a grant or credit basis.

52. We estimate that by 1957 China can increase its total exports by about 50 percent over 1952, primarily through increased exports of agricultural and mineral raw materials. This increase would probably provide adequate funds for minimum import requirements of the industrial, agricultural, and military programs. The Soviet Bloc will probably make these imports available.

53. The Chinese Communists may seek to expand trade with non-Communist countries. Relaxation of non-Communist trade controls could contribute to the fulfillment of the regime's programs and reduce China's economic dependence on the rest of the Soviet Bloc. These effects would materialize, however, only to the extent that non-Communist countries were willing and able to extend credits and supply goods not available to China from Bloc sources, or on terms more advantageous to China than those entailed in trade with the Bloc.

54. In summary, although the Chinese will face many serious difficulties in achieving their economic goals, we believe that by 1957 the regime can expand total output by 20–25 percent over 1952.

Probable Developments in the Chinese Communist Military Establishment

55. The regime apparently intends to strengthen the military establishment primarily through modernization rather than through a significant increase in manpower. Soviet assistance will continue to be essential to the fulfillment of this program.

56. The capability of the army will almost certainly improve. The number of infantry divisions will probably be reduced to provide manpower to strengthen the remaining infantry divisions, and to increase the number of service and support units. Training will be intensified and selection and utilization of personnel will improve.

57. The air force is expected to be expanded and to be developed into a more balanced force. Its personnel strength will probably be expanded to about 90,000 and its authorized aircraft strength increased to approximately 2,500, including 1,400 jet fighters and 480 jet light bombers. The extent to which aircraft are provided to fill out the authorized strength depends on Soviet supply. The over-all combat readiness of the Chinese Air Force is expected to improve appreciably during the period as a result of increases in aircraft and personnel strength, improvement in training, and an increase in supporting services and facilities.

58. Naval development will probably be relatively minor, although it may include the acquisition of a number of coastal or medium-range submarines from the USSR. It is likewise expected that the Chinese Naval Air Force will be developed to an authorized strength of 340 aircraft, including 160 jet fighters and 80 jet light bombers. New techniques in training are expected to be introduced which will enhance the capability of this force to attack shipping of all types along the China coast.

SECRET

SECRET   12

IV. CHINA'S POSITION IN 1957

59. We believe that by 1957 the Chinese regime will have further tightened its control over its people. We also believe that unless some major crisis or other unpredictable event occurs, the regime will by 1957 have attained a gross national product of roughly US $32 billion, an increase of 20–25 percent over the 1952 figure. The agricultural contribution to GNP in 1957 will probably be about 10 percent above the 1952 level. That part of the GNP accounted for by the modern industrial sector of the economy in 1957 will probably be roughly US $6 billion, a 70–100 percent increase over the 1952 level. The country will as a whole remain agrarian and underdeveloped.

60. Despite the progress made by 1957, the Communists will have only begun the task of transforming China. The country will as a whole remain agrarian, illiterate, and un-derdeveloped. Moreover, while the regime will probably have developed a modest industrial sector, China will be faced with increased difficulties in maintaining the rate of growth.

61. We believe China's dependence on the USSR will not be significantly lessened during the period of this estimate, and that maintenance of the alliance with the USSR will continue to be a dominant aspect of China's foreign policy. The Communist Chinese regime will continue to consolidate its political position, to gain in economic and military strength, and by 1957 will be a more powerful force in world affairs than at present. Certain aspects of China's development will be used to support claims that time is on the Communist side in Asia. China's increased power and prestige will present a challenge to the influence of the Western nations in Asia, and to the Asian leadership aspirations of India and Japan.

SECRET

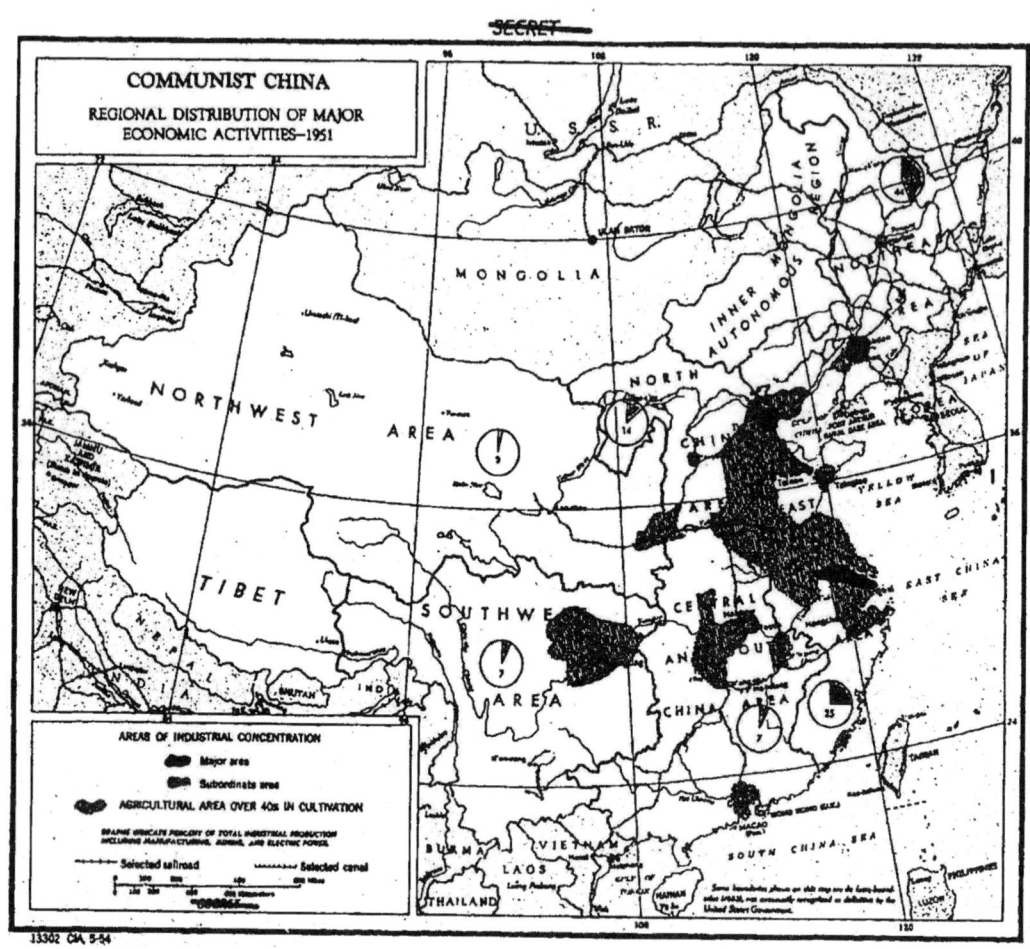

SECTION 11

NIE 13-58

Communist China

13 May 1958

APPROVED FOR RELEASE
DATE: MAY 2004

(b)(3)

NIE 13-58
13 May 1958

~~SECRET~~

N<u>o</u> 335

NATIONAL INTELLIGENCE ESTIMATE
NUMBER 13-58

(Supersedes NIE.13–57)

COMMUNIST CHINA

Superseded by 13-59

Submitted by the
DIRECTOR OF CENTRAL INTELLIGENCE

The following intelligence organizations participated in the preparation of this estimate: The Central Intelligence Agency and the intelligence organizations of the Departments of State, the Army, the Navy, the Air Force, and The Joint Staff.

Concurred in by the
INTELLIGENCE ADVISORY COMMITTEE

on 13 May 1958. Concurring were The Director of Intelligence and Research, Department of State; the Assistant Chief of Staff, Intelligence, Department of the Army; the Director of Naval Intelligence; the Assistant Chief of Staff, Intelligence, USAF; and the Deputy Director for Intelligence, The Joint Staff. The Atomic Energy Commission Representative to the IAC and the Assistant Director, Federal Bureau of Investigation, abstained, the subject being outside of their jurisdiction.

~~SECRET~~

SEC~~RET~~

COMMUNIST CHINA

THE PROBLEM

To analyze Chinese Communist domestic developments and external relations during the period of the First Five Year Plan (1953–1957), and to estimate probable trends during the next five years.

CONCLUSIONS

1. We believe that the Chinese Communist ability to exercise firm and effective control of mainland China will continue. The leadership of the party continues to demonstrate cohesion and determination and, at the same time, a considerable degree of flexibility. It is supported by a party membership of about 13 million and controls a large and efficient military and public security apparatus. We believe that the death or incapacitation of Mao Tse-tung would not endanger the regime's control of the country, although it might complicate the achieving of some objectives and reduce the party's policy flexibility. *(Paras. 43–45, 66–68)*

2. The regime apparently has made considerable progress in its efforts to recast the traditional structure of Chinese society in the Communist mold. It has collectivized almost all the peasants and has virtually eliminated private ownership in industry and commerce. Although the Chinese people have viewed with favor some of the regime's achievements, the regime's stringent curtailment of consumption and the constant pressures to conform and to work harder have provoked much dissatisfaction and disillusionment, especially among the peasants. The party's experiments during the past two years to gain wider popular support by admitting problems and encouraging their discussion—the "letting 100 flowers bloom and diverse thoughts contend" program—has been sharply cut back. *(Paras. 27–42)*

3. In its efforts to elicit a more positive popular response, the regime, because of its determination to achieve rapid industrialization, will have little to offer in the way of material inducements. Dissatisfactions and occasional popular outbursts will continue, especially among the peasantry and certain minority groups, but we believe the net effect on the regime's programs will be no more than a complicating or retarding one. Most Chinese, conscious of the regime's power and seeing no alternative, will probably continue to acquiesce in Communist rule. *(Paras. 68–70)*

SEC~~RET~~

1

SECRET

2

4. The Chinese Communists achieved a high rate of economic growth during their First Five Year Plan (1953-57), demonstrating their capability to marshal resources for investment despite the backward nature of the economy. A vital factor in their economic program was the assistance rendered by the USSR in expanded trade, credits, and technical aid. Starting from a very small base, the average annual rate of growth of industrial output was about 16 percent, but industrial output at the end of 1957 was still small compared to the industrial output of Japan or the UK. Agricultural output was adequate to meet basic needs, but its expansion fell far short of that in other sectors of the economy. *(Paras. 17-26)*

5. During the next five years, the regime will have to cope with difficult economic problems stemming from the forced pace of industrial development. However, the basic problem will continue to be the race between population growth and food production. The Chinese population is now probably about 640 million and increasing at about 2.0-2.5 percent per year; agricultural output during the next five years will, at best, probably not exceed the 3 percent per annum increase achieved during the First Five Year Plan. In the event of a series of bad crop years and of widespread lack of cooperation among the peasants, the regime would face grave difficulties. However, even in these circumstances, the regime, because of its control apparatus, probably could maintain itself in power and, at the same time, maintain industrial growth, although at a reduced rate. *(Paras. 54-57)*

6. We believe that Communist China during the next five years will probably be able to maintain a rate of economic growth roughly comparable to that of the past five years. By 1962 its Gross National Product will probably be on the order of US $65-67 billion, as compared with US $46 billion in 1957. The contribution of the industrial sector will probably have increased to about 26 percent, as compared to about 19 percent in 1957. *(Paras. 52, 53, and 59)*

7. Communist China's military power in the Far East will bulk even larger by 1962 than it does at present. The army will probably be somewhat smaller, but it will be better equipped and more mobile. The air force and navy will have increased in size and effectiveness. The Chinese Communist armament industry, with Soviet technological assistance, will probably be able to meet most, if not all, army requirements for small arms, artillery, transport, and ammunition. Shipbuilding and aircraft production will probably have increased considerably. Nevertheless, Communist China will still be dependent on the USSR for heavy and complex military equipment and for many components. *(Paras. 71-73)*

8. Although Communist China will almost certainly not have developed a missile or nuclear weapons production capability of its own by 1962, we believe that the Chinese Communists will press the USSR for such advanced weapons. By that time the USSR will probably have provided it with some varieties of missiles and other weapons adaptable to nuclear use, but with non-nuclear warheads. Unless barred by an effective international agreement, the USSR may introduce nuclear weapons into Communist China by 1962, although they will almost certainly remain under Soviet control. In any

SECRET

SECRET

3

event, even though nuclear warheads were not deployed in Communist China, they would be readily available if Sino-Soviet interests required them. *(Para. 74)*

9. Communist China will almost certainly remain firmly aligned with the USSR. Peiping will continue to acknowledge Moscow as the leader of world Communism, but as Communist China grows in strength and stature, it will probably play an increasingly important role in the formulation of general Bloc policy. Although there will almost certainly be some frictions, these are unlikely to impair Sino-Soviet cooperation during the period of this estimate. *(Paras. 75–83)*

10. In its efforts to reduce and eliminate Western influence in Asia, Communist China will probably proceed primarily by non-military means. Its foreign policy will probably display more initiative and assertiveness, while continuing to emphasize coexistence and a readiness to increase economic and political relations with other states. Without compromising its stand on basic issues, Communist China will continue to portray itself as willing to reach a rapprochement with the US. At the same time, the Chinese Communists will almost certainly continue their subversive efforts throughout the Far East. They will almost certainly continue their efforts to undermine the will of the Nationalists on Taiwan, and to discredit them internationally. They will probably not resort to overt military aggression as long as they believe it would involve them in military action with the US. Although their attitude towards the Offshore Islands may become more aggressive, a decision to initiate military action to seize these Islands would probably be contingent on an estimate that the US would not intervene militarily. *(Paras. 88–90)*

11. Japan will continue to be one of Peiping's most important targets, especially because there is a growing area of competition between Communist China and Japan. Peiping will continue to seek to reduce conservative strength and US influence in Japan by exploiting Japanese fears of becoming involved in a nuclear war, any areas of friction with the US, and Japan's eagerness to expand trade with mainland China. In pursuit of these objectives, Communist China will continue to employ both conciliatory and tough tactics. Trade between Communist China and Japan will probably increase, and Peiping will probably be able to gain at least quasi-diplomatic status for a trade mission in Japan. *(Paras. 93, 63)*

12. Assuming a general continuance of present Bloc and Western policies, we believe that intercourse between Communist China and the Free World will increase considerably during the next five years. This trend will probably involve added diplomatic recognition of Peiping by a number of states, but will occur whether or not formal diplomatic ties are established. It will also involve greater difficulty in excluding Communist China from the UN. *(Paras. 95–96)*

13. If Communist China continues its present international policy, we believe that its prestige in Asia will continue to grow during the next five years. This will occur whether or not additional countries recognize Communist China, or it is

SECRET

~~SECRET~~   4

admitted to the UN. But it does not necessarily follow that as a result of increased prestige the Chinese Communists will be able to induce non-Communist Asian countries to adopt internal or external policies desired by Communist China. Communist China's future role in Asia will be determined to an important extent by developments in five fields, in varying degrees beyond the control of the Chinese Communists:

a. The course of events in the US-USSR relationship and in the broad aspects of the cold war.

b. Developments within the Bloc such as spectacular scientific achievements or major political upheavals.

c. The extent to which local Communist parties, e.g., those in Indonesia, Laos, and India, gain or lose political strength.

d. The extent to which the growth of Communist China's power gives rise to increased apprehensions among Asian governments as to Communist China's future intentions and thus causes them to take increasingly effective measures at least to counter their own internal Communists.

e. The extent to which the US has the confidence and trust of non-Communist Asian governments, and in turn helps these governments not only to resist the Communists, but also to meet their national aspirations. *(Para. 97)*

DISCUSSION

I. INTRODUCTION

14. The Chinese Communist regime during the period of its First Five Year Plan (1953–1957) made considerable progress toward its long-run goal of transforming Communist China from a backward agricultural country into an industrialized nation. With assistance from the USSR, the Chinese Communists have achieved a high rate of increase in their Gross National Product, and especially in the output of heavy industry. The imposition of Communist institutions on society has proceeded at a rapid rate as a result of the virtual elimination of private enterprise in industry, commerce, and agriculture. These domestic achievements and the growing military power of Communist China contributed to its increased impact abroad, both in the Free World and in the Communist Bloc.

15. At the same time, the forced pace of change has created internal stresses and strains which are substantial and widespread. These stresses and strains have been produced by the rigidities and repressions which are essential features of Communist methods and programs and which hinder the development of general popular support for the regime. They were inevitable in view of the regime's efforts quickly to mold the Chinese into a disciplined Communist society. Tensions have also developed out of the intervention, at all levels of society and in all activities, of party workers who have the power to command, but who in most cases have inadequate training and experience in their duties of supervising the specific educational, social, or economic organization. Moreover, the regime's efforts to restrict consumption in order to increase investment have been felt particularly by the peasants, whose incentive to produce has been reduced. Nevertheless, as far as we can see, these tensions are not critical in the sense of threatening the position of the Communist leaders or of being likely to hamper production to the extent of seriously limiting the further growth of the Chinese Communist economy.

16. The Chinese Communists, after going through a period of pessimism engendered by the economic problems which came to a head in 1956, now appear confident that they can maintain a rapid rate of economic expansion

~~SECRET~~

SEGRET

during the next five years. This confidence is tempered by the extent of popular criticism of the regime as revealed by the recent but short-lived experiment in relaxing controls on public discussion, by the evidence that there was a growing separation between the party and the people, and by the widespread peasant dissatisfaction when collectivization failed to bring increased income. The regime's confidence is also tempered by a more realistic appreciation of the magnitude of its basic problems, particularly that of agriculture.

II. DEVELOPMENTS DURING THE PERIOD OF THE FIRST FIVE YEAR PLAN [1]

A. The Economy [2][3]

17. The Chinese Communists, during the period of their First Five Year Plan, achieved a high rate of economic growth which compares favorably with that of the Soviet Union in its First Five Year Plan (1928–1932). (See Figure 1.) This progress was achieved despite relatively crude and rudimentary planning, resulting from such factors as the limited technical personnel, the lack of reliable and comprehensive statistics, the backward state of the economy, and the rapid imposition of social change. Although the regime has made a pretense of proceeding according to an overall five year plan, it has actually operated from year to year on annual plans which have generally been aimed at correcting the excesses and defects of the previous year. Nevertheless, the regime demonstrated its capability to control the economy sufficiently to limit consumption and to marshal resources

---

[1] See Appendix A for a more detailed discussion of the First Five Year Plan.

[2] Chinese Communist statistics upon which the data and analyses throughout this estimate are based are subject to the same reservations as those of other Bloc countries, but to a somewhat greater extent, in view of the inexperience on the part of the newly established Chinese Communist statistical collection system. This inexperience probably accounts for the majority of such statistical defects as have been noted. Chinese Communist statistics are the basis for the regime's planning and we believe are not, in general, misrepresented.

[3] See maps for Communist China's railroad system and major industrial and mining centers.

for investment, despite the backward nature of the economy and the necessity of obtaining the funds for investment largely from the agricultural sector, the output of which fluctuated widely from year to year.

18. Starting from a small base, the average annual rate of growth of industrial output during the period was high, probably about 16 percent. This growth was uneven, exceeding 30 percent in 1953 and 1956, but dropping sharply in 1955 and 1957. During the five year period, production of such basic items as steel more than tripled, while the output of coal, electric power, and cement more than doubled. Despite this considerable progress, the Chinese Communist industrial output at the end of 1957 was still small compared to that of Japan or the UK. (See Figure 2.)

19. The increased industrial output was to an important degree obtained from the reconstruction, expansion, and more intensive utilization of existing plant, although a considerable investment was made in new plant, much of which will come into production in 1958–1962. The regime has directed about 56 percent of total investment into the industrial sector and has favored heavy over light industry by about eight to one. Industry became more diversified with the addition of new plant, and by the end of the period production facilities for trucks, sea-going ships, aircraft, and more complicated machine tools were put into operation, although the Chinese Communists are still dependent on foreign sources for many components.

20. The growth of industrial output was retarded by uneven development among various parts of the industrial sector, which resulted in serious imbalances. The most important of these was the failure of the output of raw materials to keep in phase with the expansion of manufacturing capacity, especially in the machine and equipment building industries. In some cases, however, the deficiencies of raw materials arose from the difficulties in developing natural resources; for example, the regime has been unable to develop sufficient sources of crude oil and copper, accessible to existing rail lines, to meet requirements. The output of light industry, dependent largely on

SEGRET

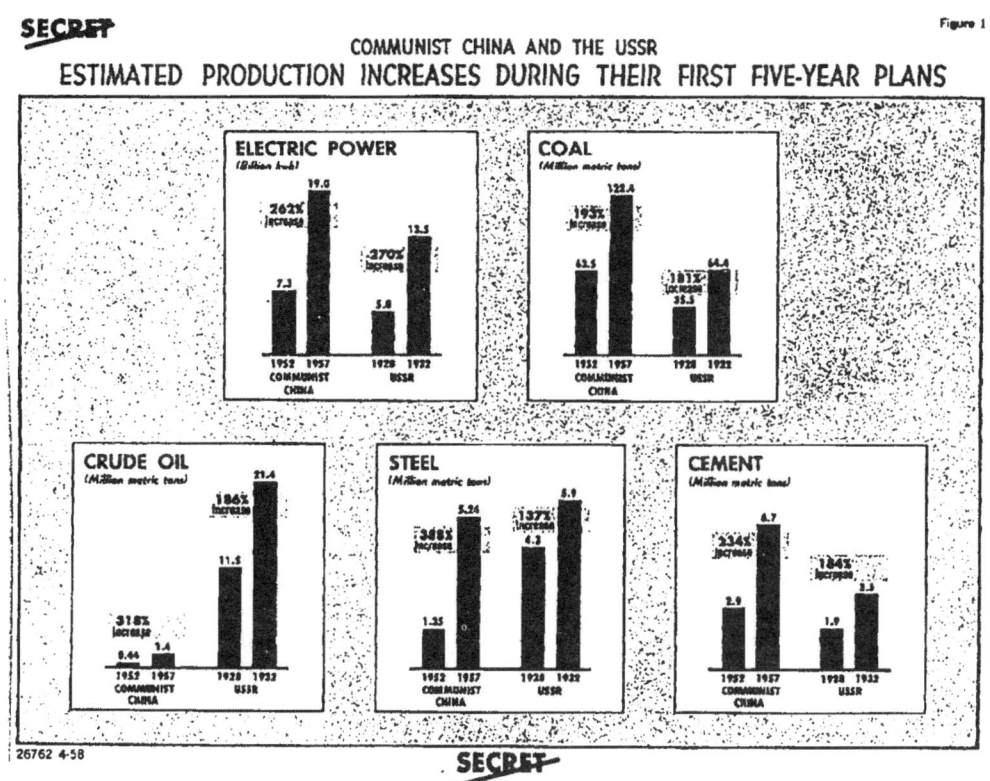

SECRET

Figure 2

COMMUNIST CHINA
ESTIMATE OF 1957 GROSS NATIONAL PRODUCT
AND PRODUCTION OF PRINCIPAL COMMODITIES
COMPARED WITH THOSE OF SELECTED COUNTRIES

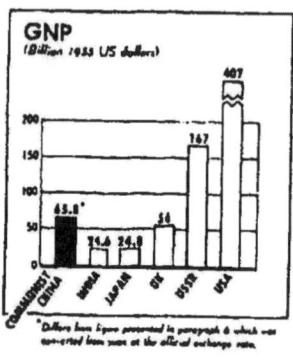

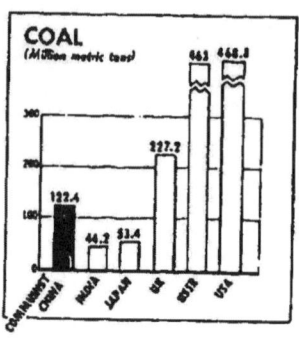

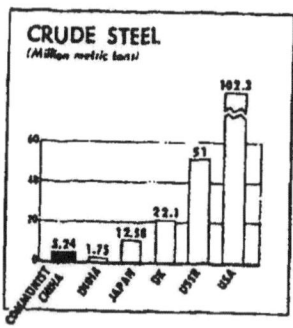

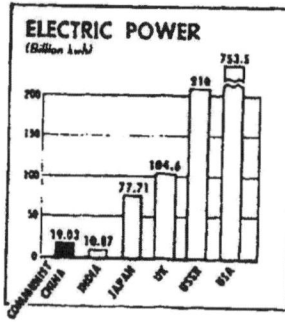

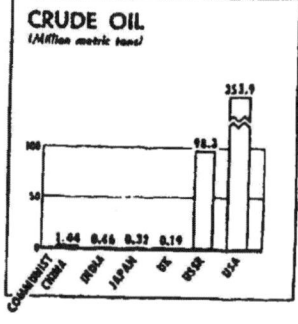

PER CAPITA

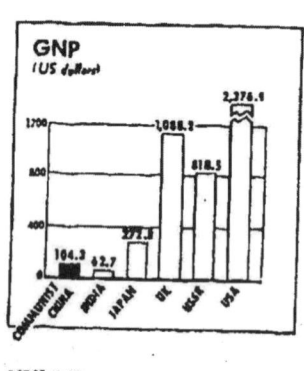

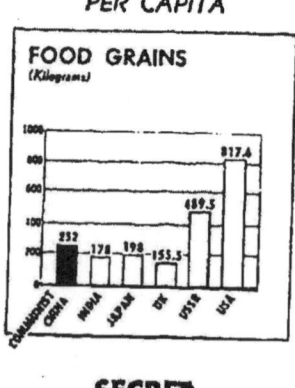

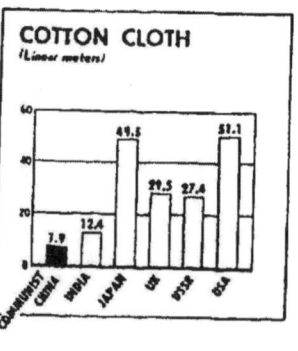

26763 5-58

SECRET

SEC~~RE~~T   6

agricultural raw materials, has not been sufficient fully to utilize present plant capacity.

21. Technical assistance from the Bloc has been of paramount importance to Communist China's industrialization. The major industrial projects, accounting for about 40 percent of total industrial investment, were designed, supervised, and placed in initial operation by Soviet technicians. In addition, Bloc, largely Soviet, advisors and technicians have worked with virtually every ministry in the government and with many individual enterprises. Technicians have provided on-the-job training for Chinese workers and some 7,000 Chinese have been sent to the USSR for training. Soviet bloc technical data have been used on a large scale.

22. The growth of agricultural output was adequate to meet basic needs, but its expansion fell far short of that in other sectors of the economy. Serious natural calamities in 1954 and 1956 and bumper crops in 1955 caused wide fluctuations in output during the five year period. Moreover, production was adversely affected by the disruption and confusion which accompanied the rapid collectivization of agriculture in 1955 and 1956. Agricultural growth was also hampered as a direct result of the regime's decision to minimize state investment in this sector and to depend on its ability to squeeze the bulk of agricultural investment funds directly from the earnings of the collectives. The large flood control and irrigation projects, undertaken by the state, were not sufficiently advanced to increase materially the acreage under irrigation, even though the amount spent exceeded the plan by 50 percent. Furthermore, State investment in the chemical industry was inadequate to increase substantially the availability of chemical fertilizer. The increases in grain and cotton production that were achieved were largely the result of direct investment by the collectives in small irrigation projects which permitted an expansion of double-cropping.

23. Economic progress during the First Five Year Plan, to an important extent, was dependent on the importation of vital machinery, equipment, and industrial raw materials. Bloc countries were Communist China's major trading partners, accounting for nearly 78 percent of total trade. There was some increase in trade with non-Communist countries, but this increase was limited to some extent by Western trade controls. The Chinese Communists were able to maintain an import surplus over the period 1953–1957 as a whole. This was made possible by Soviet credits, largely of a military nature, which accounted for about 13 percent of total imports, and, to a lesser extent, by remittances from Overseas Chinese. However, during the period, balance of payments pressures increased. Despite a doubling of exports, imports rose by only one-third, and the trade balance shifted from an import to an export surplus. This shift resulted from the exhaustion of foreign credits, mounting foreign debt service, reduced Overseas Chinese remittances, reduced Soviet expenditures in China after the force withdrawal of 1955, and the Chinese Communist foreign aid program. (See Figure 3.)

24. Despite this slim margin on which they have been operating, the Chinese Communists made a series of offers or grants of economic aid. The largest portion of Chinese Communist foreign aid has gone to other Communist countries: grants in goods and services of $325 million each to North Korea and North Vietnam, $40 million to Outer Mongolia, and $7.5 million to Hungary; and a loan of $25 million to Hungary. In addition, to non-Communist countries, Communist China has extended grants totalling $55 million, and has extended in late 1957 and early 1958 loans totalling an additional $32 million.[4] Of the total of about $810 million in grants and loans, Bloc and non-Bloc, about $630 million had actually been expended by the end of 1957.[5]

---

[4] Grants (in millions of US$): Cambodia, 22.4; Nepal, 12.6; Egypt, 4.7; Ceylon, 15.75. Loans extended (in millions of US$): Indonesia, 11.2; Burma, 4.2; Yemen, 16.3.

[5] The loans and grants to Bloc countries were in yuan currency to North Korea and North Vietnam and in rubles to Hungary. Yuan data have been converted into US dollar equivalents at the rate of 2.46 yuan per US $1 and rubles at 4 per US $1. The use of the yuan-dollar exchange rate may overstate considerably the value of aid to North Korea and North Vietnam.

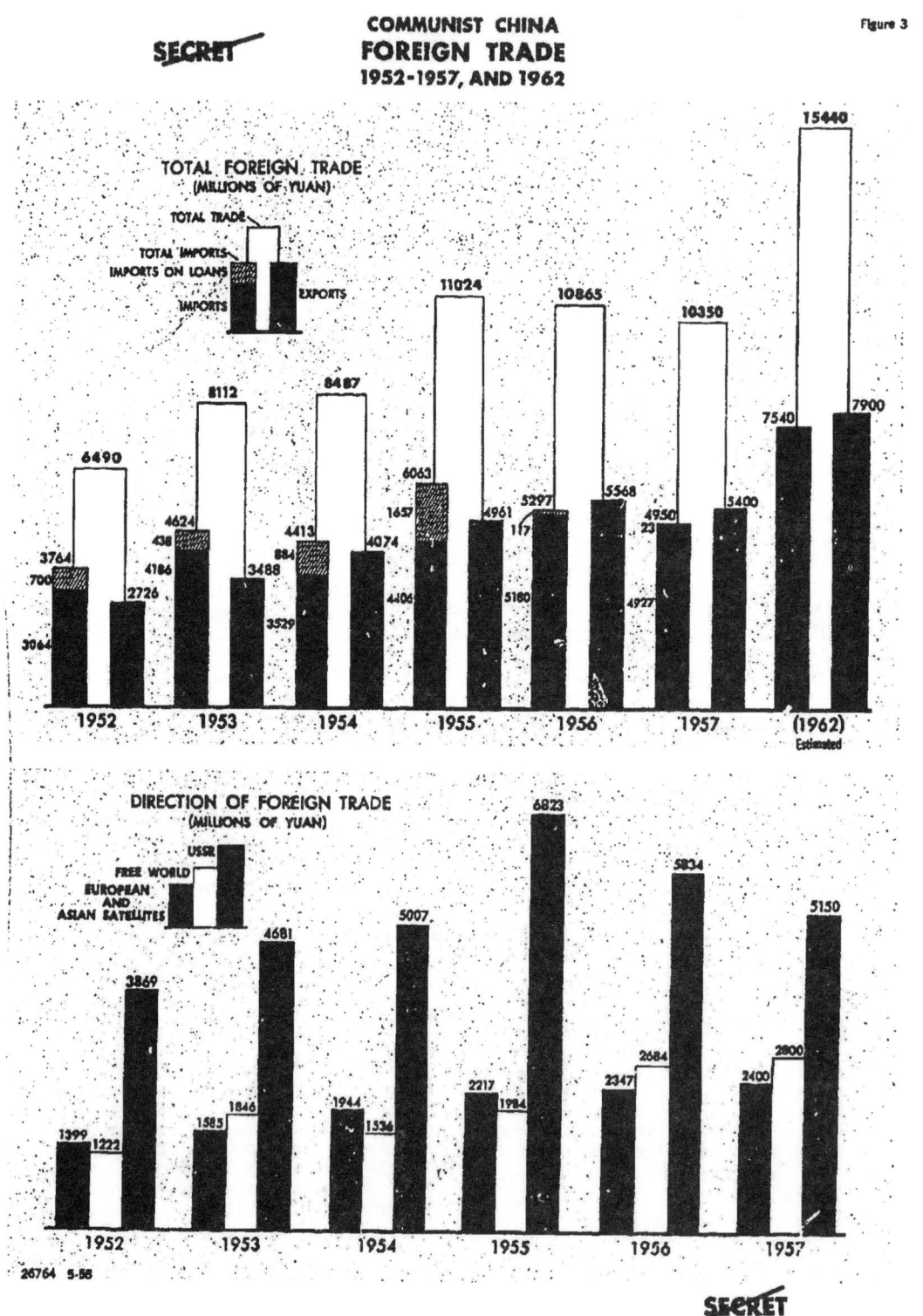

COMMUNIST CHINA
FOREIGN TRADE
1952-1957, AND 1962

SECRET

7

25. The total increase in GNP during the past five years has probably been great enough to register an average annual growth in per capita output of five to six percent, even though the population expanded at an average annual rate of about two percent. About 45 percent of the increase in output apparently was channeled into investment or government purchases of goods and services. While the remainder was absorbed by an increase in personal consumption, probably more than three-fifths of this increase went to the non-agricultural population, which comprised less than one-fifth of the population. As a result, per capita consumption of the peasant population was probably improved little, if any.

26. The fact that population growth has nearly kept pace with the increase in agricultural output has become a matter of deep concern to the regime. During the past five years, the number of mouths to feed has probably increased by some 65 million and now totals about 640 million. As a result of improved sanitation, hygiene and public health measures, better distribution of food, and the maintenance of peace within the country, the rate of increase of the population has probably risen somewhat over the period of the last five years, averaging about 2.2 percent. With an average annual increase in agricultural output during the past five years of about three percent, the margin of safety is very thin. In an effort to deal with this problem the regime is developing programs which it hopes will, in time, reduce the birth rate.

B. Reorganization of the Chinese Society

27. The regime apparently made considerable progress in its efforts to recast the traditional structure of Chinese society in the Communist mold. These efforts sprang from both Communist doctrine and from the pragmatic need to establish a high degree of organization and control in order that a relatively small group — the Chinese Communist Party — could dominate the vast Chinese population.

28. Before 1953, the power of the landlords and well-to-do peasants which had been dominant in rural areas was virtually eliminated. Subordination of youth to their elders was weakened by placing the former in positions of responsibility. Women were given equal status in society. Through centralized control of all media of communications and a cadre network, the Communists weakened the clan and regional loyalties which still existed among many Chinese. The regime sought to convince all Chinese that the welfare of the individual and of the family must be subordinated to the general good of the nation as a whole.

29. Since 1953, the regime has intensified its efforts to reorganize traditional Chinese society. By persuasion, pressure, and, in some instances, terror, the Communists increased their efforts to impose the Communist way of life on the intellectuals and the middle class. The most radical changes in the old ways of life during the past five years, however, resulted from the regime's programs to socialize all forms of economic activity. The success of these programs was surprising because of the rapidity with which the millions of peasants were shuffled into collective groupings and business enterprises were brought under government control. Moreover, there were relatively few outward manifestations of resistance, at least initially.

30. By the end of 1956, socialization had virtually eliminated all private control of industrial and commercial enterprises. The regime continued to utilize many former owners as managers and technicians, paying them liquidation dividends which may be continued for a few more years. It has also introduced measures designed to increase party control of management and labor.

31. By the end of 1957, the Chinese Communists claimed that 93 percent of peasant households were in collective farms, and that an additional four percent were in cooperatives. The remaining small fraction, except in Tibet and certain other exempted areas, had been placed under the guidance of the nearest collective.

SECRET

SECRET

8

32. Although the organizational phase of collectivization was quickly accomplished, the Communists have not realized the major benefits which they had anticipated. Despite an increase in the output of major food crops, the government's 1956 collection declined, in part because many peasants discovered that even in collectives they could circumvent government controls, especially when the local cadres sided with the peasants. Agricultural output was also adversely affected by the dislocations which accompanied the actual organization of the collectives, and by the difficulties which were encountered in establishing effective management of the larger agricultural units.

33. The Communists also had to cope with peasant disillusionment which became increasingly apparent in 1957. Many peasants were unhappy because their incomes had not increased as promised, or because they had not been adequately remunerated for their contribution of land and implements. In addition to evading government efforts to procure grain, substantial numbers of peasants withdrew from collective farms, although most of them were forced to return. The higher urban incomes continued to attract large numbers of peasants into cities where unemployment was already a critical problem. Strong measures have been taken to force these dissatisfied peasants to return home, but the problem still exists.

C. Problems in Eliciting Popular Support

34. The regime's progress in changing the form of Chinese society apparently was not matched in the realm of popular attitudes. The Chinese population as a whole appears to have ambivalent feelings toward the regime. The regime has had considerable success in its efforts to foster a sense of common identity in the population at large, in part because of the groundwork of nationalist sentiment which had been stimulated by Sun Yat-sen and the Kuomintang, and in part because of its own achievements. There has probably been a favorable response to specific programs such as public health and education which improve the lot of the individual, or road building, irrigation, and flood control which are visible community improvements. There has probably also been a favorable, but less general, response to developments which boost national pride such as the production of planes and trucks, bridging the Yangtze, and the increased world prestige of Communist China.

35. But in most Chinese these effects have in varying degrees almost certainly been offset by negative reactions to other aspects of the regime. The intellectuals have been resentful of the pressures to conform and the restrictions on discussion. The urban workers have disliked the constant orders to produce more goods faster, the compulsory attendance at innumerable indoctrination meetings in their free time, and the shortages of consumer goods. The peasants have been dissatisfied with the failure of their personal incomes to rise in proportion to their increased output, and with the regimentation of the collective system. In general, the regime has made little progress in gaining popular acceptance of the Communist dogma or in substituting, as an incentive, the prospect of a future millenium in place of more food and clothing for the present generation. Moreover, the intensification and centralization of control have probably caused previously diffused discontent to be directed against the regime. But regardless of dissatisfaction or resentment, the Chinese are aware of the power of the regime and see no alternative; their response to the regime is, for the most part, one of acquiescence.

36. To elicit greater popular support for the regime and to improve the effectiveness of the party organization, the regime undertook a venturesome experiment in the spring of 1957. It admitted the existence of problems, relaxed restrictions on public discussion, and invited criticism of the operations of the party and its programs. Although some elements within the party were apparently opposed to relaxing controls, Mao and other leaders seemed to see many advantages. Public criticism, in their view, might provide a safety valve, give the people a greater sense of participation in party affairs, and create the im-

SECRET

pression that the regime was modifying its authoritarian procedures. They apparently feared that the party had become separated from the people, a weakness they believed had been a principal cause of the outbursts in Hungary and Poland. Moreover, public criticism, they thought, would reveal to the leaders the weaknesses in the operations of the party and provide the basis for corrective measures. They must also have estimated that rule by the Chinese Communist regime had been generally accepted and that criticisms would be directed at the implementation of policy rather than at the basic character of the regime itself.

37. This program grew out of a largely unsuccessful effort in early 1956 to create a more positive response to its programs by a relaxation of domestic tensions and by promising an improvement in the harsh conditions of life. However, the promises and incentives directed initially to the intellectuals, and later extended to the peasants and workers, failed to evoke a significant response, and in the spring of 1957 Mao broadened the scope of the liberalization policy. As part of the 1956 measures, intellectuals had been encouraged to debate differences on non-political subjects; Mao now encouraged the population in general to participate in the greater freedom to discuss and extended the subjects of discussion to the operation of the party and its programs. At the same time he formalized his policy in a doctrinal statement which recognized that even in a Communist state there were contradictions in outlook between the leaders and the people, and within and between various groups. But these contradictions, he insisted, were largely non-antagonistic because of the disappearance of exploitation of one class by another, and, therefore, could be resolved by discussion and persuasion, rather than by force.

38. The extent and intensity of the criticism appears to have surprised the regime. It found that neither the Communist system, the party's monopoly of leadership, nor the Soviet orientation had been as fully accepted in China as it had apparently believed, especially among the very intellectuals it had courted. The regime's critics were numerous and came from many select groups, including even the party. Their criticisms almost certainly reflected the views of a body of opinion much larger than the regime has admitted.

39. In June 1957 the regime reacted by abruptly cutting off criticism, and Mao's contradictions formula was rewritten to point out clearly the categories of Communist truth which were above criticism. The regime subsequently conducted an intensive campaign against its critics and has dismissed accused "rightists" from their positions. It has apparently not felt it necessary to implement its sometimes explicit threat of punishing its critics on harsh "counter-revolutionary" grounds, however, and the erring ones have been told that they will be given a chance to redeem themselves. To counteract the criticism, the regime also launched a massive campaign designed to convince the people of the superiority of the Communist system.

40. Nevertheless, the regime did not disregard all criticism, and has taken steps to improve the operation of the party and its relations with the people generally. The regime has urged a continuation of public discussion, although, as might be expected, the response has been guarded and concerned largely with details of administration and production. The party also continued the "rectification" program which had been launched as part of Mao's original program and which seeks by persuasion and education to create conformity, tighten discipline, correct errors, and reinvigorate the party.

41. One major source of difficulty within the party was that it had apparently grown too fast for proper indoctrination of members. Total party membership is at present about 13 million. About two-thirds of its members had been recruited since 1949 and about two million since June 1956. As a result there were many who were free-riders, dead-wood, or "not steeled through labor." Traditional localist sentiments also still existed in the party, as exemplified by the many rural cadres who supported the grievances of the peasants rather than enforced edicts of the regime or who resented party personnel of

SECRET

non-local origin. Moreover, the exercise of authority and the enjoyment of special privileges led to a deterioration of the party's relations with the people.

42. Although the main emphasis of rectification has been upon reeducating members, a number of party officials and deputies to the National People's Congress have been dismissed from the party for "rightist" activities, and further dismissals of cadres for incompetency or unreliability are probable. There has also been a wholesale transfer of party and government cadres to lower levels, particularly to rural areas where large numbers were assigned to agricultural collectives. This program seems to have had a number of objectives: strengthening of the party network in the crucial agricultural field; retrenchment of non-productive personnel in party, government, and industrial organs; reduction of bureaucratic tendencies in these organs; inculcating members with an appreciation of manual labor; and punishment of errant members. It probably was also intended to meet criticisms of the material privileges enjoyed by party members. There are indications that many of those transferred resented the shifts.

D. The Regime's Ability to Control Mainland China

43. We believe that the regime has the ability to exercise firm control of mainland China. Despite the fact that problems and weaknesses within the party have been revealed by the rectification program, the party retains its basic elements of strength: a ruthless and resourceful leadership, a large membership organized to act as an instrument of control and policy implementation, and an intention and ability to enforce a high degree of discipline and conformity. The party organization continues to be backed up by large and well-disciplined police, militia, and security organizations, supplemented by a network of informers and local "resident's committees" which provide surveillance over individual family groups. Party control is reinforced by mass organizations which mobilize various social and occupational groups in the population behind Communist programs and which serve as channels for propaganda and indoctrination. The authority of the party is further enhanced by its control of all media of communication and of the distribution of the bulk of food supplies in urban areas, and by its success in corralling most peasants into collectives.

44. Behind this control mechanism stand the large Chinese Communist military forces which are effectively under the control of the party. During the revolution the party and the army were, to a large extent, an integral unit. Military personnel and veterans continue to make up a large part of the party. The regime claims that about 75 percent of the rank and file of the armed forces are members of the Chinese Communist Party or of the Young Communist League, and all receive intense political indoctrination. Because of the close identity of the party and army in the past, many senior party members have a military background; thus the 1956 enlargement of the Politburo and the Central Committee brought a significant number of such persons into the top levels of party leadership. However, there is no indication that they form a military bloc within the party leadership, or that a military group with political ambitions has emerged within the armed forces. The party appears to be fully aware of the importance of maintaining control over the military and the military appears to accept the dominant role of the party. At the time Marshal Zhukov was ousted from his positions in the Soviet Union, Chinese Communist military spokesmen publicly stated their support of a strong party role in the armed forces.

45. The regime has been able to deal effectively with sporadic outbursts of resistance which have for the most part been localized and poorly organized. Probably in part to demonstrate its power, the regime has carried out two nationwide drives against "counter-revolutionaries." The security forces have also dealt with several student riots and demonstrations against the regime, and with some civil disturbances growing out of peasant resentment against collectives. There have been indications of continuing discon-

SECRET

SECRET   11

tent in minority areas, recently including demands for genuine autonomy, but large-scale armed uprisings have been reported only in Tibet. Strong anti-Chinese sentiment in Tibet culminated in an outburst in 1956 and induced the regime to announce that the introduction of social "reforms" into Tibet would be postponed for six years. Despite this concession, sporadic incidents continue in Tibet.

E. Strengthening Its Military Establishment [6,7]

46. The capabilities of the armed forces to fulfill their internal and external functions have increased significantly during the past several years. The Korean War gave great impetus to the development and modernization of Communist China's armed forces and stimulated large-scale Soviet aid. Since the war, the trend has continued toward further modernization and a more balanced military establishment.

47. Since 1954, ground force personnel and infantry division strength have remained at an estimated 2½ million men and 114 divisions respectively. However, overall capabilities have been increased by continued modernization. Anti-aircraft and anti-tank battalions are now included in most of the infantry divisions, and a tank-assault gun regiment has been added to at least 28 of the infantry divisions. In 1955 the regime inaugurated a new military conscription and reserve program which is now providing an army composed in the main of selected conscripts. The army's effectiveness in modern warfare, as a result of current training programs, has been considerably increased. In addition, the reserves will include, on a continuing basis, about two million men who will have undergone active military service within the previous three years.

48. Since 1954, Communist China's combined air arm has increased from 65,200 to 87,000

officers and men while total aircraft in operational units have increased from 1,580 to 2,880. A more significant indicator of progress toward modernization is the increase from 850 to 2,280 jet aircraft, of which 1,835 are fighters and 445 are light bombers. Communist China has also developed an extensive radar detection system which covers the entire coast and major inland industrial centers. This system has fair to good detection capability except for aircraft at low altitudes. Its high altitude GCI capability has not been expanded to include all areas.

49. The navy has gradually increased its overall strength to 55,000 and its general service personnel strength to 48,000 officers and men. This growth was accompanied by a substantial increase in offensive and defensive capabilities. Its major surface units include four destroyers, 16 submarines, four escort vessels, 54 amphibious ships and 31 mine warfare vessels, as well as a Naval Air Arm including 435 combat aircraft.

50. Although still dependent to a large degree upon the Soviet Union for heavy and complex equipment, aircraft, and many component and spare parts, Communist China has made progress in its effort to achieve military self-sufficiency. It now produces small arms, mortars through 160-mm, and artillery through 122-mm howitzers. In addition, Communist China now has a number of airframe and aircraft parts plants, including an aircraft assembly plant at Mukden capable of series assembly of jet fighter aircraft. Mukden's monthly assembly capacity will probably reach 100 jet fighters by 1963. Communist China has a rapidly growing shipbuilding industry now assembling submarines and producing hulls for escort vessels, submarine chasers, mine warfare vessels, and motor torpedo boats. However, practically all armament for these vessels and a substantial part of components, equipment, and machinery is obtained from the Bloc. The Chinese Communists continue to be handicapped by a shortage of technological skills in both the armed forces and the armaments industry. We believe that the country has no guided missiles or nuclear weapons and, at present, lacks the capability to produce them.

[6] See Annex B for more complete discussion.

[7] See maps for the disposition of ground forces and combat jet aircraft, and for the location of naval bases.

SECRET

SECRET

51. The high cost of maintaining such a large military establishment and of developing a munitions industry has been a heavy drain on Communist China's economy. The Chinese Communists have reduced the proportion of expenditures budgeted as military from 26 percent in 1953 to 18 percent in 1957. However, this has not involved a significant decline in the absolute amount spent, and there has probably been an increase in investment in plants for producing military equipment.

III. PROBABLE TRENDS WITHIN COMMUNIST CHINA DURING THE NEXT FIVE YEARS

52. We believe that during the next five years the Chinese Communists will continue to be able to exercise effective control of mainland China and will gain some success in further imposing Communist social institutions and patterns on the Chinese people. The regime will probably be able to maintain a rate of economic growth roughly comparable to that of the last five years, but this will necessitate continued stringent control of consumption, particularly in view of the increasing population. Its efforts to gain increased popular support will be severely limited by its determination to maintain the pace of economic development and social change. There will continue to be a widespread but fluctuating feeling of dissatisfaction and discontent among the Chinese people which, while hampering somewhat the regime's programs, will probably not be translated into effective resistance.

A. The Economy

53. Although the Second Five Year Plan is still in process of formulation, the general outlines of this plan as announced in September 1956 appear to be the basis of the regime's planning. These indications are sufficiently clear to enable us to estimate that total output will probably increase by 7–8 percent annually during the period of the Second Five Year Plan, or about as rapidly as in the First Five Year Plan. The increments to production will probably cost more in terms of investment required, since gains from more intensive utilization of existing plants will be far less. However, investment during the Second Five Year Plan will probably continue to increase relative to total output. The emphasis will continue to be on industrial development, and by 1962 the industrial sector will probably contribute nearly 26 percent of total gross product as against 18 percent in 1957 and 13 percent in 1952.

54. *Agricultural Production.* In their approach to the Second Five Year Plan, the Chinese Communists have been forced to give greater priority to the expansion of agricultural production in order to provide for the minimum consumption needs of its growing population, agricultural raw materials, especially cotton, for its expanding industry, and exports with which to repay loans and to finance the import of vital capital equipment. This greater priority for agriculture will involve some reorientation of industrial development, with a greater share of investment allotted to those heavy industries which provide fertilizers, agricultural chemicals, irrigation equipment, and implements for agriculture. For example, investment in the chemical fertilizer industry will probably rise from one percent of total state investment in the First Five Year Plan to about three percent in the second plan period.

55. The Chinese Communists have announced that, in 1958, 14 percent of the state's capital investment will be in agriculture, suggesting that such investment for the entire Second Five Year Plan may be as much as four times the amount allocated for this purpose during the First Five Year Plan when it amounted to only 7.8 percent of a smaller total investment. The state's investment in agriculture is used primarily on large-scale water conservation projects. However, direct investment by the collectives in irrigation and drainage facilities, fertilizers, farm tools and machinery, livestock, and other production requisites will continue to provide the major source of funds for agricultural development. Such investment, and the related technological improvements, are considered by the regime to be the most effective way of immediately increasing agricultural production.

SECRET

SECRET   13

56. In September 1956 the regime set 1962 agricultural goals at 250 million tons of grain and 2.4 million tons of cotton, but in 1957, recognizing that these goals were far too ambitious, it lowered the targets to 240 million tons of grain and 2.15 million tons of cotton, while increasing substantially the proposed agricultural development effort. However, we believe that these goals are still too optimistic, in view of the limited amount of fertilizers that will be available and the modest proposed increases in both irrigated areas and sown area obtained through reclamation and multiple cropping. Between 1957 and 1962 grain production will probably only rise from 185 million tons to 215 million tons and cotton from 1.64 million tons to 2 million tons. About one-fourth of these production increases are expected to result from increased application of chemical fertilizer.

57. The above estimates imply a rate of increase of agricultural production of about three percent annually. This increase would provide a small margin over the probable annual increase of population of 2.0–2.5 percent. However, a number of contingencies could remove this margin. A major imponderable is the willingness of the peasants to maintain their efforts to produce under collectivization. Weather and its effect on crops are also unpredictable. Finally, we cannot completely discount the possibility that the present rate of population growth might increase. Under the worst combination of these contingencies for the Chinese Communists — a series of bad crop years, peasant apathy, and a rising rate of population growth — the regime would face grave difficulties. However, with its internal security system and its control of food distribution the regime could almost certainly maintain itself in power. Furthermore, other stopgap measures open to Peiping would include loans or aid from the Soviet Bloc, and a reduction in exports and some increase in imports of agricultural products. At the same time, the regime would have sufficient production capacity in heavy industry and construction to enable it to maintain industrial growth, though at a reduced rate.

58. Ensuring a food supply for its enormous and growing population will be Communist China's number one economic problem for the indefinite future. Arable land is relatively limited, and by far the major share of the land area is too high, dry, or hilly to be cultivated. At present about 11 percent of the land is under cultivation. Marginal lands could be brought under cultivation and double cropping extended through heavy investment and modern techniques which would increase the sown area by possibly half. With a generous water supply and a long growing season in the most important farm areas, yields can be raised through improvements in flood control, irrigation, pest control, crop types, and fertilization. In the long run and with more investment, we believe the Chinese Communists can probably double agricultural output. However, present population growth, if unaltered, would double the population in 28 to 35 years, making difficult any improvement in living standards even if all agricultural potentials were realized.

59. *Industrial Production.* No finalized Second Five Year Plan has been prepared, but the preliminary proposals put before the Eighth Congress of the Chinese Communist Party in September, 1956, provided for an increase in gross value of industrial production of about 86 percent during the Second Plan, compared to a rise of about 115 percent achieved during the First Plan. Heavy industry will continue to receive priority. Although there is evidence of considerable change in the individual industrial goals, the attainment of the overall industrial goal, as proposed, appears likely in view of the prospective level of industrial investment. (See Table 1.)

60. An increasing proportion of heavy industrial investment will be in new industrial areas in northern Manchuria and in north-central and northwest China, based upon the location of raw materials and upon strategic considerations. Increased production during the Second Plan will rely greatly on completion of new capacity, much of which was started during the First Plan. In contrast with the First Five Year Plan, in which emphasis was on large scale plants, significant proportions of

SECRET

SECRET

14

TABLE I

ESTIMATED PRODUCTION OF SELECTED COMMODITIES 1952, 1957, 1962 *

Commodity	Measure	1952	1957	% increase 1957 over '52	1962 Preliminary Goal	1962 Estimated Prod.	Estimated % increase 1962 over '57
Industry							
Electric power	Bil kwh	7	19	161	44	44	131
Crude steel	TMT	1,349	5,235	288	12,000	12,000	129
Coal	MMT	64	122	93	190–210	190–210	55–72
Trucks	Units	0	7,000	—	**N.A.	32,000	357
Merchant vessels	TGRT	7	21	200	N.A.	120	471
Cement	MMT	3	7	72	12.5	12.5	87
Turbines	T kw	7	240	3,482	N.A.	1,289	437
Electric generators	T kw	30	284	847	1,400–1,500	1,400	393
Crude oil (Nat. & Syn.)	TMT	436	1,443	231	5,000–6,000	3,500	143
Copper (refined)	TMT	8	14	70	N.A.	50	257
Chem. Fertilizer	TMT	194	803	314	5,000–7,000	6,000	647
Cotton cloth (factory)	Mil. mtrs	3,017	4,000	33	8,000–9,000	6,354	59
Agricultural							
Total grains	MMT	168	185	10	240	215	.16
Cotton (ginned)	TMT	1,305	1,640	26	2,150	2,000	22
Cattle (incl. buffalo)	Mil. head	57	74	30	90	90	22
Hogs	Mil. head	89	114	28	220	160	40

* Footnote 2 on page 5 applies also to this table.
** Not available.

the increased output of iron, steel, and coal will come from newly constructed or renovated small and medium size units. To the extent that this program is implemented, it will provide more employment, conserve scarce capital, and require less machinery imports.

61. The variety of products made by Chinese industry will continue to increase rapidly, but there will continue to be shortages, especially in chemical fertilizers and crude oil. During the Second Five Year Plan, the machine building industry will probably be able to supply at least 70 percent of machinery requirements, compared to about 60 percent in the First Five Year Plan. In addition to the priority development of the chemical fertilizer and machinery industries, it is expected that increased attention will be given to merchant shipbuilding, copper, and crude oil. Even if the regime achieves its crude oil targets, however, in 1962 it will still be heavily dependent on imports to meet its rapidly increasing requirements.

62. Shortages of trained technicians and scientists will continue to exist. In an effort to solve this problem, the regime plans to have one third of the 500,000 students, who will graduate from colleges and universities during the next five years, go into teaching in all fields. Of those who will not go into teaching, one half will be engineers, a third will be in medicine, science, agriculture, or forestry, and about a sixth in law, the social sciences, and other fields. During this period the regime also plans to double its present enrollment in primary and middle schools. Even if these goals are met by 1962, however, the regime will still be far short of the highly trained personnel needed in the scientific and technical fields.

63. *Foreign Trade.* Total exports in the Second Five Year Plan are estimated at 32.0 billion yuan, and imports at 29.2 billion yuan. This compares with 23.3 and 25.2 billion yuan, respectively, during the First Five Year Plan. We believe that the bulk of Communist

SECRET

China's trade will continue to be with the other Bloc countries, especially the Soviet Union. However, the proportion of total trade with the non-Communist world will probably increase in the Second Five Year Plan, expanding from about 22 percent to possibly 30 percent of total trade. We believe that the most important elements of this increase will be an expansion of Communist China's exports of iron ore and coal to Japan and consumers goods to South and Southeast Asia, and imports of fertilizers, industrial equipment, and steel from Japan and capital goods from Western Europe. Communist China will probably increase the use of its growing merchant marine in international trade.

64. The maintenance of the present level of multilateral trade controls will complicate Chinese Communist economic and military development by creating import problems, increasing costs, and reducing flexibility. Furthermore, present unilateral US financial controls will deny Communist China an important export market, as well as reduce dollar remittances.

65. The Chinese Communists apparently are going ahead with their Second Five Year Plan with no provision for new long term credits from the USSR. Communist China will have to finance through exports the imports required for industrialization, as well as to repay Soviet credits advanced during the First Five Year Plan and to finance their own aid program — both of which total an estimated 3.0 billion yuan. With their present capabilities, the Chinese Communists can probably carry out their planned industrial development without further Soviet credits. However, in the event of serious economic difficulties, the Chinese might seek and obtain some assistance on credit from the USSR.

B. The Party

66. The party will probably continue to face difficulties in maintaining vigor, flexibility, and internal discipline. The strains created by recent massive shifts of cadres to lower levels and the difficulty of absorbing the high post-1949 membership will continue. Difficulties that will inevitably arise in formulating the regime's program will almost certainly create policy differences at various party levels. Although these problems may force the party occasionally to resort to repressive measures, in the main the regime will probably be able, through periodic rectification programs, to resolve intra-party conflicts by discussion, persuasion, and administrative disciplinary procedures. Moreover, we believe that the party will retain a significant degree of flexibility in its policies.

67. These problems would be aggravated by the death or incapacitation of Mao. Should a succession question arise in the next five years, party authority would probably initially pass to a group, with Liu Shao-chi, Chou En-lai, Teng Hsiao-ping, and Ch'en Yun as its most likely members, and with Chu Teh as tituiar head of state. Policy disagreements and power rivalries would probably sharpen in the absence of Mao. The temptation to occupy his position would be great, and could lead to a struggle for dominance within the party. We believe that such a struggle would complicate the achieving of certain of the regime's objectives and reduce its policy flexibility, but would not threaten the regime's ability to control the country.

C. Popular Attitudes

68. We see little prospect that popular discontent can or will be translated into organized and active resistance in the near future. Unrest will probably continue at about its present level, and sporadic cases of isolated, small-scale active resistance will probably occur, particularly in rural and ethnic minority areas. Reactions to the increasing pressures of austerity and industrialization may, at times, cause the regime to clamp down, but the Chinese Communist leadership, while capitalizing on the people's recognition of the regime's willingness to utilize severely repressive measures if necessary, will probably avoid widespread or systematic use of terroristic methods. There will continue to be much dissatisfaction, but we believe the net effect on the regime's programs will be no more than a complicating or retarding one. Although the regime will continue to seek

SECRET   16

greater positive support, it will have limited success because of its determination to carry out its economic and social programs. The response of the bulk of the Chinese people to the regime will probably remain one of acquiescence.

69. The regime will continue to have problems with intellectuals. The outspoken criticisms which came from the universities in the spring of 1957 showed the regime that its efforts at indoctrination failed to force many students and professors into accepting the Communist way. The problems of winning the student generation will be made more difficult by the shortage of facilities for higher education, the limited urban employment opportunities for graduates, and the need to sharpen disciplinary measures and political controls over students. Furthermore, the regime will probably continue to force great numbers of middle school graduates to accept long-term agricultural assignments in the countryside.

70. The peasants will almost certainly continue to give the regime trouble. The regime recognizes that a major problem during the Second Five Year Period will be to improve the management of the collective farms and to obtain from the peasants a greater acceptance of the collective system. The regime will probably be able to keep the peasants in line by enforcement of tighter controls, and, in good crop years, by allowing some increases in consumption.

D. The Military Establishment

71. Communist China's military capability will almost certainly continue to improve over the next five years. Although the army will probably be reduced in size, it will be equipped with newer and better weapons, and will be more mobile and better trained than at present. The air force and navy will increase in size and effectiveness. Although the armed forces will be somewhat better balanced, the concept of a large ground army will still prevail. The Chinese Communists will probably maintain a large standing army which, in addition to its offensive and defensive missions, will provide the basic force for con-

trolling mainland China and will continue to have an intimidating effect in Asia.

72. By 1962 the combined air forces will probably have about 3,600 aircraft, an increase of more than 700. The Chinese Communists probably will have completed converting their fighters and light bombers to jets, and may by that time have some jet medium bombers. The navy will probably continue its rapid development, with principal emphasis on improved defense capability within home waters. There will probably be a significant increase in submarine strength, and the probable replacement of overage ships will increase the navy's operating effectiveness.

73. The armaments industry will increase in size and efficiency, but during the period of this estimate, Communist China will continue to be heavily dependent upon the Soviet Union for many kinds of heavy and complex military equipment and for technological assistance. During 1958–1962 it will probably be able to meet armed force needs for small arms and for nearly all artillery, transport, and ammunition, but will still be unable to meet the needs for armored fighting vehicles and more complex fire control systems. The shipbuilding industry will also continue its rapid expansion. Domestic aircraft production will probably increase considerably, but Communist China will continue to be dependent on the USSR for many components.

74. Although Communist China will almost certainly not have developed a missile or nuclear weapons production capability of its own by 1962 because of the continuing shortage of technicians and the demands of other military and economic programs upon its limited resources, we believe that the Chinese Communists will press the USSR for such advanced weapons. It is probable that during the next five years the USSR will provide the Chinese Communists with some varieties of missiles and other weapons adaptable to nuclear use, but with conventional warheads. The Chinese Communist and Soviet views on the introduction of nuclear warheads* into Communist China are less certain. Unless barred by an effective international agreement, the

---

*Including bombs.

SECRET

SECRET   17

USSR may introduce nuclear weapons into Communist China by 1962, although they will almost certainly remain under Soviet control. In any event, even though nuclear warheads were not deployed in Communist China, they would be readily available if Sino-Soviet interests required them.

IV. COMMUNIST CHINA'S EXTERNAL RELATIONS

A. With the Bloc

75. Communist China's close relations with the USSR are based on mutual objectives, reliance on Soviet military power and economic support, a common ideology, and a conviction that Bloc unity is essential in the face of a common enemy. In the Chinese Communist view, unity is crucial to the expulsion of Western, particularly US, influence from Asia and Africa, and to the ultimate achievement of economic and military superiority over the West. The Chinese Communists appear to accept the Soviet Union as the head of the Bloc because of its experience and leadership in the doctrinal, economic and technological fields, and because of its military power. They have supported Soviet policy on all international questions. Communist China has in turn sought and gained Bloc acceptance as the second major Communist power and, probably, as a participant with the Soviet Union in the formulation of general Bloc policy.

76. The Chinese Communists insist that the strength and unity of the Bloc against the West must be maintained and that the essential Communist character of each Bloc state be preserved. To the extent that it will contribute to, or is compatible with, these overriding considerations, the Chinese Communists favor flexibility in intra-Bloc relations, desiring particularly that the Chinese party have a wide area of doctrinal and policy initiative. Although there have been differences in the emphasis which the Chinese Communists have placed on various aspects of intra-Bloc relations over the past two years, their basic concept of intra-Bloc relations has remained: the USSR is the head of the socialist camp and the member states should at all times place the interests of unity among the Socialist countries above everything else; but the USSR should, in turn, refrain from excessive intervention in the internal affairs of each Communist state. These views of unity and diversity were substantially reflected in the Moscow 40th Anniversary communique, probably of joint Sino-Soviet authorship.

77. Close Sino-Soviet alignment does not appear to have been affected by the cessation of Soviet credits, although the Chinese Communists may have hoped for new credits or for more lenient repayment terms on past credits. Whatever the nature of the Peiping-Moscow discussions on this subject, the Chinese Communists appear to have accommodated themselves to the situation, and in 1957 they altered their planning for the Second Five Year Plan to take account of reduced estimates of import availabilities. The Soviet Union is still extending technical assistance and has concluded a long-term agreement which is believed to provide for an increased level of Sino-Soviet trade, including the bulk of the essential import needs of Communist China's industrial development program. Moreover, the Chinese Communists probably believe that the USSR remains a source of aid in the event of a serious crisis.

78. Sino-Soviet relations as they concern guidance to the Asian Communist parties appear to have been governed by a mutually acceptable division of responsibilities and a willingness to cooperate. Despite occasional differences of nuance in the statements of Asian Communist parties, we have little evidence of any Sino-Soviet disagreement on the character of Communist activities in Asia. Communist leaders of North Korea and North Vietnam, as well as those in non-Communist Asian countries, visit both Moscow and Peiping for consultation. The policy line, as given in newspapers and radio broadcasts of both countries, varies little if any.

79. With respect to the border areas, the USSR and Communist China apparently have overcome, or at least suppressed, their historical conflict of interests, and in Sinkiang and Outer Mongolia are cooperating in development programs. The Soviet Union is

SECRET

~~SECRET~~

18

building the portion of the trans-Sinkiang rail line from the Soviet line in Kazakhstan to Wusu in Sinkiang Province, and the Chinese Communists have accepted Soviet technicians in the area to assist in its development. The USSR, by constructing the trans-Mongolian railroad to China, has facilitated increased Chinese Communist cultural and economic relations with Outer Mongolia.

80. During the five year period of the estimate, it does not appear likely that there will be any appreciable change either in the firmness of the Sino-Soviet relationship or in China's status and role therein. Though there will almost certainly be frictions, Communist China and the USSR will probably be able to work out satisfactory solutions to problems arising out of China's status in the Bloc, its economic relations with the USSR, and the division of Communist responsibilities in Asia. Nevertheless, because of Communist China's growing stature and strength, it is possible that problems may arise which would be difficult to resolve.

81. A source of disagreement may be Communist China's possible desire to exert greater influence on general Bloc policy, both internal and external. Because of the immense value of the Sino-Soviet alliance to both partners, Soviet and Chinese Communist leaders almost certainly will consider that they must meet certain of each other's requests, be careful not to offend each other's sensibilities, and defer, at times, to the other partner. Although the Soviet leaders will almost certainly be apprehensive lest a strengthened China seriously challenge the USSR for Communist primacy at some distant date, there is no evidence that this is affecting present policy. External policy disagreements, if any, would be more likely to occur with respect to areas where the interests of one party might be considerably greater, such as the Taiwan straits, or where they differed as to the risks involved in undertaking a specific action.

82. With respect to high level Soviet negotiations with the West, the Chinese Communists probably feel that it would be inadvisable at present to press for the introduction of topics which are of primary interest to Communist China and which would require its presence, e.g., entrance into the UN and the acquisition of Taiwan. It is possible, however, that differences between Peiping and Moscow may arise in the future with respect to the substance or the mechanics of negotiations with the West.

83. Sino-Soviet cohesion would probably not be significantly affected by a Soviet-Western detente, or by Communist China's entry into the UN or recognition by the US. Communist China would probably welcome a Soviet-Western detente because its leaders would believe that this would increase Communist opportunities in Asia. They would probably also welcome a limitation of armaments agreement which convinced them that they could safely reduce their expenditures for arms, although they would probably take the position that they would not be bound to any agreement in which they did not formally participate as the representative of China. The USSR would almost certainly welcome Communist China's representation in the UN and its recognition by the US, although the Soviet leaders might have some misgivings that these developments might reduce somewhat Peiping's political dependence on the USSR.

B. Relations with the Non-Communist World[*]

84. Communist China's leaders appear to view the present world position of the Sino-Soviet Bloc with considerable confidence. They seem convinced that the world balance of power has shifted to the Bloc and that the "East Wind" is prevailing over the West. Chinese Communist optimism is based on a view of history that assumes that Communism will ultimately triumph and on specific developments such as recent Soviet weapons advances, Communist gains in the Near East and Africa, and the rapid economic growth of the Bloc. While the Chinese Communists probably do not consider that the West has suffered any decisive defeat in the Far East since the French were forced out of Indochina, they appear confident that the trend in Asia

[*] See NIE 13-2-57, "Communist China's Role in non-Communist Asia," dated 3 December 1957.

~~SECRET~~

142

SECRET

is running against the West. Peiping almost certainly considers the growth of Communist political strength and influence in Indonesia and of neutralism and anti-American feeling in some Asian countries as indications of this trend.

85. In a period of less than a decade, Peiping's leaders have seen their country become the strongest Asian power and achieve substantial progress in making its impact felt in Asia and the world. They are cognizant of growing pressure in the Free World for expanded economic and political relations with Peiping. Communist China is not handicapped by Asian racial antagonisms against the white man and it can claim common experience with the former colonial areas. The Chinese Communists almost certainly believe their economic progress can be used in their efforts to convince the underdeveloped Asian countries that Communism is the best way forward.

86. The Chinese Communists have given no indications of undue impatience in the pursuit of their objectives in Asia. They appear aware of the many problems of internal development facing Communist China, the continuing need to adjust and reconcile intra-Bloc relations, and the suspicions of Communist China which exist in much of Asia. Most importantly, they almost certainly consider the presence of US influence and military forces in Asia to be the major obstacle in their path. They almost certainly estimate that any attempt to speed up the process of communizing Asia by military aggression would involve serious risk of war with the US, but at the same time probably believe that over the long run the US will not be able effectively to counter the forces which they consider to be working to the advantage of Communist China.

87. Given these views, Communist China appears to be directing its energies toward the intermediate objective of weakening the position and influence of the US in Asia. To this end it is seeking to induce Asian countries to adopt a policy of friendship toward the Bloc, to strengthen, and if possible bring to power, indigenous Communist movements without the use of external force, and to undermine the will of the Nationalists on Taiwan to resist. Since Indochina, the principal thrust of Communist China's policy has been reasonableness and peaceful coexistence, though it has been adamant on certain basic issues, particularly Taiwan.

88. We believe that Communist China will continue essentially the outlines of its present flexible course in Asia, though displaying more assertiveness and a heightened readiness to take advantage of opportune situations. It will probably intensify its efforts to convince other nations of its peacefulness and reasonableness, and even of its willingness for a rapprochement with the US, believing that an apparent readiness to make concessions will add significantly to Free World pressures to accept Communist China as a member of the community of nations and to bring about a change in US policy.

89. Communist China will continue to seek admission to the UN and the expansion of economic and political relations with most states. It will probably make additional offers of economic assistance to other Asian countries. At the same time, it will continue its subversive efforts throughout the Far East. In its propaganda overtures, it will attempt to create an exaggerated impression of its economic growth, and, while stressing its peaceful intentions, will do nothing to dim its growing reputation in Asia as a military power. In relations with Asian states its military power will be an operating but silent factor. It will probably not resort to overt military aggression which it believes would involve it in military action with the US.

90. Peiping is probably concerned that, as an unwanted by-product of peaceful coexistence, there is a growing acceptance of a "two-Chinas" concept. The Chinese Communists will continue their efforts to disabuse the world, and especially other Asian leaders, of any idea that Communist China will renounce its intention to gain control of Taiwan. They will almost certainly not resort to military action to seize Taiwan, so long as this would involve risk of war with the US. They will almost certainly continue their present efforts

SECRET

SECRET   20

to undermine Nationalist will and to discredit the Republic of China abroad. The possibility cannot be excluded that the Chinese Communists will adopt a more aggressive policy toward the Offshore Islands, in part because of intense irritation and a sense of affront, in part to emphasize their determination to destroy the Nationalist government, and in part to test US intentions in the Taiwan area. If they should become convinced that the US would not intervene militarily, they would seek to capture these islands by military action.

91. The Chinese Communists will probably complete the announced withdrawal of their forces from Korea in order to bring pressure on the US to do the same, to enhance Communist China's chances for UN entry, and to support Moscow's efforts to create Free World pressures for summit negotiations and disengagement schemes. However, Peiping will almost certainly maintain its military forces in a position to reintervene rapidly in case of a resumption of hostilities. The Chinese Communists, in concert with the Soviet Union, will probably encourage the North Korean regime to build covert strength in South Korea and to press for the reestablishment of cultural and economic contacts across the armistice line. The Chinese Communists will probably publicly support North Korean pressure for nationwide elections under "neutral" supervision, but will continue to oppose direct UN supervision. The Chinese Communists will almost certainly not agree to unification on terms which they estimate would lead to an anti-Communist Korea.

92. Peiping's objectives in Vietnam will similarly be to strengthen the Communist regime in the north while attempting to undermine the government in the south. Peiping will continue to support Communist agitation for nation-wide elections under conditions that would favor the Communists. The Chinese Communists may believe that should South Vietnam be deprived of President Diem's leadership, the Communists might gain sufficient strength to seize control from within.

93. Japan will continue to be one of Peiping's most important targets, especially because there is a growing area of competition between Communist China and Japan. Chinese Communist policies will be directed toward reducing the degree of cooperation between Japan and the US, particularly in the military field, toward undermining the Japanese government's anti-Communist position, toward destroying the friendly relations between Japan and the GRC, and toward increasing the influence in Japan of left-wing elements, e.g., left-wing Socialists, and the Japanese Communist Party. Peiping will continue to exploit Japan's desire for peace, its fears of becoming involved in a nuclear war, any areas of friction with the US, and Japan's eagerness to expand trade with mainland China. Peiping will probably be able to gain at least quasi-diplomatic status for a Chinese Communist trade mission. In pursuit of these objectives, Communist China will continue to employ both conciliatory and tough tactics.

94. Although the majority of the Overseas Chinese will probably continue to seek to avoid entanglement in the political activities of both Communist and Nationalist China, Peiping will nevertheless continue its efforts to use the Overseas Chinese as instruments for both overt and covert activities. At the same time, these communities will continue to be a source of friction between Peiping and the host governments. The nature and effectiveness of Chinese Communist policy towards Overseas Chinese will continue to vary from country to country, but there are indications that Peiping will increase its efforts to allay Southeast Asian suspicions by emphasizing in its propaganda the responsibilities of the Overseas Chinese to the host country.

95. Assuming no significant change in the basic policies of the Bloc or of the West, in particular the US, we believe that intercourse between Communist China and the Free World will increase considerably during the next five years. This will come about for a number of reasons, including a growing belief that normal relations with Communist China should be established, a hope that such relations would reduce tensions in Asia, and a desire to exploit what many see as a major trading potential. For these reasons, addi-

SECRET

SECRET   21

tional countries will probably recognize Communist China, possibly including Canada, New Zealand, Belgium, France, and Japan.

96. It is probable that the US will experience more difficulty in seeking to exclude Communist China from the UN. Moreover, the effect of the UN's censure in generating opposition to Communist China will probably decrease with the passage of time and with the withdrawal of Chinese Communist troops from Korea. Should Communist China gain a seat in the UN, it would be taken, in Asia especially, as a mark of international acceptance of Communist China, and many of the countries not already recognizing Peiping would probably do so. Particularly in Asia, commercial and other forms of intercourse with Communist China would almost certainly increase substantially. Communist China's opportunities in Asian countries for subversion, for influencing the Overseas Chinese, and for giving covert support to indigenous Communist parties would increase.

97. If Communist China continues its present international policy, we believe that its prestige in Asia will continue to grow during the next five years. This will occur whether or not additional countries recognize Communist China, or it is admitted to the UN. But it does not necessarily follow that as a result

of increased prestige the Chinese Communists will be able to induce non-Communist Asian countries to adopt internal or external policies desired by Communist China. Communist China's future role in Asia will be determined to an important extent by developments in five fields, in varying degrees beyond the control of the Chinese Communists:

a. The course of events in the US-USSR relationship and in the broad aspects of the cold war.

b. Developments within the Bloc such as spectacular scientific achievements or major political upheavals.

c. The extent to which local Communist parties, e.g., those in Indonesia, Laos, and India, gain or lose political strength.

d. The extent to which the growth of Communist China's power gives rise to increased apprehensions among Asian governments as to Communist China's future intentions and thus causes them to take increasingly effective measures at least to counter their own internal Communists.

e. The extent to which the US has the confidence and trust of non-Communist Asian governments, and in turn helps these governments not only to resist the Communists, but also to meet their national aspirations.

SECRET

SECRET

ANNEX A[1]

THE FIRST FIVE YEAR PLAN

A1. The Chinese Communists made substantial economic progress during their First Five Year Plan 1953–1957. Gross National Product increased at an average annual rate of about 7–8 percent,[2] which compared favorably with recent rates of a little over three percent in India, eight percent in Japan, and seven percent in the Soviet Union. While the average rate of growth was fairly rapid, increases from year to year were uneven, in large part because agricultural output, which provides about 50 percent of total national income and the raw materials that determine the output of light industry, depends upon uncertain weather conditions. (See Figure 4 for Gross National Product, by sector of origin.)

A2. To achieve this rate of growth, total investment averaged 17 percent of the GNP for the five year period, a proportion roughly comparable to that in the US. Investment in capital construction accounted for about 58 percent of gross investment during the five year period; of total investment in capital construction 56 percent went into industry, 19 percent into transportation and communications, and only about 8 percent into agriculture. Nevertheless, over 50 percent of total investment funds were derived directly or indirectly from agricultural output.

A3. Communist China's budget revenues rose sharply up to 1954 as the regime consolidated its controls over the economy, but have since risen more gradually and, as a proportion of the GNP, actually declined slightly from 29 to 27 percent between 1954 and 1957. The regime's fiscal policies have been to maximize revenues and to tailor its expenditures to its expected receipts. The regime's flexible control over expenditures has generally maintained budgetary balance and economic stability, except in 1956 when the government resorted to currency issue to cover a budget deficit. However, a surplus in state revenues was reestablished in 1957, largely as a result of a cutback in investment. (See Figure 5 for state revenues and expenditures.)

Industrial Production

A4. During the First Five Year Plan, Communist China, with substantial Soviet assistance, made considerable progress in laying the foundations for industrialization. Starting from a small base, the gross value of industrial output increased about 133 percent, with heavy industry increasing more than 200 percent and light industry some 85 percent. Although the average annual rate of growth of industrial output during the period was high (16.5 percent), it was uneven, being reduced to 7 percent in 1957, which was a year of consolidation and rebuilding of inventories after the overambitious construction activity of 1956.

---

[1] Chinese Communist statistics upon which the data and analyses throughout this estimate are based are subject to the same reservations as those of other Bloc countries, but to a somewhat greater extent, in view of the inexperience on the part of the newly established Chinese Communist statistical collection system. This inexperience probably accounts for the majority of such statistical defects as have been noted. Chinese Communist statistics are the basis for the regime's planning and we believe are not, in general, misrepresented.

[2] However, in international comparisons, account should be taken of Communist China's price structure, which in terms of world prices overvalues industrial manufactures — the fastest growing sector — and thus overstates the rate of growth. If Communist China's industrial manufactures were re-valued at world market prices, the rate of growth would drop to 6–7 percent.

SECRET

22

SECRET

COMMUNIST CHINA

Figure 4

GROSS NATIONAL PRODUCT, BY SECTOR OF ORIGIN
1952, 1957, and 1962
(1956 Constant factor prices)

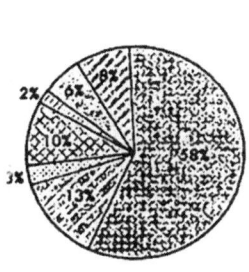

1952
73.7 billion yuan

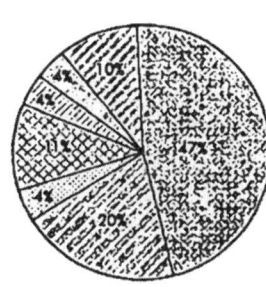

1957
103.2 billion yuan

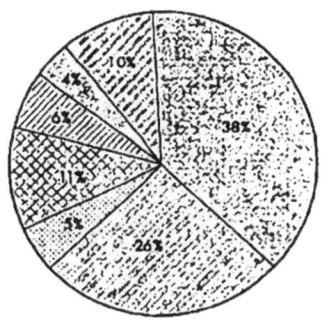

1962
148.4 billion yuan

Agriculture, Forestry, and Fisheries	State Construction
Industry	Government (including Health and Education)
Modern Transportation and Communications	Miscellaneous Consumer Services and House Rent
Trade, Native Transportation, and Other Business Services	

26806 5-58

SECRET

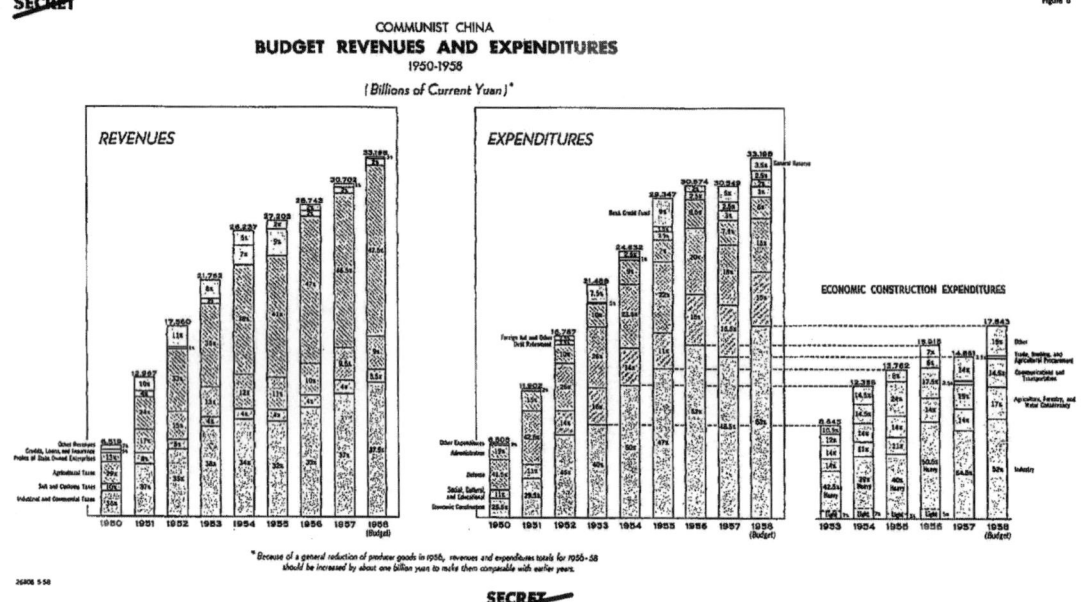

COMMUNIST CHINA
BUDGET REVENUES AND EXPENDITURES
1950-1958
(Billions of Current Yuan)*

*Because of a general reduction of producer goods in 1958, revenues and expenditures totals for 1956-58 should be increased by about one billion yuan to make them comparable with earlier years.

ANNEX A

A5. *Machine and Equipment Building.* One of the most important developments of the five year period was the rapid development of machine and equipment building industries. Whereas Communist China was formerly heavily dependent upon foreign producers for machinery, as well as for much of the industry's raw materials, its machine building industry probably was able to satisfy about 60 percent of the machinery requirements of the First Five Year Plan. Communist China now is able to produce a portion of its requirements for more complicated machine tools, mining and metallurgical processing equipment, power station equipment for medium size plants, motor trucks, aircraft, and locomotives. The naval and civil shipbuilding industries, the electronics industry, and related ferrous and non-ferrous metallurgy industries have also achieved considerable development. Although much of the recent advance has involved imitation of Russian equipment from Russian plans with substantial Russian components, Communist China now is independently able to design many items. The rapid development of machine industries in relation to other industries and services created imbalances in product demand and raw material availability which led to production cutbacks and under-utilization of capacity in a number of machine building industries in 1957 (e.g., trucks, locomotives, freight cars, machine tools, and agricultural and textile machinery).

A6. *Iron and Steel.* During the past five years, pig iron output increased from 1.9 million tons to 5.9 million tons and crude steel rose from 1.35 million tons to 5.24 million tons. Increased production was obtained mainly through the development of existing facilities, but in the next five years the plan is to establish new iron and steel bases and to improve facilities to provide an increased variety of steels. Construction is under-way on two large integrated plants, one at Pao-t'ou and one at Wuhan, and on some 25 small and medium size non-integrated plants based on nearby coal and ore deposits.

A7. *Non-Ferrous Metals.* China has become self-sufficient in most non-ferrous metals, with exports of these commodities increasing.

A significant aspect of non-ferrous mineral production has been the rapid development of the aluminum industry which will support aircraft production and provide a partial substitute for copper. Further development of non-ferrous metal production is planned, with particular emphasis on the expansion of copper output, presently inadequate in the Bloc.

A8. *Chemicals.* Production in the chemical industry tripled during the Five Year Plan. Important commodities now produced in China include basic industrial chemicals, chemical fertilizers, insecticides, antibiotics, plastics, and organic synthesized dyestuffs. However, the industry still is far from meeting the needs of agriculture and other industries in either volume or variety of products. Development of the chemical industry during the Second Five Year Plan appears to have a high priority. As an integral part of the drive to solve China's pressing agricultural production problem, the chemical fertilizer industry is to be developed as fast as possible and, to aid the tight situation in the supply of raw cotton, the synthetic fiber industry is also to be emphasized.

A9. *Petroleum.* Production of crude oil, although underfulfilling the Plan goal by some 25 percent, still achieved the high growth rate of 230 percent during the Plan period. Development of existing and new producing fields, and construction of new processing and transport facilities during the Plan, have laid the groundwork for future large increases in production. However, the Chinese Communists are planning large-scale investment in high cost production of oil from shale and coal, suggesting that they are pessimistic over the potential crude oil output. Whatever the increase in production that is achieved, it will almost certainly be insufficient to meet the increased requirements for petroleum products, and Communist China will remain heavily dependent upon imports.

A10. *Coal.* Coal production nearly doubled during the First Five Year Plan and generally kept pace with industrial and power requirements. However, urban and rural household demand increased faster than anticipated and the regime was forced to introduce rationing

SECRET   ANNEX A

in 1956 and 1957. Increased emphasis on small and medium size workings should help to meet the increasing demand for household use.

A11. *Light Industry.* Light industry, although becoming more diversified, progressed much more slowly than heavy industry during the First Five Year Plan, although most production goals were attained. Most increases in light industry production during the First Five Year Plan came from a greater utilization of existing facilities. Although additional capacity has been developed in the cotton textile industry, there has been considerable under-utilization of capacity during the last three years because of shortages of raw materials.

A12. *Regional Dispersion of Industry.* The Chinese Communists plan a more balanced distribution of economic activity throughout the territory of China within a period of three Five Year Plans (1953-1967). But they made relatively little headway toward this goal during the First Five Year Plan. There was an even greater concentration of industrial production in the old industrial areas as a result of reconstruction of existing industrial plant and of building of new industry in these areas. New construction was apparently guided largely by the fact that these areas have known sources of raw materials and fuel, developed transportation facilities, and a supply of skilled labor. More than 80 percent of total investment in China's iron and steel industry was allocated to northeast China during the Plan and half of the 156 industrial projects carried out with Soviet aid are being located in this one region.

A13. *Transportation.* Despite recurrent traffic congestion, the transport system has been able to support the growth of the economy. The transportation system has been utilized at close to capacity, and all branches of the sector have experienced high growth rates. The railroads have been primarily responsible for the support of the industrial sector but the other types of carriers are increasing their proportionate share of the load. The following tabulation of estimated total freight ton-kilometers carried exclude inland and coastal junks and carts and pack animals:

TABLE II

	1952 (Billion ton kilometers)	%	1957 (Billion ton kilometers)	%
Railroads	60.2	86.6	134.6	81.5
Roads	.678	1.0	3.79	2.3
Inland Waterways	3.64	5.2	15.7	9.5
Coastal Shipping	5.0	7.2	11.1	6.7
TOTAL	69.518	100	165.19	100

A14. By domestic merchant ship construction and acquisition from Poland and elsewhere, the Chinese Communists are continuing to expand their shipping fleet at a substantial rate. The Chinese Communists probably intend not only to expand their coastal merchant marine operation, but also to enter to a limited extent into the carriage of their international trade, especially with other Asian countries. The regime is also apparently planning an expansion of Yangtze River traffic and Yellow Sea coastal shipping to relieve strain on the railroads.

A15. Chinese Communists now have a civil air system which provides direct connections between Peiping and most of the major cities. The Chinese Communists have made considerable investment in civil aviation and there has been an almost complete modernization and changeover of planes and equipment. During the next five years, the network will probably be expanded to include the other major cities, but the goal of a nation-wide air network is not expected to be reached until the third Five-Year Plan.

A16. During the first four years of the First Five Year Plan emphasis was placed on building new rail lines, particularly in the West and Northwest. (See map.) The rail line to the Soviet Union through Sinkiang province has progressed beyond Yu-men, the area which contains the largest proved indigenous source of crude oil. The trans-Mongolian line to the Soviet Union has been completed, which in addition to providing a shorter rail connection between China proper and the European USSR, has permitted an increase in Chinese economic relations with Outer Mongolia. Another portion of the future north-south

SECRET   24

trunk line in the west has been completed between Pao-chi, on the Lanchow line, and Cheng-tu in Szechwan Province. The regime also completed the strategic rail line from Ying-tan (on the rail line between Shanghai and Changsha) to the east coast port of Amoy. However, the regime was forced to curtail work in 1957 on new lines and to put emphasis on repairing and increasing the capacity of existing lines in the high density use sectors in the North and Northeast. In part, this was done to alleviate the critical tie-ups which had developed in certain sections of the system in 1956, and in part because of the necessity generally to reduce investment spending in 1957.

A17. The supporting role of native transport in China remains very important. A recent article by the Minister of River Fleet of the Soviet Union, reporting on his inspection of Chinese inland waterways, presents a percentage breakdown of freight carried by all of the various types of transport in 1956:

TABLE III

	Tons carried	Ton/km
Railroads	33.0	78.7
Inland Waterways		
Modern Ships	4.7	8.5
Native Ships	9.9	3.6
Coastal Shipping	1.5	5.7
Motor Vehicles	10.7	2.3
Carts and Pack Animals	40.2	1.2
TOTAL	100.0	100.0

This table emphasizes the important part junks, carts, and pack animals play in short-haul local movement of goods. Such transport in 1956 carried over 50 percent of the freight tonnage, but less than 5 percent of the ton-kilometers.

Agricultural Production

A18. During the First Five Year Plan, we estimate the output of food rose 10 percent[1] to 185 million tons grain equivalent, with grain crop area increasing about 3 percent (including double cropping) and per hectare yields rising about 7 percent. Cotton production in-

[1] The official Chinese Communist figure is 20 percent, which we believe overstates the actual rate of growth.

creased by about 25 percent, with the area planted in cotton expanding by about 3 percent and the yields per hectare increasing by about 22 percent.

A19. The main factor to which this agricultural expansion is credited has been the mobilization of idle and underemployed rural labor for increased cultivation work and land improvements, which was accelerated after collectivization. Irrigated land reportedly increased by one-fifth to 37,000,000 hectares, and extensive flood control and soil conservation measures were undertaken. In addition, chemical fertilizer supplies were raised from 333,000 tons to a peak of 2,000,000 tons in 1956, providing a small but important addition to soil fertility. Rural coal supplies were more than tripled to a peak of over 25,000,000 tons in 1956, permitting greater use of straw and other by-products as feed and fertilizer. Improved seeds were developed and by 1957 were reportedly sown on 40 percent of the grain acreage, 80 percent of the cotton acreage, and 30 percent of the oil seed acreage. There has also been an increase in the supply of farm tools, and some progress was made in controlling crop pests.

A20. The growth of agricultural production was adversely affected in certain respects by the collectivization of the peasants. It upset the production and market organization in the farm areas and reduced the production of certain subsidiary products. Moreover, there has been a sharp decline in draft animal power per crop hectare, due to an increase in the acreage under cultivation without a corresponding increase in draft animals, and to the lack of care given them by the collectives.

A21. The Chinese Communists have had considerable difficulty in raising livestock production. Cattle are the major source of draft power on China's farms and hogs are the major source of meat in the diet of the population. Official concern has been great, but planned increases have not been realized. Although the number of hogs increased from a low of 84 million in 1956 to 114 million in mid-1957, it still fell short of the 1957 target of 138 million.

Foreign Trade and Economic Relations

A22. Foreign trade has been an important factor in Communist China's First Five Year Plan, and has supplied important quantities of military equipment, capital goods, and essential raw materials. To obtain the necessary imports, the foreign trade policy was to expand exports as rapidly as possible in order to finance a greater volume of imports, and to limit imports to essential commodities. During the period 1953 to 1957, balance of payments pressures increased, reflecting the cessation of Soviet loans, a rise in foreign debt service, continuing high foreign-aid commitments, and declining receipts from foreign expenditures in China and from Overseas Chinese remittances. As a result, although exports approximately doubled between 1952 and 1957, imports rose by only a third. Trade with the Bloc accounted for about 78 percent of total trade.

A23. Imports during this period totalled almost 25.2 billion yuan. Of this total, approximately 3.2 billion yuan was financed by Soviet credits — military credits accounted for 2.2 billion yuan, or roughly 9 percent of total imports, and economic credits accounted for about 1 billion yuan, or 4 percent of total imports. The composition of imports is estimated approximately as follows: machinery and equipment (including military equipment), 60 percent; raw materials, 30 percent; and consumer goods, 10 percent.

A24. Exports are estimated at approximately 23.3 billion yuan during 1953–1957. Agricultural products and products processed from agricultural raw materials accounted for about 75 percent of total exports, with exports of mining products, machines, and industrial products contributing the remaining 25 percent. The small decline in exports in 1956–1957, which apparently caused the Chinese Communists to decrease imports in some degree in 1957, was partially due to a drop in exports of foodstuffs, exports which largely would have gone to the USSR.

Population, Manpower, and Consumption

A25. According to the Chinese Communists, the population of China at the end of 1957 was 640 million, compared to about 575 million at the end of 1952. It was not until about 1956 that recognition of the dangerously narrow margin between the rates of growth of agricultural output and population caused Communist China's leaders to change their doctrinal outlook from one of pride in greater population to the need for population control. They are now developing programs to reduce the birth rate. We expect population growth rate to level off at about 2.0 to 2.5 percent. At this rate the population in 1962 would be about 706–724 million and, by 1967, 780–818 million. In any event, the population increase during the Second Plan period will continue to press heavily on the supply of food and consumer goods.

A26. This population growth not only poses a problem of food supply but also the problem of maintaining full employment with equitable income distribution. The employment category of factory workers and office staff — the only category open to major percentage increase — is still limited to 24 million, and only 5.2 million persons were added to these categories during the First Five Year Plan against a total population increase of 65 million. The Communists have evidenced awareness of their growing employment problem and have plans to use more investment funds on projects which maximize employment. Various steps have been taken to stiffen the policy preventing peasant migration into the cities and even to transfer large numbers of present urban residents back to the countryside. The latter policies will serve to lower average income of the rural population but will not increase agricultural output since rural labor is already excessive.

Scientific Development

A27. During the past year Communist China has reemphasized its policy of vigorous development of scientific research. Although there was retrenchment in most other fields in 1957, the Chinese Academy of Sciences budget was raised one third, and it established over a dozen new research institutes and laboratories. Such emphasis has also been expressed in organizational changes, expansion, and in

SECRET   ANNEX A

revised policies in higher education and training of researchers. However, the amount of significant research work continues to be small. Scientific manpower resources have improved only slightly, and the regime has acknowledged that educational policies have not produced sufficient numbers of graduates qualified for advanced scientific training.

A28. Educational policies in higher education have been revised to place more emphasis on quality. Curricula are expected to be redesigned to provide a broader and more fundamental education rather than the present highly specialized type. The Chinese Academy of Sciences sent 129 students to the USSR in 1956. In addition, the Ministry of Higher Education sent about 500 post-graduates last year, of whom perhaps 200 may be trained as potential researchers.

A29. Training programs in the Academy of Sciences, the universities, and the USSR will probably expand gradually so as to produce by the end of the estimate period some 3,000–4,000 new people with potential for being productive in scientific research and development. This gradual expansion would double

the number now believed to be of research and development caliber. Highly competent scientists will, however, emerge much more slowly; the present estimate is that only a few hundred will be added by 1962 to the less than 1000 now available.

A30. We believe that a transition period has now arrived in which the utilization of Communist China's scientific resources in support of economic and military development will gradually change. Whereas the scientific effort is now concerned with low-level industrial testing, trouble shooting, and assimilation of imported foreign technology, we expect that Communist China's developmental capability by 1962 will be compatible with the level of its imported foreign technological processes. This work will be concentrated in the applied fields listed in the 12-year plan for research and development: nuclear energy, electronics, metallurgy, power, etc. By 1962 we may also expect some basic research results which will go somewhat beyond the backlog of research experience brought back by Chinese scientists from Western laboratories.

SECRET   27

SECRET

ANNEX B

COMMUNIST CHINA'S MILITARY ESTABLISHMENT

A. Ground Forces

B1. During the period 1955–1957 Communist China's system of internal military regions was reorganized to provide twelve, rather than the previous six regions, and to orient them strategically and functionally to present day requirements. This represents a considerable improvement in the administrative and command structure. Also during the past year there has been a trend toward creating a better balanced army through an increase in the proportion of support units to infantry units. There are continued indications of a possible shift in tactical doctrine to meet problems of modern military operations. For example, continuing atomic and some chemical warfare exercises emphasize individual and unit protective measures similar to those of the Soviet army, and there appears to be increasing emphasis on mobility and dispersion and somewhat decreased emphasis on the offensive doctrine of mass attack. It is unlikely that there is any significant degree of operational integration or coordination between the Soviet and Chinese ground command except in the logistical fields, where it is required because of Communist China's continued dependence on the Soviet Union for much of its military equipment.

B2. In January 1958, about 26 percent of Communist China's ground force strength was in Korea and Manchuria, 23 percent in the area bounded by Shanghai, Hankow, Canton, and the coast, and about 17 percent in the north China plain area. The remainder provided coastal defense in the areas north of Shanghai and south of Canton or was disposed in the central, western and northwestern areas as internal and border security forces. This general deployment represented little change from that of the previous year. (See map.)

B3. However, in February the Chinese Communists announced their intention to withdraw all their forces from North Korea by the end of 1958. Two armies have already been withdrawn, and it appears probable that the remaining forces, which include three armies and total about 200,000 men, will be withdrawn in 1958 as announced. A survey of present troop dispositions indicates south and central China as feasible locations for at least part of the forces withdrawn. Strategic considerations suggest the probable retention of a significant part of the force in north and northeast China. However, there is no firm evidence as to where withdrawing forces will actually be stationed. Although immediate Communist defensive capabilities in Korea are weakened by the withdrawal of Chinese Communist troops, the speed with which forces in Korea could be reinforced from China leaves the relative capabilities of UN and Communist forces in Korea essentially unchanged.

B4. There has been a considerable turnover of ground force personnel as older and physically unfit men have been replaced by conscripts. The military Service Law of 1955 provides for a three-year term of service under the military conscription system and the establishment of a reserve. The ground force enlisted personnel, with the exception of a nucleus of non-commissioned officers, now consists of selected conscripts, who are trained in modern warfare with modern weapons. The training cycle begins with basic training in the spring and appears to progress to regimental and divisional size maneuvers by the following winter. The service school system for officers and non-commissioned officers appears to be concentrating on retraining in the refinements of modern warfare. Higher-level staff colleges are also in operation and both junior and senior officers may be detailed to

SECRET

28

SECRET
ANNEX B

TABLE IV

THE CHINESE COMMUNIST GROUND FORCES

	Units	Estimated Strength
		2,575,000 Total
Armies	36	47,900 each
Divisions		
Infantry	114	14,900 each
3 Infantry Regiments		
1 Artillery Regiment		
24 light & medium field artillery pieces		
12 medium mortars		
1 AA battalion		
12 light AA pieces		
12 AA machine guns		
1 AT battalion		
12x57-mm AT guns		
*1 tank-assault gun regiment		
32 medium tanks		
12 self-propelled assault guns		
—Support units		
Armored	3	6,600 each
80 medium tanks		
10 heavy tanks		
8 self-prop guns		
Parachute	1 (possibly 3)	7,000 each
Cavalry	3	5,000 each
Artillery		
Field Artillery	13	5,500 each
108 pieces up to 152-mm		
Rocket launcher	2	3,300 each
72x132-mm multiple rocket launchers		
Anti-tank	3	3,400 each
72 AT guns		
Anti-aircraft	6	4,800 each
108 light & medium guns		
Public Security	20	7,000 each

* To date only 28 of the 114 infantry divisions are believed to have the tank-assault gun regiment.

(In addition, the ground forces are believed to include a number of public security and artillery divisions not yet identified, and approximately 68 independent regiments including artillery, engineer, motor transport, and public security.)

appropriate military schools in the Soviet Union. The reserve includes conscripts who have completed their military service, graduates of reserve training programs in the high schools and universities, and officers released from active duty. After 1958, the reserve will contain at all times about two million men who have had active military service within the previous three years. The Chinese Communists are probably capable of effectively and rapidly mobilizing this reserve for active duty.

B. Air Forces

B5. Communist China's air arm is heavily dependent upon the Soviet Union for planes, equipment, supplies and training. Consequently, its tactical doctrines and command and logistic relation closely resemble those of the Soviet Union. The air force and the naval air force constitute a reasonably developed and improving air arm. Their personnel are young and vigorous. Morale is high. The air forces are organized into bomber, fighter, attack, and transport units which could operate

SECRET
29

ANNEX B

from many points on Communist China's periphery. The Chinese Communists now have 104 airfields suitable for jet operations and 285 other bases. They have developed a reconnaissance capability, at least in the photographic field. In equipment, training, and deployment, the air forces are oriented toward defensive and tactical operations.

B6. The Chinese Communist air defense is concentrated in areas containing major military and industrial targets, with the Shanghai area the most heavily defended. They have a radar system with a central control, which covers the entire coast as well as these major centers. This system provides a fair to good capability to detect penetration of coastal and major target areas, except by aircraft at low altitudes: however there are still some areas not adequately covered by GCI. Air interception capability is hampered by a shortage of adequate GCI radars, by a serious shortage of airborne intercept equipment, by inadequate pilot experience in night and all-weather flying, and by only fair but improving standards in ground controlled interception procedures. (See map.)

B7. The air arm is gradually increasing in size and converting rapidly to jet aircraft. During the past year, the total number of aircraft increased by 475 and the number of jets increased by 540. Piston fighters will probably be phased out entirely by the end of 1958 and we estimate that by 1962 the Chinese Communists will have about 2,900 jet fighters. By mid-1959 piston light bombers will probably be completely replaced. The piston medium bombers will probably increase to about 60 by 1961, and by 1962 the Chinese Communists may have a few jet medium bombers. Communist Chinese air interception capability will improve during the next five years as the programs are carried out to improve communications, to acquire additional high altitude GCI, and to develop further their all-weather interception capabilities. However, the effectiveness of Communist China's air defenses could still be substantially reduced by well planned and coordinated multiple attacks, and by electronic countermeasures. Air force ability to support ground operations is being enhanced through operational train-

ing. Operational effectiveness of the bomber force is reduced by such factors as electronic equipment of limited capability, which under other than visual or ideal radar conditions affects bombing accuracy, and by the lack of combat experience.

TABLE V

THE CHINESE COMMUNIST AIR ARM

A. Air Force

	Jets		Non-Jets
Total Personnel 79,000			
Fighters	1,300		35
Attack, fighter	180		70
Light bomber	230		165
Medium bombers	—		20
Transport	—		170
Helicopter, large	—		30
Reconnaissance	30	(5 light	—
Utility/Liaison	—	bomber; 25	65
Trainer, fighter	115	fighters)	—
TOTAL	1,855		555
TOTAL AIR FORCE	2,410		

B. Naval Air Force

	Jets	Non-Jets
Total Personnel 8,000		
Fighter	200	—
Light bomber	205	—
Transport	—	20
Helicopter, large	—	10
Reconnaissance, lgt bomber	5	10
Utility/Liaison	—	5
Trainer, fighter	15	—
TOTAL	425	45
TOTAL NAVAL AIR FORCE	470	
TOTAL AIRCRAFT ALL TYPES	2,880	

C. Navy

B8. The principal strength of the Chinese Communist Navy consists of four destroyers and 16 submarines. All of these vessels, with the exception of three submarines assembled in China, were transferred from the Soviet navy during 1954–1955. Large-scale exercises, including anti-submarine and probably amphibious operations, have been held in the Yellow Sea. During 1957, units of the fleet were at sea more often and for longer periods of time than previously, indicating a probable increase in operating effectiveness. Rocket

SECRET
ANNEX B

installations on landing craft have been confirmed, and there is evidence that training in atomic, biological and chemical warfare has been initiated.

B9. Communist China has begun a significant shipbuilding program with large-scale technical assistance from the Soviet Union. At first, component sections prefabricated in the Soviet Union were assembled in Chinese shipyards; however, increasing numbers of component parts are being produced in China, including propulsion equipment, steel plates, and electronic gear. Five classes of new ship construction, all based on basic Soviet designs, have been identified. By far the largest and most important of these ships are the "W" class submarines (SS) and the "Riga" class escort vessels (DE). Other identified new construction includes "Kronstadt". class submarine chasers (PC), T-43 class fleet minesweepers (MSF), and "P-6"

class motor torpedo boats (PT). Nearly all of this new construction is concentrated in the Shanghai shipbuilding complex. The only known naval shipbuilding outside of the Shanghai area is submarine chaser construction at Whampoa and possible PT boat construction at Wuchang on the Yangtze River and Whampoa. In addition, the Chinese shipyards are rapidly increasing the numbers and size of merchant ships under construction.

TABLE VI

THE CHINESE COMMUNIST NAVY *

Officers and men	55,000	(includes 8,000 naval air)
Destroyers	4	
Submarines	16	
Patrol	216	(including 110 PT's, 4 DE, and 25 PC)
Mine warfare	31	
Amphibians	54	

* For naval air strength see Table V.

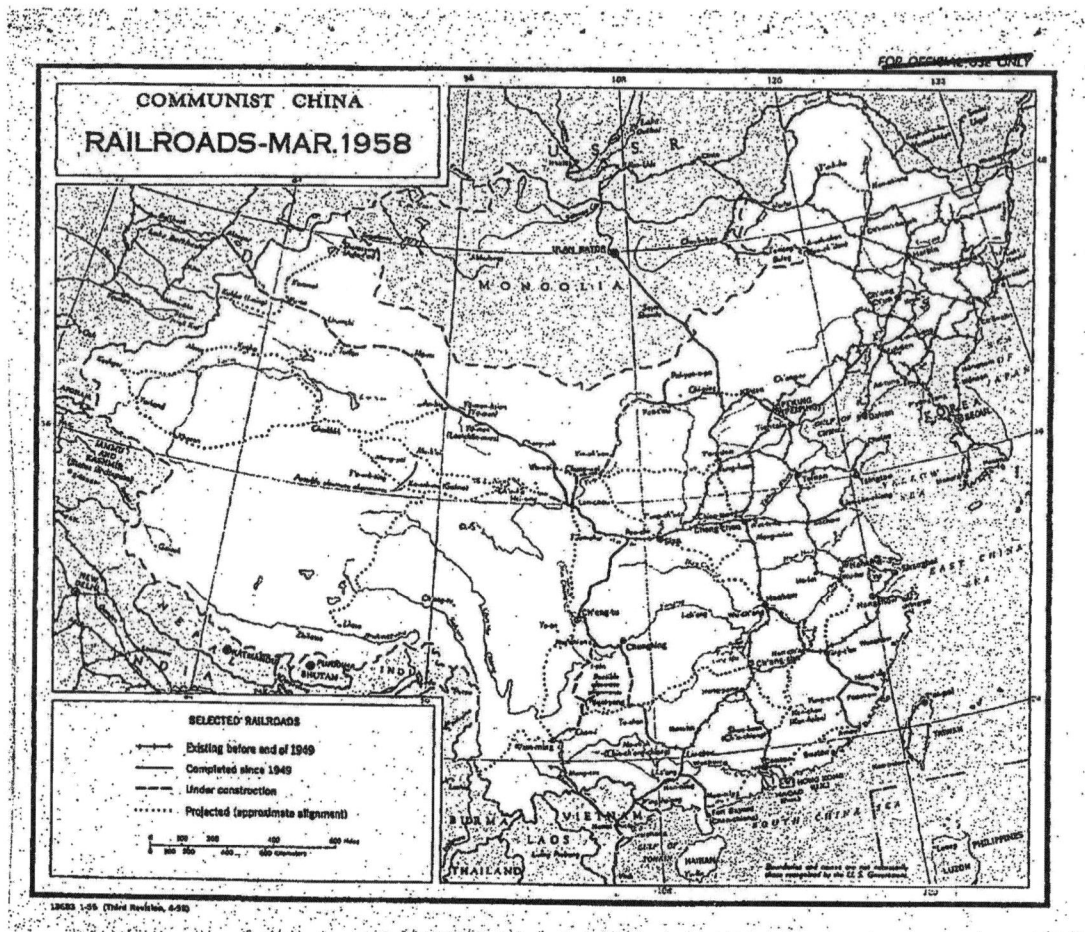

COMMUNIST CHINA
AIR DEFENSE DISTRICTS and
DISPOSITION OF COMBAT JET AIRCRAFT

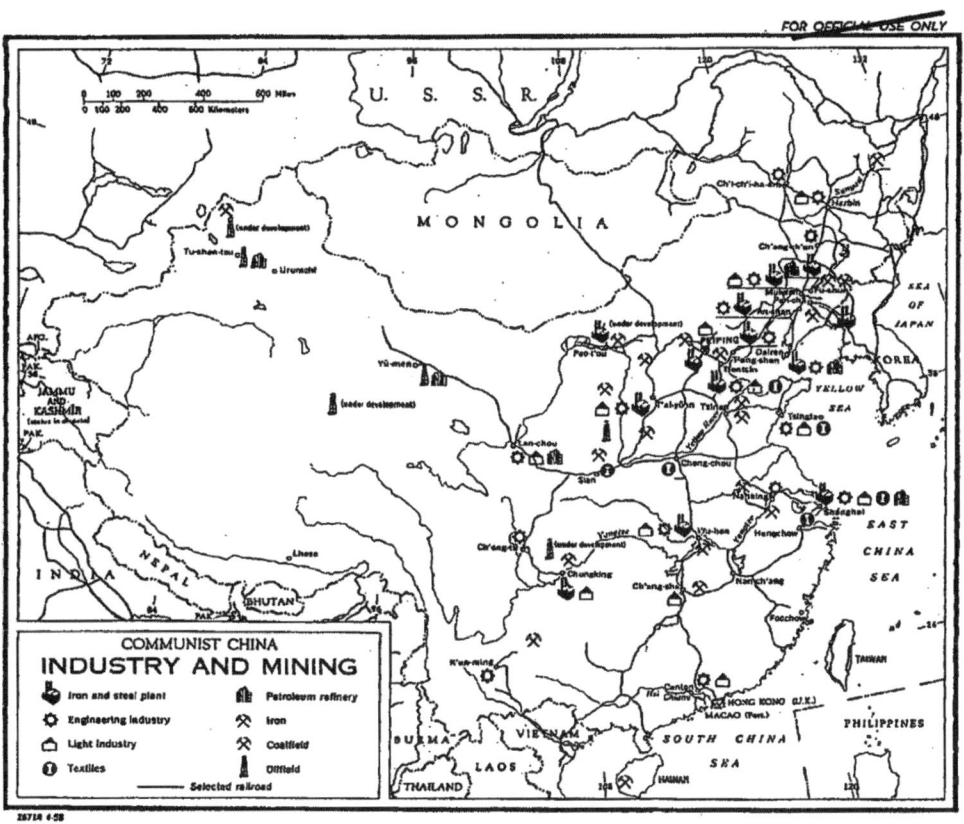

SECTION 12

SNIE 100-9-58

Probable Developments
in the Taiwan Strait Area

26 August 1958

APPROVED FOR RELEASE
DATE: MAY 2004

SNIE 100-9-58
26 August 1958

~~SECRET~~

N.º 342

SPECIAL

NATIONAL INTELLIGENCE ESTIMATE

NUMBER 100-9-58

PROBABLE DEVELOPMENTS IN THE TAIWAN STRAIT AREA

Submitted by the

DIRECTOR OF CENTRAL INTELLIGENCE

The following intelligence organizations participated in the preparation of this estimate: The Central Intelligence Agency and the intelligence organizations of the Departments of State, the Army, the Navy, the Air Force, and The Joint Staff.

Concurred in by the

INTELLIGENCE ADVISORY COMMITTEE

on 26 August 1958. Concurring were The Director of Intelligence and Research, Department of State; the Assistant Chief of Staff for Intelligence, Department of the Army; the Director of Naval Intelligence; the Assistant Chief of Staff, Intelligence, USAF; and the Deputy Director for Intelligence, The Joint Staff. The Atomic Energy Commission Representative to the IAC and the Assistant Director, Federal Bureau of Investigation, abstained, the subject being outside of their jurisdiction.

~~SECRET~~

SECRET

PROBABLE DEVELOPMENTS IN THE TAIWAN STRAIT AREA

THE PROBLEM

To estimate probable developments in the Taiwan Strait area over the next few months, with particular reference to (a) Chinese Communist capabilities, (b) Chinese Communist courses of action, (c) Chinese Nationalist courses of action, and (d) Chinese Communist reactions to Chinese Nationalist and/or US measures to maintain control of the Nationalist-held offshore islands.

CONCLUSIONS

1. We believe that Communist China's principal purpose in stepping up its military pressures in the Taiwan Strait area is to test the intentions of the US and of the Republic of China (GRC) with respect to the offshore islands. Communist China probably expects that the resultant increase in tensions will also increase pressures for its participation in world decisions, arrest any drift toward acceptance of a *de facto* "two Chinas" situation, and, especially if the US should seem reluctant to take strong measures to hold the offshore islands, accelerate the erosion of Nationalist morale. *(Paras. 13–18)*

2. In view of US commitments to defend Taiwan and our estimate that neither Communist China nor the USSR is willing to risk a major war at present, we believe that Communist China will not attempt to seize Taiwan or the Penghus during the next six months at least. *(Para. 19)*

3. Although Communist China might risk a sudden assault upon the major offshore islands, we believe it more likely that it will not attempt to do so in the immediate future, because of its fear of possible US intervention. Communist China will probably continue to exert military pressures against the Chin-men (Quemoy) and Matsu groups, seeking to avoid a clear point of military showdown. Depending on US reactions, these pressures could include intensive and sustained artillery harassment of Chin-men (Quemoy), aggressive air and naval action in the Strait area, provocative overflights of Taiwan, seizure of lightly-defended offshore islands, and a serious effort to interdict supply of the Chin-mens and Matsus. If US reactions to these pressures should lead the Chinese Communists to believe that the US would not intervene, they would probably then attempt to seize Chin-men or Matsu, or both. *(Paras. 20–24)*

SECRET

1

SECRET

2

4. If opposed only by Chinese Nationalist forces, the Chinese Communists have the capability to deny the Taiwan Strait to the Chinese Nationalist air force, interdict supply of the offshore islands, or seize these islands. Timely warning might not be available that preparations had been completed for an assault on either the Chin-men or the Matsu groups. *(Para. 10)*

5. We believe that the Chinese Communists will not be deterred from increasing their military pressures by US moves which stop short of either an explicit guarantee of the offshore islands or the commitment of US air or naval forces at least to the protection of the supply of these islands. However, if the US gave an explicit guarantee or committed its forces to the defense of the major offshore islands, the Chinese Communists would probably not attempt to seize those islands or interdict their supply. *(Paras. 32-33)*

6. Nevertheless, Communist China's activation of its coastal airfields and aggressive attempts to deny its airspace to overflights are probably here to stay, regardless of Chinese Nationalist and US actions. To a somewhat lesser degree, so are Chinese Communist air sorties and other probing actions in the Taiwan Strait area. *(Para. 31)*

7. The Chinese Nationalists will probably not resort to unilateral action against the mainland so long as Chinese Communist pressures stop short of a heavy and sustained air or artillery bombardment of the offshore islands, or a determined effort to interdict supply of Chin-men or Matsu. Should the Chinese Communists take such steps, the chances are better than even that the Nationalists would take whatever military action they could against the mainland. They might then bomb mainland targets, even in the face of explicit US objections. *(Paras. 28-29)*

DISCUSSION[1]

I. INTRODUCTION

8. In recent weeks, the Chinese Communists have suddenly stepped up military pressures in the Taiwan Strait area after more than two years of relative quiescence. Following a temporary burst of propaganda during the latter part of July reemphasizing the liberate Taiwan theme, they progressively activated six of the seven jet airfields in the Foochow-

[1]See NIE 100-5-56: "Chinese Communist Capabilities in the Taiwan Strait Area and Probable Courses of Action over the Next Six Months" of 22 May 1956. For data and analysis concerning Communist China's overall military strength, see also NIE 13-58: "Communist China" of 13 May 1958. See also SNIE 100-7-58 (Limited Distribution)

Swatow area which were rushed to completion in 1956 but not made operational until now. At present approximately 200 jet fighters are based on these fields. Several air engagements with Chinese Nationalist aircraft have followed from the increased frequency and strength of Communist air patrols along the coastal area. In the last few days, there have been aggressive Chinese Communist naval actions in the Strait, intensive artillery bombardments of the Chin-men (Quemoy) group, and air action in the immediate vicinity of Chin-men. Chinese Nationalist officials, worried over the possible threat these actions pose to the security and position of the Republic of China (GRC), are seeking additional US commitments.

SECRET

SECRET   3

9. The heightened tension in the Taiwan Strait coincided with the Middle East crisis and the recent meeting in Peiping between Khrushchev and Mao and their defense ministers. Furthermore, Communist China's actions in the Strait must be considered against the background of the belligerent tone of its statements during the past year concerning world policy in general. These developments present major questions, discussed below, concerning Chinese Communist intentions, Chinese Nationalist intentions, and the likelihood of expanded hostilities in the Taiwan Strait area.

II. CHINESE COMMUNIST CAPABILITIES [2]

10. Assuming a situation in which the Nationalists continue to receive US military supplies (possibly in increased amounts), but have the responsibility for the delivery of supplies and reinforcements to the offshore islands and for their actual defense, the Chinese Communists have the following capabilities:

(a) The Chinese Communist Air Force (CCAF) could establish and maintain air superiority over the Nationalist air force in the area of the Taiwan Strait. Through the combined use of artillery, air, and naval forces, the Communists could interdict the supply of Nationalist garrisons on the offshore islands.

(b) The Chinese Communists could seize any of the smaller, lightly-defended offshore islands with the forces they now have in place. An assault on these islands could be launched quickly and probably without prior detection.

(c) The Chinese Communists have had for several years sufficient ground forces in the Foochow area (estimated 48,000) to seize Matsu. Little redeployment of naval forces would be required to support such an assault. A successful assault on Chin-men would probably require a minimum of 200,000 troops. About 80,000 are estimated to be in the Amoy area opposite Chin-men, and additional troops

[2] See Annex for Chinese Communist and Chinese Nationalist military strengths and capabilities in the Taiwan Strait area.

could be moved in quickly, possibly without detection. Considerable artillery to provide cover for an assault is already emplaced. Little, if any, further aircraft redeployment would be necessary to make possible bombing operations with fighter cover, or jet close support. Sufficient improvised lift could readily be assembled for an assault against either island group. Timely warning might not be available that final preparations for either operation had been completed.

11. The Chinese Communists have the ability to organize, launch, and support logistically a large-scale assault against Taiwan or the Penghus. Before undertaking such an operation, they would have to stockpile additional materiel in the vicinity of embarkation points, deploy additional troops to East China, and concentrate most of the required troops in the vicinity of the embarkation points. They would have to concentrate the bulk of their naval and amphibious strength in the area between Shanghai and Canton. Activation of additional airfields near the coast would not be necessary. The initial bombing of Taiwan preceding an assault would probably be launched without redeploying bombers. The preparations for a major assault on Taiwan probably could be identified, at least in their later stages. In view of the US commitment to defend Taiwan and the Penghus, we have not attempted an assessment of the outcome of such an assault.

III. PROBABLE CHINESE COMMUNIST INTENTIONS

A. Chinese Communist Motives

12. As part of their basic and continuing objectives, the Chinese Communists seek to eliminate the GRC as a rival and extend their control to Taiwan. Their efforts to accomplish this objective in the past have included military pressures against the offshore islands and psychological pressures directed at Taiwan. To date these efforts have been stymied by US commitments to the GRC — explicit and implicit — which have faced the Chinese Communists with unacceptable risks in the military field and which have served to main-

SECRET

SECRET

4

tain Nationalist morale and will to resist at a sufficiently high level to limit the impact of Chinese Communist threats and inducements.

13. The Chinese Communists probably have become more impatient and frustrated as the passage of time has failed to visibly advance them toward their goal of ending the existence of the GRC. Over the past two years their tactics have failed to stimulate defection on Taiwan, or to prevent wider international acceptance of a *de facto* "two China" situation. They have also failed to displace the GRC as the representative of China in the UN or to gain the participation of Peiping in world decisions.

14. Thus, the Chinese Communists probably feel that a period of tension in the Taiwan Strait would be useful in reminding the world of Peiping's strength and determination to achieve its objectives. Beyond this, they probably believe that world trends and the passage of time have brought some weakening in Nationalist morale and determination, and they may hope that the US has become less resolved to assist in the defense of the offshore islands. They have probably set out to test these propositions and may view the occupation of the coastal airfields as a significant first step, since the Nationalists had openly threatened in 1956 to retaliate if such a move took place.

15. Broader considerations may also be influencing the Chinese Communists in the present situation. In recent months Chinese Communist leaders and their propaganda have indicated impatience with some of the results of the general Bloc line of peaceful coexistence. The Chinese Communists have argued that the present world balance of power is highly favorable to the Bloc, that the West is a "paper tiger," that the Bloc could destroy the West in nuclear warfare without receiving mortal damage, and that the present world situation is one of "revolutionary opportunity" for the expansion of Bloc influence. We do not suggest that the Chinese Communists are now prepared to push the Bloc into general war or that the Chinese Communists are urging this policy on Moscow. However, we do believe that the Chinese Commu-

nists now rate the risks involved in local wars to be somewhat less than they did immediately prior to the sputnik era. We also believe that they are less sensitive than previously to opinion in the Free World, less concerned to maintain a peaceful pose, and more inclined to seek to gain their ends by reminders of their growing power.

16. A desire to discuss Taiwan Strait problems was probably responsible in part for the recent meeting of Khrushchev and Mao. In addition, Chinese Communist uneasiness regarding Khrushchev's fast footwork toward a summit meeting may also have been a factor. In any event, it is almost certain that both partners felt that the pace of world developments required closer coordination of their policies. Moreover, they probably reached new agreements concerning the nature and extent of future military cooperation, possibly including missiles and nuclear weapons.

17. The USSR probably has no objection to the heightening of tension in the Taiwan Strait; indeed it may consider this development as serving its interests. We believe that the USSR and Communist China are in general agreement on policy in the Taiwan Strait. However, if the Chinese Communists were to adopt courses of action involving substantial risk of a major military clash with US forces, the USSR would almost certainly seek to restrain Peiping.

18. We believe that Peiping will continue for some time to test US and GRC intentions and to maintain an atmosphere of tension. Chinese Communist leaders will not expect to quickly achieve their basic objectives by this course of action. However, they probably expect that a demonstration of their power will serve to undermine Nationalist morale, discredit talk of a "return to the mainland," and make some Nationalists more receptive to psychological pressures and inducements, particularly if the US should fail to give strong support to the Nationalists. Moreover, they probably hope that increased tensions in the Taiwan Strait will generate pressures for international meetings in which Communist China would be an indispensable participant.

SECRET

SECRET   5

B. Possible Chinese Communist Courses of Action

19. In view of US commitments to defend Taiwan and our estimate that neither Communist China nor the USSR is willing to risk a major war at present, we believe that Communist China will not attempt to seize Taiwan or the Penghus during the next six months at least.

20. The Chinese Communists might assault Chin-men or Matsu, or both, within the near future. They have the capability to seize the islands but are probably deterred because of their fear of possible US intervention. If the Chinese Communists were to attempt to seize these islands, they would probably strive for a quick military victory. This, they would probably estimate, would give the US too short a period for political countermeasures or for effective military intervention by non-nuclear means. The decision to launch such an attack would probably be based on an estimate that the US would not use nuclear weapons in defense of the offshore islands. Moreover, the Chinese Communists probably would estimate that, even if the US employed nuclear weapons, it would do so on a limited scale, and that the adverse international political and psychological consequences of any use of nuclear weapons would seriously damage the position of the US and work to the long-run advantage of Communist China.

21. However, we believe it more likely that the Chinese Communist plan is to apply a broad range of military and psychological pressures, designed so as to avoid a clear point of military showdown. These pressures will be intended to intensify the war of nerves in the Taiwan Strait and to test US intentions with respect to the offshore islands. If the US reaction to these pressures should lead the Chinese Communists to believe that the US would not intervene, they would probably then attempt to seize Chin-men or Matsu, or both.

22. Although the Chinese Communists may temporarily revert to lower levels of military pressures, we believe that they intend to expand their present level of military activity. They could do this by aggressive air action

seeking to deny the Strait area to Nationalist aircraft, by increased naval activity, and by intensive and sustained artillery harassment of the Chin-men island group. In this case, the Communists would probably intercept Nationalist patrols over the Taiwan Strait and conduct air raids on the offshore islands. They might conduct provocative overflights of Taiwan. These operations could result in accidental clashes with US aircraft operating in the area. Such levels of activity could lead to numerous air engagements with the Nationalists which, if continued, would cause serious attrition of the Nationalist air force, and increase considerably the sense of insecurity and uncertainty among Nationalist leaders and armed forces. The Communists might hope that the levels of activity would discourage the Nationalists and perhaps even lead them to evacuate the offshore islands.

23. Concurrent with such increased activity, and as a further step to test US intentions, the Chinese Communists might seize one or more of the lightly-defended offshore islands. This could be done quickly and with little or no prior warning. Such a development would have serious adverse psychological impact on the Nationalists generally, and especially those on the major offshore islands of Chin-men and Matsu. In determining the degree of risk involved, the Chinese Communists might make a distinction between those small islands often considered a part of the Chin-men and Matsu groups, and the more isolated islands.

24. The Chinese Communists might make a serious effort to interdict supply of the major offshore islands. If the Communists took this course of action they would probably estimate that they were running serious risk of US intervention, even though there had been no prior indications of explicit US intentions. The isolation of the offshore islands could be accomplished by a combination of air, artillery, and naval action. Artillery action alone could seriously hamper resupply of Chin-men. However, it would probably take two or three months of intensive effort to interdict supply of the offshore islands to the point where reserve stocks on these islands became criti-

SECRET

170

SECRET   6

cally low. In the event that the Chinese Communists had conducted interdiction operations against Chin-men and Matsu over a period of time without encountering a clear indication of US intention to defend these islands, we believe that they would probably then invade them if surrender did not seem imminent. The Nationalists do not have the capability to evacuate their garrisons in the face of Communist opposition.

IV. PROBABLE CHINESE NATIONALIST COURSES OF ACTION

25. Thus far, the Nationalist reaction to increased Communist pressures has been moderate. The Nationalists have reemphasized their determination to hold Chin-men and Matsu. They have challenged some Communist aircraft over the coastal area and have continued their reconnaissance effort. However, they have refrained from bombing the newly activated Communist airfields. They have increased their efforts to secure additional military aid and firmer defense commitments from the US.

26. The Chin-mens and Matsus have immense importance to the GRC. About one third of its combat troops are committed to their defense. These islands are a vital element in the Taiwan early warning system. They are also a symbol of GRC prestige. They sustain the hope of a return to the mainland, and some Nationalist officials may consider them instruments which might be used to embroil the US in war with Communist China. The GRC is probably convinced at present that it must hold Chin-men and Matsu in order to keep alive the hope of a return to the mainland, to prevent a disastrous blow to morale, to preclude any further decline in the prestige and international position of their government, and to assist in the defense of Taiwan.

27. We believe, therefore, that the loss of the offshore islands would under any circumstances have a severe effect on Nationalist morale. The impact of such a loss would be of the greatest severity if the US withheld its support and the Chinese Nationalist troops stationed on the islands were defeated by a Chinese Communist assault. The impact of

the loss would be of less severity if the troops were evacuated with US assistance. In any case, the Nationalist government, if it is to survive, would require new and convincing demonstrations that the US was still determined to protect Taiwan and to preserve the GRC's international position.

28. The major courses of action open to the Nationalists, without US participation, are very limited. The most important would be to launch air attacks against mainland targets. In view of Taiwan's vulnerability to retaliation, and in the absence of US approval, the Nationalist leaders probably will not resort to this course of action so long as Communist military pressures stop short of a heavy and sustained air or artillery bombardment of the offshore islands or of a determined effort to interdict supply of Chin-men or Matsu.

29. However, should the Chinese Communists take such steps, we believe that the chances are better than even that the Nationalist leaders would take whatever military action they could against the mainland. They might bomb the mainland even in the face of explicit US objections, with the expectation that the resulting situation would force the US to intervene.

V. PROBABLE CHINESE COMMUNIST REACTIONS TO CHINESE NATIONALIST AND/ OR US MEASURES TO MAINTAIN CONTROL OF THE OFFSHORE ISLANDS

30. The Chinese Communists probably hope that their military initiative in the Taiwan Strait can be conducted in such a way as to put the onus of aggressor on the US or the GRC for any counteraction they take. Communist China's leaders probably estimate that while their increased pressures will cause some world sympathy to develop for the plight of the beleaguered offshore islands, the predominant world reaction will be fear of war and a desire that the US take steps to lessen tensions and end a threat to peace. Peiping and Moscow probably conclude that any additional moves by the US to maintain Nationalist control of the offshore islands will tend to isolate the US diplomatically on this issue. Thus it should be anticipated that Bloc diplo-

SECRET

171

SECRET   7

macy and propaganda will seek international political gains from any such US moves; the greater the US commitment, the more vigorous the Communist political effort.

31. Communist China's activation of its coastal airfields and aggressive attempts to deny its air space to overflights are probably here to stay, regardless of Chinese Nationalist and US actions. To a somewhat lesser degree, so are Chinese Communist air sorties and other probing actions in the Taiwan Strait area. Thus, even though certain US/GRC reactions may cause the Chinese Communists to refrain from attempting to seize the offshore islands or interdict their supply, some Communist pressure will continue.

32. The Chinese Communists will probably not be deterred from increasing military pressures against the Nationalists by US moves which stop short of either an explicit guarantee of the offshore islands or the active commitment of US air or naval forces to protection of the supply of these islands. Although the Chinese Communists might become a lit-

tle more cautious, we do not believe that they would abandon their program of pressures as a result of lesser measures such as the more frequent appearance of US ships and aircraft in the area, the provision of improved weapons to the GRC, or the issuing of warnings in general terms to the Chinese Communists.

33. However, the Chinese Communists would probably not attempt to seize the major offshore islands or interdict their supply in the face of an explicit US guarantee or the active participation of US naval and air forces in the protection of these islands or their supply. We still think that the Chinese Communists wish to avoid large-scale clashes with US forces. Moreover, Moscow would probably be urging restraint on the Chinese Communists at this point. Nevertheless, there would be considerable risk of occasional clashes between US and Chinese Communist ships and aircraft. The possibility should not be excluded that such clashes might be invited in order to create an incident which could be brought before the UN or some other international forum.

SECRET

SECRET

8

ANNEX

CHINESE COMMUNIST AND CHINESE NATIONALIST MILITARY STRENGTHS AND CAPABILITIES IN THE TAIWAN STRAIT AREA

I. Chinese Communist Ground Forces

1. The Chinese Communists have an estimated 894,000 ground troops organized into 12 armies and supporting units in the Nanking, Foochow, and Canton military districts. Of these armies, all of which are probably first class units, three are stationed in the immediate Taiwan Strait area in the vicinity of Swatow, Amoy, and Foochow. The estimated strength of these armies is 46,000 each. Within the Foochow Military Region there are 11 combat divisions with a total strength of 107,300. In addition, there are 20 combat divisions in Nanking Military Region with a strength of 244,700 and 16 combat divisions in Canton Military Region with a strength of 223,000. We have no confirmed reports that additional units are being moved to the coastal areas. However, such troop movements could take place rapidly and possibly without detection.

2. The reorganization of the Chinese Communist Army, which has occurred since 1954, has given them a more balanced force which is better able to carry out a coordinated amphibious assault. In any amphibious assault against the offshore islands it is believed that the Chinese Communists would be capable of attaining at least a three to one numerical superiority, although they would not necessarily employ all such forces. The actual numerical size of the assault force would, of course, depend upon the particular objective attacked. The Communists would probably employ no more than a reinforced regiment against a lightly defended island such as Kaoteng (700 men). They would undoubtedly amass 200,000 men for an attack on Chinmen (Quemoy). Such forces would be capable of successful assault operations provided the Communists also had air and naval superiority in the area.

3. The Communists are estimated to have over 400 field artillery pieces in the Chin-men area, including at least 36 152-mm howitzers and/or gun/howitzers and 120 122-mm guns and/or howitzers. These weapons can completely cover Chin-men Island from positions around Amoy Harbor. Effective interdiction, however, is restricted by the extreme range and the limited number of pieces that can reach all targets on the island. Moreover, the Communists probably could not interdict resupply operations without effective aerial observation.

4. There are an estimated 184 Chinese Communist field artillery pieces in the Matsu area including 24 122-mm guns and/or howitzers. The relatively small number of Communist pieces that can reach the Matsu Islands limits the effectiveness of interdiction in this area.

II. Chinese Nationalist Ground Forces

5. Nearly a fourth of Nationalist China's 450,000-man Army (one third of its combat strength) is deployed on the offshore islands — 86,000 on the Chin-men group and 23,000 on the Matsu group. Of the remainder 16,000 are on the Penghus (Pescadores) and 331,000 on Taiwan itself.

6. The defensive position of Nationalist forces is good. Mines have been laid in the waters off Chin-men. Beaches on both island groups are protected by multiple belts of barb wire and concrete and steel hedge-hogs and by land mine fields. Dug in positions along and behind the beaches are mutually supporting. Both island groups probably have 30 days of all supplies except ammunition. There is probably a 40-day stock of ammunition on the Chin-mens and a 50-day stock on the Matsus. Moreover, the state of training and morale of Nationalist forces on the offshore

SECRET

SECRET   9

islands is good. They possess the will to fight, and in the event of attack will undoubtedly receive the strongest support from Taiwan which the GRC is capable of giving.

7. There are serious weaknesses in the Nationalist position, however. On Chin-men, defensive positions are concentrated in a crust along the beaches; the interior of the island is only lightly held. The southeast portion of the island is relatively weakly defended, and the excellent beach in that area is used for off-loading supplies. Nationalist forces are out-gunned by the Communists' 393 field artillery pieces (estimated — based on TO&E) 210 of which can be positioned to cover part or all of the area of the Chin-men group. The Nationalists have only 308 artillery pieces. On the Matsu Island group, also, the Nationalists are out-gunned. As shown above, the Communists have an estimated (based on TO&E) 184 field artillery pieces, 68 of which can reach Kaoteng and Peikan. In addition, there are an unknown quantity of artillery pieces capable of firing on Nankan. Of the Nationalists' 80 artillery pieces, only 8 155-mm guns can reach Communist positions. With the islands of the Matsu group separated by from three to eight miles, Nationalist positions on one island cannot be supported from another. For these reasons, and because of the proximity of the islands to the mainland, the Nationalists, without air and naval superiority, could not hold them for more than a few days against a determined Communist assault.

8. Chinese Nationalist strength figures on the offshore islands occupied by regular Nationalist forces are as follows:

(1) Chin-mens
  a. Chin-men — 74,100
  b. Little Chin-men — 10,450
  c. Ta-tan — 1,300
  d. Erh-tan — 250

(2) Matsus
  a. Nankan — 11,500
  b. Peikan — 5,000
  c. Kaoteng — 700
  d. Tungchuan — 2,300
  e. Hsichuan — 3,300

III. Chinese Communist Navy

9. The personnel strength of the Chinese Communist Navy totals 58,000, including 8,000 in naval aviation. Its operational units include the following:

Destroyers (DD)	4
Submarines: *	
Short range	4
Medium range	4
Long range	10
Escort Vessels (DE)	4
Patrol Vessels	249
Includes:	
Patrol Escort (PF)	16
Sub-Chaser (PC)	29
Motor Torpedo Boat (PT)	120
Mine Vessels	31
Includes:	
Fleet Minesweeper (MSF)	4
Landing Ships	53
Service Craft (approx)	300

* Submarine strength is being increased by new construction at the rate of 4 per year.

10. The naval air arm includes 490 combat aircraft.

11. The navy has growing capabilities for medium, short and long range submarine operations and for surface activity in coastal waters. It has an extensive capability for both offensive and defensive mining operations. Coupled with Communist air power, the navy has a significant capability against Chinese Nationalist forces in coastal waters.

12. With aerial support in the Taiwan Strait, the navy has the capability for operations in the Matsu and Chin-men areas. We believe that with a southward deployment of units currently assigned to the Yellow Sea Fleet, it could effectively interdict the supply lines to the offshore islands.

13. In an amphibious assault against Chin-men or Matsu it is unlikely that larger amphibious units (LST, LSM) would be employed due to the extremely adverse beaching conditions. The Communists have the capability, however, of launching a strong assault employing lesser amphibious units (LCU, LCM) and such non-naval craft as might be required. Naval combat units (DI, Gun Boats, etc.) would probably be employed off the seaward side of Chin-men. The deep, less re-

SECRET

SECRET   10

stricted waters off Matsu would permit a freer employment of such combat units in support of an assault particularly after the heavier Nationalist shore batteries were reduced.

14. In an amphibious operation against the Penghus and Taiwan with relatively unrestricted waters and more extensive beaches, all available strength afloat could be employed. Using available amphibious shipping, including merchant landing ship types, a balanced force of approximately three rifle divisions could be lifted in such an assault.

IV. Chinese Nationalist Navy

15. The personnel strength of the Nationalist Navy (GRCN) totals 58,000 including 25,400 marines. The navy, scheduled to be augmented by 1 DD and 2 LST within the next year, consists of the following:

Destroyer (DD)	4
Escort Vessel (DE)	5
Patrol Escort (PF)	7
Escort (PCE)	2
Sub-chaser (PC)	16
Motor Gunboat (PGM)	2
Motor Torpedo Boat	6

Mine Vessels

Minelayer Coastal (MMC)	2
Fleet Minesweeper (MSF)	5
Coastal Minesweeper (MSC)	2

Miscellaneous

Amphibious Vessels	39
Aux. and Service Craft	71

16. The general state of training is good. Logistical support of the offshore islands is adequate for present requirements. Over-all combat effectiveness has continued to improve, with operational availability on the increase due to improvements in maintenance and supply, overhaul and improved operating procedures.

17. The navy is primarily a defensive force with limited capabilities. It can conduct limited ASW and mine warfare. It can provide lift for amphibious counterlandings on the offshore islands in strength up to one division. However, the GRCN would be unable to oppose successfully the relatively large force of Chinese Communist PT boats and submarines, which is capable of operating in the Taiwan Strait. Lack of cooperative air sup-

port by the Nationalist air force has hampered the navy in operations requiring such support. In the light of Chinese Communist air strength in the Taiwan Strait, this deficiency could become critical.

18. The Marine Corps with a personnel strength of 25,400 has the men, equipment and skill to make it capable of executing modern amphibious operations. The Marine Corps continues to have the capability of planning and executing an amphibious operation at division or brigade level against light to moderate resistance providing adequate naval and air support is available.

V. Chinese Communist Air Force (CCAF) and Naval Air Force (CNAF)

19. Communist China's air forces comprise a strong, modern tactical force. Their equipment, training and deployment are oriented toward air defense and tactical support operations. They have a nucleus of battle experienced fighter pilots who gained experience against US air tactics in the Korean War.

20. Chinese Communist air defense is organized around a good early warning system, with a good ground control intercept capability in daylight and clear air. The CCAF night and bad weather intercept capability is limited somewhat by a shortage of electronic airborne intercept equipment and a poor height finding capability at higher altitudes. In the coastal area between Hong Kong and Shanghai, their ground controlled intercept capability probably would be good.

21. The combined Chinese Communist air forces include 2,460 jet aircraft of which 1,785 are fighters and 450 are high bombers. In the coastal area opposite Taiwan, there are seven airfields that could sustain jet operations. Of these, six are presently operational and the other could quickly become operational. There are no bomber aircraft operating from airfields directly opposite Taiwan. However, Taiwan is well within range of Chinese Communist jet light bombers stationed at airfields outside the immediate area. The redeployment of some piston and light bomber forces to rear areas directly behind the coastal airfields is expected.

SECRET

SECRET

11

22. There can be little doubt that the vastly outnumbered Chinese Nationalist Airforce would be quickly overcome by Chinese Communist air power in any decisive contest, unless the Nationalist forces were supported by US air power.

CCAF — CNAF
(Total Inventory)

Jet Fighter	1,785
Piston Fighter	275
Jet Light Bomber	450
Piston Tactical Attack	505
Land Based ASW	20
Piston Medium Bomber	20
Piston Transport	290
Other Jet	225
Other Piston	810
Total	4,350

VI. Chinese Nationalist Air Force

A. CURRENT STRENGTH

23. The Chinese Nationalist Air Force (CAF), a separate service on a par with the other Nationalist Chinese military services, is the strongest indigenous non-Communist air force in Asia.

CAF
(Total Inventory)

Jet Fighter	450
Jet Light Bomber	1
Piston Tactical Attack	9
Land Based ASW	10
Piston Transport	143
Other Jet	46
Other Piston	167
Total	826

24. The CAF has an inventory of over 800 aircraft, of which almost two-thirds are in operational units; of these aircraft, an excess of 450 combat type permits fully equipped combat units. Personnel strength totals nearly 88,000 and includes almost 1,300 trained pilots (there are, in addition, almost 800 trained pilots occupying command and staff positions not requiring frequent flying); an additional 250 pilots are in training.

B. CURRENT CAPABILITIES

25. The principal tactical capability of the CAF at present is photo reconnaissance within a 750-mile range of Taiwan, and limited night reconnaissance up to a 1,000-mile range. Missions are currently regularly flown over the Communist Chinese mainland by the RB–57 and RF–84F aircraft (and occasionally by RF–86F's) of the CAF's two tactical reconnaissance squadrons.

26. A fairly good organization for the control and functioning of air-ground support, modeled after that of the USAF, has recently been activated. Considerable practice will be required to insure technical effectiveness of this system and its components.

27. Despite the existence of a well organized early warning/ground controlled intercept system and 6 F–86F squadrons with day fighter capability, the CAF could be expected to offer only delaying action against an air assault by Communist China. This defense would be limited to daylight hours and would be of short duration, pending the arrival of USAF support.

28. The CAF has no strategic air capability nor are any aircraft programmed through MAP that would provide a capability. The CAF would be capable of giving limited support to amphibious landings or to defense against such landings, as well as harassing hostile shipping within the Taiwan Strait. The capability of the 33d Bomb Squadron (10 P4Y-2's) is limited to patrol activities over the Taiwan Strait.

29. The air transport capability of the CAF has been enhanced considerably over the last two years. Airdrop techniques have improved with the training derived in joint operations and in pamphlet and food airdrops in South China. The two air transport groups — one specializing in air transport and the other in troop carrier operations — are capable of performing rear area air supply, supporting initial amphibious operations limited with airdrops and paratroop operations, and assisting in psychological warfare operations through food and pamphlet drops on the Chinese mainland.

SECRET

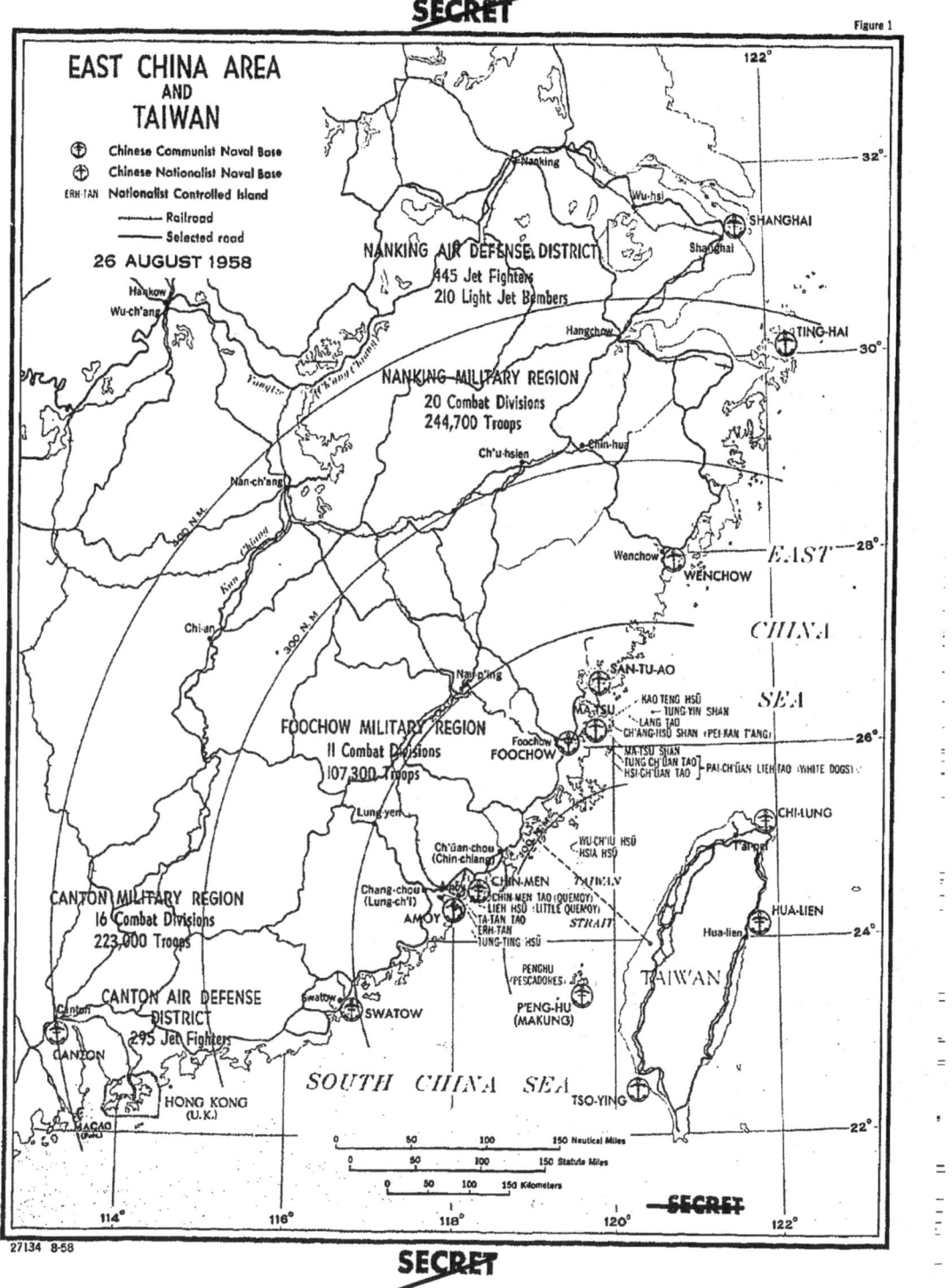

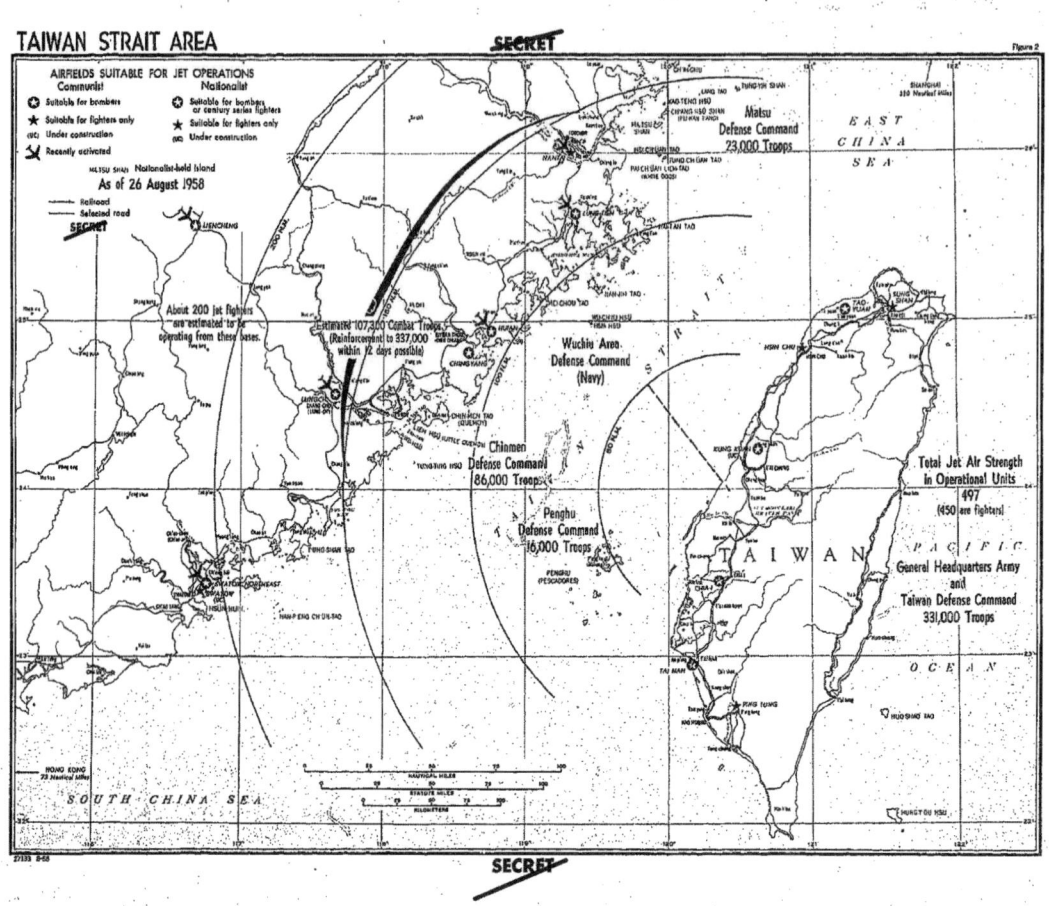

SECTION 13

SNIE 100-11-58

Probable Chinese Communist and Soviet Intentions in the Taiwan Strait Area

16 September 1958

SECRET

SPECIAL

NATIONAL INTELLIGENCE ESTIMATE

NUMBER 100-11-58

(Supplements SNIE 100-9-58)

PROBABLE CHINESE COMMUNIST AND SOVIET INTENTIONS IN THE TAIWAN STRAIT AREA

Submitted by the

DIRECTOR OF CENTRAL INTELLIGENCE

The following intelligence organizations participated in the preparation of this estimate: The Central Intelligence Agency and the intelligence organizations of the Departments of State, the Army, the Navy, the Air Force, and The Joint Staff.

Concurred in by the

UNITED STATES INTELLIGENCE BOARD

on 16 September 1958. Concurring were The Director of Intelligence and Research, Department of State; the Assistant Chief of Staff for Intelligence, Department of the Army; the Director of Naval Intelligence; the Assistant Chief of Staff, Intelligence, USAF; the Deputy Director for Intelligence, The Joint Staff; the assistant to the Secretary of Defense, Special Operations; and the Director of the National Security Agency. The Atomic Energy Commission Representative to the USIB and the Assistant Director, Federal Bureau of Investigation, abstained, the subject being outside of their jurisdiction.

SECRET

SECRET

PROBABLE CHINESE COMMUNIST AND SOVIET INTENTIONS IN THE TAIWAN STRAIT AREA [1]

THE PROBLEM

To reassess the probable intentions of Communist China and the Soviet Union with respect to the Taiwan Strait area in the light of the most recent evidence.

THE ESTIMATE

I. COMMUNIST CHINA

1. We believe that the most likely Chinese Communist course of action in the immediate future is to continue military harassment and interdiction of supply of Chinmen. The Chinese Communists probably expect this course to make the island untenable, and thereby to put the next move up to the US. The US has a limited range of choices: it can allow the island to fall by attrition; it can assist the Chinese Nationalists to withdraw from the island; it can agree to Chinese Nationalist attacks on the mainland; it can undertake to maintain resupply of Chinmen by all-American convoys; or it can itself take the military action necessary to assure resupply of the island by the Chinese Nationalists. Any of the latter three courses of action eventually would probably involve US attacks on the mainland, and the US could be charged before world opinion with expanding the scope of armed conflict.

2. In pursuing this course, it is likely that the Chinese Communists are willing to take actions involving considerable risk of major armed conflict with the US. If US ships move close in-shore in the course of escorting Na-tionalist supply convoys, the Communists will probably not desist from their artillery barrages against unloading operations. If the US attempts to prevent by force the interdiction of supply, US forces so engaged will almost certainly be attacked within the limits of Chinese Communist capabilities. If the US were to announce that it would resupply Chinmen with all-American convoys (supported by appropriate combat strength ready to defend against attack) we believe that the Chinese Communists would probably attack the US force, although there is a chance that they would not. In any event, the Communists will demand that world opinion condemn US aggression and force a political settlement favorable to Communist China.

3. In addition to the continued interdiction of Chinmen, the Chinese Communists might seize, with little or no warning, one or more of the smaller offshore islands. This would be calculated to fall outside the scope of any US commitments to GRC defense and would serve further the Communist objective of eroding the Nationalist position. The effect would be further calculated as not prejudicing the Chinese Communist position of negotiation, but, rather, as increasing the international sense of urgency for a peaceful settlement and, at the same time, placing added political pressure on the US.

[1] This estimate supplements SNIE 100-9-58: "Probable Developments in the Taiwan Strait Area," 26 August 1958.

SECRET

1

SECRET

2

4. The Chinese Communists may not maintain a continuous interdiction of supply of the islands. It may be that they will let occasional convoys go through, and will thereby seek to prolong the present crisis rather than bring it to the earliest issue. Such action might be related to the ambassadorial talks in Warsaw, or to moves in the General Assembly of the UN. But we believe that such interruptions in the Chinese Communist interdiction would be only a temporary measure.

5. Another Chinese Communist course of action, though we consider it unlikely, is that the Chinese Communists will gradually call off the interdiction of the Chinmens. If they did so, it would be because they had decided, or had been persuaded by the Soviets, that the dangers inherent in maintaining interdiction were too great, and that another opportunity should be awaited at some future date.

6. Finally we consider it possible, though unlikely, that the Chinese Communists will assault one or more of the major offshore islands. We consider this unlikely because, in their view, (a) it would be almost certain to involve them in major hostilities with the US, (b) it would diminish the political and propaganda advantage they now have, and (c) it would probably be unnecessary because they could get the islands by other means.

II. USSR

7. The Soviet perspective on the Taiwan Strait situation is almost certainly based upon substantial knowledge of Chinese Communist plans and intentions. It is probable that the Soviet leaders, at least since the Mao-Khrushchev talks, have not only been informed but have also generally concurred in Chinese Communist actions in the Strait area. The Soviet public commitment to support the Chinese Communists, accompanied since August 31 by a rising volume of propaganda, is in part intended to deter the US. Moreover, we believe that this commitment was almost certainly made on the basis of calculations that activities in the Taiwan Strait area would fall short of provoking US intervention on such a scale as to call for overt Soviet military participation.

8. The Soviet leaders cannot be greatly concerned with the fate of the offshore islands, and, having less directly at stake than the Chinese Communists, may be inclined to favor a more conservative course. Their principal objectives are political — to discredit the US, to comply with the wishes of their Chinese ally, and to enhance the power and prestige of the Sino-Soviet Bloc. They believe that the opportunity to put the US in the dock under accusations of jeopardizing peace should be utilized to the maximum, and that support for the US would be far less than it was in the Middle East crisis. They also believe that if the US backs down from its position on the offshore islands or acts in defiance of world opinion, they will have inflicted a serious political defeat on the US.

9. While the Soviets probably do not wish to see the scale of hostilities expanded and the risk of their involvement magnified, they will be aware that the US may be led by Chinese Communist actions to engage Chinese Communist forces. If such hostilities are initiated, but limited to conventional weapons and confined to the mainland area adjacent to the Taiwan Strait, the Soviets would probably consider that the Chinese Communists did not require direct military assistance and would provide moral, political, and material assistance. Thus, they would almost certainly not intervene militarily, at least in an overt manner risking a direct confrontation of Soviet and US forces.

10. If hostilities continued for long, or particularly if they were expanded in area and scale, at some point the Soviets would probably feel that they would have to go further in support of Communist China. With respect to Soviet reactions to the US use of nuclear weapons, much would depend upon the scale of the US attacks, the extent of territory over which they would be delivered, and the entire context of events. The Soviets might conclude that more could be gained at less cost and risk by exercising military restraint and leading a political campaign to condemn the US before world opinion. They would have many supporters. On the other hand,

SECRET

SECRET

3

the Soviets might conclude that such a challenge could not be passed by without nuclear retaliation. Particularly if the US extended the area of nuclear attack for a considerable distance into mainland China, there would be a better than even chance that the Soviets would provide the Chinese Communists with capabilities for nuclear retaliation under Soviet control. And, at some point high on a scale of increasing damage and danger to the Chinese regime, the Soviets might directly attack US forces engaged in China, including the bases from which such forces were operating, in the face of the attendant risk of general war.

III. THE PROSPECT FOR NEGOTIATIONS

11. In each of the contingencies discussed above the USSR will make every effort to exploit the situation politically and at the same time to prevent the spread of hostilities. The Chinese Communists are now engaged in discussions with the US on the Taiwan Strait question in the ambassadorial talks. However, they probably hope that world opinion and the continuing military threat to Chinmen will force the US to agree to higher-level discussions, such as a bilateral foreign ministers conference or a multilateral conference, possibly even at the summit level. They may fear that an attempt at a solution in the UN would solidify opinion in favor of an acceptance of "two Chinas." However, both Moscow and Peiping apparently deem it advantageous to raise the issue in the General Assembly, either to forestall a US initiative or in hopes of furthering their aims of pillorying and isolating the US.

12. Regardless of the forum, it is clear that the Chinese Communists are in no mood for any negotiated settlement which would restore the *status quo ante*. They will oppose any proposal that smacks of "two Chinas," that commits them to accepting the principle that they have no right to "liberate" the territory held by the GRC, or that grants the US a right to individual or collective self-defense in the Taiwan Strait area. While it is possible that they would permit a temporary cease-fire to develop during the negotiations in order to enhance their propaganda posture, they would be unwilling to commit themselves to an indefinite cease-fire. They would refuse any proposal which seemed to tie their hands more than those of the GRC. They might accept some type of "neutralization" of the offshore islands as an interim move, hoping that the negative effect on GRC morale would be greater than the restriction on Communist activities. However, they almost certainly would not regard this as a permanent solution. Sino-Soviet insistence upon a resolution of the entire Taiwan problem favorable to Communist China will remain strong, and it is likely that they will continue to take a considerable risk in utilizing military pressure as a means of undermining the strength and determination of the Chinese Nationalists.

SECRET

SECTION 14

SNIE 100-12-58

Probable Developments in the
Taiwan Strait Crisis

28 October 1958

SNIE 100-12-58
28 October 1958

~~SECRET~~

Nº   340

SPECIAL

NATIONAL INTELLIGENCE ESTIMATE
NUMBER 100-12-58

PROBABLE DEVELOPMENTS IN THE TAIWAN STRAIT CRISIS

Submitted by the
DIRECTOR OF CENTRAL INTELLIGENCE

The following intelligence organizations participated in the preparation of this estimate: The Central Intelligence Agency and the intelligence organizations of the Departments of State, the Army, the Navy, the Air Force, and The Joint Staff.

Concurred in by the
UNITED STATES INTELLIGENCE BOARD

on 28 October 1958. Concurring were The Director of Intelligence and Research, Department of State; the Assistant Chief of Staff for Intelligence, Department of the Army; the Director of Naval Intelligence; the Assistant Chief of Staff, Intelligence, USAF; the Director for Intelligence, The Joint Staff; the Assistant to the Secretary of Defense, Special Operations; and the Director of the National Security Agency. The Atomic Energy Commission Representative to the USIB and the Assistant Director, Federal Bureau of Investigation, abstained, the subject being outside of their jurisdiction.

~~SECRET~~

SECRET

PROBABLE DEVELOPMENTS IN THE TAIWAN STRAIT CRISIS

THE PROBLEM

To estimate probable Chinese Communist courses of action with respect to the crisis which has existed in the Taiwan Strait since August; and probable Chinese Communist, Chinese Nationalist, and non-Communist East Asian reactions to various possible developments in the Taiwan Strait area.

THE ESTIMATE

I. THE CHINESE COMMUNISTS AND THE TAIWAN STRAIT CRISIS

A. Chinese Communist Objectives and Motives in Initiating the Crisis

1. In initiating the present crisis, Communist China has shown greater boldness in probing US intentions in the Taiwan Strait than at any time heretofore. This shift in tactics has taken place against a background of generally increased Chinese Communist assertiveness and confidence since the advent of sputnik. In general, however, we believe that the shift in tactics in the Taiwan area does not portend any basic change in the over-all conduct of Chinese Communist foreign policy as described in NIE 13-58 (16 May 1958).[1]

2. The Chinese Communists regard continued GRC control of the offshore islands as an affront to their national prestige and dignity. They may still regard the GRC position on the offshore islands, backed as it is by the US, as a military threat. However, we do not believe that the Chinese Communists initiated the present crisis with the firm intention of obtaining the offshore islands regardless of GRC, US, and world reactions. Such recent actions in the present crisis as the failure to use the CCAF for offensive action, the less than maximum possible artillery effort, the emphasis on the undermining of Chinese Nationalist morale, and the cessation of the bombardment between 6 and 20 October almost certainly indicate that Peiping's leaders are using military power primarily as a political weapon, and that they are not committed to the immediate capture of the islands at all costs.

[1] NIE 13-58 (16 May 1958) held that: the Chinese Communists view the present world position of the Bloc with considerable confidence; they feel the trend in Asia to be running against the West; they are not impatient to achieve their goals; they are directing their energies toward the intermediate objective of weakening the position and influence of the US in Asia; the principal thrust of their policy will continue to be reasonableness and peaceful coexistence, though they will display more assertiveness; they are concerned about the growth of "two Chinas" sentiment; they will probably not resort to overt military aggression which they believe would involve them in military action with the US; they will continue their efforts to undermine Nationalist will; and "the possibility cannot be excluded that the Chinese Communists will adopt a more aggressive policy toward the Offshore Islands, in part because of intense irritation and a sense of affront, in part to emphasize their determination to destroy the Nationalist Government, and in part to test US intentions in the Taiwan area."

SECRET

1

SECRET

2

3. Nor do we believe that the Chinese Communists viewed the acquisition of the offshore islands as their fundamental objective. Their primary purpose in increasing military and political pressure in the Taiwan Strait area was undoubtedly to further their ultimate goal of eliminating the GRC and bringing about the withdrawal of US forces from the Taiwan area. They probably believed that their action would serve this purpose: (a) by probing US determination to support the GRC; (b) by driving a wedge between the US and the GRC; (c) by discrediting the GRC and the US before world opinion; (d) by reminding the world that Communist China must be reckoned with; (e) by preventing a drift toward wider acceptance of a *de facto* "two Chinas" situation; and (f) by straining Nationalist morale. Although domestic considerations probably played some part in the timing of the Chinese Communist initial attack, we believe that these considerations were of secondary importance in the reaching of the decision to initiate the attack.

4. Available evidence, albeit inconclusive, indicates that the USSR did not initiate the crisis by encouraging the Chinese Communists to their actions. However, the Soviets clearly acquiesced in it and have supported it, almost certainly in the belief that it would not lead to large-scale hostilities between Communist China and the US. There is no evidence as to what role the USSR played, if any, in the temporary suspension of shelling.

B. Present Chinese Communist Intentions

5. Whatever the expectations of the Chinese Communist leaders in July and August, they have probably become convinced that the US itself would fight rather than permit the offshore islands to fall in the face of direct military pressure. In these circumstances, the Chinese Communists, apparently unwilling to risk resort to those increased military measures which would be necessary to effect a complete interdiction of the islands, probably estimate that they can best pursue their objectives at the moment by emphasizing the political aspect of their effort, while maintaining a measure of military pressure. They probably retain considerable confidence that a course of shelling and intermittent "truces" will still serve to aggravate US–GRC relations, erode Nationalist morale, and exert world and domestic pressures on the US to effect a withdrawal of Nationalist troops from the offshore islands, as a step towards Communist China's aim of eliminating the GRC.

6. The Chinese Communists almost certainly consider that their position is a strong one and that there is little compulsion on them to make concessions. They probably intend to maintain in the Warsaw talks that the only issue negotiable with the US is a withdrawal of US forces from the Taiwan area, insisting that the question of the offshore islands and Taiwan is a purely Chinese affair. However, they probably view a continuation of these talks as desirable in order to give the world the impression that they are willing to negotiate, to forestall UN or other international consideration of the crisis, to arouse doubts in the GRC's mind regarding US policy, and to reap whatever prestige benefits result from direct talks with the US. At the same time, they will probably continue to offer to negotiate with the GRC, suggesting to the Nationalists openly and through covert contacts that they had better make a deal soon before the US abandons them. They will almost certainly prefer such negotiating channels to any discussion of the crisis in the UN or in any other international forum, since this would probably involve resolutions which would not fully endorse Peiping's position and which might have "two Chinas" connotations.

7. Peiping's negotiating position is limited by its concern that acceptance of any concessions might prejudice its claim to Taiwan and the offshore islands. It may hope that the US will exert pressure on the GRC to withdraw from the offshore islands, calculating that such pressure will exacerbate US–GRC relations. However, the Chinese Communists would not accept such a withdrawal as a permanent solution to the Taiwan problem, although they may suggest that if they were given the offshore islands and if the US were

SECRET

SECRET

3

to withdraw its forces from the Taiwan area, they would not use force against Taiwan for a certain period. They certainly do not view a *de facto* neutralization or a reduction of the Nationalist garrisons as acceptable solutions, and it is most unlikely that they would respond to such proposals by offering any concessions. Certainly they would not agree to such reciprocal measures as a demilitarization of the coastal area opposite the offshore islands.

8. The specific actions which Communist China will pursue within the limits indicated above — refraining from both extreme risks and major concessions — are difficult to estimate. Chinese Communist tactics will depend in large measure on Soviet attitudes and on Nationalist and particularly US actions. The Chinese Communists will probably move up new and improved aircraft and other weapons into the immediate coastal areas, but we believe that they will continue to refrain from launching a direct assault to capture the major offshore islands as long as they believe that this would involve them in hostilities with the US. Nevertheless, this does not rule out, especially in the event that their present tactics fail to advance their cause, the resumption of serious interdiction efforts and more aggressive employment of air and naval units in the Taiwan Strait. Although the Chinese Communists probably now believe that the US would fight rather than permit the islands to fall in the face of direct military pressure, they probably also believe that the US would exercise considerable restraint short of a direct and flagrant Chinese Communist challenge. Consequently, they probably believe that it would be safe again to create a high degree of military tension in the Strait area. In such a situation there would always remain a serious chance of miscalculation, from which hostilities could develop between US and Chinese Communist forces.

9. On balance, we feel that for the near future the chances favor a prolongation of the present situation of no maximum interdiction effort, no serious negotiation, no solution. Assuming the Nationalists remain on the offshore islands, the Chinese Communists will probably maintain an atmosphere of crisis and tension in the Taiwan Strait for some time to come. In any event, they will not give up their efforts to split the US and the GRC, to cause the collapse of the GRC, and to undermine US prestige in Asia.

10. We do not anticipate that the Chinese Communists will take overt military action against other Far Eastern countries during the near future. In the event that the offshore islands were lost by the Chinese Nationalists, we would foresee heightened Communist pressures against other areas of Asia.

SECRET

SECTION 15

SNIE 100-4-59

Chinese Communist
Intentions and Probable Courses of
Action in the Taiwan Strait Area

13 March 1959

SECRET

SPECIAL
NATIONAL INTELLIGENCE ESTIMATE
NUMBER 100-4-59

CHINESE COMMUNIST INTENTIONS AND PROBABLE COURSES OF ACTION IN THE TAIWAN STRAIT AREA

Submitted by the
DIRECTOR OF CENTRAL INTELLIGENCE

The following intelligence organizations participated in the preparation of this estimate: The Central Intelligence Agency and the intelligence organizations of the Departments of State, the Army, the Navy, the Air Force, and The Joint Staff.

Concurred in by the
UNITED STATES INTELLIGENCE BOARD

on 13 March 1959. Concurring were The Director of Intelligence and Research, Department of State; the Assistant Chief of Staff for Intelligence, Department of the Army; the Assistant Chief of Naval Operations for Intelligence, Department of the Navy; the Assistant Chief of Staff, Intelligence, USAF; the Director for Intelligence, The Joint Staff; the Assistant to the Secretary of Defense, Special Operations; and the Director of the National Security Agency. The Atomic Energy Commission Representative to the USIB and the Assistant Director, Federal Bureau of Investigation, abstained, the subject being outside of their jurisdiction.

SECRET   N<u>o</u>   380

SECRET

CHINESE COMMUNIST INTENTIONS AND PROBABLE COURSES OF ACTION IN THE TAIWAN STRAIT AREA

THE PROBLEM

To assess Communist China's capabilities, intentions, and probable courses of action with respect to the Taiwan Strait area over the next year.

CONCLUSIONS

1. We believe that Communist China broke off the Taiwan Strait crisis last October primarily because it believed that to increase military pressures to the point necessary for a successful interdiction effort against Chinmen carried unacceptable risk of hostilities with the US. Furthermore, relations between the US and the Government of the Republic of China (GRC) had not been impaired, Nationalist morale remained high, and the tensions created by Peiping's actions were proving damaging to Communist China's international prestige. Peiping was also concerned over moves by some Asian countries toward compromise proposals it considered unacceptable. (*Paras. 15–18*)

2. There has actually been little change since last October in the military picture in the Taiwan Strait area. The Chinese Communists do not have the capability to prevent resupply of the Matsus or Big and Little Chinmen by artillery fire alone. They could at any time create considerably greater havoc on the Chinmen group than they did during the previous crisis should they choose to exercise their full artillery capability. Moreover, by supplementing artillery bombardment with attacks by aircraft and motor torpedo boats, possibly along with offensive mine-warfare, they could make resupply and reinforcement of the Chinmen and Matsu garrisons virtually impossible unless US air and naval forces were committed to keeping the supply lines open. The Chinese Communist forces remain capable of taking any of the smaller coastal islands quickly and with little or no warning. Barring US intervention, they also could seize the larger coastal islands. (*Paras. 23–25, 27*)

3. There are presently no indications of any Chinese Communist preparations for increased military pressures in the Taiwan Strait. There is no firm evidence that additional troops, heavier artillery, missiles, additional aircraft, additional motor torpedo boats, or minecraft have been moved into the Strait area. However, Communist forces could be quickly and heavily reinforced, and quite possibly without detection prior to their employment. (*Para. 31*)

SECRET

1

2

SECRET

4. The Chinese Communists will almost certainly seek to avoid hostilities with the US. We believe that they will not attempt to seize Chinmen or undertake an all-out effort to prevent its resupply. We also believe such actions unlikely against the Matsus, though the Chinese Communists may in this case be somewhat less certain of US intentions and possible reactions. However, we believe that the Chinese Communists will continue to employ military pressures in support of their essentially political and psychological campaign in the Taiwan Strait. They will probably attempt to keep the Strait issue alive and probably will not relax their military pressures to such a degree as to permit the situation to become quiescent over an extended period of time. (*Para. 37*)

5. There are a number of military pressures open to the Chinese Communists. They may engage in periodic heavy shelling and limited air and/or sea operations to harass the Nationalists in the Chinmen and Matsu areas; if the CCAF improves its proficiency, it might more aggressively engage the CAF. The Chinese Communists might attempt to seize one or more of the small, lightly-held offshore islands, particularly Ta-tan and Erh-tan, which could probably be taken by a surprise operation before effective counteraction could be mounted. (*Paras. 38-39*)

6. In the course of the Berlin crisis the Chinese Communists may exercise their ability to heighten tensions in the Taiwan Strait, either as a part of co-ordinated Bloc strategy or in furtherance of their own objectives in the Far East. We believe that the Chinese Communists would not heighten tensions without prior consultation with the Soviets. In either case, the Soviet position would almost certainly depend on the course of the negotiations or on events in the Berlin crisis itself. The Soviets will probably desire to keep tensions in the Far East about as they are at present so long as they judge that the Berlin situation is progressing according to their liking. Should the Soviets estimate that the Berlin situation is going badly for them, they may advise the Chinese Communists to increase tensions in the Far East. The Chinese Communist response to such Soviet advice would be influenced not only by the Berlin situation and Soviet desires but also by Peiping's own estimate of the advantages or disadvantages of heightening tensions in the Taiwan Strait or possibly elsewhere in the Far East. Any moves to heighten tension in the Taiwan Strait, however, would almost certainly be calculated to fall short of provoking major hostilities. (*Para. 34*)

SECRET

SECRET

3

DISCUSSION

I. INTRODUCTION

7. The past few months have seen a shift in the apparent mood of Chinese Communist foreign policy. During most of 1958, Peiping's over-all conduct of foreign policy was marked by truculence and toughness, and in August Communist China suddenly undertook the most aggressive action in the Taiwan Strait since 1949. Peiping has let up on its military pressures in the Strait since last October, however, and has softened the belligerent tone of its foreign policy pronouncements.

8. Nevertheless, the issues involved in the Taiwan Strait crisis have not been resolved. Communist China's basic objectives in the Taiwan Strait area remain unchanged: to eliminate US influence and power, to destroy the GRC, and to assume control of all Nationalist-held territories. The purpose of this paper is to examine the initiation and the course of the 1958 Strait crisis, the Chinese Communist breaking off of the crisis, and the developments which have occurred since that time to see what light they throw on Communist China's probable courses of action in the Strait area over the next year.

II. THE 1958 TAIWAN STRAIT CRISIS

9. We believe that a number of considerations were behind the Chinese Communist decision to step up their military activity in the Taiwan Strait in August 1958. In the most general sense, the operation reflected the apparent confidence with which the regime viewed the external situation during 1958. Under the impact of Soviet progress in rocketry, Peiping's leaders appeared to have been convinced that a decisive shift in the world balance of power had occurred in the Bloc's favor. Peiping's propaganda appeared to reflect some impatience to move more forcefully to exploit the Bloc's favorable power position. It's "peaceful coexistence" line had failed to advance Communist China's interests in the Taiwan Strait; this line had in fact contributed to a sense of international complacency and a tendency in world opinion to accept a *de facto* "two Chinas" situation.

10. In this general atmosphere Peiping's leaders probably believed that the time was ripe for a new blow at the GRC. Communist China probably estimated that the US would be diplomatically isolated on the offshore island question, and that the USSR's progress in advanced weapons might deter the US from accepting great risks in local war situations. Accordingly, Peiping probably believed that the US, already committed at the time in the Middle East, might be unwilling or unable to prevent the loss of the offshore islands. Peiping apparently set out to test this estimate by probing US reactions, in the expectation that if the US did not intervene, the offshore islands could be gained through interdiction, evacuation, or, perhaps, mass defections. The fall of these islands, Peiping believed, would seriously undermine the morale and staying power of the GRC on Taiwan, drive a wedge between the US and the GRC, and cause the US to suffer a major loss of prestige and influence in Asia.

11. Peiping probably anticipated that it could not lose in such a probing action, believing that even if the US did make a firm stand in the Strait, the resulting tension would create serious problems for the US in its relations with its allies and with the neutral nations of Asia, increase pressures for world acceptance of Communist China, and halt any tendency toward world acceptance of a *de facto* "two Chinas" situation.

12. In any event, Communist China's leaders probably did not intend to take measures which would seriously risk US counterattack against the mainland. Intense artillery bombardment was probably considered to be the principal arm which could be safely employed. The extent to which other military means would be committed was probably contingent upon US and GRC responses.

13. We continue to believe that foreign and Bloc policy considerations were primary in

SECRET

4   SECRET

Communist China's decision to initiate hostilities in the Taiwan Strait. However, the regime must have considered the interplay between such a military crisis and its domestic "leap forward" and commune programs in its planning. The Strait venture proved a useful instrument in pressing for accelerated economic efforts and in organizing the populace into communes. The regime probably had planned to take advantage of the Strait action to push these domestic programs, but we do not believe that this action was undertaken because of any compelling internal need.

14. The role of the USSR in the 1958 Strait crisis is still not clear, though we continue to believe that the USSR did not initiate the crisis by encouraging the Chinese, but, instead, acquiesced in and supported Chinese initiative. We are confident that the idea of the thrust in the Strait was Chinese, that it had been in the process of planning and maturing for some time, and that some kind of timetable existed for its activation. The fact that Khrushchev left Moscow for a trip to Peiping at the height of the Middle East crisis seems to indicate that the two allies felt a need at the time for closer over-all coordination of Sino-Soviet policies. The subsequent events of August suggest that there was agreement with the USSR on the timing of the Strait venture and on the extent to which it would be pushed. The Mao-Khrushchev meeting may also have included an agreement that diversionary pressures in the Strait could advance Bloc interests in the Middle East, and that a high state of tension might be maintained simultaneously on two fronts, Far East and Middle East.

III. COMMUNIST CHINA'S BREAKING OFF OF THE TAIWAN STRAIT CRISIS

15. *Peiping's Assessment of the Crisis.* We believe that Communist China broke off the crisis last October primarily because it had found that to increase military pressures to the point necessary for a successful interdiction effort carried unacceptable risks of hostilities with the US. Furthermore, relations between the US and the GRC had not been impaired, and the tensions created by the push were proving damaging to Communist

China's international prestige. In sum, Communist China's leaders had found their venture in the Strait politically and militarily unrewarding, and the problem at hand had become one of how to disengage as gracefully as possible and to find new ways and means of advancing their aims in the Taiwan Strait area.

16. Communist China's leaders were undoubtedly impressed with the rapidity, scale, and nature of the US military response. Where the US intentions with respect to the offshore islands probably had earlier seemed unclear to Peiping's leaders, it probably now looked to them as if the US would intervene rather than permit Chinmen to be captured or starved out. Only with respect to the Matsus and some of the lesser offshore islands were US intentions not clearly manifested.

17. Peiping also found that it had underestimated Nationalist nerve, morale, and military capabilities. The CCAF was no match for the greater skill of CAF pilots, who, after the beginning of the intensive Chinese Communist bombardment, shot down about 30 Communist MIG's with the loss of only one or possibly two F-86's. The CAF advantage was increased with the introduction of Sidewinders. The Chinese Communists also found that artillery bombardment alone could neither elicit Nationalist defections nor prevent resupply of Chinmen against the support measures which the US/GRC had brought to bear.[1] There were no defections from the offshore island garrisons or on Taiwan, and in fact Nationalist morale seemed to improve.

18. The Chinese Communists were probably surprised to learn that a number of Asian

---

[1] The Chinese Communists found that artillery fire could be effective for temporary neutralization only and could not be decisive unless employed in conjunction with other means; that Communist fire direction means and procedures were inadequate for the reduction of Nationalist fortifications and counterbattery capability; that indirect fire techniques were inadequate to interdict determined amphibious resupply operations executed with modern equipment; and that Communist fortifications offered inadequate protection against accurate Nationalist counterbattery fire.

SECRET

197

SECRET   5

leaders condoned the US counteractions and considered the onus of aggression to be on Communist China. Peiping was concerned over moves by some Asian countries towards compromise proposals it considered unacceptable. Its leaders also found that its military activities in the Strait were having a damaging effect on its influence in Asia, especially since its aggressive action occurred at a time when its commune revolution and its generally tough foreign policy were encountering adverse reactions in Asia.

19. *Peiping's Tactics Since the Crisis.* Communist China's retreat from its earlier military and psychological warfare pressures has almost restored the general pattern of precrisis activity. The principal differences are that the coastal airfields are now occupied and that the level of artillery effort is somewhat greater than that in the weeks immediately preceding the crisis.

20. The principal Chinese Communist effort with respect to the Strait since October has been the attempt to undermine Nationalist morale and to induce Nationalist defections, through sporadic shellings, propaganda appeals, negotiation offers, and the covert passing of letters to contacts and old friends in Taiwan. The present campaign, like similar ones in the past, seeks: (a) to separate by any means the close alliance and defense relationship between the US and Nationalist China—primarily by implying that each is being undercut or sold out by the other; (b) to weaken popular confidence in Nationalist long-term ability to survive as contrasted to Communist China's growing might and "inevitable" victory; (c) to convince officials and technicians on Taiwan that there is a place for them in the "New China"; and (d) to convince the world that Communist China will never accept a "two Chinas" solution and that Communist China's growing strength dictates acceptance of the Communist solution for ending the continuing crisis: US withdrawal from the Taiwan area and no outside interference in the "domestic" struggle between Peiping and Taipei.

21. We have no evidence that the Nationalists are receptive to these Communist overtures or have made clandestine responses to them. We do not believe that the Communist campaign has in fact made much headway. The Nationalists are aware of the many unattractive aspects of communal life on the mainland, the limited role permitted non-Communists there, the greater freedom and the higher standard of life on Taiwan, and the continuing support which Taiwan is receiving from the US. It is possible, however, that some two-way communication, between individuals, may be going on unknown to us.

22. In continuing the Warsaw ambassadorial talks, Communist China has almost certainly not anticipated that they would lead to a surrender of the offshore islands. It has probably continued these talks to create the impression that it is willing to negotiate outstanding issues, and to avoid the onus of breaking off the talks. It probably also hopes to create doubts about the US in the minds of the Chinese Nationalists, and to extract whatever prestige value there may be in holding direct negotiations with the US.

IV. CHINESE COMMUNIST CAPABILITIES [2]

23. There has actually been little change since last October in the military picture in the Taiwan Strait area. Both the Communists and the Nationalists have increased their air strength slightly, and the Nationalists have reinforced their artillery on Chinmen, but the balance of forces remains about the same as it was in August–September. Perhaps the most important change has been an improvement in Chinese Communist resupply and reinforcement capabilities opposite the Matsus as a result of the completion of the rail line to Foochow.

24. Assuming no US intervention, we believe that the Chinese Communists could seize the Matsus or the Chinmens,[3] although at considerable cost. A successful assault against the Matsu Islands could be mounted with the troops already stationed in the Foochow area (an estimated 47,600). We estimate that the

---

[2] See Military Annex and maps (Figures 1–6).

[3] For details concerning the various offshore islands, see maps and paragraph A1 of the Military Annex.

SECRET

6 SECRET

Chinese Communists would consider that 200,000 combat troops would be required for a successful attack on the Chinmens. Although this would necessitate the movement of more than 100,000 additional ground force troops into the Amoy area, such a movement could be made quickly and quite possibly without detection. The degree and nature of US military involvement would be the decisive factor in the outcome of a battle for the larger coastal islands.

25. The Chinese Communists do not have the capability to prevent resupply of Big and Little Chinmen by artillery fire alone.[4] However, the Chinese Communists could make resupply much more difficult and could create considerably greater havoc on the Chinmen group than at any time in the previous crisis should they choose to undertake the intensive and all-target bombardments of which they were and are capable. There are no major logistic limitations to effective resupply of the Communist artillery in the Amoy area.

26. The Chinese Communists do not have the capability to prevent resupply of the Matsus by artillery fire alone. Although the Chinese Communists have an estimated 90 artillery pieces capable of reaching the three northern-most islands, limited observation even during periods of good visibility would preclude effective interdiction.

27. The Chinese Communists could seize any of the small, isolated offshore islands quickly and with little or no warning: specifically, Tung-ting, the Wu-chiu's, and the Tung-yins. Although the Nationalists could support the defense of the Tan Islands (in the Chinmen complex) more effectively than in the case of the more isolated islands, the Chinese Commu-

nists could seize the Tans and deny them to Nationalist recapture. Should Peiping decide to garrison the Tan islands, the Nationalists could seriously harass the defenders.

28. Given the demonstrated superiority of the CAF fighter units, Peiping would have to be prepared to accept disproportionate losses in any air engagements with the Nationalists unless the quality of the Communist fighter units had improved. These losses could become very costly if the battle were prolonged. Despite this qualitative difference, the great numerical advantage of the Chinese Communists over the GRC in aircraft, along with the large number of airfields in close proximity to the offshore islands, give the CCAF the capability to effectively attack Nationalist resupply operations in the offshore island area. The Chinese Communists also have the capability to protect their own surface operations in the area from decisive interference by the Nationalist Air Force. The introduction of Soviet air-to-air missiles and appropriate training would lessen the qualitative difference.

29. By supplementing artillery bombardment with attacks by aircraft and motor torpedo boats, possibly along with offensive minewarfare, the Chinese Communists could make resupply and reinforcement of the offshore island garrisons virtually impossible unless US air and naval forces were committed to keeping the supply lines open.

30. The Chinese Communists have the capability to launch an air or amphibious attack against Taiwan or the Penghus (Pescadores), but could not neutralize or seize these islands against US resistance.

31. There are presently no indications of any Chinese Communist preparations for increased military pressures in the Taiwan Strait. There is no firm evidence that additional troops, heavier artillery, missiles, additional aircraft, additional motor torpedo boats, or minecraft have been moved into the Strait area. However, troops, ships, and aircraft could at any time be committed quickly to operations against the offshore islands, quite possibly without prior detection.

---

[4] The supply situation on the Chinmens at no time reached a dangerous stage during the Taiwan Strait crisis, quantities even of critical items always remaining at about 30 days supply. By the time of the cease-fire, deliveries by sea and air, except as limited by weather, had risen to tonnages exceeding the minimum daily requirements. The supply situation on the Chinmens has been further improved since October. See also Military Annex.

SECRET

SECRET

7

V. PROBABLE CHINESE COMMUNIST COURSES OF ACTION

A. General Considerations

32. We believe that Communist China's basic objectives in the Taiwan Strait area will remain unchanged. After the experience of last year's crisis, however, Communist China's leaders may well estimate that no feasible course of action is likely to lead to an early achievement of their principal objectives. Yet they almost certainly believe that time is on their side and that they will be able to exploit new opportunities which may arise in the Taiwan Strait area in the normal course of events or which may result from their continued pressures.

33. Meanwhile, the present situation must seem to them to offer at least some advantages. They can increase or decrease tension in the Strait area to capitalize on international developments or to serve domestic needs. Their post-October insistence that the offshore islands and Taiwan constitute a single problem which must be solved at one time is probably designed in part to rationalize their inability to capture the islands; clearly they are sensitive to the charge that they backed down during last year's crisis. Nevertheless, they probably also believe, as they have stated, that as long as the Nationalists hold the offshore islands the Taiwan Strait does not form a natural dividing line which might appeal to world sentiment as a basis for a "two Chinas" solution. They may also consider that the present situation contains some opportunities for undermining Nationalist morale and for disturbing US-GRC relations.

34. In the course of the Berlin crisis the Chinese Communists may exercise their ability to heighten tensions in the Taiwan Strait, either as a part of co-ordinated Bloc strategy or in furtherance of their own objectives in the Far East. We believe that the Chinese Communists would not heighten tensions without prior consultation with the Soviets. In either case, the Soviet position would almost certainly depend on the course of the negotia-

tions or on events in the Berlin crisis itself. The Soviets will probably desire to keep tensions in the Far East about as they are at present so long as they judge that the Berlin situation is progressing according to their liking. Should the Soviets estimate that the Berlin situation is going badly for them, they may advise the Chinese Communists to increase tensions in the Far East. The Chinese Communist response to such Soviet advice would be influenced not only by the Berlin situation and Soviet desires but also by Peiping's own estimate of the advantages or disadvantages of heightening tensions in the Taiwan Strait or possibly elsewhere in the Far East. Any moves to heighten tensions in the Taiwan Strait, however, would almost certainly be calculated to fall short of provoking major hostilities.

35. We do not believe that domestic considerations would by themselves cause Communist China to go so far as to undertake a major military effort in the Strait area during the next year. However, Peiping could create greater tension in the Strait area at any time as a means of rallying greater public sacrifice and enthusiasm for its domestic programs of rapid, forced economic development and the communalization of society.

36. Several other factors may influence Peiping's course of action in the Taiwan area. Despite some moderation in recent months of the bellicose tenor of Peiping's general foreign policy statements, some of the assertiveness which characterized its outlook during 1958 is still present. The Taiwan Strait situation provides the easiest outlet for this assertiveness, but if the Chinese Communists saw such opportunities elsewhere, they might feel less inclined to increase pressure in the Strait area. Peiping's action would of course also be affected by any developments which might lead it to see an increased likelihood of a change in US or GRC policies. Continuation of the Warsaw talks might inhibit but will not prevent the Chinese Communists from taking more forceful actions should they so choose.

SECRET

8 SECRET

B. Probable Courses of Action

37. The Chinese Communists will almost certainly seek to avoid hostilities with the US. We believe that they will not attempt to seize Chinmen or undertake an all-out effort to prevent its resupply. We also believe such actions unlikely against the Matsus, though the Chinese Communists may in this case be somewhat less certain of US intentions and possible reactions. However, we believe that the Chinese Communists will continue to employ military pressures in support of their essentially political and psychological campaign in the Taiwan Strait. These pressures will probably not repeat the pattern of last year's unrewarding military activities. However, Peiping will probably attempt to keep the Strait issue alive, and will probably not relax its military pressures to such a degree as to permit the situation to become quiescent over an extended period of time.

38. There are a number of military pressures open to the Chinese Communists. They may engage in periodic heavy shelling and limited air and/or sea operations to harass the Nationalists in the Chinmen and Matsu areas. They might attempt to seize one or more of the small, lightly-held offshore islands, particularly Ta-tan and Erh-tan. Peiping might execute such an assault to support a political move or to provide specific evidence of progress for domestic political and propaganda purposes.

39. Though we believe it unlikely, it is possible that the Chinese Communists may resume intensive and sustained artillery bombardment of the major offshore islands, perhaps using heavier guns. They might initiate aggressive aerial activity over the offshore island area and, possibly, the Strait. We believe, however, that they would be reluctant to expose their air force to the possibility of another humiliating defeat by the CAF, and hence we think them unlikely to initiate such air activity until they have considerably improved the proficiency of their pilots. Sufficient improvement might be accomplished by a few CCAF regiments with present equipment during the next few months. Moreover, during the period of this estimate the CCAF will probably have more advanced aircraft and may also acquire air-to-air missiles.

40. Peiping will probably intensify its political and psychological warfare campaign against the GRC. This can be done with little risk and with minimum demands upon Communist China's leadership or resources. In particular, Peiping might increase its campaign of rumors regarding secret negotiations with GRC leaders. It might renew the offer to negotiate in formal and concrete terms which might win support from some non-Communist countries.

41. Peiping might renew its demand that the US discuss the Taiwan problem and other questions at the ministerial level, perhaps citing the lack of progress in the Warsaw ambassadorial talks to demonstrate the need for higher-level discussions. Peiping would almost certainly rebuff any over-all consideration of Taiwan Strait questions by an international group, particularly by the UN.

42. Although we believe that the Chinese Communists are not likely during the period of this estimate to undertake actions which they believe would run great risks of involvement with US forces, they almost certainly will not change their basic objectives in the area. Over the longer run, as Communist China's economic and military strength grows, its leaders will probably become increasingly audacious in pursuing those objectives.

SECRET

SECRET

9

ANNEX A

MILITARY ANNEX

A. GENERAL

1. The 100-mile wide Taiwan Strait separates the island of Taiwan from the mainland of China.[1] The Penghus (Pescadores), an archipelago of 64 islands, lie about 25 miles west of Taiwan, and like the main island, receive the protective benefits of the relatively wide strait. The offshore islands are not so fortunate, geographically speaking, from a defensive standpoint. These islands consist of two major groups and three lesser groups. The largest is the Chinmen (Quemoy) group consisting of: (1) Chinmen (Quemoy) Island, 47 square miles, garrisoned by five divisions plus supporting troops; (2) Little Chinmen (Little Quemoy, or Lieh Hsu) 6.7 square miles, garrisoned by one division and supporting troops; and (3) the eight small, rocky Tan islets, three of which are garrisoned with lightly armed troops of the Chinmen forces, about 1,200 on Ta-tan, 215 or Erh-tan, and perhaps 70 on Hu-tzu Hsu. The military significance of the Tans (aside from morale considerations) is confined to their usefulness as posts for observation of the Amoy port area. The other major group consists of the Matsu complex, including the Pai-ch'uan or White Dog Islands. The largest island, Matsu, about four square miles, is garrisoned with about 11,500 well-armed regular army troops; Chang-hsu, three square miles, has 5,000 regulars; and Kao-teng, about one square mile and northernmost of the Matsus, has 750 regulars. The southern islands of the complex, the Pai-ch'uans (White Dogs), still have some guerrilla forces, but are mainly manned by regulars: 3,300 on the one square mile of Hsi-ch'uan and 2,300 on the slightly smaller Tung-ch'uan. The other islands of the Matsu complex are not regularly garrisoned.

2. Largest of the somewhat isolated lesser groups is the Tung-yin group. Lying about 26 miles[2] ENE of the nearest island garrisoned by Nationalist regulars (Chang-hsu, in the Matsus), the two rugged small islands (1.8 and 0.6 square miles) comprising the group are held by about 2,000 lightly armed guerrillas. Lying about halfway between Chinmen and Matsu and about 14 miles SE of the mainland are the two Wu-chiu Islands, the larger of which is 250 acres. About 600 lightly-armed guerrillas hold this group. Tiny Tung-ting (Chapel) Island, about 14 miles south of Chinmen and eight miles off the mainland is held by about 70 regulars from a Chinmen division.

3. In the Foochow area the Chinese Communists have an estimated 47,600 troops facing the 23,000 GRC troops in the Matsu Island group. In the Amoy area they have an estimated 86,900 ground force troops facing about 86,000 GRC troops on the Chinmen Island group. The GRC garrisons on the Chinmens and the Matsus are now at or about optimum strength. Artillery strength in the Chinmen and Matsu areas is approximately as follows:

COMMUNIST		NATIONALIST	
Chinmen Area			
152-mm	108	8 inch Hows	11
122-mm	264	155-mm Guns	20
76, 75 and 57-mm	237	155-mm Hows	84
		105-mm Hows	122
		75-mm Hows	80
TOTAL	609[3]	TOTAL	317
Matsu Area			
152-mm	2	155-mm Guns	8
122-mm	88	105-mm Hows	60
76 or 57-mm	15	75-mm Hows	12
TOTAL	105	TOTAL	80

[2] All over-water distances in this note are given in *nautical* miles.

[3] All but 63 of the Communist artillery pieces in the Chinmen area are believed to be within range of Nationalist positions. In addition to the pieces listed there are 274 covered positions in the area, the occupancy of which cannot be determined. (See Figures 3 and 4)

[1] See maps (Figures 1–6).

SECRET

10

SECRET

4. Prevailing weather conditions in the Taiwan Strait determine to a great extent the Nationalist capability for resupply and reinforcement of any of the offshore islands, and also are a limiting factor in any attempted invasion of Taiwan and the Penghus by the Communists. The gentle, variable winds and light seas of spring (April through June) provide optimum conditions for movement across the Taiwan Strait. During the summer (July through September), when the typhoon risk is high, traffic from Taiwan to the offshore islands may be completely disrupted for relatively long periods. The strong northeasterly winds in the fall and winter cause a period of heavy seas which also restrict movement and confine offloading to a few especially favorable, leeward beach sites. Seasonal variations in weather are of far less significance for amphibious operations from the mainland against the offshore islands.

B. THE CHINESE NATIONALISTS

5. *Logistical Considerations.* The Communist interdiction of the Chinese Nationalist efforts to resupply the Chinmen garrison created the outstanding problem of the Taiwan Strait crisis. However, the supply situation on Chinmen (Quemoy) never degenerated to a dangerous stage during the Taiwan Strait crisis. The Communists' interdiction of the resupply effort influenced the extent of the Nationalists' counterbattery artillery fire, and undoubtedly initiated a general austere supply consumption program. However, by 6 October 1958 (when the Communists announced their unilateral cease-fire), Nationalist resupply had reached a point where adequate supplies were being delivered despite the interdiction effort. The amount of resupply to support the Chinmen garrison was computed by MAAG Taiwan to be a daily average of 320 tons, which included 900 rounds of counterbattery artillery ammunition. For the four days immediately prior to the cease-fire, air deliveries alone averaged 240 tons daily. For the period 14–30 September, despite interdiction and bad weather, daily deliveries averaged approximately 175 tons. Individual

day's efforts of 553 tons (27 September) and 422 tons (1 October) were recorded. During the two-week period immediately following the cease-fire a total of about 40,000 tons of supplies was delivered.

6. The valuable experience gained in continuing to resupply the island despite the Communist artillery fire has greatly improved the amphibious and aerial delivery capabilities of the GRC. The supply status of both Chinmen and Matsu as of February 1959 indicated that the garrisons have stocks of supplies on hand sufficient for approximately three months.

STATUS OF SUPPLY ON CHINMEN IN DAYS OF SUPPLY

Class	7 Sep 58 [*]	14 Feb 59
I ....(Rations)	33	94
II–IV ...(Equipment)	46–60	90–129
III ......(POL)	53	96
V ....(Small Arms)	90	90
V ....(Artillery)	33–78	84

CHINMEN STOCKS OF ARTILLERY AMMUNITION BY ROUND AS OF 14 FEBRUARY 1959

8 inch Hows	30,081
155-mm Hows	296,797
155-mm Guns	60,620
105-mm Hows	491,812
90-mm Guns	11,155

7. The amphibious craft of the Nationalist Navy, supplemented by the BARCs (barge, amphibious, resupply cargo) assigned the Army, can transport more than the minimal level of 320 tons daily to resupply the offshore islands. The Chinese Nationalist Air Force has the capability of delivering approximately 300 tons of supplies daily to the offshore islands.

8. *Naval Forces.* The naval losses sustained by the GRC during the 1958 hostilities have been partially replaced, and additional US ships are programmed for the next six months.

PRESENT GRC NAVAL FORCES
60,800 personnel, including 25,000 marines

Destroyers	4	Subchasers	15
Escort vessels	14	Amphibious vessels	61
Minelayers	2	Auxiliaries and	
Minesweepers ..	7	service craft	67

[*] Prior to receipt of resupply.

SECRET

SECRET   11

Although GRC ship strength is slightly below the August 1958 level, losses have not been major, and will be exceeded by replacements. There have been no significant changes in deployment. The amphibious capability of the GRC Marine Corps continues to improve as newer equipment is received, particularly tanks, and more landing exercises are conducted. It is now considered capable of mounting raiding operations against the mainland.

9. *Air Forces.* The decisive victories scored by Nationalist F-86F's over Communist MIG's in the August-October air battles clearly demonstrated the high level of training and excellent caliber of CAF fighter units. Their F-86F fighter squadrons must be ranked among the world's finest air combat units in daylight operations. This excellent fighter capability is being improved as increasing numbers of Nationalist pilots are being trained in the use of the Sidewinder air-to-air missile. Since the easing of tensions in the Strait, the CAF has also attempted to improve its airground support capability through extensive training. The CAF's transport and troop carrier squadrons performed well in resupplying Chinmen during the recent crisis and further such training is being achieved as the airlift of supplies and personnel to Chinmen continues. Lastly, training in paratroop drops has also been extensive in the past few months.

10. The over-all capability of the CAF has been improved in recent months by the receipt of new equipment from the United States. Installation of Sidewinder equipment on additional fighters has increased the CAF's combat capability; it is expected that a total of 155 Nationalist fighters will be equipped with these missiles by the end of 1959. Fighter capabilities are also being improved as the more advanced F-86F replaces the F-84G's in Nationalist fighter squadrons. About 90 F-100's will probably become operational during 1960. The loan of 16 C-119's for an indefinite period has augmented the CAF's airlift capabilities.

11. The GRC's present total aircraft inventory in operational units is as follows: [5]

	Operational
Jet Fighters	397
Jet Fighters (Reconnaissance)	21
Jet Light Bombers (Reconnaissance)	3
Land-Based ASW	4
Piston Transport	117
Other Jet	—
Other Piston	10
TOTALS	552 [*]

12. *Missiles.* The GRC antiaircraft strength has been enhanced by the movement of a US Nike-Hercules battalion into the Taipei area. This has allowed the redeployment of the Nationalist AAA units which formerly defended Taipei to other strategic areas. There is also a US Matador squadron on Taiwan.

13. *Offshore Islands Defense.* Major emphasis has been given to improving the Nationalist counterbattery artillery capability of the offshore islands during and following the Taiwan Strait crisis:

a. *Chinmen:* At the beginning of the crisis in August 1958, the Nationalist artillery units assigned to the Chinmen Defense Command consisted largely of the light artillery organic to the six infantry divisions of the Command, totalling 308 pieces. Of these, only the fifty-six 155-guns and howitzers were capable of delivering effective counterbattery fire against the more than 600 Communist artillery pieces being employed against the island complex. By 1 November 1958, however, GRC artillery on Chinmen and Little Chinmen capable of counterbattery fire had been about doubled. This had been accomplished by a shift in emphasis from light to medium and heavy artillery even though the total number of guns had increased by only nine during this period. In addition, twelve 240-mm howitzers are now being readied on Taiwan for Nationalist use on Chinmen; however, date of deployment is uncertain. Further, the Nationalists are improving their observation capability with action already underway to provide equipment

---

[5] There is no GRC naval air force.

[*] In addition there are about 237 aircraft in non-operational status: training, storage, or obsolescent.

SECRET

204

12   SECRET

and training for sound and flash bases, and electronic meteorological sections for the offshore islands. (See Figures 3 and 4)

b. *Matsu:* The artillery inventory in the Matsu Defense Command in August totaled 32 guns and howitzers, and has been increased to 80 since that date. The Communists have approximately an 11 to 1 ratio of counterbattery weapons compared to the Nationalists in the Matsu area, while the ratio in the Chinmen area is only 3 to 1. The Matsus have a much lower priority than the Chinmen complex; however, plans call for an augmentation of the heavy artillery. (See Figure 5)

14. The military position of the GRC on the offshore islands, particularly the main island of Chinmen, has shown substantial improvement since the Taiwan Strait crisis in the fall of 1958. The Nationalist troops on Chinmen still number about 86,000; however, the GRC has agreed "in principle" to a reduction of about 15,000 men. The agreed reduction in personnel is to be offset by increases in artillery and automatic weapons, so that the overall defensive capability of the islands will be strengthened. If this were accomplished, the number of divisions deployed on the Chinmens would be reduced from six to five. The present Chinese Nationalist infantry division has approximately 63 percent of the personnel, 33 percent of the vehicles, and less than 50 percent of the artillery and crew-served weapons of the US World War II type division. The newly adopted "Forward Look" infantry division of the GRC (seven divisions of a total of 21 are scheduled to be reorganized by December 1959) will have about 57 percent of the personnel, 50 percent of the vehicles and crew-served weapons, and the same artillery as the US World War II type division. One or more of these new divisions will probably be committed to Chinmen during 1959. Neither of the GRC type divisions has organic armor assigned. Morale of troops on the offshore islands, including the small Tan Islands, is reported as excellent.

15. Nationalist capabilities for defense of the offshore islands could probably not be significantly impaired by local subversion or sabotage. With full US support brought to bear in time, Chinese Nationalist forces probably could hold the major offshore islands indefinitely; without such support, they probably could not long withstand an all-out attack.

C. THE CHINESE COMMUNISTS

16. *Logistical Considerations.* Although the Taiwan Strait is a substantial barrier affording protection to Taiwan and to the Penghus, there are no significant logistical difficulties in operations against the offshore islands, except, probably, in the supply of POL. The Communist surface transportation system will accommodate a maximum of 7,500 tons per day into the Amoy-Foochow area. The two cities share the rail (5,000 tons) and river (2,000) capacity. In addition, there is a road capacity of 500 tons per day. An indication of the adequacy of this transportation capacity is seen in the estimated weight of artillery ammunition expended during the first six weeks of the bombardment of Chinmen. In August-October 1958 the average daily expenditure of artillery ammunition was 450 tons and the total expended was approximately 20,000 tons—consumed from an estimated 220,000 ton stockpile and an annual production rate by Communist China of about 44,000 tons. The daily supply requirements for a Chinese Communist Army in combat is 509 tons, again indicating the adequacy of the mainland transportation system in the Foochow-Amoy area to support military operations. Interior bottlenecks, an over-all shortage of rolling stock, and POL shortages, however, would develop during an extended operation.

17. *Naval Forces.* The over-all naval strength of the Chinese Communists has improved slightly during the past several months, but this improvement is believed part of the programmed naval buildup that has taken place over the past several years and is not related directly to the Taiwan Strait crisis.

PRESENT CHINESE COMMUNIST NAVAL FORCES
57,000 personnel, not including 8,000 in naval aviation

Destroyers	4	Patrol vessels (including 125 motor torpedo boats)	209
Submarines	21		
Escort vessels	4		
Mine vessels	33	Landing ships	53
		Service craft (appx.)	300

SECRET

SECRET   13

In the offshore islands area, the strength of Chinese Communist Naval Forces appears to be about the same as at the climax of the recent crisis, no known permanent deployments of submarine, major surface or landing ship units into the Strait having taken place. The relatively shallow water in the Taiwan Strait makes the effective use of submarines more difficult, and greatly increases their vulnerability to ASW operations.

18. It is difficult to fix the number of small Chinese Communist vessels in the area at present. Based on the demonstrated ease with which motor torpedo boats can be introduced undetected, the strength of small patrol and landing craft types could be covertly augmented over a relatively short period of time. Moreover, in view of the relatively short distances involved, the bulk of major naval strength could be deployed into the Straits over a 24–48 hour period with little or no prior indication. There have been no authenticated instances of the employment of mine-warfare by the Chinese Communists; neither have there been positive indications of mine stockpiles along the Strait. However, the emphasis which the Chinese Communist Navy is known to place on such doctrine, coupled with an appreciable capability for mine delivery from all types of vessels, makes the occurrence of offensive mining a possibility to be reckoned with in the event of a renewal of hostilities.

19. *Air Forces.* With the possible exception of a small increase in fighter strengths, Chinese Communist Air Force levels have remained about the same in the Taiwan Strait area as they were during August–October 1958. At present, there are approximately 200–250 jet fighters based on the airfields in the Foochow-Swatow area. While there are no bomber aircraft operating from these fields, the Chinese Communists continue to have jet light bombers based at airfields well within striking range of Taiwan. It is possible that the Chinese Communists have some bomber forces in areas directly behind the coastal airfields.

20. The Chinese Communists must have been highly displeased with the performance of their fighter pilots during the crisis, and we consequently believe that they must be conducting an intensive training effort to rectify this weakness. However, we have no direct evidence of any such effort. It is estimated that it would take about four months of intensive training to make a CCAF regiment combat proficient (with existing equipment).

21. It is possible that the Chinese Communists have received some MIG–19 aircraft from the Soviet Union; several months would probably be required, however, before Chinese pilots would be capable of effectively using this aircraft in combat.

22. We consider it likely that the embarrassing air losses suffered by the Chinese Communists last fall, along with the glimpse they had of the effectiveness of the Sidewinder air-to-air missiles, have led the Chinese Communists to press the USSR for similar weapons. We have estimated that the Soviets have developed several types of short-range air-to-air missiles, equipped with HE warheads. These could be made available for use by Chinese Communist jet fighters; we have no evidence, however, to confirm or deny the existence of such weapons in mainland China.

23. The combined Chinese Communist Air Force and Naval Air Force include 2,395 operational jet aircraft, of which 1,795 are fighters and 460 are light bombers. The present total aircraft inventory in operational units is estimated to be:

	Operational
Jet Fighter	1,795
Piston Fighter	35
Jet Light Bomber	460
Piston Light Bomber/Tactical/Attack	235
Land-Based ASW	10
Piston Medium Bomber	20
Piston Transport	190
Jet Trainers	140
Other Piston	150
TOTALS	3,035 *

24. *Reinforcement Capability.* Within 12 days the forces in the Amoy-Foochow area can be reinforced by approximately 255,000 troops, including three airborne divisions (of 7,000

---

* In addition there are about 1,385 aircraft in non-operational status: training, storage, or obsolescent.

SECRET

14

SECRET

troops each), quite possibly without detection by GRC or US forces. Within 21 days an additional 46,000 troops could be deployed to the Amoy-Foochow area, making an estimated total force of 24 infantry divisions assembled there. These moves would not involve any redeployment of those coastal units now stationed outside of the immediate Amoy and Foochow areas (which presumably would be kept in position against the possibility of a Nationalist counterattack). Compared with a World War II type US infantry division, the Chinese Communist infantry division has approximately the same personnel strength (about 17,000), but only 50 percent as much artillery, and 25 percent of the tanks and motor vehicles. Morale of the Chinese Communist forces is considered good.

25. *Lift Capabilities.* In an amphibious assault against Chinmen or Matsu it is unlikely that larger amphibious units (LST, LSM) would be employed due to the extremely adverse beaching conditions. However, by employing lesser amphibious units (LCU, LCM) and readily available native craft, in successive waves, the Chinese Communists have the capability of launching assaults with forces numerically superior to the defenders on either the Chinmens or the Matsus. Timely warning might not be available that final preparations for either operation had been completed.

26. Utilizing assigned transport aircraft, together with available civil transport, and disregarding normal maintenance and operational attrition, as well as combat attrition, it is possible that a maximum Chinese Communist airborne force of up to 10,200 men could be dropped on the offshore islands in two lifts on D-Day, followed by 5,100 men on D+1 Day, and the remaining 5,700 men of the three airborne divisions on D+2 Days. This airborne force is essentially light infantry, since the Chinese Communists do not have the aircraft or the capability to drop vehicles, or artillery larger than the pack 75-mm howitzer. Sufficient airfields are available in southeast China to mount such an operation within close range of the Nationalist positions. The use of helicopters to move personnel from the mainland to the Chinmen or Matsu Islands could increase the total force available by a considerable number, depending on the number of lifts flown. The Chinese Communists have an estimated 40 helicopters capable of carrying 16 troops each.

27. *Missiles.* There is no present evidence to corroborate recent low-level reports that the USSR has supplied short-range ballistic missiles to Communist China, and there are no confirmed indications that the Chinese Communists have any type of missile in the Taiwan Strait area. The absence of firm evidence does not, of course, preclude the possibility that the Chinese Communists may have received Soviet missiles and may have deployed some to the Taiwan Strait area, though we believe it unlikely.

SECRET

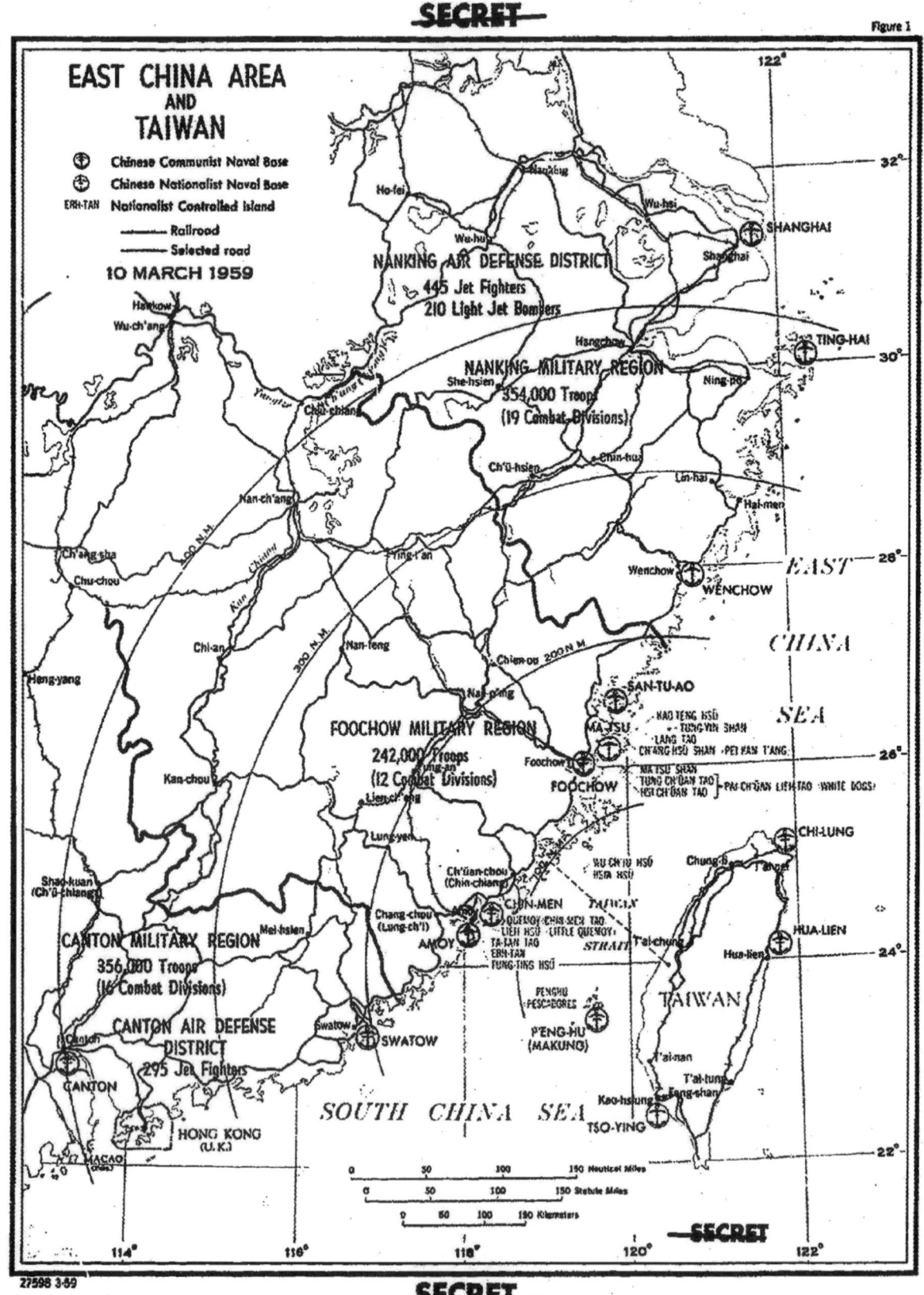

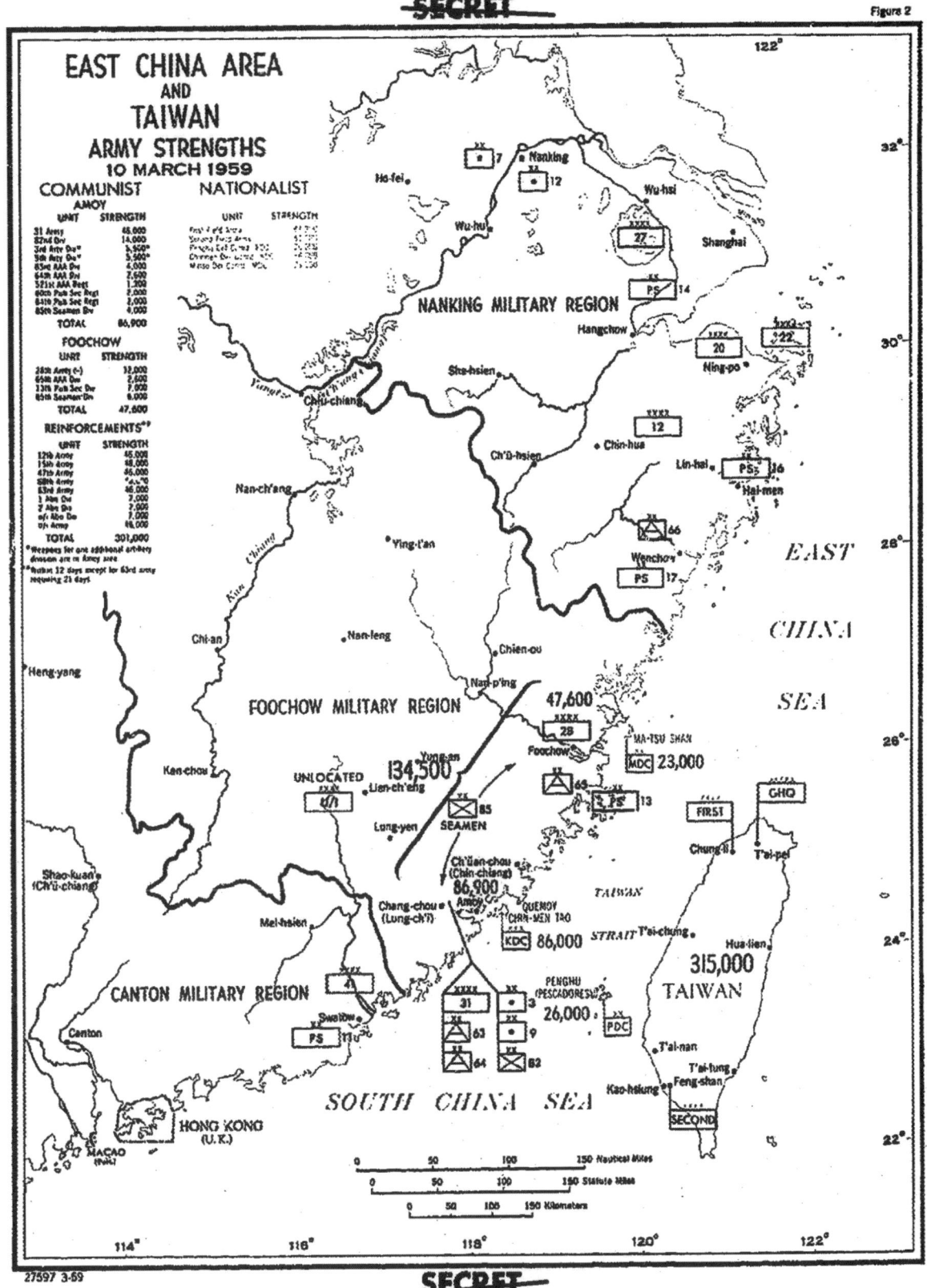

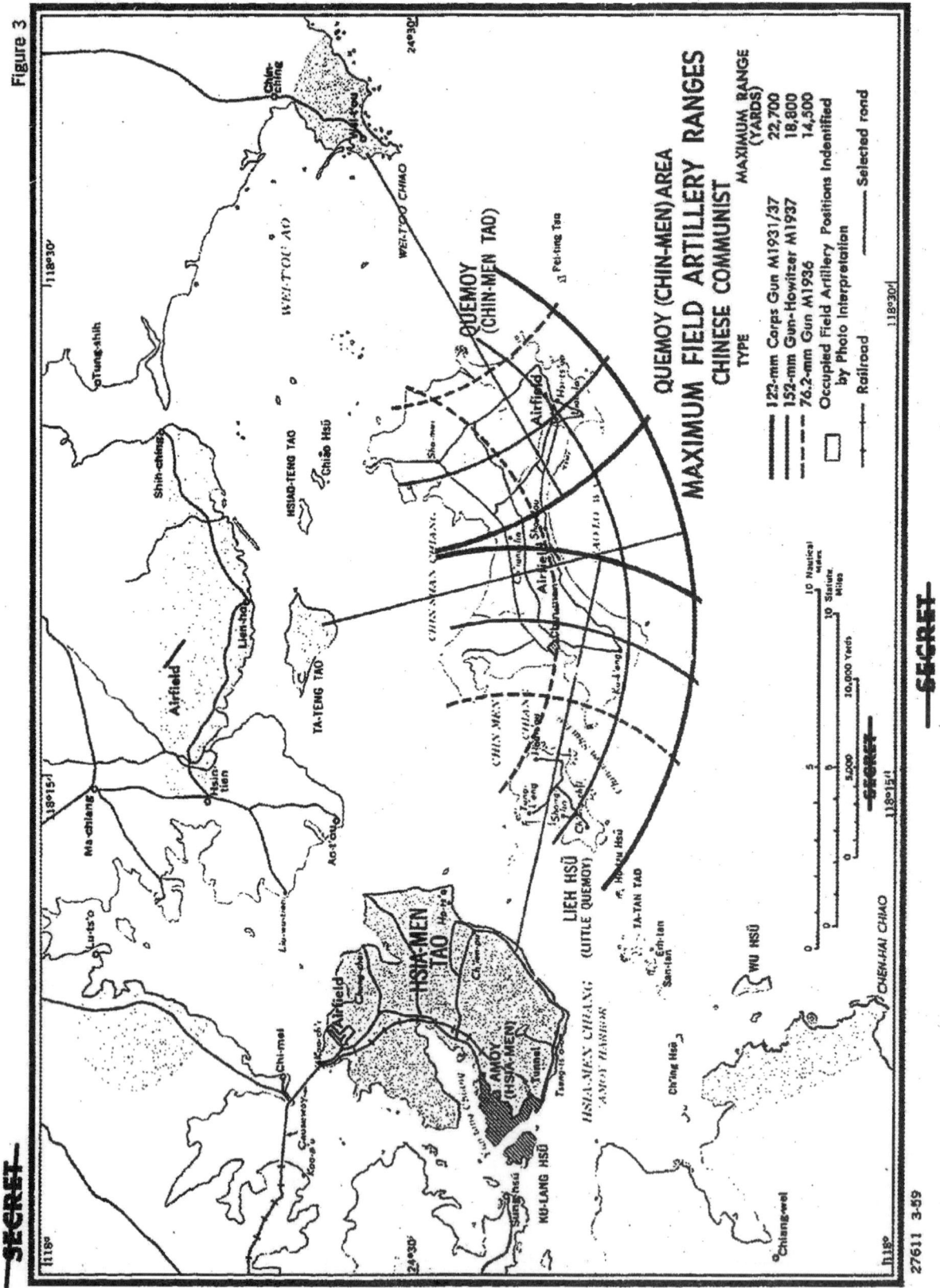

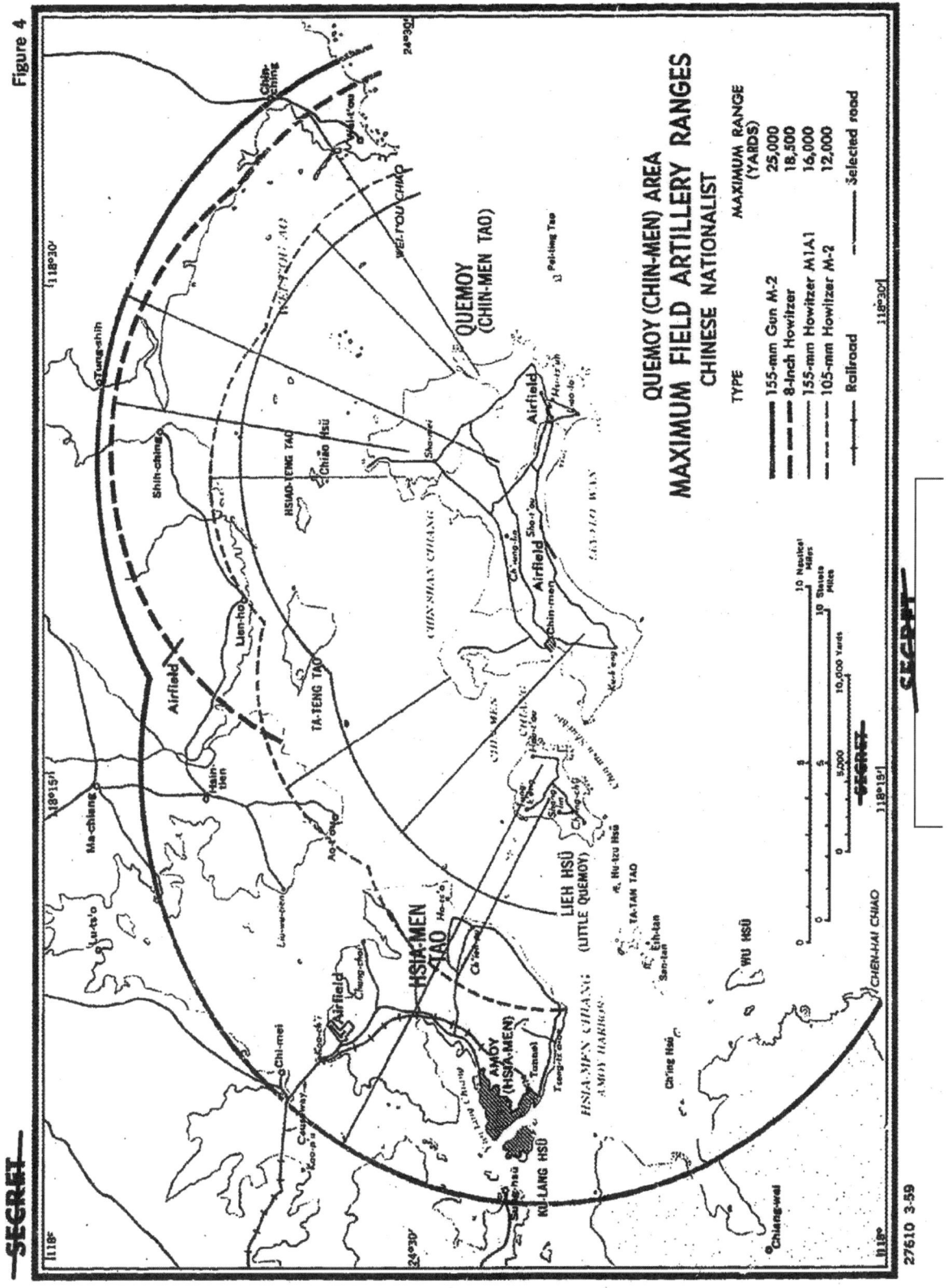

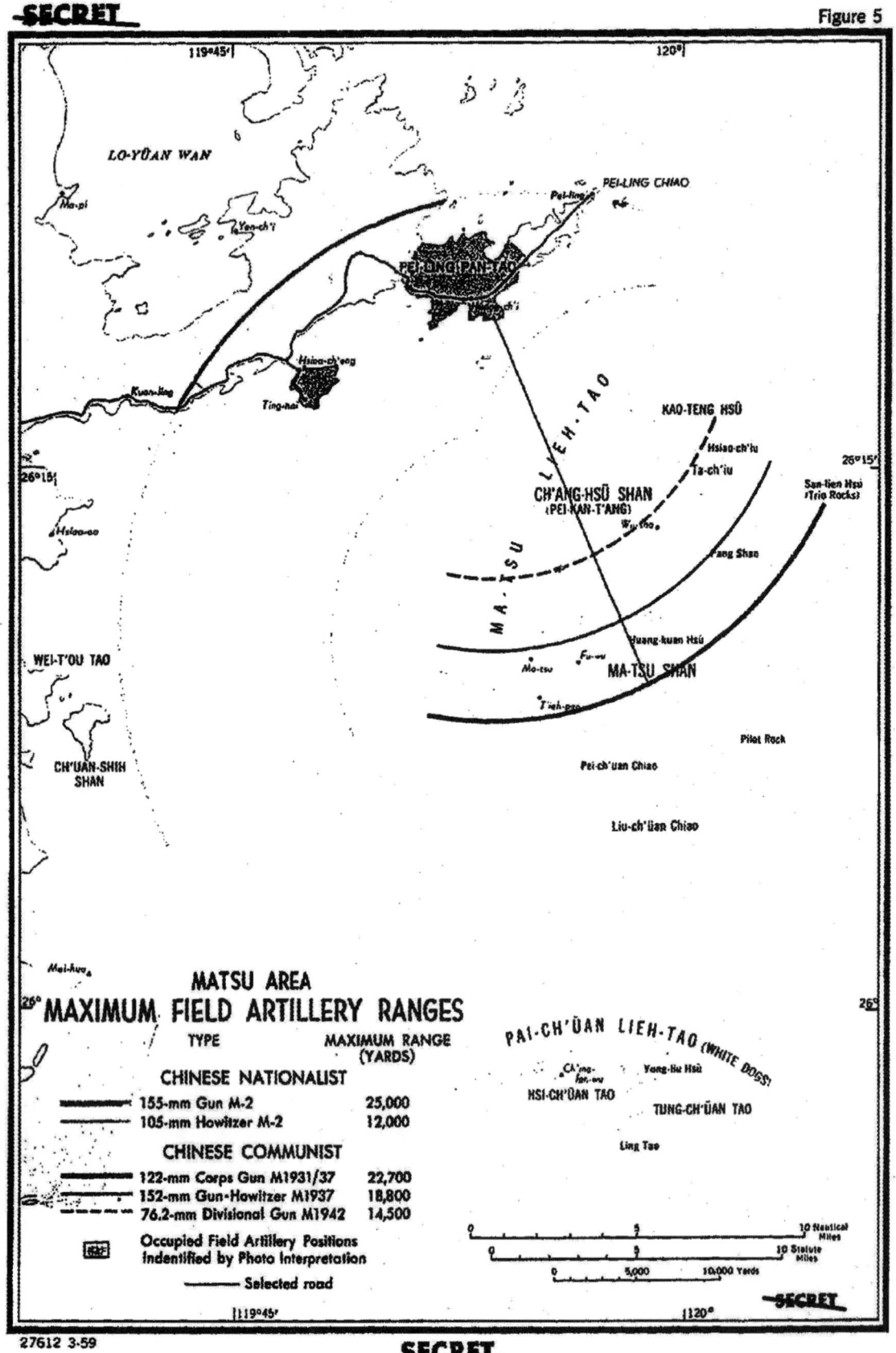

Figure 5

SECRET

MATSU AREA
MAXIMUM FIELD ARTILLERY RANGES

TYPE	MAXIMUM RANGE (YARDS)
CHINESE NATIONALIST	
155-mm Gun M-2	25,000
105-mm Howitzer M-2	12,000
CHINESE COMMUNIST	
122-mm Corps Gun M1931/37	22,700
152-mm Gun-Howitzer M1937	18,800
76.2-mm Divisional Gun M1942	14,500

Occupied Field Artillery Positions
Indentified by Photo Interpretation

Selected road

27612 3-59

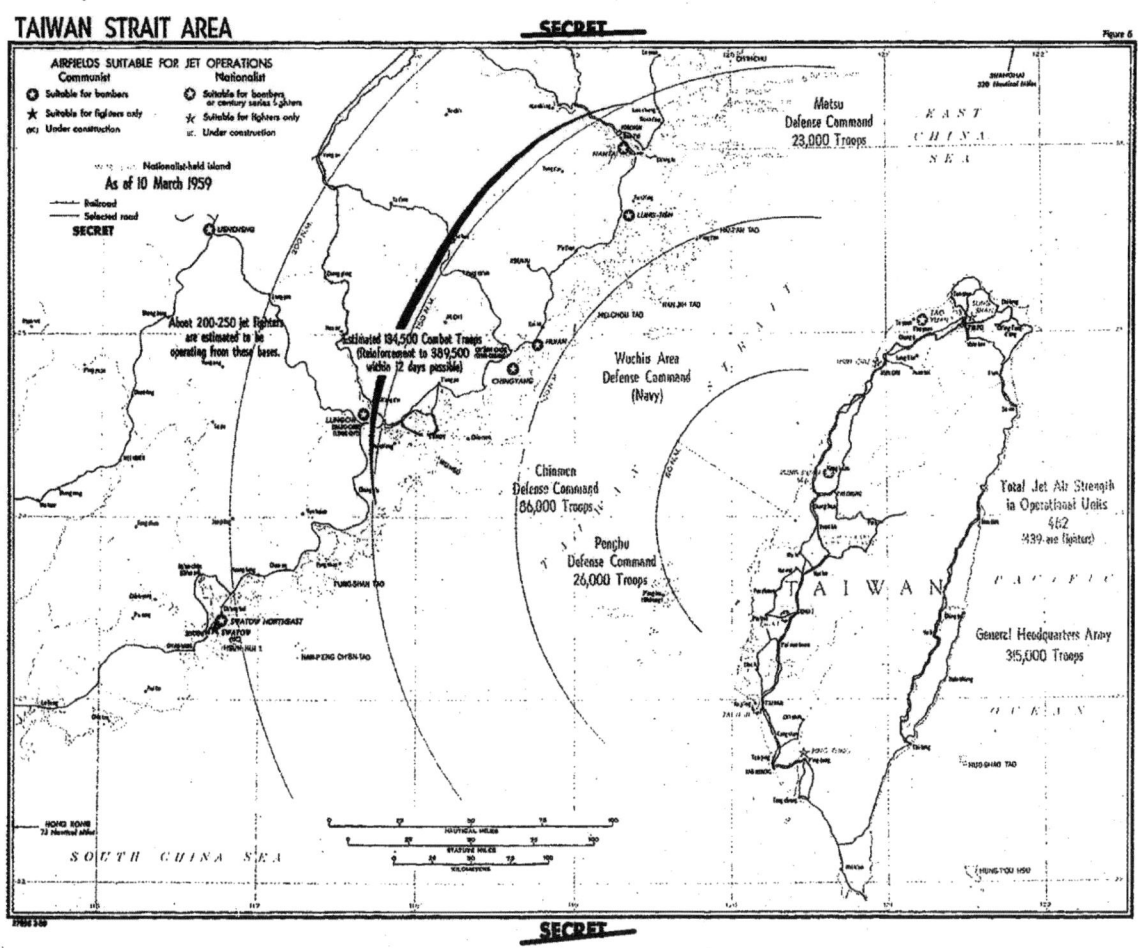

SECTION 16

NIE 100-3-60

Sino-Soviet Relations

9 August 1960

APPROVED FOR RELEASE
DATE: MAY 2004

NIE 100-3-60
9 August 1960

~~SECRET~~

NATIONAL INTELLIGENCE ESTIMATE
NUMBER 100-3-60

SINO-SOVIET RELATIONS

Submitted by the
DIRECTOR OF CENTRAL INTELLIGENCE

The following intelligence organizations participated in the preparation of this estimate: The Central Intelligence Agency and the intelligence organizations of the Departments of State, the Army, the Navy, the Air Force, The Joint Staff, and AEC.

Concurred in by the
UNITED STATES INTELLIGENCE BOARD

on 9 August 1960. Concurring were The Director of Intelligence and Research, Department of State; the Assistant Chief of Staff for Intelligence, Department of the Army; the Assistant Chief of Naval Operations for Intelligence, Department of the Navy; the Assistant Chief of Staff, Intelligence, USAF; the Director for Intelligence, The Joint Staff; the Atomic Energy Commission Representative to the USIB; the Assistant to the Secretary of Defense, Special Operations; and the Director of the National Security Agency. The Assistant Director, Federal Bureau of Investigation, abstained, the subject being outside of his jurisdiction.

~~SECRET~~   N⁰ 391

SECRET

SINO-SOVIET RELATIONS

THE PROBLEM

To examine the Sino-Soviet relationship, and to estimate probable developments therein over the next five years.

CONCLUSIONS

1. The growth of Communist China's power and self-confidence has brought to the Sino-Soviet relationship an increased Chinese assertiveness and a consequent sharp increase in discord, particularly concerning outlook and attitude toward the non-Communist world. There is still one Communist faith, but there are now two voices of Communist authority. As a consequence, the Sino-Soviet relationship is in process of difficult change. (*Paras. 7–9*)

2. The Sino-Soviet relationship is not a Communist monolith. Instead, it contains elements of both cohesion and division, and varying degrees of unity are displayed in the relations of the two powers in ideological, foreign policy, economic, and military affairs. Although joined in the pursuit of broad Communist objectives, the Soviet and Chinese partnership is subject to many of the separatist forces that have traditionally confronted alliances and coalitions. (*Paras. 58–63*)

3. We believe that cohesive forces in the Sino-Soviet relationships will remain stronger than divisive forces at least through the period of this estimate. The strongest of the cohesive forces will be a mutual awareness of the heavy damage to their national interests and to the Communist cause which a substantial impairment of the alliance would inflict. The two partners will almost certainly continue to share a common hostility to the West and a belief that through their common effort in advancing international communism they can someday participate in dominating the world. Their relationship will also continue to find cohesion in the political, economic, and military advantages each receives. This will have particular force for the Chinese who, in view of their continuing military and economic dependence on the USSR, will probably feel that they have no genuinely acceptable alternative to maintaining their alliance with the Soviets. (*Paras. 13–14, 64–65*)

SECRET

1

SECRET   2

4. Divisive forces continue to be present, however, and may increase. Differing national interests and characteristics, and the wide disparity in the development of the USSR and Communist China as Communist societies, will continue to exert basic stresses on the Sino-Soviet relationship. Communist China's relative weight in the Bloc is likely to grow over the next five years. This growth will diminish the leverage Moscow can bring to bear through Peiping's military and economic dependence. The Chinese Communists will be more inclined to pursue their own interests and to question Soviet leadership than they have during the first decade of the alliance. (*Paras. 15–17, 66*)

5. We do not rule out the possibility that the two powers may during the period of this estimate either come to an open break or reach a more fundamental integration of interests than now exists. We believe it much more likely, however, that there will be no fundamental reconciliation of differences, that discord will ebb and flow, and that the growing duality of power in the Bloc will become increasingly incompatible with the present Bloc structure which has been based on a single source of authority. However, differences will be unlikely to force the USSR and Communist China so far apart that they cease to look to each other for support in their common drive against the West. (*Paras. 67–69*)

6. The threat which the Sino-Soviet allies pose to US security and US interests is of great dimensions and is more likely to increase than to diminish during the period of this estimate. Nevertheless, since the alliance is a changing and evolving relationship, it offers possibilities for favorable as well as unfavorable developments from the US point of view. Stresses and strains in the Sino-Soviet relationship will tend to weaken the hostile combination, and may provide situations and opportunities which can be exploited by the West. At the same time, Chinese Communist pressure may on occasion influence the Soviets to pursue a more militant course toward the West than the Soviets would otherwise choose on tactical grounds. (*Paras. 70–71*)

DISCUSSION

I. INTRODUCTION

7. The Sino-Soviet relationship has of late been publicly displaying greater signs of apparent strain than at any time in its decade of existence: most importantly, the USSR and Communist China have been engaged in a controversy over global strategy in which each claims to be preaching the true doctrine. Disputes of this magnitude raise the question as to whether the Sino-Soviet relationship can long maintain its present character or its present degree of coordination.

8. The history of the Communist movement has been marked by controversies and schisms. These have occurred not only within the Communist Party of the Soviet Union, but between parties and between Communist regimes as well. Where disputes have reached serious proportions they have generally been settled by an exercise of Moscow's power. Occasionally, however, Moscow has either not sought or has not been able to exert such power, and schisms have occurred. The most notable example is Yugoslavia.

SECRET

SECRET

3

9. Until Communist China began to emerge as a great power, the Communist movement had not experienced a serious controversy involving a major potential rival to the USSR. Since Communist experience provides no clear precedent for settling such a dispute between major Communist powers, the present contention between Moscow and Peiping foreshadows a difficult test for the Sino-Soviet relationship in offsetting inherent schismatic forces. The outcome will in the long run significantly influence the future course of world communism, internally and externally. It will also have profound implications for the interests of the US and the West. The discussion which follows seeks to examine the nature of the Sino-Soviet relationship and to estimate its future course.

II. THE BASES OF THE SINO-SOVIET RELATIONSHIP

A. Evolution of the Relationship

10. The present Sino-Soviet relationship has been molded by an association—sometimes harmonious, sometimes discordant—of nearly 40 years' standing between the Communist Party of the Soviet Union and the Chinese Communist Party. Beginning with the founding of the Chinese Communist Party in 1921, the two groups shared a belief both in revolutionary communism, and in the goals of overthrowing existing Chinese regimes and destroying Western influence in China. It was to the interests of the USSR to sponsor the nascent Communist movement in China. To the Chinese Communist Party, in its early years a weak and disparate assortment of intellectuals, labor leaders, and military figures, the USSR was initially the only source of guidance and support.

11. There have been difficulties inherent in this relationship from the outset. Stalin's faulty comprehension of the Chinese scene led to a degree of misguidance that at times almost wrecked the Chinese Communist Party.[1] The USSR continued historic Rus-

---

[1] Chinese Communist media continue occasionally to criticize the courses taken, especially in the years 1931–1934, by "misguided" Chinese leaders who "automatically copied foreign experience."

sian efforts to obtain special rights and influence in China. China lacked even the economic base and administrative-technical skills which the Bolsheviks inherited in the Russia of 1917. Marxism, which had once been transplanted to the Russian scene, then required even more radical adaptations to fit it to an agrarian Chinese setting.

12. These problems were fairly manageable as long as the Chinese Communist Party was only a revolutionary instrument for pulling down the existing Chinese state, but the situation began to take on a new aspect once the Chinese Communist Party had firmly established its authority in China. To a far greater extent than the Soviet Satellites, it won its victory by its own efforts. The Peiping regime had developed its own sources of political and military power, independent of direct Soviet control. The terms of the Sino-Soviet Alliance (14 February 1950) accorded it special status within the Bloc, and it soon became clear that Peiping could in some respects set its own course. Mao had already gained a reputation as a doctrinal innovator; the foundation had been laid for Peiping to become a unique second source of authority in what had been a monolithic Bloc.

B. Underlying Forces

13. A number of very strong ties bind Communist China and the USSR. The leaders of both countries share a common core of philosophy and confront a common enemy. They join in perceiving the world powers as divided into two hostile camps and in placing their two countries on the same side. The Soviet and Chinese Communist leaders declare that there is an overriding need to preserve the unity of the Bloc in carrying on the struggle against the common enemy, and especially against its leading element, the US, the arch-enemy by definition.

14. Each nation derives great practical benefits from its association with the other. The USSR and Communist China both appreciate the great increase in strategic strength that derives from their alliance. Their possession of a large land mass fronting on two oceans obliges the West to disperse its military

SECRET

SECRET   4

strength widely in opposing the Bloc. The fact that Communist China opposes the West in Asia immobilizes a considerable portion of Western armed forces, diverts Western political and economic assets, and enables Moscow to concentrate its forces elsewhere. It was demonstrated in Korea that in certain circumstances Chinese Communist armed forces may serve Soviet interests without necessarily involving Soviet armed forces in direct conflict with the West. For its part, Communist China has received economic backing and technical support which has been essential to its industrial development. It has also received guidance in the establishing and administering of a Communist totalitarian state, support from the Soviet Union in international forums, equipment for a powerful military establishment, and the protection of the Soviet nuclear capability.

15. Basic stresses, however, underlie the relationship. National identity—that is, the whole spectrum of peculiarly national interests and national characteristics—is a powerful separatist force. Russia and China are nations with long and proud traditions, and the Russians and the Chinese are very different peoples whose relations with one another have often been marked by enmity and reciprocal contempt. The Chinese Communists, in particular, continue to manifest traditional Chinese extreme pride and sense of superiority. Although both the Soviet and Chinese Communist leaderships preach that "nationalist thinking" is an evil to be overcome, their primary appeals to their publics are overwhelmingly keyed to national pride and aspiration. "Proletarian internationalism" has not bridged the gulf that exists between the heritages, cultures, and psychological outlook of the Russians and the Chinese.

16. The wide disparity in the development of the USSR and China as Communist societies also places important stresses on their relationship. The immediate needs and objectives of the two countries differ in many respects. Communist China is in the early stages of building an industrial base; it feels compelled to drive its people, squeeze its capital from their output, and prolong extreme

austerity. The prevailing mood is revolutionary. On the other hand, the relatively mature and affluent Soviet Union has reached the stage where it is giving greater attention to the working conditions and living standards of its people in order to achieve the planned expansion and qualitative improvement of its economy. In addition, the Soviet people almost certainly have an increasing stake in preserving the gains in living standards and freedom from terror that they have experienced since Stalin's death.

17. The greatly different status of the two partners in international affairs also exerts a separatist force. The foreign policy outlook of Communist China is heavily influenced by the fact that it does not itself play a central role in international councils and it lacks many of the attributes of the great power status it covets. Because of relative isolation in international affairs and its geographical position, Communist China is an Asian power with immediate interests concentrated in that area and with little opportunity or capability for realistically assessing the situation in the West. Its foreign policy aspirations are frustrated not only by Western opposition but also by Soviet restraints.

III. THE CHARACTER OF THE SINO-SOVIET RELATIONSHIP

A. Communist Relations

18. *Ideology.* The leaders of both countries draw upon the same Marxist-Leninist system of thought for their appreciation of international and domestic affairs. They share a common faith in the ultimate world triumph of communism, believing themselves to be riding the crest of inevitable historic development. They are unalterably opposed to what they consider to be the decadent system of capitalism, which has in their view reached its final stage in imperialism. They believe that their efforts can hasten the destruction of capitalism. In addition, the Soviet and Chinese leaders also agree that Communists must gain and hold power in other countries, and that a "dictatorship of the proletariat" must be established, led by the Communist Party, to oversee forced development of the

SECRET

SECRET

economy through state planning and state ownership of the means of production.

19. In practice, however, the interpretation and application of ideological "truths" is at times a divisive force in the Sino-Soviet relationship. Although in both regimes all policies are conceived within the Communist frame of reference and some may be largely motivated by doctrinal concepts, we believe that most major policy decisions are primarily directed by practical considerations. In any case, every important switch and turn of policy in the Communist world must be accompanied by doctrinal justification. In the past few years both the Soviet and Chinese Communist leaders have endeavored to sanctify widely differing policies by citing selected excerpts from the vast and often contradictory mass of Communist scripture, claiming in the process that their leaders, Khrushchev and Mao, are "creatively developing" classic Communist doctrines. In this colloquy, Mao Tse-tung and his colleagues appear in a sense as fundamentalist "prophets" who consider that the "established church" has become too worldly and urbane, and that a return to original militancy is necessary for invigorating the common faith. Moreover, they deny status to Khrushchev as a great developer of communism on a level with Marx, Engels, Lenin, Stalin, and Mao. They appear to consider Khrushchev a second-generation Communist and a backslider from Leninism.

20. As long as Chinese policy initiatives and doctrinal pretensions were confined to relatively minor domestic matters, the Soviet attitude was favorable. However, as early as 1956 the Chinese began to make grand pronouncements on Bloc matters, and have since become increasingly assertive on both domestic and world affairs, differing flatly and openly with the Soviets on an increasing range of questions of doctrinal interpretation. The Soviet leadership is affronted by the departure from Soviet policy and the Chinese challenge to Soviet authority. Thus, Sino-Soviet debates on the proper interpretation of Communist scriptures reflect serious disputes both on fundamental policies and on the authority of the interpreters to formulate such policies.

21. In the past few years Moscow and Peiping have at times been in strong disagreement on a number of questions of ideological interpretation. Among these have been the Chinese emphasis on "uninterrupted revolution," the Chinese view that "contradictions" can exist between the leaders and the led in a Communist state, and the Chinese claim that political awareness is as important in stimulating productive effort as is a system of economic rewards. Although these matters are of considerable importance among Communists, they have been largely overshadowed by two especially significant areas of disputation. These concern ideological support for variant foreign policies and the theoretical "correctness" of the Chinese communes.

22. The most serious question of foreign policy for Moscow and Peiping is which policy should be followed toward the West and toward revolutionary movements outside the Bloc. In general, the Chinese interpret Leninist literature to justify a much harder and more aggressive line in these respects than does Khrushchev. The differences concern interpretation of the present historical epoch, the degree to which modern weaponry introduces new elements into the historical process, the proper definition of coexistence, the possibility of eliminating war, and, most importantly, the proper risks to be run. The USSR and Communist China publicly state their present bitter differences in ideological terms—which, among Communists, indicates that the dispute has become acute.[2]

23. The other principal dispute has concerned the Chinese Communist commune program, which runs completely counter to Khrushchev's plans for organizing and raising agricultural production in the USSR and Eastern Europe. Apparently without any previous discussion with the Soviets, the Chinese launched this radical program in August 1958. Individual comments in the controlled Chinese press built a crescendo of doctrinal claims which gave the impression that through the develop-

---

[2] These differences, as they apply specifically to foreign policy and to the world Communist movement are discussed below in paragraphs 32–39.

SECRET

SECRET

6

ment of communes, the stage of "communism" was just around the corner in China. The Chinese thereby implied not only that they had found a way to get there ahead of the USSR and the rest of the Bloc, but that the Chinese Communist commune might well serve as a model for certain other countries.

24. Partly as a result of Soviet displeasure, the Chinese, toward the end of 1958, backed away from their more extravagant ideological claims for the communes. At the same time, internal considerations also dictated a number of retreats in the commune system. The Chinese accepted the Soviet position that no society could advance to communism without following the Soviet experience of greatly developed industry and high productivity, and they temporarily abandoned their claim that the commune idea was relevant to other countries. The initial Chinese assertiveness almost certainly played an important part in moving Khrushchev, at the XXI Congress of the Communist Party of the Soviet Union in February 1959, to make new ideological pronouncements of his own. These clearly seemed calculated to make unequivocal the primacy of the Soviet Union's position in the march toward communism, and at the same time to concede that all Bloc countries, including China, would achieve the ultimate goal of communism at approximately the same time.

25. The commune dispute has not yet been resolved. Soviet criticism of the communes has continued, and the Chinese Communists have moved slowly to regain some of the ground lost in their retreat of December 1958. In addition to reasserting the objectionable claims that the communes represent the beginnings of China's transition to communism and are relevant to other countries, the Chinese Communists have undertaken a program of urban communalization as well. Articles in the Chinese press have revealed, moreover, that the issue of Soviet experience and its relevance to the Chinese commune program has become a subject of dispute within the Chinese Communist Party and that opponents of the program have seized on Soviet criticisms and the Soviet example to buttress their own positions.

26. *Leadership Within the Bloc.* Peiping began to take an active, independent role in Bloc affairs in 1956. China's reluctance to go along fully with de-Stalinization, its initial encouragement of the Poles and Hungarians in 1956, and its criticism of Soviet "great power chauvinism" added to Soviet problems, even though Peiping subsequently supported Soviet actions in Hungary and assisted the Soviet leadership in reaffirming unity in the Bloc. More recently, the Chinese Communists have more directly challenged Soviet leadership by lobbying among representatives of other Bloc members against the course of Soviet foreign policy.

27. Nevertheless, Peiping continues to pay formal allegiance to Soviet leadership of the Bloc and world communism. The Chinese leaders accept the importance for Communist unity of a single locus of leadership, and they recognize that at least for the foreseeable future it must lie in Moscow. However, they have insisted that Soviet policies must reflect Chinese Communist interests and Peiping's views on certain fundamentals of Marxism-Leninism: in particular, (a) unremitting struggle against the clearly defined enemy (the US), and (b) more militant revolutionary policies in the world Communist movement.

28. The existence of an independent Chinese position on key issues encourages elements within the European Satellites to become more assertive. On a number of occasions, various satellites have failed to echo Soviet disapproval of Chinese statements and policies, and have sometimes given the Chinese open support.[a] Initially there was some evidence of support in Eastern Europe, especially in Bulgaria, for the communal organization of the countryside. East Germany has been publicly

[a] For example, three weeks after the USSR had published its neutral stand on the Sino-Indian border dispute in the autumn of 1959, East Germany began public support of the Chinese Communist position. This lasted about six weeks, being abruptly switched on 9 November to match the Soviet position. Czechoslovakia for a briefer time gave even stronger support to Peiping on the border issue and had earlier joined Peiping in attacking Indian "imperialism" for causing the revolt in Tibet. North Korea and Albania gave early support to Peiping's opposition to Moscow's detente tactics.

SECRET

223

SECRET

7

sympathetic with Peiping's praise of Mao's contributions to Marxism-Leninism, has emulated certain Chinese economic innovations, and has at times joined in criticizing the Soviet line of coexistence with the West. The Chinese *Red Flag* articles of April 1960 were almost certainly designed in part to encourage and support any party members who disagreed with Khrushchev's policies toward the West.

29. All three of the Asian Satellite areas—North Korea, North Vietnam, and Outer Mongolia—have strong historical and cultural ties with China, and the Chinese Communists have retained a keen interest in these areas. However, Moscow also has interests in these areas, and there appears to be a Sino-Soviet division of authority in these satellites. Moscow-dominated Communist regimes in Outer Mongolia and North Korea were an established fact by the time the Peiping regime came into being. Moscow continues to dominate these areas, although Peiping's influence in North Korea has appreciably increased since Communist China's intervention in the Korean War. Chinese influence is probably predominant in North Vietnam, but even in this case, Moscow has retained considerable influence. Both Moscow and Peiping have substantial economic aid programs in the Asian Satellites, with Soviet aid predominating in Outer Mongolia and North Korea, and the Chinese leading in North Vietnam.[4] This division of authority is almost certainly a delicate matter, but we have no indication of serious Sino-Soviet frictions on this score.

---

[4] Economic Assistance Commitments of Communist China and the USSR to the Asian Satellites, as of 11 July 1960:

	(Million US $)	
	Communist China	USSR
North Korea	225	458 [a]
Outer Mongolia	115	375 [b]
North Vietnam	300	253
TOTAL	640	1,086

[a] Including debt cancellations amounting to $132 million.

[b] Including debt cancellations amounting to $100 million, but excluding assistance committed in February 1960 for which no value has been announced.

30. *Leadership of Communism Outside the Bloc.* The Chinese Communists believe that their experience uniquely equips them to provide guidance to Free World Communist parties in the colonial or semicolonial countries, which in Communist parlance includes most of Asia, Africa, and Latin America. Communist China has recently made conspicuous efforts in these areas to increase its influence both with local Communist parties and with the non-Communist governments. In some of these countries, local Communists appear to be more receptive to Chinese than to Soviet guidance, and in some cases, at least, the USSR appears at present to favor an important role for the Chinese Communists. Nevertheless, Soviet influence remains dominant among the world's Communist parties. Even in non-Communist Asia, the three largest Communist parties—those in India, Japan, and Indonesia—still look principally to the USSR for guidance, although there is presently a tendency among their leaders to consult both Moscow and Peiping.

31. Despite the forcefully expressed differences of view in Moscow and Peiping regarding the tenor and pace at which communism should be pushed in the colonial or semicolonial countries, we have seen few signs of a Sino-Soviet struggle for dominance in these areas. It is probable that as long as there is a prospect of a workable compromise or reconciliation of views between Moscow and Peiping, neither wants to start a course of overt action abroad which might severely reduce this prospect. Nevertheless, if Sino-Soviet differences continue without a real settlement, instances of competitive efforts to guide Communists, front groups, and leftward-leaning neutralist governments are likely to become more frequent and increasingly sharp.

B. Strategic Relations

32. *World Outlook and Foreign Policy.* The Soviets and the Chinese Communists picture the world as now divided into three groups of states: (a) the Communist Bloc; (b) the anti-Communist, "imperialist" nations; and (c) the uncommitted nations and underdeveloped nations. They agree in viewing the latter group as affording the main opportunity for advanc-

SECRET

SECRET
8

ing the Communist struggle against the West, although constant pressure and efforts to erode the West's position in other areas continue. On these general questions the Soviets and the Chinese Communists agree. It is on questions of method, pace, and risk that they differ.

33. The Soviet leaders, headed by Khrushchev, believe that to push as forcefully for international Communist goals as Peiping desires is to take political and military risks which could jeopardize the achievement of those goals. The Soviets and the Chinese agree that Soviet advances in science and modern weapons have altered the world balance of power, but the Soviets are more concerned than are the Chinese over the possibility that "adventures" by the Communists could develop into a general war. Such a war, in the Soviet view, would be catastrophic to all participants, because of the destructive potential of modern weapons. The Soviets feel under these conditions that war should and can be avoided. In their view, the most effective approach for the attainment of world Communist goals is a flexible one, combining example, propaganda, and aid to existing regimes in newly independent countries (even though this involves cooperating in some cases with bourgeois nationalists) with subversion and on occasion the application of military pressure.

34. At the same time, internal factors in the Soviet Union reinforce Moscow's interest in avoiding serious risk of hostilities with the West. The Soviets strongly believe that their present economic plans, if unobstructed, will decisively strengthen the Socialist countries in competition with the anti-Communist group of nations, and will help considerably in demonstrating to all the superiority and desirability of the Soviet system. Moreover, current Soviet internal policies place stress on incentives, rather than coercion, and continued attention to the lot of the worker and peasant, whose production is vital to the program.

35. The Chinese believe that the Bloc should push more boldly and aggressively toward Communist world goals. They hold that Soviet achievements in advanced weaponry have so altered the world balance of power that

more forceful action should now be taken, even at the risk of local wars. In the Chinese view, if local war should develop into general war, not only would world communism triumph, but enough would remain of the world to make the victory worthwhile. Any relaxation of tensions meanwhile will dull Communist fighting spirit and allow the West a breathing space in which to prepare for war against the Bloc. The Chinese Communists are thus less inclined than Moscow to favor negotiations as a tactical method of struggle against the West.

36. The Communist Chinese not only consider the US as their prime enemy on ideological grounds, they also consider the US an immediate national enemy which is preventing them from gaining Taiwan and thus completing their victory in the Chinese civil war. They also consider that the US is blocking the expansion of Chinese Communist influence in Asia and in international affairs generally. This causes Peiping's enmity for the US to be more passionate and inflexible than is the case in Moscow. The "hate America" spirit which pervades Peiping's propaganda is also useful in justifying sacrifices by the Chinese people.

37. The Chinese also hold that many of the "oppressed peoples" of Latin America, Africa, and non-Communist Asia are ready for nationalist revolution, and that wars against "imperialist oppression" in these areas are inevitable, just, desirable, and deserving of Bloc encouragement and support. Although it may be expedient to support bourgeois national revolutions in these areas, revolutionary pressure should be applied where the opportunities exist and the bourgeois national regimes replaced by Communist ones as soon as practicable. They place less emphasis than do the Soviets on the possibility of attaining Communist power by parliamentary or other means short of armed revolution.

38. These differences have been building up since late 1957 and reached considerable dimensions in October 1959 when Khrushchev's speeches in Peiping clearly implied disapproval of Communist China's truculent foreign policy. They became openly bitter in April 1960 with the Chinese attacks on Soviet detente tactics preceding the Summit. Although the

SECRET

SECRET

9

failure of the Khrushchev-inspired Summit brought joy to Peiping, the Chinese Communists continued to criticize Soviet policy and lobbied for their own cause before such bodies as the World Federation of Trade Unions. In the Chinese Communist view, proof of the validity of its great expectations from a generally hard line is to be found in recent revolutionary events in Korea, Turkey, and Japan, which Peiping interprets as blows against US-supported reactionary regimes and indications that the natives are restless.

39. At the Bloc conference in Bucharest in June, the USSR apparently outlined its harder and more militant line toward the West, including at least temporary abandonment of negotiations as a major tactic. This switch to harsher tactics had probably been motivated in part by the Chinese Communist attitudes on world policy, and the Soviets probably attempted at Bucharest to extract in return Peiping's promise to fall in line with Moscow on ideological and other questions. The change in Soviet tactics may have partially assuaged Chinese Communist discontent with Bloc foreign policy. Such accommodation as may have been reached in recent weeks, however, almost certainly does not eliminate the basic factors which originally led to differences.

40. *Borderland Areas.* There has been considerable enmity in Russian-Chinese history regarding the borderland areas of Sinkiang, Mongolia, and Manchuria, and we believe that some sensitivity may continue on this score. The USSR secured Outer Mongolia as a puppet in 1924, and acquired temporary hegemony in Sinkiang province in the 1930's and 1940's. In ousting the defeated Japanese from Manchuria in 1945, the Soviets reclaimed part of Tsarist Russia's special rights concerning Dairen, Port Arthur, and the Manchurian railroads. They also sacked the Manchurian industrial complex of over three quarters of a billion dollars worth of plants and equipment. Since the Communist takeover of China, however, and especially since the USSR gave up its special status in Manchuria in 1955, these issues appear to have played little noticeable role in Sino-Soviet relations.

C. Military Relations

41. *The Military Alliance.* Since its inception in 1950, the Sino-Soviet Alliance has had an important military component. Although its text [a] is focussed on Japan, both Moscow and Peiping view their military alliance in broader terms. For example, the Chinese Communists have stated in effect that they would enter any hostilities involving the Warsaw Pact; and the Soviets, in making supporting statements during the 1958 Taiwan Strait crisis, specifically referred to their commitment to Communist China under the 1950 treaty. The existence of the alliance greatly increases the military power of the entire Bloc and enhances the position of each power in world affairs.

42. Despite the existence of the military alliance and the high degree of materiel standardization of the Soviet and Chinese Communist armed forces, there has been no evidence of joint maneuvers of Sino-Soviet forces, land, sea, or air. They do, however, coordinate their air defenses. We lack direct evidence and are unable to ascertain the scope and nature of Sino-Soviet joint military planning. The Chinese continue to stress the military thought of Mao, and some Chinese military leaders have occasionally been criticized for following alien (Soviet) military doctrine too closely. There also appears to be little intimacy or a camaraderie between Soviet and Chinese military personnel.

43. *Communist China's Dependence on the Soviet Union.* Communist China attaches great importance to its military alliance with the Soviet Union. The protection provided by the military alliance with the USSR in 1950 enabled the Chinese Communist regime to set out upon its ambitious domestic programs with little fear of outside molestation. Lack-

---

[a] The formal basis for military cooperation was established by the Treaty of Friendship, Alliance and Mutual Assistance, of February 1950. This treaty, which is valid until 1980, provides that if one of the parties should be "attacked by Japan or any state allied with it, and thus be involved in a state of war, the other contracting party shall immediately render assistance with all means at its disposal."

SECRET

SECRET   10

ing a nuclear strike capability of its own, Peiping obtains increased foreign policy maneuverability from Soviet possession of modern nuclear weapons. China has relied almost entirely on Soviet materiel to convert its primitive mass army of 1949 into a powerful semimodern army, backed by a sizable jet air force and a navy with more than a score of medium and long-range submarines. Military deliveries from the USSR appear to have declined as Communist China has increased its armament production capability,[*] but Peiping is still heavily dependent on the USSR for many items which are essential to the maintenance of its present military establishment and to the further development of its modernization program.

44. *Nuclear Weapons and Missiles.* Communist China is totally dependent upon the USSR for military support with nuclear weapons and missiles. We believe it unlikely that the Soviets have stationed nuclear weapons in China, but even if they have, such weapons would almost certainly be held under strict Soviet custody. The USSR could give China nuclear weapons from its own stockpile, but it almost certainly has not done so, and we do not believe that the Soviets intend to do so within the foreseeable future. Similarly, we have no evidence that the USSR has equipped the Chinese with surface-to-surface ballistic missiles. There are indications, however, that the Chinese may have received some Soviet air-to-air missiles.

45. The USSR is aiding Communist China in basic nuclear research, but such aid does not appear to include direct assistance in fissionable materials production or nuclear weapons development. The Chinese are currently dependent on the Soviets for supplies of slightly-enriched uranium and heavy water for the research reactor which the USSR made available to Peiping in 1958. In the same

manner, the development of uranium mines and processing plants under way in China for several years is also a product of Soviet scientific and technical assistance.

46. The USSR is almost certainly reluctant to see the Chinese Communists acquire nuclear weapons under their own control. Probably the most important consideration to the Soviets is that Chinese acquisition of a nuclear weapons capability would reduce Soviet leverage in controlling Chinese independent action, particularly action which might involve China in hostilities with the US. At the same time, the Chinese desire to achieve a nuclear weapons capability is very strong. Attainment of even a minimal capability would not only greatly augment Chinese military and technological prestige throughout the world, particularly in Asia, but would also enlarge Chinese freedom of action in pursuing their national objectives.

47. We are unable to assess with confidence the impact of these fundamentally opposing interests upon the Sino-Soviet relationship. We do not believe that either party wishes to push its own concern to a point where this issue will irreparably damage their relationship. On the other hand, given the key importance of the problem to both sides, this issue is almost certainly a source of friction. We believe that the Soviets are deliberately moving slowly in assisting the Chinese to acquire a nuclear weapons capability, while seeking to hold Chinese impatience and discontent at a level consistent with the best interests of the Sino-Soviet relationship. At the same time, the USSR has probably given the Chinese generalized assurances of Soviet protection with its nuclear weapons capability.

48. Although we cannot estimate the likelihood of such a development, it is possible that the Soviets may decide to assuage the Chinese desire for a nuclear weapons capability by providing the Chinese with a simple nuclear device and assisting them in detonating it. This would enable the Chinese to claim they had acquired a nuclear capability and to derive great prestige benefit from a widely publicized detonation. Although this action would probably assist the Chinese somewhat

---

[*]From 1950 through 1955 about $820 million in military deliveries to China were financed by Soviet loans. All deliveries since have been on a cash basis, and the Chinese have repaid over half the amount loaned. Most of the materiel consumed in the Korean War was probably donated by the USSR, while China supplied the manpower. See also Annex C.

SECRET

SECRET   11

in their nuclear weapons program, it would not, for the Soviets, run the risk of greatly accelerating the Chinese attainment of a separate nuclear weapons capability. Such an arrangement might permit the Soviets to delay further in providing the more advanced assistance the Chinese would need to obtain a nuclear weapons capability.

49. Chinese attainment of the capability to detonate their own nuclear device in the near term, say within two or three years, rests almost entirely upon the nature and extent of Soviet aid. If Soviet aid continues at its present apparent pace and character, the Chinese might attain the capability to detonate their own nuclear device by about 1964. However, if the Soviets have, in response to Chinese pressure, provided a great deal more aid than we have detected, a nuclear device of Chinese manufacture might be detonated a year or two earlier. Given direct Soviet supply of designs and fissionable material, and assistance in fabrication of the device, a nuclear detonation could be produced in China at almost any time in the immediate future. Even after the Chinese do test a device, it would take them several additional years to produce a small stockpile of weapons, since they do not possess the requisite highly advanced scientific, technical, and industrial establishment.

50. *Disarmament, Test Bans, and Atom-Free Asia.* The USSR's dramatic gestures toward unilateral reduction in armed forces have not been imitated by the Chinese. Peiping has praised the Soviet decision, but has defended its present force levels, and has made clear its belief that true disarmament is impossible prior to the universal triumph of communism. Proposals for an "atom-free zone for Asia"[7] have also received occasional Chinese Communist propaganda support. That they are considered by the Chinese to be nothing more than propaganda is indicated by Peiping's insistence that no treaty with the West can be meaningful.

---
[7] This is the popular catch phrase for the idea of banning all nuclear weapons, development, and production from Asia. It also has been presented as for "Asia and the whole Pacific Basin," "Asia and Africa," and other forms.

51. Peiping has stated that it favors the cessation of nuclear testing and has given propaganda support to the Soviet position in the test ban negotiations. If these negotiations should approach agreement, we believe that Peiping would make its adherence conditional on certain demands on the West and probably also on the Soviet Union. Peiping might set these demands so high—for example, on such matters as UN seating, the Taiwan question, and US bases in the Far East—as to make it unlikely, in Peiping's view, that the West would accept them. On balance, however, we believe that there would be prior Sino-Soviet discussions and that the Chinese would not have as their major goal the sabotaging of an agreement against Soviet wishes.

D. Economic Relations

52. *The Economic Model.* For the first few years of its existence, Communist China closely followed the Soviet course of economic development and relied upon the advice of Soviet experts for the planning and direction of its own economic plans. By about 1957, however, the Chinese Communists had recognized that the Soviet model was not adequate to meet the conditions existing in China. During the next few years, therefore, and most dramatically in 1958, the Chinese introduced economic policies that had no counterpart in Soviet practice and which, in some cases, dismayed the Soviets. The Chinese innovations, according to their own formulation, consist of three major policies: the communes, the "great leap forward," and "walking on two legs" (i.e., accompanying the rapid development of big industry with the concurrent development of vast numbers of small local plants and the use of simple equipment, and also the simultaneous development of agriculture and industry). These new policies were added to, but not substituted for, the Soviet capital-intensive model.

53. *Economic Benefits.* Economic cooperation between Communist China and the USSR has been an important aspect of their rela-

SECRET

SECRET   12

tionship ever since the Peiping regime was established. Both parties have benefited from this cooperation, although the economic effect on the Soviet Union has been much less than that upon China. The Soviet Union has exported a very small part of its industrial output to China (never more than two percent) in exchange for foodstuffs and industrial raw materials. Soviet importation of products requiring high labor input in exchange for goods requiring low labor input has aided its labor-short economy.

54. Chinese gains from this exchange have been much greater. The Chinese have benefited in all fields from support provided by Soviet technology and science. Soviet know-how in economic organization, finance, industrial engineering, and in science has been invaluable. The machinery and technical assistance received from the USSR and the Eastern European Satellites in the past decade have been vital to Communist China's industrialization program. Given the unavailability of Western materials, it would have been otherwise impossible for China to have achieved the extremely high rate of industrial growth (23 percent annually) which we estimate it attained through 1950-1958. China's economic ties to the USSR and the Bloc are obviously strong.

55. The USSR has made available for purchase by China 291 major installations, valued at more than $3 billion. About one-half of these installations, which form the core of China's industrial development program have been completed and are now in operation.[s] Soviet trade has been of particular value to China in that it has meant guaranteed deliveries of investment equipment, industrial raw materials, transport equipment, and petroleum products. Soviet support also has been extended in the form of modern technology, the services of Soviet experts, and loans of about $1.3 billion, 1950-1956, of which $430 million was for economic development and the remainder primarily for military purchases.

---
[s] See Table 1.

TABLE 1
USSR PROJECT CONSTRUCTION AGREEMENTS WITH COMMUNIST CHINA, 1950-1959

Date of Agreement	Economic Credits (Million US$) [a]	Number of Projects	Value of Complete Sets of Equipment [b] (Million US$) [a]
February 1950	300	50	1,300 [d]
September 1953	0	91 [c]	
October 1954	130	15	100
April 1956	0	55	825
August 1958	0	47	N.A.
February 1959	0	78	1,250
Total	430	291 [c]	3,275

[a] Converted from rubles at the official rate of 4 rubles to US $1.

[b] Including technical assistance related to these projects.

[c] Agreement signed to deliver equipment for a total of 141 projects.

[d] This sum includes the value of equipment and technical assistance for all of the 141 projects contracted through September 1953.

[e] The Chinese announced in April 1959 that the 211 major Soviet assisted projects agreed upon through April 1956 were reduced in number to 166, as a result of merging of some projects during their construction.

56. The Sino-Soviet economic relationship has been conducted in extremely business-like terms. The USSR has at no time given China financial grants; indeed, China has committed more in economic grants and credits to other countries than it has received in economic loans from the USSR. Since Soviet credits expired in 1956, China has paid for all its imports from the USSR with current exports. In order to repay previous credits, China since 1956 has annually shipped more goods, by value, to the USSR than it has received from it.[s] We believe that the terms, and possibly even the level, of Soviet aid and trade are sore points for Peiping. The Chinese leaders probably find it difficult to look with equanimity on fairly sizable Soviet aid to neutral states while China has had to deny itself

---
[s] See Figures 1 and 2.

SECRET

SECRET   13

needed foodstuffs and other goods in order to pay for such Soviet aid as it receives.[16]

57. The Chinese Communists have no intention of participating in any scheme for economic integration, such as CEMA, which would gear their economy to that of the USSR and make them more dependent on Moscow. To the contrary, they are determined to develop as complete and autarkic an economy as possible, and, in view of the vast economic potential of China, they regard the development of all major industries, rather than specialization in a few, as the more realistic policy. The Soviets appear to accept this approach as proper for China at this time. It is probable, nonetheless, that specific aspects of economic cooperation and the exchange of goods and services within the Bloc have occasioned some friction in Sino-Soviet economic relations.

E. Summary Analysis of the Sino-Soviet Relationship

58. The nature of the Sino-Soviet relationship cannot be described in simple terms. No single descriptive term characterizes the behavior of the two Communist states toward one another or their joint demeanor toward the rest of the world. The two countries do not, to take an extreme example, conduct themselves as though they comprised a solid, unitary bloc, a Communist monolith which disregards national boundaries and interests and pursues Leninist precepts in perfect consonance. They do not, at the opposite extreme, behave in the manner of classical nineteenth century great powers, viewing their problems and their relationships strictly from the viewpoint of national interests. Instead, their relationship occupies a position somewhere between these poles and contains elements of both. The Communist ideology

which pervades their relations both modifies the urgent nationalism of the two countries and is in turn modified by national considerations.

59. The Sino-Soviet relationship also does not display uniform cohesion in all respects. Varying degrees of intimacy and cohesion are exhibited in the relations of the two powers in ideological, foreign policy, economic, and military affairs. In economic matters, for example, the USSR and China are pursuing long-term programs which have among their goals the industrialization of China and the growth of Sino-Soviet economic strength. At the same time, the two countries transact the actual business of exchanging Soviet industrial products for Chinese agricultural and mineral products on terms which closely resemble trade negotiations in the capitalist world. In military affairs, the two powers have undertaken to modernize the Chinese military establishment and presumably seek to increase their combined power in support of the military alliance. Yet, the military relationship between the USSR and Communist China is not as close as that between the US and its NATO allies. Moreover, in the keen Chinese desire to obtain a nuclear weapons capability there is a strong potential for disunity.

60. The Sino-Soviet relationship appears most solidly unified on matters of broad Communist objectives. On the central core of Communist thought—the view of a world divided between capitalist-imperialist and socialist-proletariat camps, the belief in the eventual triumph of communism everywhere, and the faith in Marxist-Leninist precepts as a basis for building a new human society—China and the USSR appear in firm agreement. However, in the interpretation and application of these broad beliefs and concepts the two Communist states diverge in many respects, and, as they have demonstrated in recent months, they can on occasion disagree sharply and quite fundamentally. Paradoxically, the very Communist ideology which joins the two powers together also provides a source for disagreement and potential disunity.

---

[16] In comparison with Soviet economic loans to China of $430 million, 1950–1956, the USSR since 1950 has extended loans or grants, for economic development, of $684 million to India, $621 million to the UAR, and $211 million to Afghanistan. To date, however, the utilization of these Soviet offers has amounted only to the following: India, $139 million, the UAR, $85 million, and Afghanistan, $69 million.

SECRET

SECRET   14

61. In the realm of foreign policy, relations between the two Communist powers display on occasion a striking lack of cohesion and uniform direction. They find in their common enmity to the US a single point of departure, but in their approach to the US and in other foreign relations, notably in dealing with influential neutral powers, they sometimes take quite different paths. The actions of Communist China toward India and Indonesia during the past year clearly embarrassed the USSR and were unmistakably out of key with the tone of coexistence and detente the Soviet regime was then seeking to establish. It is impossible to advance any analysis of such behavior as the single correct one, but it appears most likely that the Chinese on these occasions were motivated more directly by considerations of their national interest than by concern for Bloc harmony and unity.

62. Divergences in foreign policy derive both from differing national interests and from doctrinal differences between the two Communist states. The Chinese differ sharply with the Soviets as to the pace, vigor, and manner of combating the West; Peiping clearly disdains the slower, more subtle formulas of Khrushchev. Some lack of harmony also exists in the approach of the two Communist powers to the methods and short-term goals of establishing communism in neutral and undeveloped countries.

63. In sum, the Sino-Soviet partnership is not a monolith but a structure of several kinds of relationships which vary in strength and intimacy and contain within themselves elements of both cohesion and division. Though joined by Communist thought, the partnership is subject to many of the separatist forces that have traditionally confronted alliances and coalitions. The future of this relationship will be determined by the interplay of these elements and the success of the Communist leaders in containing conflicting forces.

IV. PROSPECTS

64. We believe that the cohesive forces in the Sino-Soviet relationship are stronger than the divisive forces and are likely to remain so throughout the period of this estimate at least. It is probable that for some time to come both the Soviet and Chinese leaders will value the alliance so highly that they will make strong efforts to keep discord from wrecking it. There will be a powerful tendency on each side to stop short of any irrevocable act which would force a permanent split.

65. The strongest of the cohesive forces throughout this period will be a mutual awareness of the heavy damage to their national interests and to the Communist cause which a substantial impairment of the alliance would inflict. The two partners will almost certainly continue to share a common hostility to the West and a belief that through their common effort in advancing international communism they can someday participate in dominating the world. Their relationship will also continue to find cohesion in the political, economic, and military advantages each receives. This will have particular force for the Chinese who, in view of their continuing military and economic dependence on the USSR, will probably feel that they have no genuinely acceptable alternative to maintaining their alliance with the Soviets.

66. Divisive forces will continue to be present, however, and may increase. The distinct national characteristics and the disparate developmental stages of the two states discussed in this estimate will continue to exert a disruptive force. Judging from the experience of recent years, there will continue to be a trend, though a somewhat uneven one, toward modifying the more arbitrary and stringent features of Soviet society and institutions; the Chinese Communists, however, will still be in the throes of forcefully engineering a vast economic and social upheaval with all the internal tensions this entails. Communist China's relative weight in the Bloc is likely to grow over the next five years. This growth will diminish the leverage Moscow can bring to bear through Peiping's military and economic dependence. Peiping's foreign policy outlook will probably continue to be less flexible and more aggressive than Moscow's, and this will at times place heavy strains on the relationship. Peiping will be more inclined to pursue its own interests and to question Soviet leadership than during the first decade of the alliance.

SECRET

SECRET

67. The future nature of the Sino-Soviet relationship will be shaped in part by developments which cannot be known at present: changes in Soviet or Chinese Communist leadership; the compulsions or restraints which developments within the USSR and China will exert on the respective leaderships; the strength and policies of the West; the opportunities which occur for the Communist movement throughout the world; and the failures and successes of various Communist ventures.

68. The interplay among these contingent developments and the broad forces of cohesion and division in the Sino-Soviet relationship will determine its precise future form. We do not rule out the possibility that the two powers may either come to an open break or reach a more fundamental integration of interests than now exists. We believe it much more likely, however, that there will be no fundamental reconciliation of differences, that discord will ebb and flow, and that substantial though not complete cooperation between Moscow and Peiping will continue. Complete unity appears inherently improbable between two centers of vigorous Communist authority and national pride, each backed by so much power as to make it difficult for either one to impose its will on the other and each having strong reasons for continuing to hold its own views. At the same time, such discord is unlikely to force the USSR and Communist China so far apart that they cease to look to each other for support in their common drive against the West.

69. The tensions inherent in the Sino-Soviet relationship could eventually lead to a basic reformation of the structure of the Bloc. It is even possible that the Sino-Soviet relationship will begin to take on more of the aspects of a traditional alliance between two powerful nation-states, perhaps extending to the development of tacitly acknowledged spheres of influence. In any event, over the next five years the growing duality of power in the Bloc will become increasingly incompatible with present Bloc structure which has been based on a single source of authority. As a consequence, quick and effective coordination of policy against the West may become

more difficult. Moscow may face difficulties in successfully denying its European allies an increased measure of authority and initiative and in preventing satellite officials from attempting to use Sino-Soviet differences as leverage against Moscow. The cohesion of the world Communist movement may suffer as a result of confusing and at times contradictory counsel from both Moscow and Peiping and of probable Chinese attempts to increase its influence in the guidance of other Communist parties.

70. The interplay of Sino-Soviet differences may well have an important effect on Bloc policies toward the West. Elsewhere we have estimated that the Soviets are likely, during the next few years, to mingle elements of accommodation and of pressure in their foreign policy. The Chinese will seek to minimize the former and maximize the latter. This tendency will be particularly strong in matters directly related to Communist China's national interests, especially those concerning the Taiwan question and Peiping's position in the international community. We do not believe that their efforts will decide the course of Soviet policy, but they will influence it. The Soviets will not be quite as free to reach agreements with the US, if they wish to do so, as they would be if they were not allied to the Chinese. Moreover, Chinese Communist pressure may at times cause the Soviets to pursue a more militant course toward the West than the Soviets would otherwise choose on tactical grounds.

71. Since the Sino-Soviet alliance is a changing and evolving relationship, it offers possibilities for favorable as well as unfavorable developments from the US point of view. Stresses and strains weaken the hostile combination, and possibly can be exploited to the advantage of the West. Public manifestations of Sino-Soviet disagreement damage the facade of Communist unity and diminish, to some degree, the forward thrust of world communism. Nevertheless, despite these mitigating considerations, the threat which the Sino-Soviet allies pose to US security and US interests is of great dimensions, and we believe that it is more likely to increase than to diminish during the period of this estimate.

SECRET

SECRET

ANNEX A

THE IMPACT OF SOVIET TRADE AND TECHNICAL ASSISTANCE ON COMMUNIST CHINA'S ECONOMY

1. During the past 10 years, actual Soviet deliveries to Communist China of complete installations and other capital equipment have amounted in value to more than $2 billion. In a series of agreements negotiated since 1950 the USSR has agreed to provide China with complete installations for 291 major projects, which form the core of China's industrialization program. These projects include complete sets of factory equipment for the large, modern, industrial plants—steel mills, a large petroleum refinery, aircraft and truck factories, and machine-building plants—and electric power installations, which form the core of the Chinese industrial development program. About one-half of these installations have been placed in full or partial operation. By importing complete factories from the USSR, China has received a relatively standardized basic plant and has gained the advantage of integrated planning by experts who are familiar with the demands of a socialist planned economy. These are not "aid" projects in the sense of economic grants, but they have helped China's industrial growth greatly by providing long-range guaranteed deliveries and by providing ready availability of modern Soviet technology and the services of Soviet experts who have supplied necessary guidance in all phases of plant construction and initial operation. The Soviet role in building these projects was especially comprehensive during the First Five-Year Plan (1953–1957).

2. The Chinese now claim to be more capable of coping independently with the building of modern industrial plants, and perform much of the planning and construction work on aid projects formerly done by Soviet experts. As the Chinese advance in technical competence, however, they are attempting more complex types of production—aircraft, electronics equipment, and steel-making equipment—and Soviet assistance continues to be vital, although on a much higher technical level.

3. Soviet "aid" has taken various forms. The USSR loaned China about $1.3 billion, 1950–1956, of which $430 million was for economic development and the remainder primarily for military purchases. The credits had been almost fully utilized by 1955 and China now has repaid about two-thirds of the total indebtedness. A vast amount of Soviet technical data appears to have been made available free of charge over the past decade. The USSR has sent technicians and equipment which were in some cases in short supply at home. It has also coordinated its shipments with China's development programs and has been willing to make economic commitments years in advance.

4. China has also benefited from the extensive economic relations it has formed with the Eastern European Satellites, particularly Poland, East Germany, and Czechoslovakia. Agreements have been negotiated with certain of these countries calling for technical assistance and equipment for the construction in China of at least 100 large industrial installations, about two-thirds of which have been finished and placed in operation. Including these projects, the total value of machinery and equipment paid for and received by China during 1950–1959 from the European Satellites was about $1.7 billion, approximately 40 percent of China's imports of these items from all sources.

SECRET

SECRET

17

5. Figures for the First Five-Year Plan indicate that the joint projects involving Soviet capital equipment and technicians, but also Chinese materials, equipment, and labor, accounted for 44 percent of all state investment in industry during that period. In absolute figures, China invested 11 billion yuan [11] in Soviet projects during the First Five-Year Plan out of a total industrial investment program of 25 billion yuan.

6. The original Second Five-Year Plan proposals, which continued the emphasis on large-scale industry and on the Soviet-assisted industrial construction projects, probably were based on the assumption that the proportion of state industrial investment in Soviet-assisted projects would be maintained at about the level of the First Five-Year Plan. The leap forward drive, however, which greatly increased investment in small-scale home-grown industries, has radically changed the pattern of investment. The trend established in 1958 and 1959, and in the 1960 plan suggests that industrial investment during the Second Five-Year Plan may be twice as large as originally planned—100 instead of 50 billion yuan. Meanwhile, investment in Soviet-assisted projects, even though it seems to have been expanded, probably will not exceed 25 to 30 billion yuan. According to these figures, the proportion of investment in Soviet-assisted projects to total industrial investment will

decline from 44 percent during the First Five-Year Plan to about 25 to 30 percent during the Second.

7. In addition to equipment for the 291 Soviet-assisted projects, China imports from the USSR a substantial additional amount of investment equipment and other items for industrial plants not included in the assistance agreements. Also vital to the running of China's economy are imports of Soviet industrial raw materials, transport equipment, and petroleum products. [12]

8. Petroleum products from the USSR are of particular importance, for even in 1959 Communist China's domestic production was able to meet only about half of its requirements, and more than 90 percent of its total imports were obtained from the USSR. Out of total imports of 3.3 million tons of crude oil and refined petroleum products in 1959, aircraft fuels and other fuels and lubricants for military uses may have comprised about 1 million tons. For these products China is still almost wholly dependent upon foreign supplies. In spite of considerable growth in domestic production of crude oil and in domestic refining capacity expected in the next five years, China's demand is growing so rapidly that annual petroleum imports are expected to rise to about 5 million tons in 1965. Imports will continue to consist mainly of refined petroleum products including a sizable quantity of military fuels.

[11] This figure includes the value of the investment goods imported from the USSR for these projects.

[12] For a commodity breakdown of Sino-Soviet trade, 1950–1958, see Table 2.

SECRET

SECRET

TABLE A-2

IMPORTS BY COMMUNIST CHINA FROM THE USSR AS REPORTED BY THE USSR [a] 1950–1958

Million US $ and Percentages

Imports	1950 [b] Value	%	1951 [c] Value	%	1952 [b] Value	%	1953 [b] Value	%	1954 [c] Value	%
Equipment and machines ..	41	11	108	23	157	28	161	23	199	26
Complete installations ...	(1)	(0.3)	(32)	(7)	(41)	(7)	(49)	(7)	(93)	(12)
Ferrous metals	20	5	50	10	66	12	68	10	88	12
Nonferrous metals	3	1	17	4	16	3	14 [d]	2	22	3
Petroleum and petroleum products	11	3	39	8	33	6	45	6	45	6
Paper	4	1	11	2	17	3	9	1	6	1
Miscellaneous [e]	23 [d]	6	51	11	19 [d]	4	10	2	25	3
Unaccounted for [f]	286	73	200	42	246	44	391	56	374	49
Total	388	100	476	100	554	100	698	100	759	100

Imports	1955 Value	%	1956 Value	%	1957 Value	%	1958 Value	%
Equipment and machines	230	31	305	42	272	50	318	50
Complete installations	(142)	(19)	(217)	(30)	(209)	(38)	(166)	(26)
Ferrous metals	76	10	61	8	33	6	61	10
Nonferrous metals	13	2	18	2	8	1	16	3
Petroleum and petroleum products ...	79 [d]	11	86	12	90	17	92	14
Paper	7	1	6	1	3	1	neg	neg
Miscellaneous [e]	16	2	15	2	15	3	31	14
Unaccounted for [f]	237	43	242	33	123	22	114	18
Total ....,.........	748	100	733	100	544	100	634	100

[a] All data contained in this table are from source [aa], except where otherwise indicated.

[b] 80

[c] 84

[d] 77

[e] Including such categories as chemicals, building materials, pharmaceuticals, and cultural and consumer goods.

[f] Representing the value of goods not listed by Soviet sources and believed to be primarily of military and strategic origin.

SECRET

TABLE A-2 (Continued)

EXPORTS FROM COMMUNIST CHINA TO THE USSR AS REPORTED BY THE USSR [a] 1950-1958

Million US $ and Percentages

Exports	1950[b]		1951[c]		1952[b]		1953[b]		1954[c]	
	Value	%	Value	%	Value	%	Value	%	Value	%
Raw materials of agricultural origin	67	36	86	26	125	30	122	26	116	20
Foodstuffs	22	12	23	7	57	14	89	19	149	26
Raw materials of animal origin	10	5	17	5	32	8	13	3	25	4
Nonferrous and alloy metals.	20	11	46	14	73	18	101	21	107	19
Textile raw materials	17	9	30	9	39	9	58	12	56	10
Textiles	N.A.	N.A.	4	1	15	4	17	3	37	6
Miscellaneous [d]	52	27	126	38	73	17	75	16	88	15
Total	188	100	332	100	414	100	475	100	578	100

Exports	1955		1956		1957		1958	
	Value	%	Value	%	Value	%	Value	%
Raw materials of agricultural origin	130	20	139	18	129	18	102	12
Foodstuffs	179	28	201	26	128	17	219	25
Raw materials of animal origin	22	3	26	3	21	3	22	2
Nonferrous and alloy metals	118	18	126	16	142	19	123	14
Textile raw materials	60	9	59	8	49	7	38	4
Textiles	59	9	96	13	136	18	194	22
Miscellaneous [d]	76	13	117	16	133	18	183	21
Total	644	100	764	100	738	100	881	100

[a] All data contained in this table are from source [a], except where otherwise indicated.
[b] [a]
[c] [a]

[d] Miscellaneous includes industrial goods, industrial raw materials, chemicals and rubber, and cultural and consumer goods.

SECRET

9. The trend toward greater Chinese self-sufficiency is also characterized by the growth of the Chinese machine-building industry. Although China must continue to rely entirely on imports for some types of machines, it officially claims that it is now able to fulfill from internal production about 80 percent of its overall requirements for machinery, as compared with a production rate during the First Five-Year Plan which met only 60 percent of such requirements. This advance has not been uniform in all lines of production, however, and much of the additional machinery produced in China has been of simple types, for example, irrigation pumps for agriculture, or simple equipment for small factories.

10. The impact of Soviet equipment on Communist China's economy has been greatly enhanced by the employment of a large number of Soviet experts, most of whom have been on Chinese Communist payrolls or included in the cost of the Soviet assistance to major aid projects. By late 1959 about 11,000 Soviet economic and technical experts reportedly had worked in China at one time or another. These experts have included not only top-notch Soviet industrial specialists but also economic advisers who have helped formulate economic planning in all sectors in the Chinese economy. In the past two or three years the number of Soviet technicians has dwindled, and the remaining technicians are mostly in the background as technical advisers and

trouble shooters rather than as managers and operating engineers. Another mechanism for transmitting Soviet technology to Communist China has been the training program for Chinese students in the USSR. By 1958 China reportedly had sent 14,000 students to the Soviet Union for study and 38,000 individuals to Soviet industrial establishments for on-the-job training. Most of those receiving practical training were assigned to plants similar to ones under construction in China, to prepare them for serving as the initial group of skilled workmen and technicians in newly completed Chinese factories.

11. Although less tangible than technical assistance in the form of expert advice and training, Soviet transfers of technical information have been of considerable importance in the industrialization program of Communist China. Under the Sino-Soviet Scientific and Technical Cooperation Agreement of October 1954, the USSR has provided China with blueprints for the construction of 600 kinds of factories and enterprises, designs for 1,700 sets of machinery and equipment, and substantial information on production processes. Additional agreements for further technical cooperation were negotiated in 1958 and 1959, for application during the Second Five-Year Plan (1958-1962). Knowledge and data obtained in this manner from the USSR have been useful to China even on projects with which the USSR has not been involved.

SECRET

SECRET

ANNEX B

SINO-SOVIET SCIENTIFIC AND TECHNOLOGICAL RELATIONS

A. Scale and Nature of Communist China's Dependence on the Bloc

1. Communist China is capable, without organized foreign aid, of gradually expanding its scientific and technological capabilities, utilizing a small group of very able Chinese scientists who have access to the international literature in their fields. To reach world levels of effort in a significant number of selected fields by 1967, the Chinese would require considerable outside aid, particularly in advanced academic training. The dependence at present, however, is for the most part at everyday, practical levels. Aid is required, for example, for organizing the national research establishment, planning a research program, providing the latest in scientific know-how and solving problems quickly, furnishing materials for research, and training new scientists. As progress is made, personnel at increasingly higher scholastic and scientific levels will be sought. This pattern has been followed in other countries and is not new. To date, the Chinese have requested aid from the Soviet Union and other Bloc countries in a wide variety of fields and have received aid in a number of them. The Chinese also have followed Western technological developments and made use of them as far as practicable.

B. The Scale, Nature, and Terms of Soviet Assistance

2. By 1958, the Soviets had largely satisfied the Chinese need for organization, planning, and undergraduate education. Most of the aid was on a practical level with little participation in research and development. Personnel furnished up to this time were primarily teachers, short-term lecturers, advisors, and industrial types. Starting in 1958, a few hundred researchers began to work jointly with Chinese scientists in China for periods of several months to a year or two.

3. Since January 1958, when a 5-year protocol was signed under the Sino-Soviet Scientific and Technical Agreement of 1954, Soviet aid has stepped up. This protocol clarified Sino-Soviet relations in research and development and the training of scientists, for which purpose over 120 programs were to be carried out jointly or with Soviet assistance to support China's 12-year Plan for Scientific Development. We believe some of this work also supports the Soviet research program.

4. Connected with the 1958 step-up was an agreement made in December 1957 between the academies of the two countries which provided for direct communications, joint research and expeditions, and coordination of work in important problems of science and technology. Similar agreements were executed in January 1958 between the academies of agricultural sciences of the two countries and between the ministries concerned with higher education. These were 5-year agreements with executive plans to be made yearly. The agreements were associated with the protocol mentioned above. Research and development and training in all fields and all pertinent agencies of government were encompassed in these documents.

5. Training in the Soviet Union is one of the most important ways that the Soviet Union is aiding China. Training in China has not progressed well and only a handful of qualified new scientists has been produced in China. The growth of qualified scientists in China has come almost entirely from those returning

SECRET

21

SECRET   22

after graduate study in the Soviet Union (other than the 200 or more who returned from the US and Europe after the Communist takeover). Postgraduate training began to receive increased emphasis starting in 1955, and, by 1957, a policy was adopted whereby only graduate students would be sent abroad. With this new policy, the number sent each year is believed to have dropped from the 2,000 and over for 1955 and 1956 to a few hundred per year. The number studying in the Soviet Union appears to be declining, but the level of study is rising. There are probably about 4,500 Chinese currently studying in the Soviet Union, mostly in scientific and technical fields.

6. The expenses of Soviet experts who stay in China up to three months reportedly are paid by the Soviet Union; those who stay up to six months have their travel paid by China; and those who stay longer have both salaries and expenses paid by China. It is believed that the expenses of Chinese students in the Soviet Union are borne by China. Scientific apparatus and instruments are also paid for; in 1958, this trade item was reportedly 100 million yuan.

C. Net Worth to the USSR

7. Benefits to the Soviet Union are not obvious, although a number of Chinese researchers and graduate students working in Soviet research institutions have contributed to the overall research and development output in the USSR. Some research done in China in a few fields is probably of a level that would be of interest and value to Soviet scientists. Close contact with China's research and development has given the Soviet Union an opportunity to keep informed on China's progress and prospects. The Soviet access to the geographical area of China gives some advantage to the Soviet Union in such fields as geophysics. Advantages in satellite tracking also derive from this access.

SECRET

SECRET

ANNEX C

COMMUNIST CHINA'S MILITARY DEPENDENCE ON THE USSR

A. Ground Forces

1. *Equipment.* Communist China's dependence upon the USSR for equipment has progressively lessened over the last 10 years. Nevertheless, China is still dependent upon the Soviet Union for many types of equipment for its armed forces.

2. At the time of the Korean War, Communist China was making mainly infantry weapons and ammunition. The USSR supplied armor, artillery, ammunition, and vehicles on a large scale, although Communist China was also using a variety of captured Japanese and US weapons. Shortly after the end of the Korean War, Communist China decided to develop a munitions industry with Soviet aid and geared to the production of Soviet-type weapons. Since then, China has gradually expanded its production to include Soviet-type artillery and artillery ammunition, medium trucks, the new type Soviet small arms and ammunition, and, most recently, medium tanks. It is believed that Communist China now produces enough of these items to supply the current peacetime replacement requirements of its armed forces. For all other items of equipment, especially heavy armor, specialized artillery, some kinds of complex signal and electronic equipment, and a variety of trucks and special purpose vehicles, Communist China is completely dependent upon the USSR or other members of the Bloc.

3. The quantities of equipment which may have been sent to China are unknown. However, sufficient equipment has been identified in the hands of troops to indicate that these shipments have been substantial. Little is known of the possible stockpiles of equipment in Communist China, but it is probable that if stockpiles exist that they consist primarily of Soviet items. Estimated production of military items in Communist China indicates that output would hardly have been sufficient for the accumulation of stockpiles. Also, during the heavy Chinmen shelling, the artillery ammunition which was recovered and analyzed was mainly of Soviet manufacture, which suggests that ammunition stocks are certainly of Soviet origin.

4. In the last few years, the nature of Soviet assistance to Communist China has shifted. Instead of supplying mainly finished military equipment and supplies, the USSR is now chiefly providing technical aid and industrial facilities for munitions manufacture. By this means, China has been able to initiate production of a fairly extensive number of up-to-date weapons. More importantly, these industrial plants provide the base which can be expanded so that Communist China will ultimately become self-sufficient in the output of many types of military equipment.

5. But for the present, and for some years to come, Communist China's ability to modernize its forces with items of its own production will be very limited. At current estimated production rates, for example, of such a basic item of equipment as the T-54 tank, it will be five years before the T-34 tanks now assigned to units in the armored divisions and tank regiments of infantry divisions can be replaced, even at the modest levels now carried in the current TE.[13]

6. China does not now have and is not likely to have for a number of years a domestic capability to meet all of its requirements at wartime consumption levels for conventional weapons and the more complex types of radar and electronic equipment now essential for a modern ground force. The Chinese, even in peacetime, are dependent on the Soviets to

---

[13] See tables C-1 and C-2.

SECRET

23

SECRET

24

supply replacements and spare parts for many weapons now in use, and must rely on the Soviets for much of their communications equipment, radar, and early warning devices.

7. Chinese Communist ground forces dwarf all non-Communist Asian military forces, but the level of equipment of the Chinese forces is still far short of advanced modern standards. For example, in the Soviet tank divisions, there are more than eight times the number of tanks in the Chinese armored divisions; in the tank regiments of infantry divisions, the Soviets are over twice as strong as the Chinese in numbers of tanks. The Soviets have 25 times more tanks than the Chinese and most of them are larger and newer models.

8. Thus, even in a nonnuclear war, the time is not in sight when the Chinese Communists will be able to sustain major military operations against a modern armed force without substantial quantities of additional Soviet weapons and equipment. The Chinese will also need help in meeting their increasing POL requirements.

9. The lack of a major military research and development program will further extend the time before Communist China will achieve "military self-sufficiency." The Chinese have demonstrated a capability to make improvements on blueprints and plans of the relatively simple military equipment they are now manufacturing, but seem not yet to have undertaken any serious program of research and development of a truly "Chinese" weapons system, or of native Chinese support equipment.

10. *Training.* The Soviets have made a significant contribution to the Chinese Communist armed force strength by permitting them to attend Soviet training schools and through the Soviet advisory program in China. Here again, limited data indicate that the Soviets are withdrawing some of their personnel from lower units, probably because the Chinese can run their own training programs for their current organizations and weapons. However, the Chinese undoubtedly realize the importance of continuing to send as many personnel as possible to advanced Soviet schools

to prepare for further modernization of their forces.

11. *Logistics.* The Chinese Communists were unable to support their effort in Korea without a large-scale Soviet logistics effort, and, despite considerable work and progress, this portion of the Chinese Communist military organization remains basically weak. The weakness is found in the transportation system's limited capacity and its vulnerability to interdiction, in the logistical organization structure which provides this service to the combat forces, and in the lack of materiel, e.g., spare parts, POL, and other essential items, to permit the Chinese Communist forces to engage in modern warfare. They would be dependent on the Soviet Union for logistic support in any military operation against an enemy which included a modern Western military force.

B. Air Forces

12. Communist China is today heavily dependent upon the Soviet Union for aircraft, air weapons, air logistic items, electronic equipment, and training; and it is likely to remain so for a long time to come. As China lacks the two essential ingredients for a long-range strike power (nuclear weapons and long-range delivery capability), it must perforce rely upon Soviet capabilities. In addition to this dependence, China must also rely upon its Soviet ally for the maintenance and further development of the defensive and offensive air capability it now has in being.

13. Today, Communist China's aircraft inventory totals more than 3,000 aircraft in operational units including about 1,850 jet fighters and about 400 jet light bombers. The great bulk of these aircraft has been supplied to China by the Soviet Union. This aid undoubtedly constitutes the major direct Soviet contribution to Communist China's present military power. In addition to this support the Soviets have also helped the Communist Chinese to establish facilities for the local production of Soviet-designed aircraft. The Chinese Communists began series production of Soviet-designed fighters (FRESCO-

SECRET

SECRET   25

MIG–17) and utility aircraft (COLT–AN-2) in 1957 and have been producing helicopters (HOUND–MI–4) in series since the fall of 1959. Series production of FARMERs (MIG–19) has probably recently begun. Soviet support of this production has been extensive, but has decreased from initial levels as the Chinese have been able to supply more and more of the raw materials, components, and qualified personnel required in production. While this trend is likely to continue, it is probable that the Chinese Communists will have to depend on the USSR to supply certain components for these aircraft for some time to come.

14. Communist China remains heavily dependent on the Soviet Union for air logistic items. While Peiping's overall dependence on the USSR for air logistic materials has decreased moderately since 1950, the volume of its imports has increased substantially as a result of increases in Communist China's aircraft inventory. At present, it is estimated that China must depend upon the USSR for approximately 80 percent of its total air logistic requirements. China is particularly dependent on the USSR for the higher grade petroleum products required for its air forces. It is believed that all such products, including all aviation fuels, are now imported from the USSR and European Bloc countries. Even with the expected improvements in China's petroleum industry, Peiping will probably continue to rely on the USSR for the major portion of these petroleum products for some time. Thus China's military air capability will continue to be directly dependent upon the Soviet supply line.

15. Soviet training assistance has included both extensive supervisory and materiel support and has resulted in the development of an air training establishment in China closely patterned after that of the Soviet air forces. At the time of the Korean War, a large number of Soviet advisors and instructors were employed throughout the Chinese Communist Air Force. Since that time, the number of Soviet personnel assigned in China has markedly decreased but a few still remain in an advisory capacity. Today the Chinese Communists are capable of meeting most of their annual training requirements through their own resources and probably rely upon the Soviets only for advanced technical equipment and for the training of highly skilled technicians.

C. Naval Forces

16. *Materiel Assistance.* Only through the extensive assistance of the Soviet Navy has the rapid development of the Chinese Communist Navy (CCN) been possible, and ships transferred from the USSR [14] and those assembled in China from largely Soviet-supplied components [15] today provide the principal combat potential of the navy. Most CCN naval materiel, especially ordnance, electronics, and propulsion machinery, and petroleum products, has also originated in the USSR. Much recent Soviet technical assistance has been directed toward the establishment of programs for local Chinese production of naval equipment.

17. *Soviet Naval Advisory Mission.* Equally important assistance in the development of the CCN has been furnished by the Soviet Naval Advisory Mission. This mission was instituted to impart Soviet naval experience, methods, and technical skills to the Chinese. It consists of the Soviet Advisory Section at Naval Headquarters, Peiping, and of a network of representatives attached to every major subordinate command or installation. Initially set up in 1950, this network became so extensive as to include every ship and tactical organization in the navy. It is estimated that by about 1954, upwards of 500 Soviets were assigned to various naval missions with the CCN, with about 100 serving with the Soviet Advisory Section in Peiping. Gradually, as the CCN developed and gained practical operating experience, the number of Soviet advisors was reduced. At the present time, the number probably does not exceed 150; the advisory section in Peiping has been reduced to about 30 persons with the remaining 120 on duty with the fleet and district commands, the naval academy at Dairen, and specialized training commands.

[14] See table C–3.
[15] See table C–4.

SECRET

SECRET

18. For psychological reasons the Soviet Naval Advisory Mission is integrated into the CCN organization so as to cloak even the slightest outward appearance of Soviet control or domination. Most of the personnel wear civilian clothing or CCN uniforms without badges or rank insignia. Relations between the Chinese and their Soviet advisors are generally described as "polite" with little evidence of serious ethnic friction on any level. Customarily the local Soviet advisors give specific advice only when it is requested. They do, however, make periodic reports to the head of the Soviet Advisory Section, Peiping, who in turn can recommend general remedial measures to the national CCN high command. The Soviet Naval Advisory Mission not only provides beneficial guidance to the CCN but also enables the Soviet Navy to evaluate adequately the professional competence of its Far Eastern ally.

19. Numerous other Soviet personnel have been provided to the Chinese to give technical guidance in the establishment of shipbuilding programs. Additional technicians have been sent to instruct the Chinese in the proper operation and maintenance of modern naval equipment.

20. *Training.* During the earlier stages in the development of the CCN large numbers of Chinese officers were sent to the USSR for senior and specialized naval schooling. Small numbers of senior naval officers are still being sent annually to the Order of Lenin Naval Academy at Leningrad for command and staff training. A limited number of junior officers and enlisted personnel are enrolled each year for specialized technical training at several other Soviet naval schools in the Leningrad area and in the Vladivostok-Nakhodka naval complex.

21. In addition to technical and materiel assistance in developing the CCN, the USSR has taken several measures which have enhanced the prestige of China as a new naval power. In 1955, the USSR ceded Kuan-tung Pan-tao (Kwantung Peninsula) to China, together with its important naval and industrial complex of Port Arthur-Dairen. Port Arthur has since become one of the two largest bases of the CCN. In the summer of 1956 the Soviet Pacific Fleet made an official visit to Shanghai, the first visit of foreign warships to mainland China since the defeat of the Chinese Nationalists. To date the Chinese Communists have not paid the customary return visit.

SECRET

SECRET

27

TABLE C-1

COMMUNIST CHINA

ESTIMATED CURRENT ANNUAL PRODUCTION OF ARMAMENTS AND MILITARY VEHICLES

Small Arms

7.62mm Pistol, type 51 (Copy of Sov TT-33)	10,000
7.62mm Carbine, type 56 (Copy of Sov SKS)	250,000
7.62mm SMG, type 56 (Copy of Sov AK)	180,000
7.62mm Light MG, type 56 (Copy of Sov RPD)	15,000
7.62mm Heavy MG, type 53 (Copy of Sov Goryunov)	1,000
12.7mm Heavy MG, type 54 (Copy of Sov M38 DShK)	1,000
	457,500

Mortars

82mm (Copy of Sov 82mm M1937)	4,000
120mm (Copy of Sov 120mm M1938/43)	2,000
160mm (Copy of Sov M43)	500

Recoilless Rifles

57mm, type 36 (Copy of US M18) Production ceased at end of 1957	
75mm, type 52 (Copy of US M20)	2,000

Rocket Launchers

90mm, type 51 (Copy of US M20) Production ceased at end of 1957	
102mm, type 50	100

Artillery

37mm AA gun, type 55 (Copy of Sov M1939)	50
57mm AT gun, type 55 (Copy of Sov M1943)	50
76mm Div gun, type 54 (Copy of Sov M1942)	175
122mm How (Copy of Sov M1938)	25
152mm How (Copy of Sov M1943)	10

Tanks

T54 (100) Medium (Copy of Sov Model)	100

Trucks	15,000
Jeeps	500

Ammunition

Artillery and Mortar	1.4 million rounds
Small Arms	150 million rounds

SECRET

SECRET    28

TABLE C-2

MAJOR ITEMS OF EQUIPMENT—CHINESE COMMUNIST GROUND FORCES

	Item	Quantity Now in Inventory	Country of Origin
Arty:	100mm Fld/AT Gun	70	USSR
	122mm How	1,800	USSR, China
	122mm Gun	500	USSR
	152mm How	400	USSR, China
	152mm Gun/How	400	USSR
	130 Gun	75	USSR
AAA:	37mm AA Gun	1,450	USSR, China
	57mm AA Gun	250	USSR
	85mm AA Gun	1,350	USSR
	100mm AA Gun	250	USSR
Rkt Lnchr:	132mm Rkt Lnchr	150	USSR
	140mm Rkt Lnchr	35	USSR
Armor:	M Tk, T-34/85	2,600	USSR
	M Tk, T-54	100	USSR, China
	H Tk, JS-2	60	USSR
	Aslt Gun, SU-76/100	800	USSR
	Aslt Gun, JSU-122	100	USSR
	Aslt Gun, JSU-152	100	USSR
Radar:	Radar Devices	600	USSR, China

TABLE C-3

SOVIET SHIPS TRANSFERRED TO COMMUNIST CHINA

Type/Class	Number	Date	Remarks
SS/"M-II"	1	1953	Nonoperational
SS/"S-1"	4	1954–1955	
SS/"M-V"	4	1954–1955	
SS/"SHCH-II"	4	1955	Nonoperational
DD/"GORDYY"	4	1954–1955	
PC/"KRONSHTADT"	6	1955	
PT/"P-4"	80	1953	
MSF/T-43	2	1954	

TABLE C-4

SOVIET NAVAL DESIGNS CONSTRUCTED IN COMMUNIST CHINA

Type/Class	Number	Date*	Remarks
SS/"W"	17	1955	Additional units under construction or fitting out.
DE/"Riga"	4	1955	Program terminated with launching of 4th unit in 1957.
PC/"KRONSHTADT"	18	1955	Program terminated with launching of 18th unit in 1957.
PT/"P-6"	60	1956	Still under construction.
MSF/T-43	8	1956	Still under construction.

*Date construction program started in Communist China.

SECRET

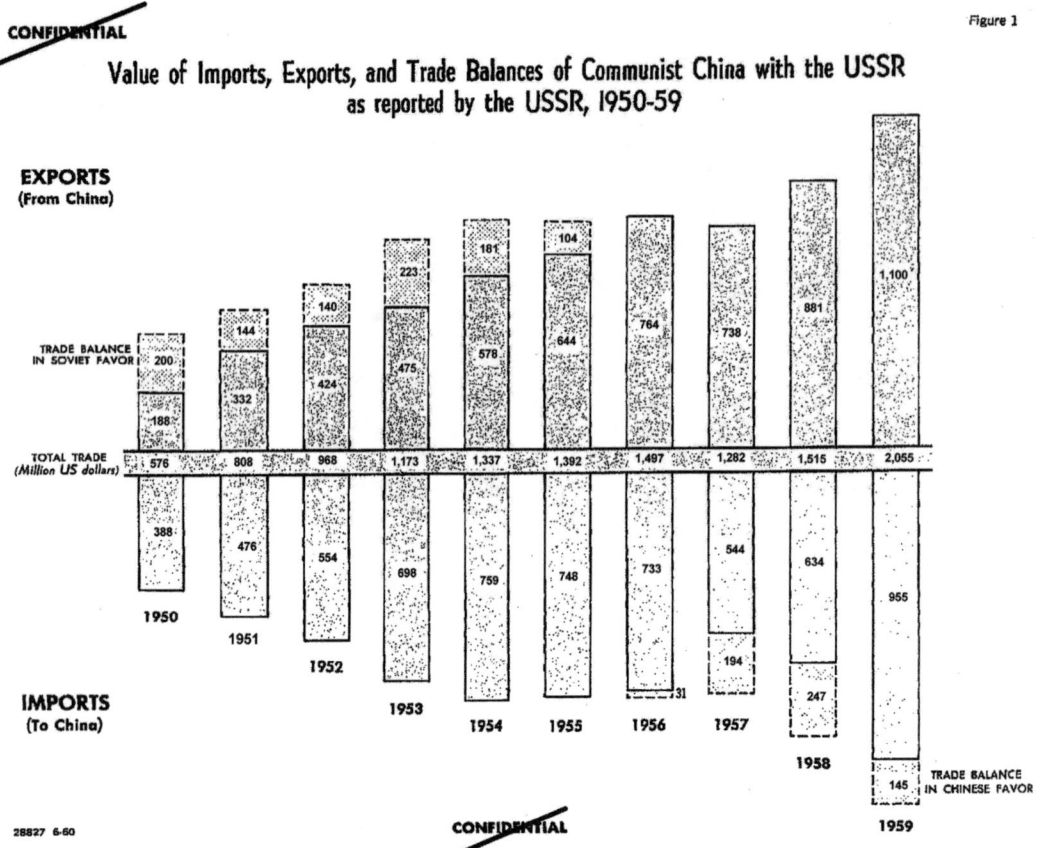

Figure 1

Value of Imports, Exports, and Trade Balances of Communist China with the USSR
as reported by the USSR, 1950-59

CONFIDENTIAL

EXPORTS
(From China)

TRADE BALANCE
IN SOVIET FAVOR

TOTAL TRADE
(Million US dollars)

IMPORTS
(To China)

TRADE BALANCE
IN CHINESE FAVOR

28827 6-60

CONFIDENTIAL

CONFIDENTIAL

Figure 2

Estimated Utilization and Repayments of Soviet Loans by Communist China, 1950-59
Million US dollars*

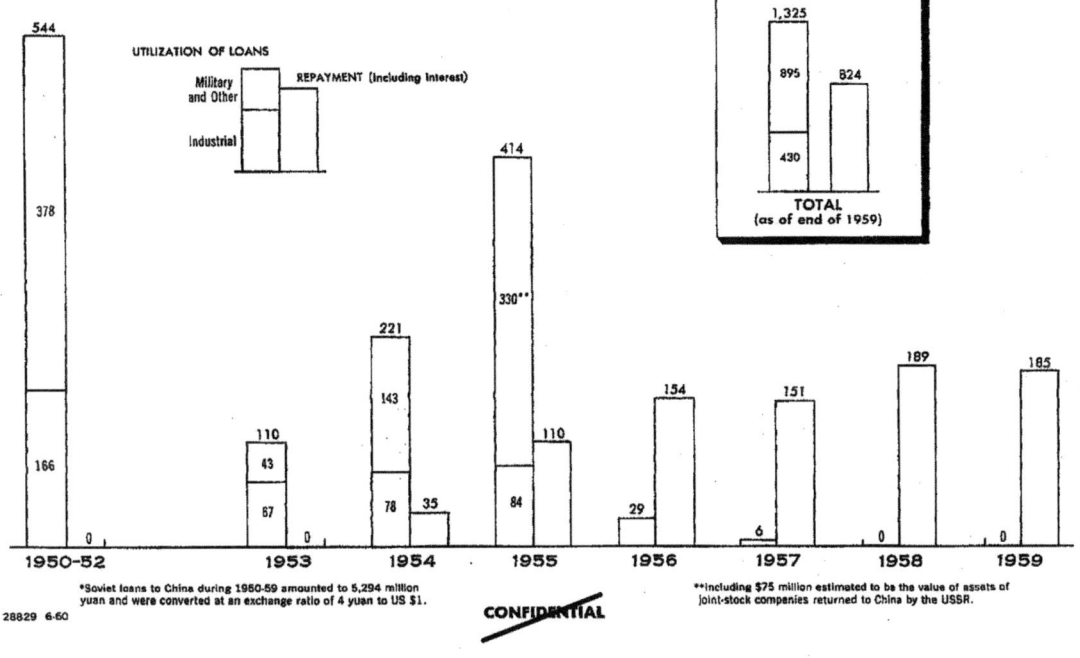

*Soviet loans to China during 1950-59 amounted to 5,294 million yuan and were converted at an exchange ratio of 4 yuan to US $1.

CONFIDENTIAL

**including $75 million estimated to be the value of assets of joint-stock companies returned to China by the USSR.

28829 6-60

SECTION 17

NIE 13-60

Communist China

6 December 1960

APPROVED FOR RELEASE
DATE: MAY 2004

(b)(3)

NIE 13-60
6 December 1960

~~SECRET~~

NATIONAL INTELLIGENCE ESTIMATE
NUMBER 13-60

Supersedes NIE 13-59

COMMUNIST CHINA

Submitted by the
DIRECTOR OF CENTRAL INTELLIGENCE

The following intelligence organizations participated in the preparation of this estimate: The Central Intelligence Agency and the intelligence organizations of the Departments of State, the Army, the Navy, the Air Force, The Joint Staff, and the Atomic Energy Commission.

Concurred in by the
UNITED STATES INTELLIGENCE BOARD

on 6 December 1960. Concurring were The Director of Intelligence and Research, Department of State; the Assistant Chief of Staff for Intelligence, Department of the Army; the Assistant Chief of Naval Operations (Intelligence), Department of the Navy; the Assistant Chief of Staff, Intelligence, USAF; the Director for Intelligence, Joint Staff; the Atomic Energy Commission Representative to the USIB; the Assistant to the Secretary of Defense, Special Operations; and the Director of the National Security Agency. The Assistant Director, Federal Bureau of Investigation, abstained, the subject being outside of his jurisdiction.

~~SECRET~~   N° 440

SECRET

COMMUNIST CHINA

THE PROBLEM

To analyze Chinese Communist domestic developments and external relations, and to estimate probable trends during the next five years.

CONCLUSIONS

1. The leaders of Communist China are determined to make China a leading world power as rapidly as possible. Over the past 11 years Communist China has made impressive gains in industrial and military strength and in the organization and regimentation of the Chinese people. These gains, together with a conviction that world trends strongly favor the Communist cause, have been increasingly manifested during the past year in aggressive self-confidence towards both the West and the USSR. (*Paras. 11–14*)

2. We believe that over the period of this estimate, Communist China's economy will continue to grow rapidly, especially in heavy industry, although at a less rapid rate than 1958–1960. Communist China's dependence on the rest of the Bloc for economic and military equipment and for technological assistance will have been substantially reduced. By 1965 Communist China will probably be the world's leading producer of coal, the third ranking producer of crude steel,

a major producer of electric power, and it will have a merchant marine of significant size. It will also have made substantial progress toward becoming a modern power in science and technology, though its relative standing will remain well behind that of the advanced nations. However, if Sino-Soviet relations should deteriorate to the point where Bloc sources of industrial equipment and technical assistance were greatly reduced, Communist China's economic growth would be slowed, expansion into more complex fields of industry inhibited, and military development retarded. (*Paras. 17–20, 34, 36*)

3. Peiping will continue to face major economic problems for many years to come. It will continue to be dependent upon foreign sources for some key items of industrial and military equipment and for specialized technical knowledge. Communist China's petroleum requirements will grow rapidly during the next five years, and even the expected tripling

SECRET

1

SECRET

2

of domestic production will not end China's dependence upon petroleum imports. Transportation will remain overburdened. Agricultural production will still be meager in relation to domestic and export needs. Per capita supplies of food and other consumer goods will not have risen enough to enable material incentives to replace coercion and political pressures as the chief spurs to production. An increasingly urgent population problem will confront the regime with difficult policy decisions. (Paras. 16, 18-20, 24-25, 29, 31, 33)

4. There will probably be growing dissatisfaction and disillusionment among the Chinese masses concerning the heavy burdens they will be forced to carry, and the regime will face increasing problems in overcoming public apathy, fatigue, and passive resistance. In addition, there may be an increase in party factionalism when Mao Tse-tung dies. Such developments, however, will not threaten the regime's ability to control and direct the country. Furthermore, there is positive support from some millions of people who have made real advances under Peiping's rule, and among many there is a feeling of pride in Communist China's rapid advance as a world power. In any case, we now see no serious threat, either internal or external, to the continuance of the regime. (Paras. 42-43, 49)

5. Peiping's conventional military capabilities will probably continue to grow, and will increasingly threaten the non-Communist Asian periphery. The rate of increase in Communist China's military capabilities will be determined in large part by the economic demands of the regime's overall economic develop-

ment program and by the nature and extent of Soviet assistance. Communist China will probably have exploded a nuclear device during the period of this estimate and may have produced a small number of elementary nuclear weapons. It may also have produced a jet medium bomber. However, unless there is a great increase in Soviet aid in the missile field, which we believe is unlikely, China will be unable to develop and produce even medium-range guided missiles by 1965. (Paras. 50-64)

6. The most important development of the past year in Communist China's affairs has been the breaking out of the long-smouldering Sino-Soviet dispute over Communist world policy and authority within the Bloc. We believe that the differences between Peiping and Moscow are so basic and are so much a product of the different situations and problems in the two countries that any genuine resolution of the fundamental differences is unlikely. Although the possibility of a complete break cannot be excluded, we believe that the alliance against the West will hold together. Nevertheless, the estrangement will probably continue, with ups and downs as new issues arise.[1] (Paras. 70-73)

7. A basic tenet of Communist China's foreign policy—to establish Chinese hegemony in the Far East—almost certainly will not change appreciably during the period of this estimate. The regime will continue to be violently anti-American and to strike at US interests wherever and whenever it can do so without paying

---

[1] The judgment of this paragraph appears to be consistent with such information as we now have on the recently adjourned conference in Moscow.

SECRET

253

SECRET

3

a disproportionate price. It will continue and almost certainly step up its efforts to create trouble and confusion in Asia, Africa, and Latin America and to subvert anti-Communist and, probably, non-Communist governments in these areas. (*Paras. 82, 86–88*)

8. During the period of this estimate Peiping's policies will range between relative moderation and outright toughness. Peiping will probably again increase its military pressures in the Taiwan Strait area. However, we believe that Peiping does not intend to advance its aims by overt military action elsewhere, although it probably will react forcefully to challenges and opportunities. Its arrogant self-confidence, revolutionary fervor, and distorted view of the world may lead Peiping to miscalculate risks. This danger would be heightened if Communist China achieved a nuclear weapons capability. (*Paras. 89–90*)

9. Even before the explosion of a nuclear device, Peiping's military power and potential may increasingly complicate the international disarmament problem. Peiping will exploit this situation in an effort to enhance its international status, but at the same time may attempt to prevent the conclusion of any disarmament agreement, at least until it becomes a nuclear power. (*Para. 91*)

10. In 1965 Communist China will be playing more fully the role of a leading world power, whether or not it is a member of the UN. Its arrogance, pretensions, and capabilities for independent action will remain a source of concern to the USSR. At the same time the danger posed by Communist China to US interests, particularly in Asia, will have increased. (*Para. 92*)

DISCUSSION

I. INTRODUCTION

11. As Communist China enters its twelfth year, the balance sheet shows both impressive assets and formidable liabilities. China's continuing rapid economic growth and its steadily increasing military strength are moving the regime closer to its goal of becoming a leading world power. At the same time, the regime is facing some of the greatest difficulties, domestic and foreign, it has yet encountered.

12. Although there is much discontent and apathy, especially among the peasants, the general aspect of Communist China is marked by regimented energy on the part of the people, and self-confidence on the part of the leaders. In the reports of returning travelers the word "arrogance" appears with striking regularity. Even Communist visitors report that the dedication and drive of the Chinese are in conspicuous contrast to the situation in other Communist countries.

13. Despite these manifestations of self-assurance, Peiping confronts a serious domestic weakness in agriculture and an external crisis in relations with Moscow. In 1960 the nation's diet is still at a precariously low level and the regime has been unable to meet all of its export obligations from the domestic harvest. The year has been even more conspicuously marked by Peiping's open challenge to Moscow's authority in the Communist Bloc. This action has brought upon Peiping the severe disapproval of the USSR and most of the rest of the Bloc and has raised the possibility that Bloc economic and technical support, which are essential for China's rapid growth as a great power, might be seriously reduced or even cut off.

SECRET

SECRET

4

14. The small group of men who run Communist China have almost unlimited ambitions for their regime and country. They explicitly assert that China shall become thoroughly communized as rapidly as possible, and they apparently believe that China will eventually become the greatest nation in the world. Belief in the reality and attainability of these goals has led this handful of zealots to drive themselves and to be prodigal with the lives and energies of the Chinese people; they have cajoled and coerced the workers and peasants of the country to do a maximum of work in return for minimal compensation and promises that the rapid growth in production will ultimately bring much greater material rewards. The leaders themselves are inspired by a mixture of Communist idealism and Chinese nationalism. They promote communism to hasten China on the road to power and glory, and exploit Chinese nationalism to hasten the building of communism.

II. DOMESTIC BASE

A. Economic[2]

15. *General.* The Chinese Communist regime during 1958–1960 has greatly accelerated its efforts to catapult the country into the ranks of the chief industrial powers in the shortest possible time. As a result of this effort the gross national product (GNP) of Communist China increased by about 18 percent in 1958, 12 percent in 1959, and about 12 percent in 1960.[3] The latter two years would have shown greater rises but for the abnormally bad weather which crippled agricultural output. A tremendous input of labor and capital investment was concentrated upon the expansion of the economy, especially heavy industry. Although still labeled the "Great Leap Forward," the regime's economic policies at the

end of 1960 are relatively conservative compared to the extreme programs of 1958.

16. Despite its successes Communist China has a long way to go before becoming a modern industrial power. Industrial production in 1959 was less than 10 percent of that of the US, while the general level of technology and the general quality of product in Chinese industry were still far below the standards of the industrialized nations of the world. Moreover, 80 percent of the population is engaged in agriculture, and per capita GNP in 1959 was only about US $120,[4] or roughly a quarter of that of Japan. The Chinese Communist regime has been able to sustain its rapid economic growth only through imposing severe hardships on the Chinese people and through restraining rises in their already meager standard of living. In result, there is widespread disillusionment among the people.

17. Thus Communist China's economy faces the next five years with both greater assets and greater liabilities. The economy is now organized to sustain heavy investment, and the percentage of GNP invested, which rose from 20 percent in 1957 to about 33 percent in 1960, will probably reach about 40 percent in 1965.[5] At the same time, many serious economic difficulties will challenge the regime.

---

[a] During the First Five-Year Plan (1953–1957) the average annual increase in GNP was seven percent.

[4] A number of different methods may be employed to convert one country's GNP into the currency of another country for purposes of comparison. These different methods will frequently yield widely differing results, particularly when the structures of the two economies are so dissimilar as are the US and Chinese economies. Any one of the methods has defects in providing international comparison; thus the above figure should be regarded only as a rough approximation.

[5] Prices of capital goods in China, where capital is scarce in comparison to labor, are high compared to prices of capital goods in the US. If investment were valued in terms of the US price structure, these percentage shares of investment as a portion of Chinese GNP would be reduced by about one-third; even so, investment would still be an impressively high percentage of GNP. The higher prices for capital goods also result in a slightly higher growth rate of GNP.

---

[2] The Chinese Communists, like their Soviet mentors, have made it difficult for foreign observers to use official data in gaining a clear understanding of the workings of the economy. They have released only partial data and in various ways presented misleading comparisons in reporting economic production and activities. This requires that Chinese Communist statistics be viewed critically and in some cases substantially discounted. See Appendix II.

SECRET

SECRET

5

It is probable, however, that the leaders will be able to find sufficiently effective solutions to keep the economy growing rapidly, even though occasionally faltering and always under great pressure, especially in agriculture. On balance, we estimate that over the next five years the annual growth in GNP will average 10 to 11 percent, provided the flow of equipment and technology from the rest of the Bloc continues.

18. *Dependence on the Bloc.* Until recently the number of Soviet technicians in Communist China was gradually reduced by common agreement as Chinese technical capabilities improved; the number of Soviet technicians in China at the beginning of 1960 was about half the peak reached in 1954. In the summer of 1960, however, Moscow unilaterally withdrew the majority of its remaining technicians from China. If these are not replaced, the movement of Chinese industry, technology, and weaponry into more complex fields will be slowed. Moreover, a major reduction in deliveries from the Bloc would alter the magnitude and structure of Communist China's economic growth. The annual growth in GNP would fall somewhat, although it would still be large because of the high level of investment. The regime would be forced to alter its development program, reducing emphasis on sectors requiring more advanced technology and more complex equipment.

19. Branches of heavy industry which are especially dependent on outside aid for equipment, technology, or both, include: the finishing stages of aluminum and steel, large electric power stations, cement, selected chemicals (fertilizer, plastics, and synthetic fibers), heavy and complex machine tools, selected electronic equipment, naval shipbuilding, jet aircraft, heavy ordnance and engineer equipment, and nuclear energy. In addition, China now imports about half its POL from the Bloc.

20. Several sectors of the Chinese economy have never received substantial Soviet Bloc support or have outgrown the need for much outside aid: i.e., agriculture, transportation, light industry, mining, and some branches of heavy industry. Heavy industry should be able to satisfy nearly all of Chinese planned needs through 1965 for the following goods: equipment for smelting and refining of copper and aluminum, machinery for small and medium iron and steel furnaces and steel rolling mills, coal mining machinery of the less advanced types, oil drills, equipment for refining petroleum (except by catalytic cracking), heavy industrial chemicals, small and medium turbogenerating equipment, rubber tires, lathes, trucks, small merchant vessels, small transport aircraft, radios, and television sets.

21. *Agriculture.* Agricultural achievements in 1955 and 1958 provided opportunities for instituting collectivization and communalization, respectively. The real increases of food production in 1958 were greatly magnified by false statistics. Misled by these spectacular figures, the regime in late 1958 allowed food to be consumed through free supply in the commune messhalls at a rate which could not be sustained. Moves were also made toward reducing acreage with the expectation of producing more crops on less land by new Communist methods of intensive agriculture. By the end of 1958 food reserves were already running low, and there were serious local shortages in many parts of the country. Since then the problem has been greatly aggravated by two successive bad crop years. Production of food grains in 1959 was probably about 10 percent less than our estimate of 212 million tons for 1958. The 1960 harvest is likely to be little, if any, better. And in these past two years the population increased by about 30 million.

22. As a result, rationing has had to be intensified. In addition, the regime has felt it necessary to supplement the food supply with city garden plots and an intensive nationwide program to collect wild foods and fibers. Despite such moves, by the autumn of 1960 Peiping was falling behind on export commitments and was even buying grain abroad in an effort to meet them. Serious hunger and malnutrition were reported from several parts of the country, and it is likely that food conditions will further deteriorate through the spring of 1961 before the early summer harvests. The cotton crop has also

SECRET

SECRET

6

fallen short, temporarily halting growth in the textile industry and bringing on even stricter rationing of cotton cloth.

23. The regime has belatedly come to a realization that more effort and investment are needed to enable agricultural production to keep up with growing demands upon it. During the past three years Peiping has given increasing attention to agriculture. The share of capital investment devoted to agriculture in the national budget has increased from a little over 8 percent in 1957 to nearly 12 percent in 1960, while under the commune organization peasant investment has more than doubled in the same period. In the latter part of 1960 vigorous efforts were made to increase the labor force available in the countryside. Cadres and civil servants were sent to the rural areas and all nonproductive units such as teams for welfare, culture, and athletics were dissolved for the duration and sent to work in the agricultural "front lines."

24. Unless 1961 should turn out to be a third successive year of bad weather, the present food and export emergencies will be largely ended by the 1961 harvest. Given average weather, the regime will probably be able to meet its minimum needs for agricultural production for the next five years and perhaps for a considerable time beyond that. Although there will probably be 90 million more Chinese to feed in 1965 than in 1960, we believe that the regime will invest enough in agriculture in the form of fertilizer, irrigation, mechanization, and manpower to meet the increased demand and, possibly, to provide a little improvement in the average diet. Nevertheless, throughout the next five years and indeed for the foreseeable future, the industrial priorities of the regime's program will limit the agricultural effort. This suggests that the balance between consumer needs and agricultural production will be a precarious one, always subject to being drastically upset by the vagaries of weather and agricultural policy. Another poor crop year in 1961 would probably force substantial cutbacks in the development effort and a further reorientation of investment from industry to agriculture.

25. *Population*. We estimate Communist China's population in mid-1960 at about 690 million and at 762 to 780 million in mid-1965. This population growth rate of 2 to 2.5 percent annually reflects the effect of a vigorous public health program that has increased life expectancy from about 30 years before 1949 to 54 years in 1958, an increase which Western nations required about 50 years to achieve in their demographic transitions. As a result, the population growth in the absence of curtailed fertility can be expected to accelerate, leading to a doubling of the population in about 25 years. However, the Chinese leaders, we believe, are aware of the long-run dangers of rapid population growth. At the same time, it is probable that an effective program to curtail fertility would involve considerable coercion and would encounter significant ideological and social resistance, resulting in adverse effects on party unity and public morale. In any event, the critical nature of the population problem will become increasingly clear to the regime and it may begin to take more effective action during the period of this estimate.

26. *Industry*. Industrial growth over the last three years has been rapid but uneven. There were two great surges: one in the last half of 1958, the other covering the last quarter of 1959 and the first quarter of 1960. In part these rapid increases resulted (especially in 1958) from a greatly intensified exploitation of China's greatest natural resource, manpower. People worked longer and harder, and millions were added to the industrial labor force. Existing plant facilities were utilized more extensively, and there was great expansion of the fuel and raw material sectors, such as mining and building materials, which could use large amounts of unskilled labor.

27. Increased labor input, however, is only part of the explanation for the rapid growth of industrial output. The Chinese Communists are now receiving the payoff from 10 years of intensive effort to expand capacity in heavy industry. Large industrial plants have been built with equipment and technology acquired from other members of the Bloc, primarily the USSR. Many of these plants

SECRET

SECRET

have come into production in the past three years, and, starting from a low base figure, the addition of the output of these large factories resulted in striking percentage increases. Supplementing the increase in output from the large plants, a smaller but appreciable increase has come from the establishment of a large number of modern, small, domestically-built plants using labor-intensive methods of production.

28. In 1958 industrial production increased by about 40 percent over 1957, and by another 33 percent in 1959. We anticipate that the 1960 increase will be about 25 percent. We believe that the production of crude steel, which has received especial emphasis from the regime, rose as follows (in millions of metric tons):

1957	5.4
1958	8.0
1959	13.4
1960 (planned)	18.4

Production of crude steel in 1960 was scheduled to level off at the rate of the last quarter of 1959, probably because it is out of balance with rolling mill capacity and the rest of heavy industry. Coal production has risen from 130.7 million tons in 1957 to an estimated 425 million in 1960, although there has been a drop in the quality.[6] Output of electric power has likewise more than tripled in three years: 1957, 19.3 billion kilowatt-hours; 1960, an estimated 58.3 billion kilowatt-hours. Other basic industries have also increased greatly.

29. Although the production of crude oil in Communist China increased from 1.7 million tons in 1957 to an estimated 5.2 million tons in 1960, there have been indications of a widespread shortage in the latter part of 1960. At present China produces about half of the crude oil and petroleum products it uses and relies on imports (primarily from the USSR) for the other half, including virtually all of its aviation fuel. By 1965 domestic crude oil pro-

duction may reach 18 million tons, with a corresponding growth in refining capacity. Even so, demand will probably have grown so much that imports will be required to meet a quarter of the nation's needs of petroleum products.

30. Chinese efforts have been most effective when they concentrated on accelerating the Soviet-style program established in the First Five-Year Plan and least successful when they involved a radical (Chinese) departure from this established program. Planning and the organization of industrial production is likely to resemble more closely the Soviet model as the development of a complex modern industrial society progresses.

31. The rate of industrial expansion, however, although remaining high, is expected to decline during the next five years for a number of reasons. The recent practice of stressing a narrow and simple product mix[7] will of necessity give way to greater diversity, complexity, and specialization. This greater diversity and complexity will require larger amounts of investment and longer lead times between investment and the completion of industrial facilities. Moreover, industrial investment will decline as a share of total investment, because agriculture and transportation will necessarily claim an increasing share of investment. Also, with material incentives for workers and peasants continuing to be severely limited, Peiping will probably face difficulties in sustaining labor effort and in increasing labor productivity.

32. Assuming no drastic reduction of Soviet trade deliveries and technical support, we estimate that Communist China's industrial growth, which averaged a little over 15 percent during 1953–1957 and about 35 percent during 1958–1959, will drop from about 25 percent in 1960 to as low as 12 percent in 1965. Production in heavy industry will expand considerably faster than light industry, and by

---

[6] This places Communist China ahead of the US and second only to the USSR in coal production, but coal is still the main source of energy in China. In petroleum, natural gas, and electric power, Communist China ranks far down on the list of producers.

[7] For example, China's steel industry now produces only a few kinds of alloys and a limited number of rolled or extruded shapes. As the economy turns to the production of more advanced types of sophisticated machines, a wide range of special alloys and a great variety of shapes will be required.

SECRET

SECRET

8

1965 it will probably be more than three times the 1959 level. Production in heavy industry will probably grow by nearly a third in 1960, but by 1965 the annual growth rate may decrease to about one-sixth. Production in light industry will increase by an estimated 10 percent in 1960, dropping to about half that by 1965.

33. Although Peiping will probably increase its investment in modern transport to enable an approximate doubling of capacity by 1965, this rate of expansion would still leave the transportation situation very tight. Railroads, the primary means of transport, will be substantially extended, improving the network in the areas now served and completing the trans-Sinkiang line to the USSR, the network in the southwest, and possibly even a railroad to Lhasa. Truck transport will also be expanded to handle shorthaul traffic, while coastal and inland shipping transport will be rapidly developed to supplement both road and rail transport. It is also expected that Communist China will greatly expand its merchant marine through construction and purchase, and will probably carry a substantial proportion of its foreign trade in its own vessels. China's telecommunications facilities, which have developed rapidly in the past few years, will continue to expand and will provide increasing support to the regime's economic, military, and political programs.

34. By 1965 Communist China's gross industrial output will probably rank with that of the UK, West Germany, France, and Japan. It will lead the world in the production of coal and will be a major producer of electric power.[8] It will probably rank third in crude steel output.

35. In terms of quality and diversity of output, however, Communist China will still be in the third echelon of industrial powers. A sizable technological gap will still exist be-

tween China and Japan. Evaluated in terms of per capita GNP or by the standard of living of its people, China will still be a backward nation. Although the income of the average citizen will probably have risen slightly above the 1960 level, the per capita production of food and other consumer goods will not have risen sufficiently to replace coercion and political pressures as the chief spurs to production.

36. *Science and Technology.*[9] The Peiping regime considers scientific and technological progress of major importance in developing Red China into a world power. The country is making significant progress in a well conceived 12-year program to raise its scientific and technological level in vital areas by 1967. The effort is concentrated in 11 broad technological fields, such as electronics and atomic energy, and at the same time a beginning has been made in associated fundamental research. Notable success is already evident in several key technological areas, and we believe general scientific and technological capabilities will be increased significantly by 1967. Communist China's relative standing will remain well behind that of the advanced nations, however, primarily because of a general lack of scientific manpower, the most limiting factor in the Chinese effort.

B. Social-Political

37. *The Party.* The members of the Chinese Communist Party (CCP) face tremendous problems in seeking to cajole and coerce the workers and peasants to serve the ambitious goals the regime has set. Such problems are especially acute for the working level party cadres who, whatever their energies or skills, are caught between the demands of the party leaders and the desires of the Chinese people. It is they who have to spur on the peasants and workers day after day, insisting that they produce to the limits of physical endurance in return for pitifully inadequate rewards. The position of these

---

[8] Provided construction of the 30 large hydroelectric projects now on the books proceeds on schedule, by 1965 China will be producing close to 200 billion kwh a year. This is more than the estimated combined production of the European Satellites by that year and about the same as US production in 1940.

---

[9] A further discussion of Communist China's science and technology appears in Appendix I, and nuclear weapons capabilities are discussed in paragraphs 56–62 below.

SECRET

COMMUNIST CHINA
GROSS NATIONAL PRODUCT, BY SECTOR OF ORIGIN
1954, 1959, AND 1965

(Billion yuan in 1957 prices)

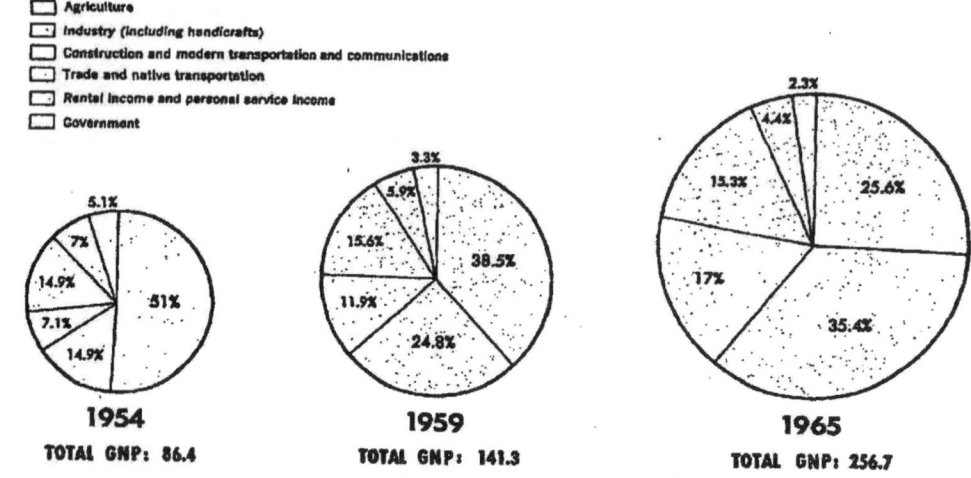

☐ Agriculture
☐ Industry (including handicrafts)
☐ Construction and modern transportation and communications
☐ Trade and native transportation
☐ Rental income and personal service income
☐ Government

1954
TOTAL GNP: 86.4

1959
TOTAL GNP: 141.3

1965
TOTAL GNP: 256.7

Gross national product, at factor cost, does not include indirect taxes.

29370 11-60

FOR OFFICIAL USE ONLY

COMMUNIST CHINA
ESTIMATED ANNUAL PRODUCTION
OF SELECTED MAJOR COMMODITIES, 1957-65

TOTAL GRAINS
Million metric tons

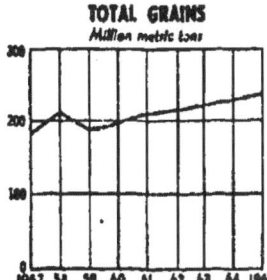

CRUDE STEEL
Million metric tons

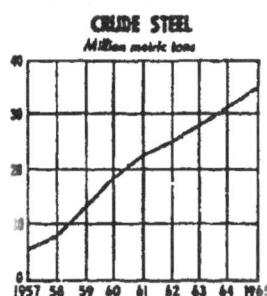

ELECTRIC POWER
Billion kilowatt-hours

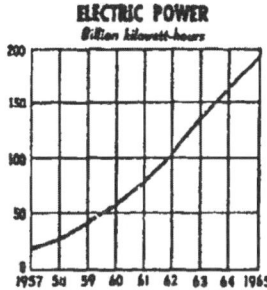

COAL
Million metric tons

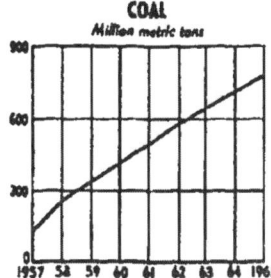

CRUDE OIL
Million metric tons

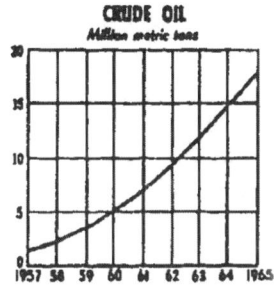

CEMENT
Million metric tons

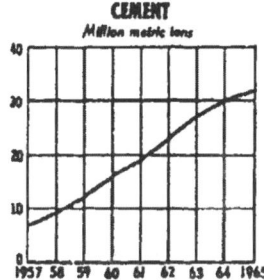

CHEMICAL FERTILIZER
Thousand metric tons

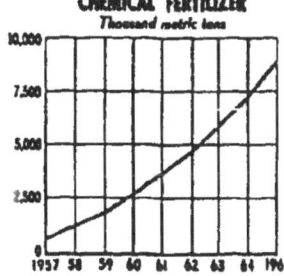

TRACTORS
Thousand units

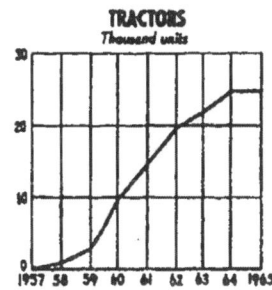

RAILROAD FREIGHT CARS
Thousand units

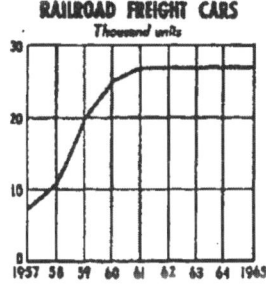

MEDIUM TRUCKS
Thousand units

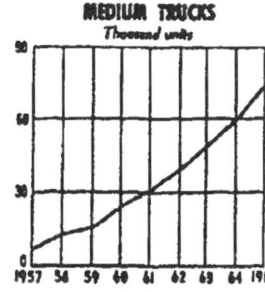

MERCHANT VESSELS
Thousand gross register tons

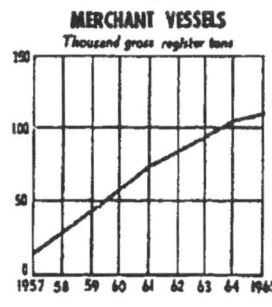

COTTON CLOTH
Million linear meters

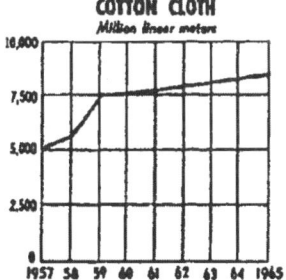

29371 11-60

FOR OFFICIAL USE ONLY

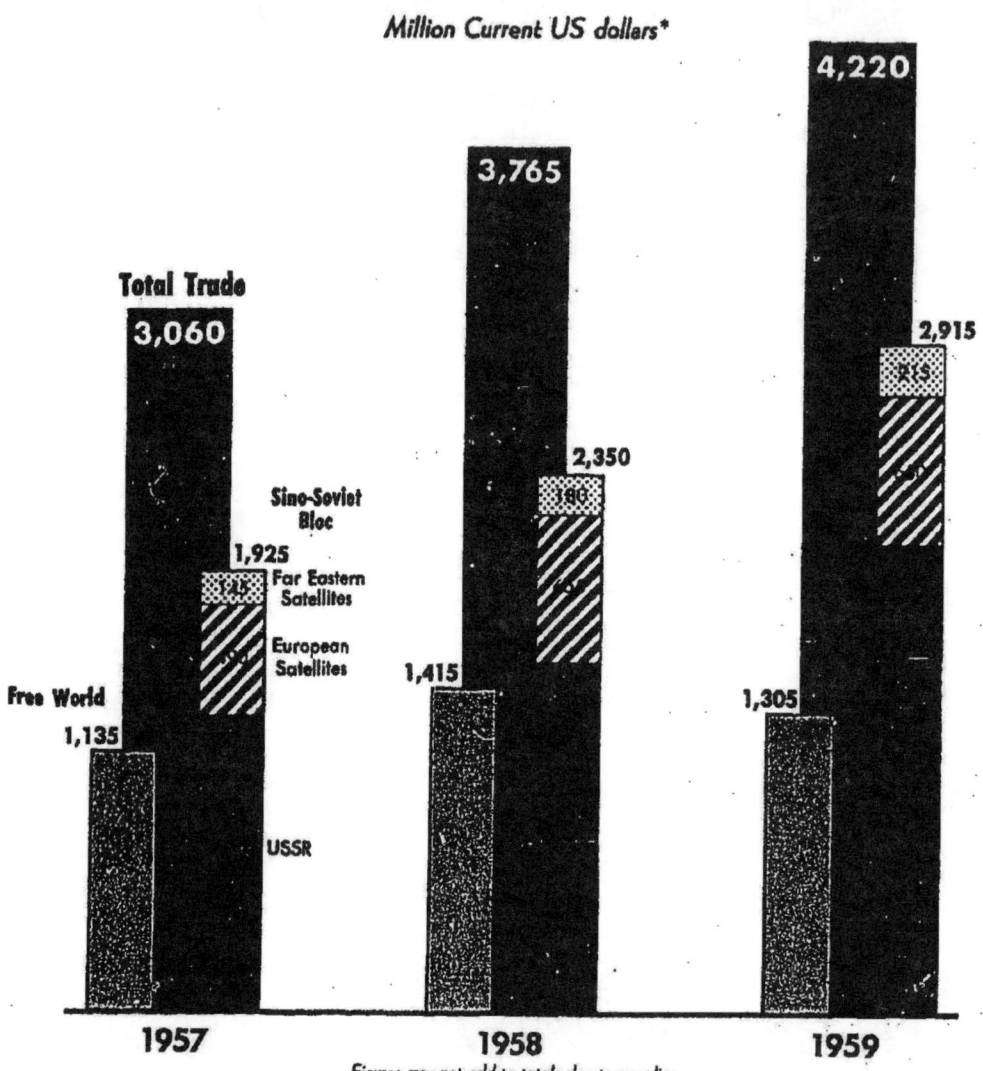

COMMUNIST CHINA
DIRECTION OF FOREIGN TRADE, 1957-59

Million Current US dollars*

Figures may not add to totals due to rounding.

*Yuan values have been converted to dollar values at dual conversion ratios: 1 yuan to US$ 0.40 for Free World trade, and 1 yuan to US$ 0.25 for Bloc trade.

29372 11-60

FOR OFFICIAL USE ONLY

SECRET

9

party cadres has become even more difficult in the past three years as the party leadership has abruptly and repeatedly changed course. For example, the party leaders confessed that many of the original claims of advances made in 1958 were exaggerated, and they suddenly abandoned the deep-plowing and backyard steel-making programs upon which so many millions of people so frantically expended their energies. Moreover, party leaders have publicly criticized the cadres for doing the very things Peiping had only a few months before been directing them to do. As a result there has been some sag in party spirit, and Peiping has felt it necessary to infuse new enthusiasm and discipline into the party.

38. Various measures have been taken in an effort to gain the positive, enthusiastic support of party members. In the 18-month period ending in June 1960, nationwide recruitment was undertaken to reinvigorate the party at the lower levels. About 2.5 million new members were added, bringing the total membership to over 16 million.[10] The party continues to be fairly successful in promoting the idea that membership is a privilege and honor, and in stimulating rank-and-file members with the concept that they are a part of an elite vanguard.

39. Nevertheless, renewed disciplinary measures within the party have become evident. A continuous series of campaigns has been directed against the members since the summer of 1959. A drive against "rightist opportunists" sought to chastise and silence those critics who had questioned the party's extremist policies of 1958–1959 and to reestablish the infallibility of the party leaders. The cadres have also been subjected to a "3-anti" drive directed against bureaucratism, corruption, and waste, and the transfers of cadres to the lower levels serves as another disciplinary tool.

[10] Already the world's largest Communist Party, the COP is now larger by some four million than the Communist Party of the Soviet Union, although it represents a much smaller proportion of the total population (about 2.3 percent in Communist China; 3.8 percent in the Soviet Union).

40. Another effort to establish the absolute authority of the party has been a nationwide movement in the past year to have all Chinese—party and nonparty alike—embark upon intensive study of the works of Mao Tse-tung, which have become canonized as "the ideology of Mao." Mao has also been credited personally with originating the regime's major policies, and the recent publication of the fourth volume of Mao's works has given new impetus to the "cult of Mao" trend. In addition to reinforcing party authority and unity, this buildup of Mao probably reflects an outcropping of the leadership's nationalist pride and confidence in their superiority as developers of Marxism-Leninism, and challenges the Kremlin by exalting a Chinese as the foremost living Communist theoretician.

41. Although prolonged and acrimonious intraparty debates have occurred in the past three years, party discipline at the top level has enabled the regime to maintain its essential unity and the party has not been forced to resort to Stalin-style open purges. The removal in 1959 of Defense Minister P'eng Teh-huai and Chief of Staff Huang K'o-ch'eng was probably the result of their questioning of party policies, and some others may have fallen from grace or suffered a loss of influence, including Politburo members Ch'en Yun (economic expert) and Chang Wen-t'ien (specialist on foreign policy, including Sino-Soviet relations). In general, however, the party leadership has not been beset by acute factionalism, and Mao appears to continue in control of the party and its policies. Mao's authority, together with the active support he receives from many others in the leadership group, makes it likely that his views will continue to prevail and that factionalism will not be a serious problem while he lives.

42. It is possible that Mao, now 67, will die during the period of this estimate. If so, his influence as the patron saint of Chinese communism will still remain strong, particularly since his heir apparent, Liu Shao-ch'i, appears to favor Mao's policies. Moreover, the tradition of party unity will still carry considerable weight. However, neither Liu

SECRET

263

SECRET   10

nor any other successor would inherit Mao's personal authority and prestige. As a result, there may be at least a temporary trend toward more collective leadership, perhaps involving compromises on some controversial policies. Alternatively, it is possible that with the disappearance of the centripetal force which Mao exerts, disagreements over policies or power struggles would become more frequent and serious, and the views of the professional military leaders may carry more weight. Moreover, party leadership will begin to devolve upon the second generation.[11] Mao's death may thus have considerable repercussions but we believe on balance that it will not cause basic changes in Chinese Communist policy or in the party's ability to enforce its dictates.

43. *The People.* In general the attitude of the overworked, underfed people of China toward the regime is probably best described as resignation. Bitterness is widespread, but it is impossible to say what proportion of the populace it characterizes. The only sustained overt resistance comes from the national minorities, most conspicuously in Tibet. There has been evidence of brave but futile uprisings among the Moslems of China's great Western regions, and there have been isolated instances of hunger-driven attacks on government granaries by peasants. None of this, however, adds up to a serious threat to the regime. The watchfulness of the party, the pervasiveness of the secret police, and the haunting fear of informers preclude the organization of dissidents except in remote areas. Furthermore, there is considerable positive support for the regime. Millions of people have made real advances under Communist rule, and among many there is a feeling of pride in China's rapid advance as a world power.

44. Executions and condemnations to labor reform battalions are not resorted to as much as they were in the early 1950's because more effective methods of control have been developed which have the added virtue of bring-

ing less international disapprobation upon the regime. The use of overwhelming social pressures including accusation and confession meetings is a principal device employed. An effective damper upon dissidence is also provided by the extreme degree of regimentation which is imposed upon the people: they haven't the time, energy, or privacy to organize any kind of antiregime activities. Two new devices of regimentation introduced in the past three years are the commune system and the universal militia.

45. The great economic promises which the regime made for the commune system have remained unfulfilled, but the system has been retained in diluted form throughout the countryside, partly for social and political reasons. "Freeing" the housewife from household chores to work in the fields and factories, caring for children in communal child-care centers, and feeding the people in communal messhalls have all worked to weaken the family and to improve opportunities for surveillance and indoctrination. It is likely that during the period of this estimate the regime will move toward the reinstitution of some of the early commune features.

46. Social-political motivation is even more evident in the case of the urban communes. This program, which was postponed in 1958 when difficulties were encountered, was finally launched in March of 1960, and by July the regime claimed that nearly 55 million urban dwellers had been enrolled. The pattern of organization for urban communes is less standardized than that of the rural ones, but the chief characteristics appear to be the institution of communal messhalls and child-care centers and the release of women to various kinds of subsidiary industrial work. This unpopular program is of dubious economic value, and it has brought few if any real benefits to its members. Like the rural commune, however, it improves the regime's capabilities for regimentation and indoctrination. The use of service teams to do the housecleaning provides a continuing inspection of the workers' quarters and their few personal possessions.

---

[11] The average age of CCP Politburo members is over 60. Mao is 67; Chou En-lai, 62; and Liu Shao-ch'i, about 62.

SECRET

SECRET 11

47. The new militia organization is likewise a potent instrument of control. Although a body of militia outside the army has existed for many years, the present nationwide framework for the militia dates from 1958. At that time it became an integral part of the "Great Leap Forward" and commune programs. From about five million members in 1950, the organization has grown to an estimated 220 million,[12] and includes women as well as men. According to Mao, the militia is not solely, or even primarily, an adjunct of the army, but is intended to serve many purposes: military, labor, educational, and physical culture. The primary tasks of this greatly expanded militia clearly lie in economic and political fields at present. It provides a means of organizing under military discipline a mobile labor corps which can be readily moved wherever it is needed. Units have been engaged in irrigation, flood prevention, cultivation, and construction projects. The organization of these peasants and workers along military lines and subject to military discipline adds one more means of regimenting the individual and preventing the organization of resistance.

48. To the leaders, however, these institutions of control represent only a beginning of the processes of creating a new "Chinese Communist man." The Chinese Communists have published articles praising the prospect of further decline of the family and claiming that love of the state is a far greater and more rewarding thing than love of family. How far they can actually go in changing the Chinese people remains to be seen, but they have already gone much further in regimenting the reputedly individualistic Chinese than most students of China had thought possible.

49. We believe it unlikely that antiregime activities will threaten the regime's ability to control and direct the country during the next five years. The Soviet experience of the early 1930's demonstrated that even mass starvation may not generate resistance that can upset a ruthless totalitarian regime. The majority of people will probably be dissatisfied with their personal lot under communism, but they will lack any effective means of translating their discontent into active resistance. As disillusionment and the pressures toward dissidence increase, the sophistication and pervasiveness of Peiping's control mechanism will also grow. Peiping's chief problem will be not so much the suppression of dissidence as the overcoming of apathy, fatigue, and passive resistance. In any case, we now see no serious threat, either internal or external, to the continuance of the regime.

C. Military [13]

50. *General.* There have been no dramatic changes in the size, equipment, or deployment of Communist China's military forces during the past year. Progress toward improving the capabilities and modernizing the equipment of the armed forces has been steady, but not spectacular. Communist China's own munitions industry is growing principally as the result of industrial machinery and technical assistance from the USSR, and Soviet shipments of military equipment to China began to decrease in 1956. Peiping is still dependent upon Moscow for many kinds of military equipment and supply, particularly POL and the more complex items associated with a modern and balanced conventional force. However, during 1960 Soviet shipments of military equipment and machinery for the production of military supplies to China appear to have dropped off sharply.

51. The concept of a large ground force continues to dominate Chinese Communist military doctrine. There are more than 2.8 million men in the military establishment, which is capable of defeating any other non-Soviet Asian force or combination of forces. About 95 percent of them are assigned to the army, making it the largest in the world. In addition to its traditional mission of defending Communist China, the army has important internal security, economic, and political

[12] Only a small percentage of these are militarily effective. See paragraph 52.

[13] See charts and maps, pages 27ff. for details concerning Chinese Communist military strengths and dispositions.

SECRET

S̶E̶C̶R̶E̶T̶

12

functions. In fulfilling its functions the army is backed up by a large trained reserve and a huge People's Militia.

52. A few select Militia units have achieved a fair degree of military effectiveness. However, on the whole, the militia lacks the weapons, training, and support that are required in the development of military capabilities. In the strict military sense, the principal value of the militia lies in its potential as a source of partially trained manpower for replacements for the regular armed forces or to free the regular forces from routine internal security tasks.

53. The Chinese Communist Air Force and Naval Air Force have a combined personnel strength of about 82,500 and about 2,300 jet aircraft in operational units. The air force now has about 30 advanced fighters (FARMER/MIG-19) in tactical units. Its air defense capability has improved through modernization of its aircraft control and warning network and an intensified training program for fighter pilots. The air offensive capability lies in a light jet bomber (BEAGLE/ IL-28) force of about 420 aircraft, 20 piston medium bombers (BULL/TU-4), and about 145 piston light bombers (BAT/TU-2). The Chinese Communist Navy (including its air force) has an estimated 78,500 men. Its principal strengths are its submarine force (29 ships, including 21 "W" Class), a large and effective motor torpedo boat force, and an extensive minelaying capability.

54. *Relations Between the Party and the Military.* Communist China's senior military and political leaders have worked closely together for many years. At least a third of the members of the Central Committee of the CCP have had extensive military experience, and nearly all of the remaining two-thirds have had some military experience. Every key position in the Ministry of National Defense and in the armed forces is held by a party member whose background includes continuous party activity since the 1920's or 1930's. Until recently there had been no indications of serious differences of opinion among the top leaders.

55. However, in September 1959 the Minister of Defense and the Chief of General Staff were replaced under conditions which strongly suggest that differences of view had developed among the top leaders on a number of important questions. We believe that these questions include the relative priority of military modernization versus economic development, party interference in professional military matters, and the constant involvement of the armed forces in nonmilitary activities like the commune program. In addition, it is likely that there are high-level disagreements concerning strategic concepts and the nuclear weapons issue. No widespread purge within the military appears to have followed the replacement of the Minister of Defense and the Chief of Staff, and it is likely that the present incumbents will attempt to close any gaps which may have developed between military and political thinking. However, as younger military technicians and specialists emerge and assume more responsible positions, it is likely that military-party differences will continue and perhaps increase.

56. *Sino-Soviet Cooperation and Advanced Weapons.*[14] Communist China does not have as yet a missile or nuclear weapons capability of its own. Peiping is giving high priority to a nuclear weapons development program. Until the Chinese Communists develop their own nuclear capability they will remain dependent upon the USSR for military support with nuclear weapons. We believe it unlikely that the Soviets have stationed nuclear weapons in China, but even if they have, such weapons would almost certainly be held under strict Soviet custody. The USSR could give China nuclear weapons from its own stockpile, but it almost certainly has not done so, and we do not believe that the Soviets intend to do so within the foreseeable future. Similarly, we have no evidence that the USSR has equipped the Chinese with surface-to-surface ballistic missiles. There are indications, however, that the Chinese may have received some Soviet air-to-air missiles.

[14] Paragraphs 41–51 of NIE 100-3-60, "Sino-Soviet Relations," dated 9 August 1960, discuss this question in more detail.

S̶E̶C̶R̶E̶T̶

SECRET   13

57. We are almost certain that the Chinese Communist desire for a nuclear weapons capability and Soviet reluctance to provide the Chinese such a capability is a major issue in Sino-Soviet relations. The Chinese Communists almost certainly consider that a demonstration of their capability to produce nuclear weapons would confirm their claim to great power status, and they will probably carry their nuclear weapons program forward as rapidly as feasible.

58. Our evidence with respect to Communist China's nuclear program is fragmentary as is our information about the nature and extent of Soviet aid. In what we estimate to be the present state of Chinese Communist competence, the carrying out of fissionable materials production programs requires significant Soviet assistance in the form of technicians, designs, and equipment. As we have estimated earlier, we believe that the Soviets have been moving at a deliberate pace in assisting the Chinese in the nuclear field, seeking to hold Chinese impatience and discontent at a level consistent with the Soviet view of the best interests of the Sino-Soviet relationship. Recent evidence strongly suggests that in the past the USSR has given the Chinese Communists more technical assistance toward the eventual production of nuclear weapons than we had previously believed likely. This evidence is insufficient to establish how much assistance has actually been given, although we believe the aid has been fairly substantial and increasing over the years, at least until recently.

59. The USSR has provided Communist China with a nuclear research reactor and is training nuclear scientists in the Joint Institute for Nuclear Research in Dubna, USSR. The exploitation of native uranium resources has been underway, with Soviet assistance, since 1950. At least 10 deposits are now being worked, and we believe that ore with a uranium metal equivalent of several hundred tons is being mined annually and retained in China. The Chinese Communists have probably initiated the processing of uranium ores into metals, and this leads us to believe they are currently building a plutonium production reactor. Although there is no conclusive evidence, there are strong indications that they may also be building a U-235 gaseous diffusion plant.

60. On the basis of the fragmentary evidence available, we now believe that the most probable date at which the Chinese Communists could detonate a first nuclear device is sometime in 1963, though it might be as late as 1964, or as early as 1962, depending upon the actual degree of Soviet assistance.[15][16] Given direct Soviet assistance in fissionable materials, designs, and fabrications, the Chinese could produce a nuclear detonation in China at almost any time in the immediate future. On the other hand, if as a result of Sino-Soviet dissensions there were a lessening of Soviet assistance in the nuclear field, the Chinese Communist progress would be substantially retarded.

61. While the explosion of a nuclear device would give the Chinese Communists political and propaganda rewards, they would almost certainly proceed to create an operational nuclear capability as quickly as feasible. However, at least two years would probably be required after the first test to produce a small stockpile of elementary weapons. Moreover, given economic limitations and the reali-

---

[15] This paragraph is from NIE 100-4-60, "Likelihood and Consequences of the Development of Nuclear Capabilities by Additional Countries," dated 9 September 1960. See paragraphs 37 to 41 of that estimate for a fuller discussion of this question. See also NIE 13-2-60, to be published in mid-December 1960.

[16] The Assistant Chief of Naval Operations (Intelligence), Department of the Navy, believes that information on the nature and extent of Soviet aid to Communist China is as yet insufficient for a reliable estimate of the year in which the Chinese Communists could detonate a nuclear device. He considers, however, that certain basic evidence should have become available to us by this time if the Chinese Communists were progressing toward detonation of a domestically produced nuclear device very much before the final stages of this five-year estimate.

The Assistant Chief of Staff, Intelligence, USAF, contingent upon continuation of the present level of Soviet assistance, believes that the Chinese will probably detonate their first nuclear device in 1962, and possibly as early as late 1961.

SECRET

SECRET

14

ties of geography, they would probably rely initially on aircraft as delivery vehicles. They have a few piston medium bombers of the BULL type, which could reach Japan, Taiwan, Okinawa, South Korea, and South Vietnam, as well as additional areas in Southeast Asia. In addition we believe that by 1965 they may have a substantial number of jet medium bombers, assuming continued Soviet assistance.

62. The Chinese Communist missile program, we believe, is in the early research and development phase. The initial production effort will probably be air-to-air rockets with a simple type of radio or infrared guidance system. We believe that they will also go forward as rapidly as they are capable with the development of ballistic missiles, probably concentrating in the first place on a missile with a range of 200–500 n.m., capable of carrying a fission warhead. Such missiles would give them coverage of most of the targets mentioned above. If deployed in Tibet, such missiles would also give coverage of the major cities of northern India. We believe that they could develop such missiles by the late 1960's or, with considerable Soviet assistance, much earlier. We do not believe they could, by themselves, produce the 6,500 n.m. missile necessary to give them a capability against the US until well after 1970.

63. *Trends in the Military Forces.* In addition to pushing its program to attain a nuclear capability, Communist China will probably continue to increase its conventional military capability over the next five years. The rate of increase in Communist China's military capabilities will be determined in large part by the economic demands of the regime's overall economic development program and by the nature and extent of Soviet assistance.

64. By 1965 the Chinese Communist leaders will be more aware of the implications of nuclear weapons and this may have some effect on their strategic thinking. However, Communist China will probably still maintain a mass army. The offensive and defensive capabilities of the air force and naval air force will probably have improved considerably by 1965. Their jet fighter strength will gradually increase and higher performance aircraft will

be introduced. Offensive strength may be further enhanced by the introduction of jet medium bombers. Although Communist China's aircraft industry is becoming less dependent upon imported components, its assembly and production program is still dependent upon the Soviets for original blueprints, technical assistance, and training, and for the more complex electronic and specialized equipment. At present Chinese factories are turning out about 2 MIG–19's [17] and 12 light piston transports (COLT) per month. MIG–19 aircraft and engine production will probably build up to about 18 per month by 1962. We believe that the Chinese Communists are planning to build BADGER (TU–16) and/or CAMEL (TU–104, the transport version) aircraft. Assuming continued Soviet assistance, we estimate that production could begin in the last quarter of 1961. The Chinese Communist Navy will also increase in size and improve its capabilities over the next five years. The shipbuilding industry will almost certainly continue to grow, producing additional and improved ships, primarily of Soviet design, for both the navy and the rapidly increasing merchant marine. Naval construction will include submarines as well as surface ships no larger than destroyers.

D. Summary

65. Despite the difficult problems the regime will encounter, domestic developments during the next five years will provide a stronger base for the regime's pursuit of its ambitious objectives. Its economic dependence upon the rest of the Bloc will be considerably reduced and its military dependence, though still critical in some respects, will lessen somewhat. Although throughout the period the effective striking range of its military forces will be limited to nearby Asian countries, Peiping's

---

[17] We believe that the Mukden aircraft plant is producing MIG–19 airframes and engines from domestically produced components. The metallurgical industry in Communist China has not yet mastered the technology involved in producing and fabricating the high-grade and high-temperature alloys—including chrome and nickel alloys—used in the manufacture of jet engines. Such alloys must still be imported from Bloc countries.

SECRET

SECRET

15

ability to assert international influence will increase. Peiping's growing impact on world affairs will be greatest in the political field. Its capabilities in economic warfare will also increase, but not to the same extent. The steady growth of the domestic base will probably encourage continued confident aggressiveness of the regime in striving for the rapid advancement of Communist China's international position.

III. COMMUNIST CHINA'S INTERNATIONAL POSITION

A. Peiping's View of the World Situation

66. The Chinese Communists tend to have an astigmatic view of the world and of their own position in it. This distorted image is due in part to their limited exposure to the outside world. Probably of more importance, however, is their tendency to create a picture of the world that gives continuing validity to their own revolutionary experiences and successes, justifies the policies they feel they must pursue to solve their special domestic and international problems, and remains true to certain fundamental Communist precepts. Some of their foreign policy actions continue to demonstrate considerable pragmatic flexibility, and they probably overstate some of their views for polemical purposes. Nevertheless, their interpretation of world developments seems to have a strong doctrinaire and China-centric bias, leading Peiping to an overly optimistic appraisal of the prospects for communism in general and Communist China in particular.

67. In their picture of the world, the Chinese Communists see the alliance of the anti-Communist "imperialist" nations as weakened and divided and the US as frustrated and nearing political bankruptcy in world affairs. Since the advent of Sputnik in late 1957, the Chinese have apparently believed that Soviet weaponry developments have tipped the balance of world military power to the Bloc. They also appear convinced that the Bloc has surpassed the West in political influence in many areas of the world and will overtake the West in economic power within a few years.

68. The Chinese Communists appear to view the uncommitted and underdeveloped countries as providing the greatest opportunity to hasten the collapse of the capitalist world. They portray the peoples of Asia, Africa, and Latin America as increasingly restive and disillusioned with their governments and with Western imperialism. They appear convinced that the time has come to encourage and support nationalist and Communist revolutions in these areas. This, they apparently believe, would isolate the US, lead to the disintegration of its alliance system, and deprive it of essential markets and raw materials.

69. With this view of the West on the run and the peoples of the uncommitted countries turning toward the Bloc, the Chinese have apparently concluded that unremitting Bloc pressure must be maintained, particularly on the chief enemy, the US, and that the world situation is ripe for exploitation by bold and militant Communist policies, even if a risk of war is involved. Accordingly, during the past year, the Chinese have argued with vigor that: (a) the unchanged and unchangeable nature of "imperialism" will inevitably breed new wars as the imperialist nations are pressed to the wall; (b) serious negotiation with the West is foolhardy, inasmuch as any detente or lessening of tensions would only provide the US a breathing space in which further to increase its preparations for war, and moreover would confuse the people of the world and lull their will to fight against imperialism; (c) emphasis should be placed on supporting revolutionary leftist movements, rather than on wooing nationalistic bourgeois governments; and (d) Bloc policy should not be seriously inhibited by fear of war, because even a nuclear war would not be disastrous. Indeed, the Communist Chinese claim to believe that the horrors of nuclear war are overrated, that at least 300 million Chinese would survive, and that a nuclear war would result in the universal triumph of communism.

SECRET

SECRET   16

B. Sino-Soviet Relations [18]

70. These Chinese Communist views of the world situation and Peiping's efforts to propagate them within the Bloc during a time when Soviet leaders were pursuing a more moderate policy emphasizing economic and political competition and minimizing risks of war, led to a sharp dispute between Moscow and Peiping. About June 1960 Khrushchev took the offensive and has since maintained strong pressure on Peiping. Moscow has intensified public attacks on Peiping's "dogmatism" and "narrow nationalism." It has also insisted, although in some cases unsuccessfully, that other Communist parties around the world back the Soviets in the dispute. However, the Chinese have not dropped their criticisms of the Soviets or abandoned their views, and have indeed hinted that they are prepared to rely on their own resources, if necessary, for future economic development.

71. A number of fundamental issues are at stake in the dispute. Foremost is Peiping's challenge to Soviet dominance of international communism. Contributing to this are sharp differences on the basic nature of Bloc policy, a clash of Russian and Chinese national pride, and the personal prestige of Mao and Khrushchev. In short, the controversy has achieved such momentum and involves such basic issues that a serious strain has developed.

72. Nevertheless, the cohesive forces in the alliance remain strong. Moscow and Peiping continue to share common broad objectives, and the recognition of a common enemy and of the many strategic advantages they derive from their alliance. There is almost certainly an acute awareness on both sides of the serious damage that a continued breach would inflict on their respective na-

tional interests and on the prospects of international communism. In addition, while the Soviet leaders cannot condone Chinese obstinacy or accept Chinese policy preferences without weakening their control of the Communist movement, they cannot allow an overt and formal breach to occur without a further serious loss of influence over the Chinese and without gravely weakening the international Communist movement as a whole. The Chinese, on the other hand, despite their revolutionary zeal and arrogance, need the continuing economic, political, and military support of the Soviet Union to achieve their ambitious foreign and domestic goals. Moreover, there is strong pressure from the other Communist parties for a resolution of the dispute.

73. However, since the Sino-Soviet disagreement involves such fundamental issues, it seems to us virtually impossible that there can be a return to the relationship of earlier days, with the Soviets dominating a closely-knit alliance. On the other hand, an overt and formal breach like that between the USSR and Yugoslavia in 1948, while possible, seems unlikely. Consequently, we believe that the alliance against the West will hold together, but that the estrangement will continue, with ups and downs as new issues arise. Even if some nominal Sino-Soviet accommodation is reached, the bitterness and suspicions engendered by the present dispute will continue to color the Sino-Soviet relationship. Neither will trust the other as fully as before, and policy coordination will be more difficult. In time—though not necessarily within the next few years—the problems inherent in the relationship could lead to even more serious crises in Sino-Soviet relations.

C. Communist China's Foreign Relations

74. Despite its arrogance and tough talk, in practice Peiping has been following essentially low-risk policies during the past year. This apparent contradiction suggests that Chinese Communist policy is neither irrational nor inflexible. One of Mao's fundamental

[18] The judgments in this section appear to be consistent with such information as we now have on the recently adjourned conference in Moscow. NIE 100-3-60, "Sino-Soviet Relations," dated 9 August 1960, and Chapter V of NIE 11-4-60, "Main Trends in Soviet Capabilities and Policies, 1960-1965," dated December 1960, contain a more detailed discussion of this subject.

SECRET

concepts has been that a total and irrevocable commitment of forces should not be made unless there is overwhelming superiority over the enemy. Mao and his colleagues are almost certainly aware that Communist China does not possess such superiority at present.

75. The gap between Communist China's words and actions probably corresponds to the gap between its ambitions on the one hand and its own present power position on the other. Communist China's foreign policy will reflect this gap, with both tough and moderate tactics continuing to be applied, at times with little apparent consistency, to the various opportunities and challenges at hand. Though Peiping will assume a pose of sweet reasonableness in many instances, we do have some concern that Peiping's arrogant self-confidence and revolutionary fervor may increase the danger of Chinese miscalculation in Asia.

76. *Policy Toward the US.* The most intense element in Peiping's foreign policy is unremitting hostility toward the US. The Chinese Communists view the US as the major obstacle to their own ambitions and to the general expansion of Communist power and influence in the world. The Chinese Communist leaders have made the US the symbol of evil and maintained a "hate-America" campaign within China which at times has reached a near-frenzied pitch.

77. Still being in a real sense outside the international political arena and unable to challenge the US militarily or economically, Peiping has attempted to undercut US power and influence in the Far East, concentrating its pressures against the offshore islands, Taiwan, Southeast Asia, and Japan. Thus far, however, Communist China has won no clear victories in these areas, and has not been able to increase its own power and influence as rapidly as it has hoped. Especially evident in Chinese Communist foreign policy is a great element of frustration caused by US denial to Peiping of both Taiwan and acknowledged world status as a near-great power which governs China.

78. *The Taiwan Issue.*[19] Much of Peiping's "hate-America" campaign revolves around the Taiwan issue. Peiping has never deviated from its views that the Taiwan question is purely an internal Chinese matter and that, consequently, support of the Nationalist government is "foreign intervention" and "aggression" against Communist China. Peiping will almost certainly not change its objective or views with respect to Taiwan and will remain vehemently opposed to a "two China" solution. It almost certainly will not renounce the use of force in the Taiwan area and will continue to maintain that the only peaceful solution would be for the US to withdraw its military commitments to the Nationalists and its military forces from the Taiwan Strait area.

79. The Chinese Communists are not likely to attempt to take Taiwan by force in the face of strong US defense commitments to the Nationalists. Peiping probably believes that the continued strengthening of its international position and a deterioration of the situation on Taiwan will eventually lead to the collapse of the Nationalists and the recovery of Taiwan. However, Peiping is anxious to speed up the process of acquiring Taiwan.

80. Accordingly, we believe that the Chinese Communists will again initiate a high level of military pressure in the Taiwan Strait area, within the next year or so. The form and nature of this pressure cannot be predicted with assurance. We believe that it will be primarily a probing action designed to test again Nationalist strength and morale and US resolve concerning the defense of the offshore islands and to exacerbate relations between the US and its allies. This action, however, will probably be at a level below that which Communist China estimates would lead to major hostilities with the US. The Soviet

---

[19] The question of Taiwan and the likelihood of renewed Chinese Communist military activity in the Taiwan Strait area are considered in detail in the following estimates: SNIE 43-60, "The Offshore Islands," dated 6 September 1960; and SNIE 100-4-59, "Chinese Communist Intentions and Probable Courses of Action in the Taiwan Strait Area," dated 13 March 1959.

SECRET   18

estimate of the US response would be the key factor in determining the nature of any prior Soviet commitments to the Chinese and of the restraints the Soviets would seek to impose upon them.

81. *Communist China and the UN.* Communist China has made no concerted drive of its own for membership in the UN, but has relied upon the Soviet Union and several neutralist nations of the Afro-Asian group to present its case. Communist China wants the China seat at the UN both as a symbol of recognition of its big power status, as a blow to the Chinese Nationalists, and as a major defeat of US policy. Peiping would almost certainly refuse to take a seat under any arrangement which provided for continued Nationalist Chinese representation. The future policy of the USSR with respect to the UN is not entirely clear, and Moscow may seek to use the representation issue to embarrass the organization and the US. In any event, the China representation issue will probably become acute next year, since it now appears that the US will have serious difficulty in maintaining the moratorium.

82. *Policies in Asia.* Peiping's policies in Asia have not followed a consistent line. At the Bandung Conference in 1955, their hard, militant approach gave way to a "peaceful co-existence" line. In 1958 and 1959, Peiping reverted to a hard line in Indonesia, India, Japan, and the Taiwan Straits. Apparently realizing they had pushed too hard, the Chinese Communists have again shifted back toward the pre-1958 coexistence theme: they have accommodated Burma in settling the border issue, concluded friendship treaties with Burma, Nepal, and Afghanistan, revived proposals for an Asian peace pact and atom-free zone, and adopted a less adamant and arrogant attitude toward India and Indonesia. Peiping's less belligerent approach towards its Asian neighbors has occurred at the very time that Peiping has been trumpeting for a militant Communist world policy and almost wrecking its relations with Moscow in the process.

83. In Asia, Japan is a priority target for Peiping. The immediate Chinese objective is to weaken Japan's ties with the US and to stimulate Japanese neutralism. Peiping gave strong propaganda support and some covert financial aid to the demonstrations in Japan against the security treaty, and probably believes that its efforts contributed substantially to the cancellation of President Eisenhower's visit and the resignation of the Kishi government. The most significant Communist assets, from Peiping's point of view, are the neutralist sentiments in Japan and the continuing widespread belief among Japanese that more normal relations with mainland China are necessary for Japan. As it has in the past, Peiping may miscalculate Japanese reactions to attempts to influence its policies. However, unless Peiping overplays its hand, an increase in Sino-Japanese trade and cultural relations is probable, and the establishing of diplomatic relations is possible within the period of this estimate.

84. Communist China's growing power will increasingly threaten the stability and orientation of the states of Southeast Asia. In spite of Communist China's militant view of the world situation, we do not believe that Peiping intends to advance its aims in Southeast Asia by overt aggression with its own troops, or those of North Vietnam (DRV). Nevertheless, depending on the circumstances, the Chinese might sponsor the committing of DRV troops, or commit Chinese "volunteer" troops, in the event of US or SEATO military intervention in the Indochina states area. Peiping almost certainly believes at the present time that much of Southeast Asia can eventually be subverted without need of Chinese or DRV invasion, and will almost certainly continue clandestinely to supply equipment, training, and funds to Communist movements in the area. Peiping also may gain a greater degree of direction of these movements than it now appears to enjoy, and its militant outlook may accordingly be reflected in increased revolutionary activity on their part. In any event, awareness of the growing power of Communist China will probably cause certain Southeast Asian governments and leaders to become

SECRET

SECRET   19

more responsive than they now are to Bloc pressures.

85. Unsatisfactory relations with India now constitute one of Peiping's major policy problems in Asia—a problem for which it can find no easy solution. The border dispute is not likely to be resolved soon, although an eventual settlement may be achieved involving Chinese recognition of India's claims in NEFA and Chinese retention of the area it now controls in Ladakh. Even if such a settlement is reached, Communist China's relations with India are likely to remain cool and their rivalry in Asia is likely to intensify.[20]

86. *Policies Elsewhere.* Peiping has been giving great attention to Africa. In the past year Communist China has continued to give strong support to the Algerian revolutionary regime. It signed a treaty of friendship, a trade agreement, and extended a $25 million credit to Guinea during President Sekou Toure's visit to Peiping. Chinese Communist trade and cultural delegations have visited a number of new African countries. To date, Peiping's efforts have not met with conspicuous success in terms of diplomatic recognition.[21] However, the failure of any of the new African states at the 1960 General Assembly session to support the US-sponsored moratorium on UN consideration of Chinese representation almost certainly buoys Peiping's expectation of future African diplomatic support. The Chinese Communists undoubtedly also estimate, not without justification, that the confusion, inexperience, anticolonialist sentiment, and racialism which exist in Africa can be exploited not only for Communist, but for Chinese Communist benefit. Increasing Chinese activity is likely and it will constitute a potential source of Sino-Soviet friction.

---

[20] For a fuller discussion of these problems, see NIE 100-2-60, "Sino-Indian Relations," dated 17 May 1960, and NIE 51-60, "The Outlook for India," dated 25 October 1960.

[21] In 1959-1960 it obtained recognition from Guinea, Ghana, and Mali. Of the 17 African nations which have achieved independence during 1960, 1 has recognized Peiping, 6 have recognized the GRC, and the remaining 10 have taken no formal stand. Throughout Africa and the Middle East, 10 states recognize Peiping, 15 recognize the GRC, and 12 recognize neither.

87. In general, Communist China has slackened its efforts in the Arab World. Its relations with several of the countries in the area, notably the UAR, have cooled. Peiping appears to have switched interest to Africa, and its influence in the Middle East is likely to rise more slowly than in Africa.

88. In the last several years, the Chinese Communists have greatly stepped up their activities in Latin America. They have been particularly busy in Cuba and have effected a breaking of Cuban relations with the Republic of China and the establishing of diplomatic relations with Peiping. The Chinese Communists apparently pin their hopes in Latin America more to a belief that revolutionary and anti-US sentiment will increase, than to any expectation of soon establishing friendly relations with existing governments other than that of Havana. Peiping will almost certainly further increase its activities in Latin America and may well exert a growing appeal, due in part to China's rapid economic progress from underdeveloped status. Peiping appears even now to have assumed, or been accorded, an increasing role in the guidance of Communist movements in Latin America.

D. Foreign Policy Outlook

89. Despite their impatient and bellicose attitude, we do not believe that the Chinese Communists plan to initiate overt military action in non-Communist Asia in the near future except perhaps in the Taiwan Strait (as discussed in paragraphs 78-80 above). Peiping probably believes present trends in underdeveloped areas generally are moving along lines favorable to Chinese Communist interests and objectives. However, they are anxious to speed up these trends. While retaining a belligerent stance, the Chinese Communists will probably continue to follow policies which they estimate would not run high risk of war with the West, unless they have the backing of the USSR. However, Communist China will probably not hesitate to act tough from time to time, seeking to impress upon the people's of Asia its growing power and presence. At the same time, the Chinese Communists will probably be increasingly

SECRET

SECRET

20

active in encouraging and supporting indigenous left-wing revolutionary movements throughout the underdeveloped world. Governments aligned with the US will continue to be the objects of periodic Chinese Communist villification and pressure.

90. We believe that once Communist China detonates a nuclear device, and particularly when it attains a nuclear weapons capability, its foreign policy will become more truculent and militant. A nuclear explosion would also have a strong impact on other countries. The dominant reaction would be a fear that the chances of war had increased, and there would be stronger pressures for full acceptance of Communist China as a member of the world community. While some countries in Asia would increasingly look to the US to provide the counterbalance to Communist China's military strength, there would also be a heightened inclination toward accommodation with Peiping.

91. Even before the explosion of a nuclear device, Peiping's military power and potential may increasingly complicate the international disarmament problem. If Western disarmament negotiations with the USSR make significant progress, international pressures will probably grow greatly for Communist China's participation. Peiping's leverage with respect to disarmament will become even greater once China has become a nuclear power. Peiping will exploit this situation in an effort to enhance its international status, but at the same time may attempt to prevent the conclusion of any disarmament agreement, at least until it becomes a nuclear power.

92. In 1965 Communist China will be playing more fully the role of a leading world power, whether or not it is a member of the UN. Its stature in Asia will have grown, and its military, economic, and subversive pressures will increasingly threaten the non-Communist Asian periphery. Peiping's policies will have ranged between a relatively moderate approach and outright toughness, but intense hatred for the US and an eagerness to push the Communist world revolution will probably still be dominant elements of Peiping's outlook. Communist China's arrogance and pretensions will almost certainly remain a source of concern for the USSR. At the same time the danger posed by Communist China to US interests, particularly in Asia, will have increased.

SECRET

SECRET

APPENDIX I: SCIENTIFIC AND TECHNOLOGICAL

93. Education in China is now closely focused on the technological needs of the state. Out of a total of about 630,000 students graduated from college by mid-1959, an estimated 300,000 were in scientific and technological fields. However, the quality of scientific and technical education in China is still poor, and the training of most graduates in recent years has been along very narrow specialized lines which ill suit them for creative or independent developments in their fields. Only a very few highly trained scientists are available, probably about 1,000,[22] most of them Western-trained. About 30,000 researchers and technicians in all are employed by research organizations. There also is an undetermined but probably much higher number of technically trained persons engaged in engineering development or other technical work primarily related to production. Currently, most new, high-caliber scientific and technical personnel are those trained in the USSR, but by 1965 the Chinese program should be producing some well trained men.

94. The major Chinese effort over the next five years therefore will be devoted to building up a scientific and technological base while channeling their present capabilities into areas essential to national development—improvement of the food supply, public health, heavy industry, and military technology. During this period, they will need and will continue to procure foreign technological aid and exploit Western and Soviet Bloc designs and practices.

95. The expanding biological and agricultural research and development programs related to food supply are not likely to improve greatly, but some gains in agricultural output will probably result from the institution of modern practices. Achievements in health have been impressive in reducing infectious and epidemic diseases, but the level of health and individual medical care will remain poor. Areas important to raising the level of industrial technology, such as chemistry and metallurgy, will continue to show marked weakness despite vigorous efforts. Strong electronic capabilities are now emerging and, by 1965, Chinese capabilities should be approaching those of the more advanced European Satellites.

96. Military modernization is receiving strong emphasis. A fair capability to produce most kinds of conventional armaments is rapidly emerging. Little effort is yet expended on fundamental research in military fields, however. Both naval and aeronautical research facilities are supporting production of aircraft and ships primarily of Soviet design and more advanced models probably will be forthcoming in the next few years, still primarily of Soviet design. While we believe the present chemical warfare capability of Communist China is small and primarily defensive in nature, there is recent evidence of increasing activity in this field. Some CW agents are probably produced and a small but significant research program is believed to be underway. There is little evidence of activity in biological warfare. The Chinese are capable of achieving a modest BW program and a fairly substantial CW program by 1967, if they so desire.

97. In the atomic energy field, as in other fields, there is only a small corps of highly qualified scientists, most of whom received their training in the US, UK, France, or Germany. Although they are probably somewhat hampered by the administrative and training responsibilities which are imposed

---

[22] This is roughly two percent of the number available in the USSR.

SECRET

SECRET   22

upon them, they are capable of carrying forward work in nuclear weapons design. In addition to stepped-up training at home, Peiping is expanding its nucleus of skilled personnel by sending advanced students to the USSR and the Satellites, particularly to the Joint Institute for Nuclear Research at Dubna in the USSR.

98. There is evidence of a growing awareness in Communist Chinese scientific and military circles of the importance of guided missiles in modern warfare, and it can be assumed that an increasing amount of basic scientific effort in China is being directed toward the ultimate development of a native missile capability. There are several outstanding Chinese Communist scientists, some of whom are US trained in missile technology or related fields.

99. Because both the technical and industrial requirements for a missile program are so great and so complex, and because of the lack of intelligence indicating any integration of these requirements toward a guided missile capability, we believe that the Chinese Communists are not yet ready to engage in the testing or production of any type of guided missile. It is possible that they are now in the theoretical or early planning stages.

100. They are believed capable of developing and producing unguided rockets for use with nonnuclear warheads by 1965. Such an endeavor is probable in order to provide the means for delivering large HE warheads at ranges in excess of conventional artillery.

101. A Chinese Communist official has stated that the regime will eventually launch an earth satellite, and there are indications that Chinese personnel are studying rocket technology with Soviet assistance. The Chinese would value highly the political and propaganda gains resulting from a launching. Using Soviet launching equipment, and with Soviet guidance throughout the project, Soviet-trained Chinese Communists could probably perform a successful earth satellite launching about one or two years after initiation of the project. The satellite itself, including scientific instrumentation, could be of Chinese design and manufacture. There is as yet, however, no evidence of the initiation of any projects to launch earth satellites from the territory of Communist China. Any launching from Communist China during the period of this estimate will be the direct result of Soviet participation and the decision to do so would be based on political factors.

SECRET

SEC~~R~~ET

APPENDIX II: RELIABILITY OF CHINESE COMMUNIST ECONOMIC STATISTICS

102. The Chinese Communists, like their Soviet mentors, have made it difficult for foreign observers to use official data in gaining a clear understanding of the workings of the economy. They have released only partial data and in various ways presented misleading comparisons in reporting economic production and activities. This requires that Chinese Communist statistics be viewed critically and in some cases substantially discounted.

103. Since 1958 observers have been faced with a complication in the form of agricultural crop reporting which grossly overstated actual production. Our analysis of Peiping's agricultural statistics between 1954 and 1957 indicates that they have been generally consistent and reasonably accurate. However, the patent impossibility of the production claims since 1958 has made it necessary in describing agricultural developments, to construct separate estimates based on evaluation of production factors, marketing and supply availabilities, and government policy directives. While we believe our estimates are consistent with all of these various indicators, they cannot by their nature be considered precise.

104. We believe that political influences, which sought to justify the communes and to spur rural localities to greater production efforts, debauched rural statistical reporting in 1958 and 1959 and inhibited the central statistical authorities from modifying and rationalizing the local data. When the Chinese Communists withdrew their extravagant agricultural claims in August 1959, they lowered the figures for grain and cotton production by one-third. At the same time, production targets for 1959 were correspondingly reduced. Even though top leaders, by their act of recanting in August 1959, seemed genuinely to want to face

facts, they took no effective measures to eliminate political domination of the rural statistical reporting system, which after the 1959 harvests again proved incapable of providing even reasonably accurate crop yield and production data. Whether the reporting system of the 1960 crops is still hopelessly corrupted by politics is unknown. Moreover, even if it were obtaining reliable data, the regime would be reluctant to admit its exaggerations by publishing them.

105. Chinese statistics for industrial production for 1958–1959 also became somewhat more difficult to interpret, although the Leap Forward psychology of these years did not corrupt the official data for industry as seriously as it did for agriculture. Large-scale modern industry, which had a relatively sophisticated accounting system providing reasonably accurate data, contributed most of the increased industrial output. Although the regime appears to have exaggerated the expansion of small-scale, "native" industrial output, its magnitude was not such as to cause major distortions in the total production estimates.

106. Chinese Communist claims for the production of several major industrial commodities and for the performance of the modern transport sector have been evaluated by examining their consistency with the capacity of the industry concerned and with inputs of labor and raw materials. In some instances, the existence of new plants or the expansion of old plants could be confirmed by reports of Western observers. In other cases it has been impossible to assess the practical meaning of claimed increases: for example, the quantity and quality of the three million tons of alleged steel produced in backyard furnaces

SEC~~R~~ET

23

SECRET   24

in 1958 or the quality of the coal mined in the greatly increased production of 1958–1959. In general, however, this evaluation suggests that the official claims of great achievements in industry and transportation are plausible. Our estimate that the overall value of Chinese industrial production increased 33 percent in 1959 over 1958 was made by weighing and combining the results of this evaluation of claims for individual industrial products. The estimate that industrial output would increase by 25 percent in 1960 over 1959 is based on the 1960 production targets which we believe will be substantially fulfilled.

SECRET

SECRET

APPENDIX III: TABLES AND MAPS

Table I

GROSS NATIONAL PRODUCT, BY END USE 1957-1959

End Use	Billion Yuan in Current Market Prices [a]			Percentage Distribution		
	1957	1958	1959	1957	1958	1959
Personal consumption expenditures	79.4	86.4	91.2	69.3	63.2	59.6
Gross domestic investment	23.4	39.3	47.9	20.4	28.7	31.3
Net foreign investment	1.0	0.7	0.7	0.9	0.5	0.5
Government purchases of goods and services	10.7	10.4	13.3	9.4	7.6	8.6
Gross national product	114.5	136.8	153.1	100.0	100.0	100.0

[a] The estimates of GNP in constant 1957 prices are as follows (billion yuan): 1957, 114.5; 1958, 135.6; 1959, 151.5.

Table II

AGRICULTURAL AND NONAGRICULTURAL
EMPLOYMENT [a] 1957-1965

Million Persons

	1957	1958	1959	1960	1961	1962	1963	1964	1965	Percent Increase 1957-1965
Total	287	292	315	321	327	333	339	345	351	22.3%
Agricultural	244	248	260	262	264	266	268	270	272	11.5%
Nonagricultural	43	44	55	59	63	67	71	75	79	83.7%

[a] Mid-year figures. Figures include civilian employment only.

SECRET

25

SECRET

26

Table III

COMMODITY COMPOSITION OF IMPORTS AND EXPORTS
1957–1959

Percentage Distribution by Major Trading Areas

	1957			1958			1959		
	Total	Free World	Soviet Bloc	Total	Free World	Soviet Bloc	Total	Free World	Soviet Bloc
Exports	100.0	100.0	100.0	100.0	100.0	100.0	100.0	100.0	100.0
Agricultural products	53.3	62.1	47.8	53.1	63.0	46.7	48.5	60.1	42.9
Minerals and metals	16.2	9.3	20.6	13.2	6.9	17.2	11.5	7.8	13.3
Chemicals	6.6	4.3	7.8	5.7	4.8	6.3	3.9	3.5	4.1
Industrial products	20.1	20.9	19.6	24.3	23.2	25.1	30.3	24.3	33.1
Miscellaneous	3.8	3.4	4.2	3.7	2.1	4.7	5.8	4.3	6.6
Imports	100.0	100.0	100.0	100.0	100.0	100.0	100.0	100.0	100.0
Agricultural products	9.9	25.6	0	8.6	19.2	0.7	5.7	16.1	0.2
Petroleum products	6.9	0	11.3	5.6	0	9.8	6.4	neg.	9.7
Chemicals	15.3	35.8	2.3	14.1	29.1	3.0	13.2	34.6	2.0
Minerals and metals	7.4	8.4	6.7	20.0	34.1	9.5	13.9	29.6	5.7
Machinery and equipment	43.4	14.3	61.9	39.6	9.9	61.6	47.3	9.6	67.0
Other manufactured goods	6.7	14.2	1.9	3.9	6.9	1.7	3.7	8.8	1.1
All other (mainly Military goods)	10.4	1.7	15.9	8.2	0.8	13.7	9.8	1.2	14.2

Totals do not necessarily equal sum of parts because of rounding.

Table IV

PERFORMANCE OF MODERN FREIGHT TRANSPORT
1957–1965

Sector	1957	1958	1959	1960	1961	1962	1963	1964	1965
	billion ton-kilometers								
Performance									
Railroads	134.59	185.52	263.4	350.0	422	495	565	635	700
Motor trucks	3.94	6.96	12.0	18.9	23	27	31	35	39
Inland waterways	20.12	25.07	40.2	55.4	68	80	92	105	125
Coastal shipping	14.27	18.84	28.6	39.5	49	58	67	76	85
TOTAL	172.92	236.39	344.2	463.8	562	660	755	851	949
	million metric tons								
Tons carried									
Railroads	274.20	381.09	542.0	720.0	870	1,020	1,170	1,320	1,470
Motor trucks	83.73	176.30	344.0	540.0	655	770	885	1,000	1,115
Inland waterways	40.49	56.66	91.4	126.1	155	183	212	240	269
Coastal shipping	13.28	19.70	31.8	43.9	54	64	74	85	95
TOTAL	441.70	633.75	1,009.2	1,430.0	1,734	2,037	2,341	2,645	2,949

SECRET

SECRET   27

Table V
THE CHINESE COMMUNIST GROUND FORCES

	Units	Estimated Strength
		2,681,000 Total [a]
Armies	36	7 @ 49,000
		16 @ 48,000
		6 @ 47,000
		6 @ 46,000
		1 @ 21,000
Divisions		
Infantry	115 [c]	70 @ 15,000
		45 @ 6,000–
		14,000
3 Infantry Regiments		
1 Artillery Regiment		
24 light and medium field artillery pieces		
12 medium mortars		
1 AA battalion		
12 light AA pieces		
12 AA machine guns		
1 AT battalion		
12 x 57/76-mm AT guns		
1 tank-assault gun regiment [b]		
32 medium tanks		
12 self-propelled assault guns		
Armored	3 [c]	6,600 each
80 medium tanks		
10 heavy tanks		
8 self-propelled guns		
Airborne	3 [c]	7,000 each
Cavalry	3 [c]	5,000 each
Artillery		
Field Artillery	14	5,500 each
108 pieces up to 152-mm		
Rocket Launcher	2	3,300 each
72 x 132-mm multiple rocket launchers		
Antitank	3	3,400 each
96 AT guns		
Antiaircraft	5	1 @ 4,000
1 @ 84 light and medium guns		5 @ 2,700
5 @ 52 light and medium guns		
Public security	17	7,000 each
TOTAL NUMBER OF COMBAT DIVISIONS	166	

[a] Figure includes support and miscellaneous elements not shown in this Table.

[b] To date, 70 of the 115 infantry divisions are believed to have the tank-assault gun regiment. (In addition, the ground forces include approximately 68 independent combat regiments including artillery, cavalry, tank, and public security.)

[c] Counted for purposes of comparison or measurement of line division strength, we consider, on this basis, that the Chinese Communists have an estimated total of 124 line divisions.

SECRET

SECRET

28

Table VI

CHINESE COMMUNIST AIR FORCE AND NAVAL AIR FORCE

Estimated Operational Strength—1 October 1960

Personnel	NAVY 13,500	AIR FORCE 69,000	Total 82,500
Fighter			
Jet	270	1,410	1,680
Attack			
Jet (Ftr)	0	180	180
Prop	0	40	40
Light Bomber			
Jet	180	240	420
Prop	20	125	145
Medium Bomber			
Prop	0	20	20
Transport			
Prop (Light)	10	145	155
Prop (Small)	0	2	2
Helicopter			
(Light)	10	30	40
Reconnaissance			
Prop (ASW)	10	0	10
Trainer			
Jet (Ftr)	20	105	125
TOTAL	520	2,297	2,817

Table VII

CHINESE COMMUNIST NAVY ESTIMATED SHIP AND PERSONNEL STRENGTH

1 January 1961

Personnel	78,500 (Includes 13,500 Naval Air Force)
Principal Combatants	
Destroyers (DD)	4
Escort Ships (DE)	4
Submarines (SS)	29
Long-range W-Class ..	21
Long-range S-1-Class.	4
Short-range	4
Patrol	247
Mine Warfare	36
Amphibious Warfare	259
Auxiliary	48
Service	300

SECRET

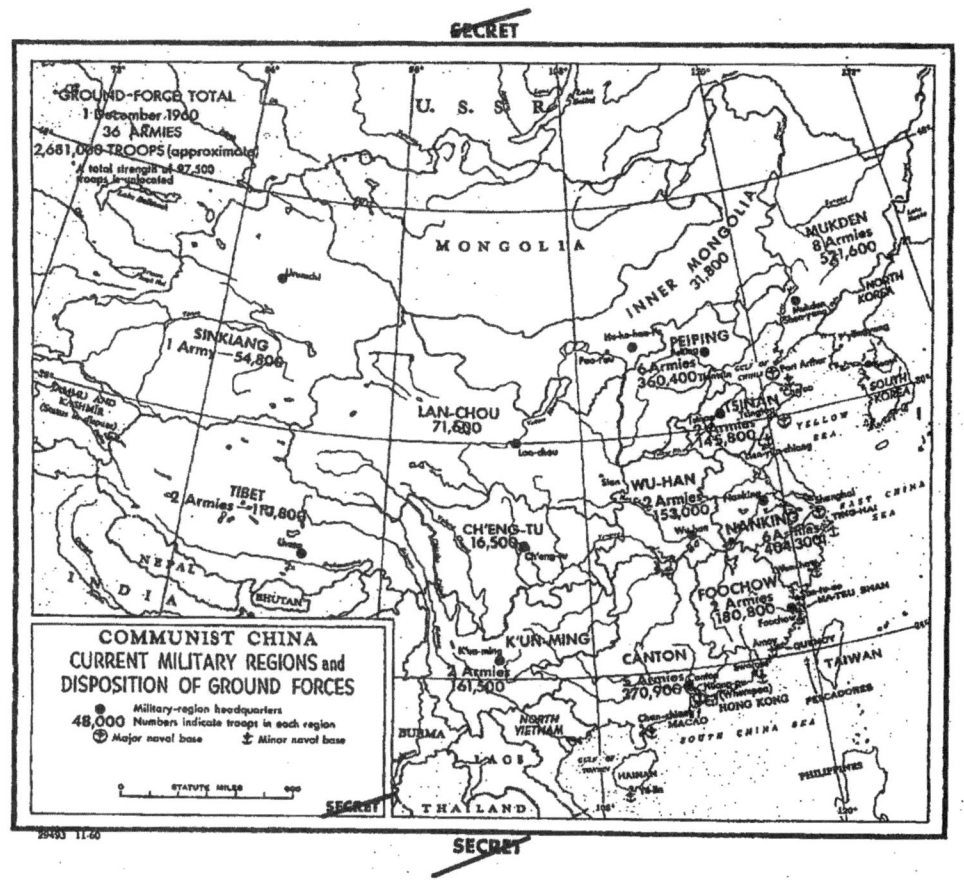

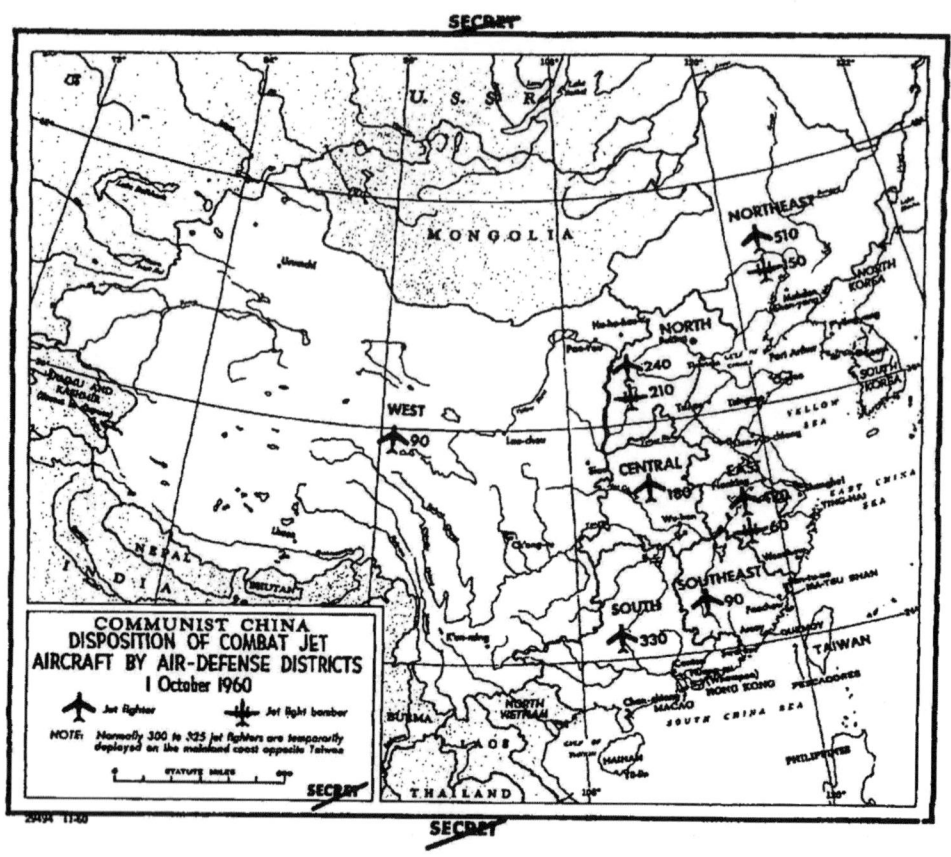

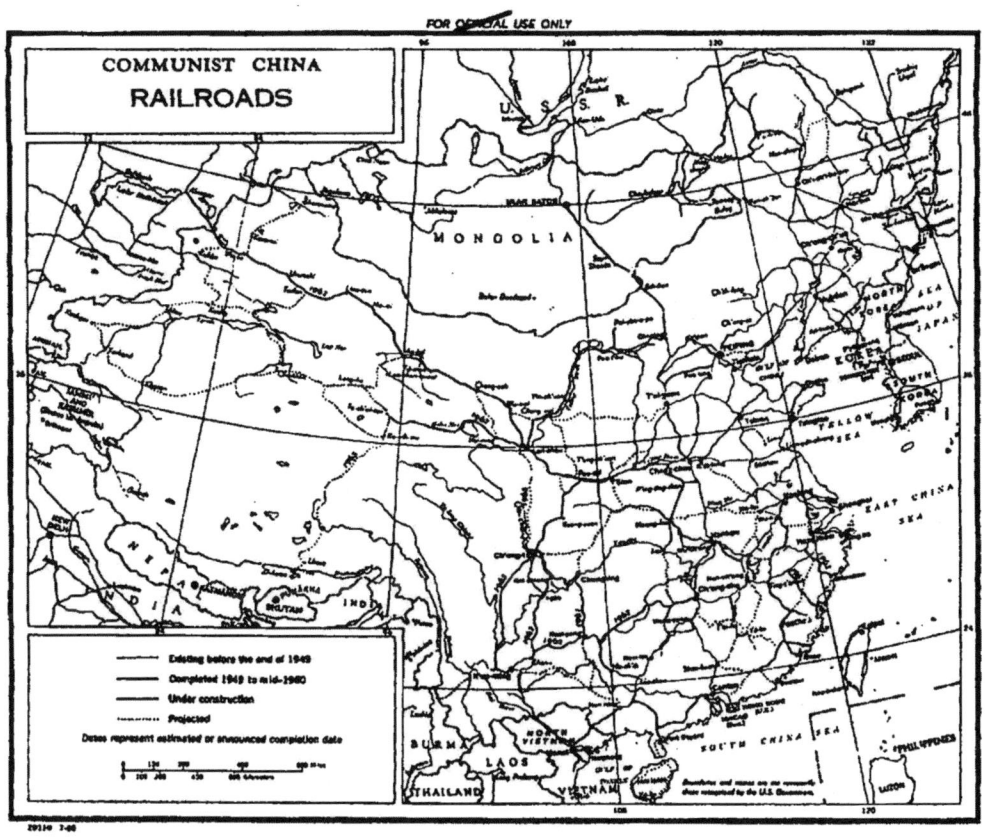

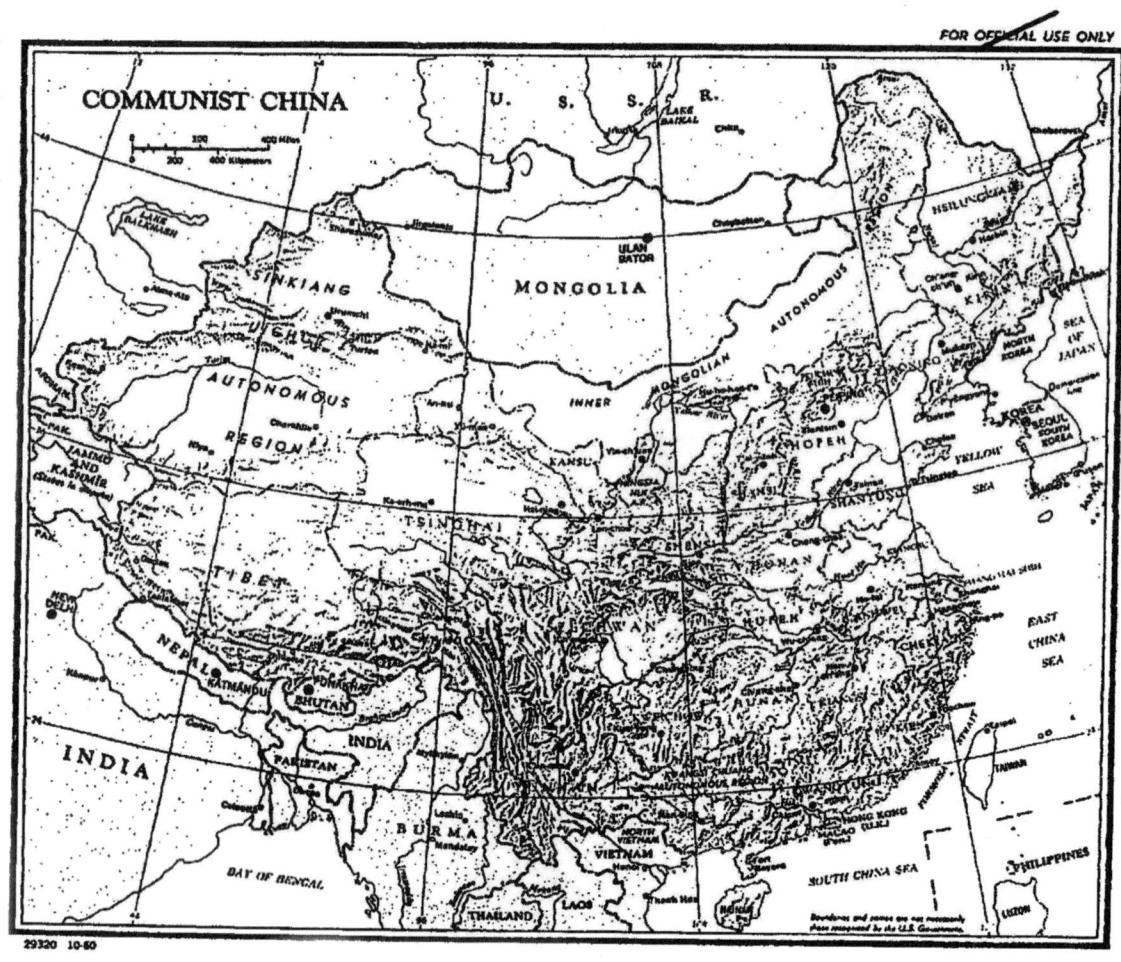

SECTION 18

NIE 13-2-60

The Chinese Communist
Atomic Energy Program

13 December 1960

APPROVED FOR RELEASE
DATE: MAY 2004

TOP SECRET

(b)(1)
(b)(3)

NIE 13-2-60
13 December 1960

NATIONAL INTELLIGENCE ESTIMATE
NUMBER 13-2-60

THE CHINESE COMMUNIST ATOMIC ENERGY PROGRAM

THIS DOCUMENT CONTAINS CODE WORD MATERIAL

Submitted by the
DIRECTOR OF CENTRAL INTELLIGENCE
The following intelligence organizations participated in the preparation of this estimate: The Central Intelligence Agency, the National Security Agency, and the intelligence organizations of the Departments of State, the Army, the Navy, the Air Force, The Joint Staff, Defense, and the Atomic Energy Commission.

Concurred in by the
UNITED STATES INTELLIGENCE BOARD
on 13 December 1960. Concurring were The Director of Intelligence and Research, Department of State; the Assistant Chief of Staff for Intelligence, Department of the Army; the Assistant Chief of Naval Operations for Intelligence, Department of the Navy; the Assistant Chief of Staff, Intelligence, USAF; the Director for Intelligence, The Joint Staff; the Assistant to the Secretary of Defense, Special Operations; the Atomic Energy Commission Representative to the USIB; and the Director of the National Security Agency. The Assistant Director, Federal Bureau of Investigation, abstained, the subject being outside the jurisdiction of his Agency.

Copy No. **107**

TOP SECRET

TOP SECRET

THE CHINESE COMMUNIST ATOMIC ENERGY PROGRAM

THE PROBLEM

To determine the current status and the probable future course of the Chinese Communist atomic energy program to mid-1965.

SUMMARY AND CONCLUSIONS

GENERAL

1. Communist China is energetically developing her native capabilities in the field of atomic energy. Since the early 1950's she has been making a concerted effort to develop the corps of scientists and technicians and establish the research facilities essential to the exploitation of nuclear energy. The over-all effort has progressed steadily since 1955 with the benefit of a substantial amount of Soviet aid. This assistance has been obtained by the Chinese Communists via negotiated, formal arrangements under which they apparently have maintained a considerable degree of autonomy. However, we believe that the Soviets have provided this aid at a deliberate pace, hoping to postpone the attainment of a native Chinese nuclear weapons capability as long as possible.

ORGANIZATION

2. Control of the Chinese Communist military atomic energy program and direction of much of the total atomic energy program is currently vested in the Second Ministry of Machine Building (SMMB), which was established in February 1958. This ministry is probably patterned after its Soviet counterpart, the Ministry of Medium Machine Building. The peaceful uses aspects of the program, covering nuclear research, training, and isotope applications, are largely under the control of the Scientific and Technological Commission of the State Council, with the Institute of Atomic Energy of the Academy of Sciences as the most prominent research establishment.

TECHNICAL CAPABILITIES

3. The Chinese Communists have acquired a small but highly competent cadre of Western-trained Chinese nuclear specialists. Their nuclear research effort has expanded rapidly since the early 1950's and more than twenty nuclear research facilities have been established at institutes and universities. In addition to the Soviet-supplied research reactor and cyclotron, there are a variety of cyclotrons and other accelerators, most of which are of Chinese manufacture. The Chinese have access, through the Joint Institute for Nuclear Research, to the large Soviet accelerators at Dubna. China's share of the financial costs of the institute is 20 percent, a share exceeded only by that of the Soviet Union. We believe that the widespread Chinese training and research effort is coordinated to the needs of the military atomic energy program. The Chinese Communists are now capable of comprehending and exploiting the large body of open scientific literature in the nuclear sciences. However, the present shortage of

TOP SECRET

1

TOP SECRET

2

trained scientists and engineers will probably persist throughout the period of this estimate. This shortage would hamper Chinese efforts to design, construct, and operate facilities for the production of fissionable materials and would be particularly serious, should the Soviets decide to reduce or terminate their technical aid.

URANIUM ORE PRODUCTION

4. During the period 1950–1954 the Chinese Communists, with some Soviet aid, explored a number of areas for uranium resources. In 1955 this quest for uranium, as well as the supporting Soviet aid, was intensified.

Soviet ore concentration plant designs developed for the Chinese in 1957 were probably intended for the exploitation of these southern deposits and expansion of Sinkiang operations.

5. Although we have no information on the actual grades of the ore, we estimate that Communist China is currently producing ore equivalent to about 500 tons of recoverable uranium metal per year (see Table 3, page 16), and by 1963 will be capable of producing more than a thousand tons per year. We have no evidence that any Chinese Communist uranium ore has been supplied to the USSR, and believe that it has all been retained for domestic use.

URANIUM METAL

6.   evidence that a uranium metal facility was constructed dur-

ing the 1957–1960 period.

Accordingly, we estimate that a Chinese uranium metal plant came into operation in late 1960.[1]

FISSIONABLE MATERIALS

7. Chinese development of uranium resources and the construction of ore concentration and uranium metal plants certainly imply an intended use for the uranium in plutonium production. Although uranium metal is not required for U–235 production, the first stages of the process could also supply feed for U–235 separation. Planning and design of fissionable materials production facilities could have been in progress in China as early as 1957.

8. We estimate that a first Chinese production reactor could attain criticality in late 1961, and the first plutonium might become available late in 1962.[1] Since there is no conclusive evidence for the date of the uranium plant startup, and since the construction of reactor and chemical separation facilities has not been directly established, the actual start of plutonium production could be a year earlier or several years later.

9. It is possible that a U–235 plant is now under construction. Considering the magnitude of the developmental work and industrial support required for the construction of a gaseous diffusion plant, however, it is improbable that the Chinese could produce highly enriched U–235 earlier than late 1962.[1]

---

[1] The Assistant Chief of Staff, Intelligence, Department of the Air Force, disagrees with the uranium metal and fissionable materials production schedule in paragraphs 6, 8 and 9. An alternative interpretation

is that a plutonium separation plant came into operation in late 1960. See his footnote to paragraph 10, page 3.

TOP SECRET

NUCLEAR WEAPONS

10. On the basis of all available evidence, we now believe that the most probable date at which the Chinese Communists could detonate a first nuclear device is sometime in 1963, though it might be as late as 1964, or as early as 1962, depending upon the actual degree of Soviet assistance.[2][3] If the Soviets provide fissionable materials, and assist in the design and fabrication of a nuclear device, the Chinese could produce a nuclear detonation in China at almost anytime in the immediate future. On the other hand, if there were a lessening of Soviet assistance in the nuclear field as a result of current Sino-Soviet dissensions, progress would be substantially retarded.

11. While the explosion of a nuclear device would give the Chinese Communists political and propaganda rewards, they would almost certainly proceed to create an operational nuclear capability as quickly as feasible. However, at least two years would probably be required after the explosion of a nuclear device to produce a small number of elementary weapons.

---

[2] The Assistant Chief of Staff, Intelligence, Department of the Air Force believes that the Chinese will probably detonate their first nuclear device in 1962, and possibly as early as late 1961. The great political, psychological, and military advantages to be gained are such that the Chinese would accord top national priority to the development of a nuclear weapons program. He interprets the available evidence on the production schedule of uranium metal and fissionable material to indicate that in 1959 a uranium metal plant started producing fuel elements for the production reactor which is believed to have gone critical in 1960. The first nuclear device will probably use plutonium from this reactor. Finally, he believes that after late 1961 highly enriched U-235 will be available for subsequent devices.

[3] For the view of the Assistant Chief of Naval Operations (Intelligence), Department of the Navy, see footnote 8, page 19.

NUCLEAR POWER

12. Since the Chinese nuclear program appears to be weapon-oriented, we believe that production reactors would be given precedence over reactors designed for nuclear power. Further, we do not believe that the Chinese would complicate the design of their first production reactors in an effort to extract by-product power. We estimate that the Chinese will not construct nuclear power stations in the 1960–1965 period.

SOVIET ASSISTANCE

13. Soviet assistance has been an important factor in the Chinese atomic energy program. Under an agreement for cooperation concluded in 1955, the Soviets have provided to the Chinese a research reactor, cyclotron, technical assistance and training. A Sino-Soviet Scientific and Technical Agreement for the years 1958–1962 was concluded in 1958. Other known Soviet aid has been largely concerned with uranium prospecting and the preparation of designs for uranium ore concentration and uranium metal facilities.

14. We have no firm evidence of Soviet assistance in designing or constructing fissionable materials production facilities or in supplying the materials or equipment needed for such production.

15. There is some evidence that Soviet aid may have been curtailed.  reports that a general withdrawal of Soviet technicians from China took place in mid-1960.

TOP SECRET

TOP SECRET

DISCUSSION

I. INTRODUCTION

16. There is ample evidence that Communist China is placing great emphasis on atomic energy in its quest for the scientific and military stature essential to a major world power. Two major related efforts are being accorded a very high priority:

    a. The development of schools and laboratories required for the training of scientists and engineers and the conduct of research essential to the understanding and exploitation of the nuclear sciences;

    b. The development of the scientific and industrial base which would be needed for the development and production of nuclear weapons.

17. A large body of information is available concerning the Chinese quest for trained manpower and research facilities, and how this effort is organized and controlled. Information on their military atomic energy program is quite scanty; however, their large scale exploitation of their uranium resources and statements by key Chinese Communist officials are strong evidence that they intend to develop a native nuclear weapons capability.

II. HISTORY AND ORGANIZATION OF THE CHINESE COMMUNIST ATOMIC ENERGY PROGRAM

GENERAL

18. Control of the Chinese Communist military atomic energy program and direction of much of the total atomic energy program is currently vested in the Second Ministry of Machine Building (SMMB) (see Figure 1). This ministry is probably patterned after its Soviet counterpart, the Ministry of Medium Machine Building. The peaceful uses aspects of the program, covering nuclear research, training, and isotope applications are largely under the control of the Scientific and Technological Commission (STC) of the State Council, with the Institute of Atomic Energy (IAE) of the Academy of Sciences as the most prominent research establishment.

MILITARY ATOMIC ENERGY PROGRAM

19. Evolvement of the organization of the military aspects of the Chinese Communist atomic energy program can be traced through several stages of development. Early in 1955, widespread activity by uranium prospecting/mining units

In 1956, Liu Chieh, the Deputy Minister of Geology and Deputy Head of the Third Bureau, was the one with whom Soviet atomic energy advisers in China had to deal, an indication that Liu was in over-all control of the program. In addition, Liu headed the Chinese delegation to the March 1956 conference in Moscow which resulted in the formation, by eleven Bloc countries, of the Joint Institute for Nuclear Research (JINR) at Dubna, USSR. It is evident that his atomic energy responsibilities were not limited to uranium procurement.

20. In November 1956, the Third Ministry of Machine Building (TMMB) was established under General Sung Jen-ch'iung. A third ministry had been originally established in April 1955 to handle the manufacture of machinery and electric generators, but was abolished in May 1956 when its responsibilities were taken over by the Ministry of Power Equipment Industry. The functions of the new Third Ministry were not made public,

4

TOP SECRET

TOP SECRET

21. In April 1957, the Chinese press announced that Liu Chieh had been relieved of his duties in the Ministry of Geology and the Third Office of the State Council without mention of the reasons for his relief or of his future assignment. It is reasonable to assume that Liu assumed a comparable position with the TMMB.

22. In February 1958, the TMMB was renamed the Second Ministry of Machine Building. We do not believe that this change in name represented any real change in the nature or functions of the former TMMB. This belief is supported by an announcement in the Chinese press on 18 September 1959 that Liu Chieh was Deputy Minister of the SMMB, and on 13 September 1960 he was appointed minister.

23. Some of the elements of the present SMMB have been identified

The First and Seventh Bureaus, referred to in the Chinese Communist press in December 1957 as being under the TMMB, may have continued to function after establishment of the SMMB. A list of these elements is given in Table 1.

ORGANIZATION OF NUCLEAR RESEARCH

24. Promotion of science was an announced policy of the Chinese Communist regime after its takeover in 1949, and emphasis was accorded to nuclear studies from the outset. The new regime established the Chinese Academy of Sciences in November 1949 (with 15 to 20 institutes), by reorganizing and consolidating the various institutes and laboratories of the Chinese Nationalist's Academia Sinica and the National Academy in Peiping. The new Academy's Institute of Modern Physics (later named the Institute of Physics and then renamed the Institute of Atomic Energy in early 1957) was assigned nuclear studies as a priority mission. The Chinese have stated that the research program of this institute did not begin until 1953. In March 1954, they announced their intention of asking the Soviet Union for aid in their nuclear program, and in April 1955, an agreement was signed under which the Soviets were to supply a research reactor, cyclotron, and technical assistance and were to train Chinese specialists (see paragraph 69).

25. The nuclear research and training effort was intensified during the years 1955 to 1957. The goals of scientific and nuclear policy were clarified, local resources and capabilities were surveyed, the necessary steps were taken toward setting up a nuclear research organization, and a number of basic research projects in nuclear science and technology were launched. The nuclear energy program was given a further boost with the completion of the research reactor and cyclotron at the Institute of Atomic Energy, Peiping in mid-1958.

26. In May 1956, the State Council of the CPR established the Scientific Planning Commission, composed of high-level scientific, communist party, and military members. The commission formulated a Twelve Year Plan for Science (1956–67), wherein stress was given to research in certain broad fields of endeavor, the leading field to be atomic energy.

27. Chinese nuclear research is also being assisted by China's membership in the Joint Institute for Nuclear Research (JINR) at

TOP SECRET

6

TOP SECRET

Table 1
SOME ELEMENTS OF THE SECOND MINISTRY OF MACHINE BUILDING

UNIT		REMARKS
First Bureau		Per Chinese press, existed under TMMB before it was renamed SMMB
Third Bureau	December 1956 (Subordinate to Min. of Geology), October 1957 (Subordinate to TMMB), February 1958 (subordinate to SMMB)	Control of ___ units throughout China, engaged in uranium prospecting and mining
Sixth Bureau	16 June 1959	As supplier of atomic energy related instruments
Seventh Bureau		Per Chinese press, existed under TMMB before it was renamed SMMB
Twelfth Bureau		
	17 July 1959	As contracting organization for the Tientsin Municipal Chemical Industry Bureau for the delivery of deep-well water pumps

Dubna, USSR, since 1956. China's share of the financial costs of the institute is 20 percent, a share exceeded only by that of the Soviet Union.

28. Currently, the nuclear energy research and development program is controlled and directed by two main bodies, the Scientific and Technological Commission (STC) and the Academy of Sciences (AS). (See Figure 1). The STC is the most powerful organization for controlling scientific research in Communist China. Formed in 1958 by merger of the Scientific Planning Committee and the State Technological Commission, it supervises closely the cooperation and coordination of research between the AS and other research organizations. The Academy of Sciences is the chief organization for research in Communist China (see Figure 2). Certainly, the most important nuclear research is carried out by the Academy's Institute of Atomic Energy's two

locations in Peiping. We believe that the SMMB also exerts considerable influence in the area of nuclear research and training.

29. More than twenty different installations for nuclear energy research have been identified (see Annex A), and there is good reason to believe that the Chinese will continue to stress nuclear energy research through the establishment of additional facilities. A number of institutes of the AS, dealing with physics, chemistry, mathematics, geology, and electronics are known to be engaged in various aspects of the Chinese Communist atomic energy program.

III. TECHNICAL CAPABILITIES

NUCLEAR RESEARCH

30. The Communist Chinese have steadily advanced their nuclear research effort since the early 1950's. Principally under the IAE the

TOP SECRET

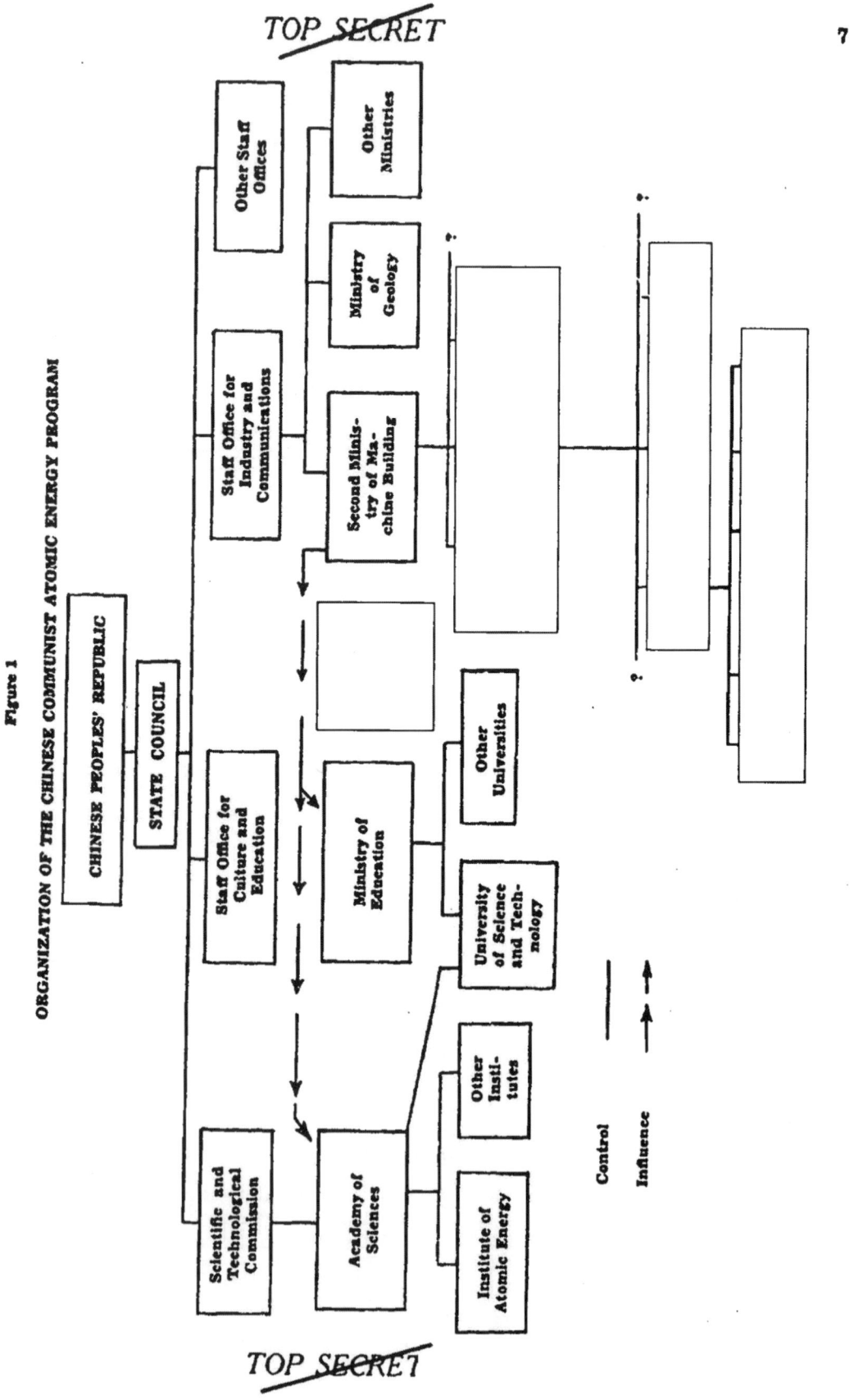

Figure 1

ORGANIZATION OF THE CHINESE COMMUNIST ATOMIC ENERGY PROGRAM

TOP SECRET

TOP SECRET

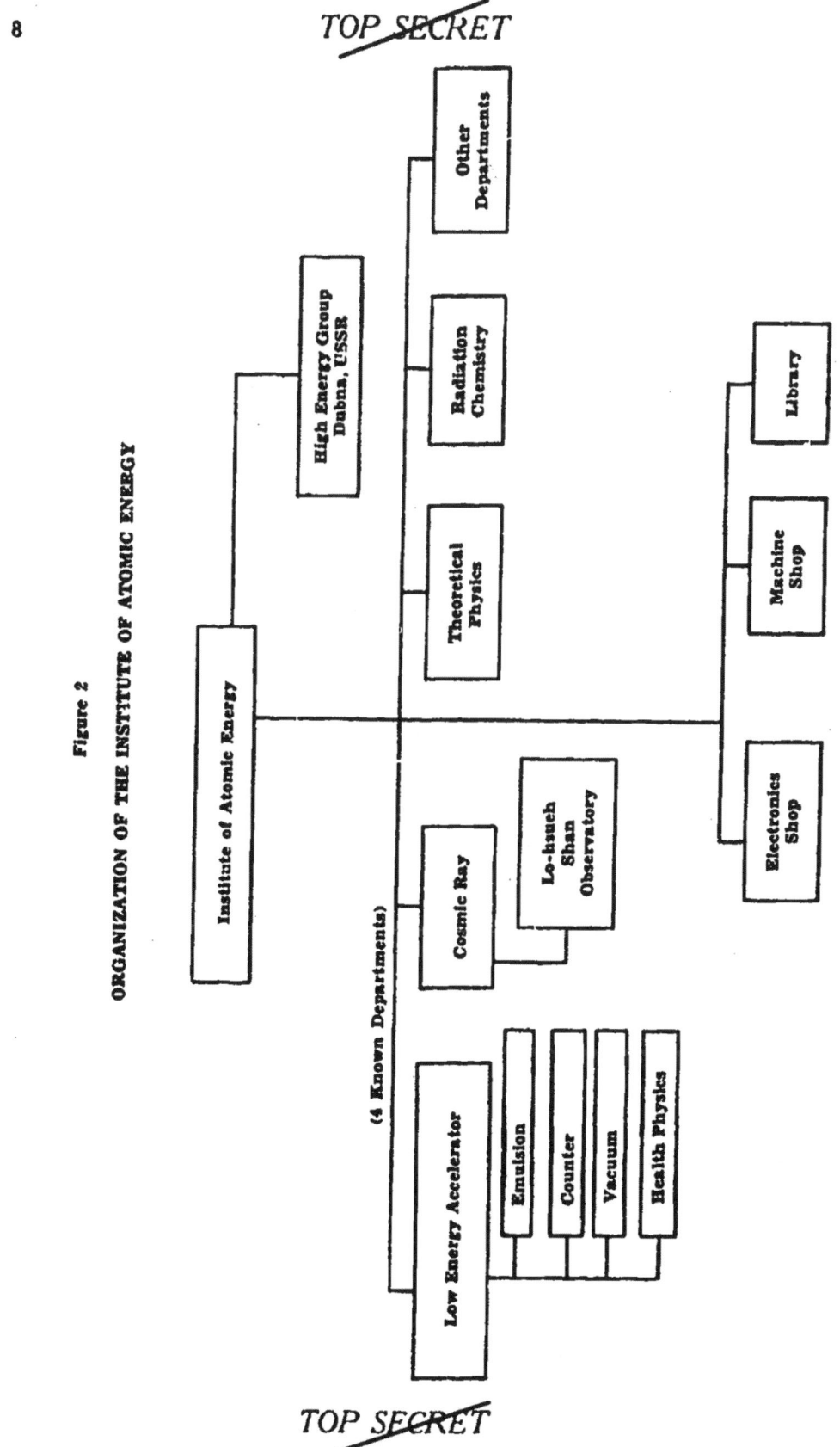

Figure 2

ORGANIZATION OF THE INSTITUTE OF ATOMIC ENERGY

TOP SECRET

TOP SECRET

TOP SECRET

Communist Chinese, with varying degrees of Soviet assistance, have established more than twenty facilities engaged in nuclear research in various parts of the country (see Figure 3). The major institute, located in the suburbs of Peiping (see Figure 4), about 20 miles southwest of the city, houses the Soviet-supplied 7.5 to 10MW research reactor and the 25 Mev cyclotron (Figures 5 and 6). The reactor uses two percent enriched uranium fuel and heavy water as moderator. It has been one of the less successful examples of Soviet assistance to the Chinese. For nearly one and one-half years after the reactor became critical in 1958 its operations were suspended because of mechanical difficulties.

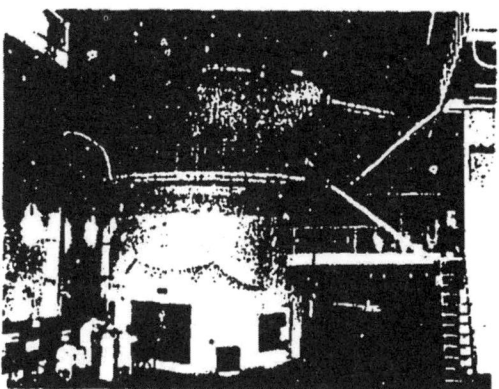

Figure 5

Research reactor at the IAE, Peiping, 1958

Figure 4

Research reactor and cyclotron building of the IAE, Peiping, 1958

31. Chinese high energy physics research is carried out at the Joint Institute for Nuclear Research at Dubna, USSR. Nuclear reactions of high energy mesons and protons are studied utilizing the 10,000 Mev synchrotron and the 680 Mev synchrocyclotron, bubble chambers, emulsions, and Cherenkov counters. Wang Kan-ch'ang, leader of the Chinese scientists at Dubna, and also Deputy Director of JINR, recently has been credited as being one of the discoverers of a new nuclear particle, the anti-sigma minus hyperon.

32. Theoretical research in cosmic rays is conducted by a department of the IAE. Experimental data are gathered at the Lohsueh Shan Observatory in Yunnan Province (see

Figure 6

The IAE's 25 Mev cyclotron, Peiping, 1958

TOP SECRET

TOP SECRET

Figure 7), which is equipped with multi-plate and magnetic-field cloud chambers (see Figure 8). There are also facilities for the observation of cosmic ray strength, including a cubical-shaped meson monitor, a neutron recorder, and a large-sized, Soviet-furnished ionization chamber. Closely allied to the theoretical research in cosmic rays is the work conducted by a small group of scientists at the IAE in nuclear physics, which is similar to that conducted in a number of other countries. This includes calculations of energy levels, utilizing the shell-model concept, and studies of the inter-actions of nucleons and the characteristics of fundamental nuclear particles.

RESEARCH EQUIPMENT

33. Although the Communist Chinese have received large quantities of laboratory equipment from the USSR, they have been quite successful in building scientific apparatus for their research. (Major items of nuclear research equipment are listed in Table 2). They have built two accelerators at the IAE's location about eight miles northwest of Peiping, (Figure 9), which is primarily concerned with theoretical nuclear physics and low energy acceleration. These machines are a 2.5 Mev electrostatic proton accelerator and a 6.75 Mev Van de Graaff accelerator. Other native equipment includes the 1 Mev cyclotron at the Physics Department of Southwest Normal Colleg the 2 Mev cyclotron at Tientsin University, a 10 Mev induction-electron accelerator (betatron) at the Central China Engineering Institute in Wuhan, and a 5 Mev induc-

Figure 7

Lohsueh Shan Observatory for cosmic ray research, Lohsueh Shan, 1957

Figure 8

Multiplate equipment for cosmic ray research at Lohsueh Shan Observatory, 1957

TOP SECRET

12   TOP SECRET

Table 2
MAJOR ITEMS OF NUCLEAR PHYSICS RESEARCH EQUIPMENT IN COMMUNIST CHINA

Item	Location	Research Facility	Rating	Remarks
Reactor	Peiping (SW)	IAE	7.5–10 MW	Soviet Supplied
Reactor	Peiping (NW)	Tsinghua University	2 MW	
Reactor	Tientsin	Nank'ai University	3 watt	
Accelerator	Peiping (SW)	IAE	25 Mev	Soviet Supplied Cyclotron
Accelerator	Peiping (NW)	Tsinghua University	5 Mev	"Induction Electron Cyclotron"—Betatron
Accelerator	Tientsin	Tientsin University	2 Mev	Cyclotron
Accelerator	Chungking	Southwest Normal College	1 Mev	Cyclotron
Accelerator	Ch'engtu	Szechwan University	.06 Mev	
Accelerator	Peiping (NW)	IAE	2.5 Mev	Electrostatic Proton
Accelerator	Peiping (NW)	IAE	0.75 Mev	Van de Graaff
Accelerator	Peiping (NW)	Peiping University	30 Mev	"Induction Electron Cyclotron"—Betatron
Accelerator	Peiping (NW)	Peiping University	0.7 Mev	Electrostatic
Accelerator	Tientsin	Nank'ai University	2 Mev	Electrostatic
Accelerator	Canton	Chungshan University	(unknown)	Rotary
Accelerator	Hsian	Chiaotung University	1.5 Mev	Electrostatic
Accelerator	Luta (Dairen)	Institute of Petroleum AS	2 Mev	Van de Graaff
Accelerator	Wuhan	Wuhan Atomic Energy Research Institute	2 Mev	

Figure 9

The IAE research establishment, Peiping, 1958

Figure 10

5 Mev betatron designed and built at Tsinghua University, Peiping, 1958

tion-electron cyclotron at Tsinghua University in Peiping (see Figure 10).

34. The Chinese have made considerable progress in establishing a broad capability to manufacture a wide range of necessary equipment for training young nuclear scientists and for supporting the nuclear research of their institutes and universities. An intensive effort has been made to provide from domestic sources a sufficient quantity of nuclear radia-

tion detectors, high grade emulsions, scintillating crystals, photomultiplier tubes and accessory electronic equipment (see Figure 11). More recently, Chinese developments with pulse height analysers and micro-second measuring equipment might imply future work in neutron time-of-flight studies or even in nuclear weapon development. By about 1967,

TOP SECRET

TOP SECRET

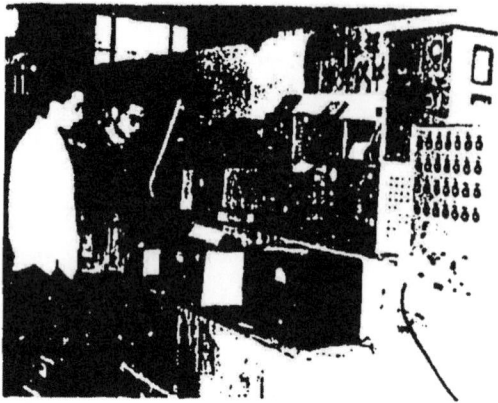

Figure 11

Examples of electronic equipment built by the Chinese, Peiping, 1958

Figure 12

Chinese-produced radioactive deep-well surveying equipment

the Chinese could be as well provided with laboratory equipment for research in nuclear physics as are the larger western European countries at the present time.

NUCLEAR CHEMISTRY

35. Studies in nuclear chemistry are conducted in a number of institutes of the Academy of Sciences. The IAE is concerned with the production of radioactive isotopes in the Soviet-supplied reactor, and with the production of radioactive isotopes in the Soviet-supplied reactor, and with the separation of stable isotopes using the ion exchange method. The reactor reportedly has produced over 30 different radioactive isotopes, including cobalt-60, sodium-24, phosphorus-32, and calcium-45. Isotopes are being used in industry in conjunction with Chinese-produced gamma-ray instruments for detecting flaws in machinery; in geology, to detect types of rock and the geological formations of strata (Figure 12); in medicine, in radioactive cobalt apparatus for treating tumors and cancer (Figure 13); and in agriculture, to improve fertilization and cultivation of crops. Academy of Sciences institutes, other than the IAE, are conducting studies on reactor corrosion problems, uranium and thorium chemistry, and the separation of the rare-earths. In 1957, it was reported that Communist Chinese scientists had ob-

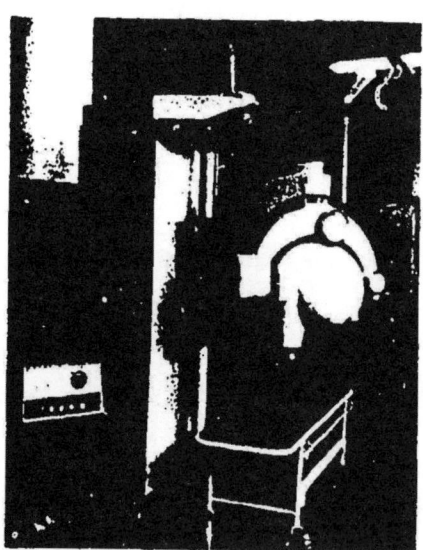

Figure 13

Radiocobalt unit for medical therapy, Shanghai, 1958

tained pure uranium and thorium on a laboratory scale.

MANPOWER AND TRAINING

36. When the Communists came into power in China in 1949, only about ten scientists were engaged in nuclear physics research. Since 1949, Communist China has made an intensive effort to train scientists and engineers in the

TOP SECRET

14　　　　　　　　　　*TOP SECRET*

numbers necessary to support a comprehensive atomic energy program, building from a core of highly competent, Western-trained scientists. Nevertheless, the present shortage of trained scientists and engineers will probably persist throughout the period of this estimate. This shortage would hamper Chinese efforts to design, construct, and operate facilities for the production of fissionable materials and would be particularly serious should the Soviets decide to reduce or terminate their technical aid. Annex B contains a listing of leading Chinese Communist nuclear scientists.

IV. NUCLEAR MATERIALS PRODUCTION

URANIUM ORE

37. In March 1950, a Sino-Soviet Non-Ferrous and Rare Metals Stock Company was established, with headquarters at Urumchi, for the development of resources including uranium in the Sinkiang-Uighur Autonomous Region.

　　　　　　　　　　　　　sources report uranium prospecting and mining activity in the area. Chinese Communist open literature indicates that the company was operated until 1954 when it was dissolved as a joint stock company. Apparently, Soviet participation in Chinese uranium problems continued under different arrangements, however,

38. Chinese uranium prospecting and mining units, to which Soviet geologists and technicians were attached (see Section VII)
　　　　　　　　　　　　　　　Until early 1957, these units were subordinate to the Third Bureau of the CPR Ministry of Geology; they are now subordinate to the Third Bureau of the SMMB.

39. Although uranium deposits of varying size are known to exist in a number of areas throughout the CPR, very few specific mining locations are known. The Chinese are believed to be working two deposits in the Haich'eng district of Liaoning Province.

TOP SECRET

TOP SECRET

TOP SECRET

16 TOP SECRET

signed and helped to construct a pilot chemical concentration plant in Peiping.

Nothing is known of the grade of any of the Chinese ores. However, assuming that the average grade permits economical mining operations,

The high priority accorded this experimental installation suggests that a similar urgency was attached to the construction of the larger ore concentration plants.

URANIUM METAL

Our estimate of Chinese Communist recoverable equivalent uranium metal production for the years 1952 through 1963 is presented in Table 3, below.

Table 3

ESTIMATED CHINESE COMMUNIST RECOVERABLE EQUIVALENT URANIUM METAL PRODUCTION 1952-1963
(Metric Tons)

Year	Annual	Cumulative (Rounded)
1952	40	40
1953	40	80
1954	60	140
1955	60	200
1956	80	300
1957	100	400
1958	200	600
1959	400	1,000
1960	500	1,500
1961	700	2,200
1962	1,000	3,200
1963	1,200	4,400

42.

Soviet specialists who have published on subjects related to both ore concentration and uranium metal production have been noted at the Ch'angsha Mining and Metallurgical Institute.

46. Assuming the construction time required to be two to three years, the uranium metal plant could have been completed in 1959 or 1960.

43. Currently

the Soviets de-

TOP SECRET

TOP SECRET

On this basis, we estimate that a Chinese uranium metal plant came into operation in late 1960, probably in the Ch'angsha area.[4]

OTHER NUCLEAR MATERIALS

47. There is evidence that the Chinese produce other materials such as thorium, heavy water, graphite, etc., which have nuclear energy applications. Some of these products are now exported, but could be diverted to internal use.

48. Thorium deposits have been reported at various sites in China, but the most likely areas appear to be in the Ch'aitamu Basin in Tsinghai province; Hsinhua, in Hunan province; Hainan Island; and near Paot'ou, in Inner Mongolia. Present information does not permit an estimate of thorium production. In the past they have imported thorium, probably for non-nuclear uses, for example, the manufacture of gas mantles.

49. Chinese interest in heavy water production was indicated by an October 1959 statement by Ch'ien San-ch'iang, Director of the IAE, that an analysis of heavy water concentration in various waters had been made, and that the deuterium content of some oil field waters offered the most promise. The possibility that the Chinese may be following the Soviet practice of associating small heavy water production plants with nitrogen fertilizer producers is indicated by Chinese statements that the SMMB has supplied various types of equipment for the Szechwan Chemical Plant, a large new nitrogen fertilizer plant located near Chengtu, which began trial pro-

duction in October 1959. There is evidence of atomic energy activity in the Szechwan Basin.

Thus it is possible that a small-scale heavy water production program is in progress in China.

50. Certain other raw materials, useful in an atomic energy program, have been noted in numerous shipments from China to the USSR. Notable among these are large quantities of beryllium, lithium, and fluorite ores. Molybdenum, niobium and tantalum ores have also been exported to Russia.

---

[4] For the view of the Assistant Chief of Staff, Intelligence, Department of the Air Force, see footnote 1, page 2.

TOP SECRET

18   TOP SECRET

53. From 1955 to 1960 the Communist Chinese attempted to obtain from foreign sources many materials required in an atomic energy program. The pure metals included uranium, thorium, beryllium, lithium, boron, and some of the less known rare earth metals.

54. The quantities desired were initially very small, sometimes amounting to only a few grams but hundreds of kilograms of metals such as beryllium, cerium, and zirconium were specified by the Chinese in international trade requirements in 1960. It may well be that the Chinese focussed their effort on production of uranium metal and could not satisfy their requirements for supplementary nuclear metals from domestic sources. The Chinese may not be able to become self-sufficient in their production of supplementary nuclear metals until the early to mid-1960's.

FISSIONABLE MATERIALS PRODUCTION

55. Chinese development of uranium resources and of ore concentration and uranium metal facilities strongly implies an intended use for the uranium in plutonium production. Although uranium metal is not required for U-235 production, the first stages of the process could also provide feed material for U-235 production. Since provision for these uranium users would ordinarily coincide with or even precede that for the feed materials plant, planning and design of fissionable material production facilities may have been in progress in China as early as 1957.

56. *Plutonium.* We have no evidence of the planning or subsequent construction of production reactors. However, the lack of such evidence cannot be considered conclusive.

the Peiping Research Reactor, an overt project which must have required extensive correspondence with Moscow.

57. Our estimate of when the Chinese may attain a plutonium capability must be based on the estimated startup date of the Chinese uranium metal plant. Allowing a year of uranium plant operation to perfect technology

and to produce enough uranium to supply a small plutonium production reactor, reactor criticality might occur in late 1961, and the first plutonium might become available late in 1962.[3] Since there is no conclusive evidence for the date of the uranium plant startup, and since the construction of reactor and chemical separation facilities has not been directly established, the actual start of plutonium production could be a year earlier or several years later.

58. *U-235.* It is possible that a U-235 plant is now under construction. In this case, a somewhat shorter delay between feed availability and fissionable materials production could be effected. Considering the magnitude of the developmental work and industrial support required for the construction of a gaseous diffusion plant, however, it is improbable that the Chinese could produce highly enriched U-235 earlier than late 1962.[5]

V. NUCLEAR WEAPONS

59. Although we have no conclusive direct evidence of a Chinese nuclear weapons program, we believe that such a program exists and has been given priority by the Chinese. We believe that the Chinese would almost certainly consider that a demonstration of their capability to produce nuclear weapons would confirm their claim to great power status.[4] While we believe that the Chinese Communists will carry their nuclear weapons program forward as rapidly as possible, success will depend in large measure upon the degree of assistance received from the Soviets. Recent evidence strongly suggests that the USSR may have given the Chinese Communists more technical assistance leading toward the eventual production of nuclear weapons than we had previously considered likely. However, we believe that the Soviets have provided this aid at a deliberate pace, hoping to postpone the

---

[3] For the view of the Assistant Chief of Staff, Intelligence, Department of the Air Force, see footnote 1, page 2.

[4] For a discussion of Chinese incentives for a nuclear weapons program see NIE 100-4-60, 20 September 1960.

TOP SECRET

TOP SECRET

19

attainment of a native Chinese nuclear weapons capability as long as possible.

60. On the basis of all available evidence, we now believe that the most probable date at which the Chinese Communists could detonate a first nuclear device is sometime in 1963, though it might be as late as 1964, or as early as 1962, depending upon the actual degree of Soviet assistance.[7,8] If the Soviets provide fissionable materials or assist in the design and fabrication of a nuclear device, the Chinese could produce a nuclear detonation in China at almost any time in the immediate future. On the other hand, if there were a lessening of Soviet assistance in the nuclear field as a result of current Sino-Soviet dissensions, Chinese Communist progress would be substantially retarded.

61. After the explosion of their first nuclear device, the Chinese would almost certainly proceed to create an operational nuclear capability as quickly as feasible. However, at least two years would probably be required after the first test to produce a small number of elementary weapons.

VI. NUCLEAR POWER

62. The Chinese Communists announced in 1956 that "atomic power stations would be built." However, such stations were not in-

---

[7] For the view of the Assistant Chief of Staff, Intelligence, Department of the Air Force, see footnote 2, page 3.

[8] The Assistant Chief of Naval Operations (Intelligence), Department of the Navy believes that information on the nature and extent of Soviet aid to Communist China is as yet insufficient for a reliable estimate of the year in which the Chinese Communists could detonate a nuclear device. He considers however, that certain basic information should have become available to us by this time if the Chinese Communists were progressing toward detonation of a domestically produced nuclear device very much before the final stages of this five-year estimate. In the absence of what he considers to be any evidence pertaining to or indicative of the production of fissionable materials in Communist China and in the light of the relatively elementary state of known nuclear research facilities, he is unable to accept the time schedule for nuclear weapons as given in this paper.

cluded in the Second Five Year Plan (1958-1962), and there is no present evidence for a power program. Since the Chinese nuclear program appears to be weapon-oriented, we believe that production reactors would be given precedence over reactors designed for nuclear power. Further, we do not believe that the Chinese would complicate the design of their first production reactors in an effort to extract by-product power. We estimate that the Chinese will not construct nuclear power stations in the 1960-1965 period.

VII. SOVIET ASSISTANCE TO THE CHINESE COMMUNIST ATOMIC ENERGY PROGRAM

63. Soviet assistance has been an important factor in the Chinese atomic energy program to date, ranging from participation in uranium prospecting and processing to the supply of a research reactor and cyclotron. This aid has been furnished under formal contractual agreements under which the Chinese Communists have apparently maintained a considerable degree of autonomy.

64.   a number of Soviet organizations have participated in aid to the Chinese atomic energy program, including several groups from the Ministry of Medium Machine Building (MINSREDMASH), the organization in charge of the Soviet military atomic energy program. The Soviet organizations and their sub-units known to be participating in the Chinese atomic energy program are shown in Figure 13.

The USSR Chief Directorate (now called State Committee) for Utilization of Atomic Energy (GLAVATOM) has carried out overt aid programs

TOP SECRET

20

TOP SECRET

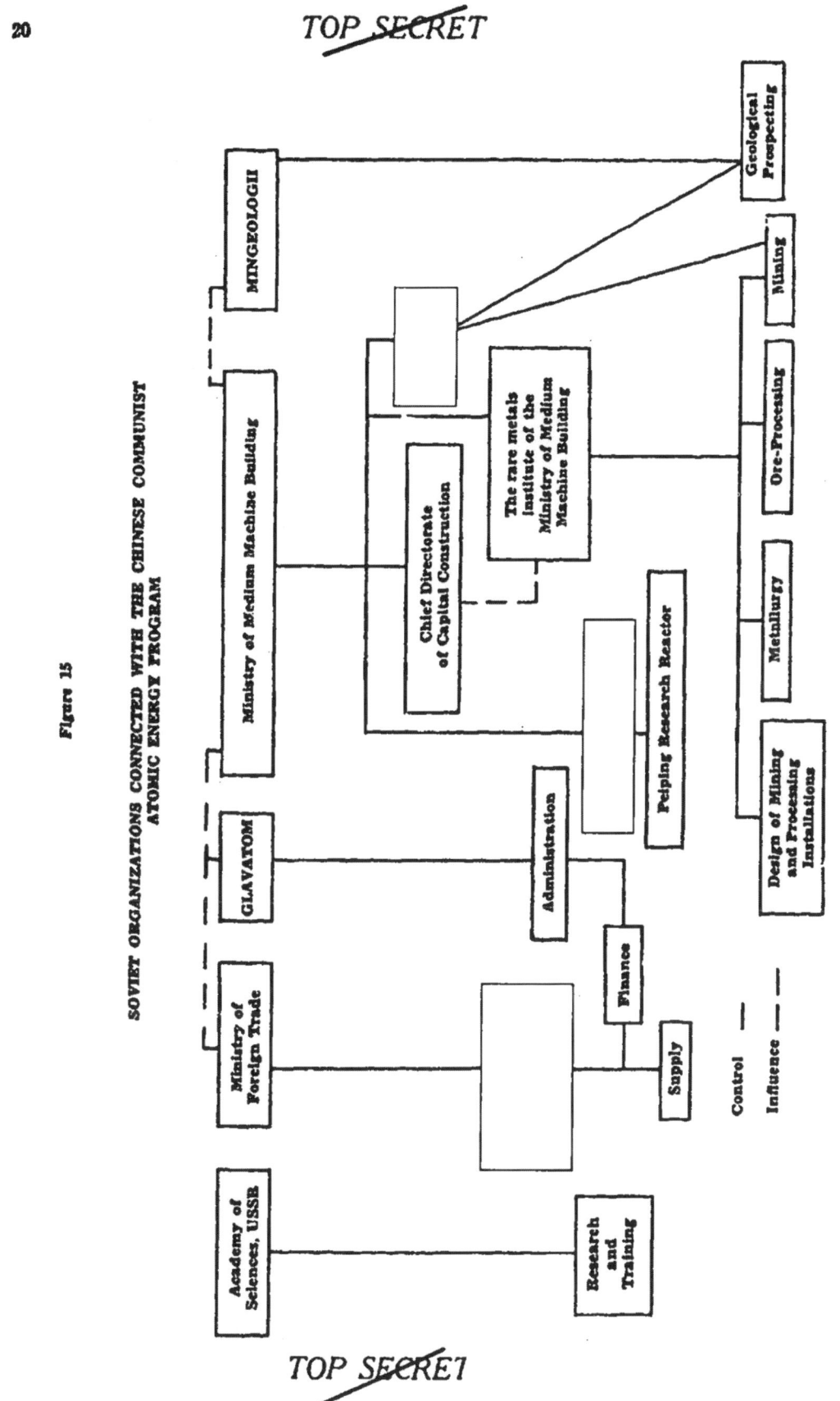

Figure 15

SOVIET ORGANIZATIONS CONNECTED WITH THE CHINESE COMMUNIST
ATOMIC ENERGY PROGRAM

TOP SECRET

TOP SECRET

The Chief Directorate of the Civil Air Fleet (GUFVF) of the Moscow AVIA group has conducted aerial prospecting surveys for the Chinese atomic energy program since 1955. The USSR Academy of Sciences has furnished much of the known scientific research and training assistance and may have assisted in Chinese prospecting for rare metals.

65. The earliest Soviet participation in the Chinese atomic energy program was concerned with exploration for and exploitation of uranium resources. The Sino-Soviet Non-ferrous and Rare Metals Stock Company organized in 1950 may have been intended to develop ore resources for ultimate Soviet use. However, we have no evidence that Chinese uranium ore was ever supplied to the USSR, and at least since 1954, when the company was dissolved as a joint operation, the Chinese uranium appears to have been intended for domestic use only. Soviet participation in the Chinese ore program has included field assistance as well as technical guidance. The degree of Soviet aid to the uranium ore production program apparently decreased after mid-1957.

Soviet participation in uranium prospecting continued, however, at a reduced level

66. There is some evidence that Soviet aid may have been curtailed. a general withdrawal of Soviet technicians from China took place in mid-1960,

67. The Soviets have also assisted the Chinese by designing uranium ore concentration and uranium metal facilities.

The main body of personnel appears to have been active in China until mid-1957, but a smaller group concerned largely with ore-processing technology was noted in China as late as January 1958, when it was winding up its affairs.

68. Aid in the peaceful uses of atomic energy has been largely provided by GLAVATOM and the USSR Academy of Sciences,

69. A Sino-Soviet Nuclear Energy Agreement was signed in 1955, and published to the world. Under its terms the USSR agreed to:

a. Provide an experimental heavy-water moderated research reactor with thermal capacity of 7.5-to-10 megawatts, and a 25 Mev cyclotron; render scientific and technical assistance in building, assembling,

TOP SECRET

TOP SECRET

adjusting and starting the reactor and cyclotron; and to assist in the design of the scientific and experimental installation to house these pieces of equipment; and

b. Supply the Chinese with fissionable and other materials for the reactor and for carrying out research in nuclear physics, train Chinese specialists in nuclear physics in the USSR and supply Soviet speci. .ts to work in China.

70. On 18 January 1958, after nearly ten weeks of negotiations in Moscow by a Chinese scientific delegation led by Kuo Mo-jo, president of the Academy of Sciences, a Sino-Soviet Scientific and Technical Agreement, covering th. ,ears 1958–62, was signed. None of the details of this agreement have been made known, yet it is likely that certain aspects of Soviet aid to the Chinese Communist atomic energy program were provided for.

71. Soviet specialists have also assisted the Chinese with the installation of an ASK–1 ionization chamber, with a volume of 1,000 liters, filled with argon at 10 atmospheres, and screened by a 12 cm layer of lead. This chamber, which was a gift of the Soviet Union, was probably installed at the Chinese Institute of Atomic Energy's location northwest of Peiping, for the use of the Cosmic Ray Department of the Institute.

TOP SECRET

SECTION 19

NIE 10-61

Authority and Control in
the Communist Movement

8 August 1961

APPROVED FOR RELEASE
DATE: MAY 2004

392

15 AUG 1961

~~SECRET~~

NIE 10-61
8 August 1961

NATIONAL INTELLIGENCE ESTIMATE
NUMBER 10-61

AUTHORITY AND CONTROL IN THE COMMUNIST MOVEMENT

Submitted by the
DIRECTOR OF CENTRAL INTELLIGENCE

The following intelligence organizations participated in the preparation of this estimate: The Central Intelligence Agency and the intelligence organizations of the Departments of State, the Army, the Navy, the Air Force, The Joint Staff, and the Federal Bureau of Investigation.

Concurred in by the
UNITED STATES INTELLIGENCE BOARD

on 8 August 1961. Concurring were The Director of Intelligence and Research, Department of State; the Assistant Chief of Staff for Intelligence, Department of the Army; the Assistant Chief of Naval Operations (Intelligence), Department of the Navy; the Assistant Chief of Staff, Intelligence, USAF; the Director for Intelligence, Joint Staff; the Assistant to the Secretary of Defense, Special Operations; the Director of the National Security Agency; and the Federal Bureau of Investigation. The Atomic Energy Commission Representative to the USIB, abstained, the subject being outside of his jurisdiction.

~~SECRET~~

N.° 437

APPROVED FOR RELEASE
DATE: MAY 2004

SECRET

AUTHORITY AND CONTROL IN THE COMMUNIST MOVEMENT

THE PROBLEM

To assess the cohesion of the Sino-Soviet Bloc and among the parties of the world Communist movement, to identify trends in the degree of Soviet control, and to estimate the future implication of these trends.

SUMMARY AND CONCLUSIONS

General Considerations

1. According to Communist doctrine, it would be impossible for conflicts of interest to disturb in any basic way the relations between Communist parties in the international movement. This is so, it is argued, because the class interests which are the source of international conflict among non-Communist states have been suppressed by the new social order, and have been replaced by the fundamental identity of views and harmony of interests of the "classless" society. In fact, however, the appearance of unity in the Communist movement has been due, not so much to the absence of conflicts of interest, as to the overwhelming authority exercised by Moscow. This authority has rested on the great military and economic power of the USSR, on its historical precedence as the first Communist state, on the long personal ascendancy of Stalin over the international Communist movement, and on the tradition of dictatorial centralism in that movement. (*Paras. 13–18*)

2. In the period since World War II a number of developments have demonstrated the falsity of the simplistic Communist theory of natural harmony among Communist parties. When the Communist parties of Eastern Europe achieved state power they naturally acquired new interests and attitudes different from those they had reflected as small conspiratorial groups wholly dependent on the protection and support provided by Moscow. Yet they were small states in Moscow's immediate sphere of power; therefore, whatever pretensions to independence they may have had were bound to be extremely circumscribed. The achievement of state power by the Chinese Communists was a different matter, however, because it meant that for the first time Communist theory on state relations had to be applied to the relations between two great powers. (*Paras. 14–16*)

SECRET

1

SECRET

2

3. Beyond this, there was in the postwar period a considerable growth in the number and in the size of Communist parties all over the world. Among them there were wide variations in the cultural and political environments in which they operated, in their tactical problems, and in the degree of their Marxist-Leninist sophistication and training. Over the years, moreover, there has been a tendency for a number of the more important non-Bloc parties to be increasingly concerned to see that their own local points of view are considered in policy deliberations of the international movement. (*Paras. 14, 39–40*)

4. All these developments have tested not only the theory of unity, but also the authority of the Soviet Party over other parties which was the practical reality on which the appearance of unity was built. In the best of circumstances it was bound to become increasingly difficult for Moscow to maintain the unity of so large and varied a movement with so wide a range of differing views and interests. In addition, these events have aggravated the frequent conflicts between the requirements of the foreign policy of the Soviet state and those of the international Communist movement. Altogether, it is evident that Communist political institutions, like all other institutions, are subject to pressures for change and are in fact changing. (*Paras. 13–21, 34–40, 59*)

Disciplinary Problems in the Communist Movement

5. Stalin's authority over the international Communist movement was tested almost as soon as the new Communist states came into existence at the end of World War II. Challenged by Yugoslavia in 1948, he failed either to impose discipline or to prevent Yugoslavia's subsequent survival as an independent Communist state. When the Chinese Communists achieved state power in 1949—like the Yugoslavs, largely by their own efforts—they inevitably acquired a special status in the Bloc. After Stalin died and his awesome aura of personal authority over the parties disappeared, his less eminent successors attempted to overcome the abuses of his brutal and open control by substituting a more flexibly exercised but still decisive influence. These experiments were cut short, however, by the Eastern European upheavals of 1956, which showed that the balance between influence and outright control would be a difficult one to strike. (*Paras. 13–15, 19–21*)

6. Since 1956, when Peiping helped Moscow to restore its badly shaken authority in Eastern Europe, China has become an increasingly important factor in the direction of the movement, and has developed pretensions as an authoritative source of Communist doctrine. When the Chinese leaders resorted in 1960 to open polemics in their policy disagreements with Moscow, and also lobbied openly among Communists against Soviet policies, the Soviets responded by, in effect, putting the Chinese on trial before the other parties, first at Bucharest and later at the November conference in Moscow. Nevertheless, during the Sino-Soviet dispute of 1960 the Chinese were able to bring a successful challenge to Soviet authority and to establish the formal principle of mandatory consultation among the parties on matters of general Communist policy. (*Paras. 16, 21–28*)

SECRET

SECRET

3

Prospects for Soviet Authority

7. Since the 81-party conference of November 1960, the Soviets and the Chinese have continued, within limits, their separate efforts to preserve and expand their own authority in the movement. It seems to us unlikely that the two major parties will be able for some time to come to resolve their differences and achieve a stable arrangement for directing the Communist movement. On the other hand, an open rupture between them appears to us equally unlikely. We believe that the course of their relations will be erratic, cooperative at some times and places, competitive at others. *(Paras. 35, 38, 59–62)*

8. In this situation the Soviet Party possesses enormous advantages, because of its greater military and economic power, and also because of its traditional authority and prestige within the movement. The ability of the Chinese Party to contend for leadership is currently limited by China's serious internal difficulties. The Soviets retain some opportunity to exert pressure by virtue of China's relative economic and military weakness, though this apparently was not very effective in the dispute of 1960. Because of the present preponderance of Soviet power, Moscow will probably be able, though with increasing difficulty, to maintain its primacy in the Communist movement for some time to come. The Soviet leaders will endeavor to maintain the substance of their former authority by exercising pressure and influence bilaterally upon other parties, by confronting their rivals with strong majority coalitions at international gatherings, and sometimes by shrewd adjustments of Soviet policies in order to undercut Chinese

criticisms. Because the role of personalities has figured in some degree in the Soviet-Chinese difficulties, the appearance of new leaders in either country could have an important influence on the further course of their relations. *(Paras. 60–62)*

9. In these circumstances, the other parties will almost inevitably be tempted to bargain between Moscow and Peiping in order to obtain greater advantages for themselves. Within certain parties which develop serious prospects of achieving power, and which therefore must make important tactical choices, conflicting brands of advice may tend to intensify factionalism. In the long run, some of the parties in Eastern Europe, or factions within them, may attempt to develop further the autonomy conceded by Stalin's successors. In the Asian satellites, where Chinese influence is already strong and has a good prospect of increasing if China's power continues to grow, the regimes will be better able to bargain with both Communist great powers for economic and political support. *(Para. 63)*

Implications for Policy Toward the West

10. It is evident that the international Communist system, for decades little more than an instrumentality of Soviet policy, is being changed, because of the forces of nationalism and diversity within it, into a movement reflecting an appreciable diffusion of power. While the altered relationships within the Communist movement and the decline in Soviet authority have not altered the fundamental hostility of the Communists toward the non-Communist world, we believe that these developments are having

SECRET

318

SECRET   4

an important influence on Communist policy. They have already diminished to some extent the flexibility of Soviet policy towards the West, and the Soviet Party will probably encounter increasing difficulties in its efforts to coordinate general Communist policy. These difficulties may not be as serious in times when events generally favor Communist interests, but they may again erupt into open polemics during periods of adversity, or even at times when fundamental decisions are required for the exploitation of unfolding opportunities. (*Paras. 59, 65*)

11. The development of the relationship between the USSR and China, and the evolution of the international Communist movement generally, will obviously be of profound significance for the security and interests of the West. In the long run Chinese power, assertiveness, and self-interest might increase so far as greatly to impair the common policy with the USSR, and even lead the Soviets to believe that they had more in common with the ideological enemy than they have today. For some time to come, however, the most likely prospect is that the USSR and China will maintain their relationship in something like its present form. It will be an alliance which is from time to time troubled and inharmonious, but which nevertheless preserves sufficient unity to act in concert against the West, especially in times of major challenge. However, present trends as described in this paper point to an increasing complexity, diversity, and interplay of forces within the Communist system, and to a remarkable survival of old-fashioned impulses of nationalism. (*Para. 67*)

12. These trends may have various effects. They may from time to time result in more aggressive anti-Western policies intended to hold the forces of disunity in check. They may enable certain parties, free from the restrictions of a rigid, general Communist line, to pursue more effective policies in local situations. But eventually, if such trends persist, they may considerably diminish the effectiveness of the Communist movement as a whole. This would give the West opportunities for maneuver and influence which could provide important advantages in the world struggle. (*Para. 68*)

DISCUSSION

I. DEVELOPMENT OF RELATIONS AMONG THE COMMUNIST PARTIES

A. The Comintern Period

13. The Comintern (Third International) was at the outset, for a brief period, a collection of independent parties and groups which shared a bond of unity in dedication to common revolutionary goals. Immediately after the Russian Revolution and the end of World War I, Communists lived in the expectation of imminent revolutions in Western Europe, and even Lenin anticipated that his own party would share leadership of the international movement with the victorious parties of Western Europe. As these illusions died, however, the Soviet Party was not long in establishing its ascendancy, and in making the Comintern over in its own Bolshevik image. In the twenties, international Communist policy was increasingly subordinated to the needs of Soviet foreign policy, and the parties were gradually placed under increasingly stringent supervision by Moscow through the vast international bureaucracy of the Comintern. Subsequently, through repeated purges and

SECRET

SECRET

other means of pressure, Stalin acquired almost complete control over all the parties except the Chinese. At the same time, he dispensed more and more with formal institutional organs, and in the mid-thirties distrust and suspicion moved him to decimate the entire headquarters apparatus of the Comintern. Long before it was formally abolished in 1943, the Comintern had in fact lost its practical importance, though Stalin's tight control of the Communist movement remained unimpaired.

B. The Emergence of New Communist States

14. World War II, which disrupted party communications with Moscow, nurtured autonomous tendencies among the parties and helped the French, Italian, and several East European parties to develop greater mass support in the partisan struggles and to become increasingly self-reliant. The most important effect of the war, however, was the fundamental alteration it wrought in the Communist movement by the creation of new Communist states outside the Soviet Union. Previously, Soviet control over the movement had been relatively simple, involving only parties out of power whose very existence often depended on Moscow's political and financial support. Now the Communist system, still based on a single source of power and authority, had to embrace not just parties, but also national states, each of which had its own particular national interests.

15. Stalin was not disposed to give much play to these national interests. As soon as the Communist Parties in Eastern Europe were securely established in power, he took steps to impose complete, all-pervasive control, tieing the new states tightly to Moscow and treating them as mere extensions of the Soviet state system. The Yugoslav Party, however, refused to submit to such treatment, and subsequently was able to survive expulsion from the Cominform and to establish itself as a continuous, glaring contradiction of Soviet claims that membership in the Bloc best serves the national interests of its individual members. In the rest of Eastern Europe, despite the ensuing crackdown, secret police methods of rule could only repress, but not eliminate, disaffection and nationalist resentment which often infected the local parties as well as the population.

16. The establishment of Communist control in China created an additional problem for Moscow, but one of far greater magnitude. By virtue of its size, population, and the traditional influence of its civilization, China was a great power. Moreover, the Chinese Party, unlike most parties in Eastern Europe, achieved its revolutionary victory largely by its own efforts and established its own basis of power in a country far too large and remote to make the imposition of direct control practicable for Moscow. Its leader, Mao Tsetung, knew from experience that Stalin had little comprehension of local problems in China, which differed greatly from those in the Soviet Union. He did not hesitate to interpret Communist doctrine independently to suit the needs of Chinese internal policy; thus even before Stalin's death Mao gained the reputation of a doctrinal innovator. Thus, whatever Stalin's wishes may have been, China inevitably acquired a special status in the Bloc.

C. The Death of Stalin

17. Nevertheless, until the death of Stalin, Soviet authority was largely unquestioned, and the Soviet Party possessed manifold assets for asserting its control. It had been the first party, and for decades the only one, to achieve power and provide a secure base for the international movement. It had built a powerful state, developing in the process an internal system which came to be the model of socialism for other parties. Its ideological pronouncements had become dogma, and its publications served as the basic indoctrination material for Communists everywhere. The other parties were in great part dependent upon the USSR for psychological and financial support, while those which had been brought to power in Eastern Europe knew that Soviet military might was their sole guarantee of survival against a hostile populace. The leaders of the more important parties were usually selected by the Soviets,

SECRET

SECRET   6

trained in Soviet Party schools, and then installed and maintained in positions of leadership by the Soviets; frequently they were also purged or liquidated by the Soviets.

18. This system of control depended on Stalin's enormous personal authority, an element of great strength but also one which concealed a major vulnerability. It was Stalin who determined policy, who defined socialism, who pronounced doctrine, who selected leaders. Soviet prestige among Communists was in great part identical with the respect and genuine regard which they felt for Stalin personally. None of his colleagues had a following among the other parties; in fact, the only man who approached him in prestige was in the Chinese Party. Thus his death in early 1953 diminished at a stroke Moscow's authority within the Communist movement, and this at a time when China's power was rising, and when difficulties were accumulating in Eastern Europe.

D. Khrushchev's New Approach

19. Even before his death, some of Stalin's lieutenants were acutely conscious of the deleterious effects of his policies toward the other Communist parties and of the necessity to adopt a new approach which would combine less direct, though still effective methods of control with toleration of a limited amount of local autonomy. The intent behind Khrushchev's new approach was not to allow genuine autonomy, but to employ a more flexible policy in order to maintain the maximum amount of *effective* Soviet control.

20. This new approach had the effect in Eastern Europe of releasing pent up forces crying for reform, as well as repressed bitterness over Soviet arbitrary treatment and exploitation, stimulated still further by the reversal of Stalin's policy toward Yugoslavia and the acknowledgment of a Communist party's right to follow a "separate road." The destruction of the Stalin myth, which severed an important thread of authority and caused confusion and soul-searching among the parties, was the final blow. The result in Poland was a resurgence of nationalist feeling which swept a party leader to power who personified this

outlook and which led Moscow to grant Poland an important measure of bona fide internal autonomy. In Hungary, the result was a deep division within the party which opened the way to revolt. Though the military repression in Hungary abruptly checked the trend toward liberalization in Eastern Europe and made it clear that the Soviets would deal ruthlessly with any attempted defection from the Bloc, the Communist movement as a whole was badly shaken and there was a clear need for authoritative political and ideological guidance. It required strenuous Soviet efforts, including substantial economic aid and concessions to injured nationalist feelings in Eastern Europe, before the Moscow Conference of November 1957 could meet this need with an agreed reaffirmation of basic principles of "socialist development" for Communist countries, based on Soviet experience.

E. China's Entry into Bloc Affairs

21. Meanwhile, the Chinese Communists perceived in the upheavals of 1956 both a problem and an opportunity. They were fully as concerned as the Soviets to restore unity and stability to the Bloc. But at the same time they found themselves, in the wake of Soviet mistakes, in a position to influence the reestablishment of that unity on a new basis. Having built up their own strength and confidence since coming to power in 1949, and already exercising some influence over the Asian Parties within and outside the Bloc, they were now in a position to contribute significantly to the Soviet effort to restore order in Eastern Europe while at the same time increasing the weight of their own influence in the movement as a whole. Thus, both in their important doctrinal statements of this period and Chou En-lai's tour of the European Satellites, they managed to convey the idea that Soviet leadership should be respected because they, the Chinese, said so. The result, despite Peiping's public insistence upon Moscow's primacy, was to nudge both the Bloc and the international movement toward a greater sharing of leadership, and to show that Chinese influence and authority in the movement were now considerable.

SECRET

SECRET

II. CURRENT RELATIONS AMONG THE BLOC PARTIES

A. The Sino-Soviet Dispute of 1960

22. We have in previous estimates examined the causes of the Sino-Soviet dispute and the issues to which it has given rise.[1] During 1958 and 1959, both sides limited themselves, at least in public, to setting forth their positions in seemingly abstract ideological discussions, which in fact reflected policy disagreements over a growing range of specific issues. In the spring of 1960, however, China finally dropped this restraint and by June was openly lobbying against the USSR among the delegates to the World Federation of Trade Unions (WFTU) meeting in Peiping. Moscow responded sharply by, in effect, putting the Chinese on trial at a meeting of a number of the Communist Parties in Bucharest later in the month. The Chinese held fast, and even obtained open support from the Albanian Party. The two sides agreed finally to a plenary session of the entire Communist movement at which disputed matters would be debated again when all the parties sent representatives to the November celebration in Moscow.

23. Between June and November, each side became increasingly aggressive. Both tried to line up support by circularizing the entire movement with lengthy attacks on the other. With Moscow employing all its powers of influence and control, most parties fell readily into line behind the USSR, but a few stayed on the fence or leaned toward China on certain issues. Meanwhile, polemics in the Bloc press became increasingly explicit, and the USSR exerted strong pressure on China in various aspects of their state relations.[2] All these

---

[1] Paragraphs 122–130 in NIE 11-4-60, "Main Trends in Soviet Capabilities and Policies, 1960–1965," dated 1 December 1960; NIE 100-3-60, "Sino-Soviet Relations," dated 9 August 1960.

[2] This pressure included the withdrawal of the bulk of Soviet technicians at the end of July (an estimated 2,000 to 3,000), suspension of Chinese publications in the USSR, diplomatic protests, the expulsion of certain Chinese officials, and ominous warnings in the press. There is also considerable evidence suggesting border difficulties between the two countries during this period.

measures failed to deter the Chinese, and the November meeting became a direct confrontation. What was at stake there was not only a range of disputed policy issues, but the more fundamental question of how and by whom Communist policy was to be determined—in other words, the question of leadership in the international movement.

24. In the most general sense, therefore, the question of authority was involved in every issue debated at the Moscow proceedings. The final document in general gave preference to Soviet propositions on world strategy and internal Communist policy, and in signing it the Chinese subscribed to many formulations which they had vigorously contested in the preceding months. But in order to obtain this Chinese agreement, the Soviets had at many points to allow Peiping to include its formulations as well, although these usually received less prominence than the Soviet statements. The result was a compromise document which stated both sides of numerous questions and thereby clearly conveyed to the other parties that Chinese demands for a real voice in policymaking for the Communist movement had, however reluctantly, been granted by the Communist Party of the Soviet Union (CPSU).

25. But the issue of authority was joined even more directly in a series of proposals designed specifically to assert Soviet primacy and bind the Chinese to future obedience. Foreswearing any aspirations to truly Stalinist leadership, but confident that they could still command a majority in the international movement, the Soviets fell back on a proposal for majority rule as a means of forcing the Chinese into formal submission. In another maneuver, they sought to have the document acknowledge their leading role by endorsing the decisions of the 20th and 21st CPSU Congresses, which had been called into question by the Chinese. Again, they proposed that the parties formally condemn "factionalism," a clear reference to Chinese efforts to form anti-Soviet coalitions with other parties, and "national communism," a phrase injected to

SECRET

SECRET

8

lay the basis for future attacks upon Chinese deviations.

26. Although the Chinese had been willing to compromise on points of doctrine, they proved adamant in their opposition to these disciplinary proposals. They insisted that neither they nor any other party should be bound by the decisions, even if they were correct, of Soviet Party Congresses. They contended that majority rule, while correct for the individual parties, was intolerable for the movement and that only unanimous decisions of all the parties could have universal validity. Lastly, they refused to agree to the condemnations of "factionalism" and "national communism."

27. In the end, the Chinese prevailed on these central issues of authority because the Soviets found no way of imposing their will upon the Chinese. The two offending phrases were excluded from the document. The Soviet Congresses were praised, but only in limited terms, and the contributions of "other parties" were commended in the same breath. As for the mechanism for international decisionmaking, the USSR had to abandon majority rule in favor of a formal undertaking to observe those decisions which were "jointly worked out" at bilateral and multilateral conferences, a formulation which came close to providing a veto power to the Chinese or any other party.

28. Thus, despite the commanding majorities which the Soviets had, they failed to gain their major points on what is to them a vital issue—the USSR's dominating role in the Communist world. The measure of this failure was actually greater than the textual compromises and losses which they had to accept in producing a unanimous statement. Not only did they fail to coerce the Chinese, but in the voting they were actively opposed by Albania and on several occasions lost the support of North Korea, North Vietnam, and a number of other Asian parties. In addition, they had to undergo, in full view of the entire movement, the unprecedented experience of freewheeling debate and even outright vilification of their leader.

B. Effect of the Dispute on the European Bloc Parties

29. The Sino-Soviet dispute produced widespread uneasiness within the Bloc. The USSR had the support of most Communists in the Satellites, but some sympathy for certain Chinese methods and attitudes had been manifested in 1958-1959 in the Bulgarian, East German, and Czech Parties. This ambivalence quickly disappeared, however, as soon as the Soviets invoked their authority in coming out directly against the Chinese. The performance of all the East European Communists at the Moscow Conference, except the Albanians, was thoroughly obedient.

30. Albania, however, turned out to be a dramatically different case. The Albanian Party is in the hands of unreconstructed Stalinists who are obsessed with the fear that Yugoslavia will re-establish its former tutelage over the Albanian Communist movement. Accordingly, this leadership was gravely alarmed when, in 1955 and 1956, Khrushchev launched his attack upon Stalin, including in the indictment Stalin's attempts to subvert Yugoslavia, and took up the cultivation of Tito. Even after the post-Hungarian hardening of Soviet policy, the Albanians continued to see a threat to their independence in Khrushchev's advocacy of "peaceful coexistence" and his reluctance to accede to an all-out attack on Tito. Thus, when the Chinese appeared as the champions of a hard, antirevisionist line, Albania broke ranks and during meetings of the Communist Parties in 1960, openly joined the Chinese side with virulent attacks upon the CPSU.

31. Chinese support offers some protection for the Albanians, since the USSR must recognize that direct moves against Tirana risk the further worsening of its already delicate relations with Peiping. The Albanians enjoy two other advantages, however, which are probably more important in the defense of their new anti-Soviet stance. One is their physical separation from the Bloc, which makes it difficult for the USSR to apply physical force without greatly damaging its international position. The other is the unity of

SECRET

SECRET

9

the Albanian top leadership, dating from wartime partisan combat and secured by a series of purges which cleansed it first of members sympathetic to its former mentor, the Yugoslav Party, and then, in 1960, of pro-Soviet elements. As a result, the Soviets have had to restrict themselves to indirect methods which thus far have proven embarrassingly ineffectual. Moscow's failure to punish the defiance of another Communist state is especially ignominious in view of Albania's size and hitherto complete subordination.

C. The Asian Satellites

32. Among the Asian Satellites, Peiping has cultural and geographic advantages which enable it to compete with the Soviets on a nearly equal basis. As a result, North Vietnam, North Korea, and Outer Mongolia have found themselves in a position between the two great Communist powers that is delicate, but at the same time rewarding. In North Vietnam, most of the top leaders are Soviet-trained, but Communist China played an important role in advising, training, and supplying the Vietminh revolution against the French. Furthermore, the geographical location of North Vietnam and the similarity of many of its problems make close cooperation with Peiping a natural course for Hanoi. On the other hand, the North Vietnamese leaders appreciate that the only way for them to avoid being completely dominated by their giant neighbor is to retain a strong Soviet presence in North Vietnam. These conflicting tendencies have not impaired the essential unity with which Moscow, Peiping, and Hanoi have pressed their objectives in Laos.

33. The Outer Mongolian and North Korean Communist regimes were both placed in power by the Soviets before there was a Communist China. During the past decade both regimes have undergone purges that were apparently aimed, at least in part, against leaders who looked toward Peiping for guidance or support. At present Soviet dominance seems secure in Outer Mongolia in spite of Peiping's considerable efforts to enhance its influence there. Even though the present leaders of North Korea are nearly all Moscow-trained,

they exhibited a pronounced affinity for Peiping's forced-draft industrialization and commune programs in 1958 and 1959. Subsequently the party backed away from emulating Chinese methods when the Soviets indicated their displeasure. At the present time Soviet influence probably continues to exceed that of China.

34. Outer Mongolia did not back any of the Chinese positions during the Sino-Soviet dispute. North Korea and North Vietnam sought to steer a middle course supporting most of the Soviet propositions, but joining the Chinese on the critical issue of discipline. The fact that these two Asian states no longer automatically and unhesitatingly follow all Soviet leads constitutes a considerable setback to Moscow's authority. In addition, Peiping and Moscow appear to have become engaged in a competition to win support by pumping economic aid into the three Asian Satellites.

D. Continued Strain in Bloc Relations

35. Despite Soviet and Chinese efforts after the Moscow conference to portray interparty harmony and fraternal solidarity, it is evident that important differences of view persist. Each party has made its own tendentious interpretation of the December Statement, stressing those portions which correspond most closely with its views during the dispute. The Chinese, moreover, are making the most of the advantages gained in Moscow by stressing the special responsibilities of the "two largest parties" in the movement. Differences also continue to be apparent in the interpretation of contemporary world developments.

36. The Albanians have been by no means as restrained as their Chinese allies since the conference. They have gone to great lengths to endorse the anti-Soviet behavior of their leaders at Moscow and to affirm that their party line had been correct before, during, and after the dispute. They continue to criticize in indirect but unmistakable terms contemporary Soviet policy, especially toward Yugoslavia. Continued strain in Sino-Soviet relations, moreover, was most clearly indicated at the Albanian Party Congress, held in Febru-

SECRET

SECRET

ary, which became the occasion for another confrontation, though on a far lesser scale, of parties in the movement who endorsed the Soviet or Albanian-Chinese positions.

37. Following this Congress, Albania has continued to receive staunch support from China, including extensive economic aid, while relations with Moscow have steadily deteriorated. A show trial staged in Tirana, involving Albanian naval officers among others, and ostensibly directed at a Greek-Yugoslav-US plot, was in fact an anti-Soviet demonstration. It was followed by the evacuation by the Soviets of their important submarine base at Valona.

38. There have been few indications that the many serious problems in Sino-Soviet state relations which were evident in 1960 have been resolved. Though a trade agreement was signed in April which eased China's debt burdens appreciably, the Soviet commitments under the agreement were far from generous, especially in view of China's serious economic problems. Moreover, the Chinese economy continues under the handicap created by the withdrawal of Soviet technicians, and there is no evidence of any agreement to send them back in their former numbers. The lack of detail in the June communique following the talks on economic, technical, and scientific cooperation suggested that, though some Soviet assistance would continue, there is little likelihood that the former degree of economic cooperation will be restored.

III. THE NON-BLOC PARTIES

A. General

39. World War II and its aftermath brought about substantial and in some cases radical changes in the circumstances of Communist Parties outside the Bloc. In Western Europe, the French and Italian Parties developed considerable popular support and some independent financial resources, and even in the smaller countries the parties became an established part of the local political landscape. During the same period, in the countries which first gained independence after the war, many Communist parties rapidly came to ac-

quire real domestic prospects and, therefore, became more preoccupied with problems of domestic politics.

40. These advances were, of course, gratifying to the Soviet leaders. At the same time, the USSR has continued to pursue its own interests in ways which have often conflicted with those of local Communist parties; in particular, Khrushchev has made it a major point of policy to court newly independent governments, even when the local parties are seeking to discredit and replace them. The non-Bloc parties have thus become increasingly concerned to have their own interests considered in the formulation of the movement's policies. China's success has probably given them some encouragement in this endeavor. Equally important, China's rise has weakened the concept of monolithic authority in the individual parties, making it easier for differences within these parties to develop into open factionalism.

B. Western Europe and the US

41. The Western European Parties, still led by tested veterans of the Comintern period who have always maintained a firm Soviet orientation, have remained responsive to Soviet control. Nevertheless, the relationship of the individual parties to the CPSU has changed considerably since the days of the prewar period. The widespread discrediting of parliamentary democracy before the war and the underground struggles of World War II enabled the parties to develop such strength that a number of them were later able to withstand prolonged adversity and political isolation.

42. The altered status of these parties was not particularly apparent until 1956, when Khrushchev's de-Stalinization speech had a profound effect causing demoralization and in some cases large-scale defections. The response of the leaders of the Italian and French Parties provided a clear measure of the change which had occurred. Togliatti reacted to the Khrushchev speech by openly advocating "polycentrism" in the movement, by which he meant autonomy for the parties. The French

SECRET

SECRET   11

leaders responded in a different way, by asking Khrushchev to tone down his denigration of Stalin. Though Togliatti soon ceased to advocate his proposal, both initiatives, different as they were, showed an assertiveness which would have been inconceivable in Stalin's time.

43. Khrushchev's speech also stimulated short-lived demands for increased autonomy in the other West European parties, especially in the Danish Party, where a faction under Aksel Larson took a more extreme position even than Togliatti, and finally had to be expelled. An effect of these developments was that the Soviet leaders subsequently were more attentive to the local problems and desires of the parties. At the same time, the Soviets recognized that greater autonomy was necessary if these parties were to play their role in the "peaceful coexistence" strategy. Thus the Rome conference of Western European parties in 1959 resulted in a policy agreement giving the individual parties considerable leeway in implementing the general line.

44. Despite this loosening of discipline, the Western European parties have been among Moscow's strongest supporters in the dispute with Peiping, and Chinese attempts to influence them were unavailing. These parties have been greatly assisted in their internal campaigns by the Soviet line on nonviolent methods of achieving power and the avoidance of war, and they saw China's advocacy of violence and high risks as threatening their prospects for winning popular support. Some groups within these parties have at times sought to use various Chinese arguments for factional purposes, but at the Moscow Conference the interventions of the West Europeans were all in support of Soviet positions. However, their leaders did not behave at Moscow in the obsequious manner of former days and even showed some evidence of resenting Soviet pressure. They showed reluctance to commit themselves to accept future Soviet guidance unreservedly, and were bolder than they had ever been before in urging the movement to give greater heed, in working out general policy, to their own local problems.

45. With its traditional deference to Soviet guidance, the Communist Party, USA (CPUSA), gave the Soviet Union its unqualified support at the Moscow Conference. In addition, the CPUSA has enthusiastically supported Soviet "peaceful coexistence" tactics as most favorable to its efforts in the US. Adoption of the more militant, revolutionary Chinese position would place the party under still more handicaps in operating in the US. At present, there appears little prospect that the Chinese position will gain any significant support in the CPUSA.

C. The Middle East

46. The Communist movement in the Middle East historically has been under close Soviet direction, especially those parties which, banned at home, are forced to operate from bases within the Bloc and thus are completely dependent upon Soviet support. In recent years, however, signs of friction have become visible in the Syrian and Iraqi Parties. Both these parties were strong enough to nourish immediate political ambitions, and both have been hampered by Soviet cultivation of their domestic opponents, the "national bourgeois" regimes of Nasser and Qasim.

47. The formation of the United Arab Republic (UAR) in 1958 was facilitated by the danger of an imminent Communist bid for power in Syria. Since that time, Syrian Communist leader Bakdash has been unable fully to reconcile himself to Soviet policy toward Nasser and has resisted acceptance of the Syro-Egyptian union. In Iraq, traditional factionalism in the Communist Party became bitter in 1959 when the Communists overreached themselves in a campaign of violence, bringing on a governmental repression from which the party still has not recovered. The USSR disapproved of this tactic, regarding it not only as premature but as likely to spoil its own relations with Qasim. The Chinese, however, probably encouraged it and thereby gained the sympathy of the radical faction within the Iraqi Party. Chinese attempts to broaden their influence among Middle Eastern Communists have, however, brought few results to date. At the Moscow meeting Bakdash, the

SECRET

SE̶C̶R̶E̶T   12

most influential Communist in the area, expressed his resentment of Chinese attempts to proselytize members of his own party, and violently criticized Chinese disobedience. The other parties also lined up behind the Soviet position.

D. The Asian Parties

48. Among the non-Bloc parties of Asia, Soviet authority is far less secure. Among the smaller parties Chinese influence is strong and in a few cases outweighs that of the USSR. The larger ones, those of India, Indonesia, and Japan, contain pro-Chinese elements and, in addition, are reluctant to come out openly against the major Communist power of the region. When put to the test at the Moscow Conference, some of the Asian parties extended a degree of support to the Chinese, and none of them lined up solidly behind the Soviets in the manner of their European and Arab colleagues. Further, this pattern was repeated at the Albanian Party Congress in February 1961.

49. In Japan, after the Communist Party had thoroughly discredited itself in the eyes of the Japanese public by its violent and illegal activities between 1950 and 1953, the post-Stalin trends in Soviet foreign policy have favored the efforts of the Japanese Communist Party (JCP) to rehabilitate itself. The party can the more convincingly portray itself to the people as independent, and in favor of peaceful accession to power, and thus pursue its current strategy of advocating a broad national front against American imperialism and domestic monopoly capitalism. Support for China exists among minority elements within the Communist Party and among certain radical student and trade union groups outside the party. The JCP is likely to retain its pro-Soviet orientation as long as the present leaders remain in control of the Japanese Party. However, recent Soviet and Chinese moves suggest that each is seeking to strengthen its influence in the JCP.

50. The domestic position of the Indonesian Communist Party (PKI) is unique. It is one of the largest Communist parties outside the Bloc, has an important popular following, and enjoys the protection of Sukarno, who has drawn it, along with the anti-Communist Army, into the national leadership. Thus the Soviet line on the nonviolent, parliamentary road to socialism is far better suited to the PKI's needs than the more radical and revolutionary approach advocated by China, which at this stage could only serve to forfeit Sukarno's protection against the army and diminish the party's popular support as well. Soviet foreign policies—cultivation of Sukarno, provision of economic and military aid, and support of Indonesia's claim to West New Guinea—harmonize ideally with the PKI's internal tactics and enhance its domestic position. Despite all those factors, a Chinese-oriented faction does exist within the party, and had sufficient strength to influence the conduct of the PKI delegation in Moscow.

51. Soviet foreign policy has had a much more mixed effect upon the prospects of domestic Communists in India, where Moscow's aid and encouragement has been extended to a government which treats the local party as an opponent rather than a partner. While Moscow's "peaceful coexistence" tactics have given communism some respectability in India, it has been difficult for the local party to reconcile Soviet courtship of Nehru with his ousting of the Communist Government in Kerala and the current trend of Indian foreign policy, which the party regards as pro-Western. These tactics have intensified the traditional factionalism in the Indian Party, with a minority frankly sympathetic to China and anxious to steer the party to a more revolutionary course. This minority received a severe check, however, when the Tibetan revolt and the Sino-Indian border dispute aroused Indian national feelings against China and placed the Communists in an exceedingly awkward position. Suslov, attending the Indian Party Congress in April 1961, found it more important to keep the Indian Party together behind a vague and generally moderate political line than to try to impose discipline on the pro-Chinese faction, and as a result the party remains uncertain, divided, and subject to serious disputes in the future.

SE̶C̶R̶E̶T

SECRET

13

52. In contrast with the larger parties, the interests of a number of the smaller Asian parties—for example, those of Malaya, Burma, and Australia—are not in their view furthered by gradualist tactics generally advocated by Moscow. For many of them prospects for achieving power via parliamentary methods are exceedingly remote. They therefore feel frustrated by Soviet "peaceful coexistence" and "united front" tactics, and are anxious to abandon this approach for more direct revolutionary methods. The effect of this attitude was evident during the discussions in Moscow in November, and afterward, at the Albanian Congress, where several of these parties sided with the Chinese against the Soviet positions.

E. Africa

53. The Communist movement in Africa is still insignificant, and the focus of Soviet strategy there is the radical nationalist leadership with which the USSR can cooperate in antiwestern policies. The longer term Communist objective is the conversion of radical nationalist states to communism, and the Bloc has devoted much more effort to this than to the buildup of Communist parties from scratch. While the Sino-Soviet clash over strategy in underdeveloped areas is potentially significant for the African Communist movement, there is at present little specific evidence of rivalry or friction. There have been vague reports, for example, that at the November 1960 Moscow Conference, the Soviet and Chinese delegates clashed over specific details of African policy, but the nature of these differences—if they actually exist—is not known. The four African parties represented at Moscow (South Africa, Tunisia, Morocco, and Sudan) all appear to have supported the Soviet side of the ideological dispute with China.

F. Latin America

54. The leaders of the Latin American parties are in nearly all instances veteran Communists who were trained in the USSR and still must look to Moscow for material support. After Stalin's death the Soviets began to take a more active hand in directing Communist activities in Latin America. At the Moscow Conference of November 1957, and again at the 21st CPSU Congress in January 1959, the Latin American parties were given direct, detailed instructions on tactics in support of the "peace campaign" in their countries.

55. In recent years the Chinese Communists have enlarged their efforts to acquire influence among these parties. They have been handicapped by their lack of official representation in most of the Latin American countries. By bringing Latin American Communists to Peiping for visits and extended training, however, and by greatly stepping up their propaganda in the area, they have succeeded in making known their divergent views. Chinese revolutionary tactics have won some admiration, particularly among younger Communists, but Chinese influence has to date not become an important factor within these parties.

56. As the Sino-Soviet dispute developed, Soviet-oriented party leaders managed to minimize the differences and to prevent discussion among their memberships. During the early stages of the Moscow Conference, there were some indications of support for Chinese views in some of the smaller parties (Honduras, Nicaragua, Panama, Peru) which felt that they had no prospects for achieving power by nonviolent means, and a serious split developed in the Uruguayan Party. On the other hand, the important Cuban and Brazilian parties were among the strongest Soviet supporters on the key issue of discipline within the international movement. In the last analysis, all the Latin American parties, in certain cases under some pressure, stood firm in support of the Soviets against the Chinese.

57. The success of the Cuban revolution has introduced a new factor of major importance into the structure of Communist authority and control in Latin America. Cuba is heavily dependent upon Soviet material support, and the Cuban Communists look primarily to Moscow rather than Peiping. At the same time, the Cuban Communists apparently feel that their revolutionary success had unique features which allow them a certain pride and independence, and they also consider that their success in Cuba has provided a model and

SECRET

SEET   14

inspiration for the other parties in Latin America. At the Moscow Conference, both the Cubans and the Brazilians initially voiced reservations about the Soviet concept of a "national democratic state"—of which Cuba is the first example—showing reluctance to bind themselves to any rigid policy formulation which might not fit future conditions elsewhere in Latin America.

58. Havana has a special importance as a secure base for Communist activities in Latin America. For one thing, it has provided the Chinese with a point of entry into an area where they have found it difficult to obtain a foothold. For another, it has become the logical meeting place and training ground for Latin American Communists. Some of these, however, apparently are concerned that the great prestige of the Cubans in their own parties may weaken their own leadership, and they may suspect their Cuban comrades of ambitions to lead the movement in the area. Thus the future interaction of Soviet, Chinese, and Cuban aspirations and interests in the Communist movement of Latin America is at present far from clear.

IV. THE OUTLOOK

59. It is evident from the foregoing account that the international Communist movement, for decades little more than an instrumentality of Soviet policy, is being changed, because of the forces of nationalism and diversity within it, into a movement reflecting an appreciable diffusion of power. The real distribution of authority is at present uncertain and shifting. We believe that in spite of the present show of harmony the Soviet and Chinese leaders are not agreed upon the future structure of relations among the parties. The Chinese have carefully avoided making any claim to primacy and have insisted only upon an enlarged role for themselves with the CPSU in the direction of the movement. But it is not at all certain that their ambitions end at that point. During the struggles of 1960, it appeared that the Chinese were making a bid for codetermination of policy in the Communist movement, in part because they believe that they have better preserved the purity of

Communist doctrine. We believe that, though in future they may exercise more judicious tactics, they will miss few opportunities to advance their claims. For the present, however, they are refraining from open challenges to the CPSU, but are nonetheless continuing to develop their coterie of supporters among the other parties.

60. The Soviets, for their part, are finding it difficult to reconcile themselves to the impairment of their control over the Communist movement. At the same time they recognize that the rise of Communist China, the proliferation of non-Bloc parties, and the drawbacks of Stalin's coercive techniques require them to adopt a new approach to the problem of authority and control in the Communist movement. They have experimented with looser methods of supervision, especially in Eastern Europe, and have tried to establish the idea that there exists a "comity" of equal Communist nations. But in all this they have merely been seeking new forms for maintaining their authority undiminished. Thus they did not hesitate, when confronted with a direct challenge, to use coercion in state relations with China and Albania and, on a party level, to try to railroad through international meetings their views on ideology and global strategy. Though they have renounced formal leadership of the movement, they hope to retain the substance of their former authority by exercising pressure and influence bilaterally upon other parties and by confronting their rivals with strong majority coalitions at international gatherings.

61. It seems to us unlikely, therefore, that the Soviet and Chinese parties will soon find a way to resolve their differences and achieve a stable arrangement for directing the Communist movement. For one thing, the relations between the two states are already cluttered with a series of political, economic and military issues which keep mistrust alive. For another, there appears to be no intimacy, and little regard, between the leaders of the two powers. Most important, however, each has strongly-held views on the strategy which can best serve both its own interests and those of

SECT

SECRET

15

the movement, and the differences in these views go deeper than personal jealousies.

62. On the other hand, each side is aware of the immense damage that would result from an open rupture. It may be that both will take the events of 1960 as a warning not to allow their relations to become so openly bitter in the future. But, we believe that the course of these relations will be erratic, cooperative at some times and places, competitive at others. This course will also be influenced by external and even fortuitous factors. Western policy, for example, might act either to drive the USSR and China closer together or to widen the breach between them. Again, a major change in the leadership of either party, while it probably would not affect the fundamentals of their relationship, could alter the vigor with which one or the other prosecutes its claims.

63. Under these circumstances, with authority diffused and both Peiping and Moscow soliciting their support, the other parties will almost inevitably be tempted to bargain between them in order to obtain a greater measure of independence for themselves. Some of the parties in Eastern Europe, or factions within them, may attempt to develop further the autonomy conceded by Stalin's successors. In this connection, Yugoslavia, which stands as an example of a successful Communist state enjoying full independence, would exercise an increasingly strong attraction, particularly if Khrushchev's policies toward Belgrade belie the formal proscription of Yugoslavia as deviationist. In the Asian Satellites, where Chinese influence is already strong and has a good prospect of increasing, the regimes will be better able to bargain for economic and political support.

64. The parties outside the Bloc, even those still closely tied to Moscow, will also find their positions affected by Sino-Soviet competition. Some of these parties, particularly those which are less doctrinaire and less accustomed to close Soviet tutelage, will be inclined to select from differing Soviet and Chinese tactical advice whatever happens to fit their particular needs of the moment. Those smaller parties

of Asia, in which pro-Chinese inclinations are already strong, will probably tend to solidfy their ties with Peiping. The sharpest effects will probably be felt in those parties in the underdeveloped countries, such as India and Indonesia, which enjoy real political prospects and therefore must make important tactical choices. The two brands of advice, often sharply different, now being urged upon those parties will probably intensify the factionalism which already plagues their ranks.

A. Policy Effects

65. While the altered relationships within the Communist movement and the decline in Soviet authority have not altered the fundamental hostility of the Communists toward the non-Communist world, we believe that these developments are having an important influence on Communist policy. The Chinese Party, through the disputes of the past year, has already diminished to some extent the flexibility of Soviet policy toward the West, and the Soviet Party will probably encounter increasing difficulties in coordinating general Communist policy. Soviet and Chinese differences of view on general tactics for the parties as well as the differences in the national interests of the two states, are important enough to make the working out of an agreed course of policy more, rather than less, complicated. These difficulties may not be as serious in times when events generally favor Communist interests, but they may again erupt into open polemics during periods of adversity, or even at times when fundamental decisions are required for the exploitation of unfolding opportunities. This would be especially true if the Chinese thought the Soviets showed signs of making concessions to the West on important matters, or if the Soviets felt that Chinese actions threatened to involve the USSR in war.

66. The hardening of Soviet policy over the past year or so almost certainly owes something to the CPSU's desire to counter Chinese charges of insufficient revolutionary zeal. We think that this effort is partly responsible, for example, for the vigor with which the Soviets have attacked the West on the issues of

SECRET

colonialism and the structure of the UN. It may have played a part in their reversal of position in the nuclear test talks and their total subordination of disarmament policy to political struggle. This is not to say the Chinese can now exercise a veto power over Soviet policy. Moscow's present tactics appear to be guided by much the same calculations of risk which the Chinese earlier criticized as overly cautious. Nor has Khrushchev been deterred from renewing personal diplomacy with the US or reviving contacts with Yugoslavia, leaving Peiping to swallow its objections. But the Chinese probably have succeeded in limiting somewhat the USSR's freedom to engage the West on any basis other than militancy.

67. The development of the relationship between the USSR and China, and the evolution of the international Communist movement generally, will obviously be of profound significance for the security and interests of the West. In the long run Chinese power, assertiveness, and self-interest might increase so far as greatly to impair the common policy with the USSR, and even lead the Soviets to believe that they had more in common with the ideological enemy than they have today. For some time to come, however, the most likely prospect is that the USSR and China will maintain their relationship in something like its present form. It will be an alliance which is from time to time troubled and inharmonious, but which nevertheless preserves sufficient unity to act in concert against the West, especially in times of major challenge. However, present trends as described in this paper point to an increasing complexity, diversity, and interplay of forces within the Communist system, and to a remarkable survival of old-fashioned impulses of nationalism.

68. These trends may have various effects. They may from time to time result in more aggressive anti-Western policies intended to hold the forces of disunity in check. They may enable certain parties, free from the restrictions of a rigid, general Communist line, to pursue more effective policies in local situations. But eventually, if such trends persist, they may considerably diminish the effectiveness of the Communist movement as a whole. This would give the West opportunities for maneuver and influence which could provide important advantages in the world struggle.

SECRET

SECTION 20

NIE 13-63

Problems and Prospects
in Communist China

1 May 1963

APPROVED FOR RELEASE
DATE: MAY 2004

~~SECRET~~

NIE 13–63
1 May 1963

(b)(3)

NATIONAL INTELLIGENCE ESTIMATE

NUMBER 13–63

(Supersedes NIE 13–4–62 and
NIE 13–4/1–62)

Problems and Prospects
in Communist China

Submitted by the
DIRECTOR OF CENTRAL INTELLIGENCE
Concurred in by the
UNITED STATES INTELLIGENCE BOARD
As indicated overleaf
1 MAY 1963

~~SECRET~~

Nº 425

SECRET

PROBLEMS AND PROSPECTS
IN COMMUNIST CHINA

THE PROBLEM

To establish where Communist China now stands in its domestic situation and foreign policies, to identify the major problems it faces, and to estimate probable developments over the next two years or so and, where possible, further ahead.

CONCLUSIONS

A. Communist China's domestic situation appears slightly improved from its recent grievous state. To a considerable extent this improvement reflects relatively moderate, pragmatic policies which have replaced the excesses of the "leap forward" and commune programs. With good luck and good management, the economy could within the next couple of years resume a rapid rate of growth approaching that of the First Five-Year Plan, though it is likely to fall short of this. A critical question over the next five years will be whether the Chinese Communist leadership will sustain a pragmatic course in the face of its strong ideological compulsions. Unsound doctrinaire policies, bad weather, and other unfavorable factors could combine to cause complete economic stagnation. *(Paras. 1–6, 11–17)*

B. Though discontent will persist and could increase if the economic situation deteriorates, we do not believe that dissidence will pose any serious threat to the regime in the next two years. *(Para. 10)*

C. Communist China's economic difficulties and the drastic reduction of Soviet cooperation have lessened the relative effectiveness of Communist China's military establishment. Nevertheless, Peiping still has by far the strongest Asian army, and this is sufficient to support the kind of relatively cautious foreign

SECRET

1

SECRET

policies Peiping has actually been conducting or is likely to conduct during the next two years. It will almost certainly not have a militarily significant nuclear weapons system until well beyond this period.[1] *(Paras. 18–23)*

D. Peiping's dispute with Moscow springs from basic issues of incompatible national and party interests, and the Chinese Communists show no signs of relenting. Public polemics may be damped down on occasion, but we do not believe a fundamental reconciliation will take place. The Chinese will almost certainly continue to attempt to expand their influence at Soviet expense in the underdeveloped countries and to turn Communists throughout the world against Khrushchev and his policies. A formal schism could occur at any time, although the chances are reduced by each party's great anxiety to avoid the onus of having split the world Communist movement. *(Paras. 24–30)*

E. Communist China's foreign policy will probably continue generally along current lines. Peiping will remain passionately anti-American and will strive to weaken the US position, especially in east Asia, but is unlikely knowingly to assume great risks. China's military force will probably not be used overtly except in defense of its own borders or to assert territorial claims against India. Subversion and covert support of local revolutions will continue to be Peiping's mode of operation in southeast Asia and, to a necessarily more limited degree, elsewhere in Asia and in Africa and Latin America. *(Paras. 31–40)*

DISCUSSION

I. THE ROAD TO 1963

1. The situation in Communist China is a little better than it has been during the past two years. However, the effects of ill-advised policies and the almost total loss of Soviet support, intensified by a long spell of bad weather, have left a China that is far different from the one which, five years ago, so exuberantly undertook the risks of the economic "leap forward" and of assertive independence of Moscow.

2. By 1958, the Chinese Communist leaders had concluded that the country's rate of economic progress was unsatisfactory. Despite impressive growth in the industrial sector, China's agricultural produc-

---

[1] This question will be discussed in detail in NIE 13-2-63, "The Chinese Communist Advanced Weapons Program," (TOP SECRET) to be published soon.

2   SECRET

SECRET

tion had not increased sufficiently to feed a growing population, repay the Soviet credits, finance current imports, and provide capital for rapid industrial development. China's leaders apparently concluded that they could meet their economic problems only by a radical departure from Soviet techniques of economic development. Deciding to rely chiefly on manpower, their only readily available surplus resource, they suddenly and summarily organized the peasants in mid-1958 into huge super-collectives—communes—that were to regulate every phase of productive activity in the rural areas. At the same time they embarked on an all-out, frenetic drive for industrial and agricultural development under the banner of "the great leap forward."

3. This sharp divergence from the Soviet model was part and parcel of a developing Sino-Soviet dispute over a broad spectrum of military, economic, diplomatic, and ideological questions. By mid-1958, the Chinese leaders had apparently become convinced that the USSR did not intend to satisfy Chinese desires respecting advanced weapons, industrial development, and great power status. They initiated sharp new departures not only in economic development but in military programs. What was particularly galling to the USSR was Peiping's growing ideological assertiveness. Communist Chinese leaders became increasingly critical of Moscow's international policies. By the end of 1960 the USSR had responded by withdrawing most of its technicians, Soviet deliveries were declining sharply, and the rift between China and the Soviet Union had become wide and deep.

4. Communist China has paid a staggering price for these assertions of Chinese political and economic independence and the decisions of its leaders to force the rapid emergence of a great new China by radical means. The new Chinese theories of development created economic and psychological chaos. The drastic reduction of Soviet cooperation critically increased the regime's difficulties, and led to technical breakdown and disorganization in industry and drastic setback to Peiping's modern weapons programs. By the end of 1962, the nation's economy was generally no further along than it had been at the end of 1957. The Chinese people have spent five strenuous, painful years on a treadmill. And whereas the regime had entered 1958 with a great reservoir of respect and popular support, it now has to call upon a weary and disillusioned people to move the country forward.

5. The past several months have shown signs of improvement. The food situation eased somewhat in the summer of 1962, as a result of better weather, agricultural decentralization, and an increase in private plots and "free markets." There has been a rise in the production of agricultural support goods (e.g., tools, pumps, and fertilizer). These developments, and others such as the one-sided victory over Indian forces on the Himalayan border, appear to have improved popular morale somewhat and have probably reduced the dissidence potential.

SECRET

3

SECRET

6. Peiping's leaders have entered 1963 in a mood of some confidence. Although they admit to having set overambitious goals and committed other errors, they evince no doubts about the validity of Marxism-Leninism or the correctness of their interpretation of it. They place the major blame for past disasters upon cadre errors, unprecedentedly bad weather, and Soviet sanctions. They believe that by surviving these trials they have demonstrated the soundness of their regime. Communist China can now recover on its own, they apparently believe, and without the need to rely on external aid from an untrustworthy partner.

II. PROSPECTS

A. Political

7. The leadership elite of the Chinese Communist Party has not survived the crises of the past five years unscathed. In 1959 the Minister of Defense and the Armed Forces Chief of Staff were removed from office and disgraced. A few other key figures appear to have been shoved quietly into the background. A number of provincial First Secretaries and other middle-level officials have lost their jobs. At the lower levels of the party there has been a considerable increase in cynicism and a notable loss of elan.

8. The regime nevertheless remains under the control of essentially the same group of Long-March veterans who have led Chinese communism since the mid-1930's. Ultimate power still rests with Mao Tse-tung, although basic decisions are probably reached by leadership consensus. It is unlikely that the composition of the leader group will be seriously altered during the next two years or so, although the actuarial odds will be increasingly against this group—nearly all of whom are in their 60's or 70's. If Mao, who will be 70 this year, should die, he would probably be succeeded by Liu Shao-ch'i, the present Chairman of the government and Mao's designated heir, but Liu would not enjoy Mao's prestige and pre-eminence over his colleagues.

9. The Chinese Communist regime will almost certainly continue to adhere to its own brand of communism and to remain very much anti-US. The character and direction of its domestic policies over the next two years are, however, less certain. Beginning in 1960, Chinese leaders have relaxed pressures and controls and removed many of the coercive features of the commune and "great leap forward" programs. In the past few months they have begun to intensify political pressures and controls aimed at increasing central direction of the economy and curbing private activities. This recent behavior raises a question of the extent to which they may reverse over the next few years the more permissive and pragmatic courses which have helped alleviate the consequences of Peiping's earlier policies.

4　　　　　SECRET

SECRET

10. Any significant rise in public dissidence in the near future is unlikely. The bulk of the people, especially the four-fifths who constitute the peasantry, seem prepared to work stoically for very modest, direct rewards, as they have for centuries. For the most part, they will probably continue neither to combat nor support the regime, but will strive to ignore it. Judging from the limited available evidence, they will probably remain more interested in personal survival than in revolution. The regime will have somewhat greater difficulty with the young people, who are embittered by current drastic restrictions in educational opportunities and frustrated by very limited and arbitrarily assigned job opportunities. Dissidence tendencies would increase if the regime pushed political and economic controls too harshly or too far or if food supplies decreased sharply. We doubt, however, that conditions will deteriorate so far in the near future as to precipitate widescale resistance. Taipei is unlikely to receive decisive popular support for any military efforts short of a major invasion which had established momentum. Dissidence among national minorities (e.g., in Sinkiang) will almost certainly persist but remain localized.

B. Economic [2]

11. Communist China has the potential for substantial economic growth. It has good supplies of most of the natural resources needed by modern industry and it has a huge and hard working labor force. The much greater productivity of Japanese and Taiwanese fields indicates that Chinese agricultural output could be considerably increased. Properly managed, the economy of the Chinese mainland could provide a continually improving standard of living for a number of years to come, in spite of a population growth rate that may again rise to as much as 2.5 percent a year.

12. During the past five years, however, Communist China's economy has been grievously mismanaged. The leadership has been handicapped by inadequate economic training and experience, limited by a narrow doctrine, and misled by fanaticism. The Second Five-Year Plan was abandoned in its infancy in favor of the uncoordinated frenzy of the "leap forward." In addition, several consecutive years of very bad weather and the abrupt withdrawal of Soviet economic and technical cooperation further upset the economy.

13. Following the chaos of the past five years, Peiping has apparently decided to go ahead on schedule with a Third Five-Year Plan to cover the years 1963–1967. Since the plan is hardly beyond the preliminary stage and even the annual plan for 1963 has apparently not been formulated, the chief significance of announcing the Third Plan at this

---

[2] For details, see Annex A.

SECRET

5

SECRET

time is as a signal that the regime is, for the moment at least, intent upon returning to a systematically planned economy. The one big deviation from standard Communist practice is the order of priority for planning and investment: first, agriculture and those branches of heavy industry which support agriculture and national defense; then light industry; and finally industry in general. This stress on agriculture marks a belated recognition that greater agricultural investment is necessary to enable China to feed its people and that this is a prerequisite to a vigorous and rapidly growing heavy industry.

14. In any event, the outcome of the race between growth in agricultural production and growth in population will be constantly in doubt. In 1962, population stood at 60 million above the 1957 level, while grain production had no more than regained the 1957 level. To succeed in agriculture over a period of years, Peiping must not only minimize the depressing effects of collectivization and lowered incentives but stimulate production with increasing amounts of fertilizer, improved seed, better disease and insect control, better water conservancy, and more modern tools and techniques. It takes time and money to develop these resources and utilize them effectively. In the meanwhile, the critical factor may well prove to be Peiping's management of the peasantry. The outlook is not bright in this respect. Communist agricultural management has demonstrated itself in China, as elsewhere, to be a damper on productivity.

15. In industry there has been a modest improvement in performance in recent months, according to the scanty evidence available. The current stress on quality controls, coordination among industries, and the gearing of output to actual needs will, if continued, probably place industry on a sounder, more rational basis. The need for goods to provide incentives for labor and items for export has induced Peiping to give light industry priority over those branches of heavy industry that do not directly support agriculture or national defense. What is needed for a large increase in light industrial production is not so much new investment as reactivation of presently idle capacity; this, in turn, depends on increased supplies of raw materials from agriculture.

16. The margin between success and failure will remain so slim, and the variables so great, that any estimate of Communist China's overall economic future must be general and tentative. If the regime continues to pursue relatively moderate and rational policies and if it has reasonably good luck with the weather, the Communist Chinese should enjoy continued, though modest, recovery during the next year or so. This will result largely from returning idle capacity to production, and it will probably be accompanied by improvement of product quality, more effective coordination of the allocation of resources, and better maintenance and repair of equipment. Over the longer run, the imponderables increase, and a wide range of developments is well within the limits

6

SECRET

of possibility. We believe that the upper limit of what Peiping can achieve over the next five years, with the variables generally favorable, is a resumption of substantial economic growth approaching that of the First Five-Year Plan.

17. Of the variables which, unlike the weather, are subject to Peiping's control, the one which probably is of critical importance to the economy is national economic policy. The present order of economic priorities and the use of material incentives to stimulate production run against the grain of Peiping's doctrine. Both the strong Chinese craving for "modernity" and the doctrinaire Communist compulsion toward rapid industrialization militate against lasting primacy for agriculture. As soon as the Communist Chinese leaders judge the agricultural foundation to be adequate, they will almost certainly shift their emphasis to industrial expansion, and they may do so prematurely. Moreover, to renew a program of general development entailing large capital expenditures would require reimposition of stringent controls over consumption, distribution, and procurement of agricultural output. The regime may not be successful in increasing its take from the hard-pressed countryside, and, even if it is, the substitution of political pressures for economic incentives could again depress agricultural output and stimulate dissension against the regime. With this in mind, together with the possibility of adverse trends in such other variables as crop weather and foreign economic relations, we believe that the regime's economic achievements are likely to fall short of the upper limit described in the preceding paragraph. Furthermore, it is possible that a combination of unfavorable developments could result in economic stagnation which in time could critically erode the unity and strength of the regime.

C. Military [a]

18. The modernization of the armed forces, which was progressing steadily until about 1960, has practically ended, except for the continued introduction of radar and certain other electronic equipment. No advanced aircraft, submarine components, or other items of advanced equipment have been received from the USSR in the past two and one-half years, domestic production of fighter aircraft and submarines has ceased, and inventories are being reduced by deterioration and cannibalization. During the depths of the domestic decline, the military forces suffered shortages of even routine items of supply, but this condition has apparently been alleviated in the past year. In general, the army has been less affected than the other services.

19. Peiping almost certainly intends to achieve domestic production of all necessary weapons and materiel for its armed forces. It has a

---

[a] Annex B sets forth Order of Battle figures for Chinese Communist air, naval, and ground forces.

SECRET

7

SECRET

long way to go before reaching this goal, however. The Chinese at present are probably unable to produce even MIG-17's entirely by themselves, and it will be a number of years before they can design and produce more advanced types of military aircraft. Indeed they may have chosen instead to concentrate their limited resources on missiles. Their wholly domestic naval shipbuilding capacity is likely to be restricted to surface ships of the smaller types during the next few years.

20. Our knowledge of the morale of the Chinese Communist forces is minimal. From Chinese documents we know that morale was low during the depth of the food shortages (late 1960, early 1961) when the troops were underfed and overworked and were distressed by the even greater suffering of their families. Measures taken to ease the situation of the troops and to provide special rations to their families appeared to improve morale beginning in the latter half of 1961. The Chinese troops in the recent Sino-Indian border fighting displayed no indication of poor morale. Air force and navy units have not been similarly tested, however, and the decreasing effectiveness of their equipment, along with the inadequacy of training caused by fuel stringency and lack of spare parts, may have lowered morale in these services.

21. Additionally, there have been problems at top command levels, where the military policy of the party was apparently challenged. However, dismissal of Defense Minister P'eng Te-huai and the strengthening of security measures within the armed forces appears to have insured subservience to the party.

22. Peiping's military policy has always been characterized by caution in undertaking initiatives in the face of superior power. Hence the decline in the relative effectiveness of its military equipment and weapons is likely further to temper Peiping's policy, especially in circumstances where it might confront US armed power or US-equipped Asian air forces. However, the Chinese Communist Army will continue to be the strongest in Asia and to provide a powerful backing for Chinese Communist foreign policy. The Sino-Soviet dispute will probably place additional demands on Chinese military dispositions and capabilities, since one of the consequences of China's new "independence" from the USSR will be the need to keep a closer watch than previously on the long China-Russia border—which the Chinese still consider a "difficult" and "unsettled" question.

23. *Advanced Weapons.*[4] Peiping appears determined to achieve a nuclear and ballistic missile capability, and in time it will almost certainly do so, though it is not likely to acquire a militarily significant system until well beyond the period of this estimate. In the shorter term,

---

[4] This subject will be treated fully in the forthcoming NIE 13-2-63, "Communist China's Advanced Weapons Program," (TOP SECRET).

8

SECRET

the Chinese Communists probably hope to produce and detonate a nuclear device as a step toward developing this capability and in the expectation that this would boost morale at home, strengthen the regime's
claim to world power status, and inspire fear in its Asian neighbors. For
some time to come, even a limited effort in the nuclear and missile fields
will severely tax the regime's economic and technical resources.

D. Sino-Soviet Relations

24. We believe that Peiping's continued willingness to challenge Moscow's leadership in spite of the costs and risks involved is based principally on the following elements:

a. A conviction that Moscow's policies are inimical to Communist
China's national interests, and in particular that Moscow wishes to
retard or prevent Communist China's development as a leading world
power. The Chinese Communist leaders see Moscow's unwillingness
to confront the US as involving the postponement of such national goals
as the seizure of Taiwan. These differences are compounded by the
xenophobic emotions inherent in the Chinese racial, nationalistic, and
cultural pride and practices.

b. A determination that Peiping must be accepted as an equal partner
in the formulation of Bloc policies.

c. A conviction that Moscow is becoming increasingly revisionist and
bourgeois, abandoning classic revolutionary goals and destroying the
militancy of the world Communist movement. The Chinese are particularly outraged at what they interpret as attempts to temporize with
the US arch-enemy.

d. A conviction that in the present historical stage the victory of
communism will be won chiefly in the underdeveloped areas of the
world, and that the militant "path of Mao Tse-tung" provides the best
blueprint for the struggle in these areas.

e. A conviction that Moscow's "revisionist" policies are unacceptable
to significant elements in other Communist parties (particularly those
parties out of power) and even in the Soviet Party itself. This factor,
together with restiveness in many parties to Soviet domination, probably nurtures the conviction of the Chinese Communist leaders that
they will inevitably prevail.

25. The present Sino-Soviet relationship can be characterized as one
of *de facto* break. The two regimes have long been at odds on a wide
range of issues. Party and state contacts between them are minimal.
They are engaged in competitive proselytizing within the world Communist movement. During the past year, polemics have become increasingly bitter and explicit. There are even some indications of growing tensions along the Chinese-Russian borders.

SECRET

9

SECRET

26. Nevertheless, both parties have been at pains to avoid a formal break.[5] Each continues to preach the unity of the Communist movement. This is in part a device to throw on the other the blame for the disunity now apparent; both parties wish to avoid a situation which might involve a formal renunciation of the alliance and to avoid the onus for having forced such a break if it does in fact ensue. They share a mutual concern for the advantages that a formal break would give their common enemies, and for the damage it would do the world Communist movement. Additionally they wish, in view of their long common border, to keep some limits on hostility. Both sides probably hope that eventually, perhaps after the departure of the rival leadership, the other will see reason and make the critical concessions necessary to restore unity.

27. Bilateral Sino-Soviet discussions of differences may take place in the immediate future, but in any discussions that transpire the Chinese are likely to be truculent and assertive. Moscow will endeavor to temporize and avoid a dramatic and adverse denouement of the Sino-Soviet conflict, but will feel obliged to react forcefully if pushed hard enough. Thus a formal break is possible. It is also possible that at any time negotiations may result in a temporary damping down of the public aspects of the dispute, but the fundamental issues will persist. Sino-Soviet relations will continue to be plagued with tensions that will lead to continuing estrangement and have correspondingly adverse effects for Bloc and international Communist unity.

28. The practical effects of the dispute on Communist China will continue to be serious. China's industrial plant and military establishment will continue to suffer from lack of Soviet cooperation. Petroleum products now make up about half of China's imports from the USSR, and a further cutback here, especially in aviation fuel and high quality lubricants, would for a time seriously reduce Peiping's military capabilities. A cutoff of spare parts for Soviet equipment would also handicap both military and industrial progress. New foreign and domestic sources of supply could, however, probably be developed, in some cases fairly rapidly.

---

[5] Some confusion has surrounded assessments of the Sino-Soviet "break" and of its consequences. This paper seeks to make the following distinctions:

1. A break already exists in Moscow-Peiping relations—and may have existed since at least 1960: this we call a *de facto* break (paragraph 25).

2. Most discussions of whether or not a Sino-Soviet break will occur have been directed, in our view, to what should be called a *formal* break. Such a formal break could take many forms: unlike the Soviet-Yugoslav situation of 1948, there is, technically, no international Communist body from which to expel the CCP, or the CPSU. There could, however, be a severance of party relations, a formal and specific denunciation (possibly emanating from separate international Communist conferences), or any circumstances in which at least one of the protagonists states officially that a formal break now exists.

10   SECRET

29. Continuing estrangement will almost certainly cause Khrushchev increasing embarrassment within the CPSU, and also lead to more competition for adherents and influence throughout the world Communist movement, with China tending increasingly to assert itself as a rival center of truth, authority, and example. Peiping already appears to have displaced Soviet influence in North Korea. North Vietnam will continue to attempt to profit from its "neutralism," but it appears to be drifting toward Peiping. In Cuba, it is likely that the Chinese posture encourages Castro to reject Soviet advice which conflicts with his own predilections. Peiping will press its campaign to win over the leftist militants throughout non-Communist Asia, Africa, and Latin America, lining up the *ad hoc* support of parties where it can and settling for splinter factions elsewhere, e.g., Brazil. Further Chinese gains are probable in the Japanese and Indonesian Communist parties, at the expense not only of pro-Soviet factions but of Soviet interests and influence in those countries. We definitely do not expect the balance in the world Communist movement to shift to Peiping in the next two years—or, perhaps, ever.

30. Peiping may attract enough adherents in the underdeveloped areas of the world to cause the Soviets to adopt a somewhat more militant public posture in these areas, in an effort to outbid the Chinese for the support of selected revolutionary movements and to prove themselves true Marxist-Leninists. However, the USSR's actions in the Far East (as elsewhere) will almost certainly continue to spring principally from considerations of Soviet security and interests, not the status of relations with Peiping. Indeed, even if there were a formal Sino-Soviet break, the USSR would almost certainly intervene in any US–Chinese hostilities which threatened to establish a non-Communist regime in China along the USSR's borders.

E. Foreign Affairs

31. Peiping is engaged in a struggle with Moscow for influence in the Communist Parties of the underdeveloped nations of Asia, Africa, and Latin America. The Chinese Communists believe that they are uniquely fitted to lead this major portion of the world's peoples into communism because of their own experience, their correct interpretation of Marxism-Leninism, and their status as a nonwhite, non-European people who have been victims of imperialism. According to Peiping's reasoning, when these nations are brought into the "Socialist camp," the Western capitalists, deprived of their captive markets, will be unable to retain their positions of power, and socialism will triumph.

32. Peiping recognizes that this is a long-term objective which at present it lacks the capability to bring about. It can provide very little material aid to Communist revolutions except in countries on which it borders, e.g., Laos. Thus a limited and somewhat opportunistic policy

11

SECRET

is followed, with the aim of reducing the US and Western presence in Asia and (with lesser priority) the rest of the underdeveloped world.

33. Peiping's foreign policy objectives can be roughly distinguished by the amount of risk the regime is prepared to take to carry them out. The obvious first rank objective is the preservation of the regime and the protection of its existing boundaries. For these purposes Peiping is willing to go to war, almost regardless of the odds. If US or SEATO troops approached its borders through Laos or North Vietnam, Peiping would almost certainly be ready to commit its forces openly, unless in the particular circumstances it saw greater advantage in more covert military operations. The acquisition of Taiwan falls in the second rank of objectives—those for which Peiping is fully prepared to use overt military force, but only when the prospects of success are judged to be high. To achieve this goal, Peiping is prepared to run fewer risks and is particularly anxious to avoid direct conflict with the US. Peiping almost certainly will not attempt to seize by military force either Taiwan or any of the major offshore islands which it believes the US would help Taipei to defend.

34. For its broader and longer range goals of spreading communism throughout the underdeveloped world, Peiping is probably not prepared to accept any substantial risk, although it must be noted that Peiping tends to estimate the risks involved in supporting "wars of national liberation" much lower than does Moscow. Peiping apparently does not intend to undertake overt conquests of foreign lands in the name of communism, but intends to let indigenous revolutionaries do the fighting and the "liberating." Peiping is prepared to train foreign nationals in guerrilla and political warfare, and will back revolutionary movements to the extent of its limited capabilities with equipment, funds, propaganda, and support in international affairs.

35. Peiping's approach to world affairs is strongly influenced by Chinese nationalism. Chinese nationalistic feelings have been an asset to the regime domestically and have shaped certain courses of foreign policy quite apart from, and sometimes contrary to, the interests of communism. The Sino-Indian confrontation in the Himalayas is a case in point. Here, Chinese national interests and motivations took precedence over the interests of the Indian Communist Party.

36. During the next two years, Peiping will remain active in southeast Asia. In Laos, Peiping will continue to encourage and aid North Vietnamese and Pathet Lao efforts to dominate the country. There is already a Communist Chinese presence in the country, and the nucleus of a Chinese-built road network is designed to increase ties to mainland China. These roads could also facilitate the movement of Chinese troops if an eruption of fighting in Laos were to bring US or SEATO forces into the area. Peiping will encourage and support subversive

12

SECRET

SECRET

activities in Thailand, and will probably try to exploit racial and other tensions in the emerging Federation of Malaysia. In some parts of southeast Asia, the overseas Chinese provide an instrument for Peiping, but they are unpopular in the host countries and in many areas appear to be less responsive than formerly to Peiping. Peiping's long-range goals almost certainly envisage the gaining of dominant influence over the area and the exploitation of its economic riches.

37. Communist China's policies toward its two greatest Asian neighbors, India and Japan, are likely to continue along approximately the present lines through the next two years or so. The Chinese Communist leaders wrote off Nehru some time ago as a bourgeois nationalist whose usefulness to them has passed and who therefore need no longer be courted. They now are aiming to diminish India's stature as an alternative model of development and to undermine its status as a leader of the nonaligned and Afro-Asian blocs. They almost certainly have no intention of invading India beyond Chinese-claimed territory during the next two years, though they will respond vigorously to anything they consider a provocation. In any case they will carry on a continuous political campaign against the Indian leadership. In the case of Japan, Peiping will simultaneously strive to gain dominant influence in the Japanese Communist Party; nudge the Socialists and other leftists into more militant and anti-US courses; bid for Japanese businessmen's support, by dangling trade prospects before them; woo the Japanese public with propaganda and people-to-people diplomacy; and demand recognition from the existing Japanese Government.

38. Communist China will continue to exert considerable influence in Asia, almost regardless of developments in its domestic and foreign policies. The depressed conditions of life in China have somewhat tarnished the image of China held widely in Asia. However, this effect will probably prove short-lived, especially if mainland China regains some of its former economic momentum. More important, fear of Communist China will almost certainly continue and may grow. Even now, the policies of several Asian countries, especially Burma and Cambodia, are conditioned in important measure by desire not to provoke Peiping.

39. Fear will also be increased by detonation of Communist China's first nuclear device, though the psychological impact will not be as great as would have been the case had the Chinese detonation come suddenly a few years ago. Initially at least, most Asian governments will make new and most earnest inquiry into US intentions for the defense of east Asia and the western Pacific.

40. Peiping's intense anti-Americanism is deeply rooted both in Communist doctrine and in militant Chinese nationalism. This attitude will almost certainly persist as long as the present group of leaders remains in control, and there is no reason to anticipate a softening by their suc-

SECRET

13

SECRET

cessors. Peiping remained antagonistic toward the West even in the winter of 1961–1962, when the regime's fortunes were in many ways at their lowest ebb and it had fears for its own security. The regime might make minor concessions for expediency, but in the foreseeable future it will almost certainly not abandon its basic anti-American attitude.

14

SECRET

SECRET

ANNEX A

ECONOMIC

I. ECONOMIC PERFORMANCE IN 1962

1. In 1962, the moderate economic policies adopted in the winter of 1960–1961 were continued. Private activity in agriculture and in rural trade was still permitted. Major industrial goals included the expansion of production to support agriculture and the expansion of output in light industry, handicrafts, and the mining and timber industries. Emphasis was placed on improvement of quality, on cost reduction, on increases in output per worker, and on better care of equipment.

2. The communique issued after the 10th Plenum of the 8th Party Congress, which met secretly in Peiping on 24–27 September 1962, suggests that the retrenchment and consolidation prevailing in 1961 and 1962 will be generally continued for the time being, but that some tightening up of discipline in economic affairs is considered necessary to direct and mobilize resources as a condition for a more organized development effort. To these ends, the party appears to have decided (a) to retain recent emphases on more conservative management policies for industry, policies which are similar to those that prevailed in 1957; (b) to retain the "leap forward" and "communes," at least as concepts; and (c) to permit no further retreat in collectivization of agriculture, and as a corollary, to restrict private "capitalist" tendencies in the countryside.

3. Economic information, either officially released or independently acquired, continues to be extremely fragmentary. Official claims note advances in some areas of production in 1962; refugee, diplomatic, and traveler reports indicate improvement in the supply of some foods and other consumer goods; and weather data suggest slightly better growing conditions during the year for the country as a whole. These bits and pieces, together with Peiping's more optimistic outlook since September, suggest moderate improvement in an extremely difficult situation. Even with improvement in 1962, serious problems still remain in every major sector of an economy that probably is no more productive than it was in 1957.

A. Agriculture

4. A slight increase in production of grain appears to have occurred in 1962,* but from 1960 and 1961 levels which were abnormally low. Production of grain in 1962 is estimated to have been on the general order

---

*Our estimates of output are based primarily on weather data, although the probability of somewhat larger acreage of fall grain crops and slightly increased supplies of chemical fertilizer also have been taken into consideration.

SECRET

15

SECRET

of the 185 million metric tons harvested in 1957, when the population was about 10 percent smaller. The average diet in the 1962–1963 consumption year has probably improved above that of the previous consumption year, largely as the result of increased production on private plots. The food situation remains stringent, but no longer desperate.

5. The expected level of grain imports by China in the 1962–1963 consumption year (July–June) suggests that domestic production and stocks are far from comfortable. Contracts have already been signed for delivery of about 3.3 million metric tons of grain during the first six months of 1963—about the amount imported during the same period of 1962. We estimate that five million tons of grain will be imported during the 1962–1963 consumption year. This is a million tons less than in the previous year but still amounts to about four percent of total food grain consumption. By comparison, China exported about one million tons of grain in 1957.

6. The acreage planted to cotton in 1962 was about half that planted in 1957, and the output was correspondingly only about half the 1.64 million tons produced in 1957.

B. Industry

7. In 1962, the Chinese Communists seem to have achieved moderate success in industry. Compared with 1961, there appear to have been increases in the output of priority goods such as chemical fertilizer, some farm implements, and many types of light industrial and handicraft products. Output per employed worker probably increased somewhat, although in large part this resulted from laying off excess labor and thereby adding to the problem of unemployment. Technical and managerial personnel were accorded greater prestige and responsibility. Problems of quality, cost, and maintenance of equipment eased somewhat, but still persist as obstacles to industrial efforts.

8. The available evidence, which is fragmentary, suggests that total industrial production in 1962 was about equal to that of 1957, or roughly half the 1959–1960 peak. Production of agricultural chemicals, some farm equipment and tools, and a number of light industrial products was considerably above the level of 1957, but production of the machine building and textile industries was below that of 1957. Production of steel and electric power may have been at roughly the level of 1958.

9. Shortages of food for industrial workers, the insufficient supply of agricultural raw material, and the regime's shift to priorities in favor of agriculture account for only part of the difficulties in industry. In addition the industrial sector has been severely damaged by the excesses of the "leap forward," which produced neglect and abuse of equipment, shoddy construction, and wasteful imbalances in the capacity of inter-

16

SECRET

SECRET

dependent enterprises and industries. Greatly compounding all these problems was the withdrawal of Soviet technicians, the drop in Sino-Soviet trade, and the drying up of opportunities for study in the USSR and Eastern Europe. The cumulative effect of these handicaps has been serious.

10. Many industrial plants are producing far below capacity. The reason for this situation in light industry is clear: the inability to obtain the necessary raw materials from agriculture. The explanation for idle capacity in heavy industry is more complex. Some heavy industrial plants—for example, aircraft, shipbuilding, truck, and chemical fertilizer plants—are producing below capacity because of the lack of spare parts, key components, raw materials, or technical expertise. These deficiencies exist in the plants themselves or in industries supplying components and raw materials. In addition, the drastic cutback in the investment program and the sharp decline in industrial output has lessened the need for basic heavy industrial items such as steel, electric power, construction materials, and some types of machinery. In the industries supporting agriculture, however, especially the chemical industry, additional plant and managerial-technical personnel are sorely needed.

11. We believe that factories producing military equipment have been able barely to keep up with peacetime attrition on some important items of military equipment. Production rates at some existing facilities may have recovered somewhat from the low levels of 1960–1961, but except in the electronic field we believe that little or no headway was made in the program to modernize the equipment of the armed forces. Almost certainly, no significant additions were made to the capacities of industries producing conventional armaments.

12. It is estimated that the total availability of petroleum products in Communist China in 1962 was slightly less than in 1959, the last year for which there is reliable data, but supplies apparently were adequate to meet the essential needs of both civilian and military consumers, though on an austere basis. Of the total supply, about 70 percent was produced domestically, as compared with 50 percent in 1959. Communist China, as far as is known, has not produced aircraft fuels except on a trial basis, and continues to rely on imports from the USSR. The Chinese, however, have the capability of producing jet fuel, although such production would necessarily reduce output of other petroleum products, and difficulties with quality probably would be encountered. China probably does not have the capability to produce high-test aviation gasoline and certain high-quality lubricants.

C. Foreign Trade

13. The reduction in agricultural products available for export, the deterioration in Sino-Soviet relations, the cutback in investment, and the decline of industrial output have combined to lower China's total

SECRET

SECRET

volume of trade and to alter its direction and composition sharply. Total trade in 1962 may have amounted to as little as $2.5 billion, compared with $4.2 billion in 1959. Trade with the USSR declined from a peak of $2.0 billion in 1959 to perhaps as low as $600 million in 1962. Imports of petroleum products, almost all from the USSR, declined from 3.2 million metric tons in 1961 to 1.9 million tons in 1962, although imports of aircraft fuels and high-quality lubricants in 1962 continued at the level of 1961. The regime is now concentrating on imports of foodstuffs and raw materials; machinery and equipment imports fell off about 85 percent between 1959 and 1962. In November 1962, the Chinese Communists concluded a long-term trade agreement with Japan and throughout the year were actively contacting Western suppliers of industrial products, but few deals of any size or importance have been concluded as yet. China's foreign exchange position remained tight in 1962, but the regime managed to meet its obligations promptly.

D. Transportation

14. In 1962 all forms of transportation in Communist China appeared to be operating at about the 1961 level or lower, with the possible exception of coastal shipping, which is reported to have been more active during the latter part of the year. Although efficiency and capacity continued to be hampered by poor administration, low worker morale, insufficient and low-quality fuel, and lack of materials for maintenance, the transport system is apparently supporting the economy with less difficulty than in recent years, largely because decreased economic activity has greatly reduced demands on the system. The impressive earlier program for extending China's transportation network, which was abandoned in the collapse of the "leap forward," remained in abeyance during 1962. Except for construction on militarily significant roads in Yunnan and Tibet, there was little construction during 1962 on major railways and highways. Production of locomotives, freight cars, and trucks remained at very low levels. Maintenance and production of spare parts for transportation equipment probably improved little if at all.

E. Education and Science

15. In the fall of 1962, the regime drastically curtailed student enrollment at all levels and closed many substandard schools. As a result, some five million high school and college-level students were thrown on the already saturated labor market. This has caused great disappointment among students and their parents. The drastic decision to retrench was undoubtedly a difficult one for the regime to make; it was probably taken to avoid a further diminution in the quality of education, but it may eventually lead to even greater disillusionment and resentment.

18   SECRET

SECRET

16. A comprehensive 12-year plan for science, which was to have run from 1956 through 1967, has been at least revised and possibly abandoned. In 1962, the regime began to woo the Western-trained scientists who had been ignored or suppressed during the "leap forward." Emphasis is now being placed upon quality in scientific training and research, and political interference in the scientific and academic community has been markedly reduced. The call for scientific support of agricultural development seems to be increasing.

II. PROSPECTS

A. Short-Term Prospects

17. The Chinese Communist leaders seem to have drawn confidence from having weathered the extreme crisis of the past three years and have entered 1963 in a mood of cautious optimism. However, they forecast no major increases in production in 1963, and are hoping for an "upsurge" in 1964 if all goes well, hinging on their success in securing further increases in grain output while restoring production of industrial crops. Their foreign trade negotiations also seem pointed towards 1964; their trade missions in western Europe have frankly stated that they are exploring equipment availabilities on which firm import decisions will not be taken before the fall of 1963.

18. While only modest economic growth at best is expected in 1963, the outlook for 1964 and 1965 is obscure. The generally depressed agricultural situation still colors the entire economic outlook, although, given average weather, further moderate agricultural recovery seems likely. The prospects are fair for restoring industrial crop production, and the resulting light industry expansion could increase industrial output by about five percent annually in 1964-1965. Even greater increases in industrial output might be secured if the regime can reorient its foreign trade to support a substantial expansion in capital construction. With an apathetic population, low food stocks, unsettled foreign trade relations, and heavy foreign debt service obligations, it seems unlikely that China can organize the domestic and foreign resources for a rapid increase in investment. But even without increased investment, greater utilization of presently idle capacity could increase industrial output by 5-10 percent a year in 1964-1965.

B. Future Economic Policy

19. Communist China's economic prospects depend heavily on whether the leadership in Peiping will postpone its goal of transforming China into a modern industrial and military power long enough to insure a safe margin in agricultural production. A Communist state has never before given first priority to agricultural development. The leaders

SECRET

19

SECRET

have certainly been burned by the catastrophic failure of the 1958–1960 "leap forward" and will presumably be extremely chary of risking a repetition. The composition of the leadership's top echelon remains essentially unchanged, however, and its record is such that a return to radical, politically charged programs cannot be ruled out. The likelihood of a return to such programs will increase in the longer term if progress toward cherished goals appears to lag.

20. In November 1962, several high-ranking officials, including four Politburo members, were appointed to the State Planning Commission, which suggests that a high-level task force has been formed to draw up a Third Five-Year Plan. The plan, when and if it appears, is likely to be more of a political than a planning document, for the uncertainties confronting the regime would seem to preclude detailed long-term planning. Its goals are likely to be general and qualitative rather than specific, and the regime would probably view it as an important instrument for attempting to inspire confidence, unify the country, and galvanize support.

C. Agriculture

21. The regime intends to continue to give priority to agriculture, and Peiping appears to be thinking in terms of an agricultural modernization program that will require 20 to 25 years. Certain elements of this program seem reasonable and feasible for expanding farm output, such as the emphases on research and extension facilities, promotion of chemical fertilizer, electrification, and irrigation. Other pronouncements calling for rapid mechanization, strengthened collectivization, and "politics leading economics" could lead to adverse effects on farm output through inflexible management, lack of peasant production incentives, and a concentration on releasing rural manpower for industry.

22. Even if the reasonable elements in the leadership prevail, there still can be no speedy solution in agriculture. If increased supplies of chemical fertilizer and other inputs are to yield maximum results, they must be accompanied by improved varieties of seeds and improved farming practices. Research and extension services (and, above all, the trained technicians to man them) cannot be created overnight, nor can they be expected to bear fruit on any scale within less than a decade. Furthermore, it remains to be seen just how much effect the recent steps toward centralization will have on the crucial question of peasant incentives.

D. Industry

23. Current emphasis on industries producing goods for agriculture and for consumers is likely to continue for at least the next year or so. Some branches of heavy industry that cannot now produce enough to meet the requirements of the priority sectors of the economy are likely to

20

SECRET

SECRET

be allocated increased resources for expansion of plant and technical competence. These are likely to include mining, producers of chemicals and machinery for agriculture, producers of some chemical raw materials for light industry, and industries that will help to broaden Chinese technological capabilities. The latter group of industries will be needed to develop a native capability for producing a wide variety (though not necessarily a large volume) of complex machinery and selected metals and chemicals, which in turn will be needed in the development of chemical fertilizer industries and the production of nuclear weapons and guided missiles.

24. Prospects for resuming industrial growth are contingent on recovery in agriculture. If agriculture recovers, even to a level representing less than the per capita output attained in 1957, industrial production could be pushed rapidly for a year or two because idle capacity exists in many industries. After existing capacity is put to use, however, growth in industrial production would slow down if present goals—which stress variety and quality rather than quantity—are retained. Yet if present goals are reversed, agriculture and, possibly, popular responses, will suffer. In any event, the slogan of overtaking Great Britain in 10 to 15 years in total production of basic industrial items is now dead. Similarly, the regime has dropped its one-time goal of producing 40 million tons of crude steel by 1967, and probably would now be satisfied if it attained half that amount.

E. Foreign Trade

25. Prospects for major increases in foreign trade are poor, partly because of Peiping's heightened desire for autarky. Present evidence suggests that Sino-Soviet trade in 1963 will continue at no more than the low level of 1962. Although China plans to turn to the non-Communist world to replace some Bloc sources of machinery, such purchases probably will be selective. Moreover, because of foreign exchange stringency, the Chinese will probably seek to import technology mainly by importing prototypes, including whole plants, to be copied in China. Yet the Chinese machine building industry is too backward to undertake a rapid buildup of industrial capacity.

26. Further disruptive effects on China's economy would follow a complete Sino-Soviet break, but the Chinese could recover from this break if they were willing to pay the economic and political costs of increasing their trade with non-Bloc countries. Of the total Chinese exports to the Soviet Bloc in 1961 ($700 million), approximately $350–$450 million could be sold in non-Bloc countries and another $170 million would represent Chinese debt repayments to the USSR, no longer required. The Chinese could import from non-Bloc countries all of the chemicals and metals imported from the Soviet Bloc in 1961, and nearly all of the machinery and equipment, the POL, and the

SECRET

SECRET

industrial raw materials. Japan would represent a complementary trading partner for the Chinese, although Western Europe would be a keen competitor for the Japanese. Large-scale diversion of Chinese trade from Bloc to non-Bloc countries would involve initial costs to the Chinese of developing new markets for their exports and new sources for their imports, and would require costly and time-consuming adjustments to Western specifications for most machinery imports. More important, such a diversion of trade would place restraints on Chinese foreign policy, including the subordination of political goals in trade with Japan, and the willingness to supply technical data to foreign businessmen, to accept non-Bloc technicians in China, and to send Chinese personnel outside the Bloc for training.

27. The outlook for trade with Japan is obscure, in spite of the signing of a long-term trade agreement in November 1962. Japan could be a highly profitable market for low-price, bulky minerals such as salt, magnesite, coal, and iron ore that are hard for China to sell elsewhere. But erratic and unstable political relations have discouraged potential Japanese industrial users from regarding Communist China as a source for large quantities of such products. Nevertheless, Sino-Japanese trade has been rising slowly and may continue to expand.

28. Peiping would probably wish to reserve a substantial amount of foreign exchange for future grain purchases during 1963–1965, but during this period Peiping is obligated to liquidate a Soviet trade debt of about $500 million, and to pay nearly another $500 million on outstanding grain credits and on existing food purchase commitments. These figures suggest little margin for an increase in imports.

F. Education and Science

29. Although it has done much to correct damaging excesses in the fields of education and science, the regime now faces the difficult and delicate task of stretching the limited resources of the intellectual community to achieve immediate production results—in such fields as the mechanization of agriculture and the modernization of weapons. At the same time training and development programs of sufficient depth and scope must be undertaken to overcome China's backwardness across a wide range of disciplines. Communist China has isolated itself from much current scientific development throughout the rest of the world, except indirectly through scientific journals.

30. Communist China's research and development effort still suffers from a very critical shortage of scientific and technical manpower in the upper levels of competence and experience. Almost as critical is the shortage of experienced scientists capable of independent research but with abilities below those of the top rank; these are the men who form the main body of researchers in a mature scientific community. On the other hand, China is much better supplied with persons trained

22   SECRET

as technicians and highly specialized engineers. China had a great need for such types and has used them in providing technical services to the economy, particularly in engineering development work aimed at adapting foreign designs and p...cesses to conditions in China.

31. The total number of college graduates by itself is impressive— over one million, with nearly 600,000 in scientific and technical fields, inclu...'ng medicine and public health. These figures in themselves, however, are n?t true indicators of China's research and development capabilities because the average quality of the graduates is not high. Communist China is believed to have some 2,000 to 3,000 highly quali- fied scientists in research and development. Among the scientific lead- ers and the main body of experienced scientists and technologists, there exists a useful degree of competence in practically all scientific and engineering fields. The regime thus has the resources to assemble a team of researchers competent to attack almost any objective, but not enough to man many teams effectively at the same time.

32. The regime's new attitude toward research and training is prob- ably producing an improved environment for research and development and should permit reasonably effective scientific and technological sup- port during the next few years.

G. Population

33. Regardless of what approach the Chinese Communists may take to economic recovery in the next five years, the population pressure on food resources will continue to be a major underlying problem. The rate of population growth averaged an estimated 2.4 percent from 1953 through 1958, slowed down to 1.5 to 2.0 percent in recent years, and probably will rise if average diets improve. Marxist doctrine would make it awkward for the regime to push an all-out birth control cam- paign. Even if this were not so, Peiping may feel it could do little to control the birth rate effectively, especially in rural areas where social beliefs are hard to change and medical services are poor. Since the spring of 1962, a low-key campaign has been conducted in urban areas to encourage late marriages and family planning, but this policy will have only a negligible effect on the national birth rate within the next decade.

[p 24 omitted -- nonsubstantive]

SECRET

ANNEX B

ORDER OF BATTLE TABLES

TABLE 1

AIR FORCES
(As of 1 April 1963)

CCAF

TYPE OF AIRCRAFT	ROLE	NUMBER [a]	TOTAL
FAGOT (MIG–15)	Fighter (Day)	690	—
FARMER (MIG–19)	Fighter (Day)	60	—
FRESCO (MIG–17)	Fighter (Day)	815	—
FRESCO D (MIG–17D) [b]	Fighter (Day)	145	1,710
BEAST (IL–10)	Ground Attack [c]	40	40
BAT (TU–2)	Light Bomber, piston	100	—
BEAGLE (IL–28)	Light Bomber	175	—
BULL (TU–4)	Medium Bomber, piston	15	290
C46/C47	Transport	30	—
CAB	Transport	35	—
COACH	Transport	35	—
COLT	Transport	25	—
COOT	Transport	2	—
CRATE	Transport	45	172
TOTAL			2,212

CCNAF

FAGOT	Fighter (Day)	170	—
FRESCO	Fighter (Day)	70	—
FRESCO D	Fighter (Day)	30	270
BAT	Light Bomber	5	—
BEAGLE	Light Bomber	150	155
CAB	Transport	15	—
COLT	Transport	5	—
CRATE	Transport	5	25
MADGE	Reconnaissance	10	10
TOTAL			460

TOTAL AIR FORCE PERSONNEL 82,000

---

[a] Figures rounded to nearest five.

[b] FRESCO D has a limited all-weather capability.

[c] In addition, a unit of 30 MIG–15 (FAGOTs) is specially trained in ground attack. All FAGOT/FRESCOs are adaptable to ground attack, but have poor range and load-carrying characteristics.

SECRET

25

SECRET

TABLE 2

NAVAL FORCES
(As of 1 April 1963)

SHIPS

TYPE/CLASS	TOTAL	ORIGIN	REMARKS
Old Destroyer/"GORDYY"	4	Soviet transfers	Obsolescent; built in 1941.
Destroyer Escort/"RIGA"	4	Chinese-built	Extensive Soviet technical and material assistance involved.
Submarine/"W"	21 or 23	Chinese-built	Extensive Soviet technical and material assistance involved. Completion of 4 units following Soviet withdrawal is believed to have been accomplished by the Chinese.
Submarine/"S-1"	4	Soviet transfers	Obsolescent; built in 1941.
Submarine/"M-V"	3	Soviet transfers	Coastal submarine. Obsolescent.

PATROL

TYPE/CLASS	TOTAL	ORIGIN	REMARKS
Patrol Escort/Various Classes	15	Taken over in 1949	All of WW-II (or earlier) design.
Submarine Chaser/ "KRONSHTADT"	25	6 units Soviet transfers; 19 units Chinese-built	Soviet aid needed for Chinese-built units.
Motor Torpedo/"P-6" "P-4"	80+ 70+	Chinese-built Soviet transfers	Soviet aid needed for Chinese-built units.
Fast Patrol Boat/ "SHANGHAI"	12	Chinese-built	Chinese design.
Motor Gunboat	44	Chinese-built	Some Soviet components used for Chinese-built units.

MINESWEEPERS

TYPE/CLASS	TOTAL	ORIGIN	REMARKS
Fleet Minesweeper/ "T-43"	14	12 Chinese-built 2 Soviet transfers	Soviet aid involved in Chinese program.
Minesweepers, Coastal (Old)	4	Taken over in 1949	US WW-II design.
Minesweeper, Auxiliary	20	Some Chinese-built; some taken over in 1949	Limited to in-shore minesweeping.

26   SECRET

SECRET

TABLE 3

GROUND FORCES
(As of 1 April 1963)

	UNITS	ESTIMATED STRENGTH
Infantry Divisions	107	69 @ 15,000
		38 @ 14,000

   3 infantry regiments
   1 artillery regiment
   1 tank-assault gun regiment (in 69 divisions)
   1 AA battalion
   1 AT battalion
     Principal weapons:
       24 light and medium field artillery pieces
       39 x 57/76-mm AT guns
       120 light and medium mortars
       12 light AA pieces
       32 medium tanks
       12 self-propelled assault guns

	UNITS	ESTIMATED STRENGTH
Armored Divisions	4	@ 6,600

   2 armored regiments
   1 infantry regiment
   1 artillery regiment
     Principal weapons:
       10 heavy tanks
       80 medium tanks
       14 self-propelled assault guns
       20 light and medium field artillery pieces
       12 light AA pieces
       57 light and medium mortars

	UNITS	ESTIMATED STRENGTH
Airborne Divisions	3	@ 7,000
Cavalry Divisions	3	@ 5,000
TOTAL LINE DIVISIONS	117	
Field Artillery Divisions	12	@ 5,500
	1	@ 7,000
	1	@ 7,800

   3 gun or gun-howitzer regiments
   1 AA battalion
     Principal weapons:
       108 pieces 122-mm to 152-mm
       12 light AA pieces

	UNITS	ESTIMATED STRENGTH
Antitank Divisions	3	@ 3,400

   4 antitank regiments
   96 56-mm to 100-mm AT guns

	UNITS	ESTIMATED STRENGTH
Antiaircraft Divisions	9	various
Border Defense and Military Internal Security Divisions	15	@ 7,000
TOTAL GROUND FORCE PERSONNEL	2,632,000	

NOTE: The Ground Forces are organized into 34 armies and a number of independent divisions and other units.

28

SECRET

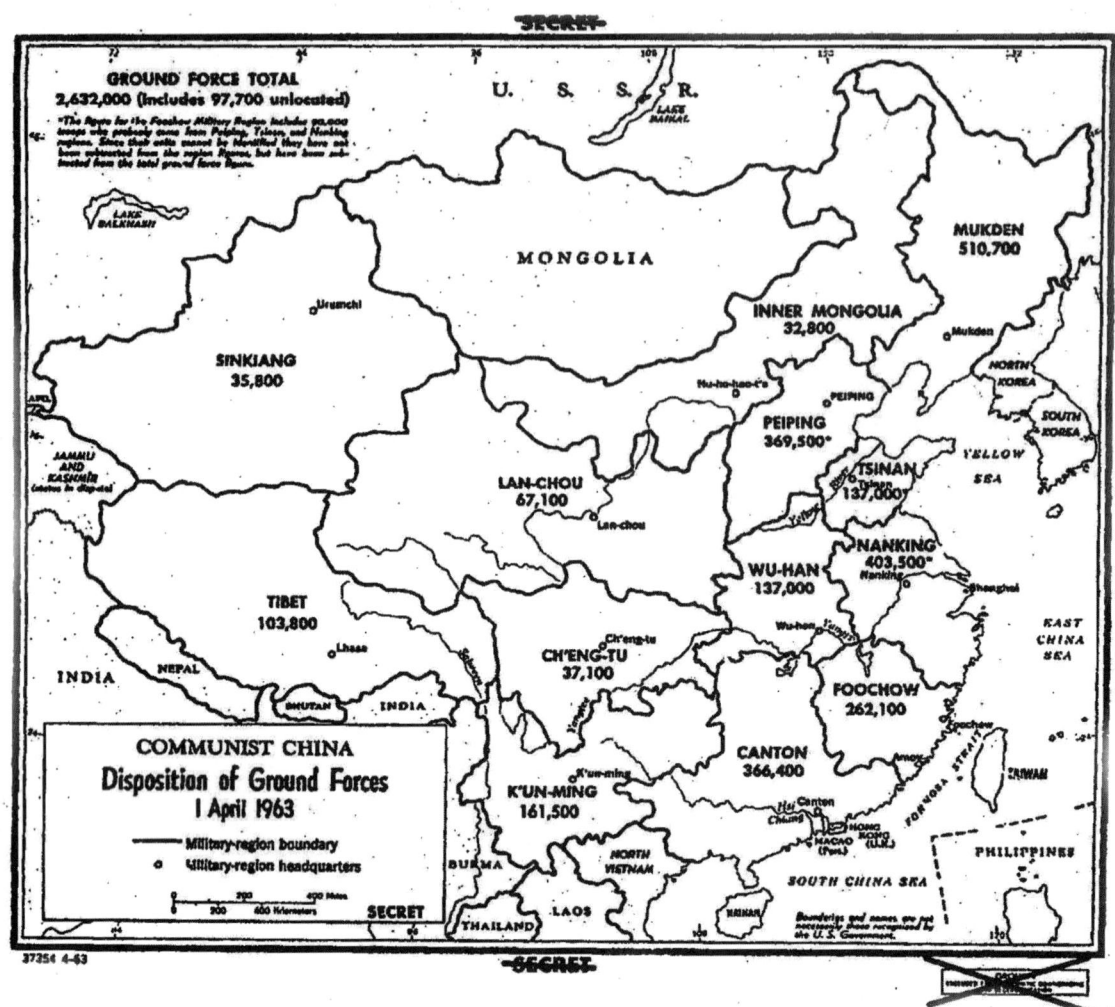

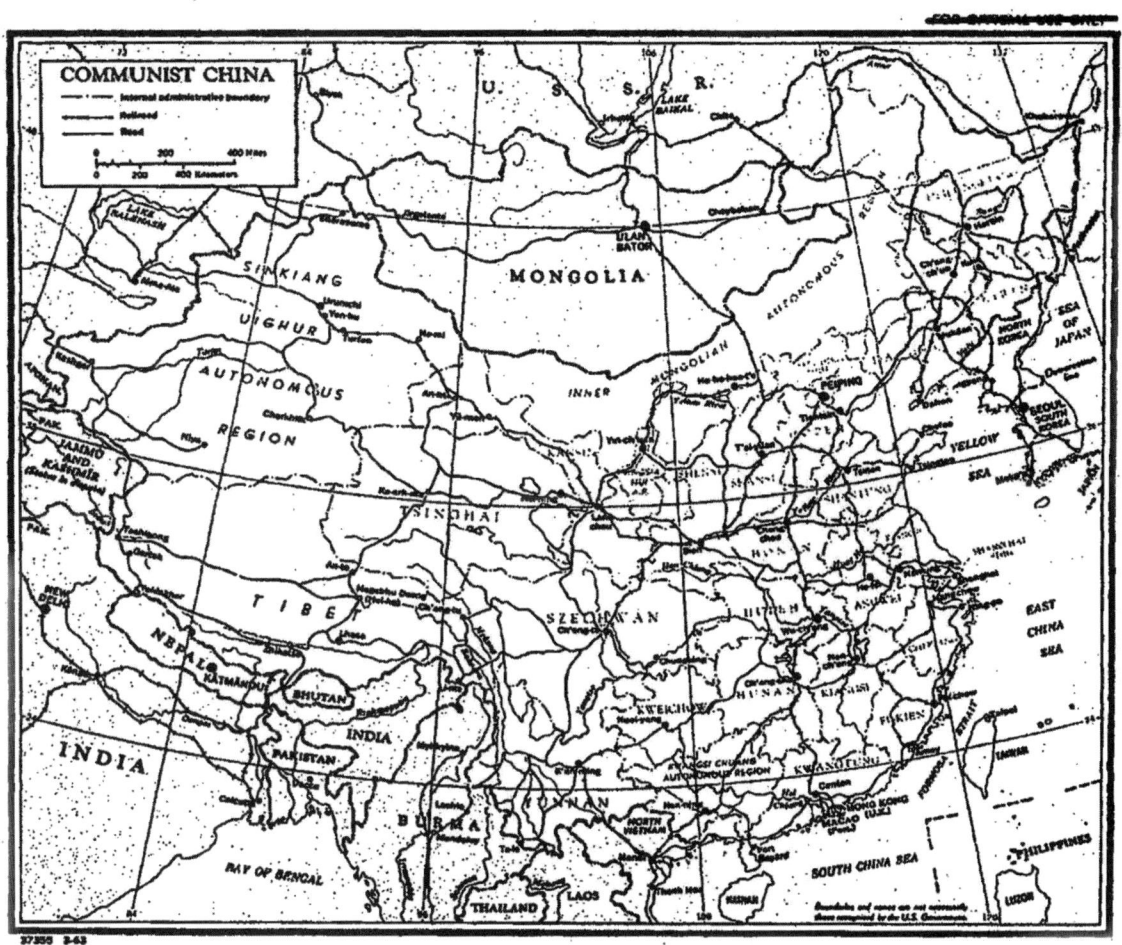

SECTION 21

SNIE 13-4-64

The Chances of an Imminent Chinese
Communist Nuclear Explosion

26 August 1964

APPROVED FOR RELEASE
DATE: MAY 2004

SNIE 13-4-64
26 August 1964

(b)(1)
(b)(3)

SPECIAL NATIONAL INTELLIGENCE ESTIMATE
13-4-64

The Chances of an Imminent

Communist Chinese Nuclear Explosion

Handle Via   Controls Jointly

NOTE: This is the estimate as approved by the
United States Intelligence Board. No
further distribution will be made.

Submitted by the
DIRECTOR OF CENTRAL INTELLIGENCE

Concurred in by the
UNITED STATES INTELLIGENCE BOARD

As indicated overleaf
26 August 1964

T-O-P ~~S-E-C-R-E-T~~

CENTRAL INTELLIGENCE AGENCY

26 August 1964

SUBJECT: SNIE 13-4-64: THE CHANCES OF AN IMMINENT COMMUNIST CHINESE
NUCLEAR EXPLOSION

THE PROBLEM

To assess the likelihood that the advanced stage of construction at a
probable nuclear test site in Western China indicates that the Chinese
Communists will detonate their first nuclear device in the next few months.

CONCLUSION

On the basis of new overhead photography, we are now convinced that
the previously suspect facility at Lop Nor in Western China is a nuclear
test site which could be ready for use in about two months. On the other
hand the weight of available evidence indicates that the Chinese will not
have sufficient fissionable material for a test of a nuclear device in the
next few months. Thus, the evidence does not permit a very confident estimate
of the chances of a Chinese Communist nuclear detonation in the next few

T-O-P ~~S-E-C-R-E-T~~

~~GROUP 1
Excluded from automatic
downgrading and
declassification~~

T-O-P S-E-C-R-E-T

months. Clearly the possibility of such a detonation before the end of
this year cannot be ruled out -- the test may occur during this period.
On balance, however, we believe that it will not occur until sometime after
the end of 1964.

DISCUSSION

1.   Overhead photography of 6-9 August shows that the previously
suspect facility near Lop Nor in Sinkiang is almost certainly a nuclear
testing site. Developments at the facility include a ground scar forming
about 60 percent of a circle 19,600 feet in diameter around a 325.-foot
tower (first seen in April 1964 photography), and work on bunkers near the
tower and instrumentation sites at appropriate locations is underway.

the outward appearance and apparent rate of construction
indicate that the site could be ready for a test in two months or so.
The characteristics of the site suggest that it is being prepared for both
diagnostic and weapon effect experiments.

2.   Analysis of all available evidence on fissionable material production in China indicates -- though it does not prove -- that the Chinese
will not have sufficient material for a test of a nuclear device in the
next few months. The only Chinese production reactor identified to date is

- 2 -

T-O-P S-E-C-R-E-T

T-O-P ~~S-E-C-R-E-T~~

the small, air-cooled reactor at Pao-t'ou. As of September 1963,

Construction was continuing
throughout the site, including some fairly substantial work around the
building which houses the reactor. Photography of March 1964 indicated
that major construction at the site -- including service roads,

and additional security provisions -- had apparently been
completed. Thus we believe the reactor went into operation possibly in
the latter part of 1963 but more probably in early 1964. We estimate that,
even if no major obstacles were encountered, it would take at least 18
months, and more likely two years, after the starting up of the Pao-t'ou
reactor before a nuclear device would be ready for testing. Thus, if the
Pao-t'ou reactor started operation no earlier than late 1963 and if it is
China's only operating production reactor, the earliest possible date
for testing is mid-1965.

3. It is, of course, possible that the Chinese have another source
of fissionable material. Such a facility might have been started with
Soviet aid as a result of the 1957 Soviet-Chinese aid agreement, probably
about the same time as the Lanchou gaseous diffusion building. We would
expect this reactor to be a fairly large water-cooled production reactor.
There are areas, particularly parts of Szechwan, which are suitable for
such a reactor and have not been photographed. Since it is doubtful that

- 3 -

T-O-P ~~S-E-C-R-E-T~~

T-O-P S-E-C-R-E-T

a reactor of this type could have been finished before the withdrawal of
Soviet technicians in 1960, its completion would have depended on a native
Chinese effort, a difficult but not impossible task. Such a reactor might
have started operations in 1962 or 1963, thus making available sufficient
plutonium for a test by the end of this year.

4.   On the other hand we have photographed much of the area around
virtually all locations where A-E activity is indicated

            and about half of all locations that might be geographically
suitable for reactor sites. Apart from Pao-t'ou, no operating production
reactor or isotope separation plant has been found. We believe it unlikely --
though clearly not impossible -- that such an operating facility exists.

5.   It is also possible that the Chinese may have acquired fissionable
material from a foreign source, e.g.,

- 4 -

T-O-P S-E-C-R-E-T

T-O-P S-E-C-R-E-T

As for the Soviets, we do not believe that
in the past they have transferred appreciable amounts of weapon-grade material
to the Chinese. In the current state of their relations with the Chinese, they
would almost certainly not furnish fissionable materials to them.

6.   Obviously, it is incongruous to bring a test site to a state of
readiness described in paragraph 1 without having a device nearly ready for
testing. It would be technically undesirable to install much of the instrumentation more than a few weeks before the actual test. We cannot tell from
available photography whether the installations have yet reached this
point -- it seems unlikely that they have, mainly because some heavy construction is still going on. However, it is possible that the basic work
will soon be completed, and that final preparations could be made this fall.

7.   On the other hand, in such a complex undertaking as advanced
weapons development -- especially when it is almost certain that there is
heavy political pressure for at least some results -- it would not be surprising if there were uneven progress among various phases of the program.
In a number of instances in the past, Peiping has been unable to prevent --
and has seemed willing to tolerate -- uneven development in various
important programs. Indeed, in other parts of their advanced weapons program
we have already observed this. Some facilities seem to be behind schedule --
notably the incomplete gaseous diffusion plant at Lanchou; others are

- 5 -

T-O-P S-E-C-R-E-T

T-O-P ~~S E C R E T~~

larger and more elaborate than present Chinese capabilities warrant --
for example, the possible nuclear weapons complex near Koko Nor.

8. As for the test site itself, Lop Nor is extremely remote, with
poor transportation and communication facilities, and we might expect to
see the Chinese taking a long leadtime in preparing this installation.
They have relatively few men with the necessary scientific competence and
and they cannot be fully confident that unexpected difficulties will not
appear. We believe the Chinese would do everything in their power to
prevent a last minute hitch on the testing facility from delaying, even
briefly, China's advent as a nuclear "power."

9. The evidence and argument reviewed above do not permit a very
confident estimate of the chances of a Chinese Communist nuclear detonation
in the next few months. Clearly the possibility of such a detonation before
the end of this year cannot be ruled out -- the test may occur during this
period. On balance, however, we believe that it will not occur until sometime after the end of 1964.#

\#   NIE 13-2-64, "Communist China's Advanced Weapons Program," scheduled
      for October 1964, will address all aspects of the Chinese program.

- 6 -

T-O-P ~~S E C R E T~~

SECTION 22

NIE 13-9-65

Communist China's Foreign Policy

5 May 1965

APPROVED FOR RELEASE
DATE: MAY 2004

~~SECRET~~

NIE 13-9-65
5 May 1965

(b)(3)

NATIONAL INTELLIGENCE ESTIMATE

NUMBER 13-9-65

Communist China's Foreign Policy

Submitted by the
DIRECTOR OF CENTRAL INTELLIGENCE
Concurred in by the
UNITED STATES INTELLIGENCE BOARD
As indicated overleaf
5 MAY 1965

~~SECRET~~

N⁰ 584

.SECRET

APPROVED FOR RELEASE
DATE: MAY 2004

COMMUNIST CHINA'S FOREIGN POLICY

THE PROBLEM

To analyze the principles and forces which shape the formulation and conduct of Communist China's foreign policy and to estimate the probable course of that policy over the next two or three years.

CONCLUSIONS

A. We believe that the principal aims of Chinese Communist foreign policy over the next few years will be as follows: (a) to eject the West, especially the US, from Asia and to diminish US and Western influence throughout the world; (b) to increase the influence of Communist China in Asia; (c) to increase the influence of Communist China throughout the underdeveloped areas of the world; (d) and to supplant the influence of the USSR in the world at large, especially in the presently disunited Communist movement. (*Para. 1*)

B. These objectives, and the method and style with which they are pursued, are shaped by ideology, by Chinese tradition, by the apparatus of power which the present Chinese Communist leaders can bring to bear to achieve their ends, and by the personalities and experience of these leaders. As a result, their foreign policy in some ways resembles an international guerrilla struggle which attempts to wear down the enemy's strength by attacking the weak points. (*Paras. 2-16*)

C. For both ideological and nationalistic reasons, China regards the US as its primary enemy. Peiping's immediate security interest and the short reach of its military power lead it to concentrate its main foreign policy efforts on undermining the US position in the Far East, though in other parts of the world the Chinese Communists are also using such means as they have to weaken the US. Among other "capitalistic" nations, which Peiping sees as in some sense victims of

SECRET

1

SECRET

US exploitation, Peiping tries simultaneously to build up recognition of China as a major power and to weaken the US position of leadership. (*Paras. 17-20*)

D. The USSR has come increasingly to rival the US as a dominant problem for Chinese foreign policy. China recognizes the USSR as a pioneer Communist nation and as the most powerful member of the Communist camp. Yet nationalistic and ideological factors join to create a strong enmity. The Chinese leaders will continue to seek the overthrow of the present Soviet leadership, but without great hope of seeing the emergence of new men who would follow the Peiping line. Elsewhere in the Communist world, Peiping will seek to dilute or supplant Soviet influence and to win over or split Communist parties and front movements. (*Paras. 21-24*)

E. Peiping has chosen the underdeveloped, ex-colonial world as its most advantageous arena of conflict. In this "Third World," the Chinese not only aim to erode US strength but to displace Soviet influence; they seek to establish themselves as the champions and mentors of the underdeveloped nations. The greatest impact of Peiping's policy is felt in Southeast Asia. The theater of primary interest is Indochina, where Peiping is seeking a decisive and humiliating defeat of the US. To date, the Chinese leaders have not made risky countermoves to the limited US attacks in North Vietnam, and they almost certainly seek to avoid a wider war. Nevertheless, they have been making preparations for at least limited engagement, and we believe that they would be prepared to risk a major military conflict with the US should they feel China's vital security interests threatened by US actions. (*Paras. 25-28*)

F. In the rest of Southeast Asia, unless the situation alters sharply, Peiping is likely to support policies designed to maintain and increase pressure against the US. Peiping seems to look on Africa as a second great area of opportunity and is likely to increase both its overt and subversive efforts on that continent. (*Paras. 29-33*)

G. As long as the present group of leaders remains in control, which is likely to be well beyond the period of this estimate, Peiping's dynamic and aggressive attitudes will persist. Moreover, though we have little information concerning the next generation of leaders, there are many reasons to believe that China's foreign policy will be assertive and uncompromising for a long time to come. (*Para. 39*)

2   SECRET

SECRET

DISCUSSION

I. THE BASES OF CHINESE COMMUNIST FOREIGN POLICY

1. The ultimate aim of Chinese Communist foreign policy is to establish a Communist world according to Peiping's militant revolutionary brand of Marxism-Leninism. But this is a distant objective; it is more a hope and a faith than an end or aim of immediate action. The more immediate aims seem to us to be as follows: (a) to eject the West, especially the US, from Asia and to diminish US and Western influence throughout the world; (b) to increase the influence of Communist China in Asia; (c) to increase the influence of Communist China throughout the underdeveloped areas of the world; (d) and to supplant the influence of the USSR in the world at large, especially in the presently disunited Communist movement.

2. These objectives, and the method and style with which they are pursued, are shaped by ideology, by Chinese tradition, by the apparatus of power which the present Chinese Communist leaders can bring to bear to achieve their ends, and by the personalities and experience of these leaders. In the following paragraphs we discuss these basic factors in more detail.

3. The Chinese leaders are dedicated, even fanatic, Communists. Belief in the righteousness of their cause, the correctness of their doctrine, and the certainty of eventual victory sustained them through the arduous and bloody 28-year struggle which brought them to control of the vast land and population of mainland China. Subsequent successes in consolidating their power at home, gaining a stalemate in Korea, challenging the USSR for leadership of the Communist movement, and humiliating India in the brief frontier hostilities of 1962 have further heightened their faith in the soundness of their interpretation of Communist doctrine. Although they have suffered a number of serious setbacks along the way, they believe that as long as these principles are correctly interpreted and applied, China can be confident of eventually gaining its long-range goal of a Communist world with its center in Peiping. This doctrinal faith gives a messianic cast to Communist China's foreign policy and provides it with great drive and staying power.

4. Peiping's world view is in large part shaped by Communist doctrine, which provides the framework for its appreciation of specific international situations. Communist ideology also influences its tactics and provides it with a particularly effective instrument for propaganda and subversion—especially important foreign policy tools for a nation which is not materially powerful on the world scene.

5. The Chinese part of the calculus brings in psychological, cultural, historic, and geopolitical factors which make Chinese Communist foreign policy a quite different thing from, say, Soviet or Polish Communist foreign policy. The Chinese leaders look back on at least three thousand years of cultural heritage. They have a strong sense of the centrality of their nation, history, and culture,

SECRET

3

SECRET

and this feeling generates an arrogant and patronizing attitude toward other nations and peoples. It also makes them highly sensitive to any real or fancied slights or disrespect. Those characteristics, already visible in China's contacts with European "barbarians" in the 18th century, were intensified by the subsequent course of those relations. The imposition of foreign enclaves, spheres of influence, and extraterritoriality in the 19th and early 20th centuries has left scars and has led the Chinese to class themselves among the victims of colonialism and racial exploitation.

6. Peiping's policy is also shaped by what the Communists call "objective circumstances." One of these circumstances is that China is a materially underdeveloped country. Its armed forces cannot reach far beyond China's boundaries nor can they conduct the kind of technologically advanced warfare of which the US and the USSR are capable; hence China poses a direct military threat only in nearby parts of Asia. China is dependent on imports of equipment and techniques to modernize rapidly its economy and industrial technology; the virtual termination of Soviet cooperation in 1960 necessitated increased contacts with Western Europe and Japan to this end. China's agriculture has proved insufficient to feed a vast and expanding population, and this has forced Peiping to make extensive purchases of grain abroad. On the other hand, the very magnitude of China's population encourages Peiping's aspiration to become a dominant world power and enables the regime to accept manpower losses with limited qualms. This, along with the geographic size of the country, makes the Chinese leaders believe that China could, if necessary, absorb a tremendous amount of military punishment and, in the long run, still envelop and defeat an invading enemy. They have even issued optimistic statements about their ability to survive a nuclear attack.

7. The unique experience of the Chinese Communist Party (CCP) in fighting its way to power in over two decades of guerrilla warfare against vast odds has strongly conditioned the thinking of the Chinese leaders. Mao Tsetung and his veteran colleagues have so adapted communism to reflect Chinese experience that in practice the Chinese and Communist ingredients are thoroughly mingled. To a considerable extent then, Peiping's foreign policy is a projection into the world arena of the principles and concepts developed in the prosecution of China's long civil war. Indeed, Communist China's foreign policy is primarily a strategy for revolutionary war. That is, it apparently is conceived in terms of conflict rather than of adjusting relations with other states by negotiations; revolutionary wars against those who align themselves with China's opponents are encouraged and supported; and any compromise or concession, except those made expedient by some tactical situation, is viewed as surrender. International politics is viewed as a great guerrilla struggle in which the opponent is to be constantly harassed and threatened.

8. The Chinese Communists have amply demonstrated their ability to concentrate on long-range goals in the face of seemingly hopeless odds and often at the expense of short-term gains. At the end of their Long March, when their forces had dwindled from over 300,000 to about 25,000, they kept working

4   SECRET

SECRET

toward the day when they would control all China. They emphasized the concept of protracted struggle, holding that a unified and determined group following correct principles could in time wear down a divided and less dedicated enemy, no matter how great his initial superiority. They believe that a succession of defeats inflicted at points of enemy weakness will gradually erode his strength and eventually reduce him to absolute inferiority. This policy of patience and long-range perspective reflects both Communist and traditional Chinese ways of thinking.

9. An important concept which helps sustain the Chinese will in the face of indefinitely protracted struggle is expressed in Mao's admonition to have contempt for the enemy strategically but to respect him tactically. This means that the weaker force must have complete confidence in ultimate victory—it must have contempt for the will and staying power of the enemy. But in all actual engagements with the enemy on the road to that ultimate victory, the weaker force must be constantly conscious of the immediately superior strength of the enemy. Following this line, Peiping's foreign policy has grand and dangerous ambitions but is almost always cautious and realistic in practice.

10. The Chinese leaders acquired their present power through decades of violence, which leads them to lay great stress on the efficacy and necessity of using violence in pursuit of national aims. They feel that it is ineffective to modify the present world order; it must be destroyed and replaced by a Communist (Chinese-style) world order. Mao has said: "All power flows from the barrel of a gun." Having no stake in either the Western or Soviet systems of world order, the Chinese are relatively free to encourage and exploit chaos wherever they are able to do so. So far, they have not been able to organize much of the world on their pattern. This leaves them with limited responsibilities, free to pursue a guerrilla offensive—sniping, harassing, and exploiting the difficulties of those who defend the *status quo*. They are in the position of political "outs" attacking the "ins," blaming them for all the evils of a very imperfect world.

11. The Chinese Communist leaders view the nations of the world as falling into three groups: the Communist world, comprising China and the other Communist states; the capitalist world, comprising the US, Western Europe, the white nations of the British Commonwealth, and Japan; and the Third World, comprising the underdeveloped, ex-colonial, mostly nonwhite nations of Asia, Africa, and Latin America. Eschewing traditional balance-of-power politics, Peiping has chosen to challenge the US and USSR simultaneously. Out of respect for their greatly superior material strength, Peiping strives to avoid a head-on military confrontation with either of them, choosing rather the Third World as its primary arena of contention. This also reflects a concept developed in the Chinese civil war, when the Communists conducted their struggle in the underdeveloped countryside rather than in the cities.

12. In the Third World, Peiping uses the full gamut of foreign policy instruments, selecting and mixing them according to local circumstances. The Chinese

SECRET

5

SECRET

apparently place particular hope on the use of insurgency in this arena, holding that it is there rather than in the advanced capitalist countries that significant revolutionary pressures can be generated under present conditions. They try to promote and assist local "wars of liberation" wherever practicable. The Chinese have raised Mao's concept of guerrilla warfare to the level of a "law" of the process of world revolution.

13. The especial virtue of this method is that it can usually be pursued at low cost and little risk to Communist China. It uses local manpower and, as far as possible, local or captured equipment. Peiping provides training, advice, a limited amount of material, and massive propaganda support. With a small investment, Peiping has caused great trouble to anti-Communist forces in Africa and in Southeast Asia. The Chinese role in the Congo has been such that, should the insurrection there collapse, Peiping could disengage with little loss. In Vietnam, a number of other factors, including geographic proximity come into play, and the risks to Peiping are much greater.

14. As a totalitarian nation, Communist China pursues a total foreign policy; every act is seen as a political act. At the same time, it remains acutely aware of the pluralistic nature of most nations and uses its policy instruments selectively against different targets within each country. Diplomacy, trade and aid, propaganda in many forms, subversion, insurrection, the implied threat of military force, the spectre of approaching nuclear weapons capabilities—all these are used simultaneously and in varying proportions as deemed appropriate. Propaganda is an instrument particularly congenial to the evangelistic nature of Chinese communism, and it is suitable to a nation whose material power is limited. The Chinese use it with great skill. As one example, their ability to turn out a spectacular reception for visiting dignitaries, including masses of apparently enthusiastic people lining the streets, has had a marked effect on even so sophisticated a guest as Pakistan's Ayub Khan. Every Chinese who travels outside the country, from the urbane and subtle Chou En-lai to the lowliest acrobat, is an active agent of Peiping's propaganda.

15. In the employment of its various means of advancing its foreign policy, Peiping is generally flexible, practical, and opportunistic. Although the influence of the socio-economic theories of communism may occasionally lead the Chinese Communists to misread a particular situation, they do not let these theories seriously inhibit their choice of means for implementing their policies. Guided by the Communist operational code that the end justifies the means, they readily employ tactics which violate particular Communist theories, as in their implicit promotion of racial prejudice against the whites—even Communist Russians.

16. By pursuing its foreign policy persistently and energetically, Communist China has had much more impact on the world than its military and economic power would seem to justify. Both Washington and Moscow are focusing much of their attention on their various problems with Peiping. This results less from the potency of Chinese policy than from the peculiar vulnerability of the

6   SECRET

SECRET

international order in present circumstances. The rapid dissolution of colonial empires in Africa and Asia has left a political vacuum, marked by uncertain and shifting national alignments and chronic instability. The new nations with their weak, inexperienced governments are highly vulnerable to Peiping's line. With large expectations and small capabilities, their people are frustrated by the *status quo* and naturally inclined to blame their woes on such external factors as colonialist exploitation and racial domination. It is not too hard to sell them radical "solutions" to their problems. And not least important is that in a war-fearing world, troublemakers who want to upset the existing order can get by with a great deal, not because of their wisdom or strength, b. ' because of the reluctance of others to take up the challenge.

II. POLICY TOWARD THE CAPITALIST WORLD

17. Ideological and nationalistic compulsions converge to make the US Communist China's primary enemy. According to Communist doctrine, the US, as the leading "capitalist imperialist" power, is the devil which must be destroyed to demonstrate the correctness of Communist doctrine and to clear the way for Communist progress. From the point of view of Chinese nationalism, the US is the power which frustrates completion of the unification of China and blocks Chinese ambitions in Southeast Asia. The US presence in the Western Pacific appears to the Chinese Communists as the major military threat to their security. If China is to dominate the Far East, it must reduce and eventually eliminate US strength in the area.

18. Communist China's immediate security interests and the short reach of its military power lead Peiping to concentrate its main foreign policy efforts on changing the balance of forces in the Far East. It works unremittingly to stir up anti-American feeling among other Far Eastern peoples and to undermine US alliances and military base agreements. It expects in time to force the US to abandon Taiwan. At the moment, however, Peiping's policies are undergoing their most violent and dangerous test in Vietnam.

19. In other parts of the world, the Chinese Communists are using whatever means they can to weaken the US. Their aim is to foster and support anti-imperialist revolution where practicable, as a means of scattering and draining US strength and establishing the US in the eyes of Asians, Africans, and Latin Americans as the white imperialist oppressor.

20. The rest of the so-called capitalist world is seen by Peiping as an intermediate zone comprised of countries which, while capitalist themselves, are also victims of US exploitation. Among these nations, Peiping tries simultaneously to build up China's position as a recognized power and to weaken the US position of leadership. Peiping has been quick to exploit and to encourage French actions disruptive of Western unity. The Chinese have played upon Western European interest in trade opportunities by sending wide-ranging purchasing missions which have aroused expectations far in excess of China's

SECRET

7

SECRET

actual ability to buy. Competition for this new market leads Western and Japanese industrialists to pressure their governments for improved relations with Peiping.

III. POLICY TOWARD THE COMMUNIST WORLD

21. In recent years, the Soviet Union has come increasingly to rival the US as a dominant problem in Chinese foreign policy. In this case, too, nationalistic and ideological factors join to create strong enmity. Peiping now sees Moscow as a rival for leadership of the world Communist movement, as a dangerously degenerate force which threatens to lead the movement into a revisionist, neo-bourgeois dead-end, and as an unfaithful ally who refuses to lend proper support to legitimate Chinese objectives. The Chinese leaders are also well imbued with traditional anti-Russian feeling; they are acutely conscious of Tsarist territorial grabs, resentful of numerous indignities perpetrated by the Communist Russians, nervously aware of their long common boundary, and on guard against Russian subversion of China's border tribes. The bitter rivalry with the USSR sometimes diverts Chinese energies from their focus on the US, but often the same course of action can serve both anti-US and anti-Soviet ends, as it does in Vietnam. We believe that, unless a major international war breaks out, Peiping will continue its attacks on Soviet leadership beyond the period of this estimate.

22. Nonetheless, Peiping's attitude toward the Soviet Union is somewhat ambivalent. The USSR is recognized as the pioneer Communist nation and the most powerful member of the Communist camp. The Chinese regret that it is being led astray by revisionists and still hope that some day it will be run by men who will use Soviet power to support the Chinese line on world Communist policy. They also cherish the great strength inherent in an undivided world Communist movement. Yet the tactics they employ to undermine the present Soviet leadership tend to split and weaken the movement. The matter is further complicated by the fact that the nationalistic aspects of China's anti-Soviet feeling are directed at the Soviet state and people, not just the leaders.

23. The Chinese attack on Soviet leadership is conducted throughout the world and at all levels. Since at least 1960, the Chinese have striven with their limited assets to promote the overthrow of the Soviet leadership. They probably believe that they played a large part in the downfall of Khrushchev, and they probably do not expect Brezhnev and Kosygin to last long. It is unlikely, however, that they expect soon to see the USSR taken over by Soviet leaders who would follow the Peiping line. Within the Bloc, they encourage independence like that of Rumania and, where possible, defection to the Chinese side, as by Albania. In some non-Communist countries, e.g., Japan and New Zealand, they have captured the local Communist party; in others they are promoting party splits.

8

SECRET

SECRET

24. In Communist front movements, such as the World Federation of Trade Unions, they try to capture the leadership and swing the organization behind China's militant policies. They have had considerable success in limiting or barring Soviet participation in various Afro-Asian organizations and conferences. For the foreseeable future they are likely to continue their campaign to replace Soviet leadership in leftist movements throughout the world.

IV. POLICY TOWARD THE THIRD WORLD

25. "Asia, Africa, and Latin America" is a phrase which occurs with monotonous frequency, not only in Peiping's propaganda, but in its theoretical journals and domestic indoctrination programs. The Chinese leaders claim that the underdeveloped nations on these three continents represent three-fifths of the world and they reason that by getting most of these nations to follow the Chinese line Peiping can assure the eventual achievement of its goals. In this Third World, the Chinese not only aim to erode US strength, but to displace Soviet leadership of leftist movements; they also take up popular causes in the area and try to establish themselves as the champions and mentors of the underdeveloped nations. Seeking the broadest common denominator, Peiping avoids emphasis on formal communism and instead stresses anti-imperialism, national liberation, and less openly, anti-white feeling.

26. The greatest impact of Peiping's policy, as might be expected, is felt in nearby parts of Asia, and the theater of primary interest at present is Vietnam. Although Peiping is undoubtedly very much interested in adding South Vietnam to the Asian Communist bloc, it is probably even more concerned about how developments in Vietnam affect Peiping's struggles against Washington and Moscow. Indeed, many North Vietnamese leaders almost certainly have doubts that Peiping's policies are consistently in Hanoi's best interest.

27. Peiping sees the Vietnam struggle as an opportunity to demonstrate to all doubters the correctness of its line that the US is a "paper tiger," and that a properly conducted "war of liberation" can be brought to a successful conclusion, in spite of US opposition, without bringing on a major international war. Peiping now appears to be seeking a decisive and humiliating defeat of the US. If a Communist victory could be brought off in South Vietnam in the face of US military power, Peiping would have made a major advance in world affairs. The Chinese line in the Communist dispute would be vindicated, Soviet pretensions to leadership of the world movement would be discredited, US capability to counter local guerrilla insurrections would be placed in doubt throughout the world, and US prestige seriously damaged. Peiping's arrogance and aggressiveness would increase, while its efforts to take over leadership in the Communist movement and in the Third World would be greatly advanced. Communist failure to achieve their objectives in South Vietnam, on the other hand, would tend to discredit the Chinese before other Communists and in the Third World and to check their momentum in world affairs. Thus, to the Chinese leaders the present struggle involves vastly greater stakes than the control of South Vietnam.

SECRET

9

SECRET

28. Peiping also is almost certainly anxious to avoid escalation of the Vietnamese struggle into a major Sino-US war, which might destroy China's painfully acquired industrial and advanced weapons facilities and prove the Chinese line on world Communist policy to have been dangerously wrong. While the Chinese may be quite confident that a wider war can be avoided, they have been making preparations for the possibility of at least a limited engagement growing out of US attacks against North Vietnam. To date, they have not made risky countermoves to the limited US air strikes in central North Vietnam. Nevertheless, we believe that the Chinese leaders would be prepared to risk a major military conflict with the US should they feel their vital security interests threatened by US actions. The Communists almost certainly feel that the tide is running strongly in their favor in South Vietnam. They therefore are almost certainly giving the Viet Cong and North Vietnam every encouragement to hold on in the face of US bombings and to sustain or stepup their pressures in the South. In the meantime, they will continue to do what they can to maximize international and US domestic pressures for cessation of US bombings and for US withdrawal from Vietnam.

29. In the rest of Southeast Asia, unless the situation alters sharply, Peiping is likely to continue its current policies. It will continue to support Indonesia's aggressive, anti-Western policies while seeking to control the costs and risks to Communist China. It will also support the growth in power of the Peiping-oriented Indonesian Communist Party. In the Indonesia-Malaysia confrontation, Peiping sees the prospect of a conflict which could further undermine the US-UK position in the area at little or no cost to China. The Chinese will continue trying to pressure Thailand; they will encourage increased dissident activity and from time to time issue threats and warnings. They also will probably continue their guarded tolerance of Ne Win's regime in Burma. Peiping will encourage Prince Sihanouk's anti-US activities but probably will stop short of any firm commitments which might involve it too deeply. In the Philippines, Peiping will continue its efforts to promote leftward trends and anti-Americanism, but probably without notable success.

30. In northeast Asia, the important target is prosperous, capitalist Japan. Peiping takes a long view and is prepared to go a step at a time toward the distant goal of a Communist Japan. During the next few months, the stress will be on disrupting Japan's relations with the Republic of China on Taiwan by such tactics as insisting on Japanese Government guarantees on loans for major Communist Chinese purchases. Peiping will support and sharpen nationalist and leftist demands for termination of the US-Japan defense treaty and removal of US military bases from Japan and Okinawa, but with little prospect of success during the period of this estimate. Peiping will continue to be the dominant influence on the Japanese Communist Party and will keep striving to increase its influence in the Socialist Party and other leftist groups and to sow dissension within the ruling Liberal Democratic Party.

10   SECRET

SECRET

31. In South Asia, China will continue to woo Pakistan and to play upon Pakistan's fear of India and the effects of US military aid to India. It will carry on its feud with India but probably will not initiate hostilities. It may encourage the leftwing Communists in India to increase their anti-government activity, and, perhaps, turn to violence. Against the small Himalayan states, which form an outer zone for India, it will continue its steady pressures in order to draw them under increasing Communist influence. Peiping, which had considerable influence in the Bandaranaike government in Ceylon, will probably promote strikes and other forms of resistance to the new government of Dudley Senanayake.

32. In Peiping's view, Africa is the second great area of opportunity. Considering that Peiping's serious bid for significant influence there is only two or three years old, its impact has been remarkable. This is in large part a function of the great vulnerability of the area; nonetheless, Peiping's flexibility in exploiting widely varied opportunities is noteworthy. In some countries, such as Congo (Brazzaville) and, until recently, Burundi, it used bribery to great advantage. In others, it has used economic aid, managing to get considerable political mileage out of its offers. China has made these offers on a no-strings basis, some in the form of grants but most in the form of credits on comparatively generous terms. Although Peiping's military aid is largely clandestine, it is known to be supplying arms to active or potential revolutionaries in several African nations, including the Congo (Leopoldville) and Mozambique.

33. Peiping has succeeded in winning recognition from many of the new African nations and will continue its efforts to win over others. Substantial African support exists for a UN seat for Communist China. Where Peiping has embassies, it uses overt diplomacy with some success. Exchange visits of national leaders have proved effective. Premier Chou En-lai has visited Africa twice in the past year, and a number of African leaders have been flattered with spectacular receptions in Peiping. Communist China subsidizes several African journals and floods the continent with Chinese propaganda literature. Africans are brought to China for training in subversion and guerrilla warfare. A few others are subsidized for study at Chinese universities. The student program has had spotty success, with many of the African students returning disillusioned and anti-Chinese. During the next few years, Peiping is likely to increase its efforts in Africa substantially.

34. In Latin America, Peiping will also seek to cause trouble for the US. It will probably also seek to improve relations with some existing Latin American governments, particularly if this involves a worsening of relations between them and the US. In general, however, Peiping faces a more stable social order in Latin America than in Africa, and there will be fewer openings to exploit. In further contrast, most Latin American countries already have long-established Communist parties with ties to Moscow; the focus of Peiping's effort among

SECRET

11

SECRET

these parties will probably be to gain footholds, to try to subvert them from Moscow where possible, and to foster splinter parties where it cannot—as it has already done in Peru, Ecuador, and Brazil. Peiping will also continue present efforts to increase its influence in Argentina's Peronista movement. Sino-Cuban relations appear to have deteriorated sharply in the last few months. If this trend continues, Peiping's Latin American program may be impeded by Castroite opposition.

V. POLICY TOWARD INTERNATIONAL ORGANIZATIONS

35. The UN at once attracts and repels the Chinese Communists. They feel a mission to occupy China's seat as one of the big five in the UN. They will continue to seek international support for their membership, partly as a matter of prestige, and partly to create problems for the US. However, they still bitterly resent the UN effort against them in Korea and are stung by the annual humiliation of being rejected for membership. They particularly object to the UNs peacekeeping activities, which they consider are performed at the behest of the US and which are aimed at damping down the very kind of disorders the Chinese wish to promote.

36. Peiping sees its fundamental interest not in being a part of an increasingly effective UN, which has no part in the Chinese Communist long-range world view, but in using the UN in the short run and eventually destroying it. It is clearly not prepared to pay a price for admission. On the contrary, it asks a price—the expulsion of Nationalist China—for joining. The Chinese Communist leaders feel that, although they can continue to get along outside the UN, the UN will be hard pressed to function as a world organization while a nuclear power controlling nearly one-quarter of the world's population remains outside. The recent addition of Indonesia's 105 million people to China's group of outsiders—a move Peiping applauded—doubtless strengthens this confidence.

37. The Chinese Communist leaders view international conferences on nuclear disarmament with similar cynicism. While they appreciate that total nuclear disarmament would greatly reduce the gap between Chinese and US military potential, they also realize that such disarmament is highly unlikely in the next few years (they would almost certainly refuse to accept meaningful inspection of their own facilities). Thus their propaganda support of complete nuclear disarmament is no more than a means of winning credit with the neutralists and have-nots who want to see US and Soviet stockpiles destroyed.

38. A significant, longer term gambit which the Chinese may be undertaking is a sort of extortion aimed at ending US protection of Taiwan. They have hinted that they may refuse to enter any agreement for the renunciation of nuclear weapons while the US stands between them and the "recovery" of the island. They hope thus to marshal increasing pressure against the US position and to weaken Taiwan's defense.

12   SECRET

SECRET

VI. LONG-RANGE PROSPECTS

39. As long as the present group of hard-line, Long-March veterans remains in control of Communist China, which is likely to be well beyond the period of this estimate, Peiping's dynamic, aggressive policies will be continued, possibly even accelerated. How the succeeding generation of leaders will act is uncertain, as we know little about them. Their lack of experience in the outside world, however, and their many years of one-sided indoctrination do not give much promise of a favorable change. Furthermore, there are no short-range solutions for China's food and population problems, and such psychological factors as the arrogance arising from the Chinese sense of superiority as a people and as the guardians of "true" communism will inhibit the development of a spirit of cooperation and compromise for a long time to come.

SECRET

13

SECTION 23

NIE 13-7-65

Political Problems and Prospects
in Communist China

5 August 1965

APPROVED FOR RELEASE
DATE: MAY 2004

(b)(3)

SE̶C̶R̶E̶T̶

NIE 13-7-65
5 August 1965

NATIONAL INTELLIGENCE ESTIMATE

NUMBER 13-7-65

Political Problems and Prospects in Communist China

Submitted by the
DIRECTOR OF CENTRAL INTELLIGENCE
Concurred in by the
UNITED STATES INTELLIGENCE BOARD
As indicated overleaf
5 AUGUST 1965

SE̶C̶R̶E̶T̶

N? 463

APPROVED FOR RELEASE
DATE: MAY 2004

SECRET

POLITICAL PROBLEMS AND PROSPECTS IN COMMUNIST CHINA

THE PROBLEM

To analyze Communist China's most significant political problems and to estimate its political character over the next few years.

CONCLUSIONS

A. The dedicated, narrowly doctrinaire men who rule China initially gained the support of the Chinese people by swiftly unifying a country in chaos. But their adventurist "Great Leap Forward" program failed disastrously, substantially reducing popular faith in the leadership and popular support of its programs. Despite their failures, the dwindling group of elderly leaders remain determined to carry through political and social programs that will produce a modernized China, and a "new Communist man."

B. This policy is the work of a remarkably small and stable group of men. Mao and his lieutenants have, over the past three decades, avoided major internal schisms and refused to admit younger blood into their ranks. In recent years the leadership has turned inward upon itself; it has virtually dispensed with formal party meetings and congresses while cloaking its operations in ever greater secrecy.

C. The party can exact obedience and compliance, but, despite its recurrent campaigns, the people attempt to improve their material lot and to avoid politics. These attitudes have widely infected the lower levels of the party apparatus as well. The regime is currently engaged in massive campaigns to "reform" or weed out errant party cadres and to "educate" the people to accept the regime's collectivist programs. It has announced that it will launch another production up-

SECRET

1

SECRET

surge, but this is likely to differ significantly from the ill-fated Great Leap Forward. The outlook is for increased tensions.

D. Mao is 71, and most of his dozen or so closest lieutenants are in their 60s. Mao's departure probably will not split the leadership, and policy is likely to continue along present doctrinaire lines. His successors will not have Mao's authority, however, and this may in time open the door to the growth of factionalism inside the party.

E. Mao's lieutenants will be succeeded in their turn by a generation of party veterans, now in their 50s. Although these men give no evidence of a broader, more moderate viewpoint, they will have to deal with a host of accumulated pressures and may perforce be more flexible and pragmatic. At least for the next several years, however, political and social problems within China are unlikely to prevent economic and military development or to force a softening of Chinese foreign policy.

2

SECRET

SECRET

DISCUSSION

I. THE LEADERSHIP

1. Mao Tse-tung has guided the fortunes of Chinese communism for more than a generation. During this time he has survived at least two factional challenges and has purged or set aside a number of his lieutenants. Nevertheless, the inner circle or 10 or 12 leaders has been fairly stable. This group is now, through age, nearing the end of the road. Mao Tse-tung himself, who is 71, is clearly declining in vigor and may be seriously ill; almost all the others appear to have medical problems, if only those incidental to advancing age. The average age of the Politboro is 65 and that of the Central Committee is 61. Since 1958, when changes in the 195-member Central Committee were last made, 15 members have died. About one-third of the remainder seem to be either in disfavor or inactive due to age or health. These losses have not been replaced.

2. The narrowing of the leadership base has been accompanied by a tendency to conduct party affairs with greater secrecy. For example, minimal publicity has been given to the operations and staffing of the party's six regional bureaus, a major alteration in the party apparatus undertaken in 1960. The regime apparently has a growing preference for *ad hoc* deliberations of the few top leaders rather than formal meetings. Under the provisions of the party constitution, a party congress, which would establish a new central committee, has been overdue since 1961. Thus a widening disparity between the formalities of party organization and the realities of power has developed, while the role and influence of those directly in charge of the party apparatus have grown.

3. The exigencies of the Sino-Soviet dispute probably explain some of this behavior. It is likely that some of those who are in disfavor opposed splitting with Moscow, while the position of those advocating a hard, unyielding line toward Moscow has probably been enhanced. By not formally dismissing and replacing the dissenters, Mao has preserved a monolithic front and denied the Soviets a polemical opening.

4. Mao is fearful and suspicious that future leaders, untempered by war and revolutionary strife, will falter in the struggle. There are indications that he is increasingly sensitive to criticism, and more and more concerned for personal loyalty to himself. Even senior party leaders, who once spoke with some originality, are now inclined to repeat chapter and verse from Mao's statements and the party line. The "cult of Mao" also serves to sanctify him and his writings in such fashion as to discourage future deviation from his policies. However, the cult has reached such levels as to suggest that Mao's egotism is becoming as overweening as Stalin's in his last years. At any rate, in Mao's efforts to get the "revolution" as he envisions it back on the track, he seems to be increasingly inflexible and arbitrary and shows a tendency to look back upon his years as a guerrilla leader for methods of coping with modern-day problems.

SECRET

3

SECRET

5. Since the purge of Defense Minister Peng Teh-huai and his sympathizers in 1959, there has been little direct evidence of dissension in the inner circle, although there have been some interesting signs of maneuvering for position. We are still unable to identify with confidence any cliques or factions within leadership circles. Yet common sense and the past history of the party persuade us that personal antipathies and rivalries exist. Friendships and associations based on regional origin, early party experience, and wartime service, as well as differences over policy, all tend to divide such a collection of men into groupings.

6. Since the establishment of the Communist regime, individual party leaders have tended to concentrate on one or two major areas of activity—party, or central government, or military affairs—and may tend to represent the special interests of these areas. There have been occasional reports of rivalry between party organizations and government ministries in Peiping, with Liu Shao-chi, Mao's heir apparent, and Chou En-lai generally regarded as the respective champions of these two groups. Over the years, Liu, party secretary-general Teng Hsiao-ping, and Politburo member Peng Chen have been advocates of a militant domestic line and have vigorously pushed Peiping's quarrel with Moscow, while Chou and Foreign Minister Chen Yi seem to be somewhat more moderate and pragmatic.

7. Mao Tse-tung has been preparing for an orderly transfer of power to the present Chairman of the government, 67-year-old Liu Shao-chi, who seems to be at least as militantly doctrinaire as Mao. Although Liu is capable and dedicated, he lacks the charisma and prestige of the almost legendary Mao. If Liu does not survive Mao, party secretary-general Teng Hsiao-ping and Politburo member Peng Chen, both about 65, seem the strongest candidates for the top position. Premier Chou En-lai, 67, has the seniority, stature, and popularity, but probably recognizes that he lacks sufficient strength within the party organization to take over. The top military leader, Lin Piao, is in chronic ill health and thus an unlikely candidate despite his relative youth (57).

8. We cannot be certain that with the demise of Mao there will not be a struggle for power among the survivors. But we see nothing to suggest that the initial transition will not be relatively smooth or that there will be immediate drastic changes in policies. Nevertheless, the passing of such a towering figure as Mao will inevitably have profound consequences. His successor will be a leader of much smaller stature and will probably have to contend with greater factional pressures. At least until he has consolidated his position, the successor is likely to have more difficulty in promulgating and carrying out extremist programs. He will be more vulnerable than Mao to criticism for any policy failures. The problem of bringing new blood into the aging hierarchy will probably devolve upon the successor. This is almost certain to cause increasing pressures from below for greater representation and accommodation of special interests and views.

9. There are enough party members in their 50s whose ties go back to the Long March days (1934-1935) to permit a continuation of the "old guard" tradi-

4

SECRET

SECRET

tion and policies for some time to come. Over the next few years, these men probably will assume positions of sufficient power to ensure their succession against any rival claims from government technicians and bureaucrats or younger military officers. This interim generation of leaders may be even more doctrinaire than the incumbents and are likely to be narrower in perspective; they will probably strive hard to continue Maoist policies. Whether they will have the abilities and staying power necessary to persevere in such a program is another—and unpredictable—matter.

II. POLITICAL PROBLEMS

10. Up until 1958, the regime had the enthusiastic support of important segments of the population and at least the general approval of the great majority of Chinese people. Since the failure of the Great Leap Forward in 1959 and the ensuing economic disasters, there has been a widening gap between the revolutionary goals of the leadership and the individual, materialistic goals of the people. The regime can command compliance and obedience, but it has been unable to arouse the population from its disillusionment and its political apathy. Although there has been substantial recovery and a general feeling that the economy is again moving forward, the former revolutionary élan has not been regained.

11. China's enormous economic problems would severely test a Chinese government of any description. But the Communist regime, through its doctrinaire excesses, has added greatly to the problem. Faced with the prospect of imminent economic collapse, the regime had to halt its program of rapid industrialization and was forced to retreat from its ultracollectivist programs and to shift to more realistic programs which were adapted to China's limited resources. Nevertheless, on a per capita basis, food production is still far below pre-Leap Forward (1957) levels. Except for the military and one or two other favored industries, industrial expansion has not resumed its earlier growth rate. Even now, the regime can only hold out to the people the prospect of austerity and painful social change over the coming decade. Moreover, to justify the continued authority of the Party, the regime must rationalize and administer its new policies along doctrinaire, and probably contradictory, lines.

12. Much of the economic improvement of the last two or three years in rural areas is due to decentralization into smaller collective units and to production from private plots and household handicrafts carried on by individuals for their own profit. Despite the resulting production gains, the Chinese leaders are dismayed by this resurgence of "spontaneous capitalism" and do not intend to let it set the pattern for future farm policy. These "capitalist" practices are, of course, antithetical to the regime's doctrinal concepts. They also interfere with the process of siphoning off resources for state investment, and impair the regime's ability to return to massive collectivist production programs. The regime is obviously anxious to tighten the commune administration and restore its control in the countryside, but for fear of disrupting production it has so far moved slowly and cautiously.

SECRET

5

SECRET

13. Following the drastic decline in industrial activity beginning in 1960, several million urban workers have been moved back to the countryside. The morale of the industrial workers fortunate enough to retain their jobs is still depressed, though undoubtedly better than a year or so ago. There are indications that workers have responded poorly to various campaigns in recent years. Visitors to Communist China have been surprised by the slow pace of work and the seeming indifference of workers in the factories they have visited, suggesting a degree of dissociation from the regime and its goals.

14. One of Peiping's main political problems stems from the disaffection of the lower-level party cadres, especially in rural areas. This development stems from the onerous and contradictory demands placed on them, the requirement to enforce unpopular policies, the demand to set an example of personal austerity, and the hazard of serving as scapegoats for the regime's mistakes. As a result of their unhappy plight, some cadres have been guilty of financial corruption. Many have come to identify themselves with the people they are supposed to control and have developed a tendency to avoid responsibility by resorting to highly bureaucratic methods.

15. One of the most striking developments of the past year in Communist China has been the bitter attack launched against China's intellectuals. Mao is reliably reported to have said that "the intellectuals have never aligned themselves with us." Judging from the regime's propaganda campaigns, these recalcitrant intellectuals would de-emphasize class struggle and close party control. They favor more moderate, practical programs oriented toward economic development and improved living standards. In foreign policy, they appear to favor Khrushchev's concept of "peaceful coexistence," would reconcile the differences in the Sino-Soviet dispute, and would reduce China's support of rebellion abroad. It is doubtful that these views have any significant support within the upper echelons of the party. Rather, what the regime apparently fears is that these views will become influential after Mao and the old guard have left the scene.

16. The disillusionment of youth is probably greater than that of other segments of the population. Once the exuberant and zealous vanguard in building a "new China," their initial expectations were high. Now, finding their educational and employment opportunities severely constricted, they seem to display pragmatic and non-revolutionary thoughts. A full-blown campaign in 1963 intended to reinstill China's youth with revolutionary spirit and to imbue a willingness for self-sacrifice failed. Rather than responding as the leadership expected, young people ridiculed this campaign and displayed a degree of cynicism that shocked and dismayed the regime.

17. There has been no outward evidence of major tension between the party and the military since 1959, when Defense Minister Peng Teh-huai was removed from office because he opposed the Great Leap Forward and commune programs, objected to the interference of political indoctrination and non-military production assignments, and opposed the policies which helped bring about the with-

6

SECRET

drawal of Soviet military and technical assistance. Since then, the regime has taken measures designed to enhance the loyalty of the armed forces. These have included increased rations, preferential treatment for the families of servicemen, and a sustained campaign of political indoctrination combined with a tightening of party control. Finally, the high level of investment in military programs has probably gone a long way toward satisfying the demands of the professional military. Nevertheless, the sudden abolition of military ranks in May 1965 suggests that the party is not fully satisfied with the "revolutionary purity" of the armed forces and that it may fear a resurgence of professionalism.

III. THE REGIME'S PROGRAMS

18. In the fall of 1962, the regime decided to halt its retreat from the original collectivist goals of the Great Leap Forward and commune programs and to launch a "socialist education" campaign. This campaign, with the objective, in the words of Mao, of "educating man anew and reorganizing our revolutionary ranks," implicitly recognized the political disrepair of the regime and the party. The extent of the political reconstruction required is indicated by the fact that it is envisaged as lasting five to seven years. It is now apparent that in mid-1964 the regime decided to elevate both its domestic and anti-Soviet campaigns to a new pitch of intensity—that of "sharp and complex class struggle on the international and domestic fronts." The revival of the class struggle theme, though largely contrived, provides a scapegoat ("class enemies") for previous failures, justifies a militant, rigid internal political program, and creates a greater contrast between the purity of Mao's communism and the back-sliding "revisionism" of the Soviet Union.

19. Although encompassing all classes and groups, the regime's campaign initially has been focused on rural areas, especially on the lower-level cadres. The regime's technique is to send into a locality a group of outsiders, including a core of disciplined and hardened cadres, to investigate misdeeds and bring erring cadres before "struggle" meetings where they must confess their crimes and engage in self-criticism. For those (and they are in the great majority) who have committed minor crimes and who willingly confess, the punishment usually consists merely of restoring misappropriated funds or paying fines, although it may also include dismissal. For more serious crimes or failure to confess, the punishment is to be labeled a "class enemy" and to be sent to a labor camp or, in the most extreme cases, sentenced to death. There is mounting evidence that the campaign is impairing, rather than strengthening, the fervor of the cadres. Their authority, effectiveness, and prestige have been eroded; many have stated that they want to resign; and some have even committed suicide. Since late spring, pressures on the rural areas seem to have abated; this may be largely in deference to production requirements, but may also reflect some recognition of these counter-productive aspects.

20. The regime has made it clear that it means to restore its rural controls and to get the revolution in the countryside back on the track. Peiping has revived the peasant associations which were used during the land-reform era (1950-1952)

SECRET

to bully and suppress landlords and rich peasants. In the past year, Poor and Lower-Middle Peasants Associations and Congresses have been formed to "supervise" cadres and to keep an eye on the suspect rural classes, including the more energetic and productive "upper middle" peasants. These organizations may be used to press for an increase in the sale of grain to the state and in the accumulation of investment funds, overcoming the objections of the better-off peasants and those cadres who favor more income for commune members.

21. In another organizational measure aimed at extending party control, the regime is establishing political offices, modeled on the political commissar system of the People's Liberation Army, in all industrial, financial, trade, and communications organizations. Peiping has stated that this measure is designed to create a disciplined labor "army" in preparation for a new upsurge in production.

22. The regime's programs to deal with its problems with youth and intellectuals emphasize the concept of "remolding through labor." Hundreds of thousands of students (300,000 in 1964 alone) have been sent to frontier regions and the countryside for an indefinite stay. Such measures can be explained at least in part on grounds of a dearth of employment opportunities. The regime's political motives, however, can be seen more clearly in a new policy of interrupting the studies of college students (except those in the physical sciences) for periods up to 18 months to participate in the "socialist education" campaign. This is supposed to provide valuable revolutionary training and to remove the students from the corrupting influence of "bourgeois intellectuals and experts" in China's institutions of higher learning. These suspect adult intellectuals are also subjected to "remolding" through extended periods of physical labor amongst the masses. Thus the regime is attempting the well-nigh impossible task of providing the sound education essential to economic and technical development and at the same time producing an intelligentsia that is receptive to simplistic and dogmatic ideology.

23. The regime, though not seeking to provoke an international crisis to distract people from domestic problems, is using the Vietnam war to stir up nationalistic feelings. A good example of this is the current program to build up and revitalize the militia. The regime is screening militia recruits carefully and is careful to put political indoctrination ahead of military training. While the militia has its military purposes, one of its main functions is to give the regime another device for political indoctrination and control. Peiping's anti-Soviet campaign is also being put to domestic use. The regime has attached to home-grown "revisionist" tendencies the added stigma of identification with the despised Soviet back-sliders.

24. The regime has called for a new "production upsurge," and many current Chinese programs suggest that Peiping may once again employ the basic theories of the Leap Forward strategy: that the basic wealth of China is its manpower, and that this manpower is available for mobilization and regimentation through political indoctrination rather than material incentives. At the same time, there is considerable evidence that the regime, remembering well the disaster of the

8   SECRET

SECRET

Great Leap Forward, is disposed toward greater caution and realism. For example, the regime has emphasized quality and efficiency over quantity in production policies and has given high priority to birth control and farm development, all of which run counter to Marxist-Leninist tenets and the underlying philosophy of the Great Leap. If and when the goals for the coming Third Five-Year Plan (1966-1970) are revealed, we will have a sounder basis for judging the regime's strategy. If, as seems likely, the plan calls for a more intensive collective effort by the workers and peasants, the people's response will also give us a clearer idea of the degree of popular disillusionment. We judge the situation to be unpropitious for the success of even a controlled Leap Forward in economic development.

IV. PROSPECTS

25. The doctrinaire and elderly men who rule China are likely to persist in, and probably intensify, their political programs aimed at producing a new breed of man that will see the world as they do. We believe such a program is unlikely to restore the former unity and revolutionary *élan*. The reaction to the Great Leap Forward disaster is still strong in all sectors of society, and there appears to be a general, unexpressed feeling that the regime's pressures will not be carried to intolerable levels and that its more extreme demands can be evaded or withstood. However, if methods of exhortation and persuasion fail, the regime will either have to back down from its revolutionary goals or rely increasingly on methods of coercion and suppression. We believe that the present leaders, who seem to be increasingly dogmatic and inflexible, will not give way. Thus the outlook for the next several years is for economic and social programs fostering increased tension.

26. Although the regime has mishandled many of its programs, it has been remarkably effective in enforcing its basic control over the country. We see little chance that this control will significantly weaken over the next two or three years. The Chinese people would almost certainly rally to the regime and fight in the event of war. Peiping is aware of this reservoir of patriotism and is increasingly using the crisis in Vietnam to justify its programs and the tightening of political and social controls.

27. A leadership as disposed to extremist enterprises as the Mao regime is susceptible to factional rifts, and we do not rule out the possibility of serious strife within the upper rank. However, we have no good evidence of policy differences or personal rivalries sufficient to crack the discipline under which the top leaders have so long operated. Thus we believe that, even if Mao were to depart from the scene, the unity of the top leaders will remain basically firm for the next two or three years. Nor is there much chance that internal difficulties will force Peiping to alter its aggressive and arrogant foreign policies. Rather, the prospect is for an accumulation of difficulties and pressures that will have to be accommodated by some future leadership. Such a leadership, on present evidence, is probably some years away.

SECRET

9

SECTION 24

SNIE 13-66

Current Chinese Communist Intentions
in the Vietnam Situation

4 August 1966

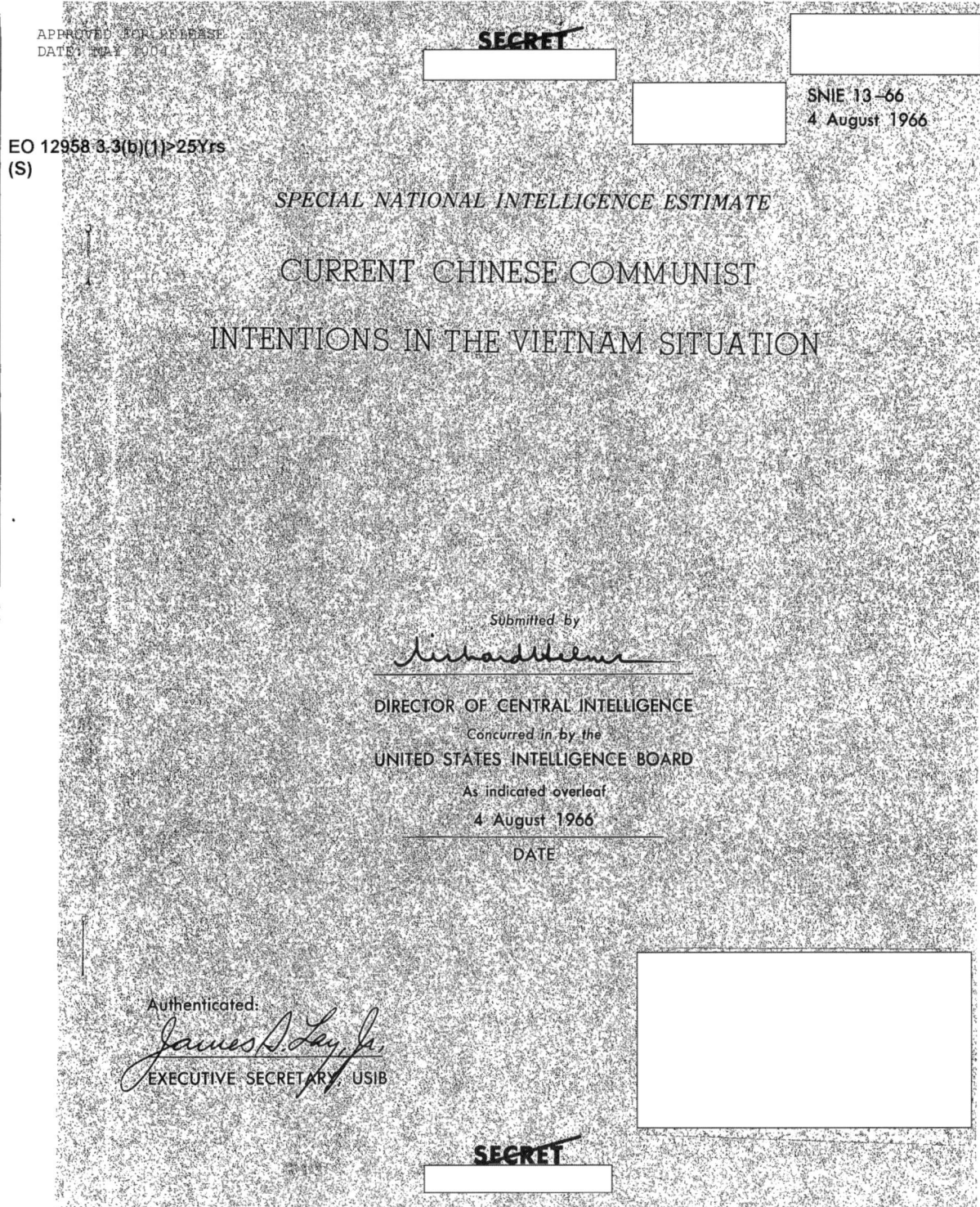

APPROVED FOR RELEASE
DATE: MAY 2004

EO 12958 3.3(b)(1)>25Yrs
(S)

SECRET

SNIE 13-66
4 August 1966

SPECIAL NATIONAL INTELLIGENCE ESTIMATE

CURRENT CHINESE COMMUNIST

INTENTIONS IN THE VIETNAM SITUATION

Submitted by

DIRECTOR OF CENTRAL INTELLIGENCE

Concurred in by the

UNITED STATES INTELLIGENCE BOARD

As indicated overleaf

4 August 1966

DATE

Authenticated:

EXECUTIVE SECRETARY, USIB

SECRET

~~SECRET~~

CENTRAL INTELLIGENCE AGENCY

4 August 1966

SUBJECT: SNIE 13-66:   CURRENT CHINESE COMMUNIST INTENTIONS IN THE VIETNAM SITUATION

CONCLUSION

The Chinese Communists have responded to recent US air action against North Vietnamese POL facilities and to Ho Chi Minh's July 17 appeal for more aid with massive propaganda demonstrations all over China. These occasions were used to renew pledges of complete support for Hanoi and to reiterate the Chinese view that the war must be continued to final victory. At the same time, the Chinese seem likely to provide more manpower for logistical and engineering functions in North Vietnam, and, for the first time, they may move some infantry troops into North Vietnam as a precautionary step against the contingency of invasion.

GROUP 1
Excluded from automatic
downgrading and
declassification

~~SECRET~~

SECRET

We do not conclude, however, that the Chinese have changed their basic policy because of the recent air strikes. We have estimated that Peking would almost certainly intervene if North Vietnam were invaded or if the collapse of the Communist regime seemed likely. But we continue to believe that, at present levels of US action against NVN, China will not commit its ground forces to the war, nor its air force to deliberate and sustained action against US forces.

DISCUSSION

1. Peking has responded to the US air strikes on POL facilities in North Vietnam and to Ho Chi Minh's July 17 appeal for more aid with massive propaganda demonstrations all over China. The burden of the declarations made on these occasions is for the most part not new; that China is no longer bound by any restrictions in aiding North Vietnam, that China is a great "rear area" in the struggle, and that Peking and Hanoi are now ready to deal "joint blows" against the US. In addition, the Chinese have warned against underestimating their willingness to support Hanoi and have stated that China was prepared to make the greatest "national sacrifice" in this effort.

the Chinese Foreign Minister indicated that increased bombing of Hanoi and Haiphong and an invasion of North Vietnam would bring China into the war. Chen Yi argued that

- 2 -

SECRET

the US was following a course which would lead to heavier bombings, then to an invasion of North Vietnam, and finally to an attack on China.

2. It may be that Peking intended these various warnings to presage a more direct involvement in Vietnam. In again asserting a right to take action at any time and in any place, and in adding to this a total denunciation of the Geneva agreements, the Chinese could be laying the political and legal foundation for certain open military steps. It is possible, moreover, that they are unfolding new courses of action worked out with Ho Chi Minh more than a month ago when he is thought to have visited Peking.

3. On the other hand, the Chinese clearly had to take a hard line in response to the Hanoi-Haiphong bombings, particularly if they were not to be outdone by the Warsaw Pact declaration sponsored by the USSR. And the North Vietnamese mobilization order, which preceded the more significant of the Chinese declarations, called for "still more vigorous support" from all Communist countries.

4. Taking Chinese statements as a whole, we note that Peking has been careful to hedge any commitment to direct action and has purposely tried to portray China in a supporting rather than a direct role. It is significant that the Chinese have reiterated the Maoist doctrine that outside aid cannot "replace" the people's struggle and that the Vietnamese people "should and can rely on themselves" to prosecute the war. It seems

- 3 -

SECRET

likely that if China planned some direct participation in the war, it would adopt a less negative position on the value of outside assistance. Such a gratuitous reminder of the limits to outside aid may also have been intended to discourage Hanoi from accepting the Warsaw Pact offer of volunteers.

5.   A complicating factor in judging Chinese intentions is the recent internal crisis. This situation has been confusing and we are far from certain as to its meaning and implications. It could be that after a period of turmoil, the Chinese leadership is now speaking with a new assurance and developing a bolder line on the Vietnam war. On the other hand, the "cultural revolution" must be creating considerable disarray in China, perhaps even within the armed forces, and this would seem to argue against a decision to go to war in Vietnam. Indeed, one theme of the campaign has been that the main enemies are inside China. Compared to the situation six months ago, there is apparently less emphasis in domestic propaganda on preparing the population for war with the US, by stressing civil defense, for example.

6.   As to recent military indicators, there is no evidence thus far of significant movements of ground or air forces to South China. Nor are there other indicators of the sort that might be expected, if the Chinese leadership intended to commit ground forces to combat at an early date. Furthermore, there have been no movements indicating an intention to threaten military action in other areas such as Laos, Taiwan, or Korea.

- 4 -

SECRET

SECRET

7.   It seems probable, therefore, that the current Chinese line on Vietnam is designed mainly to serve a number of political purposes. Peking wants to provide a dramatic reassurance to North Vietnam, now that Hanoi has again rejected all overtures for negotiations and reaffirmed its intention to fight a long war. Since Chinese actions have been cautious, Peking also probably feels that some strong words are needed to augment concern in the US and elsewhere that China's intervention is becoming more imminent. The hoped for effect would be to deter a still further increase in the scale of attack on NVN. Finally, the Chinese seem intent on destroying any lingering hopes that a negotiated settlement can be arranged. To this end Peking, unlike Hanoi, has emphasized that the Geneva agreements are dead and can no longer be thought of as a basis for negotiations.

8.   We conclude that the Chinese have not changed their basic policy because of the recent air strikes. We have estimated that Peking would almost certainly intervene if North Vietnam were invaded or if the collapse of the Communist regime seemed likely. But at present levels of US action against NVN we continue to believe that China will not commit its ground or air forces to sustained combat against the US. In our view, neither the Chinese nor the North Vietnamese regard the present situation as critical enough to justify outside intervention with its attendant risks of a much wider war, including ultimately the threat of nuclear war, which the Chinese must now reckon they would have to face without assurance

- 5 -

SECRET

SECRET

of Soviet support. Hanoi still has considerable freedom of action vis a vis both Moscow and Peking, and Ho Chi Minh's polite refusal of Communist "volunteers" strongly suggests that North Vietnam is not moving to expand the war in this way.

9.   This is not to say that Chinese involvement in the war will not grow, or that the Chinese will confine themselves to resounding phrases. Peking and Hanoi probably estimate that the war has entered a new and more intense phase with the Hanoi-Haiphong bombings and the rapid commitment of NVA troops to SVN. They anticipate a further US buildup, and Hanoi apparently intends to continue a heavy rate of infiltration into SVN. They probably also estimate that US air strikes against NVN will become more intense and widespread.

10. For some time Chinese military personnel have been present in North Vietnam; current strength is estimated at 25,000 to 45,000.[*] They include AAA troops, engineers, construction crews, and various other logistical support groups. More assistance of this nature is almost certain.

11. Hanoi and Peking may now believe that the time has come to move ahead with plans for greater Chinese support against the contingency of invasion. The Chinese are already apparently participating in the construction of a large base, perhaps including an airstrip, located some

---

[*] Lieutenant General Marshall S. Carter, Director of the National Security Agency, does not believe there is sufficient intelligence to support a numerical estimate of Chinese Communist troop strength in the DRV.

- 6 -

SECRET

SECRET

75 miles northwest of Hanoi. The ultimate purpose of this base is unknown. Beyond this, it is possible the Chinese will move some infantry troops into North Vietnam.

12. Altogether, there is some reason to believe that the Chinese presence, and consequently influence in North Vietnam may grow, consonant with Hanoi's apparent resolution to continue the war for some time. We do not believe however, that recent Chinese behavior indicates that Peking has made a decision to enlarge the war by overt involvement of their forces against the US.

- 7 -

SECRET

SECTION 25

NIE 11-12-66

The Outlook for Sino-Soviet Relations

1 December 1966

APPROVED FOR RELEASE
DATE: MAY 2004

(b)(3)

SECRET

NIE 11-12-66
1 December 1966

8 DEC 1966

NATIONAL INTELLIGENCE ESTIMATE

NUMBER 11-12-66

The Outlook for Sino-Soviet Relations

Submitted by

DIRECTOR OF CENTRAL INTELLIGENCE

Concurred in by the

UNITED STATES INTELLIGENCE BOARD

As indicated overleaf

1 December 1966

Authenticated:

EXECUTIVE SECRETARY, USIB

SECRET

Nº 463

SECRET

THE OUTLOOK FOR SINO-SOVIET RELATIONS

THE PROBLEM

To examine current developments in the Sino-Soviet dispute and their possible significance for the future relations of the two Communist states.

CONCLUSIONS

A. We believe that Sino-Soviet relations will continue to deteriorate so long as the Mao Tse-tung – Lin Piao leadership group retains authority. But we do not foresee a deliberate break in state relations; the Soviets are apprehensive about the costs of such a development within the Communist movement and the Chinese probably fear its possible impact on Hanoi.

B. Even so, we cannot completely exclude a sudden explosion of the dispute into a new and more virulent form in the near term. The Vietnamese war has added to the uncertainties and the urgency of the dispute, the emotions of the principals involved could come to have greater relevance, and unplanned incidents could provoke greater hostility and more forceful retaliations. Moreover, the situation in China is fluid; it is possible that domestic requirements or pressures might cause the leadership to force a severance of all remaining vestiges of contact with the USSR.

C. In the longer term, prospects for major changes leading either to a further deterioration or an easing of the dispute appear to rest mainly on what happens in China after Mao. The emergence of a Chinese regime even more anti-Soviet than its predecessor is certainly one of the possibilities. In this event, hostility could reach new levels of intensity. All forms of cooperation, including even the transit across China of Soviet supplies for North Vietnam's war effort might

SECRET

1

SECRET

cease. Though serious military incidents along the Sino-Soviet border are also possible, both sides would almost certainly seek to avoid war.

D. The emergence of a more flexible leadership in Peking could lead to some easing of tensions. We do not believe that any Chinese regime would offer the Soviets substantial concessions, but in exchange for certain benefits, such as renewed economic and military assistance, new Chinese leaders might be willing to damp down the dispute. Even a limited Sino-Soviet rapprochement would be likely to have some important effects on the international scene since world opinion has come to expect active discord between the two. An easing of the dispute could also lead to greater Sino-Soviet harmony vis-a-vis the Vietnamese war, assuming its continuation.

E. Nevertheless, any Sino-Soviet rapprochement in either the short or longer term is likely to have definite limits. We expect little or no positive cooperation at the party level and a continuing general atmosphere of barely suppressed suspicion and mistrust. Moreover, the Sino-Soviet relationship would remain highly vulnerable to clashes of national interests over a broad range of issues, and if China's power began to give punch to its national assertiveness, serious trouble could develop, particularly over the frontiers.

2

SECRET

SECRET

DISCUSSION

I. INTRODUCTION

1. The Sino-Soviet dispute has greatly intensified in recent months. Peking has stepped up the frequency and fury of its attacks on the USSR. Moscow, which for almost two years sought to convey an image of reason and restraint in the dispute, has since August begun to reply forcefully in kind. China accuses the USSR of acting in collusion with the US, and Moscow charges that Peking serves the imperialist cause by refusing to cooperate with the rest of the Communist world. China claims that the Soviet leadership is deliberately transforming the USSR into a bourgeois society, Moscow asserts that current developments and policies in China have "nothing in common with Marxism-Leninism." And each side now publicly contends that the other is beyond redemption so long as its present leaders are in control.

2. Hostility between the USSR and Communist China has, of course, existed for many years. Serious, though concealed, differences arose even during periods of relative harmony in Stalin's time, and open antagonism dates back at least to 1960. The reasons for Sino-Soviet friction and for the long decline in the relationship are complex, and over the years a substantial number of issues have been involved in the dispute. Underlying everything have been conflicts of national interest and ambition, some of a largely traditional nature, such as Sino-Russian competition in Mongolia and Korea, and others which have assumed a largely Communist character, such as the rivalry for political and ideological preeminence within the "socialist world." Different stages of internal development and great disparities in wealth and power have helped to create conflicting attitudes and a general feeling of ill will between the two countries. Doctrinal disagreements and quarrels over Communist strategy, cultural antipathies, and even personal enmities (as between Khrushchev and Mao) have all played important roles. Certain key moves made in the dispute have also stimulated discord and helped to give the contest a momentum of its own: for example, the USSR's refusal in the late 1950's to satisfy China's demands for the wherewithal to achieve a nuclear weapons capability, and Peking's decision in the same period to challenge Moscow's dominance in the Bloc.

3. Three developments appear to have contributed the most to the current sharpening of the dispute. First, China's internal quarrels have been accompanied by the mounting violence in polemical attacks on the USSR and its adherents in the movement. The campaign against domestic revisionists and anti-Maoists, part of an apparent struggle within the Chinese leadership, has evidently encouraged comparable attacks on Mao's principal enemies abroad as well. Secondly, China's growing isolation within the Communist movement—it is now virtually without significant allies—has frustrated and embittered Peking, and this seems to have reinforced its determination to remain arrogant and intransigent vis-a-vis the USSR. Finally, the war in Vietnam has

SECRET

3

SECRET

become a key area of dissension, since it involves the most fundamental differences over Communist strategy and tactics.

II. RECENT BACKGROUND

4. The present Soviet leaders decided late in 1964, shortly after their assumption of power, that Soviet policy toward China was sorely in need of repair. They apparently believed that Khrushchev had caused unnecessary damage to Soviet prestige and leadership of the Communist movement by his insistence on engaging polemically with Peking and his efforts to commit other parties to a formal repudiation of Chinese views. They did not wish to compromise the USSR's basic political and ideological position in the dispute, and probably had no strong expectation that relations with China could be significantly improved. But they did hope that a new approach could reverse growing support for the Chinese within the movement and eventually help to isolate Peking from the rest of the Communist world.

5. To this end, Khrushchev's successors acted with calculated restraint, avoiding polemics, retreating from demands for an anti-Chinese international Communist conference, and, in general, seeking to shift the blame for the continuing dispute onto Peking. At the same time, partly to disprove Chinese charges of Soviet unreliability and softness, and partly to contest actively with Peking for influence in Hanoi, they also sought to reestablish the USSR's credentials as a major Asian power and publicly committed themselves to increase their support of North Vietnam. And, in support of this general line, they placed stricter limits on negotiations with the West and reintroduced a number of cold-war themes into their propaganda.

6. The Chinese Communists seem initially to have misread Khrushchev's fall from power as a blow against revisionism and as a further vindication of their own harsh revolutionary line. They soon rebuffed the efforts of the new Soviet leadership to mute polemics, and were apparently unprepared for the effectiveness of the new Soviet tactics. They were also unprepared for the series of setbacks they encountered abroad: for example, the failure of their efforts to form an Afro-Asian front in 1965 without Soviet participation, highlighted by the fiasco over the Algiers conference; the loss of their position in Indonesia; the characterization of their trade policies by the previously friendly Castro as political blackmail; and, in general, their growing unpopularity among Afro-Asian neutralists.

7. The Chinese became aware that things were going against them and that some of their early supporters, such as the Japanese Communists and the North Koreans, were beginning to drift away from their camp. But rather than change course, they persisted in unyielding policies and insisted that "temporary setbacks" could not deflect them from long-term objectives. Even their growing vulnerability to Soviet allegations that only China stood in the way of unified Communist support for North Vietnam did not persuade them to modify policies. Last spring, in fact, Peking adopted a domestic line which could hardly have

4

SECRET

SECRET

been fashioned to do it more harm in the movement or render it more susceptible to Soviet ridicule and cries of alarm. Indeed, all of the world's Communist Parties have been mystified by the course of events in China, and virtually all have been alienated by the antiparty aspects of Red Guard rampages, the appearances of Maoist megalomania and Chinese chauvinism, and the general turmoil which seems to have swept over China.

III. CURRENT PROBLEMS AND DEVELOPMENTS

8. The USSR and Communist China today find it difficult to maintain even the pretense of a meaningful political and military alliance. Party contacts practically do not exist. State relations are minimal, formal, and often not polite. Cultural contacts are kept up, but on a very small scale. Trade, which reached a peak of over $2 billion in 1959, sank to about $400 million last year and will probably decline even further this year. Only negligible quantities of military supplies are still shipped from the USSR, principally certain spare parts contracted for earlier and items of equipment which the Chinese could produce themselves or obtain elsewhere. The 1950 Treaty of Friendship, Alliance, and Mutual Assistance has not been formally renounced, but both sides have expressed doubt as to its continuing validity; Peking has indicated that it does not count on—or even necessarily want—Soviet military assistance, and the USSR has clearly implied that in many circumstances it would not feel at all bound to extend such assistance. The two countries do not even cooperate easily or well on problems associated with the provision of military assistance to North Vietnam. Peking has in various ways hampered the delivery of Soviet equipment to North Vietnam.

9. *The Situation on the Border.* Tension has existed along the Sino-Soviet frontier since at least 1962 (when some 50,000 border tribesmen in Sinkiang, apparently stirred up by the Soviets, emigrated en masse to the USSR). Since 1963, Moscow has undertaken some modest reinforcement of its military and security forces in regions near China, especially opposite Sinkiang and eastern Manchuria. It has also stepped up its military assistance to Mongolia and this year began the construction of an air defense system in that country. The Chinese have apparently begun to give some attention to air defenses in areas of Sinkiang bordering the USSR. They have also sought to impose stiff new regulations governing the use of border rivers and have apparently harassed the Soviets along the land frontiers as well.

10. *Condition of the Communist Movement.* Sino-Soviet rivalry within the world Communist movement is still bitter and intense. The Chinese glorify Mao, vilify the USSR, and define their views as "universal truth;" the Soviets allow the Chinese to discredit themselves in this way and try, for the most part successfully, to block Peking's maneuvers. The character of this competition, however, has changed greatly over the past two years. The USSR must still reckon with the split, partly because of the maneuverability it gives parties which are anxious to avoid Soviet domination, and partly because a number of parties maintain a neutral posture in the dispute, including, most notably, the North

SECRET

5

SECRET

Vietnamese. But while Moscow was confronted only two years ago with a serious challenge to its leadership, today it faces a China which can count on full support only from Albania, the Communist Party of New Zealand, a handful of tiny splinter groups, and a small number of front groups which are obviously Chinese controlled.

11. *Impact of the Vietnamese War.* The Soviets have increasingly sought to use the Vietnamese war as an issue against China. They have charged, for example, that Peking's failure to cooperate had prolonged the war by preventing a "quick end" to US "outrages." And they have employed their aid to North Vietnam as a means to increase their influence in Hanoi at Chinese expense, and in this they have apparently had some success. But while thus offering the Soviets an effective tool to use against the Chinese, the war also tends to limit the USSR's maneuverability in the dispute. Moscow must contend with Hanoi's refusal to choose sides, which means also that North Vietnam is unwilling to accept Soviet political guidance on the conduct of the war. Moreover, Chinese control over direct land and air supply routes to North Vietnam is a factor limiting Soviet influence in Hanoi.

12. The eventual outcome of the war will clearly have a major bearing on the further course of the Sino-Soviet quarrel. The Soviet attitude toward the war appears to be mixed. The effect it has had in imposing strains on American resources and burdens on American relations with Europe and friendly countries elsewhere must be seen as advantageous. On the other hand, the Soviets are aware also that the situation carries some risk of direct confrontation which, in that area and under present circumstances, they must wish to avoid. For them, the optimum outcome would be one which, by a political process perhaps including a negotiation, gave Hanoi a good prospect of achieving its aims in South Vietnam and thus inflicted a major reverse on US policy. Evidently the Soviets do not think that the moment has yet come when they can set in motion a scenario which would end in this way. But should they be able to, in the face of continuing Chinese opposition to a political solution, they would strike a major blow at Peking's influence among the Asian Communists which would also go far to reestablish Moscow's ascendancy throughout the Communist movement.

13. For their part, the Chinese apparently wish for the present to see the Vietnam struggle continue. They see it as a prime example of a "people's war" waged against their main enemy, US imperialism. They hope for an outcome which would support their claim that this Maoist strategy is essential to revolutionary advance and at the same time diminish Soviet claims to give authoritative guidance to the revolutionary struggle.

IV. SHORT-TERM PROSPECTS

14. No clear pattern emerges from the most recent developments in the dispute: the mutual expulsions of the few remaining students, the Chinese demonstrations against the Soviet Embassy in Peking, the exchanges of diplomatic protest notes, the rising pitch of invective, and the hints from both capitals of growing difficulties over the transshipment of Soviet supplies to North Vietnam. Ordinarily,

6

SECRET

SECRET

an accelerating deterioration of relations such as this might be expected to lead to a complete and final break. Neither China nor the USSR, however, has allowed matters to get completely out of hand.

15. Peking seems willing to run the risk of provoking a formal break in diplomatic relations, but seems reluctant to take the final step itself. It almost certainly wants to avoid the onus for doing so. It may, in addition, wish to avoid a total rupture because of a concern that this would complicate the Vietnamese war and relations with Hanoi, and, perhaps, because of a fear that Hanoi, if forced to choose, might align itself with the USSR.

16. The Soviets probably hope to avoid a formal break in state relations. They probably find their presence in Peking useful for a number of very practical reasons, including the maintenance of a listening post. They may also feel that the continued show of the Soviet flag provides some encouragement to any elements in the Chinese Party which oppose present Maoist policies and some opportunity for contacts with such elements if future conditions permit. More important, they continue to be impressed with the probable costs of initiating a break in terms of their relations with other Communist parties.

17. A further deterioration of relations appears to be the most likely near-term prospect in Sino-Soviet relations. The Soviets for their part will wish to exploit what they perceive to be growing Chinese weaknesses. They may, for example, state publicly what they have already suggested privately: the Mao-Lin Piao regime is abandoning communism and becoming, in essence, a Fascist dictatorship. Some rise in the frequency, though probably not the magnitude, of incidents along the Sino-Soviet border also seems likely. Continued difficulties associated with the transit across China of Soviet supplies for Vietnam seem almost certain. Forced reductions in the size of diplomatic missions are possible. But we do not foresee a deliberate formal rupture in state relations between the two countries; the Soviets will probably remain generally apprehensive about its possible costs in the movement, and the Chinese will probably continue to fear its possible impact in Hanoi.

18. The Soviets are genuinely concerned about the trend of events in China. They also wish to capitalize on the apprehensions of others and to insure China's isolation in the Communist movement. For these reasons, Moscow will probably continue to seek some form of international Communist condemnation of Chinese extremism and obstructionism. But the Soviets know that many parties, though hostile to Peking, would not favor an international conference explicitly called for that purpose, or any enterprise which threatened to expel the Chinese from the movement.

19. A further intensification of the dispute is not itself likely to alter China's bellicose international stance or its foreign policies generally. It might, however, have some effects on the USSR's foreign policies. We do not believe that growing Sino-Soviet friction automatically assures a commensurate Soviet effort to improve relations with the West. But, as China has become more and more

SECRET

7

SECRET

isolated and discredited, the Soviets have become less sensitive to Chinese accusations and perhaps less responsive to Chinese pressures for militancy. Since August, for example, there have been a number of signs that the USSR has become more interested in some movement in its relations with the US. In any case, as a simple matter of prudence, Moscow's inclination to avoid crises in the West would probably be reinforced by a fear of possible major difficulties in the East.

20. We cannot completely exclude a sudden explosion of the dispute into a new and even more virulent form, even in the near term. The Vietnamese war has added to the uncertainties and has no doubt increased the sense of urgency associated with the contest. The emotions of the chief actors in the dispute could come to have even greater relevance, and unplanned incidents could provoke even greater hostility and lead to new forms of mutual retaliation. Moreover, the internal situation in China is fluid; it is possible that domestic requirements or pressures might cause the leadership to force a severance of all remaining vestiges of contact.

V. THE OUTLOOK AFTER MAO

21. Prospects for significant changes in the Sino-Soviet relationship—either a further, radical deterioration or an easing of the dispute—appear to rest in the main on what happens in China. We cannot foresee, however, what is most likely to emerge from the present turmoil in Peking, nor can we estimate the timing of possible developments.

A Radical Deterioration of Relations

22. The emergence after Mao of a Chinese regime even less flexible and more nationalistic than its predecessor is certainly one of the possibilities. Such a regime, either for its own purposes or because of miscalculation, might bring matters to a head with the USSR. The ways in which this could be done, and the consequences of such an act, are beyond counting. Hostility so intense as to lead to a severance of all forms of cooperation concerning Vietnam is certainly one possibility. Serious military incidents along the Sino-Soviet frontier are also possible, but both sides would almost certainly seek to avoid war. China probably would be constrained by its military inferiority and the USSR by its anxieties over the military and political costs.

Prospects for an Easing of the Dispute

23. The present Soviet leaders—and any likely successors to them—would look to Peking for improvements in the Sino-Soviet relationship. They are not of a mind, and see no need, for any substantial changes in their own position. While thus convinced that most of the movement toward compromise must come from China, they surely do not expect this from the existing Chinese leadership. They may calculate, however, that the successor regime will be dominated by men less anti-Soviet than Mao. The Soviet leaders may even believe that the

8

SECRET

SECRET

present radical course of Chinese policy will hasten the day when there will be a reaction against the radical Maoist line.

24. Should such a reaction occur, Moscow might then hope for some kind of grand Communist unity under Soviet sponsorship, but it almost certainly would not count on a restoration of the close relations it enjoyed with Peking in the early and middle 1950's. The Soviet leaders probably would try, however, to encourage a new leadership in Peking to end China's overt anti-Soviet campaign and its competition with the USSR in the Third World, in Vietnam, and in the international movement. As part of this program, they almost certainly would offer the Chinese economic aid.

25. A successor leadership in Peking might be interested in an improvement of relations, but we do not believe that any Chinese regime would be likely to offer substantial concessions to this end. Mao's personality certainly played an important role in setting the tone of the Sino-Soviet polemic and his views also contributed to the substance of the dispute, as did Khrushchev's. But Mao's departure from the scene and his replacement by a more flexible leadership would not heal all the wounds or remove basic issues. The Chinese leadership as a whole—not just Mao—seems genuinely to feel that it is the aggrieved party in the dispute and that it has been the victim of a double-cross, specifically, the USSR's failure to fulfill promises to give China extensive technical, economic, and especially military assistance. More important, any conceivable new leadership in Peking is likely to retain strong feelings about Chinese national independence, cultural and ideological superiority, and perhaps racial superiority as well. Divergent Chinese and Soviet national interests are likely to remain a source of friction and distrust for many years to come.

Consequences of an Improvement

26. Nevertheless, we believe that a future Chinese leadership might see advantages in a damping down of the dispute and in a resumption of some forms of cooperation with the Soviets. It might see benefits, for example, in a resumption of Soviet economic, technical, and military aid programs. It might see some virtue in attempting to revive the credibility of past Soviet commitments to defend China. And it might be willing, in exchange for such benefits, to reduce polemics and to agree to cooperate with the USSR in Vietnam if the war was still in progress.

27. Such an agreement might even include harmony among Moscow, Peking, and Hanoi concerning overall strategy and the question of the war's continuation or settlement. If, in these circumstances, the decision were made to continue the fighting, Hanoi would benefit from the establishment of Sino-Soviet cooperation in a number of ways. It would probably receive military supplies somewhat faster and perhaps in greater quantity; the establishment in China of supply bases for Soviet materiel, for example, would expedite shipment and perhaps allow an improvement in the mix of weapons delivered. Finally, a greater degree

SECRET

9

 SECRET

of unity would give Hanoi's political statements and warnings somewhat more force than in the past.

28. Even a very limited rapprochement between the USSR and Communist China would be likely to have an effect on the international scene as a whole. World opinion has come to expect active discord between the two, and world politics rests in part on the assumption of its continuation. The changes in opinion and politics which would probably flow from any such adjustment in the Sino-Soviet relationship, however, are not easily foreseen. They might be subtle and very gradual: a slow renewal of confidence within the Communist movement, for example, or a growth of anxiety in Europe about the USSR's intentions in the West, now that its frontiers in the East were more "secure." Or they could be more substantial, as in Vietnam, and perhaps as in India, which might fear that any trend toward Sino-Soviet harmony would seriously threaten its security interests. Some of these effects would probably be present even though, as we believe likely, a limited rapprochement failed to hide all evidence of continuing basic differences and clashes of interests.

The Long Term View

29. Over the long term, to the extent that China proved successful in realizing economic, technical, and military progress, Soviet fears of a strong China on its borders are likely to grow. The prospect of a powerful China is probably some way off in Soviet calculations, and would not, in any case, necessarily prevent Moscow from seeking to normalize relations. But it would serve, we think, to limit the USSR's inclination to consider China as an ally and to reinforce other alternatives in Soviet foreign policy. These alternatives will probably include continuing interest in good relations with Japan and India, as potential checkmates to Chinese influence in Asia, and, over time, a more urgent interest in a European settlement.

30. On the Chinese side, while changes in the regime and its policies may produce an interest in normalizing relations with the USSR in order to obtain economic and military assistance, Peking is not likely to be willing to pay much of a political price for such aid. It almost certainly would not accept Soviet leadership in the world Communist movement, renounce its traditional interests in border areas, or forgo its claims to a leading role in both Asian and world affairs. China's requirements, political and economic, are likely to cause any non-Maoist successor regime to look to Japan and the West as the major source of the necessary capital and technology for China's development.

31. Thus, while we believe that the Sino-Soviet relationship could come to be characterized by improved state-to-state relationships and a relaxation in the bitter ideological struggle, we expect little or no positive cooperation at the party level and a continuing general atmosphere of barely suppressed suspicion and mistrust. Moreover, the relationship would remain highly vulnerable to clashes of national interest over a broad range of issues, and if China's power began to give punch to its national assertiveness, serious trouble could develop, particularly over the frontiers.

10   SECRET

SECTION 26

NIE 13-3-67

Communist China's Military Policy
and Its General Purpose
and Air Defense Forces

6 April 1967

APPROVED FOR RELEASE
DATE: MAY 2004

(b)(1)
(b)(3)

~~TOP SECRET~~

NIE 13-3-67
6 April 1967

NATIONAL INTELLIGENCE ESTIMATE
NUMBER 13-3-67

Communist China's Military Policy and Its General Purpose and Air Defense Forces

Handle Via Indicated Controls

WARNING

The sensitivity of this document requires that it be handled with maximum security precautions on a need-to-know basis. Recipients will insure that only personnel having all proper clearances and a need-to-know will have access to this document.

Submitted by

DIRECTOR OF CENTRAL INTELLIGENCE

Concurred in by the

UNITED STATES INTELLIGENCE BOARD

As indicated overleaf

6 April 1967

Authenticated:

EXECUTIVE SECRETARY, USIB

Pages 32

Copy No. 0905

~~TOP SECRET~~

TOP SECRET    1

COMMUNIST CHINA'S MILITARY POLICY AND ITS GENERAL PURPOSE AND AIR DEFENSE FORCES

THE PROBLEM

To assess Communist China's general military policy and to estimate the strength and capabilities of the Chinese Communist general purpose and air defense forces through 1969.

CONCLUSIONS

A. Whatever the outcome of the current political crisis, any Chinese leadership will probably continue to work towards a dominant position in Asia and great power status on the world scene. It will probably continue to be concerned by the danger of conflict with the US, and possibly with the USSR. Thus China will almost certainly continue to give high priority to improving its military capabilities.

B. Although the threat of force and its actual use beyond China's borders are significant elements in Peking's outlook, Chinese military strategy places primary emphasis on defense. With the possible exception of their nuclear/missile activities, we do not see in train the general programs, the development or deployment of forces, or the doctrinal discussions which would suggest a more forward strategy. At least for the short term, the high priority nuclear program is probably viewed by the Chinese as primarily for deterrence, though Peking's successes in this field bring substantial prestige and political influence, particularly in Asia.

C. In our view, Chinese forces are capable of providing a strong defense of the mainland and launching significant offensive operations in neighboring areas. Thus far the political turmoil does not seem to have affected these Chinese capabilities or military production programs in any significant way.

TOP SECRET

2   TOP SECRET

D.   Under a broad policy of modernization, Peking is pursuing the following programs and objectives:

1. *The Army*.   Improvement of firepower, mainly by supplying new tanks and heavier artillery.   The army's organization and size has remained static: about 2½ million men in 118 combat divisions of uneven quality and strength.

2. *Air Defense*.   A growing inventory of fighters (Mig-19s), addition of better radars, and preparations for production of the SA-2, probably as part of a point defense system for key target areas. Production of the Mig-19 continues (20-25 a month) and production of the Mig-21 is expected.

3. *The Navy*.   Five R-class submarines have been produced and about 10 more will probably be built by 1970.   A construction program for guided missile patrol boats began in 1966 and is proceeding at an estimated rate of 10 per year.   The South China Fleet is being strengthened by deployment of patrol and torpedo boats and by expansion of shipbuilding and shore installations in South China.

E.   Nevertheless, the limitations and demands on China's economic and technological capacities are such that conventional forces will remain deficient in modern equipment at least into the early 1970's. There is little prospect for a significant increase in the mobility of Chinese ground forces; the air defense system will still be unable to cope with a major air attack; fighters will be at least a generation behind the US and USSR.   Naval capabilities will still be mainly limited to offshore patrol and escort.

F.   The current modernization programs for conventional forces plus even a modest effort to produce and deploy advanced weapons systems will, in our view, put pressures on an already strained economy. Thus China will face an increasingly difficult problem in allocating scarce economic resources between civilian and military needs and within the military sector.   Resolution of these problems may be a cause of continued dispute, both within the military and at the top level of national decision-making.

TOP SECRET

TOP SECRET

3

DISCUSSION

1. For well over a year China has been caught up in a great political crisis. The People's Liberation Army (PLA) has been involved, particularly in recent stages; its leadership has been shaken and present and future military policies may have been in dispute. The situation is still highly uncertain, and whatever its outcome, the PLA as a key institution is bound to be affected. For some time China may be in a period of transition.

I. FACTORS AFFECTING MILITARY POLICIES

2. From the outset, Maoist China has aspired to a dominant position in Asia, to great power status in the world, and to leadership of the world's revolutionary forces. These ambitions have brought China face to face with the US in Asia and caused Peking to view the US as its principal enemy intent on the encirclement and overthrow of the Chinese revolution. And these same ambitions led to the Sino-Soviet dispute and the eventual end of Soviet military, technical, and economic assistance.

3. In this situation, Chinese military policy has had to provide first of all for the defense of the mainland; beyond that, however, there has been a requirement to develop the military strength that would give weight to Peking's ambitions in the outside world. So far the solution seems to rest on a curious blend of the military doctrines derived from the receding revolutionary past plus some appreciation of the realities of the nuclear era.

4. Making a virtue out of the necessities imposed by limited material resources and near isolation, Chinese defense doctrine continues to emphasize the virtues of self-reliance, the supremacy of men over arms, and the tactics of people's war. Their basic strategy for defense of the mainland still relies on mass, distance, time, and superior ideology. But the Chinese recognize that material means are important, even if not paramount. Thus, support programs for the armed services have always been given a high priority and support for nuclear weapons development has had priority above all.

5. In the main, the Chinese are not building forces or developing great capabilities or theoretical doctrines for out-of-country operations. Much of the conventional equipment being produced (e.g., Mig-19s, radars, and motor torpedo boats) is best suited to air and naval defense. A system of strategic petroleum storage areas has been constructed in locations which would serve mainly to support wartime military and civilian operations within the country. Equipment programs that would improve China's ability to project its power over long distances outside its borders do not seem to have had a high priority. Not much has been done to enlarge air and sealift capacity, and there apparently has been no major effort to improve troop transport capabilities of the ground forces.

6. The positioning of the forces-in-being also reflects concern with defense. Large ground forces are stationed opposite Taiwan and adjacent to Korea, and

TOP SECRET

4   ~~TOP SECRET~~

the bulk of the ground forces are deployed within a 150-mile deep strip along China's coast. The bulk of the naval forces are positioned to defend the northern and central coastal area, probably in recognition of this area's particular vulnerability to the powerful naval and amphibious capabilities of the US. The air defense forces are oriented toward defense of coastal areas.

7. Though we cannot be sure how the Chinese view their emerging nuclear capability, it could also fit into a generally defensive strategy. Given the tremendous imbalance in strategic strike capabilities which the Chinese cannot reasonably expect to alter in the foreseeable future, their development of such weapons would presumably be aimed at deterring a nuclear attack in the hopes of confining a war within limits most favorable to China. In any event, the Chinese are almost certainly motivated by prestige considerations, by their judgment that the acquisition of nuclear weapons will have a considerable impact on their overall political position, and by their desire to establish a more favorable military posture to support their foreign revolutionary programs.

8. Maoist revolutionary doctrine taught respect for the enemy and the need to avoid direct encounters with superior forces; this basic caution continues to guide Chinese military policies today. In our view this attitude also reflects Peking's continuing awareness of its own military and economic weaknesses, the risks of provoking a major attack, and, despite some brave oratory, a recognition that nuclear attack is not only possible but would be enormously destructive for China.

9. This is not to say that Peking's military and political strategies are passive. The threat of force and its actual use are still significant elements in Peking's outlook. There are several circumstances in which resort to military action is possible. They would almost certainly fight if attacked or if they believed the security of the mainland were threatened. If the collapse of Communist power in North Vietnam or North Korea seemed likely, from whatever cause, this would probably be regarded in Peking as posing such a threat and would thus lead to intervention with armed force. In the special circumstances of Vietnam, however, we cannot be confident at what point short of a large-scale invasion the Chinese might feel compelled to use their own combat forces. In other areas, such as India, Burma, Laos, and Thailand, the Chinese also might use force, if they deemed it necessary to protect China or to advance vital interests.

10. *Future Policy Problems and Prospects.* In its broad outline, China's strategic doctrines and policies realistically reflect the hard facts of the current strategic setting, the type of forces available, and the kind of war these forces could fight best. As for the future, it seems likely that the Chinese have not yet worked out a coherent strategic concept integrating their conventional and prospective nuclear capabilities. Some aspects of present military programs suggest a lack of coordination and phasing. It is possible that some programs, particularly in the advanced weapons field, are being pushed hard for political reasons and with less regard to practical military and economic considerations.

TOP ~~SECRET~~

TOP SECRET   5

It is also possible that the Chinese underestimate the costs and complexities of building a modern military establishment.

11. Once Mao is gone, a broad range of economic and strategic questions will probably be reviewed. Chinese aspirations for great power status have created basic, long-term policy problems. Probably the most critical of these is how to divide resources between military and civilian programs. A subsidiary question is how to distribute resources between conventional and advanced weapons programs and between the various branches of the Armed Forces. And these issues cannot be separated from such potentially divisive and key foreign policy questions as Sino-Soviet relations, the proper posture toward the US, or support to "liberation struggles" on the periphery of China. That there are probably conflicting opinions on these issues within the leadership of the PLA is given added significance by the political convulsions now wracking China.

12. *The PLA's Political Position.* No one can say with much confidence when or how these political convulsions will end or what they will mean for the role of the military in national politics, for military policy, or for the capability of the Armed Forces. At present there seems to be an effort at stabilization and consolidation. It cannot be excluded, however, that disorders will again become severe. If so, the economy and central authority could be disrupted, and China's military programs, particularly those in the advanced weapons field, could conceivably suffer serious delays or even total disruption.

13. Barring such a collapse, however, the general circumstances in China would seem to favor a greater role for the military in the decision-making process. In January, the PLA was officially ordered to intervene in the political struggle, ostensibly to protect the revolutionaries in their attempt to seize power. As a result, the PLA now seems to be assuming an ever increasing role not only in administrative and control functions in the provinces, but in national politics as well. Indeed, events of the past year have so disrupted the party and other traditional control elements and created so much tension in Chinese society that it is difficult to see how any leadership—Maoist or otherwise—could reduce the heavy reliance on the Armed Forces for internal control.

14. Despite its enhanced political influence, we cannot be confident of the PLA's cohesion in advancing a common position. Factionalism has already appeared in the top command and there have been purges of important military figures. The old issue of professionalism versus political indoctrination may have contributed to the downfall of the Chief of Staff, Lo Jui-ching. But it is also possible that a broader range of issues was in dispute; for example, the Vietnam war may have provoked debate over the likelihood of war with the US, the proper strategy in the face of a confrontation with the US over Vietnam, and the advisability of "joint action" with the USSR.

15. In the provinces, the response of individual commanders to the cultural revolution has been ambiguous. Some military figures may have opposed the "cultural revolution" within the army, and others may have been reluctant to see the PLA used in the political struggle. In any case, many commanders were

TOP SECRET

6 TOP SECRET

forced to rely on their own judgments. In general, the army seems to have maintained its discipline and most of its actions in the "cultural revolution" suggest that its primary concern is with stability.

16. *Economic Problems.* Even with political stability and united councils, the Chinese will have to cope at some point with some distressing economic facts. The economic burden of China's military and military-related programs is heavy and will almost certainly become heavier. Although the data for making computations are most inadequate, we calculate that expenditures on these programs may be as high as 10 percent of China's gross national product (GNP). More significant than this highly generalized accounting is the fact that weapons programs use manpower and materials of the highest quality and absorb a very high proportion of China's modern investment. The cumulative effect over a period of time of concentrating scarce resources on weapons programs could be to threaten China's ability to solve its basic economic problems.

17. Production of major items of military equipment either slowed down or virtually ceased after mid-1960 following the collapse of the Great Leap Forward and the withdrawal of Soviet technical assistance. Research and development (R and D) costs, on the other hand, probably increased after the Soviet withdrawal and continued to climb as R and D programs expanded and matured to include actual testing programs. Annual expenditures for hardware, which during 1961-1962 must have fallen well below their pre-1960 level, probably started to climb again in 1963 and rose more rapidly in the years thereafter. Thus total expenditures for the military are now probably at an all-time high.

18. China is now at the point where it faces further and possibly steeply rising expenditures if it continues its present programs and moves on to the deployment of weapons under development. Not only will outlays for new equipment increase, but, as this more sophisticated equipment becomes operational in military units, maintenance costs will be growing at increasingly higher rates. For example, in the case of radar production it is calculated that between 1956 and 1966 the portion of total output that went into replacement and maintenance increased from one-quarter to one-half. There will be more demanding standards for the technical qualifications and training of personnel required to operate more modern equipment and this, too, will cause costs to rise.

19. *Scientific and Technological Capabilities.* The Chinese are at least investigating the problems connected with most aspects of conventional military technology, as well as the more advanced weapons such as missiles and nuclear weapons. If the project were given sufficient priority and time, China's scientific and technological manpower is probably capable of providing the R and D necessary for the production of most any type of conventional or advanced weapon. China lacks the scientific, technical, and trained manpower base, however, for the simultaneous development of a full range of weapons and their production in quantity. This will remain true at least through the early 1970's.

20. Since 1960, when China was cut off from needed technical support by the USSR, the Chinese have been able to offset some of their technological weak-

TOP SECRET

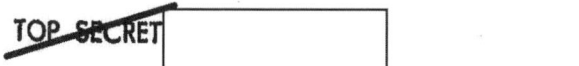

TOP SECRET 7

nesses by importing critical items that have materially assisted their military programs. China has been purchasing in increasing quantities such items as special steels, refractory metals, special purpose lathes and other machine tools, scientific instruments, and other electronic equipment. China's purchases of complete plants have also expanded considerably since 1963. Some of these plants will provide important inputs to the buildup of China's military industrial base. Moreover, the purchase of advanced Western technology and equipment for priority civilian sectors will free additional scarce Chinese scientific and technical manpower for use in military programs.

21. *Prospects.* Though China's political situation is confused and uncertain, we see little chance in the short run of a change in the basic policy of stressing military development. Given the military programs we can now identify, military expenditures will almost certainly outpace overall economic growth. This does not mean that progress in present military programs is likely to stop, but it does mean that they cannot be greatly expanded without quickly running into more serious economic difficulties.

22. At this time we cannot predict with much confidence which programs the Chinese will favor in the future nor can we predict in what quantities Peking will decide to turn out various items of equipment. There is a good chance that the Chinese themselves do not yet see the way clearly. The process of adjusting military programs may be slow and painful and itself a cause of continued dispute, both within the military and at the top level of national decision-making.

23. For the next few years, we do not foresee any basic changes in Chinese strategy, which is likely to remain essentially defensive in nature. In this strategic context, it would appear to make sense for them to proceed with a program for modernizing conventional forces at moderate rates, plus a priority program for deploying a modest number of strategic missiles to serve as a deterrent and for political purposes. On balance, we believe this is the course the Chinese will follow, particularly if a more moderate leadership emerges in Peking.

24. We have noted, however, anomolies in the size and nature of certain production facilities which suggest that the Chinese may have considerably more ambitious goals. If the Chinese do try to pursue a more ambitious course over the next few years, we believe they would risk serious long-term economic consequences and the possible disruption of the military programs themselves.

II. THE OUTLOOK FOR THE GENERAL PURPOSE FORCES AND AIR DEFENSE [1]

25. There have been no significant changes in the organization or structure of the PLA or its constituent elements, the Chinese Communist Army (CCA), Navy (CCN), and Air Force (CCAF). The Ministry of National Defense (MND),

---

[1] See Annex A for a summary of the order-of-battle for the Army, Air Defense, and Navy.

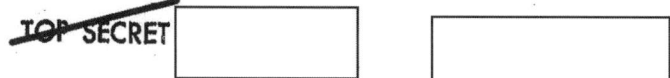

TOP SECRET

8 ~~TOP SECRET~~

under the policy control of the Military Affairs Committee of the Party Central Committee, remains the senior military authority. The chief staff components of the MND are its three general departments: the General Staff Department, the General Political Department, and the General Rear Services Department. Most combat arms and services, such as the air force, navy, armored, artillery, and selected supporting organizations, are represented at the MND level by separate headquarters. However, there is no separate headquarters for the ground forces which are apparently controlled directly by the staff of the MND proper, or through the 13 military regions.

The Chinese Communist Army

26. While China is giving highest priority to the development of a nuclear deterrent, the main strength of the Chinese Communist military establishment will rest for many years on its large army and nearly inexhaustible reserves of manpower. The organization, deployment, and size of the army has remained relatively static. It numbers some 2.4 million. We can confirm the existence of some 118 combat divisions. We also believe there are some 21 independent combat regiments, and numerous combat support and service support divisions and regiments. It is likely that the strength and level of equipment of these units varies greatly. Nevertheless, if not faced with major opposition from a modern outside power, the Chinese could overrun their neighbors in Southeast Asia or Korea in a conventional attack. Moreover, China is in an excellent position to meddle in localized situations across its southern borders, where Chinese military presence and aid could be a decisive factor supporting a "war of liberation."

27. The CCA is a conscript army, but inasmuch as only a small percent of those eligible are taken into military service, the regime is able to be highly selective. Even so, the CCA has difficulty in finding or developing technical personnel. The extension of tours of service decreed in 1965 should help raise standards of technical training and experience. We believe that the extension in service tours was directed primarily to this end. There is no firm evidence that the extension resulted in an increase in the number of major units in the CCA, though there obviously has been some fleshing out of existing units.

28. If the Chinese Army undertook to engage in open warfare against modern opposition, these strengths in manpower would be offset by serious deficiencies. Much of the heavier military hardware in general use throughout the army is obsolescent by US and Soviet standards. The army also lacks the organic unit mobility necessary in modern warfare. Furthermore, Chinese infantry divisions are weak, by Western standards, in organic armor and artillery.

29. The Chinese have designated certain "on duty" or "alert" divisions. There are indications that the firepower and training activity of a number of divisions have increased. We are not sure how many divisions are involved nor what the basis is for their selection. However, this may be a program designed to bring selected units up to a higher level of military effectiveness.

~~TOP SECRET~~

437

TOP SECRET 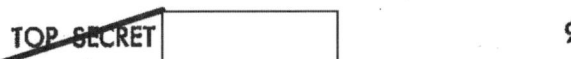 9

30. *Conventional Equipment.* The Chinese are self-sufficient in the production of small arms and ammunition and are making progress toward their goal of self-sufficiency in the production of heavier ground force equipment. Production at the Pao-t'ou tank plant picked up again after 1963 and we estimate current output at about 500 medium tanks a year. Some artillery units within the CCA have shown a steady increase in weapons of a variety of caliber. (including 85/100 mm field guns, 122 mm and possibly 152 mm howitzers, and 160 mm mortars) over the past several years, indicating a fairly substantial artillery production program. Truck production is low, however, and there is no evidence of programs to produce a wide variety of armored equipment. Despite some general progress, we believe the Chinese will not complete their current modernization programs until the mid-1970's. While this will result in a substantial improvement in mobility and firepower, the technical level of Chinese equipment at that point will still lag considerably behind that of the US and USSR.

31. *Tactical Missiles.* There was some activity in 1966 that could be interpreted to mean a Chinese interest in short-range ballistic missiles. There is currently, however, no evidence of troop firing, deployment, or series production of such missiles. The Chinese have tested at least one fairly lightweight nuclear device and probably have the capability to produce such weapons for tactical deployment. For the next few years the limited supply of fissionable material will probably be committed to the strategic weapons program. Lacking the nuclear warheads for tactical missiles, the Chinese could use chemical or high explosive warheads; however, since other more conventional and accurate means of delivery are available for these types of munitions, it is highly unlikely that the Chinese would employ missiles for such a purpose. If Chinese military doctrine does call for the deployment of tactical missiles and if they have been under development at the missile test range, the Chinese probably could begin deployment by late 1967 or early 1968. We think this unlikely, however, and we estimate that deployment of tactical ballistic missiles will be delayed for some years until there is a much greater supply of fissionable material. There is no evidence of a Chinese program to develop antitank missiles or large artillery-type free rockets.

32. *Air Support.* The Chinese have no separate tactical air command, and we have no information concerning PLA doctrine on the use of aircraft in a close support role. At present any tactical strike or ground support mission would fall principally on the 270 or so obsolescent IL-28s in the CCAF and CCNAF, although several fighter regiments appear to have a ground attack mission.

33. The Chinese have an extremely limited airborne assault capability. China has three airborne divisions, all subordinate to the CCAF, but little is known about their training, equipment, strength, or of Chinese doctrine concerning the use of such troops. The principal limitation on the employment of Chinese airborne forces is the small size of the Chinese air transport fleet and the

TOP SECRET

10   TOP SECRET

characteristics of the available aircraft. Available light and medium military transport aircraft could lift about 4,400 lightly-equipped troops or airdrop about 2,800 airborne infantry troops to a distance of about 500 n.m. Civil aircraft could augment this capability by about 50 percent. The only transport aircraft now in production in China is the single-engine AN-2 which can carry only 10 to 12 passengers. We have no evidence of preparations for producing a heavy transport aircraft. More up-to-date transport aircraft are being purchased by the Chinese on the foreign market at a rate of some 6 to 7 per year. In addition, acquisition of four AN-12/Cubs in late 1966 has increased the military airlift capability of the Chinese Communists. These aircraft are the first rear extraction aircraft in the Chinese inventory. Further purchases of this type aircraft from the Soviets would substantially increase the Chinese Communist airlift capability over the next few years.

The Air Defense Forces

34. The overall responsibility for air defense is vested in the Air Defense Command (ADC) of the CCAF. The ADC controls 9 air defense districts. It has at its command an extensive air surveillance and control network comprised of some 650 radar stations, a fighter force of about 2,300 aircraft (including some naval air), antiaircraft artillery (AAA), and a limited number of surface-to-air missiles (SAMs).

35. There has been a substantial improvement in early warning and ground control intercept capabilities with the deployment of indigenously produced radars. The radar network is now capable of providing warning against approaching aircraft flying at medium and high altitudes [   ] low altitude coverage is negligible. Radar coverage extends along the entire length of the eastern and southern approaches to China and is substantially complete on the western approaches. The northern border approach is still mostly open, although radars cover avenues of approach from that direction to all important target areas in the interior. Further expansion and improvement of the air surveillance network is anticipated. The electronics industry is one of the most sophisticated sectors of Chinese industry. It is almost completely self-sufficient in the production of existing radar types, and is actively engaged in the development of newer, more specialized equipment.

36. [   ] The Chinese have, on occasion and in response to specific situations, modified their air defense control structure in order to achieve more effective control of the air defense organization in a limited area. Such measures provided only marginal and short-term improvements. While the Chinese air defense system is capable of coping with minor incursions over its air space, we believe that the limitations [   ] would result in an almost complete disintegration of the air defense system in the event of a large, concerted air attack on the mainland. There will be improvement [   ] during the next few years. However, the costs

TOP SECRET

TOP SECRET [   ]   11

are too high, the technology too sophisticated, and the requirements too great for the Chinese to develop a system capable of coping with a major air attack over the next several years.

37. The Chinese fighter force consists of some 1,800 obsolete Mig-15s and Mig-17s, 500 or more Mig-19s, and 25-35 Mig-21s. A major improvement in the fighter capability has resulted from the resumption of Mig-19 production at Shen-yang at an estimated rate of 20-25 aircraft per month. Thus, the Mig-19 force has tripled since 1965. We think that production of the Mig-19 will continue at this rate, at least until a more modern fighter becomes available.

38. In this connection, we believe that the Ch'eng-tu plant should now be ready to produce Mig-21 aircraft. If we are correct in this judgment, Mig-21s could be entering operational service in small numbers in 1968 and in increasing numbers in 1969. The Chinese have claimed to be working on an improved version of the Mig-19. Even if this is so and they decide to produce such an aircraft in quantity, it could not be available for several years and we continue to believe that Mig-19s and Mig-21s will be the mainstay of the CCAF into the 1970's.

39. Probably less than 10 percent of the fighter force has airborne intercept equipment, but those aircraft that do are distributed among units along the southern and eastern periphery. Air-to-air missiles (AAMs) of the Soviet AA-2 type are believed to be available for use and the Chinese may be producing a limited number of them.

40. The air defense system includes, in addition to the fighter force, a point defense system involving 19 or 20 air force AAA and at least 6 army AAA divisions which are more lightly gunned. Since early 1965, China has shifted some of the weight of its AAA to the southern provinces adjoining North Vietnam and into North Vietnam.

41. In addition to the deployment of conventional, tube artillery, the Chinese have a limited SAM capability. Some 35 deployed sites have been built, but at least 13 were later abandoned. Of the remaining 22 sites, no more than 12 are believed to have been occupied at any one time. The administrative subordination of the SAM units is not known, but they are probably operationally subordinate to the various Air Defense Headquarters, and function in the same manner as conventional AAA units.

42. The Chinese are working on SAM development. The SAM R and D facilities at the Shuang-ch'eng-tzu Missile Test Range have been modified several times since 1964. A new SAM unit training site was built in 1966, the technical training facility was expanded, and a solid propellant plant large enough to support series production of SAMs is nearing completion at T'ai-yuan. There is also some evidence that the Chinese are producing a few missiles to replenish the small stock of missiles supplied by the USSR before the 1960 crisis in Sino-Soviet relations.

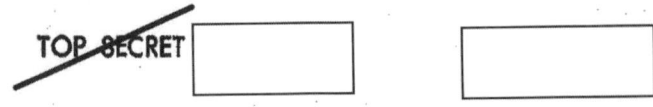

TOP SECRET [   ]   [   ]

TOP SECRET

43. We are not sure, however, that this activity presages a major deployment program. The Chinese must have learned from North Vietnam's experience that a large number of SAMs, supported by heavy concentration of AAA, are required to defend even a relatively limited area. They also have seen that the US has the capability to counter the Soviet SA-2 system with considerable effectiveness. Thus a decision regarding SAM deployment exemplifies a general dilemma facing Chinese military planners: whether to build and deploy at great cost a weapon system that at best can only partially fulfill a requirement and which would compete for resources with other high priority programs.

44. The Chinese will no doubt continue developmental work on SAMs, probably hoping to improve on the SA-2 system. In the meantime, we believe there is a fairly good chance that the Chinese will begin a program to deploy SA-2s for a point defense of a few key targets. We do not know which or how many targets the Chinese would select in the initial stages for such a defense, but facilities associated with advanced weapons program are likely candidates. This could involve at least some 20 areas and if the Chinese followed Soviet practice even this limited deployment would require 80 to 100 battalions and approximately 2,000 to 3,000 missiles. We estimate that it would take the Chinese 4 or 5 years to deploy an SA-2 force of this size.

The Navy

45. The CCN is growing rapidly but remains principally an offshore patrol and escort force. It consists of 11 principal surface ships, 34 submarines, about 525 smaller combatants and a variety of amphibious, auxiliary, and service craft. Headquarters is located in Peking and the operational forces are distributed among three major fleets.

46. Several programs now underway are contributing to the gradual development of Chinese naval capabilities. The CCN force of torpedo attack submarines continues to expand at the rate of 2 to 3 units a year. Construction of the W-class submarine has stopped and the Chinese are concentrating on production of the R-class. Five R-class have already been built and we believe that a total of about 10 more will be built by 1970. The Chinese have also _____ and commissioned at least one submarine tender, providing the CCN with some capability for supporting out-of-area submarine operations.

47. Another significant program is the construction of various types of coastal patrol craft. Since 1965, about 100 fast patrol boats of native design have been added to the fleet. A construction program for the OSA/KOMAR guided missile boats began in 1966 and is proceeding at an estimated rate of about 10 a year. _____ we believe the Chinese are producing missiles for these boats. These craft with a range of several hundred miles could extend their operations into the Tonkin Gulf and the Yellow Sea.

TOP SECRET

TOP SECRET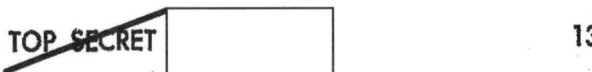

13

48. There is still no indication that the Chinese plan to develop or further deploy a land-based cruise missile for coastal defense. There are three confirmed sites: one for R and D and training, one for tactical use, and one inactive.

49. The South Sea Fleet, the weakest of China's three fleets, is being strengthened. Numerous fast patrol and torpedo boats, including a native designed hydrofoil type, have appeared in the South Sea Fleet. Shipbuilding and shore installations in South China have also been significantly expanded and modernized. In 1965, the Chinese began producing destroyer escorts of a native design (Kiangnan-class) in the Canton area, which now ranks second to Shanghai in shipbuilding capability.

50. The CCN's troop lift capability with amphibious ships and landing craft is about two infantry divisions (28,000 troops) or one infantry and one artillery division (20,200 troops), but we have not observed any troop training involving amphibious operations. In port-to-port operations, ships of the merchant marine fleet could deliver about four infantry divisions (up to 49,000 troops). In addition, in operations where the use of smaller ships and craft is feasible, the Chinese could employ literally thousands of junks for transporting troops and light equipment. The Chinese have not built any LST, LSM or large troop transports, but they are building substantial numbers of large landing craft and naval auxiliaries.

51. We believe that the CCN's program of expansion and modernization will continue and that its capabilities for operating close to China's shores will substantially increase. The Chinese lack training and experience in operations away from their own waters, however, and have as yet shown no interest in undertaking such operations. Once begun, it will take them several years before they can develop a significant operational proficiency.

The Outlook

52. The present outlook is for a gradual but general increase in the capabilities of the Chinese Communist general purpose and air defense forces as the process of modernization goes forward over the next few years. All arms and services are likely to share in this progress. Thus far we see no evidence that the political turmoil has affected the fighting capabilities or interfered with military production programs. But now the PLA is assuming more and more noncombat tasks and if this trend is long continued it would almost certainly affect the capabilities of the Chinese forces.

TOP SECRET

TOP SECRET 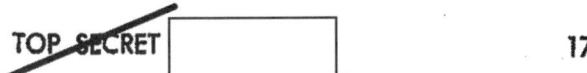   17

ANNEX A

CHINESE COMMUNIST ORDER OF BATTLE

A. Army

1. The Chinese Communist Army (CCA) is estimated to include 118 combat divisions (107 infantry, 3 airborne,[2] 5 armored, 3 cavalry), 24 combat support divisions, 20 border/internal defense divisions, 11 railway engineer divisions, and some 112 combat and combat support regiments, 36 service support regiments, and 40 border/internal defense regiments. These units vary widely in equipment and military effectiveness.

2. The main field command organization in the CCA is the army, of which there are some 35. The typical CCA army includes 3 infantry divisions and 1 artillery regiment, and probably numbers about 50,000 at full strength. There is nothing in the CCA analogous to the Soviet combined arms or tank armies.

3. For administrative purposes, mainland China is divided into 13 military regions (see map), and these are divided into subordinate districts which in most cases conform to provincial boundaries. These are territorial rather than operational commands.

4. We estimate that at full strength the standard infantry division would number about 14,000 officers and men. Its principal combat elements would be 3 infantry regiments, 1 artillery regiment, and 1 tank/assault gun regiment. Its heavy equipment, all of Soviet type, would include T-59 and T-34 tanks, and SU-76 and SU-100 assault guns. The division would have a large number of mortars (82 mm, 120 mm, and 160 mm), as well as 57 mm, 76 mm, 85/100 mm guns and 122 mm howitzers. In addition to the standard infantry division the Chinese have light divisions for use in mountainous and other difficult terrain. These type units are similar to the standard division, but do not have the tank/assault gun regiment and are equipped with lighter artillery.

5. The Chinese armored division at full strength would number about 8,000 officers and men. Its principal combat elements would be 2 armored regiments, 1 artillery regiment, and 1 infantry regiment. Its heavy equipment would include T-59 and T-34 tanks, a few JS-1 or JS-2 heavy tanks, and some JSU-122

---

[2] One army, the 10th Air Army, consisting of the three airborne divisions, is subordinate to the CCAF, but is, for the purpose of this paper, included with the CCA.

TOP SECRET

18   TOP SECRET

and JSU-152 assault guns. In addition the division would have a small number of mortars, 76 mm, 85 mm, and possibly 100 mm guns, and 122 mm howitzers.

6. The CCA has two types of field artillery divisions. The gun division would have about 5,400 men at full strength; it usually has 3 regiments equipped with 122 mm guns and 152 mm gun-howitzers. The howitzer division would have about 6,300 troops; it is normally organized into 3 artillery regiments equipped with 122 mm and 152 mm howitzers, and probably a rocket launcher regiment, equipped with 132 mm or 140 mm multiple rocket launchers.

7.   It appears likely that the so-called "alert" divisions have had priority in the modernization program. They may be at or near the personnel strength and equipment levels of the formal TO&E described above; others probably fall short of what the TO&E calls for, and some may be well below this standard.

TABLE 1

ESTIMATED NUMBER OF ARMY UNITS 15 MARCH 1967 [a]

	NUMBER OF UNITS
Army Headquarters	35 [b]
Combat Divisions	118
107 Infantry	
3 Airborne [b]	
5 Armored	
3 Cavalry	
Border/Internal Defense Divisions	20
Combat Support Divisions	24
15 Field Artillery	
3 Antitank	
6 AAA	
Service Support Divisions	11
11 Railway Engineer	
Combat Regiments (Independent)	21
5 Infantry	
6 Tank	
10 Cavalry	
Border/Internal Defense Regiments (Independent)	40
Combat Support Regiments (Independent)	61
11 Field Artillery	
6 Rocket Launcher	
35 Engineer	
9 Signal	
Service Support Regiment (Independent)	36
35 Motor Transport	
1 Railway Engineer	

[a] We estimate no substantial change in these figures through 1969.

[b] One army, the 10th Air Army, consisting of the three airborne divisions, is subordinate to the CCAF, but is, for the purpose of this paper, included with the CCA.

TOP SECRET

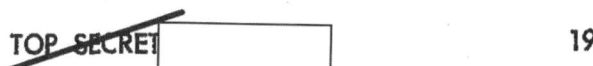

TOP SECRET
19

B. Air Force

8. The Chinese Air Force and Naval Air Force (CCAF and CCNAF), number slightly more than 214,000 men and are equipped with some 2,800 aircraft. The largest active operational unit in the CCAF is the Air Division, with each division consisting of 2 to 3 regiments. The CCAF has a total of some 89 regiments including 65 fighter regiments (Mig-15/Mig-17/Mig-19/Mig-21), 10 attack regiments (Mig-15/IL-10), 8 jet light bomber regiments (IL-28), 5 prop light bomber regiments (TU-2) and 1 medium bomber regiment (TU-4/TU-16). (See Table 2 for aircraft totals by type.)

9. Attrition is taking an increasing toll of the jet light bomber force and has already reduced the original force of some 450 to its present strength of approximately 270. The number of sorties flown per month by the average IL-28 pilot is probably barely sufficient to maintain minimum proficiency. However, the fact that many pilots have been flying these same aircraft for up to 10 years would probably provide the bomber force with sufficient experience to conduct daytime medium-altitude bombing missions. With less than 10 percent of training done at night, it seems likely that the night and radar bombing capabilities of most crews would be very marginal.

10. The strength of both bomber and fighter units has been gradually reduced during the past few years. IL-28 regiments, originally consisting of about 30 aircraft each, now are believed to possess only about 18 aircraft per unit. Fighter regiments, with a previous strength of 32 aircraft, have also been reduced due to attrition, and now have no more than 25 aircraft. With the advent of Mig-19 production, however, this trend will be reversed.

11. The Air Defense Command (ADC) is the only major command in the CCAF. For air defense purposes, both CCAF and CCNAF fighters are controlled by the ADC through its nine air defense districts. These districts are further subdivided into zones and sectors.

12. The air defense weapons system includes, in addition to the fighter force, 19 or 20 antiaircraft artillery (AAA) divisions administratively subordinate to the CCAF. The AAA divisions are operationally subordinate to the CCAF Air Defense Headquarters in the area in which they are located, just as are other CCAF air divisions. The administrative subordination of the surface-to-air missile (SAM) units is not known. Undoubtedly, however, these units are operationally subordinate to the various Air Defense Headquarters, and function in the same manner as conventional AAA units. Some 35 deployed SAM sites have been built, but at least 13 were later abandoned. Of the remaining 22 sites, no more than 12 are believed to have been occupied at any one time.

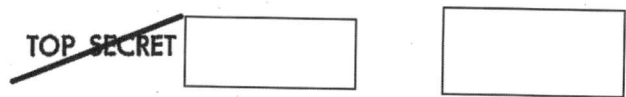

TOP SECRET

20 TOP SECRET

TABLE 2

ESTIMATED NUMBERS OF MILITARY AIRCRAFT (1967-1969)

	15 MARCH 1967			1 JANUARY 1969
	CCAF	CCNAF	TOTALS	
Fighter				
Mig-15/Fagot	330	0	330	50–100
Mig-17/Fresco	1,185	215	1,400 [a]	1,100–1,400
Mig-19/Farmer	425	105	530 [b]	725–850 [c]
Mig-21/Fishbed	35	0	35	75–125
Bomber				
TU-2/Bat	75	10	85	0–25
IL-28/Beagle	155	115	270	175–225
TU-4/Bull	13	0	13	0–10
TU-16/Badger	2	0	2	4–8
Transport				
Medium	13	0	13	25–35
Light	150	10	160	200–250
Reconnaissance				
BE-6/Madge	0	5	5	0–5
Helicopter				
MI-4/Hound	135	15	150	300–350

[a] Approximately 20 percent possess all-weather capability.

[b] Approximately 25 percent possess limited all-weather capability.

[c] We would expect this figure to be less if an intensified production of the Mig-21 occurs.

C. Navy

13. *General.* Present ship strength of the CCN includes 34 submarines, 4 destroyers, 7 destroyer escorts, and about 525 smaller combatants, including at least 8 guided missile patrol boats. Personnel strength is estimated at about 142,000, including 17,000 in the naval air force.

14. Administrative and operational control over the naval forces is exercised through the Commander-in-Chief of the Navy. Orders from the Minister of National Defense are passed to the Commander-in-Chief of the CCN via the General Staff for information and coordination. CCN Headquarters is located in Peking. The CCN is comprised of three major fleets: North Sea Fleet with headquarters in Tsingtao, East Sea Fleet with headquarters in Shanghai, and South Sea Fleet with headquarters in Chan-chiang (Fort Bayard). The North Sea Fleet is the major Chinese fleet and includes over half of the submarines and destroyers. Submarines currently operate only in the North and East Sea Fleets.

15. The CCNAF fighter regiments, charged with the protection of Chinese territorial waters, are administratively controlled by CCNAF Headquarters at Peking through the fleet headquarters. In their air defense role fighter units are operationally controlled by the ADC of the CCAF. The bomber regiments are controlled by the fleet headquarters.

16. The CCNAF includes 12 fighter regiments of about 30 fighters each, and 6 jet light bomber regiments (20 IL-28s each). Naval IL-28 bombers have

TOP SECRET

 TOP SECRET 21

been detected in activity which suggests these aircraft may have a torpedo attack capability.

TABLE 3

ESTIMATED NUMBER OF NAVAL UNITS (1967-1969)

Type	15 MARCH 1967 TOTALS	MID-1969 [a]
Principal Combatant:		
Old Destroyer (ODD)	4	4
Destroyer Escort (DE)	7	12–16
Ballistic Missile Submarine (SSB)	1	1–2
Submarine (SS)	33[b]	36–39
Patrol:		
Old Patrol Escort (OPF)	16	
Submarine Chaser (PC)	23	26–28
Fast Patrol Boat (PTF)	120	200–220
Motor Torpedo Boat (PT)	185	
Hydrofoil Motor Torpedo Boat (PTH)	20	70–80
Motor Gunboat (PGM)	87	
Old Motor Gunboat (OPGM)	3	
Guided Missile Patrol Boat (PTG/PTFG)	8–10	30–40
Minewarfare:		
Minesweeper, Fleet (MSF)	20	28–32
Minesweeper, Coastal (MSC)	35	
Minesweeper, Coastal (Old) (MSC(O))	4	
Minesweeper, Auxiliary (MSA)	20	
Amphibious:		
Tank Landing Ship (LST)	20 (8)[c]	
Medium Landing Ship (LSM)	13 (11)[c]	
Landing Ship Infantry (LSIL)	16	
Utility Landing Craft (LCU)	10	
Landing Craft Mechanized (LCM/LCT)	220	250–260
Auxiliaries:		
Miscellaneous Auxiliary (AG)	35	
Light Cargo Ship (AKL)	11	
Net Laying Ship (AN)	6	
Oiler (AO/AOL)	15	
Landing Craft Repair Ship (ARL)	1	
Small Submarine Tender (ASL)	1	
Ocean Tug (ATA)	10	
Service Craft (various types)	349	

[a] Blank spaces indicate a lack of sufficient data to make useful projections.

[b] Includes 21 "W" class, 3 "M-V" class, 4 "S-1" class, 5 "R" class.

[c] Numbers in parentheses are additional units in merchant service.

 TOP SECRET

TOP SECRET

ANNEX B

MILITARY INDUSTRIES

TOP SECRET

TOP SECRET

25

ANNEX B

MILITARY INDUSTRIES

A. Production of Ground Forces Equipment

1. At least 10 major plants are involved in the output of finished military equipment and about 30 plants are involved in explosives/ammunition production. Except principally for infantry weapons, little is known about current production rates for specific military equipment.

2. The vast majority of Chinese Communist Army (CCA) weapons and vehicles are of Soviet design, and many of the older artillery pieces and all of the T-34 tanks are Soviet manufactured. Nevertheless, the Chinese now appear to produce all of the small arms, conventional ammunition, and T-59 tanks, some of the field and antiaircraft artillery and chemical munitions, and most of the transport vehicles found in the CCA.

3. Production of small arms is believed to be more than adequate to meet CCA unit requirements as well as to provide for a large reserve inventory. Samples of Chinese-produced weapons obtained in Vietnam have shown that small arms currently in the hands of CCA soldiers are well-made, rugged, and entirely adequate for their intended use. Future production rates are contingent on several factors, the most immediate of which is the conflict in Vietnam. However, the Chinese will probably not produce above the present rate and will probably reduce small arms production over the next few years.

4. [   ] photography indicate that current production of field and antiaircraft artillery includes 57 mm antiaircraft guns, 85 mm and 100 mm field guns, 122 mm howitzers, and, possibly 152 mm howitzers. Even so, a substantial part of the CCA's total inventory of medium and self-propelled artillery was obtained from the USSR. Major Chinese artillery plants are located in Ch'i-ch'i-ha-erh, Pao-t'ou, and T'ai-yuan.

5. There is no evidence that the Chinese are now building T34s, assault guns, or heavy tanks. The T-59, currently in production, appears to be a copy of a Soviet medium tank, T-54A. The Chinese are believed to have begun producing

TOP SECRET

26

TOP SECRET

the T-59 in late 1958. In 1961 the combined effect of the Soviet withdrawal and failure of the "Great Leap Forward" caused production either to slow considerably or perhaps to stop entirely for a time. If production did stop, it probably was resumed on a limited scale in 1962, but did not recover entirely until 1965. We now believe it is producing at a rate of 400-600 a year. Major operating tank facilities include an assembly plant at Pao-t'ou, a diesel engine plant at Ta-t'ung, a refitting and parts plant in Harbin. A research and development (R and D) center is located in Ch'ang-hsin-tien.

6. The current CCA inventory of wheeled transport vehicles is believed to be in the vicinity of 150,000 vehicles and is composed of a heterogeneous collection of Soviet, Chinese, and European-built vehicles. The majority of the Chinese trucks are produced in the Vehicle Plant Number 1 in Ch'ang-ch'un which was completed with Soviet technical and material assistance in late 1956.

B. Aircraft Industry

7. The Chinese Communists have given the development of military aircraft a high priority. There are five centers of the aircraft industry in Communist China: Shen-yang, Sian, Ch'eng-tu, Nan-ch'ang, and Harbin. Three of these centers, Shen-yang, Nan-ch'ang, and Harbin are currently producing aircraft. The facility at Ch'eng-tu appeared completed by late 1964, and the facility at Sian in late 1966, although there is no indication of production as yet.

8. Chinese aircraft production began in 1956 with production of the Mig-17s at Shen-yang, where the Soviets had helped the Chinese build an airframe and jet engine plant. There is good evidence that this plant was retooled in the late 1950's, and that by 1959 or 1960, the Chinese began to assemble Mig-19s from Soviet supplied components. Assembly apparently ceased in 1960 with the Sino-Soviet rift. After a delay of several years, the Chinese resumed production of the Mig-19 at Shen-yang. This plant is currently believed to be producing at a rate of some 20-25 aircraft per month, with more than 500 Mig-19s produced since the resumption of production.

9. In the late 1950's, the Chinese began construction of a second fighter production complex at Ch'eng-tu. Construction continued at the plant in the early 1960's, and by late 1964 both the airframe and jet engine plants were apparently completed. As of 1 January 1967 the factory does not appear to be engaged in anything other than possible repair and maintenance. Older type aircraft (Mig-15/Mig-17s) have used the factory airfield, but apparently in an air defense capacity. Despite the delay in production, it is still estimated that a more advanced type of jet fighter, presumably the Mig-21, will be produced at Ch'eng-tu. The delay in the appearance of such aircraft may result from difficulties in producing this more complex aircraft.

10. A factory at Harbin is currently producing MI-4 helicopters, at a rate of about 10-12 per month. Production is believed to have resumed in 1965. The

TOP SECRET

TOP SECRET   27

aircraft plant at Nan-ch'ang which has been in production since the late 1950's, is currently producing AN-2 light transports and basic training aircraft of the Yak-18 type. While aircraft production at this plant never ceased entirely in the early 1960's, it was drastically reduced. As of 1 January 1967, the plant is estimated to be producing aircraft at a rate of some 10-12 AN-2s and 1-2 of the Yak-type trainers per month.

C. Missile Production

11. Chinese production of air defense type guided missiles (SAMs, AAMs) may be underway. [   ] several factories in the T'ai-yuan area are considered good candidates for current production. Located at T'ai-yuan are solid propellant production and testing facilities, munitions plants, and an electronics plant. These facilities are believed capable of producing both SAMs and AAMs.

12. In addition to the T'ai-yuan complex, the Chinese have built a major solid propellant production and testing facility at Hu-ho-hao-t'e, in Inner Mongolia. This new facility, currently in the final stages of construction, is probably capable of producing various solid propellant grains in substantial quantities.

D. Naval Construction

13. Naval shipbuilding in Communist China has followed a pattern similar to that of other military industries. The Soviets assisted in establishing shipyards and while the Chinese were learning the technology, the Soviets supplied components which were assembled in China. Chinese Communist construction of modern units began under Soviet supervision during the 1955-1960 period. Following withdrawal of Soviet aid, their construction was severely curtailed and remained so for several years. In late 1962 an active program of ship production resumed. The Chinese have been constructing some Soviet class ships as well as increasing numbers of indigenously designed or modified ships of various classes. The naval shipbuilding industry has progressed to a level higher than that achieved prior to 1960, and several shipyards are currently being modernized and enlarged.

14. Chinese Communist submarine construction, initiated under the Soviets, virtually ceased in 1960 due to the Sino-Soviet rift. However, the outfitting of four "W" class units previously launched continued. By 1962, 21 "W" class submarines had been constructed in China, 15 at Shanghai and 6 at Wu-ch'ang, from Soviet supplied components.

15. In 1962, construction of "R" class submarines began at Shanghai and Wu-ch'ang. Currently, five "R" class units appear to be operational. While the "R" class construction program is continuing at Wu-ch'ang, it appears to have been interrupted at Shanghai. How many of this class submarine the Chinese intend to construct is not known, but we believe that a total of about 10 more will be built by 1970.

TOP SECRET

28   TOP SECRET

16. A single "G" class ballistic missile submarine was constructed at the Luta Shipyard, Dairen, between 1962 and 1964. The Soviets almost certainly provided the hull design, and may have supplied components for the vessel, as well. We have no evidence that the Chinese are now constructing any more of this class submarine.

17. Two years after the withdrawal of Soviet assistance, the Chinese began production of a number of native-designed craft. Twelve Shanghai class PTFs appeared in production at Shanghai from 1959 to 1961; production of an enlarged version of the Shanghai class began at Dairen in 1963 and has reached the rate of about 50 units per year. Other native-designed units include the Hainan class subchaser and Huchwan class hydrofoil torpedo boat (PTH). Three and possibly four of the Hainan class subchasers were constructed at the Huangpu Shipyard, Canton, from 1964 through 1966. The Huchwan class PTHs are constructed in Shanghai. The extent of the latter (PTH) program is not known, although some 17 units had been produced by 1967. The most significant product of the Chinese naval design program is the Kiangnan class destroyer escort, the first of which completed fitting out at Shanghai in 1966. Construction of additional Kiangnans began at Canton in 1965 and is continuing. Three units are currently operational, and two more are under construction at Canton.

18. Numerous other small combatants and support units, primarily of Soviet design are under construction at the various shipyards. It became evident in 1966 that the Chinese were producing guided missile patrol boats of both the OSA and KOMAR classes. Additional T-43 class minesweepers are being constructed as are P-6 class PTs. About 12 of the latter are believed to have been produced at the Huangpu Shipyard since late 1965, and the program may be continuing.

TOP SECRET

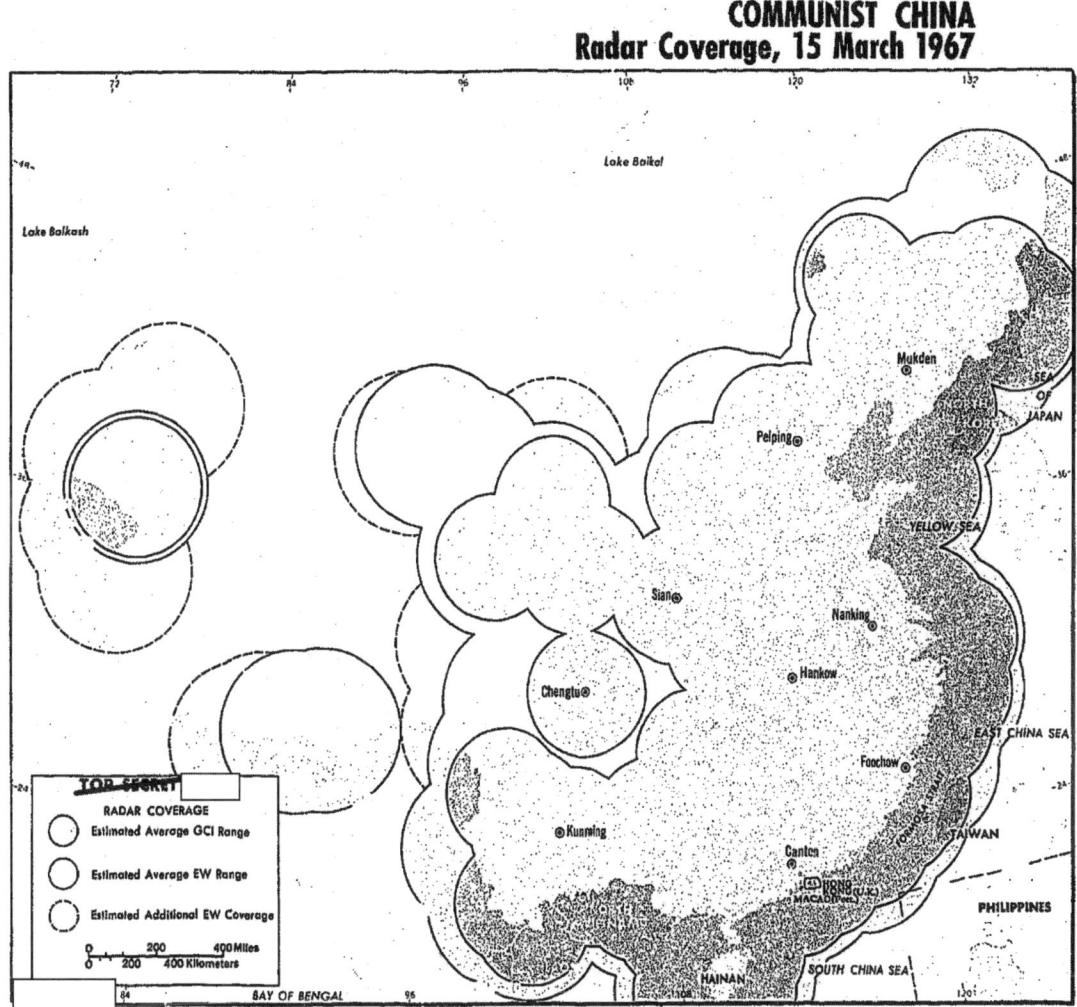

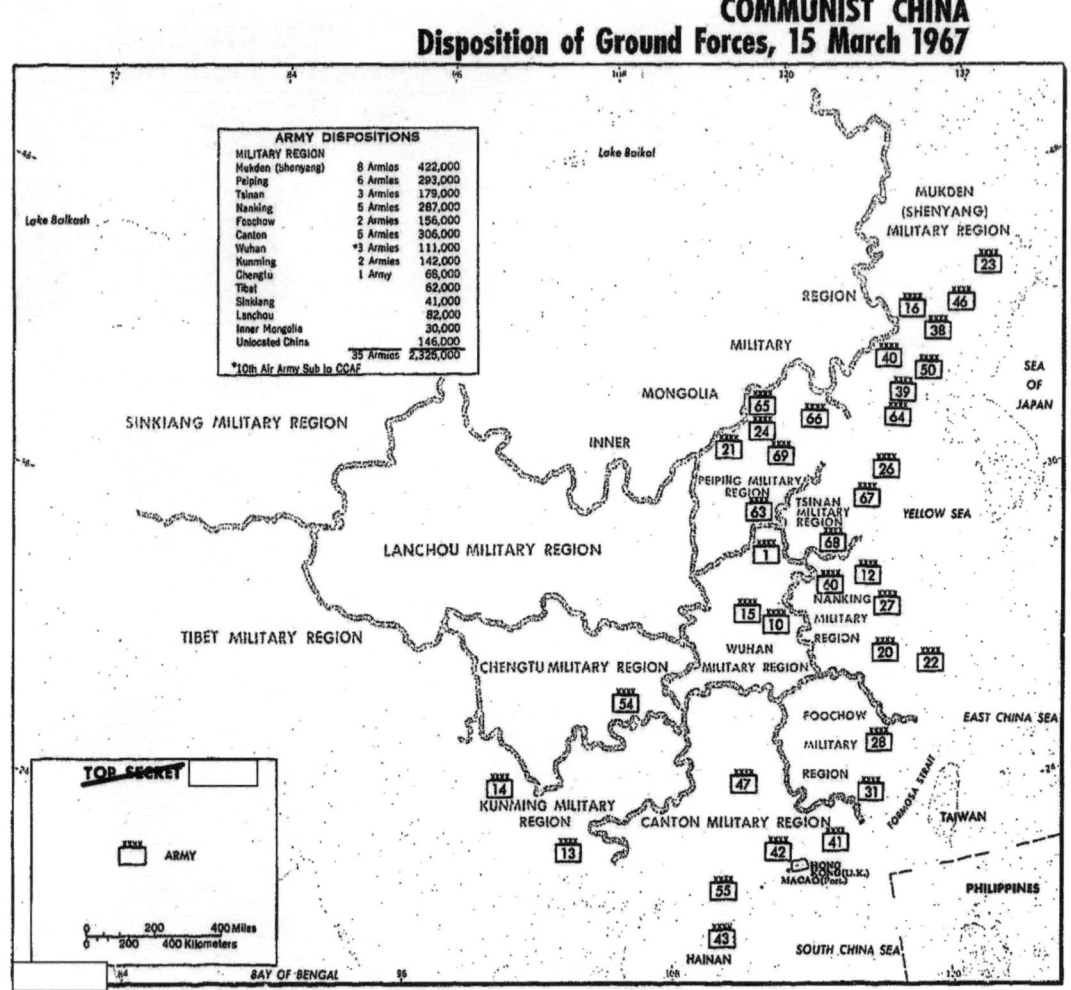

COMMUNIST CHINA
Disposition of Ground Forces, 15 March 1967

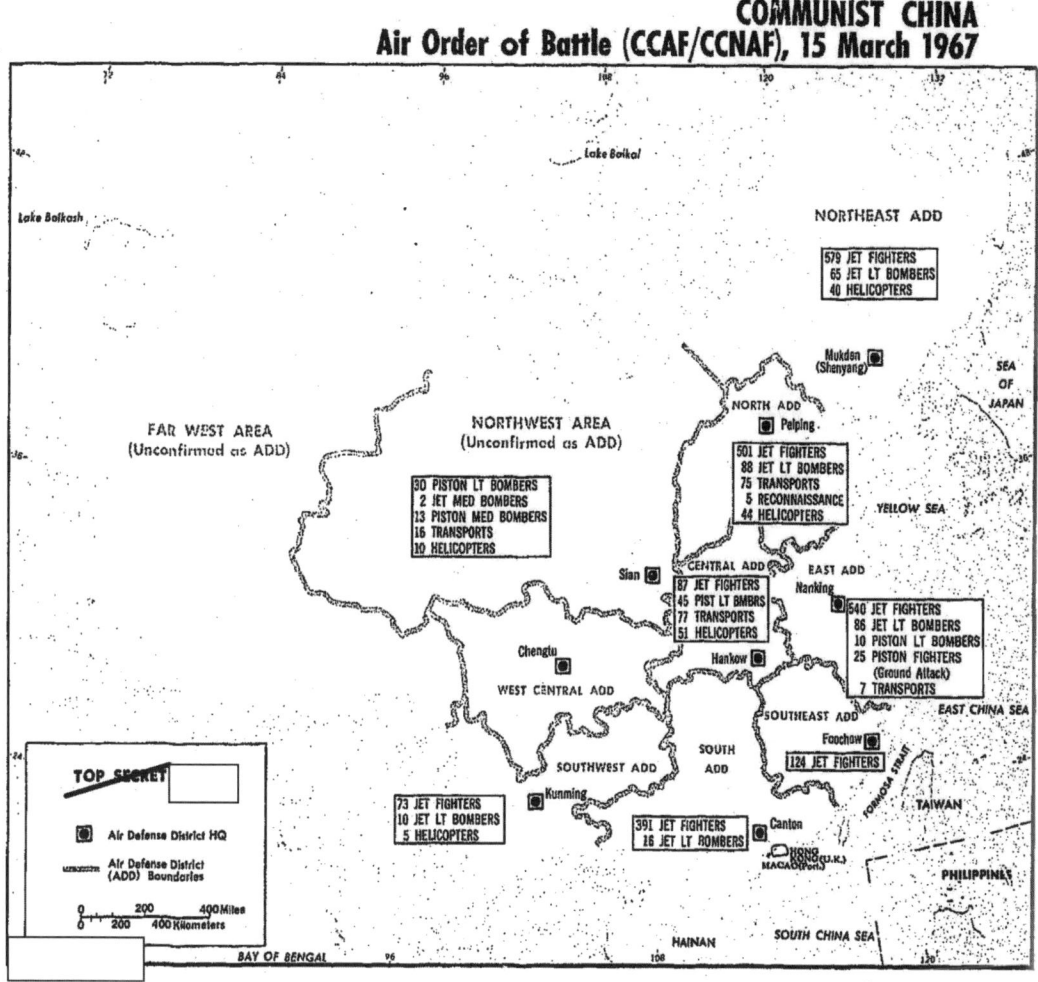

COMMUNIST CHINA
Air Order of Battle (CCAF/CCNAF), 15 March 1967

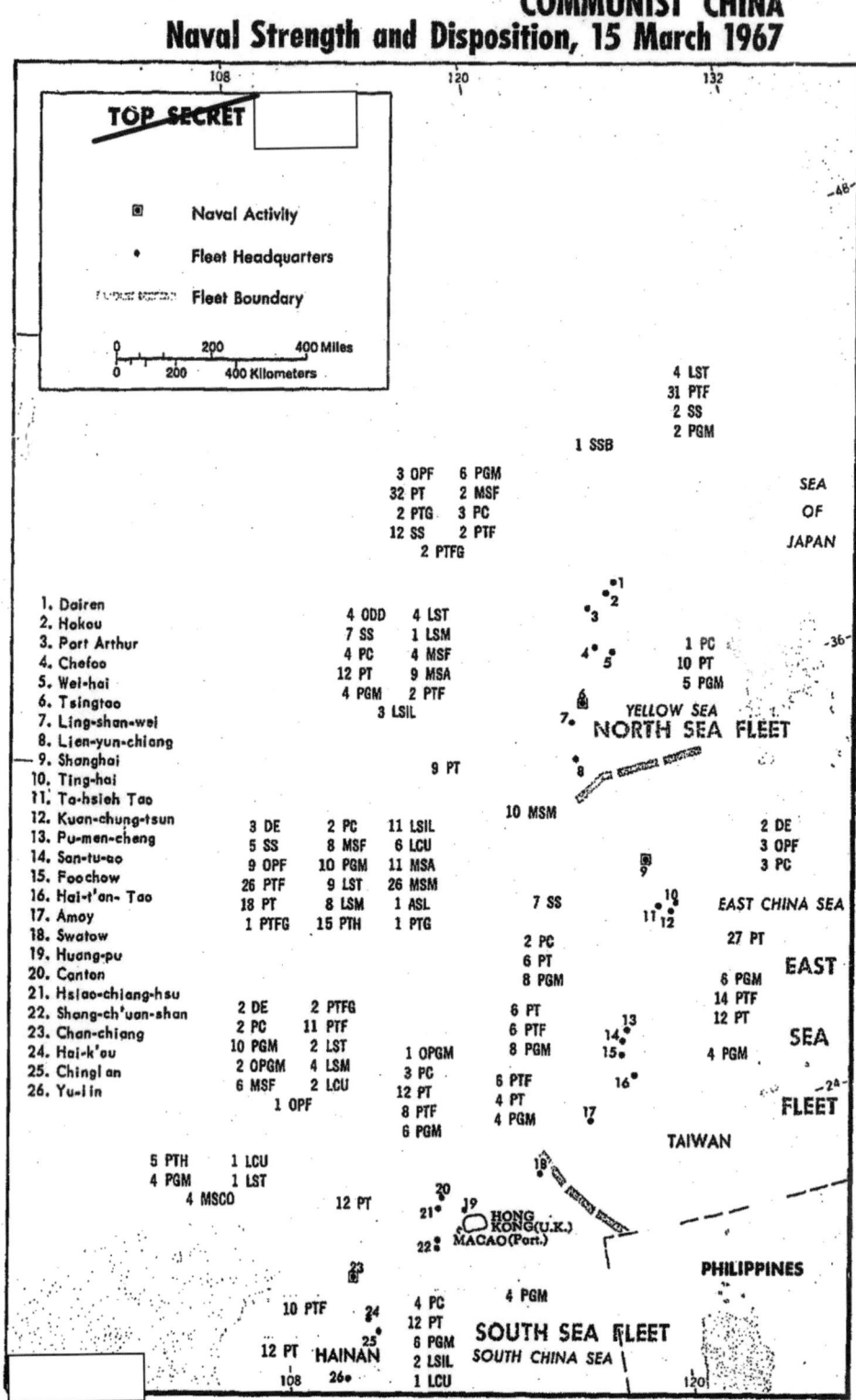

COMMUNIST CHINA
Naval Strength and Disposition, 15 March 1967

TOP SECRET

▣ Naval Activity

• Fleet Headquarters

Fleet Boundary

0   200   400 Miles
0   200   400 Kilometers

1. Dairen
2. Hokou
3. Port Arthur
4. Chefoo
5. Wei-hai
6. Tsingtao
7. Ling-shan-wei
8. Lien-yun-chiang
9. Shanghai
10. Ting-hai
11. Ta-hsieh Tao
12. Kuan-chung-tsun
13. Pu-men-cheng
14. San-tu-ao
15. Foochow
16. Hai-t'an- Tao
17. Amoy
18. Swatow
19. Huang-pu
20. Canton
21. Hsiao-chiang-hsu
22. Shang-ch'uan-shan
23. Chan-chiang
24. Hai-k'ou
25. Chinglan
26. Yu-lin

4 LST
31 PTF
2 SS
2 PGM

1 SSB

3 OPF   6 PGM
32 PT   2 MSF
2 PTG   3 PC
12 SS   2 PTF
2 PTFG

SEA
OF
JAPAN

4 ODD   4 LST
7 SS   1 LSM
4 PC   4 MSF
12 PT   9 MSA
4 PGM   2 PTF
3 LSIL

1 PC
10 PT
5 PGM

YELLOW SEA
NORTH SEA FLEET

9 PT

10 MSM

2 DE
3 OPF
3 PC

3 DE   2 PC   11 LSIL
5 SS   8 MSF   6 LCU
9 OPF   10 PGM   11 MSA
26 PTF   9 LST   26 MSM
18 PT   8 LSM   1 ASL
1 PTFG   15 PTH   1 PTG

7 SS

2 PC
6 PT
8 PGM

EAST CHINA SEA

27 PT

EAST

6 PGM
14 PTF
12 PT

SEA

2 DE   2 PTFG
2 PC   11 PTF
10 PGM   2 LST
2 OPGM   4 LSM
6 MSF   2 LCU
1 OPF

6 PT
6 PTF
8 PGM

6 PTF
4 PT
4 PGM

4 PGM

FLEET

1 OPGM
3 PC
12 PT
8 PTF
6 PGM

TAIWAN

5 PTH   1 LCU
4 PGM   1 LST
4 MSCO

12 PT

HONG
KONG (U.K.)
MACAO (Port.)

PHILIPPINES

10 PTF   24

12 PT HAINAN
108   26•

4 PC   4 PGM
12 PT
6 PGM   SOUTH SEA FLEET
2 LSIL   SOUTH CHINA SEA
1 LCU

SECTION 27

NIE 13-7-67

The Chinese Cultural Revolution

25 May 1967

APPROVED FOR RELEASE
DATE: MAY 2004

~~SECRET~~

NIE 13-7-67
25 May 1967

(b)(1)
(b)(3)

NATIONAL INTELLIGENCE ESTIMATE

NUMBER 13-7-67

The Chinese Cultural Revolution

Submitted by

DIRECTOR OF CENTRAL INTELLIGENCE
Concurred in by the
UNITED STATES INTELLIGENCE BOARD
As indicated overleaf
25 May 1967

Authenticated:

EXECUTIVE SECRETARY, USIB

~~SECRET~~

N⁰ 617

SECRET

THE CHINESE CULTURAL REVOLUTION

CONCLUSIONS

A. The political crisis in China continues. No end is in sight. Among the several possible outcomes, no one is distinctly more likely than others. But whatever its ultimate resolution, the Great Proletarian Cultural Revolution has already done immense damage to the top leadership and the party, has profoundly altered the internal power structure, has greatly unsettled all levels of Chinese society, has unleashed new forces of instability, and has contributed to China's growing isolation in the world.

B. We have no evidence that the Cultural Revolution has yet had any significant effects on the military capabilities of the PLA or on China's advanced weapons programs. But the PLA is assuming more and more noncombat tasks and if this trend long continues it would almost certainly affect its combat capabilities.

C. Instability and confusion are likely to persist so long as Mao retains sufficient power and vigor to push his designs for remoulding the party and combating real and imagined threats to his doctrines and policies. Mao could misjudge his power position and go too far. He is now heavily dependent on the military for support; too vigorous efforts to bridle the armed forces could produce a coup against Mao or even fragmentation of the country and civil war. But these are extreme cases and we think it more likely that a basic tendency toward preservation of national unity will persist, despite the divisive impact of the Cultural Revolution.

D. Looking beyond Mao, the Cultural Revolution has made it more likely that the succession will be a disorderly and contentious struggle. The military may play a decisive role, but Lin Piao would not necessarily be their candidate. A collective including Chou

SECRET

1

SECRET

En-lai, some of the military leaders, and even some of the now disgraced party figures, might emerge. In any event we believe that many of Mao's dogmas and practices are likely to be set aside. This might be a gradual process, though it could come more rapidly if unresolved internal and external problems have been aggravated during the last months or years of Mao's rule.

E. The political crisis has already focused the leadership's energies and attention on internal affairs and has at least temporarily damaged Chinese prestige abroad. Within this context, however, China has maintained a relatively active foreign policy, though it has become more rigid in international Communist affairs. For the most part Peking has maintained policy positions which were well established before the Cultural Revolution began. As long as the Maoists retain control, Peking is unlikely to make any important changes in the general line of its foreign policy. At any rate, in the short term, an unremitting hostility to the US and the USSR is likely to remain the predominant feature of Chinese foreign policy. It is possible, however, that over the longer term, internal changes in the direction of moderation, if they do occur, will create more favorable conditions for reappraising foreign policy and perhaps for introducing elements of greater moderation.

SECRET

DISCUSSION

1. Only two years ago, the fortunes of Communist China seemed to be rising. Internally, the economy was recovering from the disasters of the Great Leap Forward and the split with the USSR. Chinese scientists had already exploded their first atomic device. Even the problem of succession to the aging Mao seemed to be safely resolved in favor of Liu Shao-chi and a unified collective leadership. Externally, China was making progress in its dispute with the USSR: Khrushchev, the arch-enemy, had fallen in disgrace; several Asian Communist Parties adhered to China's bloc and there was support and sympathy from a wide variety of other Communists in Europe, Latin America, and Africa. In Vietnam, the success of the Viet Cong promised early vindication of Mao's line on armed liberation. Trends in Djakarta also held out the prospect of a Communist success that would outflank all of Southeast Asia.

2. Now the outlook for China has been drastically altered. Its leadership is in a sorry condition. The Chief of State and the General Secretary of the party are in disgrace, accused of treachery. Old revolutionary war heroes are discredited. Promising situations abroad have turned sour and foreign friends have been alienated. China is nearly isolated. For a few weeks early in 1967 there were serious and widespread disorders. The Great Proletarian Cultural Revolution has plunged China into the greatest political crisis in the regime's 17-year history.

I. THE COURSE OF THE CULTURAL REVOLUTION

3. In retrospect, it seems likely that tensions have been building up in the political leadership during the years after the collapse of the Great Leap Forward and the humiliating retreat from that policy. A degree of stability and order was achieved, but at the cost of abandoning many of Mao's programs. During this period Mao was remarkably withdrawn, though the various political and ideological campaigns came and went. It may be that Mao's political powers were partially circumscribed and his initiatives blunted. It is likely, as the posters have claimed, that some of his lieutenants did not consult him regularly and thus took some decisions out of his hands. This probably led Mao to seek means to reassert his authority and doctrines over the country.

4. Mao has an almost mystical faith in what mobilized and indoctrinated masses can accomplish. This lay behind such movements as the Leap Forward and the Socialist Education campaign, a precursor of the Cultural Revolution. His approach stresses ideological indoctrination and the inevitability of struggle in political development. Indeed, his preoccupation with "contradictions" may have led him to exaggerate the dangers of capitalistic and bourgeois remnants in China. Thus, he has insisted on "uninterrupted revolution" as the means to combat what he sees as a persistent threat from the right. Others among

3

the leadership apparently believed that these matters could and should be submerged in the interest of getting on with the business of constructing a modern China.

5. In any case, Mao's dissatisfaction with the political situation must have been growing. We know from his conversations with foreign visitors that he was brooding over China's future. He indicated his concern over how little time might be left for him to complete his revolution. He expressed particular concern over the outlook of the younger generation, untried in revolution. And he was more and more obsessed that Soviet-style revisionism might infect China, especially after his death. Many of the themes which became prominent in the Cultural Revolution were strikingly expressed in the polemics with the USSR, especially in mid-1964.

6. It was in this state of latent tensions that new policy issues must have aggravated differences within the top command in Peking. The Vietnam war in particular and the threat of a war with the US were such issues. Related to them was the question of joint action in Vietnam with the USSR. Then, there was the practical question of a third Five-Year Plan. Perhaps the debacle in Indonesia added to the strains. Mao's suspiciousness may have led him to interpret policy disagreement as disloyalty. But in any event, by September-November 1965, Mao had apparently decided to make a move against his opponents. Whether these policy differences were the reason or merely the opportunity to open the attack is unclear. Mao may have decided sometime earlier, in the aftermath of the Great Leap, that his opposition in the party had to be removed if his general line were to be implemented.

7. An underlying issue must have been the question of Mao's successor. For years it had been widely known that Mao had designated Liu Shao-chi. But as his distrust of the party apparatus grew, he began to build up the Peoples Liberation Army (PLA) as a model of orthodoxy and to enhance the prestige of its leader, Marshal Lin Piao. This situation added to the contention and struggle and became particularly acute after the Central Committee plenum last August, which confirmed Lin as the heir apparent. Those who had staked their careers on Liu were struggling to survive his decline and downfall, and those around Lin were probably trying to capitalize on his new prominence. As a consequence, political maneuvers have been tense and convoluted. Not only were leaders acting to protect their own careers, but we assume that, wherever possible, they took the opportunity to embarrass or eliminate rivals. The curious charges against implausible culprits suggests that many attacks were designed to settle old scores. We cannot completely discount repeated references to an attempted "coup" in February 1966. At that time Mao may have detected moves that he interpreted as attempts to usurp his power. Or, more likely, those leaders who saw themselves threatened by the campaign launched in the fall of 1965 may have taken defensive measures to counter Mao.

8. The Cultural Revolution has passed through various phases. When it first became public in the spring of 1966, it appeared limited to bringing down the

4

SECRET

intellectuals and the party propaganda and cultural apparatus. By June, it had claimed the powerful Peng Chen and his Peking Party apparatus as major victims. In August, the Mao/Lin Piao forces won a showdown in the Central Committee. Despite the resulting demotion of Liu Shao-chi and Teng Hsiao-ping, party opposition appeared to be widespread in the provinces. The Red Guards were then unleashed for a frontal assault on the party apparatus. The immediate results were inconclusive and in October and November the extremes of the Red Guard movement were moderated. A new escalation followed in December when the revolutionary organizations were turned loose on the hitherto exempt factories and countryside, although the impact on the latter was somewhat less. By January the revolution was at its high tide, and party leaders were being deposed on a large scale, possibly with some PLA assistance. Disorder, confusion, and resistance were growing apace.

9. A major retreat then occurred as the PLA was brought in to restore order. In the process some Red Guard and "revolutionary" organizations were suppressed in the interests of stability. In the ensuing countercurrent, even Madame Mao criticized the "anarchy" of the young revolutionaries. The party cadres were granted a temporary reprieve from attacks and some were installed in positions of authority. But for many, the respite did not last. In March, some Red Guard units that had been criticized in February resumed limited and more controlled action, and senior governmental officials were again brought under heavy attack.

10. The situation remains highly fluid. The top leadership has not been stabilized; the purge has yet to run its course and may be intensified even within the PLA; struggles over the pace and direction of the revolution continue. The shape of the governing and control institutions and their political composition is still being worked out. Mao's revolutionary followers appear to be locked in intramural struggles for position and confusion continues. The restoration of regime authority throughout China remains a serious problem for the Maoists. Above all, the mental attitudes and physical health of Mao are uncertain.

11. To the degree that the Cultural Revolution represents a last effort by Mao and his supporters to determine the future of China, then they have scored a Pyrrhic victory at best. Mao has succeeded in tearing apart the bureaucratic apparatus. It is questionable, however, whether he can find experienced or talented people who are also loyal Maoists to reinvigorate the old party machine, to replace it, or to build a parallel power structure. The young activists have been treated to a taste of revolution, but thus far they have not inherited real power. Indeed, the more traditional forces, the PLA as well as what remains of the bureaucracy, seem to have proved indispensable. Without them China might have degenerated into chaos. Thus, after more than 18 months of revolutionary turmoil, Mao is still a long way from achieving his ultimate objectives.

SECRET

5

SECRET

II. MAJOR EFFECTS ON THE SYSTEM AND THE SOCIETY

A. Consequences for the Leadership

12. The party purge has virtually demolished the top leadership. Within the Central Committee, no more than one-third of the members are apparently in good standing. Of the 25 members installed in the politburo in August 1966, only 7 are still clearly in good standing; 6 appear to have been purged, and the remainder have come under varying degrees of attack. There seems to be no clear pattern in these actions. Hard line leftists and presumably loyal Maoists have fallen, while some leaders who were thought to be more moderate have survived. The beneficiaries of one round of the purge have turned out to be the next victims. In some cases, leaders who were purged many years ago have been reinstated and assumed important posts.

13. In any event, Mao has stripped away much of the experienced command that has run China for the past decade or more. He is now relying on a small, incongruous group headed by Lin Piao and Chou En-lai, and including Mao's wife, his ghost writer and ideologue Chen Po-ta, and Kang Sheng, a party secretary with long associations with the secret police. Beyond this hard core, there has been no stable group that can be identified, and there are probably divisions and rivalry within the hard core.

14. Mao has not only demonstrated his ability to bring down prestigious leaders but also his willingness to do it regardless of their position or previous association with him. In these circumstances no one, including Chou En-lai and Lin Piao, can be sure of the future. There must be a great reluctance at all levels to assume responsibility or to take initiatives. The surviving leadership probably works in an atmosphere of deep mutual suspicion with personal survival an ever present concern. This situation must be having highly adverse effects on the decision-making process at the national level. Not only are many of the most experienced officials now in disgrace, but those remaining must find it difficult to carry on objective discussions on key economic, military, and foreign policy issues in the midst of the strain and suspicion induced by the Cultural Revolution.

B. Damage to the Party Structure

15. Mao probably launched his attack on the party not only to reduce its role, at least temporarily, but also to reconstitute its leadership. The extent and the tenacity of the opposition, however, may have forced Mao to widen his campaign beyond what he originally intended and to resort to mass action against the party by extra-party instruments. Even party officials spared in the purge have been humiliated by criticism and self-criticism. The result has been confusion in the party's chain of command, depressed morale, and a general erosion of authority throughout the apparatus.

16. It is possible that Mao intends to restore the party apparatus to its former place of authority. This could be a long and difficult process, particularly if the

6

SECRET

SECRET

central authority should itself lack strength and unity. At present the party apparatus is discredited and must contend with an atmosphere conditioned by Mao's own attacks on the principle of unquestioned obedience to party authority. By undermining one of the main props of his power, and gaining the enmity of party leaders, Mao has made himself more dependent on the military.

C. Military Involvement

17. The PLA now occupies an important, perhaps decisive role in Peking and throughout China. On the political front it has assumed a leading position in the provisional administrative organs now being set up.[1] Moreover, it has been assigned administrative and control functions in economic and public security activities throughout the country. Thus far the PLA's primary action has been to restore order and maintain stability. But in assuming much of the party's function as an organ of control, the PLA has greatly enhanced its already powerful position.

18. The chaos of recent months, however, has also raised doubts about the cohesion of the PLA's top leadership. Factionalism has already appeared at this level and there have been purges of important military figures. Although the numbers do not compare to the losses in the party, the total may be large. Some military leaders may have been implicated because of close personal ties with disgraced party figures, others may have opposed the Cultural Revolution within the army, and still others may have been reluctant to see the PLA used in the political struggle. Thus far, the PLA has generally responded to Peking directives and authority.

19. A factor which continues to be divisive in the military leadership is the old issue of whether to stress political indoctrination at the expense of professional training. It also seems likely that a broader range of issues was in dispute; for example, the introduction of large-scale US forces in the Vietnam war probably provoked debate over the likelihood of war with the US and the proper Chinese response. In this context, the advisability of "joint action" with the USSR was almost certainly debated, both within the PLA and the top political leadership. Whatever the issues, the PLA has demonstrated that it is not immune to the policy differences that are troubling the regime. While this is not entirely a function of the Cultural Revolution, the confusion of the campaign brought latent problems to the surface and accentuated the policy disputes.

20. We have no evidence that the Cultural Revolution has yet had any significant effects on the military capabilities of the PLA or on China's advanced weapons programs. But the PLA is assuming more and more noncombat tasks and if this trend long continues it would almost certainly affect its combat capabilities.

---

[1] These organs are the "three-way alliances" which are made up of military personnel, representatives of the revolutionary masses, and party and governmental cadre who are considered revolutionary.

SECRET

7

SECRET

D. Costs to the Economy [2]

21. Despite the radical tone of the Cultural Revolution, the regime's economic policies have continued generally moderate. This probably reflects, in part at least, a realistic appreciation of the dangers to the country that would result from serious disruptions in agriculture and industrial production. Therefore, the Cultural Revolution was not directed into the farms and factories until the end of 1966. Confusion was immediate and affected many areas. Workers left their jobs; rail transport was interrupted; peasants demanded more grain; and production was disrupted as workers demanded more benefits. These were partly spontaneous reactions. But, in addition, many local party authorities, fearing for their own positions, connived to encourage the workers and peasants in their demands, hoping to spread confusion and thereby force Peking to pull back.

22. For a time, Peking attempted to maintain both production and a high level of revolutionary activity. By late January, however, the serious disruptions brought a moderating response from Peking. As has come to be expected, Chou En-lai served as the voice of moderation, taking a stand that inevitably had the effect of pointing up the hazards of radical actions not only in the economy but elsewhere as well. Although this point of view has since lost ground to a resurgence of the radicals, the economy is still being protected from extreme policy shifts.

23. The army was brought in to restore order and to transmit economic directives, particularly in those areas where the party has lost control. The test of this expedient is yet to come. While the army has the power generally to maintain order and enforce rulings from above, it would be surprising if the PLA suddenly displayed talents for managing the increasingly diversified economy. Nevertheless, there appears little alternative to the PLA replacing civilian authority wherever the latter is ineffective in managing production. Based on the reports received to date, the army has more often been involved in a propaganda role. Where it has been involved in coordinating or supervisory work, the military has created frictions because of its lack of flexibility and experience.

24. We cannot quantify the costs of the relatively limited disruptions which occurred last winter or the continuing deleterious effects of uncertain or inexpert management and administration of the economy, but they surely have been significant. Transport and communications, food distribution, and foreign trade have all been adversely affected for short periods. Industry and agriculture may have been more seriously affected: industry probably showed little or no increase during the last quarter of 1966 and the first quarter of 1967, and in agriculture the disruptions during winter and early spring may have affected planning and preparations for spring farm work.

25. While the regime is now exercising prudence with respect to the economy, it is also condemning Liu Shao-chi for allegedly following the same course in

---

[2] A fuller discussion of the prospects for the Chinese economy will appear in NIE 13-5-67, "Economic Outlook for Communist China."

8

SECRET

SECRET

the past.

We cannot be sure, therefore, that the restraints now in force on economic policy are secure against further, and more serious, attacks from Mao. Chou has shown remarkable finesse, presumably with Mao's approval, in thus far blunting any radicalization of economic policy. But as long as Mao lives, such a possibility will remain a significant threat. If Mao should decide on a production upsurge in the manner of the Leap Forward, we would expect a prompt deterioration in the economy.

E. Foreign Policy

26. It is likely that foreign policy issues played a role in dividing the leadership. It is obviously absurd to credit Liu Shao-chi and his followers with all the pro-Soviet, procapitalist, and capitulationist type policies contained in current charges. Even so, it is probable that there were high-level critics of Mao's basic line, which resulted in the loss of Soviet military, technical, and economic assistance. By early 1966, China's attempt to take a leading role in the world revolutionary movement was failing, with consequent losses to Chinese prestige, particularly in the case of the Indonesian fiasco. But most critical, the Maoist line had left China with few friends or allies at the very moment when the dangers to China, because of the increased US involvement in Vietnam, were becoming the most acute since 1950.

27. The political crisis has focused the leadership's energies and attentions on internal affairs. Within this context, China has maintained a relatively active foreign policy, though it has become more rigid in international Communist affairs. In general, its actions have tended to consist of positions and policies well established before the Cultural Revolution began. The more rigid policy toward the Communist world has permitted the USSR to score heavily in the world Communist movement at China's expense. Even among Asian Communists, China has lost friends. In the rest of the world, the excesses of the Red Guards severely damaged China's image and added to its already declining prestige.

28. For the North Vietnamese, the Cultural Revolution has introduced tension and doubts about China's reliability. Moreover, the vehemence of Peking's anti-Soviet line must emphasize to Hanoi its tenuous position on the end of a long supply line maintained by bitterly quarreling allies. We cannot be very certain of how the Cultural Revolution has affected China's position on Vietnam. They almost certainly will continue to support Hanoi and to urge a protracted war.

29. As long as the Maoists retain control, Peking is unlikely to make any important changes in the general line of its foreign policy, despite its growing isolation and lack of notable successes. In fact, the Cultural Revolution can be interpreted as an effort to provide the revolutionary successors and the internal orthodoxy which will insure the continuation of the foreign policy developed over the last seven or eight years. This policy involves unrelenting and

SECRET

9

uncompromising struggle for preeminence within the international Communist camp and for leadership within the Afro-Asian world, hostility toward the US and the USSR, and selective peaceful coexistence with the rest of the world.

F. General Effects on Society

30. Even before the Cultural Revolution, the Chinese people were showing increasing disenchantment with the recurrent burdens of mass campaigns and incessant ideological exhortations. Now, the eulogies to Mao and his thought have become so extreme as to mock all belief and the use of terror against respected elders must have shocked and repelled much of the population. The intellectuals bore the initial brunt of the Red Guards, the government bureaucracy was drawn in later, and most of the urban populace has been touched in some way. Of the 600 million people who reside in rural China, relatively few felt the impact of the revolutionary activity, which was essentially an urban phenomenon. But few people in China could have escaped the message that Mao was having trouble with long trusted leaders; to some degree at least peasant faith in the wisdom and effectiveness of the leadership must have suffered.

31. The evidence of January indicates that once the workers and peasantry realized that they were being encouraged to attack the authorities, the campaign quickly degenerated into a loss of discipline and order. The swift spread of insecurity, confusion, and disrespect of authority must have jolted many in Peking, if not Mao and his most zealous supporters. At any rate, Peking promptly retreated and it was at this juncture that the PLA was called into the picture.

32. Another group that may pose a continuing problem is the students. While the excitement of "rebelling against authority" has probably distracted students temporarily, they will realize, if or when things quiet down, that they have been shunted aside and have lost educational and employment opportunities. This will add to the frustrations of this group ⬚ Perhaps equally important, the long disruption in the schools is causing China to slip behind in its effort to overcome shortages in trained manpower. This could have serious longer range consequences for research and development in both the industrial and military sectors.

III. THE OUTLOOK

33. *Internal Politics and Policies.* The prospects are that, so long as his health permits him to exercise active leadership, Mao will maintain a continuing high level of tensions while some of those around him try to moderate the pace and mitigate the damage. Autocratic though he may be, Mao appears to retain enough political flexibility to respond to forces about him and to be influenced by those colleagues who have his ear. As the creator and prime mover of the Cultural Revolution, he must feel his campaign is far from finished. Thus, there will probably continue to be fluctuations between more radical initiatives and periods of consolidation or retreat. We cannot predict precise tactics or individual victims at the top. But we can be fairly confident that as long as

10

SECRET

Mao is capable of political command, China's situation will probably be tense and inherently unstable.

34. Although the events of the past year and half have resulted in a surprising degree of political instability in China, we do not believe such drastic developments as civil war or fragmentation along regional lines are likely. We do feel, however, that if Mao and his followers attempt to purge the military with the harshness they applied to the party, there is a good chance that they would face defiance and resistance. This might lead to regional alliances and loss of control at the center, or a military coup.

35. The present prospect of continuing instability under Mao would become even more certain should Mao's health decline and a long interregnum occur. It is difficult to estimate the prospects for Mao's health. Obviously, at 73, his health is subject to sudden deterioration. If he were to linger on, as Lenin did, then factionalism would almost certainly grow as each leader sought to secure his position through appropriate alliances. The possibility of a coup would exist and its realization might depend on whether Mao could be maneuvered out without a struggle. An extremely critical situation could develop if the leaders tried to set Mao aside during a period of poor health, and he revived enough to fight back. If such a period were prolonged, one consequence might be the decline of Peking's authority throughout China.

36. If Mao dies in the near future we would still expect the succession to be disorderly and contentious. Lin Piao is the chosen heir, but he would face a severe test. We are not convinced that he has the political acumen or physical stamina to survive the tough infighting that is likely to follow Mao's death. His chances may depend to a great extent on whether he can command the political support of the PLA, particularly if at that time the party is still in a weakened state. Recent events, however, suggest that factionalism based on personal rivalries and policy conflicts have occurred in the army as they have elsewhere.

37. Also in the near term, Chou En-lai is a figure to be reckoned with. His staying power and abilities are well known. More than any other leader at present, Chou seems to have the versatility and skill to grasp the levers of power and steer the country toward more moderate policies. He too, however, would probably have to count on the PLA for political support. Indeed, it is possible that his survival thus far reflects a working arrangement between Chou and his government bureaucracy and some of the military leaders. Chou appears in good health despite his 69 years, but the past year has subjected him to long work days and incessant stress.

38. It is also possible that after a long period of domination by Mao, the political and military leaders would be inclined toward a greater measure of collective leadership. This tendency would probably be strengthened if Mao's excesses continue for some time. In any case, considerable political maneuvering is likely and almost certainly no single leader will assume the powers and wield the influence that Mao has had.

SECRET

11

SECRET

39. The composition of the post-Mao leadership will, of course, have a great bearing on the direction of Chinese policies. Once Mao leaves the scene, however, we believe many of the uniquely Maoist dogmas and practices are likely to expire with him, not only because they have been discredited in the Cultural Revolution but also because they are not relevant to the emerging realities of social and economic development. Indeed, the fact that the Cultural Revolution was necessary demonstrates that perpetuating Mao's revolution depends to a great extent on his person. Even if Lin Piao gains power, we would still expect a movement away from the extremes of Maoist internal policies. We cannot say how fast or how far this process would develop. In the near term, it might unfold gradually. If Mao stays on for some longer period, then the process might be much more rapid, particularly if unresolved internal and external problems have been aggravated during the last months or years of Mao.

40. If the party is still enfeebled at the time of change, the army would probably assume a stronger role in policymaking. In our view, there is probably a cautious group within the PLA who would be inclined to find common ground with moderate political leaders. We would not rule out that the net result of the succession struggle would be to create a military regime in China.

41. Economic constraints will impose limits on China's policies. Since the "Great Leap," Peking has used moderate policies to restore living standards and to organize its resources for renewed economic development. A continuation of these policies could probably secure modest economic growth. Most Chinese will judge any government on its ability to help them meet their basic needs of food, clothing, and shelter.

42. Radical policies which seek more ambitious economic goals could not be long maintained if, in the face of population pressure, they reduce or even interrupt the growth of production. Mao's "Leap Forward" approach, with its emphasis on political motivation at the expense of material incentives, has already been discredited. Many Chinese leaders probably feel that they have a better model in the more balanced approach of the 1960's or even in the Stalinist model in effect during the first Five-Year Plan in 1953-1957. The chances that Mao's successors will adopt revisionist economic policies may be affected by economic pressures forcing them toward a very hard line on austerity and discipline throughout Chinese society. We can be sure that any likely successor group will base its program on Marxism-Leninism, even if it is strongly influenced by military leaders. But actual programs will probably reflect increasingly the influence of Chinese culture and the Chinese environment. The resemblance to socialism as it has developed in the West will almost certainly diminish over time.

43. *China's World Role.* These various permutations in the resolution of China's political crisis cannot help but affect its world policy. But we cannot predict with any confidence how internal developments will bear on foreign

SECRET

SECRET

affairs. There is no precedent in Communist China for a succession struggle. Stalinist analogies are tempting but perhaps misleading. Much might depend on what transpires while Mao remains in control. Finally, the world scene changes and creates new situations and problems.

44. If a succession struggle is prolonged, this would probably concentrate attention on internal affairs even more than it has during the Cultural Revolution. Thus, for some time, China's unremitting hostility toward the US and USSR, accompanied by a more flexible policy toward the rest of the world, are likely to be the predominant trends.

45. Beyond this, the most we can estimate is that the forces of change inside the country could, but not necessarily would, have the same effect on international conduct; that is, a more moderate internal policy might be accompanied by some relaxation of external tensions and some moves to reduce China's isolation. The last phase of Mao and the succession, however, will probably coincide with the growth of Chinese strategic capabilities, and we are highly uncertain how the Chinese leadership expects to exploit this situation. As of now we would estimate that the sum total of the various political, economic, military factors, as well as international developments will create pressures for adjusting Chinese ambitions and resources, as defined and expounded by Mao, to the realities of world politics.

SECRET

13

SECTION 28

NIE 13-5-67

Economic Outlook for Communist China

29 June 1967

APPROVED FOR RELEASE
DATE: MAY 2004

(b)(1)
(b)(3)

~~SECRET~~

NIE 13-5-67
29 June 1967

NATIONAL INTELLIGENCE ESTIMATE

NUMBER 13-5-67

Economic Outlook for Communist China

Submitted by

DEPUTY DIRECTOR OF CENTRAL INTELLIGENCE

Concurred in by the

UNITED STATES INTELLIGENCE BOARD

As indicated overleaf

29 June 1967

Authenticated:

EXECUTIVE SECRETARY, USIB

~~SECRET~~

N⁰ 456

SECRET

ECONOMIC OUTLOOK FOR COMMUNIST CHINA

CONCLUSIONS

A. Economic activity in China, especially in the industrial sector, is being slowed by the Cultural Revolution. Nevertheless, military production and development continue to enjoy a high priority, and have been considerably aided by imports from the Free World.

B. Foreign trade has grown, and the non-Communist world now accounts for three-fourths of China's trade. China's balance of payments position has improved over the past two years. Support of North Vietnam has been substantially increased during the past year, but imposes no undue strain on the Chinese economy.

C. The economic outlook depends heavily upon the development of the political situation. During the next year or two, assuming a continuation of the present level of political turmoil, the economy seems likely to deteriorate somewhat, though probably not to the point of causing a sharp decline in industrial production, widespread unemployment, or acute food shortages. The weapons programs could be continued, though some stretch out in particular items might be necessary.

D. We think it unlikely that Mao will achieve sufficient political success in the Cultural Revolution to permit him to embark upon a new economic initiative similar to the Leap Forward. When Mao disappears from the scene, there will probably be a period of confused contesting for power during which economic recovery will be neither rapid nor sure.

E. The unfavorable food-population ratio, the economic costs and imbalances inherent in the military program, and the shortcomings

SECRET

1

SECRET

of the educational system are problems likely to persist for at least a decade. A pragmatic regime could probably surmount them, but any successor to the present regime will also inherit some of the ambitious political goals of its predecessor. These will strongly affect the allocation of resources, probably at the expense of laying foundations for self-sustaining economic growth.

2

SECRET

SECRET

DISCUSSION

I. THE POLITICAL SETTING

1. The political upheaval in China has complicated the analysis of China's economic performance, policies, and goals. The Third Five-Year Plan was to have begun in 1966, but a comprehensive plan has not yet been officially announced, and during the course of the Cultural Revolution little has been said concerning economic performance. Instead, attention has been focused on the political and social revolution. The leadership has been riven, and a new generation is beginning to assert itself. Cleavages are appearing between the young and the old, the students and the workers, the urban and the rural areas, and the regions and the center. Until a new order and consensus are established, economics is likely to be of secondary concern.

2. This situation reflects Mao's doctrines of social development. Mao fears the bureaucrat and the technician who, by their tasks and training, place a premium on stability and find reasons to halt revolutionary change. The cult of the amateur, embodied in "Mao's Thought," places more faith in arousing the talents and initiative of the common man than in following the advice of the highly trained specialist. It follows that Mao disdains material incentives for the more powerful—but ephemeral—force of ideological stimuli, and insists on the primacy of political enthusiasm over technical specialization. Prudent enterprise management in China has repeatedly found its cautious policies under attack by Mao. In brief, Mao is more a revolutionary leader than an economic planner.

3. The Leap Forward (1958-1960) stands as a stark example of carrying Mao's ideas to extreme lengths. Following Mao's order that "politics take command," a massive campaign of ideological exhortation elicited a nationwide outpouring of labor energies. Although this resulted in dramatic, but temporary, spurts in production, the lack of planning and coordination made the campaign ultimately self-defeating. Thus, faced in 1960 with crippling food shortages, cessation of Soviet aid, and a discouraged and disgruntled population, Peking had little choice but to pull back.

4. From mid-1960 to the end of 1962, Peking followed retreat and retrenchment policies to restore order and stability by curtailing investment, reducing or ending industrial subsidies, returning redundant urban labor to the rural areas, reviving private plots, restoring free markets, and decentralizing communes. Such pragmatic policies brought about a recovery of industrial and agricultural production that lasted into 1966.

5. We do not know whether Mao had to be pressured into these readjustments or whether he recognized the gravity of the situation and willingly acquiesced. Recent revelations confirm that there was continuing dissatisfaction among some leaders with Mao's leadership during the 1960's. It also seems probable that

SECRET

3

some top leaders were making decisions without first seeking Mao's approval. For his part, Mao was apparently growing more and more embittered as he felt himself being eased aside and his policies neglected. Thus, the collapse of the Leap Forward and the subsequent attempts at recovery contributed to the political tensions that erupted in the Cultural Revolution.

6. The radical policies of the Cultural Revolution have created an atmosphere conducive to radical economic initiatives similar to those of the Leap Forward. This would not be inconsistent with Mao's general notions; indeed, the political campaign was moved into the factories and the countryside in late 1966 and early 1967. However, this produced such confusion and disruptions to production that the regime moved rapidly to retreat from what seemed to foreshadow serious economic dislocations. With economic planning in a state of suspended animation, it seems likely that major economic initiatives will be postponed until some resolution of the political struggle is achieved.

7. In any event, the purge of the party and the general confusion about who is in charge have weakened the direction and control of the economy. Although the People's Liberation Army (PLA) has been ordered to help relay and enforce economic directives where the party and managerial apparatus has been discredited, the results have been less than satisfactory. The PLA has the ability to maintain order and discipline but lacks the necessary skills for administering complex economic activities. At the top, Premier Chou En-lai continues to maintain day-to-day operations in the governmental and economic bureaucracies, but only three of his 15 Vice Premiers remain in good political standing. Of the top level economic administrators, only Chou and Li Fu-chun seem to be currently acceptable to the Maoists. The weakening of the managerial and administrative apparatus is one of the major wounds inflicted on the economy by the Cultural Revolution.

II. PERFORMANCE

8. There seems little doubt that economic performance has declined this year, but it is impossible to quantify the decline.[1] Scattered indications of a gradual decline in economic efficiency are supported by Red Guard posters citing official admissions that production declined in January and February, and again in April. Nevertheless, there is no evidence suggesting that an economic crisis is near.

A. Agriculture

9. Thus far, the Cultural Revolution has had little impact on agriculture. Grain output in 1966 was at about the level of 1964 and 1965. Although grain production has recovered from the low levels of 1959-1961, it has yet to top the

---

[1] Peking has published little useful data since 1960. While detailed statistical analysis of the economy is thus out of the question, careful sifting of all available information gives us considerable confidence in detecting the general movements of the economy. With the exception of foreign trade, where good statistics are available, the conclusions of this section are drawn from analysis of what is necessarily an inadequate data base.

SECRET

4

SECRET

record year of 1958. Meanwhile, population has grown by 15 to 20 million a year. Current reports of reduced rations and rising food prices, in both state and free markets, suggest gradually tightening supplies. Caloric intake per capita is probably somewhat less than in 1957, but we see no indications of either malnutrition or serious food shortages. Since 1961, Peking has augmented domestic food supplies by an average net import of almost five million tons of grain a year. We expect imports to continue at about this level.

B. Industry

10. The Cultural Revolution has halted the recovery of industry. Steady growth over the years 1963-1966 raised industrial production to a level above that of 1958, though still below the Leap Forward peak of 1960. This growth resulted mainly from fuller use of existing capacity. Some excess capacity still exists, particularly in light industries, but capacity is insufficient in other industries producing priority products such as finished steel. The revival of the construction industry in 1966 is suggested by the fact that, for the first time since the Leap Forward, all major cement plants in China were in operation. New construction was underway at military research and production facilities, electric power plants, chemical plants, petroleum facilities, and at mining sites. The disruptions of the Cultural Revolution probably have led to a slow decline of industrial output beginning in the last quarter of 1966.

11. Industrial policy during the past several years has been aimed more at increasing the range of finished products in support of major programs than in expanding basic industries. Priority attention is being accorded modern weapons, steel finishing facilities, electronic equipment, petroleum, and chemical fertilizer. Steel output has recovered to the point where most needs for ordinary steel products are probably being met. Deficiencies exist in the capacity to produce and fabricate refractory metals, high quality alloy steels, and a variety of finished steel products. China has been carrying on negotiations with Western Europe and Japan for plant and equipment to fill these gaps. In petroleum, output of crude oil has doubled since 1962, and China is now virtually self-sufficient in petroleum products; in 1966 only one percent of the total supply had to be imported. This remaining import need is for chemical additives to improve the quality of domestically-produced aircraft fuels and lubricants. Capacity in the chemical fertilizer industry increased from about 3 million tons in 1962 to 6-7 millions tons in 1966. Current emphasis is on the construction of small and medium-size plants, which may add about a half-million tons in 1967.

C. Transportation

12. China's transport system, which was overloaded and subject to periodic congestion during the Great Leap Forward, has been able in the last few years to meet basic economic needs without undue delay. The Cultural Revolution has caused only sporadic disruptions and backlogging of cargo at major rail junctions and ports. These difficulties have inconvenienced the economy in a

SECRET

5

SECRET

fashion similar to the current agricultural and industrial dislocations, but no serious economic results have yet been identified.

D. Military Production

13. With the high priority given military production, China has developed weapons technology beyond what it received from the Soviets and is now making rapid progress. The Chinese have exploded six nuclear devices, have undertaken an ambitious missile program, and are attempting their own research and development (R&D) on a variety of weapons systems. Work on strategic missile systems is underway; MIG-19 fighter aircraft are being produced, and a follow-on aircraft will probably soon appear; an expanded surface-to-air missile deployment may be impending; medium bombers and submarine-launched missiles may also be on the way; finally, continued progress is being made on an early warning radar system and on conventional naval and land armaments.

14. China has carefully exploited the world's markets to obtain up-to-date technical data and equipment for industry. As Peking's shopping list grows, it includes a larger proportion of items that can be related to the advanced weapons program. COCOM regulations have generally prevented the Chinese purchase of military equipment, but the COCOM list does not cover many types of industrial equipment with either direct or indirect value to China's military program. Since 1961, China has purchased more than half a billion dollars worth of machinery, equipment, and scientific instruments from Japan and Western Europe, and dependence on these sources will increase.[2] These imports not only aid the weapons program but help relieve the pressure on skilled manpower and equipment throughout industry.

E. Foreign Trade

15. Foreign trade has not been significantly affected by the Cultural Revolution. It grew about 10 percent in 1966, and at $4.2 billion had almost regained the peak level of 1959. Although transport disruptions delayed shipping schedules in early 1967, the Chinese have been taking pains to meet their trade commitments.

16. Foreign trade increases in 1965 and 1966 were largely a result of continued growth in trade with the Free World, which now accounts for three-

---

[2] The following tabulation shows the value (in millions of dollars) of machinery, equipment, and scientific instruments imported by China from Japan and Western Europe. It excludes imports of transportation equipment.

Year	Total	Machinery & Equipment	Scientific Instruments
1962	13.4	12.6	0.8
1963	16.6	14.3	2.3
1964	54.4	46.7	7.7
1965	156.9	138.2	18.7
1966 (est.)	195	170	25

SECRET

SECRET

quarters of China's trade. Japan supplanted the USSR as China's main trading partner in 1965 and widened its lead in 1966. The impressive rate of growth of Sino-Japanese trade—52 percent in 1965 and 32 percent in 1966—has been roughly matched by that of Chinese trade with Western Europe. Hong Kong remains China's best source of hard currency. Total earnings from trade with Hong Kong reached $475 million in 1966, and in addition, about $75 million in nontrade earnings were received, despite a drop in remittances because of the Cultural Revolution. China's trade with Communist countries in 1966 continued the decline that began in 1960. Trade with the Soviet Union fell to about $320 million, a decline of 23 percent from 1965.

17. China's balance of payments position has improved notably over the past 2 years. Foreign exchange and gold holdings increased by about $50 million in 1966, reaching a level of $450 to $550 million. China purchased $135 million of gold from the West in 1965 and $40 million in 1966. China's indebtedness to the Free World totaled about $265 million at the end of 1965 and was probably little changed in 1966. All this indebtedness is short-term. China has chosen not to ask for long-term credits, but could probably obtain them if it wished.

18. China's economic aid commitments to non-Communist countries fell from about $310 million in 1964 to approximately $120 million annually in 1965 and in 1966. The largest commitments in 1966 were credits of $43 million to Cambodia and $28 million to Guinea, and a $20 million grant to Nepal. Actual drawings remained well below extensions, averaging about $60 million a year over the last three years. China ceased announcing aid to Communist countries in 1965, but we believe deliveries increased in both 1965 and 1966.

F. Support to North Vietnam

19. Chinese aid to North Vietnam has grown steadily over the past year. China has been supplying small arms and ammunition, trucks, industrial raw materials, semimanufactures, food, and other consumer goods. There are also four antiaircraft divisions and many thousands of engineering troops in North Vietnam, and some fighter aircraft may have been supplied. China has increased the shipment of a broad range of items to replace bombing losses, including rails, construction materials, spare parts, and drugs and medicine. Chinese Communist capabilities for providing these materials and manpower far exceed commitments made so far. This aid, together with Soviet aid transiting China, has increased the burden on the rail net, but it still preempts only a small fraction of Chinese rail capacity. To the best of our knowledge, the flow of aid has been maintained with only minor interruptions in spite of China's internal political turmoil.

20. Peking has also made substantial investment in defense and related construction in Southern China. This construction, which is part of a general program of strengthening defenses along the periphery, is concentrated on new airfields and main line railroads. Yunnan Province has now been linked to the main rail net of China, thus permitting direct shipments between the two

SECRET

7

SECRET

without a detour through North Vietnam. The new construction also provides an additional route for supplies to North Vietnam.

III. PROBLEMS AND PROSPECTS

A. The Short-Term Outlook

21. Over the past 17 years, the regime's most impressive achievement has been its use of the party as a political and economic apparatus to i.. mess the vast energy of China's enormous population. Now, with the party in disorder and the government bureaucracy under attack, this control has been enfeebled. Under these conditions, it will be difficult to keep agriculture and industry functioning as a coordinated whole. It is already evident that economic efficiency has declined. Planning and managerial control are likely to be even further weakened if the purges continue, and the military lack the adaptability to take over the functions of the disabled party.

22. Thus, any estimate of the general outlook for the Chinese economy must of necessity be conditioned by the political outlook. During the next year or two, assuming a continuation of the present level of political turmoil, the economy seems likely to deteriorate somewhat, though probably not to the point of causing a sharp decline in industrial production, widespread unemployment, or acute food shortages. The weapons program could be continued, though some stretch out in particular items might be necessary. Unless political developments upset the foreign trade patterns which have been developing, foreign trade will probably grow. Choices in allocation of resources, especially among military uses, export programs, and industrial and agricultural investment will be made more difficult because of general political chaos and the decline of central authority.

23. It is possible that the present indeterminate political situation will be ended by Mao's early reestablishment of sufficient control to embark on an economic phase of the Cultural Revolution. Should he succeed, we would expect this to be similar to the Great Leap Forward, including a reduction in material incentives and great stress on exhortation. If unrestrained by the moderates, Mao would be likely to abolish the private plots and free markets. But this would almost inevitably lead to severe food problems and thence to apathy and a decline in morale and efficiency.

24. While we certainly cannot rule out such an evolution of the economic situation, we think it unlikely. We do not believe that Mao will achieve a clear-cut resolution of the political struggle; indeed, it is possible that he intends the struggle to drag on. Even if he thought that the time had come to move the revolution into a new phase, any step in the direction of radical economics would almost certainly generate new opposition from those, such as Chou En-lai and perhaps much of the PLA leadership, who have supported Mao thus far.

25. Even when Mao disappears from the scene, political stability is unlikely and economic progress will be neither rapid nor sure. There could be a long

8

SECRET

 SECRET

period of confused contesting for power; at the very least there will be an interregnum before a new leadership is consolidated. If a coherent leadership emerged, it might adopt less grandiose national goals, make more concessions to social demands, and attempt to restore some sort of administrative order. It might to some extent scale down and stretch out China's military programs. But it would probably still give priority to advanced weapons, and China's hostility towards the US would be likely to persist.

B. Economic Considerations for the Longer Term

26. The problems characteristic of a nation seeking industrialization and modernization are present in China, but are often sharply exaggerated by China's ambitions. Never before has a nation so industrially backward and with so large and poor a population attempted so strenuously to acquire the military strength and stature of a major world power. China's gross national product (GNP) is considerably smaller than that of Japan or France; in its per capita GNP and the portion of GNP contributed by industrial output, China's economy resembles that of India. In pursuit of its goals over the past 17 years, China has utilized over one-quarter of its GNP for investment and military expenditures, and has cut corners to increase the impact of this effort. Agriculture has been slighted, and industry is disproportionately oriented toward military production. Striking progress has been made in advanced weapons development, but this success has strained China's resources and talent and has led to new calls for shortcuts. It is in this setting that China's deep economic problems must be understood.

27. *Food-Population Ratio.* China at best faces only slow progress in reducing population growth. Some success has been achieved in reducing the birth rate in the cities, but it will take a long time to accomplish a significant reduction among the peasantry, who constitute over 80 percent of the population. Moreover, even a highly successful rural birth control program would secure only a limited reduction in fertility, and this would tend to be offset by increasing life expectancies. Thus there seems little likelihood of any notable change in the rate of population growth over at least the next decade.

28. The Chinese intend to raise agricultural output over the next decade mainly by greater use of chemical fertilizer. Peking has already sharply increased the supply of chemical fertilizer, both from imports and domestic sources. In order to increase agricultural production commensurate with population growth, China needs an annual increment of roughly two million tons of chemical fertilizer. China is not currently building large chemical fertilizer plants, and unless new plans are quickly put into effect, much of the requirement will have to be met from imports. Moreover, China will shortly, say by 1970, face sharply increased requirements for farm investment to use that fertilizer, including additional irrigation, improved transport and distribution, and more intensive technical measures. China may face trouble if it is not prepared to divert the necessary resources to underwrite these investments and to sponsor suitable changes in the organization of farm production.

 SECRET

9

SECRET

29. *Economic Costs of the Military Program.* The success of the weapons program has been at the cost of withholding resources from the civilian sector and delaying the growth of a general industrial base for the broader needs of the economy. There will be some benefits to civilian industries from the spin-off of R&D in the weapons field, as well as in the stimulation of industries in ancillary fields. But these benefits are greatly outweighed by the loss in general economic development that is an inevitable consequence of the high priority given to the weapons program. In any event, the costs of the military program are now around 10 percent of China's GNP. Overall costs will substantially grow as advanced weapons systems move into production and deployment, and R&D costs will increase as the Chinese move further beyond designs furnished by the Soviets. Production costs will be high because China will have to create the industrial backup in machinery and skills that is already available to most industrialized nations. Moreover, China's limited supply of scientists and technicians has been concentrated on military R&D, and general scientific research is suffering as scarce scientific talent is applied to solving urgent practical problems of military production.

30. *Shortage of Educated Manpower.* Peking has vastly expanded school facilities and enrollments in China and for the first time has provided its young generation with an education. But at the same time it has interfered with education by recurrent political campaigns. The most recent and extreme example is the closing of China's universities and the proposed overhaul of the curriculum throughout the school system to concentrate on Mao's works. Moreover, the system of higher education is handicapped by the siphoning off of professional personnel for high priority military programs, and the balance among various types of professional and technical training is not consistent with China's specific needs. These weaknesses will necessarily slow the achievement of economic efficiency as the economy attempts to advance to levels where both professional competence and technical skills are required.

31. These problems—the unfavorable food-population ratio, the economic costs and imbalances inherent in the military program, and the shortcomings of the educational system—seem likely to persist for at least a decade. Any regime which comes to rule China will have to cope, not only with the damage which is being done by the Cultural Revolution, but with these almost intractable facts of economic life. A pragmatic regime could probably mobilize China's resources in such a way as to keep the economy moving at a moderate rate of development and provide some modest increases in the low standard of living now prevailing.

32. But any regime will inherit some of the political goals as well as the economic problems of its predecessor. It will likely try to continue the military program, compete with the USSR for influence in the Communist world, and retain its antagonism to the US. These will strongly affect the allocation of resources, probably at the expense of laying foundations for self-sustaining economic growth.

10   SECRET

SECTION 29

NIE 13-8-67

Communist China's Strategic
Weapons Program

3 August 1967

APPROVED FOR RELEASE
DATE: MAY 2004

~~TOP SECRET~~

(b)(1)
(b)(3)

NIE 13-8-67
3 August 1967

NATIONAL INTELLIGENCE ESTIMATE
NUMBER 13-8-67

Communist China's Strategic Weapons Program

Handle Via Indicated Controls

WARNING

The sensitivity of this document requires that it be handled with maximum security precautions on a need-to-know basis. Recipients will insure that only personnel having all proper clearances and a need-to-know will have access to this document.

Submitted by

DEPUTY DIRECTOR OF CENTRAL INTELLIGENCE

Concurred in by the

UNITED STATES INTELLIGENCE BOARD

As indicated overleaf

3 August 1967

Authenticated:

EXECUTIVE SECRETARY, USIB

Pages 21

Copy No. 140

~~TOP SECRET~~

TOP SECRET

1

COMMUNIST CHINA'S STRATEGIC WEAPONS PROGRAM

THE PROBLEM

To assess China's strategic weapons policy and programs and to estimate the nature, size, and progress of these programs through the early 1970's.

CONCLUSIONS

A. It is clear that China aspires to great power status and that its present leaders have given high priority to developing a substantial strategic capability as essential to such status. With wise management of their limited resources, the Chinese could continue to make steady progress toward the achievement of these goals over the next decade.

B. The probable extent of actual progress will remain in doubt, however, so long as fanaticism and disorder continue to infect China. Some adverse effects on the advanced weapons program are probable in any event; serious disruptions could result from pressures to do too much too soon or from a general breakdown in central authority.

C. China probably now has a few fission weapons in stockpile deliverable by bomber, and has demonstrated the capability to produce thermonuclear weapons with megaton (mt) yields. It will soon have the plutonium available to aid in reducing such weapons to missile warhead size as well as to facilitate the development of more compact, light weight fission devices. For the next year or two, the limited availability of fissionable material will place significant restraints on warhead production, but this will ease significantly in the following years as the Yumen plutonium production reactor reaches full output.

D. We believe that limited deployment of an MRBM with fission warheads is likely to begin in the next six months or so. After 1968

TOP SECRET

490

2 ~~TOP SECRET~~

when increasing numbers of warheads could be made available, deployment will probably proceed at a higher rate. This deployment would be designed to threaten US bases, and major cities from Japan through the Philippines, southeast Asia, and northern India.

E. We estimate that the Chinese can have an ICBM system ready for deployment in the early 1970's. Conceivably, it could be ready as early as 1970-1971. But this would be a tight schedule, and should the Chinese encounter major problems, the IOC would be later. In any event, we will almost certainly detect extended range firings once they begin, and monitoring of these tests will probably provide about one year's advance warning of IOC.

F. We have no basis at this time for estimating how far or how fast the Chinese will carry deployment of their first-generation ICBM. Assuming political and economic stability, China will probably have the resources to support a moderate and growing ICBM deployment through 1975. Beyond that time frame, there is the possibility of significant improvements to this first system or the development of a follow-on solid fuel missile system based on the large complex now under construction at Hu-ho-hao-té in Inner Mongolia. If China makes good progress in the development of solid fuels for ICBM ranges, it might limit deployment of the first-generation system.

G. Other strategic delivery means have received less priority but China may begin production of some TU-16 medium bombers this year in the now-completed plant at Sian.

H. China will probably not push ahead vigorously with the now semidormant diesel-powered missile-firing submarine program. The one G-class submarine launched in 1964 does not yet have a missile. It would probably be at least 1970 before additional missile launching submarines could be available. China has shown some interest in nuclear propulsion technology, but even if design on a nuclear submarine is already underway, the first unit probably could not be operational until the late 1970's.

I. For political effect, China will probably attempt to launch an earth-satellite as soon as possible. This might be accomplished this year using an MRBM with an added stage or a heavier payload might be orbited using an early test vehicle from the ICBM program.

~~TOP SECRET~~

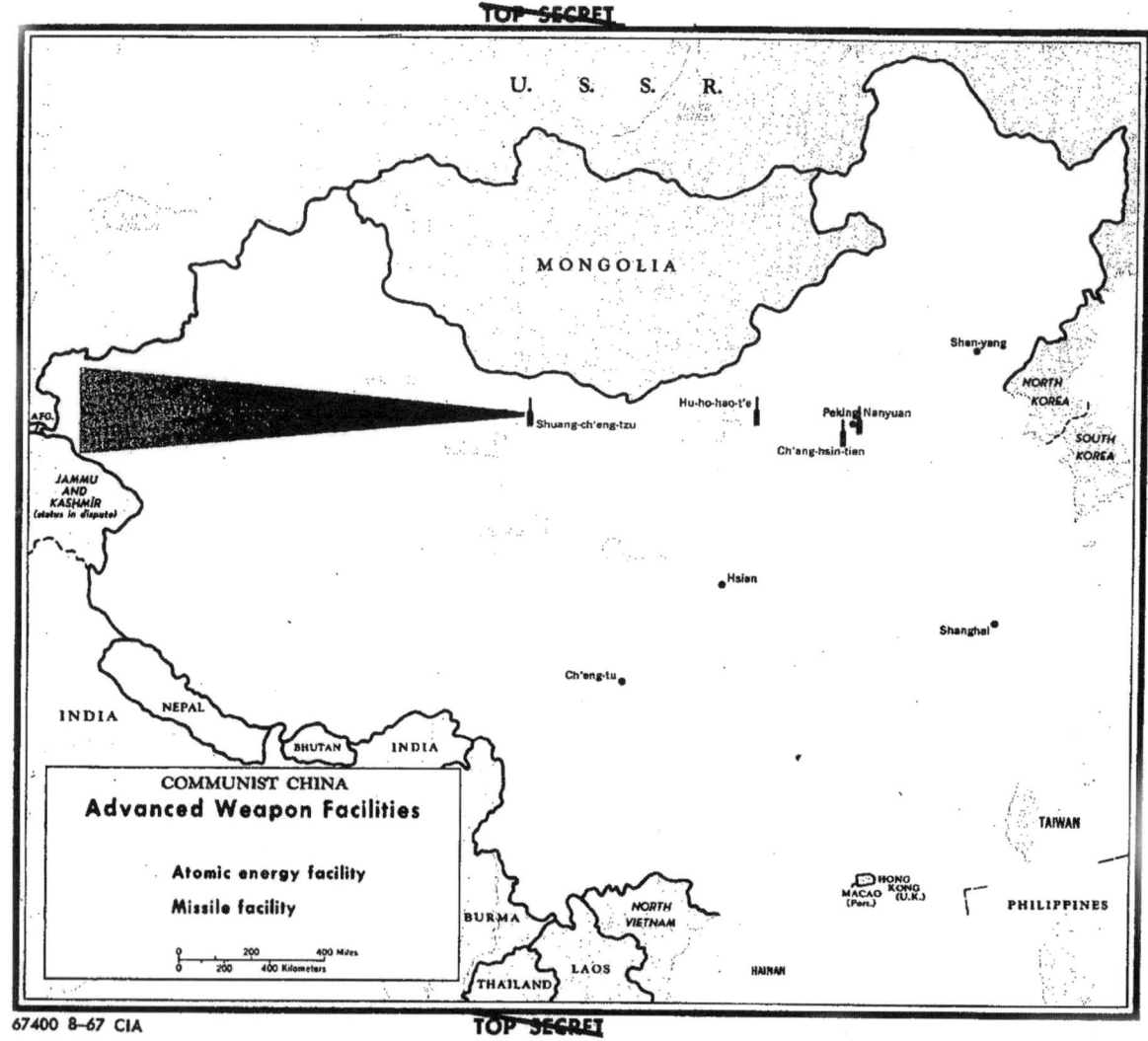

TOP SECRET

3

DISCUSSION

1. *General Considerations.* We now see more clearly the broad outlines of the Chinese strategic weapons program. It includes high priority work on an MRBM, on an ICBM, and on the production of fissionable materials and the development of both fission and thermonuclear weapons. Work in all these fields showed significant progress in the last year and these efforts clearly attest to Chinese determination. But many questions remain which bear critically on our judgments concerning the future pace and scope of the program, particularly with respect to production and deployment over the next five years. As yet there has been no obvious interference by the Cultural Revolution in the advanced weapons program, but we doubt that it has been completely immune.

2. We have little evidence on Chinese thinking with respect to the role of advanced weapons in their overall strategy. The present leaders probably believe that the successful development of strategic weapons would greatly enhance their prestige and strengthen their claims to leadership in Asia and their status as a great power. They would also hope that the possession of a strategic capability would give them greater security in supporting revolutionary struggles, particularly in Asia, and that it would serve to lessen the dangers of nuclear strikes on China itself for any reason. In other words, the Chinese may believe that the ability to strike the US and targets in Asia with nuclear weapons would serve to limit US military operations in Asia, and to keep any direct confrontation at the level of conventional arms where the Chinese would expect to enjoy many advantages.

I. NUCLEAR PROGRAM

3. *Thermonuclear Devices.* Peking has conducted six tests, three of which were related to thermonuclear development.

4.   the Chinese on 17 June 1967 detonated a thermonuclear device
This device was airdropped, probably by a TU-16. Both of China's TU-16 jet medium bombers were at the airfield serving the Lop Nor test area for several weeks before the test, and one was observed
over a weapon loading pit at this airfield. The airdrop marker used

TOP SECRET

4 ~~TOP SECRET~~

for CHIC-3 was refurbished for CHIC-6

6. *Fission Devices.* Peking announced on 27 October 1966 that it had on that day exploded a nuclear device which had been delivered by a guided missile.

There is no conclusive evidence as to the distance the missile might have flown, but we believe it probably was fired from the Shuang-ch'eng-tzu Missile Test Range (SCTMTR). Just prior to the test, a new launch complex was constructed at SCTMTR at a location well away from other facilities, suggesting a special concern for safety. This may have been the site from which the missile was fired. If so, this would mean that the missile flew a distance of about 450 nautical miles (n.m.) to the point of detonation in the Lop Nor nuclear test area. We do not know what type of missile was used, but the MRBM which has been under development for some years is the logical candidate.

Nuclear Materials Production

7. *U-235.*

our belief that U-235, the fissionable material used in all Chinese tests to date, is produced at the Lanchou uranium isotope separation plant. But we are now less confident of our estimate that the Chinese are using the electromagnetic process to "top off" the U-235 product that has been partially enriched in the gaseous diffusion cascade at Lanchou. Further analysis indicates that the Chinese could be using any one of three methods: the gaseous diffusion process only, gaseous diffusion process "topped off" with gas centrifuges, or "topping off" with electromagnetic separators.

~~TOP SECRET~~

If the production is done entirely by the gaseous diffusion process (and this would require the use of small, tightly packed stages operated in a manner to maximize enrichment at the expense of some production capacity) it is likely that the level of output is between this minimum quantity and an amount two or three times greater. If electromagnetic "topping off" is the technique used, production rates close to the lower end of the range would be probable, considering the amount of building space available at Lanchou. Higher production rates would require that the final enrichment be done elsewhere in a sizable installation. A careful search has revealed no such installation, and we think it unlikely that it could have escaped our notice.

9. *Plutonium.* A large plutonium production reactor at the Yumen nuclear complex began operation in early 1967. We had previously estimated that the Chinese would operate the reactor well below capacity for a year or two in order to gain operating experience and to minimize the chances of equipment breakdowns.

To extract this plutonium the Chinese are proceeding rapidly with construction of a chemical separation plant at Yumen. The plant should become operational during the first half of 1968. The Chinese may have pilot plant facilities that could provide some plutonium for testing before the large chemical separation plant at Yumen comes into operation.

10. *Other Nuclear Materials.* A likely candidate for the source of heavy water—from which deuterium, one of the materials used in thermonuclear weapons, is obtained—has been identified. Apparently the Chinese have followed the common practice of locating heavy water facilities at nitrogen fertilizer plants. There is an installation resembling a Soviet heavy water facility at a fertilizer plant in Kirin Province in Manchuria.

Current Nuclear Weapons Production

11. In general, the Chinese seem to be giving priority to thermonuclear weapon development. Certainly thermonuclear testing has been the greater drain on

TOP SECRET

6 ~~TOP SECRET~~

nuclear material, and the success of the program strongly implies that China's best nuclear scientists have been concentrating on this program.

The Chinese leaders almost certainly would want to have at least a few nuclear weapons on hand as soon as possible.

Thus we believe the number of weapons in stockpile is likely to be small.

13. We have identified a facility that could be China's first nuclear stockpile site. It is located about 13 miles east of the nuclear weapons development and production complex near Koko Nor and appears to be nearly complete. We have recently identified construction at a site about 10 miles north of Wushiht'ala airfield, which supports the Lop Nor test area. Its similarity to the Koko Nor facility during its early stages of construction suggests that it too may be intended for nuclear weapon storage.

II. CURRENT STATUS OF DELIVERY SYSTEM PROGRAMS

The MRBM Program

14.   the accelerated pace of missile launchings at SCTMTR, first noted in 1965, extended through 1966 and is continuing in 1967. The evidence,   is fairly conclusive that most of the testing has been related to the development of an MRBM.

~~TOP SECRET~~

TOP SECRET

7

15.

Similarly, we cannot ascertain a number of important details concerning the missile's performance characteristics. Judging from what we see at the range, the Chinese MRBM is about 70 feet long, is serviced by road-transportable equipment, probably has radio-inertial guidance, and probably uses storable propellants. We continue to estimate that the Chinese have been working on a 1,000-mile missile but at present our evidence only permits us to say that some of the firings detected apparently flew somewhere between 600 and 1,000 n.m.

16. Though the system is road-transportable, we think it will require fixed sites probably involving some permanent support facilities. Considering the generally poor road network in China, the Chinese would probably want to locate their sites near rail lines. There is no sign of any work involving silos at SCTMTR. Hence, deployment, at least initially, will almost certainly be at soft sites.

17. Though the Ch'ang-hsin-tien Missile Development Center (CHTMDC) near Peking is primarily a research and development (R&D) facility, it probably is capable of producing missiles in quantities sufficient for a limited deployment program. A plant located nearby at Nanyuan appears suitable for producing airframes and possibly other missile components as well. These two facilities are the best candidates for the production of China's MRBM. There is no evidence that the Chinese have begun series production at these facilities. Judging from our experience with Soviet missile production, it is unlikely that we will learn the quantities of missiles being produced at any particular plant.

18. The apparent frequency of missile firings at SCTMTR during May and June is greater than would be expected in the R&D phases of a missile's development. Although other explanations are possible, the evidence seems to indicate that the Chinese are conducting at least some troop training firings. If this is the case, preparation of field sites should already have begun. We have searched 1967 photography of somewhat more than half of China's rail network and have detected no such site preparation. Since we do not yet know what the deployed sites will look like, we cannot be confident that we would spot the first deployment sites early in their preparation. (See centerfold map.)

[map redacted]

TOP SECRET

10   TOP SECRET

The ICBM Program

19. There is good evidence that the Chinese are working on an ICBM system. A large new launch facility (Launch Complex B at SCTMTR) capable of accommodating a missile in the ICBM or space booster category, appears ready. Looking back over developments at CHTMDC we now believe that the Chinese have been working on the development of an ICBM since at least the early 1960's.

20. At this stage in the program, we cannot say much about the system's characteristics. Though a completely new design cannot be ruled out, it is more likely that the ICBM and MRBM programs have been closely related. For example, the clustering of MRBM-size engines would eliminate the need for the development of an entirely new propulsion system, and would be a logical approach for the Chinese to use. The missile will probably be a two-stage vehicle in excess of 100 feet in length and about 10 feet in diameter. In order to reach the principal targets in the US, the Chinese would need a missile system with a range of 6,000 n.m. Chinese test facilities appear adequate to handle engine thrusts large enough to give this range.

21. A storable propellant system has important advantages for a deployed missile system. Though the evidence is not conclusive one way or the other, we believe the Chinese probably intend to use such a propellant in their ICBM. It is unlikely that the Chinese have mastered the complex technology of all-inertial guidance, and their first ICBM system will probably have radio-inertial guidance.

22. Launch Complex B is apparently ready to support flight testing. The first tests will probably be firings of the first stage to distances of a few hundred miles, within the borders of China. The orientation of Complex B and the location of what appears to be a downrange electronic station suggest that eventually there will be firings in a southwesterly direction. ICBMs fired to full range in this direction would impact in the Indian Ocean. The Chinese would presumably desire to provide instrumentation and communication facilities within range of the impact area. This requirement could be met by land-based facilities, but for both technical and political reasons we believe the Chinese are more likely to rely on specially equipped ships. As yet, however, we have no evidence of preparations to provide such facilities.

Other Delivery Systems

23. *Bomber Program.* There is good evidence that in the late 1950's the Soviets were helping the Chinese build a plant at Sian for the production of the

TOP SECRET

~~TOP SECRET~~   11

TU-16 (Badger) jet medium bomber. Work on this plant, which was interrupted in the early 1960's, was resumed in late 1963 or early 1964 and it now appears complete. If the Chinese still intend to produce TU-16s, the plant could turn out its first aircraft late this year or in early 1968.

Missile Submarine Program

24. The Chinese apparently retain an interest in a submarine launched missile system, but there is some evidence to suggest that the program has been delayed for some reason or other. China's only G-class submarine was launched late in 1964 and began putting to sea occasionally about a year later. No new submarines of this class have been identified under construction, however, and the existing one has never been detected in anything but routine underway training. Furthermore, at about the time the Chinese were building their G-class they were also working on a special wharf facility which we believe is for missile handling, but this facility has remained in a state of semicompletion.

25. We have no direct evidence for judging what kind of submarine launched missile the Chinese may envisage or when they may have one available. We have not detected any testing of such a missile but it is possible that some of the missile engine static testing at Ch'ang-hsin-tien and flight testing at Shuang-ch'eng-tzu could be connected with a submarine missile system. While land-based tests could remain unidentified, it is less likely that a sea-based test program would long avoid detection. At least a year of sea-based launchings would probably be required to test out fully a submarine launched ballistic missile (SLBM) system.

26. *Space Program.* The acting Chief of Staff of the Peoples Liberation Army has been quoted in Red Guard newspapers as claiming that the Chinese will conduct a space launch in 1967. Primarily for political reasons, the Chinese will probably try to put something into space as soon as possible, and it could occur this year. One possibility is the launching of a small satellite using an MRBM with an added stage. Another is the launching of a heavier payload with an early test vehicle from the ICBM program.

III. PROSPECTS

27. Chinese determination needs to be taken into account when considering the likely future scope and pace of their strategic weapons program. But determination alone will not solve the many practical problems facing the Chinese. In planning, design, and testing, the Chinese no doubt have benefited from the foundations laid during the period of Soviet assistance. But in the production of MRBMs as well as in the testing of ICBMs and the fabrication of suitable

~~TOP SECRET~~

12   TOP SECRET

warheads, the Chinese are dependent primarily on their own technology and on whatever they can gain from non-Communist sources. They will continue to profit significantly from their access to Japanese and West European technology and from their ability to purchase industrial plant, sophisticated instruments, and scarce materials from these sources. But this can only partially offset the deficiencies of China's relatively limited technological and industrial base. We think it likely that they will encounter difficulties in moving from R&D to the industrial production of the components of complex weapons systems. And when the Chinese solve their production problems, they will still face an intense competition for scarce resources.

28. Chinese military planners must recognize that in the foreseeable future China cannot begin to match the nuclear striking power of the US. They probably also realize that the credibility as a deterrent of their first-generation systems will suffer because these systems would have a poor chance of surviving an offensive strike and would be vulnerable to some degree to defensive systems the US is capable of deploying. In order to concentrate on developing improved and refined systems that would have a more impressive credibility as a threat and as a deterrent, Peking might opt for only a token deployment of its earliest weapons. Against this, however, Peking would probably weigh the judgment that more than token deployment of its first ICBM would be worthwhile because it would enhance its leverage on Asian countries, would have increased deterrent effect on the US, and would generally pay important political and psychological dividends.

29. The Chinese must also strike some balance in the allocation of resources as between intercontinental and regional strategic forces and between weapons systems within the regional force. Rather than concentrating all resources on, say, an ICBM program, the Chinese probably believe that they could more quickly enhance their overall military posture by allocating some of their limited means to a force which could hold much of Asia hostage. Within the regional force concept, the idea of producing more than a few TU-16 bombers as weapons carriers might lose some of its attraction for the Chinese, if they were able to develop a reliable and mobile MRBM or an IRBM capable of delivering thermonuclear weapons.

30. To further complicate the situation, there remains the question of political and economic order in China. Thus far, the political upheaval in China does not seem to have affected the strategic weapons program; the regime has exercised particular care to insulate the nuclear and missile program from it. But gradually small bits of evidence have accumulated which suggest that some longer term harm may have been done to the administration and organization of the programs.

TOP SECRET

TOP SECRET   13

31. For example, according to Red Guard posters, revolutionary strife has occurred in the governmental ministries responsible for nuclear and missile development. The head of the National Defense Scientific and Technology Commission, Nieh Jung-chen, has come under sporadic attack. Another possible sign of political interference is the distinct "Leap Forward" flavor of Peking's propaganda treatment of the recent sixth nuclear test. Unnamed advocates of solving scientific problems step by step have been criticized while "revolutionary" scientists and technicians who were not afraid to take bold shortcuts have been extolled. Though this is no doubt partly propaganda

it could mark the intrusion of political pressures into the advanced weapons program. Thus, despite the priviledged status of these programs, it will be increasingly difficult for Peking to shield them from unrealistic demands for spectacular progress, from the unhealthy political atmosphere in China, and from the general erosion of economic efficiency and managerial control.

32. It is difficult to judge how much our basic calculations of the time required to develop, produce, and deploy various kinds of military hardware should be adjusted to take account of these weaknesses. It may be that we have considerably underestimated the Chinese, and it is possible that they will be able to bring most of their programs to fruition on a rapid schedule and to produce and deploy various weapon systems in substantial quantities. But the odds are better that the Chinese will have to make compromises, perhaps stretching out some programs and settling, at least initially, for limited deployments.

IV. PROJECTIONS

33. It is clear that China aspires to great power status and that its present leaders believe that a substantial strategic capability is essential to such status. Barring serious political and economic upsets in China, we believe the Chinese have the resources to make steady and impressive progress toward the achievement of such a capability. At the same time, we would stress that the Chinese program will be limited in scope, and in qualitative and quantitative achievements over the next decade by the industrial, technological, and skilled manpower weaknessess of China. If China should attempt too much too soon, the long-run consequences could be highly disruptive both for an orderly advanced weapons program and for the economy in general.

The Nuclear Program

34. Through 1970, at least, Chinese fissionable materials will be limited to the output from the Yumen reactor and the U-235 production plant at Lanchou. These amounts are not inconsiderable, however, and once plutonium devices have

TOP SECRET

14   TOP SECRET

been tested, it is apparent   that China will be able to build
a substantial weapons stockpile by 1970.

TOP SECRET

~~TOP SECRET~~   15

35. If the Chinese envisage a substantial ICBM deployment program with TN warheads, and if they have already made good progress in solving the considerable technical problems involved, we would expect to see efforts to expand U-235 capacity some time in the next year or two. Once construction started on a new U-235 plant, it would take about three years for production of U-235 to begin.

Delivery Systems

36. *MRBM Deployment.* As suggested above we believe that the Chinese MRBM should be ready for deployment in 1967 or 1968. Evidence respecting troop training is not conclusive, however, and evidence on other preparations for deployment is lacking. This leaves open the possibility that little or no deployment of the MRBM is planned. It could be that the principal purpose of the MRBM program was to develop technology for an ICBM.

37. We think it more likely, however, that significant deployment is intended and that it will begin within the next six months or so. For the next year or two, however, the availability of nuclear warheads is likely to limit MRBM deployment.

38. MRBM deployment will probably be designed to give coverage to targets in the arc stretching from Japan through the Philippines, southeast Asia, and northern India. The Chinese objective might be to provide coverage of important military bases and population centers within this area, hoping in this way to hold Asian countries hostage against any US threats to China. They might consider that this could be accomplished by the deployment of some 80-100 MRBM launchers in fixed, soft sites.

Barring economic or political disruptions we believe that China will proceed with MRBM deployment somewhat as above, although it may be the mid-1970's before deployment on this

~~TOP SECRET~~

503

16   ~~TOP SECRET~~

scale is achieved. For both military and political reasons we do not anticipate any early deployment of MRBMs directed at the USSR, although some of those MRBMs located in Manchuria would have the capability of hitting targets in the Soviet Union.

39. *IRBM.* If, as we believe, the Chinese are working on a 1,000-mile MRBM and an ICBM, there would be only a marginal requirement for an IRBM. Moreover, we see no evidence of any such program and consider any early Chinese efforts to develop an IRBM unlikely.

40. *ICBM Deployment.* We estimate that the Chinese can have an ICBM system ready for deployment in the early 1970's. Conceivably, it could be ready as early as 1970-1971. But this would be a tight schedule and makes allowance for only minor difficulties and delays. We have no evidence that flight testing of the ICBM has even begun. Should the Chinese encounter major problems, the IOC of an ICBM would be later. In any event, we will almost certainly detect extended range firings once they begin, and monitoring of these tests will probably provide about one year's advance warning of IOC. With further nuclear tests, the Chinese should have by 1970 a one to three mt thermonuclear warhead suitable for their ICBM.

41. We have no basis at this time for estimating how far the Chinese will carry deployment of their first-generation ICBM. In view of the requirements of other military programs and the pressure on resources, however, we believe deployment will proceed at a moderate pace and well below any possible maximums. By moderate we mean that in 1975 the number of operational ICBM launchers might fall somewhere between 10 and 25.

42. Additional information bearing on the probable scope of both the MRBM and ICBM programs should be available over the next year. In the meantime, we have some clues suggesting that the Chinese are already at work on follow-on systems. The best evidence of this is a large installation the Chinese are building at Hu-ho-hao-té in Inner Mongolia which we believe is for testing and manufacturing composite solid fuel rocket motors. This complex is still under construction and it will probably be at least three years before motors developed here could be ready for flight testing. Thus, it is too early to tell what kind of missile the Chinese are working on. But the fairly large size of the static test facilities at this installation suggests that some kind of long-range system is envisaged.

43. *Medium Bombers.* We believe the Chinese intend to produce the TU-16 bomber at Sian. Such a medium bomber with a combat radius of 1,650 n.m. would give more range than an MRBM and would provide an interim carrier for thermonuclear weapons. It would also add flexibility to China's military capabilities. Finally, the Chinese may consider it useful to follow through on the original plan (which dates from the late 1950's) for TU-16 production in order to gain experience useful in the future development of larger aircraft. Few if

~~TOP SECRET~~

any TU-16s could be available before early 1969, but by 1972 there could be 75 or so assigned to operational units. By that time, it is possible a follow-on bomber could be in the early stages of R&D and would eventually replace the TU-16 force.

44. If the Chinese plan to use their TU-16 aircraft against naval and other clearly defined radar targets, they would probably produce some of them in an air-to-surface missile (ASM) configuration. The Chinese probably have the capability to develop an ASM, with a 75 to 100 n.m. range, and given time, a compatible nuclear warhead. But in view of the pressures of other programs, we would not expect to see an operational ASM system before 1972-1973.

45. *Missile Launching Submarines.* We believe that development of an SLBM system will continue to suffer from a lack of priority for several more years.

there is no evidence that the Chinese are building G-class submarines. Thus, it would probably be at least 1970 before additional missile launching submarines could be available. The Chinese have shown some interest in nuclear-powered submarine technology, but, even if they have already started working on designing such a submarine, the first unit probably could not be operational until the late 1970's.

SECTION 30

NIE 13-9-68

The Short-Term Outlook
in Communist China

23 May 1968

APPROVED FOR RELEASE
DATE: MAY 2004

~~SECRET~~

NIE 13-9-68
23 May 1968

(b)(3)

NATIONAL INTELLIGENCE ESTIMATE

NUMBER 13-9-68

The Short-Term Outlook in Communist China

Submitted by

Richard Helms

DIRECTOR OF CENTRAL INTELLIGENCE

Concurred in by the

UNITED STATES INTELLIGENCE BOARD

As indicated overleaf

23 May 1968

Authenticated:

James S. Lay Jr.

EXECUTIVE SECRETARY, USIB

~~SECRET~~

N⁰ 439

SECRET

THE SHORT-TERM OUTLOOK IN COMMUNIST CHINA

THE PROBLEM

To estimate the main trends and outlook in China over the next year or so.

CONCLUSIONS

A. The situation inside Communist China is still highly fluid and the outlook uncertain. Disorder, confusion, and unrest continue but have been reduced since the high water mark last summer. Nevertheless, the ranks of those alienated by the Great Proletarian Cultural Revolution have grown; the costs in political control, social discipline, and economic progress have far outweighed the gains. Though Mao was successful in breaking high-level opposition in the old party apparatus, in its broader aspects his Cultural Revolution has been a failure and we believe it will be gradually phased out.

B. Mao still appears to be the central figure and source of basic policy. Mao and the regime are officially committed to the reconstruction of a new framework for administrative and political control. On balance, we believe that the trend will be toward regaining some stability, in part because of the increased influence of the moderate elements in Peking. But there still will be sharp twists and turns, occasional crises, and disorder and turmoil at various levels which will reflect strong differences among factions and leaders over policies and tactics.

C. The military will remain Peking's most reliable instrument over the coming year. As the only cohesive force with a nationwide system of command and control, the military will have to serve a variety of administrative and control functions. The scope of the rebuilding effort—political, economic, and social—may require the heavy support

SECRET

1

SECRET

of the People's Liberation Army (PLA) for some years to come. Military dominance in political life may become institutionalized, particularly if political reconstruction bogs down in violence and disarray requiring the repressive force of the PLA. The corollary to this increased political role is the diversion of the PLA from normal military routine and a consequent reduction in its military readiness.

D. The damage to the economy as a direct result of the Cultural Revolution includes depressed industrial production, a delay in modernization and economic growth, aggravated labor problems, setbacks in the training of technical specialists, and a general hiatus in the formulation of new economic policies and plans. The cumulative damage to the economy of prolonged political turmoil will not be easily or quickly repaired. Whatever the political course for 1968, agricultural output is not likely to repeat last year's very good harvests, which benefited from exceptionally good weather. At best, China can hope only to restore stability and balance to the economy in 1968, foregoing any prospect of expansion. Indeed, there is a possibility that a reduction in food output, combined with problems of collection and distribution, could cause a serious food shortage by 1969, which in turn could have serious political repercussions.

E. "Red Guard diplomacy" cost Peking last year in relations with Communist as well as non-Communist regimes. Since last summer, however, the regime has taken steps to reduce the violent and provocative influence of internal affairs on foreign relations. In the main, the Cultural Revolution has not altered the general line of Chinese policy abroad; it still remains revolutionary in tone but cautious and prudent in deeds. Preoccupation with internal affairs is likely to relegate foreign concerns to a secondary role.

F. A major uncertainty in any estimate of China's future is the problem of Mao's passing. The events of the past two years have made it more likely that Mao's departure will usher in a stormy and possibly protracted period in which policy differences and power aspirations will continue to fuel a leadership struggle. Mao's legacy is likely to be an enfeebled party, a confused bureaucracy, and a divided and harried leadership. In our view the ultimate result will be to accelerate the rejection of Mao's doctrines and policies.

2   SECRET

SECRET

DISCUSSION

I. BACKGROUND

1. The Great Proletarian Cultural Revolution is entering its third year. It has already had a profound effect on every aspect of life in China, on the country's internal and external policies, and on its probable future. The course of the revolution has been highly erratic. Moreover, the reasons behind the various twists and turns have often been obscure and confusing.[1]

2. Despite fluctuations in policy and revolutionary activity, the general trend through last summer seemed to be one of increasing violence and turmoil as the traditional forces for maintaining order were weakened. By August a climax of sorts was reached. Fighting among various revolutionary groups reached a peak. Civil disorder reached dangerous proportions. The People's Liberation Army (PLA) came under sharp political attack, and political maneuvering suggested a crisis within the top leadership over the future of the Cultural Revolution.

3. Suddenly, in early September, Peking shifted the line, demanding once again that moderate directives actually be implemented. The attack on the PLA was repudiated. The army was finally empowered to use limited force to retrieve weapons seized during the summer. Revolutionary excesses were condemned. Some of the political leaders were purged on charges of ultraleftism. Stabilization became the official program: Peking revived its call for alliances of Red Guards, PLA leaders, and trusted party cadres as the prerequisite for constructing the new "revolutionary committees," which would assume administrative responsibilities in the provinces. It reaffirmed its policies that party cadres were to be rehabilitated; factional struggle was to be halted; students were to resume classes; nationwide coordination by revolutionary groups was to be restricted. By the end of the year Peking was claiming "decisive" victory for the Cultural Revolution. There were indications that a party congress would be convened to legitimatize the changes. In short, it appeared that the "destructive" phase had ended and a "constructive" phase had begun.

4. But the reality has been far different. The "alliances" have frequently aggravated wounds rather than healed them. The revolutionary youth resent their eclipse and, as they remain in official favor, are still a volatile force in an unstable situation. Violence has not ended; severe fighting continues to erupt in scattered cities. The army remains the only effective control instrument in most of the country. The new revolutionary committees have been formed with the greatest difficulty. The new order is being built on a series of unstable compromises.

---

[1] The discussion of the origins of the Cultural Revolution contained in NIE 13-7-67, "The Chinese Cultural Revolution," dated 25 May 1967, SECRET, paragraphs 3-7, appear to be still valid.

SECRET

3

SECRET

II. FACTORS IN THE CURRENT SITUATION

A. Mao and His Adherents

5. Any estimate of China's future course must begin with the position and attitudes of Mao Tse-tung. Despite uncertainties over his health and mental capacities, he still appears to be the central figure and the source of basic policy. The Cultural Revolution has reflected Mao's concern over party bureaucratism and growing problems within the society. He has also been concerned to reassert his authority in the party and to reinstill revolutionary fervor in the country at large.

6. Mao apparently felt that the party could not be remolded, but had to be terrorized and demolished before a new order could be constructed. The record thus far suggests that Mao remains firmly dedicated to the notion that the Chinese revolution can only be kept alive by involving the "masses" in direct participation in "revolutionary action." From Mao's standpoint, moreover, the past two years have brought some notable gains. He and his coterie have broken the top level resistance that confronted him in the early 1960's. And he has brought the younger generation into direct participation in political life and revolution. But these gains have yet to be consolidated in the creation of a new revolutionary order, which is now the paramount task.

7. Thus far, Mao has displayed considerable tactical flexibility in pushing the Cultural Revolution, but his room for maneuver has been gradually narrowed for several reasons. Neither the social order nor the economy can long tolerate a political vacuum and chaotic direction, and their requirements impose a time limit on the Cultural Revolution. Moreover, Mao has not had the whole hearted support of all of his colleagues. While few have dared to confront him directly, attempts must have been made to deflect him from his more radical plans. Others probably have tried to limit the power and influence of those leaders who have risen rapidly to the top as a result of the Cultural Revolution. Mao's own plans have probably not been firmly fixed, since a major concept of the revolution has been to stimulate the "masses." Thus, at various points, new and unforeseen situations have developed which have dictated retreats as well as advances. As each radical phase has brought more damage, the ranks of those alienated by Mao's tactics and policies have grown.

8. As long as Mao is in power, a group associated with his more radical policies is likely to retain a strong position within the top leadership. Such elements will almost certainly continue to encourage Mao to push his more revolutionary ideas. They will also work against the more moderate elements and policies that seem to threaten their positions, and they may also turn against each other as has happened in the past. Such competition is likely to be undertaken particularly with a view toward the succession to Mao.

9. The position of Lin Piao is one of the great mysteries of the Cultural Revolution. He issues instructions in the name of Mao, and on the record, he is Mao's "best pupil" and selected heir. A cult of sorts has developed around Lin, and

4   SECRET

SECRET

he seems to behave in the Mao tradition of rare public appearances and pro-nouncements. Apparently, he stands above the fray of daily struggle. In such circumstances it is difficult to determine with any certainty his actual role or the extent of his political influence.

B. The Nature of the Opposition

10. Opposition to Mao and the Cultural Revolution is ill-defined and lacking in cohesion or central direction. Despite charges of plots against him, there has been no straightforward effort to depose Mao that we are aware of. The leadership has responded to Mao's purges, not by overt opposition, but rather by maneuvering for survival. This has involved evasion, passive resistance, blunt-ing of directives, and assiduous protection of vested interests. This defensive reaction has been most risky in the upper echelons where purges have been severe. But at the level of provincial officials and below, despite numerous purges, this form of opposition has been relatively effective, in large part due to the chaos that has grown as the Cultural Revolution has more and more disrupted the social order.

11. One of the principal results of the resistance to the Cultural Revolution has been the development of two wings in the top leadership. On the one hand there are those vested interest groups and leaders whose primary concern is with maintaining order, stability, and national security, and on the other those charged with the conduct of the revolution. Among the more moderate forces are the PLA, the government bureaucracy, and most of the "old guard" of the party. Probably they do not constitute a permanent faction, but rather a loose coalition in competition with the Cultural Revolution Group under Chen Po-ta, Kang Sheng, and Madame Mao.

12. As number three in the Peking hierarchy, Chou En-lai has played a major role in the Cultural Revolution. He continues to maneuver adroitly through complicated political conflicts, remaining in the fray but somehow above it, serving Mao but at the same time moderating the more extreme consequences of Maoist policies. As premier of the State Council, Chou has for many years had responsibility for administering China's economic, military, and govern-mental bureaucracy. He has thus been the spokesman for what we have come to view as the more moderate interests in China. As such, we see him as the symbolic if not actual leader of this group.

13. There is considerable evidence that there are important differences in the leadership over policy, objectives and tactics though there are probably also areas of common concern. These differences reflect the division of competing interest groups as well as political infighting for personal gain. Furthermore, conflicts are unavoidable in the bizarre situation of a regime in power trying to conduct a revolution without at the same time destroying the country and itself. These conflicts have been responsible for the twists and turns in policy and for the air of uncertainty prevailing at various times in Peking. Since September 1967, the forces working for moderation appear to have made im-

SECRET

5

SECRET

portant gains in power and in their influence over the course of the revolution. Recently, however, the campaign against right deviation has shown that the Cultural Revolution Group is by no means out of action.

14. In sum, we believe the leadership is divided on policy matters and is strained by the existence of factions with competing aspirations for power. It will retain a superficial unity as long as Mao presides over it, but the divisions will be an element of potentially great instability in the short term and especially during the post-Mao period.

C. The Instruments of Power

15. The institutional structure of China has been heavily damaged. The effective control formerly exercised by the regime through the party has been seriously weakened. No longer is it clear that Peking speaks with one voice; no longer are its institutions immutable and unassailable. Authority and discipline have suffered accordingly. By endorsing the slogan "to rebel is justified," Mao has gone far to undermine the mechanisms of control.

16. *The Party Apparatus.* The Communist Party of China has not been repudiated, and the Maoists claim it will be reconstructed and purified. Nevertheless, its organizational structure has been disrupted, its prestige badly tarnished, its authority virtually demolished, and its future therefore beclouded. The party elite at all levels from Peking to the counties had been drawn from the "old guard," or those two million members—10 percent of the membership—who had joined the party by 1948. This elite justified its status on the grounds of seniority, the sharing of pre-1949 hardships, and its unshakable loyalty to Mao and the party. But this elite has become disoriented and shaken to its roots, first, by Mao's denial of its worth and, second, by Mao's support of young revolutionaries who dispute the qualifications and relevance of the "old guard" for ruling China.

17. Top party leaders had been purged in 1966, but the full assault on the party came in early 1967 when the Red Guards were ordered to "seize power" and "to drag out the power-holders." As a result, in each organ and unit one or more of "old guard" officials were selected for severe criticism, pillory, and, in many cases, purging. This ritual symbolized the subordination of the party and the "old guard" to Mao and the revolutionaries, but it also paralyzed party operations. The party secretariat has ceased functioning; the party's six regional bureaus are being by-passed and presumably have been deactivated; provincial party committees are being replaced by the new revolutionary committees.

18. The attack on the party has demoralized and confused the cadre. Their ties with deposed party leaders, no matter how routine, have been grounds for suspicion and attack during the witch-hunts of the revolutionaries. Defensive actions on their part have been defined as opposition to Mao. Attempts to organize their own Red Guards have contributed significantly to the wide-

6

SECRET

SECRET

spread factional struggles. Longstanding working relationships between party workers and their counterparts in the local military establishments have occasionally led to mutual efforts at resisting Red Guard intrusions. Among the lower level cadres, dropouts have been common as the confused directives and contradictory policies have left them in exposed and dangerous positions.

19. *The Governmental Structure.* Many of the experienced bureaucrats have also been discredited and removed. The formerly efficient bureaucracy is showing clear signs of strain as it responds indecisively to what are, at best, confusing orders. At the provincial and local levels, governmental operations have been severely hampered by the administrative confusion. At the center, governmental ministries continue to function but Red Guard disruptions have clearly interfered with normal business. Governmental ministers have undergone criticism and many have been lost to the purges; even Chou En-lai has not been able to protect all of the key personnel in the government. As a result, administrative chaos has occurred, especially at the provincial level, which has required the intervention of the army.

20. *The Military.* Initially it seemed as if the PLA might be only lightly involved with the Cultural Revolution. The military leadership, however, has not escaped the purges, even though the full disruptive force of the Cultural Revolution has been generally kept out of the inner workings of the PLA. Most of the losses have been within the political commissar system, but commanders have been removed as well. As the authority of the party and the government declined, the PLA, as the only cohesive force with a nationwide system of command and control, was drawn in to maintain stability and order. It was assigned a wide variety of administrative and control functions throughout China.

21. Given this central role, the PLA has found itself heavily involved in local politics as well as in top level disputes. Its problems with these unfamiliar tasks have been severely complicated by vague and often contradictory directives from the center. In many instances, the PLA encouraged and supported "conservative" Red Guards. However, the most common reaction was to adopt a neutral role in the political disputes and to concentrate on restraining the violence. Even here, however, the PLA often was unable to remain neutral or to act as peacemaker between warring factions. As a result of these contrasting responses, there have been splits at various levels in the PLA at various times. Although usually extolled by the Peking leadership, the army's difficult role has brought it under attack on several occasions by the militants of the Cultural Revolution Group.

22. *The Revolutionaries.* The role of the Red Guards and more adult "revolutionary" groups, which were organized later, has fluctuated with the ebb and flow of the Cultural Revolution. As shock-troops in the initial assault on the party, the young revolutionaries were useful to Mao. The massive Red Guard rallies of 1966 had demonstrated the potency of Mao's unique ability to manipulate the "masses." The prompt and enthusiastic response to Mao's charisma was an effective warning to actual or potential opposition. More recently, ideological

SECRET

7

~~SECRET~~

fervor has declined among the revolutionaries as it has among the population at large. Evidence is accumulating that the continuing factional violence owes less to ideological motivation than to struggle between organizations representing the "haves" and "have-nots" for power, status, and material advantages.

23. As the top level control instrument of the Red Guards and other revolutionary organizations, the Cultural Revolution Group has also been unstable. The original 17 member group has been largely purged. However, the top leaders—Chen Po-ta, Kang Sheng, and Madame Mao—retain their prominent rank; with the possible exception of Kang, their rise and their survival is largely due to their close ties to Mao. Their vested interest in continuing "revolution" is no doubt reflected in their advice to Mao as well as their guidance of the Red Guard revolutionaries.

24. *The New Power Structure.* Peking has been trying since early 1967 to put together a new power apparatus incorporating the party cadres, the PLA, and the "revolutionary masses." The center has officially proclaimed that each province and city is to be governed by a revolutionary committee based on a "three-way alliance" of these elements. The first revolutionary committee was formed in Heilungkiang Province on 31 January 1967. Progress was slow and erratic last year, but the pace has quickened in recent months, and only a few major administrative areas have yet to set up the new committees.

25. The future role and powers of these revolutionary committees are quite uncertain, especially in light of a policy to rebuild the party. The committees have been described as only "provisional." Nothing has been said, however, of reestablishing the provincial governments. In any case, the regime has indicated it hopes to complete the reorganization process during 1968.

26. The process of forming a new administrative apparatus for the provinces has sharpened the very factionalism it was intended to halt. Rival Red Guard organizations have resisted mergers with old enemies, the relationship between former party cadres and the Red Guards is still greatly strained, and the PLA has been hard pressed to carry out its ambiguous orders. Even though violence has abated in the general sense, fierce political infighting and tensions continue. In effect, there will be a requirement for the PLA to remain in control until the new revolutionary committees develop unity and administrative effectiveness or until the party is itself sufficiently reconstructed to reassert authority.

D. Social Order

27. In addition to the violence directly related to the politics of the Cultural Revolution, there has been a general decline in social order and discipline in China. We cannot determine how pervasive the present lawlessness (black-marketing, bribery, profiteering, petty crime, and the violent settling of old scores) has become. But the regime's former effectiveness in suppressing such activity has clearly deteriorated. Moreover, the surplus urban population, which had been moved into the rural areas, has flowed back into the cities where it survives as best it can, often illegally. Similarly, the students have resisted

8 ~~SECRET~~

SECRET

regime orders to return to their schools, and have done so in the name of Mao. For their part, the workers have taken advantage of the confusion to push for greater material benefits and better working conditions. Unless these tendencies toward unsanctioned individual and group action can soon be contained, they could have far-reaching implications for the future of the Communist system in China.

28. Psychological coercion through propaganda and the all-pervasive party are no longer effective controls, and the PLA lacks the numbers and the organization to control society as the party did. Until an equivalent of the party's control mechanism can be rebuilt, which may take years, the regime has little alternative to accepting a reduced presence in many areas. Revolutionary excesses have created unrest and the invitation to seize authority has encouraged forceful attempts at solving problems. Sporadic violence is therefore likely to continue in 1968. Even with clear and precise orders, the PLA will need time to control the situation, and will certainly be unable to remove the underlying tensions. Ultimately, Peking may have to choose between a heavier use of military power to maintain order and a more flexible approach to social controls, such as material incentives.

E. The Economy

29. Despite Mao's radical views on economic development, economic policy has not been subjected to the extremes of the Cultural Revolution. Even though many of the existing policies are being attributed to the disgraced Liu Shao-chi, we have seen no significant departures from the relatively permissive line on private plots and free markets in the rural areas or from relatively conservative policies in industry. Thus, despite the unceasing rhetoric endorsing Mao's views and refuting those attributed to Liu, the actual policies have been relatively unaffected. As regards planning, the Third Five-Year Plan (1966-1970) is no longer referred to and is almost certainly a dead issue.

30. The disorder and turmoil had an adverse effect on the economy in 1967. Production losses in industry have been reflected in reduced construction, in declining inventories, and in depressed foreign trade. Disruptions in transport and coal shortages in particular affected the entire economy. Agriculture, on the other hand, was a bright spot due to unusually favorable weather, and this has sustained consumption, thus precluding severe personal hardship.

31. In the urban labor force, with industrial production down and the population of working age expanding, the number of unemployed and underemployed has jumped in the last 18 months. At the same time, the regime has been preaching frugality and has been attempting to cut wages and fringe benefits. These developments, coupled with the general turmoil and factionalism of the Cultural Revolution, have led to serious clashes between groups of workers and widespread discontent with living standards and employment opportunities. The regime has promised to reexamine the whole wage question at a later stage

SECRET

9

SECRET

in the Cultural Revolution. In the short term, however, no relief can be expected and popular discontent probably will mount.

32. In the longer run, the economy's need for highly trained specialists has been seriously compromised by the nearly two-year closure of the universities. The very virulence of the attack on intellectuals will make a resumption of effective higher education difficult. Indeed, if the curricula are changed in the proposed direction of eliminating foreign influences in favor of Maoist dogma, then the quality of education could suffer a further serious decline. The closure of lower and middle schools is less serious in terms of vocational skills because those schools had already graduated more students than could be absorbed by the modern economy.

F. Military Capabilities

33. The heavy commitment of troops to Cultural Revolution activities has almost certainly disrupted the training mission of the PLA; that it may also be disturbing the morale and effectiveness of the troops is more difficult to prove, but nevertheless likely. The scope of the rebuilding effort—political, economic, and social—that now faces the regime seems likely to require the heavy support of the PLA for some time to come. As a result it is unlikely that the military can recoup its losses in combat readiness. The sheer weight of the political and administrative tasks will inevitably affect the performance of its military duties. In the event of a military threat to China, however, the PLA probably could give a good account of itself.[3]

34. Construction, missile firings, and nuclear testing have continued in the modern weapons field throughout the Cultural Revolution. But there is good evidence that political turmoil has spread to organizations directing and implementing the advanced weapons program. In a speech of January 1968, Chou En-lai deplored the damage that factional strife had caused in the military industries. He referred to prolonged political struggles and damage to equipment in the ministry responsible for missiles. We have no solid information on how serious these disruptions might have been. But it seems likely that resource allocation and policy guidance must have suffered during the excesses of the Cultural Revolution.

III. PROSPECTS

A. Internal Policy

35. There are of course a number of major uncertainties affecting any estimate of China's future course. There will be unforeseen events, such as the kidnapping at Wuhan last year, or the death of some key figure such as Mao, Lin, or Chou. Personal animosities and tension among competing interest groups have intensified, they may increase to the point where they will prevent orderly resolution of major issues. Conflict will almost certainly continue over the

---

[3] A more detailed discussion of military readiness will be taken up in the forthcoming NIE 13-3-68, "Communist China's General Purpose and Air Defense Forces."

10

SECRET

SECRET

process of reconstructing the party and there will be tension over the relative influence of military and civilian leadership. Outside events, such as the war in Vietnam, could alter Peking's attitude. Popular disillusionment as well as economic disruption may preclude any early restoration of social stability, particularly if there is a sharp decline in farm output in 1968, further discrediting the present leadership.

36. It is unlikely that Mao will ever be satisfied with a general stabilization of political life at the cost of his revolutionary programs. He will probably try to keep on initiating such programs to achieve further changes in Chinese society and politics, though with some appreciation of the dangers of anarchy and economic chaos. He is likely to be suspicious of retreats and to favor periodic upsurges in revolutionary efforts. If he sees the responses as incorrect or inadequate, he may attempt further purges. This basic attitude of Mao has been and will continue to be responsible, to a large extent, for the continuing turmoil. As long as there is room for doubt over Mao's attitude toward how to continue the "struggle," there will be elements in the leadership and especially among young revolutionaries who will be encouraged to persist in their disruptive actions in the name of Mao. They will do so partly in the belief that this is actually what is wanted, regardless of official edicts to the contrary, and partly to protect or enhance their power positions.

37. Thus, the outlook for China is at best uncertain. On the basis of the record it would be prudent to allow for some sharp turns and surprises. But the trend appears to be running against the extremes of Maoism. Even though China has demonstrated remarkable tolerance for prolonged chaos, there appears to be growing recognition in Peking that it is time to cut the losses of the Cultural Revolution and to consolidate the limited gains.

38. On balance, we believe that the trend will be toward regaining stability. This is partly because the resistance to the revolution reached dangerous proportions last summer and threatened a confrontation between the army and the revolutionaries. It also reflects increased political influence of the more moderate elements in Peking. Finally, Mao himself probably concurred in the move toward moderation, since he himself hopes to reconstruct a new order out of the disruption of the old party apparatus.

39. The Cultural Revolution as such will not be repudiated, just as the Great Leap Forward was never formally discredited, but under the guise of victory statements, the more radical and destructive features will probably be set aside. This does not mean the situation will promptly return to normal. There is likely to be considerable disarray and confusion for some time. Fighting will probably break out from time to time and become severe in some areas. Political maneuvering in Peking will continue.

40. We believe that a new organizational framework will gradually evolve. Its ultimate composition and correlation of forces is uncertain. Mao at least intends that it should reflect the influence of the new revolutionary generation; the Cultural Revolution Group will seek to establish revolutionary influence over

SECRET

SECRET

the process of party building and within the revolutionary committees. The record thus far, however, suggests that the PLA and the party cadres will probably be the predominant elements. Thus, the reconstruction of the party and the evolution of the powers of the revolutionary committees will probably be the sources of continuing struggle, though perhaps not in as violent a form as in the past two years.

41. The military will remain Peking's most reliable instrument of control over at least the coming year. The PLA will have the main responsibility for carrying out the political reorganizations. Military dominance in political life may become institutionalized, particularly if political reconstruction bogs down in violence and disarray or if economic and social problems require the repressive force of the PLA.

42. Beset by many problems, China can at best hope only to restore stability and balance to the economy in 1968, foregoing any prospect of expansion. Even this hope rests on the dubious assumption that China can restore effective economic priorities and discipline at a time of continued political conflict. For example, Peking would have to reimpose effective controls over the distribution of food, wages, and movements of the population. In view of the limited progress towards economic stability so far this year, economic performance for the whole of 1968 probably will show a continued decline.

43. In any case, a decline in agricultural production is likely compared with last year's very good harvests. Weather conditions are unlikely to be as favorable as in 1967, the supply of chemical fertilizer will be reduced, and the effects of poor management in the irrigation system will be felt. The lack of firm administrative control may lead to serious problems in procurement and distribution of food. Thus, there is a possibility that severe food shortages will develop by 1969, with major political consequences. At a minimum, farm output in 1968 will probably be reduced enough to inhibit economic growth in 1969.

44. There are various indications that Mao considers the economic policies followed since the collapse of the Great Leap Forward to be revisionist; they relied too much on material incentives and discipline and too little on the inspirational, creative force of Maoist doctrine. Mao believes that only by unleashing the latent energies of the Chinese masses can China's economic problems be overcome. It may be that the Cultural Revolution was intended, in part, as a preparing of the ground for some drastic stroke by Mao in the field of economic policy.

45. If so, the situation hardly seems ripe for any such move. To attempt another Leap Forward type of experiment in the midst of the current turmoil and without an effective management and control apparatus, would invite an economic and social crisis. Peking will have its hands full in restoring order and balance to the economy and it lacks the investment resources to launch a significant long-term expansion program. We therefore conclude that major initiatives in economic policy are unlikely this year.

12   SECRET

SECRET

B. External Policy

46. "Red Guard diplomacy" cost Peking heavily in 1967. Chinese diplomats arrogantly propagandized Mao's revolutionary dogma abroad while xenophobia was encouraged at home. This truculent approach created serious problems in neutral Asian countries such as Burma, Cambodia, Nepal, and Ceylon where China had earlier built up reasonably good relations. Diplomatic representatives in Peking were exposed to the fanaticism of the mob. British, French, Czechs, Russians, Mongolians, Japanese, Indians, and Indonesians suffered physical abuse in Peking; diplomatic premises were invaded and in some cases sacked. For at least four days in August, Foreign Minister Chen Yi was displaced by one of the ultraleftists thrown up by the Cultural Revolution.

47. The violent phase was relatively short-lived, and a more balanced approach has prevailed since the excesses of August. But the verbal assault on Burma, Thailand, Malaya, the Philippines, India, and Indonesia has continued. This harsher revolutionary policy in support of insurgency, even in countries with which Peking has diplomatic relations, will probably continue at least so long as Mao and his general line dominate in China. Although domestic preoccupations will make 1968 an unlikely time for Peking to mount any major subversive effort beyond its borders, we expect Peking to continue its low-level assistance to the Thai, Burmese, and Indian insurgents. Such assistance would be consistent with Peking's past actions in those areas where the danger of confrontation with the US is slight.

48. Vietnam remains Peking's most immediate concern. Even at the height of the Cultural Revolution, China maintained its military and economic support of Hanoi, tolerated almost open political differences, and sought to portray Vietnamese developments as successes for Mao's strategy. But in Vietnam as elsewhere in the Far East, Peking has been cautious about risking military confrontation with the US.

49. In the near future, Peking's aim will be to keep Hanoi moving toward what Peking hopes will be a major foreign policy success, the defeat or withdrawal of the US from Vietnam. To this end Peking will continue to urge Hanoi to persevere in a protracted war without overt Chinese participation.

50. Peking strongly opposes the idea of serious negotiations over Vietnam at this stage in the war. It will probably press Hanoi to be as stiff and uncompromising as possible in the discussions with the US. Even so, it will probably not take coercive measures such as cutting off aid to Hanoi. Peking lacks sufficient influence in Hanoi to block full-fledged negotiation on a settlement. Should Hanoi accept a cease-fire, Peking would disapprove but would have to accept Hanoi's decision.

51. At the other focal point of China's foreign policy, relations with the Soviet Union remain frozen in bitterness. Peking's obsessive anti-Soviet line has ruled out "united action" by the Communist nations on behalf of Vietnam, and has cost China the support of formerly friendly Communist parties. The result

SECRET

13

SECRET

has been to heighten China's isolation, and together with the radical innovations of the Cultural Revolution, has damaged Peking's prestige on almost all fronts.

52. We see no basis for compromise in Sino-Soviet relations so long as Mao is alive. The Soviet build-up of military forces along China's northern border points up how far the conflict has progressed since 1960. China must be sensitive to this show of force, as well as the Soviet potential for subversion among the minority populations along the border. But we believe Peking will remain cautious about raising military tensions in border areas and will probably not undertake a comparable build-up on the Chinese side.

IV. AFTER MAO

53. If Mao dies in the next year or so, the succession will probably be disorderly and contentious. Lin Piao has received a clear mandate as successor but we believe his prospects of consolidating his position are quite uncertain. Initially Lin might take over as Chairman of the Board, with Chou En-lai as the Chief Executive. Chou's unique abilities might hold things together temporarily in a transition period. But varying attitudes and approaches of the leadership—only partially repressed by Mao's dogmatic rule—would soon erupt. We foresee a stormy and possibly protracted period in which basic pol' issues will fuel a fierce leadership struggle. Personalities will rise and fall as the leaders contest for positions in the new power structure. At this stage we are unable to say how the leadership might sort itself out. Much will depend on the balance of power which develops in the process of reconstructing a political order. Present trends suggest the military might play the central role in post-Mao China.

54. The judgment on Maoism is already coming in, and it will heavily influence the direction of future Chinese policy after Mao. Mao's legacy is likely to be an enfeebled party, a confused bureaucracy, and a divided and harried leadership. Factionalism and strife have replaced the discipline and unity that formerly characterized the regime. Mao's drive to revive revolutionary enthusiasm has had the opposite effect. It is possible that Mao may institute changes that restore some of Chinese communism's old forward momentum, but we doubt that his specific programs would long survive him. His campaign to break the hold of the past will probably have some limited success. But China's culture and traditions are already modifying Mao's communism even as Mao attempts to reshape old habits and customs. Most importantly, much of Mao's revolutionary dogma is proving irrelevant to China's problems in the modern world. It is likely that the rejection of his doctrines, though not necessarily of communism in the broadest sense, will accelerate at his passing.

SECRET

SECTION 31

SNIE 13-69

Communist China and Asia

6 March 1969

APPROVED FOR RELEASE
DATE: MAY 2004

(b)(3)

~~SECRET~~

SNIE 13-69
6 March 1969

SPECIAL
NATIONAL INTELLIGENCE ESTIMATE
NUMBER 13-69

Communist China and Asia

Submitted by

DIRECTOR OF CENTRAL INTELLIGENCE

Concurred in by the

UNITED STATES INTELLIGENCE BOARD

As indicated overleaf

6 MARCH 1969

Authenticated:

EXECUTIVE SECRETARY, USIB

~~SECRET~~

N⁰ 423

~~SECRET~~

COMMUNIST CHINA AND ASIA

THE PROBLEM

To survey recent Chinese foreign policy and alternate lines of development in the near term; to define the nature of the Chinese threat in Asia, and to estimate Chinese intentions in the area; and to estimate the longer term outlook for Chinese foreign policy.

CONCLUSIONS

A. The Chinese Communist regime has fallen far short of its aspirations for a position of dominance in East and Southeast Asia and for the leadership of the world revolution. Neither its efforts at conventional diplomacy nor at supporting revolutionary struggles have been pursued consistently or with a regard to objective realities. Mao's ideological pretensions have earned China the enmity of the USSR, and his bizarre domestic programs have cost China greatly in prestige and respect elsewhere in the world. Yet China's location and size, and the traditional apprehensions of its neighbors, ensure for it a major impact upon Asia regardless of the policy it follows.

B. As long as Mao is the dominant figure, major changes in China's international posture do not appear likely. Mao will remain an insurmountable obstacle to any accommodation with the USSR, and there is little alternative to continuing hostility toward the US. A failure by the Vietnamese Communists to achieve their aims might require some shift in tactics, but the Chinese would almost certainly not launch an overt attack, nor would they be likely to open a major new front of conflict.

C. Nevertheless, Chinese aspirations for political dominance in Asia will persist. Almost certainly Mao and his immediate successors will not expect to achieve this by military conquest, although force and violence figure strongly in Mao's doctrines. The Chinese may hope that the possession of a strategic capability will give China greater freedom

~~SECRET~~   1

SECRET

to support "people's war" or, more remotely, to engage in conventional war in Asia by diminishing the possibility of nuclear attack on China. Whatever Chinese hopes, however, the actual possession of nuclear weapons will not necessarily make China more willing to risk a direct clash with the US; indeed, it is more likely to have a sobering effect.

D. Whatever modifications in Chinese policy flow from its advance into the nuclear age, the principal threat from China will for many years be in the realm of subversion and revolutionary activity—mainly in Southeast Asia. In South Vietnam and Laos, Peking must take account of Hanoi's direct interests. China's policy toward Cambodia will be largely conditioned by Sihanouk's attitude. If he moves very far toward accommodation with the US, Peking's pressures against him—now minimal—would be increased. The Chinese may see Thailand as a more lucrative target for a Chinese-sponsored "people's war." Peking is already providing some training and support, but even the Chinese must realize that the Thai insurgency faces a long, difficult fight. The Chinese have a more clear-cut choice in Burma, and whether they significantly increase the insurgency or restore more normal diplomatic relations could be an indicator of trends in Peking's foreign policy.

E. The rest of Southeast Asia is less important in Peking's immediate scheme because the Chinese lack direct access and current prospects for insurgency in these areas are minimal. Peking seeks to weaken and embarrass India, but not to confront it directly so long as there is no threat to Tibet.

F. It is in the area of conventional diplomacy, which suffered severely in the Cultural Revolution, that Peking could most easily achieve significant changes. Restoration of normal diplomacy would facilitate a trend toward recognition of Peking, and this would in turn put pressure on other countries, particularly Japan, which does not want to be left behind in opening relations with the mainland. Taipei would undoubtedly suffer diplomatic losses in this process.

G. The departure of Mao could, in time, bring significant change in China's relations with the outside world. There could be contention and struggle for leadership that would freeze major policies during a long interregnum. But on balance, we believe Mao's departure will generate a strong movement toward modifying his doctrines.

2

SECRET

SECRET

H. A less ideological approach would not necessarily make China easier to deal or live with in Asia. Pursuit of its basic nationalist and traditional goals could sustain tensions in the area, and a China that was beginning to realize some of its potential in the economic and advanced weapons fields could become a far more formidable force in Asia than is Maoist China.

DISCUSSION

I. INTRODUCTION

1. During 20 years of rule, the Chinese Communists have not come close to realizing China's aspirations for leadership or domination in Asia. There are many reasons for this. China has of course had to operate from an economic base inadequate to support the full range of its pretensions. Maoist preoccupation with making China the leader of the world revolution has often led to policies and actions harmful to other more traditional or conventional Chinese goals in Asia. The tension and inconsistencies in the basic Chinese approach to foreign policy have been magnified by frequent shifts in actual tactics and strategy. In consequence, Peking has failed to pursue any single course with consistency and maximum effect over a prolonged period.

2. In the flush of victory in 1949, Peking joined the USSR in proclaiming Asia ripe for revolution and called for "people's war" against all existing governments in the area. But China was not ready to offer much practical assistance to this end, local communist parties lacked the strength for revolution, and the principal result was to alienate the leaders and supporters of the newly independent Asian governments who considered themselves anti-imperialist and deserving of Peking's support, not its enmity.

3. The Korean war forced China to concentrate on more immediate security concerns, and in its aftermath Peking shifted to the line of peaceful coexistence abroad while concentrating on construction at home. But this line, which had considerable promise of winning friends, diplomatic recognition, and broad commercial opportunities for China, gradually gave way to a more belligerent and revolutionary line. By the late 1950's, the dispute with the USSR began to take shape and has since consumed a good deal of China's energies and attention. During the early 1960's, China suffered a great loss of prestige as the absurdities, administrative confusion, and economic chaos of the Great Leap became evident to the world.

4. By 1964, however, China seemed to be back on an even keel and growing in strength and influence. A working balance between support for revolutionary goals and improving China's international position seemed to exist in Chinese foreign policy. China was closely aligned with North Vietnam and North Korea, commanded respect among numerous communist parties, and had established an "axis" with Indonesia. The revolutions in Vietnam and Laos were progressing.

SECRET

3

SECRET

Maneuvering was underway for a new Afro-Asian conference, which the Chinese hoped to turn against the USSR. Several noncommunist states were considering recognition, and France actually took this step. Chou En-lai embarked on an extensive tour of Africa. In October 1964, Mao's archenemy Khrushchev fell and the Chinese exploded their first atomic device.

5. But once again a combination of circumstances intervened to produce major shifts in the Chinese posture in foreign affairs. Suddenly, in 1965, the war in Vietnam became much more than another war of liberation. With the US intervention, Mao's theories on the validity of guerrilla war were being subjected to extreme test, and China itself felt the risk of direct conflict with the US. The problem was a delicate one: how to assure success in the Vietnam war without provoking an American attack on North Vietnam and ultimately China.

6. The entire question of how to confront the US was apparently the subject of a debate during 1965, a debate which was greatly complicated by changes in the USSR, where the new leadership was bent on rebuilding its position with Asian Communists, especially in Hanoi. The Soviet proposal for "united action" to support Hanoi, however, was regarded by Mao as a trap which would hamstring Chinese freedom of action and undermine Peking's claim to be the center of a new revolutionary movement. Most important, Mao saw that any accommodation with Moscow would contribute to the erosion of morale and ideological purity which he apparently feared was already spreading rapidly throughout the Chinese party and society.

7. In the rest of the world, the Chinese found that they had overestimated the revolutionary enthusiasm of their friends. Chou En-lai's African tour was cut short, after embarrassing reaction to his vivid descriptions of Africa's ripeness for revolution. With the collapse in 1965 of the "Bandung II" Conference in Algiers, China was rebuffed in its effort to form an anti-Soviet and anti-US bloc of Afro-Asians. The recognition by France was not followed by a rush of other countries. And the alliance with Sukarno collapsed in a massive bloodbath for the Indonesian Communists and a wave of violent repression of the overseas Chinese community there.

8. China reacted to these circumstances, not by muting its revolutionary propaganda, but by calling for an acceleration of the worldwide revolutionary movement. Supposedly, the various insurgencies, activists, parties, and front groups would step up their efforts in order to divert US resources and wear down the US will. At the same time, the USSR and its clients would be excluded from the new phase of intensified revolutionary activity, and China would remain the center of the movement.

9. The net effect of this line was to create an even wider gap between Chinese ideological prescriptions and objective reality. In dealing with major problems of national security, especially those involving a threat of confrontation with the US, China was forced to remain cautious and prudent. As the domestic crisis of the Cultural Revolution deepened, Peking became more and more rigid and

4

SECRET

SECRET

doctrinaire, insensitive to the advice of its friends, utterly hostile and inflexible towards its enemies, and increasingly oblivious to the deterioration of its international position.

10. Even so, the Chinese leaders might have been content with their position had it not been for new developments in 1968. The onset of negotiations over Vietnam was tantamount to a repudiation of the Chinese by Hanoi, seemed to vindicate the position of the USSR, and pointed to growing Soviet influence. And the USSR engaged in a substantial military buildup in the Far East which was clearly directed against China. The Chinese have not reacted by a similar buildup of their own along the Soviet frontier, and they probably do not expect an open Soviet attack. But they are no doubt concerned about Soviet efforts to influence internal developments in China in one way or another. All this was brought into sharper focus by the invasion of Czechoslovakia and the subsequent promulgation of the "Brezhnev doctrine."

11. In sum, by the end of 1968, the revolutionary line had failed in its principal objectives. It was becoming increasingly clear that a settlement in Vietnam was not likely to validate Mao's strategy of "people's war." The influence of the USSR in the region had not been contained but had in fact grown, both in the communist capitals of Pyongyang and Hanoi, and in South and Southeast Asia. China had failed completely to achieve a "broad united front" against the imperialist US and the revisionist USSR. Instead it found itself "encircled," as Chou En-lai acknowledged, and isolated on most key policy issues.

12. Yet Peking's lack of progress toward its revolutionary objectives has by no means completely vitiated its influence in Asia. China's location, size, and history, buttressed by the traditional apprehensions of its neighbors, ensure for it a major impact upon Asia regardless of the policy it follows. Awareness of China's existence and potential for making trouble affects the current policies of every country in the area.

II. IMMEDIATE PROSPECTS

13. In the near term, there does not appear to be much chance for a major change in China's international posture. As long as Mao is the dominant figure of the regime and the source of ideological guidance, Chinese policy will probably be confined within fairly narrow limits. He is likely to remain an insurmountable obstacle to any accommodation or modus vivendi with the USSR. Indeed, Chinese enmity for the Soviet Union has recently reached a level at least equal to that against the US; China now has two "number one enemies." With age, Mao has become less flexible and even more obsessed with revolutionary goals. There is not likely to be any slackening in his commitment to the notion that China is the center for inspiring the world revolution and that its principal allies are not to be found in the established Communist regimes and parties, but in the guerrilla movements that have accepted "Mao's thought" and intend to persist in protracted struggle. In this sense, there is little alternative to continuing hostility toward the US.

SECRET

5

SECRET

14. Yet within this fairly rigid strategic framework, there are signs of some greater flexibility in tactics. These signs are often contradictory and confusing, but they could be significant if domestic affairs are entering a new phase. The growing concern that the US and USSR are pursuing parallel, anti-Chinese policies may be a factor dictating Chinese moves to complicate or disrupt what they see as a tacit alliance. What such moves might be is not at all clear, and in the end they may be of no great significance. As long as Maoist ideology is dominant, however, the road to Moscow is blocked. Ironically, the Chinese may be coming to feel that they have more room for maneuver *vis-a-vis* the US than the USSR, though of course the Taiwan question will continue to obstruct Sino-US relations.

15. Whether shifts in Chinese tactics do occur could depend, of course, on developments in Vietnam. The Chinese already perceive that the war in Vietnam is likely to end in a negotiated settlement. They have taken some steps to mute their opposition to negotiations. And at some point in this process, they are likely to re-emphasize their broad political interest in the area, seeking to make it clear that no lasting settlement can be achieved without Peking's approval.

16. Of course, it is possible that the Chinese will choose not to adjust to developments in Indochina, but rather seek to disrupt them. However, a failure by the Vietnamese Communists to achieve their aims would probably not lead to extreme reactions by the Chinese. Almost certainly the Chinese are not going to launch an overt attack in Vietnam or seize some territory elsewhere, nor are they likely to open a major new front of conflict, using their own resources. At the other extreme, there is little likelihood that the Chinese will suddenly become quiescent because of the outcome in Vietnam. They are going to remain active in support of those movements that they believe are loyal to Maoist concepts and have some potential for effective development.

17. In any case, China's foreign policies are likely to be influenced to a significant degree by the internal crisis. Even if the extremes of the Cultural Revolution are already past, it is possible that a new phase of coercive social programs and disruptive economic initiatives may prove as debilitating as the political purge. If, on the other hand, a more moderate line in internal policies prevails, then order may also be gradually restored, and the Foreign Ministry professionals may gain greater influence over policy. But as long as Mao lives and rules in Peking, there will be an inherent instability in China. Foreign policy in a general sense will be subordinate to and reflect the internal line. Accordingly, Peking will be more likely to respond to outside events than to launch major new initiatives of its own.

III. THE CHINESE THREAT IN ASIA

18. All these considerations do not mean that China will be a negligible factor in Asia or in international politics. Chinese goals, in Asia at least, are fairly clear. Almost all Chinese—whether in Peking or on Taiwan—would agree that China's rightful position is one of political dominance on the Asian main-

6

SECRET

SECRET

land, and ultimately throughout East and Southeast Asia. Such aspirations have deep historical roots. In this sense, China poses a threat to Asia and to those outside powers which seek to play an important role in Asian affairs. The question is how the Chinese intend to accomplish their objectives.

A. Military Power

19. Almost certainly the Chinese do not expect to achieve a dominant position by military conquest, even though force and violence figure strongly in Maoist philosophy and Chinese Communist practice. In the cases where the Chinese have resorted to military means—in Korea and India—this was, in their view, defensive to protect the security of their borders. Indeed, a principal objective of China, like most states, is to insure its security against unfriendly powers ranged along its frontiers. Where the Chinese see an immediate threat to their security, they will be prepared to use force, even pre-emptively. But neither Mao nor his immediate successors are likely to believe that the Chinese revolution can be exported by the People's Liberation Army, or that armed conquest in the style of Imperial China is a safe or profitable course.

20. All this, of course, applies primarily to China as a conventional military power, but its acquisition of nuclear weapons will not necessarily increase its aggressiveness. The Chinese may hope that the possession of a strategic capability will give China greater freedom to support "people's war" or, more remotely, to engage in conventional war in Asia by diminishing the possibility of nuclear attack on China. The Chinese certainly hoped to gain such freedom in the Taiwan Strait crisis of 1958 by exploiting the Sino-Soviet alliance to deter the US. Moscow's refusal in that instance to back China with nuclear threats was probably a major factor in convincing Peking that it must have its own nuclear weapons.

21. Whatever may have been Chinese hopes in the past, however, the actual possession of nuclear weapons is likely to have a sobering effect. China has no hope of achieving parity with either the US or the USSR in nuclear weapons in the foreseeable future.[1] Despite its propaganda concerning China's ability to withstand nuclear attack, Peking will almost certainly come to realize, if it does not already, that either the US or the USSR possesses more than sufficient nuclear weapons to devastate China.

22. In these circumstances, China is likely to remain cautious in areas of possible direct confrontation with the US or the USSR, calculating that its own possession of nuclear weapons may increase, rather than lessen, the chances of a pre-emptive nuclear strike against it. For some time, China is likely to value its nuclear capability primarily as a Great Power status symbol and for

---

[1] The Intelligence Community currently estimates that the earliest possible initial operational capability for a Chinese intercontinental ballistic missile is late 1972, and that if the Chinese achieve that date, they might have between 10 and 25 launchers in 1975. A modest program for deployment of medium-range ballistic missiles will also probably be underway in the next few years.

SECRET

7

SECRET

its political effects. In sum, when China actually becomes a nuclear power during the next decade, it will probably be subjected to the same constraints and complications of policy as the other nuclear powers.

23. We cannot predict the ultimate effect of Chinese acquisition of nuclear weapons on the rest of Asia. At a minimum, China will gain greater prestige and respect; translated into political gains, this will probably mean that more countries will seek some relationship with Peking at Taiwan's expense, and that some will explore the possibility of accommodation, if Chinese policy is sufficiently flexible to permit such accommodations. However, few countries are likely to respond favorably to China's desire to monopolize nuclear power in Asia and to provide "protection" for the area against all outside powers. Indeed, the Chinese attitude may increase pressures in some Asian countries to develop their own nuclear capabilities or to cling more closely to other nuclear powers.

B. People's War

24. Whatever modifications in Chinese policy flow from its advance into the nuclear age, the principal threat from China will, for many years, be in the realm of subversion and revolutionary activity. Such activity will be conducted mainly in Southeast Asia where it relates directly to Peking's security interests in denying the US or other unfriendly powers positions close to China's borders. It also serves to satisfy the more general interest of China in establishing its own dominance in the area and in the world revolutionary movement.

25. *Vietnam and Laos.* To these ends, Peking supports and assists the Communists in Vietnam and Laos. For the present, at least, Peking has to take account of North Vietnam's direct interests in both South Vietnam and Laos. Peking could try to circumvent the North Vietnamese and open competing lines to the National Liberation Front and to the Pathet Lao. But its chances of gaining significant influence are poor and the cost in relations with Hanoi potentially so great that such a maneuver is unlikely. Though sharp disagreement could develop over tactics in Laos, in general Hanoi and Peking almost certainly share the same immediate goal: communist control of Laos, with Hanoi in the dominant role.

26. *Thailand.* As a close ally of the US and as a US strategic base, Thailand is a key object of Chinese policy in Southeast Asia and will probably receive increased emphasis after the war in Vietnam is settled. In this respect, Thailand is the most obvious target for "people's war." The political leadership of the Thai insurgency is now lodged in Peking, and the Chinese are providing some training and arms. Moreover, the Chinese have assumed a heavy propaganda commitment; recently they have announced the formation of a Thai "People's Army" supreme command and publicized the new manifesto of the Thai Communist Party.

27. The Chinese will almost certainly continue to support the Thai insurgents. Yet they must realize that the insurgency faces a long, difficult fight; it has made little progress in gaining the allegiance of ethnic Thais. And Thailand possesses

8

SECRET

SECRET

many strengths. Thus, it is possible that at some point the Chinese might want to reconsider their support, if in doing so they could induce Bangkok to draw away from its alliance with the US.

28. *Burma.* A period of cordial Sino-Burmese relations was broken by Peking in the midst of the Cultural Revolution nearly two years ago. Since then the Chinese have openly supported the Burmese Communist movement and publicly endorsed the formation of a united front with the ethnic insurgents. During much of 1968, the insurgency did increase along the Sino-Burmese border. There is, on the other hand, some evidence that the Chinese may want to restore more normal relations. Neutralist Burma would, of course, be receptive to such a move, especially if accompanied by a letup in the insurgency. Thus the Chinese have a fairly clear-cut choice between increasing the insurgency in northern Burma and restoring more normal government-to-government relations. How they decide could provide some indication concerning the extent of their commitment to the policy of insurgency in general.

29. *Cambodia.* Relations with Phnom Penh have fluctuated in recent years, partly because of Sihanouk's belief that Peking is sponsoring an insurgency, which he styles the Khmer Rouge. But the Chinese have been willing to tolerate a number of insults and taunts from Sihanouk and to furnish him arms, mainly because of the importance of Cambodia to the prosecution of the Vietnam war. The Chinese also value the fact that Cambodia is ostensibly neutral and frequently anti-American. Finally, in the long term Cambodia could be of potential significance in developing an insurgency in Thailand, with Cambodian territory possibly serving some of the same purposes it has served in the Vietnam war.

30. Thus, a major change in relations will probably depend less on Peking than on Sihanouk. He has long believed that China will become the dominant force in the Far East, and he sees value in trying to use the Chinese as a counterweight to his traditional enemies, the Vietnamese and the Thais. In these circumstances, Peking will probably continue to have considerable influence in Phnom Penh. Nevertheless, if Sihanouk feels that the tide is setting against the Communists in Vietnam, he is capable of becoming more cooperative with the US. Should he attempt to move very far in this direction, however, neither Hanoi nor Peking would be reluctant to step up political pressures against him and to increase support to dissident groups in Cambodia.

31. *Other Areas.* Insurgencies in the rest of Southeast Asia are much less important in the Chinese scheme, mainly because the Chinese have no direct access and the insurgents' prospects are currently minimal. The attempt of the Maoist-oriented Indonesian Communists to develop an insurgency in East Java last summer resulted not only in failure but in the death of key leaders. Peking occasionally publicizes the exploits of the Malayan Communist Party, which in turn pays homage to Mao. Peking, of course, has a considerable potential asset in the large ethnic Chinese population in Malaysia, but the Communist movement's overidentification with the Chinese hampers its avowed policy of forming a broadly based movement with the Malays. Peking has little influence in the

SECRET

.9

SECRET

Huk movement in the Philippines, though China periodically publicizes the exploits of Filipino insurgents.

32. *India.* In the late 1950's, China came to regard India as a competitor for leadership in Asia, especially because India seemed to benefit from the support of both the USSR and US. Thus Chinese policy has been framed to harass and intimidate India and demonstrate that it was generally incapable of taking the role of a leading Asian power. Since the border war of 1962, the Chinese have maintained some level of tension and threat along the Indian frontier; their military aid to Pakistan serves the same general purpose.

33. If China chose to, it could probably cause considerable trouble by supporting dissidents along the Indian frontier, especially in the northeast. The Chinese eagerly publicized the Naxalbari uprisings in Darjeeling, as the beginning of a Mao-inspired peasant upheaval. In Eastern India, the Chinese have propagandized and apparently have provided limited arms and training to Naga and Mizo tribesmen. Peking's aim seems to be to embarrass and worry New Delhi without becoming deeply involved, and we do not foresee much change in this attitude.

C. Politics and Diplomacy

34. In general, China's relations with the noncommunist world have suffered in consequence of the Cultural Revolution. Its extreme xenophobia and hysteria impinged on Chinese diplomatic relations. Foreign diplomats in Peking were abused and humiliated; Chinese embassy staffs abroad were reduced and ambassadors withdrawn. Even now, the functioning of the Ministry of Foreign Affairs remains disrupted by political campaigns and factional disputes.

35. Nevertheless, it is in the area of normal political relations and conventional diplomacy that the Chinese probably have the greatest room for change. Without much effort, the Chinese could resume normal diplomatic activity in Europe, Africa, and the Middle East. Moreover, there appears to be a new movement towards diplomatic recognition of China. Though the Chinese have exhibited no eagerness for such recognition, there is no doubt they would regard it as a gain, especially if such a trend adds to pressures in Japan and elsewhere for closer relations with China.

36. The next two years should present the Chinese with new opportunities for exerting some influence on Japanese politics. The tensions associated with the Okinawa question and the US-Japanese Security Treaty all lend themselves to exploitation by Peking. China could make a serious overture to restore more normal commercial relations and could encourage the visits of influential Japanese politicians. To have a significant impact in Japan, however, Chinese maneuvers would require a more skilled and flexible diplomacy than Peking has been willing to adopt thus far.

37. Eventually, a return to more normal diplomacy does seem likely. The flow of visitors to China has begun to increase, relations with the foreign em-

10

SECRET

SECRET

bassies in Peking have been eased, some new economic agreements have been concluded in recent months, and rumors recur that the Foreign Minister or Chou En-lai may visit abroad. Some reports have indicated that Chinese ambassadors are to return to their posts this spring. However, both China's internal politics and the reaction of Chinese leaders to foreign events could serve to delay moves to restore greater normalcy to Chinese diplomacy. Peking's abrupt postponement of the 20 February session of the Warsaw Talks—rationalized by references to the case of defecting Chinese diplomat Liao Ho-shu—suggests that Peking is as yet undecided about its foreign policy posture.

D. China's Vital Interests: Korea and Taiwan

38. In North Korea, the Chinese have seen their influence diminish significantly, largely because of their own rude arrogance and partly because of the consequences of the USSR's renewed cultivation of Pyongyang and Kim Il-song. Such a deterioration, however, is not likely to be a permanent state of affairs. Developments in Korea are of major importance to China, especially if tensions there continue and the danger of hostilities grows. Eventually, we expect the Chinese to repair their position and attempt to gain some influence over the Korean leadership. Probably, however, China will not pursue a policy intended to increase the risks of war. Its behavior during the past year, particularly in the Pueblo crisis, suggests that the Chinese are not about to pledge themselves unreservedly to Kim Il-song's adventurism.

39. Taiwan, of course, is a central element in Chinese foreign policy. US support for the GRC is a monumental obstacle to any Chinese reconsideration of its relations with the US. Peking will almost certainly not abandon its claim to Taiwan, and this position appears to rule out acceptance of a two-China solution. Yet there is not much Peking can do to gain possession of Taiwan as long as it is reluctant to engage in a military confrontation with the US. There is the possibility of pressure on the offshore islands (Chinmen and Matsu). Such a move might appeal to Peking as a test of US intentions in the post-Vietnam period, especially if it could be used to aggravate relations between Washington and Taipei.

IV. THE POST-MAO PERSPECTIVE

40. In some respects it is fruitless to speculate on the longer term development of Chinese foreign policy. The prospect of Mao's departure overshadows all other considerations. In many respects, the situation is analogous to that of the USSR in the early 1950's, when the death of Stalin unlocked Soviet foreign policy and led to a series of significant new departures. Naturally, this question is uppermost in China's case also. Will Mao's departure open a new era of significant change in China's relations with the outside world?

41. We believe that Mao's departure will generate a strong movement toward modifying his doctrines and jettisoning his disruptive programs. In foreign affairs, new leadership will ultimately seek to focus more effectively on national interests

SECRET

11

SECRET

understood in terms of a more realistic world view. Even if Maoist rhetoric should temporarily survive, we believe the trend will be toward moderating the Maoist line in favor of more practical diplomacy. Some modus vivendi with the USSR is possible, though anything approaching a renewal of the old alliance is most unlikely. Moreover, we would not exclude a return to the tactics of peaceful coexistence as part of an effort to undermine the US position in Asia.

42. But such a process is not inevitable and it would not in any case have to be steady and uninterrupted. If there is contention and struggle for the leadership, major policies could be frozen for a long-term interregnum. The timing of Mao's departure and the identity of the principal survivors could be important to policy. Finally, there is the response of outside powers. It would make a great difference whether a new leadership had plausible alternatives or whether it believed that its enemies were seeking to exploit China's weaknesses and uncertainties. Thus, the transition from Mao and his generation may last many years before real changes evolve. Meanwhile, support to subversive movements, if not to active insurgencies, is likely to play a continuing role in China's external policy.

43. In any case, a less ideological approach would not necessarily make China easier to deal or live with in Asia. Pursuit of its basic nationalist and traditional goals could sustain tensions in the area, and a China that was beginning to realize some of its potential in the economic and advanced weapons fields could become a far more formidable force in Asia than is Maoist China.

12

SECRET

SECTION 32

NIE 11/13-69

The USSR and China

12 August 1969

APPROVED FOR RELEASE
DATE: MAY 2004

(b)(1)
(b)(3)

SECRET

NIE 11/13-69
12 August 1969

NATIONAL INTELLIGENCE ESTIMATE

NUMBER 11/13-69

(Supersedes NIE 11-12-66)

The USSR and China

Submitted by

DIRECTOR OF CENTRAL INTELLIGENCE
Concurred in by the
UNITED STATES INTELLIGENCE BOARD
As indicated overleaf
12 August 1969

Authenticated:

ACTING EXECUTIVE SECRETARY, USIB

N⁰ 457

SECRET

SECRET

THE USSR AND CHINA

THE PROBLEM

To estimate the general course of Sino-Soviet relations over the next three years.

CONCLUSIONS

A. Sino-Soviet relations, which have been tense and hostile for many years, have deteriorated even further since the armed clashes on the Ussuri River last March. There is little or no prospect for improvement in the relationship, and partly for this reason, no likelihood that the fragments of the world Communist movement will be pieced together.

B. For the first time, it is reasonable to ask whether a major Sino-Soviet war could break out in the near future. The potential for such a war clearly exists. Moreover, the Soviets have reasons, chiefly the emerging Chinese nuclear threat to the USSR, to argue that the most propitious time for an attack is soon, rather than several years hence. At the same time, the attendant military and political uncertainties must also weigh heavily upon the collective leadership in Moscow.

C. We do not look for a deliberate Chinese attack on the USSR. Nor do we believe the Soviets would wish to become involved in a prolonged, large-scale conflict. While we cannot say it is likely, we see some chance that Moscow might think it could launch a strike against China's nuclear and missile facilities without getting involved in such a conflict. In any case, a climate of high tension, marked by periodic clashes along the border, is likely to obtain. The scale of fighting may occasionally be greater than heretofore, and might even involve punitive cross-border raids by the Soviets. Under such circumstances, escalation is an ever present possibility.

SECRET

1

SECRET

D.   In the light of the dispute, each side appears to be reassessing its foreign policy. The Soviets seem intent on attracting new allies, or at least benevolent neutrals, in order to "contain" the Chinese. To that end Moscow has signified some desire to improve the atmosphere of its relations with the West. The Chinese, who now appear to regard the USSR as their most immediate enemy, will face stiff competition from the Soviets in attempting to expand their influence in Asia.

DISCUSSION

I. POLITICAL BACKGROUND

1. The causes of the Sino-Soviet dispute are complex and, by now, intertangled. Some reflect primarily the clash of important national interests, compounded by historical and racial enmities, and the distrust of one great power for a neighboring power. These conflicting interests include, for example, the USSR's refusal in the late 1950's to satisfy China's demands for the wherewithal to achieve a nuclear weapons capability, diverging foreign policies and international priorities, Chinese dissatisfaction with the terms of Soviet economic aid and Soviet economic sanctions, Sino-Russian competition for influence elsewhere in East and South Asia, China's claims to Far Eastern and Central Asian territory ceded to Russia during the 19th century.[1] To some extent these issues would have arisen to complicate relations between Russians and Chinese almost regardless of the political systems in Moscow and Peking.

2. Ideology has also contributed to the development of the dispute. From its early stages, Peking has challenged the USSR's ideological supremacy and infallibility. Mao has rejected the Soviet model for internal socialist development; has also has rejected Soviet strategies for encouraging the spread of Communism, and he has asserted that his own doctrines must be treated with the same respect as those of Lenin. A struggle for leadership of the world's Communist Parties continues, waged in great part with ideological arguments. These ideological arguments have compounded economic and political rivalries. The ideological perspective limits the ability of the two sides to compromise their own quarrels, to agree to disagree. Misconceptions of each other's motives and behavior tend to become encapsulated in doctrinal formulae, and are thereby made rigid.

3. Personalities have played some role in the quarrel. Khrushchev and Mao found each other particularly antipathetic. After the fall of Khrushchev, probes by both governments during visits by Chou En-lai to Moscow and Kosygin to Peking in the winter of 1964-1965 convinced both sides that their differences were beyond compromise. The Chinese interpreted Khrushchev's removal as a vindication of their own ideological positions, while the new Soviet leadership would not go beyond certain limits in modifying the basic course set by Khrushchev.

---

[1] See Annex.

2

SECRET

SECRET

And while the Soviets now publicly express their hope that Mao's passing might lead to a less anti-Soviet policy in Peking, their private statements as well as their acts indicate that they expect the Chinese problem to be with them for the foreseeable future.

4. By mid-1965 the Chinese resumed their public attacks on Moscow and the new Soviet leaders moved toward a policy that might be described as the "containment" of China. This policy has several aspects: ideological isolation of China within the world Communist movement, political isolation of China by strengthening Soviet ties with Asian countries, economic isolation by drastically reducing Sino-Soviet trade, propaganda designed to warn the Soviet people and their allies of the perils of Maoism, and an impressive increase in Soviet military strength at key points along the Chinese frontier. The Chinese have tried to counter these moves by seeking support of other Communist states and Parties, by trying to establish pro-Chinese factions within Communist Parties, and by propaganda even more virulent than that of the Soviets.

5. In launching the Cultural Revolution, one of Mao's aims was to rid the Chinese Communist leadership of elements inclined towards revisionist policies attributed to Moscow. The Cultural Revolution movement was accompanied by an upsurge of anti-Soviet propaganda and maltreatment of Soviet personnel by the Chinese "masses." Judging from official Soviet propaganda, the Cultural Revolution convinced the Kremlin that the Chinese had virtually abandoned Marxism-Leninism, had eliminated moderate cadres, and had created a personal Maoist dictatorship intent on increasing its military strength. The fact that China was beginning to achieve a nuclear capability added to Moscow's fears. Thus the "containment" measures begun in 1965 were continued and even intensified.

6. From 1965 to 1969, Sino-Soviet state and economic relations declined steadily. Each country recalled its ambassador in 1966, and during the following year each unilaterally cancelled several minor agreements. Cultural contacts, ostensibly regulated by annual protocols, are in limbo. The February 1950 Treaty of Friendship, Alliance and Mutual Assistance is technically valid until 1980, but Peking has indicated that it does not count on or necessarily want Soviet military assistance, and the Soviets have implied that they would not feel bound to provide it. In the economic sphere, the total annual trade between the two countries, which reached a peak of over $2 billion in 1959, sank to less than $100 million in 1968.

7. As relations deteriorated, propaganda attacks increased. In February 1967, for example, when the Soviet embassy in Peking was under siege, the Sino-Soviet conflict accounted for about 25 percent of all Soviet propaganda, foreign and domestic, and about 50 percent of all Chinese propaganda. The Chinese were equally busy attacking the Soviets during November 1967, the 50th anniversary of the Bolshevik Revolution. Nearly as voluble was their denunciation of the Soviet invasion of Czechoslovakia in 1968. The Soviet use of force against a neighboring Socialist state was clearly disturbing to Peking. The Chinese chose this moment to protest publicly against Soviet intrusions into Chinese airspace, and

SECRET

3

SECRET

to renew charges that the Soviets were building up troops along the border and in Mongolia.

8. With the Ussuri River episodes of March 1969, the already tense and hostile relationship between the two countries entered a critical phase. The dozen or so known border clashes have involved uniformed forces as well as civilians, and appear to have produced several hundred fatalities. During March, the levels of propaganda rose to unprecedented heights—to 30 percent of all broadcasts for the Soviets and about 75 percent for the Chinese—and the tone became notably harsher. Both sides began stressing highly emotional themes— heroic deaths, funerals, patriotic letters stained with blood, and the like. Since March, the level of propaganda has fluctuated at generally lower levels, but ominous new themes have appeared. Soviet commentators, who formerly sought to convey a Soviet attitude of calm and restraint in dealing with Red Guard extremism, now stress that Maoism, "a criminal racist theory," represents a "chauvinistic intoxication" that has "reached a point of being a military threat" to the Soviet Union. In his June speech to the International Communist Conference, Brezhnev denounced the Chinese Communists at great length and alleged that Peking was preparing for nuclear war against the USSR. And although playing upon xenophobia and the threat of "foreign devils" is not a new tactic for Peking, the current campaign in China, emphasizing that the Chinese must not show "the slightest timidity before a wild beast," seems to be more extreme than in the past. Lin Piao has warned that China may have to cope with "a big war . . . at an early date—a conventional war . . . or a nuclear war."

9. Both Peking and Moscow have publicly expressed a readiness to negotiate their border disputes. Nevertheless, each side has adopted rigid positions and has made deliberately annoying statements. The Chinese deny they intend to claim thousands of square miles of present Soviet territory, but they insist that Moscow acknowledge that the treaties whereby Russian tsars gained title to those lands are "unequal." The Soviet side has shown inflexibility by claiming that an uninhabited and frequently flooded island in the Ussuri River is "age-old Russian soil," and it has suggested provocatively that Manchuria and Sinkiang are not historically part of China. The talks on navigation and border rivers which resumed in Khabarovsk in mid-June have yielded some results in the form of an agreement on navigation regulations for 1969; but no date has been set for broader talks on territorial matters, and the outlook for such talks is poor.

10. These developments outlined pose the larger question of how far the foreign policy of each regime will be affected by the continuing deterioration of the relationship. The Ninth CCP Congress did not formally demote Washington from its position as enemy number one, but the choicest vitriol was reserved for the Soviets. Chinese overtures this year to "ultrarevisionist" Yugoslavia suggest that Peking has become more flexible in pursuing a basically anti-Soviet foreign policy. There is good reason to believe that the Soviet leaders now see China as their most pressing international problem, and are beginning to tailor their policies on other issues accordingly. Brezhnev's suggestion for

4

SECRET

547

SECRET

an Asian collective security system, and Foreign Minister Gromyko's address to the USSR Supreme Soviet in July, in which a moderate tone toward the West was juxtaposed with harsh words for the Chinese, both suggest that Moscow is seeking allies, or at least benevolent neutrals, against China.

II. THE MILITARY DIMENSION

11. Until late 1965, Soviet theater forces near the Chinese border were very thin, though some steps were taken to improve their capability to handle border skirmishes. The Chinese also saw to their own border security requirements during the pre-1965 period. However, a persistent and impressive Soviet military buildup began in late 1965. At that time there were many possible reasons for the buildup: the Chinese challenge to Soviet hegemony, China's successful nuclear tests, and China's growing role in Asia. At any rate, it appears that the present Soviet force structure in the East reflects decisions taken in 1965, although Moscow may recently have raised its original military force goals.

12. As of June 1969, the Soviets had some 30 ground force divisions along the Sino-Soviet border and in Mongolia, double the figure of late 1965. About half the divisions were at combat strength, and others were gradually being raised to that status. These divisions were backed up by an unusually large complement of conventional artillery and of tactical surface-to-surface missiles. The increase in Soviet tactical air strength has kept pace with the ground force increase.

13. There has been no corresponding buildup on the Chinese side. The Chinese have only about nine ground force divisions in the border areas of Sinkiang, Inner Mongolia, and the Heilungkiang-Kirin regions of Manchuria. And although the Chinese have more than 50 divisions behind them in the Shenyang-Peking-Lanchou Military Regions, these are no match for Soviet divisions in firepower and mobility.

14. The disparity between the Soviets and Chinese in other types of forces is even more pronounced. Chinese air defenses have been improved in recent years, but remain thin, whereas Soviet air defenses are heavy and have been strengthened since 1965. The Soviets have continually maintained about 225 medium and heavy bombers in the area, and could quickly add to this force from other parts of the USSR; the Chinese medium bomber force of a dozen or so is largely obsolete. There are a considerable number of strategic missiles in Soviet Central Asia and the Far East which could be targeted against China. Finally, the Soviet Pacific Fleet is more than a match for the entire Chinese Navy.

15. In a military confrontation, the factor of space affects each country, though in different ways. The great length of the border makes linear defense along its whole extent virtually impossible. The USSR's vital Transsiberian Railroad runs close to the Manchurian border; thus defense in depth is not feasible for the Soviets in that sector. Hence, Soviet strategy requires a concentration of theater forces for rapid attack or counter-attack along traditional invasion routes into China. What we know of Soviet troop dispositions seems to bear out this analysis. In contrast, the Chinese military planner might feel that he could yield

SECRET

5

SECRET

part of Sinkiang and northern Manchuria to an attacking force. Not only does such a strategy accord with Mao's concepts of "protracted warfare," but the alternative—positioning large Chinese theater forces in those salients prior to hostilities—would offer Soviet commanders the opportunity to encircle and trap these units.

16. The Soviets also face problems of time. Ideally, a war with China should achieve its aims quickly, to avoid the dangers of protracted conventional warfare against the inexhaustible reservoir of Chinese manpower. The Soviets could simplify this military problem by using nuclear weapons, but this would enormously complicate their political problems. Moreover, from a Soviet planner's standpoint, a conflict with the Chinese, if it is to occur at all, should be initiated fairly soon, before the Chinese deploy an MRBM force.

III. PROSPECTS

17. It is almost certain that there will be no significant easing of tensions during the next two or three years. Conflicting national interests, competition for leadership of the Communist movement, and genuine fear of each other's intentions will prevent a rapprochement. Even the border problems are not likely to be resolved. While both sides may be willing to reach some temporary accommodation, neither is likely to compromise any fundamental positions.

18. The propaganda line in both the USSR and in China is very sharp. Each country now considers the other its most immediate enemy; each country accuses the other of plotting with the imperialists to encircle and destroy it. In this kind of atmosphere any act by the other side is viewed with suspicion; any military preparations appear menacing. For the first time, it is reasonable to ask whether a Sino-Soviet war could break out during the next two or three years.

19. The fact that such a question can be seriously posed is a measure of the gravity of the Sino-Soviet conflict. The potential for a war exists; to the Soviets, at least, early military action might seem to have many advantages. But a decision to attack is a political act and we have no firm evidence about the intentions of Chinese and Soviet leaders.

20. We believe that an unprovoked, major attack by China into Soviet territory is highly unlikely. This judgment is based primarily on the fact of China's disadvantage in military power, and its basic unpreparedness for large-scale war beyond its northern borders. Moreover, since the Korean War, China has avoided major military confrontation with the two great powers. It is also hard to see what advantages China could gain from an attack. Propaganda about the Soviet threat may of course be designed to foster the national unity required to rebuild the power structure shattered by the Cultural Revolution, but an actual war could imperil any gains achieved. At present the Chinese probably have two objectives: to deter a Soviet attack which they believe has grown more likely with the Soviet military buildup, and to promote national preparedness to meet the threat. Peking apparently has chosen to signal its determination by a strategy of small-scale confrontations in border areas where the Chinese legal claim is good.

6

SECRET

SECRET

21. By contrast, we see reasons why the Soviets might now, or in the near future, consider major offensive actions against the Chinese. Soviet planners, looking beyond minor border clashes, must feel that the real danger is yet to come. During the tenure of Mao, or that of his immediate successor, the Chinese will probably deploy a nuclear missile force, and a more substantial medium bomber force than they now possess. The Soviet leaders might feel that even a small number of Chinese missiles would alter the strategic situation, and that as the force grew, the Chinese would be under fewer inhibitions in using their ground forces. The Soviets might hope to prevent this development by using their air superiority to knock out Chinese nuclear and missile installations, while blocking Chinese retaliatory attacks on the ground with their own theater forces. The optimum period for exercising this option is beginning to slip away.

22. The Soviet leaders might see other important benefits in military action. A major defeat of Chinese forces would demonstrate the might of the Soviet armed forces throughout the world, and help the prestige of the Soviet leadership at home. The Soviets might even hope for the downfall of the Mao-Lin regime, or if it survived, the detachment of Sinkiang, Inner Mongolia, and Manchuria from China. They might thus be able to establish a buffer zone like that in Eastern Europe. In fact, protection of national minorities in the Sinkiang and Inner Mongolian regions against Chinese oppression might be the excuse for opening a war.

23. A body of recent evidence concerning Soviet military activity suggests that Moscow may be preparing to take action against China in the near future. Lately, there has been unusual military activity on the Soviet side of the Chinese border, including an unusually large exercise in which China was apparently the simulated enemy. Some air units were temporarily deployed from parts of the Western USSR normally considered the base for reinforcement against NATO. Also, the Transsiberian Railroad has been carrying a volume of military traffic apparently large enough to interfere with normal civilian traffic. This military activity seems disproportionate to any visible Chinese offensive threat. Meanwhile the Chinese, whose military force deployment had remained virtually static during the earlier Soviet buildup, have recently made minor adjustments in their air defenses which suggest that they may be taking a more serious view of the situation.

24. There are also political indicators that suggest that the Soviets may be preparing for a showdown with China. The Kremlin is clearly trying to ease friction with the West; one purpose is almost certainly to expand its freedom of action in the East. Soviet propaganda repeats the themes that Mao is a "warlord," a "chauvinist," a "militarist," that he thinks that war is the only solution to his problems, that like all warmongers, he falsely accuses the Kremlin of planning an attack on him in order to excuse his own evil plans. Finally, recent articles and broadcasts deplore the oppression of Uigurs, Kazakhs, and Mongolians in China, and suggest that rebellion by these peoples would be justified.

25. On the other hand, the Soviets must recognize the formidable risks of military action. From a military point of view, this rests mainly on the uncertainty

SECRET

7

SECRET

of the outcome. Even if the Soviet leaders believe that a conventional air strike would knock out Chinese nuclear and missile installations, they must surely realize that they would be starting a process which they could not be sure of controlling, and whose course would be determined as much by the Chinese as by themselves. They must also ask themselves whether, later if not sooner, it might be necessary to use nuclear weapons against Chinese troops or installations, with all the political costs of such a course, and whether the Chinese, though at a great disadvantage in modern weaponry, might still manage to deliver nuclear weapons on Vladivostok or Khabarovsk.

26. Even if the Soviets succeeded completely in destroying Chinese nuclear and missile capabilities, and were, in addition, able to establish viable buffer states on the frontier, the rest of China would remain unconquered. The Soviets have no assurance that the Mao-Lin regime would fall, or that, in any case, the Chinese would stop fighting. Regardless of the type of regime in unoccupied China, it would be even more bitterly hostile to the USSR than it is at present, and it would be even more determined to gain a nuclear capability.

27. Moreover certain political factors militate against a Soviet attack on China. The nature of collective leadership is such that the men in the Kremlin might find it easier to continue a policy of improving military and political defenses against the Chinese heresy than to reach a decision to attack. A Soviet-initiated war would certainly complicate Moscow's relations with Hanoi and might seriously reduce Russian influence there. Both Communist and non-Communist states in Europe might take advantage of Soviet involvement in Asia, particularly if the war were protracted. A war would make reconciliation with China impossible for many years, and it is by no means certain that the Soviets have given up all hope of some improvement in their relations with China after the period of Mao and Lin. Brezhnev's article in the August issue of *Problems of Peace and Socialism* reaffirmed Soviet friendship for the Chinese people and suggested that he expected a long period of tension rather than an early outbreak of hostilities. The same note has been struck in other recent statements.

28. As above noted, we do not look for a deliberate Chinese attack on the USSR. We also believe that Moscow will seek to avoid becoming engaged in a prolonged and full-scale war with China. But the Soviets have set in motion an extensive series of measures—military, political, diplomatic—to ready themselves for continuing or increasing levels of hostility. Their preparations have already reached a stage which would permit them a variety of military options. Of these, the Soviets might find the most attractive to be a conventional air strike designed to destroy China's missile and nuclear installations. The Soviets might calculate that they could accomplish this objective without getting involved in a prolonged and full-scale war. We cannot say that they are likely to reach this conclusion but we believe there is at least some chance they would.

29. In any case, it is clear that tension between the two countries has become acute. At the very least, polemics will remain strident, and the dispute in its present form will probably intensify and grow. Barring a change in Chinese

8

SECRET

SECRET

policy, armed clashes will occur periodically. The scale of fighting may occasionally be greater than heretofore, and might even involve punitive cross-border raids by Soviet ground and tactical air forces. Under such circumstances, escalation of the conflict will be a continuing possibility.

IV. IMPACT OF THE DISPUTE ELSEWHERE IN THE WORLD [2]

A. Policies Toward South and East Asia

30. In those South and East Asian nations which view China as a potential security threat, Moscow appears hopeful of gaining politically from its quarrel with the Chinese. We see the recent Soviet suggestions concerning "a system of collective security in Asia" as an effort to capitalize on an anticipated reduction in the Western presence and, at the same time, to prevent any significant Chinese gains in its wake. In trying to contain the Chinese, the Soviets can play upon Asian fear of China and Asian resentment of Chinese support of local subversive elements. These themes will be particularly persuasive in such mainland states as India, Burma, and Thailand. The Soviets may also try to exploit widespread local animosity toward the large ethnic Chinese minorities in Malaysia and Indonesia.

31. The continuation of the Sino-Soviet dispute—coupled with the Soviet effort to project its influence into South and East Asia—will work to limit Chinese options. Peking has clearly believed that the prolonged struggle in Vietnam would lead ultimately to a substantial weakening of US power and influence in East Asia. The Chinese have foreseen opportunities in the post-Vietnam period for expansion of their own influence, particuarly in such nearby states as Burma and Thailand; they may also have hoped for a far more influential role in Hanoi and, by extension, in Laos and Cambodia, once Soviet war materiel was no longer necessary to the North Vietnamese. But with large Soviet forces poised on a tense border, Peking will almost certainly find it more difficult to intimidate its southern neighbors by flexing its military muscles or rattling its nuclear weapons. The Chinese will face intensified Soviet competition in dealing with established Asian governments and in organizing leftist groups.

32. The continuing Sino-Soviet conflict will be reflected in an important way in relations with Japan. The Soviets see Japan as the emerging power center in Asia, with a serious military potential as well as an ability to provide the Chinese, via trade and aid, with the sinews of a modern industrial state. Moscow wants to forestall both developments, but its leverage in Tokyo is not very great. It can get some small advantage from Japanese hopes for the eventual return of Habomai and Shikotan and can exploit Japanese interest in investment opportunities in Siberian resources. Moscow has some influence in Japan's main opposition party, the Socialists, and even among the independent-minded Japanese Communists, though Peking also possesses allies among the leftist opposition.

---

[2] This discussion is predicated on the assumption that the dispute between the USSR and China remains at about its present level, i.e., short of major war.

SECRET

SECRET

33. The major Chinese assets in this contest for influence in Tokyo are the common cultural traditions and the longstanding Japanese distrust of Russia. In addition, Japan probably views Chinese markets as more profitable over the longer term than costly and risky joint enterprises with the Soviets in Siberia. (In any case, the Japanese are in a position to bargain for and secure both.) Japan obviously relishes its current bargaining position among the powers—the US, as well as China and the USSR—and would almost certainly not want to antagonize any of them in order to gain some transitory advantage with the USSR or China.

B. The US and the West

34. Elsewhere, the Soviets have taken the position that, because of the China problem, the USSR should generally seek to avoid provoking unnecessary difficulties—e.g., over Berlin—with the US in particular and the West in general. Since one of their greatest fears is that the US or the Federal Republic of Germany might be willing to put pressure on the USSR in collusion with China, they will try to preserve an atmosphere of detente, and to be accommodating on minor issues. Problems with China may have encouraged the Soviets to look upon arms control measures with growing interest, seeing in them a means to reduce tensions with the US and to bring additional pressures against Peking. We are not suggesting that the Soviets presently contemplate any sacrifice of essential positions—e.g., the division of Germany and the legitimacy of a Soviet sphere in Eastern Europe. Even less likely is a major revision of China's anti-US stance.

C. Other Communist Parties

35. The fragmentation of the international Communist movement which began with Yugoslavia in 1948, has been accelerated by the intensification of the Sino-Soviet quarrel. The main document of this year's International Communist Conference registers the decline of Soviet influence over other Parties by acknowledging that the Communist movement has no single center, no leading Party. Peking will continue to have some success in creating anti-Moscow factions in Communist Parties and various front organizations. Beyond that, the Chinese will be able to attract the interest, if not always the support, of young revolutionaries repelled by the USSR's status as a "have" society. Yet the Maoist model has lost much of its previous lustre, because of the self-induced domestic convulsions of the last few years, which seemed so incomprehensible and pointless to others throughout the world, both Communist and non-Communist. We do not foresee any significant narrowing of the existing fissures in the world Communist movement.

36. Indeed, we rather expect to see more Communist Parties adopt positions which support neither Moscow nor Peking. This separateness may parallel the neutrality practiced in various ways by the Romanians and the North Vietnamese. The North Koreans and many Parties in the Third World may share Castro's suspicion, expressed some time ago, that neither Moscow nor Peking is

10   SECRET

SECRET

sufficiently committed to the struggle against "imperialism." Still other Parties are likely to move toward what both Peking and most of the present CPSU leaders regard as revisionism. These Parties are likely to deprecate the use of violence by Communists as a means of obtaining power—this is the position taken by the Italian and Finnish Parties and the one toward which the Japanese Party seems to be headed. Other Parties will advocate lessening the role of ruling Communist Parties—this has been the policy identified with Dubcek and Tito. Temporary alliances may often cut across ideological boundaries completely, as seems to be indicated by Peking's recent flirtation with Belgrade. And many Communist Parties, regardless of their political complexion, may find it less difficult to co-exist with non-Communist groups than with each other.

[pp 12-14 omitted--NONSUBSTAN

~~SECRET~~

TERRITORIAL CLAIMS

1. Nearly all of the 4,150-mile Sino-Soviet border [1] derives from 19th century treaties by which an expanding Czarist Empire acquired some 590,000 square miles of territory that had been under the nominal control or domination of Manchu China. In both the western and the eastern sectors, the border traversed territory essentially unpopulated or inhabited mainly by nomadic groups—neither Russian nor Chinese. Chinese propaganda notwithstanding, both Peking and Moscow have long agreed that these treaties should serve as the basis for determining the alinement of the border and for settling other border issues.

Western Sector (See Map)

2. Most of the 1,850-mile western sector was defined by the 1860 Treaty of Peking and was demarcated in accordance with the 1864 Tarbagatay (T'a-ch'eng) Treaty.[2] Boundary modifications and territorial exchanges were made by the 1881 Treaty of Ili (or St. Petersburg). Peking refers to the loss of about 170,000 square miles through these treaties, a claim apparently based on the westernmost extension of mobile pickets sent to regulate use of pastures by nomadic Kazakhs in Central Asia (see map). Chinese control in Central Asia fluctuated greatly throughout history, however, and the westward limits of its authority were vague and usually remote from settled areas of Chinese population. When the boundary was actually demarcated in 1864, Russian officials interpreted the 1860 treaty to refer to permanent Chinese outposts located considerably east of the maximum Chinese claim. The 1881 treaty transferred about 27,000 additional square miles from the Lake Zaysan, Ili, and other areas to Russia.

3. In 1895, the southernmost sector of the border in the high Pamirs was determined, without direct Chinese participation, by an Anglo-Russian treaty designed primarily to define the boundary between British India and Russia. Although Chinese maps depict the de facto boundary in this sector, it is labeled "indefinite"—the only sector of the entire border so designated. The Chinese claim of some 8,000 square miles in the Pamirs apparently is based mainly on Manchu military operations conducted in this region during the 18th century.

4. Border incidents and tensions in the western sector have arisen frequently because of the relatively large population straddling the frontier—mainly Turkic-speaking Muslim groups such as the Kazakhs, Kirgiz, and Uighurs. Moreover, movement by these largely nomadic and semi-nomadic peoples across the frontiers

---

[1] The 2,650-mile Sino-Mongolian border is not included in this discussion.

[2] "Demarcation" refers to the actual physical marking of a boundary on the ground, usually by markers or pillars; or, in the case of a water boundary, by a set line on a map.

~~SECRET~~ 15

SECRET

has been customary. Along the northern half of the border, several natural corridors facilitate such movement.

5. The most publicized border-crossing incident of recent years occurred in April and May of 1962, when some 60,000 Kazakhs and Uighurs fled from the Ili and T'a-ch'eng areas of northwestern Sinkiang into Kazakhstan, apparently in hope of finding better economic conditions in the USSR. Peking still complains of alleged Soviet coercion of these migrants and of Moscow's persistent refusal to return them to Chinese control. Chinese concern is heightened because these frontier tracts are easily accessible from Kazakhstan and because the USSR has in the past fostered dissident sentiments among their non-Chinese inhabitants.[*]

Eastern Sector (See Map)

6. The 2,300-mile eastern sector of the Sino-Soviet border is formed primarily by the Amur and Ussuri Rivers and, except for a small segment at the extreme western end, was established by the Treaties of Aigun (1858) and Peking (1860). China claims that these treaties resulted in the loss of some 385,000 square miles, a figure derived from the amount of territory that had been acquired by China in the Treaty of Nerchinsk (Nipchu) in 1689, which defined a boundary that incorporated almost all of the Amur Basin within China. During the intervening 170 years of Chinese ownership, however, the vast forest lands of the Amur-Ussuri territories had remained unsettled by Chinese and were almost exclusively the domain of scattered Tungusic tribes.

7. *The Problem of the Amur-Ussuri Islands.* The 19th century treaties made no specific allocation of the numerous islands in the Amur and Ussuri. In the case of the March 1969 incidents, the Chinese base their claim to ownership of Chen-pao/Damanskiy on the fact that the main navigable channel lies to the east (Soviet) side of that island. Recent Soviet public statements imply, [____] [_____] that the Chinese version of [__] location of the main channel is correct. [_____] While acknowledging the principle of international law that the main channel determines riverine boundaries, the 13 June Soviet statement cites exceptions where a *riverbank* border is in effect and claims that the 1860 Treaty of Peking is "another such example." The Soviet version of the boundary, however, is based not on the wording of the treaty, but on an accompanying map. The Chinese claim that the map—which the Soviets have not chosen to produce—is at a scale smaller than 1:1,000,000[*] and cannot accurately show either the riverine boundary or island ownership.

8. The USSR's evident determination to disregard the main-channel argument reflects an unwillingness to see this principle applied to other and more strategic islands, specifically Hei-hsia-tzu Island at the Amur-Ussuri confluence near Khabarovsk. Russian sources describe the boundary here—and their maps show it—

---

[*] This area was the base for an anti-Chinese separatist regime, the "East Turkestan People's Republic," established in 1946 with the help of Soviet-trained personnel (see map).

[*] That is, one inch on the map equals approximately 15 miles on the ground.

16

SECRET

SECRET

as following the Kazakovicheva Channel at the extreme western end of the island. Chinese maps locate the boundary at the Amur-Ussuri confluence, directly opposite Khabarovsk. Hei-hsia-tzu is a low and marshy island about 25 miles long. It was occupied by the USSR in the early 1930's following the Japanese occupation of Manchuria, and permanent habitations and installations were constructed on the island. Although the USSR is in de facto occupation, the Chinese case for ownership appears to agree with the intent of the 1860 treaty as well as with the main-channel principle.

SECRET   17

CHINA-U.S.S.R. BORDER: WESTERN SECTOR

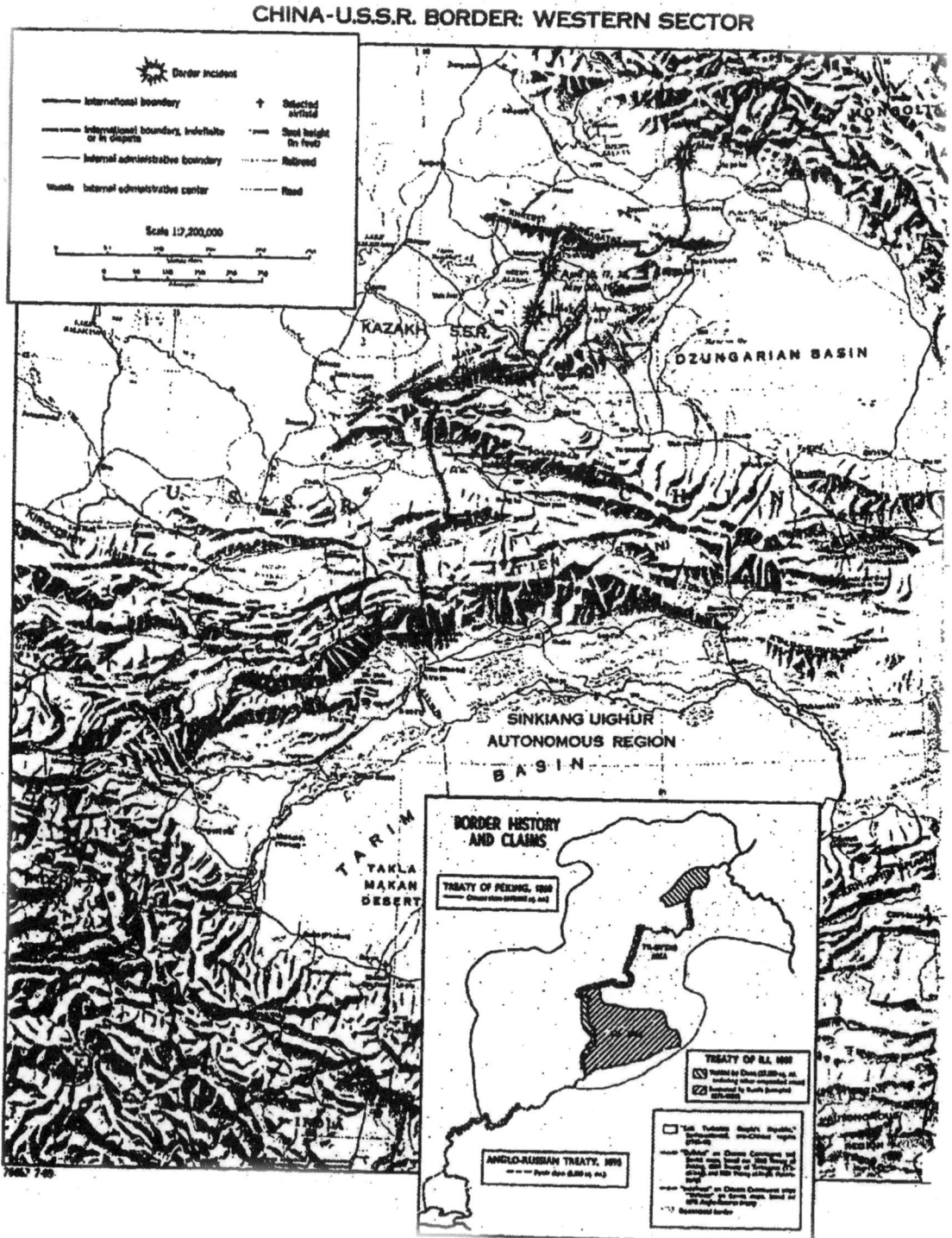

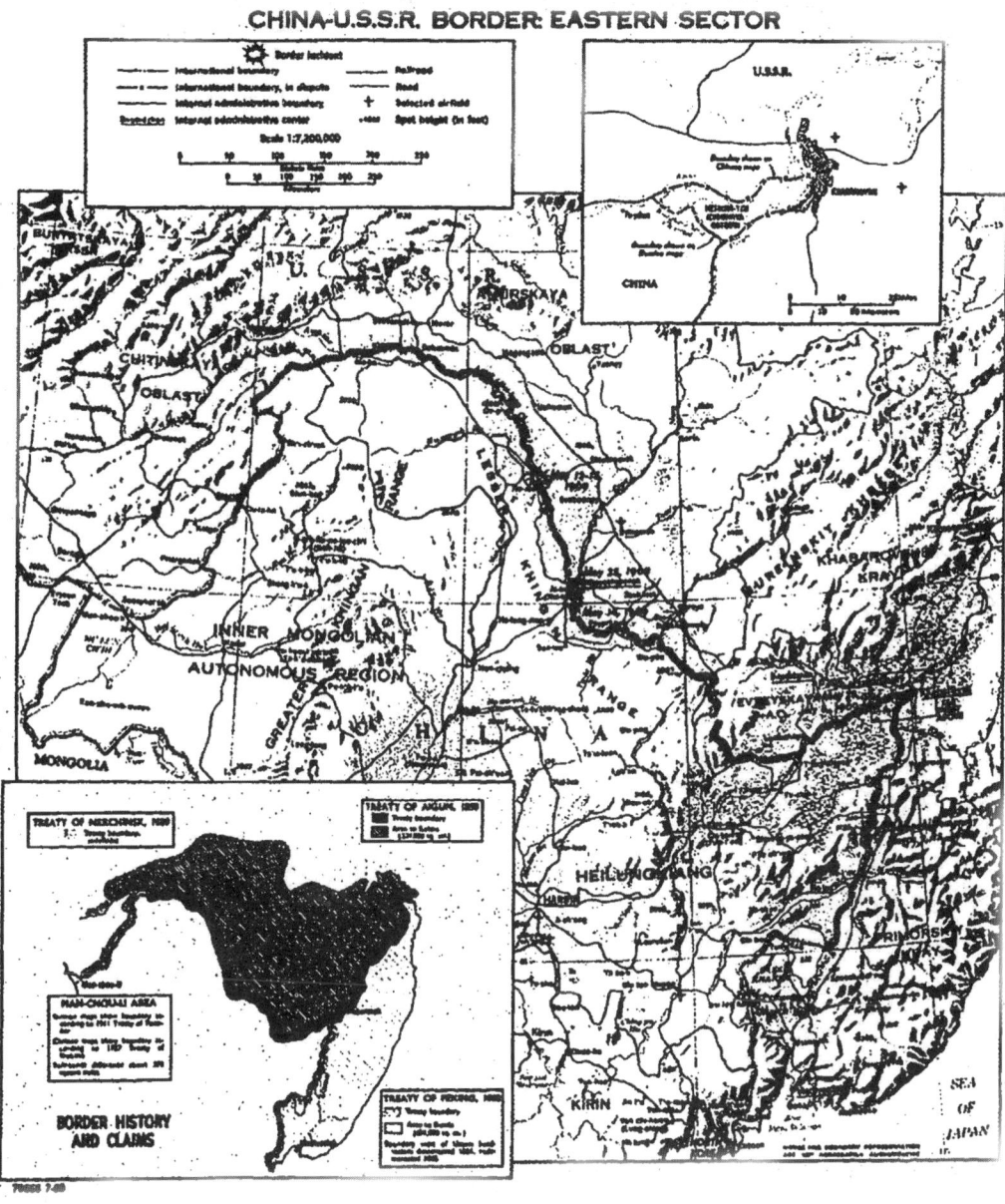

SECTION 33

SNIE 13-9-70

Chinese Reactions to Possible
Developments in Indochina

28 May 1970

APPROVED FOR RELEASE
DATE: MAY 2004

TOP SECRET

(b)(3)

TS 186127
SNIE 13-9-70
28 May 1970

SPECIAL NATIONAL INTELLIGENCE ESTIMATE
Number 13-9-70

Chinese Reactions
to Possible Developments in Indochina

Submitted by

P. E. Cushman, Jr

DEPUTY DIRECTOR OF CENTRAL INTELLIGENCE

Concurred in by the

UNITED STATES INTELLIGENCE BOARD

As indicated overleaf

28 May 1970

Authenticated:

James S. Lay Jr.

EXECUTIVE SECRETARY, USIB

Note: This is the Estimate.
No further dissemi-
nation will be made.

Copy No. 49

TOP SECRET

APPROVED FOR RELEASE
DATE: MAY 2004

(b)(3)

~~TOP SECRET~~   TS 186127

C E N T R A L   I N T E L L I G E N C E   A G E N C Y

28 May 1970

SUBJECT: SNIE 13-9-70: CHINESE REACTIONS TO POSSIBLE DEVELOPMENTS
IN INDOCHINA

NOTE

Cambodia's involvement has given a new shape to the struggle in Indochina. This paper considers how China and North Vietnam might view future hypothetical developments, particularly in the military field, which might compel them to consider a significant change in their strategy, and estimates what their reactions might be if such developments do take place. insofar as these involve military or other moves by the US and its allies, they are to be regarded as actions which the Communists might possibly anticipate, not as courses of action being entertained by the Allied side.

Group 1
Excluded from automatic
downgrading and
declassification

~~TOP SECRET~~

TOP SECRET

THE ESTIMATE

I. PEKING'S VIEW OF THE STRUGGLE IN INDOCHINA

1.   Peking has viewed events in Southeast Asia during the course of the war in Vietnam mainly in the light of its aspirations for political dominance in the area. Its perspective is long term, involves no fixed time schedule, and is an aspect of its pretensions to lead a world-wide revolutionary movement. More immediately, Peking sees the war in Indochina as a continuation of a lengthy liberation struggle; first against the French, and now against the US. Peking's advice to the Communists in Indochina has been repetitious and consistent. They are to persist in self-reliant and protracted struggle until they can destroy the enemy or his will to fight. That this may involve occasional defeats and considerable losses is a foregone conclusion. Only by a prolonged and costly struggle can they hope to achieve eventual victory, and they must carry on this struggle themselves, without reliance on outside forces.

2. On one hand, the Chinese view the fighting as a test of Mao's theory of "people's war." They believe a victory would enhance China's political prestige in Asia and would support their claims for ideological pre-eminence over the Soviet Union. On the other hand,

- 2 -

TOP SECRET

TOP SECRET

Peking has had to consider the possibility that an adverse turn in the war might lead to a security threat on China's southern border and therefore a possible direct confrontation with the US. In practice, this has meant militant advocacy of "people's war" for others, but careful maneuvering to ensure that China stays safely out of the line of fire.

3. In defining its role in this struggle, Peking has been both cautious and prudent. Thus far the policy has been to rule out any direct use of Chinese troops in the ground fighting and to reduce the risks of even an accidental confrontation with the US. There is evidence that the Peking leadership reaffirmed these basic ground rules after a long and bitter debate during 1965. This conflict, which pitted Minister of Defense Lin Piao against his Chief of Staff, was concerned with the assessment of, and possible responses to, the large-scale US intervention in Vietnam then under way. Lin Piao ended the debate with an authoritative endorsement of Mao's theories on "people's war," emphasizing defense in depth rather than moving across China's borders to meet the threat.

4. This decision not to intervene overtly in the Vietnam War was consistent with Peking's policy, at least since the Korean War, of not risking major hostilities with either the US or the USSR. There is as

- 3 -

TOP SECRET

TOP SECRET

yet no indication that the acquisition of nuclear weapons has changed this basic stance. Indeed, it may have had a sobering effect. When hostilities along the Sino-Soviet border in 1969 threatened to escalate into a nuclear conflict, the Chinese moved to calm the situation. We judge that China's troubled internal situation and its unresolved problems with the USSR incline its leaders to continue making the same cautious calculations of risk that have marked their conduct of recent years. This means that China's aims in Southeast Asia should be pursued by subversion, revolutionary activity, and diplomacy rather than by the open use of its own military forces.

5. <u>Recent Developments</u>. Recent events in Indochina are not likely to change this basic approach. As long as the US/GVN move into Cambodia does not critically affect Hanoi's ability to continue the war, Peking is likely to minimize the threat posed by the current Allied actions. Moreover, Peking probably sees immediate benefits from the political reaction aroused in the US against the Cambodian involvement. And if the US should not withdraw from Cambodia, Peking would assess the situation as one in which the US was getting more and more bogged down in an expanding war that would guarantee growing opposition both at home and abroad. In this sense, at least, it would make little difference to Peking whether the US kept to its schedule and withdrew or whether it continued its involvement in Cambodia.

- 4 -

TOP SECRET

~~TOP SECRET~~

6. In Peking's view, the US is fighting a losing war in which
Hanoi has only to be patient and persevere in order to outlast the US.
In order to preserve that patience, China will continue to supply
North Vietnam with economic and military aid. More important, Peking
is probably now better prepared to furnish steady and dependable
political support than it was during the Cultural Revolution.
Relations with Hanoi have improved considerably since last fall,
and recent events in Cambodia have brought Peking and Hanoi closer
together. The remarkable turnout in Peking for Le Duan's recent visit,
in which both Mao and Lin made one of their increasingly rare
appearances, is evidence of Chinese concern to strengthen ties with
Hanoi at Moscow's expense. Peking's careful campaign to exploit
Sihanouk, recently emphasized in a major pronouncement by Mao himself,
is also intended to diminish Soviet influence in Indochina.

7. In short, Peking has moved promptly to exploit the Cambodian
developments for its own ends. The Chinese leadership has seized the
opportunities presented to reduce Soviet influence on Hanoi and to
increase its own capability to influence Hanoi without, for the present
at least, exposing itself to greater risks or markedly higher costs.

8. At the same time, Peking may have some concern that an
intensified and enlarged scale of hostilities could weaken Hanoi's

- 5 -

~~TOP SECRET~~

TOP SECRET

will and capacity to continue. Against this possibility Peking is probably prepared to render increased aid to Hanoi, increase the level of threat in its propaganda, perhaps stimulate insurgency and tensions elsewhere in Asia, or attempt to unsettle the US by moving troops about in southern China. Judging by its past actions, however, Peking is likely to calculate carefully the risks of these moves and to prefer gestures and actions that will worry but not provoke the US.

9. The Soviet Factor. Peking's reactions in Indochina are conditioned by the terms of its bitter rivalry with the USSR. At critical points during the course of the war, the Chinese have sought to project an image of militant devotion to "people's war," partly at least to outflank politically the Soviets; the latter are constrained in Southeast Asia by geography and by some concern to avoid complicating relations with the US or offending potentially friendly non-Communist Asian regimes. Peking calculates in these situations that Moscow's position is certain to be relatively "soft," providing ample room for Chinese posturing without a requirement for risky commitments. Nonetheless, this stance carries the risk that the Soviets might be able to expose the gap between Chinese rhetoric and performance.

10. Moreover, so long as large and hostile Soviet forces threaten China's northern and western borders, there is added reason for avoiding

- 6 -

TOP SECRET

TOP SECRET

direct military involvements in Southeast Asia. In sum, the Soviet factor reinforces other considerations which make Peking want to avoid precipitate and risky action even though it continues to discourage compromise settlement of the war.

II. PEKING'S REACTIONS TO POSSIBLE FUTURE DEVELOPMENTS

11. The paragraphs above outline what has been China's fundamental position on the situation in Indochina. At this juncture, the Chinese may be preoccupied as well with future developments, particularly in the military field, which might compel them to consider a more direct involvement. In this section, we estimate Chinese reactions to each of several such possibilities. Peking's reactions to the possible cumulative effect of these various actions are discussed in paragraphs 23 through 26.

Continued Allied Military Activity in Cambodia

12. Peking probably anticipates a continuing and substantial Allied effort to exploit the political turnabout in Phnom Penh -- to include sustained operations by ARVN in strategic border areas and occasional deeper forays, all with US air and logistical support, and a naval blockade in the Gulf of Siam. Peking may also expect to see

- 7 -

TOP SECRET

TOP SECRET

continued employment of US advisory personnel with ARVN units in
Cambodia and would not be greatly surprised at reintroduction of
US combat units subsequent to 30 June 1970. Such developments,
in our view, would not lead Peking to undertake any radically new
commitment to the struggle in Indochina. Cambodia is relatively
remote from the Chinese border. Moreover, despite concern over the
immediate impact of the Allied operations, Peking would probably
not conclude that longer term prospects for the success of the
liberation struggle in Indochina were critically affected.

Allied Support of the Lon Nol Government

13. Though apparently willing to bargain on Hanoi's behalf
with Lon Nol only a month ago, the Chinese are now committed to the
destruction of his regime. In their logic, there is little doubt
that the US will provide support to Lon Nol. China almost certainly
expects continued and increased shipments of US (and other) arms
to Phnom Penh and, perhaps, the dispatch of US advisory personnel
on the Laos pattern. Even so, the Chinese almost certainly give
little weight to the capabilities -- present or future -- of the
Cambodian Army. The Chinese might attempt to counter the US move by
establishing some sort of political-military advisory presence with a
"liberation government" on Cambodian soil -- on the pattern of its

- 8 -

TOP SECRET

572

TOP SECRET

mission at Khang Khay in northern Laos. The Chinese will even draw some political comfort from the Soviet diplomatic presence in Phnom Penh as a situation which the Chinese can exploit as evidence of Soviet opposition to the forces working for Sihanouk's return.

Thai Military Commitment to Cambodia

14. The entry of Thai forces into Cambodia would further complicate the Communist military position there, but it would be equally significant, in Peking's view, as a sign of Bangkok's willingness to commit itself more firmly and overtly to an active military role in the Indochina area. The Chinese reaction would be designed as a clearcut warning to Bangkok of the perils of its course: the Thai "liberation movement" would be elevated to a more prominent position in Peking's revolutionary propaganda and insurgent forces in Thailand would be directed to increase their pressures on the Thai Government. But China would almost certainly see no need to bring its own forces to bear.

Renewed Bombing of North Vietnam

15. Additional and sustained US bombing raids on North Vietnam's panhandle area -- on SAM sites and other military targets -- would not surprise Peking which, as before, would stand aside while Hanoi coped

- 9 -

TOP SECRET

TOP SECRET

with the problem of maintaining the southward flow of troops and materiel. If the US resumed bombing of North Vietnam on the pattern of 1965-1968, the Chinese would probably, as before, provide engineer troops and AAA units to supplement North Vietnamese air defenses.

Ground Troops in Southern Laos

16. The Chinese might think it possible that the Allies will try to challenge Hanoi's control of southern Laos by sustained ground operations into that area. While small Allied military units have operated in Laos for years, their impact on the war has been relatively slight and their numbers have been small enough to permit their presence to remain largely unacknowledged -- in deference to the "neutral" status of the Lao Government. Crossing this political threshold would be read in Peking as US willingness to contemplate a far more activist course in Indochina in search of a military decision.

17. Presumably, the Allied forces in southern Laos would be targetted against VC/NVA sanctuaries, logistical bases, and infiltration routes to South Vietnam. The Chinese concern would depend on the degree of success these operations had in stemming the flow of men and supplies from North Vietnam and on the nationality of the forces involved.

- 10 -

TOP SECRET

TOP SECRET

18. The Chinese would probably view Thai entry into southern Laos as part of a longer range US plan to place the defense of the Mekong Valley in Thai hands. Although China (and North Vietnam) would be inclined to doubt that effective Thai troops in sufficient numbers would be available to have a decisive impact on the situation, the Communists might see the move as portending the eventual commitment of US ground forces to the area. The entry of US ground forces into southern Laos would raise concern in Peking because of the military effect on Hanoi's logistic system and because it would raise the spectre of later US ground operations in northern Laos. Nonetheless, so long as the deployment of US forces were confined to southern Laos, the Chinese would probably feel no need to introduce their own forces in the area. They would probably move ground forces to the Laos border, however, and might reinforce their units presently in northwestern Laos in order to signal their concern over the safety of their borders.

Ground Troops in Northern Laos

19. Northwestern Laos borders China, and Peking would be most sensitive to military activities in that region. Moreover, to help supply PL/NVA troops in the region, China is building roads from its own territory, and some 10,000-14,000 troops in engineering, AAA, and

- 11 -

TOP SECRET

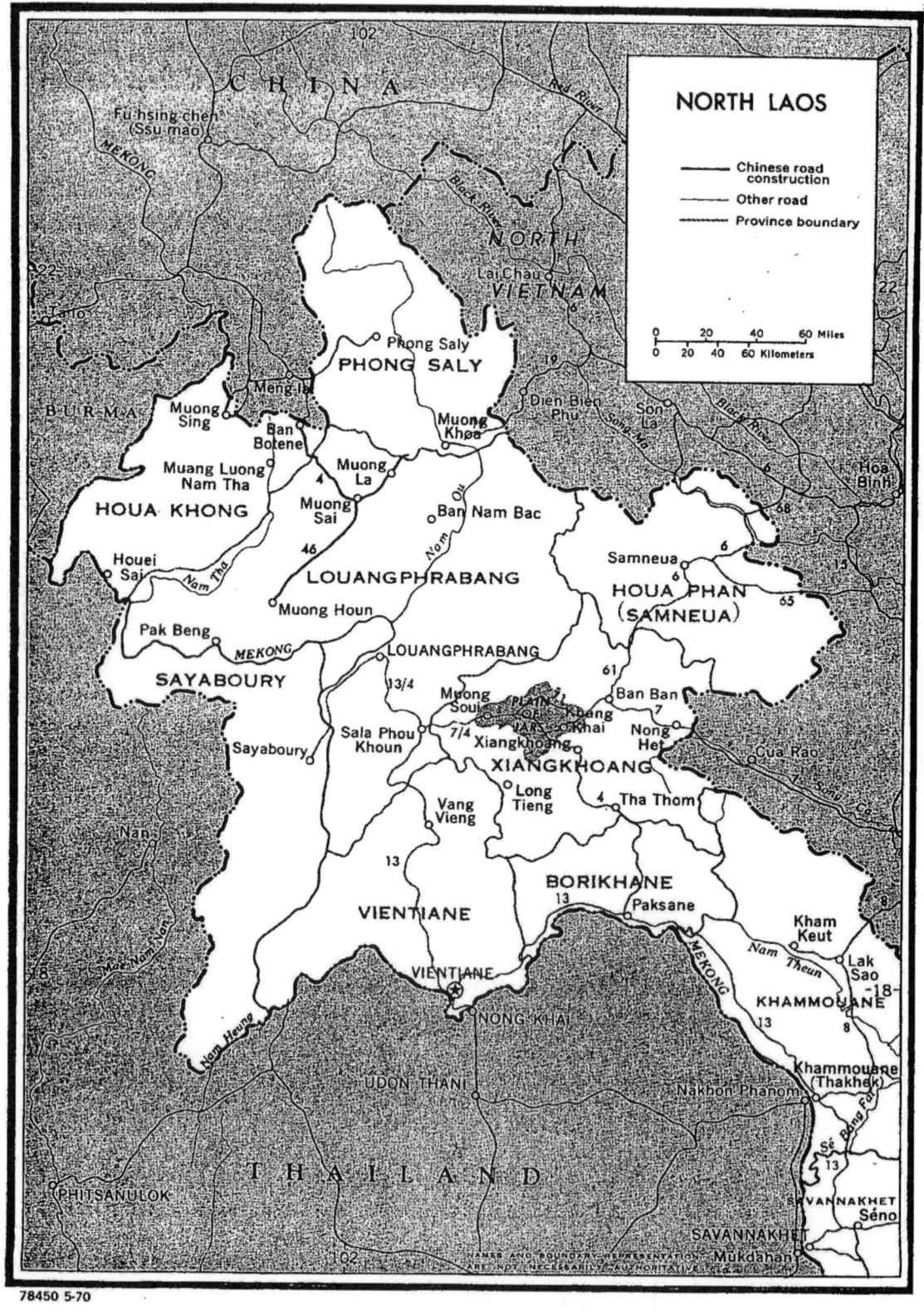

78450 5-70

TOP SECRET

security units are in northwestern Laos in connection with this activity.[1] Up to now, other Chinese security requirements in northwestern Laos have been met by PL/NVA control of the region.

20. Any direct effort -- by US, Thai, or Lao bombing or by Thai/Lao ground harassment -- to force the withdrawal of Chinese troops from northwestern Laos would be resisted. The Chinese already have AAA in place to defend against air attacks and, with PL/NVA forces, sufficient ground strength to meet small-unit probes. If necessary, they might also reinforce their own troops in the region on a limited scale or encourage PL/NVA troops to undertake diversionary moves for political and psychological effect -- e.g., feints against Luang Prabang.

21. This is not to say that the Chinese would push ahead on their road construction under any and all circumstances. The road itself -- at least the segment south of Muong Sai -- is not critical to the Communist position in the region. Thus, if PL/NVA forces proved unable to remove any Thai/Lao blocking force south of the present terminal at Muong Houn, the Chinese might choose to stop construction rather than commit their own combat forces to action in

---

[1] See map of North Laos.

- 12 -

TOP SECRET

TOP SECRET

the area. The presence of Thai forces well south of Muong Houn -- in the area of Pak Beng or south of the Mekong (in Sayaboury Province) -- would probably not result in offensive military action by the Chinese.

22. Northeastern Laos and the area of the Plain of Jars is not as sensitive as northwestern Laos from the Chinese point of view. But the dispatch of sizable Thai ground forces into this region would be viewed very seriously by Peking. If this should happen, the Chinese would probably move quickly to bolster their forces in border regions adjacent to northwestern Laos, but the initial burden of meeting the buildup would probably remain on Hanoi. If such a Thai force was, in Hanoi's view, formidable enough to threaten its vital interests in the area, the North Vietnamese might feel compelled to request direct assistance from China. In these circumstances, Peking might respond to Hanoi's request.

* * * * * *

23. Thus, in a developing situation in Indochina, Peking's first concern would be the possibility that an adverse turn in the war might lead to a security threat on China's southern border or a direct confrontation with the US. This makes military moves in Laos

- 13 -

TOP SECRET

TOP SECRET

particularly sensitive. In addition to primary concern over the direct threat to its borders in northwestern Laos, the Chinese would be apprehensive over any actions in northeastern Laos which posed a threat to the security of North Vietnam. In contrast to its direct security interest in northern Laos, actions in southern Laos and Cambodia are of concern to the Chinese primarily in terms of the way in which they affect Hanoi's capacity to prosecute the war. For Peking, Laos plays a more significant role in this respect than does Cambodia.

24. In general, as in the past, we see two circumstances in which actions such as those discussed above might provoke Chinese reactions beyond the limits of what they have done in Indochina since 1965. The first would be a situation in which military forces approached areas in northern Laos in such a way that Hanoi found it a threat to the security of North Vietnam, or Peking a threat to its own borders. The second would be a situation in which Allied actions, singly or in combination, seriously threatened Hanoi's will and ability to continue the struggle in South Vietnam.

25. In the first case, Peking would probably introduce ground combat troops to northwestern Laos to prevent the establishment of a

- 14 -

TOP SECRET

TOP SECRET

strong military presence on its borders. Peking might undertake deployments elsewhere in northern Laos if persuaded that North Vietnam's own security was threatened. Such a case might arise if large non-Lao forces overran the Plain of Jars and moved eastward.

26. In the second case, where Peking sensed that Hanoi's will and ability to persist in the struggle in South Vietnam were failing, the Chinese would attempt to encourage Hanoi to persevere and would offer generous material assistance. They would loudly threaten the Thai, the Cambodians, the South Vietnamese, and the US -- and attempt to step up guerrilla warfare in Thailand. But if Hanoi, nonetheless, concluded that it had no choice but to postpone the armed struggle, the Chinese would probably feel compelled to accept the decision. We do not believe that China would wish to alienate Hanoi by further demands that it actively continue the war, nor would Peking choose to commit its own forces to the Indochina struggle so long as territories critical to its own security or that of North Vietnam were not threatened.

- 15 -

TOP SECRET

SECTION 34

NIE 13-7-70

Communist China's
International Posture

12 November 1970

APPROVED FOR RELEASE
DATE: MAY 2004

~~SECRET~~

NIE 13-7-70
12 November 1970

(b)(3)

NATIONAL INTELLIGENCE ESTIMATE

NUMBER 13-7-70

Communist China's International Posture

Submitted by

DIRECTOR OF CENTRAL INTELLIGENCE

Concurred in by the

UNITED STATES INTELLIGENCE BOARD

As indicated overleaf

12 November 1970

Authenticated:

EXECUTIVE SECRETARY, USIB

~~SECRET~~

N? 344

COMMUNIST CHINA'S INTERNATIONAL POSTURE

NOTE

China's return to active diplomacy raises new questions about the direction of its foreign policy. After four years in which the internal preoccupations of the Cultural Revolution thoroughly overshadowed foreign relations, Peking is now moving to repair its international image and to exploit new opportunities. In attempting to estimate how China will play this new role in international politics over the next year or so, this paper will examine Peking's options in terms of those policy factors which are most likely to remain constant and those which are subject to greater variations in response to domestic or external events.

It must be acknowledged at the outset that we have remarkably little information on the decision-making processes in Peking. Thus, estimates of short-run tactical moves are susceptible to considerable error. As in the past, sudden twists and turns in Chinese policies will probably continue to surprise us. But in the broader perspective of long-range goals and basic capabilities, this paper attempts to set useful guidelines on the course that China is likely to follow in adapting to the outside world.

CONCLUSIONS

A. With the waning of the radical and frenetic phase of the Cultural Revolution, Peking has substantially recouped its earlier diplomatic position and is moving to compete for influence in new areas. Its successes to date—due in large part to the receptivity of other nations to a more normal relationship with the Chinese—have been impressive, especially in areas of secondary importance to Peking. In areas of prime concern, i.e., the Soviet Union, the US, Southeast Asia and Japan, progress has been marginal and Peking's policy less sure.

1

SECRET

B. Many domestic and foreign obstacles stand in the way of achieving Peking's basic goals, whether these be China as a great power and leader of the world revolution or as a more traditional but highly nationalistic country concerned primarily with Asian interests.

C. On the domestic side, stability and steady growth in basic elements of strength—economic, military, political—are far from assured. Even in the best of circumstances, China's marginal economy will serve to limit its maneuverability in foreign affairs. A great deal of work remains to be done to restore effective government administration, and to rebuild a communist party. So long as Mao lives, the possibility of disruptive campaigns exist and his death could usher in a period of leadership uncertainty and intense preoccupation with internal affairs.

D. Externally, China's aspirations remain blocked directly or indirectly by the realities of the international scene including: the vastly superior power and hostility of the USSR, its most immediate threat as well as rival for ideological leadership in the Communist world; the US presence and US commitments around the periphery of China; and the growth in economic strength and self-confidence of another traditional rival, Japan.

E. Even should the Chinese regime wish to alter its basic foreign policy approach and use its growing military force aggressively in peripheral areas, its options would be limited by the risk of provoking one or another of the superpowers. From Peking's point of view, military adventures in Southeast Asia, against Taiwan, in Korea, or in the Soviet Far East would be needlessly risky and the potential prize not worth the game. Peking does, however, have room, even in present circumstances, for some maneuver directly between the two great powers as well as around their flanks or under their guard in Southeast Asia, the Near East, Africa, and even in Eastern Europe.

F. At present, the Chinese see the USSR as their major military threat. By accepting negotiations with the Soviets, cooling border tensions, and improving their diplomatic image, the Chinese apparently judge that they have reduced the risk of hostilities with the Soviets. There is little prospect, however, of a genuine rapprochement emerging from the present Sino-Soviet talks. But both sides are apparently concerned that their dispute not end in a military test. Thus, as long as they both continue to exercise the present degree of military caution,

2

SECRET

SECRET

there is likely to be some improvement in diplomatic and trade relations but little movement in border talks. As long as Mao lives there is almost no chance of significant compromise on the ideological questions.

G. With the US, Peking has moved from its previous intransigence to a more flexible approach better designed to exploit the Sino-US relationship for Chinese purposes. The Chinese hope to unsettle the Soviets by playing on their fears of a Sino-American rapprochement as well as exploit the potential for changes in the balance of forces in East Asia resulting from the drawdown of the US military presence. In pursuing its new flexibility, however, Peking does not expect an early major improvement in Sino-US relations and any small improvements are likely to be limited to marginal issues.

H. Japan poses special problems to Peking because it too is an Asian power, is outstripping China in economic growth, and is strongly resistent to Maoist subversion or Chinese threats. And the Chinese, who remember Japanese imperialism in China during World War II, wonder what threat the Japanese may become to their security over the long term and fear Tokyo will one day take on the role of protector of Taiwan. The Chinese answer so far has been to continue with a rather rigid and vituperative propaganda attack on Japan's leaders, their policies, and their alleged ambitions in Asia. While this may impress the North Koreans and some people in Southeast Asia, it does little good for China's cause in Japan itself. Nonetheless, and despite the burgeoning growth in Sino-Japanese trade, any basic shift in China's approach to Japan seems unlikely in the present ideological climate in Peking.

I. In Southeast Asia, Peking's earlier fear that the Indochinese war might spill over into China seems to have lessened. Indeed, the Chinese seem to believe that the US is being forced gradually to withdraw its military presence from the region and that this process will eventually improve the prospects for Chinese influence. Rather than use overt military force to exploit possible developments in this area, Peking's more likely course will be to increase its support to subversive and insurgent activity. The Chinese will seek to maintain their role as revolutionary leaders without exposing themselves to undue cost or risk. In addition they will rely on conventional diplomacy when this suits their needs. There is abundant evidence that Peking feels no need to

SECRET

3

SECRET

set deadlines and has no schedule to fulfill; it is clearly prepared for the long haul.

J.   In the longer run, if Mao's successors follow a more steady and pragmatic course, they are likely to have greater success than Mao in expanding China's political influence and acceptance. We cannot be sure, of course, how future leaders will see their situation, and it is possible that they will be prepared to employ China's developing power in a more aggressive manner. We think it more likely, however, that they will continue to focus their foreign policy on diplomacy at the overt level and on subversion at the covert level. The open use of military force will probably be judged needlessly risky.

K.   While we do not doubt that China would fight tenaciously if invaded, we see no compelling factors moving Peking toward a policy of expansionism, or even a higher level of risk-taking. For all its verbal hostility and latent aggressiveness, neither the present nor the probable future leadership is likely to see foreign adventures as a solution to China's problems.

DISCUSSION

I. FOREIGN POLICY: SOME PRINCIPLES AND PRIORITIES

A. The Ideological Base

1. In part, Peking still perceives the outside world in traditional ways. The Sino-centric view of the Middle Kingdom has survived the advent of the communists. The past century has left a residue of bitterness and frustration among those Chinese—certainly the vast majority—whose sense of nationalism and patriotism has been outraged by what they see as unfair treatment of China by foreigners. This basic sense of injustice and frustration has facilitated the people's acceptance of enormous sacrifices and has permitted the communists to carry out revolutionary programs aimed at reaching grandiose—often unrealistic—goals. While popular expectations have been repeatedly disappointed, the basic dynamism of Chinese nationalism remains to be exploited again and again. Unlike the ideology of Maoism, which may not long survive its creator, the traditional sense of China's privileged role in the world will probably remain a constant theme in this and any foreseeable Chinese government.

2. Maoist ideology, which emphasizes the inevitability of class conflict and world revolution, adds an ingredient of violence and militance to traditional Chinese drives. It attempts to project the revolutionary experience of the Chinese civil war onto the world stage by advocating the defeat of the affluent Western Powers through the mobilization of the poor countries in the world.

4

SECRET

SECRET

Peking recognizes the limits of the revolutionary line, however, and has accepted and developed a policy of peaceful coexistence for application where this suits its needs. Analogous to the domestic united front policy which served the communists well in the Chinese civil war, the peaceful coexistence line was originally intended to be a temporary accommodation to the norms of international conduct which would be replaced as other countries followed China's revolutionary path. But as the prospects for world revolution have dimmed, peaceful coexistence has assumed a larger role in Chinese foreign policy, even while propaganda stress on the more orthodox policy of revolutionary struggle remains at a high pitch.

3. Ideology continues to play an exceptionally important role in the formulation of Chinese foreign policy. Although decision-makers may hold varying degrees of faith in revolutionary dogma, all are required to justify their proposals in its terms. Such justification has become particularly important as a result of the Cultural Revolution during which the purge and counterpurge of a divided leadership was rationalized by linking internal political deviations with external heresies. Many domestic figures deposed during the Cultural Revolution, for instance, were accused of following policies that were pro-Soviet or "social imperialist". As the excesses of the Cultural Revolution have subsided, even the return to more conventional diplomacy has been clothed in the rhetoric of Maoist ideology.

B. The Military Ingredient

4. Military strength has been a major preoccupation of a leadership long attuned to Mao's dictum that the "barrel of a gun" was the source of all political power. Moreover, the Chinese have been as sensitive to the needs of defense as they have been to the role of violence in advancing world revolution. Political concepts and programs are conceived in strategic and tactical military terms and transmitted to the Chinese masses and the rest of the world in martial rhetoric. The traditionally strong position of the military in Communist China has assumed new importance as a result of its vital role in underpinning the regime during the Cultural Revolution. As a by-product, the military appears to have increased its influence over the formulation and execution of policy.

5. Communist China's military power is impressive by Asian standards but remains markedly inferior to that of the superpowers. The People's Liberation Army (PLA), whose basic strength lies in the size and fighting ability of its ground forces, has the capability to put up a formidable defense of the mainland against any invaders. However, while persistent efforts over the past 20 years to strengthen and modernize the Chinese Armed Forces have yielded some creditable results, economic and political disruptions have left the PLA vulnerable in certain areas against a modern opponent. Some of its more evident problems are an apparent deficiency in motorized transport and heavy armament, an air defense system which probably lacks adequate communications and data processing capabilities, and a navy which remains little more than a coastal defense force.

SECRET

5

SECRET

6. Since China's intervention in the Korean War, which Peking considered a defensive move, China's military posture has remained basically cautious and prudent. Moreover, after this experience Peking appeared somewhat more restrained in the use of military threats to further its foreign policy objectives. The abortive move against the off-shore islands in 1958 and the defensive reinforcement along the Formosa Strait in 1962 both reflected Peking's concern over another confrontation with the US. Even against the demonstrably weaker power of India, Peking was careful in 1962 not to become embroiled in a lengthy campaign. Peking was probably satisfied to make the point that, in spite of severe internal difficulties, China was still ready and able to defend itself.

7. For all Peking's militance in the ideological field, the deployment of China's military forces remains basically defensive. Maoist military doctrine emphasizes defense in depth and the engagement of the entire civilian population to overcome an attack. The fear of a US attack has eased, in part because of a lessening concern since 1965-1968 that the Southeast Asian war might spill over into China, and is probably lower now than at any other time in the past 20 years. The Chinese now view the Soviet Union as posing the most immediate military threat and over the past year have been conducting an extensive campaign to prepare for the possibility of an eventual war. In accordance with this altered threat, there are indications that the Chinese are adjusting their military deployments, although there has been no wholesale movement of troops to the northern border.

8. Even though the main approach to the defense of China still emphasizes defense in depth—e.g., Mao's "people's war"—there is more to its military posture than a readiness to fight a prolonged, defensive war within China. The Peking leadership has clearly given a high priority to acquiring the military symbols of a great power, especially strategic weapons, but also conventional forces as well. Peking probably wants the strategic weapons primarily as a deterrent against a Soviet or US attack and to increase Chinese bargaining strength on international issues. There is no evidence that the achievement of a strategic capability will necessarily make the Chinese more aggressive. They will continue to be deterred by overwhelmingly superior US and Soviet power both from outright attacks and from engaging in "nuclear blackmail" in East Asia. China wants its views to have impact on the international scene and is willing to expend scarce resources to achieve this goal, but it can be expected to continue to exercise caution in employing its conventional and nuclear strength. Peking expects its political influence in Asia to grow, not from the open use of military power, but through active diplomacy and the encouragement and support of subversive and revolutionary activities, all backed by the looming presence and growing power of immemorial China on the Asian scene.

C. Domestic Constraints Affecting Foreign Initiatives

9. In addition to the ideological and military preconditions cited above, domestic factors determine and often severely restrict the range of foreign policy tactics and instrumentalities open to Peking. These domestic constraints operate

6

SECRET

SECRET

to limit the economic, psychological, and bureaucratic resources available for the conduct of foreign relations.

10. The Chinese economy during the 1960s did not even approach the high sustained growth rates of the 1950s. A combination of factors were responsible for this failure—the distorted planning and bizarre management of the Great Leap Forward at the end of the 1950s; the cessation of Soviet aid; bad agricultural conditions in the early years of the decade; and finally, the disruptions of the Cultural Revolution. At the same time, the proportion of resources devoted to the military sector increased, adding to China's technological capabilities, but further hobbling development of the civilian economy.

11. This failure to maintain a high rate of growth in the civilian economy limits China's capability to use economic leverage for foreign policy goals. China's image in the early 1950s as the economic model for Asia has been largely destroyed. The fabled potential of the "China market" has lost much of its attraction to world traders, thereby reducing the political concessions Peking can exact in exchange for trading privileges.

12. Policy ineptitude also hinders the Chinese. If Peking's intense preoccupation with internal politics had paid off in terms of rapid economic, social, and political development, the Chinese might now have a sounder domestic base for the conduct of foreign affairs. In fact, the major experiments designed to push China ahead, including both the Great Leap Forward and the Cultural Revolution, have been disasters. Although the economy has largely recovered, party organization remains disrupted, civil administration has been hampered, and lasting tensions have been created within the leadership as a result of the Cultural Revolution.

13. The foreign policy apparatus proved as vulnerable as other bureaucratic organs to the impact of the Cultural Revolution. For nearly three years, the formulation and execution of foreign policy were paralyzed by political infighting. Red Guard activities in embassies abroad and within the foreign ministry itself brought constructive activity to a virtual standstill. All ambassadors but one were recalled to Peking, embassy staffs were substantially reduced, and militant posturing was offered as a substitute for traditional diplomacy.

14. This is not to say, of course, that China's presence was not felt in the outside world during the Cultural Revolution. Trade and aid programs continued, as did support for subversion in Southeast Asia and elsewhere. And China's potential as a great power was evident to the world as the development of nuclear weapons continued despite domestic turmoil. Nonetheless, it was not until 1969 that Chinese ambassadors began to trickle back to their posts, and the current campaign to retrieve China's international status and influence started in earnest. The return to pre-Cultural Revolution diplomacy has been slow and uneven, and the balance between radical and more pragmatic influences remains delicate and potentially unstable.

SECRET

7

II. PROSPECTS AND CONTINGENCIES

A. Peking's Activist Foreign Policy

15. With its foreign affairs apparatus largely restored, Peking is moving quickly to recoup its pre-Cultural Revolution diplomatic position and to compete for influence in new areas. This drive has emphasized peaceful coexistence and has sought influence through conventional, diplomatic means. Its successes to date—due in large part to the receptivity of other nations to a more normal relationship with the Chinese—have been impressive, especially when compared to the almost total isolation at the height of the Cultural Revolution. Most of the gains, however, have come in areas of lesser concern to Peking and under circumstances which have made improvement in relations easy and relatively cheap.

16. In areas of prime interest to the Chinese, Peking's policy has been less sure. Uncertainty and cautious experimentation have been characteristic of relations with the Soviet Union, the US, Southeast Asia, and Japan. In these areas where policy decisions are more difficult, differences within the leadership apparently come to the fore and strain the entire decision-making process. This was especially marked in the fluctuations of Chinese policy toward the USSR during 1969 and the continuing holding operation pursued vis-à-vis the Soviets in 1970. Peking's handling of the recent turmoil in Cambodia—and its effect on Sino-American relations—also betrayed an initial hesitance which underscored the regime's difficulties in formulating policies on major foreign issues.

B. Sino-Soviet Relations

17. Though some of the immediate danger has been removed from the situation, the Sino-Soviet dispute remains the single most important bilateral concern for Peking. At the same time, it conditions and determines many aspects of the Chinese posture in dealing with other Communist states, the Third World, and the West.

18. Although relations between Moscow and Peking had been deteriorating markedly over the last decade, and the Soviet troop deployments along the Sino-Soviet border had been building since the mid-1960s, the Chinese did not appear to take the threat of Soviet military action seriously until after the invasion of Czechoslovakia. Even then, Peking sought to deter the Soviets by adopting a harshly militant posture, combining provocative behavior on the border with strident propaganda and an intensive war preparations campaign. Soviet pressure continued to grow in 1969, however, and after bloody clashes on the Ussuri in March and in Sinkiang during August, Soviet diplomats began to drop broad hints about a possible pre-emptive strike against Chinese nuclear and strategic weapons facilities. The Chinese, aware now that they might be faced with the choice between backing down and risking their nuclear installations, finally agreed in September to the border negotiations which opened in Peking October 20.

8

7

SECRET

19. The experience of that tense summer moved the Chinese to reassess their foreign policy tactics. Far from deterring the Soviets, their militant posture had not only raised the possibility of broad conflict with the Soviets to an unacceptable level, but also deepened Chinese diplomatic isolation. After what was apparently a prolonged debate early in the fall, the leadership decided that border talks offered the most viable means of defusing the dangerously tense situation. At the same time, the decision was apparently taken to launch a wide-ranging diplomatic campaign to restore China's world status and influence, both as a deterrent to the Soviets and in support of Chinese objectives outside the bilateral Sino-Soviet framework.

20. Since the opening of the border talks, there has been no evidence of progress on any of the basic issues confronting the negotiators. In spite of the stalemate, however, there have been no specific reports of new border clashes, which argues that the mere existence of the talks has had some stabilizing effect. For their part, the Chinese have demonstrated their concern for maintaining the talks at the highest possible level by vigorously resisting any move which might lead to their downgrading. The Soviets seem to have conceded this point, possibly because of their preoccupation with events in Eastern Europe and the Middle East, and a consequent unwillingness for now, to trigger new complications with China.

21. Despite the soothing effect of the talks, the border situation remains potentially explosive. The Soviets have continued their force build up along the border. Although the Chinese have not significantly beefed up force levels near the border, there is some evidence that they have deployed troops north into areas close enough to be readily available in an emergency. They are also trying to improve the effectiveness of their paramilitary forces. Chinese civil defense campaigns to build air raid shelters, disperse population and stockpile food— all of which are useful for domestic political reasons as well—remain in effect.

22. There have been signs of some slow, halting normalization of state relations, although the ideological gulf remains as broad as ever and questions of principle and substance are no closer to solution than before. After protracted haggling an exchange of ambassadors is in the final stages of arrangement, and discussions for the 1970 Sino-Soviet trade protocol have been completed.

23. The prospect of a genuine rapprochement growing out of the Sino-Soviet talks now seems remote. As long as Mao lives there is almost no chance of significant compromise on the ideological questions. Peking, seeing no prospect of a military advantage over the Soviets, appears committed to the long-term process of keeping tensions below the flash point while attempting to pile up political points in the communist world by embarrassing the Soviets at every opportunity. Even with a continuation of the deep national antagonism and the ideological schism, both sides are apparently concerned that the dispute not end in a military test. Over the last year both sides have had cause to estimate the costs of a prolonged military confrontation, presumably a prospect that neither finds particularly advantageous.

SECRET

9

SECRET

C. The Triangular Relationship: US/USSR/China

24. The Chinese approach to the US has been strongly affected by their political conflict with the USSR. This was apparent earlier this year when Peking moved from its previous intransigence against the US to a more flexible approach better designed to exploit the Sino-US relationship for Chinese purposes. The primary aim was undoubtedly to unsettle the Soviets by playing on their fears of a Sino-US rapprochement. By demonstrating their concern over this possibility, the Soviets have probably insured that the Chinese will continue to exploit the "triangular relationship" wherever and whenever it suits their needs. Even though events in Cambodia caused the Chinese to take a ...rder line against the US, they have clearly maintained the option to return to a more flexible posture when it serves their interest.

25. The potential for changes in the balance of forces in East Asia resulting from the drawdown of US military presence is another factor encouraging more flexible Chinese tactics toward the US. The Chinese will hope to speed American troop withdrawals from the area, especially from Taiwan. At the same time, they see possibilities for improving their relations with states now forced to rely less on American guarantees. Peking may also hope that it can exert its influence to exacerbate frictions caused by a reduction in the US posture. The Chinese probably see the US-GRC relationship as particularly vulnerable in this respect.

26. There are no indications that Peking expects to bring about an early, major improvement in Sino-US relations. The Chinese probably expect no far-reaching US concessions on Taiwan, which remains the main test for Peking. Nor are they likely to give up the US as the prime target in their ideological offensives against the capitalist-imperialist enemy. Nonetheless, Peking will wish to maintain sufficient flexibility to exploit the triangular relationship and to move promptly in whatever direction offers the maximum benefits.

27. For these reasons any early improvement in Sino-US relations is likely to be limited. For example, although recent US trade concessions have been studiously ignored by the Chinese in public, they have privately shown some interest in how far the US might move in this direction. While likely to reject any formal trading relationship, the Chinese seem ready to accept more subtle, indirect trading through third parties. Similarly they are likely to show little interest in formal diplomatic recognition so long as the US remains committed to the GRC. At the same time, however, they will probably retain an interest in keeping lines of communication open through contacts such as those at Warsaw. The pace of Chinese gestures will probably be slow and erratic, subject to pressures felt in Peking from changes in Sino-Soviet and Soviet-US relations.

28. For some years to come, Sino-Soviet relations will be Peking's major concern in foreign affairs. Peking has already shown an acute sensitivity to the possibility that the US and the USSR might find considerable common ground in opposing China. In reaction, Peking will attempt to exacerbate the existing

10

SECRET

SECRET

suspicions between Moscow and Washington; will increasingly portray itself before the world as the innocent victim of "collusion" between the superpowers; and will throw out lines to other Western Powers and the Third World in an effort to elicit new support. The more direct solution would be for Peking to seek a rapprochement with Moscow, but there seems little likelihood that Mao could accept the shifts required to move his regime closer toward the Soviets. Thus, over the next few years, or until Mao's death, Peking will probably concentrate on keeping the Sino-US-USSR relationship as fluid as possible in order to prevent any alliance against China.

D. China's Regional Aims

29. *Southeast Asia.* Peking's early fears that the Indochinese war might spill over into China seems to have lessened in recent years. Even though Peking has expressed apprehension that US frustration in Vietnam might lead to further escalation, the basic judgment of the Chinese seems to be that the US is bogged down in an indecisive effort that is more likely to lead to a withdrawal than to further expansion of the fighting. Their confidence in this judgment must have been shaken temporarily by the US move into Cambodia, but their calculation of the ensuing political costs for the US has probably persuaded them that it is still valid. Thus, what we believe to be their long-range estimate probably remains unchanged; i.e., in a protracted struggle Hanoi's patience will outlast that of the US.

30. As regards the likelihood of the PLA being sent into Southeast Asia for offensive action, the evidence of the past 20 years suggests Peking would be inclined in this direction only if China's security is seen as threatened, as on the Sino-Korean border in 1950, or if China is provoked, as on the Sino-Indian border in 1962. Thus, we continue to believe that China would use its military forces to prop up North Vietnam if it appeared that there was a real danger of that government collapsing. Similarly, China would no doubt react with the PLA to a direct military threat elsewhere along its southern borders.

31. Peking's more likely response—and almost certainly its initial response—to aggravation in this area would be to increase its support to subversive and insurgent activity. The fact that China continues its long-term improvement of its logistic capabilities along this border, including the current road building in northern Laos, illustrates Peking's desire to have support facilities ready for whatever contingencies may develop. The character of the facilities, operational considerations, and recent history all suggest that Chinese plans in this area relate to the defense of south China and the assistance of nearby insurgencies rather than to a massive push by the PLA into Southeast Asia. The objective, as before, would be to bring into existence friendly governments responsive to Peking's political influence; and, in Peking's view, this could be done better by indirection—including diplomatic pressure—than open aggression.

32. *Thailand and Burma* are already targets for a subversive effort. Thailand's close ties with the US guarantee China's continuing hostility. Thus far, Peking

SECRET

11

594

SECRET

has had little opportunity to apply diplomatic pressure on Bangkok and has been relying on a long-term campaign to encourage insurgency against the government. There is no suggestion that Peking sees this as an easy task or one that can be accomplished quickly even if given a high priority. On the contrary, Peking is consistent in advocating local self-reliance and has given little material aid to the active insurgents. Should there be a substantial reduction in the US presence in Southeast Asia, the Chinese may combine this low-level activity with more positive diplomatic blandishments.

33. In Burma, Chinese propaganda is encouraging revolutionary activity, supplemented by small amounts of aid in arms and training to dissident ethnic minorities. But diplomatic contacts with this neutralist government have been damaged rather than broken. Peking's return to moderation in other areas of its diplomacy may eventually be extended to include improved relations with Rangoon. Indeed, it now appears that both sides are prepared to resume more normal relations. Even so, Peking is not likely to abandon its support of Burma's insurgents.

34. Elsewhere in Southeast Asia, the Chinese are likely to persist in encouraging local revolutionaries, but in these relatively remote areas, significant material assistance is unlikely to be provided. The Chinese will continue to find it difficult to refuse requests for aid from any source that claims an insurgent or revolutionary capability, but they will continue to urge self-reliance rather than dependence on outside aid. Thus, the Chinese will maintain their role as revolutionary leaders but without exposing themselves to undue cost or risk. There is abundant evidence that Peking feels no need to set deadlines and has no schedule to fulfill; it is clearly prepared for the long haul.

35. *South Asia.* China's interest in India has a relatively low rank on Peking's scale of priorities. China is concerned with Sino-Indian border issues, with persistent rivalries with the Soviets over influence in South Asia, and with demonstrating that India is incapable of playing the role of a leading Asian power. Toward these ends Peking has sought to embarrass and intimidate New Delhi, but without becoming deeply involved in the effort. For instance, Peking has propagandized and provided limited arms and training to Naga and Mizo tribesmen in eastern India without, however, attempting to turn this into a major campaign.

36. On a larger scale, Peking's military aid to Pakistan—the major non-communist recipient of such Chinese aid—was born out of common enmity to India. In the process the Pakistanis have become major clients of the Chinese and Peking will probably seek to preserve and nurture this relationship even if Sino-Indian relations should improve somewhat in the coming years. Tentative feelers between Peking and New Delhi suggest both parties may be ready for a return to conventional diplomacy. While formal ties may be restored, in line with Peking's current effort to bolster its diplomatic image, the relationship will undoubtedly remain cautious and cool for some time to come

12   SECRET

SECRET

37. *The Asian Communists.* Peking now seems determined to consolidate the currently improved ties with both North Vietnam and North Korea. If only because of the primacy of the Sino-Soviet conflict, Peking is likely to go to some lengths to improve its relations with Pyongyang and Hanoi, preferably at Moscow's expense. The error of pushing Pyongyang and Hanoi, whether ideologically or politically, now seems to be clear to Peking and is unlikely to be repeated in the same gross forms as during the Cultural Revolution.

38. China's present call for "militant unity" is probably designed, in the first instance, to squeeze out the Soviet Union. It also serves to give the impression of a more active role in the "anti-imperialist" struggle than China's cautious actions warrant. Indeed, it seems likely that China will continue to tailor its role toward propaganda and material support of those on the front lines rather than expose itself to greater risk. This apparent effort to write itself belatedly into any possible settlement in Indochina, together with its sponsorship of Sihanouk, will require careful diplomacy if it is not to alienate Hanoi. Having borne the burden of the fighting, the Vietnamese are likely to be especially sensitive to any Chinese attempt to dictate strategy or tactics. Currently the Chinese are moving with finesse but their natural bent toward chauvinism is nearly as likely to erupt against the Vietnamese as against Westerners.

39. *Japan* represents a special case for Peking. Because of Japan's remarkable economic performance and US encouragement for it to assume a more active role in Asia, Peking is showing concern over Japan's potential military power, and its possible designs on another Greater East Asia Co-prosperity Sphere. This concern was heightened last fall by the signing of the Nixon-Sato communiqué on the reversion of Okinawa. Peking has always been apprehensive over Japan's expanding influence in Asia, particularly in Taiwan, and has taken the view that the Nixon-Sato communiqué signaled a more assertive and direct role for the Japanese in the area. Peking's reaction has been marked by indignation and by an unsettling conviction that as the US disengages from Asia, Japan will fill the void both economically and militarily and will assume the lead role in countering China. Adding to Peking's dilemma is the awareness that its political assets and leverage in Japan have markedly dwindled and its image has suffered from the extremes of the Cultural Revolution.

40. Despite its limitations—and past failures—Peking seems to have decided to continue on a course of limited meddling in Japan's internal affairs. Peking has also launched an intensive propaganda campaign which raises the specter of a remilitarized, imperialistic Japan, a foreign policy ploy designed to fan traditional Asian fears and to undercut Japanese influence. Moreover, the Chinese are attempting to build a case against US-USSR-Japanese "collusion," which is also intended to strengthen Peking's hand in its competition for influence in Asia. So far this approach has been successful in helping improve China's relations with North Korea, but has not had a significant impact on Peking's non-communist neighbors. Furthermore, the campaign has not been allowed to affect

SECRET

SECRET

materially China's burgeoning trade with Japan, which is expected to reach record levels again this year.

41. *Taiwan.* The continued existence—indeed thriving—of the Nationalist Chinese Government in Taiwan remains a central issue in Chinese foreign policy. This symbol of the unfinished revolution remains a highly emotional issue even after two decades. The Peking leadership faces the general frustration of knowing that they cannot take Taiwan by force, that it will not fall to them by default, and that the growing strength of the independence-minded Taiwanese could weaken Peking's claim to the island and perpetuate the issue indefinitely. The continued recognition of the GRC by many countries in the world and its presence in the UN and other international bodies blocks Peking from full international participation and remains a major irritant to the Chinese Communist leadership. Finally, the Taiwan issue is a complex obstacle to improved relations with both the US and Japan, thus severely limiting Peking's freedom to maneuver on international issues.

42. *Korea* continues to attract Chinese interest because of the strategic role of the peninsula, the quadrilateral competition for influence there, and the volatile relationship between the north and the south. Peking has worked assiduously to regain its influence in Pyongyang and has succeeded in reviving warm displays of friendship. While attempting to limit the role of the US, USSR, and Japan, however, Peking will also seek to limit North Korean adventurism. The outlook is for tough political support for Kim Il-song's propaganda outbursts combined with quiet restraint on his military excesses to avoid drawing China into another military confrontation on the peninsula.

E. China and the World Community

43. Where Peking's security interests are not directly engaged, Chinese diplomatic activity over the last year has involved far more tactical flexibility than has been shown vis-à-vis the US and the USSR. The face shown the world once again broadly resembles that displayed prior to the Cultural Revolution, a carefully nurtured image of reasonableness, but entailing little or no change in long-term goals. Sino-Soviet considerations are part of the equation in most of this diplomatic activity, and in some cases, notably in Eastern Europe, tend to dominate the Chinese approach.

44. Eastern Europe has become an attractive target for Peking because Soviet problems there seem to draw Soviet attention away from China. In addition to its close ties with Albania, Peking has been actively cultivating the Rumanians, and more recently has shown real flexibility in shelving ideology and improving long-frigid relations with Yugoslavia. Ambassadors have returned to Hungary, Poland, and East Germany. Peking is clearly preparing for long-term competition with the Soviet Union and for this reason alone is likely to give greater attention to the East Europeans. Much will of course depend on the subtlety and finesse of Peking's approach, but at this point the Chinese have apparently assessed the

14   SECRET

SECRET

opportunities as worth pursuing. In this effort as in other diplomatic endeavors now underway, Peking will likely recover ground lost during the Cultural Revolution, and, if it can hold to its new pragmatic diplomacy, achieve some forward movement.

45. Elsewhere in the world, Peking is showing revived interest in fostering better relations where the cost is cheap and the opportunities tempting. This does not rule out support for revolutionary activity, as is evident in the Near East. In contrast to the heavy arms aid from the Soviets to the Arab world, the Chinese apparently hope to sway the Arabs by concentrating their aid on the fedayeen. This will probably be mainly propaganda on "people's war" with some training and small-arms aid. This also serves to keep the pot boiling and the Soviets distracted. But while denouncing the ceasefire as an American-instigated "Munich" and declaring strong support for the fedayeen in the Jordanian crisis, the Chinese have carefully refrained from attacks on the Arab governments involved, apparently unwilling to compromise future state relations in the area.

46. In *Africa*, the Chinese will be concerned to restore diplomatic losses to the GRC in recent years. This will require more professional diplomacy and less proselytizing. Indeed, China's Foreign Ministry already seems to have accepted this retreat from Maoist missionary work. For the most part, aid projects are likely to remain modest but with special efforts to make them practical and highly visible. The construction of the $400 million Tanzania-Zambia rail line appears to be China's prestige project for Africa; the Chinese apparently also hope, through the provision of military aid, to convert Tanzania into a major beachhead in Africa.

47. In an effort which may be intended mainly to spotlight Peking's return to the world scene, the Chinese have also been displaying unprecedented interest in UN membership. In earlier years, Peking put preconditions on its membership which were clearly unacceptable to the international body. More recently, Chinese officials have dropped their extreme demands and have sent out a number of cautious feelers for support in the UN. Whereas Chinese diplomats formerly spurned such support, now they go out of their way to express appreciation for it. Despite all of this activity, Peking has not softened its opposition to any "two-China" formulation, and has continued to make it clear that the GRC must either withdraw or be dismissed before Peking would accept UN membership. Widened diplomatic recognition of Peking, such as by Canada and Italy, is steadily improving the chances for its admission to the UN; such an outcome seems likely within the next few years.

*　　*　　*　　*　　*

48. In general, and barring the contingency of military attack by the USSR, China's future international posture is likely to depend more on Chinese internal developments than on external factors. If domestic political and economic problems accumulate, so will the pressure to give them even higher priority,

SECRET

15

SECRET

with a concomitant lessening in foreign interests. Mao Tse-tung remains the key variable. So long as he retains his dominance within the leadership, Mao could attempt to reverse the present relatively moderate trends. In the past, his impatience has grown as his goals for China have been frustrated by economic reality and recalcitrant human nature. His ability to retreat and consolidate is still evident, but it is questionable whether his age and health will permit another major push toward his visionary aims. In any event, despite his deep concern over the ideological conflict with the Soviets, Mao's attention is likely to remain primarily on developments within China. Nor is he likely to abandon his caution and risk the destruction of China by provocative moves against either the US or the USSR.

49. Mao's death during this period could create succession problems that could give Peking reason to project a low posture on the international scene for some time. Almost any foreseeable combination of successors—even presumably hard-core Maoists like Lin Piao, the designated successor—would probably play for time to consolidate their positions and to strengthen China to meet possible challenges. In the longer run, as those who follow Mao face up to the needs of China, the trend is likely to be away from the ideological excesses of Maoism toward a more realistic adjustment to the difficulties—as well as the opportunities—facing China. Indeed, if the successors persist in the present movement toward greater flexibility and pragmatism, they are likely to have greater success than Mao in expanding China's political influence abroad. And for the longer run, China's traditional ethnocentrism will continue to fuel an assertive and potentially aggressive nationalism.

50. Presumably they will continue to focus their foreign policy on diplomacy at the overt level and on subversion and insurrection at the covert level. This could include "war by proxy" as well as efforts to exacerbate US relations with its Asian allies and to exploit internal tension within these countries. We cannot be sure, of course, how future leaders will see their situation, and it is possible that they will be prepared to employ China's developing power in a more aggressive manner. It now seems likely, however, that the open and offensive use of military power will continue to be judged needlessly risky and therefore counterproductive. Even the development of an operational strategic weapons system may reinforce Chinese caution rather than encourage a more reckless policy. While we do not doubt that China would fight tenaciously if invaded, or if threatened directly with invasion, we see no compelling factors moving Peking toward a policy of expansionism, or even a higher level of risk-taking. For all its verbal hostility and latent aggressiveness, neither the present nor the probable future leadership is likely to see foreign adventures as a solution to China's problems.

16 SECRET

SECTION 35

NIE 13-3-72

China's Military Policy and
General Purpose Forces

20 July 1972

APPROVED FOR RELEASE (b)(1)
DATE: MAY 2004   (b)(3)

TOP SECRET

NATIONAL INTELLIGENCE ESTIMATE

China's Military Policy and General Purpose Forces

Handle via   Control Systems Jointly

TOP SECRET
NIE 13-3-72
20 July 1972

N⁰   200

TOP SECRET

Handle via   Control Systems Jointly   1

CHINA'S MILITARY POLICY AND GENERAL PURPOSE FORCES

NOTE

This is the first estimate on Chinese theater forces to appear in the enlarged format for military estimates.

Optimism regarding our knowledge of Chinese military affairs, however, is tempered by the fact that the circumstances surrounding the 1971 purge of the top military leadership and many of its implications remain obscure. The purge has obviously altered the prospects for the succession to Mao Tse-tung and it has produced at least a temporary return to the pre-Cultural Revolution norm of the Party "controlling the gun". It may have important consequences for military morale, for military priorities, and for military policy.

TOP SECRET

2

Handle via ~~TOP SECRET~~ Control Systems Jointly

THE PROBLEM

To assess Communist China's general military policy and to estimate the strength and capabilities of the Chinese Communist general purpose and air defense forces through 1977.

CONCLUSIONS

POLICY AND STRATEGY

A.   Chinese military policy has been strongly influenced by Peking's aspirations to reclaim a leading role in Asia and to gain recognition as a major world power, and by acute concern to deter attack or invasion by the great powers. Taken together, these considerations have caused China to maintain a substantial military establishment and to bear the heavy costs of modernizing its general purpose forces and of developing an independent strategic nuclear capability. Nonetheless, Mao's insistence on a basic policy of self-reliance and China's limited technical and industrial base have insured that the process of modernizing the People's Liberation Army (PLA) would be a protracted one.

B.   Mao's primary concerns have been with the progress of the revolution in China, and the long-term development of modern military forces has taken place within the context of this overriding goal. Mao's willingness to subordinate defense and purely military considerations to the higher priority goals of politics and the continuing revolution—as in the Cultural Revolution—has had an impact on military professionalism, on combat readiness and morale, and even on military production programs. The PLA, in playing a "vanguard role" in the revolution, has been drawn deeply into politics and has been exposed to the inevitable rewards and penalties. The purge of Lin Piao and the top military leadership in 1971 is only the latest, if most dramatic, manifestation of the PLA's continuing involvement in vital issues of national policy.

C.   The policy of the People's Republic of China with respect to the use of force has been generally cautious. It has limited the use of combat forces beyond China's borders to circumstances where Peking has seen real and imminent threats to Chinese territory or to vital Chinese interests. In the 1960s, the increasingly hostile nature of Sino-

~~TOP SECRET~~

~~TOP SECRET~~   3

Handle via   Control Systems Jointly

Soviet relations radically altered China's strategic problems. Although the Chinese were careful not to show any sign of weakness, they were at pains behind this brave front to control the risks of direct military confrontation with either of the two superpowers, and, as might be expected, their military stance remained essentially defensive.

D. China's strategy for defense against a possible Soviet invasion follows Mao's principles of "luring deep" and "people's war". In the face of the much superior firepower, air support, and mechanized mobility of the Soviet Union, the Chinese have chosen not to position large forces close to the border where they might easily be cut off. The Chinese strategy seems to be to hold back their key main force units until the invading forces are overextended and weakened by the resistance of local defense forces and guerrilla harassment. In contrast to the northern border regions, the coastal areas of China have important concentrations of population and industry, and in these areas the Chinese are prepared for a forward defense employing air and naval forces. If an enemy force landed, it would be met at once by both local defense and main force army units.

E. Another example of Peking's defense-mindedness and awareness of China's vulnerability to attack from the air is the immense effort that has gone into passive defense. The Chinese are building a large portion of their new factories—especially those for military-related industries—in interior regions and have dispersed some of them in out-of-the-way valleys and canyons. Perhaps to a degree unmatched elsewhere in the world, the Chinese are building civil defense facilities, ranging from simple shelter trenches and bunkers to large tunnels with sophisticated life-support equipment in some large cities. Large tunnels now in existence or under construction at 75 or so of China's airfields will be able to shelter most of China's fighter force, and other underground facilities built or under construction will be able to shelter all of the navy's existing submarines and missile boats.

F. While the main focus of China's strategy is defensive, this is not to say that Peking has given no thought to contingencies involving offensive operations. In any case, a military force which has been developed to defend against the superpowers inevitably has a considerable offensive capability against lesser foes. China could, for example, conquer all of Southeast Asia if opposed only by indigenous

~~TOP SECRET~~

4

TOP SECRET

Handle via   Control Systems Jointly

forces. If Peking decided to take Taiwan, a considerable redeployment of its forces would be required, as well as extensive amphibious and airborne training. Once these preparations were made, China could almost certainly take Taiwan in the absence of US military intervention. If the Chinese were to participate in a major attack against South Korea, which we think unlikely, they could effectively commit as many as 35 divisions in the narrow peninsula. In the case of South Asia, the Himalayas and the vast reaches of the Tibetan Plateau would severely limit China's offensive capabilities; long and difficult supply lines would prevent the Chinese from sustaining any offensive into India beyond the Himalayan foothills. But in any of these contingencies, Peking would be constrained by the necessity of providing for defense needs elsewhere, particularly vis-à-vis the Soviet Union, and by the requirements of internal security.

THE FORCES

G. The greatest relative weakness of the Chinese vis-à-vis the US and the USSR is in the field of strategic weapons, and Peking has assigned first priority to ambitious and costly programs aimed at providing China with a credible deterrent against nuclear attack. After strategic programs, air and naval modernization has had the higher claim on resources; modernization of the army seems to have received a somewhat lower priority.

H. Even so, the ground forces remain the dominant element. The size of the force (at 3.0 million men, the Chinese Army is the largest ground force in the world), the toughness and discipline of the Chinese soldier and the quality of small arms with which he is equipped are impressive. The Chinese Army for its size and by US and Soviet standards, however, has relatively little armor, and is only moderately well equipped with artillery. Tactical air support for ground troops is limited, and shortages of vehicles and transport aircraft restrict mobility and logistic support. In a non-nuclear war on its own ground against any invader the Chinese Army would be a most formidable force. In these circumstances it would be able to capitalize upon its vast manpower reserves, its ability to mount a large-scale guerrilla effort, and its ability to use China's terrain and territory to advantage in fighting a prolonged war. In contrast, the Chinese Army would experience

TOP SECRET

Handle via ~~TOP SECRET~~ Control Systems Jointly 5

great difficulty in trying to push very far beyond China's borders against the opposition of a modern force. Here the weakness in transport, logistics, firepower, and air support could become critical.

I. While its inventory of some 4,000 combat aircraft is the third largest in the world, China's equipment is far below the standards of US or Soviet aircraft. Air defense is the primary mission of this force, with 37 of the 53 Chinese air divisions assigned to this role. The air defense system suffers from serious weaknesses because of its reliance on relatively outmoded aircraft, a very modest level of surface-to-air missile (SAM) deployment, limited air surveillance capabilities, and the lack of automatic data-handling equipment.

J. China's ground attack fighter force consists of Mig-15/17 jet fighters and a growing number (currently about 185) of F-9 fighter-bombers (a Chinese-designed aircraft somewhat larger than but resembling the Mig-19). About three-quarters of China's 540 or so bombers are obsolescent Il-28s. The Chinese also have deployed about 43 Tu-16 jet medium bombers, but we believe Peking intends to use the Tu-16s mainly as part of China's force for peripheral nuclear attack.

K. The Chinese have invested heavily in naval programs, and this effort is beginning to pay off. The fleet now includes about 53 attack submarines, 16 destroyer escorts (including 8 that are equipped with cruise missiles), about 55 missile patrol boats, and several hundred motor gunboats and torpedo boats. The coastal patrol type vessels are prepared to play a significant defensive role; the larger ships and submarines further enhance Chinese defensive capabilities but have not yet ventured any extended operations into deep waters. The Chinese Navy has only a limited air defense capability, and its antisubmarine warfare capability is rudimentary. The Chinese have only a limited sealift potential, have no amphibious shipbuilding program and have conducted no large-scale amphibious training.

PROSPECTS

L. Peking's cautious attitude respecting the use of force seems likely to continue for some time, partly because the Chinese see no advantage in risking a military confrontation with the vastly stronger superpowers, and partly because Maoist doctrine continues to hold that

~~TOP SECRET~~

6

TOP SECRET

Handle via   Control Systems Jointly

revolution cannot be sustained by external forces. We do not rule out a shift in this generally defensive and cautious policy on the use of force as China's conventional and strategic power grows and in circumstances in which nationalist sentiments may have gained ground at the expense of Maoism. But there is little in the current situation to suggest that such a shift would be likely in the next few years.

M.   We cannot foresee any weakening in the basic drive to develop China as a major military power. As in the past, however, progress in modernization and in developing military professionalism is likely to come into conflict with Maoist political and ideological goals. Moreover, because of China's limited technical base, the modernization of the PLA will necessarily be protracted, and the process will undoubtedly require numerous compromises concerning the balance of effort between strategic and conventional forces, and between near-term results and longer-term progress. While the Chinese could probably step up their efforts at military modernization somewhat, they are much nearer the margin of their capabilities than either the US or USSR.

N.   Thus the outlook for the next five years is one of continuing improvement along current lines based on programs now underway. A continuation of this persistent effort to build a formidable military establishment is unlikely to produce any spectacular breakthroughs or developments in the PLA. It will, however, permit Peking gradually to operate in the international arena with somewhat less concern for China's military weaknesses and shortcomings.

O.   The Chinese Army is receiving newer and better equipment—including improved light and medium artillery, light amphibious and medium tanks, armored personnel carriers, more modern communications equipment, and increasing numbers of trucks—that will gradually upgrade its firepower and mobility. Training is being conducted on a larger and more elaborate scale, and there may be other changes in process—e.g., more attention to arming and training paramilitary forces—that will enhance the military usefulness of China's virtually unlimited manpower. While these improvements will not be sufficient to enable Peking to project its forces much beyond China's borders against first class opposition, the PLA should be able increasingly to

TOP SECRET

TOP SECRET

Handle via   Control Systems Jointly   7

contest an invasion more effectively and in somewhat more forward positions than is now the case, especially on the northern and north-western frontiers. In short, the already formidable defensive capabilities of the Chinese Army will increase, and the prospect of engaging this force will become a more and more unattractive proposition for any potential adversary.

P. The outlook for air and air defense forces is one of substantial increases in size with qualitative improvement proceeding at a more modest pace. Peking may decide to phase out production of Mig-19 fighters in favor of Mig-21s. Chinese-produced Mig-21s evidently have not yet entered the force, but we expect this to occur in the near future. The availability of this aircraft would mark the beginning of major improvements in intercept capability, particularly as the Mig-21s would probably be armed with air-to-air missiles and be equipped for all-weather operations. The Hsian-A interceptor, a native-designed follow-on to the Mig-21 currently being tested, may be available for deployment in the mid-1970s.

Q. SAM deployment will probably proceed at a faster rate than in years past, and deployment of the Chinese version of the SA-2 may be supplemented by a low-altitude weapon during the period of this Estimate. Radar coverage will improve and expand, and new communications equipment now becoming available will improve the command and control of China's air defense system. Despite this growth and improvement, however, China will continue to be vulnerable to a large-scale attack by planes employing the latest equipment and technology.

R. The new F-9 fighter-bomber represents a significant improvement in China's ground attack capability and is likely to be deployed in fairly substantial numbers. Peking may soon conclude that the cost of building and deploying the outmoded Il-28 jet light bomber is not warranted and that production should cease. Although the Chinese will probably use the Tu-16 bomber primarily as a strategic weapon carrier, some will probably be assigned to reconnaissance and other non-strategic roles.

S. China's naval programs clearly attest to an ambition to become an important naval power. Production of attack submarines, destroyers,

TOP SECRET

Handle via ~~TOP SECRET~~ Control Systems Jointly

destroyer escorts and guided-missile patrol boats is likely to continue to be substantial. The evidence suggests that China now has one nuclear-powered attack submarine; if so, several more will probably enter the fleet during the period of this Estimate. At this point, however, the Chinese Navy's level of operational experience has not kept pace with additions of new units and advances in technology. Given the complexity of learning to operate as a deepwater navy, this situation is likely to persist throughout the period of this Estimate. Although there is a good chance that the Chinese will begin to "show the flag" in foreign waters with some of their newer units, there is little likelihood of their establishing a major naval presence in waters distant from China for some years.

T.   China's nuclear program has given first priority to the development of high-yield thermonuclear weapons for strategic attack. But the Chinese have an obvious requirement for tactical nuclear weapons, and Chic-13, which was tested in January 1972, could have been a step in filling this requirement.

Thus we feel that it is too early to conclude that China has developed a nuclear weapon for delivery by fighter aircraft. Nevertheless, we think it likely that the Chinese will acquire a tactical nuclear capability during the period of this Estimate. A bomb is the best candidate for an early capability. Somewhat later, toward the end of the period of this Estimate, the Chinese will probably be capable of deploying tactical nuclear missiles or rockets.

TOP SECRET

SECTION 36

NIE 11/13/6-73

Possible Changes in the
Sino-Soviet Relationship

25 October 1973

APPROVED FOR RELEASE
DATE: MAY 2004

Secret

(b)(3)

NATIONAL
INTELLIGENCE
ESTIMATE

Possible Changes in the Sino-Soviet Relationship

Secret

NIE 11/13/6-73
25 October 1973

№ 410

SECRET

POSSIBLE CHANGES IN THE SINO-SOVIET RELATIONSHIP

PRÉCIS

Significant improvement in Sino-Soviet relations is unlikely in the next year or two—particularly if Mao survives. A central element of the impasse at this stage is the absence of any visible inclination in Moscow to reduce its military forces along the Chinese border.

War between Moscow and Peking is a possibility, but we rate the odds as low—no higher than 1 in 10. China, clearly the weaker party, would not attack. The USSR would mainly be deterred by: China's strategic missile capability, however modest; the chance of becoming bogged down in a protracted ground war; concern over the potential impact on its economic relations with the West; and, uncertainty as to the nature and scope of US reactions.

Military action against China—particularly a disarming nuclear strike—may continue to have a certain appeal to some Soviet leaders, and arguments for a disarming strike would probably gain strength if the US appeared to move toward an anti-Soviet alliance with the Chinese. Even in this contingency, however, the counter-arguments would seem far more compelling. Thus, it is likely that Moscow will hold to a more measured course, one which does not foreclose the possibility of some accommodation over the longer term.

SECRET

1

SECRET

[DIA and Air Force would differentiate between a large-scale invasion and a disarming strike, rating the likelihood of a disarming strike as markedly greater than that of an invasion.]

Indeed, the longer the Sino-Soviet peace is maintained, the better the chances for a reduction of tension in the relationship. Mao's death, for one thing, should ease the way toward accommodation for both sides. Soviet or Chinese disappointments in dealing with the US might provide other incentives to bury the hatchet. So would the growth of Chinese nuclear strength and overall self-confidence in dealing with both superpowers. There are also the cumulative costs of years of tension and military preparedness, which may dispose both sides toward less risky, more controlled forms of competition—a new relationship in which differences are muted and third parties prevented from exploiting Sino-Soviet cleavages.

But movement beyond limited accommodations toward a genuine and durable rapprochement—broad collaboration and perhaps a new alliance—seems highly unlikely, even through 1980. National antagonism and basic clashes of interest run too deep.

*   *   *   *

A long-term improvement in the tone of Sino-Soviet relations would not necessarily mean communist unwillingness to do business with the West. There would still be strong interest in a continuing interchange of trade and technology. But there would be adverse effects. The Chinese would be less interested in improving relations with the US and less tolerant of the US military presence in the Far East. The Soviets would be less concerned with détente in Europe and more willing to compete with the US globally. Japan would have less room for maneuver between Moscow and Peking, both of which would oppose the growth of Japanese influence abroad.

The most significant result of any major reduction in Sino-Soviet strains might well be a general fear in the West and in the Third World that something like full-scale rapprochement was in the wind. This would stimulate interest in regenerating alliances with the US and could, in certain circumstances, increase resistance to further détente efforts among Western leaders.

SECRET

617

SECRET

THE ESTIMATE

I. THE ROOTS OF CONFLICT

1. *Background.* The Sino-Soviet dispute owes as much to old national rivalries as to the ideological battles of the last decade or so. Before Mao won control of the Party in the mid-1930s, however, the relationship of the Chinese communists with the Soviets resembled that of pupil and teacher. But even then, the Chinese found Soviet advice inappropriate and often hazardous, and the efforts of Moscow to control the Chinese Communist Party created a lasting mistrust and resentment. After the Chinese communists won their civil war, Mao's 1949 pilgrimage to Moscow was marked by lengthy and tough negotiations over the Sino-Soviet Treaty of Friendship, Alliance, and Mutual Assistance. Stalin was concerned that Mao might become a new Tito, and was quick to take exception to Chinese claims for Mao's doctrinal originality.

2. With this inauspicious beginning, it is surprising that the Sino-Soviet honeymoon lasted as long as it did. During the 1950s, the Korean War and its lingering effects on attitudes in Peking and Washington, and China's urgent need to develop and modernize its economy, tied Peking to Moscow. All the while, of course, Peking hoped to become self-reliant and feared that Soviet aid might freeze China in a permanent state of dependence and inferiority. In a poorly executed attempt to achieve an economic breakthrough, Peking launched its Great Leap Forward and commune system in 1958; the Soviets saw it as an ideological challenge as well as a misuse of their technical aid.

3. On yet another track, the death of Stalin in 1953 encouraged Peking to promote Mao as the top ideologue and senior leader of the communist world. The Soviets made little effort to conceal their contempt for this challenge, though it was after Khrushchev's de-Stalinization speech—at the 20th Congress of the CPSU in 1956—that this facet of the dispute began to intensify. China's interventions in the Polish and Hungarian crises of that year confirmed Peking's new assertiveness in competing with Moscow on matters concerning international communism.

4. Moscow's refusal to provide the kind of nuclear aid demanded by China, coupled with Soviet reluctance to join China in confronting the US in the 1958 Taiwan Strait crisis, further aggravated the deteriorating

SECRET

3

SECRET

relationship. The Soviet withdrawal of technicians from China in 1960 brought the conflict into the open and marked the end of attempts to develop cooperation in economic and technical fields. As the dispute worsened through the polemical exchanges of 1963-1964—and as the Chinese subsequently concluded that the fall of Khrushchev meant no softening of Soviet policy toward Peking—the stage was set for an escalation into military competition. Indeed, the Peking meeting between Mao and Kosygin in February 1965 left neither side in doubt about the depth and enduring nature of their conflict. It probably also served to give final impetus to a Soviet decision to strengthen their military forces along the Chinese border.

5. *Military Aspects.*[1] The military buildup along the Sino-Soviet border since 1965, particularly on the Soviet side, remains the most dramatic and convincing evidence of the deep hostility between the two powers. Soviet divisions near the border in 1965 numbered 13 or 14. Now there are 43 combat divisions which could be used in the early stages of a major conflict with China. In the same period, Soviet tactical air strength near the border has grown from less than 200 aircraft to some 1,150. The buildup has been relatively fast though it appears to reflect a long-range plan for methodical growth. While some experienced Soviet military personnel and some air units have been drawn from the western USSR, no ground units opposite the NATO central region have been used in the buildup. Soviet deployment of new forces to the Sino-Soviet border area appears to have tapered off.

6. For their part, the Chinese made no effort to concentrate additional troops close to the border, though aware of the Soviet buildup shortly after it began. In the period 1965-1968, China was deeply enmeshed in the Cultural Revolution, which involved the intensive participation of the People's Liberation Army. Peking was also sensitive to the threat posed by US forces in Indochina. China's relative military weakness required that it offer no serious provocation to either the USSR or the US. The chosen strategy was to hold Chinese forces well back from the frontiers—where they might easily be cut off by the superior mobility and firepower of enemy forces—in order to maintain balanced protection of vital centers against all potential threats.

7. Chinese fear of Soviet attack reached its peak in 1969-1970, following the Soviet show of force in response to Chinese-incited border incidents along the Ussuri River. Peking's immediate counter was to impose greater restraint over its frontier units, to agree to border talks with Moscow, to shift some army units northward (though still far back from the border), and to intensify the construction of underground shelters and facilities. Chinese concern over Soviet military intentions was also used at this time to justify phasing out those aspects of the Cultural Revolution that had become increasingly anarchic and troublesome. "Red Guard Diplomacy" was replaced with a new image of respectability and responsibility in the West. Peking's confidence vis-à-vis the Soviets rose dramatically in 1971 with its entry into the UN and the improvement of its relations with the US. While Chinese fears of Soviet attack are real and ever-present, these diplomatic successes—together with China's progress in the deployment of strategic weapons—have reduced their intensity relative to the peaks of 1969-1970.

8. *Current Levels of Contact.* Apparently as the result of a deliberate Soviet decision to intensify the propaganda battle, exchanges

[1] See NIE 11-13-73, "The Sino-Soviet Relationship: The Military Aspects," dated 20 September 1973, TOP SECRET ALL SOURCE, for a detailed analysis of the subject.

4

SECRET

SECRET

between Moscow and Peking have recently reached the highest level of acrimony since 1969. Soviet moves in this latest series of political exchanges have included another offer of a non-aggression treaty to Peking in June (which according to Brezhnev, "China did not even deign to answer"), and an initiative at the Crimean Conference of the Warsaw Pact party leaders in July to provoke discussion of the "China problem." These actions were followed in August by two authoritative Pravda articles which seemed to argue that China had by its own actions and policies removed itself from the socialist community. The Soviets have been moved in all this by their concern over Chinese meddling in both East and West Europe in the midst of MBFR and CSCE negotiations, by their hope to influence intra-Party debate in China, and by their desire to limit China's appeal to the non-aligned states (especially during the non-aligned conference in Algiers in August). The Soviet campaign may also reflect some maneuvering by Moscow vis-à-vis the Sinophilic Romanians and perhaps some preliminary efforts to set the stage for an international communist conference which would denounce the Chinese.

9. The Chinese, reacting to these Soviet efforts to condemn them in the eyes of Eastern Europe, to isolate them politically from the socialist world, and possibly to meddle in Chinese internal affairs, responded with predictable vehemence. In his definitive statement at the Party Congress in August, Chou En-lai left no doubt that Peking considers the Soviets as its number-one enemy. He charged that the "new czars" have restored capitalism, imposed a "fascist dictatorship," and used military force to back their foreign policies; he stated that China should remain on guard against a "surprise attack" by the Soviets. For all his bill of particulars against the Soviet leadership, Chou was careful not to rule out improved relations—or at least not to leave China vulnerable to a charge of rejecting compromise. As Chou put it, "The Sino-Soviet controversy on matters of principle should not hinder the normalization of relations between the two states on the basis of the five principles of peaceful coexistence." Despite this gesture on Chou's part, the net effect of these exchanges has been to further poison the atmosphere in the bilateral relationship.

10. Apart from these well-known polemics, there is little evidence on the structure and functioning of the current Sino-Soviet relationship. On the governmental level, trade and diplomatic matters (including border talks at the vice-ministerial level) are conducted correctly though coldly. And these governmental channels appear to be the main—if not the only—direct lines of contact between the two countries. There is no indication of any regular liaison between the two communist parties; indeed, it would be remarkable if any direct party link had survived the years of acrimony. However, the diplomatic mechanism is always available for quick and secure contacts. And if the situation should warrant, new channels could be hastily staffed for closer liaison. So long as fundamental disagreement persists, however, both sides are likely to continue to air their differences in public as well as in their private exchanges.

II. THE CONFLICT AS AN ELEMENT IN INTERNATIONAL POLITICS

11. The rupture of the Sino-Soviet relationship has helped establish the preconditions for new patterns of relations among the powers. The rivalry between Moscow and Peking now affects virtually every aspect of their foreign policies and, on balance, has exacted a heavy price from each of them in their dealings with other nations. Their attention and resources have been diverted from

SECRET

5

SECRET

other problems to deal with what has become a high priority for each—containing the influence of the other. The Soviets fear the considerable boost in economic and military strength which China could achieve over time from the unrestricted import of US and other Western technology. The Chinese fear the isolation and vulnerability that would result from US-Soviet "collusion to achieve world hegemony." Peking and Moscow are sensitive, of course, to the efforts of other powers, particularly the US, to exploit their rivalry; and this makes calculations of balance and advantage among the major powers—including Japan and Western Europe—exceedingly complex. All Chinese and Russian policy decisions must now be weighed in the light of how they might affect the balance of their rivalry.

12. For a few third parties, the Sino-Soviet competition has brought undesired complexities and disadvantages. North Vietnam was able, during the crucial years 1965-1970, to play Peking and Moscow to its own advantage. Hanoi, however, would have preferred the resolute backing of a united communist bloc during this period. And now, Hanoi finds the separate and competing approaches of the Soviets and Chinese to Washington distinctly harmful to its more parochial interests in South Vietnam. For North Korea, a degree of division between Moscow and Peking was for many years welcome; it provided Kim Il-song the opportunity to assert his independence of both these powerful allies. But the intensity of the Sino-Soviet dispute and its profound effect on Soviet and Chinese relations with the US have served to foreclose external support for any North Korean military approach to the unification issue.

13. For most of the world, the present status of the Sino-Soviet relationship brings a greater sense of opportunity and security. Japan now finds the two communist powers far less hostile as they compete, to a degree, for its favor. Peking is even prepared to accept, at least at this point, a continuing US military presence in Japan. Chinese fears of the USSR are also a major factor in Peking's more moderate posture toward local governments in Southeast Asia and in its current willingness to countenance a continued US presence in that region. These changes in Peking's posture have by no means meant assurance of Chinese restraints on North Vietnam, or Chinese collaboration with the US to achieve a negotiated settlement in Cambodia, or Chinese disengagement from the active communist insurgencies in Thailand and Burma. But the shift has opened the possibility of a less disruptive Chinese role in the area in the future, and even of some collaborative efforts with the US and the local anticommunist states, all designed to serve China's broader strategy vis-à-vis the USSR.

14. Moscow's push for détente in Europe is in part motivated by a desire to improve its ability to deal with the problem of China. Recognizing this, Peking has actively encouraged the nations of Western Europe to ignore Soviet blandishments and to strengthen their ties with Washington. Peking's encouragement of a stronger NATO as a shield against Soviet pressures is helpful to US policy. The Chinese position on MBFR, however, is opposed to that of the US; and Chinese arguments about US-Soviet "collusion" tend to reinforce suspicions of the same in places like Paris. China's relative lack of influence in Europe, though, limits the impact of its views on ongoing substantive negotiations concerning that area.

15. China's effort to shake Moscow's control over the communist parties and the states of Eastern Europe probably represents more of an irritant than a threat to the Soviet posi-

6

SECRET

SECRET

tion there. But the Sino-Soviet conflict has complicated Moscow's dealings with its Warsaw Pact allies, introducing another contentious issue and giving some of them a degree of leverage against the USSR. It has also encouraged a natural tendency among some East European states to seek as independent a foreign policy as possible without inciting Moscow's ire. Romania's ostentatious friendship with Peking and refusal to cooperate in Soviet propaganda against Peking is particularly frustrating to Moscow.

16. China's admission to the UN brought the Sino-Soviet conflict directly into that body, further complicating international efforts to achieve consensus on major issues—e.g., arms control and the Law of the Sea. While Peking continues to oppose US positions in the UN, its most biting attacks there have been directed at the Soviet Union and the "social-imperialist" threat. The US has not been able to take direct advantage of the Sino-Soviet dispute in the UN to secure favorable votes, but Peking's attacks on the Soviets have taken some of the international heat off Washington, long the favorite target for Third World rhetoric. Moreover, with the Soviets and Chinese frequently pulling their clients in different directions, anti-US forces at the UN have had more tactical difficulty mustering support for their positions.

17. Peking has regularly tried to rally Third World countries against the US as well as the USSR, however, and has attempted to warn newly independent nations of the "threat" which close relations with either power represents. Currently, for example, Peking is busily denouncing the US and the USSR for perpetuating tensions in the Middle East at the expense of the Arab cause.

18. The Sino-Soviet rivalry has also caused Peking to greatly reduce its involvements in most revolutionary and guerrilla movements in recent years, and to devote attention to cementing ties with existing power structures almost everywhere in the Third World. This has contributed to a lowering of tension in various troublespots and to better relations between Peking and many non-communist states important to Washington. China has dramatically improved relations with Iran, for example, hoping to help block the further development of Soviet influence in the Persian Gulf region. In Africa, the Chinese have been aggressively expanding state-to-state relations, in a few cases (e.g., Somalia) in direct competition with the Soviets and virtually everywhere with an eye toward weakening the influence of the superpowers. In Latin America, where Chinese interests are still limited, there has been far less maneuvering between the two communist powers for influence.

19. Peking and Moscow have backed up their competition for influence in the Third World with trade and aid. The USSR provides by far the greater amount and is engaged in a broad-based contest for influence throughout the Third World, against the US as well as China. Peking has perforce been more selective with its aid; and its substantially expanded aid programs appear designed for the most part to counter the Soviets. China has moved aggressively to edge out the Soviets when targets of opportunity arose—e.g., by offering substantial aid to Sudan after its serious rift with Moscow. Peking has also extended generous aid offers to states with which it had little previous contact, as in Zaire, despite the displeasure such initiatives raised in other, less liberally treated, client states like Congo Brazzaville. The Chinese have not abandoned their established allies, of course, and continue—by virtue of their large aid programs—to enjoy far greater influence than the Soviets in states like Pakistan and Tanzania. In fact, in most cases one or the other of the communist powers is in a clearly more

SECRET

7

SECRET

influential position vis-à-vis the other, so that despite the world-wide Sino-Soviet competition, there has not been a wild bidding war between Moscow and Peking for economic influence in the Third World.

20. Peking and Moscow still compete for the favor of selected national liberation and subversive organizations world-wide, but the fervor of their competition has dimmed dramatically in recent years. The seriousness of the Sino-Soviet competition has focused Chinese and Soviet attention on more crucial areas (e.g., Europe and the US), as well as encouraging them to deal with existing governments. In only three areas is there still a significant competition for influence with national liberation groups. In Indochina, both Moscow and Peking, while paying proper deference to Hanoi's leading role, still compete for influence with the liberation forces in Laos and Cambodia. In the two other sectors—among the Arab fedayeen and the revolutionaries of southern Africa—the competition between the two has been low-keyed, with the Soviets generally holding the upper hand without serious challenge. Since the Chinese appear unwilling to commit the resources to oust the Soviets from their dominant position, and the Soviets equally unwilling to up the ante to make the liberation groups more serious threats, the contest for influence seems likely to stay within current parameters.

III. THE FUTURE OF SINO-SOVIET RELATIONS

21. The fundamental issues and basic clashes of interest which separate the two powers appear so profound as to ensure *the prolongation of a competitive and adversary relationship*. Sino-Soviet antagonisms, rooted in history and cultural differences and nurtured on 15 years of insults, threats, and ideological disputes, have grown deep and strong. Shifts in both Soviet and Chinese

foreign policies in recent years have added new dimensions to their conflict. In particular, the efforts of each country to cultivate better relations with Washington have fed mutual distrust and helped fuel the rivalry. So have the efforts of each to expand economic ties with the West. And neither development seems to be a short-term proposition: the first reflects a belief in both Moscow and Peking that easing tensions with Washington serves their national interests and strengthens their international position, and the second is in both cases the result of basic and probably durable economic needs, especially for protein supplements and advanced technology. The current competition in contiguous areas has also heightened the level of distrust and contention. Chinese efforts to encourage East Europeans to loosen their ties with the USSR provoke Moscow's ire. Moscow's efforts to promote its Asian Collective Security concept have intensified the Chinese conviction that the USSR is determined to isolate China and check its influence throughout Asia.

22. In sum, the Sino-Soviet dispute has by now gained such momentum and has so involved the personal prestige of the leaderships, particularly on the Chinese side, that any significant amelioration seems unlikely in the near term. Thus, for the next year or two—and particularly if Mao survives—it seems most likely that the present level of tension will persist. This is not intended to imply that Sino-Soviet relations are fixed for the immediate future. The tone of the relationship will surely vary from time to time. Border frictions, domestic political needs, or unusual troop deployments could contribute at any time to eruptions in the relationship. The level of propaganda invective will vary in any case. The possibility of war, of course, will remain.

23. The Soviets have shown no inclination to respond to Chinese demands that they pull back their forces along the border. Moscow

8

SECRET

SECRET

clearly feels real concern about security in Soviet territory bordering China and has deployed what it probably considers the minimum force capable of handling any contingency on its frontiers. But the Chinese clearly see this as a disproportionate and unjustified display of strength, and are disinclined to make concessions under what they choose to interpret as a Soviet show of force. At this point, it is doubtful that either side would reduce military forces along the border for fear that this would signal irresolution or lack of staying power to the other side.

24. *Although we rate the odds of war as low, it is necessary to give serious attention to this possibility.* Because of Chinese awareness of Soviet military superiority, the chances are remote that Peking would deliberately take actions leading to war. But various motivations are conceivable for major Soviet military actions against China. In the improbable event that China engaged in persistent border harassments, the Soviets might move beyond local reprisals and cross the border in considerable strength in an effort to halt such provocations. Larger military operations, involving penetrations of several hundred miles into Manchuria and Sinkiang, might be undertaken to exert pressure on the Chinese leadership in some other context as well. Deeper penetrations, which would require more extensive mobilization of Soviet forces, would have the purpose of solving the more basic "China problem." An opportunity for such action might occur in the unlikely contingency of a China sharply divided by an internal struggle for power.[2] In this case, the Soviets

---

[2] The idea that China might suffer deep internal divisions and a severe weakening of central authority gained currency outside China during the Cultural Revolution. In retrospect, we can see that there were serious strains; but the more significant fact was the continuing responsiveness to central authority despite deep cleavages within the leadership at all levels.

might intervene with the aim of supporting or imposing a faction more favorably disposed toward cooperation with the USSR.

25. Whatever the circumstances of a Soviet move into China, Soviet leaders would almost certainly expect Chinese resistance to develop and to be stubborn. They would have no assurance that the war could be brought to an end on Moscow's terms nor that Soviet forces would not get bogged down in a protracted and costly struggle. Moscow might foresee being confronted eventually with a choice between withdrawal or the use of nuclear weapons in an effort to end the conflict. The use of nuclear weapons, even if successful, could have far-reaching adverse repercussions for the USSR's position in the world.[3] Moscow would fear that the US would turn hostile, move close to China, and attempt to rally world opinion in favor of a general policy of condemning and isolating the USSR. In any event, Moscow's general policy of détente with the West, particularly its effort to foster economic ties with the advanced Western countries, would be imperiled. Thus, a major ground attack on China, especially one involving nuclear weapons, would involve not only accepting serious new risks, but rejecting an established policy that has reduced conflict on the border with China and promised political and economic benefits elsewhere in the world.

26. While Soviet planners probably recoil at the thought of becoming bogged down in ground actions in China, there no doubt remains the temptation to deal with the more critical aspects of the Chinese threat before it is too late—i.e., to knock out China's still modest but growing strategic capability with

---

[3] The Assistant Chief of Staff, Intelligence, USAF, believes that the use of nuclear weapons against China might also be viewed by the Soviets as having desirable repercussions, either of a tactical or strategic/political nature.

SECRET

SECRET

a disarming nuclear strike. Arguments for this course as the only means of forestalling a basic and unfavorable shift in the world strategic balance would probably gain strength if, in Soviet eyes, the US appeared to move from an even-handed posture between Moscow and Peking toward an anti-Soviet alliance with the Chinese. In this event, it could be argued in Moscow that détente had failed and that a display of naked force which destroyed Chinese strategic capabilities and instilled an abiding fear among the peoples and governments of Asia, Europe, and the Middle East would bring gains that more than offset the damage to the Soviet image.

27. The counter-arguments seem far more compelling. The Soviets could not be certain that some Chinese missiles would not survive the blow or that the Chinese would refrain from launching them against Soviet cities. Nor could Moscow be certain that China would not attempt to engage Soviet general purpose forces in a protracted struggle. As in the case of a ground invasion, there would be much concern about hostile US reactions. As for discounting these reactions and shifting belligerently to a general posture designed to exploit fear of Soviet ruthlessness and power, most Soviet leaders would probably view this as bringing with it all the disabilities of the Stalin era.

28. Our judgment, based on weighing all these and other considerations, is that the chances of a premeditated large-scale Soviet attack on China—while certainly still such as to demand attention—are quite low, say on the order of 1 in 10. While Moscow is prepared to punish the Chinese at any point on the frontier where the Chinese might act forcibly to assert territorial claims, the main Soviet policy to counter China is centered on diplomatic efforts and on activities within the world communist movement. These efforts will not cause the USSR's "China problem"

to go away; and military action, particularly a disarming nuclear strike, may continue to have a certain appeal to some Soviet leaders. But when considered in light of the calculable and incalculable risks of military action, arguments for a more measured course which holds open the possibility of some accommodation and even reconciliation over the longer term are far more likely to prevail within the top Soviet leadership.

29. Most participants in this Estimate feel that the judgment above applies to both a large-scale Soviet invasion and a disarming nuclear strike. While the latter course probably rates more serious consideration by Soviet planners, the chances still seem low that such a course would actually be approved and implemented. DIA and Air Force, however, would differentiate between a large-scale invasion and a disarming strike, rating the likelihood of a disarming strike as markedly greater than that of an invasion.

30. If war does not intrude over the next few years, the odds on this contingency will decline as the Chinese deterrent grows. In the meantime, other factors may emerge to encourage *a trend toward reduced levels of tension and a more controlled competition.* An unpredictable yet potentially crucial factor affecting the future of Sino-Soviet relations is the post-Mao leadership situation in China. Given his personal involvement in the whole process of the deterioration of the Sino-Soviet relationship, Mao's passing will present an opportunity for both sides to reassess their postures.

31. It is doubtful that any single successor to Mao, even Chou, will be able to command the power and authority that Mao has wielded. A period of persistent pulling and hauling appears likely; there are bound to be disputes on matters of authority, style, pace, and priorities, and these disputes will leave casualties. Rivalries might become particularly intense

10

SECRET

SECRET

if Chou should predecease Mao. And if Mao and Chou were to leave the scene at about the same time, Chinese politics might become seriously unstable and Peking's international behavior—including the course of relations with the USSR—unpredictable.

32. Various possibilities could be imagined in the post-Mao environment. There could be a breakdown in central authority as contending factions in Peking formed alliances with regional leaders; in this event, China might cease to play an active international role until unity had been restored. A second possibility is the emergence in Peking of a faction which—with or without covert Soviet assistance—would move China back into close alliance with the USSR.

33. Extreme changes of this sort are unlikely in the light of present circumstances and the history of the Chinese Communist Party. There is a strong commitment to a unified China within the armed services and the Party, and it is likely that the appearance of a regionally based challenge to central authority would serve to unite other contending factions in defense of Peking's authority. As for a "pro-Soviet faction," there is no reliable evidence for the existence of any such group in the Chinese Communist Party since at least the early 1950s, much less information to indicate any significant Soviet capability to manipulate Chinese leaders.[4]

34. This brief discussion does not exhaust the alternatives. But the most likely composition of the leadership after Mao and Chou

---

[4] Despite allegations concerning Lin Piao and Peng Te-huai, their problems with Mao almost certainly arose from domestic policy and power issues. Foreign policy, including the proper balance of Chinese relations with the US and the USSR, may have become involved in later stages of both affairs; but even if this is the case, there is no evidence to suggest that either Lin or Peng were being manipulated by the USSR or were consciously seeking to advance Soviet interests.

will be some combination of the military leaders, party cadre, and experienced civilian bureaucrats now visible on the scene at national and regional levels. While these men reflect a range of views, the political balance appears somewhat to the right of the revolutionary activists who reached their high point during the Cultural Revolution. While these leaders would undoubtedly offer lip service to the revolutionary ideals of Mao, and almost certainly would persevere in seeking a socialist China, they would nevertheless tend to be more pragmatic than idealistic, more moderate than radical, and more concerned with China's material future than with the world's ideological struggles.

35. A leadership drawn from this group would probably retain an interest in productive relations with the US and the West. But it might also be disposed to place relations with the USSR on a more businesslike basis for a variety of strategic, political, and economic reasons.

36. On the Soviet side, leadership changes do not seem likely to result in major shifts in Soviet attitudes or policies toward Peking. While differences undoubtedly exist on how best to handle Moscow's China problem, it is not possible to discern precisely how these differences will affect decisions on the tone and pace of Moscow's approaches to China. What does seem clear is that the USSR would, at least over the longer term, welcome a less tense and more businesslike relationship with Peking.

37. Should Moscow sense that a leadership similarly disposed had emerged in Peking, it is possible—even likely—that it would take the initiative to explore the opportunities for a more relaxed relationship. The Russians might offer to make certain political gestures. They might suggest a visit to Peking by the USSR's current leader, or extend token concessions indicating respect for Chinese inde-

SECRET

11

SECRET

pendence and doctrinal originality. (There are precedents for both these actions in Soviet relations with Yugoslavia.) The Soviets might also offer to expand trade and to resume economic and, perhaps, military aid. They might even offer to reduce their competition with Peking for influence in Southeast Asia in exchange for similar Chinese restraint in Eastern Europe and the Middle East. Moscow would hope that Peking would reciprocate by suspending its anti-Soviet politicking at the UN and in diplomatic conversations with third nations, or at least quieting its anti-Soviet propaganda, restraining its missionary activities in the communist world, and tacitly accepting the status quo on the territorial issue.

38. Indeed, any genuine reduction of Sino-Soviet tension is difficult to foresee without some sort of concurrent move toward settlement of the longstanding border issue. The problem could be negotiated if China holds to its present position that the current border as defined in the "unequal treaties" of the czarist era is an acceptable basis for a settlement. In such case, the border problem is essentially one of agreement on certain territorial adjustments, in the Pamir region and, most importantly, along the riverine frontiers of Manchuria. It is just such disputed areas—e.g., the strategically important island opposite the Soviet military center of Khabarovsk—however, that Peking is prone to cite when it claims that the Soviets are occupying territory beyond that obtained under the "unequal treaties." Thus, the negotiation remains deadlocked, a casualty of the overall poor tenor of Sino-Soviet relations rather than a result of intrinsically irreconcilable territorial claims.

39. Another set of factors of possible long-range significance concerns Peking's perception of the Soviet threat. The view that the Soviet Union is the principal military threat underlies much of China's current foreign

policy. The Soviets are seen as being in an aggressive, expansionist phase while the US is described as being in a state of decline. As the development and deployment of China's strategic weapons progress, China's concern with the immediate military threat should decline. Further, the mere passage of time without an actual attack should of itself be reassuring to the Chinese. As such perceptions change, a somewhat less antagonistic relationship with the Soviets may appear better suited to China's interests in the eyes of its leaders.

40. Evolutionary trends in the complex Sino-Soviet-American political triangle may also contribute to the amelioration of the Sino-Soviet relationship. Indeed, both Moscow and Peking may one day conclude that the US has gained excessive advantage from communist intramural conflicts. Moreover, in the case of Moscow, a desire for better relations with China might be encouraged by serious setbacks in US-Soviet relations—such as might flow from difficulties in arms negotiations, trouble in trade relations, or problems growing out of third-party conflicts (e.g., in the Middle East). As for Peking, an inclination to move closer to the Soviets might be encouraged by, say, certain developments in US relations with Taiwan or Japan.

41. Less dramatically, China and the USSR might just conclude independently that, in any case, they had gotten all they could out of détente with the West, that there was not much more mileage to be gained by competing with one another for Washington's favors. A shift of this type in China's attitude would be a logical outgrowth of increasing Chinese nuclear strength; as the deterrent grew, Chinese self-confidence would increase, and concessions to US positions would appear less necessary.

42. The main theoretical line in China's current foreign policy—opposition to "super-

12

SECRET

SECRET

power hegemonism"—reflects Peking's nationalist and ideological reservations about leaning to one side and its long-run intention to undercut both Soviet and US influence. At present China's preoccupation with the Soviet threat predominates and dictates the need to lean towards the US. However, as China grows in strength and confidence, Peking's leaders may find it possible, even desirable, to oppose US and Soviet influence internationally on a more equal basis, while not necessarily sacrificing other productive aspects of its relations with the US.

43. *In sum, it appears that the Sino-Soviet relationship, while it will continue to move through varying degrees of tension, is more likely to move toward lessened tension than toward war.* In time, the cumulative cost of years of tension and military preparedness are likely to predispose the leaders in both Peking and Moscow toward less risky, more controlled forms of competition. The basic national antagonism is likely to remain as deep as ever, but rather than remain poised indefinitely on the brink of military confrontation, both parties are more likely to seek a new relationship in which the differences are muted, the virulent debates withdrawn from international forums, and third parties prevented from exploiting their conflict. Peking and Moscow have had many years to assess the potent risk of their rivalry. After Mao, both parties will probably seek to cut the costs and reduce the risks by moving the competition into safer realms.

44. *A move beyond limited accommodations to a genuine and durable rapprochement*—one in which there is a renewal of broad collaboration and perhaps reinstatement of the alliance—seems out of the question in the near term and highly unlikely in this decade. This is so not only because of all the factors which argue for continued contention, but because any major amelioration of the

contest (with its attendant implications of threat for the non-communist world) would jeopardize each side's policies and investments in the West.

45. A fundamental change from the present relationship would be likely only if there were a dramatic turnover in leadership in Moscow or Peking (which is highly unlikely), or if either party or both came to see new and significant threats from the non-communist world. It is difficult at this time to conceive of a threat of such proportions as to cause the communist adversaries to set aside their differences. Presumably, it would have to involve a threatening move by the US and some of its allies or the emergence of a militarized and aggressive Japan. The US action would have to be seen in Moscow and Peking as distinctly warlike; the souring of the present détente would not likely serve as sufficient motivation.

IV. WORLD IMPLICATIONS OF POSSIBLE CHANGES IN SINO-SOVIET RELATIONSHIP

War

46. War between the USSR and China would, of course, have global repercussions. Assuming the Soviets were the aggressor, initial world reaction would be one of awe at Soviet boldness and ruthlessness, and fear that a process had been set in train which might soon result in severe instability and disruption throughout Europe, the Middle East, and Asia—if not in time in a third World War. The attention of the nations, individually and in concert, would be focused on limiting the arena of conflict and, ultimately, discouraging any Soviet effort to pursue maximum goals vis-à-vis China.

47. In the case of a Soviet disarming nuclear strike, it would be impossible to restore anything resembling the *status quo ante*, hence

SECRET

13

SECRET

difficult to foresee any willingness on the Chinese side to set aside their outrage and discuss a settlement. Thus, there would be the prospect that military action at some level would continue following the initial nuclear strike.

48. Virtually every nation would look to the US as the only possible leader in any effort to restrain the Russians, mollify the Chinese, and halt the shooting war. While China would have the sympathy of much of the world, there would be little sentiment favoring US military intervention on Peking's behalf. But neither would a posture of rigorous neutrality on the part of the US meet approval. Rather, the US would be expected to take a firm line against the aggressor, provide reassurance to other nations against possible Soviet intimidation, and take the lead in mobilizing world efforts to contain and end the conflict. Few nations outside of NATO would care to join the US in assuming a conspicuous posture in opposition to Soviet ambitions; communist leaders in Eastern Europe and East Asia would be especially reticent.

49. If Washington were successful in a peace effort, much goodwill and respect would accrue to the US. On the other hand, even if it ended quickly, the Sino-Soviet conflict would initiate a period of generalized fear and disruption, clearly reversing the present trend toward détente among the powers and preoccupation with economic growth and social change among the smaller nations. The arms race would be given impetus all along the Sino-Soviet periphery. Japan, India, and Israel, among others, would think more seriously about achieving nuclear deterrent capabilities. US allies in East Asia and Western Europe would expend more funds on weaponry and draw closer to established alliances with the US. The US would come under heavy pressure from friends and allies to expand its own military programs.

Rapprochement

50. Global reaction to the hypothesized Sino-Soviet reconciliation would be heavily contingent on its cause. If reconciliation were to come about as a communist response to US policies or actions (initiated perhaps in collaboration with the Japanese) which appeared to menace Russian and Chinese interests, the new Sino-Soviet unity would probably be seen as essentially defensive and probably of limited durability (i.e., subject to rapid erosion once the presumed US threat had receded). But, in the interim, most world leaders would focus on peacekeeping efforts and would try to avoid giving offense to either side, especially if events seemed to be heading toward a dangerous great-power confrontation.

51. If the reconciliation had emerged, independently of actions by other powers—i.e., mainly as a consequence of arrangements between Moscow and Peking—world concerns would have a different focus. The geopolitical reality of a unified communist bloc, dominating the Eurasian landmass and far stronger than before, would be intimidating—even if accompanied by bloc protestations of peaceful and beneficent intent.

52. The world would probably return to a form of bipolarity. The US would be viewed as the only possible leader of a reconstituted military and political counterweight to communist power, though Western Europe and Japan, far stronger than 20 years ago, would be much more important components of any rebuilt security structure. While a few Third World countries might seek security from anticipated Sino-Soviet pressures in affirmations of neutrality, many more would move closer to the US and seek its protection. There would be deep concern, especially in Asia and the Middle East, that the US might not be as responsive to the security needs of small

14

SECRET

SECRET

and remote states as it was during the cold war.

53. But whether the world would then turn back into a period of tensions and troubles reminiscent of the cold war at its worst would depend not only on the power and purpose of the renascent communist alliance but also on its needs. Certainly some of the Soviet and Chinese leaders, no longer constrained by their own rivalries, would be drawn initially toward harsh and expansionist foreign policies. They would wish to use the fact of their renewed collaboration—and the image of augmented communist strength—to extort concessions from other powers, especially those on the bloc's periphery. But there would be some sobering second thoughts in both capitals. The actual *strategic* balance between the two opposing sides, East and West, would not necessarily be altered appreciably by the joining of Soviet and Chinese forces in a new alliance. This would depend essentially on when the joining took place—it will be some years before the Chinese can deploy an intercontinental force in any great strength—and what the level of opposing Western forces happens to be at that time. Moreover, some of the imperatives which have brought both Moscow and Peking into postures of détente—notably the requirement for high-quality imports from the West—would survive even complete Sino-Soviet reconciliation. Finally, even in the best of circumstances, Sino-Soviet reconciliation would not (*could not*) erase mutual distrust or eliminate the legitimate fear in both capitals that the new confederacy was perhaps destined to be short-lived.

Limited Improvement in Relations

54. A limited improvement in Sino-Soviet relations, of itself, would not imply a concurrent unwillingness to do business with the West. Particularly in the economic sphere,

Moscow and Peking would remain interested in a continuing interchange of trade and technology with the US, Western Europe, and Japan. In a situation in which the two communist powers were giving less priority to scoring points against the other, it might be possible to conduct debate and negotiations on certain international issues without the disruptive effects of Sino-Soviet polemics.

55. There would be adverse effects. The US might find the Chinese, even if not anxious to reverse courses of action already undertaken, less eager to improve the relationship and less prone to accept the maintenance of the US military presence in the Far East. It might also find the Soviets, reassured about their Chinese flank, more willing to compete with the US and less concerned about détente in Europe—feeling freer, perhaps, to raise their price or perhaps to jettison this policy altogether if it were not producing the desired gains.

56. Other powers might find some of the underlying assumptions of their policies subject to erosion as well. Japan would find its room for maneuver between the USSR and China much more limited, and its activities in South Korea, Taiwan, and Southeast Asia opposed by both countries. India and Pakistan would face reduced support from their respective communist patrons. Hanoi and Pyongyang would find it more difficult to play Moscow and Peking off against one another. In short, the premises behind the present alignment of major powers might have to be revised. Indeed, the most significant result of any important reduction of the Sino-Soviet gap might be the apprehensions generated internationally that something approaching full-scale Sino-Soviet rapprochement was in the wind. Such concerns would stimulate interest in regenerating alliances with the US and could, in certain circumstances, increase resistance to further détente efforts among Western leaders.

SECRET

15

SECTION 37

NIE 13-8-74

China's Strategic Attack Programs

13 June 1974

APPROVED FOR RELEASE
DATE: MAY 2004

(b)(1)
(b)(3)

Top Secret

NATIONAL INTELLIGENCE ESTIMATE

China's Strategic Attack Programs

Top Secret

NIE 13-8-74

13 June 1974

Copy № 226

Handle via   Control Systems Jointly.

~~TOP SECRET~~

Handle via   Control Systems Jointly   1

CHINA'S STRATEGIC ATTACK PROGRAMS

KEY JUDGMENTS

China's programs to develop and deploy nuclear weapons have slowed since 1971, probably reflecting

— a shifting of national economic priorities to emphasize agriculture and basic industry coinciding with diminished influence of the military in policy circles since the fall of Lin Piao

— a changed perception of the strategic environment resulting from some combination of: a) China's acquisition of a modest but credible nuclear retaliatory capability against the USSR, b) improved relations with the US, and c) perceived constraints on the USSR due to Soviet detente with the US.

China now has a force of about 130 nuclear delivery vehicles— half missiles and half bombers. Its stockpile of nuclear weapons is probably sufficient for ... the missiles, though perhaps not for all the bombers. These systems have the range to hit US forces and bases in Asia as well as targets in the eastern USSR but cannot attack the continental US. China's force suffers from a number of vulnerabilities, but has achieved a measure of survivability through concealment, mobility, and hardening.

China's present objective probably is to obtain a token nuclear capability to strike the USSR west of the Urals and the continental US.

— It will gain a token capability to strike European Russia when its limited-range ICBM becomes operational, possibly late this year or, more likely, in 1975.

~~TOP SECRET~~

~~TOP SECRET~~

Handle via   Control Systems Jointly

— It is developing two missile systems that could strike the continental US: a) a full-range ICBM that will not be operational before 1977, and, given the present pace of development, probably not until 1979 or later; b) a submarine-launched ballistic missile system that will not be operational before 1978 at the earliest, and probably will be later.[1]

Over the longer term, Peking almost certainly will seek to deploy a stronger deterrent force against the US and the USSR. It is also reasonable to expect China to strengthen its regional deterrent and to increase its options for responding to limited nuclear attack.

Assuming a continuation of present trends, which appears likely, China by 1980 may have some 120 missiles and well over 100 bombers for delivery of nuclear weapons against peripheral targets, including those in the USSR, and a few, say six, ICBMs and one or two nuclear missile submarines for use against the US as well as the USSR. Such a force would confer on China a somewhat improved capability to deter nuclear attack by the USSR and, for the first time, an ability to strike the continental US.

In the less likely event that China makes accelerated progress, it might have some 30 ICBMs and four nuclear missile submarines by 1980. Such a force would significantly improve China's deterrent posture against both the US and USSR.[2]

---

[1] For the position of the Director of Naval Intelligence see the footnote on page 6.

[2] For the position of the Director, Defense Intelligence Agency see the footnote on page 7.

~~TOP SECRET~~

Handle via

Control Systems Jointly

3

SUMMARY

China's nuclear weapon programs have slowed markedly since 1971. It now seems likely that China will only moderately improve its regional nuclear strike capability over the next few years and probably will not deploy full-range ICBMs or a ballistic missile submarine before the late 1970s.

Force Development Policy. The general nature of the slowdown suggests the influence of national-level policy decisions, and not solely technical problems with individual programs. Beginning in 1971, and roughly coinciding with the purge of Lin Piao and the subsequent reduction of the role and influence of the military in the government, China's national economic priorities began shifting to agriculture and basic industry and away from military procurement. China's present leadership may believe that devoting a greater share of resources to basic industry and perhaps to research and development would contribute more to China's national power over the long run than pouring large resources into the production of obsolescent aircraft and first-generation missiles.

Certain programs which could yield significant improvements in China's strategic capabilities several years hence are still moving ahead, although for the most part slowly— for example, the programs to develop solid-propellant missiles and a ballistic missile submarine and the construction of facilities for the production of nuclear materials and for R&D work on airframes and aircraft engines. On the other hand, programs which could yield quick but limited improvements in China's nuclear weapons posture are languishing— the programs for the limited-range (3,000-3,500 nm) CSS-X-3 ICBM and the TU-16 bomber, for example.

The decisions to move ahead more slowly with programs for nuclear forces probably reflect a change in the Chinese perception of the strategic environment, resulting from some combination of: (a) China's acquisition of a modest but credible nuclear retaliatory capability against the USSR, (b) improved relations with the US, and (c) perceived constraints on the USSR due to Soviet detente with the US.

~~TOP SECRET~~

4

TOP SECRET

Handle via   Control Systems Jointly

Present Forces. China's nuclear strike force has grown slightly over the past two to three years but its composition remains unchanged. Then and now the Chinese have a capability for nuclear strike by missiles and bombers all around the periphery of China at distances up to 1,650 nm. While most of this capability has a strategic orientation, some of it is intended for a theater support role within China's borders. At the present time, the Chinese are estimated to have operational:

China's present stockpile of nuclear weapons is probably sufficient for all its operational missiles, though perhaps for only a portion of the bombers.

Presently deployed Chinese missiles have a capability to strike all US bases and allies on the periphery of China, and most of them can strike Soviet targets east of the Urals. The TU-16s can reach somewhat beyond the same areas, though their capabilities to penetrate to heavily defended Soviet targets are limited. The IL-28s could attack Soviet targets close to the border, and could also reach Korea and Taiwan and, with staging from points close to the border, northern Luzon in the Philippines and nearly half of South Vietnam.

Survivability. The Chinese have attempted to achieve survivability of their nuclear deterrent through a combination of concealment, mobility, and hardening. Missile units are deployed either in a semimobile mode, moving from garrisons to temporarily occupied, inconspicuous field sites, or at fixed soft sites with tunnels to protect missiles and essential equipment but with unprotected launch pads. Camouflage and other means are used extensively to conceal the locations of these launch areas. There are indications that some further deployment of the CSS-2 IRBM may be in the semimobile mode. Provisions for the survivability of Chinese bombers are not as extensive as those for the missile force.

— about 60 TU-16 jet medium bombers, capable of delivering nuclear bombs, with an operating radius of 1,650 nm and deployed at four airfields.

— possibly a few nuclear-armed IL-28 jet light bombers, with an operating radius of 570 nm.

TOP SECRET

—In the case of the US, it rests on US fears for the security of a few US bases and cities of allies in the Far East.

Chinese Goals. The scale and variety of the nuclear and missile development and production facilities that China has established indicate that Peking's ultimate objective is to build a strategic nuclear capability befitting a major power. There is no reason to believe, however, that Peking aspires to match the capabilities of US and Soviet nuclear forces. When considered in relation to US and Soviet programs, Chinese strategic programs represent a small effort. The pace of the Chinese effort, moreover, is slow and deliberate, and programs are undertaken with an economy of means, reflecting limited Chinese resources.

China's present objective probably is to obtain a token nuclear capability to strike the USSR west of the Urals and the continental US. Over the longer term, Peking almost certainly will seek to build a force of nuclear delivery vehicles that will be a stronger deterrent to nuclear attack by either the US or the USSR. It is also reasonable to expect that China will attempt to improve and somewhat expand its regional and theater nuclear capability, both to strengthen its regional deterrent and to increase its options for responding to limited nuclear attack.

Prospects for Major Systems. The Chinese may acquire a limited capability to strike Soviet targets west of the Urals, possibly starting in late 1974 but more likely in 1975. By then, they may have completed two of the three silos in the field now being built for the CSS-X-3. An initial operational capability (IOC) for the CCS-X-3 in late 1974 or 1975 would also require either an early resumption of flight testing or that the Chinese be satis-

Chinese View of Their Deterrent. The Chinese probably believe that they have acquired a modest but nonetheless credible nuclear retaliatory capability against the USSR. At the same time, it is clear that they realize that their force remains vulnerable in important respects.

— They are working on a phased-array radar northwest of Peking, but presently have no effective means of detecting the approach of hostile ballistic missiles.

— Redundant, hardened strategic communications for the missile force are under construction, but are not complete as a nationwide system.

— Reaction time for present missile forces is several hours. The Chinese may be looking to future systems to give them faster reaction time.

China must also be aware that its present ability to deter nuclear attack through the threat of nuclear retaliation would be marginal if the stakes were high.

— In the case of the Soviet Union, it depends on Soviet fears for the security of some few cities in Siberia and the Soviet Far East, and perhaps on Soviet uncertainty about IRBM deployment in western China which might be within range of some cities in the Urals.

6   ~~TOP SECRET~~
              Handle via   Control Systems Jointly

fied with the very limited flight test program accomplished before 1971. While the missile could possibly reach Moscow

it could not reach US targets except for a portion of Alaska and several US bases in the mid-Pacific, including Guam. There is no evidence of preparations for further CSS-X-3 deployment.

The Chinese have no capability to attack the continental US directly and are unlikely to attain one for several years. The full-range (7,000 nm) CSS-X-4 ICBM now under development could not be operational until 1977 at the earliest

In their most recent test of the CSS-X-4, the Chinese attempted to use it to orbit a satellite, which could mean that the current priority of the CSS-X-4 program is its application as a large space booster.

The other system under development by China that could directly threaten the continental US is the ballistic missile submarine. Construction of one or more such units is probably under way, and the lead hull might be launched this year or next. The missile for the system probably will be a two-stage solid-propellant SLBM, comparable in size to the early US Polaris and probably capable of delivering a nuclear warhead to a range of some 1,500 to 2,000 nm. Flight testing of such a missile has not yet begun, and probably will take at least three years. Therefore, even if test firings begin soon, the missile is unlikely to be ready for system integration with the first operational SSBN before mid-1977. Allowing for a minimum of six months for full integration of the system, the earliest IOC date would be 1978. But in view of China's lack of experience in the flight testing of

solid-propellant systems, IOC might be considerably later.[3]

Prospects for Future Forces. Under alternative assumptions, Chinese prospects are assessed as follows:

— If the Chinese show little more urgency and no greater rate of development and deployment progress over the next several years than in the past few years, they may have by 1980 some 120 missiles and well over 100 bombers for use against peripheral targets, including those in the USSR, but only a few, say 6, ICBMs and one or two SSBNs capable of attacking the US.

— If the Chinese make accelerated progress in the development of intercontinental systems and second-generation regional systems, and shift resources to hasten their deployment, by 1980 they might have a regional force of about the same size as above, but qualitatively improved, and some 30 ICBMs and about four SSBNs capable of attacking the US.

The first projection is a better reflection of Chinese performance to date and we have no present basis for predicting any marked improvement. It would mean that by 1980 China would have somewhat improved its capability

---

[3] The Director of Naval Intelligence, Department of the Navy, believes that China's submarine-launched ballistic missile program appears to have made significant progress during the past year. Testing of an ejection or launch-assist device installed in the PRC G-class submarine apparently has been conducted. Some land-based testing of a SLBM could have occurred

If submarine firings begin soon and proceed smoothly and the SSBN is launched this year as expected, the SLBM/SSBN system could reach IOC in late 1976. A more likely IOC would be by mid-1977.

~~TOP SECRET~~

TOP SECRET

Handle via   Control Systems Jointly   7

to deter nuclear attack by the USSR by virtue of:

— an enlarged and improved regional strike force;

— an emergency strike capability against targets in the Far East by one or two relatively invulnerable SSBNs;

— a token and vulnerable capability to strike targets in European Russia with a handful of ICBMs in silos.

The intercontinental strike element of this force would have conferred on China for the first time the ability to strike the continental US. This would have considerable political and psychological value. But the ICBM force would be small and vulnerable and only the SLBMs would represent a survivable retaliatory force, and then only for short periods.

In the less likely event that China makes accelerated progress in the development of intercontinental systems and second-generation regional missile systems, the Chinese by 1980 could have a significant capability to deter nuclear attack by the USSR—a capability that the Chinese could feel fairly confident would deter Soviet nuclear attack unless the stakes were very high. This improved deterrent posture would be based principally on China's expanded ICBM force—some 30 ICBMs in silos, a force probably large enough for assured retaliation against large populated areas in European Russia.

This number of ICBMs would also improve China's deterrent position versus the US. Moreover, with four nuclear submarines, during periods of tension China might be able to keep one or two nuclear missile submarines on patrol in the North Pacific from where they could strike targets in the US.[4]

---

[4] The Director, Defense Intelligence Agency, believes that a third case, reflecting a lesser effort, should also be included. A third force mix would concentrate on a more limited force, and intercontinental ballistic missile systems would be sacrificed at the expense of expanding other budgetary sectors.

TOP SECRET

8   ~~TOP SECRET~~

Handle via   Control Systems Jointly

Projections of China's Strategic Nuclear Delivery Force
(NIE 13-8-74 compared with NIE 13-8-73)

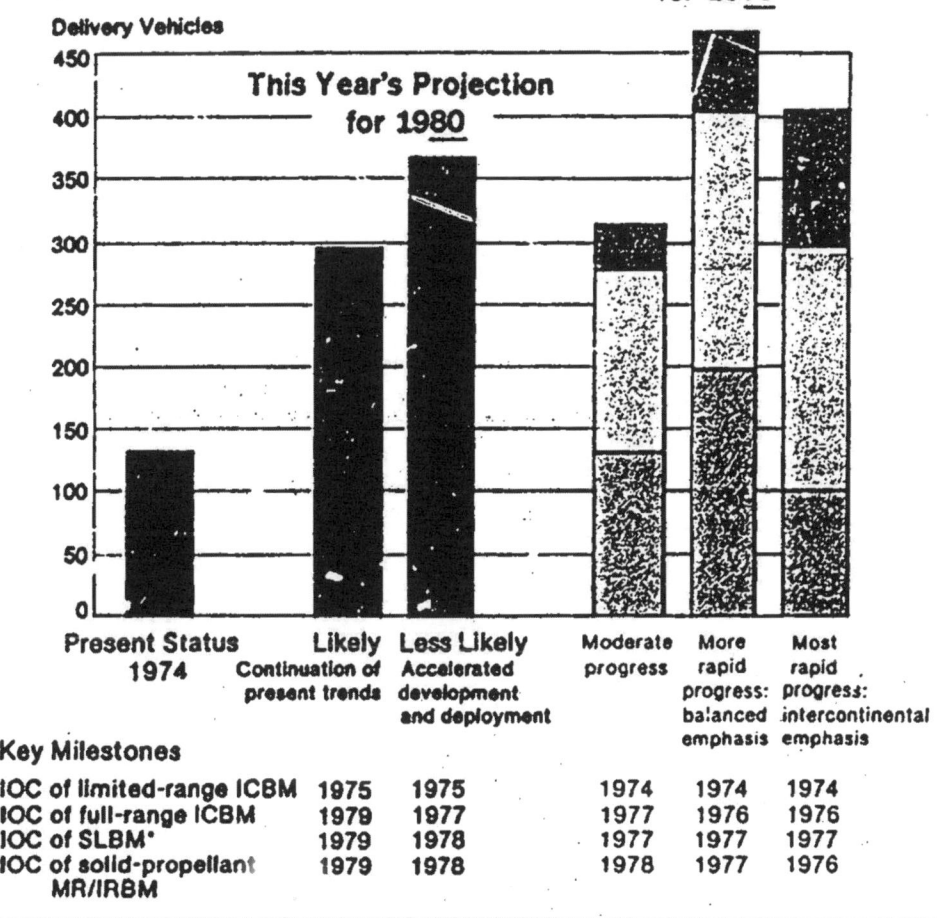

Key Milestones	Present Status 1974	Likely Continuation of present trends	Less Likely Accelerated development and deployment	Moderate progress	More rapid progress: balanced emphasis	Most rapid progress: intercontinental emphasis
IOC of limited-range ICBM		1975	1975	1974	1974	1974
IOC of full-range ICBM		1979	1977	1977	1976	1976
IOC of SLBM*		1979	1978	1977	1977	1977
IOC of solid-propellant MR/IRBM		1979	1978	1978	1977	1976

■ Missiles capable of reaching US: full-range ICBMs and SLBMs

■ Missiles capable of reaching only Asian and Soviet targets, including limited-range ICBMs

■ Bombers capable of reaching only Asian and Soviet targets: TU-16's and nuclear-equipped IL-28's

NOTE: All bars represent high sides of ranges of uncertainty under the stated conditions.

* For the position of the Director of Naval Intelligence see footnote on page 6.

~~TOP SECRET~~

~~TOP SECRET~~

I. NUCLEAR FORCE DEVELOPMENT POLICY

1. China's plans to create a nuclear force, as evidenced by analysis of its development and deployment programs, have passed through several stages. Hindsight suggests that a decision was made at an early date to concentrate initially on developing and deploying as quickly as possible a missile force with a capability against peripheral targets that would constitute the beginnings of a deterrent against attack by the US and its allies, or any potential adversary. The development effort was based mostly on the aid provided by the USSR before the Sino-Soviet split in 1960. Given the incomplete status of this assistance program and the rudimentary nature of China's technical and industrial base at the time, this was an ambitious undertaking. Nonetheless, it appears to have succeeded. There is good evidence now that a limited number of nuclear-equipped CSS-1 MRBMs and some Soviet SS-2-type short-range ballistic missiles (SRBMs) were deployed by the end of 1966.

2. By the mid-1960s the Chinese had begun to prepare for the next phase of their plan for nuclear forces. This phase coincided with a sharp rise in Sino-Soviet tension and with a period when China's military establishment was in political ascendancy. The objective during this period, apparently, was to expand China's minimal regional deterrent and to achieve a measure of strategic deterrence against both the US and the Soviet Union. Starting in the mid-1960s, the Chinese considerably expanded their R&D and production facilities. The effort progressed throughout the second half of the 1960s despite the serious turmoil created by the Cultural Revolution, suggesting that it had high priority and some degree of immunity from the political situation. By the early 1970s, CSS-1 deployment had been expanded, the CSS-2 IRBM had been developed and initially deployed, testing of the technically similar and longer range CSS-X-3 (which could reach west of the Urals) had started, and the first two Chinese earth satellites had been successfully orbited. Flight testing of a large full-range ICBM, the CSS-X-4, also began in this time period, and the foundations were laid for a major solid-propellant program, including the development of an SLBM.

3. The pattern of China's progress toward an intercontinental nuclear strike capability and an enhanced regional deterrent force began to change in a marked way in 1971.

— After November 1971, there were no further test launches of the CSS-X-3 ICBM,

Work on three operational silos for the CSS-X-3, begun in 1969 and 1970, continued at a slow pace. So far as we know, no others were started.

— After a successful test in September 1971, the CSS-X-4 full-range ICBM was test-launched once in 1972 and twice in 1973,

— After 1971, no additional fixed launch sites for the CSS-2 were started, although work continued at fixed sites already under construction.

— China's program to develop an SLBM continued to make steady, gradual progress but the program has moved more

TOP SECRET

10

~~TOP SECRET~~

Handle via   Control Systems Jointly

slowly than expected and flight testing of an SLBM still has not occurred.

— China's production of the TU-16 strategic bomber began to decline from the rate of about two aircraft per month in 1971 to one per month in 1972 and then was suspended in 1973.

— Production of IL-28 light bombers began to decline from a high of about five per month in 1971 to a current rate of two per month.

4. A year ago it seemed possible that the slow progress in some programs was a phase and that after a time all or most programs would move forward rapidly. This has not occurred and it is now clear that the strength levels projected for China's strategic forces in NIE 13-8-73 will not be achieved. That Estimate indicated that by mid-1978, assuming moderate progress, China might have some 140 missiles and an equal number of TU-16 bombers for use against peripheral targets, including those in the USSR, as well as some 15 ICBMs and one or two SSBNs for use against the US.[*] It now appears that by mid-1978, the Chinese capability is likely to fall short of even this moderate improvement in their forces.

5. Although technical or programmatic reasons can be adduced in all cases to explain each program's termination or limited progress, the overall pattern suggests the influence of more general, national-level economic and strategic factors. And indeed, there is evidence from China's economic policy debates and from developments in nonstrategic military programs that 1971 was a turning point for the country's overall defense weapons policy.

---

[*] NIE 13-8-73, China's Strategic Attack Programs, dated 7 June 1973, TOP SECRET

6. It is clear that in 1971, roughly coinciding with the purge of Defense Minister Lin Piao and a number of his military associates on the Politburo, national economic priorities were shifted to give more priority to agriculture and basic industry, apparently to some extent at the expense of military procurement. During 1971 there was a debate over the allocation of resources between the steel and electronics industries which was probably partly related to defense issues. After the fall of Defense Minister Lin Piao, a national economic planning conference was held in late 1971 and early 1972 to review the shortcomings of past policies. Little is known of any decisions made at the conference, but a long-range policy emphasizing the primacy of agriculture and the need for industry to support agriculture has been in effect since.

7. In 1972 and 1973, industrial production continued to expand at about 8 percent per year and certain sectors—petroleum, fertilizer, steel, and transportation—grew at even higher rates. During this same period, several military programs, in addition to those strategic programs already noted, slowed perceptibly. Examples are military aircraft production and destroyer construction. Not all programs slowed and indeed we have noted increases in conventional submarine and tank production. In some cases technical as opposed to policy decisions may explain the decrease in activity. Nevertheless, it seems clear that a number of important military programs slowed at a time when the other sectors in Chinese industry were expanding—a trend which implies that priorities had shifted.

8. A policy review in late 1972 led to China's purchase during 1973 of 1.2 billion dollars' worth of whole industrial plants from the West, the first such massive imports since the cessation of Soviet aid. These plant imports

~~TOP SECRET~~

TOP SECRET

Handle via   Control Systems Jointly   11

appear to supplement rather than replace on-going domestic investment programs. There has also been some increase in weapons-related imports but not on the same scale. Thus, developments of the past year in China's import policy reinforce the impression that a relative shift in resources and emphasis from military to civilian industries has occurred since late 1971. Nevertheless, it is not possible to determine whether there has been any shift of priorities or resources within the military between general purpose forces and strategic forces.

9. Within the strategic weapons category, developments during the past year seem to indicate that certain programs which could yield significant improvements in China's strategic capabilities several years hence are moving ahead, although for the most part slowly. For example, the construction of facilities for the production of nuclear materials and for research and development of airframes and aircraft engines is proceeding steadily, and work continues on programs to develop solid-propellant missiles and a ballistic missile submarine. On the other hand, programs which could yield quick but relatively limited improvements in China's nuclear weapons posture seem to be languishing. These include initial operational deployment of the CSS-X-3 system, and the TU-16 production program.

10. China's failure to move forward briskly with aircraft production and missile deployment programs could be due just as much to strategic considerations as to technical and economic ones. The current leadership may believe that devoting a greater share of resources to basic industry and perhaps to research and development would contribute more to China's national power than pouring large resources into the production of obsolescent aircraft and first-generation missiles. The Chinese may have judged that while they could moderately improve the capabilities of their regional nuclear forces, they had no hope, in the near term, of deploying nuclear delivery systems in modes and numbers sufficient to establish a credible retaliatory capability against European Russia. They may believe that future systems offer a better prospect of bolstering their capabilities against the USSR. Improved relations with the US may have reinforced China's technical and economic reasons for not moving rapidly to deploy intercontinental missile systems. Moreover, the PRC leadership may have come to believe that the retaliatory capability they had already achieved against targets in Siberia and Central Asia together with US-USSR detente had decreased the USSR's option for an outright attack on China.

II. THE STATUS AND DIRECTION OF FORCES AND PROGRAMS

The SRBM Force

11. During the past year, for the first time since 1965, an SRBM unit was observed deployed at a field launch site. The unit was observed at Mu-chia-yen in north-central China, a location enabling it to cover potential routes within China by an invader moving through Sinkiang or from Mongolia. (See Figure 1.) Although SRBM equipment had been observed at a few missile-related installations in China since 1962, their locations appeared inappropriate for operational deployment of the system. The more recent evidence suggests that the Chinese have had a few SRBMs operationally deployed since the early 1960s.

TOP SECRET

12
~~TOP SECRET~~

Handle via   Control Systems Jointly

Figure 1

Chinese Missile Units with a Theater Support Role

563403 6-74 CIA

Estimated Characteristics and Performance of
the Short-Range Ballistic Missile

IOC* .... 1962 (high-explosive warhead)
                 1966 (nuclear warhead)
Configuration ... Single stage
Propellants .... Cryogenic

12. We do not know how many SRBMs units are deployed—perhaps only a few,

It is unlikely that any new SRBM units were formed after later generation missiles became available and, since there is no evidence that the system is still in production, additional deployment is unlikely. The total force probably does not exceed 10 launchers.

* Initial Operational Capability

---

* All estimated ranges in this Estimate are expressed in terms of a non-rotating earth (NRE).

~~TOP SECRET~~

TOP SECRET

Handle via   Control Systems Jointly   13

The CSS-1 Force

13. Although it is an obsolescent and cumbersome missile system with slow reaction times, the CSS-1 appears likely to remain in China's inventory for several more years at least. Two launches were conducted recently from the Shuang-ch'eng-tzu Missile Test Range, the first since December 1971. Their purpose probably was to test operational crew proficiency and missile system reliability. Production of the CSS-1 may have ended in 1970. The deployed force—now some 20-30 launchers—probably has not increased since 1972 at the latest.

Estimated Characteristics and Performance of
the CSS-1 Medium-Range Ballistic Missile*

IOC	1966
Configuration	Single stage
Length	
Diameter	
Propellants	Cryogenic, probably liquid oxygen and alcohol

14. There is some evidence that part of the CSS-1 force is being relocated for use primarily in a theater support role.[7]

The CSS-2 Force

15. During the past year, deployment of China's CSS-2 IRBM system continued at a measured, deliberate rate. Some 30-35 launchers are estimated to be operational now. About five launchers are known to have been

Estimated Characteristics and Performance of
the CSS-2 Intermediate-Range Ballistic Missile

IOC	1971
Configuration	Single stage
Length	
Diameter	
Propellants	Storable liquid

---

*The CSS-2 has never been test-fired to a range of more than about 1,350 nm, equivalent to some 1,400 nm NRE. Although this falls short of true IRBM range—1,500 to 3,000 nm—the uncertainties about the CSS-2's characteristics leave open the possibility that it could fly to at least 1,500 nm, so it is considered an IRBM.

---

[7] That is, for employment against relatively fixed targets supporting the operations of enemy forces, such as troop concentrations, staging areas, and invasion routes. Such use is distinguished from tactical use in support of ground forces which are in direct contact with an enemy.

TOP SECRET

14

TOP SECRET

Handle via   Control Systems Jointly

brought to operational status during the past year—about average for the program.

same period.

16. The present slow rate of deployment suggests that the Chinese do not intend to increase the size of the CSS-2 IRBM force significantly. Some further expansion of the force may occur if the Chinese replace the CSS-1 system with the CSS-2 at some established sites and institute some semimobile deployment of the system. There is a growing body of evidence that China is exploring semimobile deployment of the CSS-2 and, in fact, may already have begun deployment in this mode.

Estimated Characteristics and Performance of the CSS-X-3 Intercontinental Ballistic Missile	
Configuration	Two stages
Length	
Diameter	
Propellants	Storable liquid

19. When the CSS-X-3 reaches IOC in late 1974 or, more likely, the first half of 1975, as estimated, the Chinese will have a token capability to cover targets in the European USSR, possibly including Moscow. They may consider the creation of such a capability sufficient justification for deploying a largely untested missile. The reasons behind the decision to truncate the program are unkown, but probably include political and strategic considerations as well as the costs of deploying enough CSS-X-3s to form a credible threat to the European USSR.

The CSS-X-3 Program

17. The CSS-X-3 regional ICBM program continues to be a major enigma in China's strategic weapons effort. The system has not been flight-tested in over 2½ years,

urthermore, there is no evidence that m   CSS-X-3 silos are being built. It appear   refore, that while the Chinese have r   abandoned the program, they plan to deploy the system in only token numbers.

18. The CSS-X-3 flight test program includes only two firings of the vehicle in a missile role, both from the Ching-yu rangehead to a range of some 2,000 nm, With a small third stage, the vehicle was also used to launch China's two successful satellites during the

The CSS-X-4 Program

20. China's first true ICBM-class system, the CSS-X-4, continued to run into technical problems during the past year. Of the four launches of the system made to date, only the first one—in September 1971—appears to have been completely successful.

TOP SECRET

647

TOP SECRET

15

Handle via

Control Systems Jointly

TOP SECRET

16 ~~TOP SECRET~~

Handle via   Control Systems Jointly

After an interval, on-pad exercises with a CSS-X-4 missile began in mid-January 1974 and are still continuing. (See Figure 3). The activity may involve only checkout of the launch facility or training. A launching—either one in-country or another attempt to launch a satellite—could be scheduled to occur sometime in the next few months.

Estimated Characteristics and Performance of the CSS-X-4 Intercontinental Ballistic Missile

Configuration	Two stages
Length	
Diameter	
Propellants	Storable liquid

21. It is still much too early to reach confident conclusions as to when the CSS-X-4 might reach IOC as a weapon delivery system. Continuation of work on large R&D launch silos for the system at the Wu-chai rangehead during the past year indicates that the Chinese retain their interest in using the CSS-X-4 as a weapon system. (See Figure 4.) One of these silos, started in 1968, could finally be ready to support flight testing of the CSS-X-4 by the end of this year. Construction of a second silo there, started in mid-1971, is also proceeding slowly. There is, however, no evidence of the construction of operational silos for the CSS-X-4 in the field

if construction of operational silos is started soon, the system probably could attain IOC sometime in 1977 at the earliest. If the difficulties take longer to correct, or new ones appear, IOC will be even later, say in 1979.

22. Given the history of the program to date, it seems unlikely that the program will move smoothly and uninterruptedly toward an early IOC. It is even possible that there will be no deployment of the CSS-X-4 in the period of this Estimate. The fact that the Chinese attempted to use the system to orbit a satellite could mean that the current priority in the CSS-X-4 program is its application as a large space booster. Launches of the system in a space role obviously will also provide much valuable data on its potential performance as an ICBM. Such an interim objective would be compatible with the slowness in the R&D silo construction at Wu-chai—nearly six years in duration—and the apparent absence thus far of construction of operational silos in the field.

23. There are a number of priority space applications which probably need the payload launch capability of a vehicle as large as the CSS-X-4. These include a photoreconnaissance satellite for collecting strategic targeting data and other intelligence, and a communications satellite for both military and civilian use. There is substantial evidence pointing to Chinese interest and activities in these and other types of satellite payloads. This evidence includes statements by Chinese scientists at international meetings, the construction over the last several years of a significant space-tracking network in China, and construction of some 20 probable ground stations for a domestic communications satellite program.

The Development and Production of Missile Systems

24. China has made a substantial investment over the past 15 years in developmental testing and production facilities for both liquid- and solid-propellant missile systems.

~~TOP SECRET~~

Handle via

TOP SECRET

Control Systems Jointly

17

TOP SECRET

18 ~~TOP SECRET~~

Handle via   Control Systems Jointly

Construction continued to be observed at several of these sites over the past year. In terms of the total number and variety of such facilities now available, the Chinese have the production and testing capacity for supporting a ballistic missile and space effort far larger than the one which is apparent. (See Figure 5.)

25. Current operational Chinese ballistic missile systems all use liquid propellants, and a major investment has been made in the facilities needed to develop and produce such systems. These facilities were initially concentrated in the Peking area. In the mid-to-late 1960s, however, a large production complex was built near Feng-chou in east-central China. A large developmental facility for propulsion systems was started in about 1970 near

Wu-hsing southwest of Shanghai. The Wu-hsing installation now is nearing completion and appears to be designed to develop and perform static tests of both liquid- and solid-propellant systems. At least two possible propulsion test facilities have been discovered recently near An-ning and Sui-yang.

26. Although the Chinese have not yet flight-tested a solid-propellant ballistic missile, their continuing investment in facilities capable of developing and producing solid-propellant rocket motors of various sizes up through strategic class has considerable significance for the future. The first such complex, at Hu-ho-hao-t'e, Inner Mongolia, was started in the mid-1960s and further expanded several years ago. Despite the substantial capacity of this installation, the Chinese started to build an-

~~TOP SECRET~~

TOP SECRET

Handle via   Control Systems Jointly

Figure 5

Missile Development and Production Facilities in China

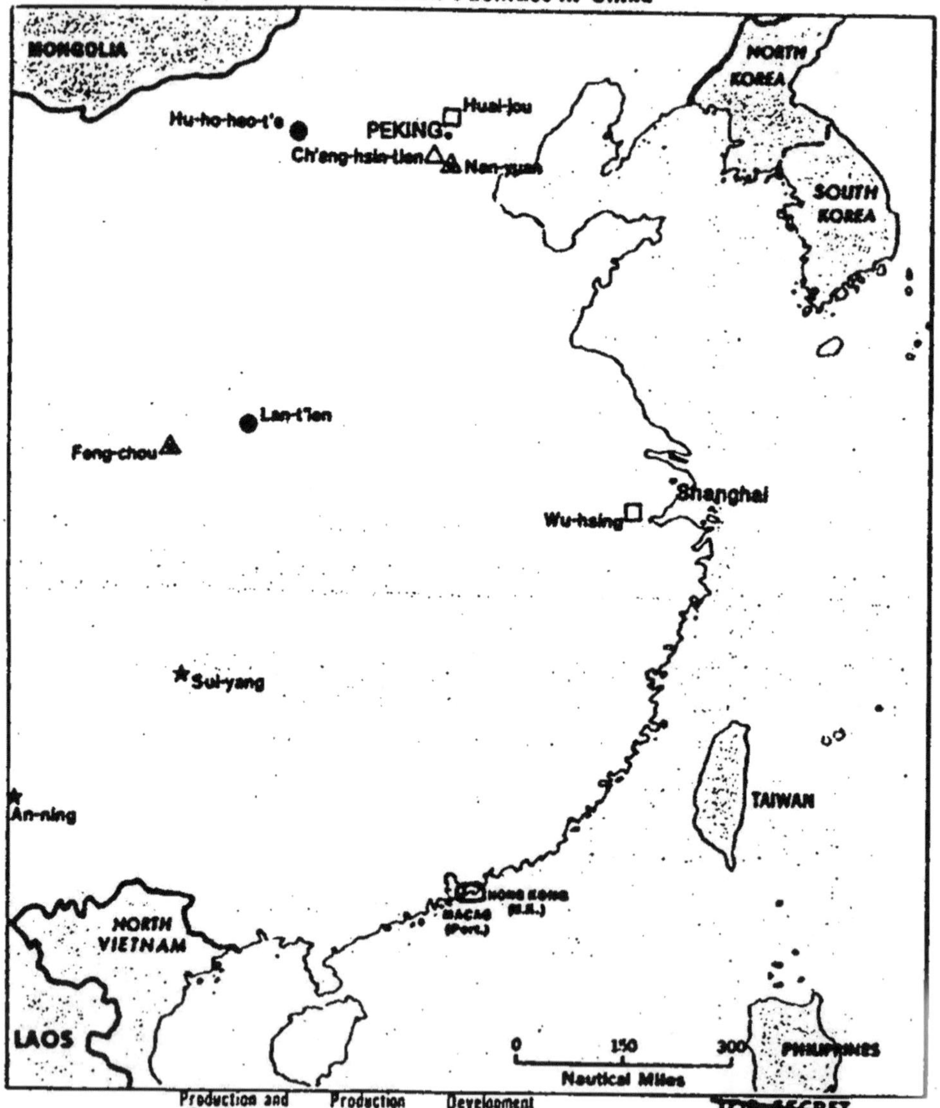

TOP SECRET
563456 6-74 CI

	Production and Development	Production	Development
Liquid propellant facility	—	△	△
Solid propellant facility	●	—	—
Facility associated with both liquid and solid propellants	—	—	□
Undetermined type of propellant facility	★	—	—

TOP SECRET

20   ~~TOP SECRET~~

other comparable large solid-propellant complex near Lan-t'ien in east-central China in the late 1960s. The overall appearance of this facility, particularly the identification there of three and possibly four static test stands, now indicates that, like Hu-ho-hao-t'e, it too is designed to develop and produce several different types of rocket motors, including at least some in the strategic class.

27. Static firing of several types of strategic-size rocket motors has been under way at Hu-ho-hao-t'e since the late 1960s. The rate of static testing appears slow and there is as yet no evidence that any solid-propellant missiles have been flight-tested. This slow progress may reflect a fairly long developmental timetable, at least by US standards. The Chinese may also have run into technical problems along the way. In any case, the Chinese have been working sufficiently long at Hu-ho-hao-t'e on large rocket motors to suggest that flight testing of a solid-propellant SLBM, as well as similar systems for use in the land-based missile program, could begin in the near future.

The Submarine-Launched Ballistic Missile Program [a]

The Missile

28. China's submarine-launched ballistic missile program made progress during the past year. Although flight testing of the missile has not yet begun, testing of a missile ejection or launch-assist device installed in China's G-class test-platform submarine probably has occurred since October 1972 in the Lu-shun area.

[a] For the position of the Director of Naval Intelligence, see the footnote on page 6.

30. On the basis of this evidence it is estimated that the first-generation Chinese SLBM will be a two-stage, solid-propellant system comparable in size to the early US Polaris and the French M-1 missiles.

The Chinese SLBM almost certainly will have only a soft target capability.

~~TOP SECRET~~

TOP SECRET

21

Handle via   Control Systems Jointly

TOP SECRET

22

~~TOP SECRET~~

Handle via   Control Systems Jointly

Estimated Performance and Characteristics of
the Chinese Submarine-Launched Ballistic Missile

Configuration	Two stage
Length	
Diameter	
Propellants	Solid

The Submarine

31. The Chinese probably intend to install their SLBM in a submarine with nuclear propulsion. China has designed and built at Hu-lu-tao a modern attack submarine, the Han class, which is probably nuclear powered. Its appearance in 1971 showed the Chinese have developed techniques for designing and building modern submarine hulls suitable for nuclear propulsion. There still is uncertainty, however, about China's success in developing a reliable nuclear propulsion system suitable for an SSBN. The Han apparently had propulsion difficulties which caused it to be returned to the shipyard for more than a year. If indeed it is nuclear powered, trouble-free operations over a longer period are needed to indicate a successful system.

32. China has adequate facilities for the assembly of SSBNs. There are at least five and possibly 11 building positions suitable for the assembly of large-diameter hulls in the construction hall at the Hu-lu-tao shipyard and two at the Kuang-chi shipyard.

Assuming that assembly of the lead SSBN takes about three or four years on the building ways, it is possible that an SSBN will be launched at Hu-lu-tao in 1974 or 1975. The construction hall at Kuang-chi is now finished, but the Chinese are not likely to launch a submarine there until late in the decade.

The System

33. It is still too early to determine with much confidence when China's first SLBM system will attain an operational capability. The pacing factor could well be the missile development effort. There is no evidence that SLBM flight testing has actually begun, but such firings could now be fairly near at hand. This testing is expected to be conducted from land-based facilities prior to any launches from a submarine. Initial launches are expected to occur from well-instrumented rangeheads such as Shuang-ch'eng'tzu or Wu-chai, especially in view of China's lack of experience in the solid-propellant area. After land-based flight tests, the G-class test submarine probably will participate in the flight test program.

34. A flight test program for an SLBM probably will take at least three years to complete, even if it is relatively trouble free. Therefore, if test firings begin soon, the missile is still unlikely to be ready for system integration with the first operational SSBN before about mid-1977. Allowing for a minimum of six months for full integration of the missile and submarine, the earliest IOC date would be 1978.[*] But, in view of the relatively lengthy flight test programs observed for land-based liquid-propellant systems and China's lack of experience in the flight testing of solid-propellant systems, IOC might be considerably later.

---

[*] For the position of the Director of Naval Intelligence, see the footnote on page 6.

~~TOP SECRET~~

TOP SECRET

Handle via

Control Systems Jointly

23

35. Thus far, there has been no evidence in China's oceanographic or geodetic activities to suggest a significant effort to support a ballistic missile submarine program. Over the past three or four years, however, some changes in Chinese marine programs have suggested the beginning of an effort to develop submarine operating areas or missile test ranges through acquisition of detailed gravity data and seabottom characteristics over an inceasingly broader sea area. Neither of the areas surveyed in detail—east of Shanghai and off south China—would substancially increase the target coverage already available to land-based missiles deployed on the mainland.

The Bomber Force

The TU-16 Strategic Bomber

36. Production of TU-16 jet medium bombers was suspended at least temporarily in 1973. The rate of production had declined from a high of about two aircraft per month in 1971 to a rate of one per month in 1972. It is too early to determine whether production will resume. If the suspension is permanent, the TU-16 may be the victim of a decision to limit investment in strategic weapons or a part of the overall cutback in aircraft production since late 1971.

Estimated Performance of the TU-16 Badger*

Load (pounds)	Combat radius (nm)
3,300	1,750
6,600	1,650
10,000	1,550

*The Chinese do not now have an aerial refueling capability. Their TU-16 is configured for refueling in flight but the Chinese have only one tanker, and there is no evidence that they are building tankers or practicing mid-air refueling.

37. About 60 TU-16s are currently operational at four bases, Wu-kung and Kung-ho in north-central China and Ta-t'ung and Sha-ho closer to Peking. (See Figure 7.) TU-16s have long been used in the nuclear testing program, and the entire force is considered capable of delivering any nuclear bomb in the Chinese inventory. The three TU-16s on the naval air force base at Sha-ho appear to have a maritime role and presumably also would be available for nuclear delivery.

38. The primary mission of the 18 TU-16s based at Ta-t'ung is not clear. They may have been based there temporarily pending completion of a new airfield at Wen-shui about 175 nm southwest of Peking. That airfield will have aircraft storage tunnels of a type built at Kung-ho and parking facilities typical of those at TU-16 bases. This suggests a plan in which almost all TU-16s would eventually be incorporated into a single force with a strategic nuclear attack mission and consisting of three elements, one each at Wu-kung, Kung-ho, and Wen-shui.

39. Alternativeiy, the TU-16s at Ta-t'ung might have a primary mission of conventional bombing, adding a longer range element to the conventional force. They would, however, retain a secondary mission of strategic nuclear attack. The absorption of the TU-16s into existing IL-28 regiments at Ta-t'ung instead of maintaining separate unit integrity supports this analysis.

40. Suspension of TU-16 production and the possible assignment of about a third of the force to a conventional bombing unit could

TOP SECRET

24 ~~TOP SECRET~~

Handle via   Control Systems Jointly

Figure 7

Strategic Missile and Bomber Deployment and Related Facilities

563404 6-74 CIA

~~TOP SECRET~~

TOP SECRET

Handle via   Control Systems Jointly   25

reflect a change in China's view of the utility of the TU-16 nuclear bomber force. Although China's original goal for the TU-16 force is unknown, a force much larger than the 50-60 aircraft now available would be necessary to penetrate to more than a few targets protected by modern air defenses such as those of the Soviet Union. There is no evidence of development of a follow-on bomber or a modification program to improve the TU-16's capabilities, but a future air-to-surface missile (ASM) program remains a possibility.

41. The TU-16 force may have been intended only to provide an interim capability for nuclear strikes at greater ranges than the first Chinese missiles could achieve. Deliveries of TU-16s to Ta-t'ung, for a possible conventional role, began in mid-1971, about the time that the CSS-2 IRBM—with range and payload comparable to the TU-16—reached IOC. Even if the TU-16 force does not grow in the future, the Chinese might elect to build tanker versions of the aircraft, or to configure some existing TU-16s as tankers. China obtained one such TU-16 from the Soviets in 1959, but has not built any. Tankers would allow the Chinese to extend the combat radius of the existing force and to use more advantageous attack profiles.

The IL-28 Light Bomber

42. The IL-28 is an old and vulnerable bomber but China still appears to consider it an important weapon system.

Estimated Performance of the IL-28 Beagle	
Load (pounds)	Combat radius (nm)
2,200	570
....	About 500

43. As yet, there is no evidence that operational units are being trained or equipped for a nuclear delivery role. There are about 100 airfields in China from which IL-28s could operate, and redeployment or staging from those airfields closest to the border would permit strategic operations against substantial portions of the Soviet Union, all of South Korea, and parts of South Vietnam and India. The limited range of the aircraft suggests that it might also be used in a theater support role within China. If it is to be used in that role, a weapon with a yield lower than the device tested in 1973 would be desirable.

The F-9

44. China currently has some 300 operational F-9 fighter-bombers, almost all of them assigned to ground attack units. The F-9 can carry a payload of some 2,200 pounds to a radius of nearly 450 nm, using external fuel. These capabilities are consistent with possible use in a theater nuclear role. The F-9 is the most likely aircraft in China's current operational inventory to receive tactical nuclear weapons. There is no convincing evidence, however, that the aircraft now has a nuclear capability.

The Nuclear Weapons Program

Nuclear Testing and Weapons Development

45. Developments since late 1972 indicate that there may have been some shifting of pri-

TOP SECRET

26 ~~TOP SECRET~~
Handle via   Control Systems Jointly

orities in China's nuclear weapons test program for the purpose of developing a weapon for delivery by the IL-28 light bomber against strategic targets.

Future Availability of Nuclear Weapons

49. China's capacity to produce fissionable materials is expanding. Construction is proceeding at its second gaseous diffusion plant, at Chin-k'ou-ho, and it is likely that this plant will become fully operational sometime in 1975. The Kuang-yuan plutonium reactor is continuing its cooling system tests prior to startup and should begin producing later this

~~TOP SECRET~~

year, and the new nuclear weapons fabrication complex at Tzu-t'ung is now complete and active. China's older nuclear sites appear to be active, and some are undergoing modest expansion. (See Figure 8.)

50. China's capacity for production of nuclear materials is roughly comparable to that of France. It is quite small compared to that of the US and USSR. Upon completion of the new production facilities in Szechwan China's annual U-235 capacity will be less than 10 percent of that of the Soviet Union, and its annual plutonium equivalent capacity no more than 15 percent of that of the Soviet Union. In terms of cumulative amounts, the Chinese stockpile is a small fraction of the Soviet and US stockpiles.

51. The future growth of the Chinese nuclear weapons stockpile will be governed not only by the availability of fissionable materials but also by the design of the nuclear weapons in the stockpile. Continued production of the type of weapons estimated now to be in stockpile—all of which use relatively large amounts of U-235—would minimize the size of the stockpile. At the same time, this would leave unused a growing surplus of plutonium, which could be used for additional weapons requiring less U-235 and more plutonium. If the Chinese were to continue to produce their current weapons and use the remaining plutonium for all-plutonium fission weapons, their future stockpile would include the all-plutonium weapons   A future stockpile combination of thermonuclear weapons with lesser amounts of U-235, composite fission weapons, and all-plutonium fission weapons would, however, appear more likely.

52. The Chinese could have many uses for the potentially large number of plutonium fission weapons that might be included in their stockpile by the end of this decade. In the light of their generally defensive posture, they might well stockpile low-yield fission weapons for tactical delivery by IL-28s, or F-9s, or for tactical missile systems that might be available by then. Other weapons for which they might want a nuclear capability include coastal defense missiles, depth charges, and quite possibly, atomic demolition munitions. There is, however, no specific evidence that they intend to develop a capability in these areas.

III. CHINA'S NUCLEAR ATTACK CAPABILITY

Forces and Capabilities

53. The Chinese now have a capability for nuclear strikes by missiles and bombers all around the periphery of China at distances up to 1,650 nm. (See Figure 9.) While most

28   TOP SECRET

Handle via   Control Systems Jointly

TOP SECRET

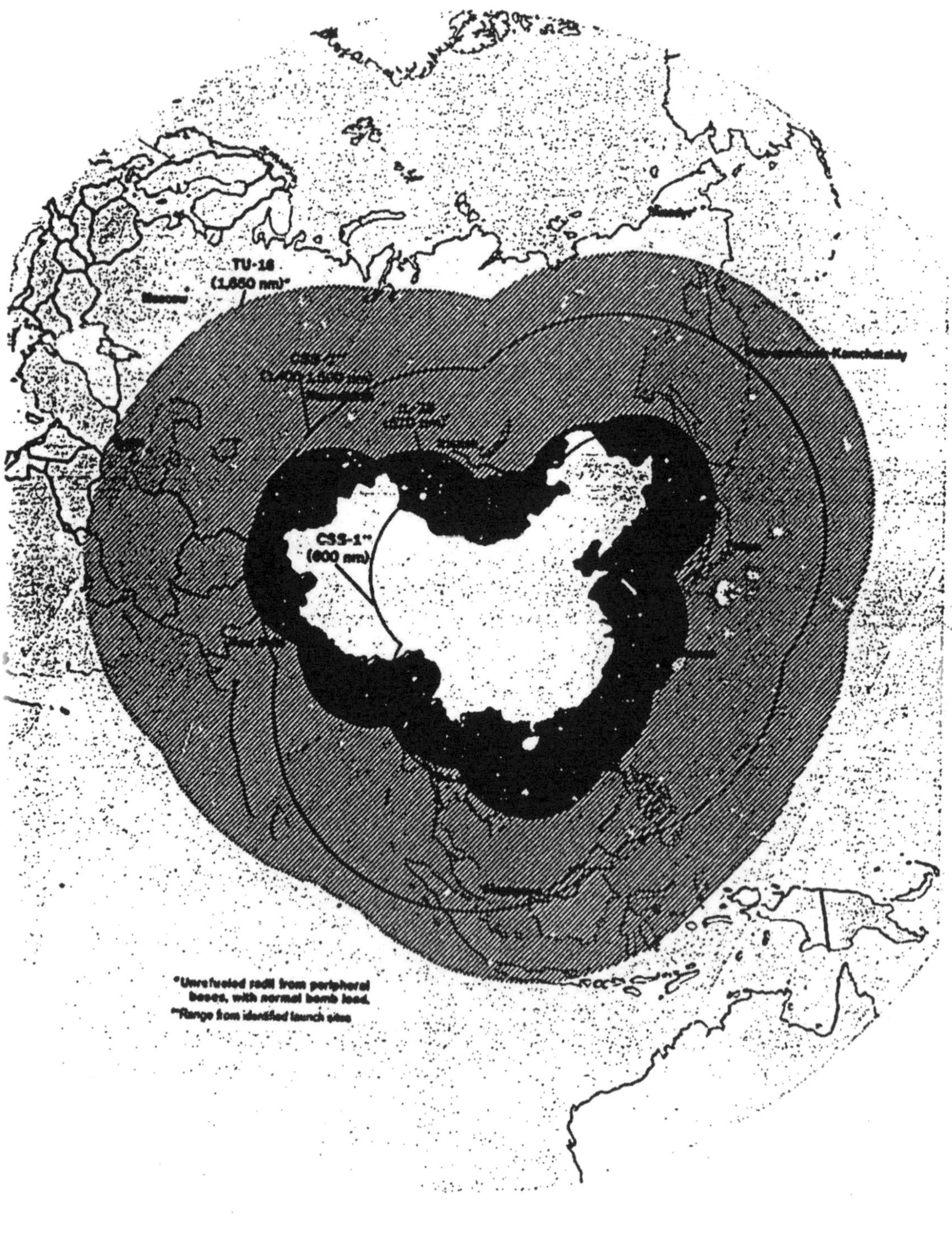

30

~~TOP SECRET~~

Handle via   Control Systems Jointly

of this capability has a strategic orientation, some of it is intended for a theater support role, including use within China's borders. At the present time, the Chinese are estimated to have operational:

—

—

—

— some 60 TU-16 Badger jet medium bombers, with an operating radius of 1,650 nm, deployed at four airfields. Although all of the force could be used for delivery of fission and thermonuclear bombs, about a third of this force might have conventional bomb delivery as its primary mission.

— a few of China's more than 400 IL-28 Beagle jet light bombers, with an operating radius of 570 nm, also may have a nuclear delivery capability.

The Chinese probably have enough nuclear warheads to equip all of the missiles, but it

may be that so far only some of the TU-16s and only a very few of the IL-28s have actually been allocated nuclear weapons.

54. Presently deployed Chinese missiles have a capability to strike all US bases and allies on the periphery of China. Launch sites for the CSS-1 and CSS-2 are grouped opposite South Korea and Japan, opposite Taiwan and Okinawa, and opposite the Philippines and Southeast Asia. While the CSS-1 covers only targets in the immediate area, CSS-2s are located so that the ones opposite Taiwan can cover Korea and much of Southeast Asia, and those opposite Korea and Indochina can cover Taiwan. The TU-16 bomber could cover all of these areas, as well as reconnoiter and attack US naval forces in the western Pacific. IL-28s could reach targets in Korea and Taiwan and, with staging from points close to the border, northern Luzon in the Philippines and nearly half of South Vietnam.

55. Most of China's presently deployed missiles can strike targets within the USSR. A number of CSS-1s in north and northeast China can hit the Soviet Union, including major bases and populated areas such as Vladivostok and Ussuriysk, and all the CSS-2s except a handful in southwest China can reach some part of southern Siberia and the Soviet Far East. The TU-16s have the range to reach targets in the USSR as far as the Urals from forward bases in China, though their capabilities to penetrate to heavily defended areas are limited. IL-28s could attack targets closer to the border.

56. A token capability to strike Soviet targets at greater ranges may be acquired, possibly by late 1974 or, more likely, in 1975. By then the Chinese may have completed two of the three silos under construction in central China and installed CSS-X-3 missiles in them.

~~TOP SECRET~~

TOP SECRET

31

Handle via   Control Systems Jointly

the CSS-X-3 has an estimated range of 3,000 to 3,500 nm. While the missile possibly could reach Moscow from two of the three silos, the missile could not reach any part of the US except a small part of Alaska. It could, however, reach several US bases in the central Pacific, including Guam. There is no evidence of preparations for deployment beyond the three silos now under construction.

57. The Chinese have no capability to attack the continental US directly and are unlikely to attain one for at least several years. The CSS-X-4 could not be operational until 1977 at the earliest. And an SSBN system will probably not be operational until 1978 at the earliest.[19] The Chinese do not seem to be pushing either of these programs with any particular urgency, and even if no technical difficulties develop, the actual IOCs of these systems are likely to be at least a year or more beyond these dates unless the pace of development increases markedly.

[19] For the position of the Director of Naval Intelligence, Department of the Navy, see the footnote on page 6.

TOP SECRET

32

~~TOP SECRET~~

Handle via   Control Systems Jointly

Strategy Underlying Deployment

64. The exigencies of China's security requirements have changed drastically over the years. Begun with Soviet assistance, the Chinese strategic program at first was predicated on the idea that the US was the main enemy. This probably held more or less true until the mid-1960s. But as Sino-Soviet relations worsened to the point where large Soviet forces were positioned on the border and bloody border clashes erupted in 1969, the Soviet Union became the chief threat. Chinese leaders make this fact clear by their frequently expressed concerns about Soviet intentions and by the thrust of their international policy.

65. To date, however, the deployment of Chinese strategic forces shows no overriding concentration on the Soviet threat. In part this is probably a reflection of the fact that a substantial part of the construction and other preparations for presently identified deployment was begun before Peking's perception of the threat shifted. The Chinese may also have feared that an obvious and extensive reaction to the Soviet threat would have been

~~TOP SECRET~~

TOP SECRET

Handle via   Control Systems Jointly   33

dangerous during a period of high tension. Still, in the several years since the Soviet threat became uppermost, there is no evidence of a resulting change in the pattern of deployment. The most recently started fixed missile launch sites are at Lien-k'eng-wang, where CSS-2s are optimally located for hitting both the USSR and US bases in Asia. Within the past two years, other CSS-2s have continued to be deployed at fixed sites in southwest China where they can reach US bases and India, but not the USSR. Thus it appears that the Chinese deployment programs have been influenced less by a particular threat and more by a general determination to develop a strike capability around the entire periphery of China.[11]

66. The Chinese have shown that they consider survivability to be crucial to the effectiveness of their nuclear deterrent. They have attempted to achieve survivability through a combination of concealment, mobility, and hardening. Currently operational missile units are deployed in a semimobile mode, moving from garrisons to temporarily occupied, inconspicuous field sites, and at fixed soft sites with tunnels to protect missiles and essential equipment but with unprotected launch pads.

---

[11] The Assistant Chief of Staff for Intelligence, Department of the Army, and the Assistant Chief of Staff, Intelligence, Department of the Air Force, disagree with paragraphs 64 and 65. They believe that the Soviet Union had replaced the US as China's primary strategic adversary well before the mid-1960s. They believe that all MRBM, IRBM, and TU-16 deployment has taken place during a period of primary concern for defense against Soviet attack. Present deployment patterns should be viewed not as an attempt to simultaneously threaten every potential adversary, but rather as an attempt to provide for a moderate amount of targeting flexibility while still deploying virtually every operational delivery vehicle against the threat of Soviet attack.

Concealment and camouflage are extensively employed at these launch areas. The protection from nuclear and conventional blast provided by the tunnels cannot be confidently estimated.

67. The Chinese are making some provision for survivability of their bomber force. They have dispersal airfields and have constructed tunnels for the protection of bombers at one of four existing TU-16 bases and at another base under construction. However, the force does not appear to have an operational alert system or an adequate warning system to enable aircraft to disperse on short notice. In the case of the IL-28s, the Chinese may be counting on the size and dispersion of the force to complicate enemy targeting.

68. Since 1971 the Chinese have not begun construction of any additional fixed missile sites. They may believe mobility, whenever feasible, offers a better probability that missiles would survive an attack than does deploying them at fixed sites subject to multiple coverage by many enemy weapons. While about 10 fixed sites for the CSS-2 are still under construction, there are indications that further deployment of the system may be in the semimobile mode.

TOP SECRET

666

34   ~~TOP SECRET~~

Handle via   Control Systems Jointly

and that some units, deep in their tunnels, could survive a Soviet nuclear attack. They may also believe that the Soviets could not count on destroying all of the nuclear delivery elements of the widespread Chinese bomber force. Consequently, the Chinese probably believe they now have acquired a modest but nonetheless credible nuclear retaliatory capability against the USSR.

72. But the Chinese no doubt feel that their deterrent force remains vulnerable in important respects:

— They have no effective means of detecting the approach of hostile ballistic missiles. They are working on a phased-array radar northwest of Peking that should provide some warning of attacks from most Soviet ICBM complexes. However, the short flight time of missiles launched from the Soviet Union would limit the amount of warning possible, and Soviet missile complexes in eastern Siberia are outside the radar's coverage.

— Missile force reaction times would range from less than an hour to several hours, depending on the system involved and its readiness condition.

71. How Peking judges Soviet ability to pinpoint all Chinese missile launchers is not known; the Chinese might, conservatively, overestimate Soviet abilities to locate missile sites. Even so, they probably believe that some of their semimobile units could not be targeted

73. Even a limited capacity for nuclear retaliation represents a major gain for a country which confronts powerful adversaries. Nevertheless, China might well judge that its present ability to deter nuclear attack by the Soviet Union or the US through the threat

~~TOP SECRET~~

~~TOP SECRET~~

Handle via   Control Systems Jointly

35

of retaliation posed by its nuclear strike force would be marginal if the stakes were high.

a. In the case of the *Soviet Union*, China's ability to deter nuclear attack would rest on Soviet fears for the security of some few cities in Siberia and the Soviet Far East, and perhaps on Soviet uncertainty about the existence of IRBM deployments in western China which might bring some cities in the Urals into range. China has no capability at present to threaten targets in the USSR west of the Urals, though it may soon acquire a token capability with the CSS-X-3.

b. In the case of the *United States*, China's ability to deter nuclear attack would rest on US fears for the security of a few US bases and cities of allies in the Far East. Although with the CSS-X-3 the Chinese could strike part of Alaska, the Chinese have no near-term prospect for a nuclear strike capability against the continental United States.

74. The Chinese have increased their options for deterring nuclear attack at the tactical end of the nuclear strike spectrum by establishing a capability to attack enemy targets on Chinese territory with nuclear weapons. This capability is probably intended both to deter an invading force and to provide an option to respond in a limited way to tactical use of nuclear weapons by an enemy without risking the political and military consequences of attacking targets on foreign soil.

IV. FUTURE FORCES

75. The current status of development and deployment programs permits reasonably confident estimates of the composition and size of China's nuclear delivery force within the next two years or so. Through at least 1976 the force will consist of some 40 short- and medium-range missiles and, by that year, the Chinese will probably have about 50 CSS-2s and a few CSS-X-3s in operational silos. As for bombers, most if not all of China's 60 TU-16s and a small fraction of its more than 400 IL-28s probably will have a strategic attack role. The total number of aircraft of these types probably will not increase much but that portion of the IL-28 force configured to deliver nuclear weapons probably will grow slowly, as will the number of nuclear weapons available for delivery.

76. An estimate of longer term prospects must take into consideration:

— that the CSS-X-4 and SLBM intercontinental systems still have major technical hurdles to surmount in their development programs before they can achieve IOC.

— that, by comparison with the US and Soviet programs, Chinese advanced weapon programs represent a small effort and slow progress.

— that the pace of the effort has been slowed further by Chinese decisions to adjust priorities in favor of building the economic base of the country.

— that Chinese judgments about priorities may have been influenced by a reappraisal of what was strategically feasible in the near term, and reinforced by their perception of a changed relationship among the US, USSR, and China.

— that, because of fundamental deficiencies in technical manpower and resources, China's ability to speed up its advanced weapons effort is limited.

~~TOP SECRET~~

TOP SECRET
Handle via

Control Systems Jointly

— that, nevertheless, the Chinese advanced weapons effort has ambitious long-term goals, as evidenced by the extensive facilities that have been established for the development and production of nuclear weapons and liquid- and solid-propellant missiles.

77. The scale and variety of the nuclear and missile development and production facilities that China has established indicate that its ultimate objective is to build a strategic nuclear capability befitting a major power. This is suggested by the breadth of the Chinese effort, which includes all the elements of a balanced strategic capability, as much as by its size. There is no reason to believe, however, that Peking aspires to match the capabilities of US and Soviet nuclear forces.

78. Subject to the constraining influences enumerated above, China's present objective probably is still to obtain a token nuclear capability to strike the USSR west of the Urals and the continental US. It is possible, however, that the Chinese will not carry out even this limited objective within the period of this estimate. For example, the Chinese might conclude that the present strategic environment requires an ICBM threat against the western USSR, but not a comparable capability against the US. In such a case, they might deliberately forego deploying a full-range ICBM, while continuing to use their large ICBM booster as a space launch vehicle and building a few SSBNs.

79. But their gradual past progress and the evidence of more ambitious longer term goals make it almost certain that the Chinese will work toward a force of nuclear delivery vehicles that, because of its size and surviva-

bility, will be a stronger deterrent to nuclear attack by either the US or the USSR. It is also reasonable to expect that China will seek to improve and somewhat expand its regional and tactical nuclear capability both to strengthen its regional deterrent and to increase its options for responding to limited nuclear attack.

80. In pursuing these objectives, it is not yet clear whether the Chinese will concentrate on liquid- or solid-propellant missile systems, or employ both; whether they will continue to emphasize systems suitable for a regional force, or stress their program to develop an intercontinental capability; or whether, to enhance force survivability, they will concentrate on missile systems suitable for semimobile or mobile deployment, or on systems relying on hardened facilities. The success of R&D efforts currently under way probably will have an important bearing on these decisions.

81. Guided by these considerations, two illustrative force mixes for the period mid-1974 through mid-1980 have been projected (see next two pages).

— The first (Case A) assumes continuation of present gradual deployment trends and eventual success with current development programs for an ICBM and an SSBN system. It assumes that continued slow progress with the CSS-X-4 ICBM might cause Peking to move ahead with some further deployment of the CSS-X-3. It also postulates that by the end of the decade the Chinese will have developed and will deploy a solid-propellant land-based system in the MRBM/IRBM category.

— The second projection (Case B) assumes earlier success with the systems currently

TOP SECRET

TOP SECRET

Handle via   Control Systems Jointly   37

in development, as well as with follow-on systems, and a somewhat faster rate of deployment. It also assumes that earlier deployment of second-generation systems will affect levels of deployment for the CSS-1 and CSS-2 and that the Chinese will not increase their deployment of the CSS-X-3, particularly in view of the likely availability of the CSS-X-4 to provide coverage of both Soviet and US targets.

Both projections assume that the Chinese will configure a growing number of IL-28s for a nuclear delivery mission and that there will not be a new strategic bomber during the period

of this estimate, although some limited further production of the TU-16 might occur.[13]

---

[13] The alternative force developments presented here represent possible directions that Chinese strategic attack forces could take. It should be emphasized that no one of them is to be considered an estimate that Chinese strategic attack forces will be composed of the particular weapon systems in the precise numbers listed. They are intended to be illustrative models of possible trends and differing emphases, and are developed primarily for broad policy use at the national level.

Case A: Continuation of Present Trends:
—Gradual Growth of Theater Support and Regional Forces
—Eventual Success with Programs to Develop Intercontinental Systems and Second-Generation Theater Support and Regional Systems

	1974	1975	1976	1977	1978	1979	1980
						(numbers at midyear)	
Land-based missile launchers							
SRBM	10	10	10	10	10	10	8
CSS-1	30	30	30	30	30	30	30
CSS-2	30	40	50	60	60	60	60
Solid MRBM/IRBM						5	10
CSS-X-3		2	3	3–6	3–6	3–12	3–12
CSS-X-4						2	6
3SBNs [a]						1	2
SLBM launchers						16	32
Bombers [b]							
TU-16	60	60–70	60–80	60–90	60–90	60–90	60–90
IL-28	3	10	20	30	40	50	50

---

[a] For the position of the Director of Naval Intelligence, Department of the Navy, see the footnote on page 6.

[b] Aircraft available as strategic weapon carriers. During the period of this estimate the Chinese probably will have available fission weapons suitable for tactical delivery by F-9 and IL-28 aircraft.

TOP SECRET

38   ~~TOP SECRET~~

Handle via   Control Systems Jointly

Case B: Accelerated Development and Deployment of Intercontinental
Systems and Second-Generation Theater Support and Regional
Systems.

	1974	1975	1976	1977	1978	1979	1980
					(numbers at midyear)		
Land-based missile launchers							
SRBM	10	10	10	10	10	10	8
2nd-generation SRBM	..	..	..	..	5	10	20
CSS-1	30	30	30	30	30	25	20
CSS-2	30	40	50	50	50	50	50
Solid MRBM/IRBM	..	..	..	..	5	10	20
CSS-X-3	..	2	3	3	3	3	3
CSS-X-4	..	..	..	2	10	20	30
SSBNs [a]	..	..	..	..	1	2	4
SLBM launchers	..	..	..	..	16	32	64
Bombers [b]							
TU-16	60	60–70	60–80	60–90	60–90	60–90	60–90
IL-28	3	19	20	40	60	60	60

[a] For the position of the Director of Naval Intelligence, Department of the Navy,
see the footnote on page 6.

[b] Aircraft available as strategic weapon carriers. During the period of this estimate
the Chinese probably will have available fission weapons suitable for tactical delivery
by F-9 and IL-28 aircraft.

82. Of the two projections, Case A is believed to approximate the more likely growth of Chinese forces in this decade. It is a better reflection of Chinese performance to date and we have no present basis for projecting any marked changes in this record of performance. IOCs and force levels on the order of those shown for Case B, while requiring more rapid progress and a larger investment of resources, are nevertheless within the bounds of China's capabilities. Both cases take account of what is known today about China's apparent mixed priorities for developing at least some operational capability to strike targets at various distances, including strategic targets in both the USSR and the US.[14]

[14] The Director, Defense Intelligence Agency, believes that there is a third case reflecting a lesser effort, which, although not shown, is just as likely as Case B. Such a projection should be included to reflect the full range of possibilities for China's nuclear forces. The "lower" case judgments are briefly mentioned in the estimate but are not represented here. A third force mix would project a reduced Chinese nuclear capability that concentrated on a more limited force. Intercontinental ballistic missile systems would be sacrificed at the expense of expanding other budgetary sectors.

~~TOP SECRET~~

TOP SECRET

Handle via   Control Systems Jointly

39

83. A great many variations of these cases are possible. For example, success with one weapon system—or failure with another—could lead to a shift of resource allocations to the more successful system to hasten its deployment. In addition, changes in China's perceptions of its strategic requirements or the impact of political and economic influences could affect the pace and scope of the strategic weapons program as a whole. It is not impossible that such influences will result in still another case, involving reduced Chinese effort. For example, as indicated in paragraph 78 above, the Chinese might decide to deploy an ICBM threat against the western USSR but not against the US.

Implications of Future Forces

84. *Capabilities Against the USSR.* If present missile development and deployment trends continue, as projected in Case A, by 1980 China's capability to survive nuclear attack and retaliate against targets in the eastern areas of the Soviet Union will be enhanced somewhat by enlargement of the MRBM and IRBM force from some 60 to about 100 missiles. With the addition of IL-28s to the nuclear strike force, well over 100 bombers are likely to be available as strategic weapons carriers. The first SLBM units will provide an emergency strike capability against targets in the Far East. The small force of about 9-18 ICBMs in silos that China might have by 1980 to threaten targets in European Russia would have little prospect of surviving a Soviet first strike and thus would have limited deterrent value. All things considered, however, China will have somewhat improved its capability to deter nuclear attack by the USSR.

85. In the less likely event that the Chinese make the accelerated progress in the development of intercontinental systems and second-generation regional missile systems indicated by Case B, they could have by 1980 a significant capability to deter nuclear attack by the USSR—a capability that they could feel fairly confident would deter Soviet nuclear attack unless the stakes were very high. Under this force assumption, the ability of China's regional nuclear forces to retaliate following nuclear attack will also have improved markedly. China's regional strike capability would number some 120 land-based missiles, not many more than in Case A but about one-third of them second-generation missiles with somewhat improved survivability and reaction time. The bomber force is unlikely to be very different from that of Case A. With some four SSBNs operational, China would be able to maintain one or two missile submarines on continuous patrol in the North Pacific but not in more distant seas within range of European Russia. This would significantly increase the number of missiles that would likely survive a Soviet first strike and be able to retaliate against Soviet targets in Asia. China also would have about 30 ICBMs in silos, a number probably large enough to make it uncertain in the calculations of Soviet military planners that some would not survive for retaliatory strikes against large populated areas in European Russia.

86. *Capabilities Against the US.* If present trends continue, by 1980 China will have a few, say 6, ICBMs capable of striking the continental US and from time to time probably would be able to place one missile submarine in position to strike targets in the western United States. This force would confer on China for the first time the ability to strike the continental US. This would have considerable political and psychological value. But the ICBM force would be small and

TOP SECRET

KV-371-254

Tolley's
Company Law

Edited
by
A. L. Chapman
LL.B (Lond.), F.T.I.I., Solicitor

and

R. M. Ballard
M.A.(Cantab.), Solicitor

Tolley Publishing Co. Ltd.

Whilst every care has been taken to ensure the accuracy of the contents of this work, no responsibility for any loss occasioned to any person acting or refraining from action as a result of any statement in it can be accepted by the editors, any of the authors or the publishers.

© 1983 Tolley Publishing Co. Ltd.

ISBN Hardback 0 85459 106-0
Paperback 0 85459 069-2

Published by
Tolley Publishing Co. Ltd. 209 High Street, Croydon, Surrey CR0 1QR.

Photoset by Computape (Pickering) Ltd, Pickering, North Yorkshire
and printed at The Pitman Press, Bath.

Preface

Whatever else our membership of the E.E.C. has brought, there is no doubt that it has provided plenty of grist for the mills of accountants and lawyers. Strange new animals like the "PLC" have arrived on the scene courtesy of Brussels, accompanied by such a quantity of legislation regulating the previously unregulated that company law now rivals tax law as one of the most complex and statute-laden areas of law

However, not all the new rules bear the stamp of Brussels. The hideously complicated rules on directors' loans and insider dealing are the direct result of Parliament intervening to stop abuses that the City of London was unable or unwilling to regulate. Both these subjects receive detailed treatment in this book, as do all the recent developments, particularly those incorporated in the Companies Acts of 1980 and 1981, including, for example, the new rules on dividends, directors' duties, disclosure of directors' dealings and purchases of own shares.

Throughout, the emphasis has been on the practical rather than the theoretical, with extensive use being made of tables and charts, although where the occasion demands an attempt has been made to deal with the more difficult aspects of a particular doctrine, statutory provision or decided case. The book has been written for practising lawyers and accountants and company secretaries, and as such it should attempt to provide answers to or guidance on the problems that arise in the real commerical world, which are rarely straightforward. Thus, in the chapter on financial assistance for acquisition of shares the reader will find 37 examples of transactions that either are or are not prohibited by the 1980 code.

Wherever possible, the reader is referred to the appropriate forms or procedures, for example, for incorporating a company or making a rights issue. Moreover, for Stock Exchange oriented subjects like prospectuses and takeovers, the City's own regulations are dealt with.

The book is a compilation, with its 42 chapters being contributed by the 17 practising lawyers and accountants listed below, who were chosen, and hopefully have demonstrated, that they know a good deal about their particular topics, even if like most of us, they would not claim to be a master of the whole of company law.

It is hoped that this will be the first of many editions of a book that attempts to provide practitioners with a working guide to what is now one of the most important and difficult branches of commercial law. Comments, criticisms and suggestions for its improvement will, therefore, be gratefully received.

Apart from the contributors, with whom it has been a pleasure to work, the editors thank Miss Wyn Brown for undertaking the task of preparing the tables of statutes and cases.

The law is stated as at March 1, 1983.

A.L.C.
R.M.B.

Contributors

R. M. Ballard, M.A. (Cantab.), Solicitor.

A. G. J. Berg, M.A. (Oxon.), Solicitor.

R. F. Berner, Solicitor.

A. P. M. Croome, M.A. (Cantab.), Solicitor.

P. D. Daniels, LL.B. (Dunelm.), Solicitor.

K. N. Dierden, B.A. (Soton.), A.T.I.I., Solicitor.

A. F. Douglas, LL.B. (Edin.), LL.M. (Lond.), Solicitor.

R. G. Fentiman, M.A. (Oxon.), B.C.L., Solicitor, Fellow and Lecturer in Law, Queens' College, Cambridge.

J. A. Freedman, B.A. (Oxon.), Solicitor.

M. I. Kingston, LL.B. (Manch.), Solicitor.

P. L. R. Mitchell, LL.B., Solicitor.

D. P. Morland, M.A., F.C.A.

J. E. Parkinson, M.A., Solicitor, Lecturer in Law, University of Bristol.

S. H. Rajani, Solicitor.

A. M. V. Salz, LL.B. (Exon.), Solicitor.

J. A. Sultoon, M.A. (Oxon.), Solicitor.

K. Wright, M.A., LL.B., Lecturer in Law, University of Reading.

Contents

Contents

Contents

Contents

Table of Cases

Table of Cases

Page

Table of Statutes

Page

Table of Statutes

Table of Statutory Instruments

Accounting Reference Date

The Companies Act 1976 introduced new rules requiring companies to prepare, lay and deliver their accounts by reference to "accounting reference periods". There are restrictions on a company's ability to alter that period.

Accounting reference date and period

A company may notify the Registrar of its accounting reference date within six months from the date of its incorporation (existing companies were entitled to give this notice up to October 1, 1977, the date section 1 of the Companies Act 1976 came into force). Notice is to be given on company Form No. 2. *Failing such notification the accounting reference date is March 31 in each year until any subsequent alteration.*

The *first* accounting reference period of a company is such period ending with the accounting reference date as,

(a) begins on the day after the date to which the profit and loss account last laid before the company in general meeting before section 1 of the 1976 Act came into force was made up; or

(b) if no profit and loss account was so laid, begins on the date of incorporation (C.A. 1976, s. 2).

This first accounting reference period will normally be for a period exceeding six months but not exceeding eighteen months (C.A. 1976, s. 2(4)).

Example 1
A company is incorporated on October 1, 1981 and does not notify an accounting reference date. The company will have a first accounting reference period which runs from October 1, 198▮ to March 31, 1983. Had the company been incorporated on 30 September, its first accounting period would have ended a year earlier, on March 31, 1982.

However, it is possible for the first accounting period to be for less than six months if the company takes steps under section 3 of the 1976 Act to shorten this period (see below).

Accounting reference periods subsequent to the first period begin after the end of the previous accounting reference period and end on the next accounting reference date. Except where a company alters its accounting reference date, succeeding periods will thus be of twelve months duration. Accounting reference periods can never exceed *eighteen* months (C.A. 1976, s. 3(5)).

1

Preparation of accounts

Every company is required to prepare a profit and loss account and balance sheet beginning with the day after the date to which its last accounts ended, and ending on the accounting reference date *or* within seven days before or after this. The seven day leeway allows a company to run, for example, a 52 or 53 week accounting period which always end on the last Friday of, say, June. For a newly-incorporated company the period for its first profit and loss account and balance sheet commences with the date of incorporation (C.A. 1976, s. 1(1) to s. 1(4)).

Period for laying accounts

A company must lay the profit and loss account and balance sheet before a general meeting and deliver them to the Registrar within the following periods:

(a) ten months after the end of the accounting reference period if it is a *private* company; or

(b) seven months after the end of the accounting reference period if it is a company other than a private company.

In either case the period may be extended by three months where the company carries on business, or has interests, outside the United Kingdom, the Channel Islands and the Isle of Man. To obtain the extension the company must give notice to the Registrar claiming the extension in respect of each accounting reference period on Form No. 2.

For newly incorporated companies where the first accounting reference period exceeds twelve months from the date of incorporation, the period allowed for laying and delivering accounts in reduced by the number of days by which the accounting reference period exceeds twelve months. However, the newly incorporated company is always to have a minimum period of three months after the end of the accounting reference period to lay and deliver accounts.

> *Example 2*
> Facts as in Example 1. With a October 1, 1981 incorporation date, the company has a first accounting period of eighteen months. If it is a private company, it has four months after March 31, 1983 to lay and deliver the accounts. If it is a public company, the period will be three months.

Where a company gives notice to shorten its accounting reference period (see below), the period allowed for laying and delivering the accounts in respect of the shortened period is the seven or ten month period allowed in respect of the new accounting reference period *or* a period of three months beginning with the date of the notice, whichever period is longer.

> *Example 3*
> Facts as in Example 1. On February 15, 1983 the company serves a notice specifying June 30 as the company's accounting reference date. The company's first accounting

reference period will thus be shortened to end on June 30, 1982. The period for laying and delivering the accounts will not expire until May 15, 1983, whether the company is a public or a private company.

Section 1 of the 1976 Act provides that the above rules as to the laying and delivering of the profit and loss account and balance sheet extend to the auditors report and directors report which, by sections 156 and 157 of the 1948 Act, are to be attached to the balance sheet.

Unlimited companies are exempted from the obligation to deliver accounts to the Registrar provided certain conditions are met.

If accounts are not laid and delivered within the time limits mentioned above, every director of the company commits a criminal offence, punishable with a fine of up to £400 plus £40 for each day the default continues. It is a defence for a director to show he personally took all reasonable steps to secure compliance with the obligation to lay and deliver the accounts *before* the time limits expired. Where accounts are filed with the Registrar late, the company can also be liable to a fine of up to £450 (C.A. 1976, s. 4(4)). Where a company has not filed its accounts the Registrar, or a member or creditor of the company, may apply to the court for a default order against the directors (C.A. 1976, s. 5(5)). Failure to deliver accounts to the Registrar, or conviction under section 4 of the 1976 Act, can result in a director being disqualified to act as such under section 188 of the Companies Act 1948 (and see *Re Civica Investments Ltd., Financial Times*, June 8, 1982).

Alteration of accounting reference period

A company may alter its accounting reference date by giving notice to the Registrar (C.A. 1976, s. 3). Generally, it is only possible to alter the accounting reference date for the *current* and future periods. Section 3(1) enables a notice of change to be given at any time *during* an accounting reference period. Notice is given on Form No. 3.

In one circumstance however notice may be given *after* the end of the last accounting reference period to apply to that period and future periods (s. 3(2)). This is if,

(i) the company is a subsidiary or holding company of another company and the new accounting reference date coincides with that other company; and

(ii) the period allowed for laying and delivering accounts in relation to the previous accounting reference period has not expired before the notice is given.

Notice is given on Form No. 3a.

The Form No. 3 or 3a must state whether the current or previous accounting reference period, as the case may be, is to be treated as shortened or extended.

There is no minimum period for which an accounting reference period may run. In other words, a company can *shorten* its accounting

reference period as much as it likes, but the Form 3 must state that the
accounting reference date is being brought forward.

Example 4
A company's accounting reference date is December 31. On June 30, 1982 the
company serves notice altering its accounting reference date to May 31. The effect
will be that the accounting reference period commencing on January 1, 1982 will run
to May 31, 1982 if Form 3 states that the period is being shortened, or to May 31,
1983 if the form states that the period is being extended.

There are two restrictions on the *extension* of an accounting reference
period, whether it is a current or the immediately preceding period.
First, it is not permissible to extend a period to a length which would
exceed 18 months. Secondly, unless the Secretary of State directs
otherwise, an accounting reference period may not be extended unless,

(a) *no* earlier accounting reference period has been extended by a
    previous notice; or

(b) the notice is given at least five years after the date on which any
    earlier accounting reference period of the company which was so
    extended came to an end; or

(c) the company is a subsidiary or holding company of another
    company and the new accounting reference date coincides with the
    accounting reference date of that other company (sections 3(6) and
    3(7)).

This means that a company is not normally able to extend its accounting
reference period more than once every five years.

It is never possible for a company to alter an accounting reference
period which has already ended except for the one which has just ended.

The end of an accounting reference period will usually herald the end of
an accounting period of a company for the purposes of corporation tax,
though a tax accounting period can never exceed twelve months (Taxes
Act 1970, s. 247). Where the company is a subsidiary of a group and is
about to be sold, there may be an advantage in closing the accounting
reference period early to avoid tax group relief problems under the
anti-avoidance provisions in section 29 of the Finance Act 1973.

Overseas companies

Companies incorporated outside Great Britain, but with a place of
business within Great Britain, must also prepare accounts and deliver a
copy to the Registrar by reference to their accounting reference period.
As might be expected, there is no requirement as to the laying of the
accounts before a general meeting or equivalent. An overseas company's accounting reference period is determined as for a Great Britain
company, except that references to the date of incorporation are
substituted by the date on which the company established a place of
business in Great Britain. Notification of an accounting reference date

on or within six months of establishing a place of business in the U.K., or of a change of date (see below), is made on company Forms Nos. F7, F7a and F7b.

If in a language other than English, the accounts delivered to the Registrar must have annexed a certified copy translated into English (C.A. 1976, s. 1(7)). The accounts must be delivered to the Registrar within thirteen months after the end of the accounting reference period, otherwise the company, and every *officer or agent* of the company who knowingly and wilfully authorises or permits the default, commits a criminal offence punishable on summary conviction by a fine not exceeding £400 plus £40 per day.

An overseas company may alter its accounting reference date in the same way as a Great Britain company, except that it may extend a current or the last preceding period as often as it chooses.

Accounts

This chapter deals with the following topics:

A   Accounting records
B   Form and content of accounts: general principles
C   Balance sheet requirements
D   Profit and loss account requirements
E   Notes to the accounts
F   Holding companies and subsidiaries
G   Filing exemptions for small and medium-sized companies
H   Special classes of company
I   Transitional rules.

A separate chapter, *Directors' Report*, deals with the directors' report, including the requirements of the Stock Exchange for the directors' report of listed companies.

A   Accounting records

Section 12(1) of the Companies Act 1976 requires *every* "company" (i.e. every company within the meaning of section 455(1) of the Companies Act 1948) to keep *accounting records*. Section 12(2) states simply that those records must be sufficient "to show and explain the company's transactions". However, sections 12(3) and 12(4) go on to amplify this general obligation by imposing the following requirements:

(1) the records must disclose with reasonable accuracy the *financial position* of the company at any particular time;

(2) the records must be such as to enable the directors to ensure that any balance sheet and profit and loss account they prepare under section 1 of the Companies Act 1976 (see the chapter *Accounting Reference Date*, earlier) complies with section 149 of the Companies Act 1948. Section 149, as amended by the 1981 Act, sets out in detail the form in which a company's accounts must be prepared, and provides an overriding requirement that the accounts give a "true and fair view" (see page 11);

(3) the records must contain entries from day-to-day which show all moneys paid and received by the company and which identify the underlying transactions;

(4) the records must also contain a record of the assets and liabilities of the company;

(5) also, where the company deals in "goods", the records must include a statement of the stock held by the company at the end of each financial year (a financial year being the period to which the company's accounting reference period runs, which may not be a full calendar year: C.A. 1976, s. 1). The records must include all the stocktaking statements from which the above closing stock statement is made, and statements allowing the buyers and sellers of all goods to be identified (*except* for goods sold "by way of ordinary retail trade").

Interpretation of section 12

The Auditing Practices Committee of the C.C.A.B. has taken Counsel's opinion on certain points of difficulty arising out of section 12. Set out below is a summary of the main points covered in the opinion.

Section 12(3)

Question 1

Section 12(3)(a) requires the accounting records to "*disclose* with reasonable accuracy, *at any time*, the *financial position* at that time". What does the phrase the "financial position" of a company mean?

Answer

In requiring that the accounting records be sufficient to disclose the *financial position* of the company, the 1976 Act recognises that it is not practicable to draw up financial statements giving a "true and fair" view at any time during the year. The concept of "true and fair" is extremely wide and embraces information not necessarily contained within the accounting records themselves. Nevertheless, the Act has installed the requirement that the directors should have available to them an adequate statement "at any time" of the company's financial position, even though this is drawn up to a less rigorous standard than the "true and fair" requirement of the company's annual statutory accounts.

This subsection appears to require more than mere disclosure of the cash position (as shown in the cash book) and would seem to indicate that the directors should be in a position to prepare a statement showing, in addition, the other tangible assets, liabilities and pre-tax results with reasonable accuracy. It follows that in order to do this it will be necessary to be able to form a reasonable estimate of the company's stock position, but this does not necessarily require a physical stocktaking or maintenance of continuous detailed stock records. The method by which the estimate of stock is arrived at will be a matter for judgement, depending on the circumstances.

There appear to be three ways in which an estimate of stock may be reached, depending on the circumstances of the business:

(a) By the use of gross profit margins applied to sales arriving at a cost of stock sold (this may be appropriate if a business has a limited number of product lines and works on the basis of fixed profit percentage).

(b) By maintaining detailed records of cost of sales. In this way the cost of sales may be accurately determined and a residual stock figure arrived at.

(c) By maintaining detailed stock records so as to enable a stock valuation to be performed at any time and used in the compilation of gross margin in the form of a traditional trading account.

The Act clearly recognises that it would be impracticable for the raw data contained in the accounting records to present the true and fair view of the state of affairs and results required for annual accounts purposes.

Question 2
How is the financial position "disclosed" pursuant to section 12(3)(a)?

Answer
Records must be maintained which provide the basic information from which the financial position can be ascertained. It is suggested that "disclosure" does not mean that the financial position needs to be displayed after each transaction has been recorded, but that the information from which a statement of the financial position can be prepared is available.

Question 3
Is the phrase "at any time" in section 12(3)(a) to be taken literally?

Answer
Yes, in so far that the accounting records should be capable of disclosing the necessary information at any point in time. This information does not need to be recorded instantaneously, but should be in a form sufficient to enable a statement showing the financial position at any selected date to be drawn up.

Section 12(4)

Question 4
Section 12(4) requires the *accounting records* to show receipts and payments of money from *day-to-day*, and to contain a record of the *assets and liabilities of the company*. What are "accounting records"?

Answer
Accounting records comprise the orderly collection and identification of the information in question, rather than a mere accumulation of documents.

The accounting records need not be in book form; they may take the form of, for example, a loose-leaf binder or computer tape; it will even be sufficient if the books of prime entry are in the form of a secure clip of invoices with an add-list attached. The essence of the matter is that the information recorded is organised and labelled so as to be capable of retrieval. A carrier-bag full of invoices will not suffice.

Question 5
Does "day-to-day" mean hourly, daily, weekly or monthly?

Answer
Normally, the cash book taken together with the day books and ledger will provide the information required under section 12(4)(a). Clearly, transactions cannot be recorded instantaneously. What is necessary is that when the entries are made, each transaction is shown separately and is identified by its date and an explanation of the matter in respect of which it takes place. In the case of retail shops it is likely that a record of the total day's cash takings will suffice.

Question 6
What is meant by "a record of assets and liabilities"?

Answer
The subsection states that the accounting records shall in particular contain "a record of the assets and liabilities of the company". Therefore, details must be included of all the company's assets and liabilities, such as debtors, creditors and plant. There is no express requirement that this record should be updated on a day-to-day basis, but the requirement clearly is that a person looking at the accounting records can find recorded therein what are the assets, and what are the liabilities, of the company at any particular time. For this purpose the relevant records must be updated at frequent intervals and must contain information as to dates of acquisitions and disposals of assets and of the incurring and discharge of liabilities. This sub-section specifically excludes stocks, which are dealt with below.

Section 12(5)

Question 7
Section 12(5) requires a company dealing in goods to prepare and keep certain statements as to stock. What stock records form part of the accounting records as defined in section 12?

Answer
The need to be able to estimate stock in order to provide information from which to prepare a statement showing the company's financial position has been dealt with above. Subsection (5) requires that statement of stock held at each financial year-end be retained. For this purpose, the term "statement of stock" is taken to mean a summary supporting the amount included in the accounts in respect of stock. It is further required that the stocktaking records which support the year-end stock summary – whether these be annual, perpetual or the year-end – shall also be retained. It will be seen that the Act imposes an obligation to retain documentation supporting year-end stock valuations, but allows considerable flexibility in meeting the requirement to disclose the "at any time" financial position.

Question 8
Section 12(5)(c) requires the stock records to enable the buyers and sellers of all goods, except goods sold by way of ordinary retail trade, to be identified. How detailed should the records of transactions with sellers, goods and buyers be to comply with subsection (5)(c)?

Answer
The intention of the Act appears to be to ensure that the substance of transactions is properly recorded. In the case of products where the individual item identity of the product is irrelevant to the seller and purchaser, product type identity will normally be sufficient, whereas in the case of goods where the identity of the individual item is relevant, each particular item will need to be identified. In practical terms, this section is unlikely to impose a greater obligation than that already imposed by VAT regulations, or the commercial needs of the business. The identity of vendor and purchaser will normally be available from purchase and sales ledgers.

Location of accounting records

Generally, the accounting records are to be kept in Great Britain, either at the registered office of the company or at such other place as the directors consider fit (section 12(6)). The records must be open at all times to inspection by the officers of the company. (Note that a shareholder generally has no right of inspection, save as may be contained in the company's articles: see for instance Article 125 of Table A.)

A company is however permitted to keep its accounting records outside Great Britain. But the company must then send certain accounts and returns to be kept at a place in Great Britain, where the company's officers may inspect them. These accounts and returns must disclose the "financial position" of the business with reasonable accuracy at six monthly intervals, and be sufficient to allow the company's directors to ensure that the company's balance sheet and profit and loss account comply with section 149 of the 1948 Act (section 12(7), 12 (8)).

Preservation of accounting records

The accounting records which a company is required to keep by section 12 must be preserved for the following periods from the date they are made:

(a) *private company*: three years;

(b) *any other company*: six years.

This is subject to any direction as to the disposal of records given by rules made under section 365(1) of the 1948 Act (winding up rules). Note that, for *value added tax* purposes, records need only be kept for three years (Finance Act 1972, s. 34).

Penalties

If a company fails to prepare and keep accounting records as required by section 12 every director, manager or secretary who is in default is guilty of a criminal offence, punishable on indictment with up to two years imprisonment, or a fine or both, or with six months imprisonment or a fine of up to £400, or both, on summary conviction (section 12(10), 12(11)). It is a defence against the company not having prepared proper accounting records that the person acted honestly and that "in the circumstances in which the business of the company was carried on the default was excusable".

If a director, manager or secretary fails to take all reasonable steps to secure that the company complies with the time limits for preserving the accounting records, or intentionally causes a default by the company, he is guilty of a criminal offence, punishable in the same way as a failure to prepare and keep the records in the first place (s. 12(10), 12(11)).

Failure to comply with section 12 could in certain circumstances result in the disqualification of a director under section 188 of the 1948 Act (disqualification by court for up to 15 years for conviction of an indictable offence in connection with the management of a company).

B.   Form and content of accounts: general principles

As explained on page 2, section 1 of the Companies Act 1976 requires accounts to be prepared, laid before a general meeting and filed by every company, for each accounting reference period. The obligation extends to overseas companies. The accounts comprise a balance sheet and a profit and loss account, made up to the accounting reference date. The Companies Act 1948, as amended by the 1981 Act, lays down detailed statutory rules as to the form and content of these two accounts.

The requirements in outline

Section 149 of the 1948 Act requires each of the balance sheet and the profit and loss account to,

(1) be drawn up under either the *historic cost* convention or under certain *current cost* methods;

(2) be prepared in accordance with one of various *formats* prescribed by Schedule 8 to the Act;

(3) be drawn up in accordance with certain general *accounting principles*;

(4) contain the *information* set out in Schedule 8;

(5) provide additional information, as required by Schedule 8, by way of *notes* to the accounts; and

(6) give a *"true and fair view"*.

The provisions of section 149 and Schedule 8 are extended to group accounts, subject to certain amendments.

(1) *Historic cost and current cost methods*

Schedule 8 permits a company either to prepare its accounts under the historical cost convention (section B of Schedule 8), or under current cost methods (section C of Schedule 8). The EEC Fourth Directive, on which Schedule 8 is based, assumes that most accounts will be drawn up under the historical cost convention, but permits national legislation to allow inflation accounting. The effect of section C of Schedule 8, which is purely permissive, is to permit accounts to be prepared in any of the following three ways:

(a) under the historic cost convention;

(b) under the historic cost convention, but with selective revaluation of assets; or

(c) under current cost methods.

The alternative accounting rules in section C are not, however, simply a statutory enactment of SSAP 16, the accountancy bodies' standard accounting principles for current cost accounting. First, the section C rules permit a range of alternative accounting rules. Secondly, the section C rules apply to the accounts (balance sheet and profit and loss account) which a company is required by statute to prepare, but as explained are purely *permissive*. SSAP 16 *requires* a company within its scope to prepare current cost accounts, but these can be in a supplementary statement, not in the statutory accounts. Only where a company within SSAP 16 prepares its statutory accounts on a current cost basis must those accounts comply with section C of Schedule 8.

In broad outline, where advantage is not taken of section C and accounts are prepared under the historic cost rules in section B the following rules apply.

(a) *Fixed assets* are to be included at their purchase price or production cost. In addition:

    (i)   depreciation must be applied to write off fixed assets over their useful economic lives;

    (ii) goodwill can only be included if acquired for valuable consideration. There is no obligation to include goodwill in the balance sheet, but where it is included it must be depreciated over its useful economic life (except for goodwill arising on consolidation, in *group* accounts: see below);

    (iii) development costs may only be capitalised in special circumstances. Research costs may never be capitalised. (Note that SSAP 13, which deals with accounting for research and development, sets out detailed requirements for development costs to be capitalised.)

(b) *Current assets* are to be included at the lower of cost (i.e. purchase price or productive cost) or net realisable value.

If instead a company wishes to take advantage of the current cost rules in section C of Schedule 8 it may adopt the following basis of valuation:

(a) *intangible fixed assets*: current cost, except that goodwill can only be shown at acquisition cost, less any depreciation;

(b) *tangible fixed assets*: current cost *or* market value;

(c) *investments*: market value *or* an indexed valuation considered by the directors to be appropriate to the company's circumstances;

(d) *current assets*: current cost.

Where a company departs from the historical cost rules, it must give certain information in the notes to its accounts (see E, *Notes to the Accounts*, on page 44).

(2) *The prescribed formats*

Schedule 8 requires a company to prepare its balance sheet and profit and loss account under prescribed formats. There are two alternative formats for the balance sheet and four for the profit and loss account. A company is free to choose whichever formats it wishes, but having chosen a company may only adopt a different format if the directors consider there are special reasons for a change (when the notes to the accounts must contain certain information: see E, *Notes to the Accounts*, on page 44).

Under the balance sheet formats, Format 1 adopts the more usual vertical style of presentation, which allows net assets to be shown, balanced by share capital and reserves. Format 2 uses the horizontal style. Format 1 is as set out below. (Format 2 can be found in Appendix 1.)

Balance sheet – Format 1

A **Called up share capital not paid**

B **Fixed assets**
   I   Intangible assets
       1 Development costs
       2 Concessions, patents, licences, trade marks and similar rights and assets
       3 Goodwill
       4 Payments on account
   II   Tangible assets
       1 Land and buildings
       2 Plant and machinery
       3 Fixtures, fittings, tools and equipment
       4 Payments on account and assets in course of construction

III Investments
   1   Shares in group companies
   2   Loans to group companies
   3   Shares in related companies
   4   Loans to related companies
   5   Other investments other than loans
   6   Other loans
   7   Own shares

C   Current assets
I   Stocks
   1   Raw materials and consumables
   2   Work in progress
   3   Finished goods and goods for resale
   4   Payments on account
II Debtors
   1   Trade debtors
   2   Amounts owed by group companies
   3   Amounts owed by related companies
   4   Other debtors
   5   Called up share capital not paid
   6   Prepayments and accrued income
III Investments
   1   Shares in group companies
   2   Own shares
   3   Other investments
IV Cash at bank and in hand

D   Prepayments and accrued income

E   Creditors: amounts falling due within one year
   1   Debenture loans
   2   Bank loans and overdrafts
   3   Payments received on account
   4   Trade creditors
   5   Bills of exchange payable
   6   Amounts owed to group companies
   7   Amounts owed to related companies
   8   Other creditors including taxation and social security
   9   Accruals and deferred income

F   Net current assets (liabilities)

G   Total assets less current liabilities

H   Creditors: amounts falling due after more than one year
   1   Debenture loans
   2   Bank loans and overdrafts
   3   Payments received on account
   4   Trade creditors
   5   Bills of exchange payable
   6   Amounts owed to group companies
   7   Amounts owed to related companies
   8   Other creditors including taxation and social security
   9   Accruals and deferred income

I **Provisions for liabilities and charges**
   1 Pensions and similar obligations
   2 Taxation, including deferred taxation
   3 Other provisions

J **Accruals and deferred income**

K **Capital and reserves**
   I   Called up share capital
   II   Share premium account
   III Revaluation reserve
   IV Other reserves
       1 Capital redemption reserve
       2 Reserve for own shares
       3 Reserves provided for by the articles of association
       4 Other reserves
   V   Profit and loss account

Under the profit and loss account formats, there is again a choice between the vertical style (Formats 1 and 2) and a horizontal style (i.e. separating charges from income). In addition, expenses may be classified by *function* (e.g. cost of sales: Formats 1 and 3) or by type (e.g. raw materials: Formats 2 and 4). One of the two vertical styles, Formats 1 and 2, will probably be most commonly used. These two Formats are set out below; Formats 3 and 4 are set out in Appendix 1.

Profit and loss account – Format 1

1 Turnover
2 Cost of sales
3 Gross profit or loss
4 Distribution costs
5 Administrative expenses
6 Other operating income
7 Income from shares in group companies
8 Income from shares in related companies
9 Income from other fixed asset investments
10 Other interest receivable and similar income
11 Amounts written off investments
12 Interest payable and similar charges
13 Tax on profit or loss on ordinary activities
14 Profit or loss on ordinary activities after taxation
15 Extraordinary income
16 Extraordinary charges
17 Extraordinary profit or loss
18 Tax on extraordinary profit or loss
19 Other taxes not shown under the above items
20 Profit or loss for the financial year

Profit and loss account – Format 2

1 Turnover
2 Change in stocks of finished goods and in work in progress
3 Own work capitalised
4 Other operating income
5 (*a*) Raw materials and consumables
   (*b*) Other external charges
6 Staff costs:
   (*b*) wages and salaries
   (*b*) social security costs
   (*c*) other pension costs
7 (*a*) Depreciation and other amounts written off tangible and intangible fixed assets
   (*b*) Exceptional amounts written off current assets
8 Other operating charges
9 Income from shares in group companies
10 Income from shares in related companies
11 Income from other fixed asset investments
12 Other interest receivable and similar income
13 Amounts written off investments
14 Interest payable and similar charges
15 Tax on profit or loss on ordinary activities
16 Profit or loss on ordinary activities after taxation
17 Extraordinary income
18 Extraordinary charges
19 Extraordinary profit or loss
20 Tax on ordinary profit or loss
21 Other taxes not shown under the above items
22 Profit or loss for the financial year

In sections C and D below, which set out in detail the statutory requirements for the balance sheet and profit and loss account, the text follows the Format 1 style. Section D, dealing with the profit and loss account, also however includes references to Format 2 items, because the vertical profit and loss Format 1 and Format 2 styles differ slightly in content.

As will be noted from Format 1 above, each item in the two balance sheet Formats is preceded by either a letter of the alphabet or a Roman or Arabic numeral. As explained in section C, *Balance Sheet Requirements*, below, an item preceded by a letter or a Roman numeral must generally be shown as such on the face of the balance sheet. Items assigned an Arabic numeral may (a) be rearranged or adapted, where the special nature of a company's business so requires, or (b) combined, if not material or combination assists clarity.

The items in each of the profit and loss account formats are preceded by an Arabic number, and so the rules outlined in the preceding paragraph, permitting rearrangement, adaption, or combination, apply (see section D, *Profit and Loss Account Requirements*, below).

(3) *Accounting principles*

Schedule 8, as amended, now gives statutory effect to certain general accounting principles. Prior to June 15, 1982, these general principles, though contained in the statements of standard accounting policies ("SSAP's") issued by the accountancy bodies and thus generally adopted in accounts, did not have statutory force. There are six fundamental principles contained in Schedule 8. The first four are those previously contained, in non-statutory form, in the accounting bodies' SSAP 2, dealing with the disclosure of accounting policies. The Schedule 8 principles are,

(a) a company is presumed to be a *going concern* (paragraph 10 of Schedule 8);

(b) all income and charges for the financial year to which the accounts relate must be *accrued*, regardless of the actual time of receipt or payment (paragraph 13);

(c) *"prudence"* must be exercised so that only realised profits are included in the profit and loss account, and all liabilities and losses which have arisen or are likely to arise in respect of the relevant financial year are to be taken into account (including post-balance sheet date events; paragraph 12);

(d) accounting policies must be applied *consistently* from one financial year to the next (paragraph 11);

(e) it is not permissible to *set off* amounts representing assets or income against amounts representing liabilities or expenditure, or vice-versa (paragraph 5); and

(f) in determining the *aggregate amount* of any item in the accounts, the amount of each component item must be determined separately (paragraph 14).

The directors of a company may depart from principles (a) to (d), and principle (f), but only if there are special reasons for doing so. Those reasons, and the effect of the departure, must be given in the notes to the accounts (see section E below).

Accounting policies on matters other than those listed above are in general governed by the accounting bodies' SSAP's. These are non-statutory. However, paragraph 36 of Schedule 8 requires those policies to be disclosed in the notes to the accounts (see section E, *Notes to the accounts*, below).

Although the SSAP's are non-statutory, the U.K. accounting bodies expect their members to observe them. In general they apply to all companies, ttough some SSAP's do not apply to companies below a certain size (e.g. SSAP 10, requiring a statement of the source and application of funds, does not apply to companies with a turnover or gross income below £25,000, and SSAP 16, current cost accounting, applies only to listed companies or companies above a certain size).

They may be departed from only in special circumstances. A list of the SSAP's currently in force, and of proposed SSAP's currently at Exposure Draft (ED) stage, is contained in Appendix 2. Appendix 2 also includes the explanatory forward to the SSAP's issued by the accounting bodies.

Whilst, therefore, Schedule 8 to the 1948 Act (as amended by the 1981 Act) now lays down detailed *statutory* requirements as to the form and content of a company's accounts, it does not represent an exhaustive code of the manner in which the statutory accounts are to be prepared. It should always be remembered that there may be additional practical constraints on the manner a company prepares its accounts, imposed by the SSAP's. And there may be additional requirements – for instance SSAP 10 requires all but very small companies to include in their accounts a statement of the Source and Application of Funds, even though the preparation of this statement is not a statutory requirement.

(4) *The Schedule 8 information*

Sections C and D below set out the information which Schedule 8 to the 1948 Act requires to be included in the statutory accounts. There are transitional rules for financial years which straddle the "appointed day" of June 15, 1982 (i.e. the date when Schedule 8, as amended by the 1981 Act, came into force), or for financial years which end before June 15, 1982 but for which statutory accounts are produced after that date. These are dealt with in section I below (*Transitional Rules*).

(5) *Notes to the accounts*

Schedule 8 also requires detailed notes to be annexed to the balance sheet and profit and loss account. The Schedule 8 requirements are dealt with in section E, *Notes to the Accounts*, below. The purpose of the notes is to supplement the information given in the balance sheet and profit and loss account, and to give details of any other information relevant in assessing the state of the company's affairs in the light of the information given, or which affects the items shown in the profit and loss account (paragraphs 37 and 52 of Schedule 8).

Any information which Schedule 8 requires to be given in the notes may, alternatively, be given in the accounts themselves (paragraph 35 of Schedule 8).

(6) *True and fair view*

The obligations in Schedule 8 as to the form and content of the statutory accounts are subject to the very important, and *overriding*, requirement that the balance sheet and profit and loss account give a *true and fair view* of the state of the company's affairs (section 149(2) of the 1948 Act, and, for group accounts, section 152(2) of that Act). Some statutory guidance is given as to how a company should comply with the "true and fair view" requirement:

(a) If a balance sheet or profit and loss account which complies with Schedule 8 does not give a "true and fair view", then additional information must be provided in the balance sheet or profit and loss account, or in notes (C.A. 1948, s. 149(3)(a), 152(3)).

(b) If due to special circumstances a balance sheet or profit and loss account, even with such additional information, would not give a true and fair view, then the directors may depart from the strict Schedule 8 requirements to the extent necessary. The notes to the accounts must give details of the departure, the reasons for it and its effect (see section E, *Notes to the Accounts*, below).

Special classes of company

Banking, insurance and shipping companies

These companies are exempted from the requirements of Schedule 8, as permitted by the EEC Fourth Directive. (A separate Directive on banking and insurance companies is in the course of preparation; shipping companies are exempted from the Fourth Directive for eight years.) Banking, insurance and shipping companies *may*, if they choose, continue to prepare their accounts under what is now Schedule 8A to the 1948 Act instead of under Schedule 8 (see section H, *Special Classes of Company*).

Investment companies

Special provisions apply to investment companies, as defined in section 41(3) of the Companies Act 1980 (see section H, *Special Classes of Company*).

Unregistered companies

Schedule 8 applies to unregistered companies, the 1981 Act having amended section 435 and Schedule 14 to the 1948 Act to achieve this result.

Small and medium sized companies

Companies whose turnover, balance sheet total and average number of employees fall below certain levels may file modified accounts with the Registrar (sections 8 to 10 of the 1981 Act). This means that such companies need disclose less information to the public than other companies. However, they must still prepare accounts which comply fully with Schedule 8 for their *shareholders*, so there is no relaxation in the amount of work to which these companies and their auditors are put.

The filing exemption for small and medium sized companies is dealt with in section G, *Filing Exemptions for Small and Medium Sized Companies*.

Dormant companies

A dormant company is not required to appoint auditors and prepare audited accounts (section 12 of the 1981 Act). A dormant company is defined as one in which no "significant accounting transaction" occurred in the relevant accounting period (s. 12(6)). Any transaction which is required to be entered in the company's accounting records under section 12 of the 1976 Act (see section A, *Accounting Records*, above) is a significant accounting transaction, except for the taking up of shares by the subscribers to a newly incorporated company.

If a company qualifies as a "dormant company" it is entitled to pass a special resolution not to appoint auditors. The special resolution must be passed at the general meeting of the company at which any accounts of the company are laid (see the chapter on *Accounting Reference Date*). However, if the company has been dormant since incorporation it may pass the special resolution *before* any such general meeting (i.e. it need never appoint auditors if it passes a special resolution before its first annual general meeting).

Upon any "significant accounting transaction" occurring, the company ceases to be a dormant company. A company *cannot* be a dormant company if it itself is required to prepare group accounts under section 150 of the 1948 Act (see below). Also, the company must normally have been entitled to the filing exemptions for small companies for the immediately preceding accounting period (see above), unless it has been dormant since incorporation and is able to take advantage of the ability to pass a special resolution dispensing with the appointment of auditors before its first annual general meeting.

Where a dormant company has dispensed with the appointment of auditors, it need not file *audited* accounts, nor an auditors report. But it must still prepare and file the statutory balance sheet and profit and loss acount in the form required by Schedule 8 (subject to the small company exemptions). The directors must include a statement on the balance sheet immediately above their signatures of the following type: "The company has been dormant (within the meaning of section 12 of the Companies Act 1981) throughout the year ended ....".

Upon a company ceasing to be dormant the directors may appoint auditors at any time before the next general meeting at which the company's statutory accounts are to be laid (see the chapter *Accounting Reference Date*). If the directors fail so to appoint auditors, the company itself may do so in general meeting.

Group accounts

When group accounts are required

Section 150 of the 1948 Act requires every company which has a subsidiary, as defined in section 154 of the Companies Act 1948, to prepare a group balance sheet and profit and loss account, dealing with the state of affairs of the company and all its subsidiaries. These group accounts are treated as if they were documents listed in sections 1(6) to 1(8) of the 1976 Act – that is they must be laid before the company in general meeting and filed with the Registrar (see the chapter *Accounting Reference Date*).

However, group accounts are *not* required if the company is itself a *wholly-owned* subsidiary of another company incorporated in Great Britain: the obligation rests only with the ultimate *Great Britain* holding company. The test is applied at the end of the relevant financial year. A company is a wholly-owned subsidiary of another if it has no members except that other and that other's wholly-owned subsidiaries and its or their nominees (section 150(4)).

Example

In the following structure:

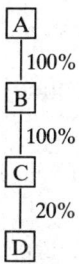

only A need prepare group accounts, in relation to B and C. But if A is, say, a U.S. company, B must prepare group accounts for it and C. Likewise if A, though a G.B. company, beneficially owns only 99 per cent of B: B as well as A must prepare group accounts (see the definition of wholly-owned subsidiary in section 150(4)). If C has the right to control the composition of D's directors, D will be a subsidiary of C (section 154(1)), and so its affairs must also be included by A or B in the group accounts, as the case may be. Note that it is irrelevant that C may be a foreign company.

Also, group accounts need not be prepared if the holding company's directors are of the opinion that,

(a) such accounts are impracticable, or would be of no real value to the members of the company in view of the insignificant amounts involved, or would involve expense or delay out of proportion to the value to members of the company;

(b) the result would be misleading, or, if the Department of Trade agrees, harmful to the business of the company or any of its subsidiaries; or

(c) if the Department of Trade agrees, the businesses of the holding company and that of the subsidiary in question are so different that they cannot reasonably be treated as a single undertaking.

Form and content of group accounts

The most usual form of group accounts is a "consolidated" balance sheet and profit and loss account. Consolidated accounts will generally eliminate intra-group transactions. These may, but need not, be wholly or partly incorporated in the holding company's own balance sheet and profit and loss account (C.A. 1948, s. 151(3)). Instead of preparing one set of consolidated accounts, it is permissible to produce more than one set, dealing with different groups of subsidiaries. Or the group accounts may be prepared otherwise than as consolidated accounts. But this is only permitted where the holding company's directors consider this is a better way of presenting the same or similar information in a way which may be readily appreciated by the shareholders (section 152(2)). (Note that SSAP 14 (group accounts) will require consolidated accounts in nearly all cases, and is more restrictive than section 152(2).)

Section 152, as amended by the 1981 Act, requires the group accounts to be prepared in accordance with Schedule 8, as amended. However, if the holding company *or any subsidiary* is a banking company, insurance company or a shipping company then the group accounts *may*, if the holding company chooses, be prepared under the less rigorous requirements of section 152A and Schedule 8A.

Schedule 8 to the 1948 Act contains certain requirements which apply only to group accounts. These are dealt with in section F, *Holding Companies and Subsidiaries*. Otherwise, the consolidated accounts must be drawn up under the normal Schedule 8 rules, governing the format, content, notes and so on. As will be seen from section F, the main difference is that the Schedule 8 requirements concerning goodwill do not apply, so that for instance goodwill arising on consolidation does not have to be depreciated over its useful economic life.

The Companies Acts do not however detail the precise methods by which consolidated accounts are to be prepared. Normally the "acquisition", as opposed to the "merger" method, is used (see also the chapter *Takeovers*, discussing *Shearer v. Bercain* and sections 36 to 41 of the Companies Act 1981). SSAP 14 contains fuller details.

Section 152 contains the same overriding "true and fair view" requirement as for individual accounts (see page 18). The Department of Trade has issued a statement on the way it considers this "true and fair view" requirement is to be reconciled with the Schedule 8 requirements, following the prosecution in 1981 of Mr. D. G. C. Webster, the finance director of Argyll Foods, for the failure of his company's group accounts to comply with sections 150 and 152 (SSAP 14 was also not followed, as it happens). (See Appendix 3 for a copy of the statement.)

A company may apply to the Department of Trade for permission to prepare group accounts otherwise than in the strict Schedule 8 form.

Other matters

Signature by directors

Every balance sheet, including a consolidated balance sheet, laid before the company in general meeting or delivered to the Registrar pursuant to section 1 of the 1976 Act must be signed by two directors (unless there is only one director, when he must sign). Failure to comply with this requirement renders the company and every officer in default liable to a default fine (C.A. 1948, s. 155).

Right to receive accounts

Subject to certain exceptions, every member, debenture-holder and person entitled to receive notices of general meetings must be sent a copy of the balance sheet at least 21 days before the general meeting at which the balance sheet is to be laid (C.A. 1948, s. 158). "Balance sheet" for this purpose includes the auditors report and the directors report, and every document required by the Companies Acts to be annexed to the balance sheet, such as the profit and loss account and group accounts (C.A. 1948, s. 156, 158(1) and C.A. 1967, s. 24). The 21 day requirement can be waived if unanimously agreed by all the members entitled to attend and vote at the meeting (section 158(1)(c)).

Every member and debenture holder is also entitled, on demand, to be furnished with a copy of the company's latest balance sheet (as defined).

Publication of accounts

Section 11 of the 1981 Act contains certain requirements as to the publication of accounts. These requirements are additional to those in section 156 of the 1948 Act, under which it is an offence to circulate, issue or publish a balance sheet without attaching the profit and loss account and, in certain circumstances, group accounts. For the purposes of section 11, accounts are "published" if the company publishes, issues or circulates them or otherwise makes them available for public inspection in a manner calculated to invite the public or any class of the public to read them.

Where a company publishes, otherwise than by delivery to the Registrar, full *individual* accounts (i.e. the full balance sheet, profit and loss account etc. sent to members or, where it is entitled to send modified accounts to the Registrar, those accounts) it must also, subject to certain exceptions, publish its full group accounts, its auditors report and its directors report. A company may "publish" its full *group* accounts without its full individual accounts, but it must publish its auditors report with the full group accounts. If a company "publishes" abridged accounts (e.g. in a financial newspaper), the accounts must be accompanied by a statement that the accounts are not full accounts, and which indicates (a) whether there is an auditors report and if so whether that report is unqualified, and (b) whether full accounts have been filed with the Registrar. The full text of the auditors' report must not be published with abridged accounts.

Penalties

Various criminal penalties are imposed on directors, and in some instances the company, where the Companies Acts accounting requirements are not met. For instance every director of a company which lays before a general meeting, or publishes, accounts which do not comply with section 149 of and Schedule 8 to the 1948 Act is liable to a fine, unless he can prove he personally took all reasonable steps to comply with the statutory provisions (C.A. 1948, s. 149(7)). A company and every officer who is in breach of section 11 of the 1981 Act (publication of accounts) is liable to a fine of up to £200. Likewise a company and every officer who breaches section 155 (signing of balance sheet) or section 158 (delivery of copy of accounts) of the 1948 Act is liable to a fine: see above. Persistent failure to file accounts with the Registrar can result in the disqualification of a director by the court for up to five years (C.A. 1948, s. 188; conviction for an offence triable on indictment which is in connection with the "management" of a company can carry disqualification under section 188 for up to 15 years).

C   Balance sheet requirements

This section sets out the statutory requirements for balance sheet items. Further commentary on certain of these items is given in the section below dealing with notes to the accounts. After describing those rules which are of general application, the information on each asset and liability item is commented on under four possible main headings:

Presentation:	describing the presentation required in balance sheet format
Accounting principles:	stating any specific accounting principle applicable to the asset or liability item
Disclosure:	indicating any information to be given about the item in the notes to the accounts
Definition:	paraphrasing any definition given in the 1981 Act

If no explanation of a balance sheet heading is given in this section it is because the heading is self explanatory.

The letters or Roman numerals assigned in Format 1 of Schedule 8 of the 1948 Act (as amended) – for the relevance of which see section B above – are given against the appropriate items. (For instance, the heading *Fixed Assets*, sub-heading *Intangible assets*, has the letter "B" assigned to the heading and the Roman numeral "I" to the sub-heading: see overleaf.) References to the relevant sections or paragraphs in Schedule 8 are given in the righthand margin. "Sch. 8, BSF" in the right-hand margin is an abbreviation for the Balance Sheet formats section of Schedule 8 to the 1948 Act, and is used below to refer to the Notes to the Balance Sheet Formats in Schedule 8.

Balance sheet – general

General rules: – Prescribed formats must be followed.   Sch. 8, para. 1

– Any item may be shown in greater detail.   Sch. 8, para. 3(1)

– Additional headings may be included for items not otherwise covered by the prescribed headings. But research costs, share or debenture issue costs or preliminary expenses must not be treated as assets.   Sch. 8, para. 3(2)

– *Items assigned letters or Roman numerals must be shown on the face of the balance sheet*   Sch. 8, para. 1(1)

– Items assigned Arabic numerals in the balance sheet formats may be rearranged or adapted where the special nature of a company's business requires such adaption. (Arabic numerals indicate detailed subdivisions of main balance sheet items such as divisions of "stocks").   Sch. 8, para. 3(3)

– Items assigned Arabic numerals may be combined if not material or where combination makes for greater clarity (in the latter case the individual amounts must be disclosed in the notes).   Sch. 8, para. 3(4)

– Amounts which are not material in a particular context may be disregarded.   Sch. 8, para. 85

– Corresponding amounts for the previous financial year must be shown.   Sch. 8, para. 4(1)

– If a corresponding amount is not comparable with the current year's amount, the corresponding amount must be adjusted and particulars of the adjustment and the reasons for it disclosed in the notes.   Sch. 8, para. 4(2)

– If there is no amount for the current year the relevant heading need not be shown unless there is a corresponding amount for the previous financial year.   Sch. 8, paras. 3(5), 4(3)

– Set-offs between asset and liability items are prohibited.   Sch. 8, para. 5

– The amounts of the components of asset and liability items must be determined separately.	Sch. 8, para. 14

Classification of assets as fixed or current

Assets are to be shown as fixed assets if they are intended for use on a continuing basis in the company's activities. Any assets not intended for continuing use are to be shown as current assets. Thus the traditional criterion of realisation within one year for classification as current assets does not apply, although debts falling due after one year must be shown separately.

Sch. 8, para. 75

A   Called up share capital not paid

Presentation:	– Called up share capital unpaid may alternatively be shown under current assets – debtors.	Sch. 8, BSF Note (1)

B   Fixed assets:

I   *Intangible assets*

Presentation: Separate disclosure (may be in notes) is required of:

	– Development costs in so far as there are special circumstances justifying their capitalisation.	Sch. 8, para. 20(1)
	– Concessions, patents, licenses, trade marks and similar rights and assets (other than goodwill), if acquired for valuable consideration or created by the company itself.	Sch. 8, BSF Note (2)
	– Goodwill if acquired for valuable consideration.	Sch. 8, BSF Note (3)
	– Payment on account for intangible assets.	
Accounting principles:	– Development costs, where capitalised, are to be written off over a period which must be stated in the notes. In so far as these costs are written off, there is a restriction on distribution of profits unless the notes to the balance sheet indicate that the amount is not to be treated as a realised loss and explain the circumstances justifying the directors' decision.	Sch. 8, para. 20(2); CA 1980, s. 42A

	– Goodwill (but not goodwill arising on consolidation) is to be written off over a period not exceeding its useful economic life.	Sch. 8, paras. 21(2), 21(3), 66
	– Others: rules as for tangible fixed assets.	
Disclosure:	– Movements as for tangible fixed assets.	
	– Additional information in notes – see section E, *Notes to the accounts*, below.	Sch. 8, para. 20(2)

II   *Tangible assets*

Presentation:	– The assets must be analysed into four categories: 1. Land and buildings 2. Plant and machinery 3. Fixtures, fittings, tools and equipment 4. Payments on account and assets in course of construction	
Accounting principles:	– Normally to be stated at purchase price or production cost, less provisions for depreciation or diminution in value where appropriate. Interest on capital borrowed to finance the manufacture of an asset may be capitalised. Current cost accounting or the revaluation of specific assets is however permitted.	Sch. 8, paras. 17, 31(1), 32(2)
	– The depreciable amount of assets with limited useful economic lives must be written off systematically over those lives.	Sch. 8, para. 32(1)
	– Provision for diminution in value must be made if any reduction in value is expected to be permanent or written back to the extent that it is no longer necessary.	Sch. 8, paras. 19(2), 19(3)
	– Tangible assets may be carried at a fixed amount where they are constantly being replaced and are neither material to the company nor subject to material variation in quantity or value (such as tools).	Sch. 8, para. 25

Disclosure:	– Movements on each of the four categories (which may be shown in notes to the accounts) giving cost or revalued amount (whichever is appropriate), additions, disposals, transfers and any revision of revalued amount. Movements on cumulative depreciation and provisions for diminuation in value must also be shown including provision for the year, the effect of disposals and any other adjustment.	Sch. 8, para. 42
	– Comparative figures for movements need not be given.	Sch. 8, para. 58(2)
	– Additional information in notes – see section E, *Notes to the accounts*, below.	
Definition:	– Purchase price and production cost – as for current assets.	

III   *Investments*

Presentation:	– The investments must be analysed into seven categories: 1. Shares in group companies 2. Loans to group companies 3. Shares in related companies 4. Loans to related companies 5. Other investments other than loans 6. Other loans 7. Own shares	
Accounting principles:	– As for tangible assets, except that the purchase price of fungible assets (i.e. those which are indistinguishable from one another) may be calculated using an appropriate method such as FIFO, LIFO or weighted average.	Sch. 8, paras. 27(1), 27(2), 27(6)
	– Provision for diminution in value may be made where an investment has fallen in value even though the fall may be temporary. Such a provision must be written back to the extent that it is no longer necessary.	Sch. 8, paras. 19(1), 19(3)
	– Investments may be stated at market value or "other appropriate value".	Sch. 8, para. 31(3)

Disclosure:	– In any case where cost is calculated using the methods appropriate for fungible assers, any material difference from market value or, if more appropriate, the most recent actual purchase price, must be disclosed.	Sch. 8, paras. 27(3) to (5)
	– Particulars of the method of determining "other appropriate value" and reasons for adopting this method must be disclosed in the notes.	Sch. 8, para. 31(3)
	– The nominal value of own shares held must be separately disclosed.	Sch. 8, BSF Note (4)
	– Movements as for tangible assets.	
	– Additional information in notes – see section E, *Notes to the Accounts*, below.	
Definition:	– Group companies are a holding company, subsidiaries or fellow subsidiaries (as defined in section 154 of the 1948 Act).	Sch. 8, para. 80
	– Related companies are companies (other than group companies) in which the investor has an equity interest, held for the long-term, with a view to exercising control or influence to secure a benefit to the investor's own activities. Where an investor holds 20% or more of the equity there is a presumption that the investee is a related company unless the contrary is shown. Most companies which are "associated companies" within SSAP 1 will be "related companies" within paragraph 91.	Sch. 8, para. 91
	– See the heading *Classification of assets as fixed or current*, above.	

C Current assets

Accounting principles:	– General rules:	
	– Purchase price or production cost, except where net realisable value is lower.	Sch. 8, paras. 22, 23(1)

	– Provisions to reduce to net realisable value must be written back if the reasons for which they were made have ceased to apply.	Sch. 8, para. 23(2)
Definition:	– Purchase price is the actual price paid plus any expenses incidental to the acquisition and includes any consideration (whether in cash or otherwise) given in respect of an asset.	Sch. 8, paras. 26(1), 89
	– Production cost includes raw materials, consumables and direct production costs. A reasonable proportion of indirect production costs and interest on capital borrowed to finance production of the asset may also be included. In the case of a current asset, distribution costs may not be included in production costs.	Sch. 8, paras. 26(2) to (4)
	– Where there is no record of the purchase price or production cost of an asset, or this information cannot be obtained without unreasonable expense or delay, the value shown in the earliest available record after the acquisition of the asset may be regarded as cost.	Sch. 8, para. 28

I   *Stocks*

Presentation:	– Four categories (which may be shown in notes). 1. Raw materials and consumables 2. Work in progress 3. Finished goods and goods for resale 4. Payments on account	
Accounting principles:	– Purchase price or production cost may be determined by FIFO, LIFO, weighted average or some similar method. The method chosen must be one which appears to the directors to be the appropriate in the circumstances of the company. The use of LIFO would not however be permitted by accounting standards.	Sch. 8, paras. 27(1), 27(2)
	– Stocks may be carried at current cost.	Sch. 8, para. 31(5)

	– Raw materials and consumables may be carried at a fixed amount where they are constantly being replaced and are neither material to the company nor subject to material variation in quantity or value.	Sch. 8, para. 25

Disclosure: – Any material difference between the balance sheet amount of stocks and replacement cost or, if more appropriate, the most recent actual purchase price, must be disclosed for each category of stocks. — Sch. 8, paras. 27(3) to (5)

II *Debtors*

Presentation: – Amounts falling due after more than one year must be shown separately for each item. — Sch. 8, BSF Note (5)

– Six categories (which may be shown in notes). — Sch. 8, BSF Note (1) Sch. 8, BSF Note (6)
 1. Trade debtors
 2. Amounts owed by group companies
 3. Amounts owed by related companies
 4. Other debtors
 5. Called up share capital not paid (may alternatively be shown under separate heading)
 6. Prepayments and accrued income (may alternatively be shown under separate heading)

Accounting principles: – As for current assets generally.

Definition: – Group companies and related companies – see *Fixed assets, Investments*, above.

– Accrued income – see *Prepayments and accrued income*, below.

III *Investments*

Presentation: – Three categories (which may be shown in notes).
 1. Shares in group companies
 2. Own shares
 3. Other investments

Accounting principles:	– As for current assets generally, but purchase price of similar investments may be calculated using an appropriate method such as FIFO, LIFO or weighted average.	Sch. 8, paras. 27(1), 27(2), 27(6)
	– Investments may be stated at current cost.	Sch. 8, para. 31(4)
Disclosure:	– In any case where cost is calculated using the methods appropriate for fungible assets, any material difference from market value or, if more appropriate, the most recent actual purchase price must be disclosed.	Sch. 8, paras. 27(3) to (5)
	– The nominal value of own shares must be separately disclosed.	Sch. 8, BSF Note (4)
Definition:	– Group companies – see *Fixed assets, Investments*, above.	
	– See also *Classification of assets as fixed or current*, above.	

IV   *Cash at bank and in hand*

D   Prepayments and accrued income

Presentation:	– May alternatively be shown under debtors.	Sch. 8, BSF Note (6)
	– Amounts falling due after more than one year must be shown separately.	Sch. 8, BSF Note (5)
Accounting principles:	– As for current assets generally.	
Definition:	– Accrued income is defined in the EEC Fourth Directive as income relating to the year but not receivable until after its expiry.	

E, H   Creditors

Presentation:	– Amounts falling due *within* one year and amounts falling due after *more than one year* must be shown separately for each item and, in the horizontal format (Format 2 in Schedule 8), the aggregate must be shown for each item.	Sch. 8, BSF Note (13)

	– Nine categories (which may be shown in notes):	Sch. 8,
	1. Debenture loans (showing convertible loans separately)	BSF Note (7)
	2. Bank loans and overdrafts	
	3. Payments received on account (if not shown as deductions from stocks)	Sch. 8, BSF Note (10)
	4. Trade creditors	
	5. Bills of exchange payable	
	6. Amounts owed to group companies	
	7. Amounts owed to related companies	
	8. Other creditors including taxation and social security	
	9. Accruals and deferred income (which may alternatively be shown under separate heading).	Sch. 8, BSF Note (10)
Accounting principles:	– Where the amount owing to a creditor is greater than the value of the consideration received (e.g. a discount on the issue of a debenture loan) the difference may be treated as an asset (rather than written off at once). The difference must be written off by a reasonable amount each year and be completely written off before repayment of the debt. The current amount not written off must be shown separately in the balance sheet or in the notes.	Sch. 8, para. 24
	– The accruals concept should be followed.	Sch. 8, para. 13
	– The aggregate amount for creditors in respect of taxation and social security must be shown separately.	Sch. 8, BSF Note (9)
Disclosure:	– Additional information in notes – see section E, *Notes to the accounts*, below.	
Definition:	– Deferred income – see *Accruals and deferred income*, below.	

F Net current assets/liabilities

Presentation:	– This item appears only in the vertical format.	
	– Prepayments and accrued income, wherever shown, must be taken into account in determining this figure.	Sch. 8, BSF Note (11)

G   Total assets less current liabilities

Presentation: – This item appears only in the vertical
                     format (Format 1).

I   Provisions for liabilities and charges

Presentation: – Three categories (which may be shown
                     in notes):
                     1. Pensions and similar obligations
                     2. Taxation, including deferred taxa-
                        tion
                     3. Other provisions

Disclosure: – Additional information in notes – see
                     section E, *Notes to the accounts*, below.

Definition: – Provisions which are for any liability or   Sch. 8,
                     loss which either is likely to be incur-   para. 88
                     red, or certain to be incurred but un-
                     certain as to amount or date on which it
                     will arise.

                   – Deferred taxation, which is not defined
                     in Schedule 8, is expected to be treated
                     as a "provision" since it is likely that
                     there will be some uncertainty regard-
                     ing either the amount required or the
                     date on which timing differences may
                     reverse. Other tax "provisions" are
                     likely to be classified as "creditors"
                     unless there is some uncertainty as to
                     either the amount of the liability or the
                     date on which it will arise.

J   Accruals and deferred income

Presentation: – May alternatively be shown under cre-   Sch. 8,
                     ditors.   BSF Note
                                                                     (10)

Accounting   – The accruals concept should be fol-   Sch. 8,
principles: lowed.   para. 13

Definition: – Deferred income is defined in the
                     E.E.C. Fourth Directive as income re-
                     ceivable before the year end but relat-
                     ing to a subsequent year.

Minority interests

This caption does not appear in the prescribed formats but in the accounts of groups containing partly owned subsidiaries it will have to be added in accordance with paragraph 3(2) of Schedule 8 to the 1948 Act.

K Capital and reserves

I *Called up share capital*

Disclosure:	– The amount of allotted share capital and the amount of called up share capital which has been paid up must be shown separately.	Sch. 8, BSF Note (12)
	– Additional information in notes – see section E, *Notes to the accounts*, below	
Definition:	– Allotted share capital is not defined but is presumed to be the full nominal value of shares allotted.	
	– Called up share capital is the aggregate amount of calls made on shares, share capital paid up without being called and share capital to be paid on a specified future date under the terms of allotment.	C.A. 1980, s. 87(1)

II *Share premium account*

III *Revaluation reserve*

Presentation:	– An alternative name may be used such as current cost reserve.	Sch. 8, para. 34(3)
Accounting principles:	– Surpluses or deficits, after providing for such matters as backlog depreciation, which arise from stating assets at market value or current cost, must be taken to the revaluation reserve. This requirement applies to surpluses or deficits which arose from revaluations in previous years.	Sch. 8, para. 34(1), 34(2)
	– The reserve must be reduced to the extent that it is no longer necessary for the purpose of the accounting policies adopted by the company (e.g. a reduction in operating capability under current cost accounting).	Sch. 8, para. 34(4)

	– A transfer to profit and loss account may be made only if the amount represents realised profit or was previously charged to profit and loss account (e.g. current cost adjustments no longer required because of a reduction in operating capability).	Sch. 8, para. 34(4)
Disclosure:	– The treatment for tax purposes of amounts taken to revaluation reserve must be disclosed.	Sch. 8, para. 34(5)
	– Movements on revaluation reserve are to be shown in notes.	Sch. 8, para. 46

IV   *Other reserves*

Presentation: – Four categories (which may be shown in notes):
  1. Capital redemption reserve
  2. Reserve for own shares
  3. Reserves provided for by the articles of association
  4. Other reserves

V   *Profit and loss account*

D   Profit and loss account requirements

This section sets out the statutory requirements for profit and loss account items. Further commentary on certain of these items is given in section E below, dealing with notes to the accounts. After describing those rules which are of general application and comparing the alternative vertical formats of the profit and loss account, the comments on each item are made under four possible main headings:

Presentation: – describing the presentation required in the profit and loss account format.

Accounting principles: – stating any specific accounting principle applicable to the income or expense item.

Disclosure: – indicating any information to be given about the item in the notes to the accounts.

Definition: – paraphrasing any definition given in the Act.

If no explanation of a profit and loss account heading is given in the chapter it is because the heading is self explanatory.

The Arabic numbers assigned in Format 1 of Schedule 8 to the 1948 Act (as amended) are given against the appropriate items (see section B,

Form and Contents of accounts: general principles, above, for the relevance of the Arabic numbers). Where an item does not appear in Format 1 the Arabic number assigned in Format 2 is given, indicated by an asterisk. "Sch. 8 PLF" is an abbreviation for the Profit and Loss Account Formats section of Schedule 8 to the 1948 Act.

References to the prescribed headings in the profit and loss account formats and to the relevant sections or paragraphs in Schedule 8 are given in the right-hand margin.

Profit and losses account – general

General rules:
- Prescribed formats must be followed. Sch. 8, para. 1(1)

- Any item may be shown in greater detail. Sch. 8, para. 3(1)

- Additional headings may be included for items not otherwise covered by the prescribed headings. Sch. 8, para. 3(2)

- All items may be rearranged or adapted where the special nature of a company's business requires such adaptation. Sch. 8, para. 3(3)

- All items may be combined if not material or where combination makes for greater clarity (in the latter case the individual amounts must be disclosed in the notes). Sch. 8, para. 3(4)

- Corresponding amounts for the previous financial year must be shown. Sch. 8, para. 4(1)

- Amounts which are not material in a particular context may be disregarded. Sch. 8, para. 85

- If a corresponding amount is not comparable with the current year's amount, the corresponding amount must be adjusted and particulars of the adjustment and the reasons for it disclosed in the notes. Sch. 8, para. 4(2)

- If there is no amount for the current year the relevant heading need not be shown unless there is a corresponding amount for the previous financial year. Sch. 8, paras. 3(5), 4(3)

- Set-offs between income and expenditure items are prohibited. Sch. 8, para. 5

Comparison of alternative vertical formats

A comparison of the alternative vertical forms of the profit and loss account (Formats 1 and 2) is set out below showing the way in which the information disclosed will differ. It seems likely that a majority of companies will adopt Format 1 (operational basis) rather than Format 2 (type of expenditure basis), or Formats 3 or 4 (which use a horizontal layout). Turnover and other operating income are shown for the sake of convenience, although there is no difference in the requirements other than the position of "other operating income".

"Operational"	*"Type of expenditure"*
1. Turnover	1. Turnover
	2. Change in stocks of finished goods and in work in progress
2. Cost of sales	3. Own work capitalised
	4. Other operating income
	5. (a) Raw materials and consumables
3. Gross profit or loss	(b) Other external charges
	6. Staff costs:
	(a) wages and salaries
4. Distribution costs	(b) social security costs
	(c) other pension costs
	7. (a) Depreciation and other amounts written off, tangible and intangible fixed assets
5. Administrative expenses	(b) Exceptional amounts written off, current assets
6. Other operating income	8. Other operating charges

The remaining vertical format items are the same for both types of presentation.

The corresponding horizontal layouts for each type of profit and loss account (Formats 3 and 4) contain the same items as the vertical layouts shown above.

1. *Turnover*

Disclosure:		
	– Notes must show turnover broken down by classes of business and by geographical markets, having regard to the manner in which the company's activities are organised, in so far as those classes and markets differ substantially.	Sch. 8, paras. 55(1), (2), (3)
	– Classes or markets which do not differ substantially must be treated as one class or market. Immaterial amounts may be combined with those of another class or market.	Sch. 8, para. 55(4)

	– This additional information on turn-over may be omitted if disclosure would be seriously prejudicial to the company's interests. The fact that such information has not been disclosed must be stated in the notes.	Sch. 8, para. 55(5)
Definition:	– Amounts derived from the provision of goods and services within the company's ordinary activities after deduction of trade discounts, value added tax and any other taxes based on turnover (such as car tax).	Sch. 8, para. 94

2. Cost of sales

Accounting principles:	– Must be stated after inclusion of any necessary provisions for depreciation or diminution in value of assets.	Sch. 8, PLF Note (14)

4. Distribution costs

Accounting principles:	– As for cost of sales.	

5. Administrative expenses

Accounting principles:	– As for cost of sales.	

6.* Staff costs

Disclosure:	– Where "operational" format is used there must be disclosure in the notes of: (a) wages and salaries (b) social security costs (c) other pension costs	Sch. 8, para. 56(4)
	– In all cases the notes must show the average number of employees during the year, wherever located, and the average number of employees in categories selected by the directors having regard to the manner in which the company's activities are organised (such as by class of business or geographical location).	Sch. 8, para. 56(1), (2), (3), (5)

7(a)* *Depreciation and other amounts written off, tangible and intangible fixed assets*

Accounting principles:	– The depreciable amount of assets with limited useful economic lives must be written off systematically over those lives.	Sch. 8, paras. 18, 32(1)
	– Provision for diminution in value must be made if any reduction in value is expected to be permanent or written back to the extent that it is no longer necessary.	Sch. 8, paras. 19(2), 19(3)
	– Goodwill (but not goodwill arising on consolidation) is to be written off over a period not exceeding its useful economic life.	Sch. 8, para. 21(2), 21(3), 66
	– Development costs, where capitalised, are to be written off over a period which must be stated in the notes.	Sch. 8, para. 20(2)
Disclosure:	– Where "operational" format is used there must be disclosure in the notes of depreciation and other amounts written off.	Sch. 8, PLF Note (17)
	– In all cases there must be separate disclosure of (a) provisions made and (b) amounts written back which relate to diminution in value of tangible and intangible fixed assets	Sch. 8, para. 19(2), 19(3)
	– Where there has been a departure from historical cost accounting the amount of depreciation included under this heading (or under cost of sales, distribution costs or administrative expenses) may be the historical cost amount provided that the additional depreciation based on the revaluation is shown separately.	Sch. 8, paras. 32(2), 32(3)

7(b)* *Exceptional amounts written off, current assets*

Definition:	– No definition is given in Schedule 8. Article 39 of the EEC Fourth Directive included an option that "exceptional value adjustments could be made to current assets where, on the basis of reasonable commercial assessment,

these are necessary if the valuation of these assets is not to be modified in the near future because of fluctuations in value." As this option was not taken up by the U.K. it is envisaged that this heading will rarely be used.

7. *Income from shares in group companies*

This caption would not normally be applicable to consolidated accounts.

8. *Income from shares in related companies*

The investor's share of the pre-tax results of related companies will usually be included under this caption in the consolidated profit and loss account where the equity method of accounting has been used.

9. *Income from other fixed asset investments*

Disclosure:	– Income and interest derived from group companies must be shown separately from that from other sources.	Sch. 8, PLF Note (15)

10. *Other interest receivable and similar income*

Disclosure:	– As for income from other fixed asset investments.

11. *Amounts written off investments*

Accounting principles:	– Provision for diminution in value of fixed asset investments *must* be made if any reduction in value is expected to be permanent or written back to the extent that it is no longer necessary.	Sch. 8, paras. 19(2), 19(3)
	– Provision for diminution in value of fixed asset investments *may* be made where an investment has fallen in value even though the fall may be temporary. Such a provision must be written back to the extent that it is no longer necessary.	Sch. 8, paras. 19(1), 19(3)
	– Provision is to be made to reduce current asset investments to net realisable value where this is below purchase price.	Sch. 8, para. 23(1)
Disclosure:	– There must be separate disclosure of: (a) Provisions made for temporary diminution in value of fixed asset investments.	Sch. 8, para. 19(1)

(b)	Provisions made for permanent diminution in value of fixed asset investments.	Sch. 8, para. 19(2)
(c)	Any amounts written back in respect of provisions for temporary or permanent diminution in value of fixed asset investments.	Sch. 8, para. 19(3)

12. *Interest payable and similar charges*

Disclosure:	– Amounts payable to group companies must be shown separately.	Sch. 8, PLF Note (16)
	– Additional information in notes – see section E, *Notes to the accounts*, below.	

Profit or loss on ordinary activities before taxation

Presentation:	– Surprisingly this heading does not appear in any of the formats but nevertheless the amount of profit or loss on ordinary activities before taxation must be shown in the profit and loss account.	Sch. 8, para. 3(6)
Disclosure:	– Show separately profit or loss before taxation attributable to each class of business.	Sch. 8, para. 55(1)

13. *Tax on profit or loss on ordinary activities*

Disclosure:	– Basis of charge for U.K. corporation tax and U.K. income tax.	Sch. 8, para. 54(1)
	– Special circumstances affecting the tax liability in respect of profits, income or capital gains for current year or succeeding years.	Sch. 8, para. 54(2)
	– Amounts included in tax on profit or loss on ordinary activities for: (a) U.K. corporation tax (b) U.K. corporation tax before double taxation relief (c) U.K. income tax (d) Foreign taxes on profits, income and (if charged to revenue) capital gains	Sch. 8, para. 54(3)

14. *Profit or loss on ordinary activities after taxation*

Minority interests

This caption does not appear in the prescribed formats but in the accounts of groups containing partly owned subsidiaries it will have to be added in accordance with paragraph 3(2) of Schedule 8 to the 1948 Act.

15, 16. *Extraordinary income and extraordinary charges*

Disclosure: – Particulars (such as amount and nature) of any extraordinary income or charges must be given in the notes.   Sch. 8, para. 57(2)

17. *Extraordinary profit or loss*

18. *Tax on extraordinary profit or loss*

Disclosure: – Amounts included in tax on extraordinary profit or loss for: Sch. 8, para. 54(3)
(a) U.K. corporation tax
(b) U.K. corporation tax before double taxation relief
(c) U.K. income tax
(d) Foreign taxes on profits, income and (if charged to revenue) capital gains.

19. *Other taxes not shown under above items*

20. *Profit or loss for the financial year*

Disclosure: – Disclose in the notes the effect of the inclusion in the profit and loss account of any item relating to a previous financial year.   Sch. 8, para. 57(1)

    – Disclose in the notes the effect of any transactions that are exceptional by virtue of size or incidence although they fall within the company's ordinary activities.   Sch. 8, para. 57(3)

Appropriations

Presentation: – The profit and loss account must show two additional items:

    – Amounts transferred or proposed to be transferred to, or withdrawn or proposed to be withdrawn from, reserves.   Sch. 8, para. 3(7)(a)

    – Aggregate amount of dividends paid and proposed.   Sch. 8, para. 3(7)(b)

E   Notes to the accounts

Schedule 8 to the 1948 Act (as amended) lays down certain minimum requirements on information to be given in the notes to the accounts, if not given in the accounts themselves. Much of the disclosure that will be necessary in the notes has been described in sections C and D above dealing with the Balance Sheet and the Profit and Loss Account, consequently this section deals only with additional items.

General matters

True and fair view

Where it is necessary to depart from a requirement of Schedule 8 in order for the accounts to give a true and fair view, particulars of the departure, the reasons for it and its effect on the accounts must be given in the notes.

C.A. 1948, s. 144(3), 144(4)

Accounting policies

The accounting policies adopted by the company (including its accounting policies as regards depreciation and diminution in value of assets) must be shown.

Sch. 8, para. 36

The basis of translation of foreign currency amounts into sterling must be disclosed.

Sch. 8, para. 58(1)

Any departure from the general accounting principles set out in Schedule 8 (broadly the fundamental accounting concepts of SSAP 2) must be disclosed, together with the reasons for it and its effect on the accounts.

Sch. 8, para. 15

Departures from historical cost accounting

A company may depart from the historical cost accounting rules so as to revalue specific assets or adopt current cost accounting. Where there is such a departure there must be disclosure in the notes of the balance sheet items affected and the bases of valuation used.

Sch. 8, para. 33(2)

The comparable amounts under historical cost rules, or the differences between the historical cost amounts and the valuations, must be shown for all balance sheet items (except stocks) affected by a departure from historical cost accounts.

Sch. 8, para. 33(3), 33(4)

Any surplus or deficit arising from a revaluation of assets, including any revaluation in previous years, must be taken to a revaluation reserve, information on which is given in section C, *Balance Sheet Requirements*, above.

Sch. 8, paras. 34(1), 34(2)

Subsidiaries, associated companies and other trade investments

The name and country of incorporation, or country of registration (e.g. England, Scotland) if incorporated in Great Britain (but only if the place of registration differs from that of the company itself), class of shares and proportion of capital held must be disclosed for all subsidiaries and all other companies in which the investing company (a) holds more than 10 per cent of any class of equity, (b) holds more than 10 per cent of the total allotted share capital or (c) holds shares which are stated in the investing company's accounts at an amount in excess of 10 per cent of its total assets. This information may be omitted, *subject to Department of Trade approval*, where disclosure would be harmful to the business of either the investor or the investee. Corresponding amounts for the previous financial year need not be given.	Sch. 8, para. 58(3) and C.A. 1981, s. 4(1), 4(2), 4(3)
Disclosure of the capital, reserves and results as shown by the latest accounts of the investee is required for all companies in which the investor owns more than 20 per cent of the allotted share capital.	
Except in the case of investments which have a material effect on the investor's assets or results, these disclosures may be made in the annual return submitted to the Registrar rather than in the accounts. Where disclosure is made in the annual return, the fact that the accounts disclosure is limited must be noted in the accounts.	C.A. 1967, s. 3(4); 4(4), C.A. 1981, s. 4(4), 4(8)

Information on the amount of the investee's capital, reserves and results may be omitted if:

– The investee does not publish its balance sheet either in Great Britain or elsewhere and less than 50 per cent of its capital is held by the investor.	C.A. 1981, s. 4(6)
– The investee is a subsidiary and its accounts have either been included in the investor's group accounts or included in or in a note to the investing company's accounts by way of the equity method of valuation.	C.A. 1981, s. 4(4)
– The investee is a subsidiary and the investor is exempt from preparing group accounts as a wholly owned subsidiary of another company incorporated in Great Britain.	C.A. 1981, s. 4(4)
– The interest in the investee exceeds 20 per cent but does not exceed 50 per cent and has been included in or in a note to the investor's accounts by way of the equity method of valuation.	C.A. 1981, s. 4(5)
– The information is not material.	C.A. 1981, s. 4(7)

Section 4 of the 1967 Act (as amended) brings within the disclosure requirements investments of more than 10 per cent of *all* the share capital (not just the equity share capital as defined in section 154(5) of the 1948 Act) of a company. In practice section 4 of the 1981 Act extends the disclosure requirements only to those companies which have material investments of more than 20 per cent of the share capital of another company which they do not include in or in a note to the accounts by way of the equity method of valuation. Most companies will be unaffected by these changes.

Equity accounting

The use of the equity method of accounting, whereby the investor's share of the results of the investee is included in the profit and loss account is permitted only in the *consolidated* accounts. This appears to create an obstacle for a company which has no subsidiaries and does not have an interest in an associated company. It is suggested that the obstacle could be circumvented merely by the formation of a subsidiary – which could even remain dormant.

Sch. 8, para. 65

The valuation of investments on an equity basis in *company* accounts will presumably be treated as a departure from historical cost accounting. Consequently any surplus or deficit which arises from stating investments by way of the equity method of valuation in the company accounts must be taken to revaluation reserve.

Sch. 8, para. 34(1)

Format of accounts

If there is any change from the previous year in the format of the balance sheet or profit or loss account, there must be disclosure of the reasons for and the nature of the change.

Sch. 8, para. 2(2)

Any items preceded in the formats by Arabic numerals which are combined together in the balance sheet or profit and loss account for greater clarity must be shown separately in the notes.

Sch. 8, para. 3(4)

Corresponding amounts

Corresponding amounts for the previous financial year must be shown for all disclosures made in the accounts except for movements on fixed assets, movements on reserves or provisions for liabilities and charges, the details of subsidiaries and other investments required by sections 3 and 4 of the 1967 Act and details of transactions with directors and officers required by sections 54 and 56 of the 1980 Act. If corresponding amounts are not compa-

Sch. 8, paras. 4(2) 58(2), 58(3)

rable with the current year's amounts the corresponding amounts must be adjusted. Particulars of the adjustments and the reasons for them must be disclosed in the notes.

Assets

Development costs

Where development costs are carried as an asset, there must be disclosure of the reasons for capitalisation and the period over which these costs are being or are to be written off (see generally SSAP 13 for the restricted circumstances where development costs may be treated as an asset).

Sch. 8, para. 20(2)

There will also be a restriction on distribution of profits where development costs are capitalised unless the notes indicate that the amount is not to be treated as a realised loss and explain the circumstances justifying the directors' decision.

C.A. 1980, s. 42A

Goodwill

Where goodwill (other than goodwill arising on consolidation) is included as an asset, there must be disclosure of the period over which it is being written off and the reasons for choosing that period.

Sch. 8, para. 21(4)

Deferred costs

The excess of the amount owing to a creditor over the value of the consideration received (e.g. discount on issue of a debenture loan) may be treated as an asset rather than written off at once. In this event the excess cost must be shown in the notes if it is not separately disclosed in the balance sheet.

Sch. 8, para. 24

Capitalised interest

If interest on capital borrowed to finance the manufacture of an asset is included in its production cost, there must be disclosure in the notes of the fact that interest has been capitalised and of the amount of interest involved.

Sch. 8, para. 26(3)(b)

Fixed assets

Where fixed assets (other than listed investments) are included at a valuation the notes must disclose:

Sch. 8, para. 43

- The years (so far as they are known to the directors) in which the assets were valued and, for each year, the value of the assets involved.

– For assets which have been valued during the financial
year, the names of the persons who valued them or
particulars of their qualifications and, in either event,
the bases of valuation adopted.

A note may be necessary in the accounts of companies   Sch. 8,
whose distributable profits are not plentiful and which   paras. 44,
have some revaluation deficits but which have not re-   82
valued all their fixed assets other than goodwill.

There must be disclosure of the division between freehold
and leasehold interests in respect of amounts shown in
the balance sheet or its related notes in respect of land
and buildings. Leasehold interests must be further sub-
divided between long leases (unexpired terms of 50 years
or more) and short leases (unexpired terms of less than 50
years).

Listed investments

For each category of investments there must be disclosure   Sch. 8,
of the book amount of listed investments. This amount   para. 45(1)
must be further sub-divided between those listed on a
recognised stock exchange in Great Britain and those
listed elsewhere.

The market value of listed investments in each category   Sch. 8,
must be given by way of note where it differs from   para. 45(2)
the balance sheet amount. The stock exchange value of
any investment must be disclosed where a market value
has been taken which is higher than the stock exchange
value.

Stocks and investments

The cost of stocks and those investments which are   Sch. 8,
indistinguishable from one another may be calculated by   para. 27
using an appropriate method such as FIFO, LIFO or
weighted average. Any material difference between cost
calculated by one of these methods and market value or
replacement cost or, if more appropriate, the most recent
actual purchase price must be disclosed in the notes.

Inclusion of earliest available value as cost

Where there is no record of the purchase price or produc-   Sch. 8,
tion cost of an asset, or this information cannot be   para. 51(1)
obtained without unreasonable expense or delay, a com-
pany may regard the value shown in the earliest available
record after the acquisition of the asset as its cost.
Disclosure is required the first time the earliest available
value of an asset has been included as its cost.

Loans permitted by section 42 or 43 of the 1981 Act

The aggregate amount of any loans made under the authority of section 42(6)(b) or (c) of the 1981 Act (i.e. loans to employees etc. assist the acquisition of a company's own shares) or under section 43 (loans amounting to financial assistance by private companies) must be disclosed in respect of each balance sheet heading in which they appear.

Sch. 8, para. 51(2)

Capital and liabilities

Share capital

The authorised share capital and, where there is more than one class of shares, the number and aggregate nominal value of each class allotted must be disclosed.

Sch. 8, para. 38(1)

Where shares have been allotted during a financial year, there must be shown:
- The reason for making the allotment.
- The class of shares allotted.
- For each class, the number allotted, their aggregate nominal value and the consideration received.

Sch. 8, para. 39

If there are any option or conversion rights in respect of the company's share capital, there must be shown:
- The number, description and amount of the shares for which there are option or conversion rights.
- The period during which these rights are exercisable.
- The price to be paid on allotment.

Sch. 8, para. 40

If there are any redeemable shares, there must be disclosed:
- The earliest and latest dates of redemption.
- Whether the redemption is obligatory or at the option of the company.
- Whether any premium is payable on redemption.

Sch. 8, para. 38(2)

If any fixed cumulative dividends on shares are in arrear, there must be shown:
- The amount of the arrears.
- The period for which the dividends are in arrear (by class of shares).

Sch. 8, para. 49

Details of the amount of allotted share capital and of called up share capital which has been paid up are required in the balance sheet – see section C, *Balance Sheet requirements*, above.

Debentures and loan stocks

Where debentures or any form of loan stock have been issued during a financial year, there must be shown:

Sch. 8, para. 41(1)

– The reason for making the issue.
– The classes of debenture issued.
– For each class, the amount issued and the consideration received.

Particulars of any redeemed debentures which the company has power to reissue must be disclosed.

Where any of the debentures are held for the company by a nominee of trustee, the nominal amount of the debentures and the amount at which they are carried in the company's accounting records must be disclosed. | Sch. 8, para. 41(3)

Movements on reserves and provisions

Where there is a movement on any reserve or provision for liabilities and charges (other than a transfer to a provision for the purpose of which it was established) there must be disclosure of the movements on that reserve or provision consisting of: | Sch. 8, para. 46
– The amount at the beginning and the end of the year.
– Transfers to or from reserve or provision during that year.
– The source and application of the amounts transferred.

Corresponding amounts for the previous financial year need not be given. | Sch. 8, para. 58(3)

Provisions

Particulars must be given in the notes of each provision included in "other provisions" where the amount of that provision is material. Where provisions for liabilities and charges include an amount for taxation there must be disclosure in the notes of the amount of that provision which is not in respect of deferred taxation. | Sch. 8, para. 47

Pensions

Particulars must be given of any pension commitments which have been provided for under "provisions for liabilities and charges" and of any pension commitments for which no provision has been made. Separate particulars are required of any commitment which relates wholly or partly to pensions payable to past directors. | Sch. 8, para. 50(4)

Indebtedness

For each category of creditors, there must be shown: | Sch. 8, para. 48(1)
– The amount which is repayable otherwise than by instalments more than five years from the balance sheet date.

- The amount which is repayable by instalments any of which are repayable after the five year period.
- The aggregate amount of those instalments which are repayable after the five year period.

The terms of repayment and the rate of interest payable should be shown for each debt which falls to be taken into account in the above disclosure. However it will be sufficient to provide a general indication of repayment terms and interest rates if compliance with this requirement would result in a statement of excessive length.

Sch. 8, para. 48(2), (3)

For each category of creditors, there must be shown the amount for which security has been given and an indication of the nature of the security.

Sch. 8, para. 48(4)

Security for the indebtedness of others

Any charge on the assets of the company to secure the liabilities of another person must be disclosed including, where practicable, the amount secured.

Sch. 8, para. 50(1)

Contingent liabilities and financial commitments

For any contingent liability not provided for in the accounts, there must be shown:
- The amount or estimated amount of the liability.
- Its legal nature.
- Details of any security provided in connection with the liability.

Sch. 8, para. 50(2)

As regards commitments for capital expenditure, there must be shown:
- The amount of contracts for capital expenditure which have not been provided for in the accounts.
- The amount of capital expenditure authorised by the directors which has not been contracted for.

Sch. 8, para. 50(3)

Any other financial commitments which have not been provided for in the accounts and which are relevant to an assessment of the company's state of affairs must be disclosed.

Sch. 8, para. 50(5)

Any security, contingent liability or commitment which has been entered into on behalf of a group company must be shown separately. Any such disclosure must distinguish between commitments on behalf of:
- a holding company or a fellow subsidiary, and
- a subsidiary

Sch. 8, para. 50(6)

Recommended dividends

The aggregate amount recommended for distributions by way of dividend must be disclosed.

Sch. 8, para. 51(3)

Profit and loss items

Interest payable and similar charges

Except for loans from group companies, separate disclo-   Sch. 8,
sure is required of the amount of interest payable on or   para. 53(2)
similar charges in respect of:
– Bank loans and overdrafts and loans (other than bank
  loans and overdrafts) which are wholly repayable within
  five years, by instalments or otherwise, whether or not
  secured.
– Loans of any other kind, whether or not secured.

Additional profit and loss account information

Disclosure in required in the notes of the amount set aside   Sch. 8,
for: para. 53(3)
– Redemption of share capital.

– Redemption of loans.   Sch. 8,
                                                               para. 53(3)

and the amount of: Sch. 8,
– Income from listed investments.   para. 53(4)

– Rents from land (after deduction of outgoings), if rents   Sch. 8,
  are a substantial part of the company's revenue for the   para. 53(5)
  year.

– Hire of plant and machinery charged to revenue.   Sch. 8,
                                                               para. 53(6)

– Auditors' remuneration (including expenses).   Sch. 8,
                                                               para. 53(7)

Information required by other Acts

Disclosures required by other Acts include: C.A. 1948,
– Directors' emoluments (note also the Companies   s. 196;
(Accounts) Regulations 1982 S.I. 1698).   C.A. 1967,
                                                              s. 6, 7

– Ultimate holding company.   C.A. 1967,
                                                              s. 5

– Higher paid employees' emoluments (note 1982 S.I.   C.A. 1967,
1698 above).   s. 8

– Transactions with directors.   C.A. 1980,
                                                              s. 54

– Transactions with officers.   C.A. 1980,
                                                              s. 56

(For further details, see pages 322 and 324.)

Corresponding amounts need not be given for transactions with directors and officers (paragraph 58(3) of Schedule 8 to the 1948 Act).

F Holding companies and subsidiaries

This section deals with those provisions of Schedule 8 to the 1948 Act which are unique to the accounts of holding companies and subsidiaries. "Holding company" and "subsidiary" are defined in section 154 of the 1948 Act.

Company's own accounts

Any balance sheet item relating to group companies must be sub-divided into:

– Amounts attributable to dealings with or interests in a holding company or fellow subsidiary.
– Amounts attributable to dealings with or interests in a subsidiary.

This information may be disclosed either by way of a sub-division of the relevant item in the balance sheet or in the notes.

Sch. 8, para. 59

The number, description and amount of any shares or debentures of its holding company held by a subsidiary must be disclosed in the holding company's accounts. This requirement does not apply to any shares which the subsidiary holds as a personal representative or as a trustee provided that neither the holding company nor any subsidiary is beneficially interested under the trust other than by way of security.

Sch. 8, para. 60

Both of these disclosures will be required in group accounts in respect of any unconsolidated subsidiaries.

Sch. 8, para. 67

Holding company profit and loss account

If a holding company prepares a consolidated profit and loss account it need not prepare its own profit and loss account provided that:

– The amount of the consolidated profit or loss for the financial year which is dealt with in the accounts of the holding company is disclosed in the consolidated profit and loss account.

C.A. 1948, s. 149(5) (b)(ii)

– The fact that the holding company has taken advantage
  of this exemption is disclosed in the notes.

C.A. 1948,
s. 149(6)

Group accounts

The 1981 Act made no change in the rules relating to the
preparation and form of group accounts contained in
sections 150 and 151 of the 1948 Act. Section 152 of the
1948 Act now provides that group accounts must comply
with the requirements of Schedule 8 to the 1948 Act (as
amended) so far as they are applicable to the form in
which the group accounts are prepared. The overriding
requirement for truth and fairness, so far as concerns
members of the holding company, remains.

C.A. 1981,
s. 2

If group accounts take the form of consolidated accounts
they should combine the information shown in the separate accounts of the holding company and the subsidiaries
but with such adjustments, if any, as the directors of the
holding company consider necessary. Group accounts
which do not take the form of consolidated accounts must
give the same or equivalent information as would be given
in consolidated accounts.

Sch. 8,
paras. 61,
68

Consolidated accounts should comply, so far as practicable, with the requirements of the Companies Acts as if
they were the accounts of an actual company, and may
deal with an investment in another company by way of the
equity method of accounting where the investee is so
closely associated with the investing group as to justify the
use of that method. The following disclosures are not
required on a consolidated basis although the information
must be given in respect of the holding company:

Sch. 8,
paras. 62,
63, 65

– Directors' and employees' emoluments etc. – section
  196 of the 1948 Act and sections 6 to 8 of the 1967 Act.

– Directors' and officers' transactions – sections 54 and 56
  of the 1980 Act.

– Interests in other companies – section 4 of the 1967 Act
  and section 4 of the 1981 Act.

*The accounting principles set out in Schedule 8 for deter-
mining the amount at which goodwill is stated in the
balance sheet, including the requirement to amortise goodwill over its useful economic life, do not apply to goodwill
arising on consolidation.*

Sch. 8,
para. 66

Information on non-consolidated subsidiaries

Where a holding company does not prepare group accounts (perhaps because it is a wholly owned subsidiary of another company incorporated in Great Britain) or has prepared group accounts which do not deal with one or more subsidiaries, the following information is to be given in the notes to the holding company's accounts:

Sch. 8, paras. 69(1), 69(2)

- The reasons why the subsidiaries are not dealt with in the group accounts.

Sch. 8, para. 69(2)(a)

- Where the holding company is a wholly owned subsidiary of another company incorporated in Great Britain, a statement that in the opinion of the directors the aggregate value of shares in and amounts owing from the subsidiaries is not less than the aggregate of the amounts at which these items are stated in the holding company's balance sheet.

Sch. 8, para. 69(4)

- In any other case, the aggregate value on the equity method of shares in the subsidiaries.

Sch. 8, para. 69(3)

- Any qualifications in the audit reports on the accounts of the subsidiaries if the subject of the qualification is not covered by the holding company's accounts and is material from the point of view of its members. This requirement also applies to any note in a subsidiary's accounts calling attention to a matter which, but for the note, would have been referred to in a qualified audit report.

Sch. 8, para. 69(2)(b)

If the information set out below is not obtainable this fact must be stated in the notes. The Secretary of State may also exempt a company for disclosure of all or part of the above information.

Sch. 8, para. 69(5), 69(6)

- N.B. Statements complying with paragraph 15(4) of Schedule 8A to the 1948 Act will not be required where accounts are prepared to comply with Schedule 8.

Non-coterminous financial years

Where a holding company has subsidiaries whose financial years are not coterminous with that of the holding company the notes must state:

Sch. 8, para. 70

- The reasons why the holding company's directors consider that the subsidiaries' financial years should not be coterminous.

– The dates on which the subsidiaries' financial years
   ended or the earliest and latest of those dates.

(Section 153 of the 1948 Act requires the directors of a
holding company to secure that the financial year of its
subsidiaries coincides with the holding company's except where there are good reasons against this. See also
section 152(4), and note paragraph 18 of SSAP 14
(group accounts).)

G   Filing exemptions for small and medium-sized companies

Small and medium-sized companies (as defined below)
which have prepared accounts complying with Schedule 8
to the 1948 Act are entitled to file a modified set of the
directors' report and accounts ("modified accounts") with
the Registrar. *However a full set of the directors' report
and accounts will still be required for submission to the
members of the company.*

C.A. 1981,
s. 5(1).
Sch. 2,
para. 7(2)

The filing exemptions

Small companies

A small company may file a modified balance sheet
showing only those items assigned a letter or a Roman
number in the balance sheet formats, supplemented by
disclosure of debtors falling due after more than one year
and creditors falling due within one year and after one
year.

C.A. 1981,
s. 6(2)(a),
6(3), 6(4)

A small company need not file:

– A profit and loss account.

C.A. 1981,
s. 6(2)(b)

– A directors' report.

C.A. 1981,
s. 6(6)

– Particulars of directors' or higher paid employees'
   emoluments.

C.A. 1981,
s. 6(2)(d)

– Notes to the accounts as required by Schedule 8 with
   the exception of those dealing with:
   Accounting policies (Sch. 8, para. 36)
   Share capital and allotments (Sch. 8, paras. 38, 39)
   Indebtedness and security (Sch. 8, paras. 48(1),
   49(4))
   Basis of translation of foreign currency (Sch. 8, para.
   58(1))
   Corresponding amounts (Sch. 8, para. 58(2))

C.A. 1981,
s. 6(2)(c),
6(5)

Note: Surprisingly perhaps the exemptions do not extend to transactions with directors and officers and, where applicable, the name of the ultimate holding company and details of subsidiaries, associated companies and other trade investments; this information will still have to be given in the modified accounts of a small company.

Medium-sized companies

A medium-sized company may make certain modifications to its profit and loss account but otherwise it is required to file a full set of accounts.

C.A. 1981, s. (7)(a)

For filing purposes a medium-sized company may combine the following profit and loss account headings into one item of "gross profit or loss":

"Operational" basis	*"Type of expenditure" basis*
Turnover	Turnover
Cost of sales	Changes in stocks
Gross profit or loss	Own work capitalised
Other operating income	Other operating income
	Raw materials and consumables
	Other external charges

C.A. 1981, s. 6(8)

The note disclosing turnover and profitability by class of business and turnover by geographical market may be excluded from the set of accounts which is filed.

C.A. 1981, s. 6(7)(b)

Definition of small or medium-sized companies

A company cannot take advantage of the filing exemptions if it is (or was at any time during the financial year to which the accounts relate):

C.A. 1981, s. 5(3), 5(4)

– A public company.
– A banking, insurance or shipping company.
– A member of an ineligible group (which is a group which includes a public company, banking, insurance or shipping company or any body corporate (such as a foreign company) which has power to offer its shares or debentures to the public or falls within the provisions of the Banking Act 1979 or Part II of the Insurance Companies Act 1974).

The general rule is that a company will qualify as small or medium-sized in respect of a financial year if it does not exceed at least two of the following limits *for both that year and the previous year*:

	Small	Medium-sized	
Turnover	£1.4 million	£5.75 million	
Gross assets at end of the year	£0.7 million	£2.8 million	C.A. 1981,
Average number of employees	50	250	s. 8(1), 8(2), 8(3)

Exceptions to this general rule are:

– Entitlement to the exemptions, once established, will not be lost unless the size test is exceeded for two consecutive years.   C.A. 1981, s. 8(5), 8(6)

– A company which is incorporated after the appointed day for Part I of the 1981 Act (June 15, 1982) may qualify as small or medium-sized for its first financial year on the basis of the figures for that year.   C.A. 1981, s. 8(7)

– There is a transitional provision whereby any company incorporated before the appointed day may qualify as small or medium-sized in respect of the first year for which accounts are prepared to comply with Schedule 8 on the basis of the figures for either that year or the preceding year.   C.A. 1981, s. 8(8)

The turnover limits are to be proportionately adjusted for any accounting period which is less than or more than a year.   C.A. 1981, s. 8(11)

After two years dormant a company will, as a consequence, qualify as a small company.

Dormant companies which are members of ineligible groups and which have resolved to be exempt from an audit may avail themselves of the filing exemptions for small companies.   C.A. 1981, s. 12(9)

The application of these rules to companies which move into and out of categories is illustrated in the examples below:

Accounts year	Established company				New company			
	Example 1		Example 2		Example 3		Example 4	
1981	P	N/A	P	N/A	--	–	--	–
1982	P	E	F	E	P	E	F	N
1983	F	E	P	E	F	E	P	N
1984	P	E	P	E	F	N	P	E
1985	F	E	P	E	P	N	F	E
1986	F	N	F	E	P	E	P	E
1987	P	N	P	E	F	E	F	E
1988	P	E	P	E	P	E	F	N

Notes
1. It has been assumed that 1982 is the first year in which the company prepares accounts which comply with Schedule 8, as amended.
2. Recognition has been given to the transitional provisions of section 8(8) of the 1981 Act.
3. Size test − P = Pass, F = Fail.
   Eligible for filing privileges − E = Eligible, N = Not eligible.

Group exemption

A holding company which is required to prepare group accounts will not be able to take advantage of the filing exemptions unless the group as a whole would qualify as small or medium-sized if it were an actual company. If the group qualifies as medium-sized the holding company is also to be treated as medium-sized even though, on its own, it would have qualified as a small company. *It is worth noting that a subsidiary of a large private company may avail itself of the filing exemptions if the subsidiary itself qualifies as small or medium-sized.* C.A. 1981, s. 9(1), 9(2), 9(3)

The figures of turnover, gross assets and average number of employees for the group are to be determined from the group accounts and, where subsidiaries are not dealt with in the group accounts for reasons other than impracticability (section 150(2)(b)(i) of the 1948 Act), from the relevant figures for subsidiaries omitted from the group accounts. C.A. 1981, s. 9(4), 9(5), 9(6)

Modified accounts — directors' responsibilities

In the case of a small company the directors must sign the modified balance sheet prepared for filing purposes as well as the full balance sheet which forms part of the accounts submitted to the shareholders. C.A. 1981, s. 7(1)

If a company takes advantage of the exemptions available to small or medium-sized companies the balance sheet which is filed must include a statement immediately above the directors' signatures that:

– The directors have relied on the exemptions for individual accounts on the ground that the company is entitled to the benefit of those exemptions as a small company (or a medium-sized company)	C.A. 1981, s. 7(2), 7(3)

and, where modified group accounts are filed, that:

– The documents filed include modified group accounts.	C.A. 1981, s. 10(5)(a)

Modified accounts — auditors' responsibilities

The auditors of a small or medium-sized company which proposes to file modified accounts have a duty to provide the directors with a report as to whether the requirements for exemption have been satisfied.	C.A. 1981, s. 7(6)

The expression "the requirements for exemption have been satisfied" is to be taken to mean that:

– The company is entitled to the benefit of the exemptions for individual accounts on the ground claimed by the directors.	C.A. 1981, s. 7(8)(a)
– The modified accounts have been properly prepared in accordance with the rules set out in section 6 of the 1981 Act.	C.A. 1981, s. 7(8)(b)
A special auditors' report must be filed with the modified accounts stating whether, in the opinion of the auditors, the requirements for exemption have been satisfied and reproducing the full text of the auditors' report on the full accounts submitted to the shareholders.	C.A. 1981, s. 7(4), 7(5)

H   Special classes of company

Investment companies

An investment company is required to prepare accounts which comply with Schedule 8 subject to certain modifications where the company has been an investment company (as defined by section 41(3) of the 1980 Act) for the whole of the financial year and has not been prohibited in that year from making a distribution because of section 41(5) of the 1980 Act (particular restrictions on distributions by investment companies). (Section 41(3) of the 1980 Act defines an investment company as a *public* company which has given the Registrar of Companies notice in a prescribed manner that it is to carry on business as an investment company *and* meets the tests in section 41(4) as to maximum size of investments, distribution of income and retention of capital profits.)	Sch. 8, para. 73

– The provisions relating to the revaluation reserve (see section C, *Balance Sheet requirements*, above) do not apply to any profit or loss arising on the revaluation of investment.

Sch. 8, para. 71(1)

– Thus the Act does not rule on the accounting for capital surpluses and deficits and so accepted industry practices may continue. The affairs of investment companies are of course already regulated by the distribution rules in the 1980 Act and by tax legislation (section 359 of the Taxes Act 1970).

– Provisions for the diminution in value of fixed asset investments need not be charged to profit and loss account, but may be charged to a reserve which has been credited with surpluses on the revaluation of investments or be shown separately in the balance sheet under the heading of "other reserves".

Sch. 8, para. 71(2)

– Disclosure must be made in the notes of any distribution which reduces net assets to less than the aggregate of called up share capital and undistributable reserves (as defined by section 40 of the 1980 Act).

Sch. 8, para. 72

Banking, insurance and shipping companies

The EEC Fourth Directive does not apply to the accounts of banks and insurance companies for which special EEC directives are being formulated, nor need it be applied to shipping companies' accounts until 1988. As a consequence the accounts of a banking, insurance or shipping company need not comply with the new requirements of Schedule 8 to the 1948 Act as amended, and may alternatively be prepared in accordance with what is now Schedule 8A to the 1948 Act (i.e. the pre-1981 Act requirements, with some minor amendments imposed by Schedule 2 to the 1981 Act). This privilege is also extended to the *group* accounts of a holding company which has a subsidiary which is a banking, insurance or shipping company.

Sch. 2, paras. 1(b), 2(b)

A "banking company" is defined as a recognised bank or a licensed institution within the meaning of the Banking Act 1979. An "insurance company" is a company to which Part II of the Insurance Companies Act 1974 applies and a "shipping company" is a company which satisfies the Secretary of State that it ought to be regarded as a shipping company in the national interest.

Sch. 2, para. 8

The 1981 Act changes to the disclosure requirements for banking, insurance or shipping companies whose accounts

are prepared to comply with Schedule 8A to the 1948 Act
are as follows:

– The accounts must state (presumably in the notes) that they are prepared in compliance with section 149A (or 152A) of and Schedule 8A to the 1948 Act.	C.A. 1981, s. 17(2)
– The disclosures concerning redeemable preference shares apply to all redeemable shares.	Sch. 2, para. 4(4)(a)
– A public company which purchases its own shares must disclose the number and nominal value of the shares purchased, the aggregate amount of the consideration paid and the reasons for their purchase.	Sch. 2, para. 4(4)(c)
– The concession for insurance companies, that wholly owned but non-insurance subsidiaries may avail themselves of the statutory disclosure exemptions available to their parent company, is withdrawn.	Sch. 2, para. 4(5)(b)
– The extended requirements for disclosure of interests in other companies introduced by sections 3 and 4 of the 1981 Act and the restriction on distributable profits in respect of development costs (section 42A of the 1980 Act) do not apply.	Sch. 2, paras. 5(1), 6(3), 7(1)
– Disclosure in the directors' report of arrangements for directors to acquire shares or debentures will no longer be required.	C.A. 1981, s. 16(2); Sch. 2, para. 5(5)
– The directors' report is not required to be considered by the auditors.	Sch. 2, para. 5(5)
– Where the company takes advantage of the exemptions in Part III of Schedule 8A, the auditor's report must state whether the accounts have been properly prepared in accordance with the Companies Acts 1948 to 1981.	1982 S.I.1092

Overseas companies

An overseas company (i.e. a foreign incorporated company which has a place of business in Great Britain) is required to file accounts with the Registrar in the form that would have been required had it been incorporated in Great Britain. Consequently the accounts of an overseas company are required to comply with Schedule 8 so far as they are not covered by exemptions granted by the Secretary of State (although the relevant legislation has yet to be brought into force: see 1982 S.I. No. 676). The	C.A. 1976, s. 9

exemptions currently in force excuse overseas companies from filing an auditors' report and a directors' report, and from certain disclosure requirements of the 1948 and 1967 Acts which are inappropriate.

Unregistered companies

The disclosure requirements of the 1981 Act apply to unregistered companies, such as chartered companies trading for profit and statutory water companies, in the same manner as they apply to companies generally. Consequently the accounts of unregistered companies are required to comply with Schedule 8, though this requirement is not yet in force.

C.A. 1981, s. 20

I   Transitional rules

For transitional years (i.e. those which straddle the appointed day (June 15, 1982), or which end before the appointed day but for which the accounts are produced afterwards), companies have the choice of preparing accounts in accordance with either the new rules as now contained in Schedule 8 to the 1948 Act, or the old rules as set out in what is now Schedule 8A to the 1948 Act. Since comparative figures will have to be shown most companies can be expected to observe the old rules in a transitional year.

Sch. 2, para. 1(a), 2(a)

The following minor modifications to the old rules apply however:

Accounts

– Such accounts must state (presumably in the notes) that they are prepared in compliance with section 149A (or 152A) of and Schedule 8A to the 1948 Act.

C.A. 1981, s. 17(2)

– The disclosures concerning redeemable preference shares apply to all redeemable shares.

Sch. 2, para. 4(4)(a)

– Where a public company purchases its own shares there must be disclosure of the number and nominal value of shares purchased, the aggregate amount of the consideration paid and the reasons for their purchase.

Sch. 2, para. 4(4)(c)

The last two disclosures provide for the rare cases of companies using the new capital reduction provisions in the Act before the end of a transitional year.

The extended requirements for disclosure of interests in   Sh. 2,
other companies introduced by sections 3 and 4 of the   para. 5(1),
1981 Act, and the restriction on distributable profits in   6(3), 7(1)
respect of development costs (section 42A of the 1980
Act) do not apply to any company which prepares
accounts in accordance with Schedule 8A.

Directors' reports

Directors' reports attached to *Schedule 8A* accounts are
not required to be considered by the auditors. Disclosure
of exports and arrangements for directors to acquire
shares or debentures will no longer be required. (C.A.
1981, s. 16(2), and Sch. 2, paras. 5(4), 5(5)). See the
chapter *Directors' Report*, page 304.

Acquisitions of Private Companies and Businesses

The assets of a limited company can be transferred for value in one of two ways. Either the owners of the shares of the company can agree to sell them, in exchange for cash, loan notes, or shares in the acquiring company or the satisfaction of existing indebtedness, in which case the transaction is commonly described as a "takeover", or some or all of the assets of the company can be sold as such while leaving the existing shareholdings intact. In the former case the net value of the company's assets and liabilities is reflected in the price to be paid for the shares transferred, while in the latter values will be ascribed to individual classes of property, for example, premises, goodwill, stock-in-trade, customer contracts, plant and work-in-progress. Where a business is being sold as a going concern the vendors will often prefer to dispose of the shares, since the element of goodwill included in the consideration is likely to be greater than on a sale of assets on a "break-up" value. In times of economic recession a purchaser prefers the "asset stripping" method, that is a transfer only of realisable assets and not liabilities, as this leaves behind the employees (subject to their redundancy rights); but with the introduction in 1982 of employment continuity regulations (see below) which transfer automatically the workers with the undertaking, one of the advantages of the asset-purchase route has been removed.

There can be significant tax differences both for the vendor and the purchaser between a share sale and an asset sale. On an asset sale, the vendor will be discontinuing the whole or part of a trade or business. There are likely to be capital allowance and stock relief clawbacks, any unutilised trading or capital losses or surplus advance corporation tax will be incapable of carry forward for use by the purchaser, and the vendor's capital gains tax liability, if any, will be dependent on the base cost to the selling company of its assets, rather than the base cost of the shares in that company. The purchaser, on the other hand, will be entitled to capital allowances and stock relief on, broadly speaking, the price it pays for equipment, industrial buildings and stock, and will acquire a capital gains tax base cost for capital assets of the price it pays. It may be entitled to capital gains tax roll-over relief on the assets it buys.

By contrast, on a share sale the existing capital allowance and stock relief position will continue (the purchaser inheriting the potential liability for clawback) and the losses will be preserved (subject to certain anti-avoidance provisions for trading losses and advance corporation tax). The purchaser cannot claim roll-over relief for a share purchase. On a share sale, stamp duty can be minimised by implementing a stamp duty saving scheme (see *Tolley's Tax Planning*), but on an assets sale the purchaser will be liable for two per cent ad valorem duty on most assets, other than those which can be transferred by delivery.

Purchase of shares

As explained in *Formation and Types of Company*, below, a private company is one which has not been registered or re-registered as a public limited company under Part I of the Companies Act 1980 and hence is prohibited by section 15 of the 1980 Act from offering its shares and debentures to the public. Consequently although there is now no limit to the number of shareholders a private company can have (section 28 of the Companies Act 1948 used to prescribe a maximum of 50), it is likely that the shares will be vested in relatively few hands. Accordingly an agreement by all the holders to sell in such a case is simpler to procure than the takeover of a public company whose shares are listed on the Stock Exchange. In the latter case, the number of shareholders necessitates the making of a formal offer instead of the shareholders getting together to negotiate and sign a sale contract. A takeover of a listed company will also involve compliance with a number of detailed statutory and non-statutory rules (see the chapter *Takeovers*, below). It is unsatisfactory for a purchaser to acquire part only of the shares of the target, even fifty-one per cent, since the minority may obstruct the management and prevent the passing of special resolutions. A purchaser will therefore usually try to buy all the issued shares, or at least enough to secure complete control at general meetings. If all but a few are willing to sell, section 209 of the Companies Act 1948 (discussed in the chapter *Takeovers*) provides power to acquire shares of shareholders dissenting from a scheme or contract approved by a majority of nine tenths of shareholders, and this procedure is available for public and private companies alike.

Preliminary stages

While a formal offer for shares is required for takeovers of companies listed on The Stock Exchange, with the offer binding the purchaser as soon as the requisite percentage of acceptances are received, it is more usual in the case of private companies for exploratory negotiations to be commenced with the majority shareholders or the board (who may often be the one and the same), culminating perhaps in initialled heads of agreement, prior to the execution of a formal contract of sale together with a deed of tax indemnity. Investigation of the underlying assets and liabilities is desirable since the acquirer of shares is purchasing obligations as well as benefits unless the vendor agrees to "clean out" the company's balance sheet prior to completion. The process of investigation is not unlike that required in a conveyancing transaction (and may indeed include enquiries as to freehold or leasehold properties owned by the target).

Accountants' report

Often an intending purchaser will, with the vendor's consent, appoint its own auditors as investigating accountants for the purposes of examining the target's books and records and ascertaining the state and value of the business. This process assists the purchaser in putting a net asset value on the shares, but the more thorough the investigation the more the vendor is likely to resist the imposition of warranties in the sale agreement on the basis that no reliance has been or need be placed on them. The better course, as far as the purchaser is concerned, may be for him to seek information on an informal basis and afterwards insist on tight warranties. If a detailed report is commissioned, the parties will want to ensure confidentiality so as not to arouse suspicion among the target's employees or customers or otherwise affect goodwill. The negotiators are, of course, "insiders" although no liability for insider dealing in the target's shares attaches under Part V of the Companies Act 1980, unless the shares are listed on a recognised stock exchange (see *Insider Dealing*, below). The purchaser should require that the report covers at least the following matters.

Contents of accountants' report

(a)　corporate structure including intra-group debts and trading;

(b)　nature of the business and any areas which show growth or recession;

(c)　details of management and other personnel, including terms of service contracts and any unusual benefits, general terms and conditions of the work force and state of labour relations at plant level (including unionisation) and pension rights;

(d)　production, marketing, distribution and accounting policies;

(e)　turnover and profits in relation to capital employed over a representative number of accounting periods;

(f)　a detailed break-down of assets and liabilities including capital and forward commitments;

(g)　taxation outstanding and suggested tax indemnities;

(h)　borrowing powers, accounting policies, insurance policies;

(i)　future prospects seen in the light not merely of the target's present position but as an integral part of the purchaser's existing business (if any). If the report is on a major scale, management consultants, credit reference agencies and even a merchant bank may be involved. The terms of appointment and division of function between the professional advisers should be as clear-cut as possible, not only to produce material of the greatest utility but also to demarcate lines of responsibility if claims for damages in negligence should subsequently arise.

If the purchaser is a listed company, The Stock Exchange's *Admission of Securities to Listing* contains various requirements concerning accountants' reports.

Investigation of title

Where a major portion of the assets of the target includes land the purchaser will, in addition to extracting property warranties in the agreement (see below), invariably require his solicitor to effect enquiries and searches.

Companies Registry

Section 95 of the Companies Act 1948 requires registration of floating charges over a company's assets, including land. If not registered within twenty-one days of creation, the charge is void as against a liquidator or creditor although it remains valid against the company itself or its shareholders (*Independent Automatic Sales v Knowles* [1962] 3 All E.R. 27). A company search revealing the existence of a charge supplies notice to a purchaser of incumbrances which, if not cleared off by completion, will seriously hamper subsequent dealings with the company's property. A company search will also reveal details of the company's share capital and shareholders, its memorandum and articles of association, the location of its registered office, the identity of the directors and secretary and so on (see *Company Searches*, below).

Other registries

The Local Land Charges Register, the Land Register and the Land Charges Register should also be searched by the purchaser for incumbrances on the property. However the relevant legislation only affords protection to purchasers of land and not to purchasers of shares in the company owning the land.

(1) *The Local Land Charges Registry.* This is maintained by the local authority in the area in which the subject property is situate. A local land charge will be enforceable against the purchaser of charged property whether registered or not, although the purchaser of an interest in land or in the proceeds of sale of it has a right to compensation if the local land charge is not revealed by a search at the Registry because of incorrect registration or non-registration (section 10(3) of the Local Land Charges Act 1975). A purchaser of shares rather than of the land itself has no such right.

(2) *Land Charges Registry*. The Land Charges Act 1972 provisions authorising guaranteed official searches of the Register and the payment of compensation when a charge is not discoverable behind the root of title, apply only to purchasers of unregistered land, again excluding purchasers of shares. Moreover any charge which has been created by the company to be purchased will be enforceable against it despite non-registration under the Land Charges Act.

(3) *Land Registry*. The vendor's consent is required before the purchaser can see the register. Again the protection designed for a purchaser for value of registered land (by section 20 of the Land Registration Act 1925) does not extend to a purchaser of shares, who will not take free from an unregistered registrable incumbrance.

Enquiries

The purchaser's solicitor may require completion of the usual conveyancing form of Preliminary Enquiries (copies of which can be obtained from law stationers). The vendor or his adviser is not bound to supply the requested information but false or misleading replies may give rise to damages if subsequently incorporated by a warranty (*Gilchester Properties, Ltd v Gomm* [1948] 1 All E.R. 493; see generally, Emmet on Title, 17th Edition, chapters 1 and 4). Since it is unlikely that a shares sale would go off as a result of preliminary enquiries, the answers thereto are invariably unhelpful ("the purchaser must rely on his own searches"), and as the affected matters can be dealt with in the contract the practice of asking for them is not universal.

Investigation of title: documents

The purchaser will obviously wish to examine or see any title documents to the company's property, although these will tell him little more about incumbrances than already discovered at the registries. If the property is *registered land*, the Land Certificate should be in the vendor's possession if there are no charges by way of legal mortgage or mortgages on the land; by section 65 of the Land Registration Act 1925 the Land Certificate must be deposited at the Land Registry while any such incumbrance is registered. The names and description of the property on the register and Land Certificate should be examined against each other.

If the property is *unregistered land* the title deeds are less illuminating than the Land Certificate in showing up any incumbrances. No evidence of leases, mortgages, estate contracts and so on is marked on them. However the deeds should be requested for inspection if only to check that they are in order, and will be available for handing over at completion.

Financial assistance

The purchaser's solicitor should check with the purchaser how he intends to pay for the acquisition, and in particular whether he hopes to use the surplus cash or assets of the target in any way. If so, the restrictions imposed by section 42 of the Companies Act 1981 on a company's ability to give financial assistance for the acquisition of its shares will require careful consideration (see the chapter *Financial Assistance*, below). Where the target company is, or can be turned into, a private company it may be possible for it to give financial assistance by taking advantage of the procedure laid down in section 43 of the 1981 Act.

The sale agreement

Warranties

In a purchase of shares, the purchaser acquires all the liabilities as well as all the assets of the undertaking. Investigation into the company's affairs may not reveal the full extent of these, so a prudent purchaser will ensure that the agreement for sale and purchase, to be signed by both parties, contains a large number of warranties given by the vendor covering areas where problems might arise. On breach of any warranty by the vendor the purchaser may claim damages, but he may not repudiate the contract as a whole unless the breach deprives him of substantially all of the benefit he would have received thereunder (see generally *Hong Kong Fir Shipping Co. v Kawasaki* [1962] 2 Q.B.26 and the cases, following that decision). The measure of damages for breach will sometimes be written into the agreement. This will probably be the direct and attributable loss suffered by the purchaser as a consequence of breach, because the alternative measure – the amount of the diminution in the value of the purchaser's shares – may pose great difficulties in quantification. A right of rescission for pre-completion breach of warranty may also be written in.

In *Levison v Farin* [1978] 2 All E.R. 1149, Levison sold her fashion design business to Farin, the agreement containing a warranty that between the balance sheet date and completion there would be no material adverse change in the overall value of the net assets of the company. In fact, due to Levison's illness, by completion there was such a material adverse change, the balance sheet figure of £44,000 having been reduced by £8,600. Farin recovered damages in the sum of £5,560 which represented the direct loss suffered of £8,600 less the £2,940 tax benefit obtained by off-setting the trading loss which had resulted in the reduction of the balance sheet figure against later profits.

Misrepresentation

If a false statement of fact which was material in inducing the purchaser to enter the contract is continued in a warranty, a right of rescission will arise whether written into the agreement or not, at common law if the misrepresentation is fraudulent and in equity and under the Misrepresentation Act 1967 if it is negligent or innocent. An agreement for purchase of shares is not a contract *uberrimae fides*, so the failure to disclose a material fact will not amount to misrepresentation unless some part of the matter is referred to in the agreement and non-disclosure amounts to distortion. If there is no such distortion, the purchaser may instead hope to rely on the rule in *Hedley Byrne & Co v Heller & Partners* [1964] A.C. 565 that, where a duty of care arises between negotiating parties with a "special relationship", damages may be awarded in tort for negligent mis-statement, which may perhaps be stretched to cover negligent non-statement. It may also be possible to proceed against, for example, a negligent professional adviser such as an auditor, if reliance has been placed on audited accounts to the knowledge of the adviser (see *JEB Fasteners v Bloom* [1981] 3 All E.R. 289 and *Auditors*, below). If the misrepresentation is made fraudulently, that is,

(a) with knowledge of its falsity; or

(b) without belief in its truth; or

(c) recklessly, not caring whether it is true or false,

the purchaser may rescind and bring a common law action for deceit and can recover the whole loss flowing from the misrepresentation whether foreseeable or not (*Doyle v Olby (Ironmongers) Ltd* [1969] 2QB 158).

If the misrepresentation contained in the warranty is negligently or innocently made, the purchaser's remedies are now largely governed by the Misrepresentation Act 1967. Before the Act was passed rescission was not possible (a) if a misrepresentation was incorporated as a term in a contract or (b) once the contract had been executed. Section 1 of the 1967 Act makes rescission possible in both cases. However this right may be lost if the representee (the purchaser) affirms the contract after discovery of the misrepresentation, or if it is impossible to restore the parties to their original positions, or if an innocent third party has acquired rights for value in the subject matter of the agreement. This is always true of rescission, but by section 2(2) of the Act the right to rescind may be removed altogether by a court, which may award damages instead where there has been an innocent misrepresentation. If the right to rescind has already been lost as above, damages will be awarded under section 2(2). Section 2(1) of the Act provides in effect that damages may be claimed for negligent misrepresentation if the representee would have been so entitled had the misrepresentation been fraudulent, i.e. that a misrepresentation was relied on and loss was suffered. The question of *reliance* on the misrepresentation is an interesting one, particularly if the purchaser has conducted his own full investigation into the vendor's affairs, but the misrepresentation need not have been the only factor inducing entry into the contract, providing it was material (see *Barton v Armstrong* [1975] 2 All E.R. 465).

In practical terms the purchaser who discovers that a negligent or innocent misrepresentation has been made in a warranty has several possible remedies open to him. Although the misrepresentation may by then be an incorporated term in an executed contract, he may rescind the contract and be indemnified, unless on general principles he has lost his right to rescind. Alternatively, if the misrepresentation was innocently made, the court may grant damages instead if the rescission would cause the vendor excessive hardship. If the misrepresentation was negligently made, the purchaser may claim damages under section 2(1) as well as or instead of rescission, at his option. The Act does not indicate the measure of damages for either section and this has led to some confusion in the courts. In *Andre & Cie v Michel Blanc* [1979] 2 W.L.R. 429 a tortious measure of damages has been advocated for section 2(1) by the Court of Appeal, with the aim of putting the representee in the position he would have been in had the misrepresentation not been made. However in an unreported 1980 first instance case, *Errington v Martell-Wilson*, a contractual measure of damages, calculated to put the representee in the position he would have been in had the representation been true, was awarded. This confusion has also surrounded the measure of damages for section 2(2). Section 2(3) provides that there shall be no double recovery if damages are awarded under both sections, so section 2(2) perhaps either involves an indemnity measure or is *sui generis*.

In view of this uncertainty a purchaser might be well advised to view the whole issue as a breach of contract rather than as a misrepresentation problem. He could thus claim damages for breach, which might be far more substantial than those awarded under section 2(2). He could also repudiate if the breach was one which deprived him of substantially the whole benefit of the contract. This is completely different from rescission *ab initio* for misrepresentation and so no question arises of a court invoking section 2(2) (damages in lieu). The purchaser in such a case has more control over the outcome of the breach.

In recent years some vendors have tried to include a warranty in their agreements excluding the provisions of the Misrepresentation Act altogether. However section 3 of the Misrepresentation Act, as amended by section 8 of the Unfair Contract Terms Act 1977, prohibits *contracting out of liability* by such terms unless it is 'reasonable' to do so. In *Cremdean Properties v Nash* (1977) 244 E.G. 547 the Court of Appeal showed itself prepared to take a hard line on this issue and it is likely that no circumvention of section 3 will be allowed.

Clauses in the vending agreement which attempt to limit the vendor's liability for breach to the purchase price or any other figure are not required by the Unfair Contract Terms Act 1977 to be "reasonable", because the Act does not apply to contracts for the sale of securities (U.C.T.A. 1977, Sch. 1, para 1(e)).

Standard warranties

There are numerous widely used standard warranties which a purchaser's solicitor will introduce (assuming, as is conventionally the case, that he is preparing the sale agreement). These may be incorporated into the main text, but are frequently added as a schedule. No single aspect of the transaction invites more contention than the final format of warranties. The purchaser's adviser will ritually assert that full, unqualified warranties covering every part of the business transferred as well as the status of the transferors are essential for the protection of the purchasers interest; he is buying the shares "blind" having no knowledge or control of the company's management and the right to sue if the business is worth less than the consideration price remains his only weapon. On the other hand, the vendor's advisers, if the purchaser has already conducted an investigation into the target's affairs, will try to limit post-completion responsibilities either by deletion of probing warranties altogether or by the insertion of qualifications, for instance "so far as the warrantors are aware," or "to the best of the warrantors' knowledge information and belief" (which affords a higher duty of care). The contracting parties themselves, having reached agreement in principle at an early stage by exchanges of letters, may be bewildered by this approach and may not understand why the lawyers cannot adopt a brisker timetable. In seeking to protect one's client's interest therefore, it is advisable to remember:

(a) that where the adviser is suggesting the insertion of particular warranties, it should be explained to the client why these are thought to be needed;

(b) a prolonged insistance on unqualified warranties that cannot reasonably be given by the other side may cause the sale to go off;

(c) where warranties are included to "probe" for information by way of disclosure (see "Disclosure Letter" below), they should not be drawn wider than is necessary to discover the state of the business to be sold;

(d) a timetable should be set by which the process of bargaining on warranties and other contentious matters is resolved. Too often last-minutes changes to the wording of a sale agreement can cause considerable difficulties and may even delay completion.

Frequently the vendor will seek to limit the life of the warranties to a specified period, arguing that if there are undisclosed liabilities and the like these should all have come to light within a few years, and that he should not be left with an indefinite liability. He may also seek to limit the maximum amount recoverable under the warranties to the total purchase price, or some aggregate thereof. And he may seek to set a *de minimis* amount (say, £5,000) below which no claim under any specific warranty will lie. The purchaser, whether or not he accepts any of the above restrictions, may seek to withhold part of the purchase price for a period of, say, six months or a year, giving him a period to see whether the warranties are untrue and, if they are, enabling him to recover out of the retention rather than relying on the future credit-worthiness of the vendor.

The following basic warranties can be regarded as "usual" where a commercial business is being sold. Often a large number of additional warranties are called for; in addition detailed tax warranties will usually be requested. If the company being sold is a member of a group of companies, a large number of additional tax warranties are likely to be called for.

Status of the
target company

1. That all documents and returns have been duly made to the Registrar of Companies.

2. All legal requirements affecting the formation and operation of the target have been met and no breaches of the Companies Acts have occurred. No undisclosed resolutions have been passed.

Accounts

3. Balance sheet and profit and loss account present a true and fair view of the target's affairs, and have been prepared in accordance with the statutory requirements.

4. Net asset value as at completion date not less than as shown the accounts. All liabilities are taken account of, including taxation. Stock in trade and work in progress has been included at realisable value.

5. Proper provision has been made for contingent and other debts and liabilities.

6. Since the balance sheet date no dividends have been paid, no loan or share capital repaid, no material commitments entered into and there has been no departure from conducting the business in the ordinary course.

7. No unusual or long-term contracts, no major capital expenditure, no assets disposed of at less than the higher of book value or market value.

Assets

8. Target is sole beneficial owner of and has a good and marketable title to the assets included in the accounts, free of any charge, equity lien or encumbrance. All debts owed will be collectable in full.

9. Target has good title with vacant possession to leasehold properties the present user of which has planning permission and is not subject to any statutory notice or restriction.

Tax

10. All tax returns have been made and such returns are not the subject of disputed assessment by the Inland Revenue (other major tax warranties will include PAYE, VAT, N.I., capital gains tax base values, roll-over relief claims, shortfall clearances, development land tax liabilities).

Employer

11. Particulars of existing pensions schemes are those which have been disclosed to the purchaser.

12. Written statements of the terms of service of every employee of the company pursuant to the Employment Protection (Consolidation) Act 1978 are as disclosed and there are no employees engaged in the business except as set out in a separate schedule.

13. No alterations to salaries or other terms and conditions will be made prior to completion without written consent of the purchaser.

14. There is no trade union recognition agreement other than as disclosed and no facts exist which could give rise to any industrial dispute in the business.

Miscellaneous

15. Books and records of the target company have been accurately kept; all documents of title are in possession of the target and are properly stamped.

16. There is no actual or pending litigation or arbitration affecting the company nor are there any facts or matters in existence which could give rise to the same.

17. The target has adequate insurance cover against all risks which a company in its type of business normally covers.

18. The target has all consents licences and permits it requires to carry on its business. None of its agreements or arrangements is registrable under the Restrictive Trade Practices Act 1976 or infringes the Fair Trading Act 1973 or the Treaty of Rome.

	19.	On completion the Vendors will have the right to sell their shares in the target company free from any lien or incumbrances.

Information   20. All information relating to the Company which is material to a purchaser of the shares has been disclosed; information supplied by the vendors, the directors of the company, and its professional advisers is true and accurate in all material respects.

The warranties will be given by the vendors accepting liability in proportion to the number of shares they presently hold. If the liability is joint and several, a claim can be brought for breach of warranty against one vendor who must then seek contribution from his co-warrantors. Vendors of a business who are not directly concerned in management may require the directors to participate as warrantors, at least as regards those warranties which concern the day to day operation of the undertaking. Where the vendor is the parent company of the target, the purchaser will normally be satisfied with a corporate warrantor only. If the vendor is an intermediate company within a group, the purchaser may require a guarantee by the ultimate parent.

Disclosure letter

A vendor is extremely unlikely to be able to offer unqualified warranties in the terms suggested above. Nor is a purchaser likely to expect this. The warranties are therefore a vehicle for requiring total disclosure of all matters which may affect the operation of the business in the purchaser's hands. The vendor's solicitor should carefully take his client through each warranty, pointing out its pitfalls, to establish whether it can be given without reservation. Clients are generally most willing to co-operate in this exercise but sometimes do not understand, without guidance, what sort of material they are required to bring to light, for example, disputed accounts, personal injury claims by employees, change in treatment of a particular item in the accounts, adverse factors affecting sales, staff problems, and debts due where there is the likelihood of non-payment. All these should be set out in a disclosure letter delivered to the purchaser's solicitors prior to the signing of the formal contract. The purchaser should insist on delivery well before he becomes liable to pay any part of the purchase consideration, in case there are revealed matters which justify a rescission of the bargain.

Other terms

To define all the possible clauses in the sale and purchase agreement is beyond the scope of this work. The reader is referred to Knight, *The Acquisition of Private Companies*, 3rd edition, and Wine, *Buying and*

Selling Private Companies and Businesses, both of which contain various precedents. The basic structure of the agreement will normally be as follows:

(1) The parties.

(2) Recitals: status of company, its capital, new shares to be issued if stamp duty saving scheme to be adopted, any special circumstances.

(3) Definitions.

(4) Agreement by the vendor to pass any necessary resolutions.

(5) Agreement to purchase.

(6) The consideration.

(7) Completion and documents to be delivered on completion.

(8) Special terms applying to any properties.

(9) Special conditions.

(10) Post-completion obligations of vendor and purchaser.

(11) Warranties and indemnities (cross referencing to a schedule).

(12) Employees (cross referencing to a schedule).

(13) Restrictive covenants.

(14) Announcement and notices.

If the target company is itself the parent of one or more subsidiaries being sold, the agreement will be adapted so that the representations and warranties apply equally to group accounts, group employees, and group management. It is not necessary to have a separate agreement for each subsidiary.

Restrictive covenants

Covenants restraining the vendor from competing with the business transferred are common, but must be carefully drafted to avoid being excessive in extent or duration and thus unenforceable. All covenants in restraint of trade are *prima facie* void as contrary to public policy, and will only be enforceable if they are reasonable with reference to the interests of the parties concerned and of the public. A typical covenant might involve the vendor of the shares in a company promising not to take up similar employment or set up a similar business in a geographical area associated with the existing business for a certain length of time (e.g. 3 years). Even if the parties are not in dispute, the court maintains a jurisdiction to declare the provision illegal and unenforceable. However the court will generally look benevolently on a reasonable restrictive covenant if a purchaser is buying the goodwill as well as other assets from the covenanting vendor. The goodwill would be worthless if the vendor could compete without hindrance with the purchaser. Further, if one part of the covenant is unreasonable but severable, the court will usually apply the "blue pencil test", and enforce the remainder if it will stand on its own (*Goldsoll v Goldman* [1914] 2 Ch. 603).

Stamp duty saving scheme

Often the purchaser will persuade the vendor to implement a stamp duty saving scheme to minimise the purchaser's stamp duty on the shares it acquires. In essence, this involves a bonus issue by the target of shares on renounceable letters of allotment (the handing over of which does not attract stamp duty) and a conversion of the existing shares into deferred shares of almost negligible value (the transfer of which accordingly attracts only nominal stamp duty). The vendor will usually require an indemnity from the purchaser protecting him from any adverse tax effects of the scheme. Stamp duty saving schemes are dealt with in detail in *Tolley's Tax Planning*.

Indemnities

An indemnity is another type of promise given by the vendor that he will bear financial loss in specified circumstances. An indemnity may be included in the main agreement against any loss, damage, expense or liability resulting from any of the warranties being untrue, but a vendor would probably resist this potentially very wide promise. Liability under an indemnity will be for the indemnified amount, which may not correspond with the actual economic loss to the purchaser (this amount being, broadly speaking, the sum recoverable for breach of warranty).

The most common indemnities will be those in the Deed of Indemnity concerning tax. This deed, executed contemporaneously with the sale agreement, may be a short "catch-all" deed wherein the vendor agrees to indemnify the purchaser in respect of any claim for (a) taxation arising from any transaction effected or any income earned before completion; (b) capital transfer tax arising from the sale.

Alternatively the vendor may only accept the obligation to indemnify in respect of certain taxes, which will be listed in a longer deed. If there is more than one vendor, they will usually agree to indemnify jointly and severally; the purchaser may claim from all or any of them should the need arise and it is up to the vendors to apportion the amount payable amongst themselves. Under either form of indemnity, the purchaser is concerned particularly with tax liabilities which, though primarily those of the vendor shareholders, can also be recovered from the target (eg certain of the close company tax liabilities).

Consents and approvals

Once an agreement satisfactory to both parties has been drawn up, all necessary consents to and approvals of the sale and purchase agreement must be obtained and all those interested must be informed before completion can take place.

(1) *Third party consents to the purchase of shares.* Consent is required where the purchaser, vendor (or the undertaking itself) has entered into contracts with third parties which may affect or be affected by the transaction. Thus if the main agreement includes a clause that all office equipment will be transferred with the undertaking, such equipment being the subject of a hire purchase contract, the vendor (if he is the hirer or guarantor) will have to obtain the consent of the owner to substitute the purchaser or the target for himself as the obligor. Occasionally a hire contract made with the target itself will require novation if there is a provision requiring this on a change of control.

(2) *The shareholders of the purchasing company.* These may have to consent before a share transfer can proceed, particularly if the articles of the target specify this. This is unlikely if there are a large number of shareholders, but even in this case consent may still be required if the transfer is for a consideration of shares in the purchasing company and an increase in the authorised capital is necessary. Even if there is sufficient authorised share capital which is at the disposal of the directors, section 14 of the Companies Act 1980 provides that allotments are permissible only if authorised by the company's articles or by an ordinary resolution in general meeting for a maximum duration (five years) and amount (see the chapter *Shares*).

(3) *Vendor or purchaser a listed company.* The Quotations Department of The Stock Exchange may require the approval of shareholders to the transfer to be sought (see the chapter on *Takeovers* for The Stock Exchange requirements as set out in the *Admission of Securities to Listing*). Circulars to shareholders, or public announcements, may be required.

(4) *Mergers of two or more commercial undertakings.* These are a special case sometimes requiring the consent of the Monopolies and Mergers Commission (see *Takeovers*).

(5) *Statutory consents.* There is legislation regulating transfer activity in insurance, banking, unit trust management, investment and other ventures. The consent of the Secretary of State or other government Department may be required before a purchaser may take over the running of the company. The acquisition of a business may also, if it reduces the number of competitors in a particular trading activity, require the consent of the Office of Fair Trading.

Completion

Prior to completion

A press announcement of the share transfer may be made if it is one which will have a significant impact on suppliers and customers. There is no firm rule about this, although listed companies may be required by The Stock Exchange to inform their shareholders or even, if the transaction is a Class 1 transaction for the purposes of chapter 4 of the

Stock Exchange's *Admission of Securities to Listing*, to put out a circular (see the chapter *Takeovers*).

Once a draft contract is finalised the parties may proceed at once to signature, although if this is too far in advance of the projected completion date (eg more than 28 days) it may be made subject to the fulfilment of certain conditions and the obtaining of relevant consents. Often contract and completion take place on the same day to enable an efficient transfer of management. The agreement will be only one of several documents to be completed and the purchaser's solicitors will usually draw up a completion agenda. This agenda will usually list,

(a) the people who should be present (and whether they should attend with any company seals);

(b) the documents to be produced;

(c) drafts of company and board resolutions passed both pre- and post-completion, to authorise the transfer and any stamp duty saving scheme.

At the completion meeting the vendor must usually deliver,

(a) share transfers duly executed in favour of the purchaser or his or its nominees;

(b) renounceable allotment letters duly executed (if a stamp duty saving scheme is being implemented);

(c) resignations of directors (see below);

(d) resignations of secretary and auditors (see below);

(e) waiver of pre-emption rights;

(f) the deed of indemnity, if any; and

(g) powers of attorney.

The statutory books of the company (particularly the register of members) may be checked. The purchaser will complete the registration application forms on the allotment letters if a stamp duty saving scheme is being implemented. Service agreements will be executed if resigning officers of the company are to be re-engaged. Finally the purchaser will deliver the consideration in whatever form has been agreed:

(a) share certificates; or

(b) allotment letters for consideration shares; or

(c) bankers draft.

A share-for-share consideration does not require a valuation of assets prior to allotment of new shares, provided the offer is made to all the vendor shareholders (section 24(2) of the Companies Act 1980, as amended).

Post completion

After completion the purchaser's solicitor will attend to miscellaneous matters of reorganisation, produce conformed copies of the purchase agreement, make any requisite alterations to banking arrangements including mandates and prepare and deliver to the Registrar of Companies, within 14 days, notices of change of directors and secretary (Form 9b) and of registered office (Form 4a). There will also be stamp duty on the share transfers and probably various tax matters to be dealt with.

Effect of the share transfer on employees

The transfer of control of the shares will have no effect on the contracts of employment between the target company and its employees. The employees need not be consulted, even though the new owners may alter non-contractually regulated working conditions, or have completely different plans for company growth, promotion chances and so on. If the identity of the employing company is changed, then broadly that of itself does not trigger an obligation to give to each employee a written statement under section 4 of the Employment Protection (Consolidation) Act 1978, provided the continuity of employment is not altered. A change of employer within the purchaser's group does create such an obligation. If the target's employees have been employed directly by a corporate vendor or another group company, subsequent employment by the target itself or by a corporate purchaser involves a dismissal (which will have redundancy payment and other implications), unless the continuity provisions in the Employment Protection (Consolidation) Act 1978 apply.

Share premium account and pre-acquisition profits

If the purchaser pays for the target company not with cash but with its own shares, it will, subject to section 37 of the Companies Act 1981, be required to open a share premium account equal to the excess of the market value of the target's shares over the nominal value of the shares the purchaser issues as consideration. The result is to reduce the profits per share available for distribution by the parent and generally to prevent the purchaser using the target's pre-acquisition profits to pay out dividends. Section 37, however, excludes the obligation to open a share premium account if, broadly speaking, the purchaser acquires at least 90 per cent of the target company, though the application of section 37 does not automatically mean that pre-acquisition profits of the target company are then available for distribution by the purchaser once these have been passed up by way of dividend. (This topic is dealt with in greater detail in the chapter on *Takeovers*, below).

Effect of the share transfer on directors and officers

A purchaser of the majority of shares of the target company will wish to exercise control by appointing his own board of directors and other officers. Thus the directors, company secretary and auditors will usually tender their resignations at a board meeting just prior to completion. At the same time the purchaser must have appointed its own directors and officers to avoid a lacuna. The purchaser may of course offer further appointment to the resigning officers and will often do so if the vendor has been the proprietor of the business and it is desired to maintain know-how and goodwill.

On resignation directors will become entitled to any contractual benefits accrued during their services to the company (for instance arrears of salary and pension), but other forms of compensation on loss of office are strictly regulated by sections 191 to 193 of the Companies Act 1948 (see page 259). Any such payments will not be lawful if they are not disclosed to the shareholders and approved by the company in general meeting. Section 192 provides that any transfer of any part of the property of the company to a retiring director must be similarly disclosed and approved. Section 193 provides that in certain types of share transfer, a director is under a duty to take all reasonable steps to ensure that details of any proposed payment to be made to him are sent to shareholders.

Any director can be removed from office by ordinary resolution at a general meeting under section 184 of the 1948 Act, whether or not his contract or the company's articles permit this (see page 246). Such removal does not prejudice entitlement to compensation for loss of office, section 184(6) or other statutory or contractual benefits, since removal or resignation as a director does not of itself determine any underlying service contract, which will have to be treated like any other service contract. To avoid difficulty a director's service contract may provide for automatic termination on ceasing to hold office, without the necessity for periods of notice.

Purchase of assets

General considerations

The phrase "purchase of assets" is used rather loosely to describe both a purchase of particular assets of a company and a purchase of an entire business or undertaking. Where a company is not to be sold as a going concern, its saleable parts are severed from the obsolete stock, defective premises, potential liabilities and surplus staff. The Transfer of Undertakings (Protection of Employment) Regulations 1981 only protect employees on the transfer of an "undertaking", a term usually applied when a purchaser buys assets including goodwill such that the vendor can no longer continue in the same business (but defined in Regulation 2 to include "any trade or business"). As the Regulations represent an important additional obligation, purchase of assets proper and purchase of a business should be carefully distinguished and explained to clients, even though the method of acquisition is similar for both.

A purchase of assets (which in the text below includes the purchase of a business unless otherwise stated) is often less complicated in procedure, or at least requires less lengthy acquisition documents, warranties and indemnities, than a purchase of shares. It is advantageous for the purchaser because he need take on only selected assets and liabilities, which makes investigation far simpler. As briefly mentioned earlier, there can also be tax advantages to the purchaser in buying assets. There may also be benefits to a vendor of retaining a charge on the assets if the payment of the consideration is deferred in whole or in part.

Preliminary stages – investigation

Investigation of title is even more essential in a purchase of assets than in a purchase of shares, but results in a greater degree of legislative protection. Where land is being sold the purchaser must examine the Land Register, the Land Charges Register and the Local Land Charges Register, but as a purchaser of actual interests in land, he will be protected by the statutory provisions whose benefits are denied to the purchaser of shares (see above). The title documents to all property, real, personal or intellectual where appropriate must also be examined.

Charges against the company itself may be discovered by carrying out a company search (see page 219). All charges – like Inland Revenue charges and debentures – should be removed by the vendor from the assets prior to completion. The purchaser will require to see a certificate of discharge and will normally insist on the insertion of a related indemnity in the sale agreement.

Valuation

It is vitally important in a purchase of assets that what is actually being bought is carefully defined and valued. Anything which is not specifically mentioned in a schedule to the sale agreement may become the subject of later dispute and lazy stocktaking and drafting could leave the vendor with assets for which he has no further use. The transaction may also involve several stages. Thus there will almost inevitably be a period between contract and completion, particularly if licences and leasehold properties are to be transferred and consents are required. The date at which a valuation of stock or plant is to take place must be decided by the parties, and where this takes place at or shortly before completion provision is required in the sale agreement for a "final payment date" at which refunds or further payments are made.

The risk and duty to insure may pass to the purchaser on exchange of contracts, whilst an agreed sum for the stock is paid over at completion when the assets pass, with a balancing of payments taking place on the final payment date.

Valuation may be a complicated process; the more so as the final consideration may be re-apportioned with an eye to tax and stamp duty consequences (see below). The purchaser will normally appoint a valuer who will work closely with the vendor in stocktaking and examination of accounts. However as differing valuations, even by professional valuers, are possible, it is wise to provide in the agreement for the settlement of disputes, either by independent reporting accountants agreed on by the parties or by an arbitrator appointed in accordance with the Arbitration Acts, whose decision shall be binding.

The assets of a business can be roughly divided into eight categories, all of which require different approaches for valuation.

(1) *Premises and property*
Land and buildings will be treated as fixed assets by the valuer. If the buildings have been so adapted as to constitute specialised premises, only suitable for carrying out the business being sold, the value will be the net current replacement cost including site works. If the buildings are non-specialised the value will be the current open market value for the existing use with vacant possession. The land will also be valued at current open market value for the existing use. Obviously the parties are free to negotiate other figures.

Some integral plant and machinery, like air conditioning, space heating, fire hydrants, drainage systems and lifts, installed for the benefit of the building rather than the business, will be included in the valuation of the building at net current replacement cost value (determined with reference to depreciation and the proportion of working life remaining).

(2) *Plant and machinery*
The valuer must draw up an inventory of plant and machinery, which as a general rule and unless otherwise specified will not include dies, moulds, patterns, jigs, drawings designs and similar items (or spare parts which are normally counted in with stock). To avoid stamp duty any fixed plant will wherever possible be unbolted or otherwise severed so that it can be transferred by physical delivery.

The valuer's report must clearly define what is being valued and the date of valuation. The plant and machinery will generally be valued at open market value on the assumption that it will continue in its existing use in the business of the company. Allowance must be made for the cost of installation, wear and tear, age and obsolescence.

(3) *Stock in trade*
An inventory should be prepared of the stock which includes raw materials, work-in-progress, and finished goods. It is important to verify the physical existence of the stock, and for the valuer to agree on the basis of stock valuation with the parties, who may take differing views as to the treatment of values of raw materials and have different attitudes to obsolete stock.

The vendor's employees will normally perform the stock taking, under the supervision of the valuers to ensure it is systematic, well-informed, efficient in the identification of slow-moving, obsolete or defective stock, and in accordance with any specific instructions. It is helpful if the vendor has kept continuous stocktaking records as a rapid one-off stocktake may be less efficient and important items missed off the inventory. The stock taking should identify articles and ownership, count, measure or weigh all stock, report any damaged or defective stock, and record all this information. The actual measure ent may be very rough, based on approximate trigonometric calculations if the stock is stored in heaps, or on proportions if in containers. Work-in-progress may be either physically counted or calculated with reference to the movement of stock; it is undesirable to rely solely on accounting records. Customers' contract files may also be checked.

Normally all the stock will be valued at the lower of cost and net realisable value. Surplus stock must be valued as scrap, as must any work in progress or finished goods which are obsolete.

(4) *Goodwill*
Goodwill is difficult to define and even more difficult to value. Lord Eldon described it as "nothing more than the probability that the old customers will resort to the old place even though the old trader or shopkeeper has gone". It is important to remember that an assignment of goodwill is subject to stamp duty, so that the purchaser will want to ascribe a purely nominal value to it if the purchase consideration can realistically be apportioned between the other assets.

(5) *Benefit of contracts*
The assignment for value of existing customer and supply contracts attracts stamp duty, so although it is likely that the purchaser will want to secure the benefit of such contracts, he should avoid direct assignment. The benefit can be transferred by the vendor cancelling and the purchaser novating the agreements, with third parties' consent. However as cancellation may give rise to liabilities for the vendor, it is probably better to draw up completely new contracts with the other parties. Thus if the purchaser wishes to ensure that a particular director will stay on, he may enter into a new service agreement with that director. Valuation of the benefit, if any, transferred is really a matter for the parties, but if assignment is used, stamp duty will be minimised if a nominal value only can properly be attributed.

(6) *Intellectual property and know-how*
A purchaser must check any patents or trademarks and similar intellectual property for proof of title. Know-how is an intangible asset which will usually only be transferred if the vendor is to continue in the running of the business. Valuation of intellectual property will really be a matter of agreement – the initial cost of obtaining patents and the like will probably have already been offset against income from them.

(7) *Hire purchase and similar liabilities*
The purchaser may wish to be substituted for the vendor in various hire purchase agreements, credit sales, leases and rental contracts. If some part of the consideration is properly apportionable to the benefit, if any, transferred by this substitution stamp duty will be payable if it can be said that there is an assignment of that benefit. The consent of the other party to the agreement will have to be obtained, and specific

provision in the sale agreement will be necessary, together with warranties and undertakings on both sides to ensure transfer and fulfilment of obligations.

(8) *Debtors and creditors*

It is unusual for a purchaser to take on the collection of book debts, as the assignment of these attracts stamp duty. Similarly a purchaser will not usually take on the burden of creditors. Instead, chiefly for stamp duty purposes, the purchaser will act as agent for the vendor in collecting the book debts and will apply these against the vendor's liability to creditors. However if debts are to be assigned it is important for the valuer to verify the debts by examination of the ledger account for evidence of written-off bad debts, unusual transfers, excessive discounts, loans to directors and employees and particulars of any local authority loans.

Warranties

Asset purchase agreements generally contain fewer warranties than share purchase agreements, as there are normally fewer uncertain liabilities to be provided for. No letter of disclosure is usually given. Apart from standard warranties promising that the accounts are correct, that all written information given prior to contract is true and so on, the most important warranty is to title; and the purchaser must be sure that good title will pass – for example that no licences have been granted over any asset, or that assets are not subject to mortgages or charges.

A clause may provide for rescission in the event of breach of warranty to title, and the purchaser may also disaffirm for any other breach if this causes the loss of sustantially the whole benefit of the contract. Where damages will be an appropriate remedy, other clauses may be inserted. Thus it will usually be provided that in the event of late payment or failure to pay the balance payable on the final payment date, the defaulting party will pay interest on any sum due, at a rate to be determined by the parties and incorporated in the contract. The agreement may also set up a retention fund of part of the consideration to cover claims for breach of warranty. Alternatively if quantification is difficult and liquidated damages would be better, a clause may provide for abatement of the purchase price unless the vendor fulfils his obligations.

Other common warranties include a promise by the vendor to carry on the business unchanged between exchange of contracts and the completion date or final payment date. This protects the purchaser, who might otherwise find that his purchased stock, capital commitments and so on have changed dramatically during the period.

The purchaser may also get a warranty that the goods acquired will be in no worse condition than at contract when they finally pass into his ownership, but by section 13 of the Sale of Goods Act 1979 goods sold by inventory description must anyway correspond with that description.

There will usually be no deed of tax indemnity attached to the purchase agreement but covenants to hold harmless may be included in the latter. Either party may agree to indemnify the other for loss caused by any default, and there may also be more specific indemnities (as for example where a vendor agrees to indemnify the purchaser for all obligations to customers or creditors of the company, if for instance these are not being paid off at completion out of a fund set up with some part of the purchase price to ensure payment).

Consents and approvals

As with a purchase of shares agreement, (a) there may be Stock Exchange requirements if either company is listed; (b) the Monopolies and Mergers Commission may have to give consent; (c) statutory consents may have to be given for transfer of assets in a regulated industry. Further, the consents of parties to contracts with the vendor, the benefits of which are to be assigned, are required unless the nature of the contract is such that mere notice is sufficient (for example trade supply or computer services). If the vendor has been granted any loans under the Local Employment Acts or the Industry Act 1972, these will be repayable on change of ownership of the assets unless the purchaser obtains Department of Industry consent and gives suitable undertakings. Also, regulation 10 of the Transfer of Undertakings (Protection of Employment) Regulations 1981 (see below) provides for a consultation process with recognised trade unions representing employees whose services are being transferred. While not a "consent" in the strict sense, non-consultation is a relevant factor for the purposes of regulation 11 in dealing with a complaint to an industrial tribunal.

Apportionment of the consideration

As mentioned, the stamp duty payable on the transfer and the tax benefits available to the purchaser will depend on the amount of the total consideration properly apportionable to the various assets. A transfer of land and buildings, the benefit of contracts, or assignment of goodwill attracts two per cent stamp duty on the value; no duty is payable on stock in trade, work-in-progress or moveable plant and machinery which is transferred by delivery (see section 59 of the Stamp Act 1981). For stamp duty purposes an apportionment of the consideration should be made on Form 22. Where the purchaser's solicitor is in any doubt about the apportionment and the duty payable, he should submit the contract and any assignment for adjudication by the Controller of Stamps. The capital allowances on, for instance, plant and machinery, or to a lesser extent the stock relief on stock, available to the purchaser will depend on what proportion of the total consideration is apportionable to those items. The amount apportioned to capital assets will determine the purchaser's chargeable gain or allowable loss on a subsequent sale. Often the purchaser's interest in allocating a high price to one item will be counterbalanced by the vendor's desire, again for tax reasons, for the allocation of a low price. And for stamp duty and most other tax purposes an artificial apportionment can be adjusted by the Inland Revenue. To avoid disputes in the future, it is advisable for the vendor and purchaser to set out an agreed apportionment in the sale agreement.

Value added tax may be payable on specific classes of assets transferred (including goodwill, see Customs and Excise press release, December 10, 1982). However, where the whole or part of the business is being transferred, the sale will not generally be treated as a supply of goods or services and is therefore exempt from V.A.T. (V.A.T. (Special Provisions) Order 1981 S.I. No. 1791).

Completion

Completion will involve basically the same procedure as for a purchase of shares with a few obvious differences – thus no share transfer documents will be exchanged and there will be no necessity for board or company meetings dealing with appointment or resignation of officers. Where transfer of the business is geared to take place on a particular date, but some part of the transaction is delayed, for example completion of the conveyance of properties, part of the consideration may be appropriated to a designated joint deposit account under the control of both parties' solicitors. This may also occur where there is an agreed retention pending stocktake or where some customer contracts are regarded as being of doubtful enforceability.

Employment continuity

The regulations

The Transfer of Undertakings (Protection of Employment) Regulations 1981 entered fully into force on May 1, 1982. They implement the EEC Council Directive 77/187. The principal provisions are as follows:

(a) the regulations apply where a person transfers a *commercial undertaking* or part thereof to another person (regulation 3);

(b) such a transfer will not operate to terminate the employees' contracts of employment but any such contract which would otherwise have been terminated by the transfer will continue as if made between the transferee and the employees (regulation 5). Provision is made for the continuance of collective agreements (regulation 6). Regulations 5 and 6 do not apply to occupational pension schemes (regulation 7);

(c) provision is made for the application of the remedies for unfair dismissal contained in the existing law where an employee of the transferor or transferee is dismissed by reason of the transfer (regulation 8);

(d) a trade union recognised by the transferor is deemed after a transfer to be similarly recognised by the transferee (regulation 9);

(e) the representatives of the employees who may be affected by the transfer are to be informed by the transferor and the transferee of the date of and the reasons for the transfer and its implications for them. Where the transferor or the transferee envisages that he will be taking measures in relation to the affected employees, he must enter into consultation with their representatives (regulation 10). A complaint may be presented to an industrial tribunal that these duties have not been performed and the tribunal may award compensation (regulation 11); and

(f) in the case of transfers by receivers and liquidators in a "hive down" to a subsidiary company, the transfer is not deemed to take place until the transferee company ceases to be a wholly owned subsidiary of the transferor or the relevant undertaking is transferred by the transferee company to another person, whichever occurs first (regulation 4).

Effect of transfer of business on officers and employees

Where the shares of the company whose undertaking is being sold are not themselves transferred, the company remains as a shell and its directors and officers do not automatically cease to have office. The vendor will make his own arrangements according to whether the appointments continue within the context of any part of the business which is retained. Senior personnel may indeed remain with the vendor but be seconded under consultancy arrangements to merge the assets into the purchaser's organisation, or to maximise goodwill.

Where directors or other officers are also engaged under service contracts, their position will be no different from any other employee in the case of a transfer of assets. Until May 1982 such a transfer had the consequence that all the employees working in the business were made redundant at completion. The purchaser was able to select such staff as were required for the continued operation of the business either on the same terms or upon new ones. In such cases redundancy pay was still available since there had been a dismissal by reason of redundancy (section 81 of the Employment Protection (Consolidation) Act 1978). There were, however, breaks in continuity for the purpose of holiday or pension entitlement which had adverse consequences even for those employees who were lucky enough to redeem their jobs.

After May 1982, the Transfer of Undertakings (Protection of Employment) Regulations do away with the necessity of dismissing and re-employing the employees involved in the transfer of a commercial business. The effect of regulation 5, referred to above, is that such a transfer will operate to continue the existing service contract of every employee as if it were made not with the vendor, but with the purchaser of the business. If the vendor wishes to retain specific employees he must transfer them out of the business before the main transfer takes place. The purchaser may still, of course, enter into new agreements with key employees on enhanced terms if it is desirable to retain them. The effect of the regulations is that the vendor will no longer be liable to claims for damages for wrongful dismissal, compensation for unfair dismissal and redundancy payments in respect of employees who "go across" with the undertaking. They thus become the purchaser's responsibility. A prudent vendor will, however, provide in the sale agreement for an indemnity against any claim brought by a former employee. It is axiomatic that there must be a transfer of the "undertaking", since a mere transfer of assets will not invoke regulation 5 and the vendor remains the employer, with attendant liability. It is suggested that because of the difficulty of deciding in advance whether the sale is one to which the regulations apply (there is no correlation, for example, between these regulations and the VAT Special Provisions Order referred to above), the parties should give the most careful expression in the contract documents to who shall bear the liability for any consequent claims for unfair dismissal, redundancy etc.

Regulation 8(1) provides that any employee of the vendor or the purchaser who is dismissed because of the transfer or a related reason will be treated as having been unfairly dismissed. However, regulation 8(2) qualifies this to remove much of its sting, because there will have been no unfair dismissal, and only redundancy, if the reason was "an economic, technical or organisational reason entailing changes in the work force". This rather ambiguous expression will almost certainly give rise to dispute. In principle it provides for a legitimate rationalisation of the business – which may be its only means to profitability – consequent upon the sale. On the other hand, if employees find themselves surplus to requirements merely because the undertaking is operated more efficiently without any reorganisation as such, it is not clear whether they may make a claim. There is also a problem in interpreting regulation 5. The intention of the regulation is that the contract of every employee be transferred in its existing state, so that all the terms and conditions that previously applied will continue to do so (excepting pensions). This extends to pay, conditions of service, holiday entitlements, locally negotiated bonuses, and other special conditions. It is, however, a criticism of the regulation that it does not allow to lapse those terms which are personal to the vendor or inconsistent with the business now carried on by the purchaser. For example, if an employee has enjoyed the benefit of a share incentive scheme with the vendor, must the purchaser continue to honour it and go out in the market to buy shares in the holding company? Or again, if an employee has been entitled to the use of a company bus to his place of work, but is relocated consequent upon the transfer and such transport is not available (or is not needed because of proximity), is there a breach by the purchaser of the existing terms? Since these are matters which will have to be resolved by an industrial tribunal, the only interim advice is that the parties should take all possible care to demarcate responsibilities in the event that subsequent claims by employees arise. It should however be noted that regulation 12 provides that any provision of any agreement (whether a contract of employment or not) shall be void insofar as it purports to exclude or limit the operation of regulations 5, 8 or 10, or to preclude any person from presenting a complaint to an industrial tribunal under regulation 11.

Annual Return

The statutory provisions governing annual returns are contained in sections 124 and 126 of the Companies Act 1948 and in the Sixth Schedule to that Act. Section 124 requires every company having a *share capital* to make an annual return, in the form set out in Part II of the Sixth Schedule, at least once in every year. An explained below, the date to which the annual return is made up will be governed by the date of the company's annual general meeting. "Year" means a calendar year, that is the period from January 1 to December 31 (*Gibson* v. *Barton* (1875) L.R. 10 Q.B. 329). The rules are relaxed for new companies. A company is not required to submit an annual return in the year (i.e. calendar year) of its incorporation. Nor need it submit an annual return in the following year if it was incorporated after 1 July in the year (this is the effect of sections 124(1)(a) and 131(1) of the 1948 Act).

A similar obligation is imposed on companies not having a share capital (C.A. 1948, s. 125). But the contents of the annual return need, broadly, include only the details listed under paragraphs 1, 2, 4 and 6 below. A newly-incorporated company without a share capital is granted the same exemptions as a company with a share capital (section 125(2)).

Contents of annual return

In outline, the annual return of a company having a share capital is required to contain the following information:

(1) The address of the registered office of the company.
(2) (a) The address of the place where the register of members is kept if different from the registered office.
    (b) The address where the register of holders of debentures is kept if different from the registered office.
(3) A summary, distinguishing between shares issued for cash and shares issued otherwise than in cash, with the following particulars:
    (a) the amount of share capital and the number of shares into which it is divided;
    (b) the number of shares taken from the commencement of the company up to the date of the return;
    (c) the amount called up on each share;
    (d) the total amount of calls received;
    (e) the total amount of calls unpaid;
    (f) the total amount (if any) paid as commission in respect of any shares or debentures;
    (g) the discount allowed on the issue of any shares issued at a discount or so much of that discount as has not been written off at the date on which the return is made;

    (h) the total amount of the sums (if any) allowed by way of discount in respect of any debentures since the date of the last return; and

    (i) the total number of shares for which share warrants are outstanding at the date of the return and of share warrants issued and surrendered respectively since the date of the last return, and the number of shares comprised in each warrant.

(4) The total amount of the indebtedness of the company in respect of all mortgages and charges required to be registered under the 1948 Act. (For a company registered in Scotland, this *includes* mortgages and charges which would be required to be registered if the company had been registered in England.)

(5) A list,

    (a) containing the names and addresses of all persons who, on the fourteenth day after the company's annual general meeting for the year, are members of the company and of persons who have ceased to be members since the date of the last return;

    (b) stating the number of shares held by each of the existing members at the date of the return specifying shares transferred since the date of the last return by persons who are still members and have ceased to be members respectively and the dates of registration of the transfers; and

    (c) if the names are not in alphabetical order, having annexed an index sufficient to enable the name of any person to be easily found.

Where the company has converted any of its shares into stock and given notice to the Registrar, the list must state the amount of stock held by each of the existing members instead of the amount of the shares and particulars relating to the shares (C.A. 1948 s. 124(1)(b)).

If the annual return for *either* of the previous two years has listed all the particulars in (a) to (c) above, then it is only necessary to include in the return those particulars which relate to persons ceasing or becoming members since the date of the last return, to shares transferred since then or changes in the stock held by a member (C.A. 1948, s. 124(1)(c)).

There are special provisions governing the inclusion of details in any Dominion register of the company (s. 124(2)).

(6) Particulars of persons who at the date of the return are directors and secretary of the company.

Time for completion of annual return

The annual return must be completed within 42 days after the annual general meeting for the year. It must be made up to the fourteenth day after the annual general meeting. It must then be signed by both a director *and* secretary of the company and sent "forthwith" to the Registrar (section 126). Section 179 of the 1948 Act prevents the same person signing both as director and secretary.

Penalties

If an annual return is not properly completed, then the company, and every director, manager, secretary or person in accordance with whose directions or instructions the directors of the company are accustomed to act is guilty of a criminal offence and liable to a fine, on summary conviction, not exceeding the statutory maximum (currently £1,000). A conviction after continued contravention carries a fine of up to one-tenth of the statutory maximum (C.A. 1948 s. 124(3), 125(3) and C.A. 1981, Sch. 3, para 4).

Failure to complete and forward the annual return in the time referred
to above renders the company and the persons listed in the previous
paragraph liable to a default fine. The fine may be up to one-fifth of the
statutory maximum (currently £1,000), or up to one-fifteenth of that
amount after continued contravention (C.A. 1980, Sch. 2).

Completion of annual return

For a company having a share capital, the annual return must be made
on Companies Form No. 6A. A filing fee of £20 is payable. For
companies without a share capital, the relevant form is Form No. 7.

(1) As the annual return is required to show only the position at the
     date to which it is made up, it is not necessary to include an
     explanation reconciling the share capital details with those in the
     previous return, even though the relationship may be difficult to
     follow where, for example, there have been several capital reorga-
     nisations during the year.

(2) If shares have been issued with renunciation rights but the period of
     renunciation is still running at the date of the return, it is necessary
     only to specify the number of such shares at the end of part five of
     the Form (as well as including the shares in the details at part
     three), and to add a note giving the date of issue of the shares and
     the date by which renunciation may be registered.

(3) The details of the company's indebtedness at part four of the return
     need only cover debts relating to *registered* charges (or charges
     which should be registered under the Companies Acts).

(4) According to the Chartered Institute of Secretaries and Adminis-
     trators, the Registrar is unlikely to object if any of the following
     departures from the strict requirements of the Sixth Schedule are
     made:

     (a) The number of stock units being shown instead of the amount
          of stock.

     (b) Present and past members being shown in separate alphabetic-
          al lists without an index being annexed.

     (c) Shares transferred by any person being aggregated and the
          total shown against his name with the word "various" in the
          column for date of registration, instead of the details of each
          transfer by that person being shown separately.

     (d) The omission of past members and the number of shares
          previously held by them in the case of a class of shares having
          been cancelled since the last return under the terms of a
          scheme of arrangement, provided that the return includes a
          note giving details of the cancellation and the date on which
          the scheme was approved by the court.

(e) The omission of past members whose shares have been acquired as a result of a take-over bid, provided that details of all transfers prior to the bid are shown and the return is accompanied by an explanation signed by a director and the secretary.

(5) If an annual general meeting is held at which the annual accounts are not presented, an annual return made up to the date of the meeting should include a note explaining this. If the meeting is adjourned so that the accounts can be presented, the return should still be made up to the fourteenth day after the date of the original meeting.

(6) A useful guide on completing the two annual return forms is produced by the Companies Registration Office. The guide for completion of Form No. 6A (companies with a share capital) is reproduced below.

Annual return guide

The following notes are for use in connection with the completion by companies of their annual returns on Form 6A. The note references appear against the relevant items on the form. Any queries on these matters should be addressed (in the case of companies in England and Wales) to Companies Registration Office, Crown Way, Maindy, Cardiff, or (for those in Scotland) to Companies Registration Office, Exchequer Chambers, 102 George Street, Edinburgh.

Notes

(1) Include payments on application and allotment and any sums received on shares forfeited.

(2) Include also any mortgages and charges which would have been required to be so registered if created after July 1, 1908.

(3) Give list of persons holding shares or stock in the company on the fourteenth day after the holding of the annual general meeting. Show also those persons who have held shares or stock in the company at any time since the date of the last return, or if this is the company's first return, since the date of incorporation.

(4) If the names in the list are not arranged in alphabetical order, an index sufficient to enable the name of any person to be readily found must be annexed.

(5) If the return for either of the two immediately preceding years has given as at the date of that return the full particulars required as to past and present members and the shares and stock held and transferred by them, only such of the particulars need to be given as relate to persons ceasing to be or becoming members since the date of the last return and to shares transferred since that date or to changes as compared with that date in the amount of stock held by a member.

(6) The aggregate number of shares held by each member must be stated, and the aggregates must be added up so as to agree with the number of shares stated in the "summary of share capital and debentures" (paragraph 2) to have been taken up.

(7) When the shares are of different classes these columns should be sub-divided, so that the number of each class held, or transferred, may be shown separately. Where any shares have been converted into stock the amount of stock held by each member must be shown.

(8) The date of registration of each transfer should be given as well as the number of shares transferred on each date. The particulars should be placed opposite the name of the transferor and not opposite that of the transferee, but the name of the transferee may be inserted in the "remarks" column immediately opposite the particulars of each transfer.

(9) Section 110 of the Companies Act 1948 refers. In the case of a register kept otherwise than in a legible form reference should also be made to section 3(3) of the Stock Exchange (Completion of Bargains) Act 1976 and Regulation 2 of and Schedule 1 to the Companies (Registers and other Records) Regulations 1979.

(10) If any such register or part of any such register is kept outside Great Britain, insert the address in Great Britain where any duplicate thereof is kept.

(11) If the columns give insufficient space the particulars must be continued on a separate sheet. "Director" includes any person who occupies the position of a director by whatsoever name called, and any person in accordance with whose directions or instructions the directors of the company are accustomed to act.

(12) Full names must be given. In the case of an individual, his present Christian name or names and surname must be given. "Christian name" includes a forename and "surname" in the case of a peer or person usually known by a title different from his surname means that title. In the case of a corporation, its corporate name must be given.

(13) In the case of an individual, any former Christian names and surname must be given in addition.
"Former Christian name" and "former surname" do not include,

    (a) in the case of a peer or a person usually known by a British title different from his surname, the name by which he was known previous to the adoption of or succession to the title; or

    (b) in the case of any person, a former Christian name or surname where that name or surname was changed or disused before the person bearing the name attained the age of eighteen years or has been changed or disused for a period of not less than twenty years; or

(c) in the case of a married woman, the name or surname by which she was known previous to the marriage.

(14) Dates of birth need only be given in the case of directors of a company which is subject to section 185 of the Companies Act, 1948, namely a company which is a public company or, being a private company, is a subsidiary of a public company or of a body corporate registered under the law relating to companies for the time being in force in Northern Ireland as a public company.

(15) Usual residential address should be given or, in the case of a corporation, the registered or principal office.

(16) The names of all bodies corporate incorporated in Great Britain of which the director is also a director should be given, except bodies corporate of which the company making the return is the wholly-owned subsidiary or bodies corporate which are the wholly-owned subsidiaries either of the company or of another company of which the company is the wholly-owned subsidiary. A body corporate is deemed to be the wholly-owned subsidiary of another if it has no members except that other and that other's wholly-owned subsidiaries and its or their nominees.

(17) In the case of a Scottish firm, the firm name should be shown.

(18) Where all the partners in a firm are joint secretaries, the name and principal office address of the firm alone may be stated.

(19) Usual residential address should be given, or, in the case of a corporation or Scottish firm, the registered or principal office.

(20) Banking companies. A banking company, in order to avail itself of the benefit of section 432 of the Companies Act 1948, must add to the annual return a statement of the names of the several places where it carries on business (on Form 24).

Documents to be annexed to annual return

All *limited* companies must annex to the annual return filed with the Registrar every balance sheet and profit and loss account laid before the company in general meeting during the period to which the return relates, plus the notes to the profit and loss account, the auditors report and the directors report (C.A. 1948, s. 149, 156, 157). Unlimited companies are under the same obligation unless exempted by section 47 of the Companies Act 1967.

Articles of Association

As is explained briefly on page 401 (*Formation and Types of Company*), the constitution and internal regulations of a company are set out in its memorandum and articles of association. Whereas the memorandum establishes the basis of the company's existence in accordance with the Companies Acts and includes the objects which it is permitted to pursue, the articles are essentially concerned with the company's internal management and administrative structure. A company's articles cannot, subject to the Companies Acts, modify or have priority over its memorandum. Those qualifications apart, the articles are the primary means of regulation by a company of its affairs and constitute a contract between each member and the company (section 20 of the Companies Act 1948 and *Welton v. Saffery* [1897] A.C. 299).

Format and contents

Acknowledging the importance of the role of the articles of association of a company, the legislature has offered guidance by the provision of model regulations for limited companies (whether limited by share capital or guarantee) and unlimited companies. The model forms applicable to companies incorporated on or after June 15, 1982 are set out in the First Schedule to the Companies Act 1948 as amended by the Companies Acts of 1967, 1976, 1980 and 1981, the Decimal Currency Act 1969, The Stock Exchange (Completion of Bargains) Act 1976 and the Insolvency Act 1976. The relevant provisions of the First Schedule now apply equally to all limited companies with a share capital (whether public or private) incorporated on or after December 22, 1980. (Prior to that date Table A Part I of the First Schedule applied to public companies and Table A Part II (which incorporated the whole of Table A Part I with the exception of regulations 24 and 53) to private companies. Table A Part II was repealed by the Companies Act 1980 but continues to apply to private companies incorporated before December 22, 1980.)

Choice of Table A

A company limited by shares may register, with its memorandum of association, articles of association signed by the subscribers to the memorandum and prescribing the regulations of the company (C.A. 1948, s. 6). The company may adopt as its articles all or any of the regulations contained in Table A of the First Schedule to the Companies

Act 1948 (C.A. 1948, s. 8(1)). However, its promoters may, alternatively or additionally, adopt such provisions as they wish on incorporation (subject to statute and the common law), and its shareholders can subsequently make alterations. If a company limited by shares elects not to register articles with its memorandum, or, insofar as the articles which are registered do not exclude or modify the statutory regulations applied by the Act under which the company was incorporated, those regulations will, as far as possible, be the regulations of the company just as if they were contained in duly registered articles (C.A. 1948, s. 8(2)).

Companies limited by guarantee, with or without a share capital, and unlimited companies having a share capital, do not enjoy the same freedom of choice; not only must they register articles of association with their memorandum of association but those articles must accord with the respective forms set out in Tables C, D and E in the First Schedule to the Companies Act 1948, or must be as near to the relevant form as circumstances permit (C.A. 1948, s. 11).

Articles of association must be printed, divided into paragraphs numbered consecutively and, in the case of the articles of a company delivered for the purpose of its incorporation, signed by each subscriber of the memorandum of association in the presence of a witness who must attest the signature (C.A. 1948, s. 9).

Which form of Table A applies?

Over the years there have been several forms of model regulations prescribed by statute or statutory instrument. The form which applies to a company is, to the extent that the company has not by special resolution excluded or modified its application, the form contained in and applied by the Act under which the company was incorporated. This will include any amendments made to the statutory form prior to the date of incorporation of the company. Unless the statutory form in force at the time of incorporation of a company is expressly and validly disapplied, the form will still operate as the articles of the company to the extent it is not inconsistent with any special articles which have been adopted. Even so, it is common in practice to find articles of a company incorporated prior to July 1, 1948 which now purport to disapply Table A in the First Schedule of the 1948 Act – even though this form of Table A, unless specifically adopted by special resolution, cannot apply to that company. Where specific articles are proposed to be adopted, the date of incorporation of a company should always be ascertained and the statutory form applicable at that date adopted, excluded or modified, as necessary.

Modification of statutory form

As explained, a company limited by shares may elect to disapply Table A in whole or in part. The decision to disapply or vary the provisions of

Table A often depends on the circumstances regarding the membership of a particular company. For example, companies which have their share capital quoted on The Stock Exchange in London or which have a "listing" on the London Unlisted Securities Market generally disapply the whole of Table A and adopt "long form" articles of association. The adopted articles frequently follow the substance and pattern of Table A, incorporating the special requirements of The Stock Exchange (see page 103) and specific non-Table A articles. They are printed in full for convenience, enabling both members and public to have easy access to a single document containing all the applicable articles. This "long form" of articles is also commonly adopted by a UK subsidiary of a foreign corporation or a company which has a significant proportion of non-resident members. In those cases, both members and management – particularly if the company is administered from outside the United Kingdom – find it convenient to have the regulations of the company set out in a single document, rather than to have to cross refer to the regulations contained in an unfamiliar statute which may not be readily available.

On the other hand, a substantial number of companies choose to adopt Table A, subject to specific modifications and additions set out in "short form" articles of association. In such a case, Table A is incorporated expressly into the articles, usually by the first article, but subject to the modifications then set out in the special articles. (This express incorporation is not strictly necessary if the Table A to be adopted is the form which was applicable at the date of incorporation of the company, since it automatically operates as the regulations to the extent that it is not specifically excluded (C.A. 1948, s. 8 and page 99 above).

Use of "short term" articles is the preferred approach where, for example, the regulations adopted by a company do not depart significantly or to a material extent from the form set out in Table A, or where the company secretary and other officers charged with the administration of the company are familiar with, and have ready access to, the contents of Table A. Subsidiary members of a group of companies will often have standard "short form" articles, enabling consistency of administration by the parent company and central group control systems when dealing with the management and affairs of each subsidiary. "Short form" articles are also preferred by many companies because of the cost saving involved in printing.

Whether the articles of association of a company are in "long form" or "short form", they will, in most cases, modify the regulations of Table A. The current Table A is largely in the same form as that originally adopted by the Companies Act 1948. As a result of the development of the commercial sector since that time, a number of modifications are commonly made. Table A sets out the basic management and administrative structure of a company limited by shares and accordingly contains provisions for the regulation of the following general matters which are common to all such companies:

(1) share capital and class rights;

(2) allotment, transfer and transmission of shares;

(3) meetings of members;

(4) appointment and removal of directors;

(5) powers of directors;

(6) meetings of directors;

(7) borrowings;

(8) general administration – for example use of the common seal, the giving of notices, winding up; and

(9) financial administration – dividends, reserves and accounts.

Common modifications to Table A

Modifications to Table A which are frequently made are set out in the table below.

---

(1) The *allotment of shares* by directors pursuant to and in accordance with section 14 of the Companies Act 1980 (see the chapter, *Shares*).

(2) The *class rights* attached to different categories of shares. Separate class rights may either be set out in the memorandum of association or the articles; because of the difficulties attaching to any future variation of class rights once they are incorporated into the memorandum, the latter approach is the more common.

(3) *Pre-emption rights* in favour of existing members in respect of any allotment or transfer of shares. Such a provision is particularly common in small family companies or where a company is a vehicle for a joint venture or has a comparatively small number of members. Sales or other transfers to third parties will be made subject to a right of existing members to a first refusal (see the chapter *Shares*, below). A special article is likely to continue to be used notwithstanding section 17 of the Companies Act 1980 (pre-emption rights on allotment of equity securities) because of the limited scope of that section (see page 810). For example, it applies only to allotments not to transfers of shares and, in its application to allotments, does not cover, amongst other things, any allotment of shares which are wholly or partly paid up otherwise than for cash. Nor does it provide pre-emption rights in respect of allotments of shares other than equity securities (as defined in section 17) (Note that public limited companies having their share capital quoted on The Stock Exchange will be subject to the pre-emption rights contained in the Listing Agreement and, additionally, the guidelines set out in the practice statement of the Council for the Securities Industry dated July 16, 1981 and the related statement by the Investment Protection Committee of the British Insurance Association (see page 810). Companies on the Unlisted Securities Market are subject to similar extra-statutory limitations).

(4) *The appointment and removal of alternate directors.* The use of alternate directors is helpful to enable the management of a company to be carried on with the maximum of flexibility in the absence of individual directors. The idea is particularly convenient if companies have a widespread board of directors, such as in a group where a subsidiary's board is largely made up of

representatives of the holding company. The use of an alternate is also helpful in situations where it is desirable to maintain the balance of a board of directors in the absence of one or two individuals as in the case of a joint venture.

(5) In the case of subsidiaries, *the appointment and removal of directors*. Acknowledging the relationship existing between a holding company and its subsidiary, the articles of a subsidiary may provide for the appointment and removal of the directors of a subsidiary merely by the delivery of notice in writing to that effect signed by or on behalf of the registered holders of a majority of the issued shares of the company. This procedure recognises the *de facto* control of a holding company and obviates the need for the parent company, as a member of the subsidiary, to have to resort to formal resolutions of either the shareholders or of the directors to make changes in the directorate of the subsidiary.

(6) The means by which *resolutions of the board* are passed. Article 106 of Table A provides that a resolution in writing, signed by all the directors for the time being entitled to receive notice of a board meeting, is as valid and effective as if it had been passed at a duly convened meeting of the directors. This can be unduly restrictive as the resolution has to be *signed* by *all* the directors entitled to receive notice. In effect, it is often as easy to convene and hold a meeting to pass the resolution. To provide the flexibility intended by Article 106, articles of a company commonly state that the resolution is effective if *agreed* by all the directors or, in some cases, by a number of directors sufficient to constitute a quorum of the board. Such an article may be drafted to allow the directors to take effective decisions by telephone, telex (although the identity of the sender should be verified) and other means of communication, and for those decisions to be valid and effectual decisions of the board without recourse to a formal board meeting or written resolution. (As a matter of practice, however, it is preferable that such decisions should subsequently be documented and confirmed by the relevant directors.)

(7) The *quorum* of meetings of directors. Such an article, like the previous example and the use of alternate directors, is intended to enable effective decisions of the directors to be taken at short notice. It is possible for companies to vary the quorum requirements to allow directors in contact with a meeting by telephone to be counted among the number of directors present.

(8) *The destruction of original documents*. Recent advances in the field of information processing and retrieval – for example microfiche recording – have led to the increasingly widespread practice among larger, primarily quoted, companies of adopting articles enabling the destruction of original documents such as stock transfers, cancelled share certificates and other title documents to securities after a specified period of time. The combination of the improved information recording systems and the ability to destroy the originals can result in material savings to companies whose storage costs would otherwise be substantial because of the significant numbers of documents involved.

As will be seen from the examples in the above table, the ability of a company limited by shares to adopt articles specifically tailored to its requirements is extremely wide. In essence, the only limitation is that the articles of a company are always subject to overriding statute, the common law and the conditions contained in its memorandum. For instance, an article empowering a company to give financial assistance for the purchase of its own shares contrary to section 42 of the Companies Act 1981, or to distribute profits in excess of the limits in sections 39 to 45 of the Companies Act 1980, will be ineffective. The certainty involved in the adoption of Table A is among the primary reasons, however, why the model statutory regulations tend to form the substance of any articles (whether by repeating them in "long form" articles or incorporating them by reference in "short form" ones); a significant advantage in adopting Table A regulations is that they cannot be *ultra vires* the company since a company is authorised by section 8 of the Companies Act 1948 to adopt Table A, in whole or in part (*Lock v. Queensland Investment and Land Mortgage Co.* [1896] 1 Ch. 397).

Companies having their capital quoted on The Stock Exchange, London are also obliged to conform their articles of association to the requirements of the listing agreement to which each such company becomes a party as part of the procedure of admission of its share capital to the Official List. The Council of The Stock Exchange currently requires the articles of each quoted company to comply with the provisions set out in its book "Admission of Securities to Listing", otherwise known as "the Yellow Book". The table below outlines the main requirements dealt with.

Stock Exchange requirements

(1) the transferability and registration of shares;

(2) the issue and replacement of share certificates;

(3) dividends;

(4) borrowings;

(5) directors' conflicts of interests;

(6) the appointment and removal of directors;

(7) accounts;

(8) capital structure and class rights;

(9) proxies; and

(10) notices.

Effect as a contract

The nature of the contract established by the articles of association of a company is set out by section 20(1) of the Companies Act 1948:-

> "Subject to the provisions of this Act, the memorandum and articles shall, when registered, bind the company and the members thereof to the same extent as if they respectively had been signed and sealed by each member, and contained covenants on the part of each member to observe all the provisions of the memorandum and of the articles."

Thus, whatever form they may take, whether Table A or otherwise, the articles of association for the time being of a company will be binding on both the company and its members respectively. Any alteration duly made in accordance with section 10 of the Companies Act 1948 has effect as if originally contained in the articles. (Note that by section 9 of the European Communities Act 1972 a company cannot rely on the articles of association against a third party if the alteration has not been filed with the Registrar of Companies and published by him in the London or Edinburgh Gazette. The contract created by the articles has, however, been the subject of a significant degree of judicial review, as section 20 provides that the company and members are bound by the articles only to the extent as if they had been signed and sealed by the members, not by the company. The cases have not always appeared consistent in settling the nature of the obligations created between a company and its members, and between one member and another by the memorandum and articles of association of the company. The generally accepted principle outlined by Astbury J. in *Hickman v. Kent or Romney Sheep-breeders' Association* [1915] 1 Ch. 881, who attempted to reconcile the disparity between previous judgments of the courts, is that the articles of association of a company evidence a contract between the company and its members in their capacity, and with respect to their rights and obligations, *as members* (see further page 240).

Company and members

Following that principle, a company is obliged to its members to comply with the terms of its articles of association insofar as they affect the rights and obligations of the members as members; and a court will, upon the application of a member, grant an injunction to prevent a company infringing its articles accordingly. Thus in *Wood v. Odessa Waterworks Co.* [1889] Ch.D. 636 a company was restrained by injunction from acting contrary to its articles pursuant to an ordinary resolution of its members to distribute debenture bonds instead of a cash dividend. Similarly, each member in his capacity as member of a company is obliged *to the company* to comply with its articles.

If rights are conferred on a member by the articles of association of a company otherwise than in his capacity as member, he cannot sue on the contract constituted by the articles but must, if he is to have direct legal remedy, establish a collateral contract independent of the articles. For example, in *Eley v. Positive Government Security Life Assurance Co.* (1876) 1 Ex.D. 88 the plaintiff, a member of the company, sought unsuccessfully to enforce the right which was embodied in its articles to be employed for life as solicitor to the company. Similarly, in *Beattie v. Beattie* [1938] Ch. 708 an article referring a dispute between the company and a member to arbitration was held not to be an agreement to submit a dispute to arbitration, because the dispute involved the company and a member in his capacity as director and not as a member.

Member and members

Equally limited is the judicial interpretation of section 20(1) and its forerunners concerning the relationship created by the articles of association between one member of a company and another member. Whilst the courts appear to have acknowledged that the articles constitute a contract between the members themselves, as well as between the company and its members, there is conflicting judicial authority whether one member may only enforce the articles against another member through the company. On the one hand, there is authority that the articles do not constitute a contract between the members themselves and so can only be enforced by one member against another through the medium of the company,

> "the articles constitute a contract between each member and the company, and there is no contract in terms between the individual members of the company; but the articles do not, any the less in my opinion, regulate their rights inter se. Such rights can only be enforced by or against a member through the company or through the liquidator representing the company; but I think that no member has, as between himself and another member, any rights beyond that which the contract with the company gives" (Lord Herschell in *Welton v. Saffery* [1897] A.C. 299 at 315).

On the other hand, there are decisions of lower courts, both before and after *Welton v. Saffery*, which support the opposite view: see *Eley v. Positive Government Security Life Assurance Co.* (1876) 1 Ex.D. 88; *Browne v. La Trinidad* (1887) 37 Ch.D. 1; *Borland's Trustee v. Steel Bros & Co.* [1901] 1 Ch. 279. In *Rayfield v. Hands* [1960] Ch. 1, Vestey J. first decided that an article requiring any member of a company proposing to transfer shares in the company to inform the directors "who will take the said shares equally between them at a fair value" was an article regulating the relationship between the plaintiff as a member and the defendants as members rather than as directors since the directors were in effect specified members of the company. He then addressed the question of the dicta of Lord Herschell in *Welton v. Saffery* cited above and the following dicta of Astbury J. in *Hickman v. Kent or Romney Marsh Sheepbreeders' Association*,

> "the articles of association are simply a contract as between the shareholders inter se in respect of their rights as shareholders. They are the deed of partnership by which the shareholders agree inter se."

On the basis of Astbury J.'s dicta and the decisions in *Dean v. Prince* [1954] Ch. 409 and *Borland's Trustee v. Steel Bros & Co.*, Vestey J. decided that, in the circumstances before him and by applying the maxim that he should validate, if possible, the articles as a commercial document (see below), the articles were enforceable by one member directly against another.

The decision in *Rayfield v. Hands* should not however, be taken too far. Certainly, it is widely accepted by the authorities that Lord Herschell's words in *Welton v. Saffery*, even if obiter, still represent the general principle. Vestey J. himself acknowledged this in *Rayfield v. Hands*:

> "The conclusion to which I have come may not be of so general an application as to extend to the articles of association of every company, for it is, I think, material to remember that this private company is one of that class of companies which bears a close analogy to a partnership."

The essence of the decision in *Rayfield v. Hands* is therefore that if one member accepts, through the articles of a company, a personal obligation to another member, that other member may seek to enforce that personal obligation directly against him. In the absence of further judicial consideration of the apparently conflicting authorities, however, and apart from the limited circumstances prevailing in the case of a quasi-partnership, it appears that a member cannot enforce the articles of association of a company against another member except through the company itself.

Interpretation

The articles of association, comprising the regulations for the internal management and administration of a company, should be read together with the memorandum of association. Section 20 of the Companies Act 1948 contemplates this by establishing the relationship of the company with its members by reference to both the memorandum and articles. Whilst the articles may serve to resolve any problem of construction of the memorandum or to supplement the memorandum (*Angostura Bitters (Dr. J.B. Siegert & Sons) Ltd v. Kerr* [1933] A.C. 550), the memorandum will always prevail (*Re Duncan Gilmour & Co Ltd* [1952] 2 All E.R. 871 and *Ashbury v. Watson* (1885) 30 Ch.D. 376).

In construing the articles of a company, they should be regarded as a business document and should therefore be construed to give them reasonable business efficacy, where that result is admissable on the language, in preference to a result which would or might prove unworkable (*Holmes v. Keyes* [1959] Ch. 199).

Alteration of articles

By section 10 (1) of the Companies Act 1948, a company may, subject to the Companies Acts 1948 to 1981 and to the conditions contained in its memorandum, alter its articles of association by special resolution. Apart from these restrictions, there is no limitation on the capacity of a company to alter its articles and the company may not deprive itself of or fetter its ability to alter its articles by any arrangement contained in the articles in favour of either its members or a third party (*Allen v. Gold Reefs of West Africa* [1900] 1 Ch. 656 and *Punt v. Symons & Co* [1903] 2 Ch. 506). Thus, any attempt in a company's articles to elevate any specific article to the status of being unalterable or requiring a greater majority than that necessary to pass a resolution will be contrary to section 10(1) and void (*Malleson v. National Insurance Corporation* [1894] 1 Ch. 200).

In practice, rights may be entrenched in articles either by using the concept of separate classes of shares to which are attributed the rights which are sought to be protected (and which can only be varied or abrogated with the separate consent of the holders of the shares of each separate class: section 72 of the Companies Act 1948), or by increasing the voting power of specific shares in the article which embodies the special rights if and to the extent that a special resolution is proposed to alter that article, thus enabling the protected shareholder to defeat the special resolution if he wishes (there may, however, be limitations on this: see *Bushell v. Faith* [1969] 2 Ch. 438 at 448.) Alternatively the rights to be protected could be set out in the memorandum of association and declared to be unalterable. The effect of sections 4 and 23(2) of the Companies Act 1948 is to prohibit the alteration of such a condition.

The inability of a company to fetter its freedom to alter its articles of association is such that a company cannot be prevented from altering its articles, even if to do so would occasion a breach of contract between itself and a third party. The aggrieved party would nonetheless have a prima facie action for damages for breach of the contract:

> "A company cannot be precluded from altering its articles, thereby giving itself power to act upon the provisions of the altered articles – but so to act may nevertheless be a breach of contract if it is contrary to a stipulation in a contract validly made before the alteration." (Lord Porter in *Southern Foundries (1926) Limited v. Shirlaw* [1940] A.C. 701 at 740).

Lord Porter proceeded to say that a court will not, by injunction, restrain a company from altering its articles in breach of contract with a third party; it was considered that such a third party would have an adequate remedy in damages.

The point is not, however free from doubt. Lord Porter's observations were *obiter* and were preceded by two conflicting decisions, *British Murac Syndicate Limited v. Alperton Rubber Co. Limited* [1915] 2 Ch. 186 and *Baily v. British Equitable Assurance Co.* [1904] 1 Ch. 374. The latter case (which was subsequently reversed in the House of Lords on a different point) was not cited in *Southern Foundries (1926) Ltd v. Shirlaw*.

Bona fide for the benefit of the company

Whilst the position regarding the position of third parties affected by an alteration of the articles of association may be uncertain, as regards the members any alteration must be made, not only in the manner required by law, but also *bona fide* for the benefit of the company as a whole (*Allen v. Gold Reefs of West Africa Limited* [1900] 1 Ch. 656 – see Lindley M.R. at 671, and *Sidebottom v. Kershaw, Leese & Co. Limited* [1920] 1 Ch. 154). If an individual shareholder is therefore prejudiced by an alteration to a company's articles, he may not be bound by the alteration and may be able to restrain it or set it aside, even though made in the manner required by law and in accordance with any conditions set out in the company's memorandum, if he can show that the alteration was not *bona fide* for the benefit of the company as a whole.

The courts will not allow the majority of members to benefit to the disadvantage of the minority if any decision to alter the articles of association is not taken *bona fide* for the benefit of the company as a whole (*Brown v. British Abrasive Wheel Co.* [1919] 1 Ch. 290). The courts will leave it to the members to ascertain what is considered to be *bona fide* for the benefit of the company as a whole, and will not upset a resolution of the members unless it is considered that to have taken such a decision would have been unreasonable in all the circumstances,

> "The absence of any reasonable ground for deciding that a certain course of action is conducive to the benefit of the company may be a ground for finding lack of good faith or for finding that the shareholders, with the best motives, have not considered the matters which they ought to have considered. On either of these findings, their decision might be set aside," per Scrutton L.J. in *Shuttleworth v. Cox Bros & Co. (Maidenhead) Limited* [1927] 2 K.B. 9 at 23.

If, however, there is evidence to show that the decision was not taken in good faith, but was influenced by malice, a court will be prepared to intervene to prevent the wrongful exercise of the company's power (*Sidebottom v. Kershaw, Leese & Co. Limited* [1920] 1 Ch. 154).

The courts have also considered what should be regarded as being for the benefit of the company as a whole. Broadly, the consensus of the decisions is that a distinction must be drawn between the company itself as a separate commercial entity and the company in the form of its members as a body, and that the latter is the important aspect for the purposes of determining whether an alteration benefits the company as a whole,

> "A special resolution ... is liable to be impeached if the effect of it were to discriminate between the majority shareholders and the minority shareholders, so as to give the former an advantage to which the latter were deprived" (Evershed M.R. in *Greenhalgh v. Arderne Cinemas Limited* [1951] Ch. 286).

In this respect, it is not necessary for each member to take a purely objective view and he need not disregard his own interests; a member must consider whether the alteration is for the benefit of the company as a going concern even if, in doing so, he is mindful of his own position. If the consensus of the majority is such that it can be said that, even with regard to the personal interests involved, the decision was made in good faith and on reasonable grounds, a court will not overturn that decision.

In considering the possibility of an alteration of the articles of association which could be prejudicial to the interests of certain members, regard should also be had to the rule in *Foss v. Harbottle* (1843) 2 Hare 461 and section 75 of the Companies Act 1980 (see *Shareholders*, page 770), since a court will be prepared to grant relief in the case of fraud on the minority or where members are unfairly prejudiced.

Informal alterations

Notwithstanding that there may have been no formal alteration of the articles of the company in accordance with section 10 of the Companies Act 1948, a court may have regard to an alteration evidenced by the acquiescence of the members of the company over a long period of time or made expressly by the agreement of those members (*Ho Tung v. Man On Insurance Co* [1902] A.C. 233). This concept has been recently extended by the decisions promulgating the "assent principle" in *Re Duomatic Limited* [1969] 2 Ch. 365 and *Re M.J. Shanley Contracting Limited* (in voluntary liquidation) (L.S.G., March 26, 1980). The latter case involved the validity of a winding-up resolution passed at a "meeting" of one member (holding proxies from the other members). It was held by Oliver J., applying *Re Duomatic*, that, while there was not a valid meeting, the commencement of the winding-up of the company took effect as at the date of the purported meeting because of the agreement of all the members of the company which was evidenced by the particular circumstances.

This principle has been extended to give validity to an alteration of the articles of association of a family company where, notwithstanding the absence of a special resolution, the court upheld that an agreement by all the members of the company was sufficient to override the articles and was therefore valid (*Cane v. Jones* [1981] 1 All E.R. 553). It is understood that this principle is supported by the Registrar of Companies on behalf of the Department of Trade. The Registrar of Companies has accepted that the unanimous assent of the members of a company is an effective alternative in all cases in which a particular kind of resolution is prescribed by the Companies Acts. Accordingly, the Registrar of Companies will accept for registration an alteration to the articles of association which is evidenced by the agreement of all the members entitled to attend and vote at a general meeting of a company notwithstanding that a special resolution as defined by section 141(2) of the Companies Act 1948 has not been passed. If so satisfied, the Registrar of Companies will treat such an assent as being as binding as a resolution passed in general meeting, on the basis that while section 10 of the Companies Act 1948 lays down the procedure whereby a majority of the shareholders of the company may effect an alteration of the articles, the section does not override the fundamental principle that all the members of a company, acting together, may do anything which is *intra vires* the company.

If this procedure is followed to effect an alteration of the articles of association of a company, it should be borne in mind that the publicity requirements (see below) apply to any informal agreement in the same way as to a special resolution passed in general meeting.

Disclosure and publicity requirements

Generally, articles of association must be registered at the Companies Registration Office on the incorporation of a company. However, for companies limited by shares the regulations in the statutory form applicable to the Act under which the company is incorporated will apply if special articles are not registered (C.A. 1948, ss. 6 and 8).

By virtue of section 143 of the Companies Act 1948, a printed copy of every special resolution of the members of a company effecting a change in its articles of association must be delivered to the Registrar of Companies for registration within fifteen days after it has been passed. The section also applies to any other resolutions agreed by all the members but which, if not so agreed, would not have been effective for their purpose unless, as the case may be, they had been passed as special resolutions or as extraordinary resolutions. By section 14(6) of the Companies Act 1980, section 143 is also extended to any resolution of a company to give, vary, revoke or renew an authority to allot relevant securities. Such an authority may be contained in the articles of a company.

A copy of every resolution or agreement which is required to be delivered to the Registrar of Companies by section 143 of the Companies Act 1948 must be embodied in or annexed to every copy of the articles of association of the company which is issued after the passing of the resolution or the making of the agreement (C.A. 1948, s. 143(2)).

Section 9(5) of the European Communities Act 1972 requires that, in addition to the resolutions required to be delivered pursuant to section 143 of the Companies Act 1948, a company must also deliver within fifteen days after an alteration is made to a company's articles of association, a printed copy of the articles as altered. As mentioned earlier, section 9(3) of the 1972 Act obliges the Registrar of Companies to cause to be published in the London or Edinburgh Gazette notice of the receipt by him of any document making or evidencing an alteration in the articles of a company. By section 9(4), a company is not entitled to rely against other persons in respect of any alteration of its articles in two circumstances. First, if the alteration had not been published under section 9(3) at the material time and is not shown by the company to have been known by the person concerned at that time. Secondly, if the material time fell on or before the fifteenth day after the day of publication in the Gazette and it is shown that the person concerned was unavoidably prevented from knowing of the alteration at that time.

Companies listed on The Stock Exchange should send a copy of the altered articles to The Stock Exchange.

Each member of a company is entitled to a copy of its memorandum and articles of association upon payment of the sum of 5p or such lesser sum as the company may prescribe (C.A. 1948, s. 24). The articles of a company may be inspected at the Companies Registry (see *Company Searches*); any person is entitled to obtain from the Registrar a sealed copy or extract from the filed articles (C.A. 1948, s. 426).

Auditors

Every company formed or registered under the Companies Acts must each year prepare accounts which disclose to members the company's current state of affairs. Nothing less than a full and unbiased examination of the accounts prior to their issue would be likely to justify the reliance placed on disclosure as a fundamental concept of U.K. company law and, to this end, the Companies Acts demand that a company's accounts be examined and reported on by an independent person who must say whether they meet the detailed requirements of the Companies Acts and give a "true and fair" view of the company's affairs. The company auditor is charged with this duty.

The Companies Acts contain a number of provisions designed to safeguard the auditor's independence, to secure his position against the possibility of interference from the directors, to ensure that he is qualified for the task and to empower him to make a thorough check of the company's books and records. The auditor must discharge his duty with reasonable skill, care and caution, practical guidance on which can be found in the Statements of Auditing Standards approved by the Councils of the Accountancy Bodies, but ultimately the standards of which fall to be tested by the courts. If the auditor fails properly to discharge his duty he may find himself liable to the company or perhaps to its members for any loss or damage occasioned by his neglect and may be liable to third parties who have relied upon his negligently prepared report.

Auditor's duties

The auditor's report

For each accounting reference period, the directors must prepare and lay before the company in general meeting a profit and loss account and balance sheet (and group accounts, if any) and, by virtue of section 14 of the Companies Act 1967, it is the duty of the auditor during his tenure of office to report to the members on these accounts. He must also report on the consistency of the directors' report with the accounts (section 23A of the 1967 Act) and, where necessary, make a statement on non-compliance with the provisions of sections 54 to 57 of the Companies Act 1980 requiring disclosure of directors' dealings (C.A. 1980, s. 59). (The provisions of sections 54 to 57 are discussed in the chapter *Disclosure of Directors' Dealings*). Save in the cases of those banking, discount, shipping and insurance companies which may still take advantage of the exemptions from full accounting disclosure conferred by Part III of Schedule 8A to the 1948 Act (see the chapter *Accounts and 1982 S.I.* 1092), the report is required to state whether in the auditor's opinion the balance sheet and profit and loss accounts (and group accounts) have been properly prepared in accordance with the Companies Acts and give a true and fair view of the company's state of affairs for the financial year. This report must be annexed to the accounts (C.A. 1948, s. 156). For these companies which can and do avail themselves of the benefits of Part III of Schedule 8A, all that is required is that the auditor reports that the accounts have been properly prepared in accordance with the Companies Acts. (Prior to the Companies Act 1967, a "true and fair" opinion on the accounts of excepted companies had to be given but this was dropped on the recommendation of the Jenkins Committee, on the basis that accounts which did not disclose certain matters could have presented a view that was neither true nor fair and, if those words were used, they might have been misunderstood.)

The auditor will comply with his duty by reporting to the directors, who will normally ensure that the report is circulated to members prior to the annual general meeting at which it will be read out and at which it will be made available for inspection. If for any reason no general meeting is held or the report is not laid before it or the report is misrepresented, the auditor will not be in breach of his statutory duty (*Re Allen Craig & Co. (London) Limited* [1934] Ch. 483). In order to ensure that his report cannot be conveyed improperly or misrepresented, the auditor is entitled to attend any general meeting of the company and to receive all notices and any other communications and to be heard at such meetings on any part of the business which concerns him as auditor.

Duty to investigate

Section 14(4) of the Companies Act 1967 provides that in making his report the auditor must carry out investigations which will enable him to form an opinion on whether proper accounting records have been kept, and proper returns adequate for the audit have been received from any branches of the company not visited by him. In addition, the investigations must be such as to enable the auditor to form an opinion on whether the company's accounts are in agreement with the accounting records and returns. If the auditor is not satisfied on both points then he must state so in his report and, in making any qualification to the accounts, must state clearly and unequivocaly the true state of the company's affairs. It is not sufficient for him merely to make some oblique reference to a problem and to leave it to the members to draw a conclusion on the truth of the matter (*Re London & General Bank Limited (No. 2)* [1895] 2 Ch. 673).

Investigations are unlikely to be meaningful unless the auditor is in a position to have access when he wishes to the books, accounts and records of the company or to such information and explanations as might be necessary from the directors and other officers of the company. The right to such access is provided specifically by section 14(5), entitling the auditor to the books and so on which he thinks necessary for the performance of his duties. Further, in order to prompt the directors to give full and honest explanations when required, section 19 of the Companies Act 1976 provides that any officer who knowingly or recklessly makes a misleading, false or deceptive statement to the auditor will be guilty of an offence and liable to the penalties set out in section 19(3). If the auditor fails to obtain access or does not receive the requisite co-operation he must state so in his report. In the case of a holding company with subsidiaries incorporated in Great Britain, each subsidiary and its auditor(s) must give any information and explanation which the auditor of the holding company requires but, where subsidiaries are incorporated overseas and are therefore outside the territorial scope of the Companies Acts, the duty to take all reasonable steps to obtain information and provide such explanation as is required by the auditor falls on the holding company. Any failure on the part of the auditor of a subsidiary or of the holding company itself will be an offence under section 18 of the Companies Act 1976.

The Companies Acts nowhere set out what the auditor must do properly to discharge the duties laid down by section 14, and it is here that the auditor must exercise his professional skills with such caution and care that, when his report is considered in relation to the true state of affairs of the company, no charge of neglect or breach of duty can be levelled against him. In the words of Lord Denning, an auditor is not merely an "adder-upper and subtractor" and each audit will present problems which will require the judgment of the auditor to be exercised in that particular context. Accordingly, no uniform practice can be adopted which will ensure that each auditor can in every case properly discharge his duties. Accountancy Standards and Guidelines drawn up by the accountants' professional bodies go some way towards laying down acceptable practices, but these must be interpreted and applied by each auditor using his subjective judgment to the case in hand. (The "Auditing Standards" issued by the CCAB set out basic principles and guidelines which members of the various accountancy bodies are expected to follow in conducting an audit. The "Auditing Guidelines" give guidance on the procedures by which Auditing Standards may be applied and their application to specific items in financial statements, and deal with current auditing techniques and particular audit problems.) Ultimately, only the courts are able to judge whether the auditor has done sufficient to discharge his duties. If he is negligent, the auditor may be liable to the company for breach of contract or in tort, or misfeasance proceedings may be brought against him under section 333 of the Companies Act 1948 (power of court to assess damages against delinquent officers in a winding up). The auditor cannot be exempted or indemnified in respect of any such liability by the company (C.A. 1948, s. 205), but relief might be granted by the court in certain cases (C.A. 1948, s. 448). The auditor may also be liable in tort to the members, or in certain circumstances to third parties, who have suffered loss through reliance on the auditor's report. The following section of this chapter examines some of the general principles which have so far been laid down by the courts in determining what the duties of an auditor are and the standard of care and skill which he must exercise.

Watchdog or bloodhound?

Although a number of the leading cases on auditor's duties and the standard of care were heard towards the end of last century, the statements of principle which they contain are still to a large extent relevant today. In *Re London & General Bank Ltd.* the auditor's duties (and those matters which were not his responsibility) were considered in detail. Lindley, L.J. had this to say:

> "It is no part of an auditor's duty to give advice either to directors or shareholders, as to what they ought to do. An auditor has nothing to do with the prudence or imprudence of making loans with or without security ... It is nothing to him whether dividends are properly or improperly declared, provided he discharges his own duty to the shareholders. His business is to ascertain and state the true financial position of the company at the time of the audit and his duty is confined to that.... But he does not discharge his duty by [examining the books of the company] without enquiry and without taking any trouble to see that the books themselves show the company's true position. He must take reasonable care to ascertain that they do so.... An auditor, however, is not bound to do more than exercise reasonable care and skill in making enquiries and investigations. He is not an insurer.... What is reasonable care in any particular case must depend upon the circumstances of that case. Where there is nothing to excite suspicion very little enquiry will be reasonably sufficient.... Where suspicion is aroused, more care is obviously necessary; but, still, an auditor is not bound to exercise more than reasonable care and skill, even in a case of suspicion...."

In *Re London & General Bank Ltd.* dividends had been paid out improperly because the assets of the company had been overstated in the balance sheet. It was found that the auditor had been negligent in respect of a particular year's report where certain loans were entered in the accounts at face value but were not realisable and the auditor had failed to draw sufficient attention to this fact. The members relied on the accounts when resolving to pay out a dividend and because the auditor had breached his statutory duty in preparing the accounts he was held liable to repay those dividends.

In *Kingston Cotton Mill Co.* [1896] 2 Ch. 279, a case reported in the year following the *Re London & General Bank Ltd.* case, Lopes L.J. added the following oft-quoted remarks on the standard of care to be exercised by an auditor:

> "It is the duty of an auditor to bring to bear on the work he has to perform that skill, care and caution which a reasonably competent,

careful and cautious auditor would use. What is reasonable skill, care and caution must depend on the circumstances of each case. An auditor is not bound to be a detective, or, ... to approach his work with suspicion, or with a foregone conclusion that there is something wrong. He is a watchdog, but not a bloodhound. He is justified in believing tried servants of the company in whom confidence is placed by the company. He is entitled to assume that they are honest, and to rely upon their representations, provided he takes reasonable care. If there is anything calculated to excite suspicion, he should probe it to the bottom, but in the absence of anything of that kind he is only bound to be reasonably cautious and careful."

The decided cases further indicate that the auditor must be aware of the contents of a company's memorandum and articles (*Leeds Estate Building & Investment Society Limited v. Shepherd* (1887) 36 Ch. D 787; and that he is responsible for dereliction of duty by his employees and that these employees are required to exercise the same standard of skill and care as the appointed auditor *(Henry Squire (Cash Chemist) Limited v. Ball, Baker, & Co.* (1911) 106 LT 197). Further, an auditor cannot make excuses such as shortage of time for failure properly to discharge his duties *(Re Thomas Gerrard & Son Limited* [1967] 3 W.L.R. 84).

With regard to the physical checks which the auditor must make, the Accountancy Standards and Guidelines set out what is currently thought to be good practice by supplementing and augmenting propositions laid down in a number of cases, including, for example *Fox & Sons v. Marrish Grant & Co.* [1918] 35 T.L.R. 126 (reconciling bank statements with cheque counterfoils) and *Re City Equitable Fire Insurance Co. Ltd.* [1925] Ch. 407 (verifying ownership of securities).

Whilst these and other cases might still be followed in determining the duties of an auditor, it should be appreciated that auditing standards today are considered to be much higher than they were in the past and therefore that the auditor should be cautious in placing reliance on the older cases on questions of standard of care. Although in some of the older cases the auditor was not found to have failed in his statutory duty, on the same or similar facts the courts today might well find him negligent. In *Re Thomas Gerrard & Son Limited*, Pennycuick J. stated clearly that according to expert evidence auditing standards were much higher today, and the accountants' bodies recognise that standards have improved. In particular, in relation to fraud, where the older cases seem to indicate that the auditor need not approach an audit with suspicion that something might be wrong, it is thought that, save perhaps for the most ingenious of frauds, failure on the part of the auditor to spot defalcations which could be revealed by a more thorough audit would not pass unpunished. Indeed, in relation to the attitude or approach which the auditor must take, the Guidelines issued by the accountants' bodies recommend a much stronger line than that taken by Lopes L.J. in the *Kingston Cotton Mill Co.* case. In the explanatory foreward to the Guidelines, it states that the auditor should recognise the possibility of material irregularities or fraud which could, unless adequately disclosed, distort the results or state of affairs shown by the financial statements. The auditor must, accordingly, plan his audit so that he has a "reasonable expectation of detecting material mis-statements in the financial statements resulting from irregularities or fraud."

Liability of auditors

The civil liability of an auditor covers first, liability to the company in tort where he is negligent in carrying out his duties or for breach of contract under the terms of his engagement with the company, an implied term of which would be that he would exercise reasonable skill and care in discharging his duties. Secondly, it is considered that the members could have a claim against an auditor in tort where he is negligent in discharging his duties to the members or for breach of his statutory duty. Thirdly, a claim could be made in tort for negligent mis-statement by a third party who had suffered damage or loss by relying on the auditor's report. And, finally, an action for misfeasance or breach of trust under section 333 of the Companies Act 1948 might be made. (Section 333 provides that any officer who has been guilty of any misfeasance or breach of trust in relation to the company, may be ordered by the court in the course of winding up the company on the application of the liquidator or official receiver to repay money in respect of the misfeasance or breach of trust. *Re Kingston Cotton Mill Co.* provides authority for the proposition that an auditor is an "officer" for the purposes of section 333.)

It is important to note that the discussion of auditors' liability in this chapter is limited to auditors appointed for Companies Acts purposes only and not in respect of other ancillary services. In many cases a firm of accountants acting as auditors will also be engaged to provide advice on other financial matters, such as accounting services and tax advice and any negligence in carrying out these tasks could give the company grounds for action. Similarly, where an "auditor" is appointed to carry out other tasks for a third party, such as share valuation or to investigate a company prior to acquisition, then that party would have grounds for an action in tort or for breach of contract if the auditor was negligent. In such cases the choice of remedy is likely to depend on the different measures of damage for tortious and contractual liability.

Hedley Byrne

The question whether a third party might bring a claim against an auditor centres on whether a duty of care is owed to that third party who relies on a negligently prepared auditor's report. Prior to the House of Lords' decision in *Hedley Byrne & Company Limited v. Heller & Partners Limited* [1964] A.C. 465, the authorities were against the proposition that auditors could be liable to third parties for the tort of negligent mis-statement, on the basis that no duty of care existed. In *Hedley Byrne*, a very definite development of the law took place with the House of Lords overruling the Court of Appeal decision in *Candler v. Crane, Christmas & Co.* [1951] 1 All. E.R. 426 and approving the dissenting judgment of Denning L.J. in that case. In his judgment in *Candler*, Denning L.J. made the following remarks on whether accountants owed a duty to persons other than those with whom a contractual relationship exists:

> "Let me now be constructive and suggest the circumstances in which I say that a duty to use care in making a statement does exist apart from a contract in that behalf. First, what persons are under such duty? The answer is those persons, such as accountants..... whose profession and occupation it is to examine books, accounts, and other things and to make reports on which other people – other than their clients – rely in the ordinary course of business. Their duty is not merely a duty to use care in their reports. They have also a duty to use care in their work which results in their reports. Herein lies the difference between these professional men and other persons who have been held to be under no duty to use care in their statements, such as promoters to issue a prospectus.... those persons do not bring, and are not expected to bring, any professional knowledge or skill into the preparation of their statements. They can only be made responsible by the law affecting persons generally, such as contract, estoppel, innocent mis-representation or fraud. It is, however, very different with persons who engage in a calling which requires special knowledge and skill. From early times it has been held that they owe a duty of care to those who are closely and directly affected by their work apart altogether from any contract or undertaking in that behalf.... [Accountants] are not liable, of course, for casual remarks made in the course of conversation, nor for other statements made outside their work, that are not made in their capacity as accountants..... but they are, in my opinion, in proper cases, apart from any contract in the matter, under a duty to use reasonable care in the preparation of their accounts and in the making of their report. Secondly, to whom do these professional people owe this duty? I will take accountants, but the same reasoning applies to others. They owe their duty, of course, to their employer or client, and also, I think, to any third person to whom they elect themselves to show the accounts, or to whom they know their employer is going to show the accounts so as to induce him to invest money or take some other action on them. I do not think, however, the duty can be extended still further so as to include strangers from whom they have heard nothing and to whom their employer without their knowledge may choose to show their accounts. Once the accountants have handed the accounts to the employer, they are not, as a rule, responsible for what he does with them without their knowledge or consent..... In my opinion accountants owe a duty of care not only to their own clients, but also to all those whom they know will rely on their accounts in the transactions for which the accounts are prepared."

In *Candler* the accountants knew that the accounts were to be given to

the plaintiffs for a particular purpose and Denning L.J. was not required
to deal specifically with the position where the accountant had no actual
knowledge that the accounts would be shown to a third person who
would rely on them. Denning L.J. did, however, approve the dicta of
Cardozo C.J. in the American case of *Ultramares Corporation v.
Touche* (1931) 174 N.E. 441, indicating that it would be going too far to
impose a duty of care in such circumstances. In *Ultramares* the
accountants had no prior knowledge of the plaintiffs, who were creditors of the company in question, and were therefore held not liable in
negligence to the plaintiffs which had extended credit in reliance on the
audited accounts. The range of the transactions in which the certificate
of audit might be used was not confined in that case in any way, and in
such a situation Cardozo C.J. felt precluded from confirming that a duty
of care was owed to third parties who could be foreseen as likely to
sustain damage if carelessness existed. He said:

> "If liability for negligence exists, a thoughtless slip or blunder, the
> failure to detect theft or forgery beneath the cover of deceptive
> entries, may expose accountants to a liability in an indeterminate
> amount for an indeterminate time to an indeterminate class. The
> hazards of a business conducted under these terms are so extreme as
> to enkindle doubt whether a flaw may not exist in the implication of a
> duty that exposes these consequences."

JEB Fasteners

Since *Hedley Byrne*, the extent of a duty of care in respect of negligent
mis-statement has been the subject of much academic discussion and a
gradual development of the principle became discernible in a number of
cases both in the U.K. and the Commonwealth, culminating in the firm
acceptance of a new principle in the recent case of *JEB Fasteners* [1981]
3 All E.R. 289. In this case in the High Court, Woolf J. reviewed certain
decisions since *Candler* and, in the light of them felt it was now possible
to say that the appropriate test for establishing whether a duty of care
existed was whether the defendants knew or reasonably should have
foreseen at the time the accounts were audited that a person might rely
on those accounts and could suffer loss if they were inaccurate.
According to Woolf J., this test would place a limitation on those
entitled to contend that there had been a breach of duty owed to them,
in that they must have relied on the accounts and, secondly, that they
must have done so in circumstances where the auditors either knew that
they would or ought to have known that they might. If the situation was
one where it would not be reasonable for the accounts to be relied on
then, in the absence of express knowledge, the auditor would be under
no duty and thus, there would be an acceptable limit to the circumstances in which, and the period during which, the audited accounts could
be relied upon.

On the facts of the case, Woolf J. found that as the defendants knew of
the need for financial support from outside for the company in question,

they ought to have realised that the accounts could be relied upon until the next audit by the commercial concerns to whom the company would look for financial assistance. The auditor would not know precisely who would provide the financial support or what form it would take and could not have known that the support would come by way of a take-over offer by the plaintiffs. However, this was one foreseeable method, and Woolf J. held that it would therefore not be right to exclude the duty of care merely because it was not possible to say with precision what machinery would be used to achieve the necessary financial support. However, notwithstanding the negligence of the auditor, Woolf J. went on to find that it was not causative of any loss which the plaintiffs suffered as a result of taking over the company and therefore that no liability arose.

When the case went to the Court of Appeal, the question of liability was not in issue and no consideration was given to the development of the law since *Hedley Byrne*, nor, it must be said, was any doubt thrown on Woolf J.'s judgment. (The subject matter of the appeal was whether, if the plaintiffs relied on the accounts and the accountants were negligent, it was open to the judge to find in favour of the defendant on the basis that there was no causal link between the negligence and the loss. The Court of Appeal found that what Woolf J. meant was that while the contents of the accounts were observed and considered by the directors of JEB Fasteners, it did not in any material degree affect their judgment in deciding whether or not to take over the other company and for this reason no liability would exist.)

It seems that the door has now been opened for creditors, investors and other third parties who might rely on accounts to take action against negligent auditors, provided the injured party can point to some reason why the auditors should have foreseen that the accounts could be relied on and that loss could in consequence be suffered. It is thought that because credit is such an every day part of a company's business, it would be reasonable in almost every case to expect an auditor to foresee that his report might be relied upon by a third party creditor and therefore that creditors should be able to bring an action against the auditor for loss if it can be shown that reliance was in fact placed on the auditor's report. Investment in private companies is a much less frequent occurrence, and so it is considered likely that special circumstances will have to be present which put the auditor on notice that an investment is an imminent possibility before the auditor will owe a duty of care to the potential investors.

The position of the auditor of a quoted company is, it is suggested, different in that he must foresee that investment in such a company will be made from day to day and, accordingly, that he may always owe a duty of care to potential investors who rely on his report to invest in that company. In Scotland too, it seems that the new principle enunciated by Woolf J. has become a part of the law of delict according to the two recent cases of *Twomax and Goode v. Dickson McFarlane and Robertson* and *Garden v. Dickson, McFarlane and Robertson* (as yet unreported). In these cases, which were heard together, Lord Stewart held that a firm of accountants were liable to make reparation to three investors who had purchased shares on the strength of accounts which had been negligently audited. In making their share acquisitions, the pursuers argued that they relied upon the balance sheets and accounts prepared and audited by the defenders. It was later found that there had been errors in the accounts to such an extent that the accounts were misleading and produced a seriously distorted picture. Lord Stewart followed the Woolf J. principle which he felt contained "the simplicity of the proximity or neighbour principle with a limitation which has regard to the warning against exposing accountants to indeterminate liability". On the facts, the auditors did not know of the interests of the pursuers but knew that the company needed fresh capital, that a director wished to sell his shares and, further, that the accounts were being made available to creditors. Lord Stewart concluded that the auditor should have realised that there would be dealings in shares of the company and that his certificate would be relied upon. Damages were awarded against the defenders for the full amount paid for the shares, Lord Stewart accepting that the shares would not have been purchased at any price had the accounts been accurate.

According to the press, the *JEB Fasteners* case has caused some alarm to the accountancy profession and it will be interesting to see whether any further development of the law in this area takes place, either to confirm or further clarify just how "indeterminate" the auditor's liability now is.

Appointment of auditor

Prior to the Companies Act 1976, an auditor could be re-appointed automatically at a company's annual general meeting unless he was no longer qualified, his appointment was expressly or impliedly terminated or he had given written notice that he was unwilling to be re-appointed. In the Jenkins Report it was noted that where auditors were appointed in the name of a firm, it was wrong in law to allow for automatic re-appointment if the firm did not comprise the same individuals who were initially appointed (as is often the case due to partnership changes). Partly in order to meet this legal difficulty, section 14 of the 1976 Act was introduced requiring a specific resolution appointing or re-appointing auditors to be passed at every annual general meeting held after June 18, 1977 at which accounts are laid before members. The resolution must provide that an auditor's term of office should run from the conclusion of the general meeting at which accounts are laid until the conclusion of the next.

The first auditors of a company may be appointed by the directors at any time before the first general meeting of the company at which accounts are to be laid to hold office until the conclusion of that meeting. The directors likewise may fill any casual vacancy but, if the directors fail to appoint an auditor, the company in general meeting may do so. Where a company fails to appoint an auditor, it must give notice to the Secretary of State within seven days of the general meeting at which the auditor should have been appointed and in those circumstances the Secretary of State may appoint an auditor.

Section 12 of the Companies Act 1981 permits a dormant company to dispense with the appointment of auditors (see the chapter *Accounts*).

Where a new auditor is to be appointed, special notice (28 days) is required for the resolution and the notice, together with a copy of the resolution, must be sent by the company to the person to be appointed.

Removal of auditor

An auditor can be removed by ordinary resolution of the company notwithstanding anything set out in any agreement or letter of engagement between the auditor and the company. This does not, however, deprive a sacked auditor from claiming compensation or damages for loss of his office or in respect of any other appointment which terminates with his removal as auditor (C.A. 1976, s. 14(10)).

Special notice (28 days) is required for a resolution removing an auditor before the expiration of his term of office and a copy of the notice must be sent to the person to be removed. The auditor may make representations in writing to the company in respect of his removal and request that the company sends copies to all members and states that representations have been made in the notice of the resolution for his removal. If copies of the representations are not sent out to members because they are received too late or because of the company's default, the auditor may require that his representations be read out at the meeting. Where representations have been made which contain defamatory matter, the company or any other person who claims to be aggrieved may apply to the court for an order that the representations need not be sent or read out.

Finally, an auditor who has been removed is entitled to attend the general meeting at which his term of office would otherwise have expired and any other general meeting at which it is proposed to fill the vacancy caused by his removal. He may also be heard at any meeting which he attends on any part of the business of the meeting which concerns him as a former auditor of the company. A copy of the resolution removing an auditor must be registered within fourteen days of it being passed with the Registrar of Companies.

Resignation of auditor

Prior to section 16 of the Companies Act 1976 being introduced, there was no specific statutory provision dealing with the right of an auditor to resign. Differences of opinion existed on whether an auditor could resign during his tenure of office only with the consent of the company in general meeting or whether he should be expressly permitted to resign with the consent of the directors. The danger was, of course, that as no specific provisions existed an auditor could terminate his appointment by arrangement with the directors where he wished to resign because of a disagreement over the accounts and nothing of the dispute or circumstances surrounding it would be disclosed to the members. Jenkins felt that whilst a right to resign should be recognised, the question whether an auditor had improperly resigned should be left to the recognised professional bodies to deal with as a matter of professional conduct.

The legislature were not convinced by the Jenkins proposal and section 16 of the 1976 Act provides the auditor with a specific right to resign coupled with a duty either to state that there are no circumstances connected with his resignation which he considers should be brought to the attention of the members or creditors or to make a statement of any such circumstances. If neither statement is given the auditor's resignation is not effective. A copy of the auditor's resignation must be registered by the company within 14 days with the Registrar of Companies, and if it contains a statement of matters to be brought to the attention of members or debenture holders, a copy must be sent to each of those persons. As with section 14 (removal of auditors), a court order can be obtained to the effect that no copies need be circulated if the statements are defamatory, but notice to this effect must be given to the members and debenture holders. If there is default in complying with the requirement to register and circulate the notice of resignation, the company and every officer of the company who is in default will be guilty of an offence and liable to the penalties provided for in section 16(7) of the Companies Act 1976. Further, the court may enforce the duties of the company by order under section 428 of the Companies Act 1948.

To emphasise or explain the circumstances giving rise to his resignation the auditor may requisition through the directors an extraordinary general meeting of the company to hear his reasons. Alternatively, the auditor may request the company to circulate a statement setting out the reasons for his resignation. If such a request is made, the directors are obliged to circulate the statement to any person to whom notice of the meeting is sent and to mention the fact that a statement has been made in the notice of the meeting. If the directors fail within 21 days from the date of receipt of the requisition notice to requisition a meeting for a day not more than 28 days after the date on which the notice convening the meeting is given, all directors who failed to take reasonable steps to procure the convening of the meeting will be guilty of an offence and liable to the penalties contained in section 19(3).

If a copy of the auditors statement is not sent out because it was received too late or because of the company's default, the auditor may require that the statement be read out at the meeting. This right is in addition to the auditors' right to attend and be heard at any meeting on any part of the business of the meeting which concerns him as former auditor of the company.

Remuneration

Section 14(8) of the Companies Act 1976 provides that where the directors appoint the auditor as first auditor then they will be entitled to fix his remuneration. Similarly, where an auditor is appointed by the Secretary of State under section 14(2) where the company fails to appoint or reappoint an auditor, the Secretary of State will decide on the remuneration. In other cases, the auditor's remuneration is to be fixed by the company in general meeting or in such a manner as the company decides. The normal approach is for the general meeting to resolve that the directors alone may decide on the auditor's remuneration.

With regard to making sure that his fees are paid, an auditor has, at least, a particular lien over books of accounts, records and so on which the company has delivered to the auditor, and also over other documents which have come into his possession in the course of acting as his client's agent in the course of his ordinary professional work. Authority for this proposition can be found in *Woodworth v. Conroy* [1976] Q.B. 884.

Qualification

The qualifications which an auditor must have are either that he is (a) a member of a body of accountants recognised for this purpose by the Department of Trade; or (b) is a person for the time being authorised by the Department of Trade to be appointed as an auditor (C.A. 1948, s. 161; C.A. 1976, s. 13). Whilst there has been some pressure on the Department of Trade to admit other accountancy bodies (which it could do by statutory instrument), at present, only members of the Institute of Chartered Accountants in England and Wales, the Institute of Chartered Accountants of Scotland, the Association of Certified Accountants and the Institute of Chartered Accountants in Ireland are recognised for Companies Acts purposes (C.A. 1976, s. 13(1)). Under category (b), a person can only be authorised if he has similar qualifications obtained outside the United Kingdom; or has obtained adequate knowledge and experience in the course of his employment by a recognised body; or was practising as an accountant on August 6, 1947 and applied for recognisition before January 27, 1968. New admissions under the "adequate knowledge and experience" qualification were stopped on April 17, 1978. Overseas accountants with similar qualifications may be refused authorisation if reciprocal arrangements do not exist for U.K. accountants to practice as auditors in their countries.

Disqualified persons

In order to ensure that the auditor is wholly independent of the company certain persons are disqualified from acting. Section 161 of the Companies Act 1948 provides that no officer or servant of the company or person who is a partner of, or in the employment of, an officer or servant of the company or another company may be an auditor. Thus, an accountant who is, for example, the secretary of a company may not also be auditor. The "disqualification" extends to any person disqualified from acting for a subsidiary or holding company of the company in question. A body corporate cannot be appointed as an auditor. A Scottish firm can be appointed as an auditor provided all its partners qualify (C.A. 1948, s. 161(4)).

Any person who acts as an auditor while he knows he is disqualified or fails without reasonable excuse to vacate his office when he becomes disqualified will be guilty of an offence under section 13 of the Companies Act 1976. However, it is important to note that ignorance of the law appears to be a defence to a charge under section 13(5) and (6). In the recent case of *Secretary of State v. Hart* [1982] 1 W.L.R. 481 the respondent acted as the auditor of two companies at a time when he was disqualified from acting because he was a director of the companies. He was charged with acting as an auditor of a company knowing that he was disqualified. The magistrate found that the respondent had been ignorant of the law and as section 13 required actual knowledge of the offence he dismissed the case. On appeal it was held that on a true construction of sections 13(5) and (6), ignorance of the law was a sufficient defence to the charge since these subsections could reasonably be interpreted as meaning that a person was not guilty of the offence unless he not only knew the facts which disqualified him from being an auditor but also knew in law that he was so disqualified.

Bonus Issues

Whatever a bonus issue of shares or debentures may be, it could hardly be accurately described as an issue by way of bonus. That expression is misleading, implying as it does some element of gratuitous intent on the part of the company. A company cannot make a gift of its shares, and it would be wrong to suppose that a bonus issue in any way involved a depletion of the assets of the company. A more accurate description of the procedure is a *capitalisation issue*. Essentially, what is involved is a capitalisation of reserves and the issue of shares or debentures treated as fully-paid. In this way the permanent capital of a company can be increased without further cash or assets being introduced. One liability of the company is replaced by another; in the balance sheet the shareholders' funds may change their character, but they do not alter in extent. Another common description of the procedure is "scrip issue".

Nature of bonus issue

The power of a company to make bonus issues is derived in most cases from article 128 (as amended) of Table A to the Companies Act 1948. A company incorporated under legislation prior to the 1948 Act and whose Articles have not been updated since may not have the requisite authority, and an alteration of the Articles will in that case be necessary. Article 128 has been supplemented by article 128A, which was inserted by paragraph 36(9) of Schedule 3 to the 1980 Act. The importance of that new regulation is discussed later. Broadly, under article 128 the company in general meeting (i.e. by ordinary resolution of the members) is empowered, upon the recommendation of the directors, to resolve to capitalise certain reserves or profits and apply the sum so capitalised in paying up *in full* unissued shares or debentures of the company. Those shares or debentures are to be allotted and distributed credited as fully paid to the members of the company entitled to dividend distributions in the proportion in which they would have been so entitled.

An allotment of bonus shares to the members of a company does not contravene the general rule, contained in section 20(1) of the 1980 Act, that shares allotted by any company should be paid up in money or money's worth (C.A. 1980, s. 20(5)). However, even bonus shares must not be issued at a discount, that is otherwise than out of funds or profits applicable to that purpose (C.A. 1980, s. 21). In an early case, where bonus shares were issued to subscribers for debentures, it was held that this was ultra vires even if authorised by the Articles, and the shareholder was not thereby relieved from liability as a contributory in a winding-up. In other words the full nominal value of the share then had to be paid (*Welton v. Saffery* [1897] A.C. 299). Under section 21(2) of the 1980 Act the amount of any discount must be paid to the company by the allottee, together with interest at the appropriate rate (i.e. five per cent. per annum or as specified by statutory instrument).

As indicated earlier, an issue of bonus shares under article 128 of Table A does not permit payment of the nominal amount of those shares otherwise than in full. Nevertheless, there is nothing to prevent bonus shares being issued partly paid provided the requisite power is taken in the Articles. This is subject, in the case of a public company, to the restrictions contained in section 22 of the Companies Act 1980. That section provides that a *public company* shall not allot a share except as paid up at least to one quarter of its nominal amount and the whole of any premium on it. This restriction applies equally to bonus shares as to any other. However, by section 22(3), the requirement on the allottee to pay up the minimum amount plus interest does not apply in relation to the allotment of a bonus share in contravention of the general rule unless the allottee knew or ought to have known that the share was so allotted. Furthermore, any shares (including bonus shares) can be issued under an employees' share scheme without regard to the minimum payment requirement (section 22(4)). If bonus shares *are* issued otherwise than fully paid, the allottee cannot be compelled to accept them; if he does he remains liable to pay up the balance of the nominal amount.

Finally under this heading, there are two further particular provisions relating to bonus issues which deserve mention. First, the allotment of any bonus shares (but not debentures) is not prohibited under section 42 of the 1981 Act as being financial assistance for the acquisition of shares. It would appear that even an issue of *redeemable* shares would not contravene this prohibition. Secondly, it has now been confirmed, by a 1981 amendment to section 24 of the 1980 Act expressed to be for the avoidance of doubt, that an expert valuation is *not* required on a bonus issue by a public company (see now section 24(11A) of the 1980 Act).

Available profits

At common law it was permissible to capitalise any profits otherwise available for distribution as a dividend for the purpose of issuing bonus shares or debentures. This included a surplus on capital account resulting from a revaluation of fixed assets made in good faith by competent valuers, and not likely to be liable to short-term fluctuations (see *Dimbula Valley (Ceylon) Tea Co. Limited v. Laurie* [1961] Ch. 353). To this common law rule were added certain statutory variations for capitalisation referred to below.

The general rules for distributions have been modified by section 39 of the Companies Act 1980. Distributions are restricted to the excess of a company's undistributed, accumulated, realised profits over its current accumulated, realised losses. Under section 45(2) of the 1980 Act, however, an issue of shares, whether fully or partly paid, is excluded from the definition of a "distribution" for this purpose. Accordingly, issues of bonus *shares* may be made out of non-distributable profits (for example, unrealised appreciations on a revaluation). This does not extend to bonus issues of *debentures* which cannot be made out of a capitalisation of unrealised profits (C.A. 1980, s. 39(3)). These statutory rules are recognised in practice by article 128A of Table A, which was introduced by the 1980 Act with effect from December 22, 1980. Although that article does not apply to companies incorporated prior to December 22, 1980 (unless the articles of those companies are subsequently updated), there is nevertheless a saving provision in section 45(1) of the 1980 Act which enables such companies to rely on any pre-existing authority to issue bonus shares out of unrealised profits.

In addition to the common law powers of capitalisation, there are two statutory funds or reserves which can be used to pay up bonus shares (but not debentures). They are the share premium account (section 56(2) of the 1948 Act as amended) and the capital redemption reserve (section 53(3) of the 1981 Act). The power to apply these capital funds in paying up bonus shares is conferred on a company by article 128 of Table A, subject to the proviso (as amended) to that regulation. The amendment (which was inserted by paragraph 36(8) of Schedule 3 to the 1980 Act) together with corresponding substantive amendments operates to enable companies to *allot* as opposed to *issue* bonus shares so paid up. It is thought that this facilitates the issue of such shares on renounceable letters of allotment and their subsequent renunciation. Technically, an allotment of a share on a renounceable letter does not of itself constitute an *issue* of shares (*Oswald Tillotson v. I.R.C.* [1933] 1 K.B. 134), so that if any share were renounced by the allottee the use of a share premium account or capital redemption reserve would it seems strictly be *ultra vires*. This defect is therefore remedied but, again, only in relation to companies whose Articles are adopted or modified after the 1980 Act.

Uses of a bonus issue

The primary purpose of a bonus issue is to increase the capitalisation of a company so that the permanent capital available to it can more realistically reflect the assets employed by the company. Any bonus issue results in a dilution of the equity in the existing ordinary shares, but a shareholder retains that value overall albeit in a different form. A more substantial share or loan capital account can often enable a company to obtain further finance from outside sources. A capitalisation issue can also be used as an effective defence against a takeover, because the bidder cannot thereby obtain control and distribute the company's reserves.

Bonus issues are also employed for other, perhaps more specialised purposes. Those include the following:

(a) A bonus issue of preference shares followed by a placing with institutions or an offer for sale is an attractive means of enabling members of a company (particularly the successful family company) to raise cash without relinquishing control or diluting their equity stake. The preference shares so issued may be listed on The Stock Exchange or through the Unlisted Securities Market.

(b) A capitalisation issue can to a certain extent be regarded as a stock dividend, and this is certainly a common procedure, for example in the United States. In the United Kingdom, although a straightforward bonus issue will generally be regarded as a capital receipt for tax purposes (*I.R.C. v. Blott* 8 T.C. 101), certain bonus issues can be treated as cash dividends of an equivalent amount in the hands of the recipient shareholders (see section 34 of the Finance (No. 2) Act 1975).

(c) The issue of bonus preference shares or debentures can sometimes be used effectively to "freeze" the current value of a company, thus enabling new shares to be issued at par or with a less substantial premium than would otherwise be the case. This can be useful especially where the value of a company's freehold property artificially inflates the value of the ordinary shares. A revaluation of the property, followed by a bonus issue of preference shares (*not* debentures) can shift value out of the ordinary shares and render them more marketable.

(d) A bonus issue is also commonly used both by private and public companies, listed and unlisted, as a means of reducing stamp duty on a transfer of shares. The bonus shares are issued on renounceable letters of allotment (or renounceable certificates) on which no stamp duty is payable provided renunciation can take place no later than six months from issue (see sections 59(1) and 65(1) of the Finance Act 1963). For a full explanation of the mechanics and tax implications of such schemes see *Tolley's Tax Planning*.

Although detailed consideration of taxation is outside the scope of this book, the making of a bonus issue, whether of shares or debentures, should not be carried out without reference to the tax implications. In particular, attention should be paid to the distribution provisions in sections 234 and 235 of the Taxes Act 1970, and the anti-avoidance legislation contained in section 460 (cancellation of tax advantages from certain transactions in securities) of the Taxes Act.

Prospectus requirements

The prospectus requirements of the Companies Acts do not generally affect bonus issues, in spite of the wide definition of "public" in section 55(1) of the 1948 Act. A "subscription or purchase" within the definition of "prospectus" in section 445 connotes a payment in cash in each case (see *Governments Stocks and Other Securities Investment Co. Limited v. Christopher* [1956] 1 W.L.R. 237). Shares or debentures issued by way of capitalisation are generally fully paid up, in accordance with articles 128 and 128A of Table A, and no further payment is therefore required.

It is of course possible, and indeed where bonus securities are allotted in a renounceable form likely, that the new shares or debentures issued by way of bonus will be purchased from the allottees other than by existing members of the company. In such a case, however, the documents issued by the company purely as an element of the capitalisation would not of themselves amount to an "offer for sale". On the other hand, a subsequent offer to the public of the new bonus securities, particularly where it is made within six months after the allotment (see section 45(2) of the 1980 Act) will normally be deemed to be a prospectus issued by the company for all purposes, including therefore those stated in the Fourth Schedule to the 1948 Act.

Stock Exchange requirements

Where the company is listed on The Stock Exchange regard must always be had to the requirements of the Listing Agreement.

One of the stated means by which securities may be brought to The Stock Exchange is by means of a capitalisation issue to holders of securities, by which further securities are credited as fully paid up out of the company's reserves in proportion to existing holdings, and not involving any monetary consideration. Under the Listing Agreement any alteration in the capital structure of a company must be notified to The Stock Exchange. This will involve the delivery of proof documents and ultimately final printed documents, together with full details of the posting of renounceable letters or certificates.

Where a listed company issues bonus securities, permission will normally be given to deal in those securities (subject to allotment) shortly before the general meeting at which the capitalisation issue is approved. Under fairly complex dealing arrangements, existing securities are not normally made "Ex" until the first business day following posting of the relevant document. This ensures that a shareholder can at all times deal with his whole stake in the company. However, this does not prevent claims to rights (i.e. to the new shares) arising because the register will be closed some time before the document is posted in order to ascertain entitlement. Nevertheless, it is possible after early consultation with the Department of Trade for the old securities to be made "Ex" soon after the proposal becomes firm. In such a case dealings in the new securities begin at the same time as the old securities are made "Ex" with special settlement immediately following the day on which the documents of title are posted.

The Stock Exchange prefers capitalisation issues (and rights issues) to be timed so that dealings in the new securities can be commenced on the first day of an account. For bonus issues this effectively means that the renounceable documents should be posted on the last dealing day of an account. This is in order to avoid dealings both "Cum" and "Ex" in the same account.

On a capitalisation issue it often occurs that a shareholder's entitlement will include a fraction of a share. Under Stock Exchange rules that fraction must be sold for the benefit of that shareholder unless the value of the fractional entitlement is small in which case it may, if the Council of The Stock Exchange agree, be sold for the benefit of the company provided that the articles of association permit this procedure, or it is approved by the shareholders in general meeting.

Outline procedure for public company

Not every public company will have a listing on The Stock Exchange. However, many of the procedural elements that are required under the Listing Agreement are also commonly adopted in the case of many public companies, particularly those which intend seeking a quotation at some time in the future.

1. The first step is to check the articles of the company to ensure that it has the relevant powers to capitalise profits and issue bonus shares. This is particularly important in view of the alterations made by the Companies Act 1980 which were referred to in more detail earlier. It is also of course vital that the company has sufficient authorised capital to enable the issues of shares to be made. (For the procedure on an increase of share capital see the chapter, *Shares*.)

2. A capitalisation issue requires the consent of the company in general meeting. It will be necessary, therefore, for there to be a board meeting to convene an extraordinary general meeting of the company. What is required is an *ordinary* resolution (see the chapter, *General Meetings*). At this board meeting the directors will also approve the draft documentation.

3. If the company is listed, it will be necessary to observe The Stock Exchange requirements as to information to be provided. This will include the filing of draft documents, and the giving of preliminary information on the proposed issue.

4. In order to give publicity to the proposed issue, a press announcement will generally be made at this stage. This will simply contain details of the proposed issue (subject to the approval of shareholders).

5. It will then be necessary to arrange the printing of the required documents. These will include the notice of extraordinary general meeting together with forms of proxy, and the renounceable certificates. There are certain Stock Exchange requirements in relation to any document which is to be circularised to the shareholders. For example, it must state that application has been

made to the Council of the Stock Exchange for the new securities to be admitted to the Official List, and full details of the shares to be issued and the pro rata entitlement to them must be given. If the document is a renounceable document of title, it must show *as a heading* that the document is of value and negotiable and that in all cases of doubt, or if prior to receipt the addressee has sold (other than *ex* rights) all or part of his registered holding of the existing securities, a stockbroker, bank manager, or other professional adviser should be consulted immediately.

6. The extraordinary general meeting is held at which the ordinary resolution necessary for a capitalisation issue is approved by the shareholders.

7. The register of members is closed and shareholdings are balanced as at the record date. This enables the entitlements of shareholders to be ascertained.

8. A listing for the new securities is obtained from The Stock Exchange.

9. The renounceable documents are posted to the shareholders. In general, in the case of capitalisation issues the renounceable documents take the form of renounceable certificates. Until the last day for renunciation has passed, the new securities can be dealt in without the usual transfer formalities, and without payment of stamp duty.

10. Dealings in the new securities commence on the next working day after the renounceable certificates have been posted. Fractions are generally sold in the market immediately dealings commence.

11. Once the time for renunciation has passed, new share certificates are issued to the renouncees. The original allottees who do not renounce merely retain their certificates which at that time automatically cease to be renounceable. Dealings thereafter are conducted under the normal transfer system, subject to stamp duty.

12. Finally, a return of allotments must be made to the Registrar of Companies on form PUC 7, accompanied by a form 52 simply giving particulars of the amount of reserves capitalised in respect of the bonus issue. No capital duty is payable since no assets are contributed to the company.

Borrowings

For the obligations of a company in respect of a borrowing made by it to be valid, four main conditions have to be satisfied,

(a) subject as stated below, the company has to have the power to make the borrowing and incur the related obligations;

(b) subject as stated below, the directors of the company have to have the power to authorise the making of the borrowing and the incurring of the related obligations;

(c) subject as stated below, the contract relating to the borrowing has to be validly entered into on behalf of the company; and

(d) the borrowing must not be unlawful and, subject as stated below, must not contravene any contract or obligation binding the company.

Power of company to borrow

Every trading or commercial company has an implied power to borrow money for the purposes of its business if such borrowing is not expressly prohibited (*Re David Payne & Co Limited* [1904] 2 Ch. 608, *Re Badger* [1905] 1 Ch. 568). It is, however, almost invariable for the memorandum of association of a commercial company to include an express power to borrow money. But such an express borrowing power, like an implied power, can only be exercised for the purposes of the company's business (*Re David Payne*, above). Even if the company's memorandum contains a *Cotman v Brougham* clause, declaring each of the objects set out in each sub-clause of the memorandum to be an independent object of the company (see page 567), that will not convert a power to borrow into an independent object of the company, exercisable otherwise than for the purposes of the company's business (*Re Introductions Limited* [1970] Ch. 199; *Re Horsley & Weight Limited* [1982] 3 W.L.R. 431). A lender is not, however, required to enquire what is the purpose of the borrowing. However if the lender does know the purpose of the borrowing, and if the purpose is one which is not authorised by the company's memorandum of association, then the lender is not protected, unless he can bring himself within the provisions of section 9(1) of the European Communities Act 1972 (*Re Introductions, Re Horsley & Weight*; for section 9(1) see page 574).

Power of directors to borrow

The articles of association of a commercial company will normally include a general clause providing that the business of the company shall be managed by its directors (see, for instance, Article 80 in Part 1 of Table A). In addition, articles of association usually contain a specific clause stating that the directors may exercise all the powers of the company to borrow money, to mortgage its property and to issue securities (see, for instance, Article 79 in Part 1 of Table A).

Borrowing articles of this type frequently limit the amount of debt which can be outstanding at any given time, at least without the prior consent of the shareholders.

A limit of this kind is contained in the proviso to Article 79 in Part 1 of Table A. The effect of this proviso is that, except with the previous sanction of the company in general meeting, the amount for the time being remaining undischarged of "moneys borrowed or secured by the directors as aforesaid" shall not exceed the nominal amount of the company's then issued share capital. But "temporary loans obtained from the company's bankers in the ordinary course of business" are to be excluded in calculating the company's borrowings. The words "borrowed or secured by the directors as aforesaid" refer back to the earlier part of Article 79 and therefore include not only money borrowed, but also amounts contingently outstanding under any guarantees issued by the directors. It is thought that the exclusion of "temporary loans obtained from the company's bankers" extends also to temporary overdrafts, although it has been held that an overdraft is not a loan (*Waterlow v Sharp* L.R. 8 Eq. 501, but contrast *Brooks & Co. v Blackburn Benefit Society* 9 App. Cas 857).

In the case of a listed company, The Stock Exchange requires that its articles of association should provide that the directors shall be under an obligation to restrict the borrowings of the company and, so far as the directors can do so, its subsidiaries. The required restriction is that the aggregate amount outstanding of all moneys borrowed by the same group shall not, except with the consent of the company in general meeting, exceed an ascertainable amount.

The borrowing restrictions contained in the articles of listed companies are invariably in a more detailed form than the proviso to Article 79. These restrictions usually limit outstanding borrowings to a multiple (generally between two and three times in the case of trading companies) of the adjusted amount of share capital and reserves of the company. They also usually specify what items are to be treated as borrowings and how the amount of adjusted share capital and reserves is to be calculated. In addition, the restrictions frequently contain provisions designed to avoid the limit's being exceeded as a result of a temporary fall in the rate of sterling as against a foreign currency in which borrowings have been incurred.

Articles which contain a borrowing limit generally include provisions to the effect that no lender to the company shall be concerned to enquire whether the limit is being observed and to the effect that no debt incurred in excess of the limit shall be invalid, unless the lender had express notice at the time of the loan that the limit was being exceeded.

Even apart from such provisions, where articles require an ordinary resolution of the company or the consent of the company in general meeting, for the company to make a borrowing in excess of the limit, the lender (if he is an "outsider" and unaware of any fact putting him on enquiry) has a right to infer that the necessary resolution has been passed or the necessary consent given (*Royal British Bank v Turquand* 6 E. & B. 327). But, if the articles state that the limit can only be exceeded with the sanction of a special resolution or an extraordinary resolution, the lender is not entitled to assume that the required resolution has been passed. This is because, unlike ordinary resolutions, special and extraordinary resolutions are public documents. Section 143 of the 1948 Act requires these resolutions to be recorded with the Registrar of Companies, and the lender would therefore have constructive notice of the fact that the necessary special or extraordinary resolution had not been passed.

Moreover, if the borrowing limit is contained in the company's articles, the lender may be in a position to avail himself of the protection of section 9(1) of the European Communities Act 1972 (see page 574).

Despite the protections which would normally be available to a lender who had made a loan in excess of a borrowing limit, the normal practice, at least where substantial loans are involved, is to obtain a certificate from two directors of the company – or from its auditors, in the case of public issues of loan stock – that the loan will be within the limit.

It is to be noted that if the loan carries a right to subscribe for shares in the borrower or another company or to convert the loan agreement into shares in the borrower, then the provisions of section 14 of the Companies Act 1980 will be applicable. The result is that, unless the articles of the company whose shares are to be acquired contain an authority which is effective under section 14, the directors of that company will require to obtain the authority of the company in general meeting before they can grant the subscription or conversion right concerned. Nevertheless, as a result of section 14(8), a failure to comply with the requirements of section 14 will not affect the validity of the grant of the right to subscribe or convert, and it seems clear that the obligations of the borrower with respect to a loan carrying such a right will not be affected by a contravention of the section. (Reference was made above to a power to convert a loan agreement into shares of the borrower. Although this may be an unusual transaction, a position whereby the lender can require the borrowing company to issue shares to him in exchange for and the satisfaction of the loan agreement would probably fall within section 14.)

It should also be borne in mind that, if the loan carries a right to subscribe for, or convert the loan agreement into, "equity securities" of any company, the pre-emption right provisions of sections 17 to 19 of the Companies Act 1980 will be applicable. (Section 17(11) probably applies to a right to convert a single security, even though section 14(10)(b) (definition of "relevant securities") refers to a right to convert "any security" into shares and the definition of equity security in section 17(11) refers to a right to convert "any securities".) If the requirements of these provisions are not complied with, it appears from section 17(10) that the sole consequence will be that the company and its officers who knowingly authorised or permitted the contravention will be liable to compensate persons entitled to the pre-emption rights concerned who suffered loss as a result. Although there is no provision corresponding to section 14(8) (breach of section 14 not to affect validity of a contract), it seems that the grant of the right to subscribe or convert will not be avoided. In any event, it seems clear that a contravention of the section will not affect the obligations of the borrower with respect to the loan carrying the subscription or conversion right concerned.

The validity of the loan contract

The loan agreement, debenture or other relevant document has to be validly entered into on behalf of the company. This will mean that the execution or signature of the document should have been duly authorised by the directors (or by a committee of directors or a managing or executive director to whom the directors have delegated their authority), and that the document should have been executed in the manner or signed by the persons so authorised.

The common practice is for lenders to request a certified copy of the minute of the meeting of the directors at which the resolution authorising the execution or signature of the loan agreement was passed.

Illegality, etc.

As with other contractual obligations, the obligations of a borrower under a loan agreement may be void or unenforceable if the loan agreement is unlawful or affected by illegality. In addition, the Companies Act 1980 renders voidable transactions or agreements which contravene section 48 or 49 of that Act.

In this connection, the following provisions are of particular relevance to loan transactions:-

(a) Section 49, which is subject to section 50, prohibits a company from making a loan to a director of the company or of its holding company and from providing a guarantee or any security in connection with such a loan. In the case of "a relevant company" these prohibitions are extended to transactions in favour of "a person connected" with such a director. For example, a loan of over £2,500 by "a relevant company" to another company in more than one-fifth of whose equity share capital a director of the lending company was interested could fall within section 49 unless both companies were members of the same group or section 50 was otherwise applicable. (See *Directors' Loans*, page 269.)

(b) Section 48 of the 1980 Act prohibits any arrangement whereby a director of a company or its holding company or a person connected with such a director is to acquire a non-cash asset of the requisite value from the company, or whereby the company acquires such a non-cash asset from such a director or connected person, unless the arrangement is first approved by a resolution of the company concerned – and, in certain cases, its holding company – in general meeting. See *Directors' Duties*, page 248. Since section 87(4)(b) extends the meaning of "the acquisition of a non-cash asset" to cover the creation of an estate or interest in or a right over any property, it is thought that section 49 might be applicable to a case where a company does not transfer a non-cash asset outright to a director, but merely grants him a mortgage or charge over it.

(c) Section 42 of the Companies Act 1981 prohibits a company from giving, in certain circumstances, financial assistance for the purpose of the acquisition of any of its own shares or any of the shares in its holding company, or for the purpose of reducing or discharging any liability incurred by a person for the purpose of such an acquisition, see *Financial Assistance*, page 372. In relation to loan transactions, section 42 is more likely to apply to a guarantee or a charge which a company gives in order to secure the obligations of a purchaser of its shares to pay the purchase price, or to repay a loan raised to pay for its shares, rather than to any loan made to the target company itself. It seems clear that securities given in contravention of these sections are void despite some authority to the contrary (see page 397).

(d) Section 482 of the Income and Corporation Taxes Act 1970 makes it unlawful, except with the consent of HM Treasury and subject to certain exceptions and exemptions, for a body corporate resident in the United Kingdom to cause or permit any body corporate not so resident over which it has control to create or issue any debentures.

In the case of a company listed on The Stock Exchange, Chapter 4 of "Admission of Securities to Listing" – the Yellow Book – normally makes it a requirement of The Stock Exchange to obtain the approval of the company's shareholders to a transaction, a principal purpose or effect which is the granting of credit (including the lending of money) by the company or any one of its subsidiaries to, or to an associate of, a director or substantial shareholder. The terms director and substantial shareholder have extended meanings and include a person who occupied that position within the preceding twelve months. However this requirement does not apply to a granting of credit upon normal commercial terms in the ordinary course of business and is frequently waived where the amounts involved are insignificant.

Other provisions

The Consumer Credit Act 1974 does not apply to an agreement for the provision of credit to a company, unless the agreement is for the provision of credit jointly to the company and one or more individuals and the amount of the credit is £5,000 or less (sections 8 and 188(5) of the Consumers Credit Act 1974).

The Control of Borrowing Order 1958, 1958 S.I. No. 1208 as amended, does not apply to any transaction effected by or on behalf of a company resident in the United Kingdom, except that in the case of an issue of sterling securities (which does not include the signature of a single loan agreement) to raise £3 million or more, the time at which the securities are to be issued has to be approved by the Bank of England. However, section 1(3) of the Borrowing (Control and Guarantees) Act 1946 provides that the rights of the persons concerned in any transaction shall not be affected by the fact that the transaction was in contravention of any Order made under that Act, although such a contravention constitutes an offence.

Although the Exchange Control Act 1947 has not been repealed, since October 23, 1979 almost no exchange controls have been in operation (see the Exchange Control (General Exemption) Order 1979 S.I. No 1660).

Contracts with third parties

Loan agreements and loan stock trust deeds frequently contain an undertaking by the company to keep its borrowings, and those of its subsidiaries, within a specified limit, such as a given multiple of its share capital and reserves. Such restrictions are often similar in form to the borrowing limits to be found in the articles of listed companies. If a lender makes a loan which causes a borrowing limit in another loan agreement to be breached, is his loan (and the agreement governing it) valid? On general principles, it seems that the loan will be valid provided that he had no notice of the borrowing limit – although the lender under the loan agreement containing the borrowing limit will have his remedies against the company, and probably its directors (or those who authorised the offending loan). If a lender is aware of a borrowing limit in another loan agreement and knows that his loan will cause that limit to be breached, it seems clear that he will be liable to the other for any loss (which is not too remote) which the other lender suffers as a result of the breach, on the basis of having procured a breach of contract.

It also seems clear that the second lender's loan agreement will be invalid (see *Clerk & Lindsell* on *Torts* at 15–08). What, perhaps, is unclear is whether and, if so, how far, a lender who is aware of a borrowing limit in another loan agreement owes any duty of care to the other lender to check whether his loan will breach the limit. In principle, it seems that such a duty of care may well exist, although the extent to which a lender is bound to check whether his loan will be within a borrowing limit will probably depend upon the circumstances of the particular case. If an intending lender is under such a duty of care, it follows that he will be liable for any loss suffered by the other lender as a direct and foreseeable result of the duty not having been discharged (see, for instance, *Anns v Merton LBC* [1978] A.C. 728 and *Junior Books Limited v Veitchi Co Limited* [1982] 3 All E.R. 201).

Guarantees

The considerations mentioned earlier in this chapter are also of relevance to guarantees. In addition, guarantees raise, in a somewhat more acute form than borrowings, questions regarding the powers of the company concerned, particularly if it derives no direct benefit from giving the guarantee.

It is doubtful whether even a commercial company has any implied power to give guarantees (*Colman v E.C. Rly* (1846) 10 Beav 1; compare *Re Friary Breweries* (1922) W.N. 293). But, even where a company's objects clause contains an express power, the validity of guarantees given under such a power has, in certain circumstances, been open to question. These questions have arisen largely because of a passage in Eve J's judgment in *Re Lee Behrens & Co. Ltd.* [1932] 2 Ch. 46 at 51, which indicates that the exercise of even an express power is invalid and ultra vires, unless the following three questions can be answered affirmatively: (i) Is the transaction reasonably indicidental to the carrying on of the company's business? (ii) Is it a bona fide transaction? (iii) Is it done for the benefit and to promote the prosperity of the company?

The third question, primarily, fell to be considered in *Charterbridge Corporation Ltd. v Lloyds Bank Limited* [1970] Ch. 62. There, Penny-cuick J. said that he thought that this question was quite inappropriate to the scope of express powers. He held that, where the objects clause of a company contains an express power to give guarantees, the fact that the directors of the company who authorised the guarantee were not acting with a view to the benefit of the company does not render the guarantee ultra vires.

Charterbridge was considered by the Court of Appeal in *Re Horsley & Weight Limited* [1982] 3 W.L.R. 431. It is considered that the effect of the latter case is that, despite Pennycuick J.'s statement in *Charterbridge*, the test of whether a transaction is done for the benefit and to promote the prosperity of the company is relevant where the express power concerned is, on a proper construction of the memorandum of association, either (a) not an independent object of the company, but merely an ancillary power, or (b) an independent object,but one which is subject to an express or implied limitation that it only extends to acts which benefit or promote the prosperity of the company, or to acts which are done for the benefit and to promote the prosperity of the company (see also pages 569 to 571).

It was this qualification which was effectively (although not expressly) applied in *Rolled Steel Products (Holdings) Limited v British Steel Corporation* [1982] 3 W.L.R. 715. In that case, Vinelott J. held to be ultra vires a guarantee which he found to have been, to the knowledge of the person to whom the guarantee was given, clearly detrimental to the company's commercial interests. The grounds of this decision were first, that the provision in the memorandum which authorised the giving of guarantees represented – despite the separate objects clause contained in the memorandum – not an independent object, but only a power ancillary to and to be exercised when expedient in furtherance of the substantive objects or purposes of the company; and second, that the recipient of the guarantee was aware that the guarantee was not entered into by the company for any purpose of the company, but was a gratuitous disposition of its property and was entered into for the benefit of its majority shareholder and another company which he owned.

Turning now to the first question referred to above, Pennycuick J. said in *Charterbridge* (at p. 71) that the question whether a transaction is reasonably incidental to the carrying on of the company's business is probably appropriate to the scope of the implied powers of a company where there is no express power. It is thought, however, that this statement was *obiter*, since Pennycuick J. held (at p. 69) that it could not be asserted on the facts of the case that the guarantee in issue was not reasonably connected with the company's business. The correct position, it is considered, is that the "reasonably incidental test" is applicable where the relevant power in the objects clause is, on its true construction, merely ancillary to the dominant or main objects of the company, but not if the relevant power is truly a substantive or independent object which can be pursued in isolation as the sole activity of the company (compare *Re Horsley & Weight* at 437E).

In the light of *Charterbridge*, *Horsley & Weight* and *Rolled Steel Products*, it is thought that the position with regard to a guarantee given under an express power is as follows:

(a) One must first determine whether the power to give guarantees is a substantive object or merely an ancillary power; for this purpose, a substantive object is an object which is capable of standing as an independent object of the company which can be pursued in isolation as the sole activity of the company; an ancillary power, on the other hand, is something which cannot be a substantive object and which is only ancillary to the dominant or main objects of the company.

(b) Whether a power is a substantive object or an ancillary power is a question of construction of the memorandum of association read as a whole; sometimes, for instance in the case of a guarantee company or a banking company, it will be obvious that the power to give guarantees is a substantive object; but, in the case of an ordinary trading company, the matter will normally be less clear;

and, in such a case, the following guidelines are relevant in construing the company's memorandum:

(i) if there is no separate objects clause declaring each of the objects listed in the memorandum to be a separate and independent object, a power to give guarantees will usually be an ancillary power;

(ii) if there is such a separate objects clause, a power to give guarantees will, it is believed, normally be a substantive object unless the subclause conferring the power contains no words showing that it is only an ancillary power; for example, in *Rolled Steel Products*, Vinelott J. indicated that a power to give guarantees for any such persons, firms or companies "as may seem expedient" would be construed not as a substantive object, but as an ancillary power to be exercised when expedient in furtherance of the objects of the company; the "expedient" wording would negative the effect of any separate objects clause. In addition, it may be noted that, even if the wording of the power contains nothing to suggest that it is only of an ancillary nature, a separate objects clause will not result in the power being treated as a substantive object unless the activity covered by the power is, in fact, capable of standing alone as an independent object. A power to borrow money and a power to promote the company's interests by advertising its products, for instance, cannot be independent objects. It is thought, however, that a power to give guarantees (unless its wording indicates the contrary) is capable of being pursued in isolation as a company's sole activity, and can therefore constitute a substantive object. Some support for this view is provided by the finding in *Horsley & Weight* that a power to grant pensions to past and present directors and employees and to make charitable subscriptions which was contained in the objects clause of a commercial company could and did constitute a substantive object of the company. Nevertheless, it has to be said that in *Rolled Steel Products* Vinelott J. appears to have considered that a subclause of the objects clause of a trading company which authorises the lending of money, the giving of credit and the giving of guarantees can, of necessity, only amount to an ancillary power.

(c) Even if the power to give guarantees constitutes a substantive object of the company, a further question arises if a guarantee is gratuitous, that is to say, if the company receives no payment or other benefit from giving it: does the memorandum extend to gratuitous guarantees, or is it confined to authorising guarantees for which the company receives some payment or other benefit? If the latter, a gratuitous guarantee would be ultra vires. It is thought that this is, in essence, merely a different formulation of the qualification made by Buckley L.J. in *Horsley & Weight* (at 440H) that, if the memorandum of association expressly or by implication provides that an express object only extends to acts which benefit or promote the prosperity of the company, regard must be paid to that limitation. As a matter of general principle, there seems no reason why the giving of gratuitous guarantees cannot be a substantive object of a company. This is because the objects of a company need not be commercial – they can be whatever the original incorporators wish, provided that they are legal. Nevertheless, it is felt that there may be a risk that, unless it includes words making it apparent that gratuitous guarantees are authorised, a power to give guarantees which is contained in the memorandum of a commercial company would be construed, in the context of the memorandum as a whole, so as not to extend to gratuitous guarantees.

(d) If, as a matter of construction, the power to give guarantees is a substantive object, then, subject to the gratuitous guarantee point mentioned in (c) above, a guarantee given in accordance with the power cannot be ultra vires; this is because the doing of an act which is a substantive object must be intra vires, for it is by definition something which the company is formed to do. In particular, the third test formulated by Eve J. in *Lee Behrens* (is the transaction done for the benefit and to promote the prosperity of the company?) is not relevant to the exercise of a power expressly made an independent object upon a proper construction of the memorandum: *Horsley & Weight* at 442H.

(e) But if the power to give guarantees is only an ancillary power, it must be the case that the giving of the guarantee is in fact ancillary or incidental to the pursuit of some dominant or main object of the company. It seems clear that this requirement entails that the giving of the guarantee must be, in some sense, reasonably incidental to the carrying on of the company's business – Eve J's first test. Moreover, it appears from the judgment of Vinelott J. in *Rolled Steel Products* that the guarantee must be entered into for the benefit and to promote the prosperity of the company or, putting it at its very lowest, that the giving of the guarantee must not be clearly detrimental to the company's interests. In other words, *Rolled Steel Products* suggests that, if a power is merely an ancillary power, that means that it is only conferred for the furtherance of the company's commercial purposes and so only authorises transactions which are entered into for the benefit and to promote the prosperity of the company – Eve J's third test.

(f) In *Rolled Steel Products*, Vinelott J. indicated that, even if a guarantee given in pursuance of an ancillary power is ultra vires because it is given for a purpose which is not authorised by the company's memorandum of association (i.e. it is not given for the furtherance of the company's commercial objects), it may still confer rights on the person to whom it was given, if he can show that he entered into the transaction in good faith and for valuable consideration, and did not have notice of the fact that the guarantee, while ostensibly within the company's powers, was entered into in furtherance of a purpose which was not an authorised purpose. It may be noted that this formulation differs in some respects (particularly as to where the onus of proof lies) from the views expressed by Pennycuick J. in *Charterbridge* to the effect that, while the state of mind of the recipient of a guarantee is irrelevant to the question of ultra vires, it may be material to an action against him on the ground that he had notice that the transaction was entered into by the directors in breach of duty. It may also be noted that under section 9(1) of the European Communities Act 1972 a guarantee decided on by the directors of the guarantor company is to be treated in favour of a third party dealing with the company in good faith (as to which see *International Sales & Agencies Limited v Marcus* [1982] 3 All E.R. 551) as within the capacity of the company.

Where a company gives a guarantee, or a collateral charge to secure the liabilities of another person, the normal practice has been for the party to whom the guarantee or charge is given to request a certified copy of the minutes of the meeting of the directors at which the transaction was authorised showing that the directors considered that the giving of the guarantee or charge was "in the best interests" of the company giving it. It is felt that this practice may still serve a useful purpose for the following reasons:-

(a) if, on a proper construction of the memorandum, the power to give guarantees is not an independent object of the company, the fact that the directors have considered it to be in the best interests of the company to give the guarantee should normally go some way to satisfy the test that the guarantee should be given for the benefit and to promote the prosperity of the company;

(b) if the power to give guarantees is, in fact, an independent object but one, nevertheless, which is subject to an express or implied requirement that it can only be exercised to promote the prosperity of the company, the view formed by the directors should be prima facie evidence that this requirement was met; and

(c) if the guarantee is nevertheless ultra vires, the fact that the third party was given a copy of a board minute recording that the directors considered the guarantee to be in the best interests of the company might, depending on the circumstances, assist him in claiming rights under the guarantee on the basis outlined in (f) above.

Debentures

No one seems to know exactly what "debenture" means. The term has a variety of connotations according to the context in which it is used. In a banking or commercial context, it normally connotes an instrument executed under the common seal of a company under which the company (i) covenants to pay all moneys from time to time becoming due to a bank or other lender – an "all-moneys" debenture – or to repay a specific loan with interest and (ii) creates fixed charges over the company's freehold and leasehold properties (and usually certain other assets) and a floating charge over all its other property, including its business.

So far as the common law meaning of the term is concerned, in general a debenture is a document of which it can usually be said that it creates or acknowledges an indebtedness: but there is no hard and fast definition (*Slavenburg's Bank v Intercontinental Limited* [1980] 1 All E.R. 955 at 976, *Levy v Abercorris Slate and Slab Company* (1887) 37 Ch. D. 260.). In *Topham v Greenside Glazed Fire-Bricks Company* (1887) 37 Ch. D. 281 at 292, it was held that a memorandum of a deposit of title deeds by a company with its bankers as security for the balance for the time being owing on the company's current account was not a debenture – the memorandum containing no acknowledgement of a debt or covenant to pay. And it has been said that the word "debenture" as ordinarily employed in legal and commercial circles did not in the year 1908 include an ordinary mortgage of land: *Knightsbridge Estates v Byrne* [1940] A.C. 613 at 628. However, the term has more recently been given wider interpretations. Thus, in 1925, the Court of Appeal held to be a debenture a certificate in respect of an issue of "income stock" which certified that the company was indebted to the registered holder of the certificate in a specified sum, payable only out of profits, and which stated that three-quarters of the net profits of the company for every year were to be applied in paying off such sum. The court reached this conclusion while leaving open the question of whether the debt referred to in the certificates would be repayable in a liquidation of the company (*Lemon v Austin Friars Investment Trust* [1926] 1 Ch. 1; and see *R v Findlater* [1939] 1KB 594). In 1979, Lloyd J. said in the *Slavenburg* case that, if it had been necessary for his decision, he would have been prepared to hold that the following documents (all in the Dutch language and governed by Dutch law) were all debentures:

(i) a general credit agreement by which a bank was to provide a company with credit facilities by way of current account and the company was to provide certain collateral securities;

(ii) a general agreement of assignment whereby the company agreed to assign to the bank all the company's present and future debts; and

(iii) an assignment by way of security to the bank of the entire business of the company.

It seems clear, therefore, that a formal loan agreement – whether containing security or not – entered into by a company is to be regarded as a debenture. It may well also be the case that where, as frequently happens, the repayment and other terms of a proposed facility are set out in a facility letter from the bank to the company, the company countersigning a duplicate of the facility letter by way of confirmation, the duplicate countersigned by the company would nowadays be held to constitute a debenture.

Section 455(1) of the Companies Act 1948 contains a definition of "debenture" which generally applies for the purpose of the Companies Acts (and applies also for the purposes of section 482 of the Income and Corporation Taxes Act 1970). The statutory definition is:

> "debenture" includes debenture stock, bonds and any other securities of a company, whether constituting a charge on the assets of the company or not".

The application of this definition is very wide. This is because the words "any other securities" are not to be construed as referring only to securities *ejusdem generis* as the genus (if any) to which debentures belong. They include all other securities (except presumably shares and stock) of any kind whatsoever, for example, a mortgage of freehold properties (*Knightsbridge Estates v Byrne* [1940] AC 613 at 628). As a result, the meaning of "debentures", where the statutory definition applies, is practically as wide as the meaning of "securities". In this connection, it may be noted that a guarantee has been held to be a security (*Temperance Loan Fund v Rose* [1932] 2 K.B. 522; *I.R.C. v Henry Ansbacher & Co* [1963] A.C. 191). So too, in a stamp duty context, has an agreement for the payment of part of the purchase price at a later date (*I.R.C. v Henry Ansbacher, I.T.A. v I.R.C.* [1961] A.C. 427). On the other hand, it should be borne in mind that, as with most general statutory definitions, the definition of "debentures" in section 455(1) is subject to the formula "unless the context otherwise requires".

Types of debenture

Debentures, in the sense of instruments which describe themselves as such (and not other instruments, for example, loan agreements which are debentures within the common law or statutory meanings of the term) fall into the following main categories:-

(a) *Single debentures*: that is, a debenture issued to one person alone. An example is the "all moneys" debenture containing fixed and floating charges of the type commonly issued to banks by their company customers. Single debentures usually contain charges over the assets of the issuing company, but this is not an essential characteristic.

(b) *Debentures in a series*: these take the form of a number of single debentures issued to different persons. The debentures or, as is more usual, the conditions endorsed thereon will state that each debenture is one of a series of so many debentures each for a given sum and, particularly where the debentures are secured, will provide that all the debentures in the series are to be payable *pari passu* and will rank equally without any preference or priority one over another (as to whether a *pari passu* clause of this type has any meaning in the case of unsecured debentures, see *Re Colonial Trusts Corp* (1880) 15 Ch. D. 465 at 468).

(c) *Registered debentures*: these mean that the legal title to the debentures is vested in the persons whose names appear in a register of the holders of the debentures which is maintained by the company. The conditions endorsed on the debentures normally specify the manner in which they may be transferred, and, in any event, by section 1 of the Stock Transfer Act 1963 fully paid up debentures issued by a company within the meaning of the Companies Act 1948 (except a company limited by guarantee or an unlimited company) may be transferred by a stock transfer form of the type provided for by the 1963 Act. The legal title to a registered debenture does not pass until the name of the transferee is duly registered as the holder of it in the register of debenture holders, although a transferee for value may well acquire an equitable interest in the debenture at an earlier stage. As a result of section 126 of the Finance Act 1976, transfers of debentures issued by companies formed in the United Kingdom, or by non-United Kingdom companies if the debentures are denominated in sterling, are normally exempt from United Kingdom stamp duty, unless the debentures carry a right to convert into or acquire shares or other securities. If a debenture, though outside section 126, is secured, but is not a marketable security as defined in section 122(1) of the Stamp Act 1891, a transfer at full value is normally exempt from duty: section 64 of the Finance Act 1971, which abolished "Mortgage, Bond, Covenant" head of charge.

(d) *Debentures to bearer*: these are transferable by delivery. If a debenture to bearer does not qualify as a negotiable instrument by virtue of being a promissory note within the meaning of section 83(1) of the Bills of Exchange Act 1882, it will nevertheless normally qualify as a negotiable instrument by usage (See *Bechuanaland Exploration Company v London Trading Bank Limited* [1898] 2 Q.B. 658 and *Edelstein v Schuler & Co* [1902] 2 K.B. 144). One factor which may prevent a debenture from qualifying as a promissory note may be a right given to the holder to demand immediate repayment if certain events of default should occur (see sections 11 and 89 of the 1882 Act.) Under the Exchange Control Act 1947, the issue of bearer debentures required the consent of H.M. Treasury, though this is not currently the case. See sections 59 to 61 of the Finance Act 1963 for the stamp duty position on issue.

(e) *Convertible debentures or, more frequently, loan stock:* these give the holders the right to convert their debentures into shares of the company, and contain special provisions designed to protect the conversion rights from being diluted by rights issues and similar transactions. The fact that the debenture holders are given potentially advantageous conversion rights normally permits the company to pay a lower rate of interest than would otherwise have been necessary.

(f) *Irredeemable and perpetual debentures*: a company may issue debentures which do not have any final date for redemption and which the company is only obliged to redeem upon the happening of certain contingencies, for instance, a default in the payment of interest or a winding up. But the company must be authorised by its memorandum to do this: *Re Southern Brazilian Railway Co Limited* [1905] 2 Ch. 78. The validity of such debentures is expressly confirmed by section 89 of the Companies Act 1948. Alternatively, debentures may provide that they are redeemable only at the option of the company, so that the holder has no right to require repayment.

Trust deeds

Debentures issued to a large number of persons are commonly secured by a trust deed. The main advantages of a trust deed are:

(a) to provide for a trustee for the debenture holders who can take action, speedily if necessary, on their behalf;

(b) to give the company a single person with which it can deal in connection with matters arising out of the debentures;

(c) to provide for machinery, such as the holding of meetings, whereby decisions taken by the holders of a majority of the debentures, including decisions to modify the debenture holders' rights, can be made binding upon all of them (though registered debentures in a series may provide for such meetings without the need for a trust deed; see also section 206 of the 1948 Act); and,

(d) if the debentures are secured, to vest the security and the power to enforce it in a single person.

Section 87(3) of the Companies Act 1948 gives a debenture holder the right to request a copy of the trust deed securing the debentures.

Section 88 of the 1948 Act provides that any provision in a debenture trust deed shall be void in so far as it would exempt the trustee from or indemnify him against liability for breach of trust where he fails to show the degree of care and diligence required of him as trustee, having regard to the provisions of the trust deed conferring on him any powers, authorities or discretions. The validity of such provisions is also subject to the Unfair Contract Terms Act 1977.

Debenture stock and loan stock

Where loan capital is to be issued to a large number of persons, it is nowadays more common to issue debenture stock or loan stock than debentures. Debenture stock has been defined as "borrowed capital consolidated into one mass for the sake of convenience". Instead of each lender having a separate bond or debenture, he has a certificate entitling him to a certain sum, being a portion of one large loan (*Murray v Herring* [1908] 2 Ch. 493 at 497). So, while a debenture is not divisible, divisibility is of the essence of debenture stock; and a transfer of debenture stock may be for any amount, subject to the terms of issue. Similarly, whereas a debenture constitutes a contract between the company and the holder of the debenture for the repayment of the loan, in the case of debenture stock, the stock certificate does not necessarily constitute such a contract, for the only covenant for repayment may be contained in the instrument constituting the stock.

Debenture stock is normally constituted by a trust deed. This will include a covenant by the company with the trustee to pay to the trustee the principal amount of the stock and interest thereon. However, the covenant will be followed by a proviso to the effect that the company's obligations to the trustee will *pro tanto* be satisfied by every payment which the company makes to any stockholder.

A debenture stock certificate will generally contain on its face a statement certifying that the person named therein is the registered holder of so many pounds of the stock. On the back of the certificate there will usually be set out the "conditions", namely the repayment and other main terms of the stock.

Often the debenture stock certificates do not give any undertaking for payment with the stockholders direct, so that the only payment undertaking is the covenant with the trustee contained in the trust deed. In these circumstances only the trustee, and none of the stockholders, will be a creditor of the company and so entitled to present a winding up petition. This will be the case if the debenture stock certificates state that the stock is issued subject to the provisions contained in the trust deed without also stating that the stock is issued subject to the conditions endorsed on the certificates (*Re Dunderland Iron Ore Co. Limited* [1909] 1 Ch. 446; see the stock certificates on pages 1221 and 1226 of Volume 6 of the *Encyclopedia of Forms and Precedents*, which are in this form).

Normally debenture stock is secured by a trust deed, and The Stock Exchange requires that, unless otherwise agreed by the Council, there shall be a trustee or trustees of listed loan capital. However, in some instances where The Stock Exchange requirements do not apply, it may be unnecessary to go to the lengths of providing for a trustee. In such cases, the practice is for the stock to be constituted by a deed poll executed by the company. Such deed polls normally contain a covenant for payment which is made with, or for the benefit of, the stockholders for the time being. It is thus thought that, in these cases, the stockholders are creditors of the company, whether or not the stock certificates also incorporate a repayment undertaking with them.

The term "debenture stock" is usually reserved for stock which is secured by a mortgage or charge; if the stock is unsecured, it is normally called "loan stock", and it is a requirement of The Stock Exchange that securities constituting an unsecured liability be entitled "unsecured".

The foregoing comments regarding debenture stock are, however, equally applicable to loan stock.

Issue of debentures

The considerations which are relevant where debentures or other loan capital securities are issued to the public are outlined in the chapter *Prospectuses and Public Issues*.

Debentures or loan stock may be issued at a discount, unless they are convertible into shares (at all events if the conversion right is not exercisable only at some future date) and the possibility exists that the shares may therefore be issued at a discount (*Mosely v Koffyfontein Mines Limited* [1904] 2 Ch. 108). Where secured debentures are issued at a discount, section 95(9) of the Companies Act 1948 requires the particulars of the relevant charge delivered under section 95 to include particulars of the discount.

Debentures and loan stock may also be issued at a premium.

Section 92 of the Companies Act 1948 provides that a contract with a company to take up and pay for any debenture of the company may be enforced by an order for specific performance.

By virtue of section 90 of the 1948 Act, a company has power to re-issue debentures which it has previously redeemed, unless the company's articles or any contract entered into by it provides to the contrary or the company has manifested its intention that the debentures shall be cancelled. Under that section, the persons to whom the debentures are re-issued will, normally, have the same priorities as if the debentures had never been redeemed.

Debenture holders' remedies

The main remedies of the holder of an unsecured debenture in default of payment are no different from those of any other creditor: he may sue for his money, and, on obtaining judgment, levy execution on the company's property; and, under sections 222 and 223 of the 1948 Act, he can present a petition for the winding up of the company. The holder of a secured debenture is in the position of a mortgagee or chargee and his main remedies (in addition to those of an unsecured creditor) are his power to appoint a receiver and his power of sale. A debenture containing a floating charge over a company's undertaking normally provides that the receiver may also be a manager and gives him wide powers to carry on the company's business (see the chapter *Receivers*). Where there is a trust deed (whether covering unsecured or secured loan stock or debentures) the enforcement steps are generally taken by the trustee. However, very occasionally, a debenture holder may bring a debenture holders' action against the company, with any trustee also being joined as a defendant. This is a representative action under Order 15 Rule 12 of the Rules of the Supreme Court which is brought by the plaintiff on behalf of himself and all the holders of all other debentures in the same series. It seems that such an action can be maintained by the holder of debenture stock as well as by a holder of a debenture – see *Palmer's Debentures* at p. 412 – but loan stock trust deeds often expressly provide for this.

Subordinated debt

In recent years, it has become common for companies to create (or attempt to create) a type of debt which, in a winding up, will rank behind all or certain other debts of the company (for a consideration of subordination in an international context, see Philip Wood, *The Law and Practice of International Finance 1980*, chapter 17). To take a common example, a bank may agree to make a loan to one of the subsidiary companies within a group provided that the parent company makes a loan to the subsidiary which will rank behind the bank's loan in any winding up of the subsidiary. The chief advantages of subordinated debt are that it provides a method of increasing a company's capital base but, unlike share capital it does not attract capital duty and its repayment is not subject to the reduction of capital provisions of the Companies Acts.

The main difficulties surrounding such arrangements are presented by sections 302 and 317 of the Companies Act 1948. Section 302 is in that part of the Act headed "Provisions applicable to every Voluntary Winding Up". It provides that, subject to the provisions of the Act as to preferential payments, the property of a company shall, on its winding up, be applied in satisfaction of its liabilities *pari passu*. The 1948 Act contains no express provision in similar terms which applies in a non-voluntary winding up. But, in a winding up of an insolvent company, section 33(7) of the Bankruptcy Act 1914, which provides that subject to the provisions of that Act all debts proved in the bankruptcy shall be paid *pari passu*, is applied by section 317 of the 1948 Act (*Re Jessel Securities Limited* (1978) (C.A.) unreported in which it was held that section 317 incorporates section 66 of the Bankruptcy Act, and in which *dicta* in *Re Whitaker* [1901] 1 Ch. 9 were applied.

The question is whether these provisions affect the validity of an agreement between a debtor company and any two or more of its creditors which is not made under the provisions of section 206 (or section 306) of the 1948 Act and which provides that, in a winding up of the debtor company, a debt due to one creditor shall rank not *pari passu* with, but after, the company's other debt. Is the agreement valid so as to oblige the liquidator to pay the other debts in full before the debt which is the subject of the agreement? In short, is it possible by contract to oblige a liquidator to follow an order of distribution different from that prescribed by statute? In *British Eagle v Air France* [1975] 1 W.L.R. 758 at 771 and 780, it was said that a "contracting out of" section 302 must be contrary to public policy, but that statement was made in the context of an agreement which would have placed the creditors concerned in a position analogous to that of secured creditors without the need for the creation and registration of charges. In other words, the *British Eagle* agreement would have placed the creditors in question ahead of, and not behind, the other creditors. On the other hand, in *National Westminster Bank Ltd. v Halesowen Presswork Limited* [1972] A.C. 785 it was held that it was impossible for a creditor to contract out of the set off provisions of section 31 of the Bankruptcy Act 1914, even though the effect of such a contracting out would have been to benefit the other creditors. In the light of these two cases – and the latter case applies by analogy to section 302, *British Eagle* at 771 – it seems doubtful whether an agreement for a debt to rank not pari passu with, but behind, the other debts of a company would be binding upon a liquidator of the company. This view is supported by *Re Orion Sound Limited* [1979] 2 NZLR 574 in which Mahon J declined to follow *Re Walker Construction Co Limited* [1960] NZLR 523 (upholding the validity of a moratorium agreement in view of the *Halesowen* and *British Eagle* cases). He held that a deed of compromise purporting to establish classes of deferred and preferred creditors was contrary to public policy. The present state of the authorities is, therefore, such that subordination agreements have to operate within, and not as variations of, the insolvency and liquidation legislation.

The legislation, however, affords two possible methods of making a subordination agreement binding upon a liquidator. The first method is to provide that the debt to be subordinated shall become due and payable only if and when the company's other debts, or one particular other debt, have, or has, been paid in full. It is widely thought that such a provision is effective to make the debt concerned a contingent debt for the purposes of section 30(4) of the Bankruptcy Act 1914 (made applicable in the winding up of an insolvent company by section 317 of the Companies Act 1948). Thus the debt would be provable only at its value estimated by the liquidator or the court which, if the company were clearly insolvent, would be nil or minimal. Further, it is believed that such a debt, which by its terms could not have become due at the commencement of the winding up, would not fall within the mandatory set off provisions of section 31 of the 1914 Act, as incorporated, in the case of an insolvent winding up, by section 317 of the 1948 Act (cf. *Re A Debtor* [1956] 1 W.L.R. 1226 but for a contrary view see the Cork Report, paras. 1352 to 1355).

The second method of ensuring that a debt will be subordinated in a manner binding upon a liquidator – at least in an insolvent winding up – is to provide that it will carry interest varying with the profits of the business of the debtor company (note however that the interest may be treated as a distribution under section 233(2)(d)(iii) of the Taxes Act 1970 (subject to section 60 of the Finance Act 1982), and thus not deductible by the borrower). Section 3 of the Partnership Act 1890 (made applicable in the winding up of an insolvent company by section 33(9) of the 1914 Act and section 317 of the 1948 Act) provides for a statutory postponement of the claims of a creditor who has advanced money "by way of a loan" upon a contract providing that the lender shall receive a rate of interest varying with the profits of the business of the borrower, or a share of such profits. This method is accordingly available only where the debt to be postponed is a debt in respect of a loan. And it seems that this statutory postponement does not affect the lender's right to enforce any security which he may hold for the loan or to avail himself of any statutory right of set off to which he may be entitled: *Ex p. Sheil* (1877) 4 Ch. D. 789 and *Badeley v Consolidated Bank* (1888) 38 Ch. D. 238, cases on the slightly different wording of section 5 of Bovill's Act.

In deciding which of these two methods to use, it will normally be necessary to consider what will be the position if the junior creditor, as well as the debtor company, is wound up. The first method seeks to provide that the moneys owed by the debtor company to the junior creditor should not be recoverable by the junior creditor, or its liquidator, if the debtor company is insolvent. The effect of this is not merely to prevent the junior creditor from proving in a winding up of the debtor company; it also means that the moneys which the junior creditor would otherwise have recovered in a winding up of the debtor company will go to the senior creditor and the other creditors of the debtor company to the extent that their claims are outstanding, with a corresponding reduction in the amounts available to the junior creditor's own creditors.

Thus, the contingent debt scheme produces a financial effect which is similar, if not identical, to the financial effect which would be produced if the junior creditor were to create a charge over the moneys owing to it from the debtor company, such charge to secure whatever might be outstanding from the debtor company to the senior creditor and its other creditors. However, on balance, it is thought that the contingent debt scheme does not amount to a charge created by the junior creditor over its property, because the subordination agreement does not itself confer on the senior creditor and the other creditors of the debtor company any interest in the sums to which the junior creditor would otherwise be entitled. Rather, it provides that the junior creditor shall have no such entitlement if the other creditors have not been paid. It is also believed that the risk of the subordination constituting a charge is lower if the junior creditor originally makes its loan to the debtor company on subordinated terms than if an attempt is made to subordinate a loan originally made on non-subordinated terms. Be that as it may, the point is clearly an arguable one. It could also be contended, on the basis of certain remarks in the *British Eagle* case at page 780, that the contingent debt scheme is vulnerable on grounds of public policy. This is because, in a winding up of the debtor company and of the junior creditor, it puts the senior creditor and the other creditors of the debtor company in a position analogous to that of secured creditors of the junior creditor without the need for the creation (and, if applicable, the registration) of a charge over the debt from the debtor company to the junior creditor.

The difficulties which may arise if a subordination arrangement constitutes a charge created by the junior creditor are described below. Having regard to those difficulties and to the fact that a contingent debt contract seems more vulnerable to attack as a charge or quasi-charge than a loan made at a rate of interest varying with profits, it may be that, on the current state of the authorities, the second method of subordination is safer than the first. But this is subject to the qualification that, where the second method is used, the junior creditor's loan is, so it seems, liable to be discharged by set off to the extent of any debt owing by the junior creditor to the debtor company, being a debt to which section 31 of the Bankruptcy Act 1914 applies.

Because all general creditors rank *pari passu* in a winding up, there is no method by which a debt can be subordinated to another unsecured debt of the company (unless the other debt has priority by virtue of section 319 of the 1948 Act), but not to the company's unsecured debts generally. Frequently, however, the junior creditor undertakes with the senior creditor that, if the junior creditor receives any dividend in respect of its debt in a winding up of the debtor company, it will hold the amount which it receives upon trust for the senior creditor to the extent that the debt owing to the senior creditor has not been paid. This is designed to give the senior creditor an advantage which it will not have to share with the other creditors.

The effect of such a trust is to give the senior creditor a right to recover any amount still owing to it from the company out of any dividends received by the junior creditor in the company's winding up. In other words, the trust amounts to a charge created by the junior creditor over any dividends which it may receive – the charge securing the outstanding balance of the senior creditor's debt. This produces a number of difficulties. First, if the junior creditor has entered into undertakings with third parties (as, for instance, in the standard clause contained in floating charges, considered under *Company Charges*, not to create charges over its property), a trust of this kind may be unenforceable, or rank behind any such floating charge. Similarly, the senior creditor may find itself postponed if the junior creditor has already given a fixed charge over its present and future debts, for instance, under an all-moneys debenture in favour of its bank.

Secondly, if the dividends which are the subject of the trust or charge relate to book debts of the junior creditor, the question will arise as to whether the trust is registrable under section 95 of the Companies Act 1948 as a charge on book debts. Moreover, if the junior creditor is subordinating itself to the holders of loan stock or bonds issued by the debtor company, it seems that the subordination trust is registrable under the section as a charge for the purpose of securing an issue of debentures.

The position regarding book debts is not entirely clear. But it has been argued that, if the terms of the trust are such that it covers only the amounts actually received by the junior creditor in the winding up, and not its rights to receive those amounts, the trust does not extend to any debt. Further, it is, perhaps, arguable that a liquidator's duty to pay a dividend to a creditor does not represent a debt owing to the creditor (compare *Prout v Gregory* (1889) 24 QB 281 and *Macks v Ward* [1884] W.N. 16). It might also be possible to postpone any requirement to register the trust or charge under section 95 by drafting the provision as an agreement by the junior creditor that, in the event of a winding up of the debtor company, it will, at that point, create a charge over any dividends he may receive. It is thought that, under a provision of that type, the charge, if registrable at all, would only be created, and therefore require registration, in the event of the winding up of the debtor company.

The third difficulty relates to the priorities as between the senior creditor and any subsequent assignee or chargee of the company's debt to the junior creditor, or the junior creditor's rights to prove for the debt, who has no notice of the trust in favour of the senior creditor. The subsequent assignee or chargee will gain priority over the senior creditor if it gives notice to the company (or liquidator) of its assignment or charge before the senior creditor gives notice to the company of the trust in its favour or, possibly, if the subsequent assignment or charge is a legal assignment under section 136 of the Law of Property Act 1925 (see *Ward v Duncombe* [1893] A.C. 369 at 391 and *Chitty on Contracts* at 1184). It seems that the most the senior creditor can do is to take from the junior creditor a covenant against subsequent assignments (compare *Helstarz Securities Ltd. v Herts. C.C.* [1978] 3 All E.R. 262) and forthwith to give notice to the company of the subordination trust.

Finally, since the subordination trust amounts to a collateral, or surety-type security for the company's debt (compare *Re Conley* [1938] 2 All E.R. 127), it is liable to be discharged by any of those events which have the effect of releasing a surety. Examples are a material variation in the contract between the company and the senior creditor which is neither insubstantial nor clearly to the benefit of the junior creditor, or the senior debtor's entering into a binding agreement to give the company further time for payment, in each case without the junior creditor's consent. It follows that subordination trusts should be – although they not always are – accompanied by the protective provisions usually inserted in guarantees to guard against these contingencies.

The Cork Report

The Report of the Review Committee on Insolvency Law and Practice (Cmnd 8558) recommended the inclusion of an appropriate proviso to section 33(7) of the Bankruptcy Act 1914 (made applicable to insolvent liquidations by section 317 of the 1948 Act) to allow effect to be given to subordination agreements (paragraphs 1448 and 1449 of the Report). If this were done, many of the problems discussed above would disappear.

However, the Cork Report also recommended (paragraphs 1953 to 1965) that, in a liquidation, loans to a company from other companies in the same group which appear to the court to represent all or part of the "long-term capital structure" of the borrowing company should be subordinated to the claims of its other creditors. These proposals would impact particularly on amounts advanced by parent companies to "thinly capitalised" subsidiaries. These proposals may be relevant to persons lending to parent companies whose assets mainly consist of shares in, or debts from, subsidiaries, in circumstances where no guarantee is taken from the operating subsidiaries.

Charges over Shares

This chapter deals with the creation and enforcement of mortgages and charges over shares, debentures and similar securities and related questions of priorities.

Creation of legal mortgages of registered securities

Where shares or debentures are in registered form – as opposed to bearer form – the legal title is vested in the person whose name is for the time being entered on the register of members or debenture holders maintained by the company. It follows, therefore, that a legal mortgage of registered shares or debentures can only be effected by the mortgagee being entered on the relevant register as the holder of the mortgaged securities.

A legal mortgage of registered shares or debentures normally involves the execution of –

(a) a *stock transfer form* under the Stock Transfer Act 1963 (unless the securities are partly paid or issued by a company limited by guarantee or an unlimited company or are securities to which the Stock Transfer Act 1982 applies). The form transfers the securities to the mortgagee and enables him to become the registered holder. Transfers by way of security for a loan are only subject to the fixed stamp duty of 50p, but the certificate printed on the back of the stock transfer form to the effect that the transfer falls with that category must be completed and signed; and

(b) an *agreement* between the mortgagor and the mortgagee, the main terms of which,

  (i) set out the mortgagor's obligations as to the repayment of the mortgage debt and the payment of interest;

  (ii) record that the securities have been or are to be transferred by way of security only and provide for the mortgagee to retransfer the mortgaged securities, or to transfer an equal number of securities of the same class, to the mortgagor when the mortgage debt has been duly repaid;

  (iii) provide for the circumstances and manner in which the security may be enforced;

  (iv) usually provide that, until default, the mortgagor shall be paid the dividends or interest on the securities and the mortgagor

155

shall be able to control the exercise of the voting rights attaching to the securities; and

(v) frequently, contain a "topping-up clause" obliging the mortgagor to mortgage further securities, if the market value of the securities originally mortgaged should fall below the outstanding amount of the mortgage debt plus a certain margin.

It appears that where such an agreement is executed under seal, then, even if the stock transfer form is not sealed – although bodies corporate should execute stock transfer forms under their common seal – the mortgage will probably be a mortgage "made by deed" within section 101 of the Law of Property Act 1925. Consequently the mortgagee will acquire the power of sale (and of appointing a receiver of income) conferred by that section. It also appears that the agreement, if under seal (as well, probably, as the stock transfer, if sealed) will be "the mortgage deed" for the purposes of section 101(3) of that Act (variation of statutory powers).

Creation of equitable mortgages of registered securities

An equitable mortgage over registered shares or debentures may be created by a mere deposit of the relative certificates by way of security for a debt (*Harrold v Plenty* [1901] 2 Ch. 314). But usually the mortgagor also executes a "memorandum of deposit" which records the fact that the securities have been deposited by way of mortgage and contains other terms similar to those mentioned above (except for the provision for re-transfer on redemption). The memorandum will also contain an undertaking by the mortgagor to execute any transfers or other documents which the mortgagee may require to vest the securities in himself, his nominee or a purchaser, and/or a power of attorney authorising the mortgagee to do so.

If, as is common, the memorandum of deposit contains a clause whereby the mortgagor expressly charges the securities deposited (together with any moneys or other property which may in the future be derived from them), then the charge is created by the memorandum, and not the deposit (compare *Re White Rose Cottage* [1965] Ch. 955D). Moreover, if there is an express charge over the securities, it is not necessary, in order for the charge to be valid against the chargor, that the certificates be deposited with the chargee. In such a case, the main object of taking up the certificates is to preserve the chargee's priorities as against third parties (see page 165).

A legal mortgagee of securities, being the registered holder, is himself able to execute the transfer of the securities which will be necessary if he should sell them in the exercise of his power of sale. There are two methods of putting an equitable mortgagee in a position to deliver the transfers required on the exercise of the power of sale, without having to rely on the mortgagor's co-operation or to obtain a court order.

First, at the time the mortgage is originally effected, the mortgagor signs and delivers to the mortgagee a "blank transfer", i.e. a signed but undated stock transfer form with the name of the mortgagor filled in as the registered holder and the details of the shares or debentures completed. The name of the mortgagee (or his nominee) may or may not be filled in as the transferee; if it is, then the mortgagee (or his nominee) will have to execute a further transfer when it comes to exercise its power of sale. The mortgagee has an implied authority to fill up the blanks over the signature of the mortgagor, unless the articles of association of the company require its shares to be transferred by deed (*Re Tahiti Cotton Co.* (1874) L.R. 17 Eq. 273). The main difficulty about relying on blank transfers, particularly in connection with mortgages of shares, is that they will not cover other securities which may be issued in respect of the original securities, for instance, on a capitalisation issue. (Also, if the articles only permit transfer by deed, the mortgagee will be unable to complete the blanks unless he is authorised to do so by a power of attorney under seal: *Powell v London & Provincial Bank* [1893] 2 Ch. 555.). From the mortgagor's point of view, there is the disadvantage that, if the transfer leaves the name of the mortgagee blank and covers a larger number of shares than, in the event, need to be sold to pay off the mortgage debt, the mortgagee is entitled to sell all the shares comprised in the transfer (accounting to the mortgagor for the surplus after repaying the mortgage debt), and has no obligation to transfer the shares into his own name first so as to be able to execute a transfer for just the number of shares which have to be sold (*Stubbs v Slater* [1910] 1 Ch. 632).

The second method is for the memorandum of deposit to be executed under seal and to contain an irrevocable power of attorney given by way of security pursuant to section 4 of the Powers of Attorney Act 1971. Under this, the mortgagee will be appointed the attorney of the mortgagor to execute, on his behalf, any transfers which may be required in the event of the mortgagee's exercising the power of sale or which may be necessary to enable the mortgagee to have the securities registered in his name. Occasionally, the mortgagor also declares that he holds the securities upon trust, by way of security, for the mortgagee, and the mortgagee is given power to appoint a new trustee in the place of the mortgagor (compare *London and County Banking Corporation v Goddard* [1897] 1 Ch. 642). But this advice is of limited value because the mortgaged securities cannot be vested in the new trustee automatically on his appointment (section 40 of the Trustee Act 1925 not applying to registered securities) and, to do this, a transfer executed by the mortgagor is required.

It is generally considered that a mortgagor of shares who remains the registered holder must, in the absence of agreement to the contrary, vote as his mortgagee directs (see e.g. *Buckley's Companies Acts* at p. 972). *Wise v Landsell* [1921] 1 Ch. 420 is usually given as the authority for this proposition, but the relevant observations in that case appear to have been based on the fact the "real owners" of the shares were the mortgagees, the equity of redemption being worthless.

Bearer securities

It would seem that the deposit of bearer securities (without a memorandum of deposit) in order to secure the repayment of a debt is a mere pledge of chattels, and not an equitable mortgage, so that the depositee acquires no right of foreclosure (see *Carter v Wake* (1877) 4 Ch. D. 605, and *Harrold v Plenty* [1901] 2 Ch. 314 which indicates that the securities in *Carter* were bearer bonds. The two cases are not easy to reconcile.) However the position may well be different if a covering document transfers to the depositee by way of mortgage the absolute legal interest in the securities and provides that the depositee is to have all the remedies of a mortgagee.

On general principles, there seems no reason why an equitable charge should not be created over bearer securities by express agreement, although the position of the chargee will not be particularly strong if the securities remain in the possession of the chargor.

The above considerations apply to renounceable letters of allotment (or renounceable share certificates) which may be treated as bearer documents, if the form of renunciation has been signed and no name has been inserted in the registration application form.

Consequences of legal and equitable mortgages

Registered shares

Where a *legal* mortgage of registered shares is taken, there are five main consequences of the mortgagee's being entered in the register of members as the member in respect of the shares.

(1) If the shares are not fully paid, the mortgagee becomes a contributory, liable, in the event of the company being wound up, to contribute to the assets of the company to the extent of the amount unpaid on the shares. Also, if the mortgage debt is repaid and the shares are re-transferred into the name of the mortgagor, the mortgagee's name may still be placed (as a past member) on the "B" list of contributories in respect of the shares, unless the transfer back to the mortgagor was registered one year or more before the commencement of the winding up (*Weirkersheim's Case* (1873) 8 Ch. App. 831). By the same token, a legal mortgagee of shares will be liable for any calls made by the directors while the shares stand in his name in respect of moneys unpaid on the shares (and these may include any premium which is payable), or any sum which under the company's articles is deemed to be a call duly made (see, for instance, article 19 of Table A). Any right of indemnity which the mortgagee may have against the mortgagor for sums paid or payable by the mortgagee in respect of the shares may prove to be of little actual value.

(2) Any dividends and other distributions will go in the first instance to the mortgagee; but, if the articles of the company concerned

contain a provision in the terms of article 121 of Table A, the mortgagee will be able to send a dividend mandate to the company directing it to pay to the mortgagor "any dividend, interest or other moneys payable in cash" in respect of the shares.

(3) Similarly, the mortgagee will receive directly all documents which are sent to the shareholders of the relevant company, for instance, its annual report and accounts, letters of allotment issued in connection with rights and bonus issues and circulars relating to take-overs.

(4) In the ordinary way, where shares are transferred to and registered in the name of a mortgagee it follows, from his position as owner in law of the shares, that the ownership carries with it the right to vote vested in the owner of the shares (*Siemens Brothers v Burns* [1918] 2 Ch. 324). It requires a contract to control the exercise of that right, thus, subject to the terms of any such contract, the mortgagee may vote the shares as he deems best, irrespective of any directions of the mortgagor as to how the voting rights should be exercised, whether or not the security is yet enforceable (*Siemens Bros. & Co Limited v Burns* and see *Musselwhite v C. H. Musselwhite & Co Limited* [1962] Ch. 964). But, if there is an agreement whereby the mortgagee undertakes to vote as directed by the mortgagor, the agreement can be enforced not only by a prohibitive injunction, but also by a mandatory injunction (*Puddephat v Leith* [1916] 1 Ch. 200).

(5) If both the mortgagor and the mortgagee are bodies corporate, and the mortgaged shares represent more than half in nominal value of the equity share capital of a third body corporate, then section 154 of the Companies Act 1948 may operate. However, registration of the shares into the name of the mortgagee will only result in the body corporate in which the shares are held becoming the mortgagee's subsidiary under section 154 if none of the following conditions is satisfied,

  (a) the mortgagee holds the shares "in a fiduciary capacity" – it is thought likely, but not certain, that this would cover an institution holding the shares as a trustee under a debenture stock trust deed;

  (b) the shares are held by virtue of the provisions of any debentures of the subsidiary company – not the mortgagor company – or of a trust deed for securing the issue of any debentures of the subsidiary company;

  (c) "the ordinary business" of the mortgagee includes the lending of money and the mortgagee holds the shares "by way of security only for the purposes of a transaction entered into in the ordinary course of that business."

In addition, the following considerations should be borne in mind when taking a mortgage of shares, whether legal or equitable:

(1) Although the point is not entirely free from doubt, it is possible that, where a financial or investment company creates a charge on shares, the charge may be registrable under section 95 of the Companies Act 1948. This could be so where the charge extends, whether expressly or by implication, to any dividends which may in the future be declared on the shares or any debentures which may subsequently be issued in respect of the shares. The charge could then be registrable as a charge on book debts, but only so far as regards such future dividends (or at least final dividends: see *Potel v I.R.C.* [1971] 2 All E.R. 504) or debentures – see the chapter, *Company Charges*.

(2) Taking a mortgage over shares, whether legal or equitable, may also trigger the notification provisions of section 27 of the Companies Act 1967 with respect to interests of directors or, unless the mortgage is an exempt security interest under section 71, the provisions of Part IV of the Companies Act 1981 as to disclosure of interests in voting shares in public companies (see the chapters *Disclosure of Directors' Dealings* and *Disclosure of Shareholdings*).

(3) The United Kingdom tax implications of taking a mortgage over shares in a company, particularly where the shares represent a controlling interest, have to be taken into account. The main problem is that, subject to any agreement with the mortgagee as to the exercise of voting rights, a legal mortgagee of shares will have the right to vote the shares, and so may have "control" of the company for the purposes of sections 302 and 534 of the Income and Corporation Taxes Act 1970 (see generally the comprehensive article by M.J. Gammie in [1977] B.T.R. 342 to 361). Possible problems include the loss of group relief (F.A. 1973, s. 29) and other adverse consequences flowing from a company being or not being connected, grouped or linked with another company. A transfer of shares by way of security does not constitute a capital gains tax disposal, unless and until the security is enforced (section 23 of the Capital Gains Tax Act 1979). It is believed that the Inland Revenue consider that permission does not generally have to be obtained under section 482 of the Income and Corporation Taxes Act 1970 for a company resident in the United Kingdom to create a mortgage, including a legal mortgage, over shares or debentures of a company not so resident over which it has control, although it may be necessary to obtain such permission in order to enforce the mortgage, for instance, by selling the shares or debentures. The Revenue's views should however be checked, particularly given the severe consequences of a breach of section 482.

Private companies

Where a charge is to be taken over shares in a private company, it is necessary to give special consideration to any restrictions upon the transfer of shares which are contained in the company's articles of association. It will be recalled that, under section 28 of the 1948 Act, it used to be necessary for the articles of a private company to contain such restrictions. Despite the repeal of the section, the articles of private companies still commonly contain such restrictions (see the chapters *Articles* and *Formation and Types of Company*). These tend to be of two main types,

(a) an article giving the directors power to decline to register any transfer of any shares;

(b) a "pre-emption" article, to the effect that any shareholder desirous of transferring his shares must first offer them to the other shareholders, so that he can only transfer his shares to an outsider to the extent that they have not been taken up by the other shareholders. Even then, the shareholder's right to transfer his shares is often made subject to a power for the directors not to register the transfer.

It is often provided that these restrictions shall not apply to a transfer from one shareholder to another, or, in the case of pre-emption restrictions, from one shareholder to his relatives. The exact meaning and scope of such restrictions are often matters of difficulty and these problems are compounded by the fact that the articles seldom make express provision for, or even contemplate, the creation and enforcement of mortgages over the shares concerned. Subject to that, and to the fact that the position in any particular case will depend upon the true construction of the relevant articles, it is thought that the following represents the general position.

(1) An article giving the directors an absolute power to decline to register any transfer of any shares, for instance what was formally article 3 in Part II of Table A, will apply,

(a) to any transfer made upon the mortgagee exercising his power of sale or pursuant to a foreclosure order obtained by the mortgagee; and

(b) almost certainly, to a transfer of shares into the name of the mortgagee in order to effect a legal mortgage of them.

(2) A pre-emption article which contains a general statement that no member shall be entitled to transfer any share otherwise than in accordance with certain provisions, those provisions not mentioning transfers by way of security, will be breached if the shareholder transfers his shares by way of legal mortgage, unless the requirements of the article are complied with or are waived by the other shareholders. (This view is based on the High Court and Court of Appeal decisions in Mrs E. Hunter's action as they appear from *Hunter v Hunter* [1936] A.C. 222.) In addition, it is thought that a pre-emption article which does not contain any such general prohibition but which is brought into play when a member is "desirous of transferring" any of his shares, will probably apply if a shareholder actually executes a transfer (and possibly even a blank

transfer) by way of security (see *Hunter v Hunter*, above, though it was said in *Lyle & Scott v Scott's Trustees* [1959] A.C. 763 at 777 that the purpose of the article under consideration was to prevent sales to strangers as long as other shareholders were willing to buy them at the prescribed price – but mortgages were not being considered there.) Such a pre-emption article will also arguably come into operation if a shareholder creates an equitable mortgage over his shares by depositing the share certificates by way of security for a debt, even if he does not execute a blank transfer or a document containing an undertaking to execute a transfer at the mortgagee's request. This is because a deposit of the certificates as security amounts to an agreement to execute a transfer of the shares by way of mortgage – *Harrold v Plenty* [1901] 2 Ch. 314 – and it is not open to a shareholder who had agreed to do a certain thing and is bound to do it to deny that he is desirous of doing it (*Lyle & Scott v Scott's Trustees* [1959] A.C. 763 at 774. *Safeguard v National Westminster Bank* [1982] 1 All E.R. 449 seems inapplicable as there the shareholder involuntarily came under the obligation to transfer). But in *Champagne Perrier–Jouet v Finch* [1982] 1 W.L.R. 1359, an equitable mortgage did not trigger the pre-emption article.

Such a pre-emption article will clearly apply where a legal mortgagee, having become registered as member in respect of the shares, takes steps to exercise his power of sale (*Hunter* and *Perrier–Jouet* at 1369). If, contrary to the view expressed above, the article is not brought into play by an equitable mortgage of the shares, it may be the case that it will not apply if the mortgagee proposes to exercise his power of sale, because that is not a case of "a member" being desirous of selling his shares – unless, perhaps, the sale is effected under a power of attorney granted by the mortgagor, in which case the acts of the mortgagee may be capable of being attributed to his principal, the mortgagor.

Public companies

Under section 38 of the Companies Act 1980 a lien (see below) or other charge of a public company on its own shares is void, unless it is one of the permitted charges, the main categories of which are as follows.

(a) A charge on shares in the company which are not fully paid for any amount payable in respect of the shares.

(b) In the case of a company whose ordinary business includes the lending of money or consists of the provision of credit or the bailment of goods under a hire purchase agreement, or both, a charge on the company's own shares which arises in connection with a transaction entered into by the company in the ordinary course of its business.

(c) In the case of a company (except an old public company which failed to apply for re-registration until after fifteen months from December 22, 1980), which is re-registered as a public company, a charge on its own shares which was "in existence" immediately before its application for re-registration. The exact meaning of the words "in existence" is not entirely clear. It is thought that if, immediately prior to its application for re-registration, a company's articles gave it a lien over its shares, it is arguable that the lien would have then been "in existence", as an equitable charge, as against the persons who were then the registered holders at least as regards any shares then in issue, even though, at that time, there were not owing any moneys which could have then been secured by the lien. (In this respect, *New London and Brazilian Bank v Brocklebank* (1882) 21 Ch.D. 302 indicates that the company's lien is effective as soon as the shareholder is registered as the member in respect of the shares, even though his debt to the company arises at a later time.) The above argument may be re-inforced by the fact that a charge taken by a company over its own shares otherwise than under its articles, for instance, an ordinary equitable charge under a memorandum of deposit, would be "in existence" once it had been created even though no liabilities had as yet been incurred for the charge to secure (compare *Esberger's Case* [1913] 2 Ch. 366).

In any event, it may be noted that, even before the Companies Act 1980 came into force, it was a requirement of The Stock Exchange that fully-paid shares in a listed company should be free from all liens.

Liens

Almost invariably a company's articles will give it a lien over its shares for certain amounts which may become due to the company from the holders of such shares. As noted above, section 38 of the Companies Act 1980 provides that, in the case of a public company, such a lien, unless "in existence" immediately before the company applied for re-registration as a public company, may only extend to shares which are not fully paid and may only secure amounts payable in respect of such shares. Article 11 of Table A (as amended by the Companies Act 1980 in relation to companies registered after December 21, 1980) gives a company "a first and paramount lien" on every share, not being a fully paid share, for all moneys called or payable at a fixed time in respect of that share.

The articles of a private company may, however, give it a lien over its shares for all moneys payable to the company by the holder of the shares, whether or not in respect of the shares concerned. Before it was amended by the 1980 Act, article 11 of Table A conferred such a lien, but only over shares which were not fully paid and which were registered in the name of a single person, and only for moneys which were presently payable.

Many companies' articles embody article 10 of Table A (now deleted by the Companies Act 1981). This provided that the company should not make a loan for any purpose whatsoever on the security of its shares. It has been held that a company's payment of a number of bills for a shareholder-director did not amount to the company making a loan to him, so that the prohibition contained in article 10 did not prevent the operation of another provision of the company's articles which gave it a lien on every share registered in the name of a person "indebted or under liability to the company": *Champagne Perrier–Jouet S.A. v H. H. Finch Limited* [1982] 1 W.L.R. 1359 (see also section 49 of the Companies Act 1980).

A lien over a company's shares which is conferred on the company by its articles amounts to an equitable charge over the shares, and does not merely give a right to hold the shares (*Re General Exchange Bank* (1871) 6 Ch. App. 818). The lien is a "mortgage" for the purposes of the Law of Property Act 1925 (see L.P.A. 1925, s. 205 (i)(xvi) and *Everitt v Automatic Weighing Machine Company* [1892] 3 Ch. 506). However, it will usually be unnecessary for the company to rely on the enforcement rights given to a chargee of shares under the general law, since the company's articles will normally provide how the lien may be enforced and will give the company an express power of sale – see, for instance, articles 12 to 14 of Table A.

An article may validly provide that, where shares are held by joint holders, the company shall have a lien on the shares for any moneys owing by all or any of the shareholders alone or jointly with any other person. Where the shares are registered in the names of trustees, the company's lien under such an article for a debt due to it from one of the trustees in his personal capacity prevails over the interest of a beneficiary under the trust (*New London and Brazilian Bank v Brocklebank* (1882) 21 Ch. D. 302). This is unless, at the time the debt was incurred, the company had notice that the shareholders held the shares as trustees. Section 117 of the 1948 Act and, it appears, such an article as article 7 of Table A, do not protect a company which, in the face of notice that a shareholder is not the beneficial owner of the shares, makes advances or gives credit to the shareholder (*Mackereth v Wigan Coal and Iron Company* [1916] 2 Ch. 293; there the article did not purport to relieve the company from equities even where it had notice – cf. article 7, but see *Perrier–Jouet* at 1367). Conversely, a lien on shares held by any shareholder for debts due to the company by or on behalf of such shareholder gives the company no lien as against a person indebted to the company on whose behalf a registered holder holds shares in the company (*Re Ystalyfera Gas Co* [1887] W.N. 30). Likewise, where the beneficial owner of shares under a bare trust is indebted to the company, and the company's articles give it a lien on the shares for all moneys due from the registered holder of the shares "or other the person for the time being entitled thereto as against the company", the policy of the Companies Acts is such as to free the company from any obligation to recognise the interest of the beneficial owner, and it may therefore present a bankruptcy petition against him upon the footing that it holds no security upon his estate (see *Re Perkins* (1890) 24 Q.B.D. 613, but note *Bradford Banking Co Limited v Briggs* (1887) 12 App. Cas. 29 at 31, 32, 38 and 40).

The priorities as between a company having, under its articles, a lien on its shares and a mortgagee of such shares are considered in the next part of this chapter.

Priorities

Mortgages and charges

On general principles, the title of a bona fide legal mortgagee of securities (including negotiable securities) will prevail over a prior equitable interest, for instance, that of a prior equitable chargee or that of a beneficiary under a trust pursuant to which the shares are held by the mortgagor, unless, at the time he made his advance, the mortgagee had notice, actual or constructive, of the prior equitable interest (*Shropshire Union Railways and Canal Company v The Queen* (1875) L.R. 7 H.L. 496; *Sheffield v London Joint Stock Bank* (1888) 13 App. Cas. 333). Moreover, where a lender takes an equitable mortgage without notice of an earlier equitable interest and later, after acquiring such notice, converts his mortgage into a legal mortgage by registering a transfer of the shares into his name, then his title will prevail over the prior equitable interest. It seems there is an exception, however, if before the transfer is sent to it for registration, the company acquires notice of the fact that the transfer involved a breach of trust (*Dodds v Hills* 2 H&M 424; *Roots v Williamson* (1888) 38 Ch. D. 485 at 497, 498). Where the contest is between an equitable mortgage or charge of shares and another equitable interest, the equitable title which is prior in time prevails, subject to two exceptions. The first is if the equities are not equal, because there has been some positive conduct of the owner of the prior interest such as to disentitle or estop him. Such conduct must amount to something tangible and distinct, and the conduct of the beneficial owner of shares in allowing the share certificates to remain in the possession of a sole trustee (the registered holder) is not sufficient to take away his pre-existing equitable title as against a later equitable mortgagee (*Shropshire Union Railways*, above). However, where the owner of the prior equitable title is not a beneficiary under a trust of the shares, but an equitable mortgagee of them, it may well be that his allowing the mortgagor to retain the share certificates will result in his being postponed to a subsequent equitable mortgagee who takes up the certificates (compare *Rice v Rice* (1854) 2 Drew 73). The second possible exception is if the owner of the subsequent interest holds a completed transfer of the shares and all necessary conditions have been fulfilled to give him, as between himself and the company, a present, absolute, unconditional right to have the transfer registered before the company is informed of the existence of a better title (see *Société Generale de Paris v Walker* (1885) 11 App Cas. 20 at 28, 29; *Roots v Williamson*, above; *Peat v Clayton* [1906] 1 Ch. 659 at 664; contrast *Ireland v Hart* [1902] 1 Ch. 522 at 529).

Liens

A lien given to a company by its articles of association over shares in the company for any debt due to the company by the holder of the shares will prevail over the title of a legal or equitable mortgagee of the shares, subject to two exceptions.

First, by registering a legal mortgagee as the holder of the shares, the company will normally be regarded as having by its conduct precluded itself from setting up its lien (an equitable interest) as against the mortgagee (*Re Northern Assam Tea Co* (1870) L.R. 10 Eq. 458). This is unless the transfer to the mortgagee was passed under a mistake and the register is shortly rectified (*Anderson's Case* (1869) L.R. 8 Eq. 509). It is thought that the likelihood of the lien being taken to have been waived will be greater where the articles expressly entitle the directors to decline to register a transfer of shares on which the company has a lien – see, for instance, article 24 of Table A.

Secondly, the company's lien will not have priority over a mortgage in favour of a third party as regards advances which the company makes to the shareholder or debts which the shareholder incurs to the company after the company received notice of the third party's mortgage. This is so even though the company's articles give its "a first and paramount lien and charge" and the third party mortgagee knew, or ought to have known, of this article when the shares were mortgaged to him: *Bradford Banking Co Limited v Briggs* (1886) 12 App. Cas. 29. It seems that a company cannot lose its lien by failing to take up the share certificates (*Re National Bank of Wales* [1899] 2 Ch. 629 at 676).

Two further points with respect to priorities may be noted.

Dearle v Hall. First, the rule in *Dearle v Hall* (3 Russ. 1) is inapplicable to shares in companies (*Societé Generale de Paris v Walker* above). Thus, a person having an equitable interest in shares cannot obtain or protect his priority by giving the company notice of his interest, subject to the fact that the company may be unable to claim priority, as regards advances it makes after receipt of such a notice, for any lien on the shares given to it by its articles. (See the references to *Mackerett v Wigan Coal and Iron Company* and the *Bradford Banking* case above.)

Stop notices. Secondly, under Order 50, rule 11 of the Rules of the Supreme Court, a person claiming to be beneficially entitled to an interest in any securities of the kinds set out in section 2(2) (b) of the Charging Orders Act 1979 (other than securities in court) who wishes to be notified of any proposed transfer or payment of those securities may file a stop notice, either in the central office of the Supreme Court or in a district registry. This must be addressed to the company (or other entity) in which the securities exist and must be filed with an affidavit containing the information specified in that rule. Section 2(2) (b) of the 1979 Act extends to (inter alia) United Kingdom government stock, securities of any body incorporated within England and Wales and securities of any body incorporated outside England and Wales which are registered in a register kept within England and Wales. Under Order 50, rule 12, where a stop notice has been served on a company, it may not register a transfer of the securities, or take any other step restrained by the stop notice, until 14 days after the company has sent a notice to the person on whose behalf the stop notice was served.

The stop notice procedure thus provides a means whereby an equitable mortgagee of registered securities may obtain some protection for his interest. But the effect of a stop notice is purely temporary, and the person serving it has to proceed to obtain a restraining order under Order 50, rule 15 against the company concerned or an injunction against the registered holder of the securities. Accordingly, a stop notice will, of itself, only give the person serving it a brief opportunity to assert his claim before the securities are transferred or a payment in respect of them is made to another person.

In practice, it is rare for an equitable mortgage of shares to be protected by a stop notice. If such protection is thought necessary, a legal mortgage is usually taken – unless the shares are not fully paid.

Enforcement

The three principal methods by which a mortgage or charge over securities may be enforced are, briefly stated, as follows.

Sale

If the charge is made by deed, then the chargee will, when the money secured by the charge has become due, have the power of sale conferred by section 101 of the Law of Property Act 1925, subject to section 103 of that Act. This is subject to the terms of the deed not providing otherwise. Whether or not the mortgage is made by deed, but the contract fixes a date for the payment of the debt, and the date passes without the debt being paid, then the mortgagee may at once proceed to sell the mortgaged securities (*Deverges v Sandeman Clarke & Co* [1902] 1 Ch. 579). And, where no date is fixed for payment, the mortgagee has an implied power of sale upon giving reasonable notice requiring payment (*Deverges v Sandeman Clarke & Co; Stubbs v Slater* [1910] 1. Ch. 632). Moreover the fact that the notice, by mistake, demands more than what is actually due is not a ground for invalidating the exercise of the power of sale: *Stubbs v Slater*.

As regards the statutory power of sale given to an equitable mortgagee, doubts still persist, despite dicta in *Re White Rose Cottage* [1965] Ch. 940, as to whether the Law of Property Act 1925 authorises an equitable mortgagee, even one whose mortgage extends to all the interest, both legal and equitable in the mortgaged property, to transfer the legal interest in the mortgaged property (see for instance *Fisher and Lightwood, The Law of Mortgages*, at 380). The position is not made any easier by the observations in *Hunter v Hunter* [1936] A.C. 222 to the effect that the ordinary express power of sale does not authorise a disposition of the equitable interest divested of the legal title. Accordingly, in order to place the position beyond doubt, equitable mortgages commonly contain an irrevocable power of attorney authorising the mortgagee to execute any necessary transfers. But, if *Re White Rose Cottage* cannot be taken as establishing that an equitable mortgagee has a statutory power to transfer the legal interest, it seems equally doubtful whether that case establishes that an equitable mortgagee has power, under section 104 of the 1925 Act, to overreach interests ranking after his mortgage. And it is not clear whether the device of a power of attorney would enable the mortgagee, in the exercise of his power of sale, to transfer the legal interest (otherwise than to a purchaser for value without notice) free of such a subsequent interest. Whatever the true position, however, it seems clear that an equitable mortgagee by deposit of share certificates has an implied power of sale and does not need to rely on the statutory power of sale, as distinct from the statutory power to overreach subsequent interests (see the cases cited in the previous paragraph and *Deverges v. Sandeman* [1901] 1 Ch. 70 at 73). So far as liens are concerned, as noted above, the articles of a company normally specify the manner of enforcing any lien which they give the company over its own shares. Where the lien is to be enforced by sale, the effect of the articles may be to require the company to go through any pre-emption procedures laid down by the articles by first offering the shares to other shareholders before selling them on the open market (*Champagne Perrier – Jouet S.A. v H.H. Finch Limited* [1982] 1 W.L.R. 1359).

Foreclosure

A mortgagee of shares, including an equitable mortgagee of registered shares under a deposit of the share certificates, is entitled to an order for foreclosure, as well as having a power of sale (*Harrold v Plenty* [1901] 2 Ch. 314). It is thought that, under section 35 of the Companies Act 1980, a limited company will normally be prohibited from enforcing by foreclosure any charge or lien over its own shares (assuming that the remedy of foreclosure would otherwise be available to it). Similarly, it also appears that the effect of section 35 (4) (c) is to render unenforceable any power given by a limited company's articles to forfeit shares for failure to pay any sum due to the company otherwise than in respect of the shares concerned (see also *Hopkinson v Mortimer Harley & Co* [1917] 1 Ch. 646).

Appointment of receiver

Unless extended by the mortgage deed, the power to appoint a receiver under section 101(1)(iii) of the Law of Property Act 1925 only enables a receiver to be appointed of the income of mortgaged securities, and not over the securities themselves (and see *Marshall v Cottingham* [1981] 3 All E.R. 8 at 10).

Company Charges

This chapter deals with the law relating to mortgages and charges created by companies. It should be read in conjunction with the chapter on *Borrowings*.

Power to give security

The general rule is that a company has power to mortgage its property for past or future debts incurred in the course of its business, unless prohibited by its memorandum of association from doing so (*Re Patent File Co.* (1870) L.R. 6 Ch. App. 83). Nevertheless, it is almost invariable for the objects clause in a company's memorandum of association to contain a sub-clause authorising the company to give security. The terms of such a provision need careful examination, both as to the items which may be made the subject of the security – thus a reference to all the company's property whatsoever, both present and future, will not include uncalled capital, *Re Streatham and General Estates Co.* [1897] 1 Ch. 15; *Re Russian Spratts Patent* [1898] 2 Ch. 149 – and also as to the liabilities which may be secured. For example, the clause may only authorise the giving of security in respect of borrowings made by the company, and may not extend to security for guarantees given by the company or for liabilities incurred by other persons. The considerations relating to the powers of the directors to borrow money which are noted in the chapter on *Borrowings* are equally applicable to the powers of the directors to grant security.

As regards mortgages and charges, there is the additional point that companies frequently agree to their powers to grant security being restricted by loan agreements, loan stock trust deeds and other contracts with lenders. These restrictions generally result from the fact that persons lending to a company on an unsecured basis usually stipulate that the company is not to grant security to another lender or, at least, not unless the first lender is given equivalent security.

The main types of restriction are as follows:-

(a) *a negative pledge*: an undertaking by a company with a lender not to give any security to any third party at all, or not to give such security without also granting equivalent security to the lender to whom the negative pledge is given;

(b) *a pari passu clause*: an undertaking by a company with a lender that its liabilities in respect of the loan will rank at least *pari passu* with

169

all its other liabilities (except those having preference under the
general law). Where the loan concerned is unsecured, the pari
passu clause is contravened if the company grants security for any
other liability;

(c) *restrictive clauses in floating charges*: these are considered under the
     heading *Other Charges* below and prohibit a company from grant-
     ing any security ranking ahead of or pari pasu with the floating
     charge.

It is also common for guarantees to contain a clause which prohibits the
guarantor from taking any security from the principal debtor, at least in
respect of the amount payable under the guarantee.

There is authority for the proposition that restrictions of the first and
third type, at least those of the kind contained in floating charges, will
be construed strictly (*Robson v Smith* [1895] 2 Ch. 118).

Although there does not appear to be any direct English authority
concerning restrictions of the type described in (a) and (b) above, it may
be doubted whether security knowingly taken in breach of such a
restriction would be valid as regards the lender entitled to the benefit of
the restriction. The judgment at first instance in *Swiss Bank Corporation v. Lloyds Bank* suggests that the lender entitled to the restriction
could obtain an injunction to restrain the granting or enforcement of the
security ([1979] 2 All E.R. 853 at 874 b and c), although an observation
in the Court of Appeal ([1980] 2 All E.R. 422 at 428e) indicates that this
part of the first instance judgment may be open to some question.
Whether the lender entitled to the restriction could assert that the
lender who obtained the security held the security upon a constructive
trust for him seems doubtful (see *Goode's Commercial Law* at p. 723).

Fixed and floating charges

It may be said that a fixed or specific charge is a charge over present or
future property which fastens on that property when the charge is
executed (*Illingworth v Houldsworth* [1904] A.C. 355); or in the case of
future property, when it comes into existence (*Independent Automatic
Sales v Knowles & Foster* [1962] 1 W.L.R. 974). See *Re Yorkshire
Woolcombers Association* [1903] 2 Ch. 289 at 294, *Independent Automatic Sales v Knowles & Foster*, above, and *Siebe Gorman v. Barclays
Bank* [1979] 2 Ll. Rep. 142 at 159 in relation to future property. It
follows that from the time the charge fastens on the property the person
who gave the charge is unable to deal with the property without the
consent of the person to whom the charge was given (*Re Florence Land
& Public Works Co.* (1878) 10 Ch. D. 530 at 541; *Re Yorkshire
Woolcombers Association Limited*, above). On the other hand, a
floating charge, although an immediate and a present security, and not a
future one (*Evans v Rival Granite Quarries Limited* [1910] 2 K.B. 979
at 999), is a charge which hovers over and floats with the property
which it is intended to affect, until some event occurs or

some act is done which causes it to fasten on the subject of the charge within its grasp. Until that time the chargor can deal with the property without the consent of the chargee (*Illingworth v Houldsworth; Re Yorkshire Woolcombers Association Limited*). When such an event or act takes place, the charge is said to affix or "crystallise". At that point, the chargee becomes entitled to a fixed charge over the property which is at that time the subject of the charge and any subsequent dealing with that property requires the chargee's consent.

It was said in the *Re Yorkshire Woolcombers* case (page 295) that, if a charge contains the following three characteristics it is a floating charge, although the fact that a charge does not contain all these characteristics does not necessarily mean it is not a floating charge:

(a) it is a charge on a class of assets of a company present and future;

(b) that class is one which, in the ordinary course of the business of the company, would be changing from time to time;

(c) the charge contemplates that, until some future step is taken by or on behalf of the chargee, the company may carry on its business in the ordinary way as far as concerns the particular class of assets in question.

A floating charge need not be on the whole undertaking nor on the whole property of the company (*Re Yorkshire Woolcombers* at page 298). Thus it may cover assets merely of a specified category or categories: *Re Bond Worth* [1980] 1 Ch. 228 at 266. It has been suggested that it must embrace both present and future property (*Re Yorkshire Woolcombers* at page 298). But it has been held that a charge over exclusively present assets of a company may be a floating charge, as may be a charge over exclusively future assets (*Re Bond Worth* at 267). It may be noted that a floating charge created by an English company and extending to land in a foreign country is, as regards such land and the proceeds of any sale of it, a valid equitable security according to English law, even if the concept of a floating charge is unknown to the law of the foreign country and even if the formalities required by the laws of that country in relation to mortgages have not been complied with: *Re The Anchor Line (Henderson Brothers) Limited (No. 2)* [1937] 1 Ch. 483; see *Re Maudslay* [1900] 1 Ch. 602 and *Re Vocalion (Foreign) Limited* [1932] 2 Ch. 196 as to the position of competing creditors.

The two essential requirements of a floating charge are first, that it should reserve either expressly or by necessary implication a right to the company to deal with the property subject to the charge for a certain time as though the charge had never been executed (*Re Yorkshire Woolcomber* at 298); and secondly, that it should be intended to fasten upon and specifically bind the assets concerned which are in existence at the time when the chargee intervenes (or some event occurs) so as to crystallise the charge (*Tailby v Official Receiver* 13 App. Cas. 527 at 541; *Illingworth v Houldsworth at 358*).

A document may take effect as a floating charge, despite the fact that it is in the form of an assignment or a mortgage; although, if the parties have specified that a charge is to be a fixed one, the court will take that into account: *Siebe Gorman v Barclays Bank* at 159. Thus, a bill of sale containing an assignment by way of mortgage over all the trade assets for the time being of the mortgagor has been held to be a floating security (*Tailby v Official Receiver*), as have an assignment of present and future book debts (the *Re Yorkshire Woolcombers* and *Illingworth* cases; contrast the *Siebe Gorman* case), and an assignment of furniture and loose effects from time to time placed on certain premises. (*National Provincial Bank v United Electrical Theatres Limited* [1916] 1 Ch. 132).

The approach of the court is to treat the charge as a commercial document, and to consider whether the intention of the parties was that the assets charged should remain at the command of the company which would be able to deal with them and dispose of them in the ordinary course of business, or whether it was intended that the assets should pass to the chargee so that the company would be unable to use them without the chargee's consent (see the *Re Yorkshire Woolcombers* and *Illingworth* cases and *Re Florence Land* at 541 and *Re Bond Worth* at 267E to 268C). *Re Bond Worth* concerned a condition incorporated into a contract for the sale of goods which provided that, until full payment had been received, the "equitable and beneficial ownership" (but not the legal title) in the goods would remain the vendor's. It also provided that the vendor would have a corresponding equitable interest in any proceeds of sale of the goods, any products manufactured from the goods, and any proceeds of sale of such products. In view of the substance of the transaction, as appearing from the wording of the whole of the retention of title clause, and the other provisions of the relevant contracts of sale, the condition was held to create, as regards each of the four categories of asset, an equitable charge. And because of the implicit freedom of the purchaser to use those assets as it pleased for its own benefit in the course of its own business, this could only be a floating charge.

Crystallisation

A floating charge crystallises –

(a) upon the winding up of the company (*Re Panama, New Zealand and Australian Royal Mail Co.* (1870) 5 Ch. App 318 at 322; *Hodson v Tea Company* (1880) 14 Ch. D. 859; *Wallace v Universal Automatic Machine Co.* [1894] 2 Ch. 547, *Re Crompton* [1914] 1 Ch. 954);

(b) upon the appointment of a receiver (*Biggerstaff v Rowlatt's Wharf Limited* [1896] 2 Ch. 93 at 103; *Evans v Rival Granite Quarries* [1910] 2 K.B. 979; and see *Re Christonette International Ltd.* [1982] 3 All E.R. 225); and

(c) upon possession being taken under the charge of the company's assets (*Biggerstaff v Rowlatt's Wharf* at 105).

It has been held in the New Zealand case of *Re Manurewa Transport Limited* [1971] N.Z.L.R. 909 that a floating charge crystallises automatically, without any act or intervention on the part of the chargee in certain circumstances. These are that the instrument provides that, upon the occurrence of a specified event (for instance, the charging of the company's assets in favour of a third party contrary to the provisions of the instrument) the moneys secured shall immediately become due and payable and the floating charge shall immediately attach and become affixed as the specified event occurs. That decision, which was largely based on *Davey & Co v Williamson & Sons* [1898] 2 Ch. 198, a not wholly satisfactory case (see the comments in *Evans v Rival Granite*), has not escaped adverse comment, e.g. [1979] J.B.L. 231. Thus the validity of automatic crystallisation clauses cannot, it seems, be regarded as entirely free from doubt (*Re Horne and Hellard* (1885) 29 Ch. D. 736, which has been cited as authority for the validity of automatic crystallisation charges (40 Conv. (N.S.) at 397) must it seems be overruled by *Governments Stock Investment Co. v Manilla Railway Co.* [1897] A.C. 81.) It is thought, however, that a provision whereby the holder of a floating charge may, in certain events, by written notice to the company, convert the charge into a fixed charge as regards any assets specified in the notice is more likely to be valid. This is because it does at least necessitate some "intervention" by the chargee, which is consistent with various dicta in the English cases (the *Governments Stock* case at 86, and *Evans v Rival Granite* at 993). A clause of this type appears in *Palmers Debentures*, page 238.

Assuming, nevertheless, that an automatic crystallisation clause is valid, it would appear that, at least if the crystallising event is some act done by the company, the fixed charge thereby created by the company would (if it fell within one of the categories specified in section 95(2)) require registration under section 95 of the Companies Act 1948 within 21 days after the occurrence of the crystallising event (compare *Cornbrook Brewery Co. Limited v Law Debenture Corp. Limited* [1904] 1 Ch. 103). The extent to which registration of the *floating* charge would make it unnecessary to register the *fixed* charge appears to be an open point. (In *Re Manurewa Transport*, above, it was held, apparently without argument, that registration of the floating charge amounted to registration of the fixed charge.) A floating charge containing an automatic crystallisation clause may still be a floating charge for the purposes of section 322 of the 1948 Act, even if a crystallising event is subsisting on the date when the charge is executed: *Re Port Supermarket Limited* [1978]] 1NZLR 330.

The effects of crystallisation

Upon crystallisation, the floating charge becomes affixed and the right of the company to deal with its assets in the ordinary course of business without the consent of the holder of the floating charge comes to an end. In other words, the incomplete assignment constituted by the floating charge is converted into a completed equitable assignment or charge

(*Biggerstaff v Rowlatt's Wharf*, above; *George Barker (Transport) Limited v Eynon* [1974] 1 W.L.R. 462). This assignment or charge extends to assets which the company acquires after crystallisation, for instance, debts arising to the company after a receiver has been appointed: *N.W. Robbie & Co. Limited v. Witney Warehouse Ltd.* [1963] 1 W.L.R. 1324. Although this assignment becomes complete when a receiver is appointed, it only becomes effective as against third parties when they receive notice of the receiver's appointment and so notice of the assignment: *Business Computers Limited v Anglo-African Leasing Limited* [1977] 1 W.L.R. 578 at 582A. Thus, a creditor of a company cannot, after receiving notice of the receiver's appointment, set off against a debt owed by him to the company a debt which only accrues due to him from the company after the date of the notice, unless the two debts arise out of connected transactions (*Business Computers Limited v Anglo-African Leasing Limited*).

The disadvantages of a floating charge: section 322

By section 322 of the Companies Act 1948, in a winding up of a company, a floating charge created within twelve months of the commencement of the winding up is invalid, "except to the amount of *any cash paid* to the company *at the time of* or subsequently to the creation of, and in consideration for, the charge." But this result is excluded if it is proved that the company was "solvent" immediately after creation of the charge. Where section 322 applies, the exception for cash paid to the company extends to interest thereon currently, five per cent per annum (see also page 521).

Under section 229 of the 1948 Act, a winding up by the court is deemed to commence at the time of the presentation of the petition (or the passing of any earlier winding up resolution) and, under section 280, a voluntary winding up is deemed to commence at the time of the passing of the resolution for voluntary winding up.

To be solvent for the purposes of section 322, the company must satisfy two tests:-

(i)   its assets must exceed its liabilities (compare *Re European Life Assurance Company* (1870) L.R. 9 Eq.122 at 128);

(ii) it must be able to pay its debts as they fall due (*Re Patrick and Lyon Limited* [1933] Ch. 786 at 791).

It may be noted that, whilst the necessity of satisfying both tests is stated in *Palmer's Debentures* (p. 60) and *Gore-Browne* (34–23, note (u)), the Cork Report (para. 1556 *et seq.*) suggests that, under the present law, only the second test is applicable.

The onus of proving the company's solvency is on the holder of the floating charge (*Re Patrick and Lyon Limited*). Accordingly, where no money is paid to the company giving the floating charge – for instance, where a subsidiary gives a charge to secure a guarantee given by it for money advanced to its parent – the common practice is for two directors (or sometimes the auditors) of the charging company to be asked to certify that the company will be solvent immediately after the creation of the charge.

Whether in any particular case there was "any cash paid to the company" depends on the facts of that case, looking at the substance, and not the form, of the transactions concerned: *Re Matthew Ellis Limited* [1933] Ch. 458. Thus, where three directors who had guaranteed a company's overdraft, the repayment of which was being pressed for by the bank, sent cheques to the company on terms that the company should hand those cheques to the bank in reduction of the overdraft and issue debentures to the directors, it was held that there had not in fact and in substance been any cash paid to the company. All that had happened was that the directors had, using the company as a conduit pipe, paid the cash to the bank (*Re Orleans Motor Company Limited* [1911] 2 Ch. 41; *Re Matthew Ellis* above. The position would have been different had the directors not been liable for the overdraft: *Re Thomas Mortimer Limited* [1965] Ch. 186 at 189; cf. *Re Destone Fabrics, Limited* [1941] 1 Ch. 319.). However, it is not the case that in order for a payment to be treated as "cash paid to the company" for the purposes of the section, the money must go to swell the assets of the company and become available for its creditors or that the cash must be absolutely and unconditionally paid to the company. Nor is it the case that money cannot in any circumstances be cash paid to the company if it is applied in discharge of an antecedent debt (*Re Matthew Ellis*, above, disapproving earlier dicta). Nevertheless, although it is very difficult to lay down a precise test for the application of the section, it may be said that the court will tend to apply the section if the company received no advantage from the transaction and the transaction was not a bona fide one intended for the benefit of the company, but was designed merely to secure a past debt of the company to the prejudice of its other creditors (see *Re Matthew Ellis* at 473, 474, 476, *Re Destone Fabrics* and *Re Mataura Motors Limited* [1981] 1 N.Z.L.R. 289).

As indicated above, the cash must be normally paid to the company which gives the floating charge, and not, for instance, to its holding company. But where the holder of the charge, at the request of the company, makes a payment direct to another creditor of the company (without going through the form of paying the money to the company to enable the company to make the payment), such a payment constitutes cash paid to the company, provided that the holder of the floating charge has no liability to the payee creditor in respect of the debt which the payment discharges (*Re Thomas Mortimer Limited* [1965] Ch. 186 at 189; *Re Yeovil Glove Co. Limited* [1965] Ch. 148). So, subject to that proviso, when a company's bank honours cheques of the company in favour of creditors, and the company's account is overdrawn, on each occasion the bank makes a payment in cash to the company within the meaning of the section.

The cash has to be paid *at the time* of (or subsequently to) the creation of the charge. For the cash to be paid "at the time of" the creation of the charge, it does not have to be paid at the same moment as the security was created, or even within the same twenty four hours. It is a question of what are the circumstances of the particular case and what is the real substance of the transaction. Thus a payment on account of the consideration for the security, in anticipation of its creation and in reliance on a promise to execute it, although made some days before its execution, is made at the time of its creation within the meaning of the section: *Re Columbian Fireproofing Co. Limited* [1910] 1 Ch. 758 and 2 Ch. 120. So, where an advance was made "on account of debentures to be issued as arranged", debentures which were not issued until fifty-four days later – and only five days before the company went into liquidation – were upheld. The very long delay had not in any true sense been acquiesced in by the lenders who had pressed for the debentures to be executed: *Re F & E Stanton Limited* [1929] 1 Ch. 180. But, as a rough guide, a delay of about four or five days between the advance of the loan and the execution of the floating charge can be permitted as the time required to complete the necessary formalities. If the lender allows much more time to elapse, his charge may start to become open to challenge (see *Re F & E Stanton* at 193 and 194 – in the *Re Columbian* case a ten day delay was permitted).

Under the section, the cash has to be paid "in consideration for the charge". But these words are not used in a strict contractual sense; they will apply to payments made in reliance upon and because of the existence of the charge (*Re Yeovil Glove Co. Limited* [1965] Ch. 148 at 178).

It is to be noted that, if at the time a company gives its bank a floating charge, the company's account is already overdrawn and the bank does not rule off the account at that time, then the rule in *Clayton's Case* (1816) Mer. 572 will apply. The bank will, in the absence of any appropriation by the company, be entitled to apply any amount paid into the account by the company after the date of the charge against the company's pre-charge indebtedness (for which the charge could be vulnerable under the section, because such indebtedness would relate to advances made by the bank prior to the charge's creation), before applying such payment against indebtedness of the company arising after the date of the charge (*Re Yeovil Glove*). So, if a company is already substantially overdrawn at the time the bank takes its floating charge and the company gets into further difficulties shortly thereafter, it could be in the interests of the bank to allow the company to continue to operate (subject to any question of fraudulent trading) within a suitable overdraft limit. This enables the company's trading receipts to be applied in reducing its pre-charge indebtedness in respect of which the floating charge might be invalidated in the event of a liquidation commencing within twelve months of the date of the charge. The Cork Committee has recommended (para. 1562 of the Report) that the decision in *Re Yeovil Glove* be reversed.

The main points arising from section 322 which should be borne in mind when it is proposed to take a floating charge may be summarised as follows:

(1) If the charge is to secure not cash to be paid to the company but, for instance, a past debt or a guarantee, consideration should be given to taking a fixed charge, unless it is plain that, immediately after the charge is executed, the company will be solvent, both in the sense of being able to pay its debts as they fall due and in the sense of having a positive net worth. The reason for this is that, if an otherwise valid fixed charge can be obtained, section 322 will be inapplicable, and the charge will only be liable to avoidance under section 320 (fraudulent preference) if,

(a) a liquidation commences within six months of creation of the charge – under section 322 the company has to survive for twelve months;

(b) the liquidator can show that the dominant intention of giving the charge was to prefer the chargee to other creditors of the company (see e.g. *Re F.L.E. Holdings Limited* [1967] 3 All E. R. 553 at 558) – no such intention has to be shown under section 322; and

(c) at the time of the creation of the charge the company could not pay its debts as they fell due from its own money – under section 322 the holder of a floating charge has to show that the company could pay its debts and, in addition, that the company had a positive net worth.

(2) If the floating charge is to secure an overdraft, and there is already an amount overdrawn, then, in order to obtain the benefit of *Clayton's Case* referred to above, the account should not be ruled off when the charge is created.

The disadvantages of a floating charge: preferential debts

Section 319(5)(b) of the 1948 Act provides that, so far as the assets of a company available for payment of general creditors are insufficient to meet the preferential debts specified in section 319, those debts shall have priority over the claims of holders of debentures under any floating charge created by the company. Accordingly the debts shall be paid out of any property comprised in or subject to such a floating charge. These preferential debts are considered below.

Section 319 applies where a company is being wound up. If a company is not being wound up, and a receiver is appointed on behalf of the holders of debentures secured by a floating charge, or possession is taken by or on behalf of such debenture holders of any property comprised in or subject to the floating charge, section 94 of the 1948 Act applies. That section provides that the preferential debts of the type referred to above shall be paid out of any assets coming to the hands of the receiver or the person taking possession of the property in priority to any claim for principal or interest in respect of the debentures.

Sections 317 and 94 give preferential debts priority over the claims of the holder of a floating charge, but not over those of a holder of a fixed charge. So, where a receiver was appointed by a bank under a debenture containing both a fixed charge and also a floating charge, it was held that the preferential debts only had priority in respect of assets derived from the subject of the floating charge, and not in respect of assets subject to the fixed charge: *Re Lewis Merthyr Consolidated Collieries Limited* [1929] 1 Ch. 498. But it seems that a fixed charge ranking in point of priority behind a floating charge, will rank behind the floating charge not only to the extent of the claims of the holder of the floating charge, but also to the extent of the preferential debts which have priority over the floating charge (see *Gore-Browne on Companies* at 18–28).

The postponement to preferential debts is, perhaps, the main weakness, in practical terms, of the floating charge, and this fact has been one of the principal reasons why banks' standard debentures nowadays seek to take fixed charges over as many categories of asset as possible, notably book and other debts.

The Cork Committee has recommended (at paragraph 1538 et seq. of the Report) that a fund equal to ten per cent of the net realisations of assets subject to a floating charge should be made available for the distribution among the ordinary creditors. For this purpose, there would be an extended statutory definition of "a floating charge" (see paragraphs 1585–6 of the Report), which would include any charge which extends to future property and which leaves the company substantially free to deal with the assets subject to the charge in the ordinary course of business. Under this definition, the type of fixed charge over present and future book debts which featured in *Siebe Gorman v. Barclays Bank Limited* [1979] 2 Ll.R.142 would be classed as a floating charge. However, the Cork Committee took the view that the effects of the "ten per cent fund" proposals would be counter-balanced by their proposals to reduce the number and amount of preferential debts (see Chapter 32 of the Report).

The disadvantages of a floating charge: priorities

It is of the essence of a floating charge that, until the charge crystallises, the company retains the power (unless the charge provides to the contrary) to deal with the assets subject to the charge in the ordinary course of its business. As a result, the holder of a floating charge is liable, subject as mentioned below, to be postponed to interests in the charged property which are created or arise in the ordinary course of the company's business. The main types of such interests are described below.

Other charges

In the absence of some provision to the contrary, a floating charge leaves the company free to create specific charges over the charged property which will have priority over the floating charge, even if the floating charge is stated to be "a first charge" (*Re Colonial Trusts Corporation* (1880) 15 Ch. D. 465 at 472 and *Wheatley v Silkstone and Highmoor Coal Company* (1885) 29 Ch. D. 715). In addition, although the company will not be entitled to create a second floating charge ranking ahead of or *pari passu* with the first charge if the second charge covers the same property as that subject to the first charge (*Re Benjamin Cope & Sons Limited* [1914] 1 Ch. 800), the company may create a second floating which will rank ahead of the first charge, if the second charge only covers some of the assets which are subject to the first charge (*Re Automatic Bottle Makers, Limited* [1926] 1 Ch. 412).

However, for many years it has been normal for floating charges to contain a provision restricting the right of the company to create other charges, or at least prior or pari passu charges. Such a provision is usually along the following lines:

"The Company shall not without the consent of the Bank create any mortgage or charge upon all or any part of the undertaking or property hereby charged and no lien is, without the prior written consent of the Bank, to arise in any manner thereon [which would, in any such case, rank in priority to or pari passu with the charge hereby created]'.

But even a clause of this kind leaves the holder of the floating charge vulnerable at a number of points.

(1) *Purchase money mortgages*: where a company agrees to purchase property on terms that part of the purchase price should remain outstanding to the vendor on a mortgage of the property to be executed in his favour, the interest which the company acquires in the property is subject to that of the unpaid vendor or mortgagee. Thus the floating charge will also be subject to his interest: *Wilson v Kelland* [1910] 2 Ch. 306. The position is similar if a company, which wishes to borrow part of the purchase price for an asset, enters into an agreement with the lender which provides for him to have a charge over the asset for the amount lent by him and then enters into the contract to purchase the asset. The company will only acquire the asset subject to the lender's security (notwithstanding that the charge to the lender is executed some days after the date of the conveyance to the company), so that the floating charge will also be subject to the lender's security (*Re Connolly Brothers, Limited (No 2)* [1912] 2 Ch. 25; *Security Trust Co. v Royal Bank of Canada* [1976] A.C. 503 at 518). In other words, the floating charge only bites on property which is already fettered by the agreement to give the other charge (the *Security Trust Co.* case at 520A).

(2) *Liens*: a clause which merely provides that the company is "not to be at liberty to create any mortgage or charge" in priority to the floating charge does not apply to a lien, if the lien is given by the general law and arises through the company carrying on its business in the ordinary course and not so as to give the person claiming the lien any advantage by a direct act of the company. An example is a solicitors's lien to retain deeds and papers until his bill of costs is satisfied. This is because in such a case the lien arises by operation of law and is not created by the

company: *Brunton v Electrical Engineering Corporation* [1892] 1 Ch.
434; cf. *London and Cheshire Insurance Co. v. Laplagrene Co.* [1971]
Ch. 499 at 514.

For this reason, it has become common for the protective clause to be
extended with a view to precluding such liens arising, but it may be
doubted whether this would be effective unless the person claiming the
lien had express notice of the prohibition. It is also arguable that these
clauses, in order to have business efficacy, must be read subject to an
implied exception for liens arising in the ordinary course of trading,
since, otherwise, some very normal transactions would be prohibited
(for example, the delivery of a vehicle to a garage for repairs, which
could result in the garage's having a lien on the vehicle for the
reasonable cost of the repairs completed).

Moreover, even if the clause is so extended, it will have no application
to a *Mareva* injunction, because it is not the case that any rights in the
nature of a lien arise when a *Mareva* injunction is made (*Cretanor
Maritime Co. Limited v. Irish Marine Limited* [1978] 1 W.L.R. 966).

(3) *Garnishee proceedings*: similarly a clause prohibiting the company
from creating charges does not apply to a garnishee order obtained by a
creditor of the company who attaches a debt owing to the company – or
to other forms of execution – because the word "charge" in a provision
of this class is construed strictly. (*Robson v. Smith* [1895] 2 Ch. 118, and
see *Execution Creditors*, below).

(4) *Persons taking charges without notice of the prohibition*: notwithstanding that a floating charge prohibits the creation of prior charges, a
charge over property subject to the floating charge which is obtained by
a third party will rank ahead of the floating charge –

(a) where the third party acquires a legal mortgage of the property, if
    he had no actual or constructive notice of the prohibition at the
    time of making his advance (*English Scottish & Mercantile Invest-
    ment Company Limited v. Brunton* [1892] 2 Q.B. 700); or

(b) where the property is land and the third party acquires an equitable
    mortgage, if he had no actual or constructive notice of the
    prohibition and obtained a deposit of the title deeds, these having
    been left in the company's possession by the holder of the floating
    charge (*Re Castell & Brown Limited* [1898] 1 Ch. 315; *Re Valletort
    Sanitary Steam Laundry Company Limited* [1903] 2 Ch. 654; these
    cases may also apply by analogy where the third party obtains a
    charge over shares or other securities the relevant certificates being
    deposited with him).

In 1892 it was held that actual knowledge that a company had issued
debentures did not involve constructive knowledge of the prohibition
which they contained against prior charges (*English & Scottish Mercantile Investment Company Limited v. Brunton*), and this case was followed
in another case where all that was known was that debentures had been
issued, with no actual knowledge that these contained a floating charge:

Re Valletort [1903] 2 Ch. 654. In 1907 it was stated that if a bank had notice of the existence of debentures requiring registration under the forerunner of section 95 of the Companies Act 1948, that did not mean that the bank had notice of a prohibition contained in the debenture against other charges, as the bank could not have discovered this prohibition by inspecting the register (*Re Standard Rotary Machine Company Limited* 95 L.T. 829). In 1910, it was stated *obiter* in *Wilson v. Kelland* [1910] 2 Ch. 306 at 313 that, although the particulars of a floating charge registered under an enactment corresponding to section 95 of the Companies Act 1948 amounted to constructive notice of a charge affecting the property in issue, they did not give constructive notice of the special provisions contained in the charge which prohibited the creation of prior charges. But nowadays the inclusion of such a prohibition is extremely common – banks' standard form debentures invariably contain one – and it may therefore be questioned whether these cases can still be safely relied upon. However, in view of the statement in the case last referred to, it has become the practice to include a note of the prohibition in the particulars of the floating charge delivered under section 95. But as yet there appears to be no authority that this will be effective to give constructive notice of the prohibition. In any event, the overall state of the law is such that a person proposing to take any charge over a company's assets should first search at the Companies' Registration Office to see whether the company has created any floating charge and, if it has, should ask for a copy of the floating charge to ascertain whether it restricts the company's liberty to create other charges.

Sales of assets

It has been held that the fact that a company has given a floating charge over all its undertaking and assets does not prevent it from selling substantially all its assets, including goodwill, to a new company formed for the purpose in exchange for shares and debentures in the new company. But this is only the case provided that the objects clause of the vendor company contains a provision authorising the sale and provided that, notwithstanding the sale, the vendor company continues to carry on business, even if it is not the business on the security of which the holder of the floating charge relied (*Re Borax Company* [1901] 1 Ch. 326). Accordingly, debenture stock trust deeds usually contain provisions preventing companies disposing of a substantial part of their assets – generally thought to mean about 10 per cent – without the trustees' prior consent, and frequently more detailed restrictions on disposals are included. Such provisions will not, however, bind a purchaser who has no actual or constructive notice of them, and, in this context, the considerations mentioned above in relation to the effectiveness as against third parties of prohibitions on prior charges are of relevance.

Execution creditors

The rights of the holder of a floating charge will prevail against those of a creditor who levies execution over property subject to the charge, at least until the sheriff sells the goods: *Re Standard Manufacturing Company* [1891] 1 Ch. 627 at 640; *Re Opera* [1891] 3 Ch. 260. However this is the position only, it seems, if the floating charge crystallises before the goods are sold, albeit after they are seized. (The main authorities for this view are *dicta* in *Evans v Rival Granite* [1910] 2 K.B. 979 at 995 and 1000, *Taunton v Sheriff of Warwickshire* [1895] 2 Ch. 319 and *Norton v Yates* [1906] 1 K.B. 112. On the other hand, neither the *Re Standard* nor the *Re Opera* cases state this expressly, and the tone of the remarks by Lord Halsbury L.C. and Fry L.J. in *Re Standard* is to the contrary – in this connection see *Simultaneous Colour Printing Syndicate v Fowermaker* [1901] 1 Q.B. 771 (particularly the argument of the plaintiff's counsel). Note that in *Buckley on Company Law*, 14th edition page 266, it is stated that the rights of the debenture holders prevail at any rate until the sheriff has sold, whether or not a receiver has been appointed.)

Similarly, the rights of the holder of a floating charge will prevail against a creditor who seeks by garnishee proceedings to attach a debt due to the company only if a receiver is appointed or the charge otherwise crystallises before the garnishor obtains payment of the debt attached, albeit after a garnishee order nisi (*Norton v Yates* [1906] 1 K.B. 112; *Cairney v Back* [1906] 2 K.B. 746, *Evans v Rival Granite* at 997 and *Geisse v Taylor* [1905] 2 K.B. 658). And a floating charge will only prevail against a distress by the landlord if the charge crystallises before the distress is made (*Re Roundwood Colliery Company* [1897] 1 Ch. 373).

Thus, if the holder of a floating charge is to ensure that his rights prevail against execution creditors of this type, he may need to take prompt action to appoint a receiver so that his charge crystallises before the execution can be completed.

Sellers under title retention clauses

As a general rule, the holder of a floating charge can acquire no interest in an asset which, although in the possession of the company, is in fact owned by someone else.

In the *Romalpa* case, aluminium foil was sold to a company upon an express term that ownership therein – which meant the full legal ownership as well as the equitable and beneficial ownership, *Re Bond Worth* [1980] 1 Ch. 228 at 263F – would only pass to the company when it had met all that was owing to the suppliers. The sale was also upon the implied term that the company could sell on the foil to third parties, provided that such sales were made for the account of the suppliers to whom the company was to account on a fiduciary basis for the proceeds. It was held that the suppliers were able to trace and recover the proceeds of sale from a receiver/manager of the company's business appointed by its bankers (*Aluminium Industrie B.V. v Romalpa Limited*

[1976] 1 W.L.R. 676; see also *Re Nanwa Gold Mines Limited* [1955] 1 W.L.R. 1080 and also *Re Kayford Limited* [1975] 1 W.L.R. 279).

However, the *Romalpa* case possessed three special features which limit the scope of its application.

First, the contract reserved to the suppliers the full legal title to the foil, and not merely equitable ownership thereof, and made the purchaser a bailee of the foil, while it was in possession of it, until all money which it owed to the suppliers had been paid. In contrast, a contract which merely reserves the equitable or beneficial ownership and so creates no bailor – bailee relationship is liable to be construed as creating an equitable charge over the materials supplied. Such a charge is registrable under section 95 of the Companies Act 1948 as a floating charge, or, depending on the terms of the contract, as an instrument which, if executed by an individual, would require registration as a bill of sale: *Re Bond Worth* at 246H to 247B and 263F to H.

Secondly, it was held in the *Romalpa* case that the purchaser had been on-selling the materials supplied as agent of the suppliers. The situation is different where a supply contract (i) reserves only the beneficial ownership in the materials supplied and (ii) provides that, if the purchaser resells them while amounts remain owing to the suppliers, the beneficial entitlement of the suppliers will attach to the proceeds of sale or to the claim for such proceeds, and (iii) does not stipulate that the purchaser can only resell as agent of and for the account of the supplier. Here the contract is again liable to create a registrable charge in relation to the proceeds of sale – either a floating charge, or possibly a charge on book debts (*Re Bond Worth* and *Borden (U.K.) Limited v Scottish Timber Products Limited* [1981] 1 Ch. 25 at 38G).

Thirdly, the proceeds of sale which the suppliers traced and recovered in the *Romalpa* case were the proceeds of selling the material supplied in its raw unprocessed state. The aluminium foil had not been mixed with any other goods nor manufactured into other products (and the proceeds of the sale of the foil had been kept separate). And even if a supply contract succeeds in imposing on the purchaser the fiduciary obligations of a bailee/agent necessary for the tracing remedy to be available, that remedy can only be asserted to the extent that the property to be traced can be identified at every stage in its journey through life, and can be identified as property to which a fiduciary obligation still attaches in favour of the supplier (*Borden* at 46F). In *Borden* resin was sold on reservation of title terms. The intention was that the purchaser should use it in the manufacture of chipboard. The resin ceased to exist and the suppliers' title to the resin became meaningless when the resin was incorporated in the chipboard. It was held that the resin could not subsequently be traced into the chipboard which was a wholly new product.

Generally, it seems clear that, if the intention of the supply contract is that the item supplied should be mixed with heterogeneous goods in the manufacturing process so that it will lose its character and what will emerge will be a wholly new product, the only way in which the supplier can acquire rights over the finished product or the proceeds of its sale is by an express contractual stipulation. This is liable to involve a charge which is registrable as a floating charge or as an instrument which, if executed by an individual, would require registration as a bill of sale (provided that it gives the supplier a right to seize or take possession of the finished product) or as a charge on book debts, according to the terms of the contract (*Borden* at 42C and D. Templeman L.J. suggests at page 45 that the interest of the supplier may be a registrable charge even where tracing is available).

Existing contractual rights, rights of set off and Mareva injunctions

The equitable assignment of a company's assets to the holder of a floating charge which is brought about by the appointment of a receiver is subject to the rights already given by the company to other persons under ordinary trading contracts (*George Barker (Transport) Limited v Eynon* [1974] 1 W.L.R. 462 at 473). It is also subject to the rights of third parties to set off against amounts payable by them to the company (i) amounts which accrued due to them from the company before they received notice of the receiver's appointment, or (ii) amounts subsequently accruing due from the company if these are closely connected with the claims of the company against the third parties concerned (*Business Computers Limited v Anglo-African Leasing Limited* [1977] 1 W.L.R. 578).

The position is similar if a *Mareva* injunction has been granted, the effect of which is to restrain the company from removing a certain asset outside the jurisdiction. If a receiver is subsequently appointed under a floating charge which covers that asset and which also provides for the receiver to be the agent of the company, the receiver, as the company's agent, is bound by the injunction. But the holder of the floating charge is not so bound and, in his capacity as an equitable assignee of the asset concerned, he may be able to assert a right to have the asset discharged from the injunction (*Cretanor Maritime Co Limited v Irish Marine Management Limited* [1978] 1 W.L.R. 966).

Registration of charges

Part III of the Companies Act 1948, that is to say, sections 95 to 106 inclusive, contains provisions regarding the registration of certain kinds of charges affecting companies which are registered in England or companies incorporated outside Great Britain which have an established place of business in England.

The principal provision is section 95(1). This provides that every charge to which the section applies which is created by a company registered in England shall, so far as any security on the company's property or undertaking is conferred thereby, be void against the liquidator and any creditor of the company *unless* the prescribed particulars of the charge together with the instrument, if any, by which the charge is created or evidenced are delivered to the Registrar of Companies for registration within 21 days after the date of the charge's creation. Section 95(1) also provides that when the charge becomes void, the money secured thereby shall immediately become payable.

It should be noted that section 95 does not make registration of the charge a condition of its validity. What the section requires is the delivery to (or receipt by) the Registrar of Companies of the prescribed particulars, together with the instrument, if any, by which the charge is created or evidenced: *N.V. Slavenburg's Bank v Intercontinental Ltd.* [1980] 1 All E.R. 955 at 963H.

Where the charge is created by an English company the prescribed particulars have to be completed on a Form No. 47. However if the charge secures a series of debentures to the benefit of which the holders of the debentures in that series are entitled *pari passu*; the relevant form is Form No. 47a.

Section 95(2) lists nine kinds of charge to which the section applies. These are:-

(a) a charge for the purpose of securing *any issue of debentures*;

(b) a charge on *uncalled share capital* of the company;

(c) a charge created or evidenced by an instrument which, if executed by an individual, would require registration as a *bill of sale*;

(d) a charge on *land* wherever situate, or any interest therein, but not including a charge for any rent or other periodical sum issuing out of land;

(e) a charge on *book debts* of the company;

(f) a *floating charge* on the undertaking or property of the company;

(g) a charge on *calls made* but not paid;

(h) a charge on a *ship or aircraft* or any share in a ship;

(i) a charge on *goodwill*, on a *patent* or a licence under a patent, on a *trademark* or on a *copyright* or a licence under a copyright.

To decide whether section 95 applies to a transaction, the following questions have to be considered:

(1) does the transaction constitute a *charge* – rather than, for instance, an outright sale or an agreement for a future security?

(2) does it constitute a charge *"created"* by the company?

(3) is the charge one to which the *section applies*?

Question One – Does the transaction constitute a charge?

Section 95(10) provides that the expression "charge" includes mortgage, but apart from that there is no definition of the term. A charge may be said to be created where property is expressly or constructively made liable, or specially appropriated to, the discharge of a debt. A mortgage may be said to be created where property is conveyed or assigned to a creditor subject to an expressed or implied right of redemption in the debtor or where a specifically enforceable agreement is made so to convey or assign property (See generally *Swiss Bank Corporation v. Lloyds Bank Limited* [1980] 2 All E.R. 419 at 425, *Re Bond Worth Limited* [1980] 1 Ch. 228 at 250, and *Snell's Equity*, 28th edition, pages 386 and 437. Generally a mere *chargee* cannot foreclose, but see *Sadler v Worley* [1894] 2 Ch. 170.)

In determining whether a transaction constitutes a mortgage or charge, it is the substance and not the form of the transaction which has to be considered. Where the transaction is the subject of a written agreement, the substance of the transaction evidenced by the agreement must be looked at, and not its mere words. (This is demonstrated by *Helby v Matthews* [1895] A.C. 471 at 475. Thus the fact that an assignment is expressed to be given "as security" does not necessarily mean it is a charge: *Siebe Gorman v Barclays Bank* [1979] 2 Ll. Rep. 142 at 161.) It follows that it is impossible for the parties to a transaction by way of mortgage or charge to alter the effect of section 95 by adopting a form which does not accord with the real transaction between them (*Saunderson v Clark* (1913) 29 T.L.R. 579). But it should be noted that the fact that the transaction was one of financing is immaterial to the question of whether it constitutes a charge, because financing can be done by means of a mortgage or, for instance, by means of a sale (*Re George Inglefield Limited* [1933] 1 Ch. 1 at 27; *Manchester Railway Co v North Central Wagon Co.* (1888) 13 App. Cas. 554 at 567). In other words, the question is not with what object the alleged lenders employ their money, but the method they have of employing it (*Olds Discount Co. Limited v Cohen* [1938] 3 All E.R. 281F, cited with approval by Lord Scarman in *Lloyds & Scottish Finance v Cyril Lord Carpets*, 1979 H.L. (unreported)). "If the method employed constitutes a sale, the mere fact that its purpose is an advance of money will not convert the transaction into a loan" (per Lord Scarman in *Lloyds & Scottish*: see also *Olds Discount Co. Limited v Playfair Limited* [1938] 3 All E.R. 275 at 277A).

These principles generally fall to be applied in two types of case, the question typically being whether the transaction concerned was an outright sale, or a mortgage or charge with an equity of redemption being left in the grantor.

Sham document. In a normal case, the court will consider the documents as they stand, treating them fairly, and approach them without a sinister desire to impute to them something which they do not contain (*Re George Inglefield* at 20 and 22). Nevertheless, if, upon an examination of all the relevant circumstances, the court finds, as a matter of fact, that the real transaction was one of loan and security, and that a document taking the form of an outright transfer on sale was a "sham", or a mere pretence intended to conceal or disguise the true nature of the business, the court will disregard the form of the document and decide the case by reference to the real transaction (see for example *Madell v Thomas* [1891] 1 Q.B. 230). But, for a document to be held to be a "sham", it must be shown that there was another independent contract which the document purported to conceal, that the parties really made some other and different contract between them (*Garnac v Faure and Fairclough* [1966] 1 Q.B. 650 at 672A and 684A; see also *Barton v Bank of New South Wales* [1890] 15 App. Cas 379). Further, both, and not just one, of the parties to the transaction must have intended the documents to mask a loan (*Stoneleigh Finance Limited v Phillips* [1965] 2 Q.B. 537); see generally the chapter on shams in *Tolley's Tax Planning*. Thus, even where the original documented intention of the parties was to enter into a loan, but on receiving legal advice that a loan would be unlawful the parties drop the idea of a loan and decide that the transaction should be, for instance, a sale and leaseback, with an option to purchase for £1, the sale and leaseback documents will not be held to be shams, provided that the parties bona fide substituted the sale and leaseback transaction for the loan transaction, and intended to act accordingly (*Yorkshire Railway Wagon Company v Maclure* (1882) 21 Ch. D. 309, *Stoneleigh* at 579).

Implied equity of redemption. Although the document in question may take the form of an absolute or outright conveyance or assignment of the type made on a sale, the court will hold the document to be one of security if it discovers, on the face of the document, either in express words or by necessary implication, an equity of redemption in the grantor (*Re Kent and Sussex Sawmills Limited* [1947] 1 Ch. 177). Thus in the *Re Kent and Sussex Sawmills* case, the company instructed a third party to pay to the company's bank to which the company was indebted all moneys payable to the company under a supply contract between the company and the third party. The instructions stated that they were to be regarded as irrevocable unless the bank should consent to their cancellation. The court held that this language disclosed by implication an equity of redemption and that the transaction was one of charge (see too *Sanderson v Clark* (1913) 29 L.R. 579 and contrast *Re George Inglefield*, above).

Distinction between a sale and a charge. In *Re George Inglefield Ltd*, Romer L.J. pointed out the essential differences between a transaction of sale and a transaction of mortgage or charge:

(a) in a sale, the vendor is not entitled to get back the property by returning to the purchaser the money that has passed between them, but in a mortgage the mortgagor is entitled (until he has been foreclosed) to get back the property by returning the money that has passed between them;

(b) in a sale, if the purchaser resells the property for more than he paid, he does not have to account to the vendor for the profit; but if a mortgagee realises the property for a sum in excess of the amount he advanced (plus interest and costs) he must account to the mortgagor for the surplus; and

(c) in a sale, if the purchaser resells the property for less than he paid
     for it, he cannot recover the difference from the vendor; but if a
     mortgagee realises the property for less than the amount advanced
     by him (plus interest and costs), he can recover the balance from
     the mortgagor (though see *Siebe Gorman v Barclays Bank*, below
     for other indications of a mortgage, and see Lord Harworth M.R.
     at page 21 in *Re George Inglefield* and *Snell's Equity*, 28th edition,
     page 389).

However, the findings in *Siebe Gorman v Barclays Bank* [1979] 2 Ll.
Rep. 142 are noteworthy. There a company executed a deed of
assignment of certain bills of exchange in favour of a creditor, the
assignment being expressed to be "in consideration of the extension of
credit facilities on the part of the assignee to the assignor and as security
for the aforementioned debt" of the assignor to the assignee. The bills,
and a letter of credit also assigned, had a total face value lower than the
amount of the company's debt. It was held, against the factual background of the case and in the light of the actual words used, that the
assignment was not a charge. Nor was the assignment, although
outright, a sale. Instead it amounted to an agreement that the company's debt should be discharged to the extent of what the assignee
actually received from the bills assigned.

Where a company sells property in a financing transaction but is given
the option to repurchase the property for the original price, it is liable to
be argued that the option to repurchase is really an equity of redemption. This is particularly so if the documents provide for the option to
terminate on the occurence of those "events of default" in which
security under a debenture is commonly made to become enforceable.
However, *prima facie*, an absolute conveyance does not become a
mortgage merely because the vendor stipulates that he shall have a right
to purchase, provided that the conveyance contains nothing to show that
the relationship of debtor and creditor is to exist between the parties:
Alderson v White 2 D & J 105; *Manchester Railway Co. v North Central
Wagon Co.* (1888) 13 App. Cas. 554 at 568. Moreover, as regards their
legal incidents, there is all the difference in the world between a
mortgage, and a sale with a right of repurchase, despite the fact that if
the transaction is completed by redemption or repurchase as the case
may require there is no difference in the actual result (the *Manchester
Railway Co.* case and *Becket v Tower Assets Co. Limited* [1891] 1
Q.B.1; compare *Olds Discount v Cohen* at 283 B, but note L.P.A. 1925
s. 205(1) (xvi)). Thus, in the absence of other factors, a right of
repurchase should not, of itself, result in a conveyance or assignment
being treated as one made by way of mortgage. If, however, there is also
a right for the purchaser to require the vendor to repurchase the
property for the original price – particularly if the documents provide
for this right to be enforceable in what would be the normal "events of
default" in a debenture – the likelihood of the transaction being treated
as a mortgage is greatly increased, because the effect of such a right is to
give the so-called purchaser an entitlement to recover the amount paid

by him. In short, if the "vendor" has a right to get back the property transferred by him by paying an amount based on the original purchase price plus interest, and the "purchaser" has a right to get back the money paid by him by requiring the "vendor" to repurchase that property, it may be difficult to explain the true nature of the transaction otherwise than in terms of a mortgage (see *AA v Australian Secured Deposits [1973]* 1 NZLR 417 and *Fisher & Lightwood on Mortgages*, 9th edition, page 10).

Present not future right. In order to be registrable under section 95, an agreement has to be so expressed as to create a present equitable right to a security. If it is so expressed as to be merely an agreement that in some future circumstances a security shall in the future be created, it does not require registration, at all events, not before the specified circumstances have arisen (*Re Jackson & Basford Limited* [1906] 2 Ch. 467 at 477, applied in *Williams v Burlington Investments Limited* (H.C.) (1977) 121 S.J. 424; see also *National Provincial and Union Bank of England v Charnley* [1924] 1 K.B. 431 at 449). Thus in the *Burlington Investments* case it was not necessary to register a contract by a purchaser of land to create in future on request by the vendor a legal charge on so much of the land as should not at the time of the request have been sold on by the purchaser, the charge securing, inter alia, any extra sale price that might be or become due on the purchaser obtaining planning permission (cf. *Property Discount Corp. v Lyon Group* [1981] 1 W.L.R. 300 at 311). But an agreement for value to create security, for instance, to execute a charge of land by way of legal mortgage, may constitute a present equitable mortgage. Further, where a company agrees for valuable consideration to issue secured debentures to a person, or to issue them to him when called upon to do so, the person may be held to be entitled to the security and to occupy the position of a secured creditor, notwithstanding that the debentures concerned have not actually been issued (*Pegge v Neath & District Railway Co. Limited* [1898] 1 Ch. 183; *Simultaneous Colour Printing v Fowermaker* [1901] 1 K.B. 771; *Levy v Abercorris Slate Co.* 37 Ch. D. 260). In such instances, it is thought that the agreement, while still executory, would be registrable because it creates, subject to sections 40 and 53 of the Law of Property Act 1925, a present equitable right to a security (*Re Jackson & Basford Limited* [1906] 2 Ch. 467 at 477; *Re Port Supermarket Limited* [1978] 1 NZLR 330; cf. *Re Gregory Love & Co.* [1916] 1 Ch. 203 at 211).

But it has to be borne in mind that, where a creditor making an advance takes from the debtor a promise to execute a charge at the request of the creditor, the court will, in the absence of any other circumstances, readily infer that the purpose of the parties – i.e. the debtor as well as the creditor – was to give the creditor a right to be preferred on request. Such an arrangement, although for value, is fraudulent and unenforceable, and when the debtor in performance of his promise in fact creates the charge at the request of the creditor, the court again, in the absence of any other circumstances, will readily infer that the intention of the debtor is to prefer the creditor (*Re Eric Holmes Property Limited* [1965]

Ch. 1052 at 1067). Despite this, a charge created in pursuance of such a fraudulent arrangement cannot be set aside as a fraudulent preference if the winding up of the company commences more than six months after the creation of the charge, nor can the charge be avoided under section 172 of the Law of Property Act 1925 (*Re Lloyds Furniture Palace* [1925] Ch. 853). It is clear, however, that these considerations do not apply to the undertaking of the kind normally included in an equitable mortgage or charge to execute a legal mortgage upon demand. It also seems that the legal mortage, when executed, does not have to be registered if the original equitable mortgage was registered (*Re William Hall (Contractors) Limited* [1967] 1 W.L.R. 948).

Question Two: Did the company "create" the charge?

By its terms, section 95(1) applies only to a charge "created" by a company. Accordingly, the lien of an unpaid vendor does not require registration, because it is the creature of the law and does not depend upon contract; it is a charge arising by operation of law (*London and Cheshire Co. v Laplagrene Co* [1971] Ch. 499). Similarly, it seems clear that if a company's solicitor has a lien over the company's papers in his possession until his bill of costs is paid, such a lien is not registrable because it arises under the general law. (The position may be otherwise where the company has not acted according to the ordinary course of business but so as to give their solicitor an advantage by its own direct act.) It also seems that such a lien – being a mere right to retain possession of the papers – is not a mortgage or charge: *Brunton v English Electrical Corporation* [1892] 1 Ch. 434. Likewise, a charging order on land imposed by the court does not required registration (*Re Overseas Aviation Limited* [1963] Ch. 24). By contrast, an equitable mortgage or charge created by deposit of title deeds requires registration, because it is a contractual charge and does not arise by operation of law (*Re Wallis and Simmonds (Builders) Limited* [1974] 1 All E.R. 561). But where a contract for the sale of land provides that the purchaser should give the vendor a legal charge on the land for such of the purchase price as is to remain outstanding, the vendor's lien for the unpaid purchase price must be taken to have been abandoned when the legal charge is executed on completion. Thus it will not be available to the vendor if his legal charge subsequently becomes void for non-registration (*Capital Finance Co. v Stokes* [1969] 1 Ch. 261; *Burston Finance Limited v Speirway* [1974] 3 All E.R. 735). Moreover, when an equitable charge is created by deposit of title deeds, the implied right of the chargee to retain the deeds does not constitute a separate or independent lien which will survive the avoidance of the charge under the section (*Re Molton Finance Limited* [1968] Ch. 325).

Finally the terms of section 95(1) make it clear that a charge is registrable, notwithstanding that there exists no instrument by which the charge is created or evidenced. An exception to this is section 95(2)(c). For a charge to be registrable under that provision, it must be created or evidenced by an instrument which, if executed by an individual, would require registration as a bill of sale.

Question Three – Is the charge one to which the section applies?

Not every charge created by a company requires registration. To be registrable a charge must fall within one of the categories specified in section 95(2), when read with sections 95(6) and (7). Thus, if a company gives a fixed charge over shares which it holds in another company, the charge will not be registrable, unless it is given for the purpose of securing an issue of debentures. Certain of the specified categories will now be considered in turn.

(1) *A charge for the purpose of securing any issue of debentures*
The term "debenture" is defined in section 455 of the Act, and the scope of this definition has been considered in the chapter on *Borrowings*, page 142. The better view is that there is not "any *issue* of debentures" within section 95(2)(a) if a debenture is issued to a single person. The phrase "issue of debentures" refers to a number of debentures issued at a particular time or so connected together in some other way as to form a collective group. Thus the word "issue" must be read as referring in a collective sense to the aggregate of a number of individual debentures issued by a company (*A.A. v Australian Secured Deposits Limited* [1973] 1 NZLR 417). A charge securing an issue of debentures is registrable whatever the nature of the charged property. Moreover, such a charge is registrable whether the debentures are issued by the company creating the charge or by some other person. If the charge secures a series of debentures, and the holders of the debentures of that series are entitled to the benefit of that charge *pari passu*, section 95(8) will apply. Consequently delivery of the deed containing the charge or, if there is no such deed, of one of the debentures of the series (together with a Form No. 47a giving the particulars mentioned in that section) will be sufficient. But this is subject to the proviso to section 95(8) (as substituted by the 1980 Act), which requires there to be sent to the Registrar a Form 48 containing particulars of the date and amount of each issue in the series.

(2) *A charge on uncalled share capital of the company*
The "property" of a company does not include uncalled capital: *Re Russian Spratts Patent Limited* [1898] 2 Ch. 149. Accordingly, if a charge on uncalled capital is to be taken, the company's objects clause and the debenture should include an express reference thereto (though note *Palmer's Debentures* at page 40). Moreover, before a charge of uncalled capital is taken, one should check to see whether the company has passed a special resolution under section 60 of the Companies Act 1948 to the effect that a part of its uncalled capital shall only be capable of being called up in a liquidation, since any uncalled capital which is subject to such a resolution cannot later be charged (*Re Mayfair Property Co.* [1898] 2 Ch. 28. This case indicates that a section 60 resolution cannot be revoked by another special resolution). In the

absence of a court order, a receiver will have no power to make calls, unless the charge gave him authority to do so and the company's articles enable the directors to delegate to a receiver the power to make calls. If the company is wound up, a receiver can only make calls by using the name of the liquidator (*Re Westminster Syndicate Limited* 99 L.T. 924 and *Sadler v Worley* [1894] 2 Ch. 170).

(3) *A charge created or evidenced by an instrument which, if executed by an individual, would require registration as a bill of sale*
The relevant statutes are the Bills of Sale Act 1878 and the Acts of 1882, 1890 and 1891. Section 4 of the 1878 Act, when read in the light of section 3, contains an elaborate definition of "bill of sale". Very broadly, however, the term will include (i) every document transferring property (or an equitable interest) in personal chattels or giving a charge on them, where the transferee or chargee does not take *possession* of the chattels but is given power to do so, and (ii) any document giving an authority to take possession of personal chattels as security for any debt. But "transfers of goods in the ordinary course of business of any trade or calling" are excluded from the section. So too are "documents used in the ordinary course of business as proof of the possession or control of goods". The same section (in conjunction with section 5) defines "personal chattels". The main items are goods and other articles capable of complete transfer by delivery and fixtures. But fixtures, other than trade machinery, which are assigned together with the land or building to which they are fixed, are excluded. And the term does not include choses in action.

Generally, therefore, any document creating a charge over goods of a company will require registration under the section, provided that the document is one whereby the chargee has power to seize or trace possession of the goods (as to which see *4 Halsbury's Laws*, para. 608, note 6 and para. 613, note 9), unless the transaction falls within one of the following exceptions:

(a) The section will not apply if possession of the goods concerned passes immediately to the chargee independently of any document, by their being delivered, actually or constructively, to the chargee (*Dublin City Distillery Limited v Doherty* [1914] A.C. 823, *Wrightson v McArthur* [1921] 2 K.B. 807 and *Re David Allester* [1922] 2 Ch. 211). If as a result of another transaction the person claiming the security is already in possession of the chattel, no further delivery or overt change in possession is necessary. However, it must be shown that the security was intended to be by way of pledge, and not some other form, such as a bill of sale or equitable charge: *R.A. Barrett & Co Limited v Livesey* (C.A.) (1980) (unreported).

(b) Where possession does not pass, the section will not apply if either the document containing the charge is a document "used in the ordinary course of business as proof of the possession or control of the goods" (*Re Hamilton Young & Co.* [1905] 2 K.B. 772), or constitutes a transfer of "goods in the ordinary course of business of any trade or calling".

(c) The Act of 1891 (amending that of 1890) provides a general exemption for instruments creating any security on imported goods, provided the document is executed before the goods are deposited in a warehouse or factory, reshipped for export or delivered to a purchaser (other than the charging company). But this exemption does not cover a document which purports to create a general charge on all future goods, whether imported or not. The exemption seems to be limited to charges over particular goods which can be identified at the time of the creation of the charge, for example a consignment of goods arriving by a particular ship (*N.V. Slavenburg's Bank v Intercontinental Ltd.* [1980] 1 All E.R. 955 at 976).

(d) Section 4 of the 1878 Act excludes "bills of sale of goods in foreign parts or at sea" and it seems that this section, when taken with section 24, excepts bills of sale over goods situate in Scotland or Northern Ireland (*Coote v Jecks* (1872) L.R. 13 Eq. 597).

The Bills of Sale Acts apply to individuals only, and not to corporations at all (*N.V. Slavenburg's Bank v Intercontinental Ltd.* [1980] 1 All E.R. 955 at 975).

(4) *A charge on land, wherever situate, or any interest therein, but not including a charge for any rent or other periodical sum issuing out of land.*
It is not possible to consider here the numerous cases as to what has been held to constitute an "interest in land" for the purposes of various enactments. It may, however, be noted that a right to be granted leases under a building agreement, conditional upon the grantee's completing the development, seems to be an interest in land for the purposes of section 95 (*Property Discount Corporation Limited v Lyon Group Limited* [1981] 1 W.L.R. 300). Also, an option to purchase land (which vests in the grantee the right to call for a conveyance of the land without any further act by the grantor, creates an equitable interest in the land (*Pritchard v Briggs* [1980] Ch. 388). But section 95(7) provides that the holding of debentures entitling the holder to a charge on land shall not for the purposes of section 95 be deemed to be an interest in land.

It is to be noted that, by section 3(7) and (8) of the Land Charges Act 1972, a land charge for securing money which is created as a floating charge does not require registration under the Land Charges Act 1972 if it is registered under section 95 (see the *Property Discount Corporation* case, where registration under section 95 against the chargor company was sufficient although it was not the estate owner). So far as registered land is concerned, the registration of a charge under section 95 does not affect dealings with such land (*Ruoff and Roper on Registered Conveyancing* at 689).

In the recent Canadian case of *Royal Bank of Canada v Madill* 120

D.L.R. 17, doubts were expressed as to whether a charge over "any other real property hereafter acquired by the company" could take effect as a valid fixed charge, because, among other reasons, it was said that there was not a sufficient description of the property for the purposes of the Statute of Frauds.

(5) *A charge on book debts of the company.*

This category of charge frequently gives rise to difficulties because the Companies-Act 1948 does not define "book debts". The leading case on the matter is *Paul & Frank Ltd. v Discount Bank Overseas Limited* [1967] Ch. 348 which provides authority for the following propositions. *First*, a debt is a book debt if it arises in the course of a business and, as a matter of practice, such a debt would, in the ordinary course of the business, be entered in well-kept books relating to the business. *Second*, although the case contains no *express* authority for this, it is thought that *Paul & Frank* supports the view that the debt must be such as is commonly entered in the relevant books *as a book debt* (or, at least, as a debt) (see pages 359G to 360A and 362A of the report). *Third*, the question whether any item is a book debt will generally resolve itself into a question of fact. Is accountancy practice such that the item is ordinarily entered as a book debt – or as a debt – in well kept books relating to a business of the type in question? If that is the accountancy practice, whether the debt was actually entered as such in the company's books is irrelevant. *Fourth*, a charge which covers future book debts under a future contract which, when that contract comes to be made, will constitute book debts (e.g. an ordinary contract for the sale of goods on credit) has to be distinguished from a charge of the benefit of an existing contract, if the benefit of that contract does not, at the date of the charge, comprehend any book debt. e.g. an insurance policy or a guarantee under which no moneys have become payable. The first type of charge is registrable. The second is not, because section 95(2)(e) does not apply to an existing contract which does not at the date of the charge comprehend a book debt notwithstanding that the contract may ultimately result in a book debt. However, in *Contemporary Cottages (NZ) Limited v Margin Traders Limited* [1981] 2 NZLR, it was said that it was illogical to distinguish in this way between debts under contracts which are in existence at the date of the charge and debts under contracts which are not. This distinction would involve the consequences that charges over the latter category of debt would be registrable, but charges over the former not registrable. In the New Zealand case, it was held that a charge over sums which would become payable under an existing construction contract when the work was completed was a charge on book debts. The debts were debts existing at the date of the charge, conditional upon completion of the work. Alternatively, they were "future debts", in the sense of debts which would only come into existence when the work which made them payable was completed, and the observations by Buckley J. in *Independent Automatic Sales Limited v Knowles & Foster* [1962] 1 W.L.R. 974 at 985 showed that such debts could be classified as "book debts". See also *Re Brush* (February 1983).

A bill of exchange given in respect of a book debt itself constitutes a book debt, whether or not it has been entered in the company's bills receivable book (*Dawson v Isle* [1906] 1 Ch. 633; *Siebe Gorman v Barclays Bank* [1979] 2 Ll. Rep. 142 at 158). But section 95(6) provides that where a negotiable instrument has been given to secure the payment of any book debts of a company, the deposit of the instrument for the purpose of securing an advance to the company shall not, for the purposes of section 95, be treated as a charge on those book debts.

Frequently, a bank will issue a bond or a guarantee, or will make advances against a charge over moneys standing to the credit of a company's account with it. (Note that in *National Westminster Bank v Halesowen Presswork* [1972] A.C. 785 it doubted whether a debtor could have a lien over his own indebtedness to his creditor; but see *Swiss Bank Corpn. v Lloyds Bank* [1981] 2 All E.R. 449 at 452). Such a credit balance represents a debt from the bank to the company (*Foley v Hill* [1848] 2 H.L. Cas 28; *Parker v Marchant* 1 Ph. 356 at 361). Is such a debt a book debt for the purposes of the section? There is no English case directly in point, but, in three cases at first instance, none of which concerned section 95 or any comparable provision, it has been held that cash at bank did not constitute a book debt (*Re Stevens* [1888] W.N. 110, 116, *Re Haigh* [1907] 51 S.J. 345 – cases on construction of wills – and the case referred to in *Dawson v Isle* at 634). Morover, in a New Zealand case concerning a charge which excluded "book and other debts" from the charged property, it was held that a balance lying to the credit of the company with its bankers was not a book debt, although it fell within the expression "other debts" (*Watson v Parapara Coal Co. Limited* [1915] 17 GLR 791). It is therefore thought that, at least in the case of a normal trading company, a company's bank balance is not a book debt in so far as ordinary accountancy practice is to enter such a balance in the books concerned as "cash at bank" and not as a debt.

It has been held that bonds of railways companies belonging to a firm constituted book debts of the firm (*Re Stevens*, above, but the report does not indicate the nature of the firm's business). However it is felt that it is only in the case of an investment or financial company that securities of this kind are likely to be book debts, and then only if accountancy practice is such that securities of that type are ordinarily entered in the books of such companies as debts, and not, for instance, as investments.

There are many ways in which a charge over a book debt may be created; and to operate as an equitable assignment or charge no particular form of words is required in the document (*Durham Brothers v Robertson* [1898] 1 Q.B. 765 at 769; *William Brandt's v Dunlop* [1905] A.C. 454 at 462). In particular, an agreement between a debtor and a creditor that the debt owing shall be paid out of a specific fund coming to the debtor, or an order given by a debtor to his creditor upon a person owing money or holding funds belonging to the giver of the order, directing such person to pay such funds to the creditor, will create a valid equitable charge upon such fund. But this is only if the agreement, as well as providing that the fund shall be applied in a particular way, also imposes an obligation in favour of the creditor to pay the debt out of the fund (*Rodick v Gandell* [1852] 1 De GM&G 763 at 778; *Palmer v Carey* [1926] A.C. 703; *Swiss Bank Corporation v Lloyds Bank Limited* [1981] 2 All E.R. 449 at 453). Thus, an undertaking to pay a specified sum out of the first moneys to be received on a future sale of certain rights constituted a good equitable assignment of the moneys (*Cotton v Heyl* [1930] 1 Ch. 510). And a letter from a company to its customer instructing the customer to pay to the company's account at its bank all amounts payable by the customer, and stating that the instructions were to be regarded as irrevocable without the bank's consent, constituted a charge on the book debts of the company (*Re Kent & Sussex Sawmills Limited* [1947] 1 Ch. 177, *Walter & Sullivan Limited v Murphy Limited* [1955] 2 Q.B. 584, *Paul & Frank Ltd v Discount Bank (Overseas) Limited* [1967] Ch. 348 at 364).

The question also arises whether an agreement giving a bank an express right to set off its customer's deposits or balances with it against its customer's debts or liabilities to it, amounts to a charge created by the customer over its deposits or balances. There are differing opinions, but the more widely held view seems to be that such an agreement does not constitute a charge. The basis of this view is that such an agreement only gives the bank simple contract rights of set off, and does not give it any security interest in the customer's balances (see, for instance, *Goode's Commercial Law* at p. 719). Some support for this view may be provided by the fact that the contractual settlement arrangements in the *British Eagle* case ([1975] 1 W.L.R. 758) were held not to create charges, although it should be borne in mind that the British Eagle clearing house system for multilateral settlements was of a somewhat different nature from that of a bilateral set off agreement between a bank and its customer. The real difficulty of such set off contracts arises from certain dicta in the *British Eagle* case. These dicta can be taken to suggest that, if or to the extent that such a contract gives the bank wider (or more preferential) rights of set off than those conferred by section 31 of the Bankruptcy Act 1914, the contract may be void for reasons of public policy, at least in an insolvent winding up of the customer. This is on the ground that it would achieve a distribution of the customer's property which runs counter to the principles of English involvency legislation; or, at least if a charge on the customer's balances would have been a charge on book debts (as to which question, see above), on the ground that the contract would give the bank a position analogous to that of a secured creditor without the need for the creation and registration of a charge over the customer's book debts.

It is now clear that it is legally possible to create a fixed charge over future book debts. Further, where a company gave its bank an all-moneys debenture containing fixed mortgages or charges over the company's premises, goodwill, uncalled capital and over "all book debts and other debts now and from time to time due or owing to the Company" and a floating charge over all other assets of the company, the court rejected a contention that the charge of the book debts could only amount to a floating charge (*Siebe Gorman v Barclays Bank* [1979] 2 LL. Rep 142. The company undertook to pay into its account with the bank all moneys which it might receive in respect of the book and other debts which were charged, not to charge or assign the same in favour of any other person without the bank's prior consent and to execute a legal assignment of such debts to the bank, if required. By contrast, in *Re Armagh Shoes Ltd.* (1981) N. Ireland (unreported), a charge expressed to be a fixed charge over receivables, debtors, plant, machinery, fixtures, fittings and ancillary equipment was held to be a floating charge as regards all the assets concerned, *Siebe Gorman* being distinguished on the ground that the company had not been given any such undertakings as were given in that case).

An assignment by way of mortgage of any entire debt with a proviso for redemption and re-assignment, and an assignment of an entire debt expressed to be by way of continuing security, are absolute assignments (not purporting to be by way of charge only) for the purposes of section 136 of the Law of Property Act 1925 (*Tancred v Delagoa Bay Railway Co.* (1889) 23 Q.B.D. 239; *Hughes v Pump House Hotel Co.* [1902] 2 K.B. 190, respectively). The House of Lords has confirmed that a normal "block discounting" scheme for hire purchase debts, where, in return for an immediate advance, the hire purchase company sells to the finance house at a fixed discount the debts arising from its hire purchase agreements constitutes a sale, and not a charge, of the debts concerned: *Lloyds & Scottish Finance Limited v Cyril Lord Carpets* [1979] (unreported).

(6) *A floating charge on the undertaking or property of a company*
The characteristics of a floating charge have been considered under *Fixed and Floating Charges*, above. A floating charge on part only of the undertaking or of the property of a company is registrable (*Re Yorkshire Woolcombers Association Limited* [1903] 2 Ch. 284 at 298). A charge which does not cover property of the type referred to in the other paragraphs of section 95(2) is registrable if it is a floating charge.

The remaining three categories of charge specified in section 95(2) are listed on page 185 above.

Foreign property

Section 95 applies to a charge created by a company registered in England, even if the charged property is not situate in England. If it is situate outside the United Kingdom and the charge is also created out of the United Kingdom, then section 95(3) applies. This provides that it is sufficient if a copy of the instrument creating the charge (certified as correct in accordance with paragraph 6 of the Companies (Forms) Regulations 1979) is delivered and received by the Registrar of Companies within 21 days after the date on which such instrument or copy could, in due course of post and, if despatched with due diligence, have been received in the United Kingdom.

Section 95(5) applies where a charge comprises property situate in Scotland or Northern Ireland and registration of the charge is necessary in that country. It provides that delivery to the Registrar of Companies in England of a Form No. 47c certifying that the charge has been presented for registration in Scotland or Northern Ireland has the same effect as the delivery of the instrument itself.

Date of creation

Where a charge is created by an instrument executed by the company, the charge is created on the date on which the company executes the instrument, and not on any subsequent date on which the money to be secured is advanced (*Esberger & Son Limited v Capital and Counties Bank* [1913] 2 Ch. 366). The position is similar if a charge is given of future property, for instance, of book debts which may accrue in the future. Although the charge is not effective until property comes into existence on which the charge can operate, it seems that the charge is created when the instrument containing it is executed, for no further action on the part of the grantor is required to bring the charge to life (*Independent Automatic Sales Limited v Knowles & Foster* [1962] 1 W.L.R. 974 at 985; but see *Security Trust Co. v Royal Bank of Canada* [1976] A.C. 503 at 521C). *Re Spiral Globe (No. 2)* [1902] 2 Ch. 209 concerned a case where bearer debentures, without a trust deed and containing a floating charge, were not issued to and deposited with the company's bankers until more than three months after they had been sealed by the company (their having remained in the company's possession during that time). It was held that the charge was created on the date of sealing and not when the debentures were issued. It is thought that a charge will be created when the charge document is signed by the company, even though there are other partners who have not yet signed. The question is the date on which the charge under the document becomes effective in favour of the chargee. Leaving the date on the document blank until all partners have signed is of no relevance.

Where a trust deed securing an issue of debentures contains a charge in favour of the trustees, then the relevant date for the purposes of section 95(1) and (2)(a) is the date of the execution of the trust deed and not of the issue of the debentures: *Re New London Omnibus Co.* [1908] 1 Ch. 621. It makes no difference that a similar charge is also contained in the body of the debentures themselves.

A specifically enforceable agreement to execute a charge on the occurrence of a specified future event (except, probably, a mere demand for the charge by the intended chargee) will, it is thought, only become registrable when the specified event occurs, for at that point, and no earlier, the beneficiary of the agreement becomes entitled in equity to the charge (*Re Gregory Love & Co* [1916] 1 Ch. 203 at 211). This assumes the agreement does not otherwise constitute a present security (see *Re Property Discount Corporation v Lyon Group* [1981] 1 W.L.R. 300). But once the formal charge is executed, the conception of the equitable charge (and its abortion under the section) will not affect the position regarding the executed charge (*Williams v Burlington Investment Limited* (H.L.) (1977) 121 S.J. 424).

Substituted property

What is the position when property originally comprised in a duly registered specific charge is withdrawn and a specific charge is executed over other property to replace it? If the original charge was contained in a trust deed securing a series of debentures and section 95(8) was otherwise applicable, it seems clear from *Cunard Steamship Co. Ltd. v Hopwood* [1908] 2 Ch. 564 that the registration of the original charge protects the charge of the substituted property. But it is not certain how far that decision is applicable where the charges are given in favour of a single lender. In such a case it is thought that the prudent course is to register the charge of the substituted property, unless the original charge and the particulars delivered in respect of it extended and expressly referred to any substituted property. This is because in the *Cunard* case, the section required only "a general description of the property charged" (see now section 95(8) and Form 47a). By contrast, the form applicable where a single person is entitled to the charge (Form 47) requires "short particulars of the property charged."

Consequences of non-registration

If a charge and the required particulars are not delivered for registration within the specified period, three consequences follow. *First*, the charge becomes void as against the liquidator and any creditor of the company, but only so far as any security on the company's property or undertaking is conferred by the charge. This is without prejudice to any contract or obligation for the repayment of the money thereby secured. The charge is thus void in the event of a winding up. But if the charge is spent before the liquidation, the liquidator cannot defeat it under the section. Thus, if, before the liquidation, book debts assigned by way of charge are paid to the chargee or goods subject to a charge are seized by the chargee, the avoidance of the charge under the section does not enable the liquidator to reclaim the money received or goods seized by the chargee (*Slavenburg's Bank v Intercontinental Ltd.* [1980] 1 All E.R. 955 at 967). The charge is also, even before a winding up, void against any creditor including a subsequent registered incumbrancer who had express notice of the prior charge at the time when he took his own security: *Independent Automatic Sales v Knowles & Foster* [1962] 1 W.L.R. 974 at 981. It may follow that, if the company subsequently transfers the property subject to the charge to another company, then, unless the charge is not binding on the transferee for some other reason, for example for non-registration under the Land Charges Act 1972, the charge will no longer be liable to attack under section 95, even if the transferee company does not register it under section 97 (see *Acquisition of property subject to a charge*, below). This view is supported by the fact that the express terms of section 95(1) only make an unregistered charge void so far as it confers any security on the property or undertaking of the company which created the charge.

The *second* consequence of a failure to register is that when the charge becomes void the money which it secures becomes immediately payable. What is the position where the unregistered charge was given as a security for the debt of a third party? If the company which gave the charge gave no guarantee of the debt, it would seem that the debt, being the money secured by the charge (see *Re Conley* [1938] 2 All E.R. 127), immediately becomes payable under section 95(1) when the time for registration expires without the charge having been registered. But the position may be different if the charging company gave a guarantee of the debt, so that the money secured by the charge is not the debt itself but the amount which may become due under the guarantee. Here it is thought that the section does not operate so as to make that amount immediately payable under the guarantee if the principal debtor has not defaulted in making payment of the sums guaranteed.

The *third* consequence of non-registration is that the company and every officer who is in default becomes liable to a fine under section 96(3).

Remedying the position

If a charge and the required particulars are not delivered for registration within the specified time, the matter can be remedied in two ways. First, a fresh charge can be taken and duly registered. The new charge, though subject to any other charges or interests previously created by the company, should not be liable to be set aside as a fraudulent preference if the intention in creating it was to correct the omission to register the previous charge (compare *Re Tweedale* [1892] 2 Q.B. 216). Alternatively, if it can be shown that the omission to register was accidental or due to inadvertence or some other sufficient cause, or is not of a nature to prejudice the position of the creditors or shareholders of the company or that on other grounds it is just and equitable to grant relief, an application to the court may be made under section 101 for an order that the time for registration shall be extended. Normally, such an order will not be made after a company has gone into liquidation (*Re Mechanisations (Eaglescliffe) Limited* [1966] Ch. 20 at 36). This principle was confirmed in *Re Ashpurton Estates Ltd.* (1982) 126 S.J. 380, which also confirmed that, where a liquidation is imminent, that is a relevant factor to be taken into account by the court in considering an application for an extension of time under the section. An order extending the time for registration will now usually provide that it is to be without prejudice to the rights of parties acquired during the period between the date of the creation of the charge in question and the date of its actual registration. Where a company withdraws its opposition to an application under section 101, this may involve a fraudulent preference, but only if the requisite intention to prefer can be proved (*Peat v Gresham Trust Limited* [1934] A.C. 252).

Registrar's certificate

It is to be noted that section 98(2) provides that a certificate given by the Registrar of Companies of the registration of any charge shall be conclusive evidence that the requirements of Part III of the Act as to registration have been complied with. This means that once the Registrar's certificate is issued the charge cannot be set aside under section 95. This is so even if (a) the date inserted in the charge and the particulars delivered in respect of it was a date some three months later than the true date of the charge's creation (*Re C.L. Nye Limited* [1971] Ch. 442), or (b) the particulars delivered failed to mention some of the charged property (*National Provincial Bank v Charnley* [1924] 1 K.B. 431, but n.b. page 454 and compare *Re Eric Holmes (Property) Limited* [1965] Ch. 1052 at 1072A), or (c) or mentioned only the principal sum, and not interest or other sums, secured by the charge (*Re Mechanisations* above).

Acquisition of property subject to a charge

Section 95 applies only where a company *creates* a charge. If a company acquires property which is already subject to a charge of a kind which, if it had been created by the company after the acquisition of the property, would have been registrable under section 95, then section 97 applies. This requires the company to deliver to the Registrar of Companies the prescribed particulars and a certified copy of the charge within 21 days after the date on which the acquisition of the property is completed. There is a proviso that, if the property is situate and the charge was created outside Great Britain, the 21 days is to run from the date on which the particulars and copy of the charge could in due course of post, and if despatched with due diligence, have been received in the United Kingdom.

The consequence of failing to register a charge under section 97 is that the company and every officer of the acquiring company who is in default is liable to a fine under section 97(2). In contrast to the position under section 95, a failure to register a charge subject to which a company acquired property (and which it did not create) does not result in the charge becoming void or in the money which it secures becoming immediately payable. In the case of an English company, the relevant form is Form No 47b.

Section 97 only applies to what can truly be said to be a purchase of an equity of redemption, for instance, a purchase of land already subject to a mortgage created by someone else (*Security Trust Co v Royal Bank of Canada* [1976] A.C. 503 at 520). Contrast the case where a company agrees to buy property on terms that part of the purchase price will be left outstanding and will be secured by a mortgage of the property. In accordance with the ordinary conveyancing practice, the entirety of the property is conveyed to the company which then charges it in favour of the vendor by way of legal mortgage. Here it is not true to say that all that is purchased is the equity of redemption. Accordingly, the charge,

since it is created by the company, is registrable under section 95
(*Security Trust Co*, above, and *Capital Finance Co. Limited v Stokes*
[1969] 1 Ch. 261). Also, if a transfer of property to a company excepts
and reserves to the transferor an interest in the nature of a charge, it is
doubtful whether such an exception can operate otherwise than as an
implied grant back by the company of a charge to the transferor, which
will be registrable under section 95 (*Re Bond Worth Limited* [1980] 1
Ch. 228).

Other provisions of Part III

Certain of the remaining provisions of Part III of the 1948 Act may be
briefly noted. Section 99 requires the company to endorse a copy of the
Registrar's certificate of registration on every debenture or certificate of
debenture stock which is issued by the company, otherwise than before
the relevant charge was created, and which is secured by the charge
concerned.

Section 100 provides for the Registrar of Companies to make an
appropriate entry on the company's file upon receipt of a statutory
declaration in the prescribed form stating –

(a) that the debt for which the charge was given has been paid or
     satisfied in whole (Form No. 49) or in part (Form No.49a); or

(b) that part of the property or undertaking charged has been released
     from the charge (Form No.49a) or has ceased to form part of the
     charged property (Form No.49b).

It cannot be said that the forms which have been prescribed for the
purposes of section 100 (or indeed the wording of the section itself) are
entirely satisfactory. There is no prescribed form which clearly covers
the case where all the charged property is released, without the debt for
which the charge was given having been paid or satisfied in whole, or the
case where all the charged property is sold by the charging company.
The practice in such cases is to modify the prescribed forms appropriately.

Section 103 requires the company to keep at its registered office a copy
of every instrument creating any registrable charge. However, in the
case of a series of uniform debentures, a copy of one of them is
sufficient. Section 104 requires the company to keep at its registered
office a register of all charges specifically affecting property of the
company – this includes charges not of a type requiring registration
under section 95 or 97 (see *Re Overseas Aviation Limited* [1963] 1 Ch. 24
at 50). The register must also record all floating charges on the
undertaking or any property of the company. Section 105 gives any
creditor or member of the company a right to inspect the copies of the
instruments creating registrable charges and the register of charges kept
by the company, and provides that any other person may inspect the
register of charges.

Foreign companies

Section 106, as amended, provides that the provisions of Part III of the 1948 Act shall extend to charges on property in England which are created, and charges on property in England which is acquired, by a company incorporated outside Great Britain which has an established place of business in England. Certain points arising out of this section (but not what amounts to "an established place of business in England") were decided in *N.V. Slavenburg's Bank v Intercontinental Natural Resources Ltd* [1980] 1 All E.R. 955. First, section 106 applies to any company incorporated outside Great Britain which has an established place of business in England, and not just to companies incorporated in Northern Ireland. Secondly, it applies to such a company even if it has failed to register under Part X of the Companies Act 1948. Thirdly, it applies if the company had an established place of business in England at the date of the creation of the charge, even if it ceases to have one the next day. Fourthly, the section does not only apply to charges on property which is in England at the time the charge is created or the property acquired – it also applies in the case of future property in England. Finally, the expression "the liquidator" when used in section 95(1), as extended by section 106, is not confined to a liquidator in an English winding up under Part IX of the 1948 Act, but includes the foreign equivalent (whether in the place of incorporation or elsewhere) of an English liquidator. In other words, section 95 is applicable where there is a foreign proceeding in the nature of a winding up, and it is not necessary that there should also be a winding up in England under Part IX of the 1948 Act.

The main point to emerge from this case concerns the lender who takes a charge from a foreign company over present or future property in England (for instance, a charge over book debts owing to the charging company by persons resident in England). He will find that, under English law, his security over the assets in England will be void in the event of a foreign winding up, if he fails to register his charge and it subsequently transpires that, at the time the charge was created, the company had an established place of business in England. And this can happen, at least in the case of a charge covering future property, if the assets concerned are sent to England after the charge is created.

The *Slavenburg* case did not throw any further light on what is necessary for a company to have "an established place of business" in England. In the *Huron* case (1911 S.C. 612) it was said that the company must have "a local habitation of its own". This case (with which Cohen J. agreed in the *Rabenek* case [1944] 1 Ch. 404) shows that "establishing a place of business" is not the same as "carrying on business", and that a corporation will not be treated as having established a place of business in England merely because it carries on business in England through agents located there. In *Deverall v Grant Advertising* [1954] 3 All E.R. 389, an American company had an English subsidiary which carried on business at an address in London. The plaintiff had been the chairman of the English subsidiary and also "regional director" of the American company in the Sterling area. In the latter capacity, the plaintiff's functions were those of a consultant and co-ordinator; but there was no evidence that he carried on, on behalf of the American company, at the London address any trading or business activities, or entered into any contract on their behalf or did any other specific act of that sort. Moreover, the London premises were the offices of the English company, and there was no visible sign or physical indication that the American company was doing business at that address or had any connection with the premises. On those facts, it was held that the American company had not established a place of business in Great Britain (see also *Overseas Companies*).

The prescribed forms applicable to charges which are made registrable by section 106 are Forms No.F8 to F12b.

Scotland

The law in Scotland relating to company charges differs in several material respects from that in England and Wales. The rules as to the security which can be given, and the remedies available to lenders, differ. Also, the ability of a Scottish company to grant floating charges is governed by statute law, introduced for the first time in 1961 (see now the Companies (Floating Charges and Receivers) (Scotland) Act 1972). All Scottish companies may now create floating charges, and the Scots legislation now recognises floating charges created by English companies over assets in Scotland. The 1972 Act sets out a detailed code concerning floating charges, providing for instance that a floating charge can "crystallise" only on a winding up or on the appointment of a receiver and lays down the rules of priority between fixed and floating charges.

Part III A of the Companies Act 1948, added by the 1972 Act, contains provisions similar, but not identical, to those of Part III for the registration with the Registrar of Companies in Scotland of charges on property created or acquired by incorporated companies registered in Scotland and also, as regards property in Scotland, by companies incorporated outside Great Britain which have a place of business (not only an "established" place of business) in Scotland. Accordingly, a charge over Scottish property created by an English company with a place of business in Scotland does not require to be registered in Scotland under section 106K, whereas before the amendment to section 106 under the 1981 Act took effect on December 22, 1981, a charge over English property created by a Scottish company with an established place of business in England had to be registered in England under section 106 as well as in Scotland under section 106A.

Company Contracts

Preliminary contracts

A limited company has no legal existence prior to its registration and the issue by the Registrar of a certificate of incorporation. A company's promoters will, however, often enter into commitments in advance of incorporation to enable business to be commenced or a prospectus to be issued as soon as limited liability is achieved. (This is subject to restrictions imposed on public companies by section 4 of the Companies Act 1980, prohibiting the commencement of business if the company's share capital is less than the authorised minimum.) There will also be legal and accountancy costs generated by the company's formation, which may be sought to be attributed as a debt of the company itself. The problem attaching to these obligations is that they are incurred by agents on behalf of a non-existent principal, and the other contracting party is concerned to know who, if anybody, and when, he can sue to enforce his rights.

Common law

A contract by a non-existent company and the execution of supporting documents by its purported officers in its name is a nullity: *Newborne v Sensolid (G.B.) Ltd* [1954] I Q.B. 45. There is no-one in authority to enable legal relations to be created, nor anything for the company to ratify later in general meeting. It is immaterial that the intention or understanding of the company representative is that incorporation will afterwards take place. Nor does it matter whether the agent acts in the capacity of promoter or director: the company will not be bound.

If it was sought to make the agent personally liable, this could only be on the basis of a contract not with or on behalf of the company, but with the agent himself assuming the mantle of principal. It might be expected that this liability would be confined to contracts where the agent manifestly, by his words or actions, assumed a primary responsibility. But in *Kelner v Baxter* (1867) L.R. 2 C.P. 174 it was held that even though the proposed directors intended to act in an agency role the liability of principals was to be imputed to them, since there was no other way the agreement could be kept alive. Much depended, however, on the construction of the particular contract.

European Communities Act 1972

Section 9 (2) of the European Communities Act 1972 now provides that where a contract purports to be made by a company, or by a person as agent for the company, at a time when it has not been formed, then subject to any agreement to the contrary the contract has effect as one entered into by the person acting for the company or as agent for it, and he is personally liable accordingly. This removes the fine distinctions on the older authorities. The agent is liable whatever hat he wears. As the provision is subject to contrary agreement, it is open to the parties expressly to defer liability until the newly-formed company is available to adopt or novate the transaction: *Phonogram Limited v Lane* [1981] 3 All E.R. 182. The operation of section 9 (2) is not restricted to cases where the company is already in the process of formation. Neither does liability depend upon a representation that the company is already in existence, since the claim is not merely for damages for breach of warranty of authority.

Making the company liable

The following methods are commonly adopted to ensure that the *company* afterwards becomes an effective party to a pre-incorporation agreement:

(1) The contract can be made with a trustee for the company, and the memorandum or articles drafted to include a provision binding the directors to adopt it. There must, however, be a distinct new agreement, made by or on behalf of the company with full capacity, to enter into the terms of the previous obligation. At that point only is the original contract superseded and the personal liability of the trustee negatived.

(2) A new contract can be inferred from the conduct of the parties. If an agreement has been initialled for identification before incorporation and then the company treats itself as bound by it, the other party may be able to show that this amounts to a novation. This is, however, a risky course, since in *Howard v Patent Ivory Co.* (1888) 38 Ch.D 156 it was held insufficient that money had been spent and work done in the belief that a contract was in being. Facts sufficient to establish a replacement contract must point unequivocally to its existence.

(3) The promoters can prepare a draft contract showing the company as a party, but have it executed by the other party only. There will in the objects clause of the memorandum be a provision binding the company to execute upon incorporation, and indeed the text of draft resolutions may be annexed to the agreement. This method avoids the interim liability of a trustee, and is appropriate where the other contracting party is himself the promoter.

Provisional contracts

Before the coming into force of the Companies Act 1980, any contract made by a registered company before it was entitled to commence business was regarded as provisional, and became binding only upon the company commencing business. A private company was entitled to commence business as soon as it was incorporated, but a public company could only do so after complying with the requirements of section 109 of the Companies Act 1948. Section 109 is, however, repealed by Schedule 4 to the Companies Act 1980, consequent upon the abolition by Part I of that Act of the old distinction between public and private companies. The present position is governed by section 4 of the 1980 Act. This provides for the issue by the Registrar to a company registered as a public company of a certificate evidencing that the nominal value of the company's allotted share capital is not less than the authorised minimum (presently £50,000).

To secure a certificate there must be delivered to the Registrar a statutory declaration stating:

(a) the nominal value of the company's allotted share capital is not less than the authorised minimum;

(b) the amount paid up, at the time of the application, on the allotted share capital;

(c) the amount, or estimated amount, of the preliminary expenses of the company and the persons by whom any of those expenses have been paid or are payable; and

(d) any amount or benefit paid or given or intended to be paid or given to any promoter, and the consideration for the payment of the benefit (section 4(3)).

A certificate issued under this provision is conclusive evidence that the company is entitled to do business and exercise any borrowing powers. Contravention of section 4 is a criminal offence.

The provisions are stated to be without prejudice to the validity of any transaction entered into by a company. But if a company enters into a transaction unlawfully and fails to comply with its obligations to obtain a certificate within 21 days of being called upon to do so, the directors of the company are jointly and severally liable to indemnify the other party to the transaction in respect of any loss or damage suffered by him by reason of the failure to comply (section 4(8)). Thus the old rule of non-enforceability is abrogated since it was capable of causing hardship to a third party, and instead the contract remains valid and the officers assume a personal responsibility if, for example, the company subsequently goes into liquidation without discharging its indebtedness on the transaction.

The form of contract

Section 32 (1)(b) of the Companies Act 1948 provides that any contract which if made between natural persons would by law require to be in writing, signed by the parties to be charged, may be made on behalf of the company in writing, signed by any person acting under its authority, express or implied. Thus a contract disposing of an interest in

land, for which writing is required under section 40 of the Law of
Property Act 1925, requires the signature of an officer who, by board
resolution or otherwise, is empowered to bind his principal. Such a
contract may in the same manner be varied or discharged. Oral
contracts can, similarly, be made on behalf of the company by its
authorised agents (section 32(1)(c); a similar provision extends to other
corporations under the Corporate Bodies Contracts Act 1960, which
does not however apply to Scotland).

Board minutes

Many commitments of this kind will not require a board resolution,
since the agent will have a general authority, particularly if he is an
executive director or manager, to conduct certain aspects of the
company's business. In cases where transactions are of unusual value or
otherwise outside the usual course of business, it is a worthwhile
precaution to obtain a board minute in support of the executed
document or the oral arrangement. By section 145 of the Companies
Act 1948, where board minutes are made the board meeting is deemed
to have been duly held and convened, all proceedings duly carried
through and all directors validly appointed, until the contrary is proved.
A bill of exchange or promissory note shall be deemed to have been
validly made, accepted or endorsed on behalf of a company if the
transaction takes place in the company's name or on its behalf by any
person acting under its authority (C.A. 1948, s. 33).

If a document requires to be authenticated by a company, it may be
signed by a director, secretary or other authorised officer, and need not
be under its common seal. Thus where, for instance, certified copies of
documents are required for filing or stamping, a general authority to
sign vested in the company secretary is sufficient. Again, although
power to effect a transaction may require a board resolution, the ability
to execute a valid document in support is invariably trusted to persons
with usual authority of a continuing kind. Provided any requirements of
the articles have been met, it will be unnecessary to show that a
particular authority had been given to execute the document (*Duck v
Tower Galvanising Co* [1901] 2 K.B. 314).

The seal

Every company must have a common seal, engraven with its name, and
the use of a seal without a name is an offence (C.A. 1948, s. 108). The
seal is the official signature of the company, and is impressed upon those
documents which would, if executed by natural persons, be required to
be made by deed (C.A. 1948, s. 32(1)(a)). The number of documents
required under English law to be executed under seal are now few, but in
practice a company will affix its seal to a wide range of documents, for
example share certificates, debentures, mortgages, and contracts the
consideration for which is not clearly evidenced on the face of the
document. In Scotland the seal is required to be placed on all company

deeds: section 32(4). The articles of association will usually provide for the affixing of the seal to be evidenced by a director and the secretary, and an outsider will be on notice of the irregularity if this attestation does not appear. There is no legal requirement, however, that the seal be affixed in the presence of witnesses. As a matter of good company practice the secretary will record in a seal book each occasion of the seal's use; an automated record will be substituted where a mechanical process is employed for sealing a large number of share certificates each day. Where manuscript amendments are made to a typed deed, it is usual practice for each amendment to be initialled by the persons who evidenced the affixing of the seal. This is obviously good practice, though it appears not to be essential in the case of documents under seal, as there is a presumption that any manuscript or similar amendments were made prior to execution. There is not, however, a similar presumption for documents under hand.

If the sealed instrument appears regular on its face and not inconsistent with any restrictions imposed in the articles, an outsider is entitled to assume that due formality has been observed in the sealing (see *County of Gloucester Bank v Rudry* [1889] 1 Ch.629; *Re Barned's Banking Co* (1867) L. R. 3 Ch.105). This protection is, however, only an aspect of the "indoor management" principle of company law discussed below, and does not apply where the document is not merely irregularly executed, but has no authenticity at all. Thus if an officer of a company forges a share certificate and convinces outsiders of its validity by affixing a seal which it is within his power to do, the company is not prevented from aserting that the document is a forgery or otherwise invalidated *(Ruben v Great Fingall Consolidated* [1906] A.C. 439).

Where the requirements of the articles for the sealing or attestation of a deed are not met, a purchaser is protected under section 74 of the Law of Property Act 1925, if, nevertheless, the seal is affixed by the company's "clerk, secretary or other permanent officer or his deputy, and a member of the board of directors, council or other governing body". There must thus be two signatures of persons whose status can be verified. Although the Act speaks of a "purchaser", section 74 is not confined to a purchase deed (see definition (xxi) in section 205 of the 1925 Act). Conversely, some documents to which company seals are affixed do not qualify as deeds, e.g. a certificate of title to shares.

Conventionally, a deed executed by an individual requires to be delivered. This is not so in the case of corporations where the placing of the seal is itself evidence of delivery. The traditional words "signed, sealed and delivered" in the testatum of a deed are therefore replaced in the case of a company by the words "the common seal was affixed hereto in the presence of". The presumption of delivery causes a problem: how is a company to execute a deed in escrow, holding back its obligation until the fulfilment of some condition? This is said to be a matter of the intention of the parties, but the authorities appear to require that some positive act of retaining possession be proved to prevent the deed having immediate force *(Mowatt v Castle Steel Co.*

(1886) 34 Ch.D 58). It may be safer if the company executes a separate escrow agreement specifying the time and place at which the principal deed is to become operative.

Powers of attorney

Articles commonly provide for appointment by the directors of attorneys to discharge their functions in particular circumstances. In addition, section 34 of the Companies Act 1948 gives a specific power to appoint attorneys to execute deeds on a company's behalf outside the United Kingdom. In such a case the appointment must be made under seal. The attorney then signs with his own seal and binds the company thereby. The form and effect of powers of attorney is governed by the Powers of Attorney Act 1971. Such powers do not have to be deposited at the Central Office of the Supreme Court if executed after October 1, 1971. A power may be either general or special. If general, it will be strictly construed against the donee, and should therefore be drafted in sufficiently broad terms to cover every eventuality. Thus, if directors execute powers appointing fellow directors to give effect to a rights issue of shares by approving the form of circular to shareholders, it will be prudent to vest the donees with such other powers as are requisite for completing the matter (e.g. signing any prospectus for registration with the Registrar of Companies or in compliance with The Stock Exchange rules). A power is required to be stamped with fifty pence nominal duty.

Capacity to contract

Memorandum of association

A limited company only acts through its agents, primarily its directors. Their ability to create legal obligations on its behalf depends upon the authority with which they are vested. There are thus two problems, first, does the company itself have power to enter into a proposed transaction? Secondly, have the agents been clothed with sufficient power to carry it through? These questions were once of fundamental importance, since if a contract was outside the capacity of the company it was completely unenforceable, a fact which often operated to the detriment of third parties (see *Re Jon Beauforte (London) Limited* [1953] Ch. 131). Moreover, if the transaction was within the power of the company it might yet be beyond the scope of authority of the particular officers who were engaged in effecting it, so that outsiders were faced with the unenviable task of assessing the status of the company officer with whom they were dealing to ensure he was a fully-fledged agent. These difficulties are considerably reduced by section 9 of the European Communities Act 1972.

A company must act within the powers expressed or implied in the objects clause of its memorandum of association. Any transaction outside the objects clause is *ultra vires* and void. The impact of the ultra vires rule is considered in the chapter *Memorandum of Association*, but section 9 (1) of the 1972 Act provides,

> "in favour of a person dealing with a company *in good faith*, any transaction *decided on by the directors* shall be deemed to be one which it is within the capacity of the company to enter into, and the power of directors to bind the company shall be deemed to be free of any limitation under the memorandum of articles of association; and a party to a transaction so decided shall not be bound to inquire as to the capacity of the company to enter into it *or* as to any such limitation on the powers of the directors, and shall be presumed to have acted in good faith unless the contrary is proved."

Effectively this negatives the *ultra vires* rule, provided the third party acts in good faith and can show that the transaction has been arrived at by the directors in a regular manner, i.e. by board resolution, and not by one or some of them acting without the authority of their peers. However, the principle will not apply in favour of a constructive trustee: *International Sales and Agencies Ltd v Marcus* [1982] 3 All E.R. 551; see [1982] C.L.J. 244.

Articles of association

It will be seen that section 9 of the 1972 Act operates to bestow authority on the directors as well as the company itself, i.e. it affects the application of the agency principle as well as the *ultra vires* rule. In most cases, this will be sufficient, but prior to 1972 there was a body of law which defined the extent to which the articles of association could be treated as validating or invalidating contracts made by directors and officers in purported exercise of some authority. These provisions are still of relevance in respect of transactions which are not "decided on by the directors" or in which the outsider is not acting in good faith. In these circumstances, section 9 cannot apply.

Agency and apparent authority

Under the general law, a principal (the company) is liable for the acts of his agent (a director or employee) if the agent enters into a transaction which he has been authorised to perform. The principal will also normally be liable if the transaction is either one that an agent of his type would normally have authority to perform, or is one in respect of which the principal has held out the agent as having authority, even though he has not in fact been awarded actual authority. But for the principal to be bound on this "apparent authority" or "holding out" basis – as contrasted with the case where the agent has actual authority – the third party must not know that the agent is exceeding his actual authority.

Thus, a person appointed managing director is given by most articles, such as articles 107 and 109 of Table A, a wide power of management which in practice enables outsiders to treat him as having the conduct of the business of the company. As such, it would be virtually impossible for the company to refuse to adopt a transaction, other than one not made in the ordinary course of business, which the managing director has entered into. An individual director, without further executive qualification, has no such power. He is simply regarded as a member of a board. Where a director has a service agreement which requires him to perform a particular task, such as finance director, he will possess the usual authority that his function demands. An ordinary director held out by the company as exercising special powers, or appearing to be in de facto control, will have an effective authority based on estoppel (*Freeman & Lockyer v Buckhurst Park Properties Limited* [1964] 2 QB 480; *Hely-Hutchinson v Brayhead* [1968] 1 QB 549). The outsider is protected whether or not he has read the company's articles (unless, of course, the articles clearly show that the director or officer could not have had authority, in which case the outsider will have constructive notice of the limitation and the company will not be bound).

Thus, in *Freeman & Lockyer v Buckhurst Park Properties* the articles contained a power to appoint a managing director, although no individual was appointed to this office. Two directors allowed a third to undertake the management of the company's business, who engaged on his own authority architects to obtain planning permission for certain properties which the company wished to develop. The architects performed their work and submitted their bill, but the company refused to pay, alleging that the director had no authority. The Court of Appeal held that the company was bound. Provided there was a power of delegation contained in the articles, it was reasonable for an outsider to assume that a person having the appearance of such a delegate should be a person with whom the outsider could do business. Where the outsider was induced by a representation contained in the articles to enter into the contract, the company was estopped from arguing that the terms of the articles had not been fulfilled. The *Hely-Hutchinson* case shows that a director who acts without authority may be liable to a third party in damages for breach of an express on implied warranty of authority.

Section 180 etc.

Section 180 of the Companies Act 1948 provides that "the act of a director or manager shall be valid notwithstanding any defect that may afterwards be discovered in his appointment or qualification". A similar rule is repeated in article 105 of Table A. It might be thought that this provision offers an additional protection to a third party where a director or other officer has acted beyond his authority. However, in *Morris v Kanssen* [1946] A.C. 459, the precursor of this section was given a very limited operation. The court distinguished between (a) an appointment in which there is a defect or, in other words, a defective appointment and (b) no appointment at all. Thus where an appointing instrument contains a culpable omission the court may infer that the parties intended it to be filled; but where, for example, authority exists in the articles or by virtue of a board or members' resolution to appoint a person to a particular function, and that appointment is never made, section 180 cannot apply to a person who in fact fills the office. In practice therefore, the cases considered above dealing with the agency principle, or the indoor management rule in *Royal British Bank v Turquand*, into which the agency principle blurs and which is discussed below, will offer a better protection.

As far as concerns borrowings, an article such as article 79 of Table A may give a third party protection if the directors borrow an amount in excess of that authorised by the articles (e.g. in excess of the nominal capital of the company where article 79 applies).

Turquand's rule

The memorandum and articles of association are registered, and therefore public documents giving all persons dealing with the company constructive notice of the company's powers and, to some extent, those of its officers. There are, however, many matters of "indoor management" which do not become documents of record and which an outsider has no means of discovering, even though they may have a bearing on agreements made with him. For example, although section 145 of the Companies Act 1948 provides that every company shall cause minutes of proceedings of directors and managers to be kept in books provided for that purpose, section 146 requires disclosure to the public of books containing the minutes of proceedings of general meetings only. Any other rule, indeed, would seriously impair the confidentiality of the company's management and its decision-making processes, but it does have the result that documents conferring or restricting the authority of officers or employees are seldom available to an outsider, except where the company itself wishes to ensure that a decision is binding.

As discussed above, an outsider deals with a company through its agents and is therefore concerned to enquire whether such an agent has authority either express, implied, usual, or ostensible. The general commercial rules of agency have, however, received a gloss in relation to corporate contracts which has arisen out of attempts to mitigate the severity of the *ultra vires* rule. This gloss has come to be known as the rule in *Royal British Bank v Turquand* (1856) 6 E&B 327, although it has received much embellishment since its nineteenth-century enunciation. It should also be borne in mind that the rule has no application where the contract or obligation sought to be enforced is *ultra vires* the company, i.e. beyond the powers given in the memorandum of association: we are concerned only with its effect in relation to agency.

Actual or usual authority

The rule is based on the proposition that if what the company and its officers propose to do is not inconsistent with anything stated in the memorandum and articles, an outsider is bound to enquire no further: he can assume that the transaction is regular and legitimate. In *Turquand*, the board of directors were authorised to borrow on bond such amounts as the company might from time to time authorise in general meeting. The directors borrowed from a bank on a sealed bond without any resolution being passed, and the company afterwards refused to acknowledge the indebtedness. The court held that the company was bound, since there was nothing to suggest that the authority was wanting, and no facts to put the outsider on enquiry. The fact that the restrictions were contained in a registered deed (equivalent to today's memorandum and articles) did not allow the company to avoid liability: the public documents did not prohibit the directors undertaking the transaction but merely required an act of indoor management. The decision is based on business convenience, since commerce would be impossible if every creditor or trader was bound to probe a company's internal workings before dealing with particular officers.

Actions outside usual authority

An outsider is also protected under the *Turquand* rule if an individual without actual or usual authority is represented by the company to have a power which he does not in fact possess. Again, this is really little more than an application of the general agency rule of "holding out" referred to above, applied to the specific situation of a company. As shown by the decision in the *Freeman & Lockyer v Buckhurst Park Properties Limited* case, the company will be bound if,

(a) the outsider can prove an inducement to make the contract by the agent being held out as occupying a certain position;

(b) that the representation, whether express or implied, comes from persons within the company who have actual authority to make it; and

(c) the transaction is one which would be within the normal scope of the authority of the individual held out as having it, if he had in fact been appointed.

In *Mahony v East Holyford Mining Co* (1875) L.R. 7 H.L. 869, the articles of a company empowered the subscribers to appoint directors but no such appointments were ever made. The articles further provided that cheques should be signed in such manner as the board determined. The company's bank was informed that the board had resolved that cheques should bear certain signatures, and the bank honoured these. It was held that the cheques were valid, the company being estopped from denying the validity of the representation about a signatory's authority, notwithstanding that a board of directors had never been appointed.

On the other hand, in *Houghton & Co v Nothard, Lowe & Wills Limited* [1927] 1 K.B. 246, a director entered into an agreement for the sale by a third party of certain of the company's goods under which the third party was entitled to retain the proceeds as security for a debt due from another company. The third party had not inspected the articles of association, but assumed the director possessed an authority he did not have. It was held that the company was not bound, since the transaction was so unusual as to put the outsider on notice as to whether the power to carry out business of this kind had actually been delegated to the person in question. Again, in *Rama Corporation Limited v Proved Tin Limited* [1952] 2 Q.B. 147 a director entered into a contract on behalf of his company and received monies as agent for it. He had in fact exceeded his authority, and the other party reclaimed the monies, alleging that the company was estopped from denying the validity of the transaction because the articles contained a power enabling delegation to one or more directors. It was held that because the other party had not inspected the articles they could not use this in evidence as a representation that the director concerned had apparent authority, and accordingly the contract was unenforceable.

Exceptions to Turquand

It is clear that the *Turquand* principle does not apply in a number of situations,

(a) where the memorandum or articles of association indicate un-equivocally that the director or officer was not empowered to enter into the transaction (but where section 9(1) of the European Communities Act 1972 applies this constructive notice rule is overriden);

(b) where the outsider knows or ought reasonably to have known of the lack of actual authority (*Howard v Patent Ivory Manufacturing Co* (1888) 38 Ch.D 156);

(c) where the document relied on is a forgery and beyond the powers of the individual officer to execute (*Ruben v Great Fingall Consolidated* [1906] A.C. 439);

(d) where the outsider is put on inquiry by any suspicious circumstances (*Kreditbank Cassel G.m.b.H. v Schenkers Limited* [1927] 1 K.B. 826; *Underwood Limited v Bank of Liverpool* (1924) 1 K.B. 775).

Exceptions (b) and (d) are relevant where an individual's position either as an insider, or a person having frequent dealings with a company, is such as to permit him to assess whether a director or other officer is genuinely empowered to proceed to contract.

Practical implications

The company's position

The following notes of guidance will assist a company's officers and advisers in ensuring that their contract documents are validly executed without giving rise to any personal liability.

(1) On any bill of exchange and promissory note the complete name of the company must appear together with the word "limited" or "p.l.c." as the case may be (section 108 (1)(c) of the Companies Act 1948). Where the name is incorrectly set out or there is no reference to the company's limited liability, directors and other officers can be personally liable: *Atkins & Co v Wardle* (1889) 61 L.T. 23; *Durham Fancy Goods Limited v Michael Jackson (Fancy Goods) Limited* [1968] 2 Q.B. 839.

(2) In order to establish agency, it is important that the director or other officer signs manifestly "for" or "on behalf of" the company. A failure to do so will not give rise to personal liability in all cases, especially if the company's headed notepaper is being used and it is otherwise clear from the context that only a representative capacity is intended. However, in the case of negotiable instruments, section 26 of the Bills of Exchange Act 1882 provides that "the mere addition to his signature of words describing him as agent, or as filling a representative character, does not exempt him from personal liability". It must be clear for whom the representative is acting, although even here section 26(2) of the 1882 Act may result in personal liability in certain circumstances. Where a more junior employee is signing the letter or bill, and signs "per pro" the officer, the status of the officer and his relation to the company should be set out. If the company's management have any doubt about this requirement being accurately implemented, they should require that all letters go out in the name of the director or officer concerned, in a pre-determined format.

(3) As a matter of internal administration, the chain of authority down to the person actually writing the letter and purporting to bind the company should be clearly established in writing. Where the board delegates an authority to a manager, this should be minuted unless it is clearly within the manager's ordinary and usual scope of activity. Where a manager delegates to a junior employee, ideally two sets of authority should exist. In cases where an outsider may doubt the status of a company employee to execute a particular document, the employee should produce a form of authority or attorney which shows his right to do so. In a sale of assets by a company, the sale agreement may be signed by a director or by the company secretary, and there will be a warranty in favour of the purchaser that due authority exists to effect the disposal. Where solicitors are acting for both parties, a purchaser will normally assume that the vendor has such authority without requiring to see it, but it is nonetheless advisable for it to be available at the completion meeting.

The third party's position

From the point of view of a person dealing with a company, the following should be observed.

(1) Wherever possible the outsider should ascertain the status of the company representative. He will then be entitled to assume that the representative is empowered to enter arrangements of a sort which officers of similar status conduct in other companies. Of course, a company secretary in one organisation may be vested with considerably more authority than one in another, and in such a case the outsider must judge by reference to his commercial experience. For example, it is within the usual authority of company secretaries to negotiate for contracts involving office services, but not usual for such officers to enter into agreements for the sale and purchase of trading assets (see the chapter *Secretary*). If the outsider has any reason to believe that the authority has been exceeded, or the proposed transaction is beyond the scope of the officer's powers, he must seek clear evidence of authority in the form of a board or committee minute, or power of attorney, because the rule in *Turquand's* case will not protect him.

(2) It is a counsel of perfection to suggest that every outsider should, before dealing with a company, inspect its articles. This is undoubtedly prudent where the proposal is to enter into a transaction of some size. Although the articles are a constructive notice, the outsider will not be prejudiced if he has not read them unless either they clearly indicate that the director or officer has no authority (but section 9(2) of the European Communities Act will normally override this), or unless the outsider seeks to rely specifically on some power therein contained. If, for example, matters appear to be delegated to an officer whose usual responsibility would not include them, a third party is put on inquiry and ought to inspect the articles to see whether such a power of delegation exists; and if it does, to call for the instrument effecting the appointment.

(3) A company search (see page 219) will often prove revealing in discovering who has the appearance of authority, since particulars of directors and secretaries must be filed with the Registrar together with any changes; and every company must also keep at its registered office a register of directors and secretaries which is open to public inspection (C.A. 1948, s. 200). The fact that a person is shown as a director is capable of amounting to a representation by the company that the person concerned has an apparent authority appropriate to his position. An outsider will be protected even if there is some internal irregularity, for instance if shareholders have removed the directors but particulars of the change have not been filed.

Ratification

An act or transaction which is *intra vires* the company but outside the authority of the directors can be ratified by a subsequent adoption of the proper procedure (eg. holding a full board meeting, obtaining approval in general meeting, or whatever).

Criminal liability

Where the entering into of a contract or transaction by a company would, if it were entered into by an individual, give rise to criminal liability, questions arise as to whether it is possible to attribute to the company's agent the necessary *mens rea* to secure a conviction. As a limited company is an abstraction and can have no corporate mind of its own, liability can attach only by (a) making the officer personally responsible, or (b) treating him as the *alter ego* of the company so that his wrongdoing is vicarious. There are many cases where the Companies Acts provide for personal liability of directors and officers (for example for fraud under section 330 or failure to keep accounts under section 331 to the 1948 Act), but normally liability will be attributed to the company itself if the wrongdoing is that of the management or board of directors who can properly be described as having the conduct of the company's affairs (see *Moore v Bresler Limited* [1944] 2 All E.R. 515). As Lord Reid explained in *Tesco Supermarkets Ltd. v Nattrass* [1972] A.C. 153, "It must be a question of law whether, once the facts have been ascertained, a person in doing particular things is to be regarded as the company or merely as the company's servant or agent. In that case any liability of the company can only be a statutory or vicarious liability".

In certain cases both the company and the officers are liable. For instance, under section 18 of the Theft Act 1968, if a company commits an offence under section 15 (obtaining property by deception), section 16 (obtaining pecuniary advantage by deception) or section 17 (false accounting), then any officer knowingly involved commits an offence and may be made a co-defendant with the company. If an officer of the company or any person on its behalf:

(a) uses or authorises the use of any seal on which its true name is not engraven; or

(b) authorises the issue of any business letter or other official publication, or signs any bill of exchange, prommisory note, cheque or order for goods or issues any invoice receipt or letter of credit where the name of the company is not set out,

he commits an offence and is personally liable to the holder of any bill of exchange or whatever for the amount thereof, unless it is duly paid by the company (section 108 (4) of the Companies Act 1948).

Company Searches

An important aspect of English company law is the means by which certain information regarding the constitution and continuing affairs of a company is made available to the public. The concept has long been promoted by the legislature that adequate protection is given to the public, including the existing and prospective members and creditors of a company, if sufficient information relating to a company is made available for the public to make a proper assessment of its financial position and affairs together with its authority and powers, its capacity (and that of its management) to enter into arrangements of the nature contemplated by the interested third party, and the ability and experience of its directors.

Legislation has made provision for the disclosure of this information through,

(1) the maintenance by the company of registers and records and the disclosure to its members of adequate financial information on a regular basis;

(2) the delivery to the Registrar of Companies of documents for registration, these documents often duplicating the information required to be kept by the company in its own registers and records, and the maintenance by the Registrar of those documents on files to which the public is given access; and

(3) the publication of the more important information regarding the constitution and standing of the company in the London Gazette or the Edinburgh Gazette, depending on the place of registration of the company concerned.

In addition, any company having all or any part of its share or loan capital listed on The Stock Exchange is subject to the disclosure requirements of the Listing Agreement.

The following pages are primarily concerned with the information to be found on the register of a company which is required to be maintained by the Register of Companies, and the way in which that information is made available to the public in England and Wales. The remaining disclosure requirements of the Companies Acts, including the compulsory maintenance by a company of various registers and records, the preparation and delivery of audited financial information and the directors' report, and the concept of official notification by the Registrar of Companies in the Gazette are discussed elsewhere in this book.

Establishment of registration offices

To enable the due registration of companies, the Companies Act 1948 provides, by section 424(1), for the establishment and maintenance of files in England and Scotland at such places as the Department of Trade thinks fit. The three Companies Registration Offices have been established, two in respect of companies registered in England and Wales and the other in respect of companies registered in Scotland. Searches of the public register of companies registered in England and Wales can be made at either,

Companies Registration Office, Crown Way, Maindy, Cardiff CF4 3UZ. Tel: 0222–388588; or London Search Room, Companies House, 65–71 City Road, London EC1. Tel: 01–253–9393.

The remainder of this chapter is primarily concerned with the information which is generally available to the public upon application to the Registration Offices in England and Wales and the means by which that information is produced. Searches against companies registered in Scotland can be made at, and guidance regarding the procedures involved obtained from, Companies Registration Office, Exchequer Chambers, 102 George Street, Edinburgh EH2 3DJ. Tel: 031–225–5774.

Following the reorganisation of the public search facilities in recent years as part of the transfer of the major clerical function from London to Cardiff, it is now possible to search in either London or Cardiff against all existing companies registered in England and Wales as well as against the bulk of such companies which have been dissolved since 1976. Information in both centres is primarily made available to the public in the form of microfiche copies of the original documents which have been delivered for registration. In addition, files containing the original documents delivered for registration for existing companies and for those which have been dissolved since 1975 are maintained at the Cardiff office. Files containing the original documents delivered for registration concerning companies which were dissolved prior to 1976 are stored in the London office. Information which is available for public inspection and which is not on the microfiche system may be inspected at the office at which the relevant original file is kept.

Information available for inspection

The information recorded at the Registration Offices is compiled from the documents which each company incorporated under the Companies Acts is required by statute to deliver (in most cases in prescribed form) to the Registrar of Companies. The Registration Offices also hold available for inspection the information which is required to be delivered to the Registrar of Companies by companies or corporations which were not incorporated under the Companies Acts, but which are otherwise subject to the statutory registration and disclosure obligations. Such companies or corporations are those overseas companies which have established a place of business within Great Britain, and which are therefore registered under Part X of the Companies Act 1948 (see *Overseas Companies*), and British statutory and chartered corporations, except those which were not formed for the purpose of gain or which are specifically exempted from compliance by the Department of Trade. (C.A. 1948, s. 435 and Sch. 14, as amended by C.A. 1967, s. 54).

As indicated earlier, the information which is kept available for inspection at the Registration Offices basically duplicates much of the information which a company is required to maintain in its registers or records, or which it is otherwise obliged to make available to its members, such as the information required to be provided in the audited accounts and directors' report which must be laid before the members each year by the company in general meeting. By virtue of such information being made available for inspection at the Registration Offices, the public at large (and not only the members) is thereby given access to substantially the whole of the statutory records which a company is obliged to maintain.

In essence, the public file of a company contains documents which have been filed by or on behalf of, or notices which have been entered against, the company and which fall into three broad bands of classification. The following summarises and emphasises the general nature and scope of the public register within those classifications. The statutory requirements for filing documents are dealt with throughout this work in relation to the particular section or statute.

(1) General information relating to the constitution and management of a company

In this category are included the original registration documents of a company – the memorandum and articles of association duly subscribed (section 12 of the Companies Act 1948 and sections 2 and 3 of the Companies Act 1980), the statement of the names and particulars of the first directors and secretary of the company and of the intended registered office on incorporation (section 200 of the Companies Act 1948 and sections 21 and 23 of the Companies Act 1976 and Form 1), the statement of allotment of the capital subscribed on incorporation (section 52 of the Companies Act 1948 and Form PUC 1), the declaration of compliance (section 3 of the Companies Act 1980 and Form 41a) and, upon registration, the certificate of incorporation signed by or on behalf of the Registrar of Companies. In addition, in the case of a company registered as a public limited company on incorporation, the register will also show the certificate issued by the Registrar of Companies enabling it to do business (section 4 of the Companies Act 1980).

In order to update the information on the public register, any changes to the documents or information reflected in the documents filed on incorporation also appear on the register once filed. These include all resolutions or orders effecting an alteration to the memorandum and articles of association of the company, together with the copies of the memorandum and articles, as altered from time to time (section 5 of the Companies Act 1948 and section 9 of the European Communities Act 1972), other resolutions of the company required to be delivered to the Registrar of Companies (section 143 of the Companies Act 1948 and section 14(6) of the Companies Act 1980), any changes of the particulars filed regarding the directors and secretary of the company, including any resignations, removals or appointments (section 200 of the Companies Act 1948 as amended by section 22 of the Companies Act 1978 and s. 95 Companies Act 1981 and Form 9b), any change in the registered office of the Company (section 23(3) of the Companies Act 1976 and Form 4a), and any certificate of incorporation on change of name or re-registration which may from time to time be issued by the Registrar of Companies.

Further, if a company has a share capital, the public register will reveal those documents which have been filed by the company pursuant to its obligations to make returns regarding any increase in its nominal capital (section 68 of the Companies Act 1948 and Form 10), any consolidation of shares, and any subdivision, redemption or cancellation of shares (section 63 of the Companies Act 1948 and Form 28). In addition, any allotment or issue of shares, the consideration given and the amount paid up or credited as paid up, will be revealed by the returns of allotments which a company is obliged to make (section 52 of the Companies Act 1948).

The public register will also set out a copy of any prospectus which is delivered to the Registrar of Companies in accordance with section 41 of the Companies Act 1948 (or, in the case of an overseas company, section 420 of the Companies Act 1948) in connection with any proposed issue of shares or debentures by a company. To a third party, whether one who is considering an investment in the securities of the company or one who is interested in the company from the viewpoint of a creditor, the prospectus will provide useful general and financial information given at the date of its issue and which is beyond that normally to be found in the company's public documents. This is because in the case of a registrable prospectus the company must comply with the requirements of the Fourth Schedule to the Companies Act 1948 and, if the company is quoted on The Stock Exchange, the provisions of the Listing Agreements (see the chapter *Prospectuses and Public Issues*).

Other general information which is recorded on the public register of a company includes details of any,

(a) accounting reference date adopted by the company (sections 2 and 3 of the Companies Act 1976 and Forms 2, 3 and 3A);

(b) removal or resignation of the auditors of the company (section 14 of the Companies Act 1976 and Form 14);

(c) reduction of capital (section 66 and 143 of the Companies Act 1948) or a reconstruction approved by the Court (sections 206–207 and section 287 of the Companies Act 1948); and

(d) appointment of a receiver over all or any part of the assets of the company, or resolution or order for the winding-up of the company, together with the notice of appointment of a liquidator and all subsequent returns by the liquidator.

(2) Financial information of a company

Whilst the general category of documents which are available for public inspection primarily concerns the details of the constitution and management of the company and of its shareholders' commitment in the way of equity, the second category is based on the premise that the public should have access to a regular report on the financial condition of the company and its business in the same form as such information is provided to the members.

The public therefore has access to the audited balance sheets (together with the applicable directors' reports) and profit and loss accounts of a company which are required to be laid before the members in general meeting and subsequently delivered to the Registrar of Companies (section 1 of the Companies Act 1976). This is subject to relaxations for small and medium sized companies (see the chapter *Accounts*) and an exemption for unlimited companies (see the chapter *Formation and Types of Company*).

In addition to the financial information which is contained in the accounts and directors' report, a company is also required to deliver to the Registrar of Companies for registration an annual return which must be completed within forty-two days after the annual general meeting for that year (sections 124–126 of and Schedule 6 to the Companies Act 1948 and the chapter *Annual Return*). The annual return sets out, and to some extent repeats, certain information for the purposes of the public register regarding the financial condition, management and structure of the company including,

(a) the registered office;

(b) the situation of the registers of members and debenture holders, if not at the registered office;

(c) a summary of the share capital of the company, distinguishing between shares issued for cash and shares issued as fully or partly paid up otherwise than in cash;

(d) particulars of the indebtedness of the company in respect of all registerable mortgages and charges;

(e) a list of those persons who were members of the company on the fourteenth day after the annual general meeting for the year, together with those persons who have ceased to be members since the date of the last return, and including details of shares held and transferred (as the case may be); and

(f) particulars of the directors and secretary of the company as at the date of the return.

(3) Information relating to the registerable charges of a company

The third category is, like the second, primarily aimed at the protection of creditors rather than the distillation of information for the benefit of actual or prospective members. Whereas the purpose of the publication of the annual audited financial statements of a company is to set out, in generally accepted form, a means by which a third party can take an objective view of its financial condition, the purpose of disclosing the secured interests of other creditors is to enable a trade creditor to assess the risks involved in dealing with the company and to establish his priority in the order of repayment should the company be wound up. Unlike a trade creditor, a loan creditor will usually be in a sufficiently strong position to investigate the financial condition of a borrowing company before making an advance and therefore incurring any unwarranted risk. Without the benefit of the public mortgage register, a trade creditor would find it difficult to take a view on the chances of receiving payment on a subsequent winding up.

The information in this category which is available for inspection by the public is solely concerned with details of registrable charges which are delivered to the Registrar of Companies (see the chapter *Company Charges*). For each applicable company, the public records will contain a register of mortgages and charges, together with a copy of each mortgage and charge and the statutory particulars delivered with the original document at the time of its lodgement for registration. The mortgage register will also be accompanied by copies of each certificate of registration of mortgage and charge issued against the company by the Registrar of Companies, and of any memorandum of satisfaction filed in respect of any existing registered mortgage and charge.

Slavenburg Register

The Registrar of Companies also maintains, independently of the general companies' register, an alphabetical index which is known as "the Slavenburg Register" (named after the decision in *N.V. Slavenburg's Bank v. Intercontinental Natural Resources Limited* [1980] 1 All E.R. 955, see the chapters *Company Charges* and *Overseas Companies*). This details the particulars of any charge over property in England and Wales which have been delivered for registration pursuant to section 106 of the Companies Act 1948 by or on behalf of an overseas company or corporation which, although not registered under Part X of the Companies Act 1948 as having established a place of business in England and Wales, has nevertheless registered a charge, perhaps at the insistence of the lender. This register, which is contained in a bound volume, is available upon request at the General Counter at either Companies House in London or at Companies Registration office in Cardiff.

In the case of charges over a company's land, it may also be necessary to carry out a Land Charges or Land Registry Search.

Inspection of information

The means of inspection of the public records of a company is effectively by personal attendance at the Search Rooms of one of the Registration Offices.

Company search agents

As there is no means by which an official search can be carried out by post, the use of company search agents is common. The leading company formation agents have branches close to each Registration Office. If it is inconvenient or not possible to carry out a personal search at a Registration Office, company search agents will upon application, either by post or telephone, carry out the required search and forward the results against payment of fee (which will include the official search fee).

The use of professional company search agents has its merits. Apart from the close proximity of the agents to the Registration Offices and the obvious saving in time, the agents will be familiar with the procedures involved in effecting a search and will be able to obtain the required information with the minimum of inconvenience as far as the client is concerned. Search agents offer an efficient alternative to personal attendance and will present a written or, in some cases if required by the client, a telephonic report (followed by a written confirmatory report) of the information required with a minimum of delay, often with copies of the applicable documents filed on the public register.

The system is not without its disadvantages, however. Company search agents may be instructed generally to present the latest relevant information on a company as evidenced by the public register, or they may be asked to search for and report on the existence of specific information. In the former case, the search agents will usually present a report on the basis of the most recently filed operative documents. Personal attendance by the client might result in a more subjective and complete overall assessment of the company, or of notice being taken of information available on the public register which, although not the latest or even operative, would have some importance to the particular searcher. Similarly, if instructions are given to the agents to detail specified information, documentation which might otherwise be considered relevant and which is available on record might be disregarded. At best, either disadvantage merely results in delay in discovering the complete position as far as the client is concerned, since the client is frequently given the microfiche and the documentation obtained by the agents to enable personal verification. At worst, if the client is not supplied with the original microfiche or does not have the means of making full use of it by placing it on a viewer or otherwise obtaining copies, the client could take a decision which is not based upon all the information disclosed by the public register.

Company's name and number

Before a search of the public register can be made against a company, whether by personal attendance or by company search agents, the full name and registered number of the company must be known. The name and number of a company on the index contained at each Registration Office is as set out on its certificate of incorporation or, if it has changed its name, on the latest certificate of incorporation on change of name issued by the Registrar of Companies. Alternatively, if a copy of the certificate is not available, each company is required to set out its registered title and number on its letterhead and other business letters (section 108 of the Companies Act 1948 and section 9(7) of the European Communities Act 1972).

If the full title, but not the registered number, of a company is known, the registered number can be ascertained by scanning the public index of all companies which is maintained by the Registrar of Companies at the Registration Offices. This index is divided into a main index dealing with existing companies and subsidiary indices giving the numbers of dissolved companies and details of changes of name. It is updated on a daily basis. As a matter of practice, companies which are dissolved or removed (indicated by the prefix "D"), or change their name (indicated by the prefix "C"), during a calendar year remain on the main index until the end of that year after which their name is removed and placed on the relevant subsidiary index. The main index also lists limited partnerships, Part X registered overseas companies and companies registered in Scotland or Northern Ireland in addition to those registered in England and Wales, and differentiates between them by the addition of the prefix "L" in the case of a limited partnership, "F" in the case of an overseas company, and "SC" or "NI" in the case of a Scottish or Northern Ireland company. The public register in England and Wales does not, however, contain the registered documentation of Scottish or Northern Ireland companies. A search must be made in Edinburgh or Belfast, as the case may be, against such a company. Copies of this name index can be purchased from the Registrars of Companies, enabling solicitors' firms, for example, to have readily available a full list of company names and numbers.

Armed with the registered name and number of the company to be searched against, a search application must be purchased (official search fee £1 per application) at the Index Room (at the Registration Office in London) or Control Counter (at the Registration Office in Cardiff). Once completed with the name and number of the company which is the subject of the search together with the identity of the searcher (which is required for the internal purposes of the Registration Office), the form must be presented to the Search Room Counter (in London) or returned to the Control Counter (in Cardiff). Upon presentation of the completed form, the searcher is issued with a number corresponding to a seat in the Reading Room where the records of the company are delivered.

The public records available for inspection are delivered on microfilm contained in a separate envelope for each company. The microfilm is divided into three categories corresponding to the three classifications discussed earlier in this chapter. Each classification is given one or more microfiche, which is essentially a form of microfilm, approximately the size of a postcard, containing up to sixty pages of documentation on each fiche. Each microfiche is headed with the registered number of the company and carries a suffix as follows:

"G" or "GEN"   – the general documents relating to the incorporation, constitution, structure and management of the company;

"A", "AC" or "AR"   – the financial and other information contained in the audited accounts and annual returns of the company; and

"MD" or "MR"   – the details of the mortgages and charges of the company including, where applicable, notice of the appointment of a receiver or liquidator.

A searcher may occasionally find a consolidation fiche headed "CF". The full fiche is available for inspection on request.

Documents which have been filed for registration are microfiched in chronological order under the appropriate classification and the fiches in each classification are numbered consecutively.

The searcher is given on microfiche the entire public record of a company, except accounts and annual returns which were more than three years old at the time at which the original documents were filmed, and changes of directors, secretary and registered office effected more than seven years before the original filming although the latest, no matter how old, will be on the microfiche. Records which are not on microfiche are available for inspection upon application by the searcher to the Search Room Counter (in London) or the Control Counter (in Cardiff).

Warning fiches

As there is invariably a delay between the delivery of documents for registration and their appearance on the relevant microfiche, the Registrar of Companies alerts the searcher to the existence of certain important recently filed documents which have not been filmed. This warning is given by the insertion of a special fiche in the company's fiche envelope. The warning fiche indicates that a document relating to either a mortgage, charge, liquidation, receivership or court order for the restoration of a company to the register has been received for registration. Upon enquiry at the General Counter (in London) or at the Control Counter (in Cardiff) the searcher will be given details of the new document.

For those people who do not have private access to suitable microfiche viewing equipment, the Reading Room in each Registration Office is fitted out with viewers. Searchers can therefore examine the microfiche at the time of the search and take whatever notes are required. The Reading Rooms also have viewer-printers from which copies of the microfiche can be made upon presentation of the appropriate form (to be found in the Reading Room) identifying the company and microfiche and the information to be copied and upon payment of the fee which is charged per page. Since the microfiche is non-returnable, the searcher may alternatively retain it and view the contents on any compatible viewer away from the Registration Office.

Registered offices

To facilitate the service of legal process or other notice on companies, which may generally only be served on a company at its registered office or, in the case of an overseas company, at the address of the person authorised to accept service on behalf of the company, the relevant address can be obtained from a separate index which is maintained by the Registrar of Companies at both London and Cardiff. If the registered office is the only information required by the searcher, it is not necessary to effect a full search. Personal attendance at the Registration Office is nonetheless still required.

Certificate of good standing

Public authorities regulating the operations of corporations or companies incorporated or registered outside Great Britain are often empowered to issue certificates of good standing in respect of corporations or companies within their authority. This facility is commonly used in credit transactions where the existence and good standing of the borrower is clearly of prime importance to the lender.

The Registrar of Companies recognises the desire of non-residents to have, if possible, a form of quasi-governmental assurance regarding the existence of English registered companies. The Registrar will, upon application to the Registration Office at Cardiff and upon receipt of the appropriate fee (currently £3.50 per application) issue a certificate, numbered C.16, in respect of any registered company setting out its name, registered number and date of incorporation. The certificate also confirms, as at the date it is issued, that according to the documents on the file in the custody of the Registrar of Companies, the named company has been in continuous and unbroken existence since its incorporation and that there is no document on the public file showing any proceedings for the winding up of liquidation of the company or that it is not in operation.

Enforcement

The clear disadvantage of the system of disclosure and registration advocated by the legislature to enable the public to monitor the registration and performance of companies, is that the protection of the public depends on full and prompt disclosure in accordance with the statutes and on the rapid transmittal on to microfiche of all information once delivered to the Registration Offices.

It is acknowledged that, despite the efforts of the staff of the Registrar of Companies, a significant number of companies do not comply fully with the disclosure requirements, with the consequence that the statutory information is incomplete. Section 428 of the Companies Act 1948 enables the Court, on the application of any member or creditor of a company or the Registrar of Companies, to make an order directing the company and any officer thereof to make good any default in complying with any provision of the Act requiring the company to file with, deliver or send to the Registrar of Companies any return, account or other document or to give notice of any matter. Such an order of the court may be granted in addition to and without prejudice to any penalty or default fine payable under the Act (C.A. 1948, s. 428(3)).

Failure to comply with an order made under section 428 could lead to a company and its officers being charged with contempt of court with the possible consequences of a fine and imprisonment. While the levying of penalties and default fines, and the possibility of contempts proceedings, are an obvious incentive to procure compliance with the statutory requirements, the procedures open to the Registrar have not been enforced as widely or as publicly as are necessary to persuade all companies to make their returns when, and in the form, required. Nor, given the number of existing companies and the amount of information required from them for disclosure, is it likely that all but an acceptable minimum of companies will comply in all respects with the statutes so far as the public register is concerned.

A further sanction open to the Registrar of Companies against defaulting companies is his power, contained in section 353 of the Companies Act 1948, to strike the name of the company from the register of companies, upon compliance with the applicable notice provisions, if he has reasonable cause to believe that the company is not carrying on business or in operation. However, this sanction is not available if the company is carrying on business or in operation even if it continues to default in respect of its disclosure obligations. In such an event, the Registrar must resort to the default fine or court order procedures to procure compliance.

Another aspect of the system is that, given the number of returns made by existing companies, there is invariably a delay from the time a document is delivered to the Registrar of Companies to the time it is available for public inspection on the microfiche. As indicated earlier, warning is given of the more important documents which have not been filmed, but equally important documents from a commercial point of view, such as increases in share capital and alterations to the memorandum or articles of association are not the subject of warning notices. The failure to keep the public register completely up to date with these documents could have unfortunate consequences for a third party relying on the contents of the public record alone.

Unless there is a substantial shift on the part of the legislature, it is unlikely that the public will be fully protected from these drawbacks. If, as in some jurisdictions, matters requiring compulsory notification and public disclosure were not effective until so disclosed, companies might be encouraged to see the urgency and desirability of maintaining public records up to date.

If the legislature is inclined to consider reform in this area, it might also give consideration to the concept of an official postal search. Personal attendance at one of the two official centres is not always easy for the average trade creditor or prospective member; nor is the use of company search agents the ideal alternative. If the fundamental basis for the protection of the public is the disclosure of information, it is submitted that adequate efficient access to that information should be given. At the moment, access is difficult for all but a comparatively few professionals and search agents within a reasonable distance of London and Cardiff, or members of the public having a reasonable means of attendance at the Registration Offices. Postal searches with the results being made available in immediately transmittable form would give more force to the legislature's intent.

Directors

Although there are many references to directors in the Companies Acts, there is not a full definition of the term "director". Section 455(1) of the 1948 Act merely provides that '"director" includes any person occupying the position of director by whatever name called'. There is no magic in the term "director"; those occupying that position may be designated, for example, governors or managers by the company's constitution. Thus a director is to be recognised by his function. However, it is impossible exactly to define what it is that a director does, for this varies according to the nature of the company, the constitution of the company and any contract between the company and the director. In a "one man company" the one man is often operating much as a sole trader, albeit through the medium of a company, while many small "family" companies are functionally similar to partnerships with all those interested in the company being involved in its running so that, at least while things go smoothly, the distinction between shareholders and directors will be of little significance to those involved. In larger companies, quite different types of directorships may exist within a single board: there will be full-time managing directors who, in addition to their directorship, will usually have a service contract with the company and will often be regarded as employees of the company. Other directors may be appointed not so much to work for the company as such but rather to bring their general advice, skill and business experience to the board-room table – such individuals will often hold many such directorships. Still others may be appointed solely to allow the company to benefit from the supposed kudos attached to their name. The only uniting factor is that all these individuals have the right to sit on their company's board and participate in the affairs of the company there conducted, subject, of course, to the company's memorandum and articles of association.

It should be noted that in various provisions of the Companies Acts (e.g. in relation to the register of directors under section 200(9)(a) of the 1948 Act) the term "director" is used to include not only a person who holds that office, but also "any person in accordance with whose directions or instructions the directors of a company are accustomed to act". Such a person is termed a "shadow director" by section 63(1) of the 1980 Act for the purposes of certain provisions in that Act, though the same definition, without the designation "shadow director," is found in various provisions in the 1948 and 1967 Acts. However, by section 63(1) such an individual will not be regarded as a "shadow director" for the purpose of the 1980 provisions, if the directors are accustomed to act in accordance with his instructions "by reason only that the directors of the company act on advice given by him in a professional capacity"; this exclusion is not contained in all of the equivalent provisions in the 1948 and 1967 Acts.

Nature of the director's office

In *Re City Equitable Fire Insurance Co. Ltd.* [1925] Ch. 407 Romer J. observed that: "It is indeed impossible to describe the duty of directors in general terms, whether by way of analogy or otherwise". Nevertheless, the nature of a directorship is often characterised by way of analogy to other relations known to the law. Four of these will now be considered. All are valid up to a point but none is totally accurate and the applicability of each will depend on the nature of the company and its constitution.

(1) *The director as agent*

In *Ferguson* v. *Wilson* (1866) L.R. 2 Ch.App. 77 Cairns L.J. stated that: "The company itself cannot act in its own person, for it has no person; it can only act through directors, and the case is, as regards those directors, merely the ordinary case of principal and agent".

However, although the general rules of agency do apply, a director may become personally liable in ways peculiar to company law, for example where he signs a cheque on the company's behalf which does not contain the correct full name of the company and which the company fails duly to honour (C.A. 1948, s.108(4)). For various purposes, e.g. criminal responsibility, the mind of the director may be regarded as the mind of the company according to the "organic theory" originating in *Lennard's Carrying Co. Ltd.* v. *Asiatic Petroleum Co. Ltd.* [1915] A.C. 705. Further, the director's scope of authority is generally much wider than is usual for an agent for, as Walton J. remarked in *Northern Counties Securities Ltd.* v. *Jackson & Steeple Ltd.* [1974] 1 W.L.R. 1133 "... a director is an agent, who casts his vote to decide in which manner his principal shall act..."

(2) *The director as managing partner*

In *Automatic Self-Cleaning Filter Syndicate Co. Ltd.* v. *Cunninghame* [1906] 2 Ch. 34 Cozens-Hardy L.J. observed that "I do not think it true to say that directors are agents. I think it is more nearly true to say that they are in the position of managing partners..." While this may describe the factual reality as perceived by the participants in a small family company, there are, of course, major differences. The directors need not hold any shares in the company unless qualifying shares are required by the articles, their powers are limited by the terms of the company's constitution and, most fundamentally, a director, *qua* director, is under no liability for the company's debts unless the company's memorandum provides for the unlimited liability of its directors under sections 202 and 203 of the Companies Act 1948.

(3) *The director as trustee*

Many early cases refer to directors as trustees. This is again, however, not wholly accurate for their duties are in some respects quite different from those of trustees. It is of the nature of a director's task to take greater risks than would be permitted a trustee and the standard of care and skill applicable to directors is considerably lower than that which applies to trustees. Directors may, however, be described as fiduciaries (see further the chapter *Directors' Duties*). As Lord Porter stated in *Regal (Hastings) Ltd.* v *Gulliver* [1942] 1 All E.R. 378: "Directors, no doubt, are not trustees, but they occupy a fiduciary position towards the company whose board they form." Thus directors do owe fiduciary duties closely akin to those owed by trustees, although these duties are owed solely to the company (*Percival* v. *Wright* [1902] 2 Ch.421 – but on very special facts it may be possible to argue that the duties are owed to individual shareholders: *Coleman* v. *Myers* [1977] 2 NZLR 225, 298).

(4) *The director as employee*

If a director is appointed managing director he will usually have a service contract and may be regarded as an employee of the company for the purpose of the unfair dismissal and redundancy legislation. The director's status as employee is, however, quite distinct from his status as director. Thus in the case of *Lee* v. *Lee's Air Farming* [1961] A.C. 12 the Privy Council held that Lee was operating "in dual capacities" both as governing director of the company and as its servant while flying the aeroplane.

Appointment

Minimum number

Although there is no maximum number of directors which a company can have, section 176 of the 1948 Act does establish a statutory minimum. A private company may have a sole director but a public company must have at least two directors unless it was registered before November 1, 1929, when it too may have a sole director.

However, the 1948 Act seeks to ensure that even where a company is permitted to have a sole director, at least two people must be involved in running the company. Section 177(1) provides that "every company shall have a secretary and a sole director shall not also be secretary", and section 179 provides that "a provision requiring or authorising a thing to be done by or to a director and the secretary [e.g. the signing of the annual return under section 126(1) of the 1948 Act] shall not be satisfied by its being done by or to the same person acting both as director and as, or in place of, the secretary."

It should also be noted that a director need not be an individual. There is nothing to prevent a limited company being appointed director of another limited company (*In re Bulawayo Market and Offices Company, Limited* [1907] 2 Ch. 458). This fact is recognised by the provision in section 200(2)(b) of the 1948 Act that if a director is a company the entry in the register of directors must include its corporate name and its registered office. (Clause 40 of the lapsed 1973 Bill would however have provided that "no body corporate . . . shall be capable of being appointed a director".) To prevent abuse of the principle that sole management should not be vested in one pair of hands through the use of corporate directors, section 178 provides that no company "shall have as sole director of the company a corporation the sole director of which is secretary of the company".

The first directors

The choice of the first directors is usually left to the subscribers to the memorandum (article 75 of Table A), although they may be named in the articles. The articles may also give to outsiders the right to nominate directors as, for example, in *British Murac Syndicate Ltd.* v. *Alperton Rubber Co. Ltd.* [1915] 2 Ch. 186.

In any case a statement naming the first director or directors must, by virtue of section 21 of the Companies Act 1976, be delivered to the registrar at the same time as the proposed company's memorandum is delivered under section 12 of the 1948 Act. This is made on Form 1. The statement must contain the same particulars as must appear in the register of directors maintained under section 200 of the 1948 Act (see the chapter *Disclosure of Directors' Dealings*), and must contain a signed consent by each of the directors to act as such. The purported appointment, for example by the articles, of a person not mentioned in this statement is void (C.A. 1976, s. 21(5)).

Subsequent directors

The articles usually contain wide powers to appoint extra directors or to fill vacancies. Thus article 95 of Table A provides that: "The directors shall have power at any time . . . to appoint any person to be a director, either to fill a casual vacancy or as an addition to the existing directors". A "casual vacancy" was described by Lord Coleridge C.J. in *York Tramways Co. Ltd.* v. *Willows* (1882) 8 Q.B.D. 685 as "any vacancy not occurring by effluxion of time, that is any vacancy occurring by death, resignation or bankruptcy". A vacancy created by the removal of a director under section 184 of the 1948 Act (see below), if not filled at the same meeting, is also to be filled as a casual vacancy (section 184(4)). On the appointment of a new director (or retirement of an existing director), notification must be given to the Registrar of Companies on a Form 9b. The director must signify his consent to act by signing a consent declaration on the form.

Mode of election

The mode of electing the directors is primarily determined by the company's articles. However, in relation to public companies as defined in the Companies Act 1980, section 183 of the 1948 Act provides that, unless previously agreed to by the meeting with no vote against, "a motion for the appointment of two or more persons as directors of the company by a single resolution shall not be made". The purpose of this provision is to allow individual directors to be rejected so that the meeting cannot merely be presented with the option of electing a "team" to the board. However, since a cumulative voting system is not used a majority in the meeting can still ensure the election of its candidates with no proportional representation for the minority.

Although a resolution passed in breach of section 183 is stated to be void it is not totally without effect. First, section 183 is without prejudice to the effect of section 180, which provides that the acts of a director or manager shall be valid notwithstanding any defect that may afterwards be discovered in his appointment or qualification. Secondly, the void resolution is regarded as "another appointment" so as to exclude the application of a provision for the automatic reappointment of directors in default of another appointment (e.g. article 92 of Table A).

Qualification

No general qualifications need to be possessed in order to act as a company director, although certain events do disqualify a person from acting as director, e.g. insolvency (see below). However, the articles will often specify qualifications; a most common stipulation is that each director must hold a certain number of shares in the company. The reason usually advanced for such a requirement is that it will give the director "a personal interest in the affairs of the company, and induce him to attend to them in a way very different to what he would do if he had no interest at all" (per Lindley L.J. in *In re North Australian Territory Company (Archer's Case)* (1892) 1 Ch. 322). In reality however, the qualification is usually so small as to amount to little more than a token holding in the company.

The Companies Acts do not require directors to hold any shares in their company and article 77 of Table A merely provides that the shareholding qualifications for directors may be fixed by the company in general meeting, and unless and until so fixed no qualification is required. If such a qualification is imposed, careful drafting should be employed, for many problems have arisen in the cases concerning the construction of such clauses, some of which will now be considered.

(1) *Is the shareholding a condition precedent of holding office?*

The qualification provision may take one of two basic forms. First, it may be phrased as a condition precedent to a person's appointment that he should hold a certain number of shares in the company. An illustration of such a construction is provided by *In re Percy & Kelly Nickel etc. Mining Company (Jenner's Case)* (1877) 7 Ch.D. 132, where the relevant article stated: "No person shall be qualified to be a director who is not the holder of shares or stock in the company to the nominal value of £500". If such phraseology is adopted the appointment of a person who does not hold the requisite shares is void even if he later acquires shares.

Secondly, the article may allow the appointment of an individual who does not hold any shares but requires him to obtain shares within a certain time; this will be the case if the article merely states that "a director's qualification shall be . . . . ". Where such a provision is used section 182 of the 1948 Act requires the director to obtain the stipulated holding within two months or such shorter period as the articles may specify. One problem which has arisen out of this provision was the exact date from which the two months began to run. In *Holmes* v. *Keyes* [1959] Ch. 199 a poll was taken at a general meeting held on December 23, 1957; the counting took place on December 24 when the company was informed of the result. The defendant who was thus elected was registered with his qualifying shares on February 24, 1958 and the question for the Court of Appeal was whether he had obtained those shares within the permitted two months. It was held that the director was appointed only when the result of the poll was known and accordingly that the two months did not begin to run until midnight on December 24.

(2) *Where may the shares be obtained?*

The shares need not be obtained from any particular source (e.g. by direct allotment from the company) unless the articles so specify. Problems may arise, however, where the qualifying shares are given to the director. In *In re Canadian Oil Works Company (Hay's Case)* (1875) L.R.10 Ch. App. 593 it was agreed by the vendors that in return for Hay agreeing to become a director they would provide him with his forty qualifying shares. When the purchase money was paid by the newly formed company, part was handed to Hay who used it to pay for his qualifying shares. James L.J. held that the money used to pay for Hay's shares was "never intended to be, and never did become, under the control or power of the vendors. It never . . . ceased to be the property of the company". Thus Hay had not paid for the shares and was liable to that extent as a contributory in the company's winding up. *Hay's Case* may be contrasted with the case of *In re Dover Coalfield Extension, Limited* [1908] 1 Ch. 65. The Dover Company transferred certain shares which it held in another company to Cousins (a Dover director) to qualify him as a director of the latter company. This was held to be "a perfectly proper transaction", since all was done 'with perfect propriety' and with full disclosure.

(3) *Holding shares "in his own right"*

The article may provide that the director must hold the shares "in his own right". This does not mean, however, that the director must hold the shares beneficially, as it is the form of the entry on the register which is all important. In *Bainbridge* v. *Smith* (1889) 41 Ch.D. 462 Lindley

L.J. observed that "I do not think the test is beneficial interest, the test is being on or not being on the register as a member . . . " Thus such an article was not satisfied in the case of *Boschoek Proprietary Company Ltd.* v. *Fuke* [1906] 1 Ch. 148, where Fuke's holding of 500 shares was registered in the form: "Fuke, liquidator of the Heidelburg Company".

(4) *Does the acceptance of office imply an offer to acquire the qualifying shares?*

There is much old authority as to when an offer to purchase the shares will be implied from the conduct of the director and as to what is required on the part of the company to accept such an offer (e.g. *In re Issue Company (Hutchinson's Case)* [1895] 1 Ch. 226). It seems that such an offer could not now be implied, however, since section 182(3) of the 1948 Act expressly provides that a director failing to obtain the qualification shall vacate his office. Nevertheless, the effect of a director's automatically becoming a member at the expiry of the qualification period may presumably still be achieved by the use of a specially worded clause such as that in *In re Anglo-Austrian Printing and Publishing Union (Isaac's Case)* [1892] 2 Ch. 158. This provided that if a director failed to acquire the qualification holding of shares of £1,000 nominal value within one month of his appointment he should be "deemed to have agreed to take the said shares from the company, and the same should be forthwith allotted to him accordingly". By virtue of this article, although shares had not actually been allotted to him, Sir Henry Isaacs was held liable to be placed on the list of contributories in the company's winding up.

(5) *Ceasing to hold shares*

An article requiring a director to hold qualifying shares will usually provide that the director shall vacate his office forthwith if he ceases to hold those shares (and see s. 182(3)). However, in *Molineaux* v. *The London, Birmingham and Manchester Insurance Co. Ltd.* [1902] 2 K.B. 589 the director's qualification was raised from 50 to 250 shares on an increase in the company's capital. The Court of Appeal held that when this was done the plaintiff had not ceased to hold the qualification for to hold otherwise might in such cases "instantaneously cause the vacation of office of every director".

Performance of the directors' functions

The power to run a company is vested in the board of directors, and *prima facie* it is the board which must exercise those functions through resolutions passed at duly convened board meetings. On the face of it, a single director has little power (assuming he is not the only director of the company). However, the running of a large company would be practically impossible if all decisions required a board meeting. In reality board meetings in large companies are infrequent affairs to discuss and formulate general policy, whilst the day-to-day decision making is delegated to managing directors or committees of directors under empowering provisions in the company's articles (hence the criticism of the phrase "any transaction decided on by the directors" in section 9(1) of the European Communities Act 1972). The chapter *Directors' Meetings* discusses the procedural and other requirements for board meetings.

Delegation by the board

(1) *To committees*: The articles usually allow the board to delegate powers to committees of directors (e.g. article 102 of Table A). Such a committee may consist of one director (*Re Fireproof Doors* [1916] 2 Ch. 142), and this is expressly provided for by article 102 of Table A. It is essential that the articles and empowering resolutions should be clearly drafted to specify the exact duties and powers of the committee and the rules for its functioning (see articles 103 and 104 of Table A)

(2) *To managing directors*: The managing director has no specific powers accorded to him by law; his authority is based entirely on the terms of the delegation by the board and his service contract (if any). Thus article 107 of Table A provides: "The directors may from time to time appoint one or more of their body to the office of managing director for such period and on such terms as they think fit ..." Accordingly, subject to his service contract, a director is at the mercy of the board. This is nicely illustrated by the case of *Re Richmond Gate Property Co. Ltd.* [1965] 1 WLR 335 where a managing director was appointed on the basis of an article equivalent to article 108 of Table A. (i.e. that "A managing director shall receive such remuneration ... as the directors may determine"). The company went into liquidation before any decision on remuneration had been taken by the directors. The managing director's claim for remuneration failed; he could not recover on a *quantum meruit* basis as there was an express contract and since the express contract provided for such remuneration as the directors may determine, "if they do not determine to pay him anything, he does not get anything".

(3) *To non directors*: In the above cases it is assumed that the committee members and managing directors are also directors. The articles may, however, permit certain functions to be delegated to individuals who are not directors. Somewhat confusingly these individuals are sometimes designated directors (e.g. sales directors) but they are not members of the board and are not directors within section 455(1) of the 1948 Act. Where such delegation is permitted by the articles its exercise will not involve a breach of the directors' duties of care and skill. In *Re City Equitable Fire Insurance Co. Ltd.* [1925] Ch. 407 Romer J. observed that "In respect of all duties that, having regard to the exigencies of business, and the articles of association, may properly be left to some other official. a director is, in the absence of grounds for suspicion, justified in trusting that official to perform such duties honestly ...".

Assignees and alternates

The articles may allow a director to assign his office to another person: however, where this is permitted, such an assignment is ineffective unless and until approved by a special resolution of the company (C.A. 1948, s. 204).

Assignment must be distinguished from the right to appoint an alternate to act in one's place during temporary absences. A director has no statutory right to appoint an alternate nor does Table A include such a power. If such a power is desired to be contained in a company's articles it is important that it is carefully and precisely drafted so as clearly to define the rights, duties and powers of the alternate (and see the chapter *Directors Meetings*).

Remuneration

"It is not implied from the mere fact that he is a director that he is to have a right to be paid for it" (per Bowen L.J. in *Hutton* v. *West Cork Railway Company Ltd.* (1883) 23 Ch.D. 654). However, the company's articles will usually allow directors' fees to be paid. Alternatively or in addition, a director may work for the company under a contract of service or under a contract for services (i.e. as employee or as independent contractor) under which he is to receive payment. Such a contract will often expressly or impliedly incorporate terms from the company's articles. It should also be noted that, in the absence of such a contract, a director may be able to recover on a *quantum meruit* basis for work done for the company. In *Craven-Ellis* v. *Canons Ltd.* [1936] 2 K.B. 403 Green L. J. in the Court of Appeal observed that the fact that the plaintiff's appointment as managing director was a nullity, since the plaintiff himself and the directors purporting to appoint him did not hold the required share qualification, "presents no obstacle to the implied promise to pay on a *quantum meruit* basis which arises from the performance of the services and the implied acceptance of the same by the company" (cf. *Re Richmond Gate Property Co. Ltd.*, above, where the right to remuneration depended on the board's resolution.)

Before looking in more detail at the director's right to remuneration three general points may be made:

First, under section 319(1)(b) of the 1948 Act, in the winding up of a company, priority is given, *inter alia*, to debts comprising "wages or salary ... of any clerk or servant". This will include salary due to a director under a service contract but not directors' fees.

Secondly, section 189 of the same Act prohibits the payment of a director's remuneration free of income tax; any such agreement is to have effect as if it provided for payment as a gross sum subject to income tax and surtax, of the net sum for which it actually provides.

Thirdly, under section 196 of the 1948 Act, details of directors' emoluments must be disclosed in the company's accounts. (This topic is dealt with in the chapter *Disclosure of Directors' Dealings*.)

Remuneration under the articles

The generally accepted view of the effect of section 20 of the Companies Act 1948 is that no article giving a person a right otherwise than in his capacity as member may be enforced by that person against the company, even if he is, in fact, a member (*Hickman* v. *Kent or Romney Marsh Sheepbreeders' Association* [1915] 1 Ch. 881; this interpretation of section 20 has been forcefully and repeatedly criticised by Professor Wedderburn based on the authority, *inter alia*, of *Quin & Axtens Ltd.* v. *Salmon* [1909] A.C. 442). Thus if an article appoints X as director and provides for his remuneration he may not sue to recover that remuneration on the basis of the article, even if he holds shares in the company, since that provision does not form part of his contract of membership under section 20 because it concerns him *qua* director. However, as will be seen, it is often possible to imply a service contract between the company and the director which incorporates the terms of the articles and by virtue of which the agreed remuneration may be recovered.

A company's articles will generally allow the company to vote fees or remuneration for its directors. Thus article 76 of Table A provides that "the remuneration of the directors shall from time to time be determined by the company in general meeting". If such an article is adopted it is the general meeting and not the board which must determine the remuneration (although the informal agreement of all the members could be equally effective – *Re Duomatic Ltd.* [1969] 2 Ch. 365 and *Cane v Jones* [1981] 1 All E.R. 533). In *Kerr* v. *Marine Products Ltd.* (1928) 44 T.L.R. 292 the plaintiff had been appointed by the board to act as "overseas director" at a salary of £1,800 per year; it was held that he could not recover this salary since the agreement was beyond the powers of the board, the articles requiring a determination of the general meeting. The articles may, however, allow the directors to vote their own remuneration. This is the case as regards managing directors under article 108 of Table A (see *Re Richmond Gate Property Co. Ltd.* [1965] 1 WLR 335, above).

The details of the director's entitlement to fees will depend on the company's articles. The directors may be entitled to a percentage of the company's profits, or to a fixed total amount which they may then allocate among themselves as they see fit, or to a fixed individual amount. Where the director's entitlement is to, for example, £10,000 per annum, problems have arisen as to whether an apportionment can take place if the director works for only part of the specified period. Article 76 of Table A provides that remuneration "shall be deemed to accrue from day to day", but in the absence of such a provision doubt has arisen as to whether directors' fees constitute "annuities" (defined as including 'salaries and pensions' by section 5) within section 2 of the Apportionment Act 1870. The cases on this point are inconclusive and unsatisfactory, the point being left open by the Court of Appeal in *Moriarty* v. *Regent's Garage and Engineering Co. Ltd.* [1921] 2 K.B. 767. If the Act does not apply it is simply a matter of construction of the particular article.

Remuneration under a contract outside the articles

Here we are concerned with the case where a director's service is terminated by the company and the claims he may have. A vital distinction which must be made is whether the director is an employee of the company or not. Only if the director is an employee will he qualify for the protection of the law relating to unfair dismissal and redundancy in Parts V and VI of the Employment Protection (Consolidation) Act 1978. The term "employee" is defined by section 153(1) of that Act as "an individual who has entered into or works under . . . a contract of employment". Thus it must be established whether a director's service is under a contract of service (making him an employee) or under a contract for services (making him an independent contractor). While it is clear that a director's contract may be a contract of service there is no clear way of recognising when this will be the case.

In *Folami* v. *Nigerline (U.K.) Ltd.* [1978] I.C.R. 277 the Employment Appeal Tribunal stated that "It seems to us that where it is established that a person has been appointed managing director of a company, that his duties include the effective management of the affairs of the company in all its respects, that he has discharged those duties, and that he has been recompensed by that company in the sense that he has received a salary from the hands of the company, the *prima facie* conclusion to be drawn is that he is an employee of the company." However, in *Parsons* v. *Albert J. Parsons & Sons* Ltd. [1979] I.C.R.271 the Court of Appeal reached the conclusion that the director in question was not an employee for the purposes of unfair dismissal. The applicant worked full-time as a director of the family company receiving remuneration which was referred to in the company's accounts as "directors' fees and emoluments" (the director being treated as self-employed in relation to national insurance contributions). Shaw L.J. remarked that "They saw as the reality of the matter that this was a family business and that the members of the family were utilising the companies concerned as agencies to carry on that business rather than the other way round". Thus in a large company, managing directors will generally be regarded as employees. *Parsons*, however, suggests that in a small family company even a full-time director may not enjoy the statutory protection because the company is in the nature of a quasi-partnership. The director may therefore be less well protected if he has a large personal stake in the business.

If a company terminates a directorship in breach of its contract with the director an action for damages will lie, and in the case of a director who is also an employee this will be in addition to any statutory claims. In order to establish if such a breach has occurred it is necessary to determine the terms of the contract, which may be express or implied. Problems often arise where the termination has resulted directly or indirectly from an alteration of the company's articles. Whilst it is a fundamental principle that a company cannot be precluded from exercising its statutory power to alter its articles under section 10 of the 1948 Act, the exercise of this power does not allow the company to justify a breach of contract. A frequent difficulty, therefore, in such cases is to determine whether it is an implied term of the contract that its content may be affected by a valid alteration of the company's articles.

The cases are not wholly consistent. In *Southern Foundries (1926) Ltd.* v. *Shirlaw* [1940] A.C. 701 Shirlaw was appointed managing director of Southern Limited for ten years. Later Southern Limited was taken over by Federated Limited and new articles were adopted for Southern Limited giving it the power to remove its managing directors. Shirlaw was removed from office under this new article and he sought damages for wrongful repudiation of contract. Viscount Maugham (in the minority) held that it was an "implied term of the contract that the company by altering its articles could give powers to a third party, including a power to dismiss the company's directors". The majority, however, held that Shirlaw could recover, not so much on the basis that the contract contained an implied term that the original articles should continue to govern Shirlaw's service, as on the basis of the positive rule of law expounded in *Stirling* v. *Maitland and Boyd* (1865) 5 B & S 840. In that case Cockburn L.J. stated that "if a party enters into an agreement which can only take effect by the continuance of a certain existing set of circumstances, there is an implied agreement on his part that he shall do nothing in his own motion to put an end to that state of circumstances under which the arrangement can be operative". This approach was followed by Diplock J. in *Shindler* v. *Northern Raincoat Co. Ltd.* [1960] 1 WLR 1038. This may be contrasted with *Read* v. *Astoria Garage (Streatham) Ltd.* [1952] Ch. 637 where the managing director was held to have been appointed under an implied contract which incorporated a term from the articles that the appointment should be subject to termination by the general meeting.

Thus it appears that if a managing director is appointed under an express contract it is unlikely that the company will be held to have the power to arrogate to itself, by a change in the articles, a right to terminate the contract without incurring liability. However, if the contract is an implied one it is likely to incorporate provisions from the articles and this may well include a term that it is to vary according to the company's articles.

Section 47 of the 1980 Act

The company in general meeting has the statutory power under section 184 of the 1948 Act to remove any director by ordinary resolution. If the exercise of this power involves a breach of contract, however, the director's right to recover damages is preserved by section 184(6). This could be a considerable disincentive to the exercise of the statutory power if the director in question is serving under a long service contract. The opportunity for abuse is particularly apparent where directors' contracts are settled by the board. Section 47 of the 1980 Act therefore seeks to curb this potential abuse by requiring approval of the general meeting for directors' (including shadow directors') contracts of employment of over five years duration. "Employment" for the purposes of this section is defined as including employment under a contract for services (section 47(7)(a)), so that the distinction between a director who is an employee and a director who is an independent contractor is irrelevant for section 47. Section 47 is aimed at:

"any term by which a director's employment with the company of which he is the director . . . is to continue or may be continued, otherwise than at the instance of the company . . . for a period exceeding five years during which the employment –

(a) cannot be terminated by the company by notice; or

(b) it can be so terminated only in specified circumstances" (section 47(2)).

To this, section 47(3) adds an anti-avoidance provision which requires the aggregation of the period of a new contract with the unexpired period of an earlier contract where a new contract is entered into containing such terms as are specified in section 47(2) more than six months before the expiration of the earlier contract. If this combined period is more than five years the arrangement is caught by the section.

As regards holding companies, section 47 applies to any employment by a director of a holding company in the group consisting of the holding company and its subsidiaries, and it is the approval of the general meeting of the holding company which must be sought. Section 47 does not, however, apply to the employment of a director of a company which is a wholly owned subsidiary (within the meaning of section 150 of the Companies Act 1948), although if the director is also a director of the holding company then approval by its general meeting will be required.

The Act does not *prohibit* such lengthy contracts, it merely requires that they be "first approved by the company in general meeting", that is by ordinary resolution. Before such a resolution can be passed, a written memorandum setting out the agreement must be available for inspection by the members of the company (apparently even by those with no right to vote at the meeting) at the company's registered office for at least fifteen days immediately preceding the meeting and at the meeting itself (section 47(4)). The object of the section may, however, possibly be defeated by the adoption of a variant of the weighted-voting article such as that in *Bushell* v. *Faith*, giving extra votes to the directors' shares on resolutions under this section. One may doubt whether the courts would sanction such blatant avoidance (but see the discussion of *Bushell* v. *Faith* below).

If an agreement contains a clause which contravenes section 47 this is not fatal to the whole agreement. The effect of the section is merely to render the offensive term void to the extent that it contravenes the section; in addition the agreement is deemed to contain a term entitling the company to terminate it at any time by giving reasonable notice (section 47(5)).

In the case of companies covered by the City Code on Takeovers, there are now extra-statutory rules prohibiting directors voting themselves new service contracts after an offer has been made for their company.

The 1967 Companies Act contains certain publicity requirements for directors' service contracts; these are dealt with in the chapter *Disclosure of Directors' Dealings*.

Termination of a director's office

Resignation

A director may resign his directorship at any time (*Glossop* v. *Glossop* [1907] 2 Ch. 370). A director's resignation may, nevertheless, be in breach of his service contract which will render him liable in damages to the company.

Retirement by rotation

A company's articles usually provide for a certain proportion of the directors to retire each year. A typical example is article 89 of Table A, which provides that:

"At the first annual general meeting of the company all the directors shall retire from office, and at the annual general meeting in every subsequent year one-third of the directors for the time being ... shall retire from office."

Such retirement is often, however, a mere formality. The directors will be eligible for re-election (article 91 of Table A) and a director presenting himself for re-election will be deemed to have been re-elected unless "it is expressly resolved not to fill such vacated office or unless a resolution for the re-election of such director shall have been put to the meeting and lost" (article 92 of Table A).

Retirement due to age

Section 185 of the 1948 Act establishes an upper age limit for directors. This section, however, only applies to public companies or to private companies which are subsidiaries of public companies (section 185(8)). Even as regards these companies the section has effect subject to the company's articles and, in any case, the age limit does not apply if the director's appointment is approved by a resolution of the general meeting of which special notice (within section 142 of the 1948 Act) stating the age of the director has been given (section 185(5)).

Where section 185 does apply subsections (1) and (2) provide that a person may not be appointed a director once he has attained the age of 70, and if already a director he must vacate his office at the next annual general meeting following his seventieth birthday.

A person appointed or proposed to be appointed as a director of a company subject to section 185 is under an obligation to inform the company of his age if he has attained the retiring age (C.A. 1948, s. 186). This does not apply to reappointments, since the director's date of birth will already be contained in the company's register of directors under section 200 of the 1948 Act.

On the resignation or retirement of a director, notice must be given to the Registrar of Companies on Form 9b (and to The Stock Exchange if the company is listed); see the chapter *Disclosure of Directors' Dealings*.

Disqualification

Under the articles

The articles usually contain provisions for a director to vacate his office on the occurrence of various events, e.g. becoming of unsound mind or absenting himself voluntarily for more than six months from board meetings without permission (see article 88 of Table A). Also where a director is required to hold qualifying shares, ceasing to hold those shares will usually be stated to cause vacation of office (see above). In such cases the office is *ipso facto* vacated on the occurrence of the disqualifying event (*Re Bodega Co. Ltd.* [1904] 1 Ch. 276).

By statute

Various statutory provisions provide either for automatic disqualification or allow the court to make a disqualification order. First, section 187 of the Companies Act 1948 provides that an undischarged bankrupt commits a criminal offence if he, without the leave of the court, acts as a director or liquidator or takes part directly or indirectly in the promotion, formation or management of any company. If leave is sought to allow an undischarged bankrupt so to act, notice of such application must be given to the official receiver, who is under an obligation to oppose the application if he feels that to allow it would be contrary to the public interest (section 187(2)).

Secondly, section 188 of the 1948 Act allows the court to make an order disqualifying a person from acting as director if one of three things is established:

(a) the person is convicted of an indictable offence in connection with the promotion, formation, management or liquidation of a company;

(b) the person appears to have been persistently in default regarding the statutory requirements in relation to returns, accounts, etc (see section 188 (2C) for the meaning of persistently – broadly three or more defaults);

(c)   the person appears to have been guilty in the course of the winding up of a company of an offence under section 332 of the 1948 Act or of some other fraud or breach of duty as officer, liquidator, receiver or manager.

The effect of such a disqualification order is that the person against whom it is made may not, without the leave of the court, be a liquidator or a *director* or a receiver or manager of the property of a company or in any way, whether directly or indirectly, be concerned or take part in the promotion, formation or management of a company. To act in contravention of such an order again constitutes a criminal offence (section 188(6)). The maximum length of disqualification which can be ordered is five years if the order is made by a summary court or if it relates to persistent failure to make returns, but in other cases is fifteen years. (See Appendix 4 for a Home Office circular dealing with disqualification orders under section 188.)

Thirdly, section 9 of the Insolvency Act 1976 allows for a similar disqualification order to be made against a person who has been a director of two or more companies which have gone into liquidation within five years, if it appears to the court that the director's conduct as director of any of those companies makes him unfit to be concerned in the management of a company. The maximum disqualification period here is five years and the application for an order under this section must be made either by the official receiver or by the Secretary of State.

Under section 29 of the 1976 Act the Secretary of State must maintain a register of disqualification orders made under section 188 of the 1948 Act and section 9 of the Insolvency Act 1976.

Removal of a director under section 184

Notwithstanding any provision to the contrary in a company's articles or in its contract with a director, the company may remove that director by ordinary resolution by virtue of section 184 of the Companies Act 1948. This section applies to all directors except a director of a private company who held office for life on July 18, 1945.

Where it is proposed to remove a director under this section special notice of such resolution is required (under section 142 of the 1948 Act). The director affected has the right to be heard at the meeting and if the director so requests the company is obliged to circularise his written representations to the members before the meeting (sections 184(2) and (3)), although the company may be relieved of this obligation if the court is satisfied that the right is being abused to secure needless publicity for defamatory matter (section 184(3)).

Although the company has the legal right thus to terminate a director's office, two important legal consequences for the company may flow from the exercise of that right.

First, the director so removed may petition for the company's winding up on the "just and equitable" ground under section 222(f) of the Companies Act 1948, on the authority of the decision of the House of Lords in *Ebrahimi* v. *Westbourne Galleries* [1973] A.C. 360. Such a petition may well be successful where the director has a substantial stake in a small family company (often formerly a partnership) "formed on a basis of personal relationship, involving mutual confidence", for here the individuals' "rights, expectations and obligations *inter se* . . . are not necessarily submerged in the company structure".

Secondly, where a director is removed in this way, section 184(6) states that he is not thereby deprived of any compensation or damages payable in respect of the termination of his appointment.

Section 184 was introduced on the recommendation of the Cohen Committee to give the shareholders greater power over the directors. This object may, however, be circumvented by the adoption of an article which provides for the director's shares to carry extra votes on a resolution under section 184. Such a clause was upheld by the House of Lords in *Bushell* v. *Faith* [1970] A.C. 1099 in what has been described by Professor Schmitthoff as "one of the most remarkable instances of judicial interpretation defeating the clear intention of the legislator" ([1970] J.B.L. 1).

The 300 issued shares in a private company had been allotted equally to the defendant and his two sisters and article 9 of the company's articles provided that in the event of a resolution being proposed at a general meeting of the company for the removal of a director, any share held by that director should carry three votes. The two sisters sought to remove their brother and claimed that the resolution had been passed by 200 votes to 100; the brother, however, claimed on the basis of article 9 that the resolution had been defeated by 300 votes to 200. The majority of the House of Lords held that a company is at liberty to allocate its voting rights in any way it sees fit, and this freedom is unaffected by section 184 (Lord Morris dissenting argued that to sanction such a scheme "would be to make a mockery of the law"). Lord Donovan felt that Parliament may have left this freedom with companies deliberately, for "there are many small companies which are conducted in practice as though they were little more than partnerships, particularly family companies running a family business; and it is, unfortunately, sometimes necessary to provide some safeguard against family quarrels having their repercussions in the boardroom". It has been suggested, following these *dicta*, that the *ratio* of the case does not extend to public companies; the *ratio* is not, however, expressly restricted to private companies or "partnership companies". In this latter case the remedy of "just and equitable" winding up may well be available in any case. Lord Reid observed that the novel practice of adopting weighted voting provisions "may not have been contemplated in 1948 and it may be that the whole practice will be reviewed when amendments to the Companies Acts are being proposed". No such amendment has yet taken place although clause 44 of the lapsed 1973 Bill would have outlawed such clauses.

Directors' Duties

Rational treatment of the law on directors' duties is impeded for at least two reasons. First, the law does not present, and should not be regarded as, a consistent code of conduct for directors. Though courts speak of the existence of duties the discovery of a duty is often merely a step to providing a remedy. Secondly, directors' conduct may be impugned under more than one so-called head of duty. For both reasons, it is helpful and accurate to view directors' duties from the point of view of the remedies available to a company against allegedly defaulting directors. But it is conventional and probably right to separate directors' fiduciary duties and those of skill and care. By pointing to the former a company can say that directors have done something they ought not to have done. By pointing to the latter it can be said that they have done badly what they may legitimately do.

General considerations

The duties of directors may be owed by people who are not expressly appointed directors and by those who are not actually called directors. This is particularly so in relation to duties imposed by the Companies Acts rather than under general company law. For some purposes of the Companies Acts directors' duties are owed by "any person occupying the position of director by whatever name called" (C.A. 1948, s. 455(1) and C.A. 1967, s. 56(1) respectively). For the purposes of many Companies Acts' provisions (e.g. sections 124, 200, 201, 407 to 409, 414 and 415 of the 1948 Act, and sections 25, 27, 29 and 30 of the 1967 Act), and notably in Part IV of the Companies Act 1980 ("Duties of Directors and Conflicts of Interest": see pages 260 to 264) "any person in accordance with whose directions or instructions the directors of a company are accustomed to act" is a director (called a "shadow" director in the 1980 Act). Reference to shadow directors prevents avoidance of duty by, for example, someone who appoints a nominee director or is a substantial shareholder and who controls the company at one remove. Professional advisers, such as solicitors and accountants, may not be shadow directors by virtue only of the advice they give as professional advisers (e.g. C.A. 1981, s. 63(1)). A holding company is not a shadow director of a subsidiary by virtue only of section 63 of the Companies Act 1980 (section 63(5)). Section 63(3) and (4) imports the concept of a shadow director into section 26 of the Companies Act 1967 (directors' service contracts) and section 199 of the Companies Act 1948 (directors' disclosure of contractual interests).

248

Directors' duties are the duties of directors singly, though the duty to act in the company's interests is a requirement that directors make corporate decisions properly which typically affects directors as a body. Where several directors are liable for a default they are jointly and severally liable (see, for example, *Re Englefield Colliery Co* (1878) 8 Ch.D.388). Knowledgeable third party participants in directors' breaches may be liable as constructive trustees in some circumstances (*Belmont Finance Corporation Limited v Williams Furniture Limited* [1978] 3 W.L.R. 712).

Orthodoxy has it that directors' duties are owed to the company and not to its shareholders, employees or creditors. Support for this is given by *Percival v Wright* [1902] 2 Ch. 421, and section 46 of the Companies Act 1980, which imposes a duty on directors to consider employee interests, but states that this is owed to the company alone. The practical point of this analysis is that a minority shareholder can only exceptionally sue to enforce a company's rights (*Foss v Harbottle* (1843) 2 Hare 461; see generally page 788). It also means that the directors of a company do not owe any duties to a subsidiary, at least if the subsidiary has different directors (*Lindgren v L & P Estates Limited* [1978] Ch. 572).

Fiduciary duties

Very crudely, and rather unhelpfully, it can be said that a director must not abuse his position as a director or, in those cases where duties are analysed in such terms, as a trustee of company property. The roles of director and trustee both generate the same fiduciary duties so far as directors are concerned.

It is generally considered that, as a fiduciary, a director must not put himself in a position where his personal interests and those of the company conflict. However it seems a director will not be liable merely for getting into a position of potential abuse (see *Swain v Law Society* [1981] 3 All E.R. 797, 813 per Oliver L.J.). Thus, it is not without more a breach of duty for a director of one company to be a director of another company even where the companies compete (*London and Maschonoland Exploration Co Limited v New Maschonoland Exploration Co Limited* (1891) W.N. 165), or to otherwise work for or prosecute the interests of some outsider.

Fiduciary duties are talked of, first, when a company wants to invalidate the actions of directors supposedly taken on the company's behalf and, secondly, when a company wants to recover a loss or prevent a director's unjust enrichment. These two circumstances are dealt with in turn.

Invalidation of directors' decisions

Directors must act "bona fide in what they consider – not what the court may consider – is in the interests of the company, and not for any collateral purpose" (*Re Smith & Fawcett Limited* [1942] Ch. 304, 306 per Lord Greene M.R.). This is the overriding duty.

The essence of the duty is that directors must do what is right for the company, and there are three main possible ways of impugning directors' actions for not so doing.

(1) *They might not have considered the company's interests.* This is not so much to do with directors' deliberations before acting, but is more an implication of law from their conduct. It could mean any one of four things. First, that they did not give their mind to the matter at all, either because it never occurred to them or because they acted unthinkingly on another's instructions (*Selangor United Rubber Estates Limited v Cradock* [1967] 1 W.L.R. 1168) or advice (*Re W & M Roith Limited* [1967] 1 W.L.R. 432, where a solicitor gave advice that the impugned action was the right thing to do). Secondly, and amounting to much the same thing, that they acted in their own or some third party's interest (e.g. that of the wife in *Re Roith, supra*, who benefited by the pension arrangements contained in the director's impugned service contract with the company). Thirdly, that they could not possibly have considered the company's interests because they had fettered their discretion to do so by (a) promising an outsider or co-director or a shareholder to do something (e.g. to vote a certain way) or (b) by being or getting into a position of actual or potential conflict of interest (*Re Englefield Colliery Co* (1878) 8 Ch. D.388, where directors agreed before a company's registration to pay sums to a promoter out of company funds). A director's liability for fettering his discretion is sometimes said to give rise to a duty in its own right. Fourthly, that they might have done something which an intelligent and reasonable man could not reasonably have considered was in the company's interests (*Gething v Kilner* [1972] 1 W.L.R. 337, 342 per Brightman J; *Charterbridge Corporation v Lloyds Bank* [1970] Ch 62, 74 per Pennycuick J). Each of these ways of interpreting directors' duties may be interchangeable in a given case. The last is a route to the courts' objective control over standards of directors' conduct. A director could, of course, defend himself in each case by showing that, in the particular circumstances, he had acted in the company's interests.

(2) *They might not have acted bona fide (i.e. honestly and in good faith).* This is not an independent requirement of directors' liability. In *Re Roith supra* the director acted in good faith but his action was invalidated nonetheless.

(3) *They might have acted for a collateral purpose.* An action is clearly invalid if *ultra vires* or illegal. But *intra vires* and legal actions may be invalid if carried out for what a court considers as an improper or collateral purpose. Though a court will not expressly substitute its own for the directors' view of a purpose it may override the directors' view if it decides that in the circumstances they could not have acted on that purpose. In *Howard Smith Limited v Ampol Limited* [1974] A.C. 821 Lord Wilberforce said that a court in deciding what a purpose was should view the matter objectively and "if it finds that a particular

requirement [i.e. of the company] though real, was not urgent, or critical, at the relevant time, it may have reason to doubt, or discount, the assertions of individuals that they acted solely in order to deal with it" (*ibid*, p. 832).

The case of *Howard Smith Limited v Ampol Limited* illustrates these principles at work:

> Both litigant companies wanted to take over X Limited. Ampol and an associated company already owned 55 per cent of X Limited's shares. The majority of X Limited's directors resolved to issue new shares to Howard Smith Limited. Ampol challenged the share issue. The court said (i) that the shares had been issued for the purpose of destroying Ampol's majority not (as was argued) for the purpose of providing capital for X Limited (the former was a more pressing and, therefore, a more likely purpose in the circumstances than the need for capital), (ii) that the purpose was improper because the primary (though not exclusive) purpose of issuing shares was the provision of capital, (iii) that it was irrelevant that the directors had not acted out of self-interest (cf. *Hogg v Cramphorn* [1967] Ch. 254 where it was said to be irrelevant that directors who tried to preserve their position on the board did so honestly believing it was in the company's interests).

It is permissible for directors to promote their own interests (*Hirsche v Sims* [1849] A.C. 654, 660 per Lord Selborne) or those of anybody else (*Parke v Daily News* [1962] Ch. 927), where to do so is in the company's interests. This permits the promoting of employees' interests (see C.A. 1980, s. 48) or those of a group of companies of which the directors' is one (*Charterbridge Corporation v Lloyds Bank* [1970] Ch. 62). However, there is a danger that where directors could be seen to be acting for several purposes a court will say they acted for one that was collateral. Where a director fails to consider the employees' interests, section 46 of the Companies Act 1980 confirms the employees' limited remedy in this way:

> "(1) The matters to which the directors of a company are to have regard in the performance of their functions shall include the interests of the company's employees in general as well as the interests of its members.
>
> (2) Accordingly, the duty imposed by subsection (1) above on the directors of a company is owed by them to the company (and to the company alone) and is enforceable in the same way as any other fiduciary duty owed to a company by its directors."

The practical effect of the section is to deny an employee a direct remedy against defaulting directors, and to permit a shareholder such an action only if he argues himself into an exception to the rule in *Foss v Harbottle* (see page 790) or brings himself within section 75 of the Companies Act 1980 (see page 803).

The interests of the company as such need not be the same as those of its shareholders. It would probably be a failure to act in the company's interests for directors to accumulate profits for the benefit of the company as a corporate body if that meant failing to pay shareholders' dividends. As Lord Evershed M.R. said in a different context in *Greenhalgh v Arderne Cinemas* [1951] Ch. 286, 291:

> "The phrase "the company as a whole" does not mean the company as a commercial entity distinct from the corporators; it means the corporators as a general body."

Directors must balance fairly the different interests of different classes of present shareholders (*Henry v G.N.R.* (1857) 1 De G & J 606, 638 per Lord Cranworth) and those of present and future shareholders (see Savoy Hotel Investigation, H.M.S.O. 1954).

The difficulty of balancing sectional and long and short-term interests exposes directors to the risk of inadvertent breach of duty. But their position is made easier by the possibility of relief from liability (see page 216). Moreover, an Australian case suggests that the courts may be realistically lenient in establishing the existence of a breach. In *Mills v Mills* (1938) 60 C.L.R. 150, 164, Latham C. J. said that directors are not,

> "... required by law to live in an unreal region of detached altruism and to act in a vague mood of ideal abstraction from obvious fact which may be present to the mind of any honest but intelligent man when he exercises his powers as a director."

Anything done by directors or a director in making corporate decisions, or exercising the powers conferred on him by the company's articles, which is not bona fide in the company's interest is void and may be declared so by the company. An agreement with a third party will be set aside only if the third party knew that the director was acting in breach of duty (*Charterbridge Corporation Limited v Lloyds Bank* [1970] Ch. 62, 69 per Pennycuick J and *Rolled Steel Products (Holdings) Limited v British Steel Corporation* [1982] 3 W.L.R. 715). A director, or directors jointly and severally, may be personally liable for any loss or profit flowing from their actions.

Loss recovery and the prevention of unjust enrichment: duties as director

Liability for causing loss to the company

A director may be a fiduciary by virtue of his position as a director. As fiduciaries directors are liable to compensate those to whom their duties are owed for loss resulting from their defaults (see *Knot v Cottee* (1852) 16 Beav. 77). The most conspicuous example of loss that may be caused by directors acting as such is the misuse of corporate property. Usually the duty of directors in relation to property is said to be owed *qua* trustee of company property rather than *qua* director. For a recent example of a director misusing company property, see *International Sales & Agencies v Marcus* [1982] 3 W.L.R. 551 (where it was held that the recipient of the misapplied property held it as constructive trustee).

Liability for profits made

Where a director profits personally from his position, the courts will often give a remedy to a company not on the basis that he has acted in breach of trust, but simply because of his fiduciary position as a director (cf. the cases on page 255).

Possibly most abuses of position are attributable to use of corporate information, but the way in which a profit is made is irrelevant in establishing liability under the present heading. The basis of liability in such cases is not that a director has mishandled property, but that he has enriched himself unjustly by abusing his fiduciary position as a director: "The liability arises from the mere fact of a profit having ... been made." This comment was made by Lord Russell in *Regal (Hastings) Limited v Gulliver* [1942] 1 All E.R. 378, which is a typical case. Regal owned one cinema, wanted two more and intended to sell all three as a going concern. The deal was structured so that the company and its directors (in their own right) subscribed for the shares of a subsidiary company set up to take the two new cinema leases. The directors made a profit on the subsequent sale of the subsidiary's shares. The company (now controlled by its purchasers) wanted to recover that profit. It won. The directors had to account to the company for their profit.

The basis of liability is summed up by Lord Russell as follows:

> "The rule of equity which insists on those who by the use of a fiduciary position make a profit, being liable to account for that profit, in no way depends on fraud or absence of bona fides; or upon such questions or considerations as whether the profit would or should otherwise have gone to the plaintiff, or whether he took a risk or acted as he did for the benefit of the plaintiff, or whether the plaintiff has in fact been damaged or benefited by his action." (*ibid* p. 386)

The directors were liable even though they had caused no loss to the company, and neither the profit-making opportunity nor the profit itself was fixed with a trust or said to belong in equity to the company.

Thus, under the present law, a director's enrichment need not be at the company's expense. If directors attract a contract to themselves by virtue of their position (and profit thereby), they are liable even though the other party had refused to contract with the company (*Industrial Development Consultants Limited v Cooley* [1972] 1 W.L.R. 443, 453 per Roskill J.). Nor does it matter that the company was financially or legally unable to acquire the benefit in question. In *Boston Deep Sea Fishing and Ice Co v Ansell* (1888) 39 Ch. 339, account was ordered of directors' profits from bonuses paid to them although the company could not have received them, not being a shareholder of the bonus-paying company. Moreover, it would seem not to matter that the company had refused to agree to the arrangement which generated the enrichment. However, there is a case for arguing for the introduction into English law of the principle revealed in the Canadian case of *Peso Silver Mines v Cropper* (1966) 58 D.L.R. (2d) 1, where a director was held not to be liable for a benefit which the company had refused to acquire.

One area in which a director may make an unjustifiable profit otherwise than at the company's expense is by dealing in the company's shares as a result of obtaining confidential price sensitive information, for example, as to an imminent takeover bid or the company's financial results. The ability of a director with confidential information to deal in listed shares or to deal in any shares on a recognised stock exchange is now severely curtailed by Part V of the Companies Act 1980 (see *Insider Dealing*, page 473).

Although there is little authority on the point, it is probable that a director who uses confidential information to deal in shares could be liable to account for his profit on the basis of the principles just discussed. In this respect, the cases discussed under *Misuse of information*, below, will often be relevant. In practice, of course, it is not the company which suffers loss and therefore there is little incentive for a company to bring proceedings – particularly where the director is punishable for his actions under the criminal law.

Exceptions to prohibition of personal profit

The principal limitations on this head of liability are these:

(1) "The plaintiff has to establish . . . that what the directors did was so related to the affairs of the company that it can properly be said to have been done in the course of their management and in utilisation of their opportunities and special knowledge as directors" (*Phipps v Boardman* [1967] 2 A.C. 46, p. 391 per Lord Macmillan).

(2) In principle, a director can escape liability if the impugned action was performed qua individual not qua director, but, in practice, this may be hard to establish. A director has "one capacity and one capacity only" in which to carry on business and that is as a director-fiduciary (*Industrial Development Consultants Limited v Cooley supra* p. 451 per Roskill J.).

(3) Where it is argued that a director has profited from the use of information, the question to ask ought to be whether the information would have been in the director's knowledge but for his directorship. Whilst this is equivalent to the question whether confidential information is property (discussed below), it would detract from the purity of the principle described in this section if anything were to turn on the nature of the profit-producing information. So when Roskill J. in *Industrial Development Consultants v Cooley, supra*, says that a director has a duty in respect of information of "concern to the plaintiffs and . . . relevant to the plaintiffs to know" he should be taken as meaning no more than that a director makes a profit from his position when he uses information he has by virtue of his position.

(4) Arguably, a constructive trust should not be fixable on an enrichment obtained in breach of duty except where company property has been misapplied and the director is in breach of trust as a result (see *Lister v Stubbs*, discussed below). If a company's only remedy in the absence of a substantive trust of company property is an account of profits that would mean that a director could retain, say, shares obtained in breach of duty. But some cases defy orthodox principle, and treat as company property shares obtained as bribes by directors (*Re Morvah Consols Tin Mining Co* (1875) 2 Ch. 1, 6, 7 per Mellish L. J. and Brett J.; *Eden v Ridsdales Railway Lamp Co Limited* (1889) 23 Q.B.D. 368).

Liability for non-disclosure of contractual interests

A director's statutory duty to disclose such interests is discussed in the chapter *Disclosure of Directors Dealings*, page 311. Where a director is personally interested in a contract to which the company is a party and has not disclosed the interest, the company will be entitled to any profit made under the principles already discussed. The company may also discontinue the source of the director's enrichment by setting aside the contract, as it is voidable at its option against all but bona fide third parties without notice of the breach of duty (*Transvaal Lands Co v New Belgium etc. Co* [1914] 2 Ch. 488). A breach of the disclosure duty is ratifiable.

In practice, virtually all company's include a provision in their articles allowing a director to be interested in a contract with the company (see e.g. article 84 of Table A). The article will normally provide that the director is not liable for any profit made, and will often allow him to count towards the quorum for, and vote at, the board meeting which considers the contract. It appears that an article of this type is not prohibited by section 205 of the 1948 Act (see further below).

Loss recovery and the prevention of unjust enrichment: duties as trustee

However desirable and accurate it is to say that all financial recovery of a non-contractual kind from defaulting directors rests on the principles already described, and that a director's trusteeship of company property is simply another source of fiduciary duties, there are cases in which the courts have held that directors are trustees and provide a remedy on that ground (see, for example, *Selangor United Rubber Estates Limited v Cradock (No. 3)* [1968] 1 W.L.R. 1555, 1575 per Ungoed-Thomas J.). The practical significance of this is that proprietary remedies become available to the company (it also lets the courts show the importance of preserving corporate assets). Availability of proprietary relief allows recovery in rem of misapplied property or its product, not merely from a defaulting director but by way of tracing from third parties who hold the property other than as bona fide purchasers for value. This is advantageous to a company where any personal claim against a director is ineffective. For example a director's default may not give rise to a debt and a personal action as in *Sinclair v Brougham* [1914] A.C. 398. It is also advantageous where the holder of the property is insolvent (in which case the company would be a secured creditor). It allows recovery not merely of the property but of any profits flowing from its use which are said to belong in equity to the company (*Keech v Sandford* (1726) Sel. Cas. Ch. 261; *Cook v Deeks* [1916] 1 A.C. 554). Where a director's or a third party's enrichment from the property's use takes the form of shares or contractual rights they are held on trust for the company (*Cook v Deeks, supra*).

The position in the simple case of loss arising from default is as follows:

"As soon as the conclusion is arrived at that the company's money has been applied by the directors for purposes which the company cannot sanction, it follows that the directors are liable to replace the money however honestly they have acted." (*Re Sharpe* [1892] 1 Ch. 154, 165 per Lindley J.)

Re Sharpe has the typical pattern of this kind of case. A company's articles prohibited payment of dividends except out of profits. Its directors paid interest to shareholders out of capital. The Court of Appeal held that the directors' action was ultra vires the company and they were in breach of their duties as trustees of company property. The company recovered the amount of the wrongful payments (plus interest).

The purposes which the company cannot sanction are those which are illegal, ultra vires the company, improper or pursued by directors otherwise than bona fide in the company's interests. Directors must handle corporate property "for the company's purposes in accordance with their duties, powers and functions" (*Selangor United Rubber Estates Limited v Cradock* [1967] 1 W.L.R. 1168).

A director will be liable even in the absence of bad faith (*Re Sharpe, supra*, p. 158 per North J.). Examples of breach of trust when property is applied for illegal purposes are payments made in contravention of statute (e.g. C.A. 1948, ss. 190 and 191; and C.A. 1981, s. 42).

Mis-use of information

The mis-spending of company money is the clearest case for granting proprietary relief by applying a trust analysis of a defaulting director's duty. The aim in such a case (as in *Re Sharpe, supra*) is to restore a company's loss. More difficult is the application of a trust analysis to profits made by directors' misuse of information. A trust could be imposed on such profits or other kinds of benefit such as shares or contractual rights where directors use information in breach of fiduciary duty. In some cases that fiduciary duty derives from a director's position as director and a trust is imposed on the profit or benefit he receives (*Cook v Deeks* [1916] 1 A.C. 554; *Re Morvah Consols Tin Mining Co* (1875) 2 Ch. D. 1; *Eden v Ridsdales Railway Lamp and Lighting Co Limited* (1889) 23 Q.B.D. 368). In most it derives from a director's trusteeship of property (cf. *Phipps v Boardman* [1967] 2 A.C. 46).

Both derivations of the trust of the enrichment achieve the same practical result of allowing proprietary remedies against directors for the enrichment's recovery. Both could helpfully be seen as alternative routes to the provision of a particular kind of remedy. But the law does not conventionally regard them as such. Where there is a substantive trust of property it will fix profits from the property's misuse with a trust, but where the director's duty derives merely from his position as director a company has only the personal remedy of an account of profits (*Lister v Stubbs* (1890) 45 Ch. D. 1). If a substantive trust of property is necessary to fix a trust on a director's enrichment from the use of corporate information it is critical to see whether and to what extent information is property.

It is not certain that information ought to be treated as property (see *Jones* (1970) 86 L.Q.R. 463; *Phipps v Boardman, supra*, p. 127 per Lord Upjohn). But several cases assume that it is (*Phipps v Boardman, supra*, p. 107 per Lord Hodson, p. 115 per Lord Guest; and *Bell Houses v City Wall Properties Limited* [1966] 2 Q.B. 656). If it is accepted that it is, it is not clear whether all information to which a director has access qua fiduciary is property and fixed with a trust (*Phipps v Boardman, supra*, p. 114 per Lord Guest), or only either that which is confidential (*ibid* p. 114 per Lord Guest) or that which is of value to the company (*Bell Houses v City Wall Properties Limited, supra*, p. 680 per Danckwerts L.J.; p. 693 per Salmon L.J.), or that which is of concern to the company (*Industrial Development Consultants Limited v Cooley, supra*, p. 451 per Roskill J.); or whether these alternative tests are – functionally at least – the same. Probably they are and the true test is no more than that the information from which the profit was made derived from the director's special position and knowledge as director. This mirrors the sole requirement for liability to account for profits, which is that any enrichment must derive from a director's special knowledge and opportunity (cf. *Phipps v Boardman, supra*, p. 391 per Lord Macmillan).

Cases on confidentiality indicate the kinds of information the law protects. That a unifying principle of practical use is hard to find, and that cases are to be viewed on their facts, is suggested by Ungoed-Thomas J. He was confident that courts recognise what information is confidential (*Duke of Argyll v Duchess of Argyll* [1967] Ch. 302, 330). But it seems that to be confidential information must not be public knowledge (*Saltman Engineering Co Limited v Campbell Engineering Co Limited* [1963] 3 All E.R. 413, 415 per Lord Greene M R), or merely a matter of the ordinary skill and ability ("know-how") of directors (cf. *Herbert Morris Limited v Saxelby* [1916] 1 A.C. 688, 704 per Lord Atkinson). However, it need not, in the case of inventions, be in relation to anything novel or specially commissioned (*Cranleigh Precision Engineering Limited v Bryant* [1965] 1 W.L.R. 1293).

It may be that recovery of a defaulting director's enrichment analysed in terms of a director's trusteeship of corporate assets mirrors the recovery of profits where no substantive trust is in question. However it is said that a director's liability in respect of corporate information is stricter than that of a non-director employee (*Baker v Gibbons* [1972] 1 W.L.R. 693, 700 per Pennycuick V C), presumably because of the proprietary aspects of the matter. It is possible that the additional requirement that the information must be property might be used as a bar to a recovery which might otherwise be possible in the absence of that requirement (cf. *Industrial Development Consultants Limited v Cooley* [1972] 1 W.L.R. 443, 451 per Roskill J.).

Result of breach of trust

Whatever it takes to make a director liable, and whether the trust of the enrichment derives from an existing trust of corporate property or is merely remedial, the result is the same, and critically different from the effect of the liability under the principle preventing unjust enrichment (page 252). The company is entitled to proprietary relief, which allows a company to follow its property into third parties' hands and obtain an order for its preservation pending trial (R.S.C. Ord. 50, r. 3), and recover any profit made as a result of its use. Had a trust analysis been invoked in *Regal (Hastings) Limited v Gulliver, supra*, the shares purchased by the directors on the basis of the information they had at their disposal as directors would have been fixed with a trust. This would have permitted the recovery of the shares from purchasers from the directors – subject to the usual defences to restitutionary claims such as bona fide purchase for value – in addition to recovery of any profit on their sale from the directors. Persons into whose hands the company's property comes as a result of a breach of trust may be liable as constructive trustees: see *Selangor United Rubber Estates Limited v Cradock* [1968] 1 All E.R. 1093; *Belmont Finance Corporation v Williams Furniture Limited* (No. 2) [1980] 1 All E.R. 393 and *International Sales and Agencies Limited v Marcus* [1982] 3 All E.R. 551.

Example

The following example illustrates the law's response to directors' use of corporate information, and the difference between liability as a director and liability as a trustee.

X, Y and Z are directors and majority shareholders of Mega Limited. For some time Mega has supplied goods and services to Macro Limited. Knowing of Macro's requirements, X, Y and Z contract to supply goods and services to Macro of the kind which Mega remains ready and willing to supply. They make a profit from doing so. There is no suggestion of misrepresentations having been made by X, Y and Z to Macro.

Mega is entitled to the directors' profits on one of two grounds. First, because the contract and any profit from it is fixed with a constructive trust (*either* because the information as to the profit-making opportunity is Mega's property, in respect of which the directors are in breach of trust *or*, controversially, because a constructive trust flows from the directors' breach of a fiduciary duty stemming from their positions as directors). Alternatively, because the directors must account for the profits from their abuse of fiduciary position as directors. In addition to these fiduciary remedies, X, Y and Z, had they had service contracts with the company, would be liable (i) to summary dismissal for so enriching themselves even if their default is an isolated act (*Boston Deep Sea Fishing and Ice Co v Ansell* (1888) 39 Ch.D. 339), and (ii) for damages in respect of the company's lost business opportunity, the measure of damages reflecting the likelihood of the company itself getting the contract (*Industrial Development Consultants Limited v Cooley* [1972] 2 All E.R. 162, 176 per Roskill J.).

Statutory duties

Statutory provisions have extended the principles discussed. A director has a considerable number of statutory tasks to perform under the Companies Acts, with failure being punishable by fines and in some cases imprisonment, or disqualification from acting as a director under section 188 of the 1948 Act, as amended. For a recent example, see *Re Civica Investments Limited*, Financial Times Law Reports, June 8, 1982, where a director was disqualified under what is now section 188 for failing to deliver accounts. In addition, the Companies Acts have in certain areas extended or modified the common law rules, concerning breach of trust or fiduciary duty, and it is these extensions and modifications with which this section is concerned.

(1) Option dealings

Section 25 of the Companies Act 1967 prohibits a director (and anyone in accordance with whose directions the director is accustomed to act, and the director's spouse and children) from buying – though not from selling – options to buy or sell the listed debentures or shares of his company or of a company in the same group (sections 25(1) and (2)).

The options in question are stated to be the right to make or call for delivery of shares or debentures or the right to elect to do so (the time limit for exercise and the amount and number involved having been specified (section 25(1)(a)(b)(c)).

The penalty for non-compliance is a fine or imprisonment for a term not exceeding three months on summary conviction and two years on indictment (section 25(1)).

A director's freedom to buy convertible debentures or options to subscribe for them is expressly preserved (section 25(4)).

(2) Loss of office payments

Section 191 of the Companies Act 1948 requires disclosure to members and approval by the company of a company's payments to a director for loss of office or as consideration for or in connection with retirement from office. The section requires (a) disclosure to all members (i.e. voting and non-voting; *Re Duomatic Limited* [1969] 2 Ch. 365) before any payment is made, and (b) approval by the company by assent of all voting members or by resolution in general meeting (*Re Duomatic Limited, supra*). It applies only to uncovenanted payments and does not affect contractual obligations to pay (*Tampoa Tatara Timber Co Limited v Rowe* [1977] 3 All E.R. 123 (P.C.)).

Section 192 of the 1948 Act imposes a similar requirement in respect of payments to a director for loss of office made not by the company but from some other source in connection with a transfer of the company's undertaking or property. Undisclosed and unauthorised payments are to be held in trust for the company (section 192(2)). In this connection a quite properly disclosed payment by a third party might be attacked as a bribe (for example, where on the transfer of a business a bonus is to be paid to directors of the selling company; *Southall v British Mutual Life Assurance Society* (1871) 6 Ch. Ap. 614).

Section 193 of the Companies Act 1948 imposes a duty on recipient directors to disclose payments of a similar kind made in connection with the transfer to "any persons" of a company's shares, being a transfer resulting from (a) an offer made to the general body of shareholders, (b) an offer made by or on behalf of some other body corporate with a view to the company becoming its subsidiary or a subsidiary of its holding company, (c) an offer made by or on behalf of an individual with a view to its obtaining the right to exercise or control the exercise of not less than one-third of the voting power at any general meeting of the company, or (d) any other offer which is conditional on acceptance to a given extent (section 193(1)). The statutory disclosure requirements are met if particulars of the payment, including its amount, accompany any notice of the offer to the shareholders, or if reasonable steps are taken towards disclosure (section 193(3)). The penalty for non-compliance with the section is a fine not exceeding £200 (section 193(2) and C.A. 1980, Sch. 2). Any sum received by a director in the absence of disclosure or general meeting approval is to be held in trust for any persons who have sold their shares as a result of the offer, the expense of the distribution of such sums having to be borne by the director (section 193(3)). The section regulates in detail the procedure for any meeting called to approve the payments (sections 193(4) and (5)).

Section 194 of the 1948 Act amplifies sections 191, 192 and 193. It deals first with proceedings for recovery of payments treated as received on trust under sections 192, 193(1) and (3). Where it can be shown that the payment was received pursuant to an arrangement entered into as part of the agreement for the transfer of property or shares in question, or within one or two years thereafter, and the company or any transferee was privy to that arrangement, the payment is deemed, unless the contrary can be shown, to be one to which section 192 or section 193(1) and (3) applies (section 194(1)). It deals secondly with any payment potentially within sections 191, 192 and 193, and provides that those sections do not apply to bona fide payments by way of damages for breach of contract or to a pension or superannuation payments paid to a director (section 194(3)). Non-monetary consideration or excess payment for shares are within sections 192 and 193 (section 194(2)).

(3) Substantial property transactions

Section 48 of the Companies Act 1980 in certain circumstances prohibits substantial property transactions (called "arrangements" in the section) between a company and a director of that company. It extends to transactions between a company and a director of its holding company (but not of a subsidiary), and between a person connected with any such director. It applies to private as well as public companies. The prohibition is removed if the transaction is approved by the company (or, if appropriate, by the holding company) by ordinary resolution in general meeting. Importantly, the section does not apply to arrangements between a company and a director of a wholly-owned subsidiary (as defined in section 150 of the 1948 Act) or a person connected with the director. Nor does it apply if the company is disposing of a non-cash asset and the director or connected person acquires it in his capacity as a member of the company (sections 48(6) and 48(8)).

Arrangements

The "arrangements" in question are those whereby a director of a company or of its holding company or a "*connected person*" is to acquire one or more "*non-cash assets*" of the "*requisite value*" from the company, or the company acquires the same from a director or a connected person (section 48(1)). Section 48(3) refers to "arrangements" and "transactions" entered into pursuant to "arrangements". Not only contracts are arrangements. Agreements binding in honour only and situations where it appears that various parties are acting in accordance with some pre-arranged scheme would seem to be included. So too are schemes whereby property is channelled through a number of hands in an attempt to disguise the nature of the arrangement (e.g. a director transfers property to X who transfers it to Y who transfers it to the company).

Non-cash asset

A "non-cash asset" includes any property, real or personal, tangible or intangible, or any interest in property other than cash (including foreign currency) (section 87(1)).

Requisite value

To be of the "requisite value" a non-cash asset must amount to £50,000 or ten per cent of the company's net assets as disclosed in its latest financial statements or (where there are no such statements) of the company's called-up share capital, subject to an overriding minimum of £1,000 (section 48(2)).

Directors and connected persons

A director is defined to include a "shadow director" within the meaning of section 63 of the 1980 Act. This term is considered on page 269 (*Directors' Loans*), but includes broadly a person in accordance with whose directions or instructions a director is accustomed to act. Connected persons are defined, in a very complex fashion, by section 64. Again, the definitions are considered in the chapter *Directors' Loans*, but in summary include the following:

(i)   *Family members.* The director's spouse, child or stepchild (including any legitimate or illegitimate child under 18 (sections 64(1)(a) and 64(2)).

(ii) *Associated companies.* A body corporate "associated" with the director (section 64(1)(b)).

Broadly, a director is *associated* with a body corporate if he and any
connected persons are (a) *"interested"* in shares comprising at least 20
per cent in nominal value of the equity share capital of that body
corporate, or (b) entitled to exercise or to control the exercise of 20 per
cent of the voting rights at any general meeting of that body corporate
(section 64(3)(a)).

"Equity share capital" means a company's issued share capital other
than share capital that carries the right, as to both dividends and capital,
to participate only up to a specified amount (section 64(4)(a); C.A.
1948, s. 154). Whether a person is "interested" in shares is determined
by the detailed rules in section 28 of the 1967 Act, but with certain
modifications set out in section 64(4).

A director controls voting rights where their exercise is controlled by a
body corporate which is itself controlled by the director (section
64(4)(b)).

A body corporate is controlled by a director where (i) the director (or a
connected person) is "interested" in any part of the equity share capital
of the body corporate within the meaning of section 28 of the 1967 Act,
as modified, or has the right to exercise, or control the exercise of, any
part of the voting rights of the body corporate's general meeting (section
64(3)(b) (c)), and (ii) the director, together with connected persons and
the company's other directors, is interested in over 50 per cent of the
equity share capital, or is entitled to exercise, or to control the exercise,
of over 50 per cent of those voting rights (section 64(3)(b)(ii)).

As a result, where a director of one company in a group is associated
with the holding company, such that the holding company is connected
with him, other companies in the group may be connected with him. On
the face of it, the effect is that arrangements made between companies
in a group may fall foul of section 48. However, section 48(7),
introduced by the 1981 Act, excludes those arrangements where the
companies concerned are a holding company and a wholly-owned
subsidiary, or each are wholly-owned subsidiaries.

(iii) *Trustees.* A person who is trustee of a trust that (a) has the director
or certain connected persons among the beneficiaries, or (b)
confers on the trustees a power that may be exercised for the
director's or certain connected persons' benefit (section 64(1)(c)).

(iv) *Partners.* A director's or connected person's partner (section
64(1)(d)).

Breach of section 48

(i) *Effect on the arrangement.* It, and any transaction forming part of
it, is voidable at the instance of the company (section 48(3)) except
where, in relation to the arrangement:

(a) restitution of any property transferred is impossible (section
48(3)(a)); or

(b) the company or a person nominated by it has been indemnified for any loss or damage suffered (section 48(3)(a)); or

(c) its avoidance would prejudice rights acquired by third parties bona fide for value without actual notice of the breach of statute (section 48(3)(b)); or

(d) it is ratified within a reasonable period (unspecified) by the company or, where appropriate, a holding company in general meeting (section 48(3)(c)).

(ii) *Effect on the director (and any connected person).* They are liable together with any other director (but only of the company itself) who authorised the arrangement or a transaction entered into pursuant to it to account to the company for any profit arising from the arrangement or transaction, or to indemnify the company for any loss or damage similarly arising, or both (section 48(4)). A director who is not himself a party to the arrangement or a transaction will be excused if he shows that he took all reasonable steps to ensure compliance with the section. A connected person and any other director involved will be excused if he can show that he did not know of the relevant circumstances of the breach at the time the arrangement was made (section 48(5)).

(4) Contracts in which director has an interest

As mentioned briefly above, section 199 of the Companies Act 1948 imposes an obligation on a director to disclose any direct or indirect interest in a contract or proposed contract with the company. (This provision is dealt with in more detail in the chapter *Disclosure of Directors' Dealings*, page 321.) Breach of the section can result in heavy fines (section 199(4) and C.A. 1980, Sch. 2). In addition, it appears that if section 199 is not observed the normal protection in the articles permitting the director to be interested in the contract and allowing his profit (see above) is removed, with the result that his profit is recoverable and the contract can be avoided by the company (*Hely-Hutchinson v Brayhead Limited* [1968] 1 Q.B. 549).

(5) Service contracts

Section 47 of the Companies Act 1980 introduced statutory controls preventing directors abusing their powers in voting themselves long-term service contracts which were not in the interests of their company. Section 47 requires any contract giving a director five or more years service to be approved by ordinary resolution of the company, failing which it is void. The provisions of section 47 are discussed in the chapter *Directors*, page 242. Section 26 of the Companies Act 1967 requires disclosure to be made of a director's service contracts with the company and its subsidiaries. Section 189 of the 1948 Act prevents a director taking advantage of his position by granting himself tax-free remuneration (see pages 239 and 328).

(6) Directors' loans

Detailed statutory provisions now restrict the ability of a director, and in certain cases persons connected with him, from taking loans or similar arrangements from his company or group. These are dealt with in the chapter *Directors' Loans*, page 269.

Extra-statutory duties

In the case of companies listed on The Stock Exchange, The Stock Exchange Listing Agreement restricts the ability of a director or his circle of associates from contracting with or obtaining benefits from his company or companies in the same group (see the provisions of chapter 4 of the Listing Agreement, and in particular the Class 4 transaction conditions). Often a transaction will only be permitted with shareholder approval or after a disclosure to and waiver from The Stock Exchange.

Where a takeover of a public company is involved directors' operations may also be restricted by the CSI's Takeover Code. The Institute of Directors have issued a Code of Practice for non-executive directors: [1983] 4 Co. Law 32.

Duties of skill and care

The classic statement of the duty's nature and extent is Romer J's in *Re City Equitable Fire Insurance Co* [1925] Ch. 407, 427:

> "... a director need not exhibit in the performance of his duties a greater degree of skill than may reasonably be expected from a person of his knowledge and experience. A director of a life insurance company ... does not guarantee that he has the skill of an actuary or of a physician ... a director is not bound to give continuous attention to the affairs of his company. His duties are of an intermittent nature to be performed at periodical board meetings ... He is not, however, bound to attend such meetings, though he ought to attend whenever he is reasonably able to do so ... In respect of duties that, having regard to the exigencies of business and the articles ... may properly be left to some official, a director is, in the absence of grounds for suspicion, justified in trusting that official."

These dicta are often and mistakenly given the status of statutory words.

Cases in point are few and old, but a director's duty to show care may not be as limited as sometimes thought. In *Dorchester Finance Co Limited v Stebbing* (unreported; (1980) 1 *Co. Law*. 38) Foster J suggests that there ought to be no difference between the skill demanded of an executive and a non-executive director, at least where the latter is professionally qualified (in *Dorchester* both non-executive directors had accountancy experience though only one was professionally qualified).

The three limbs of Romer J's test may be stated as follows:

(1) *Skill.* The subjective formulation of required skill means that directors must display such skill as their personal qualifications warrant. More is expected of experienced men of business (*Dorchester Finance Co Limited v Stebbing, supra*) than the amateur (*Re Denham & Co Limited* (1883) 25 Ch. D. 752).

A director's service contract might import an objective standard by providing for reasonable skill to be shown by directors (though such a term might be implied). Whatever the standard, it has been held that a director will not be liable for a mere error of judgment (*Re Brazilian Rubber Plantations Co Limited* [1911] 1 Ch. 425, 437 per Neville J). Section 13 of the Supply of Goods and Services Act 1982, which comes into force on July 4, 1983, would have the unintentional effect of substituting an *objective* requirement of skill for non-executive directors (directors with service contracts are outside section 13). But [1982] S.I. 1771 will exclude all company directors from section 13.

(2) *Diligence.* The degree of diligence required of a director depends on the facts of cases. One director among many (*Marquis of Bute's Case* [1882] 2 Ch. 100), or a director who is not vested by the articles with much, or any, effective power (*Re Denham & Co* (1883) 25 Ch. D 752), need not be as diligent as one on whom the company relies, though it may be that an executive or experienced non-executive director must show appropriate diligence (*Dorchester Finance Co Limited v Stebbing, supra*).

(3) *Liability for others' acts.* A director is not solely by virtue of his position liable for the acts of co-directors or company officers. But he will be if he participated in the wrong and its takes little to make out participation. Merely signing minutes approving a misapplication of property attracts liability (*Re Lands Allotment Co* (1884) 1 Ch. 617). So does unquestioningly signing a cheque for what turns out to be an unauthorised payment (*Re City Equitable, supra*), though a director is not liable for signing a cheque for an authorised payment put to unauthorised use. But it is not enough to escape liability that an executive or experienced non-executive director missed a board meeting (*Dorchester Finance Co Limited v Stebbing, supra*). A director is liable though actually ignorant of another's wrong where he ought to have supervised the activity or ought to have known that it was wrong (*Selangor United Rubber Estates Limited v Cradock* [1967] 1 W.L.R. 1168).

Remedies

Reference has already been made to the duty of a director to account for secret profits or other unjust enrichment, or to restore the company's property. Where liability is founded on breach of trust, proprietary remedies – the tracing of property in particular – become available to the company.

Other remedies which may be available for the company include:

(a) damages for breach of the duty of care;

(b) an injunction or declaration, chiefly to prevent a threatened breach;

(c) recission of a contract, subject normally to the rights of third parties acting bona fide without notice;

(d) removal as a director by the company in general meeting (and dismissal from any executive office).

The nature of the action will decide what period, if any, of limitation applies beyond which liability ceases. A *liquidator* may be able to bring a misfeasance summons against a delinquent director under section 333 of the 1948 Act.

Relief from liability

Honesty and reasonableness

If a director is or will be liable for negligence, default, breach of duty or breach of trust to his company (but not to a third party – *Customs and Excise Commissioners v Hedon Alpha Limited* (1981) 125 S.J. 273) a court may relieve him wholly or partly from liability (C.A. 1948, s. 448). It must appear to the court that the director "has acted honestly and reasonably and that, having regard to all the circumstances of the case, including those connected with his appointment, he ought fairly to be excused" (section 448(1)). The three requirements that the director be honest, reasonable and ought fairly to be excused are conjunctive: all three must be made out. The third provides the court with a discretionary long stop for the prevention of relief. This discretion might operate to make it hard for a remunerated director to obtain relief (*National Trust Company of Australasia v General Finance Company of Australasia* [1905] A.C. 373, 381 per Sir Ford North).

An impugned director might want to rely on his ignorance in his defence. In some cases the law requires that he must rely on the knowledge of others. Thus, he will not be excused liability for a breach which would have been avoided had legal and, presumably, other professional advice been sought (*Re Duomatic Limited* [1969] 2 Ch. 365; *Re J Franklin & Son Limited* [1937] 2 All E.R. 43, though that is not to say that he can escape liability in all cases by delegating his responsibilities to third parties: see *Re Civica Investments Limited*, Financial Times Law Reports June 8, 1982). But he may be excused for relying on advice which turns out to be wrong (*Re Claridges Patent Asphalte Co Limited* [1921] 1 Ch. 543). In other cases he must think for himself. He must not unthinkingly do as he is told by an outsider when that involves (albeit unknowingly) misapplying funds (*Selangor United Rubber Estates Limited v Cradock* [1967] 1 W.L.R. 1168).

An impugned director might want to say that his default was a mere technicality. A director will be excused liability for omitting accidentally to obtain general meeting approval for something as required by the articles (*Re Duomatic, supra*) but not invariably where the default is technical (e.g. not where a court decides in all the circumstances that he ought not to be: *Re J. Franklin, supra*). Relief will not necessarily be denied though his action was far more than a technical default, for example, in respect of an ultra vires transaction (*Re Claridges Patent Asphalte Co Limited, supra*).

Section 448(2) allows a director to apply to the court in respect of future proceedings. Application under section 448 is by way of petition (R.S.C. Ord. 102, r. 5(1)k).

Expressly defined duties

Section 205 of the Companies Act 1948 provides that, subject as therein provided,

> "any provision, whether contained in the articles of a company or in any contract with a company or otherwise for exempting any officer of the company ... from, or indemnifying him against, any liability which by virtue of any rule of law would otherwise attach to him in respect of any negligence, default, breach of duty or breach of trust of which he may be guilty in relation to the company shall be void."

(1) *Provisions in the articles.* It is possible for a company's articles to define the extent of a director's duties. It is not possible for them to modify the extent of a statutorily defined duty or to exempt a director from liability for breach of any duty (see section 205). They may provide that a director is to be indemnified against loss arising out of proceedings against him in which he obtained judgment or was acquitted (section 205(b)). It is possible that a company's articles may not abridge a common law duty in circumstances where it would not be possible to ratify the director's actions in general meeting (see below), but there is no authority on the point. It is generally considered that article 84(3) of Table A to the 1948 Act, permitting directors' interests in company contracts, overrides section 205 and that waiver provisions in articles therefore also override section 205 (and see (1982) 98 L.Q.R. 413).

(2) *Contracts with the company.* The same principles apply here mutatis mutandis to clauses in director's service contracts or other arrangements. Unresolved is the problem of a company's contractual release of a director from a particular liability he has incurred. Before the rule contained in section 205 existed this was possible (*Re Joint Stock Trust and Finance Corporation Limited* (1912) 56 S.J. 272). There is no authority on whether the resemblance of such a release to a conventional compromise or settlement of a claim takes it out of the range of section 205.

Ratification by the company

A company might by ordinary resolution in general meeting ratify what a director has done. What may validly be ratified is to some extent uncertain. The following are kinds of unratifiable breach.

(1) Breaches of duty involving the abridgement of the rights of individual shareholders (e.g. a refusal to register a share transfer in *Re Smith & Fawcett* [1942] Ch. 304), or a class of shareholders (e.g. cases of fraud on a minority). The principle prevents ratification of breaches involving misapplications of corporate property (as it did in *Cook v Deeks, supra*) as that entails an infringement of mem-

bers' rights. (For that reason the choice of a proprietary approach as described above might be critical.)

(2) Breaches of duty involving acts which a company cannot lawfully do. This principle applies where the articles or general law forbids acts of a certain sort and the breach means acting unlawfully or ultra vires. It also applies where the articles establish a procedure for doing something (e.g. obtaining a special resolution) which is not followed. In *Re Exchange Banking Co* (1882) 21 Ch. D. 519, it was held that even had shareholders known all the facts when they ratified a transaction they could not validly do so where the transaction was ultra vires.

(3) Breaches involving actions which are fraudulent or dishonest (see page 250). In *Mason v Harris* (1879) 11 Ch.D. 97 a sale to promoters could not be ratified where a director had acted fraudulently (cf. *Pavlides v Jensen* [1956] Ch. 565, 575).

The making of a secret profit (*Regal (Hastings) Limited v Gulliver, supra*) or a failure in skill and care (*Pavlides v Jensen, supra*) are ratifiable.

Directors' Loans

This chapter deals with the restrictions governing loans to directors, and similar transactions. The relevant legislation is now contained in the Companies Act 1980. This tightened up the law in three areas of potential conflict of interest between directors and their companies, namely directors' service contracts, substantial property transactions involving directors, and directors' loans. The first two topics are dealt with in other chapters. A number of amendments to the directors' loans provisions in the 1980 Act were made by the Companies Act 1981, and these were brought into force on December 22, 1981.

The legislation draws a fundamental distinction between, first, most *private companies* and, secondly, *public companies* (and private companies in a public company group). For most private companies, the broad position is that *loans* or *guarantees* to directors are prohibited. The prohibition is extended to *indirect arrangements*, such as assignments of loans or back to back loan transactions, which result in a director obtaining a loan or guarantee. The legislation then lays down a number of carefully-drawn exceptions to these prohibitions.

Public companies (and private companies in a public company group) are subject to additional restrictions, of two types. First, the prohibition on loans and guarantees is extended to include transactions referred to as *"quasi-loans"* and *"credit transactions"*. The prohibition against indirect arrangements extends to these two additional classes of transaction. Secondly, the restrictions are extended to apply not only to transactions entered into with or for a director, but also to transactions entered into with or for a wide circle of persons *connected* with that director. The same exemptions afforded to private companies are afforded to public companies. In addition, there are further exemptions dealing with the "quasi-loan" and "credit transaction" prohibitions. Public companies and their directors, but not most private companies or their directors, may commit a criminal offence if the prohibitions are breached.

Cutting across the broad division of companies into private and public companies are special relaxations for money-lending companies and recognised banks.

The 1980 Act restrictions on directors' loans are closely linked with the disclosure provisions in that Act, which are dealt with on page 324. Those provisions require disclosure in a company's statutory accounts of permitted, as well as prohibited, loan transactions. This may well cause

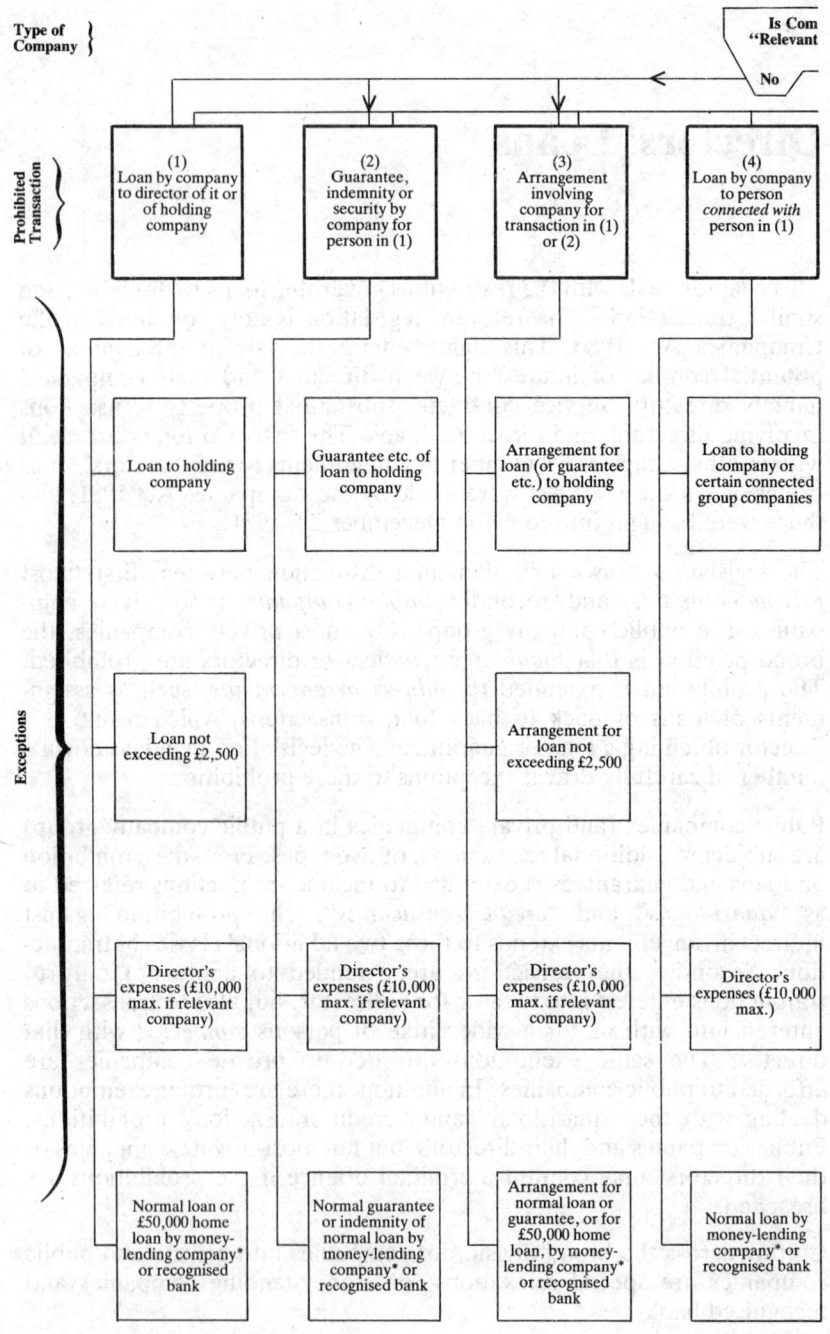

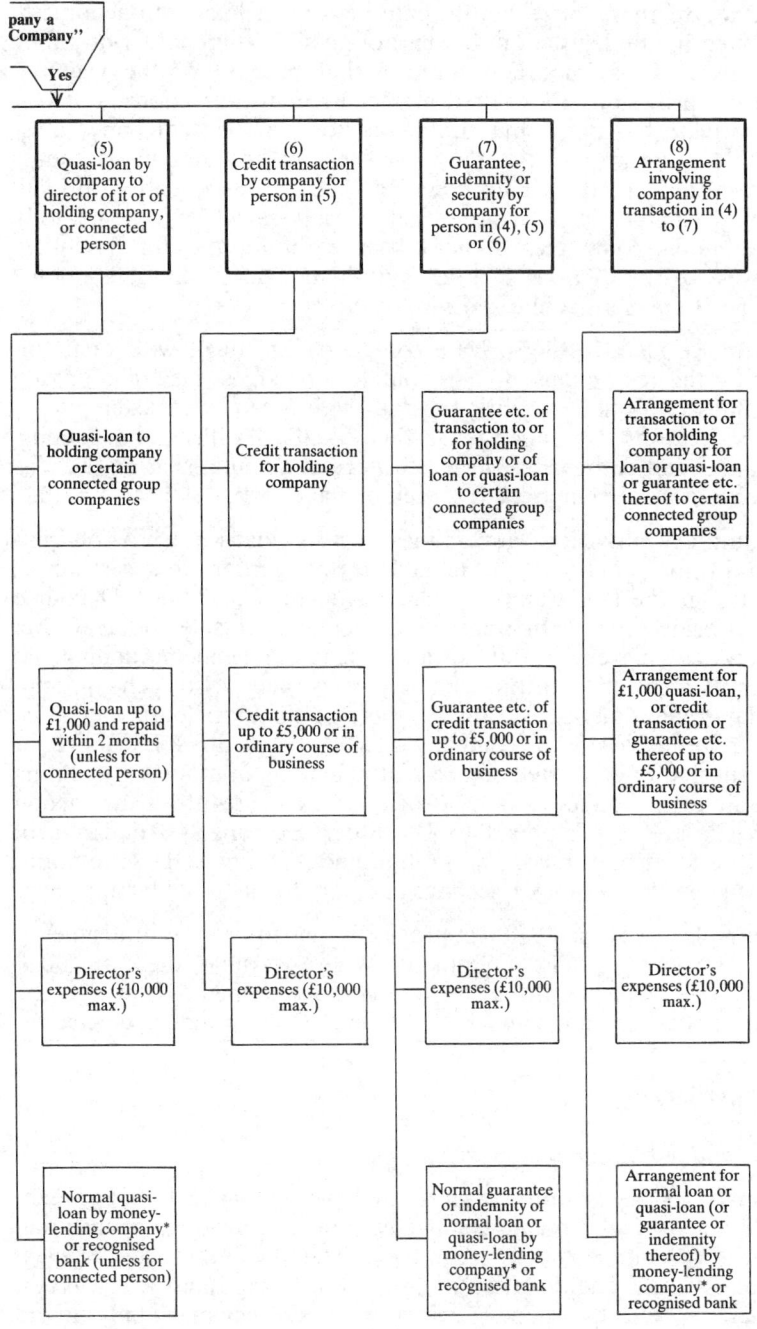

a director to think twice before entering into a loan transaction not prohibited by the legislation, because of possible shareholder or public disapproval. It is important to note that because of the way the disclosure provisions are drafted, it appears that transactions *permitted* for a private company, but prohibited for a public company, must nevertheless be *disclosed* in the private company's statutory accounts (see section 54 of the Companies Act 1980). Consequently a private company cannot simply ignore the restrictions which operate only against public companies; it must keep careful track, for disclosure purposes, of transactions such as quasi-loans and credit transactions, and loans to persons connected with its directors.

The restrictions affecting private companies are dealt with first, followed by the restrictions affecting public companies (including private companies in a public group), together with the relevant exemptions. This is followed by separate sections dealing with money-lending companies and recognised banks. A diagram summarising the various prohibitions and exemptions is set out on pages 270 to 271.

The statutory provisions governing directors' loans are now all contained in the 1980 Act, as amended (the earlier, less restrictive, legislation in the 1948 Companies Act having been repealed). Of course when considering a loan transaction that falls outside the 1980 Act prohibitions, reference should always be made to the memorandum and articles of association of the company concerned. Also, general company law requirements, like those governing directors' duties, must be borne in mind. Where the company is listed on The Stock Exchange, or is the subsidiary of a listed company, the lending of money or granting of credit to a director or any associate may constitute a transaction within Class 4 of Chapter 4 to The Stock Exchange's Admission of Securities to Listing. If so, it will require notification to the Quotations Department of The Stock Exchange and perhaps shareholder approval.

The complexity of the 1980 Act provisions has forced the draftsman to use a number of detailed definitions. Where possible, these are dealt with in the text, but three need separate treatment. They are the definitions of "relevant company", "director" and "connected person".

Relevant company

Private and public companies and groups

Although the legislation draws a fundamental distinction between, broadly, private and public companies, not *all* private companies fall into the "private company" category. The Act refers to *"relevant companies"*; the additional restrictions concerning quasi-loans, credit transactions and transactions with connected persons apply to all "relevant companies". All public companies are relevant companies but so are certain private companies. As will be seen, the existence anywhere in a *group* of companies of a non-private "company" will normally make every group company a "relevant company".

The definition of "relevant company" is contained in section 65(1). (The definition was amended by the Companies Act 1981; as originally drafted any private company which had a subsidiary incorporated abroad would have become a "relevant company", subject to the Companies Act 1980 (Commencement No. 2) Order 1980. The full definition of "relevant company" in section 65(1) as amended by the 1981 Act was brought into force on December 22, 1981.) Four categories of company are "relevant companies":

(1) a company which is not a private company;

(2) a company which although a private company is a subsidiary of a company which is not a private company;

(3) a company which although a private company has as *one* of its *subsidiaries* a company which is not a private company; and

(4) a company which is a subsidiary of a company which although itself a private company has as another subsidiary a company which is not a private company.

The wording in (3) suggests that a private company which has *only* one subsidiary, which is not a private company, is not a relevant company, though section 6(c) of the Interpretation Act 1978 (plural to include singular *unless* context otherwise requires) indicates to the contrary.

Company

The definition of relevant company refers to a "company". By section 455(1) of the Companies Act 1948 a "company" is a company formed and registered under the Companies Acts 1948 to 1981 or under certain earlier Acts (and see section 86 of the 1980 Act). Companies incorporated outside Great Britain (i.e. including Northern Ireland companies) are excluded. Consequently such companies are neither subject to the directors' loans provisions in the 1980 Act, nor does their existence in a group determine whether a Great Britain incorporated "company" is a "relevant company" (even though such companies can be "subsidiaries" as defined in section 154 of the Companies Act 1948: see below).

"Company" does however include an unlimited company. It appears that unregistered companies, such as most chartered companies and statutory companies, are not themselves subject to the directors' loans prohibitions but are subject to the disclosure provisions and the definition sections in Part IV of the 1980 Act, for instance the "connected persons" definition in section 64 (see section 67, the Companies (Unregistered Companies) Regulations 1975 S.I. No. 597 and *Official Report*, February 26, 1980, col. 1159).

Private company

By section 1(1) of the Companies Act 1980, a private company is any company other than a "public company" (as also defined in that section). "Private company" thus includes both pre-1980 Act private companies and post-1980 Act private companies. But as from June 23, 1982 the term does not include an "old public company" (see C.A. 1980, s. 8(2)).

Subsidiary

The definition in section 154 of the Companies Act 1948 applies, so that a company's "subsidiaries" include all its sub-subsidiaries, and so on (section 154(1)(b)). The definition of "subsidiary" includes foreign companies not incorporated under the Companies Acts. Consequently, in applying the "relevant company" test, shareholding or board control can be traced through a foreign subsidiary to a Great Britain incorporated sub-subsidiary.

Example

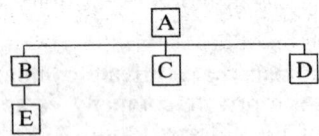

Situation 1. A, B, C, D and E are all G.B. incorporated companies; A owns 100 per cent of the equity share capital of B, C and D and B owns 100 per cent of the equity share capital of E.

If *any one* of A, B, C, D or E is not a private company, each and every company will be a "relevant company".

Situation 2. As Situation 1, except that B is a Delaware incorporated company; all the other companies are G.B. incorporated private companies. None of A, C, D or E is a "relevant company". Likewise if E, not B, is the Delaware company: none of A, B, C or D is a "relevant company". But if, in the first case, E is a public company, all of A, C, D and E will be "relevant companies".

Situation 3. A, B, C, D and E are all G.B. incorporated companies, but B and E are public companies. A owns 100 per cent of the equity share capital of C and D (as does B of E). But B's share capital comprises 100 voting ordinary shares and 900 non-voting participating preference shares (with an upper limit on the participation in dividends and capital); A owns all the preference shares and 50 of the ordinary shares in B (but does not have control of the composition of B's board). B is not a "subsidiary" of A, so that none of A, C, or D is a "relevant company".

It may happen that a private company which has already made directors loans becomes a "relevant company". This will occur if the company is re-registered as a public company, or another company in its group re-registers, or a new subsidiary is incorporated as a public company. In this case, the additional prohibitions which apply to "relevant companies" will apply as from the date of re-registration or incorporation, but transactions already lawfully entered into will not be invalidated. However any "continuing" transactions, such as the provision to a director of a company credit card in respect of which a "quasi-loan" may arise whenever the card is used (see below), will need to be carefully reviewed.

Director

The Companies Act 1980 restrictions apply to loans to *directors* and, in the case of relevant companies, to persons "connected" with directors. By section 455(1) of the Companies Act 1948 "director" is defined non-exhaustively to include "any person occupying the position of director by whatever name called". This includes for instance an alternate director. To restrict avoidance, section 63 of the 1980 Act extends this definition to include "shadow directors". For the purposes of the directors' loan provisions, a "director" is to include any person "in accordance with whose *directions or instructions* the directors of a company are *accustomed* to act". There are two exceptions:

(a) the extension does not apply to a person, such as a solicitor or accountant, who gives advice in a professional capacity, where the directors are accustomed to act on his directions or instructions *by reason only* of such advice; and

(b) the extension will not, *by itself*, result in a holding company being treated as a director of any subsidiary or sub-subsidiary company (the holding company might of course be appointed formally as a director).

Although section 63 extends the meaning of "director", it is nevertheless necessary, for the section to apply, that,

(a) the directors must be acting on directions or instructions – mere *suggestions*, with no express or implied requirement that these be adopted, are insufficient;

(b) the directors must be *accustomed* to act on directions or instructions – a one-off direction from a controlling shareholder would not count; and

(c) it is not enough that a person is a director in all but name, or that a person appoints a nominee to be a director in his place to carry out his wishes; *the directors*, as a body, must be acting on *that person's* directions and instructions, rather than taking decisions as a body or group which includes that person (or his nominee).

The type of person who may be caught by the "shadow directors" rules includes:

(i) the controlling shareholder who instructs the directors how to act, or who appoints a nominee director (or directors) whose wishes tend always to be followed by the board;

(ii) possibly, the director who resigns his directorship for a week, takes a loan from the company and is then reappointed (see *Official Report*, Standing Committee A, December 7, 1979 col. 481), though this seems rather doubtful in the majority of cases in view of (c) above;

(iii) perhaps, in certain circumstances, the general manager or similar employee of a company on whose "advice" the board of directors tend to act. An example might be a U.K. subsidiary of a foreign parent, where non-U.K. individuals appointed as the directors of the foreign parent tend to act on, or ratify, the decisions of the general manager of the U.K. subsidiary.

Connected persons

As mentioned, for public companies or other "relevant companies" the loan restrictions extend to transactions with a wide circle of persons "connected" with a director (or shadow director). Section 64 sets out the tests for determining when a person is "connected" with a director. There are four categories of connected person, all but the last of which (associated companies) are relatively straightforward. The tests exclude persons who are themselves directors, since a loan transaction entered into with such a person would be caught anyway. This exclusion is of importance when considering certain of the exemptions which operate by reference to monetary maximums (see the references to "relevant amounts", later). The four categories are as follows:

Category	Notes
(1) *Family* Any spouse, and any child under 18, unless that person is himself a director	Spouse does not apparently include a former spouse. Child includes step-child and illegitimate child. Perhaps surprisingly, a son or daughter of 18 or over is not treated as "connected" – so a public company can lend to a director's 20 year old son, but not to the director's wife
(2) *Trustees* Any person *acting in his capacity* as a trustee of a trust and who is not himself a director	Trust to have beneficiaries which include or may include the director, his spouse, any children under 18 (including step-children and illegitimate children) or any body corporate "associated" with the director (see (4) below). Trustees of an employees' share scheme, as defined in section 87(1) of the 1980 Act, or of a pension scheme, are excluded. Thus it is not intended that executive directors be precluded from participating in share incentive schemes (*Official Report*, Standing Committee A, December 4, 1979 col. 536)
(3) *Partners* Any person *acting in his capacity* as a partner of certain specified persons, unless that partner is himself a director	The specified persons are the director, or any individual or company "connected" with the director under the tests in (1) and (2) above or (4) below
(4) *Associated companies* Any body corporate with which the director is "associated", that is where:	Two provisos attempt to restrict to manageable levels the degree of aggregation of share interests and votes required under (a). First, it is not necessary to count interests in shares or votes held by any other associated company (which because of test (4) itself is of course a "connected person"), unless that company is a trustee or partner within test (2) or (3). Secondly, it is not necessary to aggregate share interests or votes held by

(a) the director, and persons "connected" with him under the tests in (1) to (3) above;

trustees of a trust which is "connected" with the director under (2) above solely because the beneficiaries include or may include an associated company (s. 64(3) as amended by C.A. 1981, Sch. 3, para. 54).

(b) are together *"interested"* in 20% or more of the shares of the company; *or*

In calculating the 20% share interest limit it is the *nominal* value of the *equity share capital* in the company which is to be taken. Equity share capital is defined in section 154(5) of the Companies Act 1948 and, broadly, includes ordinary shares and most participating preference shares, but not fixed-rate preference shares. To determine whether a director and those connected with him are "interested" in the shares in question, it is necessary to apply the very wide rules set out in section 28 of the Companies Act 1967 (except that references in section 28(4A) and 28(4B) are to read as "more than one-half" instead of "one-third or more" so as to equate these rules with the 50% voting test in section 64(3)(b)(ii), discussed in the next paragraph). The terms of section 28 are dealt with elsewhere (see page 316), but broadly a person has an interest in shares (i) if he is the registered holder (unless a bare trustee) or (ii) if, even though not the registered holder, he is a non-discretionary and non-reversionary beneficiary of any trust which itself has any interest in the shares or an interest in them is held by a company of which he has directly or indirectly at least 50% of the votes or control of the board, or (iii) if he has entered into a contract to purchase the shares or has any option over the shares or has rights over the votes or dividends on shares.

(c) are together entitled to exercise or to *control* the exercise of more than 20% of the voting power in general meeting of the company. Again, the associated company is not "connected" if it itself is a director of the company in question

In determining whether the director and those connected with him can exercise more than 20% of the *voting power* of a company in general meeting, any votes held indirectly by a director through another company are to be included in the calculation, but only if the director "controls" that second company. To decide this one has to apply another, similar, range of complex tests to the second company. By section 64(3)(b), the director will "control" the second company if (a) the director *or* certain connected persons* are "interested" in *any* equity share capital of that second company or can exercise or control the exercise of any votes in general meeting AND (b) the director, certain connected persons* *and* the directors' fellow-directors are together "interested" in more than 50% of the equity share capital or are entitled to exercise or control the exercise of more than 50% of the voting power (*the two provisos already mentioned apply to exclude associated companies "connected" by virtue only of the 20% shareholding or voting tests).

Examples

(1) A is a director of P Limited, a public company. A owns 5 per cent of the equity share capital of X Limited and 20 per cent of the equity share capital of Y Limited. Y Limited itself owns 15 per cent of the equity share capital of X Limited:

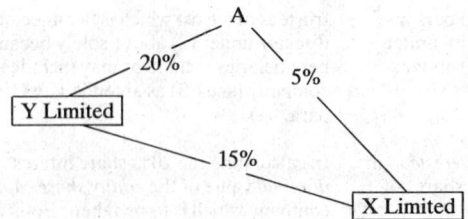

Because of A's 20 per cent holding in Y Limited, Y Limited is connected with A and therefore a loan from P Limited to Y Limited would be within the 1980 Act restrictions. But a loan from P Limited to X Limited would be outside the restrictions, because in deciding whether X Limited is a person "connected" with A, Y Limited's shareholding in X Limited is to be disregarded when calculating the 20 per cent limit.

(2) As in (1) above but A owns 51 per cent of Y Limited (giving him 51 per cent of Y Limited's votes). A transaction between P Limited and X Limited would now be caught, because Y Limited's interest in X Limited can now be aggregated with A's direct interest.

(3) As in (1) above but A is one of the limited partners in a partnership of which Y Limited is the general partner. X Limited will now be "connected" with A (though only if Y Limited is "acting in its capacity" as A's partner – it is not clear what this means in the present case).

(4)

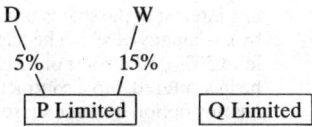

D owns 5% of the equity share capital of P Limited and his wife owns 15%. D is also a non-executive director of Q Limited, a third party public company which supplies goods to P Limited. Q Limited's supplies, if made on credit terms, may be credit transactions (see below) and as such could be prohibited because Q Limited will be entering into credit transactions with a person connected with one of its directors.

Private companies

The rules restricting loans to directors of companies which are *not* relevant companies (i.e. private companies which are not members of a group in which a non-private company exists) prohibit three main classes of transaction. The restrictions are set out in section 49 of the 1980 Act.

Prohibited transactions

(1) *Loans.* Subject to certain exceptions, a private company may not make a *loan* to a person who is,

(a) a director of the company; or

(b) a director of its *holding* company (s. 49(1)(a)(i)).

"Loan" is not defined, but as a matter of general law involves a payment of money to or for someone on condition that it will be repaid (*M.S.D.*

Speirs Limited v. Fahey [1973] 1 N.Z.L.R. 478). Whether interest is payable is not relevant. Probably the asset loaned must be money: *Champagne Perrier – Jouet S.A. v. H. H. Finch Limited* [1982] 1 W.L.R. 1359. The essential element is the promise of repayment (*Pannam on the Law of Moneylenders*, page 6). "Making" a loan would seem to involve actually providing the borrower with money so that the mere grant of an overdraft facility would not, prior to a drawdown on the facility, involve the making of a loan. But a drawdown would result in a "loan" – *Brooks v. Blackburn Building Society* (1884) 9 A.C. 857; cf. *Waterlow v. Sharp* L.R. 8 Eq. 50. The fact that the governing law of the loan may not be a U.K. law is irrelevant for section 49 purposes (s. 65(8)).

"Holding company" is defined by section 154 of the Companies Act 1948 to include not only the immediate parent of a subsidiary but more distant parents. If company D is a Companies Act subsidiary of company C, which in turn is a subsidiary of company B, whose holding company is company A, then section 49 prohibits company D from making a loan to a director of any of companies A, B, C or D. But if D was a *foreign-incorporated* subsidiary it could make any of those loans (it will not be a "company").

(2) *Guarantees.* Again subject to certain exceptions, a private company may not enter into any *guarantee* or provide any *security* in connection with a *loan* made by *any* person to,

(a) a director of the company; or

(b) a director of its holding company (s. 49(1)(a)(ii)).

"Guarantee" is defined to include indemnity (s. 65(1)), but "security" is not defined. The identity of the person making the loan itself is irrelevant. The giving of the guarantee or the provision of security need not be cotemporaneous with the making of the loan, though it must be "in connection with" this. "In connection with" probably means a substantial relationship in a business sense (see for instance *Clarke Chapman Limited v. IRC* [1976] Ch. 91; *Custom & Excise v. Top Ten Productions* [1969] 3 All E.R. 39).

(3) *Arrangements relating to loans and guarantees.* The third prohibition is designed to prevent a company achieving indirectly that which the first two prohibitions prevent it achieving directly. By sections 49(3) and 49(4) a company shall not,

(a) *arrange* for the assignment to it or the assumption by it of any rights, obligations or liabilities under a loan, guarantee or security transaction for a director of it or any of its holding companies. (The transaction itself is treated as having occurred on the date of the *arrangement*. This is of relevance when calculating certain of the financial limits provided for in the exemption provisions.); or

(b) *take part in* any *arrangement* which satisfies two tests. First, the arrangement involves someone else entering into *either* a loan, guarantee or security transaction for a director of it or any of its holding companies, *or* an arrangement for the assignment or assumption of any rights, obligations or liabilities thereunder. Secondly, that other person has or will obtain some *benefit* under the arrangement from the company, any holding company of it, *or any subsidiary of the company or any of its holding companies* (see Example (3) below).

Examples

Sections 49(3) and 49(4) are designed to prevent the following types of transaction:

(1) A director arranges a loan from a third party bank, with his company (or a subsidiary) subsequently taking an assignment of the loan: section 49(3). (If the company and the bank *novated* the loan, section 49(3) would probably not apply, but then the company would itself normally be making a loan and so would be caught by section 49(1).)

(2) A director arranges a loan from a third party bank, guaranteed by an independent party. His company, or a subsidiary, takes over the guarantee: section 49(3).

(3) Company A has two subsidiaries, B and C. Company B enters into an understanding with an insurance company that if it makes a house loan to one of its directors, company C will place insurance business with the company: section 49(4).

(4) A company, X, enters into back-to-back arrangements with an independent company, Y, whereby Y makes loans to X's directors and in return X makes loans to Y's directors: section 49(4).

(5) Company A makes a loan at low interest to a director of its subsidiary, company B. Company B makes up company A's shortfall on the interest received by paying to A amounts designated as "management fees": section 49(4).

(6) Perhaps, the entry into of a directors' pension scheme between a company and an insurance company, where the scheme offers "loan back" facilities to participating directors (the Department of Trade are currently considering the position here: *Official Report*, Written Answers, November 13, 1981 col. 189). Although the insurance company must receive a "benefit" "in pursuance of" the arrangement (see further below), the insurance company presumably benefits simply by virtue of the company entering into the pension scheme, regardless of whether the company also makes employer's contributions to the scheme.

Sections 49(3) and (4) refer to "*arrangements*". These are not defined, but clearly extend beyond agreements having binding force in law. For instance, in *Pilkington Brothers v. I.R.C.* [1981] S.T.C. 219 at 236 Nourse J. said " 'arrangements' is in both ordinary and statutory parlance a word of wide import by no means confined to relationships having contractual force and effect" (see also the House of Lords' decision in *Pilkington* [1982] S.T.C. 103 and *Re British Basic Slag* [1963] 1 W.L.R. 727, a case on section 6 of the Restrictive Trade Practices Act 1956; cf. *Registrar of Restrictive Trading Agreements v. Schweppes (No. 2)* [1971] 1 W.L.R. 1148). The Department of Trade clearly considers that the word is of wide application. In a consultative document issued by the Department on September 23, 1981, dealing with possible amendments to section 54 of the 1980 Act, it is stated that the term arrangement "is intended, by avoiding the specificity of the word "contract", to cover any understanding entered into by two or more parties on the basis of which a series of transactions may be carried out between them". And in the parliamentary debates on section 49 a Government spokesman explained "an arrangement .... may cover a number of agreements and cover a number of parties" (*Official Report*, Standing Committee A, November 29, 1979, col. 439).

Section 49(4) provides that a company shall not "*take part in*" any arrangements; elsewhere the phrase "enter into" tends to be used. The phrase "take part in any arrangements" is also used in section 13(1)(b) of the Prevention of Fraud (Investments) Act, where it has been given a wide meaning:

> "Taking part in arrangements is not confined to a single act which can only be done at a single point of time. Depending upon the nature of the arrangements, it may include a whole variety of acts done over a period .... Anything a person does to [enable the prohibited transaction to occur] thus constitutes taking part in the arrangements .... It is not necessary that everything should be done by [that person]." (*R. v. Markus* [1976] A.C. 35 at 62)

Section 49(4), although widely drawn, is not however without limitation. In particular, it is necessary that the third party has or will obtain a *benefit* from the arrangement, *and* that this is obtained *in pursuance of* the arrangement. The Government stated in the parliamentary debates on section 49(4) that the section is only intended to apply where the benefit conferred by the company is a quid pro quo for the facilities obtained by a director. Thus where a director banks at the same bank as his company, a loan from his bank will not of itself trigger the section simply because the bank continues to receive business from the company (*Official Report*, Standing Committee A, November 29, 1979, col. 439; according to the parliamentary debates the burden of proof of an "arrangement" is on the person alleging its existence). On this basis the pension loanback arrangements discussed in Example (6) above would not fall within section 49(4) if for instance the company was unaware of the loanback facility at the time the pension scheme was set up.

Exceptions

(1) *Loans and guarantees to directors of subsidiary or sister companies*

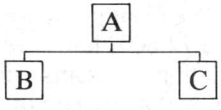

Section 49 does not prohibit company A making a loan to or giving a guarantee for a director of company B, *provided* the director is not also a director of company A. Likewise company C may make a loan to or give a guarantee for that director, *provided* he is not also a director of company C.

It follows that company A or company C may take part in section 49(3) or 49(4) "arrangements" in relation to a loan to or guarantee for the director of company B, *provided* broadly company B is not a party to these (see for instance Example (5) above).

Where the loan, guarantee or arrangement is permitted under the above rules, disclosure of the transaction will not normally be required (see section 54, though note section 54(7)(b)).

(2) *Loans to persons connected with a director.* In the case of private companies which are not "relevant companies" there is no prohibition on loans to or guarantees for anyone "connected" with a director (subject to the possible application of some wide dicta by Lord Denning in *Wallersteiner v. Moir* [1974] 1 W.L.R. 991 at 1015, a case concerning section 190 of the 1948 Act, if the loan is made to a company wholly-owned by the director).

(3) *Meaning of "loan".* Reference has already been made to the meaning of "loan". Although the word may be capable of a fairly wide interpretation, it clearly does not, in the context of Part IV of the 1980 Act, extend to "quasi-loans" and "credit transactions" as defined in the Act (and see *Champagne Perrier – Jouet S.A. v. H. H. Finch Limited* [1982] 1 W.L.R. 1359). So normal season ticket purchase and credit card arrangements for directors of private companies are not prohibited (unless the companies are "relevant companies" or the arrangements are structured as loans. Disclosure may nevertheless be required). Moreover, it is established that the sale of an asset on deferred terms does not amount to the making of a loan (*Ramsden v. I.R.C.* 37 T.C. 619 at 625). Likewise if a company meets an obligation of a director to a third party, the company has not made a loan to the director even though the director is thus indebted to the company: *Potts v. I.R.C.* 32 T.C. 211; *Champagne Perrier – Jouet v. H. H. Finch Ltd.*

(4) *Loans up to £2,500.* Section 50(2A), introduced with effect from December 22, 1981, provides that section 49(1)(a) does not prevent a company making a loan to a director provided the aggregate of the *"relevant amounts"* does not exceed £2,500. This is a useful exemption, though the £2,500 limit may mean it is of only limited use – for instance it will be of little use in relation to house purchases (see below), or loans for management buyouts. The exemption does not extend to *guarantees* and the like of loans up to £2,500, but does apply to section 49(3) or 49(4) "arrangements" relating to loans not exceeding £2,500. The procedure for determining the "aggregate of the relevant amounts" is a complex one, laid down in section 51 and sections 65(4) to 65(6). The "relevant amounts" procedure is designed to aggregate all existing transactions and arrangements of a particular type (small loans in the present case) entered into by the director and his circle of connected persons with his company and other companies in the group. The purpose is to prevent the mis-use of exemptions by fragmentation techniques. An illegal transaction does not however require aggregation. Nor do most transactions entered into before December 22, 1980 (see (7), *Timing of loans*, below). In the present context the "relevant amounts" are computed as follows.

Sums to be added	*Notes*
(1) Principal amount of the proposed loan	If principal is unascertainable, it is deemed to exceed £50,000 (s. 65(5)). This applies for (2) and (3) below, also
(2) Principal amount of any earlier loans made in reliance of the section 50(2A) exception, *less* any principal repaid	This includes earlier loans made to the director *or any person connected with him** (s. 51(2) and 51(3)) by the company *or any subsidiary* which is still a subsidiary (and, if the proposed loan is for a director of the company's holding company or a person connected with him*, earlier loans so made by that holding company or *any* of its subsidiaries which are still subsidiaries (s. 51(2), 51(4) and 65(6)))
(3) Principal amount of any earlier loans by third parties which involved section 49(3) or 49(4) "arrangements" if the "arrangements" relied on the section 50(2A) exception, *less* any principal repaid	This includes earlier loans by third parties which involved the "arrangements" specified opposite where the loans were made to any of the persons listed in (2) above

*But a loan by a non-relevant company to a *connected* person will not have been made by virtue of the section 50(2A) exception, and so can be ignored in the aggregation |

The idea is to prevent a group of companies abusing the £2,500 limit by each of a number of companies lending £2,500 to a director. Note that section 54 will nevertheless require disclosure of the loan.

(5) *Intra-group transactions.* Section 50(4)(a) provides that section 49 will not prevent a company making a loan to, or giving a guarantee or security for, any holding company (where for instance the holding company is a director). It follows that also exempted is a section 49(3) or 49(4) arrangement by a company which involves a loan, guarantee or security for its holding company.

(6) *Director's expenses.* Commonly a director is provided with money to meet expenses to be incurred in his company's business. A difficult question is whether expenses arrangements amount to the making of a loan. Where a director is provided with a sum to pay a specific and ascertained company expense, this almost certainly does not amount to the making of a loan. If the director is given a lump sum, out of which to meet the company's expenses, and on condition that any surplus is returned, then arguably the surplus is a "loan" (though the alternative and better argument is that the director is acting as agent or trustee for the company and is not a "borrower"). The Department of Trade consider that a lump sum provided to meet expenses which, if paid by the director himself, would have been reimbursed, is not a "loan" (see *Accountancy*, June 1982, page 8). Much may turn on the particular facts, and in particular on the amount of expenses provided in relation to the anticipated expenditure, the period for which the expense allowance is in the director's hands, and whether the director is able to use the expense allowance to meet his own personal expenses (with subsequent reimbursement to the company).

If the provision of an expense allowance does amount to a "loan" it will nevertheless fall outside the section 49 prohibitions if it falls within the "directors' expenses" exclusion in section 50(4)(c). (It might alternatively be excluded under another head, such as the £2,500 exemption. Note that even if within one of the exclusions, as a "loan" the transaction will be disclosable under section 54, so it may still be important to decide whether the transaction is in fact a "loan".) Section 50(4)(c) provides an exclusion for loans, and guarantees or arrangements relating thereto, where,

(a) a company provides any of *its* directors (but not directors of its holding company) with funds;

(b) to meet expenditure incurred or to be incurred;

(c) for the *purposes of the company* or for the purpose of enabling the director *to properly perform his duties as an officer* of the company;

(d) provided *either*,

   (i) the company's action is given prior approval by the shareholders in general meeting, at which the purpose and amount of the expenditure and any liability of the company is disclosed (s. 50(5)(a)); *or*

   (ii) the funds are provided on the condition that they will be repaid within six months after the next annual general meeting of the company unless at that meeting the approval referred to in (i) is given (s. 50(5)(b)).

The exclusion extends to anything done by the company for the purposes specified in (c) above to enable a director to avoid incurring expenditure (section 50(4)(c)).

The phrases "for the purposes of the company" and "for the purposes of enabling [the director] properly to perform his duties" are not defined. Clearly travelling expenses between different places of work, and normal entertainment expenses, are covered. Arguably a loan of money made to a director, who applies the loan in purchasing a season ticket for travelling from his home to work, falls within the second, and maybe even the first, phrase (though contrast, in a different context, the income tax cases of *Ricketts v. Colquhoun* [1926] A.C. 1 and *Burton v. Rednell* 35 T.C. 435; cf. *Pook v. Owen* 45 T.C. 571). On the other hand a loan to a director for house-purchase would seem, except in exceptional circumstances, to be outside the exclusion. And the exclusion does not extend to cash advances used by a director to meet private expenses (with subsequent reimbursement).

(7) *Timing of loans.* The prohibitions in section 49 do not apply to transactions or arrangements entered into before December 22, 1980 (though a loan or guarantee before that date may have been prohibited by section 190 of the Companies Act 1948). This should be borne in mind when calculating "the aggregate of relevant amounts" under

section 51. Where however a section 49(3) or 49(4) "arrangement" is involved the transaction to which the arrangement relates is to be treated as having been entered into after December 22, 1980, so as to catch the "arrangement" if this itself is entered into after that date (s. 65(7)). (If the "arrangement" was entered into before then and the company does nothing further in relation to that arrangement (such as confirming its existence or otherwise "taking part" in it) after that date, then the arrangement is not caught. The section 54 disclosure requirements are more onerous.) Note that some transactions, though set up some time ago, may involve a continuous series of loans (e.g. directors' overdrafts or current accounts).

For a loan, guarantee or arrangement to be caught, the person concerned must be a "director" at the time the transaction or arrangement is entered into. So a company may, subject to its memorandum and so on, make unlimited loans to a senior employee just before he is appointed a director (this tactic has received parliamentary blessing: see *Official Report*, Standing Committee A, December 4, 1979, cols. 480, 482). And as discussed earlier, the "shadow director" rules may not be wide enough to prevent a person resigning his directorship for a period to take a loan. Such transactions will however normally require disclosure under section 54.

(8) *Money-lending companies and recognised banks.* Additional exemptions apply, both to "private" companies and to relevant companies, which are money-lending companies or recognised banks (see below).

Public companies and companies in public groups

All the above prohibitions, and exclusions, apply equally to *relevant* companies, subject to a few minor amendments. In addition, two further categories of restriction are imposed. First, quasi-loans and credit transactions are prohibited (subject to their own exclusions). Secondly, transactions with a director's circle of connected persons are caught.

Prohibited transactions

(1) *Loans and guarantees.* Thus the prohibitions described above in relation to non-relevant companies apply, but with an added restriction on loans to, or guarantees and the like for, persons "connected" with the director (section 49(1)(b)(ii) and (iii)). Furthermore, the prohibition on guarantees and security arrangements extends to guarantees and security for "quasi-loans" to, or "credit transactions" for, a director or a person connected with him.

(2) *Quasi-loans.* Section 49(1)(b) prohibits a relevant company from making a "quasi-loan" to a director of the company or of any holding company (or anyone connected with such a director). Quasi-loan is widely defined by section 65(2) as,

"A transaction under which one party ("the creditor") agrees to pay, or pays otherwise than in pursuance of an agreement, a sum for another ("the borrower"), or agrees to reimburse, or reimburses otherwise than in pursuance of an agreement, expenditure incurred by another party for another ("the borrower")

(i) on terms that the borrower (or a person on his behalf) will reimburse the creditor; or

(ii) in circumstances giving rise to a liability on the borrower to reimburse the creditor."

A transaction can thus be a quasi-loan if it is a reimbursement of expenditure already incurred, and whether or not made in pursuance of an "agreement". References in the legislation to a person to whom a quasi-loan is made are references to the borrower. The borrower's liabilities under a quasi-loan include the liabilities of anyone who has agreed to reimburse the creditor on the borrower's behalf (section 65(2)(b) and (c)). Note that for a quasi-loan to exist the "borrower" must be under an *obligation* (either by agreement or by operation of law) to reimburse the "creditor", though it is irrelevant whether the creditor was legally obliged to make the payment or reimbursement.

Examples

The following transactions constitute quasi-loans:

(1) A public company purchases an airline ticket for a director's spouse who is accompanying him on a business trip, with the director subsequently reimbursing the company.

(2) A public company pays a travel agent's account, which includes amounts owing for private travel by a director of its parent company.

(3) The private subsidiary of a public company lays out money for furniture and decorating work for a director's house, on the basis that the director will make reimbursement later.

(4) A director of a public company uses a company credit card to pay for personal goods or services. (Use for business purposes only would not however result in a quasi-loan being made. Similarly, no quasi-loan would arise if the credit card was in the director's own name, the company reimbursing him for any business expenditure incurred. This may however have VAT disadvantages for the company. If the company has authorised the director to use the credit card for private expenditure, the fact that the director reimburses the company before the company pays the credit card company will not prevent a quasi-loan arising. Even if the director agrees always to "reimburse" the company before it receives a payment demand from the credit company (when the company has probably not agreed to *pay* any sum), the company will have agreed to reimburse the credit card company for the expenditure it has incurred to suppliers on behalf of the directors' personal expenditure. In practice the £1,000 exemption discussed below removes many of the problems relating to company credit cards (except that *disclosure* is still required). Alternatively directors can take two cards; a company card which is used only for business expenditure, and a personal card used for private expenditure. No quasi-loans will then arise.)

(5) A company purchases a season ticket from British Rail and hands this over to a director on terms that he repays the price over the following twelve months (or alternatively the company hands the director a cheque made payable to British Rail on terms that the amount of the cheque be repaid over time).

(3) *Credit transactions.* By section 49(2) a relevant company is prohibited from entering into a "credit transaction" as *creditor* for a director

of the company or any holding company, or a person connected with such a director. Section 65(3) defines a credit transaction,

"as a transaction under which one party ("the creditor"):

(a) supplies any goods or sells any land under a *hire-purchase agreement* or *conditional sale agreement*;

(b) leases or hires any land or goods in return for periodical payments;

(c) otherwise disposes of land or supplies goods or *services* on the *understanding* that payment (whether in a lump sum or instalments or by way of periodical payments or otherwise) is to be deferred."

By section 87(2) and section 189(1) of the Consumer Credit Act 1974,

"hire-purchase agreement means an agreement other than a conditional sale agreement, under which –

(a) goods are bailed or (in Scotland) hired in return for periodical payments by the persons to whom they are bailed or hired, and

(b) the property in the goods will pass to that person if the terms of the agreement are complied with and one or more of the following occurs –

(i) the exercise of an option to purchase by that person,

(ii) the doing of any other specified act by any party to the agreement,

(iii) the happening of any other specified event";

and

"conditional sale agreement means an agreement for the sale of goods or land under which the purchase price or part of it is payable by instalments, and the property in the goods or land is to remain in the seller (notwithstanding that the buyer is to be in possession of the goods or land) until such conditions as to the payment of instalments or otherwise as may be specified in the agreement are fulfilled."

"Services" are defined to mean anything other than goods or land (section 65(1)).

Examples

Section 49(3) catches the following types of transaction.

(1) A public company leases a car or a flat to a director (*unless*, in either case, the lease is rent-free).

(2) A private company sells hi-fi and electrical equipment to the wife of its public parent company's chairman under a hire-purchase agreement.

(3) A public company sells furniture to a director on terms that payment be deferred for twelve months (note there need only be an "understanding" that payment will be deferred, which implies less than a legally binding agreement).

(4) *Arrangements relating to loans, quasi-loans, credit transactions and associated guarantees.* The prohibitions in sections 49(3) and (4) against indirect transactions such as the assignment of transactions and back-to-back transactions, discussed in detail earlier, apply equally in the case of relevant companies, and are extended to include indirect arrangements relating to quasi-loans and credit transactions (and associated guarantees or security provisions). The prohibition also catches indirect arrangements involving loans, quasi-loans and credit trans-

actions (and guarantees etc. thereof) for persons *connected* with a director of the company in question or of any holding company.

Exceptions

(1) *Transactions with directors of subsidiary or sister companies.* The exemption explained above for transactions by a company with a director of a subsidiary company or a sister company applies to all loans, quasi-loans and credit transactions, and guarantees thereof, entered into by a relevant company to or for such a director (or a person connected with him). But as before the director must not also be a director of the subsidiary or sister company. Likewise a subsidiary or sister company may enter into or take part in "arrangements" under section 49(3) or 49(4), provided, broadly, the director's company is not a party to these.

(2) *Meaning of loan, quasi-loan, credit transaction.* Because of the inclusion, for relevant companies, of prohibitions against quasi-loans and credit transactions, there is little scope for relevant companies arranging loan-type transactions which are outside the prohibitions. For instance, the sale of an asset on deferred terms, mentioned earlier in relation to non-relevant companies, will be caught as a "credit transaction".

(3) *Loans up to £2,500.* As for non-relevant companies, a company may make *loans* (but not quasi-loans, credit transactions or guarantees) of up to £2,500 to a director. Section 54 will require disclosure of the loan. *The exclusion does not extend to loans to persons connected with a director.* In deciding whether the £2,500 limit is observed the "aggregate of the relevant amounts" is to be computed as follows (C.A. 1980, s. 51, 65(4), 65(5) and 65(6)):

Sums to be added	*Notes*
(1) Principal amount of proposed loan to the director	If principal is unascertainable, it is the deemed to exceed £50,000 (s. 65(5)). This applies for (2) and (3) below, also
(2) Principal amount of any earlier loans made to the director in reliance of the section 50(2A) exception, *less* any principal repaid	This includes earlier loans made to the director or any person "connected" with him* (s. 51(2) and 51(3)) by the company or any subsidiary which is still a subsidiary (and, if the proposed loan is to a director of the company's holding company or a person "connected" with him*, earlier loans so made by that holding company or any of its subsidiaries which are still subsidiaries (s. 51(2), 51(4) and 65(6)))
(3) Principal amount of any earlier loans by third parties to the director which involved section 49(3) or 49(4) arrangements if the arrangements relied on the section 50(2A) exception, *less* any principal repaid.	This includes earlier loans by third parties which involved the "arrangements" specified opposite where the loans were made to any of the persons listed in (2) above

*But a loan by a non-relevant company to a *connected* person will not have been made by virtue of the section 50(2A) exception, and so can be ignored in the aggregation.

(4) *Quasi-loans up to £1,000.*   Section 50(2) permits a relevant company to make a quasi-loan to a director or a director of any holding company (*but not to a person connected with such a director*) if two conditions are satisfied. First, the quasi-loan must contain a term requiring the director (or someone on his behalf) to reimburse the *"creditor"* (i.e. the company of which the director is a director, or a subsidiary company, which makes the quasi-loan) within two months of it being incurred. Secondly, the amount of the quasi-loan must not exceed £1,000. If there are other quasi-loans made to the director under the section 50(2) exemption still outstanding, and these have been made by the company of which the director is a director, *or by any* subsidiary (including sub-subsidiaries) of that company, then the outstanding liabilities of the director under those quasi-loans must first be deducted from the £1,000 limit (section 50(2); the "relevant amount" test in section 51 is not used here).

This exception is chiefly of relevance in relation to company credit card transactions (see earlier). The two month time limit is too short to exempt most season ticket arrangements which constitute quasi-loans. The exemption does not extend to guarantees of quasi-loans, but does include section 49(3) or 49(4) "arrangements" relating to quasi-loans. A quasi-loan covered by the £1,000 exemption may still require disclosure.

(5) *Intra-group transactions.*   By sections 50(4)(a) and (b) a relevant company is permitted to make a loan, quasi-loan or credit transaction to its holding company (or companies). Likewise a relevant company may enter into a guarantee or provide security in connection with any such transaction made by another person with its holding company. This covers intra-group transactions where a parent company is a director of a subsidiary, or the parent company is "connected" with one of the subsidiary's directors, as where the director owns 20 per cent of the parent's equity share capital. Note that in the case of *credit transactions* the exemption only applies if the subsidiary company enters into a credit transaction as "creditor" (see below).

Section 50(1) provides a further exemption for intra-group transactions between relevant companies. Sections 49(b)(ii) and 49(b)(iii) prohibit a relevant company making a loan or quasi-loan, or giving a guarantee or security for such a transaction, to persons *connected* with a director of the company or its holding company. Where a director is "associated" with another company – by for instance holding 20 per cent of its equity share capital – that other company will be "connected" with the director, as explained earlier. Section 50(1) nevertheless permits loan, quasi-loan and guarantee or security transactions (but *not* credit transactions) to be entered into with that company provided two conditions are satisfied:

(a) the company is "connected" *only* because it is associated with the director; and

(b) the company is in the same *group* as the relevant company making the loan, quasi-loan or guarantee. A "group" is defined to mean a section 154 Companies Act 1948 holding company and its subsidiaries.

In relation to both the section 50(4) and the section 50(1) intra-group exemptions, section 49(3) or 49(4) arrangements, such as assignments or back-to-back agreements, relating to the relevant type of transaction are also exempted.

The exclusion of credit transactions from section 50(1) means that, for instance, a lease of property by a parent company to a subsidiary in which a director of the parent has a 20 per cent holding is caught. The section 50(4)(b) exemption only applies to credit transactions in which the subsidiary, not the parent, is "creditor". See, however, exemption (7) below.

(6) *Director's expenses.* The section 50(4)(c) exemption in relation to funds provided to meet expenditure for the purposes of a company's business or to enable a director properly to perform his duties applies equally to relevant companies, extending to quasi-loans and credit transactions. The exemption includes anything done by a company to enable a director to avoid incurring such expenditure, such as the provision of goods or services to enable a director to perform his duties. This might perhaps include a credit transaction such as the renting of a London flat to a director to enable him to carry out entertainment obligations.

As with a non-relevant company, the company must either obtain prior approval for the transaction in general meeting or impose a condition for repayment or discharge of any loan or liability within six months after the next annual general meeting. For a relevant company, however, there is an additional requirement. The "aggregate of the relevant amounts" must not exceed £10,000. For these purposes the "relevant amounts" are to be computed as follows:

Sums to be added	Notes
(1) "Value" of the proposed transaction or arrangement	Values are broadly as follows: loan: principal; quasi-loan: maximum amount to be reimbursed; credit transaction: reasonably expected price of goods, land or services in an ordinary course of business transaction; guarantee or security: amount guaranteed or secured; section 49(3) or 49(4) arrangement: value of underlying transaction less any amount by which liabilities thereunder reduced (see s. 65(4)). If value is unascertainable, it is deemed to exceed £50,000
(2) Value (as in (1) above) of any earlier transactions made in reliance of the section 50(4)(c) exception,* *less* any amount by which that value has been reduced	This includes earlier transactions entered into with the director, or any person "connected" with him, by the company or any subsidiary which is still a subsidiary (and, if the proposed transaction is *for* a director of the company's holding company, or a "connected" person, earlier transactions so made by that holding company or any of its subsidiaries which are still subsidiaries. Section 65(6) determines whether transactions are made *for* a person)

| (3) Value (as in (1) above) of any earlier transactions* with third parties which included section 49(3) or 49(4) arrangements if the arrangements relied on the section 50(4)(c) exception, *less* any amount by which the liabilities under the transaction have been reduced | This includes earlier transactions by third parties which involved the arrangements specified opposite where the transactions were made with any of the persons listed in (2) above |

*This will include any guarantee or security arrangements.

(7) *Permitted credit transactions.* Section 50(3) contains two exemptions for credit transactions entered into by a relevant company. These exemptions extend to credit transactions with connected persons, to guarantees of and security for all such credit transactions, and for any section 49(3) or 49(4) arrangements which relate to such credit transactions. Such transactions may however still require disclosure. (A third exemption for credit transactions is contained in the intra-group exemptions, discussed in (5) above.)

The first of the two exemptions applies where a relevant company enters into a credit transaction (a) "in the ordinary course of its business" and (b) the *value* of the transaction (as defined in section 65(4)) is not greater, and its terms not more favourable, than would be reasonably expected in a transaction with a person not connected with the company but of the same financial standing as the director or his connected person. Thus a company whose ordinary course of business includes supplying goods on hire purchase or leasing terms is not precluded from dealing with its directors on arm's length terms. But the exemption would not permit goods to be provided at artificially low rates. Similarly a relevant company can supply goods on trade credit to other companies who happen to be "connected" with a director of the first company provided the supply is in the ordinary course of business and on arm's length terms. "Ordinary course of business" is not defined (but see the references to *Steen v. Law* below). In the parliamentary debates on section 50(3) a government spokesman considered that in the case of hire purchase sales and similar transactions the "ordinary course" test restricted the exemption to sales of items which were part of a company's existing or forthcoming product range or an ancillary item (*Official Report*, Standing Committee A, December 4, 1979 col. 475).

The second exemption permits credit transactions "for" a director of a relevant company or anyone connected with him if the "aggregate of the relevant amounts" does not exceed £5,000 (section 50(3)(a)). A credit transaction is "for" a person if the relevant goods or services are supplied to him or land is sold or disposed of to him (section 65(6)(b)). The "aggregate of the relevant amounts" is to be calculated as follows:

Sums to be added	Notes
(1) The price which could reasonably be expected for the proposed goods, land or services in an arm's length deal	Section 65(4) postulates a transaction entered into at the same time in the ordinary course of business and on the same terms (except as to price) as the actual transaction. If the price cannot be ascertained, it is deemed to exceed £50,000
(2) The price (as in (1) above) of any earlier transactions made in reliance of the section 50(3)(a) exception*, *less* any amount by which this "price" has been reduced	This includes earlier credit transactions entered into with the director, or any person "connected" with him, by the company or any subsidiary which is still a subsidiary (and, if the proposed credit transaction is for a director of the company's holding company, or a "connected" person, earlier transactions so entered into by that holding company or any of its subsidiaries which are still subsidiaries)
(3) The price (as in (1) above) of any earlier credit transactions* made with third parties which included section 49(3) or 49(4) "arrangements" if the "arrangements" relied on the section 50(3)(a) exception, *less* any amount by which the liabilities under the transactions have been reduced	This includes earlier third party credit transactions which involved the arrangements specified opposite where the transactions were made with any of the persons listed in (2) above

*This will include any guarantee or security arrangements.

An example of the type of transaction excepted by the £5,000 limit is repairs to a director's car carried out in the company's workshops where payment is deferred.

(8) *Timing of transactions.* The comments made earlier in relation to the timing of non-relevant company loans, guarantees and arrangements apply equally to loans, quasi-loans, credit transactions, guarantees and arrangements made by relevant companies.

(9) *Money-lending companies and recognised banks.* The additional exemptions which apply to such companies are discussed in the next section.

Money-lending companies and recognised banks

Special exemptions apply to money-lending companies. Such companies, whether relevant companies or non-relevant companies, are subject to the normal restrictions and exemptions described above, but enjoy additional exemptions for loans, quasi-loans and guarantees of loans and quasi-loans.

A money-lending company is defined as a company whose *ordinary business* includes the making of loans or quasi-loans or the giving of guarantees in connection with loans or quasi-loans (section 65(1)). This includes not only recognised banks under the Banking Act 1979 but other companies such as licensed deposit-takers. For a person to carry on the *business* of money-lending there must be a system, repetition and continuity of the lending of money (*Edgelow v. MacElwee* [1918] 1 K.B. 205; *Chow Young Hong v. Choong Fah Rubber* [1962] A.C. 209). Cases on the Moneylenders Acts tend to suggest that the lending must also be with a view to profit.

The section 50(4)(d) exemption

The exemption for money-lending companies covers loans and quasi-loans made by the company, and guarantees of or indemnities for loans or quasi-loans made by other companies or persons. The loan, quasi-loan, guarantee or indemnity can be to or for a person connected with a director. But the exemption does not extend to credit transactions, or to the provision of security. However section 49(3) or 49(4) arrangements relating to loans, quasi-loans and guarantees or indemnities for such transactions are exempted. But two, and in most cases three, conditions must be met for the exemption to apply.

First, the loan, quasi-loan or guarantee must be entered into in the *ordinary course of the company's business* (section 50(6)(a)). This phrase is not defined, but in *Steen v. Law* [1963] 3 All E.R. 770 at 776, a case on the meaning of the phrase in a section concerning financial assistance for share purchases in the New South Wales Companies Acts, the Privy Council held that to qualify a transaction must be consistent with the normal course of business and be of a kind and scale which the company ordinarily practices. Also, the money should be at the borrower's free disposition and not be confined to special uses or restricted to particular and defined purposes. The decision in *Steen v. Law* was followed by the Divisional Court in *Fowlie v. Slater*, March 23, 1979. Similarly in the Australian case of *Downs Distributing Co. v. Associated Blue Star Stores* (1948) 76 C.L.R. 463 it was held that the phrase means that "the transaction must fall into place as part of the undistinguished common flow of business done, that it should form part of the ordinary business as carried on, calling for no remark and arising out of no special or particular situation".

Secondly, the loan quasi-loan or guarantee must not be greater in *amount* or on *more favourable terms* than that or those which the company could reasonably be expected to have offered to a person not *connected* with the company but of the same financial standing (section 50(6)(b)). Subject to an exception for certain house loans (see below), this means that a money-lending company cannot lend to a director of it or of its holding company (or to persons connected with those directors, if it is a relevant company) at a cheap rate of interest, or in excessive amounts. The use of the phrase "more favourable terms" in section 50(6)(b) suggests that a company lending to a director on favourable terms may nevertheless be lending in the "ordinary course of its business" under section 50(6)(a), which would represent a widening of the meaning generally adopted for that phrase before the introduction of the 1980 Act. This is of particular relevance when considering the special provisions relating to house loans (see below).

Thirdly, for all money-lending companies *except* recognised banks and companies which are *not* relevant companies, there is a limit of £50,000 of loan, quasi-loan and guarantee per director. The £50,000 limit is applied by reference to the "aggregate of the relevant amounts", which are computed pursuant to sections 51 and 65 as follows:

Sums to be added	*Notes*
(1) The principal amount (for a proposed loan or loan guarantee) or the maximum amount to be reimbursed (for a proposed quasi-loan or quasi-loan guarantee)	If the principal amount or amount to be reimbursed is unascertainable, it is deemed to exceed £50,000. This applies for (2) and (3) below, also
(2) The principal amount or amount outstanding under any earlier loan, quasi-loan or guarantee transactions made in reliance of the section 50(4)(d) money-lenders exemption,** *less* any amounts repaid or reimbursed	This includes earlier loans etc. made with the director, or any person "connected" with him*, by the money-lending company or any subsidiary which is still a subsidiary (and, if the proposed loan etc. is for a director of the money-lending company's holding company or a "connected" person*, earlier transactions so made by that holding company or any of its subsidiaries which are still subsidiaries (s. 51(2), 51(4) and 65(6)))
(3) The principal amount or amount outstanding under any earlier loan, quasi-loan or guarantee transaction made with third parties which included section 49(3) or 49(4) "arrangements", if the "arrangements" relied on the section 50(4)(d) money-lenders exemption, *less* any amount repaid or reimbursed	This includes earlier third party loans etc. which involved the "arrangements" specified opposite where the transactions were made with any of the persons listed in (2) above

*Except that, by section 50(6), a company "associated" with a director but over which the director does not have 51% control under section 64(3)(b) is *not* to be treated as "connected" with the director; see *Official Report*, Standing Committee A, November 29, 1979 for the reasoning behind this relaxation.

**This will include any home loans made under section 50(7): see below.

Home loans

Section 50(7) permits money-lending companies, including recognised banks, to make house-purchase loans to directors on "cheap" terms provided a number of conditions are satisfied. Quasi-loans, and guarantees of loans, are not covered. In theory it may be possible for a money-lending company to enter into "arrangements" for a home loan which meet the section 50(7) requirements, but this is unlikely to arise in practice. By section 50(7), the requirement in section 50(6)(b), that the loan must not be greater in *amount* or *on more favourable terms* than in arm's length deals, is not to apply,

(a) in the case of a *loan* to a *director* of the company or of its holding company (but not to persons connected with the director);

(b) which is made in the *ordinary course* of the company's business;

(c) which is for the purpose of facilitating the purchase of (or for the purpose of improving) the whole or part of any dwelling-house together with *any* land to be occupied and enjoyed therewith;

(d) for use as the *director's* "only or main residence";

(e) provided similar loans are *ordinarily* made by the company to its employees on terms no less favourable;

(f) and the "aggregate of the relevant amounts" does not exceed £50,000.

A loan in substitution for an existing loan from any source which met conditions (c) and (d) also qualifies.

The phrase "only or main *residence*" is not defined, but some assistance can be gained from the capital gains tax cases, such as *Batey v. Wakefield* [1981] S.T.C. 521 and *Frost v. Feltham* [1981] S.T.C. 115, on the meaning of the identical phrase in the capital gains tax legislation (see *Tolley's Tax Planning*).

Although the *terms* of the loan must not be more favourable than those of similar loans granted to employees, it does not matter that the amounts advanced are greater than would be advanced to employees or (subject to the overriding "ordinary course of business" test) to third parties. From the drafting of sections 50(6) and 50(7) it would appear that a large loan at a low interest rate may be a loan in the "ordinary course of business", even though cases such as *Steen v. Law*, discussed above, tend to indicate to the contrary.

In calculating "the aggregate of the relevant amounts" it is necessary to include in the £50,000 aggregation any loans, quasi-loans or guarantees made by the money-lending company on "normal" terms, whether for house-purchase or other terms. But this rule does not apply in the case of loans etc. by recognised banks, who suffer no fixed upper limit on their "normal" loans (see sections 50(6) and 51(2A)). Such banks may thus loan up to £50,000 to a director on "cheap" terms for house-purchase plus further amounts, without limit and whether for house-purchase or other purposes, which satisfy the "normal" loan requirements, particularly the "ordinary course of business" requirement, in section 50(6). It also appears that up to £50,000 may be lent on "cheap" terms by a recognised bank (or any other moneylending company) after December 22, 1980, regardless of the amount lent on "cheap" terms before that date. This is because neither section 50 nor section 51 applies to loans made before that date (section 65(7); confirmed in *Official Report*, Standing Committee A, December 4, 1981, col. 488). (But a money-lending company which, although *not* a relevant company and so not subject to the £50,000 limit on "normal" loans, is not a recognised bank is not excluded from the aggregation rule and thus cannot lend more than £50,000 for house-purchase unless the *whole* of the loan satisfies the section 50(6) "normal" loan tests. The only exceptions appear to be where a "cheap" loan was made before December 22, 1980 (where a further £50,000 on "cheap" terms can now be lent) or if a "normal" loan (for house-purchase or otherwise) is made *after* the "cheap" house loan.)

Subject to the above comments, the general rules for determining the "aggregate of the relevant amounts" for the purpose of the £50,000 limit on home loans are as follows:

Sum to be added	*Notes*
(1) The principal amount of the proposed "cheap" loan	If this amount is unascertainable, it is deemed to exceed £50,000. This applies to (2) and (3) below, also
(2) The principal amount (for loans or loan guarantees) or the maximum amount to be reimbursed (for quasi-loans or quasi-loan guarantees) under any earlier loan made in reliance of the section 50(4)(d) money-lenders exemption (whether pursuant to sections 50(6) or 50(7))*, *less* any amounts repaid or reimbursed	This includes earlier loans etc. made with the director or any person "connected" with him,** by the money-lending company or any company which is still a subsidiary (and, if the proposed loan is for a director of the money-lending company's holding company, earlier transactions so made by that holding company or any of its subsidiaries which are still subsidiaries (s. 51(2), 51(4) and 65(6))
(3) The principal amount or amount outstanding under any earlier loan, quasi-loan or guarantee transaction made with third parties which included section 49(3) or 49(4) arrangements, if the arrangements relied on the section 50(4)(d) money-lenders exception, *less* any amount repaid or reimbursed	This includes earlier third party loans etc. which involved the arrangements specified opposite where the transactions were made with any of the persons listed in (2) above

*See text for position of recognised banks and money-lending companies which are not relevant companies.
**Except that, by section 50(6), a company "associated" with a director but over which the director does not have 51% control under section 64(3)(b) is *not* to be treated as "connected" with the director.

The ability of money-lending companies to make "cheap" house loans to directors provided a general house-loan scheme exists represents something of an anomaly, but in the debates on the 1980 Act the Government resisted parliamentary attempts to remove the exemption or to extend it to all companies. It should be remembered that the 1980 Act does not prevent a company making house loans to directors of a subsidiary or to directors of "sister" subsidiary companies (provided in both cases the individuals are not also directors of the company). Moreover it is permissible, so far as the 1980 Act is concerned, to provide a senior employee with a house loan shortly *before* he is appointed as a director. In such a case, however, problems will arise if the individual, once a director, chooses to move house. It may though be possible to avoid the making of a fresh "loan" by arranging for a new house to be substituted as security for the *existing* loan (when the director's ability to obtain tax relief on any interest paid on the loan will need to be examined). One method used by some non-money-lending companies to provide house loans to directors, involving back-to-back arrangements with loans from a third party bank or insurance company, is no longer effective (sections 49(3) and 49(4)), though pre-December 22, 1980 transactions generally remain valid.

Civil and criminal liability

Sections 52 and 53 set out the civil remedies and criminal penalties for the entering into of transactions or arrangements prohibited by section 49.

Civil remedies

Any loan, quasi-loan, credit transaction or guarantee, or an arrangement relating thereto, which is entered into in breach of section 49 is voidable at the option of the company – and no-one else – entering into the transaction (section 52; without this provision the transaction, rendered illegal by section 53, would probably be void). As a result the company will be able to rescind the transaction and recover any money or other asset with which it has parted. There is no time limit imposed within which the company must rescind (confirmed by *Official Report*, Standing Committee A, December 4, 1981 col. 493, although note the general law on rescission). There are three exceptions to the general rule allowing the company to rescind,

(a) restitution of the money or other asset is no longer possible (section 52(1)(a));

(b) the rights of a bona fide purchaser for value without *actual* notice of the section 49 contravention would be affected (section 52(1)(b)). But the person for whom the transaction or arrangement was made cannot fall within this exemption; or

(c) the company is indemnified by a director (or where relevant a person connected with him) for the loss or damage suffered, pursuant to the terms of section 52(2) (section 52(1)(a)).

Section 52(2) goes on to impose obligations on the director *for* whom the prohibited transaction or arrangement was entered into. In the case of a relevant company, these obligations extend to connected persons for whom the transaction or arrangement was entered into. The rules for ascertaining "for" whom a transaction or arrangement is made are set out in section 65(6).

By section 52(2) the director or connected person, *and any other director* of the company which entered into the transaction or arrangement who *authorised* it, is liable to account for any direct or indirect gain he has made out of the transaction or arrangement. In addition any such person is jointly and severally liable, with any other director or connected person caught by section 52(2), to indemnify the company, for any loss or damage suffered. This liability does not extend to loss or damage suffered by a third party. But the liability is without prejudice to any other liability the person may be under (e.g. *Wallersteiner v. Moir* [1974] 1 W.L.R. 991 indicates that a director receiving a loan in breach of section 49 would be liable to compensate the company under general law). There are however two exclusions from the liability under section 52(2).

First, any director who authorises a transaction or arrangement will not be liable if he can show that he did not know the "relevant circumstances" (not defined as such) constituting the contravention. This test is to be applied at the time the transaction or arrangement is entered into.

Secondly, where a *relevant* company enters into a transaction or arrangement with a person *connected* with a director of it or its holding company, then (a) that director is not liable if he can show he took all reasonable steps to comply with section 49, and (b) the connected person is not liable if he can show he did not know the "relevant circumstances".

Criminal liability

A director involved in a prohibited transaction or arrangement may also be guilty of a criminal offence. Criminal liability extends to the company which enters into the transaction or arrangement. In both cases, however, it is only *relevant* companies and their *directors* who can be liable. The only circumstance where a connected person, or a non-relevant company or any of its directors, can be liable is if that person procures a *relevant* company to enter into a transaction or arrangement *knowing or having reasonable cause* to believe that the company was breaching section 49 (section 53(3)). This liability extends to *any* person who so procures the entering into of a prohibited transaction or arrangement.

A director of a relevant company commits an offence if he authorises or permits his company to enter into a transaction or arrangement "knowing or having reasonable cause to believe" that the company was breaching section 49.

The relevant company itself is always guilty of an offence unless either,

(a) the transaction or arrangement is not for a director of it or its holding company, but for a *connected person*; or

(b) the company can show it did not know of the "relevant circumstances" at the time the transaction or arrangement was entered into. Presumably a director's knowledge of the relevant circumstances will be imputed to his company (see *Bolton Engineering v. Graham* [1957] 1 Q.B. 159; *Belmont Finance Corporation Limited v. Williams Furniture Limited* [1979] Ch. 250).

Conviction on indictment under section 53 carries a maximum prison sentence of two years or a fine; summary conviction a maximum sentence of six months or a maximum fine of £1,000 (see sections 28(2) and 61 of the Criminal Law Act 1977).

Directors' Meetings

In contrast to the rules relating to shareholders' meetings, relatively little formality is required to convene and conduct a board meeting. It is interesting to compare the number and complexity of the regulations of Table A governing shareholders' meetings (articles 47 to 74) with those regulations governing the conduct of board meetings (articles 98 to 106). This is largely the result of the very general opening sentence to article 98 which provides that "The directors may meet together for the despatch of business, adjourn, and otherwise regulate their meetings as they think fit". Obviously it would be open to a board of directors so to regulate their meetings that they are beset with formality, but this would be unusual.

Notice

There is no set period of notice that has to be given to directors of proposed board meetings (in contrast to the minimum periods prescribed by statute for general meetings of the company). Notice here simply needs to be reasonable notice having regard to the practice of the company and other surrounding circumstances (*Browne v. La Trinidad* (1887) 37 Ch.D.1). Thus, for the average private company where board meetings are infrequently held and convened with little formality, notice of a few hours or minutes even would be sufficient provided that it gave all directors a reasonable chance to attend the meeting. In the absence of express provision in the Articles or in regulations made under article 98 of Table A (or an analogous provision) to the contrary, there is no need for the notice to be in writing, nor for it to state the nature of the business proposed to be transacted. Notice must however be given to *all* directors for the time being of the company, as business done at a meeting of which some directors only have notice is invalid and a director has no power to waive his right to notice. By way of exception to this rule, a company's Articles will usually provide that it shall not be necessary to give notice of a directors' meeting to any director for the time being absent from the United Kingdom (see e.g. article 98 of Table A).

Quorum

A company's Articles usually provide that a specified number of directors shall form a quorum (see e.g. article 99 of Table A), and if this is the case it is not then necessary for all the company's directors to attend a board meeting provided that they have been given notice of that meeting. Generally, the Articles will provide that questions arising at any meeting shall be decided by a majority of votes of the directors present (see e.g. article 98 of Table A), votes in this case being cast on the basis of one man one vote, although typically the chairman may have a second or casting vote in case of an equality of votes if the Articles so provide (see again article 98 of Table A). In reckoning a quorum for a particular resolution, directors who are not entitled to vote on that resolution, perhaps because they are interested in a contract the subject of that resolution and are prevented by the company's Articles from voting on contracts in which they are interested, cannot be counted towards that quorum. A problem that the small private company sometimes meets in practice is how best to pass board resolutions where the number of directors has fallen to one. The first point to check here is that under the company's Articles the number of directors holding office has not been allowed to fall below the prescribed minimum set by the Articles. If it has, then typically (see e.g. article 100 of Table A) the continuing director may act solely for the purpose of increasing the number of directors to the requisite minimum (or for summoning a general meeting of the company), but for no other purpose. This would then be the first step to take. In some cases the Articles may already provide (which however Table A does not) something along the following lines:

"The number of the directors shall be determined by ordinary resolution of the Company, but unless and until so fixed there shall be no maximum number of directors and the minimum number of directors shall be one. In the event of the minimum number of directors fixed by or pursuant to these Articles or Table A being one, a sole director shall have authority to exercise all the powers and discretions by Table A or these Articles expressed to be vested in the directors generally and article 99 in Table A shall be modified accordingly."

In this latter case the sole director will still have to surmount the problem of how to hold a meeting of directors at which he is the only director present in the light of the generally held view that it is impossible to have a meeting of one. It is submitted that in these circumstances the simple and correct solution is for the sole director to act by written resolution rather than to attempt to argue that he is capable of holding a meeting by himself. Articles (e.g. article 106 of Table A) usually provide that a resolution in writing signed by all the directors shall have the same effect as a resolution passed at a meeting of the directors.

Conduct of meetings

As outlined earlier, the construction of rules for the conduct of board meetings is a matter largely left to be determined by the directors. If any standing orders have been made by the board under a provision like article 98 of Table A concerning the conduct of meetings, then obviously these should be adhered to. However, outsiders dealing with the company in good faith are unlikely to be affected by a departure from such a standing order in view of the protection afforded by section 9 of the European Communities Act 1972 and the rule in *Royal British Bank v. Turquand* (1856) 6 E. & B. 327. A much greater degree of formality is likely to surround the board meetings of a large public company than those of a small private company, which may be convened only very infrequently. A large number of small private companies only ever hold a board meeting either to convene the annual A.G.M. or at the suggestion of the company's solicitors or accountants to tackle some matter requiring a formal board resolution, like the alteration of a bank mandate or the affixation of the company's seal to a conveyance.

Typically the chairman of the board will chair board meetings and may or may not have an agenda prepared by the secretary to guide him through the business to be discussed. Minutes should be taken (see below) and it will usually fall to the secretary to write these up. The secretary should also take a note of the attendance of directors at board meetings and record this on the minutes themselves.

All directors willing and able to attend board meetings should be given the opportunity to do so, and a director wrongfully excluded from board meetings can obtain an injunction restraining further exclusion (*Pulbrook v. Richmond Consolidated Mining Co* (1878) 9 Ch. D. 610.

Where the Articles of Association permit a director who is going to be absent from board meetings to appoint an alternate to represent him in his absence, with entitlement to receive notices of all board meetings, then notices of such meetings should certainly be given to the alternate director who will have the same rights to attend as his appointer. As the appointer himself remains a director of the company, the better view seems to be that notice of board meetings should be given to him as well as to his alternate unless the articles specifically provide that in such circumstances notice need not be given to the appointer.

Typically (see e.g. article 102 of Table A) the directors will be able to delegate any of their powers to committees consisting of such of their number as they think fit. It is open to the directors to make appropriate regulations for the procedural operation of a committee. Further provisions regulating the conduct of committee meetings are set out in articles 103 and 104 of Table A. The use of committees is to be recommended where difficulty in giving notice of full board meetings to all directors is anticipated, provided of course that the full board is prepared to delegate its powers on the matters in question.

Minutes

Minutes of all proceedings of the directors at board meetings must be taken and entered in the company's minute book (C.A. 1948, s. 145(1)). Such minutes, if signed by the chairman of the meeting at which the proceedings minuted took place or by the chairman of the next succeeding meeting, are evidence of the proceedings (section 145(2)). Where minutes have been made in accordance with section 145, then until the contrary is proved the meeting minuted is deemed to have been duly held and convened and all proceedings at that meeting deemed duly had and all appointments of directors, managers or liquidators deemed to be valid (section 145(3)).

Care should be taken to ensure that minutes kept are accurate, as there is a presumption that a matter was not brought before the board in the absence of any reference to that matter in the minutes of the relevant board meeting. This presumption may be rebutted by express evidence to the contrary.

Disclosure of interests in contracts and arrangements

Almost invariably a company's articles will release a director from the prohibition at general law that he may not contract with his company (see e.g. article 84(3) of Table A and the chapter *Disclosure of Directors' Dealings*). He may however be prevented from voting on that contract or arrangement (see e.g. article 84(2)), and nothing in the company's articles can release a director from the provisions of section 199 of the Companies Act 1948, as amended and supplemented by section 60 of the 1980 Act. Section 199 is discussed in greater detail in the chapter *Disclosure of Directors' Dealings*. As explained there, under section 199 (as amended), any director of the company who is in any way, whether directly or indirectly, interested in a contract or proposed contract with the company is under a duty to declare the nature of his interest at a meeting of the directors of the company. Section 60(1) of the 1980 Act has extended the meaning of the term "contract" here to include any transaction or arrangement (whether or not constituting a contract) entered into since December 22, 1980. The phrase "transaction or arrangement" is deliberately wide. Section 60(2) of the 1980 Act also extends the scope of the director's duty to declare the nature of his interest in loan and quasi-loan transactions and arrangements as referred to in section 49 of the 1980 Act made by a company for its director *or a person connected with him*. Thus for example it is necessary for a director to disclose the nature of his interest in any loan by the company to his wife or child.

It should be remembered that for the purposes of the duty to make disclosure a director is interested in a contract or proposed contract and arrangement under the section whether his interest arises "directly or indirectly". It is self evident that a director is directly interested in his own service contract with the company, and although it seems ludicrous that he should be required to declare the nature of his interest in such service contract to his co-directors, for the sake of good order the formal disclosure should be made. Indirect interests can arise in a number of ways – for example through the director holding shares in another company (even if only as trustee) or by being a partner in a firm where the other company or firm is a party to the contract with the director's company.

Directors' Report

As is further explained on page 63 (*Accounts, Transitional Rules*), a company's accounts in respect of any financial year (as defined in section 1 of the 1976 Act) beginning before June 15, 1982 may comply with the provisions of section 149A of Schedule 8A to the Companies Act 1948, rather than with the new provisions in section 149 of, and Schedule 8 to, that Act (substituted by the 1981 Act). Furthermore, the accounts in respect of *any* financial year of a banking, insurance or shipping company (whether or not that financial year begins before June 15, 1982) may, at that company's option, be prepared in accordance with the old rather than the new provisons.

A directors' report attached to any section 149A/Schedule 8A accounts must comply with the provisions of the Companies Acts 1948 to 1980 without reference to the amendments relating to directors' reports introduced by the 1981 Act, whereas a directors' report attached to section 149/Schedule 8 accounts must take account of the amendments (C.A. 1981, Sch. 2, paras. 4(2), 4(3), 5(4) to 5(6) and 6(2)).

Accordingly, any consideration of the legal requirements relating to directors' reports must be in two stages: first, by reference to the position under the Companies Acts 1948 to 1980 and, secondly, by reference to the position under the 1981 Act.

Companies Acts 1948 to 1980

Under section 157 of the 1948 Act (as amended by section 1 of the 1976 Act), "there shall be attached to every balance sheet prepared under section 1 of the Companies Act 1976 (or under that section taken with section 150 of this Act (group accounts)) a report by the directors with respect to the state of the company's affairs, the amount, if any, which they recommend should be paid by way of dividend, and the amount, if any, which they propose to carry to reserves within the meaning of the Eighth Schedule to this Act". In addition, the 1967 Act (particularly section 16) requires that a considerable amount of further information be contained in the directors' report. Table 1 below sets out the combined requirements of section 157 of the 1948 Act and section 16 of the 1967 Act.

Table 1

Contents of directors' report (pre-1981 Act)

(1) Directors' statement as to the state of the company's affairs (section 157).

(2) The amount, if any, of dividend they recommend should be paid (section 157).

(3) The amount, if any, they propose to transfer to reserves (section 157).

(4) The names of the persons who, at any time during the financial year to which the report relates, were directors of the company (section 16(1)).

(5) The principal activities of the company and of its subsidiaries and any significant change in those activities during the year (section 16(1)).

(6) Any significant changes in the fixed assets of the company or of any of its subsidiaries, and any significant difference between the market value of any land included as one of those assets and the value at which it is included in the balance sheet "with such degree of precision as is practicable" (section 16(1)(a)). (Banking, discount, insurance or shipping companies as referred to in Part III of Schedule 8A to the 1948 Act do not have to disclose details of significant changes in fixed assets (section 16(2)).

(7) The reason for making any issue of shares or debentures during the year, the class or classes and amounts issued and the consideration received by the company (section 16(1)(b)).

(8) In respect of the first financial year of the company ending after December 22, 1980 (and only as regards loans from and contracts with the company in which any director was interested and which were entered into before December 22, 1980 but did not subsist after that date) the information required by section 16(1)(c) of the 1967 Act (for all other purposes section 16(1)(c) has been repealed by the 1980 Act).

(9) Particulars of any arrangements to which the company is a party and which subsist or have subsisted at any time during the year whose objects are, or one of whose objects is, to enable directors of the company to acquire benefits by means of the acquisition of shares or debentures of the company or of any other company, the particulars being sufficient to explain the effect of those arrangements and to give the names of the persons who at any time in the year held shares or debentures pursuant to those arrangements (section 16(1)(d)).

(10) A statement in respect of each director of the company at the end of the financial year as to whether or not, according to the register kept by the company for the purposes of sections 27 and 29 of the 1967 Act, any interests in the shares or debentures of the company or any of its associated companies are recorded, and particulars of any interests so recorded together with a statement of such interests at the beginning of the financial year (or the date during such year on which any new director first joined the board) (section 16(1)(e)).

(11) Particulars of any matters (other than those which should be dealt with under the categories described at paragraphs (6) to (10) above or elsewhere in the 1967 Act as to matters which have to be included in directors' reports) so far as they are material for the appreciation of the state of the company's affairs by its members, being matters the disclosure of which will not, in the opinion of the directors, be harmful to the business of the company or any of its subsidiaries (section 16(1)(f)).

(12) Any information required under regulations made by the Secretary of State about the arrangements in force (for the year to which the report relates) for securing the health, safety and welfare at work of the employees of the company and its subsidiaries and for the protection of other persons against risks to health or safety in respect of the activities at work of employees (section 16(1)(g)). This last requirement was added by section 79 of the Health & Safety at Work Act 1974.

(13) Where the company (or group in the case of a holding company) has carried on businesses of more than one class during the year which, in the opinion of the directors, are substantially different from each other, and the company's turnover exceeds £1 million, or it is a member of a group of companies, the proportions in which the turnover is divided amongst those classes, and the extent or approximate extent to which the business of each class contributed to, or restricted, the profit or loss of the company or group (section 17).

(14) Where the average number of persons employed in the United Kingdom by the company (or in the case of a holding company, by the group) during the year (calculated week to week) was not less than 100, the actual average number employed and the aggregate remuneration (inclusive of all bonuses) paid to employees (section 18).

(15) Where a company (not being the wholly-owned subsidiary of a company incorporated in Great Britain) has in a financial year given money in excess of £200 for political or charitable purposes a statement of the amount of money given and, in the case of political purposes, the name of the person or identity of the political party receiving the money and the amount so given (section 19 as amended by the Companies (Directors' Report) (Political and Charitable Contributions) Regulations 1980).

(16) Where its business consists in or included the supply of goods, and the company's turnover exceeds £1 million (or where the company is a member of a group, £50,000) a statement of the value of the goods exported during the year or a statement of the fact that no goods have been exported, unless the Department of Trade have been satisfied by the directors that it is in the national interest that the information should not be disclosed (section 20).

(17) Where information required to be given in the accounts but permitted to be given in a statement annexed is in fact given in the directors' report under the proviso to section 163 of the 1948 Act, a statement of the corresponding amount for the immediately preceding financial year, except where that amount would not have to be shown had the information been shown in the accounts (section 22).

(18) Where the average number of employees exceeds 250 a statement as to the company's policy during the year for the employment, training, career development and promotion of disabled persons (Companies (Directors' Report) (Employment of Disabled Persons) Regulations 1980).

Companies Act 1981

There are a number of different and additional provisions to observe for directors' reports prepared in conjunction with accounts which comply with the new Schedule 8 to the 1948 Act as introduced by the 1981 Act.

For the general requirement in section 157 of the 1948 Act that the directors' report be with respect to the state of the company's affairs, there is substituted a requirement that the report should contain "a fair review of the development of the business of the company and its subsidiaries during the financial year" and of their position at the end of it (C.A. 1981, s. 13(1)). No definition is given of "fair review" but this must at least encompass a general review of the prominent features of the company's financial year.

New specific disclosures

The requirement for the disclosure of particulars of any matters material for the appreciation of the state of the company's affairs by its members (see paragraph (11) in Table 1 above) is removed and replaced by a more precisely defined requirement for the disclosure of,

(a) particulars of any important events affecting the company and its subsidiaries which have occurred since the end of the company's financial year;

(b) an indication of likely future developments in the business of the company and its subsidiaries; and

(c) an indication of the activities (if any) of the company and its subsidiaries in the field of research and development (C.A. 1981, s. 13(3)).

There are also new provisions relating to the acquisition by a company of its own shares. Section 14 of the 1981 Act provides that where shares in a company are acquired by the company by purchase, forfeiture or otherwise or, in the case of a public company by a nominee for the company, or where shares in the capital of a company are charged by it, there must be disclosed,

(i) the number and nominal value of shares so acquired and, where such acquisition is by purchase, the consideration paid and the reason for the purchase;

(ii) the *maximum* number and nominal value of shares so acquired or charged (whether in the year to which the report relates or not) which were held during the year;

(iii) the number and nominal value of shares so acquired or charged which were disposed of or cancelled during the year and, where disposed of for value, the consideration in each case; and

(iv) the amount of the charge in each case where the shares have been charged.

Where the number and nominal value of such shares has to be stated so does the percentage of called up capital which they represent.

Disclosures no longer required

A number of matters which required disclosure in the directors' report under the 1967 Act will not under the 1981 Act have to be disclosed there. This is because similar information will, by and large, but with the notable exception of export details, be given in the accounts themselves and notes thereto. These are,

(i) turnover and profitability by class of business (see paragraph 13 of Table 1 above);

(ii) the number of employees and their remuneration (paragraph 14; see now Companies Act 1948, Schedule 8, paragraph 56);

(iii) the issue of shares or debentures (paragraph 7);

(iv) arrangements for directors to acquire shares or debentures (paragraph 9);

(v) details of exports (paragraph 16; repealed with effect from December 22, 1981);

(vi) additionally, disclosure of directors' interests in shares and debentures (paragraph 10) may now be given in the notes to the accounts instead of in the directors' report.

In those rare cases where a subsidiary's accounts have been prepared to comply with the new Schedule 8 to the 1948 Act, and the group consolidated accounts have been prepared in accordance with Schedule 8A (as could be the case where a group holding company has a banking, insurance or shipping subsidiary), disclosure of turnover and profitability by class of business and details of UK employees will still have to be given in the directors' report.

Table 2

Contents of directors' report (post-1981 Act)

(1) Directors' "fair review" of the development of the business of the company and its subsidiaries during the financial year, and their position at the end of it (C.A. 1948, s. 157(1) as amended).

(2) The amount, if any, of dividend they recommend should be paid (section 157).

(3) The amount, if any, they propose to transfer to reserves (section 157).

(4) The names of the persons who, at any time during the financial year to which the report relates, were directors of the company (Companies Act 1967, section 16(1)).

(5) The principal activities of the company and of its subsidiaries and any significant change in those activities during the year (section 16(1)).

(6) Any significant changes in the fixed assets of the company or of any of its subsidiaries, and any significant difference between the market value of any land included as one of those assets and the value at which it is included in the balance sheet "with such degree of precision as is practicable" (section 16(1)(a)). (Banking, discount, insurance or shipping companies as referred to in Part III of Schedule 8A to the 1948 Act do not have to disclose details of significant changes in fixed assets).

(7) Particulars of any important events affecting the company and its subsidiaries which have occurred since the end of the company's financial year (section 16(1)(f)).

(8) An indication of likely future developments in the business of the company and its subsidiaries (section 16(1)(f)).

(9) An indication of the activities (if any) of the company and its subsidiaries in the field of research and development (section 16(1)(f)).

(10) Any information required under regulations made by the Secretary of State about the arrangements in force (for the year to which the report relates) for securing the health, safety and welfare at work of the employees of the company and its subsidiaries and for the protection of other persons against risks to health or safety in respect of the activities at work of employees. This last requirement was added by section 79 of the Health & Safety at Work Etc. Act 1974.

(11) Where a company (not being the wholly-owned subsidiary of a company incorporated in Great Britain) has in a financial year given money in excess of £200 for political or charitable purposes a statement of the amount of money given and, in the case of political purposes, the name of the person or identity

---

of the political party receiving the money and the amount so given (Companies Act 1967, section 19 as amended by the Companies (Directors' Report) (Political and Charitable Contributions) Regulations 1980).

(12) A statement in respect of each director of the company at the end of the financial year as to whether or not, according to the register kept by the company for the purposes of sections 27 and 29 of the 1967 Act, any interests in the shares or debentures of the company or any of its associated companies are recorded, and particulars of any interests so recorded together with a statement of such interests at the beginning of the financial year, or the date during such year on which any new director first joined the board (n.b. this information *may* instead now be shown in the notes to the accounts: Companies Act 1981, section 13(4)).

(13) Where the average number of employees exceeds 250 a statement as to the company's policy during the year for the employment, training career development and promotion of disabled persons (Companies (Directors' Report) (Employment of Disabled Persons) Regulations 1980).

(14) Where the company purchases its own shares, or acquires shares by forfeiture or surrender, or shares are acquired by another person where sections 37(1)(c) or (d) of the 1980 Act apply, or shares are made subject to a lien or a charge under sections 38(2)(a) or (d) of the 1980 Act, the directors' report shall include the details set out in section 16A(2) of the 1967 Act, which in outline are:

(a) the number* and nominal value of shares so acquired or purchased and, where such acquisition is by purchase, the consideration paid and the reason for the purchase;

(b) the *maximum* number* and nominal value of shares so acquired or charged (whether in the year to which the report relates or not) which were held during the year;

(c) the number* and nominal value of shares so acquired or charged which were disposed of or cancelled during the year and, where disposed of for value, the consideration in each case; and

(d) the amount of the charge in each case where the shares have been charged.

(15) For financial years beginning after December 31, 1982 of a company employing more than 250 people in the UK, a statement describing steps taken to introduce, maintain or develop arrangements concerning employee information and consultation, employee share schemes and the like, and employee awareness of financial and economic factors affecting the company's performance (The Employment Act 1982 (Commencement Order) 1982 S.I. 1656)).

*(Stating also the percentage of called up share capital which those shares represent.)

Auditors' responsibilities

Section 15 of the 1981 Act introduces a major new requirement that auditors are duty bound to consider whether the information given in the directors' report is "consistent" with the accounts, and if in their opinion the information is not "consistent" they must state that fact in their report. It is interesting to note the choice of the word "consistent" here, which presumably means that provided consistency is established it will not be necessary to check the accuracy of additional information which does not conflict with the accounts, although out of prudence this is likely to be done.

Miscellaneous

It is no longer permissible for certain information to be given in the

directors' report instead of in the accounts, because the proviso to
section 163 of the 1948 Act has been repealed. Failure to annex the
directors' report to the statutory accounts, to send it to members and
debenture holders, and to lay it before a general meeting and file it with
the Registrar, can lead to fines on the directors (C.A. 1948, s. 158 and
C.A. 1976, ss. 1 to 4).

Distribution of directors' report

Every person entitled to receive a copy of the company's balance sheet
is entitled to receive also a copy of the directors' report (C.A. 1948, s.
158 and C.A. 1967, s. 24).

Stock Exchange requirements

For companies listed on The Stock Exchange, the listing agreement
specifies certain additional disclosure requirements in the directors'
report. It is not clear whether these requirements will be modified to the
extent that the information · must now be contained in the accounts
themselves. In outline these are set out in Table 3 below:

Table 3

Outline of Stock Exchange requirements

(a) The reasons for any material departure in the accounts from Statements of
    Standard Accounting Practice.
(b) An explanation of any material difference in the trading results shown in the
    accounts from any forecast published by the company.
(c) A geographical analysis of turnover and trading results of operations carried
    on outside the United Kingdom.
(d) The principal country in which each subsidiary operates.
(e) Information regarding each company in which the group has an equity interest
    of 20 per cent or more (country of operation, share and loan capital, reserves,
    percentages of each class of loan capital held).
(f) The interests of each director in the share capital of the company and its
    subsidiaries, distinguishing between beneficial and non-beneficial interests.
(g) Substantial interests in the share capital held by persons other than directors.
(h) The "close company" status of the company, and investment trust status where
    applicable.
(i) Significant contracts in which directors are materially interested.
(j) Waivers of emoluments by directors.
(k) Waivers of dividends by shareholders.
(l) Amounts of bank loans and overdrafts and other borrowings repayable within
    periods of one year or less (or on demand), between one and two years,
    between two and five years, and within five years or more.
(m) Interest capitalised during the year and amount and treatment of related tax
    relief.
(n) For any director proposed for re-election, the unexpired period of any service
    contract.

Disclosure of Directors' Dealings

"If there is one key word which more than any other sums up the underlying principles of company law in this country, it is *disclosure*" (Sealy, (1981) 2 Co. Law. 51).

However, while the philosophy of maximum publicity and disclosure is central to company law, its mechanics have evolved in a haphazard manner. For example, some information must be recorded at the company's registered office, other information must be delivered to, and recorded by, the Registrar of Companies, whilst other information must be presented in the company's accounts. Often the same information will be available at different places and will be contained in various different documents causing considerable additional work and expense. One illustration is the details of the directors' names, addresses, nationalities, business occupations and the like. This information is to be recorded in the company's register of directors and secretaries which must be kept at the company's registered office (C.A. 1948, s. 200). This same information must be communicated to the Registrar of Companies (as regards the first directors by virtue of C.A. 1976, s. 21 and as regards subsequent changes by virtue of C.A. 1948, s. 200(4), and any change in the directors must be notified by the Registrar in the Gazette (European Communities Act 1972 s. 9(3)(c))). In addition, the same information must also appear in the company's annual return (C.A. 1948, s. 124, s. 125(1)(d) and Sch. 6).

This chapter is concerned with disclosure in relation to directors. Publicity must be given in different ways to a variety of information concerning the directors: e.g. who they are, what other directorships they hold, what they earn, the terms of their service contracts, their interests in the company's shares and debentures and details of any loans or similar transactions made to or with them by their company.

Publicity is achieved primarily by two methods, the keeping of registers by the company and the furnishing, by the company, of notes to its accounts.

The *registers* which must be kept by the company are:

(a) the registers of directors and secretaries (C.A. 1948, s. 200); and

(b) the register of directors' interests in the company's shares and debentures (C.A. 1967, ss. 27–29).

The information which must appear in the *company's accounts* relating to directors is:

311

(a) details of the directors' emoluments (C.A. 1948, s. 196 and C.A. 1967 s. 6); and

(b) details of various transactions and arrangements involving directors (C.A. 1980, ss. 54–58).

In addition, certain disclosures must be made to the *company*. Disclosure of directors' interests in contracts with the company is required to be made to the general meeting in consequence of the director's fiduciary position, unless he is exempted therefrom by the company's articles; disclosure must, in any case, be made to the board of the company under section 199 of the 1948 Act.

Information relating to directors is also provided in two other ways. First, section 26 of the 1967 Act requires copies of directors' service contracts to be available for inspection by the company's members, and secondly, the use of directors' names on business letters of the company is regulated by section 201 of the 1948 Act.

Registers: the register of directors and secretaries

By section 200(1) of the Companies Act 1948, every company incorporated in Great Britain must keep a register of its directors and secretaries at its registered office, and failure so to do constitutes a criminal offence (section 200(7)). The term "director" here includes "a person in accordance with whose directions or instructions the directors of a company are accustomed to act" (section 200(9)(a), subject to section 455(2)).

Details required

The details which must be included in the register in relation to each director are listed in section 200(2) and are as shown below.

---

(1) *If the director is an individual*

(i) His present forename and surname (or title if a peer).

(ii) Any former names. This does not, however, include a married woman's maiden name or a name which was changed or disused before the director was eighteen or more than twenty years ago (section 200(9)(d)).

(iii) His usual residential address.

(iv) His nationality.

(v) His business occupation (if any).

(vi) Any other directorships presently held by him. A directorship in another company need not be mentioned if that other company is either "dormant" or a "relevant company" in relation to the company keeping the register and, in either case, has been such for the whole of the period that the individual has held the directorship during the preceding five years (C.A. 1948, s. 200(2) as amended by C.A. 1981, s. 95). A company is "dormant" during any period when no significant accounting transaction (within C.A. 1976, s. 12 and C.A. 1981, s. 12(6)) has occurred. This exception is to prevent

---

the register being cluttered with references to "shelf" companies, the directors of which will, in all probability, resign and be replaced when the company is activated. A company is a "relevant company" in relation to another company, for the purposes of this section, if "it is a company of which that other company is a wholly owned subsidiary or if it is a wholly owned subsidiary of that other company or of another company of which that other company is a wholly owned subsidiary." This exception is intended to avoid unnecessary duplication of information in the registers of the companies in a single group.

(vii) Any other directorship held by him in the preceding five years. This provision was added by section 95(2) of the Companies Act 1981; its aim is to assist in the provisions allowing disqualification orders to be made (C.A. 1948, s. 188 and Insolvency Act 1976, s. 9). The identity of the other companies with which the director has been involved in the previous five years must thus be revealed, and their performance may then easily be ascertained. Again the directorship need not be mentioned if it was in a company which, for the whole of the period within the last five years that he held the directorship, was either "dormant" or a "relevant company" in relation to the company keeping the register.

(viii) His date of birth if the company is subject to the age limits in section 185 of the Companies Act 1948 (i.e. if it is a public company or a private company which is a subsidiary of a public company).

(2) *If the director is a corporation*

(i) Its corporate name.

(ii) Its registered or principal office.

Inspection

The register must be available for inspection during business hours for at least two hours each day. Any member of the company has the right to inspect the register free of charge while any other person may be charged up to 5p for each inspection (section 200(6)). Failure to permit such inspection is an offence by the company and any officer in default and the court may order an immediate inspection of the register (sections 200(7) and 200(8)).

Other disclosure of directors

Further publicity is given to the details of the directors listed in section 200(2) in three other ways (see also the chapter *Publicity Requirements*).

(1) *The Registrar of Companies.* By virtue of section 21 of the Companies Act 1976, when a company's memorandum is delivered for registration under section 12 of the 1948 Act it must be accompanied by a statement containing the particulars required by section 200(2) in relation to the first directors. Any subsequent change in the directors or in their particulars must be notified to the Registrar of Companies within 14 days, stating the date of the occurrence of the change (s. 200(4)). Thus if a person holds a large number of directorships his resignation

from any one will necessitate a change in the register of each company and a notification to the registrar by each company.

(2) *The annual return*. A company's annual return must contain "all such particulars with respect to the persons who at the date of the return are the directors of the company ... as are required by this Act to be contained ... in the register of the directors ..." (C.A. 1948 s. 124 and Sched. 6 if the company has a share capital; s. 125(1)(d) if the company does not have a share capital; see also page 93).

(3) *The Gazette*. Section 9(3)(c) of the European Communities Act 1972 requires the Registrar of Companies to cause to be published in the Gazette notice of the receipt by him of any document notifying him of a change among the directors of a company. By section 9(4)(c) the company is not entitled to rely, against any other person, on such a change if the event has not been officially notified in the Gazette at the material time, unless that person knew of the change.

It should also be noted that companies incorporated outside Great Britain which establish a place of business in Great Britain must, within one month of that date, deliver to the registrar, *inter alia*, a list of their directors (C.A. 1948 s. 407 (1)(b) and page 599). The particulars which must be provided in relation to the directors are listed in section 407(2) and are similar, although not identical, to those listed in section 200(2).

In addition The Stock Exchange's *Admission of Securities to Listing* requires a listed company to notify The Stock Exchange immediately of any change in its directors.

Registers: the register of directors' interests

Every company must, under section 29 of the Companies Act 1967, keep a register containing the information given to it by its directors in consequence of section 27 of that Act. Section 27(1) sets out various share and debenture interests, and events relating to shares and debentures, notification of which must be given to the company by a director. "Director" for these purposes includes a person in accordance with whose directions or instructions the directors of a company are accustomed to act (section 27(11); this is a slightly different definition to the "shadow director" definition introduced by section 63 of the 1980 Act for various other of the disclosure requirements discussed in this chapter). (Note that, in addition to the *disclosure* requirements concerning directors' share interests, discussed below, the Companies Act 1981 now restricts a director's *dealing* in his company's shares where he has inside information – see the chapter *Insider Dealing*.)

Interests held at the time of appointment.

A director must inform the company of any interest (as defined in sections 28 and 31; see below) which he has at the time of his appointment in the shares or debentures of the company. This notification must be in writing and must be expressed to be given in fulfilment of the obligation imposed by the section (section 27(1)(a)). The notice must include the number of shares of each class and the amount of debentures of each class in which the interest subsists. Notices will normally be addressed to the secretary of the company.

The director must also inform the company of any such interest "in any other body corporate, being the company's subsidiary or holding company or a subsidiary of the company's holding company." Interests in wholly owned subsidiaries are, however, excluded. Section 154 of the 1948 Act gives the meaning of "holding company" and "subsidiary". A company is treated as the wholly owned subsidiary of another company if "it has no members but that other and that other's wholly owned subsidiaries and its or their nominees" (section 27(13), the same definition as in section 150 of the 1948 Act).

This obligation must be fulfilled, if the director knows of the interest when he becomes a director, within five days (excluding Saturdays, Sundays and bank holidays – section 27(12)), commencing on the day after his appointment. If he only later finds out about the existence of the interest it must be notified within the same period from the date when he discovers the existence of the interest (section 27(3)(a)).

Events occurring while a person is a director

Section 27(1)(b) lists the events the occurrence of which must be notified to the company by the director. Again this must be done in writing, must be stated to be in fulfilment of the statutory obligation and must state the number or amount and class of shares or debentures involved. The four events are as follows:

(a) "Any event in consequence of whose occurrence he becomes, or ceases to be, interested in shares in, or debentures of, the company or any other body corporate, being the company's subsidiary or holding company or a subsidiary of the company's holding company." If the event is the entering into of a contract to purchase such shares or debentures the notice must include the price to be paid (section 27(5)). Section 28(11) sets out certain rules as to when a director is treated as ceasing to be interested in shares or debentures.

(b) "The entering into by him of a contract to sell any such shares or debentures." Again the notice must include a statement of the price to be received.

(c) "The assignment by him of a right granted to him by the company to subscribe for shares in, or debentures of, the company." Here the notice must include a statement of the consideration for the assignment or of the fact that there was no consideration (section 27(6)).

(d) "The grant to him by another body corporate, being the company's subsidiary or holding company or a subsidiary of the company's holding company, of a right to subscribe for shares in, or debentures of, that other body corporate, the exercise of such a right granted to him as aforesaid and the assignment by him of such a right so granted." If the event is the grant of such a right the notice must include the date on which it was granted, the period during which, or time at which, the right is exercisable, the consideration for the grant and the price to be paid for the shares or debentures. If the event is the exercise of such a right the notice must include the number of shares or amount of debentures in respect of which the right was exercised and the name(s) of the person(s) in whose name(s) they were registered (section 27(7)). If the event is the assignment of such a right then the notice must include a statement of the consideration (section 27(6)).

Again the notice must be given within the same five day period of the later of the occurrence of the event or the director's becoming aware of it (section 27(3)(b)). Failure to comply with the requirements of the section or knowingly or recklessly to make a false statement is an offence (section 27(8)), although a prosecution may be instituted only with the consent of the Department of Trade or of the Director of Public Prosecutions (section 27(10)).

Interests in shares or debentures

Rules for determining when a person is "interested" in shares or debentures for the purposes of section 27 are laid down by sections 28 and 31. Section 31 deals with the interests of a director's spouse and children while section 28 lays down general and specific rules for deciding what interests are included in, and excluded from, the ambit of section 27.

(1) *Spouses and children*

Section 31 provides that, for the purposes of section 27, an interest of, or a contract, assignment or right of subscription entered into, exercised or made by, or grant made to, the spouse or minor child of a director (if the spouse or child is not also a director) shall be treated as being an interest etc. of the director himself (sections 31(1)(a) and (b)). A director is also obliged to notify his company of either of the following events:

(a) The grant by the company to his spouse or minor child of a right to subscribe for shares in, or debentures of, the company.

(b) The exercise by his spouse or minor child of such a right. The notice must include the same information as is required in relation to an event falling within section 27(1)(b)(iv) (section 31(2)), and again the notice must be given within the five day period.

(By section 31(5), children includes step-children, although a man's illegitimate children may not be included (the natural father of an illegitimate child is not generally regarded as its "parent" – see e.g. *Re M* [1955] 2 Q.B. 479). The section only includes a director's spouse and not a cohabitee (compare section 184(5) of the Consumer Credit Act 1974, where a spouse is defined as including a "reputed" spouse).)

(2) *The rules in section 28*

Section 28(2), as amended by the Companies Act 1981, gives a wide general definition of the term "interest" in section 27. It is to include "any interest of any kind whatsoever", and "any restraint or restriction to which the exercise of any right attached to the interest is or may be subject" is to be disregarded. The section then goes on to detail cases where a person is to be taken to be interested in a company's shares or debentures and to list various interests which are to be disregarded for the purposes of section 27.

Interests *included* in section 27 are as follows.

(a) A person will have an interest for the purposes of section 27 even though the shares or debentures in which he has an interest are unidentifiable (section 28(6)).

(b) Where persons have a joint interest in shares or debentures each of those persons is taken to have an interest (section 28(5)).

(c) Any beneficiary under a trust, the trust property of which includes an interest in shares or debentures, is taken to have an interest even if he would not otherwise have such an interest (section 28(3)). However, by section 28(7), as long as another person is entitled to receive the income from the trust property, an interest in reversion or remainder in the shares or debentures is to be disregarded.

(d) A person has an interest in shares etc. if he enters into a contract for their purchase (section 28(4)(a)).

(e) A person has an interest in shares etc. if, not being the registered holder, he is entitled to exercise any right conferred by the holding of those shares or to control the exercise of any such right. This extends to the case where he has an absolute or conditional right or obligation the exercise or fulfilment of which would enable him to exercise or control the exercise of the right (sections 28(4)(b), (4D) and (4E)).

(f) A person has an interest in shares etc. if a company has an interest and either the company or its directors are accustomed to act in accordance with his directions or he controls the exercise of at least one-third of the voting power at the company's general meeting. Where a person controls the exercise of at least one third of the voting power of a company, any voting power controlled by the company is attributed to that person (sections 28 (4A) and (4B)).

(g) A person has an interest in shares etc. if, otherwise than by virtue of an interest under a trust, he has a right to call for the delivery of, or acquirē an interest in, such shares, or is under an obligation to take such shares (section 28(4)(c)). This covers, for instance, put and call options. The right or obligation need only be conditional. However, rights or obligations to subscribe for shares do not count (section 27(4F)).

Interests *excluded* from section 27 are as follows.

(a) A person holding shares or debentures under English law as a bare trustee or as a custodian trustee, or under Scottish law as a simple trustee, is treated as uninterested in those shares or debentures (section 28(8)).

(b) Section 28(9) and (10) state that certain types of interest are to be disregarded; these include interests subsisting by virtue of,

   (i)   an authorised unit trust scheme (within the meaning of the Prevention of Fraud (Investments) Act 1958);

   (ii) a scheme made under section 22 of the Charities Act 1960 (common investment funds);

   (iii) a scheme made under section 11 of the Trustee Investments Act 1961;

   (iv) a scheme made under section 1 of the Administration of Justice Act 1965;

   (v)   a scheme set out in the Schedule to the Church Funds Investment Measure 1958.

(c) Section 27(1) allows the Secretary of State to make regulations by statutory instrument providing for exceptions to section 27. Three such instruments have been made, S.I. 1967 No. 1594, S.I. 1968 No. 865 and S.I. 1968 No. 1533. These exceptions exclude interests in shares or debentures of certain trustees or personal representatives where the Public Trustee is also involved, interests arising under a company's memorandum or articles limiting a persons right of disposal (e.g. pre-emption rights), interests in certain overseas companies, interests notifiable to subsidiaries where the interest is notifiable to a holding company also, interests of a trustee or beneficiary of certain pension schemes, and interests in a society registered under the Industrial and Provident Societies Act 1965.

Register

The information provided in consequence of section 27 must be recorded by the company in a register kept for that purpose (section 29(1)). Section 29(2) requires the company to enter on the register, against the director's name, particulars of any grant made by it to a director of a right to subscribe for its shares or debentures and particulars of the exercise by the director of such right.

Entries on the register must be against the name of the relevant director and must be in chronological order (section 29(3)). The entry is to include the date of its inscription, which must be within three days of the occurrence of an event under section 29(2) or in other cases within three days of the receipt of the information provided by the director. Again the three day period commences on the day after that on which the obligation arises and excludes Saturdays, Sundays and bank holidays (section 29(4)). The company must also keep an index to the register (section 29(9)).

The register must be kept at the company's registered office if the register of members is kept there. If the register of members is kept elsewhere the company may keep this register either at that place or at its registered office (section 29(7)). The register must be available for inspection by any member of the company free of charge during business hours for at least two hours each day; non-members have a similar right to inspect the register but may be charged up to 5p for each inspection (section 29(7)). The court may, if necessary, order an immediate inspection (section 29(13)). Copies of the register or parts thereof may be requested by any person; the company must provide such copy within ten days and may charge up to 10p per hundred words (section 29(10)). The register must also be available for inspection at the company's annual general meeting (section 29(11)).

If the Department of Trade considers that a breach of section 27 may have occurred, section 32 empowers it to appoint inspectors to investigate the matter.

Listed companies

An additional requirement for listed companies is imposed by section 25 of the Companies Act 1976. Where such a company receives a notification by one of its directors under sections 27 or 31 of the 1967 Act which relates to shares or debentures listed on a recognised stock exchange, that company must notify the stock exchange of that matter. This obligation must be fulfilled before the end of the day after the receipt of the information (again excluding Saturdays, Sundays and bank holidays). The stock exchange is at liberty to publish any such information.

Further, paragraph 10(h) of The Stock Exchange's *Admission of Securities to Listing* requires the directors' report of a listed company to include a statement showing the interests of the directors in shares of the company or its subsidiaries, as appearing in the register kept under section 29. The statement must distinguish between beneficial and non-beneficial interests and should note changes between the end of the financial year and one month before the AGM.

The form of the registers

Section 436(1) of the Companies Act 1948 provides that the register of directors and secretary, and the register of directors' interests, may be kept "either by making entries in bound books or by recording the matters in question in any other manner." The phrase "in any other manner" is further elaborated by section 3 of The Stock Exchange

(Completion of Bargains) Act 1976. In order to allow computerisation section 3(1) declares that registers may be kept by recording the information otherwise than in legible form so long as it is capable of being reproduced in a legible form. If this is done the obligation to allow inspection and to provide copies is taken to refer to the legible form of copy of the register (section 3(3)). Section 3(4) allows the Secretary of State by statutory instrument to make regulations governing the use of non-legible forms of register. This power was exercised in The Companies (Registers and Other Records) Regulations (S.I. 1979 No.53). These Regulations relax the requirements for keeping registers, where they are computerised for instance, otherwise than at the registered office.

Disclosure to the company

Requirements under general law

Before considering the detailed and complex disclosure provisions contained in Part IV of the Companies Act 1980 relating to the company's accounts, a brief mention must be made of the other requirements for disclosure of transactions involving directors. These are the general equitable requirement of disclosure to the general meeting, from compliance with which duty the directors are usually released by the company's articles, and the mandatory requirement of disclosure to the board under section 199 of the Companies Act 1948.

The general equitable requirement is that a director may not contract with his company, or have an interest in any contract with his company without the approval or ratification of the general meeting (see also *Directors' Duties*, page 248). In *Aberdeen Rail Company v. Blaikie Bros.* (1854) 1 Macq. 461 the company had entered into a contract to purchase chairs from a partnership. A director of the company was also a member of the partnership and because of this fact the company sought to avoid the contract. Lord Cranworth L.C. stated that "it is a rule of universal application that no-one having such [fiduciary] duties to discharge shall be allowed to enter into engagements in which he has or can have a personal interest conflicting or which possibly may conflict with the interests of those whom he is bound to protect." Such a contract is voidable at the instance of the company (and therefore dependant on *restitutio in integrum* being still possible and *bona fide* third party interests not being affected), and the director is liable to account to the company for any profit he has made out of the transaction. If, however, a director sells property to his company which he did not acquire in his fiduciary capacity, the company is not entitled to affirm the contract and treat the director as trustee of the profit. "To rescind the contract is one thing, but to force on the vendor a contract to sell at another price is a totally different thing" (per Lord Davey in *Burland* v. *Earle* [1902] A.C. 83). If the director is also a shareholder he may vote in that capacity at the general meeting which is asked to approve the contract. In *North-West Transportation Co. Ltd.* v. *Beatty*

(1887) 12 App. Cas. 589 Sir Richard Baggallay observed that "every shareholder has a perfect right to vote upon any such question, although he may have a personal interest in the subject matter", subject, of course, to the constraints of oppression of, or fraud on, the minority.

In reality a company will often need to contract with the directors, for example to give them service contracts, and it would be time-consuming and costly to call a general meeting to approve each such contract. Thus it is usual for the company's articles to exclude the operation of the equitable rule (for example, article 84 of Table A). Article 84 exempts the directors from compliance with the general equitable rule if disclosure is made to the board in accordance with section 199 of the 1948 Act which is, in any case, mandatory (see the chapter *Directors' Meetings*, and below). Note however that notwithstanding such an article and compliance with section 199, certain transactions between a director or a connected person and his company or its holding company now require approval in general meeting under section 48 of the Companies Act 1980 (see *Directors' Duties* page 260). Likewise, section 47 of the 1980 Act requires certain service contracts to be approved in general meeting, over and above the general equitable requirements, and section 199, being complied with (see the chapter *Directors*).

Section 199: disclosure to the board

Section 199 requires a director of a company who is interested in any way directly or indirectly, in a contract, proposed contract, transaction or arrangement with his company to declare his interest to the board, generally at the board meeting at which the contract, transaction or arrangement is first considered (section 199(1), as extended by section 60 of the 1980 Act). The disclosable transactions or arrangements include any transactions within section 49 of the 1980 Act (loans, quasi loans, guarantees and credit transactions to directors *and to certain connected persons* – see page 269).

Section 199 does not "prejudice the operation of any rule of law restricting directors of a company from having any interest in contracts with the company" (section 199(5)). Thus compliance with section 199 does not, of itself, validate the contract; the director must make disclosure to the general meeting unless the articles provide otherwise. A director who does not comply with section 199 is liable to a fine of up to £1,000 (section 199(4)). Although section 199 does not deal with the civil consequences of non-compliance it is generally considered that the contract will be voidable.

Section 199 is extended by section 63(3) of the 1980 Act to cover contracts and the like "involving shadow directors", i.e. certain persons in accordance with whose directions or instructions the directors are accustomed to act. However, since a shadow director has no right to attend board meetings he must declare his interest by notice in writing to the directors.

If a director becomes interested in a contract, transaction or arrangement *after* it is made he must declare his interest at the first meeting of the directors held after he becomes so interested. As regards an interest in a proposed contract, transaction or arrangement, disclosure must be made at the board meeting at which the question of entering into the contract is first taken into consideration if he is already interested in the proposed contract at that time, and if not then at the next board meeting after he does become so interested (section 199(2)).

The director is required to declare "the nature of his interest". In *Imperial Mercantile Credit Association* v. *Coleman* (1873) L.R. 6 H.L. 189, which concerned an article adopting this same wording, Coleman had stated that he had an interest in a certain contract but had not given the details of that interest. Lord Cairns observed that "a director ... must show that he has, in letter and in spirit, complied with the provisions of the clause ... a man declares his interest, not when he states that he has an interest but when he states what his interest is." However, by s. 199(3) it is a sufficient declaration of interest if a director gives a *general notice* to the effect that,

(a) he is a member of another company or firm and is to be regarded as interested in any contract with that company; or

(b) that he is to be regarded as interested in any contract with a specified person who is "connected" with him (within the meaning of section 64 of the Companies Act 1980).

Disclosure in the accounts: directors' emoluments

Section 196 disclosure

Section 196 of the Companies Act 1948 requires that a note to the company's accounts, as prepared under section 1 of the 1976 Act, must show, "so far as the information is contained in the company's books and papers or the company has the right to obtain it from the persons concerned", the information in the box below.

---

(1) *The aggregate amount of the directors' emoluments.* The term "emoluments" includes fees and percentages and any expenses paid so far as they are charged to U.K. income tax; it also includes contributions paid, in respect of directors, under pension schemes and the estimated value of any benefits received otherwise than in cash. The amount shown is to include all emoluments paid in respect of services as director of the company or, while a director of the holding company, as director of its subsidiary or paid "otherwise in connection with the management of the affairs of the company or any subsidiary". The note must distinguish between amounts paid for services as director and other emoluments (section 196(2)).

(2) *The aggregate amount of the directors' or past directors' pensions* (sections 196(1)(b) and (3)).

(3) *The aggregate amount of any compensation to directors or past directors in respect of loss of office* (sections 196(1)(c) and (4)).

If these requirements are not complied with the auditors who examine the accounts must include in their report, so far as they are reasonably able to do so, a statement giving the required particulars (section 196(8)).

Section 6 disclosure

Section 196 only requires disclosure of the total amount paid to the directors; further requirements for disclosure of directors' individual emoluments are provided by section 6 of the 1967 Act. A note to the company's accounts must reveal the following information.

---

(1) The emoluments of the company's chairman (section 6(1)(a)). The term "chairman" is used not only to include a person elected to that office by the directors but also "a person who, though not so elected, holds any office (however designated) which, in accordance with the constitution of the company, carries with it functions substantially similar to those discharged by a person so elected" (section 6(7)(a)).

(2) The number of directors receiving emoluments within each £5,000 band (i.e. the number who received below £5,000, the number who received between £5,000 and £10,000 and so on) (section 6(1)(b)).

(3) The amount received by the director who received the highest amount if that amount is greater than that received by the company's chairman (sections 6(2) and (7)(b)).

In each of these cases the company need not reveal or include the emoluments of a director or chairman who performs his duties wholly or mainly outside the United Kingdom.

A company is exempt from compliance with this section if it is neither a holding company nor a subsidiary of another company and the total amount of the directors' emoluments for the year, as shown in the note to the accounts under section 196(1)(a) of the 1948 Act, does not exceed £60,000 (s. 6(6) and Companies (Accounts) Regulations 1982 S.I. 1698).

Section 6(4) imposes the same duty on the company's auditors as section 196(8) of the 1948 Act, to include in their report any information required by section 6 which is not disclosed in the accounts.

Under section 7(1) a note to the accounts must also detail any emoluments waived by the directors.

Listed companies

Paragraph 10(m) of The Stock Exchange's *Admission of Securities to Listing* requires the directors' report of a listed company to include particulars of any arrangement under which a director has waived or agreed to waive any emoluments.

Disclosure in the accounts: Companies Act 1980

Section 54 of the 1980 Act requires disclosure, in a note to the company's accounts, of (a) the particulars stated in section 55 regarding (b) the transactions and arrangements involving directors referred to in sections 54(1) and 54(2). For this purpose, "directors" includes "shadow directors" as defined in section 63(1) of the 1980 Act.

Disclosable transactions or arrangements:

Group accounts

Group accounts prepared by a holding company must contain particulars of the following:

(a) any transaction or arrangement of a kind described in section 49 entered into by the company or by a subsidiary of the company for a person who at any time during the relevant period was a director of the company or its holding company or was connected with such a director. Section 49 deals with loans, quasi-loans, guarantees and credit transactions with directors and certain connected persons (see *Directors' Loans*, page 269);

(b) an agreement by the company or by a subsidiary of the company to enter into any such transaction or arrangement for a person who at any time during the relevant period was a director of the company or its holding company or was connected with such a director; and

(c) *any other transaction or arrangement* with the company or with a subsidiary of the company in which a person who at any time during the relevant period was a director of the company or its holding company had, directly or indirectly, a *material interest* (section 54(1); see also rule 10(l) of the Listing Agreement where the company is quoted).

Individual accounts

By section 54(2) the same transactions and arrangements must be disclosed in accounts prepared by any company which is not a holding company – transactions or arrangements involving a subsidiary being excluded of course.

Material interest

The term "material interest" in sections 54(1)(c) and (2)(c) is not fully defined and will therefore be a question of fact. However, section 54(4)(a) provides that a director is always treated as "interested" in any transactions or arrangement between him or a connected person and his company or its holding company. By section 54(4)(b), the interest is not *material* if "in the opinion of the majority of the directors (other than that director) of the company which is preparing the accounts in question it is not material ... " This is stated to be without prejudice to the question of whether an interest is material if the directors have not considered the matter. Note that the test is not whether the *transaction* is material but whether the director's interest in it is material – so the sale of a six thousand pound item to a director is always caught, however insignificant to the company, because the director's *interest* in the sale is obviously material.

Timing

These provisions apply to accounts for years ending on or after December 22, 1980 and cover transactions and arrangements entered into before then if they are subsisting on or after that day (sections 56(7) and 65(7)). The now repealed provisions of section 197 of the 1948 Act and section 16(1)(c) of the 1967 Act still govern accounts relating to financial years ending before December 22, 1980 (sections 66(2)(a) and 54(6)(c)); those sections also apply to loans and contracts entered into before December 22, 1980 in the first financial year ending after that date but not subsisting after then (sections 66(2)(b) and 54(6)(d)).

Additional rules

Section 54 requires disclosure of transactions and arrangements of a kind described in section 49 even if the transactions are not, in fact, prohibited by section 49 (section 54(7)(a); an example would be a loan to a director of less than £2,500). It also applies whether or not the person in whose favour the transaction was made was a director of the company or was connected with a director of the company at the time it was made. Thus disclosure must be made of a loan to an individual who is not a director at that time but later in the same financial year is appointed a director (section 54(7)(b)). The same applies to sub-sidiaries: if a company is a subsidiary of another at some time during the financial year it does not matter that it was not a subsidiary at the time of the transaction or arrangement (section 54(7)(b)). Moreover, as explained at page 282, section 49 does not generally prohibit the making of quasi-loans or credit transactions to directors of *private* companies, or the making of loans, quasi-loans, credit transactions or guarantee or security arrangements for persons *connected* with a director of a private company. Nevertheless, section 54 requires all these transactions to be disclosed in the accounts.

Excepted transactions

However, the following transactions, arrangements and agreements need not be disclosed:

(a) A transaction arrangement or agreement between one company and another in which a director of the first company or of its subsidiary or holding company is interested only by virtue of his being a director of the other company (section 54(6)).

(b) A contract of service between a company and one of its directors or a director of its holding company or between a director of a company and any of that company's subsidiaries (section 54(6)). It

should be noted that this exception is limited to a contract of service
and does not include a contract for services, and that even though a
contract of service is excluded from section 54 it is still subject to
section 26 of the Companies Act 1967 (see below).

(c) A transaction, arrangement or agreement which was entered into
prior to the period covered by the accounts and which does not
subsist in that period, or a transaction, arrangement or agreement
entered into before December 22, 1980 and which does not subsist
on or after that day (section 54(6)).

(d) The section does not apply to accounts prepared by any company
which is, or is the holding company of, a recognised bank in respect
of transactions or arrangements within section 49 (but "other
transactions" are included) (section 54(5)).

(e) Section 58(1) excludes from the application of sections 54(1) and
(2) certain transactions made in respect of a director and persons
connected with him if their total amount during the financial year
did not exceed £5,000. The excepted transactions are credit transactions and agreements to enter into credit transactions, guarantees
or security arrangements associated with credit transactions, and
assignments or indirect arrangements concerning section 49(1) and
49(2) transactions.

(f) By section 58(3), disclosure of "other transactions" under sections
54(1)(c) or 54(2)(c) (ie transactions outside section 49 in which a
director has a material interest) is not required if, broadly, the
value of the transaction is below the higher of £1,000 or one per
cent of the net assets of the company (subject to an overriding limit
of £5,000). However, if there is more than one transaction outstanding each transaction must be aggregated in applying the above
limits (see further section 58(3)(b)).

Disclosable particulars

The particulars which must be revealed in the accounts in relation to the
transactions, arrangements or agreements which fall within section 54
are listed in section 55. Section 55(1) states that the accounts must
contain particulars of "the principal terms" (this phrase is not further
defined) of the transaction, but, without prejudice to the generality of
this provision, it goes on to list the details which must be recorded in
relation to particular transactions. These are as shown in the box below.

(a) A statement of the fact either that the transaction was made, or subsisted, as
the case may be, during the financial year.

(b) The name of the person for whom it was made. Where it is made with a
person who is "connected" with a director under section 64, the name of that
director.

(c) The name of the director with the material interest and the nature of that
interest, if the transaction falls within sections 54(1)(c) or (2)(c).

(d)   As regards loans or arrangements for loans:

(i)   the amount of the liability at the beginning and end of the financial year;

(ii)   the maximum liability during that year;

(iii)   the amount of interest which has fallen due but has not been paid; and

(iv)   the amount of any provision (within the meaning of C.A. 1948, Sch. 8) made in respect of any failure or anticipated failure to repay any part of the loan or interest.

(e)   As regards guarantees and securities:

(i)   the amount for which the company was liable at the beginning and end of the year;

(ii)   the maximum potential liability of the company; and

(iii)   any amount or liability incurred by the company under the guarantee or security.

(f)   As regards any other transaction, arrangement or agreement, its "value." Section 65(4) sets out rules for determining the "value" of the various categories of transaction, arrangement or agreement.

Section 56 provides further detailed rules as to the particulars of amounts outstanding which must be included in the accounts, in respect of transactions within section 49 of the 1980 Act (loans, quasi-loans, credit transactions etc).

Broadly, the accounts must disclose the amounts outstanding under loans and similar transactions to persons *other* than directors who are "officers" of the company (see section 455 of the 1948 Act), subject to a de minimis exception for aggregate amounts not exceeding £2,500 and excluding loans and the like from recognised banks.

Recognised banks

As mentioned, recognized banks are not required by section 54 to disclose full details of loans and the like within section 49. However, section 56(4) requires certain details of the aggregate loans and such like to be disclosed in the accounts. In addition, section 57 requires details of the section 49 transactions which would require disclosure under section 54 if the company was not a recognised bank to be kept in a register, which must be available for inspection by members prior to the annual general meeting. But if the recognised bank is a wholly-owned subsidiary of another company which is incorporated in the United Kingdom this obligation is dispensed with (and see the £1,000 threshold in section 58(4)).

Auditors' duty

If the accounts do not comply with sections 54 or 56 the auditors who examine the accounts must include in their report, so far as they are reasonably able to do so, a statement giving the required particulars (section 59).

Inspection of directors' service contracts

By virtue of section 26 of the Companies Act 1967, directors' service contracts (including those of "shadow directors" as defined in section 63 of the 1980 Act) must be available for inspection by the members of the company. If the director's contract is in writing the company must keep a copy of it for this purpose and if the contract is not in writing a written memorandum setting out the terms of the contract must be kept (sections 26(1)(a) and (b)). The same obligation is imposed in relation to the contract of service of a director of the company with a subsidiary of the company (section 26(1)(c)). Any variation of a director's service contract effectively counts as a new contract for disclosure purposes (section 26(7) and C.A. 1980, s. 61(3)). These copies or memoranda must be kept at the company's registered office, the place where the register of members is kept or the company's principal place of business, if in England (section 26(2)). All such copies and memoranda must be kept at the same place and the Registrar of Companies must be informed of that place, unless it is the company's registered office (section 26(3)).

Section 26(1) does not, however, apply to contracts of service under which the director is required to work wholly or mainly outside the United Kingdom. As regards such contracts the company is however required to keep a memorandum, which must comply with section 26(3A). Also, copies or memoranda setting out the terms of the contract or of a variation therein need not be kept if the unexpired period of the contract is less than twelve months or if the contract can be terminated by the company within the next twelve months without the payment of compensation (section 26(8)(b)).

These copies or memoranda must be available for inspection by any member free of charge during business hours for at least two hours each day (section 26(4)). Failure to allow such inspection or to comply with the requirements of the section constitutes an offence by the company and every officer in default, and the court may order an immediate inspection (sections 26(5) and 26(6)).

For a listed company, The Stock Exchange's *Admission of Securities to Listing* requires service contracts or written memoranda thereof to be available for inspection throughout usual business hours for a period leading up to the AGM, and be available at the place of the AGM. The right of inspection is to be extended to press representatives, potential investors and other interested persons. The director's report of a listed company must state the unexpired period of the service contract of any director proposed for re-election at the forthcoming AGM.

Details of directors on business letters

Section 201(1) of the 1948 Act requires that a company shall not state the name of any director in any business letter (otherwise than in the text or as signatory) on which the company's name appears unless the name of *every* director is included. That is, directors' names are not obligatory but a company cannot give some but not others. Where names are given, the Christian names, or initials, of each director must be given as well as his surname. The term "director" here bears its extended meaning of persons in accordance with whose directions or instructions the directors are accustomed to act (section 201(4)(a)). This section applies to all companies registered in Great Britain after November 22, 1916 and to any company incorporated outside Great Britain which establishes a place of business in Great Britain after that date (section 201(2)). Any officer of a company who is in default under this section is liable to a fine under section 201(3). (See also the chapter *Publicity Requirements*.)

Disclosure of Shareholdings

A company's register of members does not disclose the beneficial ownership of shares in the company. Section 117 of the Companies Act 1948 provides that "no notice of any trust, expressed, implied or constructive, shall be entered on the register". The 1948 Act provided for disclosure regarding a director's holding in his company's shares and for Department of Trade investigations into ownership in certain cases, but is silent as to the disclosure of interests of shareholders generally. Only in 1967 were the recommendations of the Cohen and Jenkins Committees, that there should be to some extent a register of beneficial ownership, acted upon. Legislation was then introduced which, essentially, imposed an obligation on any person with a substantial interest in a company's shares to notify that company of his interest and thereafter of any changes in amount.

This legislation was soon found to be wanting and despite substantial amendments made by the 1976 Companies Act it was inadequate to deal with certain events which occurred. The most notorious of these was the secret acquisition during 1979 of a substantial shareholding in Consolidated Gold Fields Limited, by a foreign buyer, through nominee companies, each of which was instructed to acquire an interest small enough to fall outside the disclosure rules. This process was followed by a "dawn raid" on the market to increase the buyer's holding yet further, without warning and thus without giving private investors the opportunity to participate.

In August 1980, the Department of Trade reacted by publishing a consultative document which invited comments on the legal provisions already existing in respect of disclosure of interests in shares, the powers of the company and the Secretary of State to investigate the ownership of the company and the powers to impose restrictions on shares. Various proposals were made by the document itself but these were criticised as not being sufficiently far-reaching. In particular, the failure of the document to deal with "ad hoc combination(s) of persons or companies acting only by arrangement" angered the City. The Government, which had wished to leave this matter to self-regulation by the Council for the Securities Industry ("CSI") was forced to act, following comments made in the House of Lords when the Companies (No. 2) Bill (which became the 1981 Act) was debated in that House. A second consultative document was published on May 29, 1981 setting out proposed clauses for insertion into the Bill at Committee Stage in the House of Commons only two weeks later.

As a result the legislation now governing this area shows signs of being hurriedly drafted. Although there were consultations, it would seem from the reports of Standing Committee A's deliberations that not all the points raised were thoroughly considered. Nevertheless the legislation does attempt to deal with many of the criticisms made of the previous law governing the disclosure of interests in shareholdings. The discussions of the Standing Committee, which will be referred to below, are of great assistance when examining these complex provisions.

The disclosure requirements of the 1981 Act

The relevant provisions are now to be found in sections 63 to 83 of the Companies Act 1981. They came into force on June 15, 1982 and now entirely supersede sections 33 and 34 of the 1967 Act and sections 26 and 27 of the 1976 Act. References in the remainder of this chapter are to the 1981 Act, unless otherwise specified.

The principal changes to the previous legislation

– The disclosure requirements now cover all public companies rather than, as previously, only listed companies.

– The obligation to disclose now rests on knowledge of the number of shares in which a person has an interest, not knowledge of a particular acquisition or other event.

– There are completely new provisions covering persons acting together ("concert parties"). The interests of each member of a concert party are attributed to the other members.

– The company's powers to investigate interests in its own voting shares are extended.

– The Act introduces stronger penalties for failure to notify or to respond to inquiries when required.

The basic obligation to disclose

The notification obligation now applies to interests in voting shares in any public company as defined in the Companies Act 1980. This extension of the requirement, from listed companies only, reflects the increase in trading in securities in companies on markets which do not involve a full listing.

By section 63(2), the obligation to notify arises where there is a change in the percentage of "relevant share capital" (essentially voting shares in a public company) in which a person has an interest, from below to above the "notifiable percentage" or from above to below that percentage, or where the "notifiable percentage" is exceeded both before and after the transaction but the percentage level changes (fractions of a percentage level being rounded down). The "notifiable percentage" is, at present, five per cent, but may be altered by regulation introduced by the Secretary of State and approved by Parliament (section 64).

The obligation will arise whether the change in the percentage of shares in which a person has an interest occurs as a result of an acquisition or disposal, or whether it arises from some other circumstance, such as an increase or reduction of share capital or of the relevant class of share capital (sections 63(1) and 63(4)).

Liability founded on knowledge

The obligation to disclose is founded on knowledge as previously. However, the provisions in section 33 of the 1967 Act had given rise to difficulty and uncertainty in practice since the knowledge required was knowledge of the particular occurrence which took the shareholding across a relevant threshold. This imposed a heavy burden on the prosecution where, for example, a shareholding had been built up in a series of transactions. Under the 1981 Act, the obligation to notify arises wherever a person with an interest in relevant shares knows that the amount is such or has changed so that the notification requirements are applicable. This new test has itself been criticised as being as difficult to police as its predecessor. This remains to be seen but it does, at least, dispose of the need to specify a particular occurrence which is information of no practical value to the company.

The knowledge requirement does not permit a principal to shelter in blissful (and calculated) ignorance behind an agent. A principal is obliged to ensure that his agent notifies him immediately of dealings made on the principal's behalf which might give rise to a notification obligation on his part (section 72(1)). However there are situations in which a person might be genuinely unaware that he has an interest giving rise to a duty to notify; for example where he has an interest under a trust or by way of a concert party, and in such cases he is fully protected, for all facts relevant to determining whether a person has an obligation to notify at a given time are taken to be what he knows them to be at that time (section 63(3)).

Alterations to share capital

Where there is a change in the amount of share capital of the relevant company there will not necessarily be an obligation to notify, since section 63(5) requires a notification to state the number of shares in which the person making the notification is interested. Therefore, if a person who has already made a notification acquires no further shares, what he has reported will remain true regardless of the fact that there has been an increase in the share capital resulting in a change in the percentage level of shares in which he has an interest. If, on the other hand, a person has acquired further shares on the increase in share capital he will be required to make a notification even though the percentage level of shares in which he is interested remains exactly the same. This requirement is imposed in a somewhat oblique fashion by the second paragraph of section 63(7). A shareholder acquiring new shares by way of rights issue or bonus issue will need to be advised of this provision. A reduction in share capital for a shareholder retaining the same number of shares as before the reduction gives rise to an obligation to notify only where it results in the shareholder having a notifiable percentage where previously he did not.

Relevant share capital and the percentage level

"Relevant share capital" is defined in section 63(10) as issued share capital of a public company of a class carrying rights to vote in all circumstances at general meetings of the company. It is provided that temporary suspension of voting rights will not result in shares being excluded from the definition. This proviso, it seems, is intended to cover not only cases where a member is not entitled to vote because sums are due in respect of the shares or because a restriction has been imposed under section 174 of the 1948 Act, but also cases where a member is disqualified from voting on a particular issue, either under the articles or perhaps under section 47(9) of the 1981 Act. However, as the Law Society has pointed out, it is doubtful whether the proviso does cover shares with particular, as opposed to temporary, disqualifications.

The "percentage level" is the nominal value of all shares in a company in which a person is interested expressed as a percentage of the nominal value of the whole share capital of that company (section 63(7)). Fractions are rounded down. This is subject to the second paragraph of section 63(7), discussed above (see *Alterations to share capital*). Note also that where the relevant company has different classes of shares, the percentage level has to be calculated by reference to each class separately (section 82(2)).

Time limits

Generally, notification must be made within the five days next following the day upon which the obligation to notify arises (section 63(6)). According to the Government in Standing Committee, notification is made only when the company has received the notification. By section 64(3) the normal five day period is extended to ten days in cases where notification is required as the result of a reduction in the notifiable percentage. Saturdays, Sundays and bank holidays may be ignored when calculating these time limits (section 82(3)).

The contents of the notification

The notification must be in *writing* and must:

(1) specify the share capital to which it relates; and

(2) state the number of shares in which there is a notifiable interest (or that there is no longer a notifiable interest) – section 63(5);

(3) identify the notifier and give his address, and where he is a director of the company, state that it is given in fulfilment of the obligation under sections 63 to 65 – section 72(2);

(4)   where appropriate give details of the registered holder or holders of the shares and the number of shares held by each – section 65(1).

The last of these requirements was introduced in the 1981 Act in order to assist the company to keep a close watch on strategic shareholdings. It is subject to a requirement of knowledge so that the person making the notification is not placed under an unreasonable obligation, but further information coming to the knowledge of a person after he has made a notification gives rise to a further obligation to notify during the currency of the original notification, as soon as he becomes aware of it (as does any change in the above details).

The requirement in (3) above regarding directors is to distinguish a notification given under these sections from one under section 27 of the 1967 Act (see page 314). Since the director's duty to disclose his shareholdings under section 27 is quite separate from that under the 1981 Act, any director of a public company must consider both sets of requirements each time he enters into a transaction involving the company's shares.

Interests to be notified

"Interest in shares"

Section 70 defines very widely the interests in shares which are required to be notified. The range of interests to be notified is then cut down by section 71. The drafting is based on a narrow view of the meaning of "an interest in shares". According to this strict view the phrase would not, for example, cover a right to specific performance under a contract for the purchase of shares. Thus, this, and other specific cases are expressly provided for in section 70.

Contracts, and "put" and "call" options (even where conditional) are covered, in addition to other arrangements conferring present or future rights to control rights arising from shares. Persons being appointed either by proxy vote at a specified company meeting, or representatives of a corporation at company meetings are not to be taken as having an interest in shares (section 71(2)).

Contingent interests are expressly included so that arrangements may not be contrived to conceal interests until it suits the holder to reveal them. All interests under trusts are covered so that anyone, trustee or beneficiary, to whom the trust gives a discretion as to the exercise of rights arising from shares comprised in the trust, will have a duty to disclose (section 70(3) read subject to section 71, explained below). Section 70(8) provides that it is immaterial that the shares in which a person has an interest are unidentifiable, making the definition a very wide one indeed.

Clearly no type of arrangement involving relevant shares should be entered into without considering the impact of the disclosure provisions very carefully. However, the Government stopped short at defining "interest in shares" as including the interest of a person who in practice exercises control over shares – according to the Government there was otherwise a risk of casting the net too wide and catching bona fide groups of shareholders acting together, such as investment protection committees. However the concert party provisions discussed below are designed to deal with certain non-binding arrangements.

"Interests to be disregarded"

Having defined "interest in shares" so extensively, the legislation then cuts down the number of interests requiring notification.

The "interests to be disregarded" under section 71 are either necessary to avoid placing an obligation to disclose on those with no discretion over rights arising from the shares whatsoever, or are included in section 71 because holdings of that nature are not considered to pose a threat. Thus, for example, a beneficiary under a trust is not required to disclose a discretionary interest or one in reversion or remainder, and a bare trustee has no obligation to disclose his holding. These exemptions do not, however, apply to foreign trusts. Since one of the major problems in this area is enforcing disclosure provisions against foreign residents it was not wished to give them any scope for avoidance. Foreign trusts might not have exact equivalents of these interests and this could lead to difficulties. Of the other interests to be disregarded, interests under authorised unit trusts and interests held by jobbers for the purposes of their business are two of the most common types. The only change in policy in the 1981 Act, when defining interests to be disregarded, was to narrow the exemption for an interest held as security. When building up its interests in shares in Consolidated Gold Fields, de Beers relied upon the exemption in the 1967 Act for holdings of shares by way of security by anyone whose ordinary business was the lending of money. To avoid future abuse of this exemption, it is now limited to certain bodies specified in section 71(5) – including recognised banks, insurance companies and U.K. stockbrokers. Certain interests that are to be disregarded are prescribed by statutory instrument (section 71(1)(j) and Public Companies (Disclosure of Interests in Shares) (Exclusions) Regulations 1982 S.I. 677). These include interests of beneficiaries under approved or statutory retirement benefit schemes.

Family and corporate interests

The definition of "interest in shares" is, in effect, further extended by deeming a person to be interested in any shares in which his spouse or any infant child or step-child of his is interested (section 66(1)). Surprisingly this obvious anti-avoidance provision was introduced for substantial shareholders only in 1981 although it was included in the 1967 provisions for director's disclosures.

Interests in shares held indirectly through companies are also covered. Interests in shares held by a company are deemed interests also of any person in accordance with whose directions that company or its directors are accustomed to act, or of any person entitled to exercise or control the exercise of one-third or more of the voting power at general meetings of that company (section 66(2)). Section 66(3) has the effect of widening this concept yet further to take in an interest held through a chain of companies. Section 66(4) provides that a person whose shares are subject to a "put" option or with a "call" option, whether contingent or not, is to be taken to be able to control the exercise of the voting rights attaching to those shares. The combined effect of this and the extended concept of directly held interests in section 70, is that holding a series of options may result in an obligation to disclose and significant opportunities for avoidance are thus removed.

Persons acting together – concert parties

The important new provisions covering concert parties take effect, essentially, by deeming a person to be interested in shares in which another person is interested under the basic rules, where those persons are acting together. The provisions are thus a further extension of the concept of an "interest in shares".

The linchpin of the provisions contained in sections 67 to 69 is found in section 67(6). This attributes interests in shares in the "target company" held by any party to a "relevant agreement", to all other parties to that agreement, for the purpose of the disclosure obligation. All shares in the target company in which a party to the agreement has an interest are to be taken into account, not only those acquired under the relevant agreement. Clearly, if the aim is to ensure that a company is forewarned of any attempt to build up an interest in it, the legislation must be designed to reveal the whole picture, not merely pieces of a jigsaw. Section 67(7) prevents the process of attributing an interest of one party to another party to the agreement from continuing ad infinitum, but makes it clear that interests of a party under one agreement will be counted as his interests for the purpose of these provisions under any other relevant agreements. Thus a series of agreements with one common party will not be effective to avoid the provisions.

The relevant agreement

The concert party provisions do not apply to all types of agreement. The provisions will apply only where there is an agreement between two or more persons and the surrounding circumstances are as follows.

(1) The agreement must provide for the acquisition, by at least one party, of an interest in shares in a specified ("target") company.

(2) It must impose requirements in connection with the use, retention or disposal of interests in shares so acquired on at least one of the parties. "Use" covers not only the exercise of rights but also of any control or influence arising from interests.

(3) An interest in the company's shares must actually be acquired in pursuance of the agreement.

(4) The agreement must either be legally binding or involve mutuality.

(5) The agreement need not be in any particular form – in fact "agreement" is widely defined in section 67(4) so that it may include any type of arrangement, the terms of which may be implied or even be nothing more than expectations.

(6) Once the agreement falls within the disclosure provisions, then section 67 will continue to apply regardless of variations in the interests held, the parties and to the substance of the agreement, provided requirements of the type described in (2) above continue to be imposed.

As can be seen from these requirements, the legislation is not concerned with arrangements which existing shareholders come to as to the use of their existing interests. Such agreements are not perceived as a threat and may be positively useful to the company at times of crisis so that it was thought that it would be unwise to deter parties from entering into them. Condition (3) results in there being no obligation to disclose a concerted intention any more than there is an obligation upon an individual to disclose his intentions. Indeed the problems of policing these provisions, already very significant, would be greatly increased if a positive acquisition were not to be required to activate the obligation.

An agreement to purchase shares without any requirement as to what should be done with them thereafter is clearly not within the mischief which the legislation seeks to prevent and, by virtue of condition (2), will not be caught. Condition (2) makes it very unlikely that a purchase of shares on the advice of a professional adviser would give rise to a relevant agreement. However it was the case of the investment adviser which was cited in Standing Committee to explain condition (4) above. It was said in Committee that it was not enough, to create a concert party, for one person to agree with another that he would buy shares and hold them. "Only if the other person relies upon the first person to do it is there a genuine concert party case". This statement indicates that reliance by one party only is required but it must surely be read in the context of other comments in the same debate that the parties must rely on each other, as only this interpretation gives the word mutuality its full meaning. The right approach in determining whether there is a non-legally binding arrangement covered by the provisions was stated in Committee to be that of the courts when considering restrictive trade practices legislation (see *Re British Basic Slag Limited's Agreements* [1963] 2 All ER 807 where Danckwerts L. J. described the relevant provisions as "calculated to drive any accurately minded lawyer to despair"). That legislation applies to agreements "under which restrictions are accepted by two or more parties", whereas section 67(1)(a) requires obligations or restrictions to be imposed on only one of the parties for the agreement to be covered by the Act. Nevertheless, where the arrangement is not legally binding, the better interpretation would seem to be that there should at least have been a communication between the parties as a result of which *each* has intentionally aroused in the *other* an expectation that he will act in a certain way with the consequence that each party is under a moral obligation to act in that way.

Subject to this area of uncertainty, the wide definition of agreement is not in doubt; in the picturesque language of Mr. R. Eyre, Under Secretary of State for Trade – "a nod may be as good as a wink in these matters", and it was important to cover all types of arrangement.

There is one express exception, that of agreements to underwrite or sub-underwrite any offer of shares in a company, but then only if the agreement is confined to that purpose and any matters incidental to it (section 67(10)).

The notifications

Sections 67(8) and (9) set out requirements for notifications made in respect of target companies by parties to a relevant agreement, additional to those set out under *Contents of notification*, above. Such notifications must make it clear that the notifier is party to a relevant agreement, give names and addresses (if known) of the other parties and differentiate between the notifier's direct interests and his deemed interests under the concert party provisions. A person notifying a company that he has ceased to be interested in shares must make it clear if this is because he or another party has ceased to be a party to a relevant agreement and give full details of any such other person.

Obligation of persons acting together to keep each other informed of relevant facts

It is fundamental to this legislation that the obligation to notify is founded on knowledge and the concert party provisions are no exception (section 69(3) and (4)). For this reason it is essential to impose an obligation on persons acting together to keep each other fully informed of relevant facts. This is done by section 68 which requires parties to relevant agreements to inform each other in writing if they activate the agreement by making an acquisition, and thereafter of all relevant occurrences and changes in connection with the target company, whether concerning interests held pursuant to the agreement or not. The details to be provided are those which an individual has an obligation to provide to the company; the number of shares held both pursuant to the agreement and otherwise and details of registered ownership so far as is known. Addresses and changes of address must also be notified to all parties to the agreement.

The time limit for this notification is five days, which when added to the notification period under section 63 means that full details about concert parties should reach the target company within ten days.

There will clearly be much duplication of notification which will prove time consuming and expensive for notifiers and companies alike. Parties may appoint one of their number to make the notification on their behalf but this will not absolve each individual from liability. It was suggested that a "prime mover" might be identified upon whom the liability for reporting might rest, but this was rejected since it would have been almost impossible to define "prime mover" with sufficient precision and indeed there might not always be such a person.

If a notification has been made in accordance with section 68, then the person notified is regarded as having knowledge of the notifier's interest in the shares (or that the notifier's interest has ceased if that is the case) (section 69(5)).

Application of section 63 in cases within sections 66 and 67

Section 69 is a technical clause, required to link sections 66 and 67 with section 63, so that deemed interests where there is a family or corporate interest or a concert party are clearly covered by the general requirements of section 63 as to notification.

Power of company to investigate ownership of its shares

The company

The powers of the company to investigate interests in its own shares were first introduced in the 1976 Act and are extended in the 1981 Act, reflecting the government's philosophy that essentially these matters should be managed by the company itself, with an appeal to the courts or Department of Trade being a last resort. The powers of the company are now set out in section 74 of the 1981 Act. The main points to note are:-

(1) The company may make written enquiry of any person whom it knows, or has reasonable cause to believe to be or have been interested in relevant shares within the previous three years. Thus, the company's starting point does not have to be a member.

(2) The information which the company may require of a person includes details of that person's own interests in the relevant shares (if any) over the previous three years, details of the interests in the shares of any other person subsisting simultaneously with those of the person to whom the enquiry is addressed (so far as is known to him) and, where the person's own interest has ceased, details of his immediate successor so far as known to him. To complete the picture, the person of whom enquiry is made must give details of any past or present concert party agreement or arrangement relating to the exercise of any rights arising from the shares in question of which he has knowledge.

(3) The interests to be notified under section 74 are those defined in sections 66, 67 and 70 (see above), but the exceptions listed in section 71 (see *Interests to be disregarded*, above) do not apply, giving the company the maximum opportunity to discover the true

position. In addition, there is a further extension of the definition
of interest in shares to include past and present rights to subscribe
for relevant shares or to acquire such rights.

(4) The information required must be given within a reasonable time to
be specified by the notice served by the company. No period is laid
down by the legislation; what is reasonable will vary with the
circumstances.

For a sample form of request by a company under these provisions, see
Tolley's Company Secretary's Review, June 9, 1982.

Members' requisition

To deal with the situation where the very persons of whom enquiry
needs to be made are those controlling the company who choose not to
act under section 74, or where the directors are simply not taking the
action they should, section 76 empowers holders of not less than
one-tenth of the paid up capital of the company carrying the right to
vote at general meetings to requisition an investigation. The requisitioners are required to give reasonable grounds for their requisition and
details of the particulars required. The company must make an
investigation and prepare a report of its findings. This must be made
available at its registered office. If the report is not complete three
months after the requisition, an interim report must be made at the end
of three months and thereafter every three months until the investigation is concluded. There are time limits for making the report available
and informing the requisitioners that it is available once the investigation is concluded or the three month period has passed. Section 76(10)
defines the time at which the investigation is to be regarded as
concluded, as the time when all necessary or expedient enquiries have
been made by the company and either a response has been received or
the time limit for receiving it has passed.

As a last resort, dissatisfied requisitioners may still ask the Department
of Trade to investigate under section 172 or 173 of the 1948 Act. In
extreme cases, they are likely to do this immediately, without first
invoking the section 76 procedure, so that it is probable that section 76
will not be utilised very frequently.

The report (which need not include disclosure of information about
foreign holdings where the Department of Trade agrees that this would be
harmful in the context of the provisions regarding accounts in the 1967
Act) must be retained and kept available for inspection for six years.

The register of interests in shares

Sections 73, 75 and 78 to 80 set out detailed provisions about the
maintenance of a register of interests disclosed.

Two separate parts of the register are to be kept: one recording interests
disclosed under section 63 and the other recording the present interests

ascertained by the company on inquiry under its section 74 powers. Past interests discovered under section 74 need not be recorded; they are made notifiable only to assist the company in tracing present interests and building up a complete picture. The information has to be recorded in chronological order within three days of receipt. The register must either be in the form of an index or an index must be made and updated within ten days of a new entry being made in the register.

Where information about a person's interests is supplied by another person, the company must, within 15 days, notify the person about whose interest it has been informed (a) of any entry relating to him made in the register as a consequence and, (b) of his right to have any incorrect information removed. A court order may be obtained if an application for removal of an incorrect entry is wrongly refused. A person named as a party to a concert party arrangement has similar rights, on ceasing to be a party, to require that fact to be recorded.

Correct entries in the register may not be removed until six years after the facts they record have been superseded (or, six years from the date of entry, where the fact recorded is cessation of the interest). Similarly, the register has to be kept for six years after a company ceases to be a public company.

Information about foreign holdings, disclosure of which the Department of Trade agrees would be harmful, need not be made available for inspection (section 73(9)).

The register must be kept at the company's registered office, or it may be kept with its register of members if that is elsewhere. It must be available for inspection by any person free of charge at reasonable times determined in accordance with section 80(1) and copies must also be provided within ten days at a reasonable charge as provided in section 80(2). This applies also to reports of investigations made under section 76. A court order may be obtained if there is wrongful refusal to allow inspection or provide copies. Wrongful removal of entries on the register is prohibited and entries so removed must be restored as soon as practicable.

Enforcement of obligations

Offences by persons with interests.

The following acts or omissions are criminal offences under sections 72(3) and 77:

(1) to fail to give notice to the relevant company as and when required by the above provisions;

(2) to knowingly or recklessly give false information when giving notice;

(3) to fail to give notice to another person as and when required under the concert party provisions. However in this case it is a defence to

show it was not possible to contact the person to whom notice was to be given, although notice must be given as soon as that does become possible, so that the defence is a very limited one;

(4) for a principal to fail without reasonable excuse to secure that relevant information is notified to him by his agent;

(5) for any person of whom enquiry is made by the company under its section 74 powers to fail to give the information required or to knowingly or recklessly give information which is false in any material particular. It is a defence to prove that the requirement to give the information was frivolous or vexatious. In addition, the Secretary of State for Trade may exempt persons from compliance with a section 74 notice in special circumstances under strict conditions.

Penalties

The maximum penalty for all the above offences is significant, being two years imprisonment, an unlimited fine, or both. Proceedings in respect of offences (1) to (4) may be instituted only by, or with the consent of, the Secretary of State for Trade or the Director of Public Prosecutions.

These penalties should provide a real deterrent against failure to comply with the disclosure provisions. As the Jenkins Committee pointed out, a person acquiring interests in shares anonymously with a view to acquiring control of a company will find it difficult to conceal his identity once he has gained control, so that he will take these penalties very seriously indeed.

Imposition of restrictions

As important as the penalties, however, are the sanctions which may be imposed under the provisions of the 1981 Act. These will be of particular assistance in enforcing disclosure requirements where foreign parties are concerned – the problem which gave rise to the pressure for strengthened legislation prior to the 1981 Act. As a result of these sanctions a person convicted of one of the offences (1) to (4) above may find that he reaps no benefit from his interest in the shares in any event. Under section 72(6), the Secretary of State may direct that the shares in relation to which the offence was committed shall be subject to the restrictions imposed by section 174 of the 1948 Act (as amended by section 91 of the 1981 Act). These are restrictions on the transfer of shares, the exercise of voting rights, the issue of additional shares and the payment of sums due on shares. These restrictions may be lifted only as provided for in section 174.

Similarly, by section 77(1), where a person fails to give information required by a company under section 74, the company may apply to the court for an order subjecting "the shares in question" to restrictions under section 174 of the 1948 Act. However, the circumstances in which section 174 may be applied are not synonymous with those in which the offence described in (5) above is committed. Section 77(1) provides for failure to give information required within the time specified by the notice but not the giving of false information. Possibly the giving of false information would be construed by the courts as a failure to give the information required. Perhaps of more importance is the fact that section 77 applies only where a person "who is or was interested in any shares in the company" fails to give information, so providing no sanction in the very case which presents most difficulty: where the company has reason to believe, but cannot prove, that a person has or had a relevant interest.

The restrictions are to apply to "the shares in question"; isolating those shares could also prove to be a problem. Since the company must apply to the court to impose the restrictions, sections 74(3A) to (6) apply with the omission of references to the Secretary of State or Department of Trade so that responsibility lies with the company and the court only.

Imposing restrictions in the articles

Whether the power to impose restrictions arises under section 72 or section 77, it is in no way affected by any power contained in the memorandum and articles of the company to impose restrictions on its own shares. Companies should consider imposing such restrictions as a method of regulation which will escape the ambiguities, complexities and formalities of the statutory powers and give the company control over the position without having to make an application to the court. The statutory powers are nevertheless useful, particularly as the extent to which a company may impose its own sanctions is not clear.

Where section 174 restrictions are imposed the company or any person aggrieved may apply to the court for removal of the restrictions, but the discretion of the court is now cut down by the amendments made by section 91 of the 1981 Act. Subsection (3A) of section 174 allows removal of the restrictions only once full disclosure has been made and provided no unfair advantage has been obtained by failing to make that disclosure earlier or on an approved sale of the shares. This prevents a person undeterred by the criminal penalties, perhaps because he is a non-resident, from building up his interest in a company, notwithstanding section 174 restrictions being imposed, and then making full disclosure and reaping the benefits of his secret acquisition. The amendments to section 174 also make it possible for sales of the shares in question to be ordered so that the company does not have to accept a situation in which part of its capital is frozen indefinitely. In such a case the proceeds of sale are to be paid into court and the persons interested in the shares may apply for payment.

Since sections 63 and 74 impose an obligation to disclose only information of which the person obliged has knowledge, ignorance will be a defence to the imposition of restrictions under sections 72 and 77. But, where a section 172 or 173 investigation is carried out by the Department of Trade, restrictions may be imposed even where the difficulty in finding out the relevant facts about any shares is not due to the unwillingness of the persons concerned. Thus ignorance of the facts, or in the case of a resident of a foreign country, prohibition by the laws of that country from making disclosure (examples given by the Government in Standing Committee), will not necessarily prevent the imposition of restrictions under section 174 following a Department of Trade investigation.

Offences by the company and its officers

The company and those of its officers in default are punishable by fines where there is a failure to comply with one of the many burdens imposed on the company by the 1981 legislation.

In summary, the obligations and the sections imposing the penalties for failure to comply with them are,

(1)   the proper maintenance of a register in accordance with sections 73 and 75, duly kept up to date and with no wrongful deletions (sections 73(10), 78(7) and 79(3));

(2)   the investigation and preparation of a report under section 74 where requisitioned by members, making the report available and notifying the requisitionists that it is so available (section 76(12));

(3)   making registers and reports available for inspection and providing copies thereof as required under section 80 (section 80(3)).

Section 117 of the Companies Act 1948

The disclosure provisions described above are designed to protect the company, its shareholders and employees. They do not afford protection to those persons with an interest in shares whose names do not appear on the register of members. That is, disclosure under these provisions does not put the company to which disclosure is made on notice as to beneficial interests in the shares concerned (section 73(4)). It is vital to retain the fundamental rule in section 117 that no notice of trust is receivable by the company since otherwise the company would have to ensure that there had been no breach of trust before registering any transfer.

Conclusions

One recent trend in company law has been the increase in the amount of information to be disclosed, collected and made available. Doubts have been expressed about the cost effectiveness of this process (see Sealy in *The Disclosure Philosophy and Company Law Reform*, The Company Lawyer, Vol. 2 No. 2). Because of the no doubt unavoidable complexity of the provisions relating to disclosure by substantial shareholders and to concert parties, their observance will prove expensive and time consuming for all parties concerned. They will need to be very effective to convince those (including the Government) who would have preferred to leave this problem to self regulation by the companies and City institutions. The CSI has now revised its "Rules Governing Substantial Acquisitions of Shares" to restrict market raids and the City Code on Take-overs and Mergers and Stock Exchange Listing Agreements have been amended to take account of the 1981 Act. Self regulation will be of importance in this area; the Companies Acts alone will not prevent market raids.

Nevertheless, though there may be doubts about the cost effectiveness of this legislation and although it may need to be supplemented by non-statutory rules, it does provide for an impressive array of information to be made available. If the information collected is used as it intended it should be and if companies utilise their new powers of investigation and restriction to the full, these new tools should provide powerful assistance in combatting acquisitions by stealth and dawn raids, as well as providing interesting information about the ownership of companies for more general purposes.

Other shareholding disclosure requirements

Brief mention has already been made to the Companies Acts requirements as to the disclosure of *directors'* interests in shares. These are dealt with in detail in the chapter *Disclosure of Directors' Dealings* (page 314). In the case of listed companies, the statutory requirements are supplemented by The Stock Exchange's *Admission of Securities to Listing*.

Corporate shareholders also have obligations to disclose certain shareholdings in their accounts – not just holdings in subsidiary and associated companies, but also shareholdings exceeding 10 per cent (see *Accounts*, page 45).

Where a substantial acquisition of shares in listed companies, or certain other companies is involved, reference should also be made to the extra-statutory regulations referred to above and in particular the *Rules Governing Substantial Acquisition of Shares*, and the *City Code on Takeovers and Mergers*, both issued by the Council for the Securities Industry – see generally the chapter on *Takeovers*.

Dissolution and Revival

Methods of dissolution

The existence of a company incorporated in England or Scotland may be brought to an end either,

(a) by dissolution as the ultimate stage of,

   (i) a members' voluntary winding up (see section 290 of the Companies Act 1948, and *Liquidations*, below);

   (ii) a creditors' voluntary winding up (see section 300 of the Companies Act 1948, and *Liquidations*, below);

   (iii) a compulsory winding up (see section 274 of the Companies Act 1948, and *Liquidations*, below), or a winding up under the supervision of the court (see section 315 of the Companies Act 1948); or

(b) by dissolution as a result of the company's name being struck off the register by the Registrar of Companies pursuant to section 353 of the Companies Act 1948.

Striking-off by the Registrar of Companies

The procedure under section 353 of the 1948 Act may be invoked by the Registrar,

(1) where he has reasonable cause to believe that the company is not carrying on business or is not in operation (section 353(1)); or

(2) where the company is being wound up and he has reasonable cause to believe either that no liquidator is acting, or that the affairs of the company are fully wound up, and the returns required to be made by the liquidator have not been made for a period of six consecutive months (section 353(4)).

In the first of these cases the procedure is as follows:

(a) the Registrar sends the company by post a letter inquiring whether it is carrying on business or is in operation (section 353(1));

(b) if he does not receive a reply within one month, he sends the company within 14 days thereafter a reminder by registered post giving the company a further month to respond (section 353(2));

(c) if he receives an answer that the company is not carrying on business or is not in operation, or does not receive a reply to the second letter within the further period of one month referred to in (b) above, he publishes in the London *Gazette*, and sends to the

346

company by post, a notice that at the expiration of three months from the date of the notice the name of the company will, unless cause is shown to the contrary, be struck off the register and the company will be dissolved (section 353(3)). For companies registered in Scotland, the notice is published in the Edinburgh *Gazette*, not the London *Gazette*;

(d) at the expiration of the period of three months referred to in (c), the Registrar may, unless cause to the contrary is previously shown by the company, strike its name off the register, and must publish notice thereof in the London or Edinburgh *Gazette*. Upon the publication of the notice the company is dissolved (section 353(5)).

In the second case, the Registrar publishes in the London or Edinburgh *Gazette* and sends to the company or the liquidator, if any, the notice referred to in (c) above. The final step is as in (d) above (section 353(4) and (5)).

Effect of dissolution

The dissolution of a company has the following effect.

1. All property and rights vested in or held on trust for the company immediately before its dissolution (including leasehold property but not including property held by the company on trust for any other person), are deemed to be *bona vacantia*. As a result, the property and rights belong to the Crown, or to the Duchy of Lancaster or the Duke of Cornwall, as the case may be, subject to any order made by the court under sections 352 or 353 of the 1948 Act (see below), and except as provided by section 108 of the 1981 Act (see also below). However, where the property is land subject to a rentcharge, the vesting does not impose on the Crown, etc. any liability for the rentcharge except in respect of any sums accruing due after the Crown, etc. has taken possession or control of the land or has entered into occupation thereof (section 356 of the Companies Act 1948 as read with section 324).

2. Any property or rights so vested may, however, be disclaimed by the Crown, etc. by a notice executed (i) within twelve months of the date of vesting, or (ii) if any person has by written application required the Crown, etc. to decide whether or not to disclaim it, within three months after the receipt of such application, or (iii) in either case, within such further period as may be allowed by the court (section 355 of the Companies Act 1948). A notice of disclaimer is required to be filed with the Registrar of Companies and be published in the London or Edinburgh *Gazette* (section 355(6)). A disclaimer under section 355 has the same effect as if it was a disclaimer under section 323(1) of the 1948 Act made immediately before the dissolution (section 355(2) of the Companies Act 1948, and *Liquidations*, below).

3. Where the company has been struck off, the power of the court to wind up that company is not affected (section 353(5)(b)). However, the person seeking the winding up should ask for both restoration to the

register and a winding up (*Re Cambridge Coffee Room Association* [1952] 1 All E.R. 112).

4. A pending action by a company ceases absolutely and for all time on the company's dissolution and is not revived by a subsequent order, under section 352, declaring the dissolution void (*Foster Yates & Thom. v. H W Edgehill Equipment, The Times*, November 30, 1978).

5. Where a right of action was assigned by the company before dissolution, it survives in favour of the assignee insofar as he is able to sue in his own name without joining the company. Examples are where the debt is purely equitable, or section 136 of the Law of Property Act 1925 applies (absolute legal assignment by writing under the hand of the assignor).

6. A legal estate (including a leasehold estate) held by the company does not ordinarily come to an end (*Re Strathbaline Estates* [1948] Ch. 228). Where it does, section 181 of the Law of Property Act 1925 enables the court to create a corresponding estate and vest it in the person who would have been entitled to the estate which has determined.

7. In relation to any property held by the company on trust for any person the court may make a vesting order in favour of the beneficiary (see sections 44(ii)(c) and 51(ii)(c) of the Trustee Act 1925).

8. No proceedings can be taken under section 333 of the 1948 Act against the directors or officers for misfeasance unless, it seems, fraud is alleged (*Caxon v. Gorst* [1891] 2 Ch. 73).

9. A creditor may have a right in damages against a liquidator if he has wilfully or negligently distributed the assets and caused the dissolution of the company without providing for the creditor's debt (*Pulsford v. Devenish* [1903] 2 Ch. 625; *Re Armstrong Whitworth Securities Co.* [1947] Ch. 673). Where a liquidator sells and purports to convey land to which the company has no title, and then after due notice under rule 106 of the Companies (Winding up) Rules 1949 proceeds to make a distribution to creditors and contributories and the company is dissolved before the purchaser realises the defect in title, he has no right of action against the contributories (*Butler and Another v. Broadhead and Others* [1974] 3 W.L.R. 27).

10. A solicitor who continues to represent a company after it has been dissolved may be liable to an opposing party for costs incurred after dissolution.

Revival of a dissolved company

Where a company has been dissolved the court may at any time within two years of the date of the dissolution, on an application being made by the liquidator or any person who appears to the court to be interested make an order, upon such terms as it thinks fit, declaring the dissolution to have been void. This applies whether the dissolution occurs as the ultimate stage of a winding up, or under section 353)*Re Belmont & Co.* [1952] 1 Ch. 10). For a person to be "interested" he must have a proprietary or pecuniary interest in reviving the company. This does not include a solicitor to a proposed claimant (*Re Roehampton Swimming Pool* [1968] 1 W.L.R. 1693).

The court order may be made even after two years provided the application is made within that period (*Re Scad* [1941] Ch. 386). The effect of an order is that such proceedings may be taken as might have been taken if the company had not been dissolved, and all consequences flowing from the dissolution are themselves avoided (*Re C.W. Dixon* [1947] Ch. 251). However, any purported corporate activity of the company carried out during the period of dissolution is not validated (*Morris v. Harris* [1927] A.C. 252). And, as mentioned above, any action by the company which was pending at the time of dissolution is not revived. The person on whose application the order is made must within seven days after the making of the order, or such further time as the court may allow, file with the Registrar of Companies an office copy of the order (section 352).

Where a company has been struck off the register by the Registrar under section 353 of the 1948 Act, and the company or any member or creditor feels aggrieved by such striking-off, the court may, on an application made before the expiration of 20 years from the publication of the notice in the *Gazette* referred to above, order the company to be restored to the register. The court must be satisfied that the company was at the time of striking-off carrying on business or in operation, or otherwise that it is just that the company be restored to the register. Upon an office copy of the order being filed with the Registrar of Companies, the company is deemed to have continued in existence as if its name had not been struck off. The court may give such directions and make such provisions as seems just for placing the company and all other persons in the same position as nearly as may be as if the name of the company had not been struck off (section 353(6)). As to the restoration to the register of a company struck off by the Registrar of Companies after the presentation of a winding up petition but before the making of a winding up order, see *Re Thompson and Riches Ltd* [1981] Ch. 477. In that case the court granted a declaration that the dissolution, vesting the company's assets in the Crown, was void and the assets were instead to be vested in the Official Receiver as liquidator. The company may oppose an order for revival but only with the authority of a general meeting (see generally *Re Regent Insulation Co. Limited, The Times*, November 5, 1981).

An order declaring the dissolution void or restoring the company to the register under sections 352 or 353 of the 1948 Act does not affect any disposition made by the Crown, the Duchy of Lancaster or the Duke of Cornwall of property, or of any right or interest therein, vested in those bodies as *bona vacantia*. The purpose is to protect purchasers of property from those bodies. But the relevant body must account to the company for any consideration received for the property, right or interest or the value of any such consideration at the time of the disposition or, if no consideration was received, an amount equal to the value of the property, right or interest disposed of, as at the date of the disposition (see section 108 of the Companies Act 1981, which applies in relation to the disposition of property, rights or interests by the Crown, the Duchy of Lancaster or the Duke of Cornwall made on or after December 22, 1981, whether the company was dissolved before, on or after that date).

In England, notice of application for a declaration that a dissolution is void or for restoration to the register must be given to the Attorney General through the Treasury Solicitor (see *Practice Notes* [1928] W.N. 218 and [1931] W.N. 199 and *Re Belmont & Co.* [1952] Ch. 10).

Under English procedure, the company must be made co-applicant and the Registrar of Companies a respondent where restoration to the register is sought (see also *Re Walter Wright* [1923] W.N. 128).

Dividends

The law on dividends has been built up over the years from case law, much of which has now been superseded by Part III of the Companies Act 1980 (restrictions on distribution of profits and assets), as amended by the Companies Act 1981.

Part III of the 1980 Act deals purely with what profits may be lawfully distributed and the main part of this chapter examines those provisions in some detail. The first section of this chapter, however, deals briefly with some practical aspects concerning the actual payment of dividends which, on the whole, is a subject untouched by the Act.

Payment of dividends

This is governed by the memorandum and articles of association of the paying company, and, as always, they must be examined for any special provisions.

Memorandum of association

This is unlikely to contain anything of relevance, but occasionally it does, for example,

(i)   a restriction on distributions of capital profits is sometimes hidden away in a sub-clause of the objects clause (often as a proviso to the power to realise investments). This was sometimes inserted for tax reasons (particularly with property investment companies), or because its presence is required (in the memorandum or articles) by section 359(1)(d) of the Taxes Act 1970 if the company wishes to have authorised investment trust status;

(ii) under section 25(2) of the Companies Act 1981, a prohibition on the payment of dividends is required to be included in the memorandum or articles of any company which seeks exemption from the requirements of the 1948 Act relating to the use of the word "limited"; and

(iii) older companies sometimes restrict or circumscribe dividend rights in the clause dealing with share capital.

Articles of association

Under Table A articles, and under most forms of articles encountered in practice, the basic power to pay dividends lies in the general meeting, which may declare dividends (by ordinary resolution) but not exceeding the amount recommended by the directors (article 114). However, the directors, by resolution of the board, are authorised to pay "interim dividends" (article 115). Such a resolution of the board can be revoked prior to actual payment, as no debt is created (see *Potel v. IRC* 46 T.C. 658).

If dividends are to be paid otherwise than in cash, an express authority is required, as in article 120 (dividends in specie) or article 128 (capitalisation of profits and issue of bonus shares).

Article 118 provides that dividends shall be declared and paid according to the amounts *paid up* on respective shares (reversing the English common law rule, in the absence of such an article, that payment is made according to the *nominal* amount of the share irrespective of the amount paid up). Article 118 further apportions dividends according to the amount paid up during any part or parts of the period in respect of which the dividend is paid, unless the share was issued on terms that it ranked for dividend as from a particular date. If, therefore, shares are being issued which it is desired will participate in full in the first dividend following their issue (rather than a proportion thereof according to the time in which they were in issue), this should be expressly provided in the resolution of the board (or general meeting) authorising the allotment of the share.

A further point of some importance is that in the absence of anything to the contrary in the articles, dividends (and bonus shares) are payable (or issuable) to those members on the register *at the time of the declaration*. Table A contains nothing to the contrary, but well drafted modern long form articles usually permit a "record date" of not more than 28 days prior to payment. This problem has received statutory recognition in relation to section 17 of the Companies Act 1980 (pre-emption rights on issue of shares). Section 17(13), inserted by Schedule 3 to the Companies Act 1981, permits the use of record dates under section 17.

As stated earlier, express authority is required in the articles for dividends in specie, as can be found in article 120. This did not appear in pre-1948 versions of Table A and therefore old articles need to be carefully checked for such a power. With demergers becoming more popular, the point is of particular relevance, as a demerger will involve a distribution in specie (but if made in a winding up, see article 135).

Demergers are discussed more fully under the heading *Distributions in kind and demergers*, below.

Finally, out of *what* profits are dividends payable? Watch out for articles restricting payment to "the profits of the business", which would preclude capital profits. Table A now merely states that no dividend shall be paid otherwise than in accordance with the provisions of Part III of the 1980 Act (article 116). Before its amendment by the 1980 Act, it read "... otherwise than out of profits", which is not considered to be restrictive.

Other contracts

Further restrictions on distributions will often be found in contracts, in particular convertible loan stocks, convertible preference shares, options, warrants or even in a straight loan agreement entered into by the company.

Capitalisation of profits

As stated earlier, express authority is required in the articles of association for the capitalisation of profits or reserves, as can be found in articles 128, 128A and 129 of Table A (and note, in relation to articles which pre-date December 22, 1980, section 45(1) of the 1980 Act). These did not appear in pre-1948 versions of Table A and therefore old articles should be checked for such a power.

An issue of shares as fully or partly paid bonus shares is excluded from the definition of "distribution" in Part III of the 1980 Act and is therefore not subject to the Act's restrictions (section 45(2) of the Companies Act 1980). Therefore, unrealised capital and revenue profits, and realised capital profits of an investment company, can be so utilised, although they cannot be used for the payment of dividends by virtue of sections 39 and 41 of the 1980 Act (see further pages 355 and 366).

However, the above exclusion from the definition of "distribution" does not extend to the utilisation of capitalised profits in paying up amounts unpaid on *existing* shares, or in paying up bonus *debentures*. These transactions must, therefore, comply with the distribution rules in the 1980 Act (and be authorised by the articles, as under article 128 of Table A). (See also the express prohibition in section 39(3).)

Although article 128A of Table A (inserted by Schedule 3 to the 1980 Act) gives a suitable *power* for the capitalisation of profits which are not distributable by way of dividend, it covers *fully paid* bonus shares only, whereas the exclusion in section 45(2) from the *restrictions* in the 1980 Act extends to partly paid bonus shares.

Similarly, article 128 permits the use of a share premium account or capital redemption reserve for paying up fully paid bonus shares only, although in this case repeating the restrictions in sections 56 and 58 respectively of the 1948 Act, which do not extend to partly paid bonus shares.

Dividend restrictions: Companies Act 1980, Part III

The Companies Act 1980 lays down for the first time in statute form a definition of what may legally be distributed, and imposes many additional restrictions compared with the old law. The Act was amended by the Companies Act 1981.

Summary

The following is a summary of the new rules in the order in which they are considered.

Any company (*public or private*) can only make distributions out of its accumulated, realised profits so far as not previously distributed or capitalised, less accumulated, realised losses so far as not previously written off in a reduction or reorganisation of capital (sections 39(1) and (2)).

A second restriction applies only in the case of *public companies*: distributions may only be made so long as the company's net assets do not fall below the aggregate of its called up share capital and "undistributable reserves", as defined in the Act (section 40). The main effect of this requirement is that, for public companies, any excess of unrealised losses over unrealised profits must be covered by realised profits.

Distributions in kind are now covered by section 43A. Special rules apply for certain listed investment companies (section 41); in relation to long-term business of insurance companies (section 42) and to banking, insurance and shipping companies.

These tests are to be applied by reference to "relevant accounts" complying with specified requirements – usually the last audited accounts (section 43).

It should, of course, be appreciated that it is not enough just to satisfy the statutory tests when considering whether a dividend can be paid. The directors of a company must have regard to the company's best interests generally – as was the case under the old law. They could, for example, be held liable if they paid a dividend in an imprudent manner (i.e. without paying due regard to the future cash requirements of the business and to the present and future solvency of the company), even though the statutory tests may have been satisfied. In addition, the company's memorandum or articles may (but rarely do, except in the case of companies which make investments) contain further restrictions on distributions, over and above those set out in the 1980 Act (recognised by section 45(5)). Furthermore, convertible stocks, convertible preference shares, options and warrants often impose contractual restrictions on distributions. Finally, there is the old common law rule that dividends must not be paid out of capital.

Conversely, it should be noted that the restrictions in the Act apply only to "distributions" as defined in section 45(2). The definition – any distribution of a company's assets to its members – is an extremely wide one and could cover any benefits in cash or in kind, but the following are expressly excluded and are therefore not caught by the restrictions in the Act:

(a) an issue of fully or partly paid bonus shares (see also page 353);

(b) the redemption or purchase of any of the company's own shares otherwise than out of distributable profits;

(c) certain reductions of capital; and

(d) distributions in a winding up.

The new distribution rules are not merely of importance for determining what can be distributed to the members. In addition, they are utilised by the 1981 Act, in provisions authorising certain payments which were formerly unlawful, provided these are made out of, or by reference to, distributable profits. Those provisions all appear in Part III of the 1981 Act and cover,

(i) financial assistance for the acquisition of a company's shares (replacing section 54 of the Companies Act 1948); and

(ii) the purchase or redemption by a company of its own shares, and related payments (see pages 372 and 668).

Sections 54 and 60 of the 1981 Act provide for appropriate adjustments to be made to a company's accounts in respect of such matters.

Section 39: restriction applicable to all companies

Section 39 of the 1980 Act restricts distributions to "accumulated, realised profits so far as not previously utilised by distribution or capitalisation [defined in section 45(3)], less ... accumulated, realised losses so far as not previously written off in a reduction or reorganisation of capital duly made". The terms "profit" and "loss" cover both revenue and capital profits and losses (section 45(4)) – except where the context otherwise requires, notably in relation to certain listed investment companies, which are the subject of a special regime. Thus, for the vast majority of companies, *the distributability of profits is governed by the distinction between realised profits and unrealised profits*, there being no distinction between capital profits and revenue profits. The same applies to losses.

Major changes made by section 39

(1) Unrealised profits (whether revenue or capital) are no longer distributable, reversing the decision in *Dimbula Valley (Ceylon) Tea Company Limited v. Laurie* [1961] Ch. 353, which permitted (in the case of a company incorporated in England) the distribution of unrealised capital profits, although casting doubt on the commercial wisdom of such action. However, unrealised profits can still be used, as explained on page 359, to release realised profits for the purpose of paying dividends.

(2) (Because of the use of the word "accumulated" in relation to profits and losses) the profit for any particular year becomes irrelevant and the profit and loss account is to be regarded as a continuous account. This reverses *Ammonia Soda Co Limited v. Chamberlain* [1918] 1 Ch. 266, which was generally taken as authority in England for the proposition that a distribution of revenue profits may be made in one year even though there might

be an accumulated deficit on revenue account from previous years in excess of such revenue profits. A company will now either have to make good its accrued losses before paying any dividends, or, alternatively, it will have to apply to the court for a reduction of capital, thereby cancelling the loss (see further page 358). For instance,

> Year 1 – £100 trading loss
> Year 2 – £100 trading loss
> Year 3 – £100 trading profit

The company cannot now distribute the £100 profit in year 3. A further £100 profit is required before any dividend out of subsequent profits can be paid.

(3) *Ammonia Soda v. Chamberlain* also permitted the application of an unrealised capital profit in writing off realised revenue losses. For the reasons given on page 360, regarding adjustments, any realised losses which have been written off against unrealised profits will henceforth have to be added back into the total of accumulated realised losses, thereby reducing profits available for distribution under section 39 (and a similar effect will reduce the profits available under section 40).

(4) It had been the law that a dividend can usually be paid out of revenue profits without making good a capital loss, realised or unrealised (*Lee v. Neuchatel Asphalte Co.* (1889) 41 Ch. D. 1; *Verner v. General & Commercial Investment Trust* [1894] 2 Ch. 239). By virtue of section 39, if the capital loss is a *realised* loss, it will now reduce the amount of profits available for distribution. Section 40 (see below) will also result in the need to make good an *unrealised* capital loss, but this only affects public companies.

In any event, now that the 1981 Act requires provisions to be made for depreciation of fixed assets (C.A. 1981, Sch. 1, paras. 18, 19 and 32), section 39(4) (see below) will ensure that, for all companies, dividends will be restricted to allow for depreciation, subject to section 39(5).

Additional rules introduced by section 39

(1) Section 39(3) further restricts the purposes for which an unrealised profit may be applied (and more restrictions result indirectly, as explained on page 360 regarding adjustments). (Note, however, the uses which can still be made of unrealised profits – page 359). The purpose of this section is to prevent a company in difficulties from favouring its shareholders.

(2) Section 39(4) provides that any "provision" (of any kind mentioned in paragraphs 87 and 88 of the new Schedule 8 to the 1948 Act) is to be treated as a realised loss. However, there is an exception for any provision in respect of any diminution in value of a fixed asset, provided it appears on a revaluation of *all* the fixed assets, or of all the fixed assets other than goodwill (section 39(4)

as amended by the 1981 Act). Where this exception applies, it follows that a provision may be treated as an *unrealised* loss. Further, for the purposes of determining whether any such general revaluation of fixed assets has taken place, "any *consideration* by the directors" of the value at any particular time of any fixed asset is treated as a revaluation of that asset. In other words, the directors "consideration" is good enough, provided that,

(a) where any particular assets have not *actually* been revalued but are so treated because of the directors' consideration, the directors are "satisfied" that the aggregate value at the time in question of all assets so "considered" is not less than their aggregate book value (section 39(4A), inserted by the 1981 Act); and

(b) it is stated, in a note to the relevant accounts for the purposes of section 43, (i) that the directors considered the value at any time of the relevant fixed assets without actually revaluing them; (ii) that they are satisfied that their aggregate value at the time in question is or was not less than their aggregate book value; and (iii) that the relevant items affected are accordingly stated in the accounts on the basis that a revaluation of the fixed assets, including the assets in question, took place at that time (sections 39(4A) and 43(7A), inserted by the 1981 Act). No such note need be given however in the case of interim or initial accounts of a private company.

(3) Section 39(5) provides that depreciation after an upward revaluation of a fixed asset is to be treated as a realised profit insofar as it exceeds the depreciation which would have been charged if no revaluation had been made. Thus, where depreciation on the full revalued amount is charged against distributable profits (as required by SSAP 12, although this is not obligatory under the new accounting rules (C.A. 1981, Sch. 1, para. 32(3))) then the excess depreciation may be added back to distributable profits.

(4) Section 39(7) provides that where the directors are unable to determine whether a profit or loss made before December 22, 1980 is realised or unrealised, they may treat the profit as realised and a loss as unrealised.

(5) Section 39(8) formerly provided that "fixed asset" includes any asset which is not a current asset. However, this has been repealed by the 1981 Act because there is now a statutory requirement for all assets to be classified as fixed or current (the definitions of which now appear in paragraph 75 of Schedule 1 to the Companies Act 1981).

(6) The 1981 Act inserts a new section 42A. This provides that "development costs", if shown as an asset in the accounts (i.e. if capitalised), are to be treated as a realised loss except insofar as the development costs represent an unrealised profit made on a revaluation of those costs. This would therefore remove one advantage of capitalising development expenditure. This new sec-

tion does not apply to banking, insurance and certain shipping companies, nor to other companies if there are "special circumstances" which justify the directors in deciding that the amount shall not be treated as a realised loss, provided that a note to this effect, specifying the circumstances, appears in the accounts.

Section 39: practical implications

Increasing distributable reserves

Companies with past losses, whether realised or (in the case of public companies) unrealised, may be unable to pay dividends under the 1980 Act. It is therefore becoming common to see either of the following practices adopted:

(a) large dividends being paid by private subsidiaries up to the parent in order to make good the parent's losses;

(b) the parent's share capital, or share premium account, being reduced or cancelled under section 66 of the Companies Act 1948; the reduced amount may then either be used to cancel the past losses or else credited to a general reserve, available for distribution.

"Realised" profits

The question of when a profit is "realised" for the purposes of the 1980 Act originally gave rise to difficulty, since accounting practice was, in some instances, in conflict with case law on the meaning of the term.

However, the matter has now, to many a lawyer's (but not accountant's) relief, been firmly placed in the hands of the accountants by paragraph 90 of Schedule 1 to the Companies Act 1981, which declares "for the avoidance of doubt" that references in the Schedule to realised profits are to such profits "as fall to be treated as realised profits … in accordance with principles generally accepted with respect to the determination for accounting purposes of realised profits …". By virtue of section 21(1) of the 1981 Act, this rule is extended to all references to "realised profits" in the Companies Acts.

In September 1982 the CCAB issued a paper called *The determination of realised profits and disclosure of distributable profits*. This is set out in full in Appendix 6. The paper emphasises the importance, in deciding whether a profit is "realised", of applying the "accruals" and "prudence" concepts, as set out in SSAP 2 and now given statutory recognition in paragraphs 12 and 13 of Schedule 8 to the Companies Act 1945. SSAP 2 lays down the important principle that profits are recognised as realised only when realised in the form of cash or of other assets the *ultimate cash realisation* of which can be assessed with *reasonable certainty*.

In determining whether profits are "realised" account should also be taken of sections 39(5) (see page 357), 39(6) (position where no record of original cost) and 43A (see page 365).

Avoidance

Although section 39 requires that profits must be realised, it would appear to be possible "artificially" to convert an unrealised profit into a realised one (thereby permitting distribution). For example–

> A fixed asset showing an increase over book value could be sold (and, if need be, leased back or even repurchased (in effect, a company law version of "bed and breakfast")), thereby creating a realised profit. Obviously there would be tax consequences but tax – and stamp duty – might be avoided by selling to a subsidiary and taking advantage of the various tax and stamp duty exemptions for intra-group transactions. In particular, an asset could be purchased from one subsidiary by the parent company and subsequently sold to another subsidiary, again creating a realised profit.

As a result of the definition of realised profits in paragraph 90 of Schedule 1 to the 1981 Act (see page 358), it will fall in the first instance upon the accounting profession to say whether such artificial intra-group "realisations" represent realised profits of the vendor company. (Of course, such profits are not treated as realised in the *group* accounts – but this is not the point since section 39 is concerned with each *individual* company's accounts.)

Even on the assumption that an auditor will agree to treat such profits as realised in the vendor's own accounts, the following points should perhaps be borne in mind.

(a) Even in the simplest case of a straight sale from parent to subsidiary, it is possible that a court might frown on the transaction, for the simple reason that, otherwise, a company could always evade section 39 by forming a subsidiary and transferring an asset to it. The grounds for attack might conceivably include holding the directors who authorised a scheme deliberately to by-pass section 39 liable for breach of trust, in that they were misusing their powers. Furthermore, such a misuse of power might be one which was not ratifiable by shareholders at the annual general meeting approving the dividend and therefore, for example, a creditor could complain.

(b) The vendor company should receive consideration which is truly worth the amount realised, e.g. if an asset is sold for £1 million, the amount realised by the vendor will be less than this if the purchase price is left outstanding as a loan from the vendor to the purchaser if the purchaser (e.g. a subsidiary) is unlikely to be able to pay this. A provision might therefore have to be set up in the vendor's books, representing the doubtful element of the debt and this would accordingly reduce the "realised" profit.

(c) If a sale is coupled with a repurchase, it is possible, depending on the facts, that the courts might hold there had been no real change in beneficial ownership, at any rate where the vendor is controlled by, or controls, the purchaser and is thereby able to procure the repurchase. It is just possible that a court might go on to hold that, in reality, no profit had been realised, borrowing perhaps from the new principles being applied in tax cases (see *W. T. Ramsay v. I.R.C.* [1981] S.T.C. 174 and *I.R.C. v. Burmah* [1982] S.T.C. 30), though of course these principles do not yet extend beyond highly artificial schemes involving the avoidance of tax.

(d) Even assuming that profits on intra-group sales can be regarded as realised, the auditors may consider it necessary to qualify their report by indicating that some of the relevant company's profit represented surpluses which had arisen on intra-group transactions, thereby creating realised reserves of the company but which were not realised as far as the group was concerned. Such a qualification may fall within section 43(8) of the Companies Act 1980 and therefore the auditors would have to state whether, in their opinion, the matter referred to was material for the purpose of determining the legality of any proposed dividend (see s. 43(3)(c), below).

In spite of these points, intra-group realisations are not uncommon in practice. It should also be emphasised that the reservations cover only intra-group sales made for the purpose of artificially creating realised profits and there are likely to be many instances of intra-group sales made bona fide for some other motive.

Adjustments to balance sheet figures for section 39

The figures appearing in most companies' balance sheets will usually be accumulated realised profits so far as not previously utilised, less accumulated realised losses so far as not previously written off. Since section 39 qualifies "utilised" by "by distribution or capitalisation", and qualifies "written off" by "in a reduction or reorganisation of capital", two adjustments will have to be made to arrive at the appropriate figures when considering the section 39 test, namely,

(a) If in the past any realised profits have been utilised in any manner *other than* by distribution or capitalisation (e.g. to write off unrealised losses which have not subsequently been realised), these realised profits can in effect be added back to the figure for accumulated realised profits (because section 39 only refers to "accumulated realised profits so far as not previously utilised *by distribution or capitalisation*"). Thus a company which has so written off unrealised losses is not penalised as a result.

(b) Conversely, if any accumulated realised losses have in the past been written off *other than* in a reduction or reorganisation of capital (e.g. by writing them off against unrealised profits which have not subsequently been realised), then such an amount must be deducted from the figure, required by section 39, for accumulated realised profits less losses.

To this extent, section 39 is retrospective in its effect.

Bonus shares

Finally, although unrealised capital and revenue profits cannot be distributed, they may be applied in paying up unissued shares as fully or partly paid bonus shares provided that the articles permit this (section 45(2)). Even where the articles predate December 22, 1980 and are so worded as to permit only the use of, for example, "distributable" profits for bonus issues (as in article 128 of Table A), the requisite power is deemed to be present by section 45(1). New articles incorporating Table A will have the requisite power by virtue of a new article 128A (inserted by Schedule 3 to the 1980 Act), although this only covers fully paid bonus shares (see above).

Section 40: additional restriction on public companies

Section 40 of the 1980 Act applies only to *public companies*, and imposes a restriction on distributions in addition to that imposed by section 39. The restriction is that the distribution must not reduce the amount of the net assets, as shown in the relevant accounts, below the aggregate of the company's called-up share capital, as defined in section 87(1), and its "undistributable reserves". "*Net assets*" are defined as the aggregate of a company's assets less the aggregate of its liabilities (section 87(4)(c)). "*Liabilities*" includes any provision for "liabilities" or charges (defined in paragraph 88 of Schedule 8 to the Companies Act 1948; section 87(4)). Since intangible assets (e.g. goodwill) are not excluded from the definition of net assets, a company can include these for the purpose of passing the section 40 test. "*Undistributable reserves*" are defined in section 40(2) as,

(a) share premium account;

(b) capital redemption reserve;

(c) the amount by which the company's accumulated, *unrealised profits*, so far as not previously utilised by any "capitalisation", *exceed* its accumulated, *unrealised losses*, so far as not previously written off in a reduction or reorganisation of capital duly made. "Capitalisation" is defined in section 45(3), but is subject to section 40(3). (The amount calculated under (c) will presumably be zero where unrealised losses exceed unrealised profits); and

(d) any *other* reserve prohibited from distribution by the memorandum or articles or some other statute (e.g. the articles of companies which make investments often prohibit the distribution of realised capital profits).

Section 40(4) incorporates the rules contained in sections 39(4) to 39(7) (see pages 356 to 357 above).

What does section 40 really mean?

Although the effect of section 40 is in broad terms intuitively clear, the precise effect of the section, when one asks exactly what it adds to the restrictions in section 39, is not obvious. This is due to the mixed use of the term "net assets", on the one hand, and "share capital and reserves", on the other.

In order to see the effect of section 40 more clearly, and to relate it to section 39, section 40 can be reconstructed in algebraic terms and a substitution can be made for the term "net assets". This has the effect of restating the restrictions of section 40 purely in terms of reserves, thereby enabling better comparison with section 39. The algebra is a little long (mainly due to the unusual wording of section 40(2)(c), which gives either a positive or a zero, but never a negative figure) and is not reproduced here. What is of interest is the result, and this is set out below under the heading *Restatement of section 40*.

It will be seen that the most obvious effect is the one which is stated in all commentaries on the subject, namely that unrealised losses must be covered by realised profits. However, this is not the full story, in that it is interrelated to some other restrictions, as will be seen.

Restatement of section 40

(Accumulated) *realised profits** (less accumulated realised losses*) must not merely exceed zero (the effect of section 39, subject to the adjustments mentioned on page 364**) but, in the case of public companies only, they must *further cover*:

(1) whichever is the greater of (*but not both*):

(a) any accumulated *unrealised losses** (in excess of unrealised profits*); or

(b) previously distributed unrealised profits, so far as not subsequently realised *plus* unrealised profits (not subsequently realised) previously utilised otherwise than by capitalisation or distribution (e.g. by writing off against realised losses) *minus* unrealised losses (not subsequently realised) previously written off otherwise than in a reduction or reorganisation of capital (e.g. by writing off against realised profits).

AND

(2) any reserves (other than those in sections 40(2)(a), (b) or (c)) prohibited from distribution by the memorandum or articles or by some other statute.

*In the case of profits, these refer to profits not previously utilised in any manner and, in the case of losses, to losses not previously written off in any manner i.e. (usually) the balance sheet figures.

**The effect of such adjustments is of course that, instead of zero, there should be substituted the expression in (1)(b) above but omitting the words "previously distributed unrealised profits, so far as not subsequently realised". Thus, the *extra* effect of section 40, over and above section 39, amounts to three matters: inclusion of accumulated unrealised losses ((1)(a) above), inclusion of undistributable reserves ((2) above), and inclusion of previously distributed unrealised profits which are not subsequently realised. A corollary of this is that a company satisfying section 40 will automatically satisfy section 39. This is, however, a slight oversimplification since it assumes that the two examples given in brackets in (1)(b) above – writing off unrealised profits against realised losses, and writing off unrealised losses against realised profits – are the only instances of the matters dealt with by (1)(b) and the only cases where adjustments under section 39 are called for. If the actual wording of sections 39 and 40 is studied, it will be seen that there may be cases where this is not so.

Section 40: practical implications

(a) Unrealised losses (insofar as they exceed unrealised profits) must be made good out of net realised profits before a distribution can be made, whereas section 39 only requires realised losses to be made good. In practice, such unrealised losses will usually arise from the writing down (otherwise than by way of depreciation or in respect of a permanent diminution in value) of *capital* assets, since other unrealised losses will usually be charged to the profit and loss account. It should be noted that there is nothing in the Act to oblige a company to write down the value of the capital asset (otherwise than by way of depreciation, or under paragraphs 19(2) and 21 of Schedule 1 to the 1981 Act). But if this is done, section 40 will catch the resulting unrealised loss.

The effect of this is to apply a strict capital maintenance concept to public companies, for the protection of creditors. The E.E.C. Second Directive does not require, and the 1980 Act does not provide, that the same restriction be placed upon private companies.

By way of example, take a simple case of a company with £200 share capital, a £100 realised profit, net assets of £210, no unrealised profits but £90 unrealised losses. Under section 39, taken on its own, £100 would be distributable as profits. However, under section 40 this will be restricted to the excess of assets over share capital and undistributable reserves i.e. £210 − £200 = £10.

(b) A company which has previously distributed unrealised profits (which have not subsequently been realised) must cover those distributions by realised profits before any further dividends can be paid. For instance, assume a company's figures for the last two years have been:

> Year 1 – £100 trading loss
> Year 2 – £100 trading loss, but £200 unrealised profit (£100 dividend paid)

Apparently, in the financial year after the distribution provisions come into force, the company would have to make £400 trading profit in order to pay £100 dividend – the accumulated realised losses of £200 plus the £100 unrealised but distributed profit both have to be covered before a dividend is lawful. If the £100 loss in year 2 had been written off against the remaining unrealised profit it would make no difference since, although accumulated losses (as shown in the books) would be reduced, an adjustment would be necessary as explained in paragraph (a) under *Adjustments for section 40* (below) and in paragraph (b) under *Adjustments for section 39* at page 360 above.

This problem will particularly affect some property companies, because they will have been transferring increases in value of properties to profit and loss account to offset losses in respect of development expenses, particularly interest costs. Not only must they now cease the distribution of such unrealised profits (by virtue of section 39), but public companies must further, as a result of section 40, make good all previous such distributions (insofar as those profits have not subsequently been realised). (Previous and future write-offs of development expenses against such unrealised (capital) profits will produce the same result, for the reasons explained below under paragraph (a) of *Adjustments for section 40* (below), and under paragraph (b) of *Adjustments for section 39*, at page 360 above.)

However, because section 38 of the Finance Act 1981 now permits companies to obtain tax relief where it capitalises development expenses (insofar as they consist of *interest* payments), the need to charge them against profits has been removed, thereby eliminating future problems.

The 1980 Act will thus have, in this manner, retrospective application without any limitation. It will cause some companies practical difficulties in establishing (i) the extent to which dividends have in the past been paid out of unrealised profits, and (ii) the extent to which such sums have subsequently become realised.

Adjustments to balance sheet figures for section 40

(a) As already mentioned (see *Restatement of section 40*, paragraph (1)(b) above), if in the past *realised* losses have been written off against unrealised profits (which have not subsequently been realised) *or if unrealised profits (which have not subsequently been realised) have been distributed* (so that the revaluation reserve is inadequate to reflect the unrealised surpluses on fixed assets), then these must be added back to "undistributable reserves" and this will effectively mean that they reduce profits available for distribution. Goodwill written off against unrealised profits may produce the same effect.

It should be noted that the phrase above in italics applies only to section 40, and not section 39 (see page 360 above).

(b) Conversely, if any accumulated unrealised losses (which have not subsequently been realised) have been previously written off *other than* in a reduction of capital (e.g. by writing them off against realised profits), then such an amount can in effect be deducted from undistributable reserves, thereby increasing profits available for distribution.

These adjustments all demonstrate that section 40 is retrospective in effect. However, they add little or nothing over and above the effect of the adjustments required by section 39 (see above), except in the circumstance referred to in the italicised phrase in (a) above, and possibly where there have been write-offs of goodwill, or write-offs otherwise than against realised losses or profits respectively. (For an explanation as to why this is so, see the top of page 363).

Distributions in kind and demergers

A new provision, section 43A of the Companies Act 1980, which was added by the 1981 Act, has the effect that where a company distributes an asset in specie, the distribution is deemed to "realise" any unrealised profit shown in the accounts in respect of the book value of that asset. The profit is "realised" for the purposes both of the 1980 Act distribution rules and the 1981 Act accounting rules. This provision is intended to remove an element of doubt which particularly affected "demergers".

Demergers have been encouraged by recent tax legislation, but for company law purposes, they still constitute a distribution in specie and (unless made in a winding up or reduction of capital), must therefore comply with the distribution rules in the 1980 Act. But what is the *amount* of the distribution which one must satisfy from the distributing company's distributable reserves? Is it cost, book value or market value of the asset being distributed?

The answer is cost, less any amounts already written off as *realised* losses, such as depreciation. This is because any unrealised profit or loss actually shown in the books is treated as realised on the demerger (in the case of profit, as a result of section 43A, and in the case of losses, presumably on normal accounting principles). Therefore, reserves increase or decrease by this amount. But the demerger also removes, from the assets side of the balance sheet, an amount equal to book value i.e. cost (less depreciation) plus or minus any unrealised profit/loss. Therefore, the net loss to distributable reserves is (cost, less depreciation, plus/minus unrealised profit/loss) – (unrealised profit/loss) = cost, less depreciation. In other words, the net result is that the distributing company's distributable reserves are reduced by the cost (less depreciation) of the demerged asset, regardless of what the unrealised profit/loss was in respect of the demerged asset.

Section 40 will modify the general rule, outlined above, for those *public* companies whose books already record net unrealised losses (e.g. arising on a downward revaluation of some other fixed asset). *If the removal of any amount of unrealised profit already recorded in the books of the distributing company in respect of the demerged asset would result in those books showing an overall net unrealised loss (that is, if the amount calculated under section 40(2)(c) of the 1980 Act would be negative), then* this amount will *further reduce* distributable reserves, over and above the amount already described.

> *Example*
> Assume: Demerged asset cost: Nil
>   Unrealised profit on demerged
>   asset already shown in books: £1m
>   Unrealised losses in respect of
>   other assets: (£3m)
>   Realised profits: £5m
> On distribution of the asset, a profit of £1m is realised. Realised profits then become £6m but net unrealised losses are increased from (£2m) to (£3m).
> Therefore, distributable reserves go from £5m − £2m = £3m prior to the demerger to £6m − £1m − £3m = £2m after the demerger.

Conversely, if the demerged asset shows an unrealised *loss*, the net loss to reserves may be *less* than in the case of a private company, because the effect on distributable reserves of converting an unrealised loss to a realised one will be nil, if the company previously had net unrealised losses on its other assets.

Special cases

Insurance companies

Section 42 of the 1980 Act contains special rules as to what are "realised profits" in relation to long-term (i.e. life assurance) business of *any insurance company* to which Part II of the Insurance Companies Act 1974 applies (see section 12 of that Act). These rules provide that amounts properly transferred to profit and loss account from a surplus in the long-term business funds, and any deficit in such funds, shall be respectively treated as realised profits and realised losses (even though these amounts in fact contain elements of unrealised profit and loss arising from the actuarial and other valuations). Subject to the foregoing, any profit or loss arising in that long-term business must be left out of account.

Investment companies

Section 41 of the 1980 Act contains special rules for certain *listed* investment companies. The following points on section 41 are noteworthy.

1.   Section 41 gives investment companies the option of making a distribution on the basis of sections 39 and 40 or, instead, of making a

distribution out of "accumulated, realised *revenue profits* ... less accumulated *revenue* losses (whether realised *or unrealised*) ..." But the distribution must not reduce the amount of the company's assets, as shown in the company's "relevant accounts", below one and a half times its liabilities. "Liabilities" includes any provision for liabilities or charges (within the meaning of paragraph 88 of Schedule 8 to the Companies Act 1948; section 41(2)). Clearly, the advantage of falling within section 41 is that capital losses can be ignored (unlike section 39 as regards realised capital losses and unlike section 40 as regards unrealised capital losses). The price paid for this is that realised capital profits cannot be included and furthermore the above asset ratio test and the further restrictions in 2. below must be satisfied.

Thus, a company which falls within section 41 can pass on dividends or other income received, irrespective of whether the market value of its investments has fallen. This is very important to an investment trust (i.e. a company approved by the Inland Revenue under section 359 of the Taxes Act 1970) because if it failed to distribute most of its income it would lose the special capital gains tax privileges.

Little guidance is given by the 1980 Act as to what constitutes a revenue profit and what constitutes a capital profit. In such circumstances, the courts would fall back on the "ordinary meaning" of such words and such case law as there is.

Section 41(11) has been repealed for a reason similar to the repeal of section 39(8), see page 357 above. Section 42A (treatment of development costs) applies to section 41 in the same way as it applies to section 39 (see page 357).

The words "profits" and "losses" are respectively qualified by references to "distribution or capitalisation" and "reduction or reorganisation of capital", as under section 39, and accordingly the remarks on page 358 under *Section 39: practical implications* will apply here in a similar manner (but account must be taken of the difference in wording between section 39(2) and section 41(1)).

2. "Investment company" for the purposes of sections 39 to 45 means a public company which has given (and not revoked) the "requisite notice" (Form 25 – and Form 25a for revocation) to the Registrar of Companies and has since the date of that notice complied

(a) with the requirement that the business of the company consists of *investing its funds mainly in securities* (*not* in land or other assets, but see 4. below) with the aim of spreading investment risk and giving members of the company the benefit of the results of the management of its funds; and

(b) with further requirements which are similar to paragraphs (b), (d) and (e) of section 359(1) of the Taxes Act 1970 (section 41(8) expressly incorporates part of the Taxes Act for this purpose).

In addition, an investment company may not make a distribution under the special rules in section 41 unless,

(a) its shares are *listed* on a recognised stock exchange (see section 359(1)(c));

(b) since the start of the accounting reference period preceding that in which the distribution is made, the company has not distributed any capital profits or applied any unrealised profits or any capital profits (realised or unrealised) in paying up debentures or any amounts unpaid on any of its issued shares (this – and (c) below – is to prevent switching in and out of investment company status); and

(c) the company gave the requisite notice before the time specified in section 41(6).

3. It will be for the directors, in conjunction with their professional advisers, to decide whether the company meets the above criteria. The fact that it is an investment company will be publicised,

(a) by the necessary notice being given to the Registrar, as mentioned above; and

(b) on all the company's letters and order forms (as a result of an amendment to section 9(7) of the European Communities Act 1972, made by Schedule 3 to the 1980 Act).

Furthermore, if an investment company makes a distribution which, although permitted under section 41, would not be permitted under section 40 (because its net assets are thereby reduced to less than share capital plus undistributable reserves), this fact must be disclosed in a note to the accounts (paragraph 72 of the new Schedule 8 to the Companies Act 1948, as substituted by the Companies Act 1981).

4. The criteria summarised in 2. above are designed to ensure that, subject to minor variations, companies which are not approved by the Inland Revenue as investment trusts will not be able to take advantage of investment company status under the 1980 Act. In particular, the definition of "investment company" refers (like section 359(1)(a)) to the business of investing (mainly) in securities; *not* in land or other assets. (There is however a power for the Secretary of State at some future time to widen the definition in the Act to include land and other assets. The Government have indicated that this power will only be exercised if there are sound reasons and it is considered to be in the public interest). The use of the word "mainly", with reference to investing in securities, is designed to permit investment companies to have a small proportion of investments in assets other than securities, and, for example, at times of a falling market, to keep a proportion of assets in liquid form. In *Fawcett Properties v. Bucks C.C.* [1961] A.C. 636 the view was expressed that "mainly" gave rise to difficulties, but probably meant "more than half".

5. In 1. above, it was observed that section 41 gave the option *either* to make a distribution on the basis of sections 39 or 40 *or* to apply the

section 41 tests. The former option is only likely to be of use to an investment company if its distributions are held back by the "asset ratio" test i.e. if it is highly geared. This is because applying the sections 39 and 40 tests (but taking account of the restriction on distribution of realised capital profits – see sections 41(4)(c), 41(5) and 49(2)(d)) will not, on most occasions, give a better result than will the first leg of the section 41 test, namely that the company can distribute realised revenue profits, less revenue losses (realised or unrealised).

Banking, insurance and shipping companies

Certain (but not all) of the amendments made by the 1981 Companies Act to the distribution rules in Part III of the 1980 Act may not apply in respect of banking, insurance and shipping companies (as defined in paragraph 8 of Schedule 2 to the 1981 Act), with the result that the 1980 Act applies in its original form in respect of such matters.

The relevant amendments are listed in paragraph 6 of Schedule 2 to the 1981 Act.

The reason for this is that these amendments were consequential upon the introduction by the 1981 Act of new accounting requirements. These new requirements are not obligatory for such companies, since banking and insurance companies were not covered by the E.E.C. Fourth Directive and shipping companies were permitted exemption for a limited period.

Relevant accounts

It is, of course, important to establish the figures by which the restrictions in sections 39, 40 and 41 can be determined in any particular case. Section 43 provides that the restrictions shall be determined by reference to "the relevant items as stated in the relevant accounts". The relevant accounts will normally be the last audited annual accounts. However, subsequent interim accounts *may* be used instead if the proposed distribution would be found to contravene any of the sections if reference were made only to the last annual accounts. (For example, the last annual accounts might show unrealised stock profits which it is desired to distribute, the stock having subsequently been sold and the profit realised. In such a case, interim accounts will be required so as to show the realised profit but only if the last annual accounts do not show sufficient reserves available for distribution.)

Special provision is made for a company which has not yet produced any audited accounts: "initial accounts" will be required (see sections 43(2)(c) and 43(6)), but these are not considered further here.

Last annual accounts

If it is wished to rely on the *last annual accounts*, the following requirements must be satisfied:

(a) the accounts must have been laid before the company in general meeting (section 43(2)(a));

(b) they must have been "properly prepared (as defined in section 43(8)) or have been so prepared subject only to matters which are not material" for the purposes of determining the legality of the proposed dividend (section 43(3)(a));

(c) the auditors of the company must have made an *unqualified report* on the accounts. If the report is qualified, then the auditors must state in writing whether, in their opinion, the substance of the qualification is material for the purpose of determining the legality of the proposed dividend. (A material qualification will not, of itself, prevent a distribution from being made, but if the directors choose to distribute they would do so at their own risk.) The Act defines the term "unqualified report" as "a report, without qualification, to the effect that in the opinion of the person making the report the accounts have been properly prepared" (section 43(8)); and

(d) a copy of any statement by the auditors relating to a qualification must have been laid before the company in general meeting.

Since the auditors will, as a result of these provisions, be able in many cases to block a proposed dividend, the overall pressure on auditors from, and potential friction with, the company's directors will obviously be increased.

Interim accounts

If it is wished to rely on *interim accounts*, the following requirements must be satisfied:

(a) it must be possible to make "a reasonable judgment ... as to the amounts of any of the relevant items ..." (section 43(2)(b)). "Relevant item" means profits, losses, assets, liabilities, provisions, share capital or reserves (section 43(8));

(b) in the case of a public company only (section 43(5)):

(i) the accounts must have been "properly prepared" etc. as in section 43(3)(a) in relation to annual accounts (see (b) above under *Last annual accounts*); note that section 43(8)(b) requires any balance sheet to be signed by two directors in accordance with section 155 of the 1948 Act;

(ii) a copy of those accounts must have been delivered to the Registrar of Companies; and

(iii) if the accounts are not in English a certified translation is required.

It will be observed that there is *no requirement for an auditors' report* in the case of interim accounts, whereas if the last annual accounts are relied on a report is required.

Consequences of breach of Part III

No criminal sanctions are imposed in respect of breaches of this part of the 1980 Act.

Section 44 deals with the civil consequences of *receiving* an unlawful distribution but does not cover the position of directors responsible, save in cases where they are also shareholders. However, a director who is a party to an unlawful distribution could presumably be liable to the company in consequence of his existing fiduciary duties, since he is misapplying the company's funds (*Wallersteiner v. Moir* [1974] 3 All E.R. 217; *Selangor United Rubber Estates Ltd. v. Craddock (No. 3)* [1968] 1 W.L.R. 1555; *Belmont Finance v. Williams Furniture (No. 2)* [1980] 1 All E.R. 393 – these were cases on breaches of sections 54 and 190 of the 1948 Act; for a case on improper dividends see *Flitcroft's case* (1882) 21 Ch. D. 519).

Section 44(1) provides that if a member of a company knows, or has reasonable grounds for believing, at the time of the distribution that a distribution made to him is in contravention of the Act, he shall be liable to repay it (or the offending part) to the company. Finally, an illegal distribution may trigger an event of default under, for example, a loan agreement or trust deed.

Examples

These provisions are acknowledged by all to be complex. At the risk of over-simplification, the following table illustrates the position of two companies, A and B, whose accounts show:

	A	B
–Unrealised capital gain (loss) on revaluation of asset	800	(200)
–Realised capital profit	400	100
–Past accumulated realised, but undistributed, revenue profits	200	300
–Realised revenue profit (loss) for the current year	100	(50)
–Past realised revenue loss written off against past unrealised revaluation surplus	(50)	–
Former law permitted the following distribution:	1,500	350
New law permits the following distributions:		
(i) for private companies	650	350
(ii) for public companies	650	150
(iii) for investment companies	*250	**250

*(Test in sections 39 and 40 would, prima facie, give 650. However, investment companies would be unable to use the realised capital profit of 400 and, therefore, it is no help to use sections 39 and 40 instead, since they would also allow only 250.)

**(Assuming the investment company satisfies the "asset ratio" test.)

Financial Assistance for Acquisition of Shares

Section 42 of the Companies Act 1981 restricts the ability of a company to give assistance for the acquisition of shares in it or its holding company. It came into force on December 3, 1981, replacing section 54 of the Companies Act 1948. The section prohibits two types of transaction. The first is the giving of financial assistance *before or at the same time* as an acquisition of shares where the assistance is for the purpose of that acquisition. The second is the giving of financial assistance *after* the acquisition, where the assistance is for the purpose of reducing or discharging a liability incurred by anyone for the acquisition. So for instance a company may not lend money to a potential purchaser to enable him to buy shares in the company, nor may it subsequently lend money to him to discharge bank borrowings he has incurred to fund the share purchase.

The meaning of "financial assistance" is partially, but not exhaustively, defined, so that reference may be necessary to cases on the meaning of that phrase under section 54 of the Companies Act 1948.

After laying down two basic prohibitions against the giving of "financial assistance", section 42 goes on to provide four important categories of exemption. The first, which applies to all types of company, public or private, is where a company's principal or larger purpose in a transaction involving financial assistance is not the giving of that assistance. The second category, which again applies to both public and private companies, gives a blanket exemption to specified types of financial assistance, such as the payment of a dividend to a purchaser of shares, or a payment to a purchaser in a reduction of capital. This blanket exemption includes a redemption or purchase by a company of its shares under the procedures contained in sections 45 to 62 of the 1981 Act. The specific exemption for dividends is very valuable in practice, as it provides a relatively simple method of giving permitted financial assistance to a purchaser of shares.

The third category of exemption permits the lending of money by a money-lending company acting in the ordinary course of business, or by any company to enable employees to acquire fully paid shares. Any company may also provide money for certain employee share schemes. Although this exemption applies to both public and private companies, there are limitations for public companies.

The final, and most far-reaching, exemption enables a *private* company to give virtually any type of financial assistance, provided the company is solvent and provided a complicated set of pre-conditions is met. The rules are set out in sections 43 and 44 of the 1981 Act. This means that for most private companies there is no longer, for practical purposes, a restriction on their giving financial assistance. Even the bidder for a public company may be able to take advantage of this exemption, by re-registering the company as a private company once he has obtained control and then using the company's assets to help pay for his bid.

A transaction entered into in breach of section 42 is a criminal offence, and can result in serious civil law consequences.

When considering whether transactions involving financial assistance are permissible, regard must always be had not only to sections 42 to 44, but also to other restrictions. For example, the transactions must not be *ultra vires* the company, or in breach of the directors' fiduciary duties, or amount to an unauthorised reduction of capital or a fraudulent preference. And an important point to check is that a company's articles do not contain restrictions on the giving of financial assistance. In particular, any company incorporated before December 3, 1981 and which incorporates Table A of Schedule 1 to the Companies Act 1948 into its articles, will be subject to the restrictions in Article 10 of Table A. These follow the more restrictive terms of the now-repealed section 54 of the Companies Act 1948. (Companies incorporated after December 2, 1981 which adopt Table A, or companies which adopt new articles incorporating Table A after that date, will not be subject to the Article 10 restrictions: C.A. 1981, s. 119(5).)

Prohibited transactions

A transaction will be in breach of section 42 if the following circumstances exist:

(1) There is an *acquisition of shares* in a company;

(2) the company or a subsidiary directly or indirectly gives *financial assistance*;

(3) the financial assistance is not of an *exempted type*; and

(4) *either* the financial assistance is given *at or before* the acquisition and for the *purpose* of that acquisition; *or*

(5) it is given *after* the acquisition and for the *purpose* of reducing or discharging a liability itself incurred for the purpose of the acquisition.

Circumstance (1): acquisition of shares in a company

Acquisition

Section 42 refers to the *acquisition* of shares, and so covers not only the purchase of shares in a company or the subscription of shares in that company, but also an *exchange* of shares in another company for shares in that company (cf. *Re V.G.M. Holdings Limited* [1942] Ch. 235).

Shares

The acquisition must be of *shares*, so that an acquisition of debentures or loan stock is outside section 42, although the reference to shares includes stock (C.A. 1948, s. 456(1)). An acquisition of convertible loan stock is probably outside section 42, unless the acquirer proposes to exercise the conversion rights and the assistance is given directly or indirectly for that purpose. (Moreover, the giving of any financial assistance after the acquisition to reduce or discharge a liability of the acquirer may be within section 42 if at that stage the loan stock has been converted.)

Company

For section 42 to apply the acquisition must be of shares in a company formed and registered under the Companies Acts 1948 to 1981 or certain earlier Acts (see section 455(1) of the Companies Act 1948 and note section 114 of the 1981 Act). Financial assistance for the acquisition of shares in a company incorporated outside Great Britain (i.e. including Northern Ireland companies) is outside section 42. Thus a Great Britain subsidiary of a foreign company may give financial assistance for the purchase of shares in the parent (contrast section 54 of the 1948 Act). It appears that unregistered companies, such as most chartered companies and statutory companies, are not "companies" for section 42 purposes. However unlimited companies are subject to section 42 (this is deliberate: *Official Report*, Standing Committee A, June 30, 1981, col. 318).

Circumstance (2): direct or indirect financial assistance by company or subsidiary

The restriction prohibiting financial assistance extends beyond assistance given by the company whose shares are being acquired, to include assistance given by any subsidiary. "Subsidiary" is defined by section 154 of the Companies Act 1948 to include any sub-subsidiary. Moreover, although the company whose shares are being acquired must be a company registered under the Companies Acts (see above), "subsidiary" includes foreign-incorporated companies. Thus in the following group structure:

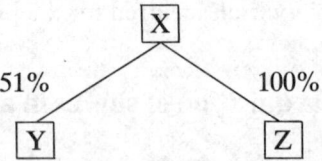

Y may not, on the face of it, give financial assistance for the acquisition of shares in X even if Y is, say, a U.S. company. This is almost certainly unintended, and neither the section 42(3) or 42(4) let outs, nor most of the section 42(5) exemptions (see below) apply to a foreign subsidiary.

Moreover the penalty provisions in section 42(12) deal only with "companies". It appears that the Department of Trade consider that the section 154 definition of subsidiary should not apply in this type of situation (*Law Society's Gazette* September 1, 1982, p. 1044), though the legal justification for this view is unclear. Returning to the example, X can, as might be expected, give financial assistance for the acquisition of shares in Y, its subsidiary. Likewise Z can give financial assistance for the acquisition of shares in Y.

Directly or indirectly

Sections 42(1) and 42(2) state that it is not permissible "to give financial assistance *directly or indirectly* for the purpose" stated. It seems clear that the words "directly or indirectly" qualify "give", not "for the purpose". That is, the sections provide that the financial assistance need not be given directly to the person acquiring the relevant shares. Thus if company A is proposing to purchase shares in company B, company B cannot lend money to company A's subsidiary for the purpose of putting company A into funds (for a more complicated example see the facts in *Wallersteiner v. Moir* [1974] 1 W.L.R. 991, a case on section 54 of the Companies Act 1948).

Financial assistance

Section 42(8) provides a partial definition of "financial assistance" by listing three particular types of financial assistance ("financial assistance" by way of gift, loan and guarantee, as defined in section 42(8)). It goes on however to state, rather unhelpfully, that "financial assistance" also means "any other financial assistance". But for such "other" financial assistance there is an important limitation: the financial assistance must result in the company's net assets being materially reduced (unless it has no net assets).

Before examining the three types of financial assistance specified, and the fourth, residual, category, one general point must be made. It is established that for financial assistance to be prohibited it is not necessary that the assistance be given to the *acquirer* of the shares. Financial assistance given to the vendor of shares (e.g. repayment of a debt owed to him) is capable of falling within section 42 (see *Armour Hick Northern Limited v. Whitehouse* [1980] 1 W.L.R. 1520; *E.H. Dey Pty Limited (In Liquidation) v. Dey* [1966] V.R. 464 (Australia), cases on the wording used in section 54 of the 1948 Act).

(A) Financial assistance by way of loan

Section 42(8)(c) specifically provides that "financial assistance" includes assistance given by way of loan. The first point to note is that the transaction must constitute "financial assistance", which is not itself defined. However a loan is probably always "financial assistance" to someone, leaving only the question whether it is directly or indirectly for the purpose of the acquisition or the discharge of a liability incurred for the acquisition.

To catch transactions similar to loans the definition refers to assistance,

(a) given by way of a loan *or any other agreement,*

(b) where any obligation of the person giving the assistance (e.g. a lender) is to be fulfilled before the obligations of any other party to the agreement (e.g. a borrower).

This catches not simply the making of a loan where the lender is required to advance money but the borrower is not required to repay for a period, for example, until a demand is made, but any other type of credit or deferred payment transaction. For instance, a sale of an asset at full value is caught if the purchaser is not required to pay the purchase price for a period, however short, or if part of the payment is to be ascertained and paid by reference to future profits. The wording used is very wide, as section 48(8)(c) applies where *any* obligation of *any other* party to the transaction remains unfulfilled. It is not clear whether "any other agreement" is to be interpreted *ejusdem generis* with "loan" to include only transactions similar to loans. Moreover, section 42(8)(c) goes on to provide that financial assistance includes assistance given by way of *novation* or *assignment* of any rights under a loan or other agreement. So the purchase by a company from a bank of a loan taken from the bank by a purchaser of the company's shares would constitute financial assistance (*Official Report*, Standing Committee A, June 30, 1981, col. 302). It is irrelevant whether there is a reduction in the company's "net assets" as a result of the giving of the financial assistance.

(B)   Financial assistance by way of guarantee or security

It is also specifically provided that "financial assistance" includes financial assistance given by way of guarantee, security, indemnity, release or waiver (section 42(8)(b)). Examples include a company guaranteeing a borrowing from a third party lender taken to fund a purchase of shares in the company, or charging its assets as security for such a borrowing. Likewise, a release of a debt owed by the purchaser to a company, or waiver of a payment due for assets sold, will constitute financial assistance. In the case of assistance by way of indemnity there is an exclusion for an indemnity given by the company or its subsidiary in respect of the indemnifier's *own* neglect or default. An example is an indemnity given to the underwriter of a rights issue of the company's shares against the issue not being taken up as a result of neglect or default on the company's part, though it is not clear in what circumstances the issuing company can be said to commit neglect or default.

(C)   Financial assistance by way of gift

This is specifically included in the definition of financial assistance by section 48(8)(a). There are certain estate duty cases which suggest that "gift" may include a sale or transfer at undervalue (see for instance *Letts v. I.R.C.* [1957] 1 W.L.R. 201; *A-G v. Kitchin* [1941] 2 All E.R. 374). If a sale at undervalue *does* constitute a gift, and not merely "other financial assistance" under heading (D) below, then there will be financial assistance even if the element of bounty is not large enough to have a material effect on the net assets of the company in question.

(D) Other financial assistance

Being a section whose breach involves criminal penalties, it might be expected that section 42, and in particular the meaning in section 42(8)(d) of "other financial assistance", would be construed narrowly. A similar expectation might be derived from an examination of the mischief section 42 is aimed at (prevention of an unauthorised reduction of capital, and also protection against the misuse of a company's assets to the detriment of minority shareholders or creditors: see in particular *Re Wellington Publishing Co. Limited* [1973] 1 N.Z.L.R. 133). But cases on the precursor to section 42, section 54 of the Companies Act 1948, suggest that section 42 is likely to be construed widely (see for instance *Wallersteiner v. Moir* [1974] 1 W.L.R. 999 and *Belmont Finance Corporation Limited v. Williams Furniture Limited* [1980] 1 All E.R. 393).

Consequently it appears that,

(i)   the phrase "any other financial assistance" is not to be construed *ejusdem generis* with the three types of financial assistance specifically identified in section 42(8) (loan, guarantee, gift);

(ii) instead, it can extend to any form of financial assistance. Lord Denning's dicta in *Wallersteiner* at page 1014 is probably still relevant: "You look at the company's money and see what has become of it. You look at the company's shares and see into whose hands they have gone. You will then soon see if the company's money has been used [to give financial assistance]". Once it is established that "assistance" is given, the mere fact that money is involved in some shape or form will make that assistance "financial assistance": *Armour Hick Northern Limited v. Whitehouse*;

(iii) in deciding the initial question whether financial assistance exists, it seems from the section 54 cases that an objective, not a subjective test is to be applied (though note Quillam J. in *Re Wellington Publishing Co. Limited* [1973] 1 N.Z.L.R. 133 at 140). Subjectivity only becomes relevant once the "purpose" test is applied (see below);

(iv) "other financial assistance" can include, therefore, (a) the purchase by the company whose shares are being acquired of an asset (whether at over value or not), (b) a similar purchase by that company's subsidiary, (c) the sale or exchange of an asset, particularly a liquid asset, by the company or a subsidiary, (d) the placing of the company's trading opportunities in the hands of a purchaser, or (e) debt set off arrangements. But dividends are generally specifically exempted, under section 42(5) (see below).

However, "other financial assistance" may not constitute financial assistance for section 42 purposes if the company giving the assistance has "net assets" (i.e. in broad terms if the company is not insolvent, though the test is not by reference to liquidity but net worth). A company with "net assets" can give other financial assistance if those net assets are not reduced to a *material extent* as a result of the assistance being given. "Net assets" are defined for this purpose by section 87(4)(c)· of the Companies Act 1980 to mean the aggregate of a company's assets less the aggregate of its liabilities. Section 87(4)(c) does not expressly state that *actual*, as opposed to book, values are to be used, but this was certainly the view of the Government (*Official Report*, House of Lords, October 27, 1981, col. 956), and the wording of section 87(4)(c) does contrast with that in section 42(11), which uses book values for the "net assets" test in section 42(7) (see below). "Liabilities" include any provision for liabilities or charges, defined to have the same meaning as "liabilities" in section 42(11)(b) (C.A. 1980, s. 87(4)(c) and C.A. 1948, Sch. 8, para. 88). "Liabilities" thus includes provision for any liability or loss which is either *likely* to be incurred, or *certain* to be incurred but uncertain as to amount or time. So a purchase by a company for cash at market value of a fixed asset from a prospective purchaser of its shares would not constitute financial assistance because the company's net assets would not be reduced. (This assumes that in arriving at the "market value" account is taken of, for example, the ease with which a fixed asset may subsequently be sold. It also assumes that section 42(8)(c) is not in point, which it would be if for example payment was deferred.) But a purchase at over value, if this was significantly above market value in relation to the size of the company's net assets as a whole, would constitute financial assistance (and might fall within section 42(8)(a), see above). In many cases, however, it will be difficult to determine whether, and if so by how much, a transaction results in a reduction of the company's net assets. No guidance is given as to what will constitute a "material" reduction, though the question is presumably an objective one based on the view of a prudent creditor or auditor.

Circumstance (3): exempted types of financial assistance

Section 42(5) exemption

Section 42(5) provides that none of the following eight transactions is to be prohibited, whether or not the company in question is a public company. Most of the transactions are ones for which specific procedures are provided for by the Companies Acts.

(1) A distribution of the company's assets by a *dividend lawfully made*. This is an important exception in practice, as it provides a relatively straightforward way of a purchaser funding his acquisition. The

distribution must actually constitute a dividend. There is no statutory or case law definition of this term, though there is some indirect authority suggesting most distributions on shares other than those involving a reduction of capital or a capitalisation of reserves will amount to a dividend (see *Hill v. Permanent Trustee Co.* [1930] A.C. 720; *Re Doughty* [1947] 1 Ch. 263; on the other hand Part III of the 1980 Act refers to "distributions" whereas section 42(5) refers only to a "dividend"). A distribution of assets in specie made out of profits will normally constitute a dividend (though express power for the dividend is required in the company's articles). To satisfy the "lawfully made" test the dividend must clearly satisfy the rules concerning available distributions in sections 39 to 45 of the Companies Act 1980. For public companies, those rules are now relatively strict. The dividend would also need to comply with the provisions of the company's articles, and so would normally have to be paid equally to all shareholders of the relevant class (*Official Report*, Standing Committee A, June 30, 1981, col. 300). In declaring or proposing dividends the directors now have a statutory duty to consider the interests of employees (section 46 of the 1980 Act). It is unclear whether a dividend is not "lawfully made" if the directors, in declaring it (if an interim dividend) or recommending it to the company in general meeting (if a final dividend), have not properly considered the working capital and solvency requirements of the company and the interests of any minority shareholders or creditors. The directors may be in breach of their fiduciary duties, and subject to an action for a misfeasance, but this itself probably does not make the payment of the dividend unlawful. Note that if the dividend is *not* lawfully made, it may still not necessarily amount to financial assistance (*Coleman v. Myers* [1977] 2 N.Z.L.R. 225 at 288; cf. *Re Wellington Publishing Company Limited* [1973] 1 N.Z.L.R. 133 at 140–1).

(2) A distribution made in the course of a winding up of the company.

(3) A reduction of capital sanctioned under section 68 of the Companies Act 1948.

(4) The allotment of bonus shares (which does of course amount to an "acquisition of shares"; a bonus issue may be used in a stamp duty saving scheme included in a take over). The exception does not extend to the paying up of amounts unpaid on partly or nil paid shares by way of capitalisation of profits or reserves, or the allotment of bonus debentures. But for a company with "net assets" this would not in any event normally constitute "financial assistance" under section 42(8)(d) (no reduction in net assets), though possibly the paying up could constitute a "gift" within section 42(8)(a). Even if the company had no net assets or the payment constitutes a "gift", it is questionable whether there is any "financial assistance".

(5) Anything done pursuant to a court order made under section 206 of

the Companies Act 1948 (compromises and arrangements with
creditors and members, including company reconstructions).

(6) Anything done under a section 287 scheme (company reconstruction involving liquidation and transfer of assets in exchange for
issue of shares to members).

(7) A redemption or purchase of shares under sections 45 to 62 of the
Companies Act 1981.

(8) Anything done under an arrangement between a company in
voluntary liquidation and its creditors which is approved by an
extraordinary resolution pursuant to section 306 of the Companies
Act 1948.

Section 42(6) exemption

Three further exemptions are contained in section 42(6), though these
are subject to certain restrictions in the case of public companies.

Lending in ordinary course of business

Section 42(6)(a) provides that a company whose ordinary business
comprises in whole or in part the lending of money is not prevented
from giving financial assistance by lending money in the ordinary course
of its business. But the decisions in *Steen v. Law* [1964] A.C. 287 (P.C.)
and *Fowlie v. Slater* (Divisional Court, March 23, 1979) show that this
exception is relatively limited. To fall within the exception the company
must not only carry on an established business of money-lending, but
the lending in question must be consistent with the company's normal
course of business and be of a scale which the company ordinarily
practices. Thus the size of the loan, its term, the type of borrower and
any security must be consistent with the company's general business.
The loan must be at the borrower's free disposition and not be confined
to special uses or restricted to particular and defined purposes (Lord
Ratcliffe in *Steen* at 301; this requirement has been criticised: N.L.J.
November 8, 1979 page 1089). In particular, it was stated by the Privy
Council in *Steen* that it is "virtually impossible to see how loans, big or
small, deliberately made by a company for the direct purpose of
financing a purchase of its shares could ever be described as made in the
ordinary course of its business". This passage was cited and followed in
Fowlie v. Slater. In that case Slater Walker Limited made a number of
loans to another company for the purpose of assisting that company to
purchase shares in Slater Walker Limited's parent company. It was held
that the loans were outside the ordinary course of business proviso and
were caught by section 54 of the Companies Act 1948 (the wording of
the proviso being identical to that in section 42(6)(a)). Although Slater
Walker Limited was an authorised bank and carried on a money-lending
business, the loans were not made in the ordinary course of that
business. The loans were not at the borrower's free disposition but were
made specifically and solely for the purchase of shares in the lender's
holding company, and in addition were not for the benefit of the

borrower. Nor could the fact that the company made fifteen loans to the purchasing company bring the exemption into operation: the repeated making of special loans for special purposes could not make lawful what was otherwise unlawful.

Thus a loan made by a bank or money-lending company for the purchase of its own shares can virtually never fall within section 42(6)(a), and a loan made by such a company for a purchase of shares in its parent company can only qualify in exceptional cases.

Funding an employees' share scheme

Section 42(6)(b) enables a company to provide money for the acquisition of shares in it or its holding company, provided the shares are fully paid and the money is provided under an employees' share scheme. The money can be made available to the trustees, if any, of an employee share scheme, or to the employees direct. The money may be provided by loan, or by other ways, such as gift or bonus. "Employees' share scheme" is defined to mean:

"a scheme for encouraging or facilitating the holding of shares or debentures in a company by or for the benefit of:

(a) the bona fide employees or former employees of *the company, the company's subsidiary or holding company or a subsidiary of the company's holding company*; or

(b) the wives, husbands, widows, widowers or children or step-children under the age of 18 of such employees or former employees".

Thus a company may make a loan to executive directors to enable them to acquire shares in the company. (This is subject to section 49 of the Companies Act 1980 (loans to directors), and to the directors not utilising their powers otherwise than for a proper purpose, see *Hogg v. Cramphorn* [1967] 2 Ch. 254.) There must actually be a "scheme", which is not itself defined.

Lending to employees

Section 42(6)(c) enables a company to lend to employees, *other* than directors, who are employed in good faith to enable those employees to acquire *fully paid* shares in the company or its holding company to be held by them as beneficial owners. The categories of qualifying "employees" are thus more limited than for the section 42(6)(b) exemption. Directors are excluded, and the company cannot make loans to employees of other group companies, such as subsidiaries, to enable them to buy shares in the company. Former employees, and relatives, are also excluded. As with the section 42(6)(b) exemption, the employees must be genuine employees. However, it is not necessary for a share scheme to exist.

Restriction for public companies

None of the three section 42(6) exemptions applies in the case of a public company unless the company has *net assets* and either,

(a) those net assets are not reduced by the transaction; or

(b) the reduction in net assets is covered by "distributable profits". "Distributable profits" are defined by section 62(1). They are the profits which could lawfully be distributed under sections 39 to 45 of the Companies Act 1980. These are to include the unrealised profits on any assets distributed in specie, which by section 43A of the 1980 Act are deemed to be available to cover that distribution. In ascertaining the distributable profits available from the latest accounts, regard must be had to section 60 of the 1981 Act (reduction for subsequent transactions).

In computing "net assets" for the purpose of (a) it is the *book* value of the company's aggregate assets less its aggregate liabilities which is to be taken (section 42(11)(a), which refers to the company's "accounting records"). For these purposes "liabilities" include provision for contingent or unascertained liabilities, because the expression "liabilities" includes amounts retained to provide for any liability or loss either likely to be incurred, or certain to be incurred but uncertain as to size or time (section 42(11)(b)). In contrast to the section 42(8)(d) test for "other financial assistance", immaterial reductions in net assets are not ignored. Presumably the reduction in the *book* value of the net assets will normally be measured by reference to the amount of the reduction in the accounts, a book figure, and not by reference to the actual value of the reduction, if different.

Given that the three section 42(6) exemptions relate chiefly to loans it is not immediately obvious how a loan of cash would result in a reduction in a company's net assets, unless the company, perhaps on the advice of its auditors, treated the loan as worth less than the principal advanced because of doubts as to its recoverability. Merely lending at a low, or even a nil, rate of interest should not result in the loan being worth less in the books than the cash it replaces. Section 42(6)(b), however, envisages the "provision of money" for an employees share scheme, and in this case, it is easier to see how a company's net assets may be reduced, as cash may be used to pay up shares to be handed over to employees rather than being advanced as a loan. In this case an amount equal to the cash paid out must be deducted from the company's profits available for distribution, whether or not the transaction constitutes a Companies Act 1980 "distribution" as such.

Private company exemption

All private companies may provide financial assistance for the acquisition of their, or their holding company's, shares, provided a complicated procedure is followed. The company must, however, be solvent (in the sense that it must have "net assets"). This exemption is dealt with in detail below.

Circumstance (4): financial assistance at or before acquisition

Section 42(1) provides that it is unlawful to give "financial assistance" *for the purpose* of an acquisition or proposed acquisition, either before or at the same time as the acquisition. It is not strictly necessary that a proposed acquisition actually takes place.

Timing

No guidance is given as to the precise time that an "acquisition" of shares takes place. However, in the case of a purchase or exchange of existing shares this is almost certainly not before a binding and unconditional purchase contract exists, and perhaps not until share transfers have been registered. In the case of an issue of new shares the acquisition probably does not take place until allotment, and perhaps not until issue.

Purpose

The giving of the financial assistance is only prohibited if it is *for the purpose of* the share acquisition. The fact that the assistance may be said to be "in connection with" the acquisition is not relevant (cf. section 54 of the Companies Act 1948). Use of the word "purpose" indicates that the company must have the object or intention of assisting the acquisition (see the *Shorter Oxford English Dictionary*), and not merely that the assistance is *in connection* with the acquisition or that it *results* in assisting the acquisition. A mere causal link is not enough (see generally *Official Report*, House of Lords, October 27, 1981, cols. 953, 959, 963). The test clearly appears to be a subjective one, based on motive. It probably connotes an intention by the assistor to achieve a result desired by him (*Sweet v. Parsley* [1969] 1 All E.R. 347 at 363). And it is the motive and intention of the company giving the assistance which must be considered, not that of the person receiving the assistance.

Moreover, section 42(3) goes on to provide that the giving of financial assistance is not prohibited *even though* for the purpose of an acquisition of shares if,

(a) the company's *principal* purpose in giving the assistance is not to give it for the purpose of the acquisition; *or*

(b) the purpose is an incidental part of some *larger* purpose of the company.

In both cases, however, the assistance must be given "in good faith in the interests of the company".

The burden of proof in relation to (a) and (b) will be on the company (confirmed in *Official Report*, Standing Committee A, June 30, 1981, col. 316). However the test is nevertheless based primarily on the company's – i.e. the board's – intention, and not a court's objective view. Board minutes will provide strong prima facie evidence of the company's intention. Even so, board minutes and other evidence may be open to review by a court, perhaps especially in the case of a subsidiary sharing common directors with its parent. Note in particular that in *Howard Smith Limited v Ampol Limited* [1974] A.C. 821 at 832, Lord Wilberforce stated that when a dispute arises as to whether directors made a decision for one purpose or another, or whether one or other purpose was a primary purpose, the court can review the position *objectively*. But given that the test is primarily subjective, and given the wide wording of the "motive" let-outs at (a) and (b) above, many transactions in which an element of financial assistance is involved are likely, as a practical matter, to fall outside the section 42(1) prohibition (see the examples below). It will, however, often be very difficult for professional advisers to sanction a transaction because they will be bound to apply a more objective test than the company. On the basis of *Howard Smith*, it is the objective view which will ultimately prevail in the event of dispute.

In good faith in the interests of the company

The requirement that, to claim the benefit of the section 42(3) "motive" let-outs, the financial assistance must be given "in good faith in the interests of the company" probably involves both a subjective and an objective test (confirmed by *Official Report*, House of Lords, October 27, 1981, col. 968). The requirement really does no more than repeat the general law (see *Re Smith & Fawcett Limited* [1942] Ch. 304 per Lord Greene M.R. at 306 and *Re Roith* [1967] 1 W.L.R. 43).

Whether the assistance is given "in good faith" is a subjective test. The "interests of the company" are the interests, primarily, of its members, but probably also of its creditors and, now, its employees (section 46 of the Companies Act 1980). Here the test is probably *objective*. One problem is that often the giving of assistance may well be in the interests of a group as a whole, but is less obviously in the interests of the company as such. A good example is guarantee and security arrangements. But provided there are reasonable grounds for believing that the assistance will be for the benefit of the company itself, as well as the group, this may be sufficient (*Charterbridge Corporation v. Lloyds Bank* [1970] Ch. 62). Clearly, however, it will be helpful if board minutes and other evidence show that the directors paid some attention to the interests of the company itself, and that some benefit would accrue to the company. Independent professional advice may be appropriate.

In deciding whether the directors, in giving the assistance, have acted in good faith in the interests of the company, it may also be necessary to ask whether they have performed their common law obligation to exercise their powers for a proper purpose (see *Hogg v. Cramphorn Limited* [1967] Ch. 254 and *Howard Smith Limited v. Ampol Limited* [1974] A.C. 821). It is not altogether clear whether this is part of the good faith test or a separate test. In any event, the court has a power to review the directors' motives (see *Howard Smith, supra*).

The nature of the "purpose" and "in good faith" tests means it is difficult for a third party, such as a lending bank, to be confident that section 42(3) is met. Some protection may be available by taking a statutory declaration from the directors that section 42(3) is met, but this will still not help if the declaration is false.

Circumstance (5): financial assistance following the acquisition

Section 42(2) makes unlawful certain financial assistance given *after* an acquisition of shares in the company or any holding company has taken place. There is no time restriction on the word "after". The section can however apply only where a *liability* has been incurred, by the acquirer or anyone else, *for the purpose* of the acquisition. But where such a liability exists, the company may not give directly or indirectly any financial assistance *for the purpose of reducing or discharging* the liability.

From this, it might be thought that if a person acquires shares in a company without incurring any liability (e.g. by using surplus cash), the company is quite free subsequently to give the acquirer financial assistance (e.g. by making him a loan). However, sections 42(9) and 42(10) extend very considerably the meaning of the phrases "liability has been incurred" and "for the purpose of reducing or discharging the liability". These two sections will always need to be examined very carefully by the advisers to an acquired company. By section 42(9) the acquirer (or any other person) is treated as incurring a liability whenever he changes his *financial position*, either,

(a) by making any agreement or arrangement; or

(b) by any other means.

The agreement or arrangement in (a) need not be an enforceable one, and need not be made on the acquirer's (or the other person's) own account.

By section 42(10) a company is to be treated as giving financial assistance "for the purpose of reducing or discharging any liability" if it gives financial assistance for the purpose of wholly or partly restoring the *financial position* of the person who incurred the liability.

A major difficulty is the reference, in sections 42(9) and 42(10), to a change or restoration in a person's "financial position". The phrase is capable of a very wide meaning. Presumably a purchase of shares at market value out of borrowed money, or even out of cash, can constitute such a change. (For a possible indication to the contrary, however, see the references to "financial position" by Schreiner J. in *Gradwell (Pty) Limited v. Rostra Printers Limited* [1959] 4 S.A.L.R. 419, cited in *Belmont Finance Corporation Limited v. Williams Furniture Limited* [1980] 1 All E.R. 395 at 401, and by Judge Mervyn Davies Q.C. in *Armour Hick Northern Limited v. Whitehouse* [1980] 1 W.L.R.

1520.) Thus the company which subsequently lends to a person who purchased its shares out of cash resources would appear to be in breach of section 42(2) by making the loan. The acquirer will have "changed his financial position" (by paying out his surplus cash in return for shares) and the company will have partly "restored his financial position" (by replacing the cash as a loan).

The position of guarantees and security arrangements is particularly obscure. Despite the width of sections 42(9) and 42(10) it appears such arrangements are normally permissible, though the contrary is certainly arguable. The question whether section 42(2) applies must arise at the time the guarantee or security is given, and not at the time, if ever, that the guarantee is called or the security enforced. On this basis, it is difficult to see how the giving of a guarantee or the granting of security by an acquired company in relation to an acquirer's borrowings either reduces or discharges any liability or restores the acquirer's "financial position" (see example (27) below).

Section 42(2), like section 42(1), contains a subjective "purpose" test. First, the liability incurred on the share acquisition must be incurred *for the purpose* of that acquisition. Secondly, the financial assistance given by the company must be given *for the purpose* of reducing or discharging that liability. Again, there is no offence if the liability is incurred or the assistance given only in *connection* with the acquisition or discharge, or if it merely *results* in the acquisition or discharge.

Moreover, section 42(4) mirrors the section 42(3) motive let-out by providing that the giving of financial assistance is not prohibited *even though* for the purpose of reducing or discharging a liability if,

(a) the company's *principal* purpose in giving the assistance is not to reduce or discharge the liability; *or*

(b) the purpose is an incidental part of some *larger* purpose of the company.

Again, however, the assistance must in either case be given "in good faith in the interests of the company".

The wide wording of sections 42(9) and 42(10) means that the directors of an acquired company will need to tread very carefully to avoid a breach of section 42. Unless and until the courts interpret sections 42(9) and 42(10), there will be considerable uncertainty as to the scope of the prohibition on financial assistance after an acquisition.

Examples

Financial assistance at or before the acquisition

(1) *Direct loan.* X proposes to buy A Limited. A Limited makes a loan to X to enable him to buy the A Limited shares. The loan is prohibited by section 42(1) (unless, in extremely exceptional circumstances, A Limited is a money-lending company: see *Fowlie v. Slater*, above).

(2) *Indirect loan.* As in (1), but A Limited lends to Y, to enable Y to lend to X: the loan to Y is prohibited by section 42(1) (indirect financial assistance; see *Selangor United Rubber Estates Limited v. Cradock (No. 3)* [1968] 1 W.L.R. 1555).

(3) *Repayment of existing loan.* As in (1), but instead of A Limited making loans to X, A Limited repays existing indebtedness owed to X. There is probably no "financial assistance" by A Limited because its net assets will not be reduced, even if the loan is not yet due and payable (section 42(8)(d); it seems doubtful whether early repayment of a debt can amount to financial assistance by way of "release or waiver" under section 42(8)(b)). If however the loan is not yet due and is at a low rate of interest early repayment may perhaps reduce net assets, when it will be necessary to determine whether the reduction is "material". Where A Limited has no "net assets" for section 42(8)(d) purposes, or there is a *material* reduction, there *may* be "financial assistance" (though the *Armour Hick* and *Gradwell* cases, mentioned below, suggest the contrary if the loan is due and payable). If there is "financial assistance", the position would then depend on whether A Limited can rely on the "purpose" exemptions, particularly the "principal purpose" and "incidental purpose" tests in section 42(3). This will be harder if the loan is not yet due and payable than if it is (e.g. if the loan is repayable on demand and X has made a demand), and the "good faith in the interests of the company" test will be a particularly difficult hurdle. (On repayment of existing indebtedness, see generally *Spink (Bournemouth) Limited v. Spink* [1936] Ch. 544 at 548; *Gradwell (Pty) Limited v. Rostra Printers Limited* [1959] 4 S.A.L.R. 419, cited in *Belmont Finance Corporation Limited v. Williams Furniture Limited* [1980] 1 All E.R. 395; *Armour Hick Northern Limited v. Whitehouse* [1980] 1 W.L.R. 1520.)

(4) *Discharge of target's indebtedness.* A Limited is a wholly-owned subsidiary of B Limited, which is a wholly-owned subsidiary of C Limited. B Limited has outstanding indebtedness to C Limited. X wishes to buy B Limited, but it is a condition of the sale agreement with C Limited that B Limited's indebtedness is paid off before the sale. Repayment of the indebtedness is capable of constituting financial assistance even though it is not assistance to X (*Armour Hick*). But if B Limited itself makes the repayment, there is probably no "financial assistance," at least provided the debt is due and payable (*Armour Hick*). And in any event, if B has "net assets" there is almost certainly no "financial assistance" within section 42(8)(d), or if B has no net assets the "purpose" exclusions may apply (see (3) above for more detail). If B Limited has to borrow to discharge the debt, this should not affect the position. However, if *A Limited* discharges B Limited's debt, this is probably "financial assistance" within section 42(8)(d) (*Armour Hick*). If A Limited has net assets and A Limited's rights, if any, against B Limited (subrogation, agreement or whatever) have an actual value close to the cash paid out, section 42(8)(d) should not apply, but the transaction would probably fall within section 42(8)(c), when the net asset test is irrelevant. If there is "financial assistance" it may be difficult for A Limited to rely on the section 42(1) and 42(3) "purpose" let-outs.

(5) *Release of loan.* Y agrees to sell his shares in A Limited to X for an agreed price provided X procures that A Limited releases Y from a debt of £1m. owed to A Limited. The release by A Limited will constitute financial assistance (section 42(8)(b)), and will be unlawful. The timing of the release (e.g. not until the acquisition is completed) probably makes no difference. (It is difficult to see how the purpose let-outs could apply unless, perhaps, X reimburses A Limited the £1m.; cf. *Curtis Furnishing Stores Limited v. Freedman* [1966] 1W.L.R. 1219.)

(6) *Guarantee or security.* X, a director of A Limited, proposes to buy 10% of A Limited's shares. He funds the purchase by bank borrowing, but procures that B Limited, A Limited's subsidiary, guarantees the borrowing and/or charges a property it owns as security for the loan. This is an unlawful transaction (s. 42(1) and 42(8)(b); the "purpose" let-out is not available in the absence of exceptional circumstances).

(7) *Purchase of asset.* X Limited intends to acquire A Limited but has no funds. It arranges for A Limited to buy for cash two properties, P and Q, P at market value and Q at overvalue. Assuming A Limited is solvent (in the sense that it has net assets), the purchase of property P will not constitute "financial assistance", however

undesirable or unnecessary it is for A Limited to acquire property P, because A Limited's net assets will not be materially reduced (section 42(8)(d); cf. the *Belmont Finance* case on section 54 of the 1948 Act, and watch that the payment provisions under the purchase contract are outside section 42(8)(c)). Whether or not property P is readily realisable appears irrelevant (assuming, as would normally be the case, that the "market valuation" of it has taken into account the nature and saleability of the property). A Limited's purpose in buying the property also appears to be irrelevant. The purchase of property Q will amount to "financial assistance", unless perhaps A Limited has net assets and the degree of overvalue is not "material" in relation to A Limited's assets as a whole – but there might nevertheless be a "gift" within section 42(8)(a), see earlier. The purchase will thus only be permissible if the purchase is justifiable from the viewpoint of A Limited's business (ss. 42(1) and 42(3)). Even if it is, however, it will be difficult for A Limited to satisfy the "good faith in the interests of the company" requirement in section 42(3), because the purchase is at overvalue.

(8) *Sale of asset.* X Limited intends to acquire A Limited but has no funds. A Limited, which has no net assets, exchanges a readily realisable asset for a less realisable asset, of the same "market" value, with X Limited, enabling X Limited to obtain cash for the acquisition by selling the asset. Because A Limited has no "net assets" under section 42(8)(d), the transaction *may* constitute "financial" assistance. If so, A Limited will have difficulty relying on the section 42(3) purpose exemption, unless there are good commercial reasons for A Limited entering into the exchange. If instead A Limited sold the readily realisable asset for cash, at undervalue, there would be "financial assistance" even if A Limited had net assets, unless the degree of undervalue was not material in relation to A Limited's total net assets. Note that if a sale at undervalue constitutes a "gift" for the purposes of section 42(8)(a), the materiality of the undervalue becomes irrelevant.

(9) *Deferred payment etc.* A Limited sells assets to X in the ordinary course of its business, but agrees that payment be deferred for a year. Shortly afterwards X acquires some shares in A Limited. The deferral constitutes financial assistance (s. 42(8)(c)), but if A Limited has no knowledge of the proposed acquisition, the assistance is probably not "for the purpose" of the acquisition. Likewise if A Limited pays a large insurance premium to its insurance company, whose life fund subsequently buys shares in A Limited's parent. Section 42(8)(c) appears capable of applying (though if this is wrong, so that only section 42(8)(d) is relevant, there might only be "financial assistance" in the first place if A Limited had no net assets, on the basis that the reduction in the company's cash is matched by an equivalent "asset" (the benefit of prepaid insurance premiums), or that any reduction in net assets was not "material".) But again the "purpose" test should provide a let-out.

(10) *Set-off.* X wishes to acquire A Limited. X owes £1m. to A Limited, but A's subsidiary, B Limited, owes £2m. to X. A Limited agrees to a contractual set-off arrangement with X in relation to the two loans, which enables X to persuade its bank to increase X's overdraft limit, giving it funds for the acquisition. Assuming A Limited has "net assets" it is difficult to see how any "financial assistance" arises (at least until rights of set-off are exercised), unless perhaps it can be said that there is a "release or waiver" by A Limited under section 42(8)(b), or unless the particular terms of the set-off agreement fall within section 42(8)(c).

(11) *Moneys left outstanding.* A Limited agrees to purchase an asset for its business from X Limited, and pays a returnable deposit of £100,000. The purchase falls through, and shortly afterwards X Limited decides to buy shares in A Limited, using the deposit. By not calling for the return of the deposit when the purchase fell through A Limited will have given financial assistance (s. 48(8)(c), loan), which is likely, depending on the precise facts, to be for the purpose of the acquisition (see generally *Wallersteiner v. Moir* [1974] 1 W.L.R. 991).

(12) *Mortgage of shares.* X buys shares in A Limited using a bank loan, and then charges the shares as security for the loan. A Limited has not given any financial assistance.

(13) *Issue of fully or partly paid shares.* A Limited issues shares to X credited as fully paid up on the basis that X will pay the subscription moneys due in cash or in specie

in 12 months time. (If A Limited is a public company then note C.A. 1980, ss. 20 to 24.) This would constitute financial assistance under section 42(8)(c) and may thus be prohibited (against this section 87(3) of the 1980 Act treats the shares as fully paid up "for the purposes of the Companies Acts"). Or A Limited issues partly-paid shares to X. Again this appears to fall within section 42(8)(c), unless it can be argued X gets no "assistance", or that no obligation arises on X until a call is made. But the "purpose" exemptions should normally apply (though a distinction must be drawn between the reason for issuing new capital and the reason for deferring payment).

(14) *Issue of shares with debentures.* A Limited issues shares and secured debentures to an institution as a "package" (i.e. the institution must take debentures as well as shares). Although A Limited is giving security this would not appear to constitute "financial assistance" within section 42(8)(b) because no "assistance" is being given to the subscriber or anyone else.

(15) *Commission for cash alternative etc.* P Limited offers to acquire the shares of A Limited in exchange for shares, and P's merchant bank offers a cash alternative whereby it will buy the shares issued by P at an agreed price. P Limited pays the merchant bank a commission for this. The commission payment may not constitute "financial assistance" at all (unless the arrangements can be said to fall within section 42(8)(c)), because P's net assets will not be *materially* reduced by the payment, but in any event P's principal purpose will not normally be the giving of financial assistance (but will be the acquisition of A Limited). (An alternative route is for the merchant bank to subscribe for shares direct, P Limited using the cash received to satisfy the "cash alternative".) The position is similar where P Limited gives an indemnity in connection with the acquisition by the merchant bank of shares in P – there may be financial assistance within section 42(8)(b) (depending on the terms of the indemnity), but again P Limited may be able to rely on the "principal purpose" exclusion. Likewise the payment of underwriters' commissions on a rights issue or placing will normally be protected (and see section 53 of the Companies Act 1948 in any event). Any indemnity given to the underwriter will only constitute financial assistance if it goes wider than covering the company's own neglect or default (s. 42(8)(b)); even then the "purpose" exemptions will normally apply. The position may be more difficult if it is desired that a subsidiary of A Limited makes the payments or gives the indemnity, because of the "in good faith in the interests of the company" test.

(16) *Intra-group transfers.* A Limited wishes to sells its subsidiary, B Limited, to X, but wishes first to transfer out of B Limited an asset, such as a factory or intellectual property, used by A Limited. Rather than making the transfer of the factory at market value (which would increase the sale price of B Limited and thus increase A Limited's capital gains tax liability), the transfer is made at book value. The transfer by B Limited may constitute financial assistance (*Armour Hick* and section 42(8)(d)), but B Limited will argue that the purpose, or principal purpose, is not to give X financial assistance. The difficulty with relying on the section 42(3) "purpose" let-out is that the transfer may not be in the interests of the company (being in the interests of A Limited). (One alternative, assuming B Limited has sufficient distributable reserves, may be to transfer the factory as a distribution in specie, though this only works if such a distribution is a "dividend" within section 42(5)(a). Or the factory could be transferred at market value and the excess over book value paid up as a dividend.) The position is similar if, say, B Limited is owed £1m. by a fellow subsidiary, C Limited, and B Limited assigns this debt to A Limited for nil consideration immediately prior to the sale.

(17) *Purchase of shares in subsidiary.* A Limited owns 90% of B Limited and wishes to buy in the minority. It procures that B Limited lends it the money to fund the purchase. This is unlawful under section 42. Instead, B Limited might pay up a dividend to A Limited. Alternatively, A Limited turns B Limited into a private company and adopts the section 43 procedure (see below).

Financial assistance after the acquisition

(18) *Loan.* X Limited acquires A Limited, having borrowed to fund the acquisition. The borrowing might be from a bank, or from its own shareholders, institutions or even A

Limited's shareholders (by the issue of loan stock). Having acquired A Limited, X borrows from A Limited and uses the borrowings to pay off its indebtedness. A Limited is in breach of section 42(2), as it will have given financial assistance for the purpose of reducing or discharging X's liabilities on the acquisition. There is no time limit after which A Limited may properly make the loan. The repayments made to X's lender will be recoverable by A Limited (see below). However, if A Limited puts X in funds by paying up lawful dividends, or reducing its capital, this is permitted. Alternatively, X Limited might procure that A Limited follows the section 43 procedure for permitted financial assistance (re-registering A Limited as a private company if necessary): see below.

(19) *Loan after cash acquisition.* X Limited acquires A Limited for cash, out of its own cash resources. One year later A Limited lends to X Limited, to fund its working capital requirements. Arguably this constitutes "financial assistance" (restoration of financial position) and so is unlawful unless A Limited can rely on the "purpose" exemptions in sections 42(2) and 42(4). The main question is whether by paying out surplus cash for shares A Limited changed its "financial position".

(20) *Loan after share for share exchange.* X Limited acquires A Limited in a share for share exchange. A Limited then lends X Limited money. Even though X Limited might be said to have incurred a "liability" on the acquisition (owed to the old A shareholders on the exchange shares issued, section 42(9)), the loan can hardly be said to reduce or discharge that liability.

(21) *Indirect loan.* X Limited's subsidiary, Y Limited, borrows to repay indebtedness owed to X Limited. X Limited uses the repayment to acquire A Limited, and A Limited subsequently lends to Y Limited. This is prohibited (section 42(2)), unless, exceptionally, A Limited can bring itself within the section 42(4) motive let-out, or the borrowing by Y Limited was not "for the purpose" of X Limited's acquisition. Alternatively, Y Limited lends surplus cash to X Limited to fund X Limited's acquisition. After the acquisition, A Limited lends to Y Limited. This will be prohibited by section 42(2) if Y Limited can be said to have "changed its financial position" by making the loan (cf. the decision in *Coleman v. Myers* [1977] 2 N.Z.L.R. 225 at 288 and see *Official Report*, Standing Committee A, June 30, 1981, col. 299).

(22) *Repayment of existing loan.* After X Limited has acquired A Limited, A Limited repays an existing debt to X Limited. This will not normally be prohibited (see (3) above).

(23) *Novation of loan.* X Limited borrows from its bank to fund the acquisition of A Limited, and A Limited subsequently enters into a novation agreement whereby it takes over the borrowing. This is prohibited (s. 42(2) and 42(8)(c)).

(24) *Waiver of existing loan.* X Limited borrows £1m. from a bank to help fund the acquisition of A Limited, a trade supplier which X owes £1m. After the acquisition, A Limited waives X's loan. The waiver constitutes financial assistance (section 42(8)(b)) and falls within section 42(2): X's "financial position" being partially restored to that before the acquisition when, as now, it owed £1m.

(25) *Loan of surplus cash.* X Limited borrows to purchase A Limited, at 16% p.a. fixed. Two years later A Limited sells a property surplus to its requirements, and wishes to invest the surplus cash. The highest return it can obtain from an outside lender is 12%; X Limited offers to borrow at 14%, to use the loan to repay its original borrowing. This will constitute financial assistance. But A Limited may well be able to argue that its "principal purpose" in making the loan is to obtain the best return possible, and that the making of the loan is not to give financial assistance to X Limited. It may also be able to argue that the making of the loan is in the interests of the company, although this could depend on the solvency of X Limited and whether the loan is repayable on demand.

(26) *Temporary loan.* X purchases A Limited, using a short term facility from a third party bank, repayable within a month. X intends to procure A Limited to pay a dividend after acquisition which he will use to repay the bank facility. Delays arise in

paying the dividend, and so X borrows from A Limited on a temporary basis to repay the bank. The temporary loan by A Limited amounts to financial assistance (s. 42(8)(c)), and although probably not made for the purpose of the *acquisition* (see *Coleman v. Myers* [1977] 2 N.Z.L.R. 225 per Mahon J. at 289), is now caught by section 42(2).

(27) *Giving of security or guarantee.* X Limited borrows to buy A Limited, and after the acquisition A Limited charges its assets as security for the borrowing. The giving of security constitutes "financial assistance", but it is difficult to see how this amounts to the "reduction or discharge" of X Limited's liabilities or the partial restoration of X Limited's financial position before the borrowing (ss. 42(2) and 42(10); one argument might however be that X Limited's ability to borrow is partially restored to the original position once it has turned its loan into a secured borrowing). Likewise if A guarantees X Limited's borrowing. If X Limited charged its own assets at the time it borrowed, and A Limited subsequently adds its unencumbered assets to the security, it could be argued that X Limited's "financial position" (of having unencumbered assets) is in effect partially restored.

(28) *Charging subsidiaries.* X Limited acquires A Limited. Under a trust deed constituting a previous loan stock issue, X is bound to procure that all its subsidiaries charge their assets as security for the stock. On A Limited becoming a subsidiary, it charges its assets pursuant to the loan stock deed. As in (27), it is difficult to see how this falls within section 42(2); and even if it does, section 42(4) may provide a let-out (see *Official Report*, Standing Committee A, June 30, 1981, col. 298). Note however that section 42(1) will also require consideration if the security is given "at the same time" as the acquisition.

(29) *Group refinancing.* One year after the X Limited group has acquired A Limited, the group reorganises its financing arrangements by consolidating all borrowings through X Limited, with all its subsidiaries (including A Limited) charging their assets as security, or giving cross-guarantees or both. Although it is possible that section 42(2) could apply, section 42(4) should normally permit A Limited to give the security (and it could be argued that the assistance was not "for the purpose" stated in section 42(2) at all).

(30) *Refinanced liabilities.* X Limited borrows from a finance house to acquire A Limited. Six months later, X Limited decides to refinance its borrowing through its bank. Six months after that, A Limited makes a loan to X Limited, which X uses to discharge the bank loan. A Limited is not discharging *the* liability incurred to purchase its shares, so arguably A Limited's loan is not within section 42(2). However, the wording of section 42(10) (restoration of X's original financial position) indicates that the transaction is caught by section 42(2).

(31) *Set-off.* X Limited borrows from its bank to purchase A Limited. After the acquisition, A Limited transfers its bank deposits to X Limited's bank, and X Limited and its subsidiaries (including A Limited) give the bank rights of set-off between the various bank accounts. Merely granting a right of set-off probably does not constitute "financial assistance" by A Limited within section 42(8), provided it has "net assets" (see (10) above), and even if section 42(2) could apply the section 42(4) motive let-out may in some cases be available.

(32) *Purchase of asset.* After X Limited has acquired A Limited, A Limited buys for cash illiquid assets from X Limited, X Limited using the cash to repay borrowings made for the acquisition. Purchases at market value (or undervalue) should be permitted provided A Limited has "net assets"; purchases at overvalue may not be (see (7) above).

(33) *Transfer of business.* X Limited borrows to fund the acquisition of A Limited, giving its bank a floating charge. A Limited's assets and business are then hived up to X Limited, at market value on loan account. X Limited services its bank borrowing partly out of the income from A's business. Whether or not A Limited has "net assets" the transfer of the business will constitute financial assistance (it will fall within section 42(8)(c), loans etc.)) and will be in breach of section 42(2) if the transfer can be said to be for the purpose of partly restoring X Limited's financial

position (e.g. by giving it the profit-earning capacity to pay off its bank borrowing). It may be difficult for A Limited to show that the transfer falls within section 42(4), as having some other purpose and being in the interests of the company. (A solution might be to hive-up the business in a liquidation of A Limited.) The position will be similar if A Limited gifts, or sells on loan account, an income producing asset, such as a lucrative patent.

(34) *Dividends and reduction of capital.*   X Limited buys A Limited for £4m., using borrowed funds, and subsequently procures that A pays a dividend of £2m. and reduces its share premium account by £2m., to enable it to repay its borrowing. This is permitted (s. 42(5)).

(35) *Section 206 acquisition.*   X Limited acquires A Limited for cash, using borrowed funds, under a section 206 scheme involving the cancellation and reissue of A Limited's shares. A Limited is nevertheless prohibited from subsequently making a loan to X Limited for the purpose of paying off its borrowing, notwithstanding section 42(5) (the subsequent loan is not made as part of the section 206 scheme).

(36) *Private company exemption.*   X Limited borrows to buy A Limited, and A Limited subsequently lends to X Limited. A's loan is permitted if A complies with the procedure contained in sections 43 and 44 of the 1981 Act, and it is a private company with "net assets" at the time of the loan. This is clearly a very valuable exemption. If A Limited is a public company, X Limited may be able to procure its re-registration as a private company pursuant to section 10 of the Companies Act 1980. It seems there is nothing to prevent X Limited giving its bankers an advance undertaking that, on acquiring A Limited, it will re-register A Limited to enable that company to make the loans.

(37) *Management buy-out.*   A Limited, a public company, owns B Limited, a private company. The management of B Limited wishes to buy the company, and forms M Limited, a private company, for the purpose. M Limited borrows to fund the purchase, and then B Limited gives security for that borrowing. Although B Limited's security falls within section 42(1), it is permitted if B Limited follows the section 43 procedure. B Limited must have net assets (on book values) and, if these can be said to be reduced by the contingent liability of giving the security, the reduction must be covered by distributable profits (see below). Or B Limited takes over M Limited's borrowing, invoking the section 43 procedure. Alternatively, M Limited liquidates B Limited and hives-up its business. Here no "financial assistance" can arise in any event (section 42(5)).

Financial assistance by private companies

Following recommendations made by the Jenkins Committee, sections 43 and 44 permit a *private* company to give financial assistance otherwise prohibited by sections 42(1) and 42(2) *provided* a complex procedure is followed. *However the private company must be solvent.* The test of solvency is by reference to net assets, using book values. The section 43 relaxation will be of particular assistance in management buy-outs. In practice, if there is any doubt as to whether a proposed transaction by a private company may breach section 42 it will be prudent to take advantage of section 43.

The procedure permits a private company to give financial assistance at or before, or after, an acquisition,

(a)   of its shares;

(b)   of shares in any holding company, *provided* the holding company is itself a private company and there is no intermediate public company (sections 43(1) and 43(3)).

Example

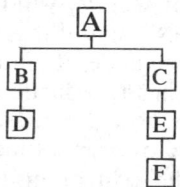

If A and D are private companies, D can give financial assistance for the acquisition of shares in either A or B if B is also a private company, but *not* if B is a public company. If C is a public company but B is a private company, D may give financial assistance for the acquisition of shares in either B or A (and in C, E or F). If E and F are private companies, F can give financial assistance in relation to E's shares, but not, if C is a public company, in relation to A's or C's shares. In all cases D can give financial assistance for the acquisition of its *own* shares.

A public company cannot take advantage of the section 43 procedure unless it is first converted into a private company under section 10 of the 1980 Act. "Private companies" are all companies *other* than public companies and old public companies (as defined in sections 1 and 8 of the 1980 Act).

Conditions to be satisfied

(1) Creditors adequately protected

A private company may only give financial assistance which is within sections 41(1) or 42(2) if,

(a) the company has "net assets"; and

(b) either these net assets are not reduced by the assistance, or the reduction is covered by distributable profits.

"Net assets" means the *book* value of the company's assets less the *book* value of the company's liabilities (including certain contingent or unascertained liabilities as referred to in section 42(11)). The "net assets" are to be determined immediately before the financial assistance is to be given. In deciding whether and to what extent the financial assistance given reduces "net assets", it will presumably be the reduction in the accounts (normally a *book* reduction), which is taken. There is no exclusion for immaterial reductions in net assets. "Distributable profits" means the profits available for distribution under sections 39 to 45 of the 1980 Act, including any unrealised profits on non-cash assets if these are included in the financial assistance (C.A. 1981, s. 62). In computing the profits available for distribution, account must be taken of any distributions already made since the latest accounts, including any financial assistance *already* provided out of distributable profits since the date of those accounts (C.A. 1981, s. 60 and C.A. 1980, s. 43(7)). A private company which, on book values, has a negative net worth can never take advantage of the section 43 procedure to give financial assistance; and a private company with no distributable profits can only do so if the assistance does not reduce its net assets.

The giving of a guarantee or security is capable of reducing a company's net assets. The guarantee or security will be a "liability" to include in the calculation of "net assets" only if it is either "likely" or "certain" that a loss or liability will arise under it. Often, therefore, the giving of a guarantee should not result in any reduction of net assets. Even where it does, it is difficult to know how the reduction is to be calculated. In relation to guarantees, the Government indicated at one stage that the appropriate reduction is the cost of insuring the liability under the guarantee (*Official Report*, Standing Committee A, June 30, 1981, col. 313), though this seems doubtful – probably the reduction if any is that shown in the accounts. The advancing of a loan should not normally reduce "net assets", unless a provision is necessary because of the poor credit of the borrower (see section 42(11)).

In all cases it may be prudent for the directors of the company to obtain an auditor's report on whether the proposed financial assistance will reduce net assets, and if so, by how much. (The report to be given by the auditors in relation to the directors' statutory declaration, mentioned below, does not deal with the "net assets" point.)

The position of creditors is further protected by a requirement that the directors give a statutory declaration as to the solvency of the company.

(2)   Statutory declaration

Each and every director of the company giving the financial assistance is required to make a statutory declaration on a Form 59. Where the financial assistance relates to shares in a holding company of the company, a statutory declaration, on Form 59A, must also be made by each and every director of that holding company and of any intermediate companies (section 43(6)). The Form 59's require details to be given of the proposed assistance, the business of the company whose directors are giving the declaration and the identity of the person to whom the assistance is to be given. In addition, a Form 59 must state that in the director's opinion,

(a)   there will be no ground, immediately following the giving of the assistance, on which the company could be found unable to pay its debts; and

(b)   the company will be able to pay its debts as they fall due within the following twelve months (or, if it is intended to liquidate the company within twelve months, that it will be able to pay its debts in full within twelve months of the liquidation commencing).

The directors are required to take account of the contingent and prospective liabilities of the company in forming their opinion (C.A. 1981, s. 43(7) and C.A. 1948, s. 223(d)). It is not clear if the *full* value of these liabilities has to be taken into account, though it seems probable that the directors need only include contingent or prospective liabilities to the extent they are likely to crystallise in the twelve month period. (This is certainly the view of the Law Society's Standing Committee on

Company Law: *Law Society's Gazette*, July 28, 1982, but see (1983) Co Law 33). One reason for requiring the statutory declaration is that a private company is not required to take account of unrealised losses in calculating its distributable profits.

(3) Auditor's report

Attached to the statutory declaration must be a report from the company's auditors stating that,

(a) they have inquired into the company's state of affairs; and

(b) they are not aware of anything indicating that the directors' opinion as to the matters in *(2)*(a) and (b) above is "unreasonable in all the circumstances".

(4) Special resolution

The giving of the financial assistance must normally be approved by the company's shareholders in general meeting. The exception is where the company is a wholly-owned subsidiary. A company is a "wholly-owned" subsidiary of another if it has no members except that company *and* its wholly-owned subsidiaries and its or their nominees (C.A. 1948, s. 150(4), C.A. 1980, s. 21(1) and C.A. 1948, Sch. 8, para. 95). In addition, if the company is giving the assistance in relation to shares not of it but of a holding company, then the holding company must approve the assistance by special resolution. So too must any intermediate companies between the holding company and the company, apart from wholly-owned subsidiaries. The special resolution or resolutions must be passed on, or within seven days of, the date on which the directors' statutory declaration is given. The resolution will only be effective if the directors' statutory declaration, with the auditors' report annexed, is available for inspection by the shareholders at the general meeting.

(5) Cancellation of special resolution

A shareholder or shareholders who do not consent to or vote for the special resolution may apply to the court for the cancellation of the resolution, provided he (or they) hold at least ten per cent of the nominal value of any class of the company's issued shares. (In the case of a company not limited by shares, the qualification is that the shareholder or shareholders comprise at least ten per cent of the members.) The application for cancellation must be made within 28 days of the special resolution being passed. An application for cancellation is governed by sections 11(4) to 11(10) of the 1980 Act. No guidance is given as to the grounds on which a court may cancel the special resolution, though the court has wide powers to deal with the application as it sees fit. In particular, it can require the company to buy out the dissenting shareholders. An aggrieved shareholder may also petition the court for relief under section 75 of the Companies Act 1980.

(6)   Timing

The financial assistance must be given within eight weeks of the making of the directors' statutory declaration (or of the earliest declaration, where more than one is required). Where a special resolution is required, the assistance cannot be given earlier than four weeks after the passing of the resolution (or of the latest resolution, where more than one is required). The four week time limit does not apply if every shareholder entitled to vote at general meetings voted in favour of the resolution, since it will not then be possible for any shareholder to seek the cancellation of the resolution. If therefore all shareholders agree with the proposed financial assistance, it is important they all vote in favour of the resolution, otherwise a four week delay arises.

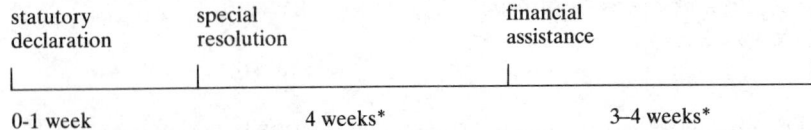

statutory declaration	special resolution		financial assistance
0-1 week	4 weeks*		3–4 weeks*

* not required if special resolution unanimous

If an application for cancellation of a special resolution is made, the assistance cannot be given until the application is finally determined, though the court then has power to extend the eight week deadline.

(7)   Filing

The directors' statutory declaration, with the auditors report attached, and any special resolution passed by the company whose directors gave the declaration, must be lodged with the Registrar of Companies within 15 days of the passing of the special resolution. If no special resolution is required – i.e. where the company in question is a wholly-owned subsidiary – the declaration and report must be lodged within 15 days after the declaration is made.

Consequences of breach of section 42

Criminal penalties

If a company gives financial assistance in breach of sections 42(1) or 42(2), then both the company, and any "officer who is in default", are liable,

(a) on conviction on indictment, to up to two years imprisonment and/or a fine;

(b) on summary conviction, to up to six months imprisonment and/or a fine not exceeding the statutory maximum (currently £1,000 – see sections 28(2) and 61 of the Criminal Law Act 1977).

The term "officer" extends beyond a director to include anyone occupying the position of a director, such as an alternate director, and also to a manager or secretary (section 455(1) of the 1948 Act). For a person to be a manager he must probably be someone who has wide powers of management of the company's business (see *Gibson v. Barton* (1875) L.R. 10 Q.B. 329). An officer's knowledge will normally be imputed to the company (*Belmont Finance Corporation Limited v. Williams Furniture Limited* [1980] 1 All E.R. 395).

Persons involved in a breach of sections 42(1) or 42(2) could also be subject to a charge of conspiracy (see particularly sections 1 to 4 of the Criminal Law Act 1977).

A director of a private company who makes a statutory declaration under section 43 without having reasonable grounds for the opinion expressed is liable to the same penalties as a person in breach of section 42 itself (s. 44(7)).

Civil consequences

The 1981 Act does not give any guidance as to the civil consequences of a breach of section 42. Reference must therefore be made to the court decisions on section 54 of the 1948 Act. These demonstrate that the consequences can be severe. In summary the position is as follows.

(1) Transaction void

The transaction in breach of section 42 appears to be void: *Heald v. O'Connor* [1971] 1 W.L.R. 497; *Selangor United Rubber Estates Limited v. Cradock (No. 3)* [1968] 1 W.L.R. 1555 at 1656; *E. H. Dey v. Dey* [1966] V.R. 464 (cf. the earlier cases of *Victor Battery Co. Limited v. Currys Limited* [1946] Ch. 262 and *Spink (Bournemouth) Limited v. Spink* [1936] Ch. 544).

This means that any property transferred in the transaction, such as loan moneys or an asset sold at undervalue, is irrecoverable (though see (4) below), and that any guarantee or security given is unenforceable. But if the guarantee is simply a guarantee by a third party of a loan which is in breach of section 42 the guarantee itself may be enforceable, depending on its terms (*Heald*).

(2) Severance of illegal element

However, it may in certain cases be possible to sever the illegal part of a transaction and leave the rest of the agreement enforceable (see *South Western Mineral Water Co. Limited v. Ashmore* [1967] 1 W.L.R. 1110 and note the two Australian cases of *Vam Limited v. Macdonald* [1970] 3 N.S.W.R. 3 and *Nieman v. Smedley* [1973] V.R. 769).

(3) Breach of fiduciary duties

Any director who procures that the company enters into the illegal transaction will be in breach of his fiduciary duties to the company. He can be sued by the company for breach of trust and required to make good any loss suffered by the company (*Belmont Finance Corporation Limited v. Williams Furniture Limited* [1980] 1 All E.R. 395; *Wallersteiner v. Moir* [1974] 1 W.L.R. 991). The breach of trust action extends to agents of the director who acted in awareness of the breach. An action can be brought not only by the company, but by its liquidator or, generally, a minority shareholder (*Re Smith & Fawcett* [1942] Ch. 304). An honest belief that the transaction is not in breach of section 42 is no defence (*Belmont*).

(4)   Liability as constructive trustee

The company or its liquidator may be able to recover property from a third party who has acted with knowledge of the facts, on the basis that the third party is a constructive trustee (*Belmont, Selangor* and *Karak Rubber Co. Limited v. Burden* [1972] 1 W.L.R. 602). A bank or other third party which receives a company's funds with actual or constructive knowledge of the breach must return the funds (unless he has "some better equity" against the company: *Belmont* at 405). The fact that the third party is acting without any fraud or dishonesty is not a defence. Moreover, a third party who participates in a transaction which is in breach of section 42 may be liable as a constructive trustee even where no property comes into his hands, if he has knowingly participated in a dishonest design (*Belmont; Barnes v. Addy* [1874] 9 Ch. App. at 251).

(5)   Liability for conspiracy

Where there is a scheme or arrangement involving a breach of section 42, the company can, as an alternative to an action for breach of trust, sue either or both of the directors and *any other participants* in tort, for conspiracy (*Belmont*). It is probably not a defence to such an action that the participants have acted on Counsel's, or other legal advice and/or have an honest belief that no breach of section 42 is involved (*Belmont*). The company need only show (a) a combination by the participants (b) to effect an unlawful purpose (c) which results in damage to the plaintiff. A sincere but erroneous belief in the *facts* may however give a defence. Damages recoverable in tort may be slightly wider than those in contract. Simple or compound interest may be added by the court to any damages awarded.

(6)   Misfeasance proceedings under section 333

If the company which commits a breach of section 42 is subsequently liquidated, a director or officer who has participated in the breach may be subject to misfeasance proceedings under section 333 of the Companies Act 1948.

Other points

(a)   If financial assistance is given in contravention of section 42, then for certain purposes the company's distributable profits are to be reduced to the extent the assistance reduces net assets or increases net liabilities (section 60(1)). But where unlawful financial assistance is given which is also an unlawful distribution under the 1980 Companies Act, section 44 of the 1980 Act (return of unlawful distributions by recipient) will not apply.

(b) In certain circumstances shares in a public company acquired with financial assistance (whether or not unlawful and even if the assistance is only "in connection" with the acquisition) are to be cancelled (section 37(1) of the 1980 Act).

(c) A minority shareholder who objects to an act or proposed act of financial assistance (lawful or unlawful) may have a wide range of remedies under section 75 of the 1980 Act (relief where shareholders are unfairly prejudiced).

(d) The Court of Appeal judgments in the *Belmont* case emphasise the importance of directors obtaining independent professional advice in relation to any transaction which could infringe section 42. This extends not simply to legal advice (and incorrect advice will only ameliorate and not avoid the criminal and civil consequences of breach), but also to financial advice, for example as to the value of property or assets to be bought or sold.

(e) Solicitors and other professional advisers acting for a company in a transaction where a breach of section 42 could arise should ensure that the company is fully advised of the legal position, the importance of the purpose tests and the serious criminal and civil consequences arising on a breach of section 42. Particularly where the purpose tests may be relevant the company should be advised to consider the matter carefully at full board level, with detailed minutes being kept where appropriate.

(f) Banks and other third party lenders must keep a watchful eye on how repayment is made of a loan advanced for the purpose of acquiring a company's shares. If the loan is repaid in breach of section 42, for example out of a loan made by the acquired company, the bank may be liable as constructive trustee to repay the funds received if it has actual or constructive knowledge of the breach. This means that banks can be in a very vulnerable position. *Some* protection may be afforded if the loan agreement contains a covenant requiring the borrower to notify the bank if payments are made out of funds received otherwise than in a specified manner (and see *Official Report*, House of Lords, April 7, 1981, col. 481). Where a company is relying on the "purpose" exceptions this may result in the bank being forced to decide for itself whether the "principal or larger purpose" and "the good faith in the interests of the company" tests are met.

Formation and Types of Company

This chapter is divided into the following sections,

(a) the nature of a company and how it differs from an unincorporated business;

(b) lifting the veil of incorporation;

(c) types of companies (including public companies, private companies, companies limited by guarantee, unlimited companies, holding and subsidiary companies);

(d) practical steps on the incorporation of a private limited company; and

(e) ready made companies.

The nature of a company

Separate legal identity

A company is, from the date of incorporation, a separate legal entity distinct from its members. This fundamental principle of company law was established by the House of Lords in the case of *Salomon v. Salomon* [1897] A.C. 22. From it can be derived the main characteristics of a company.

First, a company's property belongs to it alone and not to its individual shareholders. The converse is also true. A company's debts and liabilities are its obligations alone and cannot generally be enforced against its members. This contrasts with the position of a partnership. Here the property belongs to the partners and they are personally liable for the firm's debts (there is an exception in the case of limited partnerships registered under the Limited Partnerships Act 1907).

From this principle stems the concept of limited liability, a concept which is sometimes mistakenly believed to refer to the liability of the company. A company is always liable without limit for its own debts, and so long as it has assets to pay such debts, it can be forced to pay them. However the liability of its shareholders may, depending on the type of company, be limited. In the case of a company limited by shares the shareholders are generally only obliged to contribute to the company the amount (if any) which is not paid up on the shares that they hold and, in the case of a company limited by guarantee, they are only obliged to contribute the amount they have guaranteed to contribute to

400

the company in the case of its being wound up. (The liability of shareholders in an unlimited company to contribute to its assets is however unlimited.)

Secondly, a company has perpetual succession unless it is wound-up or dissolved. Neither death of its members nor any other changes in its membership affect its continued existence as a separate person.

Thirdly, a company can sue and be sued in its own name. The same is also true of a partnership (Rules of the Supreme Court, Order 81). However, in the latter case, the action is still brought by the partners and their liability in respect of the firm's debts is not affected by this.

Fourthly, the interests which members of a company have in it (i.e. their shares) are a separate form of intangible property which can be transferred to others without affecting the continued existence of the company. By contrast, a change of partners terminates a partnership. Even if the remaining partners agree that the firm will continue, the partnership is different from that which previously existed.

This characteristic of companies is frequently utilised when a business run by a company is to be disposed of. It is more common for the members of the company to sell their shares in it (thereby avoiding a cessation of the company's business and the tax consequences which arise on cessation) instead of arranging for the company to sell the various assets of the business. On the other hand a sole trader or partnership has no such choice (unless the business is incorporated before sale).

Fifthly, a company is subject to the *ultra vires* rule. It may therefore be restricted by its memorandum of association from carrying out certain activities (see the chapter *Memorandum of Association*).

Sixthly, a company, unlike a sole trader or partnership, has the power to give security for its borrowings by creating a floating charge over all its assets, or any class of assets.

Memorandum and articles

As a separate legal entity a company can only act through agents. The activities of a company and its agents are regulated by its memorandum and articles of association.

Broadly, the memorandum governs the company's external affairs; its purpose is primarily to state what the company has been formed to do. In practice, however, a company's predominant activity will often not be immediately apparent from an inspection of its memorandum – this is the result of determined attempts by draftsmen to avoid the *ultra vires* rule. It also indicates, amongst other things, the amount of share capital which the company is authorised to issue and the extent of each shareholder's liability to the company, that is, whether the company is limited by shares or guarantee, or is unlimited (see *Memorandum*).

The articles, on the other hand, regulate the company's internal affairs (see the chapter *Articles of Association*). The day to day management of a modern company is invariably vested in its directors and the articles deal with their appointment, powers and removal (see further page 470). They will also lay down procedures for board meetings, including quorums, notice and voting. Ultimate control of a company is vested in the general meeting of shareholders, though in practice the diversity of the shareholdings in large public companies often makes it difficult for such control to be effectively exercised. In particular the Companies Acts specifically provide for the general meeting to exercise certain powers in relation to the allotment of shares, alteration of the company's articles, the declaration of dividends and voluntary winding up. The conduct of such meetings will also be governed by the articles (subject to the provisions of the Companies Acts).

Lifting the veil of incorporation

Whilst generally it is not possible to look behind the separate personality of a company, there are exceptions to this principle. In certain circumstances the actions and property of a company are treated as those of its members and the members can be made liable for the company's debts. This is commonly referred to as "lifting the veil of incorporation". An example would be where a person wishing to avoid an existing agreement to sell his land to a third party conveys the land to a company which he controls. In such a case the courts might grant a decree of specific performance to the third party against the company on the basis that the company is the alter ego of the vendor (see *Jones v. Lipman* [1962] 1 W.L.R. 832).

The circumstances in which the veil of incorporation will be lifted can be split into two categories,

(a) under express statutory provision; and

(b) under case law.

The first category is comparatively well established. Examples of it include the following.

Statutory provisions

Section 31 of the Companies Act 1948

This section, as amended by the Companies Act 1980, provides that if a company carries on business for more than six months with less than two members, any person who (i) is a member (not a director) of the company during the time that it carries on business after those six months, and (ii) knows that it is carrying on a business with only one member, is jointly and severally liable with the company for the company's debts contracted during that period. It is possible for two persons to be so liable in respect of different periods.

The requirement in section 31 that a company should have a minimum of two members is often effectively nullified in practice by arranging for one of two members to hold a single share as a nominee for the other member. It should be noted that this section does not remove the separate legal personality of the company – it simply makes the member or members jointly and severally liable with the company for its debts.

Section 332 of the Companies Acts 1948 (fraudulent trading)

Section 332 provides that if in the course of the winding-up of a company, it appears that any business of the company has been carried on with intent to defraud creditors or others or for any other fraudulent purpose, the court, on the application of the official receiver, the liquidator, a creditor or member (including certain former members), may declare that any persons who were knowingly parties to the carrying on of the business in such a manner shall be personally responsible without limit for all or any of the debts or other liabilities of the company. (The section also contains criminal sanctions which can be invoked whether or not the company is being wound-up; C.A. 1981, s. 96.)

To be a "party to" the carrying on of business within the meaning of the section a person must take some positive steps in the carrying on of the company's business in a fraudulent manner; mere omission to take steps to prevent its doing so is not enough (*Re Maidstone Building Provisions Ltd.* [1971] 1 W.L.R. 1085).

Section 108(4) of the Companies Act 1948

This section provides that where an officer of a company or any other person acting on its behalf signs or authorises the signature of any cheque, bill of exchange or order for money or goods on which the name of the company is not properly set out, the officer is personally liable to the holder of the cheque or similar item for the amount of it unless it is paid by the company. This includes the omission of the word "Limited" at the end of the name (see *Atkins & Co. v. Wardle* [1889] 5 T.L.R. 734, and *Durham Fancy Goods Ltd. v. Michael Jackson (Fancy Goods) Ltd.* [1968] 2 Q.B. 839. See also *Hendon v. Adelman* (1973) 117 S.J. 631 (omission of ampersand in name fatal), *British Airways Board v. Parish* (1979) 2 Ll. Rep. 361 (omission of "Limited" fatal); *Maxform SpA v. Mariani* (1979) 2 Ll. Rep. 387 and *Banque de l'Indochine et de Suez SA v. Euroseas Group Finance Co.* [1981] 3 All E.R. ("Co" instead of "Company" not fatal) and *Barber & Nicholls Ltd. v. R. & G. Associates (London)* [1981] CAT 455 (omission of "London" fatal).

Section 4(8) of the Companies Act 1980

This section operates where a *public* company enteres into a transaction before it has obtained from the Registrar of Companies a certificate confirming he is satisfied that the nominal value of the company's allotted share capital is not less than the authorised minimum (currently £50,000). If the company fails to comply with its obligations in connection with the transaction within 21 days of its being called upon to do so, the directors of the company will be jointly and severally liable to indemnify the other party to the transaction if the company fails to comply with its obligations.

Taxation

The veil of incorporation is frequently lifted under express statutory authority in matters involving taxation. For instance, the income of a close company may be treated for income tax purposes as belonging to its members (F.A. 1972, s. 94 and Sch. 16) and, for capital transfer tax purposes, a transfer of value by a close company may be apportioned among its "participators" (F.A. 1975, s. 39). Similarly, where companies form part of a 75 per cent group within the meaning of section 532 of the Taxes Act 1970, one member of the group may set against its trading profits trading losses incurred by another member (T.A. 1970, s. 258) and companies within the group can be made liable for one another's tax liability (see, for example, sections 277 to 279 of the Taxes Act 1970).

Case law

It is only when the second category, case law, is considered that the scope of the doctrine of lifting the veil becomes less clear. The decided cases do not provide a general principle under which the courts will permit the veil to be lifted – they merely indicate that in certain circumstances the judiciary will refuse to apply the principles laid down in *Salomon's* case. Some of these cases are difficult to reconcile with others where the courts have refused to lift the veil. Examples may be split into three main categories.

Fraud

It is well established that the courts will not permit the veil of incorporation to be used for the purpose of fraud or dishonesty, or for any improper purpose, for example to avoid legal obligations. The most often cited example of this principle is the case of *Gilford Motor Company v. Horne* [1933] Ch. 935 where Horne, a former employee of the plaintiff, attempted to avoid a restrictive covenant imposed on him by his former employer by forming a company which provided his services. The courts described the company as "a mere cloak" for his activities and granted an injunction to enforce the restrictive covenant against Horne and the company he had formed. A further example is the case of *Jones v. Lipman* (see above).

Agency

Where there is an agency arrangement between a company and its members, the courts are prepared to lift the veil of incorporation and treat the acts of the company as those of its members. This possibility was recognised by Lord Halsbury in the *Salomon* case. But in reality this is not an example of veil lifting under the principles of company law but merely an application of the general rules of principal and agent.

An agency may be constituted by express agreement (see *Southern v. Watson* [1940] 3 All E.R. 439 and *Rainham Chemical Works Ltd. v. Belvedere Fish Guano Company Ltd.* [1921] 2 A.C. 465). Alternatively, the courts may be asked to *imply* an agency arrangement to permit the veil of incorporation to be lifted. In the case of *Smith, Stone & Knight Ltd. v. Birmingham Corporation* [1939] 4 All E.R. 116, Atkinson J. held that a business belonged to the plaintiff company although it was carried on in the name of its subsidiary; accordingly, the plaintiff was in occupation of premises at which the business was carried on and was entitled to compensation for the disturbance of *its* business when the premises were compulsorily purchased by the local authority.

Similarly, in *Wallersteiner v. Moir (No. 2)* [1974] 1 W.L.R. 991, Lord Denning M.R. viewed various companies through which Mr. Wallersteiner had operated as "puppets". He continued:

> "He controlled their every movement. Each danced to his bidding. He pulled the strings. No-one else got within reach of them. Transformed into legal language they were his agents to do as he commanded. He was the principal behind them. I am of the opinion that the court should pull aside the corporate veil and treat these concerns as being his creatures – for whose doings he should be, and is, responsible".

However, in a number of other cases the courts have refused to lift the corporate veil despite the apparent existence of an agency relationship. (Examples include *Wm. Cory & Sons Ltd. v. Dorman Long & Co.* [1936] 2 All E.R. 386, *Ebbw Vale UDC v. South Wales Traffic Area Licensing Authority* [1951] 2 K.B. 366 and *Tunstall v. Steigmann* [1962] 2 Q.B. 593.)

More recently, in the capital gains tax avoidance case of *Burman v. Hedges & Butler* [1979] S.T.C. 160, Walton J., in rejecting the Inland Revenue's argument that a subsidiary was the agent of its parent, indicated that this conclusion could not be arrived at simply because a subsidiary conformed to the wishes of its parent or pursued policies which commended themselves to the parent company. He also stated that the question of whether a subsidiary company was an agent of its parent was one to be determined by a consideration not merely of the position of the subsidiary but of the whole of the facts of the case, including the relationship between the parties and the documents and engagements which each of them had entered into. Similarly, in the case of *I.R.C. v. Burmah Oil Co. Ltd.* [1982] S.T.C. 30 (which also involved a tax avoidance scheme) the Special Commissioners refused to accept that the roles played by Burmah's subsidiaries in the scheme were those of nominees or agents. This was despite their finding that the relevant transactions were preplanned and would, having regard to Burmah's status as parent of the other companies concerned and the composition of the boards of directors of those companies, have almost inevitably been carried out precisely according to plan. (This did not prevent the House of Lords finding in the Inland Revenue's favour on the basis of the principle applied in *W. T. Ramsay Ltd. v. I.R.C.* [1981] S.T.C. 174, indicating that the "form and substance" principle applied in *Ramsay* and *Burmah* is a separate and wider concept than that of "lifting the veil".)

In the absence of an express nominee or agency relationship, the position therefore appears to be that the veil will only be set aside on the ground of agency where the evidence clearly and unambiguously shows that a person so closely controls and directs the activities of a company, that the company is as a matter of fact merely acting as an agent on behalf of that person.

Associated companies

There is some evidence that in the case of associated companies the courts have, in addition to the possibility of construing an agency relationship, been prepared to lift the corporate veil by reason of the commercial and economic inter-relationship that exists between them. Lord Denning in particular has shown a willingness to treat separate members of a group of companies as one economic entity. This approach can be seen in such cases as *Littlewoods Mail Order Stores Limited v. IRC* (45 T.C. 519) and *D.H.N. v. London Borough of Tower Hamlets* [1976] 1 W.L.R. 852.

However, this approach has been doubted in the subsequent cases of *Woolfson v. Strathclyde Regional Council* [1977] S.L.T. 159 and *Rakusen Properties Limited v. Leeds City Council* (1979) S.J. 848, and it seems that there is no general principle of English law that a group of companies will be viewed as one entity by reason only of a group relationship.

Other cases where the corporate veil may be lifted include "overriding public interest" and trusteeship. However, these are of limited scope. Most of the examples falling within the first category concern questions of nationality in wartime. The trusteeship cases, which involve construing a trust between a company and its members so that the company as trustee holds its property on trust for the members, are somewhat exceptional, and again may be no more than the application of general trust law.

It therefore seems that, in the absence of express statutory provision, the courts will generally only lift the corporate veil if there is fraud or improper purpose, or clear factual evidence of an agency relationship.

Types of company

Section 1(2) of the Companies Act 1948 provided for three types of companies: companies limited by shares, companies limited by guarantee and unlimited companies. The latter two categories could under that Act be formed either with or without a share capital and, in addition, each type of company could be formed either as a public or a private

Types of companies capable of incorporation under C.A. 1948	Whether capable of incorporation under C.A. 1980	Whether may continue to exist after March 21, 1982	Obligations (if any) during re-registration period
Public companies limited by shares	Yes	Yes	Obliged to re-register as a PLC or a private company
Private companies limited by shares	Yes	Yes	No action required
Public companies limited by guarantee without a share capital	No	No	Automatically became private
Private companies limited by guarantee without a share capital	Yes	Yes	No action required (must remain private)
Public companies limited by guarantee with a share capital	No	Yes	Obliged to re-register as a PLC or a private company
Private companies limited by guarantee with a share capital	No	Yes	No action required
Public unlimited companies without a share capital	No	No	Automatically became private
Private unlimited companies without a share capital	Yes	Yes	No action necessary (must remain private)
Public unlimited companies with a share capital	No	No	Automatically became private
Private unlimited companies with a share capital	Yes	Yes	No action necessary (must remain private)

company. Thus, in total, ten different types of company could exist under that Act.

The Companies Act 1980 has substantially simplified the position. Some types of company can no longer *exist* and other types of company can no longer *be formed*. To facilitate the changeover, the Act provided for a fifteen month re-registration period which ended on March 21, 1982. During the re-registration period old public companies which were limited by shares or limited by guarantee and with a share capital were obliged to re-register as either public or private companies under the 1980 Act. Public companies limited by guarantee without a share capital and any unlimited public companies automatically became private companies.

The position following the expiry of the re-registration period is summarised in the table on page 407. (Voluntary re-registrations, which are permitted under the 1980 Act and which continue to be available after March 21, 1982, are considered below.)

Public companies

Prior to the 1980 Act a public company was defined by exclusion; it was any company which did not satisfy the definition of a private company contained in section 28 of the 1948 Act. This is now reversed. Section 1 of the 1980 Act defines a public company as one (i) limited by shares or limited by guarantee and having a share capital (ii) whose memorandum states that the company is to be a public company and (iii) which is registered or re-registered as a public company under the provisions of the 1980 Act. Thus, unlimited companies and companies limited by guarantee without a share capital will now be private companies. Companies limited by guarantee with a share capital may no longer be formed, although the few companies of this type that existed prior to the 1980 Act may continue to do so.

This definition gives little indication of how a public company differs from a private company. The main differences of *form* between the two arise from the requirements with which a public company must comply in order to register under the 1980 Act. There are three main differences.

First, the company's name must end with the words "public limited company" or, if it is a Welsh company, the Welsh equivalent, "cwmni cyfyngedig cyhoeddus." (A company is a Welsh company if its memorandum states that its registered office is to be in Wales: C.A. 1980, s. 2(2).) The abbreviations p.l.c. and c.c.c. respectively are permitted by section 78 of the 1980 Act, and the former is now widely used.

Secondly, the company's memorandum must be in the form set out in Schedule 1 to the 1980 Act, or as near to it as circumstances permit (C.A. 1980, s. 2(4)). Companies limited by shares should adopt the form set out in Part 1 of the Schedule and the form for any companies limited by guarantee with a share capital is now contained in Part II.

Effectively, the new requirement is for a specific clause stating that the company is to be a public company.

Thirdly, the nominal value of the company's allotted share capital must be not less than the authorised minimum (C.A. 1980, s. 4(2)). This is at present fixed at £50,000, but the Secretary of State has power to vary that figure by statutory instrument. At least one quarter of the allotted share capital must be paid up before the company can commence business.

Public companies are no longer required to have a minimum number of seven members – two is sufficient, as in the case of private companies.

Subject to section 2(4) of the 1980 Act (form of memorandum, see above), the documents that must be lodged with the Registrar of Companies in order to incorporate a public company have not altered. Provided they are in order and the Registrar is satisfied that all the requirements of the Companies Acts relating to incorporation and registration have been met, he will issue a certificate of incorporation. This is conclusive evidence that all the requirements have been complied with (C.A. 1980, s. 3(4)). However, a *newly incorporated* public company will require from the Registrar a further certificate, similar to the old trading certificate required under section 109 of the Companies Act 1948, before it is able to do business or exercise borrowing powers (C.A. 1980, s. 4). To obtain this certificate it must satisfy the Registrar that its share capital is adequate. This may be done by filing with the Registrar a statutory declaration, on Form 8, made by a director or the secretary of the company, stating that the nominal value of the company's allotted share capital is not less than the authorised minimum. Form 8 must also give the following details,

(a) the amount paid up, at the time of application, on the allotted share capital (shares allotted must be paid up at least as to one-quarter of the nominal value and the whole of any premium);

(b) the amount (or estimated amount) of the preliminary expenses and the persons by whom these expenses have been paid or are payable;

(c) any amount or benefit paid or given (or intended to be paid or given) to the promoters of the company and the consideration for the payment of the benefit.

Failure to obtain the certificate before a company commences business renders both the company and its officers in default liable to a fine. The validity of any transaction that has been entered into is not affected, although the directors will be jointly and severally liable to indemnify the other parties to the transaction if the company fails to comply with its obligations in connection with that transaction within twenty-one days of its being called upon to do so. If the certificate has not been issued within one year of the company's registration, the company may be wound-up by the court under section 222 of the 1948 Act.

Why be a public company?

The only advantage of a public company over a private company under the 1980 Act is that the former has the right to (i) offer shares or debentures to the public (for cash or otherwise) or to (ii) allot such securities with a view to their being offered for sale to the public, or both (C.A. 1980, s. 15).

In return for this benefit, public companies are subjected to far more stringent controls than private companies. These include, in addition to the restriction on minimum share capital mentioned above, the following.

Pre-emption rights on allotment of shares

The statutory pre-emption provisions which apply on the allotment of shares (contained in sections 17 to 19 of the 1980 Act) may, in the case of a private company, be excluded by a provision contained in its memorandum or articles (C.A. 1980, s. 17(9)). Both public and private companies can, however, avoid the statutory pre-emption provisions by giving the directors authority to allot shares in accordance with section 14 of the 1980 Act and including in that authority a power to allot in disregard of the statutory provisions (C.A. 1980, s. 18(1) and the chapter *Shares*). However, the authority must be renewed every five years (C.A. 1980, s. 18(3)).)

Payment for share capital

Sections 20 to 31 of the 1980 Act contain a number of detailed rules concerning the payment for shares allotted by companies, most of which relate only to public companies. These are dealt with in greater detail in the chapter *Shares*, but in outline the position is as follows.

(1) A public company may not allot shares unless at least 25 per cent of the nominal value and the whole of any premium has been paid up (section 22(1)).

(2) A public company is prohibited from accepting an undertaking to *do work* or *perform services* as consideration for the allotment of shares (section 20(2)).

(3) Where a public company allots shares as fully or partly paid in exchange for a non-cash consideration, any undertaking which forms part of that consideration (e.g. to transfer assets to the company) must be performed within five years of the allotment (section 23). Further a prior expert's valuation and report on the consideration given will usually be required (section 24).

(4) The original subscribers to the memorandum of a public company must pay for those shares in cash (section 29).

(5) Section 26 contains special provisions dealing with the acquisition of non-cash assets from the original subscribers to the memoran-

dum of a public company (or from members at the time of registration or re-registration as a public company under the Act).

Maintenance of capital

If at any time after December 21, 1980 the net assets of a public company are reduced to 50 per cent or less of its called up share capital, the directors must convene an extraordinary general meeting within 28 days of the date on which any one of them becomes aware of the fact (C.A. 1980, s. 34). The meeting is to be held within 56 days. The purpose of the meeting is to consider what measures, if any, should be taken to deal with the situation – there is no obligation to undertake specific measures.

Distribution of profits

A public company is subject to additional restrictions on the distribution of profits to those applicable to *all* companies set out in section 39 of the 1980 Act. A distribution can only be made by a public company if its net assets do not fall below the aggregate of its called up share capital and its "undistributable reserves" (C.A. 1980, s. 40; see the chapter *Dividends*).

Loans to directors

Where a group of companies includes a public company, the rules concerning loans to directors are extended (in relation to each company in the group). Broadly, the effect of these provisions is to prohibit or restrict transactions in the nature of or in substitution for loans (C.A. 1980, s. 49; see the chapter *Loans to Directors*).

Purchase of own shares

Both public and private companies may issue redeemable shares. They may also purchase their own shares (C.A. 1981, ss. 45 and 46). However, only a private company can apply capital in the purchase or redemption of its shares where it has insufficient profits available (C.A. 1981, s. 54; and see the chapter *Purchase and Holding of Own Shares*). Note that section 53 of and Schedule 9 to the Finance Act 1982, which remove some of the tax disadvantages where a company purchases its own shares, apply only to *unquoted* companies, as defined in the 1982 Act.

Financial assistance for acquisition of shares

The prohibition against companies providing financial assistance for the purchase of their shares contained in section 42 of the 1981 Act is relaxed in the case of private companies. Section 43 of the 1981 Act has introduced a procedure whereby, in certain cases, private companies may provide financial assistance, subject to various safeguards for creditors and shareholders being complied with (see the chapter *Financial Assistance*).

Accounting requirements

Public companies cannot take advantage of the provisions contained in sections 5 to 10 of the 1981 Act permitting "small" and "medium sized" companies to file with the Registrar less detailed accounts, nor can they qualify as "dormant" companies so as to dispense with auditors (see pages 19 and 20).

Other items

Other differences between a public and a private company include rules governing the age and number of directors, voting on directors' appointments, and the ability of proxies to speak at general meetings.

Any company considering whether to register as a public company should weigh up the above matters carefully. There is little point in a company assuming the more onerous obligations of a public company unless it is likely in the fairly near future to offer its securities to the public.

Private companies

A private company is now defined as any company that is not a public company (C.A. 1980, s. 1(1)). Section 28 of the 1948 Act, which formerly contained the definition of a private company, has been repealed.

The effect is to free private companies from two of the three restrictions previously contained in section 28. They need no longer insert provisions in their articles limiting the number of their members to fifty; neither need their articles restrict members' ability to transfer shares. However private companies are still generally prohibited from offering their shares or debentures to the public. (This prohibition, which is now contained in section 15 of the 1980 Act, does not extend to companies limited by guarantee which do not have a share capital; such companies have no shares to offer but they are not precluded from seeking to borrow from the public.)

New private companies, that is those incorporated after December 21, 1980, are in practice likely to dispense with any restriction in their articles on the maximum number of shareholders, but in many cases they will no doubt continue to adopt articles restricting the transfer of shares. Shareholders will often continue to require clauses giving pre-emption rights to enable them to prevent control of their company passing to "outsiders".

As the repeals are not retrospective, articles of old private companies, that is those incorporated prior to December 22, 1980, will continue to contain the restrictions required by section 28 unless positive steps are taken to alter them. Where pre-emption rights on transfer are to be retained (which will normally be the case), alteration will only be *necessary* if the restriction on the number of members is becoming burdensome. However, where private companies are intending to alter the articles anyway, for example to take account the new restrictions on allotment of shares contained in sections 14 and 17 of the 1980 Act, they may well want to take the opportunity to remove the limit on the number of members at the same time.

Offers to the public

Section 15 of the 1980 Act makes it a criminal offence for a private limited company (other than a company limited by guarantee not having a share capital),

(a) to offer to the public, for cash or otherwise, any of its shares or debentures; or

(b) to allot or agree to allot, for cash or otherwise, any such shares or debentures with a view to all or any of them being offered for sale to the public.

It is clearly important to establish what is an "offer to the public". These words are used in sections 45(2) and 55 of the 1948 Act and both the sections will apply for the purpose of determining whether there has been a breach of section 15. This question is considered in greater detail in the chapter *Prospectuses and Public Issues*, but in outline the position is as follows.

By virtue of section 45(2) of the 1948 Act, there is in effect a presumption that an allotment or an agreement to allot shares or debentures is made with a view to them being offered for sale to the public, if

(a) a subsequent offer for sale of any of the shares or debentures is made to the public within six months after the allotment or the agreement to allot; or

(b) at the date when the offer was made the whole of the consideration to be received by the company had not been received.

By virtue of section 55(1), references to the public include *any* section of the public. However, section 55(2) provides that an offer is not treated as made to the public if it can properly be regarded "in all the circumstances" as being *a domestic concern* of the persons making and receiving it (section 55(2)). The meaning of this phrase has been clarified by the 1980 Act by the addition of a new section 55(3), the effect of which is to create a presumption that an offer of shares or debentures in a private company to, broadly, existing members or employees is not an offer for sale to the public. By virtue of section 55(3) there is a *rebuttable* presumption that an offer of shares or debentures of a private company is the domestic concern of the persons making or receiving it if it is,

(a) an offer made to (i) an existing member of the company or (ii) an existing employee of the company, or (iii) a member of the family (as defined by section 55(4)) of an existing member or employee or (iv) a debentureholder; or

(b) an offer of shares or debentures to be held under an existing employees' share scheme, as defined by section 87 of the 1980 Act; or

(c) an offer falling within (a) or (b) above and made on terms permitting renunciation in favour of a person mentioned in (a) above or, where there is an employees' share scheme, a person entitled to hold shares under such a scheme.

It should be noted however that an allotment by a company to its members on renounceable letters of allotment may be treated as an offer to the public, unless the renouncement is limited to its existing members or employees or their families.

If a company contravenes section 15, both it and every officer in default are liable to a fine. Any allotment or sale of shares or any agreement to allot or sell remains valid.

The formation procedures for a private company have not altered as a result of the changes introduced by the 1980 Act, save that a new statutory declaration of compliance is required and, where Table A is adopted, the articles will be different. (The 1980 Act made a number of modifications to Table A as set out in the 1948 Act.)

Re-registration of a private company as a public company

Sections 5 and 6 of the 1980 Act, which came into force on December 22, 1980, provide for the re-registration of private companies as public companies (other than private companies which have no share capital or are old public companies). As explained above, the distinction between the two is now more significant than it was prior to 1980 and this is reflected in the re-registration procedure.

A private company wishing to re-register is required to pass a special resolution. However, it must also be able to satisfy the conditions laid down by the 1980 Act relating to its share capital. These are as follows.

(a) the nominal value of the company's allotted share capital must not be less than the authorised minimum, at present £50,000 (C.A. 1980, s. 6(1)(a));

(b) not less than 25 per cent of the nominal value of each share allotted, together with the whole of any premium, must be paid up (C.A. 1980, s. 6(1)(b));

(c) where any of the company's shares or any premium payable on them have been fully or partly paid up by an undertaking to do work or perform services for the company or a third party, the undertaking must have been performed or otherwise discharged (C.A. 1980, s. 6(1)(c)); and

(d) where any of the company's shares have been allotted as fully or partly paid as to either the nominal value or any premium for a non-cash consideration, and the consideration consisted of or included an undertaking other than one described in paragraph (c) above (e.g. an undertaking to transfer assets), that undertaking must either have been performed or discharged or there must be a contract which requires the undertaking to be performed within five years (C.A. 1980, s. 6(1)(d)).

For the purpose of determining whether these requirements are complied with, two types of shares may be disregarded. The first type is shares allotted in pursuance of an employee share scheme which are not 25 per cent paid up or the premiums (if any) on which are unpaid. The second type is shares allotted before June 22, 1982, provided that the aggregate of all the shares that it is proposed to disregard by virtue of this exception does not exceed 10 per cent of the nominal value of the company's allotted share capital, excluding employee share scheme shares of the type referred to above (C.A. 1980, s. 6(2)).

Further, if the company has allotted any shares for a non-cash consideration between the balance sheet date – a date not more than seven months before the company's application for registration – and the passing of the special resolution to re-register, the consideration for the allotment must have been valued in accordance with the provisions of section 24 of the 1980 Act (experts' report on non-cash consideration before allotment of shares). Also, a report as to the value of the consideration must have been made to the company in accordance with those provisions during the six month period immediately preceding the allotment (C.A. 1980, s. 5(5)).

Provided it satisfies these requirements, the company must then pass the appropriate special resolution and deliver an application to the Registrar in the prescribed form, Form R5.

The special resolution

The special resolution which a private company re-registering as a public company is required to pass by section 5(2) of the 1980 Act must,

(a) state that the company should be re-registered as a public company;

(b) alter the company's memorandum to state that the company is to be a public company;

(c) otherwise alter the memorandum to comply with Schedule 1 to the 1980 Act – this will involve changing the company's name to indicate that it is a public limited company; and

(d) alter the company's articles as required, e.g. to remove any articles inserted under section 17(9) of the 1980 Act and, possibly, to remove any restrictions on transferability.

A copy of the special resolution must be sent to the Registrar within 15 days.

The application for re-registration

Section 5(3) of the 1980 Act requires the application for re-registration to be signed by a director or the secretary of the company, and to be accompanied by,

(a) a printed copy of the memorandum and articles as altered by the special resolution;

(b) a copy of a written statement by the auditors of the company that, in their opinion, the relevant balance sheet (a balance sheet prepared as at a date not more than seven months before the company's application for re-registration) shows that at the balance sheet date the company's net assets were not less than the aggregate of its called-up share capital and undistributable reserves (these terms are defined by sections 87(1) and 40 of the 1980 Act).

(c) a copy of the relevant balance sheet together with a copy of an unqualified report on that balance sheet by the company's auditors. An unqualified report is defined by section 5(10). Broadly it is a report without material qualification and, for this purpose, a qualification is not material if the person who makes the report states in writing that the matter giving rise to the qualification is not material for the purpose of determining whether, at the balance sheet date, the company's net assets exceeded the aggregate of its called up share capital and distributable reserves (section 5(11));

(d) a copy of an expert's report in respect of any non-cash consideration received for shares allotted since the balance sheet date;

(e) a statutory declaration in the prescribed form (Form R6) by a director or the secretary of the company confirming that (i) the requirements as to the special resolution, the share capital and the valuation of any non-cash consideration have been satisfied, and (ii) between the balance sheet date and the application for re-registration there has been no change in the company's financial position that has resulted in the net assets of the company becoming less than the aggregate of its called up share capital and undistributable reserves.

If all the documents are in order the Registrar will issue a certificate of re-registration as a public limited company.

Re-registration of a public company as a private company

The process whereby a public company can *voluntarily* re-register as a private company is less demanding. The relevant provisions are contained in section 10 of the 1980 Act. ("Old" public companies which wished to re-register as private companies had to do so before March 22, 1982 in accordance with the provisions in section 8 of the 1980 Act.)

The company must pass a special resolution resolving to re-register as a private company. The resolution must also remove the words "public limited company" or "p.l.c." from the name and replace them with the words "Limited" or "Ltd.", and make any other alterations to the company's memorandum and articles as are required. In particular, all reference to the company being a public company must be removed. The company should then send the special resolution to the Registrar together with an application in the prescribed form (Form R10), signed by a director or the secretary of the company and a printed copy of the memorandum and articles of the company as altered. The special resolution should be filed within 15 days. However, the Registrar will normally be unable to issue a certificate of re-registration until 28 days have elapsed since the passing of the special resolution. This is because the 1980 Act contains provisions enabling minority shareholders to apply to the court within this 28 day period for cancellation of the resolution. (It is not necessary for the full 28 days to elapse before issue of the certificate if (i) an application for cancellation has been made and subsequently withdrawn, or (ii) the court has made an order confirming the resolution and a copy of the order has been delivered to the Registrar.)

An application for cancellation may be made only by,

(a) the holders of not less than five per cent in nominal value of the company's issued share capital (or any class of capital if more than one); or

(b) not less than fifty of the company's members.

No application may be made by a person who has consented to, or voted in favour of, the resolution. Such an application would only appear to be likely if it is thought that the loss of public company status will adversely affect the marketability or perhaps the value of the shares. Where an application for cancellation of the special resolution has been made, the company must give notice of this to the Registrar of Companies; it must also deliver to him an office copy of any order cancelling or confirming the resolution. This must be done within 15 days of the making of the order (or such longer period as the court directs). Failure to do so renders both the company and any officer in default liable to a fine. A court hearing an application for cancellation will make an order either cancelling or confirming the resolution. However, it may do so on such terms and conditions as it thinks fit. In particular, it may order the purchase by the company of any member's shares, thereby reducing the company's capital, and make any consequential amendments to the company's memorandum and articles of association. It may also make an order requiring the company not to make any, or any specified, alteration in its memorandum or articles (C.A. 1980, s. 11(7), (8)).

If the Registrar is satisfied that the company may be re-registered as a private company, he will issue a certificate of re-registration. The company will become a private company and the alteration to its memorandum and articles of association contained in the special resolution will take effect on the issue of the certificate.

Re-registration as a private company will generally be a voluntary act of the company. However, in two circumstances re-registration is compulsory. First, if at any time the court makes an order confirming a reduction of capital of a public company which has the effect of bringing the nominal value of the company's allotted share capital below the authorised minimum, the company must cease to be a public company. The court may *order* that the company shall be re-registered as a private company and, if it does, it must also specify the alterations to be made to the company's memorandum and articles of association in connection with that re-registration. This effectively dispenses with the requirement that the company must pass a special resolution to re-register. If the court does not make such a direction, the Registrar of Companies must refuse to register the order under section 69(1) of the 1948 Act (thereby depriving it of any effect), until the company has been re-registered as a private company.

Secondly, where a public company cancels shares under section 37 of the 1980 Act, and this results in the company's allotted share capital being reduced below the authorised minimum, the company must apply to be re-registered as a private company.

Companies limited by guarantee

Companies limited by guarantee are generally formed for charitable, social or other non-trading purposes. They are widely used by schools and colleges, professional and trade associations, clubs supported by annual subscriptions and management companies for blocks of flats in which all the tenants are members.

Prior to the 1980 Act, they could be formed either with or without a share capital. However, in practice the former type was rarely used because it had few advantages. Their use imposed a double liability on the members: a liability to pay up the amount (if any) unpaid on their shares *and* a liability to honour their guarantee in the event of the company being wound up. It also rendered the company liable to capital duty both on the issue of shares and on the making of calls in respect of the guarantees. Now, by virtue of section 2(1) of the 1980 Act, new companies limited by guarantee must be formed *without* a share capital. This means that they must also be private companies.

The effect of the 1980 Act on guarantee companies incorporated prior to its coming into force is as follows. The small number of such companies that were incorporated with a share capital may continue to exist despite the provision in section 2(1). Guarantee companies with a share capital that were public companies were obliged to re-register as public limited companies or private companies before March 22, 1982, and any such companies without a share capital automatically became private companies. Private companies limited by guarantee *with* a share capital may re-register as public limited companies and vice versa. The procedure to be adopted is described above.

Many companies limited by guarantee have in the past taken advantage of the provisions contained in section 19 of the Companies Act 1948 and obtained a licence from the Department of Trade to dispense with the word "Limited" from their names. This section has now been replaced by section 25 of the 1981 Act, which has altered both the class of companies that may be exempted from the requirement to use the word "Limited" and the procedure for obtaining exemption.

Under section 25, a company which is or is about to be registered as a company limited by guarantee will be permitted to omit the word "Limited" from its name, provided,

(a) the objects of the company are or will be the promotion of commerce, art, science, education, religion, charity or any profession (including anything incidental to or conducive to any of these objects); and

(b) the memorandum or articles (i) require its profits (if any) or other income to be applied in promoting its objects, (ii) prohibit the payment of dividends to members, and (iii) require all the assets that would otherwise be available to the members on a winding up to be transferred to another body that either has similar objects or has objects concerned with the promotion of charity.

To obtain an exemption a statutory declaration in the prescribed form must be submitted to the Registrar of Companies.

The guarantee

The memorandum of a guarantee company must contain a clause stating that each member undertakes to contribute to the assets of the company in the event of its being wound up while he is a member (or within one year after he ceases to be a member). The contribution is the amount required to discharge the company's debts and pay the costs of winding up, up to a specified maximum. The amount of the guarantee must be included in the memorandum, but the Act does not specify minimum or maximum limits. In practice, the sum stated is often £1. The effect of the guarantee is that a member is not obliged to pay the sum guaranteed while the company is a going concern, the liability only arising if a contribution is needed to pay the company's debts when it is being liquidated. (In the case of a guarantee company with a share capital a member is also liable in respect of calls made on unpaid capital in the normal way.)

The amount which members have agreed to contribute in a winding up is not an asset of the company, but merely a contingent liability of members to contribute in the event of the company being wound up. Accordingly, it cannot be mortgaged or charged by the company while it is a going concern (*Re Irish Club* [1906] W.N. 127).

The memorandum and articles

Both a memorandum and articles of association *must* be filed on incorporation of a company limited by guarantee. There is no provision, as in the case of companies limited by shares, that a model set of articles will apply unless excluded. The memorandum and articles should be in the "form" set out in Table C of Schedule 1 to the 1948 Act, as amended by the 1980 Act. (Table D applies to "old" guarantee companies *with* a share capital.) In practice, however, the diversity of organisations that operate as companies limited by guarantee means that articles vary widely to take account of individual circumstances. The word "form" does not in this context include content (*Gaiman v. National Association for Mental Health* [1971] Ch. 317). The articles must, however, state the number of members with which the company proposes to be registered (C.A. 1948, s. 7(2)).

Unlimited companies

Unlimited companies are not widely used. The reason for this is very apparent: members may be required to contribute all their assets to the company in a winding up to the extent the company is unable to pay its debts.

However, as many small businesses are well aware, the protection of limited liability is often more apparent than real – major creditors of a company, such as banks, will frequently seek from the company's shareholders personal guarantees of its debts. With this in mind, the fact that unlimited companies are generally freed of the obligation to file accounts with the Registrar of Companies has made them more attractive in recent years. They are utilised where secrecy in relation to financial affairs is important and the loss of limited liability will not in practice be material – examples include personal service companies (where the only activity is the provision of a service through the medium of a company) and service companies for professional persons. Where limited liability is discarded it may be important to ensure that adequate insurance is available to cover liability arising from the business activities.

A further advantage of unlimited companies is that they are not subject to capital duty on the allotment of shares. They can therefore also be useful as investment companies, particularly within a group of companies. Thirdly, unlimited companies are not subject to the normal rules relating to reduction of capital.

Following the 1980 Act, unlimited companies may only be private companies, although they may still be formed with or without a share capital.

Unlimited liability

Members of an unlimited company can be made liable without limit for the debts and obligations of the company. As in the case of companies limited by guarantee, this liability is contingent on the company being wound up. While the company is a going concern its members can only be called upon to contribute to the company any capital unpaid on their shares, if any. Further, during the winding up only the liquidator of the company can claim against the members, who will then be liable to contribute the company's assets an amount sufficient for the payment of its liabilities together with the expenses of winding up (C.A. 1948, s. 212(1)). Creditors of the company can only petition for its winding up if debts owed by it to them are unpaid – they cannot sue the members directly.

As in the case of limited liability companies, a past member is also liable to contribute to the assets of the company if he ceased to be a member within the twelve months preceding the commencement of the winding up. However, such liability only arises if the debt or liability in respect of which his contribution is sought was contracted before he ceased to be a member and it appears to the court that existing members are unable to make the contributions required of them (C.A. 1948, s. 212(1)).

Filing of accounts

An unlimited company must file an annual return. It must also prepare audited accounts in respect of each accounting reference period (C.A. 1948, ss. 124 and 125; C.A. 1976, s. 1(1)(b)). However, those accounts need not be sent to the Registrar of Companies in respect of an accounting reference period if during that period,

(a) the company was not, to its knowledge the direct or indirect subsidiary of a limited company; or

(b) there were not, to its knowledge, held or exercisable by or on behalf of two or more limited companies, shares or powers which if they had been held or exercisable by one of them, would have made the company the direct or indirect subsidiary of that company; or

(c) it was not the holding company of a limited company (C.A. 1976, s. 1(8)).

"Limited company" is defined to include foreign companies the liability of whose members is limited.

Thus to retain the benefit of not filing accounts, an unlimited company must not form part of a group of companies which contains a limited company.

Capital duty

An unlimited company is not a capital company for the purposes of the capital duty provisions in the Finance Act 1973. Consequently, it is not liable to pay capital duty of one per cent on the issue of shares.

In practice, the capital duty benefits of using an unlimited company are sometimes enjoyed without the disadvantage of loss of limited company status by interposing a limited liability company with a minimal share capital between the unlimited company and its ultimate shareholders.

This is not appropriate where secrecy is important because the exemption in connection with the filing of accounts is lost.

Return of capital to members

An unlimited company can, provided it is authorised by its articles to do so, reduce its issued share capital and return the excess to members. Alternatively, it may permit its members to withdraw from membership altogether by purchasing its own shares (see *Re Borough Commercial and Building Society* [1893] 2 Ch. 242). If at the time when the company acquires its own shares it knows that its existing assets, together with the amounts which it would expect to obtain from members on a winding up, will be insufficient to satisfy its liabilities, the acquisition of shares will be set aside as a fraud on its creditors (*Mitchell v. Glasgow Bank* [1879] 4 App. Cas. 624).

By contrast, a limited company cannot reduce its share capital unless the prior consent of the court is obtained (C.A. 1948, ss. 66 and 67). Neither until recently could it purchase its own shares (by virtue of the rule in *Trevor v. Whitworth* [1887] 12 App. Cas. 409), although it could issue and subsequently redeem redeemable preference shares (see now section 35 of the 1980 Act and the chapter *Redeemable Shares*).

Limited companies may now purchase their own shares and issue redeemable shares provided the requirements in sections 45 to 52 of the 1981 Act are complied with. However, this does not negative the advantage of using an unlimited company as difficulties may be encountered in satisfying the 1981 Act requirements (see the chapter *Purchase and Holding of Own Shares*). Unlimited companies can still provide greater flexibility when a company wishes to purchase its own shares.

Other matters

As in the case of guarantee companies, both a memorandum and articles of association must be filed on incorporation. The appropriate model form is Table E in Schedule 1 to the 1948 Act. The articles must state the minimum number of members with which the company is to be registered. They must also state the amount of the proposed share capital (C.A. 1948, s. 7(1)). Other minor differences between limited and unlimited companies are,

(a) an unlimited company is not required to file a return of allotments under section 52 Companies Act 1948;

(b) an unlimited company need not keep a register of mortgages and charges on its assets at its registered office, although such mortgages and charges must be registered at the Companies Registry; and

(c) an unlimited company has no statutory power to issue redeemable preference shares but, since it may purchase any of its shares, there seems to be no reason why it should not issue preference shares or any other class of shares on terms that they will or may be redeemed at a future date. (Sections 45 and 46 of the 1981 Act (power of a company to issue redeemable shares and purchase its own shares) do not apply to unlimited companies.)

Re-registrations involving unlimited companies

Section 43 of the Companies Act 1967 provides for the re-registration of a *private* limited company as an unlimited company (see paragraph 43 of Schedule 3 to the 1980 Act). All the company's members must approve the re-registration, and the memorandum and articles of the company must be altered to bring them into conformity with Table E of Schedule 1 to the 1948 Act. Consent of the court is not required.

Once the memorandum and articles of association have been altered and the consent of the members have been obtained, an application to re-register as an unlimited company, signed by a director or the secretary of the company, should be made in the prescribed form (Form R1). The application should be accompanied by the following documents,

(a) the prescribed form of assent (Form R2) subscribed to by all the members;

(b) a statutory declaration by the directors that Form R2 has been signed by all the members (Form R4); and

(c) a printed copy of the altered memorandum and articles. (The application on form R1 must itself set out the alterations in the memorandum and articles.)

On receipt of these documents the Registrar of Companies will issue a revised certificate of incorporation.

It is also possible for an unlimited company to re-register as a private limited company (section 44 of the 1967 Act). This requires the passing of a special resolution of the company and the making of an application to the Registrar of Companies (Form R3), together with the payment of capital duty. However, it is only possible to re-register once. Thus, a limited company that has re-registered as an unlimited company *cannot* re-register with limited liability.

Other possible re-registrations involving unlimited companies which are rare in practice, are the re-registration of an unlimited company as a public limited company and the re-registration of a public limited company as a private unlimited company. The procedure to be adopted in the former case is the same as that applicable to the re-registration of a private *limited* company as a public limited company, save that additional steps are necessary to convert the company re-registering into a company limited by shares (see section 7 of the 1980 Act). In the second case two steps are necessary. The company must first re-register as a private *limited* company in accordance with section 10 of the 1980 Act (see above); it must then re-register as a private unlimited company under section 43 of the 1967 Act.

Holding and subsidiary companies

The definitions of "holding company" and "subsidiary company" are contained in section 154 of the 1948 Act. This provides that one company ("A") is the holding company of another company ("B") and B is A's subsidiary if,

(a) A is a *member* of B and *controls the composition* of B's board of directors; or

(b) A holds more than half of the *equity share capital* of B; or

(c) B is a subsidiary of a third company ("C") and C is itself a subsidiary of A.

Controlling the composition of the board

A is deemed to control B's board only if, by the exercise of a power exercisable by it without the consent of any other person, A can appoint or remove all or a majority of the directors of B (C.A. 1948, s. 154(2)). A is deemed to have power to appoint a director of B if,

(a) a person cannot be appointed as a director of B unless A exercises a power exercisable by it without the consent of any other person; or

(b) a person's appointment as a director of B follows necessarily from his appointment as a director of A; or

(c) A itself or another of its subsidiaries is a director of B.

A might have a power exercisable without the consent of any other person to appoint a director of B by virtue of a contract between A and B, or between A and other members of B. Note that A need only be a member of B and a holding of one share (even a non-voting share) would suffice.

Holding more than half the equity share capital

Equity share capital is defined by section 154(5) as the issued share capital of a company, excluding any part which, neither as respects dividends nor as respects capital, carries any right to participate beyond a specified amount in a distribution. This definition will often exclude preference shares.

Convertible debentures and options to subscribe for shares are not taken into account until the option to convert or subscribe is exercised.

It should be noted that any shares held or power exercisable by a nominee for A, or by a nominee for another subsidiary of A, are treated as held or exercisable by A (C.A. 1948, s. 154(3)). However, any share held or exercisable by A in a fiduciary capacity is treated as not held or exercisable by it. Also, any share held or power exercisable by any person by virtue of the provisions of any debentures of B, or of a trust deed for securing any issue of such debentures, are disregarded. Further, any shares held or power exercisable by, or by a nominee for,

A or another of its subsidiaries, are treated as not held or exercisable by A, if (i) the ordinary business of A or the other subsidiary includes the lending of money, and (ii) the shares are held or the power is exercisable by way of security for the purposes of a transaction entered into in the ordinary course of such business.

The most significant result of a company being a holding company within section 154 is that it is obliged to prepare and submit group accounts to the Registrar of Companies. The existence of a group relationship is also significant for the purposes of, amongst other things, section 27 of the 1967 Act (obligation of director of a company to notify it of interests of his in shares in, or debentures of, the company or associated companies), section 49 of the 1980 Act (prohibition of loans, etc., to directors and connected persons) and section 42 of the 1981 Act (prohibition of financial assistance for acquisition of shares).

Companies not formed under the Companies Acts

Generally, the provisions of the Companies Acts 1948–81 will only apply to a corporate body if it is "a company" as defined by section 455 of the 1948 Act, i.e. it is, broadly, a company *formed and registered* under that Act or one of the earlier Companies Acts which preceded it (a "registered" company). Companies may, however, be formed in other ways. Although this is unusual today, a number of such "unregistered" companies, formed largely in the nineteenth century, do still exist. The two most significant examples are companies incorporated by royal charter, known as chartered companies, and companies incorporated by private Acts of Parliament, known as statutory companies. Certain provisions of the Companies Acts apply to unregistered companies.

Chartered companies

Chartered companies were at one time often formed for trading purposes. However, this practice declined when the concept of the limited liability company incorporated by registration under the Companies Acts became established. A number of old trading companies incorporated by royal charter do however still exist. Today this method of incorporation is generally used only for non-trading organisations, particularly those formed for charitable or quasi-charitable purposes.

The charter fulfils the role of the memorandum and articles of a company registered under the Companies Acts. It will generally state the objects of the company and regulate its internal affairs. A chartered company is, however, not subject to the *ultra vires* doctrine; it has power to deal with its property and to incur liabilities in the same way as an ordinary individual, even though it is not authorised to do so by its charter (*Sutton's Hospital Case* [1612] 10 Co. Rep.), although in such a case its charter may be revoked.

Members of a chartered company are only liable to contribute towards payment of the company's debts if such an obligation is imposed upon them by the charter. Where such a provision has been made, they are only obliged to make a contribution up to the amount provided for in the charter.

Statutory companies

Statutory companies were commonly used in connection with public utilities such as gas, water, electricity and railway undertakings. This was because they would generally require compulsory powers, e.g. to acquire land. Most of these statutory companies were taken over as a result of the nationalisation of these industries. However, a number do still exist today. These are largely water supply companies, although others include insurance companies and banks.

The constitutions of statutory companies are generally closely analogous to those of registered companies, although the relevant statute should always be referred to as variations do occur. The *ultra vires* rule applies to them (subject to the application of section 9 of the European Communities Act 1972 (Companies (Unregistered Companies) Regulations 1975, para 4)), and the liability of their members is limited.

Unregistered companies and the Companies Acts

Some provisions of the Companies Acts (and other related Acts) are drafted so as to cover unregistered companies. Examples include section 187 of the 1948 Act (provisions as to undischarged bankrupts acting as directors), section 206 of the 1948 Act (power to compromise with creditors and members) and section 1 of the Stock Transfer Act 1963 (simplified transfer of securities).

In addition, section 435 of the 1948 Act provides that the sections listed in Schedule 14 to that Act (which include provisions relating to prospectuses and allotments, annual returns, accounts, audits and Department of Trade investigations) apply to all corporations incorporated in, and having a principal place of business in, Great Britain unless, (i) they are incorporated by or registered under a public general Act of Parliament or, (ii) they are, broadly, not formed for the purpose of gain by the corporation or its members or (iii) they are exempted by the Department of Trade. The scope of Schedule 14 has been further extended by subsequent Companies Acts to include, amongst other things, the provisions relating to new accounting formats (C.A. 1981, s. 21), contents of directors' report (C.A. 1967, s. 54) and transactions involving directors (C.A. 1980, s. 67). (See also section 9(8) of the European Communities Act 1972 and section 4 of the Stock Exchange (Completion of Bargains) Act 1976.)

It should also be noted that Part VIII of the 1948 Act provides a process whereby certain unregistered companies may register under that Act. Where an unregistered company does so register, all the provisions of the Act, subject to certain exceptions contained in section 394(3), apply to it as if it were a company as defined by section 455. Section 13 of the

1980 Act further enables a company which wishes to register under Part VIII to apply to register as a public company.

Incorporation of a private limited company: practical steps

When a new private limited company is required two initial points should be borne in mind. First, when must the company be ready to commence operations? If it is needed quickly because, for example, it must enter into a contract by a specified date, there may be insufficient time to file the necessary documents with the Registrar of Companies *and* obtain a certificate of incorporation. If so, it will normally be necessary to buy a "ready-made" or "off-the-shelf" company from one of the company formation agents (see page 435 below).

Secondly, delays in preparing a new company to commence business can be reduced by ensuring that all the information required is available at the outset. (This applies equally when a ready-made company is to be used.) A checklist of the necessary information is set out at the end of this chapter and the more important points contained in it are considered below.

Information required

Name

It is generally advisable to have at least one alternative to the proposed name in case the first choice is unavailable. The availability of the proposed name should be checked before incorporation documents are filed with the Registrar of Companies. It is generally no longer possible to obtain from the Registrar of Companies provisional approval for a proposed company name, (except where the prior approval of the Secretary of State to a name is specifically required – see section 22(2) of the 1981 Act). However, a check can be made by inspecting, without charge, the index of company names which the Registrar of Companies is required to keep (C.A. 1981, s. 23). Copies of the index are kept in the public search rooms at Cardiff, Edinburgh and London. Where a personal inspection is not possible, use may be made of company name clearance services now offered by some company agents.

Unless an application for exemption is to be applied for, the last words of the company name must be "Limited", or its Welsh equivalent ("Cyfyngedig"), or abreviations of these words.

Provided the proposed name is not the same as one already on the index, and does not require the approval of the Secretary of State or is not otherwise unacceptable, it should be registered (see further the chapter *Names*). It is possible that, between the time when the index of company names is checked and the time when the incorporation documents are dealt with by the Registrar of Companies, the chosen name is allotted to another company. But this is unlikely to occur very often in practice and the risk of such an occurrence can be considerably reduced by making a final check of the index of company names immediately prior to lodging the incorporation documents.

As the Registrar is generally no longer obliged to give provisional approval to proposed names, it is possible that names will be registered which are very similar to names of existing companies. However, the Secretary of State has power to require a company to change its name within twelve months of its registration if it is the same as or "too like" a name appearing on the index at the time of registration (C.A. 1982, s. 24(2)). Section 46 of the 1967 Act (power of the Department of Trade to require company to abandon misleading name) also continues in force.

Business name

Where it is important for a company to commence business under a particular name by a specified date, it is still possible for it to trade under a business name. This may be appropriate where a ready-made company has been acquired and an application for change of name lodged with the Registrar, but no certificate of incorporation on change of name has been received. The Registration of Business Names Act 1916 was repealed with effect from February 26, 1982 and the Registry of Business Names has been abolished. It is therefore no longer necessary to register a business name which does not reflect the name of the proprietor of that business. However, sections 28 to 38 of the 1981 Act, which also came into force on February 26, 1982, must be complied with. Broadly a company which carries on business under a name other than its corporate name is required to include on all business letters, invoices and similar documents, details of its corporate name, together with an address in Great Britain for service of documents (this will normally be the company's registered office). It must also display a notice containing this information at each place of business and supply a similar written notice to anybody requesting one in the course of its business (see further the chapter *Names*).

It should be noted that registration of a name with the Registrar does not affect any proprietory rights which a person may have in a particular name; a passing-off action may be brought in respect of a name which the Registrar has placed on the index of company names, and the acceptance by the Registrar of a particular name is not an indication that no trademark rights exist in it (see the chapter *Names*).

Registered office

Every company registered in Great Britain must also have a registered office in Great Britain at which legal process may be served on it. The address of the registered office must be stated on the company's letters and order forms (E.C.A. 1972, s. 9(7)).

The company's memorandum will only state whether the registered office is to be situated in England, Scotland or Wales. It does not contain the address of the registered office. This is contained in Form 1 (statement of first directors and secretary and intended situation of registered office), which is filed on incorporation, and may be altered by a board resolution and filing of Form 4a.

Principal likely activities of the company.

This information is required to ensure that the objects clause in the memorandum covers this purpose for which the company is formed (see page 430 below).

Amount of initial authorised share capital.

Companies are most frequently formed with an authorised share capital of £100 divided into shares of £1 each. However, there is no legal maximum or minimum amount of authorised capital and since 1973 there has been no capital duty saving in having a small authorised share capital as, broadly, capital duty is paid on an issue of shares, not an increase in the authorised capital of a company. This should be taken into account if it is anticipated that the company will require a substantial issued share capital either on incorporation or in the near future – it will avoid the need to hold a general meeting to increase the authorised capital later on.

Form of articles of association.

Articles of association may be either long or short form. Long form articles contain all the regulations of the company. Short form articles adopt Table A except to the extent that the articles state otherwise. The latter form of articles is more widely used. However, where directors or members of the company, or both, have little experience of company law the former can be of greater assistance to them. Alternatively, Table A can be bound into the Articles for ease of reference. Modifications to Table A are considered below (see also the chapter *Articles of Association*).

Details of directors, secretary and shareholders.

These details are required to complete (a) Form 1, and, (b) where it is intended that the proposed shareholders will also be the subscribers, the subscription clause to the memorandum, and (c) the following registers which the company is obliged to keep: the register of directors and secretary (see section 200 of the 1948 Act), the register of directors' interests in shares or debentures of the company (see section 29 of the 1967 Act) and the register of members (see sections 110 to 111 of the 1948 Act). It also enables the obligations imposed on directors by section 27 of the 1967 Act (obligation of directors of a company to notify it of their interest in shares or debentures of the company and associated companies) to be complied with.

Details of auditors and banking arrangements.

The first auditors may be appointed by the directors at any time before the first annual general meeting at which the accounts are laid before the company. However, it is advisable to arrange for appointment of the auditors at the first meeting of the directors after incorporation. Similarly, to enable the company to commence business as soon as possible after incorporation all necessary bank mandates should be approved at the same time.

Omission of directors' names from notepaper.

Section 201(1) of the 1948 Act, which used to require the names of all directors of the company to be stated on all business letters, trade catalogues etc. has been altered by the 1981 Act. It is no longer necessary for directors' names to appear on business letters. However, if the name of any director does appear (except in the text of a letter or as a signatory) the names of all directors must be shown (see also the chapter *Publicity Requirements*).

Documents and forms required

The following should be sent to the Registrar of Companies together with the appropriate fee (currently £50):

(a) the memorandum and articles of association of the company;

(b) Form PUC1 (statement of capital on formation);

(c) Form 1 (statement of first directors and secretary and intended situation of the registered office); and

(d) Form 41a (declaration of compliance with the statutory requirements of the Companies Act).

Memorandum of association

The memorandum of association must state,

(a) the name of the company;

(b) whether the registered office of the company is situated in England, Wales or Scotland;

(c) the objects of the company;

(d) that the liability of the members is limited (if the company is limited by guarantee the amount which each member undertakes to contribute to the company in a winding up must also be stated); and

(e) if the company has a share capital the amount of the share capital with which it proposes to be registered and the division of it into shares of a fixed amount.

The memorandum may also contain optional provisions which could have been inserted in the articles, for example, a clause detailing the rights attaching to different classes of shares.

Items (a), (b), (d) and (e) will in practice cause few difficulties. Care should be taken, however, in adopting an objects clause to ensure that the effects of the *ultra vires* doctrine are avoided (see the chapter *Memorandum of Association*). The practice widely followed is to insert, as the first sub-paragraph to the clause, an object designed to cover the business for which the company has been formed, any business reasonably incidental to such business and any business which might be connected with it. This sub-paragraph is then followed by up to thirty other standard paragraphs conferring the power to engage in most transactions which the company might wish to enter into. In addition, it is normal practice to insert, after the main objects clause, a clause authorising the company to "carry on any other trade or business which, in the opinion of the directors, can be advantageously carried on in connection with or ancillary to any of the above mentioned businesses" (see *Bell Houses Ltd. v. City Wall Properties Ltd.* [1966] 2 Q.B. 656) and, at the end of the objects clause a further sub-paragraph stating that no paragraph within the objects clause is to be restrictively construed or construed as subsidiary or ancillary to any other paragraph (see *Cotman v. Brougham* [1918] A.C. 514). This will in practice ensure that the vast majority of transactions are within the objects clause. However, where unusual transactions are contemplated it is advisable to check the objects clause beforehand.

The memorandum must be signed by each subscriber in the presence of a witness who must attest the signature. Each subscriber should write in his own hand opposite his name the number of shares which he subscribes for. The minimum is one each. The name, address and occupation of each subscriber should be stated in full.

The memorandum may be subscribed by the persons who are to be the ultimate members of the company. Alternatively, the persons involved in the formation of the company may be the subscribers where, for example, it is anticipated that a general meeting will be required before the company is able to commence business and time is of the essence.

The articles of association

It is not necessary to file articles on incorporation of private companies limited by shares. If they are not filed, the regulations in Table A Part 1 of Schedule 1 to the 1948 Act (as amended by the 1980 Act) will apply (see the chapter *Articles of Association*). Table A Part II, which could be adopted by companies incorporated prior to December 22, 1980 has now been repealed but will still apply to those companies which adopted it on incorporation.

The normal practice is to file articles which adopt Table A except as otherwise modified by the filed articles. Modifications to Table A will depend on the circumstances; the modifications required for a "one man company" will differ from those required where the company is being formed in order to incorporate a partnership (the question of control will be a critical one in the latter case), and articles of a subsidiary company will be different again. Common alterations are set out in the chapter *Articles of Association.*

Statement of capital on formation (Form PUC1)

On the formation of a company limited by shares – but not a company limited by guarantee – capital duty at £1 per £100 or part of £100 is chargeable on the greater of (i) the nominal value of the shares allotted on incorporation, and (ii) the actual value of assets of any kind contributed by the members less the liabilities which have been assumed or discharged by the company in consideration of the contribution (F.A. 1973, Sch. 9, paras 4(1)(iii) and 7(1)). If duty on the subscriber shares is to be accounted for either when a call is made on them (they are nil paid at the time of incorporation), or when the company proceeds to allot all its shares, including the subscriber shares, to other persons, then, although the number of shares taken on incorporation will be shown in box C of Form PUC 1, the amount paid or due and payable on each (box E), and accordingly the amount of capital duty payable, will be nil.

Form 1

This contains the particulars which are required to be given by sections 21 and 23(2) of the 1976 Act concerning the first directors and secretary and the intended situation of the registered office of the company. It must be signed by the proposed directors and secretary as well as by or on behalf of the subscribers. Each of the proposed directors and secretary named on the form who has signed it is deemed to be appointed on incorporation.

Form 41a

This is a statutory declaration stating that the requirements of the Companies Acts have been complied with. It may be signed by a solicitor engaged in the formation of the company or a person named in Form 1 as a director or the secretary of the company (C.A. 1980, s. 3(5)).

Post incorporation matters

The Registrar of Companies will, provided the filed documents are in order, issue a certificate of incorporation. Until the certificate is issued it is possible that the application will be rejected because, for example, the proposed name is unacceptable. It is therefore unwise to order business stationery or the company seal prematurely. Nevertheless, employment contracts for directors, business transfer agreements, declarations of trust in respect of nominee shareholdings and applications for allotment of shares may be prepared in draft, statutory registers, minute books and shares certificates obtained, and auditors and banks approached.

It is advisable to complete the incorporation formalities immediately after the certificate of incorporation is received from the Registrar of Companies. This ensures that all the Companies Acts requirements have been complied with and that the company is ready to commence business. A meeting of directors should be held to deal with the following matters:

(a) adoption of the company seal;

(b) appointment of a chairman (if appropriate), managing director and any additional directors, and (subject to section 47 of the 1980 Act (contracts of employment of directors)) approval of any employment contracts. (If for any reason persons other than the intended directors of the company were named on Form 1, for example the company advisers, their resignations should be produced and recorded with effect from the end of the meeting);

(c) appointment of auditors;

(d) approval for registration, subject to stamping, of stock transfer forms transferring the subscribers shares to the intended members of the company, if appropriate, allotment of further shares in accordance with sections 14 and 17 of the 1980 Act (if required) and issue of share certificates. (If all the shares are fully paid up, distinguishing numbers in respect of the issued share capital may be dispensed with (see section 74 of the 1948 Act).);

(e) approval of banking arrangements, including agreeing authorised signatures in respect of the company's bank account and passing the resolutions required by the bank (see article 85 of Table A);

(f) approval of any business contracts, subject to section 48 of the 1980 Act (substantial property transactions involving directors);

(g) disclosure by directors of their interests in any contracts made with the company in accordance with section 199 of the 1948 Act and article 84(1) of Table A (see also section 60 of the 1980 Act). Provided Articles 84(2) and 84(4) of Table A have been altered, this will enable them to be counted in a quorum and vote at meetings at which contracts in which they have interests are discussed. It is sufficient if directors make a general disclosure to the board of their interest in any contract with specified companies or firms; this avoids having to give notice of their interest every time a contract with the firm specified is considered;

(h) disclosure in writing by the directors of their interests in shares of the company in accordance with sections 27 and 31 of the 1967 Act (obligation of directors of a company to notify it of their interests in shares or debentures of the company and associated companies);

(i) adoption of an accounting reference date, to which date the company's accounts will be prepared. Failure to notify the Registrar of Companies of an accounting reference date within six months of incorporation will result in the company's accounting reference date becoming 31 March.

It should be borne in mind that, as a result of the 1980 Act, it may now also be necessary to hold a first general meeting of the company. By virtue of section 48 of that Act, any substantial property transactions between the company and any of its directors must be approved by a general meeting; there will invariably be such a transaction whenever an existing business is being incorporated, unless the business is worth less than £1,000 (see the chapter *Directors' Duties*). Secondly, a general meeting will be required if, broadly, any director's service contracts are to be entered into for terms exceeding five years (C.A. 1980, s. 47 and the chapter *Directors*). Thirdly, unless the articles have been suitably drafted, a resolution will be required to authorise an allotment of shares; and any shares which the directors wish to allot will have to be offered to the initial subscribers first.

After the first board meeting the following returns should (where appropriate) be made to the Registrar of Companies together with any capital duty in respect of the allotment of shares:

(a) Form PUC2 where shares are allotted for cash;

(b) Form PUC3, together with the contract constituting the title of the allottee to the allotment, where shares are issued for a non-cash consideration. If there is no such written contract, Form 52 (particulars of a contract relating to shares allotted as fully or partly paid up otherwise than in cash) should be filed instead;

(c) Form PUC5 (statement of amounts or further amounts paid on nil paid or partly paid shares) if the nil paid subscribers shares are paid up. The Registrar no longer requires this form to be filed with the Stamp Office;

(d) Form 9b (notice of change of directors or secretaries or their particulars), signed by any new appointees;

(e) Form 2 (notice of accounting reference date);

(f) A copy of any resolution passed giving the directors authority to allot shares pursuant to section 14 of the 1980 Act (section 143 of the 1948 Act applies to such a resolution by virtue of section 14(6)); and

(g) Form 26 (notice of place where copies of directors' service contracts or memoranda thereof are kept) and Form 27 (notice of place where register of directors' interests in shares etc. is kept) where appropriate (see sections 26(3) and 29(8) of the 1967 Act).

Any stock transfer forms in respect of the subscriber's shares and declarations of trust should be produced for stamping, minutes of the first board meeting prepared, share certificates issued by the company and the company's statutory books written up.

Depending on the reason for incorporating the new company, other matters may require attention. First, where an existing business is being transferred to the company, the following matters will be relevant:

(a) registration of the company for VAT;

(b) notification of transfer to be given to customers and suppliers, insurance companies, public utilities, etc.;

(c) employment contracts of employees and notice to trade unions;

(d) pension and life assurance arrangements for directors and employees;

(e) patents and trade marks owned or used under licence agreements;

(f) transfer of premises to the company;

(g) the obtaining of consent to the transfer of long term contracts, for example hire purchase agreements and leases; and

(h) payment of stamp duty on any business transfer agreement (see section 59 of the Stamp Act 1891).

Secondly, where a group reorganisation is involved, relevant matters include,

(a) making a group election under section 256 of the Taxes Act 1970 in respect of dividends;

(b) claims for stamp duty relief (if available) under section 55 of the Finance Act 1927 or section 42 of the Finance Act 1930; and

(c) claims for exemption from capital duty under paragraph 10 of Schedule 19 to the Finance Act 1973.

Ready-made companies

It will often be necessary to use a ready-made company where time is of the essence, for instance, where a contract must be entered into by the company before a specified date. This is because a company has no power to contract prior to the date of its incorporation, and attempts to overcome this by arranging for a contract to be entered into before incorporation by a third party as "agent" for the company will fall within the ambit of section 9(2) of the European Communities Act 1972. This provides that, where such an arrangement is made, the "agent" is, unless otherwise agreed, personally liable on the contract. (For a recent case on this, see *Phonogram Ltd. v. Lane* [1981] 3 All E.R. 182; see the chapter *Company Contracts*). Where there is sufficient time to incorporate a company, it may still be appropriate to use a ready-made company if few changes in its memorandum and articles are likely. However, where this is not the case, preparation of documentation to comply with the statutory requirements can be time consuming and consideration should be given to incorporating the company in the required form.

Where a ready-made company is required, company formation agents will generally require details of the main activity of the proposed company to ensure that a suitable objects clause is obtained. The purchaser will then normally receive, in addition to the certificate of incorporation of the company and copies of the memorandum and articles, a certificate to confirm that the company has not traded since incorporation and has no outstanding debts or liabilities, stock transfer forms duly completed in blank by the subscribers (forms of renunciation are sometimes used instead) and, depending on the formation agents used, a company's register and seal, draft board minutes for the first board meeting and Companies Registry forms. To ensure that they can sever their connections with the company before they lose control of it, the formation agents will commonly require a completed Form 4a (notice of change in situation of registered office) and Form 9b (change of directors and secretary) to be returned to them beforehand. They will then also send to the purchaser a resolution of the first director or directors appointing as directors and secretary the persons named in the Form 9b and a letter of resignation of the first director and secretary. (Other methods of severance are also used.)

The normal post incorporation matters will need to be carried out. In addition however it may be necessary to,

(a) change the company's name (it is advisable to check the index of company names beforehand);

(b) alter the company's objects clause (if a suitable objects clause could not be obtained in the time available);

(c) adopt new articles (the existing articles should be checked carefully to ensure that matters relating to control etc. are appropriate);

(d) increase the company's authorised share capital (the authorised share capital of ready-made companies is generally £100).

A general meeting of the company will be required for any of these. Alterations to the company's name, objects clause and articles all require special resolutions. An increase of capital will only require an ordinary resolution unless article 44 of Table A has not been adopted.

Where speed is important and the shareholders or directors, or both, are not available to attend these meetings at short notice, they may appoint proxies to attend the meetings on their behalf. Alternatively, other persons, for example those engaged in the formation of the company, may be appointed as directors by the company formation agents to carry out the required alterations. They can then approve transfers of the subscribers' shares to themselves at the first board meeting, adjourn the board meeting to hold a general meeting of the company, at short notice if required, to pass the necessary resolutions altering the company's constitution and subsequently re-convene the board meeting to complete the post-incorporation formalities. After these have been carried out they can, at the resumed board meeting, approve stock transfer forms transferring shares held by themselves to the intended shareholders of the company, appoint new directors and secretary, and resign.

In addition to the board minutes, the following documents may be needed:

(a) notice of the extraordinary general meeting containing details of the resolutions proposed (special resolutions should be stated in full);

(b) an "agreement to short notice", that is an agreement to the extraordinary general meeting being called by less than the statutory minimum period of notice, signed by members who together constitute a majority in number of the members having a right to attend and vote at the meeting *and* hold not less than 95 per cent in nominal value of the shares giving a right to attend and vote at the meeting (C.A. 1948, s. 133 – in practice, where the two subscribers are the only members of the company, both should sign);

(c) proxy forms (where appropriate).

(d) minutes of the extraordinary general meeting recording the passing of each resolution referred to in the notice of the meeting;

(e) letters of resignation of directors and secretary and Form 9bs in respect of the new directors (where appropriate); and

(f) stock transfer forms (where the transferees from the subscribers are not to remain members of the company).

Within fifteen days after the resumed board meeting signed copies of the following should be filed with the Registrar of Companies,

(a) the special resolution changing the company's name (C.A. 1948, s. 143) together with the appropriate fee (currently £40);

(b) the resolution to increase the company's nominal capital together with Form 10 (C.A. 1948, s. 63(1));

(c) the special resolution amending the company's objects clause (C.A. 1948, s. 143);

(d) the special resolution amending the company's articles together with a printed copy of the articles as amended (C.A. 1948, s. 143; E.C.A. 1972, s. 9 (5)); and

(e) Form 9b (notice of change of directors). Section 200(4) of the 1948 Act requires this to be filed within *fourteen* days of the general meeting.

A printed copy of the memorandum as altered must also be filed with the Registrar of Companies between 22 and 36 days after the passing of the special resolution making the alteration (this assumes that no application is made to the court for the alteration of the objects clause to be cancelled; C.A. 1948, s. 5(7); E.C.A. 1972, s. 9(5)). The Registrar of Companies' current practice in connection with alterations to the memorandum and articles is as follows. Where the amendment is small, for example a change in the authorised capital, a rubber stamp may be used. Alternatively, the alteration may be permanently affixed to a copy of the original document, provided the new version obscures the words to be amended. (Manuscript amendments are not accepted.) Where more substantial amendments are made, the altered pages may be removed from a copy of the original, amended pages inserted and the pages collated.

The inserted material should be printed and all alterations be validated by the seal or an official stamp of the company.

Checklist of information required to incorporate a private limited company

1. Date on which the company is to commence operations.

2. (a) Proposed name of the company.
   (b) Alternative name(s).
   (c) Whether a business name is to be used.

3. Where will the registered office of the company be?

4. Principal likely activities of the company.

5. Is the company to be limited by guarantee? If so:
   (a) What amount will each member guarantee to contribute to the company in the event of a winding up?
   (b) Is an application for exemption from the requirement to use the word "limited" to be made?

6. Amount in £'s of the initial authorised share capital of the company and the denomination of each share (e.g. £100 divided into 100 shares of £1 each).
   (N.B. guarantee companies can no longer be formed with a share capital.)

7. Whether a full or short form of articles of association is required. (The latter is more common.)

8. What provisions are required in the articles relating to allotment of shares and pre-emption rights on allotment?

9. Are pre-emption rights on transfer of shares required?

10. Are any special provisions required in the articles relating to the question of control?

11. Details of provisions in articles of association as to minimum and/or maximum number of directors (if any).

12. Should directors be empowered to appoint "alternate directors" to act in their absence.

13. Are directors to retire by rotation?

14. Details of any limits to be placed in the articles on the directors' power to borrow?

15. Details of any special provisions as to quorums at either meetings of the board of directors or meetings of the company.

16. Details of each of the proposed shareholders of the company:
    (a) full name;
    (b) address;
    (c) number of shares to be held by each;

(d) if any shareholder is to be a nominee, name of person on whose behalf the share(s) are to be held.
NB: a minimum of two shareholders is required.

17. Details of each of the proposed first directors of the company (on separate sheets if necessary):
(a) full name (including all forenames *in full*);
(b) any former names;
(c) nationality;
(d) usual *residential* address;
(e) business occupation (if any);
(f) the names of any other companies registered in Great Britain of which the director is also a director (other than (i) a company of which the company will be a wholly owned subsidiary or (ii) a wholly owned subsidiary of such a holding company).

18. Except to the extent that the information is given in 16 above, details of the interests of the directors, their wives/husbands (unless also directors) and children under 18 in the shares or debentures of,
(a) the company;
(b) the holding company (if any) of the company;
(c) any other subsidiary of such a holding company.

19. Which director is to be chairman of the board of directors? Is he to be given a casting vote?

20. Which director (if any) is to be managing director of the company?

21. Details of any service contracts required.

22. Details of the proposed secretary of the company:
(a) full name (including all forenames *in full*);
(b) any former names;
(c) usual *residential* address.

23. Details of the proposed auditors (in Great Britain) of the company:
(a) name;
(b) address;
(c) an individual in the firm who will primarily be responsible.

24. Have the auditors been asked to act? If not, who is to contact them?

25. Name and address of the branch of the company's proposed bank.

26. Has the bank been informed? If not, who is to approach them?

27. Who is to obtain the form of resolution and specimen signature form required by the bank in connection with the opening of an account for a limited company?

28. Details of arrangements to be stated in the resolution for signing of cheques (e.g. by any two directors).

29. Who is to obtain the following:
    (a) common seal;
    (b) book containing the statutory registers;
    (c) book of share certificates;
    (d) minute book.

30. What is the company's accounting reference date to be?

31. How many copies of the memorandum and articles are required?

32. Are the names of the directors to appear on the notepaper etc. of the company?

33. Other matters.

General Meetings

The general meeting is the formal occasion at which the business assigned to the members by statute or the company's constitution is conducted. The nature of the proceedings varies considerably, depending on the size and type of the company, from the carefully planned showpiece of the large public company, to the often casual discussion, not always recognised as a general meeting by the participants, of the small family business. The rules governing the conduct of general meetings are largely the same, however, regardless of the size of the company, though there are several concessions to informality from which a company with a small number of shareholders may benefit.

Meetings of members fall into two categories. All members may attend and vote at *general meetings*, unless they only hold shares of a class which do not confer that right. *Class meetings* may only be attended by holders of shares of the relevant class. Meetings of debentureholders and creditors are also often regulated in a similar way to meetings of members.

What is a meeting?

In the nature of things, a "meeting" normally requires the presence of at least two people. In one case it was held that there had not been a valid meeting where there was only one member present, even though he held proxies for other members (*Re Sanitary Carbon Co.* [1877] W.N. 223). Subject to quorum requirements being satisfied, there may be a meeting where there are two or more proxies present, but no members present in person. There will be a valid meeting, even though there is only one person present, where the meeting is an annual general meeting called by the Department of Trade under section 131(2) of the Companies Act 1948 or a general meeting called by the court under section 135(1) of that Act and an order to this effect is made in either case. A class meeting may be held with only one person present if all the shares of the class in question are held by him (*East v. Bennett Bros.* [1911] 1 Ch. 163; see also C.A. 1980, s. 32(6)(a)).

Types of general meeting

There are two types of general meeting, namely the annual general meeting ("A.G.M.") and the extraordinary general meeting ("E.G.M.").

Annual general meeting

Every company must hold an A.G.M. in each calendar year and meetings may not be more than fifteen months apart (C.A. 1948, s. 131(1)). A newly incorporated company need not hold its first A.G.M. in the first or second calendar year of its incorporation, so long as it holds it within eighteen months of incorporation. An A.G.M. must be specified as such in the notice calling it, and the holding of a meeting which is not an A.G.M. will not satisfy the obligation to hold an A.G.M. in the relevant year.

If a company fails to hold an A.G.M. as required by section 131(1) the company and every officer in default will be liable to a fine (section 131(5)). Any member may apply to the Department of Trade for the Department to call or direct the calling of a general meeting where the company has failed to hold an A.G.M. within the relevant period (section 131(2)). The Department of Trade may give such ancillary or consequential directions as it thinks fit in order to facilitate the holding of the meeting, even though the directions given may be at variance with the company's articles. A meeting convened under this procedure will normally be deemed to be an A.G.M.; where the meeting is not held in the year in which the default occurred it will not be treated as the A.G.M. for the year in which it is actually held unless the company resolves otherwise, in which case the one meeting will be treated as the A.G.M. for both years. If such a resolution is passed, it must be registered at the Companies Registry (section 131(3) and (4)). Voting rights are determined as at the date of the actual meeting (*Musselwhite v. Musselwhite* [1962] Ch. 964).

Attendance at A.G.M.'s is notoriously low, in the case of most public companies being less than one per cent of the members. There is, however, evidence to suggest that the offer of a free lunch will result in a significant increase in the numbers attending! Meetings often start at 12 noon in order to provide a natural incentive to the efficient administration of business.

Business of the A.G.M.

The Companies Acts do not state what business must be conducted at an A.G.M. and hence this is entirely dependent on the articles. Article 52 of Table A provides that the ordinary business of an A.G.M. is the declaration of a dividend, consideration of the accounts, balance sheets and reports of the directors and auditors, the election of directors in place of those retiring and the appointment of auditors and the fixing of their remuneration. Under Table A any other business conducted at an A.G.M. is "special business" and will only be valid if previous notice is given to the members of its general nature (Article 50). There is nothing to prevent a special or extraordinary resolution from being passed at an A.G.M. so long as the notice requirements have been fulfilled; the practice of calling an E.G.M. for this purpose immediately after the conclusion of the A.G.M. is unnecessary.

The Acts do not require the accounts to be presented at an A.G.M. rather than at an E.G.M., but unless they are for some reason unavailable this is the usual practice. Section 1(6) of the Companies Act 1976 provides that the directors must "lay before" the company the directors' report and accounts, but there is no obligation to read them out and there is no necessity to resolve that the accounts be accepted. Article 52 of Table A refers to the "consideration" of the accounts, however, and it is common to resolve that they be "received". If a dividend is to be paid a resolution to this effect must be passed. It is open to the meeting to reduce the dividend recommended by the directors, but not to increase it (Article 114). A resolution that a smaller dividend be paid may be put without specific notice having been given, since this will fall within the scope of the business for which notice has been given. The chairman may, however, rule out of order any proposal to use the amount of the reduced dividend for some alternative purpose, for example for a charitable donation, unless notice of the intention to move such a resolution has been given, since this would constitute special business. The auditors' report must be read out at the meeting and be open to inspection by the members (C.A. 1967, s. 14(2)).

The auditors must be appointed by resolution at each general meeting at which accounts are laid before the shareholders in accordance with section 1(6) of the Companies Act 1976, to hold office from the conclusion of that meeting until the conclusion of the next meeting at which those requirements are complied with. The auditors are, therefore, normally appointed from one A.G.M. to another. Any attempt by a shareholder to appoint other auditors would be out of order unless special notice had been given (section 15 of the Companies Act 1976). Section 14(8) of the 1976 Act provides for the auditors' remuneration to be fixed by the company in general meeting or in such manner as the general meeting determines. The usual course is for the meeting to resolve that the directors should settle the fees, but it is open to the general meeting to fix them, however inpracticable this may be.

As stated earlier, where Table A applies, and under most common forms of articles, the ordinary business of an A.G.M. includes the election of directors in place of those retiring. By section 183 of the Companies Act 1948 multiple appointments may not be made under the same resolution, in the case of a public company, unless the contrary is first agreed upon at the meeting without dissent. In major companies appointments are usually voted on separately. It is open to the members to put forward the names of alternative candidates for election at the meeting without the names having been included in the notice, even where the other candidates have been named (*Betts & Co. v. Macnaghten* [1910] 1 Ch. 430). The matter will only remain ordinary business, however, to the extent that the number elected does not exceed the number retiring. Articles also commonly include a provision to the effect that a person (other than a director retiring at the meeting) may not be nominated for election unless notice of the intention to propose him has been given to the company in advance (see, e.g. Article 93). If the members wish to put forward a candidate at the meeting, therefore, they must comply with the necessary preliminaries. Further, they cannot remove a director unless special notice has been given (C.A. 1948, s. 184(2)).

In the case of a company listed on The Stock Exchange, copies of all directors' service contracts of more than one year's duration (or where they are not in writing, written memoranda) must be available for inspection at the company's registered office or transfer office from the date of the notice calling the A.G.M. until the date of the meeting. The contracts or memoranda must also be made available at the meeting and for at least fifteen minutes before its commencement (Listing Agreement, paragraph 11(b)). The company must allow any interested person to inspect the documents (cf. C.A. 1967, s. 26).

Where proper notice of a members' resolution has been given in accordance with section 140 of the Companies Act 1948, that resolution forms part of the business of the A.G.M. despite anything to the contrary in the articles (section 140(6)).

Extraordinary general meeting

Where business cannot wait until the next A.G.M., or it is for some other reason inappropriate to deal with it at that meeting, it will be necessary to call an E.G.M. Under Table A all business conducted at an E.G.M. is "special", even though if it were dealt with at an A.G.M. it would come within ordinary business. Notice of all the business to be conducted at the meeting must, therefore, be given. E.G.M.'s may be convened in the following circumstances.

(a) The articles normally authorise the directors to call an E.G.M. whenever they think fit (e.g. Article 49). As with other powers, the directors must exercise their discretion in good faith, and hence may not, for instance, select a time and place for the meeting with the intention of making it difficult for certain members to attend. As with the A.G.M. it is usually the secretary's responsibility to send out notices of the meeting, but he must be authorised to do so by the board. In the absence of that authority the meeting will be invalid, though notice sent out without authority may subsequently be ratified by the board.

(b) Pursuant to section 132 of the Companies Act 1948, the members may requisition a meeting. The provisions of this section prevail over any contrary regulations of the company to the extent that those regulations attempt to cut down the rights conferred by section 132. The directors must "proceed duly to convene" an E.G.M. on the requisition of members of the company who hold at the date on which the requisition is deposited not less than one tenth of the paid-up capital of the company which carries the right to vote at general meetings (or where the company has no share capital, of members with one tenth of the shares). The requisition must state the objects of the meeting, must be signed by the requisitionists and be deposited at the registered office of the company.

Whilst the directors, on being requisitioned, must "forthwith" convene a meeting, section 132 does not impose any time limit within which the meeting must actually be held. So the directors might be tempted to try to frustrate the aims of the requisitionists by calling the meeting for some distant date, although in these circumstances a court might exercise its inherent jurisdiction. But once the directors have convened the meeting the requisitionists cannot call the meeting themselves under the procedure discussed in the next paragraph, even where the date is a distant one (see *Re Windward Islands Enterprises (UK)* July 29, 1982, where the delay was over four months). Unless the articles provide otherwise, the directors need not include in the notice calling the meeting any information other than the objects of the meeting, as stated in the requisition (*Ball v. Metal Industries* 1957 S.C. 315).

If the directors do not within 21 days from the deposit of the requisition convene a meeting, the requisitionists, or any of them representing more than half of their total voting rights, may convene a meeting themselves to conduct the business referred to in the requisition. A meeting convened by the requisitionists must as nearly as possible be convened in the same way as a meeting convened by the directors. The meeting must be held within three months of the deposit of the requisition. The requisitionists are entitled to be repaid by the company their reasonable expenses in calling the meeting and the company may recover any sums so paid from the remuneration of the directors who were in default.

(c) Section 134(b) of the 1948 Act provides for a further means of calling an E.G.M., but it only applies "in so far as the articles of the company do not make other provision". The section allows a meeting to be called by two or more members holding not less than one tenth of the issued share capital, or not less than five per cent in number of the members where the company does not have a share capital. Table A does make "other provision"; by Article 49 any two members (without reference to the size of their shareholdings) may convene an A.G.M., but only where there are insufficient directors available in the United Kingdom to form a quorum for the purpose of resolving to call a meeting.

(d) By section 17 of the Companies Act 1976 a resigning auditor, who considers that there are circumstances surrounding his resignation which should be brought to the attention of the members or creditors, may deposit with his resignation a requisition calling on the directors to convene a general meeting for the purpose of receiving and considering an explanation of those circumstances. The directors must within 21 days from the date of deposit of the requisition convene a general meeting for this purpose for a date not later than 28 days from the date on which the notice convening the meeting is given. An auditor resigning in these circumstances also has the right to have a statement made by him, concerning the reasons for his resignation, sent out with the notice of meeting (see page 121).

(e) Section 34 of the Companies Act 1980 requires the directors of a public company to convene an E.G.M. on becoming aware of a "serious loss of capital", for the purpose of considering whether any, and if so what, measures should be taken to deal with the situation. A "serious loss of capital" occurs when the value of the company's net assets falls to half or less of its called-up share capital. The directors must convene the meeting not later than 28 days from the earliest date on which this fact is known to any director of the company, and the meeting must be held within 56 days of that date. The section does not dispense with the need to give proper notice of the business to be conducted at the meeting (section 34(3)), so unless proposals have been formulated in advance and sufficient notice of them given the meeting can only perform a consultative role. It may be noted that section 34 does not fully correspond with Article 17 of the Second EEC Directive on Company Law, on which it is based, which requires the general meeting to consider specifically whether the company should be wound up, as well as any other measures to deal with the situation.

(f) The court may order a meeting if it is for any reason impracticable for a meeting to be convened in accordance with the ordinary procedures, for example, because the number of members has fallen to one (C.A. 1948, s. 135). The court may order the meeting of its own motion or on the application of a director or any member who would be entitled to vote at the meeting. The court also has an inherent jurisdiction to direct the calling of a meeting, for example, to enable the company to determine whether an action brought in the company's name by a member should be continued (*Re Paris Skating Rink Co.* (1877) 6 Ch.D. 731; *Pender v. Lushington* (1877) 6 Ch.D. 70).

Notice

To whom notice must be given

Every member of the company is entitled to notice of a general meeting unless the articles provide otherwise (C.A. 1948, s. 134(a)). Table A does not provide otherwise except as regards members who do not have a registered address in the United Kingdom and have not given the company an address within the United Kingdom where notice may be sent (Table A, Article 134(a)). Where this is the case notice need not be given. Notice must be given (unless the articles provide to the contrary) to the holders of a particular class of shares even though the shares do not confer the right to attend and vote at the meeting. (Where a class of shares do not have voting rights it will normally be provided that holders of the shares do not have the right to attend meetings and it appears that this will be the case even though the latter right is not expressly excluded: *Re Mackenzie & Co.* [1916] 2 Ch. 450.)

Article 134(b) provides that notice must be sent to a deceased member's personal representatives or a bankrupt member's trustees in bankruptcy. Article 133 requires the notice to be sent to the address provided by the personal representative or trustee, but where they have not provided an address notice may be given in the same way as if the death or bankruptcy had not occurred (i.e. normally by sending it to the address of the deceased or bankrupt). In the absence of Article 134(b) or its equivalent there is no need to give notice to a personal representative or trustee in bankruptcy unless they are registered, since they are not otherwise members. As a result of section 134(a) of the Companies Act 1948 the provisions of Table A will apply except in so far as the articles adopted by the company do not otherwise provide; section 134(a) is concerned with the method of service and not with who is entitled to notice and hence it is not necessary for the articles to make alternative provision in order for Article 134(b) to be excluded.

Finally, by section 14(7) of the Companies Act 1967 the auditors are entitled to attend any general meeting of the company and to receive notice and other communications relating to the meeting which any member is entitled to receive. Under section 15(6) of the 1976 Act, an auditor who has been removed is entitled to attend and receive notice of the general meeting at which his term of office would have otherwise expired and also any general meeting at which it is proposed to fill the vacancy caused by his removal (note also Article 134(c) of Table A).

Effect of failure to give notice

Failure to give notice to all those entitled to receive it will invalidate the meeting (*Smyth v. Darley* (1849) 2 H.L.C. 789) and hence it is desirable for a company to include in its articles a provision such as Article 51, which prevents the accidental omission to give notice or the non-receipt of notice from having this effect. "Accidental omission" has been held to cover the situation where a notice was accidentally not posted (*Re West Canadian Collieries* [1962] 1 All E.R. 26), but not where notice was not sent because of a mistaken belief that a member was not entitled to attend (*Musselwhite v. Musselwhite & Son* [1962] Ch. 964).

Method of giving notice

Apart from the requirement that notice be in writing (C.A. 1948, s. 133), the method of giving notice is entirely dependent on the articles. It is possible, therefore, for a company to adopt articles which do not require it to give individual notification to its members; for example, they might provide for notice by newspaper advertisement only.

Article 131 of Table A sets out the means of giving notice in a company which has adopted Table A, but the general meeting may prescribe an alternative method (Article 50). In accordance with Article 131 notice is to be served either personally or by post to the member's registered address. Where notice is sent by post, a properly addressed and pre-paid letter is deemed to be served 24 hours after posting. For the purpose of this provision a notice sent by second class post is arguably not properly pre-paid, given that it is deemed to be served 24 hours after posting, and hence it is desirable to amend Article 131 to provide that notice shall be deemed to be served 48 hours after posting if it is intended to use second class post. If Table A has been excluded and the articles do not make other provision, section 7 of the Interpretation Act 1978 will apply and notice will be deemed to be effected at the time when the letter would be expected to be delivered in ordinary course of post, provided it is properly addressed and pre-paid.

Where share warrants to bearer have been issued it is normally provided that notice may be served by newspaper advertisement. In the case of a listed company any notice given by advertisement must be placed in at least one London daily newspaper (Admission of Securities to Listing, Schedule VII A.H).

Length of notice

Section 133 of the Companies Act 1948 lays down minimum periods of notice and any provision in a company's articles providing for shorter notice is void. Articles may provide for longer notice. The required period of notice is:

(a) in the case of an A.G.M. or a meeting at which it is intended to propose a special resolution, 21 days;

(b) for any other meeting, 14 days' notice, unless the company is an unlimited company, in which case the required period is seven days.

It has been held by the English courts (but otherwise in Scotland) that "days" means "clear days", that is, the day of service and the day of the meeting are excluded from the required number of days. Table A expressly provides this (Article 50) and accordingly care should be taken to ensure that the day of service (or deemed day of service) and the day of the meeting are not counted.

By section 133(3) of the 1948 Act a meeting may be held on shorter notice than that required by section 133(1) if, in the case of an A.G.M., this is agreed by all the members entitled to attend and vote at the meeting, and in the case of any other meeting, by a majority holding at least 95 per cent in nominal value of the shares giving the right to attend and vote at the meeting (that is, whether they attend or not). As regards a company which does not have a share capital the subsection is rather awkwardly drafted, but presumably means that those holding 95 per cent of the total voting rights must agree. It is not necessary for the consent to short notice to be given at the meeting or for all those consenting to attend the meeting. It is, however, usual for a company holding a meeting on short notice to obtain the written consent of the appropriate proportion of members. It should also be noted that section 133(3) does not dispense with the need to give notice altogether (though this may be a mere formality) nor does it validate a notice which is in some other respect defective. The fact that a meeting is held on short notice must be made known to those attending; section 133(3) will not be satisfied where this is not known to those present (*Re Pearce, Duff & Co.* [1960] 3 All E.R. 222). It is, however, possible for the members to dispense with the notice requirements entirely, as an aspect of the general power of the shareholders to waive irregularities by unanimous assent.

It should be noted that under section 293 of the Companies Act 1948, as amended by section 106 of the 1981 Act, a company must give at least seven days' notice of a meeting at which a resolution for voluntary winding up is to be proposed, notwithstanding any power of the members to waive notice requirements. Failure to do this will not invalidate the proceedings, however, but the company and any officers in default will be liable to a fine.

Contents of notice

At common law a notice convening a meeting must state the time and place at which it is to be held (see also Article 50). If a meeting is an A.G.M. it must be described as such in the notice (C.A. 1948, s. 131(1)). Every notice calling a meeting of a company with a share capital must state with reasonable prominence that a member entitled to attend and vote at the meeting has the right to appoint a proxy, or where permitted, more than one proxy, to attend and vote instead of him. The notice must also state that the proxy need not be a member (C.A. 1948, s. 136(2)). Subject to a number of minor exceptions, where the accounts are to be presented at a meeting, section 158 of the 1948 Act requires a company to send a copy of the balance sheet and profit and loss account, auditors' report and directors' report (C.A. 1967, s. 24) to every member of the company (whether or not entitled to receive notice of general meetings) and to every holder of debentures and anyone else entitled to receive notice. These documents must be sent at least 21 days before the meeting at which they are to be presented, but this requirement may be waived if all those entitled to attend and vote at the meeting agree.

Listed companies must state in the notice of an A.G.M. the time and place at which copies of service contracts (or memoranda) which fall within paragraph 11(b) of the Listing Agreement may be inspected. If there are no such contracts, the notice must state that fact (paragraph 11(c)).

Ordinary and special business

At common law, no business may be conducted at a meeting unless sufficient notice of the nature of the business has been given to those entitled to receive it. Where a company's articles divide business into ordinary and special business, and set out what constitutes ordinary business (either expressly or by implication) the notice of meeting need not specify what ordinary business is to be conducted, since what this may include will be apparent from the articles (see, e.g. Article 52).

A notice calling a meeting at which special business is to be conducted must indicate the "general nature" of the business with sufficient particularity to enable a member to decide whether it is worthwhile attending. It has been held that a notice setting out the names of proposed directors was sufficient to enable additional, unnamed, directors to be elected, since a reasonable shareholder on reading the notice would realise, for instance, that those nominated might not be elected and hence others would be put up in their places (*Betts & Co. v. Macnaghten* [1910] 1 Ch. 430). The mere statement that the purpose of a meeting is to increase the company's nominal capital is not sufficient, however, since the effect on the company and the shareholders will vary depending on the size of the increase (*MacConnell v. E. Prill & Co.* [1916] 2 Ch. 57). Where the directors have an interest in the passing of the resolution they must be particularly scrupulous in making full disclosure of that interest in the notice (or accompanying circular, which will be construed with the notice), since the conferment of a benefit on the directors is something to which a member might legitimately take objection and wish to vote against (see, e.g. *Normandy v. Ind, Coope & Co.* [1908] 1 Ch. 84; cf. C.A. 1948, s. 207(1)).

Ordinary, special and extraordinary resolutions

If it is intended to move a special or extraordinary resolution at a meeting, notice specifying the resolution as special or extraordinary must be given (C.A. 1948, s. 141). It has recently been confirmed in *Re Moorgate Mercantile Holdings* [1980] 1 All E.R. 40 that notice of a special resolution must contain the "entire substance" of the resolution; this results from the requirement in section 141(2) of the Companies Act 1948 that the resolution passed be "*the* resolution" set out in the notice. A resolution will only be regarded as "the resolution" where it is identical or the differences result from the correction of grammatical or clerical errors, or reduction to more formal language or other rephrasing, so long as there is no departure whatever from the substance. The *de minimis* rule does not apply. As a result, the only amendment which can be validly made to a special resolution is one which does not involve any departure from the substance of the resolution as set out in the notice. The inclusion in the notice, therefore, of such expressions as "with such amendments and alterations as shall be determined on at the general meeting" does not increase the scope for amendment. These principles doubtless also apply to extraordinary resolutions, since the notice requirement in section 141(1) of the 1948 Act for extraordinary resolutions is the same as that in section 141(2) for special resolutions.

It is not necessary for ordinary resolutions to be set out verbatim in the notice (see *Re Moorgate Mercantile Holdings*, above, at p. 54), and hence amendments may be validly moved so long as they are within the scope of the business of which notice has been given. It is quite common, however, for ordinary resolutions to be set out in full in the notice, with the statement that the resolution may be passed with such amendments as are appropriate (though the latter is not strictly necessary).

Member's resolutions

Members who fulfil the requirements of section 140 of the Companies Act 1948, may have notice of any resolution which they wish to be put at an A.G.M. sent out by the company, and they may also require a statement relating to any proposed resolution or the business to be dealt with at any general meeting to be dispatched by the company. Unless the company resolves otherwise, these operations will be at the expense of the requisitionists, though this will not be great where a members' resolution is simply included in the notice of meeting.

The requisitionists must deposit a copy, or copies, of the resolution signed by all the requisitionists at the company's registered office not less than six weeks before the meeting, where the requisition requires notice of a resolution to be given, and not less than a week before the meeting in the case of any other requisition. There must also be deposited or tendered with the requisition a sum reasonably sufficient to meet the company's expenses in giving effect to it. The requisitionists must between them represent not less than one twentieth of the total voting rights or be at least one hundred members on whose shares an average of at least £100 per member has been paid up. A requisition requiring notice of a resolution will be deemed to be served in time if after the requisition has been deposited the company calls a meeting for a date less than six weeks away.

Section 140(3) requires notice of a members' resolution requisitioned under the section to be given in the usual manner to all members of the company entitled to receive notice by serving a copy of the resolution on them. Notice is to be given to any other members by informing them of the general effect of the resolution. Notice of the resolution must be served, where practicable, at the same time as the notice calling the meeting, and if not, as soon as possible thereafter.

It would appear that a members' resolution requisitioned under section 140 may (where it is an ordinary resolution) be amended at the meeting so long as the amendment falls within the scope of the notice. Whilst section 140(3) requires a "copy" of the resolution to be served, notice of the precise wording of the resolution is not made a precondition of validity (cf. *Re Moorgate Mercantile Holdings* [1980] 1 All E.R. 40). Were it otherwise, the usefulness of the section to members would be severely restricted.

Section 140 is not exhaustive of the members' right to give notice of a resolution to be proposed at a general meeting, but where the members do not or cannot rely on the section they will have to give notice themselves to all the members. The practical difficulties and expense may make this impossible where the company is of any size.

Stock Exchange requirements

In the case of a company listed on The Stock Exchange proofs of notices of meetings (including newspaper advertisements), proxy forms and circulars must be sent to The Stock Exchange for approval (Listing Agreement, paragraph 6). Proof documents (four copies) should be submitted by the company's brokers in sufficient time for approval prior to final printing. It is not necessary to submit a proof notice and related proxy form for an A.G.M. at which only routine A.G.M. business is to be conducted. Six copies of notices and other related documents in their final form must also be submitted at the time they are issued (paragraph 7).

Special notice

In respect of the following resolutions (which are all ordinary resolutions) special notice must be given, namely:

(a) a resolution appointing as auditor a person other than a retiring auditor, removing an auditor before the expiration of his term of office, filling a casual vacancy in the office of auditor or reappointing as auditor a retiring auditor who was appointed by the directors to fill a casual vacancy (C.A. 1976, s. 15);

(b) a resolution to remove a director under section 184 of the Companies Act 1948 or to appoint someone else instead of a director so removed at the meeting at which he is removed; and

(c) a resolution appointing or approving the appointment of a director over 70 years of age where section 185(5) of the 1948 Act applies.

Where special notice of a resolution is required, notice of the intention to move the resolution must be given *to* the company at least 28 days before the meeting at which it is to be moved. The company must then give notice of the resolution to the members at least 21 days before the meeting, at the same time and in the same manner as it gives notice of the meeting, or where that is impracticable, by placing an advertisement in a newspaper with an appropriate circulation, or by any other method allowed by the articles (C.A. 1948, s. 142). In order to prevent the intention of the person serving the notice on the company from being frustrated, if the company calls a meeting 28 days or less after that notice has been given, the notice will be deemed to have been properly given for the purposes of the section. It would seem that a resolution of which special notice has been given may not be amended at the meeting since the reasoning in *Re Moorgate Mercantile Holdings* would appear to apply.

By section 184 of the Companies Act 1948 and section 15 of the Companies Act 1976, the company must also give notice of the relevant resolution to a dismissed director and to a dismissed, retiring or resigning auditor (and his replacement), respectively. These will then have the right to make representations of a reasonable length in writing to the company and to require these statements (as long as they are not received too late) to be sent with the notice of the relevant resolution to the members; the notice must state that the representations have been made. Where this is not done, the director or auditor in question may require the representations to be read out at the meeting, without prejudice to his right to be heard orally.

Circulars

Where the business to be conducted at a meeting is other than routine it is common for the directors to send out a circular with the notice of meeting explaining why the steps to be taken at the meeting are necessary, and often attempting to defuse any actual or likely opposition. The circular will be read in conjunction with the notice in order to establish whether sufficient notice of the business to be conducted has been given (*Re Moorgate Mercantile Holdings* [1980] 1 All E.R. 40). Any interest which the directors have in the passing of a resolution will normally be disclosed in a circular rather than in the notice itself, but as with a notice, the shareholders must not be mislead and in the event of a circular being found to be "tricky" the resolutions passed at the meeting will be liable to be set aside. It is permissible for the directors to join a "battle of circulars" with an opposed group of shareholders or outsiders, and for the directors to finance their campaign from company funds, since they are entitled to encourage the members to support policies which they believe to be in the company's interests and to resist counter-proposals. The directors will be in breach of duty, however, if their policies are designed, for example, merely to keep themselves in office (*Peel v. London & N.W. Railway* [1907] 1 Ch. 5).

The right to have circulars dispatched by the company is not confined to the board. Section 140 of the Companies Act 1948 requires the directors to circulate a statement of not more than one thousand words which has been prepared by the appropriate number of requisitionists. The statement may be concerned with a proposed resolution or other business to be dealt with at any general meeting, not merely an A.G.M. (as is the case with the right to require notice to be given of a members' resolution under section 140). The circular must be sent to all those entitled to receive notice of the meeting. If, however, the court is satisfied that the requisitionists are abusing their rights under section 140 in order to publicise defamatory material, the court may relieve the company of its obligation to circulate the statement. An application to the court may be made by the company or a person claiming to be aggrieved by the statement.

The costs of a circular requisitioned under the Section must be borne by the requisitionists unless the company resolves otherwise, and hence there is normally little advantage as far as the requisitionists are concerned in using their rights under section 140. There will be a saving if the circular is sent out at the same time as the notice of the meeting, but this will not always be possible, for example where the statement is issued in opposition to proposals by the directors which have been set out in the notice calling the meeting. The opposing members may also regard it as tactically unwise to reveal their argument to the board before it reaches the members or to lose control over timing or to be confined to one thousand words.

It should be noted that in the case of a listed company, where the company issues a circular to the holders of a particular class of security, a copy of the circular, or a summary of its contents, must be sent to the holders of all other listed securities unless the contents of the circular are irrelevant to them (Listing Agreement, paragraph 14).

Proxies

The term "proxy" refers both to the agent appointed by a member to vote on his behalf at a meeting of the company and to the document appointing that agent.

Right to appoint a proxy

A member's right to appoint a proxy is governed by section 136 of the Companies Act 1948; the provisions of that section may be made more generous to the members by the articles, but not less so. Any member entitled to attend and vote at a meeting may appoint a proxy, who need not be a member. There is no right to appoint a proxy in a company which does not have a share capital. By section 136(2), members must be informed of their right to appoint a proxy in the notice calling the meeting, which must also state that the proxy need not be a member. This information must be given reasonable prominence.

Section 136(1)(b) provides that a member of a private company is only entitled to appoint one proxy to attend on the same occasion, subject to the articles. This may mean that a member may not appoint a second or further proxies to vote in respect of different shares held by him or that he may not appoint a second proxy as an alternative to the first (that is, the latter to attend if the first is unable). The first interpretation seems preferable, since the appointment of a proxy to attend in the alternative is totally unobjectionable and in this case both proxies will not be attending "on the same occasion".

Validation of proxies

Articles normally provide that for the purpose of checking the validity of appointments, proxy forms must be lodged with the company within a certain period before the meeting. By section 136(3), any provision in the articles which requires the instrument appointing a proxy or other evidence of the validity of the appointment to be received by the company more than 48 hours before a meeting or adjourned meeting is void. Where the articles do not include a provision of this kind lodgement is unnecessary. Article 69 of Table A provides that the instrument appointing a proxy must be deposited with the company "not less than 48 hours" before the time for holding the meeting or adjourned meeting, and at least 24 hours before the taking of a poll, where this is deferred.

Stamp duty

If a form of proxy is only capable of being used at one meeting, it is exempt from stamp duty. A proxy which may be used at more than one meeting is a "general proxy" and must be stamped 50 pence (F.A. 1949, s. 35 and Sch. 8). A proxy which is required to be stamped, but which has not been, may be rejected by the chairman, but it is not void and he is not obliged to reject it. If the chairman allows an unstamped proxy the votes cast under it will be valid (*Marx v. Estates & General Investments* [1976] 1 W.L.R. 380).

Requirement for validity

The articles normally prescribe the form a proxy must take. If the appointment does not comply with the mandatory requirements in the articles it is invalid and the chairman must not allow the proxy to vote. Where the articles require a proxy to be witnessed, for example, it will be invalid if it is not witnessed (*Harben v. Phillips* (1883) 23 Ch.D. 14). Trivial non-compliance will not, however, invalidate a proxy (*Oliver v. Dalgleish* [1963] 1 W.L.R. 1274). Article 68 of Table A requires a proxy to be in writing and signed by the appointer or someone exercising a power of attorney on his behalf. Where the appointer is a company the appointment must be under seal or signed by an authorised officer or attorney. Articles 70 and 71 set out two model proxies and require proxies to take one or other form or as near thereto as circumstances allow. This requirement is directory only and it seems that any form of proxy which would be otherwise effective will be valid (*Isaacs v. Chapman* (1915) 32 T.L.R. 183).

Proxy forms are often given without the name of the appointee being filled in. Such forms are valid so long as someone is authorised to fill in the blank. The authority need not be in any particular form (*Re Lancaster* (1877) 5 Ch.D. 911).

Solicitation of proxies

The Companies Acts do not require a company to provide its members with proxy forms to fill in and return in advance of a meeting, but where proxies are solicited at the company's expense and the invitation to appoint a proxy specifies a particular person who is willing to act as proxy, the company must make a similar invitation to all members entitled to appoint a proxy for the meeting (C.A. 1948, s. 136(4)). In other words, the directors may not only solicit proxies from those members who they think will be favourable to their cause. Officers in breach of section 136(4) will be liable to a fine, but they will not be in breach where they have merely supplied to a member, at his request in writing, a proxy form naming the proxy, or with a list of persons willing to act as proxy, so long as the form or list is available to every member entitled to vote at the meeting, if requested. It is quite legitimate for the company's money to be used to invite members to appoint proxies, in the hope that this will increase the liklihood of the directors' proposals being accepted at the meeting, because the directors are entitled to promote policies which they consider to be in the company's interests. Experience shows that the number of proxy forms returned will normally be greatly increased if postage is pre-paid by the company.

If a company is listed it must send a two-way proxy form with the notice convening a meeting to everyone who is entitled to vote at the meeting; that is, the appointer must be able to direct the proxy to vote for or against each resolution (Listing Agreement paragraph 12; see Article 71). It is not, however, necessary to provide a two-way proxy form for purely procedural resolutions. The Stock Exchange requires the form to state that if the appointer does not indicate whether the proxy should vote for or against a resolution, the proxy may vote as he thinks fit.

Rights of proxy

The scope of the authority conferred on a proxy is, within the confines of what the articles permit, to be determined by construing the form of appointment (*Re Waxed Papers* [1937] 2 All E.R. 481). A proxy has the right to speak at a meeting of a private company, but unless the articles provide otherwise, not at a meeting of a public company (C.A. 1948, s. 136(1)), and hence a proxy may not move a resolution or an amendment. Whether a proxy counts towards a quorum depends on the articles. Under Article 53 of Table A (as amended by Companies Act 1980), a proxy must be counted. Subject to contrary provision in the articles, a proxy may only vote on a poll (that is, not on a show of hands), but a proxy does have the right to demand a poll to the same extent as if he were the member he represents. Any provision in the articles purporting to exclude this right will be void (C.A. 1948, s. 137). A proxy appointed by five members may, therefore, demand a poll on his own.

Obligation of proxy

In the absence of a contract or some fiduciary obligation, a proxy is not bound to attend and vote at the meeting for which he is appointed. If the proxy does attend it is not clear what the consequences would be, as between the proxy and his appointer, if he were to vote contrary to his instructions, or whether this would affect the validity of the votes cast. (These questions are briefly discussed in *Oliver v. Dalgleish* [1963] 1 W.L.R. 1274). Where a proxy contracts with his appointer to attend and vote at the meeting he will, as regards his appointer, be bound to attend and vote as directed, and likewise if he stands in a fiduciary relationship to his appointer. The directors do not owe a fiduciary duty to the members, without more, but it is likely that where a director is appointed proxy he must vote in accordance with his instructions if he votes at all (otherwise two-way proxies would be pointless), though it is not clear whether a director-appointee is bound to attend the meeting (see *Second Consolidated Trust v. Ceylon Amalgamated Estates* [1943] 2 All E.R. 567 and *Re Dorman Long & Co.* [1934] Ch. 635).

Revocation

As between appointer and proxy the authority to act may be revoked at any time unless the appointer is contractually bound not to revoke, or the proxy has an interest in the subject of the meeting and has given value for the right to act as proxy, for example where the proxy is an unregistered transferee. In order to avoid the difficulties which the company would face if the authority were revoked but the proxy nevertheless voted, articles usually provide that a proxy will not be invalidated by revocation unless the company has been notified of this before the start of the meeting. If the articles do not make provision for notification after the meeting has begun but before an adjourned meeting or a poll, notification will only be effective if it is received before the start of the meeting, since the adjourned meeting and poll are regarded as continuations of the meeting. Article 73 of Table A provides that a vote cast by proxy will be valid where the proxy has been expressly revoked, or on the death or lunacy of the appointer, or on the transfer of the shares in respect of which the proxy is given, unless notice in writing is received at the company's registered office before the meeting or any adjourned meeting at which the proxy is to be used has begun. A member may vote at a meeting despite his having appointed a proxy. If the member votes before the proxy, the proxy's authority will be impliedly revoked, and if the proxy also votes his vote will be invalid. The votes cast by the member in person will be valid in these circumstances even where the articles require advance notification of revocation to be given to the company, as the company is regarded as not needing this protection where the member is present at the meeting in person (*Cousins v. International Brick Co.* [1931] 2 Ch. 90).

Corporate representatives

Section 139 of the Companies Act 1948 empowers a corporation, whether or not a company within the meaning of the Act, to appoint a natural person to act as its representative at any general meeting or class meeting of a company of which it is a member. A corporation may also appoint a representative for creditors' meetings held in pursuance of the Act or the provisions of a debenture or trust deed. The representative must be appointed by resolution of the directors or other governing body of the corporation. Where the appointing company is in liquidation the liquidator will be the "governing body" for this purpose, so long as he is in effective control.

It is desirable from the point of view of the appointing company to appoint a representative rather than a proxy, since a representative has the same rights at a meeting as if he were registered with the shares held by his appointer. Hence, the representative must, for example, be counted in a quorum, and may speak at the meeting and may vote on a show of hands. There is also no need to notify the company of the appointment of a representative before the meeting, though the company may subsequently require proof of appointment. A company may, if it so desires, appoint a proxy rather than a representative, who will then be in the same position as if he had been appointed by an individual member.

Conduct of meetings

It is essential that meetings be conducted in accordance with the general law and the company's regulations, since an irregularity may render the proceedings invalid. Where a company is of any size its legal adviser will normally attend meetings to assist the chairman with any points of procedure which may arise, and this is prudent in any case where it is anticipated that there will be opposition to the board's proposals, since those opposed may try to create, or at least subsequently rely on, an irregularity.

Quorum

In so far as the articles do not otherwise provide, a quorum at a general meeting of a public or private company is two members personally present, that is, not present by proxy (C.A. 1948, s. 134(c)). Where the articles require two members to be "present" this means present personally (*M. Harris Ltd.* 1956 S.C. 207). By Article 53 of Table A, two members present personally or by proxy will constitute a quorum. A personal representative of a deceased shareholder who has not been registered does not count towards the quorum, unless the articles provide otherwise, since he is not a member (*quaere* whether a shareholder with no voting rights may be counted in the quorum; *Young v. South African etc. Exploration Syndicate* [1896] 2 Ch. 268, 277). A member who holds shares in his own right and as trustee will, however, count as two members as far as the quorum is concerned, as he holds the shares in two different capacities.

Where Table A applies a quorum need only be present at the start of the meeting, and not for its entire duration (*Re Hartley Baird* [1955] Ch. 143), but the proceedings will only be valid as long as they still constitute a meeting. It is not clear whether a quorum must be present throughout where the articles are not specific on the point. Where a meeting is called by the court or the Department of Trade under sections 135 or 131(2) of the Companies Act 1948, respectively, it may be declared that one member constitutes a quorum. An application might be made to the court under section 135 where, for example, a minority are abusing the quorum requirements by refusing to attend a meeting, in order to make it impossible for any business to be validly undertaken at it (see, for example, *Re H. R. Paul & Son* (1973) 118 S.J. 166).

Article 54 provides for automatic adjournment of a meeting if half an hour from the time scheduled for its commencement a quorum is not present. The meeting then stands adjourned until the same time a week later at the same place, or at such other time and place as is decided by the directors, since the former may prove inconvenient. Where the meeting has been requisitioned by the members it is automatically dissolved. Article 54, as amended by the Companies Act 1980, no longer provides that at the adjourned meeting the members present after half an hour from the time appointed for commencement shall constitute a quorum, even though the quorum requirements are not otherwise satisfied. Where a company has adopted the pre-1980 Act Table A, arguably "members" may be read as "member" (see section 6 of the Interpretation Act 1978), but it does not follow that a valid meeting could be held with only one person present, since there may well not be a meeting. There would be a valid meeting, however, where there was one member present in person and another by proxy (*Daimler Co. v. Continental Tyre & Rubber Co.* [1916] 2 A.C. 307).

Chairman

Unless the articles provide otherwise, any member of the company may be elected chairman of a meeting by the members present (C.A. 1948, s. 134(d)). The articles normally state that the chairman of the board (if any) will preside at a general meeting, or failing him, any director (see, e.g. Article 55). Article 56 provides that if no director is willing to act as chairman, or no director is present within fifteen minutes of the time arranged for the start of the meeting, the members present may choose one of their number to be chairman.

The function of the chairman is to ensure that the business of the meeting is got through in an efficient manner. It is the chairman's duty to preserve order and if he is unable to do so he has the inherent power to adjourn the meeting until it can be restored. The chairman must act in good faith and the adjournment must not last longer than is reasonably necessary for the restoration of order (*John v. Rees* [1969] 2 W.L.R. 1294). It is also the chairman's responsibility to ascertain the true sense of the meeting with regard to the questions under consideration. In this connection, Article 58(a) provides that the chairman may, of his own motion, require a poll to be taken if he has reason to believe that the result on a poll would be different from that on a show of hands (*Second Consolidated Trust v. Ceylon Amalgamated Tea & Rubber Estates* [1943] 2 All E.R. 567).

In larger companies it is usual for the chairman at an A.G.M. (who will be the chairman of the board or someone standing in for him) to make a formal speech reporting on the activities of the company over the preceding year and commenting on its future prospects. The meeting will normally be thrown open to the members to speak after the resolution that the directors' report and accounts be adopted is moved and seconded. The members may ask questions of the chairman and directors, who are not bound to reply if they do not consider it to be in the company's interests. Every member entitled to attend and vote at the meeting has, prima facie, the right to speak and voice his opposition to any proposed resolution, but the chairman must keep the discussion within reasonable bounds and may put a stop to further consideration of a particular matter once it has been sufficiently debated and a fair cross-section of views has been heard. He must not use this power capriciously, or to stifle discussion, or, in particular, to prevent the views of a minority being effectively expressed. The majority may resolve to require the chairman to put an end to further discussion, so long as they are not acting oppressively towards a minority (*Wall v. London & Northern Assets Corp.* [1898] 2 Ch. 469).

Article 57 of Table A provides that the chairman may adjourn the meeting with the consent of the members, and must adjourn if directed to do so. If the articles are silent, the chairman may only adjourn if an ordinary resolution to this effect is passed (*National Dwellings Society v. Sykes* [1894] 3 Ch. 159). Occasionally the articles confer on the chairman a discretion to adjourn without the consent of the meeting; where this is the case the chairman, so long as he acts in good faith, may refuse to adjourn, even though a majority of members present demand this (*Salisbury Gold Mining Co. v. Hathorn* [1897] A.C. 268). If the chairman improperly refuses to adjourn, or adjourns when he is not entitled, the members may elect a new chairman to replace him (*National Dwellings Society v. Sykes*, above).

The chairman does not have a casting vote in the event of equality of voting, unless the articles state the contrary. Article 60 of Table A provides that the chairman shall have a casting vote, both on a show of hands and on a poll.

The chairman may dissolve a meeting when the business for which it was called has been completed.

Resolutions

A resolution formulated by the board will normally be proposed by the chairman, and in the case of a members' resolution the chairman should invite an appropriate member to propose it. Unless the articles so provide, there is no need for a proposed resolution to be seconded, though this is the usual practice. The chairman should not allow a resolution to be proposed which is not covered by the notice convening the meeting. Regardless of the origin of a resolution, it should be put to the meeting by the chairman, who must clearly indicate what the proposal is, preferably by reading the resolution out, and after allowing time for discussion, put it to the vote.

The chairman must be particularly scrupulous with regard to the acceptance or rejection of amendments to resolutions, since a mistake will result in the resolution which is eventually carried being invalid, even though the chairman acted in good faith (see, for example, *Henderson v. Bank of Australasia* (1890) 45 Ch. D. 330). An amendment may be validly put where it is within the scope of the notice calling the meeting. The freedom to amend resolutions will vary, therefore, according to whether the original resolution forms part of ordinary business, and whether it is an ordinary resolution, or a special or extraordinary resolution. Since specific notice of ordinary business need not be given where the articles distinguish between ordinary and special business, any amendment may be made to a resolution which is part of ordinary business, so long as it does not take the resolution outside the category of ordinary business. No amendments of substance may be made to special or extraordinary resolutions.

In the case of special business, the more general the terms of the notice, the wider the scope for amendment. Where an ordinary resolution is set out verbatim in the notice, the resolution may nonetheless be amended in so far as the resolution as set out gives sufficient notice of the general nature of the business to be conducted. So, for example, where a notice names persons to be appointed directors or as liquidator, others may be appointed in addition or instead (*Betts v. Macnaghten* [1910] 1 Ch. 430; *Re Trench Tubeless Tyre Co.* [1900] 1 Ch. 408, respectively). The test of sufficiency of notice is that it should enable a member to decide whether or not to attend to protect his interests, and hence an amendment should not be allowed where it would affect a member's decision not to attend. Accordingly, an amendment to a resolution increasing the directors' remuneration which reduced the amount of the increase would be in order, but an amendment to increase remuneration by an even larger amount would not.

The chairman should only allow an amendment which is genuinely relevant to the resolution under consideration. He should not allow an amendment which negates the main substance of the resolution; the members should be given the opportunity to accept or reject the resolution, as they see fit. Where several amendments to the same resolution are proposed, they should be put to the meeting in the order in which they were proposed, unless overlapping or inconsistency suggests a more efficient ordering. An amendment which is inconsistent with one already accepted by the meeting should not be put, since it should be regarded as having been implicitly rejected.

Voting

The common law rule is that voting shall be by show of hands and this rule will apply in the first instance unless the articles exclude it. Article 62 of Table A provides that subject to the rights attached to any particular class of shares, each member has one vote, regardless of the number of shares he holds. It is the duty of the chairman, usually assisted by the secretary, to count the number of hands raised. Unless the articles provide otherwise, proxies may not vote, though it may be difficult to distinguish proxies from members where they are not physically separated. By section 141(3) of the Companies Act 1948, a declaration by the chairman that a special or extraordinary resolution is carried is, unless a poll is demanded, conclusive evidence of that fact, without the proportion of votes cast in favour of the resolution needing to be proved. Article 58 provides similarly with regard to all types of resolution, and as to the particular majority, where a declaration is made by the chairman and this is entered in the minutes.

Voting by show of hands is an unsatisfactory way of determining the sense of the meeting and hence, except where the matter is uncontroversial, a poll will normally be held instead of, or more usually, after, a show of hands, in which case the result of the show of hands is nullified. The right to demand a poll is a common law right; the articles usually specify the conditions subject to which a poll may be requested, but the articles may not cut down the rights conferred by section 137 of the Companies Act 1948. Where the articles are silent, any member may demand a poll (see *Wimbledon Local Board* (1882) 8 Q.B.D. 459). Pursuant to section 137, it must be possible to demand a poll at any general meeting on any question except the election of the chairman and adjournment, and the articles are void to the extent that they curtail the right to demand a poll made:

"(i) by not less than five members having the right to vote at the meeting; or

(ii) by a member or members representing not less than one tenth of the total voting rights of all the members having the right to vote at the meeting; or

(iii) by a member or members holding shares in the company conferring a right to vote at the meeting, being shares on which an aggregate sum has been paid up equal to not less than one tenth of the total sum paid up on all the shares conferring that right."

Section 137(2) provides that a proxy may make, or join in making, a demand for a poll to the same extent as could the member he represents. Article 58 of Table A is more generous, in that it allows a poll to be demanded by two members, rather than five, as in section 137(1)(b)(i). That article also permits the chairman of his own motion to require a poll to be taken.

Notwithstanding anything in the articles, any member, or his proxy, may demand a poll at a meeting at which a special resolution in connection with the purchase or redemption by the company of its own shares in accordance with Part III of the Companies Act 1981 is to be put (C.A. 1981, ss. 47(9), 47(11), 48(3), 50(3), and 55(7)).

The extent of the voting rights attached to shares is governed by the company's regulations or the terms of issue. In the absence of specific reference, section 134(e) provides that a member shall have one vote per share or £10 of stock held by him in the case of a company originally having a share capital, and in every other case each member shall have one vote. Article 62 provides that each share carries one vote, subject to class rights; it is not uncommon, for example, for preference shares to have no voting rights (but see Admission of Securities to Listing Schedule VII A,F1). Voting rights may also be enhanced in certain situations (see, for example, *Bushell v. Faith* [1970] A.C. 1099).

Article 63 states that in the case of jointly held shares, the vote of the senior only (whether he is voting in person or by proxy) may be accepted. Seniority is determined by the order of names in the register.

A member need not cast all his votes the same way, as, for instance, where he is nominee for several others who wish him to vote in different ways (C.A. 1948, s. 138).

Where a special resolution is to be put to a meeting in connection with the purchase or redemption by the company of its own shares in accordance with Part III of the Companies Act 1981 (see sections 47(9), 47(11), 48(3), 50(3) and 55(7)), a member who holds shares to which the resolution relates may not vote the shares, and the resolution will be invalid if it would not have been passed but for the votes cast by him. This will be the case both on a poll and on a show of hands. A member who holds other shares which are not the subject of the resolution may exercise the voting rights attached to them on a poll only.

Article 61 requires a poll demanded on the election of a chairman, or as to whether the meeting should be adjourned, to be taken immediately. Otherwise the poll may be taken at such time as the chairman directs, and in the manner he directs (Article 59). Where there are not too many members present, it may be convenient to take the poll immediately. Whether this is done or the poll is taken at a later date, the meeting will be regarded as having continued until the result of the poll is declared, and the resolution in question will not be passed until then. Members may vote in the poll, even though not present at the original meeting. The usual method of voting is for the voters to sign a sheet indicating whether they are for or against the motion and how many votes they are casting. Scrutineers may be appointed to count the votes, and it is good practice to draw representatives from both sides. It should be noted that both on a poll and on a show of hands, the requisite majority is of those entitled to vote and actually voting, not of those present at the meeting. Article 66 prevents the validity of votes cast being questioned after the conclusion of the meeting; objections may only be made at the meeting and the chairman's decision is final (subject to fraud on his part: *Wall v. London & Northern Assets Corp.* [1899] 1 Ch. 550).

In the absence of an article allowing it, postal voting is not permissible.

Defamation

A general meeting is a privileged occasion and hence statements made at a meeting relating to the affairs of the company will only be actionable in defamation if malicious. As regards reports of the proceedings of general meetings, section 7 of the Defamation Act 1952 provides a defence to a defamation claim in respect of a "fair and accurate" report of a meeting of a public company, again in the absence of malice.

Adjournment

It may be necessary to adjourn a meeting because it is inquorate, or because there is insufficient time to complete the business for which it was called, or for a wide variety of other reasons. Article 54 of Table A provides that if there is not a quorum present after half an hour from the time appointed for the start of the meeting, it shall be adjourned until the same time, one week later, at the same place. In other circumstances, the articles normally give power to the chairman to adjourn with the consent of the meeting, and to the meeting to direct the chairman to adjourn (see Article 57). The chairman has inherent power to adjourn as a last resort, in the event of disorder (*John v. Rees* [1969] 2 W.L.R. 1294). Where the articles are silent, the right to adjourn is vested in the members (*National Dwelling Society v. Sykes* [1894] 3 Ch. 159). Under Table A, were a poll is demanded on the question of adjournment, it must be held immediately (Article 61).

An adjourned meeting is treated as a continuation of the original meeting and hence, subject to contrary provision in the articles, no notice of the adjourned meeting is necessary. (If the meeting is adjourned for thirty days or more, Article 57 requires notice to be given in the ordinary way.) No business may be conducted at the adjourned meeting which could not have been dealt with at the original meeting. Proxies given for the original meeting may vote at an adjourned meeting. The articles may not forbid the lodging of new proxies up to 48 hours before the adjourned meeting (C.A. 1948, s. 136(3), and see Article 69).

Resolutions passed at an adjourned meeting are to be treated as passed at the date they are actually passed and not on the date of the original meeting (C.A. 1948, s. 144), contrary to the earlier common law rule. Unless the articles provide otherwise, a meeting of which valid notice has been given cannot be cancelled or postponed: the meeting must be commenced and then adjourned, if appropriate (*Smith v. Paringa Mines* [1906] 2 Ch. 193).

Minutes

There is a statutory obligation on the company to make minutes of general meetings, and it is in the company's interests to keep accurate minutes since these may be of great value as evidence in any litigation which might arise out of a general meeting.

Section 145 of the Companies Act 1948 requires minutes to be made of all general meetings, which are to be entered in "books kept for that purpose". By section 436 of the 1948 Act, entries may be made in bound books or may be recorded in any other manner, so long as adequate precautions are taken to guard against falsification and to facilitate its discovery. A loose-leaf minute book is, therefore, permissible. The usual practice is for the secretary to make notes at the meeting and for the minutes to be subsequently written up in the minute book. The minutes are then normally signed by the chairman at the beginning of the next general meeting, in which event they will constitute evidence of the proceedings at the meeting in question (section 145(2)). The minutes only constitute prima facie evidence, however, and hence may be contradicted by conflicting evidence. Evidence may be adduced, for example, of a resolution which was passed at the meeting, but does not appear in the minutes (*Re Fireproof Doors* [1916] 2 Ch. 142). The articles might provide, however, that the minutes shall constitute conclusive evidence of the proceedings, in which case their accuracy may not be questioned except where they have been fradulently written up or there is an error on their face (*Kerr v. Mottram* [1940] Ch. 657; *Re Caratal (New) Mines* [1902] 2 Ch. 498). The chairman may make manuscript amendments (which he should initial) before he signs the minutes, but nothing should be erased since this may give rise to a suspicion .of falsification. Once signed, the minutes should not be altered; amendment should be made by an entry in the minutes of a subsequent meeting.

Where minutes have been made in accordance with the requirements of section 145, a rebuttable presumption arises that the meeting was duly held and convened and that the proceedings and all appointments of directors, managers and liquidators are valid (section 145(3)).

Inspection of minutes and reports of meetings

The provisions concerning the inspection of minutes are contained in section 146 of the Companies Act 1948. The minutes must be kept at the company's registered office and be open to inspection by the members for at least two hours on each business day, free of charge. A member is entitled to have a copy of the minutes supplied to him within seven days of his request, at a rate not exceeding 2.5 pence per 100 words. If the company refuses to allow inspection, or to supply the copy requested, the court may order the company to give effect to the member's rights, and the company and every officer in default will be liable to a fine.

Companies are not obliged to report the proceedings of general meetings and reporters have no right to attend. However, public companies generally invite the press to be present and occasionally circulate their members with an account of the meeting.

Types of resolution

Ordinary resolutions

The term "ordinary resolution" is not defined in the Companies Acts, but is the form in which formal decisions of the general meeting are expressed, unless the Acts or the company's memorandum or articles require a special or extraordinary resolution. An ordinary resolution will be passed if a simple majority of those voting (not of those present) vote in favour of it. It is not necessary for an ordinary resolution to be set out verbatim in the notice calling the meeting at which the resolution is to be proposed.

Extraordinary resolutions

The requirements for the passing of an extraordinary resolution are set out in section 141(1) of the Companies Act 1948. They are as follows:

(i) the notice calling the meeting (which must be given at least 14 days in advance) must state that the resolution is an extraordinary resolution;

(ii) the resolution must be set out in the notice and only that resolution may be passed at the meeting, that is, no amendments of substance may be made (*Re Moorgate Mercantile Holdings* [1980] 1 All E.R. 40); and

(iii) 75 per cent of those voting must vote in favour of the resolution (on a poll, 75 per cent of the votes cast must support the resolution).

By section 141(3), unless a poll is demanded, a declaration by the chairman that an extraordinary resolution is carried is conclusive, in the absence of fraud, unless it contains an error on its face, for example, where the chairman states the number of votes cast for and against the motion and it is evident that there is not a 75 per cent majority (*Re Caratel (New) Mines* [1902] 2 Ch. 498).

The company's articles may require an extraordinary resolution for any purpose other than one for which the Companies Acts require a special resolution. The 1948 Act requires an extraordinary resolution to be passed in connection with certain aspects of winding up. For example, where a company wishes to go into voluntary liquidation under section 278(1)(c) it must declare by extraordinary resolution that by reason of its liabilities it cannot stay in business (see also sections 303, 306 and 341). It should be stressed that there is no particular connection between an "extraordinary" resolution and an "extraordinary" general meeting. An extraordinary resolution may be passed at both an E.G.M. and an A.G.M.

Special resolutions

The requirements for a valid special resolution are the same as those for an extraordinary resolution, save that the notice calling the meeting must specify that the resolution is a special resolution and at least 21 days' notice of the intention to propose it must be given (C.A. 1948, s. 141(2)). Article 50 of Table A provides that 21 days' notice is needed. However, if it is so agreed by a majority holding at least 95 per cent in nominal value of the shares giving the right to attend and vote at the meeting, or where the company does not have a share capital, representing at least 95 per cent of the total voting rights, the resolution may be passed as a special resolution, even though 21 days' notice has not been given (section 141(2)). The members consenting must agree to the specific resolution being passed on short notice (*Re Pearce Duff & Co.* [1960] 1 W.L.R. 1014). As with an extraordinary resolution, the text of a special resolution must be set out in the notice calling the meeting and no amendments of substance may be made to it. Likewise, a declaration by the chairman that a special resolution has been passed will be conclusive (section 141(3)).

The articles may require any matter to be dealt with by special resolution. The Companies Acts require a special resolution in a wide variety of situations, normally where some constitutional change is involved (for example, section 5 and section 10 of the Companies Act 1948, altering the objects or articles, respectively), or some other matter of considerable importance to the company (for example, section 66 of the Companies Act 1948, reduction of capital, or section 222 of that Act, resolving that the company be wound up by the court).

Registration of resolutions

Section 143 of the Companies Act 1948 requires certain resolutions which are of concern to third parties to be sent to the Registrar of Companies for registration within fifteen days of their passing. The company and officers in default are liable to a fine where this is not done. The resolutions which must be registered are as follows:

(i)   special resolutions;

(ii) extraordinary resolutions;

(iii) resolutions which are effective because they have been agreed to by all the members, but which would otherwise be ineffective unless passed as special or extraordinary resolutions, as the case may be;

(iv) all resolutions or agreements which have been agreed to by all the members of a class, but which would not otherwise have been effective unless passed by a particular majority or in a particular manner, and all resolutions which effectively bind all the members of a class, although not agreed to by all those members; and

(v)   resolutions under sections 8(3) or 37(2) of the 1980 Act, and for voluntary winding up under section 278(1)(a) of the 1948 Act.

(Also, by section 63 of the 1948 Act an ordinary resolution increasing share capital must be registered within 15 days.)

By section 51(2) of the Companies Act 1967, resolutions or agreements which must be sent to the Registrar under section 143 of the 1948 Act need not be printed, so long as the copy is in a form approved by the Registrar. Details of the methods of reproduction acceptable to the Registrar are set out in *Board of Trade Journal*, 20 October 1967, p. 960.

Section 143(2) requires a copy of every resolution or agreement for the time being in force which falls within section 143, to be embodied in or annexed to every copy of the articles which are issued after the passing of the resolution, or making of the agreement, where the articles have been registered; where they have not, a copy of every such resolution or agreement must be forwarded to any member at his request, on payment of a maximum fee of five pence.

Sections 9(5) and (6) of the European Communities Act 1972 contain provisions requiring the registration of amended memoranda and articles of association.

Where a company is listed, all resolutions passed by the company (other than those concerned with routine business at an A.G.M.) must be submitted to The Stock Exchange.

Written resolutions

Whilst the Companies Acts refer generally to resolutions being passed at meetings, this is not essential. Article 73A of Table A, for example, provides that subject to the provisions of the Companies Acts, a resolution in writing, signed by all the members entitled to receive notice of, and to attend and vote at, a general meeting, shall be as effective as if it had been passed at a duly convened meeting. This article was incorporated into Table A by the Companies Act 1980, and hence now applies both to private companies and (in theory) to public companies. In practice, written resolutions will only be feasible in companies with a small number of shareholders.

It appears that written resolutions will be effective regardless of the type of resolution, that is, whether it is an ordinary, extraordinary or special resolution, or is a matter which requires an extraordinary or a special resolution. This point is not entirely free from doubt, as the definition of extraordinary and special resolutions in section 141 of the 1948 Act refers to such resolutions being passed at a general meeting. However, section 143(4) requires resolutions to be registered which have been agreed to by all the members, but which would otherwise only have been valid if they had been passed as extraordinary or special resolutions. This, therefore, envisages resolutions taking effect as extraordinary or special resolutions, even though not passed at a meeting. This interpretation has been confirmed by *Cane v. Jones* [1981] 1 All E.R. 533.

Exceptionally, it may be that the powers conferred by section 61 of the Companies Act 1948 to alter share capital may only be exercised at a general meeting, since subsection (2) unambiguously states that "the powers conferred by this section must be exercised by the company in general meeting". It is difficult to see, however, why these particular powers should be treated differently from any other matters on which the members might decide.

Informal resolutions and agreements and waiver of irregularities

A resolution (or a matter which ought to be dealt with by resolution) may be valid even though there is some irregularity in the meeting or no meeting at all. The power to make resolutions in writing is a particular example of the wider power of the members to dispense with certain formalities. The operation of the principle depends on the unanimous agreement of all those entitled to vote on the matter in question, and hence it will normally only apply in companies with a small number of shareholders. The assent of those not entitled to vote is not necessary (*Re Duomatic* [1969] 2 Ch. 365).

A resolution may be valid where proper notice has not been given provided it is passed unanimously (*Re Oxted Motor Co.* [1921] 3 K.B. 32). A distinction should be drawn between the waiver of irregularities by unanimous assent, and the power to hold meetings and to pass special resolutions on short notice under sections 133(3) and 141(2) of the Companies Act 1948, respectively; the latter do not dispense with the need to give notice altogether. The principle will also apply where there has been no meeting at all (see, for example, *Parker & Cooper v. Reading* [1926] Ch. 975, where the members were held to have informally ratified an act of the directors which was beyond the latter's powers). In *Cane v. Jones* [1981] 1 All E.R. 533 it was held that an agreement entered into by all the members (which was not signed in each other's presence) was effective to override the articles, and hence operated as a special resolution, even though no meeting had been held. (*Quaere* whether an agreement, as opposed to a resolution, must be registered under section 143(4)(c); see *Cane v. Jones*, above, at page 540.)

Where a resolution is invalid because of some irregularity at the meeting at which it is passed, the resolution may be ratified at a subsequent meeting by the appropriate majority, or informally where all the members agree.

It may, in any event, be difficult for a member to challenge the validity of a resolution because of the procedural difficulties created by the rule in *Foss v. Harbottle* (see page 788) and further, a member may be precluded from questioning an irregularity where he had acquiesced in it (see, for example, *Re Bailey Hay & Co.* [1971] 1 W.L.R. 1357).

Whilst resolutions, or agreements having the affect of resolutions, may be valid where there is an irregularity in the meeting or no meeting at all, this does not mean that a company is free to dispense with general meetings altogether. The company must hold an A.G.M. every year on penalty of a fine (C.A. 1948, s. 131). There are also other circumstances in which a meeting must be held, for example, when requisitioned by the members under section 132 of the 1948 Act, and where there has been a serious loss of capital (C.A. 1980, s. 34).

Limitations on the powers of general meeting

The general meeting is entitled to resolve upon any matter assigned to it by the Acts or the company's memorandum or articles. The articles will normally confer exclusive powers of management on the directors, and hence except in certain exceptional circumstances (for example, where the board is deadlocked, see *Barron v. Potter* [1914] 1 Ch. 895) the general meeting will not have the right to interfere with matters of management (see Article 80 and *Automatic Self-Cleansing Filter Syndi-*

cate Co. v. Cunninghame [1906] 2 Ch. 34; *Quin & Axtens v. Salmon* [1909] 1 Ch. 311).

There are also a number of restrictions on the power of the general meeting within its area of competence. The general meeting may not alter the memorandum or articles in such a way as to require a member to take more shares, or to increase the liability on his existing shares, after the date on which he joined the company, unless he agrees otherwise in writing (C.A. 1948, s. 22). Where an application has been made under section 75 of the Companies Act 1980 (complaining of conduct prejudicial to some part of the members) the court may order that certain alterations may not be made to the memorandum or articles without the court's consent (see also the court's power to make similar orders under section 5(4B) of the CompaniesiAct 1948 and section 11(8) of the Companies Act 1980, and the power of the court to cancel an alteration under section 23 of the 1948 Act).

It is possible for the rights of the members to be protected from alteration by the general meeting by inserting them in the memorandum and specifying that they are unalterable. Where members' rights are contained in the memorandum, but are not expressed to be unalterable, they may be altered in general meeting, but subject to the right of a dissenting minority of 15 per cent to apply to the court to have the alteration set aside.

Subject to the points made above, and the general protection against "unfairly prejudicial" conduct afforded by section 75 of the 1980 Act, together with the rather vague principles which prohibit a "fraud on the minority" (see page 791), the general meeting is free to alter the company's memorandum and articles despite any adverse effect this may have on the interests of the members (see, for example, *Allen v. Gold Reefs of West Africa* [1900] 1 Ch. 656). Where the company's shares are divided into different classes, however, there is a greater measure of protection against the alteration of class rights (see page 815).

Whilst a shareholders' agreement is not, as such, a restriction on the powers of the general meeting, where such an agreement has been made, a party to it may be restrained by injunction from voting inconsistently with it (*Greenwell v. Porter* [1902] 1 Ch. 530), or may be obliged by mandatory injunction to vote the way he has contracted to do (*Puddephatt v. Leigh* [1916] 1 Ch. 200).

Rights of third parties

The rights of third parties who have entered into a contract with the company, for example debenture holders, may not be unilaterally varied, and hence should the general meeting pass resolutions which are inconsistent with third party rights the company will be in breach of contract. In the event of loss, the third party will, therefore, have a right to damages, and a secured creditor will normally have the right to enforce his security.

It is not so clear, however, whether a third party may obtain an injunction to prevent the company from changing its memorandum or articles in breach of contract. Section 10 of the Companies Act 1948, for example, confers on the general meeting the right to alter the articles, and it has been held that the company cannot contract out of this right (*Punt v. Symons & Co.* [1903] 2 Ch. 506). There is, however, other, inconsistent, authority (see, for example, *Baily v. British Equitable Assurance Co.* [1904] 1 Ch. 374; cf. *Southern Foundries v. Shirlaw* [1940] A.C. 703). The more widely held view is that an injunction may not be granted to prevent a company altering its memorandum or articles, even though this might result in the company being in breach of contract (see page 107).

Class meetings

Where the company's shares are divided into different classes, it may be necessary to convene separate class meetings to consider matters relating to the interests of holders of those shares, in particular, where a variation of class rights is proposed (see page 815).

The procedure relating to the convening and holding of class meetings is usually similar to that of general meetings. By section 32(6) of the Companies Act 1980, the provisions of section 133 (length of notice), section 134 (general provisions as to meetings and votes) and section 140 (circulation of members' resolutions) of the 1948 Act, and the provisions of the articles relating to general meetings, will apply to class meetings at which a variation of the rights attached to the shares is proposed, subject to necessary modifications. The quorum in these circumstances, however, is two persons holding or representing as proxy at least one third in nominal value of the issued shares of the class in question; at an adjourned meeting one person or a proxy holding shares of the class in question constitutes a quorum. Any holder of shares of the class, present in person or by proxy, may demand a poll. Sections 136 (proxies), 139 (corporate representatives) and section 144 (resolutions passed at an adjourned meeting), expressly apply to class meetings generally. Strictly, class meetings should only be attended by members of the class, but it may prove more convenient to hold a combined company general meeting and class meeting. So long as voting is separate and no objection is made at the meeting, this is permissible (*Carruth v. I.C.I.* [1937] A.C. 707).

Provisions similar to those regulating general meetings and class meetings are often incorporated into debentures for the regulation of meetings of debenture holders.

Insider Dealing

The provisions of the Companies Act 1980 on insider dealing were welcomed by the guardians of the City establishment as a means of governing an aspect of market malpractice which the self-regulatory machinery was unable to control. It has long been generally accepted that insider dealing was, at least, unfair, an abuse of the insider's position of trust and confidence and harmful to the securities market, and since the early 1960's recommendations have repeatedly been made for protective legislation for the insider's victim. The Conservative government was first to attempt to legislate specifically on insider dealing and included proposals for criminal and civil liability in the 1973 Companies Bill (which did not pass into law). This impetus for the introduction of legislation was maintained by the Labour government but it was not until the succeeding Conservative government took office that legislation was enacted, as Part V of the Companies Act 1980.

Recognising the need for new measures to sustain investors' confidence in the market, the City's governing bodies greeted the new legislation with some enthusiasm. But those more familiar with the difficulties of successfully prosecuting criminal matters were less than optimistic about the legislation's chances of success – principally because of the many and detailed requirements of Part V which would have to be satisfied before a crime could be proved. A further cause for scepticism on the potential effectiveness of the legislation was the absence of provision for its policing and enforcement, save to the extent that proceedings were to be instituted by the Secretary of State or by, or with the consent of, the Director of Public Prosecutions in England and Wales.

To date, it is impossible to determine whether the new legislation has had any significant effect as the extent of insider dealing has never really been known. The small number of prosecutions since the legislation was introduced might be explained by fewer insider deals being carried out now that penal sanctions exist, rather than by reference to the inability or unwillingness of the Secretary of State to prosecute in cases which are brought to his attention. However, rumours continue to circulate and comment is made from time to time in the financial press suggesting that insider information may have prompted dealings prior to significant share price movements and questions remain where Stock Exchange enquiries, particularly in connection with price movements relating to takeover announcements, result in matters being taken no further.

Since Part V of the Companies Act 1980 was brought into force on 23 June 1980, only two cases have been successfully prosecuted – in both cases the accused pleaded guilty – and another case involving a husband and wife, respectively charged with insider dealing (in shares of Joseph Stocks and Son (Holdings)) and counselling or procuring to deal, was sent for trial in April 1982 to Croydon Court. It is, however, understood that the Department of Trade are actively considering proceedings in connection with insider dealing in a number of other cases, including certain transactions carried out in the shares of Suter Electrical before it announced its acquisition of Prestcold.

Whilst there may be valid reasons explaining the small number of prosecutions, a real cause for concern on the application of the legislation which was not contemplated by its critics (nor one might imagine, by Parliament) is the attitude of the court in the first case which was successfully prosecuted. The case, which was heard in Scotland, involved a partner in a firm of investment managers (Baillie Gifford) who was accused of insider dealing in shares in Winterbottom Trust, a trust company for which Baillie Gifford was investment manager and secretary. The accused purchased shares in the trust company knowing that it was soon to be reorganised and in the event, the price of the shares rose by 40p giving the accused a profit of £1,400. On being brought to trial, the accused was admonished (i.e. convicted of the offence but no penalty was imposed) after his plea of guilty had been tendered, on the basis that he was willing to repay his illicit profits to the jobber who had suffered and, in mitigation, his plead that he was ignorant of the law. There may be a little room for giving the Sheriff the benefit of any doubt because this was the first case involving the new legislation, but it would seem very unusual to regard a new statutory crime as different from any other crime where neither the repayment of its fruits nor ignorance would release the guilty party from the full force of the law. In the second case, involving an option contract taken out for shares in Harris and Sheldon Limited while a takeover and management buy-out were under discussion, the director concerned was sentenced to six months imprisonment but suspended for two years by Sutton Coldfield magistrates court.

The 1980 Act

Eleven separately identifiable offences are specified in Part V: these can, however, be divided into three principal criminal activities. The first is where an individual who has insider information ("an insider") or an individual who has received information from an insider ("a tippee") *deals* in securities; the second is where an insider or tippee *counsels or procures another person to deal* in securities; and, thirdly, a criminal offence is committed where an insider or tippee *communicates* insider information if the recipient is likely to use that information for dealing or for counselling or procuring some other person to deal.

The legislation contains detailed provisions on who can be an "insider", to be found by reference to circumstances where a person is in possession of *unpublished price sensitive information* (see page 484 below). In addition to the basic insider dealing prohibition, special provisions apply to individuals who are party to take-overs and their tippees. Crown servants and former Crown servants are brought within the scope of the general prohibitions but they are treated as a separate category of insiders. Jobbers, managers of international bond issues, trustees and personal representatives are, in differing circumstances, excluded from the Part V provisions. Although the legislation is primarily aimed at preventing insider dealing on The Stock Exchange and other investment exchanges, certain dealings "off-market" but on other anonymous securities markets are brought within the ambit of the general prohibitions. Finally, a number of statutory defences are provided in answer to any charge. These matters, together with the penalties for insider dealing, are discussed below.

Dealing as an insider

Who is an "insider"?

The starting point for determining whether any crime has been committed is to find out whether an "insider" exists. No crime can take place without his direct or indirect participation. Sections 68(1) and (2) of the 1980 Act set out the circumstances in which a person will be treated as an insider and provide, first, that only an *individual* can be an insider. A company (or any other separate legal entity) can never be an insider although, in theory, it is possible that it could commit a separate crime by acting as an accomplice or by taking part in a conspiracy to commit one of the insider dealing crimes. That is not to say that dealing in securities through a company is a way to circumvent the legislation as, in so doing, the insider would commit one or both of the two other principal crimes of counselling or procuring another person (i.e. the company) to deal, or communicating insider information.

Secondly, to be an "insider" in relation to a particular company, the individual must at the time the offence is committed (or within the preceding six months) be *knowingly connected* with the company. The insider who is able to sever his connection with a company for a period of more than six months can thereafter deal freely with the securities of that company even if he is still in possession of insider information. There seems to be no particular reason why a six month period was chosen as being the appropriate time lapse but, in most circumstances, this should be long enough to ensure that the price sensitivity of information is a spent force by the time the insider is entitled to deal.

Thirdly, to be an insider, the individual must hold the insider information *by virtue of being connected* with the company in question (section 68(1) (a)) *and* it must be reasonable to expect him not to disclose that information except for the proper performance of the functions attaching to his position (section 68(1)(b)). Lastly, he must know that the information is "unpublished price sensitive information", as defined by section 73(2).

Where an individual meets those requirements (and subject to the defences provided for in section 68(8) which are dealt with on page 488 below), he is prohibited from *dealing* on a recognised stock exchange in securities of the company, that is he is prohibited from buying, selling, or agreeing to buy or sell – whether as principal or agent (section 68(1)). He is not, however, forbidden to continue to "hold" securities, even if he would have sold them had he not been in possession of the insider information.

An insider of one company will also be prohibited from dealing in securities of any *other* company in circumstances where he holds insider information on the latter's securities through his connection with the first company, but only where that information relates to transactions between the two companies or transactions in securities of one by the other (see page 479 below).

"Knowingly connected"

The primary requirement for being an insider is that the individual must be knowingly connected with the company in question and in order to be so connected for the purposes of section 68, an individual must have sufficient *mens rea* and fall within one of the categories of persons listed exhaustively in section 73(1).

To begin with, a *director* – perhaps the most obvious candidate for being an insider – will be connected with the company of which he is a director and with any "related" company (defined in section 73(5) as a subsidiary or holding company or other subsidiary of the company's holding company). It is thought unlikely that a court would have much difficulty over the question whether a director has the necessary *mens rea* to meet the requirement of being *knowingly* connected and that even the most out of touch non-executive director would be hard pressed to prove beyond reasonable doubt that he was unaware of all the related companies of the company of which he is a director (particularly as securities of companies dealt in on anonymous securities markets only will be within the scope of the provisions).

Next, an individual will be connected with a company if he is an *officer* (which would include the company secretary and any manager – section 455, Companies Act 1948) or *employee* of the company or a related company. Again, it is unlikely that such a person would be unaware of his relationship with a particular company, although it is possible that an officer or employee might be unaware of the fact that a company is *related* to his employer company where both are members of a large group. Lastly, an individual will be connected with a company if he occupies a position involving a *professional or business relationship* between himself (or his employer or a company of which he is a director) and the company or a related company (section 73(1)).

In all cases, save for that of a director, the position must, in addition, be reasonably expected to give the individual access to information which, in relation to securities of the company or a related company, is unpublished price sensitive information and which it would be reasonable to expect a person in his position not to disclose except for the proper performance of his functions, that is, the position must envisage a relationship which involves the expectation of confidentiality. The exception for a director from having to satisfy the additional tests is based on the assumption that a director, merely by virtue of his position as such, will meet those requirements.

The additional requirements to be met by officers, employees and those in a professional or business relationship with a company are thought likely to become the subject of dispute in the courts not because of the inherent difficulty in determining what is "reasonable" but because of section 68(1). This section requires that the individual subjectively must *know* of his connection and therefore must know that it was reasonable to expect his position to afford him access to insider information and know that it was reasonable that such information should not be disclosed by a person in his position except for the proper performance of his functions. In some instances contracts of employment and in-house rules or guidelines might put a person on notice that there is a requirement of confidentiality in relation to information received by a person in his position and so to some extent shift the onus back on to that person to disprove that he did not realise the character of his position. However, circumstances can be envisaged where a junior employee might escape prosecution if he deals on the basis of insider information obtained by virtue of his connection with the company by relying on his own subjective lack of knowledge of the character of his employment for the purposes of section 73(1). For example, where an office messenger in a merchant bank or solicitors' firm obtains price sensitive information by virtue of his connection with his employer and deals on that basis, even if a court were to accept that it was reasonable to expect that person not to disclose the information except for the proper performance of his functions (so that the test in section 68(1)(b) is met), it would seem to be quite plausible that the messenger himself would not *know* that it was *reasonable* to expect him not to disclose that information. If the court were to accept his subjective understanding of his position, the requirements of section 73(1)(b) would not be met and the "insider" would be outside the scope of the criminal sanctions. Whether such a safeguard for the accused (or hurdle for the prosecution) is appropriate in addition to relying on the objective *reasonableness* of the court (as required by section 68(1)(b)) is doubtful.

Professional or business relations

Although directors, officers and employees are easy to identify and so to "connect" with a company for the purposes of section 73, the "professional or business relationship" connection has no clear meaning and is capable of being interpreted to encompass a broad spectrum of commercial relationships, not all of which might have been intended to come within the "insider" net. Whilst a Chancery court might be given to construe the phrase widely, the rule that criminal provisions should, if their meaning is unclear, be construed in favour of the accused and the fact that the interpretation of the phrase will be left to the criminal courts should be borne in mind in determining the limits of this category of connected persons.

Solicitors and accountants (and others of that ilk) in a direct professional relationship with a company are likely always to come within the scope of section 73(1)(b) as such relationships clearly envisage that price sensitive information will become available to professional advisers and it would be expected by all concerned that such information should be treated as confidential. Similarly, commercial and merchant bankers, brokers and other advisers whose relationships with client companies are based on confidentiality but where no fiduciary duty necessarily exists are likely to be within the scope of section 73(1)(b).

The position is not so clear in relation to other section 73(1)(b) business relationships where confidentiality is not so readily considered to be a key element. In cases where, for example, an individual or his employer is buying from or selling goods or services to a company, the business relationship will be obvious but the requirement for confidentiality for the purposes of section 73(1)(b) is unlikely to be present, even if the individual knows that the magnitude or importance of the order will move the company's share price.

Further, it is not clear whether all relationships of a commercial or contractual nature will fall within the scope of the subsection. Where an individual is a shareholder in a company, would he be outside the scope of the criminal sanctions because no *business* relationship exists even if he were in a position to obtain and did obtain information through the shareholder relationship? It is thought that a business relationship should have been more precisely defined and, in particular, that there should have been clarity on the question of shareholder status as often price sensitive information, such as management accounts, is made available to a substantial minority shareholder in his capacity as such. It is suggested that the relationship of a shareholder to the company of which he is a member should not, of itself, be treated as a business relationship (although it is a contractual relationship), but it may be necessary in determining this matter to analyse more closely the precise nature of the shareholder relationship in any particular case. A distinction might, for example, be drawn between a "portfolio" investment, where shares are acquired merely as an investment, and a "trading" investment where shares are acquired either to foster or to support a trading relationship between the shareholder and the issuing company. Whilst the rights of the shareholders in both cases will be the same, it is thought that there might be more scope for arguing that in the case of the trading investment there could exist the necessary *business* relationship for the purposes of section 73(1)(b).

Finally, before leaving the question of connection, it must be emphasised that the insider information must be obtained by an individual *by virtue of* his connection before an infringement of the prohibitions can occur. An individual who is connected to a company but obtains his insider information from another source will not be prohibited from dealing by section 68(1) although, of course, the tippee provisions might then have to be considered. However, once the "connection" is established and it can be shown that the insider obtained the information by virtue of his connection, there is no further requirement to show that the insider dealt on the basis of that information. The mere fact of possession of the information will prohibit his dealing.

Transactions with other companies

As mentioned briefly on page 476, the section 68(1) prohibition on insider dealing in securities in a company with which an individual is connected is extended by section 68(2) to prohibit dealing in shares in any *other* company where the insider has obtained price sensitive information relating to certain transactions involving that other company by virtue of his connection with the first. Subject to the defences specified in sections 68(8) and (10), section 68(2) provides that an individual who is (or at any time in the preceding six months has been) knowingly connected with a company may not deal on a recognised stock exchange in securities of any *other* company if he has information which he holds by virtue of being connected with the first company *and* it would be reasonable to expect a person so connected and in a position by virtue of which he is so connected not to disclose that information except for the proper performance of the functions attaching to his position. As with section 68(1), the insider must also know that the information is unpublished price sensitive information in relation to the securities of that other company. However, not all price sensitive information about the other company or its activities will prohibit the insider from dealing – the information must relate to transactions involving *both* the first company and the other company or involving one of them and securities of the other or to the fact that such transactions are no longer contemplated.

Thus, the individual who knows through his connection with one company that the fortunes of another will be affected by a transaction between the two companies (e.g. the placing of a substantial order with the other or bringing or settling a claim for damages against the other) will be prohibited from dealing in the shares of the other company. Similarly, he will be prohibited from dealing if the first company is involved in the purchase or sale of the securities of that other company. If any such transactions are no longer contemplated he will be prohibited from dealing so long as that information is price sensitive. The insider will not, however, be committing an offence if he deals while he is aware of price sensitive information involving a transaction between the other company and a third party (subject, of course, to the possibility that he might fall within the scope of section 68(1) if he is connected with the other company, say, by virtue of his employer's business relationship with the other company or within the tippee prohibitions of section 68(3)).

Tippees

The prohibition on dealing is extended by section 68(3) to dealings by "tippees" that is, individuals who have obtained information from insiders.

Sections 68(3) provides (subject to the defences stated in subsections (8) and (10)), that where an individual ("the tippee") has unpublished price sensitive information which he knowingly obtained (directly or indirectly) from another individual who is connected with a particular company or was at any time in the six months preceding the obtaining of the information so connected; and, who the tippee knows or has reasonable cause to believe held the information by virtue of being an insider; and, the tippee knows or has reasonable cause to believe that, because of the insider's position, it would be reasonable to expect the insider not to disclose the information except for the proper performance of the functions attaching to his position, then he is prohibited from dealing in securities of that company on a recognised stock exchange. In order to mirror the prohibitions on the insider, the tippee is also prohibited from dealing in securities of any *other* company if he knows that the information is unpublished price sensitive information in relation to securities of the other company and it relates to any transaction (actual or contemplated) involving the company with which the insider is connected and the other company or involving one of them and securities of the other or to the fact that any such transaction is no longer contemplated.

It should be noted that the time period in section 68(3)(a) refers to the connection between the *insider* and the company existing within the six months preceding the time when the tippee obtained the information and not to the expiry of time between the tippee receiving the information and his dealing. The tippee is prohibited from dealing at *any time* if he obtained the inside information prior to or during the six month period mentioned above, subject to the information still being unpublished and price sensitive. Although the tippee will not be able to deal so long as the information remains unpublished and price sensitive, the insider himself will be able to deal provided he has not been connected with the company during the preceding six months.

A further detail of some significance in section 68(3) is the extension of the prohibition to persons who receive insider information *indirectly* from an insider so that where information is passed along a chain of tippees each will be prohibited from dealing. The requirements of section 68(3) that the tippee *knowingly* obtained the information from an insider *and* that the tippee knew or had reasonable cause to expect the insider not to disclose the information because of his position and connection will restrict the scope of the sub-section so that where a person is unaware of the original insider's specific connection with a company he will be free to deal on the strength of a tip even where the price sensitive information is provided in detail. The prohibition on dealing by a tippee will only come into effect where price sensitive information is actually passed on, so that the tippee will be free to deal where the extent of the "information" is merely advice to buy or sell without any explanation. As will be seen below, although a tippee in such circumstances will be free to deal without transgressing the penal provisions, the "tipper" will be subject to the rigours of section 68(6) in respect of "counselling and procuring" the tippee to deal.

Takeovers

Rumour, press comment and intuition may all take credit as bounty providers to those who are able so to order their affairs as to be in a position to sell large quantities of recently acquired shares when a takeover offer suddenly appears over the horizon. On the other hand, the cynical reader might be justified in suggesting that the abuse of insider information might account for at least a small percentage of the transactions entered into prior to a bid and such a suggestion might well be justified by reference to the flurry of price activity which often occurs prior to the announcement of an offer. The legislature too was concerned over abuse in this particular area and has therefore made specific provision for takeovers, in order to prevent certain dealings by an individual where the insider information held is that he is contemplating, or no longer contemplating, a takeover bid.

Section 68(4) provides (subject to the defences in subsections (8) and (10)) that where an *individual* is contemplating, or has contemplated making, whether with or without another person, a takeover offer for a company in a particular capacity, he is prohibited from dealing in securities of that company in *another* capacity if he knows that the information that the offer is contemplated or is no longer contemplated is unpublished price sensitive information in relation to those securities. A "takeover offer" is defined by section 73(5) as an offer made to all shareholders (or all the holders other than the person making the offer and his nominees) of the shares in the company to acquire those shares or a specified proportion of them.

Section 68(5) goes on to provide that the offeror's direct or indirect tippee is also prohibited from dealing if he knows that the information that the takeover is contemplated or no longer contemplated is unpublished price sensitive information, again, subject to the defences in subsections (8) and (10).

The effect of subsections (4) and (5) is that in a takeover, in addition to the restrictions contained in section 68(2) and 3(ii) which would prohibit a director or the like of an offeror company from dealing in shares in a target company, an individual who has no connection with a company but is *himself* contemplating (or no longer contemplating) a takeover of that company is prohibited from dealing in any other capacity. Whilst the wording of section 68(4) and (5) which refers to a takeover offer "with or without another person" is not entirely free from doubt, it is considered that the prohibitions will only apply where the individual is acquiring the beneficial ownership of shares in the target company so that if the shares are being acquired through a company any individual procuring the company to do so will not be caught by subsections (4) and (5). In such circumstances, the individual will, however, have to consider the provisions of section 68(2).

Counselling or procuring

The second principal criminal activity is for an insider or tippee (including those associated with a takeover under sections 68(4) and (5)) to *counsel or procure* other persons (not only individuals) to deal in securities to which his insider information relates. Section 68(6) provides (subject to the defences stated in subsections (8) and (10) that where an individual is prohibited by section 68 from dealing in securities, he must not counsel or procure any other person to deal in those securities, knowing or having reasonable cause to believe that the person would deal in them on a recognised stock exchange).

The "counselling or procuring" offence is primarily aimed at bringing an insider who does not actually pass on insider information within the scope of the prohibition so that where he advises another person to buy or sell without saying why, he will commit an offence. No offence will be committed by the person dealing on the strength of such a tip, even if he knows that the tip was given by an insider, as the person dealing will not be in possession of price sensitive information (which, as mentioned above, is a requirement necessary to commit the offence of dealing as a tippee under section 68(3)). Further, no breach of any provision will take place if the recipient passes the tip on to any other person as, again, neither the recipient nor the next recipient in line will be prohibited from dealing.

It is particularly important for directors (or other persons in control of a company) to note the full import of the phrase "counselling or procuring". In directing his company to deal in shares, the director will be committing an offence of counselling or procuring the company to deal if he is in possession of unpublished price sensitive information (subject to the availability of any of the defences in section 68(8) and (10)). Where, for example, Company A has a shareholding in Company B and a Company A director also sits on the board of Company B, then if that director possesses unpublished price sensitive information on Company B securities by virtue of his Company B directorship, he would commit an offence if he counselled or procured Company A to buy or sell shares in Company B – even if the decision was not based on any insider information. This prohibition must be very carefully considered by directors if a partial bid is made which is sufficient to secure a place on the target company's board and a full bid is likely to be made at any time thereafter.

In contrast with subsections 68(1), (2) and (3), the "counselling or procuring" crime may be committed even if no dealing in securities takes place – although it is unlikely that any offence would ever come to light in such circumstances.

Communicating insider information

The third principal crime is contained is section 68(7). This provides than an *individual* who is for the time being prohibited from dealing by reason of his having any price sensitive information (i.e. an insider, tippee or individual who is party to a take-over and his tippee) is prohibited from *communicating* that information to any other person if he knows or has reasonable cause to believe that or some other person will make use of the information for the purpose of dealing or of counselling or procuring any other person to deal on a recognised stock exchange. The prohibition is subject to the defences contained in sections 68(8) and (10) which are discussed below.

No infringement of section 68(7) will take place unless price sensitive information (and not merely advice to deal) is passed on and, like section 68(6), a crime will be committed even if no dealing takes place. It is unlikely that any person would be caught for this offence where no dealing takes place as there would be no reason for anyone conducting an enquiry to find out whether a crime had been committed and, indeed, it would be difficult to prove that the accused knew or had reasonable cause to believe that dealing would take place if none in fact did.

Other points

Crown servants

Crown servants, who may or may not have a "business relationship" with a company for the purposes of section 73(1), will often hold unpublished price sensitive information on the securities of a company by virtue of the government's relationship with that company. For this reason, the legislature saw fit to extend the insider dealing provisions to Crown servants, former Crown servants and individuals who knowingly obtain insider information from those persons. "Crown servants" for the purposes of section 69 are individuals who hold office under, or who are employed by, the Crown and, therefore, local authority officers or employees of nationalised industries will not fall within the scope of section 69. Those persons outside the ambit of section 69 will have to be "connected" within the meaning of section 73(1)(b) if they are to be treated as insiders.

Section 69 provides that Crown servants and former Crown servants (or their tippees) holding unpublished price sensitive information in relation to securities of a particular company ("relevant securities") shall not deal on a recognised stock exchange in those securities nor counsel or procure any person to deal knowing or having reasonable cause to believe that the other person would deal on a recognised stock exchange. Section 69 also provides that the Crown servant or former Crown servant (or his tippee) may not communicate to any person his insider information if he knows or has reasonable cause to believe that the recipient of the information or some other person will make use of the information for the purpose of dealing or of counselling or procuring any other person to deal on a recognised stock exchange.

No specific connection between the Crown servant and the company whose securities are in question is required for section 69 purposes: all that is needed is that the Crown servant holds his insider information *by virtue of his position* or former position as such. For the tippee of a Crown servant to be in a position to transgress, the individual must knowingly have obtained (directly or indirectly) the insider information from a Crown servant or former Crown servant who he knows or has reasonable cause to believe held that information by virtue of his position. Like section 68, section 69 will apply only to information which it would be reasonable to expect an individual in the position of the Crown servant or former Crown servant not to disclose except for the proper performance of the functions attaching to that position and the individual holding it must know that it is unpublished price sensitive information in relation to the securities of a particular company.

It is worth noting that no "six month rule" applies to Crown servants and, accordingly, the former Crown servant will not be allowed to deal, counsel or procure or communicate insider information, until that information is no longer unpublished or price sensitive.

The defences available to a Crown servant or former Crown servant under section 69(4) and (5) are dealt with on page 490 below.

Unpublished price sensitive information

In order to fall foul of any of the outlawed activities, the information which the insider or tippee exploits must be "unpublished price sensitive information", as defined in section 73(2). The intention of the legislature was to restrict the information to which Part V would apply to fairly major events giving rise to sharp price movements but, as will be seen below, the meaning of unpublished price sensitive information and the scope of the phrase is far from clear.

Section 73(2) provides that any reference to unpublished price sensitive information is a reference to information which "(a) relates to specific matters relating or of concern (directly or indirectly) to that company, that is to say, not of a general nature relating to or of concern to that company; *and* (b) is not generally known to those persons who are accustomed or would be likely to deal in those securities but which would, if it were generally known to them, be likely materially to affect the price of those securities".

As a matter of construction, it is not entirely clear whether section 73(2)(a) refers to information relating to specific matters or to matters specifically relating or of concern to the company. In other words, does "specific" qualify the "matters" rather than whether those matters relate or are of concern to the company? The final phrase of sub-section (2)(a) (". . . . that is to say, is not of a general nature relating to or of concern to that company . . . .") suggests that the information should be restricted to information specifically relating or of specific concern to the company, and it is thought that this is the better interpretation. If this is correct, then information, for example, regarding the future availability of a particular commodity is a specific matter relating to and of concern to any particular commodity dealing company, but because that information is also of a general nature relating to or of concern to all commodity dealing companies, it should not be within the scope of section 73(2)(a) and, accordingly, an "insider" in possession of such information would be free to deal in shares in a commodity company with which he is knowingly connected.

A further question on the definition of insider information relates to the precise time when information is no longer "unpublished". As a practical matter, this point may often be crucial, as a person who is an insider will be unable to deal where rumour and press comment or other factors unrelated to the insider information in his possession are forcing a price movement which he might normally follow by dealing even if he possessed no insider information. In order no longer to be "unpublished", the information must be generally known to persons who are accustomed or would be likely to deal in the securities (section 73(2)(b)). This class of persons would, first of all, encompass professional dealers or investors who are "accustomed" to deal. However, the latter part of section 73(2)(b) deals with information also being generally known to those who would be "likely" to deal in securities i.e. any persons likely to buy or sell securities. As the public are likely to (and do) deal in securities, it is suggested that the information must not only be known to those professional dealers and investors with elaborate networks for obtaining information on securities but also to the general public. If this is the case, then information would have to be passed on by some form of public announcement such as an announcement in the press before it became unpublished. Indeed, it is by no means clear that even an announcement on the floor of The Stock Exchange would ensure that the price sensitive information was then *generally* known by persons likely to deal in securities. It is thought, however, as a practical matter that an announcement on the floor of The Stock Exchange would be sufficient to enable an insider then to deal.

Securities

The provisions of Part V are concerned only with dealings on anonymous securities markets so that private "face to face" deals are not affected – even if the shares so dealt in are listed securities.

The limitation on the transactions to which Part V of the 1980 Act applies is achieved by prohibiting dealings (or counselling or procuring dealings or communicating information for the purpose of dealings) on "a recognised stock exchange". This means a stock exchange recognised by the Department of Trade under section 15 of the Prevention of Fraud (Investments) Act 1958 (section 87(5) and section 455 of the Companies Act 1948) and, at present, only The Stock Exchange is so recognised. However, for the purposes of section 73, a recognised stock exchange is also deemed to include an "investment exchange" where anonymous dealings only take place. Section 73(5) provides that an "investment exchange" means an organisation maintaining a system whereby an offer to deal in securities made by a subscriber to the organisation is communicated, *without his identity being revealed*, to other subscribers to the organisation and whereby any acceptance of that offer is recorded and confirmed. Thus, ARIEL and any other organisation of that type would be an investment exchange and insider dealings in shares on such exchanges are prohibited.

In addition, to bring within the scope of the legislation the burgeoning market in "unquoted" shares dealt in on the USM, under rule 163 and on M.J.H. Nightingale's over-the-counter market, section 70 provides that dealings in "advertised securities" through an "off-market" dealer (as defined by section 70(3)) who is making a market in those securities will be within the scope of the insider dealing provisions of sections 68 and 69.

"Advertised securities" are either those securities which are listed on a recognised stock exchange (so that dealings in listed securities other than on a recognised stock exchange through an "off-market dealer" will be caught) or securities in respect of which, not more than six months before the occurrence of the breach of sections 68 or 69, information indicating the prices at which persons have dealt or were willing to deal has been published for the purpose of facilitating deals in those securities.

For the purposes of Part V, "securities" means "listed securities" (i.e. securities listed on The Stock Exchange) and any shares, debentures or options on shares or debentures of any company formed under the Companies Act 1948 (or its predecessors), registered under Part VIII of the 1948 Act or incorporated in and having a place of business in Great Britain – even if the securities are not listed. Thus unlisted shares, options and the like would have to be dealt in through an off-market dealer and would have to be advertised securities in order to come within the scope of the prohibitions. In addition, it would seem that only listed securities of overseas companies are "securities" and so dealings on overseas anonymous markets in securities of overseas companies which are not listed on The Stock Exchange will not be prohibited.

Dealings outside Great Britain

It would be relatively simple to avoid the restrictions of Part V if dealings within the United Kingdom only were outlawed as many securities falling within section 73(5) are traded on foreign exchanges. The legislation foresaw the problem of dealing on markets abroad and provided that activities relating to certain dealings overseas would also be prohibited. The legislature did not choose to attempt to extend its territorial jurisdiction to offences committed abroad and did not therefore attempt to prevent *dealing*, as such, abroad. It recognised, however, that in order to deal abroad, a U.K. based individual would virtually always have to get someone else to deal as agent in order to carry out the transaction. Section 70(2) provides that a person who is prevented from dealing in securities by section 68 or 69 on a recognised stock exchange is also prohibited from counselling or procuring any other person to deal in those securities in the knowledge or with reasonable cause to believe that the person would deal outside Great Britain on any stock exchange other than a recognised stock exchange. An individual who is prohibited from dealing on a recognised stock exchange by section 68 or 69 is also prohibited from communicating information to any other person in the knowledge or with reasonable cause to believe that or some other person will make use of the information for the purpose of dealing or of counselling or procuring any other person to deal in those securities outside Great Britain on any stock exchange other than a recognised stock exchange.

Accordingly, counselling or procuring a person to deal, say, on the New York Stock Exchange, in securities which were listed on The Stock Exchange (or were securities as defined in section 73(5)) would be prohibited although the crime would have to be committed in the United Kingdom for the criminal courts to have jurisdiction. Section 70 does not specifically provide that the insider must not himself deal outside Great Britain on a stock exchange but it is thought that in almost every instance where an insider deals outside Great Britain he will be counselling or procuring another person to deal.

Section 70 does not extend the prohibitions to dealings in securities of overseas companies not listed on The Stock Exchange, so, from a U.K. viewpoint, insider dealing on a foreign stock exchange in such securities would be permissible.

Finally, the defences specified in sections 68(8) and (11) and 69(5) will be available in respect of section 70(2) offences.

International bond issues

A late amendment was made to the 1980 Companies Bill to allow existing practice on the issue and market making of international bonds to continue virtually untrammelled by the new legislation. The particular aspects of the international bond market which the amendment, now contained in section 71(1), was aimed at, were the market support activities of issue managers whose practice is to deal whilst in possession of insider information on the bonds, particularly in the first few months of issue.

Section 71 contains detailed provisions defining an international bond issue and who is an issue manager for the purposes of the exemptions and provides that the prohibition of section 68 will not (by virtue of section 70) apply to an individual doing anything in relation to any debenture (or debenture option) if the thing (i.e. the prohibited act under section 68) is done by the issue manager in good faith in connection with an international bond issue not later than three months after the issue. Further, the prohibition will not apply to anything done in a case where the issue is not proceeded with before the decision is taken not to proceed with it. Secondly, where an issue manager is making a market in the bonds he will not be prohibited from doing any act by virtue of section 68 where that thing is done in good faith as a person making a market. No time period restrains this aspect of the market maker's activities.

A number of amendments were made in the 1981 Companies Act to tidy up the slack drafting of section 71. In particular, a new subsection (1A) was added to allow an issue manager to counsel and procure persons to deal on stock exchanges outside Great Britain. It seems that relief from this prohibition was inadvertently missed out of the original section 71.

Section 71(3) allows the Secretary of State to make regulations by statutory instrument extending the scope of section 71 in a number of ways including extending the exemptions of subsections (1) and (1A) to other "things done" in relation to advertised securities other than international bonds. At the date of writing, no such regulations have been made.

Defences

If an individual satisfies the numerous conditions required to commit an offence, he might still find himself outside the scope of the penal provisions if he can avail himself of one of the defences or exemptions provided for in section 68(8), (10), (11) and section 69(5). The scope of the defences which should be available was the subject of much comment during the passing of the 1980 Companies Bill through Parliament and attempts were made by a number of representative bodies, including the Law Society, to provide exclusions for certain categories of persons who, it was thought, might often be in the position of being insiders and would therefore find themselves unduly restricted in carrying out their day-to-day activities. Few of the representations by interested parties found a sympathetic ear.

The first defence which applies to dealing, counselling or procuring and to communicating insider information provides that an individual shall not be prohibited from doing any of these acts if it is otherwise than with a view to the making of a profit or avoiding a loss (whether for himself or any other person) by the use of his insider information (section 68(8)). The scope of this defence is far from clear but it seems to be intended to exclude dealing where the motive of the person was not to benefit financially from the particular action taken in relation to the securities. For example, it has been suggested that a forced sale of securities to meet a debt or a purchase to increase a minority holding for the purpose of retaining control of a company might come within the scope of this defence.

There is, it is suggested, a fundamental problem in this "motive" defence in relation to the acquisition of securities in that the purpose behind buying must always be, at least in part, to make a profit (or avoid a loss) whether in the short term by resale of even in the long term by, say, protecting the value of the investor's minority stake in a company. The fact that the timing of acquisition may be governed in part by different motives does not remove the basic element of a desire to make a profit (or avoid a loss) and any other reason for acquiring securities can only be seen as *part* of the reason for the transaction. The defence would, however, seem appropriate to the disposal aspect of dealing where factors wholly unrelated to the insider's profit motive may force a sale.

The second defence, contained in section 68(8)(b), is open to a liquidator, receiver or trustee in bankruptcy. Where that person enters into a transaction in the course of the exercise in good faith of his functions as such, then the prohibitions contained in section 68 will not apply. (It is questionable whether the words "in good faith" are necessary as a liquidator, receiver or trustee must always act in this way.)

The third defence is open only to a "jobber", that is an individual, partnership or company dealing in securities on a The Stock Exchange and recognised by the Council of The Stock Exchange as carrying on the business of a jobber. Section 68(8)(c) provides that section 68 will not prohibit an individual by reason of his having any information from doing any particular thing if the information (i) was obtained by him in the course of a business of a jobber in which he was engaged or employed; and (ii) was of a description which it would be reasonable to expect him to obtain in the ordinary course of that business; and (iii) he does that thing in good faith in the course of that business. The final phrase of subsection 68(8)(c) "in the course of that business" will prevent the jobber from taking a profit in a capacity other than as a jobber.

A further defence is provided by section 68(10) in relation to matters prohibited by section 68(2), (3)(ii), (4) or (5) (dealing) and by subsections (6) and (7) (counselling, procuring and communicating information). Section 68(10) provides that an individual will not be prohibited from doing any act by reason only of having insider information if he does that thing in order to facilitate the completion or carrying out of the transaction. The defence seems apt only to a takeover situation where shares are being bought on the market and will allow that transaction to go ahead where the purchasing company is being counselled or procured by its directors to buy shares in the target company and the information or knowledge that the takeover is planned is itself price sensitive information or where an individual who plans a takeover is within the scope of the takeover provisions by virtue of his knowledge of the imminent takeover.

It is of particular importance to note that the defence available under subsection (10) does not apply to dealing prohibited by section 68(1) and therefore that counselling or procuring or communicating information in respect of securities the dealing in which is prohibited by section 68(1) will likewise not benefit from the defence. Accordingly, the director of Company A in the example given on page 482 above could not rely on the defence in connection with Company A buying further securities of Company B, even if it could be argued that Company A had intended to make a full takeover of Company B at the outset and the purchase of further securities was to complete that transaction.

Furthermore, a director may find himself in difficulty by virtue of section 68(6) (counselling or procuring) if his company decides to buy in its own shares debentures on the market – if this is unpublished price sensitive information – as the defence of section 68(10) will not be available to him as he will be prohibited from dealing by virtue of section 68(1).

Finally, section 68(11) deals with the insider in the position of a trustee or personal representative (or where a trustee or personal representative is a body corporate, an individual acting on behalf of that body corporate) who would, apart from availing himself under sub-section (8)(a) above, be prohibited from dealing or counselling or procuring any other person to deal in securities. The insider will be presumed, if he does deal, counsel or procure, to have acted with a view otherwise than to the making of a profit or avoiding a loss if he deals on the advice of a person who appeared to him to be an appropriate person from whom such advice should be sought and did not appear to him to be prohibited from dealing in those securities. A trustee or personal representative may therefore deal where he has insider information if he seeks third party advice on whether to carry out a particular transaction.

The defences contained in sections 68(8) and (11) will apply for the purposes of section 69 (Crown servants) and the provisions of section 68(10) are mirrored in section 69(5) in their application to Crown servants. In relation to the prohibitions contained in section 70(2) (counselling or procuring or communicating information for the purposes of dealing outside Great Britain) the defences of sections 68(8) and (11) and 69(5) have effect (section 70(2)).

Penal sanctions

The penalties for infringing the prohibitions of Part V are severe although the question remains whether the courts will consider the insider crimes to be serious enough to warrant imposition of the full penalties. Section 72 provides that any individual who contravenes the provisions of sections 68 or 69 may be liable on indictment to imprisonment for a term not exceeding two years or a fine or both and, on summary conviction to imprisonment for a term not exceeding six months or a fine not exceeding the statutory maximum of £1,000 or both. An injured party may be entitled to compensation under the Powers of Criminal Courts Act 1973.

Procedure

In order to prevent frivolous or vexatious cases being taken, section 72(2) provides that no proceedings can be taken in England or Wales except by the Secretary of State or with the consent of the Director of Public Prosecutions. No such restriction is made for Scotland, but in practice the Crown Office alone will control prosecutions. Whilst in theory it is possible for a private individual to institute criminal proceedings against another in Scotland, the procedure requiring an application to the courts for permission to prosecute almost without exception results in the application being turned down.

Any person who has been injured by or suspects insider dealings to have taken place may complain to the Department of Trade who will consider the facts and determine whether matters should be taken further. In practice, however, references to the Department are most likely to come from The Stock Exchange which investigates all dealings where sharp price movements occur and monitors dealings prior to takeovers.

Civil liability

There was much debate prior to the legislation being introduced on the question whether provision should be made to enable injured parties to reclaim the wrongdoer's dealing profits. Eventually, however, it was decided that no specific civil liability should be imposed.

Part V makes no provision for any claim for recompense for the insider's victim but states that any insider dealing transaction shall not be void or voidable by reason only that it was entered into in contravention of sections 68 or 69. This removes the argument that the transaction would be void or voidable as an illegal transaction. The provisions of Part V will not prevent an injured party seeking compensation under the residual common law principles. The law in this area is not well developed and has not so far been applied in relation to transactions on anonymous securities markets (as opposed to non-disclosure in specific direct personal dealings where a fiduciary relationship exists). However, if a director makes use of insider information relating to his company for his own profit, he may be liable in law to account to the company for that profit (see the chapter *Directors' Duties*).

Other constraints on insider dealing

The prohibitions imposed by Part V are superimposed on other statutory and extra statutory constraints. The statutory inhibitions imposed prior to the 1980 Act dealt principally with directors' dealings in securities and are contained in sections 25 (options) and sections 27 to 31 (notification of interests in securities) of the Companies Act 1967 (see pages 259 and 314).

The other restraints to be considered are, first, the "Model Code" which applies to dealings by directors (and indirectly to dealings by employees and persons "related" to directors) in securities of companies listed on The Stock Exchange (whether or not incorporated in the United Kingdom) and which prohibits such dealings in the two month "close seasons" and at any other time when the "insider" is in possession of price sensitive information. The code adopted by any particular listed company may, of course, impose higher standards or more rigid rules.

Secondly, the City Code on Takeovers and Mergers prohibits insider dealings in securities of public companies by persons in possession of price sensitive information who are privy to takeover, merger or offer discussions involving such a company.

Thirdly, where securities are dealt in by an "off-market" dealer, it will be usual for that dealer to require as a condition of being admitted to the market that an undertaking be given including prohibitions on insider dealings much the same as required by the Model Code (e.g. M.J.H. Nightingale's "General Undertaking").

In addition, a director involved in insider dealing may be in breach of the fiduciary duties he owes to his company: see the chapter *Directors' Duties*.

To conclude, the provisions of Part V of the 1980 Act must be seen as a positive attempt by the legislature to stop the abuse of insider dealing by certain categories of individuals. The effectiveness of the prohibitions, and whether the categories of individuals who cannot deal require to be added to, will not be known until the provisions have been in force for a number of years and, more importantly, a sufficient number of cases have been brought before the courts. Only then will it be possible to judge whether the provisions are capable of any real and effective application.

Liquidations

In this chapter, the expressions "winding up" and "liquidation" are used interchangeably, and "company" is mainly used in the context of the winding up in England of a company formed and registered in England under the Companies Acts 1948 to 1981 and the previous companies legislation. Wherever appropriate, mention has been made of provisions affecting companies incorporated in Scotland, companies or bodies formed outside but having a relevant connection with Great Britain, and special enactments applicable to the winding up of companies or bodies carrying on particular types of business or activities. However, the treatment of these is not comprehensive.

Solvent and insolvent companies

The company to be wound up may be solvent or insolvent. This distinction is important in two main respects: first, the reasons for winding up a solvent company and those for winding up an insolvent company may be different and, secondly, the applicability of some of the winding up provisions depends on whether the company is solvent or insolvent.

Modes of winding up

A company may be wound up voluntarily or by the court. A voluntary winding up may be a members' voluntary winding up or a creditors' voluntary winding up. Even in the latter, the creditors have no say in the initiation of the winding up, as distinct from the choice of liquidator and the conduct of the winding up. A members' voluntary winding up is, however, only available if the directors of the company are able to make and file with the Registrar of Companies a statutory declaration of solvency within the prescribed time limits. Voluntary winding up (of either type) is not available for certain types of companies, e.g., insurance companies carrying on long-term business and companies incorporated outside Great Britain. Winding up by the court is often referred to as compulsory winding up.

The applicable practice and procedure and, to a lesser extent, the substantive provisions, may differ depending on the mode of winding up. The procedure in a compulsory winding up is more onerous than in a voluntary winding up because of the detailed involvement of the court and the Department of Trade and of the number and types of forms to be used. For this reason a voluntary winding up is more common.

A company may also be wound up under the supervision of the court. This fourth mode, which is somewhat halfway between a voluntary winding up and a compulsory winding up, is so rare in practice that it is ignored in this chapter.

Future law reform

A report of the Insolvency Law Review Committee under the Chairmanship of Sir Kenneth Cork was published on June 9, 1982. The Committee, which was appointed by the Secretary of State for Trade on January 27, 1977, made a comprehensive study of the whole of the law and practice relating to insolvency, both corporate and personal. In addition to measures aimed at simplifying the existing law and procedure, the Report recommends a number of radical reforms. Among those which relate to liquidations are the following:

(1) That up to ten per cent of the net proceeds from assets comprised in a floating charge should be available to the liquidator for the benefit of unsecured creditors.

(2) That for the purposes of section 322 of the Companies Act 1948 (floating charge created within twelve months of winding up), a floating charge should be redefined so as to cover all future assets comprised therein even if the charge thereon is expressed to be a fixed charge. Further, the test of solvency should be whether the value of the company's assets exceeded the amount of its liabilities, taking account of contingent and prospective liabilities, and "fresh advances" should be redefined as the amount of net increase in the borrowings since the creation of the charge (notwithstanding the rule in *Clayton's Case*).

(3) That the law should allow the appointment of an administrator by the court with a view to reorganising the company to restore profitability or maintain employment, achieving the most profitable realisation of the assets or carrying on business in the public interest.

(4) That a small company should be able to enter into an out-of-court composition or moratorium binding on all its creditors.

(5) That all preferential claims, except reduced amounts in respect of PAYE, National Insurance contributions and Redundancy Fund contributions, should be abolished; and the subrogated preferential claim of a lender of advances for payment of salaries (etc.) should be more restricted;

(6) The public utilities should treat a liquidator as a new consumer and, accordingly, should not refuse to continue supplies because of non-payment by the company.

(7) That contracts for goods under which title is reserved to the supplier should be registered to be valid.

(8) That debts (secured or unsecured) in the nature of a long term capital loan due to a "connected person" should be deferred to the claims of other creditors.

(9) That the onus of proof in respect of fraudulent (or undue) preference should be shifted more towards the creditor preferred, anda i iei f "wrongful trading" which will be easier to prove than fraudulent trading should be introduced.

(10) That the provisions relating to delinquent directors should be strengthened.

(11) That only members of a recognised professional body with at least five years experience in general practice who provide a suitable security should qualify for appointment as a liquidator.

It could be several years before any of the recommendations are given legislative effect.

Finally, an Advisory Committee has been set up under the existing legislation to keep under review the bankruptcy and winding up rules and to make recommendations to the Lord Chancellor as to any changes to these.

Principal legislation

The principal legislation is mainly contained in Part V (sections 211 to 365) of the Companies Act 1948, as amended or modified by, inter alia, section 35 of the 1967 Act, sections 63 to 69 and 125 of the Employment Protection (Consolidation) Act 1976, section 125 of the Insolvency Act 1976, the Companies Act 1981 and various fiscal enactments. Part V is divided as follows:

Section	Subject
211–216	Certain preliminary matters.
218–277	Winding up by the court.
278–283	Preliminary matters relating to voluntary winding up generally.
284–291	Member's voluntary winding up.
292–300	Creditors' voluntary winding up.
301–310	Either type of voluntary winding-up.
311–315	Winding up under the supervision of the court (not dealt with in any detail in this chapter).
316–365	Every mode of winding up.

Some provisions applicable to a winding up by the court may be invoked in a voluntary winding up (of either type) by virtue of section 307, which empowers the court on an application to determine any question arising in the voluntary winding up or to exercise, as respects the enforcing of calls or any other matters, all or any of the powers exerciseable if the company were being wound up by the court.

Section 317 provides for the application for certain purposes of the rules in force under the law of bankruptcy to the winding up of an *insolvent* company registered in England. "Rules" have been held to include sections in this context (*Re Theo Garvin Ltd.* [1969] 1 Ch. 624). (As to Scotland, see section 318.)

Special provision is made elsewhere in the Companies Acts and other legislation for the winding up of certain types of unregistered company, including overseas companies, and bodies like insurance companies and charities.

Delegated legislation

The main delegated legislation is contained in the Companies (Winding up) Rules 1949 as amended by the Companies (Winding up) (Amendment) Rules 1957–1981 ("the rules"). Rules 1 to 25 are devoted to preliminary matters, mainly concerning court proceedings, and rules 26 to 60 almost exclusively to the procedure in a compulsory winding up. The rest of the rules, that is, rules 61 to 230, apply to every or a particular mode of winding up depending on the nature, subject matter or the headlines above the group in which they are contained. A list of county courts having jurisdiction is contained in the County Courts (Bankruptcy and Winding up Jurisdiction) Orders 1971–1977.

The Department of Trade has issued general orders or regulations pursuant to rule 224 for the purposes of regulating certain matters of an administrative nature.

For delegated legislation in Scotland, see the Rules of the Court of Session 1965, Chapter IV, section 3 and, as regards the sheriff court, Act of Sederunt, March 20, 1930, as amended by Act of Sederunt (Sheriff Court Liquidations), October 12, 1948.

Forms

The Appendix to the rules contains over 100 prescribed forms for use in a winding up, but a large number of them apply only to a compulsory winding up. Three further forms (39c, 39d and 39e) for use in voluntary winding up are prescribed by the Companies (Forms) Regulations 1979.

Pre-liquidation considerations

The winding up of a company is mainly initiated for two reasons,

(a) to ensure a just distribution of its assets, and

(b) to terminate its existence by its eventual dissolution.

In the case of an insolvent company a just distribution is the primary objective, the termination of existence being merely a by-product. Where the company is solvent, the reverse may be the case.

Just distribution

The winding up provisions may enable a just distribution in the following ways:

(1) The company's assets and affairs pass into the hands of a liquidator, usually an experienced chartered accountant, whose powers, duties, and functions are regulated by statute. He is in a fiduciary position vis-a-vis the company's creditors and members generally, and certain statutory aids facilitate his task.

(2) The company's financial position is virtually "frozen" upon the commencement of the winding up. Further deterioration of its financial position and proliferation of its liabilities may thus be averted. Ordinary liabilities are discharged on a pari passu basis.

(3) It may be possible for the liquidator to "clawback" some of the advantages received from the company by a creditor at the expense of the other creditors.

(4) The liquidator may be able to call into question the past conduct of the company's officers and others in relation to the company's affairs and make appropriate recovery from them.

Termination of company's existence

The winding up of a solvent company, with the primary object of terminating its existence, may be desired, for example, as part of a corporate or financial restructuring of the group to which the company belongs, or as a subsidiary device to minimise tax liabilities or maximise tax advantages for the group, or may be a natural sequel to the winding down or disposal of its business or cessation of its activities.

Some other considerations which could affect the decision as to whether or when to commence a winding up are summarised below.

Taxation

In the case of a solvent company, particularly as part of a scheme of reconstruction, tax questions may be important. The following tax points (which are by no means exhaustive) might affect the decision on whether or when to liquidate a solvent company:

(1) On commencement of liquidation a new accounting period starts (Taxes Act 1970, s. 247(7)). This may affect the company's ability to make use of group relief and capital allowances, and the calculation of losses available for set off against profits and gains etc.

(2) Liquidation may entail cessation of trading, if not immediately then by the end of the winding up. Terminal relief may not be as attractive as the relief which might have been available on the basis of continued trading.

(3) Liquidation severs a group relationship with subsidiaries and that traced through the company (*I.R.C. v. Olive Mills Ltd.* [1963] 1 W.L.R. 712; *Ayerst v. C & K (Construction) Ltd.* [1976] A.C. 167). This could affect group relief and the ability to transfer losses

within the group and, possibly, the non-close company status of a subsidiary. (However, the group relationship continues for the purposes of corporation tax on capital gains – see section 272(4) of the Taxes Act 1970.) Payment of dividends within the group without ACT may no longer be possible.

(4) The period for determining preferential claims for outstanding taxes (as also for certain other types of preferential claims) under section 319 of the Companies Act 1948 (as amended) is fixed by reference to the date of the winding up order or the appointment of a provisional liquidator (whichever is earlier), or the passing of the winding up resolution, as the case may be.

Alternatives to liquidation

In the case of an insolvent or potentially insolvent company, practical alternatives to liquidation depend on the nature and extent of the financial problems and the likely attitude of the creditors. Possibilities (apart from appointment of a receiver by a debenture holder, see *Receivers*) are:

(1) a compromise under section 206 or, where it is intended to eventually put the company into liquidation, section 306 of the 1948 Act; or

(2) subject to the provisions relating to fraudulent trading and misfeasance, (a) agreement with all the creditors for an informal moratorium, followed by an orderly run-down of the company's business, usually under the control of an accountant and the supervision of an informal committee of the principal creditors or (b) injection of fresh capital or (c) reorganisation of its borrowings; or

(3) in the case of a defunct company without any assets and any liabilities (except, perhaps, intercompany indebtedness), to have it struck off by the Registrar of Companies under section 353 of the 1948 Act (for which see the chapter *Dissolution and Revival*).

Pre-liquidation "hive-down"

It may be possible to improve the prospects of selling the profitable parts of the company's business as a going concern if they are "hived down" into a clean subsidiary. This may also enable the tax benefit of any accumulated trading losses to be preserved for the benefit of the subsidiary and, hence, the purchaser thereof. Assets on the disposal of which a chargeable gain would arise may be left in the parent to enable the gain to be set off against any available losses. The consideration for the transfer is either paid in the form of shares in the subsidiary or is left outstanding on an open loan account. As liquidation usually means cessation of trading and certainly means the end of group relationship in this context, the hive down must be effected before the commencement of liquidation. There are, however, some possible pitfalls. First, if the relevant assets are subject to a charge which is potentially void as against a liquidator or a creditor of the company for non-registration under section 95 of the 1948 Act and are transferred before liquidation, the transfer could validate the charge as against the acquiring company because the charge is valid against the transferor company itself before liquidation and the acquiring company can have no better title than that which the transferor company had. And whilst the acquiring company should register the existing charge under section 96, failure to do so does not (unlike failure to register under section 95) invalidate the charge. Secondly, the Transfer of Undertakings (Protection of Employment) Regulations 1981, made under the European Communities Act 1972, provide that the transferee company would succeed to the transferor company's liabilities and obligations to its employees (except in respect of pensions). This would happen either immediately upon the hive down or, if the hive down is effected by a receiver (or a liquidator in a creditors' voluntary winding up) of the transferor company, when the transferee company ceases to be the subsidiary of the transferor company.

Timing of liquidation

As explained, tax considerations have an important bearing on the timing of liquidation. But in the case of an insolvent company it may not be possible to delay commencement of liquidation without the risk of falling foul of the provisions relating to fraudulent trading and misfeasance. In fact, the urgency of the situation might make it necessary to put an insolvent company into a creditors' voluntary winding up immediately. This may in some cases be achieved by the use of the "Centrebind procedure" (as to which see page 504).

Jurisdiction in a winding up

In England the High Court has jurisdiction in all cases to wind up a company compulsorily, but where the amount of the paid up share capital of a company does not exceed £120,000, the county court (having jurisdiction in bankruptcy) of the district in which the registered office of the company is situated has concurrent jurisdiction with the High Court, unless the particular county court has been expressly excluded from having jurisdiction or the jurisdiction has been conferred on the county court of another district. Appeals from the court of first instance lie to the Court of Appeal.

In Scotland, the Court of Session and Sheriff courts have jurisdiction similar to the jurisdiction of the High Court and county courts respectively.

Relationship between England, Scotland and Northern Ireland

A company registered in Scotland cannot be wound up in England, and vice versa (C.A. 1948, s. 218(1)). However, a company registered in Northern Ireland which has a principal place of business in England or

Scotland may be wound up under Part IX of the Companies Act 1948 in England or Scotland, as the case may be (C.A. 1948, s. 399(2)).

Any order made in England "for or in the course of a winding up in England" (which includes any order staying proceedings pending against the company made after the presentation of a winding up petition and before the making of a winding up order – *Re Dynamics Corporation of America* [1973] 1 W.L.R. 63) is enforceable in Scotland or Northern Ireland, and any such order made in Scotland is enforceable in England and Northern Ireland. However, reciprocal treatment is not accorded to any such order made in Northern Ireland (C.A. 1948, s. 276). Provision is also made for the avoidance of attachments on property in England of a company being wound up in Scotland (section 228(2)), and for the effect of diligence on property in Scotland of an English company (section 327(2)).

The effect of winding up in England (or Scotland) of an English (or Scottish) company extends to assets and proceedings in Scotland (or England), but not to Northern Ireland, which is for these purposes a separate jurisdiction.

Other companies

Companies formed or registered under pre-1948 Acts. The winding up provisions of the 1948 Act apply to such companies subject as provided in Part VII of that Act.

Companies not formed under Companies Act 1948 but authorised to register under it. The winding up provisions of the 1948 Act apply subject as provided in Part VIII of that Act.

Unregistered and overseas companies. An "unregistered company" (see section 398) may be wound up compulsorily (but not voluntarily or under the supervision of the court) under the provisions of Part V of the Companies Act 1948, subject as provided in Part IX, on any of the grounds stated in sections 399(5) and (6).

Where a company incorporated outside Great Britain which has been carrying on business in Great Britain ceases to carry on business there, it may be similarly wound up as an unregistered company, notwithstanding that it has been dissolved or has otherwise ceased to exist as a company under or by virtue of the laws of the country of its incorporation (C.A. 1948, s. 400). No winding up order will be made in England (or Scotland) if the company has no assets in England (or Scotland) (*Banque des Marchands de Moscou v. Kindersley* [1951] Ch. 112). It is not necessary to show that the overseas company has a principal place of business within the United Kingdom (although the location of a place of business may help to determine the part of the United Kingdom whose court has jurisdiction – see sections 399(2) and (3)). A petitioner must show that the company has some assets within the jurisdiction and that there are claimants for those assets over whom the court has jurisdiction. He need not show that the assets will be distributable by a liquidator among creditors generally; it is sufficient that the relevant assets will be available to the petitioning creditor (*Re Compania Merabello San Nicholas S.A.* [1973] Ch. 75). Where the only alleged asset is a cause of action, that is sufficient to give the court jurisdiction without proof that the action is certain to succeed (*Re Allobrogia Steamship Corporation* [1978] 3 All E.R. 423). The asset does not have to be in the company's ownership. It is sufficient if there is a reasonable possibility of the petitioner obtaining payments from a source of assets directly related to his employment by the company such as the Redundancy Fund (*Re Eloc Electro-Optieck and Communicatie BV* [1981] 2 All E.R. 1111).

Initiation of members' voluntary winding up

Winding up commences upon the members passing a special resolution under section 278(1)(b) of the Companies Act 1948 that the company be wound up voluntarily. The first step would be for the company's board of directors to meet to direct the convening of the requisite extraordinary general meeting of the company. They may specify in their direction two dates in the alternative; an early date if the requisite consent to short notice under the proviso to section 141(2) of the 1948 Act is received by that date or, otherwise, a later date which allows time to give the usual 21 days' notice under section 141(2). They may make the necessary declaration of solvency at that meeting or may postpone that step until a later meeting.

Declaration of solvency. The process does not qualify as a members' voluntary winding up unless, within the period of five weeks immediately preceding the date of the passing of the resolution or on that date but before the passing of that resolution, the majority of the directors (or all of the directors where there are no more than two) at their meeting have made a statutory declaration as to the company's solvency in the prescribed form (Form 108; see C.A. 1948, s. 283 as amended by C.A. 1981, s. 105). "Solvency" in this context means that the company would be able to pay its debts in full within a specified period not exceeding twelve months from the commencement of the winding up (section 283(1)). A director making the declaration as to solvency without reasonable grounds for his opinion renders himself liable to imprisonment or a fine or both. It is advisable for the directors to consult the company's auditors and to obtain a "comfort letter" from them before making the declaration. An error in the statement of assets and liabilities embodied in the declaration does not render the declaration void provided that the statement can reasonably and fairly be described as such a statement (*De Courcy v. Clement* [1971] Ch. 693).

Appointment of liquidator. Section 285 *requires* the company in general meeting to appoint one or more liquidators. This can be done at the same meeting, even without notice, as soon as the resolution to wind up has been passed (*Bethell v. Trench Tubeless Tyre Co.* [1900] 1 Ch. 408). The appointment can be made by an ordinary resolution but is usually made as part of the special resolution for winding up. A separate ordinary resolution may be considered preferable where, for example, votes as to the choice of liquidator are likely to be divided but not as to the decision to wind up.

The articles of association of a company usually provide that the liquidator may, with the sanction of an extraordinary resolution of the company (and any other sanction required by the 1948 Act), divide among the members *in specie* or kind the whole or any part of the assets of the company and for such purposes set a fair value on the property (see, for example, article 135 of Table A). It is usual to pass such an authorising resolution contemporaneously with or as part of the resolution to wind up.

A liquidator so authorised may wish to obtain appropriate indemnities from the shareholders in relation to and in consideration of making the distribution *in specie*.

Procedure for winding up meeting. The company's articles apply, subject to sections 133 to 139 and 141 of the 1948 Act as regards (i) notice of the extraordinary general meeting, (ii) the procedure thereat and (iii) the requisite majority for the special resolution (rules 127 to 156 do not apply here). The meeting can be validly held at short notice as permitted by section 141(2). A special resolution approved by all the members (or, where the company has an article similar to article 73A in Table A, a special resolution in writing signed by all the members having a right to vote) would have the same effect as if it was duly passed at a meeting (*Re M.J. Shanley Contracting Ltd.* [1980] 124 S.J. 239).

Filing requirements. The declaration of solvency must be filed with the Registrar of Companies within 15 days after the date of the winding up resolution (C.A. 1948, s. 283 as amended by C.A. 1981 s. 105). The winding up resolution must be filed by the company with the Registrar of Companies within 15 days after it is passed and advertised by it in the *Gazette* within 14 days after it is passed (C.A. 1948, s. 143 and s. 279).

Finally, the liquidator must, within 14 days after his appointment, publish in the *Gazette* and file with the Registrar of Companies a notice of his appointment (C.A. 1948, s. 305; Forms 39e and 39c in Appendix B to the Companies (Forms) Regulations 1979). Until publication the company is not entitled to rely against other persons on the appointment of the liquidator (European Communities Act 1972, s. 9(3) and (4)).

Initiation of creditors' voluntary winding up

Winding up commences upon the members, at a meeting convened as authorised by the board of directors, passing an extraordinary resolution under section 278(1)(c), "that the company cannot by reason of its liabilities continue its business, and that it is advisable to wind up" and that, accordingly, the company be wound up voluntarily. This form of winding up is appropriate where the company is insolvent. It is possible to commence a creditors' voluntary winding up by a special resolution in the same form as that in the case of a members' voluntary winding up under section 278(1)(b), that is, "that the company be wound up voluntarily". The text of that resolution could create a misleading impression that the winding up is either a solvent or a members' voluntary winding up. For this reason, and because until the coming into force of section 106 of the Companies Act 1981 a longer period of notice of meeting for passing a special resolution for winding up was required, this course has been rare.

Unlike in the case of a members' voluntary winding up, no declaration of solvency is made, and the creditors do have a say in the choice of liquidator and the conduct of the winding up and a right to appoint a committee of inspection to oversee the liquidator's activities. The creditors' wishes generally override the members' wishes.

Nomination of liquidator by members. The members at their meeting at which the winding up resolution is passed may also nominate a person to be liquidator (C.A. 1948, s. 294). This may be done by an ordinary resolution but is usually done as part of the extraordinary resolution referred to on page 502.

The winding up meeting of members or any subsequent meeting of the members may also appoint, by an ordinary resolution or as part of the extraordinary resolution to wind up, up to five persons to act as members of any committee of inspection that may be appointed by the creditors. This is subject to the right of a creditors' meeting to resolve that the persons appointed by the members should not be members of the committee) (C.A. 1948, s. 295).

Meetings. Unless the short notice procedure referred to on page 501 is used, at least 14 days' prior notice of the members' meeting specifying the intention to propose the winding up resolution as an extraordinary resolution must be given (C.A. 1948, s. 133(1)(b), s. 141(1), s. 293 as amended by C.A. 1981, s. 106). The rest of the requirements and procedure are as in the case of a special resolution for a members' voluntary winding up.

A *creditors'* meeting is required to be convened by the company for the day, or the day next following the day, on which the winding up meeting of the members is to be held. Notice must be sent by post to the creditors simultaneously with the sending of the notice of the members' meeting and must be advertised once in the *Gazette* and once in two local newspapers circulating in the district where the registered office or principal place of business of the company is situated (C.A. 1948, s. 293, as amended by C.A. 1981, s. 106). Where the members' meeting and creditors' meeting are convened for the same day, the creditors' meeting should be held after the members' meeting on that day. If the members' meeting is adjourned and only passes the winding up resolution at the adjourned meeting, any resolution passed by the creditors in the meantime becomes effective when the members' winding up resolution is passed (section 293(5)).

The "Centrebind" procedure. The requirement for the holding of the creditors' meeting on the day, or the day next following the day, on which the members' winding up meeting is to be held, may be impossible of compliance where the members' meeting is held at short notice. Until section 106 of the 1981 Act came into force it was the practice to convene the creditors' meeting for the earliest day on which the members' meeting could have been held but for the short notice procedure. The liquidator appointed by the members at their meeting would have all the powers of a liquidator until the time of the creditors' meeting (*Re Centrebind* [1967] 1 W.L.R. 377, approved in *Roberts Petroleum v. Kenny, The Times,* February 15, 1983 (HL). This enables the appointment of a "caretaker" liquidator pending the creditors' meeting and is known as "the Centrebind procedure." (A similar procedure could be adopted where the members' meeting had been dispensed with altogether under the written resolution procedure referred to on page 502.) The period between that appointment and the creditors' meeting was called "the Centrebind fortnight" (i.e. the minimum period of notice required for the members' meeting but for the short notice procedure) and the "caretaker" liquidator "the Centrebind liquidator". Section 106, which amended section 293 of the 1948 Act, accords statutory recognition to this procedure but reduces the Centrebind fortnight to seven days (for which see *Saxton v. Miles, The Times,* March 2, 1983).

Statement of affairs and list of creditors. The directors must lay before the creditors' meeting a full statement of the company's affairs and a list of creditors as required by section 293 (3)(a) (see Form 109).

Appointment of liquidator and committee of inspection by creditors. The purpose of the creditors' meeting is to avail itself of an opportunity of appointing a liquidator or liquidators, and a committee of inspection consisting of not more than five persons, in either case in substitution for or in addition to any person or persons appointed by the members' meeting (C.A. 1948, s. 294 and s. 295). Any resolution of the creditors requires a majority both in number of the creditors present and entitled to vote and in value of their claims (rule 134). If such a majority is not achieved on a resolution for the appointment of liquidator, the person appointed by the members continues as liquidator. If no resolution for the appointment of a committee of inspection is validly passed, the appointment of the persons appointed by the members for such committee lapses.

Filing requirements. The requirements for the filing and advertisement of the winding up resolution and the appointment of the liquidator are the same as for a members' voluntary winding up as outlined on page 502 (except that for the liquidators' appointment the forms are Forms 39e and 39d).

Initiation of winding up by the court

The initiation of a winding up by the court involves the presentation of a winding up petition to the court under section 224 of the 1948 Act by the company itself, a creditor, a contributory or, in certain cases, a government authority on one or more of the grounds specified in section 222. A petition founded upon the company's inability to pay its debts may have been preceded by the service by a creditor, to whom a sum exceeding £200 is due, of three weeks' notice of demand under section 223(1) upon the company and failure by the company to comply therewith. Inability to pay can, however, be proved by other means as well (see page 506). The petition is followed by the court making a winding up order some weeks after the presentation. Between presentation and the making of the winding up order the court may appoint a provisional liquidator. Upon the making of a winding up order the Official Receiver becomes provisional liquidator. The winding up order is followed by separate meetings of the creditors and contributories ("the first meetings") and confirmation by the court of the appointment of a substantive liquidator and, perhaps, a committee of inspection. The date of the presentation, the date of the appointment of a provisional liquidator and the date of the winding up order are each relevant for different purposes of the winding up.

The winding up is deemed to have commenced upon the presentation of the petition or, if the company was already in voluntary liquidation at that date, upon the passing of the voluntary winding up resolution (C.A. 1948, s. 229). (As to the significance of this relation back of the commencement, see page 541.)

Grounds for the petition

Subject to the enactments applicable to special types of company, the petition must be founded on one or more of the grounds specified in section 222. The grounds most frequently relied on are those set out in paragraphs (e) and (f) of that section, namely,

"(e) that the company is unable to pay its debts;
  (f) that the court is of the opinion that it is just and equitable that the company should be wound up."

(See also Companies (Floating Charges and Receivers) (Scotland) Act 1972, s. 4(1) – additional circumstances in which a company may be wound up by the court in Scotland.)

Ground (e) — inability to pay

Inability to pay debts may be established by its proof to the satisfaction of the court, regard being also had to the company's contingent and prospective liabilities, or by proof of repeated demands for payment not having been met. Alternatively, it may be established by proof of any of the following specific circumstances:

(a) a creditor (by assignment or otherwise) to whom a sum in excess of £200 is already due has served on the company, by leaving it at its registered office, a written demand requiring the company to pay the sum so due and the company has for three weeks thereafter neglected to pay the sum or to secure or to compound for it to the *reasonable* satisfaction of the creditor;

(b) if in England or Northern Ireland, execution or other process issued on a judgment, decree or order of any court in favour of a creditor is returned unsatisfied in whole or in part; or

(c) if in Scotland, the induciae of a charge or payment on an extract decree, or an extract registered bond, or an extract registered protest have expired without payment being made (section 223).

Ground (f) — "just and equitable ground"

This ground is interpreted flexibly and is not confined to particular instances nor construed *ejusdem generis* with the other grounds (*Ebrahimi v. Westbourne Galleries* [1973] A.C. 360). Some examples are:

(1) Fraudulent, mala fide or other improper element in the formation or running of the company or the need for full investigation (*T.E. Brinsmead & Sons* [1897] 1 Ch. 406; *Re Peruvian Amazon Co.* [1913] 29 T.L.R. 384).

(2) Disappearance of the justification of the company's continued existence (see e.g. *Re Eastern Telegraph Co.* [1947] L.J.R. 1247; *Re Kitson & Co. Ltd.* [1946] 1 All E.R. 435).

(3) Refusal by majority shareholder to produce accounts or pay dividends (*Loch v. John Blackwood Ltd.* [1924] A.C. 783; see also *Re Newman and Howard Ltd.* [1962] Ch. 257).

(4) Complete deadlock in the management of the company (*Re Yenidje Tobacco Co.* [1916] 2 Ch. 426).

(5) In the case of a small company which is formed or continued on the basis of personal relationship involving mutual confidence and is in substance a partnership, if the petitioning contributary is excluded from all participation in the business or if such relationship or confidence is broken and the facts are such as would have justified the dissolution of a partnership (*Ebrahimi v. Westbourne Galleries, supra; Re A & B.C. Chewing Gum Ltd.* [1975] 1 W.L.R. 579; *Re Yenidje Tobacco Co., supra*).

A petitioner on this ground must come with clean hands; for example, the breakdown in confidence must not be due to his own misconduct (*Ebrahimi v. Westbourne Galleries, supra*). Refusal by directors holding half the shares to register as members the executors of a deceased shareholder holding the other half, in exercise of their discretion under the articles, does not necessarily constitute a "just and equitable" ground (*Charles Forte Investments Ltd. v. Amanda* [1964] Ch. 240).

The winding up of a profitable company may not be in the best interests of an aggrieved shareholder. He may wish to consider the alternative of invoking section 75 of the Companies Act 1980 (power to grant relief where any shareholder is unfairly prejudiced). In any case, the court may, in exercise of its power under section 225(2), refuse to make a winding up order if it is of the opinion both that some other remedy is available to the petitioner (e.g. C.A. 1980, s. 75) and that the petitioner is acting unreasonably in seeking the winding up order instead of pursuing that other remedy.

Who may petition

The petition may be presented by the company, a creditor, a contributory or by all or any of those parties, together or separately, and, in specified circumstances, by the Secretary of State, the Official Receiver or the Attorney-General.

1. Company's own petition

Directors cannot exercise the right of the company to present a winding up petition without the authority of a special resolution contemplated in section 222(a) (or, subject to the articles of association, without the authority of an ordinary resolution of the company in general meeting). However, no such special resolution is needed if the petition is presented on its behalf by or at the direction of the receiver and manager of the company (*Re Emmadart Ltd.* [1979] 1 All E.R. 599). Further, the company in general meeting can ratify the action taken.

2. Creditor's petition

Here "creditor" includes,

(a) the assignee of the whole or part of a debt, whether at law or in equity (section 223(a): *Re Steel Wing Co.* [1921] 1 Ch. 349);

(b) a secured creditor even if he has obtained the appointment of a receiver in an action (*Re Borough of Portsmouth Tramways Co.* [1892] 2 Ch. 362);

(c) a local authority in respect of rates remaining unpaid after an unsuccessful distress (*Re North Bucks Furniture Depositories* [1939] Ch. 690); and

(d) a contingent or prospective creditor (section 224(1)).

A person whose claim is disputed on substantial grounds is not a "creditor" and the court may restrain him from presenting the petition, or refuse to make a winding up order. A petition based on a solicitor's bill of costs before it is taxed may be disallowed (*Re Laceward Ltd.* [1981] 1 All E.R. 254). The court does, however, have a discretion in appropriate cases to determine the dispute so as to preserve the petitioning creditor's remedy, where, for example, there is a danger of the company's assets being put out of reach of its creditors. In such a case it is sufficient if the creditor has a "good arguable case" (see *Re Claybridge Shipping Co. SA., The Times*, March 14, 1981).

A creditor is not entitled to base his petition solely on a claim for unliquidated damages or for an unquantified sum (*Re Humberstone Jersey Ltd.* (1977) 74 L.S.G. 711). Where, however, only the amount of the debt is disputed, the court may make a winding up order without requiring the creditor to quantify his debt precisely (*Re Tweeds Garages Ltd.* [1962] Ch. 406).

Where the debt is not presently due, or there is a dispute as to whether it is presently due, the petitioner will not be allowed to proceed except as a contingent creditor (see *Re Stonegate Securities Ltd. v. Gregory* [1980] 1 All E.R. 241). A contingent or prospective creditor must give such security for costs as the court thinks reasonable, and also establish a prima facie case for winding up, before the court gives him a hearing (section 224(1)(c)). A misrepresentation as to the precise nature and position of a contingent claim may result in the petition being struck out (*Re A Company* [1973] 1 W.L.R. 1556).

A secured creditor does not, by petitioning for winding up without deducting the value of his security, lose the benefit of his security. (He may, however, subsequently lose it by proving his claim in the winding up without disclosing and deducting the value of his security, see page 546.)

If the petitioning creditor's debt is £200 or less and his petition is founded on the company's inability to pay its debts, that inability or deemed inability must be established otherwise than under paragraph (a) of section 223.

A petitioning creditor who cannot get paid his presently due debt has, as against the company, a right *ex debitio justitiae* to a winding up order. However, the court makes its decision in the light of all the relevant circumstances.

That the company to be wound up by the court is already in voluntary liquidation will not necessarily prevent the petitioning creditor from succeeding.

The court will have regard to the wishes of the majority in value of the creditors and may refuse a winding up order if they oppose the petition for some good reason (see, e.g., *Re. A.B.C. Coupler and Engineering Co. Ltd.* [1961] 1 W.L.R. 243). The court's decision does not depend solely on the wishes of the creditors. If the facts disclose a strong prima facie case for an investigation into the company's affairs, the court may make a winding up order in the interest of commercial morality irrespective of the creditors' opposition (*Re Clandown Colliery Co.* [1915] 1 Ch. 369).

Greater weight is attached to the creditors' wish to have a voluntary liquidation instead of a compulsory winding up than to their wish to have no liquidation at all (*Re J.D. Swain Ltd.* [1965] 1 W.L.R. 909).

As to the court's attitude where a creditors' petition is opposed by contributories, see *Re Camburn Petroleum Products Ltd.* [1979] Ch. 297.

3. *Contributory's petition*

The term "contributory" (which also occurs in the provisions relating to voluntary winding up) is not necessarily synonymous with "member" or "shareholder". A "contributory" is a person liable to contribute to the assets of the company in the event of its being wound up, or a person alleged to be a contributory before the names of contributories are determined (C.A. 1948, s. 213). Section 212 of the 1948 Act (read with sections 43(6) and 44(7) of the 1948 Act), sets out the extent and the circumstances in which various categories of persons are liable to contribute. The categories include past members. Apart from their potential liability to contribute and potential rights of adjustment as against other contributories, the involvement of the contributories who are not existing members is tenuous.

A contributory cannot present a petition unless the shares in respect of which he is a contributory, or some of them, either were originally allotted to him or have been held by him, and registered in his name, for at least six months during the eighteen months before the commencement of the winding up, or have devolved on him through the death of a former holder (section 224(1)(a)). This requirement does not apply where the Secretary of State petitions under section 224(1)(d) (see page 510).

The shares must be standing in the name of the petitioner (*Re Wala Waynaad Indian Gold Mining Co.* (1882) 21 Ch.D. 849), but if the company itself is in default in allotting shares or registering a transfer it is arguable that the allottee or transferee is entitled to bring the petition (see *Re Gattopardo Ltd.* [1969] 1 W.L.R. 619). If the allotment or the allottee's entry on the register is disputed he would not be allowed to petition (*Re JN2 Ltd.* [1977] 3 All E.R. 1104). As to a bankrupt shareholder, see *Re Wolverhampton Steel & Iron Co. Ltd.* [1977] 1 W.L.R. 860; *Re K/9 Meat Supplies (Guildford) Ltd.* [1966] 1 W.L.R. 1112; and *Re H.L. Bolton Engineering Co. Ltd.* [1956] Ch. 577.

The court's attitude towards a contributory's petition is as follows:

(1) If his shares are fully paid, he must show some tangible interest in the winding up, such as the probability that there will be a substantial surplus for distribution among the shareholders (*Re W.R. Willcocks & Co. Ltd.* [1973] 3 W.L.R. 669), or that because of the failure by the company to supply accounts and information he is unable to say whether there will be such surplus, or that the company's affairs require an investigation that is likely to produce such surplus (see *Re Newman and Howard Ltd.* [1962] Ch. 257; *Re Argentum Reductions (U.K.) Ltd.* [1975] 1 W.L.R. 186). This means that the petition must be founded on the "just and equitable ground" rather than on the company's inability to pay its debts. If his share is partly paid he may not have to show the possibility of a surplus, but only that his interest would be prejudiced if the company continued to trade.

(2) Mismanagement by directors is not necessarily a good ground, particularly if the petitioner has not exhausted his other remedies (see C.A. 1980, s. 75).

(3) A petitioning contributory who is in arrears of calls may be

required to pay the calls into court or give appropriate undertakings in respect thereof (*Re Diamond Fuel Co. (No. 2)* (1879) 13 Ch.D. 400; *Re Crystal Reef Gold Mining Co.* [1892] 1 Ch. 408).

(4) If a voluntary winding up is already in progress, the court may refuse to grant the contributory's petition if the voluntary winding up represents an honest exercise of the shareholders' wishes (*Re Haycraft Gold Co.* [1900] 2 Ch. 230), unless the court is satisfied that the rights of the contributories will be prejudiced by the voluntary winding up (C.A. 1948, s. 310).

4. Petition by Secretary of State

The Secretary of State may present a winding up petition in specified circumstances, namely,

(a) against any company (see sections 222(b) and (bb), 224(b) and (d), 169(3) and C.A. 1967, s. 36);

(b) against an insurance company (see I.C.A. 1974, s. 46); or

(c) against a company advertising for deposits (see Protection of Depositors Act 1963, s. 16, as preserved by C.A. 1980, s. 83).

As to the court's attitude to a petition by the Secretary of State, see, inter alia, *Re Lubin Rosen and Associates Ltd.* [1975] 1 W.L.R. 122; *Re Armvent Ltd.* [1975] 1 W.L.R. 1679; *Re Bamford Publishers Ltd. The Times* June 4, 1970; and *Re Golden Chemical Products* [1976] Ch. 300.

5. Petition by Official Receiver

A company being wound up voluntarily or under the supervision of the court can be wound up by the court not only on an application by a creditor or contributory but also by the Official Receiver. But the court will only make an order if it considers, on balance, that the winding up already in process cannot be continued in the proper interests of the creditors or contributories (section 224(2) and *Re J. Russell Electronics Ltd.* [1968] 1 W.L.R. 1252).

6. Petition by Attorney-General

The Attorney-General can petition to wind up a charitable company under section 30 of the Charities Act, 1960.

The presentation of the petition and the ensuing proceedings

A winding up petition must be made on Forms A4, 5 or 5A with such variations as circumstances may require (rule 26). (See also *Practice Note* [1958] 2 All E.R. 124.) If the petition does not allege a case for winding up within section 222 it is liable to be dismissed with costs unless the court allows it to be amended (*Re Wear Engine Works Co.* (1875) 10 Ch. App. 188).

A petition to the High Court is presented at the office or chambers of the Registrar of the Companies Court, who will fix the time and place for the hearing of the petition (rule 27). A *Practice Direction* (see [1979] 1 W.L.R. 1413) allows, inter alia, presentation of winding up petitions to be effected by post.

Unless the court directs, the petition must be advertised once in the *London Gazette* not less than seven clear days after it has been served on the company (see rule 29 and Forms 6, 6A, 7 and 8) and not less than seven clear days before the day fixed for the hearing (rule 28). Failure to comply may result in the petition being struck out (*Practice Note* dated October 10, 1977 by Templeman J – (1977) 121 S.J. 708); (see also *Practice Note* [1980] 1 W.L.R. 657.) Delaying the advertisement for at least seven days after service of the petition enables companies which allege the petition to be vexatious, groundless or an abuse of the process of the court to apply to restrain the advertisement of the petition, as the advertisement may seriously damage the company's business and financial position even if the petition is subsequently rejected (see *Stonegate Securities Ltd. v. Gregory* [1980] 1 All E.R. 241, and *Holt Southey v. Catnic Components* [1978] 1 W.L.R. 630).

An affidavit on Form 8A verifying the petition made by the petitioner (or one of the petitioners), or some person (including a solicitor) who has been concerned in the matter on behalf of the petitioner(s) must be filed within seven days after the petition has been presented. The prescribed form must be adhered to as far as possible. Longer or supplementary affidavits, notice of which must be given to the company, may be necessary where,

(a) fraud or misconduct is alleged (*Re A.B.C. Coupler and Engineering Co. Ltd. (No. 2)* [1962] 1 W.L.R. 1236); or

(b) the quasi-partnership analogy is invoked or a deadlock in the management is claimed (*Re Davis Investments (East Ham) Ltd.* [1961] 1 W.L.R. 1396, C.A.; *Re W.R. Willcocks & Co. Ltd.* [1973] 3 W.L.R. 669); or

(c) The Department of Trade inspector's report is relied upon (as to which see *Re Armvent Ltd.* [1975] 1 W.L.R. 1679 and *Re St. Piran Ltd.* [1981] 3 All E.R. 270). Unreasonably or unnecessarily long affidavits or hearsay statements on substantive matters are generally discouraged (see *Re Koscot Interplanetary (UK) Ltd; Re Koscot A.G.* [1972] 3 All E.R. 829).

Appointment of provisional liquidator. The court may on application appoint a provisional liquidator at any time after the presentation of the petition and before the hearing thereof (rules 32 and 41; Form 11). The Official Receiver or any fit person may be appointed (*Re Croftheath, The Times*, February 18, 1975). The court may restrict or limit his powers on appointment and impose other terms (C.A. 1948, s. 238). A special manager may also be appointed (see page 514). Where the proceedings are in Scotland, the appointment of a provisional liquidator may be made at any time before the first appointment of liquidators (section 238(3)).

Powers of court on hearing petition. The court may dismiss the petition, adjourn the hearing conditionally or make any interim or other order that it thinks fit. A winding up order cannot be refused merely because the company has no assets or its assets have been mortgaged to an amount equal to or in excess of those assets (s. 225(1)). The court is reluctant to grant long or repeated adjournments even if they are unopposed (see statement of Brightman J. [1977] 1 W.L.R. 1066). As to adjournments to allow defaulting companies to file annual returns and the like, see *Practice Note* [1974] 1 W.L.R. 1459.

Substitution of petitioner. Rule 37 empowers the court to substitute as petitioner any other creditor or contributory, who would have a right to present a winding up petition against the company, if the original petitioner does not diligently or expeditiously prosecute or wishes to withdraw his petition. Following substitution, the winding up is still deemed to have commenced from the date of presentation of the petition by the original petitioner. This provision has an important practical significance. If the original petitioner has received payment of his debt after the presentation (perhaps as an inducement to not prosecuting his petition) the payment may be set aside under section 227 (see page 517). It also prevents time running between the date of the presentation and substitution for the purposes of the antecedent transactions referred to on page 519, such as fraudulent preference and invalid floating charges.

Winding up order. When a winding up order or an order appointing a provisional liquidator before the winding up order has been made, the procedure as to completion, notification and transmission thereof as laid down in section 230 and rules 38–42 must be followed. Until the order is gazetted the company is not entitled to rely on it against other persons (European Communities Act 1972, sections 9(3)(f) and 9(4)(a)).

Costs. Upon disposing of a winding up petition, the court has a wide discretion on the question of costs of the proceedings. Usually a successful petitioner and the company would be awarded their costs payable out of the company's assets, subject to any encumbrances. For cases on the question of costs see, inter alia, *Re A.E. Hayter & Sons (Porchester) Ltd.* [1961] 1 W.L.R. 1008; *Re M. McCardy & Co. (Builders) Ltd. (No. 2)* [1976] 2 All E.R. 339; *Re Lanaghan Bros Ltd.* [1977] 1 All E.R. 265; *Re Dramstar, The Times,* 30 October, 1980. Where, after presentation of the creditors' petition, but before its advertisement, the debt on which it was founded has been paid without an offer to pay the petitioner's costs, the petitioner must elect either to have the petition struck out with no order for costs, or seek an adjournment to allow an advertisement to take place so that he ultimately gets his costs (*Re Shusella Ltd., The Times,* June 23, 1982).

Recission of winding up order. The court has an inherent power to rescind a winding up order provided an application is made promptly (and, in any event, before the winding up order has been perfected).

The power is exercised cautiously (see *Practice Notes* [1971] 1 W.L.R. 4 and 757).

Proceedings subsequent to winding up order

On the winding up order being made the Official Receiver becomes provisional liquidator and continues until he or another person becomes substantive liquidator and is capable of acting as such (C.A. 1948, s. 239(a)). The Official Receiver acts as liquidator where there is no liquidator appointed or there is a vacancy in the office of liquidator (section 239(d) and (e)).

Upon the appointment of the provisional liquidator, or the making of the winding up order by a court in England, the provisions of section 235 and rules 52–57 as to the submission to the Official Receiver of a statement of affairs of the company must be complied with by the company's officers and others. That statement may be used in evidence against its maker (C.A. 1967, s. 50).

Where a winding up order has been made, the Official Receiver must submit a preliminary report, and may submit a further report, to the court as provided by section 236 of the 1948 Act.

First meetings of creditors and contributories. The Official Receiver summons separate meetings of the creditors and contributories ("first meetings") for the purpose of determining whether an application is to be made for appointing a liquidator or liquidators in the place of the Official Receiver, and for appointing a committee of inspection and deciding who are to be members of the committee if appointed (see section 239(b); rules 121–156 and Forms 71–81). The determination at each meeting is made by ordinary resolution. Voting rights at the meeting of the contributories are as provided by the company's articles, subject to sections 136 to 139 of the 1948 Act. An ordinary resolution at either meeting requires the majority both in number and in value of the contributories or creditors (as the case may be) present and voting (rule 134). The Official Receiver or the chairman files with the Registrar of the court any resolutions (rule 135) and reports the results of the meetings to the court (rule 58(5); Form 23). The court holds a hearing to decide any difference between the determinations of the two meetings, and the order is gazetted by the Department of Trade.

Appointment of liquidators. Section 237 of the 1948 Act provides that for the purposes of conducting the proceedings in the winding up the court may appoint a liquidator or liquidators. Normally this will be the Official Receiver or a chartered accountant of at least five years' standing or having adequate experience in corporate insolvencies (*Re Icknield Development Ltd.* [1973] 1 W.L.R. 537). Where a person other than the Official Receiver is appointed liquidator he cannot act until he has notified his appointment to the Registrar of Companies and given security in the prescribed manner (see section 240; rules 59 and 60; and Form 26) to the satisfaction of the Department of Trade. The Official

Receiver continues to have limited supervisory and administrative functions. The appointment of a liquidator is required to be gazetted and advertised after he has given security, where applicable (rule 58(5), (6); Forms 24, 25 and 107). As to the appointment of liquidators in Scotland, see section 241.

Appointment of committee of inspection. The provisions for the appointment of the committee of inspection in a compulsory winding up in England differ from the corresponding provisions for a creditors' voluntary winding up in at least two respects. First, the members of the committee in the former must be creditors, contributories or persons holding general powers of attorney from them rather than any "persons"; and secondly, the maximum number of the members of the committee and the proportion in which creditors and contributories may be appointed thereon is not laid down but is left entirely to the court's discretion. The appointment of a committee is required to be advertised (rule 58(6)).

Appointment of special manager. Where in a winding up by the court in England the Official Receiver has been appointed, whether provisionally (before or after the making of the winding up order) or as substantive liquidator, he may at any time apply to the court to appoint a special manager (section 263; rules 50–51; Form 21).

Miscellaneous points on all forms of winding up

Liquidators — disqualification and restrictions. The codes of ethics of certain accountancy bodies forbid their members to accept an appointment as liquidator of an insolvent company for which their firms have acted as auditors (see generally C.A. 1948, s. 187 and s. 335, C.A. 1981, s. 93 and s. 94, and rule 168). In any case, no liquidator should accept an appointment which involves a conflict of interest (section 336, corrupt inducement affecting appointment as liquidator, and rule 151, solicitation for appointment as liquidator, should also be noted). A holder of a general or special proxy cannot vote in favour of a resolution which would directly or indirectly place himself, his partner or employer in a position to receive any remuneration out of the estate of the company. However, in a compulsory winding up the holder of a special proxy which gives him a mandate to vote for an application to the court in favour of himself as liquidator may use the proxy and vote accordingly (rule 153).

Procedure for initial meetings of creditors. The following points in relation to the first meeting of creditors in a compulsory winding up and the section 293 meeting of creditors in a creditors' voluntary winding up should be noted.

Proxies. Forms (see Forms 80 and 81) of general and special proxies must be sent to the creditors and contributories with the notice. Neither the name nor the description of the Official Receiver, the liquidator or any other person must be printed or inserted in the body of the forms (rule 148). A creditor or contributory may vote in person or by proxy (rule 146), and may give a general or special proxy to any person (rules 149 and 150). As to the time for lodging a proxy for use at a meeting of creditors or contributories in a compulsory winding up, or at a section 293 meeting of creditors in a creditors' voluntary winding up, see rules 154(1) and (2). Where a corporation is represented by a representative under section 139, a copy of the resolution under that section, certified by the secretary or a director, must be produced to the chairman of the meeting (rule 146).

Proofs of debts. In a compulsory winding up, a creditor is not entitled to vote unless he has lodged with the Official Receiver, not later than the time specified for that purpose in the notice of the meeting or adjourned meeting, a proof of the debt (rule 139, see also rules 91–105 and Forms 59, 59A and 60). This restriction does not apply to any creditors or class of creditors exempted therefrom by a court order, or to any voluntary liquidation meeting (rule 139).

Debts which may restrict the right to vote. A creditor is not entitled to vote in respect of any unliquidated or contingent debt, or any debt the value of which is not ascertained (rule 140). A secured creditor, unless he surrenders his security, must, in a compulsory winding up, include in his proof of debt and, in a voluntary liquidation, lodge before the meeting, a statement of his security (rules 141 and 144) and s assessment of its value. He is entitled to vote only in respect of the balance (if any) due to him after deducting the value of his security. If he votes in respect of his whole debt, he is deemed to have surrendered his security, unless the court on application is satisfied that the omission to value the security has arisen from inadvertence (rule 141).

The chairman may admit or reject a proof for the purpose of voting, but his decision is subject to appeal to the court. If he is in doubt as to its admissibility, he should mark it as objected to and allow the creditor to vote subject to his vote being declared invalid in the event of the objection being sustained (rule 143). Since a proof is not required to be lodged before the meeting (or, unless the liquidator otherwise decides, at all) in the case of a voluntary winding up (rule 139), it seems that the references to proof in rules 140 and 143 are references to the amount which the creditor orally claims at the meeting to be due to him.

Effect of winding up: general

The effect of a winding up is mainly determined, in the case of a members' or creditors' voluntary winding up, by reference to the date of the winding up resolution (the date on which the winding up is deemed to have commenced) and, in the case of a compulsory winding up, by reference either to the date of the presentation of the winding up petition (which in most cases is the date on which the winding up is deemed to have commenced) or to the date of the winding up order.

Effect of winding up: voluntary

Cessation of business. The company must, upon commencement, cease to carry on its business, except so far as may be required for the beneficial winding up thereof.

Cessation of directors' powers. On the appointment of a liquidator all powers of the directors cease, unless these are preserved, in the case of members' voluntary winding up, by the company in general meeting or the liquidator (section 285(2)), or, in the case of a creditors' voluntary winding up, by the committee of inspection, or if there is no such committee, the creditors.

Transfer of shares etc. Any transfer of shares without the liquidator's sanction, and any alteration in the status of the members of the company, made after commencement is void (C.A. 1948, s. 282).

Stay of actions and proceedings. The court has, by virtue of sections 226 and 307 of the 1948 Act and its inherent jurisdiction power to stay actions and proceedings against a company after the commencement of its voluntary winding up (see *Anglo Baltic Bank v. Barber & Co.* [1924] 2 K.B. 410).

Execution, distress etc. After a winding up resolution is passed the provisions applicable to compulsory liquidation referred to on page 517 may be invoked by virtue of section 307.

Effect of winding up: compulsory

Stay of actions and proceedings. At any time after the presentation of the petition and before the making of a winding up order, the appropriate court may, upon application, stay any action or proceedings pending against the company in England, Scotland or Northern Ireland (section 226; and see *Re Dynamics Corporation of America* [1973] 1 W.L.R. 63). "Proceedings" includes executions (*Re Artistic Colour Printing Co.* (1880) 14 Ch.D. 502; *The Constellation* [1966] 1 W.L.R. 272) and interpleader summonses (*Eastern Holdings Establishment of Vaduz v. Singer & Friedlander Ltd.* [1967] 1 W.L.R. 1017). If a provisional liquidator is appointed before the winding up, or once a winding up order is made, the stay is automatic and no new action or proceedings may be commenced unless the court otherwise orders (section 231; see also section 350 in Scotland). A writ served on a company after a winding up order is made without the leave of the court is a nullity (see *Wilson v. Banner Scaffolding Ltd.*, *The Times*, June 22, 1982 and *Roberts Petroleum v. Kenny*, *The Times*, February 15, 1983 (HL)).

On the principle that the plaintiff is entitled to choose his tribunal, the court may allow an action to continue unless there is sufficient reason not to, for example, that expense will be saved or that the existence of the liability is substantially admitted (*Currie v. Consolidated Kent Collieries Corpn* [1906] 1 K.B. 134; *Cook v. "X" Chair Patents Co. Ltd.* [1960] 1 W.L.R. 60).

Secured creditors are generally allowed to proceed with any action to enforce their security (*Lloyd v. David Lloyd & Co.* (1877) 6 Ch. D. 339).

Where a company in liquidation has no defence to a landlord's claim for possession the court may make an order for possession even though third parties' rights are involved as such rights are protected by R.S.C. Ord. 45, r. 3 (*Re Blue Jeans Sales Ltd.* [1979] 1 All E.R. 641).

Execution, distress etc. Any attachment, sequestration, distress or execution *put in force* against the estate or effects of a company registered in England, or, as regards any estate or effects situated in England of a company registered in Scotland, *after* the commencement of a compulsory winding up is void to all intents (section 228). Section 228 also applies to distress levied without the aid of the court. The section does not prima facie apply to execution, distress (etc.) *levied but not completed before* the commencement of the winding up; nor do sections 226 and 231 (see page 516) apply to a distress. It seems, however, that where a winding up order has been made, the combined effect of sections 228 and 231 is that even a distress levied before the commencement of winding up is automatically stayed upon the making of a winding up order, subject to the discretion of the court to allow it to proceed (see *Armorduct Manufacturing Co. v. General Incandescent Co.* [1911] 2 K.B. 143).

Disposition of property etc. Section 227 of the 1948 Act provides that any disposition of the property of the company and any transfer of shares, or alteration in the status of the members of the company, made after commencement shall, unless the court otherwise orders, be void. An indirect disposition of the company's property made by a third party falls within the section (*Re Leslie Engineering Co. Ltd.* [1976] 1 W.L.R. 292). The court may validate a disposition even before a winding up order is made (*Re A.I. Levy (Holdings) Ltd.* [1964] Ch. 19) and may authorise the making of a disposition. The court is guided by what would be just and fair in the circumstances of the case, having special regard to the good faith of the person concerned (*Re Clifton Place Garage Ltd.* [1970] Ch. 477). Other things being equal, the court leans in favour of giving effect to transactions in the ordinary course of business completed after presentation of the petition but before the winding up order (see *Re Park Ward Co.* [1926] Ch. 828 where a debenture given in return for a loan while the lender was aware of the presentation of the petition was declared valid). (See also *Re Oriental Bank Corporation* (1884) 28 Ch.D. 634; *Gorringe v. Irwell India Rubber Works* (1886) 34 Ch.D. 128.) No claim will lie against a bona fide purchaser for value without notice (*Re Leslie Engineering Co. Ltd, supra*). Payments into and out of the company's overdrawn bank account may constitute dispositions, and the bank may be ordered to restore the diminution in the amount which would otherwise have been available for distribution to the creditors, less any amounts recovered from the creditors who may have received payments out of the bank account (see *Re Grays Inn Construction Co. Ltd.* [1980] 1 W.L.R. 711). A shareholder has sufficient locus standi to make an application for validation (*Re Argentum Reductions (UK) Ltd.* [1975] 1 W.L.R. 186).

A court will generally approve a disposition by a solvent company where

it is satisfied that the directors took the view that the disposition was in
the interests of the company, and an intelligent and honest man could
reasonably take this view – even if a contributory is objecting (see *Re
Burton & Deakin Ltd.* [1977] 1 W.L.R. 390).

Effect of winding up: all forms

Goods and chattels taken in execution

Section 326(1) of the 1948 Act applies where goods or chattels of the
company are taken in execution, and, before sale or the completion of
the execution by the receipt or recovery of the full amount of the levy,
notice is served on the sheriff (or any other officer charged with the
execution) that a provisional liquidator has been appointed, or that a
winding up order has been made, or that a resolution for voluntary
winding up has been passed. The person on whom notice is served must,
on being so required, deliver to the liquidatory the goods and chattels,
and any money seized or received in part satisfaction (see also rule 143).

Section 326(2) requires the sheriff who has sold the company's goods or
chattels under an execution in respect of a judgment debt exceeding
£250, or who has received money in order to avoid the sale (as to which
see *Marley Tile Co. v. Burrows* [1978] Q.B. 241), to retain the proceeds
of sale or such money (after deduction of the costs of execution) for
fourteen days. If within that period notice is served on him of the
presentation of a petition for the company's winding up, or of the
convening of a meeting of the company at which a resolution for the
voluntary winding up is to be proposed, he must pay it to the liquidator
who is entitled to hold it as against the execution creditor.

Section 326(2), unlike section 326(1), applies to a notice of the
convening of a voluntary winding up meeting. A notice is not invalid
merely because it states that a meeting of creditors has been convened
"in connection with the winding up". The section is not to be construed
literally but according to its object and intent (per Lord Denning M.R.
in *Engineering Industry Training Board v. Samuel Talbot (Engineers)
Ltd.* [1969] 2 Q.B. 270). Where money is paid to the bailiff to avoid
"sale", the 14 day period runs from the time of its receipt by the bailiff,
not from the time he hands it over to the sheriff (*Re Walkden Sheet
Metal Co. Ltd.* [1960] Ch. 170). Section 326 does not apply to a winding
up in Scotland; instead section 327 of the 1948 Act applies.

Execution creditor having notice of impending liquidation

Section 325 prevents a creditor who has issued execution against the
goods or chattels, or (unlike in section 326) lands of the company, or
(again unlike in section 326) has attached any debt due to the company,
from retaining the benefit of the execution or attachment unless he has
completed it before the earlier of,

(a) (in a voluntary winding up) the receipt by him of a notice of the
    winding up meeting of the company having been called; or

(b) (in any type of winding up) the commencement of the winding up.

(In Scotland section 327 applies, and not section 325.)

An execution against goods is completed by seizure and sale or by the making of a charging order under section 1 of the Charging Orders Act 1979. An attachment of a debt is completed by the receipt of the debt. An execution against land is completed by seizure, by the appointment of a receiver, or by the making of a charging order under section 1.

A bona fide purchaser of goods from the sheriff (or other authorised officer) is protected by section 325(1)(b) and by the Sale of Goods Act 1893 (see sections 21(2)(b) and 26).

The "benefit of execution" means the benefit of the charge obtained by the issue of execution, and does not include money actually received thereunder before notice of the convening of a winding up meeting (*Re Caribbean Products (Yam Importers) Ltd.* [1966] Ch. 331). Money paid to the sheriff or his officer to avoid sale is not a "benefit of the execution" and can be retained by the creditor (*Re Walkden Sheet Metal Co. Ltd.* [1960] Ch. 170), unless it falls within the provisions of section 326(2) discussed earlier.

Power of court to grant relief to execution or distraining creditors

The rights conferred by sections 228, 325(1), 326(1) and 326(2) on the liquidator may be set aside by the court in favour of the creditor to such extent and subject to such terms as the court thinks fit (sections 325(1)(c); 326(3)). The court has a free hand to do what is right and fair according to the circumstances of the case (per Vaisey J. in *Re Grosvenor Metal Co.* [1950] Ch. 63, 65), but the court may require to be satisfied that the creditor has been unfairly treated by the company before it interferes with the ordinary rule that all unsecured creditors should rank equally (*Re Caribbean Products (Yam Importers) Ltd.* [1966] Ch. 331). The court, in exercise of its discretion, would not normally restrain a distress levied before the commencement of the winding up. The property of the company directed to be distributed amongst its creditors (subject to preferential claims) by the winding up provisions is subject to such rights as were exercised prior to the winding up (*Re Herbert Berry Associates Ltd.* [1976] 1 W.L.R. 783). However, a distress may be restrained where preferential debts will exhaust the assets (*Re South Rhondda Colliery Co.* [1928] W.N. 126).

Fraudulent preference

Section 320 of the 1948 Act (read with section 44 of the Bankruptcy Act 1914) is aimed at preventing a creditor, or contingent creditor, from retaining the benefit of any payment or security received from the company within six months before the commencement of the winding up with intent on the part of the company to prefer that creditor over the other creditors. The ingredients are,

(i) a conveyance, mortgage, delivery of goods, payment or other act relating to property made or done by or against the company;

(ii) in favour of a creditor (or a surety or guarantor) or his agent;

(iii) within six months immediately preceding commencement;

(iv) at a time when the company was unable to pay its debts as they fell due; and

(v) with a view on the part of the company to preferring the creditor over the other creditors.

In the application to Scotland of section 320, "fraudulent preference" includes any alienation or preference which is voidable by statute or at common law on the ground of insolvency or notour bankruptcy. "Bankruptcy petition" means a petition for sequestration and the period for the purposes of (iii) above is 60 days.

Practical application of section 320

(1) Good faith or the state of knowledge on the part of the creditor or other party preferred is irrelevant. It is the intent on the part of *the company* through its directors that is material.

(2) The word "fraudulent" is misleading. There need not be any fraud in the company or the preferee. Provided the five ingredients are established the transaction is deemed to be fraudulent.

(3) "View" means intent rather than motive (*Sharp v. Jackson* [1899] A.C. 419).

(4) Preference need not be the sole view but must be the dominant, substantial or effectual view on the part of the company through its directors (*Ex p. Hill; Re Bird* (1883) 23 Ch. D. 695; *Sharp v. Jackson supra*). The fact that the company genuinely believed that it would be able to pay its debts at some future time does not itself negative the intent to prefer (*Re FP & CH Matthews Ltd.* [1982] 1 All E.R. 338).

(5) The act must be voluntary on the part of the company and evidence of pressure may negative the voluntary nature of the act. The pressure must, however, be genuine, e.g. a threat of legal proceedings. The element of "deliberate selection" was strongly canvassed in *Re Cutts* [1956] 1 W.L.R. 728 (see also *Re Fletcher* (1891) 9 Mor. 8).

(6) Where the transaction is entered into for bona fide overriding commercial reasons, e.g. payment to key suppliers in respect of past supplies to ensure continuity of supplies or payment to a bank so as to maintain the line of credit (see *Re F.L.E. Holdings Ltd.* [1967] 1 W.L.R. 1409), intention to prefer may be negatived.

(7) Where the company creates a charge to secure new monies advanced to it there is no preference to the extent of the new monies.

(8) The onus of proving inability to pay and intent to prefer is on the liquidator (*Peat v. Gresham Trust* [1934] A.C. 252). In this respect

section 320 looks to the factual position at the time of the transaction in question (*Re FP and CH Matthews Ltd., supra,* where intent to prefer a bank was established).

On the question of intent to prefer, the following cases give some guidance.

Where intent established

(a) *Re W. Blackburn & Co.* [1899] 2 Ch. 725 (debtor acting from a mere moral sense of duty).

(b) *Re M. Kushler Ltd.* [1943] Ch. 248 (preference of bank for the benefit of guarantor; intent inferred from circumstances; see also section 321(3)).

(c) *Re Eric Holmes (Property) Ltd.* [1965] Ch. 1052 (right to be preferred on request).

(d) *Re Allen Fairhead & Sons Ltd.* [1971] 115 S.J. 244 (unreality of alleged pressure by directors on their own company).

Where intent not established

(a) *Sharp v. Jackson* [1899] A.C. 419 (demand by creditor; pressure; fear of legal proceedings).

(b) *Hartshorn v. Slodden* (1801) 2 B. & P. 582 (pressure, even though debt not yet due and payable).

(c) *Re Clay & Sons* (1896) 3 Mans. 31 (ordinary course of dealing and anticipation of benefit).

(d) *Re Vautin* [1900] 2 Q.B. 325 (obligation believed to be legal).

(e) *Bulteel and Colmore v. Parker and Bulteel's Trustee* (1916) 32 T.L.R. 661 (antecedent engagement).

A transaction which constitutes a fraudulent preference is void, and the liquidator is entitled to recover the property the subject matter of the preference, or its equivalent value, from the creditor preferred for the benefit of the creditors generally. Money recovered by the liquidator under section 320 is not covered by a floating charge, even though it has crystallised by reason of the liquidation. Interest on the money recoverable is payable from the date of commencement of the winding up (see *FP and CH Matthews Ltd., supra*).

As to fraudulent preference in favour of a third party which has mortgaged or charged its property to secure the company's debt, see section 321.

Invalid floating charge

As explained in greater detail on page 174, section 322 applies where a floating charge on the undertaking or property of the company is created within twelve months preceding the commencement of the winding up is. Unless it is proved that immediately after the creation of the charge the company was solvent, the charge is invalid except to the amount of any cash paid to the company at the time of or subsequently to the creation of, and in consideration for, the charge (plus interest thereon at five per cent per annum, or such other rate as may be prescribed by order of the Treasury). (As to Scotland, see also section 322(3).)

Practical application of section 322

(1) Unlike section 320 (fraudulent preference), intent is irrelevant.

(2) The vulnerable period is twelve months, instead of six months as in the case of fraudulent preference.

(3) The section applies only to a floating charge. Where the same charge contains a fixed charge over some assets and a floating charge over others it only applies to the latter. The fixed charge may, however, fall within section 320.

(4) The section invalidates only the floating charge; the debt remains, but only as an unsecured debt (*Re Parkes Garage (Swadlincote) Ltd.* [1929] 1 Ch. 139).

(5) The onus is on the holder of the charge to prove that the company was solvent (see page 174 for the meaning of solvent).

(6) "Cash paid to the company" means that if the charge secures moneys advanced to another party (e.g. to a parent company or a subsidiary or fellow subsidiary), it is invalid except to the extent that money was on-lent or otherwise passed to the company. The test is whether it can be said that in substance and not merely in form, the money was paid to the company. The mere fact that it was paid into the company's account is not conclusive; the payment must have been intended to benefit the company and not some other person (*Re Destone Fabrics Ltd.* [1941] Ch. 319). Cash may include cheques paid by a bank on the company's behalf out of money advanced to the company (*Re Yeovil Glove* [1965] Ch. 148. A replacement advance is not "cash paid": *Re Whyte* (1983) (unreported)).

(7) The words "at the time of or subsequently to and in consideration for the charge" have been interpreted to apply to money advanced a few days before the creation of but in reliance upon a promise to create the charge (*Re Columbian Fireproofing Co.* [1910] 2 Ch. 120; *Re F. & E. Stanton Ltd* [1929] 1 Ch. 180 and page 175).

(8) Where a floating charge is given to secure an existing overdraft, and there are subsequent debits and credits therein to reflect further advances and receipts into the account, the rule in *Clayton's case* (1816) 1 Mer. 572 applies and the receipts would be applied first in payment of the pre-charge indebtedness regardless of the consequence of the charge (*Re Yeovil Glove Co. Ltd.* [1965] Ch. 148). The section would not of course apply to the post-charge advances.

Period of limitation

It was held in *Re General Rolling Stock Co.* (1872) 7 Ch. App. 646 that on the commencement of compulsory winding up the period of limitation ceases to run against a creditor. The general reasoning of the judgment in that case seems to be equally applicable to a voluntary winding up. As to the circumstances in which a company's balance sheet can be an effective acknowledgment for the purposes of the statutes of limitation see *Re Gee & Co. (Woolwich) Ltd.* [1974] 2 W.L.R. 515 and *Re Compania de Electridad* [1980] 1 Ch. 146. In *Re Overmark* [1982] 3 All E.R. 513 a liquidator's statement of affairs operated as an acknowledgement, but only as at the effective date of the statement. A period of limitation continues to run in favour of the company's debtor and the liquidator must take action to recover the debt before the period runs out. The period of limitation for an unclaimed dividend declared before liquidation is six years, not twelve (*Re Compania de Electridad, supra*).

Employees and agents

The making of a winding up order constitutes notice of termination of employment to all employees of the company (*Measures Bros. Ltd. v. Measures* [1910] 2 Ch. 248). It seems that the passing of a voluntary winding up resolution has a similar effect since the ongoing nature of the company's business comes to an end, although the business may be temporarily continued.

The authority of an agent will automatically determine. A power of attorney under seal given to secure a proprietary interest of, or an obligation owed to, the donee or the person under whom he derives title, and expressed to be irrevocable, e.g. a power contained in a mortgage or a debenture stock trust deed, will not be revoked by the winding up (Powers of Attorney Act 1971, s. 4). A power of attorney granted to a receiver does not fall within that Act unless, perhaps, the debenture contains a covenant by the company expressed to be in favour of both the debenture holder and the receiver to do all such acts and things as either of them may require in exercise of the powers conferred on them and the covenant is linked with the power of attorney conferred on the receiver. It has, however, now been held in *Sowman v. David Samuel Trust Limited* [1978] 1 W.L.R. 22 and *Barrows v. Chief Land Registrar, The Times* October 20, 1977, that a power conferred upon the receiver by a debenture to sell and convey the property as agent and in the name of the company continues to be exercisable after liquidation independently of the Powers of Attorney Act and notwithstanding section 227 of the Companies Act 1948 (see page 517). The receiver's agency to incur debts on behalf of the company ceases, and he may be personally liable for costs of an action incurred after the winding up (*Bacal Contracting Ltd. v. Modern Engineering (Bristol) Ltd.* [1980] 2 All E.R. 655).

Property

Application of property. The property of the company falls to realised and applied in payment of the following in the following order:

(i) the costs of the winding up (see *Re Mesco Properties* [1979] S.T.C. 778 and *Re Christonette International Ltd* [1982] 3 All E.R. 225);

(ii) preferential claims pari passu;

(iii) the company's other liabilities, except deferred liabilities, again pari passu;

(iv) deferred claims of creditors pari passu (e.g. interest in excess of five per cent by virtue of the combined effect of C.A. 1948, s. 317 and B.A. 1914 s. 66);

(v) any deferred debt due to a member of the company in his capacity as such, pari passu; and

(vi) unless the articles otherwise provide, in distribution among the members of the company according to their rights and interests in the company (see C.A. 1948, s. 232, 257, 265, 267, 302, 309.)

The following points should be noted.

(1) Pari passu discharge of liabilities is mandatory and cannot be contracted out of (*British Eagle International Airlines Ltd. v. Compagnie Nationale Air France* [1975] 2 All E.R. 390). This principle could extend to and render unenforceable an agreement whereby a creditor subordinates a debt owed by the company to him to the debts owed by it to the other creditors in the event of the company's liquidation; and, accordingly, could enable the sub-ordinated creditor still to receive payment from the liquidator on a pari passu basis. It may be possible to achieve the desired result by the creation of a carefully drafted trust before the commencement of the winding up.

(2) The words "unless the articles otherwise provide" and "persons entitled thereto" are subject to the general principle that the memorandum or articles cannot authorise payment of any surplus funds for purposes which cannot be said to be in furtherance of the objects of the company as a going concern. In *Parke v. Daily News Ltd.* [1962] Ch. 927 the proposal by a company after the cessation of the major part of its business and continuation of its other business, to make large ex gratia payments to its former employees was held to be ultra vires. Section 74 of the Companies Act 1980 goes a considerable way towards counteracting the effect of that case, by permitting provision being made for the benefit of employees or former employees in connection with the cessation of the company's undertaking out of the assets which are available to the members, but the general principle continues to apply to other cases. As to the resolution by directors on the eve of liquidation to make an ex gratia payment to one of their number, see *Gibson's*

Executor v. Gibson 1980 S.L.T. 2. (See also *Re Merchant Navy Supply Association Ltd.* [1947] 1 All E.R. 894; *Liverpool and District Hospital for Diseases of the Heart v. Attorney-General* [1981] 1 All E.R. 994.)

Ownership of property. A winding up order does not divest the company of the *legal* ownership of its assets, unless a vesting order in favour of the liquidator is made under section 244 of the 1948 Act. However, the company ceases to be the *beneficial* owner of its property (*I.R.C. v. Olive Mill Ltd.* [1963] 1 W.L.R. 712; *Ayerst v. C. & K. Construction Ltd.* [1975] 1 W.L.R. 16). This may have important tax consequences (see page 497).

Liabilities

Date for determination. All liabilities of the company fall to be determined (subject to section 319 regarding preferential claims – see page 541) as at the date of the winding up order or the voluntary winding up resolution.

The "act of bankruptcy" analogy. The rights of an unsecured or partly secured creditor of an *insolvent* company may be affected by the "available act of bankruptcy" analogy. Sections 30(2) and 31 of the Bankruptcy Act 1914, as read with section 317 of the 1948 Act, respectively disentitle a creditor from proving or setting off in the winding up a debt contracted by the company after the creditor had notice of "an available act of bankruptcy". There is a conflict between judicial authorities in England and in Australia on what is an analogous "available act of bankruptcy" in relation to a company. *Re Eros Films Ltd.* [1963] Ch. 565 suggests that one must look to section 1 of the 1914 Act (which, as read with section 4(1)(a), sets out formal acts on any one of which a bankruptcy petition may be founded if the act occurred within three months preceding the petition), and then ascertain an analogous formal act in relation to the company that may have occurred within three months preceding the commencement of the winding up. It was held that in the case of a creditors' voluntary winding up the issue of notices of winding up meetings within that period was such an act. By contrast, *Law v. James* [1972] 2 N.S.W.L.R. 573 suggests that, rather than looking at the Bankruptcy Act, one must directly look at sections 222 and 223 of the 1948 Act, which set out the grounds on which a petition for a compulsory winding up may be founded. One such ground is that "it is proved to the satisfaction of the court that the company is unable to pay its debts and, in determining whether the company is unable to pay its debts, the court shall take into account the contingent and prospective liabilities of the company". Accordingly, if at the time the debt was contracted the creditor was aware of the company's inability to pay debts, he would not be entitled to set off or prove for that debt in the subsequent liquidation (compulsory or voluntary). If the Australian case was followed in England there could be far-reaching implications with regard to the provision of unsecured finance to companies in a rescue situation.

Conduct of winding up: general procedural aspects

Members' voluntary winding up

Liquidator's remuneration.   The remuneration of the liquidator is fixed by the company in general meeting (C.A. 1948, s. 285(1)).

Vacancy in the office of liquidator.   Any vacancy by death, resignation or otherwise in the office of liquidator appointed by the company may be filled by the company in general meeting, as provided by section 286 of the 1948 Act.

Creditors' meeting in the case of insolvency.   If the liquidator is at any time of the opinion that the company will not be able to pay its debts in full within the period stated in the declaration of solvency, he must forthwith summon a creditors' meeting and lay before it a statement of the company's assets and liabilities (C.A. 1948, s. 288). It should be noted that, unlike in a winding up that originates as a creditors' voluntary winding up, a creditors' meeting has no automatic right to replace the liquidator by one of their choosing.

Annual meetings and accounts.   The liquidator must hold a general meeting of the company (and, in a case of insolvency, also a meeting of creditors) within three months of each anniversary of commencement and lay before it an account of his acts and dealings and of the conduct of the winding up during the preceding year (see sections 289, 291, 299 and 342; rules 197, 198 and 201; and Forms 92 to 97).

Creditors' voluntary winding up

Liquidator's remuneration.   This is fixed by the committee of inspection, or, if none, the creditors in general meeting (C.A. 1948, s. 296(1)).

Vacancy in the office of liquidator.   Any vacancy in the office of liquidator, other than a liquidator appointed by or by the direction of the court, may be filled by the creditors' meeting (section 297).

Annual meetings and accounts.   There are provisions similar to those applicable in a members' voluntary winding up concerning the holding of annual meetings and accounts, except that the accounts must be laid before both a general meeting of the members and a general meeting of creditors.

Members' and creditors' voluntary winding up: points common to both

Where several liquidators appointed.   Where several liquidators are appointed, the powers given to a liquidator by the 1948 Act may be exercised by such one or more of them as may be determined at the time of that appointment, or, in default of such appointment, by any number not less than two (section 303(3)).

Appointment or removal of liquidator by court.   If from any cause whatsoever there is no liquidator acting, the court may appoint a liquidator. Moreover, the court may, on cause shown, remove a liquidator and appoint another in his stead (see section 304).

Sale in exchange for shares etc. Sections 287 and 298 of the 1948 Act empower the liquidator, subject as provided therein, to sell the whole or any part of the business or property of the company to another company in return for shares, policies or other like interests in the transferee company or participation in the profits of or receiving any other benefit from the transferee company.

Compulsory winding up

Office and remuneration of the liquidator. A liquidator appointed by the court may resign or, on cause shown, be removed by the court (C.A. 1948, s. 242(1) and see rules 58(7) and 167). A vacancy in the office of such a liquidator must be filled by the court. Where a liquidator other than the Official Receiver is appointed, he is entitled to receive such salary or other remuneration by way of percentage or otherwise as the court may direct (section 242(2); see also rules 159, 160, 194 and 195).

Records to be maintained by liquidator. In England, the liquidator must maintain in the prescribed manner records and accounts and his receipts and payments accounts are required to be audited, filed and circularised (C.A. 1948, s. 247 and 249; rules 173-181; and Forms 86–89).

Department of Trade. In England, the Department of Trade has a supervisory role over the conduct of the liquidator. Where there is no committee of inspection the Department may, on the application of the liquidator, do any act or thing or give any direction or permission which is authorised or required by the Act to be done or given by the Committee (C.A. 1948, s. 250).

Creditors' voluntary and compulsory winding up: points common to both

Functions of committee of inspection. For the appointment of a committee of inspection see pages 504 and 514. No committee can be appointed in a members' voluntary winding up. The functions of the committee have not been exhaustively defined in the winding up provisions. Among the specific areas in which the committee is involved are sanctioning the exercise by the liquidator of some of his powers; fixing the liquidator's remuneration; issuing certificates to secure re-lease of money from the Insolvency Services Account (see below); and directing the manner of disposal of books and papers (see below). The committee's wider role is recognised, at least in the case of a compulsory winding up, by section 246(1), which requires that in the administration and distribution of the assets the liquidator must have regard to any direction given, inter alia, by the committee, and by section 252(1) which envisages that the committee will "act" with the liquidator. It seems that the committee has the same wider role in a creditors' voluntary winding up by the indirect effect of section 295(2) as read with section 253. It is generally recognised that a committee's function is to assist the liquidator and supervise his proceedings.

Conflict of interest. Rules 161 and 163 to 165 contain restrictions on members of the committee or their associates purchasing the company's assets, or directly or indirectly deriving any profit from any transaction arising out of the winding up or reciving any remuneration, or the like.

All forms of winding up

Notification on invoices etc. Each invoice, order for goods or business letter, issued by or on behalf of a company in liquidation or its liquidator or receiver or manager, on which the name of the company appears must contain a statement that the company is being wound up (C.A. 1948, s. 338). Where the company is in receivership, there should also be a statement to that effect (section 370).

Stay of winding up. At any time after an order for a compulsory winding up, the court may, on application and on relevant proof to its satisfaction, make an order staying all the winding up proceedings, either altogether or for a limited time, on such terms and conditions as it thinks fit (C.A. 1948, s. 256). This provision may be invoked in a voluntary winding up by virtue of section 307. In exercising the discretion the court applies the analogy of rescinding a receiving order in bankruptcy. It will consider the interests of commercial morality and not merely the wishes of creditors. It may refuse a stay if there is evidence of misfeasance or irregularities requiring investigation (*Re Calgary & Edmonton Land Co.* [1975] 1 W.L.R. 355).

Position of liquidator. A liquidator occupies a fiduciary position but is not a trustee for each individual creditor (*Knowles v. Scott* [1891] 1 Ch. 717, 723). In a compulsory winding up he is an officer, and subject to the control, of the court. A liquidator's duty is to the general body of the company's creditors and contributories; but as he is an agent employed for the purpose of winding up the company, charged with important statutory powers, duties, discretions and, to some extent, even quasi-judicial functions, he must treat each creditor and contributory fairly. He may be personally liable in damages to creditors for beach of his statutory duty if he does not use proper diligence. But a liquidator who, keeping within the limits of his agency and acting in good faith, inadvertently disposes of trust property is not liable as constructive trustee, even if he is negligent (*Competitive Insurance Co. Ltd. v. Davies Investments Ltd.* [1975] 1 W.L.R. 1240). (See also rules 161 and 162 as to restrictions against deriving personal profit, etc.)

Powers of liquidator. Section 245 of the 1948 Act lists the liquidator's specific powers in a compulsory winding up. Section 303, dealing with the liquidator's powers in a voluntary winding up, incorporates section 245, with modifications. In a compulsory winding up some of the powers can be exercised only with the sanction either of the court or of the committee of inspection (or, if there is no committee, the Department Trade). The exercise by the liquidator in a compulsory winding up of the powers contained in section 245 is in all cases subject to the control of the court and any creditor or contributory may apply to the court concerning his activities. In a members' voluntary winding up the exercise of some of the powers requires the sanction of an extraordinary resolution of the company and, in a creditors' voluntary winding up, the sanction of the court or the committee or (if there is no committee) a meeting of the creditors. It is submitted that in a compulsory or creditors' winding up the liquidator should prefer the court's sanction where the proposed exercise is likely to have a fundamental or substantial effect on the course or result of the winding up or where the members of the committee have some special interest in the subject matter of the exercise. In Scotland, the liquidator has, subject to general rules, the same powers as a trustee of a bankrupt estate (section 245(5)). Sections 245 and 303 are not exhaustive as to specific powers – see also, for example, section 246(2) (summoning meetings of creditors and contributories to ascertain their wishes), sections 246(3) and 307 (application to court for directions), sections 287 and 298 (sale of assets in exchange for shares etc. in a voluntary winding up), section 323 (disclaimer) and section 74(5) of the 1980 Act (provision of benefits for employees). The court would generally not sanction a proposed compromise by the liquidator with the creditors under section 245(1)(f) which involves the distribution of the company's assets otherwise than strictly in accordance with the creditors' rights. The proper way to do this is by a scheme of arrangement under section 206.

Liquidator to have regard to wishes of creditors and contributories. In England, the liquidator must, in the administration of the assets of the company and in distribution thereof among the creditors, have regard to any directions that may be given by the creditors or contributories at any general meeting or, subject thereto, by the committee of inspection (see C.A. 1948, s. 246 and s. 346).

Regard is had, in the case of creditors, to the value of each creditor's debt and, in the case of contributories, to the number of votes conferred on each contributory by the Companies Acts or the articles. The liquidator may apply to the court for directions in relation to any particular matter arising under the winding up. Subject to the Acts, the liquidator must use his own discretion in the management of the estate and its distribution among the creditors. Any person aggrieved may apply to the court which may confirm, reverse or modify the act or decision, and make such order as it thinks fit (C.A. 1948, s. 246 and s. 307).

Conduct of winding up: realisation of assets

General aspects

Collection. Section 257(1) of the 1948 Act requires the court in a compulsory winding up to cause the assets of the company to be collected, and applied in discharge of its liabilities. This duty is delegated to the liquidator by rule 78, which also provides that for the purpose of acquiring and retaining possession of the property of the company the liquidator is in the same position as if he were a receiver of the property appointed by the High Court. Moreover, the court may on his application enforce such acquisition or retention accordingly. Section 258 provides that the court may require any contributory for the time being on the list of contributories and any trustee, receiver, banker, agent or officer of the company to pay, transfer etc. to the liquidator, any money, property or books and papers in his hands to which the company is prima facie entitled (see also sections 261 and 262). This power is delegated in England to the liquidator by rule 79. Section 243 requires a liquidator or provisional liquidator, as the case may be, to take into his custody or under his control all the property and things in action to which the company is or appears to be entitled. (In a compulsory winding up in Scotland, where there is no liquidator all the property of the company is deemed to be in the custody of the court (section 243(1)). All these powers may be invoked in a voluntary winding up by virtue of section 307. The liquidator's powers and duties to collect the assets in a voluntary winding up are also implicit in sections 302, 303 (as read with section 245), 285 and 294.

Sale.   The liquidator has power to sell the real and personal property and things in action of the company by public auction or private contract, with power to transfer the whole of the property to any person or company or to sell it in parcels (C.A. 1948 s. 245(2)(a) and s. 303).

Vesting order.   Section 244 of the 1948 Act enables the court in a compulsory winding up to vest any assets of the company in the liquidator in his official name. It also enables the liquidator, after he has given any indemnity as directed by the court, to bring or defend in his official name any action or proceeding relating to the assets, or which is necessary for the purpose of winding up the company and recovering its property. (The section can also be invoked in a voluntary winding up under section 307.) Vesting under section 244 is not normally necessary because the liquidator can deal with the assets in the name of the company and use its common seal (C.A. 1948, s. 245(2)(b) and s. 303(1)(b)). However, a vesting order may assist, for example, where the seal is not immediately available or an unincorporated body is being wound up under Part IX of the 1948 Act, or it is more convenient for the liquidator to deal with the assets in his official name, say in relation to proceedings in a foreign country.

Private examination.   Under section 268 the court may, at any time after the appointment of a provisional liquidator or the making of a winding up order, summon before it and examine on oath any person known or suspected to have in his possession any property of the company or supposed to be indebted to the company, or any person whom the court deems capable of giving information concerning the promotion, formation, trade, dealings, affairs or property of the company (see also rules 72–74 and Forms 32–34). (Section 268 can be invoked in a voluntary winding up by virtue of section 307.) As to the attitude of the court on a liquidator's application to examine a defendant or potential defendant in an action by the company or the liquidator, see *Rolls Razor Ltd. (No. 2)* [1970] Ch. 576; *Re Bletchley*

Boat Co. Ltd. [1974] 1 W.L.R. 630; *Re Castle New Homes Ltd.* [1979] 1 W.L.R. 1075; and *Re Spiraflite Ltd.* [1979] 1 W.L.R. 1096.

Public examination. Where in a compulsory winding up any further report submitted by the Official Receiver under section 236 (see page 513) alleges fraud in the promotion or formation of the company, or by any officer of the company since its formation, the court may also hold its public examination (see C.A. 1948, s. 270; rules 61-66, 71–73 and Forms 27–34, 61–67). The further report of the Official Receiver must disclose at least a prima facie case of fraud, but, where several persons are to be examined, it is not necessary to attribute to each of them some particular aspect of the fraud (*Tejani v. Official Receiver* [1963] 1 W.L.R. 59). Section 270 can be invoked by originating summons under section 307 in a voluntary winding up, a "further report" under section 236 referred to above not being required (*Re Campbell Coverings Ltd. (No. 1)* [1953] Ch. 488; (No. 2) [1954] Ch. 225; *Re Serene Shoes Ltd.* [1958] 1 W.L.R. 1087).

Exemption from stamp duty. Certain types of documents entered into in the course of a winding up are exempt from stamp duty (see section 339).

Recovery of assets in respect of antecedent transactions. The liquidator must take appropriate action to have any antecedent transactions set aside and to recover any money or assets that are consequently recoverable. "Antecedent transactions" as used here includes the following.

(a) Execution, distress etc. (see pages 516 and 517).

(b) Disposition of property after commencement of compulsory winding up (see page 517).

(c) Fraudulent preference (see page 519).

(d) Invalid floating charge (see page 521).

Unauthorised or prohibited company transactions. It may be possible to obtain restitution or compensation from another party in respect of past transactions that were in breach of the Companies Acts, like ultra vires transactions or unlawful loans to directors.

Unregistered charge. Certain charges created by a company are void as against the liquidator or a creditor of the company unless they are registered with the Registrar of Companies under section 95 of the Companies Act 1948. Examples of "borderline" cases are:

(i) *Retention of title clauses.* A "Romalpa" clause might constitute a registrable charge (as a limited floating charge, or a charge under the "bill of sale" analogy or over book debts) to the extent of any proprietary interest sought to be reserved by the vendor in assets other than the goods in their original form (and, perhaps, other than the proceeds in respect of the goods sold in their original form). (See *Borden (UK) Ltd. v. Scottish Timber Products Ltd* [1979] 3 W.L.R. 672; *Re Bond Worth Ltd.* [1979] 3 W.L.R. 629; c.f.

Aluminium Industrie Vaassen BV v. Romalpa Aluminium Ltd.
[1976] 1 W.L.R. 676; see the chapter *Company Charges*, page 182.)

(ii) *Factored book debts.*   If under a factoring agreement the assignment of book debts by the company to the factoring company is in
substance a charge rather than an absolute assignment, the transaction is registrable. In *Lloyds & Scottish Finance Ltd. v. Cyril Lord
Carpet Sales Ltd.* (1979) 129 NLJ 366, assignments under a block
discounting agreement were held on the facts to be absolute
assignments, even though only 80 per cent of the debts were
actually taken by the bank in return for the advances (and see page
197).

(iii) *Sale and leaseback.*   An arrangement to raise finance by selling
fixed assets to a finance company for cash, and having them leased
back for a periodic charge with an option to repurchase them at a
price to be determined, could be held to be in reality a registrable
charge (see *Stoneleigh Finance Ltd. v. Phillips* [1965] 2 Q.B. 537,
574, per Russell L.J., see further page 187).

(iv) *"Pledge" of goods in warehouse.*   A transfer by the company of its
goods in a warehouse as security may constitute a registrable charge
under the "bill of sale" analogy if the transfer is not accompanied
by actual or constructive possession of the goods (*see Dublin City
Distillery v. Doherty* [1914] A.C. 823; and *Wrightson v. McArthur
and Hutchinson* [1921] 2 K.B. 807, see further page 192).

(v) *Contractual set off.*   A contractual right of set-off greater than the
right of set-off available under statute or general law, may constitute a registrable charge over book debts (see further page 196).

(vi) *Subordination of debt.*   If the company has subordinated a debt
owing to it to the rights of another creditor or other creditors of the
debtor, the subordination could constitute a registrable charge over
book debts (see also pages 152 and 194).

Fraudulent trading

Section 332 of the Companies Act 1948 (as modified by section 96 of the
1981 Act), enables the court in any form of winding up to declare that
any persons who were,

(i) *knowingly party* to carrying on the business of a company,

(ii) *with intent* to defraud creditors of the company or creditors of any
other persons or for any fraudulent purpose,

to be personally responsible without limitation of liability for all or any
of the debts or liabilities of the company.

The leading case is *Re William C. Leitch Bros.* [1932] 2 Ch. 71. The
respondent sold his business to the company in consideration of shares
and a debenture over all assets, present and future, and had been
appointed managing director. At a time when the company was making

losses he continued to order goods which became subject to the charge under his debenture. He was held liable. Maugham J said: "If a company continues to carry on business and to incur debts at a time when there is to the knowledge if the directors no reasonable prospect of the creditor ever receiving payment of those debts, it is in general a proper inference that the company is carrying on business with intent to defraud." This statement was approved and explained by Buckley J in an unreported judgment – *Re White & Osmond (Parkstone) Ltd.* (June 30, 1960) – where on the facts the directors were held not liable because they had genuinely believed that matters would improve.

It must be shown that there was active or positive participation by the person concerned in the carrying on of the business. The secretary or financial adviser of a company is not, merely because he fails to draw the insolvent state of the company to the attention of the directors, so concerned (see *Re Maidstone Building Provisions Ltd.* [1971] 3 All E.R. 363).

Whether a person who advances money to enable a company's business to be carried on in the circumstances mentioned is a party to "carrying on" the business is undecided. It is suggested that a mere provider of finance would not be caught by the section, unless he actively participated in the decision making. Where a bank has nominated directors of and has been providing finance for the company, it would seem that any fraudulent participation by those directors cannot be vicariously imputed to the bank, as the directors have independent functions (statutory and otherwise).

Intent to defraud creditors, or some other fraudulent purpose, must be proved and the onus is upon those seeking to prove it. The section is a punitive one and "fraud" has its criminal law meaning. There must be evidence to justify a finding of actual dishonesty; "chasing of the rainbow" cannot necessarily be described as an intent to defraud (*Re Patrick and Lyon Ltd.* [1933] Ch. 786). It was held in *Re Sarflax Ltd* [1979] 1 All E.R. 529 that a mere intent to prefer one creditor to another, where a person knew or had grounds to suspect that he would have insufficient assets to pay all creditors in full, could not constitute "fraudulent" trading within section 332. It should also be noted that the section refers to carrying on any *business*, and not any *trade*, and a person was carrying on business until he had performed all the obligations imposed upon him by the fact of trade (*Re Sarflax Ltd., supra*). The use of the word "knowingly" implies that if the person concerned had a reasonable expectation that things would turn out all right – for example, that financial support would be forthcoming – he would not be liable unless he continued to be concerned in carrying on the business after that expectation was disappointed. A single transaction may constitute fraudulent trading: see *Re Gerald Cooper Chemicals Ltd.* [1978] 2 W.L.R. 866, where it was also suggested that a creditor is a party to the carrying on of business with intent to defraud creditors if he accepts money which he knows has been procured by carrying on a business with such intent for the very purpose of making the payment.

Recovery under section 332 is not limited to debts incurred as a result of the fraud. Any sum recovered forms part of the general assets available to the liquidator, or perhaps to a debenture holder having a general charge on the assets, but see *Re Cyona Distributors Ltd* [1967] Ch. 889 where a creditor (the Inland Revenue), at whose instance an award was made against the directors, was held entitled to retain the amount of the award.

Where the court declares the directors liable, it may charge their liability against any securities they may hold against the company (section 333(2)).

Misfeasance

Section 333 of the 1948 Act provides an effective remedy against directors who have been delinquent. It creates no new liability, but provides a speedier procedure for enforcing certain rights which might have been enforced by an action before winding up.

The section allows the Official Receiver, a liquidator, a creditor, or a contributory standing to benefit, to recover money or damages for the benefit of the company in liquidation from the promoters, or past or present directors or officers of the company, who have misapplied or retained or become liable or accountable for any money or property of the company or been guilty of misfeasance or breach of trust.

The court may examine the conduct of such persons and compel them to repay or restore the money or the property with interest, or to contribute money to the assets of the company by way of compensation.

The term "misfeasance" does not cover every misconduct by an officer of the company for which he might have been sued apart from the section. Further, it is necessary to show pecuniary loss. An ordinary claim for damages based exclusively on common law negligence is not within the section (*Re B. Johnson & Co. (Builders) Ltd.* [1955] Ch. 634; and see also *Re Etic Ltd.* [1928] Ch. 861; and *Selangor United Rubber Estates Ltd. v. Craddock* [1967] 1 W.L.R. 1168).

Subject to the above points, section 333 covers a variety of wrongs, including improper payment of dividends, application of moneys for *ultra vires* purposes, application of moneys contrary to sections 42 to 44 of the 1981 Act, and unauthorised loans or payment of unauthorised remuneration to directors. (See further, *Re Reliance Wholesale (Toys) Ltd., Patterson v. Mills*, LSG, July 18, 1979.) No set off is allowed to a director who is in breach of the section.

A secretary is an "officer" (per contra in the case of fraudulent trading). Auditors may be officers where the company has articles similar to those of Table A. On the other hand, section 448(1) of the 1948 Act recognises that an auditor is not necessarily an officer. An accountant may not be so where he is merely called in to audit the accounts of the company. A subordinate manager may be "an officer", which includes anyone who exercises supervisory or management control reflecting the general policy of the company or relating to its general administration (*Re A Company* [1980] 1 All E.R. 284). A receiver and manager appointed by debenture holders is not an officer nor are the company's bankers, nor, prima facie, is the company's solicitor, but he may be when he does all the work for a fixed salary.

A bona fide error of judgment is not sufficient to make directors liable. An officer who has acted honestly and reasonably may be granted relief from liability if the court considers that he ought fairly to be wholly or partly excused (section 448).

Void transfers

By section 172 of the Law of Property Act 1925, a conveyance of property made with intent to defraud creditors, otherwise than for valuable consideration and in good faith, or upon good consideration and in good faith to any person not having, at the time of the conveyance, notice of the intent to defraud, is voidable at the instance of any person thereby prejudiced. The section applies regardless of whether the company is insolvent or is in liquidation and to both real and personal property. As to a claim against a stranger by way of third party proceedings see *Re Shilena Hoisery Co.* [1979] 2 All E.R. 6.

By section 320(2) of the Companies Act 1948, any conveyance or assignment by a company of all its property to trustees for the benefit of all its creditors is void for all purposes. This prevents evasion of the winding up provisions. (A floating charge for the benefit of all creditors is within the section: *London Joint etc. Bank v. Herbert Dickinson* [1922] W.N. 13.)

Dealing with specific types of assets

The following may be of assistance in dealing with or realising specific types of assets.

1. Disclaimer

(1) Section 323 (which does not apply to a winding up in Scotland) allows a liquidator, with leave of the court, by writing signed by him to disclaim any part of the company's property which consists of,

(a) land of any tenure burdened with onerous covenants; or

(b) shares or stock in companies; or

(c) unprofitable contracts;

or any other property that is unsaleable or not readily saleable by reason of it binding the possessor thereof to the performance of any onerous act, or to the payment of any sum of money (see also rules 75–6 and Forms 35 and 36).

(2) The disclaimer must be effected within one year after commencement or, where the property has not come to the knowledge of the liquidator within one month after commencement, within twelve

months after he has become aware thereof, or, in either case, within such extended period as may be allowed by the court. He may, however, be required to reach a decision earlier by any person interested as provided by section 323. The mere fact that the liquidator has endeavoured to sell, or taken possession of the property, or exercised any act of ownership in relation thereto, does not deprive him of the right to disclaim.

(3) The disclaimer operates to determine the rights, interests and liabilities and property of the company in or in respect of the property disclaimed, but does not affect the rights or liabilities of any other person, except in so far as is necessary for the purpose of releasing the company and its property from liability.

(4) The court has wide powers on any application for leave to disclaim to make such orders as it deems just, including an order vesting the disclaimed property in, and requiring payment in respect of a rescinded contract to, any party adversely affected.

(5) Any person injured by the operation of a disclaimer is deemed to be a creditor of the company to the amount of the injury, and is entitled to prove for that amount in the winding up.

(6) The court will not, however, allow disclaimer to the prejudice of other parties, for example, a landlord entitled to sue another party on a guarantee for the rent, etc., if the guarantee is so framed as to apply only whilst the lease remains vested in the company (see *Re Katherine et Cie* [1932] 1 Ch. 70.)

2. Sale of business and assets generally.   Attention is drawn to sections 13(1) and 14(1) of the Prevention of Fraud (Investments) Act 1958, which restrict the distribution, etc. of circulars that may induce any person to take part or offer to take part in certain types of arrangement with respect to property (including acquisition of property). Where it is necessary for the company's name to be changed as a condition of the purchase of its business, the liquidator in a members' or creditors' voluntary winding up may convene a meeting of its members for the purpose (C.A. 1948, s. 303(1)(e)).

3. Cash

(1) Cash in hand or at bank may be subject to third party rights in the nature of a trust or tracing remedy, which arise from, inter alia,

(a) receipt of proceeds of sale covered by valid "Romalpa type" clauses (see page 531);

(b) receipt of factored book debts (see page 532);

(c) receipt of advances from customers paid into a separate bank account under circumstances similar to those in *Re Kayford Ltd.* [1975] 1 W.L.R. 279;

(d) receipt of money under a mistake of fact (see *Chase Manhattan Bank N.A. v. Israel-British Bank (London) Ltd.* [1979] 3 All E.R. 1025); or

(e) money borrowed and set aside for specific purpose, as in *Barclays Bank Ltd. v. Quistclose Investments Ltd.* [1970] A.C. 567.

(2) In the case of a compulsory winding up in England, the provisions of section 248 of the 1948 Act as regards payment of money into the Insolvency Services Account at the Bank of England should be observed (see also rules 169–170 and Forms 82 and 83).

(3) In any form of winding up, section 343 should be observed with regard to payment into the Insolvency Services Account of money representing assets unclaimed or undistributed for six months and any money held by the company in trust in respect of dividends, etc. due to any member (see also rules 169 and 199 to 204 and Forms 92 to 97). Moneys paid into that account may be invested through the Department of Trade in accordance with rule 173 (see Forms 84 and 85). Interest at the rate from time to time fixed by the Treasury (currently 3 per cent per annum – Companies Liquidation Account (Interest) Order 1965 S.I. 1965 No. 920) is allowed on any amount in excess of £2,000 held in the Account. (See also Insolvency Services (Accounting and Investment) Act, 1970 and, for Scotland, C.A. 1948, s. 344.)

4. Book debts, stocks, chattels and fixtures. Book debts and stocks may be subject to valid third party rights in favour of factoring companies, or "Romalpa" suppliers (see page 531). Sales of products to the public may involve defective product liability, and plant, equipment, fixtures, motor vehicles, etc. may be subject to third party rights under hire purchase, leasing or rental agreements.

5. Freehold and leasehold property. Where forfeiture of a lease is threatened, action should be considered to obtain relief under section 146(2) or (10) of the Law of Property Act 1925 (in which "bankruptcy" includes liquidation – see section 205(1) of that Act). Where appropriate, disclaimer of the lease should be considered.

If a lease is disposed of by the liquidator by way of assignment, the company will continue to be liable (concurrently with the assignee) to the landlord on any future breaches of covenant, unless the landlord expressly releases the company from such liability. Where such release is not granted, the liquidator may have difficulty in concluding the winding up during the remainder of the term of the lease unless he has a suitable indemnity from a financially sound party. A solvent company will not be permitted to distribute its assets amongst its shareholders without regard to the landlord's right to future rent (*Lord Elphinstone v. Monkland Co.* (1886) 11 App. Cas. 332). Further, if the liquidator takes or remains in possession of a leasehold property for the purposes of the better realisation of the assets, the landlord will be entitled to payment of the rent in full as part of the winding up expenses properly incurred by the liquidator. Moreover, the liquidator becomes responsible for the repairs and performance of all the obligations under the lease (see *Re Downer Enterprises* [1974] 1 W.L.R. 1460; rule 99).

6. *Building contracts.* Some standard forms of building contract contain provisions as to termination in the event of the liquidation of the builder or the employer, valuation of works, calculation of damages, set-off and the right of the employer to use the builder's plant and machinery on the site (subject to any third party rights). There may also be special provisions imposing a trust in favour of nominated sub-contractors in respect of any money attributable to the work done by them and included in the amount paid or payable to the builder and giving a right to the employer to pay any such money direct to the nominated sub-contractors. (See *Re Tout and Finch* [1954] 1 W.L.R. 178). If the contract is outstanding, a disclaimer may be appropriate (see page 535).

7. *Unpaid share capital.* A call made before commencement and remaining unpaid is a debt due to the company and can be recovered as such by the liquidator (see page 509). Section 259 of the 1948 Act contains restrictions against set-off. To the extent that any unpaid capital is not subject to an outstanding call, the liquidator may exercise the power of the court to make calls in respect thereof, but in a compulsory winding up he must request the leave of the court or the sanction of the Committee of Inspection (C.A. 1948, ss. 260, 273 and 303(1)(d) rules 86 to 90; and Forms 46 to 58). The call may be made on the contributories to the extent of the amount required to satisfy the debts and liabilities of the company and the costs, charges and expenses of the winding up, and may be made even before the liquidator has ascertained the sufficiency of the assets. However, in the case of a limited liability company the call on the contributory concerned must not exceed the amount unpaid on the relevant shares (section 260). "Contributory" includes certain categories of past members, but they will not be required to contribute,

(i) unless the existing members are unable to satisfy the contributions required; or

(ii) in respect of any debt or liability of the company contracted after they ceased to be members or, in the case of directors or managers with unlimited liability, after they ceased to hold office (section 212(1)(b) and (c)); or

(iii) after the approval a scheme of arrangement providing for partial payment of creditors and releasing present members from a portion of their liability.

Any excessive contribution they make will be returned (*Re City of London Insurance Co* [1932] 1 Ch. 226).

Before the call is made it will be necessary for the liquidator to settle a list of contributories in accordance with rules 80 to 85 (see Forms 38 to 45). The list is made out in two parts: part A for the present members and part B for persons who have ceased to be members within twelve months before the commencement of the winding up, and certain other categories of past members. The liquidator may seek the aid of the court (under rule 90) in enforcing payment of the calls; or (under section 271) to have an absconding or evading contributory arrested or his books, papers and movable assets seized. In determining the amount of call, regard may be had to the probability that some of the contributories may partly or wholly fail to pay the call (section 260(2)). After the liquidator has made calls he may have to adjust the rights of the contributories among themselves so as to ensure that the loss of capital is borne by them in proportion to the nominal capital respectively held by them (unless the articles otherwise provide; *Ex p. Maude* (1870) L.R.6 Ch. App. 51; *Re Driffield Gas Light Co.* [1898] 1 Ch. 451). This would be necessary where shares are unequally paid up. If necessary, another call to equalise the position must, unless the articles otherwise provide, be made (*Ex p. Maude, supra*).

Conduct of the winding up: establishment of liabilities

General aspects

Notice to prove. Rule 106 empowers the liquidator from time to time to issue, unless the court otherwise orders, a notice requiring creditors to prove their debts or claims and establish any title to priority under section 319 within a period specified in the notice, which should not be less than fourteen days from the date of the notice. The notice should state that any creditor who does not prove his debt or claim within that period will be excluded from the benefit of any distribution made before the debt or claim is proved, or from objecting to the distribution. The liquidator can augment this provision by obtaining an order of the court under section 265. Although rule 106 is merely an enabling provision, the liquidator should not dispense with the notice (even in a voluntary winding up) except in a clear case (*Re Compania de Electridad* [1980] 1 Ch. 146). "Creditors" include present and former shareholders having a claim in respect of dividends or repayment of capital (*ibid*).

Mode of giving notice. The notice must be advertised in such newspapers as the liquidator considers convenient. In addition, he must send the notice, in a compulsory winding up, to every creditor or preferential creditor listed in the statement of affairs who has not proved his debt or established his claim and, in any other winding up, to the last known address of every person who to the liquidator's knowledge claims to be a creditor or preferential creditor whose claim has not been admitted (rule 106). Before making any distribution, the liquidator must use every means to satisfy himself that all creditors are paid or provided for, not only by advertising, but by writing to those creditors or possible creditors of whose existence he knows (see *Pushford v. Devenish* [1903] 2 Ch. 625; *Re Armstrong Whitworth Securities Ltd.* [1947] Ch. 673).

Proof of debt.   In a compulsory winding up, every creditor must prove his debt but the court may direct any creditors or class of creditors to be admitted without proof. In any other winding up, a creditor need only prove his debt if the liquidator so requires – this is generally required where the company is insolvent or its books and papers do not appear to be in a reliable state. The proof may be by an unsworn claim to the debt unless the Official Receiver or the liquidator requires it to be verified by affidavit (see rules 91 to 105 and Forms 59, 60 and 62). In practice, an affidavit is required only in the case of a contentious claim. The liquidator must scrutinise every proof of debt and must in writing admit or reject it in whole or part or require further evidence in support (rule 107; Form 61). If he rejects it, he must state the grounds. As to the time within which a proof of debt must be so dealt with in a compulsory winding up, see rule 117. A notice of dividend sent to a creditor is sufficient notification of an admission. A proof of debt must state whether or not the creditor is a secured creditor (rule 95).

Appeal from liquidator.   A creditor or contributory who is dissatisfied with the liquidator's decision may appeal to the court, but a notice of appeal must be given within 21 days of the notice of rejection (rule 108). In a compulsory winding up, the liquidator must file with the court the proof and a memorandum of disallowance within three days after receiving the notice of appeal (rule 115). A proof improperly admitted may be expunged by the court on the application of the liquidator or, if he declines to interfere, of a creditor or contributory (rules 109 and 110).

Filing of proof.   In a compulsory winding up the liquidator must comply with rules 113 and 114 (see Form 62) as to filing of proofs, etc. with the court.

Application to court to exclude late claimants.   A liquidator may also apply to the court (see sections 246(3) and 307) for an order allowing distribution of the assets without regard to claims which are made, or the possibility of which is notified to the liquidator, after the period specified in the notice to prove has expired but before distribution is made. The test to be applied is whether in all the circumstances it is just to make such an order. The claimant does not have to show that he had not been guilty of wilful default or want of diligence, although the presence or absence of such default or lack of diligence may be an important factor in determining what is just. Further, where the order is sought to facilitate a distribution among members, the court will be more reluctant to grant it than if the distribution is to be made among creditors (see *Re R-R. Realisations Ltd.* [1980] 1 All E.R. 1019).

Right of creditor who is excluded from interim dividend.   A creditor is entitled to prove his claim at any time before a final distribution of the assets is made, and to participate in any distribution made after he has proved his claim. However, he cannot disturb any dividend already paid (*Re General Rolling Stock Co.* (1872) 7 Ch. App. 646; *Re Metcalfe, Hicks v. May* (1879) 13 Ch. D. 236). In an insolvent liquidation he is entitled, by virtue of section 317 (as read with section 65 of the Bankruptcy Act 1914) to be paid out of any money for the time being in the hands of the liquidator, any dividends he may have failed to receive, before that money is applied to the payment of any future dividend or dividends. But again, he is not entitled to disturb the dividends already paid.

Rule against double proof. In an insolvent winding up, there can not be more than one claim (whether from the same claimant or from different claimants) in respect of the same debt (see *Re Hoey* (1919) 88 L.J.K.B. 273). Thus, a surety cannot prove if the principal creditor has already proved (see *Re Moss* [1905] 2 K.B. 307).

Various categories of liability: preferential creditors

A list of preferential debts is contained in section 319 of the Companies Act 1948 (as amended). These must be discharged out of the assets *before* any other debts except debts secured by fixed – but not floating – charges, and rank *pari passu* among themselves, but *after* the costs of winding up, including the liquidator's remuneration (see also page 708). Preferential debts are ascertained by reference to "the relevant date" which means (i) in a compulsory winding up, the earliest of the date of the winding up order or the date of the appointment of a provisional liquidator or, where a voluntary winding up has gone before, the date of the voluntary winding up resolution, and (ii) in a voluntary winding up, the date of the winding up resolution. (In *Re Barleycorn Enterprises Ltd.* [1970] Ch. 465 it was held that the costs of preparing a statement of affairs under section 235 take priority over preferential debts (see rule 195), not only against assets available for general creditors but also against the assets comprised in a floating charge. That decision was based on the argument that the expression "assets" in sections 267 and 319(5) includes all the assets of the company.)

In a compulsory winding up, the preferential claims are a first charge on the goods or effects distrained by a landlord or other person within three months next before the date of the winding up order. However, the landlord or such other person would then be subrogated to the preferential rights of the claimants to whom the payment is made (section 319(7)). The priority conferred on these debts is in addition to the priority conferred on them by section 94 (enforcement of a floating charge), under which the debts are ascertained by reference to the date on which a receiver was appointed, or possession of the assets was taken. There may thus be two sets of preferential claims and some overlapping between them, but by section 94(5) any payments made under section 94 must be recouped as far as may be out of the assets of the company available for payment of general creditors. Some of the most important types of preferential debts are dealt with below.

1. Local rates. These are preferential to the extent that they were due at the relevant date, having become due and payable within twelve months next before that date. An amended rate is payable when amended and not before (*Kershaw, Leese & Co. v. Stockport* [1923] 2 K.B. 129 but see *Re Airedale Garage Co.* [1933] Ch. 64). A director who pays the rates under a guarantee is entitled to be subrogated to the right to preferential payment of the principal creditor (*Re Lamplugh Iron Ore Co. Ltd.* [1927] 1 Ch. 308).

2. Income tax or other assessed taxes. All income tax and other assessed taxes assessed on the company up to April 5 next before the relevant date are preferential. "Assessed taxes" includes corporation tax (*Re Winget Ltd.* [1924] 1 Ch. 550), tax deducted from annual payments not payable out of profits brought into charge for tax, tax deducted from annual interest (see Taxes Acts 1970, s. 53(3) and s. 54(3)), and development land tax. The assessment need not actually be made before the relevant date (*Gowers v. Walker* [1930] 1 Ch. 262).

The Crown may select *any year* up to April 5 prior to the relevant date and claim priority for that year, and may select different years for different taxes provided that the tax has been assessed and is recoverable at the relevant date (see Taxes Management Act 1970, sections 34 to 39 and 41). As to claims by the Inland Revenue generally, see the Board of Trade Regulations of May 7, 1965 (issued under rule 224), Part II.

In the case of P.A.Y.E. and deductions from payments to subcontractors in the construction industry (see F. (No. 2) A. 1975, s. 69(7)), the priority is limited to deductions for the twelve months before the relevant date.

3. VAT and car tax. The priority is limited to tax which became due or is treated as having become due within twelve months before the relevant date (F.A. 1972, s. 41, Sch. 7, para. 18). Value added tax due by one member of a "group registration" may be preferential in the liquidation of another such member (*Re Nadler Enterprises Ltd.* (1980) 124 S.J. 374).

4. Social security contributions etc. All debts specified in section 153(2) of the Social Security Act 1975, Schedule 3 to the Social Security Pensions Act 1975 and any corresponding provisions in force in Northern Ireland are preferential to a similar extent as for VAT (except where the company is being wound up voluntarily merely for the purposes of reconstruction or of amalgamation with another company). Contributions under section 28 of the Redundancy Payments Act 1965 are also preferential to a similar extent.

5. Salaries, holiday remuneration, etc: (1) employees' claims

By section 319(1)(b), all wages and salaries, including commission, of any clerk or servant in respect of services rendered during four months next before the relevant date and all wages of any workman or labourer in respect of services so rendered are preferential up to £800 in the case of any one claimant. All accrued holiday remuneration becoming payable to any such employee on the termination of his employment before or by the effect of the winding up order or resolution is preferential without limit as to the amount. The following should be noted.

(a) Under sections 63 to 69 of the Employment Protection (Consolidation) Act 1978, certain entitlements of employees are deemed to be wages for the purposes of section 319 of the 1948 Act.

(b) A secretary of a company who devotes himself exclusively to its business may be a "clerk or servant" (*Cairney v. Back* [1906] 2 K.B. 746) as may a director employed as editor of a paper (*Re Beeton & Co. Ltd.* [1913] 2 Ch. 279; see also *Lee v. Lee's Air Farming Ltd.* [1961] A.C. 12). A managing director as such is not a "clerk or servant" (*Re Newspaper Proprietary Syndicate* [1900] 2 Ch. 349), but it seems that the position would depend on the facts of each case. A "labour only" sub-contractor is not a servant (*Re C.W. & A.L. Hughes Ltd.* [1966] 1 W.L.R. 1369).

(c) A claim for redundancy payment as such is not preferential, nor is any claim for compensation for loss of office or breach of a contract of employment (but see (a) above and (2) below).

(d) It is not clear whether the limit of £800 in respect of salaries and wages is gross or net of any P.A.Y.E. or employee's National Insurance contributions deductible therefrom. In the writer's view the limit is gross.

(2) *Subrogated claim of Secretary of State for Employment.* By section 125 of the Employment Protection (Consolidation) Act 1978, the Secretary of State is subrogated to the rights (preferential or not) of an employee in respect of any payments made pursuant to section 122 of that Act, which entitles an employee to claim certain payments, due from an "insolvent" employer, out of the Redundancy Fund. To the extent that the employee's rights would have ranked as preferential claims in the winding up the Secretary of State is entitled to be paid in the winding up "in priority to any other unsatisfied claim of the employee". Moreover, for the purpose of computing any limit under section 319 on the amounts ranking as preferential debts, sums paid to the Secretary of State under section 125 of the 1978 Act are to be treated as if they had been paid to the employee. The effect appears to be that if, for example, a bank advances money to the company in respect of which it would have a subrogated preferential claim (see (3) below), its right of subrogation would be postponed to the claims of the Secretary of State and that the amounts for which the bank can claim to be subrogated may be reduced.

(3) *Subrogated claim of lender.* Where any payment has been made to an employee on account of wages, salary or holiday remuneration out of money advanced by some person for that purpose, he is entitled to a preferential claim in respect of the money so advanced and paid to the extent to which the employee's preferential claim has been diminished by reason of such payment (section 319(4)). The purpose need not be

agreed before or at the time of the advance; it is enough that the money is in fact used for the purpose contemplated by the section (see *Re Primrose (Builders) Ltd* [1950] Ch. 561; *Re Rampgill Mill Ltd.* [1967] Ch. 1138). A bank can, by making the advances for wages, etc. from a specially set up wages account and requiring that all other advances are made from, and all receipts from the company are paid into, the general account, ensure that the rule in *Clayton's Case* does not operate so as to appropriate the receipts towards reduction of its potentially preferential claim. The proceeds of any security held by the bank in respect of advances may be applied by it first towards the discharge of those advances which are not preferential (*Re William Hall (Contractors) Ltd* [1967] 1 W.L.R. 948). It seems that in the absence of such security, any credit balance arising in the general account must be set off primarily against the preferential advances in the wages account (see *E.J. Morel (1934) Ltd.* [1962] Ch. 21).

Non-preferential creditors (secured and ordinary) generally

Section 316 of the Companies Act 1948, which applies to every form of winding up and both to solvent companies and insolvent companies, provides that all debts payable on a contingency, and all claims against the company, present or future, certain or contingent, ascertained or sounding only in damages, are admissible to proof, a just estimate being made, so far as possible, of the value of such debts as may be subject to any contingency or sound only in damages, or for some reason do not bear a certain value. The "just estimate of the value" is made by the liquidator, not the creditor (see *Re Dodds* 25 Q.B.D. 529, 533). The section is supplemented by rules 97 (costs of proof), 98 (discount), 99 (periodic payments) and 100 (non-contractual interest).

Section 316 is modified by section 317, which provides that in the winding up of an *insolvent* company registered in England the rules under the law of bankruptcy (see page 495) with regard to (i) the respective rights of secured and unsecured creditors, (ii) debts provable and (iii) the valuation of annuities and future and contingent liabilities, shall prevail and be observed. The effect of this section in an insolvent winding up is to import the following provisions of the Bankruptcy Act 1914: section 30 (debts provable), 31 (mutual credit and set-off) and the Second Schedule, rules 10 to 17 (proof by secured creditors) and rule 18 (no creditor to receive more than 100p in the £ plus interest as provided). In the winding up of a company (solvent or insolvent) registered in Scotland, the Bankruptcy (Scotland) Act 1913, sections 45 to 62 (voting and ranking for payment of dividends) and sections 96 and 105 (reckoning of majorities and interruption of prescription) apply with modifications (C.A. 1948, s. 318).

Sections 316 and 317 thus give rise to certain differences between the position of secured and unsecured creditors in a solvent liquidation on the one hand, and those in an insolvent liquidation on the other.

For the purposes of a proof in a winding up, the company's liabilities are ascertained as at the date of the winding up order or resolution. A notional line is drawn at that date. Liquidation and distribution (and, therefore, the discharge of liabilities) are treated as notionally simultaneous. "The tree must lie where it falls" (*Re W. W. Duncan & Co.* [1965] 1 Ch. 307; see also *Humber Ironworks and Shipbuilding Company* (1869) L.R. Ch. Appl. 643, 646; *Re Dynamics Corporation of America (No. 2)* [1976] 1 W.L.R. pp. 762–763; and *Re Lines Bros Limited* [1981] Com. L.R. 214 (affirmed on appeal [1982] 2 All E.R. 183; and, in relation to insolvent companies, Bankruptcy Act 1914 s. 30(3)). There are, however, certain possible exceptions to these principles, as will be seen later.

Secured creditors

Meaning. A "secured creditor" is a person holding a mortgage, charge or lien on the property *of the company* or part thereof, as a security for a debt due to him from the company (see Bankruptcy Act 1914, s. 167).

Creditors who are secured. An execution creditor (including one who has obtained the appointment of a receiver of land or a charging order in respect of land by way of execution), or a creditor who has levied distress, whose claim is not defeated by any of the provisions referred to on page 517 is a secured creditor (see *Re Printing and Numerical Registering Co.* (1878) 8 Ch. D. 535, 538; *Anglo-Italian Bank v. Davies* (1878) 9 Ch.D. 275; see also section 325(2) (as amended)); so also is a solicitor holding a lien on the company's documents for his costs (*Re Safety Explosives Ltd.* [1904] 1 Ch. 226). A party to an action for whose benefit money has been paid into court or a plaintiff who has issued a writ in rem against the company's ship may be a secured creditor (*Re Aro Co.* [1980] 2 W.L.R. 453).

Creditors who are not secured. A landlord is not a secured creditor merely because he has a power of distress (*Thomas v. Patent Lionite Co.* (1881) 17 Ch.D. 250, 257), nor is a creditor who has arrested a ship of the company in exercise of a maritime lien (*The Zafiro* [1960] P.1; cf. *The Constellation* [1966] 1 W.L.R. 272).

A creditor who has a valid reservation of title to assets supplied by him to the company, is not a secured creditor where the effect of such reservation is that the assets continue to belong to him rather than that he has a charge over them. He cannot both prove for the amount of his debt and take the assets; the value of the assets must be set-off against his debt. Where the effect of the reservation is to constitute a charge, he is a secured creditor, unless the charge is invalid for lack of registration under section 95 of the 1948 Act (see page 531). Where building materials supplied on retention of title terms by a creditor have become annexed to the company's land and have lost their identity, the creditor ceases to have any security or other interest therein and must prove as an unsecured creditor for their value (*Re Yorkshire Joinery Co. Ltd* (1967) 111 S.J. 701). A creditor who holds a security from a third party in respect of the company's debt is not a secured creditor of the company.

Position of secured creditor. A security which has been valued for the purposes of voting under rule 141 (see page 515) can be redeemed by the Official Receiver or liquidator, within 28 days after such valuation, at the value so assessed plus, unless the creditor has corrected the original valuation, 20 per cent (rule 142). Subject to this, the creditor has several alternatives in an *insolvent* liquidation (see Bankruptcy Act 1914, Sch. 2, rules 10 to 17 – they do not apply to solvent liquidations; a creditor who does not comply with these rules is excluded from any dividend).

(1) He may rest on his security and not prove (at all or for the time being).

(2) He may value his security and prove as an ordinary creditor for the balance of his claim. The liquidator may redeem the security on payment to the creditor of the assessed value. If the liquidator is dissatisfied with the value assessed, he may require the property comprised in the security to be sold. The liquidator must exercise the right of redemption or sale not later than six months after any notice is served on him by the creditor requiring him to make up his mind. A creditor may amend his valuation and proof if he satisfies the liquidator or the court that the valuation and proof were made bona fide on a mistaken estimate, or that the value of the security has diminished or increased.

(3) He may realise the security and prove as an ordinary creditor for the balance of his claim after deducting the net amount realised. Where he does so after having previously valued his security and proved for the balance, the net amount realised is substituted for the assessed value and the proof is amended and any dividends paid or payable adjusted accordingly. (Note, however, section 110(1) of the Law of Property Act 1925 as read with section 205(1)(i), which disentitles a mortgagee to sell the mortgaged property or appoint a receiver in respect thereof by reason solely of the mortgagor's liquidation, unless he has obtained the leave of the court.)

(4) He may surrender his security to the liquidator and prove as an ordinary creditor for the whole of the amount of his claim.

Rights of secured creditor to interest

If the secured creditor wholly relies on his security, he can appropriate the proceeds of his security to all principal and interest and any other sums to which he is entitled in accordance with the terms of his security, and needs only return to the liquidator any balance that remains after such appropriation.

Where, in an insolvent liquidation, he proves for any deficiency in his security (as to which he will rank only as an ordinary creditor), his right to appropriate the security towards interest or to prove for interest is affected as follows:

(a) he cannot prove for any interest accruing after the date of the winding up order or resolution (see page 548);

(b) any payments received by him from the company, or from the realisation of the security, before the date mentioned in (a), and the net amount realised from the security, or assessed by him to be the value of the security, after that date must be appropriated pro rata to principal and interest calculated up to that date (Bankruptcy Act 1914, s. 66(2)(b) and (c)); and

(c) he will be entitled to prove for the balance of principal and interest remaining after the appropriation but the amount of interest in excess of an amount equal to five per cent per annum will be a deferred claim (Bankruptcy Act 1914, s. 66(1)).

Ordinary creditors

A statute barred debt is not provable neither is a debt which itself constitutes a fraudulent preference. A debt contracted after notice of an analogous "act of bankruptcy" may not be provable.

Unliquidated damages. In an *insolvent* liquidation, unliquidated damages arising otherwise than by reason of a contract, promise or breach of trust are not provable (Bankruptcy Act 1914, s. 30(1)). Thus, unliquidated damages in tort are not provable, but once they become liquidated by judgment during the course of winding up, they are then provable on the basis that the claimant cannot disturb the dividend already paid to the other creditors before he proved his claim, but is entitled to receive any dividend which he missed out of the assets for the time being in the hands of the liquidator before any further dividend is paid to him and the other creditors (*Re Berkley Securities (Property) Limited* [1980] 1 All E.R. 1589). In a *solvent* liquidation, it seems that such a claim is provable ab initio and the liquidator must make a just estimate of the amount thereof (C.A. 1948, s. 316).

Claims with no ascertained value. In an *insolvent* liquidation, the liquidator must make an estimate of the value of any provable liability which by reason of it being subject to any contingency, or for any other reason, does not bear a certain value (Bankruptcy Act 1914 s. 30(6) and 30(4)). A debt or liability which in the opinion of the court is incapable of being fairly estimated ceases to be provable. In a *solvent* liquidation, all such debts and liabilities must be justly estimated by the liquidator "so far as possible" (section 316). Presumably, the words "so far as possible" would enable the liquidator to reject the claim if it cannot be so estimated. In all cases, an appeal lies to the court against the liquidator's determination.

Debt under a void charge. A debt secured by a charge which is void under section 95 (unregistered charge), section 320 (fraudulent preference), section 322 (invalid floating charge), or section 227 (disposition of property after commencement of compulsory winding up) is provable as an unsecured debt unless the debt itself is void. Where a charge is void under section 95, the money secured thereby becomes immediately payable (section 95(1)).

Periodic payments.   A proportionate part of any rent or other payment falling due periodically may be proved up to the date of the winding up order or resolution as if the payment was due from day to day (rule 99).

Debt payable at a future time.   A debt not due at the date of the winding up order or resolution may be proved, subject to a deduction of a rebate of five per cent per annum from the declaration of a dividend to the due date (rule 101).

Damages for breach of contract.   Damages for breach of a contract by the company before or by the effect of the winding up order or resolution are provable subject to a just estimate being made by the liquidator, and subject to the duty of the claimant to mitigate the damages. For example, in the case of damages for premature termination of an employee's contract of employment, deduction may be made in respect of,

(a)   the prospects of the employee finding and retaining an alternative employment or occupation;

(b)   income tax saved by the employee under the "golden handshake" statutory provisions (see *British Transport Commission v. Gourley* [1956] A.C. 185; *Bold v. Brough, Nicholson and Hall Ltd.* [1963] 3 All E.R. 849); and

(c)   a discount for early notional payment of his whole claim in one lump sum.

As to contracts of employment providing for index-linked increases in salary, see *Re Crowther & Nicholson Ltd.* LSG July 22, 1981, p. 841.

Claims expressed in foreign currencies.   A debt payable in foreign currency will be converted into sterling at the rate of exchange in force at the date of the winding up order or resolution (*Re Lines Bros. Limited* [1981] Com. L.R. 214, affirmed on appeal, [1982] 2 All E.R. 183.

Lessor's claims.   Subject to what is said on pages 537 and 538, a lessor can only prove for rent as it accrues (*Re New Oriental Bank Corporation* (No. 2) [1895] 1 Ch. 753). Where the lease has been assigned either before or after liquidation, the landlord can prove for the difference between the value of the lease with and without the benefit of the covenants on the part of the company (*Re House Property and Investment Co.* [1954] Ch. 576). The lessor is also entitled to prove for damages for any breaches of covenant which may have occurred.

Claim for interest.   The position varies according to whether there was a contractual obligation on the part of the company to pay interest.

(1)   Where there was no such obligation, statutory interest at four per

cent per annum from the date of the commencement of winding up may be allowed on the principal amount of the debt, as provided by rule 100. No interest is claimable in respect of any period after the date of the winding up, even if there is a surplus of assets (see *Re Rolls-Royce Ltd.* [1974] 1 W.L.R. 1584) except perhaps where any specific statute allows such interest to be claimed (e.g. Judgments Act 1838), but see 2(b) below.

(2) Where there was such an obligation,

    (a) any unpaid contractual interest will, for the purposes of ranking for dividend with other ordinary claims in any insolvent liquidations, be restricted to five per cent per annum up to the date of the winding up order or resolution (as to the method of calculation of such interest, see *Re Jessel Securities Ltd.* (1979) 129 NLJ 171);

    (b) if there is a surplus of assets after all claims have been fully discharged, the balance of contractual interest up to the date of the winding up order or resolution and, then, post-liquidation contractual interest may be paid out of the surplus pari passu with other similar deferred claims for interest, including those arising by virtue of the Judgments Act 1838 (see *Re Fine Industrial Commodities* [1956] Ch. 256; *Re Rolls-Royce Ltd, supra*).

Concurrent claims in two or more liquidations. Where companies A and B, both in insolvent liquidation, are jointly and severally liable (whether presently or contingently), to C, C's position would be as follows:

(1) Subject to (2) and (3) below, C is entitled to prove for the full amount of his claim in both the liquidations and rank for dividend accordingly up to a stage when his claim is fully satisfied.

(2) In proving his claim in A's liquidation, C must (subject to (3) below) allow credits for any amount received or recovered by him on account of the debt from,

(i) B, before B's liquidation;

(ii) B's liquidator by way of dividend;

(iii) net proceeds of any security given by B realised before or after B's liquidation;

(iv) A, before A's liquidation;

(v) the net realised or estimated value of any security given by A.

(3) C need not allow credit in A's liquidation for,

(a) any payments or dividends received or recovered, *after* he has proved his claim in A's liquidation, from or from the realisation of any security given by B (see *Re Blakeley* (1892) 9 Mor. 173);

(b) any of the amounts referred to if (2)(i), (ii) or (iii) above if pursuant

to the terms of the relevant contract or security, C has held such
amounts in a suspense account without appropriating them to the
debt (see *Commercial Bank of Australia Ltd. v. Official Assignee*
[1893] A.C. 181);

(c) any amount, realised by a receiver appointed by C under the
security given by B, not yet passed by the receiver to C – realisation
by a receiver is not realisation by the holder of the charge (see
White v. Metcalf [1903] 2 Ch. 567). The charging document may
provide that the money need only be passed when so required by
the holder of the charge (see also Law of Property Act 1925, s.
109(8)(v));

(d) the value of any security given by B to C (as distinct from any
security given by A to C) not then realised and appropriated (see
page 546).

(4) The position in B's liquidations would be mutatis mutandis similar.
C can thus (subject to other considerations) derive maximum
advantage by proving in both liquidations as early as possible.

Set off

In the winding up of an insolvent company, claims arising under mutual
dealings must be set off (C.A. 1948, s. 317; Bankruptcy Act 1914,
s. 31). Set off is mandatory and cannot be contracted out (*Rolls Razor
Ltd. v. Cox* [1967] 1 Q.B. 552; *National Westminster Bank Ltd. v.
Halesowen Presswork and Assemblies Ltd.* [1972] A.C. 785). Any debt
contracted in favour of the other party after he had notice of an
analogous act of bankruptcy cannot be set off (see page 547). All claims
provable in a winding up may be set off against similarly provable
claims, provided there is mutuality and each claim results in a liability to
pay money (*Rolls Razor Ltd. v. Cox, supra; Peat v. Jones* (1881) 8
Q.B.D. 147).

An unsecured debt may be set off against a secured debt (*Ex parte
Barnett, re Deveze* (1874) 9 Ch. App. 293; *McKinnon v. Armstrong*
(1877) 2 App. Ca. 531). A debt due to one department of the Crown has
been allowed to be set off against a debt due by another (*Re Cushla*
[1979] 3 All E.R. 415; *Re D.H. Curtis (Builders) Ltd.* [1978] Ch. 162).

A party whose claim in the liquidation is partly preferential and partly
non-preferential must first set off any debt due by him to the company
against the preferential part (*Re E.J. Morel (1934) Ltd.* [1962] Ch. 21).
In certain circumstances the value of goods of the company held by a
salesman for the purposes of converting them into money may be set off
against a debt owed by him to the company (*Rolls Razor Ltd. v. Cox,
supra*). The requirement of mutuality means that a joint debt cannot be
set off against a several debt (see *Re Pennington and Owen* [1925] Ch.
825). Money held for a specific purpose or on a trust cannot be set off
against a debt (*Re City Equitable Fire Insurance (No. 2)* [1930] 2 Ch.
293; *National Westminster Bank Ltd. v. Halesowen Presswork and
Assembly Ltd., supra*, per Lord Simon). In applying the test of

mutuality the real right to a debt will be taken into account and it is sufficient if the debts are in equity in the same right (*Brown and Gregory* [1904] 1 Ch. 627; 2 Ch. 448). An assigned debt may be set off but the assignee takes subject to all equities. As to a set off against calls, see section 259 of the 1948 Act.

Damages for misfeasance recoverable from a director, officer or promotor of the company cannot be set off against a debt due to him (*Re Carriage Co-operative Society* (1884) 27 Ch. D. 322). A payment made to a creditor constituting a fraudulent preference and ordered to be repaid cannot be set off against any other debt due to that creditor (*In Re a Debtor* [1927] 1 Ch. 410). A contingent debt may be the subject of a set off (see *Rolls Razor Ltd. v. Cox, supra*), but not a contingent claim by a surety who has not paid off the principal debt (*Re Fenton* [1931] 1 Ch. 85).

Distribution of assets

Dividends to creditors

The order of distribution of proceeds of assets is summarised on page 541. The realisation of all assets and the ascertainment of all liabilities usually takes a long time. Meanwhile the liquidator may consider paying interim dividends, but he must maintain a prudent balance between the desirability of making the maximum distribution at the earliest opportunity and the need to retain sufficient reserves to meet the costs of the winding up (including his remuneration and post-liquidation tax) down to the conclusion of the winding up, and all preferential claims and dividends on all ordinary claims or possible claims, known to him which have not been finally dealt with or excluded.

In a compulsory winding up, he must issue a notice of an intended dividend specifying the time by which proofs must be lodged by those who have not done so (rule 119; Forms 63 and 64). After that time any appeal against the rejection by the liquidator of a proof must be lodged within seven days of the rejection (subject to the power of the court to extend the time). If an appeal is lodged, the liquidator must make provision for the dividend on that proof and costs of any successful appeal. After the expiration of the time for appeal, the liquidator proceeds to declare a dividend and give notice of dividend to the Department of Trade (so that it may be gazetted), and to each creditor whose proof has been admitted (Forms 65 to 68). If it becomes necessary to postpone the dividend beyond two months, a fresh notice of intention to declare a dividend must be given to the Department of Trade, but need not be given to the creditors who have not lodged their proof: in all other respects the procedure has to be repeated (rule 119). In a voluntary winding up, the dividend may be declared and paid without any formalities (but see page 547). As to late claimants, see page 540.

In a compulsory winding up, the costs of a solicitor and other agents employed are required to be taxed (rules 183 to 193), but the rules were amended in 1981 to enable payment on account to be made before taxation in certain cases.

Distribution to members

Any surplus remaining after payment to all the ordinary and deferred creditors must be distributed among the members of the company in accordance with their rights under the company's memorandum and articles of association, after the rights of the contributories among themselves are adjusted to take account of any disparity in the amounts of their contributions in respect of shares held by them. In a compulsory winding up, a court order is required for such a distribution because the power of the court under section 265 is not delegated to the liquidator (see also rule 120 and Forms 69 and 70).

A distribution of assets remaining after repayment of the share capital is regarded as a capital distribution irrespective of the source of the assets represented in the distribution (*I.R.C. v. Pollock & Peel* [1957] 1 W.L.R. 822).

Conclusion of the winding up

Members' and creditors' voluntary winding up

Calling final meetings.   As soon as the affairs of the company are fully wound up, the liquidator calls a general meeting of the members and in the case of a creditors' voluntary winding up, or of a members' voluntary winding up where section 288 applies, a meeting of creditors to lay before them his final accounts. The meeting is called by advertisement in the *Gazette* published at least one month before the date of the meetings (sections 290, 291 and 300). Rule 129 requires individual notices to be sent by post at least seven days before the date of the meeting (Rule 129 applies to the final meeting of members in a members' voluntary winding up under section 290, but not to the final meeting of creditors under section 291 (which is linked to section 300), or of members or creditors under section 300 in a creditors' voluntary winding up). In all cases the members are presumably entitled to receive postal notice by virtue of the provisions of the articles of association. In practice, even creditors are sent the postal notice.

Return of final meetings and dissolution.   If there is no quorum, the meetings are not required to be adjourned to another day. Within one week after the meetings, the liquidator sends to the Registrar of Companies a copy of the accounts together with a return of the final meeting stating either that the account was duly presented or that no quorum was present. On the expiration of three months from the date of registration of these, the company is deemed to be dissolved but the court may on the application of the liquidator or any other interested person make an order deferring the date of dissolution. Any such order is required to be filed by the applicant with the Registrar of Companies within seven days (C.A. 1948, ss. 290, 291 and 300; rule 182; Forms 110 to 112; see the chapter *Dissolution and Revival*).

Compulsory winding up

Release of liquidator. In a compulsory winding up in England, when the liquidator has realised all the property (or so much thereof as can, in his opinion, be realised without needlessly protracting the liquidation) and has made final distributions and adjustments of the rights of the contributories or has resigned or has been removed from his office, the Department of Trade may, after taking into consideration the objections of any creditor or contributory and certain other matters, either grant or withhold release of the liquidator. Where the release is withheld, the court may on application make an order charging the liquidator for the consequences of any act or default by him. The release operates to discharge the liquidator from all liability, but may be revoked on proof that it was obtained by fraud, suppression or concealment of any material fact. The release also operates to remove the liquidator from office (C.A. 1948, s. 251; rule 205; Forms 98 to 100).

Dissolution of the company. When the affairs of the company have been completely wound up, the court, if the liquidator makes an application in that behalf, may make an order dissolving the company from the date of the order. A copy of the order must be forwarded by the liquidator to the Registrar of Companies (section 274).

All forms of winding up

Disposal of books and papers. Section 341 and rule 206 contain provisions for the disposal of the books and papers of the company and the liquidator when the company has been wound up and is about to be dissolved.

Gazetting of dissolution, etc. Sections 9(3)(g) and (h) of the European Communities Act 1972 require the Registrar of Companies to gazette any order for the dissolution of a company on a winding up and any return by a liquidator of the final meeting of a company on a winding up.

Memorandum of Association

The constitution of a company incorporated under the Companies Acts is contained in its memorandum of association. The memorandum establishes the basis of the company's existence and sets out the fundamental provisions which are necessary, under statute, for its incorporation and continued operation. These fundamental provisions include the objects which the company may pursue. The regulations governing the manner in which those objects may be achieved, and the conduct of the internal management and affairs of the company, are the concern of its articles of association (see the chapter *Articles of Association*). The articles, being primarily the means of regulation of the affairs of the company, are, in general, relatively flexible in the manner in which they may be altered by the members in general meeting to meet the particular circumstances of the company. By contrast, the memorandum of association, because of its importance as the constitution of the company, must contain the minimum provisions prescribed by statute which may only be altered in limited circumstances. Since the memorandum is the document which contains the conditions which are fundamental to the incorporation and existence of a registered company, the memorandum has priority over the articles, which cannot modify it.

The statutory background

Section 1(1) of the Companies Acts 1948 establishes the memorandum of association as the primary document in forming an incorporated company,

"Any two or more persons, associated for any lawful purpose may, by subscribing their names to a memorandum of association and otherwise complying with the requirements of the Companies Acts 1948 to 1981 in respect of registration, form an incorporated company, with or without limited liability."

The memorandum may limit the liability of the members of the company to the amount, if any, unpaid on the shares respectively held by them (in which case the company will be a company limited by shares), or to such amount as the members may respectively undertake to contribute to the assets of the company in the event of its being wound up (in which case the company will be a company limited by guarantee), or not place any limit on the liability of the members of the company (in which case the company will be an unlimited company) (see section 1(2) of the 1948 Act and the chapter *Formation and Types of Company*).

554

The importance of the memorandum of association of a company in relation to its members and creditors (actual and potential) is acknowledged by section 2 of the 1948 Act, which provides that the memorandum of a company must state,

(a) the *name* of the company, with "limited" as the last word of the name in the case of a company limited by shares or by guarantee (except that the name of a public company, as defined by section 1(1) of the 1980 Act, must end with the words "public limited company" (or the Welsh equivalent), or the permitted abbreviation);

(b) whether the *registered office* is to be situate in England or Wales, or both, or in Scotland (see also C.A. 1976, s. 30 and C.A. 1980, s. 77);

(c) the *objects* of the company;

(d) in the case of a company limited by shares or by guarantee, that the *liability of its members is limited*;

(e) in the case of a company limited by guarantee, that each member undertakes to contribute up to a specified amount should the company be wound up while he is a member, or within one year after he ceases to be a member, towards payment of the debts and liabilities of the company contracted before he ceases to be a member, and of the costs, charges and expenses of winding up, and for adjustment of the rights of the contributories among themselves; and

(f) in the case of a company having a share capital, other than an unlimited company, the *amount of share capital* with which the company proposes to be registered and the division of that share capital into shares of a fixed amount.

In addition, the memorandum of association must be in the form prescribed by statute, or as close to that form as circumstances permit. In the case of a company limited by shares or by guarantee and having a share capital (other than a public company, in either case), the memorandum must respectively be in accordance with the form set out in Tables B and D in Schedule I to the Companies Act 1948 (C.A. 1948, s. 11). The memorandum of a public company limited by shares or by guarantee and having a share capital must respectively be in accordance with the forms set out in Parts I and II in Schedule I to the Companies Act 1980 (C.A. 1980, s. 2(4)). In essence, the material difference is that the memorandum of both types of public company must contain an additional provision stipulating, as clause 2, that the company is to be a public company. The memorandum of association of a company limited by guarantee and not having a share capital, and of a unlimited company having a share capital, must respectively be in accordance with the forms set out in Tables C and E in Schedule I to the Companies Act 1948 (see the chapter *Formation and Types of Company*).

These six or, in the case of a public company, seven specific clauses required by statute to be contained in the memorandum of association of a company are considered individually later in this chapter.

In addition to those provisions which have to be stated in the memorandum of association, other provisions may be included. This is most commonly done where it is desired to entrench the conditions attaching to certain share rights. If the memorandum itself prohibits the alteration of all or any of those conditions, they are incapable of alteration (C.A. 1948, s. 23(2)). To the extent that they are not expressed to be incapable of alteration, any additional optional conditions may be altered by special resolution, since they could lawfully have been contained in the articles of association instead of the memorandum (C.A. 1948, s. 23(1)). The restrictions on the alteration of a memorandum of association are considered under the heading *Alterations*, below.

Subscription and registration

For the purposes of the incorporation of a company under the Companies Acts, section 12 of the Companies Act 1948 requires that the memorandum and articles, if any, shall be delivered to the Registrar of Companies for England if the memorandum states that the registered office of the company is to be situated in England and Wales, and to the Registrar of Companies in Scotland if it states that the registered office is to be situated in Scotland. The memorandum of association delivered to the Registrar of Companies must be subscribed by at least two persons, who each must take at least one share (C.A. 1948, ss. 1(1) and 2(4)). "Subscription" means the signature by each subscriber in the presence of at least one witness who must attest the signature, attestation being sufficient in Scotland as well as in England and Wales (C.A. 1948, s. 3). Each subscriber must also, in the case of a company having a share capital, write opposite his name the number (in words or figures) of shares he is to take upon the incorporation of the company (C.A. 1948, s. 2(4)). It is important to note that the actual signature of each subscriber (or of his duly authorised agent) and witness is required. Also, each subscriber (or agent) must physically write under hand the number of shares to be taken. It is not sufficient for either the name of each subscriber and witness, or the number of shares, to be printed or similarly set out in the subscription copy of the memorandum which is delivered to the Registrar of Companies for registration. The address and description of each subscriber and witness may, however, be printed or written by a third party and any copy of the memorandum which is subsequently delivered to the Registrar of Companies in compliance with the disclosure and registration requirements of the Companies Acts, or which is made available by the company to its members or the public, may set out the relevant details in print.

The subscription is made at the end of the memorandum of association immediately after the statutory form of declaration of association appropriate to the type of company which is being incorporated. The declarations of association are set out as part of the model forms contained in the Tables in Schedule I to the Companies Act 1948 or 1980 (as the case may be), and are followed by a table for the actual subscription. The model form requires the name, address and description of each subscriber and these details should be set out in full. In particular, the description of the subscriber should be adequate, otherwise the memorandum will be returned by the Registrar of Companies. Imprecise epithets such as "Gentleman" or "Retired" should be avoided.

Subscription by companies or firms

The memorandum of association may be subscribed by any "person". All or any of the subscribers may be non-residents or foreigners (*Re General Company for Promotion* of *Land Credit* (1870) 5 Ch. App 363). A memorandum may be subscribed by or on behalf of a corporate body, or a firm. In the former case, the Registrar of Companies will require evidence of the power of the corporate body to subscribe shares and of the authority of the person completing the subscription on behalf of the corporate body. In the latter case, unless all the members of the firm sign the subscription page and therefore subscribe jointly, evidence of the authority of the person subscribing on their behalf will also be required. Similarly, if a subscription is made by an agent or nominee of the subscriber, the Registrar of Companies will require evidence of the authority given by the principal where the agent declares the capacity in which he is acting on the face of the subscription. In practice, the Registrar of Companies normally requires production of a written authority stamped 50p as a power of attorney.

As regards the witnessing of the signatures by the subscribers, it is sufficient to have a single witness for all the signatures. However, if the same witness does not attest all the signatures, details of each attesting witness must be set out explaining which writer attested the subscription by each subscriber. The memorandum must also give the address and description of each witness in the same manner as the equivalent details of the subscribers.

Registration

Section 12 of the 1948 Act requires delivery of the memorandum of association to the Registrar of Companies, together with the additional prescribed particulars required before a company may be registered and the registration fee (see pages 430 to 432 of the chapter *Formation and Types of Company*). On receiving the memorandum, the Registrar of Companies must satisfy himself that all the requirements of the Companies Act in respect of registration and of matters precedent and incidental thereto have been complied with (C.A. 1980, s. 3(1)). This includes, in the case of a public company, that the share capital stated in the memorandum is not less than the authorised minimum (see the chapters *Shares* and *Formation and Types of Company*). For the sake of clarity and to avoid unnecessary delay, the memorandum and, in particular, the subscription should be as legible and complete as possible. The Registrar of Companies will refer incorporation documents back to the subscribers, or their advisers, for clarification or rectification if they are not clear or are incomplete or wrong (see C.A. 1980, s. 3). Once satisfied in all respects, the Registrar of Companies registers the memorandum and issues a certificate pursuant to section 13 of the 1948 Act that the company is incorporated and, in the case of a limited company, that the company is limited. The certificate of incorporation is conclusive evidence that the requirements of section 3(1) of the Companies Act 1980 have been complied with, and that the association is a company authorised to be registered and is duly registered (C.A. 1980, s. 3(4)).

The memorandum of association may be in writing, although any subsequent alteration requires the delivery for registration of a *printed* copy of the memorandum, as altered (E.C.A. 1972, s. 9(5)). Because of this requirement regarding an altered memorandum, and as section 9 of the 1948 Act requires any articles of association which accompany a memorandum for registration to be printed, it is the almost universal practice that the memorandum is printed (the meaning of "printed" is discussed on page 585 below).

The effect of the memorandum

By section 26(1) of the Companies Act 1948, the subscribers to the memorandum of association of a company are deemed to have agreed to become members of the company, and on its registration must be, and are entitled to be, entered as members in the register of members of the company. By signing the memorandum, a subscriber contracts that, on the incorporation of the company, he will take the number of shares he has written opposite his name, and subject to the articles, pay for these. The subscriber automatically becomes a member in respect of his shares, even if the company does not allot the shares to him or does not enter his name in the register of members in respect of those shares (*Evans' Case* (1867) 2 Ch. App 427). It has become the practice of some company formation agents to transfer "off-the-shelf" companies to the ultimate purchaser by having the subscribers renounce their respective rights to the subscription shares in favour of the purchaser. This does not relieve the subscribers of their obligations as members, nor the company from its duty under section 26(1) to enter the names of the subscribers as members in the register of members. It follows that to acquire such a company and to terminate the membership of the subscribers, it is necessary to use duly executed stock transfers from the subscribers which are approved and registered in accordance with the articles of association of the company.

As in any other case in which a member agrees to subscribe shares in a company, a subscriber to the memorandum of association is, as indicated earlier, obliged to pay the full amount for the shares he has agreed to take when it falls due. In the case of a private company, payment may be made in cash or in kind as agreed with the directors. Subscribers to a public company must, however, pay in cash (C.A. 1980, s. 29). However, in each case, the obligation runs with the shares, so that nil or partly paid shares transferred by a subscriber bear the obligation to meet any call for payment made by the company in accordance with its articles of association.

Notwithstanding the right and obligation of a subscriber to take up his shares, the subscriber is not liable to take up his shares if the company does not allot them to him and the whole of the share capital is allotted to other persons (*Mackley's Case* (1875) 1 Ch. D. 247 and *Baytrust Holdings Limited v. IRC* [1971] 1 W.L.R. 1333). This is because the company cannot perform its side of the bargain. It is likely in this case that the subscriber would have an action for damages against the company.

A subscriber cannot avoid his obligations by seeking to establish misrepresentation on the part of the promoters of the company before its incorporation, since any misrepresentation made prior to the existence of the company cannot be attributed to it and, once the company is incorporated, the contract made by the subscription to the memorandum of association is for the benefit of the other subscribers and members (*Lord Lurgan's Case* [1902] 1 Ch. 707).

The nature of the contract established by the memorandum of association is set out in section 20 of the Companies Act 1948. Under that section, the memorandum and articles of association, when registered, bind a company and its members to the same extent as if they respectively had been signed and sealed by each member, and contained covenants on the part of each member to observe all the provisions of the memorandum and articles. The judicial review of this section, and of the contract created by it, has largely involved the articles of association, and is discussed in the chapter *Articles of Association*, but the principles explained there are equally applicable to the memorandum of association.

The articles of association are, however, subordinate to the memorandum and cannot modify or have priority over the memorandum. When interpreting a memorandum, the articles may be considered in order to resolve any ambiguity as to the meaning of the major document, but such an interpretation may be used only to clarify the memorandum not to widen the authority or objects conferred by it (*Re Wedgwood Coal and Iron Co., Anderson's Case* (1877) 7 Ch. D. 75 and *Guinness v. Land Corporation of Ireland* (1882) 22 Ch. D. 349).

The name clause

The first of the clauses which the memorandum of association of any company registered under the Companies Acts 1948 to 1981 must have is the name clause. This must set out the name of the company ending, where relevant, with the word "limited" or, in the case of a public company within the meaning of section 1(1) of the 1980 Act, "public limited company". In either case, certain abbreviations are permitted (see sections 2(2) and 78(3) of the 1980 Act). If the registered office of the company is to be in Wales, the Welsh equivalents may be used (C.A. 1976, s. 30 and C.A. 1980, s. 78).

It is important that the name in the clause should be exactly in accordance with the wishes of the promoters. Unless the proposed name is undesirable or the same as one already on the index kept by the Registrar of Companies under section 23 of the Companies Act 1981, the company will be registered by the Registrar of Companies, and the certificate of incorporation issued, following that precedent precisely. From the date of issue of the certificate of incorporation the proper name of the company, and the only name which the company will be entitled to use as its registered name, will be the one contained in its certificate. The use of any other name as the registered name, including the rectification of an existing name to correct an error, will involve the passing of a special resolution and the issue of a new certificate of incorporation on change of name by the Registrar of Companies (C.A. 1981, s. 24). A company may abbreviate the statutory suffix of its name by using the permitted abbreviations – "ltd" for "limited" and "p.l.c." for "public limited company". The Welsh equivalents are "cyf" as an abbreviation of "cyfyngedig" (limited) and "c.c.c." for "cwmni cyfyngedig cyhoeddus" (public limited company).

Restrictions on use of names

The regulation of the adoption of names, whether for registration or for use as business names, by companies is now governed by Part II of the Companies Act 1981. The rules are discussed in the chapter *Names*.

Exclusion of "limited"

One section of Part II of the Companies Act 1981 has particular relevance to the memorandum of association of certain private companies since they may be exempted from the requirement to use the word "limited", or the abbreviated or Welsh equivalents. Section 25 of the Companies Act 1981 applies to private companies limited by guarantee, which have been or are about to be registered, or to private companies limited by shares the names of which did not immediately prior to February 26, 1982 include the word "limited", by virtue of a licence granted under section 19 of the Companies Act 1948. In either case, however, it is a pre-condition that,

(a) the objects of the company are or, in the case of a company about to be registered, are to be, the promotion of commerce, art, science, education, religion, charity or any profession and anything incidental or conducive to any of those objects; and

(b) the memorandum or articles of association of the company,

(i) requires its profits, if any, or other income to be applied in promoting its objects;

(ii) prohibit the payment of dividends to its members; and

(iii) require all the assets which would otherwise be available to its members generally to be transferred on its winding up either to another body with objects similar to its own, or to another body the objects of which are the promotion of charity and anything incidental or conducive thereto (whether or not the body is a member of the company) (C.A. 1980, s. 25(2)).

A company meeting these conditions is exempt from the requirements of the Companies Act 1948 relating to the use of the word "limited" as any part of its name. If it takes advantage of this and does not include "limited" as part of its name, it is also exempt from the requirements of the 1948 Act relating to the publication of its name and the sending of lists of members to the Registrar of Companies. However, there is no consequent exemption from the requirements of section 9(7)(c) of the European Communities Act 1972, thus a limited company which is exempt from the requirements mentioned above must nonetheless state in all its business letters and order forms that it is a limited company.

A statutory declaration in the prescribed form sworn by a solicitor engaged in the formation of a company, or by the officers of the company, under section 25(4) of the Companies Act 1981 that the company is one to which the section applies may be delivered to the Registrar of Companies. He may refuse to register a company by a name which does not include "limited" unless such a declaration has been delivered to him, although there is no positive obligation on him to demand such a declaration, or to accept it, once delivered (C.A. 1981, s. 25(4)).

Once registered without "limited" as part of its name, the company may not alter its memorandum or articles of association if by doing so it would cease to qualify for exemption under the section (C.A. 1981, s. 25(2)). Further, if the Secretary of State is satisfied that a company to which the section applies, and the name of which does not include "limited", has carried on any business other than the promotion of the permitted objects, or has applied any of its profits or other income otherwise than in promoting those objects, or has paid a dividend to any of its members, he may direct the company to change its name by resolution of the directors within a specified period so that the name includes "limited". Failure to comply with section 25 of the Companies Act 1981 may lead to fines being levied on the company and any officer in default.

The public company clause

In the case of a public company, whether limited by shares or guarantee, the second clause of the memorandum of association must state that the company is a public company (C.A. 1980, s. 2(4) and Sch. 1). This requirement applies whether the memorandum is delivered for registration on the original incorporation of the company, or on the re-

registration of a private company as a public company (C.A. 1980, s. 5(3)).

The registered office clause

This clause must be contained in the memorandum of association in the case of every company registered under the Companies Acts 1948 to 1981 (C.A. 1948, s. 2(1)). It must state whether the registered office of the company is to be situated in England or in Scotland. If the promoters of the company have decided the registered office is to be situated in Wales, the clause may alternatively state that the registered office is to be situate in any of England, England and Wales or Wales alone (C.A. 1976, s. 30). The distinction is important, since the country in Great Britain specified in the clause dictates where the company is to be registered and the country which is capable of exercising jurisdiction over it. In addition, only a company electing in its memorandum that the registered office is to be in Wales, or in England and Wales, may take advantage of the Welsh language provisions of the Companies Acts affecting the memorandum, including the name of the company, for so long as the actual address of the registered office remains within Wales.

The decision, once taken, is final, except, to a limited extent, for a Welsh company. A company may not elect to move its registered office to another country within Great Britain since, to do so, would involve a change in the nationality and domicile of the company (which is determined by the situation of its registered office), and therefore of jurisdiction over the company. Accordingly, except in the case of a Welsh company, there is no provision in the Companies Acts which allows the registered office of a company to be situate in a country other than the one in which it was registered on its incorporation.

Section 23 of the Companies Act 1976 requires that every company shall at all times have a registered office to which all communications and notices may be addressed. The intended situation of the registered office on the incorporation of a company must be specified in the particulars delivered to the Registrar of Companies for the registration of the company. Although it is not generally possible to change the country in which the registered office is to be situate, the management of a company may at any time change the situation of the registered office to another address within the country of registration. For this purpose, if the clause provides that the registered office is to be situate in England, England includes Wales but not vice versa. Notice of any change in the situation of the registered office must be delivered, on Form 4a, within fourteen days of the decision (C.A. 1976, s. 23(3)). The company and any officer in default are liable to a default fine (section 23(4)). The Registrar of Companies must also officially notify any change of registered office in the London Gazette, (or the Edinburgh Gazette for a Scottish company), the change being fully effective after the expiry of fifteen days from the publication in the Gazette (E.C.A. 1972, ss. 9(3), 9(4)).

In addition to the publication of the situation of its registered office in the Gazette and in its public records, a company must also have, in legible characters, on all business letters and order forms, inter alia, the place of registration, and the address of its registered office (E.C.A. 1972, s. 9(7) and the chapter *Publicity Requirements*). Ideally, the place of registration should follow the equivalent statement in the memorandum of association of the company – e.g. "Registered in England and Wales" or "Registered in Scotland" but the Department of Trade will accept "Registered in Cardiff" or "Registered in Edinburgh" as compliance with the section. ("Registered in London" would probably not be sufficient as the registration of companies is no longer effected at Companies House in London. The office is maintained for public search facilities and the delivery of documents). If the only address shown on the business letter or order form is that of the registered office, an indication should be made that the address given is that of the registered office.

One of the main reasons why it is so important to disclose the situation of the registered office, and to keep that information up to date, is that by section 437 of the Companies Act 1948 a document may be served on a company by leaving it at or sending it by post to its registered office. Any company registered in Scotland, and carrying on business in England, may be served with the process of any court in England by leaving it at or sending it by post to the principal place of business of the company in England, addressed to the manager or other head officer in England of the company; a copy must also be sent by post to the registered office of the company (C.A. 1948, ss. 437(2) and 437(3)).

The documents which are required by statute to be kept at the registered office of a company are set out in the chapter *Publicity Requirements.*

The objects clause and the doctrine of *ultra vires*

The objects clause in the memorandum of association of a company registered under the Companies Acts is the single most important provision concerning the existence and business of the company. The clause delimits the nature and extent of the business which the company may transact. The company may not do any act or conduct any business which is not expressly or impliedly authorised by the objects set out in its memorandum,

"no object shall be pursued by the company, or attempted to be attained by the company in practice, except an object which is mentioned in the memorandum of association" (*Ashbury Railway Carriage and Iron Co. Limited v. Riche* (1875) L.R. 7 H.L. 653, per Lord Cairns L.C.)

It is, therefore, important that the promoters of a company should anticipate the requirements and scope of the business to be transacted by the company following its incorporation and draft the objects clause accordingly. Section 1 of the 1948 Act permits a company to be formed for any lawful purpose, and the objects may, within that restriction, contain whatever provisions are thought to be necessary or desirable for the conduct of the business of the company.

The statutory form of objects clause for a private company limited by shares is set out in the First Schedule to the 1948 Act. The statutory form for a public company is set out in the First Schedule to the 1980 Act. These statutory forms are relatively straightforward and simple in content and length, containing in a single paragraph a statement of the primary business followed by a general enabling power "and the doing of all such other things as are incidental or conducive to the attainment of the above object". This trend was set by earlier Companies Acts. However, the doctrine of *ultra vires* as defined by *Ashbury Railway Carriage and Iron Co. Limited v. Riche* and subsequent decisions of the courts, has led to the universal practice of drafting an objects clause of a company to include, in addition to the "main" objects of the company's business, some twenty or thirty specific objects which the company may wish to pursue even though, in some cases, no advantage of these "subsidiary" objects is ever taken.

The *ultra vires* doctrine

The *ultra vires* doctrine is concerned with the capacity of a company itself to enter into particular transactions. A distinction must immediately be drawn between two types of transaction. First, those which are beyond the capacity of the company, and therefore *ultra vires*, because they are not authorised by the objects clause of the memorandum of association. Secondly, those transactions which are authorised by the objects clause and which are thus *intra vires* and within the capacity of the company, but which fall outside the authority of the particular organ of the company, such as the board of directors or a simple majority of the members of the company, which is purporting to enter into those transactions on its behalf. The distinction is at times less than clear, since if a matter is beyond the capacity of a company it must also be beyond the authority of the directors of the company. Further, the attempt in section 9(1) of the European Communities Act 1972 to conform the *ultra vires* doctrine with the requirements of the First Council Directive on Company Law Harmonisation of the EEC, sought to protect third parties dealing with a company not only against the lack of capacity of the company but also against the lack of authority of the directors. The question of the authority of the directors and officers of a company and the effect of the rule in *Royal British Bank v. Turquand* (1856) 6 Ex. B. 327 are considered in the chapter *Company Contracts*.

The *Ashbury Railway Carriage* case confirmed that a company registered under the Companies Acts is only incorporated for the objects and purposes expressed in its memorandum of association, and that any transaction which was not authorised by the memorandum was void ab initio and therefore incapable of ratification, even if by all the members of the company. In the case itself, a company was formed with the objects "to make and sell, or lend on hire, railway-carriages and wagons, and all kinds of railway plant, fittings, machinery and rolling-stock; to carry on the business of mechanical engineers and general contractors; and to buy and sell any such materials on commissions, or as agents". The company agreed to provide Riche with finance for the construction of a railway in Belgium. Having repudiated the agreement, the company was sued for damages and pleaded it was *ultra vires* the company to enter into such a contract. The House of Lords emphasised that certainty of the objects which may be pursued by a company was necessary for two reasons. First, to protect the shareholders of the company for the time being, and those persons who may subsequently become shareholders. Secondly, to protect the public, and particularly those persons who may become creditors of the company. Further, since there was some evidence that the contract had been purportedly ratified by the members of the company in accordance with its articles of association, the House of Lords confirmed that a distinction should be drawn between unauthorised acts of the directors which could become effective upon ratification by a higher body, the members, and those acts which were beyond the capacity of the company itself and therefore incapable of ratification,

"The question is not as to the legality of the contract; the question is as to the competency and power of the company to make the contract. Now, I am clearly of the opinion that this contract was entirely, as I have said, beyond the objects in the memorandum of association. If so, it was thereby placed beyond the powers of the company to make the contract. If so, my Lords, it is not a question whether the contract ever was ratified or was not ratified. If it was a contract void at the beginning, it was void because the company could not make the contract" [per Lord Cairns L.C.].

Thus, the basic and apparently inflexible rule was established. However, since the Companies Act 1948, the members of a company have been able to procure the alteration of the objects contained in its memorandum of association without necessarily seeking court approval (C.A. 48, s. 5; see page 580 below). Whilst a company in general meeting may by special resolution alter its objects, the members still have no capacity to ratify an *ultra vires* transaction; an alteration of the objects cannot be made retrospectively to ratify, directly or indirectly, an *ultra vires* transaction. But the statutory power to alter the objects clause is a recognition of the undesirability of an inflexible *ultra vires* rule. Indeed, the drawbacks of an inflexible rule was recognised by the courts themselves as early as 1880, merely five years after the *Ashbury Railway Carriage* decision. In *Attorney-General v. Great Eastern Railway* (1880) 5 App. Cas. 473, the House of Lords reaffirmed the doctrine of *ultra vires* as explained in the earlier case. Lord Selborne L.C., however, went on to say that,

"this doctrine ought to be reasonably, and not unreasonably, understood and applied, and that whatever may fairly be regarded as incidental to, or consequential upon, those things which the legislature has authorised, ought not (unless expressly prohibited) to be held, by judicial construction, to be *ultra vires* ..."

The "reasonably incidental" rule

In the *Great Eastern Railway* case, the company in question was a statutory corporation, but the principles laid down by Lord Selborne have since been applied to registered companies and their objects (see *Bell Houses Limited v. City Wall Properties Limited* [1966] 2 Q.B. 656 and *In re Horsley & Weight Limited* [1982] 3 W.L.R. 431). As a result, it is now accepted that anything which is reasonably incidental to the attainment or pursuit of any of the express objects of a company will, unless expressly prohibited, be within the implied powers of the company and not *ultra vires*. There are a considerable number of examples of the courts invoking the "reasonably incidental" rule.

Incorporation by reference

As indicated earlier, the decisions of the courts have precluded a short general declaration of the objects of a company, and have led to the draftsmen of objects clauses combining precision with comprehensiveness in an attempt to avoid the doctrine of *ultra vires* attaching to any extension of the business of a company. In this connection, it is not sufficient to incorporate by reference, as the objects of a company, the terms of another document (*Proprietors of Royal Exchange Buildings, Glasgow* [1911] S.C. 1337). Each of the objects must be set out clearly and its meaning capable of being derived from a reasonable construction of the wording used. It may however be possible to incorporate certain minor matters by reference.

General concluding words

It is common practice to conclude the objects clause with words like "to do all such other things as are incidental or conducive to the attainment of all or any of the above objects", but it seems doubtful whether this adds much. By adding to the phrase the additional words "in the opinion of the directors", however, it seems that a purely subjective test is introduced as to whether the company can extend its business (see *Bell Houses Limited v. City Wall Properties* [1966] 2 Q.B. 656).

Powers and the "main objects" rule

This desire to have the objects clause as comprehensive as possible, has led to the practice of incorporating into the objects clause not only the principal objects of the company but also the powers which it can exercise in pursuance of those objects. This is despite the not inconsiderable number of decisions since *Attorney-General v. Great Eastern Railway* indicating, in the view of the courts, what powers may be implied in the cases of particular businesses and what may be reasonably incidental to the express objects of a company (see Buckley L.J. in *Re Horsley & Weight* [1982] 3 W.L.R. 431 at 436 for a recent example). The practice has however been criticised by the courts (see for example Lord Finlay L.C. in *Cotman v. Brougham* [1918] A.C. 514 and Buckley L.J. *Re Horsley & Weight Limited* [1982] 3 W.L.R. 431), on the basis that the real objects of the company should be made intelligible to the public, but never proscribed.

But the difficulty in setting out in the objects clause of a company's memorandum of association the powers exercisable by a company in pursuance of its objects, is that the powers are of necessity ancillary and incidental to the "main" objects and do not therefore stand alone. The exercise of the powers themselves will be *ultra vires* unless done for the purpose of furthering the objects of the company. The courts have also developed the "main" objects test, which holds that some of the express objects may upon construction fall to be treated as no more than powers which are ancillary to the dominant or "main" objects of a company (see *Re German Date Coffee Co* (1882) 20 Ch. D. 169).

Separate and independent objects rule

The memorandum must, however, be construed as a single document and if it provides that each paragraph is to constitute a separate and independent object not limited by references in other paragraphs, the courts will uphold such a provision (*Cotman v. Brougham* [1918] A.C. 514). As a result, an objects clause will not be construed restrictively in accordance with the "main" objects rule if a "separate and independent" provision is contained in the memorandum.

The "separate and independent objects" trick thus enables a company with a wide objects clause in its memorandum to extend its business in pretty much any way it likes without fear of the *ultra vires* rule. This was confirmed by the decision of the Court of Appeal in *Bell Houses Limited v. City Wall Properties Limited* [1966] 2 Q.B. 656. The plaintiff sued for the payment of a fee which it claimed for arranging the introduction of the defendant to a financier to provide a bridging loan to the defendant. The plaintiff was a property developer and the defendant argued that the mortgage broking transaction was *ultra vires* the plaintiffs who could not, therefore, recover the fee. The Court of Appeal held that the objects clause of the plaintiff authorised the carrying on of the particular type of business. The court relied on sub-clause (c) of the objects clause,

"To carry on any other trade or business whatsoever which can, in the opinion of the board of directors, be advantageously carried on by the company in connection with or as ancillary to ... the general businesses of the company."

Provided the directors genuinely believed that the business could be carried on advantageously in connection with or as ancillary to the general business of the company, the business was within the plaintiff company's objects and powers. Nor was it necessary for the directors to have been correct in their view that the extension of the business was to the advantage of the company; they merely had to form the view honestly,

"It may that the directors take the wrong view and in fact the business in question cannot be carried on as the directors believe. But it matters not how mistaken the directors may be. Providing they form their view honestly, the business is within the plaintiff company's objects and powers. This is so plainly the natural and ordinary meaning of the language of sub-clause (c) that I would refuse to construe it differently unless compelled to do so by the clearest authority. And there is no such authority" (Salmon L.J. at p. 690).

On the other hand, the courts have also recognised that *powers* as opposed to objects may be incapable of independence, even if the objects clause of a particular memorandum of association contains the *Cotman v. Brougham* declaration that each provision is to be independent and not ancillary to or dependant upon another. In *Introductions Limited v. National Provincial Bank Limited* [1970] Ch. 199, the Court of Appeal had to consider a provision in the objects clause allowing the company to borrow or raise money in such manner as it thought fit. The objects clause also contained the *Cotman v. Brougham* provision that each sub-clause "shall be construed independently of and shall be in no way limited by reference to any other sub-clause and that the objects set out in each sub-clause are independent objects of the company". The company had been formed originally to offer facilities to overseas visitors in connection with the Festival of Britain. It subsequently took up pig breeding, an activity which was outside the scope of its objects clause even on the most liberal interpretation. The overdraft of the company, which was incurred as a result of its pig breeding business, was secured by two debentures in favour of the plaintiff bank. Before the security was granted, the bank had been given a copy of the memorandum and became aware that pig breeding was the sole business of the company. The bank, in attempting to ensure the validity of its security, sought to argue that there was an express power to borrow money contained in the memorandum; that this power was converted into an object by the *Cotman v. Brougham* clause; and that there was not therefore any need to enquire into the purposes for which the loan was to be used. The Court of Appeal held that borrowing was not an end in itself and, since the borrowing was for an *ultra vires* purpose, it too was *ultra vires*. This principle was confirmed in *Re Horsley & Weight* [1982] 3 W.L.R. 431.

Thus, notwithstanding the wording of a memorandum of association, a distinction must still be made between the objects and powers contained in an objects clause. If, despite the wording of the memorandum, a provision is incapable of being an independent object, the courts will not construe it as such and will accordingly seek to ensure that the exercise of such a power is for the purposes of the company. To the extent that it is not exercised for the legitimate purposes of the company's business, any purported exercise of the power will be *ultra vires*.

By contrast, if a company has the power to borrow money for the purposes of its business, there is no obligation on the proposed lender to establish how the company intends to apply the loan proceeds (*Re David Payne & Co Limited* [1904] 2 Ch. 608). A court will not set aside a loan as against a lender where the lender had no knowledge that the company intended to apply the proceeds for an *ultra vires* purpose. Unless the objects clause expressly limits a borrowing power, the court will go no further than to imply a limitation that the power to borrow is for the purposes of the lawful business of the company (*Charterbridge Corporation Limited v. Lloyds Bank Limited* [1970] Ch. 62). This must be balanced by the fact that any person dealing with the company has constructive notice of the contents of its objects clause as registered, since the memorandum of association as a publicly available document (see the chapter *Company Contracts*). Accordingly, if the third party is aware of the purpose behind his dealing with the company, and that purpose is *ultra vires*, he was not able under the common law to claim that he was unaware of the contents of the objects clause and therefore that a transaction was *ultra vires* the company.

For example, in *Re Jon Beauforte (London) Limited* [1953] Ch. 131, a company authorised to carry on business as costumiers and gown-makers undertook the business of veneered panel makers, which was *ultra vires*. The company ordered coke on paper headed "Veneered Panel Manufacturers" and it was held that the supplier of the coke had actual knowledge of the business which the company was carrying on and for which coke was required and that, by virtue of the *constructive* notice which the supplier had of the contents of the memorandum of association, it had notice that the transaction was *ultra vires* the company and, therefore, unenforceable against it (for the usual position following the enactment of section 9(1) of the European Communities Act 1972, see page 474 below).

Ultra vires in the wider sense

This leads on to a difficult area. As Vinelott J. explained in a comprehensive review of the case law in *Rolled Steel Products Limited v. British Steel Corporation* [1982] 3 W.L.R. 715, the phrase "*ultra vires*" tends to be used in two senses. First, it is used in the narrow sense to describe a transaction which is outside the scope of the express objects or powers in the memorandum and the powers which can be implied as reasonably incidental to these. Secondly, it is often used to describe a transaction which, although within the express or implied objects and powers of the company, is entered into in furtherance of a purpose which is not an authorised purpose.

The second use crops up particularly in cases concerning gratuitous payments by a company. Here an objective test has tended to be applied. This follows the often cited dicta of Bowen L.J. in *Hutton v. West Cork Railway Co.* (1883) 23 Ch. D. 654 that "charity cannot sit at the board room table ... The law does not say that there are to be no cakes and ale, but that there are to be no cakes and ale except such as are required for the benefit of the company".

The objective test in determining whether a gratuitous payment by a company is *ultra vires* was laid down by Eve J. in *Re Lee, Behrens & Co. Limited* [1932] 2 Ch. 46, where the court was called upon to decide whether an annuity voted by the directors to the widow of the company's former managing director was *ultra vires*. In deciding that it was, Eve J. held that the company's money could only be spent for a purpose reasonably incidental to the company's business. In determining the validity of the transaction, the court had to be satisfied by the answers to the following three questions:

(a) is the transaction reasonably incidental to the carrying on of the company's business;

(b) is it a *bona fide* transaction; and

(c) is it done for the benefit and to promote the prosperity of the company?

Eve J. held that the third test was not satisfied because the only considerations operating in the minds of the directors concerned the desire to provide for the widow and the question of what, if any, benefit would accrue to the company was never considered.

The decisions in *Hutton v. West Cork Railway Co.* and *Re Lee, Behrens & Co. Limited* were applied in *Parke v. Daily News Limited* [[1962] Ch. 927] by Plowman J.:

"The conclusions which, I think, follow from these cases are: first, that a company's funds cannot be applied in making ex gratia payments as such; secondly, that the court will enquire into the motives actuating any gratuitous payment, and the objectives which it is intended to achieve; thirdly, that the court will uphold the validity of gratuitous payments if, but only if, after such enquiry, it appears that the tests enumerated by Eve J. in *In Re Lee, Behrens & Co. Limited* are satisfied; fourthly, that the onus of upholding the validity of such payments lies on those who assert it."

The court then went on to hold that a proposal to distribute part of the proceeds arising from the sale by the company of the whole of its newspaper business among its former employees, who would be made redundant as a result of the sale (over and above any contractual entitlement which the employees might have in respect of lack of notice) was based on the desire to treat the employees generously. It was not, however, in the interests of the company; having sold its entire newspaper business, it could not be maintained that the company's reputation within the industry would be damaged. (Section 74 of the Companies Act 1980 now enables a company, which is authorised by a resolution in general meeting or which has an authority contained in its memorandum or articles of association, to make provision for the benefit of employees or former employees of the company, or any of its subsidiaries, in connection with the cessation or transfer of the whole or part of its undertaking. The realities inducing companies to make other gratuitous payments have been recognised by statute and have been the subject of recent judicial comment. Section 19 of the Companies Act 1967 requires disclosure in the directors' report of a company of any contribution made for political or charitable purposes or both in excess of £200 in any financial year. In addition, it is accepted that it is for the benefit of the company for it to make gratuitous payments to its employees or former employees if the company is to continue in business since not to do so could be detrimental to the commercial reputation of the company itself.)

However, the correctness of Eve J.'s three tests in *Re Lee, Behrens* has been severely doubted, particularly by Pennycuick J. in *Charterbridge Corporation Limited v. Lloyds Bank Limited* [1970] Ch. 62 and by the Court of Appeal in *Re Horsley & Weight Limited* [1982] 3 W.L.R. 431.

In *Charterbridge* Pennycuick J. held that the third test (benefit to the company) is quite inappropriate to the scope of express objects. This was approved in *Re Horsley & Weight* (and see also the judgment of Oliver J. in the unreported case of *Re Halt Garage Limited*, discussed in *Rolled Steel Products Limited v. British Steel Corporation*). In the *Charterbridge* case Pennycuick J. decided that the state of mind of the parties concerned was not a matter which should be taken into account in deciding whether or not a transaction was *ultra vires* the company,

"The memorandum of a company sets out its objects and proclaims them to persons dealing with the company and it would be contrary to the whole function of a memorandum that objects unequivocally set out in it should be subject to some implied limitation by reference to the state of mind of the parties concerned".

Thus it did not matter that a transaction involving a gratuitous guarantee by the company in favour of its parent company and fellow subsidiaries was not necessarily for the benefit of the company itself.

The true position now appears to be that the "benefit to the company" test is not an essential part of the *ultra vires* rule at all, but is really directed to whether the directors of a company are making proper use of their powers (particularly where the provision is an enabling power, not an independent object). This is consistent with the decisions in *Charterbridge* and *Re David Payne*, mentioned above. The test will, however, come into the *ultra vires* issue where the object of the company which is in question is one which is expressly or impliedly restricted to furtherance of the company's commercial objects (as contrasted to an object enabling gratuitous payments to be without restriction). This is the analysis adopted in the *Rolled Steel* case, relying on the *Charterbridge, Re Halt Garage* and *Re Horsley & Weight* cases. Thus in *Re Horsley & Weight* the Court of Appeal decided that a provision authorising the company to provide pension benefits for present and former employees was an independent object rather than a power, and that there was no reason why a company should not part with its funds gratuitously or for non-commercial reasons if to do so was within its declared objects. The company's declared objects need not be commercial; they could be charitable or philanthropic. But this was subject to the qualification just mentioned (Buckley L.J. at page 440):

"Of course, if the memorandum of association expressly or by implication provides that an express object only extends to acts which benefit or promote the prosperity of the company, regard must be paid to that limitation, but, where there is no such express or implied limitation, the question whether an act done within the terms of an express object of the company will benefit or promote the prosperity of the company or its business is . . . irrelevant".

A detailed analysis of the effect of *Charterbridge, Re Horsley & Weight* and *Rolled Steel* in relation to guarantees can be found on pages 138 to 142.

Effect of *ultra vires*

Following the enactment of section 9(1) of the European Communities Act 1972, many of the more draconian effects of the *ultra vires* doctrine

on third parties have been removed. Since, however, section 9(1) has
not taken away all the consequences under the common law of a
transaction being *ultra vires*, the common law position remains important. The basic position at common law has always been that any act
done by a company which is not authorised, expressed or impliedly, by
its memorandum of association is *ultra vires* the company and void *ab
initio*. No legal relationship is established by the *ultra vires* transaction
and it cannot be ratified by the company in general meeting, even if all
the shareholders agree (*Ashbury Railway Carriage & Iron Co. v. Riche*
(1875) L.R. 7 H.L.). As a result of the strict application of the *ultra vires*
doctrine, one of the reasons for its existence in fact often worked to the
detriment of those parties which the doctrine was intended to protect.
Thus in *Re Jon Beauforte (London) Limited*, discussed above, creditors
of a company who had dealt with it in good faith had no right of action
against the company since the transaction was *ultra vires* the company.

Constructive trusteeship

However, in order to seek to restore a degree of protection for third
parties in respect of an *ultra vires* transaction, the courts have been
prepared to grant remedies either against the company or against its
officers in favour of a third party entering into an *ultra vires* transaction
with the company. At law, it is accepted that persons making *ultra vires*
loans to a company may not sue to recover the amount of the loan in
contract or in quasi contract (*Sinclair v. Brougham* [1914] A.C. 398).
However, if the borrowed money is applied in paying off legitimate
indebtedness of the company (whether the indebtedness is incurred
before or after the money was borrowed) the lender is entitled to rank
as a creditor of the company to the extent to which the money was so
applied; in effect, the lender is subrogated to the rights of the legitimate
creditors who have been paid off. In addition, the lender in an *ultra vires*
loan transaction has a right to a tracing order. As a result of any *ultra
vires* act being void, any money borrowed remains the property of the
lender, so that the directors of the company purporting to act on its
behalf effectively hold this as constructive trustees. Likewise the recipient of funds paid out by a company *ultra vires* will hold the funds as
constructive trustee if he is aware that the transaction is *ultra vires:
International Sales and Agencies Limited v. Marcus* [1982] 3 All E.R.
551 (where it was held that section 9(1) of the European Communities
Act – see below – did not override the constructive trusteeship because
the section only protected "innocent" parties). Following on from the
existence of this constructive trusteeship, the legal and equitable
principles of tracing would apply to borrowings or other moneys used or
paid out *ultra vires*, to the extent they have not been dissipated. But the
right of subrogation does not confer upon a lender whose *ultra vires*
borrowing is used to repay legitimate debts incurred by a company the
right to any security over those legitimate debts (*Re Wrexham, Mold
and Connah's Quay Railway Co* [1899] 1 Ch. 440 and *Blackburn
Building Society v. Cunliffe, Brooks & Co* (1882) 22 Ch. D. 61); the

problem of *ultra vires* in loan transactions is discussed in more detail in the chapter *Borrowings*).

Position of the company

As regards the right of the company itself to enforce an *ultra vires* transaction, the contract will be void from its point of view as well as the other contracting party. Accordingly, the company may not sue in contract or in debt to cover any amounts paid in respect of the transaction. However, there is support for the proposition that the company may have a right of action in quasi contract for money had and received, if it is able to establish that the other party was unjustifiably enriched at the expense of the company (see Mocatta J. at first instance in *Bell Houses Limited v. City Wall Properties Limited* [1966] 1 Q.B. 207). Such a remedy in favour of the other party was, however, denied by the House of Lords in the earlier case of *Sinclair v. Brougham* on the basis that this would be an indirect means of enforcing the *ultra vires* rule in respect of a loan made to the company.

Remedy against directors

Both the company and third parties may have rights of action against directors of a company who engage in *ultra vires* transactions. A director entering into a transaction which is *ultra vires* the company on its behalf, is also in breach of his duty to the company so that if the company suffers a loss, the director could be liable to the company in that respect. As against the third party, the director may be liable for breach of warranty of authority since he is acting as agent of the company in effecting the transaction. If the director merely mis-represents the powers of the company to enter into the transaction, this will be a mis-representation of law and, under general contractual principles, will not be the subject of an action against the director for breach of warranty. However, if the mis-representation is one of fact, such as regarding the business of the company, a claim for breach of warranty could lie against him. Further, if the mis-representation is deliberate and fraudulent, an injured third party could sue a director in tort for deceit. Alternatively, a negligent mis-representation could lead to an action by a third party against the director under the principle established in *Hedley Byrne & Co v. Heller & Partners* [1964] A.C. 465.

Ultra vires as a defence

As some of the cases discussed earlier demonstrate, a company may raise the argument of *ultra vires* in order to avoid compliance with a transaction entered into on its behalf. But it seems this only applies in contract and property transactions and not, for instance, to criminal liability or liability in tort. Since one of the stated purposes of the existence of the *ultra vires* doctrine is the protection of the members of a company, any member may also apply to the court for an injunction to restrain the company from what would otherwise be an *ultra vires* transaction (*Parke v. Daily News Limited* [1962] Ch. 806). The second body of persons which it was intended to protect by the establishment of the *ultra vires* doctrine, the creditors of a company, have no such right.

Although a company may plead *ultra vires* as a defence, it is unclear whether the other party to a transaction may similarly plead *ultra vires* as a means of avoiding its obligations under the transaction. Such a plea was allowed at first instance in *Bell Houses Limited v. City Wall Properties Limited* [1966] 1 Q.B. 207, although the Court of Appeal subsequently left the point open whilst reversing the decision on other grounds.

This problem, and various other problems arising as a result of the application of the *ultra vires* doctrine, have in part been solved by section 9(1) of the European Communities Act 1972.

Section 9(1)

Section 9(1) of the European Communities Act 1972 was enacted in an attempt to reconcile English law with the requirements of the First Council Directive on Companies of the EEC. The Directive seeks to preserve the rights of third parties in respect of acts done by the organs of a company, even if those acts are not within the objects of the company or the powers of the organs of the company are otherwise restricted under its constitution. Section 9(1) does not however afford complete protection to third parties, providing,

"In favour of a person dealing with a company in good faith, any transaction decided on by the *directors* shall be deemed to be one which it is within the capacity of the company to enter into, and the power of the directors to bind the company will be deemed to be free of any limitation under the memorandum or articles of association; and a party to a transaction so decided on shall not be bound to enquire as to the capacity of the company to enter into it or as to any such limitation on the powers of directors, and shall be presumed to have acted in good faith unless the contrary is proved."

The section does not enable the company itself to enforce an *ultra vires* transaction against a third party. However, if a third party wishes to enforce the transaction, he cannot have it both ways. As the third party must be seen to have acted in good faith, it would seem contrary to the intention of the section if a third party could rely on the protection granted by the section, and at the same time fail to perform its own obligations under the relevant transaction.

The requirement that the person must deal with the company in good faith is fundamental to the section (and see *International Sales and Agencies Limited v. Marcus* [1982] 3 All E.R. 551). It is however, presumed that any third party dealing with the company is acting in good faith unless the company establishes the contrary. If the third party has actual notice of the lack of capacity of the company entering into the transaction, he can hardly be said to be dealing in good faith. On the other hand, bearing in mind that the section is intended to protect the innocent third party dealing with the company, it would appear that constructive notice of itself would not be sufficient to enable the company to establish that the third party was not dealing with the company in good faith. Thus the coke supplier in *Re Jon Beauforte (London) Limited* would now be protected because he only had constructive notice of the company's memorandum, but the bank in *Introductions Limited v. National Provincial Bank* would still lose out because it had been sent a copy of the memorandum (see page 568).

The second fundamental point for consideration in deciding whether a third party may rely on the protection afforded by section 9(1), is that the transaction must be one which is "decided on by the directors". Although the point has not been decided by a court, it is accepted by most authorities that the phrase must mean the directors acting as a board, and that it will not be sufficient for a third party to deal with a single director unless that director is the sole director of the company, or the dealing is one which has been approved, or is subsequently ratified, by the board as a whole. Furthermore, transactions which are not decided upon by the directors but which, for example are approved by the members in general meeting or decided on by an officer other than a director of the company, are outside the protection of the section.

A person dealing *bona fide* with a company in a transaction which has been decided upon by the board of directors of that company, will therefore be protected against any claim that the transaction was *ultra vires*. Further, the directors will be deemed to have power to bind the company notwithstanding any limitation on their powers contained in either the memorandum or articles of association. The section is, however, concerned with a "dealing" involving a "transaction". This involves a limitation on the scope of the section, since arguably the section may not be used to assist a person seeking to enforce, for example, a gift against the company which would otherwise be *ultra vires*. The third party is also still subject to the risk of a minority shareholder in the company obtaining an injunction against the company preventing it from acting *ultra vires*.

Ratification of *ultra vires* act

As mentioned earlier, an *ultra vires* transaction cannot be ratified, even by all the members in general meeting. It is clear that this rule applies to transactions which are *ultra vires* in the wider sense as well as the narrower sense: see *Rolled Steel Products Limited v. British Steel Corporation* [1982] 3 W.L.R. 715 and page 571 above.

The limited liability clause

The memorandum of association of a company limited by shares or by guarantee, with or without a share capital, must have as its fourth clause (or, in the case of a public company, the fifth clause) a statement that the liability of the members of the company is limited (C.A. 1948, s. 2(2)). This serves two purposes. First, it is fundamentally important that the creditors of the company should know that the liability of its members is limited. Secondly, it is equally important to the members to know the extent of their liability within that limitation.

In the case of a company limited by shares, a member is obliged to pay the full amount of the nominal value, and the share premium (if any) which he has agreed to pay, in respect of the shares registered in his name, to the extent that such amount has not been paid by any previous holder of those shares. A member of a guarantee company is obliged to contribute the amount specified in the memorandum of association to the assets of the company if it is wound up while he is a member or within a year of his ceasing to be a member.

In acknowledgement of the importance of the concept of the limited liability of its members, no limited company may re-register as an unlimited company without the consent of all its members (C.A. 1967, s. 43). Nor can the rights and protection of limited liability of any member be taken away by the company or the majority of its members. No member of a company shall be bound by an alteration to the memorandum or articles of association after the date on which he became a member, if and so far as the alteration requires him to take or subscribe for more shares than the number held by him at the date on which the alteration is made, or in any way increases his liability as at that date to contribute to the share capital of, or otherwise to pay money to, the company (C.A. 1948, s. 22).

A member may, however, agree in writing, either before or after an alteration to the memorandum or articles of association is made, to be bound by the alteration and any consequential increase in his liability (C.A. 1948, s. 22).

There are a number of statutory exceptions to the doctrine of limited liability of the members of a limited company. Thus if a company carries on business while having less than two members for more than six months, the remaining member is liable, jointly and severally, with the company for the debts of the company contracted during the relevant period, if he knew that it was carrying on business with only one member (C.A. 1948, s. 31). Also, if a company with less than two members makes a distribution which is unlawful under the Companies Act 1980, any member receiving the distribution who, at the time of the distribution, knows or has reasonable grounds for believing that it is an unlawful distribution is liable to repay it to the company. If the distribution was made otherwise than in cash, he is liable to pay to the company a sum equal to the value of the distribution (C.A. 1980, s. 44).

The Companies Act 1948 also extends the period during which a member can remain liable to the company. The general rule in the case of transfers of nil paid or partly paid shares is that the obligation to pay the amounts due to the company, as and when called, passes to the purchaser with the shares upon his becoming a member in respect of those shares. However, if the company is wound up within one year of a person ceasing to be a member, he may be required to contribute towards the payment of the debts and liabilities of the company contracted *before* he ceased to be a member and the costs of the winding up. However, for a company limited by shares the liability cannot exceed the amounts unpaid on the shares. Past members are only liable to the extent existing members cannot satisfy their contributions (C.A. 1948, s. 212).

The nominal capital clause

The memorandum of association of any *limited* company having a share capital, including a company limited by guarantee, must state the amount of share capital with which the company proposes to be registered and the division of the share capital into shares of a fixed amount (C.A. 1948, s. 2(4)). These are the only details relating to the share capital which are required to be set out in the memorandum. Share rights are matters which may be, and preferably should be, regulated by the articles of association, unless there is a good reason why they should be contained in the memorandum.

The amount and the composition of the nominal capital of a company is a matter for its promoters, subject to the minimum capital requirements of the Companies Acts. In particular, the par value of each share may be freely determined by the promoters. The promoters should anticipate the expected working and reserve capital requirements of the company and the amount which is expected to be contributed by each of the subscribers and subsequent members. Within that framework, the nominal capital once determined may be divided into whatever denomination of shares is decided upon by the promoters as being necessary or desirable in the particular circumstances of the company, its structure, and business.

One restriction on the freedom of the promoters is laid down by section 4 of the Companies Acts 1980, which provides that a company registered on incorporation as a public company shall not do business or exercise any borrowing powers unless the Registrar of Companies has issued it with a certificate. Before he issues such a certificate, the Registrar of Companies must be satisfied that the nominal value of the allotted share capital of the company is not less than the authorised minimum. This is currently £50,000. The amount paid up must comprise at least one-quarter of the nominal capital and the whole of any premium (C.A. 1980, s. 6). The company may not commence business until this minimum amount is paid up (see further page 409). There are similar restrictions on the re-registration of a private company as a public company.

It is not unusual for a company to have more than a single class of shares. Examples of the varying share rights and the implications as far as the members are concerned, together with the means of the alteration of the share capital and attached rights, are discussed in the chapter *Shares*. To facilitate the variation of the rights attaching to different classes of shares, these are usually set out in the articles of association of the company. There is no requirement that they be set out in the memorandum. However, if the class rights are embodied in the memorandum, and the memorandum itself does not authorise any variation or abrogation of the special rights of any class of members, those rights are unalterable (C.A. 1948, s. 23(a)).

The declaration of association

As indicated above, the specific provisions of the memorandum of association of each company registered under the Companies Act 1948 to 1981, are followed by the declaration of association in the form prescribed in the various parts of Schedule I to the Companies Act 1948 or 1981, depending on the type of company concerned. The declaration of association is in turn followed by the details of the subscription which has to accord with the requirements of section 2(4) of the Companies Act 1948. By the declaration of association, the subscribers declare that they are desirous of being formed into a company in pursuance of the memorandum of association and, in the case of a company with a share capital, agree to take the number of shares in the capital of the company set opposite their respective names.

Companies having registered office in Wales

By section 30 of the Companies Act 1976, the memorandum of association of a company registered after April 18, 1977 may contain a statement that its registered office is to be situated in Wales, as opposed to England or Scotland as was required by section 2(1)(b) of the 1948 Act. Section 30 originally contained transitional provisions allowing a company already registered on April 18, 1977, and having its registered office in Wales, to alter its memorandum by special resolution within twelve months of that date to reflect that the office was in Wales. The time limitation was repealed by the Companies Act 1980, which enables a company with a Welsh registered office to alter at any time the registered office clause in its memorandum by special resolution.

If a limited company has registered, or altered, its memorandum of association in the above manner, the memorandum may in addition state as the last word of the name of the company, the word "cyfynge-dig", instead of "limited" or "cwmni cyfyngedig cyhoeddus" or the permitted abbreviations "cyf." or "c.c.c", as the case may be (C.A. 1976, s. 30(3); C.A. 1980, ss. 2(2), 78).

A company using the Welsh equivalent, or the permitted abbreviation, as part of its name, must state in English and in legible characters that the company is a limited company or public limited company (as appropriate) in,

(a) all prospectuses, bill heads, letter paper, notices and other official publications of the company; and

(b) a notice conspicuously displayed in every place in which the company's business is carried on.

The company and every officer in default are liable to a fine on summary conviction in the event of a breach (C.A. 1976, s. 30(5) and C.A. 1980, s. 77 and page 588).

The memorandum and articles of association of a Welsh company delivered to the Registrar of Companies may be in the Welsh language, but must be accompanied by a certified translation into English (C.A. 1976, s. 30(6)). In addition, such a company may comply with any provision of the Companies Acts requiring it to deliver a document to the Registrar of Companies, by delivering a document in Welsh (or, if it consists of a prescribed form, completed in Welsh), together with a certified translation into English. If the document is one which makes or evidences an alteration to the memorandum or articles, it must be in the same language as the memorandum and articles originally registered, and, if that language is Welsh, be accompanied by a certified translation into English (C.A. 1976, s. 30(7)).

Alteration

Since the memorandum of association of a company is a document to which considerable importance is attached by the legislature, and as it effectively comprises the fundamental basis under which a company operates, the general principle adopted by the legislature is that the memorandum should only be capable of alteration under certain specified circumstances and then only in accordance with statute. The object is to protect third parties dealing with, and the members of, the company by promoting a degree of certainty within its constitution. The general rule is set out in section 4 of the Companies Act 1948,

"A company may not alter the conditions contained in its memorandum except in the cases, in the mode and to the extent for which express provision is made in the Companies Acts 1948 to 1981."

This apparently inflexible restriction may be compared with the relative ease with which the articles of association may be altered, namely by special resolution passed in accordance with section 10 of the Companies Act 1948 (see the chapter *Articles of Association*). This acknowledges that, as the essence of the articles is the internal regulation by the company of its management and affairs, the members of the company should be able to vary the internal regulations without undue difficulty.

However, the Companies Acts now provide for the alteration of the conditions contained in each of the clauses which are required by the Companies Act 1948 to be set out in the memorandum of each company, where such a change is necessary to meet a permitted variation in the actual or proposed circumstances of the company.

The name clause

The manner in which the name of a company may be changed is discussed in the chapter *Names*. Although the change of name by a company is not specifically referred to in section 24 of the Companies Act 1981 as an alteration of a condition contained in the memorandum of association for the purposes of section 4 of the 1948 Act, it is accepted that this is a necessary and integral result of a change of name. Section 2(1)(a) of the Companies Act 1948 requires every company to state its name in its memorandum. If the intent of the legislature that no public document is to be misleading is to be followed, the name which should be contained in the name clause is the name under which it is incorporated from time to time.

As a matter of practice, upon a change of name either the relevant alteration should be made to clause 1 of the memorandum of association and a footnote added to explain the history of the change of name of the company, or the contents of clause 1 should be left unchanged and an appropriate footnote added to explain the apparent discrepancy between the memorandum and the current name of the company. It is submitted that the former practice is the better of the two.

A change of name certainly evidences an alteration in the company's memorandum for the purposes of section 9(5) of the European Communities Act 1972, and should therefore be followed, within fifteen days of the change, by the delivery to the Registrar of Companies of a printed copy of the memorandum as altered.

The headnote is not a statutory part of the memorandum of association, and this can be altered freely. The model forms contained in Schedule I to each of the Companies Acts 1948 and 1980 do not contain specimen headings, but these are traditionally appended to the memorandum and articles of association.

The public company clause

If a public company proposes to be re-registered as a private company, it must, among other things, pass a special resolution to alter its memorandum of association so that it no longer states that the company is to be a public company. It must also make such other alterations in its memorandum and articles as are requisite in the circumstances (C.A. 1980, s. 10 and page 416).

The registered office clause

Although this clause is, in general, unalterable, a company having its registered office in Wales may by, special resolution, alter its memorandum of association to contain a statement that, for the purposes of section 2(1)(b) of the Companies Act 1948, the registered office of the company is to be situated in Wales – see page 578 above.

The objects clause

Despite the apparent inflexibility of the *ultra vires* rule, section 5 of the Companies Act 1948 provides a means by which the objects contained in the memorandum of association of the company may be altered in order to extend or restrict its business activities. Such an alteration must, however, fall within one of the seven specified purposes permitted by the section. The section provides that a company may, by special resolution, alter its objects so far as may be required to enable it to,

(1) carry on its business more economically or efficiently;

(2) attain its main purpose by new or improved means;

(3) enlarge or change the local area of its operations;

(4) carry on some business which under existing circumstances may conveniently or advantageously be combined with the business of the company;

(5) restrict or abandon any of the objects specified in the memorandum;

(6) sell or dispose of the whole or any part of the undertaking of the company; or

(7) amalgamate with any other company or body or persons.

However, if an application is made to the court to have the alteration cancelled in accordance with the remaining provisions of the section, the proposed alteration is not effective except insofar as it is confirmed by the court. Application may be made to the court by the holders of not less than, in aggregate, fifteen per cent in nominal value of the issued share capital of the company, or any class thereof. If the company is not limited by shares, the figure is not less than fifteen per cent of the company's members. Alternatively, the application may be made by the holders of not less than fifteen per cent of the company's debentures entitling the holders to object to alterations of its objects. However, application to have an alteration satisfied may not be made by any person who has consented to or voted in favour of the proposed alteration (C.A. 1948, s. 5(2)). The application must be made within 21 days of the date the special resolution altering the company's objects was passed.

Upon an application, the court may make an order confirming the alteration either wholly or in part and on the terms and conditions as it thinks fit and may adjourn proceedings to enable an arrangement to be made, to its satisfaction, for the purchase of the interests of the dissentient members. A court may give any directions and make any orders as it may think expedient for facilitating or carrying into effect such an arrangement. The court may, if it thinks fit, provide for the purchase by the company of the shares of any members of the company, together with the resultant reduction of the company's capital and any consequential alterations in the memorandum and articles (C.A. 1948, s. 5(4)). Any alteration to the memorandum or articles required by an order of the court has effect as if duly made by a resolution of the company (C.A. 1948, s. (4C)).

If no application is made to the court within the twenty-one day time limit the alteration cannot subsequently be cancelled. After expiry of the time limit without an application being made, the company must deliver to the Registrar of Companies a printed copy of its memorandum of association as altered by the special resolution. This must be delivered within fifteen days from the end of the original twenty-one day notice period. The Registrar of Companies will not, generally, accept delivery of the memorandum of association before the expiry of that period unless he is satisfied that there are no persons who are entitled to make an application to the court within that time (e.g. if all the members and, where relevant, debenture holders, voted in favour of the special resolution altering the objects).

If an application is made by a dissentient minority, the company must immediately give notice to the Registrar of Companies in the prescribed form. Within fifteen days from the date of any court order cancelling or confirming the alteration, the company must deliver to the Registrar of Companies an office copy of the order and, in the case of an order confirming the alteration, a printed copy of the memorandum as altered. The court may extend the time for delivery of documents to the Registrar of Companies in consequence of an application made for the cancellation of an alteration for such period as it may think proper (C.A. 1948, s. 5(7)). If the company defaults in giving notice or delivering any document as required, it and every officer in default is liable to a default fine (C.A. 1948, s. 5(8)).

If no application is made to the court concerning an alteration of the provisions of the company's memorandum with respect to its objects within twenty-one days from the date of the passing of the special resolution, the validity of the alteration cannot be questioned on the ground that it did not fall within one of the seven grounds in section 5(1) of the 1948 Act. This, coupled with the liberal attitude adopted by the courts in relation to jdr4 ii,2alterations of the objects of a company, effectively means that once all the members (and debenture holders, if appropriate) have consented to a proposed change in its objects, the company has virtually unlimited power to alter its objects.

In fact, there is only one comparatively recent reported case in which the application by a dissentient minority was accepted and the proposed alteration cancelled on the ground that the alteration was outside section 5. In *Re Hampstead Garden Suburb Trust Limited* [1962] Ch. 806 the memorandum provided that the balance of assets on a winding up should be given to an institution having objects similar to the objects of the company or, failing that, to some charitable object. A special resolution was passed altering the objects to provide that the surplus should be transferred to a specific company, whose objects were charitable but were not similar to those of the existing company. Pennycuick J. held that the purpose of the resolution was to seek to exclude altogether any institution or institutions having objects similar to the objects of the company and to direct the balance to a specified charity instead. This was not within the ambit of the words "to restrict or abandon any of the objects specified in the memorandum", the only provision in section 5 of the 1948 Act within which the proposed alteration could fall. The court accordingly refused to confirm the alteration. An alteration which is not within the terms of section 5(1) in respect of which an application is made to the court to have it set aside cannot, therefore, be confirmed.

There are, however, various older cases where the courts have refused to permit an alteration which falls within the terms of section 5 as a result of the representations of a dissentient minority (see for example *Re Cyclists' Touring Club* [1907] 1 Ch. 269 and *Re Waverley Hydropathic Co.* [1948] S.L.T. 152).

The limited liability clause

A limited company may re-register as an unlimited company in accordance with the Companies Act 1967 (as amended by the Companies Acts 1980 and 1981) and vice versa (C.A. 1967, ss. 43 and 44). The application required for the purposes of the re-registration must provide for the making of such alterations in the memorandum and articles of association of the company as are necessary to bring them, both in substance and in form, into conformity with the requirements of the Companies Acts 1948 to 1981. Further details concerning re-registration are contained in the chapter *Formation and Types of Company*.

The capital clause

The nominal share capital of the company may be altered by increasing, consolidating or dividing the shares, or by converting them into stock, or by cancelling unissued shares (C.A. 1948, s. 61). It may also be altered by means of a formal scheme involving a reduction in the nominal capital which is confirmed by the court (C.A. 1948, ss. 66, 67). Further details are contained in the chapter *Shares*.

As in the case of a change of name, any alteration of the nominal capital of a company should be reflected in its memorandum of association. Section 61 of the Companies Act 1948 states that a company limited by shares or by guarantee and having a share capital, may alter the conditions of its memorandum in accordance with the remaining provisions of that section. Similarly, section 67 of that Act permits the alteration of the memorandum of such a company if and so far as is necessary to reduce the amount of its share capital and shares consequent upon an approved reduction.

The factors considered on page 580 in respect of a change of name regarding the alteration of the memorandum of association, are therefore equally relevant in relation to the alteration of capital.

Optional clauses

Any provisions which the promoters or subsequent members of a company choose to have inserted in the memorandum of association of the company, over and above those required by the Companies Acts, and which could lawfully have been contained in the articles of association of the company instead of the memorandum may, in general, be altered by the company by special resolution. The alteration, as with an alteration to the objects clause, may be cancelled by the court upon an application by the same persons who may apply to cancel an alteration of the objects clause under section 5 unless the memorandum provides to the contrary (see page 581 above and C.A. 1948, s. 23). The ability to alter the optional conditions contained in the memorandum does not, however, apply where the memorandum itself prohibits the alteration of all or any of them, and no authority is conferred enabling the variation or abrogation of the special rights of any class of members (C.A. 1948, s. 23(2)).

If an optional provision is contained in the objects clause rather than elsewhere in the memorandum of association, the procedure which must be followed as regards any proposed alteration is that laid down by section 5 of the 1948 Act rather than by section 23 of that Act (*Re Hampstead Gardens Suburb Trust Limited* [1962] Ch. 806).

Disclosure and publicity requirements

As mentioned earlier, the memorandum of association must be registered at the Companies Registration Office on the incorporation of a company. In order to ensure that the memorandum reflects any alteration which is made to it both insofar as the public records are concerned and in relation to any copies which are subsequently circulated, whether to the members of a company or otherwise, the Companies Acts provide for disclosure in full of the alteration.

It has already been noted that section 5 of the Companies Act 1948 requires a printed copy of the memorandum of association of a company whose objects clause has been altered to be delivered to the Registrar of Companies within fifteen days from the alteration taking effect (see page 581).

Further, section 123 of the Companies Act 1948 requires that a printed copy of every special resolution a company passes, including one which makes, or evidences, an alteration to the memorandum of association of the company, must be forwarded within fifteen days to the Registrar of Companies and recorded by him. Other resolutions which, although not special resolutions, increase the nominal share capital and therefore alter, or evidence an alteration to, the memorandum of the company, must be delivered within fifteen days after the passing of the resolution to the Registrar of Companies, who must record the increase (C.A. 1948, s. 63).

When an alteration is made in the memorandum of association of a company, every copy of the memorandum issued after the date of the alteration must be in accordance with that alteration. If the company at any time after that date issues any copies of the memorandum which are not properly amended, it and every officer in default is liable to a fine (C.A. 1948, s. 25). In addition, a copy of every resolution which is required to be delivered to the Registrar of Companies by section 143 of the Companies Acts 1948 must also be embodied in or annexed to every copy of the articles of association of the company which is issued after the passing of the resolution.

As indicated earlier, section 9(5) of the European Communities Act 1972 requires a printed copy of the altered memorandum to be delivered to the Registrar within 15 days of the alteration. This is in addition to delivery of the amending special resolution required to be delivered pursuant to the Companies Acts. But where the objects clause is amended a printed copy of the altered memorandum need not be delivered under section 9(5) – as explained section 5 of the 1948 Act already imposes this requirement, but applies different time limits.

Each member of a company is entitled to a copy of its memorandum and articles of association upon payment of the sum of 5p or such lesser sum as the company may prescribe (C.A. 1948, s. 24).

As has been seen, there are a number of circumstances in which it is necessary to deliver a printed copy of the memorandum or articles of association of a company, or both, to the Registrar of Companies. For the purposes of satisfying these obligations, the Registrar of Companies has indicated in a Department of Trade notice that "printed", for all the purposes of the Companies Acts, includes in the context of printed documents those produced by letter press, gravure, lithography, "office" typeset, offset lithography, electrostatic photocopying, "photostat" or similar processes which are properly processed and washed, or stencil duplicating using wax stencils and black ink. However, no document will be acceptable if, in general appearance, format or durability, it is unsuitable for publication and use on the company's file. The notice states that experience has shown that documents produced by dye-line copying, spirit duplicating or thermo-copying are unsatisfactory.

Where the amendment to the memorandum and articles of association is small in extent, such as a change of name or change in the nominal capital, the Registrar of Companies will accept a copy of the original document amended by rubber stamping, typing or in some other permanent manner (but not a manuscript amendment). An alteration of a few lines or a complete short paragraph may be similarly dealt with, provided that the alteration is permanently fixed to the copy in such a way as to obscure the amended words. Alternatively, for more substantial amendments, pages may be replaced in a copy of the original provided the inserted material is "printed", although not necessarily in the same way as the original. In all cases, the alterations must be validated by the seal or an official stamp of the company.

Names

A registered company is, of course, a separate legal person and as such must have a name of its own. Naming a company is not, however, as straightforward as naming a child; the freedom of choice of the promoters is restricted in two ways. First, the name must include certain words, thus the final words of the company's name must be those designated by the Act to show its limited liability and indicate whether it is a public or a private company. Secondly, there are restrictions on the words that can be used. These limitations are designed to avoid confusion between different companies, and, to some extent, confusion as to the company's attributes. Thus a name may not be used if another company is already registered by that name, and the use of certain words which would tend to imply something about the status of the company requires the consent of the Secretary of State or of some other person or body nominated by him.

A company must be given a name before its independent legal existence can begin, for the name must appear in the memorandum of association (C.A. 1948, s. 2(1)(a)) and it is by this name that the company is incorporated (C.A. 1948, s. 13). A company's name is therefore of fundamental importance and provision is made to ensure that maximum publicity is accorded to the name (C.A. 1948, s. 108).

Fundamental changes have been introduced in the law governing company names by the Companies Act 1981. These changes are intended to implement the policy outlined in the Department of Trade's Consultative Document, *Companies Registration and Business Names: Proposals for Reducing the Functions of the Department of Trade*. As will be seen, this policy is to reduce civil service manning by minimising the discretionary powers left to the Secretary of State. At various points reference is made to the index of names kept by the Registrar of Companies under section 23 of the 1981 Act. It should be noted that the index is not restricted to companies' names but contains the names of the following bodies:

(a) companies within the meaning of the 1948 Act;

(b) overseas companies within the meaning of section 23(2) of the 1981 Act;

(c) bodies to which any provision of the 1948 Act applies by virtue of section 435 of that Act;

(d) limited partnerships registered under the 1907 Act;

586

(e) companies within the meaning of the Companies Act (Northern Ireland) 1960 (for which note 1982 S.I. 1654); and

(f) societies registered under the Industrial and Provident Societies Acts.

This chapter considers the rules governing the choice of a company's name and the changing of a company's name, followed by a short consideration of the common law restriction on the choice of names through the tort of passing off. Then, finally, the limitations on the use of business names by companies and the provisions requiring publicity to be given to a company's name are dealt with.

Use of "limited" and "public limited company"

The general requirements

The final words of the name of a registered company reveal both that the company enjoys limited liability status and, since the reclassification adopted by the Companies Act 1980, whether the company is public or private. The name does not, however, distinguish between a company limited by shares and one limited by guarantee nor, if the terminal word "limited" is missing, does the name indicate whether the entity is an unlimited company or some other form of association.

A private company, whether limited by shares or by guarantee, must, subject to section 25 of the 1981 Act, end its name with the word 'limited' (C.A. 1948, s. 2(1)(a) and C.A. 1980, Sch. 3, para. 3). A public company must end its name with the words "public limited company" (C.A. 1980, s. 2(2)). These final words may be abbreviated to "ltd." and "p.l.c." respectively (C.A. 1980, s. 78) and the name may be registered either in the full or the abbreviated form. Section 78 does not however, expressly authorise the abbreviations "plc", or "PLC" "Plc" or even "P.L.C.". Furthermore these words may be used only by the relevant type of company and even then only as the final words of its name. Thus sections 22(1)(a) and (b) of the 1981 Act provide that a company shall not be registered by a name which includes otherwise than at the end the words "limited", "unlimited" or "public limited company". Also the unauthorised use of these suffixes constitutes a criminal offence under section 439 of the 1948 Act in the case of "limited", and section 76(1) of the 1980 Act in the case of "public limited company". Moreover section 76(2) makes it an offence for a public company to use a name which may reasonably be expected to give the impression that it is a private company in circumstances where the fact that it is a public company is likely to be material to anyone.

The section 25 exemption

A private company will be exempt from the requirement to terminate its name with the word "limited" if it satisfies the conditions in section 25 of the 1981 Act (this exemption does not extend to public companies: CA 1980, Sch. 3 para 5.) Previously this could be achieved only by obtaining a licence under section 19 of the Companies Act 1948, each application for which involved an individual exercise of discretion. Section 25, however, provides for automatic exemption if the statutory conditions are satisfied. The exemption is available only to private companies limited by guarantee or to private companies limited by shares which had obtained a licence under section 19 before that section was repealed. The conditions which must be complied with are listed in section 25(2). These are first that the company's objects must be "the promotion of commerce, art, science, education, religion, charity or any profession and anything incidental or conducive to any of those objects". Secondly, the company's constitution must contain provisions requiring that any profits be used solely to promote those objects, prohibiting the payment of dividends and providing that if the company is wound up its assets are not to be returned to its members but rather are to be transferred to another similar body.

If a company satisfying these requirements wishes to register or re-register by a name which omits the word "limited" a statutory declaration in the form prescribed by section 25(4) should be made. The Registrar may accept this declaration as sufficient evidence of compliance with the statutory requirements and, indeed, may refuse registration unless such a declaration is made. Once a company is registered by a name which omits the word "limited" it is forbidden to change its constitution in such a way that it no longer complies with section 25 (sections 25(5) and (9)). Furthermore, if the company breaches any of the requirements of section 25(2) the Secretary of State may order that its name be changed by resolution of the directors so as to terminate with "limited". After such an order has been made the company's name may be changed once more to exclude "limited" only if the approval of the Secretary of State is obtained. Even if a company enjoys the section 25 exemption it is still subject to section 9(7)(c) of the European Communities Act 1972, which provides that despite the exemption all business letters and order forms of the company must include a statement that it is a limited company (see also page 561).

Welsh registered office

A company's memorandum must state whether its registered office is to be situate in England, in Scotland or in Wales (C.A. 1948, s. 2(1)(b) and C.A. 1976, s. 30(1)). Where the memorandum states that the registered office is to be in Wales the Welsh equivalents of the prescribed terminal words may be adopted. These are "cyfyngedig" for "limited" and "cwmni cyfyngedig cyhoeddus" for "public limited company" which may in turn be abbreviated to "cyf." and "c.c.c." (C.A. 1980, s. 78). It should be noted, however, that even if the Welsh form of nomenclature is adopted the fact that it is a private limited company (C.A. 1976, s. 30(5)) or a public limited company (C.A. 1980, s. 77), as the case may be, must be stated in English on all prospectuses, bill heads, letter paper, notices and other official publications of the company and a notice to like effect must be conspicuously displayed in every place where the company's business is conducted (see also page 578).

Restricted words and expressions

By section 17 of the 1948 Act a company could not be registered by a name which was, in the opinion of the Secretary of State, "undesirable". This discretion was exercised according to the non-binding guidelines contained in the Practice Note (No. C 186) of September 7, 1972, which included the stipulation that a name would be considered undesirable if it was "too like" that of an existing company. Thus an individual decision involving the exercise of discretion had to be made concerning each application for registration, and in 1979 nearly 63,000 companies were incorporated in England and Wales. The Companies Act 1981, however, seeks to revert to a more objective approach with the result that in the great majority of cases a company's promoters should be able to decide for themselves whether the proposed name will be accepted. Thus the previous practice of obtaining at an early stage a non-binding indication of the acceptability of a particular name is now unnecessary.

The classes of words and expressions the use of which is controlled by the 1981 Act may be divided into four groups. The first two are absolute prohibitions, whilst use may be made of words in the third and fourth categories if the consent of the Secretary of State or of some other body nominated by him is obtained.

Names which are the same

A name will not be accepted for registration if it is the same as one already appearing in the index kept under section 23 (C.A. 1981, s. 22(1)(c)). The Jenkins Committee (Cmnd. 1749 para. 450) recommended that promoters should be able to reserve a name for 30 days so that they could, with assurance, proceed to order printed stationery etc. prior to incorporation. This recommendation has not been implemented and thus until the actual date of registration the promoters run the risk of another business getting in first with the name. In deciding whether two names are the same certain minor differences are to be disregarded by virtue of section 22(3). These are the definite article where it is the first word of the name, and "company", "and company", "company limited", "and company limited", "limited", "unlimited" and "public limited company" or their abbreviations or Welsh equivalents where they are the final words of the name. Type and case of letters, spaces between letters, accents and punctuation marks are also to be ignored and "and" and "&" are treated as being the same.

Although two names which are very similar may now be registered three points should be remembered in such cases. First, a company may still be called upon to change its name within twelve months on the ground that its name is too like that of an existing entry on the index (C.A. 1981, s. 24(2)). Secondly, the fact that a corporate name has been registered affords no protection in an action for the tort of passing off (see below). Thirdly, since the Registrar does not check the Index of Trade Marks, registration under the Companies Acts does not guarantee that there has been no trade mark infringement. The promoters should, therefore, make a separate search at the Trade Mark Registry.

Names which are offensive or unlawful

A name will not be accepted for registration if the Secretary of State is of the opinion that it is offensive or that its use would constitute a criminal offence (sections 22 (1)(d) and (e)). In this case, therefore, some discretion does remain but the number of cases in which it is likely to be activated will be very small.

Names suggesting a governmental connection

A name may only be registered with the approval of the Secretary of State if, in his opinion, it is likely to give the impression that the company is connected with Her Majesty's Government or with any local authority (section 22(2)(a)).

Other restricted words

Certain words may be used only with the consent of the Secretary of State or of some other person or body appointed by him. Some words are already controlled by other statutes. Thus, for example, under section 36 of the Banking Act 1979 only a person authorised under that section is permitted to use a name which may "reasonably be understood to indicate that he is a bank or banker or is carrying on a banking business", and section 6 of the Geneva Convention Act 1957 forbids the use of certain emblems and designations including "Red Cross" without the consent of the Army Council. In addition the Secretary of State may now make regulations under section 31 of the Companies Act 1981 restricting the use of other words or expressions. The Secretary of State has exercised this power by 1981 S.I. No. 1685 and 1982 S.I. No. 1653. In the table set out below words in column (1) require his approval for use in a company's corporate name (or in a business name, see below). Column (2) lists the government department or other body which may object to the use of the name (and to which an approach must therefore be made under section 31(2) before the Secretary of State can give his approval).

(1)	(2)
Abortion	Department of Health and Social Security
Apothecary	Worshipful Company of Apothecaries or Pharmaceutical Society of Great Britain

(1)	(2)
Association	
Assurance	
Assurer	
Authority	
Benevolent	
Board	
Breed ⎫	Ministry of Agriculture, Fisheries and
Breeder ⎬	Food
Breeding ⎭	
British	
Building Society	
Chamber of Commerce	
Chamber of Industry	
Chamber of Trade	
Charitable ⎫	Charity Commission or Scottish Home
Charity ⎭	and Health Department
Charter	
Chartered	
Chemist	
Chemistry	
Contact Lens	General Optical Council
Co-operative	
Council	
Dental ⎫	General Dental Council
Dentistry ⎭	
District Nurse	Panel of Assessors in District Nurse Training
Duke	Home Office or Scottish Home and Health Department
England	
English	
European	
Federation	
Friendly Society	
Foundation	
Fund	
Giro	
Great Britain	
Group	
Health Centre ⎫	Department of Health and Social
Health Service ⎭	Security
Health Visitor	Council for the Education and Training of Health Visitors
Her Majesty ⎫	Home Office or Scottish Home and
His Majesty ⎭	Health Department
Holding	
Industrial and Provident Society	
Institute	
Institution	
Insurance	
Insurer	
International	
Ireland	
Irish	
King	Home Office or Scottish Home and Health Department
Midwife ⎫	Central Midwives Board or Central
Midwifery ⎭	Midwives Board for Scotland

(1)	(2)
National	
Nurse } Nursing }	General Nursing Council for England and Wales or General Nursing Council for Scotland
Nursing Home	Department of Health and Social Security
Patent	
Patentee	
Police	Home Office or Scottish Home and Health Department
Polytechnic	Department of Education and Science
Post Office	
Pregnancy Termination	Department of Health and Social Security
Prince } Princess } Queen }	Home Office or Scottish Home and Health Department
Reassurance	
Reassurer	
Register	
Registered	
Reinsurance	
Reinsurer	
Royal } Royale } Royalty }	Home Office or Scottish Home and Health Department
Scotland	
Scottish	
Sheffield	
Society	
Special School	Department of Education and Science
Stock Exchange	
Trade Union	
Trust	
United Kingdom	
University	Department of Education and Science
Wales	
Welsh	
Windsor	Home Office or Scottish Home and Health Department

Where two Government departments or other bodies are specified in the alternative in Column (2) of the above table, the second alternative is to be treated as specified,

(a)   in the case of the corporate name of a company,

(i)   if the company has not yet been registered and its principal or only place of business in Great Britain is to be in Scotland or, if it will have no place of business in Great Britain, its proposed registered office is in Scotland, and

(ii)   if the company is already registered and its principal or only place of business in Great Britain is in Scotland or, if it has no place of business in Great Britain, its registered office is in Scotland, and

(b) in the case of a business name, if the principal or only place of the business carried on or to be carried on in Great Britain is or is to be in Scotland,

and the first alternative is to be treated as specified in any other case.

Changing a company's name

Voluntary change

A company may at any time change its name by special resolution (C.A. 1981, s. 24(1)). There is no longer any need for the approval of the Secretary of State but the new name must, of course, comply with all the requirements dealt with above. The Registrar will issue an altered certificate of incorporation, which must be published in the *London Gazette* (European Communities Act 1972, s. 9(3)). It is only from the date of issue of the altered certificate that the alteration is effective (C.A. 1981, s. 24(1) and (6)). Despite the change of name the company remains the same legal person as it was before the change and therefore s. 24(7) provides that "a change of name by a company under this section shall not affect any rights or obligations of the company or render defective any legal proceedings by or against the company. . . ".

The procedural requirements for a name charge are discussed at pages 579 and 584.

Compulsory change

The Secretary of State has the power to call on a company to change its name in the following circumstances:

(1) *Section 24(2)*: If a company is registered by a name which is the same as or too like a name already appearing on the index or which should have appeared in the index the Secretary of State may, within 12 months, direct the company to change its name. The Act does not specify how the change is to be effected, thus it is arguable that an ordinary resolution would suffice. Even though two similar names may now be registered this section will presumably allow aggrieved companies to make representations to the Secretary of State to persuade him to exercise this power.

(2) *Section 24(3)*: The Secretary of State may, within five years of the date of registration, direct a company to change its name if he believes that misleading information was provided for the purposes of registration.

(3) *C.A. 1967, s. 46*: This section allows the Secretary of State to direct a company to change its name at any time if the name by which it is registered "gives so misleading an indication of the nature of its activities as to be likely to cause harm to the public". Unusually section 46(3) allows the company concerned to apply to the court, which has an unfettered discretion to set aside or confirm the order. (Elsewhere there

is no appeal against the exercise of the Secretary of State's powers, although it was held in *R* v. *Registrar of Companies* [1912] 3 K.B. 23 that mandamus would issue in an appropriate case).

(4) *Overseas companies*: If an overseas company has a corporate name which would not be permitted a company registered under the Companies Act 1948, it may be called upon to use a different name in Great Britain. Section 31 of the 1976 Act, as amended by section 27 of the 1981 Act, provides that if the name would not have been allowed under section 22.of the 1981 Act, or if the name is too like a name appearing in the index the Secretary of State may, within 12 months of the date on which the overseas company complied with section 407 of the 1948 Act (delivery of documents on commencement of business in Great Britain) serve a notice on the overseas company stating why its corporate name is considered objectionable and directing the company not to carry on business in Great Britain under its corporate name. The company may then register an alternative name approved by the Secretary of State for use in Great Britain, and this alternative is treated as its corporate name for all purposes of the law applying in Great Britain.

Swopping names

In group reorganisations or take-overs it is sometimes desired for two companies to swop their respective names. This can be achieved with the assistance of the staff at the Registrar of Companies, an explanatory letter in advance of the date of swopping usually being all that is required.

The tort of passing off

The registration of a company's name should prevent another company being registered with the same name but will not prevent a company being registered with a similar name or a business other than a company operating under a similar name. In the former case the simplest first step will be to seek to persuade the Secretary of State to exercise his power under section 24(2) of the 1981 Act, but an alternative, and in the latter case probably the only effective procedure will be to institute an action for the tort of passing off. This is essentially an action based on the loss of goodwill associated with a name as a result of the use by another of a name so similar as to be likely to mislead the public. Damages may be recovered but the most useful remedy is an injunction to restrain the use of the similar name by the newcomer; indeed if the facts are discovered at an early enough stage an injunction may be obtained to prevent a company being registered by the objectionable name (e.g. *Tussaud* v. *Tussaud* (1890) 44 Ch.D. 678).

In *Warnink* v. *Townend* [1979] 2 All E.R. 927, 932–3 Lord Diplock identified the requirements essential to success in establishing a cause of action for passing off: there must have been a misrepresentation made by a trader in the course of his trade to his prospective customers or the ultimate consumers of his goods or services and damage to the goodwill of the plaintiff's business must have resulted or be likely to result therefrom, such damage being a reasonably foreseeable consequence of the misrepresentation. The action will only succeed, therefore, if there is "a common field of activity" so that the public could reasonably be misled into confusing the two businesses. In *McCulloch* v. *May* [1947] 2 All E.R. 845 the radio broadcaster known as Uncle Mac failed to prevent the defendants marketing a product named Uncle Mac's Puffed Wheat, and the same hurdle defeated the plaintiffs in *Wombles* v. *Wombles Skips* [1977] R.P.C. 99 and in *Tavener Rutledge* v. *Trexapalm* [1977] R.P.C. 275. The need for there to have been some misrepresentation is illustrated by the recent case of *Cadbury-Schweppes* v. *Pub Squash* [1981] 1 W.L.R. 193 (P.C.); the tort of passing off had not been committed for although the defendant had deliberately taken advantage of the plaintiff's efforts to develop a new market in soft drinks and create a new demand he had never suggested that his product was in any way connected with the plaintiff. The Judicial Committee of the Privy Council also stressed that such cases involve an element of public policy; the court must balance the individual's right to protect the goodwill engendered by his product against the public interest in fair competition.

Business names

Despite vigorous parliamentary opposition the Companies Act 1981 abolished the register of business names kept under the Registration of Business Names Act 1916. This register had, by virtue of section 58 of the Companies Act 1947, included the business names of companies where these differed from their corporate names. The index kept under section 23 of the 1981 Act does not include business names; the Act deals with business names by controlling the names which can be used and by requiring that publicity be given to the correct corporate name where the company is trading under a business name (the Act also includes similar restrictions and controls in relation to the use of business names by partnerships and sole traders).

Choice of business name

Where a company capable of being wound up under the Companies Act 1948 has a place of business in Great Britain and carries on business in Great Britain under a name other than its corporate name, the business name must not suggest a connection with the government or any local authority, or contain any of the words prescribed in regulations under section 31 without the written approval of the Secretary of State (section 28). The regulations made under 1981 S.I. No 1685, referred to on page 590 above, cover business names as well as company names, and approval of both the Secretary of State and the bodies listed in column (2) of the table on pages 590 to 592 must be obtained before a business name can include a word or expression set out in column (1) of that table.

Publicity to be given to corporate name

A company using a business name must state its corporate name in a legible form, on all business letters, orders for goods and services, invoices, receipts and written demands for payment of business debts and must also state therein an address in Great Britain where the service of documents will be effective. A notice containing the same information must also be prominently displayed in any premises where the business is carried on and to which customers or suppliers have access (section 29). This duplicates section 108 of the 1948 Act to a large extent for it was held in *Maxform* v. *Mariani and Goodville* [1979] 2 Lloyd's Rep. 387 that the publicity requirements of section 108 referred to the corporate name rather than the business name of the company. It should be noted, however, that section 29 is wider than section 108 in that it applies to orders for services which are apparently outside the scope of section 108 (see *East Midlands Electricity Board* v. *Grantham* [1980] C.L.Y. 271).

Disclosure and publicity

Section 108 of the Companies Act 1948 seeks to ensure that maximum publicity is given to a company's name. It provides that the company's name must be fixed in a conspicuous position on the outside of every place where the company does business; furthermore the name must be mentioned "in all business letters of the company and in all notices and other official publications of the company, and in all bills of exchange, promissory notes, endorsements, cheques and orders for money or goods. . .". In addition to the criminal sanction for a breach of this section, it is provided by section 108(4) that the officer responsible shall be "personally liable to the holder of the bill of exchange, promissory note, cheque or order for money or goods for the amount thereof unless it is duly paid by the company". The original intention of this provision seems to have been to protect those who, because of a breach of the section, did not realise they were dealing with a company of limited liability (see *Penrose* v. *Martyr* (1858) El. Bl. & Bl 499). Since then, however, the section has been interpreted in a "strict and even rigid . . . and Draconian" way (per Lord Hunter in *Scottish and Newcastle Breweries* v. *Blair* 1967 S.L.T. 72, 74), even to the extent that the section was activated where an ampersand was omitted from the company's name on its cheque in *Hendon* v. *Adelman* (1973) 117 S.J. 631 (see also *British Airways Board v Parish* [1979] 2 Lloyd's Rep 361 and, for a case where the court refused to apply section 108(4), *Banque de l'Indochine et de Suez v Euroseas Group Finance Co. Limited* [1981] 3 All E.R. 198. See also the cases referred to on page 403 and the article (1982) 3 Co. Law 156).

Overseas Companies

With the constant emergence and growth of multi-national corporations and the ever-increasing popularity of the United Kingdom as a base for the multi-national executive, the various provisions in United Kingdom legislation regarding foreign companies assume increasing importance. The general statute law governing the registration by a foreign company of a place of business in Great Britain, and other matters like the issue of securities by such a company to persons in Great Britain are embodied in Part X of the Companies Act 1948. However, it is also necessary in considering some of the sections in Part X to take into account the provisions of the Prevention of Fraud (Investments) Act, 1958, and accordingly this chapter also touches on the relevant sections of that Act.

Place of business

Part X of the 1948 Act applies to all "overseas companies", which section 406 defines to mean companies incorporated outside Great Britain which have established a place of business within Great Britain. The expression "place of business" is not defined in the Act – the question whether such a place exists in Great Britain is primarily one of fact. One must look for a place occupied by the overseas company from which it conducts its business. Occupation of a place for business purposes must mean a relatively permanent arrangement. The mere fact that a director resides in a hotel when he comes to Great Britain and transacts business there, was not considered a place of business in the case of *Re Tovarishestvo Manufactur Liudvig-Rabenek* [1944] Ch. 404. Nor is it considered that an overseas company acquiring and holding property in Great Britain for investment purposes will have established a place of business merely by virtue of that fact. However, section 415 of the 1948 Act states that the expression "place of business" includes a share transfer or share registration office. Care should therefore be taken not to keep share register books or share transfer books of an overseas company at an office in Great Britain, unless it is proposed to register a place of business of that company under Part X of the Act. This could apply, for example, to property holding companies incorporated in jurisdictions where companies may be acquired "off the shelf", and where share transfer and register books are not kept in that jurisdiction but instead sent to the purchaser of the company with the incorporation documents, including, in many cases, transfers signed in blank by the incorporators. If those books and registers were to be kept at an address in Great Britain for the purpose of maintaining up to date records of shareholders, that could constitute a share transfer office requiring registration as a place of business under the Act. Subject to that point, it seems that the overseas company must, in order to have a place of business in Great Britain, occupy premises here which, or part of which, it lawfully occupies and from which its employees carry on activities in furtherance of the purpose for which the company exists.

By carrying on business through an agent with offices in Great Britain, an overseas company is not itself establishing a place of business there (*Lord Advocate v Huron & Erie Loan Co* [1911] S.C. 612). In that case, the Lord President, commenting on the same phrase in section 274 of the Companies (Consolidation) Act 1908, stated that "when the legislature selected the phrase 'establishes a place of business' it meant something other than 'carrying on business'." The company must have a 'local habitation' of its own. Although the company carried on business in this country by canvassing for loans, the loan contracts, comprising the issue of debentures and so forth, were executed by the overseas company in its foreign domicile. The services of agents, who were paid commissions, were used here and they distributed prospectuses and supplied information in respect of the terms of the loans. Nevertheless, it was held that this activity did not constitute the establishment of a place of business in Great Britain. If the agents in question had described themselves as "representatives" of the overseas company and had operated from a "representative office" of that company in Great Britain, it is submitted that this decision would have gone the other way.

If an overseas company were to carry on business in Great Britain through a subsidiary company, that would not necessarily involve its establishing a place of business in Great Britain (*Deverall v Grant Advertising Inc*. [1954] 3 All E.R. 389). In that case a number of factors were considered as leading to this conclusion. First, there was "no visible sign or physical indication" that the premises were a place of business of the overseas company. Secondly, although the premises were let by the president of the overseas company to various other companies, and the subsidiary was allowed to occupy part of the premises, the subsidiary carried out only its own business in the premises. It was the place of business of the subsidiary and it was not suggested that the subsidiary was carrying on any business other than its own. Thirdly, although the overseas company appointed a regional director who also used the premises, Jenkins L.J. decided that the regional director's functions were those of a consultant and adviser and, perhaps, were those of a "watch dog for the interests of" the overseas company. The regional director was found not to have carried on any trading or business activities, or to have entered into any contracts on behalf of the overseas company of which it could be said that the company had established a place of business within Great Britain.

It must be noted that not only does the establishment of such a place of business require an overseas company to comply with the provisions of

Part X, but it also constitutes a submission by that company to the jurisdiction of the English courts (*The Madrid* [1937] 1 All E.R. 216).

Registration and similar obligations

There is no obligation on an overseas company to register under Part X until it has actually established a place of business here. Section 407 of the 1948 Act requires all overseas companies to deliver to the Registrar for registration, within one month after the establishment of the place of business:

(1) a certified copy of the instrument defining the constitution of the company, and a certified translation if it is not in English;

(2) a list, in the prescribed form (Form F2), of the directors ("directors" being widely defined by section 415 to include any person in accordance with whose directions or instructions the directors of the company are accustomed to act) and secretary (or any person occupying the position of secretary by whatever name called), specifying,

    (a) (i) in the case of a director who is an individual, his full name and usual residential address, and his nationality and business occupation (if he has no occupation, particulars of any other British directorships should be stated), and

      (ii) in the case of a secretary who is an individual, his full name and usual residential address;

    (b) in the case of a corporation, its corporate name and registered or principal office;

(3) a list, in the prescribed form (Form F3), of the names and addresses of one or more persons resident in Great Britain authorised to accept on behalf of the company service of process and any notices required to be served on the company; and

(4) a list, on Form F1, of the documents referred to above, plus a statutory declaration on Form F14 of the date the place of business was established.

If any alteration is made in these documents, the company must register the particulars of the alteration within the prescribed time in accordance with section 409 of the 1948 Act (see Appendix 5). Paragraph 5 of the Companies (Forms) Regulations 1979 provides a prescribed time, in the case of an alteration to which section 409(1)(c) applies, of twenty-one days after the making of such an alteration, and in any other case of twenty-one days after the date on which notice of such alteration or change could, in due course of post and if despatched with due diligence, have been received in Great Britain.

Service of process

An overseas company can be "sufficiently served" by any process or notice required to be served being sent to the address of the person or persons mentioned in section 407(1)(c) of the 1948 Act. Even if the company does not have a place of business in Great Britain at the time of service, service on the person described in section 407(1)(c) of the Act is good service (*Employers' Liability Assurance Corp. v Sedgwick, Collins & Co.* [1927] A.C. 95). In this case, the overseas company was put into liquidation by the government of its place of incorporation and yet service was allowed. The requisite person's name had been left on the file and no attempt had been made to remove it – only a notification of the liquidation had been given. However, evidence existed to show that, even after cessation of business, that person had conducted correspondence on behalf of the overseas company.

The law stated above does not apply in cases where section 412(b) of the 1948 Act (which deals with a person who cannot be served) applies: *Deverall v Grant Advertising Inc.* [1954] 3 All E.R. 389. However, if the company's authority had been withdrawn prior to the person being served, service upon him would not constitute good service on the company. Section 412 provides that, where the company defaults in notifying the Registrar of the name and address of a person authorised to accept service, or where the person cannot be served for any reason, service on the company can be effected by sending the notice to any place of business established by the company in Great Britain. However, the decision in *Deverall's case* indicates that the notice must not be sent to a former place of business. The place of business must exist at the time of service. In the case of *The Madrid* (1937) 1 All E.R. 216, the person named on the file was abroad, but it was held to be proper service in those circumstances to leave the particular notice at the place where the share transfer office of the company was established at the time. Finally, as pointed out by the Jenkins Committee Report (Cmnd. 1740, para. 516), there seems to be no procedure for removing the person's name from the register except by substituting another.

Publicity

Section 411 provides that every overseas company having a place of business in Great Britain, must state its name and country of incorporation on all its bill-heads and letter paper, and in all notices and other official publications of the company. The company must also "conspicuously exhibit" its name and country of incorporation at every place where it carries on business in Great Britain. Furthermore, if the liability of the members of the company is limited, notice of that fact must be stated on all the company's business stationery, and must be affixed on every place where it carries on business in Great Britain.

Delivery of documents and penalties

Section 413 requires that all documents to be registered by an overseas company must be delivered to the Registrar at the registration office in England and Wales or Scotland, depending on where the company has established its place of business. If the company ceases to have a place of business, it must notify the Registrar in accordance with section 413(2), and the date when the notice is received is the date when the obligation of the company to deliver any documents to the Registrar ceases.

The penalty, albeit nominal, for a breach of any of the provisions of sections 407 to 413 is laid down in section 414. Every officer or agent of the company, "who knowingly and wilfully authorises" the default by the company is liable to the penalty prescribed in Schedule 2 to the Companies Act 1980.

Regulation of name

Section 31 of the Companies Act 1976, as amended by section 27 of the Companies Act 1981, allows the Secretary of State to regulate the name under which an overseas company may carry on business in Great Britain. The Secretary may serve a notice on the company to the effect that the company's name should not have been registered, where it is a name which would be precluded from registration by section 22 of the 1981 Act had the company been formed under the Companies Acts, or is too similar to a name in the index of names kept by the Registrar under section 23 of the 1981 Act (see page 594). This notice (accompanied by reasons) must be served within twelve months after the "relevent date", or if that date was before February 26, 1982, six months after that date. The relevant date means the date of compliance by the company with section 407 of the 1948 Act or, if there already has been a change of name, with section 409 of that Act.

Business name

An overseas company which has a place of business in Great Britain and which carries on business here under a business name, is subject to the provisions in section 28 of the Companies Act 1981 restricting the use of certain names (see C.A. 1981, s. 28(1)(c) and C.A. 1948, s. 400). It follows that such a company is also required to comply with the same publicity requirements in section 29 of the 1981 Act (see generally the chapter *Names*).

Charges

Section 106 of the 1948 Act, as amended, requires the registration of charges by an overseas company with an established place of business in England or Scotland if the charge is on English or Scottish property. As explained in the chapter *Company Charges*, at page 203, a lender may need to ensure a charge is registered even if the borrower itself has not registered under Part X, because registration or non-registration is not conclusive as to whether there is a "place of business" in Great Britain: *N.V. Slavenburg's Bank v International Resources Limited* [1980] 1 All E.R. 955. The Registrar of Companies has now established a

Tolley's Company Law

"Slavenburg" register (see generally *Law Society's Gazette*, September 2, 1981 and *Gazette Digest*, No 82/1). This is an index of companies which have not registered under Part X, but which have admitted a place of business in Great Britain for section 95 Companies Act 1948 purposes.

Channel Islands and Isle of Man Companies

Where a company is incorporated in the Channel Islands or in the Isle of Man and has a place of business in England or Scotland, section 416 of the 1948 Act, as amended by the 1981 Act, provides that all the provisions of the Companies Act requiring documents to be forwarded or delivered to or filed with the Registrar, shall apply to the company as if it were registered in England or Scotland (or in both England and Scotland if it has places of business in both England and Scotland). But the company is *not* required to file a printed copy of any altered memorandum under section 5(7) of the 1948 Act or section 9(5) of the European Community Act 1972, or of resolutions effecting changes to the memorandum or articles under section 143 of the 1948 Act. Nor need it notify changes of directors or secretary under section 200(4) of the 1948 Act, though see *Registration obligations*, above.

It seems however that a contract would not be rendered illegal merely by reason of the failure of such a company to comply with sections 407 or 416 of the Act: *Curragh Investments v Cook* [1974] 1 W.L.R.1559. This case concerned a company incorporated in the Isle of Man which entered into a written contract to sell property in England. The purchaser refused to complete the contract when he discovered that the vendor company had not complied with sections 407 and 416 of the Act. Megarry J. (as he then was) held that there was not a sufficient nexus between the failure to comply with the statutory provisions and the contract – the breach of sections 407 and 416 of the Act was totally unconnected with the covenants of title in the contract, and did not therefore render the contract illegal.

Prospectus requirements

Every prospectus of an overseas company inviting subscription for its shares or debentures in Great Britain must, in accordance with section 411 of the 1948 Act, state the country in which the company is incorporated and if the liability of the members of the company is limited, the fact that it is so limited.

Section 417(1) prohibits the issue, circulation or distribution in Great Britain by any person of any prospectus offering for subscription shares in or debentures of an overseas company, unless the prospectus is dated and complies with various provisions, most of which are contained in Part X of the Act and in the Fourth Schedule to the Act. The prospectus provisions are wider than the other sections of Part X, in that section 417 applies to companies incorporated or to be incorporated outside

Great Britain *and whether or not the company has established, or when formed will establish, a place of business in Great Britain*. Any condition requiring an applicant for shares or debentures to waive compliance with the requirement in section 417(1) is rendered void by section 417(2). Furthermore, section 417(3) provides that no form of application for shares in or debentures of such a company may be issued to any person in Great Britain, unless the form is accompanied by a prospectus complying with the 1948 Act. There is an exemption from the provisions of section 417 where a prospectus or form of application is issued to existing shareholders. The provisions are also relaxed where a prospectus is issued in respect of shares which are in all respects uniform with shares previously issued and for the time being dealt on The Stock Exchange, London. Section 417(5) provides that, in such circumstances, only the requirement in section 417 that the prospectus be dated need be observed. In addition to complying with the various requirements as to the contents of the prospectus, the prospectus must first be registered in accordance with section 420 by lodging a copy, certified by the chairman and two other directors as having been approved by the board of directors or the managing body of the company, with the Registrar.

Section 417(4) relieves from liability, for non-compliance with or contravention of the requirements as to the contents of a prospectus, a director or other person responsible for the prospectus, (a) if he was not aware of the non-disclosure, or (b) if the non-compliance or contravention was due to an honest mistake on his part, or (c) if the court excuses him on the ground that the breach was immaterial or that he ought reasonably to be excused. Further, no liability is incurred for failure to disclose in the prospectus a director's interest unless he had actual knowledge of the matter not disclosed.

On the request of the applicant under section 418, an exemption from compliance with the requirements of the Fourth Schedule to the Companies Act may be given by or on behalf of The Stock Exchange if compliance is regarded as being unduly burdensome.

Where the prospectus includes a statement made by an "expert", the expert must give his written consent to the inclusion of the statement in the form and context in which it is included (section 419(1)(a)). "Expert" is defined by section 419(2) to include any person whose profession gives authority to a statement made by him. In practice, this provision is construed to require any statement contained in a prospectus which is attributed expressly to an authoritative source to be accompanied by a written consent including such matters as graphs or statistical data prepared by and attributed to the organisation which prepared them. Moreover, section 419(1)(b) makes it unlawful to issue or circulate the prospectus if the prospectus does not have the effect, where an application is made in pursuance thereof, of rendering all persons concerned bound by all the provisions (other than penal provisions) of sections 50 and 51 of the 1948 Act as far as applicable.

Where the prospectus is destined for "professionals" only – that is, "any person whose ordinary business it is to buy or sell shares or debentures whether as principal or agent" – section 423(2) removes it from the definition of "prospectus" for the purposes of Part X, and it is not therefore deemed to be an offer to the public. As such, it may be circulated to professionals without infringing section 417. Whilst there is no statutory guidance as to what constitutes a person whose business involves the acquisition and disposal of shares or debentures, it would probably cover bankers, insurance companies, discount houses, stock-brokers, institutional investors and investment managers. It should also cover insurance brokers, solicitors and accountants where, in actual practice, their business involves acquiring and disposing of securities, for example, in connection with the administration of trusts and of estates. The test is wider than looking to whether such a person holds a licence to deal in securities. Many persons who might otherwise have required such a dealer's licence, may nevertheless carry on such a business on behalf of a firm of recognised stockbrokers or may effect dealings with or through the agency of a stockbroker or licensed dealer in a manner covered by the terms of section 2 of the Prevention of Fraud (Investments) Act 1958. That section enables such business activities to be carried on without the need for a dealer's licence as required under section 1 of the 1958 Act; and it is precisely that range of transactions within the saving provisions of section 2 which are likely in practice to be effected by "professionals" of the kind listed above.

It is not possible to avoid the provisions of section 417 by having the "professional" forward the prospectus material on to his client. Such a practice would contravene section 14 of the Prevention of Fraud (Investments) Act 1958.

Under section 14 of that Act, it is an offence to distribute circulars if they contain either an invitation to persons to enter into an agreement to do any of the acts specified in section 13 of that Act, or information calculated to lead to entry into such an agreement (see *Hudson v Bishop Cavanagh (Commodities) Limited* [1981] 131 N.L.J. 1238 for a recent case on the meaning of "circular"). The distribution of circulars to professionals does not contravene section 14 because of the provision, similar in effect to section 423(2) of the Act, which is contained in section 14(5). But, first, the professional is prohibited from distributing the circular in question to his client, other than at that client's specific request (in which case it would seem to be stretching the meaning of the word to call that a "distribution" by the professional of the circular in question). Secondly, section 14(1)(a)(ii) makes it clear that, where any information is provided in such a circular which is calculated to lead directly or indirectly to the doing of any of those acts described in section 13 by the recipient of the information, then the distribution will be unlawful. If it were the intention of the party distributing the prospectus that its contents should be imparted to the clients of the professional concerned, the Department of Trade would probably take the view that the distribution of the circular, albeit to a profes-sional, contravened section 14. The provision of material exclusively for professionals is not therefore of very great help in reaching the public at large.

It is important to recognise that not every circular which may be lawfully distributed to the public under the Prevention of Fraud (Investments) Act 1958 can necessarily be lawfully distributed in compliance with the provisions of the Companies Act. However, section 14(2) of the 1958 Act does remove the restriction on distribution of circulars in relation to a prospectus which complies with the relevant contents provisions of the Companies Act.

As regards the application of the Prevention of Fraud (Investments) Act to acts taking place outside the U.K., although there is a presumption against the extraterritorial application of statutes, there have been newspaper reports of prosecutions where, for example, unauthorised material was prepared in the U.K. and sent to Holland, and there would probably be a prosecution if unauthorised material were sent from outside the U.K. to the public in the U.K. For example, the posting in Northern Ireland of letters to England to obtain property by deception was held in *R v Baxter* [1971] 2 All E.R.359 to constitute a crime committed in England. In the latter case there is of course the problem of how to prosecute the offending party if he is not within the jurisdiction (although, as stated earlier, the establishment of a place of business within England would constitute submission to the jurisdiction of English courts).

Section 421 of the 1948 Act imposes liability of any person who is knowingly responsible for the issue, circulation or distribution of a prospectus, or for the issue of a form of application for shares or debentures, in contravention of sections 417 to 420 inclusive. And the civil liability for mis-statements in prospectuses contained in section 43 of the 1948 Act, is extended by section 422 to every prospectus offering for subscription shares in or debentures of a company incorporated or to be incorporated outside Great Britain, whether the company has or has not established, or when formed will or will not establish, a place of business in Great Britain.

Apart from the Companies Act and the Prevention of Fraud (Investments) Act, the Borrowing (Control and Guarantees) Act 1946 also applies to dealings in securities and gives the Treasury the power to make orders requiring permission of HM Treasury to be obtained by persons involved in the borrowing and raising of money, the issue of securities and the circulation of offers of securities for subscription. Although the terms of The Control of Borrowing Order 1958, were fairly wide-reaching, subsequent amendments have reduced its importance and, apart from the requirement of consent for the timing of issues of sterling securities in excess of £3,000,000, the provisions of the Order are of little commercial significance.

Accounts

The duty on an overseas company to prepare and deliver accounts is contained in sections 9 to 11 of the Companies Act 1976. As explained in the chapter *Accounting Reference Date*, earlier, section 9 requires every overseas company, in each accounting reference period of the company, to prepare and deliver to the Registrar a balance sheet and a profit and loss account and, if the company is a holding company, group accounts. Generally, the accounts must be in the form required of Great Britain companies under the 1948 Act: see *Accounts*, earlier (but the amendments to Schedule 8 to the 1948 Act introduced by the 1981 Act have yet to be brought into force for overseas companies – see the Overseas Companies (Accounts) (Modifications and Exemptions) Order 1982 S.I. 676). The overseas company may (within a specified period of time) notify the Registrar on Form F7 as to the date on which in each successive calendar year an accounting reference period of the company is to be treated as coming to an end. If no such notice is given, section 10 deems the date to be March 31. For being in default of section 9, the company and every officer or agent of the company who knowingly and wilfully authorises or permits the default, is liable to the penalty prescribed in section 11 of the 1976 Act.

Winding up

Where a company incorporated outside Great Britain which has been carrying on business in Great Britain ceases to carry on business there, section 400 allows it to be wound up as an unregistered company under Part IX of the Companies Act 1948, notwithstanding that it has already ceased to exist under the laws of the country under which it was incorporated. On winding up, the rules relating to English companies will be applied in the administration of its foreign assets which fall within the English jurisdiction: *Re Suidair International Airways Ltd* [1951] Ch. 165. According to rule 29 of the Companies (Winding Up) Rules 1949, the winding up petition can be served at the principal or last known principal place of business of the company within the jurisdiction. As long as the overseas company has assets in the jurisdiction (a place of business is not necessary), and there is someone concerned in the proper distribution of those assets, then, provided there is a likelihood of benefit to the creditors of the company, an English court would have jurisdiction to make a winding up order (see *Re Compania Merabello San Nicholas S.A.* [1972] 3 All E.R. 448). However, it should be noted that where a company holds English assets at the time of its dissolution, those assets vest in the Crown as "bona vacantia" (see *Re Banque Industrielle de Moscou* [1952] Ch.919). For other points concerning the winding up of any overseas company, see page 500.

Preference Shares

The share capital of a company may be divided into a number of different classes. Commonly, a company will issue both ordinary shares and preference shares. The term "preference share" is a generic one. It is not possible to apply a universal definition of a preference share; it all depends on the precise rights as set out either in the memorandum or articles of association, or both, of the company, or else in the resolution providing for the issue of preference share capital. It would be trite to say that a preference share is any share enjoying preferential rights over another class of shares; it would also be inaccurate. It is quite possible that the ordinary shares of a company would have preference over another class of (say) deferred shares, and yet it would not be correct thereby to term the ordinary shares as "preference shares". A rather more precise general definition of the term would therefore be that it comprises any share conferring preference as to income or capital, or both, over the ordinary share capital of a company.

In issuing preference shares the drafting of the precise rights that are to attach to that class is of the utmost importance. The general rule is that all shares rank equally as to capital and dividend (*Birch v. Cropper* (1899) 14 App. Cas. 525). This rule must be displaced in order for the preference share capital to be created. But once preference shares have been issued, the rights attached to them will be exhaustive (see *Scottish Insurance Corporation v. Wilsons & Clyde Coal* [1949] A.C. 462). The rule in *Birch v. Cropper* does not mean any more than that the rights of the parties – the shareholders – must be ascertained from, and only from, their agreement with the company (i.e. usually the articles).

In purely commercial terms, it is tempting to think of preference shares as being largely equated with debentures or loan capital of the company. This is to some extent strengthened by the modern tendency for institutional investors, particularly in private companies, providing finance by subscription for preference share capital. In many ways the law has tended to follow the commercial world in this respect, especially as regards the rights of preference shareholders in a scheme for the reduction of a company's capital (see the chapter *Reconstructions*). This analogy cannot be taken too far, however. Preference shares remain part of a company's *share* capital and as such are subject to all the general characteristics attaching to shares as opposed to debt. In particular, unless issued as redeemable shares, they can only be repaid on a reduction of capital (with the consent of the court) or on a purchase by the company itself under sections 54 to 62 of the Companies

Act 1981 (see the chapter *Purchase and Holding of Own Shares*), and the manner in which an income return is derived from a preference share is fundamentally different from the receipt of interest on a debenture.

As indicated, a preference share may confer priority as to the receipt of dividend income or repayment of capital on a winding-up, or both.

Dividend

In general, a preferential dividend on a share will be expressed as a fixed percentage of par value, although it is not uncommon for certain institutional investors (such as I.C.F.C.) to require a preferential dividend based on a percentage of net profits. This is achieved by providing for a total dividend of such percentage to be paid to the whole class of preference shareholders, to be distributed among the members of that class on a pro rata basis.

Prior to the introduction of the imputation system of corporation tax in 1972, the fixed rate dividend on a preference share was its gross amount from which income tax was then deducted. After April 6, 1973, the amount of such a dividend was its *net* amount based on the rate of advance corporation tax in force on that date i.e. three-sevenths. Thus, a 5 per cent preference share in 1972 was transformed into a 3.5 per cent preference share after the relevant date. The provision by which this was brought about (paragraph 18 of Schedule 23 to the Finance Act 1972) caused some confusion, and was later clarified by section 46 of the Finance Act 1976 which reversed the decision in *Sime Darby London Limited v. Sime Darby Holdings Limited* [1976] 1 W.L.R. 59, where it was held that the net dividend should fluctuate with the rate of ACT. It is now the case (and is deemed always to have been the case) that the net preference dividend is fixed, and that the tax credit available to a shareholder (and consequently the gross amount of the dividend in his hands) will fluctuate with the rate of ACT.

There is a basic presumption that dividends on preference shares are *cumulative*. This means that if a dividend is not paid in one year it will be payable in a later year when profits are distributed. However, this presumption may be rebutted by the terms on which the preference shares are issued. For example, in *Staples v. Eastman Photographic Materials Co.* [1896] 2 Ch. 303 the right to the preferential dividend was expressed to be an entitlement "out of the net profits of each year". It was held that this provision did not entitle the preference shareholders to a cumulative dividend, but that only the profits of each year could be taken. If there were no profits, or insufficient profits in that year, then the right to the dividend would lapse to that extent.

Even where the preferential dividend is cumulative, the preference shareholder has no absolute right to that dividend unless and until it is declared. For this reason, a preference dividend cannot be equated with interest on a debenture. The preference shareholders simply have a prior right to receipt of a dividend if such is declared. If no dividend is declared then no debt arises between the company and the preference shareholder. This is the general rule but it can of course be displaced by special provision in the articles or in the resolution authorising the issue. Sometimes – and this may well be the case where preference shares are subscribed by a financial institution – the articles will provide for a mandatory declaration of a dividend if sufficient distributable profits (within the meaning of the Companies Act 1980) arise.

It is a logical consequence of this rule that dividends when ultimately declared are not related back to the years when no dividend was paid, but instead constitute dividends for the year of declaration. Thus in *Re Wakley* [1920] 2 Ch. 205 it was held that no right to a dividend arises until profits are made and a dividend declared, and that each dividend is declared in respect of the current year. Arrears are not truly arrears of dividend but an accrual of a right to a dividend. When the dividend is finally declared and the so-called arrears are paid, it is income of that year and is not apportioned over the whole of the arrears period. Expressions such as "arrears of dividend" and "back dividends" are grammatically incorrect (see also *Weymouth Waterworks Co. v. Coode and Hasell* [1911] 2 Ch. 520).

It follows from the decision in *Re Wakley* that shares issued at different times should not have different priorities. Those issued earlier (on which arrears have built up prior to the later issues) should not be paid their arrears before arrears on other shares. The available profits should be distributed rateably among the shareholders according to the respective amounts of the arrears of dividend payable on the shares held by them respectively (*First Garden City Limited v. Bonham-Carter* [1928] 1 Ch. 53).

Winding-up

Having dealt with the position of preference dividends during the effective life of the company, what of the position at the end of that life on a winding-up? In *Re Walter Symons Limited* [1934] Ch. 308 the preference shares were expressed to "rank" both as regards dividends and capital in priority to the ordinary shares, but did not confer the right to any further participation in profits or assets. It was held that arrears of cumulative dividend were payable in a winding-up for the following four reasons:

(i)   the word "rank" suggests some priority which would not have been necessary while the company remained a going concern;

(ii) there was reference to capital which was not distributable otherwise than in a winding-up;

(iii) the reference to further participation pointed strongly to a winding-up; and

(iv) the construction of "dividends" as meaning "arrears of cumulative preferential dividend".

It had been argued by Counsel for the ordinary shareholders in that case that surplus assets did not mean capital, income or profits and that the preference shareholders could not therefore participate at all in the surplus assets. The point was not there specifically considered, but in *Re Wharfedale Brewery Co. Limited* [1952] Ch. 913 it was clearly decided that surplus assets formed the only fund to be considered on a winding-up, and that all assets (and not merely profits) were available for payment of arrears of cumulative preference dividends. However, in the absence of specific provision, there will not be conferred on the holders of preference shares the right to any arrears beyond the date of the liquidation, thus distinguishing cumulative preference dividends from interest (see *Re E. W. Savory Limited* [1951] 2 All E.R. 1036).

Capital

It was for many years imagined that, whilst the rights of holders of preference shares as stated in the memorandum or articles, or in the resolution creating the shares, were exhaustive, the preference share-holder was entitled to share in surplus assets on a winding-up even if no specific reference were made to such participation. The case of *Birch v. Cropper* was often cited as authority on this point, holding as it did that there was an underlying presumption that all shares should rank equally.

This assumption was exploded once and for all in the case of *Scottish Insurance Corporation v. Wilsons & Clyde Coal* [1949] A.C. 462. In the course of his speech Lord Normand said (at page 496):

"I see no ground on which it may be supposed that the declaration of rights as regards dividend is exhaustive, but the declaration of rights as regards property is not exhaustive."

Thus it was held that unless rights of participation are expressly stated, the preference shareholders will have no rights in a winding-up beyond arrears of dividend and repayment of capital. The *Scottish Insurance Corporation* case was followed in *Re Isle of Thanet Electricity Supply Co.* [1950] Ch. 161, where it was held that the onus is on the preference shareholders to establish that they are entitled to claim in a surplus on a winding-up, and that the earlier case of *Birch v. Cropper* did not mean that the ordinary shareholders were required to prove otherwise.

Participating preference shares

If the preference shareholder is able to discharge the burden of showing that he is entitled to participate in surplus assets on a winding-up, then his shares can be described as participating preference shares, or sometimes preferred ordinary shares. Preference shares having such rights of participation are less commonly found now than in the past. The basic right is to participate in surplus profits after a certain amount has been paid on the ordinary shares. As has been discussed, this right must be fully expressed in the company's constitution, and cannot be implied.

If there is a right to participate, then the question arises as to what assets of the company that right will extend to. Surplus assets on a winding-up will constitute a mixed fund of accumulated profits and capital, and it could be argued that the rights of the preference shareholders should be limited to the capital element of the fund on the basis that distributable profits over and above the preferential dividend could have been declared by way of dividend on the ordinary shares, thus defeating the rights of participation of the preference shareholders. This argument was rejected in *Dimbula Valley (Ceylon) Tea Co. Limited v. Laurie* [1961] Ch. 353. The fact that while the company is a going concern the ordinary shareholders are in control of the profits, that is they can resolve to distribute them subject to the provisions of the Companies Act 1980, is not necessarily inconsistent with another class of shareholders having a right to participate in profits which the ordinary shareholders choose to leave undistributed until after the commencement of a winding-up. If no distribution has taken place then the preference shareholders can participate even to the extent of accumulated profits. As with all cases on the subject of preference shares, it must be remembered that these general principles can be rendered inapplicable by appropriate drafting.

Whether the rights of preference shareholders recognised in the *Dimbula* case can be defeated by a distribution immediately prior to the resolution for a winding-up must be open to some doubt, at least having regard to the wider remedies now afforded to minority shareholders by section 75 of the Companies Act 1980. Depending upon the judicial interpretation of conduct "unfairly prejudicial", a preference shareholder may have recourse to the courts in such an event. However, if the courts take a narrow view and concentrate primarily on the inherent rights attaching to the preference shares (as is the case on a reduction of capital), it might prove very difficult for a preference shareholder to claim that his interests had been prejudiced, even where the motive for a distribution is partially to defeat his rights to share in a surplus on a winding-up. (Section 75 is discussed on page 803).

Redeemable preference shares

Section 58 of the Companies Act 1948, which enabled a company having the requisite power in its articles to issue redeemable preference shares, has now been superseded by sections 45 and 53 of the 1981 Act, and has ceased to have effect. Nevertheless, preference shares issued by a company before June 15, 1982 which could, but for the repeal of section 58, have been redeemed under that section are now subject to redemption in accordance with the 1981 Act provisions (see section 62(2) of the Companies Act 1981). Similarly, any capital redemption reserve fund established before June 15, 1982 by any company for section 58 purposes is now to be known as the capital redemption reserve and is to be treated as if it had been established under the 1981 Act. Any reference in the articles of any company or in any other instrument to a capital redemption reserve fund is, accordingly, to be construed as a reference to the company's capital redemption reserve.

The provisions of section 45 of the 1981 Act are not limited to preference shares, and are considered separately in the chapter *Redeemable Shares*.

Voting

Preference shareholders normally have no right to vote except on a resolution for the winding-up of the company or on a proposed modification of the rights attaching to the preference shares, either in accordance with the memorandum or articles of the company or under section 32 of the Companies Act 1980 (see the chapter *Shares*). It is nevertheless common practice in the case of preference shares having a right to a cumulative dividend to provide for voting rights if the dividend is in arrear for a specified period. For this purpose, it is usually provided that the preferential dividend shall be deemed to be due on a certain date or dates in a year in order to forestall any argument on the basis that a preferential dividend cannot technically be *in arrear* until it is *due*, and that it cannot be *due* until it is actually declared (see *Re Roberts & Cooper Limited* [1929] 2 Ch. 383).

Stock Exchange requirements

All listed companies issuing preference shares must have regard to the usual Stock Exchange regulations. There are certain specific provisions governing preference shares, the most important of which are noted below.

1. In relation to the admission of securities to listing, there are particular rules as to placings of fixed income securities (i.e. including preference shares) including requirements as to publicity and registration with Extel Statistical Services Limited at least 24 hours before the hearing of the application for listing (the 24-hour rule).

2. Where listing of any fixed income securities is required, the prospectus or circular offering them must contain particulars of the profits cover for dividends/interest, and of the net tangible assets.

3. Adequate voting rights are required to be secured to the preference shareholders in appropriate circumstances.

4. On a reduction of capital the ordinary (and generally prejudicial) treatment of preference shares is often modified by use of the *Spens formula* entitling preference shareholders to at least the quoted market value of their shares on a reduction, together with voting rights on the special resolution under section 66 of the Companies Act 1948.

Prospectuses and Public Issues

The present system of investor protection is being reviewed by Professor Gower. Within a year or so we may see a different system with entirely new legislation. Pressures are also coming from outside the United Kingdom – under the pretext of harmonisation within the EEC. For the moment, however, the most significant legislation on the offering of securities continues to be the Companies Act 1948 and the Prevention of Fraud (Investments) Act 1958. In addition, there is also the common law and support from some criminal legislation.

The Jenkins Committee on Company Law, which reported in 1960, decided that on the whole no radical changes to the prospectus provisions of the Companies Act were necessary. It acknowledged that the approach of relating the provisions to "offers to the public" was unclear and was therefore the subject of criticism. In practice, however, the system works well, which is probably due more to the requirements of issuing houses and other advisers involved in connection with prospectuses and the potential consequences for all involved of issuing a misleading prospectus, than to the prospectus legislation itself.

One suggestion which seemed to appeal to the Jenkins Committee was that the Registrar of Companies should have greater power to refuse to accept a prospectus for registration, thereby providing some regulatory control over compliance with the Companies Acts. This hints at a role more similar to the United States Securities and Exchange Commission. This is also, in broad terms, the approach which the EEC Commission seems to have in mind to inflict upon each member state (with an appropriate regulatory body in each member state to deal with prospectuses for shares which are not to be listed on any stock exchange). At present the Registrar of Companies normally merely accepts delivery of a prospectus and checks a very few basic requirements (for example that it has been dated and is accompanied by the documents referred to in it in accordance with section 41(2) of the Companies Act 1948). The Stock Exchange reviews prospectuses for securities which are to be listed, or to be traded on its Unlisted Securities Market, but would no doubt insist that it should not thereby be taken as having approved the document in terms of compliance with content requirements. Such a determination would seem to require access to the issuing company and its directors, in order to acquire a more detailed knowledge of the company's activities.

This chapter deals primarily with the law and practice relating to the documentation for the issue of securities, particularly equities. It also covers sales of securities insofar as they are made with documentation which constitutes an offer to the public. It does not in any detail deal with other aspects of the regulation of the securities markets, nor does it deal in detail with rights issues or issues by foreign companies (for which see the chapters *Rights Issues* and *Overseas Companies* respectively). Reference should be made to the chapter *Shares* for the provisions in the Companies Act 1980 which give existing shareholders certain pre-emption rights and which lay down rules for the payment for new share capital. This chapter also deals with the rules governing the issue of shares at a premium or discount. (The chapter *Formation and Types of Company* deals with the 1980 Act provisions that prevent a public company commencing business until shares up to the authorised minimum have been subscribed for and paid up as to least one quarter of their nominal value).

Offers to the public

It is important at an early stage to determine whether a proposed issue or sale of shares or debentures will fall within section 38 of the Companies Act 1948. If it does, then unless one of the exceptions contained in subsection (5) applies, or a certificate of exemption is obtained under section 39, the offering document will need to contain the information and reports specified in the Fourth Schedule to the 1948 Act. This can have significant implications on the costs and timing of an issue.

Section 38 and offers to the public

Subject to a number of exceptions, section 38 applies to every prospectus issued by or on behalf of a company, or by or on behalf of any person who is or has been engaged or interested in the formation of the company. "Company" as used here means a company formed and registered under the Companies Act 1948 or under certain prior companies legislation (but the provisions can extend to other bodies corporate – see page 647 below). "Prospectus" is defined in section 455 to mean:

"any prospectus, notice, circular, advertisement, or other invitation, offering to the public for subscription or purchase any shares or debentures of a company".

The definition (in the context in which it is used) clearly requires some form of document to be issued. The phrase "offering to the public" is explained in section 55 of the 1948 Act, as amended by the Companies Act 1980. The phrase is important not only in relation to section 38, but also in relation to section 15 of the Companies Act 1980, which prohibits absolutely a *private* limited company from offering its shares or debentures to the public, or allotting any of its shares or debentures with a view to any of those shares or debentures being offered for sale to the public. (Thus a private limited company wishing to issue its shares to the public must first convert itself into a public company under the procedure described at page 414.)

Section 55 provides, in effect, the statutory description of a "private placing". An offer or invitation need not be treated as made to the public if:

"it can properly be regarded, in all the circumstances, as not being calculated to result, directly or indirectly, in the shares or debentures becoming available for subscription or purchase by persons other than those receiving the offer or invitation, or otherwise as being a domestic concern of the persons making and receiving it" (section 55(2)).

Some difficulty in construing section 55(2) arises from the use of the words "or *otherwise* as being a domestic concern. . .". It is sometimes suggested that this requires that for any offer to come within section 55(2) there must be some link between the recipients of the offer, for example as members of a club. This is not the view generally taken by issuing houses and their advisers. It seems to be widely accepted that an offer will fall within section 55(2), and therefore not give rise to a prospectus, if the following conditions are satisfied (regardless of whether there are any links between the offerees):

(a) each offer is made to a particular addressee and may only be accepted by that addressee;

(b) each addressee who takes up an offer warrants that he is acquiring the securities for his own account for long term investment purposes and not with a view to resale, and it would be reasonable for the issuer in all the circumstances to believe such a warranty from each addressee;

(c) non-renounceable documents of title are issued to successful applicants (i.e. definitive share certificates); and

(d) the offer is not associated (either immediately or fairly soon after the placing) with an application for listing on The Stock Exchange or for some other facility for trading the securities offered.

The last of these conditions may not be essential if the listing or other trading facility can be explained in a way that does not cast doubt upon the investment representations referred to in paragraph (b) above.

By virtue of section 55(1) an offer to a section of the public, for example to the company's members or debenture holders or to the clients of the person issuing the prospectus, can constitute an offer to the public. However, the introduction of the distinction between private companies and public limited companies by the Companies Act 1980, brought with it two new sub-sections to section 55. As a result, where a *private* company makes certain offers of its shares or debentures, they are regarded, unless the contrary is proved, as being a "domestic concern of the person or persons making and receiving the offer". In particular, this provision covers offers by private companies to existing members or debenture holders, or to existing employees. However, it would appear, by virtue of section 55(3)(c), that such an offer would not be regarded as being a domestic concern under these new provisions if the right to allotment could be renounced in favour of someone who does not fall within the restricted group referred to in sub-section (3) (i.e., basically, members and employees and their families, and existing debenture-holders). As regards employees, it should be noted that, in order to come within the restricted group, the person must be an employee of the company making the offer (rather than, say, of one of its subsidiaries), unless the shares are to be held under an employees' share scheme (as defined in section 87 of the Companies Act 1980).

An offer document issued in a takeover, whereby the offeror offers its shares in exchange for the transfer of shares in the target company, was held in *Government Stock and Other Securities Investment Co. v. Christopher* [1956] 1 W.L.R. 237 not to fall within the definition of "prospectus", since the shares in the offeror company were not offered either for subscription or for purchase. It is therefore unnecessary for such offer documents, even if they offer shares to the public, to be registered as prospectuses or to comply with any of the provisions contained in sections 38 to 51 of the 1948 Act. (The Jenkins Committee considered that the "prospectus" definition should be widened to cover share exchanges, see para. 237 of their report.)

Applications for shares

Section 38 also prohibits the issue of any *form of application* for shares in or debentures of a company, unless that form is issued with a prospectus giving the information required by the Fourth Schedule to the 1948 Act. There are two exceptions to this requirement. It does not apply in the case of shares or debentures which are not offered to the public. Secondly, it does not apply in connection with a *bona fide* invitation to a person to enter into an underwriting agreement with respect to the shares or debentures. As a result of the prohibition, even where a prospectus has been registered in connection with an offer of shares, no application form may be distributed without a copy of the prospectus. This is one reason why application forms are frequently bound into the offering document. Otherwise there is inevitably a practical risk that application forms will be handed out alone.

Exceptions from the Fourth Schedule requirements

Section 38 does not apply, and there is, therefore, no obligation to include in a prospectus the information required by the Fourth Schedule,

(a) where the prospectus or form of application is issued to existing members or debenture holders (whether or not the applicant is given the right to renounce his right to allotment in favour of other persons); or

(b) where the prospectus or form of application relates to shares or debentures which are, or are to be in all respects, uniform with shares or debentures previously issued and for the time being listed on The Stock Exchange (section 38(5)).

The rights issue exception referred to in paragraph (a), strictly only applies where the documents are issued to *existing* members or debenture holders. It would seem, therefore, that it might well not apply where a company uses as a record date a date some time before the issue of the prospectus, and does not close the register between that record date and the time of actual issue of the prospectus. By the time that the prospectus is issued some of the people who were members on the record date may have ceased to be members. It is perhaps worth noting that a similar practical problem arose in relation to section 17 of the Companies Act 1980 (which contains provisions giving pre-emptive rights on new issues of shares), and that it was thought necessary in that instance for section 17 to be amended by the Companies Act 1981, so that references in section 17 to a "holder of shares" included references to any person who held shares within the 28 day period prior to the making of the offer.

Where the issuing company already has fully listed securities, a rights issue will frequently fall within the second exception. Here it is thought that the words "which are or are to be in all respects uniform" would cover shares of the same class as those already listed, but which do not rank for a particular dividend which is to be paid to the holders of the existing issued shares only. On the other hand, it is not thought that the words are sufficient to cover an issue of convertible debentures where the only listed securities are the shares into which the debentures may be converted. This exception for listed securities will not of course be available for shares which are traded on The Stock Exchange's Unlisted Securities Market, or only on a foreign stock exchange.

Types of offers

Offer for subscription

The term "offer for subscription" is used to describe an offer by or on behalf of a company to persons who will subscribe directly for the shares or debentures in the company, without there being any intervening contractual involvement of a merchant bank or similar intermediary. A merchant bank may well still underwrite the issue (in which case it will probably be involved in the preparation of the prospectus). However, the significant distinction from an offer for sale, is that the merchant bank will not act as a principal in relation to any contracts concluded under applications made pursuant to the prospectus.

Offer for sale

An offer for sale is an offer to sell shares (or the right to the allotment of shares) rather than an offer of shares for direct subscription. It is often made by a merchant bank or stockbroking firm which immediately prior to such offer has agreed to purchase the shares from one or more existing shareholders, or agreed to subscribe for the shares. The expression is, however, equally applicable to a sale by a substantial shareholder who has held all (or some) of the shares over a period. Section 45 will often operate to treat a document used in an offer for sale as a prospectus issued by the company, and as a result there will be only a limited number of differences in the requirements as to the content of such a document. Without section 45, an offer for sale would avoid many of the prospectus provisions of the Companies Acts.

Most significant public offers of shares which are to be listed on The Stock Exchange are made as offers for sale rather than offers for subscription. Typically such offers are made by merchant banks, but recently there have been a number by the Government as part of its privatisation programme. In the case of an offer of new shares by a merchant bank, the arrangements between the issuing company and the merchant bank are contained in some form of agreement, probably called an offer for sale agreement or perhaps, if only new shares are involved, a subscription agreement. This agreement will provide for the new shares to be allotted to the merchant bank provided that certain conditions are satisfied. If existing shares are involved, the vendor or vendors of those shares will be a party to the agreement, agreeing to sell the shares subject to similar conditions. Other parties (such as directors of the company whose shares are to be sold) may be added to give warranties or indemnities.

As mentioned, those who successfully apply for the shares will be entering into a contract with the merchant bank (or other person making the offer), rather than with the "issuer". As a result, the merchant bank is seen to put its name more emphatically behind the offer. Certainly it would seem that the merchant bank's potential exposure is increased where it has a direct contractual relationship with successful applicants. Where a merchant bank acts as agent for the issuer in a direct offer or invitation on behalf of the issuer, it will have significant potential liabilities under (among other things) section 43 of the Companies Act 1948 (civil liability for mis-statements) and, possibly, in tort following *Hedley Byrne & Co. Ltd. v. Heller & Partners Ltd.* [1964] A.C. 465. In the case of an offer for sale, it may also have a liability under the Misrepresentation Act 1967 and may find that the contract of sale with successful applicants is liable to be rescinded.

The wording of section 38(1) of the Companies Act 1948 does not of itself bring a prospectus for an offer for sale within the scope of that section, unless the person issuing it has been engaged or interested in the formation of the company. However, section 45 provides that where a company allots or agrees to allot any of its shares or debentures with a view to all or any of those shares or debentures being offered for sale to the public, any document by which the offer for sale to the public is made, shall for all purposes be deemed to be a prospectus issued by the company. The section goes on to provide that all enactments and rules of law as to the contents of prospectuses, and to liability in respect of statements in and omissions from prospectuses, or otherwise relating to prospectuses, shall apply and have effect accordingly, as if the shares or debentures had been offered to the public for subscription. Furthermore, unless the contrary is proved, it will be evidence that an allotment (or agreement to allot) shares or debentures was made with a view to them being offered for sale to the public if,

(a) those shares or debentures are offered for sale to the public within six months after their allotment (or the agreement to allot); or

(b) at the date when the offer for sale to the public was made, the whole consideration to be received by the company in respect of the shares or debentures had not been received.

Where a document falls within section 45, it must, in addition to containing the information and reports specified in the Fourth Schedule, state the net amount of the consideration received or to be received by the company in respect of the shares or debentures to which the offer relates, and the place and time for inspection of the contract under which the shares or debentures have been or are to be allotted (section 45(3)).

Vendor placings

It is important to note that section 45 bites on the *document* being used. Where it is possible to sell the shares without any document, there need not be any prospectus. This is often the case, for example, on a "vendor placing". Where a listed company wishes to purchase assets with its shares, but the seller wants to receive cash, the purchaser may well be able to persuade the seller to accept the purchaser's shares if, at the time the sale agreement is signed, the purchaser's merchant bank (amongst others) will agree to purchase the consideration shares from the seller. If the merchant bank does this, it will normally intend to place the consideration shares through the stock market as soon as they are allotted. Sometimes a document will be needed to achieve this, for example giving details of the acquisition. This is particularly likely where the issuer is under a Stock Exchange obligation to issue a circular to its shareholders in connection with a shareholders' meeting to approve the proposed transaction. If that document is required to be used in the placing, it will probably require to be registered as a prospectus (through a combination of section 45 and section 38). It is unlikely, however, that the Fourth Schedule will need to be complied with; the exception in section 38(5) for pari passu issues is likely to be applicable (assuming fully listed shares). If no document is required for the placing because it can be done simply by the stockbrokers on the telephone, then section 45 will have no document to apply to.

Secondary offerings

The term "secondary offering" is used to describe an offer for sale where section 45 does not apply to treat the document by which the offer for sale is made as a prospectus issued by the company. An example of such an offer would be one made by a substantial shareholder to dispose of shares he has held for some time. Where the company's shares are not already listed (for example, where a holding company wishes to "spin-off" a subsidiary to the public), it will often be necessary to reorganise the company's capital structure before the public offer (for example, to ensure an appropriate value per share). This may result in new shares being allotted "with a view to" their being offered to the public for the purposes of section 45. If the reorganisation can be achieved by a division of existing shares (pursuant to section 61 of the Companies Act 1948) the section 45 problem can be avoided. However, one advantage of allotting new shares is that they can be transferred to successful applicants free of stamp duty (by renunciation of letters of allotment), and this may increase the net proceeds of sale.

If it is considered that section 45 does not apply, it remains necessary to consider which of the various other prospectus provisions apply. First, it should be noted that the "prospectus" definition does not require the offer to be made by the company. Accordingly, any offering document which is distributed to the public will be a "prospectus" for Companies Act purposes. However, some of the prospectus provisions apply only where the prospectus is issued (or deemed to be issued) by or on behalf of the company (which is taken to mean the issuer, so that they do not apply solely because a vendor of issued shares is a company). The wording in the prospectus provisions of the 1948 Act is somewhat inconsistent, and it is therefore necessary that each section be examined separately. In particular, the wording of section 38 makes compliance with the Fourth Schedule necessary (subject to various exceptions), even where section 45 does not apply if the prospectus is issued by or on behalf of any person who is or has been engaged or interested in the formation of the company.

In summary, the following prospectus provisions of the Companies Act 1948 will normally not apply to a secondary offering (i.e. an offer for sale to which section 45 does not apply):

(a) there will be no requirement to register the prospectus (section 41) or to comply with section 40 as to experts' consents;

(b) the matters specified in the Fourth Schedule need not be set out in the prospectus, unless the prospectus is issued by or on behalf of a person engaged or interested in the formation of the company (section 38); and

(c) section 43 (civil liability for mis-statements), section 47 (minimum subscription) and section 49 (irregular allotment) will not apply.

On the other hand, section 44 (criminal liability for mis-statements), section 50 (timing for dealing with applications and revocation of applications) and section 51 (application for listing on any stock exchange) will apply.

On a literal reading of section 38(3) (which requires an application form to be accompanied by a prospectus complying with the Fourth Schedule), the use of a form of application in a secondary offering would seem to make it necessary to comply with the Fourth Schedule.

However, it is considered that this interpretation would not be given to the provision because otherwise the scope of section 38(1) would be considerably extended. This view appears to have been accepted recently in at least one large public offering.

Fixed price or tender

There is something of a fashion at the moment for offering shares at a price to be determined by tender. The fashion has gained ground from the spate of privatisations and the political concern to minimise the risks of short term profits being made by people stagging an issue. However, it is often said that the complexity involved in the tender application process is inclined to have a dampening effect on an issue, and that a conventional fixed price issue where the share price goes to a (small) premium when dealings start is for all concerned the most successful public flotation. A discount at the start of dealings (indicating that the issuing company or vendor has raised more than the market would have given it) does not necessarily mean that the issuing company has made the most of a flotation. Subsequent financing arrangements can become more difficult as a result.

As in many other areas, much of the mystery (and apparent complexity) disappears once the terminology is clear. The "minimum tender price", as the term suggests, is the minimum price at which tenders may be made and therefore also the minimum price at which shares may be acquired pursuant to the prospectus. The expression "striking price" is the price at which shares are eventually sold, as determined by the tender process. If applications are received for less than the total number of shares offered (and assuming the issue is not conditional on a greater level of acceptances), the striking price will be the minimum tender price; if the number of shares applied for exceeds the number offered, the striking price is usually determined to be the highest price at which sufficient applications are received (at that or a higher price) for all the shares being offered. Each share is sold at the striking price even if an applicant has tendered more (those who have tendered less will be unsuccessful). In the case of an offer for sale by tender where the shares are first being subscribed by a merchant bank, the subscription by the bank will normally be determined by reference to the striking price. The "tender price" is the price which an individual applicant includes in his application form. Of course, some applicants will put in a number of applications at different prices.

A tender offer can take several forms. For instance it may require a fixed amount to be paid on application, this being the minimum tender price specified in the offer, and the balance of the striking price to be paid once it has been determined. Alternatively, the offer may require all of the shares applied for to be paid for on application at the tender price. In this case any excess of an applicant's tender price over the striking price will be returned. Recent privatisation issues have refined the process a little further – presumably with the intention of making the tender process a little less confusing for the smaller investor. In one instance small applications were permitted "at the striking price". In other words, there was no need to pick a tender price and risk it being too low. On the other hand, the applicant did not know how much he would eventually have to pay. In the particular circumstances this was less important because the striking price was to be payable in two instalments, the first instalment being a fixed amount. Although contractually each applicant would remain liable for the second instalment, he could at least sell his shares before the second instalment fell due. (This route gives rise to different risks in terms of the impossibility (in practice) in Stock Exchange transactions of an original applicant going against a purchaser of his "partly paid" shares. A solution which is sometimes available is to pay up the second instalment in advance and to sell fully paid.)

In another instance, the procedure permitted certain applications to be made on the basis of a monetary amount to be invested (rather than a number of shares). Accordingly, the number of shares received by an applicant adopting this route was determined by dividing the amount he indicated he wished to invest by the striking price. This procedure was only adopted in relation to employees. Although attractively simple for the applicant, it could create significant difficulties for those who had to work out the striking price and allocations if a large number of people were able to use this procedure.

Questions are sometimes raised as to whether a tender offer is permitted by the Companies Act 1948 where section 38 applies. This is because it is suggested that paragraph 6 of the Fourth Schedule (disclosure of the amount payable on each share including the premium) and, in the case of offers for sale, section 45(3)(a) (disclosure of net amount of consideration received for the shares) requires a precise amount to be identified. As the price will not be determined until after the application list has closed, this would be impossible. It is considered, however, that these references do not require a definite amount to be specified so long as the amount is capable of determination (e.g. by reference to some formula). Accordingly, compliance with paragraph 6 should be fulfilled by an appropriate explanation of how the striking price will be determined, and compliance with section 45(3)(a) should be achieved by reference to a formula geared to the striking price.

Private placing

Where there is no offer to the public for the purpose of section 55, there will not be a prospectus so far as the Companies Act 1948 is concerned. What is and what is not an offer to the public is a question which has to be decided according to the precise circumstances of each particular case (for some working guidelines see page 615). For small companies and small amounts of money, it may well be important to ensure that a document is not a registrable prospectus requiring full compliance with the Fourth Schedule (e.g. because of the considerable cost of a five year accountant's report).

Other matters

Certificates of exemption

Although the Fourth Schedule to the 1948 Act may not appear to require a great deal of information to be included in a prospectus, compliance can sometimes be impossible or extremely difficult. Section 39 provides a mechanism for exemption from compliance with the Schedule's requirements if the securities which are being offered are to be listed on The Stock Exchange. The exemption is not available if the securities are to be traded on The Stock Exchange's Unlisted Securities Market or to be listed only on another stock exchange. The Jenkins Committee supported the flexibility offered by section 39 and felt that it would be broadly desirable for it to be extended to cover situations where a listing was not involved. This, however, raises the question of who should determine the availability of the exemption (the Jenkins Committee suggested the Department of Trade). Presumably The Stock Exchange would only be appropriate for its Unlisted Securities Market.

For the section 39 exemption to be available the distribution of the prospectus must not be limited to people who are existing members or debenture holders – but this seems somewhat academic given that such offers would in any event normally fall outside section 38. Where section 39 can apply, application may be made to The Stock Exchange for a certificate that, having regard to the proposals (as stated in the request) as to the size and other circumstances of the issue, and as to any limitations on the number and class of persons to whom the offer is to be made, compliance with the requirements of the Fourth Schedule would be unduly burdensome. Although a certificate may be given, it will only have the effect of relieving the company concerned from compliance with the Fourth Schedule if the proposals stated in the request are adhered to, and the particulars and information required to be published in connection with the application for listing are so published.

If a certificate of exemption is given, any prospectus which contains the particulars and information required by The Stock Exchange is deemed to comply with the Fourth Schedule so that, for example, a form of application issued with such a prospectus will satisfy the requirements of section 38 (section 39(2)(a)). Section 39(2)(b) goes on also to provide that, where the required particulars and information are published, section 38 does not apply to any issue, after The Stock Exchange's permission is granted, of a prospectus or form of application relating to the shares or debentures. It is not entirely clear why both section 39(2)(a) and section 39(2)(b) are needed. However, it would seem that the latter probably has the effect of making compliance with section 45(3) (see page 619 above) unnecessary in the case of an offer for sale where a section 39 certificate of exemption is granted. The relevant wording in section 45(3) is "Section [38] ... as applied by this section shall have effect as if ..." If section 38 does not apply by virtue of section 39(2), then on the wording of section 45(3), it seems the latter section cannot apply either.

The exemption procedure contained in section 39 is frequently used to avoid compliance with particular parts of the Fourth Schedule. A certificate of exemption will often be accompanied by a Stock Exchange requirement that, notwithstanding the certificate of exemption, the Fourth Schedule must be complied with except as regards the particular provision or provisions in respect of which compliance was considered to be unduly burdensome. In this way, for example, it may be possible to avoid disclosure of a highly sensitive contract which would otherwise require to be listed as a material contract and to be delivered to the Registrar of Companies under section 41. (But see *Material contracts* below.)

Treatment of applications

Applications made pursuant to a prospectus which is issued generally (i.e. issued to persons other than existing members or debenture holders), may not be accepted until the beginning of the third working day after the prospectus is first issued, or until such later time as may be specified in the prospectus. This time, which is referred to as "the time of the opening of the subscription lists", must be stated in the prospectus (C.A. 1948, Sch. 4, para. 5). The word "issue" is given a particular meaning for the purpose of this section where the prospectus is issued as a newspaper advertisement. If it is so issued before the third day after it is issued in some other manner, the date of issue is taken as the date on which it first appears as a newspaper advertisement. Otherwise the date of issue is the date on which it is first issued in any manner (C.A. 1948, s. 50(1)). This provision ensures that applicants have a reasonable opportunity to consider the prospectus and return their application forms before the application list opens.

The Companies Acts do not specify a date by which application lists must be closed, and in theory it would be possible for a company to issue a prospectus and seek applications for its shares on the basis of that prospectus over a long period. However, the directors and other people responsible for the prospectus would need to ensure that the prospectus remains accurate up until the time of allotment of shares pursuant to it. Otherwise they will run the risk of civil liability under section 43 (see below). (By section 87(2) of the 1980 Act an allotment is made when a person acquires the unconditional right to be included in the register of members in respect of the shares in question.)

Linked with the provisions regarding acceptance of applications is section 50(5) of the 1948 Act, which deals with the revocation of applications. This provides that applications pursuant to a prospectus issued generally shall not normally be revocable until after the expiration of the third working day after the opening of the subscription lists. Accordingly, applications – which in contractual terms normally amount to offers – should where possible be validly accepted before the end of this third day. Revocation may take place earlier if before then a person responsible for the prospectus under section 43 of the 1948 Act gives a public notice so as to limit or exclude his responsibility under section 43 (see page 636 below).

Although the reason is not clear, section 50(7) specifically provides that the provisions of section 50 restricting the acceptance and revocation of applications do not apply where a certificate of exemption has been given under section 39 and as a result there is no requirement to comply with the Fourth Schedule. In many public issues it will be difficult to process applications to the stage of being able to post acceptances before the results of an issue become public knowledge. It can therefore be important to ensure that, if the issue is undersubscribed, applicants will not be able to revoke their applications (i.e. withdraw their offers) before the time when it is expected that acceptances will be posted. Section 50(5) will often provide this protection – but where it does not (e.g. because there is a certificate of exemption or a longer period is needed after the opening of the subscription lists), issuers frequently write into the application form a provision that the application is to be irrevocable until a specified date. Such a provision is presumed, as a matter of contract law, to be ineffective unless it forms part of a separate contract supported by consideration moving from the issuer. In an attempt to show that this requirement has been satisfied, the agreement as to irrevocability is sometimes expressed to be given in consideration of the issuer agreeing to consider applications.

Application for listing

Many prospectuses are issued in connection with shares that will be listed on a stock exchange. This is often an important factor for an applicant. If there were no listing, the consequential limitations on marketability could seriously affect the value of the shares concerned. This is recognised by section 51, which applies where a prospectus, whether issued generally or not, states that application has or will be made for listing on any stock exchange. In these circumstances, any allotment made in pursuance of the prospectus is void if either (a) the application has not been made before the third working day after the prospectus is first issued, or (b) listing is refused before the expiration of three weeks from the closing of the subscription lists. The three week period may be extended to up to six weeks by a notification to that effect within the three week period by the relevant stock exchange.

In practice an issuer will normally have received prior to the issue of the prospectus a fairly clear indication from the relevant stock exchange that its shares will be admitted to listing. Unlike some other references to stock exchanges in the Companies Acts (e.g. in section 39), the reference in section 51 encompasses any stock exchange and is not therefore limited to listing on The Stock Exchange, London. However, it does not apply to The Stock Exchange's Unlisted Securities Market, although the underlying reasons for the provision would seem equally applicable.

Experts' consents

In the early twentieth century prospectuses appeared which purportedly contained statements by leading experts praising the company's assets or objects. In reality those experts had often not examined the matters in question. The 1929 Companies Act contained provisions to prevent this abuse; these are now contained in section 40 of the Companies Act 1948. The section provides that a prospectus which contains a statement by an expert, shall not be issued unless the expert has consented to the inclusion of his statement in the form and context in which it is included, and has not withdrawn this consent before the prospectus is delivered to the Registrar of Companies for registration. This requires any expert who is named in the prospectus to provide a short letter giving such confirmation. The prospectus must contain a statement that the required consent has been given and not withdrawn.

Most prospectuses will contain at least one expert's report: by auditors as required by the Fourth Schedule. However, it is not always easy to determine whether a statement purports to be made by an expert. "Expert" is defined to include an "engineer, valuer, accountant and any other person whose profession gives authority to a statement made by him". Where a substantial part of the value of shares in an issuing company depends upon the value of certain assets, it will often be advisable (and may be a stock exchange requirement) to include in the prospectus a detailed report by an expert. Examples are a petroleum geologist's report in the case of an oil company (typically required by Schedule II, Part D of the appendix to The Stock Exchange's "Admission of Securities to Listing", – known colloquially as the "Yellow Book") and property valuations in the case of a property company (Chapter 6 of the Yellow Book).

The requirement that such a consent be obtained is also of considerable importance in the context of civil liability for mis-statements under section 43 of the Companies Act 1948 (see page 636 below). Provided that an expert has given and not withdrawn his consent to the inclusion of statements made by him as an expert, the expert will have primary liability for those statements, and the directors and other persons responsible under section 43 will, subject to a number of other conditions, have a defence if any such statements turn out to be untrue or misleading.

Section 14 of the Prevention of Fraud (Investments) Act 1958

Besides the prospectus provisions of the Companies Acts, it may be necessary to consider whether or not a document can properly be circulated without a breach of section 14 of the Prevention of Fraud (Investments) Act 1958. Section 14(1) makes it a criminal offence to distribute any documents which are circulars containing, among other things, (a) any invitation to enter into an agreement to subscribe for, or acquire, securities or (b) any information calculated to lead, directly or indirectly, to the recipient entering into such an agreement. However, if the document is a prospectus to which section 38 applies, section 14 will not apply to the distribution of that prospectus (section 14(2)(a)). Similarly, section 14 will not apply to a form of application issued with a prospectus which complies with section 38. The same exceptions operate if section 38 does not apply because of the application of section 38(5)(b) (shares ranking pari passu with existing listed shares) or because of a certificate of exemption under section 39 (page 616). In the case of a rights issue where section 38(5)(b) is inapplicable, the distribution is normally permitted under section 14(3)(a)(iii), because the distribution is being made by the issuing company to its own shareholders. Therefore, in most cases of a "new issue" of equity securities, the Prevention of Fraud (Investments) Act will not present a problem where a Companies Act prospectus will be required. It is worth noting that where an application form is involved, the prospectus must *comply* with section 38 where it is required to do so under the Companies Act 1948. Curiously perhaps this is not the case where there is no application form; it is simply necessary that section 38 applies or would apply but for the particular exemption. There are a number of other exceptions to the restriction in section 14 of the Prevention of Fraud (Investments) Act 1958, which are of importance in the case of private placings, take-over offer documents and "secondary offerings" of shares.

Contents of prospectuses

Companies Act 1948

Most prospectuses follow a fairly similar format, covering much the same basic information, the exact format depending on the circumstances. Much of the information required by statute is often condensed into an appendix near the end of the document.

The most significant statutory content requirements result from section 38 of the Companies Act 1948, which requires a prospectus to contain the matters and reports specified in the Fourth Schedule to that Act. As already mentioned, the requirements of section 38 do not apply in a number of circumstances, one of which is where a certificate of exemption is obtained under the section 39 (see page 623). Such a certificate exempts the issuer from compliance with section 38 provided that The Stock Exchange's requirements for listing are complied with. The Stock Exchange will, however, often require compliance with all the provisions of the Fourth Schedule other than those which it considers would place undue burdens on the issuer.

The Fourth Schedule is split into three parts – Part I deals with general information to be specified in the prospectus, Part II deals with the accountant's reports to be contained in the prospectus and Part III explains the application of some of the provisions contained in Parts I and II.

The Jenkins Committee recommended various additions to the Fourth Schedule. These included:

(a) a requirement to provide information on the nature of the company's business, and on its loan capital, overdrafts and directors' borrowing powers;

(b) a requirement to provide details of turnover in respect of five financial years as part of the accountant's report; and

(c) where debentures are offered, a requirement to provide details about interest, terms of redemption and security.

None of these recommendations has yet been taken up. Most of the points are frequently covered in practice, often because they are required to be dealt with by The Stock Exchange requirements. On a general level the Jenkins Committee recommended greater flexibility with regard to the requirements for the contents of prospectuses by suggesting that the Department of Trade should have power to amend the Fourth Schedule by statutory instrument. This suggestion has also not yet been taken up.

Many of the Fourth Schedule requirements are fairly straightforward and unlikely to give rise to problems. The following are some of the paragraphs which in some circumstances can give rise to difficulty.

Accountants' report

The most significant requirement of the Fourth Schedule is for an accountants' report covering the company's profits and losses for the five "financial years" preceding the issue of the prospectus (or such shorter period as the company has been in business). Apart from profits and losses, the report must provide a statement of the assets and liabilities of the company at the last date to which the accounts of the company were made up. Where the company has subsidiaries, their profits and losses and their assets and liabilities must also be shown, either separately or combined. It will normally be very difficult for a company to issue a prospectus less than about two months after its year end, because its auditors will be unable within that period to report on the profits or losses for the year which has just ended. Part III of the Fourth Schedule explains that "financial year" means the period in respect of which the company's accounts are made up. Accordingly, it would theoretically be possible to alter the issuer's accounting reference period to avoid this problem (see the chapter *Accounting Reference Date*). The accountants who give the report must be the company's auditors at the time of the prospectus. Sometimes it is felt desirable for one of the leading international accounting firms to give the report. Where such a firm is not to act as the company's auditors, this can be achieved by appointing joint reporting accountants, the other of whom are the company's auditors.

If any of the proceeds of the issue are to be applied directly or indirectly in the purchase of a business or of shares in a company as a result of which the company will become a subsidiary of the issuing company, the prospectus must include an accountants' report covering the profits and losses and the assets and liabilities of that business or company (including its subsidiaries). This accountants' report need not be made by the company's auditors. In the case of profits and losses the report must also cover each of the five financial years of the business or company immediately preceding the issue of the prospectus.

Apart from the Fourth Schedule requirements, The Stock Exchange also requires an accountants' report where a company seeks a full listing for its shares – although there is no such requirement where the shares are only to be traded on its Unlisted Securities Market. From an investor's point of view, the accountants' report will often be of particular significance and it is therefore important that the figures reported on should not be too dated. The Stock Exchange will generally not approve a prospectus for shares which are to be listed if the latest financial period reported upon ended more than six months prior to the date of the prospectus. In addition, it is likely to be important for those involved in the issue to receive some assurance that the previous profits record as shown in the report does not give a misleading impression of the current state of the issuer's business. Such an assurance is sometimes provided by a profit forecast.

Neither the Fourth Schedule nor The Stock Exchange regulations actually requires a profit forecast. However, when one is included, The Stock Exchange requires that it be reported upon by the issuer's accountants and issuing house.

Proceeds and expenses of the issue and working capital

The prospectus must state the minimum amount of money which, in the opinion of the directors, must be raised to provide for the following:

(a) the purchase price of property purchased or to be purchased which is to be defrayed wholly or partly out of the proceeds of the issue;

(b) any preliminary expenses and commissions;

(c) the repayment of any moneys borrowed for any of the foregoing matters; and

(d) working capital (C.A. 1948, Sch. 4, para. 4).

If the amounts required for the above are to be provided otherwise than out of the money raised by the offer to the public, particulars must be given of the sources out of which such amounts are to be provided. Paragraph 4 of the Fourth Schedule is tied into section 47 of the Companies Act 1948 and section 16 of the Companies Act 1980. Broadly, section 47 prohibits the allotment of shares offered to the public for subscription, unless the minimum amount which must be raised by the issue of shares to provide for the matters specified in paragraph 4 has been subscribed, and the minimum amount payable on application for the amount so stated has been paid to and received by the company. As regards "paid to and received", receipt of a cheque is good enough so long as the company has no reason to suspect that it will not be paid. Section 16 prohibits allotment of share capital of a public company offered for subscription unless either the capital is subscribed in full or the offer states that, if it is not fully subscribed, the amount which is subscribed may be allotted in any event or in the event of the conditions specified in the offer being satisfied.

In addition, the prospectus must state the estimated amount of issue expenses and who will be paying them (paragraph 12 of the Fourth Schedule). Prior to its repeal, section 54 of the Companies Acts 1948 made it unlawful for a company to give financial assistance in connection with the subscription or purchase of its shares. Notwithstanding this, it was not unusual for the issuing company to pay a large proportion of the costs associated with a flotation, even where the shares were being made available by existing shareholders. This was presumably considered justifiable on the basis of the clear benefits which would accrue to the company from the flotation. Such an approach has been made easier by the provisions which have replaced section 54 and are contained in sections 42 to 44 of the Companies Act 1981. Financial assistance may now be given where the giving of the financial assistance is but an incidental part of a larger purpose (i.e. to enable the company to become a listed company, with an ability to raise money by rights issues and to make acquisitions with its shares), and is given in good faith in the interests of the company (see the chapter *Financial Assistance*).

The Stock Exchange requires the prospectus to contain a statement by the directors that in their opinion the working capital available is sufficient for the company's requirements or, if it is not, how it is proposed to provide the additional working capital which the directors consider necessary. This statement is backed up by a requirement that the sponsors of an issue write to The Stock Exchange confirming that they have satisfied themselves that the statement in the prospectus as to the sufficiency of working capital has been made by the directors after due and careful enquiry. The Yellow Book goes on to say that the letter will normally be required to state that there is written confirmation from those who are being relied on for finance that the relevant facilities exist.

Paragraph 9 of the Fourth Schedule requires certain details to be given of any property which is to be paid for wholly or partly out of the proceeds of the issue, or the purchase or acquisition of which has not been completed at the date of issue of the prospectus. Included in the details to be given are short particulars of any transaction relating to the property completed within the two preceding years in which any vendor of the property to the company or any person who is, or was at the time of the transaction, a promoter or a director or a proposed director of the company had any interest, direct or indirect. This paragraph can present difficulties where a significant number of properties is acquired shortly before the issue of a prospectus.

Promoters

In addition to the provision already referred to regarding transactions in property in which a promoter is interested, there are two other paragraphs in the Fourth Schedule which require disclosures in relation to promoters. The first is paragraph 13. It requires details to be given of any amounts or benefits paid or given within the last two preceding years, or intended to be paid or given, to any person who is a "promoter". Details are also required of the consideration for the payment or the giving of the benefit. Although some of the paragraphs of the Fourth Schedule do not apply where more than two years have elapsed since the date when the company was entitled to commence business, this is not the case with paragraph 13. The provision is not limited to payments and benefits arising in the course of promotion. Paragraph 31 of Schedule II, Part A of the Appendix to The Yellow Book contains a provision similar to paragraph 13, and in addition requires the promoters to be named. Secondly, if the prospectus is issued less than two years after the date when the company is entitled to commence business, full particulars of the interest of each director in the promotion of, or in the property proposed to be acquired by, the company must be disclosed (paragraph 16).

"Promoter" has been defined as someone who "undertakes to form a company with reference to a given project and to set it going, and who takes the necessary steps to accomplish that purpose" (*Twycross v. Grant* (1877) 2 C.P.D. 469). This definition might appear to limit the word to persons who are involved in the company's formation. If that were the case, the problems could be overcome by buying a ready made company, but it is considered that the definition would be applied as if the purchase were the formation of the company.

It is often very difficult to decide who is a promoter in any particular case and therefore what information needs to be given to comply with the Fourth Schedule and the Yellow Book. A parent company floating off a subsidiary would usually be a promoter. Any initial subscriber, or director, who has taken most of the initiative in setting up the company will probably be one. An issuing house will not usually be a promoter solely by virtue of its responsibilities as a sponsor and underwriter – although it may cross the line and become a promoter if it actively participates in setting up the company, has representatives on the board and is otherwise significantly involved in the decision to float the company.

A determination as to who is a promoter may also be relevant in the context of liability for the prospectus. This is because a promoter may have a potential civil liability for the prospectus under section 43 of the Companies Act 1948. In many instances a promoter will in any event have this potential liability in another capacity, so that the determination may be unnecessary. The question of liability is considered in greater detail below.

In addition to the Companies Act requirements, a promoter has fiduciary duties under common law which require, among other things, full disclosure to an independent board, or to the members or potential members, in order to avoid contracts between the promoter and the company being voidable, or the promoter incurring a liability to account for any profit made by him pursuant to such a transaction. This disclosure must extend to all transactions between the promoter and the company following the commencement of the promotion, irrespective of when any relevant property or interest was acquired by the promoter.

Material contracts

Details must be given of every "material contract", other than a contract entered into in the ordinary course of the business of the company or a contract entered into more than two years before the date of issue of the prospectus. Copies of such contracts are required to be attached to the prospectus when it is delivered to the Registrar of Companies for registration under section 41 of the Companies Act 1948. Where there is no written contract, a memorandum giving full particulars of the contract must be filed. There is also generally a Stock Exchange requirement for material contracts to be on display for examination by the public for a period of fourteen days after the issue of the prospectus. Where compliance with the Fourth Schedule is not required because of a certificate of exemption under section 39, there will be no statutory requirement to list material contracts – unless this is required by The Stock Exchange as a condition to listing (see section 39(2)). Section 41 provides that where The Stock Exchange requires a copy of a contract (or a memorandum of a contract) to be available for inspection in connection with the application made under section 39, a copy (or a memorandum) of that contract must be delivered to the Registrar with the prospectus.

If a company which is proposing to issue a prospectus considers that because of confidentiality it is important that a contract should not be available to the public, such publicity can be avoided if The Stock Exchange can be persuaded (a) that it is appropriate for it to provide a certificate of exemption under section 39, and (b) that it should not require a copy of that specific contract to be made available for inspection in connection with the application for listing. In some cases The Stock Exchange will agree to a modified version of the contract being made available for inspection – omitting the part or parts which are commercially sensitive (see the note to paragraph 35 of Schedule II Part A of the Appendix to the Yellow Book). It is also worth mentioning that in the cases of issues that fall within section 38(5) of the 1948 Act (i.e., broadly rights issues and issues of shares which rank *pari passu* with existing listed shares), there is no requirement to register material contracts. This is because there is no requirement to comply with the Fourth Schedule. The registration requirement does not apply even if The Stock Exchange requires such contracts to be available for inspection.

It is often difficult to determine whether contracts are material and whether they have been entered into in the ordinary course of the company's business. The 1948 Act does not contain any definition of what should be considered a material contract. The relevant case law dates back to the nineteenth century. It would seem to indicate that materiality should be looked at from the point of view of the potential investor rather than of the company. However, in many cases these two approaches will reach the same conclusion. In *Sullivan v. Metcalfe* (1880) 5 C.P.D. 455 it was considered that a contract which "upon a reasonable construction of its purport and effect would assist a person in determining whether he would become a shareholder in the company", would be regarded as a material contract. (See also *Twycross v. Grant* (1877) 2 C.P.D. 469 and *Broome v. Speak* [1903] 1 Ch. 586 (C.A.).) The Fourth Schedule does not specifically indicate that paragraph 14 only applies to contracts to which the issuing company is a party. It is felt that a contract may fall to be disclosed under paragraph 14 where the company is not a party if one of the parties is someone who has a direct connection with the company, such as a promoter, significant shareholder or director. In *Watts v. Bucknall* [1903] 1 Ch. 766 it was held that a director who knew of the existence of a contract, could not escape liability for its non-disclosure by professing ignorance of its contents or materiality. In cases of doubt it is clearly preferable for a contract to be disclosed.

A description of material contracts in compliance with the Fourth Schedule does not necessarily mean that no other contracts need be disclosed in order to ensure that the prospectus is not misleading or contains all relevant information. In particular, there may be important contracts which were entered into more than two years before the prospectus, such as a vital long term supply contract which might be nearing the end of its term.

Other requirements

Apart from the Fourth Schedule, Part II of the Companies Act 1948 contains a number of other content requirements. For example, section 37 requires every prospectus issued by or on behalf of a company, or in relation to an intended company, to be dated. This date will often appear at the end of the last appendix, before the procedure for application and an application form. Another example is provided by section 41(2), which requires every prospectus, on the face of it, to state that a copy has been delivered for registration and to specify, or to refer to statements included in the prospectus which specify, the documents required by section 41 to be endorsed on or attached to a copy of the prospectus so delivered. These documents are experts' consents, material contracts and any statement of adjustments.

Failure to comply with section 38

It would seem that any subscriber who suffers damage as a result of a failure on the part of the directors of the issuing company to comply with section 38, may recover damages from the directors for breach of statutory duty. Except in the case of section 38(3) (application form not to be issued without a Fourth Schedule prospectus), section 38 does not indicate what liability should result from a failure to comply with it. However, it is clear from section 38(4) that the section was intended to impose a potential liability on directors. Section 38(4) specifically provides that in the event of non-compliance with, or contravention of, any of the requirements of section 38, a director or other person responsible for the prospectus will not incur any liability by reason of the non-compliance or contravention if,

(a) as regards any matter not disclosed, he proves that he was not cognisant thereof; or

(b) he proves that the non-compliance or contravention arose from an honest mistake of fact on his part; or

(c) the non-compliance or contravention was in respect of matters which in the opinion of the court dealing with the case were immaterial or was otherwise such as ought in the opinion of that court, having regard to all the circumstances of the case, reasonably to be excused.

As in the case of liability under section 43 (see page 636 below), the burden of establishing the defence is placed upon the director. However, there is a specific exception to this rule where paragraph 16 of the Fourth Schedule is concerned (director's interest as a promoter).

Stock Exchange requirements

A number of The Stock Exchange's requirements have already been mentioned. In addition there are various regulations which are dependent upon the type of issue concerned, or the method of issue, or both. They vary, among other things, according to whether or not the issuer already has listed securities. Details of the content requirements can be found, in the case of a full listing, in Schedule II of the Yellow Book and, in the case of its Unlisted Securities Market, in Section C or D of the leaflet entitled "Unlisted Securities Market" issued by The Stock Exchange and known colloquially as the "Green Book". These regulations generally provide for much greater disclosure than the Fourth Schedule.

There are certain additional requirements (set out in Schedule II, Part D of the Appendix to The Stock Exchange's Yellow Book) for a listing for the first time of securities of a company whose activities include to a material extent the exploration of natural resources. These requirements also apply where the issuer already has listed securities, but is moving into the natural resources field. Probably the two most important additional requirements in this context are an expert's report on the estimated mineral reserves, and a more detailed analysis of the company's working capital projections.

Where application is being made for a listing on The Stock Exchange or for permission for dealings to take place in the Unlisted Securities Market, the final form of the prospectus will need to be approved by The Stock Exchange (as will various other documents, such as the company's articles of association). Usually, once a fairly presentable proof is available, that and subsequent proofs will be submitted by the sponsoring brokers to The Stock Exchange's "Reading Department" which determines whether The Stock Exchange's requirements are being met in a satisfactory manner.

A prospectus issue of shares which are to be traded on The Stock Exchange's Unlisted Securities Market is subject to similar but, in certain areas, less demanding regulations than for full listing. The differences between the two sets of regulations were intended principally to result in a reduction in the costs of obtaining a Stock Exchange quote. The most significant difference is in the area of financial information. The Unlisted Securities Market does not require an accountants' report. However, this difference is only of any practical help where the Fourth Schedule does not apply, since otherwise an accountants' report under the Fourth Schedule is required. It is doubtful whether much of the saving in joining the USM as against obtaining a full listing results from the difference in the prospectus content regulations. Of greater significance is the absence in the case of the USM of a requirement to publish the full prospectus in the press. It is to be hoped that the degree of disclosure to the investor is substantially the same in each case.

Most, if not all, prospectuses which are issued in connection with a listing of shares on The Stock Exchange will be drafted in conjunction with a merchant bank, the sponsoring stockbroker, the company's solicitors and the solicitors to the issue. The team of lawyers and advisers will seek to ensure that the prospectus complies with the necessary regulations on the basis of the information provided to them by the company. However, at the end of the day the ultimate responsibility rests primarily with the directors of the issuing company.

Licensed Dealers' Rules

If the prospectus or other document offering shares for subscription or purchase is issued by a licensed dealer under the provisions of the Prevention of Fraud (Investments) Act 1958, the provisions of The Licensed Dealers (Conduct of Business) Rules 1960 will apply. As a result, the prospectus or other document will have to comply with the requirements specified in the Second Schedule to the Rules (though this is subject to certain exceptions contained in rule 17 of the rules). These rules are in the process of change and, at the time of going to print, draft rules and regulations have been circulated by the Department of Trade.

Liability for prospectuses and verification

The directors of the issuer and other persons connected with the issue of a prospectus, can incur liability in a variety of ways under statute, common law and contract. So far as actions for damages are concerned, the two most useful remedies to a shareholder will be those available under section 43 of the Companies Act 1948 and under section 2(1) of The Misrepresentation Act 1967. Remedies under section 43 will lie against the directors, and possibly others. Remedies under section 2(1) will lie against the vendor in the case of an offer for sale, or against the issuer in the case of a direct subscription (subject to the rule in *Houldsworth v. City of Glasgow Bank* (1880) 5 App. Cas. 317, see page 640 below). Under both these sections the burden of establishing a defence is thrown onto the defendant.

The following section summarises the principal areas of liability (excluding liability for breach of section 38, which has already been dealt with on page 634). At the outset it is worth noting that more limited remedies are available to those who purchase shares in the market after a prospectus issue, than to those who subscribe for, or purchase, shares pursuant to the prospectus itself.

Section 43 of the Companies Act 1948

The primary responsibility for the accuracy of a prospectus rests with the directors. They (and others) have a potential liability under section 43 to pay compensation to all persons who subscribe for shares or debentures on the basis of the prospectus for any loss or damage sustained by reason of any untrue statement therein. By section 46(a) a statement is treated as being untrue if it is misleading in the form and context in which it is included. In addition, a statement is deemed to be included in a prospectus if it is contained in any report or memorandum appearing on the face thereof, incorporated by reference therein or issued therewith (section 46(b)).

The following also have a potential liability under section 43:

(a) every promoter;

(b) every person who has authorised himself to be named in the prospectus as having agreed to become a director; and

(c) every person who has authorised the issue of the prospectus (section 43(1)).

For this purpose the expression "promoter" is given a special meaning. By section 43(5) it means "a promoter who was a party to the preparation of the prospectus, or of the portion thereof containing the untrue statement, but does not include any person by reason of his acting in a professional capacity for persons engaged in procuring the formation of the company". Thus a promoter who is not involved in the preparation of the prospectus, or the part of it which contains the untrue statement, will have no liability under section 43.

An issuing house which is involved in the preparation of the prospectus for an offer for subscription, and whose name appears prominently in the prospectus, is likely to be treated as a person who has authorised the issue of the prospectus and thus within section 43(1). A person acting as a vendor on an offer for sale will also fall within this category (he might also be a promoter).

Defences

The principal defence provided by the section is that the person concerned had a "reasonable ground to believe, and did up to the time of the allotment . . . believe, that the statement was true". Each director should therefore ensure that he has considered every statement made in a prospectus, that he believes each statement to be true and not misleading, and that the ground for this belief is reasonable. In the case of experts' statements, there is a different, less onerous, defence for those other than the expert himself.

Obviously, each director cannot be expected to know every fact relating to the company. With respect to some statements, it will be perfectly proper for a director to rely on others, including the company's advisers, to check particular parts of the prospectus. In these cases it is considered that reliance upon an appropriate person to have carried out the detailed verification will give the director reasonable grounds for his belief that the statement is true. Nevertheless he should have taken steps to ensure that (a) the person on whom he relied was a person on whom it would be reasonable to rely in the circumstances (i.e. in relation to the particular statement), and (b) there are reasonable grounds for him, the director, to believe that the person on whom he is relying has verified the statement. Accordingly, in every case each director should have read with care the entire prospectus in substantially its final form, and should have satisfied himself that the information in the prospectus has been the subject of sufficient verification to afford him a "reasonable ground to believe" that it is true.

It is often very difficult to impress upon directors of a company the extent of their individual responsibility for a prospectus and the significance of verification in terms of limiting the risk of liability. It is up to the company's advisers to ensure a simple and efficient verification process whereby all the directors of the company can be satisfied that reasonable steps have been taken to ensure that each statement in the prospectus is accurate and not misleading. This process is also important as providing a basis for others who have authorised the issue of the prospectus, such as an issuing house, to establish that they had reasonable grounds to believe that the statements were true (see further under *Verification* on page 641 below).

Position of experts

There is a special provision dealing with experts, who might otherwise be considered to have authorised the issue of the prospectus because their consent is required under section 40. The giving of such consent is only to be treated as making an expert a person who has authorised the issue of the prospectus in relation to statements made by him as an expert (C.A. 1948, s. 43(4)). If the expert's statement is untrue, others who potentially have liability under section 43 will not be liable if they prove two things. First, that the statement included in the prospectus fairly represented the expert's statement. Secondly, that they had reasonable ground to believe, and did up to the time of the issue of the prospectus believe, that the person making the statement was competent to make it, had given his consent as required by section 40 and had not withdrawn it at the time the prospectus was registered or – to the relevant defendant's knowledge – before allotment (C.A. 1948, s. 43(3)).

Who can invoke section 43?

Only subscribers can bring an action. For these purposes, "subscriber" will include a purchaser of shares pursuant to an offer for sale falling within section 45 of the Companies Act 1948. It will often encompass a wider group than simply those who are the original applicants pursuant to a prospectus. Where arrangements are made for the shares to be traded for a period of time free of stamp duty, this will often be done by the issue to successful applicants of a renounceable allotment letter. It is considered that people who become registered as shareholders by renunciation of such an allotment letter will be treated as subscribers. In the case of an offer for sale, a renounceable letter of acceptance will typically take the place of the renounceable allotment letter. The position here is less clear, because purchasers are only treated as subscribers for the purposes of section 43 by virtue of section 45. Section 45 provides that in the case of an offer for sale falling within the section "all enactments and rules of law ... in respect of statements in and omissions from prospectuses ... shall apply and have effect ... as if persons accepting the offer in respect of any shares or debentures were subscribers for those shares or debentures". It may be argued that the renouncee of a letter of acceptance succeeds to the rights of the original applicant so that he would be able to make use of the remedy under section 43 if it were available. If a renouncee manages to establish that he should be treated as a subscriber for the purposes of section 43, then, like any subscriber, to succeed he will also have to establish that he subscribed for the shares or debentures "*on the faith of* the prospectus."

Right to indemnity

A director is entitled to indemnification under section 43(4) if he has not authorised or consented to the issue of the prospectus. It is therefore desirable that all directors confirm in writing that they authorise and consent to the issue of the prospectus. Similarly, a section 40 expert is entitled to be indemnified if he has not given his consent or has withdrawn it before the issue of the prospectus.

Section 44 of the Companies Act 1948

Section 44 provides for criminal liability for mis-statements in a prospectus. Any person who "authorised the issue" of a prospectus containing an untrue statement, is liable to imprisonment for up to two years and a fine unless he proves either (a) that the statement was immaterial, or (b) that he had reasonable grounds to believe and did at the time of the issue of the prospectus believe that the statement was true. The onus of proof is on the defendant. Full verification notes and board minutes should help the directors (and others) to establish this defence if a statement turns out to be untrue. There is no need for there to be an intention to deceive; negligence is sufficient.

Prevention of Fraud (Investments) Act 1958

Section 13 of the Prevention of Fraud (Investments) Act 1958 provides that any person who,

(a) by any statement, promise or forecast which he knows to be misleading, false or deceptive; or

(b) by any dishonest concealment of material facts; or

(c) by the reckless making (dishonestly or otherwise) of any statement, promise or forecast which is misleading, false or deceptive,

induces or attempts to induce another person to agree to subscribe for or purchase shares shall be guilty of an offence. This provision relates not only to statements which are made but also to omissions amounting to "dishonest concealment". The penalty under this section is imprisonment for a term not exceeding seven years.

Negligent mis-statement

Hedley Byrne & Co. Ltd. v. Heller & Partners Ltd. [1964] A.C. 465 established the possibility of an action in tort for negligent mis-statements provided that a duty of care is owed to those who rely upon the mis-statements. Such a duty of care will only exist if there is a "special relationship" between the makers of the statement and those to whom it is made. There has not yet been any case following *Hedley Byrne* in the area of prospectuses, but it is thought possible that the necessary "special relationship" is established between directors and prospective subscribers or purchasers pursuant to a prospectus. The existence of a duty of care for the directors would appear to be reinforced where a "responsibility statement" is contained in a prospectus (for example to meet The Stock Exchange's requirements). The Stock Exchange's present form of responsibility statement, as required by paragraph 2 of Schedule II, Part A of the Appendix to the Yellow Book, is as follows,

"The directors have taken all reasonable care to ensure that the facts stated herein are true and accurate in all material respects and that there are no other material facts the omission of which would make misleading any statement herein whether of fact or of opinion. All the directors accept responsibility accordingly."

It is worth noting that it covers omissions only to the extent that they make a statement misleading, but specifically covers matters of opinion as well as matters of fact. It is possible that the *Hedley Byrne* principle could also be applied to others involved in the preparation of a prospectus, such as an issuing house.

It is possible that a subsequent purchaser of shares may be able to show that the prospectus was issued in the knowledge that he would rely on it, and that he can therefore establish the necessary link to be able to bring an action in tort. In practice, the statements in a prospectus will underly the market in the shares for some time after the offer. If the prospectus is subsequently discovered to be incorrect in a material respect, there could well be a significant fall in the quoted price.

Contract and the Misrepresentation Act 1967

Actions for damages for breach of contract will only be available to those who have privity of contract and have suffered damage. These people may also be able to rescind their contracts. Where the prospectus offers the shares for subscription, the contract will be with the issuer. Here the rule in *Houldsworth v. City of Glasgow Bank* (1880) 5 App. Cas. 317 will apply. In this case it was held that an allottee could not claim damages unless he had first rescinded the contract of allotment. In the case of an offer for sale, the contract will be with the merchant bank which, in the case of new shares, will have a contract with the issuing company.

The remedies in relation to misrepresentations which induce a person to enter into a contract were advanced considerably by the Misrepresentation Act 1967. Before then a contract induced by a material misrepresentation could be rescinded but damages would only be available if there was a breach of a term of the contract. The remedy of rescission is lost if the subscriber fails to take action within a reasonable time after learning the truth or before the company goes into liquidation. Furthermore, the right only applies to the particular person who was induced to enter into the contract by the misrepresentation. It would not extend to a purchaser from that person. As regards a claim for damages, the courts are unlikely to accept that an incorrect statement in a prospectus amounts to a breach of a term of the contract.

As in the case of an action for breach of contract, an action under the Misrepresentation Act will be against the other party to the contract and not, for example, against the directors (even though they may be the persons responsible for making the statement).

There are two possible heads of claim under the Misrepresentation Act which have particular relevance for prospectuses,

(a) section 2(1) gives a right to damages to a person who has entered into a contract after a misrepresentation has been made to him by another party to the contract, and as a result thereof he has suffered loss, unless the defendant proves that he had reasonable ground to believe, and did believe up to the time that the contract was made, that the facts represented were true; and

(b) section 2(2) gives a discretion to the court (or arbitrator) to award damages in lieu of rescission if a misrepresentation, even if wholly innocent, would otherwise entitle a plaintiff to rescission, and the court (or arbitrator) considers that in the circumstances an award of damages is in the interest of justice.

There is therefore no *right* to damages in the case of an innocent misrepresentation. Furthermore damages can only be awarded where rescission is available. It is not clear whether the rule in the *Houldsworth* case has been displaced by the Misrepresentation Act as regards claims made under that Act. In the case of an offer for sale, it might be argued that section 45 of the Companies Act 1948 makes the company (rather than the issuing house) the other party to the contract of sale. It would seem, however, that the wording at the end of section 45(1) ensures that the issuing house will have a potential liability under section 2(1) (the wording reads "but without prejudice to the liability, if any, of the persons by whom the offer is made, in respect of mis-statements contained in the document or otherwise in respect thereof").

Theft Act 1968

Section 19 provides that,

"an officer or person purporting to act as an officer of a body corporate who, with intent to deceive its members or creditors about its affairs, publishes or concurs in publishing a written statement or account which to his knowledge is or may be misleading, false or deceptive in a material particular"

commits an offence. If an officer intends to deceive potential subscribers or purchasers, it would seem that he will not be caught by this section because the subscriber or purchaser will not at the relevant time be a member. It is therefore of limited importance in connection with new issues, although it will have some relevance for rights issues.

Verification

To assist the directors and others to show that reasonable care has been taken in the preparation of the prospectus, and therefore to avoid liability under section 43 (or otherwise) should a statement subsequently be found to be untrue or misleading, the practice has grown up of preparing "verification notes" as part of a verification process. This process as a whole should involve,

(a) the identification of at least one suitable source for the verification of every statement of fact;

(b) a written record being kept of this source;

(c) a written record being kept of a reasonable basis for each statement of opinion;

(d) each of the directors having sufficient time to consider and comment upon the prospectus and the notes (so that they may be corrected and amplified if necessary); and

(e) the notes, including copies of documents resulting from the verification process, being presented to the board meeting at the time when the prospectus is finally approved and being kept with the company's records.

It is obviously desirable that every director should be given adequate opportunity to consider the prospectus and the verification notes and to discuss them with his colleagues and the company's advisers. It is also desirable that a full board meeting attended by every director should consider the prospectus in substantially its final form. Although this will follow a number of extensive drafting sessions involving one or more director, and the distribution of earlier proofs to every director, it should nevertheless take place before it is too late conveniently to make any alterations which may be thought by the meeting to be desirable.

It must be emphasised that the responsibility of the directors (and therefore the scope of the verification process) does not end with the issue of the prospectus. Section 43 specifically requires that each director "did up to the time of *allotment* . . . believe . . .". Section 2(1) of the Misrepresentation Act is similar: "and did believe up to the time that the contract was made . . ." The directors and other persons with responsibility should, therefore, be prepared to reconfirm the statements in the prospectus at or just before the time any applications are accepted.

Underwriting

If an issuing company wishes to be certain that all the shares offered will be subscribed it will normally arrange for the offer to be underwritten. A selling shareholder will normally make similar arrangements to ensure all his shares are sold. Under a typical underwriting agreement the underwriter or underwriters will agree to subscribe for or to purchase, or to procure subscribers or purchasers for, any shares which are not taken up in the public offer. The price to the underwriters will normally be the same as the price in the prospectus. In return for taking this risk the underwriter will be paid a commission on the total value of the shares underwritten, calculated on the offer price. The commission is effectively similar to an insurance premium and is payable whether or not the underwriters actually have to take up any shares. Commission arrangements can vary according to the circumstances. However, the normal underwriting commission is 2 per cent, out of which the underwriter or underwriters will pay a commission of 1.25 per cent to sub-underwriters and a fee to the brokers to the issue. The issuing house which sponsors the issue may also charge a fee, depending upon the size of the issue and the amount of work involved.

In the case of an offer for sale where an issuing house is involved as principal, the issuing house will agree to subscribe for, or purchase, the shares. Apart from certain provisions reflecting this significant difference, an offer for sale agreement will be similar in many respects to an underwriting agreement, especially in the area of warranties, indemnities, conditions to the issuing house's obligations and rights of termination. The issuing house may take its remuneration either in the form of a discount on the share price (so long as the shares are not thereby issued at a discount), or in the form of a commission. If it is taken as a commission, it will normally be subject to value added tax.

Section 53 of the Companies Act 1948

A company's power to pay commissions for underwriting is restricted by section 53 of the Companies Act 1948. This states that such commissions can be paid if,

(a) the payment of the commission is authorised by its articles;

(b) the commission does not exceed ten per cent of the price at which the shares are issued or the amount or rate authorised by the articles, whichever is less;

(c) the commission is –

(i) in the case of shares offered to the public for subscription, disclosed in the prospectus; or

(ii) in the case of shares not offered to the public for subscription, disclosed in a statement in the prescribed form (Form 58a) signed by every director of the company and delivered before the payment of the commission to the Registrar of Companies for registration, and, where a circular or notice, not being a prospectus, inviting subscription for the shares is issued, also disclosed in that circular or notice; and

(d) the number of shares which persons have agreed for a commission to subscribe absolutely is disclosed in the same manner.

Unless the above provisions are adhered to, the company cannot pay underwriting commissions out of its capital. Nor may it pay out of capital a discount or allowance as consideration for an underwriting. It would seem (although it is not absolutely clear) that these restrictions do not apply to payments out of profits or non-capital reserves. It was decided in *Andreae v. Zinc Mines of Great Britain* [1918] 2 K.B. 454 that the filing of the prescribed form after payment of the commission will not render the commission payment lawful. In order to avoid any questions as to whether a commission payment is lawful, it is essential, in the case of an offer which is not an offer to the public for subscription, for an underwriter to ensure that the form is duly filed before the commission is paid. This would normally be necessary on private placings.

Warranties and indemnities

An underwriting agreement for a public issue will normally be subject to the condition that the shares are admitted to listing or, in the case of the Unlisted Securities Market, that The Stock Exchange grants permission for the shares to be dealt in on the Unlisted Securities Market. It will also, typically, contain various warranties and indemnities and provide for termination by the underwriter if any of the warranties are discovered to be inaccurate.

Two problems which frequently arise in practice are who should give the warranties and indemnities, and how extensive they should be? The answer will vary according to the circumstances of each offer. As a general rule, however, it is undesirable for the issuing company to give any warranties or indemnities. The remedies would merely serve further to deplete the company's assets and consequently reduce its value. One of the purposes of warranties from the issuing house's point of view is to provide evidence that it has taken care to ensure that the prospectus is accurate. It is not unusual or necessarily unreasonable (given the statutory liabilities that fall on directors) for the directors to be required to give warranties to the issuing house which impose personal liability upon them.

Indemnities essentially fall into two categories: those in favour of the issuing house to protect it against liability to others, and those in favour of the company and its subsidiaries in respect of certain specific possible tax liabilities. Examples of tax indemnities are indemnities against capital transfer tax, for which see paragraphs 33 and 34 of Schedule II, Part A of the Appendix to The Stock Exchange's Yellow Book, and, possibly other liabilities, for instance in respect of corporation tax not disclosed in the prospectus.

Supervening event

A further problem which often gives rise to some difficulty is whether or not the issuing house should have a right to terminate the agreement if there is some political or economic change before a given date and, if so, what that date should be. Some would take the view that this is a risk which the issuing house is being paid for taking. However, in some cases the issuing house may not be prepared to proceed without such a right, at least until it would normally have completed its sub-underwriting.

Acceptance and allotment

A prospectus will normally invite the public to apply for shares, on the basis of the prospectus, by returning an application form. The prospectus will state the time by which application forms must be sent in (normally the time when the application list opens and may immediately afterwards close), and to whom they should be sent. In the case of large public offers they will usually be sent to receiving bankers who are appointed specifically to receive and deal with applications. The application form must normally be accompanied by a cheque for the shares applied for and the issuer or vendor will probably reserve the right to clear all cheques. As a result, anybody stagging the issue will have to arrange for funds to be available to meet his cheque or cheques, and this can involve expense, if nothing else in lost interest. The issuer or vendor should also reserve the right to reject any application or, if it considers it appropriate, to aggregate multiple applications.

An application will probably constitute, in contractual terms, an offer. Accordingly, once it is validly accepted, there will be a contract between the company or the vendor and the applicant. Acceptance will usually be effected by the posting of a renounceable letter of allotment or a renounceable letter of acceptance. The use of renounceable documents has now become standard practice for a number of reasons:

(a) a letter of allotment is transferable within a specified period without the usual payment of 2 per cent ad valorem stamp duty due to an exemption to the Stamp Act 1891 provided by section 65(1) of the Finance Act 1963. This provides that, where the rights under letters of allotment are renounceable not later than six months after the issue of the letter, no stamp duty will be payable;

(b) it allows the registrars more time, among other things, for the preparation of definitive share certificates; and

(c) in the case of an offer for sale it provides a relatively convenient mechanism whereby the shares can be made payable by instalments.

The letters of allotment will specify a date on which they cease to be valid, and this date will be within the six month period referred to in (a) above. Definitive share certificates will usually be sent on that date to those persons to whom the renounceable letters of allotment or acceptance were sent, unless before the expiry date the relevant letter has been returned duly renounced, in which event the definitive certificates will be sent to the renouncees or their lodging agents.

Within one month of making an allotment of shares, a return must be made to the Registrar of Companies (normally on Form PUC 2), and the appropriate capital duty due under section 47 of the Finance Act 1973 paid.

Timing consent

If the money to be raised by the issue of shares or debentures is in excess of £3 million, the time at which the securities are to be offered must be approved by the Bank of England on behalf of the Treasury. This requirement arises from the Control of Borrowing Order 1958 (as amended).

Timing consent is obtained through the government broker who, in order to ensure an orderly new issues market, operates a queue system of issues wishing to come to the market. The date for which consent is obtained is referred to as "impact day" – and is the first day on which the size and terms of the issue may be made public. The Yellow Book states that it is essential for sponsors to ensure that there is no publicity given to an issue before "impact day". Either the merchant bank or the stockbroker involved in the issue will take responsibility for obtaining timing consent. It is often necessary to book a place in the queue well in advance of the proposed impact day.

Registration of the prospectus

Section 41 provides that a prospectus must be filed *on or before* the date of publication. Section 41 provides for only one copy of the prospectus (and other documents) to be delivered, but since the move of a substantial part of the Companies Registry to Cardiff, two copies of all documents are required to be delivered. Because the prospectus may not be issued until after it has been delivered for registration, it is important to know the time of registration. It is therefore usually desirable for a prospectus to be delivered by hand to Companies House in London. Since the requirement in section 41 is merely to deliver the prospectus for registration, it would seem that the Registrar has no authority to refuse delivery. However, the Registrar's staff tend to run through a check list before accepting the documents for registration. This seems to consist of the following:

(a) that the prospectus is dated (C.A. 1948, s. 37), and that the prospectus states that a copy has been delivered to the Registrar (C.A. 1948, s. 41(2));

(b) that any experts' consents that are referred to in the prospectus (usually in the statutory and general section) are attached to the prospectus (C.A. 1948, s. 41(1)(a));

(c) that the prospectus is signed by every person who is named in it as a director, and in the case of an offer for sale by the persons making the offer, i.e. usually by two directors on behalf of the merchant bank or stockbroker (C.A. 1948, ss. 41, 45). If the stockbroker is a partnership, section 45(4) of the 1948 Act requires the prospectus to be signed by or on behalf of not less than half of the partners. If the directors (or others) have not signed personally but by power of attorney, two copies of the power of attorney must be lodged. The original, which must be duly stamped, must be shown but will not be retained. If the arrangements go wrong, stamped telexed powers of attorney will usually be accepted;

(d) that copies of all material contracts listed in the prospectus are attached to the prospectus (C.A. 1948, s. 41 (1)(b)(i)); and

(e) that, if the auditors reporting pursuant to Part II of the Fourth Schedule have made any adjustments under paragraph 29 of the Schedule, a signed statement setting out the adjustments and giving the reasons for them is attached to the prospectus (C.A. 1948, s. 41(1)(b)(ii)).

Although there is no statutory requirement to produce a section 39 certificate of exemption where one has been granted, it is recommended that copies of this too be delivered, if nothing else to explain any failure to comply with the Fourth Schedule. However, it is understood that The Stock Exchange sends a copy of each section 39 certificate to the Registrar at the time the certificate is sent to the company.

If the documents pass this process, a receipt is issued stating that the prospectus "has been provisionally accepted . . . for registration" (again implying a greater role for the Registrar of Companies than appears from the Companies Act).

Foreign and unregistered companies

The law applicable to the issue of prospectuses by foreign companies is contained primarily in Part X of the Companies Act 1948 and is dealt with in the chapter *Overseas Companies*. It is perhaps worth noting here that the prospectus provisions of Part X apply whether or not the foreign company has a place of business in Great Britain.

Certain bodies corporate which are not registered companies under the Companies Acts, are brought within the Acts to a specified extent by section 435 of the Companies Act 1948 and the Fourteenth Schedule to that Act. The section applies only to bodies corporate which are incorporated in, and have a principal place of business in, Great Britain. These entities are deemed to be companies registered under the Act for the purposes of the specified provisions. Certain bodies corporate are exempt (examples are bodies incorporated by public general Act of Parliament, and charities). The provisions of the 1948 Act relating to prospectuses which are applied to these bodies are sections 37 to 46, 50, 51 and 55 and the Fourth Schedule, but their application is subject to any limitations specified by regulations made by the Department of Trade (see The Companies (Unregistered Companies) Regulations 1979, S.I. 597).

Publicity Requirements

Publicity is fundamental to United Kingdom company legislation. Considerable amounts of information are required to be made available in various ways to protect potential investors, members and third parties, as well as employees. The availability of certain information has led to the application of a doctrine of constructive notice, with the result that sometimes "the supposed boon of publicity unjustly backfires upon an unsuspecting third party" (Sealy, (1981) 2 Co Law 51). Much time and energy must be invested by a conscientious company management to ensure that the requirements are satisfied, but the usefulness of some of the information collected and made available is in doubt. It may be questioned whether the cost of meeting these obligations is justified in all cases.

Nevertheless, the requirements must be observed and some undoubtedly do serve a useful and even vital purpose. The main publicity requirements imposed upon registered companies are dealt with below under three heads – documents and information to be filed at the Companies Registry, information to be made available at the company's offices and information to be shown on business communications. In addition, various further publicity requirements are imposed upon companies listed on recognised stock exchanges (under the Companies Acts and the Stock Exchange Listing Agreement).

Documents and information to be filed at the Companies Registry

The legislation requires certain information to be filed with the Registrar of Companies at Companies House, either at Crown Way, Maindy, Cardiff CF4 3UZ or at 55–71 City Road, London EC17 1BB. Scottish companies are dealt with at Exchequer Chambers, 102 George Street, Edinburgh EH2 3DJ. Forms are prescribed by statute for the filing of information (see Appendix 5 for the Companies Registry Forms currently in use).

Information relating to each company is microfilmed and the fiches are available to the public in Cardiff or London (see the chapter *Company Searches*). Where the copy is illegible, the original may be inspected (C.A. 1948, s. 426, as amended by C.A. 1981, s. 98).

Some of the more common matters requiring registration at the Companies Registry are set out in the Table on page 650.

Table 1

Table 1 covers the activities of a company during its lifetime only; therefore it does not include documents requiring filing in relation to incorporation and commencement of business, re-registration, appointment of a receiver and liquidation. For the requirements in these situations, and for detailed explanations of the requirements which are noted in Table 1, the relevant specific chapter of this book should be consulted (i.e. *Formation and Types of Company, Receivers, Liquidation*). For detail concerning foreign companies with a place of business in Great Britain, see the chapter *Overseas Companies*.

Table 1

Matter requiring registration	Documents to be delivered	Time limit	Statutory authority
(1) Annual return	Annual Return Form 6A for companies having a share capital	Must be completed within 42 days of AGM and sent to Registrar forthwith – interpreted by Registrar as meaning must be filed within 42 days of AGM	C.A. 1948, s. 126
	Form 7 for those not having share capital		
(2) Allotment of shares	(i) Cash consideration — Form PUC2 Non-cash consideration – Form PUC3 Bonus issue – Form PUC7 and particulars of contract and/or resolution to capitalise (ii) Where consideration is given, capital duty is normally payable at the rate of £1 per £100 or part of £100 on the greater of the total nominal value of the shares allotted or the total amount paid or due and payable, or treated as paid in respect of the shares allotted. A cheque should be sent with the PUC form and the Registrar will arrange for stamping by the Inland Revenue	Within one month of allotment	C.A. 1948, s. 52, as amended by C.A. 1976, Sch. 1, Sch. 2 F.A. 1973, s. 47 and Sch. 19

Matter requiring registration	Documents to be delivered	Time limit	Statutory authority
	If the allotment is an exempt transaction under Part III of Schedule 19 to the Finance Act 1973, a claim for exemption must be sent to the Stamp Duty Adjudication Office in Worthing together with a copy of the PUC form; the original PUC form should be sent unstamped to the Registrar with an explanatory letter		
	(iii) Where non-cash consideration is given the PUC form must be accompanied by a contract in writing constituting the title of the allottee to the allotment, together with any contract of sale or (in the case of a private company) contract for services relative to the making of the allotment. If there is no written contract, the prescribed particulars must be given on Form 52. The contract (or Form 52) should be stamped as necessary before being delivered to the Registrar		
	(iv) Where an expert's report on non-cash consideration is required under section 24 of the 1980 Act this must be delivered together with the above		C. A. 1980, s. 25

Matter requiring registration	Documents to be delivered	Time limit	Statutory authority
	(v) Where a claim for credit or relief from capital duty is made under section 49(5) of the Finance Act 1973, a Form PUC4 should accompany the appropriate PUC form		
(3) Amounts, or further amounts, paid on nil paid or partly paid shares	Form PUC5	Within one month of transaction	F.A. 1973, s. 47 and Sch. 19
(4) Chargeable transaction of capital company not covered by another PUC form	Form PUC6	Within one month of transaction	F.A. 1973, s. 47 and Sch. 19
(5) Registration of particulars of special rights attaching to shares where not otherwise registrable	Forms 33, 33a, 33b for new shares allotted, rights varied or new name assigned to class respectively	Within one month of relevant event	C.A. 1980, s. 33; and see C.A. 1981, s. 102
(6) Commission payable in connection with subscription for shares where shares not offered to public	Form 58a	Before payment of commission	C.A. 1948, s. 53 (1)(c)(ii) and (d)

Matter requiring registration	Documents to be delivered	Time limit	Statutory authority
(7) Passing of special or extraordinary resolution and of other resolutions specified in section 143 of the 1948 Act	Copy of resolution (plus copy of the altered memorandum or articles of association if altered unless it was special resolution under section 5 of the 1948 Act – see below)	Within 15 days of resolution being passed	C.A. 1984, s. 143 E.C.A. 1972, s. 9(5)
(8) Alteration of memorandum of association under section 5 of the 1948 Act	(i) Special resolution and (ii) Copy of memorandum as altered *or* (iii) If application is made to court to cancel alteration: notice of application on Form 101 and office copy of Court Order (with altered memorandum if any)	(i) Copy resolution within 15 days, as above (ii) Copy memorandum within 15 days from end of period within which an application to the court to cancel the alteration may be made (unless application is actually made, when see (iii) below). The period for application is 21 days from the passing of the relevant resolution, therefore if no application is made the copy memorandum must be delivered between the 22nd and 35th day. The Registrar will not usually accept a copy any earlier than this (see page 582)	C.A. 1948, s. 143 C.A. 1948, s. 5 E.C.A. 1972, s. 9(5)

Matter requiring registration	Documents to be delivered	Time limit	Statutory authority
		(iii) If an application is made, section 5(7) of the 1948 Act applies. The application must be made within 21 days of the passing of the resolution and the company must notify the Registrar forthwith. An office copy of the Court Order cancelling or confirming the alteration must be sent to the Registrar within 15 days of the order (together with altered memorandum if any)	
(9) Increase of capital	(i) Copy of resolution authorising increase (ii) Form 10 giving particulars of increase	Within 15 days of resolution being passed	C.A. 1948, s. 63

Matter requiring registration	Documents to be delivered	Time limit	Statutory authority
(10) Consolidation of share capital, conversion of shares into stock or stock to shares, subdivision or redemption of shares, cancellation of shares otherwise than under section 66 of the 1948 Act	Notice on Form 28	One month after alteration	C.A. 1948, s. 62 as amended
(11) Accounts and directors' report	For requirements, which vary depending upon the type of company concerned, see the chapters *Accounts* and *Directors' Report*		
(12) Accounting reference date	Form 2	Within 6 months of incorporation – but if no date notified there is no default; the accounting reference date is then treated as 31 March	C.A. 1976, s. 2
(13) Change in accounting reference date	Form 3 or 3A	See the chapter *Accounting Reference Date*	C.A. 1976, s. 3

Matter requiring registration	Documents to be delivered	Time limit	Statutory authority
(14) Removal of auditor before expiry of his term of office by resolution at AGM	Form 14 – Notice of passing of resolution	Within 14 days of passing of resolution	C.A. 1976, s. 14(6)
(15) Auditor's statement on resignation where there are circumstances to be brought to attention of shareholders or creditors (see the chapter *Auditors*)	Copy of statement	Within 14 days of resignation	C.A. 1976, s. 16
(16) Change of director or secretary or particulars in the register of such persons	Form 9b	Within 14 days of change	C.A. 1976, s. 22, amending C.A. 1948, s. 200
(17) Directors' service contracts or memoranda thereof – place kept	Form 26 – Notice of place where contracts are kept or any change in that place, unless they have at all times been kept at company's registered office	Within 14 days of change	C.A. 1967, s. 26

Matter requiring registration	Documents to be delivered	Time limit	Statutory authority
(18) Registers of directors' interests and substantial interests	Form 27 (or 27A if the register is kept in non-legible form). Notice of place where registers kept and any change in that place, unless they have at all times been kept at company's registered office	Within 14 days of change	C.A. 1967, s. 29 and C.A. 1981, s. 73
(19) Charges created by companies registered in England	Form 47 or 47A and the original instrument (if any) creating or evidencing the charge (this is returned to the applicant after checking)	Within 21 days after date of creation (time for registration may be extended under section 101 of the 1948 Act by the court in some circumstances). For consequences of failure to register within time limit see the chapter *Company Charges*	C.A. 1948, s. 95
(Charges involving Scottish companies or property may involve other requirements see C.A. 1948, Part IIIA)*	(Where there is more than one issue of debentures in a series, particulars of each further issue must be delivered on Form 48)		

* Sections 95 and 97 of the 1948 Act are applied to a company incorporated outside England with an established place of business in England in respect of charges on property in England, even where the company is not registered under Part X of the 1948 Act; section 106 of the 1948 Act as amended by 1981 Act and see *N. V. Slavenburg's Bank v. Intercontinental Natural Resources Ltd.* [1980] 1 All E.R. 955. There is now a special register of such charges. On registration requirements for overseas companies generally see the chapter *Overseas Companies* (and note also the chapter *Company Charges*)

Matter requiring registration	Documents to be delivered	Time limit	Statutory authority
(20) Charges existing on property acquired by a company registered in England (for Scottish companies or property see Part IIIA of the 1948 Act and the footnote on page 657)	Form 47B and certified copy of instrument, if any, creating the charge	Normally within 21 days after the date on which the acquisition is completed, and see comments on time limits under (19) above	C.A. 1948, s. 97
(21) Satisfaction and release of property from charge in whole or part – memorandum of satisfaction may be filed	Statutory declaration on Forms 49, 49A or 49B, signed by two officers of the company and sealed	There is no obligation to apply for registration	C.A. 1948, s. 100
(22) Register of debenture holders (if kept)	Notification (on Form 102, or 102a if register in non-legible form) of address of place kept and any changes in that place unless always kept at registered office	—	C.A. 1948, s. 86
(23) Register of members	Notice on Form 103 (or Form 103a if in non-legible form) of place where register kept and any change of place unless at all times at registered office	Within 14 days of change	C.A. 1948, s. 110
(Dominion Register)	(Form 29 or 29a – Notice of place kept and of discontinuance)	(Within 14 days of opening of office, change or discontinuance)	C.A. 1948, s. 119

Matter requiring registration	Documents to be delivered	Time limit	Statutory authority
(24) Change of registered office	Form 4a (intended situation of office must be specified on application for registration of company)	Within 14 days of the change	C.A. 1976, s. 23
(25) Prospectuses	Two copies of prospectus, duly dated and signed, and certain other documents – see the chapter *Prospectuses and Public Issues*	On or before date of publication	C.A. 1948, s. 41
(26) Increase of members registered number; unlimited company or company limited by guarantee	Form 11	Within 15 days from date of increase or resolution to increase number of members	C.A. 1948, s. 7
(27) Details of purchase by company of own shares	See the chapter *Purchase and Holding of Own Shares* – the information to be returned depends on the type of company	Within 28 days from the date of purchase	C.A. 1981, s. 52

Notes to Table 1

(1) *Consequences of default*

The court may order compliance with the filing requirements under section 428 of the Companies Act 1948. This is without prejudice to the penalties imposed on the company and its officers in respect of the default. Each obligation to file is backed by penalties specified in the same section. Many of the penalties were increased by the 1980 Act; Schedule 2 of that Act sets out the increased penalties in convenient tabular form. It is no defence that the preparation of the returns was delegated to professional advisers. Persistent default may result in disqualification of an officer or officers – see section 188 of the 1948 Act as amended by section 93 of the Companies Act 1981. The Registrar maintains a public register of disqualified persons (section 29 of the 1976 Act).

(2) *Publication in Gazette*

In addition to publication by filing on the public file certain matters must be publicised by publication in the London *Gazette* (or the Edinburgh *Gazette* for Companies registered in Scotland). It is the responsibility of the Registrar of Companies to cause to be published in the *Gazette* notice of the issue or receipt by him of the documents specified in section 9(3) of the European Communities Act 1972 as amended by the Companies Acts 1976 to 1981. These documents include those altering the company's memorandum or articles and those relating to change of the company's directors or the situation of its registered office. It is very much the company's concern that these requirements should be satisfied. This is because section 9(4) of the 1972 Act prevents the company from relying on the events specified above in relation to section 9(3), or on the making of a winding-up order in respect of the company, or the appointment of a liquidator in a voluntary winding-up of the company, unless the event has been notified in the *Gazette* when the transaction in question is entered into, or the company can show that the third party had actual knowledge of the event at that time. In addition, the company may not rely upon the change for 15 days following publication in the *Gazette* where the third party is "unavoidably prevented" from knowing of the event (see also the chapter *Company Contracts*).

(3) *Form of documents*

The Department of Trade leaflet "Notes for the guidance of registered companies" gives details of the printing and copying requirements which must be satisfied in respect of documents filed. The leaflet can be obtained from Companies House in London and from Cardiff.

The altered articles and memorandum of a company are required to be "printed" by the legislation; various processes are acceptable including electrostatic photocopying, offset lithography, and stencil duplicating using waxed stencils. Section 51 of the Companies Act 1967 gives the Registrar power to approve forms of copy other than printed copies in the case of special and extraordinary resolutions and ordinary resolutions increasing capital. The Registrar will accept typed copies of such resolutions as well as copies produced as required for the memorandum and articles.

Other documents for use on the company's file must be suitable in general appearance, legibility, format and durability for that use. Regulations may be made for this purpose and failure to comply may lead to penalties being imposed as if no document had been delivered (section 35 of the 1976 Act).

Information to be made available at the company's offices

Much of the information to be filed at the Companies Registry must also be kept available by the company, together with certain additional information. Table 2 sets out the main requirements.

Table 2

Information to be made available	Place to be kept	Availability	Statutory authority
(1) Register of members (for dominion registers for companies with branches in overseas dominions see sections 119–123 of the 1948 Act)	(i) Registered office (ii) *or* other office of company where register kept up (iii) *or* office of person who has undertaken to make up register Office must be in country of registration (i.e. England and Wales, or Scotland)	Free inspection for members; not more than 5p for others; at least two hours per day during business hours – with power to close for up to 30 days in each year. Copies must also be provided, subject to certain conditions	C.A. 1948, ss. 110, 113, 115
(2) Register of debenture holders (if kept)	As in (1) above	As in (1) above – no fee for members or debenture holders	C.A. 1948, ss. 86, 87
(3) Register of charges	Registered office	Free inspection for members and creditors; others – maximum 5p; at least two hours per day during business hours	C.A. 1948, ss. 104, 105

Information to be made available	Place to be kept	Availability	Statutory authority
(4) Copy instruments creating charges	Registered office	As in (3) above	C.A. 1948, s. 103
(5) Register of directors and secretaries	Registered office	Free inspection for members – not more than 5p for others, for at least two business hours per day	C.A. 1948, s. 200
(6) Directors' service contracts or memoranda thereof	Registered office *or* other place where register of members kept *or* principal place of business provided this is in England and Wales (or Scotland for companies registered in Scotland)	Free inspection for members of the company only, for at least two business hours per day	C.A. 1967 s. 26 as amended
(7) Register of directors' shareholdings and debentures	Registered office or other place where register of members kept	As (5) above. Copies may be required under certain conditions	C.A. 1967, s. 29 as amended by C.A. 1976, Sch. 1
(8)(i) Register of substantial interests in shares	(i) With register in (7) above	Open to inspection to any person without charge for at least two business hours per day. Copies to be made available on certain conditions	C.A. 1981, ss. 73, 76, 80
(ii) Reports under sections 74 and 76 of the 1981 Act on requisition of members with respect to interests in shares	(ii) Registered office		

Information to be made available	Place to be kept	Availability	Statutory authority
(9) Accounting records – to be kept for three years from date on which made in case of private companies, six years for others	Registered office or such other place as the directors think fit (but the information must be available in Great Britain)	Open to inspection by officers of the company	C.A. 1976, s. 12
(10) Minutes of general meetings in minute books	Registered office	As in (6) above. Copies to be made available on certain conditions	C.A. 1948, ss. 145, 146
(11) Memorandum and articles of association as amended and such resolutions and agreements registrable under section 143 of the 1948 Act as are in force	—	Copy to be sent to member on request, subject to nominal payment	C.A. 1948, ss. 24, 25, 143(2)
(12) Copy contract (or written memorandum of its terms) relating to purchase of own shares, and any variation thereof (to be kept until ten years from completion of purchase)	Registered office	Available for free inspection by members and, if a public company, any other person, for at least two hours per day during business hours	C.A. 1981, s. 52 (and see C.A. 1981, ss. 47 and 56 for special provisions concerning off-market purchases, and purchases out of capital)

Note to Table 2

As to the form in which information is to be kept, see section 436 of the 1948 Act, as amended by Schedule 2 to the 1976 Act and section 3 of the Stock Exchange (Completion of Bargains) Act 1976 (use of computers for records).

Information to be given on business communications

The name of the company

Section 108 of the 1948 Act

This requires the name of the company to be shown clearly on:

(i)   the outside of every office or place of business of the company;

(ii) the company's seal (upon which it should be engraved);

(iii) its business letters, notices, official publications, bills of exchange, promissory notes, endorsements, cheques and orders for money or goods, bills of parcels, invoices, receipts and letters of credit.

Use of limited, p.l.c. etc.

The name of the company must have as its last words "limited" (for private limited companies) or "public limited company" where appropriate. The Welsh equivalents may be used but if that is done, the fact that the company is limited must be stated in English on business communications and nameplates (C.A. 1948, s. 2; C.A. 1976, s. 30; C.A. 1980, s. 2). The abbreviations "Ltd." and "p.l.c." and the Welsh equivalents may be used (C.A. 1980, s. 78). The above appellations must not be used so as to mislead the public into thinking that a company's nature is other than its true one (C.A. 1948, s. 439; C.A. 1980, s. 76). Some charitable and similar types of company may be exempted from using the word "limited" in their name (C.A. 1981, s. 25; see generally the chapters *Memorandum* and *Names*).

Business names

A company may use a business name provided it complies with sections 28 to 30 of the 1981 Act. Registration of business names is no longer required (see the chapter *Names*). In this way, a limited company may trade under a name not including the word "limited", but most of its business communications must nevertheless have stated on them in legible characters the name of the company and an address for service of documents. In addition, this information must also be displayed in a prominent position where it can easily be read by customers and suppliers in any premises in which the business is carried on and to which all or some of those persons have access (section 29 of the 1981 Act). Thus a company is obliged to publicise its status even if it uses a business name.

Additional information

Section 9(7) of the European Communities Act 1972

This requires every company to mention the following in legible characters on its business letters and order forms (a narrower range of documentation than that to which section 108 of the 1948 Act applies):

(i)   the place of registration (that is, England, Wales, or Scotland – London, Cardiff and Edinburgh are also acceptable);

(ii) the registered number as shown on the certificate of incorporation;

(iii) the address of the registered office – if the address used on the business stationery is the registered office in any event, this should be stated;

(iv) if the company is exempt from using the word "limited" as part of its name, the fact that it is a limited company must be stated;

(v)   where applicable, the fact that the company is an investment company within the meaning of Part III of the Companies Act 1980; and

(vi) where there is any reference to share capital (which is permitted but not required), the reference must be to paid-up share capital.

Section 201

Section 201 of the 1948 Act, as amended by Schedule 5 to the Consumer Credit Act 1974 and Schedules 3 and 4 to the Companies Act 1981, provides that a company must not state the name of any of its directors (otherwise than in the text or as a signatory) on any business letter, unless the name of every director is shown on the letter. This applies to companies registered in Great Britain since November 23, 1916 and overseas companies with established places of business within Great Britain, unless established before that date. Thus a company must show the names of all or none of its directors on its notepaper; it cannot be selective as to which directors' names it displays.

If the names are stated the christian names or initials of individual directors must be shown and the corporate name of every corporate director. It is no longer necessary to specify the nationality of directors. "Director" for this purpose includes any person in accordance with whose directions or instructions the directors of the company are accustomed to act. Although the section's heading refers to "trade catalogues and circulars", the section as amended now deals only with "business letters".

Company in liquidation or receivership

Where a company is in liquidation, or a manager or receiver has been appointed, every invoice, order for goods or business letter issued by or on behalf of the company or the liquidator, receiver or manager of the company must contain a statement that the company is being wound up or that a receiver or manager has been appointed (C.A. 1948, ss. 338, 370).

Overseas companies

Section 411 of the 1948 Act requires publicity to be given to the name, country of incorporation and, where appropriate, the limited liability of a company incorporated outside Great Britain which has an established place of business within Great Britain (see the chapter *Overseas Companies*).

Penalties for default

Both the company and its officers are liable to penalties if they fail to comply with the above requirements. The penalties are dealt with in each relevant section. Those penalties contained in legislation prior to the 1980 Act were updated by Schedule 2 to the 1980 Act and are set out there, in tabular form.

Purchase and Holding of Own Shares

The maintenance of capital is a long-established principle of English company law and it was on the basis of that principle that the case of *Trevor v. Whitworth* (1887) 12 App Cas 409 held that a limited company may not purchase its own shares, as that would amount to an unauthorised reduction of capital. This chapter primarily examines the significant changes made to that basic rule by Part III of the Companies Act 1981.

The basic rule: Companies Act 1980

The rule that a *limited* company may not purchase its own shares is now contained in legislative form in section 35 of the Companies Act 1980. This provides, subject to certain exceptions, that no company limited by shares or limited by guarantee, whether public or private, is permitted to acquire its own shares, whether by purchase, subscription or otherwise. There are a number of exceptions to this rule, which are as follows.

Acquisition other than for valuable consideration

A company is permitted to acquire any of its own *fully paid* shares otherwise than for valuable consideration (section 35(2)). Examples are acquisitions by way of gift or testamentary bequest (see *Re Castiglione's Will Trust* [1958] Ch. 549 and *Kirby v. Wilkins* [1929] 2 Ch. 444). A *public* company is subject to an additional restriction in this case, since, under section 37 of the 1980 Act, shares acquired in this way must be disposed of or cancelled within three years (see the chapter *Shares*).

Redemption or purchase under Companies Act 1981

A company may redeem or purchase any of its own shares in accordance with Part III of the 1981 Act (see the chapter *Redeemable Shares* and below).

Acquisition in a reduction of capital

The acquisition of shares in a reduction of capital is permitted (see the chapter *Reconstructions and Amalgamations*).

Purchase pursuant to court order

A company may purchase shares in pursuance of a court order under section 11(7) of the Companies Act 1980 (on an application related to a resolution resulting in a company becoming a private company), section 75 of the 1980 Act (unfairly prejudicial conduct), or section 5 of the 1948 Act (alteration of objects).

Forfeiture or surrender

Finally, the forfeiture and surrender of shares for failure to pay any sum payable in respect of those shares is permitted (see the chapter *Shares*).

Apart from these exceptions, any purported acquisition by a limited company of its own shares is void. In addition, there are criminal sanctions applicable against the company and any officer in default (C.A. 1980, s. 35(3)).

As explained in the chapter *Shares*, sections 36 and 37 of the Companies Act 1980 contain certain rules and restrictions governing the acquisition of shares by a *nominee* for a company. To a large extent these restrictions mirror the previous common law rules, and where the sections do not apply the common law will generally prevent a nominee acquiring shares (e.g. a nominee cannot acquire fully paid shares for any form of consideration, see *Kirby v. Wilkins* [1929] 2 Ch. 444 at 449).

Unlimited companies

An unlimited company has always had power to purchase its own shares (see Table E of the First Schedule to the Companies Act 1948), since the protection derived from the maintenance of capital in such a company is not required. However, an unlimited company is, like a limited company, precluded from holding shares in its holding company (C.A. 1948, s. 27 and page 693 below).

Purchase of own shares

The question whether a company should have the power to acquire its own shares was considered, and rejected, by the Jenkins Committee in 1962 (Cmnd 1749 of 1962), basically on the ground that there was little public interest in the possibility. That position having altered, in June 1980 the Government issued a consultative document *The Purchase by a Company of its Own Shares* (Cmnd 7944 of 1980), in which it set out the following principal reasons for examining a possible change in the law,

"The Government attaches particular importance to the principal economic arguments in favour of a relaxation of the present law. For private companies, a change should make investment and participation in such companies more attractive, by providing shareholders with a further means of disposing of their shares and by permitting the remaining members to maintain control and ownership of the business. Different considerations apply to companies whose shares are dealt in on a market. Public companies with surplus cash resources could find it useful to be able to buy their own shares and thus return surplus resources to shareholders, thereby removing the pressure on such companies to employ those surplus resources in uneconomic ways, and enabling shareholders to deploy the resources to better effect."

The Consultative Document comprises an analytical framework for consultation on the issues involved compiled by Professor L. C. B. Gower. It represents an admirable summary of the previous legal framework and, in its discussion of possible solutions and the experiences of other jurisdictions, is of great value in comprehending the background to the new rules.

Uses of the new provisions in the 1981 Act

It was recognised that a change in the law to permit the purchase by a company of its own shares would principally benefit the small family-controlled company by providing in effect an additional market for the shares, although advantages can also be discerned for public (and, subject to safeguards, even listed) companies. Some of the principal uses to which the new provisions may be put are listed below.

(1) *The buying out of dissident shareholders.* The presence of a vociferous, or simply uncooperative, minority shareholder can be greatly detrimental to a company's business. This can be particularly so in the family-controlled concern where two or more branches of the family fail to agree.

(2) *The purchase of the shares of a disinterested shareholder.* This can, for example, help stave off the threat of a take-over bid. The committed shareholders are thereby able to consolidate their control of the company.

(3) *The buying out of the shares of a deceased shareholder from either the personal representatives or legatees.* Shares falling into an estate might otherwise prove unmarketable if no other shareholder is able or willing to purchase. Without this power, a legatee might be "locked in" as a minority shareholder or else be obliged to sell to an outside investor, possibly a financial institution.

(4) *Employee share schemes.* The provisions enable shares issued under an incentive scheme (otherwise than under the conventional trust) to be re-purchased by the company on the employee ceasing to be employed.

(5) *Short-term equity funding.* A major drawback to the introduction of equity finance was the prospect of there being no market for the shares at the end of the investment period. It is now possible to grant an outside investor an option to sell his shares back to the company (see *Contingent purchase contracts* below).

(6) *Accelerating redemption.* If redeemable shares are quoted at below the redemption price, a company is enabled to save money by buying up those shares in advance of the redemption date.

(7) *Open-ended investment company.* The possibility of the open-ended investment company has been suggested as an alternative to the more conventional unit trust. However, the provisions governing the maintenance of capital on a purchase by a public company, and certain tax disadvantages, may make this impractical.

(8) *Market support.* The power might be used (subject to Stock Exchange rules) to support the market for the shares if this is thought to

be unduly depressed, thus preserving for the shareholders the value of their shares as marketable securities.

(9) *Reduction of capital.* Arguably, the provisions provide a cheaper and more straightforward means for *private* companies to reduce capital. Whether this will prove so in practice is perhaps open to some doubt, having regard to the stringent and complex provisions governing payments out of capital (see below).

It appears that there is nothing to prevent a private company giving itself power in the articles to *compulsorily* purchase its own shares (the 1981 Bill contained a restriction but this was not incorporated into the Act), although it is possible that the principle in cases such as *Brown v. British Abrasive Wheel Co. Limited* [1919] 1 Ch. 290 and *Dafen Tinplate Co. Limited v. Llanelly Steel Co* [1920] 2 Ch. 124 might be extended to restrict the company's powers here.

Taxation

Without major changes in the tax regime, the practical use of the new company law provisions would have been severely limited. The excess of the amount of the payment for the shares over their nominal value plus any premium paid on subscription would be treated as a distribution, thereby giving rise to a charge to advance corporation tax on the company and, in the case of an individual vendor shareholder, a liability to income tax under Schedule F.

Recognising this fact, the Finance Act 1982 contains detailed provisions enabling the purchase price for the shares in *unquoted trading companies* to be treated as a capital payment, subject to capital gains tax in the hands of the individual shareholder. There are numerous conditions to be satisfied before this treatment can be applied to any particular purchase (F.A. 1982, s. 53(1); section 53(2) provides tax relief where shares are bought in to meet a capital transfer tax liability on death and section 54 allows a share dealer to sell shares back to the company without a Schedule F charge). The detailed tax rules are outside the scope of this book but are dealt with in full in Tolley's *Purchase or Redemption by a Company of its Own Shares.*

Redemption of shares

The own-share purchase provisions in the 1981 Act are tied in very closely with the provisions permitting a redemption of shares, and as explained below many of the procedural and maintenance of capital requirements are the same. The chapter *Redeemable Shares* deals specifically with the rules governing redemption.

Companies Act 1981

The provisions permitting a company to purchase its own shares (in the case of a *private* company out of capital) are contained in sections 46 to

62 of the 1981 Act. The provisions took effect from June 15, 1982. Recognising that the new rules effect a revolutionary change to company law in Great Britain, the Government has, in section 61, reserved to itself power to make regulations altering certain of the provisions, including those affecting the following,

(a) the authority required for a purchase;

(b) the authority required for a release by a company of a purchase contract or contingent purchase contract;

(c) returns to the Registrar of Companies;

(d) the statutory declaration of the directors required where a private company proposes to purchase shares out of capital; and

(e) the auditors' report required to be annexed to that declaration.

The power to purchase

Subject to compliance with a number of procedural provisions which are considered below, section 46 of the Companies Act 1981 gives power to a public or private company, provided it is limited by shares or limited by guarantee and having a share capital, to purchase its own shares (including any redeemable shares). Redeemable shares can thus be bought in prior to their due date for redemption.

Authority in articles

Specific authority must be reserved in the articles of association of the company. Table A does not contain any general provision enabling a company to purchase its own shares. For companies incorporated prior to December 3, 1981, it is also necessary to eliminate the prohibition on the giving of financial assistance by a company for the acquisition of its shares, which before that date was incorporated into a company's articles by article 10 of Table A, and represented the former wide prohibition on such transactions contained in section 54 of the Companies Act 1948 (now repealed and replaced by section 42 of the Companies Act 1981 – see the chapter *Financial Assistance*). Section 42 of the 1981 Act expressly permits a purchase of own shares, which supports the view, that unless removed or amended by special resolution, the general prohibition contained in the pre-December 3, 1981 version of article 10 of Table A would operate to preclude such a purchase.

It is possible, particularly in the case of a private company, that the articles, or a shareholders agreement, may contain pre-emption or other provisions restricting the transfer of shares by a member. If there is such a provision, steps should be taken to obtain a waiver or consent from all interested parties.

The authority taken in the articles may be general, or limited for example to particular transactions, classes of share, or time within which the purchase may be made. However, in contrast to the treatment of redeemable shares, the terms and manner of purchase need not be determined by the articles.

The basic conditions

The basic conditions, apart from those relating to purely procedural matters, which are required to be satisfied by a company in making a purchase of its own shares largely follow the corresponding provisions applicable to an issue of redeemable shares under section 45 of the 1981 Act (see the chapter *Redeemable Shares*). The conditions are as follows.

(1) The shares must be fully paid.

(2) The terms of purchase must provide for payment on purchase. Apart perhaps from avoiding valuation difficulties, a factor suggested in the 1980 consultative document Cmnd 7944, the purpose of this condition is perhaps not so clear in the case of a *purchase* of shares as it is where shares are redeemed. In the latter case, the terms of redemption are effectively fixed at the outset by the company and the object of the provision is to prevent redeemable shares being exchanged at the option of the company, for shares of a different class or, for example, loan stock. On the other hand, where shares are purchased it seems unreasonable to restrict in any way the possible bargains between the company and the vendor shareholder, particularly where such a shareholder might be willing to accept payment by instalments or otherwise on deferred terms. However, there is nothing to prevent the vendor shareholder agreeing to accept cash on completion of the purchase and then immediately applying that cash, for example, in the subscription for new securities of a different class, the purchase of assets of the company, or simply leaving the purchase consideration on loan account.

(3) Generally, and subject to special rules applying only to *private* companies, the purchase monies can only be found out of distributable profits or out of the proceeds of a fresh issue of shares made for the purposes of the purchase. The expression *distributable profits* is given its Companies Act 1980 definition (C.A. 1981, s. 62; see the chapter *Dividends*). Any premium over the nominal value of the shares purchased *must* be found out of distributable profits except where the shares in question were originally issued at a premium. In this case, the premium element may be paid out of a fresh issue of shares up to *whichever is the lesser* of,

(i) the aggregate of the premiums received by the company on the issue of the shares purchased; or

(ii) the *current* amount of the company's share premium account (including any sum transferred to that account in respect of premiums on the new shares).

In such a case, the share premium account is reduced by a sum corresponding to the payment out of the fresh issue, although this does not of course result in an overall reduction of capital.

(4) Once purchased, the shares must be treated as *cancelled* and the issued share capital of the company reduced by their nominal amount. The authorised capital is not reduced. Where a purchase is contemplated, the company can issue new shares up to the nominal amount of the shares to be purchased without first increasing its authorised capital. Relief from capital duty is available in respect of new shares issued in place of shares purchased, up to the *actual value* of those shares at the date of purchase, although in the case where new shares are issued *before* the purchase, this relief is only applicable where the old shares are purchased within one month after the new issue (C.A. 1981, s. 45(10)).

The requirement that shares are to be cancelled on purchase means that the shorthand expression *"purchase* of own shares" is not strictly accurate. What this amounts to effectively is a redemption of non-redeemable shares, or redeemable shares prior to the due date for redemption. The system, common in the United States, of shares purchased by the company being held *in treasury* has not been adopted in the United Kingdom. This avoids the accounting problems that such shares might otherwise give rise to and, by providing that the purchased shares may not be re-issued, helps protect the rights of the remaining shareholders under section 14 (power of directors to issue shares) and section 17 (pre-emption rights) of the Companies Act 1980.

The cancellation of the purchased shares does not, except in the case of a purchase out of capital (see below), result in a reduction of the company's capital. The capital attributable to the cancelled shares is replaced either by a fresh issue of shares or by an amount transferred to capital redemption reserve (a topic dealt with more fully below).

(5) Following the purchase, there must be at least one member of the company holding non-redeemable shares (section 46(3)). This is an important requirement as it prevents a company effectively buying in all its shares and thereby effecting an informal winding-up. It should not of course be forgotten that it is still necessary for a company to have at least two members (C.A. 1948, s. 31).

Shareholder sanction: general

Without special rules, the control of the purchase by a company of its own shares would effectively rest with the directors. It was evidently considered that this might lead to abuses. The directors might either procure the purchase of their own shares by the company thus leaving minority shareholders with a balance sheet stripped of its assets, or else engineer purchases in order to secure majority control of the company. The 1980 consultative document considered the existing safeguards of (a) the directors' duties of care, skill and good faith and (b) the protection of minorities afforded by a winding-up order under section 222(f) of the 1948 Act on the ground that it is just and equitable, or the alternative remedy under section 75 of the 1980 Act available to minorities who are unfairly prejudiced, but concluded that further safeguards were required.

It was also necessary to incorporate disclosure and notification requirements into the new provisions. A potential creditor, and, more particularly a potential shareholder, could be prejudiced by an undisclosed contract of purchase or option over the company's shares.

In dealing with these additional safeguards, the scheme of the Companies Act 1981 is to divide the possible transactions into three categories,

(a) off-market purchases;

(b) contingent purchase contracts; and

(c) market purchases

Special rules are also applicable in the case where a private company seeks to purchase its shares out of *capital*, that is, otherwise than out of distributable profits or a fresh issue of shares.

Shareholder sanction: off-market purchases

An "off-market purchase" of shares is defined in section 47(2) of the 1981 Act as one where the shares are either purchased otherwise than on a recognised stock exchange, or where they are purchased on such an exchange but are not subject to a marketing arrangement. Shares are only subject to a marketing arrangement where either,

(i) they are listed on the stock exchange in question; or

(ii) they can be dealt in on that stock exchange *without prior permission* for individual transactions from the authority governing that stock exchange and without time limits on those dealings.

Off-market purchases will therefore exclude shares with a full listing on The Stock Exchange where the purchase takes place on that Exchange, and purchases on the Unlisted Securities Market (these are categorised as "market purchases" and are dealt with below), but will include shares dealt in under rule 163(2), or on the over-the-counter markets. A company is only permitted to make an off-market purchase in two cases:

(a) where the transaction is in pursuance of a "contingent purchase contract" already approved by shareholders under section 48 of the 1981 Act (see below); or

(b) where the terms of the proposed contract of purchase have received prior authorisation by a *special resolution* of the company. In the case of a *public* company, the authority cannot be open-ended; the resolution must state a date on which the authority is to expire, and that date cannot be later than 18 months after the passing of the resolution. Thus, for a public company the purchase contract must be entered into not more than 18 months after the resolution (unless the authority is renewed), although if a contract is so made it is immaterial whether or not it is actually completed within the specified time.

There are special rules as to certain formalities required for the passing of an effective special resolution. First, a copy of the proposed contract must be made available for inspection by shareholders at the registered office of the company for a period of at least fifteen days ending with the date of the meeting, and at the meeting itself. If the contract is not in writing, then a written memorandum of its terms must be made available in the way just described. Any written memorandum is required to include the names of the vendor shareholders, and there must be annexed to any copy of the contract any such names which do not appear in the contract itself. The requirement for these documents to be displayed effectively imposes on the company an additional notice period which runs in conjunction with the ordinary period of notice (21 days) required for a special resolution. There is, however, no power for the shareholders to waive the requirement as to inspection of documents, so that even if short notice of the meeting is agreed upon under section 133(3) of the Companies Act 1948, the 15-day display period must still be rigidly observed.

Secondly, the shares which are the subject of the purchase resolution are effectively disenfranchised. The special resolution cannot be treated as effective if votes are cast in respect of those shares (whether or not on a poll and whether by the member himself or his proxy) and the resolution would not have been passed otherwise than by the casting of those votes. Thus, the shares which are not to be purchased are in practice treated as a separate class; the special resolution will be carried if there is a 75 per cent majority of votes cast in respect of shares of that "class". What this means is that a vendor shareholder cannot vote at all on a show of hands (whether or not he owns other shares in the company) and, on a poll, can only vote in respect of shares which are not the subject of the purchase contract.

Where a number of vendor shareholders are involved, it may facilitate the transaction for there to be separate purchase contracts and correspondingly separate resolutions. Thus, vendor A would be entitled to vote in respect of contract B, and vendor B could vote on resolution A. There are no provisions inhibiting collaboration in this way.

If the above procedural requirements are not observed, the resolution is ineffective and any contract entered into by the company in reliance upon such resolution will be *ultra vires* and void. Presumably too, the company and any officer in default would be liable in such a case to penalties under section 35(3) of the 1980 Act.

Once a special resolution has been passed, it may be varied, revoked or renewed, again by special resolution. The special rules outlined above as to the passing of a resolution conferring the authority are equally applicable to a resolution to vary, revoke or renew. The contract itself, once entered into, may also be varied, provided prior authorisation is obtained by special resolution. Again, all the special rules apply, and in addition to the display for inspection of the proposed variations, the original contract (together with any previous variations) must also be made available to shareholders. Also, the company may, with the sanction of a special resolution, release its rights under the contract; any release purported to be made without such sanction is void (C.A. 1981, s. 50). However, the company cannot in any circumstances assign its rights under the contract.

Shareholder sanction: contingent purchase contracts

It may be that a company will wish to enter into a future obligation to purchase some of its shares. Full conversion of an irredeemable share into a redeemable share remains impossible (see the chapter *Redeemable Shares*) but, in this way, a company may effectively convert a share which is not *per se* redeemable into one which in practice may be redeemed (or purchased) at the option of the company or shareholder.

A contingent purchase contract is one,

(a) which does not amount to a binding contract to purchase the shares; but

(b) under which the company may, subject to conditions, become entitled or obliged to purchase those shares (C.A. 1981, s. 48).

Before a company can enter into a contingent purchase contract (and so purchase shares under it) the contract must receive the prior authorisation of a special resolution. All the conditions described above which apply to such a resolution on the conferring of an authority for an off-market purchase apply equally to a resolution approving or varying a contingent purchase contract, and any release by the company of its rights under the contract must also be authorised by special resolution. Like a purchase contract, a contingent purchase contract cannot be assigned.

The most obvious application of these provisions is to put and call options, whereby either the shareholder or the company can enforce a purchase. This could be especially attractive to institutions, or third party investors, who would then be able to provide short- or medium-term equity finance to a company whilst retaining an "escape route". It could also be used to give a company the right to re-acquire shares on the death or retirement of a director or other employee.

In practice, tax considerations may militate against contingent purchase contracts. It will not be clear until the time of the actual purchase of shares whether the tax reliefs afforded by the Finance Act 1982 will, or will not, be available. An alternate solution might be for the parties to enter into a shareholders' agreement embodying the usual put and call options as between the members themselves (and *not* the company) but providing that, subject to tax clearances, the vendor shareholder shall accept a purchase by the company if the other shareholders procure it. In this way, no contingent purchase contract is entered into and the usual provisions as to off-market purchases would have to be observed.

In some ways a purchase pursuant to a contingent purchase contract can give a company greater flexibility. Since it is the terms of the *first* contract which require approval, the terms of the purchase contract itself need not be fully set out. In addition, in the case of a public company, the time limit under section 47(8) of 18 months on the duration of the authority applies only to the contingent purchase contract; the actual purchase contract can be entered into outside that period.

Shareholder sanction: market purchases

Different rules apply to purchases on a recognised stock exchange which are subject to a marketing arrangement (C.A. 1981, s. 49). These include ordinary listed bargains and transactions through the Unlisted Securities Market. Occasional transactions under Rule 163(2) of The Stock Exchange are excluded as are dealings on the over-the-counter market.

In contrast with the special resolution required to sanction an off-market purchase, a *market purchase* requires only the authority of an *ordinary* resolution (although, like a special resolution, a copy must be registered under section 143 of the 1948 Act). The resolution may confer general authority sanctioning any purchase in the market, or authority limited to a particular class or description of shares. The authority may be unconditional or subject to conditions, but it must,

(a) specify the maximum number of shares authorised to be acquired;

(b) determine both the maximum and the minimum prices which may be paid for those shares; and

(c) specify a date, being not later than 18 months after the date of the resolution, on which the authority is to expire.

The maximum and minimum prices for the shares fixed by the resolution may be determined in either of two ways,

(i) by specifying a fixed sum; or

(ii) by providing a fixed basis or formula for calculating the price i.e. one that is without reference to any person's discretion or opinion (for example, an auditor's valuation would not be sufficient).

Because the authority given by the ordinary resolution may be general and need not specify any particular shares, there is no restriction on any shareholder exercising his votes on the resolution. Furthermore, whilst the special resolution authorising an off-market purchase must approve a specific *contract* of purchase, it is the *purchase* itself which is sanctioned under this head. For this reason, section 49(8) expressly provides that a purchase outside the time limit imposed by the resolution is valid provided a *contract* for the purchase was concluded before the expiry of the authority *and* the terms of the authority permitted the company to make a contract of purchase which would or might be executed wholly or partly after the authority expired.

There are provisions for the variation, revocation or renewal of the authority to purchase. Again, an ordinary resolution is required and that resolution is subject to the same provisions as apply when the authority is first conferred on the company.

Although a listed or USM company may under these provisions possess general authority to purchase shares on the market, the insider dealing rules contained in Part V of the Companies Act 1980 may operate in practice to inhibit many transactions. The directors of a company, on whose authority the market purchase would be made, are inevitably from time to time in possession of unpublished price sensitive information in relation to the company's shares. As such, they would not be permitted to *procure* any other person (including the company itself) to deal in those securities, unless for example the making of a profit or avoidance of a loss was not one of the purposes (C.A. 1980, s. 68; see further the chapter *Insider Dealing*).

Stock Exchange requirements

In addition to the general rules for market purchases contained in section 49 of the 1981 Act, The Stock Exchange itself published in June 1982 some notes on procedures to be adopted under the normal Listing Agreement. The text of that release is reproduced below. Although the notes refer in terms to listed companies, the requirements are equally applicable to USM companies.

Stock Exchange notes on procedure

"Immediate notification of board decision to submit proposals to shareholders for purchase by a company of its own shares

Immediate notification to The Stock Exchange should be made of any decision by the board to submit to the company's shareholders a proposal for the company to be authorised to purchase its own shares. An indication should be given as to whether the proposal relates to specific purchases, or to a general authorisation to make purchases.

Circulars to shareholders

The circular seeking shareholders' authority should be treated as a Class I circular for Stock Exchange purposes where the exercise in full of the authority sought would result in the purchase of 15% or more of the share capital. In that case it should be in accordance with Schedule II Part B of Admission of Securities to Listing ("the Yellow Book"), and the working capital statement thus required should be based on the assumption that the authority sought would be used in full at the maximum price allowed thereunder. This assumption should also be stated. Additionally, where the authority sought relates to specific proposals, the names of the shareholders who will be parties to the proposed contract should be stated together with all other material terms of the proposal. Where the board is seeking general authority to purchase shares in the market, they should state their intentions with regard to the authority thus conferred. Shareholders should be notified if the company intends to "stand in the market" for a given period, or until such time as a specified number of shares has been acquired.

A purchase on the market by way of a "put through" from a person with whom the company has a Class 4 relationship (typically a director or substantial shareholder) should be treated in accordance with the customary procedure for such transactions, and shareholders' specific approval sought (see paragraph 8 of Chapter 4 of the Yellow Book). The terms of a purchase from such a person made outside The Stock Exchange would in any event be required by the Act to have such prior consent by reason of the fact that it would be an "off-market" purchase.

Immediate notification should be made of the outcome of the shareholders' meeting, and four copies of the relevant resolutions forwarded to The Stock Exchange as soon as possible thereafter.

Convertible securities, warrants and options to subscribe for ordinary shares

Where there are in issue convertible securities or warrants or options to subscribe equity capital, a separate class meeting of the holders should be held and their approval by extraordinary resolution obtained before the company enters into any contract to purchase its own shares or first exercises a general authority to make purchases in the market. Such approval is required, whether or not there are provisions in the relevant trust deed or terms of issue regarding adjustments to be made if the company were to purchase its own shares.

The circular containing the notice of meeting must set out clearly the apparent effect on the conversion or subscription expecttions of the holders, in terms of attributable assets and earnings, if the company were to exercise in full the authorisation which it is seeking to purchase its own shares. Additionally any special adjustments which the company may propose should be set out, and the information above restated on the revised basis.

Purchase of 5 per cent or more

Purchases within a period of 12 months of a significant amount of a company's share capital, that is to say, five per cent or more, should be made either by way of a tender offer or a partial offer to all shareholders.

The tender offer should be made on The Stock Exchange at a stated maximum price. Notice of the offer should be given by paid advertisement in two national newspapers at least seven days before the offer closes. Companies are advised to consult their stockbroker for advice on the procedures for such offers.

Model code for securities transactions by directors of listed companies

The model code for directors should be regarded as applicable to purchases by a company of its own shares. Thus the company should not purchase shares at any time when the directors would not be free to do so on their own account.

Notification to The Stock Exchange of purchases

Notification of all purchases by a company of its own shares should be made by 12 noon on the following dealing day. The notification should include the number of shares purchased and the purchase price per share or the highest and lowest prices paid, where relevant. Details of these notifications will be published in The Stock Exchange Weekly Official Intelligence.

Particulars in directors' report of company's existing powers of purchase

The company's annual directors' report should contain particulars of any authorities or approvals given to the board by the shareholders to purchase the company's own shares existing at the end of the financial year. In addition to the information required under section 14 of the Act, equivalent information should be given of any purchases of its own shares, or options or contracts to make such purchases, entered into since the end of the year covered by the report. The information should also include names of the sellers in the case of all purchases made, or proposed to be made, otherwise than through the market, or made by tender or by partial offer to all shareholders."

In addition, a company proposing to purchase or redeem its own shares should discuss the matter with the Take-Overs and Mergers Panel in advance (amendment to the *City Code on Take-Overs and Mergers* dated June 3, 1982). It is not clear whether the Panel intend this requirement to include unlisted public companies as well as companies listed on The Stock Exchange (see also page 692).

Disclosure requirements

The special resolution authorising an off-market purchase or a contingent market purchase must be filed with the Registrar within 15 days in the usual way (C.A. 1948, s. 143). And although a market purchase can be sanctioned by ordinary resolution alone, the same registration requirement applies (C.A. 1981, s. 49(10)). These are normal filing requirements. But section 52 of the 1981 Act imposes additional requirements in the case of own-share purchases under section 46.

First, within 28 days after delivery to the company of the shares in question, the company must deliver to the Registrar a return on Form 64 stating with respect to each class of shares purchased,

(a) the number and nominal value of the shares;

(b) the date on which they were delivered to the company; and

(c) in the case of a *public* company only,

(i) the aggregate price paid for *all* classes of shares; and

(ii) the maximum and minimum prices paid in respect of each class.

Where purchases are effected on different dates and under different contracts a single return is acceptable. In such a case the requirement for a public company to state the aggregate price refers to all the shares to which the return relates.

Secondly, copies of certain documents must be made available for inspection. A copy of the purchase contract (market or off-market), any contingent purchase contract, and any variation agreement, or if the contract is not in writing, a memorandum of its terms, must be kept at the registered office of the company from the date of conclusion of the contract until ten years after completion of *all* share purchases under it or, if earlier, the date on which the contract otherwise determines.

The copies retained at the registered office must be available for inspection during business hours, without charge, to any member of the company and additionally, in the case of a public company, any other person. The company is entitled, by means of an ordinary resolution, to impose reasonable restrictions on times of inspection, but at least two hours in each day must be allowed.

There are financial penalties for contravention of the above requirements, and, where a company refuses to allow inspection of a contract (or memorandum of it), the court may compel an immediate inspection.

Finally, section 16A of the Companies Act 1967 (as inserted by C.A. 1981, s. 14) requires the directors report to state certain particulars relating, among other things, to a purchase by a company of its own shares, including details of the reasons for the purchase.

Failure to purchase

If a company enters into a purchase contract, or contingent purchase contract (e.g. a put option) under which it becomes bound to purchase, the normal rules of contract do not apply in the event of a breach (C.A. 1981, s. 59). First, the company will not be liable in damages for failure to purchase any of the shares. Secondly, specific performance of the contract will not be granted where the company can show that it is unable to meet the cost out of distributable profits.

Provided the purchase is due to take place not later than the date of commencement of a winding-up of the company, the purchase may then be enforced against the company, unless in the period from the due date for purchase to the commencement of the winding-up the company could not have made a distribution equal to the purchase price. The shares which the company has agreed to purchase will rank behind ordinary debts and liabilities of the company but will have preference over shares of the same class.

Payments apart from purchase price

It has already been mentioned that, in order to preserve the capital of the company, payment of the purchase price for its shares can generally only be effected out of distributable profits or, to a limited extent, out of a fresh issue of shares. (There is one major exception to this rule which is considered below.)

Clearly, this rule would be ineffective if, for example, a company could enter into an option to purchase its own shares for a purely nominal sum and effectively pay the whole of the premium element as the price for obtaining the option. Without special provision, that "option fee" could be found out of undistributable reserves.

For this reason, section 51 of the 1981 Act provides that certain ancillary payments can only be made out of distributable profits of the company. The rules cover any payment made by a company in consideration of,

(a) acquiring any right with respect to the purchase of any of its own shares under a contingent purchase contract;

(b) the variation of any off-market purchase contract or contingent purchase contract; or

(c) the release of any of the company's obligations under a purchase contract (market or off-market) or a contingent purchase contract.

If, despite these rules, such payments are made otherwise than out of distributable profits, then in the case of (a) and (b) any subsequent purchase under the contract will be unlawful, and in the case of (c) the purported release is void.

Purchase of own shares out of capital

The important exception to the general rule that purchases (or redemptions) of a company's own shares must be made out of distributable profits or out of a fresh issue of shares, relates solely to *private* companies. A private company limited by shares or limited by guarantee and having a share capital may, if authorised to do so by its articles, redeem or purchase its shares out of capital (C.A. 1981, section 54). A duly authorised purchase out of capital cannot be impugned as an unlawful distribution under section 44 of the 1980 Act (C.A. 1981, s. 60(2)). It appears that this power does not extend to payments made to acquire a contingent purchase contract (e.g. the price of a call option), or payments to vary off-market or contingent purchase contracts (see the terms of section 51).

It is important to note at the outset that specific power to purchase (or redeem) shares out of capital must be reserved in the articles of association of the company. There is no such power in Table A, nor is a general power to purchase its own shares sufficient. The article must expressly enable the company to make a payment for the purchase of those shares otherwise than out of distributable profits or a fresh issue of shares (i.e. out of capital).

The basic rule is that a company is permitted to resort to capital to make a purchase of its own shares to the extent, and *only* to the extent, that the purchase price exceeds the aggregate of,

(a) any available profits of the company; and

(b) the proceeds of any fresh issue of shares made for the purpose of the purchase.

It is thus necessary for "available profits" to be exhausted before any payment out of capital can be made. The excess of the purchase price over these items is referred to as the *permissible capital payment*.

Available profits

The available profits of a company are basically its distributable profits within the meaning given to that expression by the 1980 Act, but the question of the availability of those profits is not determined in accordance with the normal rules (C.A. 1980, s. 43) but under special conditions contained in sections 54(8) to (10) of the 1981 Act.

Broadly, the question whether there are available profits must be determined by reference to profits, losses, assets, liabilities, provisions, share capital and reserves as disclosed in such accounts of the company are necessary to enable a *reasonable judgment* to be made as to the amounts of those items. The accounts need not be audited, nor are they required to conform to any particular standard; they must however be sufficient to enable both the directors and the auditors to satisfy themselves as to the position, as both are required to give written confirmation of that fact. The accounts must be prepared as at a date not exceeding three months prior to the directors' statutory declaration under section 55(3) – the declaration is the first step in the authorisation procedure (see below). Any distributions lawfully made by the company between the date of the accounts and the date of the making of the statutory declaration (including any financial assistance and payments for the purchase of shares out of distributable profits) must also be taken into account, and go to reduce the level of available profits for this purpose.

Procedural requirements

By virtue of section 54 of the 1981 Act, a private company thus has the power to reduce its capital without seeking the sanction of the court under the traditional procedure set out in sections 66 to 71 of the 1948 Act. The ability of the court to refuse to sanction schemes which are unfair to members or creditors is therefore lost. For this reason, detailed procedural requirements must be followed where a company wishes to purchase its shares out of capital, which are intended to give dissentient members and creditors an opportunity to object, and also place a potential liability on the directors and vendor shareholders in the event of subsequent insolvency.

An outline of the procedural steps is set out in the table on page 685 below.

Assuming that the company has the necessary power in its articles (see above), the first stage is for the directors to make a statutory declaration on Form 65, specifying the amount of the permissible capital payment and stating that, having made full enquiry into the affairs and prospects of the company, they have formed the opinion,

(a) that, taking into account contingent and prospective liabilities, there will be no ground on which the company could, immediately after the payment, be found to be unable to pay its debts; and

(b) that, as regards the prospects for the year following the payment, and having regard to their intentions as to management of the company's business during that year and to the amount and character of the financial resources which will in their view be available to the company during that year, the company will be able to carry on business as a going concern (and will accordingly be able to pay its debts as they fall due) throughout that year.

The statutory declaration is required to state whether the company is a recognised bank or licensed institution within the Banking Act 1979, or is authorised to carry on insurance business in the United Kingdom. It must in addition have annexed to it a report addressed to the directors by the auditors of the company stating that,

Purchase out of capital

Time or period	Action	Reference (C.A. 1981 unless otherwise stated)
	Accounts prepared to ascertain *available profits*	s. 54(8)
Not more than 3 months before statutory declaration	Copy or memorandum of purchase contract at registered office, *unless already authorised*	s. 47(10)
Not less than 15 days before special resolution	Statutory declaration (Form 65) with auditors' report annexed	s. 55(3), (5)
Not more than 3 months after date of relevant accounts	Special resolution(s)	
Not more than 1 week after statutory declaration	– altering articles *where necessary*	s. 54(1)
	– authorising purchase contract, *unless already authorised*	s. 47(5) s. 55(6) s. 56(1)
	– approving payment out of capital	
Not more than 1 week after special resolution	*Gazette* notice	s. 56(4)
Not later than earlier of *Gazette* or other notice	Notice to creditors or national advertisement	
Not more than 15 days after special resolution(s)	Copy statutory declaration and auditors' report to Registrar	
	Copy resolutions to Registrar	C.A. 1948, s. 143(1)
Between date of earlier of *Gazette* or other notice and 5 weeks after special resolution	Original statutory declaration and auditors' report available for inspection at registered office	s. 56(5)
Not more than 5 weeks after special resolution	Application to court by dissentient shareholder or creditor	s. 57(1)
On receipt of notice of application to court	Notice to Registrar (Form 66)	s. 57(3)
Within 15 days after court order (or longer if court directs)	Deliver office copy order to Registrar	s. 57(3), (5)
Before payment out of capital	Entry into purchase contract	–
Date of entry into purchase contract	Lodge copy or memorandum of contract at registered office	s. 52(4)
Not more than 28 days after completion of purchase	Return to Registrar (Form 64)	s. 52(1)
Not less than 5 weeks nor more than 7 weeks after special resolution (subject to court order)	Payment out of capital	s. 55(6), s. 57(5)
One year after payment out of capital	Latest date for commencement of winding-up giving rise to directors' and vendor shareholders' liability	s. 58

(a) they have enquired into the company's state of affairs;

(b) the amount of the permissible capital payment has been properly calculated; and

(c) they are not aware of anything to indicate that the opinion expressed by the directors in the declaration as to the immediate and future prospects for the company is unreasonable in all the circumstances.

There are criminal penalties (including possible imprisonment for a maximum of two years) if any director makes the statutory declaration without having reasonable grounds for the opinion expressed therein. It is clear that thorough investigations of the company's affairs are vital, and the directors will no doubt look to the auditors for some comfort on the solvency (and future solvency) of the company. It is clearly essential that the directors obtain a written auditors' report on the company prior to making the declaration in order to show that they took all reasonable care in expressing their opinion.

The payment out of capital must be approved by *special* resolution, passed on the same day as the declaration is made, or within one week of it. The resolution is additional to any other resolution authorising the purchase contract in respect of the shares in question. It is of course possible that the purchase contract has been previously authorised, or that the purchase is being undertaken by virtue of an existing contingent purchase contract. Just as for special resolutions under section 47 (off-market purchase) and section 48 (contingent purchase contract), the shares which are subject to the purchase out of capital are disenfranchised for the purposes of the special resolution. In addition, the statutory declaration and auditors' report must be available for inspection at the general meeting at which the resolution is passed.

The payment out of capital itself must be made not earlier than five nor more than seven weeks after the date of the resolution. This gives a "breathing space" to enable dissentient members and creditors to apply to the court under section 57 (see below), but also ensures that delay in payment is not allowed to prejudice the declaration made by the directors and the financial information on which it was based.

Publicity

As might be expected where a company is effectively reducing its capital, a number of notices and advertisements are required. These are set out in section 56 of the 1981 Act. In common with the other procedural requirements, there are strict time limits.

Three of the requirements must be effected within one week after the passing of the special resolution approving the payment out of capital. First, a copy of the statutory declaration of the directors and the auditors' report must be delivered to the Registrar of Companies. Secondly, a notice must be published in the *London Gazette* or (for companies incorporated in Scotland) the *Edinburgh Gazette*,

(a) stating that the company has approved a payment out of capital for the purpose of acquiring its own shares by redemption or purchase or both (as the case may require);

(b) specifying the amount of the permissible capital payment for the shares in question and the date of the resolution for payment out of capital;

(c) stating that the statutory declaration of the directors and the auditors' report are available for inspection at the company's registered office (see below); and

(d) stating that any creditor of the company may, at any time within the five weeks immediately following the date of the resolution, apply to the court for an order prohibiting the payment (see below).

Thirdly, the company must either give notice to each of its creditors, or else publish in an *appropriate national newspaper*, a notice to the same effect as the *Gazette* notice. The appropriate national newspaper is one circulating throughout England and Wales, or Scotland, depending on where the company is incorporated.

The filing of the statutory declaration and auditors' report must be effected not later than the first to occur of the *Gazette* notice, or the national advertisement or creditors' notice. Also, the statutory declaration and auditors' report must be kept at the company's registered office throughout the period beginning with the date on which the *Gazette* or other creditors' notice was published or given and ending five weeks after the date of the resolution for payment out of capital. The documents must be open to inspection of any member or creditor of the company without charge during normal business hours. In contrast to the disclosure requirements regarding purchase contracts (C.A. 1981, s. 52) the company is not allowed to restrict inspection in any way. There are criminal sanctions if an inspection is refused, and the court can compel an immediate inspection.

Objections by members or creditors

As mentioned earlier, the 1981 Act provides some protection for dissentient members and creditors in cases where a company proposes to purchase its shares out of capital. Following the special resolution approving the payment out of capital, a member of the company other than one who has consented to or voted in favour of the resolution, and any creditor, may within five weeks apply to the court for a cancellation of the resolution (section 57). The application need not be made by *every* dissentient member or creditor; a representative action may be taken by any one or more of the persons entitled to make an application as those persons may appoint in writing. As soon as the company receives notice of such an application, it must in turn give notice to the Registrar on form 66.

The court has various powers in considering an application under section 57. It may make an order, on such terms and conditions as it thinks fit, either confirming or cancelling the resolution. Where it confirms the resolution it may in particular alter or extend any date or time period affecting the purchase of shares under the resolution. In addition, the court has power to sanction an arrangement for the purchase of the interests of dissentient members or for the protection of dissentient creditors, and it may give such directions and make such orders as it thinks expedient for facilitating or carrying into effect any such arrangement. For example, the court might require the interests of creditors to be secured, perhaps by means of a bank guarantee as is commonly found in a reduction of capital scheme under section 66 of the 1948 Act. It is possible too that the court may insist on the interests of dissenting members being acquired as a condition of its confirming the resolution (compare the rights of dissenting members under section 287 of the 1948 Act and the powers of the court under section 208 of that Act, discussed in the chapter *Reconstructions and Amalgamations*). The court also has specific power to order a company not to make any, or any specified, alteration in its memorandum or articles; this effectively means that the company cannot make any such alteration without leave of the court.

Within 15 days from the making of any order of the court, or such longer period as the court may direct, the company must deliver an office copy of the order to the Registrar of Companies.

Liability of past shareholders and directors

Unlike the corresponding procedure for a reduction of capital under section 66 of the 1948 Act, there remains, for a period of one year after the date of the payment out of capital, a possibility that the vendor shareholders and the directors may be called to account to the company for any shortfall on a winding-up. This is so even where the court has confirmed the resolution for payment out of capital under section 57.

Where the winding-up of the company is commenced within one year of the payment out of capital, and the aggregate of the amount of the company's assets and any amounts paid by contributories is insufficient for payment of its debts and liabilities and the expenses of winding-up, the vendor shareholders and any director who joined in the making of the statutory declaration on which the payment was based are jointly and severally liable for the insufficiency of assets, up to the amount of the payment out of capital. Exceptionally, a director may avoid liability if he shows that he had reasonable grounds for forming the opinion (i.e. as to present and future solvency) set out in the declaration. This therefore emphasises the importance of a director insisting upon full examination of all the company's affairs prior to making the statutory declaration.

If a vendor shareholder or director is obliged to contribute to the assets of the company he is permitted to apply to the court for an order directing any other person who is jointly and severally liable in respect of that amount to indemnify him so far as the court considers just and equitable. In addition, a person who is potentially liable to contribute to the assets of the company in this way is entitled to petition the court for a winding up, either on the grounds that the company is unable to pay its debts, or that it is just and equitable for the company to be wound up. This enables such a person in effect to limit the extent of his liability by himself initiating a winding-up prior to the company's assets being further dissipated or otherwise lost.

Maintenance of capital

Except in the special case of a private company purchasing shares out of capital, the scheme of the own-share purchase legislation is to maintain the capital of the company. It achieves this in two ways. First, it provides that in general a purchase may be effected only out of distributable profits or a fresh issue of shares. Secondly, the legislation requires certain amounts to be carried to a capital reserve, known as the *capital redemption reserve*. The capital redemption reserve is treated as share capital (so that the ordinary rules as to reduction of capital apply to it), except that it may be used to pay up fully paid bonus shares to be allotted in a capitalisation issue. (It is thus similar to the share premium account required by section 56 of the 1948 Act, except that the share premium account can be used to pay off the premium on debentures and to meet expenses commissions or discounts on share issues and the preliminary expenses of the company.)

The basic rule (which is contained in section 53 of the 1981 Act) is that,

(a) where shares are purchased wholly out of profits, the amount, *in nominal value*, by which the issued share capital of the company is diminished (i.e. by cancellation of the shares) must be transferred to the capital redemption reserve; and

(b) where shares are purchased wholly or partly out of the proceeds of a fresh issue, the amount (if any) to be transferred to capital redemption reserve is the difference between the nominal value of the shares purchased and the amount of the *proceeds* of the fresh issue.

Example 1

ABC Ltd. has an issued share capital of £1,000 and distributable reserves of £5,000. It proposes to purchase £200 nominal of its share capital at a price of £1,200. A fresh issue of £30 nominal of shares is made for the purpose at an aggregate subscription price of £180

	Before	After
Share capital	1,000	830
Share premium account	—	150
Capital redemption reserve	—	20
Reserves	5,000	3,980
	6,000	4,980

The net cost to the company of purchasing the shares is thus met wholly out of distributable profits and the capital remains intact.

Purchase out of capital

Different rules apply where a private company obtains approval for a payment out of capital.

First, if the aggregate of the permissible capital payment and the proceeds of any fresh issue is *less than* the nominal amount of the shares purchased, the difference must be transferred to capital redemption reserve. This means that capital is reduced only to the extent of the permissible capital payment.

Example 2

ABC Ltd. has an issued share capital of £1,000 and distributable reserves of £200. It proposes to purchase £350 nominal of its share capital at a price of £500. A fresh issue of £100 nominal of shares is made and the subscription proceeds amount to £150

	Before	*After*
Share capital	1,000	750
Share premium account	—	50
Capital redemption reserve	—	50
Reserves	200	—
	1,200	850

The capital is thus reduced by £150 only, i.e. the amount of the permissible capital payment.

Secondly, if the aggregate of the permissible capital payment and the proceeds of any fresh issue is *greater than* the nominal amount of the shares purchased, the difference is found by reducing any of the following: capital redemption reserve, share premium account, fully paid share capital, and unrealised profits standing to the credit of the revaluation reserve. The revaluation reserve is the separate reserve required to take account of unrealised profits and losses (C.A. 1948, Sch. 8, para. 34). The Act lays down no rules as to the order in which these reserves should be reduced.

Example 3

ABC Ltd. has an issued share capital of £1,000 and no distributable reserves. It does however own a freehold property which, on a revaluation, shows an unrealised appreciation of £10,000. It is proposed that ABC Ltd. purchase £200 nominal of its share capital at a price of £2,500. A fresh issue of £100 nominal of shares is made, the subscription proceeds of which are £1,000.

	Before	*After*
Share capital	1,000	900
Share premium account	—	900
Revaluation reserve	10,000	7,700
	11,000	9,500

Thus, the capital has been reduced by £1,500, i.e. the permissible capital payment.

In Example 3, the company may prefer to debit the share premium account created on the fresh issue of shares. A share premium account has limited uses (C.A. 1948, s. 56) whereas unrealised profits in the revaluation reserve may be set free for distribution once the asset in question is sold. The following would then be the position:

	Before	After
Share capital	1,000	900
Share premium account	—	—
Revaluation reserve	10,000	8,600
	11,000	9,500

Other matters

Effect of purchase

In every case of a purchase by a company of its own shares, regard should be had to the position not only of the company itself and the vendor shareholders, but also the remaining holders of shares in the company. The purchased shares must be cancelled (C.A. 1981, s. 45(8)), thus proportionately increasing the interests of the remaining members.

One obvious effect of this can be to give a particular shareholder or group of shareholders power to procure the passing of an ordinary, or special, resolution without relying on the support of any other member.

Example

ABC Ltd. has three shareholders, Mr. X (45%), Mr. Y (40%) and Mr. Z (15%). With such shareholdings Mr. Z could combine with either Mr. X or Mr. Y effectively to control the company. If the company purchases Mr. Y's shareholding, the revised holdings will be,

Mr. X	75%
Mr. Z	25%

Mr Z thus loses any possibility of having voting power over the affairs of the company.

Accounting requirements

Where a company is a member of the purchasing company, and its proportionate holding of shares is increased, new accounting requirements may arise. Thus, a company which becomes the holding company of another (as defined in SSAP 14) will in general come under an obligation to prepare group accounts. A similar increase, at a reduced shareholding level, may also give rise to a corresponding liability to account for the results of the purchasing company as an associated company, where it is considered that the increased ownership has given rise to an ability to exercise significant influence (SSAP 1).

Disclosure of interests in shares

Part IV of the Companies Act 1981 contains detailed obligations on holders of a certain percentage of voting shares in a public company to notify the company of that interest. Particularly in the case of a market purchase, a holder of shares may find his proportionate interest in the company increased beyond the notifiable percentage by a purchase outside his control and, possibly, without his immediate knowledge. In such a case the notification requirement will arise, but only after the shareholder in question becomes aware of the increased percentage level of his interest (C.A. 1981, s. 63 and the chapter *Disclosure of Shareholdings*).

City Code

Rule 34 of the *City Code on Take-Overs and Mergers* broadly provides that, except with the consent of the Take-Over Panel, a person who acquires shares which carry 30 per cent or more of the voting rights of a public company or who, having already between 30 per cent and 50 per cent, acquires in any twelve-month period more than an additional 2 per cent, is required to extend a general offer for all such voting shares.

Given the ability of a listed company having the necessary authority to go into the market and effect a purchase of its own shares without further reference to its shareholders, the possibility can clearly be envisaged of a holder of a significant number of voting shares (say, 29 per cent) unwittingly going through the 30 per cent. barrier. Such a shareholder may well be completely unaware of the intention of the company to effect a market purchase at that particular time even though he may have voted on the necessary ordinary resolution under section 49(3) of the 1981 Act.

There have been no general guidelines published by the Panel as to the application of the Code in cases of a purchase by a company of its own shares, although a company proposing to do so should in all cases notify the Panel and seek its guidance. However, it is understood that in the case envisaged above the requirement to make a bid will not be enforced at the time of the increase in voting capital attributable to the own share purchase, although if the shareholder later acquires any further interest in the company (even one share) he will then be regarded as consolidating his control and will be required to make a general offer.

It often happens that a substantial minority holder will have representation on the board. In such a case that shareholder will have advance knowledge of the proposed purchase. Where this occurs, it is understood that the Panel regard the proper procedure to be the so-called "whitewash" under paragraph 9 of *Practice Statement* 15 of the Code. This involves the question of a shareholder acquiring a further percentage of voting shares without having to make a general offer being put to an independent vote of shareholders i.e. with the relevant shareholder disenfranchised for this purpose. In practice, even in cases where a shareholder is not aware of the purchasing intentions of the company, the proper course would seem to be for the company to obtain an independent vote and a formal waiver from the Panel of Rule 34.

Holding by subsidiary of shares in its holding company

Since a company cannot, save in the cases described earlier in this chapter, acquire its own shares, it would be anomolous if a company were nevertheless able to hold shares in its holding company. Section 27 of the Companies Act 1948 accordingly provides that a body corporate (an expression which includes a company not incorporated under the Companies Acts, and an unlimited company) cannot be a member of a company which is its *holding company*, and that any allotment or transfer of shares in a company to its subsidiary shall be void. The expressions "holding company" and "subsidiary" are defined by section 154 of the 1948 Act: see the chapter *Formation and Types of Company*.

The section cannot be avoided by shares being held by, or issued or transferred to, a nominee (section 27(4)). Furthermore, the prohibition extends equally to companies which have no share capital, the reference to shares in such a case being construed as a reference to the interest of the members as such, whatever the form of that interest.

There are however a number of exceptions to the basic rule. Section 27 does not apply,

(a) where the subsidiary is concerned as personal representative or trustee, unless the holding company or any of its subsidiaries has a beneficial interest under the trust, and is not so interested only by way of security for an ordinary business transaction, where the business includes the lending of money; or

(b) so as to prevent a subsidiary which, at the commencement of the 1948 Act (July 1, 1948) was a member of its holding company from continuing as such, but – unless the holding is as personal representative or trustee as above – the subsidiary then has no voting rights. It should be noted that this exception does not enable the subsidiary to acquire further shares from its holding company; any subsequent acquisitions, even if bonus issues or rights issues, will be void.

What section 27 does not cover is the case where a company which *already* holds shares in another company becomes a subsidiary of that other company after July 1, 1948. There is no obligation to dispose of the shares, nor is there any restriction on the continued holding of those shares. However, section 27(1) nevertheless provides that the first company "cannot" be a member of its new parent – so it is not clear whether the first company can vote its shares (one argument is that the only sensible interpretation is that section 27 does not apply at all in the situation under discussion, in which case the shares can be voted).

Cross holdings

Section 27 only applies to holding companies and subsidiaries. There is no restriction on cross-holdings of shares to a lesser degree. It is accordingly possible for two or more companies to have substantial holdings in the capital of the other or others, provided that none of them becomes a 51 per cent subsidiary of any other, and that none can be regarded as controlling the composition of the board of directors of any other (C.A. 1948, s. 154(2)).

Receivers

Functions and appointment

A receiver of a company's property is an *individual* appointed by persons having the right to do so, usually secured creditors, to protect their interests (corporate receivers are prohibited under section 366 of the Companies Act 1948). The appointment can be made by a competent court of jurisdiction on the creditor's application by originating process, in which case the receiver is an officer of the court and subject to its supervision, or an appointment can be made "out of court" either (a) under statutory powers or (b) under express powers contained in the document creating the lender's or creditor's security. The latter mode is by far the most common, and by the security document it is invariably provided that a receiver so appointed becomes an agent of the company, not of the lender. His rights and duties are as defined by the instrument appointing him and by the general law of agency. Frequently the receiver is an accountant, though any individual can be appointed (except an undischarged bankrupt or, as a broad rule, someone closely interested under the debenture or other loan instrument). There can be joint receivers.

The object of a receivership is to obtain a realisation of assets for the secured lender as quickly as possible but with due regard to the rights of other creditors, employees and shareholders. The appointment of a receiver does not put the company into liquidation, although since his powers normally include the assumption of control of all the secured assets, the existing management of the company will cease to have effect and the directors, while not relieved of their statutory responsibilities, will only have residual executive power (see *Newhart Development Limited v Co-operative Commercial Bank Limited* [1978] 2 All E.R. 896). If, after the appointment of a receiver, the company is put into liquidation, the receiver is entitled to retain control of the assets for the purposes of his appointment, but otherwise the company's property vests in the liquidator (*Sowman v. David Samuel Trust Limited* [1978] 1 W.L.R. 22 and the chapter *Liquidations*, page 523).

Debenture trust deeds creating charges on property, whether specific or floating, conventionally contain express power for the trustee to appoint a receiver (who will also act as a manager where there is a crystallisation of a floating charge). The appointment takes effect as soon as the instrument of appointment is delivered and accepted by the person who is to act. An appointment will usually be sought in one or more of the following circumstances,

(a) where the company fails to comply with the terms of the debenture in relation to repayment of principal and interest;

(b) where some part of the principal monies are recalled by the debenture holder and the company fails to pay;

(c) where borrowing limits under a secured banking advance are exceeded and notices requiring reduction are not complied with within the prescribed period; or

(d) where there is some other breach by the borrower or a subsidiary company of the borrower of the provisions of the debenture trust deed which the trustee is not prepared to waive.

As explained on page 172, appointment of a receiver results in the crystallisation of any floating charges given by the company. All the assets comprised in the charge including future assets then become subject to a fixed equitable charge in favour of the chargee, subject to any prior charges or equities.

Statutory powers

Section 101 of the Law of Property Act 1925 empowers a mortgagee, where the mortgage is by deed, to appoint a receiver of the income of the mortgaged property when the mortgage money has become due and the mortgagee has become entitled to exercise the statutory power of sale – that is, when the conditions of section 103 have been satisfied. A mortgagee of specific property, as opposed to a debenture holder with a floating charge, will normally prefer to rely on the statutory power to appoint even though the circumstances of such appointment may be varied by express agreement. The powers of a receiver appointed under section 101 are defined in section 109, but again may be extended. An extension will be necessary where the mortgagee wishes to exercise the power to sell assets or to receive capital moneys, as opposed to receiving income.

Validity of appointment

Before accepting appointment or entering on to the company's property, the receiver should ensure that the charge pursuant to which the appointment is made has been validly constituted, and that the power to appoint has in fact arisen. A receiver will normally require an express indemnity from his appointor in case he is sued by the company or any creditor for interfering with its assets. The following matters could affect the validity of the charge,

(a) non-registration of a floating charge under section 95 of the Companies Act 1948 within twenty-one days of its creation renders it void against the liquidator and any creditor;

(b) the creation of the charge may be beyond the powers either of the company as defined in its memorandum of association, or of the directors as set out in the borrowing clauses of the articles. In the former case, section 9 (1) of the European Communities Act 1972 will protect the chargee if he acts in good faith on a transaction "decided on by the directors". In the latter case, articles commonly provide that outsiders shall not be concerned to see whether borrowing limits imposed therein have been complied with (e.g. see article 79 of Table A);

(c) the creation of a charge could constitute a fraudulent preference under section 320 of the Companies Act 1948 (see page 519). This only applies to a fixed charge; and

(d) a floating charge is invalid if the company is placed into liquidation within twelve months of its creation, unless it can be shown that the company was solvent at the time of creation (C.A. 1948, s. 322 and pages 174 and 521).

Thus if a receiver is appointed within six or twelve months of the creation of a charge, he should, depending on its type, pay only essential outgoings until the requisite time periods have elapsed or until he is satisfied that the charge cannot be challenged.

Appointment by the court

The High Court has a statutory jurisdiction to appoint a receiver in all cases where it appears to be just and convenient to do so (section 37 of the Supreme Court Act 1981). The court may impose such terms and conditions as it thinks fit. A county court has an equivalent jurisdiction over assets within its monetary limits. The power of the court to appoint a receiver is not limited to cases where the principal or interest on the debenture is in arrears. The normal practice is to appoint whenever the security is in jeopardy, for example because the company has become insolvent (*McMahon v North Kent Iron Works* [1891] 2 Ch. 148). It is not, however, a sufficient ground for an appointment that the assets of the company are presently not enough to pay the debenture holders in full, if the company is not itself in default of any obligation.

Being an officer of the court, the receiver must abide strictly by his terms of appointment and apply for directions if in any doubt as to how to proceed or if further powers are required. He is neither agent of the company nor agent of the debenture holders. On his appointment all the company's powers are suspended. He is personally responsible for his actions and is normally required to give security. Any interference with him is a contempt of court. Appointment by the court usually results from a debenture holders' action. The trustees of the debenture stock will normally bring the action, but this does not prevent an individual debenture-holder from doing so.

Powers and duties

General powers

Floating charges normally confer full powers on a receiver, but fixed charges commonly contain inadequate powers, in which case reliance on the provisions of the Law of Property Act 1925 will be necessary. A receiver can also apply under section 369 of the Companies Act 1948 to the court for directions (even if appointed out of court), and while not amounting to an enlargement of his powers, a direction so given will validate what might otherwise be a questionable method of proceeding. The designation "receiver" connotes a power merely to collect and realise assets, but in fact a debenture may give specific power for carrying on the business, even if the appointee is not named as "manager" as well. A managerial power is desirable in the trust deed if the charge includes goodwill, as this may only be realisable if the company can continue trading long enough to dispose of it for value.

Although debentures and the like will invariably express the receiver to be an agent of the company, he is personally liable on any contract entered into by him in the performance of his functions unless the contrary is expressly stated. Although entitled to an indemnity out of the assets, the safer course is for the receiver to contract manifestly as representative for the company, and so avoid personal responsibility. Contracts already entered into by the company prior to appointment can be continued without liability, although if they are onerous the receiver is well advised to disclaim them. A receiver appointed under a debenture or similar instrument is not a manager or officer of the company for the purposes of section 333(1) of the Companies Act 1948, so he cannot be liable to misfeasance proceedings brought under that section. The protection of acting as agent of the company ceases if the company is placed in liquidation, since the liquidator is the only person lawfully empowered to act on its behalf. But the receiver does not thereupon become agent of the lender. As mentioned, his power to deal with the property comprised in his charge is not affected by the liquidation, and he can still act in the name of the company (*Barrows v. The Chief Land Registrar, The Times*, October 20, 1977). A receiver may, if authorised by the court or the debenture deed, borrow money to carry on the business or to protect the company's property, with the borrowing ranking in priority to the debentures.

Stated in general terms, the duties of the receiver are to preserve the company's assets so as to affect a maximum realisation for the benefit of the secured creditors. These apart, the traditional view has been that a receiver owes no general duty to any other creditor or shareholder, except to ensure that if any assets remain after payment of principal, interest and costs to the secured creditors, these are not wilfully or negligently depleted (though see, in relation to the power of sale, *Cuckmere Brick Co. Limited v. Mutual Finance Limited* [1971] 2 All E.R. 633; and see page 704 below). A receiver has a general liability to account for all money which comes into his hands in his capacity as receiver. He will be liable for any loss which arises out of his own negligence or wilful default, though he is under no obligation to take greater care of the company's property than he would of his own.

Actions following appointment

A receiver must notify his appointment to the company and call for a statement of affairs (C.A. 1948, s. 372). Notice of appointment must be given to the Registrar of Companies within seven days on Form 53 (C.A. 1948, s. 102). He should immediately instruct a solicitor for advice on the validity of the charge. It is also necessary to establish as a prerequisite that there are sufficient assets to pay costs and expenses, unless the debenture holder himself gives an indemnity for the shortfall. The receiver should notify the company's bank and any other parties who are likely to be in receipt of moneys on behalf of the company. A new bank account should be opened, "XY receiver and manager, ABC Company Limited". Instructions will be given to transfer any balance standing to the credit of the company to the new account. A cash flow forecast must be prepared to see if there are sufficient moneys available for payment of wages or salaries. If there is a cash flow difficulty, the receiver may turn to the company's bankers upon the giving of security. No security will be necessary where the bankers are already the debenture holders. Movements of goods in and out of the company's premises should be halted to enable an assessment of stock to be made. Deliveries can be recommenced once the stock check is complete and the credit worthiness of customers cleared. The receiver should write to all suppliers notifying them of his appointment, and informing them that no goods will be accepted and no liabilities incurred by the company except against orders signed by the receiver or his authorised representative.

Effect on contracts

If contracts for the supply of goods have been made by the company before appointment, and title has already been acquired, the receiver will be entitled to the goods. Moreover, since the receiver has a right to disclaim existing contracts he may not be liable to pay for the goods. If title has not been acquired, or is only acquired on payment, then the receiver may disclaim the contract (*Airlines Airspares Limited v Handley Page Limited* [1970] 2 W.L.R. 163), but he will have to arrange for the return of any goods actually delivered. It is now a common occurrence for suppliers to insert a condition in the contract of supply reserving title until payment is made. A receiver cannot be in any better position vis-a-vis the third party supplier than the company itself, and if he deals with property or the proceeds of sale thereof in a manner inconsistent with the rights of the owner, he may be liable for conversion or wrongful interference. Reservation clauses sometimes extend the rights of the supplier beyond the material supplied to a proportion of the work-in-progress or finished goods, but their validity will turn on the precise construction of the clauses: see *Aluminium Industrie Vaassen B.V. v Romalpa Aluminium Limited* [1976] 2 All E.R. 552, and the cases of *Borden Limited v Scottish Timber Products* [1979] 3 W.L.R. 672 and *Re Bond Worth* [1979] 3 W.L.R. 629, discussed at page 182. In addition to so-called "Romalpa" clauses, a supplier of goods or services may be able to exercise a general lien over goods of the company for sums due before the appointment of the receiver.

Any property or rights of the company claimed by the receiver will be subject to any prior charge or encumbrance, and to any right of lien or set-off which could be asserted at the date when a third party receives notice of the appointment. After the appointment the assets of the company become assigned in equity to the debenture holders and any subsequently-incurred debt cannot usually be the subject of a set-off. If the company has assigned by way of charge the benefit of a contract, the assignment and consequently the rights of the chargee will be subject to equities existing at the date of the creation of the charge, in addition to any rights of set-off in respect of liabilities arising out of the particular contract both before and after the assignment (see *Re Ind Coope Limited* [1911] 2 Ch.223).

Goods or equipment used by the company which are the subject of hire purchase obligations are likely to be sought to be recovered by the owner. The receiver may be able to avoid this if the goods are necessary for the continued operation of the business, provided the hire purchase agreements have not been breached, the payments are up to date, or the assets concerned have become fixtures. In an ordinary hire purchase agreement there is unlikely to be any "acceleration" clause whereby a breach of covenant under one bank loan is evidence of default under the hire purchase agreement.

Position of directors and employees

The position of directors has been mentioned above. Their appointment does not cease and their liabilities continue, but they have no executive power over the assets under the receiver's control.

The appointment of a receiver does not automatically terminate the employment of the company's employees unless their continued employment is inconsistent with the receivership (see for instance *Re Mack Trucks Limited* [1967] 1 W.L.R. 780). Where employees are to be retained, they should continue to receive wages and salaries in accordance with their existing terms and conditions. Where there are to be lay-offs, the receiver can either simply cease payment or else issue formal termination notices, which in each case will operate as a dismissal for the purposes of the Employment Protection (Consolidation) Act 1978. If employees are re-engaged, or it is for any reason convenient that their contracts should be novated, the receiver should try to protect his representative capacity and avoid personal liability for payment of wages.

Appointment of a receiver by the *court* does, however, automatically terminate contracts of employment: *Reid v. Explosives Co. Limited* (1887) 19 Q.B.D. 264.

Where it becomes necessary to make employees reduntant, employment legislation requires the selection for the redundancy process be exercised fairly. A "last-in, first-out" system is usually accepted by Industrial Tribunals; an attempt to force out workers who have been troublesome, or are considered undesirable, is not generally acceptable.

The maximum possible notice of impending redundancies must be given to any recognised trade union and to the Secretary of State for Employment. Failure to comply with statutory requirements may lead to the receiver incurring personal liability for protective awards. If the position on redundancy is uncertain upon the receiver taking over (as is likely), he should safeguard the position by giving notice of termination to all the company's employees.

Where the receiver is able to achieve a "hive-down" of assets, i.e. the transfer of the maintainable part of the business to a new company, the transfer is deemed for the purposes of the Transfer of Undertakings (Protection of Employment) Regulations 1981 not to have been effected until immediately before,

(a) the transferee company ceases (otherwise than by reason of its being wound-up) to be a wholly owned subsidiary of the transferor; or

(b) the relevant undertaking is transferred by the transferee company to another person,

whichever occurs first. In such cases there is continuity of employment for the staff concerned.

Employees will be entitled, as against the company, to all statutory and contractual rights which have accumulated prior to any termination of employment. In addition, they are entitled to rights arising on the termination and on redundancy. The receiver is required to agree with each employee the amounts due under the various headings, and submit these amounts to the Department of Employment for payment out of the Redundancy Fund. In the case of claims met by the Department which are preferential under section 319 of the Companies Act 1948, the Department will rank as a preferential creditor in the receivership in place of the employee, in accordance with the rights of priority granted by sections 121 and 125 of the Employment Protection (Consolidation) Act 1978. If an employee is made redundant but re-engaged elsewhere as a result of the receiver's efforts, he is nonetheless entitled to redundancy pay. So also if there is a transfer of assets not amounting to a transfer of an undertaking within the meaning of the 1981 Regulations.

Powers over particular types of property

(1) *Leaseholds.* The right of a landlord to distrain, in respect of arrears of rent, on goods located on the company's premises which are owned by him prevails over the rights of the receiver, except where the company has also gone into liquidation and the arrears relate to a period prior to the commencement of the liquidation.

Where land has been leased by the company as a dwelling house, the Rent Acts may prevent the receiver from exercising any power of sale over the dwelling house if it is let on a regulated tenancy.

In general, the receiver should notify his appointment to all tenants to ensure that rents are paid to him. He must avoid the possibility of framing the notification in such a way that a new tenancy between himself and the tenant is created. This is achieved by making it clear that he has been appointed by the debenture holder as the agent of the company, and that he is acting solely on that behalf.

If the receiver wishes to dispose of leasehold property, he may try to procure a surrender to the landlord or, if this is not effective, make a disclaimer of the lease. In some cases the appointment of a receiver is expressed in the lease to allow the landlord to terminate it. If, on the other hand, it is desired to continue occupation of the premises, and the landlord invokes a forfeiture, the receiver may apply to the court for relief (*Scala House & District Property Co Limited v Forbes* [1973] 3 All E.R. 308). The receiver must avoid adopting the lease personally, as he will become liable for claims for dilapidation and the like.

(2) *Factored book debts.* The company may have disposed of part of its property by for instance factoring book debts. If the assignment is outright (reserving no equity of redemption) it will not have required registration under section 95 of the Companies Act 1948. Moreover, an equitable assignment is effective against the assignor and its liquidator without notice to the debtor. This also applies to a receiver. It is sometimes difficult to distinguish between a charge over the assets and an outright assignment of them (see for example the unreported case of *Lloyds & Scottish Finance Limited v Cyril Lord Carpet Sales Ltd* (1979), and pages 197 and 532).

(3) *Rateable property.* If the company continues trading it might be thought that there is no change of possession or occupancy. However, the terms of the instrument defining the receiver's powers may give him the right to take immediate possession of the charged property, where he is the person to which the local authority would look for payment of general rates (*Richards v Overseers of Kidderminster* [1896] 2 Ch. 212.) During the period of a "work-in" by the company's employees, where access to the premises is denied to the receiver, both he and the company may escape liability on the grounds that there was no "actual and exclusive occupation" on their part for the purposes of section 16 of the General Rent Act 1967: see *Re Briant Colour Printing Co Limited* [1977] 1 W.L.R. 942.

(4) *Assets in hands of third parties.* Goods in transit, assets on hire or loan, stocks held by employees, motor vehicles in repair and so on, remain the property of the company (subject to any right of lien, set-off or reservation of title considered above), and are able to be reclaimed by the receiver. He should therefore not leave these items out of account of any stock-take or inventory for the purposes of valuing the assets and offering them for sale to a purchaser of the undertaking. Where the receiver is unable to recover the goods, he has a sufficient authority to bring proceedings to do so.

Effects of supervening winding-up

A mortgagee and debenture holder is still entitled to exercise his powers over the charged property, and to convey it as mortgagee without the concurrence of the liquidator, with the benefit of section 104 of the Law of Property Act 1925. Thus the receiver can after liquidation contract to sell property, and may execute conveyances and transfers as agent for the mortgagee (for which purpose the mortgagee may appoint him as attorney). Alternatively he may, if so authorised by the charging instrument, convey under his own seal as agent for the company. Floating charges automatically crystallise on a resolution to wind-up or on an order for compulsory winding-up, but this is somewhat academic since the appointment of the receiver will have already crystallised the charge. For the receiver's status on the winding up, see page 698.

Various statutory provisions apply. Thus, section 227 of the Companies Act 1948 provides that any disposition of the property of the company made after the commencement of a winding-up by the court is void unless the court otherwise directs. This provision does not however affect any disposition of property validly charged; such property has been effectively disposed of by the company on the creation of the charge. Again, under section 243, the liquidator in a winding-up by the court is to take under his control and custody all the property and things in action to which the company is or appears to be entitled; and under section 258 the court may require any receiver to deliver to the liquidator any money, property, books and papers in his hands to which the company is *prima facie* entitled. However, it seems unlikely that the court would permit applications under these sections where a mortgagee or receiver is actually in possession of the assets charged, unless and to the extent that such assets are surplus to the requirement to satisfy the charge in full (see the chapter *Liquidations* for more detail).

Remuneration

Contractual provisions

There are two methods of dealing with the receiver's remuneration. First, section 109 (6) of the Law of Property Act 1925 provides for remuneration of up to (but not exceeding) five per cent of gross receipts for receivers *appointed under that Act*. Section 109 was, however, originally designed to apply to receivers collecting rents, and it became recognised that this level of remuneration was inappropriate in the case of receivers and managers appointed under floating charges, whose responsibilities cover a wider area. In the case of appointments which are subject to section 109, it is normally also agreed that the receiver may make an additional charge for management based on the time occupied in the business, in addition to the receiver's routine duties of realising assets. Secondly, and as an alternative, the mortgage or debenture trust deed may simply stipulate that the receiver's remuneration shall be such amount as may be agreed between the debenture holders and the receiver himself.

The remuneration of a receiver appointed by the court is fixed by the court.

On liquidation

A liquidator is empowered by section 371 of the Companies Act 1948 to apply to the court to fix the amount of receiver's remuneration, and the court may require repayment by the receiver of any amount drawn in excess of that which the court feels is justified. Where the liquidator asserts an overcharging, the receiver will be obliged to prepare schedules of work carried out and the number of hours worked by himself and his staff. The court in fixing the level of remuneration is entitled to have regard to any relevant figures: it may rely on section 109 (6) of the Law of Property Act 1925, or the Companies (Department of Trade) Fees Order 1975, which sets out the fees and charges which would be made by the Official Receiver. These vary from 20 per cent on the first £2,500 of net realisations, to 5 per cent on figures in excess of £100,000.

Where a liquidator proposes to take no action on the amount of a receiver's remuneration, it is still open to, for example, a second mortgagee to bring proceedings for an account. As regards land, if the receiver has disposed of the property on behalf of the first mortgagee he is entitled to deduct under section 105 of the Law of Property Act 1925 "all costs charges, and expenses properly incurred by him as incident to the sale". He will thus be required to justify to the court that the charges are "properly incurred".

Realisations and accounts

Valuations of fixed assets

A mortgagee (and by analogy, a receiver) owes a duty to the mortgagor to take reasonable care and to obtain a proper price for the assets under his control (*Cuckmere Brick Co Limited v Mutual Finance Limited* [1971] 2 All E.R. 633 and *Bank of Cyprus v. Gill* [1980] 2 Ll. Rep. 51. The duty extends to a guarantor of the mortgagor: *Standard Chartered Bank v Walker and another* [1982] 3 All E.R. 938). Once assets have been collected in, therefore, and before realisation, the receiver should establish what their value is on the open market. Where assets are sold at an auction dealing in the type of goods in question, the receiver is unlikely to be challenged on valuation (though note *Standard Chartered Bank v. Walker*, above). A sale by private treaty, particularly of an asset whose value is probably different from book value, presents more problems. In the case of leasehold and freehold properties the receiver should obtain a valuation in every case, on both an "existing use" and "alternative use" basis, but assuming an open market transaction; a forced sale value will also need to be calculated. As to methods of valuation, see the chapter *Acquisitions of Private Companies and Businesses*, page 83.

Conveyances and transfers

If assets are being sold piecemeal, the receiver will be required to make title to a purchaser. In cases of assets transferable by physical delivery, no document of title is required. For other types of property, the receiver is generally able to effect a conveyance by using the power of attorney on behalf of the company with which he is invariably invested by the debenture under which he has been appointed. Once such a power in the usual form has been given to the receiver, he is able to execute valid deeds himself in the name of the company and it is not necessary for the company seal to be applied to the documents (section 74 (3) of the Law of Property Act 1925).

Alternatively, there is nothing to prevent the board of directors of the company affixing the company's seal to a conveyance at the direction of the receiver and title to be made in the ordinary way. Where there are subsequent mortgagees of the property realised, they will have to consent to the release of property from the charge. In cases of difficulty, a third method is possible, i.e. completing the sale in the name of the debenture holder acting as mortgagee, using the power contained in section 101 of the Law of Property Act 1925. There is no *statutory* power for a receiver, as opposed to the debenture holders, to sell mortgage property.

Sales as going concern

Instead of the receiver selling the undertaking and assets to a purchaser piecemeal, he may enter into a contract to "hive down" these by way of sale to a subsidiary company in exchange for shares in the subsidiary. He will then sell the shares in the subsidiary to the purchaser. This enables the business to be sold "clean", i.e. free from liabilities, and often for the benefit of tax losses to be passed on to the purchaser (subject to section 483 of the Taxes Act 1970). However, if liquidation is commenced before the hiving down operation is executed, the benefit of tax losses may in certain circumstances disappear (*Ayerst v C. & K. Construction Limited* [1975] 3 All E.R. 16), as it will if there is a binding contract to sell the subsidiary before the hive-down is effected. The main risk involved in a hive-down carried out before liquidation is that this may have the consequence of validating as against the new company an unregistered charge over the assets previously owned by the transferor company, which would have been invalid as against the liquidator of the transferor company (see page 499).

Where a purchaser of assets prefers to take them in specie rather than through the medium of shares in a subsidiary, the receiver has power to enter into a contract for sale and hand over the goods on completion. However, a sale agreement often contains warranties both as to the title of goods and the state of the business, and a receiver should consider whether the circumstances are such that, in addition to any general disclaimer of personal liability, he should indicate in the contract that he will not be personally responsible for warranting the assets. The purchaser may seek to substitute warranties by the company itself (or even the directors), but these are unlikely to be satisfactory in view of the overall financial position. It should be noted that neither the company nor the receiver is able to contract out of liability for negligence which causes death or personal injury. Liability for negligence which causes other types of loss may perhaps only be avoided by exemption clauses which satisfy the requirements of reasonableness. Exclusion clauses in relation to the goods themselves *may* be unenforceable if it can be shown that it is not fair or reasonable to allow reliance on them (Unfair Contract Terms Act 1977 and Sale of Goods Act 1979).

Accounts

It is good accounting policy to "freeze" the accounts of the company as at the moment the receiver is appointed, and to open a completely new set of accounting records to cover all transactions effected thereafter. Balances should not be brought forward from the company's pre-appointment records. Where the size of business makes it impossible to impose a new accounting system, the receiver should nonetheless take such steps as are necessary to ensure that all transactions and records affecting his receivership can be separately identified.

During receivership a company remains liable to comply with section 12 of the Companies Act 1976 as to the keeping of accounting records, and the receiver, as the company's agent, has a duty to have available, and to produce to the company when required, the information to ensure compliance (*Smiths Limited v. Middleton* [1979] 3 All E.R. 842). Control of cash and other incoming monies, together with the receivership cheque book, should be in the hands of the receiver's own staff unless he is satisfied that the company's own system of internal control can continue to be relied on.

Notification of appointment and statement of affairs

The first statutory requirement of a receiver or manager of the property of a company is that under section 370 of the Companies Act 1948, every invoice order for goods or business letter issued by or on behalf of the company or the receiver or the liquidator being a document on which the name of the company appears, must contain a statement that the receiver or manager has been appointed. In addition, under section 372 (1) (a) the receiver is obliged to send to the company notice of appointment in prescribed form. Within 14 days after receipt of the notice, there must be made out and submitted to the receiver a statement in the prescribed form as to the affairs of the company. Within two months after receipt of the statement, the receiver himself must send,

(a) to the Registrar of Companies and to the court, a copy of the statement and of any comments he sees fit to make thereon, and also in the case of the copy sent to the Registrar of Companies, a summary of the statement and of his comments (if any);

(b) to the company, a copy of such comments or, if he does not see fit to make any comment, a notice to that effect; and

(c) to any trustees for the debenture holders on whose behalf he was appointed and, so far as he is aware of their addresses, to all such debenture holders, a copy of the summary.

Section 373 sets out the requirements of the statement, which must be delivered by one or more of the directors and the secretary of the company who are in office at the date of the receiver's appointment. In some cases the auditors will be responsible for the physical preparation of the documents. The statement is required to be supported by a statutory declaration. The costs and expenses incurred are to be paid by the receiver. The basic purpose of the statement is to provide an estimate of what those preparing it consider should be realised for the various classes of assets, from which are then deducted the amounts which they consider to be due to the various classes of creditors. The prescribed Form 109 is extremely detailed and consists of a main statement and a number of lists and schedules. Since there is a two month delay between the delivery of the list to the receiver and its forwarding by the receiver to the Registrar of Companies, the receiver will have the opportunity to realise some of the assets and to cause valuations of the remainder to be carried out such as to reveal any discrepancies between the gross values contained in the statement and the market values. This is the purpose of enabling the receiver to make comments.

Although the statement of affairs may amount to an acknowledgement of a debt, it is no more than an admission of past, not continuing, indebtedness for the purposes of the Limitations Act 1939: *Re Overmark Smith Warden* [1982] 1 W.L.R. 1195.

Section 372 (2) of the Companies Act 1948 requires the receiver to submit to the Registrar, abstracts or summaries of his receipts and payments covering the period of his appointment as receiver. The receiver does not have to submit full sets of accounts in the form required by Schedule 8 to the Companies Act 1948, as amended. A separate abstract must be prepared in respect of each period of twelve months during which he acts as receiver, and must be submitted within two months of the end of the period. The format of the abstract is set out in the Companies (Forms) Regulations 1979, Form 57. There is no requirement to provide a full list of every receipt and payment and often the receiver will summarise the information under headings, for example debtors, sales of assets, sundry receipts, wages and salaries, supplies of goods and services, disbursements and fees, sundry payments and pre-appointment creditors. Copies of the abstract should be sent to the company and the debenture holders. On the final abstract at the conclusion of the receivership, the total receipts must equal the total payments, and this is achieved by the inclusion of the payment by the receiver of the balance remaining in his hands to those entitled. A receiver is bound to supply details of the figures on which his abstracts are based if required to do so by the company.

Payments

A receiver appointed on behalf of the debenture holders secured by a floating charge, is bound to pay out of the first assets coming into his hands creditors who would be entitled to preferential payments in a winding-up in priority to any claim for principal or interest on the debentures (sections 94 and 319 of the Companies Act 1948). A distribution of assets or deployment of them in the business of the company without provision for these will render the receiver personally liable: *I.R.C. v Goldblatt* [1972] Ch. 498. If a winding up supervenes, the costs thereof are payable before the preferential debts, and the costs and expenses of the receiver and his own remuneration also achieve first priority (see *Re Christonette International Ltd.* [1982] 3 All E.R. concerning the liquidator's costs). These preferential payments do not, however, have priority over property comprised in a fixed charge, even though the debenture also contains a floating charge: *Re Lewis Merthyr Consolidated Collieries* [1929] 1 Ch. 498).

Order of priorities

The various preferential claims may be summarised as follows:

(1) *Creditors having preference over a fixed charge:*

    (i)   creditors holding a prior fixed charge over a particular asset;

    (ii) creditors claiming a right of set-off;

    (iii) creditors holding a repairer's lien or general lien over the assets of the company;

    (iv) creditors claiming title to assets (e.g. under a hire-purchase agreement or in respect of goods supplied under reservation of title);

    (v) a landlord;

    (vi) a statutory undertaking.

(2) *Creditors having preference over a floating charge by virtue of sections 94 and 319 of the Companies Act 1948 as amended:*

    (a) local rates which have become due and payable within a year before the appointment of the receiver;

    (b) all income tax, corporation tax, development land tax or other assessed taxes on the company up to April 5 next before the appointment of the receiver and not exceeding on the whole one year's assessment (but not necessarily the *last* year of assessment or accounting period, and different years or periods can be taken for different taxes);

    (c) P.A.Y.E. to the extent that deductions have been or should have been made during the year before the appointment of the receiver and not paid over to the Inland Revenue;

    (d) VAT and car tax having become due within the twelve months before appointment of the receiver;

(e) all arrears of wages or salary becoming due to any employee (but not a director as such) during the four months before the relevant date up to a maximum of £800. Under sections 63 to 69 of the Employment Protection (Consolidation) Act 1978 certain entitlements of employees under the employment protection legislation are assimilated to wages;

(f) accrued holiday remuneration payable to any employee on termination of his employment;

(g) any sum owed on account of Class 1 or Class 2 National Insurance contributions becoming payable in either case in the period of twelve months immediately preceding the date of the relevant event;

(h) any sum owed on account of an earner's contribution to an occupational pension scheme under sections 40 and 55 of the Social Security Pensions Act 1975, being contributions deducted from earnings paid in the period of four months immediately preceding the date of the receivership, or otherwise due in respect of earnings paid or payable in that period (see further page 541).

Subject to the above, the receiver will apply the proceeds of sale of the company's property in discharge or reduction of the principal and interest and costs of the first mortgagee and of any subsequent mortgagee who has also appointed him receiver. Since the mortgagee is beneficially entitled to the property after the deductions have been made, the mortgagee may call for it to be conveyed to him in specie, although the receiver cannot require this. There is no time limit for payment, and the receiver should not make a final payment until all actual or contingent liabilities have been discharged or adequate insurance against further claims has been taken. Any balance remaining in the receiver's hands is money belonging to the company, or if a liquidation has supervened, is money to be retained by the liquidator for the benefit of the ordinary or deferred creditors.

Discharge

A receiver appointed by the court may only be discharged by an order, which may be obtained whenever the appointment has been fulfilled or become unnecessary. It is sometimes convenient that the same person should both be receiver and liquidator; but a liquidator will not be appointed if the assets are clearly insufficient to meet the claims of the debenture holders. The application to discharge is normally made by the receiver himself. But it can be made by other persons on the ground of misconduct or incompetence, in which case the court may impose further conditions.

In the case of a receiver appointed out of court, all that is necessary is the filing with the Registrar of Companies of Form 57A pursuant to section 102(2) of the Companies Act 1948, stating that the receiver has ceased to act. The receiver should also give formal notice to the company and to his appointor, and may even require the instrument of his appointment to be endorsed with a discharge executed by the appointor. It sometimes happens that the first mortgagee will execute the discharge because he has been paid out, but a subsequent mortgagee may wish the receiver to continue with his realisation. There remains the question of books and papers in his possession, of which there may be a considerable volume. Accounts prepared in parallel to the company's accounts should be placed at the disposal of the liquidator or the directors. Papers which relate to the receiver's personal records should be retained for a period of up to twelve years (being the statutory period of limitation). He is not required to deliver any documents to the mortgagee other than in satisfaction of the mortgagee's interest or under section 372 of the Companies Act 1948 (see page 707).

Under section 93 of the Companies Act 1981 a person may be disqualified from acting as a receiver in certain circumstances, such as conviction for an indictable offence concerning a receivership or management, fraud, or persistent default in filing documents.

Position in Scotland

The Companies (Floating Charges and Receivers) (Scotland) Act 1972 introduced the facility of appointing a receiver of property belonging to a Scottish company (prior to 1972 receivers could not be appointed to Scottish companies). This materially strengthens the position in Scotland of the holder of a floating charge, who would otherwise be obliged to petition for winding-up on the grounds of insolvency, but the office of receiver is unfamiliar to the Scottish jurisdiction and there are major differences from English law, for example,

(a) only the holder of a floating charge may appoint the receiver (i.e. the trustees under a debenture trust deed do not have the power of appointment);

(b) the statutory powers conferred on a Scottish receiver are such that it is usually unnecessary to add further express powers in the appointing instrument; and

(c) it is not necessary to have an express power to appoint to receiver.

A body corporate, an undischarged bankrupt or a Scottish firm cannot be a receiver (section 11 of the 1972 Act).

When a receiver may be appointed

The circumstances in which the power to appoint may be exercised are set out in section 12 of the 1972 Act. If the instrument creating the charge specifies the circumstances in which the holder may either appoint a receiver or apply to the Court of Session for such an appointment, these will govern. If the instrument is silent, the following are the grounds for an appointment by the holder of the floating charge,

(a) the expiry of twenty-one days after the making of a demand for payment of the whole or any part of the principal sum secured by the charge, without payment having been made;

(b) the expiry of a period of two months during the whole of which interest due and payable under the charges has been in arrears;

(c) the making of an order or the passing of a resolution to wind up the company; or

(d) the appointment of a receiver under any other floating charge created by the company.

The court may also appoint a receiver on grounds (a) to (c), or if it is satisfied on the application of the holder that his position is likely to be prejudiced if no such appointment is made. the instrument of appointment may be executed either by the holder or by any person duly authorised in writing to execute it on his behalf (section 13 (4)(a)). The appointment must be notified to the Registrar of Companies and to the company itself. If there is an application to the court, the procedure involves service of a petition on the company.

Effect of appointment

The effect of appointment of a Scottish receiver is that the charge over which the property is secured crystallises at once and attaches to it as a fixed security (that is, the effect is identical to crystallisation on the commencement of an English winding-up). Section 15 of the 1972 Act vests in the receiver a large number of specific powers and he has a wide discretion as to whether they should be exercised and in what manner. A duly appointed receiver takes precedence over a liquidator, from whom he has power to recover the property charged (section 15 (1)(a)). Since there may be several floating charges created by one company, the Act provides for rules of precedence among different receivers appointed by the holders of the charges.

A Scottish receiver is the agent of the company in relation to the property attached by the charge. He is personally liable on contracts entered into by him unless he contracts as agent or unless the contract otherwise provides (section 17). A receiver does not incur personal liability on contracts entered into prior to his appointment which continue in force thereafter.

After realisation, the receiver must pay out of any assets in his hands, in priority to the claims of a holder of the floating charge, claims which would have ranked as preferential debts in a winding-up. The receiver is required to advertise for any claims, and cannot safely make payments to the holder of the floating charge for at least six months thereafter (section 19). In addition to the preferential creditors, the claims of the holders of the floating charge are deferred to certain other creditors, namely,

(a) holders of prior or *pari passu* fixed securities over the properties subject to the floating charge;

(b) persons who have successfully executed diligence over such property;

(c) creditors in respect of liabilities incurred by the receiver himself;

(d) the receiver in respect of his remuneration, expenses and liabilities.

Sections 25 and 26 of the 1972 Act provide for statements and returns to be made by a receiver in much the same way as required in England. When the receiver desires to be discharged, he must give notice within seven days to the Registrar of Companies. A receiver appointed by the court may resign only with the authority of the court and on such conditions as it may impose. On his appointment ceasing, the receiver has a right of indemnity in respect of his expenses, charges, and liabilities out of the property subject to the charge (section 22 (4) of the 1972 Act).

Reconstructions and Amalgamations

For the vast majority of transactions that a company will undertake the powers vested in the directors or, through the general meeting, in the majority shareholders, will be more than sufficient. As discussed in the chapter *Shareholders*, minority shareholders are afforded various remedies, for example under section 75 of the Companies Act 1980 where they have been or might be unfairly prejudiced. However, where the acts of the majority shareholders, viewed objectively, cannot be considered unfair, lack of consent or co-operation from the minority will not generally act as a restraint.

The flexibility thus afforded to controlling shareholders is not, however, without its limitations. Except in special cases (such as under section 209 of the Companies Act 1948) a minority holder cannot be compelled to sell or dispose of his shares; nor can his rights as a member of the company be modified without his consent. A debenture holder or secured creditor will no doubt have entrenched rights under a trust deed or loan instrument; even an ordinary creditor may be able to forestall a corporate scheme if novation of his debt is required. Furthermore, the overriding company law principle of the maintenance of share capital might also present insuperable problems in a reorganisation.

Where the ordinary powers of the company will not suffice, special provisions exist to enable schemes to proceed. This chapter examines those provisions with particular reference to the rules governing schemes of reconstruction and amalgamation.

Definitions

In common with many other expressions whose meaning is of considerable legal significance, neither "reconstruction" nor "amalgamation" is defined by statute. The meanings to be attached to those terms are important not only in the context of certain of the provisions to be considered below (for example the powers of the court under section 208), but can also have a significant effect on the tax and stamp duty consequences of a scheme. Although by concession the capital gains tax rules can be relaxed for reorganisations which do not satisfy all the case law criteria (see Statement D.14 in Index of Statements issued before July 18, 1978), the inflexible treatment for stamp duty purposes has resulted in several cases where the expressions "reconstruction" and "amalgamation" have been considered.

713

What is a reconstruction?

A reconstruction is an arrangement whereby the undertaking of a company is preserved and carried on by substantially the same persons who carried it on prior to the reorganisation. This is the "substantial identity" test enunciated by Buckley J. (as he then was) in *Re South African Supply and Cold Storage Company* [1904] 2 Ch. 268 at page 286. It is not necessary that *all* the assets pass to the new company or that *every* shareholder remains the same; nor is it essential for the new company to take over the liabilities. What is essential is that an undertakiñg or at least a part of an undertaking is transferred – a mere transfer of assets cannot constitute a reconstruction, employing as a test the ordinary use of language (see *Baytrust Holdings Ltd. v. I.R.C.* [1971] 3 All E.R. 76). Likewise the shareholders must remain substantially the same; if the reorganisation results in effect in a cash takeover, that will not be a reconstruction.

The objectives of a reconstruction include a reorganisation of the structure of the company, perhaps by means of the issue of different classes of shares, a reduction of capital (which, as will be seen below, is subject to the scrutiny of the court), tax planning considerations (although attention must now be paid to specific anti-avoidance provisions such as are contained in section 87 of the Capital Gains Tax Act 1979) and the raising of fresh capital, for example by the issue of new shares to existing holders partly paid only and then engineering a call on those shares.

Partition

The substantial identity test operates to exclude from the ambit of the term "reconstruction" a scheme to partition a company. This often occurs where two or more branches of a family wish to continue separately a like number of separate trades currently carried on by a single company. This is commonly referred to as a "company divorce" and is generally effected under section 287 of the Companies Act 1948 (which does not refer in terms to "reconstruction").

Demerger

The expression "demerger" is a creation of tax law under provisions contained in Schedule 18 to the Finance Act 1980. Those provisions afford certain exemptions from tax and stamp duty where trading activities are "demerged" or effectively placed under independent management. From a company law point of view, the primary effect of the 1980 rules is to encourage straightforward distributions in specie of trades or shares in trading subsidiaries, and to facilitate the use of sections 206 to 208 of the Companies Act 1948 where previously a distribution problem might have arisen. A full explanation of the tax implications of demergers can be found in *Tolley's Tax Planning*.

What is an amalgamation?

Whereas a reconstruction constitutes the reorganisation of one company, an amalgamation by definition involves two or more companies or businesses being brought together under the one umbrella. Again, the judgment of Buckley J. in *Re South African Supply and Cold Storage Company* is instructive:

"The difference between reconstruction and amalgamation is that in the latter is involved the blending of two concerns one with the other, but not merely the continuance of one concern."

It is not necessary that there should be a new company. Thus where shareholders in one company (Company B) exchange their shares for shares in another (Company A) with the result that Company A then owns all the issued shares in Company B, that is an amalgamation, and remains so even though there may be a pre-existing obligation on certain of the old Company B shareholders to part with their new Company A shares (see *Crane Freuhauf Ltd. v. I.R.C.* [1974] 1 All E.R. 811; [1975] 1 All E.R. 429 C.A.). However, there will be no amalgamation in the true sense of the word if the consideration for the Company B shares consists of cash alone (*I.R.C. v. Ufitec Group* [1977] 3 All E.R. 924).

Amalgamations are employed for a variety of reasons. They are certainly not limited to the much publicised public takeovers and mergers where reference might be required under Part V of the Fair Trading Act 1973 to the Monopolies and Mergers Commission. Until the enactment of section 40 of the Finance Act 1977 (now sections 87 and 88 of the Capital Gains Tax Act 1979) the share-exchange amalgamation was widely used as a tool in tax avoidance schemes. Amalgamations remain common in small corporate groups where historically businesses have been carried on separately but where a single company structure would result in increased efficiency.

Distributions in specie

One of the most straightforward forms of reconstruction is the distribution in specie of shares in a subsidiary or the whole or part of an undertaking. Thus, where Company A has a subsidiary, Company B, a reconstruction can be carried out by the distribution of the shares in Company B to the Company A shareholders pro rata to their existing holdings of shares in Company A.

The attraction of the use of the distribution in specie as a means of reconstruction has improved as a result of the tax exemptions afforded by the Finance Act 1980 to demergers of trading businesses. Previously the combination of a Schedule F and advance corporation tax charge tended in practice to rule out such distributions, unless they could be achieved in a winding-up or on a reduction of capital. However, the Finance Act 1980 provisions do not affect the ordinary *company law* rules applicable to such transactions.

The general rules relating to distributions of profits apply to distributions in specie (unless, for example, by way of a reduction of capital). Accordingly, power to make such distributions must be incorporated in the articles of association. The usual power is found in article 120 of Table A, under which on the authority of an ordinary resolution payment of a dividend may be effected by a distribution of specific assets. The dividend itself is declared as a cash amount, to be satisfied by the distribution of assets. It is for the directors of the distributing company to satisfy themselves as to the value of those assets.

The fact that a distribution may be satisfied by the transfer of capital assets does not affect the principles regarding the payment of dividends. Under section 39 of the Companies Act 1980, a company may not make any distribution (as defined) except out of profits available for the purpose. The detailed questions relating to dividends and distributions are discussed elsewhere (see the chapter *Dividends*), but the effect is to restrict reconstructions by way of distribution in specie to where the value of the shares or undertaking effectively to be "demerged" exceeds the distributable reserves of the company concerned. Two methods by which this problem might be overcome (and which have been used in practice) are, first, by a cancellation of share premium account and a transfer of the resulting credit to general reserve and, secondly, by a realisation of a distributable profit on a sale of an asset intra-group. Additionally, where the asset distributed itself contains an element of unrealised profit, the amount of that profit is treated as though it were a realised profit (see section 43A of the 1980 Act). This provision (inserted by the Companies Act 1981) further facilitates distributions in specie as a method of reconstruction.

Provided a company has the necessary powers in its memorandum it may, for example, sell its entire undertaking to a new subsidiary in exchange for shares and then distribute those shares to its shareholders. However, the courts will not allow such a scheme where the company itself is to be placed in liquidation, since this would effectively nullify the protection afforded to minority shareholders under section 287 of the Companies Act 1948 (considered below). In *Bisgood v. Henderson's Transvaal Estates Limited* [1908] 1 Ch. 743 it was held that such a scheme, which involved a proposed capital distribution by the liquidator of partly-paid shares in the new company (thus obliging the members to accept a liability and nothing else) was *ultra vires*. Accordingly, reconstructions of this nature can only be contemplated under section 287, or under sections 206 to 208 of the Companies Act 1948.

Section 287 schemes

Where a reconstruction cannot be effected by a simple distribution in specie or the transfer of an undertaking is associated with a liquidation (see *Bisgood* above), the scheme may be carried out under section 287 of the Companies Act 1948. Section 287 remains a popular means of reconstructing a company or group of companies, particularly in the case of private, or family controlled, concerns. Where a dissenting minority is unlikely to be a consideration, section 287 offers a relatively inexpensive route, avoiding as it does the necessity of an application to the court (cf. section 206 schemes, discussed below). Furthermore, where for any reason the tax exemptions for "demergers" are not available, section 287 may often represent the only means of reconstruction available to the shareholders if a prohibitive tax charge on distributions is to be avoided.

The single most important point in relation to section 287 is that it can only apply in cases where a company is proposed to be, or is in the course of being, *voluntarily* wound up. All the usual consequences of liquidation must therefore follow, and this can lead to practical problems, both with creditors and with the physical transfer of assets and property. Depending upon the precise nature of the reconstruction an elegant solution which is often adopted is the prior incorporation of a "shell" holding company which is itself wound up passing *shares* in subsidiary companies to the shareholders whilst leaving the underlying assets intact. It is only in the case of a members' voluntary winding up that an application to the court can be avoided; a special resolution under section 287 is not valid without the sanction of the court if, within one year of its being passed an order is made for compulsory winding up or a winding up subject to the supervision of the court (section 287(5)). In the case of a creditor's winding up, section 298 of the 1948 Act provides that section 287 can apply as in a voluntary winding up, with the modification that the powers of the liquidator (discussed below) may not be exercised except with the sanction either of the court or of the committee of inspection.

Under section 287 the liquidator of a company is empowered, with the sanction of a special resolution, to transfer the whole or part of the transferor company's business or property to another company in exchange for shares (or other interests) in the transferee company. Those shares are then distributed to the members of the transferor company in accordance with their rights. In practice the transferor company in liquidation will enter into an agreement with the liquidator and the transferee company under which shares in the transferee company are effectively issued direct to the holders of shares in the transferor company. Provision can also be made in the agreement for the payment by the transferee company of the expenses of winding up and for the payment out of dissentient members (as to which see below).

In order for section 287 to apply the following conditions must be satisfied.

(a) The transferor company must be a company registered under the Companies Acts (C.A. 1948, s. 445). Thus, a foreign registered company cannot be the subject of a section 287 scheme, even if it has a place of business in the U.K., and so is registered under Part X of the 1948 Act. (The residence of the company for tax purposes is immaterial.)

(b) The transferee must be a *company*, and not an individual (*Bird v. Bird's Patent Sewage Co.* (1874) 9 Ch. App. 358). However, unlike the transferor company, section 287(1) expressly provides that the transferee company need not be a registered company; a foreign company therefore falls within these provisions (cf. section 206 – see below).

(c) A special resolution must be passed authorising the liquidator to accept shares in the transferee company as consideration for the sale of the transferor company's undertaking. It is necessary to comply strictly with this rule as was illustrated in *Etheridge v. Central Uruguay Northern Extension Railway Company Limited* [1913] 1 Ch. 425 where an ordinary resolution sanctioning the sale and a special resolution for the winding up and distribution of consideration shares were held to be outside the requirements of the section.

Special notice of the resolution must be given to the members. If the directors are to derive any special advantage, this must be disclosed. In practice it is common to find a specific statement in the notice of general meeting (or accompanying document) to the effect that the directors will obtain no greater benefit from the scheme than any other shareholder.

Scope of section 287

It must be admitted that section 287 is suitable only for certain types of reconstruction. Not only can it be rendered impractical by a significant absence of unanimity among the members of the affected company, but there are restrictions on the detailed provisions of the scheme which can be adopted under section 287. Those restrictions have been laid down by the courts under successive Companies Acts as a means of protecting the rights of dissenting shareholders and are now contained in sections 287(3) (4) and (6) and in section 287(5), which enables a creditor to nullify the section 287 resolution by obtaining a winding up order.

Provisions which can validly be inserted in schemes under section 287 are as follows (per Buckley L. J. in *Bisgood v. Henderson's Transvaal Estates* above at page 760),

(1) that the shares for distribution are to be partly-paid shares. Section 287 provides no power enabling a liability to be imposed on a shareholder without his consent (*Clinch v. Financial Corporation* (1868) 4 Ch. App. 117). If the scheme is to involve such an issue and any members are unwilling to consent they must either be paid out by the liquidator or else a section 206 scheme – and an application to the court – will be necessary;

(2) that if a shareholder wishes to accept the shares he must apply for them within a limited time;

(3) that shares unapplied for may be sold for the benefit of the company or the shareholder concerned; and

(4) that the shares shall not go to the company but direct to the members.

Rights of dissenting members

"Any sale or arrangement in pursuance of [section 287] shall be binding on the members of the transferor company" (section 287(3)). In theory, therefore, holders of 75 per cent of the voting power of a company can effect a section 287 scheme binding on the minority shareholders. In practice, however, there is a sting in the tail in the form of specific statutory rights available to dissenting members.

Provided a member did not vote in favour of the special resolution (i.e. the section 287 resolution) he may within seven days of the general meeting express his dissent *in writing* to the liquidator, left at the registered office of the company. The liquidator can then be required to abstain from carrying the resolution into effect, or else to purchase the interest of the dissenting member at a price to be determined by agreement or arbitration (section 287(3)). The choice of the two alternatives is the liquidator's; so much follows from the provisions of subsection (4). Even if no notice under subsection (3) is given, a dissentient cannot be compelled to accept shares in the transferee company; those shares will either be held by the transferor company or the liquidator on trust for the member or else sold and the proceeds of sale passed to the member.

Under section 287(4) if the liquidator elects to purchase the dissenting member's interest, the purchase money must be paid before the transferor company is finally dissolved, and must be raised by the liquidator in such manner as may be determined by special resolution. In practice this will often be recoverable under the agreement with the transferee company.

What then can the dissentient member expect to be paid for his interest? In general the provisions are only likely to apply in the case of a member with a relatively small minority interest. Where there is no market for the shares the value of a minority holding will generally be small in comparison to a net asset valuation. On the other hand the value attributed to the undertaking of the transferor company for the purposes of the reconstruction might well exceed a break-up valuation. The answer is that the dissenting shareholder is entitled to be paid what he would have received in an ordinary winding up of the company, i.e. the break-up price (see *Re Mysore West Gold Mining Company* (1889) 42 Ch. D. 525). This may involve a valuation of the assets of the company, and the court has power to order the examination of witnesses for this purpose, although the dissenting shareholder himself (on whom the burden of proof lies) cannot examine the directors or obtain access to the company's books.

It is not possible to restrict the rights of dissenting shareholders under section 287 by means of provisions in the articles of the transferor company. Those rights can in practice lead to the abandonment of schemes of reconstruction before the winding up. Clearly, the earlier the major shareholders can be satisfied as to likely approval of the scheme, the more likely it is to succeed. One possible answer to this problem is to circularise all shareholders at an early stage with details of *all* the steps in the reconstruction scheme and with an invitation to the shareholders to approve the scheme as a whole. The objective is to create a contract between the shareholders (outside the articles) by means of a covenant on the part of all shareholders to vote in favour of the section 287 resolution. The form of covenant required would be such as to effect the appointment by each shareholder of the directors of the transferor company by irrevocable proxy to vote in favour of the winding up and the sale of the undertaking in return for shares in the transferee company.

Disadvantages of section 287

Section 287 is commonly employed as a means of effecting schemes of reconstruction. Certain restrictions on its flexibility and other disadvantages have already been referred to. These include,

(a) the rights of dissenting shareholders, discussed above;

(b) creditors of the transferor company cannot be bound by the section 287 resolution. They are entitled to prove in the liquidation in the ordinary way, and have the power to invalidate the resolution by applying to the court for the company to be wound up compulsorily (section 287(5));

(c) there is no power under section 287 analogous to that in section 208 (discussed below) enabling the court to make a vesting order. Thus, all assets of the transferor company must be formally transferred, and stamp duty will require to be considered; and

(d) section 287 requires a formal winding up of the transferor company. This in itself can prove expensive and time-consuming.

As mentioned earlier, the disadvantages listed at (b) to (d) might be overcome by the use of a new holding company as the ultimate transferor company. Since the holding company is a mere "shell" the winding up should be relatively straightforward. Underlying assets and liabilities of the subsidiary or subsidiaries transferred are unaffected. As regards the rights of dissentient members, it is often sought to overcome this problem by adopting a scheme under section 206, considered in the next section of this chapter. However, as will be seen, this approach may fail if the court exercises its discretion to impose extra-statutory conditions as to the protection of dissentients in exchange for the sanction of the scheme.

(At the end of this chapter there will be found an outline agenda for a reorganisation scheme under section 287. The object of the scheme, which does not fall strictly within the definition of "reconstruction" given earlier, is effectively to demerge a trading subsidiary B from its non-trading parent company A, certain of the shareholders taking control of B whilst the remaining members retain their interest in A. H Limited is a new holding company formed as the transferor company for section 287 purposes. It should perhaps be noted at this stage that there is an argument to the affect that section 287 cannot apply to "partitions" of the sort envisaged by this scheme. This is on the ground that the section presupposes that *all* shareholders in H Limited end up with the same or equivalent considerations. This point is largely academic since in practice such partitions are regularly carried out as section 287 reorganisations.)

Section 206 schemes

The scope of section 206 is by no means limited to schemes of reconstruction or amalgamation. It covers any "compromise or arrangement" between a company and its creditors or members. Its functions are therefore considerably wider than those of section 287. "Arrangement" is a word of wide import, not necessarily analogous to "compromise", and by section 206(6) expressly includes a reorganisation of share capital by the consolidation of shares of different classes or by the division of shares into shares of different classes or by both those methods. Thus, the procedure under section 206 can be adopted, for example, to alter the terms of a company's debenture stock or to replace that stock with stock in another company (in the course of a reconstruction). Such arrangements with creditors are not possible under the limited powers contained in section 287.

A scheme can still constitute a scheme of arrangement *between* a company and its members within section 206 even where it is clear that persons holding a majority of the votes are opposed to the scheme. All that is necessary is that the rights and obligations existing between the company and its members are sufficiently affected by the scheme (*Re Savoy Hotel Limited* [1981] 3 W.L.R. 441 and see below).

However, a scheme cannot be a scheme of "arrangement" unless there is an element of accommodation on each side. Where the rights of members are merely being expropriated without any compensating advantage it cannot be said that they are entering into a compromise or arrangement with the company (*Re NFU Development Trust Limited* [1973] 1 All E.R. 135).

The detailed procedural requirements of section 206 are considered below, but broadly the section enables an arrangement or compromise to be put into effect if the following steps are taken,

(1) the company or the creditors or members, or the liquidator if it is in the course of winding up, apply to the court;

(2) the court *may* (i.e. it has a discretion) order a meeting of the creditors or class of creditors, or of the members or class of

members as the case may be, to be summoned in such manner as the court directs;

(3) if at the relevant meetings a majority in number representing three-fourths in value of the creditors or class of creditors, or members or class of members, present and voting in person or by proxy, agree to the compromise or arrangement, it is then, if sanctioned by the court, binding on all the creditors or members or the classes as the case may be, and on the company; and

(4) before the scheme can have effect an office copy of the court order sanctioning the scheme must be filed with the Registrar of Companies

Exercise of the court's discretion

The provisions of section 206 afford the court discretion at two distinct stages. First of all the court has discretion as to the calling of meetings; secondly, it has discretion whether or not to sanction the scheme following the holding of the statutory meetings.

The vesting of this discretion in the court is for the overall protection of the members and creditors, particularly those in a minority. For this purpose, a creditor includes a debenture holder, and also a foreign creditor whose rights are in England. (There is nothing to prevent a foreign creditor with overseas rights seeking to enforce those rights in the appropriate jurisdiction; if that is considered a problem it may be possible to seek an analogous sanction to the scheme in the foreign court.)

In relation to the calling of the requisite meetings, it was held in *Re Savoy Hotel Limited* (above) that the court ought not to exercise its discretion in favour of convening the meetings if it was clear that, having regard to the opposition to the scheme by the holders of the majority of the votes, the meetings could serve no useful purpose. The court has no jurisdiction to sanction an arrangement under section 206 which does not have the approval of the company either through the board, or, if appropriate, by means of a simple majority of the members in general meeting.

As regards the sanctioning of the scheme itself, the courts have in general adopted an objective test as propounded by Maugham J. in *Re Dorman Long and Company Limited* [1934] 1 Ch. 635 at page 657:

"In my opinion ... what I have to see is whether the proposal is such that an intelligent and honest man, a member of the class concerned and acting in respect of his interest, might reasonably approve."

In an earlier case (*Re Alabama* [1891] 1 Ch. 213) a similar test was adopted in the case of debenture holders. Provided there is no element of bad faith and the majority voters view the scheme with regard to the interests of those they represent, and take a view which *can reasonably be taken* by business men, then the scheme will be capable of sanction.

In practice, the mere fact of approval of a scheme will often suffice for the purpose of obtaining sanction. Where a member or creditor receives full information about the scheme and is given sufficient time to consider his position, the court will not generally interfere, except where a dishonest motive is apparent (*Re English Scottish and Australian Chartered Bank* [1893] 3 Ch. 385), or where class interests are not fairly represented (see below). It is accepted that creditors, for example, are likely to be much better judges of what is to their commercial advantage than the court can be, although this is only a guide, and not a rule, and is of little value when it is proved that the majority of a particular class have voted or may have voted in the way they did because of their interests as shareholders of another class (*Carruth v. I.C.I.* [1937] A.C. 707 per Lord Maugham at p. 769). The court must be satisfied that the interests of creditors are properly protected (*Re Bramall & Ogden Limited, Law Society's Gazette*, May 22, 1981), though it seems this question is to be addressed not on the original petition under section 206, but on an application for the court to apply the provisions of section 208 once the scheme has been sanctioned by the members (*Re Clydesdale Bank Limited* [1950] S.C. 30; see below).

The objections to the scheme of dissenting members or creditors are clearly important factors in the exercise of the court's discretion: however, if no assets are available in any event for the dissenting class, their dissent will be ignored and the scheme treated as a scheme between the company and its creditors and other contributories who have an interest (*Re Tea Corporation Limited* [1904] 1 Ch. 12).

Although the scope of section 206 is wide, it cannot encompass schemes the provisions of which fall outside the general law. Thus, the court has no jurisdiction to sanction a scheme which is *ultra vires* (*Re Oceanic Steam Navigation Company Limited* [1939] 1 Ch. 41). In the *Oceanic* case the scheme involved the transfer of the undertaking of an insolvent company to a new company which was then to issue shares to the creditors of the old company. There was no power to sell the undertaking contained in the memorandum. It was held that the scheme could not be sanctioned. It is important therefore that the corporate powers of the company are wide enough to cover all aspects of the scheme *before* it comes before the courts; defects can then be remedied by special resolution. Likewise, in *Re Bramall & Ogden Limited* (above) a scheme whereby assets were transferred to a new company in consideration of a share issue by the new company direct to the shareholders could not be sanctioned under section 206 until the petitioning company amended its memorandum to permit its shareholders, rather than the company itself, to receive the consideration.

A scheme which involves an overall reduction of capital must comply with the specific provisions in that regard: see sections 66 to 71 of the Companies Act 1948 (considered below). A scheme will not be sanctioned if it involves the issue of shares at a discount, and in *Re St. James' Court Estate Limited* [1944] 1 Ch. 6 it was held that a scheme for the *conversion* (as opposed to the *issue*) of preference shares to redeemable shares could not be sanctioned as the resolutions passed at the requisite meetings did not amount to a reduction of capital and immediate increase (which would have been capable of sanction). On the other hand, in spite of the mandatory provisions of section 32 of the Companies Act 1980, alterations in class rights can be sanctioned under section 206 (see section 32(10) of the 1980 Act).

The court will exercise its discretion in favour of a scheme under section 206 which could equally well have been effected under the more restrictive rules contained in section 287, unless, perhaps, the scheme represents no more than a sale (*Re Anglo-Continental Supply Co.* [1922] 2 Ch. 723: in these circumstances the court is unlikely to sanction a scheme brought under section 206 rather than section 287 simply to evade the rights dissentients have under section 287). However, the court will in such a case generally (though not inevitably) impose a condition requiring dissentient members to be given equivalent rights to those contained in section 287(3) (see *Re Canning Jarrah Timber Company (Western Australia) Limited* [1900] 1 Ch. 708 and section 208(1) (e) below). Such a condition would, it is thought, be likely to be imposed where (as in *Bisgood v. Henderson's Transvaal Estates Limited*, above) the shares in the new company were to be issued partly-paid thus obliging the shareholders to accept a liability. Schemes under section 206 which involve the transfer of an undertaking in return for shares or debentures or both issued direct to members or creditors of the old company often incorporate such protective provisions.

The ability of the court to impose conditions as the price of its sanction was well illustrated in *Re Canning* (above) where the liquidator of the company concerned was persuaded by the court to abandon certain questionable underwriting agreements, to provide for dissentient members, and to pay out unsecured creditors in full before passing assets to the new company. In addition to this power (which effectively operates to modify schemes) it is also prudent practice to provide in the scheme itself the ability for the company to agree to any modifications which the court may approve.

Meaning of "class"

The essential purpose of section 206 is to facilitate compromises or arrangements between the company and/or groups of members or creditors or both. It is therefore of vital importance that each class of members or creditors should be accurately identified for the purpose of the various meetings which the court has power to call under section 206(1). It is only if these class meetings fairly represent what divergent interests there may be that the court will be able to apply the "business reality" test referred to in the previous section. The responsibility for ensuring that the requisite class meetings are correctly convened and constituted falls squarely on the applicant, and if there is a defect in this regard the court may well refuse to sanction a scheme if the petition is opposed (see *Practice Note* [1934] W.N. 142).

The modern approach to the question of class meetings is perhaps illustrated by the case of *Re Hellenic & General Trust* [1975] 3 All E.R. 382. In that case, a minority shareholder opposed a scheme of arrangement whereby the target company was to be taken over and members compensated in cash, on the basis that the requisite resolution under section 206(2) could not have been carried but for the support of a wholly-owned subsidiary of the purchaser. It was held that the subsidiary was to be treated as having a community of interest with its parent as purchaser and therefore as constituting a separate class for section 206 purposes. Because no separate class meeting had been held the petition failed.

In earlier cases the courts had tended to concentrate on the respective rights attached to the shares rather than to look through to the economic reality. Thus, in *Re Alabama* (above) Bowen L. J. expressed the view that, whilst it was quite proper that every member of a class of members or creditors (basing the test of "class" on rights) should attend the requisite class meeting and vote as he saw fit, the duty of the court was to recognise that other interests of a predominant kind might well affect the way in which that vote was cast, and to decide in the light of the facts whether what was proposed was reasonable and just as regards the interests of the whole class. A similar position was adopted by Lord Maugham in *Carruth v. I.C.I* (above).

It seems reasonable to suggest that the courts might in general continue to identify a class by reference to the rights attached to shares or debts, whilst reserving to itself, on the *Alabama* principle, an overall discretion to refuse sanction for a scheme which no *unprejudiced* man of business would reasonably approve. Only in exceptional cases (such as *Re Hellenic*) will the courts recognise a class distinction among shareholders of equal standing.

In the Scottish case of *Singer Manufacturing Co. v. Robinson* [1971] S.C.11 a company owning 92 per cent of a subsidiary sought to acquire the minority shares. The parent company effectively treated its own shares as a separate class and did not cast their votes. The scheme was sanctioned by the court.

Shareholders who have paid up different amounts on their shares must be regarded as a separate class and a failure to hold proper class meetings in those circumstances is fatal (*Re United Provident Assurance Co. Limited* [1910] 2 Ch. 477). Similarly, as in *Sovereign Life Assurance Company v. Dodd* [1892] 2 Q.B. 573, holders of policies which have matured are creditors and constitute a different class from policyholders whose policies have not yet matured. However, it is not necessary for a class meeting to be called if members of that particular class cannot benefit in a winding up (*Re Tea Corporation Limited*, above).

Reconstructions and amalgamations

The ability, by means of a court order sanctioning the scheme, to bind a minority of members or creditors makes section 206 an attractive vehicle for reconstructions and amalgamations. (The use in practice of section 206 for reconstructions was at one time impaired by transfers of assets in the course of the scheme being liable to be treated as distributions (with Schedule F and ACT consequences), but the tax exemptions afforded by the Finance Act 1980 in respect of "demergers" for genuine reasons of trade have remedied this defect, at least in that limited class of case.)

Under section 208, where a section 206 compromise or arrangement involves a reconstruction of any company or companies or the amalgamation of any two or more companies, *and* under the scheme the whole or any part of the undertaking or property of the company concerned ("the transferor company") is to be transferred to another company ("the transferee company") the court *may* make provision for all or any of the following:

(a) The transfer to the transferee company of the whole or any part of the undertaking and of the property or liabilities of any transferor company. This is achieved – under section 208(2) – by means of a vesting order, which in practice can save time and expense where significant assets are to be transferred. However, the order cannot affect contracts of service, although these may nevertheless be treated as continuous under the Transfer of Undertakings (Protection of Employment) Regulations 1981. Equally, capital allowances, stock relief etc. cannot be *transferred* under section 208 (but see section 252 of the Taxes Act 1970 and paragraph 20 of Schedule 9 to the Finance Act 1981).

(b) The allotting or appropriation by the transferee company of any shares, debentures, policies or other like interests in that company which under the compromise or arrangement are to be allotted or appropriated by that company to or for any person.

(c) The continuation by or against the transferee company of any legal proceedings pending by or against any transferor company.

(d) The dissolution, without winding up, of any transferor company. It is the exercise of this power – and the absence of a winding up – which (a) except in cases of demergers, causes a transfer of an undertaking to be treated as a non-exempt income distribution, and (b) in demergers enables the various specific tax exemptions to be applied.

(e) The provision to be made for any persons, who within such time and in such manner as the court directs, dissent from the compromise or arrangement. Thus a scheme can be made conditional on section 287-type protections for a dissentient minority (see above).

(f) Such incidental, consequential and supplemental matters as are necessary to secure that the reconstruction or amalgamation shall be fully and effectively carried out.

One point to note in regard to section 208 is that its operation is restricted to *registered* companies (section 298(5)) whereas the more general provisions of section 206 extend (by virtue of sub-section (6) of that section) to any company liable to be wound up under the Companies Acts which can include companies incorporated under statute, or by charter (and see sections 399 and 400 of the 1948 Act).

Takeovers

Schemes under sections 206 to 208 have often been employed where a straightforward offer would have been equally appropriate. One of the primary reasons for proceeding by way of a scheme is the reduced level of acceptances (75 per cent) which are required to bind a recalcitrant minority as opposed to that (90 per cent) applicable under section 209. This can be even more significant where the purchaser already owns a substantial proportion of the shares in the target company (see further the chapter *Takeovers*). Another reason is the avoidance of stamp duty on the transfer of shares in the target to the acquiring company; this is achieved by the cancellation of the existing issued share capital of the target and the immediate creation and issue direct to the purchaser of the new shares thereby eliminating any transfer of shares. The significance of this point has perhaps diminished with the increasing use of stamp duty saving schemes where the target is a listed company.

The case of *Re Hellenic & General Trust Limited* [1975] 3 All E.R. 382 has already been considered with reference to the meaning of "class" for section 206 purposes. That case also served to cast some doubt on the efficacy of section 206 schemes in the case of pure takeovers where for some reason the provisions of section 209 are inappropriate.

However, the *obiter dicta* in that case on this particular question seems to indicate little more than that the nature of a takeover in practice will be an important consideration in the exercise of the court's discretion. In the course of his judgment Templeman J. (as he then was) held that the fact that an arrangement under section 206 produces a result which is the same as a takeover under section 209 is "not necessarily fatal. It is not always so unfair as to preclude the court from exercising its discretion in favour of the scheme."

In concluding thus, the judgment of Plowman J. in *Re National Bank Limited* [1966] 1 W.L.R. 819 at p. 929 was expressly accepted:

"As regards [Counsel for the opposing shareholders'] second objection, namely, that the scheme really ought to be treated as a section 209 case needing a ninety per cent majority, I cannot accede to that proposition. In the first place, it seems to me to involve imposing a limitation or qualification either on the generality of the word "arrangement" in section 206 or else on the discretion of the court under that section. The legislature has not seen fit to impose any such limitation in terms and I see no reason for implying any. Moreover, the two sections, section 206 and section 209, involve quite different considerations and different approaches. Under section 206 an arrangement can only be sanctioned if the question of its fairness has first of all been submitted to the court. Under section 209, on the other hand, the matter may never come to the court at all. If it does come to the court then the onus is cast on the dissenting minority to demonstrate the unfairness of the scheme. There are, therefore, good reasons for requiring a smaller majority in favour of a scheme under section 206 than the majority which is required under section 209 if the minority is to be expropriated."

In *Re Hellenic* the scheme could not be sanctioned because the requisite class meetings had not been held. In addition, however, the court exercised its discretion against sanctioning the scheme for the following reasons,

(a) the scheme could not succeed under section 209 because of the express provisions of that section and the size of the shareholding of the objectors (i.e. 13.95 per cent). However, this would not, of itself, mean that the scheme should necessarily fail; and

(b) the scheme could only succeed under section 206 by using the votes of the acquiring company's subsidiary (which held 53.01 per cent of the shares in the target) to secure the necessary majority.

Accordingly, in similar circumstances, it is likely to prove difficult for the promotors to persuade the court to exercise its discretion in favour of the scheme,

". . . where one has in effect a section 209 scheme, then putting it at its lowest, there must be a very high standard of proof on the part of the applicant to justify obtaining by section 206 what could not be obtained by section 209, especially where there is the added element that section 206 itself only works with the help of a wholly owned subsidiary of the parent company" (*Re Hellenic* at p. 388).

A section 206 scheme cannot be used where the bid is contested: see *Re Savoy Hotel Limited* and page 722 above.

Procedure under sections 206 to 208

The following represents no more than a brief summary of the procedural requirements for schemes under section 206. The source of these requirements is Order 102 of the Rules of the Supreme Court 1965 (as amended) to which reference should be made in all cases. Precedents for the various documents required may be found in the *Encyclopaedia of Forms and Precedents* (Volume 6), *Palmer's Company Precedents*, and *Atkin's Court Forms* (Volume 10).

On the assumption that the scheme proceeds in a relatively straightforward manner, the formalities should be completed within about two months after the first application to the court. However, this estimate may have to be revised where a court vacation intervenes. In particular, it used to be rare indeed for petitions to be heard in the Long Vacation (from August 1 to September 30 inclusive: Ord. 64): see *Re Showerings* [1968] 3 All E.R. 276. The position regarding vacation business is now governed by *Practice Direction (Companies Court: Long Vacation) (No. 2), 23 February 1978* [1978] 1 W.L.R. 429. Under that practice direction, a judge of the Companies Court is available for sitting on an early Wednesday in August and each Wednesday in September. The Companies Court Registrar must be given the earliest possible warning of a proposed application during the Long Vacation, although it is not necessary at that stage to disclose the name of any company involved.

With effect from October 15, 1979 proceedings in chambers under Order 102 may be conducted by post (see *Practice Direction (Companies*

Court: Postal Facilities) [1979] 1 W.L.R. 1413). The 1979 directions were made with a view to enabling certain formal business in the chambers of the Companies Court to be transacted by post when this is more expeditious, economical or convenient. Business may nevertheless continue to be transacted personally. The classes of business covered by the directions include the issue of summonses, the presentation of petitions and the filing of affidavits.

Stage one

Proceedings are initiated by *originating summons* in the Chancery Division of the High Court for leave to call the requisite meetings. It is most common for the company itself to apply *ex parte*, although members and creditors may make the application, and in the case of a company in the course of being wound up, the summons will generally be issued by the liquidator.

Stage two

The summons is supported by an affidavit exhibiting the scheme of arrangement itself. In order that the necessary directions can be given, the affidavit should make reference to the various classes of shareholders to be accommodated, and to the required advertisements of the meeting (for example by the use of newspaper advertisements, particularly in the case of holders of bearer securities). It is also appropriate to include suggestions as to the appointment of named individuals as chairmen of the class meetings. The affidavit is filed in the office of the Companies Court Registrar.

Stage three

The Registrar will make an order on the originating summons, following which the advertisement and notice of the meeting and proxies are settled in chambers.

Proxies. Members and creditors entitled to attend the various meetings called by the order may do so in person or by proxy. The proxy delivered with the notice of the meeting must be in the form settled in chambers, although the right of the member or creditor to use any proper form of proxy is not thereby displaced; furthermore directors who receive proxies must use them, whatever form they may be in (*Re Dorman Long and Company Limited* [1934] 1 Ch. 635).

If the articles specify particular provisions as to voting (for example, in the case of joint holders of shares) those provisions will be adopted in settling the form of proxy.

Stage four

Notice and advertisement of the meetings is then given. It is essential that the terms of the order are strictly complied with, as the court will not be slow in rejecting a petition where any procedural requirement is disregarded. It has been held, for example, that a copy of the heading to the scheme will not suffice; nor will a copy of the petition proposed to be presented to the court. A copy of the newspaper containing the relevant advertisement must be lodged in chambers.

In practice, no notice is required to be given to any class not affected by the scheme. This would include shareholders, for example, in an insolvent company whose rights were regarded as of no value whatever (*Re Oceanic Steam Navigation Company Limited* [1939] 1 Ch. 41).

Explanatory statement. Under section 207 an explanatory statement must be sent with every notice summoning the meeting or meetings to be convened under the order. The statement must explain the effect of the scheme and must in particular state any material interests of the directors (in whatever capacity) and the effect on them of the scheme, although this latter requirement is not applied where the effect is the same for the directors as for others with an identical interest (see *City Property Investment Trust Corporation, Petitioners* [1951] S.C. 570). Compensation payments to directors require the sanction of the company in the usual way: section 191 of the Companies Act 1948.

It is most important that the circular is not misleading in any way; it should not, for example, imply the consent of a section of a class who might vote for reasons not related to their membership of that class (*Re Dorman Long & Co. Limited* [1934] Ch. 635). The true significance of all statements must be sufficiently explained. Furthermore, it appears that if it can be shown that the 75 per cent majority was obtained by reason of misleading statements in the circular, the minority who might be prejudiced then might have grounds for complaint (see *Gething v. Kilner* [1971] 1 W.L.R. 337 – a case on section 209 of the 1948 Act).

If notice of the meeting is given by advertisement, the explanatory statement can either be included *verbatim* in the advertisement itself, or else the advertisement can refer to the place at which and the manner in which creditors or members entitled to attend the meeting may obtain – free of charge – a copy of the statement.

Where the scheme affects the rights of debenture holders, the explanatory statement must also contain a reference to the interests of the trustees of the debenture trust deed in the same way as for directors. There are penalties for directors or trustees who fail to provide the requisite information (as to which see below), and also for the company and any officer of the company (including for this purpose the trustees) if the provisions of section 207 are not complied with by the company, unless in this case the default was due to a director or trustee failing to supply the information.

Stage five

At the meetings the required majority for each class is three-fourths in value. The chairman of each meeting is required to report to the court on the conduct and result of the meeting. It is advisable to ensure as far as possible that members of one class are not present at a meeting of another class, although, as in *Carruth v. I.C.I.* (above), this is not a procedural objection but may influence the court in the exercise of its discretion on the hearing of the petition.

Stage six

After the meetings have been held and the necessary majorities secured, the petition is presented in chambers together with supporting affidavits proving service of the notices, the conduct and result of the meetings, and the petition itself. If necessary, liberty to apply for orders under section 208 (reconstructions and amalgamations) should be sought, although if possible all requisite orders may be made on the hearing of the petition. Otherwise the application under section 208 will be adjourned to the Registrar.

The powers and discretions of the court on the hearing of the petition have been considered above. Any shareholder or member who wishes to object should give notice of his opposition at the relevant class meeting and should appear on the presentation of the petition. A person who fails to do either will not be entitled to appeal against any order sanctioning the petition unless he first of all obtains leave of the court (*Re Securities Insurance Company* [1894] 2 Ch. 410).

Stage seven

If further orders under section 208 are required, the applicant must then issue an originating summons and serve a copy (together with a copy of the affidavit in support) on any person interested. For example, if it is proposed to provide for dissentient members, those members must be served with the summons. Service of the summons must be acknowledged.

Stage eight

Where a summons is issued seeking an order or orders under section 208, a summons for directions must also be taken out. The matters on which the court will give directions include, in particular, directions for the publication of notices and the making of any enquiry, for example, as to creditors if the company is to be dissolved. To avoid this enquiry it is customary to provide in the scheme itself provisions for creditors, perhaps by means of guarantee or indemnity.

Stage nine

On the making of an order, particularly a vesting order under section 208(1)(a), the solicitors for the applicant will be required to give an undertaking to the court to lodge the order for adjudication for stamp duty purposes and to pay any duty assessed. An office copy of any section 208 order must be delivered to the Registrar of Companies within seven days after the making of the order (see also page 862).

Stage ten

The final stage of the scheme is the filing with the Registrar of companies of an office copy of the section 206 order: until this is done the order is ineffective.

Penalties

Certain of the provisions of sections 206 to 208 above are mandatory in that there are prescribed penalties for failure to comply or contravention. The penalties were revised by the Companies Act 1980.

s.206(4)	Failing to annex to every copy of the memorandum of a company a copy of every order sanctioning a compromise or arrangement with creditors or members	On summary conviction a fine not exceeding one-fifth of the statutory maximum
s.207(4)	Failing to comply with requirements as to the information to be provided for a meeting of creditors or members	(a) On conviction on indictment a fine (b) On summary conviction a fine not exceeding the statutory maximum
s.207(5)	Director or trustee for debenture holders failing to give notice to the company of matters necessary for the purposes of section 207	On summary conviction a fine not exceeding one-fifth of the statutory maximum
s.208(3)	Failing to deliver to the registrar an office copy of an order made under section 208 (reconstruction and amalgamation of companies)	On summary conviction a fine not exceeding one-fifth of the statutory maximum or, on conviction after continued contravention, a default fine not exceeding one-fiftieth of the statutory maximum

The "*statutory maximum*" referred to means (a) in England and Wales, the prescribed sum under section 28 of the Criminal Law Act 1977 or (b) in Scotland, the prescribed sum within the meaning of section 289B of the Criminal Procedure (Scotland) Act 1975. In each case the current amount is £1,000, subject to alteration by order to take account of changes in the value of money.

The reference to a *default fine* on conviction of an offence after continued contravention means that where a person has been summarily convicted of the offence in question, and continues to contravene, he can on a second or subsequent summary conviction be liable for the default fine for each day of continued contravention, instead of the penalty which might be imposed on the first conviction for that offence (C.A. 1980, s. 80(2)).

Reduction of capital

Where, as is often the case, schemes of reconstruction involve transfers of the company's undertaking, or part of it, the provisions of section 287 and section 206 (supplemented by section 208) will normally be applicable, unless a distribution in specie is in practice a viable alternative. Other corporate reconstructions can, however, often be achieved by means of a reduction of capital. So, for example, a class or a section of a class of share capital can be repaid or cancelled, and a reduction scheme can even (where the requisite conditions are fulfilled) represent one means of eliminating a minority shareholding without making a bid. This latter use of the provisions would, however, probably better be achieved through a section 206 scheme, at least where ordinary share capital is concerned, even where the petition for a reduction is unopposed (see *Re Robert Stephen Holdings Limited* [1968] 1 All E.R. 195) or, possibly, by a repurchase by the company of its own shares.

This section deals with conventional schemes of reduction of capital. It should be read in conjunction with the chapter *Purchase and Holding of Own Shares* which considers the provisions of the Companies Acts 1980 and 1981. As noted below, the rules as to share purchase contained in the 1981 Act so far as they relate to public limited companies do not involve a reduction of capital; on the other hand the ability of a private company to purchase shares out of capital without first seeking the sanction of the court significantly affects the practical use for such companies of certain of the provisions discussed in this chapter.

What constitutes a reduction of capital?

The concept under English company law of the sanctity of capital is bolstered by a general prohibition on reductions of capital without some form of special procedure being adopted. In general the confirmation of the court under sections 66 and 67 of the 1948 Act is required. However, the following reductions of capital are permitted without prior application to the court under those provisions,

(a) forfeiture of shares and surrender to avoid a forfeiture (see the chapter *Purchase and Holding of Own Shares*);

(b) the use of share premium account under section 56(2) of the 1948 Act;

(c) the purchase by a private company of its own shares out of capital, i.e. otherwise than out of distributable profits or the proceeds of a fresh issue. Although the confirmation of the court is not required, provisions exist for creditors to apply to the court for the requisite special resolution to be cancelled;

(d) under section 37(2) of the 1980 Act a public company is obliged in certain instances to cancel shares and diminish the amount of the share capital by the nominal value of those shares. This reduction of capital can be carried out by the directors without the sanction of the court, and without the passing of a special resolution; and

(e) where, under section 75 of the 1980 Act, the court is satisfied that a member or members of a company have been unfairly prejudiced, the court has power to order the purchase of shares by the *company* and for the reduction of the company's capital accordingly.

Although similar in effect to reductions of capital, the following do *not* constitute reductions since the capital base is effectively maintained,

(1) a cancellation of shares under section 61(1)(e) of the 1948 Act. This is expressly provided not to constitute a reduction of capital: in fact, this must be so as only *unissued* shares are cancelled i.e. it is only the authority to issue new shares which is curtailed; and

(2) the redemption or purchase of shares otherwise than out of capital. Although the amount of the issued share capital is reduced, the amount of the reduction must be transferred to a *capital redemption reserve* which is effectively treated as paid-up share capital.

The 1948 Act provisions

The rules regarding reductions of share capital are contained in sections 66 to 71 of the 1948 Act. The basis of the rules is to make the reduction subject to confirmation of the court, primarily (having regard to the express provisions to that effect) to safeguard the interests of creditors where share capital is to be repaid or an unpaid liability on shares is to be reduced, but also to ensure that the interests of various classes of members are protected. In practice the rights of creditors are rarely prejudiced; however, as is discussed below, the rights of certain classes of shareholder (notably in the case of preference shares) have benefited little from the mandatory application to the court under section 67.

Under section 66(1), and subject to the confirmation of the court, a company limited by shares or a company limited by guarantee and having a share capital may, if so authorised by its articles reduce its share capital in any way, and in particular may,

(a) extinguish or reduce the liability on any of its shares in respect of share capital not paid up (e.g. where the company no longer needs to call up the capital on partly-paid shares); or

(b) either with or without extinguishing or reducing liability on any of its shares, cancel any paid-up share capital which is lost or unrepresented by available assets (e.g. where the company has sustained heavy losses – in this case a reduction followed by a new share issue may be a way of restoring the company's capital without the need to pay capital duty on the new capital subscribed, see paragraph 9 of Schedule 19 to the Finance Act 1973); or

(c) either with or without extinguishing or reducing liability on any of its shares, pay off any paid up share capital which is in excess of the wants of the company (e.g. where the company is overcapitalised for its present needs);

and may, if and so far as is necessary, alter its memorandum by reducing the amount of its share capital and of its shares accordingly.

It is clear from the wide terms of section 66(1) that the power of the court to sanction reductions of capital is not limited to the three specific instances listed (see *Poole v. National Bank of China* [1907] A.C. 229, disapproving *Re Anglo-French Exploration Co.* [1902] 2 Ch. 845). The jurisdiction of the court arises not only where, for example, capital is lost or unrepresented by available assets, but whenever a special resolution reducing the share capital of a company is passed.

As the heading to section 66 states the reduction in question is of *share* capital; there is, therefore, nothing to prevent a return of capital under sub-paragraph (c) above being funded out of the reserves of the company or out of borrowings (*Re Thomas de la Rue & Co. Limited* [1911] 2 Ch. 361).

Safeguards – shareholders

In common with the duty of the court under section 206 (above), in confirming reductions of capital the court likewise has a discretion. The questions to be considered by the court were succinctly put by Lord Macnaghten in *Poole v. National Bank of China* (above) at page 239:

(a) ought the court to refuse its sanction to the reduction out of regard to the interests of those members of the public who may be induced to take shares in the company? and

(b) is the reduction fair and equitable as between the various classes of shareholders?

The scope of the "public interest" test is by no means clear, although schemes have certainly been approved by the courts where the only motive was the avoidance of liability to tax, thereby indicating that this test must be narrowly construed.

It is in relation to the "fair and equitable" test that the majority of decisions have been given, although it must be said (and was by Megarry J. in *Re Holders Investment Trust Limited* [1971] 1 W.L.R. 583) that opposed petitions for reductions of capital are comparatively rare, the vast majority of petitions being unopposed and largely rubber-stamped. The relative ease with which reductions are carried out has in many respects contributed to the modern erosion of the maintenance of capital principle.

If a scheme is unfair, then even a few opponents (who may not be significant in relation to the whole) will prevail (*Poole v. National Bank of China*, above). But if the dissent is insignificant, this may well be a factor in assessing the overall fairness of the scheme (*Re Thomas de la Rue & Co. Limited*, above). This is an example of the rule that the court will be slow to interfere in the internal management of a company,

". . . it is no part of the business of a court of justice to determine the wisdom of a course adopted by a company in the mangement of its own affairs" (per Lord Loreburn L.C. in *Poole v. National Bank of China*, at page 236).

This concept of "the company knows best" is, therefore, an approach of the court which is common to the exercise of its discretion both under section 67 and under section 206 of the 1948 Act (see above, and *Re Dorman Long and Company Limited* [1934] 1 Ch. 635).

Class rights

The general rule is that reductions of capital should broadly correspond with the various rights attaching to each class of shares. In simple terms this effectively means that if the scheme involves a return of capital in excess of the company's wants, those shares with a preferential right to repayment of capital on a winding up should receive repayment (perhaps with a premium) prior to the ordinary shares; on the other hand, if capital has been lost it is reasonable to suppose that the equity holders should bear the loss as they would if the company were liquidated.

In applying this general rule, the courts have tended to concentrate, logically, on the respective class rights as regards *capital*, and not on the more general question of the investment value of the shares. In doing so the relative position of preference shareholders who have no right to participate in a surplus in a winding up and whose investment in a company is based on the expectation of *income* rather than capital, has been found to be somewhat precarious. Although in *Re Barrow Haematite Steel Co.* [1900] 2 Ch. 846 at first instance Cozens-Hardy J. (as he then was) decided that a scheme to reduce both preference shares and ordinary shares by 50 per cent was not fair as between the two classes because (a) the company was making large and increasing profits and had properly paid dividends, (b) the earning capacity of the company would not be increased by the reduction of capital and (c) the avowed purpose of the reduction was to relieve the ordinary shareholders from the burden of preferential interest, the Court of Appeal at [1901] 2 Ch. 746 expressly declined to consider this question, no loss of capital having been proved. And in *Re Saltdean Estate Co. Limited* [1968] 1 W.L.R. 1844, the fact that there was no present prospect of the company being wound up and that continued large distributions of profits were anticipated was of no avail to the opposing shareholders.

In *Scottish Insurance Corporation v. Wilsons & Clyde Coal Co. Limited* [1949] A.C. 462, the company decided to go into voluntary liquidation following nationalisation and the transfer of its assets to the National Coal Board. Prior to the winding up resolution, it was resolved to reduce the capital of the company by returning capital to the preference shareholders. The scheme was opposed *inter alia* on the ground that the preference shareholders would thereby be deprived of their investment. The scheme was confirmed on the basis that the preference shareholders were not entitled in a winding up to more than a return of paid up capital and that consequently the holders of those shares could not object to receiving early precisely what they would receive on liquidation. As regards the preference shareholders' loss of income, this was not considered a ground for holding that the scheme was unfair on the footing that preference shares could for this purpose be equated with loans; since a lender could not complain of loss of interest if a company lawfully repaid him, so a preference shareholder could not oppose a proper reduction of capital. This suggests that, so far as reductions of capital are concerned, a non-participating preference share can in all cases be treated as redeemable (see, for example, the dissenting judgment of Lord Morton in the *Wilsons & Clyde Coal* case, at page 509).

The preoccupation of the courts with the strict rights of preference shares in respect of capital has been confirmed in a number of cases. In *Re Saltdean Estate Co. Limited* (above) a scheme was alleged to be unfair as it discriminated against the preference shareholders by preventing them from sharing in the fruits either of the company's future or past prosperity. It was held that the proposed reduction was fair. The liability to prepayment was an incident of a preference share of which the holders should be fully aware. The real significance of this decision lies perhaps in the fact that the preference shares in question did to some extent resemble equity capital in that they were entitled to participate beyond a fixed dividend in profits declared for distribution. In the course of his judgment Buckley J. said (at page 1852):

"The fact is that every holder of preferred shares of the company has always been at risk that his hope of participating in undrawn or future profits of the company might be frustrated at any time by a liquidation of the company or a reduction of its capital properly resolved upon by a sufficient majority of his fellow members. This vulnerability is, and has always been, a characteristic of the preferred shares. Now that the event has occurred, none of the preferred shareholders can, in my judgment, assert that the resulting state of affairs is unfair to him."

The insecure nature of a preference or non-equity shareholding in schemes for capital reduction is thus clear, and there is certainly little (if any) evidence of the courts considering the wider issues on the question of fairness. In listed companies an attempt is often made to protect the interests of the preference shareholders by means of the *Spens formula* which entitles such holders to at least the quoted market value of their shares on a reduction, and gives them voting rights on the section 66 special resolution (see page 612).

It has been established that a reduction need not affect all members of a particular class in an identical fashion. Thus capital can be returned to some shareholders leaving the remaining shares outstanding (*Re Robert Stephen Holdings Limited*, above.)

A reduction of capital which is not in accordance with class rights is nevertheless regular if it is effectually sanctioned in accordance with the regulations of the company (*Re Holders Investment Trust Limited* [1971] 1 W.L.R. 583), provided also that the provisions of section 32 of the Companies Act 1980 are complied with (section 32(3) and see the chapter *Shares*). Prior to the passing of the 1980 Act, a reduction could also be effected if no such sanction had been obtained; the only difference lay in the burden of proof as to fairness which in such instance would fall on the company. Section 32(3) therefore means that in all cases where class rights are to be varied in a reduction scheme the modification of rights provision must be strictly observed; if it is, then the burden of showing that the scheme is unfair will lie on the opposition. The courts will examine the variation, and if it appears that the holders of shares of the relevant class have voted with regard to other interests (e.g. as members of another class) the scheme will not be sanctioned. In *Re Old Silkstone Collieries Limited* [1954] Ch. 169 it was held that because previous reductions of preference share capital had created special rights, so that modification of those rights was required, and a separate class meeting had not been held, the scheme could not proceed. On the other hand, where repayment of capital is involved and the shares are *cancelled* this does not amount to a variation or abrogation of class rights, and no separate meeting is, therefore, required (*Re Saltdean Estate Co. Limited*, above).

The issue of fairness on more general criteria may be examined a little more closely by the courts where shares are not repaid but exchanged for something else. The mere fact that a member of a class is not to be paid out in cash, but is to receive in exchange for his shares something he may not want to accept, perhaps bearing a reduced (or non-equivalent) rate of interest and without any corresponding advantage or addition by way of security does not of itself make a scheme unfair, but it is then the duty of the court to look at the scheme as a whole. This is a question of degree; if that which the company is offering to the shareholder is so illusory as to be no adequate consideration for the capital represented by his share the court will not confirm the scheme (*Re Thomas de la Rue & Co. Limited* [1911] 2 Ch. 361).

So also in *Re Holders Investment Trust Limited* (above), where Megarry J. held that the company had failed to show that a scheme was fair (in a case where no effectual class meeting had been held) since on the evidence the advantages of a substitution of long-dated six per cent unsecured loan stock for the same nominal amount of five per cent cumulative redeemable preference shares approaching the redemption date fell substantially short of compensating for the disadvantages.

Even where the court adopts a more positive role in assessing the fairness of the overall scheme, it is confined to examining the scheme resolved under section 66. The question is not whether it is the best scheme, but simply whether it is fair.

Safeguards – creditors

The protections afforded to creditors in a reduction of capital are governed more formally by the statutory provisions than those relating to members which, as illustrated above, largely depend on the views of the courts as to the fairness or otherwise of the scheme. Under section 68 of the 1948 Act the court is only empowered to make an order confirming the reduction,

"*if satisfied*, with respect to every creditor of the company who under [section 67] is *entitled to object* to the reduction, that either his consent to the reduction has been obtained or his debt or claim has been discharged or determined, or has been secured"

Those creditors who are *entitled to object* to the reduction are those who at the date fixed by the court are entitled to any debt or claim which, if that date were the commencement of the winding up of the company, would be admissible (section 67(2) (a)).

The court may where it sees fit direct that the provisions of section 67(2) as to creditors shall apply. However, where the proposed reduction involves either (a) diminution of liability in respect of unpaid share capital or (b) payment to any shareholder of any paid-up share capital the provisions *must* apply, *unless* the court orders otherwise in the special circumstances of the case (section 67(3)), thus throwing a negative onus on the court. The "special circumstances" must be such that, broadly speaking, the creditors affected will be in no worse position than they would be if they were permitted to attend upon the application for confirmation of the reduction and to object. This could happen where the requirements of section 67(2) (c) – see below – are satisfied in any event without the intervention of the court i.e. if the creditor is paid off or if sufficient funds are appropriated to meet the liability (see *Re Lucania Temperance Billiard Halls (London) Limited* [1966] Ch. 98).

It is most unusual to find a scheme for the reduction of capital where section 67(3) is not applied. The general practice is either to obtain the consent of creditors or to secure the liabilities or prospective liabilities by means of bank guarantee. The principles on which the court will proceed when dispensing with a list of creditors were examined in the case of *Re Lucania* (above). Broadly, a company which proposed to repay paid-up capital to certain of its shareholders had sufficient cash resources to cover those payments and all its liabilities, apart from those under certain leases. Most of the leases were beneficial to the company; the others were neither beneficial nor onerous. It was argued on behalf of the company that since on a winding up the lessors would not have any significant claims (the company being able to assign, or the lessors being able to negotiate more favourable terms in the market) only a relatively modest sum was required as provision in order to satisfy the requirements of section 67(3). It was held that,

(a) the court must be satisfied, having regard to the company's liquid assets, or for some other reason, that no creditor who might be entitled to object to the reduction of capital might be prejudiced by it;

(b) a claim for future rent or future breach of covenant was of an unascertained amount and the court was, therefore, bound to fix as provision "an amount after the like enquiry and adjudication as if the company were being wound up by the court" (section 67(2) (c) (ii));

(c) the amount for which a landlord could prove in the notional winding up depends upon how long in fact the leasehold property remains in the possession of the company before it is assigned, surrendered or disclaimed. It must be assumed, for section 67(3) purposes, that the company will for an indefinite period remain in possession of the leaseholds, during which period the landlords will be entitled to prove for all rent accruing due;

(d) nevertheless, in exercising its discretion the court must have regard to reality. Thus, where the lease is a long lease it should not *normally* be necessary to insist on provision for the full rent for the whole term; where the lease is not onerous, *normally* ten years' rent should suffice. However, each case depends on its own facts;

(e) the provisions of section 67(2) could, therefore, be dispensed with if the company had appropriated a sufficient amount (in cash and trustee securities or by satisfactory guarantee) to cover all rents prospectively payable in respect of its leaseholds during the unexpired terms, but not exceeding ten years;

(f) since the company's cover was insufficient an order could not be made, although it was possible for the defect to be remedied by means of a guarantee, or in some other way.

In all cases the circumstances having regard to which the court may make an order under section 67(3) must be *special*: the mere fact that the company is solvent does not of itself suffice (*Practice Note* [1930] W.N. 78).

Where the enquiry as to creditors under section 67(2) is not dispensed with, the court settles a list of creditors and generally advertises for any unknown creditors. If, in spite of this, a creditor entitled to object remains in ignorance, either of the proceedings themselves, or their nature and effect, and is omitted from the list, he has certain rights under section 70. Under that section, if, after the reduction, the company is unable – on the basis of a compulsory winding up – to pay the amount of his debt or claim, then,

(a) the liability of the contributories as regards that debt or claim is restored to what it would have been if the reduction had not taken effect; and

(b) if the company is wound up, and the creditor provides proof to the court of his ignorance, the court may, if it thinks fit, settle a list of such contributories and make and enforce calls and orders on those contributories as if they were ordinary contributories in a winding up.

The rights of the contributories among themselves are not affected.

Procedure under sections 66 to 69

As with section 206 schemes (and indeed other court procedure in relation to the Companies Acts) schemes for the reduction of capital are governed by Order 102 of the Rules of the Supreme Court.

Stage one

The first step in any scheme for the reduction of share capital is to check whether the company has the requisite power in its articles (section 66(1)). For companies incorporated since 1948 this authority will be found in article 46 of Table A and under the 1929 Table A article 38 is relevant. If the power does not exist the articles can be altered by special resolution at the same meeting as the reduction resolution is proposed.

Stage two

A special resolution must be passed in general meeting. (For procedure as to special resolutions see section 141(2) and (3) of the 1948 Act and the chapter *General Meetings*.) The resolution must specify the exact amount of the proposed reduction: *Re Moorgate Mercantile Holdings Limited* [1980] 1 All E.R. 40. Any class meetings must also be held (see section 32(3) of the 1980 Act referred to above and the chapter *Shares*).

Stage three

Following the passing of the necessary resolutions, a petition is presented in chambers by the company *ex parte*. There is no requirement that the petition be served on any person. The petition may be presented by post (*Practice Direction* [1979] 1 W.L.R. 1413; see under section 206 schemes). There are arrangements for the hearing of petitions in the Long Vacation; the procedure under *Practice Direction No. 2 of 1978* has already been referred to in connection with the section 206 procedure. The petition sets out *inter alia* the capital structure of the company (including any alterations since incorporation), its main objects, any relevant provisions of the articles, the financial position of the company and details of the scheme for reduction passed by special resolution.

If an application is to be made under section 67(3) for the list of creditors to be dispensed with, the "special circumstances" relied upon must also be recited in the petition.

Where the petition concerns a public company and the reduction will take its allotted share capital below the authorised minimum, an order should be sought under section 12(2) of the 1980 Act for re-registration of the company as a private company without its having passed a special resolution, and for ancillary orders as to consequent alterations to the memorandum and articles.

Stage four

The petition is supported by affidavit. This should deal with the position of creditors (exhibiting any consents already obtained) and refer to any bank guarantee such as is generally obtained. Additionally, where it is alleged that capital is unrepresented by available assets under section 66(1) (b) an affidavit of a valuer confirming this point is required.

Stage five

The next stage is the issue of a summons for directions, generally at the same time the petition is presented in chambers. On the hearing of the summons the evidence is considered, and orders are generally made as to the publication of notices and advertisements and to fix the date for hearing the petition. An order under section 67(3) to dispense with the enquiry as to creditors is also made at this time, but if no such order is made then directions are given (Ord. 102, r.7(4)):

(a) for an enquiry to be made as to the debts of and claims against the company or as to any class or classes of such debts or claims; and

(b) as to the proceedings to be taken for settling the list of creditors entitled to object to the reduction and fixing the date by reference to which the list is to be made.

If an enquiry is ordered, then stages 6 to 11 below apply. Otherwise, the hearing date is fixed on the summons for directions and stage 12 follows.

Stage six

Within seven days of the order on summons for directions, the company must file in the office of the Companies Court registrar an affidavit made by a competent officer verifying a list containing,

(i)   each relevant creditor's name and address;

(ii) the amount due or, where value is unascertained, a just estimate of the value; and

(iii) the total amount and value due.

The affidavit must state that the list is exhaustive, and the list itself must be left at the registrar's office not later than one day after the affidavit is filed (Ord. 102, r.8). Copies of the names and addresses of the creditors are to be available to the general public at the company's registered office and at the office of the company's solicitor and any London agent (r.9).

Stage seven

Following the filing of the affidavit referred to at stage six, the company must, within seven days, send by post to each named creditor a notice specifying *inter alia* the amount of the proposed reduction, details of the amount or value of his debt shown in the list, and the procedure for making a claim if he is entitled to a larger amount (r.10). It is helpful if creditors are also sent a form of consent to the reduction.

Stage eight

The company must also insert an advertisement in such newspapers and at such times as the court directs. The purpose of the advertisement is to ascertain if there are any creditors not included in the list (r.11).

Stage nine

After the time limited for the creditors' responses under stages seven and eight, the company files an affidavit in answer to the enquiry. This affidavit will set out any creditors' consents which have been obtained, together with any disputed claims (r.12).

Stage ten

If there are any disputed claims, the creditor is served with a notice requiring him to file an affidavit proving his debt or claim. The court then adjudicates on the claim (r.13).

Stage eleven

Following these procedures, the list of creditors is certified and filed by the Companies Court registrar (r.14).

Stage twelve

The petition is then set down for hearing, which must be at least eight clear days after the filing of the registrar's certificate under stage 11. Advertisements must be placed in newspapers as to the appointed day; these will usually be the same newspapers as for previous orders (r.16).

Stage thirteen

Before the order can take effect, it must be registered at the Companies Registration Office, along with a minute setting out the revised details of share capital. The certificate of the Registrar of Companies is conclusive, and the minute when registered is automatically substituted for the corresponding part of the company's memorandum (section 69).

Section 12 of the 1980 Act imposes a bar on registration of the order (but not the minute) where a reduction is confirmed which has the effect of bringing the nominal value of a public company's allotted share capital below the authorised minimum, unless the court otherwise directs or the company is first re-registered as a private company.

Stage fourteen

Finally, the reduction of capital must be advertised, again generally in the newspapers advertising the petition and notice to creditors (C.A. 1948, s. 69(3)).

Penalties

s.69(6)	Issuing copies of a memorandum not in accordance with an alteration	On summary conviction a fine not exceeding one-fifth of the statutory maximum for each occasion on which copies are issued after the date of the alteration
s.71	In relation to a reduction of share capital, concealing the name of a creditor or misrepresenting the nature or amount of a debt, etc.	(a) On conviction on indictment a fine (b) On summary conviction a fine not exceeding the statutory maximum

(For the meaning of "*statutory maximum*" see page 732 above.)

Miscellaneous company law points

As has been indicated previously, the position of schemes of reconstruction and amalgamation cannot be considered in isolation from the general body of company law. Some of the areas affected have been referred to in the main text of this chapter; this section draws together a number of other unrelated points which may require consideration in the context of schemes; for further details reference should be made to the relevant chapter in this book.

Circulars

Under section 14(1) of the Prevention of Fraud (Investments) Act 1958 ("PFIA") there exists a general prohibition on the distribution of circulars containing (*inter alia*) any invitation to enter into any agreement for, or with a view to, acquiring securities. The general prohibition is subject to a number of exceptions, one of which enables a circular to be sent by a company to its own shareholders with respect to its own securities.

In cases of amalgamation, a circular will often be required, unless the relevant shareholding is very narrow. In such a case the scheme can proceed by agreement either signed or ratified by all shareholders. In other cases, a circular will not benefit from the general exemptions in section 14(2) of the PFIA because it will constitute an offer by one company (the acquiring company) to the shareholders of another (the acquired company).

Where such a circular is required, it will either have to be issued by an exempt or licensed dealer, or with the consent of the Department of Trade.

Stock Exchange requirements

Whenever any company involved in a scheme of reconstruction and amalgamation is quoted on The Stock Exchange, regard must be had to the detailed provisions of the Listing Agreement, particularly in relation to information to be given to the Quotations Department and the shareholders.

City Code on takeovers and mergers

Reference has been made in the main text to the use of section 206 schemes in takeover situations. Where the Code otherwise applies (i.e. generally in the acquisition of public companies) it expressly relates to all takeover and merger transactions, howsoever effected (see page 884).

Distributable profits

Under section 39(2) of the 1980 Act a company must generally take into account accumulated realised losses in ascertaining its profits available for distribution. However, losses which have been written off in a reduction or reorganisation of capital duly made can be disregarded for this purpose.

Financial assistance for acquisition of shares

Section 42 of the Companies Act 1981 expressly prohibits the giving of financial assistance by a company, or any of its subsidiaries, directly or indirectly for the purpose of the acquisition of the company's shares, or to reduce or discharge a liability incurred for that purpose. In relation to reconstructions and amalgamations, there are excluded from this prohibition (a) schemes under sections 206 and 287 of the 1948 Act, and (b) distributions (whether by way of dividend or on a winding up).

Outline agenda for scheme under section 287 of the Companies Act 1948

This outline agenda traces the broad procedural requirements involved in a partition of a group comprising a holding company ("Topco Limited") and its wholly-owned subsidiary ("Subco Limited"). Neither of the companies constitutes a "trading company" within the restrictive meaning in paragraph 23(1) of Schedule 18 to the Finance Act 1980 (demergers); accordingly, a distribution in specie cannot be undertaken for tax reasons.

In order to minimise tax liabilities a conventional scheme under section 287 is engineered, designed to fall within the Inland Revenue's concessional treatment for capital gains tax and corporation tax purposes (see

Statement D.14 in Index of Statements Issued before July 18, 1978 which remain valid).

The basic steps of the reorganisation are as follows.

(1) A new holding company ("H Limited") is formed to acquire all the issued share capital of Topco. The Topco shareholders then exchange their shares in Topco for shares in H Limited. Stamp duty relief under F.A. 1927, s. 55 and capital duty relief under F.A. 1973, Sch. 19, para 10 is claimed.

(2) Topco sells the entire issued share capital of Subco to H Limited for a nominal sum. Stamp duty relief under F.A. 1930, s. 42 is claimed.

(3) The shares in H Limited are reorganised into A and B shares. The shareholders who are to take ultimate control of Subco are registered as holders of the A shares; the B shares are registered in the names of the remaining shareholders.

(4) New companies, A Limited and B Limited, are formed by the A and B shareholders respectively.

(5) Topco and Subco capitalise a part of their respective reserves, issue bonus shares on renounceable letters of allotment, and convert existing shares into deferred shares (see the chapter *Stamp Duty Saving: Share Acquisitions* in *Tolley's Tax Planning*).

(6) H Limited is put into members' voluntary liquidation.

(7) In the course of the winding up of H Limited, and pursuant to C.A. 1948, s. 287, the liquidator transfers to A Limited the shares in Subco in return for an issue of A Limited shares to the holders of A shares in Topco. Likewise, the liquidator transfers to B Limited the shares in Topco in return for an issue of B Limited shares to the holders of B shares in Topco.

It is assumed,

(i) that clearances under T.A. 1970, s. 464, C.G.T.A. 1979, s. 88 and T.A. 1970, s. 267(3A) have been obtained, and that Stage (7) does not trigger T.A. 1970, s. 278 in relation to the transfer at Stage (2) (see the chapter *Company Reorganisations* in *Tolley's Tax Planning*); and

(ii) that the shares in Topco are relatively widely held, so that a circular at Stage (1) is required. If there are only a few shareholders, the share exchange can be carried out with little formality.

Stage I
Incorporation of H. Ltd. and exchange of Topco shares

Topco Limited
Group Reorganisation

	Company	Action	Documents
1.	H Ltd. (to be incorporated or purchased off-the-shelf)	Board meeting: (a) note incorporation of company (b) appoint directors (c) appoint secretary (d) appoint auditors (e) alter registered office (f) resolve accounting reference date (g) resolve to increase authorised capital (h) convene EGM on short notice	Forms 2, 9b and 4a Notice of EGM Consent to short notice
2.	H Ltd.	EGM to increase authorised capital	Form 10; copy ordinary resolution (C.A. 1948, s. 63)
3.	H Ltd.	Board meeting: – note increase of authorised capital	
4.	Topco	Board meeting: – approve circular to shareholders re. share exchange [subject to consent of Department of Trade]	Draft circular Draft acceptance forms

Company	Action	Documents
5. Topco	Board meeting: (a) note Department of Trade permission under s.14(2) (vi) Prevention of Fraud (Investments) Act 1958* (b) resolve to send out circular to shareholders	Circular Acceptance forms
6. Topco	Board meeting: (a) note that share exchange offer has become unconditional and that acceptances have been received from all shareholders (b) register transfers	Completed acceptance forms Share certificates/letters of indemnity
7. H Ltd.	Board meeting: (a) note acceptances (b) resolve to issue shares and register allottees (c) seal and issue share certificates	Completed acceptance forms Topco share certificates/letters of indemnity H Ltd. share certificates Return of allotments (Form PUC3) Statement of exemption from capital duty Statutory declaration of exemption from stamp duty

N.B.   In the event of the offer becoming unconditional it may be necessary to rely on s.209 Companies Act 1948 to acquire remaining shares

*By s.14 Prevention of Fraud (Investments) Act 1958 it is an offence (*inter alia*) to distribute a circular offering to acquire securities. This prohibition is subject to a number of exceptions, one of which is the obtaining of the consent of the D.T.I. Alternatively, and more usually, the offer could be made on behalf of H. Ltd. by e.g. a merchant bank or stockbroker.

Stage II
Scheme of reconstruction

	Company	Action	Documents
1.	Topco	Board meeting: (a) Resolve to sell Subco shares to H Ltd. for nominal consideration (b) approve sale agreement (c) execute share and stock transfers	Sale agreement Stock transfer forms Subco share certificates
2.	H Ltd.	Board meeting: (a) note transfer of Subco shares (b) instruct secretary to complete stamp duty formalities	Form PUC 2 Sale agreement (executed) Stock transfer forms Subco share certificates Statutory declaration under F.A. 1930, s. 42
3.	Subco	Board meeting resolving to: (a) register share transfers (subject to adjudication) (b) seal and issue new certificates	Stock transfer forms Old share certificates New share certificates
4.	A Ltd.	Board meeting: (a) note incorporation of company (b) appoint directors (c) appoint secretary (d) alter registered office (e) resolve accounting reference date (f) adopt company seal (g) resolve to increase authorised capital (h) convene EGM on short notice	Certificate of incorporation Forms 2, 9b and 4a Company seal Notice of EGM Consent to short notice

	Company	Action	Documents
5.	B Ltd.	Board meeting: (a) note incorporation of company (b) appoint directors (c) appoint secretary (d) alter registered office (e) resolve accounting reference date (f) adopt company seal (g) resolve to increase authorised capital (h) convene EGM on short notice	Certificate of incorporation Forms 2, 9b and 4a Company seal Notice of EGM Consent to short notice
6.	A Ltd.	EGM to increase authorised capital	
7.	B Ltd.	EGM to increase authorised capital	
8.	A Ltd.	Board meeting: (a) note result of EGM (b) instruct secretary to file necessary documents	Form 10 Copy ordinary resolution
9.	B Ltd.	Board meeting: (a) note result of EGM (b) instruct secretary to file necessary documents	Form 10 Copy ordinary resolution
10.	Subco	Board meeting: (a) resolve to increase authorised capital, capitalise reserves and convert existing shares into deferred shares (b) convene EGM on short notice	Notice of EGM Consent to short notice

	Company	Action	Documents
11.	Topco	Board meeting: (a) resolve to increase authorised capital, capitalise reserves and convert existing shares into deferred shares (b) convene EGM on short notice	Notice of EGM Consent to short notice
12.	H Ltd.	Board meeting: (a) note receipt of Subco and Topco notices of EGM (b) appoint authorised representative to attend and vote	Notices of EGM Consents to short notice
13.	Subco	EGM	
14.	Topco	EGM	
15.	Subco	Board meeting: (a) note result of EGM (b) resolve to capitalise reserves and issue new shares on renounceable letters of allotment (c) amend existing ordinary share certificates	Forms 10, 52 and PUC7 Copy resolutions New copy Articles of Association Letters of allotment Share certificates
16.	Topco	Board meeting: (a) note result of EGM (b) resolve to capitalise reserves and issue new shares on renounceable letters of allotment (c) amend existing ordinary share certificates	Forms 10, 52 and PUC7 Copy resolutions New copy Articles of Association Letters of allotment Share certificates

	Company	Action	Documents
17.	H Ltd.	Board meeting: (a) resolve to recommend reconstruction under s.287 Companies Act 1948 (b) approve draft reconstruction agreements (c) resolve to make declaration of solvency (d) resolve to convene EGM	Notice of EGM Draft reconstruction agreements Declaration of solvency
18.	H Ltd.	EGM— (a) alter Articles to provide for A Ordinary and B Ordinary Shares (b) redesignate existing Ordinary Shares (c) appoint liquidator for purposes of winding up (d) authorise liquidator to enter into and carry out reconstruction agreements (e) approve liquidator's remuneration	Draft reconstruction agreements Declaration of solvency Notice of special resolutions Advertisement of special resolution to wind up Notices of appointment of liquidator (Forms G39c and G39e) New copy Articles for filing
19.	H Ltd. (in liquidation)	Liquidator: (a) executes reconstruction agreement (b) executes transfers and letters of allotment re. Subco and Topco shares	Reconstruction agreements Stock transfer forms Share certificates Letters of allotment
20.	A Ltd.	Board meeting: (a) approve reconstruction agreement (b) execute reconstruction agreement (c) resolve pursuant to reconstruction agreement to issue shares to holders of A Ordinary Shares in H Ltd.	Reconstruction agreement A Stock transfer forms Subco share certificates Letters of allotment New share certificates Form PUC3 Statement of exemption from capital duty (n.b. page 867)

Company	Action	Documents
21. B Ltd.	Board meeting: (a) approve reconstruction agreement (b) execute reconstruction agreement (c) resolve to issue shares to holders of B Ordinary Shares in H Ltd. pursuant to reconstruction agreement	Reconstruction agreement B Stock transfer forms Topco share certificates Letters of allotment New share certificates Form PUC3 Statement of exemption from capital duty (n.b. page 867)
22. Subco	Board meeting: (a) appoint new directors and secretary (b) alter situation of registered office (c) appoint new auditors (d) register share transfers and renunciations	Forms G9b, 4a Letter from retiring auditors (C.A. 1976, s. 16) Stock transfer forms Share certificates Letters of allotment Copy auditors' letter for filing
23. Topco	Board meeting: –register share transfers and renunciations	Form 9b Stock transfer forms Letters of allotment
24. H Ltd. (in liquidation)	Final meeting of company (C.A. 1948, s. 290)	Advertisement in *London Gazette* Accounts Return to Registrar of Companies

Redeemable Shares

The ability of a company to issue redeemable *preference* shares, which was authorised by section 58 of the Companies Act 1948, was superseded and replaced by section 45 of the Companies Act 1981. That latter section forms part of a new company law regime in Great Britain which includes power for a company to purchase its own shares; in the case of a private company, out of capital. This chapter is confined to examining the nature of redeemable shares; the purchase by a company of its own shares is dealt with separately in the chapter *Purchase and Holding of Own Shares*, which also describes the procedure for redemption out of capital in the case of a private company.

Issue

Under section 45 of the 1981 Act, any company (whether public or private) which is limited by shares or limited by guarantee and having a share capital may, provided it is authorised to do so by its articles of association, issue redeemable shares of *any* class. Previously only redeemable *preference* shares could be issued, although in practice equity shares could nevertheless be issued as redeemable under the previous law, there being no requirement that the shares should have any minimum degree of preference nor that they should exclude the right to participate in surplus assets. The shares issued under section 45 can be redeemable on a fixed or flexible date and at the option of the company or the shareholder (section 45(1)).

No redeemable shares may be issued by a company without the requisite authority in its articles. With effect from June 15, 1982, article 3 of Table A in the 1948 Act is amended so as to remove the restriction which previously confined the issue to preference shares. In its new form the article reads as follows:

"Subject to the provisions of Part III of the Companies Act 1981, any shares may, with the sanction of an ordinary resolution, be issued on the terms that they are, or at the option of the company are liable, to be redeemed on such terms and in such manner as the company before the issue of the shares may by special resolution determine."

However, the amendment (by paragraph 20 of Schedule 3 to the 1981 Act) is *not* retrospective. Thus, any companies incorporated prior to the relevant date and desiring to issue redeemable shares (other than redeemable preference shares) must first effect an alteration to their articles.

Under the Table A power it will be noted that, whilst an ordinary

754

resolution is sufficient for the *issue* of the redeemable shares, the terms and manner of redemption must be determined by *special* resolution which must – under section 45(4) – provide for payment on redemption. In addition, if there is any consequential amendment to the articles as a result of the issue, that can only be effected (under section 10 of the 1948 Act) by special resolution.

The power under section 45 is limited to the *issue* of redeemable shares; it does not, for example, permit a company to *convert* existing non-redeemable shares into redeemable shares, not even where this forms part of a scheme of arrangement under section 206 of the Companies Act 1948 (see *Re St. James' Court Estates* [1944] Ch. 6 and the chapter *Reconstructions and Amalgamations*). This objective can nevertheless be carried out under section 206 by a cancellation of the existing shares and a new replacement issue of redeemable shares.

A company may not issue redeemable shares at a time when there are no issued shares of the company which are not redeemable (section 45(2)). This rule is not prejudiced by the ability of a company to purchase non-redeemable shares, since that power is restricted if the result would be that there would no longer be any member of the company holding shares other than redeemable shares (section 46(3)).

Redemption

Subject to the specific requirements of section 45 that are considered in this part of the chapter, the method and terms of any redemption are subject to the articles of the company.

Whilst redeemable shares may be *issued* partly paid, they cannot be *redeemed* unless they are at that time fully paid (section 45(3)). This provision mirrors that which was formerly contained in section 58(1)(b) of the 1948 Act, and operates to prevent an unauthorised reduction of capital.

The general rule, contained in section 45(5) of the Companies Act 1981, is that redeemable shares can only be redeemed out of distributable profits or out of the proceeds of a fresh issue of shares for the purposes of the redemption. The expression "distributable profits" is given its 1980 Act meaning (as amended by the 1981 Act; see the chapter *Dividends*). In addition, and subject to one exception, any premium payable on redemption must also be paid out of distributable profits.

The exception (in section 45(6)) relates to the position where,

(a) the redeemable shares were issued at a premium (which in accordance with section 56 of the 1948 Act will generally be carried to share premium account), and

(b) there is a fresh issue of shares made for the purposes of the redemption.

If those conditions are satisfied, then any premium payable on redemption may be paid out of the proceeds of the fresh issue up to an amount equal to the lesser of,

(i)   the aggregate of the premium received by the company on the issue of the shares redeemed; and

(ii) the *current* amount of the company's share premium account (including any sum transferred to that account in respect of premiums on the new shares).

In each case, the share premium account is reduced by the amount so paid out of the proceeds of the new issue. This effectively means that, under the 1981 Act provisions, the share premium account can only be used to fund the payment of a premium on redemption to the extent that such premium does not exceed the premium paid on the issue of those shares. If the share premium account has been reduced (for example, by a capitalisation issue or on a reduction of capital), or if the premium on redemption exceeds the premium on issue, then any shortfall must be found out of distributable profits.

The restriction on the use of share premium account under the 1981 Act provisions contrasts with the rules contained in the 1948 Act. The power of a company to apply share premium account in providing for a premium payable on redemption of redeemable *preference* shares has been nullified by the partial repeal of section 56(2) of the 1948 Act. However, and to this limited extent only, the 1981 Act contains a transitional provision which provides that a premium payable on redemption of redeemable preference shares issued before the appointed day (June 15, 1982) may be paid out of share premium account instead of out of profits, or partly out of that account and partly out of profits (see section 62(3) of the 1981 Act).

Where a company is about to redeem shares, it is given power by section 45(9) to issue new shares up to the nominal amount of the shares to be redeemed as if those shares had never been issued. This means that it is not necessary for there to be any increase in the authorised share capital of the company prior to such issue. In practice, it is necessary to ensure that the redemption takes place within one month of the new issue, in order that the relief from capital duty afforded by section 45(10) will be available. Under that provision, no capital duty is payable if the actual value of the new shares does not exceed the value of the shares redeemed *at the date of redemption*. If it does, then duty is payable only on the excess. If the issue of the new shares is made *after* the redemption, the relief from capital duty applies to those shares up to the nominal amount of the shares redeemed, whenever the new shares are issued (section 45(11)).

Shares redeemed under section 45 are treated as cancelled on redemption, and cannot be reissued. The amount of the company's issued share capital is treated as being diminished by the nominal amount of the shares redeemed, but the authorised share capital is left intact (section 45(8)).

Redemption out of capital

The general rules as to redemption of redeemable shares described above are subject to an important extension for *private* companies, which may redeem such shares out of *capital* under section 54 of the 1981 Act. This aspect is considered in detail in the chapter *Purchase and Holding of Own Shares* (the rules governing redemption out of capital being the same as those governing purchase out of capital).

Capital redemption reserve

In order effectively to maintain the permanent capital of a company which has redeemed shares, an amount equivalent to the par value of those shares must be carried to a special reserve called *the capital redemption reserve*, except insofar as redemption is out of the proceeds of a fresh issue of shares (C.A. 1981, s. 53). This only affects the nominal value of the shares redeemed, and not any premium element.

The capital redemption reserve is treated as if it were paid up share capital of the company, so that it cannot be reduced except (a) with the sanction of the court under section 66 of the 1948 Act (see the chapter *Reconstructions and Amalgamations*), (b) where a company purchases or redeems its shares out of capital under section 54(5) of the 1981 Act, or (c) where the reserve is applied by the company in paying up unissued shares of the company to be allotted to members of the company as fully paid bonus shares (see section 53(3) of the 1981 Act, and the chapter *Bonus Issues*).

Failure to redeem

Under the rules governing the issue of redeemable preference shares in section 58 of the Companies Act 1948, it was arguable that a company could be compelled to redeem shares once the date for redemption had passed. In *Re Holders Investment Trust Limited* [1971] 1 W.L.R. 583, the resolution creating the preference shares provided that they should be issued,

"on the terms that they shall, subject to the provisions of the Companies Act 1948, be redeemed by the company at par on July 31, 1971"

The company (in a scheme for the reduction of capital) had contended that a failure to redeem would not mean that the company was in default. This view was doubted by Megarry J. (as he then was).

Section 59 of the 1981 Act seeks to resolve these doubts. Broadly, a company cannot be liable in damages for a failure to redeem, although a shareholder may obtain an order for specific performance unless the company can show that it is unable to meet the cost of redemption out of distributable profits. It would appear that, in addition, a shareholder whose shares are not redeemed on the due date may be able to obtain an injunction to restrain the payment of dividends until the redemption has been effected (see *Holders* case at page 590).

Provided the due date for redemption has arrived at the date of commencement of a winding up of a company, the terms of redemption may then be enforced against the company, unless in the period from the date for redemption up to the commencement of the winding up the company could not have made a distribution equal to the price at which the shares were to have been redeemed. The redeemable shares rank behind ordinary debts and liabilities of the company but have priority over other shares as regards repayment of capital except shares having preferential rights over the redeemable shares in that respect.

Notice and disclosure requirements

Where capital is increased by the issue of redeemable shares, notice must be given to the Registrar on Form 10, stating that the shares are redeemable, and accompanied by a copy of the resolution authorising the increase. A copy of the special resolution setting out the terms and manner of redemption must also be filed in the usual way (C.A. 1948, s. 143).

On redemption of the redeemable shares notice must be given to the Registrar on Form 28 (see section 62(1)(e) of the 1948 Act as amended).

In each case, failure to comply with the notice requirements can result in a penalty under the revised scales introduced by the Companies Act 1980. On summary conviction, the penalty is a fine not exceeding one-fifth of the statutory maximum, and if there is continued contravention, a default fine not exceeding one-fiftieth of the statutory maximum. The statutory maximum is currently £1,000.

So far as accounting requirements are concerned, the following information must be given as a supplement to the information contained in the balance sheet (see paragraph 38(2) of Schedule 1 to the Companies Act 1981):

(a) the earliest and latest dates on which the company has power to redeem the redeemable shares;

(b) whether those shares must be redeemed in any event or are liable to be redeemed at the option of the company; and

(c) whether any (and, if so, what) premium is payable on redemption.

Rights Issues

The expression *rights issue* is used to describe an issue of shares or debentures to existing members or holders of such securities in a company in proportion to their existing holdings. The method by which such an issue is carried out varies considerably between the small private company and the company listed on The Stock Exchange. In the case of the small company very few formalities need be observed, with an issue simply being made to existing members in accordance with the articles of association, those members paying for the securities in cash as they are issued. For the listed company, there are numerous Stock Exchange and other requirements, and the issue is likely to be made following a provisional allotment of shares or debentures giving the recipient the opportunity to renounce his rights to the new securities.

Under the Companies Act 1980 statutory pre-emption provisions have been introduced which in many instances impose a requirement on a company to make rights issues of equity securities (as defined) as a prerequisite to any other allotment of those securities to any person. This requirement is subject to a number of exceptions, and is discussed in the chapter *Shares*. In the case of a listed company, it is a basic Stock Exchange requirement that in the absence of very exceptional circumstances (for example an extremely small issue) new issues of equity capital should be offered to existing shareholders in proportion to their existing holdings unless otherwise resolved by the equity shareholders in general meeting.

For these reasons, the use of rights issues as a means of raising capital for a company is very widespread. Rights issues are, indeed, used for other specific reasons, including the engineering of stamp duty saving in a takeover bid where there are insufficient reserves to enable a bonus issue to be carried out, and also other more sophisticated tax avoidance schemes, at least until the enactment of section 91 of the Finance Act 1981 and the decision of the House of Lords in *I.R.C. v. Burmah Oil Co. Limited* [1982] S.T.C. 30. Nevertheless, the raising of fresh capital remains the primary purpose of a rights issue.

As indicated, in the case of a listed company the rights issue route is generally the only means of raising equity capital. If there is a market in the company's shares, there can also be a market in the rights to new shares; the new shares will generally be offered at a fairly generous discount on the current market price of the existing shares. This "bonus" or premium element on the new securities does not amount to

759

an issue at a discount for the purpose of section 21 of the Companies Act 1980, assuming that the subscription price does not fall below par value.

Prospectus requirements

A rights issue of shares or debentures on renounceable letters of allotment is felt generally to fall within the prospectus requirements of the 1948 Act. The company makes an offer for *subscription* for cash, and that offer must be treated as being made to the "public" within the extended meaning given to that expression by section 55 of the 1948 Act. Issues otherwise than in a renounceable form would fall outside the requirements having regard to the specific exclusion contained in section 55(2). This cannot however be taken as excluding issues which are renounceable (see *Governments Stocks and Other Securities Investment Co. Limited v. Christopher* [1956] 1 W.L.R. 237 and further the chapter *Prospectuses and Public Issues*, page 616).

Where the prospectus requirements do apply, the full rigour of the 1948 Act requirements (as to statement of matters specified in Part I of the Fourth Schedule) is usually mitigated by section 38(5) of that Act, which provides that the Fourth Schedule requirements shall not apply to the issue to existing members or debenture holders of a company of a prospectus or form of application relating to shares in or debentures of the company, whether an applicant for shares or debentures will or will not have the right to renounce in favour of other persons (but see page 617).

The letter of allotment and any other appropriate circular must be signed by the directors (or by an attorney) and two copies must be delivered to the Registrar of Companies in accordance with the provisions of section 41 of the 1948 Act. For civil and criminal liability under the prospectus provisions, see page 635.

Control of borrowing

Although the Control of Borrowing Order 1958 (as amended by the 1970 and 1972 Orders) allows a general exemption for the majority of borrowing transactions, including the raising of money by the issue of shares or debentures, the issue of sterling securities where the amount to be raised by the issue is not less than £3 million is subject to approval as regards timing of the Bank of England, under authority delegated from the Treasury. The purpose of this requirement is simply to ensure that the market is not flooded by substantial issues of securities (whether Government or private) on the same day (see also the chapter *Prospectuses and Public Issues*).

Stock Exchange requirements

Where the company is listed on The Stock Exchange regard must always be had to the requirements of the Stock Exchange Listing Agreement. Under the Listing Agreement it is a general requirement that all alterations in the capital structure of the company must be notified to the Quotations Department. In the case of a rights issue, this will involve prior approval of all documentation at the draft stage, and delivery of final documentation prior to the issue. The company broker or the issuing house concerned will generally have the responsibility for ensuring that all Stock Exchange requirements are fully satisfied.

Aside from the general requirements, certain specific procedural steps must be observed in the case of a quoted rights issue. These include the following:

(a) The offer of securities must be accompanied by a circular in the form required by Schedule II, Part B of Appendix 34 to the Rules and Regulations of The Stock Exchange. In other words, this involves a full Stock Exchange prospectus, a subject which is considered in more detail in the chapter *Prospectuses and Public Issues*. In particular, in relation to rights issues, the allotment letter or other document of title must describe how securities not taken up will be dealt with, and the time, being not less than 21 days, in which the offer may be accepted.

(b) The issue must normally be by way of renounceable letter of allotment or some other negotiable document.

(c) Shares not subscribed for by the holders of securities to whom they have been offered should normally be sold for the benefit of the holders entitled, unless the shareholders have specifically approved other arrangements. It is essential that the Department of Trade is consulted before any alternative method is adopted, although where the amount to which a shareholder would be entitled is very small, shares may be sold for the benefit of the company, and if there is no premium at the end of the subscription period, shares may be allotted to the underwriters. Fractions are normally sold in the market for the benefit of the company.

(d) Subscription by a director for excess shares without such shares being offered to others participating in the rights issue, will not, save in exceptional circumstances, be permitted. In view of the substantial premium element obtainable on the new securities, the practice of allowing shareholders to apply for such excess shares is only rarely permitted.

(e) Facilities for the receipt of payments should be provided in or near the City of London *and*, where a substantial market exists outside London, near the trading floor concerned.

Outline procedure for public company

(1) The first stage in any rights issue of shares or debentures is always to ensure that the company has the necessary powers to make the issue. In the case of shares it is necessary to ensure that there is sufficient unissued authorised share capital which has not been earmarked for other purposes, and in the case of debentures that

the borrowing powers of the directors are sufficient. Furthermore, in the light of the requirements of section 14 of the Companies Act 1980, the powers of the directors to allot shares or other convertible securities must be confirmed. This topic is dealt with fully in the chapter *Shares*, but it broadly necessitates the authorisation of the directors either by ordinary resolution or under the articles of association. It will also generally be advisable for the statutory pre-emption provisions contained in section 17 of the Companies Act 1980 to be modified or excluded by special resolution under section 18 of that Act (see further the chapter *Shares*, particularly concerning the approach taken by the Investment Protection Committees. If section 17 is nqt excluded, problems can arise where foreign shareholders are to be excluded from the rights issue for reasons connected with overseas securities legislation. Invoking section 18 can result in timing problems and extra underwriting expense).

(2) A board meeting will be held at the initial stages to approve the proposals and all draft documentation. If a general meeting of the company is required to increase the authorised capital, alter the articles or give the directors the necessary authority to issue the new securities, the board can at the same time convene the requisite extraordinary general meeting.

(3) If the issue is of sterling securities and the amount to be raised by the issue is not less than £3 million, timing consent of the Bank of England will be required. A date must therefore be agreed with the Government Broker.

(4) The general Stock Exchange requirements as to disclosure of the proposed issue and the filing of draft documents must be observed, and the issuing house or the company's broker will have preliminary discussions with the Quotations Department as to the proposed listing of the new securities and the procedure to be adopted for the issue.

(5) The company must then arrange printing of all the relevant documents. These will include the circular to shareholders, renounceable provisional letters of allotment, and (if appropriate) an application form for excess shares. As indicated earlier, a listed company will only in exceptional cases be permitted to deal with shares which are not subscribed for in the issue by means of excess application forms. Such shares will generally be sold in the market for the benefit of the non-participating shareholders.

(6) The register of members will be closed and shareholdings balanced at the record date in order to enable accurate provisional allotments to be made (though certain problems can arise from the use of a record date).

(7) It is customary in public issues, particularly in the case of listed companies, for information to be given to the financial press as to the proposed issue. This may be in the form of an advertisement,

but is generally carried out on a less formal basis, by means of a press release.

(8) Once the preliminary work has been carried out, the directors can meet to authorise the issue of the provisional letters of allotment. At this stage, the directors must sign the circular in order to comply with the prospectus requirements of the Companies Act 1948. The signed copy of the circular must be delivered to the Registrar of Companies *before* the issue documents are posted to the shareholders.

(9) At this time, also, it is customary for underwriting arrangements to be made in connection with the issue. The majority of rights issues by listed companies are underwritten, although having regard to the premium element on the rights issue securities most such issues are often heavily subscribed. Whether an issue is to be underwritten is a matter for the directors of each company concerned; a company which is confident in the marketability and attractiveness of its securities may well take a conscious view that a refusal to enter into underwriting arrangements is indicative of a confidence in the company. Others may regard underwriting as an essential insurance against a possible unpredictable fall in the market (for further details, see page 642).

(10) In the case of listed companies, the new securities will be granted a listing on The Stock Exchange. Under section 51(1) of the 1948 Act, permission for listing must be applied for before the third day after the first issue of any prospectus which states that application has been or will be made for permission for the shares or debentures offered thereby to be dealt in on any Stock Exchange. If this requirement is not satisfied any allotment is void and all sums subscribed must be repaid.

(11) Simultaneously with the obtaining of listing for the new securities the documents are posted to the shareholders. It is a Stock Exchange requirement that the letters of allotment should be renounceable. Until the last day for renunciation has passed, the provisional right to the allotment of the new securities can be dealt in without the usual transfer formalities, and without payment of stamp duty. The allotment itself is *provisional* only, since no allotment will be made unless an application is made to the company accompanied by the subscription price (which may be the first instalment of a larger subscription price). The Stock Exchange prefers rights issues to be timed so that dealings in the new securities can be commenced on the first day of an account. This in practice avoids dealings both "cum" and "ex" in the same account.

(12) The next working day after documents are posted dealings in the "rights" commence. This is a natural consequence of the discounting of the price of the new securities as against the market quotation of the existing shares or debentures. The shareholder

sells his rights by renouncing his letter of allotment in favour of the purchaser.

(13) It is a Stock Exchange requirement that the offer be open for at least twenty-one days to enable shareholders to consider their position. For almost the whole of this period the shareholders will be able to "split" the provisional allotment letter by returning it to the issuing house with the form of renunciation duly completed giving details of the split letters required. The split letters will then be issued carrying the endorsement "Original duly renounced".

(14) Once the twenty-one day period has expired, a press announcement will be made giving details of the result of the issue.

(15) A meeting of the board of directors (or, if more convenient, a duly appointed committee of the directors) is convened to issue certificates in respect of fully paid shares. In practice, the allotment of shares is delayed by the shareholders being given a further three-week period to renounce the fully paid letters of allotment.

(16) Finally, a return of allotments is made to the Registrar of Companies on form PUC 2. Capital duty is generally payable within one month of the receipt by the company of the subscription price or, if earlier, within one month of the allotment of the shares. However, if renunciation continues, a company may deliver the PUC 2 (together with the duty) within the one month time limit, and subsequently deliver another PUC 2, marked "duplicate", giving full details of the allotments once they are finally made. The company may either file the first PUC 2 form, with the duty, thirty days after the provisional allotment letters are posted, or file a series of PUC 2 forms, with appropriate cheques, thirty days from receiving acceptances. The latter alternative is more cumbersome administratively, but will defer what may be substantial amounts of capital duty. Capital duty will only apply to an issue of shares; the issue of loan stock (even *convertible* loan stock) is not a chargeable transaction for this purpose.

Secretary

There seemed once to be a tendency to underestimate the significance of the office of company secretary, although the *Panorama Development* case (referred to below) and, more recently, the Companies Act 1980 have helped to underline its true importance as the office held by a company's chief administrative officer.

Who may be a secretary?

No company (whether public or private) may have as its secretary,

(a) a person who is also the company's sole director (C.A. 1948, s. 177(1)); or

(b) a corporation, the sole director of which is a sole director of the company (C.A. 1948, s. 178(a)) – but subject to this, a body corporate can be a secretary. A firm may also be a secretary; or

(c) a person who is also its auditor (C.A. 1948, s. 161(2)) – this provision is in fact phrased to preclude the appointment of any officer or servant of a company as its auditor but applies equally in reverse where the existing position held is that of auditor. This prohibition extends to any partner in a firm which acts as the company's auditors.

Where the Companies Acts or the articles of association of a company (whether public or private) require a thing to be done by a director *and* the secretary, that thing may not be done by the same person acting as both director and secretary (C.A. 1948, s. 179). Thus, for example, it would not be sufficient for the purposes of article 113 of Table A (which requires the company's seal to be countersigned by a director and secretary or by two directors) for the same person to countersign a document which has been sealed by the company acting in his joint capacities as director and secretary.

Public companies

As regards public companies alone, the Companies Act 1980 created a statutory requirement for secretaries of public companies to be adequately qualified. Section 79(1) of the 1980 Act provides that it is the duty of the directors of a public company to take all reasonable steps to procure that the company secretary is a person possessing both the requisite knowledge and experience to discharge his duty *and* who falls within any one of the following categories:

(a) on December 22, 1980 he was the secretary or assistant or deputy secretary of the company; or

(b) for not less than three out of the five years immediately preceeding his appointment as secretary he was the secretary of a public company; or

(c) he is a member of one of the following,

(i) the Institute of Chartered Accountants in England and Wales

(ii) the Institute of Chartered Accountants in Scotland

(iii) the Association of Certified Accountants

(iv) the Institute of Chartered Accountants in Ireland

(v) the Institute of Chartered Secretaries and Administrators

(vi) the Institute of Cost Management Accountants

(vii) the Chartered Institute of Public Finance & Accountancy; or

(d) he is a qualified barrister, advocate or solicitor anywhere in the United Kingdom; or

(e) he is a person who "by virtue of his holding or having held any other position or his being a member of any other body appears to the directors to be capable of discharging" the functions of a secretary.

From the above it will be apparent that the rigid criteria defined at (a)–(d) are complemented by the more flexible "sweeping up" provision at (e) above. The sweeping up clause was introduced to avoid debarring the suitable candidate who has worked his way up in the business world to a position of seniority and who possesses the necessary attributes to be a suitable secretary but lacks the formal qualification. Some have questioned whether the inclusion of the sweeping up provision so qualifies the remainder of section 79 as to render it redundant, but it is unlikely in practice that many boards of public companies will be prepared to take a view on whether or not a person appears capable of discharging a secretary's functions and appoint to the office of company secretary someone who lacks the necessary paper qualifications.

Appointment and removal

Every company must have a secretary (C.A. 1948, s. 177(1)). The first secretary must be named in the statement filed with the Registrar of Companies prior to incorporation (Form 1), and that statement must contain the secretary's written consent to act signed by him. His appointment is then deemed to date from the moment of the company's incorporation (C.A. 1976, s. 21). The secretary's name and address must also be recorded in the internal register of directors and secretaries maintained by the company and any change must both be recorded in the internal register and notified to the Registrar of Companies within 14 days, on Form 9b (C.A. 1948, s. 200).

Article 110 of Table A provides that, subject to section 21 of the Companies Act 1976, the secretary is to be appointed by the directors for such term, at such remuneration and upon such conditions as they think fit and that he may also be removed by them. Even if a company's articles omit article 110 of Table A or a similar provision it seems likely that analogous powers are in any event within the board's scope of authority. In practice of course the practical freedom of the directors to dismiss their secretary may be fettered if the secretary is also an employee of the company either because of his rights under a service contract or because of his rights under the Employment Protection (Consolidation) Act 1978.

Status

The secretary is an officer of the company (C.A. 1948, s. 455). He may also be an employee of the company in the same way that an executive director may wear his dual hats of fiduciary officer and executive employee. If he is an employee his arrears of salary and holiday pay in respect of that employment will, within the prescribed limits, be a preferential debt owed by the company. In practice public companies and the larger private companies tend to employ their secretaries, small private companies by a contrast sometimes engaging their accountant or solicitor on a fee paying basis as secretary.

Where a company secretary is also an employee involved in the company's management, it will frequently happen that he has *actual* authority delegated by the board of directors to enter into commercial contracts on behalf of the company. Secondly, he may have *implied* authority to enter into such contracts, as a result of the establishment of a course of dealing. Thirdly, he has certain *ostensible* authority for acts of administration – as opposed to management. The extent of this ostensible authority is probably greater than it was in the nineteenth century (see for instance the observations in *Re Maidstone Buildings* [1977] 1 W.L.R. 1085). The Court of Appeal in *Panorama Developments (Guildford) Ltd. v. Fidelis Furnishing Fabrics Limited* [1971] 3 W.L.R. 440 held that, even where authority is not expressly conferred nor conferred by implication through course of business, the secretary nevertheless, as the company's chief administrative officer, has ostensible authority in day to day *administrative* matters. Thus, in that case the company was bound by the secretary's act of ordering hire cars, ostensibly for the company's use but in fact for his own use. In the words of Lord Denning, the secretary:

"is an officer of the company with extensive duties and responsibilities ... He is no longer a mere clerk. He regularly makes representations on behalf of the company and enters into contracts on its behalf which come within the day to day running of the company's business, so much so that he may be regarded as held out as having authority to do such things on behalf of the company. He is certainly entitled to sign contracts connected with the administrative side of a company's affairs, such as employing staff, and ordering cars, and so forth. All such matters now come within the ostensible authority of a company secretary."

Accordingly, if it is desired to negate this ostensible authority in any particular instance care should be taken to ensure that all those likely to have dealings with the company secretary are expressly made aware of the limitations placed by the company on his authority.

Scope of duties

As has been seen above the secretary is the company's chief administrative officer. Typically his duties will include the convening of board and company meetings (as directed by the board), taking minutes of meetings, keeping up to date the company's statutory books, filing all appropriate returns with the Registrar of Companies and dealing with the administrative side of share transfers (unless, as is likely to be the case with larger public companies, the company has a separate professional share registrar for this purpose). In addition, as has been seen above, the secretary has ostensible authority to bind the company in contracts relating to its day to day administration, although the scope of his express authority may vary from company to company. A list of some of the main functions performed by a secretary is set out below (in most cases there is no express requirement for the secretary to perform these functions, but failure to perform them will generally result in any "officer" of the company – which includes the secretary – being in default).

Common functions performed by the secretary

(a) the registration of charges and the keeping of the company's register of charges (C.A. 1948, ss. 96 to 105);

(b) the keeping of the register of directors and secretary (C.A. 1948, s. 200);

(c) the issue of share and debenture certificates, as well as dealing with share transfers;

(d) the keeping of the register of members and debentureholders (C.A. 1948, s. 110);

(e) the keeping of the register of material share interests (C.A. 1981, s. 73);

(f) the keeping of the register of directors' share interests (C.A. 1967, s. 29), directors' contracts (C.A. 1967, s. 26), and the collation of disclosable directors' interests (C.A. 1980, s. 54);

(g) the preparation and keeping of minutes of board and general meetings (C.A. 1948, s. 145);

(h) the posting of accounts, directors' reports, auditors reports, notices of meeting and such like;

(i) the keeping of the company's memorandum and articles up to date;

(j)   the preparation and submission of the annual return;

(k)   the filing with the Registrar of changes in directors and secretary, registered office, share capital and allotments, purchase or redemption of share capital and such like (see generally Appendix 5 for a list of the various forms which a company is required to file with the Registrar and the chapter *Publicity Requirements* for a more detailed guide to the various filing and other requirements which a company is required to comply with, and which it will generally be the secretary's job to see to);

(l)   the payment of dividends and preparation of dividend warrants.

Liabilities of the secretary

As an officer of the company the secretary will be liable with his directors to default fines and so on where the Companies Acts provide, as is often the case, that "the company and every officer of the company who is in default" is expressed to bear liability. As an officer of the company he owes fiduciary duties to the company similar to those owed by a director, and no provision in a company's articles or otherwise which purports to exempt the secretary (or any other officer) from liability in respect of negligence, default, breach of duty or breach of trust can be enforced by the secretary (C.A. 1948, ss. 205 and 333). On the other hand, the secretary will not normally be liable for a breach of trust or misfeasance by the directors, even if this is committed with his knowledge (*Joint Stock Discount Co. v. Brown* (1869) L.R. 8 Ex. 376).

As with other officers, the secretary should always take care when making contracts on behalf of his company to ensure that he does so as the company's agent if personal liability is to be avoided.

Since the secretary is a servant or agent of the company, he owes fiduciary duties to the company and is almost certainly accountable to the company for any secret profit or similar gain made from the company (see generally the chapter *Directors' Duties*).

Assistant and deputy secretaries

An assistant or deputy secretary is not, as such, the company secretary and cannot therefore normally validly perform the official functions of the secretary. However, if the office is vacant, or if there is for any reason no secretary capable of acting, anything required or authorised to be done by or to the secretary may be done by or to his assistant or deputy (or if there is no such assistant or deputy capable of acting, by or to any officer of the company authorised for that purpose by the directors; section 177(2) of the 1948 Act). A company may, however, appoint more than one person as secretary, to act as joint secretaries (C.A. 1948, s. 200(3)).

Shareholders

Shareholders span a wide range; from the individual with his savings invested in a blue chip company, to the businessman who has incorporated a business he previously carried on as a sole trader; from the employee holding shares by virtue of an employee participation scheme to the trustees of a pension fund with the duty of maintaining the value of that fund. The expectations and requirements of a shareholder will differ greatly depending upon his position and the type of company involved. Company law is thus expected to cater for and protect a wide variety of interests under one umbrella. It is hardly surprising that courts and legislature alike have experienced problems in formulating rules to protect individual shareholders whose wishes do not accord with those in control of the company. It is necessary to strike a balance between protecting a minority shareholders' investment, or perhaps even his livelihood, on the one hand, and enabling a company to function without constant threat of litigation from a minority unwilling to abide by management or majority decisions, on the other.

This chapter examines the identity of shareholders, the nature of their rights, and the remedies available to the shareholder under company law where he is in a minority. It is concerned with shareholders in companies limited by shares and registered under the Companies Acts 1948 to 1981. The rights attaching to shares themselves are dealt with in the chapter *Shares*, below.

Members of a company

The word "shareholder" is not defined in the Companies Acts. Since certain types of company have no shares, the legislation refers rather to "members". However the two words may be used interchangeably in the case of a company limited by shares (except in relation to a person holding share warrants). The terms "shareholder" or "member" are used to describe the person who is legal owner of the shares rather than the beneficial owner (see *Trustees and nominees as shareholders*, page 775 below).

Definition of member

Section 26 of the Companies Act 1948 defines a member of a company as a person who agrees to become a member *and* whose name is entered in the company's register of members. In addition, subscribers of the memorandum of a company are deemed to have agreed to become members and are to be entered as members when the company is registered. The crucial difference between a subscriber and every other member in this context is that a subscriber is a member whether his name is actually entered into the register or not (*Baytrust Holdings Ltd. v. IRC* [1970] 3 All E. R. 76 at ps. 96–97), though whether he is *actually* a member prior to registration or simply *deemed* to be one is open to dispute: see for instance (1982) 3 Co Law 99. As a matter of practice it cannot be stressed too greatly that the membership of any other person is dependent upon his name being physically entered on to the register which must be kept by virtue of section 110 of the 1948 Act. Section 110(1)(b) provides that the register must show the date at which each person was entered in the register as a member and it is that date upon which membership commences not, for example, the date of allotment. Therefore the date on which a company's register is made up can be of critical importance if, for any reason, it is necessary to show that a particular person was a shareholder (as opposed to beneficial owner of a share) on a certain date. An example is where stamp duty relief is to be claimed on a company reconstruction or amalgamation under section 55 of the Finance Act 1927.

Agreement to become a member

Agreement to membership is an essential condition of membership, but the agreement need not take specific form (*Ritso's Case* (1877) 4 Ch. D. 782) unless the articles prescribe a form, which they often do in practice, as indicated below.

There are various ways in which agreement to membership may be indicated and these include,

(1) subscription to the memorandum of association;

(2) agreement to an allotment of shares by the company;

(3) agreement to a transfer of shares by an existing member. The transfer in the form required by the articles of the company has to be presented to the company by the transferee for registration, thus signifying to the company the transferee's agreement to becoming a member;

(4) where ownership of a share is transmitted to a trustee in bankruptcy or personal representative on the bankruptcy or death of the member, agreement by the trustee or personal representative to being placed on the register must be signified. The articles usually require this to be done in writing (see article 31 of Table A), although no special form is necessary if the articles do not so provide;

(5) by behaviour – for example where a person is entered as a member on the register without his agreement but then acts in such a way as to indicate ownership of the shares, rather than insisting that his name be removed, he will be estopped from denying that he is holder of the shares (*Crawley's Case* (1869) L. R. 4 Ch. 322);

(6)   the articles may provide for directors to be deemed to have agreed
      to take up qualification shares.

Who may be a member?

(1) *Companies as members*

The basic rule is that a company may hold shares in another company if
authorised to do so in its memorandum of association (*Re Barned's
Banking Co.* (1867) L.R. 3 Ch. 105).

At common law there was a fundamental rule that a company could not
subscribe for or purchase its own shares (*Trevor v. Whitworth* (1887) 12
App. Cas. 409). This rule was intended to prevent both "trafficking" by
the company in its own shares which could have resulted in manipula-
tion of the share price, and also unauthorised reductions of capital.
These objectives were not offended where the company had given no
consideration for the shares. Thus a company was permitted to be
beneficial owner of shares held for it by a trustee where the shares had
been bequeathed to it by will (*Re Castiglione's Will Trusts* [1958] 1 All
E. R. 480). The common law rules have now been codified and
amended by sections 35 to 37 of the Companies Act 1980, which, in
turn, have been amended by Part III of the Companies Act 1981. The
basic rule that a company limited by shares may not acquire its own
shares remains, subject to various exceptions including the acquisition
of its fully paid shares otherwise than for valuable consideration, and
the redemption or purchase of any shares in accordance with Part III of
the 1981 Act (section 35 of the 1980 Act as amended and see the chapter
Purchase and Holding of Own Shares, above). Under certain of the
exceptions public companies must dispose of or cancel the shares within
a prescribed time and may not exercise voting rights in respect of the
shares (section 37 of the 1980 Act). Although section 46 of the
Companies Act 1981 initially appears to give a wide power to companies
to purchase their own shares, it is in fact subject to many qualifications.
In any event, the shares so acquired may not be held by the company as
a member, since in order to avoid trafficking in shares it is provided that
shares purchased under this section are to be treated as cancelled
(section 46(2) and section 45(8)).

Section 27 of the Companies Act 1948, which was intended to prevent
avoidance by a round about route of the rule in *Trevor v. Whitworth*,
basically prohibits a company from being a member of its holding
company other than purely in the capacity of a trustee or personal
representative (see further page 693).

The prohibition against a company providing financial assistance in
connection with the acquisition of its own shares, now contained in
section 42 of the Companies Act 1981, operates to prevent companies
from simply acquiring their own shares through nominees unless one of
the exemptions in the 1981 Act applies (see the chapter *Financial
Assistance*).

(2) *Persons lacking full contractual capacity*

Persons who are not sui juris may become shareholders with full rights, subject to the general rules of contract governing dealings by such persons. Persons under the age of eighteen years, who in England are minors by virtue of section 1 of the Family Law Reform Act 1969, may thus become members unless the articles of association of the company expressly forbid this. Although a minor's contract is voidable before or within a reasonable time after he reaches the age of majority, he will not be able to recover money paid for an allotment of shares which have some value even if they have paid no dividends, since he has nevertheless obtained the rights comprised in the shares for the period during which he has held them. Therefore there has not been a total failure of consideration (*Steinberg v. Scala (Leeds) Ltd.* [1923] 2 Ch. 452). However, repudiation will enable the minor to avoid liability for future calls. On a winding up, the minor loses his power to repudiate unless the liquidator consents to repudiation. A person transferring shares to a minor may remain liable for future calls whilst the minor holds the shares, even though the transferor was not aware that the transferee was a minor.

It should be noted that the contractual position of persons under 18 in Scotland differs from that described above.

(3) *Bankrupts*

A bankrupt may continue to be a shareholder even once the beneficial interest in his shares has vested in the trustee in bankruptcy, unless the articles provide otherwise. He must, however, vote as directed by the trustee, in the same way as any shareholder holding on behalf of the beneficial owner must usually do. A bankrupt shareholder who is on the register of members may bring a minority action (*Birch v. Sullivan* [1957] 1 W.L.R. 1247).

Frequently the articles do give the trustee in bankruptcy the right to be registered in place of the bankrupt (article 32 of Table A) and it is the trustee in bankruptcy who is entitled to be paid the dividends and to receive notice of meetings under Table A articles (see below).

(4) *Personal representatives and trustees in bankruptcy*

As mentioned above, since agreement is required of a person before he may become a member of a company, a personal representative or trustee in bankruptcy cannot automatically become a member when the beneficial interest in shares vests in him, but has a special position governed by statute and the articles of the company.

It is not necessary for the personal representative to become a member since section 76 of the Companies Act 1948 provides that a transfer shall be valid as if he was a member at the time it is executed. Therefore the personal representative may choose to transfer the share without ever being registered himself. This he might well do since if he is not registered as a member himself he is liable for calls on partly paid shares only to the extent of the deceased's assets in his hands, whereas if he is registered as a member he is personally liable for such calls (albeit with a right of indemnity against the deceased's estate (*Duff's Executors Case* (1886) 32 Ch.D. 301)).

Similarly, the trustee in bankruptcy has a statutory power to transfer the bankrupt's shares (section 48(3) of the Bankruptcy Act 1914).

Articles 30 to 32 of Table A deal with the position of both personal representatives and trustees in bankruptcy and, if adopted, provide that such a person is entitled to all the rights, including dividends, of a shareholder even if he is not registered as such, with the exception of rights relating to company meetings: that is, primarily, voting rights. Article 134, however, provides that personal representatives and trustees in bankruptcy are to be given notice of general meetings.

The company must accept, as evidence of the personal representative's title, any documentation normally considered sufficient for that purpose (C.A. 1948, s. 82).

As a result of the distinctions between personal representatives or trustees in bankruptcy holding shares as such and those registered as members, it may be beneficial to either the company or the representative or trustee, depending on the circumstances, for the representative or trustee to have his own name entered into the register. Table A articles provide both for the personal representative or trustee to have the right to registration (subject to any right to decline registration that would have applied to the member before his death or bankruptcy) and for the directors of the company to have the right to compel an election between such registration or a transfer, within ninety days of a notice requiring election. In the absence of any specific provision in the articles, the personal representative or trustee may require to be registered (*Scott v. Scott (London) Ltd.* [1940] Ch. 794), subject to any general right to decline registration in the articles. If the personal representative is not registered as member it seems that the deceased's estate is treated as member for some purposes, such as bonus issues (*James v. Buena Ventura Nitrate Grounds Syndicate Ltd.* [1896] 1 Ch. 456) but not for others, such as whether there is the requisite number of members (*Re Bowling & Welby's Contract* [1895] 1 Ch. 663). Because the position in this situation is not altogether clear, companies should include provisions along the lines of articles 30 to 32 of Table A in their articles of association and in particular directors should be given the power to put personal representatives and trustees in bankruptcy to an election as to whether they wish to transfer shares held by them in that capacity or be registered as members in their own right.

(5) *Partnerships*

Even though an English partnership is not a legal person, it may be registered as a member under its partnership name (*Weikerheim's Case* (1873) 8 Ch. App. 831).

Trustees and nominees as shareholders

The Companies Act definition of member is entirely concerned with the legal owner of the share, that is, the person appearing on the register. The legal and beneficial ownership of shares is, however, frequently separated both because shares are a common form of investment for trustees and because it is often commercially convenient for shares to be held by a trustee or nominee.

Section 117 of the Companies Act 1948

Section 117 of the Companies Act 1948 makes very clear the basic philosophy of English company legislation that the company should be concerned only with the rights of the persons appearing on its register of members. Section 117 provides that:

> "No notice of any trust, expressed, implied or constructive, shall be entered on the register or be receivable by the registrar in the case of companies registered in England".

(It should be noted that this section does not apply in Scotland.) In England, therefore, it is the shareholder whose name is recorded on the register who has rights and duties *vis a vis* the company; the beneficial owner has no special status in relation to the company. The company does, however, have to note other interests in the case of personal representatives and trustees in bankruptcy before they are registered as members (see above) and certain property of trade unions or employees associations (section 4(4) of the Trade Unions and Labour Relations Act 1974).

Section 117 is usually fortified by an article in the form of article 7 of Table A. The exact relationship between this article and the section is not altogether clear, but whilst section 117 refers only to the register, article 7 refers to recognition of a trust by the company more generally. The article provides that the company is not bound by or compelled to recognise any interest in a share other than an absolute right to the whole share vested in the registered holder, even where the company has notice of some other interest.

These provisions protect the company and facilitate transfers of its shares, since the company is not liable for registering a transfer executed by a trustee where the transfer is in breach of trust (*Simpson v. Molson's Bank* [1895] A.C. 270) and so need not engage in investigations. Section 117 also has the effect of relieving the company from concern with priorities where equitable mortgages of its shares are created. However, a stop notice can be served on the company in relation to specific shares, under Order 50 of the Rules of the Supreme Court, in which case the company must give notice to the person serving the notice before registering any transfer of those shares (see the chapter *Charges over Shares*).

The reverse side of section 117 is seen in *Re Perkins* (1890) 24 Q.B.D. 613, where it was held that a company had no lien upon shares held in it by a trustee for a debt due to it by a beneficiary under that trust.

Use and abuse of nominee shareholdings

The practical result of section 117 and the philosophy behind it was to encourage the use of nominee shareholders, and the Jenkins Committee stated that in the evidence it had received "considerable emphasis has been placed on the administrative advantages of the nominee system which greatly facilitates the efficient conduct of day-to-day business in the City". The use of a nominee shareholder is, of course, essential to the Stock Exchange Talisman system. However, as well as being convenient, the system has also been abused as the use of nominee shareholders obviously hides the true identity of the shareholder, who might be engaged in "insider dealing" or might be attempting to build up an interest in the company without publicity so that he may gain control without warning to other shareholders.

These abuses have now been countered to some extent by legislation requiring disclosure of beneficial interests in the case of directors and substantial shareholders (see the chapters on *Disclosure of Directors' Dealings* and *Disclosure of Shareholdings*). In addition, the Department of Trade has powers to investigate membership of the company in certain cases. However, none of these provisions is intended to undermine the basic principle of section 117; they make information about the beneficial ownership of shares available but this does not affect the company with notice of the beneficial interests (section 29(6) of the Companies Act 1967 and section 73(4) of the Companies Act 1981).

Rights of beneficial owners

Where all or part of a trust fund is invested in shares, the rights of the beneficiaries in relation to those shares are a matter for trust law and the trust deed governing that trust. Where a nominee holds on bare trust for a beneficial owner who is sui juris there may be no formal deed although it is always desirable that there should be a clear declaration of trust (see the discussion under *Minimum number of members*, page 780). In such a case the beneficial owner is entitled to direct the trustee in the exercise of any of the rights arising out of the shares. However, whatever the relationship between the trustee and the beneficial owner may be, the company "can look only to the man whose name is on the register" (*Re Perkins*, above).

The register of members

Detailed rules are set out in sections 110 to 123 of the Companies Act 1948 for the keeping of a register of members by every company. The register is considered to be of fundamental importance as giving publicity to the identity of the members and the extent of their liability, although as the members may, in fact, be nominees and since their liability will frequently be nominal only, this importance may be of a somewhat theoretical nature.

Particulars to be shown on the register

By section 110(1) as amended by section 101(1) of the Companies Act 1981 the information to be entered on the register is,

(1) the names and addresses of the members;

(2) a statement of the shares held, distinguishing the shares by their numbers, if any, and their class (where there is more than one class), or showing the amount and class of stock held (where shares have been converted into stock);

(3) the amount paid or agreed to be considered as paid on each class of shares;

(4) the date of entry on the register as member;

(5) the date of cessation of membership of any person.

Section 101(2) of the Companies Act 1981 added new subsections to section 110 of the 1948 Act, providing that entries relating to a former member may be removed after twenty years from the date on which he ceased to be a member. Twenty years is now also the maximum limitation period for the enforcement of any liability the company may have for an error on its register of members.

Availability of information on the register

Since the purpose of the register is publicity it must be made readily available and simple to use.

It must be kept either at the company's registered office or, if it is to be kept elsewhere, a notice must be sent to the Registrar of Companies within fourteen days specifying where it is kept and any change in that place (section 110(3) and Form 103). The register of an English company must be kept in England and, if it is not kept at the registered office, must be kept at the place where the work of making it up is carried out (section 110(2)). There are special provisions for branch or "dominion" registers where an English company transacts business outside Great Britain, the Channel Islands or the Isle of Man or any other part of H.M. dominions, but all information available on such a register must also be available alongside the company's principal register (sections 119 to 122). Sometimes, also, companies keep a duplicate register at a foreign office but the principal statutory register must be kept in England. No copy of the register is kept at Companies House although information about members is available from that source from the company's annual return.

If the company has more than fifty members an index must be maintained and kept with the register so that inspection of the register is a practical option (section 111). If the register is itself alphabetically arranged, of course, no index is needed.

The register and index are to be available for inspection during business hours (or, at any event, at least two hours per working day) by any member, free of charge, and by any other person for a fee of five pence or less. Any person may require a copy of the register or part of it, and this must be supplied for a maximum payment of 10 pence per hundred words and dispatched within ten days of the company receiving the request (section 113).

The register need not be in any particular form and indeed may even be kept on computer, provided print outs can be supplied for inspection and to serve as copies (section 3 of Stock Exchange (Completion of Bargains) Act 1976, enlarging upon section 436(1) of the Companies Act 1948).

There is a power contained in section 115 for the company to close the register for up to thirty days during each year, provided notice is given via a newspaper advertisement in the area of the company's registered office. This may be useful before payment of a dividend or a bonus or rights issue although this administrative problem is usually dealt with by the simple expedient of fixing a date upon which shareholders must be registered in order to qualify for the dividend or new shares (a "record date").

Accuracy of register

Clearly, in order to comply with section 110 and contain true particulars of the type described there, the register of members must be altered when any change of relevant facts occurs. All entries on the register require the authorisation of the board of directors (*Re Indo-China Steam Navigation Co.* [1917] 2 Ch. 100 and *Chida Mines Ltd. v. Anderson* (1905) 22 T.L.R. 27), and so will not always be made immediately upon the necessary information being communicated to the company. Strict time limits are laid down in relation to most provisions concerning the maintenance of this and other registers. For example, in the case of the register of substantial interests, the company has three days in which to register information following receipt (section 73(3) of the Companies Act 1981). However no time limit is specified for making up the register of members, although the company and its officers are liable to a default fine if they do not comply with section 110(1) (section 110(4)). Presumably a time limit is inappropriate in the case of the register of members, which is more than an administrative record. It is a document of title and it is the act of entering a person's name on the register which makes him a member.

Normally it will be in the interests of the company to keep the register as up to date and accurate as possible but situations can be imagined in which the company might wrongfully enter the name of a person as member (for example to provide credibility) or refuse to enter a name of a person entitled to be registered. These possibilities are dealt with by section 116 which gives the court the power to rectify the register. Thus, although section 118 provides that the register of members is prima facie evidence of any matters directed or authorised by the Companies Acts to be inserted in the register, it is not conclusive evidence.

Any person whose name appears on the register in error will be well advised to seek rectification immediately since, until he does so, he is held out to the public as being a holder of shares and he may therefore lose his right to have the register rectified if he delays (*Re Scottish Petroleum Co.* (1883) 23 Ch.D. 413).

Section 116 enables any person aggrieved, as well as the company or any member of the company, to apply to the court for rectification of the register if a name is, without sufficient cause, entered in or omitted from the register or if the fact that a person has ceased to be a member is not duly recorded. The jurisdiction of the court is widely construed by the courts (see, for example, *Re Imperial Chemical Industries Ltd.* [1936] 2 All E.R. 463 where it was held that the section gave the court jurisdiction to remove any name standing on the register without sufficient cause even though it may have been properly entered into the register). Section 77 enables a transferor to force registration of a transferee of his shares.

The court has discretion as to whether to rectify (*Re Diamond Rock Boring Co. Ltd., ex parte Shaw* (1877) 2 Q.B.D. 463) and may also award damages to an aggrieved party (section 116(2)). The court may decide any relevant question of title in the course of exercising its jurisdiction (section 116(3)). If the register is rectified the annual return must also be amended (section 116(4)).

A company must not rectify its register on its own initiative but must apply to the court for rectification, even though the need to rectify may be clear (*Re Derham and Allen Ltd.* [1946] Ch. 31).

Whether there has been a default or unnecessary delay in entering, removing or omitting a person's name from the register will depend upon all the circumstances, since no absolute time limits are set out in section 110. In *Re Swaledale Cleaners Ltd.* [1968] 3 All E.R. 619, rectification was ordered under section 116 by registering the applicant as transferee of shares, where no effective board meeting had been held to consider whether the transfers of shares to him should be accepted or refused within four months of the transfers being produced. Section 78(1) of the Companies Act 1948 provides that refusal to register a transfer of shares must be notified to the transferee within two months from the lodging of the transfer with the company and so, if no decision had been made by that time, Harman L. J. considered that that would normally amount to unreasonable delay (and in fact, as was held in that case, the right to refuse registration would be lost). In appropriate cases the courts might refer to other time limits when considering whether there had been unreasonable delay; for instance the requirement in section 80 of the Companies Act 1948 that share certificates should be issued within two months after the allotment of or lodging of transfers of shares would indicate an outside limit for the registration of shareholdings where there is no question of refusal to register a transfer. However a deliberate default in complying with section 110 might well be revealed before any such time limit is reached and in such circumstances the court might order rectification within a much shorter period. Thus, in *Re Stranton Iron & Steel Co.* (1873) L.R. 16 Eq. 559, the company was ordered to register transfers executed and delivered only three days before, where the motive for non-registration was to prevent the transferees from voting at a meeting two days later.

Penalties for breach of requirements concerning the register

The penalties for failure to comply with the requirements relating to the register were substantially increased by section 80 of and Schedule 2 to the Companies Act 1980. If there is a default this amounts to a criminal offence and the company and every officer of the company in default are liable as set out in that schedule. The statutory maximum, which is the measure of fine referred to in that schedule, is a sum prescribed under section 28 of the Criminal Law Act 1977 and may be varied by order so that the fines can be kept abreast of inflation. Section 17 of the Stamp Act 1891 imposes a fine on a company officer who registers a share transfer which has not been duly stamped.

Minimum number of members

Two members required

There is now no distinction between public and private companies as regards numbers of members. The Companies Act 1980 removed the upper limit of 50 members previously imposed on private companies and eliminated the requirement that a public company should have a minimum of seven members (C.A. 1980, Sch. 4). The minimum number of members for all incorporated companies is now two (sections 1 and 31 of the Companies Act 1948 as amended by the Companies Act 1980).

Whilst two persons must subscribe their names to the memorandum of association in order to form a company and two members must continue to exist if the consequences of reduction below that number, set out in section 31, are to be avoided, the company may in fact be entirely in the beneficial ownership of one person, since the definition of membership is concerned only with form and legal ownership (see *Trustees and nominees as shareholders*, above). Companies are frequently formed by sole traders or others acting alone, with one share being held by a nominee on behalf of the true owner. The same situation is to be found within corporate groups; a subsidiary may be one hundred per cent beneficially owned by its parent company but care must be taken to vest at least one share in the name of a nominee. This nominee will normally be either one of the other companies within the group, or an officer of one of the companies within the group. If the nominee is to be a company, the normal rules concerning corporate members, described above, apply and the company must be empowered by its articles to act as a trustee. If the nominee is to be an officer, complications may arise on his death, resignation or termination of employment and therefore it might be thought preferable for a company within the group to act as nominee. Quite often, however, this role is performed by directors of the company whose shares are concerned, especially since, unless the articles state otherwise, a director's qualification shares need not be beneficially owned (*Pulbrook v. Richmond Consolidated Mining Co.* (1878) 9 Ch.D. 610; and see page 235).

In any case where a nominee is appointed, but particularly where there is only one other member, a clear written declaration of trust signed by the nominee should be obtained by the true owner simultaneously with the issue or transfer of the shares to the nominee so that difficulties arising on the death of the nominee, or if there is a disagreement with him, may be minimised.

Reduction of number of members below legal minimum

Section 31 of the Companies Act 1948 provides that if a company carries on business, without having at least two members, for more than six months, then any person who for any part of that period is a member and knows that the company is carrying on its business with only one member is liable directly (jointly and severally with the company) for any debts of the company contracted whilst those circumstances were continuing. Therefore, despite the fact that the two member rule may seem meaningless because of the possibility of using a nominee, it is of importance to satisfy this formal requirement.

The reduction of the number of members below two does not prevent the company from existing since it has a separate legal personality once formed. Since section 31 applies only to make a member, and not a director, personally liable it is possible that a director could continue to carry on the business of the company without the section applying to him and indeed, if there were no members, the section would not apply at all. This is not as unlikely as it may at first appear since a deceased member's estate is not a member for this purpose and his personal representative will not be a member unless appearing on the register (see above and *Re Bowling & Welby's Contract* [1895] 1 Ch. 663). In a small family company, where the members and directors were the same persons, this could cause real difficulties since no new members could be registered without a valid director's meeting and there might be no mechanism for appointing a director without a general meeting being held. In an extreme case, unauthorised persons might have to act and rely upon subsequent ratification once an authorised person had been appointed or a general meeting had been held (see *Alexander Ward v. Samyang Navigation* [1975] 2 All E.R. 424 on the validity of such a procedure). A single surviving member might enlist the assistance of the Department of Trade under section 131(2) of the Companies Act 1948. A member or director might be able to apply to the court to order that a meeting be held if the procedure for calling or conducting such a meeting prescribed by the articles were impossible to satisfy in the circumstances (section 135(1) of the Companies Act 1948). As a last resort an application may be made to the court to wind up the company under section 222(d) of the Companies Act 1948 as amended, where the number of members is reduced below two. Section 224 details the persons who may present such a petition and these include any creditor or creditors (including a contingent or prospective creditor) and, in these circumstances, any contributory – which phrase probably includes any member (see sections 212 and 213 of the Companies Act 1948 and *Re Consolidated Goldfields of New Zealand* [1953] Ch. 89).

Nature of shareholder's interest

A shareholder's interest in a company is commonly defined in contractual terms. For example, the House of Lords stated in *Prudential v. Newman Industries (No. 2)* [1982] 1 All E.R. 354 that:

> ".... shares are merely a right of participation in the company on the terms of the articles of association".

So, in that case it was held that a personal claim by a shareholder against a wrongdoer whose action had diminished the profits of the company was misconceived because the shares themselves were not directly affected by the wrongdoing; the right of participation remained intact.

It seems clear that a shareholder does not have a proprietary interest in the underlying assets of the company. In *Short v. Treasury Commissioners* [1947] 2 All E.R. 298 in the Court of Appeal, Evershed L.J. commented:

> "Shareholders are not, in the eye of the law, part owners of the undertaking. The undertaking is something different from the totality of the shareholding".

On the other hand, as Professor Gower has pointed out, a share itself is very much a piece of property in commercial terms and it is unrealistic to describe a share as merely a personal, contractual right without more. It is at the same time a bundle of personal rights and duties governed by the articles of association and a proprietary interest in the company, rather than in the assets of the company. The shareholder has rights in the company as well as rights against the company. This dual relationship causes conceptual difficulties when the question of protecting a minority shareholder's interests arises. It can be crucial whether the appropriate action is against the company or a derivative action on behalf of the company to protect the rights of shareholders, because the availability of the latter action is more restricted than the former (see below). The conceptual confusion reaches its height where the wrong can be said to have been suffered by the shareholder in both capacities (though the decision in the *Prudential* case reduces the overlap here).

The contract: the memorandum and articles of association

The rights and duties of a shareholder are governed by the memorandum and articles of association of the company, subject to the provisions of the Companies Acts. Section 20 of the Companies Act 1948 (for a fuller analysis of which see the chapters on *Articles of Association* and *Memorandum of Association*) is construed as putting the relationship between the company and the shareholder on a contractual footing

(*Hickman v. Kent or Romney Marsh Sheep-breeders' Association* [1915] 1 Ch. 881).

"The purpose of the memorandum and articles is to define the position of the shareholder as shareholder, not to bind him in his capacity as an individual" (*Bisgood v. Henderson's Transvaal Estates* [1908] 1 Ch. 759), and so the shareholder cannot rely upon the memorandum or articles in so far as they relate to his rights only as a non-member, for example as director or as the company's solicitor (*Eley v. Positive Government Security Life Assurance Co., Ltd.* (1876) 1 Ex.D. 88). However a member suing in reliance upon his right as a member to have the articles observed may by this means indirectly enforce a right arising out of the articles and relating to him in another capacity (*Quin & Axtens Ltd. v. Salmon* [1909] A.C. 442 as interpreted by Professor Lord Wedderburn, [1957] C. L. J. 193, although precisely when he has such a right to sue as a member is far from clear (see pages 104, 240 and 784)).

The memorandum and articles also constitute a contract between the members of the company inter se in respect of their rights as shareholders (*Pritchard's Case* (1873) L.R. 8 Ch. 956), so that a shareholder may enforce rights, such as rights of pre-emption which the articles give to members generally, directly one against the other (*Rayfield v. Hands* [1958] 2 All E.R. 194 – although the reasoning in this case is open to criticism it is generally considered to be correct in principle).

Although the shareholder's rights and duties are therefore governed by contract, they are also, by virtue of section 20 of the 1948 Act, subject to the provisions of the Companies Acts. Thus this is a contract which may be varied unilaterally, since under the Companies Act 1948 both the memorandum and articles may be altered by special resolution (sections 5 and 10 and 23 of the 1948 Act). In both cases, however, minority shareholders are protected to some extent. First, section 22 of the 1948 Act provides that no alterations, either to the memorandum or the articles, can have the effect of increasing the liability of an existing member to contribute to the company's share capital or pay it money in some other way. Secondly, variations of class rights are restricted by section 72 of the 1948 Act and section 32 of the 1980 Act (see the chapter *Shares*). Thirdly, where the memorandum is altered there are general statutory safeguards for the minority contained in sections 5 and 23. Fourthly, although the limits on the general power of the majority to amend the articles are not so clear, an alteration which amounts to a "fraud on the minority" will not be permitted (see below). Fifthly, section 75 of the Companies Act 1980 now enables the court to make an order requiring the company not to make any, or any specified, alteration to the memorandum of articles and such an order is binding notwithstanding any other provision of the Companies Acts.

Despite these safeguards, a shareholder who is in the minority is clearly vulnerable for his rights may be removed from him in certain circumstances, and, even where the rights remain intact in the memorandum and articles it is not always clear to what extent they may be enforced. The

question is much disputed by academic writers. Professor Lord Wedderburn takes the wide view, that the shareholder has the right to have the
articles observed by the company (and see Gregory 44 M.L.R. 526).
Others have suggested that the right is limited to the right to have the
affairs of the company conducted by the proper organ of the company
(Goldberg 35 M.L.R. 362), or to matters relating to the power of the
company to function (Prentice (1980) 1 Co Law 179). If these limitations
on the right to enforce the articles are correct and if, as some argue, the
right to enforce personal rights is also to the same extent restricted by
the rule in *Foss v. Harbottle* (for which, see below), then the protection
afforded the minority shareholder by his section 20 contract is a good
deal weaker than would at first sight appear.

Strengthening the contract: shareholders' agreements

For the reasons described above, a shareholder without control of the
company will be in a vulnerable position if relying solely on the articles
and memorandum of association and therefore he may seek other forms
of protection. Where the company concerned is a listed company, the
shareholder's position may, to some extent at least, be safeguarded by
the Stock Exchange Listing Agreement. A person acquiring shares in a
private company without gaining control will be well advised to secure
some form of additional contract if this is practical and he is in any
position to do so. Such an agreement might be with the company itself
or, as is more common, with some or all of the other shareholders. An
agreement of the latter type, a shareholder's agreement, may cover any
aspect of the company's activities. Topics frequently covered by such
agreements include the payment of dividends, the appointment of
directors, general principles for the management of the company and
the nature of its activities and the prohibition of competition with the
company by parties to the agreement. An important clause of the
agreement will often be one restricting the transfer of shares to outsiders
and, frequently, making any transfer which is permitted subject to the
transferee becoming a party to the agreement so as to perpetuate its
effect.

Voting agreements

Shareholder agreements may include, or consist of, voting agreements.
A shareholder's vote is his property and therefore he may bind himself
to vote in a particular way if he wishes. Such a contract is enforceable by
injunction (*Puddephatt v. Leith* [1916] 1 Ch. 200). However, in accordance with the principle discussed above, that the company is concerned
only with the registered shareholder and not any other person interested
in its shares, the company will be bound to accept a vote made in
contravention of a voting agreement, so that the remedy for a breach
will lie only against the shareholder concerned, not against the company.

A shareholder's agreement may be particularly desirable where a small private company is being set up, for example, to incorporate an existing partnership. Shareholder and voting agreements may upset the balance which has been reached by the law between the rights of minority and majority shareholders, but since that balance itself may not be the right one for every situation, ut is not always undesirable to engineer some adjustment.

Minority shareholders: rights and remedies

Minority shareholders can be said to have the following three types of right,

(1) special statutory rights conferred on a specified minority group for a particular purpose;

(2) personal rights against the company and other members by virtue of their contract contained in the memorandum and articles of association (see above); and

(3) the right to enforce duties owed by directors (see the chapter *Directors' Duties*) and members.

The first of these types of rights is fairly straightforward but the second and third types present more problems. The scope of each category and the overlap between them is unclear. Any attempt to define the extent to which an individual shareholder has such rights is inextricably interwoven with the question of the availability of a remedy in respect of them, and so with the rule in *Foss v. Harbottle* and the exceptions to that rule. The minority shareholder's rights will therefore be dealt with here in three sections; first a brief summary of the statutory rights conferred on certain minority groups in special particular instances, secondly an examination of the rule in *Foss v. Harbottle* and thirdly, a short account of the main statutory remedies available to the individual minority shareholder who is seeking to enforce duties owed to him.

Statutory minority rights

In certain specific areas, special protection is afforded to minority groups of shareholders of various descriptions. The main rights of this nature, which are discussed in more detail in other chapters, are set out in the table below.

Statute also protects the minority insofar as it requires certain resolutions to be passed by qualified majorities; as will be seen below, if such requirements are not adhered to, minority shareholders may take action under one of the exceptions to the rule in *Foss v. Harbottle*.

Table of statutory minority rights

Statutory provision	*Description of right*	*Description of the type and minimum size of group required to exercise right*
Section 5 of the Companies Act 1948 as amended by the Companies Acts 1976, 1980 and 1981	To apply to the court for cancellation of alteration of objects of company. The court has wide powers to make such an order as it thinks fit.	(a) Holders of 15 per cent of the issued capital of the company or any class thereof or (b) holders of 15 per cent of certain debentures.
Section 23 of the Companies Act 1948	To apply to the court for cancellation of alteration of conditions in memorandum which could have been contained in articles. Powers of court are those contained in section 5, above.	Holders of 15 per cent of the issued capital of the company or any class thereof.
Section 72 of the Companies Act 1948 and section 32 of the Companies Act 1980	To apply to the court for cancellation of variation of class rights (i) where the memorandum or articles provide for such variations to be subject to the consent of a specified proportion of that class or a resolution passed at a class meeting of that class (ii) where class rights not contained in the memorandum, and the articles do not contain provisions for the variation of class rights.	Holders of 15 per cent of the issued shares of the relevant class, being persons who did not consent to or vote in favour of the variation.
Section 140 of the Companies Act 1948	To requisition the circulation of resolutions and notices. Resolutions of which notice is given in this way are to be dealt with at an AGM, notwithstanding anything in the articles.	(i) Members representing one twentieth of the total voting rights of all the members having a right to vote at the meeting in which the requisition relates; or (ii) not less than 100 members holding shares on which there has been paid up an average sum of at least £100 per member.
Section 132 of the Companies Act 1948	To requisition the holding of an extraordinary general meeting, notwithstanding anything in the articles of the company.	Holders of one tenth of the paid-up capital carrying voting rights at the date of the deposit of the requisition.

Statutory provision	Description of right	Description of the type and minimum size of group required to exercise right
Section 137 of the Companies Act 1948	To demand a poll-any provision in the articles preventing this is void, although the articles may give more generous rights to the minority.	(i) Five members having the right to vote at the relevant meeting or (ii) a member or members representing one tenth of the total voting rights of all members having the right to vote at that meeting or (iii) a member or members holding shares in the company conferring a right to vote at the meeting and upon which has been paid-up at least one-tenth of the total sum paid up on all shares carrying that right.
Section 164 of the Companies Act 1948 as amended by section 86 of the Companies Act 1981 (see further below)	To apply to the Department of Trade for the appointment of an Inspector or Inspectors to investigate into the affairs of the company. The right is merely to apply; the Department has discretion as to whether to make an appointment and may require security for the payment of costs.	(i) 200 members or (ii) a member or members holding one tenth of the issued shared. (The company may also make an application under this section.)
Section 172 of the Companies Act 1948	To apply to the Department of Trade for the appointment of an Inspector or Inspectors to investigate the membership of the company. The Department must make an appointment unless it is satisfied that the application is vexatious; otherwise all reasonable matters referred to in the application must be investigated.	As in (i) and (ii) under section 164 above.
Section 76 of the Companies Act 1981 (see further the chapter *Disclosure of Shareholdings*).	To requisition the company to exercise its power under section 74 of the 1981 Act to require information with respect to interests in its voting shares.	Holders of one tenth of the paid-up capital carrying the right of voting at general meeting.

Statutory provision	*Description of right*	*Description of the type and minimum size of group required to exercise right*
Section 11 of the Companies Act 1980	To apply to the court for cancellation of a special resolution by a public company to be re-registered under section 10 of the 1980 Act as a private company.	(i) Holders of five percent in nominal value of the company's issued share capital or any class thereof, or (ii) 50 of the company's members provided they have not consented to or voted in favour of the resolution.
Section 44 of the Companies Act 1981	To apply to the court for cancellation of a special resolution by a private company approving the giving of financial assistance for the purchase of shares.	(i) Holders of ten percent in nominal value of the company's issued share capital or any class thereof, provided they have not consented to or voted in favour of the resolution.
Section 57 of the Companies Act 1981	To apply to the court for cancellation of a special resolution approving any payment out of capital for the redemption or purchase by a private company of its shares.	Any member of the company other than one who consented to or voted in favour of the resolution (any creditor of the company may also apply).

The rule in Foss v. Harbottle

Although much learning and many complex debates surround the rule in *Foss v. Harbottle* (1843) 2 Hare 461, it is in essence a fairly simple procedural rule.

Many of the duties owed by directors and members of a company, set out as the third type of shareholder's right above, are in fact duties owed to the company rather than to individual shareholders. Since "the proper plaintiff in an action in respect of a wrong alleged to be done to a corporation is, prima facie, the corporation" (per Jenkins L.J. in *Edwards v. Halliwell* [1950] 2 All E.R. 1064) it follows that, as a general rule, an individual shareholder cannot bring an action in such a case.

To this rule has been added another principle borrowed from partnership law "that the court will not interfere with the internal management of companies acting within their powers, and in fact has no jurisdiction to do so" (Lord Davey in *Burland v. Earle* [1902] A.C. 83). Together these rules make up the rule in *Foss v. Harbottle* and their combined effect is that where the directors or members are guilty of a breach of their corporate duties or where there is an irregularity in the way in which the companies affairs are conducted, as a general rule only the company may bring an action. Usually, the right to use the company's name in an action lies, at least in the first instance, with the directors and this is certainly the case where article 80 of Table A governs the position without qualification by another article. Thus the remedy for a breach may be in the hands of the persons responsible for it. It seems to be generally accepted that if the directors fail to act, the shareholders in general meeting may do so (this is the view of Professor Gower, and see Professor Lord Wedderburn [1957] C.L.J. 194), but, since the directors will often be shareholders also and may exercise their votes as such in general meeting without reference to their duties as directors (*North-West Transportation, Ltd, v. Beatty* (1887) 12 App. Cas. 589), this may be of little help to the minority shareholder.

It can be seen that, had the rule in *Foss v. Harbottle* remained without qualification, those in control of the company could have acted with impunity in breach of corporate duties, as the minority would have been powerless to bring an action in many circumstances. It was therefore inevitable that "exceptions" to the rule should be evolved by the courts. Some of the so called exceptions are really instances which are outside the scope of the rule, but the position is best understood if they are dealt with alongside the true exceptions.

In addition to the exceptions established by the courts there is now a new statutory exception contained in section 75(4)(c) of the Companies Act 1980, and if this is properly utilised and developed it may be that it will substantially reduce the importance of the rule in *Foss v. Harbottle*. This is highly desirable, as the extent of these exceptions is not clear and the case law is surrounded by "controversial obscurities" (Sir Robert Megarry V–C in *Estmanco Ltd. v. GLC* [1982] 1 All E.R. 37).

Despite the clear need for exceptions, the rule is a logical one if the analysis of the company as a separate legal entity is carried to its conclusion. There are also practical advantages to the rule. It prevents similar suits from being brought by a large number of plaintiffs and it avoids the futility of a successful action being brought, only to be overturned by a resolution passed at a general meeting of the company where the act complained of is ratifiable by an ordinary majority. For these practical reasons, the development of exceptions to the rule has been limited and moves towards expansion in recent cases were rejected by the Court of Appeal in *Prudential v. Newman Industries* (No. 2) [1982] 1 All E.R. 354. Moreover the rule does preserve the rights of the majority, as the Court of Appeal commented in their judgment in the *Prudential* case, and majority rule is desirable in principle since it is important to enable the business of the company to be conducted and not thwarted by a stubborn minority attempting to protect only its own interests. A balance must be reached, but the need for the introduction of section 75 of the Companies Act 1980 is an indication that the balance reached by the courts in evolving the exceptions to *Foss v. Harbottle* has been found to be wanting in certain types of case.

Exceptions to the rule in Foss v. Harbottle

In *Estmanco Ltd. v. GLC*, Sir Robert Megarry V.C. stated "no doubt one day the courts will distil from the exceptions some guiding principle that is wide enough to comprehend them all and yet narrow enough to be practicable and workable. It may be that the test may come to be whether an ordinary resolution of the shareholders could validly carry out or ratify the act in question ...". However, this stage has not yet been reached and indeed it is arguable that the test suggested by the Vice Chancellor lacks the certainty required for a practicable and workable rule. It is therefore necessary to examine in turn the following six main "exceptions" to the rule which enable a minority shareholder to bring an action,

(1) where the act complained of is illegal or *ultra vires*;

(2) where the transaction complained of can be sanctioned only by a special or extraordinary resolution or requires a special procedure and this requirement is not satisfied;

(3) where what has been done amounts to a "fraud on the minority" and the wrongdoers are themselves in control of the company;

(4) where the act complained of infringes a personal right of the shareholder seeking to bring the action (but see below);

(5) in addition to these established exceptions, it has been suggested, although the suggestion is now discredited, that there is a residual exception from the rule "whenever the justice of the case requires it"; and

(6) where section 75(4)(c) of the Companies Act 1980 applies.

Just as the rule in *Foss v. Harbottle* has been supported by the courts for practical reasons as well as in principle, so the exceptions are based on a combination of principle and pragmatism. Certainly the first, second and third exceptions listed above could be covered by Sir Robert Megarry's suggested test. These are all examples of acts which cannot be ratified by an ordinary majority, so that any action brought by a shareholder cannot, in these instances, be immediately counteracted by a resolution of the company in general meeting, overriding the views of the minority and making the process pointless. Moreover, on principle, if the act is not ratifiable by an ordinary majority then the ordinary majority should not be in sole control of whether an action may be brought in relation to that act, since that would be to permit those controlling the company to achieve indirectly something they could not achieve directly. It is less easy to bring the fourth exception within this test on the present state of the authorities, but then it is arguable that it is not a true exception in any event.

(1) Illegal or ultra vires acts

"There is no room for the operation of the rule if the alleged wrong is *ultra vires* the corporation, because the majority of members cannot confirm the transaction": *Edwards v. Halliwell* [1950] 2 All E.R. 1064. The same reasoning applies where the act is illegal (*North-West Transportation Co. v. Beatty* (1887) 12 App. Cas. 589).

(2) Where a special or extraordinary resolution or other special procedure is required

Clearly, for the reasons set out above, a simple majority cannot be allowed to confirm a transaction which requires the concurrence of a greater majority (*Edwards v. Halliwell*). This exception can also be seen as a special example of the fourth exception.

(3) Where the act amounts to a "fraud on the minority" and the wrongdoers are in control of the company

The vexed question of what nature of act amounts to a fraud on a minority cannot be dealt with fully here. The extent of this category has not been resolved although it has been much discussed in the cases. In recent cases judges have been prepared to treat this category as sufficiently elastic to cover cases where in their view equity demanded that an action be available (see for example *Clemens v. Clemens Bros Ltd.* [1976] 2 All E.R. 268, *Estmanco Ltd. v. GLC* [1982] 1 All. E.R. 437). In this way consideration of whether a yet wider residual category (category (5) above) exists may be made unnecessary. However some limitations on this category in the context of the rule in *Foss v. Harbottle* have been made clear; there must be "fraud" alleged and the wrongdoers must be in control (see page 796). Fraud in this context is wider than fraud at common law as defined in *Derry v. Peek* (1889) 14 App Cas 337. It comprises also "fraud in the wider equitable sense of that term, as in the equitable concept of a fraud on a power" (Megarry V.C. in *Estmanco Ltd. v. GLC*). It does not, however, include negligence, however gross (*Pavlides v. Jensen* [1956] Ch. 565). In that case fraud was not alleged although the directors had sold a mine belonging to the company at undervalue. An individual shareholder was thus not permitted to bring an action. The difficulty is that fraud, being a serious allegation, cannot be pleaded where those bringing the action do not have full details of what happened, as they frequently will not do if the wrongdoers are in control. This was the position in *Daniels v. Daniels* [1978] 2 All E.R. 89. In that case Templeman J. distinguished *Pavlides v. Jensen* and held that a minority action would be permitted, since not only had the directors been negligent but they had also benefitted themselves at the expense of the company. Fraud, he said, is hard to plead and difficult to prove and so there should be a remedy available to a minority shareholder wherever directors use their powers intentionally, unintentionally, fraudulently or negligently in a manner which benefits them at the expense of the company. Whether this wide definition of fraud in *Daniels* will be followed or restricted in future remains to be seen. Vinelott J. accepted the reasoning of the case in *Prudential v. Newman Industries (No. 2)* [1980] 3 All E.R. 841 but the

Court of Appeal in the *Prudential* case [1982] 1 All E.R. 354 declined to give direct guidance, although their traditional approach would suggest that they would construe *Daniels* restrictively. However, the wide definition of fraud in *Daniels* was followed and applied to a shareholder's actions in the *Estmanco* case.

The main categories of acts of a type which may amount to fraud on the minority must now be examined and Templeman J's statement in *Daniels* must be seen also in the light of the cases discussed in relation to these categories. For convenience, the discussion below adopts the four-fold classification put forward by Professor Gower, but it must be borne in mind that this is not universally accepted and the cases themselves certainly do not discuss the principles in as clear a way as the classification suggests. Moreover, some acts falling under this head may also amount to breaches of duties owed to individuals actionable under the *fourth* category of exception to the rule in *Foss v. Harbottle* (see page 796 below).

Category one: expropriation of company's property

It is well established that the expropriation of the company's property by the majority for their benefit, at the expense of the minority, is an act which can be interfered with by the court at the suit of the minority, since it is not ratifiable by the majority. So, in *Menier v. Hooper's Telegraph Works* (1874) L.R. 9 Ch. App. 350 it was held that a minority shareholder could bring an action where the majority shareholder voted for the voluntary liquidation of the company in order to compromise an action being brought in the name of the company, the compromise being to the advantage of the majority shareholder.

This case was followed in *Cook v. Deeks* [1916] 1 A.C. 554, a case on the expropriation of property by directors. The directors wrongly took a contract in their own names. It was found that they held this as trustees for the company and could not ratify the expropriation by using their voting power as majority shareholders. They would not be permitted to make a present to themselves.

Dicta in the much debated case of *Regal (Hastings) Ltd. v. Gulliver* [1942] 1 All E.R. 378, where directors were called to account for secret profits, suggest that certain expropriations of the company's property by directors might be ratifiable by the majority, even though there is reliance on the directors' own votes. However, this will not be the case where the directors have made a profit at the expense of the minority and cannot show that they have acted bona fide in the interests of the company. Where the company's property is expropriated it will rarely be possible to satisfy this last requirement. "Fraud" must be shown if a minority shareholder is to bring an action but this will be "fraud" in the wide sense described above (see *Daniels v. Daniels*).

Catagory two: certain breaches of directors' duties

Many breaches of directors' duties are ratifiable by the majority in general meeting, and in these circumstances the minority will have no remedy. For example, where it was alleged that directors were grossly negligent, but not fraudulent, in selling property of the company at undervalue this was ratifiable by the majority: *Pavlides v. Jensen* [1956] 2 All E.R. 578. However, if a director's duty of subjective good faith is breached, ratification will not be permitted. The onus will be on those arguing effective ratification to show that the directors acted bona fide in the interests of the company.

Frequently, one result of the breach of duty will be that shares are issued to the wrongdoer directors. Clearly, if they could always ratify such an issue by virtue of these shares "it would be simply impossible to set aside a fraud committed by a director under such circumstances" (*Atwoll v. Merryweather* (1867) L.R. 5 Eq 464). In *Atwoll* an individual shareholder was permitted to bring an action where directors of a company sold to it a mine for an excessive price, part of which was satisfied by the issue of shares, giving the wrongdoers voting control. This was a fraud on the minority. However, not every wrongful issue of shares by directors will be non-ratifiable. In *Hogg v. Cramphorn Ltd.* [1966] 3 All E.R. 421 shares were issued by directors, acting bona fide, which gave them voting control. It was held that an individual shareholder could bring an action in respect of this breach because otherwise the wrongdoers would have had control by virtue of the very transactions complained of. However, ultimately no action by the minority was possible because the court stood the action over to enable the directors to convene a general meeting at which the wrongly issued shares were not to be voted and the issue was in fact ratified. It is important to note that in this case it was accepted that the board had acted in good faith, but the ratification itself could have amounted to a fraud on the minority had it been achieved by reliance on wrongly issued shares, since the whole object of the issue was to deprive certain members of their majority. That this was nevertheless for a proper purpose, and therefore ratifiable, was proved by the vote in its favour by members not relying on the wrongly issued shares. This case is also explicable as falling within the fourth exception, below.

Category three: expropriation of other members' property

Expropriation of the shares of the minority by the majority will amount to a fraud on the minority if it cannot be shown that in the honest opinion of the majority the transaction was bona fide for the benefit of the company as a whole. This test is also of relevance to the other categories of fraud on a minority to the extent described under those heads. It has been evolved and interpreted in a series of cases on the alteration of companies' articles. (See also the chapter *Articles*, and *Allen v. Gold Reefs of West Africa Ltd.* [1900] 1 Ch. 656, *Dafen Tinplate Co. v. Llanelly Steel Co.* [1920] 2 Ch. 124 and *Sidebottom v. Kershaw, Leese and Co. Ltd.* [1920] 1 Ch. 154). The proper construction of the test is still not free from doubt but it would appear to be objective in so far as reasonable men acting honestly may take different views.

Therefore, the court will not normally interfere where the majority has acted honestly but may do so if the decision is such that no reasonable men could have come to it upon proper materials (see Scrutton L.J. in *Shuttleworth v. Cox Brothers & Co. (Maidenhead) Ltd.* [1927] 2 K.B. 9). Thus the subjective test will apply to a range of activities, with the objective test marking an outer limit for extreme cases. The result of applying this test is to qualify the general rule that there is no obligation on shareholders (as opposed to directors) to consider the interests of others when voting (*North-West Transportation Ltd. v. Beatty* (1887) 12 App. Cas.. 589). If the effect of the resolution is such as to discriminate between the majority shareholders and the minority shareholders so as to give the former an advantage of which the latter are deprived, the question of whether it is bona fide for the benefit of the company will become relevant. If the resolution cannot be so described it will be liable to be impeached (*Greenhalgh v. Arderne Cinemas* [1950] 2 All E.R. 1120). In the *Greenhalgh* case it was said that the company as a whole "means not the company as a separate entity but the corporation as a general body". In other words, was the resolution for the benefit of a hypothetical member in the honest opinion of those voting? However, it was also stated that it is not necessary for the persons voting on the resolution to disassociate themselves from the prospect of personal benefit altogether. In that case, it was clear that the result of the alteration of the articles was to allow the majority to sell their shares to an outsider without offering them to the minority shareholder, who, under the old articles, would have been entitled to purchase them. Since an ordinary resolution of the company was still required to permit such a sale to an outsider, the new provision did not bestow the same benefit on the minority shareholder in practice. Nevertheless, in relation to his own shares he was no worse off than he had been previously. His property as such had not been expropriated and it was held that the resolution could not be impeached; the test was satisfied.

Category four: any case where the majority do not exercise their powers "bona fide for the benefit of the company as a whole"

It is argued by Professor Gower that there is a general principle that the majority must exercise their powers "bona fide for the benefit of the company as a whole", that test being construed subjectively as described above. Thus this test would apply to cases falling outside the three categories described above, but it would be for those alleging the fraud to show that the majority was not acting bona fide for the benefit of the company as a whole, whereas under the other three categories it seems that bona fides will be a defence, if at all, only if the majority can prove it. The much criticised case of *Clemens v. Clemens Bros. Ltd.* [1976] 2 All E.R. 26 may lend some support to the view that there is such a fourth category since there resolutions not falling clearly within any of the three categories above were set aside on the basis that the majority shareholder's right to exercise her votes was subject to equitable considerations making it unjust to exercise them in a particular way. Lip-service was paid to the test of benefit to the company but

Procedure where exception to the rule in Foss v. Harbottle applies

In the above discussion, reference has simply been made to actions being brought by individual shareholders. In fact, different forms of action are appropriate, depending upon which exception applies.

The "derivative" action

A recent import from the U.S.A., this terminology has now received judicial sanction *(Wallersteiner v. Moir (No. 2)* [1975] Q.B. 373; the *Prudential* case, above).

Where the true plaintiff is the company, but an exception to the *Foss v. Harbottle* rule is alleged to apply (essentially where there is a "fraud on the minority" falling within categories one or two above), the proper practice is for the action to be brought in the name of the plaintiff shareholder on behalf of himself and all the other shareholders apart from the wrongdoers. The company should be joined as a defendant *(Spokes v. Grosvenor Hotel* [1897] 2 Q.B. 124) so that it is bound by the court's decision and may be awarded damages. In form, this looks like a representative action under R.S.C. 1965, Ord. 15, r.12 but since it is in reality brought on behalf of the company, such an action may be brought by any registered shareholder *(Birch v. Sullivan* [1957] 1 W.L.R. 1247), even where he was not a member at the time of the alleged wrong *(Seaton v. Grant* [1867] L.R. 2 Ch. App. 459). The action is available only at the discretion of the court and therefore not to a shareholder who participates in the wrong *(Towers v. African Tug* [1904] 1 Ch. 558).

In some early cases, derivative actions were brought in the name of the company but this was undesirable since it results in the action being fought over the use of the name *(Alexander v. Automatic Telephone Co.* [1900] 2 Ch. 56). Moreover if the court decides that the minority was not entitled to use the name of the company the solicitor acting for the minority may be ordered to pay the costs personally. (This was assumed to be the rule in *Marshall's Valve Gear v. Manning Wardle* [1909] 1 Ch. 267.) Since the company's name cannot practically be used, therefore, the representative form of action is the best available.

The full implications of the action being a derivative one have not yet been worked out by the English courts although there are certain safeguards; for example, if the named plaintiff withdraws, the name of a previously unnamed but represented plaintiff may be added (R.S.C. Ord. 15, r.6). What is more, the plaintiff will not gain direct financial benefit, since the party suffering the damage is the company and therefore he will risk the costs of the action for litte or no financial gain. However, since the decision in *Wallersteiner v. Moir (No. 2)* it has been possible to obtain an order that the company should indemnify the plaintiff against the costs of the action taxed on a common fund basis whether or not the action succeeds. Normally such an order should be applied for before proceeding and the test for whether an indemnity will be given will be whether it is reasonable and prudent in the company's interest for the plaintiff to bring the action, which he must be doing in good faith.

As an alternative to, or in addition to, awarding damages in a derivative action, Templeman J. held in an unreported decision in June 1978 referred to by Boyle in (1980) 1 Co Law 7 that a receiver could be appointed to take control of the company from the board and possibly investigate the affairs of the company.

Representative action or personal action

Where an individual shareholder has suffered a personal wrong perpetrated by the majority, or the company has acted *ultra vires*, the proper form of action is a personal one with the company as true defendant. If the wrong is one suffered by all members or all members of a certain class, a personal action may be brought but so also may a true representative action under R.S.C. 1965 Ord. 15, r.12, and this is preferable as binding all relevant parties. If relief is to be claimed from the directors also, they may be added as defendants. Again, the individual shareholder will not gain financially from the action; the relief sought is normally in the form of a declaration or injunction.

Statutory remedies available to individual shareholders

The restricted protection available to the shareholder at common law as a result of the rule in *Foss v. Harbottle* has led to two main statutory remedies being created. These are, first, section 222(f) of the Companies Act 1948 and, secondly, section 75 of the Companies Act 1980. Section 75 replaces section 210 of the Companies Act 1948, which had itself proved unduly restrictive. Neither of these two remedies is restricted to minority shareholders, although they will obviously be the most frequent beneficiaries. However, a shareholder who is suffering by virtue of the dominant position of another shareholder who, although not holding the majority of the shares, has, for example, taken control of the administration of the company, might also wish to bring an action under one of these sections (see *Re Stewarts (Brixton) Ltd.* (1982) 3 Co Law 77).

Section 222(f) of the 1948 Act

This subsection provides that a company may be wound up by the court if:

> "the court is of opinion that it is just and equitable that the company should be wound up".

The provisions and procedure governing a winding up on the just and equitable ground are those applying to any winding up under section 222 and are discussed in the chapter *Liquidations*. Certain points should be made here, however, in relation to section 222(f) as a shareholder's remedy.

The petitioner

A petition may be presented by any of the persons set out in section 224 of the 1948 Act and this probably includes any member (see the definition of "contributory" in *Re Consolidated Goldfields of New Zealand* [1953] Ch. 689), as well as creditors and the company itself. Following an investigation a petition may be presented by the Department of Trade (section 224(1)(d)). A member will not succeed in his petition unless he can show that he has a tangible interest in a winding up; in other words, that on a winding up there would be some assets to be distributed (*Re Expanded Plugs Ltd.* [1966] 1 W.L.R. 514).

Exercise of the discretion by the court

In *Ebrahimi v. Westbourne Galleries Ltd.* [1973] A.C. 360, Lord Wilberforce criticised the tendency to create categories under which cases must be brought if the clause is to apply – "Illustrations may be used, but general words should remain general".

The following cases are therefore merely illustrations of the circumstances in which a winding up might be ordered.

(1) Where the company's "substratum" or principal object has failed – *Re German Date Coffee Co.* (1882) 20 Ch.D. 169.

(2) Where the company was formed for a fraudulent purpose – *Re Thomas Edward Brinsmead & Sons* [1897] 1 Ch. 406.

(3) Where there is a deadlock because shares are divided equally between members on opposing sides – *Re Yenidye Tobacco Co. Ltd.* [1916] 2 Ch. 426. This situation may well arise where the business is "in substance" a partnership "in the guise of a private company" and the facts are such as would justify the court in decreeing the dissolution of a partnership (*Re Yenidye Tobacco*), although this should not be used as a test (see *Ebrahimi*).

(4) Where there is a justifiable lack of confidence in the management of the company's affairs – *Loch v. John Blackwood Ltd.* [1924] A.C. 783. In that case the directors failed to hold general meetings, submit accounts and recommend a dividend and since this was apparently aimed at keeping the petitioners in ignorance of the truth and acquiring their shares at under value it was held that the lack of probity shown justified the lack of confidence and a winding up was ordered. Dissatisfaction at being outvoted on the business affairs or domestic policy of the company is not enough to lead to the court ordering a winding up.

(5) Where the shareholder is expelled from office in breach of some special underlying obligation of his fellow members – *Ebrahimi*.

(6) Perhaps, where the directors and majority shareholders deliberately break the CSI's Takeover Code (*Re St. Piran* [1981] 1 W.L.R. 1300).

The *Ebrahimi* case is now the leading case on section 222(f) and has widened its scope considerably. In that case, a partnership between two businessmen was incorporated. One of the businessmen brought his son into the company as both shareholder and director, putting the other former partner, Ebrahimi, into a minority position at board and general meetings. After some disagreement, Ebrahimi was removed from office as a director under section 184 of the 1948 Act and since no dividends were paid and he received no remuneration he ceased to participate in the profits. Although his removal from office was strictly legal and could not be prevented, the House of Lords held that Ebrahimi was entitled to a winding up order. This decision established that the exercise of a legal right may be "subject to equitable considerations" which will lead to a winding up order where it breaches some agreement between the members, even where no fraud or malafides can be proved. Lord Wilberforce felt that references to companies which are in substance partnerships was confusing; however small a company is, it is to be treated as such. Nevertheless there is room in company law for recognition of the fact that members of the company are individuals with rights, expectations and obligations *inter se* which are not necessarily submerged in the company structure. Equitable considerations will be superimposed on the memorandum and articles in appropriate cases, particularly where the company is formed on the basis of a personal relationship, such as a partnership, where there is some understanding as to shareholder participation in the conduct of the business, or where the member cannot sell out because of restrictions on the transfer of his interest.

Moreover the House of Lords held in *Ebrahimi* that although the petition must be brought by a person qualifying as a shareholder, he may rely on facts which do not affect him in that capacity in petitioning for a winding up, making section 222(f) a very much more useful remedy for the shareholder, whose interest as such may well be interwoven with his other interests in the company.

There has been an attempt to follow *Ebrahimi* by imposing equitable considerations upon the exercise of the legal right to vote where the claim is not for a winding up order (*Clemens v. Clemens Bros. Ltd.* [1976] 2 All E.R. 268). The more orthodox view is that the reasoning in *Ebrahimi* is confined to petitions under section 222(f) (*Bentley-Stevens v. Jones* [1974] 2 All E.R. 653).

Limitations on the remedy under section 222(f)

Although *Ebrahimi* has assisted the minority shareholder by widening the scope of section 222(f), it remains the case that, since the only action the court may take under that provision is to wind up the company, the petitioner may wish to seek an alternative remedy, one that will cure rather than kill. The existence of an alternative remedy will only prevent the court from ordering a winding up if it considers that the petitioner is, in the light of this, acting unreasonably in seeking to have the company wound up (section 225 of the 1948 Act), but usually it will be in the interests of the shareholder to use some other remedy if that is available. The Cohen Committee therefore recommended the introduction of a more flexible remedy, section 210 of the 1948 Act, which, following the recommendations of the Jenkins Committee, has now been replaced by section 75 of the 1980 Act.

The alternative remedy – section 75 of the Companies Act 1980

Section 210 of the 1948 Act was poorly drafted and restrictively construed; the greatest limitation being that it was available only if the circumstances were such as to justify a winding up order under section 222(f). Section 75 of the 1980 Act adopts the recommendations of the Jenkins Committee and the court may now make such order as it thinks fit where any member petitions and shows that:

> "the affairs of the company are being or have been conducted in a manner which is unfairly prejudicial to the interests of some part of the members (including at least himself) or that any actual or proposed act or omission of the company (including an act or omission on its behalf) is or would be so prejudicial".

The relief is available without proof that the court would order a winding up under section 222(f), and this will be particularly useful where the very conduct complained of has already driven the company into insolvency.

Some of the requirements of the section require closer attention.

"Unfairly prejudicial"

This is certainly intended to be wider than the old test, contained in section 210, of "oppressiveness" and to cover conduct falling short of illegality but "involving a visible departure from the standards of fair dealing" (Jenkins Report paragraphs 203 and 204). The Report mentions as possible examples the payment by directors of excessive remuneration to themselves, the refusal to register shares in the name of deceased member's personal representatives, the issue of shares to directors and others on advantageous terms, and the passing of non-cumulative preference dividends on shares held by the minority. The full meaning of the phrase, and indeed the scope of the section generally, awaits judicial clarification. It was held in *Re a Company* [1983] 2 W.L.R. 381 that a scheme to dissipate a company's liquid resources by investment in a partly owned subsidiary was not "unfairly prejudicial".

"The interests of some part of the members (including at least himself)"

It seems that the remedy is still restricted to the member *qua* member, despite the removal of this requirement in winding up cases (*Ebrahimi v. Westbourne Galleries*, above). Lord Granchester Q.C. took this view *Re a Company*. It is unfortunate, though understandable given the wording of section 75, that he came to this decision rather than following the lead given by the House of Lords in the *Ebrahimi* case. It is not clear whether the reference to "some part of the members" is intended to restrict the remedy to cases where there is positive discrimination between different classes or groups of shareholders. It will normally be the case that some shareholders suffer more than others because of their different circumstances, but it would be unfortunate if it was not held that the "part" should include the "whole" (Boyle, (1980) 1 Co Law 280). A restrictive interpretation could make section 75 narrower on this point than section 210. This is a point of some importance in relation to the effectiveness of the section as a means of avoiding the rule in *Foss v. Harbottle*. Conduct prejudicial to the company and to all, although not particular, shareholders is not clearly within the wording of the section and so it might be argued that a case such as *Pavlides v. Jensen* where the negligence of the directors harmed the company and all its members without benefiting the defendants was not covered. Clearly, the extent to which the common law exceptions to *Foss v. Harbottle* can be made redundant and cease to be developed, and the value of the new statutory exception to the rule, will depend greatly on the attitude of the courts in construing this section when such points arise.

Conduct of affairs and actual or proposed acts or omissions

This wording is considerably wider than that under section 210 and will cover isolated acts, such as a particular and past breach of directors' duty which has affected the value of the complainant's shareholding, as well as proposed conduct. However the act or omission must be that of the company and it is the affairs of the company with which the section is concerned. Competition with the company in question may not be sufficient to support an action under section 75 unless there can be shown a misuse of the powers of management of the company to which the order is to relate, as in *Scottish Co-operative Wholesale Society v. Meyer* [1959] A.C. 324.

Who may petition

A petition may be brought by any member and also by the Secretary of State in the circumstances set out by section 75(2). References to members in this context are to be construed as including persons who are not members but to whom shares have been transferred or transmitted by operation of law, so that trustees and personal representatives are covered (section 75(9)).

Remedies available

The court has a wide discretion to make such order as it thinks fit under section 75(3). Without prejudice to the generality of subsection (3), subsection (4) provides some specific types of order which may be made. As under section 210, the court may make an order regulating the conduct of the company's affairs in the future and providing for the purchase of shares of any members by the company or other members and consequential reductions in capital (sections 75(4)(a), 75(4)(d)).

Section 75(4)(b) enables the court to require the company to refrain from doing or continuing an act complained of by a petitioner or to do an act which the petitioner has complained it has omitted to do. This may enable the petitioner to be granted an injunction where he could not obtain one under an exception to the rule in *Foss v. Harbottle*. An alteration to the memorandum or articles may be ordered or prohibited (sections 74(5) and (6)). This could be useful where, for example, an alteration of the articles is unfairly prejudicial to an individual shareholder but cannot be shown to be a fraud on the minority (Boyle, (1980) 1 Co Law 280).

Subsection 4(c) was specifically introduced to assist the minority shareholder to overcome the rule in *Foss v. Harbottle* where the court thought fit. It enables the court to authorise civil proceedings to be brought in the name and on behalf of the company by such person or persons and on such terms as the court may direct.

The question of costs is left open where such proceedings are authorised and will be a matter for the court, but it will presumably be able to impose conditions in respect of this and other aspects of the conduct of the litigation. Where such litigation is authorised, it will enable the minority to obtain compensation for the company from the wrongdoers where they are in breach of an equitable duty.

However, since an order under section 75(4)(c) can be made only if a petition under section 75 is well founded in accordance with section 75(1), such an order will not necessarily be available to side step the rule in *Foss v. Harbottle* in every case in which a wrong is done to the company if there is not also a wrong to "part of the members". Also, as mentioned above, it is not yet known how widely "unfairly prejudicial" will be construed by the courts (though note the facts in *Re a Company*, above).

Thus the impact which section 75 will have on the rule in *Foss v. Harbottle* remains to be seen: it is to be hoped that it will be widely construed. As the Jenkins Report points out at paragraph 207, since the court will have discretion as to whether or not to make such an order, the independent majority reaching a bona fide decision is adequately protected against abuse of litigation by the minority, and this removes a major objection to the relaxation of the rule in *Foss v. Harbottle*.

To summarise, it seems that although its drafting and thus its meaning is not as clear as might have been hoped, section 75, sympathetically construed by the courts, should be a useful addition to the armoury of the minority shareholder.

Department of Trade investigations

Despite the development of common law and statutory remedies for the minority shareholder, litigation in the courts in this area is still a process which is uncertain in outcome and potentially expensive for the plaintiff unless the court is prepared to make a *Wallersteiner v. Moir* order (or similar order under section 75 of the 1980 Act). Particularly where a large company with numerous shareholders is concerned, no one shareholder may be sufficiently public spirited to take the risk upon himself. Institutional investors have not always been encouraged by the courts when taking the initiative (see *Prudential Assurance Co. Ltd. v. Newman Industries (No. 2)* [1982] 1 All E.R. 354).

The Department of Trade has powers, now strengthened by the 1981 Companies Act, to investigate where there is cause for disquiet. The extent to which this power should take over from the function of the courts in this area is an important one which cannot be done justice here. However the powers of the Department of Trade are clearly helpful in cases where insufficient information is available to found an action in the courts. Not only the minority may benefit from an investigation, and indeed the company itself may request one. The Department's powers are not at present frequently used, but could be increasingly important. Many would argue, however, that further reforms are necessary to increase the effectiveness of the department's investigatory powers. Set out below is a brief outline of the circumstances in which the Department has power to act.

Inspection of company's books and papers

Sections 109 to 118 of the Companies Act 1967 give the Department of Trade extensive powers to call for the books of the company without instituting a formal investigation, so that information can be discovered without the harmful publicity to the company that would result from the announcement of an investigation. The sections give full back up powers to the Department to enable it to obtain co-operation in its inspection.

Appointment of inspectors to investigate into company's affairs

Inspectors may be appointed under various different provisions of the Companies Act 1948 as amended by subsequent Acts.

(1) *Application by members or company*

There is a discretionary power to appoint an inspector or inspectors either on the application of the company or on that of not less than two hundred members or of members holding not less than one-tenth of the shares issued (section 164 of the 1948 Act as amended by section 86 of the 1981 Act). Where the company has no share capital the application from members must be from not less than one-fifth in number of the persons on the register of members. Before instituting an investigation, the Department may require the applicant(s) to give up to £5,000 security for costs.

(2) *Court order*

The court may order that the Department should appoint an inspector to investigate the company's affairs (section 165(1) 1948 Act as amended by section 86(3) and Schedule 4 of the 1981 Act). The company itself can no longer demand an investigation but may only request one under (1) above.

(3) *Departmental discretion in certain circumstances*

The Department has a discretion to mount an investigation under section 165(1)(b) of the 1948 Act as amended by Schedule 3 to the 1980 Act, if it appears to it that there are circumstances suggesting that the company's affairs are being conducted fraudulently or unlawfully or in a manner which is unfairly prejudicial to some part of its members. There is a similar discretion if it appears that those concerned with the formation or management of the company have been guilty of fraud, misfeasance or other misconduct in that connection, and where it seems that the company's members have not been given all the information with respect to its affairs which they might reasonably expect. The power may be exercised during the course of a voluntary winding up and "members" includes trustees and personal representatives entitled to shares by operation of law (section 165(2)).

This power may clearly be used to provide considerable protection to the minority shareholder, providing him with information to bring his own action and perhaps deterring further misfeasance. However, the minority shareholder has no rights under the section; although he may report a matter to the Department it has no obligation to take action under this section. Even once a report has been completed, the Department is under no obligation to publish it; there is a wide discretion in section 168 as to supplying copies of and publishing the report. Publication might be undesirable where further proceedings are contemplated.

The 1981 Act strengthens the powers of an inspector appointed under sections 164 or 165 to obtain the production of documents relating to the company from any person (not just officers and agents of the company) and to examine any person on oath (section 167 of the 1948 Act as amended by section 87 of the 1981 Act). An inspector's powers to require production of documents relating to directors' and ex-directors' bank accounts are also strengthened (section 167(1B)).

Investigation into ownership and control of companies

The Department of Trade may appoint an inspector or conduct its own investigation into the ownership and control of a company (sections 172 to 174 of the 1948 Act). The appointment is discretionary, except where a group of members, of the size required under section 164 (see (1) above)), applies for an investigation, when the Department must make an appointment unless it is satisfied that the application is vexatious.

Information may be required by the Department or inspector of any person whom it or he has reasonable cause to believe has relevant information. The inspector has the same powers as one investigating the affairs of the company, other than the power to require disclosure of bank accounts. Restrictions may be imposed on shares or debentures wherever the Department has difficulty in finding out the relevant facts about any shares and not merely, as before, where a person was unwilling to assist. This should prevent beneficial owners outside the jurisdiction using nominees with no knowledge of the facts so as to avoid restrictions. The restrictions under section 174 (a) prevent transfers of or agreements to transfer the shares or any right to be issued with the shares, and (b) prohibit the use of voting rights, the payment of sums due on the shares and the issue of additional shares, and so should provide a powerful sanction. The 1981 Act provided for the court to authorise the sale of shares which are subject to restrictions, the net proceeds being paid into court. The restrictions may be lifted only where the shares are to be sold and the court or Secretary of State approves the sale, or where the relevant facts about the shares have been disclosed to the company and no unfair advantage has accrued to any person as a result of the earlier failure to disclose. Section 174 may be applied in connection with the disclosure of interest provisions contained in the 1981 Act (see the chapter *Disclosure of Shareholdings*).

Investigation of share dealings

Under section 32 of the Companies Act 1967 the Department of Trade may appoint inspectors to investigate possible contraventions of sections 25 and 27 of that Act (director's share dealings; see page 314).

Costs

Costs will initially be borne by the Department, except where security has been taken under section 164. This is a major advantage of opting for an inquiry rather than instituting proceedings. However, after an investigation, costs may be recovered from any person against whom a successful criminal or civil action is brought, from any company in whose name proceedings are brought to the extent of property recovered, from any company investigated except where it was the applicant or the Department which instigated the investigation, and from the applicant or applicants under section 164.

Civil and criminal proceedings

An investigation or inquiry under the above powers may lead to civil or criminal proceedings in the courts.

The Department of Trade may itself bring proceedings under section 222(f) of the 1948 Act (winding up on the just and equitable ground) under section 75 of the 1980 Act or, if it appears to the Department that civil proceedings ought, in the public interest, to be brought by a company it may bring such proceedings in the name of and on behalf of the company (section 37 of the 1967 Act). Given this express statutory power, the rule in *Foss v. Harbottle* has no application.

The shareholder now has an array of potential remedies and in an extreme case is now unlikely to be left unprotected. His position remains unclear, however, particularly in borderline cases of negligence by directors without benefit to themselves. It is not clear that the Department could intervene in such cases. The shareholder is now dependent upon the sympathetic and sensible interpretation and development by the courts of his statutory and common law remedies and upon full utilisation by the Department of Trade of its powers.

Shares

Although its name implies a proportionate entitlement to something in respect of a company, for company law purposes a share need not entitle its holder to an interest in any underlying assets, although in the case of ordinary shares it will commonly do so. Thus, where a person is entitled to a preference share, he will be entitled in general terms not to a share in any of the underlying assets of the company but merely to a preferential right to a dividend or a return of capital. Even in the case of a share having rights of participation in the assets of the company, that share will only entitle its holder to a share of the company and not to a proportionate interest in each asset of the company. The company having its own separate legal personality is the sole beneficial owner of its assets, whereas the company can generally be said to be owned by its members or shareholders. Although, in connection with other aspects of the law the courts have sometimes been persuaded to lift the "veil of incorporation", it is clear that a company does not hold its property on trust for the shareholders, and that a shareholder cannot be regarded as having any insurable interest in the underlying assets of the company (*Macaura v. Northern Insurance* [1925] A.C. 619; see the chapter *Formation and Types of Company*).

A share has sometimes been described as a "bundle of rights". The nature of a share cannot be determined simply by its description. The rights which a shareholder is afforded under the memorandum and articles of association of the company will determine the precise nature of the share itself. Thus different classes of shares in a company will have different rights as to dividends, participation in surplus assets, and voting. As part of the principle of maintenance of capital, however, a shareholder will be required, in the case of a limited company, to pay up the nominal amount on his share; this can be regarded as a liability attached to the holding of shares in a company. As indicated by section 455 of the 1948 Act, a share will form part of the share capital of a company. That share capital can be regarded as the permanent capital of the company, subject to the special rules as to reduction, redemption and purchase of shares by the company all of which are considered elsewhere in this book. It is sufficient for the purposes of this chapter simply to note that alterations of share capital can be made only within the strict procedures laid down in the Companies Acts, since the share capital will be one of the conditions contained in the memorandum (C.A. 1948, s. 4).

Under section 2(4)(a) of the 1948 Act shares in a limited company (and this chapter is not concerned with unlimited companies) are required to have a nominal or par value. Although the Jenkins Committee (Cmnd 1749/1962) recommended that the issue of no par value shares should be permitted, this has not yet been introduced into our domestic company law. The division of share capital into shares of a fixed amount does not mean that the shares are required to be paid for at the time of subscription. Generally speaking, shares may therefore remain nil paid, be partly paid or fully paid; where shares are not fully paid up there remains the overriding liability to pay up the nominal amount in the event of a call or on a winding-up.

It is provided by section 74 of the 1948 Act that each share in a company having a share capital is to be distinguished by an appropriate number. This requirement can be dispensed with where all the issued shares in the company, or all the issued shares of a particular class, are fully paid up and rank pari passu for all purposes so long as those conditions remain satisfied. It is in practice very common for distinguishing numbers to be dispensed with by a resolution of the directors. If the shares are listed, it will be necessary to obtain a new listing from The Stock Exchange for the new, unnumbered, shares.

Classification of shares

As indicated above, it is not possible precisely to classify every type of share in a company, since this depends entirely upon the actual rights and liabilities attached to a share by the company's constitution. To this extent, careful drafting of the memorandum and articles of association is always required since the rights attached to a share are generally treated as exhaustive. If no separate rights are afforded to a particular class of shares, the common law rule is that all shares in the capital of a company are to rank equally: *Birch v. Cropper* (1889) 14 App. Cas. 525. A share will clearly be of a separate and distinct class if its dividend rights differ from those of other shares. So for example, the right of a shareholder to participate in distributions may be deferred or preferred to the rights of other holders. Similarly, the right of a member to participate in surplus assets on a winding-up may well differ from that of another member of the company. Shares may have attached to them different voting rights or no voting rights at all. The right of a shareholder to transfer his shares may also create a different class of shares (see *IRC v. Beveridge* [1979] S.T.C. 592). Bearing all these variations in mind, the following represents no more than a very broad summary of some of the more customary classifications for shares.

Ordinary shares

In general terms it can be said that every company must have ordinary share capital, since that term will refer to the class of shares forming the basis for the rights of every other class of shares. So, a preference share will have preference over an ordinary share and a deferred share will rank lower in priority to it. Where a company has only one class of shares, that class will be of ordinary shares. The ordinary shares generally carry the primary voting rights of the company, rights to dividends if declared, and rights to participate in a surplus on a winding-up.

Preference shares

As outlined above, a preference share can be described as any share having priority over the ordinary shares in a company. This priority may be conferred in respect of dividends or capital, or both. Preference shares are dealt with in detail at page 607.

Non-voting shares

Although it is relatively uncommon in the case of a private company to find non-voting share capital, the issue of non-voting shares can enable equity share capital to be issued to persons without the existing shareholders thereby losing control of the company. This can be useful in the case of a listed company or a company whose shares are traded on the Unlisted Securities Market in that it can create a market in the shares of a company whilst enabling a relatively small number of voting shares to direct the affairs of the company. It is possible to obtain a listing on The Stock Exchange for non-voting shares, but they must clearly be designated as such. Although the non-voting shares will not be able to exercise any direct influence over the management of the company, the holders of such shares are nevertheless *members* of the company and have an interest as such. That interest may be protected by action under section 75 of the Companies Act 1980 in the event of the holders of the voting shares failing to exercise their control of the company in a proper manner and to the prejudice of the non-voting shareholders.

Redeemable shares

Shares of any class may now be designated by the rights attached to them as redeemable. This topic is dealt with in detail at page 754.

Deferred shares

Deferred shares (which are also described as founders shares) are often associated with the promotion of a company. They enable the promoters to enjoy a stake in the company whilst leaving equity capital available for subscription by other investors. In more modern times, deferred shares have commonly often been linked with devices for the saving of stamp duty or estate taxes.

Where different classes of shares are concerned, and a company is listed on The Stock Exchange, it is a requirement that the capital structure should be stated in the articles and that where the capital consists of more than one class of shares it must also be stated how the various classes rank for any distribution by way of dividend or otherwise.

Alteration of capital

The share capital of a company must be stated in the memorandum, but this can be altered within the strict procedures laid down in the Companies Acts. Alterations to the *authorised* capital of a company are provided for in section 61 of the 1948 Act; alterations to the *issued* capital of a company, apart from its increase by further issues which are dealt with below, are considered elsewhere in this book (see the chapters on *Bonus Issues, Preference Shares, Redeemable Shares* and *Rights Issues*).

Increase of capital

Under section 61(1) of the 1948 Act it is first of all necessary that a company be authorised by its articles to alter the share capital conditions of its memorandum. In the case of an increase of capital this authorisation is commonly provided by article 44 of Table A to the 1948 Act. For a company whose articles adopt Table A it is permissible to increase the authorised or nominal share capital by means of an ordinary resolution in general meeting; however, it is possible for additional requirements to be placed on a company perhaps involving the passing of a special (as opposed to an ordinary) resolution. It is necessary for the proposed increase to be specified in the notice convening the meeting (*MacConnell v. E. Prill & Co. Limited* [1916] 2 Ch. 57). If the increase of capital is connected with a company listed on The Stock Exchange, it is first of all necessary to file proofs of the circular with the Quotations Department prior to final printing. Where ten per cent or more of the voting capital (unclassified shares being counted as voting capital) will remain unissued, there must be included in the circular a statement that no issue will be made which would effectively alter the control of the company without prior approval of the company in general meeting.

Once the formal resolution has been passed by the company, a notice on Form 10 together with a copy of the resolution must be filed with the Registrar, together with a copy of the revised memorandum under section 9(5) of the European Communities Act 1972. Furthermore, if a company is listed, a copy of the revised memorandum must be forwarded to the Quotations Department. The penalty for failure to register with the Registrar of Companies is on summary conviction a fine not exceeding one-fifth of the statutory maximum (currently £1,000) or, on conviction after continued contravention, a default fine not exceeding one-fiftieth of the statutory maximum (Schedule 2 of the Companies Act 1980).

Capital duty is no longer levied on the nominal amount of share capital; accordingly the former practice of issuing a small nominal amount of shares at a substantial premium to reduce capital duty is no longer appropriate.

Consolidation

Section 61 of the 1948 Act also provides a company with power to consolidate all or any of its share capital into shares of a larger amount than its existing shares. The process of consolidation involves shares of a smaller nominal value being combined to form shares of a larger aggregate nominal value. So for example 100 1p shares could be consolidated so as to become one new £1 share. This procedure is commonly adopted by a company following a reconstruction in order to readjust its share capital where unwieldy nominal amounts have been thrown up. In Table A articles consolidation is authorised by article 45, and involves an ordinary resolution of the company.

Notice of consolidation must be given to the Registrar on Form 28, accompanied by a revised copy of the memorandum of association under section 9(5) of the European Communities Act 1972.

Sub-division

Sub-division of shares is permitted by section 61(1)(d) of the 1948 Act. This is the converse process to that of consolidation involving, for example, one £1 share becoming 100 new 1p shares. This does not involve any difficulty where shares are fully paid; however, where shares are only partly paid and are then sub-divided the proportion between the amount paid and the amount unpaid on each reduced share must be the same as it was in the case of the share from which the reduced share is derived. Subject to this, however, it seems that, provided the articles of association so authorise, new rights may be attached to some (and not to all) of the new shares of smaller nominal amount.

The power to sub-divide is derived in most cases from article 45 of Table A. The primary reason for sub-division is one of marketability. In recent years, many listed companies have sub-divided £1 shares into 25p shares or 10p shares to enable dealings to take place in smaller units. This to some extent has obviated the need to convert shares into stock (see below).

Form 28 is again used to notify the Registrar of Companies of the alteration and again section 9(5) applies. If the company is listed, then a new quotation must be obtained for the newly created shares.

Conversion of shares into stock

A company is permitted under section 61 of the 1948 Act to convert all or any of its paid up shares into stock, and to reconvert that stock into paid up shares of any denomination. It is important to note that this power is restricted to *fully paid* shares or stock as the case may be. The primary attraction of stock is that it is transferable in fractions and not by reference to a number of shares, although under article 41 of Table A the directors may fix a minimum amount of stock transferable; these minimum amounts are then referred to as stock units. A further advantage is that it is unnecessary for stock to have distinguishing numbers.

It is not possible for a company to issue stock direct. Instead, the company must make an issue of shares followed by a conversion into stock. This is an uncommon procedure, basically because of the tendency for shares to be denominated in smaller nominal amounts thus making redundant the attraction of the fractional transferability of stock, and because it is possible to dispense with distinguishing numbers for fully-paid shares.

Diminution of capital

The power of a company to diminish or cancel its authorised capital is derived from section 61(1)(e) of the 1948 Act. This power is restricted to shares which, at the date of passing of the resolution in that behalf, have not been taken or agreed to be taken by any person. The procedure should not be confused with a reduction of *issued* capital (which is dealt with in full in the chapter *Reconstructions and Amalgamations*). The power to diminish capital merely provides for a diminution of authorised capital. It is not used to any great extent except perhaps in connection with an overall scheme for reconstruction and amalgamation.

Variation of class rights

Where a company has issued shares of more than one class, the rights attaching to any class of shares in that company may only be varied under the terms of sections 32 and 33 of the Companies Act 1980. These provisions apply notwithstanding anything to the contrary which appears in the articles (for example, article 4 of Table A as amended by Schedule 4 to the 1980 Act). Powers to vary class rights were, however, available to companies prior to the passing of the 1980 Act, and a certain amount of case law has built up on the subject.

Section 32(1) of the 1980 Act makes provision for the variation of the rights attached to any class of shares in the company whose share capital is divided into shares of different classes. Thus, section 32 cannot apply where there is only one class of shares; in such a case a variation can be effected by alteration of the articles under section 10 of the 1948 Act, or otherwise by a scheme of arrangement under section 206 of that Act. Furthermore, it is only a strict variation of the legal rights attaching to a class of shares which will be subject to the special rules contained in section 32. Other extraneous matters, although affecting the value or limiting the effectiveness of the rights attaching to that class of shares, will not generally constitute a *variation* of those rights. Thus, a capitalisation issue of new ordinary share capital ranking in priority to, or an issue of preference shares ranking pari passu with, existing preference shares in a company will not constitute a variation of the existing rights of the preference shareholders (see *White v. Bristol Aeroplane Co. Limited* [1953] Ch. 65 and *Re John Smiths Tadcaster Brewery Co. Limited* [1953] Ch. 308). Even if the variation of the rights of one class adversely affects the rights of another class this will not generally constitute a variation of the rights of *that* class (see *Greenhalgh v. Arderne Cinemas Limited* [1946] 1 All E.R. 512 (CA) and *Hodge v. Howell* (1959) 227 L.T. 88 (CA)). By section 32(9) a variation clearly includes an abrogation of the rights attaching to a class of shares, but it is equally clear that a cancellation of shares will not constitute a variation (see *Re Saltdean Estate Co. Limited* [1968] 1 W.L.R. 1844, discussed more fully in the chapter on *Reconstructions and Amalgamations*).

Having regard to the fact that only direct variations of class rights appear to fall within section 32, it will often be advisable for specific provisions to be inserted in the articles extending the class rights variation procedure to matters which would not otherwise strictly be treated as variations. Such matters could include the following,

(a) any alterations in authorised or issued share capital;

(b) the variation of rights attaching to *other* classes of shares in the company;

(c) the issue of debentures by capitalisation of reserves;

(d) the proposing of a resolution for the winding-up of the company or for any amendment to the memorandum or articles of association; and

(e) the sale of the company's business.

It is not uncommon to find provisions extending the ambit of the variation procedure in this way, most particularly in the case of a holding of shares by an outside investor having no direct control over the company's affairs.

Class rights may be contained in the memorandum, in the articles, or in the resolution creating the particular class of shares. There may be no variation procedure, or such a procedure may be specifically set out in the company's constitution. Apart from the statutory requirements (which are considered below), further requirements as to variation may be imposed by contract, for example, under the terms of a shareholders' agreement. This is a common element in subscriptions for shares by institutional investors.

The particular procedure in each different case for the variation or modification of class rights is set out in the table at pages 818 and 819.

Class meetings

Where a class meeting is required (see the third column of the table), it is important that such a meeting should be *separate* from any other meeting of shareholders (section 32(2)(b) of the 1980 Act, and see *Carruth v. ICI* [1937] A.C. 707).

Under section 32(6) various general provisions of the 1948 Act as to meetings and the like are imported into the class rights procedure. Notwithstanding those provisions, however, the following rules are to apply in every case of a class meeting,

(a) the necessary quorum at any such meeting other than an adjourned meeting is to be two persons holding or representing by proxy at least one-third in nominal value of the issued shares of the class in question and at an adjourned meeting one person holding shares of the class in question or his proxy; and

(b) any holders of shares of the class in question present in person or by proxy may demand a poll.

Powers of court

Although the terms of section 32 override anything to the contrary in the company's constitution, nevertheless certain powers of the court are expressed, by section 32(10), to apply notwithstanding the variation procedures. These powers include the following,

(a) to cancel or confirm a resolution by an old public company not to be re-registered as a public company or by a public company to be re-registered as a private company (section 11 of the 1980 Act);

(b) to make any order under section 75 of the 1980 Act where a member of the company petitions the court on the ground that the affairs of the company are being or have been conducted in a manner which is unfairly prejudicial;

(c) under section 5 of the 1948 Act to confirm an alteration of the objects clause in the memorandum of a company;

(d) to approve a scheme of arrangement under section 206 of the 1948 Act; and

(e) to make such orders as are set out in section 208 of the 1948 Act in the case of a reconstruction or amalgamation.

Objection to variation

Prior to the 1980 Act, where a variation procedure was contained in the memorandum or articles of a company, a dissenting shareholder or shareholders had the right under section 72 of the 1948 Act to apply to the court for cancellation of the variation. This right is expressly preserved by section 32(8) of the 1980 Act in relation to a variation carried out under the statutory procedure.

Under section 72 the holders of not less than 15 per cent in the aggregate of the issued shares of the particular class in question, provided they

Class rights — modification procedure table

No.	Class rights attached by	Variation procedure contained in	Modification procedure	Reference (C.A. 1980 unless otherwise stated)
1.	Memorandum	None (or in articles otherwise than on incorporation)	Either (a) by means of a scheme of arrangement; or (b) all the members of the company must agree to the variation. This requirement cannot be overridden by an alteration of the articles	C.A. 1948, s. 206 s. 32(5) ss. 32(4), 32(7)
2.	Memorandum	Express prohibition on variation in memorandum	No variation can be effected except by means of a scheme of arrangement	C.A. 1948, s. 23 C.A. 1948, s. 206
3.	Memorandum or otherwise	Memorandum	(a) If the variation is connected with the giving, variation or renewal of an authority for the purposes of C.A. 1980, s. 14 (allotment of certain securities by directors), or with a reduction of share capital, then the variation can be effected if – (i) the *statutory variation procedure* (see 5 below) is followed; *and* (ii) any *additional* requirements of the memorandum are complied with	s. 32(3)
			(b) *Otherwise* by means of the procedure set out in the memorandum	C.A. 1948, s. 23(2)

No.	Class rights attached by	Variation procedure contained in	Modification procedure	Reference (C.A. 1980 unless otherwise stated)
4.	Memorandum	Articles at time of original incorporation	(a) As 3.(a), except that any additional requirements of the articles must be complied with in addition to the statutory variation procedure (b) *Otherwise*, by means of the procedure set out in the articles	s. 32(3) s. 32(4) C.A. 1948, article 4 of Table A
5.	Otherwise than by memorandum	None	Both (a) *statutory variation procedure* i.e. if (i) the holders of three-quarters in nominal value of the issued shares of the class in question consent in writing to the variation; *or* (ii) an extraordinary resolution passed at a separate general meeting of the holders of that class sanctions the variation, *and* (b) any *additional* requirement (howsoever imposed) is complied with	s. 32(2)
6.	Otherwise than by memorandum	Articles (whenever first included i.e. on incorporation or otherwise)	(a) As 4.(a) (b) *Otherwise* by means of the procedure set out in the articles	s. 32(3) s. 32(4) C.A. 1948, article 4 of Table A

did not consent to or vote in favour of the resolution for the variation, have the right to apply to the court to have the variation cancelled. Where such an application is made, section 72(1) provides that it is not to have effect unless and until it is confirmed by the court.

The application must be made within 21 days after the date on which the consent was given or the resolution was passed. It is not necessary for *all* dissenting members to make the application; such one or more of their number as they may appoint in writing may apply on behalf of them all. On the hearing of the application the court has a discretion to disallow the variation, but only if it is satisfied that, having regard to all the circumstances of the case, the variation would *unfairly prejudice* the shareholders of the class represented by the applicant. The burden is therefore on the applicant or applicants to prove unfair prejudice. One particular example where unfair prejudice might be established could be in a case where the majority of the holders of the particular class in question were also holders of another class of shares, and it was established on the hearing of the application that those majority holders had voted with regard to their interests as shareholders of that other class rather than as holders of the class of shares in question (see, for example, in another context, *Re Alabama* [1891] 1 Ch. 213 and *Re Hellenic & General Trust* [1975] 3 All E.R. 382).

Registration of class rights

The rights attaching to a class of shares may be so attached by means of the ordinary resolution authorising the increase of nominal capital, by special resolution (whether or not altering the articles of association of the company) or by some other means. Where those rights are attached by means of the increase of capital itself, a printed copy of the resolution will be required to be forwarded to the Registrar under section 63(2) of the 1948 Act. Similarly, where the rights are attached by special resolution, or in the case of an alteration in the articles, a copy of that resolution together with a copy of any revised articles must be delivered to the Registrar under section 143 of the 1948 Act and section 9(5) of the European Communities Act 1972.

Where, however, a company allots shares with rights which are not stated in its memorandum or articles or in any resolution or agreement to which section 143 of the 1948 Act applies, section 33 of the 1980 Act provides that the company shall, unless the shares allotted are in all respects uniform with shares previously allotted, deliver to the Registrar within one month from the date of allotment a statement in the prescribed form containing particulars of those rights. The prescribed form is Form 33. Because newly allotted shares will often have restrictions as to the receipt of dividends in the first year of issue, sub-section (2) of section 33 provides that such shares will not be treated as different from shares previously allotted by reason only of the fact that the former do not carry the same rights to dividends as the latter during the twelve months immediately following the former's allotment.

On a variation of class rights otherwise than by an amendment to the memorandum or articles of association or by resolution or agreement to which section 143 of the 1948 Act applies, the company is required within one month of the date of the variation to deliver to the Registrar a statement in the prescribed form containing particulars of the variation. The prescribed form in this case is Form 33a.

The allocation of a name or other designation, or a new name or new designation, to any class of shares will also necessitate delivery of a notice to the Registrar within one month, unless the allocation was effected by means of an alteration to the memorandum or articles or by resolution or agreement under section 143. The prescribed form in this case is Form 33b.

Section 101 of the 1981 Act requires the register of members which a company is required to keep under section 110 of the 1948 Act to distinguish between the classes of shares held by members if the company has more than one class of shares.

Allotment of share capital

Until the allotment of share capital was regulated by the Companies Act 1980, the vast majority of companies (both public and private) vested the authority to issue shares in the directors. Article 2 of Table A provides for an issue of shares by the company by means of ordinary resolution, although it is commonplace to find Table A modified by a provision that the directors shall have control over the issue of share capital.

The control of the directors may be modified to some extent by further provisions in the articles to the effect that shares may not be issued unless they shall first of all have been offered to existing members or holders of shares of that particular class pro rata to their existing holdings in the company. In addition, for a listed company, Stock Exchange regulations require shares to be offered by way of rights issue in most cases.

The general overriding discretion afforded to the directors was tempered by the common law principle that the directors were only permitted to issue shares bona fide in the best interests of the company (see for instance *Piercy v. Mills & Co.* [1920] 1 Ch. 77). This general rule was however subject to the qualification that the company in general meeting could ratify issues of shares which would otherwise be in breach of the directors' fiduciary duty (*Bamford v. Bamford* [1970] Ch. 212).

The power of directors to issue shares is however now restricted by the statutory rules introduced by the 1980 Act. Section 14 of that Act sets out detailed rules restricting the allotment of shares, and is supplemented by section 17, which introduces a general requirement that a company may not allot new shares for cash until after it has offered them to its existing shareholders (see below). Directors are now unable to allot shares unless they have obtained specific or general authority from the company. (It must also be remembered that *private* limited companies are prohibited from offering their shares – or debentures – to the public. This topic is dealt with in the chapter *Prospectuses and Public Issues*.)

Director's powers

Section 14 of the 1980 Act regulates the authority of the directors to issue shares. Under section 14(1), the directors of a company are not permitted to exercise any power of the company to allot "relevant securities", unless they are authorised in accordance with section 14 either by the company in general meeting or under the articles. For this purpose, an "allotment" of shares is treated as the acquisition of an unconditional right to be included in the company's register of members in respect of those shares (section 87(2) of the 1980 Act).

Relevant securities

The term "relevant securities" is defined in section 14(10) as meaning,

(a) shares in the company other than shares shown in the memorandum to have been taken by the subscribers thereto or shares allotted in pursuance of an employees' share scheme (as defined in section 87(1), see below); and

(b) any right to subscribe for, or to convert, any security into shares in the company other than shares so allotted.

The reference to a right to subscribe is presumably intended to include options and the issue of loan stock convertible at the option of the stockholder. It is the *grant* of the right and not the subsequent allotment of shares pursuant to that right which is controlled by section 14. It is not clear whether the grant of a conditional right to subscribe for shares (for example an option dependent upon the results of the company) could fall within these provisions; by analogy with section 87(2) it would appear that the grant of a conditional right (in the same way as a conditional allotment) is not covered by section 14. This would mean that any allotment of shares pursuant to the exercise of a conditional right which had become unconditional would itself fall within section 14(1) and would require to be covered by the requisite authority.

Exemptions

Logically, subscribers shares are excluded. So too are shares allotted in pursuance of an employees' share scheme. Such a scheme is defined in section 87(1) of the 1980 Act as meaning a scheme for encouraging or facilitating the holding of shares or debentures in a company by or for the benefit of,

(a) the bona fide employees or former employees of the company, the company's subsidiary or holding company or a subsidiary of the company's holding company; or

(b) the wives, husbands, widows, widowers or children or step-children under the age of 18 of such employees or former employees.

The authority to allot

There are detailed provisions in section 14 concerning the authority required to enable directors to allot relevant securities,

(a) the authority may be given for a particular exercise of the power or for the exercise of that power generally, and may be unconditional or subject to conditions;

(b) the authority *must* state the *maximum amount* of relevant securities that may be allotted under it and the date on which the authority will expire. That date is not to be more than *five years* from the date of incorporation of the company where the authority is contained at that time in the articles, or *five years* from the date of the ordinary resolution by virtue of which that authority is given;

(c) any authority (including an authority contained in the articles) may be revoked or varied within the five year period, again by *ordinary* resolution;

(d) the authority may be renewed from time to time (and any number of times), again by means of ordinary resolution, for a further period not exceeding five years. The renewal resolution must state (or restate) the amount of relevant securities which may be allotted under the authority or, as the case may be, the amount remaining to be allotted. It must also specify the date on which the renewed authority will expire. In practice most major companies, including listed companies, will probably renew the authority annually at the annual general meeting; and

(e) an important point to note is that the resolution giving the directors authority may be an *ordinary* resolution even if this alters the articles. (Ordinarily, a *special* resolution is required for such alteration: section 10 of the 1948 Act.) However, it is provided that the resolution giving, varying, revoking or renewing the authority must be filed with the Registrar of Companies under section 143 of the 1948 Act, even though an ordinary and not a special resolution.

Once the authority has been given the directors have the power to allot "relevant securities". That power also extends to an allotment after the five-year period has expired provided it is pursuant to an offer or agreement made by the company before the expiry of the authority, and the authority itself allowed the company to make an offer or agreement which would or might require relevant securities to be allotted after the expiry date.

Breach of section 14

Section 14 is accompanied by criminal sanctions which provide that any director who knowingly and wilfully contravenes, or permits or authorises a contravention of, section 14 shall be liable on conviction on indictment to a fine and on summary conviction to a fine not exceeding the statutory maximum (currently £1,000). However, the allotment itself is not invalidated even if the directors do not have the requisite authority (section 14(8)), even if the allottee has actual or constructive knowledge that the directors are exceeding their authority.

As explained below, in order for the pre-emption provisions of section 17 of the 1980 Act to be overriden, it is first necessary that the directors of the company have a general or specific authority to allot the shares in question under section 17. A section 14 authority is thus a pre-requisite of a special resolution overriding section 17. Both the Council for the Securities Industry and the Investment Protection Committee of the British Insurance Association have issued memoranda dealing with sections 14 and 17 in relation to listed companies. These are reproduced on page 828 below.

A practical method of ensuring directors have reasonable powers to allot shares would be to give them authority to allot the unissued shares of the company for the maximum of five years, renewing the five year authority at each annual general meeting (waiting until the five years are about to expire may be unwise because time limits are easily forgotten). The shareholders have an effective curb over the directors abusing their powers because their sanction is required before the authorised capital can be increased (assuming the company does not have a very large authorised but unissued capital to start with). It may be worth amending the company's articles to provide that the resolution at each annual general meeting is not "special" business, to avoid having to comply each year with the notice requirements for special business.

Pre-emption rights on issue

The ability of a company, or its directors, to issue shares to persons other than existing members is curtailed by section 17 of the 1980 Act (this is in addition to any pre-emption provisions *on transfer* of shares contained in the articles, which are discussed at page 851 below).

Section 17(1) provides that, subject to certain exceptions considered below, a company proposing to allot any equity securities,

(a) shall not allot any of those securities on any terms to any person unless it has made an offer to each person who holds "relevant shares" or "relevant employee shares" to allot to him on the same or more favourable terms a proportion of those securities which is as nearly as practicable equal to the proportion in nominal value held by him of the aggregate of relevant shares and relevant employee shares; and

(b) shall not allot any of those securities to any person unless the period during which any such offer may be accepted has expired or the company has received notice of the acceptance or refusal of every offer so made.

Equity securities

The section 17 prohibition relates only to "equity securities". Section 17(11) provides that an equity security means a *"relevant share"* in the company (other than subscribers shares or bonus shares) or a right to subscribe for, or to convert any securities into, relevant shares in the company. The reference to a grant of a right to subscribe for shares is equated (as in section 14) with an allotment of shares. Similarly, the allotment of shares pursuant to the grant of such a right is not prohibited under section 17. The other important definition is that of "relevant shares", which basically means all shares in the company other than shares held under an employees' share scheme (defined as above), or shares which as respects dividends and capital carry a right to participate only up to a specified amount in a distribution. This would basically cover non-participating preference shares and shares of a similar class. Debentures and loan stock are excluded, provided they are not convertible into shares, as are subscribers' shares and bonus shares: see above.

For the purposes of the section 17(1) offer, articles 131, 132 and 133 of Table A are imported into section 17 so as to provide for service of notices etc. In the case of the holder of a share warrant, the offer may be made by notice published in the London (or Edinburgh) *Gazette*. Members with a non-U.K. address need not be given notice of the allotment.

The offer must state a period of not less than 21 days during which it may be accepted; and the offer may not be withdrawn before the end of that period. The reference to the 21-day period must be a reference to *clear* days in common with other notice provisions in the Companies Acts.

There are special provisions where shares of a particular class are proposed to be issued. For this purpose a class is defined as meaning one where the shares carry the same rights as to voting and as to participation, both as respects dividends and as respects capital, in a distribution. The shares must first be offered pro rata to the existing members of the class. But any shares not taken up must then be offered to all the members of the company, not just those of the class.

Where, in relation to shares of a particular class, there are existing pre-emption rights similar to those in section 17(1) either in the memorandum or articles which require shares of that class to be offered to members of that class in priority to other members, those provisions will prevail provided the offeree or any person in whose favour he has renounced his right to the allotment accepts the offer.

Shares issued for non-cash consideration

One important qualification to the pre-emption rights is contained in section 17(4). That section provides that the pre-emption provisions shall not be applicable if the equity securities in question are, or are to be, wholly or partly paid up *otherwise than in cash*. Thus if (subject to the special restrictions on public companies considered below) a company wishes to allot shares otherwise than for cash, the pre-emption provisions will not afford any protection to existing shareholders. For instance, the provisions do not apply to shares issued on a share for share exchange.

It is clear that shares may be allotted under the provisions of section 17 by means of renounceable letters of allotment. (This is *required* in the case of listed companies). A person in whose favour the allotment has been renounced may be allotted shares notwithstanding the pre-emption provisions (see section 17(4)).

The pre-emption provisions do not apply at all to an employees' share scheme (section 17(5)).

Exclusion of pre-emption rights

Under section 17(9) the pre-emption rights may, in the case of a *private* company, be excluded entirely by a provision contained in the memorandum or articles. In addition, any requirement or authority contained in the memorandum or articles of a private company will operate to exclude the statutory pre-emption provisions if it is *inconsistent with* those provisions. Thus, a private company may insert its own specific pre-emption provisions into the articles which will operate to exclude the section 17 rules. For many private companies this may well be an advisable step given the strict, and basically inflexible, terms of section 17 itself and also the liabilities attaching to the company and its officers under section 17(10).

Under section 17(10), the company and any officer who knowingly authorises or permits a contravention of the pre-emption provisions (or the notice requirements) is jointly and severally liable to compensate any person for any loss, damage, costs or expenses which that person has sustained or incurred by reason of the contravention. Proceedings against the company and its officers must be commenced not later than the expiration of two years from the delivery to the Registrar of Companies of the return of allotments in question or, where equity securities other than shares are granted, from the date of the grant.

Disapplication of pre-emption rights

The exclusion of pre-emption rights in section 17(9) is confined to private companies. Under section 18, however, any company, public or private, may disapply the pre-emption rights. The disapplication provisions apply in two separate circumstances. The first is where the directors have been given a *general* authority to allot relevant securities under section 14 of the 1980 Act. The second is where the directors have been given a *general or specific* authority under that section.

Where a *general* authority has been given the directors may be given a further power *by the articles* or *by special resolution* to allot equity securities pursuant to that authority either without regard to the pre-emption provisions of section 17(1) or with such modifications to those provisions as the directors may determine.

Where the directors have a *general or specific* authority, the company may by *special resolution* resolve that the pre-emption provisions shall not apply to a *specified allotment* of equity securities to be made pursuant to that authority, or that the pre-emption provisions shall apply to that allotment with such modifications as may be specified *in the resolution* (section 18(2)). Where such a special resolution is proposed, or there is a special resolution to renew such a resolution, it must be recommended by the directors and there must previously have been circulated, with the notice of meeting at which the resolution is proposed, a written statement by the directors setting out,

(a) their reasons for making the recommendation;

(b) the amount to be paid to the company in respect of the equity securities to be allotted; and

(c) the directors' justification of that amount.

Whether a general or specific authority is given to the directors under section 18, that authority has a life limited to the life of the authority of the directors to allot relevant securities under section 14 (see above – in other words a maximum life of five years). If, however, the section 14 authority is renewed, the disapplication of the pre-emption rights may also be renewed by special resolution. In common with the section 14 rules, the expiry of the disapplication resolution will not prejudice a future allotment of equity securities pursuant to an offer or agreement made within the time limit, provided that the power or resolution enables the company to make an offer or agreement which would or might require equity securities to be allotted after it expired.

It is to be expected that many companies, both public and private, will seek to disapply the pre-emption provisions contained in section 17. In the case of a listed company, there are several compelling reasons why this course should be adopted,

(1) in the case of certain overseas shareholders it is often desirable in a rights issue not to issue equity securities but instead to give those holders the money's worth of their rights;

(2) the 21 day period in section 17 (being *clear* days) does not correspond with the period required by The Stock Exchange for acceptance of a rights issue (see further page 762);

(3) in certain cases under section 17 advertisement is required in the Gazette, which is a tiresome procedure; and

(4) it may be in the best interests of the company to issue small amounts of shares in special cases otherwise than pro rata to existing shareholders (e.g. in connection with an overseas acquisition).

Where the pre-emption provisions in section 17 have been disapplied, it seems that an individual shareholder cannot complain where he is excluded from participating in a share issue provided the directors have acted in good faith in the interests of the company and have acted fairly between the different classes, if any, of shareholders (*Mutual Life Insurance Co of New York v. Rank Organisation Limited* (1982) 3 Co Law 176: U.S. shareholders excluded from preferential share issue for SEC reasons).

Guidelines for listed companies

The Council for the Securities Industry issued the following memorandum on July 16, 1981 giving some general guidance on sections 14 and 17 for listed companies.

"(1) The question has been raised how companies should proceed if, when making issues of equity securities for cash, they wish to maintain the broad principle of pre-emption rights for shareholders (as provided in s. 17(1) of the Companies Act 1980), but at the same time wish to empower directors of the company to issue equity securities for cash, in certain circumstances, without pre-emption rights.

(2) Where the directors are, for the purposes of s. 14 of the Companies Act 1980, generally authorised to allot equity securities, s. 18(1) contains provisions under which they may be empowered to allot securities pursuant to that authority as if s. 17(1) did not apply to that allotment. The use of these provisions in this way would permit s. 17(1) to be disapplied and enable any conditions which it was thought fit to attach to the exercise by the directors of the authority conferred on them in accordance with s. 14 to be imposed by the shareholders either by resolution or under the articles of association.

(3) The circumstances in which a company might wish to make allotments of equity securities (for cash), otherwise than *pro rata* to existing equity shareholders, include –

(a) small issues of shares up to (say) 5% of the authorised share capital, in special circumstances, for example, in connection with an overseas listing or with a vendor placing in respect of an overseas acquisition [for which see the *Law Society's Gazette*, September 1, 1982],

(b) to cater for certain overseas shareholders in a rights issue of equity shares by giving them instead the money's worth of the rights.

(4) The Department of Trade have indicated that, in their view, the objectives outlined above can be achieved under the existing powers in ss. 14, 17 and 18 of the 1980 Act.

(5) The precise form and content of resolutions designed to take advantage of the statutory provisions are matters which companies will wish to determine for themselves, having regard to their own particular circumstances and with any necessary assistance from their legal advisers.

(6) One possible course is for the company –

(a) by ordinary resolution under s. 14 to authorise the board of directors to exercise all powers of the company to allot relevant securities (within the meaning of s. 14) up to an aggregate nominal amount of £. . . (it is for the company to determine whether the authority should be for one year or for a longer period up to the five years allowed under the section); and

(b) by special resolution under s. 18 to authorise the board of directors to allot equity securities (within the meaning of s. 17) pursuant to the authority conferred by the previous resolution as if subs. (1) of the said s. 17 did not apply to any such allotment provided that this power shall be limited –

(i) to the allotment of equity securities in connection with a rights issue in favour of ordinary shareholders where the equity securities respectively attributable to the interests of all ordinary shareholders are proportionate (as nearly as may be) to the respective numbers of ordinary shares held by them; and

(ii) to the allotment (otherwise than pursuant to subpara (i) above) of equity securities up to an aggregate nominal value of £. . .

(7) Institutional shareholders have informed the CSI of the importance they attach to the pre-emptive rights of all shareholders. Accordingly, they will support resolu-

tions on the lines indicated in para (6) above, on the understanding that disapplications for cash issues, other than by way of rights, will be on an annually renewable basis and will not exceed 5% of the authorised equity capital which they believe to be sufficient to meet the requirements of most companies.

(8) The Stock Exchange intends to retain the requirement under the listing agreement that any issue for cash of equity capital, otherwise than *pro rata* to existing equity shareholders, has to be referred to the Stock Exchange. The Stock Exchange will normally require (except in certain special circumstances) the issue to be specifically approved by a general meeting of shareholders, notwithstanding the fact that it is within the scope of a general authority previously conferred on the basis outlined above."

With reference to paragraph (7) of the above memorandum, the Investment Protection Committee of the British Insurance Association has stated that its members will be prepared to accept resolutions of the following type (the resolutions need not follow the precise wording),

"Ordinary Resolution

(1) That the board be and it is hereby generally and unconditionally authorised to exercise all powers of the company to allot relevant securities (within the meaning of s. 14 of the Companies Act 1980) up to an aggregate nominal amount of £A[1] provided that this authority shall expire on the date of the next annual general meeting after the passing of this resolution save that the company may before such expiry make an offer or agreement which would or might require relevant securities to be allotted after such expiry and the board may allot relevant securities in pursuance of such offer or agreement as if the authority conferred hereby had not expired.

Special Resolution

(2) That subject to the passing of the previous resolution and to the provisions of ss. 17 and 18 of the Companies Act 1980 becoming applicable to the company the board be and it is hereby empowered pursuant to the said s. 18 to allot equity securities (within the meaning of the said s. 17) for cash pursuant to the authority conferred by the previous resolution as if subs. (1) of the said s. 17 did not apply to any such allotment provided that this power shall be limited –

(a) to the allotment of equity securities in connection with a rights issue in favour of ordinary shareholders where the equity securities respectively attributable to the interests of all ordinary shareholders are proportionate (as nearly as may be) to the respective numbers of ordinary shares held by them; and

(b) to the allotment (otherwise than pursuant to subpara (a) above) of equity securities up to an aggregate nominal value of £B[2]—

and shall expire on the date of the next annual general meeting of the company after the passing of this resolution save that the company may before such expiry make an offer or agreement which would or might require equity securities to be allotted after such expiry and the board may allot equity securities in pursuance of such offer or agreement as if the power conferred hereby had not expired.

[1]The figure inserted at A should be the lesser of (i) the unissued equity capital, or (ii) a sum equal to one-third of the issued capital of the company, except where special arrangements have been made.

[2]The figure inserted at B should be not more than 5% of the aggregate of the sum authorised under (1) above and the issued ordinary share capital."

Listed companies are, of course, also bound by the Listing Agreement with The Stock Exchange to obtain approval by ordinary resolution – in the absence of Stock Exchange dispensation – for the issue of shares, convertible securities, warrants or options otherwise than to existing shareholders pro rata to their existing shareholdings (and see paragraph (8) of the CSI statement above).

Issue at a premium

It has been noted above that shares in a limited company are required to have a nominal or par value, and it will be seen that, save for wholly exceptional cases, there is an absolute prohibition on the allotment of shares at a discount. However, it is clear that from time to time the shares in a company may stand at a premium viz. they may have a greater value than their nominal or par value. In such circumstances, a company is permitted to issue shares at a premium subject to the provisions of section 56 of the Companies Act 1948 (as amended).

There is no overriding rule of law that, where the shares in a company are standing at a premium, no issue may be made at a price which does not take full account of the premium element, but such an issue by a company may, in certain circumstances, involve the directors in a breach of fiduciary duty, and may afford a remedy to shareholders the value of whose holdings have depreciated as a result of an issue at an undervalue.

Section 56 of the 1948 Act provides that where a company issues shares at a premium, whether for cash *or otherwise*, a sum equal to the aggregate amount or value of the premiums on those shares is to be transferred to a share premium account. The words "or otherwise" were considered in *Henry Head & Co. v. Ropner Holdings* [1952] Ch. 124 where it was held that where shares are issued for a consideration other than cash and the value of the assets acquired is more than the nominal value of the shares issued, the excess must be transferred to share premium account. This was confirmed in the more recent case of *Shearer v. Bercain* [1980] STC 359, a case concerned with merger accounting which has been partially reversed by the Companies Act 1981 and which is considered in more detail in the chapter *Takeovers*.

In general terms, a share premium account is treated in a similar way to the chapter share capital itself. Thus, it may only be reduced under the reduction of capital procedure contained in section 66 of the 1948 Act or on an own-share purchase under section 54(5) of the 1981 Act (see pages 713 and 683). Nevertheless, under section 56(2) of the 1948 Act the share premium account may be applied by the company,

(a) in paying up unissued shares of the company to be allotted to members of the company as fully paid bonus shares;

(b) in writing off the preliminary expenses of the company;

(c) in writing off the expenses of, or the commission paid or discount allowed on, any issue of shares or debentures of the company; and

(d) in providing for the premium payable on redemption of any debentures of the company. (The former power to pay a premium on redemption of redeemable preference shares was repealed by the 1981 Act, subject to transitional provisions which are referred to in the chapter *Redeemable Shares*.)

Payment for shares

Under section 29 of the Companies Act 1980, subscribers' shares in the case of a *public* company together with any premium thereon must be paid up in cash. For payment to constitute payment in cash, the consideration must be one of the following (section 87(3) C.A. 1980),

(a) cash received by the company;

(b) a cheque received by the company in good faith which the directors have no reason for suspecting will not be paid;

(c) the release of a liability of the company for a liquidated sum; or

(d) an undertaking to pay cash to the company at a future date.

The expression "cash" includes foreign currency.

Apart from such subscribers' shares, and subject to detailed provisions concerning *public* companies which are discussed below, the shares allotted by any company together with any premium may be paid up in money or money's worth, including goodwill and know-how (section 20 of the Companies Act 1980). This requirement does not, however, preclude bonus issues (see section 20(5) and the chapter *Bonus Issues*).

In the case of a *public* company section 20(2) prohibits the allotment of shares in return for an undertaking given by any person that he or any other should do work or perform services for the company or any other person. There is no such restriction in the case of a *private* company, and the court will not go behind any such arrangement made by the company to enquire whether what is given for the shares has a cash value in the market equal to the nominal value of the shares (*Re Theatrical Trust Limited, Chapman's Case* [1895] 1 Ch. 771). However, if the consideration is illusory then the allottee will remain bound to pay up the nominal value of the shares.

Section 20(3) contains sanctions where a public company accepts an undertaking in payment up of its shares. This in effect requires the holder of the shares to make payment to the company of such amount as has been treated as having been paid up by the undertaking, together with interest at the appropriate rate. A purchaser for value without actual notice is protected by section 20(4), as is a person acquiring title through the holder; other holders are jointly and severally liable with the original holder.

Relief may be available in respect of contravention of section 20(2) under section 28 of the 1980 Act, which is considered below. In addition, it should be noted that the undertaking to perform services remains enforceable notwithstanding a contravention of the statutory provisions (section 30(2) of the 1980 Act).

A number of other provisions in the Companies Act 1980 in connection with payment for shares refer specifically to *public* companies. This expression includes companies in the course of registering or re-registering as such (section 31(1) of the 1980 Act). The provisions are as follows.

Payment for allotted shares

Except in one case (shares allotted in pursuance of an employees' share scheme), a *public* company is not permitted to allot a share except as paid up at least as to *one-quarter* of its nominal value, together with the *whole* of any premium (section 22 of the Companies Act 1980).

If a public company allots a share in contravention of this restriction, section 22(2) treats the share as paid up as to one-quarter of the nominal value and the entire premium, and the allottee is liable to pay up so much of the minimum amount which should have been received as has not already been paid, together with interest at the appropriate rate.

Subsequent holders may be jointly and severally liable with the original holder of the shares, except where they purchased for value and without notice of the contravention or they derived title from such a purchaser (section 20(4) as applied by section 22(5) of the 1980 Act).

Section 22 does not apply to a bonus share unless the allottee knew or ought to have known that the share had been issued in contravention of section 22(1): section 22(3).

Payment of non-cash consideration

Restrictions are placed on a *public* company allotting shares paid up (wholly or in part) otherwise than in cash if the consideration for the allotment is or includes an undertaking which is to be or may be performed more than five years after the date of the allotment (section 23(1) of the Companies Act 1980). It is important to note that section 23(1) refers to an undertaking which *may be* performed more than five years after the allotment; this indicates that if there is any possibility (however remote) that performance may take place after the five-year period, then the shares may not properly be allotted.

If, in fact, shares are allotted in contravention of section 23(1), then section 23(2) provides that the allottee remains liable to make payment to the company of such amount of the nominal value and premium element of the shares as has been treated as paid up by the undertaking, together with interest at the appropriate rate.

The section cannot be evaded by a company entering into a contract the performance of which will take place within the five-year period, and then varying the terms of that contract. Sections 23(3) and (4) provide that a variation of the contract (including a contract entered into before the company was re-registered as a public company) which has the effect of contravening section 23(1) is void.

A subsequent holder of shares who has given value and who does not have actual notice of the contravention of section 23 will not be liable to make the payment specified in section 23(2). This also applies to any person deriving title from such a holder (section 20(4) of the 1980 Act as applied by section 23(6)). Other subsequent holders remain jointly and severally liable.

Provisions also exist to cover the position where, at the time the undertaking is given it was to be performed within the five-year period, yet performance within that period does not in fact take place. Under section 23(5) the allottee incurs a liability at the end of the five-year period to make payment to the company of the relevant amount, together with interest at the appropriate rate, which also starts to run at the end of the five-year period.

Relief in respect of contravention of section 23 is available under section 28 of the Companies Act 1980 (see below). In addition, the undertaking in respect of which the shares are allotted will be enforceable notwithstanding any breach of the section (see C.A. 1980, s. 30(2)).

Non-cash consideration: expert's report

Except in the limited case of a share for share exchange or merger, a *public* company is not permitted to allot shares as paid up (in whole or in part) as to their nominal value or any premium *otherwise than in cash* unless,

(a) the consideration for the allotment has been valued in accordance with the provisions set out below;

(b) a report with respect to its value has been made to the company by a person appointed by the company under those provisions during the six months immediately preceding the allotment of the shares; and

(c) a copy of the report has been sent to the proposed allottee of the shares (section 24(1) of the 1980 Act).

The valuation and report must (under section 24(4)) generally be made by an *independent person*, who is defined as a person qualified at the time of the report to be appointed or to continue to be the auditor of the company. Accordingly the existing auditor may make the report. (For the provisions as to qualification to be auditor of the company see section 161(2) of the 1948 Act and the chapter *Auditors*.) The independent person may, however, find that a specialist valuation of the consideration, or a part of it, is necessary. In such a case, he is at liberty to commission or accept a valuation and report made by an expert, provided that the expert is not an officer or servant (but he can be the auditor) of,

(a) the company or any other body corporate which is that company's subsidiary or holding company; or

(b) a subsidiary of that company's holding company; or

(c) a partner or employee of such officer or servant.

Contents of report

Section 24(5) sets out the matters which must be stated in the report of the independent person,

(a) the nominal value of the shares to be wholly or partly paid for by the consideration in question;

(b) the amount of any premium payable on those shares;

(c) the description of the consideration and, as respects so much of the consideration as he himself has valued, a description of that part of the consideration, the method used to value it and the date of the valuation; and

(d) the extent to which the nominal value of the shares and any premium are to be treated as paid up (i) by the consideration, and (ii) in cash.

In addition, if any part of the consideration is valued by an expert under section 24(4), the report must state the following three additional items (section 24(6)),

(i) the fact that such a valuation was made;

(ii) the name of the expert and what knowledge and experience he has to carry out the valuation; and

(iii) a description of the part of the consideration valued by the expert, the method used to value it, and the date of valuation.

Whether or not an expert's valuation is made in addition to the report of the independent person, the report must contain or be accompanied by a note made by the independent person to the following effect (section 24(7)),

(a) in the case of a valuation made by an expert, that it appeared to the independent person reasonable to arrange for it to be so made or to accept a valuation so made;

(b) that, whoever made the valuation, the method of valuation was reasonable in all the circumstances;

(c) that it appears to the independent person that there has been no material change in the value of the consideration in question since the valuation; and

(d) that on the basis of the valuation, the value of the consideration, together with any cash by which the nominal value of the shares or any premium payable on them is to be paid up, is not less than so much of the aggregate of the nominal value and the whole of any such premium as is treated as paid up by the consideration and any such cash.

In cases where only part of the consideration given to the company is accepted in payment for the shares (or any premium on the shares), the report must cover that part of the consideration and, additionally,

(i) the independent person must carry out or arrange for such other valuations as will enable him to determine the proportion of the consideration properly attributable to the payment up of the nominal value and any premium; and

(ii) his report must state what valuations have been made in this connection and also the reason for and method and date of any such valuation and any other matters which may be relevant to that determination.

Obtaining of information

Section 25 of the 1980 Act contains supplemental provisions enabling the independent person (or an expert valuer) to obtain from officers of the company such information and explanations as he thinks necessary to enable the valuation and report to be made. False, misleading or deceptive statements can lead to criminal sanctions as set out in section 25(5).

Effect of contravention

Where a public company allots any share in contravention of section 24 and either,

(a) the allottee has not received a copy of the report; or

(b) there has been some other contravention of section 24 and the allottee knew or ought to have known that it amounted to a contravention,

then the allottee and any subsequent holder are jointly and severally liable to pay to the company in cash such part of the nominal amount of the shares plus any premium, together with interest at the appropriate rate, as was represented by the non-cash consideration. Protection is given for bona fide purchasers for value without notice, and subsequent holders of the shares who acquired the shares through a holder who was not liable under the section (see section 20(4) of the 1980 Act).

Transactions outside the scope of the section

It is specifically provided in section 24(2) that certain transactions do not fall within the provisions requiring the preparation of an expert's report. These are, broadly,

(a) acquisition situations, where there is an arrangement whereby the whole or part of the consideration for the allotment consists of the transfer or cancellation of shares (or a class of shares) or some of those shares, whether or not there is an issue of shares to the company. This would include a takeover and schemes of reconstruction or amalgamation within section 206 and section 287 of the Companies Act 1948. However, the arrangement must be open to all shareholders or holders of shares of the class in question, except that shares held by nominees of the company or its associates are disregarded;

(b) a proposed merger of the company with another company. A *merger* is defined in this context as the acquisition by one company of *all* the assets and liabilities of another in exchange for shares or other securities to be issued to the other company's shareholders, with or without any cash payment. The exception does not extend to cases where the shares are issued to the company, as opposed to the shareholders, which is selling the non-cash asset. But it seems there is nothing to prevent the assets first being transferred to a new private company, with the public company then issuing shares for the shares in the new company.

Prior to the Companies Act 1981, there was some doubt whether, having regard to the definition of "non-cash consideration" in section 87(3) of the 1980 Act, a bonus issue of shares by a public company could fall within the provisions requiring preparation of an expert's report. The position was clarified "for the avoidance of doubt" by a new sub-section (11A) of section 24 which provides that such issues fall outside these provisions.

It appears that section 24 does not prevent an allotment for cash where the cash is immediately applied in purchasing non-cash assets, even if the seller is the allottee. Nor, it appears, is the issue of a convertible debenture for non-cash assets prevented, even if the debenture is converted into equity shares almost immediately: see section 87(4) of the 1980 Act.

Registration

A copy of the independent person's report must be delivered to the Registrar of Companies at the same time as the return of allotments required under section 52 of the Companies Act 1948, i.e. within one month after the date of allotment of the shares in question.

Payment by companies for non-cash assets

Section 26 of the Companies Act 1980 contains special provisions prohibiting certain companies from entering into agreements with a *relevant person* for the transfer by that person during the *initial period* of a non-cash asset to the company (or another person), where the consideration given by the company is equal to at least one-tenth of the *nominal* value of the company's issued share capital at the time of the agreement.

Whether a person is a *relevant person* or not for these purposes, and the appropriate *initial period*, can be determined from the following table:

Company	Relevant person	Initial period
Formed as a public company under C.A. 1980	Subscriber to memorandum	Two years from date of issue of certificate under C.A. 1980, s. 4 that company is entitled to do business

Company	Relevant person	Initial period
Private company re-registered as a public company under C.A. 1980, s. 13*	Any person who was a member of the company on the date of re-registration or registration	Two years from the date of re-registration or registration
or		
Joint stock company registered as public company		
Old public company re-registered as public company under C.A. 1980, s. 8	Section 26 provisions not applicable	

*This includes a company which was formerly a public company but which re-registered as a private company under C.A. 1980, s. 10

The meaning of "non-cash asset", and whether such an asset will be treated as having been transferred, is dealt with by section 87 of the 1980 Act. A non-cash asset is defined as meaning any property or interest in property other than cash (sterling or foreign currency). The ordinary meaning of "transfer" is extended very widely by section 87(4). This provides that any reference to the transfer or acquisition of a non-cash asset includes a reference to the creation or extinction of an estate or interest in, or a right over, any property and also a reference to the discharge of any person's liability, other than a liability for a liquidated sum. This effectively covers not only outright transfers of ownership but, for example, the grant of a patent licence, a lease, or an option, and the performance of a company's obligations to a third party.

The prohibition on such agreements can be circumvented only if certain conditions are satisfied. Those conditions can be found in section 26(3) and are as follows,

(a) the consideration to be received by the company (or the advantage to be derived by the company) and any consideration other than cash to be given by the company must have been valued in accordance with section 26;

(b) a report with respect to the consideration to be received and given must be made to the company during the six months immediately preceding the date of the agreement;

(c) the terms of the agreement must be approved by an *ordinary* resolution of the company; and

(d) not later than the giving of the notice of the meeting at which the resolution is proposed, copies of the resolution and report must be circulated to the members of the company entitled to receive that notice and, if the relevant person is not then such a member, to that person.

It should be noted that the requirement for a report and valuation under section 26 does not obviate the corresponding, and more general, requirement under section 24 of the 1980 Act (considered above). In certain cases, *both* sections may be applicable.

Contents of report

In addition to satisfying the requirements of section 24(4) and (6) of the 1980 Act (as to which see above), the report of the independent person under section 26 must also,

(a)   state (i) the consideration to be received by the company, describing the asset in question, specifying the amount to be received in cash, and (ii) the consideration to be given by the company, specifying the amount to be given in cash;

(b)   state the method and date of valuation;

(c)   contain or be accompanied by a note to the following effect:

    (i)   in the case of a valuation made by a person other than the independent person, that it appeared to the independent person reasonable to arrange for it to be so made or to accept a valuation so made;

    (ii)   whoever made the valuation, that the method of valuation was reasonable in all the circumstances; and

    (iii)   that it appeared to the independent person that there has been no material change in the value of the consideration in question since the valuation;

(d)   contain or be accompanied by a note that on the basis of the valuation the value of the consideration to be received by the company is not less than the value of the consideration to be given by it.

The provisions of section 26 apply equally to cases where only a part of the consideration in question is given for the transfer of non-cash assets. In such a case, the independent person must carry out or arrange for such valuations as will enable him to determine the proportion of the consideration so attributable, and the report must set out details of that valuation (section 27(3) of the 1980 Act).

Obtaining of information

The independent person, or the expert valuer, is entitled to require from the officers of the company such information and explanations as he thinks necessary to enable him to carry out the valuation or make his report. There are criminal sanctions for false, misleading or deceptive statements.

Effect of contravention

If the company enters into an agreement with a relevant person in contravention of the prohibition contained in section 26(1) and either that person has not received a report, or there has been some other contravention which was known or ought to have been known by the relevant person then, unless the agreement is or includes an agreement for the allotment of shares in that company (when section 24(9) of the 1980 Act will apply),

(a) the company is entitled to recover from the relevant person any consideration given by the company under the agreement or an amount equivalent to its value at the time of the agreement; and

(b) the agreement is void, except insofar as it may already have been carried out.

Registration

A copy of the ordinary resolution passed under section 26(3) must be delivered to the Registrar of Companies within 15 days of the passing of the resolution, together with a copy of the report. There are penalties for failure to register (see section 27(2) of the 1980 Act).

Payment for shares provisions: relief

Reference has been made above to certain special reliefs which are contained in section 28 of the Companies Act 1980. That section provides for a person who incurs liability under various provisions to make an application to the court to be exempted in whole or in part from that liability. The relevant provisions, all of which are contained in the 1980 Act, are

(a) section 20 (undertaking to perform work or services);

(b) section 23 (payment of non-cash consideration);

(c) section 24 (allotment of shares for non-cash consideration); and

(d) section 26 (transfer of non-cash assets by relevant persons).

Where liability arises in relation to a payment in respect of shares (but not in relation to an undertaking given to the company) the court has power to exempt the applicant from the primary liability and a liability in respect of interest if and to the extent that it appears to the court just and equitable to do so. In relation to the primary liability the court is directed to have regard to the following matters,

(i) whether the applicant has paid, or is liable to pay, any amount in respect of any other liability arising in relation to the shares in question under any of the relevant sections or of any liability arising by virtue of any undertaking given in or in connection with payment for those shares;

(ii) whether any person other than the applicant has paid or is likely to pay (whether in pursuance of an order of the court or otherwise) any such amount; and

(iii) whether the applicant or any other person has performed, in whole or in part, or is likely so to perform any such undertaking or has done or is likely to do any other thing in payment or part payment in respect of those shares.

Where the liability arises by virtue of an undertaking given to the company in, or in connection with, payment for any shares in the company, the court has similar powers to exempt the applicant from liability on a just and equitable basis but is directed to have regard to the following matters,

(a) whether the applicant has paid or is liable to pay any amount in respect of any liability arising in relation to those shares under the relevant sections; and

(b) whether any person other than the applicant has paid or is likely to pay (whether in pursuance of an order of the court or otherwise) any such amount (section 28(3) of the 1980 Act).

Apart from being required to consider the various matters outlined above, section 28(4) also sets out certain overriding principles which must be observed by the court in considering its order. These are,

(a) that a company which has allotted shares should receive money or money's worth at least equal in value to the aggregate of the nominal value of those shares and the whole of any premium or, if the case so requires, so much of that aggregate as is treated as paid up; and

(b) subject to that overriding principle, that where such a company would, if the court did not grant the exemption, have more than one remedy against a particular person, it should be for the company to decide which remedy it should remain entitled to pursue.

Where a liability to the company can fall upon several persons, section 28(5) deals with the case where a person brings proceedings against another person for a contribution. Such joint and several liability arises in relation to the relevant sections referred to above (sections 20, 23, 24 and 26), and also in relation to section 21 (issue of shares at a discount) and section 22 (minimum payment). The court has power in such circumstances, having regard to the respective culpability of each person, on a just and equitable basis,

(a) to exempt the contributor in whole or in part from his liability to make such contribution; or

(b) order the contributor to make a larger contribution than, but for the order of the court, he would be liable to make.

Finally, a person can be exempted in whole or in part from liability under section 26(7)(a) of the 1980 Act (recovery from "relevant person" where no expert's report) if and to the extent that it appears to the court just and equitable to do so having regard to any benefit accruing to the company by virtue of anything done by that person towards the carrying out of the agreement mentioned in that section.

Sanctions for contravention

There are criminal sanctions attaching to the company and any officer of the company in default for contravention of any of the provisions of sections 20 to 24, 26 and 29 of the Companies Act 1980 (see section 30(1)). In addition, subject to any relief which may be obtained under section 28 (see above), an undertaking given by any person in connection with payment for shares in a company, to do work or perform services or do any other thing is enforceable notwithstanding any contravention of section 20, 23 or 24 of the 1980 Act, and an undertaking given in contravention of section 26 is also enforceable provided it is in respect of the allotment of shares (section 30(2) of the 1980 Act).

Underwriting, commissions etc.

Where shares are issued to the public, it is common practice for the issue to be underwritten by an issuing house or broker. This is one method of ensuring a successful issue. It involves the issuing house or broker agreeing, in return for a commission, to subscribe or procure subscribers for the new issue of shares. The commission is payable by the company on the total number of shares underwritten whether or not the underwriters are called upon to take up shares not otherwise subscribed. Generally, the main underwriter will offer sub-underwriting participations to sub-underwriters at a lower rate of commission than the main commission rate. The balance will represent the main underwriter's profit which may, in some cases, also be supplemented by a fee.

The general company law principle of maintenance of capital is considered below. The payment of commissions out of the company's capital could be regarded in some respects as an issue of shares at a discount. For this reason, section 53(2) of the 1948 Act expressly prohibits a company from applying any of its *shares or capital money* either directly or indirectly in payment of any commission, discount or allowance to any person in consideration of his subscribing or agreeing to subscribe, whether absolutely or conditionally, for any shares in the company. The prohibition also extends to payments for procuring or agreeing to procure subscriptions. It is not only direct payments of commission which are prohibited; indirect payments, such as by means of the company acquiring property at an over-value, are also covered.

Section 53 itself provides exceptions to this general rule. Under subsection (1) it is lawful for a company to pay commission if,

(a) the payment is authorised by the articles;

(b) the amount of the commission paid or agreed to be paid does not exceed 10 per cent of the price at which the shares are issued or the amount or rate authorised by the articles, whichever is the less;

(c) the amount or rate of the commission paid or agreed to be paid is:

    (i) in the case of shares offered to the public for subscription, disclosed in the prospectus; or

    (ii) in the case of shares not offered to the public for subscription disclosed in a statement signed by or on behalf of the directors, and before the payment of the commission delivered to the Registrar of Companies, and, where a circular or notice which is not a prospectus is issued, also disclosed in that circular or notice; and

(d) the number of shares which persons have agreed for a commission to subscribe is also disclosed.

It is also provided by section 53(3) that lawful brokerage may be paid. Brokerage should not be confused with underwriting commission. Brokerage is payable to an issuing house or broker who arranges a *placing* of shares with others. It does not involve the issuing house or broker in having to subscribe for shares. The payment of brokerage must be authorised by the articles and must be reasonable. A rate of 0.25 per cent is not thought to be unreasonable in most cases.

In the case of a listed company, the underwriting agreement will be conditional on the grant of Stock Exchange permission to deal in, and quotation for, the new shares. The company will be required to provide warranties to the main underwriter that, for example, the company has no claims of material importance threatened against it and that full disclosure of all material facts has been made in the relevant circular or prospectus.

Calls

Although a share is required to have a nominal or par value, it may on occasions be issued as partly paid. As explained above and in the chapter *Formation and Types of Company*, a *public* company cannot allot shares unless at least one quarter of the nominal value plus the whole of any premium is paid up in full, but there is no such restriction for a private company. A call is the method by which the liability of a shareholder to make payment of the nominal amount of a share (together with any premium which the shareholder has agreed to pay) is crystallised and a debt created between the company and the shareholder. Subject to the articles, or any overriding agreement with the shareholder, a call can be made at any time unless the company has passed a special resolution under section 60 of the 1948 Act creating *reserve capital* which is not capable of being called up except in the event of a winding-up. Reserve capital is rarely created.

In general, calls in respect of the shares in a company, or any class of shares, must be made rateably on all members, or members of the same class, but under section 59(a) a company may make arrangements on the issue of shares for a difference between the shareholders in the amounts and times of payment of calls on their shares, provided it has the necessary authority in the articles. Article 20 of Table A provides this authority. Where a company has incorporated Table A into its articles, article 15 of Table A prevents any one call exceeding 25 per cent of the nominal value of the share, and requires calls to be at least one month apart.

Section 59 of the 1948 Act also provides that a company may, if authorised by the articles, accept a payment from a shareholder in advance of a call. Article 21 of Table A gives the necessary power to the directors to receive uncalled monies in advance and to pay interest at a rate not exceeding 5 per cent per annum or such rate as may be directed by the company in general meeting. It must be remembered that in all aspects of a call, whether in making a call or accepting a payment in advance, the directors must act bona fide in the best interests of the company.

The debt created by the making of a call is, in England, a specialty debt and as such the limitation period for recovery is twelve years. In addition to the creation of this debt, which may be enforced by action, article 18 of Table A provides for the shareholder who is in default to pay interest on the amount of the call at a rate not exceeding 5 per cent per annum to be determined by the directors. The directors are also given power to waive payment of all or any part of such interest. Furthermore, where there is default in payment, the company will have a lien over the shares for the amount of any call unpaid. In the case of public companies, there are restrictions on liens under section 38 of the 1980 Act; however, by section 38(2) a charge on a public company's own shares, not being fully paid, for any amount payable in respect of those shares, is expressly permitted (see the chapter *Charges over Shares*).

Forfeiture

In the case of default in the payment of a call or instalment, articles 33 to 39 of Table A provide a procedure for forfeiture of the shares. The procedure is broadly as follows,

(a) a notice is served on the shareholder requiring payment on a named date of the amount of the call or instalment due, together with interest. The notice must also state that in the event of non-payment the shares in respect of which the call is made will be liable to be forfeited;

(b) if the notice is not complied with, the directors must pass a resolution forfeiting the shares;

(c) on forfeiture, the shareholder ceases to be a member in respect of the forfeited shares, but remains liable to make payment of all monies due until those monies are received by the company; and

(d) the shares so forfeited can be sold by the directors, and it is provided that a statutory declaration by a director or the secretary as to forfeiture is conclusive evidence of this fact. When the shares are sold, or reissued, the company is empowered to execute a transfer of the shares in favour of the purchaser.

It is open to a shareholder to avoid forfeiture of his shares by surrendering those shares to the company. Once the shares have been surrendered, the same procedure applies as in the case of a forfeiture.

In the case of a *public* company, it should be noted that special provisions apply where shares have been forfeited or surrendered in lieu (see section 37 of the 1980 Act, discussed below).

Maintenance of capital

The maintenance of capital in relation to a company remains one of the cardinal principles of company law in spite of certain recent changes, notably in the Companies Act 1981. These changes include the ability of a private company to purchase its own shares out of capital, and the relaxation of the restrictions on the giving of financial assistance by a private company for the acquisition of shares (see section 43 of the 1981 Act). The Companies Act 1980, however, contains certain statutory rules particularly designed to prevent an unauthorised reduction of capital.

Issue at a discount

A company limited by shares has no power to issue shares as fully paid up for a money consideration less than their nominal value. This was the decision in *The Ooregum Gold Mining Company of India Limited v. Roper* [1892] A.C. 125, which is now contained in statutory form in section 21 of the Companies Act 1980. Section 21 replaced the previous provision – section 57 of the Companies Act 1948 – which in certain circumstances enabled a company to issue shares at a discount, subject to the sanction of the court. Section 57 was repealed by section 21(4) of the 1980 Act except in relation to pre-existing applications to the court.

Under section 21, if shares are allotted at a discount the allottee is liable to pay the company an amount equal to the amount of the discount together with interest thereon at the appropriate rate. This liability extends also (on a joint and several basis) to a purchaser or subsequent holder of the shares, except a purchaser for value who, at the time of the purchase, did not have *actual* notice of the contravention or who derived title to the shares (directly or indirectly) from a person who became a holder of them after issue and was not so liable (section 20(4) of the 1980 Act as applied by section 21(3)).

The appropriate rate of interest is 5 per cent per annum or such other rate as may be specified by order made by the Secretary of State by statutory instrument (section 87 of the 1980 Act).

Acquisition of a company's shares by the company

The long-established principle of company law that a company, other than an unlimited company, could not purchase its own shares (*Trevor v. Whitworth* (1887) 12 App. Cas. 409) must now be considered in the light of the rules contained in the Companies Act 1981 which expressly permit such a course of action (see the chapter *Purchase and Holding of Own Shares*).

However, the general rule as to such acquisitions was given statutory force by section 35 of the Companies Act 1980. Subject to certain exceptions which are listed below, no company, public or private, limited by shares or limited by guarantee and having a share capital is permitted to acquire its own shares, whether by purchase, subscription or otherwise.

There are a number of exceptions to this rule, which are as follows,

(a) a company is permitted to acquire any of its own *fully paid* shares otherwise than for valuable consideration, for example by way of gift or testamentary bequest (section 35(2)). In this connection it should be noted that for a *public* company, an acquisition of shares in these circumstances will fall within section 37 of the 1980 Act which is discussed below;

(b) a company may redeem or purchase any shares in accordance with Part III of the Companies Act 1981 (see the chapters on *Purchase and Holding of Own Shares* and *Redeemable Shares*);

(c) the acquisition of shares in a reduction of capital under section 66 of the Companies Act 1948 is permitted (see the chapter on *Reconstructions and Amalgamations*);

(d) a company may purchase shares in pursuance of an order of the court under section 11(7) of the Companies Act 1980 (on an application related to a resolution resulting in a company becoming a private company), section 75 of the 1980 Act (unfairly prejudicial conduct), or section 5 of the 1948 Act (alteration of objects);

(e) the forfeiture and surrender of shares for failure to pay any sum payable in respect of those shares is permitted.

Apart from these exceptions, any purported acquisition by a company of its own shares is void. In addition, there are criminal sanctions applicable against the company and any officer of the company who is in default (see section 35(3) C.A. 1980).

Acquisition of company's shares by company's nominee

Subject to certain exceptions, where shares are issued to a nominee, or acquired in partly paid form by a nominee, of a company limited by shares or limited by guarantee and having a share capital, then for all purposes,

(a) the shares are treated as held by the nominee on his own account; and

(b) the company is regarded as having no beneficial interest in the shares (C.A. 1980, s. 36(1); possibly, the section as drafted applies *only* to partly paid shares).

This effectively means that the nominee can be called upon to pay up the shares and has no recourse against the company.

This provision does not apply in the case of shares in a public company which are acquired otherwise than by subscription by the nominee with financial assistance given to him directly or indirectly by the company for the purpose of, or in connection with, the acquisition where the company has a beneficial interest in the shares (section 36(5)). In such a case, section 37 of the 1980 Act, which is considered below, will apply; without this provision the company would have been treated as having no beneficial interest in the shares thus excluding the operation of section 37.

Under section 36(2) if the nominee fails to pay up the nominal amount of the shares or any premium within 21 days of a call, then certain persons incur joint and several liability with the nominee to pay that amount. The persons who can be made so liable are,

(a) if the shares were issued to the nominee as a subscriber to the memorandum by virtue of an undertaking of his in the memorandum, the other subscribers to the memorandum; and

(b) if the shares were otherwise issued to or acquired by him, the directors of the company at the time of the issue or acquisition.

Sections 36(3) and 36(4) enable the court to give relief to a subscriber or director who is, or might be, subject to a claim under section 36(2). It must be shown that the person in question acted honestly and reasonably, and that, having regard to all the circumstances, he ought fairly to be excused from liability.

The provisions of section 36 do not apply at all in two special cases:

(i) cases involving trusts, where shares have been acquired by a nominee and the company has no beneficial interest in those shares (disregarding any rights which the company itself may have as trustee, whether as personal representative or otherwise, to recover its expenses or be remunerated out of the trust property); and

(ii) where shares have been issued to the nominee in consequence of an application made before December 22, 1980, or have been transferred in pursuance of an agreement to acquire them made before that date.

Where section 36 does not apply (e.g. an acquisition by a nominee of fully paid shares), the common law may still prevent the nominee acquiring the shares, see *Kirby v. Wilkins* [1929] 2 Ch. 444; and note C.A. 1981, s. 42 (financial assistance).

Cancellation of certain public company shares

In certain cases a public company is obliged, within a given period, to cancel certain of its shares. The circumstances are set out in section 37 of the Companies Act 1980 and are as follows,

(a) where under the articles shares in the company are forfeited, or are surrendered to the company in lieu, for failure to pay any sum payable in respect of those shares;

(b) where shares in the company are acquired by the company in breach of section 35 of the 1980 Act (see above), or where the acquisition is otherwise than for valuable consideration, and the company has a beneficial interest in those shares;

(c) where the nominee of the company acquires shares in the company from a third person without financial assistance being given directly or indirectly by the company and the company has a beneficial interest in those shares; or

(d) where any person acquires shares in the company with financial assistance given to him directly or indirectly by the company for the purpose of or in connection with the acquisition and the company has a beneficial interest in those shares.

The question of beneficial interest is determined without regard to any right of the company (as trustee) to recover its expenses or obtain remuneration out of the trust property.

Shares which fall within these provisions have no voting rights and, unless the shares or any interest in the company are disposed of within the *relevant period*, the company must within that time (and without being required to go through the formalities associated with the reduction of capital),

(i) cancel the shares and diminish the amount of the share capital by the nominal value of the shares; and

(ii) where the effect of cancelling the shares will be that the nominal value of the company's allotted share capital is brought below the authorised minimum (as defined in section 85 of the 1980 Act), apply for re-registration as a private company, stating the effect of the cancellation.

The "relevant period" is defined to mean one year from the date of acquisition in the case of circumstance (d) above, and three years from acquisition, forfeiture or surrender in all other cases.

Power is given by section 37(2) for the directors to pass a resolution where relevant altering the company's memorandum so that it no longer states that the company is to be a public company, and making any other necessary alterations (for example, as to share capital). The normal re-registration formalities must be carried out, but if a company fails to re-register within the relevant period it continues to be treated as a public company except that it is no longer permitted to offer its shares to the public.

There are criminal sanctions for failure to cancel shares as required or to apply for re-registration (see section 37(7) of the 1980 Act).

Section 37 also applies to a *private* company which re-registered as a public company after one of the specified circumstances has arisen. In such a case, all the provisions of the section apply but the relevant period of one or three years is treated as commencing on the date of re-registration.

There is also provision for the creation of a *reserve fund* in a case where a public company or its nominee acquires shares in the company, or an interest in such shares, which are shown as an asset in the balance sheet. Section 37 (10) requires an amount equal to the value of the shares or the interest to be transferred out of distributable profits to the reserve fund, which is itself not available for distribution.

Charges by public company on own shares

Except in certain specified cases, a lien or charge in favour of a *public* company on its own shares (whether arising expressly or by implication) is void: section 38(1) of the 1980 Act; see the chapter *Charges over Shares*.

The permitted class of charges are contained in section 38(2) and are as follows,

(a) in the case of every public company, a charge on its own shares (not being fully paid) for any amount payable in respect of the shares;

(b) in the case of a company whose ordinary business includes the lending of money or consists of the provision or credit or the bailment or (in Scotland) hiring of goods under a hire purchase agreement, or both, a charge of the company on its own shares (whether fully paid or not) which arises in connection with a transaction entered into by the company in the ordinary course of its business;

(c) in the case of a company (other than a company in relation to which paragraph (d) below applies) which is re-registered or is registered under section 13 of the 1980 Act as a public company, a charge on its own shares which was in existence immediately before its application for re-registration or, as the case may be, registration;

(d) in the case of any company which after the end of the re-registration period remains or remained an old public company and did not before the end of that period apply to be re-registered under section 8 of the 1980 Act as a public company, any charge on its own shares which was in existence immediately before the end of that period.

Section 38 does not apply to *private* companies, which may therefore take an equitable charge – though not a legal charge – over their own shares.

Serious loss of capital

The Companies Act 1980 introduced, in relation to *public* companies, a novel provision which applies in cases where the net assets of such a company have been reduced below a certain minimum level.

Section 34 of the 1980 Act provides that, where the net assets of the company amount to half or less of the amount of its *called-up share capital*, then the directors are obliged to convene an extraordinary general meeting for the purpose of considering whether any, and if so what, measures should be taken to deal with the situation. The directors must act within 28 days of *any* of their number becoming aware of the position. The meeting itself must be held not later than 56 days from that time.

The expression "net assets" is defined in section 87(4) of the 1980 Act, as amended, as meaning the aggregate of the company's assets less its liabilities (including any amounts retained as reasonably necessary for the purpose of providing for any liability or loss which is either likely to be incurred, or certain to be incurred but uncertain as to amount or the date on which it will arise). The reference to called-up share capital means that there must be included in the necessary calculation shares on which a call has been made but not yet paid, and also shares which have to be paid up on deferred terms (see C.A. 1980, s. 87(1)).

Two particular points call for mention. First, it will be noted that, whilst section 34 requires an extraordinary general meeting to be convened, it does not go on to specify any particular steps which must be taken at that meeting. That decision is left to the company. One alternative would be for the company to pass a special resolution to reduce its share capital under section 66(1)(b) of the 1948 Act (cancellation of share capital lost or unrepresented by available assets), together with re-registration as a private company if appropriate. Secondly, the obligation to convene the meeting arises as soon as one of the directors knows of the loss of capital; and the penalties for failure to act arise only in the case of directors who *knowingly and wilfully* authorise or permit that failure or continued failure (see section 34(2)).

It should be noted that section 34(3) expressly provides that nothing in section 34(1) operates to exclude any or the normal requirements as to the passing of resolutions at general meetings. So, for example, if it were thought appropriate that the company should pass a special resolution for a reduction of share capital, special notice of that resolution would require to be given in the usual way. If notice has not been given for the original meeting, a further meeting would be required.

Transfer and transmission of shares

Shares constitute personal property and are transferable as such (section 73 of the Companies Act 1948). The transfer of the *legal* title to shares can only be effected by means of a "proper instrument of transfer" under section 75 of the 1948 Act. This requirement cannot be waived by anything in the articles of association; however, it does not apply to any transmission by operation of law (see below). The requirement for an instrument of transfer will generally necessitate the payment of stamp duty. However, it is possible for the *equitable* title to shares to be assigned by contract, which can be oral, and which will not be subject to stamp duty (subject to L.P.A. 1925, s. 53(1)(c) and S.A. 1891, s. 59).

Transfer procedure

The Stock Transfer Act 1963 brought into force a simplified system for the transfer of registered securities. Where the 1963 Act applies, companies may adopt the stock transfer form specified in Schedule 1 in place of the provisions of the articles (see for example articles 22 to 28 of Table A). Such transfers need only be executed by the transferor and do not require to be witnessed. The Act does not, however, invalidate transfers which would otherwise satisfy the requirements of a company's articles (section 1(3)).

The 1963 Act applies only to *fully paid-up* registered securities. Accordingly, where partly paid shares are transferred, the requirements of the articles must be observed in every case. This will generally necessitate execution by the transferee and attestation.

Where a holder of shares wishes to transfer his entire shareholding, he will generally execute a stock transfer in favour of the proposed transferee and, in exchange for the payment of the price for the shares, will hand to the transferee the stock transfer and the certificate comprising the shares. The transferee will lodge those documents with the company and be issued a fresh certificate following approval of the registration by the board of directors. Where only part of a holding of shares is to be disposed of, a share certificate will not generally be handed to the transferee but will instead be lodged with the company. Following completion of the other formalities, the secretary will issue to the transferee a certificate comprising the shares which have been sold, and to the transferor a balance certificate for the residue of his shareholding.

Stock Exchange transfers

A more complex system of transfers is required for dealings effected on The Stock Exchange. This is effected under the *Talisman* system, the purpose of which is to provide an effective centralised method of transfer. (It was previously necessary for transferors to sign "open" transfers which could encourage fraud.)

The *Talisman* system is very well explained in a guide issued by The Stock Exchange in November 1978 entitled "A Guide for Institutional and Other Investors". The primary feature of the system is the use of a Stock Exchange nominee company called SEPON Limited which operates a single undesignated shareholding account in the register of every company participating in the scheme. The main features of the scheme are as follows.

(1) All sold stock is transferred by the sellers into the "SEPON" pool account. Stock is transferred to the purchasers out of this account.

(2) When the selling broker receives the certificate and signed Talisman sold transfer he sends both documents to the Stock Exchange Centre. From there they are passed to the company registrar for registration into SEPON Limited's name as trustee for the seller.

(3) On account day, the stock is transferred to the jobbers' trading account and the selling broker receives payment for it from the Centre.

(4) Purchased and sold stock are basically matched by a process known as *apportionment* which takes place after the stock has been transferred to the jobbers' trading account. The result of apportionment is that SEPON Limited then holds the stock to the order of the buyer.

(5) Following apportionment the Centre prepares bought transfers from SEPON Limited to the buyers and lodges them for registration. The appropriate registrar then issues a certificate in favour of the buyer.

(6) Stamp duty is no longer payable on individual transfers. Instead, duty is levied on the Bought transfer and collected by The Stock Exchange from the buying broker at the time of apportionment. The Stock Exchange then accounts to the Inland Revenue under a composition agreement.

Legal position of transferor and transferee

The registration procedure transfers the legal title in the shares from the transferor to the transferee. As has already been noted, however, the passing of a beneficial interest in the shares does not depend upon registration. Basically, in the case of a sale, the beneficial ownership in the shares will pass on the making of an unconditional contract; in the case of a gift, it will pass once the transferor has done everything in his power to vest the ownership of the shares in the transferee (see *Re Rose* [1952] Ch. 499). The effect of the passing of beneficial ownership is that the transferee will immediately become entitled to any dividends declared and other distributions made after the date on which such ownership is treated as having passed. In the case of voting rights, the transferee is entitled, following payment of the price, to direct the transferor how votes should be cast (*Musselwhite v. C. H. Musselwhite & Son Limited* [1962] Ch. 964).

Pre-emption provisions

The articles of private companies very often contain complex provisions designed to prevent control of the company passing out of the hands of a few shareholders (who may perhaps be members of a family). Until its repeal by the 1980 Act, section 28 of the 1948 Act required all private companies to impose restrictions on transfer. Listed companies are not permitted to have such provisions in their articles, at least in respect to any class of shares which is quoted on The Stock Exchange, since this would clearly restrict the marketability of those shares.

The ordinary, and most common, provision in this regard is the provision enabling directors to refuse registration of any transfer. As with all powers vested in the directors, the exercise of a refusal to register a transfer must be bona fide for the benefit of the company, and not, for example, for some personal motive of the directors. If the directors wish to refuse registration under this general power, they must ensure that the specific requirements of the articles are observed. For example, a positive decision must be taken at the appropriate board meeting (see *Moodie v. W. J. Shepherd (Bookbinders)* [1949] 2 All E.R. 1044) and the proposed transferee must be notified, in accordance with section 78 of the 1948 Act, within two months after the date on which the transfer was lodged with the company.

The general power afforded to the directors to refuse registration is not effective to prevent the passing of the beneficial interest in the shares. In accordance with the rules outlined above, a transferee who is refused registration will simply be able to direct the transferor (who will have retained the legal title) to vote in accordance with the transferee's wishes. Thus, the company is effectively unable to prevent the transfer of control over the shares in question. For this reason, the articles of a private company will very often contain more complex pre-emption provisions which provide for a member wishing to transfer shares first of all to offer those shares to the existing members. Such pre-emption provisions are strictly construed in favour of the shareholder wishing to transfer his shares, and must therefore be drawn with considerable care.

Many pre-emption provisions impose obligations on a member who is "desirous of transferring" his shares. Such a provision was considered by the House of Lords in the case of *Lyle & Scott Limited v. Scott's Trustees* [1959] A.C. 763. In that case, the registered holders of certain ordinary shares in the company sought to render ineffective the pre-emption provisions by entering into an agreement with a third party under which they received the purchase price for the shares and bound themselves to vote as the purchaser desired. However, no instrument of transfer was executed, and the shareholders maintained that they did not wish to execute any transfer. It was held that the acts of the shareholders were such that it could be inferred that they were "desirous of transferring" their shares. A shareholder who has agreed to sell his shares and has received and retained the price must be deemed to be desirous of transferring them; otherwise the purpose of the article would be defeated.

The *Lyle & Scott* case was considered in the more recent High Court case of *Safeguard Industrial Investments Limited v. National Westminster Bank Limited* [1981] 1 W.L.R. 286. In that case, the Bank had acquired the shares in question as executor of a former shareholder's estate. The effect of the deceased shareholder's will was to shift the balance of control of the company away from the plaintiff, and the plaintiff therefore issued an originating summons to determine whether the Bank should serve a transfer notice on completion of the administration. The Bank filed evidence that the administration was in fact complete, and that it regarded itself as holding the shares on trust for the beneficiaries. However, it was also stated that the beneficiaries did not want the Bank to transfer the shares to them, and the Bank did not propose to do so unless so directed. It was held, on a true construction of the articles, which referred to a "proposing transferor", that the word "transfer" meant a transfer of the legal interest in the shares, and could not refer to the transfer of a beneficial interest under the will. There was accordingly no obligation on the Bank to serve a transfer notice on the company. This decision was approved by the Court of Appeal [1982] 1 W.L.R. 589, where it was held that such pre-emption provisions could not be construed so as to make a person who involuntarily came under an obligation to transfer a "proposing transferor".

Following the *Safeguard* case many existing pre-emption provisions in company articles will be inadequate to prevent the personal representatives of a deceased shareholder merely retaining the legal title to the shares vested in them by a transmission (see below). This will therefore often frustrate the intentions of family shareholders. The provisions contained in article 30 of Table A to the 1948 Act are of no assistance; they merely entitle the personal representatives to elect to be registered as holders of the shares or to transfer. To be effective in such a case, the pre-emption provisions must import a compulsion on the personal representatives either to transfer or to elect themselves to be registered as holders of the shares, with a further provision that in either case all the provisions as to transfer – including thereby the pre-emption provisions – are to apply.

Transmission

The formal requirements as to a transfer of a share do not apply in the case of a transmission by operation of law. This takes place most commonly on the death of a shareholder but can also occur on his bankruptcy or under the provisions of the Mental Health Act 1959.

On the death of a shareholder, the legal title to the shares passes automatically to the personal representatives (or, if the shares are jointly held, to the surviving holder). Where the shareholder has left a will, the transmission will occur immediately on the death and is then confirmed by a subsequent grant of probate. If the deceased shareholder died intestate, then the transmission takes place on the actual grant of letters of administration to the estate.

Registration in the names of the personal representatives, or the trustee in bankruptcy or receiver, is by letter of request; there is no prescribed form unless the articles so provide. Shares are transferable by the personal representatives whether or not they have been registered as members in their own right (section 76 of the 1948 Act).

Share certificates

The share certificate represents a shareholder's document of title in respect of his shares. Under section 80 of the Companies Act 1948, a company must within two months after allotment, or the date on which a duly stamped transfer is lodged, deliver a share certificate comprising the relevant shares, unless the conditions of issue of the shares otherwise provide.

There are criminal sanctions for failure to comply with this section, and in addition, the court can order the company and any officers of the company to make good the default.

In the case of listed companies, it should be noted that The Stock Exchange (Completion of Bargains) Act 1976 specifically excludes the provisions of section 80 of the 1948 Act in relation to transfers to a Stock Exchange nominee (i.e. SEPON Limited).

Section 81 of the 1948 Act provides that the share certificate is prima facie evidence of the title of the member to the shares. Even though the certificate may be inaccurate, the company will be estopped from denying its accuracy against any person who relies upon it, except in cases of forgery or fraud (see *Dixon v. Kennaway & Co.* [1900] 1 Ch. 833). In various circumstances a company can be estopped from denying the accuracy of a share certificate it has issued.

Share warrants

Since share warrants are nowadays uncommon, it is not proposed to deal with them in any great detail. The Stock Exchange, as a market regulator, views warrants unfavourably and listing may be difficult or impossible to obtain. Furthermore, the listing of existing securities may be prejudiced by an issue of warrants.

Under section 83 of the Companies Act 1948, a company limited by shares may, if so authorised by its articles, issue a share warrant. This represents a negotiable instrument transferable by delivery. Because of this, and the fact that therefore no stamp duty is payable on transfer, duty is levied on issue, at up to six per cent (see sections 59 to 61 of the Finance Act 1963). Special registration formalities must be carried out (see section 112 of the 1948 Act). The bearer of a warrant is entitled to delivery of the underlying stock on presentation of the warrant.

Because there is no register of holders of share warrants, dividends must be advertised in newspapers. The dividends are paid on presentation of the relevant coupon which is annexed to the share warrant. Coupons are also generally used to claim entitlement to rights or bonus issues.

By section 182(2) of the 1948 Act, a share warrant does not constitute a share for the purposes of directors' share qualifications.

Takeovers

Take-overs of public companies resident in the United Kingdom are normally governed by the rules contained in the City Code on Take-overs and Mergers. Where the shares of the offeror or the target company are listed on The Stock Exchange, London, it may also be necessary to follow the applicable regulations contained in The Stock Exchange's "Yellow Book". None of these rules or regulations has the force of law but there is an ever increasing amount of statute law which has significance for take-overs, not least at the planning stage.

There are a multitude of factors to be taken into account in answering such questions as who should make the offer, what form the consideration should take, who should make any borrowing to finance the offer and who should make market purchases. Purely commercial factors are likely to play the significant part in determining the answers to these questions in most cases; however, where there is room for some flexibility, appropriate planning can produce meaningful commercial results. One important area for planning is likely to be tax, not only in terms of the costs of the acquisition and of a subsequent structure which is tax efficient, but also in terms of the tax position of the shareholders or stockholders of the target company. Other areas would typically include the implications of market purchases, funding the acquisition (including the servicing of any borrowings) and the accounting consequences for the bidder.

This chapter deals with a selection of legal and practical points which arise in connection with the planning and implementation of a take-over. A number of problems which often arise on take-overs are not dealt with in this chapter, such as the implications of section 42 of the Companies Act 1981 (restriction on giving financial assistance) and the necessary procedures under the Companies Act 1980 for the issue of shares as consideration for a take-over, including section 24 of the Companies Act 1980. Section 42 is dealt with in the chapter *Financial Assistance*. The provisions of the 1980 Companies Act which regulate the issue of shares are dealt with in the chapter *Shares*. Section 24, which as a general rule requires an independent expert's report and valuation before a public company allots shares for a non-cash consideration, specifically excludes from its requirements cases where one company makes an offer to all the shareholders (or all the holders of a particular class of shares) to buy all or some of their shares.

One of the first decisions which needs to be taken by a proposed bidder is whether the take-over should be achieved by a scheme of arrangement under section 206 of the Companies Act 1948 or by an offer which, if the conditions are met, will most likely be followed by the compulsory acquisition procedure under section 209 of the Companies Act 1948.

Scheme of arrangement or offer

The principal difference between a scheme of arrangement and a take-over offer is that the former necessarily involves court approval whereas the latter does not. This has particular implications from the point of view of flexibility and timing.

Section 206 provides that a compromise or arrangement between a company and its members (or any class of them) will, if agreed to by the company's members and if sanctioned by the court, be binding on the members (or class of members) and on the company. In the context of a take-over, in very simple terms the arrangement will normally involve:

(a) the cancellation of the existing shares in the target company;

(b) the payment of the consideration by the acquiring company to the target company's shareholders for the loss of their shares; and

(c) the re-issue of the target company's shares to the acquiring company.

An explanation of the procedure for the implementation of a scheme of arrangement is given in the chapter *Reconstructions and Amalgamations*.

One of the most important features of a scheme of arrangement is the level of shareholder approval which is required. Section 206(2) requires the arrangement to be approved by a simple majority in number representing three quarters in value of the members (or class of members) who are present and vote, either in person or by proxy, at the meeting convened by the court for the purpose of considering the arrangement. There is no quorum requirement. The level of shareholder approval is therefore significantly less than for compulsory acquisition under section 209 (see page 894 below). However, under section 206 the court plays a more significant part in ensuring that the scheme is fair. Under section 209 the matter may well never come to the court and, if it does, the onus is on the dissenting minority to demonstrate the unfairness of the offer.

Since *Re Hellenic & General Trust Limited* [1976] 1 W.L.R. 123 there has been some doubt whether a scheme of arrangement can be used in a take-over situation. The point had been considered before in *Re National Bank Limited* [1966] 1 W.L.R. 819, where one of the objections raised by shareholders holding approximately 5 per cent of the company's shares was that the scheme was effectively a purchase by an outsider of all the company's issued shares. Accordingly, it was claimed, the acquiring company was attempting to achieve under section 206 what would have required a 90 per cent approval under section 209. In that case the court concluded that the two sections, section 206 and section 209 involved different considerations and approaches and that there were good reasons for requiring a smaller majority in favour of a scheme under section 206 than the majority required under section 209. In *Re Hellenic & General Trust Limited* the facts were rather special. A little over 53 per cent of the company's shares were held by a wholly-owned subsidiary of the acquiring company and approximately 14 per cent were held by a dissenting minority shareholder. The 53 per cent shareholder voted his shares in favour of the arrangement at the shareholders' meeting and if it had not done so the required approval would not have been obtained. Templeman J (as he then was) said:

> "The fact that an arrangement under section 206 produces a result which is the same as a takeover under section 209 is not necessarily fatal. It is not always so unfair as to preclude the court from exercising its discretion in favour of the scheme".

And later:

> "... there must be a very high standard of proof on the part of the petitioner to justify obtaining by section 206 what could not be obtained by section 209, especially when there is the added element that section 206 itself only works with the help of a wholly owned subsidiary of the petitioners".

He accepted the decision in *Re National Bank Limited* but distinguished it on the facts.

It was held that, because the interests of the wholly-owned subsidiary were different from those of the other shareholders, the shares held by the wholly-owned subsidiary constituted a different class. Section 206 schemes have since been approved as a means of achieving a take-over – although where the acquiring company (or its associates) already holds shares it will obviously be desirable for them not to be voted at the meeting to approve the scheme.

Because of the court's involvement and the 21 day notice required for the shareholders' meeting convened by the court, a scheme of arrangement is likely to take at least eight to ten weeks to implement (and longer if it involves one of the court vacations). An offer can become unconditional inside four weeks – although it will be nearer six months before the compulsory acquisition procedure is complete.

Apart from timing, a scheme provides very little flexibility – especially if there is a prospect of a competitive situation emerging. In particular, the co-operation of the target company's board is normally essential to the success of a scheme (but, of course, not essential to the success of an offer). The court has no jurisdiction to sanction a scheme which is not first approved by the target company either through its board or, if appropriate, by means of a simple majority of the members in general meeting (see *Re Savoy Hotel Limited* [1981] Ch. 351).

Until it became common to incorporate stamp duty saving schemes into public take-over offers, schemes of arrangement offered the advantage of providing a route that would not attract ad valorem duty. This now seems to be a less significant advantage. It may, however, offer some attractions where foreign shareholders are involved and an offering document would give rise to particular problems in the overseas jurisdiction concerned. In the majority of cases it is likely that a prospective bidder will prefer the timing and flexibility of a public offer, at least where there are signs of some reluctance from the target company's board (for example, in terms of ensuring that its shareholders obtain a good price for their shares) or of some competition. Although the compulsory acquisition powers for an offer require 90 per cent acceptances (see further pages 894 to 900 below), an offeror will often be prepared to allow its offer to become unconditional once acceptances give it over 50 per cent of the target company's voting rights. In practice, once this level has been achieved and the offer has become unconditional, the offeror will have a good chance of achieving the compulsory acquisition level (unless the particular circumstances indicate a likely problem). It will not often be in the interests of a shareholder to hold on to his shares in this situation.

Transfer and capital duty

The transfer of shares in a United Kingdom company normally attracts stamp duty at the rate of two per cent of the value of the shares transferred (section 54 of and Schedule 1 to the Stamp Act 1891). However, in many instances the incidence of this duty can either be reduced significantly or eliminated completely.

Stamp duty saving schemes

It is now quite common in agreed take-overs for the target company board to agree, subject to the offeror undertaking to indemnify the target company's shareholders for any tax consequences, to convene a general meeting for the reorganisation of the target company's share capital specifically to reduce the offeror's liability to this duty. Under the Stamp Act no stamp duty is payable on the renunciation of rights under a letter of allotment provided that the rights under the letter of allotment do not continue to be renounceable for more than six months after its issue (section 65(1) of the Finance Act 1963). Accordingly, the saving is achieved by a resolution of the target company's shareholders to issue, by way of capitalisation, new shares in the target company to the target company's shareholders, followed by the allotment of such shares on renounceable allotment letters, renounceable usually only for such period as is necessary to enable shares acquired under section 209 of the Companies Act 1948 to be transferred by renunciation. Such renunciation of the new shares will not attract stamp duty. Stamp duty will be payable on the transfer of the existing shares but their value will have been diluted by the capitalisation issue: so, the larger the capitalisation issue, the larger the saving.

It is also increasingly common for the reorganisation (and stamp duty saving) to be taken a stage further: the value of the existing shares (and hence the duty payable) is reduced by converting them into deferred shares with restricted rights to participate in dividends and the right to the return, on a winding up, of no more than their nominal value. This conversion will have the effect of passing more value into the new shares. The terms of the offer would reflect the reduced value by attributing only a very small part of the consideration (often only 1p) to each existing share. Assuming that this is a reasonable value for the share with its reduced rights, the stamp duty payable will be limited to two per cent of the aggregate price so paid for the existing shares.

Before deciding to implement such a "deferred scheme", the terms of any options or convertible securities should be checked to ensure that they do not contain a prohibition against such a reorganisation and that the adjustment provisions will work appropriately if the reorganisation is approved and implemented.

It will also, of course, be necessary to ensure that the target company can make a capitalisation issue. This will involve checking the target company's own accounts (rather than any consolidated accounts) and the terms of its articles (see further the chapter *Bonus Issues*). It is not essential to have sufficient profits available for distribution for the purposes of section 39(1) of the Companies Act 1980 since, by the definition of "distribution" in section 45 of that Act, the section does not apply to an issue of bonus shares. If the combination of the reserves and the share premium account is insufficient, the offeror may be prepared to make the scheme possible either by a gift or by the issue of a preferential share at a substantial premium, in each case when the offer has otherwise become unconditional.

Those involved in a take-over should also be aware that the deferred scheme, although now quite common, is inclined to make the formal offer document and the form of acceptance more difficult for the ordinary shareholder to understand. This would not appear to have a noticeably adverse effect on the success of offers adopting such schemes. The complexity is caused by (a) the need to ensure that the offer is made for the share capital in existence after the reorganisation rather than for the share capital in existence at the time the offer is made, with which the shareholder is bound to be more familiar and (b) the desire clearly to separate the offer for the deferred shares from the offer for the new shares, thereby creating two separate offers with different conditions attached to each.

As mentioned, the target company, apart perhaps from trying to share in the potential saving by negotiating a price increase, will typically ask for an indemnity in favour of its shareholders against any adverse tax consequences resulting from the implementation of the scheme. If this is to benefit not only accepting shareholders but also those who do not accept (who are at least equally, and possibly more, vulnerable to any tax), it will be necessary for the indemnity to be contained in a separate deed. Before giving such an indemnity the offeror company should, of course, assure itself that no liability is likely to arise and, in particular, that no repayment of capital has been made (see section 234 of the Taxes Act 1970, subject to the relaxations in that section and in paragraph 5 of Schedule 22 to the Finance Act 1972).

Conditions for a stamp duty saving scheme

One of the conditions of the offer for the new shares will usually be that the resolution to approve the capital reorganisation is passed *and* the new shares are allotted pursuant to that resolution. The resolution itself will only become effective once the offer has become unconditional in all other respects. The condition as to allotment of the new shares will ensure that the offer does not become unconditional before the shares for which the offer has been made exist. If this were not the case, there would be an argument that the offeror had acquired equitable ownership in the existing shares and was, as a result, liable to ad valorem duty on the total consideration payable in respect of acceptances received before the new shares were allotted.

The saving scheme condition is frequently not announced at the time of the formal announcement of the offer and its terms and conditions. In view of the Take-over Code requirement that the formal announcement states all conditions to which an offer is subject (Rule 8(2), see below) this omission can only be justified where the applicable condition will lapse if it is not satisfied by a certain time, in other words, if it is a condition which cannot ultimately prevent the offer from becoming unconditional. A provision to this effect is normally included as an additional term, tucked away in the relevant Appendix's small print.

The Take-over Code provides that, generally, a compulsory offer under Rule 34 (see page 890 below) may only be subject to the condition that it is accepted in respect of a sufficient number of shares to result in the offeror (and persons acting in concert with it) holding shares carrying more than 50 per cent of the voting rights exercisable at a general meeting of the target company. Despite this, there would seem to be no reason why the Panel should not agree to the necessary stamp duty saving condition in a Rule 34 offer provided that it will lapse if not satisfied by, say, shortly after the first closing date. If an offeror is only prepared to make an offer at a particular price if a saving scheme is implemented, the condition should not, of course, automatically lapse if the offer becomes unconditional in all other respects. In such a case the condition would require to be included in the original formal announcement and would not be permitted in a Rule 34 offer.

Revenue challenge

The scheme has been used for a long time in relation to private company acquisitions. The greater publicity given to it in the take-over context may provoke the Inland Revenue into trying to challenge a scheme. Their chances of success may have improved with the recent House of Lords decisions in *W. T. Ramsay Limited v. IRC* [1981] STC 174 and *IRC v. Burmah Oil Limited* [1982] STC 30.

Renounceable allotment letters

In practice the renounceable allotment letters will only be sent out to the target company's shareholders if the acquirer is unable to acquire compulsorily the shares of those who have not accepted the offers (under section 209(1) of the Companies Act 1948, see below). In order to avoid the need for accepting shareholders to sign the form of renunciation on the allotment letter, the form of acceptance can include an authority for it to be signed on behalf of the shareholder. This authority is often given in favour of a director or other person authorised by the merchant bank acting for the offeror.

It had been thought that the use of this stamp duty saving scheme could prevent the exercise of rights under section 209(1) on the basis that renunciation of a renounceable allotment letter would not constitute a "transfer" for the purposes of that subsection. However, in *Re Simo Securities Trust Limited* [1971] 1 W.L.R. 1455 Brightman J. concluded:

> "In the context of the present case I do not think that there is any difficulty in reading the words 'a scheme or contract involving the transfer of shares' as including a scheme or contract which involves the transfer of an absolute right to an allotment of shares. Nor do I feel any difficulty in reading approval 'by the holders of not less than nine tenths in value of the shares whose transfer is involved' as including approval by persons who have an absolute right to an allotment of shares".

Although the particular mechanics of acceptance in that case did not involve renunciation of an allotment, it is thought that by analogy a renounceable allotment letter can be treated as a transfer for the purposes of section 209.

Contested offer

It will obviously be more difficult to put together an effective stamp duty saving scheme where the target company is not prepared to convene the necessary meeting to reorganise its share capital. Even where the offeror already owns at least ten per cent of the target company's voting shares before it posts its offer document and requisitions the necessary meeting under section 132 of the Companies Act 1948, the target company board will be able so to delay convening the meeting as to make the timing very difficult, if not impossible, for the offeror. A course of action open to the potential offeror is to include a provision (probably in the appendix setting out, among other things, the additional terms required by the take-over code) whereby the terms of the offer may be adjusted to two separate offers for the reorganised share capital. Once it is clear that the offer will be successful, the target company board will hopefully abandon their objections and convene the necessary meeting.

Foreign offeror

Foreign offerors (on old Exchange Control tests as to residence) may be entitled to a reduced rate of ad valorem duty. Section 49 of and Schedule 11 to the Finance Act 1974 increased the rate of ad valorem duty from one per cent to two per cent. However, paragraph 21 of Schedule 22 provides that where shares are transferred to (or to a nominee for) a person not resident for the purposes of the Exchange Control Act 1947 in the Scheduled Territories (as specified in the

Exchange Control Act), the rate of ad valorem duty is reduced to one
per cent provided that the transfer:

(a) is for full value in money or money's worth; and

(b) is accompanied by a certificate by an authorised depositary to the
effect that (i) the transferee (or the person for whom he is the
nominee) is not resident in the Scheduled Territories, and (ii) the
transfer is for full consideration in money or money's worth.

Section 206 scheme of arrangement

Transfer duty may be avoided altogether under a scheme under section
206 of the Companies Act 1948. Under the typical "206 scheme" used in
a take-over, the shares in the target company are cancelled in consideration for the issue of shares in, or the payment of cash by, the acquiring
company. No transfer duty is payable because no share transfers are
involved. However, the Registrar of Companies will not accept for
registration an office copy of the court order unless it is duly stamped or
the Stamp Office has confirmed that no duty is payable. As a result, the
practice is to submit a draft of the scheme order to the Stamp Office
before the court sanctions the scheme, so that the Stamp Office can
arrange with the Registrar of Companies for the immediate registration
of the office copy if the scheme is sanctioned. As regards capital duty,
although the target's issued share capital would normally be restored to
its position before the scheme by the issue of the same number of shares
to the acquiring company immediately after the cancellation, no duty
will be payable if (as is normal) this is done by way of capitalisation.
Furthermore, the acquiring company may qualify for capital duty relief
on the shares it issues under paragraphs 10 and 11 of Schedule 19 to the
Finance Act 1973 (see below). It is not necessary under section 206 for
the acquiring company to be incorporated in the United Kingdom.
However, the company in which the scheme takes place (i.e. the target
company) must be a 'company' liable to be wound up under the
Companies Act 1948.

An order under a section 206 scheme may in certain circumstances
attract ad valorem duty as a transfer (see *Sun Alliance Insurance
Limited v. IRC* [1971] 1 All E.R. 135). This will not be the case in the
type of scheme outlined above.

Section 55 relief

Where the offeror is offering shares, relief from transfer duty may be
available under section 55 of the Finance Act 1927. The principal
requirements for relief are as follows:

(a) the transaction must be in connection with a "reconstruction" or an
"amalgamation" – expressions which have a very technical meaning
(see *Re South Africa Supply and Cold Storage Company* [1904] 2
Ch. 268, *Baytrust Holdings v. IRC* [1971] 3 All E.R. 76, *Brook-*

lands Selangor Holdings Limited v. IRC [1970] 2 All E.R. 76 and *Crane Fruehauf Limited v. IRC* [1975] STC 51);

(b) both the acquiring company and the target company must be formed under the laws of England, Scotland or Wales. Thus a Northern Ireland or foreign acquiring or target company is outside section 55: *Nestle Co. Limited v. IRC* [1953] Ch. 395. Also, the acquiring company must have limited liability (section 55(1)(a)). However, the target company may be an unlimited company;

(c) the acquiring company must increase its share capital or issue existing unissued shares with a view to the acquisition of not less than 90 per cent of the share capital of the target company. Accordingly,

    (i) the words "with a view to" should be included in the resolution; and

    (ii) relief is not available if the acquiring company already owns more than 10 per cent of the target company (unless it first sells its holding to another person who accepts the offer).

Furthermore, the 90 per cent test applies to the *nominal* amount of the *whole* of the issued capital of the company to be acquired – including, for example, preference shares;

(d) 90 per cent by value of the consideration must be in the form of shares (as to this valuation see *Brooklands Selangor Holdings v. IRC* [1970] 2 All E.R. 76 and *Crane Fruehauf v. IRC* [1975] STC 51) but the balance of the consideration may be of any nature;

(e) the consideration shares must be issued to the holders of shares in the target company in exchange for their shares in the target company. The consideration shares must, therefore, be issued to (i.e. *registered* in the names of) the target company's shareholders. As a result, relief will not be available if the offeror issues its shares on renounceable allotment letters: *Oswald Tillotson Limited v. IRC* [1933] 1 K.B. 134. Also the consideration shares must be issued to the *"holders"* of shares in the target company in exchange for the shares held by them. The holders are, broadly speaking, the persons in whose names the target company's shares are registered (see *Oswald Tillotson; Murex v. IRC* [1933] 1 K.B. 173 and *Baytrust Holdings v. IRC* [1971] 3 All E.R. 76);

(f) relief is lost if the acquiring company ceases to be the beneficial owner of any of the shares in the target company within two years otherwise than in consequence of a reconstruction, amalgamation or liquidation.

If fractional entitlements to shares in the acquiring company are dealt with by allotment to a nominee for sale on behalf of the shareholders otherwise entitled to them, such shares will not be issued to shareholders in the target company (see (e) above). As a result, that portion of the consideration will probably not fall to be included as being in the form of shares, when applying the 90 per cent test. Also, if the acquiring company were to accept additional obligations as part of the consideration for the transfer (e.g. payment of particular expenses), these would need to be taken into account in determining whether the test has been satisfied.

Notwithstanding that the conditions for relief under section 55 may be satisfied, the share transfers will not be properly stamped (and therefore should not be registered) unless they have been adjudicated not chargeable to duty. This requires an application to the Inland Revenue by statutory declaration.

Cash alternatives

It follows from the above that because of the "90 per cent consideration" test the requirements for relief may not be satisfied where the offeror wishes to give the target company shareholders the right to choose to receive their consideration in cash, rather than in shares. However, if the offeror wishes to raise the cash required to meet the cash element of the consideration by having its consideration shares "underwritten", the relief can still be available if this "underwriting" takes the form of an agreement by the merchant bank to offer to purchase from accepting shareholders the shares in the offeror which they do not want, provided, broadly speaking, that the merchant bank's offer is independent of the bid (see generally *Crane Fruehauf Limited v. IRC* [1975] STC 51). Whilst this may preserve transfer duty relief on the transfers of all the target company's shares in respect of which acceptances are received, transfer duty will be payable on the transfer of the offeror's shares to the merchant bank (because for relief to be available under section 55 these shares must first be registered in the name of the accepting shareholder). The merchant bank will, of course, require that this cost be borne by the offeror. It may, therefore, be cheaper for the offeror to issue its consideration shares in renounceable form and to carry out a stamp duty saving scheme in the target company, instead of claiming section 55 relief. But this will result in the loss of relief from one per cent capital duty if it would otherwise be available (see further page 868 below).

Following the decision in *Crane Fruehauf Limited v. IRC* [1975] STC 51, there was some doubt whether or not relief under section 55 would be lost (if it were otherwise available) in cases where a cash alternative was offered by a third party – for example, where the offeror's merchant bank made a separate offer to acquire the shares issued by the offeror under the terms of the basic offer. Accepting shareholders were, in that particular case, under an obligation to sell their shares to a third party, and it was held that, as a result, 90 per cent of the consideration did not consist of the issue of shares. In other words, the court came to the view that because the consideration consisted of shares subject to an obligation to sell them to a third party, it should not be treated as consisting of shares. It is thought that because, in the typical third party cash alternative offer, there is no obligation upon accepting shareholders to accept the separate cash offer from the third party (i.e. normally a merchant bank), those accepting shareholders who accept the separate cash offer will be treated as having received their consideration in the form of shares.

Capital duty

Capital duty was introduced in 1973, providing one of the early examples, so far as the United Kingdom was concerned, of attempts at harmonisation within the EEC. It is only payable by "capital companies", as defined in section 48(1) of the Finance Act 1973. These include not only companies incorporated with limited liability in the United Kingdom and companies incorporated elsewhere in the EEC, but also companies incorporated outside the EEC with their effective management in Great Britain if,

(a) their shares can be dealt in on a stock exchange in the EEC; or

(b) the liability of their shareholders is limited to their shares and such shares may be transferred without prior authorisation.

Capital duty is payable on the occurrence of one of the "chargeable transactions" specified in Part I of Schedule 19 to the Finance Act 1973. These include:

(i) an increase in capital by the contribution of any assets (for example, the issue of shares on a share exchange); and

(ii) the transfer of an overseas capital company's place of effective management to Great Britain (except that where the effective management was in an EEC member state this will only be a chargeable transaction if the company was not treated as a capital company in that member state).

It should be borne in mind that capital duty is not only payable on the issue of shares. It will also be payable on capital contributions in consideration of the issue of rights of the same kind as those of members of the company, such as voting rights, a share in the profits or a share in the surplus on liquidation. It is not, however, generally considered to be payable on gifts (even if treated as capital by the recipient) unless the gift is made in such a way as to be treated as being made in consideration of the issue of shares or the granting of rights falling within the above wording (note, however, certain observations of Nourse J in *Cambridge Petroleum Royalties v. IRC* [1982] STC 325 at 333).

The present rate of capital duty is one per cent (as opposed to the normal ad valorem stamp duty rate of two per cent). In the case of a contribution of assets, it is payable not on the nominal value of the shares issued but on the actual value of the assets contributed: so on an issue for a non-cash consideration (such as a share exchange) the duty would be payable on the value of the non-cash consideration. Where the chargeable transaction is a transfer of effective management, the duty is chargeable on the actual value (and not therefore the book value) of the assets of the capital company at the time of the transaction, less its liabilities at that time. This will only rarely apply on a take-over but there may sometimes be tax reasons why a purchaser will consider using as the offeror a foreign company with residence in the United Kingdom for tax purposes. In these cases where the company is not resident in another EEC country it will be possible to avoid a capital duty charge by incorporating in the company's constitution a restriction on the transfer or other disposal of its shares "without prior authorisation" (so preventing it from being a capital company) provided that its shares cannot be dealt in on a stock exchange in the EEC (see sections 48(1)(d) and 48(1)(e) of the 1973 Act).

Relief from capital duty

An important relief from capital duty may be available in the case of a share exchange offer under paragraph 10 of Schedule 19 to the Finance Act 1973. It is similar to the transfer duty relief in section 55 of the Finance Act 1927 but there are significant differences in detail. As a result, capital duty relief may be available in a take-over where section 55 relief is not (or the other way around).

Generally speaking, relief from capital duty is available where a capital company acquires, by virtue of a chargeable transaction, either (a) share capital of another capital company so that after the chargeable transaction not less than 75 per cent of that other company's issued share capital is beneficially owned by the acquiring company, or (b) the whole or any part of the undertaking of another capital company and (in either case) the conditions set out below are satisfied. Unlike the section 55 position, there is no need for a "reconstruction or amalgamation". The conditions are,

(i) the place of effective management or the registered office of the target company is in a country in the EEC; and

(ii) that part of the consideration (other than the assumption or discharge of liabilities of the acquired company) for the chargeable transaction which is not the *issue* of the acquiring company's shares to the holders of shares in the target company (or, on an assets acquisition, to the target company or its shareholders) is *cash*. (Note that "issue" has the same restrictive meaning as under section 55 – therefore use of renounceable allotment letters by the acquiring company will result in denial of relief); and

(iii) the cash element of the consideration for the chargeable transaction does not exceed *10* per cent of the *nominal* value of the share consideration (i.e. of the *nominal* value of the shares in the *acquiring company* issued to holders of shares in the target company).

Relief is therefore only available if the consideration consists solely of shares and cash. As a result, a consideration consisting of a mixture of shares and loan stock or loan notes will mean that relief from capital duty is not available, although relief from transfer duty under section 55 might be available. On the other hand, again unlike the position under section 55, relief is available where an acquiring company already holds a significant shareholding (for example 29.99 per cent) and by a chargeable transaction increases its shareholding to over 75 per cent. Unlike section 55, the acquiring company need not be incorporated in Great Britain but in this case it must be a capital company as defined in section 48 of the Finance Act 1973. The target company also need not be incorporated in Great Britain. However, it must either be a capital company as defined in the Finance Act 1973 or be treated as a capital company in another member state, unless it should constitute the whole or part of an "undertaking" of a company which is a capital company.

The 10 per cent cash limitation (by reference to the nominal value of the shares which make up the balance of the consideration) is likely to be much more restrictive than the section 55 requirement that, of the total consideration, at least 90 per cent by value must be in shares. In both cases the percentage of the capital to be acquired is of the whole of the issued share capital of the target company so that it would, for example, include preference shares. See also the discussion on section 55 above as regards the effects of fractional entitlements and cash alternative offers.

Relief will be lost if the acquiring company at any time within *five* years after the chargeable transaction,

(a) ceases to retain at least 75 per cent of the issued share capital of the target company; or

(b) disposes of any of the shares in the target company which it held immediately after the relevant chargeable transaction.

The only exceptions in the legislation to (a) and (b) above are disposals as part of a transaction itself qualifying for relief under paragraph 10(1) of Schedule 19 or in the winding up of the *acquiring company*. In addition, however, it appears that a disposal which occurs in the winding up of the target company and the distribution to the acquiring company of a "due proportion" of the target company's assets is excepted (see the E.E.C. Council Declaration of April 9, 1973 and *Sergeant and Sims on Stamp Duty*, 8th edition, at page 551). Accordingly even intra group transfers (not themselves qualifying for relief) may not be made within the five year period without a loss of relief. Unlike the position under section 55, loss of relief can also result from a simple dilution in the interests of the acquiring company in the target company (for example on a conversion of convertible loan stocks).

In practice there appears to be a difference between the application of section 55 and the application of Schedule 19 as regards the requirement that the consideration shares be issued to persons entered in the share register of the target company. Both provisions refer to the issue of shares to *holders* of shares in the target company in exchange for the shares *held* by them in the target company. As mentioned on page 863, there are section 55 cases indicating that the shares must be issued to, broadly speaking, the target company's registered shareholders. In practice, however, the Capital Duty office do not appear always to apply this test strictly to paragraph 10 relief claims. As a result it may be possible to qualify for capital duty relief where a stamp duty saving scheme is used to save transfer duty, even though most of the consideration shares issued to the target company's shareholders will be in respect of the rights they have to be placed on the target company's register through holding renounceable letters of allotment rather than in respect of the registered shares which they hold. The availability of relief in these circumstances (even if the other requirements are met) is, however, not certain and the Capital Duty office have been known to deny relief. The decision in *Pye-Smith v. IRC* [1958] 2 All E.R. 785 is, however, often thought to assist in the argument that an owner of a renounceable allotment letter is a "holder" – it certainly indicates that the owner is the equitable owner of the underlying shares.

As mentioned earlier, where an acquiring company wishes to offer a cash alternative, relief from stamp duty can still be preserved, despite the "90 per cent share consideration" test, by the acquiring company arranging for its merchant bank to make an independent cash offer for the shares it issues to the target company's shareholders. The difficulty, however, is that the acquiring company must issue its consideration shares definitively if section 55 relief is to be available. As a result, two per cent ad valorem stamp duty is payable by the merchant bank on purchases it makes from target company shareholders who accept the cash alternative. To get round this, the acquiring company may decide to avoid stamp duty on the take-over by procuring the implementation of a stamp duty saving scheme in the target and issuing its consideration shares in renounceable form. The cost, however, of this choice is one per cent capital duty on the share consideration given by the acquiring company – capital duty relief is no longer available because shares are not being "*issued*" to the holders of shares in the target company. The following table sets out the various permutations on the assumption that the acquiring company is not entitled to the reduced rate of ad valorem duty (see above). "A" is the acquiring company, "T" the target company, and "MB" the merchant bank:

	Stamp duty on acquisition by A	Capital duty on consideration shares issued by A	Stamp duty on purchase by MB under "cash alternative"
(1) No stamp duty saving scheme in T; A issues shares definitively	Nil (section 55)	Nil (paragraph 10)	2 per cent
(2) Stamp duty saving scheme in T; A issues shares definitively	Nominal (stamp duty saving scheme)	*Probably* nil (paragraph 10 – see text)	2 per cent

	Stamp duty on acquisition by A	Capital duty on consideration shares issued by A	Stamp duty on purchase by MB under "cash alternative"
(3) No stamp duty saving scheme in T; A issues shares on RLA's	2 per cent (no "issue" for section 55)	1 per cent (no "issue" for section 55)	Nil (RLA exemption)
(4) Stamp duty saving scheme in T; A issues shares on RLA's	Nominal (stamp duty saving scheme)	1 per cent (no "issue" for section 55)	Nil (RLA exemption)

It follows from the table, that the "break-even" point in a "cash alternative" acquisition for choosing method (4) rather than method (1) (or (2)) comes where it is anticipated that at least half the target company's shareholders will accept the merchant bank's cash alternative.

For the purposes of paragraph 10, shares in a target company which are cancelled under a scheme of arrangement under section 206 of the Companies Act 1948 in consideration of the allotment of shares in the acquiring company are treated as being acquired so that relief from capital duty may be available (paragraph 11 of Schedule 19).

Relief under paragraph 10 is obtained on application by letter to the Controller of Stamps (Adjudication Section), Inland Revenue, West Block, Barrington Road, Worthing, Sussex BN12 4SF. The relevant PUC Form which is sent to the Registrar of Companies should be accompanied by a letter stating that a claim for capital duty relief under paragraph 10 of Schedule 19 has been or will be made.

Merger accounting and pre-acquisition profits

Until the recent case of *Shearer v. Bercain Limited* [1980] 3 All E.R. 295, the proper accounting treatment to be followed on a merger was often a question of particular discomfort for lawyers. The problems posed by *Shearer v. Bercain Limited* were dealt with by provisions in the Companies Act 1981 permitting merger accounting in certain circumstances. The 1981 Act's provisions (which provide a rare example in company law of "retrospective" legislation) can best be explained against the background of the problems that previously existed (and still exist to some extent where the 1981 Act's provisions do not apply).

Different approaches

The primary question concerns the issue by an acquiring company (A) of its shares as consideration for its acquisition of a target company (T).

If the aggregate fair value of T's shares is more than the aggregate nominal value of A's shares issued as consideration, does A have to transfer the excess of the aggregate nominal value of its consideration shares over the aggregate fair value of T's shares into a share premium account? The other question, which is affected by the answer to the first question, is whether A can pay dividends to its members out of dividends paid to it by T out of profits earned prior to the acquisition.

The answers to these questions can be important for a number of reasons. The amount of depreciation required in respect of amounts arising on consolidation of the target company is likely to vary according to the cost of the target company and could affect future published earnings. A restriction on the distribution of pre-acquisition profits could affect the acquiring company's ability to maintain or increase its dividend rate per share following the merger. It may therefore be important to address these questions at an early stage. From the legal point of view, merger accounting is now permitted by the removal of the requirement under section 56 of the Companies Act 1948 to set up a share premium account in certain circumstances. Current accounting practice will determine whether it is nevertheless necessary for A to treat the cost of T as being greater than the nominal value of the consideration shares (plus any other consideration provided).

Section 56 of the Companies Act 1948 provides:

> "Where a company issues shares at a premium, whether for cash or otherwise, a sum equal to the aggregate amount or value of the premiums on those shares shall be transferred to an account, to be called "the share premium account", and the provisions of this Act relating to the reduction of the share capital of a company shall, except as provided in this section, apply as if the share premium account were paid up share capital of the company."

In *Henry Head & Co Limited v. Ropner Holdings Limited* [1952] Ch. 124 this section was interpreted as requiring a share premium account to be opened "where shares are issued for a consideration other than cash and the value of the assets acquired is more than the nominal value of the shares issued". The question of pre-acquisition profits was not specifically dealt with in the judgment. It is argued that the obligation to create a share premium account does not of itself necessarily mean that dividends cannot be paid out of pre-acquisition profits, although it may in practice often have this effect. Prior to the changes in the rules regarding dividends introduced by the Companies Act 1980, if the payment of the dividend by the subsidiary could fairly have been said not to reduce the value of the subsidiary below the value at which it stood in its parent's accounts (subject to paragraph 15(5) of the Eighth Schedule) the dividend should have been distributable. It is now a question whether that dividend can be said to be a realised profit (see below).

The Jenkins Report in 1960 took the view that section 56 did require companies to transfer premiums to a share premium account where they acquired shares worth more than the nominal value of the shares issued in consideration. The Report recommended that this rule should be modified where a *new* holding company acquired on a reconstruction or amalgamation more than 90 per cent of the share capital of one or more companies, so that the new holding company could treat part of the pre-acquisition profits of any one (only) of those companies as a reserve available for distribution to its own members.

However, there were differing views as to the proper construction of section 56. As a result, there were a number of instances in which following a merger (a) the acquiring company declined to transfer any premium to its share premium account but rather showed the cost of its new subsidiary as being the aggregate nominal value of the shares it had issued, and (b) pre-acquisition profits were paid out by the acquiring company by way of dividend and were therefore treated as coming out of income and not capital.

The accountancy profession produced an exposure draft on merger acquisitions (ED3) in January 1971. This suggested a standard accounting practice which would allow, in certain circumstances, most of a subsidiary's distributable reserves to be distributed by a company acquiring more than 90 per cent of its equity shares. Although in a number of instances this accounting practice may have been adopted, because of the uncertainty surrounding the legality of the proposals the exposure draft was never converted into an accounting standard and no further steps were taken to tackle the problem for some years.

Paragraph 15(5) of the Eighth Schedule to the Companies Act 1948 (which as a result of the Companies Act 1981 now no longer applies to most companies and, as amended, has become paragraph 15(5) of schedule 8A) provided:

> "... the profits or losses attributable to any shares in a subsidiary for the time being held by the holding company or any other of its subsidiaries shall not (for that *or any other purpose*) be treated [in the holding company's accounts as revenue profits or losses] so far as they are profits or losses for the period before the date on or as from which the shares were acquired by the company or any of its subsidiaries".

It was argued that, although this was a strange place to find a general provision, the effect of the underlined words was to prevent the distribution of pre-acquisition profits of a subsidiary.

Shearer v. Bercain

In 1980 *Shearer v. Bercain Limited* [1980] 3 All E.R. 295, a tax case concerned with a shortfall assessment, clearly re-established the legal position. Bercain Limited was incorporated as a holding company in August 1971. It subsequently issued 4,100 shares of £1 each in exchange for the issued share capitals of two companies, worth £84,000 and £12,000 respectively, thus acquiring assets of £91,900 more than the nominal value of its shares. It created a share premium account to which it transferred this amount. In December 1971 both subsidiaries paid dividends to Bercain Limited out of pre-acquisition profits and Bercain wrote down the value of its investment in these subsidiaries by the amounts of the dividends from them. The Inland Revenue made a shortfall assessment on Bercain, to which Bercain's defence was that it fell within the relieving provisions applying where a restriction is imposed by law as regards the making of distributions. The Inland Revenue agreed that, if Bercain was obliged by law to create a share premium account equal in amount to the excess of the value of the shares acquired over the nominal value of the shares issued, the shortfall assessment was inappropriate.

It was argued for the Inland Revenue that the directors of Bercain could choose how many shares to issue and could issue the shares on such terms as they thought fit. Further, provided that the directors honestly believed the assets acquired were worth the par value of the shares issued, they did not have to value the assets, they could forego making a profit on the issue of their shares and the cost of the issue of the shares was prima facie the nominal value of the shares issued. Therefore, it was argued, section 56 only applied where the premium at which the shares were issued was stated in the agreement and not to other non-cash premium cases.

Walton J. held that this distinction was unsupported by section 56, which "caters for a premium being in cash, because the shares are issued for cash, and a premium being otherwise than in cash, because the shares are issued otherwise than for cash; and in both cases these premiums have to be carried to a share premium account." He thought the case before him was indistinguishable from the case of *Henry Head* and noted that in that case Harman J., although anxious to limit the effect of the section if possible, had held that "if the shares are issued for a consideration other than cash and the value of the assets acquired is more than the nominal value of the shares issued, you have issued shares at a premium". Harman J. had also mentioned that it was incorrect to say that the section did not apply where a holding company bought shares on an amalgamation. Walton J. pointed out that the directors of a company were under a duty to act in the best interests of the company in determining the number of shares to be issued, the terms of issue of the shares, how few shares could be issued for the assets being acquired and the respective values of the shares and the assets. If a company acquired an asset worth £5,000 for 1,000 shares of £1 each, it would take the assets into its books at £5,000 and not £1,000 and he thought it an untenable proposition that the cost to the acquiring company in such a situation was only £1,000. He also considered that the effect of the wording of paragraph 15(5) of the Eighth Schedule was to prevent pre-acquisition profits being distributed as dividends.

The case provided some guidance on the valuation of the premiums. Walton J. said:

> "Of course the word value must involve a valuation of some kind; but what is a valuation but an estimation, possibly an informed and reasoned estimation, but still an estimation, of what the value is in monetary terms?"

He accepted that, in order for the accounts of the acquiring company to show a true and fair view, an asset must be shown in the balance sheet at its true value and it seems implicit in his judgment that any quantification of the value of the premium must involve a bona fide assessment of the asset acquired.

The effect of the decision in *Shearer v. Bercain Limited* was to prevent the previous practice of bringing assets into a balance sheet at a cost equal to the nominal value of the shares issued as consideration for the assets. It left in some doubt the position of those companies which had failed to create share premium accounts and had distributed pre-acquisition profits of subsidiaries by way of dividends. The Companies Act 1981 contained provisions which were enacted in response to representations from the legal and accounting professions, and from industry, to mitigate the effects of *Shearer v. Bercain Limited.*

The 1981 Act

The new statutory provisions are contained in sections 36 to 41 of the Companies Act 1981. These are essentially three distinct provisions. Section 39 gives retrospective relief for those cases where no share premium account was established before the Bill was published. Section 38 deals with group reconstructions and section 37 deals with mergers which do not fall within section 38. Also, under section 41 the Secretary of State is given wide powers to restrict, modify or enlarge the relief given by sections 36 to 40 by regulations made by statutory instrument. This will enable changes to be made if practical difficulties are encountered or if changes are necessitated by further EEC directives on group accounts.

Under section 39 retrospective relief is given for any premium on shares not transferred to a share premium account, where the acquiring company (A) issued shares at a premium as consideration either for the issue or transfer to it of shares in another company (T), or for the cancellation by T of shares in T not held by A. For the section to apply T must either have been a subsidiary of A or of A's holding company at the time of the arrangement, or must have become such a subsidiary on the acquisition or cancellation of T's shares. To the extent that premiums were not transferred to a share premium account, section 56 is to be treated as not applying to those premiums. The issue of the shares by A must have occurred before February 4, 1981 (the date on which the Companies Bill was published) for section 39 to apply. The relief provided by this section is broadly worded, whereas the relief provided by the Act for issues of shares on or after February 4, 1981 is more limited.

Section 38 grants relief from section 56 for certain group reconstructions involving the transfer of a company's shares within a group of companies. Where it applies,

(a) section 37 may not be applied; and

(b) the issuing company is not required to transfer to a share premium account more than the amount by which the nominal value of the shares allotted in consideration for the transfer is less than the lesser of

(i) the cost of the shares to the transferring company; and

(ii) the amount at which those shares are stated in that company's books immediately before the transfer.

Of more significance in the context of this chapter is section 37, which provides relief from section 56 in the case of mergers which meet certain specified conditions. Section 37 cannot apply where the group reconstruction relief in section 38 applies. Subject to this exception, section 37 will apply if A, the issuing company, secures at least a 90 per cent equity holding in company T by an arrangement under which A allots equity shares in consideration of the issue or transfer to A of equity shares in T, or the cancellation of T's equity shares not held by A. "Arrangement" is broadly defined by section 40(6) to include schemes under section 206 and 287 of the Companies Act 1948; "transfer" includes the transfer of a right to be included in the target company's register of members (e.g. a renunciation of a renounceable allotment letter). If under the arrangement A also receives non-equity shares in T, or T cancels non-equity shares not held by A, the relief is also available for the shares in A which are issued as consideration for the non-equity shares. Non-equity shares are shares, such as deferred shares, which do not, either as regards dividends or as regards capital, carry any right to participate beyond a specified amount in a distribution (section 154(5) of the Companies Act 1948). Where the equity capital of T consists of different classes, the requirements referred to above must be satisfied in relation to each class separately.

A is regarded as having secured at least 90 per cent pursuant to a section 37 arrangement if, after the acquisition or cancellation of equity shares in T pursuant to that arrangement, A holds equity shares in T of an aggregate nominal value equal to 90 per cent or more of the nominal value of T's share capital (section 37(4)). It does not matter that some of these shares were not acquired in pursuance of the arrangement (for example because A had acquired a significant holding in T for cash), but merger accounting under the new proposed statement of standard accounting practice (ED31) depends upon the share consideration overall (see below). Shares held by a holding company or subsidiary of A or by a subsidiary of A's holding company (or by its or their nominees) are treated as being held by A for the purposes of the section.

Where section 37 applies, the acquiring company need not transfer premiums to a share premium account (i.e. section 56 of the Companies Act 1948 will not apply). Furthermore, section 40(1) allows a company entitled to relief under section 37 (or under sections 38 or 39) to disregard the amount which does not have to be transferred to the share premium account in calculating the amount at which the shares in the target company are to be included in the acquiring company's balance sheet.

As regards the distribution of pre-acquisition profits, section 40(2) provides that in cases where sections 37 to 39 apply, paragraph 15(5) of the Eighth Schedule is not to be treated as having restricted the distribution of pre-acquisition profits prior to October 30, 1981 (the day on which the 1981 Act came into force). From October 30, 1981 the wording in paragraph 15(5) of the Eighth Schedule (now paragraph 15(5) of Schedule 8A) has been amended to make it clear that this wording should not be regarded as preventing the distribution of pre-acquisition profits of a subsidiary (section 40(3) of the Companies Act 1981).

The Companies (Accounts and Audit) Regulations 1982 S.I. 1092 require a company which makes an acquisition falling within section 37 to disclose certain particulars of the acquisition, including the profits and losses of the acquired company, in its accounts for the year of acquisition. In certain cases details are required in those accounts, and the following two years' accounts, of disposals of shares in or assets of the acquired company.

Section 37 is fairly broad and there will be many instances where the proposed accounting standard will nevertheless require that the acquiring company show in its balance sheet the fair value of the shares acquired as being the cost of those shares (even though a share premium account is not necessary as a matter of company law). If neither section 37 nor section 38 applies, the acquiring company will have to establish a share premium account pursuant to section 56 of the Companies Act 1948. Whether or not this will effectively prevent the distribution of pre-acquisition profits, will depend upon whether the dividend received by the acquiring company (out of such profits) can be treated as a realised profit for the acquiring company, or only the return of part of the cost to it of the target company (see below for ED31 statement on this point).

ED31

A new exposure draft on this subject, ED31, was published in October 1982. ED31 proposes stricter conditions for merger accounting than are required under the Companies Act 1981. As a result, it may be necessary (if ED31 is adopted) to account for a take-over as an acquisition even though the Companies Acts do not require the transfer of any premium on the issue of consideration shares to a share premium account. The principal test applied by ED31 in distinguishing between a merger and an acquisition is that for the former there should be a share exchange with an immaterial amount of assets leaving the group. If more than 10 per cent of the consideration for the equity capital of the target company is other than equity of the acquiring company, for accounting purposes the take-over will be an acquisition and not a merger.

ED31 puts forward a number of conditions to be met if the take-over is to be treated as a merger for accounting purposes:

(a) the business combination should result from an offer to the holders of all equity shares and the holders of all voting shares which are ~~not already held by the offeror; the offer should be~~ approved by the holders of the voting shares of the company making the offer; and

(b) the offer should be accepted by holders of at least 90 per cent of *all* equity shares and of the shares carrying at least 90 per cent of all votes of the target company; for this purpose, any convertible stock is not to be regarded as equity except to the extent that it is converted into equity as a result of the business combination; and

(c) not less than 90 per cent of the fair value of the total consideration given for the equity share capital (including that given for shares already held) should be in the form of equity capital; not less than 90 per cent of the fair value of the consideration given for voting non-equity share capital (including that given to shares already held) should be in the form of equity or voting non-equity share capital, or both.

A number of significant points arise from these conditions, some of which seem to bear little relationship to the principal test of a share exchange with an immaterial amount of assets leaving the group. Certain of the requirements do not seem to have a sufficiently convincing justification against the background of a more permissive statutory provision. First, even if the take-over is achieved entirely by a share exchange, so that no resources leave the group, merger accounting will not be applicable unless the offer has been approved by the shareholders of the acquiring company. This approval will be a Stock Exchange requirement where the acquiring company is a listed company and the value of the consideration for the acquisition or the size of the target company (on an assets or earnings test) represents 25 per cent or more of the acquiring company (see Chapter 4 of The Stock Exchange's Yellow Book and page 893 below). A shareholders' meeting may be necessary to authorise the share issue (either under section 14 of the Companies Act 1980 or in terms of increasing the acquiring company's share capital). Where no shareholders' meeting is otherwise required, this will be a significant additional requirement – sometimes raising real commercial problems for the transaction.

Secondly, merger accounting seems not to be available where the acquiring company already holds at the time of the offer more than 10 per cent of the target company. Indeed, it would appear that if the acquiring company already held 10 per cent, for merger accounting to apply its offer for the balance would have to be accepted by all shareholders. In other words, even though the acquiring company might be able to obtain 100 per cent through the application of section 209 of the Companies Act 1948, this would not constitute "acceptance of the offer". The higher the percentage of equity shares already held, the more difficult it will be to meet the condition.

There may also be some significance in how a cash alternative is structured. If cash is provided by a third party, such as the acquiring company's merchant bank, in consideration for the *purchase* of the acquiring company's shares from target company shareholders, so that no assets leave the group (except by way of commissions and fees), merger relief would seem to be available. However, if the cash is provided by subscription by the merchant bank for new shares, rather than by a separate offer to purchase consideration shares from those target company shareholders who would prefer cash, merger relief may well not be available even though overall no material amount of assets will have left the group. There will probably be a risk that the cash will amount to more than 10 per cent of the fair value of the consideration, in which case, because the cash is provided (in contractual terms) by the acquiring company, merger accounting will not apply. In the former case it would seem that the consideration will be treated as being wholly in shares whatever number of target company shareholders call upon the merchant bank for cash.

Where merger accounting is applicable, the shares of the target company are to be recorded in the books of the acquiring company at the nominal value of the shares issued in exchange. Where there is additional consideration (for example, cash) its fair value is to be added to the nominal value of the shares. If acquisition accounting is required, the shares in the target company are to be shown in the books of the acquiring company at cost, which under ED31 is taken to be the fair value of the consideration given by the acquiring company. Where full relief is available under the 1981 Act from section 56 of the Companies Act 1948, the excess of the fair value over the nominal value of the shares issued by the acquiring company is to be credited to a special reserve (instead of share premium). On consolidation, the total purchase consideration is allocated between the underlying net tangible and intangible assets, other than goodwill, on the basis of the fair value to the acquiring company (in accordance with SSAP14). Any difference will represent goodwill. ED31 also states that, under acquisition accounting, pre-acquisition profits or losses of the acquired company are reflected in the value of its net assets at the date of acquisition. Distributions to the acquiring company from pre-acquisition profits should be applied accordingly to reduce the cost of the shares acquired. According to this statement such distributions would not represent realised profits to the acquiring company.

Anti-trust laws

Merger references in the United Kingdom

The ability of the government to control mergers for such reasons as maintaining competition, protecting employment and even preventing control falling into overseas hands, is in practice very wide. The principal legislation by which this is achieved is the Fair Trading Act 1973. It is supplemented by the Industry Act 1979 in relation to manufacturing undertakings (although the powers under this Act to prevent a merger have yet to be used) and in relation to particular industries either by legislation affecting those industries or by licensing provisions. For example, before any person may become a controller of an insurance company authorised under the Insurance Companies Acts 1974 and 1981 to carry on usiness in the United Kingdom, written notice must be given to the Secretary of State for Trade, who may object if it appears to him that the person concerned is not a fit and proper person to be a controller of the authorised insurance company. As another example, the change of control of a company with interests in United Kingdom petroleum licences can enable the Secretary of State for Energy ultimately to revoke such licences (see, as an example, Model Clause 39(3) for Production Licences in Seaward licences as contained in Schedule 5 to The Petroleum (Production) Regulations 1982). In addition the European Commission may assume jurisdiction to prohibit a merger.

In general, in the United Kingdom it is the Fair Trading Act which has the most significance – with considerable assistance from the rules of the City Code on Take-overs and Mergers. The City Code requires take-over offers falling within the rules to include as a term a provision that the offer will lapse if it is *referred* to the Monopolies and Mergers Commission (see further on page 880 below). Thus, where the City Code applies (and is complied with) an offeror is effectively prevented from accepting the risks of a merger reference and any subsequent action which the Monopolies and Mergers Commission might consider necessary under the Fair Trading Act. Furthermore it (perhaps wrongly) gives added significance to the reference itself – which may never lead to a determination that the merger would operate against the public interest. An approach to the Office of Fair Trading will therefore be one of the obvious items on the agenda for any board wishing to oppose a take-over offer.

Under the Fair Trading Act 1973, the Director General of the Office of Fair Trading (OFT) is under a duty to keep himself informed about actual or prospective arrangements which may fall within the scope of the Act, and to make recommendations to the Secretary of State, who is primarily responsible for deciding whether an arrangement should be investigated by the Monopolies and Mergers Commission.

The Fair Trading Act

The Fair Trading Act singles out newspaper mergers for special treatment. Other mergers are treated alike.

Newspaper mergers are dealt with in sections 57 to 62 of the Fair Trading Act. Where the acquirer is already a newspaper proprietor and the transfer of the newspaper would result in a combined circulation of over 500,000 copies a day, reference to the Commission is generally required. The strict requirement for a reference does not apply if the Secretary of State is satisfied that the newspaper to be transferred is not economic as a going concern and as a separate newspaper, or if its average circulation is less than 25,000 copies per day. A newspaper proprietor includes someone who has 25 per cent or more of the voting shares (a controlling interest) of a company which is itself a newspaper proprietor. The acquisition by a newspaper proprietor of a "controlling interest" of a newspaper company is sufficient to fall within the provisions of the Act. A company with no connections with a newspaper could acquire a newspaper without a reference being made.

As regards other mergers, if certain stated criteria exist, the Secretary of State for Trade has a discretion to refer a merger, or proposed merger, to the Commission for investigation.

(1) Two or more enterprises must cease to be distinct (i.e. merge), and at least one of the enterprises must be carried on in the United Kingdom or by or under the control of a company incorporated in the United Kingdom (sections 64(1) and 65). Enterprises cease to be distinct if they are brought under common ownership or control, or if either of them ceases business as a result of arrangements or a transaction entered into in order to prevent competition. The Act does not define control, although it gives some examples of common control, and states that a person without a controlling interest may be treated as having control if he has the ability materially to influence policy. It is thought that the acquisition of a substantial minority interest will be sufficient for a reference, especially where there is no counteracting shareholding or where the interest is supported by board representation. For example, the Commission took the view in their report on Eurocanadian Shipholdings Limited/Furness, Withy & Company Limited and Manchester Liners Limited (1976) that in the circumstances a holding of as little as 20.6 per cent could give rise to the ability materially to influence policy. It has also been suggested that the same chairman of two independent companies supported by one or more other common directors may satisfy the test of being able materially to influence policy. For the purposes of determining control certain associated persons and companies are treated as one. People who act together to exercise or secure control are to be regarded as associated.

Although two enterprises may have ceased to be distinct, they can be also treated as ceasing to be distinct on a later occasion. See the Office of Fair Trading's booklet on Mergers at page 3:

> ". . . the acquisition of a minority shareholding which enables the holder materially to influence the policy of a company may of itself constitute a merger situation qualifying for investigation. If that shareholding is increased to a level at which the holder is able to control the policy of the company, that further acquisition may be the subject of another enquiry even though several years have passed since the shareholder first acquired a sufficient holding to permit influence. Should he at a later stage move to a position in which he has a controlling interest, the final acquisition is then again open to examination."

(2) The value of the assets taken over must exceed £15 million or, as a result of the merger, at least a quarter of the goods or services supplied in the United Kingdom (or a substantial part of it) must be supplied by or to the new entity. If such a situation exists already, the proportion must increase. The "value of assets taken over" is calculated at the book

value of all the target company's assets (both within the United Kingdom and elsewhere) less provisions for depreciation, renewals or diminution in value. In many cases it will be difficult to categorise goods or services so as to determine whether the market-share criterion is satisfied. These criteria are wide enough to cover an acquisition by a United Kingdom company of an overseas company, or vice versa, if (a) the value of the assets taken over exceeds £15 million (even though the overseas company has no business in the United Kingdom), or (b) the overseas company supplies goods or services in the United Kingdom (even though supply may be by export and the company may have no place of business in the United Kingdom).

Most references are made before a merger takes place. The Secretary of State need not and usually does not give reasons for his decision. A reference may not generally be made more than six months after a merger has taken place or, if later, after the time when the merger was made public or details of it were notified to the Office of Fair Trading or the Department of Trade (section 64(4)).

Commission's report

The Commission must usually report within six months of the reference although this period may be extended once by the Secretary of State for Trade up to a further three months (section 70). The report, which is laid before Parliament and published, will typically conclude whether the merger falls within the scope of the legislation and, if so, operates, or may be expected to operate, against the public interest. If the Commission finds that the merger does or is likely to operate against the public interest, it is obliged to specify the particular adverse aspects and may include recommendations as to the action which should be taken to remedy or prevent those adverse aspects. If the Commission concludes that the merger is against the public interest, the Secretary of State has very wide powers. These range from asking the Director General to obtain assurances from the parties as to their future behaviour, to prohibiting a merger, ordering the transfer of property and other rights before or after a merger, regulating supplies, prices and charges and prohibiting discrimination.

Take-over code

A merger reference by the Secretary of State may itself have sufficiently serious repercussions to prevent the merger proceeding. Where the take-over is governed by the rules of the City Code on Take-Overs and Mergers, rule 9 provides that if the take-over falls within the ambit of the Fair Trading Act, it must be a term of the offer that it will lapse if there is a reference to the Commission before the first closing date or the date on which the offer becomes or is declared unconditional as to acceptances, whichever is later. Where the take-over falls within the Fair Trading Act, it is usual for one of the *conditions* of the offer to be receipt of confirmation in terms satisfactory to the offeror that the proposed acquisition will not be referred to the Commission. The inclusion of such a condition does not satisfy the rule 9 obligation. An offeror will frequently reserve the right to waive this condition but in most cases the Secretary of State will have reached a decision on whether or not to refer the acquisition to the Commission before the first closing date. In this way the Take-over Panel effectively prevents an offeror from accepting the risk of a merger reference prior to its offer becoming unconditional as to acceptances. If the reference is made before this time so that the offer lapses, the offeror is precluded from making another offer for twelve months without the prior consent of the Take-over Panel. By the time that the merger has been cleared by the Commission, the commercial situation may well have changed to such an extent that a further bid is not appropriate. While this position clearly assists the Office of Fair Trading in its task, it is at least doubtful whether it operates for the benefit of the shareholders whom the take-over rules are intended to protect.

Confidential guidance

Because of the effects of a merger reference it is possible to seek confidential guidance from the Office of Fair Trading at an early stage. No public announcement is made and only the party or parties concerned are informed of the Office of Fair Trading's provisional view. Because it is impossible to obtain the reactions of other interested parties, the guidance is not definitive before the merger has been publicly announced. If no approach is made to the Office of Fair Trading before the announcement of an offer, then unless the Fair Trading Act does not apply it is worthwhile shortly after the announcement to make contact with the Office of Fair Trading and to supply it with at least the accounts of each company. In cases where there is thought to be a possibility that a reference will be made, it may be advisable to prepare a written presentation for the Office of Fair Trading, aiming to show that the take-over will not operate against the public interest and should not be referred. This will be especially important for an offeror faced with an unwilling target company which feels it may be able to persuade the Office of Fair Trading that there is sufficient doubt as to the public interest to justify a reference to the Commission.

European legislation

The Treaty of Rome contains no detailed provisions for the control of mergers. At present the European Commission does not treat mergers as falling within Article 85, although the wording is wide enough to encompass mergers and this view may change. The European Commission may treat Article 85 as applicable to the relationship between a group and individual companies where not all of a group is taken over and there is a relationship between those companies taken over and those companies not taken over. The European Commission may apply

Article 86 where a company in a dominant position strengthens its position by merger or take-over and reaches a position of dominance which substantially excludes competition.

The European Commission monitors mergers and may request further information, but it has taken no official action since the *Continental Can* case in 1972. In that case the European Court of Justice upheld the Commission's view that Article 86 can apply to mergers but held that, in the particular case, the Commission had not analysed the product markets sufficiently to back up their contention that the acquirer had a "dominant position". An informal approach may be made for advance clearance (there is no formal procedure), but because an informal clearance given on full disclosure of the facts is treated as binding on the European Commission advice will not usually be given at short notice. At present it is unusual for any approach to be made to the European Commission in connection with a take-over offer for a United Kingom company. However, such an offer will often be conditional on there being no interference by supranational authorities.

The European Commission submitted a proposal for a Council Regulation on merger control in 1973 which was approved by the European Parliament but was not implemented because of differences with the Council. An amended proposal was submitted in December 1981 as a result of concern over the lack of action.

Articles 65 and 66 of the Treaty of Paris contain similar provisions to Articles 85 and 86 of the Treaty of Rome and apply where at least one of the parties produces or distributes coal or steel. Article 66 has specific provisions relating to merger control which require prior authorisation from the Commission for a take-over or other method of obtaining control by one or more parties in the field of coal or steel production or distribution. Control is very widely defined and is not limited to control through shareholdings. There are exemptions available where one party is not involved in coal or steel production or distribution or where production or distribution capacity is small.

Industry Act 1975

Under Part II of the Industry Act 1975 the Secretary of State may prohibit a take-over of "important manufacturing undertakings" by non-residents or may acquire the assets or shares of such undertakings which have been or are about to be so taken-over. The Government has advised that these powers will be used only in extreme cases and the first such case is yet to emerge. The powers under the Fair Trading Act have so far proved sufficient. Applications for an advance ruling may be made to the Department of Industry which will co-ordinate with the Office of Fair Trading if, as is likely, the Office of Fair Trading is also conducting an investigation for the purposes of the Fair Trading Act.

Anti-trust laws in other countries

Of anti-trust legislation in other countries, the U.S. Hart-Scott-Rodino

Anti-trust Improvements Act of 1976 is of particular significance because it requires notification and the elapse of a waiting period before an acquisition. It will apply if one of the parties is involved (itself or through subsidiaries or holding companies) in commerce or activities affecting commerce and each of the parties exceeds one of various relevant thresholds in respect of assets and annual turnover. It can apply where a United Kingdom company is bidding for another United Kingdom company, if each (itself or through its subsidiaries) either has assets in, or trades with, the United States. If the Act applies, it will usually restrict the acquisition of "strategic" holdings of shares in the target company to the lower of $15 million worth of shares or 15 per cent of the target company's voting rights. The normal waiting period is thirty days after the offeror has made its filing or fifteen days in the case of a cash offer, although these periods can be shortened in some cases if convincing reasons can be produced. The periods may also be extended if the Federal Trade Commission or Department of Justice raises questions on the filing. The acquisition may not be consummated during the waiting period although the offer document may be posted. However, if an offer is posted during the waiting period, the offer must not be capable of becoming unconditional before the waiting period has expired. This may be achieved by including a condition to the offer that the Hart-Scott-Rodino waiting period should have expired. The applicability or otherwise of the Act should therefore be determined before the terms of an offer are announced. The expiry of the waiting period without action by the United States governmental authorities does not necessarily mean that no action will be forthcoming from such authorities and there may of course be additional State requirements.

There may well be anti-trust implications in other jurisdictions (for example Canada and Australia) where the offeror or the offeree, or both, have subsidiaries or significant activities. For similar reasons these should be checked at an early stage. In the case of groups with large and varied overseas interests it may only be practicable to examine the most significant jurisdictions before the terms of an offer are announced. In such cases a general condition as to governmental approvals or action is likely in most cases to provide sufficient protection.

Rules applicable to takeovers

There is very little legislation controlling the documentation to be used for take-overs and mergers. The prospectus provisions of the Companies Act 1948 are concerned primarily with the issue or sale of new securities. The Prevention of Fraud (Investments) Act 1958 and the rules made pursuant to that Act (The Licensed Dealers (Conduct of Business) Rules, 1960) provide the principal statutory regulation of the conduct of take-over bids and their documentation. Section 14 of the Prevention of Fraud (Investments) Act, in effect, restricts the persons who may circulate documents containing take-over offers. An offeror, unless one of the persons referred to in section 14(3), will generally not be able to circulate its own offer without first having the document approved by the Department of Trade. The majority of take-over offers are therefore circulated by merchant banks (or other persons referred to in section 14(3)). Documents for the implementation of a scheme of arrangement are exempted from the restriction in section 14 (by section 14(2)(c)).

The Licensed Dealers Rules tend to have greater application in practice than might be supposed. Strictly, they apply only to licensed dealers, who are rarely involved in take-over bids. However, exempted dealers (i.e. persons, such as merchant banks, who are declared to be exempted dealers pursuant to section 16 of the Prevention of Fraud (Investments) Act) are expected by the Department of Trade to observe the rules. On the odd occasions where take-over bids are made by documents circulated with the prior approval of the Department of Trade (for example, because the offeror does not wish to use an exempted or licensed dealer to send out the documents), the Department requires that the Licensed Dealers Rules be observed before approving such documents.

Leaving aside the various rules in the Companies Acts dealing with insider dealing (page 473), disclosure of interests (page 300) and compulsory acquisition (page 893), it is the City Code on Take-overs and Mergers and The Stock Exchange's Yellow Book which govern the conduct of most take-overs and mergers in the United Kingdom.

The City Code on Take-overs and Mergers

The Code comprises general principles and rules, supplemented by practice notes giving rulings on and interpretations of the general principles and rules. It is of fundamental importance that anyone needing to understand the rules should also take the time to read the practice notes: in many instances these practice notes significantly extend the apparent application of a particular rule. The Code is revised and reissued from time to time but opportunities are also taken, without the issue of a new Code, to make changes in its interpretation by the issue of a new edition of Practice Note No. 17, by the issue of statements by either the Panel on Take-overs and Mergers or the Council for the Securities Industry and, sometimes, in the annual report of the Panel on Take-overs and Mergers.

The Code is issued on the authority of the CSI (the Council for the Securities Industry). It should be noted that the major city institutions (such as the Bank of England and The Stock Exchange) and the major city associations are represented on the Council and committed to support its activities. Although the Code's requirements do not carry the force of law, they are generally complied with. The introduction to the Code states:

> "The Code has not, and does not seek to have, the force of law; but those who wish to take advantage of the facilities of the securities markets in the United Kingdom should conduct themselves in matters relating to take-overs and mergers according to the Code. Those who do not so conduct themselves cannot expect to enjoy those facilities and may find that they are withheld".

In *Dunford & Elliott Limited v. Johnson & Firth Brown Limited* [1977] 1
Ll.R. 505 the Court of Appeal gave an indication of the courts' likely
attitude to the Code. Lord Denning said: "Although this Code does not
have the force of law, nevertheless it does denote good business practice
and good business standards". As an indication of such standards, it
may well have a role where the court has a discretion whether to grant
the relief which is being sought.

In the case of foreign offeror companies, compliance with the Code was
ensured, before the ending of United Kingdom exchange controls, by
the requisite exchange control consent being made conditional on
compliance by the offeror with the provisions of the Code.

The Code applies to take-overs of listed and unlisted public companies
but does not apply to take-overs of private companies. Further, offers
for companies which are considered by the Panel not to be resident in
the United Kingdom, the Channel Islands or the Isle of Man do not
normally come within the Code. There is an exception in the case of
target companies which are resident in the Irish Republic and whose
securities are either listed on The Stock Exchange or traded on its
Unlisted Securities Market. The Panel will not normally treat a company as being resident in the United Kingdom if the company is
incorporated outside the United Kingdom, or has its head office and
place of central management outside the United Kingdom.

In view of the manner in which the Code is drafted and the fact that, as
stated in the first General Principle, it is generally accepted that the
spirit of the Code must be observed and not simply its strict wording,
questions inevitably arise as to its interpretation. Consistent with this
approach, the Take-over Panel, which administers and enforces the
Code, is available to give rulings on points of interpretation. Where an
interested party (including an aggrieved shareholder) is unhappy with
an interpretation of the Panel executive, he may ask for the matter to be
referred to the Panel. Where the Panel proposes to take disciplinary
action, the right of appeal lies, in certain circumstances, to an appeal
committee.

Among other things the Code includes rules as to periods during which
conditions to any offer must be satisfied if the offer is not to lapse, and
in certain other respects regulates some of the detailed terms to be
included in any take-over offer. It provides that an accepting shareholder should be entitled to withdraw his acceptance after the expiry of
21 days from the first closing date of the initial offer if it has not by then
become unconditional as to acceptances. It also provides that all
shareholders who accept an original offer must receive the benefit of
any revised offer.

Little purpose would be served in going through each of the General
Principles and rules of the Code. However, it is thought worthwhile to
mention a few points that can give rise to problems in practice.

Secrecy and announcements

Practice Note No. 3 states that it should be an invariable routine for advisers at the very beginning of discussions to warn clients of the importance of secrecy and security. The rules in the Code governing dealings by people with price sensitive information have, of course, now been supplemented by the statutory insider dealing provisions in the Companies Act 1980 (see also *Dunford & Elliott Limited v. Johnson & Firth Brown Limited* [1977] 1 Ll.R. 505). These provisions are dealt with in greater detail in the chapter *Insider Dealing*, but it should be borne in mind that it is possible for there to be a breach of these statutory provisions where an acquiring company makes purchases in the market of a target company's shares at a time when its directors (or other representatives) are in possession of confidential price sensitive information in relation to the target company. Indeed, it has been suggested that one effective defence tactic of an unwilling target company is to provide a potential bidder with unpublished price sensitive information so that until that information is published the potential bidder is unable to make market purchases. In practice one of the particular difficulties for practitioners is to determine whether or not particular information is price sensitive. Knowledge on the part of a potential bidder that it may make an offer or alter the terms of an existing offer will not preclude the bidder itself from making purchases.

The obligation to make an announcement in the event of any untoward movement in share prices rests not only with the target company but also with an offeror. Because the target company has available to it the remedy of seeking a suspension of dealings in its shares, as opposed to making an announcement at a time when a statement might be more misleading than helpful, ordinarily the prime responsibility must be upon the target company. If the offeror and its advisers are concerned about share movements in the target company, then they should consider formally requesting the target company and its advisers to seek a suspension. The Panel has indicated that it might expect an offeror to make a statement when the potential offeree company is the subject of rumour and speculation, and it is clear beyond reasonable doubt that it is the offeror's actions (including purchases of shares or approaches to shareholders) which have directly contributed to the situation.

Whereas most people will be aware that the Code contains rules applying to offer documents, it may be less obvious that it includes very significant rules as regards announcements of an intention to make an offer. In this respect it is of paramount importance that a bidder appreciates that where an offeror has announced a firm intention to make an offer (as opposed to an announcement that talks are taking place which may lead to an offer), the offer cannot be withdrawn without the Panel's consent. The only exception is if the posting of the offer was expressed as being subject to the prior fulfilment of a specific condition and this condition has not been met (Rule 10). Related to this is Rule 8. It requires that the announcement of a firm intention to make an offer must disclose the identity of the offeror and any existing holding in the offeree company (including those in respect of which it has received irrevocable undertakings to accept the offer). More importantly, the formal announcement must state any conditions to the posting of the offer and all conditions (including normal conditions relating to acceptances, listing and increase of capital) to which the offer itself is subject. This means that the conditions set out in the offer document should essentially be the same as they were in the formal announcement. In certain respects (such as in relation to the level of acceptances) it is permissible to use some shorthand in the announcement provided that in the offer document there is no difference of substance. Certainly, it should be assumed by the offeror that it will be unable subsequently to change any conditions which could have a material commercial bearing upon its offer without the consent of both the target company and the Panel. The approval of the target company (and its advisers) will normally be the Panel's principal concern where its consent is sought. Despite this rule, it is not customary to include as a condition in the announcement the passing of appropriate resolutions in connection with a stamp duty saving scheme. This is, however, on the basis that such a condition will automatically lapse if the resolutions are not passed within a relatively short period after the offer becomes otherwise unconditional as to acceptances.

Share purchases

Until recently the Code did not as a general rule preclude the offeror itself from dealing in the target company's shares although it did (and still does) require prompt disclosure of dealings. The following are the principal rules regarding market purchases and other dealings by an offeror in a target company's shares.

(1)   If, after an announcement has been made that take-over or merger discussions are taking place or that an approach or offer is contemplated, the discussions are terminated or the offeror decides not to proceed, neither the offeror nor any person privy to the intention to terminate the discussions or to the decision not to proceed may deal in the shares of the target company prior to the announcement of the termination of discussions or the decision not to proceed.

(2)   The Code specifically states that its rules on dealings are subject to the provisions of the Companies Act 1980 and ordinarily accepted standards of business behaviour, so that a rule permitting dealings will not apply, for example, where the offeror has been supplied with confidential price sensitive information in the course of discussions.

(3)   During an offer period (as defined in the Code) an offeror may not, except with the consent of the Panel, sell any securities in the target company unless it has publicly given at least 24 hours' notice that it may make such sales.

(4)   The latest version (April 1982) of the CSI's Rules Governing Substantial Acquisitions of Shares may apply. These rules govern acquisitions between 15 and 30 per cent. Broadly, they prevent any

person from acquiring, within any period of seven days, voting shares carrying 5 per cent or more of the voting rights in a company which, together with shares he already holds, give him voting rights of 15 per cent or more, but less than 30 per cent of that company's voting rights unless,

(a) the acquisition is from a single shareholder (which can extend to several shareholders if members of the same family or group of companies or if the CSI accepts the existence of an appropriate pre-existing common interest) and is the only acquisition within any period of seven days; or

(b) he has announced a firm intention to make an offer which is not subject to any preconditions (in such a case the Code's rules outlined below will apply); or

(c) the acquisition is made pursuant to a tender offer under the rules of the CSI to take his holding to less than 30 per cent of the voting rights; or

(d) the acquisition immediately precedes, and is conditional upon, an announcement of an offer under the Code which is not subject to any preconditions and which is recommended by the board of the target company.

These rules apply not only to acquisitions of shares but also to acquisitions of rights over shares, including options and irrevocable undertakings to accept an offer. Not surprisingly they also require that two or more people acting together in the acquisition of voting shares be treated as one – although the precise wording: "where two or more persons act by agreement or understanding in the acquisition of shares . . ." amply illustrates the difficulties which the draftsman faces in these cases.

(5) Rules 40 and 41 of the Code were introduced in April 1982 and are concerned primarily with the acquisition of 30 per cent or more of a company's voting rights. Rule 40 regulates the position prior to the announcement of a firm intention to make an offer, the posting of which is not subject to the prior fulfilment of any condition. Rule 41 applies after the announcement of such an offer. If the posting of an announced offer is subject to the prior fulfilment of any condition, Rule 40 (and the Rules Governing Substantial Acquisitions of Shares) will apply until the fulfilment or waiver of all such conditions. Then Rule 41 will apply. A brief outline of the two rules is given below. They are fairly convoluted and should be considered carefully (together with Practice Note No. 18) before any action is taken which might be covered by them. If any uncertainty arises as to the application of the rules, the Panel should be approached for guidance.

Rule 40. This applies where a person (and others acting in concert with him) does not yet hold 30 per cent or more of a target company's voting rights. Before he announces a firm intention to make an offer for the target company, he may not acquire any shares carrying voting rights in that target company which, when added to shares which he already holds, would carry 30 per cent or more of the target company's voting rights unless the conditions below are met. In calculating whether the 30 per cent limit is reached, rights over shares must be included as if the shares concerned had been acquired. The conditions are,

(a) the acquisition is from a single shareholder and is made after at least seven days have elapsed since he last acquired shares (or rights over shares) in the target company; or

(b) the acquisition immediately precedes, and is conditional upon, the announcement by the person making the acquisition of a firm intention to make an offer for the target company which is publicly recommended by the board of that company.

There is a similar restriction on acquisitions of shares (or rights over shares) carrying two per cent or more of the voting rights where the acquirer already holds between 30 per cent and 50 per cent of the target company's voting rights. A single shareholder can include more than one person where those concerned are members of the same family or group of companies. For the purposes of both Rule 40 and Rule 41, rights over shares include rights acquired by a person who has agreed to purchase or take an option to acquire shares or who has obtained an irrevocable undertaking to accept an offer to be made by him.

Rule 41. After the announcement of a firm intention to make an offer, the acquiring company (and persons acting in concert with it) may not for seven days acquire any shares carrying voting rights in the target company (or any rights over such shares) unless

(a) it already holds shares carrying more than 50 per cent of the voting rights; or

(b) its offer has become unconditional in all respects.

A competing offeror is only bound by the above rule for as long as the first offeror is bound by it and, if the target company's board publicly recommends an offer, only the seven day restriction will apply, even if the recommendation is subsequently withdrawn. Subject to this, if the offeror does not already hold 30 per cent of the target company's voting rights (or rights over them) at the time of the announcement, it may not bring such holding to 30 per cent or more until the earlier of the first closing date of its offer and the date on which its offer becomes unconditional in all respects. If the offer is a competing offer, the first closing date of any offer for the target company can be taken. If at the time of the announcement the offeror already holds shares or rights over shares carrying between 30 per cent and 50 per cent, it may not acquire any shares (or rights over shares) until the earliest of the dates just mentioned.

There are considerations in relation to, among other things, compulsory acquisition under section 209 of the Companies Act 1948 which will also have a bearing upon market purchases. So too will Rule 33 of the Code.

This applies where the offeror and any person acting in concert with it purchases shares in the target company for cash during the offer period and within 12 months prior to its commencement which together carry 15 per cent or more of the voting rights exercisable at a class meeting of that class. Except with the Panel's consent, the offer for that class must be in cash (or accompanied by a cash alternative) at not less than the highest price paid for shares of that class purchased during the offer period and within 12 months prior to its commencement. More important still is Rule 34. This applies where,

(a) a person acquires, whether by a series of transactions over a period of time or not, shares which carry 30 per cent or more of the voting rights of a company; or

(b) a person who holds between 30 and 50 per cent of a company's voting rights acquires in any period of 12 months additional shares carrying more than two per cent of the voting rights.

In these circumstances, the person is obliged to make an offer for all that company's share capital which carries votes and in which he holds shares. For these purposes such a person and people with whom he is acting in concert (as defined in the Code) are treated as one. Paragraph 9 of Practice Note No. 18 brings options and irrevocable undertakings within Rule 34. It indicates that, although the taking of an option or an irrevocable undertaking from a single shareholder will not normally give rise to a Rule 34 obligation, it can do so in certain circumstances. Where the relationship and arrangements between the two parties concerned is such that effective control over the shares passes to the taker of the option or the irrevocable undertaking, paragraph 9 indicates that such action will probably be regarded as constituting an acquisition giving rise to such an obligation. It goes on to say that the Panel will normally assume that effective control has passed where (a) the option may be exercised or (b) the offer covered by the irrevocable undertaking may be made, more than one month after the option or undertaking was obtained – unless a good reason for the longer period can be substantiated. It is therefore advisable to consult the Panel wherever an option or irrevocable undertaking would take an acquiring company into a Rule 34 obligation if it were to be treated as an acquisition.

An offer under Rule 34 has to be in cash (or accompanied by a cash alternative) at not less than the highest price paid by the offeror (and persons acting in concert with him) within the preceding twelve months and should not be subject to any conditions other than the acquisition of control of over fifty per cent of the total voting share capital. Although not subject to any conditions, it is required that such an offer include a term providing that it will lapse if the offer is referred to the Monopolies and Mergers Commission before its first closing date or, if later, the date it becomes unconditional as to acceptances. The obligation to make a Rule 34 offer may extend not only to the person making the purchase which gives rise to the obligation but also to each of the principal members of the group of persons acting in concert.

Profit forecasts

Rule 16 provides that any profit forecasts which appear in an offer document (or any other document addressed to shareholders in connection with an offer) must be reported upon by the auditors and any financial adviser mentioned in the document. Furthermore, any forecast made before the commencement of the offer period must, except with the consent of the Panel, be repeated in the document and reported on in accordance with Rule 16. While this Rule does not extend to unaudited statements of results published prior to the offer period, any unaudited profits figure published *during* an offer period must be reported upon in accordance with the Rule. However, where the offeror is offering only cash, there is no obligation for a forecast to be reported on. To prevent an application of this Rule to statements of results it should be borne in mind that, for the purposes of the Code, the offer period begins on the date when an announcement is made of a proposed or possible offer (with or without terms). In other words, it is not tied to the offer itself or even, necessarily, to the date upon which the formal announcement of the offer, including its terms, is made.

Practice Note No. 6 contains some guidelines for assessing whether or not a statement is a profit forecast. Broadly speaking, the Panel considers that a profit forecast has been made whenever a form of words puts a floor under (or, in certain circumstances, a ceiling on) the likely profits of a particular period, or whenever a form of words contains the data necessary to ascertain an approximate figure for future profits by an arithmetical process.

Partial offers and level of acceptances

Except pursuant to the CSI's rules governing substantial acquisitions of shares, the Panel does not normally permit partial offers, especially if such an offer would be for between 30 and 50 per cent of the target's voting rights. Where partial offers are made, all holders must be allowed to accept in full for the relevant percentage of their holdings. Where a target company has more than one class of equity share capital, a comparable offer must be made for each class (Rule 21(3)). There is no obligation under the Code to make an offer for non-equity capital. No offer for equity share capital may be declared unconditional unless the offeror has acquired or agreed to acquire, whether pursuant to the offer or otherwise, shares carrying over 50 per cent of the target company's voting rights.

Convertible securities

Where an offer is made for equity share capital and the target company has convertible securities, the offeror is obliged by Rule 29 to "make appropriate arrangements to ensure that the interests of the holders of the stock are safeguarded and in particular that the existence of a conversion option over a period of time is adequately recognised. Taking this into account, the offeror should make an appropriate offer or proposal to the stockholders". This rule applies equally to warrants, options and other subscription rights. There is also a General Principle that all shareholders of the same class of the target company should be treated similarly by the offeror.

Particular problems can arise with regard to acceptance levels where there are conversion or subscription rights which are capable of being exercised during or after an offer period. An offeror which has acceptances in respect of just over 50 per cent of a target company's issued share capital may after allowing his offer to become unconditional at this level find that the exercise of conversion rights brings his percentage to below 50 per cent. Practice Note No. 17 offers a general rule for determining whether the 50 per cent level has been met in these circumstances. This is that if the rights are capable of being exercised during the offer period, the 50 per cent test relates to the fully diluted share capital (i.e. the existing voting rights and any voting rights which would arise on the exercise of all rights which are capable of being exercised during the offer period). If conversion or subscription rights will only arise after the offer has become unconditional, this general rule will not apply and the 50 per cent will therefore not take account of such rights. (See also the implications with regard to section 209 of the Companies Act 1948, page 892.)

Responsibility for take-over documents

An offer document may well be considered comparable to a prospectus as regards its intended effect, particularly where the offeror is offering its shares or debentures as consideration. It is clear on the basis of *Government Stock and Other Securities Investment Co. v. Christopher* [1956] 1 W.L.R. 237 that an offer document offering shares or debentures in the offeror in exchange for the target company's shares does not constitute a prospectus for the purposes of the Companies Acts, including the provisions of those Acts dealing with civil and criminal liability for mis-statements. However, Rule 14 of the Code requires that any document or advertisement addressed to shareholders in connection with an offer must be prepared with the same standard of care with regards to statements included in it as if it were a prospectus within the meaning of the Companies Act 1948. This is extended to a requirement that such documents and advertisements include a responsibility statement following the wording set out in Rule 14. The form of this responsibility statement recognises that a director may fulfil his responsibilities "either by taking part himself in supervising the preparation of the document or by delegating that task to persons reasonably believed by him to be competent to carry it out, and by disclosing to such persons any relevant facts known to him and any relevant opinions held by him". From this it seems clear that at the very least a director must have read what is substantially the final form of the offer document so that, where it is appropriate for him to delegate responsibility for a particular part of the document, he is in a position to comment on that part to the person to whom he has delegated the responsibility. The inclusion of this responsibility statement would seem to expose each director to an action in tort if he has failed to take reasonable care. For this reason alone no offer document should be allowed to be despatched unless each director has in some form confirmed, to the merchant bank or other person issuing the document, that he accepts responsibility in terms of the responsibility statement contained in the offer document. Procedurally this confirmation is different and separate from the authority on behalf of the company to make the offer; if the articles permit, this latter authority can of course be (and often is) delegated to a committee of the board.

Yellow Book

The text of the Code is also included (although not kept entirely up to date) in The Stock Exchange's Yellow Book, as part of Chapter 5. Chapter 5 itself includes some requirements applicable to take-overs, principally concerning the documentation which is used. In addition listed companies are required by paragraph 6 of The Stock Exchange's listing agreement to submit to the Quotations Department proofs of all documents to be issued in connection with take-overs. Chapter 5 also directs a request to others (i.e. persons not bound by the listing agreement) to submit to the Quotations Department drafts of circulars proposed to be issued to shareholders, and holders of other securities, of a listed company. This request would therefore apply to a foreign company offeror not listed in London.

Reference should be made to Chapter 5 for The Stock Exchange's content requirements. There will be additional requirements if the offeror is using the offer document also to provide information to its own shareholders, for example because the size of the transaction either requires a "Class 1" circular or shareholder consent under Chapter 4 of The Yellow Book. A "Class 1" circular will be required where (in over simplified terms) on one of various tests, the size of the acquisition or disposal represents 15 per cent or more of the assets, profits or share capital of the acquiring or disposing company. Shareholder consent will be required where the size, on these tests (and one additional test), represents 25 per cent or more, or where the acquisition amounts to a Class 4 transaction. A take-over can constitute a Class 4 transaction where its acceptance could result in a significant acquisition from a director or substantial shareholder (or an associate of such a person). The provisions of Chapter 4 are fairly complex and reference should be made to them for the precise scope of The Stock Exchange's requirements and some of the circumstances in which they are likely to be relaxed.

Compulsory acquisition under section 209

Section 209 of the Companies Act 1948 breaks essentially into two parts. Section 209(1) gives the acquiring company the right to acquire compulsorily the shares of minority dissenters. Section 209(2) gives members of the dissentient minority the right to require the acquiring company to acquire their shares. Broadly speaking these rights only arise where a company has acquired 90 per cent of the target company's shares. The wording of the section gives rise to a number of problems of interpretation.

Section 209(1)

The right under section 209(1) arises where a scheme or contract involving the transfer of shares or any class of shares in a target company (referred to in the section as the transferor company), to an offeror company (referred to in the section as the transferee company), has within four months after the making of the offer by the offeror company been approved by not less than nine tenths in value of the shares whose transfer is involved (ignoring for this purpose shares held at the date of the offer by, or by a nominee for, the offeror company or one of its subsidiaries). To exercise this right the offeror company must give notice in the prescribed manner to the dissentient shareholders within two months (after the expiry of the four months). Unless within a month after such notice is given by the offeror company the court, on a dissentient's application, has ordered otherwise, the offeror company will be entitled and bound to acquire the shares of that dissentient.

A number of points arise on the wording of the subsection:

(a) there must be an offer;

(b) the offer must be for shares in a company within the meaning of section 455 of the Companies Act 1948;

(c) the offeror must be a company but it need not fall within the definition of "company" in section 455 of the Companies Act 1948. The right is therefore available to a foreign company. It is considered not to be available to a consortium of companies even if the offer is made by a single company on behalf of the consortium (see *Blue Metal Industries v. Dilley* [1970] A.C. 827). This problem could be avoided either by one of the consortium members making the offer as a principal and then transferring the shares to the other consortium members, or by the formation of a consortium company to make the offer as a principal;

(d) the right may be used with regard to shares which have been allotted but not issued, for example, as part of a stamp duty saving scheme (see page 861; *Re Simo Securities Trust Limited* [1971] 1 W.L.R. 1455); and

(e) it has been confirmed (see *Re Carlton Holdings* [1971] 1 W.L.R. 918) that rights under section 209(1) are not affected by a cash alternative being made available by a separate person.

Several classes of shares

There appear to be differing views as to the section's requirements where the target company has more than one class of shares. The question that arises is whether the nine tenths requirement must be satisfied with respect to each class for which an offer is made or with respect to the total of the shares, whatever their class. The latter view relies on the words "nine tenths in value of the shares involved". The more persuasive view, however, appears to be that the test should be applied to each class separately – thus making sense of the wording at the beginning of section 209(1), "involving the transfer of shares or any class of shares". This approach would seem more consistent with the distinction between classes adopted elsewhere in the Companies Acts ensuring that each class be treated fairly.

Partial offers

A similar question that frequently arises in practice, and on which there are differing views, is whether section 209(1) is available where an offer is made for only some of the shares in a class. The section specifically permits this where the shares are held (at the date of the offer) by or on behalf of the offeror or one of its subsidiaries. In such a case the 90 per cent is determined by reference to the remaining shares of that class of the target company. However, the proviso to section 209(1) adds additional requirements where such existing holdings exceed 10 per cent (see below). In view of the proviso and the consequences of a construction allowing partial offers (for example, excluding from the offer a substantial shareholder whom the offeror knew would not accept), it would seem likely that, if a court were ever asked to consider the point, it would take the more restrictive view and conclude that the section would not apply if an offer were made for only some of the shares in a class. This would, of course, be subject to the express exception for shares held by or for the offeror or its subsidiaries.

The question arises in practice where it is felt that the offeror may well wish to make significant purchases after the date of the offer. If the offer is phrased to include such shares, they will clearly be included in the aggregate number of shares to which the 90 per cent must be applied. However, it is generally considered that people who sell their shares in the market after the offer document is despatched cannot be said to have "approved the scheme or contract involving the transfer of shares". Therefore, if they are included in the aggregate number to which the 90 per cent must be applied, market purchases will make it more difficult to satisfy the sub-section's conditions. On this interpretation, if market purchases after the offer is made exceed 10 per cent of the shares for which the offer is made, section 209(1) would not be available to the offeror. In an attempt to avoid this problem, an offer is sometimes framed so as not to apply to such shares (i.e. the offer is expressly not made for shares acquired by the offeror during the course of the offer). If the view expressed above as to partial offers is correct, such an approach would be highly risky. One alternative approach would be to arrange for a company related to the offeror (rather than the offeror itself) to make the market purchases and then to accept the offer. This arrangement would not seem to prevent the application of section 209, but does run the risk of the court on the application of a dissentient deciding that in the particular circumstances it would not be fair for the compulsory acquisition to be permitted. It has the advantage over the other approach (of excluding shares subsequently acquired by the offeror) that the shares acquired will be treated as acceptances and therefore assist in meeting the ninety per cent test. This does not seem unreasonable insofar as a shareholder who sells in the market, even if not approving the terms of the contract, is taking the benefit of a market price which reflects such terms.

It is also possible to buy "assented" shares in the market – where the seller of the shares has accepted the offer (so that they will be included in the 90 per cent). In effect this means that the purchaser will receive the consideration if the offer becomes unconditional and will receive the target company's shares if it does not. In the case of an offeror which is subject to the Companies Acts, such a purchase will not be permissible where the consideration to which the seller is or could become entitled consists of shares in the offeror or its parent.

Proviso to section 209(1)

As mentioned, there are additional requirements where the offeror or one of its subsidiaries, or someone acting as nominee for any of them, already holds at the date when the offer is made 10 per cent in value of the target company's shares. The additional requirements are that:

(a) the offeror offers the same terms to all holders of the target company's shares (or, if separate classes are involved, to the holders of each class) other than those already held by, or on behalf of, the offeror and its subsidiaries; and

(b) the holders who approve the scheme or contract, besides holding not less than nine tenths in value of the shares (other than those already so held) whose transfer is involved, are not less than three fourths in number of the holders of those shares.

The first additional requirement would appear to imply that different terms may be offered to different holders where the proviso is inapplicable, even though it seems unlikely that this would have been intended (see the Jenkins Report, paragraphs 283 and 294(l)). Such an offer would be contrary to General Principle 8 of the Take-over Code.

Of greater practical significance, however, is the requirement of approval by 75 per cent in number. Here the denominator in the calculation is the number of shareholders on the register at the date the offer is made. Clearly the register may change during the course of the offer so that there may afterwards be a greater or lesser number of shareholders. With the increased interest of arbitrageurs in United Kingdom take-over situations, the number of shareholders may well be likely to contract after the offer is made and this proviso may make the availability of the compulsory acquisition power considerably more difficult or even impossible.

One way of avoiding the application of the proviso (which would also assist the chances of satisfying the 90 per cent test) is to arrange for the offer to be made by a subsidiary and for market purchases and other acquisitions to be made by one of its parent companies or by a sister company. So long as the offeror is not the parent of the company making market purchases, is not itself making the purchases and the person making the purchases is not acting as agent or nominee for the offeror or one of its subsidiaries, the market purchases will not be taken into account in determining whether or not the proviso applies. Although this would not seem strictly to offend the wording of the section, there might be some risk that a court hearing an application from a dissentient would form the view that it was appropriate to prevent compulsory acquisition (e.g. on the basis that there had not been a sufficient approval of the scheme or contract, compare *Re Bugle Press* [1960] Ch. 270). The extent of this risk will depend upon the circumstances.

In *Re Simo Securities Trust Limited* [1971] 1 W.L.R. 1455, Brightman J. concluded (at page 1465) that, insofar as the numerator in the calculation is concerned, the proviso requires a count of the people who do in fact approve the scheme or contract. There is no requirement that only those people who were on the register at the date of the offer can be counted. This decision sometimes leads to the question of whether or not splitting a shareholding prior to acceptance into, say, ten separate shareholdings, will permit the ten acceptances to be treated separately for the purposes of the proviso. While on the basis of *Re Simo Securities Trust Limited* this would appear to work, there must be a risk that a court would either determine that the circumstances required that the acceptances be treated as a single acceptance or require the offeror to show that the offer was fair (in the context of determining for the purposes of section 209(1) whether or not "to order otherwise").

Purchases by the offeror's merchant bank

Offerors have, on occasion, arranged for their merchant bank, acting as a principal, to make market purchases, possibly in order to avoid some of the difficulties that can arise under section 209(1) and also to prevent the loss of relief under section 55 of the Finance Act 1927. Such purchases must be reported to The Stock Exchange, the Panel and the press under Rule 31(1) of the Take-over Code and would be taken into account for the purposes of Rule 33. They may also result in additional stamp duty being paid.

The merchant bank will typically be concerned to protect itself against the risk of loss should the offer not become unconditional. An indemnity from the offeror would be contrary to Rule 36 of the Code unless a specific consent were obtained from the Panel. It is conceivable that an indemnity might also give rise to a problem under section 209 insofar as the accepting shareholder is not being treated equally with the others. It is probably more likely that the arrangement with the merchant bank would simply be treated as a factor to be taken into account by the court in determining whether or not to exercise its discretion on an application by a dissenting shareholder. If the right under section 209(1) would not have been exercisable but for the arrangement (for example because, if the offeror had made the purchase, 75 per cent in number would have been required and this test was not satisfied), the risk of the court ordering that a dissentient's shares should not be compulsorily acquired must be increased. In assessing this risk it is also necessary to take into account the likelihood of such an application and its significance in the context of section 209 as a whole.

Options and convertibles

Where the target company has outstanding options or conversion rights, the number of ordinary shares in issue may change during the offer period or at least during the four month period under section 209(1). It will normally be commercially desirable to ensure that any shares which fall to be so issued can, if necessary, be swept up under section 209. This can be done by so phrasing the offer as to include not only shares in issue on the date of the offer but also shares which fall to be issued under the terms of the options or convertibles. In order to apply section 209(1) it will, of course, be necessary to provide for a cut-off date – which would not normally be later than the end of the four month period. The shares which are issued (or fall to be issued) during this period will be taken into account for the purposes of the 90 per cent and, if applicable, 75 per cent tests. Accordingly, until the cut-off date there is a possibility that the offeror will not know whether or not it will be entitled to exercise the right under section 209(1). As regards the requirement for approval by 75 per cent in number, the denominator will consist not only of those on the register at the date of the offer but also anyone who, during the offer period, exercises his right to convert and thus becomes absolutely entitled to receive an allotment of shares (*Re Simo Securities Trust Limited*).

It may also be possible to deal with convertible securities by variation of their rights – so that the holders become entitled, in place of their right to convert, to receive a specified consideration for the cancellation of their securities. Such a variation can sometimes be done by a vote of a given percentage. This will, of course, depend on the terms of the securities. If it can, it provides a very convenient way of removing the conversion rights which otherwise might continue to exist after the end of the four month period. Such a route will not avoid the need to encompass conversions within the offer if, for example, conversions may be made before the meeting is held. Section 209(1) cannot be used to acquire convertible securities whose conversion rights have not been exercised.

Discretion of the court

The procedure for compulsory acquisition cannot be operated with respect to a particular dissentient's shares where the court orders otherwise on the application of that dissentient or where an application to the court by that dissentient is pending. Normally the onus is on the dissentient to show that the scheme or contract is unfair and that a court should therefore order that the dissentient's shares should not be acquired under section 209(1). Where the scheme or contract has been approved by the vast majority of independent shareholders this will be a heavy burden of proof. Where a substantial proportion of the accepting shareholders are not independent, the court is likely to be more easily persuaded.

Alternative considerations

It was decided in *In Re Carlton Holdings* [1971] 1 W.L.R. 918 that alternative considerations should be made available to shareholders whose shares are acquired under section 209(1). This applies even where under the terms of the offer a particular form of consideration ceases to be available after a specified date and even if it is only offered by a separate person, for example by a separate offer from a merchant bank to acquire shares issued by the offeror. The decision can give rise to a number of practical problems. In the case of a cash alternative by a merchant bank, it is necessary for the offeror to make cash available to dissentients (even though it may not have been available to shareholders who accepted after a specified date). Attempts to avoid the decision by wording in the offer document to separate the alternative offer from the main offer are thought to be ineffective.

Particular problems have been experienced in offering a "mix and match" option. This option allows accepting shareholders to elect, as between two forms of consideration, to receive more of one than of the other. Elections will usually only be satisfied to the extent that other accepting shareholders make the reverse election. The problems arise because a cut-off date is necessary to establish the entitlements of accepting shareholders to one or other consideration. There is no clear answer as to what should be made available to dissentients. Perhaps the easiest in practice is to provide dissentients with the option to elect during a period of the same length as was open under the original offer and to have their elections satisfied in the same proportions as acceptors were satisfied. The prescribed form for notification under section 209(1) (Form 100) does not make it essential to reach a decision but the cautious view favours an explanatory letter setting out the precise alternatives. By this time there is unlikely in practice to be a clamorous response from the dissentients.

The decision in *In Re Carlton Holdings* also has a bearing on dividends (and, in the case of a loan stock, interest) payable on the consideration offered by the offeror. If such amounts are to be treated as forming part of the terms on which, under the scheme or contract, the shares are to be transferred, they should be made available to dissentients. If it is not possible to pay a dividend as such, making alternative arrangements could give rise to different tax positions for the various recipients.

Section 209(2)

Broadly, subsection (2) entitles a member of a dissentient minority to require an acquiring company to buy his shares. The procedure under section 209(2) is linked to a transfer which takes the acquiring company over the 90 per cent level (taking into account shares held by its subsidiaries or by its or their nominees). Within one month from the date of the transfer, the acquiring company is under an obligation to give notice in the prescribed manner (Form 100a) to the holders of the remaining shares of that class who have not assented to the scheme or contract. Within three months thereafter, any such shareholder may require the acquiring company to acquire his shares on the terms of the scheme or contract, or on such other terms as may be agreed or as the court may order.

It is thought that the date of transfer means the transfer of the legal title to the shares (i.e. registration of the transfer) rather than simply the transfer of beneficial ownership (see the Jenkins Report paragraph 290). As a result, especially where the registration of transfers is delayed because of adjudication under section 55 of the Finance Act 1927, the section 209(1) procedure may be completed before an obligation arises to send out section 209(2) notices. If section 209(2) notices are sent out and an application is made by the dissentient shareholder under section 209(2), the court will have power to specify the terms on which the transfer shall be made. Under section 209(2) the court could improve the terms, whereas under section 209(1) it can only order that the compulsory acquisition should not take place.

Universal Checklist

The aim of this checklist is to help the busy company law practitioner to avoid overlooking "the obvious". It is clearly impossible to produce a perfectly comprehensive checklist, in particular to cover specialised transactions.

The checklist is followed by notes, which give a fuller explanation of the item concerned.

When using the checklist, particularly with complex transactions, it may sometimes be helpful to analyse the transaction into a series of "two-way deals" – in other words, a sequence of stages, each stage consisting of A giving something to B in return for B giving something to A. The checklist should then be applied twice to each stage – once for each side of the deal.

A. Memorandum and articles of association etc.

1. *Power in memorandum for company?*
2. *Power in articles for directors?* Any other relevant provision or power in articles?
3. *Any interested directors (or persons "connected with" directors)?* If so, check: articles permit interest; declaration of interest (C.A. 1948, s. 199); voting ability and quorum (refer to articles); Stock Exchange Class 4 transaction rules; substantial property transactions (C.A. 1980, s. 48); loans, quasi-loans or credit transactions (C.A. 1980, s. 49); compensation for loss of office (C.A. 1948, ss. 191–4); insider dealing (see further note C. 20); disclosure of director's interests in securities (C.A. 1967, s. 27).
4. *Dealings between company and members/subscribers* for two years after incorporation/conversion to p.l.c. (C.A. 1980, ss. 26 and 27).
5. *Shareholders* – minimum of two; any maximum?
6. *Quorum for shareholders' meeting or class meeting?*
7. *Quorum for directors' meetings?*
8. *Directors: minimum/maximum number?*
9. *Directors: shareholding qualification?*
10. *Are there any pre-emption rights* or other restrictions on *issue* or on *transfer* of shares (check: C.A. 1980, s. 17; articles; any

---

shareholders' agreements; convertible shares, convertible loans, options or warrants).
11. *Share issues* – watch: authorised capital; authority of general meeting under C.A. 1980, s. 14; allotment at a discount (C.A. 1980, s. 21); clause 5 of memorandum; class rights; breach of undertaking to Stock Exchange (para 21, p. 14 of Yellow Book); expert's report (C.A. 1980, ss. 24 and 25); minimum payment of one quarter of nominal value plus all premium (C.A. 1980, s. 22); ss. 20, 23 and 29 of the Companies Act 1980; Stock Exchange Listing Agreement, para. 13; allotment: C.A. 1948, ss. 47–53 and C.A. 1980, s. 16; F.A. 1972, s. 79.
12. *Alteration of articles* – watch: no conflict with memorandum; C.A. 1948, s. 22 (increase in liability); C.A. 1980, s. 75 (conduct unfairly prejudicial); is it a fraud on the minority?; C.A. 1980, ss. 32 and 33, C.A. 1948, s. 72 and class rights generally.

B. Registration and filing

1. *Companies House* (in England/Scotland/Northern Ireland) – Search/file (especially watch registration of charges under C.A. 1948, s. 95).
2. *Bills of Sale?*
3. *Land Registry/Land Charges Registry* – search (especially bankruptcy search at L.C.R.); file.
4. *Patents; trade marks; registered designs.*

C. Miscellaneous

1. *Restrictions*: in articles; loan agreements; stocks and trust deeds; options; guarantees; charges; other contracts? (see Note C. 1).
2. *Should one request*: security; guarantees; insurance (plus charge on policy); agreed rate of interest on default; events of default clause (immediate repayment on happening of specified events).
3. *Sale at undervalue* (see Note C. 3 for implications of this).
4. *Financial assistance* for acquisition of shares (C.A. 1981, ss. 42–44). Also check articles do not contain old prohibition (e.g. article 10 of Table A, before its repeal by C.A. 1981).
5. *Fraudulent preference* (C.A. 1948, s. 320); s. 172 Law of Property Act 1925 (voluntary conveyance to defraud creditors voidable); invalid floating charges (C.A. 1948, s. 322); fraudu-

lent trading (C.A. 1948, s. 332); Social Security Act 1975, s. 152(4) (personal liability of directors for unpaid contributions).

6. *Are notices to, or consents from, any third party required?* (e.g. in respect of authorisations or licences from, or contracts or arrangements with, third parties).

7. *Exchange control* (outside U.K.).

8. *Section 482 of the Taxes Act*: transfer of business abroad, change of residence, issues and transfers of shares or debentures in non-resident companies.

9. *Restrictive Trade Practices Acts*; Articles 85 and 86 of Treaty of Rome; foreign (particularly U.S.) anti-trust legislation.

10. *Control of Mergers* under Fair Trading Act 1973 and Industry Act 1975.

11. *Control of Borrowing Order.*

12. *Import licence.*

13. *Insurance* – is fresh cover or notification of change in ownership required; key-man insurance; loss of profits; product liability?

14. *Stock Exchange Yellow Book* – Class 4
    – Class 1/2/3
    – 100% or 25% test
    (paras 13 and 17 of Chapter 4)
    – Listing Agreement/
    General Undertaking
    – Other requirements

15. *City Code on Take-Overs and Mergers.*

16. *CSI dawn raid/15 per cent rules.*

17. *Prevention of Fraud (Investments) Act 1958:*
    – section 14 (restriction of distribution of circulars relating to investments)
    – section 1 (licensing of dealers in securities).

18. *Licensed Dealer's (Conduct of Business) Rules* 1960; C.S.I. Code of Conduct for Dealers in Securities.

19. *Is there a prospectus?* Is there an offer to the public etc. within C.A. 1980, s. 15.

20. *Insider dealing* (See Note C. 20).

21. *Is a licence required*, and have all other relevant provisions been complied with, under Consumer Credit Act 1974; Moneylenders' Acts 1900 to 1927; Banking Act 1979.

22. *Serious loss of capital*: C.A. 1980, s. 34.

23. *Disclosure* of 5 per cent interests in voting shares in public companies (C.A. 1981, ss. 63–72); disclosure by director of interests in securities (C.A. 1967, s. 27).

24. *Rules against: perpetual trusts; perpetuities; accumulations* (21/80 years).

25 *Costs* (payable by which party?).

26 *Limitation Act 1980.*
27. *Work permit; immigration rules.*
28. *Pension funds (adequate funding?)*
29. *Employment:* redundancy; consultation/notification of redundancies; unfair or wrongful dismissal; notification of terms of employment contract; Transfer of Undertakings (Protection of Employment) Regulations 1981; Factories Acts; The Health and Safety at Work Act 1974.
30. *Foreign legal advice required?*

D. Tax

1. *Is income tax, corporation tax or ACT payable?*
2. *Is capital gains tax or development land tax payable?*
3. *Is a close company involved?* If so, consider: apportionment of income; benefits to participators and associates; loans to participators; possible capital transfer tax charge.
4. *Is a group involved?* If so, note section 273 of the Taxes Act (intra-group transfers); section 278 (clawback on leaving group – see also section 21 of the Development Land Tax Act 1976); payment of dividends or charges on income free of ACT or basic rate tax (section 256 of the Taxes Act); surrender of losses and ACT (sections 258 to 264 of the Taxes Act and section 92 of the Finance Act 1972); breaking of group relief relationship (section 262 of the Taxes Act and section 29 of and Schedule 12 to Finance Act 1973; sections 92(4) and 92(9) of the Finance Act 1972; and see SP 5/80).
5. *Are payments deductible?* Is a payment deductible for income or corporation tax, or allowable expenditure for capital gains (or DLT) purposes? If interest is being paid, is it deductible as a trading expense (sections 130 and 251 of the Taxes Act), or as a charge on income (section 248 of the Taxes Act; n.b. section 48 of the Finance Act 1977). Could the anti-avoidance provisions in section 38 of the Finance Act 1976 or section 496 of the Taxes Act apply, or section 76(3) of the Finance Act 1972 apply? Could the interest be treated as a distribution (section 233 of the Taxes Act (linked to profits, other capitalisation etc.) or apportioned (paragraph 3A of Schedule 16 to the Finance Act 1972)?
6. *Is a double tax treaty relevant?*
7. *Is capital transfer tax payable?*
8. *Is deduction at source required,* for instance under sections 52, 53, 54, 89, 93 or 159 of the Taxes Act, section 40 of the DLTA 1976, or under PAYE or national insurance regulations. Is there a foreign witholding tax?

9. *Are tax clearances required*, for example under sections 460 or 488 of the Taxes Act, or section 267 of the Taxes Act and section 88 of the CGTA 1979, or under Schedule 18 to the Finance Act 1980 or section 53 of the Finance Act 1982?

10. *Are assets being transferred?* If so, consider position as to capital allowances, tax losses, trading stock, stock relief (n.b. section 252 of the Taxes Act and paragraphs 3 and 13 of Schedule 8 to the Finance Act 1971; section 137 of the Taxes Act 1970; paragraph 20 of Schedule 9 to the Finance Act 1981). Also check section 483 of the Taxes Act and section 101 of the Finance Act 1972 (loss of carried forward losses, ACT).

11. *Is stamp or capital duty payable?* Is there an agreement within S.A. 1891, s. 59? Is relief under F.A. 1930, s. 42 (n.b. F.A. 1967 s. 27), F.A. 1927, s. 55 or F.A. 1973, Schedule 19, paragraph 10 available? Is there a clawback under F.A. 1927, s. 55(6), or F.A. 1973, Schedule 19, paragraph 10(3)? Are reduced rates of duty applicable (e.g. consideration below limit; share purchases by non-residents), or is the transaction exempt (e.g. under F.A. 1976, s. 126 – transfers of loan stock)? Watch F.A. 1965, s. 90 (transfer in contemplation of sale).

12. *Is VAT payable?* Is registration necessary? Is there a group registration? Will VAT paid be fully reclaimable (partial exemption etc.)?

13. *Are there employee shareholdings etc.?* If so consider section 186 of the Taxes Act, sections 77 and 79 of the Finance Act 1972, section 53 of the Finance Act 1978, section 47 of the Finance Act 1980, paragraphs 9 and 14 of Schedule 1 to the Finance Act 1974, section 67 of the Finance Act 1976.

14. *Miscellaneous points*:

(a) National insurance.

(b) Import duty.

(c) If non-resident company involved, could CGTA 1979, ss. 15 and 16 (or F.A. 1973, s. 38) apply?

(d) Are there any anti-avoidance provisions which might apply (e.g. sections 437 to 459 of the Taxes Act (settlements – note especially section 451 if company involved) and section 478 of that Act (transfer of income abroad), sections 30, 469–471 of the Taxes Act 1970 (bond-washing etc.); paragraph 3 of Schedule 8 to the Finance Act 1971 (capital allowances). See D. 9 above also.

(e) Is there a bonus issue followed by a repayment of capital or vice versa (consider sections 234 and 235 of the Taxes Act 1970)?

(f) Are tax warranties and indemnities required?

(g) Is the transaction at undervalue – see generally Note C.3.

Notes to universal checklist

A.3 "Connected with a director" – the expression used in Part IV of the Companies Act 1980 (see s. 64). Class 4 – See Note D.14 below. Substantial property transactions (C.A. 1980, s. 48) and the compensation for loss of office provisions (C.A. 1948, ss. 191–194) would require shareholders' approval. Insider dealing – for scope of this see Note C. 20 below.

A.5 Private companies' articles will often have a maximum of 50 members, but this is no longer obligatory since the repeal of C.A. 1948, s. 28. Guarantee companies' articles must state the number of members: C.A. 1948, s. 7(2).

A.6 As to class meeting quorum, see articles and now also C.A. 1980, s. 32(6).

A.11 Clause 5 of memorandum – a reminder that restrictive provisions may appear in the memorandum. Undertaking to Stock Exchange – this relates to previously authorised but unissued capital. Expert's report – only applies to public companies and to issues otherwise than in cash. Minimum payment – public companies only. Listing Agreement, para. 13 – requires shareholders' consent to certain cash issues. F.A. 1972, s. 79 catches certain shares acquired by directors and employees.

C.1 Examples of common restrictions (which, if they would be infringed by the transaction under contemplation, would require a consent or release and, in other cases, would require some form of assurance that the appropriate restriction was not infringed), are:
   (i)   disposals of property, e.g. subsidiaries;
   (ii) borrowing or charging;
   (iii) change in nature of business or ceasing to carry on a substantial part of the business;
   (iv) payment of dividends, issues etc. of shares (common with convertible shares, convertible stocks, options and warrants);
   (v)   change in control of company;
   (vi) carrying on business "in a proper and efficient manner".

C.2 This is not merely of relevance to loans but is of relevance to any agreement in which the other party has future obligations, for instance deferred purchase or payment by instalments.

C.3 Problems which may arise from sales at undervalue (or purchases at overvalue or any other transaction having an element of gratuity, where the gratuity flows *from a company*) include:
   (i)   does the gratuity element constitute financial assistance for an acquisition of shares within C.A. 1981, s. 42?;
   (ii) it is often prudent for the directors' actions to be sanctioned by a shareholders' resolution, particularly where the directors' motives may be questioned. But if the company is a wholly-owned subsidiary and acts with the parent company's assent, a resolution is probably unnecessary;

(iii) if the gratuity element passes to members of the company, it is probably within the wide definitions of a "distribution":
    (a) in C.A. 1980, s. 45(2) and must accordingly come out of profits available for distribution within the meaning of Part III of the 1980 Act
    (b) in section 233 of the Taxes Act (see especially s. 233(3)) and could therefore result in A.C.T. being payable by the company, tax on investment income being payable by the recipient (if an individual), yet no deduction against corporation tax being available to the company.

(iv) if the gratuity would result in the company's net assets falling below the company's share capital (including share premium account and other undistributable reserves) the transaction would amount to an unlawful reduction of capital;

(v) if the gratuity element passes to a director or employee or to his family, there may be a charge to tax under Schedule E (either under general principles or, for director's or higher-paid employees, under Chapter II, Part III of the Finance Act 1976);

(vi) there may be a charge to C.T.T. under F.A.75, s. 39 (transfer of value by close company) or to C.G.T. under C.G.T.A. 1979, s. 75 (transfer of assets at under-value by close company) or C.G.T.A. 1979, s. 25(2) (value shifting). Watch the recipients' position under C.G.T.A. 1979, s. 59;

(vii) if the gratuity element passes to a participator or his associate in a close company, it may be treated for tax purposes as a distribution (T.A. 1970, s. 284);

(viii) stamp duty, if any, will be payable on the market value, if this exceeds the actual price paid, by virtue of section 74(5) of the Finance (1909–10) Act (this is not a problem if intra-group exemption under F.A. 1930, s. 42 is available);

(ix) if the parties are "connected persons" or the transaction is not by way of arm's length bargain, then market value is sometimes also substituted for C.G.T. purposes, by virtue of sections 29A and 62(2) of the C.G.T.A. 1979 (this is not usually a problem in a 75% group because of the intra-group exemption in section 273 of the Taxes Act);

(x) The anti-avoidance provisions in section 485 of the Taxes Act (transfer pricing) may be invoked to restore market value for income or corporation tax purposes. The section is mainly aimed at diverting profits to foreign associates and is not normally relevant if both parties are U.K. resident and the transaction is of a revenue nature for both of them. See also *Sharkey v. Wernher* 36 T.C. 275;

(xi) a subsequent claim for a capital loss on the sale of the company giving the gratuity element may be disallowed in whole or in part on the basis that there was a depreciatory transaction (see T.A. 1970, s. 280 and see also s. 281 (dividend stripping)). Further, section 26 of the C.G.T.A.

1979 (value shifting) may operate to reduce a loss or even to increase a gain. Note the exemptions in s. 26(7) for transfers within a group or for certain group dividends;

(xii) creditors of the company giving the "gratuity" may be prejudiced (and see C. 5 in the table).

C.8   This section creates criminal offences in relation to certain company transactions with a foreign element (n.b. the general consents).

C.11 This relates primarily to issues of sterling securities where the amount of money raised is £3 million or more (and also to certain securities issued by government and public authorities). For full details see Control of Borrowing Order 1958 S.I. 1958/1208, amended by S.I.'s 1970/708; 1972/1218; 1977/1602; 1979/794.

C.14 The Stock Exchange "Yellow Book", officially called the "Admission of Securities to Listing", contains many regulations of The Stock Exchange imposed on listed companies.

Similar regulations apply to companies whose shares are dealt in on the Unlisted Securities Market of The• Stock Exchange (although in a few cases these are less strict).

The provisions relating to Class 4 transactions (which would require a circular to be sent and shareholders' approval), Class 1 transactions (which would require an immediate announcement to be made and a circular to be sent to shareholders), Class 2 transactions (which would require an announcement only), Class 3 transactions (which would only require an announcement where there is an issue of securities for which a listing will be sought) and the 100% and 25% tests (relating to sizeable acquisitions and realisations) are all to be found in Chapter 4 of the Yellow Book. The Listing Agreement is in Chapter 2. Companies on the U.S.M. are subject instead to a similar agreement called the "General Undertaking" (to be found in Appendix 3 to "The Stock Exchange Unlisted Securities Market").

C.16 The 15% Rules are published by the Council for the Securities Industry in C.S.I. Booklet No. 2: "Rules Governing Substantial Acquisitions of Shares".

C.19 "Prospectus" is defined in C.A. 1948, s. 455 and see sections 45 and 55 of the 1948 Act. If there is a prospectus, the requirements of sections 37–46 of, and Schedule 4 to, the 1948 Act apply. See also C.A. 1980, s. 16. C.A. 1980, s. 15 makes it a criminal offence for a private company to offer shares or debentures to the public. Section 15 is wider than the definition of "prospectus" because it covers (i) oral offers; (ii) offers not in cash.

C.20 For insider dealing, check –

(1)   Part V of the Companies Act 1980

(2)   Model Code for Securities Transactions by Directors of Listed Companies (pp. 47–51 of The Stock Exchange Yellow Book), or any other code adopted by the company concerned

(3)   Statement on Insider Dealing (C.S.I. No. 5)

- (4) Guidelines for Personal Dealings by Fund Managers (C.S.I. No. 4)
- (5) Paragraph 1 of The Stock Exchange Listing Agreement and Notes thereto (pp. 23–24 of The Yellow Book)
- (6) The City Code on Take-Overs and Mergers (C.S.I. No. 3) especially Rules 5, 6, 7, 30 and Practice Notes 1 and 3
- (7) The Stock Exchange and Take-Over Panel Joint Statement on Announcement of Price – Sensitive Matters of April 14, 1977 (pp. 44–6 of the Yellow Book)
- (8) Common law duties of employees and directors to account for secret profits.

C.21 Moneylenders Acts – some provisions are still in force, particularly in relation to consumer credit agreements, although eventually the Acts will be repealed under the Consumer Credit Act 1974.

D.3 Apportionment of income (F.A. 1972, Sch. 16) was formerly known as "shortfall". For the other items referred to, see sections 284 and 286 of the Taxes Act and section 39 of the Finance Act 1975.

D.8 Sections 52 and 53 of the Taxes Act 1970 relate to any annuities and other annual payments, patent royalties and mining rents and royalties. Section 54 covers yearly interest paid *by* a company or local authority or corporate partnership or *to* a person whose usual place of abode is outside the U.K. Note the exemptions for payments to or from qualifying banks.
Section 89 covers rent paid to a person whose usual place of abode is outside the U.K.
Section 159 relates to "foreign dividends" as defined in s. 159(1) (and note s. 93, covering public revenue dividends).
Section 40 of the Development Land Tax Act 1976 covers the disposal of land by a person whose usual place of abode is outside the U.K., the purchaser being required to deduct tax from the consideration.

D.9 These clearances relate respectively to transactions in securities; artificial transactions in land; company reconstructions or amalgamations; share for share exchanges; demergers; own-share purchases.

D.10 Disposals of assets (i.e. plant and machinery) on which capital allowances have been given can give rise to a "balancing charge" or "balancing allowance": see sections 41 to 45 of the Finance Act 1971. See also, generally, the Capital Allowances Act 1968. Similarly, where stock or work in progress is disposed of, stock relief previously given can be "clawed back", though the rules are now less strict than previously (see Schedule 9 to the Finance Act 1981).

D.12 Persons registered for V.A.T. who make "exempt" supplies may be unable to reclaim all the input V.A.T. they pay.

Appendix 1

Schedule 8 to the Companies Act 1948

Balance sheet formats: format 2 (see the chapter *Accounts*)

ASSETS

A. **Called up share capital not paid**

B. **Fixed assets**
   I   Intangible assets
   1. Development costs
   2. Concessions, patents, licences, trade marks and similar rights and assets
   3. Goodwill
   4. Payments on account

   II Tangible assets
   1. Land and buildings
   2. Plant and machinery
   3. Fixtures, fittings, tools and equipment
   4. Payments on account and assets in course of construction

   III Investments
   1. Shares in group companies
   2. Loans to group companies
   3. Shares in related companies
   4. Loans to related companies
   5. Other investments other than loans
   6. Other loans
   7. Own shares

C. **Current assets**
   I   Stocks
   1. Raw materials and consumables
   2. Work in progress
   3. Finished goods and goods for resale
   4. Payments on account

   II Debtors
   1. Trade debtors
   2. Amounts owed by group companies
   3. Amounts owed by related companies
   4. Other debtors
   5. Called up share capital not paid
   6. Prepayments and accrued income

   III Investments
   1. Shares in group companies
   2. Own shares
   3. Other investments

   IV Cash at bank and in hand

D. **Prepayments and accrued income**

LIABILITIES

A. Capital and reserves
    I   Called up share capital
    II   Share premium account
    III Revaluation reserve
    IV Other reserves
        1. Capital redemption reserve
        2. Reserve for own shares
        3. Reserves provided for by the articles of association
        4. Other reserves

    V   Profit and loss account

B. Provisions for liabilities and charges
        1. Pensions and similar obligations
        2. Taxation including deferred taxation
        3. Other provisions

C. Creditors
        1. Debenture loans
        2. Bank loans and overdrafts
        3. Payments received on account
        4. Trade creditors
        5. Bills of exchange payable
        6. Amounts owed to group companies
        7. Amounts owed to related companies
        8. Other creditors including taxation and social security
        9. Accruals and deferred income

D. Accruals and deferred income

Profit and loss accounts formats: formats 3 and 4

Format 3

A. Charges
       1. Cost of sales
       2. Distribution costs
       3. Administrative expenses
       4. Amounts written off investments
       5. Interest payable and similar charges
       6. Tax on profit or loss on ordinary activities
       7. Profit or loss on ordinary activities after taxation
       8. Extraordinary charges
       9. Tax on extraordinary profit or loss
     10. Other taxes not shown under the above items
     11. Profit or loss for the financial year

B. Income
       1. Turnover
       2. Other operating income
       3. Income from shares in group companies
       4. Income from shares in related companies
       5. Income from other fixed asset investments
       6. Other interest receivable and similar income
       7. Profit or loss on ordinary activities after taxation
       8. Extraordinary income
       9. Profit or loss for the financial year

Format 4

A. **Charges**
1. Reduction in stocks of finished goods and in work in progress
2. (a) Raw materials and consumables
   (b) Other external charges
3. Staff costs:
   (a) wages and salaries
   (b) social security costs
   (c) other pension costs
4. (a) Depreciation and other amounts written off tangible and intangible fixed assets
   (b) Exceptional amounts written off current assets
5. Other operating charges
6. Amounts written off investments
7. Interest payable and similar charges
8. Tax on profit or loss on ordinary activities
9. Profit or loss on ordinary activities after taxation
10. Extraordinary charges
11. Tax on extraordinary profit or loss
12. Other taxes not shown under the above items
13. Profit or loss for the financial year

B. **Income**
1. Turnover
2. Increase in stocks of finished goods and in work in progress
3. Own work capitalised
4. Other operating income
5. Income from shares in group companies
6. Income from shares in related companies
7. Income from other fixed asset investments
8. Other interest receivable and similar income
9. Profit or loss on ordinary activities after taxation
10. Extraordinary income
11. Profit or loss for the financial year

Appendix 2

List of current SSAPs and EDs

Explanatory forward to SSAPs

Authority and scope

Statements of standard accounting practice ("accounting standards") describe methods of accounting approved by the Council of The Institute of Chartered Accountants in England and Wales (in association with the Councils of The Institute of Chartered Accountants of Scotland, The Institute of Chartered Accountants in Ireland, The Association of Certified Accountants and The Institute of Cost and Management Accountants) for application to all financial accounts intended to give a true and fair view of financial position and profit or loss.

Disclosure of significant departures

Significant departures in financial accounts from applicable accounting standards should be disclosed and explained. The financial effects should be estimated and disclosed unless this would be impracticable or misleading in the context of giving a true and fair view. If the financial effects of departures from standards are not disclosed, the reasons should be stated.

Obligation for chartered accountants to observe accounting standards or justify departures

The Council expects members of the Institute who assume responsibilities in respect of financial accounts to observe accounting standards.

Where this responsibility is evidenced by the association of their names with such accounts in the capacity of directors or other officers the onus will be on them to ensure that the existence and purpose of standards are fully understood by non-member directors and other officers. They should also use best endeavours to ensure that standards are observed or, if they are not observed, that significant departures from them are disclosed and explained in the accounts. The effect of such departures should, if material, be disclosed unless this would be impracticable or misleading in the context of giving a true and fair view.

Where members act as auditors or reporting accountants the onus will be on them not only to ensure disclosure of significant departures but

913

also, to the extent that their concurrence is stated or implied, to justify them.

The Council, through its Professional Standards Committee, may inquire into apparent failures by members of the Institute to observe accounting standards or to disclose departures therefrom.

Date from which effective

The date from which members are expected to observe accounting standards will be declared in each statement of standard accounting practice.

Exceptional and borderline cases

Accounting standards are not intended to be a comprehensive code of rigid rules. It would be impracticable to establish a code sufficiently elaborate to cater for all business situations and circumstances and every exceptional or marginal case. Nor could any code of rules provide in advance for innovations in business and financial practice.

Moreover it must be recognised that there may be situations in which for justifiable reasons accounting standards are not strictly applicable because they are impracticable or, exceptionally, having regard to the circumstances, would be inappropriate or give a misleading view.

In such cases modified or alternative treatments must be adopted and, as noted, departure from standard disclosed and explained. In judging exceptional or borderline cases it will be important to have regard to the spirit of accounting standards as well as to their precise terms, and to bear in mind the overriding requirement to give a true and fair view.

Where accounting standards prescribe specific information to be contained in accounts, such disclosure requirements do not override exemptions from disclosure requirements given to and utilised by special classes of companies under statute. Examples of such special classes of company are contained, for example, in Part III of the Second Schedule to the Companies Act 1967.

Future developments

Methods of financial accounting evolve and alter in response to changing business and economic needs. From time to time new accounting standards will be drawn at progressive levels, and established standards will be reviewed with the object of improvement in the light of new needs and developments.

Status of accounting recommendations

In so far as they are not replaced by statements of standard accounting practice, the Council's "Accounting Recommendations" will continue in effect as guidance statements and indicators of best practice. They are persuasive in intent and departures from them do not necessarily require disclosure as do departures from accounting standards.

Application of accounting standards overseas

Statements of standard accounting practice are not intended to apply to accounts prepared and audited in overseas territories for local purposes where different requirements of law or generally accepted practice prevail, but are intended to be applied where accounts of overseas subsidiaries and associated companies are incorporated in United Kingdom group accounts.

Current SSAPs and EDs

SSAP 1   Accounting for the results of associated companies (April 1982)
SSAP 2   Disclosure of accounting policies (November 1971)
SSAP 3   Earnings per share (August 1974 (revision))
SSAP 4   The accounting treatment of government grants (April 1974)
SSAP 5   Accounting for value added tax (April 1974)
SSAP 6   Extraordinary items and prior year adjustments (April 1974) (now subject to a discussion paper issued in January 1983)
SSAP 8   The treatment of taxation under the imputation system in the accounts of companies (August 1974)
SSAP 9   Stocks and work in progress (May 1975)
SSAP10   Statements of source and application of funds (July 1975)
SSAP12   Accounting for depreciation (December 1977)
SSAP13   Accounting for research and development (December 1977)
SSAP14   Group accounts (September 1978)
SSAP15   Accounting for deferred taxation (October 1978)
SSAP16   Current cost accounting (March 1980)
SSAP17   Accounting for post balance sheet events (August 1980)
SSAP18   Accounting for contingencies (August 1980)
SSAP19   Accounting for investment properties (November 1981)
ED   27   Accounting for foreign currency translations (October 1980)
ED   28   Accounting for petroleum revenue tax (March 1981)
ED   29   Accounting for leases and hire purchase contracts (March 1981)
ED   30   Accounting for goodwill (October 1982)
ED   31   Accounting for acquisitions and mergers (October 1982)

Appendix 3

Department of Trade circular dated January 15, 1981

Group accounts and the "true and fair view"

The Department of Trade has set out its view of the relationship in law between the statutory requirements on the form and content of group accounts and the requirement that accounts should give a true and fair view.

This step has been taken because of the interest and comment in the accountancy profession which followed the Department's prosecution last year of directors of Argyll Foods Ltd for breaches of the law relating to group accounts and the true and fair view.

The Department's statement has been sent with a covering letter to the Consultative Committee of Accountancy Bodies.

"DEPARTMENT OF TRADE,
  SANCTUARY BUILDINGS,
    20 GREAT SMITH STREET,
    LONDON SW1P 3DB.
      Telephone Direct Line 01-215
           Switchboard 01-215 7877

13 January 1982

T J Smith Esq
Consultative Committee of
  Accountancy Bodies
Institute of Chartered
  Accountants in England & Wales
Chartered Accountants Hall
Moorgate Place
London EC2

Dear Mr. Smith

GROUP ACCOUNTS AND THE TRUE AND FAIR VIEW

There has been considerable comment on the statutory requirements relating to group accounts since the prosecution last year of directors of Argyll Foods Ltd. for breaches of sections 150 and 152 of the Companies Act 1948. In the light of this comment, we have felt, and I understand that you agree, that it would be helpful, particularly with the impending entry into force of the relevant provisions of the 1981 Act, if the Department were to set out its view of the legal position. I accordingly enclose a statement summarising what we see as the essential features of the relationship in law between group accounts and the true and fair view.

I should like to add that the prosecution referred to above was consistent with the Department's longstanding general position with regard to enforcement of the Companies Acts. It would be impracticable, and it is not the practice of, the Department to scrutinise all accounts filed with the Registrar in order to establish that they contain no prima facie breach of any of the many legal requirements applicable. However, the Department does, and is bound to, take cognizance of an apparent default that is brought to its attention, whether by the media or otherwise. In such cases the Department has a responsibility to consider the facts and to decide in the light of them (including in a case such as this the terms of the auditors' report) whether in all the circumstances a prosecution is justified.

It would also be misleading to interpret the case as implying that accounting standards have the force of law. Whilst accounting standards may in a particular case be very material evidence on questions as to accounting principles and practice, they have no formal status in law.

Yours sincerely,

Elizabeth Llewellyn-Smith

THE TRUE AND FAIR VIEW AND GROUP ACCOUNTS

(1) The Department's view of the general effect of the law can be summarised in the following propositions:

(a) "Group accounts" must "deal with" the state of affairs and profit or loss of a holding company and all those companies that are at the end of its financial year its subsidiaries (as defined in s. 154 of the Companies Act 1948) except those subsidiaries excluded from group accounts in accordance with s. 150(2)(b).

(b) Under the 1948 Act, both before and after its amendment by the 1981 Act, the sole object in law of group accounts is to give a true and fair view of the financial position of the holding company and those of its subsidiaries that are dealt with by the accounts so far as concerns members of the holding company.

(c) Group accounts must comprise consolidated accounts or accounts in some other form which better presents the same or equivalent information (s. 151).

(d) Prior to the application of the 1981 Act, the requirement to give a true and fair view overrides the specific requirements of Schedule 8 which otherwise the group accounts would have to meet.

(e) On entry into force of the relevant provisions of the 1981 Act, the true and fair view requirement will override *both* the requirements of Schedule 8 *and* any other specific requirement in the Companies Act which relates to the information to be included in group accounts (including notes to those accounts), including s. 151.

(f) Under the new provisions, the true and fair view requirement is, if possible, to be satisfied (if provision of the statutory information is insufficient for the purpose) by giving additional information in the balance sheet or the profit and loss account or the notes. Only when this is impossible is departure from other requirements permitted, and required, to the extent necessary to provide a true and fair view (the new s. 149(3) as applied by the new s. 152(3)).

(g) Section 150 does not deal with the matters to be included in group accounts. It defines what group accounts are and which companies they deal with, and states what must be done with them. Accordingly, the new s. 152 does not enable the provisions of s. 150 as to the companies dealt with in group accounts to be overridden in order to show a true and fair view of anything other than the holding company and its subsidiaries as defined. Nevertheless where it is necessary in order to give a true and fair view of the financial position of those companies to include in the accounts information about a company which is neither the holding company nor a subsidiary, that information must be given, in accordance with sub-paragraph (f) above.

(h) Although group accounts per se are defined in s. 150, the law does not prevent the directors from accompanying group accounts with information not required by statute.

(2) It is considered that the provisions of the 1948 Act relating to the obligations in respect of group accounts remain virtually unchanged by the amendments contained in the 1981 Act. So does the object of the true and fair requirement. The 1981 Act does provide a heightened emphasis on the overriding character of the true and fair requirement and explicit guidance on how it should be fulfilled. However the overriding character is expressly confined to requirements of the Acts as to matters to be included in, or in a note to, group accounts.

(3) The practical application of the propositions set out in paragraph (1) above can only be determined by directors of companies on a case by case basis in the light of all the relevant facts. It is accepted that there are a wide range of circumstances in which it will be for consideration whether the requirement to give a true and fair view requires the inclusion in group accounts (that is, other than extra-statutorily) of financial information about companies that are not subsidiaries at the end of the financial year. For example:

— the 1981 Act makes express provision for the consolidated accounts of a holding company to deal with associated companies by the equity method. This has been hitherto considered to be implicitly provided for by the need for group accounts to give a true and fair view so far as concerns members of the holding company (or, in the words of SSAP 1, to account for its stewardship). It may be noted however that SSAP 1 requires the disclosure of the relevant information as a separate item in group accounts in consolidated form.

— SSAP 14 requires the direct inclusion in a consolidated profit and loss account of financial information relating to a subsidiary disposed of prior to the end of the financial year, and that consolidated accounts should contain sufficient information about material acquisitions and disposals to enable shareholders to appreciate the effect on the consolidated results.

— SSAP 17 requires the disclosure in financial statements of information about material post-balance sheet non-adjusting events (i.e. events which concern conditions which did not exist at the balance sheet date), such as acquisitions. The disclosure is to take the form of notes describing the transaction and giving an estimate (where possible) of its financial effect. This form of disclosure is extra-statutory. There would be no prohibition on the separate provision of full pro forma accounts of a company acquired after the balance sheet date. (Section 13 of the 1981 Act will require the directors' report to contain particulars of any important events affecting the company or any of its subsidiaries that have occurred since the year-end).

— A sale prior to the balance sheet date followed by a subsequent repurchase would fall to be considered for treatment in accordance with both SSAP 14 and SSAP 17.

(4) The Department sees nothing inconsistent between the law on group accounts and the disclosure and other requirements elaborated by Accounting Standards by way of guidance statements and indicators of best practice. It does however consider it axiomatic that any emphasis on substance over form must not be at the expense of compliance with the law."

Appendix 4

Disqualification of directors and others from managing companies: Home Office Circular No. 52

(1) Clerks to the Justices will wish to note the new powers available to magistrates' courts (see paragraphs (2) to (4)); chief officers of police will wish to take account of these powers and of the new powers being granted to the higher courts (see paragraph (5)). The attention of clerks is further drawn to their duty to inform the Secretary of State when disqualification orders are made (see paragraphs (12) and (13)). They will wish to note that supplies of the forms required for notifying the Secretary of State of such matters are available from Companies House (see paragraph (2)).

Power of magistrates' courts to make disqualification orders restraining persons from managing companies

(2) Section 93 of the Companies Act 1981 amends section 188 of the Companies Act 1948 and extends to magistrates' courts the power to make a disqualification order restraining persons from managing companies for up to five years in the circumstances described in paragraphs (3) and (4) below. (References in this circular to subsections of section 188 are references to parts of that section of the 1948 Act as now amended.)

(3) Where a person is convicted summarily of an indictable offence in connection with the promotion, formation, management or liquidation of a company or with the receivership or management of the property of a company, the court may make a disqualification order (see section 188(1)(a)).

(4) A new power is created by section 188(1A) whereby the court may disqualify on summary conviction of a "relevant offence" (defined in section 188(2D) as any contravention of any requirement in the Companies Acts to file returns, accounts or other documents with the Registrar of Companies) where a person has had made against him or been convicted of, in total, not less than *three* default orders and relevant offences in the previous five years (*including* that and any other offence of which he is convicted on the same occasion). A "default order" is defined in section 188(2D) as an order made under section 337, 375 or 428 of the Companies Act 1948 or section 5(1) of the Companies Act 1976 by virtue of any contravention of or failure to comply with any relevant requirement.

Additional powers for higher courts

(5) In addition to providing new powers for magistrates' courts, sections 93 and 94 of the Companies Act 1981 strengthen and amalgamate the powers already available to higher courts to make disqualification orders. The main changes made are:

(a) the maximum period of a disqualification order made on grounds other than persistent default in filing returns is increased from five to 15 years;

(b) the power to disqualify where it appears to the court that a person has been persistently in default in filing returns, accounts or other documents with the Registrar of Companies is extended to include not only the High Court, as at present, but also County Courts where they have jurisdiction to wind up any company in relation to which a default has been committed;

(c) the grounds on which disqualification orders may be made are extended to include conviction of an indictable offence involving the liquidation or receivership of a company or where it appears in the course of winding up a company that a liquidator or receiver has been guilty of any fraud in relation to the company or any breach of his duty as liquidator or receiver;

(d) the coverage of disqualification orders will be extended to prohibit persons from:

(i) being directors or concerned in the management of overseas companies operating in the U.K. or of other unregistered companies or large partnerships; and

(ii) from promoting or forming a company or acting as its receiver or liquidator.

Police action to draw attention to the new powers

(6) Chief officers of police will wish to note the new powers granted to the courts. They may care to advise solicitors and officers to draw to the attention of the court the powers available to it to make a disqualification order in appropriate cases.

General

(7) A disqualification order is an order that a person shall not without the leave of the court (see paragraph (8) below) be a director or liquidator of a company, a receiver or manager of the property of a company, or in any way, whether directly or indirectly, be concerned in the promotion, formation or management of a company (see section 188(1B)). Orders may be made against legal persons such as companies and other bodies corporate as well as against individuals.

(8) The effect of the definition of "the court" in section 188(2D) is that power to grant leave of a disqualification order is reserved in the County and High Courts.

(9) A disqualification order may be made against a person by the magistrates' court which convicted him or by any other magistrates' court acting for the same petty sessions areas.

(10) Breach of a disqualification order is an offence (section 188(6)).

Transitional provisions

(11) Section 93 of the 1981 Act makes a number of transitional provisions:

(a) disqualification orders for more than five years and the new provisions on disqualification on grounds of misconduct as liquidator or receiver may not be used in respect of acts committed before the coming into force of section 93 on June 15, 1982;

(b) summary conviction of an indictable offence may not be used as grounds for a disqualification order if the defendant consents to be tried summarily before that date;

(c) magistrates' courts may use their new power to make a disqualification order on conviction of a relevant offence only where that conviction is for an offence committed or which continued to be committed after June 15, 1982, and for the purpose of making such an order no account shall be taken of any offence committed or any default order made before June 1, 1977.

Duty of clerk after the making of an order

(12) When a disqualification order is made, the prescribed officer of the court is required by section 29(1) of the Companies Act 1976, as amended by Schedule 3, paragraph 36 of the Companies Act 1981, to furnish the Secretary of State with particulars of the order in the prescribed form. The Companies (Disqualification Orders) Order 1982 designates the Clerk to the Justices as the prescribed officer in the case of a magistrates' court; Schedules 1 and 2 prescribe the forms to be used for furnishing particulars to the Secretary of State. Completed forms should be sent to Companies Registration Office, Companies House, Crown Way, Maindy, Cardiff CF4 3UZ. Supplies of the forms may be obtained from Prosecution Section, Companies House.

(13) Section 29(1) does not require the prescribed officer to furnish the Secretary of State with details of the quashing or variation of a disqualification order on *appeal*. However, the prescribed officer of the court which made the original order is requested to send the relevant details to the Secretary of State at the address given above. This will enable the register of disqualification orders to be kept accurate. The relevant details are: the name of the person

against whom the order was originally made, the date on which it was made, the court which heard the appeal (specifying whether the order was quashed or varied) and the date of that quashing or variation; prescribed officers may find it convenient for this purpose to use Form D04. Supplies of this form may also be obtained from Prosecution Section, Companies House.

Register of disqualification orders

(14) A register of the names and particulars of persons against whom disqualification orders have been made is available for public inspection during the currency of those orders at Companies Registration Office in Cardiff, at its London Search Room, the Companies Registration Office in Edinburgh and the Royal Courts of Justice in London.

Appendix 5

Companies Acts Forms

(except winding up forms)

Number of form	Function/description	Companies Acts reference
1	Statement of first directors and secretary and intended situation of registered office	C.A. 1976, ss. 21, 23(2)
2	Notice of accounting reference date	C.A. 1976, s. 2(1)
3	Notice of new accounting reference date given *during the course* of an accounting reference date	C.A. 1976, s. 3(1)
3a	Notice of new accounting reference date given *after the end* of an accounting reference period	C.A. 1976, s. 3(2)
4a	Notice of change in situation of registered office	C.A. 1976, s. 23(3)
5	Notice of overseas interests	C.A. 1976, s. 6
6a	Annual return of a company having a share capital	C.A. 1948, ss. 124, 126
7	Annual return of a company not having a share capital	C.A. 1948, ss. 125, 126
8	Application by public company to commence business and declaration of particulars	C.A. 1980, s. 4
9b	Notice of change of directors or secretaries or in their particulars	C.A. 1948, s. 200
10	Notice of increase in nominal capital	C.A. 1948, s. 63
11	Notice of increase of number of members	C.A. 1948, s. 7(3)

14	Notice of passing of resolution removing an auditor	C.A. 1976, s. 14(3)
17	Application by an existing joint stock company for registration as a company limited by shares or limited by guarantee	C.A. 1948, ss. 382, 384, 386
17a	Application by an existing company other than a joint stock company for registration as a company limited by guarantee	C.A. 1948, ss. 382, 385, 386
17b	Application by an existing joint stock company for registration as a private company limited by shares or limited by guarantee	C.A. 1948, ss. 382, 384, 386
17c	Application by an existing company other than a joint stock company for registration as a private company limited by guarantee	C.A. 1948, ss. 382, 384, 386
17d	Application by an existing joint stock company for registration as a public company limited by shares	C.A. 1980, s. 13
17e	Registration of an existing joint stock company. Declaration of compliance in connection with registration as a public company	C.A. 1980, s. 13(4)
18	Application by an existing joint stock company for registration as an unlimited company	C.A. 1948, ss. 382, 384, 386
18a	Application by an existing company other than a joint stock company for registration as an unlimited company	C.A. 1948, ss. 382, 384, 386
18b	Application by an existing joint stock company for registration as an unlimited company	C.A. 1948, ss. 382, 384, 386
18c	Application by an existing company other than a joint stock company for registration as an unlimited company	C.A. 1948, ss. 382, 385, 386
19	Registration of an existing joint stock company: List of members	C.A. 1948, s. 384(a)
21	Registration of an existing joint stock company as a limited company: Statement of particulars	C.A. 1948, s. 384(c)
23	Registration of an existing joint stock company: Declaration verifying documents delivered to the Registrar of Companies with application for registration	C.A. 1948, s. 386
24	Statement of places of business of banks	C.A. 1948, s. 432

Number of form	Function/description	Companies Acts reference
25	Notice of intention to carry on business as an investment company	C.A. 1980, s. 41(3)
25a	Revocation of notice to carry on business as an investment company	C.A. 1980, s. 41(7)
26	Notice of place where copies of directors' service contracts or memoranda thereof are kept or of any change in that place	C.A. 1967, s. 26(3)
27	Notice of place where register of directors' interests in shares, etc. is kept or of any change in that place	C.A. 1967, s. 29(8)
28	Notice of consolidation, division, conversion, sub-division, redemption or cancellation of shares, or re-conversion of stock into shares	C.A. 1948, s. 62
29	Notice of the situation of the office where a dominion register is kept or of any change in, or discontinuance of, any such office	C.A. 1948, s. 119
29a	Notice of place for inspection of a dominion register which is kept by recording the matters in question otherwise than in a legible form, or of any change in that place	S.E. (C of B) A. 1976, s. 3(4)
33	Statement of particulars of rights attached to shares allotted not otherwise registrable	C.A. 1980, ss. 33(1), 33(5)
33a	Statement of particulars of variation of rights attached to shares not otherwise registrable	C.A. 1980, s. 33(3)
33b	Notice of assignment of name or new name to any class of shares not otherwise registrable	C.A. 1980, s. 33(4)
39c	Members' voluntary winding up: Notice of appointment of liquidator	C.A. 1948, s. 305
39d	Creditors' voluntary winding up: Notice of appointment of liquidator	C.A. 1948, s. 305
39e	Notice of appointment of liquidator: For insertion in London or Edinburgh Gazette	C.A. 1948, s. 305
41a	Declaration of compliance with the requirements on application for registration of a company	C.A. 1980, s. 3(5)

42	Consent to act as director of a company	C.A. 1948, s. 181
44	Declaration that the conditions of section 109(1)(a)(b) and (c) of the Companies Act 1948 have been complied with	C.A. 1948, s. 109(1)(d)
44a	Declaration that the provisions of section 109(2)(b) of the Companies Act 1948 have been complied with	C.A. 1948, s. 109(2)(b)
47	Particulars of a mortgage or charge	C.A. 1948, s. 95(1)
47	Particulars of a mortgage or charge created by a company registered in Scotland	C.A. 1948, s. 106A
(Scot)		
47a	Particulars of a series of debentures	C.A. 1948, s. 95(3)
47a	Particulars of a series of debentures	C.A. 1948, s. 106A(7)
(Scot)		
47b	Particulars of a mortgage or charge subject to which property has been acquired	C.A. 1948, s. 97
47b	Particulars of a mortgage or charge subject to which property has been acquired by a company registered in Scotland	C.A. 1948, s. 106C
(Scot)		
47c	Certificate of registration in Scotland or Northern Ireland of a charge comprising property situate there	C.A. 1948, s. 95(5)
48	Particulars of an issue of debentures in a series	C.A. 1948, s. 95(8)
48	Particulars of an issue of debentures in a series containing, or giving by reference to any other instrument, any charge, by a company registered in Scotland	C.A. 1948, s. 106A(7)
(Scot)		
48a	Particulars of an instrument of alteration to a floating charge created by a company registered in Scotland	C.A. 1948, s. 106A
(Scot)		
49	Memorandum of complete satisfaction of mortgage or charge	C.A. 1948, s. 100
49	Memorandum of complete satisfaction of a registered mortgage or charge	C.A. 1948, s. 106F
(Scot)		
49a	Memorandum of (1) partial payment or satisfaction of mortgage or charge (2) release of part of property or undertaking from mortgage or charge	C.A. 1948, s. 100

Number of form	Function/description	Companies Acts reference
49a (Scot)	Memorandum of (1) partial payment or satisfaction of charge (2) release of part of property or undertaking from charge	C.A. 1948, s. 106F
49b	Memorandum of fact that part of property or undertaking mortgaged or charged has ceased to form part of property or undertaking of company	C.A. 1948, s. 100
49b (Scot)	Memorandum of fact that part of the property or undertaking mortgaged or charged has ceased to form part of the property or undertaking of company	C.A. 1948, s. 106F
52	Particulars of a contract relating to shares allotted as fully or partly paid up otherwise than in cash	C.A. 1948, s. 52(2)
53	Notice of appointment of receiver or manager	C.A. 1948, s. 102(1)
53a (Scot)	Notice to Registrar of appointment of a receiver	C. (F.C. and R.) (S.) A. 1972, s. 13(1)
53b (Scot)	Notice to Registrar of appointment of a receiver	C. (F.C. and R.) (S.) A. 1972, s. 13(1)
53c (Scot)	Notice to company of appointment of receiver or manager	C.A. 1948, s. 372(1)(a)
57	Receiver or manager's abstract of receipts and payments	C.A. 1948, ss. 372(2), 374(1)
57 (Scot)	Receiver's abstract of receipts and payments	C. (F.C. and R.) (S.) A. 1972, s. 25(2)
57a (Scot)	Notice of ceasing to act as receiver or manager	C.A. 1948, s. 102(2)
58	Statement of the amount or rate per cent of the commission payable in respect of shares and of the number of shares for which persons have agreed for a commission to subscribe absolutely	C.A. 1948, s. 53(1)(c)(ii), (d)
58a	Statement of the amount or rate per cent of the commission payable in respect of shares and of the number of shares for which persons have agreed for a commission to subscribe absolutely	C.A. 1948, s. 53(1)(c)(ii), (d)

59	Declaration in relation to assistance for the acquisition of shares	C.A. 1981, ss. 43(6), 43(7)
59a	Declaration by the directors of a holding company in relation to assistance for the acquisition of shares	C.A. 1981, ss. 43(6), 43(7)
60	Notice of application made to the court for the cancellation of a special resolution regarding financial assistance for the acquisition of shares	C.A. 1980, s. 11(5) and C.A. 1981, s. 44(3)
61	Declaration on application for the registration of a company exempt from the requirement to use the word "limited"	C.A. 1981, s. 25(4)(a)
62	Declaration on application for the registration of a company, pursuant to Part VIII of the Companies Act 1948, exempt from the requirement to use the word "limited"	C.A. 1981, s. 25(4)(b)
63	Declaration on application for the change of name of a company for exemption from the requirement to use the word "limited"	C.A. 1981, s. 25(4)(c)
64	Return by a company purchasing its own shares	C.A. 1981, s. 52
65	Declaration in relation to the redemption or purchase of shares out of capital	C.A. 1981, s. 55
66	Notice of application to the court for the cancellation of a resolution for the redemption or purchase of shares out of capital	C.A. 1981, s. 57(3)
67	Statement by a company without capital of particulars of members' class rights	C.A. 1981, s. 102(1)
68	Statement by a company without share capital of particulars of a variation of members' class rights	C.A. 1981, s. 102(2)
69	Notice by a company without share capital of assignment of a name or other designation to a class of members	C.A. 1981, s. 102(3)
70	Statement by a company without share capital of particulars of the rights of each class of members	C.A. 1981, s. 102(4)
100	Notice to dissenting shareholders	C.A. 1948, s. 209(1)
100a	Notice to dissenting shareholders	C.A. 1948, s. 209(2)
100b	Notice to transferee company by dissenting shareholder	C.A. 1948, s. 209(2)

Number of form	Function/description	Companies Acts reference
101	Notice of application made to the Court for the cancellation of an alteration made by special resolution to the provisions of the memorandum of the company	C.A. 1948, s. 5(7)
101a	Notice of application made to the Court for the cancellation of a special resolution regarding re-registration	C.A. 1980, s. 11(5)
102	Notice of place where a register of holders of debentures or a duplicate thereof is kept or of any change in that place	C.A. 1948, s. 86(3)
102a	Notice of place for inspection of a register of holders of debentures which is kept by recording the matters in question otherwise than in a legible form, or of any change in that place	S.E. (C of B) A. 1976, s. 3(4)
103	Notice of place where register of members is kept or of any change in that place	C.A. 1948, s. 110(3)
103a	Notice of place for inspection of a register of members which is kept by recording the matters in question otherwise than in a legible form, or of any change in that place	S.E. (C of B) A. 1976, s. 3(4)
109	Statement as to affairs: in the matter of a debenture or series of debentures	C.A. 1948, ss. 372(1), 373(2)
109 (Scot)	Statement as to affairs of a company	C. (F.C. and R.) (S.) A. 1972, s. 26 (2)
109a	Statement as to affairs	C.A. 1948, ss. 372(1), 373(2)
Re-registration		
R1	Application by a limited company to be re-registered as unlimited	C.A. 1967, s. 43
R2	Members' assent to company being re-registered as unlimited	C.A. 1967, s. 43(3)
R3	Application by an unlimited company to be re-registered as limited	C.A. 1967, s. 44

R4	Declaration by directors as to members' assent to re-registration of a company as unlimited	C.A. 1967, s. 43(3)
R5	Application by a private company for re-registration as a public company	C.A. 1980, s. 5(1)
R6	Declaration of compliance with the requirements by a private company for re-registration as a public company	C.A. 1980, s. 5(3)
R7	Application by an old public company for re-registration as a public company	C.A. 1980, s. 8(3)
R8	Declaration by director or secretary on application by an old public company for re-registration as a public company	C.A. 1980, s. 8(5)
R9	Declaration by old public company that it does not meet the requirements for a public company	C.A. 1980, s. 8(9)
R10	Application by a public company for re-registration as a private company	C.A. 1980, s. 10(1)
R11	Application by a public company for re-registration as a private company following a court order	C.A. 1980, s. 12(3)
R12	Application by a public company for re-registration as a private company following cancellation of shares and diminution of share capital	C.A. 1980, s. 37(5)

Overseas company forms

F1	List of documents delivered for registration by an overseas company	C.A. 1948, s. 407(1)
F2	List and particulars of the directors and secretary of an overseas company	C.A. 1948, s. 407
F3	List of names and addresses of some one or more persons resident in Great Britain authorised to accept service on behalf of an overseas company	C.A. 1948, s. 407(1)
F4	Return of alteration in the charter, statutes, etc., of an overseas company	C.A. 1948, s. 409(1)
F4a	Return of change in the corporate name of an overseas company	C.A. 1948, s. 409(2)
F5	Return of alteration in the directors or secretary of an overseas company or in their particulars	C.A. 1948, s. 409(1)
F6	Return of alterations in the names and addresses of persons resident in Great Britain authorised to accept service on behalf of an overseas company	C.A. 1948, s. 409(1)

Number of form	Function/description	Companies Acts reference
F7	Notice of accounting reference date by an overseas company	C.A. 1976, ss. 2(1) and 10(1)
F7a	Notice by an overseas company of new accounting reference date given during the course of an accounting reference period	C.A. 1976, ss. 3(1) and 10(1)
F7b	Notice by an overseas company of new accounting reference date given after the end of an accounting reference period	C.A. 1976, ss. 3(2) and 10(1)
F8	Particulars of mortgage or charge on property in England and Wales created by a company incorporated outside England and Wales	C.A. 1948, ss. 95 and 106
F8 (Scot)	Particulars of a mortgage or charge on property in Scotland created by a company which is incorporated outside Great Britain	C.A. 1948, ss. 106A and 106K
F9	Particulars of a mortgage or charge subject to which property in England and Wales has been acquired by a company incorporated outside England and Wales	C.A. 1948, ss. 97 and 106
F9 (Scot)	Particulars of a mortgage or charge on property in Scotland which is acquired by a company which is incorporated outside Great Britain	C.A. 1948, ss. 106C and 106K
F10	Particulars of a series of debentures containing, or giving by reference to any other instrument, any charge on property in England and Wales, to the benefit of which the debenture holders of the said series are entitled, pari passu, created by a company incorporated outside England and Wales	C.A. 1948, ss. 95(8) and 106
F10 (Scot)	Particulars of a series of debentures containing, or giving by reference to any other instrument, any charge on property in Scotland, to the benefit of which the debenture holders of the said series are entitled pari passu, created by a company which is incorporated outside Great Britain	C.A. 1948, ss. 106A(7) and 106K
F11	Particulars of an issue of debentures in a series by a company incorporated outside England and Wales	C.A. 1948, ss. 95(8) and 106

Form	Description	Reference
F11 (Scot)	Particulars of an issue of debentures in a series containing or giving by reference to any other instrument any charge by a company incorporated outside Great Britain	C.A. 1948, ss. 106A(7) and 106K
F11a (Scot)	Particulars of an instrument of alteration to a floating charge created by a company incorporated outside Great Britain	C.A. 1948, ss. 106A and 106K
F12	Memorandum of complete satisfaction of mortgage or charge registered by a company incorporated outside England and Wales	C.A. 1948, s. 100
F12 (Scot)	Memorandum of satisfaction of a registered charge by a company which is incorporated outside Great Britain	C.A. 1948, ss. 106F and 106K
F12a	Memorandum of (1) partial payment or satisfaction of mortgage or charge (2) release of part of property or undertaking from mortgage or charge registered by a company incorporated outside England and Wales	C.A. 1948, s. 100
F12a (Scot)	Memorandum of (1) partial payment or satisfaction of charge (2) release of part of property or undertaking from charge	C.A. 1948, ss. 106F and 106K
F12b	Memorandum of fact that part of property or undertaking mortgaged or charged has ceased to form part of property or undertaking of company registered by a company incorporated outside England and Wales	C.A. 1948, s. 100
F12b (Scot)	Memorandum of fact that part of property or undertaking mortgaged or charged has ceased to form part of the property or undertaking of company registered by a company incorporated outside England and Wales	C.A. 1948, ss. 106F and 106K
13	Statement of name, other than corporate name, under which an overseas company proposes to carry on business in Great Britain	C.A. 1976, s. 31(3)
13a	Statement of name, other than corporate name, under which an overseas company proposes to carry on business in Great Britain in substitution for name previously registered	C.A. 1976, s. 31(3)
14	Declaration by an overseas company of the establishment of a place of business in Great Britain	C.A. 1948, s. 407

PUC forms

Number of form	Function/description	Companies Acts reference
PUC 1	Statement on formation of company to be incorporated with limited liability under the Companies Act 1948	F.A. 1973, s. 47
PUC 2	Return of allotments of shares issued for cash	C.A. 1948, s. 52(1) and F.A. 1973, s. 47
PUC 3	Return of allotments of shares issued wholly or in part for a consideration other than cash	C.A. 1948, s. 52(1) and F.A. 1973, s. 47
PUC 4	Claim for credit or relief from capital duty under section 49(5) of the Finance Act 1973	F.A. 1973, s. 49(5)
PUC 5	Statement of amounts or further amounts paid on nil paid or partly paid shares	F.A. 1973, s. 47
PUC 6	Statement relating to a chargeable transaction of a capital company	F.A. 1973, s. 47
PUC 7	Return of allotments of shares issued by way of capitalisation of reserves (bonus issues)	C.A. 1948, s. 52(1) and F.A. 1973, s. 47

Appendix 6

CCAB statements on distributable profits and realised profits

(1) *The determination of realised profits and disclosure of distributable profits in the context of the Companies Acts 1948 to 1981*

Explanatory note

The Consultative Committee of Accountancy Bodies wishes to draw readers' attention to the fact that this guidance statement does not deal with the special problems arising in connection with the determination of realised profits in the context of foreign currency translation. It is intended that these problems should be dealt with in the future by the issue of an accounting standard on foreign currency translation.

Guidance statement

The following statement of guidance on the determination of realised profits and disclosure of distributable profits in the context of the Companies Acts 1948 to 1981 is issued by the Council of the Institute of Chartered Accountants in England and Wales (in association with the Councils of The Institute of Chartered Accountants of Scotland, the Institute of Chartered Accountants in Ireland, the Association of Certified Accountants, the Institute of Cost and Management Accountants and the Chartered Institute of Public Finance and Accountancy). The guidance given in this statement may need to be amended as the law is interpreted in particular cases, or as existing Accounting Standards are revised and new Standards are issued.

The statement and its appendix have been considered and approved by Counsel. They are, however, not definitive. Interpretation of the law rests ultimately with the courts.

References to the 1948 Act, the 1980 Act and the 1981 Act are to the Companies Acts 1948, 1980 and 1981 respectively.

References to the "new Schedule 8" are to Schedule 8 to the 1948 Act as inserted by section 1(2) of the 1981 Act, and as set out in Schedule 1 to the 1981 Act.

Realised profits: the statutory framework

1. The term realised profits was introduced into UK company law statutes as a result of the implementation of the 2nd and 4th EEC directives on company law in the Companies Act 1980 (Part III) and the Companies Act 1981 (Part I) respectively:

(1) Part III of the 1980 Act imposes statutory restrictions on the distribution of profits and assets by companies. These restrictions include a prohibition on the distribution of unrealised profits (there is an exception to this rule where distributions are made in kind (see section 43A of the 1980 Act, as inserted by section 85 of the 1981 Act)).

(2) Paragraph 12(a) of the new Schedule 8 requires that "Only profits realised at the balance sheet date shall be included in the profit and loss account." Paragraph 34(4) contains a similar requirement applicable to transfers from the revaluation reserve to the profit and loss account. These requirements are extended to consolidated accounts by paragraphs 61 to 66 of the new Schedule 8. They do not apply to accounts prepared under Schedule 8A to the 1948 Act.

2. The new Schedule 8 states that "references to realised profits . . . are references to such profits . . . as fall to be treated as realised profits . . . in accordance with principles generally accepted with respect to the determination for accounting purposes of realised profits at the time when those accounts are prepared" (paragraph 90 of new Schedule 8, extended to the 1980 Act by reason of section 21(1) of the 1981 Act). The term "principles generally accepted" for the determination of realised profits is not defined in the Act.

3. This statement gives guidance as to the interpretation of "principles generally accepted" for the determination of realised profits in the context of these statutory requirements. Both the statutory requirements and the following guidance must throughout be viewed in the context of section 149 of the 1948 Act, as amended by section 1 of the 1981 Act, which states that the requirement for company accounts to give a true and fair view overrides all other provisions of the Companies Acts 1948 to 1981 as to the matters to be included in a company's accounts. Section 152 of the 1948 Act, as amended by section 2 of the 1981 Act, imposes a corresponding requirement for group accounts.

"Principles generally accepted" for realised profits

4. "Principles generally accepted" for the determination of realised profits should be considered in conjunction with, inter alia, the legal principles laid down in the new Schedule 8, statements of standard accounting practice ("SSAPs"), and in particular the fundamental accounting concepts referred to in SSAP 2.

"Disclosure of accounting policies". As stated in the Explanatory Foreword to Accounting Standards, SSAPs describe methods of accounting for all accounts intended to give a true and fair view. They must therefore, where applicable, be considered to be highly persuasive in the interpretation of "principles generally accepted" for the determination of realised profits.

5. Accounting thought and practice develop over time. This is recognised in the statutory requirement that realised profits should be

determined "in accordance with principles generally accepted . . . at the time when those accounts are prepared". Because of this, the guidance set out in this statement is itself liable to amendment from time to time.

6. In determining whether a profit is realised, particular regard should be had to the statutory accounting principles in paragraphs 12 and 13 of the new Schedule 8, and to the parallel fundamental accounting concepts of "prudence" and "accruals" as set out in SSAP 2.

7. Paragraph 12 of the new Schedule 8 requires that "The amount of any item shall be determined on a prudent basis" and, in particular, as already noted, that "only profits realised at the balance sheet date shall be included in the profit and loss account". SSAP 2 amplifies the prudence concept as follows:

"revenues and profits are not anticipated, but are recognised by inclusion in the profit and loss account only when realised in the form either of cash or of other assets the ultimate cash realisation of which can be assessed with reasonable certainty".

In the light of the new statutory requirements, it should be borne in mind that the phrases "ultimate cash realisation" and "assessed with reasonable certainty" are intended to clarify the extent to which a profit can be said to be "realised" under the prudence concept in circumstances other than where the profit has already been realised in the form of cash. "Reasonable certainty" is the limiting factor.

8. This approach is consistent with paragraph 13 of the new Schedule 8 which requires that,

"all income and charges relating to the financial year to which the accounts relate shall be taken into account, without regard to the date of receipt of payment".

The statutory requirement corresponds with the accruals concept as explained at paragraph 14(b) of SSAP 2. This states that,

"revenue and costs are accrued (that is, recognised as they are earned or incurred, not as money is received or paid), matched with one another so far as their relationship can be established or justifiably assumed, and dealt with in the profit and loss account of the period to which they relate".

9. In determining realised profits, it is also necessary to comply with paragraph 12(b) of the new Schedule 8, which states that,

"all liabilities and losses which have arisen or are likely to arise in respect of the financial year to which the accounts relate or a previous financial year shall be taken into account, including those which only become apparent between the balance sheet date and the date on which it is signed on behalf of the board of directors . . .".

This statutory requirement corresponds with the prudence concept as explained at paragraph 14(d) of SSAP 2. This states that "provision is made for all known liabilities (expenses and losses) whether the amount of these is known with certainty or is a best estimate in the light of the information available".

Realised profits: summary of guidance

10. A profit which is required by statements of standard accounting practice to be recognised in the profit and loss account should normally be treated as a realised profit, unless the SSAP specifically indicates that it should.be treated as unrealised (see the appendix).

11. Profit may be recognised in the profit and loss account in accordance with an accounting policy which is not the subject of a SSAP, or, exceptionally, which is contrary to a SSAP. Such a profit will normally be a realised profit if the accounting policy adopted is consistent with paragraphs 12 and 13 of the new Schedule 8 and with the accruals and prudence concepts as set out in SSAP 2.

12. Where, in special circumstances, a true and fair view could not be given, even if additional information were provided, without including on the profit and loss account an unrealised profit, the effect of section 149(3) of the 1948 Act (as amended) is to require inclusion of that unrealised profit notwithstanding 12(a) of the new Schedule 8. Moreover, paragraph 15 of the new Schedule 8 allows the directors to include an unrealised profit in the profit and loss account where there are special reasons for doing so. Where unrealised profits are thus recognised in the profit and loss account, particulars of this departure from the statutory accounting principle, the reasons for it and its effect are required to be given in a note to the accounts.

Distributable profits

13. The definition of realised profits contained in the new Schedule 8 is extended by section 21(1) of the 1981 Act to apply to any of the Companies Acts. It therefore applies to the provisions of Part III of the 1980 Act, dealing with distributions. In that context this guidance should be read in conjunction with the statutory rules as to what constitute distributable profits and losses in particular circumstances for the purposes of that part of that Act.

14. It is essential that all companies should keep sufficient records to enable them to distinguish between those reserves which are distributable and those which are not. While most realised profits will be passed through the profit and loss account, there may be some realised profits which will originally have been brought into the accounts as unrealised profits by way of direct credit to reserves. Similarly, while most unrealised profits will be credited direct to reserves, there may be some unrealised profits passed through the profit and loss account (see paragraph 12 above). Subsequently, when such profits are realised either in whole or in part, a reclassification needs to be made between unrealised and realised profits.

15. There is no legal requirement for a company to distinguish in its balance sheet between distributable and non-distributable reserves as such. However, where material non-distributable profits are included in the profit and loss account or in other reserves which might reasonably be assumed to be distributable, it may be necessary for this to be disclosed and quantified in a note to the accounts in order for them to give a true and fair view.

16. Distributions are made by companies and not by groups. It follows that the profits of a group are only distributable to members of the group's holding company to the extent of the holding company's distributable profits. The concept of distributable profit is not, therefore, strictly applicable to groups. However, it is reasonable to assume that the distributable retained profits of subsidiaries can be distributed to the holding company. Where this is not the case, the requirements of paragraph 36 of SSAP 14 "group accounts" should be complied with. This states,

"if there are significant restrictions on the ability of the holding company to distribute the retained profits of the group (other than those shown as non-distributable) because of statutory, contractual or exchange control restrictions the extent of the restrictions should be indicated."

Appendix: accounting standards and realised profits: examples

1. As statements of standard accounting practice are revised and as new standards are issued, it is expected that they will deal with any matters relevant to the determination of realised profits.

2. This has already been done in the case of SSAP 1 "Accounting for Associated Companies", revised in April 1982. This provides an example of the way in which the true and fair view requirements should be satisfied by giving additional information rather than by including unrealised profits in the profit and loss account (see paragraph 12 above). As far as an investing company is concerned, the profits of its associated companies are not realised until they are passed on as dividends; the true and fair view, however, requires that they should be reflected in the investing company's financial statements. There is no problem where group accounts are prepared because specific provision is made for this situation in paragraph 65(1) of the new Schedule 8. Where, however, the investing company does not prepare group accounts, the revised SSAP 1 states that it should show the information required as to its share of the associated company's profit by preparing a separate profit and loss account or by adding the information to its own profit and loss account in supplementary form in such a way that its share of the profits of the associated company is not treated as realised.

3. An example of the principle that profit recognised in accordance with an Accounting Standard should normally be treated as realised (see paragraph 10 above) is provided by SSAP 9 "Stocks and work in

progress". This requires that long-term contract work in progress should be stated in periodic financial statements at cost plus any attributable profit, less any foreseeable losses and progress payments received and receivable. There was initially some concern as to whether profit thus recognised on long-term contract work in progress would be construed as realised profit within the provisions of the Companies Acts. However, the relevant principles of recognising profits in SSAP 9 are based on the concept of "reasonable certainty" as to the eventual outcome and are not in conflict with the statutory accounting principles. Such profits should be treated as realised profits. The Department does not dissent from this view.

(2) *The determination of distributable profits in the context of the Companies Acts 1948 to 1981*

Guidance statement issued in September 1982 on behalf of the Councils of the constituent members of the Consultative Committee of Accountancy Bodies, on the determination of distributable profits. This statement gives guidance on the interpretation of Part III of the Companies Act 1980 and on the determination of the maximum amount of profit which can be legally distributed under the Act.

It should be emphasised that it does not seek to deal with the many commercial factors which need to be taken into account before a company decides on the amount of a distribution to be recommended to its shareholders. It should also be borne in mind that its guidance relates solely to the determination of profits legally available for distribution and that it does not give guidance on the recognition of profit in the accounts.

This statement should be read in conjunction with the guidance statement issued by the Councils of the constituent members of the CCAB on "The determination of realised profits and disclosure of distributable profits in the context of the Companies Acts 1948 to 1981", issued in September 1982 (see (1) above).

This statement has been considered and approved by Counsel. However, it is not definitive. Interpretation of the law rests ultimately with the courts.

References to the "1948 Act", the "1967 Act", the "1980 Act" and the "1981 Act" are to the Companies Acts 1948, 1967, 1980 and 1981 respectively. Section references without ascription refer to the 1980 Act.

References to the "new Schedule 8" are to Schedule 8 to the 1948 Act as inserted by s. 1(2) of the 1981 Act, and as set out in Schedule 1 to the 1981 Act.

Introduction

1. The 1980 Act restricts distributions of both public and private companies. Previously the determination of legally distributable

reserves and profits was governed only by a company's articles of association, sections 56 and 58 of the 1948 Act, and a significant body of case law. After the commencement of the provisions of the 1980 Act, a company must restrict its distributions to those permitted by the 1980 Act, subject to any further restrictions imposed under its memorandum or articles of association.

2. In general, companies are only able to make distributions out of realised profits less realised losses, but further restrictions are imposed on public companies (see para 6 below). The 1980 Act also includes special provisions for certain investment companies and insurance companies (sections 41 and 42): these are not discussed in this guidance statement.

Provisions of the Companies Act 1980 (as amended)

Distribution

3. A distribution is defined (section 45(2)) as every description of distribution of a company's assets to members of the company, whether in cash or otherwise, except distributions made by way of,

(a) an issue of shares as fully or partly paid bonus shares;

(b) redemption or purchase of any of the company's own shares out of capital (including a new issue of shares) or out of unrealised profits;

(c) reduction of share capital; and

(d) a distribution of assets to members of the company on its winding-up.

Profits available for distribution

4. A company may only make a distribution out of profits available for that purpose (section 39(1)). A company's profits available for distribution are stated to be its accumulated, realised profits (so far as not previously distributed or capitalised) less its accumulated, realised losses (so far as not previously written off in a reduction or reorganisation of its share capital) (section 39(2)). Realised losses may not be offset against unrealised profits. Public companies are subject to a further restriction (see paragraph 6 below).

5. A company may only distribute an unrealised profit when the distribution is in kind and the unrealised profit arises from the writing up of the asset being distributed (section 43A, as inserted by section 85 of the 1981 Act).

Public companies

6. A further restriction is placed on distributions by public companies (section 40). A public company may only make a distribution if, after giving effect to such distribution, the amount of its net assets (as defined

in section 87(4)(c)) is not less than the aggregate of its called up share capital and undistributable reserves. This means that a public company must deduct any net unrealised losses from net realised profits before making a distribution, whereas a private company need not make such a deduction (see also paras 29 to 31 below).

7. Under section 40(2) the following are undistributable reserves:

(a) share premium account (see also section 56 of the 1948 Act as amended by the 1981 Act);

(b) capital redemption reserve (see also section 53 of the 1981 Act);

(c) the excess of accumulated, unrealised profits, over the accumulated, unrealised losses so far as not previously written off in a reduction or reorganisation of its share capital;

(d) any other reserve which the company is prohibited from distributing by any enactment, or by its memorandum or articles of association (or equivalent).

Section 40 only applies to public companies. However, because of the effect of section 39(2) of the 1980 Act, section 56 of the 1948 Act, and section 53 of the 1981 Act, none of the above mentioned reserves is distributable by private companies. (The restrictions which are placed upon public companies which have distributed or utilised unrealised profits prior to the commencement of the Act are discussed at paragraph 30 below).

Relevant accounts

8. Whether or not a distribution may be made within the terms of the 1980 Act is determined by reference to "relevant items" as stated in the "relevant accounts": A "relevant item" is defined by section 43(8) as profits, losses, assets, liabilities, provisions, share capital and reserves. Thus, valuations or contingencies included in notes to the financial statements, but not incorporated in the accounts themselves, have no effect on the amount of distributable profit. There is no requirement that distributions can only be made out of distributable profits described as such in the accounts.

9. The "relevant accounts" (annual, interim or initial) are defined in section 43(2) and, except for the initial or interim accounts of private companies, must be properly prepared in accordance with section 43(8).

10. Annual accounts must be accompanied by an audit report complying with section 14 of the 1967 Act, and must have been laid before the company in general meeting in accordance with section 1 of the 1976 Act (section 43(3)). Interim and initial accounts of public companies (there is no such requirement for private companies) must have been delivered to the Registrar of Companies (sections 43(5)(b) and 43(6)(d)). Initial accounts of public companies must be accompanied by a report by the auditor stating whether in his opinion the accounts have

been properly prepared (section 43(6)(b)). The interim accounts need not be accompanied by an audit report.

11. There are requirements in section 43(3)(c)) and section 43(6)(c), where an auditor has issued a qualified report on either annual or initial accounts as appropriate, that before a distribution may be made in reliance on those accounts the auditor must issue an additional statement. In this statement he must express an opinion whether the subject of his qualification is material for the purposes of determining whether the proposed distribution complies with the requirements of the Act.

Adjustments to relevant accounts

12. Adjustments to distributable profits calculated from the relevant accounts are required where one or more distributions have already been made "in pursuance of determinations made by reference to" those accounts (section 43(7)). Adjustments are also required where a company has, since those accounts were prepared, provided financial assistance for the purchase of its own shares which depletes its net assets or made certain payments in respect of or in connection with the purchase of its own shares (section 60(1) of the 1981 Act).

Basis for calculating profits available for distribution

13. The starting point in determining profits available for distribution, the "accumulated, realised profits ... less accumulated, realised losses", will be the profit or loss recognised in the relevant accounts. That is the accumulated balance on the profit and loss account. This figure may require adjustment to take into account any items which are required to be excluded in the determination of distributable profits (e.g. see paragraph 21 below). The amount so arrived at will require further adjustment for any items taken to reserve accounts which may properly be included in the determination of distributable profits. For example, an unrealised profit on an asset revaluation will originally be credited direct to a revaluation reserve. On a subsequent disposal of the asset part or all of the profit is clearly realised notwithstanding the fact that it may not have been passed through the profit and loss account.

14. If an item has not been recognised in the relevant accounts, it cannot be taken into account in determining the profits or net assets available for distribution.

Aspects requiring special consideration

Realised losses

15. Section 39(4) as amended states that certain provisions are to be treated as a realised loss. These are provisions of any kind mentioned in paragraphs 87(1) and 88 of the new Schedule 8, namely:

"... any amount written off by way of providing for depreciation or diminution in value of assets", and ". . . any amount retained as reasonably necessary for the purpose of providing for any liability or loss which is likely to be incurred, or certain to be incurred but uncertain as to amount or as to the date on which it will arise."

16. Section 39(4) as amended makes one specific exception to the rule that any provision of any kind mentioned in these paragraphs is to be treated as a realised loss, namely a provision arising on a revaluation of a fixed asset when all the fixed assets, or all fixed assets other than goodwill, have been revalued (see paragraph 19 below).

17. In view of the requirement of s. 39(4), any loss recognised in the profit and loss account will normally be a realised loss. (An exception to this rule at s. 39(5) is discussed at paragraph 21 below).

Revaluation of assets

18. A surplus over original cost recognised on revaluation of any asset is unrealised. There is no statutory requirement specifying whether the balance, if any, of the surplus that represents the writing back of past depreciation or of provisions for diminution in value should be regarded as realised or unrealised. Moreover, there is at present no unanimity of opinion as to whether such a surplus, to the extent that it represents the writing back of a realised loss, particularly where the realised loss arises from past depreciation, constitutes a realised profit. In view of the division of opinion on this matter, and in the absence of any statutory rule or clearly decisive precedent in case law, it is considered inappropriate to offer guidance on the question in this statement. Where reliance is placed on such a profit being realised in order to make a distribution, it may be appropriate for the directors of the company to seek legal advice. To the extent that the surplus represents the writing back of an unrealised loss, it should be treated as an unrealised profit.

19. A deficit on the revaluation of an asset (unless offsetting a previous unrealised surplus on the same asset) gives rise to a provision and is required to be treated as a realised loss. A realised loss thus created cannot be reduced by being offset wholly or partially against revaluation surpluses on other assets, whether or not of the same class. However, there is an exception to the general rule where a provision for diminution in value of a fixed asset arises on a revaluation of all the fixed assets (other than goodwill) (section 39(4) as amended). Although not explicitly stated, the Act implies that such a provision may be treated as unrealised, and therefore that it does not reduce the profits available for distribution.

20. For the purpose of section 39(4), a revaluation of all the fixed assets may comprise actual revaluations of some of the fixed assets combined with consideration by the directors of the value of the remaining fixed assets. However, if an actual revaluation of all the fixed assets has not occurred, the directors must be satisfied that the aggregate value of all fixed assets considered but not actually revalued is not less than the aggregate amount at which they are for the time being stated in the

company's accounts (section 39 (4A): see paragraph 45(2) of Schedule 3 to the 1981 Act). If the accounts include revalued fixed assets which have been considered, but which have not been subject to an actual revaluation, certain additional information is required to be disclosed for the revaluation to be valid (section 43 (7A): see paragraph 47(c) of Schedule 3 to the 1981 Act).

Revalued fixed assets and depreciation

21. Provisions for depreciation of revalued fixed assets require special treatment to the extent that these provisions exceed the amounts which would have been provided if an unrealised profit had not been made on revaluation (section 39(5)). For the purpose of calculating the amount of profit which is legally available for distribution, section 39(5) requires an amount equivalent to this excess depreciation to "be treated . . . as a realised profit", thereby reducing the provision for this purpose to that relating to the original cost of the asset. As a result, while the depreciation of a surplus on a fixed asset revaluation will affect the published profits, it will not normally affect the amount of a company's distributable profits, provided of course that this revaluation surplus has not been capitalised (capitalisation in this context is defined at section 45(3)).

Disposal of revalued assets

22. On the disposal of a revalued asset any surplus over cost immediately becomes realised. Any loss which has been treated as unrealised (see paragraph 20 above) should on disposal of the asset be redesignated as a realised loss.

Development costs

23. Development costs carried forward in accordance with SSAP 13 (accounting for research and development) will not normally affect distributable profits. Although s. 42A(1) (inserted by section 84 of the 1981 Act) requires that development costs shown as an asset should be treated as a realised loss, this requirement does not apply (section 42A(3)) if the directors justify the costs carried forward not being treated as a realised loss. This they will normally be able to do if the costs are carried forward in accordance with SSAP 13. Such justification must be included in the note on capitalised development costs required by paragraph 20(2) of the new Schedule 8.

Holding company

24. It should be noted that although the whole of the distributable profits of a subsidiary are (subject to the interest of minority shareholders and tax on distributions) available to the holding company, the latter cannot distribute these profits to its own shareholders until such time as they are recognised in the accounts of the holding company.

25. It is not normal practice to take credit for dividends from invest-

ments unless the amounts are declared prior to the investing company's year-end. However, dividends receivable from subsidiaries and associates in respect of accounting periods ending on or before that of the holding company are normally accrued in the holding company's accounts even if declared after the holding company's year-end. Such dividends should be treated as realised by the holding company whether they are paid or passed through a current account, provided that, in the latter case, an appropriate reassessment of the realisable value of the current account balance is made.

26. Exchange control or other restrictions may affect the ability of overseas subsidiaries to remit dividends to the UK. In accordance with the prudence concept such dividends receivable should be treated as realised only when their eventual receipt can be assessed with reasonable certainty.

27. Whilst there is no legal requirement for a holding company to take into account its share of the net losses (if any) of its subsidiaries in determining its distributable profits, the holding company may need to make a provision against a permanent diminution in the value of its investment in any such subsidiary (paragraph 19(2) of the new Schedule 8).

Current cost accounts

28. It will normally make no difference to a company's legally distributable profit whether its relevant accounts are drawn up under the historical or the current cost convention. Where net assets under the current cost convention exceed net assets under the historical cost convention, the difference consists of net unrealised profits which form part of the current cost reserve. The remainder of the current cost reserve consists of an amount equal to the cumulative current cost adjustments charged in the profit and loss account each year. According to SSAP 16 this amount is regarded as realised (in the case of the depreciation adjustment the 1980 Act specifically requires it to be so treated). This part of the current cost reserve, being realised, is legally distributable even though there would be a reduction in the operating capability of the business as a result of making such a distribution, which might, therefore, be commercially inadvisable.

Transitional provisions

Determination of distributable profits at the commencement date

29. Where the directors of a company are, after making all reasonable enquiries, unable to determine whether a particular profit or loss made before the commencement date of the 1980 Act is realised or unrealised, they may treat such a profit as realised and such a loss as unrealised (section 39(7)). Such a position will occur when there are no records of the original cost of an asset or the original amount of a liability.

30. Where a public company has distributed or utilised (otherwise than by capitalisation) unrealised profits prior to the commencement date of the 1980 Act and such profits have not subsequently been realised, an amount equal to the unrealised profits so distributed or utilised falls to be included as part of the undistributable reserves (section 40(2) and section 45(4)). This prevents a public company which has so distributed or utilised unrealised profits in the past from making any further distribution until the shortfall has been made good.

31. If, prior to the commencement of the 1980 Act, a company has realised losses (insofar as they have not been previously written off in either a reduction or a reorganisation of capital), such losses must be made good before making any distribution (section 39(2)).

32. The part of the 1980 Act dealing with distributable profits came into operation as follows (section 45(6)):

New public companies – On their registration under Part I of the 1980 Act.

Existing public companies – On their re-registration as a public limited company under Part I of the 1980 Act, or on June 22, 1982 (18 months after the appointed day), whichever is the earlier.

Private companies – June 22, 1982.

Index

The Tolley Subscriber Service

The benefits to you are . . .

Free service
No extra cost to you.

Up-to-date books
You need never again run the risk of using out-of-date editions.

Finance Bill Memorandum
Sent to you, *free of charge,* soon after each Finance Bill is published.

Pre-publication prices
You will be able to purchase most new titles at introductory discounts.

Reduced subscriptions
Tolley's business periodicals, Partnership Management, Company Secretary's Review, and Tolley's Practical Tax are obtainable at specially reduced rates for Tolley Subscribers.

Reduced conference fees
You will be entitled to reductions in fees for Tolley conferences.

Annual confirmation
Each year we will write to you with details of your standing order. Only after you have confirmed your requirements will the book(s) be sent to you. You may also vary your order at any other time.

Free Postage
Only books on standing order will be sent post-free in the United Kingdom and Eire.

Time-saving and convenient
The next edition of books on your standing order are sent to you automatically upon publication.

Become a Tolley Subscriber by placing a standing order for the next edition of any Tolley publication.

Tolley's Practical Business Periodicals

All Tolley periodicals are sent by first class post. Each is supplied with frequent cumulative indexes, which, together with the free binders, convert single issues into updated valuable reference works to use again and again. All include free supplements from time to time on important topics such as Finance Bills and Acts.

New subscribers may cancel their subscriptions within eight weeks and obtain a full refund.

Company Secretary's Review

An eight page practical business fortnightly that covers the entire field of work of the modern company secretary/administrator: company law, accounting, employment, taxation, health and safety, insurance, energy, national insurance, export, EEC, pensions, transport, property, etc. Concise news items plus sources of further information, detailed topical articles, law reports with commentary, advance warning of key dates and many other regular features, combine to produce a uniquely practical updating service. It is indexed every four issues; a storage binder is supplied for easy reference.

Annual Subscription £54.00; All Tolley Subscribers and ICSA Members £43.20.

Tolley's Practical Tax

A fortnightly, eight page bulletin that concentrates solely on taxation matters for the busy accountant and taxation practitioner. It covers all United Kingdom direct and indirect taxes (except Customs duties) and includes all the latest statutes and regulations, statements of practice, concessions, cases, treaties and official publications. Worked examples and articles by leading authors explain new developments and our 'Points of Practice' series gives valuable information that really is unobtainable elsewhere.

Annual Subscription £48.00; CSR, FDR and PM Subscribers £33.60
Other Tolley Subscribers £40.80

Partnership Management

This twelve page monthly is devoted exclusively to practical information and guidance for partnerships, partners and those advising them. It contains articles and news on every aspect of partnership management (including personal aspects where appropriate) from taxation to staff recruitment, plus legal and parliamentary notes and regular features on provision for retirement and office technology. A special feature is In Practice, highlighting particular points of law and practice and giving advice on problem-solving. A quarterly cumulative index and a ring binder are supplied for easy reference.

Annual Subscription £40.00; All Tolley Subscribers £36.00.

Tolley Book List

Tax Annuals

Tolley's tax annuals are widely used as the work of first reference by thousands of practitioners. Each is fully revised every year.

Annual Reference Guides

The special features of each include:
☐ clear, comprehensive, concise explanation of the law ☐ chapters in alphabetical order ☐ references throughout to relevant statutes, case law, Inland Revenue statements, etc. and to related sections elsewhere in the annuals ☐ comprehensive index ☐ table of statutes ☐ distinctive cover for quick identification ☐ carefully designed, readable text.

Tolley's Income Tax 1982/83
By Eric L Harvey FCA
512pp   ISBN 0 85459 074-9   **£9.95**

Tolley's Corporation Tax 1982/83
By Glyn Saunders MA
320pp   ISBN 0 85459 075-7   **£7.50**

Tolley's Capital Gains Tax 1982/83
By David Harrington MA (Oxon) FCA and
Glyn Saunders MA
284pp   ISBN 0 85459 076-5   **£8.75**

Tolley's Capital Transfer Tax 1982/83
By Robert Wareham BSc (Econ) FCA and
Christopher Greene FCA
216pp   ISBN 0 85459 077-3   **£7.95**

Tolley's Taxation in the Republic of Ireland 1982/83
By Glyn Saunders MA and
Eric L Harvey FCA ATII
224pp   ISBN 0 85459 081-1   **£7.95**

Tolley's Taxation in the Channel Islands & Isle of Man 1982
By David Harrington MA (Oxon) FCA
184pp   ISBN 0 85459 064-1   **£6.95**

Other Annuals

Tolley's Tax Tables 1983/84
16pp   ISBN 0 85459 065-X   **£2.95**

Tolley's Tax Cases 1983
By Victor Grout CBE LLB
435pp   ISBN 0 85459 095-1   **£11.95**

Tolley's Tax Data 1982/83
By Robert Wareham BSc (Econ) FCA and
David Harrington MA (Oxon) FCA
80pp   ISBN 0 85459 068-4   **£3.95**

Tolley's Tax Planning 1982/83
Edited by A L Chapman LLB FTII
800pp   Paperback
         ISBN 0 85459 089-7   **£17.50**
         Hardback
         ISBN 0 85459 099-4   **£22.50**

Grout's Value Added Tax Cases
By Victor Grout CBE LLB
264pp   ISBN 0 85459 046-3   **£10.75**

Tolley's Tax Cards 1982/83
Compiled by G V Hart FTII
36pp   ISBN 0 85459 078-1   **£7.95**

Tolley's Tax Computations 1982/83
By Thomson McLintock & Co
Loose-leaf with updating service.
         ISBN 0 85459 079-X   **£35.00**

Taxwise Taxation Workbook 1982/83
By Arnold Homer FCA ATII, Rita Burrows
ACIS ATII and Peter Gravestock FCA ATII
472pp   ISBN 0 85459 083-8   **£10.75**

Taxwise Capital Transfer Tax Workbook 1982/83
By Arnold Homer FCA ATII, Rita Burrows
ACIS ATII and Peter Gravestock FCA ATII
232pp   ISBN 0 85459 084-6   **£7.95**

Other Tax Books

Annotated Finance Act 1982
352pp   ISBN 0 85459 072-2   **£11.50**

Chapman's Capital Transfer Tax 5th Edition
By A L Chapman LLB (Lond) FTII
600pp   ISBN 0 85459 105-2   **£12.50**

Tolley's Practical Guide to VAT Planning
By H H Mainprice LLB FTII
190pp   ISBN 0 85459 103-6   **£9.95**

Jersey: A Low-Tax Area
By Mark Solly FCA ATII
336pp   Paperback
         ISBN 0 85459 054-4   **£15.00**
         Hardback
         ISBN 0 85459 053-6   **£18.00**

Tolley's Taxation in Gibraltar 1982
By James Levy LLB and
Simon Caplan FCA FTII
165pp   ISBN 0 85459 044-7   **£8.50**

Tolley's Development Land Tax 4th Edition
By Robert W Maas FCA
256pp   ISBN 0 85459 056-0   **£10.50**

Tolley's Double Taxation Relief
By Deloitte Haskins and Sells
175pp   ISBN 0 510 49387-4   **£7.95**

Tolley's Stamp Duties 2nd Edition
By Sheila V Masters LLB FCA ATII
136pp   ISBN 0 510 49024-7   **£5.95**

Tolley's Stock Relief
By Glyn Saunders MA
49pp   ISBN 0 85459 052-8   **£3.50**

Tolley's US/UK Double Tax Treaty
By Arthur Andersen & Co
212pp   ISBN 0 510 49421-8   **£9.95**

Sotinwa's Nigerian Tax Handbook 1982
By G A Sotinwa FCA
251pp   ISBN 0 85459 055-2   **£11.50**

Company Law

Tolley's Companies Act 1981
By George Eccles and Jenny Cox
400pp   Paperback
       ISBN 0 85459 039-0   **£7.95**
       Hardback
       ISBN 0 85459 058-7   **£11.95**

Tolley's Companies Act 1980
By Mary Arden and George Eccles
291pp   Paperback
       ISBN 0 510 49415-3   **£6.95**
       Hardback
       ISBN 0 85459 059-5   **£11.95**

Tolley's Company Law
Edited by A L Chapman LLB FTII and
R M Ballard MA
pp tba   Paperback
       ISBN 0 85459 069-2   **£19.50**
       Hardback
       ISBN 0 85459 106-0   **£25.00**

Tolley's Index to Companies Legislation
Compiled by Josephine Stafford BA
74pp   ISBN 0 85459 067-6   **£3.95**

Employment Law

Tolley's Health and Safety at Work Handbook
Edited by Malcolm Dewis LLB
470pp   ISBN 0 85459 029-3   **£12.95**

**Tolley's Employment Handbook 2nd Edition
with 1980 Supplement**
By Elizabeth Slade MA (Oxon)
276pp   ISBN 0 510 49390-4   **£8.95**

Tolley's Employment Act 1982
By Andrew Hillier BA
192pp   ISBN 0 85459 082-X   **£7.95**

Tolley's Guide to Statutory Sick Pay
By Coopers & Lybrand
pp tba   ISBN 0 85459 100-1   **£3.95**

Redundancy — What to do Next
By Roger Stanway and Christopher Neill
150pp   ISBN 0 85459 096-X   **£3.95**

Social Security

Tolley's Social Security and State Benefits 1982
By Jim Matthewman and Nigel Lambert
470pp   ISBN 0 85459 080-3   **£8.95**

Insolvency

Liquidation Manual
By Paul Shewell MA FCA and
John Powell FCA
300pp   ISBN 0 85459 028-5   **£21.00**

Receivership Manual 2nd Edition
By Donald Chilvers FCA and
Paul Shewell MA FCA
150pp   ISBN 0 85459 070-6   **£ tba**

**Employees' Rights in Receiverships
and Liquidations**
By Guy T E Parsons and William F Ratford
208pp   ISBN 0 510 49396-3   **£14.95**

Accounting

Companies Accounts Check List No. 1
By Peat Marwick Mitchell & Co   **£4.20 + VAT**
24pp   ISBN 0 85459 073-0   **(per pack of 5)**

Companies Accounts Check List No. 2
By Peat Marwick Mitchell & Co   **£4.20 + VAT**
32pp   ISBN 0 85459 066-8   **(per pack of 5)**

Tolley's CCA Conversion Kit
By Michael Kirwan and John Belton
229pp   ISBN 0 85459 016-1   **£45.00 + VAT**

Tolley's Reporting under CCA
By Peat Marwick Mitchell & Co
275pp   ISBN 0 85459 048-X   **£18.00**

Tolley's Pro Forma Accounts
Prepared by Arthur Young McClelland
Moores & Co   **£9.00 + VAT**
50pp   ISBN 0 85459 094-3   **(per pack of 5)**

Financial Reporting 1982-83
Edited by L C L Skerratt and D J Tonkin
271pp   ISBN 0 85291 335-4   **£19.50**

Miscellaneous

Tolley's Expansion Kit for Business
By Touche Ross & Co
92pp   ISBN 0 85459 071-4   **£4.95**

Tolley's Survival Kit for Small Businesses
By Touche Ross & Co
43pp   ISBN 0 85459 040-4   **£2.95**
       Eire Version
       ISBN 0 85459 051-X   **£3.50**

Tolley's European Community Institutions
By Joanne S Foakes BA (Oxon)
83pp   ISBN 0 85459 060-9   **£4.50**

**Tolley's Profit Sharing and other
Share Acquisition Schemes
with 1980 Supplement**
By Francis G Sandison BCL MA (Oxon)
231pp   ISBN 0 510 49383-1   **£9.95**

The Independent Director
By R I Tricker MA FCA FCMA
104pp   ISBN 0 510 49378-5   **£4.50**

CSR Survey of Company Car Schemes 1982
By Jill Greatorex
120pp   ISBN 0 85458 101-X   **£ tba**

CSR Survey of Employee Benefits
By William M Mercer Benefits Ltd
pp tba   ISBN 0 85459 088-9   **£ tba**

Focus Series

**Capital Transfer Tax: Discretionary Trusts
after Finance Act 1982**
By Tony Sherring FCA FTII
86pp   ISBN 0 85459 091-9   **£4.75**

**The Purchase or Redemption by a Company
of Its Own Shares**
By Peter Wolstenholme, MA FCA and
Robert Willott FCA
104pp   ISBN 0 85459 093-5   **£4.75**

ORDER FORM

To: Tolley Publishing Co. Ltd.,
    209 High Street, Croydon, Surrey CR0 1QR Telephone: 01-686 9141

Please supply the following publications now (or as soon as published):—

Title	Price each	Current Editions No.	£	Future Editions No.
Tolley's Income Tax 1982/83	£9.95			IT82
Tolley's Corporation Tax 1982/83	£7.50			CT82
Tolley's Capital Gains Tax 1982/83	£8.75			CG82
Tolley's Capital Transfer Tax 1982/83	£7.95			CTT82
Chapman's Capital Transfer Tax 5th Edition	£12.50			CA83
Tolley's Taxation in the Republic of Ireland 1982/83	£7.95			R182
Tolley's Tax Data 1982/83	£3.95			TTD82
Tolley's Tax Tables 1983/84	£2.95			TT83
Tolley's Tax Cases 1983	£11.95			TC83
Tolley's Taxation in the Channel Islands & IoM 1982	£6.95			C182
Tolley's Tax Planning 1982/83 Paperback edition	£17.50			TP82
Hardback edition	£22.50			TPH82
Grout's Value Added Tax Cases	£10.75			VATC
Tolley's Practical Guide to VAT Planning	£9.95			VATP
Tolley's Tax Cards 1982/83	£7.95			TXC82
Tolley's Tax Computations	£35.00			TTC82
Annotated Finance Act 1982	£11.50			FA82
Jersey: A Low-Tax Area Paperback edition	£15.00			JLT
Hardback edition	£18.00			JLTHB
Tolley's Taxation in Gibraltar 1982	£8.50			G182
Tolley's Development Land Tax 4th Edition	£10.50			DLT82
Tolley's Double Taxation Relief	£7.95			DTR82
Tolley's Stamp Duties 2nd Edition	£5.95			SD80
Tolley's Stock Relief	£3.50			SR82
Tolley's US/UK Double Tax Treaty	£9.95			DTT80
Tolley's Companies Act 1981 Paperback edition	£7.95			CO81
Hardback edition	£11.95			COH81
Tolley's Companies Act 1980 Paperback edition	£6.95			CO80
Hardback edition	£11.95			COH80
Tolley's Company Law Paperback edition	£19.50			TCL
Hardback edition	£25.00			TCLHB
Tolley's Index to Companies Legislation	£3.95			ICL
Tolley's Health and Safety at Work Handbook	£12.95			HSW
Redundancy — What to do next	£3.95			REDUN
Tolley's Employment Handbook 2nd Edition with 1980 Supplement	£8.95			E&S80

Total carried forward   £ _____

Total brought forward £ _____

Title	Price each	Current Editions No.	£	Future Editions No.	
Tolley's Social Security and State Benefits	£8.95				TSS82
Tolley's Guide to Statutory Sick Pay	£3.95				SSP
Liquidation Manual	£21.00				LM80
Receivership Manual 2nd Edition	£ tba				RM82
Tolley's Employment Act 1982	£7.95				EA82
Employees' Rights in Receiverships and Liquidations	£14.95				ERR79
Companies Accounts Check List No. 1 pack of 5	£4.83‡				CAC1
No. 2 pack of 5	£4.83‡				CAC2
Pro Forma Accounts Pack of 5	£10.35‡				PFA5
Tolley's CCA Conversion Kit	£51.75‡				CCAKT
Tolley's Reporting under CCA	£18.00				RCCA
Financial Reporting 1982-83	£19.50				FR82
Tolley's Expansion Kit for Business	£4.95				TEK
Tolley's Survival Kit for Small Businesses	£2.95				TSK
Tolley's Business — a Survival Kit (Eire Version)	£3.50				ITSK
Tolley's European Community Institutions	£4.50				EC1
Tolley's Profit Sharing and other Share Acquisition Schemes with 1980 Supplement	£9.95				P&S80
CSR Survey of Company Car Schemes	£ tba				CCS82
CSR Survey of Employee Benefits	£ tba				SEB
FOCUS 1: Capital Transfer Tax: Discretionary Trusts	£4.75				CTTDT
FOCUS 2: Purchase/Redemption Company Own Shares	£4.75				PRCOS
Taxwise Taxation Workbook 1982/83	£10.75				TTW1
Taxwise Capital Transfer Tax Workbook	£7.95				TCTW1

Please add 5% for post & packing*

Cheque enclosed for total amount of order £ _____

Name_____ Tel. No:_____

Firm _____

Address _____

_____Postcode_____

Signed_____Date_____

Registered No. 729731 England VAT No. 243 3583 67   001 A B C D E

*Post and packing charges waived if books are placed on Standing Order, under the Tolley Subscriber service.   ‡Inclusive of VAT @ 15%.